The best defense begins right

When you're up against low-flying threats, effective defense begins as far away as possible. Right at the horizon.

That's Mk 86 territory.

The Mk 86 uses its high data rate SPQ-9 sensor to scan the surrounding area for potential threats. It detects, acquires, and tracks them. And finally it helps engage them.

The Mk 86 is now serving the U.S. Navy as a fire control system handling both surface

against sea skimmers here.

and airborne threats. It tracks multiple targets with ease. And its ability to handle low-altitude threats already has been proved.

The best protection against sea skimmers begins far from the intended target. With the Mk 86, you're covered through 360°—all the way to the horizon.

Lockheed Electronics
Leadership in Technology

Alphabetical list of advertisers

35 mm Twin Field Anti-Aircraft Guns GDF-C.03/D03

The new self-propelled field anti-aircraft guns...

...for the '90s. Another 35 mm anti-aircraft innovation from Oerlikon engineered to fulfill future military requirements.

The new self-propelled anti-aircraft guns mounted on either tracked or wheeled vehicles (GDF-C03/D03):

- Are autonomous, highly mobile, powerful and flexible.
- Automatically acquire, track and engage both fixed and rotary wing aircraft; ground target engagement capabilities are designed to assure full self-protection.
- Guarantee effective air defence for mobile columns and installations of temporary importance.
- Use an integral omnidirectional search radar to provide complete airspace surveillance with IFF.
- Achieve high hit probabilities as result of the innovative high-performance sighting system whose passive electro-optical sensors are virtually immune to jamming.
- Are equipped with newly developed 35 mm weapon and ammunition feed systems which permit rapid selection of different ammunition types.

Technical Data

● Rate of fire	1200 rounds/min
● Muzzle velocitiy v_0 (dependent on ammunition type)	1175–1385 m/s
● Ammunition supply	430 rounds
● Aiming arcs: traverse	unlimited
elevation	–5 to +85 °
● Masses GDF-C03 on tracked vehicle (modified M548)	18 000 kg
GDF-D03 on wheeled vehicle (HYKA)	22 000 kg

New types of 35 mm anti-aircraft ammunition* are being developed by Oerlikon to counter the threats of the 90s.

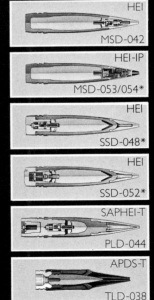

HEI
MSD-042

HEI-IP
MSD-053/054*

HEI
SSD-048*

HEI
SSD-052*

SAPHEI-T
PLD-044

APDS-T
TLD-038

OERLIKON MILITARY PRODUCTS

Machine Tool Works
Oerlikon-Bührle Ltd.
Military Products Division
Marketing (MIL-MAR)
Birchstr 155, CH-8050 Zurich/Switzerland

T

Technology for Communications International (TCI)
1625 Stierlin Road, Mountain View,
California 94043, USA . . . . [64]

&

Technology for Communications International Ltd (TCI)
41 Buckingham Palace Road, London SW1W 0PP,
England . . . . [64]

Thomson-CSF/CIMSA
10-12 avenue de l'Europe, BP 44, 78140 Vélizy,
France . . . . [29]

Thomson-CSF/DSE
Division Systèmes Electroniques,
116 avenue Aristide Briand, BP 10,
92223 Bagneux Cedex, France . . . . [9]

Thomson-CSF/SDC
Division SDC, 40 rue Grange Dame Rose, BP 34,
92360 Meudon la Forêt, France . . . . [51]

THORN EMI Electronics Ltd
Defence Systems Division, Victoria Road, Feltham,
Middlesex TW13 7DZ, England . . . . [11]

V

Vickers Instruments
Haxby Road, York YO3 7SD, England . . . . [53]

Vickers Shipbuilding & Engineering Ltd (Armaments)
PO Box 12, Barrow-in-Furness,
Cumbria LA14 1AB, England . . . . [76]

W

Walmore Electronics Ltd
11/15 Betterton Street, London WC2H 9BS,
England . . . . [21]

Against low and very low altitude threats

CROTALE
ABSOLUTE COORDINATION

The all-weather Crotale weapon system has been designed to defend sites against saturating air-attacks at low and very low altitudes.

This system ensures a perfectly coordinated and integrated defence by the use of centralized calculations and of microwave links between the acquisition unit and the firing units as well as between several acquisition units.

The Crotale system intercepts any target at more than 10 km with a reaction time of less than six seconds.

The Armies of some ten countries throughout the world are equiped with the Crotale system, proving thus the efficiency and the reliability of the units.

THOMSON-CSF
DIVISION SYSTÈMES ÉLECTRONIQUES
116, av. Aristide Briand/B.P. 10/92223 Bagneux Cedex/France
Tél.: (1) 664.13.13

5050

Classified list of advertisers

The companies advertising in this publication have informed us that they are involved in the fields of manufacture indicated below:

Accelerometers
British Aerospace Dynamics Group
Ferranti
SFIM

Acoustic equipment
British Aerospace Dynamics Group
Hughes Aircraft
Krupp Atlas Elektronik
Singer Librascope
SINTRA/ALCATEL (Dept DSM)

Acoustic equipment field tracer
DCN
Thomson CSF

Aerials/antennas
British Aerospace Dynamics Group
Elbit Computers
Elettronica
Marconi Radar Systems
SMA
TCI
Thomson CSF

AFV cupolas
Creusot-Loire
MECAR

AFV sighting systems
Barr & Stroud
British Aerospace Dynamics Group
Officine Galileo
Optische Industrie De Oude Delft
 (Oldelft)

Airborne ASW detection equipment
Alkan
DCN
Hughes Aircraft
Philips Elektronikindustrier
SINTRA/ALCATEL
SINTRA/ALCATEL (Dept DSM)
Thomson CSF
Thorn EMI Electronics

**Airborne navigation & weapon
delivery**
British Aerospace Dynamics Group
Elbit Computers
Hughes Aircraft
SFIM
Thomson CSF

Air conditioning equipment
British Aerospace Dynamics Group

Aircraft
MBB

Aircraft radar
Ferranti
FIAR
Hughes Aircraft
SMA
Thomson CSF
Thorn EMI Electronics

Air data computers
Ferranti
Thomson CSF

Air defence systems
Breda Meccanica
British Aerospace Dynamics Group
DCN
Elbit Computers
Elettronica
Euromissile
Ferranti
GIAT
Hollandse Signaalapparaten
Hughes Aircraft
Marconi Radar Systems
Matra
MBB
Oerlikon-Bührle
Officine Galileo
Selenia
SINTRA/ALCATEL
Thomson CSF

Alignment equipment
Krupp Atlas Elektronik
SFIM
Sopelem

Altimeters
British Aerospace Dynamics Group
DCN
Thomson CSF

Altitude & heading reference systems
British Aerospace Dynamics Group

Ammunition (armoured cars)
MECAR

Ammunition fuzes
Bofors
DCN
Ferranti
MECAR
Oerlikon-Bührle
PRB
Sherwood International Export
Thomson CSF
Thorn EMI Electronics

Ammunition loading
MECAR

Ammunition loading plants
Bofors
DCN
GIAT
Oerlikon-Bührle
PRB
Simmel

Ammunition test gun
Bofors
MECAR
Oerlikon-Bührle
OTO Melara
Simmel

Analysers
DCN

Anechoic chambers
British Aerospace Dynamics Group

Anti-radar weapons
British Aerospace Dynamics Group

**Anti-submarine warfare systems
equipment**
Ameeco (Hydrospace)
Bofors
British Aerospace Dynamics Group
Consorzio Sistemi Navali
 Selenia/ELSAG
Elbit Computers
Hollandse Signaalapparaten
Hughes Aircraft
Krupp Atlas Elektronik
Philips Elektronikindustrier
SFIM
SINTRA/ALCATEL
SINTRA/ALCATEL (Dept DSM)
Thomson CSF
Thorn EMI Electronics

Anti-tank weapons
Aérospatiale
Bofors
Breda Meccanica
British Aerospace Dynamics Group
Creusot-Loire
Elbit Computers
Euromissile
Hughes Aircraft
Matra
MBB
MECAR
Oerlikon-Bührle
Sherwood International Export
Sopelem

Armament systems
Alkan
DCN
GIAT
Hughes Aircraft
Lockheed Electronics
Matra
MECAR
Oerlikon-Bührle
PRB
SAMM
Sherwood International Export
Thomson CSF

Arming systems
British Aerospace Dynamics Group
DCN
Hughes Aircraft
Lockheed Electronics
Thorn EMI Electronics

Armour
Creusot-Loire

**Armoured fighting vehicles &
personnel carriers**
Creusot-Loire
GIAT
Krupp Atlas Elektronik
OTO Melara
Sherwood International Export
Steyr-Daimler-Puch

Articulated wheel loader
OTO Melara

Artillery directing radar
Philips Elektronikindustrier
Thomson CSF
Thorn EMI Electronics

A WORLD LEADER IN FUZE TECHNOLOGY

This statement is no idle boast. During the past 50 years THORN EMI Electronics has developed a total capability in fuze technology – embracing research, modelling, design, development and production. Today, the company is the largest single unit in the Western world engaged in these activities.

Since producing the world's first in-service proximity fuze in 1940, THORN EMI Electronics has supplied the majority of fuzes used by the British armed services and many of those used by other major countries. Whatever the requirement, from gun and mortar ammunition to guided missiles, THORN EMI can supply the fuze upon which the weapon's effectiveness depends.

No other European company offers such a diverse range of fuzing products. And very few companies in the world can match THORN EMI's impressive design and development capabilities, or its advanced facilities and techniques.

Fuzes are just part of the vast range of successful defence products designed and manufactured by THORN EMI Electronics. For further information, consult the experts. Call or write to our Defence Systems Division today.

Leadership in Defence Electronics

 THORN EMI Electronics
Defence Systems Division

THORN EMI Electronics Limited Defence Systems Division Victoria Road Feltham Middlesex TW13 7DZ England telephone 01-890 3600 telex 24325

A THORN EMI Company

CLASSIFIED LIST OF ADVERTISERS

ATC systems
Ferranti
FIAR
Hollandse Signaalapparaten
Lockheed Electronics
Marconi Radar Systems
Selenia
Thomson CSF

Automatic flight control systems
SFIM
Thomson CSF

Automatic rifles
GIAT
Sherwood International Export
Steyr-Daimler-Puch

Automatic test equipment
Alkan
Ameeco (Hydrospace)
British Aerospace Dynamics Group
Elbit Computers
Ferranti
Hughes Aircraft
Krupp Atlas Elektronik
Oerlikon-Bührle
SFIM
Thomson CSF

Auto-pilots
SFIM

Avionics
EL-OP

Azimuth reference equipment
British Aerospace Dynamics Group
Krupp Atlas Elektronik

Ballistic measuring equipment
Oerlikon-Bührle
Krupp Atlas Elektronik

Ballistic & tactical missiles
Aérospatiale
British Aerospace Dynamics Group
Hughes Aircraft

Batteries
Aérospatiale
Hughes Aircraft

Binoculars
DCN
Officine Galileo
Sherwood International Export

Boards, plotting
Thomson CSF

Boats, inflatable
DCN

Bombs
PRB
Sherwood International Export
Simmel

C3
British Aerospace Dynamics Group
Elbit Computers
Elektro Spezial
Hughes Aircraft
Krupp Atlas Elektronik
Marconi Radar Systems
Philips Elektronikindustrier
SINTRA/ALCATEL
Thomson CSF
Thorn EMI Electronics

Cables, electric & electromechanical
Ameeco (Hydrospace)
CSEE
Hughes Aircraft

Cameras, TV
FIAR
Thomson CSF

Camouflage nets
Oerlikon-Bührle
Sherwood International Export

Chaff
Alkan
Bofors
BPD/SNIA

Chaff dispensing countermeasure launching system
Elbit Computers

Chaff launchers
Bofors
Breda Meccanica
CSEE
Philips Elektronikindustrier
Vickers Shipbuilding & Engineering

Checkout equipment
DCN
Lockheed Electronics
MBB

Command systems & equipment
British Aerospace Dynamics Group
DCN
Ferranti
Hughes Aircraft
Lockheed Electronics
Philips Elektronikindustrier
Singer Librascope
SMA
TCI
Thomson CSF
Thorn EMI Electronics

Communication systems
DCN
Elbit Computers
Hollandse Signaalapparaten
Thomson CSF

Communications satellites (military)
British Aerospace Dynamics Group

Compasses, gyro
British Aerospace Dynamics Group
DCN
SFIM

Computerised tank fire control
EL-OP

Computers, analogue
CSEE
Ferranti
Hughes Aircraft
Officine Galileo
Thomson CSF

Computers, digital
Ameeco (Hydrospace)
British Aerospace Dynamics Group
CSEE
Elbit Computers
Ferranti
Hughes Aircraft
Lockheed Electronics
Officine Galileo
Thomson CSF

Consoles
Consorzio Sistemi Navali
    Selenia/ELSAG
CSEE
DCN
FIAR
OTO Melara
Selenia
SINTRA/ALCATEL
SMA
Thomson CSF
Vickers Shipbuilding & Engineering

Control equipment, electronic
Alkan
British Aerospace Dynamics Group
DCN
Ferranti
Lockheed Electronics
Marconi Radar Systems
SFIM
SINTRA/ALCATEL
Thomson CSF
Vickers Shipbuilding & Engineering

Converters
DCN

Countermeasure launching systems
Alkan
British Aerospace Dynamics Group
Consorzio Sistemi Navali
    Selenia/ELSAG
CSEE
DCN
Elbit Computers
Matra
Philips Elektronikindustrier
Singer Librascope

Cryogenics
British Aerospace Dynamics Group
Hughes Aircraft
Officine Galileo

Data & information processing systems
TCI

Data processing/peripheral equipment
Ameeco (Hydrospace)
CSEE
Ferranti
Krupp Atlas Elektronik
SFIM
SINTRA/ALCATEL
Thomson CSF
Thorn EMI Electronics

Delay lines
Thomson CSF

Depth charges
British Aerospace Dynamics Group

Detectors
British Aerospace Dynamics Group
DCN
SFIM

Digital data bus systems, shipborne
Consorzio Sistemi Navali
    Selenia/ELSAG
CSEE
Elektro Spezial
Hughes Aircraft
Thorn EMI Electronics

Direct drive servo systems
British Aerospace Dynamics Group
CSEE
Officine Galileo
Vickers Shipbuilding & Engineering

Direction finders, automatic
Thomson CSF

Display, alpha-numerical large scale
CSEE
SINTRA/ALCATEL
Thomson CSF

Display, cathode ray tube
Ferranti
Hughes Aircraft
Krupp Atlas Elektronik
Marconi Radar Systems
SINTRA/ALCATEL
SMA
Thomson CSF

Tactical C³I for the Combat Environment

from Librascope

CLASSIFIED LIST OF ADVERTISERS

Display, closed-circuit TV
FIAR
Hughes Aircraft
Thomson CSF

Distance measuring equipment
DCN
Krupp Atlas Elektronik
Thomson CSF

Doppler sonars
DCN
Krupp Atlas Elektronik
Thomson CSF

Drones
British Aerospace Dynamics Group
MBB

Ejector release units
Alkan
Sherwood International Export

Electronic countermeasures
Alkan
British Aerospace Dynamics Group
CSEE
DCN
Elettronica
Hughes Aircraft
Marconi Radar Systems
SATT Electronics
Sherwood International Export
Thomson CSF
Thorn EMI Electronics

Electronic fuses
Bofors
DCN
Elektro Spezial
Ferranti
Lockheed Electronics
Oerlikon-Bührle
Sherwood International Export
Thomson CSF
Thorn EMI Electronics

Electronic warning systems
Krupp Atlas Elektronik

Electro-optic systems
Barr & Stroud
British Aerospace Dynamics Group
Consorzio Sistemi Navali
 Selenia/ELSAG
CSEE
Elbit Computers
Elektro Spezial
Eltro
Ferranti
FIAR
Hughes Aircraft
Lockheed Electronics
Officine Galileo
Optische Industrie de Oude Delft
 (Oldelft)
Selenia
SFIM
Sopelem
Thomson CSF
Thorn EMI Electronics

Electro-optical directors (naval)
British Aerospace Dynamics Group

Encoders/decoders
DCN
Italtel
SINTRA/ALCATEL
Sopelem

Environmental testing
Ameeco (Hydrospace)
British Aerospace Dynamics Group
Thorn EMI Electronics

EW equipment
British Aerospace Dynamics Group
CSEE
Elbit Computers
Elettronica
Hughes Aircraft
Marconi Radar Systems
Philips Elektronikindustrier
SATT Electronics
Thomson CSF
Thorn EMI Electronics

EW systems
CSEE
Elbit Computers
Elettronica
Hollandse Signaalapparaten
Hughes Aircraft
Krupp Atlas Elektronik
Philips Elektronikindustrier
SATT Electronics
Thomson CSF
Thorn EMI Electronics

Explosives
Bofors
DCN
MBB
Oerlikon-Bührle
Sherwood International Export

Fibre optics
Ameeco (Hydrospace)
Barr & Stroud
DCN
Hughes Aircraft
Optische Industrie de Oude Delft
 (Oldelft)
Philips Elcoma

Field artillery
Bofors
DCN
OTO Melara
Sherwood International Export
Vickers Shipbuilding & Engineering

Fire-control equipment
Alkan
Bofors
British Aerospace Dynamics Group
Consorzio Sistemi Navali
 Selenia/ELSAG
CSEE
DCN
Elbit Computers
Ferranti
GIAT
Hughes Aircraft
Krupp Atlas Elektronik
Lockheed Electronics
Marconi Radar Systems
Officine Galileo
OTO Melara
Philips Elektronikindustrier
SFIM
Singer Librascope
Sopelem
Thomson CSF

Fire suppression systems
Elektro Spezial
Eltro

Flight data recorder
British Aerospace Dynamics Group
DCN
Ferranti
SFIM

Fluidics
DCN

Fluid power
DCN

Fuel cells
Hughes Aircraft

Fuel systems
DCN

Fuzes
MECAR
Oerlikon-Bührle
Sherwood International Export
Thorn EMI Electronics

Grenades (rifle)
MECAR

Ground handling equipment
Alkan
Creusot-Loire
DCN
Sherwood International Export

Ground influence mines (sea mines)
British Aerospace Dynamics Group
DCN
Thomson CSF

Guidance systems, inertial
British Aerospace Dynamics Group
DCN
Ferranti
SFIM

Guidance systems, optical
Barr & Stroud
DCN
Officine Galileo
Rank Pullin Controls
Thomson CSF

Guidance systems, radio command
DCN
Thomson CSF
Thorn EMI Electronics

Gun systems
Bofors
Breda Meccanica
CSEE
DCN
MECAR
Oerlikon-Bührle
OTO Melara
PRB
Rank Pullin Controls
Thomson CSF
Vickers Shipbuilding & Engineering

Gyroscopes
British Aerospace Dynamics Group
DCN
Ferranti
SFIM

**Harbour protection systems
(magnetic/acoustic)**
Ameeco (Hydrospace)
Bofors
DCN
Krupp Atlas Elektronik
SMA
Thomson CSF

Head-up display
FIAR
Hughes Aircraft
Optische Industrie de Oude Delft
 (Oldelft)
Thomson CSF

Heated windows
Barr & Stroud

Helicopters
Aérospatiale
MBB

The new light infantry.

The last thing a soldier wants to carry is unnecessarily heavy equipment.

At Rank Pullin Controls we have the expertise to solve this type of weighty problem.

As leaders in the development of optical technology, Rank have designed the latest generation, lightweight night sight. The SS 80.

The SS 80 has a 40% reduction in size compared to older generation sights. And that means the SS 80 weighs less than one kilo.

One thing that hasn't been reduced is Rank's ability to meet the very high standards demanded by the British Armed Forces.

The rugged construction stands up to vibration and combat. The operating temperature range of −40°C to +45°C, ensures complete reliability in any climate.

The SS 80 Night Sight makes it easy for a soldier to pull his weight.

But that's no more than you would expect from Rank Pullin Controls.

The winner in the race for arms reduction.

Rank Pullin Controls
Rank super vision. Rely on it.

RANK PULLIN CONTROLS LIMITED, LANGSTON ROAD, LOUGHTON, ESSEX IG10 3TW. TELEPHONE: 01 508 5522. TELEX: 23855.

CLASSIFIED LIST OF ADVERTISERS

Hovercraft
DCN

Hydraulic systems
British Aerospace Dynamics Group
DCN
Officine Galileo
SAMM
Sopelem
Vickers Shipbuilding & Engineering

Hydrofoils
DCN

Hydrophones
Ameeco (Hydrospace)
Thomson CSF

IFF equipment, shipborne
DCN
Italtel
Lockheed Electronics
SMA
Thomson CSF

Indicator instruments
DCN
SFIM

Indicator instruments, electro-chemical
DCN
Optische Industrie de Oude Delft
  (Oldelft)

Infantry training equipment
MECAR
Oerlikon-Bührle
Sherwood International Export
Thomson CSF

Infantry weapons
Aérospatiale
Euromissile
GIAT
Matra
Oerlikon-Bührle
OTO Melara
PRB
Sherwood International Export
Sopelem
Steyr-Daimler-Puch

Inflatable boats
DCN

Information retrieval systems
Ferranti

Infra-red detectors for thermal imaging units
British Aerospace Dynamics Group
Philips Elcoma

Infra-red equipment
Barr & Stroud
BPD/SNIA
British Aerospace Dynamics Group
DCN
Elettronica
Eltro
Hughes Aircraft
Officine Galileo
Optische Industrie de Oude Delft
  (Oldelft)
Rank Pullin Controls
Selenia
SFIM
Sopelem
Thorn EMI Electronics

Infra-red equipment materials
Barr & Stroud
DCN
Elettronica
Optische Industrie de Oude Delft
  (Oldelft)
Sopelem

Infra-red jammers
British Aerospace Dynamics Group

Infra-red thermal imaging systems
EL-OP

Infra-red warning systems
EL-OP

Instrument landing systems
Thomson CSF

Inverters
Marconi Radar Systems

Laser warning devices
Eltro
Optische Industrie de Oude Delft
  (Oldelft)

Laser rangefinders
Barr & Stroud
Bofors
CILAS
DCN
EL-OP
Eltro
Ferranti
FIAR
Hughes Aircraft
Krupp Atlas Elektronik
Optische Industrie de Oude Delft
  (Oldelft)
Selenia
Sopelem
Thomson CSF

Lasers
Barr & Stroud
British Aerospace Dynamics Group
CILAS
DCN
Eltro
Ferranti
Hughes Aircraft
Optische Industrie de Oude Delft
  (Oldelft)
Selenia

Launching equipment
Alkan
BPD/SNIA
Creusot-Loire
CSEE
DCN
Euromissile
MBB
Oerlikon-Bührle
Sherwood International Export
Vickers Shipbuilding & Engineering

Law enforcement & riot control equipment
Sherwood International Export
Steyr-Daimler-Puch

Lenses
Bofors
Officine Galileo
Optische Industrie de Oude Delft
  (Oldelft)
Sopelem

Low frequency sonars
Ameeco (Hydrospace)
SINTRA/ALCATEL (Dept DSM)
Thomson CSF

Magnetic immunisation systems
DCN
Marconi Radar Systems
Thomson CSF

Magnetometers
Ameeco (Hydrospace)
DCN

Measuring equipment
Ameeco (Hydrospace)
Bofors
DCN
Ferranti
SFIM
Sopelem
Thomson CSF

Message processing equipment
Thomson CSF

Meteorological equipment
DCN
Elektro Spezial
SFIM

Meters
SFIM
Sherwood International Export

Microwave communication equipment
Thomson CSF

Microwave landing systems
FIAR
Thomson CSF

Microwave landing systems, airborne
SFIM
Thomson CSF

Mine-hunting sonars
DCN
FIAR
Krupp Atlas Elektronik
Thomson CSF

Mine neutralisation systems
British Aerospace Dynamics Group
Consorzio Sistemi Navali
  Selenia/ELSAG
Thomson CSF

Mine-scattering systems
Alkan
MBB
Thorn EMI Electronics

Mines
Bofors
British Aerospace Dynamics Group
Sherwood International Export
Thomson CSF

Missile fuzes
Bofors
British Aerospace Dynamics Group
Oerlikon-Bührle
Sherwood International Export
Thomson CSF

Missile launchers & handling systems
Aérospatiale
Alkan
Bofors
British Aerospace Dynamics Group
CSEE
DCN
Euromissile
IMI Summerfield
MBB
Oerlikon-Bührle
OTO Melara
Selenia
Sherwood International Export
Singer Librascope
Thomson CSF
Vickers Shipbuilding & Engineering

Missile optics
Barr & Stroud
British Aerospace Dynamics Group
Oerlikon-Bührle

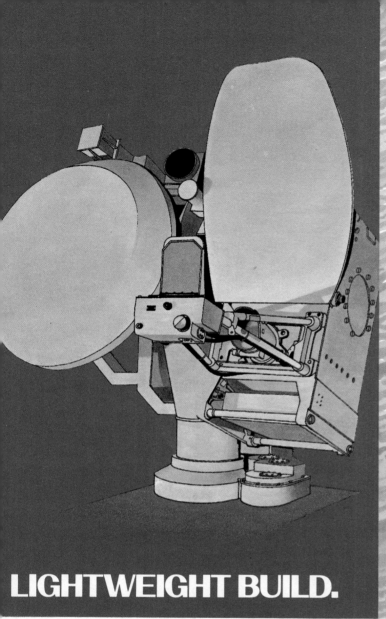

LIGHTWEIGHT BUILD.

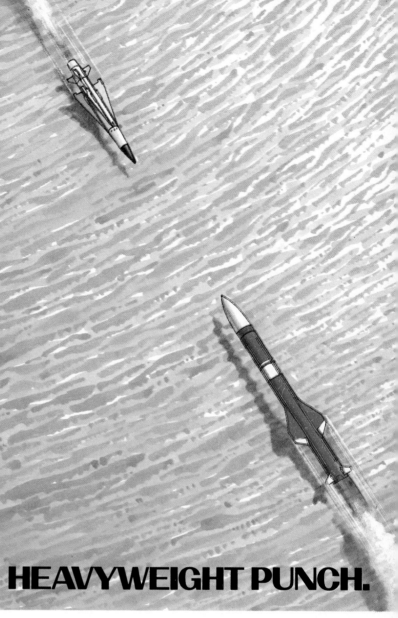

HEAVYWEIGHT PUNCH.

NEWS FLASH

SEAWOLF BLASTS EXOCET

INTERCEPTED AND DESTROYED AT MAXIMUM RANGE.

A sea-skimming Exocet missile fired from HMS Jupiter has been intercepted and destroyed by a Seawolf anti-missile fired by HMS Brilliant in a highly successful trial off the Welsh coast.

Detected and tracked by Marconi radar, the Exocet was completely destroyed at the Seawolf's maximum range of just under 3 miles. HMS Brilliant had no early warning of Exocet launch. Deta...

The Marconi Radar 805 SW.

A new, lightweight dual frequency fire control radar specially designed for use in major warships and smaller craft.

Chosen by the Royal Navy to direct the lethal punch of the Seawolf missile, and backed by the technology and experience of the largest radar manufacturer in Europe, the Marconi 805 system combats the threat of low level attack from air or sea once and for all.

For more information contact Marconi Radar Systems Limited, Writtle Road, Chelmsford, England CM1 3BN. Telephone: 0245 267111. Telex: 99108.

Marconi
Radar Systems

A WHOLE NEW GENERATION OF THINKING.

CLASSIFIED LIST OF ADVERTISERS

Missiles
Aérospatiale
Bofors
BPD/SNIA
British Aerospace Dynamics Group
DCN
Euromissile
Hughes Aircraft
Matra
MBB
Oerlikon-Bührle
OTO Melara
Selenia

Mobile workshops for maintenance service
Elektro Spezial
Eltro
Thorn EMI Electronics

Modelling of fire performance
Thorn EMI Electronics
Vickers Shipbuilding & Engineering

Monitoring stations for magnetic measurements (fixed & mobile)
Thomson CSF

Mortar locating radar
Thomson CSF
Thorn EMI Electronics

Motors, electric
Ferranti
Thomson CSF

Motors, hydraulic
DCN
Officine Galileo
SAMM
Sopelem

Mounts, antenna
CSEE
DCN
Lockheed Electronics
Marconi Radar Systems
SMA
Thomson CSF

Moving map displays
Ferranti
Hughes Aircraft
Thomson CSF

Multi sensor collection & correlation systems
TCI

Munitions & ordnance
Bofors
Lockheed Electronics
MECAR
Oerlikon-Bührle
OTO Melara
PRB
Sherwood International Export
Simmel
Thorn EMI Electronics

Naval combat systems
Aérospatiale
British Aerospace Dynamics Group
Consorzio Sistemi Navali
   Selenia/ELSAG
Creusot-Loire
DCN
Ferranti
Hughes Aircraft
Krupp Atlas Elektronik
Lockheed Electronics
Oerlikon-Bührle
Philips Elektronikindustrier
Selenia
Singer Librascope
SINTRA/ALCATEL (Dept DSM)
Thomson CSF

Naval data processing systems
British Aerospace Dynamics Group
CSEE
DCN
Elbit Computers
Hollandse Signaalapparaten
Philips Elektronikindustrier
SINTRA/ALCATEL
Thomson CSF

Naval defence systems
Bofors
Breda Meccanica
British Aerospace Dynamics Group
Creusot-Loire
CSEE
Ferranti
Hughes Aircraft
Oerlikon-Bührle
Philips Elektronikindustrier
SMA
Thomson CSF
Vickers Shipbuilding & Engineering

Naval guns
Bofors
Breda Meccanica
Creusot-Loire
DCN
Oerlikon-Bührle
OTO Melara
Vickers Shipbuilding & Engineering

Navigation aids
British Aerospace Dynamics Group
CSEE
Elbit Computers
Krupp Atlas Elektronik
Rank Pullin Controls
Selenia
SELESMAR
SFIM
Thomson CSF

Night vision equipment
Aérospatiale
Barr & Stroud
Bofors
DCN
Elektro Spezial
Eltro
Euromissile
FIAR
Hughes Aircraft
Oerlikon-Bührle
Officine Galileo
Optische Industrie de Oude Delft
   (Oldelft)
Rank Pullin Controls
SFIM
Sherwood International Export
Sopelem
Thomson CSF
Thorn EMI Electronics

Night vision equipment, components
Eltro
Oerlikon-Bührle
Optische Industrie de Oude Delft
   (Oldelft)
Philips Elcoma
Sherwood International Export
Sopelem
Thomson CSF

Noise measurement equipment
DCN

Oceanographic equipment
Ameeco (Hydrospace)
Creusot-Loire
DCN
SFIM
SINTRA/ALCATEL (Dept DSM)
Thomson CSF
Thorn EMI Electronics

Offboard countermeasures
DCN

Optical countermeasures
FFV Maintenance

Passive night vision
EL-OP

Personnel carriers
GIAT
OTO Melara
Sherwood International Export
Steyr-Daimler-Puch

Platforms, rolling
DCN

Platforms, stable
British Aerospace Dynamics Group
DCN
SFIM

Plot extractors
Marconi Radar Systems

Portable anti-tank weapons
Bofors
Breda Meccanica
British Aerospace Dynamics Group
Hughes Aircraft
MBB
OTO Melara
PRB
Sherwood International Export

Power equipment
Aérospatiale
British Aerospace Dynamics Group
DCN

Programmable fuzes
Sherwood International Export
Thorn EMI Electronics

Propellant test computer
IMI Summerfield

Propellants
Bofors
BPD/SNIA
IMI Summerfield
Sherwood International Export

Pyrotechnics
Alkan
Bofors
BPD/SNIA
DCN
MECAR
Oerlikon-Bührle
Sherwood International Export
Simmel

Racks, bomb
Alkan
Sherwood International Export

CLASSIFIED LIST OF ADVERTISERS

Radar, airborne
Ferranti
FIAR
Hughes Aircraft
Philips Elektronikindustrier
SMA
Thomson CSF
Thorn EMI Electronics

Radar, 3-dimensional (ground, mobile)
Selenia
Thomson CSF

Radar, ground
Elektro Spezial
FIAR
Hollandse Signaalapparaten
Hughes Aircraft
Lockheed Electronics
Marconi Radar Systems
Philips Elektronikindustrier
Selenia
SMA
Thomson CSF
Thorn EMI Electronics

Radar, ground ship-based
DCN
Ferranti
Hollandse Signaalapparaten
Lockheed Electronics
Marconi Radar Systems
Philips Elektronikindustrier
Selenia
SMA
Thomson CSF

Radar, high power early warning (ground)
Hollandse Signaalapparaten
Hughes Aircraft
Marconi Radar Systems
Selenia
Thomson CSF

Radar, low coverage (ground)
Hughes Aircraft
Marconi Radar Systems
Selenia
Thomson CSF

Radar reflective materials
British Aerospace Dynamics Group

Radar target illumination & tracking (ground, ship)
Hollandse Signaalapparaten
Marconi Radar Systems
Philips Elektronikindustrier
Selenia
Thomson CSF

Radio communication equipment
Bofors
DCN
Elektro Spezial
Ferranti
Hughes Aircraft
Italtel
Sherwood International Export
SINTRA/ALCATEL
Thomson CSF

Radiosounders
DCN

Radomes
British Aerospace Dynamics Group

Radomes, air supported
British Aerospace Dynamics Group
DCN

Reconnaissance equipment
Alkan
British Aerospace Dynamics Group
Hughes Aircraft
Matra
Optische Industrie de Oude Delft
(Oldelft)
OTO Melara
Sherwood International Export
Sopelem
TCI
Thomson CSF
Thorn EMI Electronics

Reconnaissance vehicles
Creusot-Loire
OTO Melara
Sherwood International Export
Steyr-Daimler-Puch

Recording equipment
Ameeco (Hydrospace)
SFIM

Remotely-piloted vehicles
Aérospatiale
British Aerospace Dynamics Group
Thorn EMI Electronics

Research & development
MECAR

Retarders, bomb
Matra

Rocket launchers
BPD/SNIA
Breda Meccanica
Consorzio Sistemi Navali
Selenia/ELSAG
Creusot-Loire
CSEE
DCN
Matra
Oerlikon-Bührle
PRB
Sherwood International Export
Vickers Shipbuilding & Engineering

Rocket motor analyser
IMI Summerfield

Rockets
BPD/SNIA
DCN
IMI Summerfield
MBB
Oerlikon-Bührle
PRB
Sherwood International Export

Secondary surveillance radar
DCN
Italtel
Thomson CSF

Self-propelled anti-aircraft equipment
British Aerospace Dynamics Group
Creusot-Loire
Oerlikon-Bührle
OTO Melara

Self-propelled field artillery
Bofors
Creusot-Loire
GIAT
Vickers Shipbuilding & Engineering

Sensors/transducers
DCN
Krupp Atlas Elektronik
SFIM
Sopelem
Thomson CSF

Servomechanics
British Aerospace Dynamics Group
CSEE
DCN
Elettronica
Lockheed Electronics
Officine Galileo
SAMM
Vickers Shipbuilding & Engineering

Servo systems
British Aerospace Dynamics Group
DCN
Officine Galileo
SAMM
SFIM
Sopelem
Vickers Shipbuilding & Engineering

Shelters, inflatable/portable
Matra

Shelters, portable
GIAT

Ship & aircraft gun mounts
Bofors
DCN
Oerlikon-Bührle
Vickers Shipbuilding & Engineering

Sights
Bofors
Consorzio Sistemi Navali
Selenia/ELSAG
Elbit Computers
Ferranti
Lockheed Electronics
Oerlikon-Bührle
Officine Galileo
Philips Elektronikindustrier
Rank Pullin Controls
SFIM
Sopelem
Thomson CSF

Remember where you saw it first

on a threat warning simulator from Walmore

The sophistication within the spectrum of the electronic battlefield continues to increase as technologies evolve.

Rapid growth in the areas of digital microelectronics, microwave, millimeter wave, and electro-optics continues to have significant impact on EW threats and their ECCM capabilities.

Yet this increasing threat sophistication is only part of the problem. The operational readiness of the free world's defence forces depends on the knowledge that EW equipment is properly maintained and personnel are properly trained in the use of sophisticated EW equipment.

At Walmore Electronics we understand these critical requirements. Through our Simulation Products Group, we produce electro-

magnetic environment simulators which offer viable solutions to the problems of test, evaluation and validation of threat warning

systems, jamming systems, reconnaissance and surveillance equipment, communications systems, as well as the training of personnel in the effective use of this equipment.

Our simulators also provide cost-effective alternatives to escalating operational expenses.

If you need to know more or have special requirements in the spectrum of threat simulation, call or write to us today:

Walmore Electronics Ltd
11/15 Betterton Street
London WC2H 9BS
Tel 01-836 1228 Telex 28752
Fax 01-240 8397

Walmore

CLASSIFIED LIST OF ADVERTISERS

Simulators
Ameeco (Hydrospace)
Bofors
British Aerospace Dynamics Group
COFRAS
DCN
Elbit Computers
Elektro Spezial
Elettronica
Euromissile
Ferranti
FIAR
Hughes Aircraft
Krupp Atlas Elektronik
Marconi Radar Systems
MBB
Oerlikon-Bührle
Officine Galileo
SINTRA/ALCATEL
SINTRA/ALCATEL (Dept DSM)
Solartron Simulation
Thomson CSF

Small arms
GIAT
Sherwood International Export
Steyr-Daimler-Puch

Sonar equipment
Ameeco (Hydrospace)
Consorzio Sistemi Navali
  Selenia/ELSAG
DCN
Ferranti
Hughes Aircraft
Krupp Atlas Elektronik
SINTRA/ALCATEL
SINTRA/ALCATEL (Dept DSM)
Thomson CSF

Sonar interceptors
Ameeco (Hydrospace)
Krupp Atlas Elektronik
SINTRA/ALCATEL
SINTRA/ALCATEL (Dept DSM)
Thomson CSF

Strategic acquisition & direction finding systems
TCI

Submarine passive listening devices
Ameeco (Hydrospace)
DCN
Krupp Atlas Elektronik
SINTRA/ALCATEL
SINTRA/ALCATEL (Dept DSM)
Thomson CSF

Submarine periscopes
Barr & Stroud
DCN
Sopelem

Submarines & systems
Ameeco (Hydrospace)
DCN
Ferranti
Krupp Atlas Elektronik
Singer Librascope
SMA

Survival equipment
Alkan
DCN
Sherwood International Export

Switching systems
DCN
Elbit Computers
Hughes Aircraft
Italtel
Thomson CSF

Synthesisers, frequency
DCN

Tactical missiles
Aérospatiale
British Aerospace Dynamics Group
Euromissile
MBB
Thomson CSF

Tank laser sights
Barr & Stroud
Hughes Aircraft
Krupp Atlas Elektronik
Officine Galileo
Optische Industrie de Oude Delft
  (Oldelft)
Rank Pullin Controls
Selenia
SFIM
Sopelem

Tanks
Bofors
Creusot-Loire
DCN
GIAT
OTO Melara
Sherwood International Export
Steyr-Daimler-Puch

Tank transporters
Creusot-Loire
DCN
OTO Melara

Target towed aircraft
British Aerospace Dynamics Group

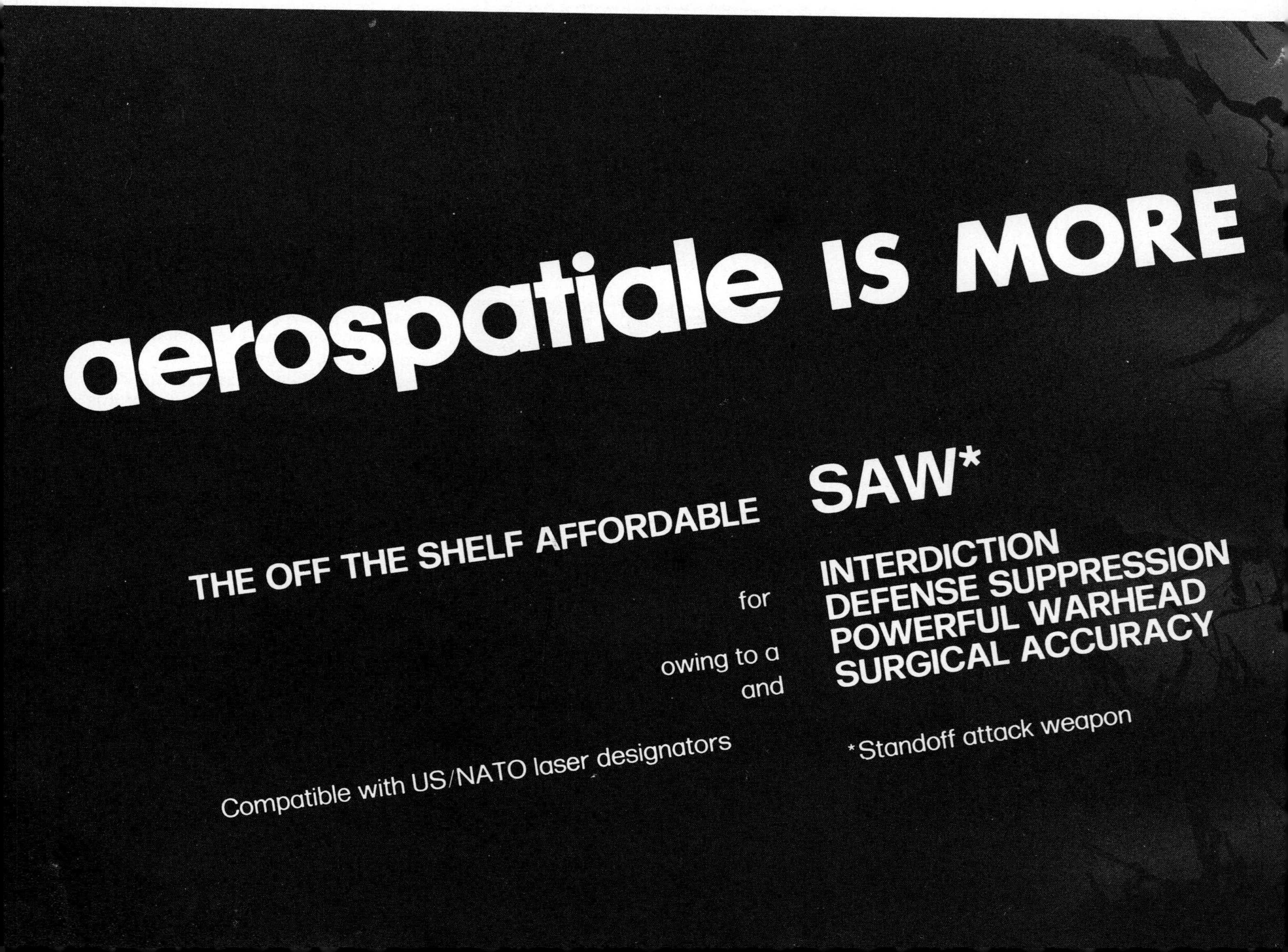

Technical assistance (operational & maintenance: tank & artillery)
COFRAS

Telemetry equipment
Ameeco (Hydrospace)
British Aerospace Dynamics Group
DCN
Hughes Aircraft
SFIM
Sopelem

Theodolites
DCN
Officine Galileo

Thermal imaging units
Elbit Computers
Elektro Spezial
Eltro
FIAR
Hughes Aircraft
Krupp Atlas Elektronik
Officine Galileo
Optische Industrie de Oude Delft
 (Oldelft)
Sopelem
Thorn EMI Electronics

Torpedo homing heads & electronics
Consorzio Sistemi Navali
 Selenia/ELSAG
DCN
Krupp Atlas Elektronik
SINTRA/ALCATEL (Dept DSM)
Thomson CSF

Torpedoes
DCN

Torpedo launching systems
Consorzio Sistemi Navali
 Selenia/ELSAG
Creusot-Loire
Philips Elektronikindustrier
SINTRA/ALCATEL (Dept DSM)

Tow target systems
Alkan

Tracking equipment
British Aerospace Dynamics Group
CSEE
DCN
Eltro
Hughes Aircraft
Lockheed Electronics
Philips Elektronikindustrier
SFIM
Singer Librascope
Thomson CSF

Trailers, tank transporter
Creusot-Loire
DCN
OTO Melara

Training
COFRAS
Vickers Shipbuilding & Engineering

Training aids & devices
British Aerospace Dynamics Group
COFRAS
Hughes Aircraft
Matra
MECAR
Sherwood International Export
Solartron Simulation
Thomson CSF
Thorn EMI Electronics
Vickers Shipbuilding & Engineering

Training & live mines
Bofors
DCN
Thomson CSF

Training & simulation
COFRAS
Consorzio Sistemi Navali
 Selenia/ELSAG
Hughes Aircraft
Marconi Radar Systems
SINTRA/ALCATEL
SINTRA/ALCATEL (Dept DSM)
Solartron Simulation

Trucks
Sherwood International Export
Steyr-Daimler-Puch

Turrets for armoured fighting vehicles
Breda Meccanica
Creusot-Loire
Euromissile
GIAT
MECAR
Oerlikon-Bührle
OTO Melara
SAMM
Sherwood International Export
Vickers Shipbuilding & Engineering

CLASSIFIED LIST OF ADVERTISERS

Ultrasonic equipment
Thomson CSF

Underwater combat control equipment
Consorzio Sistemi Navali
   Selenia/ELSAG
Krupp Atlas Elektronik
Singer Librascope
SINTRA/ALCATEL (Dept DSM)
Thomson CSF

Underwater course plotters
DCN
SMA

Underwater systems
Ameeco (Hydrospace)
British Aerospace Dynamics Group
Consorzio SMIN
DCN
Ferranti
Krupp Atlas Elektronik
MBB
SFIM
Singer Librascope
SINTRA/ALCATEL
SINTRA/ALCATEL (Dept DSM)
Thomson CSF
Thorn EMI Electronics

Underwater telephony
Ameeco (Hydrospace)
DCN
SINTRA/ALCATEL (Dept DSM)
Thomson CSF

Universal turrets & tanks
Vickers Shipbuilding & Engineering

Vehicles, military (track & wheel)
Creusot-Loire
DCN
GIAT
Sherwood International Export
Steyr-Daimler-Puch

Velocity measuring equipment
Ameeco (Hydrospace)
Ferranti
Krupp Atlas Elektronik
Oerlikon-Bührle

Video recorders
Thomson CSF

Weapons carriage & release equipments
Alkan
Sherwood International Export

Weapon systems
Aérospatiale
Alkan
Bofors
BPD/SNIA
Breda Meccanica
British Aerospace Dynamics Group
Consorzio Sistemi Navali
   Selenia/ELSAG
Creusot-Loire
DCN
Elbit Computers
Euromissile
Ferranti
GIAT
Hughes Aircraft
Krupp Atlas Elektronik
Lockheed Electronics
Marconi Radar Systems
Matra
MBB
MECAR
Oerlikon-Bührle
OTO Melara
PRB
Rank Pullin Controls
SAMM
Selenia
Sherwood International Export
Singer Librascope
SINTRA/ALCATEL
SINTRA/ALCATEL (Dept DSM)
SMA
Thomson CSF
Vickers Shipbuilding & Engineering

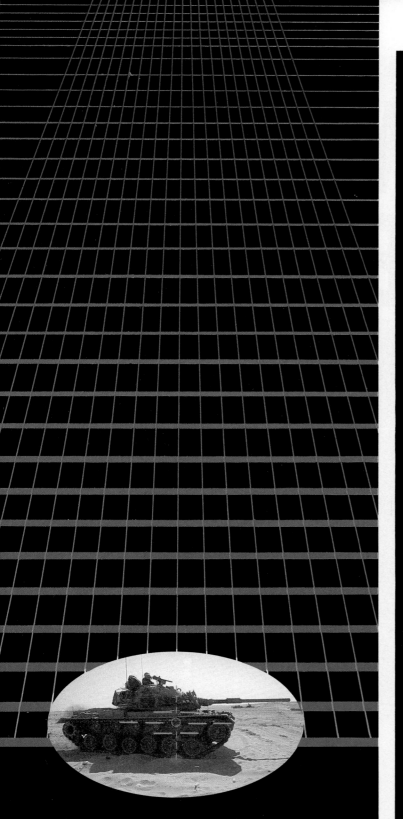

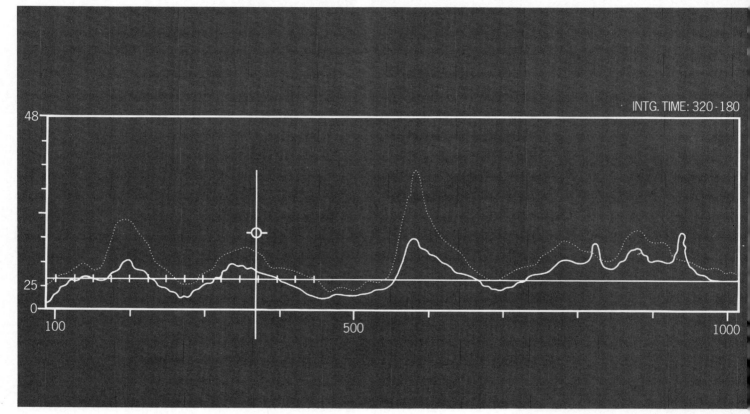

A submarine fitted with one complete system combining all the sensor, data handling, fire control and communication functions, and even platform and machinery control, if desired.

That is the submariner's dream. Such a system would finally give him the flexibility, reaction speed and technological headstart necessary to keep the edge on any adversary.

We have always been aware of this and have started to think in terms of integrated systems from the very beginning. Signaal's M8, SINBADS, GIPSY and SIASS all attest to this approach. Now that all these integrated systems have been incorporated in the highly innovative Submarine Sewaco System, the submariner's dream has come true. And what's more, we are not talking about a paper tiger: Submarine Sewaco is there and operational.

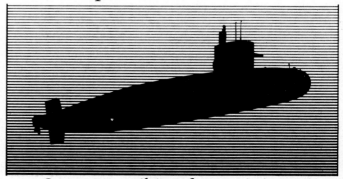

Sewaco's striking feature is its universal, multipurpose operator consoles perfor-

KE THE SUB-
AM COME TRUE

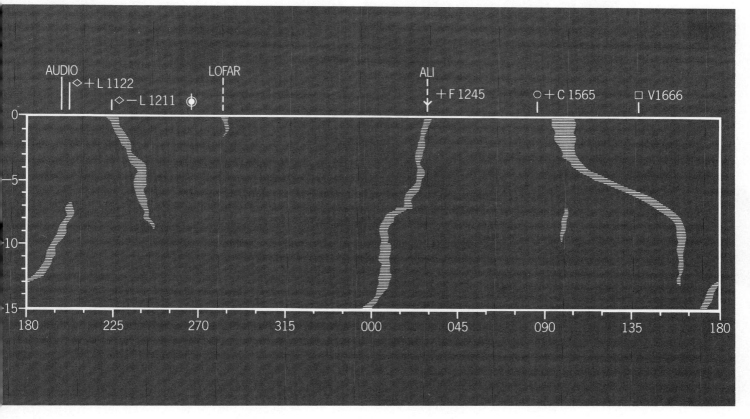

ming any combination of functions such as command display, contact evaluation plotting, sensor and weapon control.

Even a few of these consoles offer complete system reconfiguration capability and therefore optimised redundancy.

On top of that, Submarine Sewaco cuts back the manning requirement for the operational team from twelve to four men. We don't have to tell a submariner what that means.

As in so many other cases, systems integration proved to be the answer, realizing the submariner's dream. Once again it was Signaal who came up with the answer.

Hollandse Signaalapparaten B.V. P. O. Box 42 - 7550 GD Hengelo, The Netherlands. Tel. 074 -488111, telex 44310. Sensor, Combat Information, Weapon Control and Communication Systems.

SIGNAAL INTEGRATED SYSTEMS
THE WAY TO TACKLE THE FUTURE

S4E

5260

C 3 Systems
Fixed and mobile

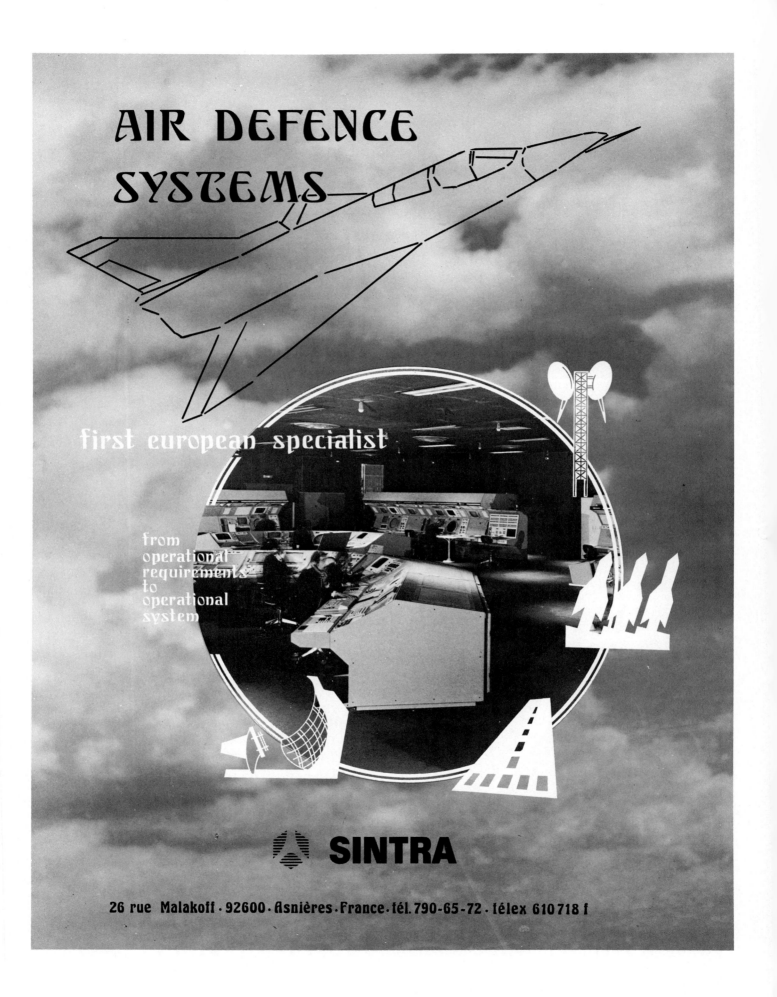

Air superiority? Bofors closes the gap

The nature of the aerial attack has changed dramatically: New types of weapon, ECM support and the changed tactics they permit mean we have to face a diversity of small targets at saturation intensity.

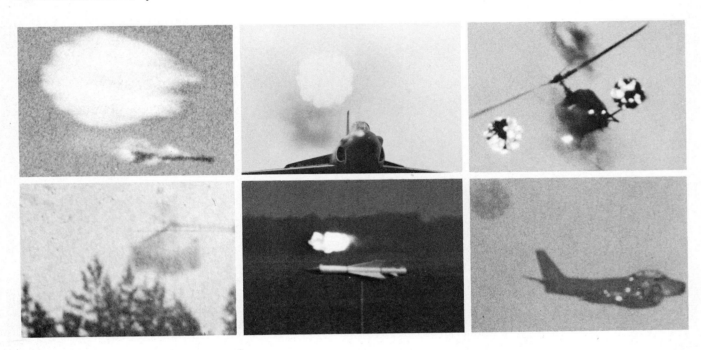

The 40 mm BOFI gun system represents a new generation of integrated fire control, guns and ammunition designed to meet the requirement of the 80's and 90's. Incorporating:

- **all-target capability, thanks to the high system accuracy and new Mark 2 proximity-fuzed ammunition**
- **all-weather and day/night capability**
- **great tactical flexibility and endurance**
- **high ECM resistance and survivability**
- **low manning requirements**

The Bofors 40 mm gun and ammunition was selected, in severe competition, for the US Army's new mobile Divisional Air Defence system (DIVAD).

IN CASE OF...

There's no substitute for experience...

Solartron simulation systems provide vital experience in naval and air defence . . . putting operators and command teams under realistic battle conditions and teaching them the skills they need . . . in a realistic scenario embracing complete environment, sensor and weapon simulators.

And with over 25 years involvement in the design and manufacture of these systems, experience is the key factor, too, in Solartron's leadership in this field.

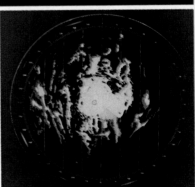

NAVAL TRAINING SIMULATION
Command and control   Navigation and blind pilotage
Aircraft control   Air defence
Electronic warfare   Anti submarine warfare

AIR DEFENCE SIMULATION
Command and control   Fighter and missile control
Air traffic control   Sector operations   Electronic warfare

Simulation by Solartron... the living image

Solartron Simulation

Solartron Simulation, Victoria Road, Farnborough, Hampshire GU14 7PW, England.
Telephone: Farnborough (0252) 544433   Telex: 858245 Solfar G

The new reality.

Fixed **MAD** for _all_ ASW aircraft – _including_ helicopters

✓ compact
✓ reliable

✓ easy to maintain
✓ cost-effective

Advanced Integrated MAD System
AN/ASQ-504 (V) Detecting Set, Magnetic Anomaly

The CAE Electronics Ltd. ADVANCED INTEGRATED MAD SYSTEM (AIMS) is the most significant development in ASW MAD technology since the introduction of MAD systems in the early 1940's.

Without AIMS, ASW helicopter crews must face the many restrictions imposed by towed MAD systems: reduced speed and manoeuverability, noise induced through towed body instability, difficult vertical gradient compensation requirements and the impossibility of achieving a true "on top" contact because of the distance separating the helicopter from the detecting head magnetometer.

CAE AIMS —

■ provides improved detection capability.

■ delivers continuous, automated feature recognition. Contact alert, visual and audible, is provided along with estimated slant range that advises the operator if he is within target acquisition range.

■ allows rapid transition from dipping sonar to MAD — impossible with a towed system.

■ eliminates hazards associated with towing MAD.

■ compensates within 8 minutes for 18 interference terms, even in a hover mode and at any altitude.

Get the complete story on AIMS — the ideal MAD system — from J.J. Elich of CAE

CAE ELECTRONICS LTD.

A subsidiary of CAE Industries Ltd.

C.P. 1800, Saint-Laurent, Québec, Canada H4L 4X4 Tel. (514) 341-6780 Telex 05-824856

The improved Phoenix missile virtually thinks for itself, thanks to advanced digital electronics. The radar-guided missile, carried by the U.S. Navy's F-14 Tomcat fighter, is the primary long-range air-to-air weapon for fleet defense. The new AIM-54C model contains 55 types of hybrid circuits—a combination of integrated circuit chips with discrete devices. They pack five or six times more computer instructions into the missile and allow it to process information hundreds of times faster. In addition, digital processing will accommodate modifications easily. As new missions are defined to meet new threats, new program memory cards can be plugged without rebuilding hardware. The missile is in low-rate production at Hughes Aircraft Company.

The antenna on the AMRAAM missile slews to such high angles that it can track enemy aircraft attempting evasive maneuvers at high g forces. AMRAAM uses the launching aircraft's radar for initial guidance and midcourse reference. A small antenna mounted in the missile's tail section receives data and relays the information over a coaxial cable to the inertial reference unit. The signals are processed and maneuvering commands are sent to four flight control fins. For terminal guidance, AMRAAM's own radar system takes over. The 4.5-inch gimballed microwave antenna in the nosecone transmits and receives signals as it closes in on the target. The Advanced Medium-Range Air-to-Air Missile is in full-scale engineering development at Hughes for the U.S. Air Force and Navy.

Production models of the infrared-guided Maverick missile are being delivered on schedule. The new AGM-65D air-to-surface weapon significantly increases the U.S. Air Force's attack capabilities by letting flight crews engage a wide variety of targets during nighttime and conditions of reduced visibility. Initial production of the first 1,100 missiles follows a rigorous flight test program during which the missile demonstrated its effectiveness against moving tanks, a hangarette, radar vans, a patrol boat, and a simulated fuel dump. Eleven of 20 direct hits in the tests were made at night. The missiles were tested in all kinds of weather and terrain, including the cold and snow of winter at Ft. Drum in New York and the forests and high humidity at Eglin Air Force Base in Florida.

The new TOW 2 antitank missile can be guided through battlefield smoke, haze, or dust—day or night—because of improvements made to the basic TOW launcher and night sight. The sight now functions as a totally independent, redundant fire control sensor, operating in parallel with the optical sight used to track the missile in daylight and clear visibility. In addition, a thermal beacon has been added to the aft end of the missile. Hughes produces the wire-guided TOW 2 for the U.S. Army and Marine Corps. In addition, more than 33 nations have fielded original TOW systems.

A laser device guided a Hellfire missile to a direct hit in firing trials involving the British Army Lynx helicopter. The tests were the first launches of the American-built antiarmor missile by a non-U.S. helicopter, proving the interoperability of NATO systems. The target was pinpointed by a Ground/Vehicular Laser Locator Designator (G/VLLD) from 4.6 kilometers away. The Hellfire, a third-generation supersonic missile, used the reflected laser light to home on the target. G/VLLD is a combination rangefinder and target designator designed for use by forward observers. It can be mounted on tripods or vehicles. Hughes builds G/VLLD for the U.S. Army.

For more information write to: P.O. Box 11205, Marina del Rey, CA 90295

TWIN 40 L 70 FIELD MOUNTING
The Weapon of Guardian System

This powerful point defence system is the first able to effectively engage, with minimum reaction time, not only aircraft but also missiles.

- *Useful intercept at very high ranges is possible, owing to the exceptional system accuracy and firing proximity fuzed ammunition.*

- *Performance has recently been improved even further by the introduction of Mark 2 Proximity Fuzed Ammunition.*

- *With a rate of fire of 1200 r.p.m. from a Guardian Unit (with Flycatcher F.C.S.) air launched and cruise type missiles can be defeated in saturation attacks, aided by large ready-to-fire magazines.*

A 1169 - STUDIO GRAFICO RESTANI, LA SPEZIA.

 **BREDA MECCANICA BRESCIANA** S.ρ.A.
2, Via Lunga - 25128 BRESCIA (Italy) - Tel. 030/31911 - Telex 300056 BREDAR I

Norinco

... affo
innova
to

Working on co
Norinco e
more bud
tradi
innovatio
timed to
of today.
profession
systems that se

Norinco engin
you need tod.
tomorrow-g
uphol
budget con

NORINCO is the trade mark of the China North Industries Corporation, a comprehensive state enterprise combining manufacture and trade with an independent commercial body operating under guidance from relevant government departments. It has a level of technology and commercial strength unique in China, and is looking out to establish and develop wide-ranging technical and commercial co-operation with other corporations worldwide.

The headquarters of NORINCO is in Beijing and branches in Guangzhou, Shenzhen, Dalian, Tianjin and Shanghai. It covers the following areas of industry:

Heavy Industry
Manufacture of complex metal parts and metal blanks such as steel castings, iron castings, finished forgings, die and free forgings. Also heavy machinery, standard and custom-built equipment, chemical processing equipment, construction equipment, heavy-duty vehicles, tools and electrical products.

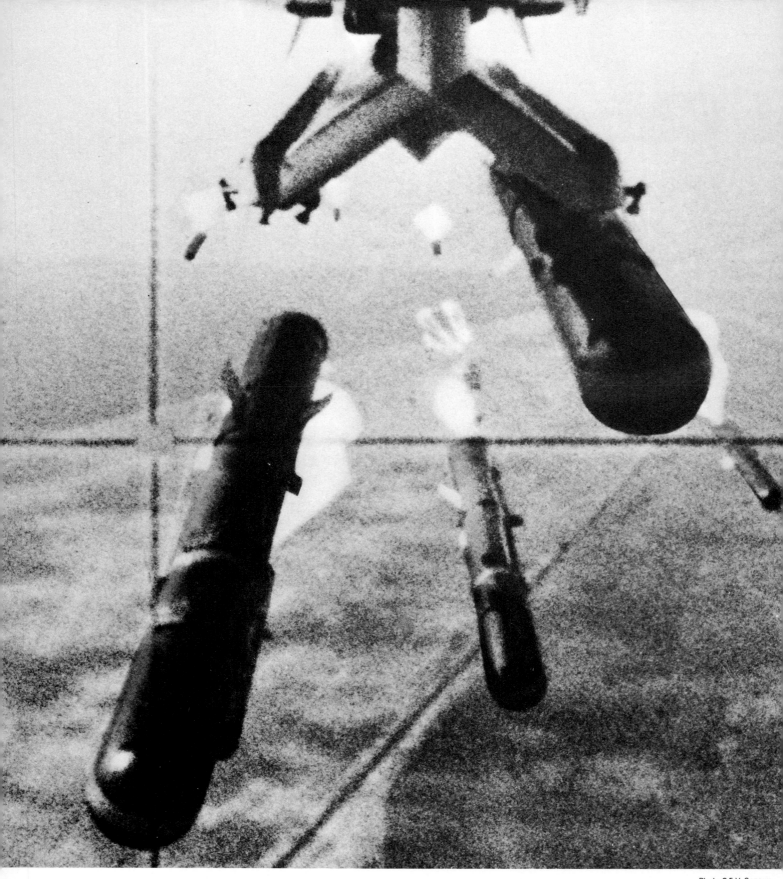

Photo C.E.V. Cazaux

Durandal: the runway destruction weapon.

The most effective way of neutralizing the enemy's air force is to ground it.
The most effective way of achieving this goal is Durandal. Capable of percing heavy layers of concrete, it explodes in depth, producing large craters and surface upheaval.
The low-altitude/high speed delivery mode creates the effect of surprise, whilst considerably limiting the vulnerability of the attacking aircraft to the enemy's anti-aircraft defence.
A single flight can this neutralize a runway for a significant period.

Missiles and aeronautical armaments.

MATRA

37 av. Louis-Bréguet 78140 Vélizy.
Tél.: 946.96.00 - Télex : 698.077.

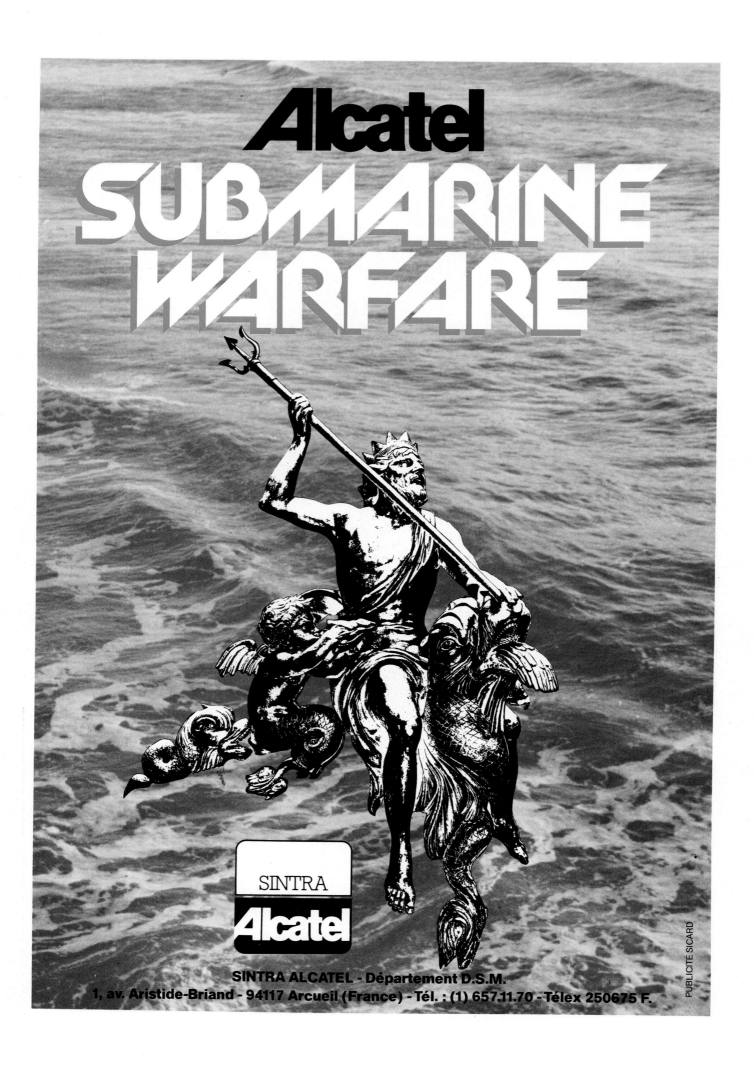

Alcatel
SUBMARINE WARFARE

SINTRA
Alcatel

PUBLICITÉ SICARD

SINTRA ALCATEL - Département D.S.M.
1, av. Aristide-Briand - 94117 Arcueil (France) - Tél. : (1) 657.11.70 - Télex 250675 F.

PEAB-DM 086 8407

Good news for air defence units: we've come up with the answer to jamming.

We've gone to a lot of time and trouble to protect our new air defence system against jamming. What have we done? Sorry, a lot of that's classified. But we can disclose that it is based on frequency agility and a combination of several types of sensor.

Anyone planning to counter our system will have to be prepared to jam on virtually all wavelengths. And we don't believe they've got the resources to do it.

SEARCH RADAR:
FISH, FOWL OR DENIZEN OF THE LAND?
Correct answer: fowl. Somewhere up there 15 metres above the ground the search radar antenna is revolving on its adjustable mast among the tree tops. You might not be able to see it at first glance, but you can be sure that it sees everything that moves.

The search radar operates in the X-band, features double lobes and can transmit an arbitrary combination of MTI and frequency agility simultaneously. And, of course, it features automatic target acquisition and threat assessment.

The search radar and fire control cabin are carried on an off-road, all-wheel drive truck.

SEVERAL EYES ARE BETTER THAN ONE.
The modular configuration of the system permits the connection of several types of sensor simultaneously. The optronic sight can be used to control all types of modern guns and missiles. It features TV target tracking as standard (together with a laser range-finder). Need night-sight capability? Just fit an IR target tracker.

Add a fire control radar to the optronic sight for all weather capability. This operates in the Ku band and, like the search radar, features frequency agility and MTI.

WE CAME ASHORE AS LONG AGO AS 1976.
At Philips Elektronikindustrier, we've always enjoyed an enviable reputation as a supplier of ship-borne fire control systems. That's no reason to think we are newcomers to the field of land-based systems. Our optronic air defence system has been operational with the Swedish Armed Forces since 1976.

On the other hand, this is the first time that we offer a complete land-based system. If you anticipate jamming, take a closer look.

Philips Elektronikindustrier AB
Defence Electronics, S-175 88 Järfälla, Sweden.
Tel. Nat. 0758-10000, Int. +46 758 10000. Telex: 115 05 PHILJA S.

20 YEARS OF ARMY SYSTEMS.

PHILIPS

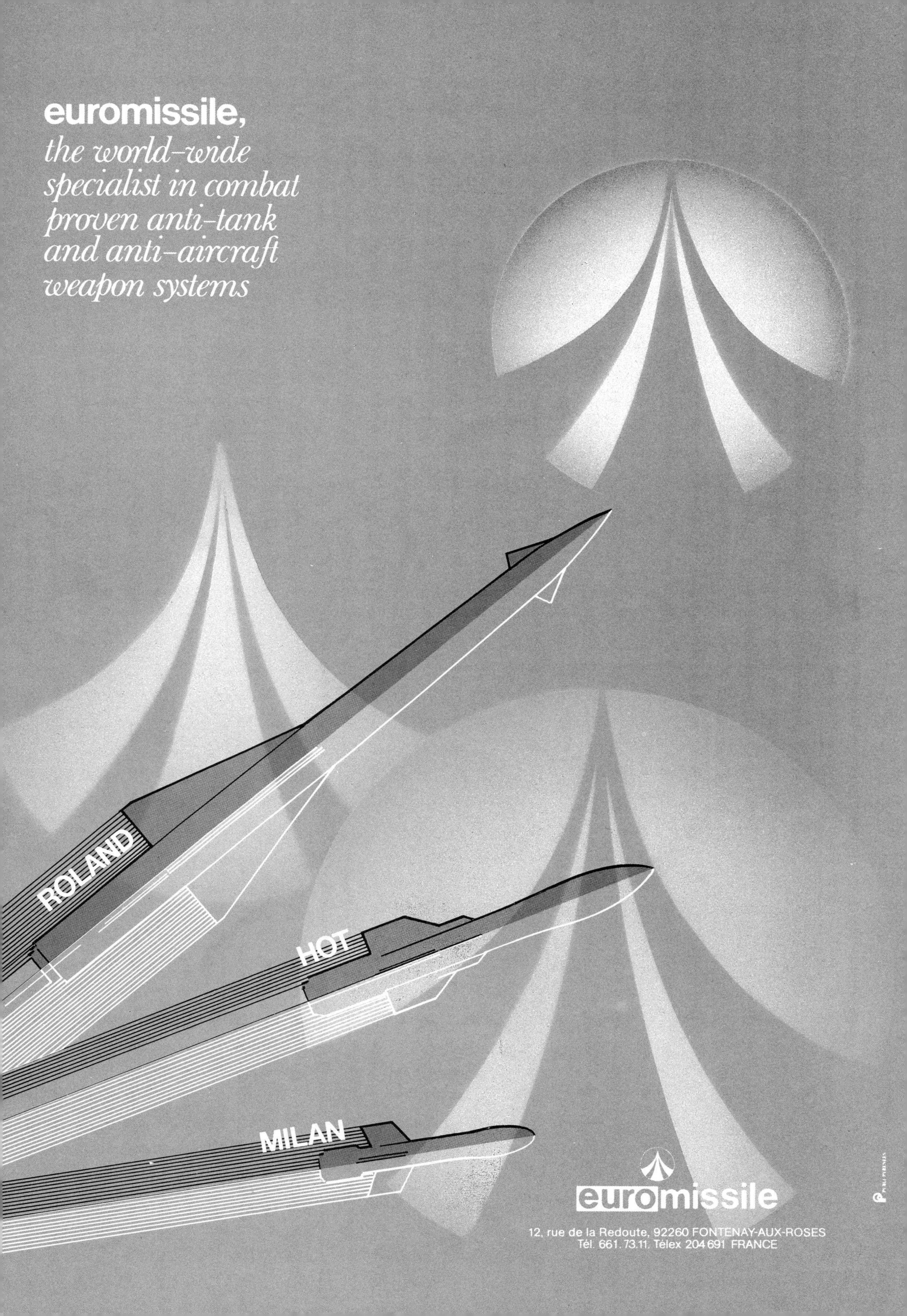

euromissile,
*the world-wide
specialist in combat
proven anti-tank
and anti-aircraft
weapon systems*

ROLAND

HOT

MILAN

euromissile

12, rue de la Redoute, 92260 FONTENAY-AUX-ROSES
Tél. 661.73.11. Télex 204 691 FRANCE

The High-Speed Generation.

The Steyr-Family of Armoured Vehicles
High top speed combined with unmatched climbing capacity and manoeuvrability — a proven generation of tracked armoured vehicles demonstrates its strong points.

The Steyr Armoured Personnel Carriers: They are exceptionally manoeuvrable vehicles. Their design concept permits them to be used for a wide range of applications — as self-propelled anti-aircraft guns, armoured command post vehicles, armoured ambulances or armoured mortar carriers.

The Steyr Tank SK 105 "Kürassier": Field-proven under the most gruelling conditions. Extremely fast and manoeuvrable. Small as a target thanks to its slim design, top-mounted gun and low profile. Large as regards its combat value, fire power and target accuracy.

The Steyr Armoured Recovery Vehicle: A powerful, dependable helper in any emergency. With a range of equipment for all fitting-, clearance- and recovery tasks that is more than complete.

The Steyr-family of armoured vehicles represents a modular construction system consisting of proven components incorporating the very latest technologies — plus the guarantee of a fully ensured spare-parts supply and simple, cost-saving maintenance.

Trucks, all-terrain vehicles, fire-arms — advanced defence systems from one source: the Steyr Defence Division.

STEYR-DAIMLER-PUCH AG
Defence Division
P.O.B. 120, A-1010 Vienna, Austria

SWAROVSKI OPTIK

A-6060 Absam, Hall in Tyrol, Austria

All optical target acquisition- and observation devices have been specially developed and designed for these armoured vehicles by Messrs Swarovski Optik.

Steyr Defence Products

1st ROUND STRIKEABILITY. 2ND GENERATION MVME-

THAT'S PACER MARK 2.

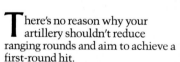

There's no reason why your artillery shouldn't reduce ranging rounds and aim to achieve a first-round hit.

But accurate muzzle velocity measurement is essential. PACER Mark 2 is the answer, being accurate to 0.1%.

PACER Mark 2 is the second generation MVM equipment from Ferranti. And it's twice as good. More versatile. More reliable. Miniaturised.

PACER Mark 2 is microprocessor-based. It measures muzzle velocity round by round in real time, and stores the answers. At the press of a button data on up to 16 rounds can be recalled, averaged and displayed.

PACER Mark 2 can cope with muzzle velocity from 100 right up to 1400 metres per sec. It will work with field artillery guns and mortars of 75mm calibre and above, and can be gun-mounted or free-standing. And with PACER Mark 2 you don't need to preset the muzzle velocity.

ECM risk is minimised because the radar transmitter is automatically switched on for no more than a second, and then off, once the measurement is made.

Designed for the battlefield and not just the firing range, PACER Mark 2 is rugged, quick into action, easy to use and easy to carry.

Aim for first round effectiveness. Get the PACER Mark 2 story now from:

Ferranti Computer Systems Limited, Cheadle Heath Division, Bird Hall Lane, Cheadle Heath, Stockport SK3 0XQ Telephone: 061-428 0771 Telex: 666803.

FERRANTI
Computer Systems

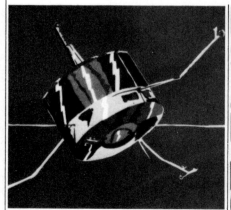
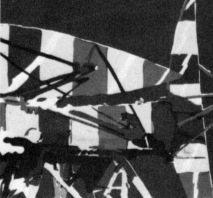

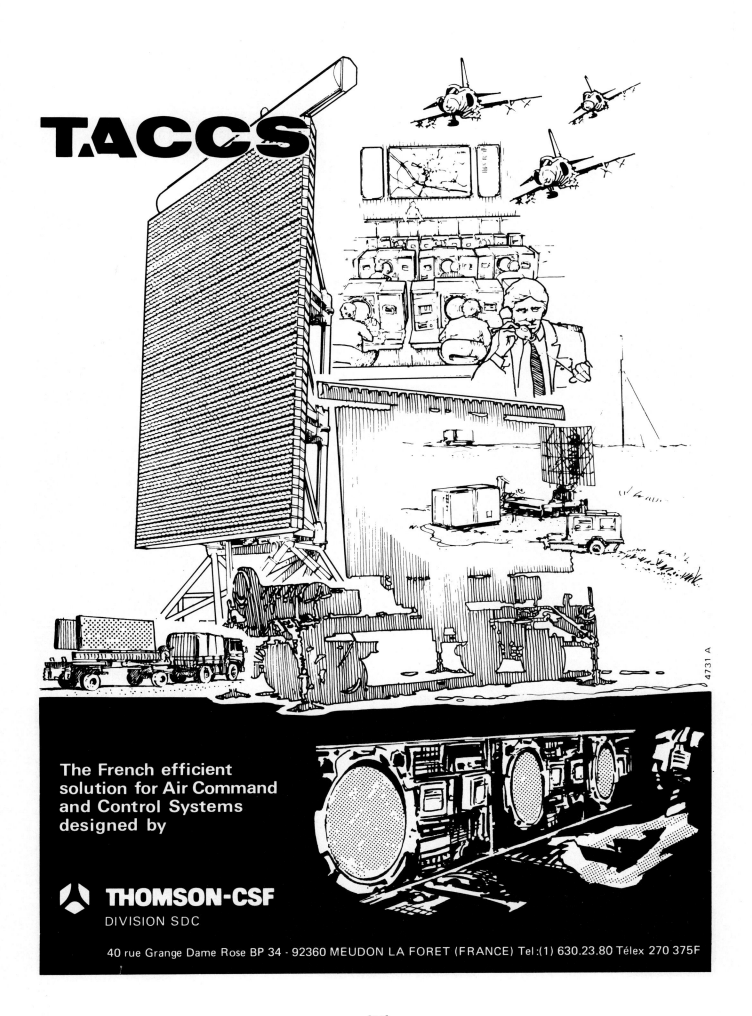

T.ACCS

The French efficient
solution for Air Command
and Control Systems
designed by

THOMSON-CSF
DIVISION SDC

40 rue Grange Dame Rose BP 34 - 92360 MEUDON LA FORET (FRANCE) Tel :(1) 630.23.80 Télex 270 375F

SIMMEL

SIMMEL FOR DEFENCE

■ THE AMMUNITION PRODUCED BY **SIMMEL** COVERS THE RANGE OF COMPLETE ARTILLERY ROUNDS FROM 155 mm TO 203 mm, (115, 155 HE-HC FOR FH 70, 175, 203), AS WELL AS SHELLS AND MORTAR BOMBS OF OTHER CALIBRES WITH SPECIAL FILLINGS (ILLUMINATING, SMOKE, ETC.).

■ **SIMMEL** IS ABLE TO SUPPLY COMPLETE ROUNDS (LOADED PROJECTILE-PROPELLING CHARGE-FUZE) OR SEPARATE COMPONENTS.

PRODUCTIONS

■ 105 HE - WP - ILL - HC
■ 155 HE - WP - ILL - HC
■ 155 for FH 70 HE - ILL - HC
■ 155 for PALMARIA HE - ILL - HC
■ 175 HE
■ 8" HE
■ MORTAR BOMBS
81 and 120 ILL - HC

SIMMEL

BORGO PADOVA, 2
31033 CASTELFRANCO VENETO (TV)
TELEFONO 0423/491241
TELEX 410127

SNIA BPD

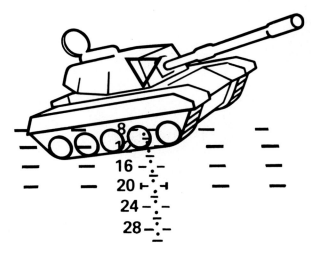

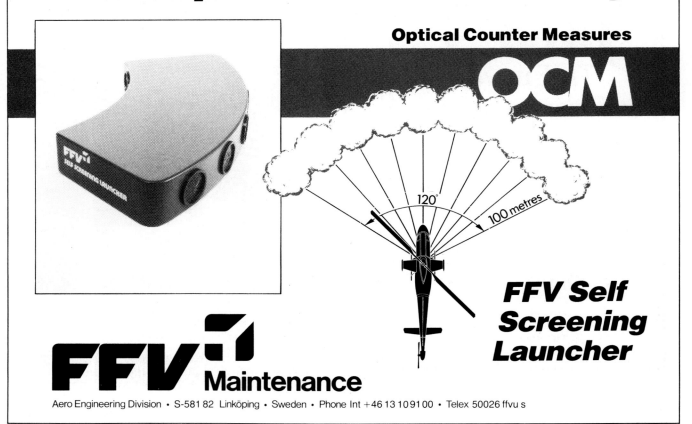

SNIA BPD

CONVENTIONAL AMMUNITION
- COMPLETE ROUNDS AND COMPONENTS FOR ARTILLERY AND MORTARS
- PROPELLING POWDERS AND BURSTING EXPLOSIVES

ROCKETS AND PROPELLANTS
- AIR TO GROUND AND SURFACE TO SURFACE ROCKETS
- ECM AND ILLUMINATING ROCKETS
- ROCKET AND MISSILE WARHEADS
- ROCKET AND MISSILE SOLID PROPELLANT MOTORS
- DOUBLE BASE AND COMPOSITE PROPELLANTS

SPACE ACTIVITIES
- APOGEE MOTORS
- STAGE SEPARATION MOTORS
- ORBITAL TRANSFER SYSTEMS
- SPACE LAUNCH VEHICLE MOTORS

UNGUIDED WEAPON SYSTEMS
- AIR TO GROUND SYSTEMS FOR USE FROM AIRCRAFT AND HELICOPTERS
- FIELD SATURATION SYSTEMS
- INFANTRY SUPPORT SYSTEMS

RESEARCH AND DEVELOPMENT
- ANALYSIS AND DEVELOPMENT OF DEFENCE SYSTEMS
- DEVELOPMENT OF NEW WEAPON SYSTEMS

TECHNOLOGIES & KNOW-HOW
- ASSISTANCE FOR MANUFACTURE OF MILITARY AND SPACE PRODUCTS AND FOR PLANT INSTALLATION

BPD

SIMMEL   SIPE NOBEL

DEFENCE AND SPACE ACTIVITIES

00187 Rome Via Sicilia 162
Tel. 06 4680 Tlx 610114 BPD RM I

M781C, 40MM PRACTICE CARTRIDGE

This cartridge is a fixed, practice-type ammunition designed as a commercial replacement for the M407 40mm Practice Cartridge to be utilized in the 40mm Grenade Launchers M79 and M203.

This cartridge consists of a thermoplastic injection molded projectile body with a rotating band filled with a high visibility yellow-orange dye. Upon impact the frangible projectile ruptures releasing the high visibility orange dye which gives the appearance of explosive impact.

MILITARY BINOCULARS MODELS NO. WMR823 & WMR723 (As Adopted By The U.S. Armed Forces)

· The 7x50mm and 8x30mm binoculars are waterproof, fog-proof and shock resistant. The binocular body is coated with tough, non-glare rubber. Lenses can be individually focused and optics are fully coated. Nitrogen filled. Strap included.
WMR823: NSN #1240-01-091-5096; 55 oz.; 7¼"x8¾".
WMR723: NSN #1240-01-091-5097; 27 oz.; 5"x7".

ELECTRICALLY OPERATED .50 CALIBER (12.7MM) AMMUNITION LINKING MACHINE

Compact, yet features heavy-duty construction for an all-around military use. Each unit is complete with Delinker M7 attachment and available for immediate delivery.
Model M5. NSN #1005-591-0118.

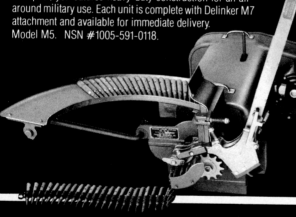

PORTABLE WATER PURIFIER (MWP-2)

The MWP-2 is a lightweight, portable, highly effective water purification unit, scientifically developed for the treatment of water contaminated by disease-laden bacteria, such as those which produce typhus, cholera and dysentery. It will remove all suspended particles — sand, metal, dust and slime, up to 5 microns. Easy to operate and maintain, the MWP-2 uses no chemicals for disinfection, and delivers pure odorless, clean, good-tasting drinking water. It can also be comfortably carried on the back over long distances.

PNEUMATICALLY OPERATED 7.62 NATO CALIBER AMMUNITION LINKING MACHINE

Linking Capacity: 60 Rds. per minute
Operates at Air Pressure: 100 PSI
Feed: Manual
Compact size. Heavy-duty construction. Immediate delivery.

CARBINE, CALIBER .30: M1

The M1 Carbine, Caliber .30: M1 is a gas-operated, self-loading, magazine-fed semiautomatic, lightweight, offensive or defensive shoulder weapon. The rear sight is adjustable for both elevation and windage. The M1 Carbine uses the Bayonet/Knife: M-4.

Length overall	2 ft. 11½ in.	Weight: 15-rd. magazine	
Length overall w/bayonet attached	3 ft. 6¼ in.	(unloaded)	5 lb. 8 oz.
		Weight: 30-rd. magazine	
Feed magazine 15 rd. or 30 rd.		(unloaded)	5 lb. 8½ oz.

M1 GARAND RIFLE, CALIBER .30 M1

The M1 Garand is a gas-operated, semiautomatic, clip-fed, offensive or defensive shoulder weapon. The M1 Garand has been standard U.S. Army issue since WWII. Its dependability and faultless construction make it a dependable infantry weapon even when subjected to the most adverse climatic conditions. Spare parts are immediately available and, should repairs be necessary, the work could be done by field personnel. The M1 Garand uses the Bayonet/Knife: M5/A1. Weight: 9.5 lb.
Length of rifle: 3 ft. 7⅝ in. Length of barrel: 24 in.

FN FAL CALIBER 7.62 NATO

The LAR is a NATO standard caliber 7.62x51mm (.308 Match) rifle with a fully locked system and gas operated by a barrel intake with gas regulator. This gives the weapon total reliability in any climatic condition and considerably reduces the recoil. Several million FNs now equip the armed forces of more than 90 free countries. These rifles are also available in a (para) version that is comparable in weight and dimensions to the .223 caliber carbines, and a heavy barrel model (LAR HB).
Overall Length 43 in. Weight (unloaded) 9.4 lbs.

M2 4.2-INCH MORTAR

A rifled muzzle-loading weapon, intended for high angle firing and used against all targets. Ideal for use in the most difficult terrain and under the most adverse weather conditions. Mortar breaks down into three (3) basic component parts: base plate, cannon tube, and elevating mechanism.

MK.669 SUPER-SUPERQUICK BOMB FUSE

Recent developments in the field of fuse design have resulted in the creation of an instantaneous bomb fuse. Known as the super-superquick fuse, its reaction time is faster — by a factor of ten — than that of the conventional "superquick" fuse. It is so rapid that it provides a new type of craterless burst effect termed a semi-airburst. The MK.669 SSQ is the first operational fuse in this category. LOT #03-0294.

We are the largest private domestic supplier and international exporter of ordnance material. We take pride in supplying materials of the highest quality, in the shortest possible delivery time. Not only does the scope of our activities cover the ordnance field, but we are also able to offer the latest in U.S. Government issue field equipment. Such as, uniforms, combat boots, canteens, tents, etc. Contact us for all your military requirements or for exclusive worldwide distributorships. You can be assured of prompt replies and immediate deliveries.

81MM MORTAR (M-29)

The M-29 81mm mortar is a smooth-bore, muzzle-loaded, high angle of fire weapon. It may be used in the conventional way or mounted in the M125A1 carrier. This is the standard 81mm mortar of the U.S. Armed Forces and very large numbers are in service.
NSN #1015-999-7794

SALADIN ARMORED VEHICLE with 76mm gun.

SHERWOOD
International Export Corporation

M3 .50 CALIBER MACHINE GUN TRIPOD MOUNT

A lightweight, portable folding mount for use with the Browning M2 .50 Cal. Machine Gun. Three telescoping tubular legs join in a tripod head for full front support of gun. NSN #1005-322-9716.

M63 AA .50 CALIBER MACHINE GUN MOUNT

Four-legged, low silhouette, medium weight, portable mount, used for antiaircraft fire. Can be easily disassembled into four compact assemblies. Used primarily with Machine Gun, Caliber .50: Browning, M2, flexible. NSN #1005-673-3246.

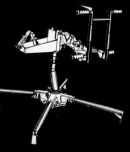

EXECUTIVE OFFICE
18714 Parthenia Street
Northridge, California 91324 USA
Phone: 818/349-7600   Telex: 66-2439
WASHINGTON, DC OFFICE
2115 Ward Court, N.W., Suite 300
Washington, DC 20037 USA
Phone: 202/293-9350   Telex: 89-2763
MIAMI OFFICE
8675 N.W. 53rd Street, Suite 108
Miami, Florida 33166 USA
Phone: 305/591-3867   Telex: 80-7818
LONDON OFFICE
The Penthouse, 21A Hanover Square
London W1R 9DA, England
Phone: 44-01-493-0636   Telex: 291741 SIEC G

ARE YOU TUNED IN WITH ALL THE LATEST DEVELOPMENTS IN MILITARY COMMUNICATIONS?

You are with Jane's.
Our 1984 Yearbook details the latest advances in military communications technology, including frequency-hopping and other anti-jamming techniques, together with just about every other system in use throughout the world. Radio communications, electronic warfare equipment, encryption and security, hardware, systems—

anything and everything to do with command, control and communications from anywhere in the world you'll find detailed in readily accessible depth.

And as a perfect complement to our Yearbook, Jane's Defence Weekly—it will keep you totally up-to-date on the latest developments in this particular field and on all defence matters internationally.

JANE'S
MILITARY COMMUNICATIONS
Where the facts are found!

For further information please contact the Marketing Department:
Jane's Publishing Co Limited, 238 City Road, London EC1V 2PU Tel: 01-251 9281 Tlx: 894689
Jane's Publishing Inc, 13th Floor, 135 West 50th Street, New York NY10020 USA

GET A GUN AHEAD.

1. The CREUSOT-LOIRE 100 mm "Compact" gun mount was designed and developed to efficiently combat air threats, in particular 1985/1990 generation missiles, as well as for firing on surface and shore targets. Now in production, it is the most versatile combat weapon on the market, with the capability to exactly meet all operational requirements.

2. The 100 mm "Compact" gun mount is a powerful weapon for the navies, providing all the units, from patrol boats to aircraft carriers, with unparalleled offensive and defensive capabilities :
– extremely high firing power with a fire rate of 90 rounds/minute.
– remarkable firing efficiency, especially against missiles, with automated ammunition selection inside the turret.

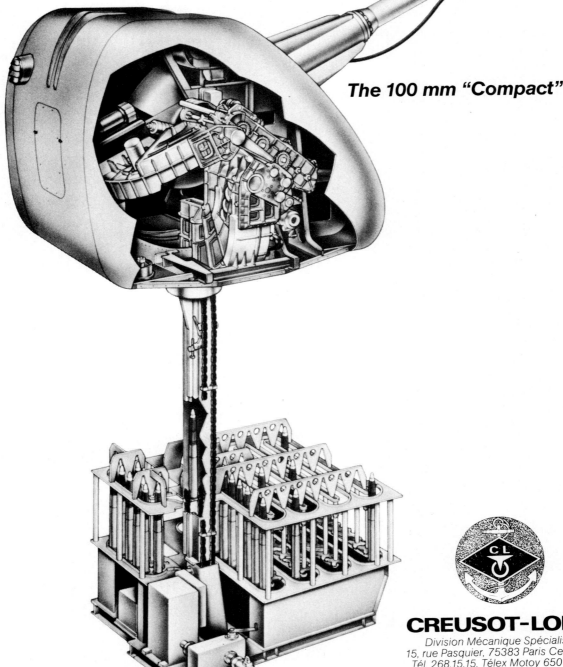

The 100 mm "Compact"

CREUSOT-LOIRE
Division Mécanique Spécialisée
15, rue Pasquier, 75383 Paris Cedex 08.
Tél. 268.15.15. Télex Motoy 650 309 F.

CRL 811

[59]

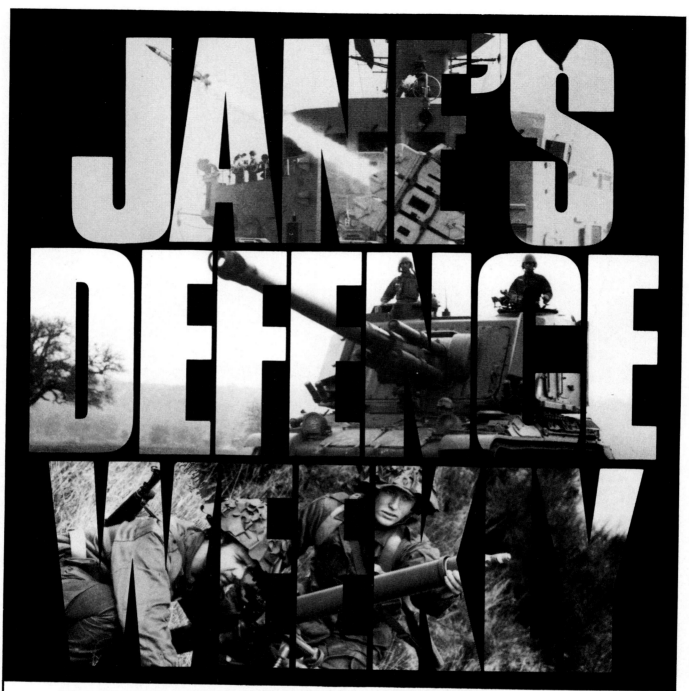

THE FACTS BEHIND THE HEADLINES AND FROM BEHIND THE LINES

The international issues of the day authoritatively reported and reviewed in-depth every week. The latest equipment, defence decisions taken worldwide, reports from behind the scenes and from behind the lines—you'll find the real facts reported first in Jane's Defence Weekly.

For details of subscription and postage rates write to:

Jane's Publishing Co Limited
238 City Road
LONDON EC1V 2PU
Tel: 01-251 9281
Tlx: 894689

JANE'S
Where the facts are found!

In the United States of America:
Jane's Publishing Inc.
13th Floor
135 West 50th Street
New York NY 10020
Tel: 212-586 7745

We also make turrets to measure.
Please send us your inquiries.

Until now, tactical HF direction-finding has been largely hit or miss. Mostly miss.

But TCI's new Series 800 Tactical DF/SSL (single station location) Systems change all that. And significantly.

They are the world's first, fully automatic, site tolerant, air or ground transportable HF COMINT systems (providing signal acquisition, signal classification, emitter location and target file management) designed for tactical operation—**in production now**. Through TCI proven advanced technologies, commanders are assured of high reliability, operational simplicity and accurate location of low power, manpack burst transmitters in seconds from a single EW site.

Additionally, the systems can be remoted, netted and integrated into larger COMINT networks. Presenting a low profile to enemy ground or air reconnaissance, they can be operational within a few hours after site selection. Speaking of sites, the System 800 can be deployed at any reasonable location, and does not require symmetrical antenna positioning.

For the complete story, write for our full scale tactical test results. They will show you how TCI's DF/SSL System 800 takes the "miss" out of tactical HF direction-finding.

TCI

Technology for Communications International
1625 Stierlin Road, Mountain View, CA 94043 U.S.A. / (415) 961-9180
Telex 348458 TECOMINT MNTV

Technology for Communications International, Ltd.
41 Buckingham Palace Road, London SW1W 0PP England / 01-828 7447 (4 lines)
Telex 261235 TCILDN G / Cable TECOMINT

COFRAS

an ally
for your defense

engineering
civil works

**operational
& maintenance**
training

**data
processing systems**
management

Compagnie Française d'Assistance Spécialisée
32, rue de Lisbonne 75008 Paris
Tél. : 561.99.33 - Télex : 660449 F.

Photos E.C.P.A.

DANIEL PIGRIT RÉALISATIONS

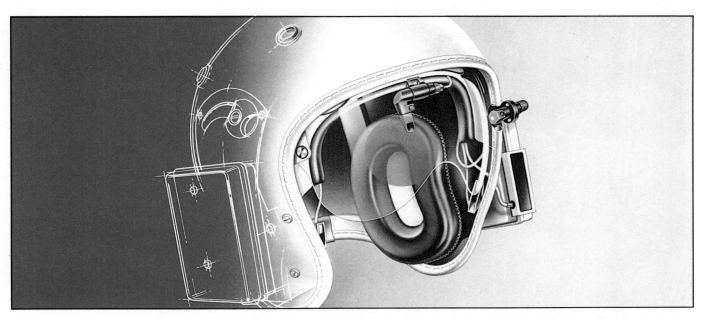

Why our Defence Force is also our creative force.

When we create weaponry, we do so with a view to innovation and improvement. Constantly adapting and refining existing technology. Closely co-operating with our major customer, our own country's Defence Force, in providing creative answers to tactical problems. So when we talk about combat-proven, we mean proven in combat.

In fact, Armscor was itself born of necessity; tested under fire. Today it embraces an entire infrastructure under the one Armscor banner. This gives us full control over everything from raw materials through manufacturing to the finished item.

And while we make an uncommonly wide range of products, we build into each the strictest quality standards we ourselves, NATO or anyone else can apply.

The reason is simply that we never forget who our biggest customer is. For our own Defence Force only the best is good enough. For you the spin-off is creative thinking applied in a wide and often custom-built product range.

Arms available for export

- Ammunition in various calibres and upwards of 140 types.
- Grenades, mines, mortars; pyrotechnic and demolition equipment.
- Range of naval, air force and army weaponry.
- Conventional and mine-protected vehicles from troop carriers to gun tractors.
- Armoured fighting vehicles.
- Advanced electronic equipment including communications and surveillance systems and components.
- All backed by individualised instruction and confidential service.

ARMSCOR
COMBAT-PROVEN RELIABILITY.

Telex Pretoria (South Africa) 3-20217.

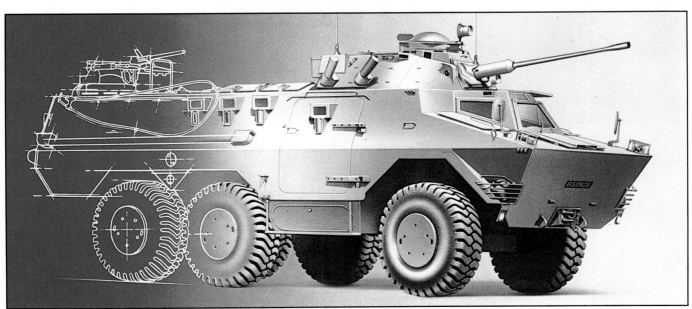

200951/5

MM/APS-705 P.P.I. display with integrated weapon guidance panel

Lupo class frigate mast, showing SMA surface search radar antennae.

HSS Series Coastal surveillance radar Antenna Group.

Radar systems for ships, aircrafts, helicopters and ground stations.

SMA
SEGNALAMENTO MARITTIMO ED AEREO

— Radars for navigation air and naval search.
— Homing and guidance radars.
— Coastal and harbour surveillance radars.
— Tactical visualization, command and control displays, missile assignment consoles.
— Graphic displays and plotting systems.
— High precision identification beacon systems.
— Signal processing and data handling techniques.
— Dedicated electronic action informations systems for above water and submarine vessels.
— Systems engineering.

P.O. BOX 200 - FIRENZE (ITALIA) - TELEPHONE: 055/27501 - TELEX: SMARAD 570622 - CABLE: SMA FIRENZE

How we can deliver quick-fire ammunition in double-quick time.

We can always be quick off the mark in meeting your ammunition needs, because we never have to wait for anyone. From raw materials to manufacturing, we ourselves co-ordinate and control every process and procedure.

Nor do we play around when it comes to packing and despatching the final product. Our major client, our own country's defence force, requires the packaging to withstand long-term storage followed by the toughest operational conditions. So when we talk about combat-proven, we mean proven in combat–in more ways than one.

One last point of interest is that we palletise our ammunition to purchasers' specifications, with delivery schedules precisely to purchasers' requirements.

Ammunition available for quick-fire and small arms.

- Quick-fire: 20 mm (HS 820-type) HEI, HEI-T, APC-T, TP and TP-T. 30 mm (DEFA-type) HEI, APCI and TP. 35 mm HEI and TP-T.
- Small arms: A wide range of ammunition in common military calibres including 5,56 mm; 7,62 mm; .22; .303; 9 mm Para.; .38 S&W; and .50 as well as 12-bore shotgun.
- All backed by confidential service.

ARMSCOR
COMBAT-PROVEN RELIABILITY.

Telex Pretoria (South Africa) 3-20217.

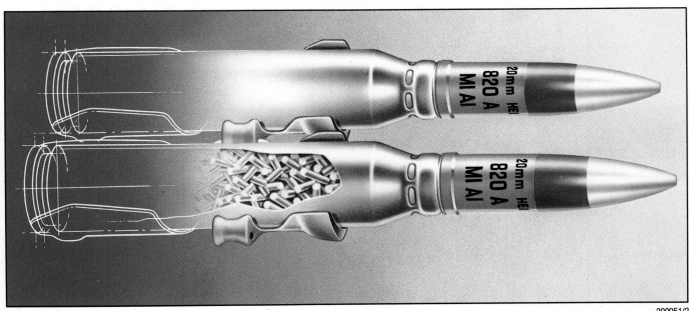

200951/2

Oldelft's nightvision image intensifier tubes link the advantages of two generations.

In the darkness of the night a good viewing is of great importance to fulfill tasks without illumination. Oldelft makes it possible with a wide range of nightvision devices: goggles, binoculars, weapon sights, and observation devices. Based on the use of second generation wafer tubes or super inverter tubes. The super inverter tube is a combination of a wafer tube with a first generation 18mm module. A unique proposition that offers you important advantages. Better image resolution. Higher image intensity. No image blooming. Little or no image smear. Oldelft's nightvision family concept of devices is more economical on the logistic level. For full details, please call or write.

Oldelft lightweight binoculars PB4SL. Designed for surveillance and reconnaissance. 18mm wafer image intensifier tube. Highspeed mirror lens. System magnification: 3.75 x. Field of view: 10.5°.

The device is also suitable for the use of third generation tubes.

Oldelft Cyclop PC1MC. Small dimensioned nightviewing device. A real lightweight: 560 g. Good wearing possibilities, also with a helmet. Highspeed optics. System magnification: 1 x. Field of view: 40°.

Oldelft weaponsight for small arms: RS4MC. Designed for accurate aiming at night. Explosions, gun flashes and such in the overall image will not cause blooming. System magnification: 4 x. Field of view: 10°.

Oldelft passive aiming device GS6MC. Suitable for medium-range crew served weapons, such as machine guns, grenade launchers, recoilless rifles and others. Explosions, gun flashes and such will not cause blooming. System magnification: 6.8 x. Field of view: 6.6°. The device is also suitable for the use of third generation tubes.

Oldelft

nv Optische Industrie De Oude Delft.
P.O. Box 72
2600 MD Delft, Holland
Telephone: (015) 14 59 49
Telex: 38345 odims nl.

How we've taken the 155 mm projectile a step further to make it go further.

Our 155 mm type M1 projectile is at the forefront of modern artillery technology, and forms the basis for our unique G5 gun-howitzer system – which itself made headlines in military circles worldwide.

One good product deserves another, so we perfected base bleed as an add-on unit for the 155 mm M1. And with this base bleed facility now fully operational, our G5 has achieved astonishing ranges in excess of 40 kilometres!

You may not have anything like our G5's. But in your own 155 mm field guns, with our projectiles, you can take combat-proven reliability to new lengths – and with greater lethality than conventional shells can offer, thanks to our high-fragmentation steel.

This same pattern of innovative thinking backed by operational testing underlies every item in our munitions arsenal. So do consult us, whatever your requirement.

Heavy-calibre ammunition
- Artillery: 155 mm type M1 family of ballistically similar projectiles including HE shell, standard or with base bleed, red phosphorous, smoke and illuminating types; also type M107 HE shell. A range of direct action, proximity and electronic time fuzes is available.
- Anti-tank: 105 mm APFSDS/T with highest quality core; and a 90 mm range that includes a novel canister round.
- Naval: 76 mm surface or anti-aircraft rounds with proximity fuze.
- Practice rounds available.
- All backed by individualised instruction and confidential service.

ARMSCOR
COMBAT-PROVEN RELIABILITY.

Telex Pretoria (South Africa) 3-20217.

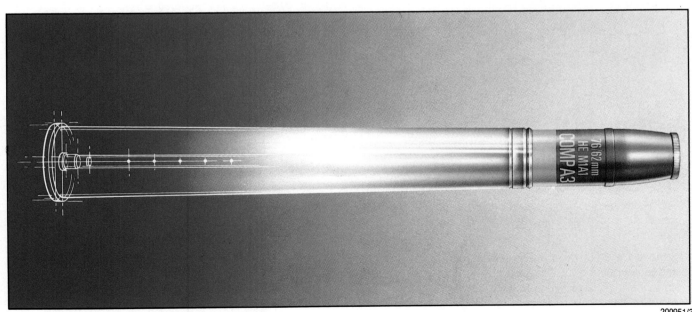

200951/3

Night or day.
seeing means efficiency.

Specialist in optronics and computer systems, Sopelem has applied its technical expertise to developing day/night sighting systems.

Besides a wide range of individual and tank equipments, Sopelem is now offering a large program of services, starting with the conception of specific systems to the training of maintenance personnel.

With their high performance and reliability, Sopelem equipments fit at the French Army specifications.

sopelem
Military Department

102, rue Chaptal 92306 Levallois-Perret - France
Tél. (1) 757.31.05 - Télex 620.111 F

Tank equipped with a night driverscope and a Soptac day/night fire control system.

OB 44 night observation binoculars

[72]

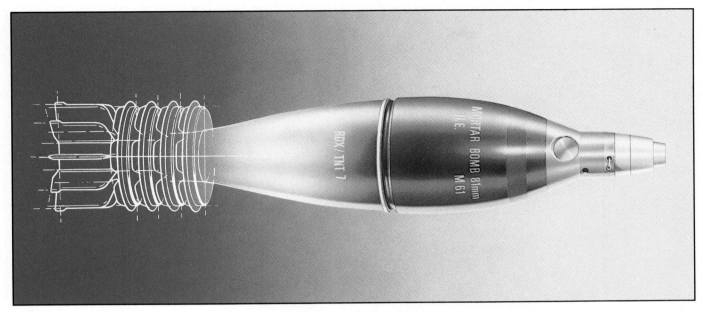

How we can make even a cheap weapon cost the enemy dear.

We see even the universally cheap mortar bomb as a challenge in cost-efficiency. So we developed proximity fuzes for our mortar bombs to ensure consistent burst height and maximum strike effectiveness—while still maintaining a competitive end price.

We can supply a range of 60 mm and 81 mm mortar ammunition covering all applications. All combat-proven in terrain where dense bush and wide-open spaces pose tremendous problems in terms of reach. Where calculated accuracy must go hand in hand with no small measure of ingenuity.

This same pattern of innovative thinking backed by operational testing underlies every item in our munitions arsenal. So do consult us, whatever your requirement.

Other stores available for export

● Pyrotechnics: a full range for army, air force and navy—from thunderflash, smoke canisters, rocket flares, trip-wire flares and coloured signals to riot-control stores and infra-red anti-missile decoys, plus an extremely effective 81 mm smoke generator for AFV's.

● Hand grenades: a comprehensive range of offensive, defensive, smoke and riot-control types.

● Rifle grenades: 5,56 mm and 7,62 mm; HE and red phosphorous smoke types.

● Mines: non-metallic; anti-personnel and anti-tank.

● Demolition equipment: a wide range for various applications.

ARMSCOR
COMBAT-PROVEN RELIABILITY.

Telex Pretoria (South Africa) 3-20217.

200951/4

Newest weapon in US strategic armoury MGM-118 Peacekeeper demonstrates mastery of 'cold-launch' technique but the programme has had its troubles and the first ten missiles deployed by December 1986 may not have completed all tests according to US General Accounting Office report

JANE'S
WEAPON SYSTEMS

FIFTEENTH EDITION

EDITED BY
RONALD T PRETTY MRAeS MRIN

1984-85

ISBN 0 7106-0799-7

JANE'S YEARBOOKS

"Jane's" is a registered trade mark

In the USA and its dependencies
Jane's Publishing Inc, 13th Floor, 135 West 50th Street, New York, NY 10020, USA

Contents

BATTLE BRED

Forged in action. Ready to strike. Elbit systems, on the move. Capabilities which have made strategy reality. Research, production and performance that is front line.

Aircraft and tank weapon delivery systems, targeting supremacy. Command, control and communications systems, maintaining the momentum of advance. Trainers, projecting officers into command. EW systems, poised for response.

Ally your forces with experience. Experience bred in battle.

 **BATTLE BRED**

ELBIT COMPUTERS LTD. • P.O.Box 5390 • Haifa 31053 • Israel • Tel: (04)517111 • Telex: 46774

Foreword

Last 15 years

Preparing, for the 15th time, to hand over to our readers another year's work in the shape of a new edition of this book, it may be appropriate to glance at some of the events of the last decade and a half. While 15 years is not a long time in relation to the development and deployment of military equipment, it is sufficient to afford us a reasonable perspective from which to view progress in the relevant technology and its application, or otherwise, with perhaps a pause to examine a few of the successes and disappointments that have been recorded in the pages of *Jane's Weapon Systems* over the period.

Referring back to the 1969-70 edition, which is the starting point for our retrospective excursion, one does not have to turn many pages before confronting the fact that the US land-based leg of the 'deterrent Triad' (of which more later) is essentially unchanged today, having been based on the force of silo-based Minuteman ICBMs from the early 1960s. The Titan II that shares this duty with Minuteman, although in markedly smaller numbers, is now almost the sole US relic of the days of the 'sheer power' generation of ICBM technology, as represented by its range of over 10 000 km with a multi-megaton nuclear payload. It was also liquid fuelled, and despite the very creditable manner in which the US Air Force (USAF) sustained an operational capability with this inherently difficult system for so long without more numerous or graver mishaps than the few that did mar Titan's service record, it was this aspect as much as any that prompted the decision to replace it.

Two other US systems that remain with us are the Lance and Pershing tactical missiles, albeit modified in varying degrees to keep abreast of modern requirements. Both now play important roles in European affairs as well as elsewhere to some extent. Lance is the basis of one proposal for the new US Army/Air Force Joint Tactical Missile System (JTACMS) programme introduced this year. This combines the former Army Corps Support Weapon System and the USAF Conventional Stand-off Weapon System, for which the now-cancelled Medium Range Air-to-Surface Missile (MRASM) based on the Tomahawk was a candidate. Britain having already cancelled its Blue Water artillery rocket well before the appearance of the first *Jane's Weapon Systems*, the sole representative on the indigenous European tactical support missile scene was the French Pluton which in 1969 was undergoing flight testing preparatory to entering operational service. A successor to the Pluton system, known as Hades, is now being studied as this latest edition records.

The Soviet side of the coin can also be seen to a degree by those readers who have the patience to study the relevant pages of successive editions of this book. Broadly, the USSR had its counterparts to Titan (the SS-9, Scarp), Lance and Pershing (Scud mobile tactical support missile); the first of these is now superseded, the latter are both still in service, although replacements are waiting in the wings as noted elsewhere. This 'echo' effect persists and this edition illustrates how the major powers tend to progress along parallel lines obeying some uncertain but still perceptible phase relationship. Thus it is that *Jane's Weapon Systems 1984-85* comes to have its first entry for a Soviet cruise missile programme. (This overlooks entries for older systems such as the various anti-ship missiles, the well-known Styx for example, which have been recorded in these pages for many years.) It is not an extensive entry admittedly. However, if finding the times of the trains from Moscow to Sverdlovsk is difficult for a Muscovite, can it ever be easy to discover what is going on in the Soviet military field? Nevertheless it is believed that the Soviet Union is engaged in the development of two distinct families of new cruise missiles, and tests of one of these was reported in the West shortly before this volume was printed.

Likely to be first on the scene is the smaller of the two new cruise missile categories. The SSC-X-4 is in the same class as the US Tomahawk and is also thought likely to enter service as a ground-based missile. Another role foreseen for the Soviet Tomahawk 'look-alike' is as a sea-launched cruise missile, SS-NX-21, to add to an already comprehensive Soviet inventory of naval cruise missiles bringing with it a nuclear payload and 3000 km range, if early assessments prove correct. While the US counterpart's air-launched version, which was last known as the MRASM project, has been dropped, the Soviet Union is thought to have the AS-X-15 air-launched version of its cruise missile.

(The US developed, albeit under a joint programme in parallel with Tomahawk, a separate air-launched cruise missile (ALCM), and has plans for a new successor under study as the Advanced Cruise Missile.)

In addition to the Soviet answer to the Tomahawk the authorities are continuing development of a larger class of cruise missiles which are possibly 60 or 70 per cent longer (up to 13 metres or so), and these are expected by the US DoD to carry nuclear payloads initially. Any decision to deploy them with conventional payloads is likely to rest on the reliability and accuracy they can achieve, since their ability to successfully engage small, hard targets relies heavily on this aspect. As yet no designation has been assigned to the newest 'large' cruise missile (although the code BL-10 has appeared in this connection), and no reliable indications of its appearance have emerged.

While on the topic of cruise missiles, this class of weapons does seem in danger of being viewed in some quarters as the missile that is 'all things to all men'. To some extent this ubiquitous mantle is no doubt due (justifiably) to the fact that cruise missiles have been demonstrated to be capable of launch from land, sea (surface ships or submarines) and aircraft. It must be acknowledged that this gives them considerable operational flexibility from the tactical point of view, and also offers the prospect of economies in production and procurement by allowing a degree of commonality between vehicles for more than one arm of a nation's armed forces. Such considerations can be relied upon to strike a sympathetic chord with both politicians and the military. Another aspect of cruise missiles as they now exist which furthers this image of universality is their ready ability to accommodate a varied range of payloads and alternative terminal guidance systems which suits the weapon for engagement of a variety of target types.

It is possibly the very versatility of cruise missiles that confuses public opinion and some professionals who are concerned with their use. At Greenham Common for instance, where USAF GLCMs are now based, the type is defined as a US nuclear strategic weapon in the minds of 'cruise-watchers' encamped there. But how, we wonder, do the Soviet military see their own new counterpart to Tomahawk, and how do they propose to deploy and use it? We doubt if they seriously contemplate dispatching two or three SSC-X-4s to 'take out' Brussels and London as an essential preliminary to the commencement of World War III – at least not while there are SS-20s, SS-22s and SS-23s on hand which could do the job in a matter of minutes where cruise missiles might take hours! No, the Soviet cruise missile in the ground-launch role is probably not regarded as of enormous strategic significance, but rather as one more means of bringing the power of the USSR's theatre forces to bear. In other words, the SSC-X-4 will be a useful and flexible shot to have in the Red Army's locker. It will also be another problem for the enemy to think about.

'Second guessing' the Soviet military mind is frequently an unrewarding game that under some circumstances can have dangerous consequences, and while there is no great danger in this instance, and although we may be wrong to aver that the SSC-X-4 has no exceptional strategic significance for the Soviet Army, such a proposition does no violence to the argument that in relation to other nuclear rocket weapons in the Army inventory the likely SSC-X-4 contribution is modest so far. An important unknown factor in this context is the accuracy and reliability that will be achieved by operational SSC-4s, and it may prove possible to deduce something of this from the numbers that eventually appear in the field. If the SSC-X-4 disappoints in this respect, US numbers can be expected to remain modest, and/or the rate of issue of missiles to units will be unhurried.

However, if the numbers do progress along similar lines to those of the SS-20, this could indicate that the Soviet Union is planning a similar role for cruise missiles as that originally stated for the US Tomahawk in the land battle context. This was an effective way of compensating for NATO's inferiority in tactical combat aircraft, and in the foreword to the 1978 edition we quoted the US intention that "the GLCM would be used for deep interdiction missions normally assigned to fighter/attack aircraft . . ." This, of course did not exclude the other possible applications of cruise missiles touched on above, and the option of using nuclear-tipped cruise missiles in a 'theatre nuclear role'

clearly had not been overlooked as subsequent Tomahawk evolution has demonstrated.

But to invest cruise missiles with too extravagant a potential, without giving due weight to limiting features, could give a false impression of their military worth under varying circumstances. Therefore, before moving on to other topics, it is worth spelling out some of the effects that arise from militarily the most significant time differential between the cruise and ballistic missile classes when considering the launch-to-target interval. The former category of weapons need much longer to reach the target area, and therefore spend much longer exposed to the defender's anti-aircraft weapons, and in the strategic context allow the defender much more time to decide on retaliatory action in response to an attack. Also, cruise missiles spend the whole of their flight time within the Earth's atmosphere, where they are consequently more accessible to defensive systems (guns, SAMs and aircraft) than are ballistic missiles that follow a trajectory which takes them above the atmosphere. The latter also travel much faster, which in itself makes the ballistic missile a more difficult target for the defender's weapons. Cruise missiles approach their targets at airliner speeds and along a more or less horizontal flight path, whereas a ballistic missile is apt to arrive from overhead with little or no warning!

Thus it was not with any great surprise that we heard as this edition was nearing completion that the US Navy (from which the Tomahawk gained considerable support in its early days, as well as when it became a joint USAF/USN system later on) is planning to deploy nuclear payload Tomahawks in a total of about 140 surface ships and submarines over the next few years. Nuclear-tipped Tomahawk submarine-launched cruise missiles (SLCMs) have already been reported aboard some submarines of the 'Los Angeles' and 'Sturgeon' clases. US sources expect most of these to be used in the land-attack role, but in addition there will be a further procurement of Navy Tomahawks with conventional warheads, of the same type as those now fitted in the recommissioned battleship *New Jersey*.

Arms control

Such moves are viewed by some US Senators as "sounding the death knell of arms control", and likely to "cause the Russians to accelerate their own (SS-NX-21 cruise missile) deployments". The Senators' mid-summer assessment could well be accurate, but it may also prove to have been overtaken by events and Soviet steps along this path could have started already. Cruise missiles are but one of a number of problems piling up to await the return of negotiators to the SALT table when and if, as everyone is assumed to hope, they can bring themselves to make this step.

Nevertheless, cruise missiles do highlight an arms limitation/reduction problem that has more than once hindered progress towards a lessening of tensions over other categories of strategic weapons, that is the question of verification. There are no obvious external differences between conventional and nuclear-armed cruise missiles, and while there are still difficulties relating to verification of ICBMs by indirect means such as reconnaissance satellites, at least a modus operandi acceptable to the US and USSR has been worked out. But it is feared that the cruise missile case will call for 'on-site inspection' to satisfy verification requirements, which the US says the Soviet side will baulk at. In any case, disclosure of information about any aspect of Soviet military capabilities is deprecated, and charges that the Soviet Union is violating the spirit, if not the letter, of the existing 'law' on verification by encrypting telemetry data transmissions of its own missile tests, interfering with US reconnaissance/surveillance satellite operations, etc, have been voiced in Washington.

Both sides have indulged in a certain amount of posturing over the mooted talks to lead to a ban on space weapons, in each case their attitude is related to the possible advantage each side hopes to gain from the negotiations and any treaty that might result. Would that it were so simple. We suspect that in addition, the parties each have in mind a long list of other desiderata attached to the proposed talks, including opportunities that could be created for pressures on powers such as Britain, the People's Republic of China and France, on the strategic sidelines; worldwide propaganda of the universal 'cry for peace' variety; any openings for favourable quid pro quo 'trade-offs' at all levels; plus the golden opportunities for horse trading during the exchanges of technical and often sensitive information that are inseparable from negotiations on such subjects. In such an environment it must be easy to lose sight of the ultimate objective, submerged as

it is in mutual suspicion and smothered in rafts of secondary considerations that are often in danger of assuming overriding significance to one side or the other. Already it seems as if just such an issue is turning out to be a major stumbling block in the way of even starting: the Soviet Union wishes to restrain any technical and operational advantages that may come out of President Reagan's wider-ranging 'space-based defence' research and development programme, while the US is thought to be principally interested in getting strategic arms limitations talks going again.

Inevitably, there is confusion in many minds where to draw the line between anti-satellite (ASAT), ballistic missile defence (BMD), and space-based defence as the US calls it, or weapons in space in Soviet terminology, or the popular 'space wars' used by the public to embrace these matters – and a lot of other things in between such as lasers and other directed energy weapons, killer satellites and ABMs. Space is too limited to undertake a detailed discussion here, but the first two types of system can be distinguished almost by definition: an anti-satellite weapon has as its target an orbiting body (ie a satellite) which may or may not be a weapon itself – it is more probably a reconnaissance or surveillance satellite; whereas the destruction of ballistic missiles is the objective of a BMD system. Because of the prohibition of nuclear explosions in space (and ergo tests of weapon systems that rely on them), alternative methods of disabling satellites, in addition to conventional explosives, are being sought such as lasers and other directed energy weapons. Although these are as yet too poorly defined (and too closely guarded secrets) to make possible any adequate entries in this volume, it is no secret that both the US and the USSR are eagerly pursuing their respective research programmes with this aim foremost. This class of weapon is also attractive for the BMD application, and if suitable lasers can be perfected it is theoretically possible to deploy them in space or on the surface for use against spacecraft. The idea of a loitering satellite equipped with a laser weapon awaiting either a hostile satellite or an incoming enemy ballistic missile clearly justifies the popular tag of 'space wars'. Banning these would satisfy the Soviets if ever the space talks get under way, while allowing their land-based directed energy weapons research to continue.

Soviet efforts in this direction are believed to date back to the mid-1960s, with large long-term commitments to the development of laser weapons as well as other directed energy weapon systems. According to official US assessments the high energy laser programme is being conducted at many closely guarded facilities costing much more than their US counterparts to run. It is claimed they have developed a rocket-driven magnetohydrodynamic generator able to produce 15 megawatts of electric power for short periods, that could be used as a compact lightweight power source for mobile or transportable laser weapons. The US source says there is no western counterpart. Other areas under development in the USSR are high-power microwave sources for weapon applications, and research into charged particle beams. Most of this work is not expected to reach fruition before the 1990s. The US directed energy programme combines efforts by the three armed services and the Defence Advanced Research Projects Agency (DARPA) to develop all three areas (laser weapons, particle beams and high-power microwave technology) for a variety of applications, if possible. One of the most important aspects is the strategic laser system technology project, which is concentrated on both laser and particle beam research to provide a foundation for both space- and ground-based weapons. These weapons might perform a number of tasks such as anti-satellite missions or ballistic missile defence.

France

At the time of the first edition of *Jane's Weapon Systems*, France was indicating its way of thinking strategically, and the first benchmarks of what has proved to be a notably consistent nuclear policy were being set out. As in the UK, submarine-launched ballistic missiles (SLBMs) had an important place in the French plan. Britain's deterrent was then completing the transfer from the RAF V-bombers to the UK Polaris submarine fleet, while the first of the new French SNLE class of nuclear submarines was engaged on trials and in 1969 firing trials of the French-developed MSBS SLBM had started. Back on land the French were also delivering prototypes of the SSBS land-based ICBM to the country's armed forces, this programme having been formally initiated as long ago as 1959. After the US pattern, France went on to create its own 'deterrent Triad', with an airborne nuclear 'force de

frappe' also. In essence, this policy has been steadfastly pursued over the ensuing years, so that the current edition contains details of what is now stated by another source* to be "the world's third largest nuclear power (with) arsenal of about 50 launchers for short-range tactical missiles, 18 silo-based IRBMs, a little more than 100 nuclear-designated aircraft and five nuclear-powered submarines with, altogether, 80 ballistic missiles". The last of these (SLBMs) are about to reach operational status with the latest, M4, version carrying an MRV payload.

The US began the period with a 'deterrent Triad' (it was not called that at the time) consisting of Minuteman and Titan ICBMs on land, B-52 bombers carrying Hound Dog and short range attack missiles (SRAM) stand-off weapons, and submarines armed with Polaris A-2 and A-3 SLMBs that were soon to be joined by Poseidon SLBMs. Of these weapons, Minuteman II and III remained in service throughout (and do so still), Polaris has been retired (although it sails on under the White Ensign until Britain gets Trident II in the 1990s), Poseidon is about to be replaced by Trident I, Hound Dog is no more and SRAM is to be joined in its last few years by the air-launched cruise missile (ALCM). New strategic systems deployed by the Soviet Union in this period included the SS-9, SS-13, SS-16, SS-17, SS-18, SS-19 and SS-20 land-based ballistic missiles, and SS-N-6, SS-N-8, SS-N-17, SS-N-18 and SS-N-20 SLBMs. The only new weapon in this category to be initiated and brought to the hardware stage by the USA is the Peacekeeper ICBM. Regular readers of *Jane's Weapon Systems* will hardly need reminding that the path of this programme has been far from untroubled, and there may yet be difficulties to overcome.

Peacekeeper

Peacekeeper's performance relative to the Soviet threat has not been re-evaluated since the original specifications were drawn up in 1979 according to a report to the US Secretary of Defense from the General Accounting Office (GAO), although officials stated that a revalidated threat assessment would be available by the time this appears. Peacekeeper performance will be evaluated against this threat, but as things now stand the GAO thinks that when it first becomes operational (December 1986) it will have to go into service with important components that have not been flight tested.

The range may also be less than was hoped because of a change in the payload to be carried (Mk 21 RV). Compensation for some of the shortfall in range is expected from the use of more northerly basing (Nebraska and Wyoming instead of Utah and Nevada as formerly planned).

It is not our aim to criticise the engineers, technicians, or even the authorities directly concerned with the programme, but rather to draw attention to some of the difficulties imposed by the system within which these people have to operate. For it is here that much of the responsibility lies for the delays that led to the lack of flight testing and also the inability to get on with accommodating the changes to the system that were felt to be necessary at various times during the chequered MX development history.

Before attempting to summarise this story, it may help us to sketch in the background to MX and the perceived need for this system. During the era in which MX, as the Advanced ICBM, had its genesis, the US authorities were speaking of a 'window of vulnerability', ie the perceived Soviet ability to launch an ICBM attack against US ICBM silos without warning, knocking out an unacceptable proportion of the US land-based strategic weapons. This 'window' arose as a result of the steady Soviet development and deployment of new generations of ICBMs with increased throwweight and better accuracy, whereas the US could already see the approaching obsolescence of its Titan II and Minuteman ICBMs.

In *Jane's Weapon Systems 1974-75* we wrote, inter alia, of the MX programme at that time, " . . . it seems likely that the following considerations will influence the final specification (of the MX Advanced ICBM).

1. SALT agreements so far do not cover air-launched nuclear weapons: the final version of MX is therefore likely to be suitable for air-launching . . . . .

2. Although SALT is taken by the US authorities to restrict deployment of land-mobile strategic missiles there is currently no objection to their development. Since mobile missiles have the advantage of presenting a potential enemy with additional targeting problems it is likely that the possibility of a mobile arrangement will be borne in mind when the MX is finally specified . . . .

3. A payload significantly larger than that of Minuteman II is regarded as important by the US authorities. Since SALT prohibits the creation of new silos for larger missiles it is almost certain that the MX will be developed to make use of the existing Minuteman silos. One way of doing this is to use a cold-launch technique – one in which the missile is ejected from the silo by cold gasses and first stage ignition does not occur until after the missile is clear of the silo". (Subsequent events can be seen here casting their shadows before them!)

The official objectives laid down for the MX programme in 1974 were as follows:

1. Selection of the preferred basing and deployment arrangements.

2. The guidance requirements for mobile missiles (air and ground launched modes).

3. Increased rocket motor efficiency.

In October 1974 what was called the Air Mobile Feasibility Demonstration programme was brought to a conclusion with the hauling of a Minuteman I ICBM from the rear door of a C-5 Galaxy strategic freighter aircraft by means of drogue parachutes, after which the missile hung for some seconds vertically until stabilised before being fired. As regular users of *Jane's Weapon Systems* will recall, in the wake of this demonstration alternative proposals for MX basing techniques followed in bewildering profusion.

Just how wide ranging (and sometimes wild) were some of these proposals was commented on in the foreword to the 1979-80 edition – they then included draping MX missiles in pairs on the hulls of conventional submarines cruising around US coastal waters; the 'multiple protective shelter' or 'shell game' land-based mobile mode and its several variants; the various protected (both hard and soft) basing solutions and taking in all sorts of suggestions that involved trenches; and machines that would bore their way from underneath mountains, before setting out to create another pile of rubble in the USSR. The air-mobile basing mode was still not forgotten, and there were plans to play the MX 'shell game' with the MX missile taking to the air at times of threat to alight at one of several thousand dispersal sites throughout the USA, there to either be launched or hide until it was time to take to the air again.

From all of this it will be fairly clear that the basing programme was in grave danger of becoming a bigger programme than the MX missile itself. But in truth this was only as it should have been, if it is recognised that the whole question was the matter of the vulnerability of the land-based leg of the US strategic 'Triad' (ie the land-based ICBMs, the other two legs being the B-52 strategic bomber force and the Polaris/Poseidon SLBM submarine fleet), and it had been stated quite clearly by Lt General Slay, USAF Deputy Chief of Staff, Research and Development, when he said, "The MX programme has as its prime objectives the preservation of the land-based elements of the American Triad concept of deterrence, and the provision of capabilities which might be needed in the future to meet an increased nuclear challenge from the USSR".

The General went on to summarise the way the MX programme was seen officially at that time, and this was quoted in the foreword to the eighth edition of *Jane's Weapon Systems*, as follows: "The main thrust of this programme is the development of an *advanced ICBM* capable of being *based* either in existing silos (our italics, Ed) or an alternative survivable basing mode. This calls for features necessary to ensure compatibility between modes of deployment to be included in the design from the outset. The alternative basing modes under consideration consist of several ground-based methods and the air mobility concept. The ground-based modes would achieve survivability through proliferation of hardened, multiple aim points, while air mobility would achieve the same end through similar means to those already employed by the bomber force, eg ground/airborne alert. The missile itself is seen as a large throwweight, MIRVed weapon having significant gains in performance over current ICBMs in such respects as accuracy, rapid response, reliability, and targeting flexibility. Among the optional basing modes considered for the MX were unprotected sites off roads, and on roads, railways, or waterways, and subterranean ones such as solid or rock tunnels. The hard aiming point options included: railway revetments, in canals or pools, covered trenches, various types of shelter, and buried trenches."

It might be argued that things could have been improved if it had not been for the SALT restrictions on the construction of new

---

The lowdown on the lowdown

Sea skimmers like Exocet come in low and fast.

They're small radar targets - often 0.1 m² or less. They hide in sea clutter. And they're usually accompanied by jamming, chaff or both.

Marconi's combat-proven experience in point defence systems provides the answer. Marconi's new ST1802 is a second generation tracker radar derived from the highly successful 800 series in service with the Royal Navy and other navies worldwide.

The ST1802 combines full random frequency agility with the most advanced techniques of moving target indication. ST1802 will supplement the ship's main surveillance sensor at low level, providing initial sub-clutter detection before automatically entering the tracking mode.

Control is instantly transferred to a co-mounted infrared/TV and laser system if any distortion is experienced when tracking low-level targets.

Marconi ST1802 tracker radar. Proven peformance. State-of-the-art technology. Frequency agility with digital MTI. Infrared/TV and laser support. For any warship down to 75 tonnes displacement.

Please ask for details from Marconi Radar Systems Limited, Writtle Road, Chelmsford CM1 3BN, England. Telephone: 0245 267111. Telex: 99108.

Marconi
Radar Systems

A WHOLE NEW GENERATION OF THINKING.

silos; this would have permitted the US to embark on a programme specifically to harden existing silos to provide increased survivability for Minuteman ICBMs. As things turned out, both survivability and renewal of the land-based ICBM force were attempted as a single programme. This offered endless scope for politicians of succeeding Administrations and assorted pressure groups to challenge whatever aspect of the overall programme that took their fancy, with the inevitable result that what has been achieved has probably cost more and taken longer to attain.

Achievements

We have studied in some detail a period of a decade and a half during which there have been instances of outstanding achievement – some of them representing a rapid transition from inception to operational deployment. In some cases minimal RDT&E times were realised, but these examples also demanded prompt and efficient management procedures for the successful attainment of their declared objective(s). Designers, engineers and technicians (whatever their intrinsic attributes and limitations) can only progress as fast as their management structure will permit – and not a great deal faster than the management's ability to understand and keep pace with achievements! Sadly, it sometimes appears that those responsible for establishing management objectives and laying down the processes for their attainment are not always aware of the close relationship between cause and effect as applied to the modification of management aims and requirements and the achievement of those objectives.

Thus, while the Soviet Union fields and later discards for newer replacements an impressive succession of weapons, the West makes do with severely aged equipment (sometimes with happy results, at other times disastrously), or makes false starts on new weapons that prove to be either ideas ahead of their time or beyond their sponsors' pockets, only to end up with nothing but a list of cancellations and a pile of bills.

The Soviet Union, to some Western eyes, appears to be able to move faster when it comes to developing and introducing new weapons and there can be little doubt that the form of government established within the Soviet bloc is more favourable to military development and procurement. Doubtless there must be more than a modicum of 'copy-cat' poaching of Western ideas and technology by the Warsaw Pact countries, and examples of parallel procurement patterns by East and West can be found quite readily. This is generally seen in the West as one of the undesirable examples of 'technology transfer'. The expression is usually well understood, but the nature of 'technology' is often less fully defined. A dictionary definition gives "the science of the mechanical and industrial arts" but this hardly goes far enough for our purposes. In the context of the design, development and manufacture of military hardware, the expression 'technology' is used to embrace almost everything from original scientific discovery (eg new principles etc), innovation by application of known principles, or refinement of existing techniques and methods, to the development of new ways of working in engineering etc, the enhancement of manufacturing processes and practices to make possible manufacture of a new system or component.

Technology

The one area of technology that has almost certainly contributed most to the advancement of military equipment of practically all kinds is electronics. Engineering techniques in this industry and the advances made in the fundamental science underpinning electronic engineering practice have undergone tremendous changes over the past 15 to 20 years. This progress has made possible numerous new types of weapon as well as providing additional capabilities or improved performance for existing ones. There have been a vast range of developments in electronic technology embracing numerous aspects of this branch of engineering, the most fundamental of these being in the area of semi-conductor devices and the other component advances that sprang from the accelerating rate of progress in solid-state physics than followed the first transistor. In all probability the applications of these advances that have had most impact on defence affairs (to say nothing of most aspects of daily life, one way or another) is the field of digital computers and data processing. With the advent of the 'computer on a chip' as the microprocessor is popularly described, all manner of possibilities were opened up to weapon designers, and increasingly systems are encountered where individual tactical missiles set out on their one-way mission with on-board microprocessors to help them find their way to target, or

to decide which of several targets to attack. This edition has examples of this sort that are designed for anti-ship missions, such as the Sea Eagle and Harpoon; for anti-aircraft roles, like the US Patriot; anti-radar missiles, such as the new UK ALARM; and the international advanced medium range air-to-air missile (AMRAAM) to be produced for NATO use.

The vastly enhanced capabilities for digital data processing that microprocessors and other computers give has yielded a host of embellishments to a wide range of systems and equipment that provide greatly increased performance characteristics thanks to the computer's ability to handle much larger amounts of information more rapidly and accurately. When allied to new electronic components, these new facilities make possible sensor systems that either have better performance than their predecessors or have characteristics which were not possible before. A typical example is the use of electronic scanning of radar beams in lieu of mechanical movement of the antenna reflector to steer the beam. Radar beams steered this way can be positioned at immensely faster rates, and there are additional gains from the electronic sophistication in terms of mechanical simplification, frequently this is also coupled with a cost advantage. The signals transmitted and received by the radar are equally enhanced by the adoption of digital signal processing. In this way both the quantity and quality of the information derived from a radar is enhanced. These new radars are often much more flexible in operation than older designs, as well as being less affected by countermeasures or natural interference.

The digital computer virtually made possible the practical realisation of what had for years been a theoretically feasible dream, over-the-horizon (OTH) radar. Without computers to steer the transmitting and receiving beams, correlate the responses and automatically carry out many other aspects of signal processing, the systems that are now capable of detecting and plotting aircraft targets hundreds of kilometres from the radar installation (which is normally limited to line-of-sight operation) would never have become a regular part of the Soviet and US defence networks.

Electronic warfare (EW) nowadays relies heavily on digital techniques for its efficiency and the past 15 years have seen this topic emerge from the obscurity that officially engulfed it and kept it as a secret 'black art' to evolve as a major sales arena for defence equipment manufacturers. Ten times as many pages are now needed in this book to reflect EW hardware as when this subject was first given a section of its own in *Jane's Weapon Systems*, which illustrates both the sales significance of EW and gives an impression of its expanded technical scope. Comparable progress has been made in other areas of military sensor systems and equipment, due to advances in electronics, component technology, and optical materials and techniques. This too is reflected in recent editions of *Jane's Weapon Systems*, and more than 100 pages are devoted to this subject in the current volume.

Systems, as much as equipment are evolving rapidly and distinct trends can be discerned here too. For instance, since the episode in the South Atlantic in 1982 the pre-existing sentiment among navies that more effective point defence weapon systems might be needed one day, has now been translated into orders from a few of them and new system projects and products from a number of manufacturers. Some of these new systems were already on the drawing board admittedly, but there is little doubt that the loss of several RN ships in the Falklands campaign gave designers and sales teams alike a prod. This is demonstrated in the pages that follow where newcomers to this naval weapons sector like the French SATAN project and the Soviet SA-N-7 and SA-N-8; development programmes such as the Spanish Meroka, US/Danish/German RAM and Israeli Barak; and fittings of recent systems like Goalkeeper and Phalanx (both ordered for the RN), Seaguard ordered by a NATO navy and under consideration by others, and Sea Chaparral are recorded together with existing weapons that are in service and still being fitted. An increasing number of systems in this category are either adopting the vertical launch technique from the outset or as a modification to enable fitting and/or operational characteristics to be improved. A good example is the Barak which in the version now being developed has VLS in place of the original combined six-round launcher and radar module that was used for sea trials.

Air-to-ground weapons are the subject of some ingenuity and energetic development, with air forces anxious to maximise the effectiveness of their aircraft and equipment while preserving them from the defenders' attention as far as possible by the use of sophisticated weapon delivery techniques. Many of the latest

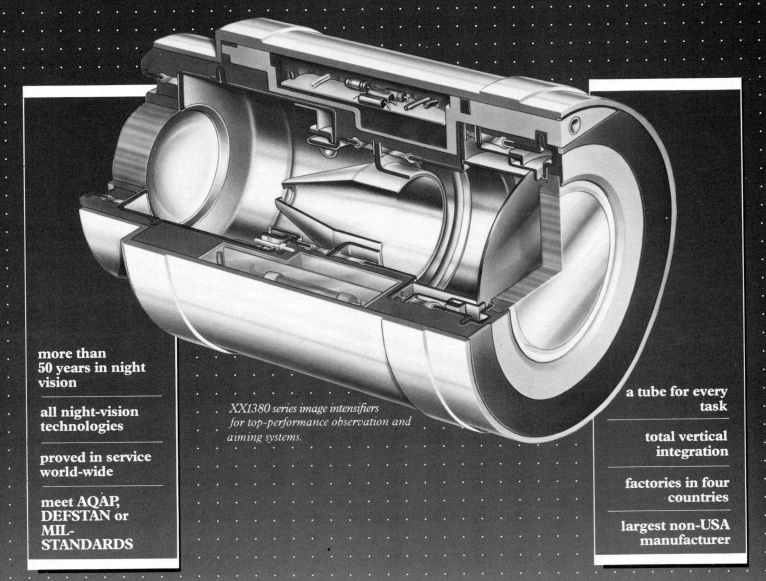

more than
50 years in night
vision

all night-vision
technologies

proved in service
world-wide

meet AQAP,
DEFSTAN or
MIL-
STANDARDS

*XX1380 series image intensifiers
for top-performance observation and
aiming systems.*

a tube for every
task

total vertical
integration

factories in four
countries

largest non-USA
manufacturer

Eight powerful reasons for specifying Philips

But, there's another – yet more powerful!
Taken together they offer you security –
in supply, in quality, in reliability – in
staying ahead!

We are first in night-vision components
because we invest – in R&D, in
technologies, in processes and in the
quality assurance procedures to support
them. We've invested for many years and
we'll keep on investing. By staying ahead
we keep you ahead. Combined forces in
night-vision technologies!

**FIRST IN NIGHT-
VISION COMPONENTS**

*Philips Electronic Components and
Materials Division,
5600 MD Eindhoven, The Netherlands.
Telex: 35000 phtc nl/nl je veo*

Electronic
components
and materials

PHILIPS

programmes in this sector are for tactical applications like airfield attack or counter-armour operations, and here European activities are well represented with such systems as the Franco-German Apache/CWS programme, Pegase and the sophisticated Vebal/Syndrom experimental project by MBB, the last of these incidentally employing a microprocessor and advanced sensors to achieve optimum results against ground armour. Laser-guided bombs (LGBs) are still being improved and the latest of the Paveway series of US LGBs appeared during 1984. A powered version of the GBU-15 glide bomb which will have about three times the stand-off range as the un-powered model is being developed in the US as the AGM-130.

As noted previously, the US MRASM programme has been dropped within the last year, but a requirement remains for what was planned for the former development of the Tomahawk cruise missile. The duties that were planned for MRASM are now to be fulfilled by the Joint Tactical Missile System (JTACMS), a project that envisages the same (or similar) missiles being used for surface and air launching as the weapon in a system that will be able to locate, track and attack fixed and moving targets deep behind enemy lines. The missile will deliver a variety of munitions, including terminally dispensed submunitions and anti-tank submunitions. JTACMS will operate with another recently defined system, the Joint Surveillance and Target Attack Radar System (JSTARS), which is an outgrowth of the earlier Pave Mover radar programme. Associated will be the Joint Tactical Fusion system, an automated system that will process, analyse and distribute intelligence reports from multiple sources for US Army and Air Force purposes. The new missile system combines the former US Army Corps Support Weapon and the USAF Conventional Stand-off Weapon (for which MRASM was proposed).

Enemy armoured formations are prime targets for this weapon, but there are other recent systems that have the same objective although the approach is quite different in most cases. For example, the first representatives of what promises to be a new and popular class of anti-tank weapons are now making their appearance. The USA has its Guided Anti-armour Mortar Projectile (GAMP) programme, while other mortar fired anti-tank systems have been designed by Sweden (Strix) and the UK (Merlin). Also new from the UK is the Lawmine, an automatic unmanned system that is deployed and left to await the approach of armoured targets which are automatically engaged with a LAW anti-tank round when they reach the optimum distance for an attack. Other US anti-armour efforts are the SADARM (Sense and Destroy ARMour) and Tank Breaker systems, while Sweden has another recent introduction to this class with the Bill anti-tank missile. The latter is designed to attack the softer top armour of its target, and this illustrates an operational requirement that is increasingly being specified in the latest anti-armour weapons. A novel modification has been devised by Israeli engineers for the well-known Hughes TOW anti-tank missile, which effectively falsifies the weapon's name by substituting a laser beam-riding guidance system for the original wire guidance that formed part of the tube-launched optically guided weapon's acronymic title. The change is claimed to give an increase in range and a new warhead has also been developed in Israel.

Changes

Readers will be pleased to note that once more Michael Badrocke has contributed a set of line drawings of the individual weapon types described in the first part of this volume, these being located at the beginning of the appropriate sections. New entries this year amount to more than 250 which is typical of the annual growth rate needed to keep pace with defence developments. Among these additions a significant number will be found that relate to emerging defence equipment manufacturing capabilities, sometimes from an unexpected quarter. Signs that the People's Republic of China is serious about its wish to enlarge the scope of commerce and co-operation with other nations include participation at various international exhibitions. Just in time for inclusion in this edition details were received of radars and other military equipment available for export from China. Elsewhere in these pages are reminders that more countries are already building up

their own capabilities in a similar fashion, and new national headings that have had to be added in recent years now include: Brazil, Chile, Greece, South Korea, Yugoslavia etc. It should also be noted that in some of these and in other countries which are not among those generally regarded as 'arms suppliers' there are notable instances of innovative projects, such as the Israeli modified TOW missile mentioned above, or the novel Meroka air defence gun system under development in Spain.

Within the last year we welcome to the appearance of our weekly companion journal, *Jane's Defence Weekly*, which provides an outlet for items of news which otherwise might have had to await the next foreword to one of the Jane's Yearbooks. This new journal also provides a platform for comment and discussion which is far more immediately and widely available than an annual summary can ever be. We hope this will prove to be a beneficial arrangement to all concerned and look forward to many years of fruitful co-operation with our new colleagues on 'the weekly' – many of whom are old friends who have joined us from elsewhere in the defence publishing field.

Acknowledgements
The 'punch-drunk' feeling at the end of 12 months' effort in preparing a new edition of a Jane's Yearbook is an amalgem of elation and exhaustion. The exact mixture is never too clear. It depends on the year and on the individual, but it is then that weariness makes concentration most difficult. This is a pity, because it is when the show is all over bar the shouting that the Editor's most satisfying task arises, remembering to thank all the many individuals who have made a contribution to this volume. In advance, the Editor begs the forebearance of anyone unwittingly slighted by any regrettable literary lacunae that may arise as a result of the euphoria of having completed another edition without provoking a visit from 'the men in white coats'.

More seriously, as we have mentioned on previous occasions, there are some of our valued correspondents who would prefer not to have their assistance to Jane's and its readers publicly acknowledged. To those whose names do not appear for this reason or because of lapses of the kind alluded to in the previous paragraph, our grateful thanks are offered. To all we add a heart-felt plea for your continued aid.

As might be expected from a product of the size of *Jane's Weapon Systems*, the total number of people who make a personal contribution or who have a direct role to play in its production in some way is enormous. Their affiliations too are correspondingly numerous and in the interests of brevity we will not attempt to record them all in the list of individuals whose assistance this year has proved of profound value.

Particular recognition is due to Bernard Blake, and Roger Villar, who compiled the Radar, Electro-optical and EW sections, and Naval Guns and Naval Armament tables of this book, respectively; Terry Gander for Inventory tables; fellow Editors of companion Yearbooks, Bob Raggett, John Taylor, Christopher F Foss, David Rider, John Moore (RN), and Ken Munson, all of whom are always ready to respond to calls for information or advice; Anne McKrill and Arthur Browne in the USA; and Thomas deFrank who has been our Washington correspondent for many years. Particularly appreciated are the letters and photographs from our numerous unofficial correspondents, among them Harrison Chen, Osame Ooe, Stefan Terzibaschitsch, Juan Taibo, Ronaldo Olive, Kensuke Ebata, Dr L J Lamb, Wilhelm Donko, Steven Zaloga, Col James Loop, G J Jacobs, all of whom deserve special mention, and thanks to all friends in the defence industry, media, embassies and armed services for their individual contributions and assistance. Our grateful thanks are also due to the Jane's production team under Production Director Kenneth Harris, and led by Christine Richards: Pat Taylor, Elizabeth Lye and Mark Alderson. Finally, sincere thanks for past support and farewell wishes have to be extended to Editorial Director Valerie Passmore who has departed for fresh challenges elsewhere.

R T Pretty   August 1984

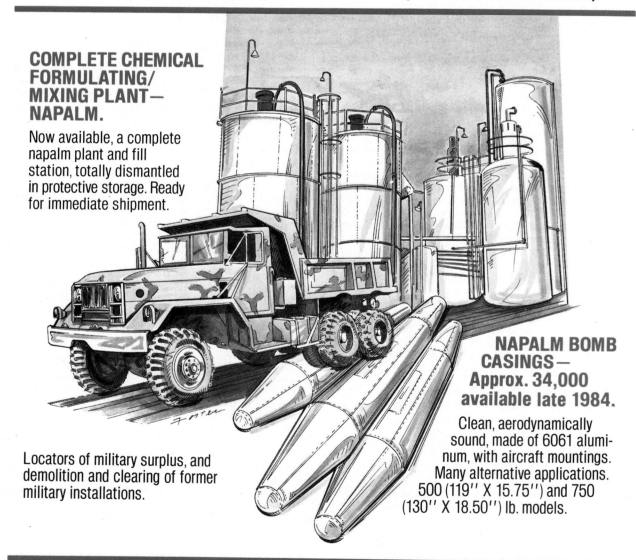

Selected glossary of acronyms and abbreviations

AA	anti-aircraft	BADGE	base air defence ground equipment
AAA	anti-aircraft artillery	BATES	battlefield artillery target engagement system
AAAW	advanced airborne anti-armour weapon	BCC	battery control centre
AAH	advanced attack helicopter	BCP	battery control post
AAM	air-to-air missile	BETA	battlefield exploitation and target acquisition
AB	assault breaker	BITE	built-in test equipment
ABM	anti-ballistic missile	BMD	ballistic missile defence
ABRES	advanced ballistic re-entry system	BMEWS	ballistic missile early warning system
ABRV	advanced ballistic re-entry vehicle	BUIC	back-up intercept control (for air defence)
ACCS	air command and control system	BVR	beyond visual range
ACE	Allied Command Europe	C³	command, control and communications
ACM	anti-armour cluster munitions, or advanced cruise missile	C³I	command, control, communications and intelligence
ACMI	air combat manoeuvring instrumentation	CAD	computer aided design
ACV	armoured cannon vehicle	CADMAT	computer aided design, manufacture and test
ADCAP	advanced capabilities	CANE	computer aided navigation equipment
ADDS	Army data distribution system	CAS	close air support
ADM	atomic demolition munitions	CASS	command active sonobuoy system
ADP	automatic data processing	CASTOR	corps airborne stand-off radar
ADPG	Air Defence Planning Group	CBU	cluster bomb unit
ADS	automatic defence system	CBW	chemical and biological warfare
AE	assault echelon	CCIS	command and control information system
AECB	Arms Export Control Board	CCTV	closed-circuit television system
AEGIS	AEW/ground environment integration system	CD	civil defence
AEW	airborne early warning	CEP	circular error, probable
AEW&C	airborne early warning and control	CFAR	constant false alarm rate
AF	audio frequency	CFV	cavalry fighting vehicle
AFAP	artillery-fired atomic projectile	CIA	Central Intelligence Agency
AFATDS	advanced field artillery tactical data system	CINCEUR	Commander-in-chief, European Command
AFB	air force base	CINCLANT	Commander-in-chief, Atlantic
AFC	automatic frequency control	CINCPAC	Commander-in-chief, Pacific Command
AFSARC	Air Force Systems Acquisition Review Council	CINCSAC	Commander-in-chief, Strategic Air Command
AFSATCOM	Air Force satellite communications system	CIR	continuous infra-red
AFV	armoured fighting vehicle	CIS	combat identification system
AGC	automatic gain control	CIWS	close-in weapon system
AGM	air-to-ground missile	CLOS	command to line-of-sight
AIAAM	advanced intercept air-to-air missile	COMINT	communications intelligence
AIM	air intercept missile	COMSEC	communications security
ALARM	air-launched anti-radiation missile	CONUS	continental United States
ALCC	airborne launch control centre	CRAF	Civil Reserve Air Fleet
ALCM	air-launched cruise missile	CRP	control and reporting posts
ALCS	airborne launch control system	CRT	cathode ray tube
ALOC	air line of communication	CSDT	control for submarine discharge torpedo
ALWT	advanced lightweight torpedo	CSEDS	combat systems engineering development site
AM	amplitude modulation	CSLT	control for surface launched torpedoes
AMCM	advanced mine countermeasures	CSMS	corps support missile system
AMRAAM	advanced medium-range air-to-air missile	CSOC	consolidated space operations centre
ANG	Air National Guard	CSW	conventional stand-off weapon
APC	armoured personnel carrier	CTBT	comprehensive test ban treaty
ARINC	Aeronautical Radio Incorporated	CV	aircraft carrier (USN)
ARM	anti-radiation missile	CVN	aircraft carrier, nuclear-powered (USN)
ARP	anti-radiation projectile	CVV	aircraft carrier, medium-sized (USN)
ARRADCOM	Army Armament Research and Development Command (USA)	CW	chemical warfare, or continuous wave
		CWS	container weapon system
ARS	automatic reporting system	CWW	cruciform wing weapon
ARSR	air route surveillance radar		
ASAT	anti-satellite (weapon or system)	DAR	Defence Acquisition Regulation
ASCM	anti-ship cruise missile	DARPA	Defence Advanced Research Projects Agency
ASM	air-to-surface missile	DCS	defence communications system
ASPJ	airborne self-protection jammer	DCU	detection and control unit
ASR	airport surveillance radar or air staff requirement	DDG	guided missile destroyer (USN)
ASRAAM	advanced short-range air-to-air missile	DEW	distant early warning
ASROC	anti-submarine rocket	DHS	data handling system
ASTAR	airborne search target attack radar	DIA	Defense Intelligence Agency (USA)
ASUW	anti-surface ship warfare	DICASS	directional command active sonobuoy system
ASW	anti-submarine warfare	DIFAR	directional frequency and ranging (sonobuoy)
ASW/SOW	anti-submarine warfare/stand-off weapon	DIVAD	Division Air Defence
ATA	advanced test accelerator	DLA	Defence Logistics Agency
ATAFCS	airborne target acquisition and fire control system	DLOS	disturbed line-of-sight
ATB	advanced technology bomber	DME	distance measuring equipment
ATC	air traffic control	DMSP	defence meteorological satellite programme
ATE	automatic test equipment	DMT	deep mobile target
ATF	advanced tactical fighter	DMTI	digital moving target indicator
ATGM	anti-tank guided missile	DMZ	demilitarised zone
ATGW	anti-tank guided weapon	DNA	Defence Nuclear Agency
AUTODIN	automatic digital network	DoD	Department of Defense (USA)
AWACS	airborne warning and control system	DOT	designating optical tracker

ARMBRUST.
The Short-Range Anti-Tank and Self-Defense Weapon.

ARMBRUST is a light, ballistic, expendable weapon. It has a combat range of up to 300 m (547 yd) with the AT projectile. Its shaped charge penetrates heavy armor.

ARMBRUST's unique features:
- Smokeless firing
- No flash or blast
- Lower report than a pistol shot
- Firing from small enclosed rooms without endangering or discomforting the gunner
- Expendable
- Maintenance-free

ARMBRUST equipped with LATAM – Laser Target Marker – also provides night combat capability against tanks and armored vehicles.

**European Defence Products
Rue du Duc 100
B-1150 Bruxelles/Belgique**

DPM	digital plotter map
DRTS	detecting, ranging and tracking system
DSARC	Defence Systems Acquisition Review Council
DSB	Defence Science Board
DSCS	defence satellite communication system
DSMAC	digital scene matching correlation
DSP	Defence Support Programme
DTOC	divisional tactical operations centre
DTU	data transmission unit
ECCM	electronic counter-countermeasures
ECIP	Energy Conservation Investment Programme
ECM	electronic countermeasures
ECR	embedded computer resources
EHF	extremely high frequency
EJS	enhanced JTIDS system
ELF	extremely low frequency
ELINT	electronic intelligence
EMC	electro-magnetic compatability
EMP	electro-magnetic pulse
EPC	electronic plane conversion
ER	enhanced radiation
ER/RB	enhanced radiation/reduced blast
ERAM	extended range anti-tank mine
ERU	ejector release unit
ESM	electronic support measures
EW	electronic warfare
EXJAM	expendable jamming system
FA	Soviet frontal aviation
FAA	Federal Aviation Agency
FACE	field artillery computing equipment
FADAC	field artillery digital automatic computer
FAESHED	fuel-air explosive helicopter delivered
FASCAM	family of scatterable mines
FAST	fuze activating static targets
FBM	fleet ballistic missile
FCS	fire control system
FDC	fire direction centres
FEBA	forward edge of the battle area
FEMA	Federal Emergency Management Agency
FET	field effect transistor
FFG	guided missile frigate (USN)
FFT	fast Fourier transform
FLIR	forward looking infra-red
FMF	Fleet Marine Force
FMS	Foreign Military Sales
FOV	field-of-view
FPB	fast patrol boat
FPR	Federal procurement regulation (US)
FRAS	free-rocket anti-submarine
FROG	Soviet free-rocket-over-ground for tactical use
FRS	Fleet readiness squadron
FSAT	full-scale aerial target
FSD	full-scale development
FTS	flexible turret system
FWE	foreign weapons evaluation
FY	fiscal year
FYDP	five-year defence programme
GAO	General Accounting Office
GBU	glide-bomb unit
GCA	ground controlled approach (radar)
GCI	ground controlled interception (radar)
GDIP	general defence intelligence programme
GDS	gun display system
GEADGE	German air defence ground environment
GEODSS	ground-based electro-optical deep space surveillance
GLCM	ground-launched cruise missile
GLLD	ground laser locator designator
GMF	ground mobile forces
GNP	gross national product
GPS	Global Position System (formerly NAVSTAR)
GWEN	ground wave emergency network
HARM	high-speed anti-radiation missile
HDD	head-down display
HE	high explosive
HEL	high energy laser
HF	high frequency
HHLR	hand-held laser rangefinder
HIPAR	high power acquisition radar
HOE	homing overlay experiment
HPI	high power illuminator
HTKP	hard-target kill probability
HUD	head-up display
HVM	hypervelocity missile
IC	integrated circuit
ICAO	International Civil Aviation Organisation

ICBM	intercontinental ballistic missile
ICC	information co-ordination control
ICWAR	improved continuous wave acquisition radar
IF	intermediate frequency
IFCS	improved (integrated) fire control system
IFF	identification, friend or foe
IFM	instantaneous frequency measurement
IFV	infantry fighting vehicle
IIR	imaging infra-red
IMINT	imagery intelligence
INF	intermediate range nuclear forces
INS	inertial navigation system
IOC	initial operational capability
IONDS	integrated operational nuclear detection system
IOS	integrated observation system
IPD	improved point defence
IR	infra-red
IR&D	independent research and development
IRBM	intermediate range ballistic missile
IRST	infra-red search and track
ITSS	integrated tactical surveillance system
IUS	inertial upper stage
IUSS	integrated undersea surveillance system
JCS	Joint Chiefs of Staff
JINTACS	joint interoperability of tactical command and control systems
Joint STARS	joint surveillance and target attack radar system
JSC	Johnson Space Centre
JSDF	Japanese Self-Defence Force
JSS	joint surveillance system
JSTARS	joint surveillance and target attack radar system
JTACMS	joint tactical missile system
JTFP	joint tactical fusion programme
JTIDS	joint tactical information distribution system
LAAAS	low-altitude airfield attack system
LAMPS	light airborne multi-purpose system
LANTIRN	low-altitude navigation and targeting infra-red night system
LAPADS	lightweight acoustic processing and display system
LARS	light artillery rocket system
LASR	low altitude surveillance radar
LAW	light anti-tank weapon
LCAC	landing craft, air-cushion
LCC	launch control centre
LCP	launch control post
LCWDS	low-cost weapon delivery system
LDS	layered defence system
LED	light emitting diode
LFICS	landing force integrated communications system
LGB	laser-guided bomb
LHA	amphibious assault ship (USN)
LLL	low-level light (television)
LLLGB	low-level laser guided bomb
LLTV	low-light television
LMTR	laser marker and target ranger
LOAD	low altitude defence
LOC	lines of communication
LPD	landing platform, dock (USN)
LPI	low probability of intercept
LRA	Soviet long-range aviation
LRAAS	long-range airborne ASW system
LRF	laser rangefinder
LRINF	longer-range intermediate-range nuclear forces
LRTNF	long-range theatre nuclear forces
LRU	line replaceable unit
LSD	landing ship, dock (USN)
LSI	large scale integration
LTD	laser target designator
LTDP	long-term defence programme
LTDS	laser target designator system
LUA	launch under attack
LWIR	long-wave infra-red
MAC	Military Airlift Command (USAF)
MAD	magnetic anomaly detector or mutually assured destruction
MANPADS	man-portable air defence system
MAP	Military Assistance Programme
MARAD	Maritime Administration
MARS	mobile automatic reporting system
MBAR	multiple beam acquisition radar
MBFR	mutual and balanced force reductions
MBT	main battle tank
MCM	mine countermeasures
MCMV	mine countermeasures vehicle
MEECN	minimum essential emergency communications network

THE TARGET:
THE MEANS:

A COMPLETE NAVAL COMBAT SYSTEM

SURVEILLANCE RADARS ● COMMAND AND CONTROL SYSTEMS FOR SURFACE VESSELS AND SUBMARINES ● RADAR AND OPTRONIC WEAPON CONTROL SYSTEMS ● SURFACE TO AIR MISSILE SYSTEMS ● ELECTRONIC WARFARE SYSTEMS ● ROCKET LAUNCHING SYSTEMS ● TORPEDO LAUNCHING SYSTEMS ● UNDERWATER SYSTEMS

Selenia Adver Dept.

MF	medium frequency
MFR	multi-function radar
MGT	mobile ground terminals
MHSV	multi-purpose high speed vehicle
MiG	Mikoyan aircraft
MILCON	military construction
MIRV	multiple, independently targetable re-entry vehicle
MLRS	multiple-launch rocket system
MMW	millimetre wave radar
MNS	mine neutralisation system
MoD	Ministry of Defence (UK)
MoU	memorandum of understanding
MPA	maritime patrol aircraft
MRASM	medium-range air-to-surface missile
MRBM	medium-range ballistic missile
MRV	multiple re-entry vehicle
MSC	Military Sealift Command
MSI	medium-scale integration
MSO	ocean-going minesweeper
MTBF	mean-time-between-failures
MTCAS	Marine Corps Tactical Command and Control System
MTI	moving target indication
MTMC	Military Traffic Management Command
MTTR	multi-target tracking radar or mean-time-to-repair
MULE	modular universal laser equipment
MX	Missile Experiment or Missile-X (advanced ICBM)
NADGE	NATO air defence ground equipment
NASA	National Aeronautics and Space Administration
NATO	North Atlantic Treaty Organisation
NAVSTAR	navigation satellite timing and ranging
NBC	nuclear, biological and chemical
NCA	National Command Authority(ies)
NDRF	National Defence Reserve Fleet
NEACP	National Emergency Airborne Command Post
NFCS	nuclear forces communications satellite
NFIP	National Foreign Intelligence Programme
NIS	NATO identification system
NMCS	National Military Command System
NNK	non-nuclear kill
NOD	night observation device
NODLR	night observation device, long-range
NORAD	North American Air Defence Command
NPG	Nuclear Planning Group
NSA	National Security Agency (US)
NSC	National Security Council
NSNF	non-strategic nuclear forces
NSR	naval staff requirement (UK)
NSWP	non-Soviet Warsaw Pact
NTC	National Training Centre
NVG	night vision goggles
O&M	operations and maintenance
OASD	Office of the Assistant Secretary of Defence
OCC	operational control centre
OED	operational evaluation demonstration
OFPP	Office of Procurement and Policy
OJCS	Office of the Joint Chiefs of Staff
OM	operations module
OSD	Office of the Secretary of Defence
OTH	over-the-horizon
OTHB	over-the-horizon backscatter
PADS	position and azimuth determining system
PAL	permissive action link
PAR	precision approach radar
PARCS	perimeter acquisition radar characterisation system
PAVE-PAWS	phased-array radars
PB	particle beam
PCU	power control unit
PGM	precision guided munition
PLRS	position location reporting system
PLSS	precision location strike system
PNVS	pilot night vision system
POL	petroleum, oil and lubricants
PPI	plan position indicator
PRF	pulse repetition frequency
PSP	programmable signal processor
PWRS	pre-positioned war reserve stocks
RAM	rolling airframe missile or random access memory
RAP	rocket-assisted projectile
RAPIDS	radar passive identification system
RAWS	remote area weather station
RB/ER	reduced blast/enhanced radiation
RCMAT	radar-controlled miniature aerial target
RD&A	research development and acquisition

RDF	Rapid Deployment Force
RDJTF	Rapid Deployment Joint Task Force
RDSS	rapidly deployable surveillance system
RDT&E	research, development, test and evaluation
REMBASS	remotely-monitored battlefield sensor system
RF	radio frequency
RFS	radio frequency surveillance
RHI	range height indicator
ROCC	region operations control centre
ROR	range only radar
RO/RO	roll on/roll off
ROTHR	relocatable over-the-horizon radar
RPV	remotely piloted vehicle
RRF	ready reserve force
RSLS	receiver side-lobe suppression
RSVP	rotating surveillance vehicle platform
RV	re-entry vehicle
RWR	radar warning receiver
SAC	Strategic Air Command
SACDIN	SAC digital network
SACEUR	Supreme Allied Commander, Europe
SACLANT	Supreme Allied Commander, Atlantic
SACU	stand-alone digital communications unit
SADARM	search and destroy armour munition
SAGE	semi-automatic ground environment (air defence)
SAL	strategic arms limitation
SALT	Strategic Arms Limitation Talks
SAM	surface-to-air missile
SAMSO	Space and Missile Systems Organisation
SAR	synthetic array radar, or search and rescue
SARS	static automatic reporting system
SDS	satellite data system
SGEMP	system-generated EMP
SHAPE	Supreme Headquarters Allied Powers, Europe
SHF	super high frequency
SHORAD	short-range air defence
SIAM	self-initiated anti-aircraft missile
SINCGARS	single channel ground and airborne (communications) system
SLCM	submarine (sea) launched cruise missile
SLEP	service life extension programme
SLMM	sea-launched mobile mine
SLOC	sea line of communication
SM	Standard missile
SNF	short range nuclear force
SNM	special nuclear material
SOSUS	sound surveillance system
SOTAS	stand-off target acquisition system
SP	self propelled
SPADOTS	spare detection and tracking system
SPAT	self-propelled acoustic target
SRAM	short-range attack missile
SSB	conventional-powered ballistic missile submarine or single side-band
SSBN	nuclear-powered ballistic missile submarine
SSKP	single shot kill probability
SSM	nuclear-powered attack submarine
SSR	secondary surveillance radar
SSURADS	shipboard surveillance radar system
START	Strategic Arms Reduction Talks
STC	satellite test centre
STIR	surveillance and target indicating/illuminating radar
STOL	short take-off and landing
STP	systems technology programme
STR	systems technology radar
SUAWACS	Soviet Union airborne warning and control system
SUBROC	submarine launched rocket
SURTASS	surveillance towed array sensor system
SUT	surface and underwater target
SXTF	satellite X-ray test facility
TAC	Tactical Air Command (USAF)
TACS	tactical air control system
TACTAS	tactical towed array sonar
TADS	target acquisition and designation system
T-AKX	commercial roll-on/roll-off ship (USN)
TALCM	tactical air-launched cruise missile
TAOC	tactical air operations centre
TAS	target acquisition system
TASM	tactical anti-ship missile
TCT	target centred tracker
TEL	transporter erector launcher (for MX advanced IBM)
TERCOM	terrain contour matching navigation system
TFR	terrain following radar
TGSM	terminally guided submunition
TICM	thermal imager common module programme
TIR	target illuminating radar

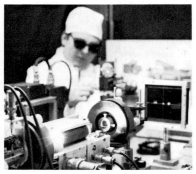

TIS	thermal imaging system		USMC	United States Marine Corps
TISEO	target identification system, electro-optical		USMCR	USMC Reserves
TLAM	Tomahawk land attack missile		USN	United States Navy
TNF	theatre nuclear forces or tactical nuclear forces		USNR	USN Reserves
TNFS³	theatre nuclear forces, survivability, security and safety			
TNW	tactical nuclear warfare		VDS	variable depth sonar
TOW	tube-launched, optically tracked, wire-guided		VHF	very high frequency
TRAM	target recognition attack multi-sensor		VHSIC	very high speed integrated circuit
TRI-TAC	joint tactical communications programme		VLA	vertical launch ASROC
TWS	track-while-scan (radar)		VLF	very low frequency
TWT	travelling wave tube		VLGM	vertical loading gun mount
			VLS	vertical launch system
UCS	underwater combat system		VRP	visual reporting posts
UHF	ultra high frequency		VSTOL	vertical/short take-off and landing
UKADGE	UK air defence ground environment			
UKADR	UK air defence region		WAAM	wide area anti-armour munitions
USAF	United States Air Force		WP	Warsaw Pact
USAFE	USAF, Europe		WRM	war reserve material
USAFR	USAF Reserves		WRS	war reserve stocks
USANG	United States Air National Guard		WSEP	Weapon System Evaluation Programme
USAR	United States Army Reserves		WVR	within visual range
USAREUR	United States Army Europe		WWMCCS	world-wide military command and control system

WHY **SELENIA** DEFENCE SYSTEMS DIVISION?

Because Selenia's PLUTO is one of the most advanced and versatile low coverage radars available on the market today.
It can operate in complex environments, countering ECM while still maintaining MTI capability.
Easily transportable by road, air on train, it can be put into operation in less than 30 minutes.
In addition, it can be fully integrated with MARS–402, a mobile automatic reporting post, making it suitable for diverse operational roles, from coastal defence to battlefield surveillance.

 INDUSTRIE ELETTRONICHE ASSOCIATE S.p.A.
DEFENCE SYSTEMS DIVISION
Via Tiburtina Km. 12,400 - 00131 ROME - ITALY
P.O. BOX: 7083, 00100 ROME
Telex: (43) 613690 SELROM I
Phone: (0039-6) 43601

STRATEGIC WEAPON SYSTEMS

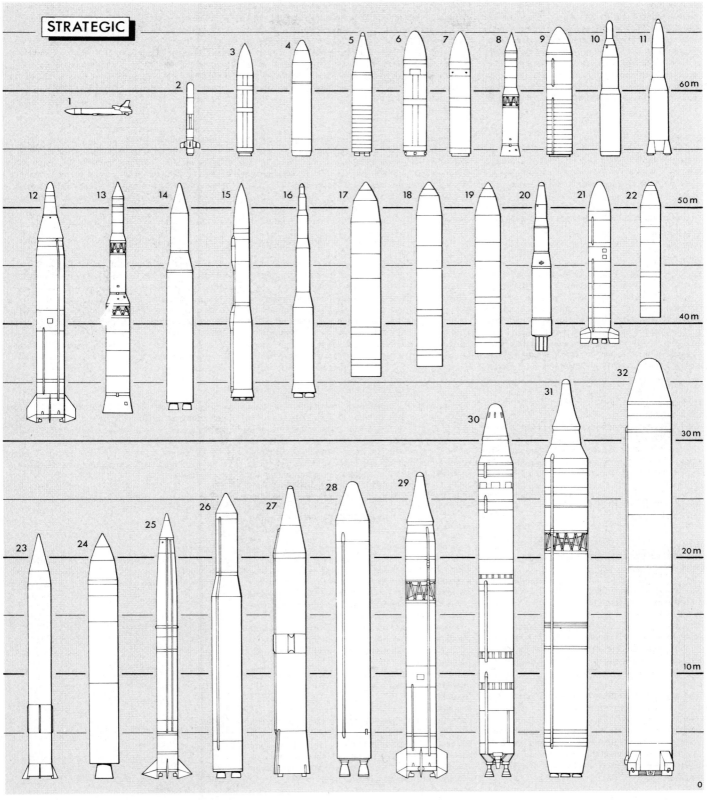

STRATEGIC

60 m
50 m
40 m
30 m
20 m
10 m
0

(1) ALCM	**(12)** CSS-2	**(23)** SS-4
(2) GLCM Tomahawk	**(13)** SS-13	**(24)** Peacekeeper
(3) Polaris A-3	**(14)** SS-11	**(25)** CSS-1
(4) SS-N-6	**(15)** Minuteman III	**(26)** SS-17
(5) MSBS (M20)	**(16)** Minuteman II	**(27)** SS-5
(6) Trident C-4	**(17)** SS-NX-20	**(28)** SS-19
(7) Poseidon C-3	**(18)** SS-N-18	**(29)** CSS-3
(8) SS-14	**(19)** SS-N-8	**(30)** Titan II
(9) MSBS (M4)	**(20)** SS-N-4	**(31)** CSS-X-4
(10) SS-N-5	**(21)** SSBS	**(32)** SS-18
(11) SS-20 (provisional)	**(22)** SS-NX-17	

CHINA (PEOPLE'S REPUBLIC)

2010.111
CSS-1 MRBM
Liquid-fuelled medium-range ballistic missiles similar to the Soviet SS-3 MRBM have been operational in north-eastern and north-western China since 1970, although recent American reports claim operational use since 1966. Like the SS-3, Shyster, these missiles have a range of about 1100 km and it is understood that some 50 were initially deployed, a total, which despite an increase of up to 100 anticipated at one time, seems to be still in the same region. The designation assigned by the American authorities is CSS-1. The first operational warheads are believed to be smaller than those carried by the Soviet missile; a figure of 20 KT has been suggested but a larger warhead may be fitted to some. In particular it is probable that those which have been most recently deployed carry thermo-nuclear warheads similar to those carried by the IRBM.

At one time it was thought that this missile would either be deployed in large numbers or be replaced by solid-fuel missiles. It now seems rather more likely, however, that the Chinese will put the majority of their effort into the ICBM and IRBM programmes and restrict the MRBM deployment to the minimum consistent with posing a significant threat to the Soviet Union while the other missiles are being deployed.

2049.111
CSS-2 IRBM
Although the Chinese IRBM and MRBM programmes have been subject to delays similar to those that appear to have affected their ICBM programme, it seems fairly clear that there has been a small-scale (15 to 20) deployment in China of a single-stage IRBM using a storable liquid propellant. This missile is understood to be similar to the first stage of the rocket which launched the first Chinese satellite in April 1970 and its range has been estimated as lying between 2500 and 4000 km. According to US sources, entry into operational service occurred in 1971 and it has been designated CSS-2.

Basing is understood to be on a basis of deployment at permanent sites from which targets in Central and Eastern Asia can be reached, although recent estimates suggest a capability for relocation of launch facilities without necessarily implying a mobile system. By late 1980 the estimated total in service had risen to about 70 missiles, with a possible national capability to add CSS-2s at a rate of between five and ten per year.

4210.111
CSS-3 ICBM
The Chinese CSS-3 long-range ballistic missile is a two-stage weapon believed to have a maximum range of around 7000 km carrying a warhead with an estimated yield of 2 MT. According to American defence analyses, two of these weapons had been deployed in silos between 1975 and 1980, by which time it was thought that another six were in the course of construction. The CSS-3 is approximately 25·5 m long and about 2·43 m in diameter and inertial guidance is assumed. Deployment is reported to be concentrated in western China, from where targets in European USSR would be accessible.

Prognostications of Chinese strategic intentions and missile production and deployment should be treated with caution, as should the observation that current practice in this area of military technology appears to be keeping abreast of significant developments, while deferring inordinate expenditure on system implementation until circumstances demand otherwise. Just what these circumstances might be are grounds for speculation, but typical examples might include deterioration of relations with the super-power neighbour to the north, or a need for a strategic initiative perceived by the Chinese themselves at some future date. Notwithstanding such considerations, the known evidence of the last 15 years or so does not indicate a Chinese stampede to achieve anything resembling nuclear parity in strategic terms with anyone.

4211.111
CSS-X-4 ICBM
In May 1980 China launched into an impact area in the Pacific Ocean two test rockets for what is provisionally understood to be a new strategic ICBM weapon designated CSS-X-4. The two launches achieved ranges of about 7000 km although the figures quoted by different observers vary quite appreciably, some higher (up to 13 800 km) and some lower, and the impact area was within the area bounded by the Solomon Islands, Fiji and the Gilbert Islands. No warheads were carried according to Chinese reports of the event, but an estimated payload weight of about 1200 kg suggests that a 5 MT warhead could be carried. Length of the CSS-X-4 has been estimated at about 33 m and two-stage liquid propulsion with inertial guidance is likely. US reports claim that CSS-X-4 missiles have been deployed in silos in central China, but this has not been confirmed. This missile is thought to bear the Chinese designation DF-5.

FRANCE

2163.111
SSBS INTERMEDIATE RANGE BALLISTIC MISSILE TYPE S-3
SSBS (Sol-Sol-Balistique-Stratégique) is a medium-range two-stage solid-propellant missile, with nuclear warhead, which is stored in and launched from an underground silo.

Launch areas are dispersed and hardened to reduce the effects of an enemy attack. Each includes the silo in which the missile is maintained in operational readiness, and an annexe housing the automatic launching equipment and servo mechanisms.

The original S-2 strategic missile force formed the main land-based element of the French 'force de frappe' from the early 1970s.

In 1973 a programme was initiated to develop the second-generation SSBS weapon system, the S-3. This programme entailed the renovation of the first two groups of S-2 silos and replacing the missiles with the S-3 model.

Retaining the same first stage as the S-2, the S-3 has a second stage of higher performance, namely, the P-6 originally developed for the MSBS. An advanced re-entry vehicle system is also included. This has a hardened thermonuclear charge and a re-entry vehicle which is hardened also against the effects of a high altitude nuclear explosion from an ABM. Other features are a new system of penetration aids designed to counter enemy defences, and a payload fairing to protect the RV during powered flight. The complete system is hardened against the effects of EMP (electro-magnetic pulse).

Improvements to the ground facilities include both equipment modernisation and system modifications to increase reliability and reduce maintenance costs.

CHARACTERISTICS
Type: Intermediate-range silo-launched, ballistic missile
Guidance: Inertial
Propulsion
First stage: SEP Type 902 motor. 4 gimballed nozzles for control. Thrust 45 000 kg
Second stage: SEP Rita II motor in wound fibreglass casing containing 6 tonnes of solid propellants. Thrust 32 000 kg. Thrust vector control by 4 freon injectors into a single fixed nozzle
Warhead: Thermonuclear (1·2 MT)
Dimensions
Length: 14 m
Diameter: 1·5 m
Range: Approx 1850 nm (>3000 km)

DEVELOPMENT
Development was covered by five contracts awarded to Aérospatiale spanning the six-year period 1974-80. Four contracts were from the Direction Technique des Engins, and one from the Commissariat à

SSBS S-3 IRBM launch from the Landes test site (Aérospatiale)

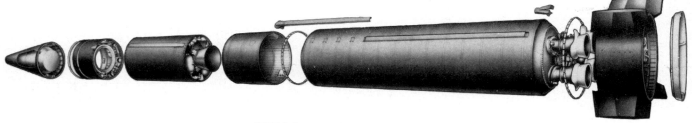

SSBS S-3 constructional layout (Aérospatiale)

l'Energie Atomique, and their combined value amounted to over $456 million. Aspects of the programme covered were: programme management; vector development; system development; experimentation and instruction for Air Force personnel; and studies, production, development, and testing related to the nuclear warhead.
STATUS
Development of the S-3 was completed and

deployment began in 1980. The first group of nine S-3 missiles and their associated silo installations on the Plateau d'Albion was officially inaugurated in May 1980 and both groups of nine silos were operational by the end of 1982.
CONTRACTORS
Aérospatiale is the prime contractor and integrator for the SSBS programme, and heads a team of some 200 French firms, under the overall authority of the

Direction Technique des Engins (a French Government body). The warhead and manufacture of the nuclear payload is the responsibility of the Commissariat à l'Energie Atomique.

1134.411
MSBS SUBMARINE LAUNCHED BALLISTIC MISSILE

MSBS (Mer-Sol Balistique Stratégique) is a medium-range, two-stage submarine-launched weapon forming a vital part of the French nuclear deterrent force. In general concept it is similar to the American Polaris missile family.

The M-1 version went into service in 1971 but was phased out in favour of the M-2 in 1974 which by mid-1977 had itself been supplanted by the M-20.

The current MSBS force is based on six nuclear-powered submarines (SLNE – Sous-marines Nucléaire Lanceur d'Engins balistique), each able to carry and launch 16 missiles. The MSBS fleet will consist of the submarines, *Le Redoutable*, *Le Terrible*, *Le Foudroyant*, *l'Indomptable* and *l'Inflexible*. Construction of the last of these began in 1978 and it will join the fleet soon.

Logistical support for the MSBS system is provided by the Ile Longue Naval Base in Brest Bay where there are the assembly and storage facilities necessary to keep the missiles in operational readiness.

The M-20 has an upgraded re-entry vehicle system which includes a thermonuclear charge, hardening against the effects of an ABM explosion at high altitude and improved penetration aids, and is now being deployed.

CHARACTERISTICS – M-20 MISSILE
Height: 10·4 m
Diameter: 1·5 m
Weight: 20 tonnes (approx)
Guidance: Inertial
Propulsion
First stage: Type 904 motor in a flow-turned Vascojet 1000 structure. Control by 4 gimballed nozzles. 10 tonnes of solid propellant. Combustion time 50 s and thrust 45 000 kg
Second stage: Rita II motor in a wound glass fibre casing containing 6 tonnes of solid propellant. Internal thrust vector system of control using freon injection into single fixed nozzle. Combustion time 52 s and thrust 32 000 kg
Warhead: Thermonuclear 1 MT
Range: About 3000 km

A completely new generation of MSBS, designated the M-4, is at the development stage. The range will be significantly increased to about 4000 km and multiple thermonuclear warheads are planned. M-4 missiles will be deployed on existing submarines after certain modifications have been carried out.

A three-stage propulsion system is employed; the first stage (M-401) has a metal casing, while the other

Loading M-4 in experimental submarine Gymnote

M-4 MSBS launch from submarine Gymnote

two motors (M-402 and M-403) have wound casings of Kevlar material produced in the USA.

The experimental submarine *Le Gymnote* is being used for M-4 tests.

CHARACTERISTICS – M-4 MISSILE
Height: 11·05 m
Diameter: 1·93 m
Weight: 35 tonnes
Guidance: Inertial
Propulsion
First stage: Type 401 motor with 20 tonnes of solid propellant and 4 flexible nozzles
Second stage: Type 402 motor with 8 tonnes of solid propellant and 1 flexible nozzle
Third stage: Type 403 1·5 tonnes solid propellant with flexible nozzle
Warhead: MRV
Range: >4000 km
STATUS
The M-20 is operational and the M-4 is in the development phase. The first M-4 test launch took place (from the Landes Test Range near Biscarosse) in November 1980 and further tests are taking place from the experimental submarine *Le Gymnote*. The 12th firing took place from *Le Gymnote* in July 1983 with successful results. Despite its larger diameter,

New generation M-4 MSBS

Current M-20 MSBS

the M-4 missile can be carried in the tubes of first generation SNLEs after certain modifications, and the earlier submarines will be converted from the M-20 to the M-4 one at a time after the M-4 enters service in *l'Inflexible*, some time after January 1985. It has been reported that an improved version, designated M-4C is being developed.

CONTRACTORS
As in the case of the SSBS, the governmental agency in control is the Direction Technique des Engins and the industrial prime contractor is the Division des Systèmes Balistiques et Spatiaux of Aérospatiale (SNIAS) whose responsibilities, in addition to the missile itself, include the on-shore assembly and

check-out operations at the naval base, as well as the command and control launch procedures aboard the submarines.

UNION OF SOVIET SOCIALIST REPUBLICS

2952.111
SS-4 (SANDAL) MRBM
Known also by the NATO code-name Sandal, the SS-4 is a low medium-range ballistic missile which is a developed version of the SS-3 (Shyster).

SS-4 was first shown in public in 1961, but was deployed originally in 1958; it became a standard MRBM in the Soviet armed forces. It was also the missile that lay at the root of the Cuban crisis in 1962. Depending on the weight of the warhead the missile has a range of between 1500 and 1800 km.

The complete weapon system comprises about 12 tractor vehicles with special trailers. Some 20 men are

required to erect and launch the missile. Official US sources report that the SS-4 has a reload capacity when fired from soft sites; it is also deployed at hardened sites but without a reload capability. The guidance system employed was originally radio command, operating on guidance vanes in the efflux nozzles, but it was observed at the time of the Cuban crisis that a changeover to inertial guidance had taken place.

CHARACTERISTICS
Type: Medium-range ballistic missile
Guidance principle: Inertial

Guidance method: By control of elevators and of guidance vanes in the efflux nozzles
Accuracy: Typically 2400 m CEP
Propulsion: 1 liquid propellant sustainer
Warhead: Optional nuclear (1 MT) or HE
Missile length: About 21 m
Missile diameter: About 160 cm
Launch weight: About 27 000 kg
Speed at burn-out: Mach 6 – 7
Range: About 1800 km
STATUS
The SS-4, with the SS-5 and an increasing number of

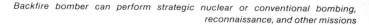

Blackjack A swing-wing strategic bomber began flight testing 1982-83 and is latest addition to Soviet deterrent

Backfire bomber can perform strategic nuclear or conventional bombing, reconnaissance, and other missions

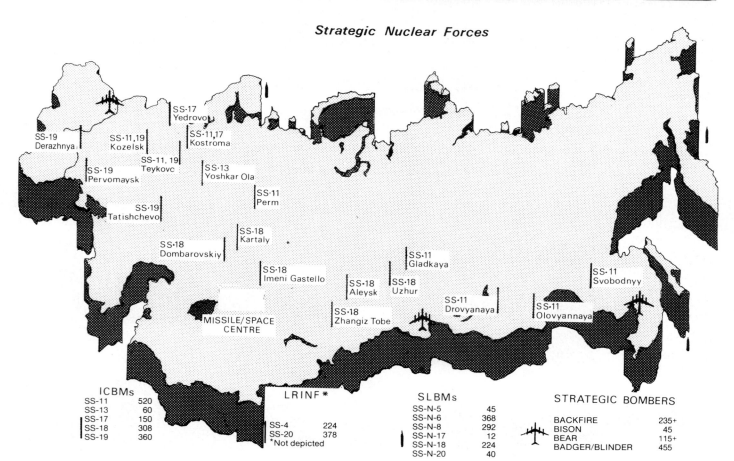

Strategic Nuclear Forces

ICBMs		LRINF*		SLBMs		STRATEGIC BOMBERS	
SS-11	520			SS-N-5	45		
SS-13	60			SS-N-6	368	BACKFIRE	235+
SS-17	150	SS-4	224	SS-N-8	292	BISON	45
SS-18	308	SS-20	378	SS-N-17	12	BEAR	115+
SS-19	360	*Not depicted		SS-N-18	224	BADGER/BLINDER	455
				SS-N-20	40		

Map summary of principal Soviet strategic assets. Note: details of longer-range IRBM force deployments and strength appear in the text

SS-20 mobile IRBMs, forms a major part of the armament of the Soviet Strategic Rocket Force. Since 1977, according to official US estimates, the proportion of SS-4 and SS-5 missiles has slowly declined as the SS-20 successor system is deployed, the SS-4 less rapidly than the SS-5. US estimates published in early 1984 suggested a total of 224, while an independent observer had put a figure of 275 as the total in late 1982. Both sources agreed on a total of 16 SS-5s, but as noted opposite this number is thought to be slowly declining still. The SS-4 is now reported to be extensively deployed in the Central Asian region of the Soviet Union and facing China.

2981.111
SS-5 (SKEAN) IRBM

Successor to the Shyster and Sandal liquid propellant MRBM weapons, the SS-5 is an intermediate-range missile also known by the NATO code-name Skean. Although similar in general configuration to its predecessors it can be identified by the absence of tail fins and its blunted nose cone. It is carried on a different trailer, towed by the latest type of heavy tractor vehicle and has been shown inside silo underground launch facilities in official Soviet films. The missile was first displayed in 1964.

CHARACTERISTICS
Type: Intermediate-range ballistic missile
Guidance principle: Probably inertial
Propulsion: Single-stage liquid propellant sustainer
Warhead: Nuclear, believed 1 MT
Missile length: About 25 m
Missile diameter: About 2·4 m
Range: Estimated 3500 km

STATUS
Operational since 1961 and deployed at both hard and soft sites. US sources state that a multiple re-fire capability is available at both types of site. Soft sites also have a reload facility. By 1984, it was estimated, all but 13 SS-5s had been retired from service, having been replaced by the SS-20 mobile IRBM system (**3219.111**).

Skean liquid-propellant MRBM

4207.111
SS-11 (SEGO) ICBM

The SS-11 Sego ICBM has been reported in four distinct versions known in official American publications as Mods 1, 2, 3 and 4. At one stage of its operational life, the SS-11 was the most widely deployed Soviet ICBM, but is now regarded as a 'third generation' ICBM. Despite having given way to replacement by newer weapons to some extent, it remains a very common member of the Soviet Union's ample strategic armoury of land-based missiles. The basic missile is a two-stage storable liquid propellant rocket with a range of between 10 000 and 13 000 km, which when it entered service around 1966 carried a single warhead payload.

The Mod 2 is thought to have become operational in 1973, although at one time the absence of any evidence of operational testing was taken as indicative of cancellation. However, firings in the latter part of 1975 suggested crew training which implied deployment of this version. Like the Mod 1, a single RV is carried, but in the case of the Mod 2 this is accompanied by penetration aids. The Mod 3 version, when it was detected soon after the Mod 2, was noted for a different RV and warhead arrangement, in particular a multiple re-entry vehicle equipped with three warheads. No details of the size of these warheads have been discovered but it has been deduced that they are unlikely to be less than the 200 KT of each of the warheads carried by the US Minuteman III.

CHARACTERISTICS
Type: Silo-launched intercontinental ballistic missile
Guidance: Inertial
Propulsion: Storable liquid
Warhead: Single nuclear (Mod 1); single nuclear plus penaids (Mod 2); 3 MRVs probably about 200 KT each (Mod 3); multiple (3 or 6) MRVs (Mod 4)
Dimensions: None available, but length believed to be about 20 m and diameter approx 2·5 m (max)
Range: 10 000 – 13 000 km

STATUS
Widely deployed with the Soviet Strategic Rocket Forces from around 1970 in various versions, but since then many SS-11 silos have been converted to house SS-17 and SS-19 missiles. The SS-11 is still deployed extensively in many parts of the USSR, and in early 1981 there were about 500 deployed operationally altogether, mostly positioned opposite the Soviet Union's borders with China, Europe, Scandinavia, and the Middle East. The two silo fields just to the east of the Carpathians house a mixture of SS-11 and SS-19 ICBMs, but the ratio between the two types is not known. It was reported that in the 1982-83 period at least 120 SS-11s, and 60 SS-19s, had been deployed at the SS-4 and SS-5 missile sites at Derazhnya and Pervomaysk. Since then opinions vary as to the number of SS-11s deployed. The official US view in early 1984 was that there were 520 in all, made up of 100 Mod 1 S-11s and 420 Mod 2 and 3 versions.

SS-11 Sego ICBM in its launch canister which is loaded into silo with the missile to aid reload and preparation for second launch

2958.111
SS-13 (SAVAGE) ICBM

First seen in public in 1965, this missile, which may be known to NATO as Savage, is a three-stage solid-propellant ICBM that has been said to be comparable with the US Minuteman.

The three stages of the missile shown here are separated by truss structures and each has four nozzles. The upper stages are believed to be identical with the two stages of the SS-14 Scapegoat missile (**2961.111**).

Although the missile has been in service for some time it has never been deployed statically on a large scale. So far as is known, moreover, it has never been equipped with other than a single warhead. One of the new generation of Soviet strategic missiles is said to resemble the SS-13 closely and this missile (the SS-16, **2990.111**) has also been reported to be limited at present to a single warhead.

CHARACTERISTICS
Type: Intercontinental ballistic missile
Guidance principle: Presumed inertial
Propulsion: 3-stage, solid-propellant motors
Warhead: Nuclear, estimated 1 MT capability
Missile length: Overall 20 m (including interstages).
1st stage 8·7 m. 2nd stage 4 m. 3rd stage 3·5 m. Nose
cone and re-entry vehicle 2·3 m
Missile body diameters: 1st stage 1·7 m. 2nd stage
1·4 m. 3rd stage 1 m. Nose cone and re-entry vehicle
1 m
Missile base diameters: 1st stage 2 m. 2nd stage
1·9 m. 3rd stage 1·4 m
Range: 8000 – 10 000 km
STATUS
Operational with about 60 deployed in early 1982.
Most of these are believed to be based in two areas:
one in the region around Ivanovo, to the north-east of
Moscow; and in the neighbourhood of Yashkar Ola,
between Gorki and Kazan. Recent official US

Savage three-stage solid-propellant ICBM

publications refer to the Mod 2 version of the SS-13 as
being the current, in-service model but no details are
given of any other versions.

2961.111
SS-14 (SCAPEGOAT) IRBM
This two-stage solid-propellant IRBM appears to
comprise the top two stages of the SS-13 Savage
(**2958.111**) missile although the warhead section
appears to be different from that of the larger missile,
and there may be other differences. Its length is
approximately 10 m overall. When loaded in its
container and transported by its tracked
erector/launch vehicle it becomes the weapon system
known by the NATO code-name Scamp (**2960.111**).
OPERATION
Before firing, the missile, still in its container, is
erected by the powerful hydraulic jacking system at
the rear of the tracked Scamp vehicle. In the process,
the cross-braced framework at the rear of the vehicle
is lowered to the ground with the missile standing
upright on it. The protective case is then opened to
free the missile, lowered and closed again leaving the
missile standing on its launching platform.

CHARACTERISTICS
Type: Intermediate-range ballistic missile
Guidance principle: Presumed inertial
Propulsion: 2-stage solid-propellant motors
Warhead: Nuclear. That of the SS-13 missile is
estimated at 1 MT but the payload of the SS-14
missile may be less and the warhead yield
correspondingly smaller
Missile length: Overall 10·6 m (including interstage).
1st stage 4 m. 2nd stage 3·5 m. Nose cone and re-
entry vehicle 2·3 m
Missile body diameter: 1st stage 1·4 m. 2nd stage 1 m.
Nose cone and re-entry vehicle 1 m
Missile base diameters: 1st stage 1·9 m. 2nd stage
1·4 m
Range: About 4000 km
STATUS
A certain amount of official confusion remains
around the precise role of this weapon system in the
overall Soviet order of battle. As recently as early 1984

the letter 'X' was incorporated in the DoD designation
(SS-X-14) which normally denotes an experimental
system or weapon.
Reported to be deployed in eastern regions of the
USSR, although the mobile nature of this weapon
system renders categoric statements of deployment
of little lasting value.

The weapon system identified as Scamp by NATO is a land-mobile IRBM. 'Iron Maiden' housing contains SS-14 missile (Novosti)

SS-14 IRBM raised to the launch position by its tracked transporter/erector/launcher vehicle

---

2991.111
SS-17 ICBM
The SS-17 is thought to bear the designation RS-16 in
the Soviet Union's own numbering system, but since
(as usual) no confirmation or denial is forthcoming
from official sources it is not proposed to use this
designation at the present time. The information is
included only in case it should be of possible use to
readers in future. Described by official US sources
(with the SS-18 and SS-19) as a 'fourth generation'
Soviet ICBM, the SS-17 two-stage storable liquid-
propellant ICBM is one of two Soviet missiles
regarded as successors to the widely-deployed SS-11
missile (**2984.111**). Both it and the other SS-11
replacement, the SS-19, have a MIRV payload
capability, improved accuracy, increased throw-
weight, and greater survivability than their
predecessor. The SS-17 is slightly longer than the
SS-11 and of increased volume. The cold-launch
technique is used, whereby the missile is ejected from
the silo by a gas generator before the main booster is
ignited, whereas the SS-19 relies upon the

conventional hot-launch technique. In a later
assessment of this aspect of Soviet ICBM force
practice, the US DoD states that all liquid-propellant
ICBMs now deployed by the USSR are contained in a
launch canister within the silo. This acts as a liner to
minimise incidental damage to the silo during missile
launch and to facilitate reloading.
The most important aspect of these new missile
developments, however, is the introduction of MIRV-
type warheads. Both the SS-17 and the SS-19 are
reputed to have on-board computers and have been
tested with such warheads; furthermore, since the
SS-17 is credited with only a four-warhead MIRV
capability whereas the SS-19 is said to be able to carry
six MIRV warheads, it would seem that two different
MIRV systems are involved. This lends colour to an
official US view that the two missiles have been
developed in competition with one another – although
this seems to be a little out of keeping with normal
Soviet practice. The SS-17 has been tested with a
single, large RV which might be allied to the potential
accuracy enhancement conferred by the post-boost

vehicle to achieve an improved hard target capability.
CHARACTERISTICS
Type: Intercontinental ballistic missile
Guidance: Inertial. Computer-controlled RV
arrangement
Propulsion: 2-stage storable liquid-propellant rocket
motors. Cold-launch
Warhead: Nuclear. MIRV system of 4 – 6 warheads.
Yield not known but probably not less than 200 KT
each (Mod 1); single high-yield RV (Mod 2); four
750 KT MIRVs (Mod 3)
Dimensions: No details known. Length appears to be
about 24 m and base diameter about 2·5 m but little
reliance can be put on these figures
Range: 10 000 km (Mod 1); 11 000 km (Mod 2);
10 000 km (Mod 3)
STATUS
Operational. Tests are said to have been observed for
the first time during the second half of 1972 and there
was intensive testing during 1973 and early 1974.
Deployment in converted and modernised SS-11
silos began in 1975. By 1980, 150 SS-17s were

deployed operationally in converted SS-11 silos and this was considered to represent the total number under present Soviet modernisation plans. The estimated total of 150 SS-17s in early 1982 apparently still holds good, although the converted SS-11 silos are now thought to contain Mod 3 SS-17s with four warheads with MIRV payloads.

2992.111
SS-18 ICBM

The SS-18 has been reported as having the designation RS-20 in a Soviet identification series, but since this cannot be confirmed the information is included only as a matter of general interest and record.

Largest of the 'fourth generation' of Soviet intercontinental ballistic missiles, the SS-18 is said to be the functional successor to the SS-9 (**2962.111**). It is a very large two-stage liquid-propellant missile with a considerable payload capacity which in one model includes a post-boost vehicle which may carry a bus-type MIRV system with an on-board digital computer. By 1983 four different versions of the SS-18 had been identified, each with a different payload/range ratio, as follows:

SS-18	Mod 1	Mod 2	Mod 3	Mod 4
Warheads	1	8/10	1	10
Max range (km)	12 000	11 000	16 000	11 000

The US authorities are sure that increased accuracy has been a major consideration in the development programme, presumably with the intention of enabling the missile to attack hardened targets successfully. Some of the more recent tests, moreover, have been carried out using a single RV, from which it is deduced that the USSR may have a continuing interest in a missile with a single very powerful warhead. However, later official assessments have mentioned the possibility of directing two of the SS-18s MIRVs against the same ICBM silo target, in which case the tests with a single large warhead might have been part of a comparative test programme designed to establish the best way of countering silos of greater hardening levels. This would be a logical step if the Soviet authorities believed that America was following a similar ICBM modernisation programme as the USSR (ie. increased hardening of own silos and infra-structure allied to improved ICBM accuracy).

2993.111
SS-19 ICBM

The Soviet designation RS-18 has been ascribed to the SS-19 by some observers but as this cannot be confirmed at present, it is not proposed to use this designation for the time being.

The SS-19 is a two-stage liquid-propellant weapon with an on-board computer and MIRV warhead system.

With the cold-launch SS-17, the hot-launch SS-19 has been designed as a successor to the SS-11 missile (**2984.111**). It has a throw-weight three or four times that of the older missile. It is also of greater volume. Its guidance system is said to combine (inertial?) navigation with a refinement of the traditional Soviet 'fly-the-wire' guidance technique. An on-board computer determines deviation from the pre-programmed course and directs correction to that course or plots a new course depending upon the attendant circumstances.

SS-18 is transported in a canister that is also used to load the missile into its ICBM silo as shown in this US sketch

Like other current fourth generation Soviet ICBMs the SS-18 is deployed in a launch canister which is inserted into the silo with the missile. Its purpose is to provide some protection to the silo launch mechanism/structure during launches to enable the silo to be reloaded and used again with minimum delay after the first firing.

CHARACTERISTICS
Type: Intercontinental ballistic missile
Guidance: Inertial. Computer-controlled RV arrangement
Propulsion: 2-stage liquid-propellant rocket motors. Cold-launch
Warhead: Single nuclear (Mod 1); 8/10 MIRV < 1MT (Mod 2); single 20 MT (Mod 3); 10 0·5 MT (Mod 4)
Dimensions: No details available. Length appears to be about 35 m and base diameter about 3 m
Range: 12 000 km (Mod 1); 11 000 km (Mod 2); 16 000 km (Mod 3); 11 000 km (Mod 4)

Slightly larger than the SS-17, it is also provided with a MIRV capability, reportedly being able to dispense four or six RVs. There is also a single RV version, Mod 2, which appeared after the MIRV model. This suggests that the Mod 2 payload may be a high-accuracy high-yield design. A Mod 3 version, which is said to combine high accuracy with a MIRV payload, was reported to have entered service in 1980, this model having a payload of six 0·5 MT warheads.

Latest of the Soviet 'fourth generation' ICBMs now operational, although a hot launch system, the SS-19 is deployed in canister launch containers which are loaded into the silos to facilitate reload and refire capability in the same way as SS-17 and SS-18 ICBMs.

CHARACTERISTICS
Type: Silo-launched intercontinental ballistic missile
Guidance: Inertial. Computer-controlled RV arrangement

STATUS
Deployed operationally in 1974 in former SS-9 silos and launch complexes converted and improved to accept SS-18s. By 1982 the task of converting SS-9 silos to house SS-18s was thought to have been completed and the number of SS-18s deployed then was estimated to be 308; the present level of deployment of this system. In late 1983 it was reported that SS-18 silos had been hardened to enable them to withstand an overpressure of 6000 psi. It was thought to have been achieved by using concrete reinforced by concentric steel rings. The geographic distribution within the Soviet Union (see map of strategic forces) suggests that SS-18s are mostly located centrally in the Dombarovskiy, Imeni Gastello, Aleysk, Zhangiz Tobe and Uzhur missile fields. The total number deployed in 1984 was estimated as 308, the majority of which are thought to be Mod 4 missiles with ten MIRVs.

Propulsion: 2-stage liquid-propellant rocket motors
Warhead: Nuclear. MIRV system of 4 or 6 warheads. Yield not known but probably 200 KT each (Mod 1); single advanced design RV (Mod 2); 6 × 500 KT MIRV (Mod 3)
Dimensions: Length about 25 m; base diameter about 2·75 m
Range: 10 000 km
STATUS
Deployed operationally in 1974. The first SS-19 test detected took place in April 1973. With the SS-17, this missile is replacing SS-11 ICBMs, the silos being improved at the same time as they are converted to receive the later type of missile.

In 1984 it was estimated that there were 60 SS-19 Mod 2 missiles and 300 SS-19 Mod 3 missiles deployed in the Soviet Union, mostly in the major Derazhnya, Kozelsk, Pervomaysk and Tatishchevo missile fields.

3219.111
SS-20 MOBILE IRBM

The SS-20 is regarded as a replacement system for the elderly SS-4 and SS-5 IRBMs (**2952.111** and **2981.111**), and its origins are generally thought to consist of two stages of the SS-16 three-stage solid-propellant ICBM programme, which apparently was not pursued to completion. SS-4, SS-5 and SS-20 deployment between 1978 and 1983 revealed a steady decrease in quantities of the first two types matched by comparable increase in SS-20 deployments, which tends to confirm the idea that the newer missile was designed as a replacement for the earlier types.

Whereas quite good photographs of its predecessors have been available for some time, photographic evidence about the SS-20 is extremely limited and generally of poor quality. Therefore open sources are mostly forced to rely upon fragmentary details culled from official (principally US)

assessments when attempting to estimate the characteristics of this weapon. The SS-20 is a two-stage solid-propellant mobile IRBM about 16·4 metres long with a multiple warhead capability and a maximum range generally accepted as between 4000 and 5000 km, although this latter parameter is the subject of various opinions as will be mentioned. Inertial guidance is employed and a figure of 400 m CEP is usually accepted, although inevitably this must rest to a significant extent on the accuracy with which the initial launch site has been surveyed and with range. Some reports claim that there are a significant number of pre-surveyed launch sites in the USSR, but that this is not absolutely essential for operation of the SS-20. An earlier report, said to be based on a secret report by the CIA, indicated that re-targeting or re-siting the launch position in the guidance system could probably be effected in seconds if the new target is within 1 or 2° of the original launch azimuth. But if the targets are widely separated it might require 20 to 30 minutes for re-targeting.

The missile is fired from a transporter/erector/launcher vehicle which is probably of the wheeled type. Recent official US reports surmise that SS-20s are deployed in groups of nine missiles, probably with their supporting command and control and support vehicles as well as supply of reload missiles (one for each launcher). Among the support vehicles there may be a meteorological unit to provide accurate local wind and other atmospheric data affecting the launch site, in the interests of system accuracy. The SS-20 is said to be capable of refiring after launching the first missile, but considerable heat is involved in each launch so that it may not be possible to prepare for a second launch in less than a few hours, according to some authorities.

The payload of the SS-20 is another feature that is

still debated. Most authorities suggest three MIRVs of 150 KT yield, with an alternative of a single larger warhead, while elsewhere the first of these is defined as the SS-20 Mod 1; SS-20 Mod 2 being the second alternative of a single 1·5 MT yield; and a third option (SS-20 Mod 3) being one 50 KT warhead with a maximum range capability of 7400 km. This last must also be debatable, as must the 'standard' SS-20 maximum range potential. The Soviet figure is 4000 to 4500 km, which is nearer to the 3700 km that has been recorded than the US estimate of 5000 km or more.
STATUS
First recorded deployments of the SS-20 took place in 1977 and by the end of 1980 it was estimated there were 180 operational launchers in use. From January 1981 onward, the pace of SS-20 base construction increased, and in May 1983 official US estimates claimed there were 351 operational SS-20s in the Soviet Union of which 243 are based in the European portion of the USSR west of the Ural Mountains. The remainder are to the east of this range and are presumed to be targeted on China, Japan and South Korea. The total of 243 facing NATO remained the same until early 1984, apparently to substantiate the Soviet moratorium on deployments that lasted until the breakdown of the Geneva arms limitation talks. However, the overall total of SS-20 deployments according to US figures in February 1984 was 378

launchers (with some additional reload missiles). Other sources quoted even higher figures.

Specific areas where it is claimed SS-20 launch complexes have been noted include the Yedrova, Yurya, Verkhnaya Salda, Omsk, Caspian Sea area, Novosibirsk, Drouyanaya and Olovyanaya regions.

The possibility that the Soviet authorities might decide to deploy SS-20s in the northeastern regions of the USSR to present a rapid threat to parts of the continental USA has been voiced by certain US observers.

US sources report SS-20 complexes of up to nine missiles, each with three nuclear warheads and with reloads for each launcher. Artist's impression shows typical deployment at unprepared sites. (Compare with earlier impression in previous edition, which showed earth revetments)

4778.111
SS-X-24 ICBM

The US code SS-X-24 has been assigned to a new fifth generation ICBM being developed by the USSR, possibly as an eventual successor to the existing SS-18 ICBM (**2992.111**). Few details beyond those revealed (or leaked) from US intelligence assessments, are available to open sources. These indicate that the SS-X-24 is probably of about the same size as the American Peacekeeper (MX) advanced ICBM, with an estimated length of between 21 and 22 metres, and up to 10 re-entry vehicles carrying payloads of unknown yield. As a successor to the SS-18 a range in the region of 12 000 to 16 000 km would be in order, but there is no evidence

concerning this parameter of the new weapon. It has been presumed by official US observers that the SS-X-24 uses solid propulsion although there are no details of the number or size of the rocket motors.

Official DoD reports have stated that the SS-X-24 is probably more accurate than either the SS-18 Mod 4 (11 000 km range version) or the SS-19 Mod 3 (**2993.111**), and it is assumed that both this and the other new ICBM being developed in parallel, the SS-X-25 (**4779.111**) will have a greater hard target kill potential (HTKP) than their predecessors. In other words they are expected to be able to redress the balance of advantage against the effects of American silo hardening programmes.

It has been estimated that both mobile

(transportable) and silo-based versions of the SS-X-24 may appear, but the silo housed model is thought the most likely to be deployed with the mobile version several years later.
STATUS
Development has probably been in progress for some years, but US officials believe the SS-X-24 could be deployed operationally in 1985. Other information advanced by different sources tends to suggest a slower pace. These report seven failures out of ten test flights, while stating that at least 12 satisfactory test flights are usual before a new Soviet missile is deployed operationally. More evidence will be needed before these two viewpoints can be reconciled.

4779.111
SS-X-25 ICBM

The designation SS-X-25 has been assigned to what is believed to be a new, 'fifth generation' ICBM now being developed as a possible successor to the existing SS-19 ICBM (**2993.111**). US intelligence estimates, upon which most of what has been revealed to date is based, suggest that the SS-X-25 is of about the same size as the US Minuteman ICBM, with a length of between 18 and 19 metres.

Solid propulsion is used and the missile has three stages. A single re-entry vehicle is thought to be carried but there have been no published estimates of the possible yield of the warhead so far. Like its contemporary, the other new Soviet ICBM SS-X-24, the SS-X-25 is thought to be capable of either silo deployment or operation in a mobile form. The latter mode of deployment is officially considered the most likely to appear in the foreseeable future. US official drawings of possible SS-X-25 deployment (see illustration), which are presumably based on satellite intelligence photographs, reveal a noticeable similarity with the now widely deployed SS-20 mobile MRBM (**3219.111**) which prompts the suggestion that the SS-X-25 might be a development of the earlier weapon.

It also raises the question of whether or not the semi-hardened shelter type deployment shown in the US artist's impression of the SS-X-25 is indicative of the major evidence of a new type of ICBM, when it could be (a) merely a more advanced method of operating the SS-20 system; (b) an improved version of the SS-20; or (c) a completely new system. More

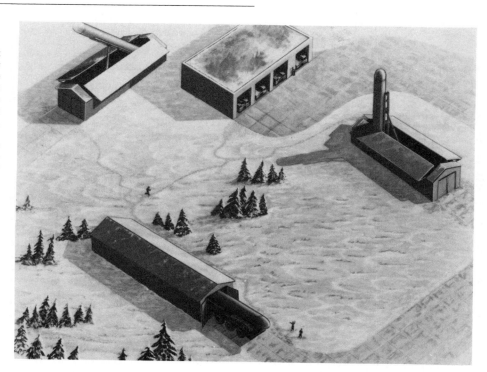

This official US artist's impression of the new SS-X-25 ICBM system in operation suggests that the now abandoned 'race-track' MX basing mode idea may live on in Soviet minds

positive evidence will be needed to allow a judgement to be made.

US DoD opinion believes that in any case the SS-X-25 will possess a greater HTKP than predecessor systems, principally by virtue of better accuracy. Any assessments of this aspect of the SS-X-25 presumably must have been derived from monitoring telemetry data obtained during test flights carried out at the Plesetsk missile range. US reports (unofficial) have stated that some of these tests were notable for the fact that telemetry was sent in encrypted form, and the legality of this in respect of the SALT II terms has also been questioned.

4819.001
SOVIET CRUISE MISSILE PROGRAMME

The Soviet Union has a long experience of cruise missile operation, admittedly mostly within a naval context, but signs have been detected that a programme to extend the areas of application of this category of weapon in Soviet service is now well advanced. Recent US analysis claims to have evidence of new air-, sea- and ground-launched cruise missiles of several types under development with one of them possibly reaching initial operational status by 1985.

The first category of cruise missile is believed to be very similar in design concept and physical parameters to the American Tomahawk (**3993.001**, **4197.221** and **4194.111**), and like that weapon, the Soviet cruise missile is expected to appear in a sea-launched version SS-NX-21 (**4796.411**), as an air-to-surface missile AS-X-15 (**3206.311**) and as a counterpart to the USAF GLCM in the SSC-X-4 ground-launched version. Insufficient data has been disclosed to make possible more than a general assessment of this class of Soviet cruise missiles, but it is thought that overall length is in the order of 7 metres and that a single warhead could be carried a distance of up to 3000 km. An air-breathing turbojet is the likely power plant, but the precise form of guidance is more open to doubt at this stage.

It has been suggested that SSC-X-4 missiles will be deployed with four-round mobile launcher vehicles, but this cannot be confirmed at present. US estimates suggest a possible operational deployment from 1985 onward, and it is thought that cruise missiles will be used in a similar fashion to Soviet Army rocket forces and SS-20 mobile ballistic missile units. The probable operational role will be in support of theatre operations. Flight tests of what is believed to be the SSC-X-4 cruise missile have been reported in 1984.

In addition to the Soviet 'Tomahawk-equivalent', the USSR is pursuing the development of a much larger class of cruise missiles, maybe about 12 or 13 metres long. These are expected to make an appearance in two or three years time, and there are likely to be both ground-launched and naval versions although no designations have been assigned as yet.

Both the new categories ('Tomahawk'-class and 'large') Soviet cruise missiles are likely to be armed with nuclear warheads at first. The decision to provide alternative conventional payloads will depend on the type of guidance system employed, and the capability to attack hard targets that its accuracy provides.

1153.411
SS-N-5 (SERB) SUBMARINE LAUNCHED
BALLISTIC MISSILE

Serb is the code-name assigned by NATO to the successor to the Sark (**1152.411**) Soviet submarine-launched ballistic missile. Serb has been described as representing the second generation in this class of missiles in the USSR.

Like its forerunner, Serb is similar in appearance to the Polaris A-2 missile in service with the USN, and it is understood to be a two-stage solid-fuel vehicle with inertial guidance. In size it conforms more closely with the dimensions of Polaris than does Sark, which is appreciably larger. According to official US information, the SS-N-5 is approximately 12·9 m in length and has a maximum diameter of 1·42 m. Launch weight has been estimated at around 18 tons. While there is fairly close agreement among the various authorities on these dimensions, there is no agreement on the missile's range capability. Estimates vary from about 1200 km to about 2400 km but the lower figure is more likely. A single re-entry vehicle with a warhead in the megaton range is carried.

When the Serb missile was displayed in the November 1967 parade, what is apparently a different ejection system to that employed in American submarine launcher tubes was revealed. At the base of the missile there is a cluster of 18 small, electrically fired cold-gas nozzles which are used to eject the missile from the sealed launcher tube. On passing clear of the submarine the section carrying these gas motors is jettisoned from the main missile body by explosive bolts fired when the first stage ignites.

Some 'Hotel' class submarines can carry three SS-N-5 SLBMs. Both boats and missiles are aged

STATUS
Operational (since 1963) in the later 'G' class (conventional) and the later 'H' class (nuclear) submarines on scales of two or three launchers per submarine. Estimates vary as to the number of SS-N-5s remaining operational. The Stockholm International Peace Research Institute (SIPRI) made an estimate of nine SS-N-5 missiles at the begining of 1984, but the distribution of these among the much-modified 'Golf' class SSBs and 'Hotel' class SSBN submarines at this time is not certain. The SS-N-5 is regarded as obsolescent.

USSR Nuclear Ballistic Missile Submarines and Missiles

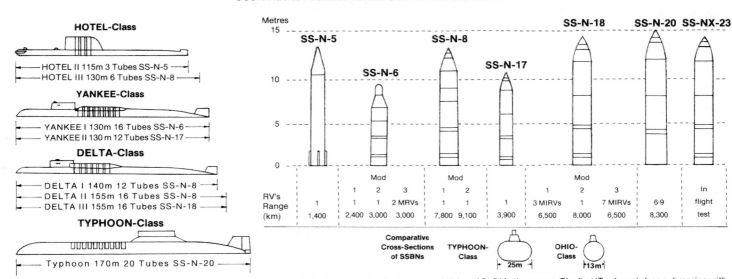

HOTEL-Class

HOTEL II 115m 3 Tubes SS-N-5
HOTEL III 130m 6 Tubes SS-N-8

YANKEE-Class

YANKEE I 130m 16 Tubes SS-N-6
YANKEE II 130 m 12 Tubes SS-N-17

DELTA-Class

DELTA I 140m 12 Tubes SS-N-8
DELTA II 155m 16 Tubes SS-N-8
DELTA III 155m 16 Tubes SS-N-18

TYPHOON-Class

Typhoon 170m 20 Tubes SS-N-20

	SS-N-5	SS-N-6			SS-N-8		SS-N-17	SS-N-18			SS-N-20	SS-NX-23
Mod		1	2	3	1	2		1	2	3		In
RV's	1	1	1	2 MRVs	1	1	1	3 MIRVs	1	7 MIRVs	6·9	flight
Range (km)	1,400	2,400	3,000	3,000	7,800	9,100	3,900	6,500	8,000	6,500	8,300	test

Comparative Cross-Sections of SSBNs

TYPHOON-Class ⊢ 25m ⊣

OHIO-Class ⊢13m⊣

Soviet SLBM capability: Diagram showing composition of Soviet strategic submarine fleet and capabilities of SLBMs they carry. The first 'Typhoon' class submarine with SS-N-20 missiles has completed sea trials and is deployed at a base on the Kola Peninsula. Production of Delta III class ships armed with SS-N-18 third generation SLBMs is believed to be nearing its end with 14 launched. Each has 16 tubes. Delta II boats have 16 SS-N-8 tubes, while earlier 'Delta I' class boats have 12 tubes. In 1984 there were four Delta II and 18 Delta Is. One 'Yankee III' class boat is fitted for SS-NX-17 tests, while 23 Yankee I & II class boats are deployed with SS-N-6 Mods 1 or 3. There is a declining number of 'Hotel II' ships which operate the ageing SS-N-5 SLBM, and one 'Hotel III' trials ship for the SS-N-8

1154.411

SS-N-6 (SAWFLY) SUBMARINE LAUNCHED BALLISTIC MISSILE

All three versions of the SS-N-6, Sawfly, submarine-launched ballistic missile are liquid-fuelled, and, based on US information, 9·65 m long and 1·65 m in diameter.

The Mod 1 is a single warhead version with a reputed range of 2400 km. In October 1972 flight tests began of a modified version which became known as the Mod 2 and this was given an increased range of about 3000 km, by virtue of an improved propulsion system. According to the American authorities the SS-N-6 Mod 2 is now capable of reaching any target in the USA from the 100 fathom contour off the coasts of the USA.

The SS-N-6 Mod 3 is the latest of the Sawfly development and has a range of some 3000 km, carrying a payload of two MRVs. These are not independently targeted.

An American DoD assessment claims that the combination of accuracy and yield of all three SS-N-6 versions is sufficient only for strikes against soft targets.

STATUS

The SS-N-6 entered service in 1968; the Mod 2 began operational service in 1973, closely followed by the Mod 3. Current deployments are all on 'Y' class nuclear submarines. It is likely that Mod 1 missiles are being replaced progressively by Mod 2 and 3 types.

'Yankee' class nuclear-powered SLBM submarines armed with SS-N-6 missiles still constitute a major proportion of the Soviet SLBM strength

Production of 'Y' class submarines ended in 1975, when there were 34 boats of this class. Several of them have since had their SS-N-6 tubes removed and the situation in 1983 was that of the 34 built, 24 boats carry either Mod 1 or Mod 3 SS-N-6s, one is fitted with the solid-propellant SS-N-17, and the remaining nine had their missile tubes removed and may be serving as SSN fleet submarines.

3078.411

SS-N-8 SUBMARINE LAUNCHED BALLISTIC MISSILE

For some time past the SS-N-8 was thought to be a possible development of the SS-N-6 (Sawfly), but recently the US Defense authorities have claimed sufficient new evidence to justify regarding this weapon to be sufficiently different to warrant another designation. As yet, no NATO code-name has been issued or leaked in open sources.

According to official US data it is about the same length as the SS-N-5 at 12·95 m, but of increased diameter, approximately 1·65 m. It is the same diameter as SS-N-6 so that its greater length gives it an appreciably larger volume. It employs liquid-fuelled propulsion and can carry a single warhead to a range of almost 8000 km. The guidance system is said to incorporate stellar-inertial techniques, capable of CEP values of 0·4 km. The American Chairman of the Joint Chiefs of Staff, General George S Brown, USAF, in 1980 said that the SS-N-8 is unique in having a range of 7800 km, exceeding by at least 3000 km the range of any other SLBM deployed in either the USA or USSR.

The existence of three versions has been reported: Mod 1 has one re-entry vehicle carrying a warhead of about 1 MT; Mod 2 has three MRVs of unspecified yield; and Mod 3 was believed to have three MIRVs, but the existence of this version of the SS-N-8 has not been confirmed.

STATUS

The SS-N-8 was operational by 1973 and is now deployed in 'D' class Soviet submarines. In mid-1983 it was estimated that the Soviet Union had a total of 22 operational Delta class submarines, with the 18 12-tube Delta Is and the 4 16-tube Delta IIs both armed with the SS-N-8. Delta III class boats are armed with the later SS-N-18 (**3357.411**).

Delta II class submarines are armed with 16 SS-N-8 SLBMs compared with the 12 carried by Delta I class boats

3356.411

SS-NX-17 SUBMARINE LAUNCHED BALLISTIC MISSILE

The SSN-X-17 is one of two new-generation Soviet SLBMs (the other being the SS-N-18, **3357.411**, below) to appear in the mid-1970s and is the USSR's first SLBM to use a solid propellant and to be equipped with a post-boost vehicle (PBV). The latter feature strongly suggests an MRV or MIRV capability, although to date only single re-entry vehicle payloads have been reported.

It began testing in 1975 and is believed to have been engaged in periodic sea trials since 1977 in a converted 'Yankee' class submarine with 12 missile tubes.

According to American official information, the SS-NX-17 is about 11·06 metres in length and 1·65 metres in diameter. Estimated range is 3900 km and inertial guidance is assumed.

The role of this weapon in the Soviet SLBM programme is far from clear from the available evidence to date. Evidence in open sources is mostly of the 'negative' sort, the most recent example being the dropping in official US sources of the 'X' (denoting experimental) from the SS-NX-17 designation. No reason has been given in support of this change and as there has apparently been no move to deploy this missile in any more submarines than the one 'Yankee' class boat that has been the sole platform for the SS-NX-17 since 1977, we see no justification for deleting the 'X' and there by implying operational status for this system.

A single submarine of an ageing class seems an unlikely basis for a new strategic weapon system, and the seeming lack of urgency and/or progress in the programme could be indicative of an essentially R & D oriented effort that may have failed to live up to expectations thus far.

3357.411
SS-N-18 SUBMARINE LAUNCHED BALLISTIC
MISSILE
The alternative Soviet designation RSM-50 has been
suggested as applying to the SS-N-18 but as this has
not yet been confirmed it is not proposed to use this
designation for the present.

The SS-N-18 SLBM began flight tests shortly after
the SS-NX-17 (**3356.411**) in 1975. It is similar in some
respects to the SS-N-8 (**3078.411**) but somewhat
larger, and is believed to be equipped with a more
sophisticated guidance system. Liquid propellant is
used and US estimates of maximum range give a
figure of about 7500 km. Like the SS-NX-17, it is
equipped with a large post-boost vehicle (PBV) and
American sources claim to have identified three
models: Mod 1 has a payload of three MIRVs and a
range of 6500 km; Mod 2 has a single RV and 8000 km
range; and the Mod 3 carries seven MIRVs with a
maximum range of 6500 km.

Official US information suggests a missile length of
about 14·1 m and a diameter of approximately 1·8 m,
which places the SS-N-18 at the top of the list of
SLBMs in terms of volume, but the projected
American Trident II (D-5) SLBM will be of comparable
size.
STATUS
Before November 1976, the SS-N-18 was tested from

*Delta III class nuclear-powered submarines are armed with 16 tubes each for SS-N-18s, most numerous of the
Soviet Union's third generation of SLBMs*

land-based launch sites in the USSR, but in early
November the first submarine launch took place in
the White Sea. There was another test in September
1978 when the SS-N-18 reached an impact area in the
Pacific Ocean. In early 1979 the US DoD disclosed the
information that deployment of the SS-N-18 aboard

'Delta-III' class submarines had commenced. This
has been confirmed and by 1983 it was estimated that
there were 14 'Delta III' class submarines (and two or
three being built), with 16 tubes each, armed with the
SS-N-18 SLBM. Entry into operational service
probably occurred in 1979.

4208.411
SS-N-20 SLBM
This submarine launched ballistic missile was first
mentioned in the 1981-82 edition of *Jane's Weapon
Systems*, when the US designation included an 'X' for
experimental or under development, i.e. SS-NX-20. In
1984 the US authorities deleted the 'X' and stated that
with the entry into service of the first of the giant
'Typhoon' class of submarines, the SS-N-20 SLBM
system that these ships fit is now considered
operational.

According to US intelligence estimates the SS-N-20
is marginally larger than the SS-N-18 (**3357.411**), but
probably carries a payload that offers more re-entry
vehicles (up to nine compared with the seven of the
SS-N-18 Mod 3) while having a greater range than the
SS-N-18 Mod 2's 8000 km, at an estimated maximum
of 8300 km.

In the 'Typhoon' class submarines, which displace
about 25 000 tons, 20 SS-N-20 missiles are stowed in
two rows of launch tubes located forward of the boat's
sail.
STATUS
Flight tests of the SS-N-20 were first detected in

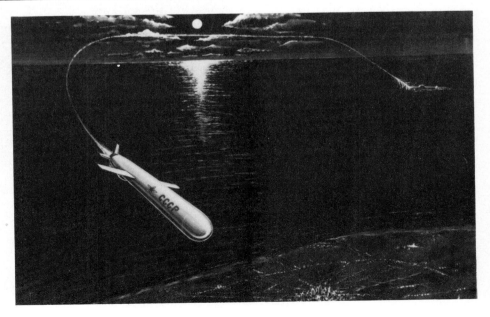

Artist's impression of Soviet 'Typhoon' class submarine armed with 20 SS-N-20 SLBMs

January 1980, reportedly with mostly unsuccessful
results. Two more successful tests were reported in
1981, and in October 1982 a simultaneous submerged
launch of four missiles took place. The first 'Typhoon'

class submarine was launched in September 1980,
and the second two years later. US authorities believe
there may be three or four more of the class now
under construction.

4795.411
SS-NX-23 SLBM
Western intelligence authorities claim to have
detected the existence of a new Soviet submarine
launched ballistic missile under development to
which the designation SS-NX-23 has been assigned.
Few details have been divulged apart from the
estimates that it has a larger throw-weight than the

existing SS-N-18 SLBM that it is thought likely to
succeed.

Like the SS-N-18, the SS-NX-23 is expected to be
deployed in 'Delta III' class submarines and to feature
multiple re-entry vehicles and warheads with
improved accuracy. Although flight tests of the new
SLBM have been reported by the US DoD, no
estimates of range or other performance

characteristics have been released. The SS-NX-23 is
thought to employ a liquid propellant rocket motor
system but the number of stages is not known.
STATUS
Development. Flight testing is thought to have started
in 1983. It has been suggested that the SS-NX-23
could enter operational service by 1985-86.

4796.411
SS-NX-21 CRUISE MISSILE
The Soviet authorities are believed by the US DoD to
be developing a new long-range cruise missile similar
to the American Tomahawk system (**4197.221** etc)
that can, like the Tomahawk be launched from
submerged submarines. The new Soviet weapon has
been given the designation SS-NX-21, the letter 'X'
denoting the fact that the system is still at the
development stage.

Little is known about the appearance or detailed
performance characteristics of the SS-NX-21, but it
has been stated that this cruise missile can be
launched from a standard torpedo tube so that a
diameter of about 53 cm can be assumed. Folding
flying surfaces are other likely features, and probably
an air-breathing turbojet power plant, possibly
coupled with a solid propellant rocket booster motor
for broaching the surface of the sea and accelerating
the missile to flying speed. These features are
illustrated in the artist's impression issued by the DoD
(see photo).

*DoD artist's impression of a Soviet SS-NX-21
submarine launched cruise missile attack*

A maximum range of about 3000 km has been suggested, and a single warhead will probably be carried. Guidance techniques that could be employed include the use of programmed inertial guidance to the target area, based on target designation co-ordinates supplied by the parent submarine, followed by one or other of the various terminal homing options available, according to the nature of the target (eg radar homing, anti-radiation etc). Readers may find it helpful to consult the entries on the US Tomahawk cruise missile in its various roles to consider the guidance technique options available.

STATUS

Development programme. It has not been confirmed but flight tests are thought to have begun, and US authorities believe the SS-NX-21 could enter operational service in 1984-85, possibly in one or more classes of Soviet nuclear attack submarines. These launch platform possibilities include particularly the newer SSNs such as the 'Sierra' and 'Mike' classes as well as existing types such as the 'Victor III' class and some of the earlier 'Yankee' class.

The Victor III class of attack submarines is seen as one possible platform for the new Soviet SS-NX-21 cruise missile

2932.131

ABM-1B (GALOSH) ANTI-BALLISTIC MISSILE MISSILE

Galosh is the NATO reporting name of the ballistic missile defence system deployed around Moscow by the Soviet authorities, based on the use of a missile thought to resemble the US Spartan anti-missile missile (**2811.131**), and designated ABM-1B under the US system of codes. In the Mosow ABM complex Galosh is used in conjunction with various radars for target detection, engagement and tracking purposes, as described in the Land-Based Air Defence Systems section of this book (**3214.181**).

Apart from photographs taken of Galosh in its transporter container, which revealed four first stage rocket motor nozzles, in a Moscow parade in 1964, the world at large has seen little of this missile. However this enabled the length of the container to be estimated (about 20 metres), from which an idea of the missile size could be derived and this led to an estimate of about 2·75 metres for the diameter.

The original single-layer ABM system for Moscow was initially completed with 64 reloadable surface launcher units for the ABM-1B located at four complexes surrounding the city, six Try Add (Triad?) guidance and engagement radars to each complex and the Dog House and Cat House target tracking radars to the south of Moscow. This is in the process of being upgraded to the total of 100 launchers permitted by the ABM Treaty of 1982.

According to official US assessments, when this upgrading is complete the new system will consist of a two-layer arrangement comprising: silo-housed modified long-range Galosh missiles designed for exo-atmospheric missile interception; silo-based high acceleration interceptors for endo-atmospheric interception; the associated engagement and guidance radars; and a large new radar at Pushkino that is designed to control ABM engagements. The silo-based launchers may be reloadable, and it is expected that the new Moscow system could be operational by the late 1980s.

CHARACTERISTICS

Type: Surface-to-air anti-ballistic missile
Guidance principle: Radar command
Propulsion: Probably 3-stage solid-propellant
Warhead: Multi-megaton nuclear
Missile length: About 20 m
Range: Estimated >300 km

Drawing of how the upgraded Moscow ABM system is expected to look when completed with silos for endo- and exo-atmospheric inteceptor missiles

Galosh anti-missile missile (Novosti)

STATUS

Operational at Moscow in four sites containing a total of 64 launchers. The Soviet Union is believed to have at least two new ABM development programmes in hand. One, designated ABM-X-3 by the American DoD, is reported to be a rapidly deployable system employing a phased array radar, missile tracking radar and a new missile. This system is described as a 'near-term' project. Far-term BMD weapon systems are also said to be in development. No clues concerning the missing ABM-2 designation have been gathered.

DoD artist's impression of an ABM-1B Galosh surface launcher of the Moscow ABM system in operation. Compare missile configuration and container with photograph of Galosh in Moscow parade

UNITED KINGDOM

2390.411
UK POLARIS MISSILES

The UK Polaris force of four submarines, each armed with 16 Polaris A-3 SLBMs have constituted the British nuclear deterrent since 1969. It is planned to continue this role until replaced by the UK Trident II system in the mid-1990s. Originally the standard US UGM-27C Polaris A-3 missile equipped with UK designed and built nuclear payload was used, but to maintain the system's effectiveness a programme to upgrade the payload was instituted under the code-name Chevaline. Missiles equipped with this system are designated Polaris A3TK.

Following retirement of Polaris from US Navy service, the Royal Navy remains the sole operator of this system.

CHARACTERISTICS

US designation: UGM-27C
Type: Submarine-launched ballistic missile (SLBM)
Guidance: Inertial
Propulsion: 2-stage, solid propellant
Warhead: 3 × 200 KT, or Chevaline (see text)
Re-entry vehicle: MRV or Chevaline (see text)
Length: 9·55 m
Diameter: 1·37 m
Launch weight: 13 600 kg
Range: 4630 km (approx)

Each standard missile is capable of a payload comprising three RVs with an estimated 200 KT yield each. Under the UK Polaris improvement programme code-named Chevaline, these are being replaced by manoeuvrable re-entry vehicles with new penetration aids. Other changes include fire control system modifications.

The Chevaline development was designed specifically to penetrate ABM defences (these surround Moscow, see **2932.131**), although it is not a

HMS Resolution, *one of the Royal Navy's four Polaris submarines. 16 missiles are carried* (Royal Navy)

MIRV system and does not involve any increase in the number of warheads associated with the Polaris force. Unofficially, Chevaline RVs are reported to have a yield of 40 KT and to be capable of separation between impact points of a maximum of 70 km; their number has not been disclosed, but on the basis of the previous Polaris payload of three 200 KT warheads and the added penetration aids of the Chevaline system, a number marginally either side of six seems a reasonable estimate.

STATUS

The Royal Navy has four nuclear-powered ballistic missile submarines, each carrying 16 Polaris missiles. They are (with launch year in brackets): HMS *Resolution* (1966), *Repulse* (1967), *Renown* (1967) and *Revenge* (1968). The UK Polaris force became fully operational in 1970. Present plans are for patrols to continue at this level until the British Trident system enters service in the early 1990s, initially with

the original Polaris missiles, but from 1982 onward progressively with the later Chevaline modified Polaris payload incorporated. In June 1981 the MoD issued a statement which said that, "The development and testing programme of Chevaline continues and is close to completion."

In 1982 it was reported that the Chevaline system had reached operational status. It was also stated that a programme costing about £300 million had been initiated for the replacement of Polaris rocket motors and some US stocks had been purchased to ensure continued availability of UK Polaris supplies.

In April 1984 Lockheed Missile and Space Company announced various contracts in support of the UK SLBM programme, including one for $138·5 million for contract modification to the UK Polaris motor restart programme.

As noted above the eventual replacement for the UK Polaris force will be the UK Trident SLBM system

(**4209.411**), a version of the system entering service with the USN (**2840.411**).

CONTRACTORS

About 800 British firms were associated with the original UK Polaris programme. Some of the major contractors are listed below.

Submarines:
 Vickers
 Cammel Laird

Nuclear reactors:
 Rolls Royce
Royal Navy Polaris School:
 George Wimpey and Co
 Vickers
 GEC-Marconi
 British Aircraft Corporation
 Sperry
 EMI

4209.411
UK TRIDENT SLBM SYSTEM

A UK Government decision to procure the American Trident SLBM system (**2840.411**) as a replacement for the British nuclear deterrent based on the Polaris SLBM system (**2390.411**) was revealed in July 1980. At that time it was intended to acquire the Trident I (C-4) missile from the USA, fit British-built warheads, and deploy it in submarines of British design and construction. The resulting system would be entirely under British ownership and operational control, but the whole force would be committed to NATO in the same way as the current Polaris force. In the event, shortly after the UK decision was made public, the US administration opted to utilise the potential offered by the larger missile tubes fitted in the new 'Ohio' class of SSBNs (Trident I can be carried in the Poseidon SLBM tube, but the tubes for Trident II missiles are both longer and of greater diameter), and procure the more powerful Trident II (D-5) missile in the 1990s. This time-scale coincided with that envisaged for the British Polaris replacement programme and it appeared sensible to adopt the SLBM planned for US service at the same time.

Where the original UK Trident programme was based on building a new class of British SSBN which would use a missile compartment based on that of the USN 640-class SSBN, adoption of the Trident II made this impossible and the solution adopted is that of employing a centre section based on that used in the USN 'Ohio' class SSBN. The British version will have only 16 missile tubes, however, compared with the American ships' 24 tubes.

The Trident II missile is expected to have an 'in-tube' life within the submarine of at least seven years, much longer than Polaris, thereby reducing the on-board maintenance considerably. If the planned fleet of four UK SSBNs is deployed, this should be adequate to provide an 'operational squadron' of three vessels continuously, so that with the fourth submarine undergoing refit there can be one armed Trident submarine on patrol at all times. Refits are planned to take place at intervals of about seven years for each submarine.

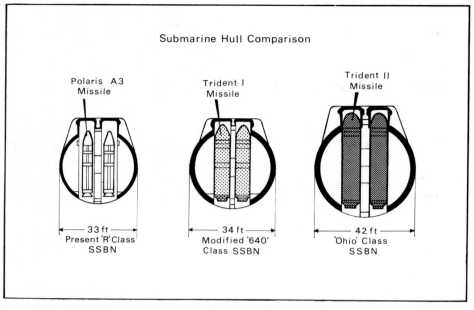

Submarine Hull Comparison

Polaris A3 Missile — 33 ft — Present 'R' Class SSBN

Trident I Missile — 34 ft — Modified '640' Class SSBN

Trident II Missile — 42 ft — 'Ohio' Class SSBN

Comparison of submarine cross-sections for Polaris, Trident I and Trident II SSBNs illustrating how hull diameter increases with missile length

STATUS

Planned for entry into service in the mid-1990s to replace the UK Polaris force. A fleet of four SSBNs, to be built by Vickers at Barrow, is planned. The Trident II (D-5) missiles will be supplied from US sources under an inter-governmental agreement. Warheads will be a British responsibility. The estimated cost (June 1982) of the programme over a period of 15 years was in the region of £7928 million.

The UK Minister of Defence, in a statement in September 1982, announced a decision to use US facilities at Kings Bay, Georgia, USA for the initial preparation for service of UK Trident missiles and for their refurbishment at the end of each British submarine's 7 to 8 year commission period. On this basis it will not be necessary to go ahead with previous plans to build the full range of facilities needed for this purpose at Loch Long in Scotland, although some new facilities will need to be constructed.

The first of the four UK Trident submarines is expected to be ordered by the end of 1985. In early 1984 it was stated that there had been no change in the cost of the Trident programme over the previous year other than for inflation and exchange rate variations. On this basis it was expected to cost a total of £8700 million.

UNITED STATES OF AMERICA

4560.111
US ICBM MODERNISATION PROGRAMME

In October 1981 President Reagan announced a comprehensive plan for modernising US strategic forces. A key part of that plan was his proposal to remedy growing deficiencies in the US land-based ICBM force. His plan called for deployment of the Peacekeeper (**4561.111**) missile with an initial operational capability in 1986. With this early deployment the President directed an aggressive research programme to identify a more survivable means of basing for the Peacekeeper missile. In November 1982, in response to a Congressional deadline, the Closely Spaced Basing plan was recommended by the Administration as the basing mode that provided the optimal survivability for Peacekeeper. Congress delayed voting on that recommendation pending a thorough review of alternatives, including a new small missile (unofficially dubbed 'Migdet man') in addition to the Peacekeeper.

The review of alternatives conducted by the President's Commission on Strategic Forces reaffirmed the necessity for a new ICBM and recommended that the Peacekeeper missile be deployed in existing silos with supporting R&D programmes to provide alternative forces for the 1990s.

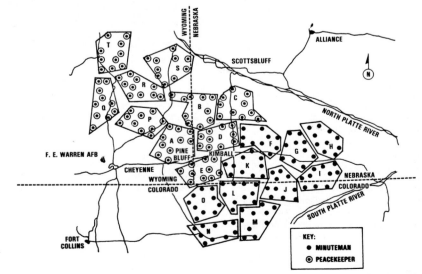

KEY:
● MINUTEMAN
◉ PEACEKEEPER

Peacekeeper deployment in existing Minuteman silos near F E Warren AFB, Wyoming. New missile will replace 100 Minuteman ICBMs

The programme for ICBM modernisation, recommended by the President's Commission on Strategic Forces and accepted by the President, calls for deployment of 100 Peacekeeper missiles in existing silos and development of a small missile suitable for either fixed or mobile development. Initial operations of the Peacekeeper system would begin in 1986, and the full force would be operational by 1989. Supporting programmes include efforts to develop superhard structures, transporters for mobile deployments, and technology for deep basing of ICBMs.

Peacekeeper

The Peacekeeper is a four-stage ICBM that carries ten independently targetable warheads which has many advantages over missile weapon systems currently in the US inventory. It will be more accurate, able to carry more warheads, with greater range and can be targeted more flexibly than the Minuteman ICBMs. Its greater resistance to nuclear effects and better guidance system provide an improved ability to destroy very hard targets. Peacekeeper is to be deployed in existing Minuteman silos as shown in the photograph. The deployment will require a minimum of modifications to the silos to accommodate new support equipment, a shock isolation system, and a more sophisticated command and control system. The deployment will be near FE Warren AFB, Wyoming, as shown in the diagram.

ICBM Technology Development Programmes

It is planned to implement additional programmes to provide alternatives for further improvement of the US ICBM force in the 1990s. Among them are the engineering and design of a small missile for mobile or fixed deployments, continued research on superhardening techniques for silos and shelters, research on different types of land-based vehicles and launchers including hardened vehicles for mobile deployment of small ICBMs, and continued work on techniques for deep basing of ICBMs.

A new small missile could carry a single warhead on two or three stages of solid-fuel motors. It would be about 11·2 m long, 106 cm in diameter, weigh about 15 500 kg, and incorporate the Advanced Inertial Reference Sphere (AIRS) or a stellar-inertial guidance system. The small missile, however, is still a concept in advanced technology development; it would not be operational before the early 1990s. The advantages of a small missile are that it could be truly mobile and, with only one warhead, it would be less inviting as a target. It is estimated $600 million would be required for design, development, and demonstration of a small missile.

Recent advances in the design of structures hardened against nuclear effects indicate considerable promise for 'superhard' missile silos. A programme to test such designs, to refine construction technology, and to validate anticipated nuclear effects will expand options for increasing ICBM survivability in fixed locations.

Supporting research will also refine designs for mobile missile transport. Concepts for road mobile operations will be explored while a hardened mobile

Artist's impression of how Peacekeeper advanced ICBMs will be deployed in existing Minuteman missile silos. Modifications will be minimal and silo will not be hardened beyond existing level

	1983	1984	1985
Peacekeeper ICBM			
Procurement	—	(21)2079·6	(40)2938·9
RDT&E	1912·6	1984·9	1716·3
Construction	45·8	31·2	114·0
Tomahawk cruise missile			
Procurement	(51)207·5	(124)326·2	(180)560·1
RDT&E	109·0	474·8	670·5
Trident I SLBM			
Procurement	(62)633·7	(52)549·9	(0)163·8
RDT&E	14·7	23·3	—
Trident II SLBM			
Procurement	—	—	(—)25·2
RDT&E	351·0	1452·7	2077·5
Trident Submarines (Ohio class)			
All-in cost	(1)1823·5	(1)2212·4	(1)2014·3
BMD Advanced Technology Programme			
RDT&E	142·8	152·9	—
BMD Systems Technology Programme			
RDT&E	376·2	316·3	—
Construction	20·0	—	12·8

transport system will be studied to see if enough protection can be provided so that mobile missiles could operate in the confines of existing military bases.

Funding contained in the US DoD fiscal year 1985 Budget relating to various aspects of ICBM programmes are listed below, together with other strategic programme funding to give an idea of the relative sizes of different aspects of the total US effort in this area (procurement quantities in brackets and funding in $millions):

4561.111

PEACEKEEPER (MGM-118) ICBM

Peacekeeper is the name assigned to the weapon that was formerly known as the Advanced ICBM, or MX, and earlier work was described in **2718.111** in previous editions. It is a major element in the US ICBM modernisation programme (**4560.111**).

The MGM-118 Peacekeeper missile is a four-stage intercontinental ballistic missile (ICBM) which has been designed to deliver 10 Mk 21 re-entry vehicles to independent targets at ranges usually greater than 8000 km. The missile is about 21·6 m long, 234 cm in diameter and weighs about 88 450 kg. Three of the four stages use solid propellant materials exhausted through a single nozzle. Hydraulically operated thrust vector actuators move the nozzles to guide the missile

Launch pad for first Peacekeeper test flight. Test stand holds missile launch canister. Cold launch technique is used whereby missile is ejected by a gas generation system and the first stage motor ignites when clear of the canister. 20 flight tests are planned, all from Vandenberg AFB, California

along its flight path. The fourth stage, called the post-boost vehicle, uses a liquid propellant to power an axial thrust engine and eight small engines which are used for attitude control. The post-boost vehicle also includes a guidance and control system, a deployment module and re-entry vehicles. The guidance function is performed by a completely self-contained inertial guidance and navigation system. During flight the missile is completely independent of ground references or commands.

The first stage solid rocket motor weighs approximately 49 000 kg and is about 9·1 m long. It will boost the missile to about 23 000 m. Stage I is equipped with a single movable nozzle which is controlled by signals from the guidance and control system.

The second stage solid rocket motor weighs approximately 27 000 kg and is about 5·5 m long. Stage II ignites after the burn-out and release of Stage I and propels the missile to an altitude of about 88 000 m. Both stages use a synthetic rubber-based solid propellant with aluminium and oxidiser additives. Stage II has a single movable nozzle which incorporates an extensible exit cone. The exit cone is folded until Stage II is ignited; it then extends. This feature allows the exit cone to enlarge so that the performance of the stage is increased without making the diameter of the missile larger. The single nozzle is controlled by signals from the guidance and control system using power provided by hydraulic actuators which receive high pressure gas from a gas generator.

The third stage solid rocket motor weighing about 7·700 kg, is approximately 2·4 m long. Stage III provides thrust to boost the missile to about 213 000 m. Stage III ignites after burn-out and release of Stage II. Stage III uses a synthetic polymer plastic-based solid propellant with aluminium and oxidiser additives. Like Stage II, the Stage III single nozzle also has an extensible exit cone to obtain performance without increasing the diameter of the missile. The solid propellants in the first three stages are contained in motor cases made of a kevlar epoxy material. The Stage III nozzle is also controlled by the guidance and control system. The nozzle is movable and positioned by a hydraulic system powered by a solid-propellant gas generator.

The fourth stage weighs about 850 kg and is 1·2 m long. Stage IV uses a liquid bi-propellant rocket propulsion system which provides velocity and attitude corrections for this phase of the missile flight. Following the burn-out and separation of Stage III, the post-boost vehicle manoeuvres and each re-entry vehicle is released. The vehicle is then moved by its propulsion systems to new positions where the remaining re-entry vehicles are deployed in sequence. The propulsion system includes the liquid propellants and tanks, an axial engine and its thrust vector actuation system, and attitude control engines. The attitude control engines use the same bi-propellants as the axial engine.

The missile guidance and control (G&C) system is contained in the post-boost vehicle. The G&C system includes the inertial measurement unit (IMU), the missile electronics and computer assembly, ground and flight software, the in-flight cooling sub-system, airborne power supply, missile interconnection cables, the missile ordnance arm switch, the power distribution switch, the missile umbilical receptacle, the supporting structure, and shields. Inside the IMU is a floated sphere containing gyros, accelerometers and some associated electronics. The gyros generate a basic computer commanded frame of reference with which all missile movements are compared. The accelerometers measure all vehicle velocities with respect to that frame of reference. Utilising the position and velocity information generated by the gyros and accelerometers, the missile and electronics and computer assembly determines all guidance and

Successful first flight of Peacekeeper (formerly the MX) ICBM in June 1983 from Vandenberg AFB, California. The unarmed missile covered a distance of approximately 4100 nm (7600 km) (USAF/DoD photo)

control functions of the missile. The G&C system also determines the correct release point for vehicles near the termination of powered flight path.

The re-entry vehicles, which contain the weapons, are conically shaped and covered with materials to protect the weapons during the flight through the atmosphere to the target. The high speed re-entry will cause extreme heating requiring a surface material to ablate or erode in a controlled manner to protect the weapon throughout its flight.

In addition to the stages and re-entry vehicles, the missile also includes a shroud and the deployment module. The shroud, often called a nosecone, protects the re-entry vehicles during the ascent phases of flight. The shroud is topped with a nose cap made of a metal called Inconel, and contains a rocket motor to separate it from the missile.

The deployment module provides the structural support for the re-entry vehicles and carries the electronics to activate and deploy them. These vehicles are mechanically attached to the deployment module. The mechanical attachment is severed by explosive units which frees the re-entry vehicles allowing them to separate with minimum disturbances from the deployment module. Each re-entry vehicle is deployed at a position which will allow it to follow a ballistic path to its target.

The ten warheads will be modified versions of the Mk 12A re-entry vehicle which is used in the Minuteman ICBM, and in this role they are given the designation Mk 21.

The change from the Mk 12A to the Mk 21 re-entry vehicle (RV) reduced Peacekeeper range, and this caused an increase in throw-weight that further

reduced RV range. The Mk 21 is heavier than the Mk 12A and not all of this increase in weight could be accommodated within the SALT II 3600 kg throw-weight limit for Peacekeeper, so that propellant had to be sacrificed, thereby further reducing range. According to the US Air Force the effects on range will be offset by the decision to site Peacekeepers in Nebraska and Wyoming rather than the original locations in Nevada and Utah further south. In this way, it is claimed, Peacekeeper with ten RVs will have the range to reach the most distant planned hard targets.

DEVELOPMENT

The US Air Force Strategic Air Command stated a requirement for a new ICBM in 1972. This weapon should be capable of destroying hardened targets and should itself be based in a survivable manner. After the requirement had been validated, the programme was initiated as the MX (Advanced ICBM), renamed the Peacekeeper in November 1982.

The Peacekeeper programme, which includes a missile and a basing system, began full-scale development in September 1979 (about two years later than intended), but the basing plans then proposed to ensure survivability were not acceptable. On taking office in January 1981, President Reagan initiated a review of the American strategic forces and alternative options for modernising those forces. In October 1981 he proposed, as part of the US deterrent modernisation programme; continuation of Peacekeeper development, with the objective of near-term interim deployment of the missile in Titan or Minuteman silos that had been modified to increase their hardness; cancellation of the MPS (multiple protective shelter) basing system; and deactivation of the Titan II ICBM force.

However, Congress rejected the proposal for interim Peacekeeper deployment, and on 22 November 1982 the President then proposed stationing 100 of these missiles in an array of 100 closely spaced 'super-hard' silos near FE Warren AFB, Wyoming (the so-called 'Dense Pack' basing mode). Congress also rejected this, allowing funds for Peacekeeper missile development but not for procurement, while restricting funds for basing mode development. Flight testing of Peacekeeper was also forbidden until the basing mode had been approved.

Consequently the President set up a Commission on Strategic Forces in January 1983, to examine basing modes for Peacekeeper. The suggestions of the Commission comprised three main elements:

(1) siting 100 Peacekeeper missiles in existing Minuteman silos
(2) development of a new small ICBM (popularly known as 'Midgetman')
(3) investigation of hardened silos, shelters, and mobile launcher systems.

The President endorsed these recommendations in April 1983 and Congress gave its approval the following month.

STATUS
After Congressional approval of the Peacekeeper basing mode in May 1983, production of Peacekeeper missiles began with a DoD request for funds for 27 missiles in the 1984 budget. This quantity was not approved however, instead Congress directed the USAF to deploy ten Peacekeepers in Minuteman silos by the end of 1986.

In a report to the Secretary of Defense by the US General Accounting Office in May 1984 it is stated that to meet the deployment date specified by Congress, some flight testing planned before deployment to verify performance of the production model will not be completed until after deployment. Also some components that are being changed or redesigned (eg the re-entry vehicle and guidance and control components) will go into production before flight testing.

The GAO also concluded that warhead range decreased as a result of using the Mk 21 re-entry vehicle in lieu of the Mk 12A, but that this limitation will be mitigated by siting Peacekeeper further north, in Nebraska and Wyoming rather than Utah and Nevada as previously planned. Meanwhile Soviet silo hardening techniques and implementation, as well as the threat have advanced since the original Peacekeeper performance specification was drawn up in 1979.

The 1984 DoD budget figures for Peacekeeper, published in February 1984 were:

	1983	1984	1985
Procurement:	—	(21)2079·6	(40)2938·9
RDT&E	1912·6	1984·9	1716·3
Construction	45·8	31·2	114·0

(Procurement quantities in brackets and funding in $ millions.)
The overall procurement plan for Peacekeeper according to GAO figures calls for a total production of 223 missiles, 100 for deployment, 108 for operational test and evaluation, and 15 to monitor the effects of ageing. The planned pattern of procurement is given in the following table:

Fiscal year	1984	1985	1986	1987	1988	1989	Total
Deployment	20	30	31	19	0	0	100
Test/evaluation	1	9	16	28	47	7	108
Ageing	0	1	1	1	1	11	15
Annual totals	21	40	48	48	48	18	223

The first flight test of Peacekeeper took place on 17 June 1983 from Vandenberg AFB, California, and the target area was Kwajalein Atoll, a distance of about 7600 km.

CONTRACTORS
Aerojet General: Second-stage.
Avco: Re-entry systems integration.
Boeing: Basing and deep basing support.
Charles Stark Draper Laboratory: Guidance and control technical support.
General Electric: Adaptation of Mk 12A warhead.
GTE Sylvania: Launch control system.
Hercules: Third-stage systems.
Honeywell: Specific force integrating receiver; gyro second source.
Martin Marietta: Missile assembly test and system support.
Northrop: Inertial measurement unit; target processor; third generation gyro.
Rockwell International: Fourth-stage system.
TRW: Targeting and analysis program.
Westinghouse: Launch canister.

Peacekeeper (MGM-118) ICBM is ejected by gas generator at base of canister before first stage motor ignites. Note sabot-like packing falling away from missile as it emerges

---

2716.111
MINUTEMAN II INTERCONTINENTAL BALLISTIC MISSILE
Minuteman II was introduced as a considerably improved version of Minuteman I. The improvements, however, took the form of an upgrading of the missile's capabilities rather than a radically new departure as, in some respects, is Minuteman III (**2717.111**). Like Minuteman I it is a three-stage ICBM carrying a single thermonuclear warhead, but it has increased range and azimuth, providing greater targeting coverage, while carrying a larger payload. A more sophisticated guidance system is capable of pre-storing the locations of a larger number of alternative targets (see **2710.111**) and the over-all accuracy of the missile system is greater than for Minuteman I. The increased payload capability enables the missile to carry a larger thermonuclear warhead together with a number of penetration aids.

The first- and third-stage motors of Minuteman II are believed to be the same as those on Minuteman I but the second-stage motor is new.
CHARACTERISTICS
Service designation: LGM-30F
Type: 3-stage, solid-propellant, intercontinental ballistic missile

Guidance: Inertial, Rockwell International Autonetics
Propulsion: First stage, Thiokol TU-122 (M-55), approx 91 000 kg st; second stage, Aerojet SR19-AJ-1, approx 27 500 kg st; third stage, Hercules, thrust approx 16 000 kg. Thrust vector control on first- and third-stage motors by 4 movable nozzles. Second-stage motor has a single nozzle with secondary liquid injection for thrust vector control
Re-entry vehicle: Avco Type 11B and 11C with Mk 1 and 1A penetration aids, the latter supplied by Tracor Inc
Warhead: Thermonuclear single warhead of a yield unofficially reported as around 2 MT
Dimensions: Length 18·2 m; diameter approx 180 cm at first stage interstage
Launch weight: Approx 31 750 kg
Speed: >24 000 km/h at burn-out
Range: >11 250 km
STATUS
Operational. According to firm plans at the time of writing, 450 Minuteman II missiles will be kept on the active strength for some years to come. In 1982 it was stated that some Minuteman II missiles are allocated to the Emergency Rocket Communications System for SIOP communications.

The Minuteman ICBM completed 20 years in operational service in October 1982, and seems destined to serve for an appreciable time yet. Additional details of historical background, deployment and development over the years have appeared under entry number **2710.111** in previous editions of *Jane's Weapon Systems*.
CONTRACTORS
Assembly, test and installations: Boeing Aerospace Company, Seattle, Washington 98124, USA.

Systems engineering: TRW Systems Group, 1 Space Park CR, Redondo Beach, California 90278, USA.

Guidance: Rockwell International Corporation, Autonetics Strategic Systems Division, 3370 Miraloma Avenue, Anaheim, California 92803, USA.

Propulsion: Aerojet-General Corporation, 9100 E Flair Drive, El Monte, California 91734, USA; Hercules Inc, 910 Market Street, Wilmington, Delaware 19899, USA; Thiokol Corporation, Bristol, Pennsylvania 19007, USA.

Re-entry vehicles: Avco Systems Division, 201 Lovell Street, Wilmington, Massachusetts 01887, USA.

Penetration aids: Tracor Inc, 6500 Tracor Lane, Austin, Texas 78721, USA.

2717.111
MINUTEMAN III INTERCONTINENTAL BALLISTIC MISSILE
Minuteman III is the most potent weapon in the land-based armoury of the United States. Like Minuteman I and Minuteman II it is basically a three-stage ICBM powered by solid-propellant rocket motors, but it

incorporates several features which make it more than a simple improvement on the two earlier members of the series.

Most of the special features relate to the final stage and re-entry system and the most significant, operationally, is the introduction of a MIRV system of three warheads. This MIRV head is essentially a

fourth stage of the missile and is powered by a 135 kg thrust motor and manoeuvred by six small pitch and yaw motors and four smaller roll motors. These motors are controlled by the fourth-stage guidance package which also organises the release of the warheads, chaff, and decoys from the General Electric re-entry vehicle. The third stage of the missile has also been considerably improved by the introduction of a new motor using fluid-injection thrust-vector control, which gives a finer control of movement than the earlier arrangement of four movable nozzles and which, with improved guidance, enables the missile to carry its large payload over a greater range and at the same time reduce the missile's CEP to about 400 m.

CHARACTERISTICS
Service designation: LGM-30G
Type: 3-stage, solid-propellant, intercontinental ballistic missile
Guidance: Inertial, Rockwell International
Propulsion: First stage, Thiokol TV-122 (M-55), approx 91 000 kg st; second stage, Aerojet SR19-AJ-1, approx 27 500 kg st; third stage, SR73-AJ-1 Aerojet and Thiokol, approx 15 500 kg st; post-boost propulsion system, Bell Aerosystems package comprising 135 kg st bi-propellant (nitrogen tetroside/MMH) engine for fore-and-aft control, 6 10 kg st engines for pitch and yaw control and 4 skin-mounted 8 kg st motors for roll control. Propellant tanks are welded shut for long-term silo storage. All motors commanded by fourth-stage guidance package
Re-entry vehicle: General Electric Mk 12. Normal Minuteman III payload is 3 MIRV warheads plus chaff and decoys. 2 or 3 Mk 12 RVs can be carried with a

yield of about 200 KT each. A Mk 12A RV with a yield of about 330 KT is being substituted for the Mk 12 on 300 Minuteman III missiles
Warheads: Thermonuclear, W-62 approx 200 KT each; or W-78, 330 KT each
Dimensions: Length 18·2 m; diameter 185 cm at first stage interstage
Launch weight: Approx 34 500 kg
Speed: >24 000 km/h at burn-out
Range: >13 000 km
CEP: <400 m
STATUS
Operational. Full planned force of 550 Minuteman III and 450 Minuteman II missiles are now operationally deployed. Considerable efforts are being sustained to maintain and enhance the operational potential of the Minuteman force, of which the Minuteman III is the principal element. These efforts embrace the Mk 12A, guidance accuracy improvements, silo upgrading and other programmes.

Replacement of Mk 12 warheads with Mk 12A RVs on some Minuteman III missiles is in progress and about 300 missiles are due to be fitted with the new RV which carries a W-78 warhead. This warhead is about 16 kg heavier than the Mk 12s and there is a consequent slight reduction in the Minuteman III range and MIRV footprint. Deployment of the Mk 12A began in December 1979. In the meantime the NS-20

guidance software improvements are scheduled for incorporation on all Minuteman IIIs.

As noted above, the Minuteman system had served as the main element of the American land-based strategic ICBM force since October 1982. Conversion of 100 Minuteman III silos in Nebraska and Wyoming to house MGM-118 Peacekeeper ICBMs will start in 1986. The first ten MGM-118s are due to be in position by December 1986.

CONTRACTORS
Assembly, test, and installation: Boeing Aerospace Company, Seattle, Washington 98124, USA.

Systems engineering: TRW Systems Group, 1 Space Park CR, Redondo Beach, California 90278, USA.

Guidance: Rockwell International Corporation, Autonetics Strategic Systems Division, 3370 Miraloma Avenue, Anaheim, California 92803, USA.

Propulsion: Aerojet-General Corporation, 9100 E Flair Drive, El Monte, California 91734, USA; Thiokol Corporation, Bristol, Pennsylvania 19007, USA.

Post-boost propulsion system: Bell Aerospace Co, Division of Textron Inc, PO Box 1, Buffalo, New York 14240, USA.

Re-entry vehicle: General Electric Co, 570 Lexington Avenue, New York, New York 10022, USA.

2826.111
TITAN II INTERCONTINENTAL BALLISTIC MISSILE

The LGM-25C Titan II is an improved version of the earlier HGM-25A Titan I intercontinental ballistic missile. It carries the largest of all US ICBM payloads and has a launch reaction time of one minute from its fully hardened underground silo.

Titan has been operational with the Strategic Air Command since 1963 and was originally deployed in three wings of 18 missiles each at Davis-Monthan AFB, Arizona; McConnell AFB, Kansas; and Little Rock AFB, Arkansas. Since entering service two missiles have been lost in silo accidents.

CHARACTERISTICS
Designation: LGM-25C
Type: Land-based intercontinental ballistic missile
Guidance: Inertial
Propulsion: 2-stage liquid propellant rocket motors. Stage 1: 195 000 kg st; stage 2: 45 000 kg st
Warhead: Nuclear. W-53, estimated 9 MT yield
Re-entry vehicle: General Electric Mk 6
Missile length: Stage 1: 21·3 m; stage 2: 6·1 m; re-entry vehicle: 4·3 m; total: 31·3 m
Missile diameter: 3 m
Launch weight: Stage 1: 117 000 kg; stage 2: 29 000 kg; re-entry vehicle: 3700 kg; total: 149 700 kg
Speed: >24 000 km/h
Ceiling: About 1500 km
Range: About 15 000 km

STATUS
Titan II is being phased out and it is planned to complete the retirement programme in 1987. Nevertheless it is arranged that those missiles on alert during the phase-out period will be in a position to contribute to the US deterrent posture. During 1982-84 the USAF made a number of improvements to enable the system to be operated safely until phase-out. Deactivated silos will be dismantled to comply with SALT terms, in step with Trident SLBM deployments. The 1985 budget requested $69.7 million for Titan system operation and winding down, and $10.3 million for silo dismantling. De-activation of the first Titans took place in Arizona in November 1982.

CONTRACTOR
Martin Marietta Aerospace, Denver, Colorado 80201, USA.

Titan II launch. Withdrawal of these weapons has started

1133.411
POSEIDON C-3 (UGM-73A) FLEET BALLISTIC MISSILE

This is a two-stage, solid-propellant strategic missile designed for launching from submerged submarines of the USN. It was a successor to the Polaris A-2 and A-3 weapons. The range of Poseidon is the same as for the Polaris A-3, 2500 nm (4630 km), but weight is more than doubled at 29 480 kg. Dimensions are correspondingly greater with length 10·36 metres and diameter 188 cm, but the later missiles were capable of deployment in the launch tubes of Polaris submarines without major modifications to the ship.

A considerably increased nuclear payload of up to 14 MIRVs carrying W-76 warheads enables a single Poseidon to be used against a number of targets. An improved guidance system was also incorporated which provided double the accuracy, it is claimed, of earlier weapons.

An improved fire control system, Mk 88, was produced for the Poseidon system by the General Electric Company. This interfaces with a later version of the Rockwell SINS (ships inertial navigation system), the missile and the launcher. Mk 88 performs target calculations, insertion of data into the guidance system, test and checkout launch order, and sequence control.

DEVELOPMENT
The first flight model of Poseidon was launched in August 1968 from Cape Kennedy, Florida. The 14th launch, in December 1969, was the first complete test of the weapons system, including the launcher, control, and missile sub-systems. Development flight testing was completed in June 1970.

STATUS
Poseidon became operational in March 1971. An undisclosed number of Poseidon warheads are assigned to NATO targets, by which is understood targets of less than global strategic importance but of greater significance than could reliably be assigned to tactical nuclear weapons, such as Lance.

The fiscal year 1984 report by the US Secretary of Defense confirmed that 12 of the original fleet of 31 Poseidon submarines had been converted to operate the later Trident I (C-4) SLBM during the 1970s, and this programme has now been completed. Unless there are any later plans to modify more Poseidon boats to operate Trident I missiles, it is intended to progessively retire the remaining C-3 Poseidon submarines between 1993 and 1999.

CONTRACTORS
Prime contractor: Lockheed Missiles and Space Company, PO Box 504, Sunnyvale, California 94088, USA.

Test launch of Poseidon

Mk 88 fire control system: General Electric Company, Ordnance Systems Division, 100 Plastics Avenue, Pittsfield, Massachusetts 01201, USA.

SINS: Rockwell International Corporation, Autonetics Marine Systems Division, 3370 Miraloma Avenue, Anaheim, California 92803, USA.

3993.001

CRUISE MISSILE PROGRAMME

The American cruise missile programme has been difficult to define satisfactorily for almost a decade, for reasons which have been discussed at some length under the above entry number in previous editions of this book. Summarised, US cruise missiles currently in, or planned for operation derive from two separate missile programmes each with their own developer and sponsoring service (USAF and USN), which subsequently were co-ordinated under DoD supervision. Since then models and applications have proliferated, thanks to a great extent to the inherent flexibility of the basic cruise missile concept and efforts of the weapons' producers and sponsoring agencies. Thus there have been air-launched versions derived from both the Boeing ALCM, AGM-86 (**1766.311**) and the General Dynamics BGM-109 Tomahawk. The latter has been developed in several versions: the MRASM (AGM-109H) medium-range air-to-surface missile (cancelled by Congress in fiscal year 1984); several ship- or submarine-launched models (**4197.221**); and the BGM-109G ground-launched cruise missile (**4194.111**). Additional details of the ALCM will be found in the Air-to-surface Missiles section of this volume, as will information on the GLCM in battlefield support context in the appropriate pages. Similarly naval applications of Tomahawk are discussed in the Shipborne Weapons section.

The extent to which any particular cruise missile model is 'tactical' or 'strategic' inevitably depends on the circumstances and the individual conventions that are adopted. However, judgements are frequently based on the parameters of range and payload capability, so that the three US cruise missiles listed in the following paragraphs normally qualify for consideration under the 'strategic' heading on this basis.

TLAM-N: The nuclear armed version of the land attack Tomahawk (BGM-109A), tactical land attack missile – nuclear (TLAM-N) which will provide the USN with a long-range tactical weapon which can be used in support of world-wide objectives, including targets within reach of covert submarines operating in waters where America has neither sea nor air control. The nuclear SLCM is claimed to match a capability that has been deployed by the Soviet Union for a long time. Launches by both submarines and surface vessels are planned, and a vertical launch Tomahawk system is planned for DDG-X, DD-963 and CG-47 ships.

ALCM: The AGM-86B air launched cruise missile (**1766.311**) is in production and will form a force of long-range nuclear-armed air-to-ground cruise missiles for use with Strategic Air Command B-52G bombers. This will provide the USAF with increased bomber routing flexibility and targeting options, and will reduce bomber exposure to enemy air defences. Initially, each bomber will have 12 ALCMs mounted externally on jettisonable pylons, with the current internal load of gravity bombs and SRAMs. In the mid-1980s, eight ALCMs will replace the internal load on each aircraft. By 1990 all B-52Gs will be loaded with 20 ALCMs each.

GLCM: BGM-109G, the ground launched cruise missile (**4194.111**) was intended as a response to Soviet deployment of long-range tactical weapons such as the SS-20 in the European theatre. The basic combat flight of the GLCM system consists of 16 Tomahawk missiles, four transporter-erector-launchers, and two launch control centres. One flight will maintain a quick reaction alert status on each main operating base during normal peacetime conditions, but during periods of increased alert status, the GLCM flights would disperse from the main base to satellite stations to ensure increased survivability if attacked. The initial operational capability (IOC) was achieved in December 1983, and construction of further GLCM basing facilities had already been started in the Federal Republic of Germany, Italy and the UK. Belgium was making basing preparations in 1983 and bilateral discussions between the Netherlands and USA were in progress. Present plans provide for 464 GLCMs to be based in Europe, deployed in 29 flights with 116 launchers; Britain and the Federal Republic of Germany have agreed to provide bases for about one third of this total each, and the remainder would be distributed

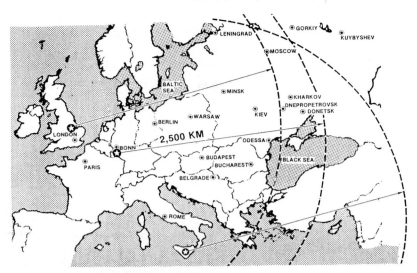

Reach of GLCMs with 2500 km range from various launch points (direct flight path)

The modernised cruiser USS New Jersey launches a BGM-109 sea launched cruise missile. USN plans to deploy nuclear tipped Tomahawk cruise missiles on surface ships and submarines for engagement of hard targets

between Italy, Belgium and the Netherlands.

The original submarine launching mode for the Tomahawk cruise missile employed the submarine's normal torpedo tubes, from which a stainless steel capsule containing the missile was ejected, but a new vertical launch system is under development by Westinghouse, under contract to the USN. Called the capsule launcher system (CLS) it is intended to add firepower to existing and future submarine fleets. Tomahawk missiles are loaded into the capsule at the factory and shipped as a unit ready for use, the capsule providing environmental protection, a means of control and communication, and facilities for a safe launch under all conditions of submarine manoeuvres. The vertical launch mode is claimed to offer an increase of up to 50 per cent in weapon loads compared with the present method which is constrained by the torpedo tubes installed. First installations will be in 'SSN 688' class submarines, within the bow section but external to the pressure hull, and a set of 12 Tomahawk missiles can be carried. These will be available for sequential launch,

in addition to the weapons carried in the torpedo room.

STATUS

The actual and planned funding for ALCM procurement in fiscal years 1983 and 1984 is $924.6 million for 570 missiles and spares. By the end of fiscal year 1984 the USAF will have deployed ALCMs on 90 B-52G aircraft, and in 1985 it is planned to modify B-52H aircraft to carry ALCMs. Development of an advanced cruise missile (ACM) to succeed the AGM-86 ALCM is planned.

In September 1982 a contract was signed making McDonnell Douglas a co-producer with General Dynamics of the Tomahawk cruise missile. Dual production began in March 1982 with McDonnell Douglas due to build ten complete missiles in its first year, and 52 in fiscal year 1983. From fiscal year 1984 the company competes with General Dynamics for up to 40 per cent of all Tomahawk production.

Planned procurement of BGM-109 GLCMs in fiscal years 1983/84/85 is as follows, with quantities in brackets and funding in $ millions.

	1983	1984	1985
Procurement	(84) 446·8	(120) 580·9	(120) 571·1
RDT&E	28·3	36·2	18·7

The comparable figures for the SLCM are:

	1983	1984	1985
Procurement	(51) 207·5	(124) 326·2	(180) 560·1
RDT&E	109·0	128·8	81·5

CONTRACTORS
AGM-86B ALCM: Boeing Aerospace Company, Seattle, Washington 98124, USA.

BGM-109 Tomahawk: General Dynamics Corporation, Convair Division, 5001 Kearny Villa Road, San Diego, California 92123, USA.

BGM-109 Tomahawk: McDonnell Douglas Astronautics Company, Titusville, Florida, USA.

Launch of GLCM during USAF tests

4562.311
US STRATEGIC BOMBER FORCE
The strategic bomber force operated by the USAF consists of B-52 and FB-111 aircraft capable of carrying nuclear or conventional free-fall bombs, the air-launched cruise missile (ALCM) (**1766.311**) or short range attack missile (SRAM) (**1107.311**) and the latest US figures on the composition of these aircraft assigned to strategic duties are as follows:

B-52D	31
B-52G	151
B-52H	90
FB-111	56

The backbone of the current strategic bomber force is the ageing B-52 fleet. The oldest version, the B-52D, first entered the inventory in 1955 and is due to be phased out. The B-52Gs now serve as an enemy airspace penetrator carrying ALCMs, and are expected to revert to conventional weapon delivery and maritime roles in the late 1980s. The latest model, B-52H, will serve in the penetration role for a number of years under present plans, and probably until the end of the century as a stand-off attack cruise missile carrier. The most modern bomber is the FB-111, the last of which was produced in 1969. With improved avionics, low-level terrain following capabilities and advanced ECM, these are effective penetration aircraft and can deliver a mixture of gravity weapons and SRAMs.

In the US view this force will continue to provide a credible deterrent for the immediate future, but by the end of the decade, when the USSR is expected to have deployed a more effective air defence system, the older B-52s will no longer be able to survive in the penetrator role. It is therefore planned to begin deploying the new B-1B bomber in 1985 to replace the B-52s in this demanding task. This will allow the B-52s to transfer to the cruise missile carrying role. Deployment of the ALCM, initially on B-52s and later on the B-1B, will improve the overall US strategic capability at the same time increasing stress on Soviet defences. An advanced technology bomber (ATB) is planned for deployment in the early 1990s.

The ALCM clearly plays a large part in the US programme to modernise the strategic bomber force capability, and by the end of fiscal year 1984 it is anticipated that ALCMs will have been deployed on 90 operational B-52Gs. Starting in 1985, as B-1B aircraft become available, B-52H aircraft will be modified to carry ALCMs. It is planned to deploy the first B-1B bombers in fiscal year 1985 with the last of a total force of 100 aircraft due for deployment in fiscal year 1988. The B-1B incorporates substantial improvements over the B-1A prototype and is expected to perform in the penetrator role principally during the 1980s. As the ATB is deployed in the 1990s, the B-1B will carry cruise missiles as part of its weapons mix and it will remain an effective part of the strategic bomber force throughout its planned operational life. As an official assessment in 1983 has it, 'Our two bomber programmes (B-52 modernisation/ALCM and the B-1) work to ensure high

B-1 bomber

B-52G with ALCMs loaded

confidence in our capability to penetrate Soviet air defences in the next century as well as complement the expanding missions of our bomber force. Rather than using the B-1B capability, for example, only in the nuclear response mission against the Soviet Union, the B-1B is a versatile plane capable of delivering a very large nuclear or conventional payload anywhere in the world. It is superbly suited for power projection, show of force, maritime missions of sea surveillance, mine laying, and anti-ship warfare. In addition, it can provide conventional firepower to remote areas to support elements of a rapid deployment force. The B-1B bridges the gap between the ageing technology of the B-52 and the radically new 'stealth' technology of the ATB. Both the B-1B and the ATB programmes continue on schedule with the first squadron of B-1Bs becoming operational in 1986.'

STATUS
The B-52Gs are expected to remain effective into the next decade. The aircraft scheduled for cruise missile

conversion will be assigned to non-penetrating or stand-off missions as the B-1B is deployed, while those not scheduled to receive cruise missiles will replace retiring B-52Ds in a conventional bomber/maritime support role. Over the next decade, as the B-1B assumes a cruise missile carrying role, DoD expects to start retiring the B-52G force. A very long operational life is foreseen for the B-52H as an ALCM carrier well into the 1990s. A number of modifications are proposed for both B-52G and H models, consistent with their planned operational life, and all are due to receive a new offensive avionics system (OAS), improved radar and other enhancements.

Proposed funding for B-1 procurement (34 aircraft) in fiscal year 1985 was $7712·3 million, the next 48 aircraft were expected to cost $5591·9 million in 1986. Development costs were similarly expected to decrease, from $508·3 million to $375·2 million in the period.

2840.411
TRIDENT C-4 (UGM-93A) STRATEGIC WEAPON SYSTEM

The UGM-93A Trident I (C-4) missile is a three-stage ballistic missile powered by solid-fuel rockets, and guided by a self-contained inertial guidance system, with a range approximately twice that of Poseidon (**1133.411**), or about 7000 km.

The guidance system for the C-4 missile, designated Mk 5, is smaller and lighter than that for Poseidon, thereby reducing inert weight and providing more space for missile propulsion. The Mk 5 guidance system is basically a functional equivalent to the all inertial Mk 3 Poseidon system. The most significant difference is the addition of a stellar sensor which takes a star sight during the post-boost phase of flight. The post-boost vehicle will correct its flight path based on data derived from the stellar sighting. This enables the Trident missile to meet Poseidon accuracy objectives at longer range. The function of the guidance system is to generate missile steering commands during powered flight that accurately direct the missile to the correct velocity, position, and altitude for re-entry body deployment to the assigned target. Control information is generated by inputs from the shipboard fire control sub-system and flight acceleration history.

The post-boost vehicle (PBV) is designed to permit corrections for errors in launch position data and manoeuvres to deploy re-entry bodies, following third stage separation.

A new Mk 4 re-entry body was developed for Trident I. In addition to the ballistic Mk 4 RV, the Mk 500 Evader manoeuvring RV was being developed as an option but the work is understood to have been discontinued. Instead, if it is decided to equip the Trident II (D-5) missile, development of a completely new Mk 5 re-entry system is more likely. Another possibility is the adoption of the Mk 12A warhead as used in some other US strategic missiles.

The launcher sub-system stows and protects the missiles aboard the submarine, pressurises the launch tube and missile before launch, and launches the missile from the submarine. The launch control group is of a new design to provide integrated control and monitoring of 24 missiles and tubes and will be collocated in the missile control centre to improve weapon system control and reduce manning to operate the equipment.

The fire control sub-system prepares the missile guidance system with targeting and launch position data and co-ordinates the preparation of the launcher and missile test and readiness equipment for the missile launch. Two basic fire control configurations are being developed: the Mk 88 Mod 2 for retrofitting to Poseidon, and the Mk 98 Mod 0 for the new Trident submarine. A new fire control computer, the Trident Digital Control Computer (TDCC), will be required to handle the increased computational work involved in providing pre-settings for the C-4 missile. A digital read-in sub-system (DRISS) will provide a digital guidance interface under the control of the TDCC. The navigation data converter will convert analogue

First launch of a US Navy C-4 Trident I SLBM from the submerged fleet ballistic missile submarine USS Ohio *off the coast of Florida (US Navy)*

navigation and optical outputs to digital. These systems are common to both fire control configurations.

The Trident navigation sub-system is basically similar in design to that of the 640-class Poseidon SSBNs with the following improvements: (1) the major addition of an electrostatically supported gyro monitor (ESGM) to lengthen the time between navigation fixes and thereby reduce submarine exposure to potential detection; (2) provision for additional closed-loop air cooling to enhance maintenance and reliability; (3) selected modifications to reduce noise, harmonics, and susceptibility to stray electromagnetic interference; and (4) re-engineering of the navigation satellite receiver and the navigation sonar system to ensure economic manufacture.

It is planned to develop a Trident II missile. This will utilise the full volume of the Trident submarine missile tube, and will provide the USN FBM force with the ability to operate beyond the areas possible with the Trident I's 7000 km range. Trident II will be able to achieve this without any reduction in payload, whereas any increase in range of the Trident I is at the cost of a smaller payload.

Two options are being considered for Trident II. One is to increase the missile diameter, as well as its length to provide both greater range and increased payload. The second option would be to use more of the additional missile volume derived from the increased dimensions for still more payload at some sacrifice in missile range. Some of the enhanced payload capability will be devoted to obtaining increased accuracies. A variety of mid-course updating techniques and terminal sensor systems are under consideration as methods of improving accuracy. Updating by means of the GPS satellite navigation system is one example of the former, and there are a number of terminal guidance techniques which might be applied. Among the warheads contemplated for Trident II are existing units such as the W-76 used in the Mk 4 RV of the Trident I missile, and the W-78 which is used in the Mk 12A RV for the updated Minuteman.

CHARACTERISTICS
Length: 10·36 m
Diameter: 188 cm
Weight: 29 500 kg
Propulsion: 3-stage solid
Guidance: Stellar-inertial
Payload: Mk 4 RV with 8 × 100 KT MIRV; or Mk 5
Range: Approx 7400 km

OPERATION
Trident may be launched from submerged or surfaced FBM submarines and is ejected by the pressure of expanding gas within the missile launch tube. After the missile has attained sufficient acceleration and reached a specified distance from the submarine, the first-stage motor is ignited, the 'Aerospike' (an extensible spike at the nose of the missile to improve aerodynamic performance) is deployed, and the boost phase begins. When the first-stage motor burns out, it and interstage are separated from the missile, the second-stage motor is ignited, and the boost phase continues. As acceleration decreases because of second-stage motor burn-out, the second-stage motor is separated and the third-stage motor ignites to continue the boost phase. Third-stage burn-out completes the boost phase, after which the post-boost control system provides equipment section thrust and control until all the RVs have been deployed.

STATUS
In 1984 the major portion of the US sea-based strategic deterrent consisted of Poseidon (C-3) and Trident I (C-4) missiles deployed in Poseidon submarines. Replacing C-3 missiles with C-4s yielded increased range and enlarged the submarine's operating areas, and thereby their survivability. But it is estimated that these submarines will reach the end of their useful lives in the mid- to late-1990s. It is therefore planned to build a force of 12 Trident submarines ('Ohio' class), all of which eventually will be armed with 24 D-5 Trident II missiles.

Eleven of the 'Ohio' class had been authorised before 1984 and funding for the 12th was requested in the 1985 budget. By early 1984 three of the class were at sea, armed with Trident I (C-4) missiles. The first 'Ohio' class boat to be fitted with Trident II missiles from new will be the ninth of the class, and this vessel was laid down in 1981. Subsequent new submarines of the class will be equipped with Trident II from the outset. The first submarine to be retrofitted to carry Trident II will be the first of the 'Ohio' class, and this is expected to take place in 1991 when the boat is due for her first overhaul.

Retrofitting of Poseidon submarines to carry Trident I was completed in 1983 when 12 boats had been converted to deploy 16 missiles each. Eight submarines of the new 'Ohio' class will also be fitted with Trident I missiles, until it is their turn to be converted to the Trident II system.

Trident II (D-5) is in full-scale development and the first submarine-launched flight test is expected to occur from the ninth of the 'Ohio' class in spring/summer of 1989. Production of the missile is planned to begin in 1987, with 27 missiles; thereafter it is expected to produce 72 Trident II missiles per year from 1988 to 1992, inclusive.

Planned funding for Trident I procurement in fiscal year 1984 was $549·9 million for 52 missiles, and this will probably be the last batch to be built. As noted above, Trident II production is not expected to commence before 1987, but development funding in fiscal years 1984/85/86 was budgeted at $1473·2, $2091·1 and $2250·5 million, respectively, and for the latter two years there were also planned preliminary expenditure on procurement of $162·9 million and $758 million.

Several years ago it was announced that the British Government had decided to purchase the Trident system for Royal Navy submarines. Originally the Trident I version was to have been procured but after the US decision to discontinue Trident I production in favour of Trident II, the British elected to follow suit and adopt the later system. Details of the UK Trident programme appear in **4209.411**.

CONTRACTORS
FBM submarines: Electric Boat Division, General Dynamics Corporation, Groton, Connecticut, USA.

Trident missile system manager: Lockheed Missiles and Space Company, Sunnyvale, California, USA.

USS Ohio *(SSBN-726) under way during sea trials. She later launched her first Trident SLBM (USN)*

3216.131

US BALLISTIC MISSILE DEFENCE PROGRAMME

Although ICBM defence is considered to be the principal role for BMD, other important applications are receiving attention. These include: defence of SAC bases (for bombers and air-launched cruise missiles), critical communications nodes, and certain command centres.

The US BMD research and development effort consists of two complementary programme elements: the ATP, and the Systems Technology Programme (STP). The first of these is devoted to the study and advance of technology relevant to BMD, while STP integrates these technologies where they are suitable for development into complete systems.

Advanced Technology Programme

The BMD ATP research effort is directed toward advancement of the technology of all BMD components and functions. The main objectives are: (1) to provide the technical basis for substantial improvements in near-term BMD systems; (2) to provide the advanced technological foundations for future BMD concepts, with emphasis on those which offer a possibility of fundamental advances in BMD capabilities; (3) to pursue research to avoid technological surprises by Soviet scientific advances; (4) to ensure that the best possible use is made of co-operation between those responsible for US strategic offensive and defensive systems planning and design; and (5) to support intelligence assessments.

The ATP is divided into six major areas of technology research: radar, optics, discrimination, data processing, interceptor missiles, and technology analysis, and these are briefly summarised in the following paragraphs.

Radar technology research is mostly concerned with technology in support of the LoAD programme, non-nuclear kill (NNK) endo-atmospheric interceptors, and advanced BMD radar concepts. Research to harden ground-based radars for low altitude BMD systems includes material development and fabrication, and thermal testing in solar facilities. Improved test facilities able to closely match the expected atmospheric nuclear effects are being investigated in collaboration with the Defense Nuclear Agency (DNA). Research into millimetric wavelength radar technology includes the design and construction of a brassboard system for the study of radar homing and fuzing techniques, and a test facility has been established at Kwajalein Missile Range to establish a data base for BMD millimetre wave technology. Among recent achievements are: the development of a 40 W E/F-band bipolar transistor (which has application to a solid-state phased array radar in that frequency band); a special analogue-to-digital converter which is being applied in the development of a high time/bandwidth product signal processor; high speed signal processing components from the Advanced Digital Signal Processor (ADSP) have been incorporated in the Cobra Judy ship-based intelligence gathering radar; a first generation optical signal processor has been built and evaluated; major progress has been made toward the development of a stable laser oscillator and a broadband heterodyne laser receiver and the appropriate components; and various microwave tube developments have been instituted.

The optics technology projects have been aimed at research into the study of optical signatures and effects leading to the design requirements of sensor hardware; an optical designation programme that evaluated the ability of optical techniques for use in endo-atmospheric BMD applications; the long-wave infra-red (LWIR) mosaic sensor programme for optical systems that can deal with heavy threats and/or nuclear induced environments; and a programme for examining the technology issues involved in the use of lasers as a weapon against ICBM or SLBM boosters. The optical field test programme is centred on the designating optical tracker (DOT) flight experiment.

The data processing technology programme is arranged to support both endo-atmospheric and exo-atmospheric BMD concepts, and design and development of an advanced distributed data processing system for endo-atmospheric BMD systems was planned for 1981.

Major endeavours in interceptor technology

include component and sub-system development for advanced interceptors, support for the endo-atmospheric NNK programme and evaluation of rapidly deployable small missile concepts. In the technology analysis programme, emphasis has been put on the defence ideas and advanced technologies that have potential for application in the high endo-atmospheric and mid-course phases of an engagement.

Major efforts were started in 1978/79 to establish the foundations for both endo-atmospheric and exo-atmospheric NNK, and the technology for the latter application is now fairly well established, and most work is now concentrated on the homing overlay experiment (HOE) which is being carried out under the STP, mentioned below. Work on endo-atmospheric NNK is on a longer time-scale and several alternative approaches to the problem are being studied. The key issues are guidance, accuracy, fuzing, warhead design and lethality, and there are various projects dealing with these aspects.

Technology in support of the LoAD system being developed as one of the STP projects includes work on hardening of LoAD components to withstand the anticipated extremely hostile environment associated with defending an MX missile and with empty shelters only a few kilometres away. Other near-term efforts are the development of the propellant and certain components of the LoAD interceptor missile, and distributed data processing, and discrimination techniques for the LoAD. Later efforts are directed at providing growth options and these include endo-atmospheric NNK ground-based optical sensors to augment the LoAD radars, and advanced techniques for discrimination and data/signal processing.

System Technology Programme

The purpose of the STP is to develop, design and test BMD systems concepts to provide deployment options for the various requirements that occur in response to the developing strategic situation. The STP provides the means for integrating advances in BMD technology and concepts into systems, and then testing and validating such systems. At present two system concepts are the main objects of the STP: AOS (Airborne Optical System) and the layered defence system. These are outlined in the following paragraphs.

LoAD is a short range system comprising low power radars and small, but fast and powerful, interceptor missiles, and its main advantage is that it is a small and simple system. It also has another advantage from the authorities' point of view, and that is the fact that it is essentially a scaled-down version of the Terminal Defence System of the former Safeguard ABM system. This means that it is a low risk option, able to take full advantage of technologies proved to be effective by field testing.

The system is comprised of an inertially guided interceptor, a small (antenna approximately 2 m diameter) phased array radar and a distributed data processor, and the system can be either on its own as a 'stand-alone' system for the protection of ICBMs or as the underlay portion of a layered defence system (see below). Another element is the LoAD engagement sensor and controller, an integrated radar and computer. This was the subject of a different contract award entrusted to Raytheon. Martin Marietta is working on the LoAD interceptor missile and McDonnell Douglas Astronautics is the prime contractor.

As mentioned above, LoAD is derived from the Terminal Defence System and the STP Terminal Defence Validation programme. This test programme arose from the site defence effort which was originally intended to be a prototype project to demonstrate solutions to BMD problems presented by a very large ICBM attack and penetration aided attacks which would severely stress a Safeguard type of system. Under Congressional direction in 1975, this effort was changed from a prototype demonstration to a technology programme, but still with the objective of validating solutions to this problem. The validation of the major issues associated with the programme enabled the BMD scheme to demonstrate the feasibility of building a BMD system that is capable of intercepting ICBM re-entry vehicles under the most stressing conditions. It showed that RVs can be discriminated among decoys, that clutter caused by ICBM tank break-up can be eliminated from consideration by bulk filtering and that large radar and data processing loads due to a heavy attack can be handled successfully. It was also shown that a BMD system can be rapidly installed using modular construction techniques. The principal tool for establishing these factors was the system technology test facility (STTF) at the Kwajalein Missile Range, where 14 target-of-opportunity tracking exercises were carried out during 1979.

Layered defence consists of two tiers of defence that operate together to minimise the number of RVs penetrating the defence area. The first tier known as ERIS (Exo-atmospheric Re-entry Interceptor Sub-system) would intercept at long range, exo-atmospherically, using autonomous interceptors with optically-homing missiles with non-nuclear warheads. The second tier, or underlay, would be a NNK system or a terminal defence system, known as the High Endo Defence System (HEDS) operating entirely endo-atmospherically. The underlay would engage only those RVs that penetrate the overlay portion of the system, so that the number of underlay radars and missiles required would be significantly reduced compared with a 'stand-alone' underlay system.

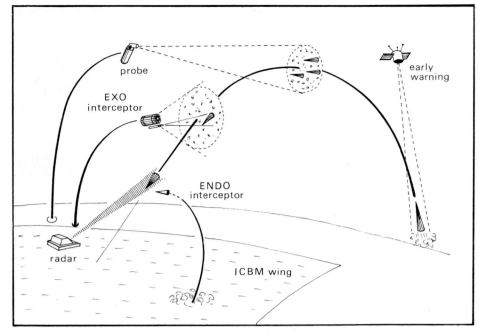

Schematic diagram of BMD layered defence system concept

The layered defence, because of its longer reach is suited for softer targets (such as SAC bases) as well as for hard targets. The real advantage seen for the layered defence concept lies in its cost-effectiveness where deceptive basing is not employed. This is made possible by: (1) the use of NNK vehicles on each interceptor missile; (2) the low leakage possible with two tiers of defence; (3) a drastic reduction in the number of underlay radars and missiles required; and (4) the use of preferential defence schemes which are possible because the overlay is able to view the whole attack at an early stage and predict the aimpoints of RVs. This makes it possible to optimise the use of defence forces with full knowledge of the threat. The layered defence is considered a higher risk BMD development than LoAD because the overlay relies on new BMD technologies which are only now reaching the validation stage. The homing overlay experiment (HOE) being conducted by the STP is the next step after DOT in the validation process.

The HOE is designed to demonstrate exo-atmospheric and non-nuclear kill techniques, and it makes the maximum use of off-the-shelf hardware. For example, both the launch vehicle and the axial propulsion engine will be modified standard units. A schedule of four HOE flights have been planned, which will have to conform to the constraints of the 1972 ABM Treaty. They will involve intercepts of special target complexes. The design of the sensor and the homing and kill vehicle had been completed by mid-1980, and work was in hand to complete the building and ground testing of the sensor and homing and kill vehicle.

STATUS

Research and development programme. Funding indicated in the 1985 Defense Budget relating to BMD was as follows:

BMD Advanced Technology Programme RDT&E in fiscal year 1983/84: $142·8 million and $152·9 million respectively.

BMD Systems Technology Programme RDT&E 1983/84: $376·2 million and $316·3 million, respectively, with $20 million for construction in 1983 and $12·8 million projected in 1985.

CONTRACTORS

Numerous contractors are involved in the BMD ATP, the BMD STP or both. Recent major contractors include:

Boeing Aerospace
General Electric
GTE
Hughes Aircraft Company
Lincoln Laboratory
Lockheed Missiles and Space
Martin Marietta
McDonnell Douglas Astronautics
MIT
Raytheon
RCA
Rockwell International
SDC
Teledyne Brown Engineering

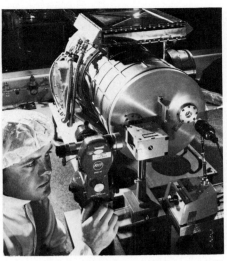

Optical alignment verification of an IR sensor to be used to detect and track ballistic missiles from the edge of space. Sensor is part of US Army's DOT programme and was developed by Hughes. It is carried by rocket to altitude of 185 km where it scans a wide volume of space and relays information on what it 'sees' to the ground. Afterwards it is parachuted into the sea for recovery and subsequent re-use

TACTICAL SURFACE WEAPONS

2283.111
INTRODUCTION
This section deals with land-based or shipborne tactical systems whose primary function is to attack surface targets. As such they inevitably include examples of several widely varying types of weapon, often differing considerably in the degrees of complexity involved in their design. Despite this, in general the entries that follow mostly fall within one or other of a few readily recognisable categories. For example anti-tank weapons are a common preoccupation and there are two broad approaches used in designing systems to counter individual tank targets or armoured formations: the small, often infantry-operated, guided missiles; and the more complex systems intended to engage multiple targets

meant to combat tanks by indirect fire techniques. As far as practicable such generic divisions of the subject matter of this section are arranged in logical groups.

For the convenience of study and reference, weapons have been divided into four groups and are listed in alphabetical order of country of origin within these groups:

Battlefield Support Weapons
Anti-tank/Assault Weapons
Coastal Defence Weapons
Shipborne Weapons

Although the majority of the entries in this section are concerned with guided missile systems, a number of important weapons that do not come into that category strictly speaking, because their significance

and operational potential makes it both sensible and convenient to treat both classes collectively. Typical of such blurring of distinctions which were once clearcut but are now hard to distinguish categorically are modern multiple rocket systems and guided mortar rounds, and new types of sophisticated artillery shells with multiple sub-munition payloads. Weapons of this sort will be found among the first two of the above groups: readers whose interests lie more with the artillery pieces which may be employed to deliver such munitions, or for whom the means of transporting and deploying multiple rocket launchers are a primary concern are directed to our companion yearbook, *Jane's Armour and Artillery*, where full mechanical, constructional and other details will be found.

Battlefield Support Weapons

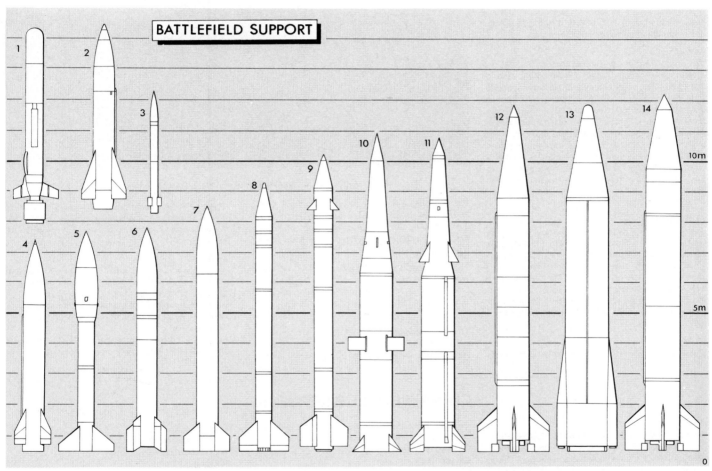

1 *GLCM*, 2 *Lance*, 3 *MLRS*, 4 *Ching Feng*, 5 *Honest John*, 6 *Pluton*, 7 *HADES*, 8 *FROG-7*, 9 *SS-21*, 10 *Pershing 1a*, 11 *Pershing II*, 12 *SS-1 Scud 1C*, 13 *SS-12 (provisional)*, 14 *SS-22 (provisional)*

ARGENTINA

3674.111
SLAM-PAMPERO MULTIPLE ROCKET SYSTEM
The SLAM-Pampero is a multiple artillery rocket system developed in Argentina. A 16-tube launcher is employed for 105 mm calibre rockets which are stabilised by four 'wrap-round' fins at the rear of the missile. A single salvo of 16 rockets will fall within an area measuring 300 × 200 m, with maximum dispersion.
CHARACTERISTICS
Calibre: 105 mm
Launch weight: 30 kg
Warhead weight: 11 kg
Propellant: Solid
Max range: 12 km

DEVELOPMENT
Development for the Argentinian Army was undertaken under contract by CITEFA, the Research and Development Institute of the Argentinian Armed Forces.
STATUS
Pre-series production began in 1979.
CONTRACTOR
Instituto de Investigaciones Cientificas y Tecnicas de la Fuerzas Armadas (CITEFA), Zufrategui y Varela, 1603 Villa Martelli, Provincia de Buenos Aires, Argentina.

Argentine mobile multiple rocket launcher SLAM-Pampero

3675.111

SAPBA-1 MULTIPLE ROCKET SYSTEM
SAPBA-1 is the designation of a new multiple rocket system under development for the Argentinian Army. Few details have been cleared for publication, but it is believed that this 127 mm rocket system is very similar in concept and certain engineering features to the Argentinian SLAM-Pampero 105 mm multiple rocket system (**3674.103**). In view of the probable all-up weight of the launcher unit with its 40 rockets

(some 3000 kg), it seems likely that a self-propelled launcher vehicle is employed, and this may be either wheeled or tracked.

CHARACTERISTICS
Calibre: 127 mm
Launch weight: 56 kg
Propellant: Solid
Launcher capacity: 40 tubes
Max dispersion for multiple launch: 500 × 400 m

STATUS
Development programme.
CONTRACTOR
Instituto de Investigaciones Cientificas y Tecnicas de la Fuerzas Armadas (CITEFA), Zufrategui y Varela, 1603 Villa Martelli, Provincia de Buenos Aires, Argentina.

BRAZIL

4146.111

ARTILLERY ROCKETS
For a number of years, Brazil has been developing unguided rockets. Pioneer work was carried out in the 1960s by the Army Departmento de Estudos e Pesquisas Tecnológicas (Department of Studies and Technological Research). At present, there is very close co-operation between the Army Instituto de Pesquisa e Desenvolvimento (Research and Development Institute) and private industry, which has resulted in a number of systems that have reached operational status with the Brazilian Army and a number of unnamed foreign forces.

Astros
The artillery Saturation Rocket System (Astros) is a mobile multi-calibre rocket system composed of launchers, fire control unit and resupply vehicles, mounted on identical 6 × 6 trucks. The rockets employed are of 127, 180 and 300 mm calibre and provide ranges of nine to 60 km, although maximum ranges of up 70 km have been reported. High explosive and cluster type warheads are available. The fire control system used is the Swiss Contraves Fieldguard system (**3314.181** in the Army Fire Control Systems section of this volume). The Astros system has been sold to a number of countries, among which, it is claimed, is Iraq.

108R (SS-06)
Designated 108-R by the Brazilian Army, this system consists of a 16-tube launcher for 108 mm, spin-stabilised rockets produced by Avibrás. These carry an HE warhead of about three kg and have a range of about 9·2 km. The launcher may be mounted on a two-wheeled trailer for towing by virtually any military vehicle, or may be vehicle-mounted. The launcher crew is said to consist of five men, and the system is fully operational.

SS-07
This system, which has also reached operational

Avibrás Astros II multiple rocket system launcher vehicle

status, comprises a 36-tube launcher for Avibrás 70 mm rockets, which are virtually standard FFARs with a four kg warhead and a range of 7·5 km. The launcher may be either trailer- or vehicle-mounted.

SBAT 127
This is an adaptation of the Avibrás SBAT-127 HVAR, with a 20 kg warhead and a range of 15 km. The launcher is a 12-round unit for trailer or vehicle mounting, and the system is operational.

X-20
This is the designation of a 180 mm artillery rocket system, known as the X-20 in the Brazilian Army. The rocket carries a 35 kg warhead and has a maximum

range of 35 km, being spin-stabilised by cruciform fins. A three-rail launcher assembly is suitable for either mounting on a tracked chassis, or towing by a 6 × 6 vehicle.

X-40
Already operational in the Brazilian Army, this system consists of a 300 mm calibre rocket capable of carrying a 146 kg warhead to ranges of 68 km. The launcher is a three-rail assembly mounted on a Bernadini X1A1 light tank known as the XLF-40.
CONTRACTOR
Avibrás – Indústria Aeroespacial SA, Caixa Postal 229, 12200 São José dos Campos, SP, Brazil.

CHINA (PEOPLE'S REPUBLIC)

5154.111

107 mm TYPE 63 MULTIPLE ROCKET LAUNCHER
The Type 63 MRL is in service in three models: mounted on a two-wheeled carriage and towed behind a light truck, mounted on the rear of a 4 × 4 or 6 × 6 truck and finally in the mountain role. In the latter it is broken down into man-pack sizes and weighs only 281 kg, assembled, when it rests on four trails, ie

two to the front and two to the rear. The rockets have a high explosive warhead and are fin-stabilised.
CHARACTERISTICS
Calibre: 106·7 mm
Number of barrels: 12
Elevation: +57°
Depression: –3°
Weight travelling: 602 kg

Weight of rocket: 19 kg
Length of rocket: 837 mm
Max velocity: 385 m/s
Max range: 8050 m
STATUS
In service in Albania, China, and Viet-Nam.
CONTRACTOR
Chinese State Arsenals.

3672.111

140 mm MULTIPLE ROCKET LAUNCHER
A 19-tube 140 mm calibre rocket launcher, mounted on the rear platform of a standard military truck, is deployed in some numbers by the Chinese People's Liberation Army. The weapon is probably of Chinese origin, although in view of the 140 mm calibre which is shared by such Soviet equipments as the BM-16-16, BM-14-17 and PRU-14, Soviet practice could well

have influenced the design. The most obvious indication of originality in the Chinese equipment is the use of 19 launch tubes, arranged in two rows: one of ten over another of nine tubes. There are likely to be other, more subtle, differences between the Chinese and Soviet hardware, but it is also likely that the performance of individual rounds of the same calibre will be very similar. This suggests a muzzle velocity of about 400 m/s and a typical range of some ten km.

The launcher is likely to be adjustable in both elevation and traverse, and the operational arrangements probably provide for rapid re-supply and reloading. All-up weight of the loaded vehicle and launcher must be in the region of 8500 kg.
STATUS
In service.
CONTRACTOR
Chinese State Arsenals.

CZECHOSLOVAKIA

5137.111
122 mm ROCKET LAUNCHER M-1972 (RM-70)

The M-1972 rocket launcher was first seen during a military parade held in Czechoslovakia in 1972. The designation RM-70 has also been associated with this weapon. It basically consists of a modified Czechoslovak Tatra 813 (8 × 8) truck chassis, on the very rear of which has been mounted the Soviet BM-21 rocket launcher (**5555.103**). The cab is of the forward control type and is fully armoured. Immediately behind the cab is a rack of 40 rockets, which enable the launcher to be reloaded in five minutes, compared with ten minutes for the Soviet BM-21 launcher. The Czechoslovak vehicle has greater cross-country capability than its Soviet counterpart and is provided with a central tyre pressure regulation system, which enables the driver to adjust the tyre pressures to suit the type of ground encountered.

122 mm rocket launcher (40 round) M-1972

CHARACTERISTICS

	Long Rocket	Short Rocket
Calibre	122 mm	122 mm
Length	3·226 m	1·905 m
Weight	77·5 kg	45·8 kg
Max velocity	not available	450 m/s
Max range	20 500 m	11 000 m
Launcher		

Capacity: 40 rounds, plus 40 in reserve
Weight: 14 000 kg (loaded)

Length: 7·76 m
Width: 2·5 m
Height: 2·7 m
Elevation: 0 to +50°
Traverse: 240°
STATUS
In service with Czechoslovakia, East Germany and Soviet Union. Yugoslavia produces its own version of

this weapon, mounted on a 12-ton FAP-2220 BS truck. The general arrangement is similar to that of the Czechoslovak system, but with a 32-tube launcher and a slightly different reloading device.
CONTRACTORS
Chassis – Tatra (Czechoslovakia). Launcher – Soviet State Arsenals.

FRANCE

4777.111
HADES TACTICAL SURFACE-TO-SURFACE MISSILE

In mid-1983 the French Ministry of Defence decided to go ahead with a new tactical surface-to-surface missile system to replace the existing Pluto weapon system (**2130.111**) and definition studies and other preliminary work was entrusted to Aérospatiale.

Definition studies were continuing in 1984 under the management of Aérospatiale, under the guidance of the Direction Technique des Engins (DGA) and in collaboration with the Commissariat à l'Energie Atomique (CEA) for the nuclear payload. Like the Pluton system it will replace, Hades will be a mobile system, and a likely configuration is shown in the nearby drawing issued by the contractor based upon the results of their definition studies. As can be seen, the missile is transported on a semi-trailer and housed in a canister which can be elevated into the firing position on arrival at the launch site. The front part of the trailer carries a shelter which is assumed to house fire control equipment and positions for the operating crew.

Range of the Hades missile is expected to be in the region of 350 km, carrying a nuclear warhead of between 10 and 25 KT. No other details are available at this early stage.

According to the 1983 French Defence Budget, the cost of developing Hades is estimated at between FFr7000 million and FFr10 000 million, and current plans envisage production of a total of 180 missiles. Hades is expected to succeed Pluto in French Army service in 1992.
CONTRACTOR
Aérospatiale, Division Systemes Balistiques et Spatiaux, BP 96 – 78133 Les Mureaux, Cedex, France.

Contractor's impression of Hades tactical surface-to-surface missile system deployed and in operation. Nuclear payload will be carried to a maximum range of about 350 km

2130.111
PLUTON BATTLEFIELD SUPPORT MISSILE

Developed to meet a French Army requirement, Pluton is a surface-to-surface tactical nuclear missile. The weapon, which has a range capability from 20 to 120 km, is installed on and fired from the AMX-30 tank chassis, the missile container being used as a launching ramp. Missile and warhead are supplied separately to operational units.

In addition to the AMX-30 launching vehicle the

system includes command vehicles containing data processing equipment organised round the IRIS 35M computer of the Plan Calcul Militaire. This is a third-generation general purpose computer capable of operation under severe environmental conditions. If operational circumstances require it, target data can be obtained in real-time from an R.20 drone (**2127.351**) equipped with a Cyclope passive IR reconnaissance system (**1070.353**). Missile guidance is by means of a simplified inertial system based on a

SFENA semi-strap-down system. Alternative warheads are available: the 25 kiloton yield AN-51 which contains the same MR50 nuclear charge as the AN-52 free-fall bomb carried by French Air Force Mirage III and Jaguar aircraft, or a 15 kiloton nuclear payload. The former is intended for important targets in an enemy's rear, while the smaller yield device would be employed for use nearer to the main battle area.

CHARACTERISTICS
Type: Land-mobile, vehicle-launched, tactical nuclear weapon system
Guidance: Inertial
Propulsion: Dual-thrust solid-propellant rocket motor. Propellant weight 1200 kg
Warhead: Nuclear 25 and 15 KT
Missile length: 7.64 m
Body diameter: 65 cm
Span: 141 cm
Launch weight: 2423 kg
Range: 10–120 km
CEP: Believed to be 150–300 m depending on range
Crew (launch vehicle): 4
STATUS
Initial production contracts were awarded in 1972, and deliveries to the French Armed Forces began early in 1974. It is now operational with four French regiments (3, 25, 60 and 74) and a fifth (32nd) is in the process of being equipped with Pluton. Each regiment has six launchers plus the appropriate support and re-supply units.

In mid-1977 General Jacques Ménard, second-in-command of the French Army planning and study department, said that consideration of a 'Super Pluton' for the period after the 1960s was already in hand. This weapon would have an appreciably higher performance with improved warhead, greater range and higher accuracy.

A later possibility to emerge (partially) was the

Aérospatiale Hades project disclosed in 1980, an air-breathing missile, possibly of the integral rocket ramjet type, which was proposed as the basis of a successor to Pluton. Various trajectories were considered including terrain following but no decisions have been announced.
CONTRACTORS
Prime contractor, project management, aerodynamic studies, structure, guidance and control system, pre-launch test and control set, vehicle integration: Aérospatiale, 37 boulevard de Montmorency, 75016 Paris, France.
    Others involved are –
    Rocket motor: SEP
    Propellants: SNPE
    Main body equipment: SFENA, Air-Equipment, Auxilec, Elecma
    Warhead equipment: SERAT
    Nuclear charge: CEA
    Launch vehicle (tank portion): DTAT/AMX
    Crane: Griffet
    Turbine: Microturbo
    Vehicle equipment: CII, CIT, SINTRA, SOPELEM
    Communication and data processing system: DTAT/GIAT
    Command vehicle: SPAIR
    Command and control equipment: CII (computer), CIT, SINTRA
    Command and control integration: DTAT/SEFT

Pluton missile on launcher vehicle

DESIGN AUTHORITIES
    Programme direction: Direction Technique des Engins.
    Nuclear warhead: Commissariat à l'Energie Atomique
    Command and control system: Direction Technique des Armements Terrestres.

2609.111

RAFALE ARTILLERY ROCKETS
Rafale is the name given to an artillery rocket concept which in general outline is similar to that of many other multiple rocket-launching systems but differs from some of them in the design of the rockets and the nature and purpose of the warheads.

Rockets are tube-launched and fin-stabilised, the fins being folded when in the launch tube. Also within the folded fin assembly are small flaps which can be set to erect when the fins open and thus act as air brakes when the missiles are required to operate at shorter ranges. Three sets of air brakes, with different surface areas, provide for three minimum ranges with an elevation angle limited to 15°.

Alternative warhead arrangements have been developed for anti-personnel and anti-armour operations. In each the main warhead contains a number of secondary charges – 35 ball grenades in the anti-personnel warhead and 63 shaped-charge grenades in the anti-armour warhead. The grenades in each are designed to detonate on impact, each ball grenade releasing 360 balls, which are said to be effective against troops at a distance of 20 m from the point of impact. Each anti-personnel grenade weighs 350 grams and ejection of grenades from the rocket warhead is accomplished at a height of about 700 m above the target area, with a timing precision of about one millisecond, by means of a series of detonating cords. By these means a total of 12 600 fragments are distributed over an area of 20 hectares. Each shaped-charge grenade has an armour-plate penetration capacity of 80 mm. Under development is a warhead which will contain five anti-tank mines.

These secondary charges are ejected from the main rocket at altitude – the ejection being timed by a fuze – so as to produce a shower of projectiles over a substantial area. Premature explosion of the main warhead is prevented by a fuze-timed safe-arm device.
CHARACTERISTICS
Rocket calibre: 147 mm
Length: 350 cm
Launch weight: 82 kg
Propulsion: Dual-thrust solid propellant motor

Rafale rocket system mock-up on Berliet 6 × 6 truck chassis (ECPA)

Tube exit velocity: 100 m/s with 5 m launch tube
Max velocity: 1050 m/s
Range: 9 – 32 km
Time of flight: 110 s max
Warhead: Anti-personnel or anti-armour, 22 kg
    The launcher comprises a 30-tube unit which can be truck- or trailer-mounted and can be trained and elevated. For each launcher carriage there is a control unit which in addition to distributing firing commands and air-brake actuation commands to the rockets contains also a drift computer and a pre-launch tester. Round-by-round or small-salvo firing are possible; the rate of fire is about two rounds/second. A crew of five is needed.

STATUS
Development. In mid-1979 it was learned that studies have been made of a version of this system using 122 mm calibre SEP rockets in place of the original 145 mm rockets. This would permit an increase in the number of tubes per launcher to 40. Individual rockets would be 2·8 m long and weigh 57·5 kg with a 20 kg warhead. The warhead could contain either eight anti-armour mines or 42 grenades each weighing 315 g and containing 336 balls for anti-personnel use.
CONTRACTOR
Société Européenne de Propulsion, Tour Roussel Nobel-Cedex 3, 92080 Paris La Defense, France.

GERMANY (FEDERAL REPUBLIC)

5577.111

LARS—110 mm ARTILLERY ROCKET LAUNCHER
The Light Artillery Rocket System (LARS) launcher comprises two groups of 18 launch tubes (4-5-5-4), which can be mechanically trained and elevated, and from which are launched 110 mm calibre rockets.

These rockets can be equipped with a variety of warheads and can be launched singly, in partial salvoes, or salvoes. The rockets are flight stabilised by fins which are folded and protected by a cover for storage and handling. A warhead has been developed which will carry either eight AT-1 anti-vehicle mines

or five AT-2 anti-tank mines.

The complete system was originally mounted on the rear of a Magirus Jupiter (6 × 6) truck chassis which was fitted with an armoured cab, but subsequently the system was removed from these chassis and fitted onto the MAN (6 × 6) truck chassis.

CHARACTERISTICS
Calibre: 110 mm
Propulsion: Single-stage, solid-propellant rocket motor
Warhead: Choice of high explosive, incendiary, or smoke
Range: 15 km. Minimum 6·5 km
Fire control: Contraves Fieldguard
Launcher
Capacity: 36 rockets in 2 groups of 18 launch tubes mounted on a 6 × 6 wheeled prime mover
Laying: Mechanical
Traverse limits: +150°
Elevation limits: 0 – 55°
Rate of fire: 36 rockets in 18 s
Weights: Rocket 25 kg. Truck and launcher 13 t. System weight in battle order 15 t
STATUS
209 supplied to Federal German Army.
CONTRACTORS
Wegmann, West Germany. Rocket by Dynamit Nobel.

LARS 2 110mm artillery rocket system on MAN 6 × 6 vehicle

ISRAEL

4098.111
ISRAELI MEDIUM RANGE ROCKET (MAR 290)
The basic 290 mm MAR 290 artillery rocket is 5·45 metres long, with a launch weight of 600 kg of which 320 kg is the warhead. Range is approximately 25 km. These rockets were originally launched from a lattice constructed four-round launcher mounted on the top of a Sherman tank chassis, the vehicle itself being manoeuvred to adjust firing azimuth, with elevation being hydraulically actuated. This model is still in use with the Israel Defence Force (IDF) but recently a new launch system has been developed based on the use of a Chieftain tank hull equipped with a new four-tube elevating and traversing launcher on a superstructure carried on the original turret ring.

Each launcher tube has an internal diameter of 700 mm to accommodate the rocket tail fin span of 570 mm. The overall height of the Chieftain with the rocket tubes in the lowered position is 3·6 metres and the vehicle weight is about 50 tons. A crew of four is carried: commander, driver, and two fire control operators. Details of the fire control system employed have not been disclosed. Rockets are launched with all four crew members inside the vehicle. Once all four rockets have been fired, the launch vehicle moves to a fresh position where reload rounds are already emplaced.

The fresh rounds are taken to this location by a truck which lowers them to the ground for the packaging to be removed. For this the truck uses its own handling crane, which is also used to lift the prepared rounds onto a special reloading frame. When the launcher vehicle approaches, it employs a system of two lugs and a bracket on the hull front to engage corresponding items on the loading frame. The frame is then connected to the vehicle's hydraulic system and a ram on the frame lifts the entire frame off the ground into a raised horizontal position until the rockets are in line with the launching tubes. The launch tubes have previously been rotated to point to the launch vehicle's rear. Using hydraulic power the rockets are then pushed into the launch tubes, and the whole sequence is carried out by one man in about ten minutes using a remote control unit. After loading, the frame is lowered to the ground, the hydraulics and mechanical systems are disconnected,

Reloading operation of MAR 290 artillery rocket system (T.J. Gander)

New tubed launcher for MAR 290 artillery rocket system mounted on Chieftain chassis (T.J. Gander)

Earlier lattice construction four-round MAR 290 launcher vehicle based on Sherman tank

and the frame may then be used for more rockets to be loaded by the supply truck.
CHARACTERISTICS
Type: Unguided, fin stabilised
Rocket diameter: 290 mm
Length: 5·45 m
Fin span: 570 mm
Weight: 600 kg (launch)
Warhead: 320 kg
Propulsion: Solid rocket motor
Range: 25 km (provisional)

Launcher
Tube diameter: 700 mm
Traverse: 360°
Elevation: 0 – 60°
DEVELOPMENT
Israel Military Industries (IMI) was instructed by the IDF to produce a version of the Soviet 240 mm BM-24 artillery rocket, using examples captured in the 1967 war as the pattern. The resulting equipment has a range of more than 10 km and is understood to be in service still with the IDF, using launchers mounted on

ZIL-157 trucks. The larger 290 mm rocket which became the MAR 290 originated in 1965 and later utilised some of the experience gathered in the course of the 240 mm artillery rocket development programme.

STATUS
The original MAR 290 with the four-round lattice launcher is still operational with the IDF and the new tube-launch version is thought to be about to enter service.

CONTRACTOR
Israel Military Industries, PO Box 1044, Ramat Hasharon 47100, Israel.

4759.111
LAR 160 LIGHT ARTILLERY ROCKET SYSTEM

The LAR 160 is a multiple launch rocket system designed to direct unguided artillery rockets at battlefield targets at ranges of up to 30 km from tubed launchers mounted on vehicles such as the M-548, M-809, AMX 15T or M-47. These are typical examples and any vehicle from a standard 6 × 6 military truck to virtually any tank chassis may be used.

The first carrier used during trails was an M548 tracked vehicle carrying 32 rounds, but the later production version used a turretless AMX 13 light tank with two 18-tube LPCs. These vehicles have a three-man crew: drive, commander and signaller/gunner operating the fire control system.

A 30 km maximum range and a warhead payload capability of 50 kg enables a wide range of warheads to be employed, including HE, illuminating, AP, and special purpose payloads such as scatterable mines, and dual-purpose submunitions. The rocket calibre of 160 mm allows virtually any payload that can be accommodated in a conventional 155 mm artillery round to be carried by the LAR 160 rocket. A radar-based fire control system is normally employed to ensure optimum accuracy, and if the Fieldguard pilot round technique is also used, maximum surprise in the target area can be achieved.

The system consists of the tracked or wheeled carrier vehicle on which is mounted an expendable multiple launcher containing fuzed, sealed-in 160 mm rockets. A typical LAR 160 battery comprises six launchers with up to 50 tubes (M-47 medium tank chassis) so that a large quantity of warheads or submunitions can be delivered to the target within about 30 seconds of opening fire. The rockets are fired from launch pod containers (LPCs) made up of varying numbers of tubes, depending on the size and type of carrier vehicle used. The tubes are filament wound in glass fibre and have integral guide rails. There is a polyurethane foam filler between the launch tube and the hexagonal aluminium outer envelope. The hexagonal section permits simple construction of LPCs of different capacities.

The LAR 160 rocket is a free flight, fin stabilised, solid propellant, surface-to-surface round comprising: a low drag aerodynamic nose section, payload section, a short burn-time solid rocket motor, and folding wrap-around stabilising fins that deploy when the rocket leaves the launch tube. The number of rockets in each LPC bundle is adjusted to suit the carrying capacity of the vehicle used, and a suitable

Model of LAR 160 on M47 tank chassis, with two 25-round LPCs

turntable with elevating mechanism is normally provided. Reloading is rapidly accomplished by replacing an empty LPC with a freshly loaded one.

Fire control systems suggested for the LAR 160 system are the Contraves Fieldguard (**3314.181**), or the Westinghouse Quickfire system based on the arrangement used in the Sgt York mobile AA gun system (**3618.131**) using a version of the F-16 AN/APG-66 nose radar (**3303.353**). In both cases, precision radar tracks pilot rockets fired to 60 – 75 per cent of their full trajectory before being detonated in mid-air to avoid alerting the target area. The computer then calculates aiming data from the trajectory information derived from the pilot shot(s) and the projected impact point(s).

CHARACTERISTICS
Rocket
Calibre: 160 mm
Length: 3·311 m
Rocket motor length: 2·032 m

Warhead length: 1·279 m
Fin span: 350 mm
Launch weight: 110 kg
Weight at burn-out: 77 kg
Propellant weight: 36 kg
Warhead weight: 50 kg
Launch pod container (18-tubes)
Lenght: 3·46 m
Width: 1·0 m
Height: 820 mm
Weight: 2522 kg (complete); 540 kg (empty)
STATUS
In production and operational with IDF. The system has been exported to an unspecified country (AMX 13 vehicle version) and arrangements have been initiated with a number of US companies with a view to adoption by American Forces.
CONTRACTOR
Israel Military Industries, PO Box 1044, Ramat Hasharon 47100, Israel.

ITALY

3764.111
FIROS 6 FIELD ROCKET SYSTEM

FIROS 6 is a field weapon system based on the SNIA BPD two inch (51 mm) rocket, capable of performing an anti-guerrilla and infantry support role within a distance of six km. The launcher of the modular type has 48 launching tubes and is installed on a light vehicle with high manoeuvrability and velocity characteristics, allowing the system to perform missions on difficult terrains (jungle, forest, desert). Each firing unit can carry the number of rockets required for firing at least two ripples. The fire control unit offers the possibility of firing partial or complete ripples of rockets with pre-selected warheads.

The rocket has high accuracy due to a special folding fin assembly unit and can carry the following types of warhead: HEI (high explosive incendiary), PFF (pre-formed fragmentation), AT-AP (anti-tank anti-personnel) SM (smoke), SP (spotting), illuminating, practice (smoke, flash and inert).

The FIROS 6 system is supplied either in the 'package' version, inclusive of the vehicle, or in a 'kit' version which can be easily installed on vehicles already in service with armed forces. SNIA BPD has developed an installation of the system with a 48-tube

Fiat 6614 APC vehicle equipped with FIROS 6 rocket launcher system

launcher on the Land-Rover Mod 109. The system has also been successfully installed and demonstrated on the FIAT Campagnola 1107AD and 6614 APC.
CHARACTERISTICS
(Typical example installed on Land-Rover 109)
Time to bring the system into action: 3 minutes
Ripple time: 5 s (48 rockets)

Disengagement time: 1 minute
Vehicle: Land-Rover Mod 109
Max speed on road: Over 90 km/h (fully loaded)
Loading capability per mission: 2 ripples (96 rockets)
Overall length: 4·46 m
Overall width: 1·65 m
Overall height: 1·95 m
Rocket launcher
Number of tubes: 48
Elevation: –5 to +45°
Azimuth: ±105°
Length: 2·00 m
Width: 0·60 m
Height: 0·91 m
Weights
Empty launcher: (including sighting and firing units) 250 kg
Payload: (96 rockets) 460 kg; empty vehicle 1850 kg; crew (3 men) 240 kg; overall weight of launch unit in combat conditions 2800 kg
STATUS
In production.
CONTRACTOR
SNIA BPD, Setlore Difesa e Spazio, Via Sicilia, 162-00187 Rome, Italy.

5230.111
FIROS 25 FIELD ROCKET SYSTEM
The FIROS 25 field rocket system has been developed as a private venture by SNIA BPD. It is an area saturation weapon system and is based on the 122 mm SNIA BPD unguided rocket. The system is intended for employment either in battery missions or isolated missions and can cover large areas in the 8 to 25 km zone.

A typical battery would consist of a command post equipped with a fire direction system, six firing units and six or more escort units. The firing unit is a modular rocket launcher installed on a heavy truck (6 × 6) vehicle or a tracked vehicle. The launcher consists of two removable modules with 20 launching tubes each. The escort unit can carry four launching modules. The loading operations are carried out removing the empty module by a jib crane fitted on the support vehicle and installing the filled one ready to fire.

The firing unit has a fire control system and a link with the command post to acquire the necessary firing data in real time. The fire control system has been designed to enable selection of the number (from 1 to 40) and type (see below) of rockets to be fired.

In isolated missions only firing units would be employed, each consisting of the launching vehicle fitted with the launcher and with fire control and fire directions systems enabling direct or indirect fire.

The rocket can carry a variety of different warheads, from the conventional types (HE, PFF, WP) to the sub-ammunition types dispensing anti-tank or anti-personnel mines and bomblets.
CHARACTERISTICS
Time to bring the system into action: 5 minutes
Ripple time: 20 s (40 rockets)
Disengagement time: 1 minute
Reloading time: 5 minutes
Launcher Unit
Number of tubes: 40 (20 per module)
Elevation: 0 to +55°
Azimuth: ±105°
Crew: 3
Landing Module
Length: 3·7 m
Width: 0·82 m
Height: 0·69 m
Empty weight: 400 kg
Loaded weights: 1470 kg (conventional W/H); 1690 kg (submunition W/H)
STATUS
Rockets and complete system are in production.
CONTRACTOR
SNIA BPD, Setlore Difesa e Spazio, Via Sicilia, 162-00187 Rome, Italy.

Replenishment/reloading of FIROS 25 artillery rocket system

FIROS 25 rocket launch

JAPAN

3673.111
TYPE 75 130 mm MULTIPLE ROCKET LAUNCHER
This weapon consists of a tracked and armoured vehicle on which is carried a 30-round launcher for 130 mm calibre fin-and-spin-stabilised artillery rockets. Sequential salvo firing is possible. The 30-round launcher unit can be elevated and traversed by power, and the vehicle can also be equipped with a 12·7 mm machine gun as secondary armament.
CHARACTERISTICS
Rocket
Calibre: 130 mm
Length: 1·9 m
Propulsion: Single-stage, solid-propellant rocket motor
Weight: 40 kg (at launch)
Range: 14 – 15 km

Launcher vehicle
Weight: 16·5 t
Road speed: 50 km/h
Crew: 3
DEVELOPMENT
The development and production of the Type 75 rocket was carried out by the Nissan Motor Company Ltd under contract from the Japanese Self Defence Agency.
STATUS
Entered service with the Japanese Ground Self Defence Force in 1975.
CONTRACTORS
Aeronautical and Space Division, Nissan Motor Co Ltd, 5-1 3-Chome, Momoi, Suginami-ku, Tokyo, Japan – Rocket and multiple launcher.
Komatsu Industries Ltd, (and others) – Vehicle.

Type 75 130 mm rocket launcher vehicle

SOUTH AFRICA

4527.111
VALKIRI 127 mm ARTILLERY ROCKET SYSTEM

Valkiri is a highly mobile artillery rocket system capable of producing high rate saturation fire on area targets at ranges of between 8 and 22 km. It can be deployed on its own or in support of more conventional artillery weapons against area targets such as camps, troop concentrations and convoys of soft skinned vehicles. Due to its high mobility, it is ideally suited to the 'shoot-and-scoot' principle of deployment, ie, to bombard the enemy and move to safety as soon as possible before he can retaliate.

The system has been designed with simplicity of operation and mobility as prime requisites, the latter being achieved by the choice of a suitable launch vehicle consisting of a 24 tube pack mounted on a light 4 ton 4 × 4 petrol driven vehicle. The elevation and traversing of the tube pack is hydraulically assisted; power for the hydraulic system being derived from the power take-off of the launcher or from the vehicle battery. During firing the launcher is stabilised by means of a pair of hydraulic supports mounted at the rear of the launcher.

Standard artillery techniques are applied to sight the launcher; the sight being mounted in the side of the launcher and stored in a special container on the vehicle when not in use. The rockets can be fired singly or in ripples of between two and 24 from within the cab of the vehicle by means of an electronic firing unit mounted inside the cab or remotely via a remote firing unit which can be connected to the launcher via a 50 metre plug-in cable.

A test circuit is incorporated in the firing unit to check the status of the rockets and associated firing circuits as regards possible open or short circuits prior to firing.

At the heart of the Valkiri system is the 127 mm calibre rocket, which consists of a missile comprised of three main sections: the nose housing warhead and fuze; the double base propellant motor; and a tail section consisting of the rocket exhaust nozzle and a folding fin assembly. Total length is 2·68 metres and the weight of each round has been estimated as being in the region of 60 kg. Both contact and proximity fuzes have been developed for the Valkiri, the latter being the most commonplace in South African service because of the nature of the particular operational needs which tend to emphasise the system's anti-personnel applications. For similar reasons the standard warhead is an anti-personnel prefragmentation type consisting of a matrix of about 8500 steel balls which are cast in epoxy resin within a thin walled cylinder surrounding the explosive. The fuze is screwed to the front of the warhead and the proximity fuze now employed represents an important operational advantage over the Soviet BM-21 according to South African sources.

Another improved proximity fuze is under development for the 127 mm artillery rocket and will be ready for production in mid-1984. This is the Valkiri radio proximity fuze which incorporates a contact back-up fuze facility and employs a system of frequency agility that is claimed to make it almost impervious to enemy jamming. It is also unaffected by smoke, dust, clouds or rain and capable of operating over a temperature range of –15° to +65°C. Arming is automatic as a result of an acceleration of 40 g for a minimum of one second, together with high airspeed; the operating airspeed range is 150 – 1000 m/s and there is a minimum impact angle of 20°. The new Valkiri fuze is powered by an internal wind turbine generator and the device is being developed by the Fuchs electronics concern for Armscor.

Only one size of propulsion rocket motor is required, this giving a maximum range of 22 km, which can be adjusted downward to 15 km by means of the launch elevation angle selected and reduced still further by use of steel drag rings affixed to the rocket body to a minimum of 7·5 km. In addition to the wrap-around aerodynamic fins at the rear of the

Valkiri MARL vehicle ready to move with 127 mm rocket on table (T. J. Gander)

rocket, spin stabilisation contributes to accuracy and spin is imparted to the round at launch by means of lugs and guides in the launch tubes. Ignition of the propulsion motor is effected electrically, and there is a test circuit to check the status of rockets prior to firing. The warhead lethal area is on average 1500 metres² and the missile accuracy at maximum range is quoted as 290 metres (standard deviation) in azimuth and 200 metres in range (standard deviation).

The Valkiri launcher has a total of 24 tubes arranged in three horizontal rows of eight, carried on a traversing and elevating mount which is operated hydraulically. This mount is integrated with a standard light four-ton Unimog 4 × 4 petrol driven chassis, the only other modification to which is the provision of two hydraulically actuated stabiliser spades which are used when deployed for firing. A canvas top cover is provided for the launcher tube assembly and apart from the inconspicuous retracted support spades there is no external evidence of the vehicle's function so that to a casual observer it appears as an ordinary truck carrying troops or supplies whilst on the move. Hydraulic power for the stabilisers and traverse and elevation of the tube assembly is derived from either the vehicle's power take-off or from the battery. Each launcher vehicle carries the firing crew of two, radio, sight and on-vehicle or remote fire control equipment.

The fundamental unit of the Valkiri system as operated by the SADF is one of the launcher vehicles described above, and this is known as a multiple artillery rocket launcher (MARL). The SADF organisational structure provides for one first line ammunition carrier vehicle to each MARL, the former being a standard SAMIL 5 ton truck fitted with a collapsible cargo stowage assembly which is also capable of fitting other vehicles. Each of these ammunition carriers transports 48 Valkiri rockets in containers, together with fuzes, tools and other ancillary equipment. Folding steps at the rear of the vehicle facilitate loading and unloading of ammunition by hand. Four MARLS and their resupply ammunition carriers comprise one artillery troop under a fire control team, which is under the direction of battery HQ. Two troops constitute one battery, batteries coming under the control of regimental headquarters. Associated with each troop fire control

is a survey team and a meteorological team, the latter having a Unimog-based support vehicle that is fitted with an anemometer and wind vane mounted on a telescopic mast for surface wind measurement to be used in ballistic computation.

In addition to the mast-mounted sensors, at the MARL sites a wind gun which fires a small calibre projectile is used to estimate the prevailing local ground wind conditions. These local meteorological data complement upper atmosphere conditions obtained by the divisional met data system based on the S700 meteorological ground station which operates in conjunction with balloon-borne radio sondes. Operationally high first-round hit capability is achieved by compensating for the prevailing upper air and surface wind conditions by means of range table correction computed from the data obtained as described above. Meteorological and upper air wind data obtained by the divisional S700 system (**4494.161**) is transmitted direct to individual troop fire control units of each battery within a division.

A MARL can be ready to fire within five minutes of arriving at a pre-surveyed site so that theoretically in under six minutes a battery can launch a total of 192 rockets carrying high explosive anti-personnel warheads to a target up to 22 km away. In accordance with the 'shoot-and-scoot' principle embraced by the system designers, each MARL can be ready to move again in a maximum of two minutes. Alternatively, in ten minutes each could be reloaded with another 24 rockets and ready to fire again. These performance factors (see also tabulated characteristics, nearby) allied to vehicles capable of road speeds up to 90 km/h, road, rail and air (C130 or C160) transportability, modest initial cost and low manning requirements add up to a remarkably cost-effective weapon system that reveals an outstanding ability to rapidly assess and define an operational requirement and react quickly and economically to meet it.

CHARACTERISTICS
Launcher
Number of launch tubes: 24
Firing rate: 1 per second
Firing mode: Singly or any ripple between 2 and 24
Elevation: 888 mils (max)
Traverse: 1851 mils
Vehicle: 4-ton 4 × 4

Max speed on open roads(loaded): 90 km/h
Crew: 2
Time to load 24 rockets: 10 minutes (max)
Time for deployment of launcher on a surveyed site:
5 minutes
Rocket
Calibre: 127 mm
Length: 2680 mm
Propulsion: Double base solid fuel rocket motor
Warhead
Type: Prefragmentation
Lethal area: 1500 m² average
Fuze: Proximity or contact
Performance
System effectivity (battery of 8 launchers) kill effectiveness on a standard 400 × 500 m
NATO target: 30%
Range: 8 to 22 km (with drag rings)

Precision at maximum range
Standard deviation in azimuth: 270 m
Standard deviation in range: 190 m
Accuracy at maximum range
Standard deviation in azimuth: 290 m
Standard deviation in range: 200 m
STATUS
Operational since 1981 with South African Defence Forces. Development began in 1977 and was completed in March 1981. In production.
CONTRACTOR
Armscor Corporation of South Africa Ltd, 0001 Pretoria, Republic of South Africa.

Valkiri 127 mm rocket system launcher preparing for operation (T. J. Gander)

SPAIN

2033.111
SPANISH ARTILLERY ROCKETS
In recent years Spain has developed a number of multiple rocket systems and brief details of these are given below.
D-10
This launcher consists of two rows each of five rockets and is mounted on the rear of a Barreiros Panter 6 × 6 truck.
E-20
This launcher has four rows each of five rockets and is mounted on a two wheeled artillery type carriage which is towed by a 4 × 4 Land-Rover.
E-32
This launcher has four rows of eight rockets and is normally mounted on the rear of a 4 × 4 truck. The rockets can be fitted with a variety of warheads including high explosive, incendiary and smoke.
E-21
This launcher has three rows of seven rockets which can be fitted with high explosive, incendiary or smoke warheads. The launcher is mounted on the rear of a Barreiros Panter 6 × 6 truck.
T-Rocket
This rocket is of the fin-stabilised type and is still under development. The rocket is 110 mm in calibre and weighs 24 kg at launch; maximum range is stated to be 12 000 m.
G-3
This launcher has a total of eight rockets and is mounted on the rear of a 6 × 6 truck. The rocket weighs 527 kg at launch and its warhead weighs 217 kg; a maximum range of 23 500 m is claimed.

D-3 rocket launchers

CHARACTERISTICS

Designation of system	D-10	E-20	E-32	E-21
Designaton of rocket	D3	E2B	R6B2	E3
Calibre of rocket	300 mm	108 mm	108 mm	216 mm
Weight of rocket	247·5 kg	16·4 kg	19·4 kg	101 kg
Max range	17 000 m	7500 m	10 000 m	14 500 m
Number of rockets in system	10	20	32	21
Mount	6 × 6 truck	2 wheeled trailer	4 × 4 truck	6 × 6 truck

STATUS
The D-10 and E-21 are known to be in service with the Spanish Army but it is believed that the E-20 has now been phased out of service.

SWITZERLAND

4123.111
OERLIKON 81 mm TYPE RWKO14 ROCKET LAUNCHER
The Type RWKO14 multi-tube rocket launcher is designed for firing Oerlikon 81 mm SNORA unguided solid fuel rockets. This rocket has folding fins and a pure internal burning propulsive element. The RWKO14 comprises two groups of 15 launch tubes mounted symmetrically on a one-man armoured turret, carried on an APC (see illustration). Loading is simple and a typical reloading time is about six minutes. Aiming in traverse and elevation is by manual operated mechanism and laying is

accomplished by means of a computer-assisted aiming periscope, Type RLK252. The firing control arrangements provide for single round firing of rockets in pairs and for salvoes, and used for ground-to-ground engagements, ranges of 4 to 10 km are attainable.
CHARACTERISTICS
Calibre: 81 mm
Rate of fire: 2 × 300 rounds/minute (max)
Length of tubes: 2000 mm
Ammunition: 81 mm SNORA rockets, with different shell types
Length: 1548-1784 mm (depending on type of shell)

Mass of shell: 15·7 – 19·7 kg (depending on type of shell)
Max rocket speed: 520 – 670 m/s (depending on type of shell)
Aiming periscope: Type RLK 252
Magnification: ×7
Field of view: 9°
Slant error correction: 10°
Aiming range
Traverse: Unlimited
Elevation: –10 to +50°
Turret weight: 820 kg (empty)

STATUS
In production.
CONTRACTOR
Machine Tool Works, Oerlikon Bührle Ltd, CH 8050
Zurich, Switzerland.

Multi-tube rocket launcher Type RWKO14 fitted on
APC

TAIWAN

4547.111
CHING FENG (GREEN BEE) SURFACE-TO-SURFACE MISSILE

This weapon made its first public appearance at a National Day parade in Taipei in October 1981 when it appeared preceded by what were reported as associated fire control and radar facilities. Little firm information from sources in Taiwan has been made available but the Ching Feng was described as a medium range surface-to-surface or surface-to-air missile with a maximum range of more than 100 km. From the photograph the weapon would seem to be carried by a transporter trailer rather than a launcher

vehicle, which to some extent leaves the method of deployment and launching procedure details unknown. The size and general arrangement of Ching Feng suggest that the nearest likely relative is the American Lance battlefield support weapon (**2682.111**) and there is a considerable degree of superficial similarity which could well be backed by internal and less visible points of similarity, or even identical features. There has been no official confirmation that Lance was ever among the items of military hardware supplied to Taiwan by the USA before the change of policy introduced during President Carter's term of office, but co-operation

between Israel and Taiwan has been noted in other instances (eg. the Hsiung Feng coastal defence missile, **4442.121**, and its obvious relationship with the Israeli Gabriel, **6019.221**) and Israel is known to operate the Lance SSM.

Lance exists in versions with either conventional HE or nuclear warheads but it seems unlikely at present that either Israeli Lance or the Ching Feng has other than a conventional payload. Therefore the latter probably most closely resembles an earlier version of Lance, with very similar performance and operating characteristics. Significant Lance characteristics in this context include: simplified inertial guidance, range of about 120 km, storable liquid-propulsion, and a launch weight of approximately 1400 kg.
STATUS
Operational with the Republic of China's Army. The Chung Shan Institute of Science and Technology is reported to have been responsible for development of Ching Feng, but the precise extent of indigenous expertise in the design of this weapon cannot be determined from available evidence at present.
CONTRACTOR
Taiwan State Arsenals.

Alternative view of Ching Feng SSM reveals similarities to US Lance. Missiles behind Ching Feng are Hsiung
Feng coastal defence missiles derived from Israeli Gabriel

A Ching Feng SSM on transporter during National
Day parade in Taipei (Photo L.J. Lamb)

4346.111
WORKING BEE-4 127 mm ARTILLERY ROCKET

The Working Bee-4 multiple artillery rocket system is believed to be related to the Working Bee-6 artillery rocket system (**4345.103**) to the extent that both systems share a common calibre of rocket, namely 127 mm. However it can be seen from photographs showing both these systems side by side that the Working Bee-4 round is much shorter than the Working Bee-6, thus indicating a shorter range. Other differences that are readily apparent are the non-training mounting for the launch tubes of the Working Bee-4 on a tracked and armoured vehicle, and their number (40, compared with the Working Bee-6's 45).

It is not known if the Working Bee-4 launcher vehicle is equipped to carry reload rockets or has any facilities for this.
STATUS
In production and operational with Taiwanese forces.
CONTRACTOR
Taiwan State Arsenal.

Kung Feng (Working Bee)-4 127 mm multiple rocket
launcher vehicle (Picture Republic of China)

4345.111
WORKING BEE-6 127 mm ARTILLERY ROCKET

Under the designation 'Working Bee-6' the Taiwan State Arsenal has developed and produced a 127 mm multiple artillery rocket system which was first revealed in the National Day Parade in October 1981. The weapon consists of a group of launch tubes comprising five rows of nine tubes carried on a trainable platform mounted on a heavy-duty military truck. The block of launchers can also be elevated, apparently by means of screw jacks, and it is estimated that the rockets are about three metres long. They are probably fin-stabilised although spin-stabilisation cannot be ruled out. No details of performance have been disclosed, nor any particulars of the firing or reloading arrangements. There is no sign of any reload facilities on the launcher vehicles themselves.

There are a number of close resemblances between this weapon and the recently revealed South African Valkiri 127 mm multiple rocket system (**4527.111**) and they may in fact share some aspects of their origin

Taiwanese Working Bee-6 127 mm multiple artillery rocket system (Photo L.J. Lamb)

although both are claimed as indigenous developments. Evidence of close collaboration with Israel in defence developments has been noted in the past (eg the Israeli Gabriel and Taiwan Hsiung-Feng naval missiles) and it is possible that the Working Bee-6 is a further example of this co-operation.

STATUS
In production and operational with Taiwanese forces.
CONTRACTOR
Taiwan State Arsenal.

UNION OF SOVIET SOCIALIST REPUBLICS

3327.111
SS-1 (SCUD) BATTLEFIELD SUPPORT MISSILE

The SS-1 family of heavy artillery rockets code-named Scud by NATO has been produced in two principal models, designated Scud A and Scud B, respectively. The more recent Scud B has been noted in two versions, one of which is thought to represent an interim stage of development leading to the standard model now widely deployed within the forces of the Warsaw Pact states and some others. Scud A is believed to have been withdrawn from first-line service. The existence of a longer range Scud C was confirmed in a US Armed Services Committee reference in hearings of April 1978 to the KY-3 Scud, when it was stated that this version was first deployed in 1965. It was added that the later version has a longer range than Scud B, but a lower CEP accuracy.

Scud is a land-mobile system, single missiles being carried on a vehicle that combines the functions of transporter and erector by means of hydraulically actuated rams which raise the missile to the upright position for launching. Scud A and Scud B have both been deployed on the tracked JS-III chassis, but from 1965 onward Scud B only has been reported on the MAZ-543 eight-wheeled transporter vehicle. The launcher vehicles can be reloaded in the field and for re-supply purposes Scud is towed tail-first by a Type ZIL-157V tractor with a special semi-trailer. Loading

onto the launcher vehicle is by means of a Type 8T210 (6.3 t) mobile crane on a Ural-375 vehicle.

The standard Scud B missile is capable of carrying either nuclear or conventional high-explosive warheads, but use of the former is probably restricted to Soviet Union formations. Liquid propulsion is employed, and the launch preparation time is quoted by Soviet sources as about one hour. Associated with Scud batteries, in addition to the re-supply and loading vehicles already noted, are a meteorological mobile unit which includes an End Tray weather radar, a ZIL-157V tanker vehicle with a trailerised pump unit, and command and control vehicles. The End Tray is assumed to be for radio-sonde tracking and data collection for use in obtaining upper-air information for ballistics computation prior to launch. A fairly lengthy survey procedure is also entailed on arrival at the firing position, and both tripod-mounted theodolites and optical devices attached to the missile/launcher by special brackets are employed for this. At least two types of theodolite have been noted.

A form of inertial guidance, possibly allied to radio command for the early stages of flight, is the generally assumed method of aiming Scud. The missile's fins are rigidly fixed to the body of the rocket, so that control is almost certain to be by auxiliary vanes or spoilers positioned within the rocket motor efflux.

Whether or not some form of control is provided for the post-burnout phase of flight is not known. In view of the trouble taken to ensure up-to-date upper-air meteorological data for ballistics forecasts, it is probable that there is no further control of Scud's trajectory after the rocket motor has stopped. If radio command over a larger portion of flight is provided, however, it may be possible to exert some control over the rocket motor to extend or curtail the distance covered, but on present evidence this seems unlikely.

Although launcher/erector vehicles for Scud are widely assumed to be of either of two types JS-111 and MAZ-543, closer study reveals that there are differences within each type. Early versions of the former, for example, had only one gas bottle on each side of the vehicle (presumed to contain compressed air for pressuring the missile fuel tanks) whereas later JS-III vehicles carried two on each side. Rather more profound differences have been noted in different versions of the eight-wheeled MAZ-543 Scud vehicle, possibly having implications on the respective missiles carried by them. The non-Soviet Union Scud launcher/erector vehicles of this type are more complex than those supplied to other users of Scud missiles. The erector cradle of the latter is noticeably less bulky and 'cluttered' in general appearance, the most obvious difference being the absence of the two long tubular actuators which run parallel with the lower third of the missile and on each side of it. Their purpose is not clear at present. Close examination of photographs reveals other variations also.

The data below refer to the standard Scud B; Scud A is roughly 0·5 m shorter and has reported range capability of some 130 km. The reputed range of the provisional Scud C model is in the region of 450 km.

MAZ 543 transporter/erector vehicles preparing for action at a launch site

Soviet SS-1 Scud deployed for action. Note crew in CBW clothing

CHARACTERISTICS
Type: Surface-to-surface, artillery missile
Configuration: Cylindrical body with conical nose and cruciform cropped delta tail surfaces
Length: 11·25 m
Diameter: 85 cm
Weight: 6300 kg (estimated)
Propulsion: Storable, liquid
Range: 180 – 300 km
Guidance: Simplified inertial
Warhead: Nuclear, optional non-nuclear warhead

STATUS
Operational in Warsaw Pact forces. In addition to the Soviet Forces, Bulgaria, Czechoslovakia, East Germany, Hungary, Poland and Romania have been reported as operating Scud. Non-Warsaw Pact countries to have received this weapon include Egypt, Iraq, Libya and Syria. All but the Soviet missiles are likely to be fitted with non-nuclear warheads.

From the numbers deployed, their length of service and the successive stages of development and improvement they have undergone, the Scud series

of weapons is well regarded within the Warsaw Pact and beyond. A successor system, designated the SS-23, is expected to replace Scud units deployed in brigades at army and front level. This will probably have improved accuracy and a range of 500 km compared with the Scud's 300 km.

2959.111
SS-12 (SCALEBOARD) BATTLEFIELD SUPPORT MISSILE

Scaleboard is the NATO name for a short medium-range ballistic missile which is identified by some sources with the SS-12 in the US series. It is a mobile missile and is normally transported on a MAZ-543 eight-wheeled vehicle similar to that sometimes used for Scud B (**3327.111**). Its warhead has been reported to be in the megaton range. This suggests that it has rather greater destructive power than its approximate equivalent in NATO, the American Pershing missile (**2965.111**).

Unlike the Scud missiles, which in transit are exposed to view as they rest in their elevating cradles, the Scaleboard missile is enclosed in a ribbed split metal casing which is elevated with the missile into the firing position.

Scaleboard appears to be approximately the same length as Scud B – rather more than 11 m – but larger in diameter. Its range has been estimated in the region of 700 – 800 km. Nothing is known about its guidance system but it is presumed to be some form of inertial guidance suitable for use with a missile that is elevated from the horizontal to the vertical shortly before firing.

CHARACTERISTICS
Type: Surface-to-surface tactical
Configuration: Scaleboard has not been publicly

SS-12 Scaleboard missile on the move

revealed outside the launcher/erector casing which completely envelopes the missile. The following dimensions are based on studies of the container and transporter vehicle (MAZ-543)
Length: 11·25 m
Diameter: 100 cm
Weight: 6800+ kg
Propulsion: Presumed storable liquid
Range: 700 – 800 km (estimated)
Guidance: Presumed inertial
Warhead: Nuclear

STATUS
Believed to be fully operational in the USSR, but there remains a marked scarcity of reliable information regarding the precise role of this weapon and the numbers and nature of its deployment. The latest available figures indicated a total (but probably diminishing) strength with the Soviet Army of 120 missiles, 70 facing the NATO area and 50 in the Soviet Far East. Steady replacement of the SS-12 Scaleboard by a more recent design, the SS-22, is presumed to be continuing.

4548.111
SS-21 BATTLEFIELD SUPPORT MISSILE

SS-21 is the designation assigned by the US to a replacement for the FROG-7 battlefield support missile (**2926.11**) and which was believed to have been under development from the early 1970s. Unofficial reports state that it is a single-stage weapon 9·44 m long and about 46 cm in diameter with a range of some 60 km, although later official US reports now quote a longer range for the FROG-7 (70 km) and as much as 120 km for the SS-21 replacement.

As with the first reports on the SS-21, the closeness of the figures then suggested for the new missile to those for its forerunner prompted questions concerning their origin and the manner in which they were derived. Were they obtained indirectly from photographs or other visual evidence, for example, or were they arrived at by deduced reckoning? The SS-21 is claimed to be a guided missile, but no indications are given of the technique employed and neither is there reliable information on the kind(s) of payload

carried. The latter are thought likely to include nuclear, conventional HE, and chemical warheads although the possibility of some kind of sub-munition warhead designed for use against specific types of target such as airfields, vehicle parks, troop concentrations etc. ought not to be ruled out.

STATUS
In early 1981 official US sources reported that only a few SS-21s had been deployed operationally, despite this weapon having been potentially ready for operation in 1976. If there was in fact any delay in introduction of this weapon it could well be simply the problems of funding and the conflicting demands of other new weapon programmes that were then gathering impetus, such as the SS-20 (**3219.111**). The existence of a very considerable 'in situ' quantity of FROG type missiles, apparently still very serviceable, must have constituted an appreciable capital investment that also represented a latent impediment to the expenditure of resources on a successor.

Official US observations in early 1984 on the then still unseen SS-21 were confined to a statement that it is a division-level weapon replacing the FROG-7. No figures of estimated deployment/production were given, but it was considered that in addition to an increased range of some 120 km, other operational benefits include better reliability and increased accuracy. The evidence for these conclusions was not divulged.

Transporter/erector/launcher vehicle for the SS-21 battlefield support missile, which according to official US sources is now replacing the FROG-7 in the Soviet Union's western theatre

---

4549.111
SS-22 BATTLEFIELD SUPPORT MISSILE

A replacement for the large, long-range battlefield support SS-12 (Scaleboard) missile (**2959.111**) has been reported in official US circles for several years under the designation SS-22. There are no confirmed illustrations of this weapon nor any published

performance data or technical details. The 1983 edition of the US Government publication *Soviet Military Power* says of the SS-22 it is expected to replace Scaleboard missiles with a range of about 900 km (a slight increase over previous estimates, Ed), but with greater accuracy.

Further speculation about the characteristics and performance of the SS-22 will have to await more adequate evidence.

4550.111
SS-23 BATTLEFIELD SUPPORT MISSILE
The SS-23 is the battlefield support missile thought by official US sources to be the successor system for the long-serving and widely deployed SS-1 Scud weapon system (**3327.111**). Scud is normally deployed in brigades at army and 'front' levels, and in Soviet service it is believed to be in the process of progressive replacement by the SS-23. The latter is reported to have an increased range of up to 500 km compared with the Scud's approximately 300 km, coupled with increased accuracy. As noted in earlier entries on the Scud system, it is considered likely that any replacement for this system would probably incorporate improvements leading to reduced reaction and re-firing times, but as yet this cannot be confirmed. Neither are there any technical details or accurate performance data available for publication.

2926.111
FROG-7 BATTLEFIELD SUPPORT MISSILE
The introduction of FROG-7, first shown to the public in 1967, marked a new departure in carrying vehicles – the vehicle used being a modern, wheeled, erector launcher (ZIL-135). The missile too, has a more modern look about it, reverting to the original single-stage design and having a cylindrical warhead of the same diameter as the missile. It has a much cleaner appearance than its predecessors. This missile is probably the last of the unguided ballistic free rocket over ground (FROG) series (see **2890.111, 2922.111, 2923.111** and **2924.111** in earlier editions), some of which were supplied to Warsaw Pact states and other friendly countries by the USSR. Mostly FROG-3s and FROG-5s, these are being replaced gradually by the FROG-7.

The main nozzle of the single-stage rocket motor is surrounded by a ring of much smaller nozzles.
CHARACTERISTICS
Type: Surface-to-surface, spin-stabilised unguided tactical missile
Propulsion: Single solid-propellant motor
Warhead: Nuclear or HE
Length: About 9 m
Diameter: About 55 cm
Launch weight: About 2 t
Range: 60 – 70 km
STATUS
Operational in the armies of several Warsaw Pact countries. Also supplied in quantity to Egypt, Iraq, Libya, North Korea, and Syria. Some missiles, supplied by the Soviet Union to Syria, were actually fired against the Israelis in the 1973 Arab-Israeli war. They were equipped with high-explosive warheads. It was at one time suggested that these particular missiles may have been a guided version (see **2927.111**) but this has not been confirmed or repeated recently; in any case they appear not to have been very effective as HE weapons.

A replacement for the FROG-7 is under development with the designation SS-21 (**4548.111**) and progressive conversion of some Soviet units to the new weapon in Western Soviet theatres has been reported by US authorities.

Positioning elevated FROG-7 missile

Crew prepare FROG-7 for launch

5555.111
ARTILLERY ROCKETS
The Soviet Union has been using multiple rocket launchers since before the Second World War, and since then has continued to develop new systems. Multiple rocket systems are used by all members of the Warsaw Pact and some members have either developed their own systems or modified Soviet equipment to meet their own requirements. Details of other Warsaw Pact multiple rocket launchers will be found under the following entries:

Czechoslovakia	BM-21/M-1972 SP	(**5137.103**)
Czechoslovakia	RM-130 SP	(**2024.103**)
Poland	WP-8 Towed	(**2611.103**)
Romania	M-51 SP	(**2612.103**)

The BM-21 is the most widely used of all of these multiple rocket launchers, and each tank and motor rifle division has a battalion of these, each battalion having three batteries of six launchers. The rockets can be fitted with a variety of warheads including high explosive, chemical, smoke, and biological.

STATUS
122 mm BM-21: Entered service in 1964 and is used by most members of the Warsaw Pact; it has also been exported to many countries, including Angola, Cuba, Egypt, Iran, Syria, and Viet-Nam.
122 mm M-1972: Entered service in 1971/72 and consists of a Czechoslovak Tatra-813 8 × 8 truck with a Soviet BM-21 launcher mounted on the rear; a special rack is carried behind the cab which contains a further 40 rockets. This enables the launcher to be

BMD-25 240 mm rockets in foreground. BM-14/17 rockets on right

quickly reloaded. It is known to be used by Czechoslovakia, East Germany, and the Soviet Union.

132 mm BM-13-16: This is the oldest of all of the Soviet multiple rocket launchers as it entered service in the Second World War. It is no longer in front line service but is still used for training. The rockets are launched from rails rather than from a frame or tube.

140 mm BM-14-16: Entered service in the early 1950s and has been used by Poland and the Soviet Union. It is no longer in front line service.

140 mm BM-14-17: Entered service in 1959 and is a development of the earlier BM-14-16; it is still used by Poland and the Soviet Union.

140 mm RPU-14: This towed multiple rocket launcher is used only by the Soviet airborne divisions and is issued on the scale of 18 per division.

200 mm BMD-20: Entered service in the 1950s but is no longer used in large numbers. Some are used by North Korea.

240 mm BM-24: Although developed in the 1950s this still remains in service with a number of countries including Algeria, East Germany, Egypt, and Syria. A number were captured by Israel and these are now used by the Israeli Army.

240 mm BM-24T: This has only been used by the Soviet Army and is the same launcher as the above but mounted on the AT-S medium tracked tractor.

BM-21 122 mm multiple rocket systems ready for action

BM-25: Entered service in the 1950s. Its rockets are believed to have a liquid, rather than a solid-propellant. The rockets are the heaviest and have the longest range of all the Soviet multiple rocket launchers.

Early in 1978 it was reported that the Soviet Union had developed a new large calibre multiple rocket system which also incorporated a rapid reload capability similar to that employed on the 122 mm M-1972 multiple rocket system.

Notes:
There are also three short rockets:
(1) length 1·905 m; weight 45·8 kg; maximum range 11 000 m
(2) with booster; range 19 000 m
(3) length 1·225 m; weight 112 kg; maximum range 6575 m.

Designation	RPU-14	BM-21	M-1972	BM-13-16	BM-14-16	BM-14-17	BMD-20	BM-24	BM-24T	BM-25
Type	Towed	SP	SP	SP	SP	SP	SP	SP	SP	SP
Chassis	—	Ural-375	Tatra 813	ZIL-151	ZIL-151	GAZ-63A	ZIL-151	ZIL-157	AT-S	KrAZ-214
Number of barrels	16	40	40	16	16	17	4	12	12	6
Rocket										
Calibre	140 mm	122 mm	122 mm	132 mm	140 mm	140 mm	200 mm	240 mm	240 mm	250 mm
Length	1·085 m	3·226 m	3·226 m	1·473 m	1·085 m	1·085 m	3·110 m	1·29 m	1·29 m	5·822 m
Weight	39·6 kg	45·8 kg	77·5 kg	77·5 kg	39·6 kg	39·6 kg	91·4 kg	109 kg	109 kg	455 kg
Max MV	400 m/s	N/A	N/A	350 m/s	400 m/s	400 m/s	N/A	465 m/s	465 m/s	N/A
Max range	9810 m	20 500 m	20 500 m	9000 m	9810 m	9810 m	20 000 m	10 200 m	10 200 m	30 000 m
Launcher crew	5	6	6	6	7	6	6	6	6	N/A
Weight loaded	1200 kg	11 500 kg	14 000 kg	6432 kg	8200 kg	5300 kg	8700 kg	8630 kg	15 240 kg	18 145 kg
Length	4·036 m	7·35 m	7·76 m	7·5 m	6·92 m	5·41 m	7·2 m	6·705 m	5·87 m	9·815 m
Height	1·45 m	2·85 m	2·7 m	3·19 m	2·65 m	2·245 m	2·85 m	2·91 m	3·1 m	3·5 m
Road speed	—	75 km/h	75 km/h	60 km/h	60 km/h	65 km/h	60 km/h	65 km/h	35 km/h	55 km/h
Range	—	405 km	1000 km	600 km	600 km	650 km	600 km	430 km	380 km	530 km
Launcher elevation	0 to +45°	0 to +50°	0 to +50°	+15 to +45°	0 to +50°	0 to +50°	+9 to +60°	0 to +65°	0 to +65°	0 to +55°
Traverse	30°	240°	240°	20°	140°	180°	20°	140°	210°	6°
Time to reload (minutes)	4	10	5	5-10	4	2	10	4	4	N/A

UNITED STATES OF AMERICA

4194.111

GLCM GROUND LAUNCHED CRUISE MISSILE

The GLCM system consists of the General Dynamics Tomahawk missile (BGM-109) integrated on an air-transportable, ground mobile-launcher unit. Together with its launch control van, it will be protected in its peacetime location within a hardened shelter. The ground mobility will lessen the risk of destruction by an enemy pre-emptive strike in the event of war. The USAF is implementing plans to deploy GLCMs and Pershing II surface-to-surface missiles (**2767.111**) in various parts of Europe as the major element of the NATO Theatre Nuclear Forces modernisation programme, initiated principally as a response to Soviet deployment of SS-20 IRBMs in Europe.

The GLCM can be used for both selective or general nuclear release options against fixed targets such as lines of communications, logistic facilities, airfields, command posts and stationary tactical targets such as staging and assembly areas.

The basic GLCM combat unit consists of 16 missiles loaded on four TELs (transporter/erector/launcher vehicle) with two mobile launch control centres. As noted above, the missile is the BGM-109 Tomahawk air-breathing cruise missile with a 2500 km range, flying at low altitude to avoid radar detection and AA defences, and carrying a nuclear warhead. An inertial navigation guidance system updated by terrain contour matching (TERCOM) information directs the missile in flight. More details

of this system have been published in earlier editions of *Jane's Weapon Systems*. Each TEL provides transport, protection, elevation and launch support for four cruise missiles, and enables rapid movement from main operating bases to remote launch locations. In combat-alert conditions, GLCMs may be moved from protective hardened shelters to areas where natural terrain offers concealment for movement and firing operations. Until launch, each missile rests in an aluminium canister which is loaded within the TEL, the wings, control fins and engine inlet being retracted during storage. To launch the GLCM, a solid-propellant rocket motor boosts the missile to cruising speed. During the boost phase fins unfold, the engine inlet and wings deploy. The turbofan engine then ignites to sustain flight; after approximately 13s the booster motor burns out and is then jettisoned.

The TEL vehicle, produced by General Dynamics also, weighs about 33 055 kg and is 16·5 m long. It is capable of off-road driving and can be carried in C-130, C-141 and C-5 transport aircraft. The design incorporates provisions for nuclear safety and protection against small arms fire.

Two launch control centre vehicles (LCCs) accompany each GLCM combat unit. The launch control sub-system consists of two launch consoles with displays and a computer and software for system

control, status monitoring, mission data storage and transfer, and missile re-targeting. The launch control sub-system is integrated with the communications sub-system within a shelter carried on the LCCs, and primary and reserve power supplies are incorporated on these vehicles. There will be redundant communications links and a lightweight fibre-optic data link between each TEL and LCC vehicle. Environmental control and protection for the crew from CBR hazards are also included. Each LCC vehicle weighs about 36 000 kg and is approximately 17·3 m long.

Within the secure main operating bases, protected buildings will provide weapon storage, maintenance and inspection. It is planned that the crews will install warheads, load TELs and undertake periodic inspection and maintenance of all GLCM combat unit parts. The missiles will be fuelled in advance and can be stored for months in their aluminium canisters without requiring scheduled maintenance or handling. Hardened concrete shelters designed to house two LCCs and four TELs protect each GLCM combat flight group from conventional attack during storage, including precision air attacks. The GLCM shelter concept divides each structure into three cells which each hold two TELs or LCCs.

GLCM will be deployed in 'flights', each consisting of a total of 22 vehicles (2 LCCs and 4 TELs carrying

16 missiles, and 16 support vehicles) manned by a total complement of 69 personnel. In transit from the main operating base (MOB) to remote launch sites it is planned to move GLCM flights in two parts called the first and second critical elements, respectively.

CHARACTERISTICS
Type: BGM-109G GLCM
Length: 6·4 m (with booster)
Max diameter: 53 cm
Wing span: 2·5 m
Weight: 1773 kg (with booster)
Speed: High subsonic
Range: 2500 km
Warhead: Nuclear W84
Propulsion: Williams International Corp turbofan; Atlantic Research Corp solid booster
Guidance: Inertial navigaton plus TERCOM

STATUS

The GLCM system is in production, with initial operating capability achieved in December 1983 and with a total of 560 production missiles planned by 1988. By then 137 TELs should have been delivered, and 79 LCCs.

Under the NATO theatre nuclear force modernisation programme it is planned to deploy 464 GLCMs in Western Europe and the UK. The anticipated programme development and production costs exceed $3000 million and the USA will pay the full cost of development and production of the GLCMs, but NATO will share the funding of the European-based storage and operating facilities. The USAF in Europe will operate the GLCM system. Two main bases for GLCM units in the UK have been designated: Greenham Common, Berkshire, which was the first with six flights and 96 missiles, and Molesworth, Cambridgeshire with a total of 64 missiles.

By the end of 1982, nearly 100 test firings of Tomahawk cruise missiles had been carried out, of which over 80 per cent were successful.

Under a contract signed in September 1982, McDonnell Douglas began building complete Tomahawk (GLCM) cruise missiles, joining General Dynamics Corporation as a producer. The first McDonnell Douglas-built missiles are expected to leave the production line in 1984.

GLCM base construction continued during 1984 in Britain and Italy, and preparations had begun in West Germany; Belgium was continuing with preparation of basing plans, and US/Netherlands discussions were in progress. Planned GLCM procurement details in the fiscal year 1985 report by the US Secretary of Defense showed provisions for 84 in fiscal year 1983 at a cost of $446·8 million, 120 ($580·9 million) in 1984, and 120 ($571·1 million) in 1985.

CONTRACTOR

General Dynamics Corporation, Convair Division, PO Box 80847, San Diego, California 92138, USA.

Ground Launched Cruise Missile BFM-109G climbs away under booster power after leaving TEL tube during a test firing (USAF)

2682.111
LANCE BATTLEFIELD SUPPORT MISSILE

Lance is a surface-to-surface guided missile designed to provide general battlefield fire support for an Army corps. It is replacing both Honest John and Sergeant missiles. It can carry either a nuclear or conventional high-explosive warhead and its range has been estimated at approximately 110 km. It requires an eight-man crew, half the number required for Honest John (**2652.111**) and Sergeant (**2940.111**).

This highly mobile missile can be delivered by aircraft or helicopter, has good mobility over ground and can swim inland waterways. Lance uses simplified inertial guidance, and is the first US Army missile to use ready-packaged and storable liquid propellants. Major ground support equipment includes a self-propelled launcher, a fully mobile lightweight launcher, and a transporter-loader.

In the field, Lance complements conventional divisional tube artillery and extends the resources for nuclear or non-nuclear supporting fire available to the divisional commander.

The Lance missile comprises a warhead section, a guidance package, fuel tankage, and an engine. The guidance package is a rugged low-cost device conceived and developed in the US Army Missile Command's Guidance and Control Laboratory. Over the operational range of the missile it is claimed to have a high degree of accuracy and reliability.

Spin-stabilisation in flight is achieved initially by venting some of the propellant gases through canted vents in the body of the missile. After initial spin has been imparted in this way it is maintained by aerodynamic pressure on the canted fins at the base of the missile.

Propulsion is by a Rocketdyne storable liquid-propellant engine comprising two concentrically-mounted sections. The outer section provides thrust during the boost phase of the missile's flight, and during this phase, which corresponds to a flight of about a mile (1600 m), the missile is under tight control by the control and guidance electronics. When the on-board inertial system detects that the predetermined velocity has been achieved, the boost motor is extinguished and the missile continues on a zero-g flight powered by the (inner) sustainer motor. At a predetermined point in the flight this motor too, cuts out, and the missile finishes its journey in free flight.

For land-mobile operations the weapon system is transported on two tracked vehicles (US Army's M113 family) one of which (M752) functions as an erector-launcher while the other (M688) carries two extra missiles and a loading hoist. Both vehicles are on the M667 chassis, with a road speed/range capability of 68 km/h/450 km. For air mobile operations the lightweight launcher will be more appropriate and this and the missile can be taken into the battle zone

by helicopter or parachuted from a fixed-wing aircraft.

CHARACTERISTICS
Designation: MGM-52C
Type: Mobile surface-to-surface tactical guided missile
Guidance: Simplified inertial
Propulsion: 2-part, concentric pre-packed storable liquid-propellant motor
Warhead: Nuclear (W70-1/2/3) or HE
Length: 6·14 m
Diameter: 56 cm
Launch weight: 1285 – 1527 kg
Speed: Mach 3
Range: 120 km

DEVELOPMENT

The Lance prime contractor was selected in 1962. The research and development contract was awarded in January 1963. The first test firing was made at White Sands Missile Range in March 1965. The first firing from the engineering model lightweight launcher was in July 1965 and first firing from the self-propelled launch vehicle came the following month. Lance development was delayed for approximately one year when problems were encountered with the propulsion system and the rocket engine, but these difficulties were subsequently overcome. The first production model was delivered to the US Army for service testing in April 1971; the first Army launch took place that August and service testing was completed in March 1972.

During development a total of 156 flight tests were conducted – including 37 Army launches, all but one of which were successful.

Nuclear armed Lance missiles were initially equipped with the W70-1 and later the W70-2 warhead, subsequent development led to initial operational capability for an enhanced radiation/ reduced blast (ER/RB) warhead for Lance, the W70-3, which was available from 1982 onward. Other alternative payloads that have been studied in conjunction with the Lance missile include a variety of multiple sub-munitions for use in the Assault Breaker programme (**3989.111**), and some of this technology is now being applied to other programmes such as the Joint Tactical Missile programme.

STATUS

Lance was type-classified 'standard' early in 1972 and the first training battalion was activated in April. The weapon was subsequently deployed with six US battalions in Europe and two in the USA as a training base. The first operational launch took place in November 1972. Lance has been purchased by Belgium, West Germany, Italy, Israel, Netherlands

Lance missile prepared for launch

and the UK. Lance is regarded as possibly being the basis of a recently revealed missile known as Ching Feng (Green Bee) (**4547.111**) in the Republic of China (Taiwan) Army by whom it is operated.

To extend the range of tactical applications of the weapons the US Army has a non-nuclear warhead which employs cluster bomblets and would be used against different targets from those for which the nuclear warhead is required. Lance production was completed in 1980, but an advanced, solid-propellant flight vehicle plays an important part in the Assault Breaker (**3989.111**) anti-armour programme as the T-22. It is possible that the T-22 might be used as a basis for a new weapon, at present known as Lance II or the Improved Lance, which in turn may become a candidate for the Joint Tactical Missile programme (see **4441.111**, below).

CONTRACTORS

Vought Corporation, PO Box 225907, Dallas, Texas 75265, USA – Prime Contractor.

American Bosch Arma Corp, Arma Division, Roosevelt, New York, USA – Gyroscope.

Systron-Donner Corporation, Donner Division, Concord, California, USA – Guidance Components.

North American Aviation Inc, Rocketdyne Division, Canoga Park, California, USA – Propulsion.

Hawker-Siddeley Canada Ltd, Toronto, Ontario, Canada – Lightweight Launcher.

FMC Corp, Ordnance Division, San Jose, California, USA – Vehicles.

4760.111

JOINT TACTICAL MISSILE SYSTEM

The joint tactical missile system (JTACMS) for the US Army will be a replacement for, or a modification of, the existing Lance missile system (**2682.111**). As such it will be used to attack targets of importance to the corps at ranges beyond those that could be engaged by conventional artillery or rockets. This missile, or similar missiles with a high degree of commonality, will be used by both the US Air Force and the Army. The former will be launched from both fighter and bomber aircraft, while the Army version will be transported and launched from a mobile ground launcher.

The operational function of JTACMS is described in the Annual Report to Congress of the US Secretary of Defence, dated February 1984, as follows: "We are developing systems that will be able to locate and track fixed and moving targets deep behind enemy lines, intelligence and fire control information will be processed by automated systems and distributed to tactical commanders for targeting decisions. Targets will be attacked by aircraft and missiles that deliver a variety of munitions, including terminally dispensed lethal submunitions. Programmes that emphasise extended-range target acquisition and deep-attack capabilities include the Joint Surveillance and Target Attack Radar System (JSTARS), the Joint Tactical Fusion programme, and the Joint Tactical Missile System (JTACMS)."

The JSTARS radar is an airborne system being developed jointly by the Army and the USAF to detect and locate targets at extended ranges, and is itself an

outcome of the previous Pave Mover programme. The JTF automated system will process, analyse, and distribute intelligence reports from multiple sources for targeting and other operational purposes. The JTACMS missile will be able to dispense terminally guided and unguided submunitions at targets well behind enemy lines to permit engagement of back-up opposing forces, air defence systems, tactical ballistic launchers, and command and control centres.

An Army Missile Command contract awarded in 1983 calls for a detailed assessment of the concept in advance of a full scale engineering development programme due to start in 1984. This study being carried out by Vought Missiles and Advanced Programmes Division includes a system design concept, missile configurations, expected performance, recommendations for the necessary test programme, and cost and time estimates. The LTV Corp is one of three competing companies participating in the study.

The JTACMS project is an outcome of earlier independent activities by the two US military services, which would have resulted in two weapons: the Army Corps Support Weapon System (CWS) (**4441.111** in the 1983-84 and earlier editions of *Jane's Weapon Systems*) and the USAF Conventional Stand-off-Weapon (CSW) for which the cancelled AGM-109 MRASM (medium range air-to-surface missile) (**4191.311**) was a candidate. The two efforts have been combined with the aim of developing a common missile.

The Vought proposal is based on an advanced

version of its Lance missile (**2682.111**), and the new weapon known as Improved Lance promises longer range, greater accuracy and payload, and lower unit costs. It retains the 22-inch (56 cm) of the standard Lance but employs a solid-propellant rocket motor, a ring laser gyro guidance system, and movable control surfaces at the rear instead of fixed fins and thrust vector control.

STATUS

The JTACMS programme is at the definition and development phase, and planned funding for fiscal years 1983/84/85/86 ($ millions) in the 1985 DoD Annual Report to Congress was 30·8, 60, 114·5 and 206, respectively.

In 1983 the British Royal Ordnance Factory signed an agreement with Vought for co-operative marketing and possible co-production of Improved Lance. It was then stated that Phase I of the Improved Lance programme would see its introduction into the US Army and USAF, with both services using available AP and anti-material warheads. Phase II would call for the introduction of a new high firing rate ground launcher, a wheeled vehicle with missiles in canisters. The nuclear warhead would be modified for installation on the Improved Lance missile. Phase III would provide for system growth, such as development of new warheads, terminal sensors, anti-ship, airfield attack and hard structure munitions etc to expand the mission capability.

CONTRACTOR

Vought Corporation, PO Box 225907, Dallas, Texas 75265, USA.

2765.111

PERSHING Ia BATTLEFIELD SUPPORT MISSILE

Pershing Ia is an improved version of the Pershing ground-to-ground guided weapon system (**2764.111**) that is now deployed with the US Army and the Federal German Republic in Europe.

The most obvious change that has taken place is the replacement of the XM474 tracked vehicles on which system components were mounted by a set of wheeled vehicles based on the M656 five-ton truck. The system now has an improved erector/launcher, an articulated truck and trailer combination that carries both the missile and its warhead (previously carried on separate vehicles) and capable of both paved road and cross-country travel. The other vehicles are a transporter for the programmer-test and power stations, the firing battery control central truck, and the radio terminal set vehicle with an inflatable antenna. All the equipment is transportable by the CS-130, C-141, and C-5A cargo aircraft.

System reaction time of the Pershing Ia has been reduced by improvements in the erector/launcher and by the introduction of automatic countdown. The radio communications system has also been expanded. There is no change in the missile itself.

Most recent of the improvements is an automatic reference system (ARS) which employs gyro compass techniques similar to those used in navigation and which enables the missile to be fired from a previously unsurveyed site. Associated with ARS is a sequential launch adapter (SLA) which permits the Pershing commander to count down and launch up to three missiles from a single control station without uncabling and recabling after each missile is launched. European-based Pershing units received ARS/SLA ground equipment in 1976/77.

DEVELOPMENT

A $66 million development contract was awarded to Martin Marietta in 1966. This was followed by two production contracts, one for $52 million in 1967 and one for $32 million in 1968. Production started in November 1967 and was completed in 1971.

Pershing Ia equipment began deployment with US and West German forces in Germany in the summer of 1969 and was completed in 1971.

CHARACTERISTICS

Military designation: MGM-31A

Type: Land-mobile air transportable surface-to-surface tactical ballistic missile system

Guidance: Inertial

Propulsion: 2-stage solid-propellant rocket motor

Warhead: Nuclear W50: these are believed to be 400KT warheads

Missile length: 10·5 m (approx)

Missile diameter: 1 m (approx)

Launch weight: About 4600 kg

Speed: Mach 8

Range: 160 – 740 km

STATUS

Operational. Funding requested for fiscal year 1976 amounted to $17 million for the final quantity of 72 automatic azimuth reference sets to extend the missile's operational life and 25 telemetry sets for training. A further $3 million requested for fiscal year 1977 was for procurement of a new safety and arming device and for a modification to the radio system to eliminate its unique signature.

Meanwhile, following successful firings in October 1974 and an Army review early in 1975, the ARS/SLA ground support equipment was classified 'standard' and a $5·4 million contract was issued to Martin Marietta Aerospace.

The ARS/SLA ground equipment was supplied to European-based Pershing units, first deliveries starting in March 1976.

In December 1977 Martin Marietta was awarded a US Army contract for about $7 million to re-open the Pershing Ia production line. Inactive since June 1975, Pershing production was recommenced to replenish the US Army inventory and is now complete.

CONTRACTORS

Complete system: Martin Marietta Orlando Aerospace, Orlando, Florida, USA.

Propulsion: Thiokol Chemical Corporation.

Communications: Collins Radio Company.

Inertial navigation: Bendix Corporation, Eclipse-Pioneer Division.

Pershing Ia surface-to-surface missiles with ARS/SLA deployed

---

2767.111
PERSHING II BATTLEFIELD SUPPORT MISSILE

The Pershing II system is a modular modernisation of the currently deployed Pershing Ia (**2765.111**).

A new inertial navigation system developed by Singer-Kearfott, and a new re-entry vehicle which incorporates a high-accuracy, terminal guidance system developed by Goodyear Aerospace are used in the later version of Pershing. Range is increased to approximately 1800 km. The enhanced accuracy combined with terminal guidance and control facilities enables warheads of appreciably reduced yields to be employed to engage small hardened targets. Earlier Pershing missiles carry W50 warheads, which are thought to be 400 KT, and these have been criticised for being excessively large and destructive for battlefield use. Pershing II will carry a single W85 warhead, with a relatively low yield.

The Pershing II terminal guidance system incorporates an all-weather radar correlation unit that compares the live radar returns with a pre-recorded and stored radar image of the target area. Continual automatic comparisons of the two provides control signals to actuate the control vanes which are a distinguishing feature of the Pershing II re-entry vehicle. The RADAG (from radar area guidance) system relies upon inertial navigation system

Pershing II missile erected from its erector/launcher vehicle and ready to fire

information from the second stage booster for position data prior to separation. Soon after re-entry, the Goodyear RADAG system is activated to sweep the target area below the rapidly descending RV, and provide accurate position updating to the inertial system. The scanner of the RADAG guidance package rotates at 120 rpm, and corrective commands are computed continuously to bring the RV back on course to its designated impact point.

Under a contract awarded by Goodyear, Norden Systems is delivering computerised systems to be used for the preparation of reference scenes that will be used to guide Pershing II missiles to their targets. Norden will supply six systems: five are miniaturised PDP-11/70Ms (also known as AN/UYK-42(V)), and one a commercial PDP-11/70 for use by Goodyear for software development. The Norden equipment is used in conjunction with digitised computer discs of possible target areas, which are supplied by the US Defence Mapping Agency (DMA). These discs, called the data base, cover such land features as terrain, elevation, rivers and buildings, and the data base is fed into the Norden computer system which predicts what the missile will see on its radar during flight.

The Norden systems are being delivered to Goodyear, apart from the two for the DMA headquarters in Washington and another for the US Army Engineer Topographic Laboratories at Fort Belvoir, Virginia. Those going to Goodyear are for mounting on government-furnished five-ton trucks.

STATUS

The Pershing II advanced development programme was completed in May 1978. Five flights of the missile were conducted successfully to test and evaluate the terminal guidance system. Full-scale development began in February 1979 with the award of a $360 million contract to Martin Marietta. Sub-contractors for Pershing II include Bendix for airborne and ground computers. Goodyear for the radar guidance sub-system, Hercules for propulsion motors, and Singer-Kearfott for the inertial measurement system.

In May 1978 it was stated that the US Army had plans to deploy a Pershing II brigade in the Federal Republic of Germany, consisting of three missile battalions of 36 missile launchers each. The brigade will require approximately 3800 men.

In December 1979, it was decided within NATO to deploy Pershing II in Europe; this is not likely before fiscal year 1984. Pershing II will be deployed in Europe in a similar fashion to Pershing Ia. This entails three American battalions of four firing batteries each with three firing platoons of three erector/launchers with missiles. The US Army now has 108 Pershing Ia launchers, but the number of missiles is classified, however replacement by Pershing IIs will be on a one-for-one basis. The initial production contract for Pershing II was signed in June 1982 and the first of 18

Close-up of Goodyear radar area guidance (RADAG) system in nose of Pershing II showing gimbal-mounted scanner (T.J. Gander)

planned flight tests took place in July. This was a failure due to faulty production techniques in the rocket motor, but the second test was successful and the programme continued on schedule.

By September 1983 the flight test programme had been completed, with 14 of the 18 missiles fired and primary test objectives achieved. Production deliveries to the US Army began in May 1983, and at 1 January 1984 production contracts awarded to Martin Marietta amounted to $725 million. That month the first Pershing II entered service in West Germany.

Planned procurement in the fiscal year 1985 DoD Budget was 70 missiles in 1984 at a cost of $404 million, and 93 in 1985 for $456 million.

CONTRACTOR

Martin Marietta Orlando Aerospace, Orlando, Florida, USA.

4440.111
GEMSS

The ground-emplaced mine scattering system (GEMSS) is a passive, primary anti-armour system. The trailer-mounted mine dispensing system, M128, provides a commander with a flexible means for

placing large quantities of anti-tank and anti-personnel mines over appreciable areas in a short time. GEMSS is the principal ground-based system of the FASCAM family of scatterable mines designed to provide lay down minefields at short notice to present obstacles to the advance or other movement of

enemy armour. The other FASCAM systems include mines sown by airborne dispensing systems and artillery delivered mines.

The M128 GEMSS dispenser can be towed by tracked or wheeled vehicles, and it holds up to 800 mines weighing about 1·8 kg each which are ejected sideways at selectable intervals of 30 or 60 metres, with their density being determined by the rate of launch and the speed of the towing vehicle.

The M75 anti-tank mine has a magnetic influence fuze giving it the ability to attack the full width of the target vehicle and the M74 anti-personnel mine is a ground blast fragmentation mine which is activated by an automatically deployed tripline sensor. Both types of mine have a built-in self-destruction

mechanism, set by the dispenser operator, to provide the choice of a long- or short-time interval. Once the SD time has elapsed, the minefield is neutralised, permitting unhindered movement of friendly forces. Using GEMSS, up to 800 mines can be emplaced in 15 minutes.

STATUS

In early 1982 the US Army reported that GEMSS was in production and would shortly be operational. This

statement was repeated in the US Army Weapon Systems report, January 1984.

CONTRACTORS

Engineered Systems Development Corporation.
Aerojet-General Corporation.
Honeywell Incorporated.

3987.111
US ROCKET ASSISTED PROJECTILES (RAP)

In common with many European countries, the United States is devoting much effort to the development of rocket assisted projectiles for tube artillery. In general these developments relate to unguided projectiles, although some attention has been given to laser guidance systems for such rounds.

As ranges increase, even if precision remains the same, absolute dispersion increases and therefore a laser guidance technique would obviously assist in overcoming this. On the other hand the greatly increased cost of the guided over the unguided round makes it desirable to explore the possibilities of unguided rounds thoroughly before abandoning them in favour of guided missiles. Results so far appear to be encouraging.

A further difficulty is the loss of payload resulting from the incorporation of a rocket motor in the projectile. In parallel with the development of the RAP rounds, therefore, there is also a programme aimed at increasing the effectiveness of the reduced payload by the use of new materials and processes in the construction of the warheads.

The rocket motors in the projectiles must be designed to withstand very large stresses. Mean accelerations in guns currently in service are typically about 5000 g for a 105 mm howitzer and about 20 000 g for a high-velocity tank gun, with 30 000 to 40 000 g in sight for the next generation of the latter. RAP rounds for field artillery may thus have to withstand chamber pressures in the order of 3000 kg/cm², acceleration in the order of 18 000 g and rotation rates up to 17 000 rpm.

To achieve increased ranges for the US Army's 155 mm and 8-inch howitzers, an RAP has been developed for each and is being procured. The 155 mm high explosive RAP round (M549) is a separately loaded projectile composed of two distinct components: the warhead, and the rocket motor. This round can be fired from existing gun systems. The 8-inch round (M650) is used with the M110A1/A2 self-propelled howitzers and the M198 155 mm towed howitzer.

DEVELOPMENT

RAP projects are controlled by (and much of the research and development work is done at) the US Army Armament Research and Development Command (ARRADCOM), Dover, New Jersey

(formerly Picatinny Arsenal). The 155 mm projects are managed by the US Army Material Development and Readiness Command's Office of the Project Manager for Cannon Artillery Weapon Systems (PMCAWS) at Dover, where that work is centred. Other projects are centred in ARRADCOM's Large Calibre Weapon Systems Laboratory.

STATUS

The fiscal year 1984 report to Congress by the US Secretary of Defense stated that in that year the USA will continue to build up its inventory of improved conventional munitions and RAPs and a total of $878 million was requested for this purpose. The budget showed a total of 98 457 155 mm RAP rounds and 33 904 8-inch RAPs. These figures incorporate production for both the US Army and Marine Corps.

CONTRACTOR

Various manufacturers will be involved, and these will be named as production contracts are awarded.

2652.111
HONEST JOHN BATTLEFIELD SUPPORT MISSILE

Honest John is a simple surface-to-surface free-flight rocket that has the accuracy of standard artillery and considerably better battlefield mobility. The unguided rocket is driven by a single-stage solid-propellant motor and can carry either a nuclear or a high-explosive warhead.

Designed to fire like conventional artillery in battlefield areas, Honest John is now the oldest missile system still fielded by the US Department of Defense. Studies were begun by US Army Ordnance in 1950, and shortly after that Douglas Aircraft (now McDonnell Douglas) submitted proposals based on the Ordnance specifications and became prime

contractor for the system. Firing tests were successfully completed in 1951 at White Sands, New Mexico.

The resultant system comprises a simple rocket and a highly mobile self-propelled launcher. Operation is simple – there are no electrical controls – and normal crew training and standard fire control techniques are employed.

CHARACTERISTICS

Military designation: MGR-1B
Type: Mobile surface-to-surface unguided tactical missile.
Propulsion: Single-stage solid-propellant rocket motor
Warhead: Nuclear (W31) or high explosive

Length: 7·5 m
Diameter: 76 cm
Launch weight: 2040 kg
Range: 7·5 – 37 km

STATUS

Honest John has been in service with the armed forces of Belgium, Denmark, the Federal German Republic, France, Greece, Netherlands, South Korea, Turkey, the United Kingdom, and the USA. Production ceased some time ago and the missile has been replaced in US Army service by Lance (2682.111). Honest John remains in service with Greece, South Korea and Turkey.

4060.111
MULTIPLE LAUNCH ROCKET SYSTEM (MLRS)

The multiple launch rocket system (MLRS) is a highly mobile automatic rocket system developed to enable a firing crew with a minimum amount of training to shoot a complete 12-rocket load, reload rapidly and fire again. Its purpose is to complement cannon artillery in engaging massed attack by enemy formations on an area basis rather than by engaging individual targets in succession. This artillery rocket

programme was initially known as the general support rocket system (GSRS), which designation applied from 1972 to December 1979 when the name was changed in the interests of uniformity and acknowledgement of the system's adoption as a NATO standard rocket. A memorandum of understanding covering the intended adoption of MLRS by Britain, France and Germany has been concluded by these states and the USA (Italy joined the group in 1982). Two teams, headed by Boeing and

LTV Aerospace and Defence Company (formerly Vought Corporation) respectively, produced competing designs for MLRS, with LTV being selected as the prime contractor in April 1980.

The MLRS configuration can be seen from the illustrations. It is designed to be operational day and night in all types of weather and to engage and defeat the following targets: tube artillery and rocket counter-batteries, air defence concentrations, trucks, light armour and personnel carriers as well as supportive troop and supply concentrations. Each Vought MLRS launcher has the capacity to neutralise one artillery battery or an equivalent target with a full 12-rocket launcher load.

Its tracked mobile launcher uses the same chassis and running gear as does the US Army's new infantry fighting vehicle (IFV) and gives MLRS cross-country capability comparable to the M1 Abrams tank; thus, MLRS can be part of a combined arms, tank-led combat team.

The self-propelled launcher loader (SPLL) is able to ripple fire two to twelve rockets. During ripple fire operations each rocket is quickly and automatically fired by the fire control system which re-positions and re-aims the remaining rockets after each shot. Successful firing tests confirm that the system can ripple fire its entire rocket load in less than one minute.

SPLL is self-laying and designed so that its three-man crew can safely stop at a firing site, conduct an entire fire mission, including rocket launches, and quickly depart the firing site without ever leaving the cab. The same crew can rapidly reload the SPLL with 12 more

MLRS self-propelled launcher/loader deployed for action

rockets. The two six-pack launch pod containers can be loaded or unloaded singly or simultaneously.

The SPLL carries two launch-pod containers, each containing six rockets. The rockets are preloaded and sealed into the launch tubes of the container. The loaded container will have a ten-year storage life without requiring any special environmental protection or field maintenance. The SPLL vehicle is a complete system containing its own fire control system, stabilised reference package, launcher drive system and self-loading and self-unloading devices. It uses its own internal system to aim the rockets and monitor system characteristics during rocket firings.

A large 25-ton tracked vehicle, the SPLL is 6·9 metres long, 2·6 metres high and 2·9 metres wide. It can get in and out of firing positions very quickly, enhancing crew survivability.

The SPLL can travel overland at 64 km/h and can accelerate from 0 to 48 km/h in 19 seconds. It can traverse a 60 per cent slope, a 40 per cent side slope, a 91 cm vertical wall and a 229 cm trench. It can also ford 102 cm of water.

It accommodates a crew of three soldiers: a driver, gunner and commander. The cab is equipped with an over-pressure ventilation system to prevent rocket exhaust fumes from entering the cab during launches. Armour protection, heating, ventilation and noise attenuation are also provided for crew safety and effectiveness.

Each finalist in the MLRS competition designed its own SPLL, but the basic carrier is the same – the fighting vehicle system carrier, manufactured by FMC Corporation, San Jose, California. It is powered by a Cummins 500 horsepower, four-cycle diesel engine. Because it is constructed from suspension and powertrain components common to the Army's new M2 infantry fighting vehicle (IFV) and the M3 cavalry fighting vehicle (CFV), logistics and maintenance in the field are simplified.

The MLRS surface-to-surface, highly accurate free-flight rockets have a range in excess of 30 km and will provide an important complement to conventional artillery systems.

Each launcher load of 12 MLRS rockets can place almost 8000 M77 sub-munitions in an area the size of six American football fields. Each M77, a derivative of the original M42, has about the same destructive power as a hand grenade and contains a shaped charge that allows it to penetrate light armour.

The low-cost solid-propellant rocket motor for the LTV Aerospace and Defence multiple launch rocket system (MLRS) is provided by the Atlantic Research Corporation of Alexandria, Virginia.

Innovative concepts were included which make the design particularly adaptable to economical high-rate production, such as use of low-cost commercially available hydroxy terminated polybutadiene (HTPB) propellant ingredients, low-cost insulation and igniter designs, use of quick-cure chemical processes to minimise tooling costs and manufacturing cycle times, an economical deep drawn 4130 steel motor case, and a net-moulded plastic nozzle. An important feature incorporated into the MLRS propulsion system design is the employment of technology which is readily adaptable to high-volume production both in the United States and in NATO countries.

MLRS includes the development of three warhead types: dual-purpose anti-material and anti-personnel munitions, scatterable anti-tank mines and guided anti-tank sub-missiles. The dual-purpose warhead is the first being developed for the system and dispenses M77 sub-munitions.

MLRS rocket launch

Rockets fired by MLRS are launched using a fire control system provided by Norden Systems who developed the fire control system using elements from the US Army battery computer system (BCS), an automated command and control system for up to 12 guns at the artillery battery level. The fire control system has four elements: the electronics unit which directs all system activities; the fire control unit which interfaces with the rockets; the fire control panel for the operator; and a small hand-held unit for remote firing and loading and unloading launch pods.

Primary functions of the fire control system include digital communications with the BCS or TACFIRE, semi-automatic processing of fire missions, re-aiming between rockets during ripple fire, ballistic computations and load/unload operations. During a fire mission these functions can be entered automatically or manually, but always under the control of the crew. The on-board system has a 256-character alpha-numeric fire control display panel that communicates to the operator in plain language rather than a code. It can communicate in any native language. The system does the firing computations and prompts the crewman to perform the next function. The system provides automatic re-targeting, thereby allowing a rapid, accurate volume of fire on many individual targets.

To eliminate the need to fire from surveyed sites (and for fresh survey after repositioning) MLRS features a new position determining system (PDS), giving greater combat mobility to the MLRS. The crew will know the position of the SPLL at all times as the PDS continuously computes the launcher position by measuring the distance and direction travelled by the vehicle. The PDS is supplied by Bendix, who provide the stabilisation reference package, part of the original MLRS aiming system. By minor adaptations to the SRP, Bendix was able to add the positioning facility to the north-seeking gyro-compass of the SRP. The first production version of the SPLL, was delivered to the US Army in August 1982.

CHARACTERISTICS

Type: Artillery, surface-to-surface
Guidance: None (free rocket)

Length: 4 m
Diameter: 227 mm
Range: 30 km+
Propulsion: Solid rocket
Warhead: M77 sub-munition, dispensing
Rockets carried: 12 per launcher
Max launch rate: Rapid ripple, 12 rounds in less than 1 minute

DEVELOPMENT

US Army MLRS concept definition study contracts were let in March 1976, and these were completed later that year. Competitive development by the Boeing and Vought teams began in 1977 and Vought fired its first MLRS demonstration rocket at White Sands Missile Range in December 1977. In April 1978 Vought began firing rockets from a prototype launch-pod container, and in December 1978 the first NATO-sized MLRS rocket was launched. The first launch from a complete SPLL was in March 1979. Firing under US Army supervision started in September 1979, this series of 24 firings being completed in December 1979. Thirty-six more rockets were launched by the Army between then and February 1980. In the period 1977-80 a total of 127 rockets was fired by Vought.

STATUS

In April 1980 the US Army selected Vought as prime contractor for MLRS. Subsequent funding awarded under four separate contracts (maturation research and development, initial production facilities, low-rate production and multi-year procurement) amounts to a total of approximately $2 billion, calling for delivery of 333 SPLLs and almost 400 000 rockets in launch-pod containers. Initial production began in early 1982. Ultimately the production rate is expected to reach 6000 rockets per month. It is planned to employ MLRS in the NATO forces of Britain, France, West Germany, and Italy as well as those of the USA.

In January 1983, Britain became the first foreign country to order MLRS when a $5·2 million contract for four launchers and 108 practice rockets plus training equipment was signed. Delivery is due in 1985. The Federal Republic of Germany followed suit in March 1983 with a $2·3 million contract for two launchers plus training hardware.

CONTRACTORS

LTV Aerospace and Defence has assembled a team of experienced Army subcontractors to develop and produce the MLRS.

Self-Propelled Loader Launcher
Sperry-Vickers: Launcher drive system
Norden Systems Inc: Fire control system
Bendix Guidance Systems: Stabilised reference package
Vought: Launcher/loader module

Launch Pod Container
Brunswick: Launch tubes
Magnavox: Platoon leader's digital message device
Vought: Launch/pod container integration

Rocket
Atlantic Research Corporation: Propulsion system
Vought: M77 munition warhead
Vought: Rocket integration

Government Furnished Equipment
FMC Corporation: MLRS carrier
US Army: M77 submunitions

LTV Aerospace and Defence Company, Vought Missiles and Advanced Systems Division, PO Box 225907, Dallas, Texas 76265, USA – Prime contractor.

YUGOSLAVIA

2266.111
128 mm ROCKET LAUNCHER M-63
Based on the Czechoslovak RM-130 rocket launcher (**2024.103**) this artillery rocket system is made in Yugoslavia. It comprises a 32-tube launcher for 128 mm spin-stabilised rockets. The launcher is mounted on a two-wheel trailer and the road wheels, together with the spread trails form the platform for the launcher when in operation. The launcher assembly can be elevated or depressed by handwheel; there is also a traverse hand-wheel, but the available traverse is limited to a few degrees for correction of aim – otherwise the launcher box would foul the road wheels. Firing is electrical.
CHARACTERISTICS
Rocket
Calibre: 128 mm
Length: 814 mm

Weight: 23 kg
Launcher
Capacity: 32 rockets
Weight: 2·5 t approx
Elevation: 0 – 48°
Traverse: 30°
Max rocket velocity: 420 m/s
System range: 8·6 km
Rate of fire: 160 rounds/minute
Time to reload: 3 minutes
Crew: 3 – 5
STATUS
Service.
CONTRACTOR
SPPR, Federal Directorate of Supply and Procurement, 1101 Beograd, 9 Nemanjina Street, Yugoslavia.

M-63 rocket launcher

5153.111
YMRL 32 128 mm MULTIPLE ROCKET LAUNCHER
The YMRL 32 was first seen in 1975 and is a modified civilian FAP 2220 BDS 6 × 4 truck chassis with a 32-round rocket launcher mounted on the rear of the body. Behind the cab is a reloading system with a further 32 rockets. In concept the YMRL 32 128 mm system is similar to the Czechoslovak BM-21/M-1972 rocket launcher (**5137.103**).

The launcher has an electric/hydraulic control system and the rockets can be fired from the cab of the truck, or away from the vehicle with the aid of a remote control system. When the 32 rockets have been fired, the launcher is swung into the horizontal position and the reloading system is raised until it lines up with the launcher. It takes about two minutes to reload the complete launcher.

The launcher can fire two types of rocket: first the older M-63 rocket and second a new rocket. The M-63 rocket is 814 mm in length and has a weight of 23 kg.

It has a maximum velocity of 420 m/s and a maximum range of 8600 metres. The new rocket has a higher velocity and a maximum range of 18 000 metres. Both rockets have a high explosive warhead.
STATUS
In service with the Yugoslav Army.
CONTRACTOR
SPPR, Federal Directorate of Supply and Procurement, 1101 Beograd, 9 Nemanjina Street, Yugoslavia.

Launch of Yugoslav YMRL 32 128 mm artillery rocket

Fire control panel in cab of YMRL32 launcher vehicle

Anti-tank/Assault Weapons

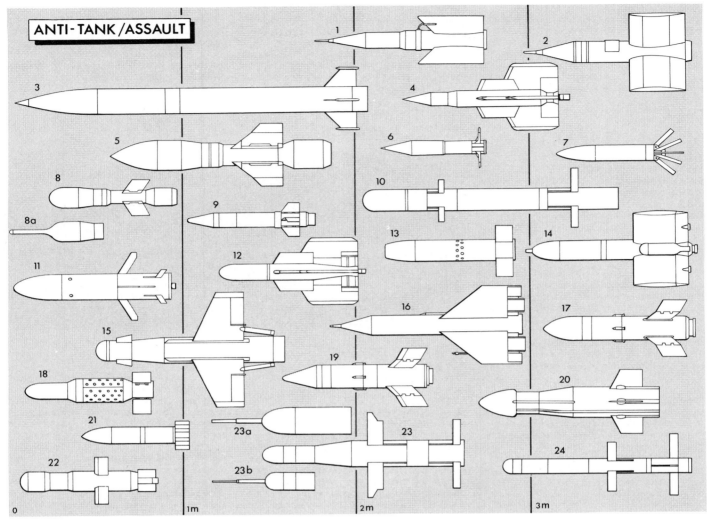

0   1m   2m   3m

1 Mamba	**9** Picket	**17** Kun Wu
2 Cobra 2000	**10** KAM-9 (T79)	**18** Dragon
3 ADATS	**11** RBS 56 Bill	**19** AT-3 Sagger
4 Mathogo	**12** Bantam	**20** Swingfire
5 HOT	**13** Strix	**21** LAW 80
6 ACL-Strim	**14** KAM-3D (T64)	**22** GAMP
7 Folgore	**15** AT-2 Swatter	**23** TOW **23a** TOW 2 **23b** Improved TOW (ITOW)
8 Milan 8a K115 long fuze version	**16** AT-1 Snapper	**24** Tank Breaker

ARGENTINA

3677.111

MATHOGO ANTI-TANK MISSILE

The Argentinian Mathogo anti-tank missile is a first-generation weapon relying upon wire guidance. It is designed to be carried and operated by an infantry soldier, but can also be launched from vehicles, helicopters or light aircraft. It is fitted with a hollow charge warhead and is reported to be able to disable the most modern tanks. In general appearance Mathogo is similar to the Swedish Bantam (**2363.111**), in particular the wing planform, but although there may be some connection between the Swedish and the Argentinian designed missiles, the weights and dimensions are not the same.

The complete system comprises: a water-tight container and launcher and 50 metres of cable; the control unit and binocular sight. Each control unit can be connected to four missiles and can be augmented by a distributor unit.

CHARACTERISTICS

Type: Surface-to-surface anti-tank guided missile with air-to-surface capability

Guidance principle: Wire-guided command to line-of-sight

Guidance method: By control of spoilers in trailing edge of wings

Gyro: Powered by solid propellant pellet

Propulsion: Booster and solid sustainer

Internal power: Thermal battery

Missile length: 998 mm

Diameter: 102 mm

Weight: 11·3 kg (missile); 19·5 kg (missile and launcher)

Effective range: 350 – 2100 m

Cruising speed: 90 m/s

A special simulator for training purposes, using moving or fixed targets, can be connected to the standard control unit. There is also a battery charger that is connected to the control unit.

DEVELOPMENT

Mathago was designed and developed by CITEFA (the Argentinian Scientific and Technical Research Institute of the Armed Forces) under contract from the Argentinian Army.

STATUS

Development was completed in 1978 after a test programme involving more than 100 launches. It is in production.

CITEFA Mathogo anti-tank missile shortly after launch. Note absence of smoke and flame plume

CONTRACTOR

CITEFA (Instituto de Investigaciones Cientificas y Tecnicas de las Fuerzas Armadas), Zufriategui y Varela, 1603 Villa Martelli, Provincia de Buenos Aires, Argentina.

BRAZIL

4193.111
BRAZILIAN COBRA 2000 ANTI-TANK MISSILE
The West German designed Cobra 2000 anti-tank missile (**2181.111**) was first supplied to Brazil some years ago, and was subsequently the subject of a licence agreement between the two countries. The co-ordinating activities of the Brazilian Cobra missile programme are the responsibility of the Army's Instituto de Pesquisa e Desenvolviment (Institute of Research and Development) in Rio de Janeiro. Following the delivery of a batch of Cobra missiles produced by MBB in Germany for evaluation and general familiarisation, IPD began a programme aimed at obtaining completely national Cobra production and support capabilities in Brazil. In 1980 this programme was reported to be almost complete, and several batches of pre-production missiles manufactured by IPD at a pilot factory have been delivered to the Brazilian Army for troop familiarisation.

No details have been obtained, but it is thought probable that in view of the age of the original design, the more recently developed Brazilian version is likely to incorporate a number of component, manufacturing, and detail changes that embody the benefits of advances made in the interim.

FRANCE

2139.111
SS 11 BATTLEFIELD MISSILE
SS 11 is a line-of-sight wire-guided battlefield missile intended for firing from land vehicles, naval vessels, and slow-moving aircraft. Normally fired from a launching ramp it may also be used with a simplified ground launcher. The designation SS 11 is applied to the surface-to-surface version; the similar air-to-surface version is known as the AS 11 (**1173.311**).
OPERATION
The operator acquires the target by means of a magnifying optical device. As soon as the missile enters his field of vision after launch, the operator commands it to his line of sight by means of a joystick. The signals are transmitted over wires trailed from the missile. Tracker flares are installed on the rear of the missile for visual reference.

When installed in a helicopter or ship the simple sighting device used for land vehicles is replaced by a special stabilised sight.
CHARACTERISTICS
Type: Surface-to-surface tactical guided missile
Guidance principle: Command to line-of-sight
Guidance method: Optical tracking and manual wire-guided remote control of missile by vectoring the thrust of sustainer efflux (TVC)
Propulsion: 2-stage solid-propellant rocket motor
Warhead: Various (see text)
Missile length: 120 cm
Missile diameter: 16.4 cm
Span: 50 cm
Launch weight: 29.9 kg
Average cruising speed: 115 – 190 m/s
Minimum turning radius: 1 km

SS 11 missile

Range: 500 – 3000 m
Armour penetration (140AC warhead): 600 mm minimum
SS 11 B1
Since 1962, the SS 11 B1 version, using transistorised firing equipment, has been in production. It is available with a variety of different warheads, including an inert type for practice: the Type 140AC anti-tank warhead capable of perforating 60 cm of armour plate, the Type 140 AP02 explosive semi-perforating anti-personnel warhead (2.6 kg of explosive) which will penetrate an armoured steel plate 1 cm thick at a range of 3000 metres and explode about 2.1 metres behind the point of impact, and the Type 140 AP59 high-fragmentation anti-personnel type with contact fuze.

HARPON
A variant of the SS 11 was produced and supplied to French, West German and Saudi Arabian forces under the name Harpon. It was an SS 11 with a modified guidance system and was described in some detail in **2095.111** in 1981-82 and earlier editions of this book.
STATUS
By mid-1980 some 174 000 of the SS 11 series of missiles had been delivered, including both ground and airborne versions and including also the Harpon (**2095.111**) version, to more than 20 customer countries. Production has now ceased.
CONTRACTOR
Aérospatiale, Division des Engins Tactiques, 2-18 rue Béranger, 92322 Châtillon Cedex, France.

2055.111
ACL-STRIM ANTI-TANK ROCKET LAUNCHER
This is a man-portable anti-tank weapon that has been adopted by the French Army where it is known as the 89 mm LRAC Model F.I.

Designed primarily for infantry use, the ACL-STRIM is a lightweight rocket launcher that fires an 89 mm rocket with an effective range of 400 metres. In the firing position the weight of the launcher and rocket is 8.6 kg; for transport, the launcher units weigh 5.4 kg and each round of ammunition in its container weighs 3.2 kg. The system is thus readily carried into action by combat troops.

The launching tube is made of glass and resin laminate and its shoulder piece and foregrip can be adjusted to suit the user. An APX M-309 sighting telescope, which is detached for transport, is clipped to the side of the launching tube.

The rocket comprises a warhead and a propulsion system. The warhead has a streamlined plastic cap in which is mounted a piezo-electric generator that detonates the charge on impact with the target. The shaped charge is contained in an aluminium alloy casing streamlined by a plastic fairing. To the rear of this is the base fuze which is at safe in the transport position and is armed in flight by gases tapped off from the propulsion system.

For transport the rocket is carried in a sealed container which in operation forms part of the launching tube and contains the electrical circuits that mate with the firing circuits in the launcher.

At normal incidence the rocket will penetrate 400 mm of armour and the weapon is effective at incidence angles up to 75° from normal.
DEVELOPMENT
Development of the ACL-STRIM was initiated by Luchaire SA and the first design study was made in 1964. The system is now in production and went into service with the French Army in 1969.
CHARACTERISTICS
Weapon
Calibre: 88.9 mm
Length: During transport, 1.168 m; in firing position, 1600 mm
Mass: During transport, with 0.5 kg sighting telescope, 5.4 kg; in firing position, 8.6 kg
Rocket
Diameter: 88.9 mm
Diameter of shaped charge: 80 mm
Total length: 0.600 m
Container length: 0.626 m
Total mass: Without container, 2.2 kg; with container, 3.2 kg
Mass of explosive of the shaped charge: 0.565 kg
Ballistic characteristics
Muzzle velocity: At +20°C, 291 m/s; at +51.5°C, 295 m/s; at –31.5°C, 287.2 m/s
Combat range: For a 1.21 s flight time (max ordinate: 1.8 m): 315 m
For a 2.3 m max ordinate (1.36 s): 360 m
Effective range: 400 – 500 m
Time of flight at 400 m range: 1.56 s
Ammunition: Anti-tank, anti-personnel/light armoured vehicles; smoke; incendiary; practice. For training, a sub-calibre barrel for firing 7.5 mm cartridges at combat ranges is available
Effectiveness of the shaped charge
Thickness of armour plating steel perforated at 0° incidence with T3 warhead: 480 mm
NATO targets 100% perforated: Single target, heavy tank, 120 mm/65°; dual target, heavy tank, 40 + 110 mm/60°
Operating limit incidence: 74 – 75°

ACL-STRIM loaded and ready to fire

STATUS
In production. In service with French and other armies. This weapon has been sold to 21 foreign states.

CONTRACTOR
The system is being produced jointly by Luchaire SA, 180 Boulevard Haussmann, 75 Paris 8e, France, and by the Manufacture Nationale d'Armes de St Etienne.

4552.111
ACCP ANTI-TANK MISSILE

The ACCP (anti-char courte porte) is a short range anti-tank missile for use by foot soldiers in the battlefield at ranges of up to 600 metres, but principally with fighting at close quarters in urban districts in mind. Now under development, the Aérospatiale concept calls for a very high penetration missile in preference to the alternative of rockets, the accuracy of which can be adversely affected with increasing range. The ACCP has an effective range of 25 to 600 metres, and a very short flight time enables the use of simple, inexpensive components. The propulsion system also is low-powered so that the weapon can be fired within a confined space.

A simple guidance system is employed that uses an IR marker on the missile which is tracked throughout its flight by a CCD camera in the firing unit so that

corrections can be signalled to it to command the missile to the line-of-sight to the target via guidance wires.

CHARACTERISTICS
Weight: 10 kg (round in tube, ready to fire): 11 kg in tactical container
Length: 930 mm
Diameter: 152 mm
Guidance: CLOS
Propulsion: Solid
Range: 25-600 m
Max speed: 300 m/s (terminal)
Penetration: 900 mm steel
Sight: CCD camera
Optical field: 200 mrad
Magnification: ×4
STATUS
Development. Initial tests carried out in 1982.

Aérospatiale ACCP short-range anti-tank missile system (Photo TJ Gander)

CONTRACTOR
Aérospatiale, Division des Engins Tactiques, 2-18 rue Béranger, 92322 Châtillon Cedex, France.

GERMANY (FEDERAL REPUBLIC)

2181.111
COBRA 2000 ANTI-TANK MISSILE

This weapon system – full designation BO 810 Cobra 2000 – comprises a small wire-guided anti-tank missile, a control box, and cable links. It is a lightweight low-cost weapon suitable for operation by one man, who can readily carry, set up, and fire two missiles.

OPERATION
Unlike many other wire-guided missiles, Cobra is not launched from a container; the missile is simply set down on the ground and, when it is fired, a booster mounted on the underside gives it a jump start that lifts it clear of even rough ground before the sustainer develops full power.

Before launching, the missile is connected to the control box by a cable. This control box contains a battery that supplies the power required to launch and control the missile and, once connected, the missile can be launched simply by pressing the launch button. By means of a junction box up to eight missiles can be connected simultaneously to the control box on which is mounted a selector switch that enables the operator to fire and control these missiles one at a time.

A target coincidence guidance technique is used. The operator has a joystick control which enables him to give lateral and vertical commands to the missile through the guidance wire trailed out behind it. Immediately after launch the missile has to be gathered rapidly into the operator's line-of-sight to the target and quite substantial movements of the joystick may be necessary to achieve this; thereafter

relatively small movements should suffice to keep the missile framed in the target. Tail-mounted flares make it easy for the operator to see the missile in flight.

An electrical testing device built into the control unit enables the controller to carry out a pre-launch check.

The cable attached to the missile is 20 metres long and that attached to the junction box is 50 metres long. The operator can thus position himself conveniently up to either 20 or 70 metres from any one missile.

CHARACTERISTICS
Type: Surface-to-surface anti-tank weapon system
Guidance principle: Command to line-of-sight wire-guidance; optical gathering and tracking
Guidance method: By control of spoilers in wings
Propulsion: Solid-propellant sustainer with separate non-jettisonable booster mounted below the missile
Warhead
(A) hollow charge type, total mass 2·7 kg: penetration 500 mm armour
(B) ATS (anti-tank/shrapnel) 2·7 kg, penetration 350 mm armour prefabricated fragmentation with destructive effect within 10 m radius
Missile length: 95 cm
Body diameter: 10 cm
Wing span: 48 cm
Launch weight: 10·3 kg
Weight at burn-out: 8 kg
Max speed: About 85 m/s
Range: 400 – 2000 m
DEVELOPMENT
Cobra was designed and developed by Bölkow

GmbH, the first design study being carried out in 1957. The system first went into service in 1960, since when more than 170,000 (including those manufactured under licence) have been supplied to the armed forces of 18 countries. A first generation missile, Cobra has been produced in two versions, the Cobra 2000 described here being slightly the heavier of the two and having a maximum range of 2000 metres whereas the earlier Cobra had a maximum range of only 1600 metres. It is still in production but its improved successor, Mamba (**2188.111**), has been so designed as to make it easy for countries using Cobra to change to the new system at whatever rate suits them best.

STATUS
In service with the forces of Argentina, Brazil, Denmark, Greece, Israel, Italy, Pakistan, Spain, and Turkey. West German production has ceased.

In 1980 it was expected that series production in Brazil of Cobra 2000 would be handed over to private industry, after several batches of missiles manufactured at a state-owned pilot factory had been handed over to the Brazilian Army for troop familiarisation.

CONTRACTORS
Originally manufactured by Messerschmitt-Bölkow-Blohm GmbH, in the Federal Republic of Germany. The warhead and sustainer motor are made by Oerlikon-Bührle, Switzerland. Manufacturing licences have been granted in Brazil, Italy, Pakistan and Turkey.

2188.111
MAMBA PORTABLE ANTI-TANK WEAPON SYSTEM

Mamba is an anti-tank missile first announced by MBB late in 1972. Of the same general type as Cobra (**2181.111**), it incorporates two major improvements in the missile, in addition to numerous other changes, and MBB have developed a completely new controller for the system. The new missile, however, will accept Cobra warheads and can be used with existing Cobra controllers by users wishing to change to the new weapon, and existing Cobra vehicle launchers can readily be modified to accept Mamba.

One of the major differences between Mamba and Cobra is that, whereas the latter used an oblique-thrust booster (to give a jump start) and an axial sustainer, Mamba has a one-cell dual-purpose oblique-thrust engine which not only retains the jump-start facility but also provides a weight compensation during the cruising phase. This saves the operator from continually having to counteract gravitational droop during the cruising phase. The other major change is the increase in maximum speed from 85 to 140 m/s.

Mamba anti-tank missile

The new controller incorporates an extremely powerful monocular with an oblique (×7) eyepiece. This permits direct transition from observation with the naked eye to telescope magnification without head movement, thus avoiding the main difficulty of

this transition. This control unit is completely independent of any power sources, batteries etc; it performs all the functions which are performed for Cobra by the test and control units, and it is operable from –40 to +60° C.

Four output sockets from the controller can be connected to single missiles and a fifth can be connected either to a fifth missile or an eight-outlet junction box, giving a total control capability of 12 missiles selected by a switch on the controller. Missile launching is by push-button and guidance by joystick, power for the ignition impulse and the joystick signals being provided by a clockwork motor operating a generator. One winding of the motor suffices for eight launches.

The Mamba system thus comprises only the missile and the control unit. It is conveniently packaged in a water-, dust-, and tropic-proof pack which is of a convenient size for carrying and stacking. Like Cobra, Mamba can be fitted with alternative shaped-charge, or training warheads and these are easily interchangeable.

Mamba is primarily designed to be launched from the ground, and since it can be laterally diverted up to 45° from its launching direction its envelope of action is very wide. If required, however, it can also be launched from a vehicle and a standard five-missile launching frame has been designed for this purpose. Any kind of vehicle can be fitted with this frame, on which the missiles are mounted in a ready-to-fire

position but from which they are easily removed. The controller can be either mounted on the vehicle or removed for remote operation.

CHARACTERISTICS

Type: Surface-to-surface anti-tank weapon system
Guidance principle: Command to line-of-sight with optical tracking
Guidance method: Wire-guidance control of wing-mounted spoilers
Propulsion: Single-cell, dual purpose solid-propellant, oblique-thrust rocket motor
Warhead: Hollow charge type total mass 2·7 kg, 500 mm armour penetration. Dummy for training. All warheads interchangeable
Missile length: 955 mm
Body diameter: 120 mm
Wing span: 400 mm
Launch weight: 11·2 kg
Max speed: 140 m/s
Effective range: 300 – 2000 m
Flight times
500 m: 6 s
1000 m: 10 s
2000 m: 17·5 s
Controller dimensions: 300 × 250 × 100 mm. 9·55 kg

Packed missile (with accessory bag): 365 × 402 × 605 mm, 18 kg
Cable system (including junction box, reel etc): 393 × 408 × 416 mm, 26 kg

TRAINING

A special training aid, Type 112/1 SU, has been designed. This is a simulator using a combat area presentation on a TV screen with superimposed symbols – which move appropriately – to represent target and missile. The trainee operates a standard controller in conjunction with this display.

STATUS

The weapon is in production and supplied to a number of other countries.

CONTRACTOR

Messerschmitt-Bölkow-Blohm GmbH, Ottobrunn bei Munich, Federal Republic of Germany.

INTERNATIONAL

4159.111
ADATS (AIR DEFENCE ANTI-TANK SYSTEM)
ADATS is the title of an international project to develop a battlefield weapon system to acquire, track and engage low-altitude high performance aircraft, helicopters, armoured vehicles and RPVs. The programme is led by Oerlikon with Martin Marietta collaborating under contract.

A modular design concept has been adopted for the fully integrated, self-contained missile system, which can be mounted on a variety of wheeled and tracked armoured vehicles. ADATS comprises a search radar, forward-looking infra-red (FLIR) and TV trackers, a laser rangefinder and a carbon dioxide laser which provides a guidance beam for the beam-riding ADATS missile, a fire control computer and control

consoles, and eight ready-to-fire missiles in their containers.

The ADATS missile has a heavy dual-purpose warhead equipped with a proximity fuze for air targets and impact fuze for use against ground targets. Smokeless propulsion accelerates the missile to speeds of over Mach 3. The complete system will provide high lethality against both air and surface targets, with availability to operate effectively in a dense ECM environment and under adverse weather conditions. Additional details of ADATS operation will be found in **4158.131** in the Mobile Surface-to-Air Guided Missile System section.

CHARACTERISTICS

Length: 2·05 m (2·2 m in canister)
Diameter: 152 mm
Weight: 51 kg (approx)
Propulsion: Solid
Range: 8 km
Ceiling: 5000 m
Speed: Mach 3 plus
Warhead: Dual-purpose 12 kg plus
Fuze: E/O proximity and impact
Penetration: 900 mm plus armour steel
Search radar: 20 km range, dual beam, search on the move capability, 360° cover.

STATUS

Unguided test launches of ADATS missiles were carried out in the USA in 1981, and all-up guided launches began in 1982. The development test phase was planned for completion in the first quarter of 1984.

CONTRACTORS

Machine Tool Works, Oerlikon-Bührle Ltd, CH-8050, Zurich, Switzerland.

Martin Marietta, Orlando Aerospace, PO Box 5837, Orlando, Florida 32855, USA.

Prototype ADATS combined air defence/anti-armour mobile weapon system on M113A2 chassis, showing the eight launcher-containers for the laser beam-riding missiles, dual beam search radar and electro-optical turret in its central position

2212.111
HOT ANTI-TANK MISSILE
HOT (Haut subsonique Optiquement téléguidé tiré d'un Tube) is a heavy anti-tank weapon being developed by Aérospatiale and Messerschmitt-Bölkow-Blohm. With low-speed spin-stabilisation like Milan (**2215.111**), it is a tube-launched, wire-guided missile of larger size and higher performance than Milan but with the same general principles of operation. HOT was planned as a replacement for the SS 11 (**2139.111**) missile and its mission profile corresponds to a NATO requirement for a missile to operate primarily from armoured or unarmoured vehicles and helicopters.

Like Milan, the missile has tail fins which fold down against the body in its launch tube and open out in flight. Guidance is automatic command to line-of-sight (CLOS) with an IR tracking system. The latter was developed by SAT and is produced in collaboration with Eltro in West Germany. Several versions are produced: for rotating tank turrets, for vehicles without turrets and for helicopters.

With the TCA system of guidance, all the operator has to do is to aim carefully at the target with an optical sighting device. When the missile is launched, IR radiation from its tracer flares is detected by a precision goniometer that is associated with the optical sight and that has its reference axis accurately parallel to the optical axis. Departure of the missile from the optical axis gives rise to an angular error signal which can be combined with an estimate of range (based on the known flight characteristics of the missile) to give a measure of the linear departure of the missile from the line of sight. This measurement is then used to generate command correction signals for the missile whose flight is controlled by means of a jet vane system.

OPERATION

To operate the system, therefore, once the target has been visually acquired, all that the operator has to do is aim carefully at the target, launch the missile, and maintain his aim steadily during the missile's flight. An advantage of this guidance system is that, because the departure of the missile from the line of sight is

Four-round HOT/Mephisto installation

measured by the system, the amount of flight correction required can be determined to a similar degree of accuracy and, as a result, the initial gathering of the missile on to the line of sight can be accomplished quickly. This has the important effect of giving the system a good short-range performance.

German Tank Destroyer with HOT Casemate vehicle launcher

HOT missile leaves UTM 800 turret launcher on M3 APC

HOT can be fired from armoured or other vehicles, from helicopters or from dug-out positions and in all conditions of visibility that permit the operator to aim at the target.

The list of vehicle types (land and airborne) to which the HOT system has been fitted is extensive and includes the following:

AFVs and Land Vehicles:
M113 series APC – 2 tubes: 11 rounds inside
AMX 10P APC (**5009.102**) – 4 tubes
Panhard M3B APC (**5022.102**) – 4 tubes; 14 rounds inside
Saviem VAB armoured car – 4 tubes; 8 rounds inside
Raketenjagdpanzer 3 (**5014.102**) – 1 tube; 8 rounds inside

Helicopters:
Bölkow PAH 1 – 6 tubes
Gazelle SA 341/SA 342L – 4 or 6 tubes
Alouette III (trials only)
Dauphin SA 361H – 8 tubes
Lynx – 8 tubes

A selection of the launch equipment employed in these various installations is described in the following paragraphs.

Mephisto
This system was specially designed to permit HOT to be installed on the Saviem VAB armoured car, but is capable of use in other vehicles of the same class. Firing is possible in all directions, and reloading is accomplished from within the vehicle as the four launchers retract while the vehicle is in the 'on-road' configuration.

The Mephisto system consists of an electrically actuated lifting module which elevates four launchers (with their HOT rounds) into either of two positions:

HCT twin-tube HOT launcher turret

(1) a high position which provides sufficient clearance to allow the module to rotate 360° in azimuth, and
(2) a low position, wherein the system is retracted within the vehicle to enable the ramps to be reloaded from inside.

Other items are the sighting system and the missile guidance electronics. The former comprises a swivelling head periscopic sight with stabilised optics, located on the axis of the launch module and partially retractable for the 'on-road' configuration. There is internal stowage for eight reload rounds. This version is in development for the French Army and claimed to be under consideration by the British and West German forces.

Launching Gear UTM 800 (Electric)
Here operation of the gear is undertaken by only one man, sitting. The movement in azimuth and elevation direction is achieved electrically. The guidance system in separated elements version is installed within the turret itself. Four missile ramps can be loaded manually. The turret has a relatively low weight and small installation volume. It can be installed on several types of vehicle. Production for the Panhard M3 vehicle is under way.

Launching Gear Lancelot (Electric)
The AMX 10 HOT vehicle is equipped with the TL HOT turret, which is served by two men. Azimuth and elevation movement is performed electrically by direct command. The guidance system is divided into small boxes and installed in the turret using a special sight for the gunner. Four launching ramps are manually loaded from the rear.

Launching Gear for Casemate Vehicle (K3S)
This consists of a retractable clamp system and a periscope guidance unit. Empty launch tubes are automatically thrown clear after launching. The reloading of up to eight missiles is automatic on retraction of the clamp system in the vehicle. Operation is entirely under NBC protection.

HCT Launching Gear (Electro-Hydraulic)
Due to the absence of a turret basket assembly, the HCT (formerly HAKO) installation exhibits reduced weight and dimensions. The standard-design guidance equipment is located at various points in the vehicle body and linked to the turret assembly by flexible cable. The operator can direct the turret through ±180° in relation to the vehicle axis for rapid

target acquisition; he has the use of a stick control to rotate the turret electro-hydraulically through ±30° in relation to its initial position. This enables precision pointing and target tracking. The stick also controls the angle of elevation of the sighting optics. A stabiliser system may be added for installation on wheeled vehicles. The turret can hold two or four ready-to-fire munitions; reloading is manual.

The HCT turret is a simple and light assembly enabling installation of the HOT anti-tank system on armoured vehicles, even of small dimensions.
CHARACTERISTICS
Type: Long-range, vehicle mounted, wire-guided, anti-tank weapon with airborne applications
Guidance principle: Command to line-of-sight. Optical aiming with automatic IR tracking.
Guidance method: Wire-guidance control of jet vane system
Propulsion: Solid-propellant booster and sustainer
Warhead: Hollow charge
Missile length: 1·275 m
Missile diameter: Warhead: 136 mm. Span: 310 mm
Launch tube length: 1·3 mm
Launch tube diameter: 175 mm
Weight: Missile and container 32 kg. Missile at launch 23·5 kg
Max speed: 250 m/s
Flight duration:
2000 m : 9 s
3000 m : 13 s
4000 m : 17 s
Range: 75 m – >4 km
Penetration: >800 mm of solid armour. NATO triple-armour target at 65° incidence. Effective against composite armour
Operating conditions: –40 to +52° C at up to 95% rh
DEVELOPMENT
The first design study for the system was made in 1964. Development is now complete.
STATUS
The system has been ordered by the French and West German forces following user trials which included the helicopter version. Several other countries have also placed contracts for HOT vehicle and/or helicopter installations, to make a total of 12 user countries in all.
CONTRACTOR
Responsibility for management, sales, and production is vested in Euromissile, 12 rue de la Redoute, 92260 Fontenay-aux-Roses, France.

2215.111
MILAN ANTI-TANK MISSILE
Milan (Missile d'Infanterie Léger Antichar) is a wire-guided, spin-stabilised, anti-tank missile system.

An advanced second-generation system. Milan incorporates a semi-automatic guidance technique that requires the gunner to do no more than maintain the cross wires of his guidance unit on the target during the missile's flight. The system comprises a missile in a container and a launch and control unit. Before the launch, the container – which also serves as a launch tube – is mounted on the launch and control unit. This in turn can be either mounted on a tripod to be fired from a ground position or, mounted on a pivot, from a vehicle.

Although heavier than some of the small first-generation anti-tank missiles, Milan is readily portable. It is also suitable for operation from armoured or unarmoured vehicles. In its simplest form operation is effective in daylight, at dawn and

Milan with K115 warhead in-flight configuration

dusk and, by means of battlefield flares, at night. It can be fired over fresh or salt water.

MILAN now has a night-firing capability through addition of the MIRA thermal imaging device manufactured by TRT and adopted by the French, German and British armies. This consists of a case weighing approximately seven kilograms which can be mounted on the standard firing post. Target

detection is possible at a range of over three kilometres, and firing the extreme range of the system.

To contend with improved tank armour making its appearance in certain theatres, the three nations collaborating in Milan production and development (France, West Germany and the UK) evolved an improved warhead (K 115) which was introduced in 1984. This has an increased diameter of 115 mm compared with 103 mm of the standard item. It also has a different configuration as can be seen from the photograph and the extended nose is arranged to ensure a greater effective stand off distance for the hollow charge payload. The launcher tube is modified to accomodate the larger diameter warhead, and the increased stand off results in appreciably enhanced armour penetration characteristics.
OPERATION
At launch the missile is ejected from its container by a piston which in turn is propelled by a gas generator

Milan firing post equipped with the MIRA night firing device

located at the rear of the launch tube and working on the recoilless principle. The ends of the tube are protected for storage and transit by caps which must be removed before firing.

As the missile emerges from the tube, the tube is disconnected from the launch unit, and the forces in the system are sufficient to throw it backwards from the launcher to a distance of about three metres, leaving the launcher ready for reloading.

When the missile is ejected from the tube its wings, which impart a slow spin to the missile, flick open. The missile then coasts forward until, at a sufficient distance from the launcher to avoid harm to the gunner, the warhead is armed.

Built into the launcher/control unit is an IR TCA guidance system similar in operation to that described above for HOT (**2212.111**). After launching, the missile is gathered to the gunner's line of sight using wide-angle detection. Detection sensitivity in

this phase is presumably relatively low but at close range the signal strength from the IR flares in the missile's tail will be high. For subsequent guidance narrow-angle detection is used. MBB in Germany with SAT in France and Eltro in West Germany are jointly responsible for production of the IR guidance system, and SNIAS for missiles. BAe and MSDS are responsible for the major portions of the appreciable quantity on order for UK forces' use.

CHARACTERISTICS

Type: Surface-to-surface, man-portable, anti-tank weapon system
Guidance principle: Automatic command wire-guidance
Guidance method: Optical tracking of target only. Automatic IR tracking of missile and control by vectoring thrust of sustainer efflux
Propulsion: Ejector in tube (gas generator). Solid-propellant boost/sustainer motor
Warhead: Hollow charge. 103 mm dia (standard); 115 mm (K115 improved)
Penetration: Against a solid target (at 90° incidence) at maximum lethality range more than 850 mm
Missile length: 0·77 m
Body diameter: 0·09 m
Fin span: 0·27 m
Weights: Missile and container: 12 kg; launcher and control unit with tripod: 16·5 kg
Max speed: 200 m/s
Range: 25 – 2000 m
Time of flight: 7·3 s to 1000 m. 12·5 s to 2000 m

DEVELOPMENT
Following the Franco-German agreement, discussion started between Nord-Aviation and Messerschmitt-Bölkow in 1962, and a design study was completed in

1963. Technical evaluation and firing demonstrations by and for the French and West German forces were completed in 1971. User trials in France, Germany, and other countries followed. In June 1972, a successful series of demonstrations was given to representatives of some 30 countries. During the official Franco-German trials, which were designed to test the weapon's efficiency in a wide range of environmental conditions, a hit probability of 88·6% was established in 665 firings.

From June 1974 to August 1983, 31 530 missiles were fired by various customers: the percentage of satisfactory technological performance of these firings overall is 94·2%, and, among the latter ones, the percentage of direct hits has been 92·1%.

STATUS
In March 1984, 165 500 Milan missiles had been ordered for use by the forces of 32 countries. Over 201 000 missiles have been manufactured, and current production is running at a rate of more than 1100 missiles and about 30 launch units per month. This can be increased to 2000 missiles and 130 launch units. Licence production for the British Army is undertaken by British Aerospace.

Series production of the K115 improved warhead was expected to begin in late 1984.

CONTRACTORS
Messerschmitt-Bölkow-Blohm GmbH, Munich, and Aérospatiale, Paris, are main contractors. BAe, TRT, Siemens, MSDS, Eltro, Luchaire-STRIM and SAT are also involved.

Management, sales, and responsibility for production: Euromissile, 12 rue de la Redoute, 92260 Fontenay-aux-Roses, France.

4545.111
EMDG PROGRAMME

Stemming from the ATEM project (**3611.111** in 1982-83 and earlier editions) of the late 1970s for the joint development of a new European anti-tank missile, a new programme to embrace that concept and also to widen its scope evolved in 1983 with the formation in Paris of the Euromissile Dynamics Group by Aérospatiale, British Aerospace and MBB. The three companies represent the participating nations, but provision exists for the later inclusion of additional companies/countries if desired.

As suggested in the entry on ATEM, this project was overtaken by events so that fresh memorandum of understanding (MOU) were drawn up between the British, French and German authorities to cover the collaborative development of two new anti-tank missiles to meet the individual requirements of all three states. These envisage the replacement in the 1990s of such weapons as Milan, HOT, Swingfire and TOW, and to do this two new missile systems are considered necessary: a short to medium range successor to Milan, and a long range weapon. Aérospatiale is to play the leading role in the development of the former, which will be a lightweight, man-portable weapon, with a range of 2000 metres using beam guidance for all-weather

day/night operation. The long range missile will be developed in both air and land launched versions. The latter will be a fire-and-forget weapon probably employing passive IR homing to permit a high rate of fire and extensive manoeuvre capability for the launch vehicle in the interests of evasive action after launch. BAe will assume a leading role for the land launched version and MBB will take a similar role in the case of the air launched long range missile. Guidance for the Milan replacement anti-tank missile will probably rely upon the laser beam-riding technique. Planned range of the long range weapon is in the region of 4500 metres.

STATUS
An MOU between France, the German Republic and the UK calling on the three to agree their operational requirements for a new anti-tank missile was signed in 1976. This resulted in the ATEM project, but progress was too slow to result in an adequate technical or industrial challenge to maintain the respective national facilities in an active state. Therefore further studies were initiated which led to new staff requirements and the formation of EMDG and the programme to develop a family of 'third generation' anti-tank missiles to meet European needs. Project definition is expected to be completed in late 1984 and development contracts have been

awarded amounting to £25 million to complete the definition phase of both weapons.

CONTRACTORS
Aérospatiale, Division des Engins Tactiques, 2-18 rue Béranger, 92322 Chatillon Cedex, France.

British Aerospace Dynamics Group, Six Hills Way, Stevenage, Hertfordshire SG1 2DA, England.

Messerschmitt-Bolkow-Blohm GmbH, Ottobrunn bei Munich, Federal Republic of Germany.

Each company will make use of the facilities and expertise within the Group and will be supported by teams of specialist contractors including:
Bodenseewerk Geräte Technik
Elektro Spezial (Philips GmbH)
Eltro
Thomson CSF
Société d'Etudes et Applications Techniques
Société d'Etudes et de Réalisations et Applications Techniques Luchaire
Télécommunications Radio Electriques et Téléphoniques
Société Nationale des Poudres et Explosifs
Thorn EMI Electronics
Royal Armament Research and Development Establishment
Royal Ordnance Factories
Rocket Motor Executive (PERME)

ISRAEL

3991.111
PICKET ANTI-TANK MISSILE

Picket is a shoulder-launched anti-tank weapon suitable for use by infantry against armoured fighting vehicles or fortified positions. It is inertially controlled along a line-of-sight to the target. In operation, the operator acquires the target through an optical sight, and within one half-second of pressing the trigger the missile is launched and the operator may then discard the launcher and take cover.

This missile consists of an armour piercing warhead, a guidance section, a single-stage sustainer rocket motor, a control section and an ejection rocket motor. The last named accelerates the missile to the initial ejection velocity and imparts spin to the round within the launcher tube. Three folding fins spring open as the missile emerges from the tube, and simultaneously a spring device separates the ejection motor from the missile which then coasts until it has reached a safe distance from the operator and before

Israel Aircraft Industries Picket anti-tank missile

the main motor is ignited. The latter provides a constant thrust throughout the entire trajectory.

The guidance and control system includes a gyroscope, an electronics package and a thrust vectoring system consisting of four jet tabs in the motor efflux. The gyro is uncaged about 100 milliseconds after the weapon is fired, and from then on the missile is locked to its inertial heading. The gyro senses and corrects angular velocities imparted

to the round at launch, due either to the gunner's movements or to tip-off and crosswinds. The round travels at supersonic speed for virtually all of its flight.

Each round consists of a missile packed in a disposable launcher tube sealed by end caps; clip-on trigger and sight units are carried separately until the Picket is prepared for action.

CHARACTERISTICS
Length: 76 cm
Diameter: 81 mm
Weight: 4·2 kg
Launcher weight: 1·8 kg
Range: 500+ m
Guidance: Gyro-stabilised to line-of-sight at launch
Warhead: HE

STATUS
Production.

CONTRACTOR
Israel Aircraft Industries Ltd, Ben Gurion International Airport, Israel.

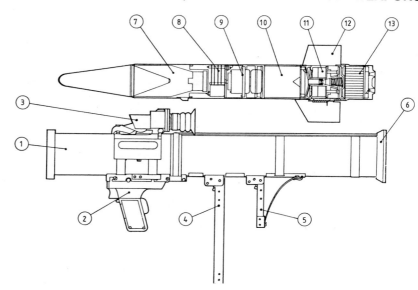

Picket anti-tank missile and its launcher, showing the main components: (1) launcher/storage tube, (2) detachable trigger unit, (3) detachable sight, (4 & 5) folding support leg and shoulder rest, (6) rear cover, (7) warhead, (8) electronics section, (9) gyro unit, (10) flight motor, (11) jet tabs, (12) stabilising fins, (13) ejector motor

ITALY

2257.111
FOLGORE ANTI-TANK WEAPON

Folgore is the name given to a light, recoilless, anti-tank rocket projector currently under advanced development in Italy by Breda Meccanica Bresciana with the collaboration of Snia Viscosa. It is a two-man system classified by its designers as a short-range system, having a maximum range of 1000 metres.

Folgore can be fired from the shoulder or from a tripod. In the tripod version two men perform the function of aimer and loader and the aimer is aided in his task by a telescopic sight fixed to the launcher which enables him to estimate target range, target speed and elevation angle in a few seconds. In the shoulder version the weapon is provided with a lighter optical device and a bipod, and if necessary, can be carried, loaded and fired by one man. The ammunition, which is the same for both versions, is composed of a rocket and a launching charge; the rocket is fin-stabilised and has a hollow-charge warhead.

In addition to the tripod-mounted and man-portable versions of Folgore, a number of designs for turret installations of this weapon for fitting in various armoured vehicles were revealed in 1982. One such, for the new OTO R3 light armoured vehicle introduced by OTO-Melara is illustrated by the accompanying general arrangement drawings, from which it can be seen that two Folgore launcher tubes are carried on the turret which also mounts a 7·62 mm machine gun and the sighting system. Other Folgore turret designs exist for use on different APCs, light tanks or other AFVs including: a power-operated turret with two Folgore tubes and a 12·7 mm machine gun; a power-operated turret with a single 7·62 mm machine gun; and a manually-operated turret with one Folgore tube and a single 7·62 or 12·7 mm machine gun.

CHARACTERISTICS
Weapon off tripod
Launcher length: 1·85 m
Launcher calibre: 80 mm
Max range: 1000 m
Minimum range: 50 m
Weapon at shoulder
Data as above except that omission of tripod and electro-optical sighting system gives a light, one-man version, intended for ranges up to 700 m.
Ammunition
Length: 74 cm
Weight: 5·2 kg
Rocket weight: 3 kg
Muzzle velocity: 380 m/s
Max speed: 500 m/s
Max trajectory height: 2·2 m at 500 m range; <3 m at 700 m range
STATUS
Development and field trials complete. Preparation for mass production in progress.
CONTRACTOR
Breda Meccanica Bresciana SpA, Via Lunga 2, 25100 Brescia, Italy

Folgore anti-tank missile system deployed for action

JAPAN

2262.111
KAM-3D ANTI-TANK MISSILE (TYPE 64)

KAM-3D is a command-controlled wire-guided anti-tank missile system which is standard equipment for the Japan Ground Self-Defence Force (JGSDF) where it is also known as the Type 64 MAT (Missile Anti-Tank).

The KAM-3D missile has an orthodox configuration, with a cylindrical metal body and cruciform metal wings incorporating full-span trailing-edge spoilers for control. Propulsion is by a two-stage Daicel Co solid-propellant rocket motor, the booster stage of which accelerates the missile to its cruising speed in 0·8 s, after which the sustainer stage maintains this speed.

The missile can be fired singly or in multiple units by infantry and is carried by jeeps and helicopters. It is launched at an elevation of 15° and the operator controls it via an optical tracking system, using a flare by day and the sustainer rocket exhaust by night as a visual reference. A gyro-stabilisation system is embodied in the missile. A three-man firing team is required to operate the system. Control is achieved by using a thumb-button control box.

CHARACTERISTICS
Type: Man-portable wire-guided anti-tank missile
Guidance principle: Command to line-of-sight with optical tracking
Guidance method: Wire-guidance control of vibrating spoilers on wing trailing edges
Propulsion: 2-stage solid-propellant rocket motor
Missile length: 100 cm
Missile diameter: Body: 12 cm. Span: 60 cm

Launch weight: 15·7 kg
Cruising speed: 85 m/s
Turning radius: 250 m
Range: 350 – 1800 m
DEVELOPMENT
Following a design study carried out in 1956, development of this missile was started in 1957, under a contract awarded by the Technical Research and Development Institute of the Japan Defence Agency. The KAM-3 weapon system was adopted as standard equipment of the JGSDF in 1964 after several hundred test rounds had been fired, and has the official designation, Type 64 ATM. Trials showed that the missile's velocity control system enabled three out of four unskilled operators to hit a target with their first round after completion of a two week training course with the ATM simulator. Skilled operators could score 19 hits in 20 firings.

A field test set (KAM-3TE) and a simulator (KAM-3TP) are made by the main contractor.
STATUS
Operational with the Japanese Self Defence Forces. No details of exports have been given.
CONTRACTORS
Manufacturers of the complete system are Kawasaki Heavy Industries Ltd, Aircraft Division, 4-1 Hamamatsu-cho 2-chome Minato-ku, Tokyo. Other manufacturers known to have been associated with the system are:
Warhead – Daikin Kogyo Co.
Rocket motor – Daicel Co; Nippon Oil & Fats Co.
Missile guidance – Nippon Electric Co.
Guidance wire – Fujikura Cable Works.

Group of JGSDF jeep-type vehicles are armed with Type 64 anti-tank missiles (left) and later Type 79 Jyu-MAT heavy missile anti-tank (right)

2263.111
KAM-9 (TYPE 79) BATTLEFIELD MISSILE
This is known also as the Type 79, Jyu-MAT, (Jyu = heavy Missile Anti-Tank), and is an extended range SACLOS anti-tank weapon having a higher performance than the KAM-3, which can be used against armoured vehicles on both land and water. The missile is launched from a tubular container, which is used also for transport and storage. A solid-propellant launch motor ejects the missile from the container to a safe distance from the operator; the flight motor then ignites and accelerates the missile to its cruising speed of 200 m/s in a few seconds.

The Type 79 has been designed to meet a requirement for a defensive weapon to engage the landing craft of an amphibious assault force, as well as tank targets. A special warhead was developed to cater for this dual role. It is basically a HEAT round but incorporates an enhanced fragmentation effect, and two types of fuze are employed: for the purely anti-tank role the contact fuze which has a piezo-electric element is used and the other is a variable delay fuze.

The missile is placed in its transport and storage container at the factory, and the container is loaded into the firing tube and subsequently fired from the container.

Prior to firing, the container is placed on the launcher which comprises the firing control device, missile checkout, tracking mechanism, and built-in sight unit. The optical sighting device is designed to be operated by one man. During the missile's flight, the operator simply keeps the optical sight trained on the target, and sensors translate the course deviation to electrical signals which are fed into a computer. The computer then feeds course corrections into the missile through the guidance cable.

Instead of a flare for IR missile tracking, an xenon lamp is used as the IR source, this being powered by a thermal battery which also provides electrical power for the missile guidance system.

The launching system has two operational modes: direct, and separate firing.
CHARACTERISTICS
Missile
Length: 1565 mm
Diameter: 152 mm
Span: 33 cm
Container: 170 × 20 cm
Weight: 42 kg (in container)
Propulsion: Solid-propellant booster and sustainer
Guidance: SACLOS. Optical sighting, IR tracking; wire command link. Manual command back-up
Warhead: Hollow charge with piezoelectric fuze or SAP HE with contact/electromagnetic fuze
Range: 4000 m (max)
Speed: 200 m/s

A complete Type 79 firing unit consists of two launcher units, a sight unit, control/guidance electronics unit, circuit breaker, and a connecting cable reel. Each launcher is normally mounted on a tripod, and one of them also carries the sight. The other launcher may be sited up to 50 metres away from the sight and is remotely operated via connecting cable. The remote facility coupled with the smokeless rocket motors used offers the operating crew good protection from enemy counter fire and enhanced operational flexibility. The complete system weighs 278 kg and requires a crew of five; it is carried on two Type 73 jeep-type small trucks.
STATUS
Operational with the Japanese Ground Self Defence Force. Reports received in 1980 indicated that work started in 1978 on a medium anti-tank missile, KAM-40 (medium-MAT) to follow existing Japanese weapons in this category. The guidance technique will probably be a semi-active laser homing system, and research and trial manufacture of the homing head and laser designator has been carried out with three competitive designs.

In late 1983 it was reported that a prototype batch of

Type 79 Heavy-MAT anti-tank weapon system on its Type 73 carrier vehicle

KAM-9 missile

eight missiles had been completed, and delivery of a laser designator, launcher and test equipment was expected in March 1984. It was also anticipated that a second batch of 60 rounds with two designators and launchers will be ready by the end of May 1985.
CONTRACTOR
Kawasaki Heavy Industries Ltd, World Trade Centre Building, 4-1 Hamamatsu-cho, 2-Chome, Minato-ku, Tokyo, Japan.

SWEDEN

4557.111
STRIX ANTI-TANK GRENADE
Strix is the name given to a joint FFV-Saab development project aimed at producing an IR homing anti-tank grenade which can be launched from 120 mm calibre mortars. As may be expected from the chosen delivery method, the Strix missile will attack targets from above, thereby engaging a less heavily armoured part of the tank or other AFV. The nearby illustration gives an indication of the configuration of the weapon and shows it to have a set of four wrap-around tail fins for projectile stabilisation, and a set of multiple side-thruster rockets arranged peripherally midway along the body length for manoeuvring in the course of terminal guidance to its target. An IR sensor located in the nose of the projectile will detect targets by their heat signature and provide correction signals which selectively actuate the side-thruster jets to ensure a hit on the target.

The developers estimate that three projectiles fired

Cutaway diagram of Strix anti-tank weapon

at a typical armoured formation would disable one or two targets.

CHARACTERISTICS
Calibre: 120 mm
Weight: 20 kg (including sustainer)
Length: 800 mm
Range: 600 m – 8 km
Guidance: IR homing, side-thrusters for manoeuvring
STATUS
Development project.

Artist's impression of Strix 120 mm mortar-launched anti-tank grenade in flight

CONTRACTORS
FFV Ordnance, S-631 87, Eskilstuna, Sweden.
  Saab Missiles AB, Linkoping, Sweden.

5557.111
84 mm RCL CARL-GUSTAV
Two versions of this weapon are described – the 84 mm RCL Carl-Gustav M2 and the more recently developed M2-550.
M2 Weapon
This is a recoilless gun intended primarily for use as an anti-tank weapon but suitable also for other assault roles. It can fire HEAT, HE, smoke, or flare ammunition and has a practical range, with HEAT rounds against moving or stationary targets, of 400 or 500 metres, and with HE rounds of 1000 metres. Smoke can be fired up to 1300 metres and flare shells up to 2300 metres. A rate of about 6 rounds/minute is easily achieved.

The weapon can be carried, loaded and fired by one man but a two-man team is standard – one carrying and firing the gun and the other carrying ammunition and assisting in the loading operation.

The gun is breech loaded and cannot be fired until the venturi has been rotated back into position and locked after the round has been inserted. The round is fired by a percussion-operated side primer, the firing mechanism being contained in a tube on the right-hand side of the barrel. This mechanism is hand-cocked, is operated by a two-pressure trigger and has a safety-catch.

Open or telescopic sights can be used: the telescopic sight has a ×2 magnification and a 17° field of view and is fitted with a temperature correction device. The weapon is fired from the shoulder, and when fired in the prone position, or over a trench or parapet, a sprung bipod mount provides support just forward of the shoulder pad.

Cartridge cases of ammunition are made of light metal alloy with a plastic blow-out disc at the rear. HE, smoke, and flare shells are spin-stabilised; the HEAT shell is aerodynamically stabilised and fitted with a slipping ring to ensure that the hollow charge performance is not reduced by excessive speed of rotation.

84 mm RCL Carl-Gustav with HEAT 551 round

Carl-Gustav with FFV 597 HEAT round loaded

M2-550 Weapon
The 84 mm RCL Carl-Gustaf M2-550, also described as the Anti-Tank System FFV 550, is a later development of the M2 weapon and features a new rocket-assisted HEAT round.

The FFV 556 telescopic sight is used with the new HEAT round. One scale is used when firing the HEAT ammunition and the other scale, in use when the range knob is pulled out, is used when firing HE and smoke ammunition.

The 84 mm FFV 551 HEAT round is stabilised by fins which unfold as the round leaves the barrel and has a rocket motor which increases the shell speed from its muzzle velocity of 260 to 350 m/s maximum. The rocket motor comes into operation when the shell is about 18 metres from the muzzle and burns for 1·5 s. The shell will penetrate 400 mm of armour, and the piezoelectric fuze system enables the weapon to function up to 80° incidence.

Like the HEAT round for the M2 weapon the FFV 551 round is fitted with a Teflon slipping ring to reduce the spin imparted by the rifling of the Carl-Gustav barrel. Practical engagement range with this ammunition is 700 metres.

The family of ammunition for the earlier M2 version is compatible with the 550 system.
CHARACTERISTICS
M2 (M2-550)
Calibre: 84 mm (84 mm)
Weapon length: 1130 mm (1130 mm)
Weight of gun and mount: 15 kg (15 kg)
Weight of sight: 1 kg (1·1 kg)
Weight of HEAT round: 2·5 kg (3·2 kg)
Anti-tank range: 400 – 500 m (700 m)
Training equipment: Sub-calibre adapters are available for both weapons to enable them to be used with small-arms ammunition for training purposes.
STATUS
In production and in service in several countries.

M3 lightweight Carl-Gustav

HEAT FFV 597
The current Carl-Gustav system is designed to defeat present-day combat vehicles, but to enable it to engage the more sophisticated MBTs in the 1990s the system will be upgraded with oversize HEAT round FFV 597. This is rocket assisted and fin stabilised. The warhead is designed to penetrate the front of compound-armour main battle tanks.

The round will be carried in two parts: warhead, and propulsion system (including rocket-motor). Loading will be carried out by inserting the propulsion system as normal Carl-Gustaf ammunition and the warhead from the front. The two parts will be joined inside the barrel by a connecting device.
CHARACTERISTICS
Calibre (outer dimension): 125 mm
Weight (complete round): 7 kg
Weight (propulsion system): 3 kg
Weight (in flight): 5·8 kg
Length (in weapon): 1·5 m
Length (warhead): 0·75 m
Muzzle velocity: 140 m/s
Maximum velocity: 375 m/s
Range (effective): > 300 m
Armour penetration: 900 mm
M3 Weapon
Carl-Gustav M3 is a lightweight version (8 kg complete) of this weapon. It is built up on a steel liner with the rifling, and covered with carbon-fibre winding. The venturi is made of glass-fibre. All external parts are made of aluminium and plastic. All existing types of Carl-Gustav ammunition can be used with the M3 with unchanged performance.
STATUS
Development. Series production beings in 1984.
CONTRACTOR
FFV Ordnance Division, S-631 87, Eskilstuna, Sweden.

2363.111

BANTAM ANTI-TANK MISSILE (BS 53)

Bantam is a small wire-guided anti-tank missile, designed for operation by a single infantry soldier, but suitable also for use when mounted in land vehicles or small military aircraft. The missile has a hollow-charge warhead and is said to be able to 'kill' the most modern heavy tank.

The complete system in its simplest configuration comprises the missile in its combined transport and launching container with carrying harness, a control unit, and 20 metres of cable. All this weighs only 20 kg, of which the launching weight of the missile is 7·5 kg.

OPERATION

Time for setting up and firing is about 25 seconds. The container is positioned on the ground with the missile pointing in the direction of interest and the operator stations himself in a convenient position up to 20 metres away (or, with extra cable, up to 120 metres away) with the control unit which is connected to the container by cable. The control unit is fitted with a sighting device and a joystick to control the flight of the missile, command signals being conveyed through the wire trailed from the missile in flight.

Each wire spool contains 2000 metres of guiding wire and in each is mounted a microswitch. One of these ignites the sustainer and up to four (as preselected by the operator) trace flares in the rear of the missile after 40 metres of flight; the other arms the warhead after 230 metres.

When the missile is launched from the container its folding wings open. These have bent rear corners to give the missile rotation in flight and vibrating spoilers on their trailing-edges which are used to control the direction of flight. The missile battery which powers the control and fuzing mechanisms is activated only when the missile starts its flight.

Also activated on firing is the missile gyro. This is energised by a powder pellet and after the missile has travelled 3 cm from the rest a pin is withdrawn that uncages the gyro. Guidance signals for the spoilers are amplified by a transistor amplifier in the missile and passed to the spoilers by way of a commutator connected to the gyro. Due to the rotation of the missile the spoilers on each pair of wings switch from traverse guidance to elevation guidance or vice versa at each quarter rotation.

The six Bantam missiles pointing forwards on the Puch-Haflinger jeep can be fired in two to three seconds after the vehicle has stopped. Six more missiles are carried at the rear of the jeep

CHARACTERISTICS

Type: Surface-to-surface anti-tank guided missile with air-to-surface capability

Guidance principle: Wire guidance

Guidance method: By control of vibrating spoilers on trailing edges of wings

Propulsion: 2-stage (booster/sustainer) solid-propellant motor

Warhead: Hollow charge; electrical fuze; weight 1·9 kg; armour penetration better than 500 mm

Missile length: 0·85 m

Missile diameter: Body: 0·11 m. Span: 0·4 m

Weights: Container with missile: 11·5 kg; minimum system with 1 missile: 20 kg

Range: <300 m – 2000 m

Hit probability: 95 – 98% at 800 – 2000 m

Cruising speed: 85 m/s

DEVELOPMENT

Bantam was designed and developed by AB Bofors as a private venture started in 1956. It is in large-scale production for the Swedish and Swiss Armies with

which it is standard equipment, having gone into service in Sweden in 1963 and Switzerland in 1967.

In addition to its use as an infantry weapon, Bantam can be used from land or other vehicles. In particular it has been designed into the Puch-Haflinger light cross-country vehicle, being available in this installation both for direct fire from the vehicle or for off-loading for use by individual infantrymen.

Bantam also has air-to-surface applications. Missiles have been fired successfully from both helicopters and light aircraft.

STATUS

In service with Swedish and Swiss forces but no longer in production.

CONTRACTOR

Manufacturer of the complete system, of associated test instruments for the missile and of a firing simulator for training is:

AB Bofors, Ordnance division, Box 500, S-691 80 Bofors, Sweden.

4544.111

RBS 56 BILL ANTI-TANK MISSILE

Bofors, under a contract awarded in mid-1979 by the Swedish Defence Materiel Administration (FMV) is developing a light anti-tank missile called 'Bill' for the Swedish Army, whose designation for it is RBS 56. Development was carried out in close co-operation with the Swedish Army.

The RBS 56 is a wire-guided command to line-of-sight weapon with an effective range capability

extending from 150 to 2000 metres, and which is fired from a container/launcher tube that can be either tripod or vehicle mounted. A sight that provides for both day and night operation is carried separately and is attached to the container tube for launching. Setting up for use can be completed in 20 s according to the manufacturer. Propulsion is by a solid-propellant rocket motor which exhausts through nozzles disposed around the circumference of the

missile body to the rear of the sustainer motor which is housed in the nose section. Cruciform wings and control surfaces flip out after launch and these are located in the tail section of the missile, where there is also a tracking signal transmitter.

A shaped charge HE warhead is carried which is normally detonated by a delayed proximity fuze. An unusual feature of the warhead is that it is angled to direct its energy at 30° downward from the missile's longitudinal datum. This, and a missile trajectory which is automatically maintained at a height of approximtely one metre above the aimer's line of sight to the target, are claimed to yield a higher kill probability. The chances of striking the less heavily armoured upper surfaces of a tank are increased, and the angled warhead means that it is less likely to strike a sloping surface at a shallow, glancing angle, thereby enhancing the pentration characteristics. The angled attack also ensures that when sloping surfaces are encountered, the thickness of armour to be penetrated is effectively lessened.

CHARACTERISTICS

Type: RBS 56. Top attack, wire-guided command to line-of-sight

Length: 900 mm

Diameter: 150 mm

Max span: 410 mm

Weights: 16 kg (missile in container); 27 kg (firing unit); 11 kg (sight and stand)

Warhead: HE shaped charge

Combat range: 150 – 2000 m (stationary targets); 300 – 2000 m (moving targets, 10 m/s crossing speed)

Time of flight: 6 s (to 1200 m); 10 s (to 2000 m)

Setting up time: 20 s

Reloading time: 7 s

STATUS

Initial test firing completed. Planned for entry into service with the Swedish Army in 1985.

RBS 56 Bill anti-tank missile unit deployed in the field

CONTRACTOR
AB Bofors, Ordnance Division, Box 500, S-691 80
Bofors, Sweden.

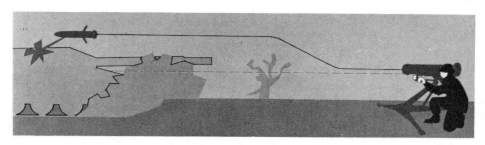

*Bill (RBS 56) anti-tank missile trajectory is
automatically maintained about 1 m above the
aimer's line-of-sight*

TAIWAN

4438.111
KUN WU ANTI-TANK MISSILE
Kun Wu is the name given to a wire guided anti-tank
missile produced by the Chung Shan Institute of
Science and Technology. It was first seen publicly in
the 20th Republic of China National Day Parade in
Taiwan during October 1981.

The Kun Wu is evidently based upon the Soviet
designed Sagger AT-3 (**2950.111**). Reports from
Taiwan state that the Chung Shan Institute, which
was responsible for Kun Wu development, is known
to have studied captured examples of the Sagger said
to have been acquired in Vietnam.

The photographs support such a contention
although it is not known if the optical guidance and
control system used with the Sagger is retained for
the Chinese version of the system or if a different
method is used for the direction of the four rounds
that are usually deployed on each vehicle. It can be
expected that Kun Wu performance will at least equal
that of Sagger, including a maximum range of up to
3000 metres with a launch weight of over 11 kg. Other
parameters are likely to be similar to those of the
Soviet missile, which is described on a later page.
Sighting arrangements are not known and it is quite
possible that the missiles are fired remotely by the
operator some distance from the vehicle. Launch
vehicles so far noted all have a prominent radio
antenna fixed to one corner of the body. Whether or
not this has some special purpose is not known.
STATUS
Production and in service.

*Kun Wu anti-tank missiles mounted on Jeep. Four rounds are carried on each vehicle in this configuration
(L J Lamb)*

CONTRACTOR
State Arsenals.

UNION OF SOVIET SOCIALIST REPUBLICS

2983.111
AT-1 (SNAPPER) ANTI-TANK MISSILE
Snapper is the NATO code-name for the wire-guided
anti-tank missile believed to be known to the Soviets
as Shmell (Bumblebee) or 3M6 and known also by the
US code AT-1. It is a vehicle-borne system, now
usually deployed on the BRDM armoured
amphibious vehicle, and is similar in general
configuration to such missiles as MBB Cobra and
Contraves-Oerlikon Mosquito.

The missile is launched from a guide rail, a triple
mounting being standard in the BRDG vehicle,
whereas quadruple mountings were used on the
GAZ-69 light cross-country vehicle on which the
missile was formerly deployed. The triple mounting is
retractable, the weapons being transported under
cover plates which open up for firing. There is also a
ground launcher for infantry use.

Provided with periscope binoculars embodying an
illuminated variable-brightness reticle with which to
sight the target, the operator uses a joystick to control
the missile, keeping it on the line of sight to the target
with the aid of tracking flares on two of the wings. The
missile can be fired and guided by an operator

Close-up of AT-1 Snapper anti-tank missile

stationed anywhere up to 50 metres from the
launcher.

Western analyses of Snapper performance report
that the missile is stable in flight but slow to respond
to control commands, indicating significant
aerodynamic or electronic damping of the control
loop. A high number of simulated or live practice
tracking exercises are claimed to be necessary to
maintain operator competence.

CHARACTERISTICS
Type: Surface-to-surface guided anti-tank missile
Guidance: Wire-guided command to line-of-sight,
optical tracking
Guidance method: By control of vibrating trailing-
edge spoilers
Propulsion: Solid-propellant rocket motor
Warhead: Hollow charge
Missile length: 1·13 m
Missile diameter: 14 cm
Launch weight: 22·25 kg
Cruising speed: 320 km/h
Range: 500 – 2300 m
Penetration: 356 – 380 mm
STATUS
Although previously thought to have been withdrawn
from service within the Warsaw Pact countries,
Snapper has been reported as deployed by
Afghanistan, Bulgaria, Czechoslovakia, Egypt, East
Germany, Hungary, Mongolia, Poland, Romania,
Syria, USSR, and Yugoslavia. Nevertheless, many
Western observers consider this missile to be
obsolete, and in the process of being replaced by the
AT-3 Sagger.

2985.111
AT-2 (SWATTER) ANTI-TANK MISSILE
Swatter is the NATO code-name for the anti-tank
missile which is known as the AT-2 in the US code and
which, like the AT-1 (**2983.111**), is carried on the
BRDM armoured amphibious vehicle.

Of similar size to the AT-1, but heavier (29·4 kg), it
is believed to be a more advanced missile – probably in
the class of the French SS 11 – and certainly has a

different configuraton. Control is by elevons mounted
on the trailing edges of the rear-mounted cruciform
wings.

The standard mount on the BRDM vehicle carries
four missiles mounted on guides, with four reload
rounds in the BRDM-2 vehicle installation. Radio
command to line-of-sight guidance is employed, the
command link having three frequencies as protection
against electronic countermeasures. There is also the

possibility of separate terminal homing (probably IR)
being provided, and this with radio guidance suits the
Swatter for airborne roles such as part of the
armament of the Mi-24 Hind attack helicopter.

As deployed on the ground Swatter does not arm
until it has flown 500 metres from the launch site. The
Swatter launcher on the BRDM has a lateral traverse
of 45°, as originally deployed. A later version,
sometimes called Swatter 2, has a different launcher

on the BRDM-2 which may well be capable of training over a much larger arc.

Swatter 2 is thought to be slightly larger than the original Swatter, with an estimated length of 1·56 metres and 16 cm diameter.

CHARACTERISTICS

Type: Anti-tank, surface-to-surface and air-to-surface
Configuration: Cylindrical body with rounded nose. Rear set cruciform wings. Two small foreplanes. Ramp launched
Length: 1·16 m
Diameter: 13·2 cm
Span (max): 66 cm
Weight: 29·4 kg
Propulsion: Solid
Range: 500 – 3500 m
Guidance: Radio command to line-of-sight, possible with terminal homing
Warhead: HEAP
Penetration: 500 mm
Average velocity: 150 m/s

STATUS

In service only with Warsaw Pact forces and those of Egypt and Syria.

Close-up of AT-2 Swatter anti-tank missile four-round launcher on BRDM reconnaissance vehicle

---

2950.111

AT-3 (SAGGER) ANTI-TANK MISSILE

Sagger is the NATO code-name for a small wire-guided anti-tank missile, also known by the US code AT-3. More compact than either the AT-1 (Snapper) or AT-2 (Swatter) missiles (**2983.111** and **2985.111**), but apparently carrying an equally powerful warhead, it is deployed in various vehicle mountings including a 2 × 3 mounting on the BRDM-1 amphibious reconnaissance car and a single mount on the BMP-1 armoured personnel carrier. A more recent installation is on the BMD light tank and it can also be deployed on the Hind helicopter. Other vehicle mountings are on the BRDM-2/BTR40PB and the Czechoslovak SKOT OT-64 Model 5 armoured personnel carrier. There is also a single manpack mounting that enables it to be fired from the ground.

In the BRDM vehicle the two clusters of three missiles are mounted retractably and are shielded when in the firing position by the cover plate that protects them when in the retracted position.

The manpack version is also known as the 'suitcase' Sagger, because the missile is carried in a glass fibre case, with the warhead separated from the rest of the missile. The lid of the case has a rail that enables it to be used as a launcher for the weapon after assembly of the missile. A control unit which incorporates a periscopic sight, a control stick, switches for missile selection, and batteries is carried in a separate container. Sagger is fired from a remote position which enables the operator to be located up to 15 metres from the missile launcher. The periscopic sight has a magnification of ×10. A three-man firing team is normally employed, with a total of four missiles per team. Either one or two men may serve as Sagger controllers, each with a sight and control unit and two missiles, while the third man deploys ahead armed with an RPG-7 for closer range protection if need be. Used in this way the effective engagement range of Sagger is considered to be between 1000 and 3000 metres, and such a team could be deployed with four missiles checked and ready to fire in about 12 to 15 minutes.

As deployed with the BRDM vehicle, the Sagger gunner can operate either within the vehicle itself or move to a position outside up to 80 metres distant. Six missiles can be rapidly fired by use of the selector switch on the control/sight unit which has a ×8 magnification. The BRDM can carry a total of 14 missiles. The larger, tracked, BMP vehicle, on which the Sagger launch rail is carried on the barrel of the 73 mm smooth bore gun, has a total capacity of four or five Saggers.

Client states of the Soviet Union on occasion evolve their own methods of mounting and deploying weapons of Soviet origin, that differ from the system(s) used by the USSR. A recent example of this is the 4×4 vehicle mounted version of the Sagger anti-tank missile introduced by Yugoslavia. The armoured vehicle is known as the BOV-1 and it is surmounted by a rotating turret on which are carried six Saggers housed in two rectangular container/launchers with three rounds in each. Sufficient

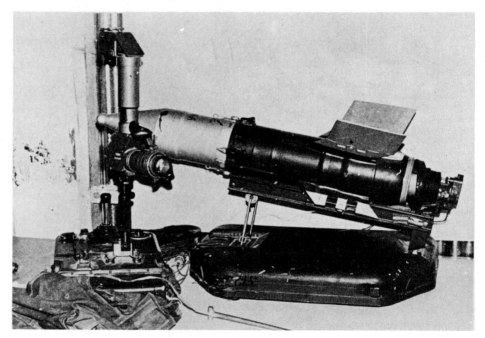

Complete AT-3 Sagger man-portable anti-tank weapon with sight on left and missile on carrying case

Yugoslav BOV-1 AFV armed with six AT-3 Sagger missiles

rounds for at least one manual reloading (ie six missiles) are reported to be carried inside the vehicle hull. Yugoslavian forces also employ Saggers in an airborne role, some Gazelle helicopters being fitted with launch facilities for four missiles.

CHARACTERISTICS

Type: Surface-to-surface guided anti-tank missile
Guidance: Wire-guided command to line-of-sight, optical tracking
Propulsion: Solid-propellant motor, 2-stage

Warhead: Hollow charge
Missile length: 86 cm
Missile diameter: 11·9 cm
Launch weight: 11·3 kg
Range: 500-3000 m
Penetration: 400 mm
Average velocity: 120 m/s
STATUS
Extensively deployed by USSR and Warsaw Pact

forces and by other nations, particularly in the Middle East and elsewhere. Used in some thousands by the Egyptian Army in 1973 with some considerable effect against Israeli tanks. The existence of a Chinese-built version of the Sagger was reported in September 1979. This is believed to be essentially identical to the original Soviet model.

In the early 1980s Taiwan introduced an indigenous anti-tank missile called the Kun Wu which bears some

obvious resemblances to Sagger and it has been reported from Taiwan sources that development of Kun Wu (**4438.111**) was based on examples of Sagger, although the warhead is thought to be different.

3638.111
AT-4 (SPIGOT) ANTI-TANK MISSILE

The designation AT-4, Spigot, was at first provisionally assigned to a man-portable, tripod-mounted version of the AT-5, Spandrel, anti-tank missile (**3608.111**). As employed by infantry, a crew of three men normally constitutes a Spigot section, between them carrying a total of four rounds plus the sight and mount.

Later information however (including an East German photograph showing a BRDM launcher for three AT-4s and two AT-5s) while confirming the similarities between these two missile types makes obvious the larger dimensions of the AT-5 Spandrel. It would therefore appear that while the basic engineering and guidance techniques may be the same for both types, the larger size of the Spandrel is mostly due to the larger propulsion motor needed for the increased range.

The sight appears to use separate optical paths which are presumed to be employed for tracking of the target (under control of the gunner) and the Spigot missile, corrections to the latter's trajectory being automatic subsequently in response to the gunner following the target.

Spigot is expected to become a replacement for the AT-3, Sagger, in the course of the next few years, although the older missile is unlikely to disappear from the scene entirely for a long time.
CHARACTERISTICS
Type: Man-portable surface-to-surface wire-guided anti-tank missile
Guidance: Semi-automatic command to line of sight; optical tracking
Propulsion: Solid
Warhead: HEAT
Launcher length: 1·2 m
Launcher diameter: 13·5 cm
Launch weight: 10-12 kg (estimated)
Range: 2000 m (approx)
Speed: 150-250 m/s (approx)
Penetration: 500 mm
STATUS
In service and observed with Soviet, Polish, East German and Czechoslovak units.

AT-4 Spigot infantry mounting modified for use on top of BMD-1 airborne fighting vehicle. Spigot anti-tank missile replaces AT-3 Sagger sometimes used in this fashion. This Spigot application first seen on parade in Moscow, October 1983

Preparing AT-4 anti-tank weapon for firing

AT-4 Spigot anti-tank missile deployed

3608.111
AT-5 (SPANDREL) ANTI-TANK MISSILE

AT-5, Spandrel, is the designation of a recent anti-tank weapon deployed on Soviet BRDM-2 AFVs. So far, only the launchers on these vehicles have been seen by Western observers. As can be seen from the adjacent illustration, five tubular launchers mounted on a presumably trainable turret are carried on each vehicle. These resemble those of the HOT and Milan anti-tank missiles (**2212.111** and **2215.111**), and while no official dimensions are available, the AT-5 is probably nearer to the latter in size.

The BRDM-2 has a hatch in the roof immediately behind the AT-5 which is probably for reloading purposes, and, according to official US estimates, the total vehicle load is 10 rounds.

A rotatable optical sighting/tracking head is incorporated in the BRDM-2, mounted in the vehicle roof above the right-hand front seat. The shape of the launch tubes has led some observers to conjecture that some form of gas generator is used to eject the missile before the propulsion motor is ignited, and, also giving cause for speculation, these tubes have always appeared to be unpainted metal of bright or light colour. The reason for this has been conjectured as being related to a need to minimise the internal temperature of the tube, possibly to protect the propellant. An East German photograph showed a BRDM-2 vehicle turret on which were mounted a mixed armament of three AT-4 Spigot anti-tank

BRDM-2 AFV with five-tube AT-5 Spandrel anti-tank missile launcher

missiles flanked on each side by an AT-5 Spandrel missile. From this photograph is was clear that the Spandrel has a larger diameter launch tube.

As the missile itself has not been displayed in public, all published estimates of performance must be regarded as speculative and the following table of characteristics are only provisional.

CHARACTERISTICS

Type: Surface-to-surface guided anti-tank missile
Guidance: Command to line-of-sight, optical tracking
Propulsion: Solid
Warhead: HEAT

Launcher length: 1·4 m
Launcher diameter: 18 cm
Launch weight: 12-18 kg (estimated)
Range: Approx 4000 m (estimated)
Speed: Approx 150-250 m/s
Penetration: 500 mm
STATUS
In service with Soviet forces

Close-up of five-round AT-5 Spandrel launcher turret

3639.111

AT-6 (SPIRAL) ANTI-TANK MISSILE

AT-6, Spiral, is the designation of a new anti-tank missile about which, at this stage, little is known. It is reported to have been deployed on Soviet Mi-24 Hind

D attack helicopters, and it is possible that this is the missile to which some sources have applied the designation AS-8. Resolution of this confusion must await the arrival of more evidence.

The AT-6 is thought to employ a semi-active

homing system which could be either IR based or of laser target-marking technique which has been suggested by some observers.
STATUS
Early operational deployment.

UNITED KINGDOM

2450.111

SWINGFIRE ANTI-TANK MISSILE

Swingfire is a long-range command-controlled anti-tank weapon system capable of engaging and destroying the heaviest armour. Armoured and soft-skinned vehicle variants are available. The missile is wire-commanded, signals being generated by an operator's joystick control, and the commands are interpreted by the missile as demands for a change of heading; thrust vector control is employed.

An important feature of the system is its indirect fire capability with the launcher concealed behind cover in such a way that there is no direct optical sight-line from launcher to target. The operator can be stationed a considerable distance (up to 100 metres) from the launcher by means of a separation cable between sight and launcher, and the missile will be gathered into his field of view by the automatic programming of the initial flight of the missile.

The system can be installed in almost any kind of military vehicle and installations have been devised for a wide range of tanks, armoured personnel carriers, armoured cars, and scout cars. In some instances provision can be made for reloading within the vehicle in which case a rate of fire can be obtained that is comparable with that of a gun system. Vehicle installations do not require traversing or elevating gear, and the missiles can be fired from launcher boxes stowed in specially prepared bins or attached externally to the vehicle at the correct launch attitude. When the separated mode of fire is being used, vehicle tilt compensation is provided by the tilt unit. In all cases emphasis has been laid on protecting the equipment and the crew so that the system has a high degree of survivability on the battlefield.

In the case of the armoured vehicle variant, two basic methods of operation are possible. In one, the missile is controlled from the launching vehicle, the operator using a periscopic sight that forms part of the main vehicle installation to engage targets in his field of view over a 90° arc – that is, 45° on either side of the direction in which the missile launcher is pointing. In the other method the operator uses a portable separation sight and stations himself in a suitable vantage point anywhere within 100 metres radius of the launcher. A variation on this latter method is the use of a pallet-mounted system. A four-missile launcher pallet is mounted on a Land Rover type vehicle. The missiles are fired with the launcher either on the vehicle or dismounted and deployed on the ground.

A typical vehicle installation comprises the separated sight and programmer and control electronics at the launcher.

CHARACTERISTICS

Type: Mobile anti-tank guided missile system. Panclimatic. Missiles prepacked in sealed launcher boxes
Guidance principle: Wire-commanded. Heading demand signals referenced to autopilot. Optical sighting with automatic initial gathering. Manual steering (direct or separated). ×1 or ×10 magnification sights
Guidance method: Thrust deflection of main motor efflux by jetavator

In its pallet configuration Swingfire anti-tank missiles can be carried and launched from soft-skinned vehicles such as the Egyptian CJ6 jeep

Swingfire Combined Sight enables this long-range anti-tank missile to be used at night or in low visibility. This is accomplished by combining thermal imaging with the optical sight using passive IR sensing to detect the target

Propulsion: 2-stage boost and sustainer solid-propellant motor
Warhead: Hollow charge powerful enough to defeat all known combinations of armour
Range: Minimum – from less than 150 m at direct fire to 300 m with max separation. Max – 4000 m

Fire arcs: Azimuth ±45° without launcher traverse. Elevation +20°, –10° relative to mounting plane
Special features: Ease of concealment. Immunity to ECM

DEVELOPMENT

British Aerospace Dynamics Group based their design, development, and production programmes on experimental work originally done by Fairey Engineering Ltd. The first design study was made in 1958 and the first public announcement concerning the system was made in 1962. The system went into service with the British Army in 1969.

A new combined sight has been developed which will permit current variants of Swingfire to be used operationally at night and in poor visibility.

Current Swingfire applications are as follows:

(1) **FV 438** – the guided weapon vehicle for Armoured Regiments and Mechanised Infantry based on the FV 432 armoured personnel carrier

(2) **Striker** – the guided weapon vehicle in the new CVR(T) series. Striker is also in service with the Belgian Army

(3) **Swingfire Pallet** – a crew-portable version which can be transported on and fired from any vehicle or trailer from a long wheel base Land Rover upwards, or fired from the ground. It can be carried over short distances (of the order of 400 metres) and deployed by its three-man crew. For this purpose it is broken down into two or three-man loads. When in action it is always used in the

'separated fire' mode and covers an arc of fire of 90° without traversing the launcher. It can be air-transported, parachuted into action, and air-dropped as a complete system. Swingfire Pallet is fully established in service with the Egyptian Army and is in production in Egypt

(4) **Micro-miniaturised (MM) Swingfire** – Development has been completed on an MM standard of

programmer and control equipment to replace the existing black boxes, ie the programmer, selector unit etc. The new standard of equipment would be compatible with the existing sighting systems including the combined sight. MM electronics will save significant space and weight and will enable Swingfire to be fitted to an ever greater range of vehicles. There is also a

lightweight alternative to the Combined Sight developed by Thorn EMI and BAe, which will fit on the separation sight base in place of the present telescope.

CONTRACTOR
British Aerospace Dynamics Group, Six Hills Way, Stevenage, Hertfordshire SG1 2DA, England.

3986.111
LAW 80 LIGHT ANTI-ARMOUR WEAPON

LAW 80 is a one-shot low cost disposable short range anti-tank weapon developed to replace existing weapons which are either light and ineffective or of a size which demands crew operation to achieve lethality. It provides a capability for the individual soldier to engage current and future MBTs over short ranges and achieve a high probability of hitting the target. The unique performance of the HEAT warhead (armour penetration well in excess of 600 mm) ensures that MBTs both current and future can be defeated from any aspect, including frontal attack. LAW 80 is stored and transported in unit load containers (ULC) containing 24 launchers. LAW 80 is issued from the ULC direct to the infantryman and is fully man portable together with his own personal weapons and pack, each launcher being provided with a carrying handle and shoulder sling.

The tactical use of LAW 80 in the British forces is to provide defence against an armoured threat at ranges out to 500 metres. In this, it complements the cover provided by medium and long range anti-tank guided weapons which suffer a minimum range problem at shorter ranges. The weapon will be operated not only by infantry but also by Royal Marines and the RAF Regiment. The system is simple to operate and does not require a dedicated gunner or specialist training.

Much attention has been placed on the need for the firer to obtain a good hit on the target, since the firing of almost all types of LAW projectile is likely to reveal the firing position. It is dangerous and time consuming to engage with a second weapon. To achieve this accuracy, a built in 9 mm spotting rifle is used. This spotting rifle contains five pre-loaded rounds, any number of which may be fired, without revealing the position of the firer. The ammunition is ballistically matched to the main projectile marked by a tracer and by a flash head to record a hit on a hard target. At any time the operator can select and fire the main projectile.

The weapon is issued as a round of ammunition, complete with its projectile and the integrated spotting rifle pre-loaded and pre-cocked. Safety is assured by the provision of detents and links which require two failures before any hazard would be caused. In deploying and operating the weapon the safety links are progressively removed automatically up to the point of firing the rocket projectile.

Shock absorbent end caps protect the weapon for carriage and storage. These also provide some side protection, in conjunction with the resilient carrying handle. The sight has its own sliding protective cover. The end caps provide sealing for the tubes to protect the projectile against the effects of water immersion, even though the projectile itself is sealed. The end caps also support the projectile against the effects of mishandling such as end drops. After removal of the end caps, the tube containing the HEAT projectile is extended rearwards from the outer tube. The launch tube is automatically locked into position. This moves the centre of gravity of the weapon from the carrying handle to the shoulder rest to provide an ideal balance suitable for any firing position.

LAW 80 anti-tank weapon ready to fire

LAW 80 anti-tank weapon sectioned

The spotting rifle is an integral part of the outer tube. Tests have shown that the five rounds of spotting ammunition sealed in the rifle are sufficient for two engagements. Also included in the external furniture is the firing handgrip/carrying handle and a folding shoulder rest. The sight is separately bonded to the front tube and a forward sliding cover allows the sighting prism to erect. The sight is of unit magnification with the graticule projected through the sighting prism into the firer's line of sight, like a head up display. The sight can be used with one or both eyes open and for low light use the graticule can be illuminated with a tritium light source selected by the firer, making the weapon effective down to starlight levels of illumination.

With the weapon extended and cocked and with the sight erected, the gunner only has to select 'Arm' on the safe/arm lever and use the trigger to fire either the spotting rifle or the rocket projectile. When the rocket projectile is to be fired the change lever is moved forward by the thumb of the firing hand. The system is completely reversible if no target is engaged with the rocket projectile. As part of the safety design, the main round cocking lever covers the detent to unlock

and close the weapon so that the weapon must be uncocked and in its spotting rifle mode before it can be closed down.

The projectile is initiated with a totally non-electric (and therefore totally EMC proof) system comprising a percussion cap in the launcher connected by a flash tube to the rocket igniter. The rapid burn of the rocket motor ensures that the efflux is contained and directed rearwards by the launch and blast tubes, leaving the projectile to coast from the muzzle to the target. No debris of afterburn is projected at the firer, the recoil is not discernible, and the noise level at the firer's ear is significantly less than 180 dB.

The forward part of the projectile consists of the HEAT warhead and its fuzing unit, and a double ogive nose switch which also provides the optimum stand-off distance. The fuzing unit generates electrical energy to fire the warhead by means of piezo crystals and contains various safety devices to ensure that the warhead does not arm until safe separation from the firer is achieved. At the rear of the projectile the composite aluminium and filament wound motor case has an extruded vane propellant. Four wrap-around fins are mounted on the rear of the motor. These are spring loaded to erect at muzzle exit to provide stability and to spin the projectile as it coasts to the target.

CHARACTERISTICS
Launcher length: 1·5 m (ready to fire); 1 m (on move)
Shoulder weight: 8·8 kg
Projectile weight: 4 kg (in launcher)
Projectile diameter: 94 mm
Armour penetration: >600 mm
Dispersion: 1 mil approx
Maximum effective range: 500 m
Rear danger area: < 20 m approx
Warhead arms at 10 to 20 m
Protected against NBC effects
Inert to RF hazards in battlefield conditions

DEVELOPMENT
It has been developed principally by the prime contractor, Hunting Engineering Ltd, and by the UK Royal Ordnance Factories on behalf of the UK Ministry of Defence who intend to make large production purchases. It is now available for approved export from Hunting Engineering Limited.

STATUS
In early 1984 the final stages of development were almost complete and production lines were being installed preparatory to introduction into service during 1984.

CONTRACTORS
Launcher, Training equipment, Sights: Prime Contractor – Hunting Engineering Ltd, Reddings Wood, Ampthill, Bedford MK45 2HD, England.
Projectile: Royal Ordnance Factories (Lead – ROF Blackburn).
Spotting rifle: Royal Small Arms Factory, Enfield.
Packaging: EPS (Research & Development) Ltd.
Indoor trainer: Hendry Electronics Ltd.
Motor design: Ministry of Defence – PERME.
Technical advice: Ministry of Defence – RARDE.
Noise cartridge: Paines, Wessex.

4757.111
LAWMINE ANTI-TANK WEAPON

In a collaborative venture, the Bracknell Division of British Aerospace and Hunting Engineering are developing a new unattended anti-tank weapon called Lawmine, which is designed to engage target automatically at ranges from under 10 metres to 100 metres or more. This weapon combines the LAW 80

anti-tank projectile (**3986.111**) with an advanced automatic target detection system that is mounted on the LAW 80 launch tube.

Any heavy tracked or wheeled AFVs crossing the line of fire are automatically sensed and the round is fired to hit the target at a point optimised to cause maximum damage. The system is unaffected by adverse weather and operates by day or night. The

mine requires a very narrow field of view which enables it to be sited within buildings or similar urban surroundings.

The Lawmine system was defined in response to a UK MoD requirement and is designed to be deployed in conditions where for logistic reasons, or because of time constraints, tactics or terrain use of conventional anti-tank mines is precluded.

STATUS
Development project.
CONTRACTORS
British Aerospace Dynamics Group, Bracknell

Division, Downshire Way, Bracknell, Berkshire RG12 1QL, England.
    Hunting Engineering Ltd, Reddings Wood, Ampthill, Bedford MK45 2HD, England.

Lawmine is a new anti-tank weapon under development by British Aerospace and Hunting Engineering. It uses the LAW 80 projectile with a new sensor system for automatic engagement of AFVs

4756.111
MERLIN ANTI-TANK MORTAR BOMB

Stemming from private venture studies carried out by British Aerospace since 1981 and a British GST (General Staff Target) relating to terminally guided mortar bombs (MORAT), BAe is now engaged on a contract valued at more than £11 million for development of an 81 mm terminally-guided anti-armour weapon for use by infantry in the 1990's. The new weapon is known as the 81 mm Merlin mortar bomb.

It is intended to provide an effective fire and forget capability for infantry confronting tanks and armoured personnel carriers, and will be compatible with existing conventional 81 mm mortars for launch, requiring no changes in weapon or personnel. The terminal guidance will give top armour penetration of targets over a wide area, and a low cost per round with low operating costs are expected to yield a low cost per kill for the system.

Millimetric wavelength radar will be used by the mortar homing head, Merlin being claimed to be the first use of this technique, and a shaped charge warhead will be employed to ensure penetration of all existing or projected top armour. In all other respects, the Merlin 81 mm mortar round is intended to be handled and stored like conventional mortar munitions, without additional logistic or training burdens.

DEVELOPMENT
British Aerospace funded development for the Merlin system from September 1981, leading to official interest culminating in the GST for MORAT of April 1983. Agreement has been reached on a contract shared equally between BAe and the UK MoD and covering project definition and the pre-development phase. The British Government has placed a contract

Test firing of Merlin 81 mm terminally-guided anti-armour bomb

worth £11 million for this joint work up to the end of 1984.
STATUS
The preparatory work by BAe has covered feasibility of the project and the first stage of the project

definition by early 1984. Some hardware had already been demonstrated.
CONTRACTOR
British Aerospace Dynamics Group, Six Hills Way, Stevenage, Hertfordshire SG1 2DA, England.

2475.111
VIGILANT ANTI-TANK MISSILE

Vigilant is a man-portable wire-guided anti-tank missile system. In its simplest configuration the system comprises a launcher box containing one missile, a sight controller, a pocket battery, and a length of interconnecting cable. The launcher box is set down on the ground with the missile inserted, pointing in the direction from which a threat is anticipated, and the operator, who carries the sight controller and its associated battery, takes up a suitably unobtrusive position where he has a good field of view. This position may be up to 63 metres from the launcher box. Thus positioned the operator

can engage targets over arcs of fire of +10° in elevation and +35° in azimuth, and at ranges of from 200 to 1375 m.
CHARACTERISTICS
Type: 1-man portable anti-tank missile system. Pan-climatic
Guidance principle: Wire-guided. Heading demand signals referenced to missile autopilot. Optical sighting. Manual or semi-automatic control
Guidance method: Servo-controlled surfaces in pairs
Propulsion: 2-stage solid-propellant motor
Warhead: Hollow-charge. Weight in excess of 5 kg with fuze

Range: 200-1375 m
Special features: Ease of concealment. Immunity to ECM
STATUS
Although now regarded as obsolescent, Vigilant remains in limited use. The system has been widely sold and went into service with the British Army and the Defence Forces of Finland and Kuwait in 1963, of Saudi Arabia in 1964, and of Libya in 1968 and to the Abu Dhabi Defence Forces in 1971. No longer produced.

UNITED STATES OF AMERICA

2573.111
DRAGON ANTI-TANK/ASSAULT WEAPON (FGM-77A/FTM-77A)

Formerly known as MAW (medium anti-tank assault weapon system), Dragon was developed for the US Army and Marine Corps. It employs a command to line-of-sight guidance system and consists of three main items: a tracker, a recoilless launcher, and a missile. The tracker includes a telescope for the gunner to sight the target, a sensor device, and an electronics package. The tracker is reusable and is attached to the launcher; the missile is never seen by the gunner and after firing the launcher is discarded.

The Kollsman-produced Type SU-36/P IR tracker

(3089.183 in 1979-80 and earlier editions) is the guidance element of the system, and consists of a six-power optical sight aligned with an IR sensor, an electronics package, the trigger, and safety catch. The IR sensor acquires a flare in the tail of the missile as it leaves the launcher. The relative angular positions of the missile and the line of sight to the target are continuously compared with the sight electronics and used to derive correction signals which are transmitted to the missile via the guidance wires.

The missile is ejected from the tube by a gas generator using a recoilless technique. When it emerges folding fins flip open and the missile starts to

roll. Thereafter propulsion and control forces are provided by the 60 small sustainers which fire in pairs on demand from the tracker. In operation, the gunner sights the target through the telescopic sight then launches the missile. While he holds his sight on the target, the tracker senses the missile position relative to the gunner's line of sight and sends command signals over wire to the missile.

As commands are sent continually to the missile, the side thrusters apply corrective control forces. The thrusters are fired at appropriate roll angles so that the missile is automatically guided throughout its flight.

CHARACTERISTICS
Designation: M47 (FGM-77A/FTM-77A)
Type: Anti-tank guided missile
Guidance: Wire-guided, command to line-of-sight
Propulsion: Recoilless launched, solid-propellant rocket motor
Warhead: Shaped charge
Launch weight: 13·8 kg (ready to fire)
Range: 1 km
STATUS
Dragon is deployed in US Army units but production for this service is now complete. A number of other countries are stated to have had procurement of this system under consideration. American users of the system also include the US Marine Corps. Some of the US Dragon inventory was suffering from a short shelf-life of the rocket thrusters, according to an Army statement of January 1982, which was repeated in 1984, when it was stated that rocket thrusters were being upgraded.

The eventual US replacement for Dragon is the subject of a programme now known as the Advanced Anti-Tank Weapon System, for which RDT&E funding of $24·9 million was sought for fiscal year 1985. This succeeds the previous Rattler (**4439.111** in 1983-84 and earlier editions) and IMAAWS (infantry man-portable anti-armour/assault weapon system) programmes, which have been dropped.
CONTRACTORS
McDonnell Douglas Astronautics Company, Titusville, Florida, USA – developer, initial production, engineering support, and night tracker.

Dragon deployed and ready to fire

Kollsman Instrument Company, Syosset, New York, USA – tracker production.
Raytheon Company, Bristol, Tennessee, USA – round production.

4551.111
GUIDED ANTI-ARMOUR MORTAR PROJECTILE (GAMP)
The US Army has a requirement for a guided projectile to be fired from existing 4·2-inch/107 mm mortars deployed by the new light divisions and the Rapid Deployment Force (RDF) and capable of use against armoured targets. The expected in-service date is 1986-87.

Raytheon has already fielded a contender for this programme known as GAMP. This is approximately 750 mm long and has folding wings set about two thirds of the way back along the body. Set in the nose behind an ejectable cover is a two-colour IR homing sensor derived from that used on the Sidewinder air-to-air missile (**3068.331**). Behind this is a Garret fluidic jet reaction control system, the gas generation system and the digital electronics package. Much of the rear third of the projectile body is occupied by the HEAT warhead. The nose-mounted seeker is understood to have a 500 metre elliptical footprint with a slant detection range of between 1000 and 2000 metres. It is designed to be effective within a 400 metre weather overcast ceiling. Range of the GAMP is expected to be between 6000-8000 metres and a top attack profile will be used.

Ballistic tests were scheduled for 1982 with firings commencing during 1983. In the long term Raytheon may offer a millimetre-wave seeker but this will not be ready for the required in-service date.

By the addition of suitable obturation devices GAMP could be fired from 120 mm mortars.

In addition to Raytheon several other contractors are expected to submit GAMP-type designs, including Martin Marietta and General Dynamics.
STATUS
Development.
CONTRACTOR
Raytheon Company, Missile Systems Division, Bedford, Massachusetts 01730, USA.

2830.111
TOW ANTI-TANK MISSILE (BGM-71)
TOW is an acronym for tube-launched, optically-tracked, wire-guided, and describes a heavy assault ground-to-ground (or air-to-ground) anti-tank guided weapon system.

The TOW launcher system, for infantry use, is made up of five elements, none of which weighs more than 24 kg, although the complete launcher weighs 78 kg when assembled and ready to fire. Two of these elements are a tripod and a traversing unit, mounted upon the tripod, to which the tripod launch tube and optical sight are attached. The gunner's optical sight is of high magnification and equipped with aiming cross-hairs which when combined with the smooth, stable motion of the traversing unit permit very accurate tracking of moving targets after very little operator training. The fifth individual element is the electronic guidance computer which sends steering commands automatically to the missile in flight.

The missile itself is contained in a sealed storage and transport container which becomes a launch tube extension when placed in the launcher breech. After the breech locks, all electronic contacts to the missile are automatically closed, and TOW is ready to fire.

The missile contains two solid-propellant motors. The launch motor ejects the missile from the launch tube and is burned out by the time the missile has left the tube. Only after the missile has flown several metres does the flight motor ignite, so that no protection is necessary for the gunner against hot exhaust gas and propellant particles. The flight motor is mounted in the centre of the missile with its two exhaust nozzles mounted on either side. This arrangement prevents interference with the guidance wires which are placed at the tail of the fuselage. Steering commands are transmitted by the two wires which uncoil from two separate spools. Short cruciform wings in the centre of the missile and the cruciform rudder surfaces all unfold after leaving the launch tube. Missile manoeuvring is done entirely aerodynamically (without jet vanes) so that TOW maintains good manoeuvrability throughout missile flight. The electronics unit is mounted between the flight motor and the armour-piercing warhead.

After the missile leaves the launch tube, a light source in the tail comes on so that the optical sensor on the launcher, which is bore-sighted with the gunner's telescope, can track the missile along its flight path. The light source is sufficiently strong to allow automatic guidance to the maximum range of the missile under all conditions in which the target is visible to the gunner.
MOBILE INSTALLATIONS
TOW can also be installed in most of the available wheeled or tracked vehicles capable of cross-country travel. The US Army is using it on armoured personnel carriers, jeeps, and AH-1S Cobra helicopters: the US Marine Corps has tested it on the 'mechanical mule'. Moreover, the American Army is equipping with a vehicle which affords greater protection to the crew whilst firing TOW. Called the Improved TOW Vehicle (ITV) (M901), it consists basically of an M113A1 armoured personnel carrier that has been modified to carry an armoured cupola or weapon station. A large pod, containing two TOW launchers, a day sight, AN/TAS-4 night sight and target acquisition sight, is attached to the base of the cupola by lifting arms. When not in use, this pod rests on the rear deck of the vehicle. The gunner operates the TOW from inside the cupola, which is designed to provide protection equal to that of the M113A1. The cupola is equipped with hand-operated power controls that allow the gunner to raise and lower the pod and rotate the cupola a full 360°. Also provided is

Israeli Laser TOW has sensor in centre of tail for laser beam-riding guidance system (T.J. Gander)

an optical system of lenses and prisms which enables him to look into the pod-mounted TOW sights.

To operate the system, the gunner raises the pod about 1·2 metres above the deck of the vehicle by extending the lifting arms. He then simply looks into the TOW sights, aims at a target, launches a missile and guides it to the target.

Two other US Army vehicles have been equipped with TOW firing systems: the M2 Infantry Fighting Vehicle, and the M3 Cavalry Fighting Vehicle. Both these vehicles evolved from the US MICV (mechanised infantry combat vehicle) programme and the TOW installation is virtually identical in each case with a two-tube launcher assembly carried on the left side of the vehicle's main armament (25 mm cannon) turret. When travelling, this launcher is retracted and lies alongside the turret; reloading can be performed from inside the vehicle, manually, and the M2 version can carry five reload rounds while the M3 has provision for 10 reloads.

Overseas countries have also adopted armoured TOW systems. The Netherlands have their own version of the M901 ITV, which is known to the Dutch as the Armoured Infantry Fighting Vehicle (AIFV), and this consists of a considerably modified M113 chassis equipped with the Emerson ITV turret. The Netherlands designation of the AIFV is YPR 765 PRAT.

In 1978 Thyssen Henschel built two prototypes of the Jagdpanzer Rakete armed with a single-tube TOW launcher, and known as the Jaguar 2. It is used with an AN/TAS-4 night sight and the launcher has a traverse of 30° left or right and an elevation of +15 to –10°. It was expected that over 150 of these vehicles might be procured for the Federal Republic German Army following evaluation.

The adaptability of TOW for the armament of fighting helicopters has been thoroughly

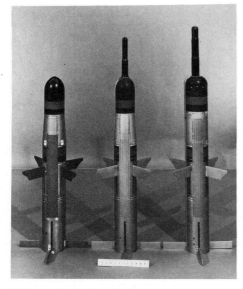

TOW missile family with (l to r): basic model; improved TOW (ITOW); and TOW 2 with larger warhead, extensible probe and higher impulse flight motor

demonstrated. For details of helicopter applications of TOW see **2831.311**.

CHARACTERISTICS
Military designation: BGM-71A
Type: Heavy anti-tank guided weapon system
Guidance principle: Automatic missile tracking and command guidance from optical target tracker
Guidance method: Wire guidance control of gas-operated aerodynamic tail surfaces
Propulsion: 2-stage solid-propellant motor. First stage quadruple; second stage single. Recoilless launch
Warhead: HEAP shaped charge
Missile length: 117 cm*
Missile diameter: 15·2 cm
Launch weight: 18 kg*
System weight: 102 kg including 1 missile
Speed: Believed to be at least 1000 km/h
Range: Minimum: 65 m; Max: 3750 m
Rate of fire: 3 launches in 90 s
Crew: 4
*TOW 2 is 140 cm with probe extended, and weight 21·5 kg at launch

DEVELOPMENT
In 1980 the US Army embarked on a two-stage programme to improve the performance of the TOW system against advanced enemy armour. The first phase of the programme involves an improved five-inch diameter warhead to increase the armour penetration characteristics; it is of the same size and weight as the standard TOW warhead but of improved design. The second phase of the programme, known as TOW 2, will incorporate a heavier six-inch diameter warhead of still greater penetration performance and this will occupy the full diameter of the missile body. Also in phase two, the missile guidance system will be improved by the use of a microprocessor based sub-system which will give greater flexibility in guidance programming and higher accuracy. To compensate for the added weight, the missile motor will have an improved propellant to provide a higher impulse.

Laser TOW
In mid-1984 Israel revealed a version of TOW that employs a form of laser guidance to replace the normal wire guidance link. Laser TOW was developed over a period of about four years by the Israel Military Industries organisation, but the production status is not known. An increased range of more than 5000 metres is claimed and a new shaped charge warhead has been developed that is said to be capable of penetrating 800 mm of armour plate.

A small booster motor is used to eject Laser TOW from the launcher tube, and this falls away after rocket motor burn out to reveal the sensor for the laser beam-riding guidance system in the centre of the missile's tail. Coded signals from the operator's sight are received by this sensor and used to actuate the four flip-out tail fins to guide the missile to the target. The increased range of Laser Tow is thought to be largely due to weight and drag reductions from deletion of the guidance wire.

TOW anti-tank missile leaving launch tube of US Army M2/M3 Bradley fighting vehicle system

Coding of the laser guidance signals permits operation of several missiles independently of each other by allocating separate channels to each launcher.

STATUS
Basic TOW has been in the US inventory for several years, and the system has been adopted by over 30 countries. By mid-1983 more than 300 000 missiles had been produced. A TOW thermal night sight and an improved warhead have been introduced into US service with the ITOW. Production of TOW 2 missiles and modification kits to convert basic launchers to the TOW 2 configuration have been delivered to the US Army since early 1983. The fiscal year 1984 report to Congress by the US Secretary of Defense, Casper W Weinberger stated that the US Army and Marine Corps will continue procurement of TOW with the improved warhead and guidance system. At the same time existing missiles will be fitted retrospectively with these improvements and initial deliveries of new TOW 2 production missiles have begun. Funded and planned TOW procurement for the fiscal years 1983-85 is as follows: 1983 – 13 000 ($161·7); 1984 – 20 200 ($216·9); 1985 – 21 822 ($296·4), all funding in millions.

CONTRACTORS
Hughes Aircraft Company, Canoga Park, California 91304, USA, is the prime contractor for the system, having developed it for the US Army Missile Command.

Emerson Electric Co, Electronics and Space Division, 8100 Florissant Avenue, St Louis, Missouri 63136, USA, are prime suppliers of the launcher, missile guidance set, optical sight, and traversing unit.

Texas Instruments Incorporated, PO Box 226015, Dallas, Texas 75266, USA, is the major sub-contractor to Hughes for the infantry ground launcher TOW 2 retrofit kits which include a digital missile guidance set and the AN/TAS-4A night sight.

4472.111

TANK BREAKER ANTI-TANK MISSILE
The Tank Breaker anti-tank missile, currently under development, is a man-portable system capable of day and night operations on a 'fire and forget' basis. It will be capable of both direct attack or top attack against armoured targets and could be the first anti-tank missile to use a focal plane array imaging IR seeker. This sensor system offers significant reductions in size, cost and complexity for tactical missile applications.

The basic Tank Breaker will be a shoulder-launched missile and a launcher with a detachable launch control unit capable of re-use. The guidance system involved will allow the gunner to acquire and lock onto a target and fire a missile in day or night conditions and in all weathers. Once the missile has locked onto the target and launched, the gunner will be able to take cover immediately or engage other targets, relying on the missile's 'fire and forget' performance to guide it to the target. One further option open to the gunner before launch is the selection of a direct attack or top attack of the target. On the target the missile's advanced HEAT warhead will be effective against modern armour, helicopters

or low performance aircraft and field fortifications. No field testing or direct support maintenance will be required for battlefield employment.

Two companies are involved in the Tank Breaker programme, sponsored by DARPA and managed under the direction of the US Army Missile Command. The companies involved are Texas Instruments and Hughes Aircraft Company.

The Hughes Tank Breaker missile is 100 mm in diameter and 1·09 metres long. The complete system will weigh less than 15·8 kg. In-flight control will be provided by proportional actuators on the tail surfaces.

The Texas Instruments submission is being developed as both a man-portable shoulder launcher and a launcher for helicopter or vehicle launching. The man-portable version uses its own dedicated launch control unit, which is re-useable, but the vehicle/helicopter version is designed for use with existing display and target acquisition systems. The man-portable version will be 1·143 metres long and weigh 15·875 kg. It will use a soft launch eject motor. The vehicle/helicopter version will be 1·27 metres long and weigh 16·78 kg. It will use an eject/booster motor at the tail to boost missile performance and

Infantry tests with Hughes Tank Breaker anti-tank missile mock-up. Air-to-ground and air-to-air versions for helicopter operations are also planned

flight control is by a combination of aerodynamic means and thrust vector control (TVC). The focal plane imaging and IR seeker array will be in the nose with the guidance electronics controlling small stub vanes for trajectory guidance just behind. The warhead will be situated in the middle of the missile body with the flight motor to the rear. At the end of the missile body are further stub vanes with larger flight control fins right at the rear. The helicopter version is intended to have a range capable of the limits of FLIR target acquisition and will be capable of use against SAM site radar emitter targets. An air target capability will permit engagement of hostile helicopters in air-to-air combat.

STATUS

The programme began in 1980 with Texas Instruments, Hughes Aircraft, McDonnell Douglas, and Rockwell International. In July 1981, after a competitive field test, Texas Instruments and Hughes Aircraft were awarded DARPA-sponsored Phase II contracts that were managed by US Army Missile Command. Phase II was completed in 1983. Both Texas Instruments and Hughes Aircraft demonstrated advanced imaging IR seekers and target trackers during captive flight tests. The programme now awaits the US Army's decision to proceed with Rattler, the medium assault weapon designated to replace Dragon (**2573.111**).

CONTRACTORS

Hughes Aircraft Company, Missile Systems Group, Canoga Park, California 91304, USA.

Texas Instruments Incorporated, PO Box 405, Lewisville, Texas 75067, USA.

3212.111

COPPERHEAD CLGP (M712)

Copperhead is the name assigned to the M712 cannon launched guided projectile (CLGP), a 155 mm round equipped with a terminal guidance system and launched from conventional howitzers into an essentially ballistic trajectory, although by means of a technique known as trajectory shaping, it is possible to use shallow flight path angles which allow Copperhead to be used with cloud ceilings below the specified 3000 feet (914 metres). This provides more guidance time below the clouds and increases projectile acquisition range. During flight the target is illuminated by a laser designator operated by a forward observer. The seeker in the nose of the CLGP acquires the semi-active laser signature and uses this signal to operate control surfaces on the projectile to cause it to follow a collision course to the target.

The origin of the system rests in the US Army requirement for a means of bringing indirect fire to bear on tanks and distant armoured targets with a high kill (preferably first round) probability using a shaped charge warhead. Indirect fire demands the use of a forward observer or a forward air controller who calls for fire in the conventional manner and designates the target during the last seconds of the projectile's flight. Several options are provided for this requirement.

Target designator systems which can be used with Copperhead include the AN/TVQ-2 ground laser locator designator (**3051.193**), the hand-held AN/PAQ-1 laser target designator (LTD) (**3157.193**), modular universal laser equipment (MULE) (**3816.193**), various RPV designator systems, and the AAH advanced attack helicopter target and designation system (TADS) (**3609.363**). A designator mounted on an armoured vehicle, such as the M113 is under consideration.

The Copperhead round is fired in an inactive state, thus simplifying the precautions needed to protect the guidance system from acceleration shocks. An acceleration-sensitive battery, initiated by firing the projectile, supplies power for guidance and control, as well as initiating and operating a timer which controls the internal operating sequence. Timer adjustment is dependent upon the required range, and therefore is similar to setting a timed fuze.

Associated with a setting of the timing switches is the selection of the trajectory mode for a ballistic trajectory or a fly under/fly out (FUFO) trajectory. The latter is intended for ranges of over 8 km and for bad weather where the projectiles travel at a lower altitude to provide a longer time beneath cloud ceiling for acquisition and guidance. The ballistic trajectory is used for shorter range shots and/or good weather conditions.

Coding of the laser signature which will be accepted by the seeker is also set in at the same time as the above selections are made. This coding will match that being used by the forward operator of the laser designator.

The Copperhead CLGP is made up of three sections; guidance, payload, and stabilisation and control. The configuration is aerodynamically controlled by cruciform in-line wings and tail fins that provide roll stabilisation and lateral manoeuvrability sufficient to provide an impact 'footprint' adequate for successfully engaging manoeuvring armoured targets.

The guidance section consists of the seeker and electronic assemblies which are housed within the nose dome and steel housing. The seeker uses folded body-mounted optics with a spin stabilised gimballed mirror (seeker gyro). The seeker gyro is spun-up mechanically by a steel spring and sustained and torqued electrically.

The payload section includes an HESH warhead in a steel structure and a fuze module. The latter incorporates six grazing sensors to detonate the warhead if the nose sensor does not directly hit the target.

The stabilisation and control section includes the flip-out aerodynamic surfaces and associated actuator mechanisms. Deployment of the fins is delayed until after the muzzle exit by the effects of launch acceleration. When deployed at their 20° sweep angle, the tail fins are canted to maintain a six to eighteen revolutions per second projectile roll rate, which aids stability and also allows liberal tolerances in vane manufacture.

CHARACTERISTICS

Type: M712
Weight: 63·5 kg
Length: 137·2 cm
Warhead weight: 22·5 kg
Explosive weight: 6·4 kg
Max range: 16 km
Minimum range: 3 km

A typical impact 'footprint' has been reported as about one kilometre radius from the nominal aim point.

STATUS

Production of Copperhead was authorised in March 1980 with the award of a $62 million contract to Martin Marietta. The fiscal years 1981 and 1982 allowed for procurement of 3125 and 4550 rounds respectively, at a cost of $117·6 million and $141·1 million, with projected procurement of 7629 rounds in fiscal year 1983 valued at $183·6 million. Initial operational capability (IOC) was scheduled for 1982, but in that year Congress withheld production funding, reportedly because the reliability factor achieved was below the 80 per cent first round hit rate specified. Since production improvements made in July 1982 the overall Copperhead firing success rate till May 1983 was 82·4 per cent, and in that month the lot acceptance test firing yielded a success rate of 90·9 per cent with ten consecutive hits out of 11 shots.

The fiscal year 1985 DoD Budget showed planned procurement of Copperhead rounds (with funding in $ millions in brackets) as follows: 1983, 1100 (55), 1984, 1415 (71·3) and 1985 2253 (102·8). The contractor reported in early 1984 that 5000 rounds of a projected total of 30 462 had been delivered.

CONTRACTOR

Martin Marietta Orlando Aerospace, PO Box 5837, Orlando, Florida 32855, USA.

3988.111

SADARM SYSTEM

The US Army SADARM (sense and destroy armour) anti-tank sub-munition system is a project to design and develop a weapon for use against massed enemy armour beyond the forward edge of the battle area (FEBA). It is intended to be delivered by conventional current eight-inch calibre artillery, although it is very probable that sub-munitions of this kind will find applications in the Multiple Launch Rocket System (MLRS) (**4060.111**) described later in this volume and adaptation of SADARM sub-munitions to the slightly smaller 155 mm calibre ammunition will greatly hasten and extend the deployment possibilities of this technique.

SADARM, in its original version, is 203 mm in diameter and about 1·14 metres long, it is cylindrical and within are contained three sub-munitions. The general concept is clear from the nearby illustration. No external guidance or control system is required and there is no need for target illumination (eg laser). The SADARM round, after reaching the target area, ejects the three sub-munition canisters over the grouped targets and a vortex ring parachute is deployed from each canister to position the latter so that during its descent a sensor can scan the target area at an angle of 30° from the vertical. The acquisition range of individual sensors is in the region of 75 metres radius, and if the sub-munition descends in an area of this size containing a vehicle, the millimetric wavelength sensor is automatically switched on. When the sensor detects its target, it fires the canister's armour-penetrating warhead at the target's top surface. The sub-munitions will incorporate the self-forging fragment (SFF) type of warhead.

Such warheads are a feature of the Avco Skeet family of sub-munitions, which were developed for a number of projects, such as Assault Breaker (**3989.111**), WAAM (wide area anti armour munitions), and in several forms which include the ESM (enhanced sensing munition), IRAAM (improved remote area anti-armour mine), SFW (sensor fuzed weapon) and ERAM (extended range anti-armour munition). By packaging six IRAAMs in an M483A1 carrier projectile equipped with an M577 fuze, a 155 mm calibre SADARM shell is obtained, designated the XM898. The Skeet warhead in this role has a novel dual (top/bottom) attack capability which enables each one to serve as either a downward firing weapon to attack tanks from above, or if a target is not presented on release from the carrier shell, the Skeet falls to the ground to remain as a run-over mine.

The 8-inch calibre SADARM projectile is designated XM836 and contains four Skeet munitions.

The ESM/SADARM deployment does not rely on parachutes, but individual sub-munitions are ejected from the rear/base end of the carrier shell and each follows a pre-computed precession-imparted search pattern caused by their rate of spin.

STATUS

A successful concept demonstration test firing of the SADARM was carried out in June 1979 at Albuquerque, New Mexico, USA.

In early 1984 Congress withheld SADARM funding until the Anti-Armour Study was completed but it was anticipated that new funding would become available after the beginning of fiscal year 1985 in October 1984.

CONTRACTORS

Aerojet Electrosystems, Azusa, California, USA.

Avco Systems Division, 201 Lowell Street, Wilmington, Massachusetts 01887, USA.

The SADARM programme is the responsibility of the US Army Armament Research and Development Command, Dover, New Jersey 07801, USA.

Operation of ESM/SADARM with armour targets detected by airborne radar or other systems being engaged from long distances by artillery. M438A1 carrier shell delivers six Skeet sub-munitions which disperse in target area. Each one seeks a target to attack from above, or to lay in wait as an anti-tank mine on reaching the ground if no target is encountered.

4758.111
XM815 HEAT-MP-T PROJECTILE

The XM815 105 mm HEAT-MP-T projectile is a multi-purpose artillery round being developed by Avco as a companion to the kinetic energy rounds M-774 and XM833. The sponsoring body is the US Army Tank Main Armament Systems Project Office, and the work is based on earlier efforts by ARRADCOM. The XM815 will replace the current 105 mm HEAT, HEP and APERS rounds.

A novel fin folding design combines high stability with low drag and this is claimed to result in significantly higher accuracy than is obtained with the M456 predecessor round. The new round incorporates the latest precision shaped charge technology, and reaches a muzzle velocity of almost 120 m/s, without excessive heating, barrel wear or muzzle blast.

The XM815 is designed for use with M68 cannon on the M48A5, M60, and M1 series MBTs against targets such as enemy BTR-60 and BRDM vehicles, or other targets such as bunkers or military structures.

The fuzing mechanism employed is the XM763 fuze system, which is a point initiating, base detonating assembly. Its major components are a crush type switch, a base element safing and arming device, and an interconnecting cable between these two elements. The crush type switch provides full frontal area impact sensitivity to the prescribed targets, while maintaining insensitivity to brush contacts, rain, and other non-impact conditions. Advanced components and energy devices enable the XM815 to survive the shock loads and other environmental stresses of launch.

STATUS

Development project. Test rounds have been fired, reportedly with good accuracy. It is stated that a high priority has been placed on getting the XM815 into

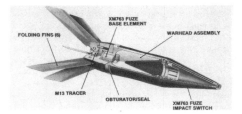

Cutaway diagram of XM815 projectile

service quickly and an initial operational capability (IOC) by the last quarter of 1986 is planned.

CONTRACTOR

Avco Systems Division, 201 Lowell Street, Wilmington, Massachusetts 01887, USA.

Coastal Defence Weapons

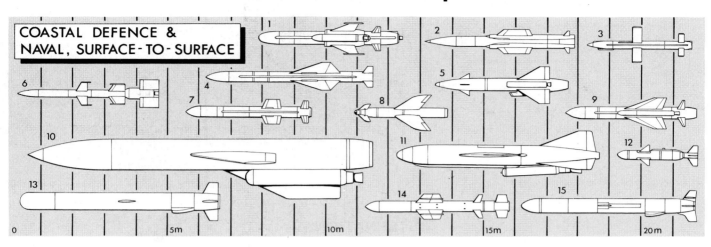

| COASTAL DEFENCE & NAVAL, SURFACE-TO-SURFACE |

1 Otomat
2 ANS
3 Gabriel
4 Exocet MM 38/9-40
5 RBS 15
6 Sea Killer II
7 Hsiung Feng
8 Penguin
9 Sea Eagle
10 Shaddock (Sepal)
11 SS-N-2 Styx
12 Sea Skua
13 SS-N-21X (provisional)
14 Harpoon
15 SLCM Tomahawk

CHINA (PEOPLE'S REPUBLIC)

3984.121
HY-2 (CSS-N-2) COASTAL DEFENCE WEAPON
Soon after it became known that the Soviet Union had supplied the People's Republic of China with SS-N-2 anti-ship missiles (**1155.221**), it was disclosed that China had embarked on a plan to deploy this missile for defence of her extensive coastline. This programme has been followed since perhaps the early 1970s, and although it is still not known to what extent it has been fulfilled, or the numbers of missiles

available for this purpose, the existence of a missile coastal defence force has now been officially confirmed by the release of a few photographs of units armed with the CSS-N-2.

More recently it was confirmed that China has its own indigenous production facilities for this weapon, which has the official designation HY-2. In 1984 the Chinese Government made this system available for export.

So far as can be gathered, the missile itself is

virtually unchanged from its shipborne configuration, and the performance must also be similar. The launcher appears to be the same as that employed by the Soviet Union for coastal defence batteries using missiles of this type. The truck-mounted radar associated with the HY-2 system provides surveillance and target detection facilities and is also stated to perform target tracking. The design apparently originates from a Soviet naval search radar and probably operates in the C-band of the spectrum.
STATUS
Operational and in production in the People's Republic of China. Available for export.
CONTRACTOR
China Precision Machinery Import and Export Corporation, 17 Wenchang Hutong Xidah Beijing, People's Republic of China.

Launch of HY-2 (CSS-N-2) coastal defence missile during training by a naval unit of the Chinese People's Liberation Army (Chinese Official)

Mobile radar for use with Chinese HY-2 coast defence missile system

FRANCE

2118.121
EXOCET COASTAL DEFENCE WEAPON
The MM40 coastal defence version of the Exocet anti-ship missile system has completed the development phase and is operational. It uses the current shipborne MM40 missile, with new propulsion arrangements that give a boost phase of 2·4 s followed by a sustainer burn time of 220 s, resulting in a longer cruise phase – about 100 s longer than that of the MM38. Another major change is in the adoption of folding aerodynamic surfaces to permit the use of much smaller tubular launcher-containers made of wound glass-fibre. The dimensions of the new tubular containers are such that four can be accommodated

in the same volume as that required for a single conventional MM38 metal housing.

The Exocet coastal defence system comprises a mobile battery, all the equipment being carried on military vehicles. The target acquisition and designation radar will usually be located on high ground to ensure adequate range. Three or four launcher vehicles will occupy predetermined locations to cover the desired firing area, with supply trucks ready to replenish them, and maintenance vehicles under cover. For engagement of targets beyond the radar horizon of the shore radar, target data supplied by a consort, (aircraft, helicopter, or ship) can be used. In this case, the consort

automatically transmits the target data to the shore radar installation.
CHARACTERISTICS
Type: MM40
Length: 5·78 m
Launch weight: 850 kg
Range: 70 km
STATUS
The MM38 and AM39 are operational with French and other navies. Development of the MM40 has now been completed. Several nations are understood to have ordered the MM40 including the French Navy.

In the basic definition configuration of the system, the radar used will be the Thomson-CSF TRS 3410

(**3273.153**) with possible over-the-horizon guidance facilities provided by Agrion 15 (**3298.353**) or ORB 32 (**1960.353**) airborne radar. Other types of radar could also be employed.

In the course of fighting to reoccupy the Falkland Isles in 1982 a Royal Navy ship was hit (albeit not disastrously) by an MM38 Exocet that apparently was launched from an improvised shore battery set up by the Argentines.

CONTRACTOR
Aérospatiale, Division des Engins Tactiques, 18 rue Béranger, 92322 Châtillon-Cedex, France.

Launch of MM40 from a coastal battery firing vehicle

INTERNATIONAL

1337.121
OTOMAT COASTAL DEFENCE SYSTEM (FRANCE/ITALY)
The Otomat coastal defence system (OCDS) uses the Otomat anti-ship missile, developed by Matra (France) in collaboration with OTO Melara (Italy), and fitted in numerous warships. An operational range of over 100 km is obtained with no more than initial target designation ('fire-and-forget'), while the use of the 'fire-and-update' technique permits ranges of more than 160 km. Salvo firing achieves similar improvement of the effective range. The 210 kg semi-armour piercing warhead has a significant destructive effect due to penetration and explosion within the target. Tactical use is facilitated by the angled firing capability (gyrodeviation) which ensures complete freedom with regard to launch axis and target azimuth.

A more detailed description and illustrations of the missile are given in the Shipborne Weapons section (**1336.221**).

The OCDS is composed of one or more Otomat coastal defence units (OCDUs) carried on cross-country vehicles. Each OCDU comprises a command group, and two to four firing groups. The command group includes one control cabin, a surveillance radar (each carried on its own truck), one command car, and an operational maintenance vehicle. The firing group consists of one firing vehicle with two missiles in containers, and one reload vehicle fitted with a hoist and two spare missiles in containers. One command group can control up to four firing groups. The basic vehicle used is the six wheel drive truck RVI GBD 6 × 6 fitted with sand-duty tyres and having an empty weight of ten tons. Maximum road speed is 75 km/h and range 1000 km.

The command vehicle houses the tactical display console, missile control panel, various communications equipments and the telecommand transmitter. The console enables the tracking of several targets, and the control panel permits the setting of initialisation data into the missiles and authorising their firing by the firing vehicles. The latter vehicles are equipped with a north-seeking gyro-compass to assist initial survey and battery setting up, and an optical sight for reversionary mode use.

VHF radio links are provided between the vehicles permitting flexible dispersion of the OCDU. The problem of over-the-horizon target designation has been solved by employing an external radar, either a relay ship, helicopter or fixed-wing aircraft. The relay platform measures target bearing and range and transmits them via data link to the control cabin. The latter measures range and bearing to the relay plaform and computes the co-ordinates with respect to the firing vehicle. A course correction transmitter allows for in-flight updating of the co-ordinates. Airborne target detection makes it possible to reach extended ranges, thus permitting a single OCDU to cover 360 km of coast line.

An Italian version of the Otomat coastal defence system was revealed in some detail at the Mostra Navale exhibition held in May 1982. In this version an Otomat coastal battery consists of six OTO C13 tracked vehicles on each of which are two Otomat missiles housed in glass-fibre launcher containers. These are linked by cables or radio to a command post vehicle on another C13 chassis, from where, it is reported, one man can control the entire battery using an SMA MM/SPQ-2F search radar mounted on top of the command post. There can be up to 20 km between the command vehicle and the others of the battery, and it is also possible to employ a naval helicopter such as the Agusta AB 212 equipped with Otomat over-the-horizon guidance facilities for engagement of distant targets. In such a role a range of more than 160 km is claimed.

STATUS
The Otomat coastal defence system is in operational service with the Egyptian Navy, and several others are contemplating acquisition of the system.

In the course of tests at the CEL (Centre d'Essais des Landes) ranges, a hit on a target at a range of more than 100 km was achieved in 1980, using the full beyond the horizon procedure (airborne detection, in-flight updating).

CONTRACTORS
Matra SA, 78140 Vélizy, France.
OTO Melara, La Spezia, Italy.

Otomat coastal defence missile leaving its container at a coastal battery

NORWAY

3074.121
PENGUIN COASTAL DEFENCE SYSTEM
The Penguin surface-to-surface anti-ship missile (**1339.221**) is in the process of being reconfigured to serve in a number of coastal defence roles, in either fixed or static versions.

The land-based Penguin missile weapon system consists of a fire control system, the missiles and missile control system. In permanent, fixed installations the system consists of a radar or optical sensor, a missile control cabinet incorporating a special purpose computer, a power supply, a firing panel, and a number of missiles. Very simple launching arrangements can be employed, largely depending on the nature of the site.

Alternatively, Penguin can be adapted as a self-contained, autonomous, mobile coastal defence unit. Vehicle-mounted surveillance radar, such as the Ericsson Giraffe (**1957.153**) which is in service and on order for the Norwegian Army, is used to provide target detection and designation for batteries of Penguin anti-ship missiles deployed on the 'flat-beds' of similar six-wheeled trucks to those carrying the radar. Three missiles can be carried, mounted transversely across the rear of the chassis, while the crew of three and the radar and missile control systems occupy the front cab. A range capability of 30 km is claimed for the Penguin in this role.

CHARACTERISTICS
Number of missiles: 4, or more
Missile data
Weight: 340 kg
Length: 300 cm
Wingspan: 140 cm
Diameter: 28 cm
Speed: High subsonic
Warhead: 120 kg
Fuze: Impact
Trajectory: Variable

Homing: Passive terminal

Range: 30 km

DEVELOPMENT

Penguin was originally developed as a ship-to-ship weapon system for the Royal Norwegian Navy by the Norwegian Defence Research Establishment and A/S Kongsberg Vaapenfabrikk.

STATUS

Studies of various configurations of coastal defence systems based on the Penguin missile have been conducted for several years by the Norwegian authories, involving a number of practical demonstrations. Giraffe surveillance radars ordered in 1983 are thought to be related to implementation of a Norwegian Penguin coastal defence system.

CONTRACTOR

A/S Kongsberg Vaapenfabrikk, PO Box 25, N-360 Kongsberg, Norway.

Schematic diagram of coastal defence system based on vehicle-mounted surveillance radar and Penguin launching units

SWEDEN

2372.121

RB 08 COASTAL DEFENCE WEAPON

The Swedish RB 08 surface-to-surface cruise missile is intended for use either as a shipborne weapon or for coastal defence.

Detailed information on this system wil be found in the Shipborne Weapons sub-section below (**2366.221**).

RB 08A boosted off its launcher

TAIWAN

4442.121

HSIUNG FENG COASTAL DEFENCE MISSILE

Hsiung Feng is the name given by the Taiwanese authorities to a missile designed to engage ship targets at estimated ranges of 30 to 40 km. It is thought that in addition to the land-mobile configuration of this weapon, which is the only one so far revealed in public, shipborne versions of it also exist. Very little in the way of performance, construction, or technical details have been released but from the few photographs which have appeared Hsiung Feng bears a very striking resemblance to the Israeli Gabriel system (**6019.221**), extending also to the container/launchers which are employed for the coastal defence version of the Taiwanese missile. Three missiles are housed, each in its own container, on a triple rotatable launcher unit which is mounted on a semi-trailer which is towed by a heavy tractor unit (see illustration), the triple launcher in the Gabriel III system having a weight of about two tonnes. Despite the Taiwanese reports that Hsiung Feng is of local manufacture, in view of the many and close similarities between this weapon and the Israeli Gabriel system, it is thought that Hsiung Feng is in reality a licence-built product manufactured in Taiwan, or a normal overseas procurement of the Gabriel system.

Two mobile coast defence missile units with triple launchers for Hsiung Feng anti-ship missiles

STATUS

In service.

CONTRACTORS

State Arsenals.

UNION OF SOVIET SOCIALIST REPUBLICS

2951.121

SAMLET CRUISE MISSILE

Like Salish, the missile known to NATO as Samlet and SSC-2B in the American system, is a surface-to-surface version of the air-to-surface jet-powered cruise missile whose NATO code-name is Kennel. It has been operational in the USSR, Egypt, Poland, and Cuba as a coastal defence weapon. When shown publicly Samlet has been mounted on what appears to be its launching ramp constructed as a trailer. But other photographs indicate that a more permanent launch emplacement also exists. For launching a JATO bottle is necessary.

Samlet, like Salish, has a radome over its jet air intake. The radome is larger than that on Salish and Samlet also has what seems to be an electronics pod mounted on its tail fin. The radome is assumed to cover a radar homing seeker: the other device may contain the receiver and associated apparatus of a command guidance link. Apart from these differences the two missiles appear very much alike and the following approximate data are probably equally true of both.

CHARACTERISTICS

Length: Approx 7 m

Wing span: Approx 5 m

Weight: Believed about 3 t

Cruising speed: Mach 0·8 – 0·9

Range (Samlet): Possibly as much as 200 km with mid-course guidance.

STATUS
An undisclosed number of Samlet missiles are reported to be operated by the coastal frontier force of the German Democratic Republic Navy.

Samlet coastal defence missile preparation

2975.121
SEPAL MOBILE CRUISE MISSILE (SSC-1B)
Sepal is the code-name (SSC-1B in the American system) for the land-based version of the shipboard Shaddock surface-to-surface weapon. Too little has been seen of this missile on public display for it to be described with confidence. The general view seems to be that it is a ramjet or turbojet-powered cruise missile with hinged wings that open out when the missile leaves its cylindrical launcher. Initial boost is provided by two rocket units under the rear of the fuselage. Length of the missile is estimated at about ten metres and the diameter of the fuselage is probably around one metre.

Shaddock is best known as a naval weapon and is described as such below (**2976.221**). It appears, however, that it is used by the land forces of the USSR, and this view is reinforced by the appearance of the container/transporter illustrated here which is clearly capable of elevating the missile to an inclined launch position.

While no doubt it could be used as a ground-to-ground weapon, however, it seems rather more likely that it would be used as a coastal defence weapon, if only because of its ability to cruise at speed at low altitude over water.

Sepal carrier with containers elevated to the launch position (Novosti)

Guidance is by radio-command with active radar homing. Range capability is in the order of 450 km, but mid-course guidance by aircraft or helicopter would be necessary for such a long mission. Each coastal defence battalion is reported to be equipped with between 15 and 18 missiles (inclusive of reloads).

STATUS
Unofficial but reliable sources have suggested that there are probably about 100 Sepal SSMs operated by the Soviet Union Navy's coastal artillery and rocket troops. These are thought to protect principal naval bases and main ports.

Shipborne Weapons

This section deals with shipborne surface-to-surface weapons for anti-ship and shore bombardment purposes. In certain cases it will be found that the missile employed in such systems has other roles, and the practice in these instances is to cross refer to the appropriate entries for other applications of a given missile. In general it will be found that the most comprehensive description of the missile as a 'round' will appear under the entry for its principal function, but adequate data for an appreciation of a missile's performance is given in the entry for each system in which it is employed.

Naval guns and unguided bombardment rockets are contained in the Equipment section of this volume, and naval fire control systems are described in a separate section.

CHINA (PEOPLE'S REPUBLIC)

3973.221
HY-2(CSS-N-2) NAVAL SURFACE-TO-SURFACE MISSILE

As a former client of the Soviet Union, the People's Republic of China received a number of SS-N-2, Styx anti-ship missiles (1155.221), and it is now confirmed that this weapon forms a major element of the Chinese inventory. It is extensively employed in both the shipborne surface-to-surface role and mounted on shore-based launchers for coastal defence purposes.

So far as can be ascertained, few if any changes have been made to the original Soviet design, although if indigenous production is being undertaken (as is the case) the possibility of internal detail changes can hardly be ruled out. Chinese-built missiles of this type are designated Hai Ying (Sea Eagle), HY-2, and they were offered for export in 1984. On the 'Luda' class and 'Anshan' class Chinese vessels on which the HY-2 is currently deployed, however, the launcher arrangements are obviously of local origin. The former class of ship has two triple trainable launchers, while the latter class has two trainable twin launchers.

STATUS
Operational and production probably continues. 'Luda' class destroyers have two triple launchers for HY-2 missiles and converted 'Anshan' class destroyers have two twin launchers although there have been reports of some of these ships having been fitted with triple launchers. Chinese 'Jianghu' class frigates have two twin launchers and frigates of the 'Chengdu' class have one twin launcher. Two main classes of fast missile boat are operated by the Chinese Navy, both derived from their Soviet 'Osa' and 'Komar' class prototypes. The former 'Hola' class, of which there are over 100, have four single HY-2 launcher/containers while the 'Hegu' class boats, numbering more than 80, have two single launchers.

One of the indigenous production centres for the HY-2 naval surface-to-surface missile which is used in both ship-launched and coastal defence roles. (Chinese Government photo)

CONTRACTOR
Chinese State Arsenals.

FRANCE

1156.221
MM 38/40 EXOCET SURFACE-TO-SURFACE MISSILE

Exocet MM38 and MM40 are surface-to-surface tactical missiles designed to provide surface warships with all-weather attack capability against other surface vessels. They can be fitted in major and minor warships including fast patrol boats and hydrofoils.

The missiles are in the form of a streamlined body equipped with four cruciform wings and four tail control surfaces in the same planes as the wings.

Propulsion is provided by a two-stage, solid-propellant motor.

The MM38 Exocet's range is about 23 nm (42 km), flying at very low altitude. Its cruising speed is high subsonic and it carries a high explosive warhead.

Missiles are stored in box-type containers which also serve to launch them. These launcher-containers are mounted on deck in suitable positions.

The missile flight consists of a pre-guidance phase during which it flies towards the target, whose range and bearing have been determined by the fire control computer and set up in the missile pre-guidance circuits before firing, and a final guidance phase during which the missile flies directly towards the target under the control of its active homing head. Throughout the whole flight the missile is maintained at very low altitude by a closed-loop control system comprising a radio altimeter and the inertial guidance platform. The radio altimeter is produced by TRT under the designation RAM.01.

Twin tubular launcher/containers for MM 40 Exocet anti-ship missile

The terminal guidance phase (approximately the last 10 km) is by means of the ADAC radar homing head developed by Electronique Serge Dassault.

Subsequent to the introduction of the original MM 38 model, a number of derivative versions evolved, several of which have been produced in quantity. The air-launched AM 39 model is described in **1770.321** which appears in the section on air-to-surface tactical weapons later in this book. The surface-launched variants are the result of combinations of alternative propulsion motor configurations, new container/launchers of wound glass-fibre construction, and folding wings and tail surfaces. The basic warhead and guidance elements remain unchanged.

The MM 40 has a longer steel-cased sustainer motor than the MM 38, thus resulting in a further increase in range. The MM 40 homing head also has a wider angle target search and acquisition 'gate' commensurate with the needs of its greater range (more than 70 km). It is carried in a tubular glass-fibre container/launcher. Four of these launchers can be mounted in the space required for one MM 38 housing.

Essential differences between the four models of Exocet are illustrated in the following table.

To launch Exocet the ship's fire control system is normally connected to the ITS (Installation de Tir Standard, or Exocet ship system). The ITS is assembled by the Ruelle establishment (DTCN) under SNIAS as prime contractor, with several British sub-contractors. Among others, ITS is fitted on the French, British, and West German ships armed with Exocet. The Thomson-CSF Vega fire control system (**1053.281**) can be used in association with an inertial platform. An updated, digital firing installation, known by the initials ITL (installation de tir légère) is now being produced. It is capable of use with both the MM 38 and MM 40 versions.

In November 1981 it was revealed that development

CHARACTERISTICS

Exocet model	MM 38	AM 39	MM 40	SM 39
Length	5·21 m	4·69 m	5·78 m	5·80 m
Diameter	35 cm	35 cm	35 cm	35 cm
Max span	100·4 cm	100·4 cm	113·5 cm	100·4 cm
Weight	735 kg	650 kg	850 kg	655 kg
Speed		Mach 0·93		
Range	42 km	50-70 km	>70 km	>50 km
Warhead	165 kg	165 kg	165 kg	165 kg
Guidance		Inertial + active radar homing		

of a submarine-launched version of Exocet had been completed, under the designation SM39. This model is to be deployed by the French Navy, for which service the SM39 is at present reserved; there are no plans to export it. The SM39 missile is essentially identical to the AM39 model, but for operation from submarines a powered and guided launcher/container known as the VSM (véhicule sous-marin) has been developed. This is 5·8 m long and can be discharged from a submarine torpedo tube. In addition to the Exocet missile, with wings folded, it contains a gas generator which powers the VSM in the water and into the atmosphere. The container then breaks up as the missile motor ignites to take the SM39 over the in-air phase of its flight to the target. Weight of SM39, in the VSM is approximately 1345 kg.

The TRT RAM.01 radio altimeter carried by the Exocet missile, in conjunction with inertial guidance, is reported to be capable of permitting safe flight at a height of between 2 and 3 m above the sea at a speed of about Mach 1. All Exocet missiles are stated to have a fire-and-forget capability in that they are entirely autonomous in operation with a claimed hit probability near 100 per cent at all distances.

DEVELOPMENT

Development has been carried out by Aérospatiale in collaboration with the French Government military research establishments, to meet a French Navy requirement.

STATUS

Manufacturer's tests were concluded in July 1972. Evaluation trials by the French Navy, with the participation of the Royal Navy and the West German Navy, began in October 1972. These led to small modifications to the firing system and missile itself during 1973, and the launch of some 30 production rounds in 1974 yielded a 91 per cent proportion of hits.

By the end of 1982, over 2000 rounds of Exocet in all its versions had been ordered by some 27 countries, among them being: Argentina, Belgium, Brazil, Brunei, Chile, Ecuador, France, West Germany, Greece, Malaysia, Morocco, Oman, Peru and the UK. More than 1300 missiles had been manufactured by January 1982.

CONTRACTORS

System manufacturer: Aérospatiale, 2 rue Béranger, 92322 Châtillon Cédex, France.

ADAC electromagnetic homing head: Electronique Serge Dassault.

Altimeter: TRT.

Radomes: British Aerospace.

INTERNATIONAL

4446.221

ANS ANTI-SHIP MISSILE

The ANS (Anti-Navires Supersonique) anti-ship missile project was initiated by Aérospatiale and MBB as a replacement for the abandoned ASSM/ASEM programme (**3331.221**) to develop a successor within NATO for the Exocet and other anti-shipping weapons. The Franco-German programme is intended to result in a missile which will rely on high speed (Mach 2 or more) and high manoeuvrability (+10 g) to penetrate ships' defence systems in the future. Other design requirements include long range engagement without requiring monitoring or guidance participation by the operator; incorporation of programmable microprocessors to permit motor adaptation to evolving operational procedures and techniques; and the ability to be used with various types of ship or aircraft launch platforms.

In order to reach the cruise speed of Mach 2 soon after launch, ANS will be propelled by a ramjet motor augmented by a powder accelerator integrated into the combustion chamber of the ramjet. A new solid propellant propulsion system is being developed by MBB, and the missile system by that company's Dynamics Division.

Two experimental vehicles were flown in 1981 for testing the solid-propellant ramjet. For these tests they were equipped with a guidance and control system that incorporated a strap-down gyro platform, a mode computer, and control vanes, all monitored by a comprehensive telemetry system. The high-energy ram jet unit uses boron propellants, and for the tests it was assisted to cruising speed by a tandem booster consisting of an Honest John artillery rocket motor. The boron propellants were developed by Bayern-Chemie.

STATUS

Pre-development project.

CONTRACTORS

Aérospatiale, 2 rue Beranger, 92322 Châtillon Cédex, France.

Messerschmitt-Bolkow-Blohm (MBB) GmbH, Postfach 801149, 8000 Munich 80, Federal Republic of Germany.

Test vehicle for the solid-propellant missile ramjet propulsion system in MBB laboratory

Launch of test vehicle with Honest John artillery rocket booster motor accelerating ramjet powered missile

1336.221
OTOMAT ANTI-SHIP MISSILE (FRANCE/ITALY)
Otomat is an anti-ship missile intended initially for launching from naval platforms of any size from fast patrol boat upwards, but also capable of land deployment (fixed or mobile). Weight is identical in both applications.

CHARACTERISTICS
Length: 4·46 m
Diameter: 46 cm
Wingspan: 1·35 m
Weight: 770 kg
Speed: Mach 0·9
Range: 60 km (effective) 180 km (max)
Warhead: 210 kg including 60 kg of explosive
Fuzes: Impact and proximity
Guidance: Inertial cruise, active radar homing
Propulsion: Solid boosters; turbojet cruise

Otomat missiles are delivered in containers which also serve as launchers, the containers being mounted on prepared locations. Propulsion during cruise is by a Turboméca turbojet engine, the four air inlets for which are in the wing roots. Two lateral jettisonable boosters are attached for the launch phase. Target information can be derived from radar, active or passive search systems, or external data sources such as data link. The ability to gyro-angle the missile through ±200° obviates the need for any ship manoeuvres at launch.

Since stemming from a common origin in a joint Franco/Italian collaborative development programme begun in 1969 (see below), the Otomat system has evolved in several distinct Italian and French versions. However, considerable commonality exists between the OTO Melara and Matra models. The following paragraphs summarise the main differences.

A new homing head produced by the Italian SMA (Segnalamento Marittimo ed Aero) company allows Otomat to follow a sea-skimming flight path up to the point of impact with the target.

A Mk II version of the Italian Otomat has been developed by OTO Melara, the principal feature of which is the provision for mid-course guidance up-dating, thus permitting increased range (up to 200 km). This version has been adopted by the Italian Navy in which Service it is designated TESEO (see below).

Subsequent to launching, the Otomat follows a cruise phase towards the target's predicted position, flying at low-level under radio altimeter control and autopilot guidance. An active homing head is used for the terminal phase.

The Otomat is compatible with any normal target designation radar and fire control system.

The Otomat Mk II as used by the Italian Navy employs a command system that provides over-the-horizon operation. The complete sub-system comprises a shipboard guidance set (TG1), a missile transponder and an aircraft transmitter (TG2). Both the shipboard and airborne elements are comprised of items from the Marconi Italiana PRT 400 Series midcourse guidance system.

The PRT401 comprises a high-gain directional antenna, stabilised in pitch and roll, and below-deck equipment. The latter includes all control command and tracking units, and a high-power microwave transmitter, a high-sensitivity receiver and a four-channel position plot data extractor, all interfaced with the system main computer. In the missile, the PRT402 equipment consists of receiver and transmitter antenna heads and a transceiver with RF

sections and signal processor facilities. The PRT403 consists of two units, a high-gain rotating microwave antenna, and a transmitter, for mid-course missile guidance purposes.

There are several additional items in the PRT 400 series to extend the Otomat range of operational facilities. A lightweight shipborne guidance system, PRT 404 consists of a solid-state transceiver unit and a two-axis stabilised high gain antenna. The former contains a receiver, four-channel position data plot extractor and a klystron-powered transmitter, all interfaced with the system main computer. The PRT 404 is suitable for Otomat installations in hydrofoils, such as the Italian *Sparviero*, or fast patrol craft.

The PRT 405 is a helicopter tracking and two-way data link for use in Otomat midcourse guidance beyond the horizon. There are three separate units: transceiver, omni-directional antenna, and a display/keyboard panel. Total weight is under 14 kg and the system is thought to have been fitted in Italian AB212 helicopters.

To enable the Otomat guidance system to be used for operation of Ikara anti-submarine missiles (**6002.241**), a missile transponder that is located in an Ikara tail fin has been developed, designated the PRT 406. This is an all solid-state unit weighing less than seven kg.

A new folding-wing version of the Italian Otomat missile, and new smaller lightweight launchers were revealed publicly in 1984. At the same event (Mostra Navale, Genoa) a project to develop a system that will combine Otomat with the Ikara ASW missile system was disclosed. For the latter scheme a different type of launcher is employed to house a folding wing version of Ikara and the Otomat guidance system is used to provide both anti-ship missile and ASW guidance facilities.

The French Otomat Compact system also employs folding wings and a lightweight launcher, and this Mk II system uses the Erato (extended range automatic targeting of Otomat) guidance system that can control up to eight or 16 missiles on four or eight launcher deck mountings. The main feature of this system is its value in utilising the full operational range of the Otomat missile by virtue of the update procedure. It allows salvo firing, with two successive missiles fired at three second intervals; several missiles in flight can be handled at the same time, attacking one or several targets.

In this technique the helicopter or maritime patrol aircraft measures the bearing and range of the surface target and transmits them by data link to the launch ship. Meanwhile the latter measures the bearing and range of the helicopter and computes the co-ordinates with respect to its own position. After firing, in the midcourse phase of missile flight, a fresh complete detection and calculation process is carried out and correction commands are sent to the missile by a telecommand transmitter. Two-axis active radar terminal homing is an advantage, permitting choice of sea-skimming or climb-and-dive attack profile.

Otomat launchers (top to bottom): standard Italian pattern, French Otomat Compact, Italian Mk II lightweight

Otomat Mk II launch from new Italian container

Italian production Otomat missile

DEVELOPMENT
Development was started in 1969 with OTO Melara and Matra working in collaboration. Manufacturers' tests were carried out from 1970 to 1974. The production of series missiles began in 1975-76 for the Italian Navy and several other customers.

Milestones in the French development include:
1979: Qualification at sea board the frigate *Le Basque*.
1980: First firing (in May) beyond 100 km in the 'fire and update' mode.

1983: In November final qualification tests at sea of Otomat Compact with the latest version of the Erato ship-to-ship FCS for export sales completed with successful 100+ km firing from *Ile d'Oleron*.
STATUS
In series production in France and Italy. Operational with a number of navies.

It is not possible to identify the respective Italian and French production or sales figures, but the total number of missiles ordered by March 1984 was well in

excess of 750 rounds which will be deployed on more than 80 ships of various classes belonging to at least seven navies. There are also coastal batteries which use Otomat (**1337.121**). The Teseo/Otomat system is being procured for Egyptian, Iraqi, Italian, Libyan, Nigerian, Peruvian, Saudi Arabian, and Venezuelan forces.
CONTRACTORS
OTO Melara, La Spezia, Italy.
    Engins Matra, 78-Vélizy, France.

ISRAEL

6019.221
GABRIEL SHIPBORNE SURFACE-TO-SURFACE MISSILE

Gabriel is a shipborne anti-ship missile developed in Israel and designed for installation in ships from about 50 tons upwards.

A sea-skimmer, the missile is transported in, stored in, and launched from hermetically sealed, reinforced fibreglass containers which also hold the missile launching rail and the hydraulically-operated container door. The missile is pre-adjusted and tested and requires no further tests or adjustments after installation. The standard launcher is a single fixed cell. An optional configuration is three missile cells mounted on a single, rotatable pedestal. The missile, whose general configuration can be seen from the accompanying photographs, is powered by a solid-propellant rocket motor.

A sophisticated guidance and homing electronics system is carried by the missile, which was developed in Israel.

After initialisation, using target data obtained from the launching vessel's own sensors, Gabriel is launched on a cruise flight path to the target area under twin-gyro platform plus radio altimeter control. The first part of the trajectory is flown at about 100 m followed by a descent to about 20 m for the major part of the flight. After target acquisition, and depending on sea state, the missile may descend to a still lower height for the terminal homing phase. Despite statements that semi-active radar homing is employed, it is thought that the basic terminal guidance mode is I/J-band (former X-band) active radar, together with additional optional modes such as 'home-on-jam', and optical plus command link. A frequency-agility capability in the radar homing system has been reported.

A manual/optical alternative control system is available for use in conditions where radar guidance is not practical, provided the ship is fitted with the requisite sensors.

Three models of Gabriel have been produced, the Mk II having approximately double the range of the Mk I model (ie about 36 km) but in most other characteristics being the same or very similar. The Mk III model ,however, has a longer range but also is larger and heavier, using active radar guidance, and has enhanced performance.

Three modes of operation have been outlined for Gabriel Mk III, known to the manufacturers as:
    (1) Fire and forget (F & F)
    (2) Fire and update (F & U)
    (3) Fire and control (F & C)

In the F & F mode, target detection is by means of the launching ship's search radar and the missile is despatched to the target area to acquire and engage a designated target without additional data or actions after launch. Using the F & U mode, target data is updated by data link during the missile flight, this reducing uncertainty of target location, increasing hit probability and decreasing the effects of enemy ECM. For the final mode, F & C, the ship's fire control radar

Launch of Gabriel III anti-ship missile

is used to provide more precise target data for use in guiding the Gabriel missile. Other ship's systems, eg optical fire directors, data automation systems, etc, may be linked with the Gabriel system in the F & C mode.

The missile control console is manned by one operator and incorporates: a PPI display of targets designated for engagement by Gabriel; search radar raw video PPI presentation; alphanumeric data display; target designation to missile facilities; and launch controls. A missile control unit (MCU) computes all pre-launch data and controls the firing sequence, and the automatic tracking computer (ATC) in the same unit computes track-while-scan data and designates targets to the FCS, using video signals from various sensors.

CHARACTERISTICS

Latest Gabriel anti-ship missile seeker uses planar scanner and modular electronics (T.J. Gander)

Model	Mk I	Mk II	Mk III
Length	3·35 m	3·41 m	3·81 m
Diameter	34 cm	34 cm	34 cm
Wingspan	1·35 m	1·35 m	1·35 m
Launch weight	430 kg	520 kg	560 kg
Warhead	c 100 kg	c 100 kg	c 150 kg
Propulsion	Solid, 2-stage rocket		
Speed	Mach 0·7		
Range	18 km	36 km	36 km +

STATUS

Developed in Israel during the 1960s, the missile is now operational in fast patrol boats of the Israeli Navy, and is in service with at least five other countries, according to Israeli sources.

Sales and fittings of Gabriel are not widely publicised but it is no secret that the Israeli Navy operates the system aboard the 'Saar' class missile boats, and the 'Reshef' class boats. Other operators

(some officially unconfirmed) are Argentina, Malaysia, Singapore, South Africa and Taiwan. One of the latest foreign users of the system to be identified was Brazil, whose new corvettes are fitted.

The Mk II Gabriel became operational in the mid-1970s and the improved Mk III version entered service in 1979/80. In the course of 1982 an air-launched version was introduced and this is illustrated and described in entry **4529.321**.

Military parades in the city of Taipei in Taiwan have revealed a number of missiles having a marked similarity to Gabriel, mounted on the backs of military trucks. These are claimed to be of Taiwanese design and manufacture, and were named Hsiung Feng (male bee). It has been stated that these were for coastal defence applications. A comparison of photographs leaves little doubt that the Hsiung Feng and Gabriel are virtually identical in design. Further details appear in entry **4442.121**.
CONTRACTOR
Israel Aircraft Industries Ltd, Ben Gurion International Airport, Israel.

ITALY

2253.221
SEA KILLER Mk 2

The Sea Killer Mk 2 is a surface-to-surface tactical missile; powered by two rocket motors it can be launched either from deck-fixed launchers or from a trainable five-round multiple launcher and uses beam-riding plus radar altimeter guidance supplemented by radio command guidance when required. The missile's ability to cruise close to the surface of the sea is operationally important.

Sea Killer Mk 2 is intended to be integrated with a conically scanning radar assisting a fire control system, the missile check out, firing, and guidance control being centralised in the missile control console. No launcher crew and no shipboard maintenance of missiles is required.

CHARACTERISTICS

Type: Shipborne medium-range surface-to-surface tactical guided missile

Guidance principle: Beam-rider/radio command/radio altimeter plus optical/radio command guidance in interference conditions

Guidance method: By control of movable cruciform surfaces at mid-point on body. Stabilisation by cruciform tail fins

Sea Killer Mk 2 launch

Propulsion: Solid-propellant booster and sustainer. SEP 4000 kg st and SEP 100 kg st

Warhead: Semi-armour-piercing HE (70 kg). Impact and proximity fuzes

Missile length: 4·7 m

Missile diameter: Body: 0·206 m. Span: 0·999 m

Launch weight: 300 kg

Speed: Transonic. Subsonic after burn-out

Range: 25 km

DEVELOPMENT

Development was initiated in 1965 and the first prototype was completed in 1969. The system was fitted in four Vosper Mk 5 frigates of the Iranian Navy but how many are operational now is not known.

The Mk 2 version is used in the Marte helicopter-launched anti-ship missile system (**1651.321**).

CONTRACTOR

SISTEL SpA, Via Tiburtina 1210, 00131 Rome, Italy.

4195.221
OTOMACH 2 ANTI-SHIP MISSILE

In mid-1980 it was revealed that OTO Melara, in collaboration with other Italian concerns, initiated a study of the development of a supersonic successor to the Otomat anti-ship surface-to-surface missile (**1336.221**), provisionally naming the new weapon Otomach 2. The figure in the title indicates the designed speed of the new missile. No details of construction or performance have been disclosed but

it is believed that an air-breathing propulsion system will be used. This will probably be supplemented by rocket boosters to accelerate the missile to cruising speed. An operating range of 100 km or more may be expected with a warhead of at least 100 kg. Guidance and control will in all probability involve most of the major Italian electronics companies, but which of these will assume the lead role is not yet known. Neither is the technique to be employed confirmed, although command and active radar methods might

be expected to be incorporated in the complete system, in the light of the intended role of the Otomach 2.

STATUS

Project study.

CONTRACTORS

OTO Melara SpA, Via Valdilocchi 15, 19100 La Spezia, Italy.

NORWAY

1339.221
PENGUIN ANTI-SHIP MISSILE

Penguin is a surface-launched anti-shipping missile primarily intended to provide small, fast naval craft with a powerful striking capability against larger vessels. It carries a 120 kg Bullpup ASM-N-7A warhead at Mach 0·8 over a range of at least 30 km. An impact fuze is fitted and the boost and sustainer motor is solid-propellant powered.

The missile is mounted on a simple launcher which is built into a container which serves as protection against weather and also serves as packing for transport to and from the ship. This unit, the box-launcher, is delivered as a sealed and tested item from the base to the ship. Combined weight of box-launcher and missile is about 650 kg. Typical ship installations comprise six or more deck-mounted box-launchers. These are located on prepared mounts which incorporate an umbilical cord connection. When fitted, the missiles are ready for immediate firing and no onboard service or repair is performed. Automatic testing can be effected from the missile control panel in the operations room.

OPERATION

The Penguin missile employs inertial guidance for the cruise phase of its flight path, with passive infra-red homing to the target for the terminal phase. After launch the missile is thus independent of the parent vessel which is thereby freed to take evasive action or engage a further target.

Design requirements include missile range comparable to the maximum effective radar range for fast patrol boats and a passive mode of operation. Target detection, acquisition, and designation is therefore by means of the launch vessel's radar and fire control system. Upon target acquisition, the fire control computer calculates the bearing to the predicted point of impact and the missile inertial guidance system is automatically slaved to the Kongsberg SM-3 computer data. The missile is then fired in the general direction of the target. After launch, the missile follows a programmed trajectory toward the predicted impact area. This programme can be varied.

USN Mk III patrol boat launching a Mk 2 Penguin missile at the USN Cape Canaveral range

Prior to acquisition of the target by the missile's infra-red homing system this operates in a search mode, scanning a sector ahead of the flight path. Upon detection of the target, the homing system tracks the target and generates signals which are used to direct the missile to the target.

The Norwegian operational requirements relating to the Penguin system call for a warhead capable of inflicting serious damage on a destroyer.

CHARACTERISTICS

Type: Shipborne surface-to-surface tactical guided missile

Guidance principle: Inertial en route guidance with infra-red terminal homing

Guidance method: Aerodynamic by moving canard surfaces

Propulsion: 2-stage solid-propellant motor

Warhead: 120 kg semi-armour-piercing. Impact fuze

Length: 3 m

Diameter: 28 cm

Span: 1·4 m

Launch weight: 340 kg

Weight with box-launcher: 650 kg

Cruising speed: Mach 0·8

Range: Mk 1, 20 km; Mk 2, 30 km (max); 2·5 km (minimum)

DEVELOPMENT

Development was initiated in the early 1960s at the Norwegian Defence Research Establishment as a response to an assessment of Royal Norwegian Navy requirements. These two bodies and A/S Kongsberg Våpenfabrikk have worked in close co-operation since the inception of the programme.

Although originally designed for deployment on smaller naval craft, the Penguin system is well suited to use on larger vessels. It is also being constructed for use in coastal defence and studies have been made of its use from helicopters. In the latter case, minor modifications only are stated to be necessary. Additionally, a redesigned version Mk 3 without the booster motor and with a smaller wingspan is now being developed for use from jet fighters such as the F-16.

STATUS
Operational in 'Storm', 'Snoegg', and 'Hauk' class patrol boats and 'Oslo' class frigates of the Norwegian Navy, and on 'Kartal' class patrol boats of the Turkish Navy. The Penguin missile system is also fitted in Royal Swedish Navy 'Hugin' class patrol boats, and in 'Combattante IIIB' fast patrol boats of the Hellenic Navy.

The USN has completed a full scale technical and operational evaluation at the Naval Weapons Centre, Dahlgren laboratory and at Noto, Cape Canaveral. Penguin installation is under study for USN ships and helicopters as well as for the US Coast Guard.

CONTRACTOR
A/S Kongsberg Våpenfabrikk, PO Box 25, 3601 Kongsberg, Norway.

SOUTH AFRICA

4444.221
SKORPIOEN ANTI-SHIP MISSILE
Skorpioen is believed to be the name under which the South African Navy operates the Israeli Gabriel II anti-ship missiles (**6019.221**) which arm the first six 'Mod' class fast attack craft serving with the SAN.

These vessels are similar to the Israeli Saar class and three of them were constructed in Haifa, reaching South Africa in July 1978. It has not been established whether or not facilities have been provided for manufacture of this weapon under licence in South Africa, but no other fittings of the system have been

reported on other SAN vessels, which suggests that to date the quantities required have not called for any alternative to supply from Israeli sources. For details of operation, performance etc readers are referred to the entry for Gabriel.

SWEDEN

3976.221
RBS 15 ANTI-SHIP MISSILE
RBS 15 is the designation of a new generation Swedish anti-ship missile system suitable for use by both Swedish Air Force aircraft and Swedish naval vessels. The first installation will be in the Royal Swedish Navy 'Spica' class fast patrol boats, each of which will have eight missiles. They will be housed in launcher/containers, and this version will be delivered first, the air-launch model following later (**3975.321**).

The general configuration of the RBS 15 can be seen from the nearby illustrations and the air intake below the missile body will be noted. An air-breathing propulsion system has been decided on to provide long range allied to a high subsonic cruise speed at sea-skimming heights. Two solid-propellant booster motors will aid launch, but these will not be required in the air-launch mode. The mission profile can include a high-level cruise phase over a preset distance, a low-level cruise phase during which the

seeker head is switched on and target acquisition takes place, followed by a sea-skimming final trajectory.

RBS 15 will have a launch and leave capability and will be provided with an ECM-resistant homing head which will be delivered by Philips Elektronik-industrier. Prelaunch operations will be minimal in scope and all calculations will be performed automatically by an on-board computer. A radar altimeter will ensure safe missile cruise at low levels above the sea surface.

CHARACTERISTICS
Length: 4·35 m
Diameter: 50 cm
Wing span: 1·4 m; 85 cm (folded)
Launch weight: 770 kg
Weight: 600 kg (without boosters)
Guidance: Probably programmed autopilot cruise with height hold, followed by active radar homing
Range: 150 km (estimated)
Cruising speed: >Mach 0·8

Four launcher/containers for the RBS 15 anti-ship missile system are fitted near stern of this Swedish fast patrol boat

STATUS
Series production. A contract worth Skr600 million for the development and production of the naval version was awarded to Saab Bofors Missile Corporation (SBMC) by the Swedish Defence Material Administration in July 1979, and in June 1982 a contract was awarded for the air-launched version. SBMC, a company formed by Saab Missies AB and Bofors, is serving as the main contractor. Saab Missiles is the prime contractor for RBS 15.

The first export order for RBS15 was placed in March 1983 when a contract for the system to be fitted in new 'Helsinki' class fast patrol boats for the Finnish Naval Forces was signed. The RBS 15 will be the main armament of this class of ship.
CONTRACTORS
SBMC, Stureplan 15, 11145 Stockholm, Sweden.
   Saab Missiles AB, 58188 Linköping, Sweden.

Launch of RBS 15 sea-skimmer anti-ship missile from Swedish Spica boat HMS Piteå

2366.221
RB 08A
RB 08A is a surface-to-surface long-range cruise missile system intended for coastal defence and ship-to-ship use.

Based on the Nord CT 20 target drone, the missile is a rocket-launched turbojet-powered monoplane carrying a warhead large enough to destroy an average freighter. The complete system comprises the missile, the fire control system, the starting box and the launchers; of these the missile and starting box are common while the fire control system and launchers used vary according to the type of system (static coastal, mobile coastal, shipborne). The missiles are easily transported: the wings fold, and the amount of other equipment required for a mobile battery is not great.

The range of the system is not disclosed, but it may be noted that the Nord CT 20 drone has an endurance of 60 minutes and a maximum speed of 900 km/h at 10 000 m. Since the all-up weight of the RB 08 is considerably greater than that of the CT 20 and since the RB 08 has the same power plant as that version of the CT 20 to which the figures above refer, a substantial reduction in endurance must be expected; nevertheless it seems probable that the system range is more likely to be limited by other factors than by the range capability of the missile.
SYSTEM DESCRIPTION
The target is detected (by radar or by other means

such as patrol boats or reconnaissance aircraft) and the target data are sent to a fire control director assisted by a computer. On the basis of these data and missile performance, the computer gives orders to the launcher.

The missile is launched by a booster unit which separates when expended. After climbing and further acceleration the missile reaches cruising altitude and speed; the climb being interrupted at a pre-set altitude which is then held by a constant altitude device. In the last part of the flight the missile is guided towards the target by the homing equipment.
AUTOPILOT
The autopilot consists of a constant altitude device, a programmer, two free gyros, one rate gyro, a signal transforming head, and logic circuits. Signals from the homing head, the constant altitude device, and the gyros are converted to steering signals fed to the wing spoilers and the elevator actuator. Pitch demands are met by elevator movement; yaw demands are met by actuating the spoilers to roll the missile and then by elevator movement.
HOMING EQUIPMENT
No details have been released concerning the operation of the homing equipment, but it seems likely that it is a radar operating in one of the higher frequency bands and capable of distinguishing between the target vessel and the surrounding sea clutter. The homing head is mounted in the nose of the missile; the warhead is mounted in the middle of

the fuselage. It has been reported in France that homing heads for the RB 08A are supplied by Thomson-CSF.
CHARACTERISTICS
Type: Surface-to-surface cruise missile system
Guidance principle: Directional launch, followed by autopilot control, terminal guidance probably active radar homing
Power plant: Turboméca Marboré IID (400 kg static thrust). Booster rocket assembly for launch
Span: 3·01 m
Length: 5·72 m
Height: 1·33 m
Missile gross weight: 900 kg
Booster unit weight: 315 kg
Total launch weight: 1215 kg
STATUS
Operational with the Swedish Armed Forces but expected to be replaced in the 1980s by a new advanced missile system (the RBS 15, **3976.221**) for fast patrol boats.
CONTRACTORS
Prime contractor: Saab Missiles AB, Linköping, Sweden.
   Missile body and autopilot: Aérospatiale, France.
   Turbojet engine: Turboméca, France.
   Electronics: Thomson-CSF, France; Standard Radio and Telefon AB, Sweden; AB Jungner, Sweden.

TAIWAN

4443.221
HSIUNG FENG ANTI-SHIP MISSILE

This is apparently a licence-built Taiwanese version of the Israeli Gabriel anti-ship missile. As described in the entry for the coastal defence application of this weapon (**4442.121**) the many similarities between the Gabriel and the Hsiung Feng include the triple launcher which originally was a noteworthy feature of the Israeli system, and therefore the main performance characteristics and other details are assumed to be essentially identical. Readers are recommended to consult the above entry and that for Gabriel (**6019.221**) to enable the performance and operational features of Hsiung Feng to be estimated.

STATUS

Hsiung Feng anti-ship missiles are reported to be fitted aboard Taiwanese destroyers of the US 'Gearing' and 'Allen M Sumner' classes, in triple launcher configuration, and in single launchers aboard two classes of fast attack craft. In many installations the missiles are associated with Selenia Orion RTN-10X fire control radars.

CONTRACTOR

State Arsenals.

Hsiung Feng anti-ship missile on parade in Taipei. The coastal defence mounting, on semi-trailer vehicle, is thought to be the same or similar to three-round mounts used aboard ship. Following vehicle is believed to carry radars and fire control equipment employed in coast defence role (LJ Lamb photo)

UNION OF SOVIET SOCIALIST REPUBLICS

1155.221
STYX SHIPBORNE SURFACE-TO-SURFACE MISSILE (SS-N-2)

The SS-N-2 Styx anti-ship missile is a short/medium range weapon which is very widely deployed by the Soviet Fleet and the navies of many of its allies. Entry into service was in 1959 or 1960, but despite the length of service this indicates, new Styx installations are apparently still being made. This weapon also has the distinction of being the first of its type to have been used operationally, in the 1967 war between Israel and Egypt, and later by Indian ships against Pakistan vessels in December 1971.

The general configuration is that of a small aircraft, with a delta planform wing and a triple tail-surface arrangement. A jettisonable booster rocket is used for the launch and acceleration phases, after which an internal motor sustains a cruising speed of about Mach 0·9. Range of early models is estimated as about 20 nm (40 km) maximum.

Three distinct versions have been reported, identified as the SS-N-2A, B, and C models,

respectively. The main known difference between the first two is that the SS-N-2A has fixed wings while those of the SS-N-2B fold, and this variation is reflected in the housing for the two different models. Less is known of the SS-N-2C apart from its performance characteristics, which are thought to include an increased range of some 80 km and a sea-skimming terminal trajectory. The latter can be preset to a limit of 300 m, and a third party (eg helicopter or fixed-wing aircraft) may be employed for guidance updating at extended ranges. The SS-N-2C is also credited with a heavier warhead.

During the relatively long service life of Styx it is probable that several guidance modes have been employed, and references probably relate to various combinations of the following alternatives: (1) the cruise phase could be carried out under either autopilot or radio command guidance; (2) the terminal phase could rely upon continuation of command guidance, active radar, or infra-red homing. Over the years, the launcher/hangars associated with Styx have undergone progressive

changes and it seems reasonable to assume that the guidance apparatus also has received periodic updating, in which case all of the above methods may be employed in different installations.

CHARACTERISTICS (PROVISIONAL)

Length: 6·25 m
Diameter: 75 cm
Span (max): 2·75 m
Weight: 2300 kg
Warhead: HE 400 kg (2A/2B); 450 kg (2C)
Range: 40 km (2A/2B); 80 km (2C)
Speed: High subsonic

STATUS

Styx has been in operational service in its SS-N-2A version since 1959 or 1960 and is now widely deployed with Soviet Navy forces and those of numerous friendly states. Most widespread are the fittings on board the 'Osa' and 'Komar' class missile boats. The SS-N-2B model appeared in 1965.

Since the appearance of SS-N-2 missiles on 'Osa' and 'Komar' boats, there have been fittings on a number of other classes of ship, both Soviet and foreign. A later class of 'Osa' missile boat has also appeared ('Osa II') on which a new missile was deployed. This was (and in some quarters still is) known as the SS-N-11 but is more correctly designated SS-N-2B to acknowledge its relationship with the earlier Styx.

A total of more than 150 'Osa' class missile boats have been transferred to foreign navies, including those of: Algeria, Bulgaria, Cuba, Egypt, East Germany, Ethiopia, Finland, India, Iraq, North Korea, Libya, Poland, Romania, Somalia, Syria, South Yemen, Viet-Nam and Yugoslavia.

The People's Republic of China is another important user of SS-N-2 and after having been supplied with initial quantities of Styx missiles and 'Komar' and 'Osa' missile boats, the Chinese have now established their own production lines. In addition, China seems to have been the first nation to add Styx to the armament of larger vessels. The 'Luda' class of destroyers of indigenous design, but based on the Soviet 'Kotlin' class in some respects, has launchers for Styx (Chinese version) amidships. China has a number of Styx missiles deployed as coastal defence weapons. (See also **3984.121** and **3973.221** for Chinese applications of the SS-N-2.)

'Osa II' class missile boat of the Soviet Fleet showing the four SS-N-2B container/launchers (Novosti)

2976.221
SHADDOCK SHIPBORNE SURFACE-TO-SURFACE MISSILE (SS-N-3)

Shaddock is the largest of the Soviet cruise missiles. It is not known to what extent, if any, the missile that is installed in many surface vessels and submarines of the Soviet Navy differs from the Shaddock missile displayed (in its container) at Moscow parades and used by Soviet land forces (NATO code-name Sepal,

2975.121), but it is generally assumed that there are some differences: moreover it appears that there are several different missiles of the Shaddock type in naval use. These have been designated SS-N-3A, SS-N-3B and SS-N-3C, while versions or derivatives fitted in later classes of ship have provisionally been numbered SS-N-12 in the American sequence and given the NATO name 'Sandbox'.

Command guidance is used, and for surface vessel

installations the missile is tracked by Scoop Pair radar (**1324.253**) and course corrections transmitted to it by radio. Soviet technical literature has described methods of terrain following for cruise missiles, without referring to any specific missile but it is quite probable that a measure of terrain following capability is provided for Shaddock in its overland role. This relies upon a radio altimeter which would also be useful in the anti-ship uses of Shaddock. For the terminal phase it is believed that infra-red homing is used: but it may be assumed with some confidence that this is one feature of the missile that will have been affected by modifications in the 10 years or so that these missiles have been in service, the most likely development being the provision of an active radar homing head.

Missile speed is believed to be transonic and range is limited mainly by radio/radar horizons. With mid-course guidance the maximum achievable range is believed to be at least 450 km, but practical ranges are nearer to 180 km for missiles launched from cruisers and less than that for submarine-launched missiles.

It is believed that the standard warhead is nuclear with a yield in the 350 KT range, although the existence of alternative warheads of about 1000 kg HE and a strategic 800 KT warhead has been reported.

One of the most interesting aspects of this weapon system is the extent to which it has been installed in submarines and the length to which the Soviet engineers have gone to find the most satisfactory form of installation. Of several types of submarine installation the most elaborate is the four-missile

'Kynda' class cruiser showing fore and aft Shaddock launcher mounts (Novosti)

arrangement in the 'W' class 'Long Bin' submarine which involves the insertion of an additional section, about 6·5 m long, into the submarine hull and constructing thereon a streamlined conning tower in which are built four forward-firing missile launchers, in two pairs both inclined to the horizontal by about 15°. Other boats of this class have what is known as the 'Twin Cylinder' fitting, in which two missile

Shaddock launchers on a 'Kresta I' guided missile armed destroyer (USN)

containers are attached to the submarine's outer casing.

STATUS

Shaddock-type missiles are installed operationally in 'Kresta I' and 'Kynda' class guided missile cruisers and in submarine classes 'E2', 'J', and 'W'. The nuclear-powered 'E2' submarines carry eight missiles in pairs, the launchers being let into the hull so as to present a smooth surface. The 'J' class non-nuclear submarines have similar launching arrangements for four missiles. In the 'W' class submarines two arrangements are still current, one being the 'Long Bin' arrangement described above and the other the 'Twin Cylinder' arrangement in which two launching tubes are mounted on the deck aft of the conning tower.

The 'Kynda' class carry quadruple launchers fore and aft and carry further missiles with which to reload the launchers. The 'Kresta' launchers and all the submarine launchers can be elevated for firing but cannot be trained. The 'Kynda' launchers, on the other hand, can be trained through about 250° and elevated up to about 30°.

Submarines are believed to be armed with the 'A' version, while the 'Kresta I' and 'Kynda' classes of surface ship have the 'B' model. The SS-N-3C is thought to be a strategic variant.

Shaddock is also deployed in a land-mobile role as a coastal defence weapon under the NATO designation 'Sepal' (**2975.121**).

2987.411

SS-N-7 SUBMARINE LAUNCHED CRUISE MISSILE

Little is known about this weapon other than that it is one of the family of cruise missiles developed in recent years in the Soviet Union, that it is carried by 'C' class Soviet nuclear submarines, on a scale of eight vertical tube launchers per submarine and that it can be launched while the submarine is submerged.

The missile is said to have autopilot control and assumed to employ a radar homing system. Range

has been variously reported between 45 and 53 km and it has been suggested that over a large part of its flight path it operates as a surface skimmer. Other provisional characteristics attributed to the SS-N-7 are a length of about seven metres, either a 500 kg HE or 200 KT nuclear warhead, and a solid-propellant rocket giving a high subsonic cruising speed.

The submarine launch capability of this missile is undoubtedly one of the causes of the recent flurry of interest in submarine-launched tactical missiles

among NATO countries. Most proposals currently under consideration in those countries, however, contemplate the use of standard torpedo tubes as launchers, presumably because of the difficulty of retrofitting anything larger without denying the submarine the option of firing conventional torpedoes. The 'C' class submarine, however, was designed from the outset to carry both missiles and torpedoes and was thus not so restricted in its choice of missile design as are the NATO designs.

1760.221

SS-N-9 (SIREN) SHIPBORNE SURFACE-TO-SURFACE MISSILE

The designation SS-N-9 has been allocated to the surface-to-surface missiles carried in the two triple launcher/containers aboard the Soviet 'Nanuchka' class missile boats which made their appearance in 1969. To date, no pictures or official details of the missiles themselves have been made public, and hence performance figures must be regarded as provisional. No other class of vessel has been definitely associated with the SS-N-9, to which the NATO code-name Siren has been assigned. It has been conjectured, however, that the anticipated new 'Papa' class of Soviet submarine may employ SS-N-9 or a derivative as its cruise missile armament, although the existing SS-N-7 may be retained for this class of boat.

The original estimated range of the SS-N-9 of up to 150 nm (about 275 km) with external mid-course guidance by co-operating aircraft or helicopter was subsequently revised downward. A normal operating range of about 40 nm (about 75 km) seems likely and American and British sources quote a maximum of 60 nm (about 110 km). The missile is estimated to be about 8·9 metres long. Autopilot, with or without radio command link guidance, is the probable method of cruise phase control and active radar homing may be the normal terminal homing technique. The

Soviet 'Nanuchka' class missile boat. Triple launchers on each side of bridge structure house SS-N-9 surface-to-surface missiles. Also to be seen is the lid of the retractable launcher for the SA-N-4 anti-aircraft missile system on the foredeck (Novosti)

associated search and fire control radar group on 'Nanuchka' class vessels is reported to be code-named Band Stand.

STATUS

Fittings so far confirmed are confined to the 'Nanuchka' class of missile boats, each of which has two triple launchers, and 'Sarancha' class hydrofoils.

However, the possibility of vertical launch SS-N-9 missiles in Soviet 'Papa' class submarines has been reported. 'Nanuchkas' have been supplied to the Indian Navy, but in place of the six SS-N-9 launchers, four container launchers for the SS-N-2B (**1155.221**) cruise missiles are fitted.

4445.221
SS-N-12 (SANDBOX) ANTI-SHIP MISSILE

The designation SS-N-12 (NATO code-name Sandbox) has been applied to the missile system that is housed in the new style of launcher noted aboard the Soviet 'Kiev' class vessels. This is generally presumed to be an improved version of the SS-N-3 Shaddock (**2976.221**), and to have a similar purpose, namely long-range anti-ship engagements. An estimated maximum range of 550 km has been suggested. So far there are no known publicly released photographs of the actual weapon housed in the SS-N-12 launcher/container so that there is little firm evidence on which to base speculative assessments of the performance. However, its considerable size can be gauged from the external appearance of the launchers and from this it seems reasonable to infer considerable payload/range characteristics. An assessment of late 1983 estimated missile length at approximately 10·8 metres, diameter 90 cm, and wing span 1·8/2·6 metres, (folded/deployed). Another source suggests a maximum speed of Mach 2·5 and, interestingly, an altitude capability of over 10,000 metres. Operating at levels such as this, a need for mid-course guidance assistance from a co-operating helicopter or fixed-wing aircraft might well be eliminated. Autopilot/inertial guidance, probably aided by a degree of command updating at intervals and active radar terminal guidance would appear to be the most likely form of operation. The relatively long range assumed would also suggest that facilities for mid-course guidance by a co-operating aircraft would be a useful capability in the SS-N-12 system.

Foredeck of new Soviet aircraft carrier Kiev, *showing eight new-type cruise missile launcher/containers believed to house SS-N-12 missiles. Note also crane for reloading on starboard side and close-in air defence weapons* (RAF)

This last feature would be particularly valuable in the case of Sandbox engagements which involve launches of SS-N-12 missiles from submarines, which would be less well equipped than major surface vessels for providing target designation facilities.

STATUS
The SS-N-12 Sandbox is understood to be deployed aboard aircraft carriers of 'Kiev' class, on which there are eight launcher containers on the foredeck, and the system has also been reported in 'Echo II' class submarines. It is believed to have become operational in 1973.

4196.221
SS-N-19 ANTI-SHIP MISSILE

SS-N-19 is the designation assigned to the vertically-launched anti-ship missile system deployed on the Soviet battle-cruiser *Kirov* and also on 'Oscar' class submarines. Both these classes have provisions for launching 20 missiles and both types of ship first appeared in 1980. They could well be intended to operate together (with other vessels) as the nucleus of an 'ocean superiority' task force able to challenge western fleets over wide areas. *Kirov* and 'Oscar' class submarines are nuclear powered.

Very few details of the SS-N-19 missile system have been disclosed by official sources in the West (still less in Warsaw Pact states) but estimates that have been made are summarised here.

The main role is that of an anti-ship weapon, with a range of up to 500 km flying at supersonic speed (at least Mach 2·5 has been quoted, but this could well be an over-estimate), and both conventional HE and nuclear warhead payloads are thought to be available. Initially it was pointed out that no radar system associated with the SS-N-19 has been identified (on either 'Oscar' submarines or the *Kirov*),

and with a range of 500 km such a sensor could be of only partial relevance, due to the line-of-sight range limitations of radar. However, later analyses have claimed an association between the SS-N-19 Sandbox and a radar code-named Trap Door, which is located in the deckhouse immediately aft of the RBU 6000 anti-submarine rocket launcher in the bow of the ship. The precise functioning of this radar is not clear as it is certainly not sited for maximum line-of-sight range performance. Possibly some form of initial 'missile' capture after vertical launch is received to ensure the missile adopts the proper approach heading to the target. Thereafter it seems probable that inertial guidance, allied to an external target detection and designation system (satellite or aircraft, for instance), with self-contained homing is the likely guidance technique. Among the imposing array of sensors and antennas displayed by the *Kirov* battle-cruiser, it is more than likely that one or other is capable of providing data link or command link facilities for an outgoing SS-N-19 missile during its mid-course phase, for such purposes as target location updating or missile course correction. Clearly submarines would have much less capability in this respect, but if the postulate that *Kirov* and 'Oscar' class submarines are intended to operate together is correct, there is no reason why the submarines should not be employed merely as launch platforms with the surface ship (and its better sensor and communications facilities) acting as the directing and controlling element. It should be noted that the *Kirov* is well provided for helicopter operations; it is estimated that four or five Ka-25 helicopters could be accomodated, possibly including both 'A' anti-submarine and 'B' missile guidance versions. Close surveillance of these vessels during exercises in the coming years may yield scraps of evidence to confirm or amend this hypothesis, but even greater patience will be required if Soviet answers are awaited.

The Soviet battle-cruiser Kirov, *despite an impressive multiplicity of sensors of all sorts appears at first glance to have little in the way of armament. This impression is aided by the fact that two of the latest Soviet weapon systems fitted in this ship (SS-N-19 and SA-N-6) are vertical launch systems and spend most of their time below decks* (RN)

4761.221
SS-NX-22 ANTI-SHIP MISSILE

The designation SS-NX-22 has been assigned to the missiles housed in the container-launchers noted aboard the recent Soviet 'Sovremenny' and 'Slava' class ships which made their appearance over the past year or two. The former class fits a total of eight launchers (in two groups of four near the bridge), and the Slava class has double that number arranged as four pairs lining the deck alongside the forward

deckhouses. In view of their newness and the small number of ships so far fitted, the letter 'X' is included in the numerical designation for this system to indicate the fact that it is most probably not yet fully operational.

The assumed role is that of a naval surface-to-surface weapon with a main operational mission of anti-shipping engagements, and until more definite evidence is forthcoming it seems reasonable to accept the general conjecture that the missile itself is

a developed version of the SS-N-9 Siren (**1760.221**) first noted in 'Nanuchka' class ships. The first of the two new types to make its appearance (Sovremenny) is also fitted with the Band Stand radar associated with the SS-N-9 on the 'Nanuchka' ships, which tends to support the suggestion of a common lineage for the SS-N-9 and the SS-NX-22. On the other hand, the later Slava does not display an obvious counterpart to the Band Stand radar, but instead appears to rely upon a radar group identified by some authorities as Front Door/Trap Door. The first of these was detected in certain Echo II class submarines in association with the SS-N-3 Shaddock anti-ship missile, and Trap Door is claimed to be used for guidance of the later SS-N-12 Sandbox (**4445.221**) which is usually assumed to be a successor to the SS-N-3. Thus there is a reasonably clear 'family' connection between the SS-N-3 Shaddock, the SS-N-12 Sandbox, SS-N-9 Siren, and the SS-NX-22 in respect of role, function, and/or guidance radar arrangements.

The presumed range of the SS-NX-22 is in the 120 km category, but this suggestion probably relates to the missile's autonomous range using own guidance and the shipboard equipment. The 'Slava' and 'Sovremenny', however, have embarked helicopter facilities available that could be employed to provide extended range capability, and this might also be used to facilitate multiple target engagements.

No estimates of missile speed or payload are possible from the extremely limited information so far available, and for similar reasons conjecture about its appearance/configuration and other characteristics is an equally unrewarding exercise.

Soviet 'Slava' class ship has 16 launchers for SS-NX-22 anti-ship missiles alongside bridge and forward deckhouses

STATUS

The two 'Sovremenny' class ships at sea with the Soviet Union's Northern Fleet are each armed with eight SS-NX-22s. Another four ships of this class have been laid down at the Zhdanov Yard, Leningrad. So far only the first of the 'Slava' class ships has been seen at sea, having appeared in 1983; 16 SS-NX-22 launchers are fitted.

UNITED KINGDOM

4447.221

SEA EAGLE SL ANTI-SHIP MISSILE

Formerly known as the P5T the Sea Eagle SL is a ship-launched version of the Sea Eagle aircraft-launched anti-ship missile (for details see entry **3630.321** in the Air-to-Surface Missiles section of this book). It is intended for the arming of ships from 200 tonnes upwards and is capable of engaging a target well beyond the horizon. The system comprises missiles, launch boxes and fire control equipment.

Sea Eagle SL has a fire and forget capability derived from an on-board computer and an active radar homing head. Just before firing, target position information is fed into the computer which after launch shapes the flight trajectory. Mid-course correction is made using a bearing reference and the terminal phase is carried out using the active radar head. The homing head is activated by the computer to ensure optimum target acquisition probability with the minimum chance of enemy detection. Two rocket boost motors are used for launch and acceleration to flight speed at which point a small gas turbine provides further propulsion.

On board ship the Sea Eagle SL round is treated as a normal piece of ammunition with no need for first-line maintenance. The missiles are housed in boxes for environmental protection and the boxes also act as launchers. Inside the box the missiles are suspended from an overhead rail with anti-roll guides on the boost motors. The boxes can be arranged in groups of one to six on launch box mountings.

Artist's impression of Sea Eagle launching from ship's deck-mounted launcher

Lightweight Sea Dart mountings can accommodate Sea Eagle SL. Salvo firing is possible.

STATUS

Late development.

CONTRACTOR

British Aerospace (BAe) Dynamics Group, Bristol Division, PO Box 5, Filton, Bristol BS12 7QW, England.

4553.221

SEA SKUA SL ANTI-SHIP MISSILE SYSTEM

The Sea Skua ship launched (SL) anti-ship missile is a variant of the Sea Skua helicopter air-to-surface missile (see entry **1530.321** in the Air-to-Surface Missiles section) intended for use on naval vessels as small as 20 metres long. Sea Skua SL comprises the Ferranti Seaspray surveillance and illuminating radar or equivalent and a control console and deck-mounted launch boxes for the missiles.

The control console is operated by one man and would normally be located in the vessel's tactical control centre or on the bridge. The deck launcher is a lightweight unit mounted on the deck and holding one or more launcher boxes for firing. The launcher boxes can be treated as conventional ammunition rounds and double as transport containers. A two-box launcher, with missiles, weighs 850 kg and would be 2·5 metres long and 1·1 metres wide. The control console weighs 140 kg.

In operation Sea Skua SL uses the radar to locate and later illuminate the target. To commence an engagement the console operator selects the missile to be fired (ripple firing is possible) and sets the missile terminal sea skim height. When the missile is armed and ready the missile can be launched using the missile's tail-mounted booster rocket. During the boost phase the azimuth and height guidance loops are closed and the homing head locks on to the target illumination radar returns. When the boost phase is complete the sustainer motor maintains flight and the missile descends to an interim sea skim height under radio altimeter control. Later in the flight path the missile descends still further to the terminal sea skim height as selected before release. Four heights can be selected by the operator. The homing head then guides the missile in azimuth to target impact. The maximum range of the Sea Skua is 15 km.

CHARACTERISTICS

Length: 2·5 m

Body diameter: 0·25 m

Wing span: 0·72 m

Speed: High subsonic

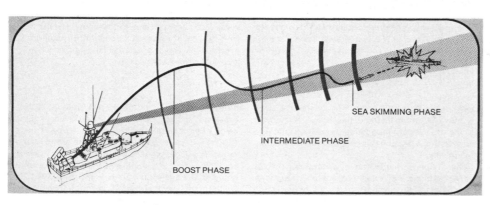

SEA SKIMMING PHASE

INTERMEDIATE PHASE

BOOST PHASE

Diagram of typical Sea Skua SL engagement

Range: Up to 15 km
Weight of two-box launcher (with missiles): 850 kg
Deck area: 2·5 m long × 1·1 m wide
Console (weight): 180 kg
Console dimensions: 975 × 600 mm × 1 m

STATUS
Possible procurement of the system by India has been reported.

CONTRACTOR
British Aerospace (BAe) Dynamics Group, Bristol Division, PO Box 5, Filton, Bristol BS12 7QW, England.

UNITED STATES OF AMERICA

4197.221
TOMAHAWK SEA-LAUNCHED CRUISE MISSILE (BGM-109)

The General Dynamics BGM-109 Tomahawk cruise missile has been chosen as the USN's long-range cruise missile. Another version is the basis of the air-launched medium-range air-to-surface missile (MRASM) (**4191.311**). Several modes of employment have been proposed for Tomahawk during the years of its development. These include a variety of 'strategic' roles, and these and the background to the US cruise missile programme in general will be found in earlier editions of *Jane's Weapon Systems* in entries **3993.011** and **1759.411**. This entry is concerned with the predominantly tactical role currently envisaged for Tomahawk by the USN, though sight should not be lost of the fact that Tomahawk has been selected for use by the USAF in NATO for the Ground-Launched Cruise Missile (GLCM) role (**4194.111**) as a major element in the NATO Theatre Nuclear Force modernisation programme.

Studies for the USN Tomahawk Sea Launched Cruise Missile (SLCM), designed for launch from submerged submarines and surface ships, were started in 1972. For submarine use the missile can be fired from a torpedo tube, while for surface ship applications armoured box launchers on deck or vertical launching systems can be employed. The Tomahawk family of cruise missiles incorporates a high degree of commonality in the basic airframe and major system components. Ahead of the mid-section on which are mounted the 'flip out' wings, a forward body contains the warhead and the guidance section, while the rear section houses the turbofan jet engine. A rocket booster motor is attached to the tail cone in the case of the SLCM and GLCM versions to propel the missiles from their tubes and accelerate them to flying speed and altitude where the turbofan can be started to sustain flight.

The SLCM is designed to be able to carry out both land attack and anti-ship missions using either nuclear or conventional high explosive warheads, and there are alternative guidance systems for each mission. These consist of the original advanced TERCOM (terrain contour matching) system which is used for both the land attack SLCM and the USAF GLCM versions of Tomahawk, and a specially modified version of the Harpoon (**2641.221**) missile

radar guidance system for use in the anti-ship version of the SLCM. The latter enables Tomahawk to be launched in the general direction of the target area to which it flies at low altitude to avoid detection by hostile radars, and at a pre-programmed distance the missile's active radar is switched on to detect and acquire the target ship. The TERCOM system used in the land attack version of Tomahawk uses inertial navigation to guide the missile to the target using the known location of the launch vehicle and that of the target, this being inserted immediately prior to launch. A pre-programmed flight path is followed to the target, with the terrain profile characteristics encountered by the missile along its flight path being compared automatically by the TERCOM equipment with computer-stored terrain data covering preselected segments of the route to confirm and adjust the Tomahawk's flight path.

For submarine launching, Tomahawk is loaded into a stainless steel capsule which provides protection during handling and underwater launch. At the moment of firing, the SLCM is ejected from the capsule and the torpedo tube. The boost motor propels the missile through the water and to the surface, and once in the air the boost motor burns out and is jettisoned. The turbofan cruise motor then sustains flight for the remainder of the mission.
CHARACTERISTICS
Length: 6·4 m
Diameter: 53 cm
Wing span: 2·61 m
Cruise engine: Williams International Corp 275 kg thrust turbofan
Boost motor: Atlantic Research Corp 3170 kg thrust solid-propellant rocket
Range: 2500 km (land attack version); 450 km (anti-ship version)
Cruising speed: 885 km/h
Guidance: TERCOM-aided inertial (land attack); modified Harpoon active radar homing (anti-ship)
Warhead: HE or nuclear (land attack); HE (anti-ship)
STATUS
In January 1981 the DoD stated that full-scale engineering development of the Tomahawk land attack missile with conventional HE warhead (TLAM/C) was going ahead for use aboard USN nuclear attack submarines, and the potential of optical scene matching area correlation terminal guidance techniques, allied to a conventional

warhead, offers a promising method of attacking fixed targets on land. Operational objectives for this variant, which will be deployed on nuclear attack submarines and surface ships, are to provide naval forces with a long-range cruise missile capable of attacking and neutralising enemy facilities and to degrade their defensive capabilities without resorting to nuclear weapons.

It was also stated that the USN intends to procure both the land attack and the anti-ship versions of Tomahawk for deployment on submarines and surface ships.

In July 1981 a BGM-109C Tomahawk cruise missile completed the first submarine-launched strike against a land target, located about 480 km from the launch position off the Californian coast. The target was at the Tonopah Test Range in Nevada, and it was reported to have been hit by the inert warhead carried by the Tomahawk, which was fully guided throughout the flight. Well over 50 previous test and evaluation flights of Tomahawk missiles, of various models, had been carried out successfully prior to this flight. Readers are also directed to entry **3993.011** in the Strategic Weapon Systems section for further information and background on US cruise missile activities.

The 1984 report by the US Secretary of Defense stated that Tomahawk had experienced some quality assurance problems in production, and that production had been slowed down from earlier projections until these problems are completely resolved. Once assured of this, it is DoD's plan to procure and deploy the missile in large numbers. The programme for fiscal years 1984-88 requested funding for procurement of 1861 missiles. Projected procurement for 1984 and 1985 was 124 and 353 missiles, respectively.

In 1982 McDonnell Douglas became a co-producer of the Tomahawk, when the Joint Cruise Missiles Project Office awarded McDonnell Douglas and General Dynamics contracts to exchange Tomahawk technology, in March 1982.
CONTRACTORS
General Dynamics Corporation, Convair Division, 5001, Kearny Villa Road, San Diego, California 92123, USA.

McDonnell Douglas Corporation, Saint Louis, Missouri 63166, USA.

On-board camera view of Tomahawk anti-ship missile striking the target after launch from a submerged submarine and flying more than 100 miles to the target. This was the first combined development/operational test of the weapon

2641.221
HARPOON SHIPBORNE SURFACE-TO-SURFACE MISSILE (RGM-84A)

Harpoon (RGM-84A) is a high-subsonic anti-ship tactical cruise missile operational with the USN.

This missile is officially regarded as the principal anti-ship weapon and has been designated for launch from P-3 and A-6 aircraft, BB-61 class battleships, FF-1052 class frigates, DD and DDG class destroyers, CG and CGN class guided missile cruisers, FFG-7

guided missile frigates, PHM patrol hydrofoils, and SSN submarines. The airborne version is described elsewhere in this book (**1301.221**) and the following description relates primarily to the shipborne version. The submarine version was described in **2441.421** in earlier editions of *Jane's Weapon Systems*, where details of the alternative launching arrangements will be found.

An all-weather system, Harpoon has been specified in a way that is intended to achieve operational

flexibility and adaptability to existing systems. The main body of the missile with its cruise-phase propulsion and guidance systems, homing and terminal manoeuvring systems, ECCM facilities and warhead is common to all applications. The aerodynamic surfaces of this part of the system exist in several forms for compatibility with various aircraft, shipboard, and submarine launchers. All surfaces are designed for quick attachment, are interchangeable, and in some cases folded for storage.

Launch of RGM-84 Harpoon missile from USS Fletcher

For all other than airborne launchings an additional boost section contains a solid-propellant boost motor. This propels the missile on a ballistic trajectory which it follows until the booster separates; after which the missile descends to a low cruise altitude, determined by its altimeter, and flies to the target under the power of its turbojet cruise engine. In the terminal phase the missile may execute manoeuvres to evade close-in enemy defences and enhance the effectiveness of its warhead. Aerodynamic control throughout is by four movable fins on the main missile body.

The weapon control system for Harpoon AN/SWG-I(V), is produced by McDonnell Douglas, with Sperry as subcontractor. Targeting data provided by shipboard systems are interfaced with the missile through this command and launch system. The Harpoon data processor, a general-purpose digital computer, receives targeting and attitude data from standard shipborne equipment (or from a third party for over-the-horizon operations) and computes the necessary missile and launcher orders. After launch, en route guidance is provided by a missile-borne system consisting of a strap-down attitude reference assembly and a digital computer; no data inputs from the ship are required by the missile after it has been launched. Cruise altitude is monitored by a radar altimeter and flight control commands are interpreted by electromechanical actuators operating on the fins. This guidance system is designed to operate satisfactorily when the missile is launched at any angle up to 90° from the required course line.

Terminal guidance is achieved by means of a Texas Instruments DSQ-28 active radar homing system which maintains its lock until final impact. Included in the terminal guidance system is provision for the terminal manoeuvre referred to above. It should be noted, also, that the high degree of manoeuvrability

CG-16, 'Leahy' class cruisers are fitted with two quadruple launchers for Harpoon anti-ship missiles

implicit in this terminal pattern also means that the missile is capable of engaging targets that are taking high-speed evasive action. The radar homing system is frequency-agile and this facility, coupled with extensive on-board computer logic circuitry, provides considerable ECCM capability to the missile in the terminal phase.

CHARACTERISTICS

Type: Shipborne surface-to-surface tactical guided missile

Guidance principle: Pre-programmed attitude reference plus radar altimeter in cruise phase; active radar homing

Guidance method: by electromechanical control of 4 moving fins (±30° travel)

Propulsion: Solid-propellant booster. Teledyne CAE J402 turbojet cruise engine

Warhead: HE penetrating blast type

Missile length: With booster 4·58 m; without booster 3·84 m

Missile diameter: 34 cm

Launch weight: With booster 681 kg; without booster 519 kg

Range: Over 50 nm (90 km)

STATUS

The USN operational evaluation was completed successfully in March 1977, and Fleet introduction was started immediately on surface ships and submarines. The airborne P-3 and A-6 application was implemented in the autumn of 1979 and 1981, respectively.

In June 1982 the USN took delivery of the first of an advanced version of the Harpoon, designated Block

1B. Based on the advanced guidance design developed for the RN, the Block 1B Harpoon flies toward its target at lower altitudes, making detection and defence more difficult for the target. In late 1982 flight test development for a still more advanced version, Block 1C model RGM-84D, was completed. This model provides increased range, waypoints, and selectable terminal trajectories.

By April 1984 more than 3400 Harpoon missiles had been ordered, of which over 2900 had been delivered. At that time it was confirmed that the Royal Navy intended fitting Harpoon in new Type 22 and 23 frigates. Submarine and aircraft launched versions already serve with British forces.

In addition to the US, 16 other countries operate the system and nine of them are NATO members.

The 1985 US DoD Budget indicated procurement of a total of almost 440 Harpoon missiles in fiscal year 1985 at a cost of $367.4 million.

CONTRACTORS

Programme Direction: US Naval Air Systems Command supported by the Naval Sea Systems Command.

Systems Contractor: McDonnell Douglas Astronautics Company, PO Box 516, St Louis, Missouri 63166, USA.

Propulsion: Teledyne CAE (turbojet), Aerojet Tactical Systems (booster).

Guidance: IBM, Lear Siegler, Texas Instruments, Northrop.

Radar Altimeter: Honeywell.

4213.211

USN 5 INCH GUIDED PROJECTILE

The USN's 5 inch guided projectile represents the initial implementation of a potential family of laser homing projectiles for use with standard USN ordnance pieces of various calibres from the 5 inch upward. The original operational requirement (OR-S0957-SH) was dated 15 April 1977 and a four- to six-year programme was envisaged. The operational objectives were to improve naval gunfire systems when used in support of army and marine corps amphibious assault operations by effectively improving accuracy against fixed and certain moving targets designated by laser target marking systems deployed on ships, aircraft or by ground forces. This would also yield considerable reductions in the number of rounds of ammunition consumed. Precision guided artillery missiles of this type will also be available for use against surface vessels, and to supplement ships' point defence anti-aircraft weapons against air targets. A range of munitions is foreseen which includes the 5 inch projectile with

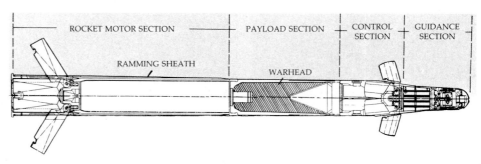

Cross-sectional diagram of the 5 inch guided projectile

which this entry is concerned, and later 8 inch and 16 inch versions.

The 5 inch guided projectile will be employed with the Mk 42 and 45 5 inch/54 calibre naval gun, and it features a semi-active laser seeker used in conjunction with laser designators such as the

Modular Laser Equipment (MULE), the new Seafire shipboard designator, or airborne equipments such as the A-6 target recognition attack multisensor (TRAM) or laser designator-equipped OV-10 aircraft. The projectile is fired from the ship into an acquisition 'basket' where its sensor acquires the reflected energy from the designator laser and automatically homes onto the target.

The projectile consists of four main sections: guidance, control, warhead, and rocket motor. A ramming sheath is provided to protect the tail fins and to assist the loading process. The guidance section houses the laser seeker head and processing electronics necessary to detect, acquire, process, track, and follow the reflected laser energy to the target. It also provides the preselected impact or height-of-burst fuzing mode for the warhead. The control section of the projectile contains a cold gas control actuation system, and batteries for the main system and timer. The payload section normally contains a 13·6 kg fragmentation/shaped charge warhead, but this space can be used for a telemetry package during tests, or trials.

The rocket motor section consists of a nozzle/fin assembly, a motor case tube loaded with liner and propellant, and a slip obturator. The rocket motor is ignited after launch from the gun barrel and provides a significant extension of the typical range of some 24 km that can be obtained with conventional 5 inch shells and Mk 42 and 45 guns.

Technical advances that were instrumental in achieving this performance included the design and development of miniaturised and shock-hardened electronics able to withstand the high loadings imposed by the firing of these shells (up to 10 000 g acceleration and 25 000 g shock) and the production of a new hardened gyro. Microminiaturisation of the seeker electronics achieved a packaging density roughly 17 per cent of the Copperhead land-based artillery laser guided shell, to fit into the 76 mm diameter nose required for automated loading into the gun aboard ship.

CHARACTERISTICS

Length: 1·54 m
Calibre: 5 in (127 mm)
Weight: 47·5 kg

USN 5 inch semi-active laser homing guided projectile

Guidance: Semi-active laser homing, proportional navigation
Control actuation: Cold gas pneumatic
Warhead: 13·6 kg dual mode, fragmentation/shaped charge
Range: >24 km

As mentioned above, 8 inch and 16 inch models have been considered and brief characteristics of these versions are included in this entry for general interest.

CHARACTERISTICS

Nominal calibres	8 in	16 in
Length	2·3 m	3·7 m
Weight	189 kg (+22·6 kg sabot)	1179 kg
Payload	61·2 kg	363 kg
Range	44 km	67 km
Launch acceleration	4000 g	3500 g

STATUS

The 5 inch guided projectile (GP) programme was started in 1977 and the planned initial operating capability (IOC) in July 1981. The latter date was allowed to slip by a few months as a result of reprogramming the funding in 1980. The 1982 DoD budget allocated funds for manufacture, test and procurement of 5 inch/54 and 76 mm rounds. Operational test and evaluation was completed in 1981 with successful results, and production contracts valued at $25 million were awarded to Martin Marietta in December 1983.

CONTRACTOR

Martin Marietta Orlando Aerospace, PO Box 5837, Orlando, Florida 32855, USA.

LAND-MOBILE SURFACE-TO-AIR WEAPONS

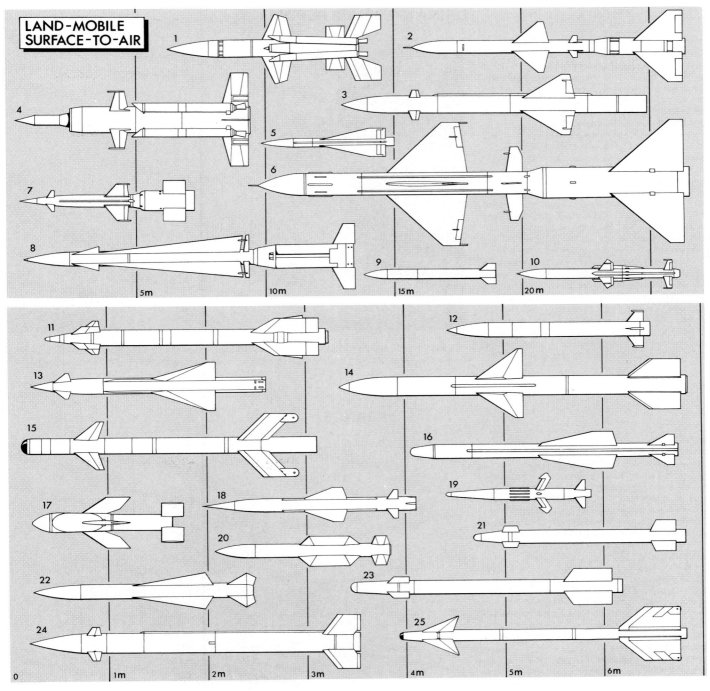

LAND-MOBILE SURFACE-TO-AIR

1 Bloodhound	**10** Gainful (SA-6)
2 Guideline (SA-2)	**11** Crotale
3 Guild (SA-1)	**12** ADATS
4 Ganef (SA-4)	**13** Roland
5 I/Hawk	**14** Spada
6 Gammon (SA-5)	**15** Low Strike
7 Goa (SA-3)	**16** Tan Sam (T81)
8 Nike Hercules	**17** Tigercat
9 Patriot	**18** Rapier

19 RBS 70
20 SA-11 (provisional)
21 SA-9 Gaskin (provisional)
22 SA-10 (provisional)
23 SA-13 (provisional)
24 SA-8 Gecko
25 Chaparral

2290.131

INTRODUCTION

Described in this section are weapons having a wide range of sizes and performance capabilities. All are suitable for use against hostile aircraft, and a few also have an anti-missile capability. All are to some extent mobile, and some are man-portable, but some of the larger systems take several hours to bring into action and are better suited to a semi-static defence role (eg of airfields or base installations) than to operations in defence of forward units.

Among the more recently developed systems there has been a noticeable emphasis on fast-reaction short-medium range weapons for defence against low-flying aircraft and tactical missiles; there have also been interesting developments in man-portable weapons capable of giving infantry units a degree of self-protection against aircraft attack that they have never previously known.

For convenience of system comparison, these mobile systems have been divided into three sub-sections - one dealing with mobile (but not portable) guided weapon systems, one dealing with mobile gun and rocket systems, and a third dealing with portable guided missile systems. While the first and third sub-sections are concerned with guided weapons which can be unambiguously distinguished from unguided weapons, there is some difficulty in defining the border between self-contained AA gun systems - which are described in the second sub-section below - and associations of AA guns with separate fire control systems. While we have endeavoured to follow a consistent line here, the reader may find it useful to consult Army Fire Control Systems in the Systems section, as well as the Land-based Air Defence Systems section where incidental references to some specific surface-to-air weapons may be found.

Mobile Surface-to-air Guided Missile Systems

CHINA (PEOPLE'S REPUBLIC)

2050.131

CHINESE ANTI-AIRCRAFT MISSILES

Little is known about Chinese developments in the anti-aircraft missile field. It is known that they possess a number of missiles supplied to them by the USSR before the two countries became estranged, and according to US statements of a year or two ago these are all SA-2 Guideline missiles (**2942.131**).

Some of these Guideline missiles have in turn been supplied by China to Albania and installed in missile sites constructed under Chinese supervision. It was at one time suggested that some such sites, as yet unequipped, would be receiving Chinese-developed missiles, but there has been no further news on the subject for a long time. It seems clear, however, that the Chinese must be manufacturing Guideline missiles at least, because according to US reconnaissance reports several hundred of the missiles had been deployed in China by mid-1973.

The Chinese preoccupation with the threat of a Soviet attack is evidenced by the overt and considerable passive/civil air defence precautions being undertaken, and it is reasonable to assume that these measures have a comparable parallel programme for the expansion of the armed air defence facilities of the Chinese mainland. These are certain to include surface-to-air missiles but no information has been made available for publication.

Chinese SA-2 Guideline air defence missile battery. This type of weapon is believed to form the mainstay of the People's Republic national air defence system and large numbers are claimed to be deployed. Fan Song radar is readily identified

FRANCE

4771.131

SAM 90 SURFACE-TO-AIR MISSILE SYSTEM

Studies have been undertaken by leading French contractors since 1983 (or earlier) into the design and development of a new surface-to-air missile system that could be suitable for use as either a land-based air defence weapon or in a shipboard configuration for naval applications. Provisional designations of the proposed new weapon are SA 90 (sol-air 90) for the land-based version, and SAN 90 (sol-air navale 90) for the naval model.

The principal collaborators in the study, Aerospatiale and Thomson-CSF, have signed a memorandum of understanding with the French Ministry of Defence providing for feasibility studies. Aerospatiale will be responsible for the missile and the launcher(s), with Thomson-CSF taking care of the search and tracking radar(s) and the guidance system (including fire control).

It has been suggested that the missile will be virtually identical for both versions of the system, with a probable weight of about 250 kg, carrying a 20 kg warhead at a speed of around Mach 3+. Range performance might differ between the two applications, with a short/medium range of some 5 to 7 km suggested for the naval variant, and a medium range/high ceiling performance more appropriate to the land-based role.

Thomson-CSF has released an artist's impression of a proposed model of a multi-purpose phased array radar for the system, in one of its land-based configurations (see illustration). Unofficial reports have suggested that this equipment will operate in the I/J-band of the spectrum to fulfil both search and tracking functions, and that the missile will be equipped with an active radar seeker to allow multiple target engagements on a 'fire-and-forget' basis.

Artist's impression of Thomson-CSF multi-purpose phased array radar for the projected SAM 90 air defence missile system, in the land-mobile form

STATUS

Feasibility study. The West German Government is known to have considered a broadly similar requirement in the land-based air defence area (**4772.131**) and the eventual possibility of a collaborative international programme should not be ruled out.

CONTRACTORS

Thomson-CSF, Division Systèmes Electroniques, 1 rue des Mathurins, 92223 Bagneux, France.

Aerospatiale, Division Engins Tactiques, 2 rue Beranger, 92320 Chatillon, France.

2074.131

CROTALE LOW-ALTITUDE GROUND-TO-AIR WEAPON SYSTEM (TSE 5000)

Crotale is the basis of a series of low-altitude surface-to-air defence systems designed for the all-weather interception of low-level targets. The system can be mounted on wheeled or tracked vehicles, on transportable shelters or on ships (see also **3972.131, 2111.231**). When vehicle or shelter housed, the complete system comprises an acquisition and co-ordination unit (ACU) linked with up to three fire units. Each of the latter is equipped with a launcher carrying four ready-to-fire containerised missiles and a tracking and guidance radar. The system is intended to counter saturation attacks on strategic or tactical positions or to ensure the protection of battlefield units. High mobility and a high degree of autonomy of logistics and operation contribute to considerable operational flexibility.

The short reaction time required of systems in this category is achieved by means of sophisticated automatic data processing and handling of the operational actions to be performed. The system can be broken down into two units to maximise the efficiency of the target designation, target signal processing and detection system by using it in association with several fire units. The automatic processing system is also capable of co-ordinating several air defence systems (eg Crotale, AA guns etc) when saturation attack protection calls for

Crotale fire unit vehicle

deployment of defence resources in depth, while not increasing risks of either over- or under-kill.

Crotale is installed on wheeled cross-country vehicles that employ electric transmission, and are of two types: the ACUs which control and co-ordinate up to three fire units and form part of an anti-aircraft defence system; and the fire units. The former vehicles are each equipped with a pulse-doppler surveillance radar with fixed echo suppression; a data processing system based on a digital computer which can handle 30 targets, automatically evaluating and tracking the 12 most dangerous targets and designating these to the most appropriate Crotale fire units or to artillery fire control posts; an IFF system; and an inter-ACU co-ordination system. The fire units each have: a turret launcher with four Crotale missiles in containers (ready-to-fire); a monopulse fire control radar that automatically tracks the target and simultaneously guides two missiles, using a very accurate differential angle-error measurement system; a digital computer; TV equipment which is used in clear weather or under jamming conditions for automatic guidance of the missile without radar transmission; and an IR angle-error measurement system for aligning the missile on the line of sight to the target immediately after launch.

All the vehicles are provided with an inter-vehicle communications system using cable and/or radio for the exchange of firing orders and data transmission, and a separate VHF radio system.

The canard-type missile is powered by a powder propulsion unit, and the rounds are housed in watertight containers which are used for transport and launching. The focused-splintering warhead weighs about 14 kg and is activated by a protected IR proximity fuze adjusted to operate according to the intercept geometry computations or on impact. Its lethal range is more than 8 metres, which is stated to be greater than the very low clearance distance provided by the accuracy of the angle-error measurement system (0·5 mrad). The system is therefore claimed to provide a kill probability of greater than 0·85 (0·96 for salvo firing).

CHARACTERISTICS

Type: Land-mobile, automatic, all-weather, surface-to-air guidance weapon system

Guidance principle: Command guidance by digital radio link

Guidance method: IR missile gathering; secondary radar missile tracking by target tracking radar; command control of missile control surfaces via autopilot

Crotale in operation. Note ACU to right of fire unit launching missile

Propulsion: Single-stage solid propellant motor

Warhead: 14 kg, HE, directed burst, fragmentation type with IR proximity fuze

Missile length: 2·94 m

Missile diameter: 16 cm

Span: 54 cm max

Launch weight: Approx 80 kg

Speed: Mach 2·3 reached in 2·3 s. 16 s time of flight to 8 km

Acquisition unit

Radar: E-band, tunable

Sub-clutter visibility: 60 dB

Target capacity: 30 processed per antenna revolution

Antenna rotation rate: 60 rpm

TWS: Automatic, 12 targets

Detection: 1 m² fluctuating target within 18·5 km

Inter-vehicle communications: up to 800 m cable; up to 3000 m radio link

Inter-sector co-ordination: 4 sectors separated by up to 10 km

Fire unit

Radar: J-band monopulse in diversity mode

Tracking: 1 m² fluctuating target within 16 km

Tracking accuracy: 0·3 mrad

Angle-error measurement accuracy: 0·2 mrad

TV tracking: 14 km range (max); field 3°

Typical target data

Speed: Mach 1·2

Altitude: 15 – 5000 m

Manoeuvre: 2 g/13 km

Radar cross-section: 1 m², fluctuating

Max engagement range: 13 km (50 m/s target); 10 km (250 m/s target)

Minimum range: 500 m

Max crossing range: Up to 6000 m against a 200 m/s target

Reaction time: 6 s from first detection to missile launch

DEVELOPMENT

Work started on the project in 1964 both at Thomson Houston and Engins Matra and a prototype missile was completed in the following year. Overall responsibility for the development lies with the Division Systèmes Electroniques of the Thomson-CSF group while full responsibility for the missile lies with Matra.

STATUS

Crotale is in production for the French Air Force and is reported to be in service or on order for the forces of about ten other countries, including Abu Dhabi, Egypt, Kuwait, Libya, Morocco, Pakistan, Saudi Arabia and Spain.

The Crotale weapon system has been developed into at least two specific export versions. Cactus (**2341.131**) was supplied to South Africa some years ago, at an early stage in Crotale's development. More recently, another version was designed and has been supplied to Saudi Arabia as the Shahine. This is described in the following entry (**3972.131**). There is also a naval version (**2111.231**) which appears in the Shipborne Surface-to-air Weapons section of this volume. Crotale in vehicle or shelter mounted configuration has four ready-to-fire missiles. Shahine has six rounds ready-to-fire in vehicle or shelter version, and Naval Crotale has eight ready-to-fire missiles. In mid-1983 a version was revealed that incorporated additional launchers for the Matra SATCP (Mistral) (**4198.131**) mounted alongside the Crotale missile launcher/containers, and training and elevating with the latter.

CONTRACTORS

Thomson-CSF, Divison Systèmes Electroniques, 1 rue des Mathurins, 92223 Bagneux, France.

Matra SA, ave Louis Bréguet, 78140 Vélizy, France.

3972.131

SHAHINE (SICA) AIR DEFENCE SYSTEM (TSE 5100)

Shahine (Sica) is a later, more powerful version of the Crotale air defence system (**2074.131**) which is being supplied to Saudi Arabia.

The system combines one or two acquisition and co-ordination units (ACUs) with two, three or four firing units each carrying six containerised ready-to-fire missiles with an effective interception range of more than 11 km. Its capability of controlling up to four independent but simultaneous interceptions, and its versatile, modular design, make Shahine (Sica) an efficient weapon system against saturation air attack.

The Shahine (Sica) system is a modular system which can be mounted on the AMX 30 type tank or any other tank similar to the ones to be protected; six-wheel armoured vehicles; or transportable

shelters for the protection of fixed installations. The last version can be moved by C 160 Transall or C 130 Hercules aircraft.

The system consists of:

(1) *ACUs* which can control and co-ordinate up to four firing units each, be co-ordinated with other ACUs and integrated with an air defence network. Each of them is equipped with a pulse-doppler acquisition radar with moving target indication (MTI); a data processing system based on digital computer providing the simultaneous display of 40 targets, automatic threat evaluation and tracking of the 18 most menacing targets and their designation to the best located firing units; a TV system featuring a TV turret concentric with and independent of the radar turret which provides ground monitoring of moving fire vehicles and optical target reconnaissance and possibly target designation

(2) *firing units* equipped with a turret carrying six

Shahine (Sica) on air-transportable shelter firing unit

containerised ready-to-fire missiles; a monopulse doppler fire control radar providing automatic target tracking and simultaneous guidance of two missiles with precise deviation measurement; a digital computer to manage the system; TV equipment designed to perform automatic tracking and missile guidance without any radar transmission, in clear weather or in case of electronic jamming; an IR localiser to gather the missile on the firing axis after launching.

All vehicles are fitted with a digital link for locating all the units of a Shahine (Sica) formation and for the automatic exchange of data and orders, and there are radio links between Shahine (Sica) units and external command posts and air defence centres.

The missile is essentially the same as that used in the Crotale system described above, but in the Shahine (Sica) application it is slightly heavier at a total weight of 105 kg. A more detailed description of Shahine (Sica) appeared under this entry number in earlier editions of *Jane's Weapon Systems*.

CHARACTERISTICS
Acquisition range: 18·5 km against 1 m² fluctuating target
Tracking range: 17 km
Service range: 0·5 – 11 km against 250 m/s target
Vehicles: Cross-country tracked type or heavy duty wheeled vehicles
Reaction time: 6 s
Missile acquisition distance: 500 m
Crossing range: 6000 m
Warhead: 14 kg
Kill probability: 0·9 (head-on target); 0·99 (two-round salvo)

STATUS
The Saudi Arabian Shahine successfully completed its trials programme with firing tests which took place in late 1978 and early 1979. Deliveries to Saudi Arabia began in late 1981.

As a significant element of a large inter-governmental contract between France and Saudi Arabia which was agreed in 1983 and known as Al Thakeb, two new versions of the Shahine system are

Shahine firing unit on AMX-30 tank chassis

being supplied. Announcing the estimated $4000 million contract in 1984, Thomson-CSF stated that of the two new Shahine versions, "one of them mounted on AMX 30 chassis for accompanying battlefield forces... while the other will be carried on air-transportable shelters for defending strategic bases and key installations. By comparison with the Shahine systems which are already operational with

the Saudi armed forces... these latest versions offer enhanced effectiveness against attacks with new weapons such as anti-radar missiles and EW."

CONTRACTORS
Thomson-CSF, Division Systèmes Electroniques, 1 rue des Mathurins, 92223 Bagneux, France.
Matra SA, ave Louis Bréguet, 78140 Vélizy, France.

GERMANY (FEDERAL REPUBLIC)

4772.131
MFS-2000 SURFACE-TO-AIR MISSILE SYSTEM
The West German programme to design and develop a successor to the existing Hawk air defence missile system in the Federal Republic is currently carried out under a collaborative study project known as the MFS-2000. This designation (which is understood to have been FMS-90) refers to a feasibility/design study for a surface-to-air missile system to operate in the 15 to 30 km range bracket. The broad requirement is thought to have many aspects in common with the French SAM 90 project (**4771.131** in this section of *Jane's Weapon Systems*) and it is possible that eventually there may be a more formal and stronger

connection between the two systems if there is a merger of the projects along the lines of other successful Franco-German weapon programmes such as Roland and Milan etc.

German contractors known to be co-operating on the MFS-2000 project include: MBB which will probably be responsible for the vehicle which is thought likely to be a solid propellant ramjet with vertical launch; and Siemens and AEG-Telefunken for the radar(s), fire control, guidance and other electronics. Siemens is reported to be working on a monopulse phased array multi-purpose planar array radar which would provide for the target detection, tracking and certain command functions, while

AEG-Telefunken's responsibilities are stated to embrace an active radar missile seeker head.

STATUS
Design/feasibility study programme. Many aspects similar to French SAM 90 project; possible eventual merger of French and German efforts thought to have been considered.

CONTRACTORS
Messerschmitt-Bölkow-Blohm GmbH, Munich, Federal Republic of Germany.
AEG-Telefunken, Postfach 1730, 7900 Ulm, Federal Republic of Germany.
Siemens Aktiengesellschaft, Hofmannstrasse 51, 8000 Munich, Federal Republic of Germany.

INTERNATIONAL

4158.131
ADATS ANTI-AIRCRAFT MISSILE
ADATS is an international project being jointly undertaken by Martin Marietta and Oerlikon with the aim of developing a highly accurate, day/night and adverse weather missile system having a true dual target capability, for engaging air targets or for use in an anti-tank role. The name derives from this dual-mode use: Air Defence, Anti-Tank System – ADATS.

The ADATS prototype configuration consists of an unmanned turret comprised of electro-optical sensor head containing FLIR, TV, laser range-finder and laser guidance sensor, and on which are also mounted a search radar and four missile launcher/canisters on each side. The complete assembly can be rotated in azimuth and elevated remotely from operator positions in the vehicle. The search radar antenna on top is free to rotate independently for surveillance purposes. Alternative mounting arrangements available allow for installation on a variety of wheeled or tracked vehicles and for shelter or container housed systems. In the prototype M113A2 system the commander and gunner sit side-by-side at the radar and E-O consoles, respectively.

ADATS firing at White Sands Missile Range, April 1984 (Martin Marietta)

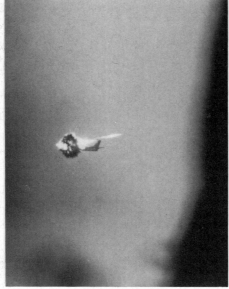
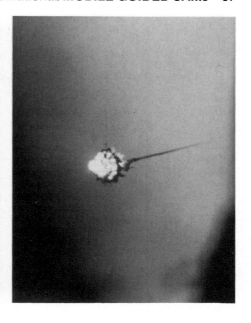

Remotely piloted target drone is destroyed by ADATS missile in tests at White Sands Missile Range, New Mexico, USA in April 1984 (Martin Marietta)

Each ADATS vehicle is regarded as a self-contained, autonomous fire unit, using its own radar for early detection of low-flying aircraft targets, or alternatively being incorporated into a network of larger radars for command and control. On detection of a target, it is handed off to the passive optical tracking system (either TV or thermal-imaging IR may be employed) which is immune to both anti-radiation missiles and ECM. Following passive tracking of the target, the missile is launched when the former is within range, subsequent guidance being by beam-riding using a coded carbon dioxide laser beam radiated from the launch vehicle. The dual-purpose warhead, with fragmentation effects against air targets and shaped charge for armoured targets, is detonated by an impact fuze or an electro-optical proximity fuze (aerial targets only).

CHARACTERISTICS
Missile
Length: 2·05 mm
Diameter: 152 mm
Weight: 51 kg (approx at launch)
Warhead: Shaped charge, dual-purpose fragmentation 12+ kg (approx)
Fuze: Impact and laser proximity
Guidance: Laser beam-riding
Propulsion: Solid, smokeless, rocket motor
Max speed: Mach 3+
Range: 8+ km
Ceiling: 5000 m
Search radar: Dual beam, integrated IFF
Search range: Over 20 km
Target acquisition: Radar, FLIR, TV, optical sight
Passive target tracking: FLIR, TV

Crew: 3 (commander, gunner, driver)
Ready to fire missiles: 8 with number of reloads dependent on vehicle type
STATUS
The first ballistic flight of an ADATS missile took place at White Sands Missile Range, New Mexico, in June 1981. This was followed by an intensive system and tactical test programme involving nearly 40 test firings, the last of which occurred in mid-1984. In 1983 helicopter mounted applications of ADATS were being studied.
CONTRACTORS
Machine Tool Works, Oerlikon-Bührle Ltd, 8050 Zurich, Switzerland
  Martin Marietta Corporation, Orlando Aerospace, PO Box 5837, Orlando, Florida 32855, USA.

2218.131
ROLAND MOBILE ANTI-AIRCRAFT WEAPON SYSTEM
The surface-to-air all-weather or clear-weather Roland weapon system is designed for defence against medium, low and very low altitude aircraft or helicopter attack. It is designed for incorporation into various types of armoured vehicles with the aim of including all operational weapon system equipment and functions within a single unit, such as: surveillance radar, tracking radar, optical sight, command computer and command transmitter link.

The weapon system is provided with two launch tubes each housing one missile, and eight missiles for reloading are stored in the magazine. After firing one or both missiles, reloading can be accomplished in about ten seconds.

Roland can be operated in either the clear-weather or the all-weather mode. Target detection is by means of a doppler surveillance radar with a PPI display. The commander sets the turret on to the designated target and then uses the tracking radar to achieve lock-on, or the gunner takes over target tracking and turret control. The target is tracked by optical line-of-sight (LOS) in the clear-weather mode, or by radar in poor visibility. The commander obtains fire authorisation from the fire control computer or passes authorisation to the gunner. The tracking radar follows the target and measures the angle between the LOS and the missile, while for optical guidance flares aid the IR sensors of the sight. Missile guidance commands are sent to the missile via a command transmitter.
CHARACTERISTICS
Surveillance radar: L-band pulse doppler
Detection velocity range: 50 – 450 m/s

FlaRakRad Roland II vehicle for West German Forces

Roland II on French AMX-30 chassis

PRF: 8·82 kHz
Scan rate: 60 rpm
Detection range: 90% on 1 m² target at 1·5 – 16·5 km
Pulse duration: 5 ms
Power: 200 W (average); 4 kW (peak)
Tracking radar: Ku-band monopulse doppler
Frequency agility: 250 MHz
Power: 10 kW
Beamwidth: 2° (azimuth); 1° (elevation)
PRF: 5 kHz
Pulse duration: 400 ns
Range: 16 km
Optical sight: Monocular
Magnification/aperture angle: ×8/10° – ×12/5° reversible
Missile tracking: IR goniometer, aperture angle reversible

Command transmitter: Ku-band, 50 kW
Roland missile
Length: 2·4 m
Diameter: 16 cm
Span: 50 cm (max)
Weight: 66·5 kg
Propulsion: 2-stage solid; 2 s boost, 13·2 s sustain
Warhead: 6·5 kg HE with proximity and impact fuzes
Range: 6000 m (max); 500 m (minimum)
Altitude: 5500 m (max); 20 m (minimum)
Speed: 500 m/s
Manoeuvrability: 12 – 16 g
Firing unit weight: 6 t
All-up weights: 32 t (AMX-30); 32 t (SPZ); 25 t (M812A)

A version known as US Roland, evolved as a result of the American decision to adopt the all-weather system for licence production in the USA. US sources state that this version is modified to give increased resistance to ECM and has a re-designed fuze. The fire unit can be mounted either on a tracked vehicle (XM975) or on a truck. The current US production configuration is on the M812A truck.

A different configuration has been evolved to meet the needs of the Federal German Republic Air Force and Navy. Known as the FlaRakRad Roland, this version is characterised by an eight-wheeled military chassis (10 T MIL GL) on which a special Roland shelter is mounted. This contains all the operational weapon system equipment, and is essentially the same as the Federal German Army version of Roland.

In the following descriptive passages, the Roland I and II versions only are considered.

OPERATION

Target detection in azimuth is performed by a Siemens/Thomson-CSF pulse-doppler surveillance radar on the launch vehicle. Threat evaluation is accomplished within a single antenna scan, and IFF facilities are provided by either a Siemens MSR-400/5 (West Germany) or an LMT (France) interrogator equipment. The former is produced under licence in the USA by Hazeltine for the US Roland.

The weapon system commander is also the operator of the acquisition radar. He selects the target and, in the Roland I configuration, directs the optical sight to the target azimuth. The gunner then searches in elevation and acquires the target, whereupon a missile may be launched. After launch the gunner maintains the LOS to the target and the missile is gathered to the LOS guided along this track by an IR guidance technique (TCA) which is described in more detail in the entry for HOT (**2212.111**).

In the Roland II configuration a Thomson-CSF tracking radar is used in addition to the periscope sight, otherwise the principle of operation is the same. Since one of the features claimed for the system is that rapid transition from radar to optical or optical to radar tracking is possible, it is reasonable to assume that the radar and optical axes are maintained in alignment.

The tracking radar is a monopulse type with a magnetron transmitting valve and doppler receiver circuits to reduce clutter returns. It is said to have a parabolic cassegrain antenna and to use circular polarisation. The antenna is gyro-stabilised in bearing and elevation – necessary because the radar is required to have a high resolving power and the weapon system is intended to be used, if necessary, on the move.

The radar deals simultaneously with the target and the missile, missile position in relation to the radar beam being established by continuous-wave transmission from the missile beacon.

Command signals are passed to the missile in flight by a radio link and the commands are interpreted as steering movements of vanes in the efflux from the sustainer motor. This command link is a microwave system.

DEVELOPMENT

In Europe a major improvement programme is in progress. For example: missile performance will be increased (range 6 to 8 km), and speed (500 to 650 m/s), and sub-systems having a direct bearing on either of these two missile parameters are to be up-graded accordingly.

US Roland leaves fire unit mounted on an Army M812A1 modified truck at White Sands Missile Range

An RCC (Roland Co-ordination Centre) is being designed to provide co-ordination for several Roland systems, and possibly guns. In a rather similar programme in the USA, tests have been carried out into the use of the Roland fire control system and its surveillance radar to provide target data for friendly air defence systems such as the IR seeking Redeye and Chaparral missiles.

STATUS

The first Roland production hardware began initial evaluation trials with live firings in March 1976 and the first fire units began deliveries in November 1977.

Euromissile handed over the first production Roland FlaRakPz to the West German Army in June 1981. In the French Army, three regiments are already equipped with Roland. A shelter version has been ordered by Argentina and two other countries. Argentina used one such system in the Falklands against British air forces in 1982.

The Brazilian Army decision to adopt the Roland system was announced in October 1972, and the first system was delivered in July 1977; the partial licence agreement is understood to remain in force.

In March 1981 Iraq was stated to have agreed to purchase a number of Roland systems, provided the political considerations will permit such a transaction.

US Roland entered production in early 1982 and was completed in 1983. The fiscal year 1985 budget contained no additional funding for procurement for the US Army. The US Army 1984 Weapon Systems handbook, issued in January 1984, stated that the US Roland programme had been restructured to field a single light battalion to be activated at McGregor Range, New Mexico by the New Mexico National Guard.

It was revealed in April 1984 that Spain has decided to procure the Roland system, the probable initial purchase comprising 18 fire units and up to 500 missiles. Other nations which have been named recently as possible Roland purchasers, though confirmed details are still awaited, are Nigeria and Saudi Arabia.

CONTRACTORS

System: Messerschmitt-Bölkow-Blohm GmbH, Munich, Federal Republic of Germany; Aérospatiale, 92-Chatillon, France.

Radars: Thomson-CSF, Paris, France; Siemens, Munich, Federal Republic of Germany.

Management, sales and responsibility for production: Euromissile, 12 rue de la Redoute, 92260 Fontenay aux Roses, France.

Hughes Aircraft Company, 8433 Fallbrook Avenue, Canoga Park, California 91304, USA – (US Roland).

Boeing Aerospace Company, Defence Systems Division, Seattle, Washington 98124, USA – (US Roland).

ISRAEL

4543.131

LOW STRIKE SURFACE-TO-AIR MISSILE SYSTEM

In mid-1983 Rafael, the Israel Armament Development Authority, revealed an air defence system for the protection of ground installations such as airfields, power stations, bridges and military bases. Limited details were disclosed but the system, called Low Strike, was declared to be capable of locating, identifying, and engaging low flying aircraft targets by day or night and under adverse weather conditions.

The system consists of three main sub-systems: surveillance radar, an optical sight, and the fire unit. The last of these is used to launch IR seeking surface-to-air missiles which are believed to be a version of the Israeli Python 3 air-to-air missile (**4185.331**), although the possibility of the earlier Shafrir (**1659.331**) missile should not be ruled out. The radar is probably the Elta EL/M-2106 point defence alert radar, or the EL/M-2106H which is principally designed for the detection and location of hostile helicopters. After detection of the target by the radar, the fire unit is automatically directed toward the approaching aircraft. Control is then passed to a manually operated optical passive sight or a thermal imaging sight for night-time use. Using the optical sight, the operator identifies the target and slaves the fire unit/launcher to the target's direction while tracking it. When the target enters the seeker's field of view, the operator can then uncage the missile seeker to follow the target. When adequate IR response from the target is detected the missile is launched, with no operator intervention, and the missile intercepts the target under its own guidance.

Each fire unit has launchers for four missiles, and the latter can be activated by either proximity or impact fuzes.

STATUS

Thought to be entering series production.

CONTRACTOR

Rafael, Israel Armament Development Authority, PO Box 2082, Haifa 31021, Israel.

ITALY

2250.131
SPADA SHORT/MEDIUM-RANGE AIR DEFENCE SYSTEM

Spada is an all-weather, short reaction time, point/area missile system designed to defend relatively small strategic areas (airports, harbours, factories, bridges, rail junctions etc) from low and very low altitude attacking aircraft flying singly, in close formation, or sequentially. The system is designed to inflict severe losses on such aircraft even when they are taking advantage of terrain masking and making use of sophisticated ECM devices.

Designed for integration with higher level air defence systems, Spada incorporates highly redundant friend/foe discriminating capabilities and employs the Aspide (**1656.331**) semi-active homing missile as ammunition. The system is modular in concept and its configuration can be adapted to optimise its deployment according to the extent of the objective, nature of the surrounding terrain, of the targets and of the threat.

The Spada system is organised around two main modules, referred to as the Detection Centre (DC), and the Firing Section (FS). The DC consists of the search and interrogation radar (SIR), which includes the SIR antenna pedestal and the corresponding equipment shelter, and the operational control centre (OCC) shelter. The FS, of which there are a number, consists of: the fire control centre (FCC) comprised of the tracking and illumination radar (TIR) antenna pedestal (including an on-mounted TV sensor), and the control unit (CU) shelter for the TIR and fire control equipment; and the missile launchers which have six missiles each.

Target detection, identification, evaluation, and designation for engagement by FSs are functions of the DC. The SIR (Selenia Pluto equipment, **3277.153**) is a low-altitude search radar particularly suited for operation in dense clutter environments and in the presence of ECM, and this provides data for the OCC. The latter consists of three operational consoles, a data processing system with two NDC-160 interconnected computers and a variety of communications links. The main functions of the OCC operators are those of checking the various system operations, setting up the zones in which automatic plot extraction and track initiation should or should not take place, manual intervention to substitute or correct automatic sequences, and selection of battery intervention criteria.

The FS represents the reaction centre of the Spada

Launch of Aspide missile from Spada system launcher at Salto di Quirra test range

system, and its principal function is to acquire and destroy assigned targets. At the FCC the TIR carries out target acquisition, tracking and illumination for missile guidance. As an additional mode of operation, the TIR provides for target search (360 degrees or sector), detection and self-designation. The TV sensor is used both as a back-up to the radar and as an aid for target identification and discrimination, as well as for kill assessment. The associated CU supervises these functions. Automatic or manual control of the firing action by means of displays and communications equipment is also monitored. The current TIR is an I-band Selenia Orion 30X monopulse radar (**1936.253**) with its own pedestal and mounted on a tower. However, at one stage a different TIR was under development specifically for Spada, and the Orion 30X (which is known as Falco in this role) will probably be succeeded by a new version, Orion 40, which will be mounted on a corner of the CU shelter roof.

The CU consists of an operational console, a data processing system that incorporates an NDC-160 digital processor, and a number of digital and telephone communications links.

A typical Spada battery would consist of one DC and its SIR, linked to two FSs with two launcher units and six missiles each. At present, most Spada systems delivered conform to this configuration of two fire units per OCC, but it is understood that the contractor has optimised the system for an arrangement of four fire units to each OCC.
STATUS
Field tests of prototype systems were completed in early 1977, with production for the Italian Air Force following in the early 1980s. Operational trials took place in 1982-83 at an Italian Air Force base. In late 1983 four Spada batteries had been ordered for the Italian Air Force, and the first of these was in place at the Italian Air Force base of Grosseto, north of Rome. Present plans indicate deployment of additional batteries at a rate of one per year until 1986, unless the programme is expedited.
CONTRACTORS
Systems and ground equipment: Selenia, Industrie Elettroniche Associate SpA, Via Tiburtina 12 400 Km, 00130 Rome, Italy.

Missile (main parts): Selenia, Rome; SNIA Viscosa, Rome; Microtecnica, Turin.

JAPAN

3619.131
TAN-SAM SURFACE-TO-AIR MISSILE (TYPE 81)

Toshiba (Tokyo Shibaura Electric) has developed for the Japanese army an IR homing air defence missile known as Tan-SAM (Tan = short, Surface-to-Air Missile) and officially designated the Type 81. The Japanese Ground Self Defence Force plans to deploy four Tan-SAM platoons of two quadruple launcher units and one fire control vehicle with each division. The quadruple launcher unit, which consists of a pair of launch ramps with a missile rail on the upper and lower surface of each, is carried on a Type 73 3·5-ton heavy truck. Each missile is loaded onto the launcher by an hydraulic loading mechanism on each side of the vehicle; the missile which is housed in a box container, is placed on the loader manually by the crew after removing the container cover. Four rounds can be loaded in three minutes.

The Tan-SAM missile is similar in appearance to the British Rapier and is powered by a solid-propellant rocket motor giving an effective range of about 7 km. The missile fuselage carries cruciform wings near the mid-point and there are cruciform control surfaces at the tail. The fire control system (FCS) is carried on a modified version of the Type 73 truck and consists of planar phased-array pulse-doppler three-dimensional radar for search and target detection and designation. The commander and radar operator are housed in a cabin equipped with three CRT displays, keyboards and other controls. The radar antenna is slewed mechanically in

Tan-SAM loaded on lower left side of standard four-round launcher unit during proving trials of the system

azimuth and elevation to face the threatened area. Each launcher vehicle can be separated from the FCS vehicle up to 1000 metres, but a distance of 300 metres is more usual; connections between the

vehicles for the transmission of target designation, firing orders etc, are by cables.

Up to six targets can be tracked by the radar simultaneously, and the radar detection range is estimated at about 20 to 30 km. All targets detected are displayed on the FCS PPI CRT and the commander selects those which are to be tracked. These are then separately displayed with threat evaluation symbols. Two targets are selected for engagement and the appropriate launcher unit receives target designation data which activates a search pattern by the missile IR homing head and at the same time inserts a pre-programmed autopilot interception course for the missile when lock-on has been achieved. After launch, the missile flies the initial part of its trajectory under automatic pilot control until homing head re-acquisition of the target is accomplished. This in-flight lock-on facility enables dual engagements and rapid engagement of additional targets during the flight of previously launched missiles before they have reached their target(s).

Each launcher vehicle is equipped with an optical

director for use as a standby target designator if ECM or other difficulties rule out radar designation. Special precautions are incorporated in the IF search pattern scanning program to reduce the problems of false acquisition due to the sun and much of this programming adjustment is performed automatically before launch by the computer in the FCS equipment.

CHARACTERISTICS

Type: Surface-to-air, short range
Length: 2·7 m
Diameter: 16 cm
Weight: 100 kg
Speed: Mach 2·4 (approx)
Effective range: 7000 m
Propulsion: Single-stage solid
Warhead: HE, contact and proximity fuzes
Guidance: Autopilot initial phase, in-flight IR lock-on and terminal homing. Radar target designation with optical director back-up

DEVELOPMENT
Development started in 1966 as a replacement anti-aircraft weapon for Japanese Ground Self Defence Force. First complete prototype constructed between 1971-76. Live prototypes produced between 1977-79. Experimental fire control radar built in 1970, with prototypes between 1972 and 1974. Development is estimated to have cost about £21 million.

STATUS
It was expected that Tan-SAM would be entering service for protection of Japanese airfields from 1982-83 onward and procurement plans have mentioned a total of 24 platoons, with deployment initially to the four northern divisions in Hokkaido.

CONTRACTOR
Toshiba (Tokyo Shibaura Electric) Co Ltd, 1-6 Uchisai-wacho, 1-Chome, Chiyoda-ku, Tokyo 100, Japan.

SOUTH AFRICA

2341.131
CACTUS
Cactus is the name given to one of the Crotale land-mobile surface-to-air guided weapon systems which is in service with the South African Air Force.

Crotale is described elsewhere in this section (**2074.131**). The Crotale system has undergone some changes in the course of development, and it may well be that the system in service in South Africa is rather different from that which has been supplied elsewhere.

It is interesting to note that the Cactus units in South Africa are linked directly to the early warning radar network which covers the north-east and north-west approaches to the Republic and which has its headquarters at Devon in the Eastern Transvaal. A Mirage interceptor squadron is also linked to the network.

In early 1981 it was reported that six Cactus units no

Cactus fire control unit vehicle

South African Cactus fire unit during a military parade

longer required by the South African forces had been re-acquired by Matra and sold to Chile for use there.

SWEDEN

3617.131
VEHICLE-MOUNTED RBS 70 ANTI-AIRCRAFT MISSILE
Bofors has produced new versions of the well-known RBS 70 anti-aircraft laser-guided missile system. One is mounted on any suitable army vehicle and is known as the RBS 70 VLM (vehicle launched missile), and another is mounted on an armoured vehicle and is known as RBS 70 ARMAD. Both systems are now completely tested and ready for production.

RBS 70 VLM is very similar to the man-portable RBS 70 (**2348.131**). It mounts on a special stand secured to the floor of the vehicle. It can be folded down when in transit and covered with a folding hood. Six missiles

are normally carried in the vehicle. The system is designed to accompany units on the move and is fitted to receive warning information from mobile search radars. When hostile aircraft are detected by the radar, an alarm is activated in the VLM vehicle and the bearing and range of approaching hostile aircraft are received by a data link from the radar, on a target data receiver mounted in the vehicle cabin.

The crew consists of the commander and the missile operator/driver. When in motion the crew sits in the cab. When alerted by an alarm they drive the vehicle to the nearest suitable site to counter the attack. The operator then erects the stand with its sight attached, loads a missile and takes his position

on the seat attached to the stand. The commander orientates the firing unit and then returns to his combat position in the cab and operates the target data receiver and his radio transceiver. The operator launches the missile and keeps his laser beam on the target while the missile is automatically guided to keep within the beam's direction. Set-up time for the VLM from the moment of a radar warning alarm of an attack can be as short as 30 seconds.

RBS 70 ARMAD consists of an armoured three-man turret mounted on any suitable APC (Bofors have used an M113A1 as prototype). The fire-control system used with ARMAD is an Ericsson solid-state 3-D radar known as HARD, which can detect and discriminate hovering helicopter targets. It provides search, acquisition and track-while-scan functions. The box-shaped antenna can be elevated and is in operation all the time the vehicle is on the alert while on the move, and is electronically stabilised. The HARD radar provides the commander and gunner inside the turret with small displays on which distinct signals are provided for helicopters and strike aircraft. The radar system provides data to a central fire-control computer, and from target acquisition to actually firing the RBS 70 missile the delay can be as little as four seconds. The radar provides ARMAD with a limited all-weather capability, for although the radar can track a target through cloud the gunner must be able to see the target in his sight to provide the missile its laser guidance.

The RBS 70 missiles themselves are stacked vertically inside the right-hand side of the turret and are loaded manually on to the launcher arm which swings up to a horizontal position above the roof passing through an automatically opening and closing armoured door. Once the missile has been fired the spent launcher tube is ejected and the arm lowers for a new round to be loaded. The turret holds seven missiles. The ARMAD crew comprises: commander, gunner and driver. The gunner uses a normal RBS 70 system laser sight. When not in use the antenna arm is lowered on to the turret roof.

RBS 70 ARMAD version on M113 chassis. Turret carries missile launcher, HARD radar, missiles and crew of 2

RBS 70 APC. In addition to the RBS 70 ARMAD version, a simpler model suitable for use in the open hatch of an APC is also being developed. This consists of a sight and loaded missile container mounted on a stand. When required for action the cover of the missile compartment is folded down and the stand and missile container is raised into the firing position.

RBS 70M under Swedish government contracts amounting to between SKr 300 and SKr 400, a night/all-weather version of the RBS 70 system has reached the full-scale development stage. This has been designated RBS 70M, where M denotes Mörker, the Swedish word for darkness. This model has an enlarged engagement envelope, larger warhead and a more powerful booster motor which is reported to

give a range extension of 30 to 50 per cent. A developmental model has been engineered and used in test firings. This has a tripod-mounted, two-round launcher with remotely operated azimuth and elevation for unmanned operation, and vehicle- and ship-mounted versions are also planned. Firings of RBS 70 were made from the deck of a Swedish naval vessel in early 1984.

The details given in the following table relate to the standard RBS 70.

CHARACTERISTICS
Length: 1·32 m (without booster)
Diameter: 106 mm (without booster)
Guidance: Laser beam-riding
Warhead: HE fragmentation
Fuze: Proximity, active laser

Range: 5 km
Altitude coverage: 3000 m
Reaction time: 5 s (RBS 70 VLM deployed); 4·5 s (ARMAD deployed)
Time of flight to 3 km: 8·5 s
ARMAD radar: HARD, 3-D pulse-doppler
Frequency: I-band
Detection range: 9-10 km (helicopters); 10-12 km (aircraft) 90% probability
STATUS
Prototypes tested and ready for production.
CONTRACTOR
AB Bofors Ordnance Division, Box 500, 691 80 Bofors, Sweden.

UNION OF SOVIET SOCIALIST REPUBLICS

2944.131
SA-1 (GUILD) SURFACE-TO-AIR MISSILE
Guild is the NATO code-name for an anti-aircraft guided missile system first shown in Moscow in 1960 and identified by the number SA-1 in the US alpha-numeric sequence.

About 12 metres long and 70 cm in diameter, this missile has no separate booster stage and is said by official sources to be liquid-propelled. Movable cruciform foreplane surfaces are another feature of the missile that distinguishes it from Guideline (SA-2, **2942.131**), which has movable tail surfaces but which is otherwise generally of much the same size as Guild. A UK MoD report of April 1976 mentions a range of 32 km for the SA-1 which is confirmed in later official US sources.

STATUS
It is doubtful if this weapon remains operational although it is possible that a small number might be retained on a reserve basis in the Soviet Union.

Guild missiles in May Day parade in Moscow (Tass)

2942.131
SA-2 (GUIDELINE) MEDIUM-RANGE SURFACE-TO-AIR MISSILE
Guideline is the NATO code-name for a medium-range, anti-aircraft guided weapon system, known also by the US alpha-numeric code as SA-2, which is standard equipment in the Soviet forces and which has been exported in large numbers to many countries outside the Warsaw Pact territory, including Cuba, Egypt, Indonesia, Iraq, Viet-Nam and Yugoslavia. Guideline missiles were used against US B-52 bombers during the bombing raids on North Viet-Nam prior to the peace settlement. Initially they scored a number of successes; but subsequently it appeared that the B-52 ECM equipment was more than a match for such ECCM equipment as the North Vietnamese had available.

The Soviet designation for the missile, or one

version thereof, is believed to be V750VK and that of the complete weapon system, including radar and power supplies, V75SM. The system is land-mobile, the missile being mounted on a Zil 157 cross-country semi-trailer transporter-erector.

Various models of the missile have been observed over the years exhibiting relatively minor changes in external appearances. The details given below relate to a type that was supplied to Egypt, but it is known that later versions exist. In particular, one that was seen in Moscow in 1967 is somewhat longer and has a larger warhead.

CHARACTERISTICS
Type: Surface-to-air tactical guided missile
Guidance principle: Radio command
Guidance method: By control of movable tail surfaces
Propulsion: Solid-propellant booster with liquid propellant sustainer

Warhead: HE 130 kg, proximity fuze
Missile length: 10·7 m
Missile diameter: Booster 70 cm; second stage 50 cm
Launch weight: About 2300 kg
Slant range: 40-50 km
Speed: Mach 3·5 (estimated)
Ceiling: 18 000 m
OPERATION
The radio command guidance system is believed to be quite straightforward. Targets are tracked by radar which feeds data to a computer: this in turn produces signals which modulate the output of the command transmitter. Two sets of four strip antennas are mounted fore and aft of the missile wings to receive these signals.

Radar used in conjunction with these missiles is generally that known to NATO as Fan Song (**2866.153** and **2868.153**). It is said that one problem with the fire control and guidance system is that the missile must be gathered to the radar beam in the first six seconds of flight or it will not be acquired at all.

According to reports published in the American press concerning Israeli experiences with Egyptian Guideline installations, it was at first found that Israeli ECM devices were adequate to deflect the beam-riding missiles. Subsequently, however, improved missiles were introduced having terminal guidance radar with a wider range of frequencies than the Israeli ECM could handle. They were, however, able to obtain improved ECM pods from the USA which they successfully used to jam the missile acquisition, tracking, and guidance systems.

Various warhead and fuze arrangements have been reported. Most of the missiles have high-explosive warheads but contact, proximity, and command fuzes have been reported. Furthermore, the larger version of the missile referred to above as having been first seen in 1967 is believed to have a nuclear warhead.

Recent reports refer to other modifications, including the introduction of optical techniques into the guidance system to give improved ECCM capabilities and low-altitude performance.
STATUS
Operational with the armed forces of the USSR since 1958, and in many other countries. Since the Soviet authorities generally appear reluctant to discard from

SA-2 Guideline medium-range AA missile on semi-trailer transporter

their inventory any weapon which continues to work reasonably well, it is likely that Guideline will remain in service for some years but the number deployed in the USSR is expected to decline in the coming years. Despite various modifications, however, it is now technologically obsolescent and unlikely to be very effective against an enemy able to deploy reasonably sophisticated ECM equipment.

In January 1976 the US Secretary of Defense reported that there had been a further decline in the number of active Soviet SA-2 sites. As Soviet use of this weapon declines (and support facilities become increasingly difficult) it is probable that its use among many of the client states equipped with it will diminish also.

Soviet client countries reported to have received the SA-2 Guideline include: Afghanistan, Albania, Algeria, Bulgaria, China, Cuba, Czechoslovakia, Egypt, East Germany, Hungary, India, Iraq, North Korea, Libya, Poland, Romania, Viet-Nam and Yugoslavia. Some of these nations may well have introduced modifications of varying degrees to suit their own purposes, and China is thought to have established its own production line at one time.

2938.131
SA-3 (GOA) SURFACE-TO-AIR MISSILE

Goa is the NATO code-name for the SA-3 anti-aircraft guided missile used both by the Soviet Army and the Soviet Navy.

Small enough to be carried in pairs on the vehicle that is used as a tractor for the trailer transporters of both Guideline and Guild, Goa is a two-stage missile that is thought to have been intended for much the same operational role as the US Hawk, that is to say, short-range defence against low-flying targets.

Control of the missile in flight is by movable foreplane surfaces, the rear mounted wings of the second stage being fixed. Considering the operational role suggested above it seems possible that the missile has some form of homing; however, it seems fairly definite that Goa is a command-guided weapon.

In addition to the original twin launcher associated with the SA-3 there is now in use a triple missile launcher, which was first noted at Yugoslav air defence batteries. It is not known if this development

was initiated by Yugoslavia or by the Soviet Union. Still more recently a four-round launcher installation of Soviet origin has made its appearance and is progressively replacing twin launchers in the USSR.

Goa is used in conjunction with an I/J-band fire control radar whose NATO code-name is Low Blow (**2884.153**) and is commonly associated with an acquisition radar code-named Flat Face (**2874.153**).

In addition to its land-based uses Goa is deployed on ships of the Soviet Navy. Further details can be found in the Shipborne Surface-to-air Weapons section (**2939.231**).

CHARACTERISTICS
Type: Shipborne or land-based surface-to-air guided missile
Guidance principle: Probably command-guided but a homing system may be incorporated
Guidance method: By control of movable foreplane surfaces
Propulsion: 2-stage solid-propellant
Warhead: HE, proximity fuze
Missile length: 6·7 m
Missile diameter: Booster 60 cm; second stage 25 – 45 cm
Launch weight: 636 kg
Range: 25 – 30 km
Speed: Mach 2+ (estimated)
Ceiling: over 13 000 m
STATUS
Introduced into service in 1961 and now widely deployed in the USSR and Warsaw Pact states.

Goa has been supplied to a number of other states, among them Egypt, Finland, Iraq, Libya, Syria, Uganda, Viet-Nam, and Yugoslavia. Its use can be expected to increase both within and beyond the Warsaw Pact.

SA-3 Goa air defence missiles are usually transported on specially converted military trucks

2934.131
SA-4 (GANEF) SURFACE-TO-AIR MISSILE

Ganef is the NATO code-name for a surface-to-air missile launched from a tracked vehicle that was first seen in public in Moscow in 1964. Its US alpha-numeric code is SA-4.

Alternative designations associated with this weapon by other sources are the Soviet name 'Krug' and the description *Zenitniy Upravlyayemiy Raket* (ZUR) or guided anti-aircraft missile. Different models are believed to have the following Soviet numbers, ZUR: 3M8, 3M8M, 3M8M1 and 3M8M2, of which the last two apply to the two versions that appear to be those now in use. The 3M8M1 model is the variant noted by Western observers and dubbed the 'long-nosed' Ganef, and this believed to have a longer range and higher ceiling than the 3M8M2. These notes refer essentially to the obvious external differences and there are likely to be significant variations internally or in performance characteristics to warrant the four designations given here.

Despite its appreciable (by most standards) range capability, the SA-4 is classed as a medium-range air defence weapon by the Soviet Union (ZRK-SD: *Zenitniy Raketniy Kompleks – Srednoye Deistvie*, anti-aircraft missile system – medium range), and is deployed with special air defence missile brigades that are allocated one to each front or army. A brigade consists of three air defence battalions, each of three batteries.

The system comprises five distinct elements, three of which are special to the SA-4 system, and the other two are employed with other Soviet weapons. The latter two are the Long Track search radar (**2937.153**) deployed at brigade level, and Thin Skin nodding height-finder radars (**3292.153**) at the brigade and

one per launcher battalion. These radars are also encountered with other air defence systems such as the SA-6 Gainful, for example.

The other (three) elements are: the SPU (*Samokhodnaya puskovaya ustanovka*) mobile launcher unit, TZM (*Transportna-zaryazhyuscha maschina*) transporter-loader vehicle, and the SSNR (*Samokhodnaya stantsiya navedeniya raket*) mobile missile guidance station, known to NATO as Pat Hand (**2936.153**).

The missiles are carried in pairs on the first of these three vehicles, and the SPU/ZRK-SD is a fully tracked, transporter- erector-launcher equipped with a 360-degree trainable mount with elevation mechanism. The two caliper clamps which support the missiles during transit are separately released by manual operation of a worm-screw on the underside of the clamps. Handles for the worm-screws are clipped to the tubular framework carrying the clamps. This frame folds forward into the horizontal position for firing. Reloading of the launcher vehicles is by means of a mobile crane, and there is a special two-point attachment yoke for lifting. Wheeled transporter vehicles may be used for re-supply purposes, each carrying one missile.

Each Ganef battery has one TZM transporter-loader vehicle, capable of carrying one reload missile and transferring it to the launcher by means of a crane. Further reload rounds are carried by the brigade, these being transported on semi-trailers which are normally distributed at battalion or brigade headquarters.

The SA-4 missile configuration is fairly typical of the period (early 1960s): a large centre body containing a ramjet main propulsion motor with a prominent nose cone unit, cruciform wings, four

wrap-around booster rockets, and four large tail fins. The boosters are solid propellant units, while the ramjet main motor uses kerosene fuel. A transponder to assist missile tracking during an engagement is located on one of the missile tail fins, and there are four interferometer antennas on the leading edges of the wings to enable the missile to home onto reflected energy from the target illuminating radar. Other missile details appear in the table below.

The Pat Hand guidance radar group operates in conjunction with the battery Thin Skin height-finder and Long Track search radar. Once a target is acquired by the latter two equipments, target data is transmitted to the Pat Hand which operates in the H-band and is thought to employ CW illumination for missile guidance as well as target tracking, supplemented by a command link.

CHARACTERISTICS
Type: Land-mobile surface-to-air tactical guided missile
Guidance principle: Command guidance, plus semi-active radar homing
Guidance method: By control of moving wings on forepart
Propulsion: Ramjet sustainer with four solid-propellant boosters
Warhead: HE, 100-135 kg proximity fuze
Missile length: 8·8 m
Missile diameter: 0·9 m
Span (tail): 2·6 m
Span (wings): 2·3 m
Launch weight: About 2500 kg
Range: About 70 km
Speed: Mach 2·5
Ceiling: 24 000 m

STATUS

Deployed operationally since the early 1960s, initially with Soviet formations only but later with Egyptian forces, before being withdrawn and replaced by the SA-6 Gainful. Within the Warsaw Pact states until recently the SA-4 has been noted only with East German and Czechoslovakian ground forces, but these have now been joined by Bulgarian units.

General arrangement drawing of SA-4 Ganef mobile launcher unit (SPU/ZRK-SD) (Steven Zaloga)

2940.131
SA-5 (GAMMON) LONG-RANGE AIR DEFENCE MISSILE

Griffon was widely accepted as the NATO code-name for a large surface-to-air weapon first displayed in public in 1963, but the practice in official US defence circles has recently been to designate this missile as the SA-5, Gammon. It has been variously described as an unmanned long-range interceptor, an anti-aircraft missile, and an anti-missile missile,' but it seems probable that although it may have some anti-missile capability it is primarily suitable for long-range anti-aircraft operations.

The nose of the missile houses a radar reflector of at least 60 cm diameter which can be combined with an active radar target seeking system.

Generally similar in size and weight to the US Nike Zeus missile, SA-5 is thought to be somewhat inferior in performance and to have a smaller anti-missile capability. The fact that it is evidently manoeuvred aerodynamically indicates that its ability to home on to targets travelling at missile speeds must be very limited.

Although the missile evidently has two stages, it has been suggested that it may in fact have three, the third being a motor built into the warhead section and used to power the warhead and homing system during the final stages of interception.

CHARACTERISTICS

Type: Long-range surface-to-air guided missile
Guidance principle: Radar homing
Guidance method: By control of moving control surfaces on wings and tail
Propulsion: 2- or 3-stage solid-propellant
Missile length: 16·5 m
Missile diameter: Booster 1 m; second stage 0·8 m
Launch weight: About 10 000 kg
Range: About 300 km
Ceiling: About 29 km

STATUS

Operational since 1967, Gammon provides point defence for a number of major areas of strategic importance. The current Soviet deployment plan appears to be based on use of Gammon as the high-altitude missile and the SA-3 Goa (**2938.131**) as the low/medium-altitude weapon for the strategic air defence of the Soviet Union. Official US sources in 1984 reported SA-5 deployments in Eastern Europe, Mongolia and Syria (see below). For further discussions of Soviet ABM and air defence systems see **3214.181, 2945.181,** and **2989.181**.

In late 1982/early 1983 the Soviet Union supplied (and reportedly manned) a number of SA-5 air defence missile installations in Syria following the earlier fighting in the Lebanon. Two sites were identified in western reports, near Damascus and the city of Homs. The SA-5s were subsequently supplemented by early warning radars and SA-2, SA-3 and SA-6 missiles according to reports of May 1983.

It is doubted that the weapons deployed in Syria are the same as the modern and sophisticated missile implied by the diagram and comments in the American 1983 edition of *Soviet Military Power* when referring to the SA-5 Gammon. Probably the SA-5 in Syria is the original SA-5 known to NATO as Griffon.

2930.131
SA-6 (GAINFUL) SURFACE-TO-AIR MISSILE

Gainful is the NATO code-name for an anti-aircraft missile system known in the US alpha-numeric code as SA-6 and first publicly shown in Moscow in 1967.

Until the 1973 Arab-Israeli war little was known about Gainful in the West. The missile system was, however, used extensively in that war – this being, so far as is known, its first operational use – and scored a number of successes in the early phases of hostilities.

Gainful is both a command guided and a homing missile and is fully mobile, both missile launchers and fire control radar systems being mounted on separate tracked vehicles. The fire control system is both sophisticated and, it would seem, effective. It comprises a primary search and acquisition radar, a target tracking and illuminating radar, a command link with secondary radar response for missile tracking and a missile-borne semi-active homing system. In ECM conditions some of the tracking functions can be performed optically.

The ground equipment of this complex is known by the NATO name Straight Flush (**2885.131**). Its limitation would appear to be restricted search capability when operating without the support of other types of surveillance radar, but it is normal practice to include such longer range radar units in combat formations to obviate this difficulty.

Other radars known to be associated with SA-6 operation include Flat Face and Long Track target acquisition radars (**2874.153** and **2937.153**) and the Thin Skin height-finder (**3292.153**). Straight Flush itself is understood to have a short-range target acquisition capability.

A typical engagement is assumed to take place as follows: after detection at long range by the Long Track early warning radar, range and bearing information (possibly supplemented with height data from the Thin Skin radar) are passed to the SA-6 battery where the Straight Flush tracker takes over when the target is acquired and in range. The SA-6 Straight Flush vehicle sometimes includes a long-range (said to be up to 30 km) electro-optical tracker for use if jamming is encountered. On target acquisition by the lower, rectangular, antenna of the Straight Flush, the target is handed over to the upper conical-scan tracker radar, and command guidance data is received by an antenna on one of the missile tail fins.

It seems fairly clear that the search/acquisition function is carried out in the 5 to 6 GHz band, the target tracking/illuminating function in the 8 to 10 GHz band and the command guidance and beacon response is also in the 8 to 10 GHz band though obviously not on the same frequencies. This sort of multiple frequency combination is of course not unlike that used in some Western missile systems of similar age.

The basic SA-6 unit is a regiment comprising five missile firing batteries. The main elements of such a battery include a Straight Flush radar for target acquisition and fire control and four TELs (transporter-erector-launchers), each of which carries three missiles. Six reload missiles are usually held in reserve on two missile transporter-loader vehicles.

The missile is constructed as a single-stage body containing a dual-thrust integral rocket-ramjet propulsion system. In the boost phase the missile is powered by a solid-propellant rocket motor which accelerates it at about 20 *g* to about Mach 1·5. With the completion of this rocket burn, the tail cone of the missile, which contains the booster nozzle, is jettisoned and the rocket propellant chamber becomes the combustion chamber for the ramjet, ram air being supplied through four intakes disposed symmetrically around the centre section of the missile. The ramjet takes the speed up to almost Mach 2·8.

Two sets of cruciform fins at the centre and tail of the missile provide stability and aerodynamic control, pitch and yaw being controlled at the centre and roll

at the tail. The tail fins also carry the command link receiver antenna and the beacon transmitter antenna. The nose of the missile is an ogival radome for the homing head.

CHARACTERISTICS
Type: Surface-to-air tactical guided missile
Guidance: Ground command plus semi-active radar homing. Aerodynamic control
Propulsion: Integral rocket-ramjet
Warhead: HE, probably 80 kg total with 40 kg HE
Fuze: Proximity and impact; possibly also command
Missile lengths: 6·2 m including tail cone; 6 m without
Diameter: 33·5 cm
Tail span: 124 cm
Launch weight: About 550 kg
Ranges: Max: high altitude possibly 60 km; low altitude probably 30 km. Max altitude about 18 km. Minimum engagement about 4 km
Speed: Mach 2·8
Ceiling: 18 000 m
STATUS
Operational with Soviet forces and supplied to Algeria, Angola, Bulgaria, Cuba (possibly), Czechoslovakia, Egypt, German Democratic Republic, Hungary, India, Kuwait, Libya, Mozambique, Poland, Romania, Syria, Viet-Nam, South Yemen and Yugoslavia.

SA-6 Gainful tactical surface-to-air missile launcher vehicle deployed

---

3209.131
SA-8 (GECKO) SURFACE-TO-AIR MISSILE

The SA-8 (Gecko) low-altitude surface-to-air missile is a command guidance system, and in addition to antennas for the search and tracking functions, the radar group (NATO designation, Land Roll) features two separate beacon tracking antennas and two transmitting horns for the command guidance signals. The main target tracking radar is a cassegrain type array, possibly using conical scan and a pulsed transmission waveform, and the two smaller cassegrain antennas flank the main tracker. They are mounted to provide a limited degree of movement relative to the main array and are assumed to be missile trackers. The command link horns for each are mounted beneath the missile tracker antennas.

Frequency use associated with the Land Roll radar group claims H-band for target acquisition and J-band for tracking purposes. Both semi-active radar and IR homing techniques have been postulated as the terminal guidance method, and either is feasible. Until better information is available it is not possible to be dogmatic about this aspect.

This arrangement indicates provision for simultaneous firing of two missiles with separate guidance for each. One possible use of this facility would be to enable simultaneous engagement of two separate targets within a formation, and another is to allow 'split engagements' with one target being tracked by the radar and another by the optical tracker which is incorporated in the system. There are other possibilities but it seems certain that a multiple target capability exists.

Both the missile launcher arms and the search radar antenna fold down for reduced transit height. The nature of the reloading arrangement cannot be ascertained from the evidence so far available, but the hull of the six-wheeled vehicles built to carry the SA-8 should be able to accommodate at least one full reload of four missiles and one source estimates as many as eight reload rounds. Two versions of the

SA-8 Gecko mobile air defence missile unit on the move. Note folded down search radar

carrier vehicle have been noted, both about 9 metres long but differing slightly in overall length.

Control is by four small canard surfaces and there is a cruciform tail assembly of about 60 cm span. The design is probably optimised for high acceleration, maximum speed, and manoeuvrability rather than range.

CHARACTERISTICS
Type: Mobile autonomous tactical air defence missile
Guidance: Radar command
Propulsion: Solid
Warhead: HE, proximity fuze
Length: 3·2 m
Diameter: 21 cm
Launch weight: 190 kg (estimated)
Range: 12 km

Speed: Mach 2
Ceiling: 6000 m
SA-8B
In a military parade in 1980 a new version of the Gecko system appeared in which the two twin missile launcher rails on the vehicle have been replaced by two triple launcher/containers, thereby increasing the ready-to-fire capacity by 50 per cent. This version was later confirmed as the SA-8B but as yet it is not known if a new NATO reporting code-name will be assigned to this model.

In appearance the six missile containers look slimmer than might be expected from photographs of the original exposed missile installation, and it is possible that the SA-8B missiles are provided with folding tail surfaces to enable their enclosure in the

Newer version, SA-8B, can be recognised by six containers which replace four exposed missiles of the SA-8a Gecko mobile AA weapon system

SA-8B surface-to-air missile system has six missiles housed in launcher containers

SA-8B fire unit, apparently photographed in an operational environment. Note search radar in operating position and only one missile container on left side of vehicle

container/launchers. A special vehicle that carries reload missiles accompanies SA-8B fire unit vehicles. Gecko is usually deployed in batteries of four vehicles, each Soviet motor rifle and tank division having five batteries forming an air defence regiment.

STATUS
In service with the Soviet forces since the mid-1970s and operating with armoured and motorised rifle divisions. The level of deployment is reported to be approximately 20 vehicles per division.

In early 1983 it was confirmed that SA-8 systems supplied to the Jordanian forces were operational, and other deployments in this region include Syria where SA-8s have been operated in company with other Soviet SAMs such as the SA-2, SA-3, SA-5 and SA-6.

3072.131
SA-9 (GASKIN) SURFACE-TO-AIR MISSILE

The SA-9 Gaskin designation refers to what at first was generally thought to be an SA-7 Grail (**2941.131**) derivative, but subsequent indications suggest this assumption to have been incorrect.

Gaskin is commonly encountered in vehicle-mounted form, on a BRDM-2 type four-wheeled cross-country vehicle. The usual installation comprises four launcher containers with an aimer's position incorporated in the base. The launcher containers are individually loaded manually on to the tubular construction mounting frame carried by the turret. When operated in an autonomous mode, the method of target acquisition is presumed to be by visual means with subsequent aiming of the weapons by optical systems. The launcher containers fold down and lie flat on the roof of the vehicle during transit, and each BRDM-2 is able to carry a full load of

eight SA-9 missiles, ie one reload round for each launcher. Although the normal configuration is with four launchers per vehicle, a small number of BRDM-2s with only two are reported to have entered service.

It has been reported that when used as part of a larger air defence column, SA-9 vehicles can be linked to search radars to assist in target acquisition, and another method could be that of using radio communications links to 'tell off' targets to individual SA-9 firing units.

It has also been reported that versions of the SA-9 have been seen equipped with the Gun Dish fire control radar (**2876.153**) mounted in front of the SA-9 turret, presumably to provide a degree of 'blind fire' capability for night and adverse weather operations. This was probably a reference to the later SA-13 system (**4471.131**, below) which externally resembles the SA-9 to which a radar antenna has been added between the two pairs of missile containers.

CHARACTERISTICS
Type: Mobile short-range tactical air defence missile
Guidance: IR homing
Propulsion: Solid
Warhead: HE
Length: 2 m (approx)
Diameter: 12 cm
Launch weight: 30+ kg
Range: 8 km (approx)
Speed: Mach 1·5+
Ceiling: 4000 – 5000 m

STATUS
US sources claim that the SA-9 was first deployed by Soviet forces in 1968, but since then this weapon has been observed with the forces of Algeria, Hungary, Poland, Syria, Viet-Nam and Yugoslavia. In Soviet formations, for regimental air defence SA-9s are deployed at a level of 16 per division (four per regiment).

SA-9 Gaskin launch vehicle with launcher complete with four missile canisters folded flat for transit

Gaskin launcher vehicle with four-canister mount in ready-to-fire position

---

3620.131
SA-10 SURFACE-TO-AIR MISSILE

SA-10 is the designation of one of the latest generation of Soviet air defence missiles, but so far no photographs or other information have been made public by Soviet sources. However, for several years this weapon has attracted a good deal of attention in official US circles suggesting that considerable importance is attached to it.

If public statements and other information issued by the US DoD are any indication, quite considerable intelligence gathering efforts have been expended on the SA-10, but while certain conclusions reached by the American evaluators have been widely distributed, the evidence on which they are based remains severely restricted. Over the past few years SA-10 has been described as having been designed specifically to engage low-level targets such as attacking cruise missiles, and as a strategic air defence missile with high performance at both high and low altitudes.

The following paragraphs are based on what constitutes the current official assessments of SA-10 capabilities and estimated characteristics.

The SA-10 is a modern advanced surface-to-air missile system apparently designed for the air defence of the Soviet Union, and is believed to be an 'all-altitude' weapon, which may exist in both semi-permanent and mobile versions. The 1984 edition of the official US publication *Soviet Military Power* states that "the Soviets are developing a mobile version of the SA-10 SAM . . . (which) could be used to support Soviet theatre forces, but, more importantly, if deployed with the territorial defence forces, would allow the Soviets to change the location of those SA-10s in the USSR. The mobile SA-10 could be operational by 1985". Elsewhere in the same document it is stated that the SA-10 is now in series production. The obvious implication is therefore that

SA-10 mobile air defence missile system includes planar array radar and transporter-erector-launcher units on wheeled chassis according to US analysts

'A' and 'B' versions of the SA-10 either exist or are about to.

The SA-10A would be the non-mobile (though probably not fixed, ie transportable or semi-permanent) model which is stated by the US DoD to be operational now at about 40 sites with nearly 350 launchers. Deployment is said to have been in progress since 1980.

The missile is understood to be about 6·25 metres long, with a diameter in the region of 45 cm and a maximum range of some 100 km. US drawings of the mobile version of SA-10 suggest that the missile is transported in tubular canisters which elevate to the vertical for launching. The canisters are carried in groups of four on a large wheeled transporter. There is apparently no provision for slewing in azimuth to aim the missile towards the target so that a vertical launch technique is implicit in the US artist's impression (reproduced here). From this drawing it will also be noted that associated with the SA-10 is a planar array guidance radar on a similar wheeled vehicle.

If the above assumptions are correct, and the vertical launch technique is employed, then the semi-permanent SA-10 installations might well utilise a form of silo launcher arrangement with a number of silos installed around important targets for their protection. The silos might or might not be permanently loaded with SA-10 missiles, and similar considerations could apply also to the associated radar(s), these items being deployed to the fixed site only at times of tension or threat, for example. At other times missiles and radars could be deployed elsewhere to meet other threats, for exercise, into hiding, or into storage etc.

Based mostly on US evaluations of intelligence data and their published findings, there is some similarity between this system (SA-10) and the possibly newer SA-X-12 system (**4774.131**), but these may have arisen by having been illustrated by the same artist as much from the similarity of the presumed roles of the two systems. Judgement must be reserved until more evidence is forthcoming.
STATUS
Believed to have been deployed in 1980 and operational with PVO Strany (Home Air Defence Command) in the USSR since 1981. In early 1984 official US sources stated that there were about 40 operational SA-10 sites with some 350 missiles. The SA-10 is in series production. A mobile version could be operational by 1985 according to the US DoD.

4470.131
SA-11 SURFACE-TO-AIR MISSILE
The Soviet SA-11 is believed to be a new land-mobile short-range surface-to-air missile system thought to have begun initial troop trials in 1978-79. No NATO reporting name has been revealed for this weapon and there are few firm details of the missile itself or its performance. The launcher vehicle is based on that employed for the ZSU-24-4 mobile anti-aircraft radar directed quadruple 23 mm gun system. In this later application the vehicle carries a turntable mounting which can be rotated through 360 degrees, on which there are provisions for the carriage of four ready-to-fire SA-11 missiles. Estimated performance figures include a speed of Mach 3 and minimum and maximum range of 3 and 28 km, respectively. Targets flying at altitudes between 30 and 14 000 metres can be engaged, and radar guidance has been assumed.

An associated vehicle, also on a ZSU-23-4 tracked chassis, carries a 3-D acquisition radar called Clamshell in the NATO designation system, and a tracking radar designated Flap Lid.
STATUS
Thought to be still under development although initial troop trials were reported in 1978-79.

4774.131
SA-X-12 SURFACE-TO-AIR MISSILE SYSTEM
SA-X-12 is the designation assigned to an air defence missile system under development in the Soviet Union that is expected to reach operational status soon. No details have been made public by the Soviet authorities, and official US sources have published only the partial results of their assessment of the intelligence data on the SA-X-12 system that has been obtained, rather than any of the evidence or photographs themselves.

The system has been identified as both a tactical surface-to-air missile and anti-tactical ballistic missile, by which is meant an ability to intercept intermediate range nuclear weapons such as the US Lance and Pershing II missiles. Unofficial US observers have apparently used this DoD assessment as a basis for an extrapolation to arrive at estimated performance characteristics that include an acceleration capability of 50 g, and a slant range of more than 550 km. (Both reasonable values, given the declared operational capability, but the DoD range estimate is lower at 100 km.)

Another possible role foreseen for the SA-X-12 is as a successor to either replace or augment the SA-4 Ganef front/army surface-to-air missile system (**2934.131**), as a tactical air defence system. An artist's impression of the SA-X-12 (reproduced here) shows the entire complex carried on a series of tracked armoured vehicles, with one type carrying two missiles in tubular launcher canisters as well as a guidance radar mounted on a retractable tower. The vertical launch technique is apparently employed as there is no provision for altering the launch azimuth once the vehicle has been halted to launch the missiles. The SA-10 surface-to-air missile (**3620.131**) in its mobile version is thought to use a vertical launch also.

With the two transporter-erector-launcher vehicles is a resupply vehicle, also tracked, which is equipped with a crane and supports for transporting and manipulating four reload missiles. Other vehicles that

Mobile SA-12 surface-to-air missile system is expected to be capable of engaging both high performance aircraft and missiles such as Lance and Pershing. Vertical launch technique is implied in this US artist's impression.

can be seen are two planar array radars which probably fulfil search/target detection and designation functions, and what could be either a crew or command and control vehicle.

US sources have likened the SA-X-12 to the US Patriot surface-to-air system (**2800.131**), which could imply an advanced type of guidance and control system. This would certainly be in keeping with the presumed design and development time-scale, and would probably be essential to fulfil the demanding performance characteristics credited to the system.
STATUS
Field trials believed to have been completed by mid-1984. No deployment information obtained, but system is thought to be operational soon.

4471.131
SA-13 (GOPHER) SURFACE-TO-AIR MISSILE
The SA-13, NATO code-name Gopher, is a low altitude air defence missile system which is intended to replace or supplement the SA-9 Gaskin system (**3072.131**) for the protection of Soviet mechanised formations. Both systems have a very similar configuration, with the SA-9 mounted on a wheeled chassis and the SA-13 on a tracked vehicle. Initially it was thought likely that the two systems shared a common missile that might have been based on an air-to-air missile such as the AA-8 Aphid (**3339.331**), but in both respects these ideas are now considered incorrect. Later evidence indicates that the SA-13 missiles are slightly larger than those of the SA-9 system (see diagram).

Two versions of the SA-13 have been noted, these being referred to as TELAR 1 and TELAR 2, where TELAR stands for transporter-erector-launcher-and-radar. This term embraces several of the main features of the system, namely: mobility; the folding retraction arrangement of the four-canister launcher; and the radar dish mounted between the two pairs of missile canisters.

The radar is assumed to be a range-only equipment that operates in conjunction with the SA-13's passive IR homing head for missile guidance, but at this stage it would be unwise to rule out other possibilities such as a target tracking mode for the radar perhaps to assist multiple target engagements. In such a mode of operation, optical fire control could be expected to provide one line-of-sight channel, and radar the other, and provided the missile IR seekers are locked onto their respective targets before launch, thereafter they would effectively operate in a 'fire-and-forget' mode.

Another function of the radar as a range-only device that has been suggested is that its use would enable the crew to ensure that only targets within lock-on range of the IR seeker would be engaged, thereby avoiding wastage of missiles.

It is believed that as many as 12 to 14 reload missiles could be carried internally in each TELAR. The TELAR vehicle is fully amphibious, and the only significant external difference between the two models is that TELAR 1 carries four small box-shaped units at the corners of its top deck which are thought to be ESM antennas for the Hat Box system, although other observers have suggested alternatives for this feature, such as a data link for communication with other vehicles of a formation. Inter-vehicle communication within formations of this kind, under battle conditions could be an important requirement, as would be some form of IFF, and these are other possibilities for the Hat Box role. TELAR 2 apparently does not have the Hat Box items.

CHARACTERISTICS
Length: 2·2 m
Diameter: 12 cm
Span: 40 cm
Launch weight: 55 kg
Speed: Mach 1·5+
Range: 10 km (max); 500 m (Minimum)
Max altitude: 5000 m
Warhead: HE 6 kg
Guidance: Passive IR homing

STATUS
Thought to have been deployed with Soviet forces since 1975, but first seen in public in 1982.

(SA-9)/SA-13 TELAR 1

SA-13   SA-9

SA-13 (launcher folded)

SA-13 TELAR 2

GA drawings of two SA-13 Gopher system versions, with SA-9 and SA-13 missiles and canisters for comparison (Steven Zaloga)

Two TELAR vehicles with SA-13 missile system with other units of a mechanised formation during Warsaw Pact exercises in 1982. Only one missile position carries an SA-13 canister

UNITED KINGDOM

4524.131
GUARDIAN AIR DEFENCE SYSTEM

Guardian is a proposed long-range surface-to-air missile system based on the Sea Dart naval missile (**6004.231**). It provides land-based area air defence against attacks from both high and low altitudes. The system can be supplied in versions either for operation from fixed sites, or as a fully mobile system capable of rapid deployment from semi or unprepared sites.

The system may also be employed in a surface-to-surface role, for instance in the defence of coastal installations against attack by surface vessels.

A Guardian air defence system consists of a number of co-ordinated batteries. Each battery typically comprises two firing troops, controlled by a battery headquarters with an associated surveillance radar. A firing troop has a troop command post and four launchers, each having four boxed missiles. Thus each troop has 16 ready to fire missiles.

Battery headquarters organisation

A battery headquarters consists of a battery command post (BCP) surveillance radar, generators and servicing facilities. A Plessey surveillance radar passes target data to the BCP. This contains display consoles and communications both to the firing troops and the surveillance system, as well as to other external networks.

Firing troop organisation

A firing troop consists of a troop command post, a tracking/illuminating radar (TIR), four launchers, missile re-supply vehicles, generators and servicing facilities.

Each troop command post includes a lightweight TIR and a weapon control console to co-ordinate the four launchers. When commanded to engage, the TIR acquires and tracks the target, having been supplied with target indication data by the surveillance radar.

The weapon control console in the firing troop command post has a single operator. The console houses a computer which determines engagement feasibility and selects launchers and missiles. The launchers each support the four boxed missiles at fixed elevation angles but can be trained in azimuth. Each launcher has missile setting equipment included to provide missile warm-up signals and power supplies before launch. When a missile is fired the TIR illuminator radiates and the missile homes onto the target by semi-active guidance.

Battery command post (BCP)

The BCP consists of a single cabin which receives target data both from the surveillance radar and other sources. It enables the battery commander to assess the threat, make tactical decisions and communicate with the firing troops.

Surveillance radar

The Plessey radar is used to detect all aircraft, missiles, helicopters and surface threats in the coastal defence role. The Guardian surveillance radar is normally an adaptation of the naval AWS-5 equipment. Built-in IFF equipment identifies hostile targets which are processed automatically into a threat priority list. Computer assisted weapon assignments are then made. The radar in mobile form features a separate antenna which can be erected quickly.

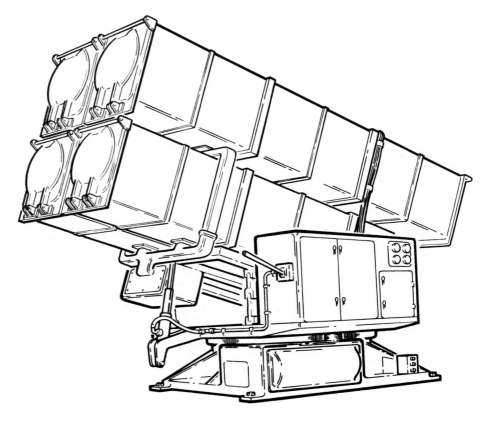

Guardian 4-box launcher

Tracking/illuminating radar (TIR)

The Marconi Radar Systems TIR provides radar tracking of the target and illuminates it during an engagement. The TIR is a land-based derivative of the 805 SD radar for Lightweight Sea Dart. The director is mounted on the roof of the firing troop command post cabin, and has a 1·4 metre diameter dish. Operation of the TIR is largely automatic and is monitored at its control console, located adjacent to the Guardian weapon control console in the firing troop command post.

Guardian control console

This unit enables a single operator to supervise a complete engagement. It contains the control computer, operator control panels, interfaces to the launcher-mounted missile setting equipment, and to the TIR and BCP. The control console selects the appropriate launcher, computes launcher pointing commands, provides command signals to other parts of the system and controls the overall progress of the engagement.

Launcher

Each launcher provides fixed elevation, 360-degree coverage with four missiles which are stored, handled and launched from their sealed air-conditioned canisters. The launcher structure consists of a pedestal base, turntable and missile canister support/elevating framework. Reloading of canisters

is achieved from the re-supply vehicle using its own hydraulic crane.

Missile

The missile is the well proven Sea Dart missile, propelled by a tandem mounted solid-propellant booster and ramjet sustainer motor. It has a cruciform wing and rear mounted control fins, with four flip-out stabilising fins mounted on the jettisonable boost section.

Deployment

Where Guardian is required as a fully mobile system, equipment is packaged in military standard containers which are transported using existing flat-bed vehicles. These vehicles are fitted with a special purpose hydraulic 'demountable pallet, off-loading and pick-up system'. Controlled from the driver's cab, each container can be off-loaded on an associated pallet which can then be quickly levelled using built-in jacks.

STATUS

The Guardian system has been proposed to various overseas countries and for use in the Falkland Islands.

CONTRACTOR

British Aerospace Dynamics Group, Bristol Division, Filton, Bristol BS12 7QW, England.

4773.131
LANDWOLF AIR DEFENCE SYSTEM

Landwolf is a short-range surface-to-air guided weapon system based on the Seawolf naval anti-missile point defence system (**2442.231**). It provides defence for sensitive ground installations against attacks by both aircraft and missiles.

The system consists of a battery headquarters and a number of firing units. The battery HQ includes a surveillance radar and a battery command post (BCP) with advanced data handling facilities. Each firing unit consists of a radar tracking and guidance system and a launching system.

The surveillance radar (eg Plessey Guardsman) detects and plots targets and feeds bearing and range data to the BCP. Here the data handling system (eg Plessey Huntsman, derived from the naval NAC 900 console) assesses the targets and allocates them

automatically to the appropriate firing units. The tracking and guidance system of each firing unit uses the Marconi Radar Systems 805 SW dual frequency radar. Following target acquisition and the firing of a Landwolf missile it automatically measures the angular displacement between the target and the missile and supplies information to the processor which generates the missile guidance signals. A weapon control console enables the firing unit to be monitored by one man.

The launching system can be supplied with either the new 4-barrel trainable launchers or with a 16-cell vertical launcher. These items are derived from the Lightweight Seawolf programme. In both cases the launcher is controlled completely automatically by the tracking and guidance system, providing extremely fast reaction times.

The Landwolf missile is propelled by a single-stage

boost motor in the first launcher option, which gives a very high initial acceleration following which the missile coasts at supersonic speed to its target. For vertical launch a tandem boost motor is fitted which is jettisoned after the turnover manoeuvre. The missile has a warhead and proximity fuze optimised against high-speed targets. Trials have included interceptions of 4·5-inch naval shells and the successful engagement of a sea-skimming Exocet missile.

Equipments are normally supplied packaged in containers and Landwolf can be deployed either as a mobile or a semi-permanent system, dependent on the user requirement.

STATUS

The Landwolf system utilises the major equipments of the Lightweight Seawolf programme, with appropriate modifications, together with a suitable surveillance radar to provide target indication data. Landwolf is currently available and has been offered to a number of overseas countries including Middle East states.

CONTRACTOR
British Aerospace Dynamics Group, Bristol Division, Filton, Bristol BS12 7QW, England.

Typical Landwolf schematic diagram

2406.131
BLOODHOUND Mk 2 SURFACE-TO-AIR WEAPON SYSTEM

Bloodhound Mk 2 is a second-generation mobile anti-aircraft guided weapon sub-system suitable for incorporation in a comprehensive air defence system. The basic unit, a missile section, typically comprises eight guided missiles and their launchers, a target illuminating radar (TIR), and a launch control post (LCP). The guidance principle is semi-active homing, the missile detecting and homing on the radiation reflected by the target when illuminated by the TIR.

Basic input required by the missile section is target location information from a surveillance radar which may be directly associated with the Bloodhound sub-system or may be part of the central equipment of a larger complex. This information is supplied to the TIR, which then searches for, acquires, and automatically tracks and illuminates the target. Simultaneously, it interrogates the target for positive identification and transmits the appropriate information to the LCP. Alternatively, the TIR may operate autonomously should data be unavailable from a surveillance radar.

At the LCP, which is the control centre of the missile section, sits the engagement controller assisted by a technical supervisor. A computer in the LCP processes the output data from the TIR to determine the optimum conditions for target engagement. This computer also performs routine tasks concerned with the state of readiness of the system; both the engagement controller and the technical supervisor are provided with displays and communications equipment to enable the former to take rapid operational decisions and the latter to maintain maximum equipment serviceability.

In the role for which it was first designed, the Bloodhound missile section is normally equipped with the Firelight TIR (**2413.153**) which is readily mobile and air-transportable. The whole equipment is contained in a single cabin and the antennas are mounted on a retractable pedestal on the roof. For static operations, or where system mobility is not a prime consideration, there is an alternative TIR, the Scorpion (**2428.153**), which is a larger radar giving a longer range. It can be broken down into transportable units but cannot be brought into or taken out of operation as quickly as the Firelight. Both radars are I/J-band CW doppler systems having good performance in the presence of natural or ECM interference.

CHARACTERISTICS
Type: Surface-to-air land-based GW system. Land-mobile. Air-transportable
Guidance principle: Semi-active homing. Receiver in missile nose detects and follows radiation reflected by target when illuminated by TIR
Guidance method: Twist-and-steer by pivoting wings
Propulsion: Ramjet with solid-propellant boosters
Warhead: HE, with proximity fuze
Launch control: From LCP by computer using data from TIR
Radar: Choice of 2 TIRs – Firelight or Scorpion
Range: >80 km
DEVELOPMENT
Bloodhound Mk 2 is the successor to Bloodhound Mk 1 which first went into service with the RAF in 1958, development having been started by the Bristol Aeroplane Co Ltd and Ferranti Ltd in 1949. Bloodhound 1 was also exported to Australia and Sweden.

The first design study for the Mk 2 version was started in 1958; the new version went into service with the RAF in 1964. In the same year the equipment also went into service with the defence forces of Sweden and Switzerland (designations RB68 and BL-84, respectively).

In late 1969 BAC was awarded a £10 million contract from the Singapore Government for the refurbishing and maintenance of the Bloodhound system previously operated by the RAF in that area.
STATUS
The RAF has Bloodhound sites in the UK as part of the NATO and UK Air Defence network, overseas Bloodhound units elsewhere having been withdrawn completely. In 1977 it was announced that the number of Bloodhound sites in the UK was being increased to strengthen the national air defence capability. This has been achieved by adding Bloodhound Mk 2 units withdrawn from service in West Germany to existing Bloodhound missiles deployed in the UK, a move completed by March 1983. In August 1978 a UK MoD programme drawn up to extend the useful operational life of Bloodhound was announced.

Bloodhound Mk 2 is also in service with the Swiss armed forces who operate about 64 launchers, and the Singapore Air Force with 28 launchers. In early 1984 BAe received a contract from the Swiss Government for a further supply of Bloodhound boost motors, indicating a significant continuation of the system's existing 15-year life in Swiss service.
CONTRACTORS
The following manufacturers are known to have been associated with the system.

Overall system, missile airframe etc (consortium leader overseas): British Aerospace Dynamics Group, Bristol, Avon, England.

Overall electronic system, missile homing system, LCP computer etc, Firelight TIR: Ferranti Ltd, Edinburgh (TIR) and Oldham (remainder).

Ramjet propulsion system: Rolls-Royce Ltd.
Missile fuze: Thorn-EMI Electronics Ltd.
Scorpion TIR: Marconi Radar Systems Ltd.

Bloodhound air defence missile at an RAF depot

2424.131
RAPIER MOBILE LOW-LEVEL ANTI-AIRCRAFT MISSILE SYSTEM

Rapier is a lightweight highly-mobile surface-to-air guided weapon system in which a supersonic, direct-hitting missile is automatically commanded to follow an optical or radar sightline to the target.

Main operational units of the standard (daylight/clear weather) system are a launcher with four ready-to-fire missiles, tactical control facility, secondary sight, an optical tracker, and a power unit. These units can be deployed in any convenient manner, according to terrain, interconnection being

by cable. Once the fire unit has been loaded with its four missiles (a two-man job) it can be left unattended and the system operated by two men until the missiles have all been fired. No cranes or mechanical handling equipment are required.

In addition to the missile launch mechanism, the firing unit contains a surveillance radar (**2425.153**) together with an IFF interrogator/decoder, a microwave command transmitter, and a computer which serves all parts of the system. When the surveillance radar detects a target the IFF automatically interrogates it to determine whether it is friendly or hostile. If the target is friendly all data on it

are cancelled and the radar continues its search; if it is hostile the tracker operator is alerted, the radar data are used to direct the tracker towards the target, and the operator will acquire it in his optical sight.

After acquiring the target optically the operator tracks it using a joystick control, thus generating an output from the tracker that is fed to the fire unit computer. On receiving a signal from the computer that the target is within range, the operator fires a missile, the launcher having been automatically aligned so that the missile will fly on the line-of-sight to the target.

While the missile flies towards the target the

operator continues tracking. A TV camera in the tracker collimated to the tracking sight detects flares mounted in the missile tail and measures any deviation from the sightline. These measurements are then fed to the fire unit computer which generates and encodes orders for the command transmitter to transmit to the missile.

Rapier is intended for both defence against fast (Mach 1+) manoeuvring low-flying targets, and slow-moving or hovering anti-tank helicopters. It has the fast reaction time necessary for the successful engagement of such targets which may appear suddenly, over terrain screening, at short range. It can also, however, be used successfully against aircraft flying at heights of some thousands of metres.

As already noted, Rapier is a direct-hitting system and it has demonstrated its capability in this respect in repeated trials. For this reason it is fitted with a semi-armour-piercing warhead and a crush fuze which detonates the HE inside the target structure.

In normal operational use the fire unit is towed by a 1 tonne Land-Rover which also carries the optical tracker and four missiles in sealed containers; a second Land-Rover tows a missile re-supply trailer which carries nine additional missiles in identical sealed containers. For continuous operation the normal detachment strength is five men, but three can deploy and man the system and, as already noted, only two men at a time are needed to operate it after deployment. A complete system can be transported by medium lift helicopters as underslung loads, or carried internally by a Chinook helicopter. Since the system 'modules' are relatively small and light, however, they can be mounted in various other ways, eg on tracked vehicles, to suit special operational requirements.

CHARACTERISTICS (System with optical tracking)
Type: Surface-to-air, land- or vehicle-based GW system. Land-mobile. Air-transportable
Guidance principle: Command to LOS
Guidance method: Optical target tracking. TV missile tracking. Computer calculates course corrections for transmission over command link. Hot gas servos actuate missile fins
Propulsion: 2-stage solid-propellant motor
Warhead: Semi-armour-piercing with crush fuze and HE
Launch control: By operator when cleared to fire by computer
Launch weight: 42 kg
Speed: Mach 2+
Range: 6·5 km

The increasing requirement for 'all-weather' and night engagement capabilities has led to a situation where most Rapier systems incorporate the Blindfire radar (see below), while preserving the excellent optical tracking facility as a back-up or alternative operating mode

Swiss Rapier
To meet the special requirements of the Swiss Army and its operating environment, a special version of the

Men of the 16th Air Defence Rgt, Australian Army loading Rapier missiles during live firing practice in South Australia

standard towed Rapier was designed in response to the contract awarded to BAe in December 1980. The Swiss Army required an improved acquisition and tracking capability in mountainous terrain, an improved ECCM capability, a tactical PPI tactical display, a Swiss IFF system, and the use of the standard Pinzgauer vehicle as the towing and support vehicles. The following significant modifications were developed to meet Swiss Army requirements:

(1) missile launcher and surveillance radar data processors, and a planar array antenna were introduced to provide multiple target plotting, threat assessment and better ECCM capabilities
(2) the launcher was modified to accommodate and operate with the Swiss IFF unit
(3) the radar tracker was modified to give better ECCM, and improved detection circuits fitted to enable operation in the presence of heavy ground clutter, such as might be generated by mountains. It was also modified to provide a lower negative tracking angle when sited on high ground to aid engagement of targets below the level of the Rapier fire unit
(4) the Swiss version is the first Rapier model to incorporate a radar PPI, giving the operator a PPI display using TV techniques. This enables him to see alternative targets, together with a number of

command functions, to enable a complex scenario to be assessed. There is also a facility that provides for presentation of ECM data to the operator. The radar display unit and launcher data processor and surveillance radar data processor are linked by a data highway
(5) the fire unit generators have been modified to suit the peculiarities of the Swiss climate, and adapted for carriage in the Pinzgauer vehicle
(6) the introduction of microprocessors into the Rapier fire unit system has been utilised to enhance the self-test and diagnostic facilities of the system.

Each of the Swiss Army mechanised divisions is responsible for its own air defence, and is being equipped with one battalion armed with 20 mm AA guns and another with the Rapier. The latter battalion is divided into a mobile headquarters battery, and two AA guided missile batteries. The mechanised divisions are responsible for the co-ordination, training and deployment of Rapier with all the other units being protected.

Tracked Rapier
Members of the M113 family of vehicles (manufactured by FMC) have been chosen for Tracked Rapier; in particular an armoured version of the M548 cargo carrier (known as the RCM 748) is used for the system. Tracked Rapier is highly mobile and can accompany tanks and other armoured vehicles over the most difficult terrain and, being amphibious, can cross inland waterways. All crew members can be provided with nuclear, biological and chemical protection devices, to enable operations to continue in hostile environments.

The launcher vehicle is based on the M548, the main alteration being the addition of an armoured cab to the front of the vehicle. This has aluminium armour which provides the crew and installed equipment with protection to APC standards. The vehicle commander is provided with a cupola which enables him to use the Ferranti helmet pointing system for passive target acquisition. An air cooling unit is positioned immediately behind the cab and the vehicle cab also has a heater. To the rear of the cab is the blast shield which protects the forward part of the vehicle from blast effects when a missile is fired.

The Rapier elements are mounted on the RCM 748 to form the launcher vehicle. The optical tracker is mounted in the cab roof and all but the top of the rotating head is armour protected. The tactical control unit and built-in test equipment are also situated in the cab. The H-30 diesel generator is situated to the rear of the vehicle engine bay. Installed on anti-vibration mounts in the rear is the launcher.

Early firing of Rapier Laserfire at MoD Test Range at Aberporth in Wales

Version of towed Rapier developed specially for Swiss Army requirements uses Pinzgauer vehicles, incorporates Swiss IFF, microprocessors and a digital highway between units, and provides enhanced ECCM, data display and diagnostic facilities

Four missiles are carried on each side with armour plate protection. The turntable and base of the launcher are also protected to APC standards by armour plate. The command antenna is mounted on an elevating mechanism which allows missiles to be fired and guided at low elevations over the cab. The Blindfire radar is fully compatible with the Tracked Rapier system.

CHARACTERISTICS (Tracked Rapier)

High battlefield survivability

Mobility: Low ground pressure. Low centre of gravity. High power-to-weight ratio. High speed across country. Amphibious. Helicopter lift by CH-53E. Air-transportable in C-130

Armour protection: For crew and equipment to APC standards

Conspicuousness: Low silhouette (height under 2·8 m). Covered surveillance radar easily disguised with tilt over rear of vehicle

Surveillance and coverage: 360° coverage by weapons systems

Firepower: 8 missiles ready-to-fire

Speed into and out of action: 15 s from coming to a halt. Out of action in under 15 s

Single shot kill probability (SSKP): Retains high lethality and SSKP of the Towed Rapier system

Day/night capability: With the add-on Blindfire radar a night and poor visibility capability is provided

Blindfire

The basic Rapier system was designed to combat the daylight/good visibility low-level threat posed by the very large numbers of ground attack aircraft and helicopters which are currently operational. The number of aircraft that can attack at low level by night or in conditions of low visibility is very much smaller, but extension of the system capability to combat this threat was considered necessary as a second priority.

To provide this added capability, Dynamics Group developed, in conjunction with Marconi Space and Defence Systems, an add-on radar (**2439.153**) which provides guidance when optical tracking is impossible.

Blindfire, as the DN181 radar is called, is mounted on the same type of trailer as is used for the Towed Rapier launcher.

Firing trials of the Blindfire system have been conducted, and at the very first attempt the target, a Meteor drone flying at Mach 0·6 at a height of 600 metres, was destroyed by a direct hit. This accuracy has been fully confirmed in subsequent trials. The manufacturers believe that this degree of success in combining a direct-hitting missile with radar tracking is unequalled elsewhere.

In daylight conditions, the addition of the Blindfire radar to the system gives the operator the option of optical or radar engagement, an option which need not be exercised until after the acquisition radar has indicated the presence of a target and, through a remote control link, has enabled the tracker to acquire the target.

Rapier Laserfire

Backed by the UK MoD, in 1983 BAe Dynamics Group introduced a new version of the system called Rapier Laserfire. This is another self-propelled model that is carried on a wheeled carriage instead of the tracked vehicle employed in the Tracked Rapier system. There are other differences from earlier Rapier

systems too, one of the most significant being the incorporation of an automatic laser tracker.

The system fits on a single pallet which can be mounted on any medium size military vehicle capable of a 3 to 4 tonne payload, and the prototype used for design proving was a standard British Army Bedford MJR1 4 × 4 equipped with a simple fold-flat modification to the cab. The latter allows a full 360-degree azimuth coverage for the turntable-mounted Rapier. The system may be vehicle or trailer mounted, or be operated from its pallet. Two vehicle-mounted systems or four palletised systems can be carried by a C-130 aircraft. The vehicle-mounted system can be transported by a Chinook helicopter and the palletised version by any medium lift helicopter, as underslung loads in both cases. The main elements of the system are: a surveillance radar; automatic laser tracker; a two-man crew cab with system controls and displays; computer associated sub-systems; four ready-to-fire Rapier missiles; and a command link. The surveillance radar is a millimetric wavelength system designed and produced by Racal Defence Systems providing target detection out to 10 km and altitude coverage to heights of 3000 metres. It is lowered from its operating position for travelling. BAe designed and manufactured the automatic laser tracker unit which includes two automatic tracking systems to track the target and missile in flight. A Ferranti laser is used for automatic target acquisition and tracking, while a standard Rapier TV system tracks the missile aided by flares mounted on the tail. The laser beamwidth is very narrow, in the order of a few milliradians, and this and the use of common optical paths for missile and target tracking ensures accurate guidance. The complete automatic laser tracker is gyro-stabilised, thereby eliminating the need for steadying jacks and time-consuming setting up procedures, and contributing to a typical 'ready-for-action' time of under three minutes.

The cab houses the crew of commander and operator, and a window in front of the former allows him to observe the progress of an engagement. A hatch in the cab roof also enables the commander to use an optical auxiliary sighting system to acquire targets under 'radar-silent' conditions. Both crew members have access to controls for manual selection or rejection of targets, setting of priority or safety zones, system status checks etc, as well as being able to operate the fire button. The computer, which controls all the Rapier Laserfire sub-systems during operations and testing, is installed in the cab, and a serial data bus is used for communication between them. This MIL Standard 1553B data highway allows other systems (eg an early warning radar) to be linked with the Rapier Laserfire.

The antenna for the command link antenna is mounted alongside the four missile launcher rails, and Rapier Laserfire uses the same command link as that used in the standard Rapier system, ie commands from the system computer are transmitted to the missile in flight where these are decoded and used to guide the missile along the laser sight-line until it strikes the target.

The engagement sequence commences with detection of a target in azimuth and elevation by the surveillance radar, which results in the system turntable automatically slewing onto the target bearing. At the same time the laser tracker and

missiles elevate to the target, if necessary, the tracker starts to search for the target. After acquiring the target, the laser tracker automatically then tracks it and the computer determines when the target comes within range. This is signalled to the operator who can then press the fire button.

STATUS

Rapier has been in operational service for some years, and has been adopted for the inventories of the armed services of about a dozen countries, as well as being under consideration for others. Those countries which are understood to have placed contracts include: Abu Dhabi, Australia, Brunei, Iran, Oman, Qatar, Singapore, Switzerland, Turkey, UK, USA and Zambia. As detailed previously, some of these have more than one version of the Rapier system in service eg towed/optical, towed/Blindfire, Tracked Rapier etc.

As noted under this entry number in *Jane's Weapon Systems 1983-84*, Rapier was credited with a number of successful engagements in the Falklands campaign of 1982, and the system has been selected for the protection of certain US Air Force missile bases in Europe.

The Australian Rapier low-level air defence system was completed in late 1983, by which time a total of 20 fire units had been supplied, supplemented by ten Blindfire radars.

The first Tracked Rapier for the British Army was handed over in early 1983, the original order having been for 50 units, but subsequent orders increased this total to 70.

A £200 million contract for a version of towed Rapier specifically configured to meet the requirements of the Swiss Army was awarded in December 1980, and the first of these systems was officially handed over in June 1984. In the course of meeting this contract, Marconi Space and Defence Systems Ltd handed over the 100th Blindfire radar supplied for use with Rapier.

In June 1984 BAe announced the development of a battery command post processor, intended primarily for users of the Rapier low-level AA system. It eliminates the manual processing associated with missile battery siting, and the software can be changed to accommodate other air defence systems, anti-tank defences, data base management or other functions.

The Rapier system, in conjunction with the Oto Melara Sidam 24 AA gun system (**4535.131**) features in a consortium response to a Canadian Government requirement for low-level air defence of its airfields and field army in Europe.

CONTRACTORS

The following manufacturers are known to have been associated with the system.

Weapon system: British Aerospace, Dynamics Group, Stevenage, Hertfordshire, England.

Safety and arming system: Marconi Space and Defence Systems Ltd.

Surveillance radar and command guidance: Racal-Decca Defence Systems (Radar) Ltd.

Secondary radar IFF: Cossor Electronics Ltd.

Servo-optical tracking system: Barr & Stroud Ltd.

Blindfire radar attachment: Marconi Space and Defence Systems Ltd.

Missile rocket motor: Imperial Metal Industries Ltd.

2465.131

TIGERCAT CLOSE-RANGE AIR DEFENCE SYSTEM

Tigercat, the land-based version of Short Brothers' widely fitted Seacat, is an autonomous ground-to-air guided missile system for low-level close-range air defence.

In the design of both Seacat and Tigercat the policy was to create a simple guided weapon capable of instant readiness. With any kind of radar warning system there is always the possibility of aircraft approach without detection to a range that permits little time for firing sequences. With Tigercat no prefiring sequences are required on the launcher and auxiliary power services within the missile are activated at launch. The system is thus capable of engaging and destroying at close range even rapidly manoeuvring targets.

Tigercat is compact and mobile and has cross-country capability. The basic fire unit comprises a director trailer, a launcher trailer, and two towing vehicles. These vehicles carry the fire-unit crew of five men, generating equipment, missiles and miscellaneous items. The launcher trailer consists of a two-wheel chassis integral with a three-missile launcher.

The principle of operation is that after a target is acquired by the aimer the missile is launched into the aimer's field of view. The aimer then directs the missile to fly along the line-of-sight to the target by manipulating a thumb-operated flight controller which applies up, down, left, and right commands to the missile by means of a radio link. Flares at the rear of the missile help the aimer to keep it in sight. As with Seacat the system is also suitable for operation using either radar or TV guidance.

Tigercat has been developed with the facility to accept a 'button-on' fire control radar to provide dark or blind fire in addition to visual operation. The director trailer in this mode incorporates the manually operated pedestal director of the lightweight Seacat system as a combined director and missile aiming sight with Seacat guidance equipment. When in radar control the 'dark fire' aimer's station is in the radar cabin where he is provided with a TV control console. The TV camera is aligned to the radar bore sight and provides optical information on the target being tracked. The system comprises a conventional camera and display and a data processing unit which permits automatic gathering of the missile to the target sightline. It can be integrated with any mobile radar system and also has the facility to receive target information via radio link when employed in the autonomous visual mode.

CHARACTERISTICS

Type: Surface-to-air close-range tactical guided missile

Guidance principle: Command link with optical or radar/TV tracking

Guidance method: Aerodynamic by movable wings

Propulsion: 2-stage solid-propellant motor

Warhead: HE

Missile length: 1·48 m

Missile diameter: 19 cm

Launch weight: 63 kg

STATUS

Tigercat is in production and is in service with or has been ordered by several overseas countries including Argentina, India, Iran, Qatar and South Africa. At least one foreign Tigercat customer is operating the radar-enhanced version of the system, the Marconi ST850 radar being supplied in 1981. Argentinian Tigercat missiles were thought to have scored hits on British aircraft during fighting in the Falkland Islands in 1982.

CONTRACTORS

Short Brothers Limited, Belfast, Northern Ireland makes the complete system including special test and training equipment. Other manufacturers known to be associated with the system are IMI Ltd which makes the rocket motor, EMI Ltd which makes the fuze and Marconi Radar Systems Ltd which supplies the ST850 radar employed in the radar-enhanced version of Tigercat.

Tigercat firing unit

UNITED STATES OF AMERICA

2542.131

CHAPARRAL SURFACE-TO-AIR WEAPON SYSTEM

Chaparral is a ground-to-air IR heat-seeking missile system which has been developed to meet US Army requirements for a low-altitude air defence weapon.

The system consists of a launch and control assembly, vehicle, and missile. The missiles are carried on and fired from a turret mounting four launch rails. Eight additional missiles are stored for ready access in the pallet. The gunner in the turret mount aims the missile at the target using an optical sight. Once locked-on to the target and fired, the missile guides itself to the target's heat source automatically. The Chaparral missile evolved from the US Navy-developed Sidewinder 1C, which has been modified for ground-to-air rather than air-to-air launch as now used by the Navy. The Navy procured the original inventory of missiles for Army use.

The launch and control assembly is a self-sustaining unit, capable of operation independent of the carrier vehicle in a ground emplacement mode. For missions requiring full-tracked mobility the fire unit is mounted on an M730 self-propelled tracked vehicle. It is amphibious when a 'swim kit' is used, will carry a crew of five, and can travel at up to 64 km per hour on the road.

One of the operational configurations is the association of Chaparral with the Vulcan air defence gun system (**2850.131**), the latter being a six-barrelled 20 mm Gatling gun adapted for ground use and mounted on a modified M113 personnel carrier. Forward area alert radar (FAAR – **1526.153**) can be deployed with Chaparral/Vulcan to provide early

warning and IFF identification within the detection area.

CHARACTERISTICS

US Army designation: M48 (self-propelled); M54 (ground emplaced)

Type: Land-mobile surface-to-air guided missile system

Guidance: IR homing after optical aiming

Missile designation: MIM-72A; MIM-72C/F (Improved Chaparral)

Propulsion: Solid-propellant rocket motor

Warhead: HE, blast fragmentation

Missile length: 2·91 m

Missile diameter: 13 cm

Span: 64 cm

Launch weight: Approx 84 kg

Speed: Supersonic

In addition to the SP and ground emplaced versions of Chaparral (M54 and M48) and improved models of this standard system, two new variants have been added: Night Chaparral and Sea Chaparral.

The former consists of a Chaparral system enhanced by the addition of a forward looking infra-red (FLIR) sensor and an associated display and control panel for the operator to give a night and adverse weather engagement capability.

Chaparral FLIR

This is a thermal imaging device designed as part of the Chaparral (M48) improvement programme. It provides considerably improved target acquisition for the operator as well as improved capabilities during daylight poor-weather conditions in addition to making night operation possible.

The Chaparral FLIR is comprised of US Army

Lightweight towed version of Chaparral air defence system

standard common modules (**3823.093** and related entries in the Electro-optical Equipment (Land) section contain additional details) specifically the following LRUs: IR receiver; receiver power supply; tracking signal processor; camera/video signal processor; control panel; video display.

The resulting Chaparral FLIR night sight is planned for installation on all M48 guided missile systems.

The Sea Chaparral employs a slightly modified launch station and can be operated either with the gunner in the mount or under the control of a remote gunner in the ship's operations room or similar fire control facility.

During 1982 a lightweight towed version of

Chaparral emerged which weighs approximately 5445 kg and is capable of being transported by cargo aircraft or helicopter, as well as towing by heavy duty vehicles. The launcher turret on the towed Chaparral has the full 360° azimuth and –10 to +90° elevation launch rail and this assembly is identical to the SP Chaparral.

STATUS

Chaparral is destined to be the US Army's forward area low-level air defence missile up to the end of this century, according to DoD.

Funding for Chaparral research and development, and procurement contained in the Report to Congress for fiscal year 1985 by the US Secretary of Defence was as follows:

Fiscal Year	R & D ($m)	Procurement ($m)
1983	24·7	52·8
1984	21·0	17·8
1985	17·6	118·3
1986	18·4	151·7

In the three years ending in 1986 it is proposed by the DoD to spend at least $47 million on Chaparral system modifications, including replacement of the propellant in the rocket motors and modifying the system with FLIR for engaging targets at night and in poor weather. A guidance system with increased resistance to IR countermeasures and which will have improved target acquisition and engagement range is being developed.

Overseas users include Egypt, Israel, Morocco, Taiwan and Tunisia, while US users are the US Army. Sea Chaparral has been selected by one foreign navy for close-in ship defence.

CONTRACTORS

Complete system and improved missile: Aeronutronic Division, Ford Aerospace & Communications Corporation, Newport Beach, California 92660, USA.

Vehicle: FMC Corporation, San Jose, California, USA.

4177.131
HAWK SURFACE-TO-AIR MISSILE

Hawk is an operational missile system providing air defence against enemy air attacks. Designed for effectiveness at medium- to low-altitude targets, Hawk uses a CW radar homing guidance system to discriminate against ground clutter and to achieve effective interception of the lowest flying aircraft.

The missile flies to intercept at supersonic speeds and is effective against the full spectrum of attacking aircraft at tactical speeds and in ECM environments. The system is mobile, helicopter transportable, and designed for use in rugged environments. The Hawk system entered service in 1960 and has served with the field units of the US Army, US Marine Corps, seven NATO nations, and 11 other countries. The system has been proven in more than 5000 flight tests. Every aspect of the system performance envelope has been verified, and the Hawk system has been used successfully in actual combat.

The system was improved in the late 1960s to counter advanced threats and to take advantage of the technological advances that had developed since the employment of the basic system described in **2640.131** in earlier editions. Two primary advances were made to the basic Hawk: (1) the no-field-test-or-repair certified round missile, and (2) the addition of a digital automatic data processor (ADP) for target processing, threat ordering, and target intercept evaluation.

There are two battery configurations of the Hawk system: the standard battery for normal field army operations and the Triad battery for situations requiring increased fire power. The standard battery includes two firing platoons, each with a tracking radar and three triple launchers. The Triad battery comprises three firing platoons. Improved assault fire units can operate autonomously when greater mobility is required.

The Hawk missile has a cruciform configuration with trailing edge control by rear elevons. Its guidance uses proportional navigation with CW, semi-active, all-the-way homing. It is a certified round requiring no field maintenance or testing. Certification is maintained through periodic batch acceptance testing, annual service firing and periodic batch sampling at special maintenance facilities operated by the contractor. The guidance system uses the latest state-of-the-art design and an array seeker antenna. The warhead is a blast fragmentation pattern design which provides a high single-shot kill probability.

CHARACTERISTICS

US Army designation: MIM-23B

Type: Mobile surface-to-air guided weapon system

Guidance: Semi-active homing with proportional navigation

Propulsion: 2-stage single chamber solid-propellant motor

Warhead: HE, blast fragmentation

Length: 5·03 m

Span: 1·19 m

Diameter: 0·36 m

Weight: 627·3 kg

Speed: Supersonic

Engagement envelope: Altitude from <30 m to >16 km. Range up to 40 km

MAJOR GROUND EQUIPMENT DESCRIPTION

Pulse Acquisition Radar (PAR)

The PAR is the primary source of high-to-medium aircraft detection for the battery. The L-band frequency allows the radar to perform in an all-weather environment. The radar incorporates a digital MTI to provide sensitive target detection in high clutter areas and a staggered pulse repetition rate to minimise the effects of blind speeds. The PAR also includes several ECCM features and uses off-the-air tuning of the transmitter.

CW Acquisition Radar (CWAR)

Aircraft detection at the lowest flyable altitudes in the presence of heavy clutter is the primary feature the CWAR brings to Hawk. The CWAR and PAR are synchronised in azimuth for ease of target data correlation. Other features include FM ranging, built-in test equipment (BITE) and band frequencies. FM is applied on alternate scans of the CWAR to obtain target range information. During the CW scan, range rate minus range is obtained. The ADP in the ICC processes this information to derive target range and range rate. This feature provides the necessary data for threat ordering of low altitude targets detected by the CWAR.

Battery Control Central (BCC)

The BCC provides the facilities for the man-to-machine interface. The tactical control officer (TCO) is in command of all BCC operations and maintains tactical control over all engagement sequences. The TCO monitors all functions and has the authority and facilities to enable or pre-empt any engagement or to change established priorities. The tactical control assistant assists the TCO in detection, identification, evaluation and co-ordination with higher commands. The tactical control console gives these two operators the necessary target and battery status information and controls required.

The azimuth-speed operator has the sole mission of earliest possible detection of low altitude targets. The azimuth-speed indicator console, a separate radar B-scope display, provides CWAR target data for this purpose. Targets selected for manual engagement are assigned to one of the two fire control operators. Each operator uses the fire control console display and controls for rapid HPI target lock, target track, missile launch, and target intercept evaluation.

Information Co-ordination Central (ICC)

The ICC is the fire control data processing and operational communications centre for the battery. It provides rapid and consistent reaction to critical targets. Automatic detection, threat ordering, and IFF followed by automatic target assignment and launch functions are provided by the ICC. The ICC contains an ADP, IFF, battery terminal equipment, and communications equipment.

The ADP is comprised of an electronic data processor (EDP) and a data take-off unit (DTO). The DTO forms the interface between the other system equipment and the EDP. With the exception of inputs from a solid-state reader and outputs to a printer, all communication with the EDP is through the DTO. The EDP is a militarised, general-purpose digital computer especially adapted to this role.

Platoon Command Post (PCP)

The PCP is used as the fire control centre and command post for the AFU. It can also be used to replace an ICC. The PCP provides manual and automatic target processing, IFF, intra-unit, intra-battery and army air defence command post communications, and the displays and fire control equipment for the three-man crew. It is essentially an ICC with a tactical display and engagement control console, a central communications unit, status indicator panel, and an automatic data processor. The tactical display and engagement control console provides the man/machine interface for the AFU. The interior of the shelter is divided into two compartments: the tactical officer, radar operator, and communications operator occupy the forward compartment with the display console, status panel, power distribution panel, and communications equipment; the rear compartment contains the ADP, air conditioning unit, and IFF equipment.

Hawk air defence missiles, here seen deployed at Twente Air Force Base, Netherlands

High Power Illuminator (HPI)

The HPI automatically acquires and tracks designated targets in azimuth, elevation and range rate. It serves as the interface unit supplying azimuth and elevation launch angles computed by the ADP to up to three launchers. The HPI X-band energy reflected off the target is also received by the Hawk missile for guidance. A missile reference signal is received directly from the HPI. Target track is continued throughout missile flight, and after intercept, HPI doppler data is used for kill evaluation. The HPI receives target designations from the BCC and automatically searches a given sector for rapid target lock-on. The HPI incorporates ECCM and BITE.

Range-only Radar (ROR)

This is a K-band pulse radar that provides quick-response range measurements whenever the other radars are denied range data by enemy countermeasures. During a tactical engagement, the radar is designated to obtain ranging information which is used in the computation of the fire command. The ROR reduces its vulnerability to jamming by transmitting only when designated.

Launcher (LCHR)

The LCHR supports up to three ready-to-fire missiles and is activated only upon the initiation of the fire cycle. When the fire button is activated in the BCC or PCP, several launcher functions occur simultaneously: the launcher slews to designated azimuth and elevation angles, power is supplied to activate the missile gyros, electronic and hydraulic systems, the launcher activates the missile motor and launches the missile. The launcher is equipped with electronic cut-outs and sensing circuits that allow firing in all emplacement situations.

PHASED PRE-PLANNED PRODUCT IMPROVEMENT PROGRAMMES (PIPs)

A series of PIPs to increase operational readiness and system effectiveness were announced by Raytheon in October 1978. In Phase I the CWAR transmitter, the Army Tactical Data Link (ATDL) and the PAR MTI performance capabilities were improved. Phase II provides reliability and maintainance improvements for the HPI and new optical tracking augmentation. Phase III streamlines the battery and reduces manpower and logistic support requirements.

Phase I: The CWAR improvements involve a new klystron transmitter, new BITE and modifications to the antenna housing and other elements of the sub-system. Advantages are: more than doubling of transmitter MTBF, a 25 per cent improvement in radar reliability; and a doubling of output power which increases detection range.

ATDL improvements include an increased memory capacity and re-formated data language. These changes provide a computer-to-computer interchange of data between a Hawk battery and a high level (battalion) fire distribution system. Modifications in this programme are to the ICC/PCP and BCC elements of the system. Benefits of this programme are more target tracks and threat ordering information, greatly reduced system reaction time, improved reliability and increased capabilities as a defensive weapon.

The PAR improvement implements a new digital MTI programme. Hardware changes include a modern solid-state control oscillator, modifications to the power distribution and the indicator azimuth range subassemblies, and addition of a digital signal processor to replace the single comparator. Performance benefits are increased detection capabilities in clutter environments, a wider range for automatic detection, a reduction in the number of adjustments and elimination of blind speeds.

Started in 1977, Phase I was fielded in 1979.

Phase II: This was approved for production in 1983. It involves modifications to the HPI. A major reliability and maintenance design was implemented that improved the reliability of the HPI by more than 300 per cent. This technology update replaced tube-type equipments with solid-state modules and the design made failure replacement much easier and reduced the number of user adjustments. Other improvements are emission control for operating in an anti-radiation

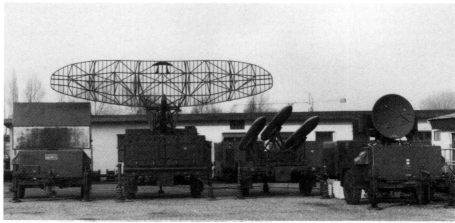
Hawk battery subject of PIP (product improvement programme) by the European 'GRIP' consortium

missile environment, an ECCM update and a new TAS.

Tracking Adjunct System (TAS)

The Tracking Adjunct System is an electro-optical tracker system developed as part of the Phase III product improvement for the Hawk fire control system. It was developed from TISEO (Target Identification System, Electro-Optical) in production and used by the US Air Force and a number of foreign countries (**1806.363**).

TAS is described in greater detail in entry **4240.183**. It provides a passive tracking capability to the Hawk fire control radar with remote real-time video viewing, and it is intended to serve as a back-up and aid to the tracking radar. Optical tracking can be coincident or independent of the radar line-of-sight, manual or automatic; acquisition and tracking, rate memory and preferential target illumination are key features. Operational benefits include positive indentification, threat assessment, kill assessment, spectre recognition, tracking in minimum doppler, silent tracking and independent tracking. The TAS operates in conjunction with the Hawk's radar and assists in the discrimination between several targets approaching at the same time or between low-flying targets and features on the horizon. It also counters some of the countermeasures which may be employed by the targets to confuse radar. TAS engineering development began in 1976. Production for the US Army and Marine Corps commenced in March 1980 and the equipment is currently being fitted to US Army Hawk batteries in the field.

Phase III: This programme increases Hawk system fire power and improves system performance while reducing manpower and logistic support requirements. The Hawk fire platoon will have fewer major items. New digital technology within the major items will allow the replacement of data cables with field wire between the radars and the PCP. The new computers used in the HPI, CWAR, tactical display and engagement control console, and ADP eliminate a large number of battery replaceable units. In addition, the new computers have common micro-computer hardware to further reduce logistic requirements.

Improved system performance will be accomplished by increased fire power, improved ECCM, enhanced operational efficiency through improved man/machine interface and a new integrated operator trainer, and upgraded air battle information throughout the C³ network.

Production approval for Phase III is planned for 1985.

DEVELOPMENT

Development of basic Hawk began in 1954 and the system first became operational in 1959, the programme having been under the control of the US Army Missile Command, Huntsville, Alabama. Engineering of the system was performed at Raytheon's laboratories at Bedford and Wayland, Massachusetts, and at White Sands, New Mexico. US production of the missile and equipment has been principally at Andover and Waltham, Massachusetts.

STATUS

Hawk systems are currently deployed throughout the world, and in the US Army and Marine Corps it will remain the mainstay of field air defences until replaced by Patriot (**2800.131**, below).

The American programme to up-grade the Hawk for the US Army and Marine Corps continues, including installation of a new missile motor and provision of a multi-engagement capability. The US fiscal year 1985 DoD budget showed scheduled and planned Hawk procurement and expenditure for 1983/84/85 as follows (quantities in brackets) and funding in $ millions: (211) 75·4, (400) 97 and (500) 125·1. A West German Air Force battalion received its first four Hawk batteries embodying modifications carried out under the European PIP in June 1982. In late 1983 Italy took delivery of its last battery of Hawk systems upgraded by the European GRIP consortium under the PIP arrangement.

Northrop received a $28·2 million US Army contract covering production of 47 launchers and 41 loaders, plus support equipment in February 1984. The company had previously delivered more than 2100 launchers. Deliveries of the latest batch begins in mid-1985. In March 1984, 61 TAS sets for United Arab Emirates Hawk batteries were ordered from Northrop.

Countries operating Hawks are: Belgium, Denmark, Egypt, France, West Germany, Greece, Israel, Italy, Japan, Jordan, Kuwait, Netherlands, Norway, Saudi Arabia, Singapore, South Korea, Spain, Sweden, Taiwan, United Arab Emirates and the USA.

CONTRACTORS

For European manufacture of the Improved Hawk air defence system Raytheon is systems contractor under the direction of the NATO Hawk Management Office (NHMO) in Paris, France. In the USA, Raytheon produced the missile guidance and control units and limited quantities of ground equipment. European contractors (see below) produced ground equipment, certain missile parts, final missile assembly, and overhaul and conversion of the basic Hawk equipment. A Raytheon subsidiary, Raytheon European Management and Systems Company (REMSCO) serves as NHMO's European programme management contractor for 16 major European industrial activities. NATO nations participating in the programmes are Belgium, Denmark, France, West Germany, Greece, Italy and the Netherlands.

Complete system development and US production: Raytheon Company, Lexington, Massachusetts, USA.

Rocket motors: Aerojet General Corporation, El Monte, California, USA.

Wings and elevons: Northrop Corporation, Beverly Hills, California, USA.

Warheads: Iowa Ordnance Depot.

NATO Improved Hawk: Belgium – ACEC; France – SNPE, SODETEG, Thomson-CSF; Federal Republic of Germany – AEG-Telefunken, MBB; Italy – Aeritalia, Aerochemie, Selenia, Sigme, MES, FIAR.

Japanese production: Mitsubishi Electric Corp and Toshiba.

2800.131
PATRIOT (XMIM-104) TACTICAL AIR DEFENCE SYSTEM

Patriot is an advanced guided weapon system intended as a replacement for the Hawk and Nike Hercules systems. The Patriot fire unit contains all the elements necessary to conduct an engagement: the radar set, engagement control station, electric power plant, and eight launching stations. Each launching station contains four missiles in their firing canisters, which also serve as shipping and storage containers. The US Army is working in collaboration with NATO countries on a joint acquisition programme. The US plans to deploy Patriot battalions in Europe and the continental USA, each battalion consisting of six batteries equipped with eight four-tube launchers (a total of 192 missile tubes). The Patriot radar set AN/MPQ-53 is a multi-function, phased array device, which performs all of the surveillance, IFF, tracking and guidance functions which currently require nine separate radars in the Hawk (**4177.131**) and Nike Hercules (**2723.131**) air defence systems. Radar target identification is performed by an AN/TPX-46(V)7 interrogator, using supplementary antenna arrays on the main AN/MPQ-53 radar antenna unit. The engagement control station AN/MSQ-104 houses the weapon control computer which automatically sequences the system through all tactical engagement operations, monitors the operational status of the hardware, conducts automated fault detection and location as required, and provides the man-machine interface for human control. The engagement control station is the only manned station and remotely controls the other elements of the fire unit. The electric power plant AN/MJQ-20 includes two 150 kW turbine-driven generators. The launching station XM-901 includes its own independent 15 kW diesel generator and radio link to the engagement control station. The guided missile XMIM-104 is a certified round, which is shipped, stored and fired from its canister without testing or maintenance in the field. Periodic lot

sampling of guided missiles on launchers and in storage will provide assurance of their capability. The tail-controlled missile carries a high explosive fragmentation warhead and is capable of outmanoeuvring and destroying any manned aircraft missile, according to the manufacturer.

CHARACTERISTICS
Type: Land-mobile, surface-to-air guided weapon system
Guidance principle: Command guidance and semi-active homing. Track-via-missile (TVM)
Guidance method: By control of 4 aerodynamic control surfaces
Propulsion: Single-stage solid-propellant rocket motor TX-486
Missile length: 5·31 m
Missile diameter: 41 cm
Warhead: Nuclear or HE
Speed: Supersonic

DEVELOPMENT
Patriot is the successor to two earlier study programmes managed by the US Army Missile Command's Research and Development Directorate. These studies were concerned with systems known as the Field Army Ballistic Missile Defense System (FABMDS) and the Army Air Defense System for the 1970s (AADS-70s).

In January 1965 the SAM-D requirement was specified and a study was directed towards defence against high-performance aircraft – at all altitudes – and short-range missiles. SAM-D was placed under project management at the US Army Missile Command in August 1965 and shortly thereafter the contract definition process was initiated by the DoD. In February 1970 the missile successfully completed its first launch environmental test. The US Army planned to begin engineering development in fiscal year 1971, but the advanced development phase was not completed until March 1972 when engineering development started.

STATUS
The Patriot engineering development programme

was initiated in 1972. In 1974 the programme was stretched to emphasise demonstration of the TVM guidance system with the minimum necessary hardware development to permit programme continuation. Authority to resume full-scale development was given in early 1976, following a successful firing programme of 12 complete successes and one partial success in 14 firings. A 49-month $425 million contract was initiated in August 1976 to complete the development programme. The firing programme was resumed in December 1976 with the first tactical prototype ground equipment. US Army developer testing, and field operational exercises conducted with troops in US Army operational tests had been completed by the end of 1981. Following completion in 1980 of the development programme, limited production of Patriot systems was authorised. Following parallel confirmation tests on development equipment in 1981 and production hardware in 1982 and 1983, authorisation of increased production was expected.

The fiscal year 1985 budget indicated allocations of $45·4, $83, $61·5 and $55·7 millions for continued development in fiscal years 1983-86. The projected procurement of fire units and missiles, and the related budget allocations for the same four years is as follows:

Fiscal Year	Fire Units	Missiles	Funding ($m)
1983	12	287	844·8
1984	12	440	963·5
1985	15	585	1202·4
1986	18	815	1354·5

In early 1983 it was stated that Belgium would no longer participate in the programme under which European member states of NATO would procure Patriot systems for air defence. The reason given was lack of funds but in April 1984 it was expected that an agreement under which the USA would supply Patriot systems without cost could be concluded. This would give Belgium 20 Patriot launchers, of which four would be deployed at each of four Belgian bases in West Germany in 1987-88.

In mid-1984 Japan was apparently still undecided whether or not to include Patriot as a candidate for the nation's Nike-J and Hawk successor system, known as SAM-X. Funding for the SAM-X programme had been dropped, and improvements to the predecessor system proposed instead, but an eventual procurement of Patriot is still thought to remain a possibility.

The Netherlands plans to deploy a similar number of Patriot systems (20) as Belgium and is likely to be the first European customer for the system. The Federal Republic of Germany is expected to field more, 28 systems, to replace Nike Hercules. The first deployment of US Army Patriot fire units in Europe were expected to occur in 1984-85.

CONTRACTORS
System: Raytheon Company, Andover, Massachusetts, USA. (Prime)

Principal sub-contractors: Martin Marietta Aerospace, Orlando, Florida, USA. (Missile airframe and launcher)

Hazeltine Corporation, Commack, New York 11725, USA. (IFF interrogator)

Patriot launch from standard 4-round firing unit

2723.131
NIKE HERCULES (MIM-14B) AIR DEFENCE MISSILE

One of the earlier surface-to-air guided weapon systems still in commission, the Nike Hercules missile, successor to the Nike Ajax, was widely deployed in the USA and other countries. It first became operational in the USA in 1958.

Nike Hercules, a second-generation missile, possesses greater destructive ability and has a better performance than Nike Ajax. It has proved successful against high-performance aircraft at a variety of altitudes and has successfully intercepted short-

range ballistic missiles and other Nike Hercules missiles in tests.

System units are a low-power acquisition radar, a high-power acquisition radar, a target tracking radar, a missile tracking radar, electronic data-processing equipment and remote-controlled launchers. A later innovation, the high-power acquisition radar (HIPAR – **2499.153**), enables Nike Hercules mobile units to get the same full target detection capability as batteries at fixed sites. The HIPAR's three vans house radar gear transmitter, receiver, and control equipment. One of its two semi-trailers hauls the 43 foot (13·1 metre) wide, fan-shaped antenna. The other semi-trailer

carries power generators. Before the mobile HIPAR was adopted more than 20 vehicles were required to move the radar system.

When a target is detected by the acquisition radar it is interrogated by the associated AN/TPX-46 IFF Mk XII interrogator and if adjudged hostile its location is transferred to the target tracking radar which pinpoints it for intercept purposes.

The Nike Hercules is launched by remote control, normally at an 85-degree angle. When the booster cluster has separated, the guidance system is activated, programming the missile to roll toward the target and dive into the intercept plane. Steering commands direct the missile to the optimum burst point. The Nike Hercules is equipped with an ECCM capability.

Each Hercules battery can operate as part of a defence network or as an autonomous unit, capable of detecting, tracking, and engaging targets. The system operators are located in a battery control trailer, a tracking radar control trailer, and a launcher control trailer. The Hercules is capable of operating in an ECM environment.

CHARACTERISTICS

Type: Surface-to-air, strategic, guided missile
Guidance: Command
Propulsion: 2-stage solid-propellant rocket motor
Warhead: Nuclear or HE
Missile length: 12·1 m
Diameter: 80 cm
Launch weight: 4858 kg
Speed: Supersonic
Range: >140 km
Ceiling: >45 km

STATUS

Major improvements were made to this system in 1961 when new radars and modifications were added to enable the system to remain operational until replaced by the Patriot (**2800.131**) missile. The number of active batteries has steadily declined since 1963, however, when there were 134 US batteries. The decline continued, and by 1980 all continental USA Nike Hercules installations are thought to have been abandoned.

A non-nuclear version of the Nike Hercules missile is being produced by Mitsubishi Heavy Industries Ltd for the Japanese Army under a licensing agreement with the American manufacturer.

A more recent possible enhancement said to be under consideration by the Japanese contractor is that known as Nike-Phoenix. This concept is based on integration of the complete guidance system of the US Navy Phoenix air-to-air missile system (**1099.331**)

Nike Hercules air defence missile launch

into the Nike System. This would entail equipping the Nike missile with the seeker from the Phoenix missile, and this would be complemented by the incorporation of the AN/AWG-9 radar (**1100.353**), modified for ground use from its original airborne application. The AWG-9 would become part of the Nike installation to replace the existing target and missile tracking radars, to provide for simultaneous engagement of up to six targets with separate missiles.

Apart from Japan, Nike Hercules is also widely deployed in NATO and other countries with which the USA has friendly military relationships. Countries believed still to have the missile in strength are Belgium, Denmark, West Germany Greece, Italy, Norway, and Taiwan. The US Nike Hercules batteries in Korea have been transferred to the Republic of Korea, where, it is believed this missile is also operated in an alternative surface-to-surface role.

Due to funding difficulties, from July 1984 the number of Belgian Nike units based in West Germany (eight) was reduced to four, but if an agreement proposed by the USA is concluded these will probably remain in service until replaced by Patriot units in the late-1980s.

In 1981 contracts were placed for a number of improvements to the existing Nike Hercules systems. McDonnell Douglas is refurbishing and modifying NATO Nike Hercules missiles, and the contract also provided for a series of test launches from the NATO test range at Salto di Quirra, Sardinia. A related element of this Nike Hercules updating programme is the digital computer system (DCS) which is being supplied by Norden Systems. The DCS is based on the PDP-11/34M mini-computer and it receives missile and target position inputs from tracking radars, solves the intercept problem and issues guidance commands to the missile. It also performs various other routines, such as fault diagnosis. By replacing the earlier analogue system with the new digital computer, reliability of the Nike Hercules system will be improved and maintenance simplified. DCS deliveries began in late 1981 for NATO batteries and supplies to Far Eastern installations are expected to follow. The complete DCS programme could cost $15 million.

CONTRACTORS

Prime: Western Electric Company, Burlington, North Carolina, USA.

McDonnell Douglas Astronautics Company, 5301 Bolsa Avenue, Huntington Beach, California 92647, USA.

Bell Telephone Laboratories, Burlington, North Carolina, USA.

General Electric Company, Syracuse, New York, USA.

AAI Inc, Cockeysville, Maryland, USA.

Raytheon Company, Wayland, Massachusetts, USA.

Mobile Gun and Rocket Systems

FRANCE

<small>FRENCH MOBILE ANTI-AIRCRAFT GUN SYSTEMS</small>

System	Chassis	Turret	Weapon(s)	Fire Control	Status	Entry No.
AA 20 (ESD)	Uses towed AA guns with transportable or mobile control unit			Galileo P56 individual gun sights, ESD RA21 radar in control unit	For protection of airfields, missile batteries, comms centres etc	**3332.131**
AMX30 SA	AMX30 (GIAT)	TG230A (SAMM)	2 × HS831A 30 mm guns (GIAT)	Oeil Vert radar (Th-CSF) APX M250 optical sight	In production	**2138.131**
Dragon (Th-CSF/Thyssen)	TH328 tank	Welded steel, 2-man (SAMM/GIAT)	2 × HSS831A 30 mm guns (GIAT)	Oeil Vert radar (Th-CSF) APX M250 optical sight	Joint project between Thomson-CSF (France) and Thyssen Henschel (West Germany)	**3679.131**
M3-VDA (Panhard)	M3 (Panhard) wheeled APC	TA20 1-man (H20R) (CNMP)	2 × HSS820SL 20 mm guns (GIAT)	RA20 radar (ESD) with Galileo P56T optical sight	In production	**2164.131**
TA20/RA20S (ESD)	VAB (Renault) wheeled armoured car	TA20 1-man (H20R) (CNMP)	2 × HSS820SL 20 mm guns (GIAT)	RA20 radar (ESD) in lead vehicle, Galileo P56 optical sight in all vehicles	Production for some overseas countries	**4502.131**
TSE 6200 (Th-CSF)	Crotale type 4-wheeled	GTS (GIAT/Th-CSF/ SAMM)	2 × F2 20 mm guns (GIAT)	Sagem stabilised optical sight. Laser rangefinder	Prototypes	**3680.131**
VDAA	Wheeled APC (Saviem)	TA20 1-man (H20R) (CNMP)	2 × HSS820SL 20 mm guns (GIAT)	RA20 radar (ESD) optical sight	Prototype	**2164.131**

3332.131
AA 20 WEAPON SYSTEM
This system is a semi-mobile configuration comprising a number of towed small-calibre anti-aircraft guns, used in conjunction with a truck-mounted fire control centre for the low-level point defence of targets such as airfields, bridges etc.

The fire control centre consists of a radar-equipped cabin mounted on a light tactical truck. The RA20 S radar is similar to that of the ESD TA20 turret which is used in other French mobile AA systems. Cable or VHF FM radio links connect the fire control centre to

up to four gun positions, each of which is equipped with a P56 weapon aiming unit comprising a sight, firing computer and hydraulic servo-drive system. Other parts of the overall system are the radar data processing and parallax computation elements.

Two firing modes are possible:
(1) autonomous, whereby each gun operates independently, firing parameters being estimated by the gunner
(2) central control mode, in which the fire control centre performs air search with the radar, threat evaluation and target designation, and

transmission of firing parameters to the computer of each gun.

The principal characteristics of the radar are a range of 11 km against a typical tactical support aircraft target, an antenna rotation rate of 40 rpm, and simultaneous tracking of up to two targets.
STATUS
Development.
CONTRACTOR
ESD – Electronique Serge Dassault, 55 quai Carnot, 92214 St Cloud, France.

4502.131
TWIN 20 mm AA WEAPON SYSTEM TA20/RA20 S
Electronique Serge Dassault has designed and manufactured the TA20 mobile gun system which, in association with the RA20 S search and target designation radar, provides the means of defending moving formations or vulnerable positions against air attack. Only one RA20 S radar is required for a two- or three-vehicle platoon, and this radar may be installed in any one of the vehicles, which then becomes the 'leader', the other one or two vehicles being the 'satellite(s)'. All vehicles are linked by an automatic radio transmission system.

The radar detects low-flying aircraft and assigns a designated target to the leader, to a satellite or both, and automatically transmits the target co-ordinates. This data is fed to the fire control system. Trajectory information is calculated by a processing unit in each vehicle. Separation between vehicles is normally less than 1000 metres. The TA20 system is operated by a crew of two: a radar operator who is also the vehicle commander and platoon commander and a gunner, alone in the turret.

The main components of the system are:
(1) two Oerlikon KAD-B rapid firing 20 mm guns delivering 2000 rounds/minute
(2) a Galileo P56T optical sight
(3) turret with a rotational speed of 80°/s
(4) gyro-stabilisation equipment for guns during firing
(5) control units for turret and gun operation.

The system is installed in the Renault VAB/VDAA; Panhard M3 VDA; AMX 13 and also the Urutu and Sibmas vehicles. It permits engagement of enemy aircraft at a range of 1800 metres, the RA20 S radar detection envelope providing for targets attacking at altitudes between ground level and 2000 metres to be acquired at a range of 12 km.

Renault VAB vehicle with ESD TA20/RA20 S twin 20 mm AA system fitted

CHARACTERISTICS
TA20 turret
Track diameter: 1500 mm
Total height: 1200 mm
Combat weight: 1940 kg
Ready use rounds: 2 × 300
Rate of fire: 1000 rounds/minute/gun
RA20 S radar: E-band pulse doppler

TWS: 2 tracks
Antenna unit weight: 60 kg
Range: 12 km
STATUS
Believed to have been ordered for export.
CONTRACTOR
ESD – Electronique Serge Dassault, 55 quai Carnot, 92214 St Cloud, France.

2164.131

M3-VDA AA GUN SYSTEM

This Panhard/ESD system combines the firepower of many heavier SP AA gun systems with the low weight and high mobility of the Panhard M3 vehicle. It comprises a one-man gun turret mounted on the specially adapted M3 and carrying a pair of HSS 820 SL guns; a weapon control system with a display for the vehicle commander; and the vehicle itself which is driven by the third member of the crew. The system is also known under the ESD designation TA20, and other variants are the AA 20 system (**3332.131**) which is a transportable version employing towed AA guns, and the VDAA (Véhicule d'Auto-Défense Anti-Aérienne) which is essentially the same as the M3-VDA but mounted on a different carrier vehicle in place of the Panhard M3.

The weapon control system comprises a radar (or alternatively an optical observation system), a computer sight, and high-speed controls for the twin guns and feed system.

The ESD radar is an I/J-band pulse doppler surveillance/acquisition device with a detection range of about 8 km (2 m² target) and a rotation rate of 40 rpm. Targets are displayed on the commander's console, and in target designation the radar feeds target bearing to the optical sighting system and range and target velocity to the Galileo computer sight. The gunner keeps the optical sight trained on the target and the computer calculates lead angle and favourable engagement conditions.

For the simpler (and cheaper) version of the equipment the radar is replaced by two optical observation posts, one for the commander and one for the gunner, with overlapping arcs of observation to give full 360° coverage. When one or other observer is tracking a target the tracking movement generates signals from which the computer calculates lead angle and engagement data as before. The absence of direct range and velocity measurements, of course, makes smooth tracking essential if reasonable accuracy is to be achieved and to this extent the non-radar version is more demanding than the other.

Panhard M3-VDA anti-aircraft vehicle

CHARACTERISTICS

Vehicle characteristics: Generally similar to the M3-VTT

Combat weight: 6300 kg

Road speed/range: 90 km/h/1000 km

Armament: 2 HSS 820 SL or similar 20 mm cannon. HSS weapon has MV 300 m/s, slant range 2000 m, maximum engagement altitude 1500 m. Rate of fire 800-1050 rounds/minute, 600 rounds (2 × 300 belts) carried

Radar: ESD pulse doppler

Computer sight: P56-Galileo

STATUS

Series production in progress for the armed forces of several foreign states.

CONTRACTORS

System: Société de Constructions Mécaniques Panhard et Levassor, 18 avenue d'Ivry, 75013 Paris, France.

Radar: Electronique Serge Dassault.

Computer: Officine Galileo.

4512.131

SABRE TWIN 30 mm AA GUN TURRET SYSTEM

The function of the Sabre AA gun system is to protect advanced battle corps units or critical points such as river crossings, transport or communications hubs, concentrations of armour in combat, rear bases and depots, target defence systems etc, against air threats posed by low or very low altitude attacks by ground attack aircraft or armed helicopters.

The Sabre turret system is designed to provide an omni-directional radar search capability and to identify, track, acquire and destroy targets. The system is capable of destroying these targets due to the following characteristics:

(1) search surveillance at 15 or 22 km of targets flying at 20 to 300 m/s

(2) quick reaction time enhanced by automatic slewing, TV tracking

(3) fire power provided by two 30 mm guns, 20 rounds/s or high-rate bursts

(4) accuracy provided by gyro-stabilised sight, low-dispersion ballistic rangefinder

(5) availability ensured by equipment reliability and easy maintenance up to second level

(6) autonomy ensured by on-board munitions (600), spare parts and electric power supply system.

System performance and short reaction time make the Sabre gun system an ideal complement to missile air defence systems. The turret is of the armoured rotating casemate type. It is equipped with two automatic Oerlikon 30 mm KCB guns, Type 230, with two link belt ammunition bearers and a burst limiter permitting the following firing modes: single-shot firing; 5- or 15-shot bursts.

The ammunition allocation is 300 rounds per weapon, making a total of 600 rounds in the turret. It also supports the Oeil Vert or Oeil Vert Plus omni-directional search radar used for threat evaluation and acquisition of targets flying at altitudes of not greater than 3000 metres and at radial velocities between 30 and 300 metres/second; the turret can also be equipped with an optional IFF system. Fire control is provided by:

Sabre twin 30 mm AA turret mounted on AMX 30 chassis

(1) stabilised electro-optical sight which ensures optical tracking of targets

(2) digital calculator which handles the data supplied by the tracking system the radar and the rangefinder

(3) automatic TV tracking system

(4) laser rangefinder which ensures highly-accurate target range measurement.

The Sabre turret is operated by a crew of two: the tank commander who controls the data provided by the radar and orders firing; and a gun-layer/firing operator who controls optical aiming and firing. The turret is autonomous in operation and can be mounted on a variety of carriers such as: tracked vehicles, eg AMX 10RC, AMX 13, AMX 30, Kurassier and Marder (see **3679.131** below); wheeled armoured vehicles by Renault or Panhard; towed and/or air transportable shelters; or casemates.

OPERATION

The different operational phases of the Sabre 30 mm twin gun system are as follows:

(1) Omni-directional search, identification, designation

Early warning is given by the radar forming part of the system or by radio information from the surveillance net. When the radar is in the 'long-range search' mode, it covers a range 1 to 15 km with Oeil Vert and 1 to 22 km with Oeil Vert Plus, from 0 to 3000 metres in altitude, for a target with a speed varying from 30 to 300 metres/second. As soon as the target is detected by the radar, the computer evaluates the threat and identifies enemy targets (optional IFF system).

(2) Target acquisition

In bearing: The tank commander selects the target by overlaying a marker on the echo using a joystick. This operation initialises automatic radar tracking of the target in range and bearing by means of a track-while-scan system. When deemed necessary by the tank commander, at 10 km for example, he slews the turret in the direction of the tracked target.

In elevation: Acquisition is carried out automatically or manually. The gun-laying/firing operator acquires the target in elevation using the stabilised electro-optical sight which includes the TV camera system installed in the turret.

(3) TV tracking and extrapolation

Target tracking is by an optical sight and a TV electro-optical system. Automatic or manual system operation is selected by the operator. For automatic operation, all turret movements are slaved by the TV angle-error measurement system which uses the camera video signal to provide angle-error data, ie the position of a target selected by the operator on the TV image with respect to the image centre. The data supplied by the tracking, radar and angle-error measurement system is processed by a digital computer which generates the fire data required to align the two guns on the future target.

(4) Final engagement

The tank commander makes the final engagement decisions demanded by the current air situation. As

Close-up of Sabre turret showing Oeil Vert radar and electro-optical sight installation

Sabre turret on air-transportable trailer/shelter. Installations of this turret on Kürassier and Dragon chassis are illustrated on later pages

soon as the target comes within the range of the weapon system and firing is authorised, the guns can engage. The guns are continuously supplied with ammunition, thereby permitting several bursts without reload.

CHARACTERISTICS
Weight: 12 t (combat ready)
Height: 2·72 m (radar retracted)
Deployment time: 3 minutes
Surveillance radar
Oeii Vert range: 15 km
Oeil Vert Plus range: 22 km
Sub-clutter visibility: >40 dB
Weapon: 2 × 30 mm KCB guns
Rate of fire: 600 rounds/minute/gun
Burst length: 5 to 20+ rounds
Effective range: 3300 m
MV: 1080 m/s
STATUS
Prototypes have been built and are under comprehensive evaluation in several configurations.

More than 50 examples of the TG 230A twin 30 mm turret, which the Sabre succeeds, were built and this earlier version was described in some detail in previous editions of *Jane's Weapon Systems*. The Sabre turret is employed in the Austrian Kürassier (**4465.131**) and the Franco-West German Dragon (**3679.131**) systems.
CONTRACTORS
Prime for system and electronics: Thomson-CSF, Division Systèmes Electroniques, 1 rue des Mathurins, BP 10, 92223 Bagneux, France.

Chassis and guns: Groupement Industriel des Armements Terrestres (GIAT), 10 place Georges Clémenceau, 92211 St Cloud, France.

Turret: Société d'Applications des Machines Motrices (SAMM), 244 quai de Stalingrad, 92130 Issy les Moulineaux, France.

Turret: Creusot Loire, 15 rue Pasquier, 75008 Paris, France.

GERMANY (FEDERAL REPUBLIC)

3681.131
WILDCAT (AAAT) TWIN 30 mm AA WEAPON SYSTEM

The Wildcat (formerly AAAT anti-aircraft armoured truck) is a highly mobile, fast road/cross-country vehicle capable of providing anti-aircraft defence for mobile formations, and key installations such as airfields. It is based on the use of a slightly modified Daimler-Benz TPZ1 six-wheeled armoured truck chassis carrying a twin 30 mm automatic cannon turret. Five versions have been considered, among them: one with a search radar and an electro-optical system that includes a TV tracker and laser rangefinder; another an all-weather version with full day/night capability, using search and tracking radars. The crew consists of three men: the commander who is in tactical control of the system, the gunner who conducts engagements, and the driver.

A search radar scans the surrounding airspace at a rate of once per second, whether the vehicle is on the move or stationary. Aircraft and helicopters within range are displayed on the radar PPI and automatically identified by IFF. After a target has been selected on the search radar display and its elevation established, it is tracked automatically by the TV tracker/laser rangefinder unit (daylight/clear weather version) or by tracker radar (all weather, day/night version). The fire control and functional sequences are controlled by a digital computer. This determines the laying of the cannon taking into account target data, vehicle cant and actual meteorological data. When the target enters the engagement zone this is signalled to both the vehicle commander and the gunner. The weapon control system is the responsibility of Hollandse Signaalapparaten. The same concern also provides the LIOD target tracker and SMR micro-computer. Details of the radar, in several applications, will be found in the Flakpanzer entry (**3330.131**) later in this section, the Flycatcher air defence fire control system (**2301.181**), the Goalkeeper naval fire control system (**3516.261**), and in entry **2302.153** in the Ground Radar section of this volume.

Prototype Wildcat (formerly the AAAT anti-aircraft armoured truck vehicle)

CHARACTERISTICS
Vehicle: TPZ1 (modified)
Combat weight: 18·5 t (approx)
Length: 6·88 m
Width: 2·98 m
Overall height: 2·74 m (radar stowed)
Ground clearance: 41 cm
Engine: Mercedes-Benz 8-cylinder, 320 hp
Max speed: 80 km/h
Operating range: 600 km approx
Cannon: 2 × Mauser Mk 30F, automatic belt fed
Calibre: 30 mm
Rate of fire: 1600 rounds/minute (combined)
Ammunition: HEI/APDS

Ammunition capacity: 500 rounds
MV: 1050 m/s (HEI)
Traverse: 360° continuous
Elevation: –5 to +85°
Fire control equipment
Search radar: Pulse doppler, digital MTI
Frequency: J-band (about 9 GHz)
Range: 18 km
Data rate: 1 Hz (60 rpm)
IFF: Integrated
Fire control computer: Digital, 24-bit
Tracking radar: All-weather version only
Frequency: Ka-band (about 35 GHz)
Range: 11 km

Antenna: Cassegrain monopulse
E-O director: (Clear weather version)
TV tracker: Militarised daylight television camera, video format to CCIR standard (625 lines, 25 frame/s, 2:1 interlace)
Field of view: 2·4° wide × 1·8° elevation
Laser rangefinder: Neodymium-YAG transmitter, 1·06 micron
Firing rate: 10 Hz
Beam divergence: 1·2 – 1·5 mil
Periscope: Fixed monocular eyepiece
Magnification: ×2, ×8
Field of view: 32°, 8°

Traverse: 360° (continuous)
Elevation: –10 to +70°
STATUS
Development project. In May 1981 the project was officially named Wildcat and it made its public debut in prototype form the following month at the Paris Air Show. No contractual details have been released. Missile versions have also been studied.
CONTRACTORS
System main contractor: Kraus-Maffei Aktiengesellschaft, Ordnance Division, Kraus-Maffei-strasse 2, 8000 Munich 50, Federal Republic of Germany.
Fire control equipment: Hollandse Signaal-

apparaten BV, Netherlands.
Twin 30 mm cannon: Mauser-Werke, Federal Republic of Germany.
Search radar: Siemens AG, Federal Republic of Germany.
Ammunition feed system: Kuka Wehrtechnik GmbH, Federal Republic of Germany.
Turret/weapon drives: AEG-Telefunken, Federal Republic of Germany.
Chassis: Krauss-Maffei AG, Federal Republic of Germany.

2182.131
20 mm TWIN GUN ANTI-AIRCRAFT SYSTEM

The AA 20 mm Twin Gun is a light highly mobile automatic system for engaging low-flying aircraft. It can also be used to engage ground targets.

Comprising two automatic rapid-fire guns with an analogue computer sight mounted on a transportable chassis that incorporates the gunner's seat, the system is suitable for rapid deployment in forward areas. The system is operated by a single gunner; to replenish ammunition two men are required and to bring the equipment into or out of action a third man is necessary.

The fire control system is the well-known P 56 computing sight and gun laying equipment made by Officine Galileo in Italy. It consists of the following main assemblies: monocular optical sight with swivelling objective prism for laying the gun against air and ground targets; electronic analogue computer for the calculation of kinematic lead values; joystick with two degrees of freedom for speed control of the line of sight; input panel for the target speed and crossing-point distance of air targets or the target distance of ground targets; hydraulic servo drive for the gun traversing and elevating gears; manual traverse and elevation mechanism; mechanical auxiliary sight.

To engage an air target the gunner first sets estimated target speed and aiming point distance on the input panel then acquires the target in his open sight using the joystick to control the gun. He then changes over to the optical sight and uses the joystick to bring the reticle into coincidence with the nose of the aircraft. Holding the sight in this relative position by means of the joystick he then presses the joystick down to put the guns under control of the computer. Thereafter he keeps the optical sight on the target and the computer points the guns with the degree of lead needed for successful firing. Firing will, however, be inhibited when appropriate by the taboo programme which can be inserted into the sight computer.

The taboo facility which can be programmed by the

Twin 20 mm gun system with MK 20 Rh 202 guns

gunner is a safety device to prevent friendly objects from being accidentally engaged. It divides the field of fire into a combat zone and a neutral zone.

When engaging ground targets it is necessary only to set the estimated range on the input panel and to bring the target into the reticle of the optical sight before firing.

The guns used in the system are Rheinmetall Rh 202 20 mm rapid-fire (**5600.103**). These are precision weapons that have a very high rate of fire (600 to 1000 rounds per barrel per minute) and a low recoil force. Both gun and ammunition feed are gas operated and independent of weapon and breech movement. In the AA weapon system, cartridges can be fed selectively so that either or both guns can be employed during an engagement.

Twin ammunition boxes containing a total of 550 ready rounds are mounted on either side of the gun assembly and fixed on the upper mount. This

ammunition supply enables the weapon to be used for long periods without replenishing the boxes. Ammunition types available are HEI, HEI-T, API-T, API, APDS-T and training and practice TP and TP-T.

Power for the computer and gunlaying systems is provided by an air-cooled engine with a centrifugal governor and a manual starter. This is installed at the rear of the mounting in a cage under the gunner's seat. The complete system is mounted as a two-wheel trailer for towing and can be towed by any vehicle capable of handling an unbraked trailer weighing 2500 kg; the wheels are removed for firing and the mounting is supported on three feet.
CHARACTERISTICS
Cannon: 2 × 20 mm MK 20 Rh 202
Laying system: Hydraulic with emergency manual controls
Elevation: –3·5 to +81·6° (hydraulic); –5·5 to +83·5° (manual)
Traverse: Unlimited
Max laying speed: 80°/s (elevation); 48°/s (traverse)
Max acceleration: 220°/s (elevation); 120°/s (traverse)
Optical system: ×5 magnification; 12° field
Length: 5·035 m (travelling)
Width: 2·36 m (travelling)
Height: 2·075 m (travelling)
Weights: Approx 2160 kg (travelling, less ammunition); 1640 kg (travelling in firing order with ammunition)
Ready rounds: 2 × 280, including 10 on each belt frame
Data input to computer: Target speed 60 – 350 m/s; crossing point distance 100 – 600 m; ground target distance 100 – 2000 m
Generator output: 5·8 kW at 4500 rpm
STATUS
In service with Argentina, Federal Republic of Germany, Greece, Indonesia, Portugal.
CONTRACTOR
Rheinmetall GmbH, 4000 Düsseldorf 1, Federal Republic of Germany.

GREECE

4511.131
ARTEMIS 30 TWIN 30 mm AA GUN SYSTEM

Following a contract awarded by the Greek MoD, Hellenic Arms Industry SA designed the Artemis 30 anti-aircraft system to meet the requirements of the Greek Army. It was first shown publicly during the Defendory Exhibition in Athens in October 1982.

The twin 30 mm cannon carriage was designed in collaboration with Kuka GmbH of the Federal Republic of Germany while the twin 30 mm cannon and the associated ammunition came from Mauser, also of the FRG. The fire control system has been designed by Philips of Sweden and the acquisition radar system by Siemens AG of the FRG.

The Artemis 30 fire unit is a twin 30 mm cannon system towed on a twin-axle split type carriage. The axle nearest to the draw bar carries the generator which powers the cannon system in action. Once deployed, this axle/generator assembly is removed and placed at a distance from the mount. The deployed mount is lowered and levelled by means of three hydraulically operated pads, two of them on outriggers, while the rear axle is power retracted upwards.

The weapons are mounted each side of a horizontal drum assembly, which elevates the two cannons. This assembly is placed on a central support which is

Diagram of typical Artemis 30 deployment showing six twin 30 mm guns, two fire control centres and E-O tracker units, and battery co-ordination post

mounted on a traversing turntable. Circular ammunition hoppers holding 500 linked rounds (250 for each gun) are also mounted on the central support. Each cannon receiver is contained in a protective housing that covers the cannon to the base of the barrel. Each of these boxes can be hinged open to reveal the mechanisms for clearing jams or for routine servicing. By removing the gun barrel the entire receivers can be swung outwards for more involved repairs and maintenance. The linked ammunition is fed from the hoppers upwards through the central drum and into the feeders from the inside. Spent links and cases are ejected through slots in the cannon housings. The weapons are the Mauser 30 mm Model F, described elsewhere in this volume. The twin cannon upper mount assembly has an unlimited 360 degree arc in traverse while the elevation arc is from –5 to +85 degrees.

The mount has three distinct modes of operation:
(1) via a remote fire control system
(2) via a gunner seated directly behind the central mount support. In this mode the gunner is provided with all necessary controls including a periscope for ground targets and also a gyroscopic angle prediction sight for air target engagement
(3) emergency operation via the gunner but with no power supplied to the mount. Weapon aiming is accomplished by means of handwheels with firing by a foot pedal. The ammunition used is the well-known GAU-8 family.

It was established early on that the Artemis 30 would not be completely dependent on radar fire control, but it was decided that any selected type of fire control would be modular so that radar could be incorporated. The simple state-of-the-art approach adopted is based on an electro-optical technique, which, despite its relative lack of sophistication, is considered to provide the weapon system with all that is required for local and area defence roles.

Philips contributed a system modified from its original design that uses a compact laser/electro-optical head mounted on a small single-axle trailer, which presents a video picture to the operator in the fire control centre. The fire control centre is usually housed in an air conditioned shelter carried on a light truck. The shelter also houses the system computer and all necessary communications equipment. The digital computer processes all incoming data and transmits gun-laying data and firing commands to the guns via land line(s). Programs for training and fault finding are handled by the digital computer and all signal processing is digital. A fire control centre usually controls three or four guns spread over an area about the size of an airfield with each gun operating over a range of 2000 to 3000 metres with a maximum engagement range of 5000 metres.

Artemis 30 field AA mount carries twin 30 mm Mauser automatic guns. Tubular containers beside carriage lower side members house replacement gun barrels to sustain operations remote from ordnance depots

Being modular in concept the Artemis 30 fire control system can be expanded and adapted to suit varying operational requirements. For use at night an infra-red sensor can be added and for all-weather use an amplitude modulation monopulse tracking radar can be installed on the director. The system may also be adapted to handle up to four twin 30 mm cannon carriages, or for use with rocket or guided missile AA systems. In the long term it has not been entirely ruled out that the Artemis 30 system will encompass some form of surface-to-air missile component. Target information is usually supplied to the fire control centre from an acquisition radar system, combined with a battle co-ordination post. All systems comprising the Artemis 30 system are fully mobile.

CHARACTERISTICS
Calibre: 30 mm
Weight: 7·1 t

Ready-use ammunition: 500 rounds
Rate of fire: 1600 rounds/minute (two guns)
Traverse: Unlimited
Traverse acceleration: 200°/s^2
Traverse speed: 100°/s
Elevation: –5 to +85°
Elevation acceleration: 166°/s^2
Elevation speed: 75°/s
Overall carriage accuracy: Better than 1·5 mrad
Max towing speed: 80 km/h
STATUS
Entering production. The company has proposed a version of the system mounted on the chassis of the Steyr 4K 7FA APC which is already manufactured under licence in Greece for the Greek Army.
CONTRACTOR
Hellenic Arms Industry SA, 160 Kifissias Avenue, Athens, Greece.

INTERNATIONAL

3679.131
DRAGON 30 mm TWIN GUN AA SYSTEM
Dragon (TH328) is the name of a joint Franco-German project to produce a twin 30 mm anti-aircraft gun system similar to the French AMX-30 SA system (**2138.131**) but mounted on a Thyssen Henschel tracked carrier vehicle instead of the AMX-30 chassis. The weapons and fire control sights and equipment are the same in both systems, but in place of the SAMM TC230A turret employed in the French system, the TH328 Dragon system has a welded steel SAMM/GIAT turret.

The system is operated by a three-man crew: commander, driver, and gunner. Its function is to provide protection from low- and very low-level air attacks against advanced battle corps units, vulnerable points and armoured formations. The chassis is a member of the TH301 medium tank family, providing excellent cross country capability over ranges of up to 600 km. It is thus able to escort tanks as well as other, faster, vehicles.

The turret is an armoured rotating casemate structure carrying two automatic HSS831A 30 mm guns. Optical observation and sighting equipment and a Thomson-CSF Oeil Vert surveillance and tracking radar (**3197.153**) are also mounted on the turret. There are two operating positions within the

Prototype TH328 Dragon 30 mm twin gun AA vehicle

turret: the commander's with a panoramic sight and radar control panel, a direct aiming periscope for air defence, an M250 for ground defence, angular vision blocks, and levers for turret steering and gun firing; and the gun-layer's station with a × 6 sight, an aiming periscope for ground engagement, angular vision blocks, and duplicated levers for turret steering and gun firing.

After optical target acquisition, the gunner keeps the reticle centre of the sight on the target by means of the gun steering control. Firing data, complemented by the Oeil Vert radar, are inserted into the fire control computer which calculates the appropriate aim-off

angles. The radar has two surveillance modes: remote, extending to a range of more than 15 km; and close-in, with a range of 7·5 km. There are five range channels in each mode, and the latter mode will be used mostly for 'pop-up' targets of opportunity. Automatic tracking in range and bearing of the target selected by the commander is possible using a track-while-scan facility, this taking place simultaneously with the surveillance function.

Firing rate of the HSS831A automatic gun is 620 rounds/minute, and the ammunition allocation is 300 rounds per weapon, giving a total of ready-use of 600 rounds in the turret, with more than 1500 rounds

accessible in the turret, backed by a reserve of about 900 rounds. Muzzle velocity is 1000 metres a second and the maximum effective range is 3500 metres, with an absolute maximum range of 10 000 metres.

STATUS

Prototype. No procurement details have been revealed.

CONTRACTORS

Thomson-CSF, Division Systèmes Electroniques, 1 rue des Mathurins, BP 10, 92222 Bagneux, France.

Thyssen Henschel, Henschel Wehrtechnik, PO Box 102969, Henschelplatz 1, 3500 Kassel, Federal Republic of Germany.

4465.131

KÜRASSIER/SABRE TWIN 30 mm TWIN AA SYSTEM

This is a combination of the Thomson-CSF Sabre twin 30 mm AA turret, a welded steel turret similar in armament and equipment to the TG 230A turret fitted on the AMX-30 twin AA system (**2138.131**) and the turret of the Franco-German Dragon system (**3679.131**), mounted on the Austrian Steyr-Daimler-Puch Kürassier chassis.

The main differences between the TG 230A turret and the Sabre are:

(1) the welded steel construction

(2) the Vassyla sight which performs the optical tracking of targets. This is a gyro-stabilised equipment which provides independent line-of-sight displacements independent of those of the turret and enabling accurate fire control of the aiming components by measurement of the line-of-sight rotation rate.

The Vassyla sight is connected to the fire control system which is based on a TMV 850 digital computer which functions as the central processor and operational co-ordination unit. The computer is linked to: a control and display console, the weapon servo-control, the radar, and the radio (via a modem). As optional equipment to the Sabre turret, the Oeil Vert pulse-doppler radar, an automatic TV tracker able to operate in low light-levels and limited visibility, and a laser rangefinder are available.

In other respects, turret performance characteristics are mostly very close to those of the Dragon and AMX-30 twin AA gun systems described above.

Twin 30 mm AA gun system with Sabre turret on 4K 7FA-FLA 30 Kürassier chassis

STATUS

At least one prototype constructed.

CONTRACTORS

Thomson-CSF, Division Systèmes Electroniques, 1 rue des Mathurins, BP 10, 92222 Bagneux, France.

Steyr-Daimler-Puch, Werke Wien, Vienna, Austria.

ISRAEL

4508.131

SPIDER II AIR DEFENCE ARTILLERY SYSTEM

The SPIDER II is a ground-based mobile fire control system designed for use against both high- and low-flying targets, aircraft, helicopters or missiles. The system searches for, designates and tracks aircraft and missiles and controls automatically the aiming and firing of six twin 30 mm cannon turrets. It is claimed to detect low altitude, small radar cross-section targets up to a maximum range of 19 km and will predict ballistics automatically for guns of calibres from 30 to 57 mm.

The basic system consists of a fire control console, tactical control console, search radar, tracking director and a processing unit. These units are normally mounted on a military truck, or housed in a standard shelter/container suitable for transport on a flat-bed vehicle. The search radar is designed primarily for detection of low-flying aircraft and uses coherent pulse doppler techniques. The tracking director is a combination of fire control radar and electro-optical systems with the latter incorporating two TV cameras and high rate and power laser rangefinder. The fire control console provides the operator with monitoring control of the system by means of a keyboard and a video display. The tactical control console is normally positioned at the commander's station, and displays essential data for

TCM 30G gun mount used in Spider II air defence system

fire control monitoring by means of a tactical display of battlefield area and targets detected by the various sensors providing information to the system.

The system is being offered currently with the TCM-30G cannon, but can be used with other weapons such as twin 35 mm Oerlikon or Bofors 40 mm guns.

During 1983 the Spider III version was revealed. This embodies missiles instead of guns to engage air targets and is described elsewhere in this edition.

CONTRACTOR

Israel Aircraft Industries Ltd, Electronics Division, Yehud Industrial Zone 56000, Israel.

4590.131

TCM MK3 LIGHT AA SYSTEM

Based on the considerable experience gained with the 20 mm twin cannon TCM-20 anti-aircraft system, Israel Aircraft Industries have developed a successor system known as the TCM Mk3. This new mount

meets all the requirements of the Israel Defence Forces for mobile air defence, and is capable of deployment in both ground-based and naval applications.

The mount itself has the simple structure, operation, and maintenance demands of the TCM-20

supplemented by advanced sub-systems such as more modern drives and the ability to employ the latest sighting systems. The new gun system can be integrated with the fire control system developed and manufactured by MBT Systems and based on a computer sight with laser rangefinder.

Using suitable adapters, the TCM Mk3 mount can accept virtually any light 20 – 25 mm AA gun, and aboard ship it may be used as either the main weapon system or as secondary armament to engage air, shore or surface targets.

Command and control of the mount is through a variable speed joystick mechanism. Mechanical movement of the joystick by the gunner is converted into electrical signals that are passed to servo amplifiers for subsequent conversion into drive commands for the training and elevating motors. The TCM Mk3 has a new drive system consisting of two separate but similar drive units (traverse and elevation), each of which includes a 24 V servo amplifier, torque limiter, gear, and feedback system. This arrangement is very sensitive to joystick demands, enabling the gunner to track fast-moving targets as easily as very slow targets.

The TCM Mk3 mount can be installed on towed or self-propelled carriages, and a wide range of guns such as the HS-404, HS-804, HS-920, Rh-202 and F-623, have been allowed for in the design. A typical

RAM V1-L combat vehicle with TCM Mk3 turret with HS-404 guns

Towed TCM 20 gun mount for AA defence

system (towed version with 2 × HS-404 guns) weighs 1350 kg ready for action. The basic version is provided with an M-18 reflex optical sight, but other options include a ×4 magnification 'starlight' sight for night operation, or the MBT FCS which incorporates a computer sight and integral laser rangefinder.

CHARACTERISTICS
Traverse: Unlimited 360°
Velocity: 0·25°/s, 75 – 80°/s max
Elevation: –10 to +90° (mechanical); –6 to +85° (electrical)

Weight: 1350 kg (2 × HS-404, towed model, ready for combat)
Power supply: 24 V DC
Primary source: 2 × 12 V DC, 80 Ah batteries
Auxiliary source: 28 V DC, 2·8 kW generator
STATUS
In production and operational with Israeli Forces.
CONTRACTOR
Israel Aircraft Industries Ltd, Ben Gurion International Airport, 70100, Israel.

ITALY

4535.131
SIDAM 25 AA TURRET
This is a one-man, powered turret mounting four Oerlikon KBA 25 mm automatic cannons, equipped with an electro-optical fire control system, and designed as the main armament for armoured personnel carriers. The system is intended to provide effective protection against air attack for troops, armoured columns and other tactically significant targets. Because of the optical sight and the gun calibre, it is also suitable for ground fire purposes.

The turret is constructed of welded aluminium alloy and carries two symetrical, externally mounted elevating masses, each of which is equipped with two 25 mm automatic guns. Each barrel has a rate of fire of 570 rounds/minute, and the rate of fire is selectable to provide single shot, 15- to 25-round controlled bursts and full rate firing. Two of the four cannon have dual feed capability for high explosive and armour piercing discarding sabot (APDS) ammunition, and 600 rounds HE and 30 APDS belted ready-to-fire rounds are provided in the turret ammunition magazines. The mode of fire (single shot, 15/25-round bursts, or continuous) can be selected from the gunner's control panel, and the system can be operated entirely from within armour protection. Selection of the types of round to be fired is performed mechanically under the control of the gunner.

The turret has hydraulically powered traverse through 360° and the elevation limits are –5 to +87°. The design allows easy installation, with minor modifications of the vehicle, in a variety of APCs and the first prototypes employed the M113, although it is understood that several other vehicles have been considered.

The system includes an Officine Galileo electro-optical sight that includes a self-stabilised optical dual periscope with a daylight TV camera, low-light TV camera and laser rangefinder, installed in the turret with an IFF device. An electronic tracking unit connected to the sight performs the angular tracking of the target, and target designation from an external source can be accommodated by a target alert display set. The fire control computer is fitted inside

Prototype Sidam 25 AA turret installed on M113 chassis

the vehicle in the gunner's console, together with an inertial attitude sensor. The fire control system is designed for two operators: the commander sitting in the turret and the gunner in the vehicle hull.

From acquisition by the commander, the target is assigned to the gunner, who carries out automatic or manual tracking by means of a joystick control. All these operations (except firing) can be carried out with the vehicle on the move. Modular design provides for the later enhancement of the system by the addition of such devices as a video compatible FLIR, an inertial navigation system, or passive IR to provide a 24-hour search and detection capability.

CHARACTERISTICS
Turret
Armament: 4 × 25 mm KBA dual-feed cannons
Rate of fire: 2280 rounds/minute (max)
Traverse: 360° continuous
Speed: 120°/s
Acceleration: 150°/s²
Elevation: –5 to +87°
Speed: 80 – 100°/s
Acceleration: 120°/s²
Fire control system: Electro-optical with laser rangefinder and computer. Attitude sensor
External designation: Automatic lock-on from

external designation via data link
Weight: 3200 kg (combat ready)
DEVELOPMENT
The turret was built by Oto Melara in co-operation with Oerlikon Italiana and Officine Galileo, under an Italian armed forces programme.

STATUS
Firings for the Italian Army were carried out in May 1983, using two prototypes on M113 vehicles.
CONTRACTORS
Turret: Oto Melara SpA, 15 via Valdilocchi 1, 19100 La Spezia, Italy.

Automatic cannon: Oerlikon Italiana, Milan, Italy.
Fire control: Officine Galileo, Florence, Italy.

4594.131

OTOMATIC 76/62 SPAAG

Oto Melara is developing a new self-propelled anti-aircraft gun system using the OF-40 BMT chassis with the Oto 76 mm 62 calibre gun as the weapon. The design also incorporates an all-weather opto-electronic fire control system by Officine Galileo, linked with an S-band surveillance and tracking radar provided by SMA. A major design consideration was an ability to detect and engage aircraft targets (ground attack helicopters in particular) at ranges greater than the anti-tank weapons the aircraft might be carrying, eg 6000 metres or more.

The general arrangement of the Otomatic 76/62 SPAAG can be seen from the drawing, from which it will be noted the radar installation is turret mounted. It is understood that this turret will also prove suitable for fitting to other chassis. The turret is constructed of welded steel, with the commander and gunner seated on the right and the loader on the left. An AA 7·62 machine gun can be fitted to the turret top for local protection.

A modified version of the Oto OF-40 tank chassis is employed, and an operating range of 600 km with a maximum speed of 60 km/h is available from a 1000 litre fuel capacity. Elevation and traverse of the 76 mm gun are hydraulically actuated, with manual mechanical operation for emergency use. Elevation limits are +60 and –5 degrees, while there is unlimited traverse (360 degrees in either direction). A total of 28 rounds of ready use ammunition is carried, with a further 52 rounds in reserve. The ready use ammunition consists normally of 25 rounds AA and three anti-tank rounds.

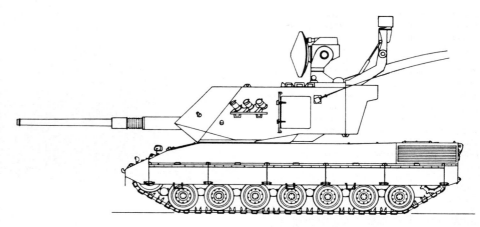

General arrangement of Oto Melara Otomatic 76/62 SPAAG

Six types of ammunition are available: HE active projectile with point detonating fuze; HE active projectile with proximity fuze; preformed fragmentation (PFF) active projectile with point detonating fuze; PFF projectile with proximity fuze; dummy with tracer and dummy fuze; and an APFSDS anti-tank projectile. The gun is capable of a cyclic rate of fire of 120 rounds/minute, and the AA projectiles have a typical muzzle velocity of 900 metres/second.

The SMA search radar operates in the S-band of the spectrum and facilities include MTI, track-while-scan (TWS), and provision for IFF. A TV camera is

associated with the tracking radar which operates in the Ka-band. Other fire control system features include a computer, the Galileo optical sight and tracking facility, and a separate system for engaging ground targets.
STATUS
The first prototype (without fire control system) is due for completion in late 1984, with a second prototype (with FCS) due about a year later.
CONTRACTOR
Oto Melara SpA, 15 via Valdilocchi 1, 19100 La Spezia, Italy.

4589.131

BREDA TWIN 40L70 AA FIELD MOUNTING

Breda Bresciana has introduced a field mounting version of its well established twin 40 mm naval anti-aircraft gun for use against low-flying aircraft and missile targets. The gun is fully automatic in operation and there is no need for any on-mount crew when the gun is in action. It is suitable for use with a wide range of fire control and target acquisition systems, for example the Signaalapparaten Flycatcher (**2301.181**).

Two Bofors 40 mm L/70 guns are combined to form a twin elevating mass within a specially designed cradle to comprise the Breda Twin 40L70. The barrels of standard Bofors guns are located 30 cm apart to reduce elevating mass recoil forces. The mounting consists of a 360-degree traverse training platform supported on a wire race bearing. The platform has parallel vertical lightweight aluminium alloy trunnion supports, and also carries the servo and ammunition feed motors together with the upper feed mechanism, firing mechanism and system junction box. The upper portion of the mounting is completely enclosed within a watertight reinforced glass-fibre cupola which is provided with three access hatches, at the rear and on each side.

Ammunition is stored in a magazine beneath the mounting platform, within the carriage, and rounds are fed to the guns via separate hoisting chains for each gun. The magazine trains with the mounting, and the system is arranged so that if either gun is out of action the other can continue to fire. The forward section of the magazine supplies the left-hand gun and the rear section supplies the right-hand gun. The system is driven by a 400 V AC motor powered from an external generator; fast or slow drive facilities are provided. The slow drive operates the magazine conveyors and the scuttle transferring the rounds to the lower chain hoist; the fast drive operates the ammunition hoists and the scuttle at the top of the hoist. Rounds are fed into the lower magazine

Towed Breda Twin 40L70 40 mm AA mount

manually via the side hatches. DC electric motors driving epicyclic gearboxes are used for gun elevation.
CHARACTERISTICS
Calibre: 40 mm
Barrel length: 2·8 m
Total weight: 9900 kg (less ammunition)
Weight of ammunition: 1100 kg
Length: 8·05 m (travelling)
Width: 3·2 m (travelling)
Height: 3·65 m (travelling)

Training velocity: 90°/s
Training acceleration: 120°/s²
Elevation velocity: 60°/s
Elevation acceleration: 120°/s²
Magazine capacity: 444 rounds
Rate of fire: 660 rounds/minute (both barrels)
STATUS
Production. In service with Venezuelan forces.
CONTRACTOR
Beda Meccanica Bresciana SpA, 2 Via Lunga, 25100, Brescia, Italy.

4536.131

BREDA LIGHTWEIGHT AA FIELD MOUNTING

The Breda twin 30 mm mounting is a new lightweight anti-aircraft towed field mounting introduced in 1983 to provide defence against air attack for troops, and other deployed ground forces. It is provided with an autonomous power supply unit and an electro-optical sighting system supplied by Officine Galileo. The latter system incorporates a laser rangefinder and infra-red facilities for night tracking of targets in addition to daylight optical tracking. Aim-off is applied automatically in optical tracking.

The guns fire standard GAU-8 high explosive ammunition at a maximum rate of 1600 rounds/minute, but API and APDS ammunition is also available for use against enemy armour and there are frangible rounds for engagement of aircraft targets.

The Breda twin 30 mm AA field mounting is suitable for integration with a variety of gun/missile air defence systems such as the Roland Co-ordination Centre (RCC).

CHARACTERISTICS

Calibre: 30 mm

Barrel length: 2·458 m

Carriage: 4-wheeled with two outriggers

Shield: Yes

Weight: 145·5 kg (gun, complete)

Length: 6·46 m (travelling)

Width: 1·76 m (travelling)

Height: 1·94 m (travelling)

Ground clearance: 0·43 m

Wheelbase: 3·5 m

Elevation/depression: +85°/–5° at 60°/s

Elevation acceleration: 90°/s²

Traverse: 360° at 80°/s

Traverse acceleration: 120°/s²

Breda lightweight twin 30 mm AA towed field mounting deployed

Flight time to 3000 m: 5·2 s

Rate of fire: 1600 rounds/minute (2 barrels)

Muzzle velocity: 1040 m/s

STATUS

Ready for production.

CONTRACTOR

Breda Meccanica Bresciana SpA, Via Lunga 2, Brescia, Italy.

JAPAN

3724.131

AW-X SELF-PROPELLED TWIN 35 MM AA GUN SYSTEM

The Japanese Ground Self Defence Force (JGSDF) initiated in 1978 the development of a self-propelled twin anti-aircraft gun system based on a pair of modified Oerlikon KDA 35 mm automatic guns, mounted on a tracked chassis. The latter has not been decided upon as yet, but it is likely to be either the Type 61 MBT hull or the Type 47 MBT chassis.

A radar fire control system based on the equipment used with Japanese Oerlikon 35 mm L 90 guns will be developed by Mitsubishi-Denki, who will also provide data processing and display equipment.

DEVELOPMENT

The AW-X was originally intended to use obsolescent Type 61 chassis for reasons of economy but maintenance problems and lack of internal space and vehicle agility have been cited as reasons for considering alternative platforms for the system. The obvious alternative of the Type 7 MBT would make possible the desirable 'fire-on-the-move' capability, but cost may rule this option out.

A contract worth about $4 million was awarded in 1978 to start the AW-X project, with modification of the Oerlikon 35 mm guns being the responsibility of Nippon Seiko-Jyo (Japan Iron Works) Company, and development of the fire control system going to Mitsubishi Electric Co.

STATUS

The first fire control system was due for delivery in March 1980. Modified KDA 35 mm guns have been delivered since September 1979, and the 1979 budget allocated a total of $1·75 million for prototype manufacture of the fire control system and display units. Prototype turret, turret stablisation and drive systems manufacture were covered by the 1980 budget. Initial operational capability is planned for service deployment in 1987.

CONTRACTORS

Nippon Seiko-Jyo (Japan Iron Works) Company.

Mitsubishi-Denki (Mitsubishi Electric) Company.

SPAIN

3208.131

MEROKA ANTI-AIRCRAFT SYSTEM

Meroka is a novel close-in air defence weapon system that has been under development for a number of years by the Spanish authorities. Both land-based and naval versions have been designed, the latter is described in entry **3176.203** in the naval ordnance section of this volume. Some of the background to the programme has appeared under the above entry number (**3208.131**) in 1983-84 and earlier editions.

The weapon used in both versions is a twelve-barrelled arrangement of 20 mm/120 calibre Oerlikon machine cannons, grouped together in two horizontal rows of six barrels. A salvo of 12 rounds can be fired in a time of 0·08 seconds, which amounts to a theoretical rate of fire of 9000 rounds/minute. The main purpose of this high rate is less the delivery of a large total of projectiles on to a target but more to meet a need for maximum density of fire when engaging certain categories of air targets, such as low-flying ground attack aircraft, and sea-skimming anti-ship missiles in the naval application. The normal practice is for each salvo to be fired as four groups of three rounds. This

minimises the total recoil force applied to the mount as well as having other beneficial operating characteristics.

The group of 12 barrels forms a single rigid unit which is traversed and elevated as a conventional gun, mechanical rigidity being aided by a number of steel bands (two in the army version, four in the naval version) that determine the spacing between the individual barrels. This feature is also used to adjust the dispersion of fire and fire pattern. Ammunition is brought to the 12 guns by two belt feeds which are supplied from a hydraulically powered rotating magazine with a capacity of 720 rounds. Elevation limits are –5 to +85 degrees, and the gun can traverse in azimuth through 360 degrees at a rate of 90 degrees/second.

A simple electro-optical fire control system that incorporates a TV camera, laser rangefinder and digital computer is used, this system being bore-sighted to the gun barrel axis. Aim-off to compensate for target motion is automatically injected when the fire button is pressed after having tracked the target for several seconds.

The prototype land-based Meroka AA gun is mounted on a towed four-wheeled carriage, and incorporates the gunner's position and a self-contained two-stroke engine that drives the hydraulic power unit for gun slewing and elevation, ammunition feed etc.

CHARACTERISTICS

Weapon: 12-barrel 20 mm Oerlikon

Barrel length: 2·4 m (120 cal)

Recoiling mass: 300 kg

Theoretical rate of fire: 9000 rounds/minute

Magazine capacity: 720 rounds

Elevation: –5 to +85°

Traverse: Unlimited 360°

Effective range: 3000+ m

Time into action: Approx 2 minutes

System weight: Approx 5 t, ready for action

STATUS

Prototype(s) completed and initial evaluation trials due to begin in late 1983.

CONTRACTOR

CETME, Centro de Estudios Técnicos de Materiales Especiales, Spain.

SWEDEN

2349.131

BOFORS 40 mm BOFI GUN SYSTEM

Based on the Bofors mobile 40 mm L/70 gun (**5228.103**) this new system incorporates an all-weather fire control instrument of the multi-sensor type, BOFI (**2378.181**), integrated with the gun. The system also includes a built-in motor generator and proximity-fuzed prefragmented ammunition. The BOFI gun system is entirely autonomous, each gun forming an individual firing unit able to engage its own targets.

As the main sensor a Ku-band (J-band) radar is used, which, after target designation from a central search radar or optical target indicator, acquires the target fully automatically on fixed frequency with MTI, and thereafter switches to frequency agility during the tracking mode to provide the greatest possible tracking accuracy. By this means the same high precision as achieved with semi-automatic electro-optical tracking using a laser rangefinder and optical sight can be maintained. The tracking radar and the electro-optical sensors are independent of each other and switching between them can be done to match any tactical situation.

For simple and easy training of the gunners, a target simulator equipment (**3593.193**) can be attached to the gun. Different flight paths can be selected and gunner performance measured.

A central search radar, such as the Giraffe (**1957.153**) or the Reporter system which also acts as a combat control centre for the battery of autonomous guns, contributes to the high effectiveness achieved. To further increase the defence potential a combat control radar can lead a mixed organisation comprised of BOFI guns and RBS 70 missile units. Such a mixed battery has considerable tactical flexibility.

Principal characteristics of the systems are:
(1) all-weather capability
(2) automatic acquisition and tracking
(3) high resistance to jamming
(4) capability of individual combat of targets

Bofors 40 mm BOFI anti-aircraft gun with the new tracking radar

(5) highly effective against aircraft, helicopters, missiles and ground targets
(6) great tactical flexibility and endurance
(7) short deployment and re-deployment times.

CHARACTERISTICS
Weight: 5500 kg
Rate of fire: 300 rounds/minute
Tactical range: 3700 m
Ammunition supply: 118 rounds on gun – sufficient for 12 engagements
System accuracy: 3 mrad
Radar accuracy: Ku-band (J-band) monopulse MTI or frequency agility
Frequency: 15·9 - 17·1 GHz
Frequency agility: 1000 Hz
Lobe width: 1·9°
Laser rangefinder: 10 Hz Nd YAG
Night sight: 3-stage image intensifier
Day sight: Telescope

Ammunition
Type: Proximity-fuzed prefragmented (PFHE)
MV: 1025 m/s
Weight of shell: 880 g
Explosive weight: 120 g
Type: High capacity high explosive (HCHE)
MV: 1030 m/s
Weight of shell: 870 g
Explosive weight: 165 g

STATUS
The fair weather version of the system has been in production since 1976. The all-weather BOFI gun system completed its design tests during 1979.

Design of proximity-fuzed ammunition was completed during 1974 and is now in large scale series production.

CONTRACTOR
AB Bofors, 691 80 Bofors, Sweden.

SWITZERLAND

4537.131

OERLIKON TWIN 35 mm AA FIELD GUNS GDF

The Oerlikon twin 35 mm anti-aircraft field gun system has been produced and delivered in considerable numbers over a long period, frequently for use in either the Super-Fledermaus or the Skyguard air defence system. The system has been described in **2374.131** in earlier editions of *Jane's Weapon Systems*, and in related entries. More recently the manufacturer has introduced a range of improvements for the Type GDF 35 mm guns and these are available as kits for updating existing guns, or the modifications may be incorporated in GDF series guns to be delivered new. Three levels of modification have been developed, referred to as Kits NDF-A, -B, or -C, and at the same time the company has introduced a new generation of 35 mm AA ammunition comprising fragmentation shells with electronic or mechanical impact base fuzes designed to ensure full detonation inside aircraft targets. The full NDF-C kit includes the following items, while omission of certain items results in the NDF-A and NDF-B modification kits:

(1) weapon cover with integrated, automatic weapon lubrication system
(2) optimised automatic cannon function which stabilises rate of fire
(3) automatic ammunition replenishers
(4) integrated power supply unit
(5) gun-King minisight with laser and digital computer for 3-D target tracking
(6) new gun control system.

The newly developed cover provides an improved, built-in protection of the automatic cannon against dust, sand, snow and water. An automatic weapon lubrication system is built into the cover. New mathematical models studied by the company based on new forms of threat from the air indicate that longer bursts of fire may be necessary in the future. The gas temperature (which is used to unlock the breech block in the 35 mm gas-operated cannon) will

Oerlikon GDF-003 twin 35 mm AA field gun incorporates NDF-C kit improvement features such as Gun-King minisight, new ammunition/reloading provisions, and power supply unit

therefore increase and cause the rates of fire to increase. This increase is held within reasonable limits by rate-of-fire regulators so that wearing parts and the weapon functions themselves are not unnecessarily overtaxed. In this way automatic fire

rate is limited to about 680 rounds/minute.

The automatic units are re-supplied with ammunition manually from the rear by the gun crew. The crew required on the gun is reduced from three to one; the gunner. The rounds are thrust into the ammunition feed system by hydraulic-mechanical devices. The barrel is elevated to 90° for the automatic replenishing cycle. Electrical and mechanical limiters prevent inadvertent firing during the replenishing procedure. The automatic replenisher substantially increases the available ready-for-firing ammunition supply. The ammunition supply on the 35 mm field AA gun is 238 rounds, 112 (56 each gun) ready-to-use rounds and 126 rounds (63 each gun) in the reserve containers. Transfer from the reserve containers into the ammunition feed is simple even while firing, provided adequate training has been given. This mode of operation requires three operators on the gun. To increase the quantity of ammunition immediately available on the gun and to reduce the men needed from three to one, the horizontally stowed automatic reloaders are mounted in place of the two reserve containers.

The power supply unit mounted on the gun is quite similar to that of the Skyguard fire control unit. When the gun is in operation, the power supply unit (which is located on the lower mount) is lowered to allow the barrel to turn freely even at the maximum angle of depression. The integrated supply unit simplifies taking up position since the single axle trailer formerly used is no longer required.

A new thyristor gun control system is located on the upper mount. Its coarse and fine transmission system operates through an on-gun microcomputer identical to that of the Gun-King sight. The new gun control system and the integrated power supply result in enhanced combat effectiveness, greater availability, assurance of continued availability etc, reduction in number of vehicles (from five to three per firing unit), and shorter times required to move into position. Diesel or petrol engines can be used (to provide power) as specified.

The minisight, known as Gun-King and developed by Contraves, is an autonomous device that carries out a 3-D electro-optical target tracking for each gun. It can be integrated in place of the XABA or the Ferranti sight. This greatly extends the autonomous operation potential of the gun under fair weather conditions. Sight operation is extremely simple; the gunner only needs to bring the periscope crosshairs into coincidence with the target. An acoustic signal indicates that firing can commence. A built-in laser measures the range of the target which, together with angular data, meteorological data and the continuously registered v_0 values, is processed by an integrated digital computer to give lead data which is then transmitted to the gun control system. The Gun-

King sight, as well as featuring in the NDF combat improvement kit for GDF 35 mm AA guns, is also a major element of the Diana 25 mm field AA gun system (**4525.131**). The main features of this new sight are as follows:

There is a common optical path in the periscope for the laser beam and for the aiming line of sight. These beams are deflected with high accuracy by a gimbaled mirror, thus a fixed eye piece is provided. The periscope has an extremely high light transmittance and is fitted with a multi-spectral optical system. Night operation is possible. Range finding is effected by a multi-divergence laser. For ground targets, the laser beam is narrowed by a divergency switch-over device, thus eliminating ground clutter.

The new Contraves high-speed computer for Gun-King calculates not only all fire control data precisely with optimum control, filter and ballistic algorithms, but also controls the periscope, laser triggering during the tracking phase and the gun drive electronics. At the moment of optimum hit probability, the operator receives an acoustic alarm to open fire. Target changes can be effected very rapidly because target data is stored in the memory. Provision is made for the insertion of muzzle velocity

and meteorological data. All data relating to weather and weapon parameters is entered into the computer and the operator can therefore immediately concentrate on precise target tracking. Sight and gun are commanded entirely by the control yoke which provides hands-on control.

NDF Series improvements can be carried out on 35 mm AA guns as follows:
GDF-001, equipped with the Xaba sight.
GDF-002, equipped with Ferranti sight.
GDF-001/002, with NDF-A improvement kit integrated. (These guns have already been improved with assemblies that are also part of the NDF-C. Further combat improvements involve the remaining assemblies.) The same applies to the GDF-003 (series production of the 35 mm AA gun with NDF-A assemblies). Guns which have been up-graded with NDF-B improvement kits cannot be modified with the NDF-C kit.
STATUS
Deliveries of NDF-C assemblies are planned for late 1985 from the Group's Zurich plant and about a year later from Oerlikon Italiana.
CONTRACTOR
Machine Tool Works Oerlikon-Bührle Ltd, 8050 Zurich, Switzerland.

Oerlikon GDF-002 twin 35 mm AA mount uses Ferranti sight and three-man crew

---

3723.131
OERLIKON 35 mm SP TWIN AA GUN GDF-CO3/DO3

The 35 mm twin AA gun GDF-CO3/DO3 system is intended as a self-propelled autonomous air defence system that fills the gap between towed mobile AA guns such as the earlier 35 mm field AA system described in **2374.131** in earlier editions (but which is still widely operated in at least 20 countries), and the more expensive and later AA tanks. Operational applications envisaged include the provision of air defence protection for: mechanised combat support troops (artillery, engineers etc) in action and during deployment; motorised formations; and sites of short-term tactical importance. Operationally, the GDF-CO3/DO3 is deployed within tactical units and engages targets independently. Primarily it is designed for deployment into reconnoitered emplacements and AA protection in an escort role is of secondary significance. The two versions, GDF-CO3 and DO3, differ only in the chassis on which the gun and sensor system is carried: a modified M548/6-Oe tracked vehicle for the CO3 model, and a 4 × 4 × 4 'giant' tyre vehicle (four wheels, all driven and steered) for the DO3 model.

The most important sub-systems are:
(1) twin 35 mm Oerlikon gun
(2) drum magazines
(3) high performance sight with FLIR
(4) search radar (consisting of sub-assemblies also employed in the ADATS system (**4158.131**)).

The gun is designed to engage aircraft, helicopters, drones and lightly armoured ground targets at ranges of up to 4000 metres. Three ammunition types with varying ballistics can be selected and fired. With

GDF-CO3 self-propelled twin 35 mm AA gun system has modified M548/6-Oe tracked chassis

regard to range, accuracy, response time and reliability, the performance of the system in airspace surveillance, target designation and fire control functions is optimised to the deployment spectrum. Even during target tracking, full airspace surveillance and IFF functions are maintained.

The GDF-CO3/DO3 mobile AA systems offer a

high fire power solution where optimal weight, mobility, and cross-country ability are required. Effective splinter protection for crew members in the vehicle and gunner's cab is provided. All operating sequences are designed to allow operation of the entire weapon system by a crew consisting of commander, gunner and driver.

CHARACTERISTICS

Calibre: 35 mm
Rate of fire: 2 × 600 rounds/minute
Ammunition: 430 rounds, up to 3 types selectable
MV: 1175 m/s (HEI); 1385 m/s (APDS-T)
Time for ammunition change: 1·5 s
Reload time: 4 minutes
Weapon range: 4000 m

STATUS

Prototypes of the basic GDF-CO2 version (tracked vehicle, without search radar), have been tested. A prototype of the wheeled version, GDF-DO3, was available in April 1984. In January 1984, deliveries of both versions were expected within 30 months.

CONTRACTOR

Machine Tool Works Oerlikon-Bührle Ltd, 8050 Zurich, Switzerland.

GENERAL DATA

Type	GD-DO3 Wheeled	GDF-CO3 Tracked
Length	8·7 m	6·7 m
Width	2·98 m	2·81 m
Height (minimum)	3·94 m	4·0 m
Wheel base	4·74 m	—
Ground clearance (max)	0·78 m	0·56 m
Minimum soil compaction	0·7 kg/cm²	0·6 kg/cm²
Engine rating	At 2300 rpm 335 kW	At 2800 rpm 155 kW
Max speed	120 km/h	45 km/h
Power/mass ratio	15·2 kW/t	8·6 kW/t
Range	1200 km (with 480 1)	480 km (with 430 1)

GDF-DO3 version is mounted on a 4 × 4 × 4 (four wheels, all driven and steered) vehicle fitted with 'giant' tyres

3330.131

FLAKPANZER 35 mm AA TANKS

The 35 mm AA tank is an armoured escorting air defence weapon system. It provides armoured formations and mechanised units on the move and in combat operations with mobile, integrated, effective low-altitude, close-to-medium range air defence in the forward battle area, particularly against attack helicopters and fighter-bombers. The system can also be rapidly deployed for other anti-aircraft tasks such as the protection of critical assets, choke points, convoys in the rear assembly areas, forward airbases, and missile sites. It is capable of engaging ground targets in a self-defence mode.

The 35 mm AA tank was designed for full combat autonomy featuring its own search radar with integrated IFF for continuous air surveillance, a tracking radar for automatic target acquisition and tracking, and two persicopes combined with a target indicator for optical target acquisition/tracking. The 35 mm twin-barrelled Oerlikon gun assures a high combat effectiveness. Own armour, environmental ruggedness and high mobility make the weapon system most suitable for battlefield deployment in extreme terrains and weather conditions as well as in a contaminated environment.

The entire fire control and gun system is integrated in an armoured turret, leaving only the auxiliary power unit and some additional units such as the land navigation equipment to be placed in the hull. This makes the weapon system particularly adaptable to various existing MBT vehicles.

The 5 PFZ-B2 Gepard and 5 PFZ-CA1 versions – both modified Leopard vehicles – differ mainly in their radar equipment. ATAK-35, a recent development, is the follow-on generation to the Gepard-CA1 family, with enhanced capabilities. The standard ATAK-35 is integrated with the Oto Melara OF-40 chassis. It integrates with other MBT chassis such as the Leopard-1, Leopard-2 and M-60.

5 PFZ-B2 (Flakpanzer 1 – Gepard)

This model has a Siemens MPDR 12/4 fully coherent pulse-doppler search radar (**3286.153**) with integrated MSR 400 IFF equipment. In addition to its own search data display it can receive and display air situation information from an external surveillance radar. The tracking Siemens-Albis radar is a monopulse-doppler type. The miniaturised and transistorised analogue prediction computer of Contraves design calculates the gun lead angles

5 PFZ-B2 Flakpanzer 1 Gepard on Leopard chassis

5 PFZ-CA1 system on Leopard chassis (Caesar)

taking into account the continuously measured muzzle velocity, the meteorological corrections and the vehicle's deck tilt. The computer furthermore gives the open-fire signal and determines the burst length of the gun for high hit probability and most economic use of ammunition.

RADAR CHARACTERISTICS
Search radar frequency: E-band
Switchable frequencies: 6
Max range: 16 km
Antenna rpm: 60
Sub-clutter visibility: ⩾57 dB
Tracking radar frequency: J-band
Switchable frequencies: 2
Max range: 15 km
Minimum range: 300 m
Sub-clutter visibility: ⩾23 dB
(for further details see **3286.153**)

5 PFZ-CA1 (Caesar)

This model has an integrated search and tracking radar of Hollandse Signaalapparaten manufacture, with a common transmitter for search and tracking. The search section is an MTI system with a digital double canceller. It too uses an integrated MSR 400 IFF system. The tracking section is of the monopulse-doppler type with a cassegrain antenna. There is an additional coaxial anti-image tracking channel. The rest of the fire control and gun system is practically identical to the B2-version.

RADAR CHARACTERISTICS
Search and tracking frequency: I-band
Max range: 15 km
Minimum range for tracking: 300 m
(for further details see **2302.153**)

ATAK-35

The combat capability of the ATAK-35 system is considerably higher than that of both 5 PFZ-B2-Gepard and 5 PFZ-CA1. The enhanced capability is mainly the result of the totally new onboard digital fire-control computer system. The radar, optical tracking and twin Oerlikon 35 mm gun systems of the CA-1 have been retained. A new generation of the Oerlikon 35 mm ammunition family can also be fired.

The new fire-control system, according to Contraves, offers the advantages of a shorter reaction time, increased hit probability against targets using tactical manoeuvring flight profiles, improved capability against attack helicopters, improved system reliability, ease of maintenance in the field by the use of automated built-in test system, reduced crew workload and further growth potential.

The ATAK-35 differs from the 5 PFZ-B2 Gepard and 5 PFZ-CA1 mainly in the following respects:
(1) Fire control computer: an advanced new digital system replaces the earlier analogue computer. Application of the modern computer algorithms based on the Kalman filtering theory makes the system capable of acquiring and engaging tactically manoeuvring air targets. High hit-probability is assured.
(2) System logic unit: a freely programmable system replaces the earlier permanently wired system. The programmable system logic unit is the nerve-centre of all logic signals resulting from the information supplied by the sub-systems.
(3) Testing facility: modern microprocessors have been employed and the built-in test equipment has been expanded. Testing in a dialogue mode is now possible. System maintenance has been made easier.
(4) Gun system: this is now capable of firing the existing as well as a new generation of the Oerlikon 35 mm ammunition family with improved combat performance.
(5) Ammunition loading: an improved concept considerably reduces the ammunition reloading time.

ATAK-35 35 mm AA tank with Oto Melara OF-40 MBT chassis. Contraves turret, Oerlikon guns, Signaal radar and Contraves optical tracking and digital FCS

(6) Growth potential: pre-planned product improvement to increase the combat capability.
(7) Tactical/technical operation: various improvements have been achieved.
CHARACTERISTICS
Max aiming rates: Turret bearing 1600 mils/s; gun elevation 1000 mils/s
Gun calibre: 35 mm
Barrel length: 3150 mm (L90)
Rate of fire: 1100 rounds/minute (twin barrels)
MV: 1175 m/s
Tactical gun range: 4000 m
Ammunition types: HEI, SAPHEI, APDS, TP
Ammunition reserves: 640 rounds AA; 40 rounds AP
Combat/empty weight: 46/42·3 t (Leopard-1); 48/46 t app (OF-40)
Length: 7·78 m (Leopard-1); 7·27 m (OF-40)
Width: 3·39 m (Leopard-1); 3·48 m (OF-40)
Height (radar retracted): 3·29 m (Leopard-1); 3·14 m (OF-40)
Road speed/cruise range: 65 km/h/550 km (Leopard-1); approx 65 km/h/500 km (OF-40)
OPERATION
An ATAK-35 fire unit is manned by a crew of three: commander, gunner and driver. The commander and the gunner perform AA operations from the fighting compartment within the AA turret, sitting in front of the operator's console. The commander evaluates threats and directs operations and the gunner engages targets. An intercom system connects the crew. The commander maintains radio communication with the higher command level and neighbouring tank units. In an emergency, one-man operation is possible.

In the primary radar operation mode, the search radar scans the airspace continuously through 360°

once a second when the vehicle is stationary and in motion. A clutter-free display of moving air targets is obtained on the search radar PPI (plan position indicator). An IFF (Identification Friend/Foe) interrogation system identifies the detected targets and displays them accordingly on the PPI.

The commander, after evaluating the threat, designates on the PPI by means of his joystick the target to be combatted. As a result, the tracking radar automatically acquires and tracks the target. The vehicle halts meanwhile. The fire control computer calculates within seconds the prediction angles, and the guns are automatically trained on the future position of the target. As soon as the target comes within the effective range of the gun, the gunner receives the signal to open fire. The fire burst length is computer-controlled, optimising the number of rounds fired.

The radars (search and tracking) and the optical system (periscopes, optical target indicator) offer redundant operation modes of the ATAK-35 system. Depending on the threat and the environment, an appropriate operation mode is chosen.
STATUS
The 5 PFZ-B2 Gepard has been in service with the Federal Republic of Germany and Belgium since 1977-78, and production is now complete. The 5 PFZ-CA1 has been in service with Netherlands Forces since 1977-78 and production of this model is also complete.

Development and validation tests of the ATAK-35 model are completed and systems are available for user trials.
CONTRACTOR
Contraves AG, Schaffhauserstrasse 580, 8052 Zurich, Switzerland.

TARGET TRACKING COMBINATIONS

Target	Mode	Range	Angles Bearing (Azimuth) & Elevation
Air	Radar	Tracking radar X-band	Tracking radar X/Ka-band
	Radar	Tracking radar Ka-band	Tracking radar X/Ka-band
	Radar-opt.	Tracking radar X-band	Periscope
	Radar-opt.	Tracking radar Ka-band	Periscope
Ground	Optical	Manual	Periscope

4525.131

DIANA TWIN 25 mm AA GUN

The Oerlikon 25 mm field AA gun Type GBF-AOB (Diana) is a towed high-performance gun intended primarily for the defence of stationary targets (eg airfields, depots etc) against low-level air attack.

The Diana system has two externally mounted Oerlikon 25 mm KBB automatic belt-fed cannons, a

gunner's cab with a sighting system for 3-D target tracking and an integral power supply. The high rate of fire of the twin cannons, the ammunition performance and the effectiveness of the sight together ensure both high hit and high kill probabilities against all hostile targets.

The gun mounting and carriage arrangement can be seen from the adjacent illustration of the system

ready for action. Conversion of the gun from the travelling to the action configuration is rapid: the mounting legs are extended hydraulically until the two wheels lift clear of the ground and swivel inwards. The location of the gunner's cab in the centre of the rotating structure between the externally mounted cannons enables both the overall length and height of the gun to be minimised, as well as reducing rotational effects on the operator.

Target acquisition and designation is carried out either optically and autonomously or by a remote radar unit such as the Skyguard central fire control system (**2377.181**), but in both cases the target is tracked by the gunner using his 3-D sight. This is normally the new Contraves Gun-King laser-computer controlled sight which can be employed for the engagement of both air and ground targets by autonomous gunfire, although the Officine Galileo P75 optical sight can be fitted as an alternative option. Precise fire control data is automatically determined and updated by a digital microprocessor developed by Contraves, and coupled with a laser rangefinder the computer controls the combat sequence of the entire gun system.

The system has two 25 mm KBB automatic cannon, each with a cyclic rate of fire of 800 rounds/minute and 250 rounds each of ready-use ammunition. The dual belt feed allows the gunner to select either of two types of ammunition. The mount has an integral power supply for both electric and hydraulic operation and it can also be operated manually if required.

The ammunition employed with the KBB gun has been designed to ensure optimum efficiency against targets of all kinds, and the high muzzle velocities and flat trajectories with short flight times give high hit probabilities. Available ammunition includes four types as follows:

The fragmentation HE incendiary shell is primarily for use against soft or lightly-armoured targets (such as aircraft, helicopters etc) and is characterised by intense blast and fragmentation effects inside the targets. The discarding sabot ammunition is most suitable for use against armoured targets such as APCs and AFVs.

CHARACTERISTICS
Gun: Twin KBB cannon
Calibre: 25 mm
Rate of fire: 2 × 800 rounds/minute
Barrel length: 2300 mm (92 calibres)
Ammunition: 250 rounds/gun
Weight: 1725 kg (less ammunition); 2100 kg (ready to fire)
Length: 4·295 m
Width: 2·1 m
Height: 2·13 m
Elevation: –5 to +85°
Traverse: 360°
Traverse speed: 1·4 rad/s (max)
Traverse acceleration: 1 rad/s²
Elevation speed: 0·85 rad/s (max)
Elevation acceleration: 1·3 rad/s²
Sight: Gun-King, Galileo P75 optional
Magnification: ×5
Field of view: 12°

Oerlikon GBF-AOB Diana twin 25 mm AA gun ready to fire. Note Gun-King sight

Laser rangefinder
Range: ≥5 km
Accuracy: ±5 m
PRF: 10 Hz
Max lead angle: ±20°
STATUS
Entering production.
CONTRACTOR
Machine Tool Works Oerlikon-Bührle Ltd, 8050 Zurich, Switzerland.

Type	NATO Designation	Round Weight	Round Length	MV
Fragmentation HE incendiary	HEI	625 g	288 mm	1160 m/s
Discarding sabot hard core projectile with tracer	APDS-T	550 g	288 mm	1460 m/s
Practice with tracer	TP-T	625 g	288 mm	1160 m/s
Practice with tracer	APP-T	550 g	288 mm	1355 m/s

UNION OF SOVIET SOCIALIST REPUBLICS

5548.131
23 mm ZSU-23-4 SP AA VEHICLE
The ZSU-23-4 has been in service with the Soviet Army since 1965, and subsequently has been built in large numbers. It is issued on the scale of four per motor rifle regiment and eight per tank regiment. The ZSU-23-4 saw extensive service in the 1973 Middle East campaign when it proved to be one of the most effective of all the low-level anti-aircraft systems employed.

It has a chassis developed from the PT-76 light tank which is almost identical to that used for the SA-6 (**2930.131**). The four ZU-23 cannons are similar to those used on the ZU-23 twin towed anti-aircraft system (**5581.103**), but are water-cooled rather than air-cooled.

Each barrel has a cyclic rate of fire of 800/1000 rounds/minute, but their practical rate of fire is 200 rounds/minute, and they normally fire in bursts of 50 rounds/barrel. A total of 2000 rounds of 23 mm ammunition is carried, 500 per barrel. Two types of ammunition are used, the HEI projectile weighs 0·19 kg while the API projectile weighs 0·189 kg; both have a muzzle velocity of 970 metres/second. The guns can be used both against ground and air targets and can be laid and fired while on the move.

The turret has full powered traverse through 360°, elevation limits being from –7 to +80°. The B-76 radar (also known in the West as Gun Dish **2876.153**) is mounted at the rear of the turret and has both target acquisition and fire control capabilities. The radar can pick targets up at a maximum range of 20 km and operates in the J-band. An MTI facility is provided, as is a computer. Optical sights are provided for use in both the ground and air roles. Day and night vision devices are incorporated, and the turret has a TPKU-2 daylight observation periscope plus two BM-190 viewers. The first type, TPKU-2 has an elevation adjustment. For night observation, the TPKU-2 is replaced by a TKN-1T infra-red periscopic sight. A generator is mounted in the forward part of the hull to provide power when the main engine is not being used.
OPERATION
The ZSU-23/4 vehicle is operated by a crew of four: commander, search/surveillance radar operator/gunner, rangefinder, and driver, the first three being

ZSU-23-4 self-propelled anti-aircraft quadruple 23 mm gun vehicle

housed in the turret. Either of the first two crew members can control gun firing, stowing and erection, and all three crew members stationed in the turret are separated from the guns by a vertical armour bulkhead which provides protection from fragments, propellant gases and flame. During live firing, guns can be positioned automatically by the radar fire control system or manually, by hand-wheels. Radar directed fire is usual against air targets, radar modes providing for search and detection, after acquisition followed by tracking. A conical scan pattern is employed for tracking and this gives angular error signals relative to the target's position from the radar boresight axis. The latter signals are

used to calculate drive signals for the turret to bring stabilised line of sight and the predicted target into coincidence. Two radar CRT displays are provided, one for the search and tracking functions carried out by the radar operator/gunner, and the other for range measurement by the ranging operator. Optical fire direction, with optical target tracking is also possible, possibly allied to radar ranging. To permit firing on the move, stabilisation is provided.
CHARACTERISTICS
Crew: 4
Weight: 14 t
Length: 6·3 m
Width: 2·95 m

Height (radar retracted): 2·25 m
Road speed/range: 44 km/h/260 km
Engine: Model V-6, 6-cylinder water-cooled diesel developing 240 hp at 1800 rpm
Agility
Max step: 1·1 m
Max trench: 2·8 m
Max gradient: 60%

Ground clearance: 0·4 m
Water crossing ability: 1·07 m
Weapon: 4 × 23 mm automatic gun
Rate of fire: 3400 rounds/minute (max combined)
Standard ammunition load: 2000 rounds
Elevation: –4 to +85°
Other equipment: NBC system and infra-red driving lights are provided

Effective anti-aircraft range: 2000/2500 m
Effective ground range: 2000 m
STATUS
In production. In service with Afghanistan, Angola, Bulgaria, Cuba, Czechoslovakia, East Germany, Egypt, Ethiopia, Finland, Hungary, India, Iran, Iraq, Libya, North Korea, Poland, Romania, Somalia, Soviet Union, South Yemen, Syria and Viet-Nam.

UNITED KINGDOM

4588.131
MARKSMAN AA GUN TURRET

In collaboration with Oerlikon and Vickers, Marconi has designed an AA turret system for installation as a direct replacement for the gun turret normally fitted in a range of main battle tanks. This will facilitate retrofitting to a number of vehicles in an existing fleet of MBTs to provide them with the mobile AA defence increasingly being demanded for armoured formations. The contractor claims that current self-propelled AA gun systems are all supplied as complete vehicles, so that the user may have to procure a new type of hull, possibly of a type that is new to the existing inventory.

The new AA turret is mounted onto the hull by means of a combined main bearing and traverse drive rack assembly with a conversion ring to allow the turret to be fitted to a range of tank hulls such as the Soviet T and US M series, Centurions and Chieftains. The system is unusual in that virtually all the equipment is housed within the gun turret itself, unlike other solutions that call for equipment stowage in the vehicle hull.

The turret is fabricated in steel armour plate, giving ballistic immunity against 14·5 mm heavy machine gun armour-piercing rounds and 155 mm airburst shell fragments. Two rapid fire Oerlikon 35 mm AA cannon are mounted, one on each side, by large diameter bearings, through which the guns are fed from two readily replaceable ammunition containers located inboard. A Marconi digital fire control system is provided, with target information supplied by a Marconi 400 Series surveillance and tracking radar, and the commander's and gunner's optical sights (the latter also incorporates a laser rangefinder). The commander and gunner sit side-by-side on the approximate centre of rotation, in front of an ergonomically designed console so that both have access to the fire control system.

Also within the turret, the solid-state stabilised turret drive system employs an electronic servo control system, with batteries and power amplifiers located on the floor to the turret basket. An auxiliary diesel generator is mounted in a separate compartment at the rear of the turret. Turret heating can be fitted, and as options an NBC pack and air

Marksman AA gun turret

conditioning are available. There is space in the turret for radios and other conventional equipment supplied by the user to be installed.

The Series 400 radar uses a single antenna for both surveillance and target tracking, and the modular radar units are mounted inboard within the bustle of the turret. Features of the radar emphasised by the manufacturer include: good ECCM performance, and freedom from the effects of secondary ground reflection (multi-path) signals, and it is claimed to be smaller and lighter than comparable radars of the previous generation. A fast reaction is achieved by fully automatic operation from the first surveillance detection of a target, through tracking and aim-off to

firing of the gun. Manual operation and optical sighting are available as reversionary modes.

The complete turret, with ammunition stowed weighs approximately 11 tonnes.

Fixed wing aircraft and helicopters can be engaged, and the stabilised system permits the turret to be used against ground targets also. The radar permits all-weather, day/night engagements, particularly of low-elevation targets.
STATUS
At least one prototype turret has been constructed.
CONTRACTOR
Marconi Command and Control Systems Ltd, Weapon Systems Division, Leicester, England.

UNITED STATES OF AMERICA

3618.131
DIVAD SGT YORK GUN SYSTEM

The DIVAD Sgt York system is the successful contender of two designs which competed for the contract to meet the US Army's Division Air Defence (DIVAD) gun system requirement. It and an alternative proposal submitted by a consortium led by General Dynamics underwent a competitive development programme following the award of contracts to the two groups of companies in January 1978. During the competition the winning Ford system was known by its developers as 'Gunfighter', but after adoption by the US Army the system was given the official name 'Sgt York'.

The new system will eventually replace the self-propelled Vulcan system (**2850.131**) now in service, and the DIVAD programme supplanted the earlier GLAADS (Gun Low-Altitude Air Defence System) programme (**2544.131**) described in previous editions of *Jane's Weapon Systems*. It is designed to provide US Army forward combat forces with an effective gun system for defence against tactical helicopters, aircraft, and engagement of some ground targets.

The weapon employed is the widely used Bofors L/70 40 mm gun, two of which are mounted in an

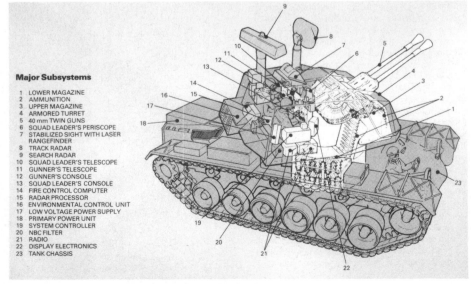

Major Subsystems

1. LOWER MAGAZINE
2. AMMUNITION
3. UPPER MAGAZINE
4. ARMORED TURRET
5. 40 mm TWIN GUNS
6. SQUAD LEADER'S PERISCOPE
7. STABILIZED SIGHT WITH LASER RANGEFINDER
8. TRACK RADAR
9. SEARCH RADAR
10. SQUAD LEADER'S TELESCOPE
11. GUNNER'S TELESCOPE
12. GUNNER'S CONSOLE
13. SQUAD LEADER'S CONSOLE
14. FIRE CONTROL COMPUTER
15. RADAR PROCESSOR
16. ENVIRONMENTAL CONTROL UNIT
17. LOW VOLTAGE POWER SUPPLY
18. PRIMARY POWER UNIT
19. SYSTEM CONTROLLER
20. NBC FILTER
21. RADIO
22. DISPLAY ELECTRONICS
23. TANK CHASSIS

Internal arrangement of Sgt York DIVAD system components

armoured turret, with a ready-use ammunition supply of more than 500 linear linkless feed, proximity-fuzed prefragmented and contact-fuzed rounds. The former type of ammunition incorporates a fuze which effectively increases the fuzing area by a factor of 40:1 nose-on, and 5:1 in side aspects. High lethality arises from 640 tungsten spheres plus additional fragments from the projectile body itself, and this has proved particularly damaging to aircraft structures. The large calibre (40 mm) of both types of round also provides high lethality against other targets, and the point detonating ammunition is very effective. The L/70 gun is a NATO standard weapon, used by 10 NATO countries as well as more than 40 other states world-wide, and production facilities for both the gun and its ammunition are also widespread within NATO and several other countries further afield.

The DIVAD system has a digital fire control system, allied to a search and tracking radar system developed by Westinghouse from the AN/APG-66 fire control radar (**3303.353**) for the F-16 aircraft. Other sensors include the vehicle commander's optical periscope, and the gunner's optical sight and laser rangefinder, and these provide a stabilised optical search and tracking capability to supplement the radar system.

The vehicle uses a modified M48A5 tank chassis and has a crew of three. The driver's position is central in the hull, while the commander and gunner have places in the turret. Most of the armament and fire control/sensor equipment is carried in or on the turret or basket. The two combat crew members sit side-by-side with the commander on the right. There is a centrally located combat display, and the controls are accessible to either crew member. Battlefield communications are handled by an AN/VRC-47 radio set.

Either of the crew members can override the automatic target engagement mode with the direct optical engagement mode and targets may be acquired optically with either periscope or gun sight. Alternative targets may be designated for radar engagement, and the gunner can optically aid the automatic radar engagement with precision thumb control tracking and laser rangefinding. For full automatic engagement the search radar detects and the fire control computer classifies and prioritises multiple targets. With crew consent, the remaining functions of target tracking, gun pointing, ammunition selection, burst length, and open fire range are also automatic. The resultant system reaction time is consequently very short. The system has an all-round (360°) engagement capability.

The radar's IFF system can interrogate and evaluate multiple targets simultaneously and these are classified as: enemy fixed-wing, enemy helicopter, enemy ground target, or friendly. The tracking radar locks onto the highest priority threat of those presented, while the search radar continues to

Sgt York DIVAD Division Air Defence gun system

alert the crew to remaining threats within detection range. The use of coherent pulse doppler radar and specially developed algorithms overcome the problem of discerning a helicopter hovering amidst ground clutter, and multi-path tracking problems are overcome by multiple-beam tracking techniques. The radar combat situation display is a plasma panel display which presents only the actual targets, target identity, target priorities and battle status information.

STATUS

The Ford system was chosen for the DIVADs production programme in May 1981 after an extended competitive evaluation by the US Army. The initial production contract for DIVAD was signed in May 1982.

The programme RDT&E phase ended in 1983. The DIVAD gun will be deployed with air defence artillery batallions of the armoured and mechanised divisions of the US Army, as well as the corps air defence artillery group and armoured cavalry regiments.

Planned procurement in the 1985 DoD budget is as follows, with quantities in brackets and funding in $ millions:

Fiscal year	1983	1984	1985
Procurement	(96)539·9	(130)559·4	(132)528·7
Spares	68·3	87·2	92·8
RDT&E	10·9		

CONTRACTORS

Prime: Ford Aerospace and Communications Corporation, Newport Beach, California 92660, USA.
L/70 guns and ammunition: Bofors AB, Sweden.
Radar: Westinghouse Electric Corporation, USA.
Turret: AAI Corporation, USA.
Optical sights: Kollmorgen, USA.
Laser rangefinder: Hughes Aircraft, USA.
IFF: Hazeltine Company, USA.
Attitude reference unit: Litton Industries, USA.

2850.131

VULCAN AIR DEFENCE SYSTEM

This is an anti-aircraft weapon system based on the Vulcan 20 mm six-barrel gun. The tracked version, M163, comprises the Vulcan gun, a linked ammunition feed sub-system, and a fire control sub-system, all mounted in an electrically-powered turret and carried on a derivative of the M113 APC. The fire control sub-system consists of a range-only radar and a lead-computing gun sight with its associated current generator. The towed VADS system, M167, contains its own batteries and is equipped with a petrol-driven generator for recharging and the whole system is mounted on an M42A1 gun carriage.

GUN

The Vulcan M168 gun, previously used as aircraft armament at rates as high as 6000 rounds per minute, has been modified for the air defence application to provide alternative firing rates of 1000 and 3000 rounds per minute. There is a burst limiting device, controlled by the gunner, which can be set for 10, 30, 60 or 100 rounds. Three muzzle clamps are available that provide different dispersion patterns for air defence and ground engagement modes. In the former a wide-angle or rectangular pattern is used to provide a high hit probability against low-flying

M163 self-propelled Vulcan air defence system on modified M113 APC (M741)

aircraft. A concentrated dispersion pattern is used in the ground role.

In the towed system a conventional belt feed is used for ammunition, the belted rounds being fed from a 500-round container. In other systems where more space is available a linkless feed system can be used and this has a capacity of 1100 rounds.

The turret is electrically driven and its drive is controlled by three solid-state servo amplifiers.

FIRE CONTROL

The fire control system consists of an XM61 gyro lead-computing gunsight and a sight current generator. The gunner visually acquires and tracks the target with the gyro lead-computing gunsight. The antenna axis of the radar is servoed to the optical line-of-sight and the radar supplies target range and range-rate data to the sight current generator. These inputs are then processed to provide outputs that are used to control the gunsight.

With inputs of range, range rate, and angular tracking of the optical line-of-sight (measured by a freely gimballed gyro), the sight automatically computes the future target position and adds the required super-elevation to hit the target.

Turret fire control is a disturbed line-of-sight system. The sight case and gun bore are physically fixed in alignment, but the sight reticle, which defines the optical line-of-sight, is positioned by the gyro and is displaced from the gun bore as the gunner tracks the target, thereby establishing the proper lead angle. The amount of optical line-of-sight displacement is dependent on the range and range rate inputs to the sight, and the required tracking time to establish the lead angle is about one second.

The range-only radar, developed by the Lockheed Electronics Company, is a coherent doppler, moving target indicator (MTI) radar. It will acquire targets up to 5000 metres away.

The fire control system may be supplemented by an AN/TVS-2B night vision and an XM134 telescope.

IMPROVED FIRE CONTROL

Lockheed Electronics Company developed an improved fire control system for the Vulcan air defence system which forms the basis of the Product Improved Vulcan Air Defence System (PIVADS), described in entry **4015.131**, below.

CHARACTERISTICS (TOWED TYPE)

Type: Land-mobile, air-transportable, light anti-aircraft weapon system

Vulcan air defence system XM167 towed version

Control: Radar ranging, optical aiming, automatic lead computation
Fire power: 6 × 20 mm guns. 3000 rounds/minute rate of fire. 1000 rounds/minute low rate of fire
Dispersion: 12 mrads; 8 × 18 mrads; or 6 mrads (80% 4 rounds fired)
Radar range: 5000 m
Weapon coverage: Azimuth 360°; elevation –5 to +80°
Turret slewing rate: Azimuth 75°/s; elevation 60°/s
Height on wheels: 2·03 m
Height emplaced: 1·73 m
Wheel track: 1·75 m
Weight: 1406 kg
Standby power requirement: 500 W
STATUS

In production for US and other governments. A towed version without radar is in production for the Belgian Air Force. The US Army's Vulcan inventory in mid-1979 consisted of about 380 tracked Vulcan air defence systems and some 220 towed models. In the

summer of 1979, firing trials of the Lockheed Electronics improved fire control system for Vulcan were undertaken. Results are understood to have been highly satisfactory.

Future US Army procurement is likely to be in the PIVADS form (**4015.131**), with light divisions having the M167A2 version and heavy divisions the M163A2 self-propelled version, until deployment of the Sergeant York system, when the M163A2 will be passed to the National Guard.

CONTRACTORS

Complete system: Aircraft Equipment Division, General Electric Company, Burlington, Vermont 05402, USA.

Radar: Lockheed Electronics, Plainfield, New Jersey, USA, and American Electronic Laboratory, Philadelphia, Pennsylvania, USA.

Vehicle: FMC Corporation, San Jose, California, USA.

4062.131

VULCAN/COMMANDO AIR DEFENCE SYSTEM

The Vulcan/Commando air defence system is a combination of the Commando V-150 wheeled armoured vehicle and the M167A1 20 mm Vulcan air defence turret. The resulting air defence system provides highly effective close-in air defence and defence against light enemy ground armour, in an armoured platform capable of both off-the-road and high-speed highway travel. The versatility of the wheeled platform allows rapid dispersal to practically all types of combat areas, and the high firing rate (1000/3000 rounds/minute) of the 20 mm Vulcan allows both air and ground targets to be engaged.

The system may be operated against targets in any of four firing modes. In the radar mode, which is the most accurate mode for engaging aircraft targets, the radar supplies continuous present range and present range rate information to the analogue computer (the sight current generator) for the computation of magnet current for the gyro lead computing sight. In the manual mode the gunner estimates engagement range and target speed and makes these settings on the control panel. In the external mode a second person, located off-mount, estimates the target's range, making the setting on a hand-held potentiometer connected to the system slip rings by a cable. In the ground mode the sight gyro is not operated and lead angle is not computed. The sight is mechanically caged at zero lead angle and 7 mils of super-elevation.

The M167A1 20 mm Vulcan turret is a 'drop-in' installation, requiring only proper location of mounting holes in the vehicle hull. The turret is totally self-contained, and remains operationally independent of the vehicle. The M167A1 VADS turret may be replaced with the basic VADS turret (without radar) with identical installation requirements.

GE/Cadillac-Gage Vulcan/Commando air defence vehicle

The Vulcan/Commando air defence system armament is the same turret, weapon and associated feed, power and radar equipment as used in the M167A1 Vulcan air defence system, in production

since 1967.

The system is made up of the 20 mm M168 Vulcan gun, a linked ammunition feed system, and a fire control system, all mounted in an electrically powered turret. The system contains its own batteries.

Firing rates for the Vulcan gun with the linked feed system are 3000 and 1000 rounds/minute. The high firing rate provides effective defence against low-flying, subsonic aircraft. The lower firing rate provides effective fire against ground targets such as trucks, boats and lightly armoured vehicles.

Fire control consists of a gyro lead-computing gunsight, a range-only radar, and a sight current generator. The gunner visually acquires and tracks the target. The radar supplies range and range-rate data to the sight current generator. These inputs are converted to proper current for use in the sight. With this current the sight computes the correct gun lead angle and adds the required super-elevation. The system uses the XM61 gyro lead-computing gunsight.

CHARACTERISTICS
Gun
Type: 20 mm 6-barrel Gatling
Length: 1864·4 mm
Max diameter: 342·9 mm
Weight: 124·7 kg
Ammunition: M50 Series
Muzzle velocity: 1030 m/s
Rate of fire: 1000/3000 rounds/minute
Dispersion: 12 mils circular; 8 × 18 mils elliptical (80% of rounds fired)
Turret
Weight: with gun 1134 kg
Ammunition capacity: 500 ready; 800 stowed
Slewing rates: Azimuth 75°/s; elevation 60°/s
Weapon coverage: Azimuth 360° continuous; elevation +80°, –5°
Modes of operation: Radar, manual, external, ground

Vehicle
Weight: 9072 kg
Max speed: Land 88 km/h; water 4·8 34 km/h
Engine: Diesel
Transmission: Automatic, 4-speed
Crew: 4 (driver, gunner, commander, radio operator)
STATUS
The only known procurement of this system was an unspecified quantity for Saudi Arabian forces.
CONTRACTOR
Armament Systems Department, General Electric Company, Lakeside Avenue, Burlington, Vermont 05402, USA.

4015.131

PIVADS (PRODUCT IMPROVED VULCAN AIR DEFENCE SYSTEM)

This improved system extends system operational life by providing improved response, acquisition and tracking to the basic Vulcan (**2850.131**) system. US Army tests of the Product Improved Vulcan demonstrated tracking accuracies within 1·25 mils rms under all conditions of approaching, crossing and manoeuvring targets. The improvement technology is applicable to new gun systems or to upgrading existing systems and uses the following techniques:

(1) replacement of disturbed line-of-sight (DLOS) gunsight configuration by a stabilised 'director' sight

(2) use of a stabilised optical sight, isolated from turret motion to provide accurate target acquisition and tracking. The tracking reticle is directly controlled by the gunner

(3) computer generated rate-aid signals significantly reduce gunner workload by driving turret to future target position based on historical position data

(4) special servos and turret drive design techniques (rate feed-forward, resonance equalisation, harmonic drives) provide the following characteristics: improved turret stiffness, minimised backlash and high bandwidth turret and sight servos, improved turret transient and steady-state tracking performance

(5) militarised digital microprocessors dramatically reduce size, cost and weight, enhance system reliability, and permit adaptive software modifications.

The PIVADS modification kit enhances system effectiveness by the use of a director-type sight, a microprocessor and improved turret drives

DEVELOPMENT
Development was undertaken as a private venture by Lockheed Electronics Company to exploit experience accumulated in the design and development of the Mk 86 GFCS (**1241.281**) and small weapon control systems simulation analysis.
STATUS
The US Army awarded a pre-production contract to Lockheed Electronics in September 1982, for the M163A2 self-propelled PIVADS, and a contract for the M167A2 towed PIVADS in November 1983. The fiscal

year 1985 budget requested $33·2 million for PIVADS procurement in FY 1985, and $21·8 million for R and D and $27·7 million for procurement in FY 1986. It is planned to deploy towed PIVADS with active light divisions of the US Army. The self-propelled version, now operated by heavy divisions, will be transferred to the National Guard as the Sergeant York air defence system (**3618.131**) is deployed.
CONTRACTOR
Lockheed Electronics Company Inc, 1501 US Highway No 22, Plainfield, New Jersey 07061, USA.

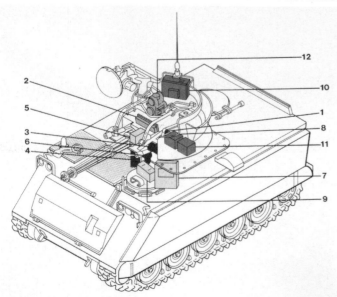
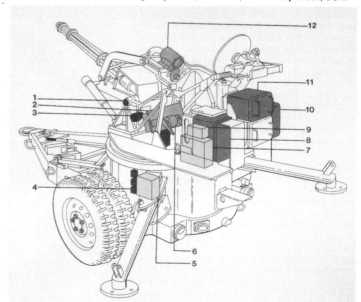

Major elements of the M163A2 self-propelled and M167A2 towed PIVADS, key for both versions: 1. elevation synchro, 2. control panel, 3. elevation drive, 4. servo amplifiers, 5. distribution box, 6. azimuth drive, 7. electronics unit, 8. radar power supply (unit 5), 9. voltage converter, 10. radar (unit 2), 11. radar (unit 4), 12. director gunsight

4466.131
GEMAG 25 AA GUN SYSTEM
The GEMAG 25 (General Electric Mobile Air Defence Gun) is a 25 mm towed mobile gun system that has been developed as an air-transportable air defence weapon similar in concept to the Vulcan towed anti-aircraft gun, and of similar size and weight but with a new gun. This is the 25 mm GAU-12/U Bushmaster which is allied to improved gun carriage drives and mountings. The 25 mm Bushmaster rotary multi-barrel gun was selected for the improvements in range and time-of-flight that it offers in comparison with the existing 20 mm Vulcan rounds. The GAU-12/U also has dual-feed facilities which permit the use of either HEI (high explosive incendiary) or APDS (armour piercing discarding sabot) rounds to be fired by the gun without altering ammunition feed arrangements. The gun is fired at rates of either 1000 or 2000 rounds per minute. The carriage has provision for a capacity of 530 rounds.

The fire control system is based on the digital system developed for the PIVADS (**4015.131** Product Improved Vulcan Air Defence System), but with provision for a number of additions including a night vision system based on the AN/TAS-6 forward-looking infra-red night observation device (**3826.193**), and a laser rangefinder. The radar provides both search and target tracking facilities and incorporates microprocessor control.

CHARACTERISTICS
Weight: 1814 kg (loaded ready for combat)
Height: 2057 mm (travel configuration); 1828 mm (emplaced)

GEMAG 25 multi-barrel anti-aircraft weapon system deployed

Length: 3683 m (travel configuration); 3589 mm (emplaced)
Gun: 25 mm GAU-12/U
Ammunition system: Linked, dual feed, HEI, APDS
Ammunition capacity: 530 rounds
Feed system: Linked hanging rail type
Firing rates: 2200/1000 rounds/minute
FLIR: AN/TAS-6
Radar: Ku-band search and track

Sight: Optical director
Computer: LSI 11M digital
IFF: AN/PPX-3 Mk XII
STATUS
Prototype.
CONTRACTOR
Armament Systems Department, General Electric Company, Lakeside Avenue, Burlington, Vermont 05402, USA.

Portable Anti-aircraft Guided Missile Systems

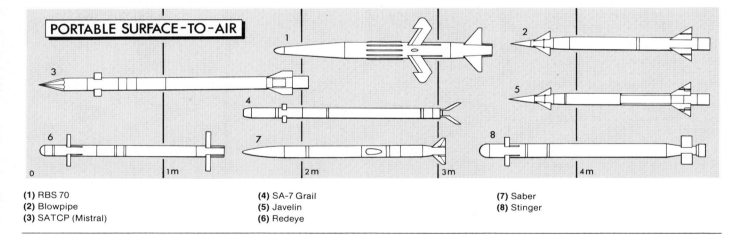

PORTABLE SURFACE-TO-AIR

(1) RBS 70
(2) Blowpipe
(3) SATCP (Mistral)

(4) SA-7 Grail
(5) Javelin
(6) Redeye

(7) Saber
(8) Stinger

FRANCE

4198.131
SATCP AIR DEFENCE MISSILE MISTRAL
The Mistral/SATCP (sol-air-très courte portée) missile project is a development programme intended to provide a short-range air defence missile system capable of production in several versions ranging from the simplest man-portable type including a variety of vehicle and AFV installations, to airborne and naval variants. The work has been entrusted to Matra, the winner from about five contractors which submitted proposals for the SATCP requirement.

The Matra Mistral SATCP system comprises, in the portable version (basic), two main elements: the missile and the firing station. The former is, of course, expendable whereas the firing unit is not, and the whole assembly can be carried by two men in separate packages.

The missile uses infra-red homing guidance, employing a passive system that is claimed to be very sensitive and capable of true 'fire-and-forget' operation. Impact and proximity fuzing is provided for the 3 kg warhead, the latter being a laser-based device, and an IFF module is available to prevent engagement of friendly aircraft and to minimise reaction time in the face of enemy targets. The system

is for defence against both fixed-wing high-speed aircraft and helicopters. The two packages comprising the man-portable version each weigh less than 20 kg. One pack consists of the missile in its launch/transport container tube, and the other includes the stand, seat and sight unit.

The SAT infra-red homing head, instead of relying on a single-cell IR receiver with consequent risks of unwanted responses from ground objects at low elevation angles etc, employs a multi-element seeker which incorporates a second 'colour' sensor operating in the ultra-violet band. This and the use of digital signal processing is stated to enhance the Mistral's performance in the face of IR countermeasures, or natural interference from the background. The sensitivity is claimed to be adequate for acquisition of a single jet aircraft target at a range of 6 km or more, or a light helicopter at 4 km, irrespective of the target aspect. Homing-head gyro run-up and head cooling preparatory to launch takes only two seconds, and weapon reaction times of less than five seconds have been achieved in tests without early warning facilities.

The firer has a sighting system that includes a clear collimator and a magnifying telescope. The former

Matra Mistral/SATCP short-range air defence missile system

allows the display of aiming data enabling the launcher to track the target while following the pre-launch sequence progress and assess azimuth and elevation lead angles. Reload time is quoted as less than 30 seconds.

In addition to the main solid-propellant rocket motor which gives the Mistral a peak speed of about Mach 2·6, there is a solid booster which gives the missile a muzzle velocity of 40 m/s, and this is jettisoned when the main motor ignites about 15 m ahead of the firer.

It is intended to employ the same missile in all versions of the system in the interests of logistic simplicity and economy. The homing head is the responsibility of SAT, and SEP and Manhurin will undertake the propulsion and warhead manufacture respectively.

CHARACTERISTICS
Length: 1·8 m
Diameter: 90 mm
Weight: 17 kg
Warhead: 3 kg

Range: 500 – 6000 m
Peak speed: Mach 2·6

It is proposed to develop imaging infra-red sighting equipment to provide a night capability for the SATCP weapon system. Five versions are understood to have been considered. The first is meant to fill French Army and Air Force requirements for portable defences for important points in the battle area or near airfields. The French Navy plans to use SATCP for the air defence of small vessels with the SADRAL (Système d'Autodéfense Rapprochée Anti-Aérien Léger), and as a supplement to existing air defence armament of large ships (**4509.231**). The Army envisages its use for air-to-air purposes on anti-tank helicopters (**4510.311**) and it is also seen as suitable for mounting on Jeeps or trucks in the dual missile launcher configuration, and on AFVs (with a six-round turret and radar) for the defence of armoured units and rapid deployment forces.

STATUS
The portable version is being developed for the French Army and Air Force.

CONTRACTOR
Matra SA, ave Louis Bréguet, 78140 Velizy, France.

JAPAN

4199.131
JAPANESE MAN-PORTABLE SURFACE-TO-AIR MISSILE
A man-portable surface-to-air missile development project was started in fiscal year 1979 by the Japanese Self Defence Force Technical Research Institute. It is understood that the intention is to develop a weapon similar to the existing generation of man-portable SAMs, such as the American Redeye, Soviet SA-7 and the British Blowpipe, but instead of relying on infra-red homing or radar guidance, the Japanese SAM will use an imaging homing system for guidance. This is claimed to be better in that it will have an all-round attack capability and high resistance to jamming. The guidance system will incorporate a CCD (charge-coupled device) to store the target image, and other important factors are the resolution characteristics of CCDs and low cost. It is hoped to achieve a unit cost of less than ten million Yen. Two types of homing head were under evaluation in 1979, and a propellant unit and a wind tunnel test model had been constructed. The former consists of a booster rocket and a sustainer motor. No other details have been made available for publication.

STATUS
Development continuing. No schedule for development or production plans have been released.

CONTRACTOR
JSDF Technical Institute.

SWEDEN

2348.131
RBS 70 ANTI-AIRCRAFT MISSILE SYSTEM
RBS 70 is a portable surface-to-air missile system operating on the beam-riding principle, and a laser beam is used rather than one of non-coherent light, which gives it substantial immunity to jamming. It has a range of about 5 km and is suitable for use against both fighter-bombers and helicopters even at the lowest levels. The engagement of targets is carried out by one man, but to fire several missiles in rapid succession a loader is needed.

The system is suitable for integration with other surface-to-air weapons or as a separate unit. Unlike many other portable anti-aircraft missile systems, RBS 70 can utilise precision target information from a search radar and it is both possible and desirable to group several RBS 70 units with one or more search radars to form an anti-aircraft battery. RBS 70 is also designed to utilise IFF signals.

A land-mobile G/H-band (former C-band) radar has been developed by LME for use with the RBS 70. It was introduced as the PS-70R but is now known under the name of Giraffe (**1957.153**). Other search radars, such as Signaal's Reporter, can also be integrated with the RBS 70.

Three packs, stand, sight, and missile in container, make up the complete firing unit which can be assembled and ready to fire in less than 30 seconds. The stand has three legs and forms the suspension device for the telescopic sight which has gyro-stabilised optics and which also contains the guidance laser beam transmitter.

To slew on to the target the operator uses coarse aiming, turning the whole sight housing in the required direction. For tracking, a thumb lever is used to operate the gyro-stabilised optics.

The missile is launched from a container which also serves for both storage and transport, the missile never being removed from the container except at the moment of firing. A starting motor ejects the missile from this launch container and separates from it at the mouth of the tube after which the missile sustainer takes over. The missile carries a receiver for the guidance beam and a small computer for calculation of control signals for the control surfaces. The warhead has both proximity and percussion fuzes but if desired the active optical proximity fuze can be paralysed before the missile is fired.

RBS 70 anti-aircraft missile firing

Among the items of test and training equipment supplied for use with the missile is a sight simulator for use in training operators. With this equipment an average AA soldier can be fully trained within 15 to 20 hours, and without a need to fire live rounds. Most of the training can be carried out indoors.

Mobile, vehicle-mounted versions of the RBS 70 are being studied and are described in entry **3617.131**.

In May 1983 it was revealed that an improved version, designated RBS 70X, is being delivered. Design changes to the missile's laser beam receiver give an increase of between 30 and 50 per cent in the engagement envelope. Weight, dimensions and maximum range remain unchanged.

CHARACTERISTICS
Type: Man-portable surface-to-air guided missile system
Guidance: Optical beam-riding on laser beam
Propulsion: Booster plus solid propellant sustainer
Warhead: Fragmentation with impact and proximity fuzes

Weight
Firing unit complete: About 80 kg
Missile in container: 24 kg
Container length: 1·6 m
Container diameter: 15 cm
Missile range: 5 km

STATUS
Development started in 1969 and the system is now in series production. In service with the Swedish and Norwegian armies, and ordered by several other nations believed to include Ireland and Singapore. Demonstrations have been given to about 20 countries, and the Swiss Government contributed to development.

CONTRACTOR
AB Bofors, 691 80 Bofors, Sweden.

UNION OF SOVIET SOCIALIST REPUBLICS

2941.131
SA-7 (GRAIL) MAN-PORTABLE ANTI-AIRCRAFT MISSILE

The SA-7, Grail (once widely known as Strela – arrow) is an extensively deployed man-portable infra-red homing light anti-aircraft missile, very similar in concept to the American Redeye (**2784.131**) but preceding the latter into service. It relies upon a tail pursuit interception to engage low-flying aircraft targets and has proved especially effective against helicopters.

Overall length of the missile is 1·29 metres and the weight is in the region of 9·2 kg. An official UK MoD report issued in April 1976 stated that the range of the SA-7 is approximately 9 to 10 km. Simple optical sighting and tracking are employed, the IR seeker being activated when the operator has acquired the target. An indicator light denotes seeker acquisition and the operator is then free to fire the missile.

Flares were for a time found to provide an effective countermeasure but it is reported that later models are equipped with filters to combat this tactic. The existence of an improved Mk 2 version of SA-7 has been confirmed, the principal difference lying in a boosted propellant charge to increase range and speed of the missile.

Over the years that SA-7 has been in use – well over ten – additional forms of deployment have been evolved, apparently by both the USSR and individual client states. In October 1975, for example, a number of Jeep-type vehicles were seen during an Egyptian military parade with a rudimentary platform and support for an SA-7 gunner at the rear of the vehicle. Four reload rounds were attached to the sides of the vehicle. Various ship fittings of this missile have been noted and the designation given to naval applications is SA-N-5.

The Soviet development is the SA-9, Gaskin, according to the British report mentioned above. In this version four missiles thought to be derived from the SA-7 are housed in rectangular launcher boxes, turret mounted on a BRDM AFV. Some observers claim that the missiles used in this system are larger and heavier, and with correspondingly higher performance, than the SA-7 Grail, but no evidence either way has been obtained. The MoD report, in fact, quotes a slightly lower range value for the SA-9 Gaskin missile than for the basic SA-7.
STATUS
In widespread use with Warsaw Pact nations, Egypt, Syria, Viet-Nam, South Yemen, and probably others including Cuba, China, Morocco and Yugoslavia.

East German troops training in the use of the SA-7 Grail anti-aircraft missile

UNITED KINGDOM

2409.131
BLOWPIPE PORTABLE ANTI-AIRCRAFT MISSILE SYSTEM

Blowpipe is a surface-to-air weapon for unit self defence in forward areas against close-range low-level air attack. To carry out this role effectively the equipment is compact, light, and simple so that it can be both carried and operated by one man.

The weapon is suitable for use in extremes of climate with no maintenance needed during long periods in the field. It can be brought into action very rapidly, and reloading time is a few seconds. Blowpipe can be used against both attacking and receding fast aircraft and helicopter targets.

The Blowpipe weapon system is entirely self-contained with no external power requirements, and consists of two main components: the missile sealed within its launching canister, and the aiming unit. The missile/canister combination is treated as a round of ammunition that can be taken out of store and fired with no preparation or testing. The aiming unit houses all the necessary equipment and controls to launch the missile and guide it towards the target.
OPERATION
To prepare the system for action all that is necessary is to clip the aiming unit to the canister, which requires only a few seconds, and the complete system, which weighs about 20 kg, is lifted to the man's shoulder. The aimer acquires his target in his monocular sight, fires the missile, and controls its flight to the target by means of a thumb-operated flight controller.

The act of pulling the trigger activates thermal batteries for power supplies in both the missile and canister (to supply the aiming unit). When these batteries have reached a sufficiently high voltage (in about one second), the missile first stage motor ejects the missile from the canister. This motor is extinguished before the missile fully emerges and the missile coasts for a safe distance from the aimer before the second stage main motor ignites to boost the missile to supersonic speed.

The missile is fitted with flares which in the early stages of flight are detected by a sensor in the aiming unit to gather the missile to the centre of the aimer's field of view. From then on the aimer guides the missile to the target by means of the controller with up/down and left/right movements. When within lethal distance of the target a proximity fuze in the nose of the missile detonates the warhead.

Commands are transmitted to the missile over a radio link, through the receiver and decoder to the missile control system. This works on 'twist and steer' principles with one pair of nose-mounted control surfaces working differentially to produce roll, and the other pair producing lateral movements.

The missile has a slim, cylindrical body and ogival-nose cone. Cruciform delta-shape canard control surfaces are mounted on the nose cone and a unique type of cruciform delta-shape tail-fin assembly is used. This consists of a sliding ring structure which, in the launching canister, is positioned near the nose of the missile, enabling the diameter of the rear of the canister to be minimised. As the missile is launched, it passes through the tail-fin assembly which finally locks on the rear of the missile. The folded wing tips open to their full span as they emerge from the canister.
CHARACTERISTICS
Type: Man-portable, shoulder-fired surface-to-air (or surface) tactical guided missile
Guidance: Radio command with optical tracking
Guidance method: Twist and steer by nose-mounted control surfaces
Propulsion: 2-stage booster-accelerator solid-propellant rocket motor
Warhead: HE with contact and proximity fuze
Missile length: 1390 mm
Missile diameter: 76 mm
System weight: 20·67 kg
STATUS
In service with the British, Canadian, Omani, Thai, and other, unnamed, forces.

A Blowpipe enhancement programme costing an

Shorts' Blowpipe close-range guided missile, although designed for low-level air defence, can also be used against lightly armoured surface targets

estimated £200 million was implemented in 1979-80, and was in full progress at June 1981. Intended to upgrade the system's performance against new threats, the programme entails improvements to the missile and the shoulder aiming unit. Blowpipe is credited with a number of successes during fighting in the Falkland Islands in 1982.

During 1982, in addition to a repeat contract from the Royal Air Force, a multi-million pound order for Blowpipe systems was placed by the Sultanate of Oman. This brought the total number of operators of the system to 16 armed forces in 11 countries. These include the British Army and Royal Marines.

Under UK MoD contract, Shorts are developing a family of Blowpipe variants for use on armoured vehicles and helicopters.
CONTRACTORS
The following manufacturers are known to have been associated with the development and manufacture of the system:

Main contractor: Short Brothers Limited, Belfast.
IFF system: Cossor Electronics Ltd.
Fuze: Marconi Space and Defence Systems Ltd.
Ignition, safety and arming unit: Royal Ordnance Factory, Blackburn.
Firing circuits: Pye Dynamics Ltd.
Thermal batteries: Mine Safety Appliances Ltd.
The co-ordinating research and development authority is the Royal Radar Establishment.

4533.131
JAVELIN/BLOWPIPE PORTABLE ANTI-AIRCRAFT MISSILE

Evolved from the very successful Blowpipe man-portable anti-aircraft missile system (**2409.131**), the Javelin shoulder-launched weapon is a surface-to-air missile system that employs a semi-automatic line-of-sight command guidance technique based on a visual system that means that the operator does not have to steer the missile in flight by means of a thumb-stick. Instead the missile is tracked to its target by keeping

the target centred in the launcher sight, command signals being generated automatically.

Javelin is a direct development from the Shorts' Blowpipe, but has a higher impulse rocket motor, a new warhead and modified fuze. The warhead is in the centre section with the fuzes in the nose. The forward part of the body contains the guidance equipment and the rear part houses the two solid-propellant rocket motors. There are four delta-shaped aerofoil surfaces in the nose for missile aerodynamic control and four at the tail to improve

ballistic stability. A feature of the missile is that the nose section is free to rotate independently of the main body, to which it is attached by a low-friction bearing. Twist and steer commands to the control fins guide the missile, resulting in a fast response rate. The new warhead relies on blast/fragmentation effects rather than penetration to effect a kill, and the improved fuze will allow remote de-activation by the operator to enable the missile to be steered away from an incorrectly engaged target without detonating.

The cannister in which the missile is factory sealed

Man-portable version of the lightweight multiple launcher with three Blowpipe or Javelin missiles in ready-to-launch position

Shoulder-launched version of Javelin close-range air defence missile system

is a lightweight environmental container designed to act as a recoilless launcher. The front cap is blown off by gas pressure when the missile gyro is fired, while the laminated rear closure is ejected at launch.

The manufacturer has designed a range of lightweight multiple launchers (LMLs) to provide the operator with a multi-fire capability when using the system in man-portable or on vehicle configurations. To suit the operational deployments required, there are three configurations of the LML. Each carries, as clip-on items, three Blowpipe canistered missiles and a standard shoulder-launch aiming unit.

The aiming unit is a self-contained firing and control pack with a pistol grip firing handle on the right-hand side. It contains a stabilised sighting system which provides manual tracking and automatic missile guidance through a solid state TV camera. Digital signals from the camera are fed to a microprocessor and the resultant guidance demands are transmitted to the missile by radio link. Controls on the handle include firing trigger, thumb-controlled joystick and system, fuze mode and super-elevation switches. Other controls are channel selector switches for the transmitter and automatic cross-wind correction switch.

The LML can be used for either Blowpipe or Javelin missiles. The three configurations are:
(1) man-portable for deployment either on the ground or in a trench with the aimer standing
(2) Land-Rover or similar vehicle mounting with a seated aimer on platform deck
(3) armoured vehicle installation consisting of a turret ring with an integral hatch cover and pintle ring for mounting of the traverse head.

The last of these configurations is suitable for mounting on a variety of armoured personnel carriers, including the M113, Cadillac Gage V-150, GKN FS 100 and Renault VAB (4×4). The aiming unit elevation axis, being below that of the missiles, permits deployment in a trench or sandbag emplacement.

CHARACTERISTICS
Length: 1·4 m
Guidance: SACLOS
Propulsion: 2-stage solid
Speed: Supersonic
Range: >4 km
Aiming unit: Standard Blowpipe type (as clip-on equipment)
Missiles on launcher: 3

Elevation: –10 to +45°
Traverse: Continuous (versions 1 & 2); ± 120° (version 3); ± 60° LML plus continuous turret ring (version 4)
Weights

Traverse head		14 kg
Tripod support		16 kg
Complete		30 kg
Vehicle mounting		
Traverse head	30 kg	30 kg
Seat assembly	10 kg	—
Support	18 kg	—
Turret with hatch		
& pintle	—	78 kg
Complete	58 kg	108 kg

STATUS
Production planned in 1983.
CONTRACTOR
Short Brothers Ltd, Missile Systems Division, Castlereagh, Belfast BT6 9HN.

UNITED STATES OF AMERICA

2784.131
REDEYE PORTABLE ANTI-AIRCRAFT MISSILE
Redeye is a shoulder-fired guided missile system designed to give a soldier an effective defence against low-flying aircraft. The US designation is FIM-43 and other users have their own nomenclature as follows: Denmark – Hamlet; West Germany – FLF-1 and Fliegerfaust; Sweden – RB69. The missile's infra-red sensing device homes on the heat of an aircraft's engines. The Redeye carries a high-explosive conventional warhead and has a two-stage solid-propellant engine. The light launching tube is also a carrying case and can be borne through brush and over rough terrain. A shipping and storage container holds one missile and three battery/coolant units.

On sighting a hostile aircraft, the gunner tracks it in an optical sight. At the same time, he energises the missile guidance system. A buzzer located in the launch tube gripstock informs the gunner when the missile is ready to fire. Upon firing, the booster charge propels the missile out of the launch tube. When the missile has cleared the launch tube muzzle by a distance sufficient to protect the gunner from blast effect (about 6 m), the main rocket ignites and propels the missile the rest of the way to its target. The missile is stabilised in flight by cruciform tail fins and steered by two movable fins close to its nose.

Redeye has no IFF facility and is limited to pursuit course engagements.

Practice firing of Redeye portable anti-aircraft missile

CHARACTERISTICS
Designation: FIM-43A
Type: Man-portable, shoulder-fired, surface-to-air guided missile
Guidance: Optical aiming, infra-red homing
Propulsion: Solid-propellant booster and sustainer
Warhead: HE
Missile length: 1·22 m
Diameter: 70 mm
Weight: 13 kg

Speed: Supersonic
Range: Not disclosed. Probably about 3 km
Crew: Normally 2

Redeye is employed in the forward battle area to protect combat troops against low-level aircraft. In the US Army the weapon is issued to Redeye teams, each made up of a gunner and assistant gunner. From four to six of these teams are assigned to a Redeye section at infantry battalion level.

STATUS
Procurement of Redeye was completed in fiscal year 1970. It has been issued to the USMC as well as the US Army and has been supplied also to the Australian, Danish, West German and Swedish armed forces. Gradual replacement by the Stinger system (**2805.131**) is in progress by the US forces.
CONTRACTOR
Prime: General Dynamics Corporation, Pomona Division, Pomona, California, USA.
Rocket motor: Atlantic Research Corporation.

4534.131

SABER PORTABLE ANTI-AIRCRAFT MISSILE

Saber is designed to engage all types of subsonic air threats and for deployment by foot soldiers. A dual-purpose shaped charge warhead is intended to provide a useful anti-armour capability also. The system is composed of three elements: the missile, launcher assembly, and a re-usable guidance unit that is easily and rapidly attached to the launcher. The missile is a simple cylindrical body with tail surfaces, and it is stabilised in all three axes. It is ejected from the launcher at low speed to minimise flashback and noise experienced by the operator, and the solid propellant rocket motor is ignited after the missile has travelled some distance from the launcher. Guidance is provided by the guidance unit attached to the launcher, which incorporates a stabilised sight line for target tracking and a guidance beam projector that provides steering signals via the guidance receiver in the missile. There is no separate seeker head in the missile itself.
STATUS
All phases of an advanced development flight test programme had been satisfactorily completed by spring 1983, and the last two guided flights were conducted against moving aerial targets with a

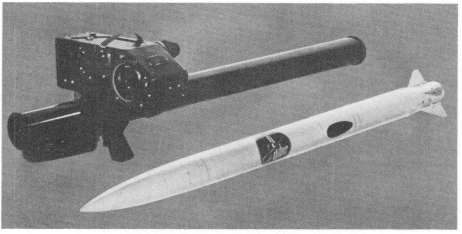

Ford Saber man-portable AA missile with launcher assembly and guidance unit

gunner tracking the target and directing the laser guidance beam at the target. Both resulted in direct hits. Demonstration firings have been carried out at various US Army establishments.

CONTRACTOR
Ford Aerospace & Communications Corporation, Aeronutronic Division, Ford Road, Newport Beach, California 92660, USA.

2805.131

STINGER PORTABLE ANTI-AIRCRAFT MISSILE (FIM-92A)

Stinger, Redeye's successor, was in engineering development from July 1972, and is the current US Army and Marine Corps' man portable air defence system (MANPADS). It is an infra-red seeking missile which enables the soldier to engage effectively low-altitude, high-speed jet, propeller-driven and helicopter aircraft. Designed for the threat beyond the 1980s, Stinger has all-aspect engagement capability, an IFF system, improved range and manoeuvrability and significant countermeasure immunity.
CHARACTERISTICS
Designation: FIM-92A
Type: Man-portable, shoulder-fired, surface-to-air guided missile
Guidance: Passive IR homing
Propulsion: Solid-propellant
Warhead: HE
Length: 1·52 m
Diameter: 70 cm
Weight: 15·8 kg
An airborne application of Stinger has been proposed, employing a two-round launcher for installation on helicopters to provide such aircraft with an air-to-air self-defence capability and an air-to-ground facility for engaging suitable radiating targets. This project has been named Air Launched

Stinger (formerly Multipurpose Lightweight Missile System, MLMS) in the former role, and ADSM (air defence suppression missile) in the air-to-ground application.
Tests have been carried out where Stinger missiles have been carried and fired from Roland surface-to-air missile system (**2218.131**) fire units. Using a special Stinger container developed by Boeing four Stinger missiles can be housed in the space of a single standard Roland launch tube.
STATUS
Stinger became operational in West Germany in February 1981, and with the US Army 82nd Airborne Division in April 1982. The improved Stinger-POST version went into production in 1983 for deployment in 1987.
In addition to the US Army and Marine Corps, it is planned for use by the USAF in small quantities for airfield defence. Projected procurement for the three US Forces as detailed in the fiscal year 1985 DoD budget is as follows, quantities in brackets and funding in $ millions:

Stinger AA missile system

Fiscal year	**1983**	**1984**	**1985**
Army	(1006) 140·8	(1205) 137·8	(2360) 209·6
USMC	(1560) 99·5	(691) 40·0	(800) 75·6
USAF	—	(60) 4·9	(156) 12·9

CONTRACTOR
General Dynamics Corporation, Pomona Division, Pomona, California, USA.

SHIPBORNE SURFACE-TO-AIR WEAPONS

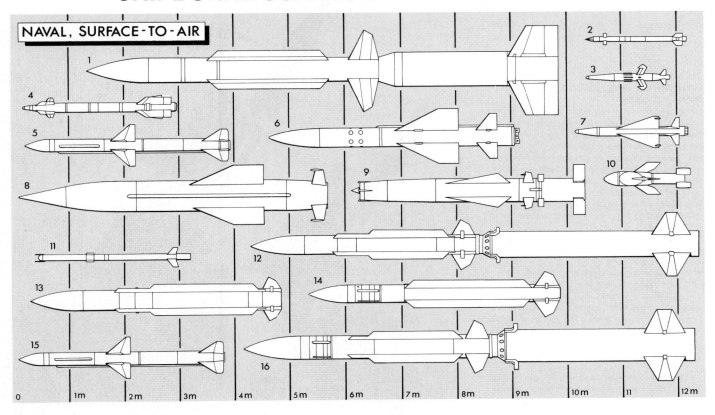

NAVAL, SURFACE-TO-AIR

1 Masurca
2 SADRAL
3 RBS 70
4 Crotale
5 Albatros
6 Barak

7 Seawolf
8 SA-N-3 Goblet
9 Sea Dart
10 Seacat
11 ASMD RAM
12 Standard II Extended Range

13 Standard
14 Tartar
15 Sea Sparrow
16 Terrier

FRANCE

1177.231
MASURCA SURFACE-TO-AIR MISSILE SYSTEM

Masurca is the surface-to-air missile system which forms the main anti-aircraft armament of the French frigates *Duquesne* and *Suffren*, whose principal role is that of escort to the aircraft carriers *Foch* and *Clemenceau*. Masurca also has armed the AA cruiser *Colbert* since 1973 when her modernisation was completed. Each of the Masurca ships is equipped with three-dimensional surveillance radar, a weapon direction system, two independent fire control systems, and a twin launcher. Aircraft and missile targets can be intercepted at ranges of 40 km or more.

The main characteristics of the missile are length (with booster) 8·6 m, (without booster) 5·29 m, diameter 41 cm, span of booster fins 150 cm, weight (with booster) 1850 kg, (without booster) 840 kg. A proximity-fuzed high-explosive warhead is carried, and both boosters and sustainer motors are solid-fuel units.

Two types of guidance system have been employed: the Mk 2 Mod 2 uses radio command, and the Mk 2 Mod 3 is equipped with a semi-active radar homing head, but the latter only is currently in service.

In addition to the missiles themselves, the Masurca weapon system contains the following main elements:
(1) a twin launcher
(2) two storage and handling systems
(3) two directors, each with a tracking radar and a target illuminator.

The DRBR 51 tracking radar has two main functions in the Mk 2 Mod 3 role:
(1) it continuously follows the target
(2) it controls the pointing of the target illuminator radar.

OPERATION
The DRBR 51 has three antennas, the main one of which is used for target tracking and as an I/J-band target illuminator radar. The missile is equipped with two antenna systems, one at the front of the vehicle, and two fixed antennas mounted on the missile body.

The latter are used to receive the illuminating radar signals direct, to provide a reference signal which can be compared with the signals reflected from the target that are collected by the forward missile antenna. This enables a doppler component to be extracted, which is used in the on-board computation of a proportional navigation interception course to the target.

DEVELOPMENT
The Masurca missile was developed by Etablissement des Constructions et Armes Navales de Ruelle in co-operation with Société des Engins Matra.

Fire control radar, missile homing head and proximity fuze were developed by Thomson-CSF. Solid propellants are manufactured by Société Nationale des Poudres et Explosifs (SNPE). Launch, storage, and handling equipments were designed and developed by Etablissement des Constructions et Armes Navales de Ruelle.

STATUS
The Masurca weapon system is operational in the Mk 2 Mod 3 version aboard the three ships named in the opening paragraph of this entry.

CONTRACTOR
Direction Technique des Constructions Navales, 2 rue Royale, 75200 Paris Naval, France.

Masurca surface-to-air missiles aboard the French ship Suffren *(DTCN)*

2111.231
NAVAL CROTALE SURFACE-TO-AIR WEAPON SYSTEM (TSE 5500)

Directly derived from the ground version of the Crotale (**2074.131**), the Naval Crotale weapon system is designed for the self-defence of ships against short range air attacks at medium, low and very low altitude, these attacks being conducted by aircraft, helicopters, air launched and sea-skimming missiles. The Naval Crotale may also be used against surface targets and is capable of artillery control.

The Naval Crotale is now operational with the French Navy and has been ordered by the Saudi Arabian Navy (8 S version).

A new version, the Modular Naval Crotale, is now available (8 MS version) for installation on board ships of 200 tons or more.

In its 8 S version, Naval Crotale is composed of:

(1) a turret assembly with two coaxial turrets: the eight-missile turret and the fire director supporting the radar antenna and receiver, the remote control antenna, the IR receiver for localisation of the missile during the first part of its flight (gathering), the differential IR tracker for guidance of the missile at very low altitude and the TV camera

(2) a shelter housing the electronic equipment data processing, radar and IR processing cabinets, launcher power control cabinet and maintenance unit

(3) an operator console in the combat information centre (CIC) for supervision of the system and sending of firing orders. Operation of the system is fully automatic, pushing the 'Fire' button being the only manual action. In the normal mode, the operator sitting in front of the data processing cabinet has just to start the system, to supervise its working and to depress the 'Fire' button.

Acquisition and tracking of the target on the target designation from the ship (surveillance radar, optical sight, radar detector or another tracking radar) are performed by the radar of the Crotale system.

After launching, the missile is gathered by the large field of the IR localiser which locks it within the radar beam. Missile guidance is performed by an improved line-of-sight guidance which optimises the manoeuvrability of the missile. A proportional navigation law is elaborated at the end of the missile flight to reduce the miss-distance in the case of a manoeuvring target. In the case of a target at very low altitude (sea-skimmer), tracking of the target and of the missile is performed by the differential IR tracker. The missile is fired and guided as in the radar mode.

The Crotale missile is boosted by a solid propellant rocket motor. The warhead, weighing about 14 kg, is triggered by an electromagnetic proximity fuze; the delay of explosion is calculated to concentrate the prefragmented splinters in the most vulnerable zone of the target.

The missile is housed inside a sealed container, which is used for transport, storage and launching. A missile inside its container forms a Crotale round. The 18-missile magazine and loading mechanism is manufactured in French Navy yards.

Modular Naval Crotale is composed of the following parts:

(1) the fire director turret, supporting the radar antenna and receiver, the remote control antenna, the IR tracker (for guidance against sea-skimmer targets) and the TV camera

(2) an independent launcher turret, supporting the IR localiser (gathering) and eight rounds

(3) the data processing cabinet, installed in the CIC

(4) the other electronic equipments (radar, IR and launcher power control cabinets) which are installed in any available compartment(s) of the ship.

Operation of the system does not differ from the Naval Crotale. The fire director of the Modular Naval Crotale, as for the Naval Crotale, can also be used for the direction of naval guns. The Modular Naval

Naval Crotale installation aboard the French destroyer Montcalm

Crotale can be installed on ships of 500 tons or more. The light eight-missile loading system is manufactured by the French Navy yards.

CHARACTERISTICS
Radar frequency: Ku-band
Range: 18 km
Differential deviation measurement accuracy: 0·1 mrad

Remote control frequency: X-band
IR tracker: 10 μ band, range 18 km
Differential deviation measurement accuracy: 0·1 mrad
Guidance: Improved line-of-sight command and proportional navigation at end of missile flight
Useful elevation: −15 to +70° (8 S); −15 to +80° (8 MS)
Useful training arc: Unlimited

Missile max speed: 750 m/s after 2·3 s
Targets for which system has been optimised
Aircraft
Speed: Mach 1·2
Altitude: 15 – 5000 m
Radar cross-section: 1 m² fluctuating
Target manoeuvrability: 2 g at 8·5 km
Missiles
Speed: Up to Mach 2
Minimum altitude: 4 m
Radar cross-section: 0·1 m²
Max interception range: 13 km (helicopter or non-manoeuvring target); 8·5 km (manoeuvring Mach 1·2 aircraft); 6·5 km (sea-skimmer)
Minimum interception range: 700 m
Vertical coverage: From 4 to 5000 m
Target max speed: Mach 2 (radial attack aircraft/sea skimmer); Mach 1·2 (crossing target)
Reaction time: 6 s (between target designation reception and first missile start)
Weight
Naval Crotale
Turret assembly: 8·2 tons with 8 rounds
Shelter + electronic equipment: Approx 10 tons
18-missile storage and loading system: Approx 15 tons with 18 rounds
Modular Naval Crotale
Fire director turret: 1 ton
8-missile turret: 4·2 tons with 8 rounds
Electronic equipment: 2·8 tons
8-missile loading system: 3·2 tons with 8 rounds
DEVELOPMENT
Development of the Naval Crotale was carried out under the responsiblity of DTCN and DTEN with Thomson-CSF as systems manager and supplier.
STATUS
The Naval Crotale, in its basic version, is now operational on 'Georges Leygues' class corvettes and 'Tourville' class frigates of the French Navy. These units are about to be retrofitted with the anti-sea-

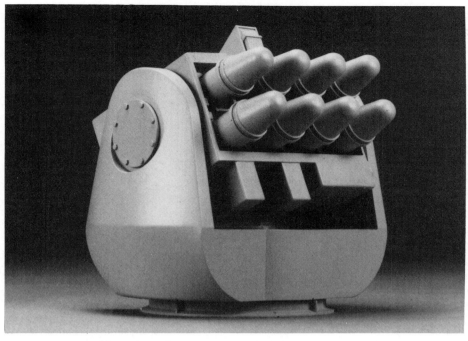
Modular Naval Crotale will employ new design 8-round launcher

skimmer capability (8 S version) and five more systems were ordered by the French Navy in 1982, bringing the total number of systems ordered by the French Navy to 14.

Five 8 S version systems were ordered by the Saudi Arabian Navy in 1980 and are now operational. Negotiations are progressing with several other naval forces for Naval Crotale and Modular Naval Crotale.

CONTRACTORS
System: Thomson-CSF, Division Systèmes Electroniques, 1 rue des Mathurins, 92222 Bagneux, France.
Missile: Engins Matra, Département Missiles, avenue Louis Breguet, 78140 Velizy-Villacoublay, France.

4776.231
SATAN CLOSE-IN WEAPON SYSTEM
SATAN (Système Autonome Tout temps d'Auto-defense Naval) is a new project for the design and development of an entirely autonomous all-weather close-in defence system for ships to provide protection against aircraft and missiles. The design is intended for fitting in ships which may already be equipped with one or more longer-range missile

Castor II J director is main sensor for new SATAN autonomous naval CIWS

systems such as the Naval Crotale (**2111.231**), or as the main anti-missile defence in other types of ship. It is completely automatic from detection to firing and has a very short reaction time.

A modular design has been chosen to permit easy installation and rapid changes to accommodate developments in the threats anticipated, and advancing technology. The main elements are:
(1) a doppler frequency-agile surveillance radar which is capable of automatic detection of missile targets in sea or rain clutter and in a heavy jamming environment. An automatic extraction system is associated with an automatic plot tracking device
(2) a data processing system with a VDU for threat evaluation, co-ordination with other weapon systems, electronic warfare and target designation
(3) a Castor II J Ku-band director radar, with an added continuous target-to-shell radar angle tracking facility. An associated digital computer generates the firing data and uses the target-to-shell angle tracking information to produce an efficient automatic firing correction closed control loop. (In many cases this IR tracking facility will be provided by a ship's Crotale system, but where this is not the case, separate E-O sensors are provided for TV or IR target tracking)

(4) one or more 30 mm Gatling EX 83 multi-barrel guns by General Electric.

By adopting an off-mounted solution for the surveillance radar and the Castor II J fire control radar, it is possible to site the various sensors aboard the ships in the optimum fashion for accurate detection and tracking. The surveillance antenna can be placed at a height that offers maximum sea-skimmer detection range, given the problems posed by geographical range and particularly the interference fringes. (Against a 500 m/s target, every kilometre gained in early detection gives three seconds more for use of defensive weapons.)

As the fire control radar is separate from the gun, it is free from problems such as vibration and debris associated with firing, and may be installed above the gun to improve the field of view or to provide autonomous search facilities. The additional errors introduced by platform movements between the mounting and the radar aiming system are corrected in the firing control loop, and the computer system integrates all platform movements by measuring the various parameters, positions and speeds.
STATUS
Development project.
CONTRACTOR
Thomson-CSF, Division Systèmes Electroniques, 1 rue des Mathurins, Bagneux 92222, France.

4509.231
SADRAL NAVAL AIR DEFENCE SYSTEM
SADRAL (Système d'Autodéfense Rapprochée Anti-aérienne Léger) is an air defence system based on the Matra Mistral land-based SATCP missile system, modified for naval applications and proposed for the French Navy. The Mistral itself is described in entry **4198.131** and the following entry is concerned with its application to 'close-in' defence of ships from aircraft or anti-ship missiles.

The equipment consists of a remotely operated stabilised mount which carries six SATCP rounds and a closed circuit TV camera. The mount can be trained in azimuth and elevation under the control of the operator who mans a simple control desk below deck. The TV camera is used for target acquisition, and this

component can be supplemented by an IR thermal imaging camera for night operations.

For the majority of its components, the SADRAL system uses equipment already certified for marine environments and in use for Otomat systems or those derived from the Totem remote-aiming system. The mass of the carriage fitted with its six rounds of ammunition is approximately 700 kg. Total mass of the SADRAL system (carriage, servos and control desk) is about 1300 kg. It is thus possible to mount two SADRAL systems on low-tonnage vessels, with a mass which is still more than 50 per cent less than that, for example, of a single Phalanx system, according to the manufacturer.

Due to missile accuracy and the penetrating power of the fragments of its charge, SADRAL's efficiency is

claimed as superior to that of a gun-based system. In addition, the SADRAL system permits interception of targets at distances much greater than those of gun-based systems, thus offering greater safety for ships. Finally, the time required to pass through the firing envelope being much greater, SADRAL permits engaging several missiles against the same target, or against a wave of aircraft, which a gun-based system does not permit.

Although the priority mission assigned to SADRAL by the French Navy is anti-aircraft defence of small vessels (patrol-boats, mine-sweepers, etc) it will also be mounted on logistic backup and transport ships. It may also be mounted in ships already equipped with a surface-to-air system, such as anti-aircraft corvettes, where its firepower would extend the threshold of saturation of the threat. In addition to defence against helicopters or airplanes, the SATCP could be used to engage sea-skimmer-type missiles flying at low altitude above the sea surface.

Target designation may be performed, according to circumstances, by using the ship's surveillance radar or an electro-optical surveillance system (IR or optical), or, if necessary, simpler designation systems (navigation radar or a lightweight optical sighting system now under study).

CHARACTERISTICS
Mount: 6-round, stabilised
Weight: Approx 700 kg (with 6 rounds)
System weight: Approx 1300 kg
Missile: SATCP (Mistral)
Length: 1·8 m
Diameter: 90 mm
Weight: 17 kg

Warhead: 3 kg
Fuze: Impact, laser proximity
Guidance: IR homing (2-colour)
Range: 500–5000+ m
Peak speed: Mach 2·6
STATUS
Development began in 1981. The French Navy is reported to have plans to procure several dozen systems for its vessels with entry into service planned for 1987.
CONTRACTORS
Prime: Matra SA, avenue Louis Bréguet, 78140 Velizy-Villacoublay, France.
Homing Head: SAT.
Propulsion: SEP.
Thermal batteries: SAFT.
Warhead, weapon canister: Manhurin.

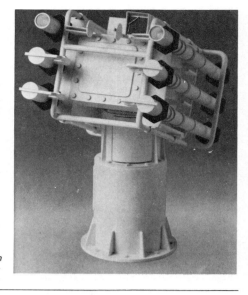

SADRAL, the version of the SATCP Mistral system under development for the French Navy

INTERNATIONAL

4775.231
NATO SEASPARROW SURFACE-TO-AIR MISSILE SYSTEM
The NATO Seasparrow Surface Missile System (NSSMS), originally known as the Point Defence Missile System, is a shipboard air defence system employing the Sparrow family of missiles. The system is designed to counter the threat of anti-ship cruise missiles and aircraft. The original shipboard use of the Sparrow missile was in the Basic Point Defense Missile System (BPDMS) which became operational aboard US ships in 1969 and in 1984 was being phased out of service. The NATO Seasparrow Surface Missile System (NSSMS) became operational in 1973 using RIM-7H missiles. Modifications to the NATO Seasparrow missile systems to accommodate the improved Sparrow AIM/RIM-7M monopulse missile began in 1983. In 1981 Seasparrows were successfully fired from Vertical Launchers aboard a Canadian destroyer. This Seasparrow Vertical Launch System will be operational aboard the new Canadian Patrol Frigates.
Basic Point Defence Missile System
The BPDMS was assembled urgently from existing hardware. It features the Sparrow AIM-7E missile launched from a modified eight-tube ASROC missile launcher. The launcher is housed on a modified 3-inch 50 calibre automatic gun carriage. Total weight of the system is 17 690 kg.

A CW semi-active radar homing system is used. Target data from the combat information centre is

supplied to the manually operated Mk 115 fire control system and the target is acquired and illuminated for homing guidance by a Mk 51 director/illuminator radar.
STATUS
BPDMS development began in 1964. In March 1983 USN ships with BPDMSs total 46: (31 in 'Knox' class ships (one system each); two LCCs with two systems each; seven LPHs (two each); five LHAs (two each); and one CV (two systems)).
CONTRACTOR
Sparrow missile: Raytheon Company.
Solid-state power drive for fire control system: General Electric.
Fire control system: Frequency Engineering Laboratories.
NATO Seasparrow Surface Missile System (NSSMS), Mk 57
The NSSMS incorporates a lightweight eight-cell launcher (Mk 29), and a fire control system (Mk 91) utilising digital computers, and powered director/illuminator(s). The RIM-7H and AIM/RIM-7M Sparrow missile family is used in a modified form with folding wings that enable them to fit into the smaller, lighter launcher. NSSMS possesses a range of operational modes from manual to fully automatic with operator intervention.

The new digital Sparrow (AIM/RIM-7M) medium

range missile features all-aspects, all-weather, crossing target capability. The 7M Sparrow incorporates an advanced inverse monopulse seeker and a digital computer. This provides substantial performance improvements in seeker sensitivity and enhances target discrimination in heavy clutter, ECM conditions, and extreme low altitude intercepts.

The onboard digital computer, besides being reprogrammable, gives greater immunity in the changing ECM threats, while providing for proportional navigation. Proportional navigation directs the missile to fly a lead angle course to the intercept point, which provides NSSMS equipped ships with the ability to protect other ships in the vicinity. The AIM/RIM-7M also includes a larger boost sustain rocket motor and blast fragmentation warhead.

The NATO Seasparrow programme was established by a Memorandum of Understanding in 1968 between Denmark, Italy, Norway and the US. Belgium and The Netherlands joined in 1970, the Federal Republic of Germany in 1977, and Canada and Greece acceded in 1982.

The contract definition phase began in 1968 and in 1969 Raytheon Company was awarded a $23 million prime contract for engineering and development, requiring the production of three engineering and development systems. One system was to be tested

Vertical Launch of Seasparrow from HMCS Huron

Artist's impression of the new Canadian Patrol Frigate fitted with Vertical Launch Seasparrow

by the US Navy, one sent to Norway for operational environment testing, and one remained at Raytheon for systems evaluation.

The first successful shipborne launch took place in March 1972 when a NSSMS on the frigate USS Downes (FF-1070) acquired and tracked an incoming target and successfully fired its missile. Another prototype Seasparrow System was installed on the Royal Norwegian Navy ship KNM Bergen (F-301) in 1973.

NSSMS entered full scale production in 1973 as a co-operative effort by the US and other NATO countries – Belgium, Denmark, Italy, The Netherlands and Norway. The US is expected to purchase approximately half of all systems produced. At autumn 1983, 111 systems had been installed with a total of 143 systems being ordered worldwide. Of this total, 87 systems are for the US aboard CV/CVN, DD, AOE and AOR class ships.

All NATO ships which will have NSSMS installations are frigates. Three NATO countries use the full system similar to the US configuration. Denmark has dual director systems in five frigates and a single director system at a land-based site. Italy has single director systems in four frigates. Norway has a single director in five frigates and one land-based site.

Five other NATO countries use the NSSMS launcher, transmitter and Seasparrow missile, but with their own fire control systems: Belgium has four, Greece with two, The Netherlands will have 14 plus one land-based site. The Federal Republic of Germany will have six plus two land-based sites, and Turkey will have four.

Japan (five systems) and Spain (four systems) have also purchased NSSMS.

Seasparrow, Guided Missile Vertical Launch System (GMVLS)

The Raytheon Company was awarded a contract in 1983 to supply the Seasparrow Vertical Launch Missile Systems for the Canadian Patrol Frigates programme. The first ship of this new class, which is scheduled for delivery in 1988, will carry 16 Vertical Launch Seasparrow cells.

Vertical Launch Seasparrow was demonstrated aboard the Canadian destroyer HMCS Huron with the successful interception of missile targets during a joint at-sea test in 1981 (**2036.231** in the 1983-84 Edition)

The vertically launched AIM/RIM-7M Seasparrow missile is modified with the addition of a Jet Vane Control (JVC) unit. The JVC provides for initial missile tip-over, orientation, and course control after

NATO Seasparrow firing from the carrier USS Kennedy

vertical launch prior to the normal Sparrow guidance control. The GMVLS vertically mounted missile launching canisters are designed to function as the transport and storage units as well as the launch cells.

STATUS

In production.

The AIM/RIM-7M, developed by Raytheon Company, completed a full-scale development test in 1982 and is now in full rate production, with total production awards of 3400 missiles. This missile system entered the US Navy inventory in 1983. RIM-7M deliveries to NATO countries also began in 1983.

In 1982 General Dynamics was awarded a second source contract for the production of 690 AIM/RIM-7M missiles. General Dynamics missile deliveries are expected to begin during mid 1984.

Under a $76 million contract awarded to Raytheon

in early 1984 the company is to supply Seasparrow VLS missile systems and AN/SPS-49 long range surveillance radars for the Canadian Patrol Frigate programme. In addition Raytheon is to receive a $16 million contract for modifications to the RIM-7M Seasparrow missile. Both contracts were issued by Paramax Electronics Inc, of Canada, a division of Sperry responsible for integrating the combat systems aboard the Canadian vessels. First ship of the new class is due for delivery in 1988.

CONTRACTORS

Raytheon Company, Equipment Division, Wayland, Massachusetts, USA.

Raytheon Company, Missile Systems Division, Bedford, Massachusetts, USA. (RIM-7H, AIM/RIM-7M, RIM-7M vertical launch missiles)

General Dynamics Corporation, Pomona Division, Pomona, California, USA (AIM/RIM-7M missile)

3616.231

GOALKEEPER NAVAL AIR DEFENCE SYSTEM

The Goalkeeper naval air defence system is an autonomous ('stand alone') radar-directed automatic weapon system developed for use aboard the Royal Netherlands Navy's 'Kortenaer' class frigates for their defence at short range against high speed missiles and aircraft. The system has been developed under contract to the Royal Netherlands Navy by Hollandse Signaalapparaten BV (Signaal) in the Netherlands and the General Electric Company (GE) in the United States.

The system has all its elements integrated on a single mount and consists of a surveillance radar, a dual-frequency tracking radar, fire control and a high rate-of-fire seven-barrel GAU-8/A 30 mm Gatling gun. Operation of the Goalkeeper system is completely automatic from target detection to target destruction, termination of firing and engagement of the next target.

For the surveillance radar Goalkeeper uses an I-band (3 cm) high power, pulse-to-pulse coherent search radar to provide a high detection probability of small targets in all weather conditions and under ECM conditions. A synthesizer-driven travelling wave tube transmitter is used to provide high power for burn-through and to permit flexibility in frequency and PRF to counteract jamming. A 30° vertical beamwidth antenna is stabilised in two modes to ensure detection and track information is obtained independent of the ship's movements. The antenna has a rotation rate of 60 rpm. Detection probability is further enhanced by the application of processing techniques such as digital pulse compression and fast Fourier transformation. Digital moving target

Goalkeeper naval air defence system with GE 30 mm GAU-8/A Gatling gun and Signaal radars combined on a single mounting

detection is used for range indication in clutter conditions and further ECCM features include PRF stagger and frequency diversity. Dual receiver channels are used to speed processing, plot extraction, track build-up, threat evaluation and target selection, followed immediately by priority target designation indication for the tracking radar and weapon. Continuous search allows rapid engagement of any subsequent targets.

After target designation the target is acquired by the dual frequency (I- and K-band) tracking radar. The narrow K-band beam provides accurate and continuous track data down to very low altitudes and continuous automatic comparison is made of the signal to noise ratios of the I- and K-band returns to maintain tracking in clutter or degraded conditions. This system has been used against missile targets flying as low as 5 m. Digital processing is used to predict the hit point and automatic calibration and closed-loop hit point correction are used to compensate for bias errors and inaccurate ballistic data. There is an automatic kill assessment sub-system for use in multiple attacks and the tracking radar has the ability to engage high-elevation targets.

The 30 mm GAU-8/A gun has a rate of fire of 4200 rounds per minute. It and the prototype EX-83 naval mounting are described in entry **4042.203** in the Naval Guns section. The Goalkeeper mount has an ammunition capacity of 1190 rounds carried in a linkless system using a feed and storage drum. To reload the gun system a bulk loading system is employed but manual loading is possible using a manual loading tray. Spent cases are returned to the drum to prevent deck debris after firing. The ammunition capacity is stated to be sufficient for several target engagements before reloading is necessary. The feed drum and much of the ammunition feed system is protected below deck. Under development by NWM de Kruithoorn in collaboration with Armatechnica Corporation in Santa Barbara, California, is an APDS round for use with Goalkeeper. For soft targets HEI will be used and a TP round is available. The APDS round will have a high density tungsten alloy penetrator.

Using computer modelling, extensive simulations of Goalkeeper performance have been carried out by Signaal, using simulated targets with armour-protected warheads. Based on the results of these simulations supersonic targets have been destroyed at a range of 500 m with second, immediate, targets being destroyed at a range of 400 m.

CHARACTERISTICS

Gun type: 30 mm Gatling-type GAU-8/A, seven barrels
Muzzle velocity: 1021 m/s
Rate of fire: 4200 rounds/minute
Feed system: Linkless, 1190 rounds capacity
Ammunition: APDS, HEI, TP
Weight: 6730 kg (all-up with 1190 rounds)
Elevation/depression: +85/-25°

Radar (search): I-band
Antenna: Slotted waveguide, 2050 × 250 mm
Beamwidth: 1·5° (horizontal); 30° (vertical)
Stabilisation: 2-axis
Rotation speed: 60 rpm
SLS antenna: Omni-directional
Radar (tracking): Dual frequency, I-/K-band
Antenna, Cassegrain: 1000 mm diameter
TV camera: Compatible with CCIR Type B

STATUS

Demonstrations of the GE EX-83 prototype gun and mount for the SGE-30 Goalkeeper were carried out in the Netherlands at Erfprins Naval Base, at least 80 NATO observers attending firings against sleeve targets in November 1979. In December 1980 the Royal Netherlands Navy and Signaal signed a contract for one prototype and two pre-production systems. In May 1983 the Netherlands Minister of Defence signed a contract for ten more systems for installation on 'S' class frigates for the Royal Netherlands Navy. At the same time proposals for Goalkeeper systems for fitting in the planned 'M' class frigates were invited. The system is also planned for fitting in the Royal Netherlands Navy's 'L' class frigates.

Ordered for Royal Navy in early 1984.

CONTRACTORS

General Electric Company, Armament Systems Department, Lakeside Avenue, Burlington, Vermont 05402, USA.

Hollandse Signaalapparaten BV, PO Box 42, 7750 GD Hengelo, Netherlands.

4016.231

SEAGUARD CIWS

Seaguard CIWS (close-in weapon system) is one configuration of the modular Seaguard naval equipment range (**3509.281**) and consists essentially of fire control modules integrated with the Sea Zenith 25 mm multiple-barrelled gun module (**4017.203**). The main elements are an above deck sensor mount, a gun mount with below-deck ammunition feed, below-deck operator console and associated below-deck electronic cabinets. The fire control element of the CIWS, the tracker module (CIWS-TM), uses a three-axis tracker mount having Ku-band radar, forward looking infra-red (FLIR) and laser sensors for the acquisition and tracking of missile targets. The Ku-band radar includes a patented mirror effect suppression technique. This radar together with the FLIR and laser are intimately combined with specialised and innovative signal processing and advanced control algorithms into a missile target tracking system which can adaptively counteract the disturbances of the mirror effect and the effects of bad weather as well as those arising from severe ECM. The naval three-axis sensor and gun mounts each have a wide dynamic performance range appropriate for defence systems intended to defeat sea-skimming and diving anti-ship missiles. A valuable feature of the three-axis mounting technique is its ability to provide hemispherical cover which includes the 'zenith cone'.

The gun element of the CIWS, the gun module (CIWS-GM) is a four-barrelled 25 mm gun mount (**4017.203**). Each gun is independently fed from below decks where sufficient on-mount ammunition is available to engage 14 targets without reloading. A unique feature of the reload system is that of on-line replenishment of ammunition which can take place without interfering with the gun module availability for firing, and indeed it may be replenished during firing. The axis configuration of the gun mount allows an elevation range of –20 to +125° for hemispherical engagement coverage.

The kill-mechanism relied upon is based on a single hit detonating the warhead and resulting in a single-round kill. This is achieved by the use of APDS with a

Picture of Seaguard CIWS at Farnborough Air Show shows Plessey Dolphin search radar module (left), CIWS-TM radar with laser rangefinder and FLIR (centre) and CIWS-GM gun module (right)

non-exotic material as the sub-calibre penetrator. The high energy level required to achieve this ultimate kill mechanism results from an ammunition development programme by Oerlikon where the boundaries of ordnance technology have been considerably advanced. A full range of other ammunition types may be used according to target or usage requirements. The overall kill probability of the Seaguard CIWS has been assessed as greater than 90 per cent against a single missile whose terminal trajectory may be from 0° (sea-skimmer) to 90° (zenith threat) with a speed of up to Mach 3. Additionally this performance is valid when evasive or pre-programmed manoeuvres are superimposed upon the basic terminal approach, and engagements can be continued at extremely close-in ranges against targets with speeds of up to 900 m/s by both the tracking and gun mount modules.

DEVELOPMENT

Development was initiated in 1977 as a joint private

venture by Contraves and Oerlikon, with co-operation from other manufacturers in Switzerland, Italy, the UK and USA.

STATUS

In full series production following a contract from a West German shipyard for Seaguard systems to be fitted in four frigates under construction for the Turkish Navy. Other contracts were under negotiation in May 1984.

CONTRACTORS

Contraves AG, Schaffhauserstrasse 580, 8050 Zurich, Switzerland.

Contraves Italiana SpA, Via Affile (Km 13150 Via Tiburtina), 00131 Rome, Italy.

Machine Tool Works Oerlikon-Bührle, Birchstrasse 155, 8050 Zurich, Switzerland.

Plessey Radar Ltd, Addlestone, Weybridge, Surrey KT15 2PW, England.

British Manufacture & Research Co Ltd, Springfield Road, Grantham, Lincolnshire NG31 7JB, England.

ISRAEL

4200.231

BARAK SHIP POINT DEFENCE SYSTEM

In June 1981 Israel Aircraft Industries announced a new naval self-defence system designed to be effective against sea-skimming missiles, aircraft, and 'other anti-ship threats'. Described as a compact modular lightweight system, Barak is capable of multiple target engagement under all weather conditions by day or night. Using two launchers, a ship can engage four simultaneous targets according to the manufacturer, and both autonomous and manual modes of operation are possible. High resistance to ECM is claimed and command guidance is employed.

The early development system comprised three main units: a deck launcher containing eight Barak missiles on which was mounted an autonomous radar, a fire control console mounted below decks in the ship's combat information centre, and a processing unit. The radar on the launcher unit, in

Barak point defence missile

addition to pointing with the launcher, had its own rapid scanning capability. It was a dual-band radar with a single antenna providing both monopulse tracking and target illumination facilities. Eight missiles were carried in the launcher unit, each of these being supersonic and highly manoeuvrable and carrying a blast fragmentation warhead equipped with contact and proximity fuzes. Missile propulsion is by a solid-propellant rocket motor, and semi-active radar homing was used. The missile configuration incorporates cruciform wings and tail control surfaces, the former being positioned in the rear portion of the missile body, close to the tail fin leading edges. The eight-round launcher was provided with training and elevation facilities, and the radar moved in azimuth with the missile mount but had its own search scan pattern also.

This configuration was apparently dropped after sea trials which confirmed many of the design parameters, in favour of the current arrangement which is based on the use of vertical launch magazines and separate search and fire control sensors.

Barak 1 is the latest version of this system and was publicly revealed for the first time at the 1983 Paris Air Show. It differs in configuration from the original Barak where target tracking and illuminating radar and missile launchers were combined on one mount, by adopting the latest vertical launch technique for the missiles and siting the guidance radars higher up on the ship's superstructure. Apparently, the Barak point defence missile (PDM) is virtually unchanged, apart from modifications to produce the necessary pitch-over movement when clear of the launching ship toward the target.

Vertical launch units (VLUs) containing up to eight missiles each can be fitted anywhere on the vessel to provide a total of 32 missiles per Barak 1 system, operated from a single below-deck console.

Missile range is about 10 km and both aircraft and anti-ship missile targets can be engaged within 360° in azimuth and between –25 and +85° elevation.

Barak point defence missile launch from early development model of the system aboard an Israeli ship. Current Barak uses vertical launch magazine(s)

A large warhead is fitted, complemented by a sophisticated adaptive proximity fuze system. Flight control of the missile appears to be by a combination of moving tail surfaces which operate aerodynamically and four vanes mounted internally in the rocket motor efflux, the latter probably being necessary to accomplish the initial pitch-over movement as well as assisting in missile manoeuvrability over-all. The aerodynamic tail controls are probably necessary to ensure missile control after rocket motor burn while the missile is 'coasting'. A complete Barak PDM round weighs about 85 kg. One VLU with eight missiles weighs 1300 kg and the radar and fire control gear accounts for a similar weight.

STATUS
By May 1984 there had been several successful firings of the vertical launch system and it was understood that presentations had been made to a number of potential purchasers of Barak. A version of the original Barak system has been adapted as the basis of a possible transportable air defence missile system for land-based use.

CONTRACTOR
Israel Aircraft Industries Ltd, Ben-Gurion International Airport, 70100, Israel.

4563.231
TCM 30 NAVAL AIR DEFENCE SYSTEM
The MBT Weapon System plant, part of the Electronics Division, Israel Aircraft Industries Ltd include among its range of air defence products a version of the Spider AA gun-based air defence system that is intended for use aboard ships of all sizes. The principal weapon employed is the TCM-30G twin 30 mm gun mount (**3729.203**), and up to six of these mounts are combined with a search radar, an optical sight, a tracker-director unit, and control consoles to consititute a flexible autonomous naval version of the Spider II land-based air defence system (**4508.131**). The twin 30 mm gun mount is incorporated in an electrically driven turret, the two automatic cannon and their feed systems being carried on a high angular acceleration slewing and elevating mounting.

It is probable that combined installations have been designed in which both TCM-30G turrets and Barak point defence missiles (**4200.231**) are integrated to form a single ship's air defence system. It is also likely that the recently introduced Elta automatic missile detection radar (AMDR) will make an appearance in combination with either or both the gun and missile naval point defence systems. The AMDR is a shipborne radar designed to automatically detect incoming sea-skimming missiles in addition to the normal function of air surveillance with automatic detection and track-while-scan facilities. This will provide rapid and reliable automatic alarm of incoming missiles; automatic detection and tracking of all high speed targets; threat evaluation,

Twin 30 mm automatic cannon on TCM-30G mount as used in naval air defence system

designation and data transmission to other defensive systems, such as a ship's ESM and command and control.

STATUS
No firm information on fittings has been received, but it is believed that certain vessels of the 'Saar 4·5' and

'Saar 5' classes and the 'Flagstaff 2' class hydrofoils are fitted with the TCM-30G twin 30 mm guns. No details of export sales have been disclosed.

CONTRACTOR
Israel Aircraft Industries Ltd, Ben-Gurion International Airport, 70100, Israel.

ITALY

2228.231
ALBATROS NAVAL DEFENCE SYSTEM

The Albatros weapon system design is based on the concept of combining the air defence potential of a medium range surface-to-air missile with the fire power of conventional gun armaments. The Albatros system makes use of the Aspide missile (**1656.331**) and can be fitted to integrate with various gunfire control systems. The resultant ship's anti-air defence capability is greatly enhanced owing to the wide coverage envelope and high kill probability of the missile, while retaining all conventional gunfire roles. Missile performance contributes to an all-weather capability against anti-ship missiles of either sea-skimming or 'diving' types.

The Albatros missile system consists of:
(a) Missile guidance
(b) Missile launching
(c) Missile magazine
(d) Aspide missiles.

Details of inter-relationships with the gunfire control section are illustrated in **1551.281** under the Naval Fire Control and Action Data Automation section. Missile guidance is by semi-active radar homing and the missile path to the target is a collision course with proportional navigation. Target illumination for missile homing is provided by the missile guidance section.

The missile launching section comprises either the standard eight-cell or a four-cell launcher so as to meet different operational and installation requirements. The eight-cell missile launcher is a self-contained mount manufactured by OTO-Melara and utilising the same power driver as the 76/62 compact gun mount. The four-cell launcher is a compact unit on which four separate canisters are mounted. Each canister is used both as container, for missile handling, and as a launching cell. A missile magazine, allowing for storage and reloading at sea, is associated with the eight-cell launcher on request. Storage and reload of canisters for the four-cell launcher is implemented by means of standard shipborne facilities.

A missile magazine, allowing for storage and reloading at sea, is associated with the eight-cell launcher on request. This magazine (manufactured by Riva Calzoni) is a 16-cell unit and can be installed below or behind the Albatros launcher; the magazine is hydraulically operated and allows for fast loading and unloading of missiles even in a severe sea environment.

The missile launching section can be associated with either a single or a double missile guidance section (Type 1/1/ or Type 2/1 respectively). The latter configuration involves the use of two directors and enables launcher sequential assignment to either director so that two distinct targets, respectively tracked by the relevant director, can be simultaneously engaged by missiles.

STATUS

The Albatros missile system was designed and developed by Selenia under contract from the Italian MoD (Navy) in the early 1970s. The first of class Albatros Mk 1 Mod 1 system, for which the missile section was fitted to integrate with an Elsag GFCS,

Launch of Aspide surface-to-air missile from Albatros 8-cell launcher

Riva-Calzoni 16-cell missile magazine for Albatros system

underwent an extensive series of operational trials aboard the Italian Navy ship *Aviere*, successfully completed in 1973.

The latest version of the system, Albatros Mk 2 is now in series production and first trials, in an Italian Navy 'Maestrale' frigate, were successfully carried out in October-November, 1983. This series of trials were to verify missile intercept capability at the extremes of the missile performance envelope, and overall capability was demonstrated against a Rushton sea-skimming target. To date, 15 countries have adopted the Albatros weapon system and it was revealed that the Japanese Navy had signed a contract with Selenia for the supply of equipment and manufacturing know-how for licence production in Japan of the complete missile launching system.

Albatros 4-cell canister launcher on corvette

CONTRACTOR

Selenia-Elsag Consortium for Naval Systems, Via Panama 52, 00198 Rome, Italy.

4497.231
DARDO CLOSE-IN WEAPON SYSTEM

The Dardo system, specifically dedicated to close range anti-missile defence, has been designed and developed by Elettronica San Giorgio – ELSAG, in collaboration with Selenia. Its prime purpose is to counter effectively high speed, late detection attacks requiring very rapid response, and especially attacks by sea skimming missiles, missiles with a diving attack profile, and aircraft launching rockets and missiles.

Thanks to a direct electronic link with the ship's own main surveillance radar, the Dardo system can operate without human intervention as soon as it is triggered by the detection of a fast low flying target. Manual operation, as a conventional FCS, is also possible. Specifically, the Dardo system carries out automatically the following functions:

(1) correlation of successive target echoes to plot the flight trajectories

(2) assignation of a priority index, continuously updated, based on time remaining to reach own ship, of a significant number of threatening targets

(3) selection of the most threatening target

(4) auto-designation of the target to the system tracking radar

(5) automatic acquisition and tracking initiation

(6) automatic opening of fire at the maximum effective firing range permitted by the tactical situation

(7) auto-spotting on the burst of rounds fired.

The tracking radar, a Selenia Orion RTN 20X (**1935.253**), has an X-band monopulse antenna, employing a coherent MTI, with frequency agility and staggered PRF. A TV camera is mounted on the same tracker pedestal, which is normally installed in a location remote from the gun.

The Selenia Orion RTN 20X is a modern X-band radar mounted separately from the gun and performs

the following functions: automatic acquisition of very low flying and fast targets; autonomous detection of targets at low elevation with a 'guard ring' for target lock-on; automatic target tracking; effective reduction of the 'image effect'; auto-spotting of the burst of rounds fired.

These functions are performed despite clutter and or a hostile ECM environment thanks to: an X-band monopulse antenna system; employment of a coherent MTI for fixed echo cancellation; high PRF; frequency agility and staggered PRF; digital processing of the video inputs.

The data processing and interfacing unit includes a digital computer, specially adapted to fire control problems with special fixed routines; an interfacing electronic module assembly to link the processing section to the peripherals; and a full range of system ON/OFF line test facilities.

This unit is directly connected to the ship's surveillance radar, processes the information received, evaluates the threats and performs a decision on which target is to be engaged.

A supervision console, which also allows the operator to carry out a manually assisted firing, is associated with the system for control and supervision of correct operation.

STATUS
In series production and operational with the Italian and several other Navies.
CONTRACTOR
Selenia-Elsag Consortium for Naval Systems, Via Panama 52, 00198 Rome, Italy.

Typical Dardo CIWS shipboard installation with 4OL70 gun and Orion 20X fire control radar with on-mounted TV camera

SPAIN

4564.231
MEROKA NAVAL CIWS
Meroka is the name of a novel type of close-in air defence weapon system that has been under development for a number of years by the Spanish authorities. Both land-based and naval versions have been designed; the former is described in entry **3208.131** in the mobile guns and rocket systems section of this volume. Some of the background to the programme has appeared under that entry number in previous editions.

The weapon used in both versions is a twelve-barrelled arrangement of 20 mm/120 calibre Oerlikon machine cannons, grouped together in two horizontal rows of six. A salvo of 12 rounds can be fired in a time of 0·08 seconds, which amounts to a theoretical rate of fire of 9000 rounds/minute. The main purpose of this high rate is less the delivery of a large total of projectiles on to a target but more to meet a need for maximum density of fire when engaging certain categories of air targets such as low-flying ground attack aircraft and sea-skimming anti-ship missiles in the naval application. The normal practice is for each salvo to be fired as four groups of three rounds, minimising the total recoil force applied to the mount as well as having other beneficial operating characteristics.

The group of 12 barrels forms a single rigid unit which is traversed and elevated as a conventional gun, mechanical rigidity being aided by a number of steel bands (two in the army version, four in the naval version) that determine the spacing between the individual barrels. This feature is also used to adjust the dispersion of fire and fire pattern. Ammunition is brought to the 12 guns by two belt feeds which are supplied from an hydraulically powered rotating magazine with a capacity of 720 rounds. Elevation limits are –20 to +85 degrees, and the gun can be traversed in azimuth through 360 degrees at a rate of 90 degrees/second.

The radar selected for target detection was the Selenia RAN-12L L-band search radar, a frequency-agile equipment with a range of about 15 km. Target assessment, threat evaluation and related functions are aided by a 16-bit miroprocessor, which can handle data for up to four Meroka turrets. Individual targets are designated to weapons which are automatically laid-on by direct links between the computer and the guns control systems.

The digital fire control system was designed by Lockheed Electronics who have been associated with the Meroka programme from a very early stage, and the antenna of that company's AN/PVS-2 doppler tracker radar (as used in land-based Phalanx air defence gun system) is mounted on top of the Meroka turret. This X-band radar will automatically track targets from a range of just over five km. A secondary line-of-sight for target tracking is provided by a General Electric low-light TV camera, boresighted to the gun axis. The latter can be used by an operator using a joy-stick control for manual target tracking in an emergency.
CHARACTERISTICS
Search radar: RAN-12L
Tracking radar: AN/VPS-2
Optical system: GE low-light TV
Weapon: 12-barrel 20 mm Oerlikon
Barrel length: 2·4 m (120 cal)
Recoiling mass: 300 kg
Theoretical rate of fire: 9000 rounds/minute
Magazine capacity: 720 rounds
Elevation: –20 to +85°
Traverse: Unlimited 360°
Effective range: 3000+ m
Turret weight: 4·5 t
STATUS
Prototype(s) of the land version completed and initial evaluation trials due to begin in late 1983. It is understood that the Spanish Navy may require additional development work to be carried out before initiating production, possibly also involving a larger calibre weapon based on the same principle.
CONTRACTOR
CETME, Centro de Estudios Tecnicos de Materiales Especiales, Spain.

SWEDEN

4546.231
RBS 70 SHIP LAUNCHED MISSILE SYSTEM (SLM)
The RBS 70 ship launched missile system is a recent proposal to adapt the well-established RBS 70 missile system for use on naval vessels. RBS 70 SLM is capable of combatting incoming aircraft at long range. The sight as used on the land-based RBS 70 (**2348.131**) has been retained, and gyro-stabilised optics have been added. The low weight and small dimensions of the system allow it to be fitted on very small vessels eg patrol boats and minesweepers.

During 1983, tests, arranged by the Swedish navy in collaboration with Bofors Ordnance Division, were carried out on a Swedish coastal minesweeper under varying weather conditions and included live firings. The firings took place with the vessel, an 'Arko' class coastal minesweeper, under way at normal speed. A prototype of the RBS 70 SLM installation was mounted on a platform above the large sweeping winches on the after deck.

The stand for the army version of RBS 70 has been replaced by one specially designed for naval use, and this is fitted directly to the deck. SLM can also be fitted on a fixed, or gyro-stabilised platform. Compared with the army version, SLM has a greatly increased resistance to cross-winds during the initial launching stage.

The system has been provided with firing limits which prevent the missile being launched on a course which would endanger the vessel or its crew. SLM is operated by one man who sits on the stand seat and operates the sight in exactly the same way as the army version. Reloading can be carried out either by the operator or a member of the ship's crew. The operator receives information on incoming targets from a suitably placed look-out.
CHARACTERISTICS
Range: 5 000 m
Height coverage: 3 000 m
Reloading time: Up to 20 s
Time from target detection to launch: From 5 s
IFF: Optional
STATUS
Prototype tested and ready for production by early 1984.
CONTRACTOR
AB Bofors Ordnance Division, Box 500, 691 80 Bofors, Sweden.

UNION OF SOVIET SOCIALIST REPUBLICS

2939.231
GOA SHIPBORNE SURFACE-TO-AIR MISSILE (SA-N-1)

Known also by the US alpha-numeric code SA-N-1, the missile, whose NATO code-name is Goa, is the principal surface-to-air missile of the Soviet Navy. It is fitted to the 'Kanin', 'Kashin', 'Kotlin', 'Kresta', and 'Kynda' classes on scales ranging from one to four twin launchers.

The shipborne Goa missile is assumed to be identical with the ground-to-air missile (**2938.131**) but the equipment associated with it is very different. The standard launcher is clearly roll-stabilised as can be seen from the accompanying illustration. Rather different, and not obviously stabilised, launchers have also been observed, but these are most probably not for Goa. The launcher is mounted on top of the missile magazine and is reloaded vertically through small hatches.

Associated with the missile in all installations is a compound radar system known by the NATO code-name Peel Group (**1323.253**) and described in the Naval Radar section. Guidance is probably by radio command.

There is, of course, no definite information on Goa's performance but it is generally taken to have a maximum slant range of about 15 km and a ceiling of some 12 000 m. Length is estimated at about 5·9 m and the maximum span at 1·2 m. A moderately sized HE warhead of about 70 kg is thought to be carried.

STATUS

Entry into service with the Soviet Fleet was in 1961-62. According to the latest available figures, Soviet vessels are equipped with a total of 66 SA-N-1 Goa systems, each system having one twin launcher. There are single systems on each of eight SAM 'Kotlin' class, eight 'Kanin' class, and four 'Kynda' class ships, while 19 'Kashin' class, and four 'Kresta I' class vessels each have two twin launcher installations. One Polish, ex-Soviet 'Kotlin' class, ship is fitted with Goa.

Goa naval air defence missiles in firing position

2943.231
GUIDELINE SHIPBORNE SURFACE-TO-AIR MISSILE (SA-N-2)

Guideline, also known, in its shipborne application, by the US alpha-numeric code SA-N-2, has been installed in only one Soviet ship, so far as is known at present, the cruiser *Dzerjinski*.

It has been suggested that one reason for this is the difficulty of providing suitable stable platforms on smaller vessels for the flapping Fan Song (**2866.153**) radars used to guide these missiles. It could also be that the relative difficulty that there appears to be in gathering these missiles to the required flight path presents even more of a problem in shipborne installations than it does on the ground.

So far as is known the general performance of Guideline as a shipborne missile is substantially the same as that described in the entry for the ground-based version.

2947.231
GOBLET SHIPBORNE SURFACE-TO-AIR MISSILE (SA-N-3)

The helicopter-carrier *Moskva* and the 'Kresta II' class cruisers were the first ships of the Soviet Navy to be seen equipped with a new surface-to-air missile that is similar in size to Goa (**2939.231**) but possibly larger and certainly launched from a different launcher and directed by a different radar complex. It has since appeared on other classes.

Although there was confusion concerning this missile it now seems to be agreed that it is that classified in the American code as SA-N-3; it is also widely believed – without, of course, any official confirmation – that its NATO code-name is Goblet.

The launcher, illustrated here, does not appear to be roll-stabilised – suggesting that the missile gathering is efficient. The missile is of conventional configuration (see photograph) and is about six metres long, weighing approximately 540 kg. A conventional high explosive warhead of about 40 kg (other estimates, however, suggest a figure of over 200 kg) is carried and the missile is powered by a two-stage solid-propellant rocket motor. Command guidance is employed, and the associated radar fire control group has the NATO code 'Head Light' (**1328.253**). The early version, aboard 'Moskva', 'Kresta III' and 'Kara' classes, has a range of 30 km and can intercept targets at between 150 and 25 000 m. The SA-N-3 missile has been credited with a maximum speed of over Mach 3.

The four reload hatches associated with the Goblet launcher are generally accepted as indicating that the launcher is a dual-purpose device and that the magazine below deck contains both Goblet, SA-N-3, anti-aircraft missiles and possibly SS-N-14 anti-submarine weapons also.

STATUS

The SA-N-3 Goblet air defence missile system entered service in 1967, and it is fitted in ships of the 'Kiev' and 'Moskva' classes of aircraft carrier, and 'Kara' and 'Kresta II' classes of cruiser.

SA-N-3 Goblet air defence missiles on their twin launch ramp

SA-N-3 Goblet air defence missile firing, with another round on the ramp

2954.231
SA-N-4 SHIPBORNE SURFACE-TO-AIR MISSILE

Since it became operational some time after 1970, very little has been divulged about the appearance or performance of the SA-N-4 naval surface-to-air missile. The system quickly became noted for its drum-shaped container magazine/launcher mounting with its 'pop-up' twin ramp launcher, and the associated radar group which earned itself the NATO reporting name of Pop Group (**1897.253**). Each SA-N-4 silo or 'bin' is believed to have a magazine capacity of 20 rounds.

The SA-N-4 missile is estimated by reliable sources to be about 3·2 metres long and to have a range in the region of 12 km, carrying a warhead of some 13 kg. Allowing for a possible underestimate of the warhead weight, the SA-N-4 appears to fall into a broadly similar category to the Western Naval Crotale (**2111.231**) and Seawolf (**2442.231**) naval SAMs, and the comprehensive nature of the associated Pop Group radar tends to confirm the sophistication of the guidance system employed. It is therefore not unreasonable to ascribe a similar operational function to the Soviet missile. This is borne out by the pattern of ship fittings noted for the SA-N-4.

Shortly after the SA-N-4 was seen in the West, the obvious visual similarities with the Soviet land-based SA-8, Geckco mobile SAM (**3209.131**) were noted, especially where the radar guidance groups were concerned, and this has been commented upon in previous editions of this book. Other assumptions that have been made include the use of radio command guidance and a missile speed of around Mach 2, although confirmation is still awaited.

STATUS

Operational since the early 1970s and fitted in a wide variety of ship classes over a relatively long period. Major classes, such as the 'Kiev', 'Kirov', 'Slava' and 'Kara' aircraft carrier and cruiser classes are each fitted with two SA-N-4 silos equipped with a total of 40 rounds per ship, and the numerous 'Krivak' destroyers have the same size of SA-N-4 installation. Still more numerous are the 'Grisha' I and II and 'Nanuchka' light missile craft all of which have single silos with 20 rounds. The system is also used to provide air defence for certain important vessels such as the replenishment ship 'Berezina', and the two amphibious warfare ships of the 'Ivan Rogov' class.

SA-N-4 missile launcher outside its silo. The associated Pop Group radar can be seen on the raised platform to the left; Drum Tilt radars are for gun fire control

4201.231
SA-N-5 SURFACE-TO-AIR MISSILE

SA-N-5 is the designation allocated to the naval version of the man-portable anti-aircraft missile SA-7, Grail, (**2941.131**). For use aboard ships the four-round multiple version, which has been seen also on certain vehicles of the Warsaw Pact states, is employed. It is a relatively simple conversion of the original man-portable battlefield weapon, basically consisting of a framework on which four Grail rocket launcher tubes can be fixed side-by-side and supported on a central pedestal which permits the gunner to slew and train the missiles manually. Performance of the missile is likely to be substantially the same as in land-based use, although the task of manually acquiring the target and aiming the weapon cannot have been made any easier for the operator by being mounted on a platform subject to sea motion as well as the ship's own course changes during any engagement.

Nevertheless its potential as a deterrent to close investigation by hostile air forces (especially helicopters), is probably well worth the modest cost of such fittings.

STATUS

Now very extensively fitted in a wide variety of ship classes. Our companion volume *Jane's Fighting Ships* reports at least 169 Soviet vessels fitted with SA-N-5 installations that consist of one, two, three or four quadruple launchers for the system, although fittings of two quadruple launchers per ship are most common.

The most numerous classes of vessel fitted with this system are those built for amphibious operations, such as the Ropucha class (17 ships) some of which have four quadruple mountings, the Alligator class (14) with two or three twin mountings, Polnochny ships (14) with two or four quad mountings, and the two Ivan Rogov ships which each have two quad SA-N-5 mountings in addition to their SA-N-4 missile silos. Intelligence gathering vessels of many types have been given SA-N-5 installations for their protection; such ships include those of the 'Balzan', 'Primorye', 'Nikolay Zubov', modified 'Pamir', 'Moma', 'Mirny', 'Mayak', and 'Okean' classes. Most of these have two quadruple mountings and between them these classes amount to a total of between 40 and 50 ships.

Other important vessels with SA-N-5 systems are seven 'Ugra' submarine support ships (some with two quad mountings) and 'Lama' class (seven vessels) missile support ships with either four or two quad mountings. Certain light missile craft, such as the 'Tarantul' and 'Pauk' classes are equipped with SA-N-5 mountings also.

4206.231
SA-N-6 SURFACE-TO-AIR MISSILE SYSTEM

SA-N-6 is the designation provisionally assigned to the vertically launched air defence missile system first noted aboard the Soviet cruiser *Kirov*. The amount of officially released information about this weapon system (from either Soviet or Western sources) is extremely slight, and to date observers have been forced to rely upon what can be deduced from the external features of the system revealed by photographs of the ship itself. No photographs of the missile have been released so far. Some examples of photographs of the vessel are reproduced nearby. It has been conjectured that the system has an anti-missile capability for defence against anti-ship missiles, and that the track-via-missile guidance technique is employed. The possiblity that the SA-N-6 is a naval version of the advanced SA-10 land-based air defence missile has been suggested.

Summarised, external features of the SA-N-6 system that can be discerned on these photographs include: the 12 hatch covers for the vertical launchers on the foredeck (forward of the 20 hatch covers for the SS-N-19 surface-to-surface launchers); two Top Dome radar director groups (**4088.253**), fore and aft; and numerous other sensors, both passive and active types, some of which undoubtedly provide target detection and designation services for the air defence fire control system. Interpretation of such details is assisted if some assumptions are made concerning the likely operational role of the SA-N-6 system. While by no means necessarily inspired by the American Aegis naval area air defence system (**2507.231**), it is a reasonable guess that the Soviet requirement was for a system to meet a very similar potential threat environment. This envisages aircraft, aircraft-launched anti-ship missiles, stand-off jamming aircraft, reconnaissance aircraft, and anti-ship missiles launched by both surface vessels and submarines. All-round hemispherical cover is required out to long ranges with a multiple target detection and tracking capability, coupled with high resistance to ECM and jamming. In the Aegis system, the missiles are equipped with mid-course guidance

Soviet battle cruiser Kirov shows the varied range of sensors available for use in detecting targets for the SA-N-6 air defence missile system. Top Pair and Top Steer radar groups high on the superstructure give early warning of air targets, while the Top Dome radar director groups (fore and aft) track both target and missile (Royal Navy)

and terminal homing facilities, and these may be expected in the Soviet SA-N-6. Other characteristics of the latter which have been estimated include an operating ceiling of at least 30 000 m, a range of up to 60 km at a speed of Mach 6, carrying a 90 kg warhead, and a missile length of about 7 m. We have received no information which causes us to disagree violently with these estimates at present, with the single proviso that the range claimed seems on the low side and may well prove to be appreciably greater when more is known of the SA-N-6. Also, at least one respected authority has revised the estimated maximum missile speed downwards to Mach 3.

Certain aspects of the numerous sensors fitted on the *Kirov's* superstructure suggest various other possibilities relating to the SA-N-6. Target detection is technically possible by a wide selection of sensors: the Top Pair (**4087.253**) and Top Steer (**4086.253**) air search radar groups are capable of long range air target detection and position fixing and enjoy high placings on the ship, thereby maximising their range potential; also located high on the ship's structure there are dual installations of Round House and Rum Tub passive ESM antenna arrays which obviously provide 360° detection facilities. Lower down on various parts of the upperworks are numerous other shorter-range sensors of different types which could serve for target detection and/or tracking at closer ranges and lower elevation angles. The two Top Dome director radar groups (**4088.253**) are complex systems incorporating a number of different antenna elements, clearly denoting multipurpose operation. The largest of these is that which is concealed behind the large dome from which the group derives its NATO code-name and this probably serves to track both targets and outgoing missiles. Carried on the same, trainable, pedestal is a group of three hemi-cylindrical antennas, the precise function of which is not clear, and above these is a small 'thimble'-shaped unit which might house a command antenna.

STATUS

Operational in 1979. Fitted in 'Kirov' and 'Slava' class ships.

View from low-level astern of Kirov shows clearly the supplementary antennas on the Top Dome pedestal. Round House and Rum Tub ESM arrays can also be seen high among the upperworks (Royal Navy)

4473.231

SA-N-7 SURFACE-TO-AIR MISSILE SYSTEM

SA-N-7 is the number assigned to the latest Soviet naval air defence weapon system to have been detected. As yet little of the missile itself, or of specific details of the overall system, have been disclosed. Vessels that are believed to have been fitted with the system are the new 'Sovremennyi' class destroyers, possibly 'Slava' class ships, and a modified 'Kashin' class ship, *Provorny*, which was used as a trials ship for the SA-N-7 weapon system and possibly other equipment fitted in 'Sovremennyi' class ships. US observers have stated that the SA-N-7 is a naval equivalent to the land-based SA-11 air defence missile, which is described as a low- to medium-altitude weapon with a range of about 28 km, a speed of Mach 3, and an altitude capability of 30 to 14 000 m. Other authorities have assigned a point defence missile system function to the SA-N-7.

Evidence in the shape of associated hardware aboard the ships mentioned above, and which cannot be hidden, does not appear to conflict with such an estimated performance envelope, and also provides one or two additional clues to the likely function and method of operation. Of these other pieces of evidence, the associated radars are among the most useful. *Sovremennyi* is reported to have six fire control/target illuminating radars (said to carry the NATO code-name Front Dome) for an SA-N-7 installation that comprises two launchers, fore and aft, each of which is believed to have only a single rail. The trials ship *Provorny* was seen with eight of these radars. These facts, if confirmed, imply that the SA-N-7 is designed to cope with multiple targets, and this in turn means that each single rail launcher must be capable of rapid firing and reloading. A further reasonable conjecture might be that the overall fire control system has a high level of sophistication, possibly based on digital computers, to ensure

Soviet modified 'Kashin' destroyer Provorny, which was used as trials ship for the SA-N-7 naval air defence system

optimum co-ordination of such aspects as target designation, threat evaluation, radar assignment, launcher pointing, reloading etc. If, as the above would seem to suggest, a number of simultaneous target engagements are contemplated, by means of a launcher system able to fire several missiles in quick succession, it is therefore likely that tracking radars are assigned to targets individually and the missiles home by semi-active radar, operating virtually autonomously after launch.

Further conjecture regarding the operation of the SA-N-7 system, as well as details of its appearance and performance, must await the receipt of further intelligence.

4565.231
SA-N-8 NAVAL SURFACE-TO-AIR MISSILE

SA-N-8 is the number assigned to the as yet unseen new missile system associated with equipment noted aboard the recently revealed 'Udaloy' class of large anti-submarine ships. External visible evidence is so far confined to vertical launching silo hatches located on the foredeck near the bow and aft inboard of the port and starboard multiple torpedo tube mountings.

The forward launcher installation appears to consist of four silos grouped together, apparently all of the same size (about 2 m diameter lids), but closer scrutiny of photographs shows that the aft pair of this group of four lack the central protuberance that can be discerned on the others. The reason for this discrepancy is not known.

Also noted in pictures that have so far been obtained, of the incompletely fitted out Udaloy and

thought in some quarters to be associated with the SA-N-8 system, are platforms forward and aft that are believed to be the future sites of radar installations that may eventually be housed within protective radomes. At this stage there is no way of confirming or denying this suggestion, and the available evidence for further speculation on such aspects as the precise role of the missile, its operation, performance and other characteristics remains extremely slender. The Udaloy is fitted with a CWIS installation amidships consisting of four 30 mm Gatling-type gun barbettes directed by port and starboard Bass Tilt radars. The ship's main armament comprises two quadruple SS-N-14 missile launchers for anti-submarine operations, and these are associated with two Eye Bowl director/guidance radars mounted on top of the bridge house. Two single 100 mm guns controlled by a Kite Screech radar mounted forward comprise the surface engagement armament. Two Helix helicopters are embarked, and with an estimated displacement of 8 500 tons (full load), this class of vessel clearly constitutes a 'high value' target for opposing aircraft and so it would be reasonable to assume a correspondingly elaborate and effective air defence system for its protection. On the basis of this information and with, at first glance, an apparently limited scope for fitting more than one radar group each for the forward and aft SA-N-8 installations, together with the knowledge of the vertical launch technique that has been assumed from the layout of the missile launcher silos, a short- to medium-range performance with high speed missiles using a sophisticated semi-active or active radar plus IR homing guidance technique might be a reasonable basis for further speculation on the system's operation.

It was revealed in 1984 that the second ship of the 'Kirov' class of cruisers is fitted with an SA-N-8 system as a point defence missile, but no other details have been obtained.

Bow view of Udaloy *shows forward SA-N-8 missile installation with four VLS hatch covers and the two 100 mm gun turrets*

Aft SA-N-8 missile launcher installation consists of 'silos' located inboard of port and starboard torpedo tubes and RBU 6000 AS rocket launchers. Note also platform on top of helicopter hangars which is expected to carry a radar for SA-N-8 guidance in the future. Flyscreen 'B' is for helicopter recovery assistance

Udaloy *anti-submarine ship armed with SS-N-14 missiles in two quadruple launchers below bridge house, two single 100 mm guns forward, two Helix ASW helicopters, RBU 6000 AS rocket launchers, and forward and aft silo-type vertical launchers for SA-N-8 air defence missiles. Among the comprehensive electronic warfare fit, port and starboard Round House, Bell Shroud and Bell Squat arrays can be detected.*

UNITED KINGDOM

1019.231
SEACAT SHIPBORNE SURFACE-TO-AIR MISSILE

Seacat is a close range, shipborne, guided missile system for anti-aircraft defence which may also be used against surface targets within visual range. The system has been designed to provide a simple and low-cost anti-aircraft capability, and represents a very cost-effective system. The guidance system is based on the use of optical tracking and a radio command link, but the system is capable of various degrees of sophistication and this has in fact been undertaken in a number of instances. Generally, such improvements take the form of integrating Seacat with ships' fire control systems. An advantage of this is that disablement of the fire control radars, or other part of that system, still leaves the option of the optically guided mode.

OPERATION

The basic form of the system, introduced into the Royal Navy as Guided Weapons System Mk 20 (GWS 20), consists of separate launcher and operator mounts, the latter carrying sighting binoculars with which the aimer first 'gathers' the missile after launch and subsequently tracks it to the target. A thumb joystick control is provided for missile guidance.

Shorts Seacat installed on an RN ship. The system is scheduled for service well into the 1990s

Movements of the joystick are converted into command signals which are transmitted to the missile from an antenna unit on the launcher mounting to maintain the missile on the line of sight to the target.

Seacat has since been deployed with the RN GWS 22 (**1242.281** and **1563.253**) fire control system in which a lock and follow tracking radar is linked to the aimer's binocular sight. Subsequent operation is the same as for the GWS 20 system. It has also been combined with Contraves Sea Hunter, San Giorgio NA9, and Signaal M 40 series fire control systems. A later development is a system that replaces the optical sighting binocular with a closed circuit television (CCTV) system produced by Marconi-Elliot Avionic Systems as the 323 Series (**1021.293**). This enables the aimer to be placed in a much less vulnerable position and also results in important improvements in efficiency. The missile gathering phase has been reduced from about seven seconds (conventional optical technique) to six seconds or less with the aid of CCTV.

A lightweight version of Seacat has been developed for installation in such vessels as 30 m fast patrol boats and inshore minesweepers, giving them guided-weapon defence against low-flying aircraft. It is in service with the Brazilian Navy and the Iranian Navy, and has attracted interest from other navies, some of which already have the standard Seacat system.

It employs a new three-round launcher (based on the Short Tigercat launcher) which weighs only 2007 kg with all its ancillaries instead of the 4700 kg of the standard four-round Mk 20 launcher. Binoculars mounted on the head of a single manually operated pedestal director form a combined director and missile aiming sight.

The latest Seacat improvement is the introduction of a height control capability which enables the missile to be flown at heights down to 4 m above the sea against surface or sea skimming targets without danger of ditching. This modification provides a 'cushion' between missile and sea, the clearance distance being automatically adjusted according to the sea state encountered. The height control facility is incorporated in one of the missile's four guidance

wings and can be readily fitted to existing Seacat installations. The missile's proximity fuze is not disturbed by being close to sea or land surfaces, and its fuzing system – both proximity and contact – in conjunction with its highly potent warhead provide a most effective counter to low level missile attack, and also permit ship or shore targets to be successfully engaged at all ranges up to maximum.

The surface skimming modification can be easily introduced to existing Seacat installations with virtually no disturbance of components, providing a highly flexible close-range defence system with the ability to engage air, shore and surface targets.

CHARACTERISTICS

Max effective range: Approx 5500 m
Warhead: HE
Solid fuel motor
Length: 1·48 m
Max span: 65 cm
Estimated weight: 63 kg

DEVELOPMENT

Development work started in the late 1950s and the first sea trials took place on HMS *Decoy* in 1962. The basic system has proved itself adaptable to other roles and a land-based version has been developed as the Tigercat (**2465.131**).

STATUS

In addition to the RN, Seacat has been ordered by 15 other navies including: Argentina, Australia, Brazil, Chile, West Germany, India, Iran, Libya, Malaysia, Netherlands, New Zealand, Sweden, Thailand and Venezuela. A fresh multi-million pound contract was awarded in 1982 for additional Seacat equipment for the RN.

A number of Argentinian aircraft were believed to have been shot down by Royal Navy Seacat missiles in the Falklands conflict of 1982, and the land-based version of the system, Tigercat, operated by Argentinian forces are reported to have claimed some British aircraft attacking Port Stanley airport in the same campaign.

CONTRACTOR

Short Brothers Limited, Castlereagh, Belfast BT6 9HN, Northern Ireland.

6004.231
SEA DART SURFACE-TO-AIR MISSILE

Sea Dart (GWS 30) is a third-generation area defence weapon system, capable of intercepting aircraft, at both very high and extremely low altitudes, and air and surface launch missiles. It is also effective against surface vessels thus giving it a triple-role capability. Launch rate is rapid and the weapon system is capable of dealing simultaneously with many targets. Despite all this the system can be installed in a variety of fighting ships from small frigates upwards, including some vessels that would be too small to accept, for example, Seaslug (**6003.231**).

The missile is launched from a twin launcher. Performance data is classified and only the linear dimensions have been released for publication, other data in the accompanying table is taken from published unofficial estimates.

The missile is virtually a thick-walled cylinder built around the Rolls-Royce (1971) Ltd Odin ramjet engine. The guidance equipment (Marconi Space and Defence Systems), the proximity fuze (EMI), the control system (BAe Bracknell division), and the fuel tanks and engine controls are all wrapped around the central air duct and ramjet in the annular space between them and the missile's outer skin.

The guidance system is one of a semi-active 'homing all-the-way' nature. It uses a proportional navigation law. The ramjet engine enables the missile to fly at controlled speeds throughout its flight envelope. The guidance system will detect very small changes in target movement. This capability, combined with very fast control responses, enables very small miss distances to be achieved.

CHARACTERISTICS

Designation: GWS 30
Type: Shipborne area defence, surface-to-air, surface-to-surface, and anti-missile guided weapon system

Guidance principle: Radar guidance and semi-active homing using tracker illuminator radar Type 909
Guidance method: By control of movable tail surfaces
Propulsion: Solid-propellant booster and ramjet sustainer
Warhead: Presumably HE
Length: 4·36 m

Body diameter: 42 cm
Span: 91 cm
Launch weight: 550 kg
Range: At least 30 km

OPERATION

A fully automatic below decks magazine is provided. Missiles are stowed vertically and are hoisted through

Launch of a Sea Dart missile from the British Type 82 destroyer HMS Bristol. Sea Dart is an area defence system against high and low flying aircraft, with an anti-missile and surface-to-surface capability. A lightweight Sea Dart system has been developed using the existing missile with lighter and simpler ship equipment. Deck mounted boxes which both protect the missile during its life on board ship and act as the missile launcher enable Lightweight Sea Dart to be fitted in ships down to 300 tons

an intermediate position onto the electrically driven twin beam launcher. Targets are designated to the system in three co-ordinates by radar. The system automatically tracks the target and points the launcher. Radar illuminates the target to provide the missile with the RF signal for self-guidance on to the target. The Type 909 target tracking and illuminating radar (**1559.253**) produced by Marconi Radar Systems has been developed from the equipment used with certain Bloodhound and Thunderbird missile systems. The missile is boosted to speed by a solid fuel tandem boost and speed is sustained by an Odin ramjet burning a liquid fuel.

Lightweight Sea Dart

In 1978 British Aerospace announced the Lightweight Sea Dart system, intended for ships down to 300 tons in size. In place of the GWS 30 missile launcher and missile magazine, the lightweight system employs fixed deck-mounted launchers, each carrying four missiles in sealed launch boxes. The boxes also serve to protect the missile during all stages of transportation and handling. The number and siting of these units depends on particular ship configurations and customer/operational requirements, but typically a small craft might fit two groups of four missiles. A firing equipment cabinet provides the interface between the missiles and a 1412AL

digital computer which is dedicated to the Sea Dart system. The computer and control panels form a single equipment console requiring only one operator. The Marconi 805 SD (**4302.253**) is in production as the system fire control radar. It provides target tracking and illuminating channels, with the signals being radiated by a single antenna. The ship's surveillance radar is used to provide initial target detection and to 'lay on' the tracker. The performance of Lightweight Sea Dart is dependent on the capabilities of the surveillance and tracking radars fitted. Studies of modern naval radars in combination with the 805 SD have shown that in the surface-to-surface role Sea Dart will match other missiles while providing better performance in the air defence role. The system retains the original triple-role capability of the Sea Dart GWS 30 and is intended to eliminate the need to fit a number of alternative systems in a warship to gain a similar capability.

DEVELOPMENT

Development started August 1962. Test firings began in 1965 and the first production order was announced in November 1967.

In mid-1982 BAe revealed a proposed long-range land-based air defence system designed around Sea Dart missiles and called Guardian (**4524.131**).

STATUS

Development is complete and the system is at sea in HMS *Bristol* and all RN Type 42 destroyers. It is also in service with the Argentinian Navy in ARA *Hercules* and ARA *Santisima Trinidad* Type 42 ships. Sea Dart also provides area defence for the new class of anti-submarine cruiser, HMS *Invincible*, and HMS *Illustrious* being operational and HMS *Ark Royal* nearing completion in early 1984. In the course of the fighting for the Falkland Islands, Sea Dart missiles fired from British ships claimed eight Argentinian aircraft.

CONTRACTORS

System contractor: British Aerospace Dynamics Group, Bristol Division, PO Box 5, Filton, Bristol BS12 7QW, England.

Other contractors associated with the system include:

Marconi Space and Defence Systems Ltd – guidance; Rolls-Royce (1971) Ltd – Odin ramjet; EMI – fuze; Vickers Shipbuilding and Engineering Ltd – launcher magazine and handling equipment; Marconi Radar Systems, Ltd – Type 909 tracker illuminator radar; Ferranti Ltd – computer and data handling; Plessey Radar Ltd – operations room equipment.

6003.231

SEASLUG SURFACE-TO-AIR MISSILE

Seaslug is a long-range beam-riding shipborne surface-to-air guided missile system.

Targets are detected at long range by radar (3-D or surveillance plus heightfinder) and their co-ordinates are supplied to the missile system control which commands the launcher. A twin ramp launcher is used and is reloaded from a between-decks magazine.

There are two versions of the missile, the Mk 2 having a rather longer range and better performance against low-flying aircraft. Both missiles have a surface-to-surface capability, but again that of the Mk 2 is better than that of the Mk 1.

CHARACTERISTICS

Type: Shipborne surface-to-air tactical guided missile. Surface-to-surface capability

Guidance principle: Beam-riding using Type 901 M shipborne radar with coded transmissions

Guidance method: By control of tail surfaces

Propulsion: Solid-propellant sustainer with 4 wrap-round solid-propellant boosters

Warhead: HE with proximity fuze

Missile length: 6 m

Missile diameter: 41 cm

Range: Probably better than 45 km. Targets engaged at heights above 15 000 m in trials

OPERATION

Fully automatic magazine handling and loading arrangements. Electrically driven twin launcher. Targets are designated to the system in three co-

Seaslug surface-to-air missile launch

ordinates by radar. The system automatically tracks the target and points the launcher. When the target comes within range the missile is fired and intercepts the target using beam-riding guidance techniques. Typical radars are the RN Type 965 (**1560.253**) for primary long-range surveillance, Type 277 for height-finding, and the Type 901 which is the Seaslug tracking and illuminating radar. It has an HE warhead with DA and proximity fuzes and four wrap-round boosters.

DEVELOPMENT

Development started in the early 1950s. Prototype trials carried out in HMS *Girdleness* during late 1950s. First fitted in 'County' class destroyers in 1961.

STATUS

Mk 2 systems remain in HM ships *Glamorgan* and *Fife*, in the Chilean ships *Prat* and *Almirante Cochran* (the former RN *Norfolk* and *Antrim*). The former HMS *London*, now serving with the Pakistan Navy as PNS *Babur* retains its Mk 1 Seaslug although it is thought there are plans to remove it.

CONTRACTORS

British Aerospace Dynamics Group, Bristol Division, Filton House, Bristol BS99 7AR, England.

Sub-contractors include:

Marconi Space and Defence Systems – missile guidance; Vickers Shipbuilding and Engineering Ltd – magazine handling gear and launcher.

2442.231

SEAWOLF SURFACE-TO-AIR MISSILE

Seawolf is the missile used in the RN's short range point defence guided weapon system, GWS 25 Mod 0. The system is currently installed in all Type 22 and some Leander class frigates. A complete single-headed system comprises surveillance radars, tracking and guidance radar and fire control, six-barrel trainable launcher and missiles. It is capable of being installed in vessels down to about 500 tons. A derivative of this system, designated GWS 25 Mod 3, employs a new lightweight dual frequency tracker designated Type 911. Developed by Marconi Radar Systems in order to give improved performance down to sea level, it will be retrofitted to ships of the Type 22 Broadsword class.

Development of the Seawolf system has produced a family of subsystem options known as Lightweight Seawolf, enabling installation in ships down to a few hundred tons. The tracking and guidance function is provided either by the Marconi 805 SW radar, derived from the Type 911, or the Hollandse Signaalapparaten VM 40 equipment. The launching system can comprise either a low mass, trainable 4-barrel launcher, based on the Seacat mounting, or the new Vertical Launching System. The latter employs the

existing Seawolf missile fitted with a tandem boost motor which is jettisoned after turnover.

The Seawolf missile employs line-of-sight guidance with radar differential tracking or TV, both with radio command. Speed and manoeuvrability characteristics are suitable for the engagement of small Mach 2 missile and aircraft targets under severe weather conditions and sea states.

Seawolf GWS 25 Mod 0

The complete system comprises the following units:

(1) air and low-air surveillance radars, Type 967 and 968

(2) radar trackers, Type 910, and TV trackers (GWS 25 Mod 0); radar trackers, Type 911 (GWS 25 Mod 3)

(3) command transmitter

(4) launcher and firing system

(5) missile and handling frame

(6) data handling

(7) guidance shaping unit

(8) operations consoles

(9) magazines.

The Type 910 tracking radar is produced by Marconi and is described more fully in the Equipment Section (**1562.253**). The TV system is produced by

Initial development of the point defence system which became the current Seawolf, incorporated a vertical launch capability. In 1968 a Seawolf type missile was launched in this way from HMS Loch Fada, *seen here. At that time, not a priority feature, vertical launch was not pursued though the concept was proved in operation.*

New four-round lightweight Seawolf launcher is based on the Seacat pedestal and weighs about 2·1 tons

Development standard Seawolf missile launched vertically from a simple launch canister during Royal Aircraft Establishment trials

Marconi Avionics. The Type 911 tracking radar is described more fully in entries **1508.253** and **2439.153** in the Equipment Section. The Type 967 and Type 968 surveillance radars provide both high and low cover, and are also produced by Marconi (**1561.253**). They are of modern design and incorporate features for air target detection up to high elevation angles as well as high performance against low-level and surface targets. Comprehensive precautions against sea and land clutter, as well as natural and man-made interference are incorporated, as is IFF.

The line-of-sight to a target is established by either the tracking radar or the TV system. Error signals proportional to Seawolf missile deviations from this datum are derived from the differential tracking radar or the TV system, and these signals are processed by a guidance shaping unit. Coded correction signals for missile guidance are produced and transmitted by microwave command link to bring the missile to the required flight path. In the GWS 25 system the data processing required to interpret the tracking data and calculate the correction demand signals is based on the use of a Ferranti FM 1600B computer (**1433.063**), which has been adopted as a standard.

A multiple launcher developed by VSEL is common to both standards and consists of six rectangular launch-tubes disposed in two banks of three, one on each side of an azimuth/elevation mounting. Reloading is manual, presumably to avoid the complexity and, particularly, the weight of an automatic system which might undesirably limit the number of ships which can carry the full Seawolf system. The launcher is separate from the tracking radar. High slewing rate and pointing accuracy are important features of the Seawolf launcher which is equipped for fully automatic firing sequence, with command override.

The Seawolf missile weighs approximately 80 kg at launch, is about 2 m in length, and has four fixed wings and four moving tail fins. A solid booster motor is designed to give minimal launch drop and speed is quoted as being in excess of Mach 2. Successful techniques employed in Rapier (**2424.131**) have been incorporated, and no on-board test or repair facilities for missiles are called for. The HE warhead is provided with both proximity and contact fuzing.

OPERATION

For the successful interception of an incoming anti-ship missile great accuracy and an extremely short reaction time are required of the system. To achieve this it is arranged that, once a target has been identified as hostile, all subsequent phases of the launch and guidance operation will be carried out automatically and without further manual control.

Other relevant features include the ability to fire salvoes, immediate readiness capability maintained over long periods, and extremely fast data handling facilities in all parts of the system.

Automatic radar guidance is the normal operating mode, with TV tracking by an aimer for low angle of sight and surface target engagement in GWS 25 Mod 0.

VARIANTS

Seawolf GWS 25 Mod 3

The most recent lightweight Seawolf system to be devised uses a Marconi 805SW tracking radar director to produce a Seawolf system suitable for fitting in ships with displacements of less than 1000 tonnes. The 805SW, designated Type 911 in RN service, is a lightweight dual frequency differential tracker that can be used in single or multifire channel installations. The major components are taken from the basic Marconi 805 range of radars (**1508.253**) to which is added the millimetric wavelength DN181 Rapier Blindfire radar (**2439.153**) and elements of the original RN GWS 25 system. The millimetric radar provides accurate tracking at low elevations, and in a series of live firings of Seawolf against small and large targets close to the sea surface in trials at a RN range, a high rate of successes was recorded.

The Mod 3 system incorporates a number of simplifications based on the experience gained in the long proving trials of GWS 25, and the opportunity was taken of modernising the data processing equipment to take advantage of the RN Crocodile and CACS projects while retaining the basic proven software and adding improvements to give a full low-level blindfire capability. Such simplifications were carefully considered to ensure they did not impair the target kill probability. Tracking a missile at I-band would simplify the receiving system, but data gathered during firing trials indicated that the risk of seriously reduced signal returns during the motor burn did not warrant this approach, particularly when salvo firings are contemplated, and so the fully proven tracking of the missile by beacon has been retained.

Two complete differential tracking radars are included, with one operating in the I-band and the other in the millimetric band, both antennas being carried on the same mounting. The J-band command data link also uses the millimetric tracking antenna. Height diversity for the command link transmissions to ensure good guidance data to the missile when flying at low level is achieved by independently illuminating the upper and lower parts of the main tracking antenna. The I-band signal processing uses Fast Fourier Transform techniques to ensure effective operation in the face of severe clutter.

The system operates with the six-round launcher of GWS 25 Mod 0, as used in the RN Type 22 frigates, and will be retrofitted to this class.

Containerised Seawolf

In 1981 British Aerospace Dynamics Group announced the introduction of a containerised version of the Lightweight Seawolf system, intended for rapid installation either on warships, or normally non-combattant vessels such as containerships or auxiliaries. A complete Seawolf installation is configured for housing within standard ISO 6 m containers.

Lightweight Seawolf

The evolution of the system has resulted in a family of lightweight subsystem options to suit different customer applications. The subsystems comprise:

(1) Tracking and Guidance System. Either the Anglo/Dutch VM40 tracking radar based on the HSA STIR tracker used in the Dutch 'Standard' frigates for Sea Sparrow guidance can be provided, or the Marconi 805 SW. Both trackers are well matched to the missile performance and offer the following features:

(a) A computer which interfaces directly with the ship's action information system, automatically controls the acquisition of the target by the tracker, lays on the launching system, decides when a missile should be launched and gathers and guides the missile to the target.

(b) A dual frequency band tracking radar with narrow beams which virtually eliminates multi-path effects, provides excellent tracking accuracy, reduces jamming sensitivity and enables low-level target engagement. Modern techniques allow rejection of clutter effects giving good separation of incoming target and intercepting Seawolf missile.

(2) Launching System

(a) 4-barrel Launcher. The lightweight 4-barrel launcher has been developed using the rotating and elevating structure of the well proven Seacat launcher. The launcher carries four Seawolf missiles contained in light alloy barrels which are designed to be semi-permanent, being able to fire many missiles before needing replacement. They are retained using a mechanism similar to an aircraft bomb mount. When reloading, Seawolf missiles are moved singly from a nearby ready-use magazine using a handling frame, and are inserted into the barrel with a loading aid. Protective end covers ensure that the missile can remain on the launcher for extended periods. An associated launcher control console derived from the Seacat equipment controls launcher movement and contains the missile firing unit. A crew safety and load panel is situated close to the launcher to inhibit it in the loading position.

(b) Vertical Launching System. Development of a vertical launch version of Seawolf in which missiles will be loaded aboard the ship in individual launch/containers was confirmed in early 1982. The container is also employed for transport and is fitted with a frangible cover and integral vertical exhaust ducting. For ship fitting, canisters can be installed singly, in groups, or in silos, above or below deck. Modifications to the Seawolf missile for vertical launch are minimal and include the addition of a tandem boost motor with integral thrust vector control to perform the pitch-over manoeuvre, and possibly the inclusion of a microprocessor in the missile itself.

The VL concept was demonstrated in 1968 and it promises faster reaction, much lower installed weights, no on-board handling and the ability to react to multiple targets from all aspects.

Target indication data for all versions of Lightweight Seawolf is supplied from a suitable surveillance radar/action information organistion source, which does not usually form part of the Seawolf system.

DEVELOPMENT

Development of Seawolf was begun by BAe and Marconi Radar to meet a UK MoD requirement, and in 1979 the latter instigated a development programme by Marconi to improve the system. This was planned for completion in 1984 but was cancelled in July 1981 after an MoD decision to opt for a lighter system which could be fitted in smaller ships. A formal requirement for this lighter system was stated in a Naval Staff Requirement issued in February 1981, based on use of the VM40 radar. As an alternative to VM40 Marconi offered the 805SW radar/director and was awarded a contract for this in March 1982.

STATUS

Seawolf GWS 25 entered RN service in 1979 aboard HMS *Broadsword*, first of the Type 22 class of frigates. The system has been installed on 'Leander' class frigates, as well as subsequent Type 22 ships. RN firing trials using the BAe Seawolf anti-missile system have been successfully completed off Aberporth, Cardigan Bay, West Wales. Two Seawolf firings were made from HMS *Broadsword*. In the first trial a shell fired from the Royal Aircraft Establishment, Aberporth, by RN crewmen was aimed to narrowly miss HMS *Broadsword*. Seawolf was fired and scored a direct hit on the shell which was intercepted at the top of its trajectory some 2000 ft above the sea.

Seawolf proved an effective defensive system against low-level air threats in the naval/air engagements between Argentinian and British forces in the Falklands conflict of 1982, and no Seawolf-fitted ship was lost. However, too few ships were fitted with the system to prevent some ships being lost to multiple air attacks. It is probable that the RN will take steps to expedite fittings following the experiences of the Falkland Island encounters.

In late 1982 a standard operational Seawolf missile was successfully launched vertically from a simple launcher/container during trials at the Royal Aircraft Establishment, Larkhill. This trial satisfied the Seawolf VL operational specification, which includes vertical launch and turn-over onto interception path when well clear of ship's superstructure. This system,

designated GWS 26 Mod 1 and including Type 911 trackers, will be operationally available for the first of the RN Type 23 frigates. The launching system could take the form of a 32-missile silo mounted forward of the bridge.

A MoD contract awarded to BAe Dynamics Group Bristol in mid-1983 covers a feasibility study of the possibility of fitting the Seawolf system in the RN's Type 42 destroyers to give these ships the best possible self-defence while retaining the Sea Dart area defence system. Ferranti and Marconi Radar are collaborating with BAe in this study, which may make use of the lightweight 4-barrel launcher.

In late 1983, a Seawolf missile fired from a Type 22 frigate. *HMS Brilliant*, successfully destroyed an MM 38 Exocet anti-ship sea-skimmer missile in a trial designed to prove Seawolf's performance at near maximum crossing range.

A UK Government contract has been awarded for final development and production of Vertical Launch Seawolf for the RN Type 23 frigates. Estimated value of the GWS 26 Mod 1 contract is in excess of £130 million.

CONTRACTORS

Missile: British Aerospace Dynamics Group Ltd.
Radar: Marconi Radar Systems Ltd.
Television: Marconi Avionics System Ltd.
Computer: Ferranti Ltd.
Launchers: Vickers Shipbuilding and Engineering Ltd (six-barrel), Rose Forgrove Ltd (four barrel); British Aerospace (VL).

UNITED STATES OF AMERICA

2507.231

AEGIS SURFACE-TO-AIR WEAPON SYSTEM

Aegis is a surface-to-air weapon system primarily designed to defend against anti-ship cruise missiles and missile launcher platforms. It is the USN's primary defensive missile system for the 1980s. Present plans call for its installation aboard a new class of guided missile cruiser. Aegis is designed to destroy small, fast targets in hostile environments such as severe weather or countermeasure conditions. As an area defence system, Aegis will be capable of defending a task force which includes a carrier and several other types of ship. The system complements the Tartar (**6006.231**) and Terrier (**6005.131**) missile systems.

Major components of the Aegis system are the missile, its launching system, the fire control, and weapon control systems, the multi-function array radar with its computer control, the system command

and control, and the operational readiness test system.

The missile used is the SM-2 version of the Standard (**1122.231**), which uses the same airframe and propulsion system developed for the SM-1 but incorporates significant additional facilities. The SM-2 has a command guidance capability, a self-contained navigation capability provided by an inertial reference unit, and a new terminal homing receiver.

This particular combination of guidance techniques imparts considerable operational benefits. The ability to navigate the SM-2 missile to the target area by means of inertial navigation, plus command corrections, followed by terminal homing, results in a much more efficient trajectory which effectively doubles the range. It also means that the demands on the ship-based fire control/guidance system are appreciably reduced. For example, the target illuminating radar needs to be directed at the

target for the homing phase only, leaving it free to engage other targets at other times. Similarly, the command guidance system can be shared between a number of SM-2/targets because the inertial reference unit permits the missile to perform its own mid-course navigation and the telemetry link is used to report missile position back to the ship.

The SM-2 is available in MR and ER models, but the current SM-1 Standard is available in the MR version only.

It is launched from the Mk 26 fully automatic dual-purpose launcher which can be used to launch Asroc (**6001.241**) anti-submarine missiles.

This launcher has a digital interface with the Mk 1 weapons control system. One of the three computerised sub-systems of Aegis, all of which use the AN/UYK-7 digital computer, the Mk 1 system accepts weapon assignment commands and special threat criteria from the Mk 1 command and decision

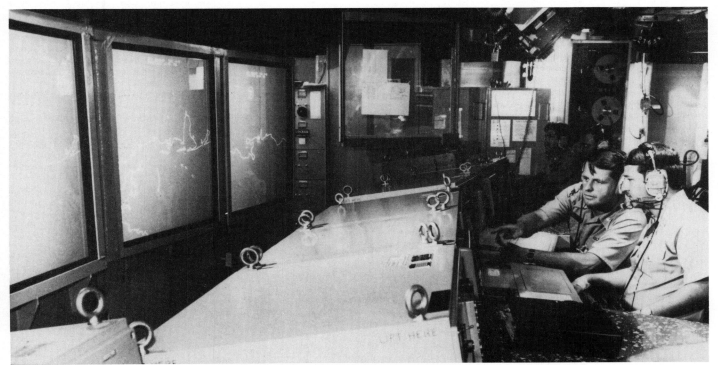

Part of Aegis cruiser USS Yorktown, *second of the class, operations room showing system display facilities*

system and tracking data from the multi-function radar. These inputs are processed to determine the possibility of engaging the target and then to generate commands for the Mk 26 launcher and pre-launch orders for the missile, commands for the Mk 99 fire control system for target illumination, commands to the multi-function radar, if mid-course guidance is required, and reports to the Mk 1 command and decision system.

The function of the Mk 99 fire control system is to illuminate the target. To do this it uses the AN/SPG-62 (slaved) radar. Inputs to the system come from the Mk 1 weapons control system which, in the case of slaved radar operation is passing on data from the multi-function radar system.

The multi-function phased-array radar, the AN/SPY-1A (described in **1570.253**) is high-performance electronically-scanned equipment capable of surveillance and the simultaneous detection and tracking of multiple targets; it has been described as the heart of the Aegis system. Associated with it are four AN/UYK-7 computers. The primary function is to search for and acquire targets and track them to whatever extent may be necessary. Beam scheduling for this and other tasks is organised by the computer. The system also handles the two-way link with the missile for mid-course guidance when requested by the Mk 1 weapons control system. Certain special facilities can be provided such as 'burn-through' facility for use in ECM conditions or passive angle tracking. The system accepts general operational commands from the Mk 1 Aegis command and decision system and mid-course guidance commands from the Mk 1 weapons control system; its operational outputs are processed signals giving target detection data to the Mk 1 command system and target and missile track data to the Mk 1 control plus mid-course guidance commands to one or more missiles. Like all other operational sub-systems in the Aegis system the radar control system is also connected to the Mk 1 operational readiness test system.

Together with the AN/SPY-1A radar system and the Mk 1 weapons control, the Mk 1 command and decision system make up the detection and decision loops of the Aegis system. The Mk 1 system is the ship's command and control centre, and targets enter the detection and decision loop from the AN/SPY-1A radar, from other ship's own sensors or from data supplied by other ships or aircraft. What happens next depends on which of the four Aegis operating modes has been selected. The modes are automatic special, automatic, semi-automatic, and casualty. In the automatic special mode targets meeting certain predetermined threat criteria are automatically fired upon unless manual override is invoked; in all other modes positive human action to initiate firing is needed.

In these three modes the Mk 1 weapons control system inserts targets into the engagement queue and schedules equipment for launching and terminal illumination. Trial intercepts are computed and a time to fire predicted. Resulting data are fed back to the Mk 1 command and decision centre which is also receiving target detection data from the radar control system, operational readiness data from the Mk 1 operational readiness test system, and electronic warfare and other data from the ship's command and control centre. Incorporated in the Mk 1 command system is another four-bay AN/UYK-7 computer and a comprehensive display system, the AN/UYA-4. On the basis of all these data, threat evaluation and weapon assignment processes are carried out so that the engagement decision can be taken.

The final major element of Aegis is the Mk 1

US Navy's second Aegis cruiser, Yorktown, *at sea during builder's trials. Ship was commissioned on 4 July 1984*

operational readiness test system (ORTS). This is linked to all the other major elements of the system and has the functions of monitoring actively and continuously the state of readiness of each, and of reporting the results of this process to the Mk 1 command and decision centre.

DEVELOPMENT

Initial planning for Aegis began in 1964 and RCA was awarded the engineering development contract for $252 930 400 in December 1969.

STATUS

At the end of April 1972 the USN and RCA jointly announced completion of the system design phase. Early in 1973, RCA announced satisfactory completion of the SPY-1A phased-array antenna tests.

The single-quadrant Aegis engineering development model completed successful land based testing in 1973, was installed in USS *Norton Sound*, and started sea trials in early 1974. By mid-1975 major test objectives had been met.

At sea, flight tests using the Standard SM-2 were successfully completed in mid-1977. This also marked the completion of the SM-2 development programme.

In mid-1978 a USN contract valued at $224 million was awarded to RCA to build, integrate and test the first Aegis weapon system which became operational aboard the lead ship of the new 'Ticonderoga' CG47 class Aegis cruisers.

In 1983, after completing sea trials and operational tests of Aegis in USS *Ticonderoga*, this ship began operations with the fleet. Over the next few years, 12 additional ships will enter service, and the 1985-89

shipbuilding programme includes 13 more, to give a total of 26 Aegis cruisers by the early 1990s.

Authorisation was sought in the fiscal year 1985 defence budget for the lead ship of the DDG-51 guided missile destroyer programme. These ships are planned to have the Aegis system. In April 1984 RCA announced the receipt of a $233 million contract for the design and development of an Aegis system for the DDG-51 class. The lead ship, *Arleigh Burke*, is due for commissioning in 1989. These ships' Aegis will incorporate the AN/SPY-1D radar and the new AN/UYK-43 computers.

In July 1984 USS *Yorktown*, the second ship of the 'Ticonderoga' class of Aegis ships was commissioned, while the third of the class, *Vincennes*, had been christened in April 1984. The fourth ship, *Valley Forge*, was launched in June 1984.

CONTRACTORS

Prime contractor: RCA Government Systems Division, Moorestown, New Jersey, USA. (Three major RCA divisions are engaged in the project.)

FCS Mk 99, radar and SPY-1A high-power transmitter: Raytheon Company.

AN/UYK-7 computers: Univac Division of Sperry Rand.

Mk 26 launcher: Northern Ordnance Division, FMC Corporation.

SM-2 missile: General Dynamics Corporation, Pomona Division.

Computer software: Computer Sciences Corporation.

Technical advice to USN: The Johns Hopkins University, Applied Physics Laboratory.

Also more than 600 other suppliers.

2543.231

Mk 15 CLOSE-IN WEAPON SYSTEM (PHALANX)

The purpose of Phalanx is to provide last ditch defence against anti-ship missiles. In its primary mode Phalanx provides continuous surveillance and defence within its engagement envelope independent of other ship systems. Phalanx is an automatic gun fire control system that uses projectile spotting coupled with closed-loop aiming to provide multiple target hits and subsequent target destruction. The principal technical feature of the Phalanx system is the closed-loop electronic spotting technique. Aim

correction is based on the ability to track both the incoming missile and the outgoing projectile in the vicinity of the missile, and to eliminate the error. The system uses a pulse doppler radar which shares a single transmitter to accomplish the search, acquisition, track and electronic spotting functions.

Incorporating the widely used and service-proven M61A1 Gatling gun used in the Vulcan land mobile system (**2850.131**), Phalanx provides a high fire rate of 3000 rounds per minute. During firing, the ammunition feed system removes rounds from the front of the magazine drum, located under the gun,

and feeds them through the chute conveyer system to the gun breech bolt assembly. After each round is fired, the empty case is extracted from the breech and conveyed back into the rear of the magazine. The gun can fire continuously under the control of the system's computer against air targets, or in the operator controlled burst mode against surface targets.

Phalanx is a total weapon system, and as a single modular package, automatically carries out search detection, threat evaluation, tracking, firing, and kill assessment. The system consists of six major assemblies and components: radar-servo assembly, gun assembly, mount and train drive platform, barbette equipment assembly, electronics enclosure and a pair of control panels. Supported by a high-speed digital computer, the fire control assembly performs these functions: target search, detection and declaration, target acquisition, target track and measurement of range, velocity and angle, projectile tracking, and measurement of projectile velocity and angle.

The gun assembly is composed of five major sub-assemblies. The gun, electrically controlled and hydraulically driven, consists of a rotating cluster of six barrels with a breech bolt for each barrel. The ammunition sub-system includes components that store, and transport rounds within the system. The gun's effectiveness is due to its firing a high kinetic energy penetrator made of high density metal. Destruction is caused by penetration of the 20 mm projectile into the warhead (of the incoming missile) and the imparting of kinetic energy into it, causing it to blow up before striking the ship.

The dual motor mount drives are torque biased to reduce system backlash, and friction is minimal. The lightweight structure has high stiffness-to-weight ratio in order to minimise impact of vibration on servo performance. The structural design will withstand all shipboard environments, including wave impact and blast forces from adjacent guns.

STATUS
In production for the USN and the naval forces of

Phalanx naval close-in weapon system combines on a single mount a six-barrel gatling gun and fire control radars

Australia, Japan, Saudi Arabia and UK. Since completion of the first Phalanx system in 1979, production contracts amounting to 249 units have been awarded and by December 1983, more than 249

systems were delivered. In November 1983 the manufacturer announced that the 135th USN Phalanx had just been declared operational. It was also reported that the battleship *New Jersey* has four systems fitted and the 'Aegis' class cruiser *Ticonderoga* has two systems. Fittings will be made in 39 classes of ship and the USN plans to install it in over 360 ships ranging from aircraft carriers to frigates. The US Secretary of Defense, in his fiscal year 1984 report, proposed funding of \$130·2 and \$169·1 million for the procurement of 40 and 49 Phalanx systems, in fiscal years 1984 and 1985 respectively.

Responding to an evident insufficiency of air defence firepower in the course of the Falkland Islands conflict of 1982, the Royal Navy urgently acquired a quantity of Phalanx CIWS and the system is installed and operational in the aircraft carriers, HMS *Invincible* and HMS *Illustrious*. There is also an RN requirement for an anti-missile defence system for fitting in other ships and the Phalanx has been proposed, in competition with other systems. General Dynamics, in association with the Bracknell Division of BAe submitted a bid in a competitive contract for this RN requirement.

CONTRACTORS
CIWS system contractor: General Dynamics Corporation, Pomona Division, PO Box 2507, Pomona, California 91769, USA.
  Vulcan gun: General Electric.

3983.231

SEA CHAPARRAL SURFACE-TO-AIR MISSILE SYSTEM

The Sea Chaparral surface-to-air missile system is an adaptation of the Chaparral land-based mobile air defence missile system (**2542.131**), which uses a version of the Sidewinder, AIM-9 (**1103.331** etc) air-to-air missile.

The launcher is a modification of that used in Chaparral in the self-propelled (M48) and ground emplaced (M54) land-based systems, but with provisions for operation either with the gunner in the mount, or with control by a remote gunner in the ship's operations room or other fire control facility.

As with the standard Land Chaparral, the Sea Chaparral system can be enhanced by the addition of forward looking infra-red sensors to provide a night engagement capability, and provisions can be made for target designation to be carried out by other ship's sensors, such as radar or optical target acquisition sights etc.

Details of the missile and its performance will be found in the above-noted entries in this volume.

STATUS
Few details have been released of fitting programmes for the Sea Chaparral system, but in February 1980 the US DoD was proposing the sale of 284 Sea Chaparral missiles and the necessary supporting and

associated hardware to Taiwan at a cost of about \$35 million.

In July 1983 it was proposed to supply Taiwan with 120 MIM-72F Sea Chaparral missiles.

CONTRACTOR
Aeronutronic Division, Ford Aerospace Communications Corporation, Newport Beach, California 92660, USA.

3017.231

ASMD RAM SYSTEM

The RAM (rolling airframe missile) programme is a joint development programme carried out under a memorandum of understanding (MOU) signed by the United States, Denmark and the Federal Republic of Germany in 1979, with the intention of producing a lightweight, high rate of fire missile which will provide a system for anti-ship missile defence (ASMD).

There is a possibility of wider NATO participation,

or of an eventual merging of this effort with a new NATO requirement for a supersonic anti-ship missile defence weapon. It is intended to supplement the anti-missile capabilities of other systems such as CIWS/Phalanx (**2543.231**), the various point defence missile systems based on the Sparrow (**2770.231**), and the longer-range capabilities of the US Fleet's other anti-air missiles. The prime threat which is to be countered by the overall ASMD weapon programme is the cruise missile. Seasparrow is cited as the ship's

main battery for point defence, soon to be complemented by the ASMD RAM system, with the CIWS/Phalanx forming the secondary battery.

For those systems without a Sea Sparrow launcher, an ASMD autonomous launcher has been developed which is designated EX-31 GMWS. This consists of a two-axis yoke mount with geared motor drive, based on the CIWS/Phalanx system. The launcher is a bolt-down item which requires connection only of power, launcher train, and elevation orders and missile orders. It has about 80 per cent of the weight of the NATO Sea Sparrow (NSS) launcher.

Those ships already fitted with NSS launchers for ASMD missiles will use insert racks which fit into the NSS cells and hold the ASMD missile canisters which act as launch tubes. The racks will be attached to hard points in the cell and will distribute missile electrical signals from the launcher to the launch tubes. Five of the new ASMD missiles will be housed in each NSS cell. Two of the eight cells in each launcher will be used for ASMD missiles, thereby doubling magazine capacity. This configuration of the system is known as RAM ORDALT, and it is planned to carry ten RAMs in the two lower centre cells of the Sea Sparrow launcher.

The RAM EX-31 version of the system employs a launcher consisting of a production Phalanx mount and elevation and train driver assemblies (see **2543.231** above) carrying a launcher guide assembly which holds 21 missiles. An alternative model has been designed with a capacity of 8 rounds, called the Very Lightweight RAM launcher and intended for fitting on smaller vessels.

It is planned to use existing command and control systems wherever possible. Ships fitted with tactical data systems will need modifications to digital programs similar to those for other anti-surface missile defence equipment such as Chaffroc. Additional conversion equipment will be required for

Test firing of ASMD RAM from an EX-31 launcher at a land-based test site

transmission of ESM data and launcher orders, and receipt of missile and launcher data.

The ASMD missile in its initial configuration consists of a 5 inch rolling airframe with dual-mode passive radio frequency mid-course and IR terminal homing. In this version the Stinger IR seeker, the AIM-9L fuze (Mk 20) and warhead (WDU-17B), and the Chaparral/Sidewinder propulsion motor are used. This guidance technique is target dependent in that it requires both active radar and IR signals from the attacking missile to function. However, a significant proportion of the Soviet inventory is of such a type and is thought likely to be so for some time to come.

CHARACTERISTICS

Length: 2·79 m
Diameter: 127 mm
Weight: 70 kg
Speed: Supersonic
Guidance: Proportional navigation. Dual-mode, passive RF, IR homing
Launcher: RAM EX-31
Weight: 5738 kg (above deck); 726 kg (below deck)
Elevation: –25 to +80°
Train: 360°
Capacity: 21 rounds

STATUS

Two engineering development models of the RAM EX-31 launch system successfully completed proof of performance testing in Europe in March 1982. Two more of these mounts are being used in the USA, one at White Sands Missile Range for firing tests and the other for environmental qualification tests and at-sea firing trials in early 1983.

A series of flight tests is continuing at White Sands Missile Range, New Mexico. In October 1982 a RAM missile successfully intercepted a remotely controlled drone representing an anti-ship missile. This test verified performance in poor visibility. The first of a series of over-water tests took place at the Pacific Missile Range later that month and by February 1983 there had been three consecutive successful interceptions of remotely controlled drone targets that represented anti-ship missiles. In February 1983 it was announced that a RAM had successfully intercepted a remotely controlled supersonic, low-altitude Vandal missile target drone (**3240.391**). The Vandal is a converted Talos naval air defence missile designed to represent typical anti-

RAM EX-31 EDM-2 aboard West German ship S-69 Habricht *during at-sea testing*

ship missiles. Additional tests are planned to continue into 1985 when a full-scale production decision is due.

In the fiscal year 1984 report by the US Secretary of Defense it was stated that the RAM system was nearing the end of the development phase and would soon be available for retrofitting in selected NATO Sea Sparrow installations. Funding for fiscal years 1984 and 1985 indicated $4·2 million and $6·5 million for R and D, respectively, followed by $18·0 million for procurement of 30 sets in 1985.

It is expected that the US funding plan for this system will be matched proportionately by Denmark

and Germany for their procurement shares. Development of RAM is funded equally by the US Navy and the German Navy with the Royal Danish Navy contributing two per cent. Series production deliveries of the first RAM systems to the German Navy are scheduled for 1987.

CONTRACTOR

General Dynamics Corporation, Pomona Division, PO Box 2507, Pomona, California 91769, USA.

1122.231
STANDARD (RIM-66 AND RIM-67) SURFACE-TO-AIR MISSILE

The Standard shipborne surface-to-air missile began life as a two-model range of anti-aircraft weapons, intended to replace gradually Terrier and Tartar with the US fleet. The original two versions are the medium-range RIM-66A, and the extended-range RIM-67A. It was the first to be solid-state and is all electric with no pneumatic or hydraulically powered controls. Power for guidance and control is derived from a 'one-shot' battery which is activated just prior to missile launch.

For both types, fully automatic magazine and loading facilities are provided for twin electrically driven launchers. The RIM-66A had a dual-thrust solid-propellant booster, and the RIM-67A used solid-propellant booster and sustainer rockets. Both versions are equipped with conventional high explosive warheads, with direct action or proximity fuzing.

CHARACTERISTICS

	RIM-66A	RIM-67A
Speed	>Mach 2	>Mach 2·5
Ceiling	>20 000 m	>20 000 m
Range	>18 km	>55 km
Length	4·47 m	8·23 m
Diameter	34·3 cm	34·3 cm
Weight	Approx 610 kg	Approx 1360 kg

Subsequent developments have somewhat altered the original plan and versions of Standard have been, or are, in the process of development for surface-to-surface, air-to-surface, and new surface-to-air applications. The following list is arranged in logical rather than chronological order.

(1) Medium-range and extended range

All existing and most contemplated variants of the original missile can be made in either MR or ER versions. This possibility should therefore be borne in mind when examining the variants listed below.

Standard 2 missile firing from USS Wainwright *near San Juan, Puerto Rico*

(2) Standard 1 Missile (SM-1)

This is the original missile. Its principal advantage over the earlier Terrier or Tartar is that it has a (horizon-limited) surface-to-surface capability. It was expected to remain in production until 1975, but was still being procured in 1978 and is operational in over 70 missile ships and attack carriers.

(3) Standard 2 Missile (SM-2)

This missile completed development in 1977 and has entered the initial phase of production. The SM-2 approximately doubles the range of SM-1 in both MR and ER versions. Lengths of the two versions are 4·47 and 8·23 m. An inertial reference is provided, and to

satisfy the requirements of the Aegis system the missile-borne equipment is augmented by a two-way link for the mid-course command guidance. Other improvements include a new semi-active terminal guidance receiver with greater resistance to ECM.

The most important changes embodied in the SM-2 are: the replacement of the SM-1 conical-scan semi-active radar homing receiver by a monopulse receiver; the provision of an inertial reference unit for mid-course guidance; a communications link for mid-course guidance correction/target position data updating and missile position reporting; and a digital guidance computer instead of the SM-1's analogue computer. These improvements make possible a far more efficient trajectory to the target, resulting in an effective 60 per cent increase in range for the MR model and more than 100 per cent increase in that of the ER model.

In the late 1970s, it was decided to expand the number of USN ships capable of employing the added capability of the SM-2 missile, beyond the 'Aegis' class vessels for which it was initially intended. This led to the CG/SM-2 weapon system programme under which it was planned to replace Terrier missiles (**6005.231**) on board 20 ships of the CG-16 and CG-26 classes (33 ships were equipped with Terrier, others being the DDG-37 class of ten vessels, one CG(N)-9 and 2 CV class carriers) with SM-2 Extended Range missiles. This programme entailed modifications to the ships' weapons control systems and radar etc, and computer software and is now largely complete.

By means of the inertial reference unit in the SM-2 missile it flies a mid-course phase wherein the missile navigates itself to the vicinity of the target. Semi-active terminal guidance, supported by the target illumination from the original Terrier fire control system, is used to complete the engagement.

The inertial reference unit and guidance computer in the SM-2 are initialised by the new weapon direction system Mk 14. Target data are derived from the modified AN/SPS-48 radar (**1252.253**) and ship attitude and velocity are provided by new shipboard gyro-compass equipment. The Navy Tactical Data System is modified to accommodate the command and control interface facilities required.

This system results in significantly decreased target processing time. Originally, a series of sequential and manual operations was involved between target detection and missile launch, and this can occupy several minutes. With the CG/SM-2 system, all target detections are passed to NTDS and those selected for engagement by the Terrier systems are automatically passed to the weapon direction system. Subsequent to launch, the fire control radar is assigned to provide target illumination for the terminal phase of flight.

The SM-2 monopulse homing receiver is also to be fitted to SM-1 MR missiles intended to be used in upgrading existing Tartar-fitted ships (see **6006.231**) in a broadly similar fashion to the CG/SM-2 programme. Additional information on the Terrier missile system will be found in **6005.231**.

(4) Standard ARM

Essentially an airborne version (see **1123.331**) this has also been adapted for use in a surface-to-surface role as part of the Interim Surface-to-Surface Missile System (**2669.221** and **2808.221**).

(5) Standard Active

The original intention was for this missile to serve as an interim anti-ship weapon until completion of Harpoon development, but delays with Active Standard made both missiles more or less contemporaries. The position at mid-1974 was that Active Standard would be maintained in development only until it was confirmed that it would no longer be required as a back-up to Harpoon. Progress with Harpoon development has led to cancellation of Standard Active.

Brief details of various Standard models and their US Service designations are given in the following list:

YRIM-66A: Standard-1 (MR). Basic development model to replace Improved Tartar. Mk 27 Mod 0 motor
RIM-66B: Standard-1 (MR). Similar to RIM-66A but with improved motor, Mk 56 Mod 0, for better performance
RIM-66C: Standard-2 (MR). Similar to RIM-66B but adapted for Aegis system
RGM-66D: Standard SSM (ARM). Similar to RIM-66B

but modified for surface-to-surface anti-radiation roles
RGM-66E: Standard SSM (ARM). Similar to RGM-66D but adapted for use with Asroc launcher
(Y)RIM-67A: Standard (ER). Replacement for Terrier. Uses Mk 30 Mod 1 sustainer to give extended range
RIM-67B: Standard-2 (ER). Similar to RIM-67A but used with CG/SM-2 weapon system

DEVELOPMENT

Further increases in performance and capabilities for the Standard family are under development. The improvements will be denoted by new block numbers to designate the upgraded missiles. Upgraded SM-2 will be designated SM-2 Block II.

After the SM-2 missile and CG/SM-2 (see above) completed design and had almost finished engineering development, the Americans identified a new threat to the US fleet, described as a 'high altitude supersonic cruise missile launched in a heavy electronic countermeasures environment'. Other references allude to saturation attacks, and cruise, manoeuvre and dive phases of an attack by the new threat missile. The SM-2 Block II programme represents the initial step towards meeting this threat. The improvements include higher power propulsion systems for increased speed and altitude performance; autopilot modifications to enable it to cope with higher speeds, provide greater stability during mid-course guidance and to increase manoeuvrability during the terminal phase; changes in the homing receiver bandwidth to reduce miss-distance in the presence of strong stand-off jammers; a modified radome to withstand the temperatures of higher missile speed; a modified fuze to cater for the increased closing speed between missile and target; and a change in warhead to ensure a target kill during the extremely short intercept interval.

An advanced missile project is aimed at meeting the increased threat of the late 1980s and 1990s, including air-launched anti-ship missiles and certain ship-launched weapons. An integral rocket ramjet (IRR) is a propulsion candidate for this missile.

STATUS

Since the Standard missile entered service in the late 1960s more than 10 000 have been delivered by General Dynamics to the USN and other navies. Almost 100 USN combat vessels and 29 ships of foreign navies are armed with Standard air defence missile systems. In early 1982 a Standard 2 Block II

missile was launched successfully to hit a drone target at White Sands Missile Range. In late 1981 contracts were awarded for Standard guidance and control group production. One of these related to the extended range (ER) version of the SM-2, the other was for production of an improved version of SM-1 Block VI missiles for use aboard USN destroyers. The latter version of Standard is an improved Block V missile with a new monopulse receiver and a digital guidance computer.

In April 1983 an extended range Standard SM-2 using a new Thiokol Mk 70 booster motor set a new altitude record for a tactical kill of an incoming target drone during operational tests. More than 40 SM-2 (ER) Block II missiles are due for delivery to the USN in 1984, before full production is established. In June 1983, the manufacturer announced delivery of the 1000th SM-1 Block VI missile to the USN.

In the fiscal year 1984 report of the US Secretary of Defense it was revealed that development had begun of an improved surface-to-air missile for use with the Aegis naval air defence system (**2507.231** in 1977 and earlier editions and **1834.281**). This was thought to be a reference to studies that had been carried out of a nuclear warhead version of the Standard SM-2 that might carry a warhead based on the W81 fission payload. It was confirmed in the 1985 report which stated that a nuclear warhead for the SM-2 is under development, with initial deployment scheduled for the late 1990s.

The Secretary's report also stated that funding provisions had been made for conversion of cruisers and destroyers armed with Terrier missiles to operate the Standard SM-2, and for similar treatment for ships with Terrier and Tartar missiles. Planned or proposed procurement and funding for Standard missiles in fiscal years 1983, 84, 85 and 86 is (missile quantities in brackets) $608·1 million (1150), $625·6 million (1190), $732·0 million (1380) and $1184·1 million (2430), respectively.

In July 1983 it was stated that 170 SM-1 standard missiles had been offered for sale to Taiwan at a cost of $105 million. These were for use on ex-US Navy destroyers operated by Taiwan.

CONTRACTOR

General Dynamics Corporation, Pomona Division, PO Box 2507, Pomona, California 91766, USA.

6006.231
TARTAR SURFACE-TO-AIR MISSILE (RIM-24)

Tartar is a medium-range, supersonic surface-to-air shipboard guided missile system. It provides primary air defence for USN destroyers and destroyer escorts and secondary air defence for cruisers. The missile booster and sustainer rockets are combined in a single solid-propellant motor, thus facilitating installation on smaller ships.

OPERATION

Tartar employs a fully automatic magazine handling

RIM-24 Tartar surface-to-air missile on Mk 13 GMLS of nuclear-powered cruiser USS California (USN Photo)

and loading system. Targets are designated to the system in two or three co-ordinates by radar. The tracker/illuminator radars automatically follow the targets and a computer provides missile launcher pointing orders. Guidance is semi-active homing, probably operating in I/J-band. The missile carries a high explosive warhead with DA and proximity fuzes.

The rocket motor has two levels of thrust to achieve rapid acceleration. The guidance system computes a collision course, then steers to intercept by means of four hydraulically actuated tail fins.

CHARACTERISTICS

Range: >16 km
Speed: Mach 2
Length: 4·6 m
Diameter: 34·3 cm
Weight: 680 kg
Motor: Dual-thrust solid-propellant
Guidance: Semi-active homing

DEVELOPMENT

Developed shortly after Terrier system and first entered USN service in 1961.

At mid-1977 there were 49 USN ships deployed with the Tartar weapons system and with Standard SM-1 (medium range) missiles. This includes nuclear-powered cruisers, guided missile destroyers, and guided missile frigates. This fleet could grow to more than 100 vessels in the 1980s with the introduction of the FFG-7 class. This factor and the evolving threat seen in such Soviet weapons as the Backfire bomber/AS-6 air-to-surface missile combination, require a continuing programme of ship system and missile improvements. This is applicable in principle to the considerable number of non-US ships fitted with the Tartar/Standard missile system, at present some 29 ships with 11 more planned.

The improvement plan being implemented is similar to that adopted for Terrier-fitted ships and

described in the entry for the Standard missile system (**1122.231**), and officially known as the CG/SM-2 (ER) programme. In the case of Tartar ships, such as the DDG-2 class, improvements in the ship's system will entail addition of the AN/SPS-52 three-dimensional radar (**1248.253**), the AN/SPS-65 radar, modifications to the AN/SPS-40 radar (**1746.253**), and integrated automatic detection and tracking of all radar targets by the SYS-1 plot extraction equipment. Control improvements will be provided by the weapons direction system Mk 13 and the DDG tactical data system, which are based on already deployed systems. Engagement from the ship's system aspect is improved by modification to the basic Tartar Mk 74 missile fire control system and addition of the Mk 86 FCS (**1241.281**) with gun and missile capability.

A similar updating and improvement programme will be applied to the SM-1 MR missiles employed. Some of these changes have been implemented and already SM-1 rounds have been deployed incorporating the new, improved Mk 45 fuze and the Mk 90 warhead. Other projected missile improvements include substitution of the SM-2 monopulse seeker receiver for the original conical scan seeker of the SM-1.

Additional details on the Standard Missile programme will be found in **1122.231**, above.

STATUS

Tartar is no longer in production but is still operational in a large number of USN ships and in the Australian, French, Iranian, Italian, Japanese, Netherlands, Spanish and West German navies. Replacement by the Standard missile (**1122.231**) has begun.

CONTRACTOR

Prime contractor: General Dynamics Corporation, Pomona Division, PO Box 2507, Pomona, California 91766, USA.

6005.231

TERRIER SURFACE-TO-AIR MISSILE (RIM-2)

This is a surface-to-air anti-aircraft missile for shipboard use. The Terrier series of missiles has been operational since 1956 and since then it has been the subject of continued development and improvement. The US military designation is RIM-2 and successive models have been denoted by letter suffixes running from RIM-2A to the latest version, the RIM-2F. The latter is also known as the Advanced Terrier.

CHARACTERISTICS
Range: >35 km
Ceiling: >20 000 m
Speed: Mach 2·5
Overall length: 8 m
Length without booster: 4·6 m
Body diameter: 34·3 cm
Weight: 1400 kg (approx)
OPERATION
Beam-rider guidance is employed to direct the missile against a target designated by the ship's tactical data system. A twin launcher is supported by automatic magazine and loading arrangements. Terrier is launched by a solid fuel rocket booster and propelled by a solid fuel sustainer.

The normal warhead is of the HE type with direct action or proximity fuze, but one version of Terrier (RIM-2D) has been produced with a nuclear head.
DEVELOPMENT
Development started about 1951, under the former military designation SAM-N-7, and Terrier was based upon the experimental LARK vehicle. First Terrier became operational in 1956.

Advanced Terrier (RIM-2F) became operational in 1963 and is carried by USN cruisers, frigates, and attack carriers. It has also been purchased by the Italian Navy. The system is progressively being replaced by the Standard missile system (**1122.231**). See this entry also for additional details of Terrier weapon system status, in particular in regard to the CG/SM-2 (ER) programme.
CONTRACTORS
Prime contractor: General Dynamics Corporation,

Launch of Terrier surface-to-air missile from aircraft carrier USS Constellation (USN)

Pomona Division, PO Box 2507, Pomona, California 91766, USA.
System co-ordination: Vitro Corporation.

4202.231

US MISSILE LAUNCHER SYSTEMS

The Northern Ordnance Division of the FMC Corporation, as well as providing most of the naval tubed ordnance requirements of the USN and many friendly navies elsewhere, supplies the launcher systems for most of the guided missiles employed by the USN. Guided missile launching systems (GMLS) are fully automatic systems comprising the missile launcher arms complete with slewing and elevation mechanisms, and reloading facilities appropriate to the missile types carried by the ship. FMC believe the GMLS Mk 4, produced about 25 years ago for the USN, to have been the first entirely automatic missile launching system in the world. Since that date the company has designed and produced six different marks of GMLS, each of them in several models, and the main details are outlined in the following paragraphs.

GMLS Mk 4

This system was produced for ships fitted with the Terrier surface-to-air missile system. The GMLS Mk 4 Mods 0 and 1 were fitted in the USS *Boston* and *Canberra* (both now withdrawn) while the Mk 4 Mod 4 was fitted in the Italian cruiser *Nave Garibaldi* (also decommissioned). Twin-ramp launchers were reloaded vertically through two hatches from a magazine below deck, in which the missiles were also stored vertically.

No Mk 4 Terrier missile systems remain in active service although a few are used on missile test ranges.

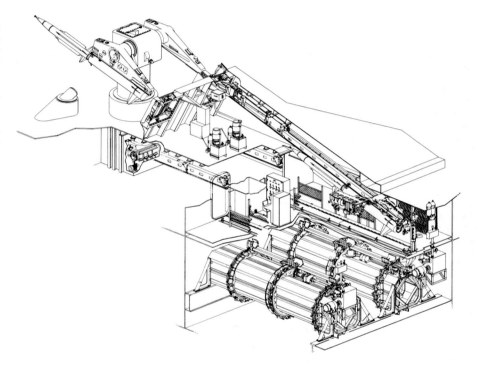

FMC Mk 10 Mod 5 missile launcher and magazine. More rotary horizontal magazine drums are provided in other models for different classes of ship

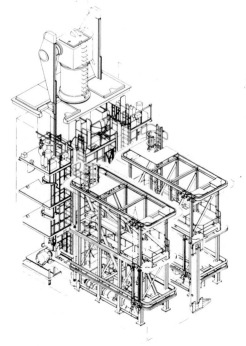

General arrangement drawings of FMC Mk 4 Mod 4 GMLS

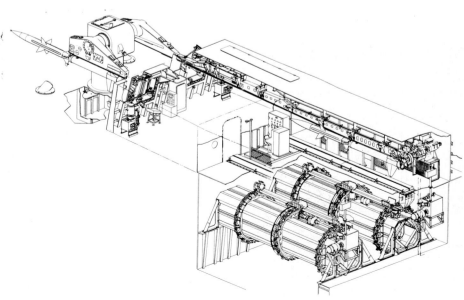

Mk 10 Mod 0 GMLS with two horizontal magazine drums for reload missiles. Other models have more drums

GMLS Mk 7

Also developed for large ship installation, the Mk 7 missile launcher system is now retired from active service, with a few systems in use on missile test ranges. The Mk 7 was designed for use with the heavy long-range Talos surface-to-air missile system. Missiles were stored horizontally in the magazine and the twin launch ramps were reloaded in a horizontal, or near horizontal position. Obsolete.

GMLS Mk 10

There are numerous models of the GMLS Mk 10, a twin-ramp launcher system designed for use with Terrier and Standard (ER) surface-to-air missile systems. This design continues the horizontal storage and reloading pattern set by the GMLS Mk 7, although certain installations differ by the amount the conveyor track deviates from the true horizontal along the route from the magazine to the missile launch ramp. Mods 2, 5, and 7 are those models which most exhibit this characteristic. Various models of the system are found on numerous ships of lesser tonnage and the capacity of the magazines for reload missiles also varies between models, although all employ a similar form of horizontal drum storage for the rounds to permit mixed salvoes.

Substantial control system and performance improvements are in progress for the Mods 0, 1, 2, 5, 6, 7 and 8. When these are complete the Model designations of these systems will be changed to Mk 10 Mods 10, 11, 12, 13, 14, 15 and 16.

The Mk 10 models 3 and 4 systems originally installed aboard CVAs have been retired from active service.

CHARACTERISTICS

Launcher type: Mk 10 Mods 0-8 (except where otherwise indicated)
Missile(s): Terrier, Standard (ER), Standard SM-2 (ER), ASROC (Mods 7 & 8 only)
Ready-use rounds: 40; 80 (Mod 2); 60 including up to 20 ASROC (Mods 7 & 8 only)
Target capability: Air and surface; air, surface, u/water (Mods 7 & 8 only)
System weight (without missiles): 1·251 t (Mod 0); 1·258 t (Mod 1); 2·416 t (Mod 2); 1·291 t (Mods 3 & 4); 1·304 t (Mod 5); 1·247 t (Mod 6); 1·641 t (Mod 7); 1·652 t (Mod 8)
System weight (full missile load): 1·816 t (Mod 0); 1·823 t (Mod 1); 3·154 t (Mod 2); 1·856 t (Mods 3 & 4); 1·869 t (Mod 5); 1·812 t (Mod 6); 2·479 t (Mod 7); 2·491 t (Mod 8). (Missiles assumed 1360 kg each and launcher complete with all fluids.)
Training limits: Unlimited; 180° due to ship's structure (Mod 3)
Training velocity/acceleration: 30°/s; 60°/s²
Elevation limits: –10 to +90°; –3 to +90°, Mods 3 & 4
Elevation velocity/acceleration: 20°/s; 40°/s²
Total crew: 12 (3 panel operators, 8 assembly men, 1 safety observer)
Ship fittings
Mod 0, 'Farragut' class, aft
Mod 1, CG(N)-9 *Long Beach*, forward
Mod 2, CG(N)-9 *Long Beach*, forward
Mod 5, 'Leahy' class, forward
Mod 6, 'Leahy' class destroyers, aft
Mod 7, some 'Belknap' class destroyers, forward
Mod 8, CG(N)-35 *Truxtun*
System interface: WDS Mk 14, GMFCS Mk 76, UBFCS 114 or 116 (Mods 7 and 8 only)
Misfire removal: Automatic jettison, air actuation
Anti-icing system: Steam
Power requirements: 440 V, 60 Hz, 3-ph
Average standby load: 52·6 kW
Average continuous operation load: 124·9 kW
Peak continuous operation load: 202·7 kW

In addition to the USN fittings of the Mk 10 GMLS listed above, the Italian Navy aircraft carrier *Vittorio Veneto* is fitted with a Mk 10 Mod 9 GMLS forward, and the Italian cruisers *Andrea Doria* and *Caio Dilio* were fitted with the Mk 10 Mod 0. The Peruvian ship *Aquirre* was fitted with a Mk 10 Mod 5, but this was removed and returned to the USA.

GMLS Mk 13

The GMLS Mk 13 series marks a return to vertical stowage and reloading of missiles, as well as representing a changeover to single-ramp launcher, embodied in a modular design which combines the launcher, reloading mechanism and magazine in a single unit which can be installed in the ship as an entity. This system has been used by the USN since

FMC Mk 13 single-ramp launcher in use

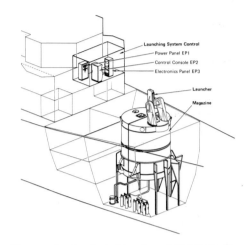

Diagram showing typical location of GMLS Mk 13 Mod 4 components

1962 in various models (from Mod 0 to 3) and a total of at least 41 had been supplied to the USN and the navies of six friendly states by 1979, when the Mk 13 Mod 4 was introduced. This version incorporated improvements in all elements of the electrical control system while retaining the basic Mk 13 mechanical and hydraulic design. Among the benefits from these improvements were reduced reaction time because of remote start and fire capabilities that permit remote operation; reduced manning requirements; ability to fire a wide range of missiles; and ability to withstand inadvertant ignition of the 'hotter' Mk 56 rocket motor by virtue of the addition of ablative material in the magazine plenum chamber. The Mk 13 Mods 0 to 3 were designed to accommodate RIM-24 Tartar and Standard 1 (MR) missiles, but the Mod 4 version handles the later Standard 2 (MR) and Harpoon surface-to-surface missiles also.

Three main groups of components comprise the Mk 13 Mod 4 GMLS; the launching system control Mk 162 Mod 0, the launcher Mk 126 Mod 4, and the magazine Mk 109 Mod 0, plus certain ancillary units. The first of these electronically directs and monitors operation of the overall GMLS and includes the power panel (EP1), control console (EP2) and electronics panel (EP3). Control of the GMLS normally takes place remotely from the ship's fire control system, but local loading and pointing are possible from EP2, permitting various reversionary modes of operation and exercise functions. The Mk 126 single-ramp launcher receives missiles from the ready service ring (RSR), part of the Mk 109 magazine that rotates to present missiles from the magazine via inner and outer rings which provide a total of 40 missiles. A single electric motor and hydraulic pump provide the power to drive either the RSR or the hoist used to position missiles in the magazine or offer them to the launch ramp. Electric motors and hydraulic power transmission trains are used for actuation of the launcher in train and elevation.

CHARACTERISTICS

Launcher type: Mk 13 Mods 0-7 (except where otherwise indicated)
Missile(s): Tartar, Standard 1 (MR), Standard 2 (MR), Harpoon (Mods 4-7)

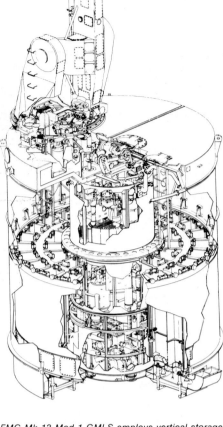

FMC Mk 13 Mod 1 GMLS employs vertical storage and launcher reloading. This mark permits modular ship fitting of missile launcher and magazine

Ready-use rounds: 40, any mixture
Target capability: Air or surface
System weight (without missiles or fluids): 6·022 t (Mod 0); 6·137 t (Mods 1 & 2); 6·133 t (Mod 3); 6·110 t (Mod 4)
System weight (with missiles and fluids): 8·432 t (Mod 0); 8·547 t (Mods 1 & 2); 8·543 t (Mod 3)
Training limits: Unlimited
Training velocity/acceleration: 90°/s; 200°/s²
Elevation limits: –15 to +95°
Elevation velocity/acceleration: 45°/s; 120°/s²
Tactical crew: 2 (1 panel operator, 1 safety observer)
Ship fittings
Mod 5/Mod 0: USN missile destroyers, DDG 15-24; 9 foreign ships
Mod 6/Mod 1: 4 USN (DDG 31-34) and 8 foreign missile destroyers
Mod 7: 2 USN cruisers, CGN 36 & 37
Mod 4: 30+ 'Oliver Hazard Perry' class frigates
System interface: GMFCS Mk 74; GMFCS Mk 92 (Mod 4)
Misfire removal: Automatic jettison
Anti-icing system: Dry steam
Power requirements: 440 V, 60 Hz, 3-ph
Average standby load: 22·9 kW; 25·7 kW (Mod 4)
Average continuous operation load: 43·9 kW; 46·7 kW (Mod 4)
Peak continuous operation load: 210·7 kW; 209·2 kW (Mod 4)

By 1981, 41 GMLS Mk 13 Mods 0 to 3 had been built and installed for the USN and the navies of six other countries: Australia, France, Italy, Japan, Netherlands, and West Germany. By 1984, 51 GMLS Mk 13 Mod 4 had been built and installed for the USN and the navies of three other countries: Australia, Japan and Spain. Fifteen more are planned for delivery during 1984 and 1985 for the USN, Australia, Japan, Italy and The Netherlands.

The USN Mk 13 Conversion Programme is currently upgrading Mods 0, 1, 2 and 3 systems to include features found on the Mk 13 Mod 4. The refurbishment programme adds ablative materials to the magazine plenum chamber, improves sprinkling characteristics, provides a solid state control system with built-in test equipment, and alters the power system from high to low voltage. When the programme is completed, the Mods 0 and 2 GMLS will be designated Mod 5; Mods 1 will become Mods 6 and Mods 3 will become Mods 7. The navies of Australia and France are also currently planning to upgrade GMLS Mk 13.

GMLS Mk 22

The GMLS Mk 22 is a lightweight version of the Mk 13, above, and is designed on an identical concept having much the same performance and configuration. Only the magazine size has been reduced, primarily to facilitate fitting in smaller vessels. Operated from a remote fire control station, the Mk 22 will direct and launch a ready-use complement of 16 Tartar or Standard missiles for surface-to-air applications and can be modified to launch the surface-to-air Standard 2 (MR) and Harpoon missiles for surface-to-surface engagements.

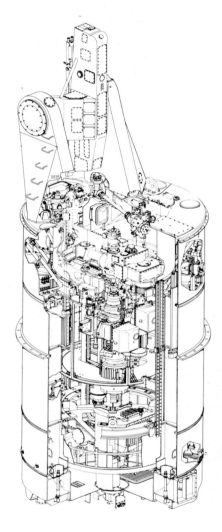

Mk 22 Mod 0 GMLS offers the same modular ship fitting possibilities as the Mk 13, for smaller vessels

CHARACTERISTICS
Launcher type: Mk 22 Mod 0
Missile(s): RIM-24 Tartar, Standard (MR), Standard 2 and Harpoon with modification
Ready-use rounds: 16, any mixture
Target capability: Surface or air
System weight (without missiles and fluids): 4·190 t
System weight (with missiles and fluids): 5·193 t
Training limits: Unlimited
Training velocity/acceleration: 88·5°/s; 132°/s²
Elevation limits: −15 to +95°
Elevation velocity/acceleration: 49°/s; 135°/s²
Tactical crew: 2 (1 panel operator, 1 safety observer)
Ship fittings
6 USN 'Brooke' class missile frigates
5 Spanish F-70 'Baleares' class frigates
System interface: GMFCS Mk 74
Misfire removal: Automatic jettison
Anti-icing system: Dry steam
Power requirements: 440 V, 60 Hz, 3-ph
Average standby load: 20·6 kW
Average operation load: 39 kW
Peak operation load: 164 kW

GMLS Mk 26

The Mk 26 GMLS is the latest and most versatile launching system in operational use by the US fleet and is capable of automatic handling and launching a mixed complement of Standard surface-to-air and ASROC anti-submarine missiles. Modular design and construction enables installations with magazine capacities of 24, 44 or 64 rounds to be fitted. The Mk 26 is credited with the shortest reaction time and fastest weapon launch rate of any existing US area defence shipboard launching system. The Mk 26 Mod 5 is the main launching system on the USN's new CG-47 Aegis class cruisers.

CHARACTERISTICS
Launcher type: Mk 26 Mods 0-5 (except where otherwise indicated)
Missile(s): Standard (MR), RUR-5A ASROC
Ready-use rounds: 24 (Mods 0 & 3); 44 (Mods 1, 4, 5); 64 (Mod 2), any mixture
Target capability: Air, surface, u/water
System weight (without missiles and fluids): 7·303 t (Mod 0); 9·385 t (Mod 1); 12·056 t (Mod 2); 7·210 t (Mod 3); 9·237 t (Mods 4 & 5)
System weight (with missiles and fluids): 8·685 t (Mod 0); 11·920 t (Mod 1); 12·056 t (Mod 2); 8·604 t (Mod 3); 11·792 t (Mods 4 & 5). (Missiles assumed average weight 580 kg each.)

Standard missile launch from GMLS Mk 26 aboard USS Norton Sound

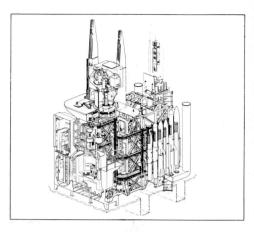

FMC Mk 26 Mod 1 GMLS is a modular system which can be configured with magazine capacities of 24, 44 or 64 missiles

Training limits: Unlimited
Training velocity/acceleration: 90°/s; 180°/s²
Elevation limits: −10 to +90°
Elevation velocity/acceleration: 50°/s; 100°/s²
Tactical crew: 3 (control console operator, 2 fin assembler/folders)
Ship fittings
Mod 0: USS *Norton Sound*, 4 USN cruisers
Mod 1: 4 USN nuclear cruisers
Mod 2: Land based test unit
Mod 3: 4 USN 933 class destroyers
Mod 4: 4 USN 993 class destroyers
Mod 5: USN Aegis cruisers 47-50
System interface: GMFCS Mk 74 Mod 5; Mk 116 underwater FCS
Misfire removal: Automatic jettison
Anti-icing system: Steam
Power requirements: 440 V, 60 Hz, 3-ph
Peak standby load: 105 kW
Peak running load: 480 kW

STATUS
The GMLS Mk 4 is now obsolete and few installations remain in service. The situation with the Mk 7 employed for the large Talos air defence missile is also related to the obsolescence of that weapon system. The many existing installations of the various models of the Mk 10 GMLS are likely to remain in service for a considerable period to come, with the systems being updated to accommodate the Standard SM-2 (ER) surface-to-air missile as part of the USN's CGN/New Threat Upgrade programme. FMC was awarded a $36·6 million USN contract in 1983 for continued Mk 13 Mod 4 system production, including two more launchers for FFG-7 class frigates and one launcher for Japan, and with these FMC will have supplied 107 Mk 13 systems since the early 1960s. Deliveries are scheduled to January 1986. The Mk 22 is no longer in production, but is being considered for modernisation to accommodate the Harpoon missile. The Mk 26 is currently in production for the first five Aegis cruisers.

CONTRACTOR
FMC Corporation, Northern Ordnance Division, 4800 East River Road, Minneapolis, Minnesota 55421, USA.

4204.231
MK 41 VERTICAL LAUNCH SYSTEM

The USN's vertical launch systems (VLS) programme has now reached the production stage with the Mk 41 VLS which will provide an improved missile launching system for surface vessels of the US fleet.

The system is based on a modular design, the basic unit being a launcher module containing eight missile cells. Each module, which consists of a structure, independently operating armoured hatch-covers, a gas-management system and requisite electronics, power supplies and support equipment, is assembled ready for installation aboard ship. Each of the eight cells in a module is designed to house a missile canister, and the system design allows any missile adapted for vertical launch to be fired from any cell. The cell is of corrugated steel construction and is both protective and reusable, thus serving as the shipping container and as the launcher rails for the

missile. The basic eight-cell module is designed as part of a Mk 41 VLS magazine. Each of the two magazines for the Aegis cruisers (CG-47 class) consists of seven eight-cell modules, plus one five-cell 'strikedown' module, thus giving the ship a total capacity of 122 missiles. A complete Mk 41 VLS magazine of seven eight-cell modules and one strikedown module, containing 61 missiles in all, occupies the space required for one Mk 26 Mod 0 conventional GMLS with a capacity of 44 missiles.

The strikedown, or replenishment, module is almost identical to the standard eight-cell module except that a hoist supporting an articulating crane is contained in the space of three cells. The inclusion of this module in each VLS magazine provides a capability for underway replenishment of the system.

Two launch control units (LCUs) consisting of AN/UYK-20 USN digital processors and associated peripheral equipment, are located at the ship's

weapons control station. These interface digitally with the appropriate ship's weapon control systems and control the launch of missiles. The Mk 41 VLS is designed to be able to interface simultaneously with up to three fire control systems, ie for air defence, surface engagement, and anti-submarine warfare systems. The initial missile compatibility specified calls for an ability to handle mixtures of Standard missiles, although provisions have been made throughout the programme for the inclusion of additional missile types later, and an important example of this is the inclusion of a requirement to accommodate missiles of 5·58 metre length and 1134 kg weight. An early addition to the VLS programme is the Tomahawk cruise missile.

The hatch covers of each eight-cell module are individually heated for anti-icing and provided with an electric motor for opening and closing, these being remotely controlled. A deluge system with individual valves for each cannister provides a water deluge to the missile warhead in the event of over-heating or accidental motor ignition. A separate sprinkler system provides fire protection for the other magazine spaces. Each module contains a plenum and uptake to vent the exhaust gases from a fired missile. The plenum and uptake are lined with ablative material to protect the structure against missile exhaust, and each module is capable of a minimum of 64 firings before ablative repairs are needed.

The missile, when ignited, pressurises the canister breaking the lower end cover allowing the gases to fill the plenum and exhaust vertically through the open uptake hatch at deck level. Double elastomeric seals are provided to form gas-tight joints at both ends of the canister to prevent gases entering the magazine spaces.

STATUS

Developed for the USN by Martin Marietta Aerospace under contract N00024-77-C-5104 to development specification WS 18968A, the Mk 41 VLS is in production. Firing tests of a prototype launcher module at White Sands Missile Range were completed in January 1981 when six Standard missiles were successfully launched, three as single launches and the other three as a ripple firing to evaluate rapid fire capabilities. In related tests, Tomahawk cruise missiles were launched vertically from a VLS module at Point Mugu, California. Pre-production Tomahawk-capable VLS modules have been installed in the USS Norton Sound the integration of Tomahawk/Aegis. The full Tomahawk launch capability is scheduled for all VLS ships. Procurement of Tomahawk-capable VLS for installation in "DD-963" class ships is planned to start in 1983, with all 31 ships of the class to be fitted. Installation in 'Arleigh Burke' class (DDG-51) destroyers is also planned.

In March 1984 it was announced that FMC Corporation, Northern Ordnance Division had been

Impression of how CG-47 class ships will look if completed with Mk 41 Vertical Launch Systems for their Aegis area defence missile systems, showing two 61-round magazines, fore and aft

designated as a second source for VLS. Under an initial $56 million contract, FMC becomes an independent competitive source, and is to supply a trainer and two VLS magazines for the Aegis programme.

CONTRACTOR

Martin Marietta Aerospace, Baltimore Division, 103 Chesapeake Park Plaza, Baltimore, Maryland 21220, USA.

AIR-TO-SURFACE MISSILES

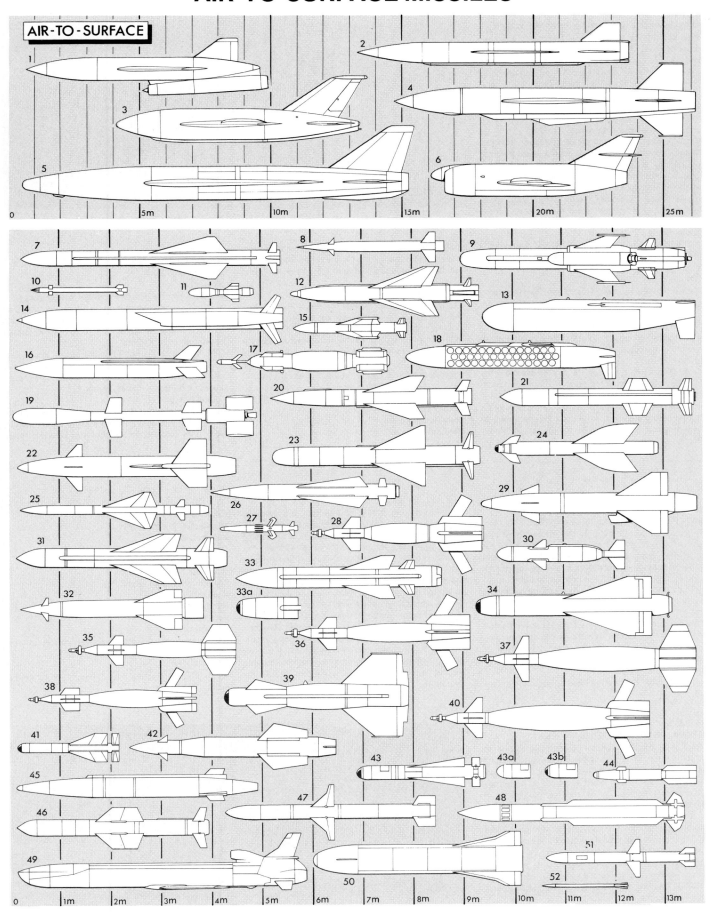

AIR-TO-SURFACE

1 AS-2 Kipper; 2 AS-6 Kingfisher; 3 AS-5 Kelt; 4 AS-4 Kitchen; 5 AS-3 Kangaroo; 6 AS-1 Kennel; 7 Exocet AM.39; 8 Martin Pescador; 9 Otomat; 10 HATCP; 11 HOT; 12 AS-30 Laser; 13 Pegase; 14 ASMP; 15 AS.15 TT; 16 Apache; 17 Matra LGB; 18 CWS; 19 Marte; 20 Kormoran Mk 1 & 2; 21 Gabriel Mk III; 22 RB 04E; 23 ASM-1; 24 Penguin Mk III; 25 ALARM; 26 RB 05A; 27 RBS 70; 28 Paveway II (Mk.13/18); 29 RBS 15; 30 Sea Skua; 31 Sea Eagle; 32 AS-7 Kerry; 33 Martel ARM; 33a Martel TV; 34 Walleye; 35 Paveway I (GBU-12); 36 Paveway II (GBU-16); 37 Paveway I (GBU-10); 38 Paveway II (GBU-12B/B); 39 GBU-15(V); 40 Paveway II (GBU-10); 41 Wasp; 42 Bullpup; 43 Maverick (AGM-65B) TV; 43a Maverick laser; 43b Maverick IR; 44 Hellfire; 45 SRAM (AGM-69A); 46 Harpoon; 47 HARM; 48 Standard ARM; 49 ALCM; 50 LAD; 51 Shrike; 52 HVM (provisional)

ARGENTINA

3678.311

MARTIN PESCADOR AIR-TO-SURFACE MISSILE

The Martin Pescador is a supersonic aircraft-launched tactical missile for use over short to medium ranges (2·5 to 7·9 km), maximum ranges being dependent upon aircraft speed at launch. It is powered by a single-stage solid-propellant rocket motor, and carries a conventional high explosive warhead weighing 40 kg. The motor exhausts through a bell-shaped nozzle, and the warhead is actuated by a direct action fuze.

The configuration of the Martin Pescador consists of the following major components: the fore-body containing radio receiver, power source, control mechanisms and logic devices; centre section with warhead and fuze; aft body section containing the rocket motor, propellant and flares; four wings attached to the aft body; and four canard control surfaces actuated by the fore-body control sub-system.

The maximum speed is Mach 2·3 and the speed at impact is Mach 1·1. The approximate time of flight is 13 s.

OPERATION

Radio command is used to direct and steer the Martin Pescador to its target. Launching is possible from any aircraft capable of a speed of Mach 0·5 or more. Launch from a hovering helicopter is possible also, in which case a range of 4·3 km can be achieved with a missile impact speed of Mach 1·1. The rear of the missile carries three flares to assist in tracking. Command signals are sent to the missile from the launching aircraft which carries the command radio transmitter. The pilot has to keep the missile on his line of sight to the target during its flight time and a button on the aircraft control column is provided for this purpose. In order that a number of Martin Pescador missiles can be launched simultaneously

Launch of Martin Pescador air-to-surface missile

from several aircraft, co-ordinated changes of radio command frequency have to be taken into account; facilities for this are provided on a missile control panel in the cockpit.

DEVELOPMENT

The Martin Pescador missile has been developed by the Instituto de Investigaciones Cientificas y Tecnicas de las Fuerzas Armadas (CITEFA) on behalf of the Argentinian Forces. It should be noted that the word 'Martin' does not signify any connection with the well-known US defence contractor, or any of the missiles produced by the American concern; *Martin Pescador* is Spanish for 'Kingfisher'.

CHARACTERISTICS

Length: 294 cm
Diameter: 21·85 cm
Wing span: 73 cm
Total weight: 140 kg

Warhead: HE 40 kg
Speed: Mach 2·3 (max)
Range: 2·5 – 7·9 km

STATUS

It is possible that *Martin Pescador* was employed in A-4 Skyhawk anti-shipping strikes against the Royal Navy during the Argentinian occupation of the Falkland Islands in April-June 1982, but this cannot be confirmed at present.

In full production. New versions are under development, with increased range and with a heavier warhead. Other developments include helicopter-launched models with longer range.

CONTRACTOR

Instituto de Investigaciones Cientificas y Tecnicas de las Fuerzas Armadas (CITEFA), Zufriategui y Varela, 1603 Villa Martelli, Provincia de Buenos Aires, Argentina.

FRANCE

4510.311

AATCP HELICOPTER MISSILE SYSTEM

This is a project to employ the short-range anti-aircraft SATCP Mistral missile (**4198.131**) for helicopter applications such as air-to-air combat between battlefield helicopters, or the engagement of ground targets such as tanks or other vehicles etc.

The concept is similar to that embraced by the American HVM programme (**4448.311**) and the Soviet use of SA-7 Grail missiles with the Hind helicopter. This heliborne version of the Mistral missile can be mounted on a support protection helicopter as main armament with a gun as the complentary weapon. It can also be mounted on anti-tank helicopters as self-protection armament.

The possibility of homing head pre-pointing makes

the missile firing easier, and further improvement derives from the ability to choose the scanning pattern of the homing head. Thanks to the 'fire and forget' guidance employed by the Mistral, the launching helicopter is free to manoeuvre immediately after firing the missile. Other significant operational characteristics are the 3 kg warhead and proximity fuze, short system reaction time, high missile velocity, and these limit the target's ability to take cover before missile arrival.

The missiles are carried in a twin-round launcher and the number of these launchers fitted depends on the type of helicopter and other weapon/equipment loading factors. Typically, four launchers with eight missiles would be fitted on a support protection helicopter.

CHARACTERISTICS

Missile: SATCP (Mistral)
Length: 1·8 m
Diameter: 90 mm
Weight: 17 kg
Warhead: 3 kg
Fuze: Impact, laser proximity
Guidance: IR homing
Range: 500 – 6000 m
Peak speed: Mach 2·6

STATUS

Development project. Pre-development studies took place in 1982.

CONTRACTOR

Matra SA, 37 avenue Louis-Bréguet, 78140 Vélizy, France.

4189.311

MATRA LASER-GUIDED BOMBS (LGB)

Matra is developing a series of laser-guided bombs (LGB) similar to the American Paveway munitions (**1534.311**) in which laser seeking guidance packages are added to standard bombs to provide increased accuracy when used against laser-marked targets. In the Matra system target illumination may be either by an aircraft-mounted laser marker or by a ground laser transmitter. In the former case a version of the ATLIS II target designator pod (**3820.393** in 1981-82 and earlier editions) is normally used, and the laser guidance sub-system for fitting on the bomb is a version of the Ariel seeker for the AS.30 laser missile (**3335.311**, below) known as the TMV 630 EBLIS and also produced by Thomson-CSF.

In the LGB application, the EBLIS is fitted in an aerodynamically shaped housing equipped with a wind-vane and carried on the nose of the bomb. The laser error detector measures the angle between the bomb velocity vector and the line between the aircraft and the target, and makes corrections by actuating electric motors to move the fins or flying surfaces to adjust the bomb's trajectory to bring it to the target. Other guidance components in the package are a guidance order computer and a roll gyroscope. These are housed in a streamline container mounted on the

Matra LGB on Jaguar aircraft. Semi-folding rear fins enable bombs to be carried under the wings of most aircraft types. The laser seeker is in the small 'thimble' with two aerodynamic vanes and the guidance and control electronics are in the larger housing with four control surfaces on the nose of the bomb itself. Note laser designator pod on fuselage centre-line.

fore-part of the bomb and with four control vanes disposed on it in a cruciform fashion. Another package of the LGB kit consists of four larger aerofoil surfaces mounted on an extension fitted to the rear of the bomb body; these too are arranged in a cruciform pattern.

Kits have been designed for fitting to several types of bomb, eg 400 kg and 1000 kg types, and for some types semi-folding wings facilitate carriage on the underwing armament stations of most aircraft types.

A feature of the Matra LGB system emphasised by the manufacturer is its ability to be used in a low-level

delivery mode, in level flight and at speeds up to Mach 0·9, enabling stand-off ranges of 4 to 10 km. There may also be a lateral offset of several degrees without impairing accuracy. Weapon flight times of up to 30 s after release are provided in the design, power for control actuation and electronics etc being supplied by a battery.

STATUS
The Matra LGB programme was started in 1978 in response to a French Government requirement, and the first phase of development was completed in late 1980 with a number of successful launches of 400 kg

LGBs. A special 1000 kg bomb body has been designed, specifically for the destruction of hard targets, as a French Air Force requirement. This LGB was engaged on final development trails in early 1984 and is due to enter service in 1985.

Several hundred Matra LGBs have been ordered by foreign customers.

CONTRACTORS
Matra SA, 37 avenue Louis-Bréguet, 78140 Vélizy, France.

Thomson-CSF, 1 rue des Mathurins, 92222 Bagneux, France.

3335.311
AS.30 LASER AIR-TO-SURFACE MISSILE
Successor to the command-guided AS.30 (**1171.311** in 1982-83 and earlier editions) tactical missile which has now ceased production, the AS.30 Laser is a supersonic, self-propelled, self-rotating homing missile designed for attacking surface point targets such as ships, bridges, etc.

The missile is in the form of a streamlined body,

fitted with cruciform, dart-shaped wings which provide lift and impart rotation. Propulsion is by two-stage (boost and sustainer) solid-propellant motors.

CHARACTERISTICS
Length: 3·65 m
Diameter: 342 mm
Wing span: 1 m
Launch weight: 520 kg

Warhead weight: 240 – 250 kg
Max range: 10-12 km, depending on initial conditions
Homing by laser illumination gives the weapon system high accuracy and allows the launch aircraft to take evasive action after launch, to remain outside the effective range of enemy defences. The missile flight path comprises two phases: the pre-guidance phase which is conducted by gyro reference; and homing onto the laser-marked target by means of a Thomson-CSF Ariel homing head. The laser target designation pod is the ATLIS equipment (**3136.393**).

STATUS
The French Air Force has ordered a number of AS-30 Laser missiles for use with Jaguar aircraft, target designation being provided by the ATLIS pod equipment (**3136.393** in the Electro-optical (Air) section of this volume). Adaptation to Mirage F1 and Mirage 2000 is under development for export customers. By the end of 1983 more than 400 missiles had been ordered.

CONTRACTOR
Aérospatiale, Division des Engins Tactiques, 2 rue Béranger, 92322 Chatillon Cedex, France.

Aérospatiale AS.30 Laser missile launched from French Jaguar aircraft just before striking laser-designated target during trials

---

1173.311
AS.11 AIR-TO-SURFACE MISSILE
This is a wire-guided multipurpose, lightweight air-to-surface missile. The SS-11 was originally conceived as a general-purpose battlefield weapon for deployment on surface vehicles, but it has been successfully adapted for use with helicopters, hovercraft, and surface vessels. Designation of the former version is AS.11.

Principal characteristics are: length 1·2 m, diameter 16·4 cm, wing span 50 cm, weight 29·9 kg.

Engagement ranges are between 300 and 3000 m and speed about 160 m/s when launched from a helicopter at the hover. Time of flight is between 18 and 20 s. The SS.11 B1 can be equipped with three types of warhead: anti-tank, a 'high-effect' high explosive warhead, or fragmentation type.

OPERATION
Using a stabilised optical sight, the operator gathers the missile after launch (aided by tracer flares attached to the missile), and then uses a control stick to transmit command signals to the missile via wires

to align the missile flight path with the target. Maintaining this alignment results in the missile hitting the target.

STATUS
By the end of 1982, nearly 180 000 of the various versions of the SS.11 series had been supplied to more than 30 different countries.

CONTRACTOR
Aérospatiale, Division des Engins Tactiques, 2 rue Béranger, 92322 Chatillon Cedex, France.

1174.311
AS.12 AIR-TO-SURFACE MISSILE
This is an airborne version of the SS.12 (which see) to provide an air-to-surface general-purpose lightweight missile. Principal characteristics are: length 187 cm, warhead diameter 21 cm, wing span 65 cm, launch weight 75 kg, weight of warhead 28·4 kg. The AS.12 can be equipped with a variety of different warheads to meet a range of operational requirements. The OP.3C has penetrating power sufficient to pierce over 40 mm of armour plate with a delayed action detonation, and other types include a powerful shaped charge, and a fragmentation head although these types have not so far been produced in series.

OPERATION
Guidance is by command signals fed to the missile via

wires, the missile operator in the aircraft usually being provided with a stabilised sighting system, and a control stick for steering the missile. Installed in a helicopter, the AS.12 is reported to be highly accurate when used with such a sight at ranges out to 6000 m. Use of a sight of this type also permits the launch aircraft to manoeuvre during missile flight. Maximum range of the AS.12 when launched from an aircraft providing 200 knots forward speed is 8000 m..

DEVELOPMENT
While the SS.12 and AS.12 are based on the highly successful techniques employed in the earlier SS.11 series of missiles, the former weapons have been designed with much greater versatility and kill-power in view. Range is approximately doubled, and the warhead is stated to be four times as powerful as that of the SS.11. The SS.12 range of missiles is capable of

being launched from the several types of launcher developed for the SS.11 missiles.

STATUS
The AS.12 is in operational service with at least eight different types of aircraft, including the ASW Atlantic, Alizé, Neptune and Nimrod aircraft, French Alouette III and Gazelle, RN Wasp, Lynx, and Wessex helicopters and the Bell SH3D and Augusta AB212 helicopters operated by other nations. By the end of 1982 more than 9500 of these missiles had been ordered and produced.

CONTRACTOR
Aérospatiale, Division des Engins Tactiques, 2 rue Béranger, 92322 Chatillon Cedex, France.

3359.311
AS.15 TT AIR-TO-SURFACE MISSILE
The AS.15 TT (TT: tous temps – all weather) is a new anti-ship missile under development for use on maritime helicopters, but which will also be suitable for alternative modes of deployment such as slow-flying fixed wing aircraft, fixed or mobile coastal batteries, or small surface craft. A coastal defence system based on the AS.15 TT has been designed jointly by Aérospatiale and Thomson-CSF, but further work has been suspended for the time being.

This system was described in entry **3974.121** in 1980-81 and earlier editions of *Jane's Weapon Systems*.

The AS.15 TT has the same warhead arrangement as the AS.12 (**1174.311**), which it is intended to replace, and can accommodate payloads weighing up to 30 kg. Range is over 15 km.

The guidance system is command-to-line-of-sight in azimuth with the missile slaved to the aircraft radar for azimuth guidance. The radar, Thomson-CSF Agrion (**3298.353**), incorporates pulse compression and frequency agility, and is equipped for automatic

tracking of the target and differential target/missile range and bearing measurements required for guidance of the missile. The guidance signals from the aircraft are passed in coded form within the radar's normal transmissions. A sea-skimming trajectory is followed in the vertical plane, with guidance data obtained from a radio altimeter.

CHARACTERISTICS
Length: 2·3 m
Diameter: 18 cm
Wing span: 53 cm

Naval Dauphin II helicopter armed with AS.15TT missiles and equipped with Agrion radar

Weight: 96 kg
Warhead: 30 kg
Range: 15 km +
Guidance: Radar tracking. Radio altimeter
Propulsion: Solid
STATUS
Announced in late 1976, development began in 1978, and flight tests began in 1980. The first flight of the missile took place on 22 June 1981. The AS.15 TT will be deployed on Dauphin 2 helicopters and the AS 332 Super Puma which will be able to carry AS.15 TT and AM 39 Exocet missiles at the same time. At the beginning of 1981 there were 200 AS.15 TT missiles on order for use by Saudi Arabian forces. A successful live firing took place on 28 June 1983 at the Centre d'Essais de la Mediterranée, when a direct hit was made on an old 300 ton patrol vessel at a range of 10 km from the firing platform, a naval Dauphin 2 helicopter. The first production AS.15TT missile launch from an SA365 Dauphin naval helicopter took place in February 1984.
CONTRACTOR
Aérospatiale, Division des Engins Tactiques, 2 rue Béranger, 92322 Chatillon Cedex, France.

1770.321
AIR-LAUNCH EXOCET (AM 39)
AM 39 is the air-to-surface version of the all-weather anti-ship Exocet missile. It is designed to be launched against naval surface targets from helicopters, maritime patrol aircraft and coastal surveillance aircraft, and jet strike/attack aircraft.

The Exocet AM 39 weapon system comprises:
(1) a command panel for insertion of operational and tactical data, and orders
(2) a missile adaptor kit which allows missile selection, initiates the firing sequence, and translates for the missile the information coming from the command panel and aircraft sensors

(3) one or more missile launchers under the aircraft wings, or alongside the fuselage, depending on aircraft type.
The weapon system uses the target range and bearing given by the aircraft's air-to-surface radar, which can be of the current type and an inertial platform or a doppler radar navigator system.

More details of the missile itself will be found in the entries dealing with the ship and land-based applications of Exocet (**2118.121** and **1156.221**).
CHARACTERISTICS
Length: 4·7 m
Diameter: 35 cm
Wing span: 1·1 m

Weight: 655 kg
Propulsion: 2-stage solid rocket motor
Range: 50 – 70 km, depending on the height and speed of launch aircraft
Flight speed: High subsonic
DEVELOPMENT
By late 1979 the AM 39 had reached operational status and tests with the Sea King and Super Frelon helicopters, and Super Etendard naval attack aircraft followed. Details of earlier development history appeared under this entry in previous editions of *Jane's Weapon Systems*
STATUS
The decision to arm aircraft of the French Navy with the AM 39 Exocet was taken by the French Government in May 1974. At present those aircraft are the Super Etendard and the Atlantic G2 maritime patrol aircraft. Six foreign governments have ordered the system for their own helicopters and for Super Etendard and Mirage strike aircraft.

The AM 39 scored its first successes in the course of the Argentinian invasion of the Falkland Islands when several Royal Navy and British merchant ships were hit by Exocets launched by Super Etendard aircraft.
CONTRACTOR
Aérospatiale, Division des Engins Tactiques, 2 rue Béranger, 92322 Chatillon Cedex, France.

AM 39 Exocet anti-ship missile on AS 332 Super Puma helicopter

---

3635.311
ASMP AIR-TO-SURFACE MISSILE
ASMP is the acronym under which the French Air-Sol-Moyenne-Portée project to develop a new tactical nuclear stand-off missile is known. In general concept it is similar to the American SRAM (**1107.311**), although there are naturally certain differences in performance and in other respects.

The project was given formal approval in April 1978 when a design and development contract for an air-to-ground medium range missile for the French Air Force's nuclear tactical force was awarded to the Tactical Missile Division of Aérospatiale. Initially the ASMP will arm the new Mirage 2000 aircraft, but it will probably be deployed with other types such as the Mirage IV aircraft of the French deterrent 'force de Frappe' aircraft, and it might replace the AN-52 nuclear bomb on the naval Super Etendard.

The ASMP is a supersonic ramjet powered missile with pre-programmed inertial guidance and capable of a stand-off range of about 100 km. It is understood that several flight profiles will be possible which may include flight at about Mach 3 at high altitudes, carrying a nuclear warhead of an estimated yield of 100 to 150 KT. The last item is being developed by the government agency CEA-DAM.

The propulsion system is a liquid-fuelled ramjet with integral booster. The latter, which is used to

ASMP air-to-surface missile test vehicle beneath Mirage 2000 aircraft

accelerate the missile to supersonic speed at which ramjet action can be sustained, is ignited in the main combustion chamber of the motor and is meant to burn away completely so that the chamber can be used for ramjet fuel burning. A smaller exhaust nozzle is employed for the acceleration phase and this is

rapidly enlarged for ramjet propulsion. Two inlets are provided to admit air for combustion and to derive the necessary pressurisation.

Guidance is being developed by ESD and SAGEM and will include an inertial platform and digital computer.

STATUS

Development flight tests began in 1980, and entry into service is planned for 1985-86. The ASMP programme was officially initiated in 1978, following studies which began in 1974. Aérospatiale became prime contractor with the award of a contract valued at Fr500 million.

Operational deployment was expected to begin around the start of 1985 on up-graded French Air Force Mirage IV bombers, 18 of which are planned. French Navy Super Etendards are expected to be similarly equipped and about 50 of them may be converted by 1988. This missile may also be deployed on a number of French Air Force Mirage 2000s.

CONTRACTOR

Aérospatiale, Division des Engins Tactiques, 2 rue Béranger, 92322 Chatillon Cedex, France.

4555.311
PEGASE

Pegase is the name given by its developers, Brandt Armements, to a modular stand-off ground attack weapon designed to meet potential French Government requirements. The Pegase vehicle is based on an essentially rectangular cross-section container equipped for carriage beneath the parent aircraft and equipped with fold-out wings and control surfaces to permit launch at low altitudes. The container portion of the vehicle is modular with optimised submunitions and a dispenser system to suit engagement of various categories of targets and missions. Payloads that have or are being studied include:

(1) runway cratering projectiles derived from the BAP 100 bomb (**3152.303**)
(2) anti-vehicle and equipment warhead submunitions, derived from the ABL BAT 120 bomb (**3863.303**)
(3) anti-light armoured vehicle warhead submunitions, derived from the ABL BAT 120
(4) anti-armour modules of the BM 400 modular bomb (**3865.303**)
(5) 70 mm HEAT grenades
(6) TACED sensor-aided anti-armour warhead submunitions
(7) PPGT terminally guided anti-armour warhead submunitions
(8) area denial submunitions
(9) fuel-air explosive (FAE) ammunition for blast effects.

Various types of container, of standard dimensions but internally configured to suit the different payloads, are planned to form the major portion of the Pegase vehicle. Other modules that would be used with the payload module(s) are a power module containing either a solid rocket motor or a turbojet, and either an autonomous guidance package or a target sensor/guidance package. Various combinations of these optimal propulsion and guidance options could be employed to configure the complete weapon to suit the type of target or anticipated operational environment. The current options under consideration are set out in tabular form (right), and they permit a combination of five configurations with differing payloads and maximum ranges.

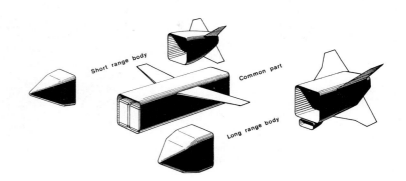

Pegase modules

CHARACTERISTICS

Version	Pegase I	Pegase II	Pegase III
Range	6 km (15 km with propulsion)	8 km (15 km with propulsion)	60 km
Mission altitude	50 – 1000 m	50 – 1000 m	50 – 100 m
Speed	High subsonic		
Max launch weight	720 kg	1300 kg	1300 kg
Propulsion	None or rocket	None or rocket	Turbojet
Store mounting	NATO 14 in	NATO 30 in	NATO 30 in
Length	3·4 m	4·2 m	4·2 m
Section	570 × 620 mm	570 × 620 mm	570 × 620 mm
Span	2·8 m	3·2 m	3·2 m
Guidance	inertial	inertial	inertial + position update
Payload capacity	450 kg	760 kg	760 kg
AB modules	4	8	
AMV/ABL 120 mm	24	36	
PAP 100 mm	14	28	14
Mines	154	224	
70 mm grenades	234	342	
Sensor-aided weapons			
TACED	14	20	10
PPGT	14	28	14
TGSM	24	36	24

STATUS

Development project.

CONTRACTOR

Brandt Armements, 52 avenue des Champs-Elysées, 75008 Paris, France.

GERMANY (FEDERAL REPUBLIC)

1180.321
KORMORAN AIR-TO-SURFACE ANTI-SHIP MISSILE

Kormoran is an advanced air-to-surface missile, designed principally for strikes against surface shipping. The guidance system employed provides a useful stand-off capability for the launch aircraft. Main characteristics of the missile are: length 440 cm, diameter 34·4 cm, wing span 1 metre, weight 600 kg, speed Mach 0·95, and range about 20 nautical miles.

Propulsion is by solid-fuel motors, and a hybrid guidance system is employed. Cruciform, broad chord swept wings are located just aft of the cylindrical missile body midpoint, and these are followed by a set of four in-line tail fins. A specially developed high explosive warhead is carried.

The Kormoran is roll stabilised and is steered by aerodynamic control surfaces at the rear. The missile is constructed in three main sections: the nose, containing the homing head; warhead; and motor, which also includes the rear structure and the main navigation package that is carried ahead of the sustainer motor.

The 160 kg warhead is designed to penetrate hulls without being damaged, and detonation is initiated by an impact fuze with a pyrotechnic delay set to explode the warhead approximately in the centre of the target.

Liners arranged around the warhead form projectiles on detonation and their resultant kinetic energy is stated to be sufficient to penetrate up to seven bulkheads. The basic explosive effect of the warhead is sufficient to cause extensive damage, not least because of a special system of simultaneous ignition at three places, which results in detonation of the entire explosive in a shorter time.

The navigation package consists of a twin-gyro platform, an inertial computer, associated electronics, and a time switch. There is a separate course and position computer in the tail section and also a radar altimeter.

The radar homing head fitted is based on the RE 576 developed by Thomson-CSF. This is stated to be capable of either active or passive homing, and the assumed mode of operation is that when the missile has reached a height to bring it within line-of-sight range of the target, the radar receiver is switched on for an initial period during which it searches for radar signals emanating from the target. If such signals are received, the homing head will lock on and the missile will operate in a passive homing mode. In the absence of signals, the radar transmitter in the missile will be switched on and a target search, lock on, and tracking sequence will follow to enable the missile to intercept the target.

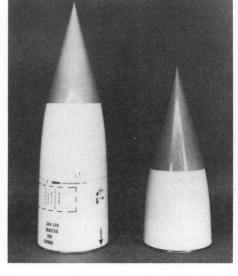

Comparison of the radar seeker heads of Kormoran 1 and 2 anti-ship missiles. Kormoran 2 head on right is all solid-state

OPERATION

A typical Kormoran sortie envisages a low-level approach to a known target followed by a brief climb to above the radar horizon when the aircraft radar is turned on briefly to acquire the target. Upon acquisition, the pilot transmits the relative position of the target into his autonomous navigation system and turns off the nose radar. The aircraft then manoeuvres into an appropriate attack position and when this has been reached another brief radar transmission is made to establish target position. This and other necessary initial data are then automatically inserted into the Kormoran's navigation system. On reaching a predetermined launching range the missile is released and the aircraft makes an immediate break away.

After launch, the missile descends to its programmed flight level. In the first part of its flight it is under inertial guidance, aided by the radar altimeter. At a prescribed distance the inertial system of the missile homing head is activated and an active radar search pattern is initiated. After lock-on has been achieved, the inertial guidance is slaved and corrected in azimuth and range by the seeker head and the missile heads for the target. At a short distance from the target, the missile descends to its final flight level in order to hit the target just above the water line. This is the standard mode, but others are possible.

DEVELOPMENT

Kormoran is the largest missile project so far undertaken in West Germany, and was initiated in 1964 to meet a Navy requirement. Development started in 1967-68 with MBB as prime contractor.

Production was completed at the end of 1983, by which time, studies and design work on a Kormoran 2 version had been in progress for several years. The new missile is principally intended to arm Bundesmarine Tornado aircraft in the late-1980s and 1990s. Kormoran will have a digitised active radar seeker head, now under development by Thomson-CSF. It will be an all solid-state system, including the emitter. Comparable improvements will be incorporated to other missile sub-systems such as the warhead, propulsion and guidance.

German Naval Air Arm Tornado armed with four Kormoran air-to-ship missiles

STATUS

The first air launch, from an F-104G, took place successfully in March 1970. Kormoran 1 has been used initially to arm West German F-104 G aircraft, followed by Tornados of the Naval Air Arm, until Kormoran 2 becomes available in the late 1980s. A total of 350 Kormoran 1 missiles were ordered for West German use, these are all believed to have been delivered. Kormoran has also been ordered for the Italian Air Force, where it will be deployed on Tornado aircraft.

Development of an improved version, Kormoran 2 had already started following a series of studies of a successor to Kormoran 1 which had been in progress since 1975. The development contract for Kormoran 2 was announced in June 1983, when the following improvements were listed: increased hit probability and penetration, better ECM protection, optimised trajectory, target selection, multiple launch, increased range, and simpler operation. Quantity production of Komoran 2 is thought likely to begin in 1990.

CONTRACTORS

Prime contractor: Messerschmitt-Bölkow-Blohm (MBB) GmbH, Postfach 8011 49, 8000 Munich 80, Federal Repubic of Germany.

Aérospatiale, Division des Engins Tactiques, 2 rue Béranger, 92322 Chatillon Cedex, France.

Thomson-CSF, Division des Matériels d'Avionique, 178 boulevard Gabriel Peri, 92240 Malakoff, France.

Airborne computer, inertial navigation: Bodenseewerk Gerätetechnik GmbH, Überlingen, Federal Republic of Germany.

4770.311

VEBAL/SYNDROM AIRBORNE ANTI-TANK WEAPON

Vebal/Syndrom is the name of an experimental airborne anti-tank weapon system being studied in West Germany under a Ministry of Defence contract awarded to MBB. The name derives from the contractions VErtical BALlistic (VEBAL) and the system is intended to provide an aircraft with a capability to carry out top attacks on multiple armour targets on a single pass over the target area.

It differs from cluster weapons and other area weapons in that a relatively small number of unguided anti-tank projectiles is used to combat whatever armour is encountered within a swath of terrain on each side of the aircraft's flight path, rather than dispensing large numbers of specialised submunitions which have varying degrees of sophistication. To achieve this the VEBAL/Syndrom system requires two pods which are mounted beneath the aircraft: one houses a multi-sensor package for detecting, classifying and accurately locating the target(s), while the other carries anti-tank projectiles which are launched downward and rearwards to attack the target's vulnerable top surface.

Sensors incoporated in the detector/locator pod include an IR linescan equipment, laser and radar, and a radiometer. The last of these plays an important part in identification of the target by means of its thermal characteristics. This process and other signal processing and data handling functions are performed by digital micro-processor, which also is responsible for carrying out the calculations needed to ensure the precise instant to fire the projectiles to ensure hitting the target(s) on the first pass.

A typical projectile pod would contain about 30 tubes and would be suitable for carriage on standard NATO mountings on most types of aircraft.

Experimental installations have been made on a Luftwaffe F-4F aircraft.

Reports state that operation is fully autonomous after the system is armed by the pilot prior to commencing his run over the target area, at low level and high speed. Any target encountered thereafter is automatically acquired and attacked. At a flight level of 250 feet (76 metres) the sensor pod scans a band of terrain about 100 feet (30 metres) wide.

STATUS

Development was started in 1977 under a contract thought to be worth about DM7 million. By late 1983 more than 500 trial sorties had been flown by the contractor, in the course of which some 100 live firings were made.

CONTRACTOR

Messerschmitt-Bölkow-Blohm (MBB) GmbH, Postfach 8011 49, 8000 Munich 80, Federal Republic of Germany.

3517.311

MW-1 MULTI-PURPOSE WEAPON

The MW-1 (Mehrzweckwaffe) is a multi-purpose cluster weapon designed and developed to engage battlefield targets such as soft- and hard-skinned vehicles moving in tactical formations over open ground; vehicles, bunkers and personnel in various battlefield or support structures or bunkers; vehicles, aircraft, runways and hardened shelters on airfields. To compensate for the limitations of the majority of earlier cluster weapons which normally carry only one type of single-purpose submunition, and often have only a limited distribution pattern, the MW-1 is provided with a range of six types of submunition, and the distribution pattern can be readily varied to suit the nature of the target(s) and the operational environment.

As employed with the Tornado aircraft, the system consists of: a single dispenser 5·3 metres long and

MUSPA area denial submunition for use with MW-1 system

MIFF anti-tank mine submunition

large enough to contain sufficient submunitions to successfully engage a tactical target (in the anti-tank role one dispenser on a single aircraft can deploy 4700 anti-armour projectiles). The dispenser consists of four sections each containing 28 transverse tubes, ie 112 tubes with 224 apertures. To ensure uniform distribution of submunitions laterally, four different ejection charges are used. This results in different ejection velocities and thus a varying spread of the submunitions on reaching the surface. The submunitions are ejected from both sides of the dispenser without recoil effects. The width of cover from a single pass can be preset between 200 and 500 metres and the length of pattern is variable between 200 and 2500 metres. This linear variation can be adjusted in flight by the pilot who can therefore select the required density of cover for a given target.

The MW-1 system includes six types of submunition, which can be dropped in any combination. These are:
(1) KB 44 armour piercing bomblet
(2) MIFF anti-tank mine
(3) MUSA fragmentation munition
(4) MUSPA, and airfield denial munition similar to the MUSA except for a complex sensor system
(5) STABO runway penetrator
(6) ASW hardened shelter penetrator.

Like the submunitions for the British JP233 system (**5218.303**) fuze details are classified. Other known features of each are summarised in the following paragraphs.

KB 44 This AP bomblet is claimed to be capable of penetrating the top and side armour of all known tanks and is a sub-calibre projectile. Seven of them are bundled together to fill the dispenser tube cross-section, each tube containing three bundles on each side, ie 42 bomblets per tube or a total of 4704 per dispenser.

MIFF is a small anti-tank mine with two plate charges, which is fired either by magnetic sensors in response

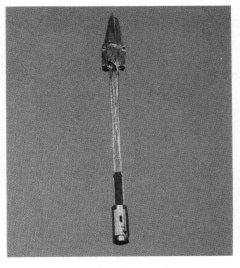

STABO runway cratering bomb for MW-1

KB 44 shaped charge anti-armour bomblet

to a tank hull or in response to ground vibration. Eight mines are housed in each tube making a total of 896 per dispenser. The mine is automatically stabilised, (either end uppermost) on impact. It will detonate after an initial delay of a few seconds whenever the sensor systems are activated. There is no self-destruct time.

This weapon is not designed to create a tank barrier but to be employed in conjunction with the KB 44 against a tank formation, or with other submunitions against an airfield.

MUSA is a fragmentation submunition for destroying soft-skinned and semi-hardened targets and is suitable for use against depots or airfields where aircraft or vehicles might be in the open. The lethality range claimed for it is more than 100 metres, and it is also suitable for anti-personnel roles. It is parachute retarded in flight and rights itself on reaching the ground for maximum fragmentation effect, and then detonates. Each dispenser can carry 672 MUSA submunitions.

MUSPA This is an airfield denial submunition with an identical warhead to the MUSA, above, and it is dispensed in the same fashion. However, initiation is a far more complex matter. It has an acoustic sensor that will detect aircraft landing, taking off or taxying, and if the aircraft comes within its effective range it will detonate. There is also a self-destruct device with a random time delay to deter airfield clearance personnel.

STABO is a runway penetrator and cratering munition. Its operating sequence begins with its ejection, stabilisation in flight and parachute retarded descent. During this phase a small sensor is exposed at the bottom of the charge, which when it touches the ground results in detonation of the charge. This opens up a hole in the concrete through which a follow-through projectile is fired to detonate beneath the surface to generate heave and create a crater. 234 are carried in one dispenser.

ASW is a hardened shelter penetrator designed for attacking aircraft, ammunition and other stores inside hardened shelters protected by overburden. The operating sequence begins with ejection and stabilised descent until the ASW hits the overburden, which causes ignition of a booster rocket that projects the submunition until it reaches a harder surface such as structural concrete. At this point a shaped charge is initiated to create a hole in the concrete, through which a projectile is accelerated to detonate within the shelter.

STATUS
In production for the West German forces.
CONTRACTORS
RTG Raketen-Technik GmbH-RTG, Oberweg 8, D-8025 Unterhaching, Federal Republic of Germany (jointly owned by Messerschmitt-Bölkow-Blohm (MBB) GmbH and Diehl GmbH & Co.)

Tornado dispensing submunitions from MW-1

4449.311
CONTAINER WEAPON SYSTEM (CWS)
Revealed at the 1982 Hanover Air Show by MBB, the container weapon system (CWS) is apparently a continuation of the SOM stand-off missile project (**4050.311** in 1981-82 and earlier editions) which originally involved MBB, British Aerospace and McDonnell Douglas in the development of a new conventional stand-off multipurpose ground attack weapon. The project now appears to be solely an MBB programme, the American and British partners presumably pursuing various national programmes individually.

The CWS is a modular system in which various payloads are made up of appropriate modules to meet a variety of operational requirements, and which can

be deployed on standard NATO 30-inch weapon lugs beneath most types of NATO military aircraft. In many ways the CWS is similar to the MW-1 multipurpose weapon (**3517.311**) developed for the Tornado, but the CWS is slightly smaller and lighter to enable it to be carried on a wider range of aircraft types. Another important difference is the provision in the CWS for free flight after release from the parent aircraft; the MW-1 container is an inert container which may or may not be jettisoned at the pilot's discretion.

The CWS is equipped with four tail surfaces and a pair of wings which unfold after release from the aircraft to permit gliding flight. There is also a version of the CWS which is fitted with a solid-propellant rocket motor to increase the effective range by extending the gliding distance. In all, four versions of

Close-up of free-flight version of MBB CWS showing 42 tubes for ejection of submunitions (T J Gander)

the CWS have been revealed and their main characteristics are detailed below. The four versions are: freight container, submunition dispener, unpowered free-flight weapons container, and a powered free-flight weapons container. The weapons employed in both the free-flight versions consist of 42 tube-launched submunitions of the same type as those for the MW-1 system, namely runway cratering, anti-tank, anti-material and anti-personnel types. The aerodynamic design is suitable for carriage at high subsonic airspeeds and the system is intended for low-level use.

CHARACTERISTICS
Length: 3·91 m; (4·15 m, powered free-flight version)
Fuselage width: 630 mm
Wingspan: 2 m (free-flight versions)
Tail span: 1·18 m
Weights: 900 kg (freight container); 950 kg (drop-container); 1000 kg (unpowered free-flight); 1200 kg (powered free-flight)
Aircraft release height: 50 – 70 m
Mission altitude: 50 – 100 m
Submunition ejection altitude: ⩾50 m
Range: 20 km (approx)
Aircraft speed: High subsonic

STATUS
Development. In mid-1983 a collaborative project between MBB and the French Matra concern was announced. Called Apache/CWS (**4554.311**) this envisages joint development of a family of ground attack stand-off weapons based on the MBB vehicle.

Completion of the development phase and production start-up is projected for 1986.

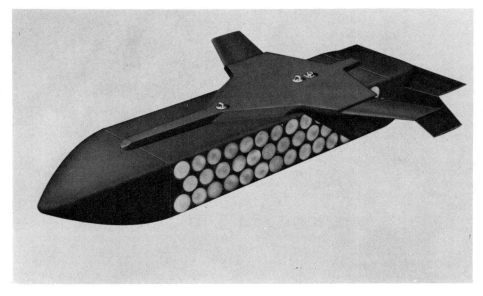

MBB CWS air-to-ground glide weapon for use against area targets

CONTRACTOR
Messerschmitt-Bölkow-Blohm (MBB) GmbH, Postfach 8011 49, 8000 Munich 80, Federal Republic of Germany.

INTERNATIONAL

4450.321
AIR-LAUNCHED ANS
This is an air-launched version of the supersonic anti-ship missile, ANS (Anti-Navire Supersoñique) being developed jointly by France and the Federal Republic of Germany as a successor to the AM 39 Exocet and Kormoran, respectively. The new weapon is an air-breathing ramjet powered missile which is intended to reach speeds of Mach 2 at sea level and 2·5 at altitude. Other operational requirements are an ability to manoeuvre at 10 g, long range and autonomous operation.

The two contractors leading the project for the French and West German governments are Aérospatiale and MBB, respectively. The division of responsibilities places airframe and seeker/guidance system design with Aérospatiale, while MBB's main duties are the propulsion system and warhead. Project management is understood to be in the hands of the French company.

Additional information will be found in the entry for the ship-launched model (**4446.221**), together with photographs of a test vehicle.

STATUS
Project definition; this phase is expected to continue to 1986, with possible entry into service in the 1990s.

CONTRACTORS
Messerschmitt-Bölkow-Blohm (MBB) GmbH, Postfach 8011 49, 8000 Munich 80, Federal Republic of Germany.

Aérospatiale, Division des Engins Tactiques, 2 rue Beranger, 92322 Chatillon Cedex, France.

Mock-up of ANS supersonic anti-ship missile beneath West German Tornado aircraft

1022.311
MARTEL AS.37/AJ.168 AIR-TO-SURFACE MISSILE
Martel is an air-to-surface tactical missile with two alternative terminal guidance systems capable of offering a considerable stand-off capability. Both versions are designed to operate in an ECM environment, to which a high resistance is claimed. The two forms of terminal guidance are: passive homing on to electromagnetic radiation in the AS.37, anti-radar version; and visual guidance to a selected target by means of a nose-mounted TV camera and a data link over which both video and command signals are passed between aircraft and missile, in the AJ.168 variant. The Martel system is the product of a joint Anglo/French development programme with prime responsibility for the AS.37 resting with Engins Matra, and for the AJ.168 with British Aerospace Dynamics Group.

General configuration of the missiles can be seen from the photograph adjacent to this entry. Length of the AJ.168 is 390 cm, and of the AS.37, 420 cm; body diameter and wingspan, respectively, for both versions are 40 and 120 cm. No details of performance have been revealed, but range has been officially stated both as 'several tens of miles' and 'several tens of kilometres'. This suggests a range of about 60 km although maximum range will be to some extent dependent upon the height of launch and subsequent trajectory.

Both versions of Martel probably employ the same basic autopilot which provides guidance until either TV or radar homing systems assume control for the terminal guidance phase. There are some indications that the autopilot can be pre-programmed to provide several options of mission profile. A fundamental difference, in addition to the guidance system, is related to the two-stage propulsion assembly, which is adapted to the mission requirements specific to each version.

ARMAT
Preliminary development work on a new anti-radar missile derived from the AS.37 radiation homing version of Martel has been commenced by Matra, the project being known as Anti-Radar Matra (ARMAT). No other reliable details have been revealed to date.

STATUS
In service with the British and French forces. The Martel system is used on the Mirage IIIE, Atlantic, and Buccaneer Mk II.

Use of both anti-radiation and TV-homing versions is apparently restricted to British Forces; the TV-homing AJ.168 is not used on French aircraft.

In mid-August 1977 the UK MoD announced an RAF requirement for a new anti-ship missile to arm

Buccaneer and Tornado aircraft. This led to the Sea Eagle (P3T) development (**3630.311**).
CONTRACTORS
Prime Contractors:
British Aerospace Dynamics Group, Manor Road, Hatfield, Hertfordshire AL10 9LL, England.
Engins Matra, 37 avenue Louis-Breguet, 78140 Velizy, France.
TV guidance system: Marconi Avionic Systems Ltd, Basildon, Essex, England.
AS.37 homing head: Electronique Serge Dassault, 55 quai Carnot, 92214 Saint-Cloud, Paris, France.

Buccaneer armed with one anti-radiation Martel and two TV-guided Martels. Note Martel data-link/control pod on starboard inner wing section

1338.321
OTOMAT ANTI-SHIP MISSILE (FRANCE/ITALY)
In addition to the ship launched and coastal defence versions of the Otomat anti-ship missile, the air launched role for this missile has also been taken into account during its development. Matra is continuing with the study of the missile's application to this role

Air-to-surface version of Otomat anti-ship missile

on classic maritime patrol aircraft types and also to a number of smaller twin-engined types suitable for EEZ (200 nautical mile zone) operations. Studies also embrace helicopters such as the Sea King and certain strike aircraft.

The missile is the same as in the other roles (**1336.221** in the Shipborne Surface-to-Surface Weapons section), but thanks to the higher forward speed of the aircraft launch platform, smaller boosters can be used to accelerate the missile to its normal cruise speed. The airborne system consists of a control panel, harmonisation box, selection box and launcher. Two missiles are normally carried by a helicopter, twin-engined aircraft or strike aircraft.

Target designation is fed to the selected missile from the airborne radar, and the harmonisation box computes the firing envelope and controls the firing sequence. After launch the missile descends to its normal low-level trajectory automatically. The two possible modes for the final approach to the target (sea skimming or climb-and-dive) can be selected prior to launch.

The present system provides for ranges of up to 100 km, using a normal modern airborne radar for target designation, in a 'fire and forget' technique. The maximum autonomous range remains the missile's typical maximum of 180 km (with growth potential).
STATUS
Development and studies continuing.
CONTRACTORS
Engins Matra, 37 avenue Louis-Breguet, 78140 Velizy, France.
OTO-Melara SpA, 15 via Valdilocchi 1, 19100, La Spezia, Italy.

1771.311
HOT AIR-TO-SURFACE MISSILE
The relatively recent increase in interest regarding the use of helicopters in a specifically anti-tank role has led to the development of a helicopter installation for the HOT anti-tank weapon. The basic HOT missile is described in **2212.111** in an earlier section of this book, and the following refers to the helicopter version.

Depending upon the type of helicopter used, four, six or eight launcher ramps to accept the HOT combined container-launch-tube can be fitted, and these are elevation-slaved to the line-of-sight. For helicopter operation, a stabilised optical sighting system, APX M397, is used, this being derived from the APX M334 sight described in **7032.393** in the Equipment Section of this book.

The guidance system includes a triple-field IR 'localiser', with a 10° acquisition field, a 5° tracking field, and a 1° tracking field. The function of the IR localiser is to establish the position of the HOT missile relative to the line-of-sight (which normally will be maintained on target by the operator using his optical sight). Appropriate guidance signals are computed and transmitted via the command wire to maintain the missile on the line-of-sight to the target.

A prototype night-firing device is currently undergoing trials. This is the VENUS system (viseur écartométrique de nuit stabilisé) designed for installation on Dauphin type helicopters. A photograph of this equipment appears nearby and additional details will be found in entry **3856.393** later in this volume.
STATUS
In November 1983 more than 53 000 HOT missiles (of all versions) were on order and almost half that number had been produced.

Night view of Dauphin helicopter equipped with two quadruple HOT anti-tank missile launcher pods and VENUS night firing equipment in ball turret

CONTRACTOR
Management, sales, and production responsibilities rest at: Euromissile, 12 rue de la Redoute, Fontenay-aux-Roses, France.

4554.311
APACHE/CWS

Under an international agreement announced in May 1983 between MBB of the Federal Republic of Germany and Matra in France, the two concerns will embark on a collaborative programme leading to a stand-off weapon system for use by tactical aircraft against a variety of targets including airfields, aircraft and vehicle concentrations, armoured formations, etc. The project will combine the German container weapon system (CWS) (**4449.311**) work that MBB has been carrying out since 1978 with the Matra company's Apache project to develop a multi-purpose modular weapon to succeed existing Durandal (**1999.303**) and Belouga (**3150.303**) weapons. It is envisaged that a modular family of ejectable-charge glider weapons will evolve capable of stand-off ranges of from ten to several tens of kilometres, suitable for dispensing a range of submunitions for attacking different types of target. The full range of submunitions available with the MW-1 system (**3517.311** in this section) ie KB44, MIFF, MUSA, MUSPA and STABO, can be deployed with the CWS.

The basic vehicle will probably be largely based on the MBB CWS, with a weight of about one ton and overall length of about 4 metres, with a 2 metre centre section designed to house and dispense the submunitions. The weapon is equipped with an inertial navigation system. Folding wings will deploy after release to give a high-wing monoplane configuration. The guidance package will also differ according to the mission.

Initially, a short wing-span glider dropped from high or low altitude, and with or without a short ascending ballistic phase, is likely to give operating ranges of 7 to 15 km. Later a folding wing glider giving ranges of 25 to 30 km may follow, with the eventual objective being a powered vehicle capable of release from very low altitudes, possibly equipped with terminal guidance, with a range of up to 50 km.

STATUS

Development project. First version planned to enter service in 1988.

CONTRACTORS

Messerschmitt-Bölkow-Blohm (MBB) GmbH, Defence Systems Group, Postfach 8011 49, 8000 Munich 80, Federal Republic of Germany.

Matra SA, 37 avenue Louis-Bréguet, 78410 Vélizy, France.

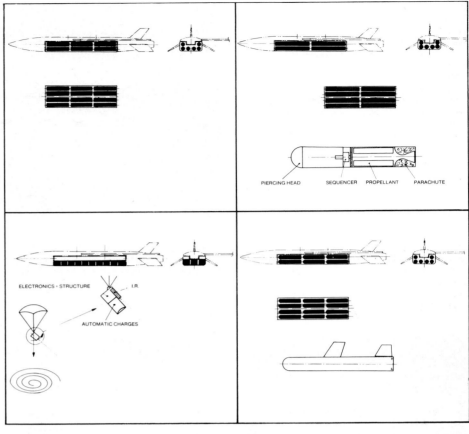

Examples of projected Apache/CWS configurations

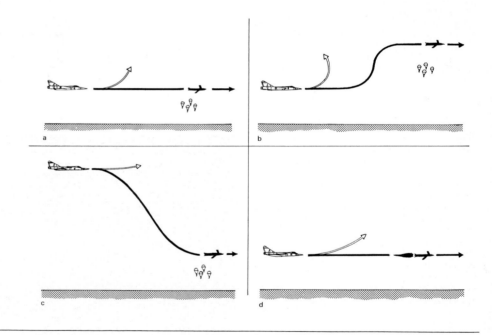

Four modes of operation with Apache/CWS vehicles:
(a) low-level launch (7-10 km range class) (b) low-level zoom launch (15-20 km class) (c) high-level launch (range speed/altitude dependent) (d) low-level launch with propulsion (range up to 50 km)

ISRAEL

4529.321
GABRIEL MK III AIR-LAUNCHED ANTI-SHIP MISSILE

An air-launched version of the successful Gabriel III anti-ship missile (**6019.221**) was revealed by the Israeli manufacturers in the last quarter of 1982 as the Gabriel Mk III A/S, together with photographs of test and development models on an Israeli Phantom aircraft. The weapon can also be carried by A-4 Skyhawk, Kfir C2, Sea Scan and other aircraft types, principally for use in anti-shipping roles.

The missile itself was derived directly from the ship-launched Gabriel mentioned above and the developers specified two configurations. That closest to the basic Mk III missile has different aerodynamic surfaces, more suitable for carriage and launching from high performance aircraft, but with the same

propulsion rocket motor as the ship-launched Gabriel III. This gives a range of approximately 40 km. The second derivative has the same aerodynamic modifications, but additionally uses the space normally occupied by the sustainer and booster motors in the surface-launched Gabriel to house a new sustainer motor which gives the Gabriel Mk III A/S a range of more than 60 km. The speed of the launch aircraft obviates the need for a missile booster motor.

The system provides all-weather, day/night, anti-ship capability against targets ranging from small fast patrol boats to destroyers and larger ships. The Gabriel Mk III A/S is an active homing, sea-skimming missile with 'fire-and-forget' and 'fire-and-update' operating modes. The I-band frequency agile radar seeker performs data processing and control

Gabriel Mk III A/S air-launched anti-ship missile

functions, providing good all-weather and ECCM performance. Inertial components, a radar altimeter and a digital processor are employed for missile guidance, and four tail control surfaces steer the missile and control its flight path. A high explosive warhead weighing 150 kg ensures maximum target damage.

The solid-propulsion motor provides over-the-horizon ranges at low level and the terminal attack altitude is set before take-off in accordance with the prevailing sea state to one of three values. Other characteristics of the missile are given below and can be gathered from the adjacent illustrations.

The complete system comprises one or more missiles (depending on the aircraft type, but typically two) and the missile fire control system (MFCS) fitted in the aircraft. In the case of a Gabriel Mk III A/S installation in a fighter aircraft the main MFCS elements include: a pilot fire control panel (PFCP), missile processing unit (MPU), power supply unit (PSU), and armament interface hardware (AIH). Built-in test facilities are incorporated and operate automatically as part of the firing sequence. The AIH units are incorporated in missile loading hardpoints and the other MFCS items are fitted in various fuselage locations.

OPERATION

As mentioned briefly above, there are two operating modes. 'Fire-and-forget' missiles, to accomplish their objective with high probability of target acquisition have to accommodate wide search areas. The actual size of the search area depends on the missile-target range at launch. To minimise the uncertainty of target position at the time of missile seeker activation, a 'fire-and-update' facility is provided in the Gabriel Mk III A/S system in addition to the basic 'fire-and-forget' mode. 'Fire-and-update' is used on larger maritime patrol aircraft as an optional mode of deployment, and relative missile/target locations are monitored, calculated and transmitted by the MFCS to the missile in flight. For this mode, in addition to the track-while-scan facilities of the aircraft's surveillance radar, a command link to the missile is added to the MFCS installation on the aircraft.

By this technique the seeker search zone in bearing and range is reduced considerably, so that the updating facility ensures that each missile is directed toward its designated target and not against 'potential targets' (which may or may not be significant) which may be close to the actual target area. After launch, data transfer between missile and launch aircraft are entirely automatic. Thus, 'fire-and-update' is an enhanced version of 'fire-and-forget' with the advantage of a reduced search zone and improved target lock-on.

In the vertical plane, at high altitudes, the missile pitch angle is controlled by a preset angle program for the descent to the midcourse phase. At low level the

Gabriel air-launched anti-ship missile mounted under wing of F-4 Phantom aircraft

missile guidance system switches to altitude command to maintain a midcourse cruise altitude of about 20 metres, before descending to 1·5, 2·5 or 4 metres for the terminal phase under pre-programmed control. In the horizontal plane, inertial guidance is used for the initial and midcourse phases for 'fire-and-forget' operation, and inertial is also used in the 'fire-and-update' mode for the midcourse phase. For both modes, seeker switch-on is under the control of pre-programmed logic in the computer. Target detection in the search area, lock-on and terminal homing are by active radar, operating in the horizontal plane only.

Target data (range/bearing) can be supplied from sensors aboard the launch aircraft, or from external sources. Altitude, speed and attitude data required for missile launch are provided from aircraft systems. The MFCS is operated by the pilot, using the PFCP, the other units (MPU, PSU and AIH) compute and supply the power and pre-launch data required by the missile. Missile release is activated by the pilot, by pressing a missile fire button on the control stick.

Missiles operated from fighter aircraft use the 'fire-and-forget' mode for one of the following procedures:
(1) radar-range and bearing launch (RBL)
(2) manual RBL
(3) bearing only launch (BOL)

Radar RBL For this technique, the aircraft radar detects potential targets and the range and azimuth data are transferred to the MPU by using the appropriate push-button on the PFCP. Target position, relative to the aircraft, is then calculated automatically and fed into the missile up to the moment of launch. The pilot receives an indication that the predetermined launch criteria have been met, by the flashing of a fire indicator light on the PFCP.

Manual RBL This method allows target location information to be fed to the missile by manual means, by either reading this information from aircraft navigation displays etc, and entering it manually on the PFCP, or receiving target data from an external source (eg a maritime patrol aircraft, ship, or other aircraft), entering this on the PFCP, while present aircraft position is updated by using an initiation point (entered via the PFCP before take-off). The MPU will continue to calculate the target location and transfer the required target range and bearing data to the missile. When the aircraft reaches the release range (as calculated by the MPU and indicated on the PFCP) the pilot can initiate missile firing.

Bearing Only Launch In this mode the pilot uses an estimated range together with a defined target bearing. Both estimated bearing and measured range are entered via the PFCP and transferred to the missile via the MPU. The estimated range is defined as Low, Medium, or High, corresponding to 20, 20 to 40, or 40+ km respectively. This operating mode is automatically selected if no other choice is made, as a fall-back mode, and in this case the aircraft is aligned to the target direction and for range the minimum weapon range is chosen.

CHARACTERISTICS

Length: 3·85 m
Diameter: 34 cm
Max span: 1·1 m
Launch weight: 600 kg
Warhead: HE 150 kg
Fuze: Impact, delayed action
Propulsion: Solid
Range: Over 60 km
Cruise speed: Mach 0·73
Launch altitude: 90 – 9000 m
Cruise altitude: 20 m
Terminal phase altitude: 1·5/2·5/4 m (pre-set)
Guidance: Inertial (plus optional command update) midcourse; active radar homing

STATUS
Entering production.

CONTRACTOR
Israel Aircraft Industries Ltd, Ben Gurion International Airport 70100, Israel.

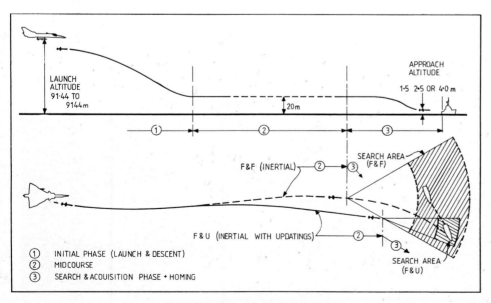

Gabriel launch and attack profile and plan

ITALY

1651.321
MARTE HELICOPTER ANTI-SHIP MISSILE SYSTEM

The purpose of the Marte system is the destruction or disabling of naval craft in 'all weather' conditions by means of Sea Killer missiles launched from helicopters in a stand-off position.

The helicopter-borne missile used in conjunction with the Marte System is the Sea Killer Mk 2 (20 km range with 70 kg warhead for the Marte version).

Installation of the Marte weapon system has been carried out on the Agusta/Sikorsky SH-3D helicopter, but the system is also suitable for installation on light shipborne helicopters, such as the Agusta AB 212.

In addition to the two Sea Killer missiles, the Marte Mk 1 equipment carried by the helicopter consists of an SMA MM/APQ-706 I-band radar (**3309.353**) for target search, acquisition and missile guidance; auxiliary launch and guidance equipment (ALGE) which includes the missile control console (MCC); command transmitter and antenna; optical tracker and 'joystick' control; and a pilot's display unit. An Elettronica ESM system is also normally fitted to provide passive detection and other electronic warfare facilities.

The APQ-706 radar provides two different operational modes, one for operations not involving the launching mission, and the other for missile guidance. There are back-to-back antennas and two transmitter/receivers with different output powers. The radar includes a data distribution and processing sub-system and a tactical PPI display with true and relative motion presentation and a micro-B display.

The MCC is part of the tactical display PPI console and contains the operational firing panel, synchro clock unit, launching computer and power supply. Using this and other ALGE items the crew are able to either perform or monitor pre-launch sequences, and radar or optical launches. Provisions are also made for elaboration of data. The pilot's display is used to select the optimum course during the launch approach. Radar and optical command guidance modes were available in the original Marte Mk 1 system, but the newer Mk 2 system (see below) employs a different technique incorporating active radar homing.

MARTE Mk 2

Essentially, the Mk 2 version of Marte consists of the Mk 1 missile to which an active radar homing head based on that of the Otomat anti-ship missile (**1336.221**) is added to replace the command guidance system employed in the Marte Mk 1 system. Thus the Mk 2 weapon becomes a 'fire-and-forget' missile using radar homing, leaving the launching helicopter free to take evasive manoeuvres immediately after weapon release. The complete Marte Mk 2 system consists of two or four missiles, a missile firing box, a pilot's display and a data processing unit (DPU), and the system is interfaced with the aircraft search radar, gyrocompass, altimeter and doppler navigator.

Marte Mk 2 anti-ship missile loaded on Italian naval helicopter

The Marte Mk 2 missile is a medium range sea-skimmer based on the Sea Killer Mk 2 (see above) which has been provided with a new guidance system. The missile employs a booster motor during the launching phase and a sustainer during the cruise. It is subsonic with an average speed of about 250 m/s, and the range is in excess of 20 km. The payload is an HE semi-armour piercing warhead weighing 70 kg which is of the fragmentation type, activated by an impact/influence fuze. In the latter of these two fuzing modes, activation is by means of a proximity sensor associated with the missile radio altimeter, which provides the necessary signal when over-flying the target.

Guidance in the vertical plane is by means of the CW radio altimeter which keeps the missile at a controlled constant height above sea level up to the moment of impact. This height selected between 3, 4 and 5 metres depends on sea state and target dimension. Guidance in the horizontal plane during the initial inertial phase of flight is gyroscopically controlled towards the target, following preset direction data already provided by the system DPU before launch. After the initial phase, the missile follows a ballistic flight trajectory for a period of time corresponding to the burn time of the boost motor (approximately 1·7 s), and after booster separation, the sustainer motor is ignited automatically and missile control is initiated (roll control, accelerometric autopilot insertion etc). Vertical plane (altimeter) guidance allows the missile to follow a preset descent path to the final cruise altitude. Gyroscopic horizontal guidance maintains the missile on an optimal trajectory for detecting and tracking the target in the final phase of the attack and this occupies approximately the first 14 km of flight.

The active radar homing head, after target acquisition, is responsible for control in the horizontal plane for the last 6 km or so until impact.

Other modes of operation can be employed according to tactical circumstances, for example: launch on ESM data (in radar silence conditions), or launch on radar data from another co-operating helicopter.

CHARACTERISTICS
Type: Marte Mk 2
Length: 4·48 m (with booster)
Wing span: 0·98 m
Diameter: 316 mm (max)
Launch weight: 330 kg
Propulsion: 2-stage solid, booster and sustainer
Range: 20 km
Average speed: High subsonic
Warhead: High explosive, semi-armour piercing
Fuze: Impact/proximity
Guidance: Gyro-pilot and radio altimeter, active radar homing
Aircraft launch speed: 50 – 100 knots
STATUS

The Italian Navy received the first operational prototype of the Marte system, in the SH-3D helicopter, at the end of 1977. Marte with Sea Killer Mk 2 entered production during 1978.

The Marte Mk 2 project was revealed in mid-1983 and on March 23, 1984 a 'fire-and-forget' test launch at the Salto di Quirra, Sardinia range, resulted in a successful hit on a ship target at a range of 19 km.
CONTRACTORS

Sistemi Elettronici SISTEL SpA, Via Tiburtina 1210, 00131 Rome, Italy.

OTO-Melara SpA, 15 via Valdilocchi 1, 19100 La Spezia, Italy.

JAPAN

1653.311
ASM-1 AIR-TO-SURFACE MISSILE (TYPE 80)

Under the designation ASM-1 the first Japanese tactical air-to-surface anti-ship missile has been formally introduced as the Type 80 for use with the Mitsubishi F-1 close-support aircraft. No official details have been obtained but provisional characteristics are: range approximately 50 km, speed about Mach 1. It has been officially stated that the ASM-1 will also be capable of ship or ground launching by the addition of a rocket booster motor. An inertial system is used for mid-course guidance and an active radar seeker for terminal homing.

JASDF ASM-1 air-to-surface missile on laboratory support trolley. The stencilled designation on the missile suggests US practice, in which case this is probably an early experimental round, denoted by the prefix letter 'X'

STATUS
In November 1973 Mitsubishi Heavy Industries Ltd was selected as prime contractor for the development of the ASM-1. Development was completed in 1979 and production commenced in 1980 to meet the requirements of the Japan Defence Agency only.

In mid-1981 a proposal to construct a new coastal defence system envisaged the use of a ground-launched version of the ASM-1 anti-ship missile which would have increased range to permit the system to be based inland but be able to reach targets 50 km off-shore.

CONTRACTOR
Mitsubishi Heavy Industries Ltd, 5-1 Marunouchi 2-chome, Chiyoda-ku, Tokyo 100, Japan.

NORWAY

3070.321
PENGUIN MK 3 AIR-TO-SURFACE MISSILE
The Penguin Mk 3 missile is a growth development of the existing Penguin Mk 2 surface-to-surface missile (1339.221). This missile is already in service with several navies as main armament on fast patrol boats. The Penguin Missile System Mk 2 has demonstrated its ability to successfully attack surface targets in both open and confined waters with minimum exposure of the launching platform. It is being developed for the Royal Norwegian Air Force. The missile fuselage is slightly longer at 3·176 metres and the span is reduced to 1 metre. Another part of the redesign of the weapon involved the canard control surfaces, and BAe Dynamics Group, Bracknell Division, is developing a new gas actuation system under contract to Kongsberg Våpenfabrikk.

Penguin Mk 3 missile is a 'fire-and-forget' weapon allowing aircraft break-off immediately after launch. Following the trajectory instructions the missile will find its way to the future target position using inertial navigation plus altimeter for reference. The missile can be launched over land and programmed to fly via a waypoint where it may descend to sea-skimming altitude and turn up to more than 90° on to its final heading. Once in the target area the target seeker is activated. When the target is acquired, the seeker locks on and guides the missile to target impact. The Penguin missile imposes very limited penalty on the aircraft performance due to its lightweight and minimal drag.

The Penguin Mk 3 missile system is designed to interface with existing aircraft fire control systems with minimum aircraft modification requirements. This is achieved by utilising an adaptor between the missile and the aircraft weapon station. The adaptor containing the retention and release mechanism for the missile, also provides space for the avionic components and attachment hardware for interface with the parent aircraft. This solution makes interface with various aircraft types possible with little or no impact on either missile or aircraft.

The air-launched version of Penguin is expected to have a useful range of at least 55 km. The modified Bullpup warhead has been retained. The missile is equipped with one solid-propellant rocket motor only. Using aircraft in the high subsonic speed range allows the booster motor to be omitted.

CHARACTERISTICS
Length: 3·176 m
Diameter: 28 cm
Wing span: 1 m

Penguin Mk 3 air-launched anti-ship missile mounted on an F-16 and showing the adaptor between the missile and the aircraft weapon station. This provides space for the avionic and other interface equipment

Weight: 360 kg
Warhead: Modified Bullpup, 120 kg
Propulsion: Solid sustainer, A/S Raufoss/Atlantic Research Corp
Range: 50 km +
Guidance: Programmed inertial, IR homing
OPERATION
Target designation to the missile can be accomplished using the launch aircraft radar, by placing a marker over the target on the display and pressing a button to insert this data into the missile. The same technique can also be employed to insert additional waypoints into the missile guidance system program. A similar technique can be used with the aircraft head-up display, in which case the pilot first acquires the target optically. This method can also be adopted using an aircraft gunsight in lieu of the head-up display. After release the Penguin missile follows an inertially guided flight path to either designated waypoints or to the target area. In the case of reaching a waypoint, the missile then changes

course and possible altitude, to fly on to the target area. On reaching the target area the IR seeker is switched on and the missile commences the terminal homing phase. This employs one of several alternative search patterns which can be selected by the pilot before the missile is launched.
STATUS
Studies for an air-launched version of Penguin were carried out in the mid-1970s, using an F-104 as the weapon platform. Following competitive evaluation, Penguin Mk 3 was chosen by the Norwegian authorities in 1979 to arm F-16 aircraft. The possibility of using it with the P-3 Orion maritime patrol aircraft has also been studied.

Full-scale development was decided on in 1980 and contracts were awarded in that year. First live air launches were planned for mid-1984. Entry into service is expected in 1987.
CONTRACTOR
A/S Kongsberg Våpenfabrikk, Post Box 25, 3601 Kongsberg, Norway.

SWEDEN

4188.311
RBS 70 HELICOPTER SELF-DEFENCE MISSILE
In mid-1981 Bofors revealed a new application of the successful RBS 70 portable air-defence missile system (2348.131), in which a helicopter mounted installation comprising two four-round launcher pods and a special version of the RBS 70 sight/guidance unit is carried to provide self-defence facilities for ground attack helicopters. The helicopter also has the usual anti-tank or reconnaissance sight, including a laser designator. The system has a 'dark firing' capability also if the sight includes a night vision facility.

Targets are initially acquired using the normal helicopter sight, and the gunner tracks the target.

Simultaneously the pilot is given both target indication and bearing and turns the helicopter towards the target. When the system is armed, the stabilised mirror in the control unit is slaved to the gunner's sight. On firing, the laser beam is activated and projected from the control unit mirror. After launch the missile is gathered into the guidance beam which it follows to the target. As the missile nears the target the laser in the gunner's sight is activated to illuminate the target. This locks the guidance beam onto the target, ensuring a hit. A more detailed outline of the RBS 70 guidance and control technique is given in the entry for the ground-mobile version of the system (3617.131), in the Mobile Surface-to-Air Guided Missile Systems section of this volume.

CHARACTERISTICS
Length: 1·32 m
Diameter: 12 cm
Wing span: 33 cm
Propulsion: Solid, booster plus sustainer
Weight: 137 kg (pod + 4 missiles); 54 kg (control unit); 15 kg (missile)
Guidance: Laser beam-rider
Range: 5 km
Speed: Supersonic
Time of flight: 8·5 s (to 3 km)
Reaction time: < 5 s
Reloading time: < 60 s (4 rounds)

STATUS
Development project. Flight trials were expected to begin in 1981 using a test installation in a Westland Lynx helicopter.
CONTRACTOR
AB Bofors, 691 80 Bofors, Sweden.

Bofors RBS 70 helicopter self-defence missile system installed on a Westland Lynx

3975.321

RBS 15F ANTI-SHIP MISSILE

RBS 15F is the designation of a new Swedish anti-ship missile for use by both Swedish aircraft and Swedish naval vessels. The latter role (**3976.221**) is being addressed first with deployment aboard 'Spica' class fast patrol boats envisaged by 1985.

The general configuration of the RBS 15F can be seen from the illustration, and the air intake for the turbojet engine will be noted beneath the missile body. An air-breathing propulsion system has been decided on to provide long range with a high subsonic speed at sea-skimming heights. In the surface-launched mode, the RBS 15F is assisted by two solid-propellant booster motors, but these will probably not be required in the air-launched mode.

The RBS 15F will have a launch and leave capability and will be provided with an ECM-resistant homing head developed by Philips Elektronikindustrier. This company is producing the system fire control

Drawing of RBS 15F anti-ship missile on new JAS multi-role combat aircraft

computer in addition to the frequency-agile radar seeker. The homing head is digitally programmable with selectable search patterns, target choice logic, and variable ECCM. The trajectory can be altered in accordance with operational demands. Prelaunch operations will be minimal in scope and all

calculations will be be performed automatically by an on-board computer. A radio altimeter will ensure safe missile cruise at low levels above the sea surface. A 'heavy' warhead is produced by Förenade Fabriksverken for the RBS 15F.
CHARACTERISTICS
Length: 4·35 m
Diameter: 50 cm
Wing span: 85 cm (folded); 1·4 m (unfolded)
Weight: 595 kg (without boosters)
Guidance: Programmed autopilot cruise with height hold, followed by active radar homing
Range: 150 km (estimated)
STATUS
On order for Swedish Air Force.
CONTRACTOR
Saab Bofors Missile Corporation AB, Stureplan 15, 111 45 Stockholm, Sweden.

1189.321

SAAB 04E AIR-TO-SURFACE MISSILE

This is an air-to-surface missile developed principally for anti-shipping strikes. The version in current Royal Swedish Air Force service is the Saab 04E which has been developed at Saab-Scania since 1968 under the SAF designation RB 04E. Principal characteristics are as follows: length 445 cm, body diameter 50 cm, wing span 2 m, and total weight about 600 kg. These figures are the same as for the earlier models but the RB 04E is stated to be technically very advanced. After launch, the missile acts independently of the launch aircraft and is automatically guided to a low-level altitude where target search and acquisition are performed at a high subsonic speed.

Guidance in the approach phase of an anti-shipping attack with the 04E is by means of a high-quality autopilot towards the target area. Precision terminal homing is by an advanced homing head, produced by Philips in Sweden.
DEVELOPMENT
The Robot RB 04 series of missiles was initiated in the 1960s and developed by the Missile Bureau of the Swedish Air Force Board (now the Defence Material Administration – Missiles Directorate). This organisation was responsible for the development of the 04C and 04D versions, but subsequent R & D has been performed by Saab-Scania.
STATUS
The RB 04E is intended for use with the AJ 37 Viggen all-weather attack aircraft, which can carry three missiles. The missile production schedule was

Saab 04E anti-shipping missile

completed in 1977 and the missile is now operational at Swedish AFBs.
CONTRACTOR
Saab Missiles AB, Linköping, Sweden.

1190.311
SAAB 05A AIR-TO-SURFACE MISSILE
The Saab 05A is a radio-command guided, manually controlled tactical air-to-surface missile. It is for use against both sea and land targets but may also be used in certain air-to-air roles. Principal characteristics are: wing span 80 cm, diameter 30 cm, length 360 cm, and total weight about 305 kg.

The airframe of the Saab 05A is made of conventional aircraft materials and consists of a pointed cylindrical body with long-chord cruciform wings and aft-mounted cruciform control surfaces. A liquid rocket motor is centrally located and the motor casing forms part of the outer skin and load-carrying

structure of the missile. The armament system is located in the nose and most of the control equipment at the rear of the missile. The VR 35 rocket motor is fitted with a tail-pipe which passes through the rear of the body. A pre-packaged liquid-propellant motor, supplied by Volvo Flygmotor AB, is used. The propellant tanks are placed around the centre of gravity to avoid CG-shift. Electrical power is supplied by a thermal battery. Before launching, some necessary electrical preheating of the missile is supplied from the aircraft. The hot gas for the control surface actuators is provided from a solid-propellant gas generator. An effective proximity-fuzed armament system is used.

The auxiliary airborne missile system equipment comprises a control stick, coding unit, transmitter, and antenna.

After launching, the missile is guided manually by the pilot who visually lines up the missile tracking flares and the target. The control signals are transmitted over the radio link with the transmitter in the aircraft and the receiver in the missile aft section. The guidance transfer function, from control stick force to the missile's transverse acceleration, is specially designed to provide a high degree of guiding accuracy for both small and large off-set angles. The command link is difficult to jam because both coded signals and a very high transmitter output are used. Guidance signals received by the missile are converted by an autopilot to control surface deflections through the medium of four hot gas actuators. The autopilot initially guides the missile into the pilot's field of view.
DEVELOPMENT
Developed by Saab-Scania on behalf of the Swedish Air Force, the system entered advanced testing in 1968-69. In June 1969, Saab was awarded a large contract by the Swedish Government for further development and production.
STATUS
The RB 05A is in service with the AJ 37 Viggen aircraft, and various versions of the Saab 105. Quantity production was completed in 1977 and the missile is operational with certain Swedish Air Force wings.
CONTRACTOR
Saab Missiles AB, Linköping, Sweden.

Saab 05A air-to-surface missiles carried by AJ 37 Viggen aircraft

UNION OF SOVIET SOCIALIST REPUBLICS

1148.311
KENNEL AIR-TO-SURFACE MISSILE (AS-1)
Kennel is the NATO code-name assigned to a Soviet stand-off air-to-surface weapon carried by Tu-16 (Badger) aircraft, one beneath each wing. According to recently released American DoD figures, the AS-1 is 8·44 metres in length, and the wing span is thus approximately 4·8 metres. It is powered by turbojet motor, and its general appearance is almost identical

with the Samlet coastal defence missile, and the two weapons may in fact be versions of the same missile. Estimated range is up to 50 nautical miles (90 km).

A probable operational role is anti-shipping strike missions, and external evidence of electronic equipment carried by Kennel missiles suggests that either beam-riding radar or radio command link guidance is used for the major portion of the trajectory, with either passive or active radar homing

for the terminal phase. The parent Badger aircraft are provided with at least two radars on the underside of the fuselage which could serve such a mode of operation.

In addition to the Soviet forces, the Badger/Kennel combination has been supplied to various client nations of the USSR. Although now obsolete, the AS-1 probably remains in service with some of these countries.

1150.311
KIPPER AIR-TO-SURFACE MISSILE (AS-2)
Kipper is the NATO code-name of another Soviet stand-off missile, which with Kangaroo (**1147.311**) was first seen in 1961. Official US information recently obtained indicates a length of 10 metres, which makes the AS-2 about two thirds the size of the AS-3, Kangaroo. Kipper, with a wing span of about 4·6 metres, also has an aircraft-like configuration with swept wing and tail surfaces. Propulsion is by a

turbojet motor suspended beneath the missile fuselage. Most Western estimates of Kipper's range give a value of between 180 and 210 km. In general appearance Kipper resembles the American Hound Dog, AGM-28 (**1093.111** 1980-81 and earlier editions), stand-off strategic bomber weapon (now out of service with US forces).

Recent analyses have deduced that Kipper flies to its target area under control of a programmed autopilot, to which there are command override

options available. Terminal homing is thought to rely on active radar homing, possibly with the alternative of passive radar guidance in some models. A high explosive warhead is carried.

Kipper is generally considered by observers in the West to be essentially an anti-shipping missile, but the possibility that it could be used for strategic bombing of land targets should not be completely discounted. The weapon is associated with the Tu-16 Badger-C bomber aircraft.

1147.311
KANGAROO AIR-TO-SURFACE MISSILE (AS-3)
Kangaroo is the NATO code-name assigned to the largest Soviet air-to-surface missile so far revealed. First shown in public in 1961, it is associated with the Tu-95 Bear bomber aircraft and is generally assumed to have retained operational status though its operational importance has probably declined significantly as newer weapons have been deployed.

As the photograph shows, the Kangaroo has the configuration of a conventional swept-wing fighter aircraft and similar dimensions, approximately 15 metres (US official sources quote 14·96 metres) in length and with a span of 9 metres. The propulsion used has not been confirmed but is probably a turbojet engine. There is no reliable information available as to the ratio in which the relatively large payload potential of Kangaroo is allocated between range and warhead, as is borne out by the wide variation in range estimates published by different specialist sources. These extend from 185 to 650 km, and it is likely that all these ranges are possible but without access to trustworthy data of the type and weight of warhead, guidance method(s), and performance, the true range figure must remain conjectural. (A recent American Senate report stated that a nuclear warhead could be carried over a distance of 350 nautical miles (648 km), which

Kangaroo stand-off missile beneath Tu-95 Bear bomber aircraft

corresponds to the higher of the two figures above.) A nuclear warhead payload of about 800 KT yield is assumed, and the maximum speed has been estimated at around Mach 2. Recently obtained information suggests that mid-course guidance is controlled by an autopilot with command override

facilities for navigational corrections, but no terminal homing facilities are thought to be carried.

In view of these considerations, the most likely role of the AS-3 Kangaroo is that of a medium/long-range stand-off strategic nuclear weapon for use against area targets, such as major cities or ports.

1151.311
KITCHEN AIR-TO-SURFACE MISSILE (AS-4)

Kitchen appears to be one of the most technically advanced Soviet air-to-surface missiles yet revealed. It has a fuselage of about 11·3 metres long to which are attached a pair of delta planform wings and a cruciform tail assembly. Propulsion is by rocket motor, liquid-fuel burning according to American sources, and inertial guidance is assumed for the mid-course phase of flight, after which an active radar homing provides for terminal guidance to the target. In 1981 the existence of a passive radar homing version was reported. American DoD sources have stated that a number of AS-4 versions are in use, of which two have been identified for strategic and naval roles, respectively. Alternative warheads exist for these roles, the former being nuclear with an estimated yield of about 200 KT, and the latter a conventional high-explosive payload for anti-ship or tactical missiles. Estimates of range vary widely from 300 to 800 km, and the aerodynamic features of Kitchen suggest a high cruising speed. A UK MoD statement in early 1976 gave a maximum range of 298 km but this is thought to have been an underestimate.

First seen carried by the Tu-22 Blinder, the AS-4 has since been reported as arming the Tu-95 Bear, and the Tu-26 Backfire B variable-geometry aircraft. On the Bear, the AS-4 is carried beneath the aircraft wings, and on the Tu-22 Blinder and Tu-26 Backfire in a semi-recessed position on the underside of the fuselage.

AS-4 Kitchen is carried in a semi-recessed position under the fuselage of Backfire strategic aircraft

1149.311
KELT AIR-TO-SURFACE MISSILE (AS-5)

Kelt is the NATO code-name of a Soviet air-to-surface weapon, first seen on a Tu-16 Badger bomber aircraft. It has superficial but pronounced similarities with the Kennel (**1148.311**) which also is used with the Badger, and with the Styx shipborne surface-to-surface missile (**1155.221**). A length of 8·59 metres has been officially reported for Kelt in an American government publication, with wing span about 4·3 metres. The fuselage centre-body and wings of Kelt appear to be the same or very similar to those of Kennel, while the nose section (and presumably the guidance system it carries) of Styx is employed. A rocket propulsion motor is used and the tail control surface arrangements of Kelt differ from those of both Styx and Kennel. Western estimates of range vary between 160 km and more than 320 km, but a British MoD report issued in April 1976 quoted the former figure as maximum range for the AS-5 (Kelt).

Propulsion is by a single-stage liquid-fuelled rocket motor, and guidance arrangements include an (inertial) autopilot for the mid-course phase of flight followed by active radar homing for the terminal phase. A passive radar, anti-radiation missile version of Kelt has been reported.

Applications of the AS-5, Kelt are thought to be confined to service with Soviet Naval Air Forces in anti-ship and other tactical roles.

AS-5 Kelt air-to-surface missile loaded on to underwing pylon of Egyptian Air Force Tu-16 Badger aircraft

3633.311
KINGFISH AIR-TO-SURFACE MISSILE (AS-6)

Kingfish, AS-6 in the American numerical sequence, is a high performance air-to-surface missile carried by Tu-16 Badger aircraft of the Soviet Naval Air Forces, and was also thought to arm the Tu-26 Backfire variable geometry aircraft on occasion, although it is more likely to have been mistaken for the AS-4, Kitchen (**1151.311**). The configuration is similar to that of the AS-4 (although it is impossible to say if this indicates either a line of development, or even a 'family' likeness) with a cylindrical fuselage supported by short-span, long-chord stub wings of delta planform. Provisional dimensions are: length 10·5 metres and maximum span 2·5 metres. Liquid propulsion has been assumed, and estimated performance gives a range of about 200 km and a maximum speed of Mach 3. US official sources have confirmed that the Kingfish is capable of supersonic flight.

The same report also revealed that one role for this missile is anti-shipping missions in which a high-altitude supersonic cruise approach trajectory is

AS-6 Kingfish missiles carried beneath the wing of a Soviet Tu-16 Badger (JASDF)

followed by a diving attack onto the target. Another reliable source has quoted a release altitude of 11 000 metres, which is followed by a climb to a cruise height of up to 18 000 metres. Inertial mid-course guidance is employed with an active radar terminal homing phase although it is possible that a passive radar homing variant exists to provide anti-radiation missile (ARM) capabilities. More recent information has confirmed use of the AS-6 Kingfish with aircraft of the Soviet Naval Air Force, and there is said to be the option of conventional HE or nuclear warheads. The latter is reported to have a yield of some 350 KT.

3634.311
KERRY AIR-TO-SURFACE MISSILE (AS-7)
Kerry is the NATO reporting name of the air-to-surface missile numbered AS-7 in the US series. It is known to be deployed on the Su-24 Fencer variable geometry fighter-bomber aircraft, and is thought to arm other types of Soviet close support aricraft also, such as Fitter or the Forger naval VTOL machine. A solid propellant rocket motor is believed to power the AS-7, carrying an HE warhead estimated to weigh about 100 kg. Precise details of the AS-7 configuration are still awaited but early information suggests a relatively large diameter weapon with large cruciform wing surfaces set well back on the missile body, with four small canard control surfaces. Initial estimates were of a heavy missile possibly weighing as much as 1200 kg, but later assessments revised this to between 300 and 400 kg and the latter figures appear more likely. It is credited with a range of about 10 km, and radio command guidance is thought to be employed, although this has not been confirmed.

Further analysis must await more evidence, either in the form of further leaks of official intelligence reports or photographic data issued by the Soviet authorities themselves.

Yak-36 Forger carrier aircraft armament includes AS-7 Kerry tactical air-to-surface missiles

3206.311
NEW SOVIET AIR-TO-SURFACE MISSILES
Official hints and leaks of less certain origin leave little doubt that successors to the above well-known (by name, if not in detail) Soviet air-to-surface missiles are on the way, and in some instances they may well be in service already. Of the established and well-known Soviet air-launched cruise missiles described in entries above, the AS-5 (Kelt) is the most widely deployed of these missiles and is fitted on the Tu-16 (Badger), while the AS-4 (Kitchen) is fitted on Tu-95 (Bear) and Tu-22 (Blinder) bombers.

The designation **AS-9** is thought to apply to an anti-radiation missile arming the SU-19 Fencer attack aircraft although other sources attribute an anti-ship role to this weapon. Estimated range is about 80 to 90 km, and official US reports claim that this weapon is at the development stage, in which case the designation applied is **AS-X-9**. The designation **AS-X-10** has been assigned provisionally to what is thought to be a Mach 0·8 laser-guided air-to-surface missile reported as being carried by MiG-27, Su-17 and Su-19 aircraft. It is estimated to be about 3 metres long and to have a range of about 10 km, using a solid-propellant rocket motor. But, again different sources suggest an anti-radiation role for the AS-10 and indicate a range of up to 40 km, possibly being deployed on the Su-24 Fencer aircraft.

Several other new air-to-surface missiles are rumoured to be under development by the Soviet Union, and the main features attributed to three of them are as follows: the first is an approximate Soviet equivalent to the US Maverick, using electro-optical guidance with a command link, and with a probable maximum range of about 40 km (this has been provisionally designated **AS-X-11** by some sources); another is a possible replacement for the AS-4 Kitchen with a speed of Mach 3·5 and a maximum range of up to 800 km; and the last is thought to be roughly equivalent to the American air launched cruise missile (ALCM) using an air-breathing turbojet with a maximum range of up to 1200 km. In mid-1981, development of a 500 kg laser-guided bomb was also reported, but no details have emerged.

Little has been added to the above by official sources since publication of the previous edition, other than the appearance of a new US designation **AS-X-15,** which is stated to refer to a new cruise missile belived by American officials to be under development for deployment on Soviet Bear H aircraft. It has been suggested that this new air-launched weapon might be a derivative version of a new small naval cruise missile that is so far only known by its US designation, SS-NX-21. It is further suggested that there may be a land-based model of the same weapon, thereby putting it broadly into a similar category to the US BGM-109 Tomahawk cruise missile which is capable of launch from aircraft, ships, submarines or ground bases.

The US reference to an AS-X-15 unfortunately still leaves the question of what weapons the assignments AS-12, AS-13 and AS-14 apply to. These numbers have presumably been assigned to new airborne weapons that have been detected by the US intelligence organisations, but they are as yet either too little known to justify public disclosure or the US authorities do not yet wish to reveal the extent of their knowledge of the new systems.

4556.311
SOVIET AIR-LAUNCHED ANTI-TANK MISSILES
As numerous Western air forces, the Soviet Union and several client states have adopted the practice of deploying anti-tank guided missiles on certain types of helicopter for battlefield operations and ground attack missions. The AT-2 Swatter (**2985.111**) is operational in its manually-guided B version with

Loading Soviet AT-3 Sagger anti-tank missile on Yugoslav Gazelle helicopter

Gazelle military helicopters operated by Yugoslavia are equipped to carry Soviet AT-3 Sagger anti-tank missiles. Note optical sight in cockpit roof to aid weapon guidance

Hind A and D helicopters and is in the process of being replaced with the later Swatter B version with semi-automatic command-to-line-of-sight guidance missiles. Users of Swatter (in addition to the USSR) include Hungary, Iraq, Libya and Syria. The Hind E ground attack helicopter has been noted equipped with AT-6 Spiral (**3639.111**) launch tubes, two being carried on the aircraft's stub wings. The frequently sighted AT-3 Sagger (**2950.111**) can be deployed on the Soviet Hoplite armed helicopter and is operated on Yugoslav Gazelle military helicopters. In the latter installation the gunner/co-pilot occupying the left-hand seat is provided with a roof sight to assist in missile guidance.

UNITED KINGDOM

4528.311
ALARM AIR-TO-SURFACE MISSILE

ALARM is the air-launched anti-radar missile being developed by British Aerospace (BAe) Dynamics Group and Marconi for the RAF to enable it to meet an essential requirement to provide a deep penetration strike capability. ALARM is designed to counter enemy surface-to-air gun and missile defences by destroying their associated radars. Work on the Air Staff Target (AST 1228) has been proceeding for some time and culminated in a fixed price bid for development and production which was submitted to the UK MoD early in December 1982. Two competitive solutions were considered and ALARM selected in July 1983. The alternative was procurement of the American AGM-88A, HARM (**1769.311**) with some licence production in the UK.

BAe Dynamics Group in association with Marconi Space and Defence Systems (MSDS) and other sub-contractors are working on the design and development of the system and have produced sub-systems which are undergoing ground tests and trials.

Other significant contributors are Thorn EMI Electronics who won a contract worth more than £4 million for the development and supply of the proximity fuze, and MBB of the Federal Republic of Germany who are stated to be involved in the missile's warhead.

The fuze being developed by Thorn EMI will be based on the company's laser experience and at least two years private-venture research had already been completed before the contract award in May 1984. The new generation fuze will provide autonomous classification of targets and precise trigger point selection.

ALARM is a microprocessor-based software-controlled missile which does not require complex aircraft systems or interfaces, and it can be updated to meet changing threats and scenarios by software changes alone. The Marconi anti-radar seeker exploits UK investment in seeker technology and EW.

The complete seeker head will be programmable, enabling operators of the ALARM system to react autonomously and rapidly to threat changes as they arise. This facility derives from the employment at the core of the seeker receiver of a complex digital processor that incorporates modern LSI techniques and new microwave IC materials. All software is produced in house by MSDS. The seeker package can be programmed before a mission with a list of target types and priorities. Re-programming during flight is also possible. The associated broadband microwave receiver is the first in the UK to utilise novel RF processing techniques, similar to those employed in EW radar homing and warning receivers.

The weight of ALARM is half that of the competing HARM's 354 kg which will allow up to four ALARM missiles to be carried by the Tornado IDS in addition

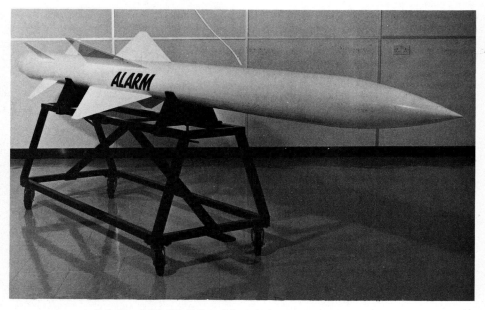

Full-size model of the British air-launched anti-radar missile (ALARM)

to its normal attack payload. ALARM does not require dedicated aircraft, and has been designed from the outset with a high degree of autonomy. It makes small demands on the carrying aircraft and does not require complex and therefore costly aircraft modification or interfaces. It can also be fitted to fixed-wing aircraft down to BAe Hawk size as well as large aircraft and helicopters.

Two operating modes have been reported: a direct fire mode where the ALARM seeker locks onto an enemy radar and is released from the aircraft immediately; and a so-called parachute mode. No details of the latter have been disclosed officially, but it has been suggested that this mode could be employed to counter enemy tactics involving temporary shut-down of the radar target. The ALARM missile would be released and allowed to drift down in the target area, remaining in the target area after the aircraft which dropped it has passed. When the subject radar transmits again, this would trigger the ALARM to re-activate its homing head and ignite the propulsion motor. There have been no details of the seeker cleared for publication but it is assumed to be a broad-band device and probably employed a fixed antenna.

STATUS

A detailed joint feasibility study by BAe and MSDS was completed in 1982 and a submission was made to the UK MoD after certain company-funded development work had been carried out. The choice

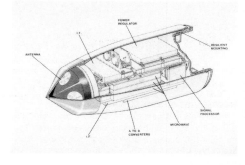

Schematic diagram of Marconi seeker head for ALARM

between ALARM and HARM procurement to meet AST 1228 was announced in July 1983 and a contract formally signed the following month. A UK requirement for about 750 missiles has been quoted with entry into RAF service some time in 1987.
CONTRACTORS
Marconi Space and Defence Systems Ltd, Chelmsford, Essex CM1 3BN, England.

British Aerospace, Dynamics Group, Hatfield Division, Manor Road, Hatfield, Hertfordshire AL10 9LL, England.

1530.321
SEA SKUA HELICOPTER AIR-TO-SURFACE MISSILE

Sea Skua is an all-weather, helicopter-launched, sea-skimming anti-ship guided weapon system which is in operational use with the RN. Primarily designed for fitment to the naval variant of the Westland Lynx helicopter fitted with the Ferranti Seaspray radar, it will be the RN's principal air-to-surface light strike weapon for use against a variety of targets ranging from missile-firing fast patrol boats to coastal escorts, frigates and destroyers. Sea Skua is also suitable for fitting on other types of helicopter and fixed wing aircraft. Studies have also been carried out on a ship-launched version and this is described in entry **4553.221**.

The helicopter/Sea Skua combination provides a cost-effective, rapid-reaction, surface attack capability up to, and well beyond, the radar horizon of the parent ship which retains the option of remaining passive and therefore undetected. Such a combination represents a valuable complement to long-range ship-to-ship missiles.

The missile is light enough to permit a four-Sea Skua fit on a small helicopter. Solid-propellant boost and sustainer motors are used to give the missile a range in excess of 15 km, sufficient to provide a good 'stand-off' capability for the helicopter with consequent protection from counter attack. To commence an engagement the helicopter would close the target to enable its radar to lock on and automatically track. While in this automatic tracking mode, the radar will illuminate the target with radio frequency energy, which, when reflected, provides the source onto which the Sea Skua semi-active radar homing head locks. On release from the helicopter

the missile drops for a short distance under autopilot control maintaining attitude angle stabilisation in roll, pitch and yaw before the rocket motors are ignited. The Sea Skua missile then descends in stages, under control of a radio altimeter, to one of four terminal sea-skimming heights selected by the pilot prior to missile release, depending on the sea state or size of target. The missile, guided by the homing head in azimuth will fly on a proportional navigational course to hit the target. The warhead is designed to explode within the target to give high lethality. Sea Skua missiles can be fired in rapid succession if required and the helicopter is free to manoeuvre after the last missile release within the limits required to maintain target illumination.

System control equipment associated with armed release of the missiles has been designed for rapid removal and replacement, thereby reducing to a minimum any weight penalty to the helicopter when it is not required to operate in the strike role. The missile can be treated as a round of ammunition as no 'onboard' testing is required. It is delivered in a wheeled 'palletrolley' fitted with a shock absorbing system suitable for shipborne magazine stowage.

CHARACTERISTICS

Length: 2·5 m
Diameter: 28 cm (max)
Span: 72 cm (max)
Weight: 145 kg
Range: >15 km
Warhead: HE 20 kg (estimated)

STATUS

In June 1981, a multi-million pound contract for Sea Skua production for the RN was announced, and it was confirmed that initial deliveries were already being made. In May 1982 the weapon scored its first operational successes in the fighting to regain the Falkland Islands, despite not having completed the RN's formal acceptance procedure.

CONTRACTORS

Prime contractor: British Aerospace, Dynamics Group, Hatfield Division, Manor Road, Hatfield, Hertfordshire AL10 9LL, England.

Homing head: Marconi Space and Defence Systems Ltd, The Grove, Warren Lane, Stanmore, Middlesex HA7 4LY, England.

Royal Navy Lynx helicopter armed with Sea Skua anti-ship missiles

---

3630.321

SEA EAGLE AIR-TO-SURFACE MISSILE

The Sea Eagle (formerly P3T) missile is described by its originators as a second generation air-launched sea-skimming anti-ship missile. It is intended as a successor to Martel and will arm Buccaneer and Sea Harrier aircraft employed by UK forces for anti-shipping operations. It may later arm RAF Tornado GR1 aircraft. A zero speed launch version for use with helicopters or as a ship-launched weapon has also been developed (**4447.221**). Active radar guidance is used and the Sea Eagle is powered by a Microturbo TRI 60 gas turbine engine which is expected to give the missile a range of about 100 km. A new multi-role radar homing head has been developed by Marconi Space and Defence Systems Ltd, specially for use against ship targets and incorporating a digital computer that provides for over-the-horizon capability against multiple targets. In addition, this fully active seeker's computer serves as the central processor for controlling pre-launch information, management of the transmit and receive functions, target detection, acquisition and tracking. This enables the Sea Eagle to engage a single designated target within a convoy of other, but potentially less valuable, targets. Certain ECCM functions are also under the control of the missile computer.

Flight trajectories of the Sea Eagle will also be under computer control, the computer's re-programming facility being of value in this regard, and possible flight paths will include a variety of sea-skimming modes of cruise, acquisition, and terminal guidance modes. A digital inertial autopilot/navigation system is employed, with a radar altimeter for height data. Sperry Gyroscope is under contract for the gyroscopic attitude sensor for Sea Eagle and this consists of a twin gyro unit that provides roll, pitch and azimuth information to the missile control computer. The radar altimeter was developed by the Royal Signals and Radar Establishment and Plessey, and will be produced by the latter. The Ferranti F100-L microprocessor is used in the Sea Eagle to carry out the digital data processing and control functions mentioned above.

The turbine used to power the Sea Eagle is the French Microturbo TRI 60 turbojet which has a thrust of 3 kN at 28 500 rpm. The Sea Eagle airframe is probably very similar to that of the Martel (**1022.311**), and the same warhead developed by the Royal Ordnance Factories may well be retained. The zero speed launch and ship-launched versions employ a slightly modified Sea Eagle missile with two strap-on booster rockets.

CHARACTERISTICS

Length: 4·1 m
Wingspan: 120 cm
Diameter: 40 cm
Speed: High subsonic
Range: Up to 100 km (provisional)
Guidance: Inertial navigation plus active radar homing
Propulsion: Microturbo TRI 60 turbojet

STATUS

Development was started in 1979. Flight tests began in 1981, and the first control and propulsion test firing was completed successfully in April 1981. Planned for use with Tornado, Buccaneer, and Sea Harrier aircraft, it may also be deployed with the Tornado GR1. The go-ahead for full production was announced on 10 February 1982.

A salvo firing of two missiles from a Buccaneer took place successfully in October 1982 at a range of more than 50 km. In July 1983 an Indian Navy contract estimated at about £200 million was announced for the supply of 12 Mk 42B Sea King helicopters (with an option on eight more) which will have Sea Eagle missiles as their armament.

Deliveries of evaluation missiles for trials by No 31 Joint Service Trails Unit from Buccaneer and Sea Harriers began in early 1984. Sea Eagle will enter service on these two aircraft types with the RAF and RN in the mid-1980s. The missile has also been flown successfully on the BAe Hawk.

CONTRACTOR

British Aerospace, Dynamics Group, Stevenage, Hertfordshire, England.

Sea Harrier with two Sea Eagle anti-ship missiles leaves ski-jump ramp at RNAS Yeovilton during trials

UNITED STATES OF AMERICA

1766.311
ALCM (AGM-86) AIR-LAUNCHED CRUISE MISSILE

The ALCM is the result of an initiative by the US Air Force to provide an air-launched strategic weapon for deployment on the B-52 bomber, and possibly other types.

Current development is concentrated upon the AGM-86B ALCM. This is larger than the original AGM-86A which was designed to be compatible with the SRAM (**1107.311**) rotary launcher. Dimensions were increased and a larger fuel tank was fitted to produce the AGM-86B, and in addition the wing sweep angle was changed from 35 to 25°. For internal stowage, all flying and control surfaces are folded or retracted, being deployed automatically after release from the aircraft. Dimensions in flying configuration are: length 6·3 metres, span 3·65 metres, and weight about 1270 kg. The engine is Williams International Corporation F107-WR-101 turbofan developing about 600 lb (272 kg) of thrust for a weight of 66 kg. Operating speed is 'high subsonic'. An internal rotary launch rack enables eight long-range ALCMs to be launched in rapid succession. The design is intended for high-speed cruise flight at very low altitudes for distances of up to 2500 km, and to aid penetration of opposing defences a very low radar cross section has been achieved.

A W-80-1 nuclear warhead of the type carried by the follow-on SRAM B (**1107.311**) short range attack missile is used. The missile has an inertial navigation system which is updated by using a map-matching position updating technique called TERCOM (Terrain Contour Matching). A terrain-following system is also incorporated which allows low-level flight. The complete navigation package is integrated by the Boeing Aerospace Company into the ACLM. Boeing also provides the complete software for the system. The navigation hardware consists of a gimballed inertial platform and digital computer, both provided by Litton Industries, a radar altimeter, provided by Honeywell or Kollsman; a pitotstatic probe, air data computer and temperature probe provided by Rosemount.

The terrain correlation updates are provided by software which processes the outputs of the air data system, radar altimeter, and the inertial platform and compares the resultant sampled terrain elevation data to a stored terrain elevation map. The correlation of the elevation profile data with the reference map provides the missile with an axis position update. The terrain correlation updates provide a very accurate position update to the missile. The inertial navigation accuracy is further improved by processing the position update through a Kalman filter in the software which refines the platform alignment, its

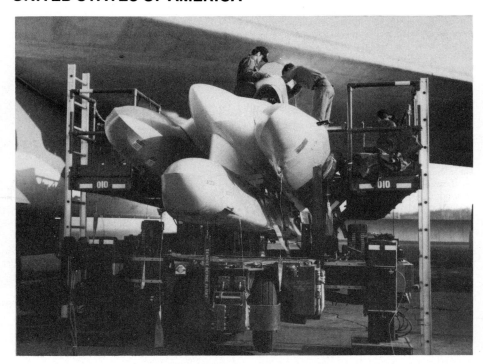

B-52 G at Griffiss AFB, New York being loaded with pylon carrying six ALCMs by airman of SAC's 416 Bombardment Wing

velocity, and its instrument error sources. The initial alignment of the platform is done by an in-air Kalman filter transfer alignment to the B-52 OAS (Offensive Avionics System).

The ALCM terrain-following system is a hybrid analogue/digital system. It uses a rate gyro and body accelerometer package supplied by Northrop and a Boeing-supplied electronics package. The principal input to the terrain-following system is the radar altimeter but the air data system and inertial system also provide inputs.

STATUS

The first powered ALCM flight was made from a B-52G release over the White Sands Missile Range in March 1976. In March 1980 the Boeing ALCM was selected for deployment with the US Air Force.

The first squadron became operational in December 1982, each aircraft carrying 12 ALCMs.

By early 1984 there were three operational squadrons equipped with cruise missiles, and since the December 1982 entry into service there had been 12 ALCM flight tests – nine successes and three partial successes. By the end of 1984 it was planned

that 90 B-52s would be operational with the ALCM, and in 1985 a start was to be made on modification of B-52H aircraft to carry the ALCM.

In July 1982, the US Air Force concluded an assessment of its requirements for a new generation cruise missile, and the President approved development and deployment of an advanced cruise missile (ACM) in August 1982. This was followed by a competition between Boeing, Lockheed and General Dynamics that ended in April 1983 when the last of these companies was selected to develop the ACM.

The fiscal year 1985 Report by the US Secretary of Defence stated that development of the ACM would incorporate the so-called 'stealth' technology to defeat enemy radar and other sensors, and would have a longer stand-off range than the ALCM.

ALCM funding in the 1985 Budget allocated sums of $28 million for development and $80·5 million for production, respectively.

CONTRACTOR

Boeing Aerospace Company, PO Box 3999, Seattle, Washington 98124, USA.

1280.311
BULLPUP (AGM-12) AIR-TO-SURFACE TACTICAL MISSILE

The Bullpup AGM-12 series of missiles relates to a now largely obsolete range of air launched missiles for attacking tactical surface targets on land or sea. Guidance is by radio command link from the launching aircraft, with optical tracking to target, aided by flares attached to the missile.

Bullpup model designations run from AGM-12A to AGM-12E, and within this group quite considerable variations of payload (and hence dimensions) exist. There are also Bullpup trainer versions carrying ATM-12 designations. These are essentially inert rounds for pilot training.

The several variants of Bullpup carry either 250 lb (113·4 kg) or 1000 lb (453·6 kg) conventional high

explosive warheads, or a nuclear warhead. Maximum speed is variously quoted by the manufacturers and the US Air Force as over Mach 2, Mach 1·8, and 1400 mph. Range quotations also vary but are approximately 11 and 17 km for the small and large versions, respectively.

Bullpup is launched on the appropriate line of sight from the aircraft to the target, and is then visually tracked by the pilot who uses a radio-command link to direct the missile to impact. Two high-intensity flares in the aft end of the missile aid tracking.

STATUS

Bullpup became operational in 1959 and has been used by the US Navy, US Air Force, and US Marine Corps, and numerous NATO services although it is no longer in the active inventory of any US service at present.

Foreign users include the Royal Navy which selected the AGM-12B as standard strike armament for the Buccaneer aircraft. This version of Bullpup has been manufactured under licence in Europe for the armed forces of Denmark, Norway, Turkey, and the UK by a consortium headed by Kongsberg Våpenfabrikk. American production has ceased and has probably been discontinued elsewhere.

CONTRACTORS

Martin Marietta Orlando Aerospace, PO Box 5837, Orlando, Florida 32805, USA.

Maxson Electronics Corporation, Sunrise Highway, Great River, Long Island, New York 11739, USA.

Prime contractor for European consortium: A/S Kongsberg Våpenfabrikk, Norway.

1129.311
WALLEYE (AGM-62A) AIR-TO-SURFACE MISSILE

The Walleye weapons family was one of the forerunners of the current (extensive) range of 'smart' air-to-surface munitions. It is believed to be now obsolete or obsolescent but is described briefly in the following paragraphs until its preceise operational status is confirmed. Originally the range comprised three models of unpowered, guided bombs,

designated Walleye Mks I and II and Extended Range, Data Link Walleye. Walleye I has the following main characteristics: length 344 cm, diameter 38·1 cm, wing span 114 cm, weight 499 kg, conventional Mk I Mod 0 850 lb (385 kg) high explosive warhead. There is also a Mk 1 Walleye model equipped with a W-72 nuclear warhead.

Walleye II, which has the US Navy designation Guided Weapon Mk 5, Mod 4, is a much larger missile

than the AGM-62A Walleye. Length of Walleye II is 404 cm, body diameter 45·7 cm, and weight 1061 kg. A warhead in the 2000 lb (907 kg) class is carried, and the weapon was designed for the destruction of large semi-hard targets such as bridges, air base facilities, and ships.

The latest version is Extended Range, Data Link Walleye II (ER/DL WE II) which has the US Navy designation Mk 13 Mod 0. This is essentially a

Walleye II fitted with larger wings to extend the glide range and data link equipment.

OPERATION

A gyro-stabilised TV camera in the nose of the weapon is aligned with the target prior to launch by the pilot. He is aided in this by a CRT monitor screen, and for target acquisition the fire control radar may be used.

When the target has been identified by the pilot, the missile TV camera is locked on and after release the missile guidance and control system uses signals from the TV head to produce control surface movements to direct the bomb to the target. The aircraft is thus free to quit the area immediately after releasing the weapon.

STATUS

Thought to be obsolete or obsolescent.

CONTRACTORS

Martin Marietta Orlando Aerospace, PO Box 5837, Orlando, Florida 32805, USA.

Hughes Aircraft Company, Missile Division, Canoga Park, California, USA.

1107.311
SRAM (AGM-69A) SHORT RANGE ATTACK MISSILE

The Short Range Attack Missile (SRAM) is a supersonic air-to-surface nuclear weapon carried by B-52 G/H and FB-111A bombers of the US Air Force. The former type of aircraft can carry up to 20 missiles, 12 on wing pylons and eight internally, and the FB-111A is able to load two missiles under each wing with two more in the weapons bay.

SRAM is designed to attack and neutralise enemy terminal defences, particularly the Sqviet surface-to-air missile (SAM) defences. The weapon is capable of penetrating terminal defences and striking mission targets while the bombers stand off outside the range of enemy defences. It can also attack enemy SAM and anti-aircraft sites so that bombers can strike primary targets with other SRAM or conventional bombs.

The missile is 425 cm in length, 45 cm in diameter and weighs approximately 1000 kg. Range varies between 60 and 160 km, depending upon the flight profile employed, and a speed in excess of Mach 3 has been quoted.

The W-69 nuclear warhead carried is stated to be of the same size as that of the Minuteman 3 but later models are believed to be armed with W-80 warheads.

A KT-76 inertial guidance system is used, and the propulsion system is a two-stage solid rocket motor developed by Lockheed. The first stage provides initial acceleration; the second stage is activated as the missile approaches its target. Trajectory can be changed in mid-flight, and the missile can be launched to hit targets in any direction regardless of the bomber's flight path. The missile can be launched from either a high or low attack mode. The high mode is said to yield the greatest range but also increases the missile's vulnerability to enemy defences.

Four basic modes of flight trajectory can be employed: semi-ballistic, altimeter-controlled terrain following, pull-up from behind radar screening terrain followed by inertial, and a combination of inertial and terrain following. Lateral deviations in flight profile can also be programmed.

STATUS

The first production SRAM was delivered to the US Air Force in March 1972. The 750th production missile was delivered in February 1974, and a total of 1500 SRAMs have been deployed with Strategic Air Command units.

The US Air Force fiscal year 1985 report to Congress stated that the Air Force had a need to supplement and eventually replace the ageing SRAM. There was also a need for more modern warhead safety, and accordingly development of an Advanced Air-to-Surface Missile (AASM) is planned, with a funding of $55 million requested.

CONTRACTORS

Main contractor: Boeing Aerospace Company, PO Box 3999, Seattle, Washington 98124, USA.

Inertial guidance sub-system (inertial platform, guidance and control electronics, guidance computer, power conditioner, rate gyros): Kearfott Division, The Singer Company, 1150 McBride Avenue, Little Falls, New Jersey 07424, USA.

Aircraft pre-launch computers, B-52, FB-111: Rockwell International Corporation, Autonetics Strategic Systems Division.

Inertial measurement unit B-52: Litton Industries, Guidance and Controls Division.

Missile computer: Delco Electronics.

Radar receivers/transmitter: Stewart-Warner, Electronics Division.

Strategic Air Command B-52 bombers can carry 20 AGM-69 SRAMs, eight internally and another 12 on the wings

---

1102.311
SHRIKE (AGM-45A) AIR-TO-SURFACE MISSILE

This is an anti-radiation air-to-surface missile for the destruction of ground defensive radar installations. Official details include: length 304·8 cm, diameter 20 cm, wing span 91·4 cm, weight 177 kg, solid-propellant rocket motor. Estimated speed and range are: Mach 2 and 12 to 16 km. A 66 kg high-explosive fragmentation warhead is carried.

OPERATION

Initial warning of illumination of Shrike-carrying aircraft by ground defence radars is obtained from ESM/ECM receivers installed in the aircraft. When within appropriate range, the Shrike sensor heads are switched on and the missiles fired when target acquisition has been achieved. After release, the missile radar receiver continuously senses the direction of arrival of radar radiation from the target and generates command signals for the missile guidance system to home it on to the radar.

Shrike guidance heads have been developed that are effective against enemy early warning, ground control intercept, and SAM guidance radars, each of which covers a different frequency range. The frequency range of a particular Shrike version is denoted by a suffix number to the AGM-45A designation, and there are at least 13 of these. Based on the specific radar to be attacked, the operational commander selects the most appropriate weapon option. The US Air Force use Shrike on modified F-105 and F-4 aircraft, termed Wild Weasel aircraft, with special radar homing and warning equipment. The US Navy employs the missile on A-4, A-6 and A-7 aircraft.

STATUS

Up to fiscal year 1978 about 24 000 Shrike missiles of all models had been procured and the 1978 budget allowed for the purchase of another 600. A similar procurement was planned for fiscal year 1979.

Future anti-radar missile requirements of the US forces are likely to be met by the High-speed Anti-Radiation Missile (HARM **1769.311**). Therefore Shrike must be regarded as obsolescent but nevertheless it is probable that appreciable stocks of these missiles (with ample support facilities) still exist and would be available for operational use.

CONTRACTORS

Joint prime contractors: Texas Instruments and Sperry Rand/Univac.

Shrike AGM-45A air-to-surface anti-radar missile prepared for flight testing at China Lake, US Naval Weapons Centre (USN)

1098.311
MAVERICK (AGM-65) AIR-TO-SURFACE MISSILE SYSTEM

The AGM-65 Maverick is a precision guided tactical missile in the 225 kg class. It was developed by Hughes Aircraft Company under contract to the US Air Force for use against hard targets such as tanks, armoured vehicles, field fortifications, gun positions, concrete communication centres and aircraft shelters. The system is currently operational on the F-4, A-7, A-10, F-111, F-16, F-5 and AJ 37 aircraft.

CHARACTERISTICS
Length: 2·49 m
Diameter: 30·5 cm
Wing span: 72 cm
Weight: 210 kg (288 kg with alternative warhead)
Guidance: TV (A/B models); Laser (E model); Infrared (D/F models)

The basic warhead is a 57 kg forward-firing shaped charge, designed for penetration through heavy armour and reinforced concrete. An alternative kinetic energy penetrator blast-fragmentation warhead has completed development and test phases. It weighs 136 kg and has a design optimised for effectiveness against major combatant ships and buried concrete fortifications. The weapon is powered by a two-stage solid fuel rocket motor and is rail launched from either single-missile or triple launcher units. Variants of the Maverick are described separately below.

TV Maverick (AGM-65A/B)

This basic missile is precision guided by a miniature TV homing system in the nose section. On his TV monitor, the pilot sees the picture transmitted from the missile seeker. He slews the seeker to the target, locks the TV tracker on target, and launches the missile. The aircraft can take immediate evasive action (launch and leave) or fire successive missiles while the first missile homes automatically on to the target.

Tracker logic steers the missile for impact at the centroid of the target in order to maximise kill probability. The B model has a modified optics system with a 2·5° field of view for greater magnification of the target area and longer range identification of small targets.

More than 30 000 Mavericks have been produced, and more than 1800 launched in test, training and combat, of which 85 per cent have been direct hits. Of the total, 100 were combat firings, which yielded 87 per cent direct hits. In addition to the USA, TV Maverick has been ordered by: Egypt, Federal Republic of Germany, Greece, Iran, Israel, Morocco, Saudi Arabia, Singapore, South Korea, Sweden, Switzerland, Taiwan and Turkey.

Laser Maverick (AGM-65C/E)

Laser Maverick will provide close air support against laser-designated targets in support of ground forces. Mounted forward of missile centre and aft sections that are common to all Mavericks, the laser guidance section homes on to the energy reflected off the target by the designator.

The C model, containing the basic shaped-charge warhead, completed development flight testing with over 90 per cent direct hits on target. Targets were illuminated with various laser designators. This version did not go into production.

The production E model utilises laser guidance with the alternative 136 kg warhead in order to meet operational requirements of the US Marine Corps. Operational flight testing of that configuration was completed in the summer of 1982 with a score of 15 out of 15 direct hits.

US Air Force analysis indicates that Laser Maverick effectiveness in the close air support role is dependent on the availability of stabilised ground target designators such as the Ground Laser Designator (GLLD) or airborne laser designators, such as the A-6E TRAM, the OV-10D NOS or the US Air Force Pave Tack system. The capability of hand-held designators is adequate for use with Laser Maverick against large or static targets. This model will be integrated with A-4M Skyhawk, A-6E Intruder, AV-8B Harrier and F/A-18 Hornet aircraft.

IR Maverick (AGM-65D)

An infra-red (IR) system provides autonomous launch-and-leave guidance both day and night, and under low visibility conditions. IR Maverick retains hardware commonality with the TV and Laser Mavericks. In addition, IR Maverick's pilot operating

Production model AGM-65D IR Maverick

US Navy A-7E Corsair with new Navy IR Maverick (AGM-65F)

procedures are similar, allowing the AGM-65D to be used on all aircraft types already equipped to operate TV Maverick. It can be used autonomously to locate and strike targets in the combat zone, or in the traditional night interdiction of roads and railroads; or it can be precisely slaved to other target acquisition aids such as forward looking infra-red (FLIR), radar, INS, LORAN, or radiation direction finders (anti-SAM).

Target recognition ranges with IR, day or night, are about twice the range for corresponding daylight visual recognition of typical tactical targets. The IR seeker has performance superior to TV or laser in low visibility. The long wave spectrum used penetrates battlefield smoke and dust which is opaque to visual systems. Thermal signature also provides unique advantages in detection of hidden/camouflaged targets and the determination of live from dead (cold) targets.

The missile has been successfully flight tested through US Air Force initial operational test and evaluation (IOT&E) on F-4, A-7, F-16, F-111 and A-10 aircraft. A variant of the IR seeker has also

successfully completed US Air Force development test and evaluation (DT&E) on the GBU-15 glide bomb launched from an F-4.

Navy Maverick (AGM-65F)

In late 1980 Hughes received a contract for the development of anti-ship algorithms to be incorporated in the IR seeker to give the IR Maverick additional capabilities against ship targets. Designated the AGM-65F, this model combines the IR guidance unit of the US Air Force AGM-65D modified with additional tracking logic for ship targets, with the warhead and propulsion sections of the AGM-65E model. IR guidance will allow US Navy pilots to undertake attacks in darkness and poor weather, and the heavy blast penetration warhead will be used with a selectable fuze for optimum effectiveness against various types of target. Flight test launches from A-7 aircraft were in progress in early 1984. Integration of the AGM-65F with A-6E and F/A-18 aircraft is scheduled.

STATUS
AGM-65D: Hughes is delivering production IR Maverick missiles against the fiscal year 1982 US Air

Force procurement of 200. The 1983 fiscal year contract for a further 900 missiles has been signed, allowing for an increase in the production rate of up to 115 missiles per month. Congress has approved the fiscal year 1984 budget request for 1382 production missiles and long-lead funding for another 600.

AGM-65E: Long-lead production approval was given in November 1982 and the full go-ahead in August 1983. First deliveries are due in March 1985, and Hughes has received fiscal years 1983 and 1984

contract awards for up to 275 missiles. The fiscal year 1985 DoD budget indicates a sum of $110·7 million for procurement of a further 600 missiles.

AGM-65F: The US Navy has completed a three-round DT&E flight test programme of the Navy IR Maverick, which resulted in three direct hits against ship targets. The Navy's operational test and evaluation (OPEVAL) programme began in 1984. The fiscal year 1985 US Navy budget indicates $29·8 million for 190 production missiles.

In May 1983 Raytheon was selected by the US Air Force as the second source for production of AGM-65D IR Maverick missiles, and was awarded a $49·6 million contract for evaluation and test missiles. Options for follow-on production provide for 500 more missiles.

CONTRACTOR
Hughes Aircraft Company, Canoga Park, California 91304, USA.

4190.311
GBU-15 MODULAR GLIDE BOMB
In the latter half of 1972 the US Air Force, with industry, instituted studies of possible ways of further enhancing the smart bomb concept by the provision of blind attack facilities and extending the effective range to permit stand-off operations by ground attack aircraft engaging high value fixed land targets.

The US Air Force refers to these later developments of electro-optical (EO) weapons as the Modular Glide Weapon System, which has now been designated GBU-15(V), a variable designator which is used for a family of weapons modules. These can be configured in various combinations to provide for various attack and target conditions. The base module set comprises those items needed to convert standard munitions, such as the Mk 84 bomb, to EO smart bombs of the sort which were extensively used in SE Asia.

The full list of major components comprises:
(1) two warhead options: Mk 84 'iron' bomb, SUU-54 dispenser
(2) wing and tail surface packages: cruciform wing module
(3) two guidance modules: EO; imaging infra-red (IIR)
(4) two adaptors to join the warhead to the guidance package
(5) a control module
(6) a data link module.

The two terminal guidance modules are interchangeable so that a weapon can be provided for specific conditions: day, night, high- or low-visibility attack. The EO seeker, DSU-27A/B which is an improved version of the TV seeker used in SE Asia, is used for daylight attacks. The pilot can use a direct attack mode if he can see the target prior to launching the weapon. By adding the data link module, an indirect attack is possible. In this case, the seeker TV data are transmitted back to the aircraft after launch,

while command signals are sent to the weapon in the opposite direction over the data link, so that the weapon can be flown by the air crew on to the target.

The IIR terminal guidance module, WGU-10/B, which is the same as that being developed for Maverick, will provide a night attack capability.

Both warhead modules weigh 2000 lb (907 kg), the Mk 84 being intended for targets such as railways, buildings, and bridges, while the SUU-54 dispenser is intended for use against area targets such as surface-to-air missile sites. The SUU-54 disperses 1800 grapefruit-sized bomblets: initial deliveries of production models of this munition began in January 1976 and tests were carried out later that year with the CBU-75 which consists of the SUU-54 dispenser filled with BLU-63 and/or BLU-86 bomblets.

CHARACTERISTICS
Type: GBU-15(V)/B
Length: 3·91 m
Diameter: 45 cm
Wingspan: 1·49 m
Weight: 1111 kg

The AN/AXQ-14 data link developed for the GBU-15(V) is designed for D-band operation.

The cruciform wing was developed to improve the small wing configuration used in SE Asia. This design gives the weapon increased manoeuvrability at low altitudes and, used with the data link module, permits attacks from stand-off ranges.

The first GBU-15(V) weapon configuration to complete development is the Cruciform Wing Weapon (CWW) that combines the EO Mk 84 and cruciform wing modules. As already stated, there is the option of exchanging the Mk 84 warhead for the SUU-54 dispenser munition, in which case the FMU-123/B fuze is used.

The data link allows TV signals to be transmitted from the weapon to the aircraft so that the aircrew can command the weapon while leaving the launch area and flying directly away from hostile territory. The

weapon has demonstrated a low-level, blind launch capability with target acquisition and target lock-on accomplished after weapon release.

Modification kits have been produced by Rockwell International's Missile Systems Division for two standard US bombs, the 2000 lb (900 kg) Mk 84 and the 3000 lb (1360 kg) M118E1. Kit designations are KMU-353A/B, KMU-390-/B, and KMU-359/B, the first two being TV and the last IR. The KMU-353 A/B has since been redesignated GBU-8. Each kit consists of a guidance section for mounting on the nose of the bomb; a tail assembly with four stabilising vanes having control surfaces on their rear edges, and containing batteries; and a set of strakes and metal straps which serve to attach and locate the guidance and control packages on the body of the bomb.

Aircraft types equipped to carry GBU-15 are the F-4E (two plus data link pod, Pave Tack, and Loran), B-52D (three plus pod), and F-111F (four plus pod and Pave Tack). Integration of the GBU-15 with the F-15 and F-16 aircraft has been started and Rockwell's Missile System Division is under contract to integrate the weapon with Royal Australian Air Force F-111Cs. Extending use of the GBU-15 to other aircraft types in continuing and fitting arrangements have been checked on the Viggen, Tornado and F-18.

AGM-130
A powered version of the GBU-15, designated AGM-130, is under development which is expected to provide up to three times the range of the un-powered glide-bomb. The number and type of booster(s) is not decided at this stage but possible sources that have been mentioned include Aerojet General and Atlantic Research. Payload/warhead options also are as yet open, among the new possibilities being the BLU-106 boosted kinetic energy penetrator (BKEP) which was intended for use with the now-cancelled MRASM (**4191.311** in 1982-83 and 1983-84 editions). Other matters which are still undecided are what altitude sensing/terrain following facilities should be incorporated.

STATUS
Rockwell delivered the first GBU-15 production units to the US Air Force in January 1982 and production deliveries of the AN/AXQ-14 data link followed shortly after. Under a $38·7 million US Air Force contract awarded on 21 December 1982 Rockwell is producing 250 cruciform wing GBU-15 guided bombs.

In May 1984 Hughes was awarded a $21 million contract for immediate and follow-on production of additional AN/AXQ-14 data links, this order bringing the total to over 1500 units.

CONTRACTOR
Rockwell International, Missile Systems Division, Defence Electronics Operations, 1800 Satellite Boulevard, Duluth, Georgia 30136, USA.

Two GBU-15 CWW carried beneath the wings of US Air Force F-111 aircraft

---

1534.311
PAVEWAY LASER-GUIDED BOMBS
The family of laser-guided bombs (LGBs) uses a common laser guidance and control sub-assembly, with only the aerodynamic surfaces (control fins and aerofoil group) changed to match the particular size warhead. The system allows for stand-off capability while providing precision weapon delivery against a wide spectrum of targets.

The original LGB conversion kits have become known as Paveway I, following the introduction of a new set of components in 1978, the latter being known as Paveway II. One notable feature of the later system is the substitution of extending tail fins for the original fixed fins of Paveway I conversions. This and other differences are shown in the accompanying diagrams and tables.

OPERATION
The guided-bomb kit directs the weapon toward a target which has been illuminated by laser energy. The desired target can be selected by the bombing aircraft, a companion aircraft, or a ground observer. The laser energy is reflected from the target and detected by the laser guidance system. The system processes the information, computes appropriate control commands, and applies these commands to movable surfaces to effect changes in trajectory, thereby guiding the weapon to the target.

The system requires no electrical connection to the unmodified delivery aircraft and is delivered in the same manner as a conventional bomb. There is no requirement for tracking or lock-on before launch, which minimises the time required for delivery with

concomitant reduction in aircraft exposure to hostile ground fire.

DEVELOPMENT
The US Air Force Armament Development and Test Centre (ADTC), Eglin AFB, initiated a competitive evaluation of two laser guidance concepts for standard bombs in 1965; the first LGB flight occured in April 1965. This evaluation proved the feasibility of the concept and was followed by establishment of the Paveway programme office at Wright-Patterson AFB. Texas Instruments was selected to conduct engineering development to supply additional laser guidance kits for M117 GP bombs.

Utilising the laser guidance kit developed by Texas Instruments, two additional GP bombs (Mk 82 and Mk 84) and the M118 demolition bomb were later successfully adapted to laser guidance and operationally deployed. Evaluations were initiated in 1971 for application of the kit to the Pave Storm cluster munition and, during 1971, both cluster weapons were successfully tested, utilising laser guidance.

The Paveway II version was developed in the mid-1970s and production began in 1977. Similar to Paveway I in appearance and operational concepts, Paveway II has more advanced electronics and a folding wing aerofoil group which improved sensitivity and manoeuvrability. Paveway II also incorporates many cost-reduction features such as plastic lenses instead of glass, a moulded-plastic ringtail instead of metal, and intergrated circuitry to improve reliability and reduce manufacturing time. The folding wings also permit increased load density on the delivery aircraft.

STATUS

The US Air Force and US Navy utilise the GBU-10E/B (Mk 84), GBU-16B/B (Mk 83), and GBU-12D/B (Mk 82) versions of Paveway II LGBs. These weapons are compatible with the F-4, F-111, F-5, A-6, A-37, A-7, A-4, A-10, F-16, AV-8A (Harrier) and B-52 aircraft. The F-14, F-15, F-18, Mirage Tornado, Buccaneer, and Jaguar aircraft types have also been added to this list.

The LGB has been introduced into the RAF inventory and also other NATO countries. The RAF system for the Mk-13/18 1000lb warhead was developed jointly by the Royal Aircraft Establishment, Texas Instruments and Portsmouth Aviation Ltd.

The development of the third generation of LGBs began in 1980-81. Known as the low-level laser-guided bomb (LLLGB) or Paveway III, this weapon is designed to be delivered from very low altitudes and significant stand-off ranges. The LLLGB incorporates state-of-the-art microprocessor technology, high-lift folding wings, and an improved scanning seeker. After a successful development flight test programme, the system has undergone initial operational test and evaluation (IOT&E) and production approval was granted in mid-1983.

In addition to US and UK operators of Paveway LGBs, Australia, Greece, the Netherlands, Saudi Arabia, South Korea, Spain, Taiwan and Thailand are reported to have been supplied.

CONTRACTOR

Texas Instruments Incorporated, 2501 South Highway 121, PO Box 405, Lewisville, Texas 75067, USA.

3637.311

WAAM PROGRAMME

The Wide Area Anti-armour Munitions programme (WAAM) is a high priority US Air Force effort designed to provide tactical air forces with a weapon system that will be capable of multiple kills against tanks and other armour from a single aircraft pass. The system is to be suitable for use under all weather conditions and by day or night. The goal is to improve the current US armour kill-per-pass capability by a factor of four to eight times. Initially the system is being considered for the A-10 ground attack aircraft but it will be suitable for use with other types of aircraft engaged in operations against concentrations of armour.

The WAAM system(s) will be complementary in use to the US Army/Air Force Joint Tactical Missile System (JTACMS) (**4760.111**), which project succeeds the Assault Breaker (**3989.111**)/US Army Corps Support Weapon System (CSWS). The primary objective is to counter second echelon armour concentrations. Initially, four WAAM concepts were studied but this number was reduced to the three described in the following paragraphs. The Cyclops proposal, which is not now being pursued, was described under this entry number in the 1980-81 *Jane's Weapon Systems*.

ACM (Anti-armour Cluster Munitions)

This was an evolution of existing cluster-bomb technology and the aircraft would normally employ a low-level delivery pass to release the cluster-bomb canister. The latter contains a large number of sub-munitions which are allowed to drift to the ground supported by parachutes. In this way, several hundred submunitions could be delivered on a single aircraft pass. This project suffered the same fate as Cyclops (above) and was cancelled in 1982-83.

	PRESENT APPLICATIONS		CCG-MAU		AFG-MXU				FUZES						
WEAPON	WARHEAD		169-D/B	*169-C/B	650/B	651/B	667/B	TYPE M120	M905	FMU-26B/B	FMU-81/B	FMU-124	MK-344	MK-376	M947 (UK)
GBU-10	E/B	2000-LB (MK84) (900 KG)	•			•			T	N/T	N/T	N/T	T	T	
	F/B			•		•			T	N/T	N/T	N/T	T	T	
GBU-12	D/B	500-LB (MK82) (225 KG)	•		•				T	N/T	N/T	N/T	T	T	
	E/B			•	•				T	N/T	N/T	N/T	T	T	
GBU-16	B/B	1000-LB (MK83) (450 KG)	•				•		T	N/T	N/T	N/T	T	T	
	C/B			•			•		T	N/T	N/T	N/T	T	T	
MK 13/18 UK		1000-LB MK 13/18	•	•				•							T

* PAVEWAY II MK II CCG

N - NOSE FUZING
T - TAIL FUZING

CCG DATA	MAU	169C/B	1325-01-085-6022
		169D/B	1325-01-098-2812
AFG DATA	MXU	650/B	1325-00-427-9099
		651/B	1325-00-427-9097
		667/B	1325-01-048-9811

TORQUE WRENCH	5180-00-477-0301 AQ
WRENCH ADAPTER	5120-01-082-1002 AQ
HYDRAULIC PUMP AND ASSEMBLY	4925-01-044-1723
WING RETRACTOR (MK82)	4925-01-010-0159
WING RETRACTOR (MK83)	4925-01-053-3121
WING RETRACTOR (MK84)	4925-01-015-2896
FLIGHT LINE TEST SET (AN/GJM-51)	4925-00-348-0798
DIGITAL TEST SET (TTU-373/E)	4925-01-064-8470
DIGITAL TEST SET (TTU-394/E)	4925-01-085-4648

Paveway II munition configurations

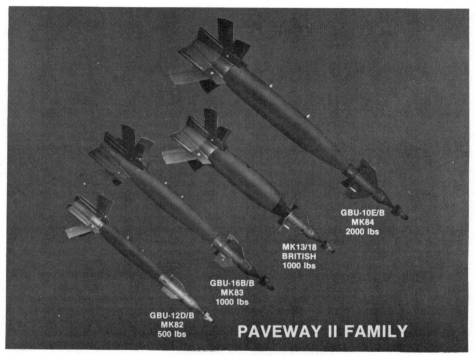

Current Paveway II family of weapons

Folding wing assembly of Paveway II LGBs enables increased load to be carried as on this F-5

ERAM (Extended Range Anti-armour Mine)

This concept is apparently an enhancement of the ACM system, with a very large number of mines being emplaced by an aircraft making a single low-level pass over the anticipated line of advance of the enemy armoured formation. Several hundred such mines could be emplaced in this way by day or night and in any weather conditions. ERAM submunitions are delivered by parachute from dispensers released by tactical aircraft, and the submunition is engineered to fit into the US Air Force tactical munitions dispenser (TMD) SUU-65/B and the combination of TMD and ERAM submunitions is designated CBU-92/B by the US Air Force. Once released, the TMD splits open low over the target area and ejects the ERAMs to fall and disperse randomly. Each ERAM has a sensor that detects the passage of an armoured vehicle at ranges of possibly up to 150 metres, whereupon the mine is projected into the air again by an explosive charge, and if the target is locked onto, the SFF warhead is detonated. According to official US sources, multiple shots for each mine are possible.

Other DoD comments concerning the ERAM concept include:
Low-level delivery
Hundreds of mines per aircraft

Multiple shots per mine
Tank kills from points distant from the tank's actual path
All weather and night capability
Can be used against armour for direct or indirect attack

WASP (Mini-missile)

This is the most advanced of the WAAM concepts and entails loading miniature missiles, each with its own new-technology seeker into cluster-bomb containers for low-level stand-off delivery by the ground attack aircraft. The WASP mini-missiles would be capable of individual independent target acquisition and tracking, and would probably employ a shaped charge warhead for armour penetration, although the SFF warhead will remain as an alternative. The GBU glide-bomb (**1597.311** in 1980-81 and earlier editions) has been named as one possible carrier vehicle for WASP submunitions.

Wasp is intended to give the launch aircraft almost complete freedom of the need to directly see the intended target(s) or to designate them for the WASP missiles. After launch, each Wasp missile will be programmed to fly to the target area where enemy armour has been located; a terminal guidance seeker will then take over control to identify the target and direct the Wasp to its target. This will take place by day or night and in adverse weather. Both millimetric wavelength radar and IR guidance techniques were studied but the former was deemed more appropriate. It was intended that Wasp missiles would be fired in clusters of ten or more. On-board computers would direct each missile in the swarm to a different target as long as there are more targets than missiles.

STATUS

The WAAM programme was started in 1975 and work is concentrated at Eglin AFB, at the Armament Development Test Centre there.

In April 1982 Hughes announced that captive flight tests of a millimetric wavelength seeker for the Wasp anti-armour missile had successfully demonstrated the ability to detect, lock-on, and track military targets autonomously. These tests were followed by successful flights in April and May of 1983 when Wasp missiles autonomously engaged and hit tank targets after launch from an F-16 aircraft. Wasp was due to go into full-scale development in fiscal year 1984 but funds were withdrawn and the project deferred.

Actual or planned development funding for the WAAM programme in fiscal years 1983-1986, in millions, is as follows (year in brackets): $13·7 (83), $23·5 (84), $27·3 (85) and $12·6 (86).

4530.311
LAD LOW ALTITUDE DISPENSER

The low-altitude dispenser (LAD) system is under development by Brunswick Corporation in collaboration with the US Air Force to perfect a means of enabling low-flying tactical and other aircraft to deliver a variety of submunitions at stand-off ranges against targets such as airfields, armoured formations, vehicle concentration etc. The concept has much in common with a number of previous projects, such as the West German Stand-Off Weapon (SOW) (**4050.311** in 1981-82 and earlier editions) and Container Weapon System (CWS) (**4449.311**), British AST 1227 (**3900.311** in 1982-83 and 1983-84 editions) and JP233 airfield attack weapon (**5218.311**).

LAD is designed as an aircraft store in the 1000 to 1400 kg class for carriage on standard NATO weapon lugs, and the configuration is simply that of a rectangular-section container housing the sub-munitions and equipped with aerodynamic surfaces for controlling its flight path after release from the aircraft. Provision is made for the addition of a 180 kg st class propulsion motor if required which typically increases the stand-off range from between 9 and 19 km to up to 24 km. Aided by an on-board microprocessor, the latter facility enables the LAD to manoeuvre after release and fly back to engage a ground target previously over-flown by the attacking aircraft. It also permits offset target attacks and is valuable for engaging targets of opportunity.

Various methods of target designation can be employed with LAD, ranging from location co-ordinates inserted into the launch aircraft's navigation/attack system from external sources such as Precision Location Strike System (PLSS) or Pave Mover etc, or targets located by on-board targeting aids, or a pilot's helmet mounted sight. Guidance of the LAD after release may be either programmed or

A-10 aircraft with Brunswick LAD weapon on wing station during technology demonstration flight series

inertial and the former can also include climb and descent manoeuvres appropriate to the nature of the target(s) and attack.

Programming of the submunition ejection timing, LAD attitude and altitude, permits considerable adjustment of the ground pattern, with further variations being possible by means of adjustments to the lateral ejection velocities and sequencing of ejection events and use of variable retarder devices on individual submunitions. The dispensing method depends on submunition characteristics, and the more sophisticated sensor-fuzed devices can be precisely delivered with tube or air-bag dispensers.

Submunitions without pattern forming devices could require a secondary dispersal system. It is understood that by 1982 at least six submunitions had been test flown and 15 types investigated, all of which were suitable for use in the LAD vehicle. Among the submunitions tested were bomblets used in the West German MBB tube-dispenser system.

STATUS

Advanced development under DoD contract for US Air Force Armament Laboratory, Eglin AFB, Florida.

CONTRACTOR

Brunswick Corporation, 3333 Harbour Boulevard, Costa Mesa, California 92626, USA.

4448.311
HVM SYSTEM

Under a US Air Force contract awarded in late 1981 Vought Corporation is engaged on the design and development of a guided air-to-ground hypervelocity missile (HVM) with the objective of demonstrating a capability of defeating all types of vehicle in an advanced armoured assault force, using small, low-cost missiles which rely on kinetic energy derived from their speed for penetration. Both air- and surface-launched versions of the HVM are expected to be produced eventually, and the land-mobile version is already known as the Bushwhacker weapon system.

Preliminary studies of the airborne system indicate a pod-housed weapon, this containing launching tubes for up to 40 HVMs and a laser radar guidance system. The last of these items would employ a carbon-dioxide laser to provide 3D ranging and doppler information, and would perform the functions of multiple target detection, classification,

identification and prioritisation in under one second. The rockets will be equipped with a track-while-guidance system, and the laser will provide a coarse beam for rocket capture, and a fine beam for terminal guidance. The use of laser guidance is intended to make the system almost impervious to enemy countermeasures.

The rocket missiles weigh less than 22 kg and are expected to cost less than $5000 per round. They will have no moving parts and will be stabilised in flight by spin imparted by the launch tube, aided by a gyro roll sensor and a series of 'squib' rocket motors that will be used for attitude control. The rockets will reach a speed of more than 1500 m/s and will carry an inert warhead of high density, possibly a depleted uranium rod weighing 2·2 to 2·7 kg able to penetrate most modern armour plate. Estimated maximum range is about 6000 metres.

Multiple target engagement is an important capability and it is hoped to be able to demonstrate firing of several missiles delivered simultaneously against separate stationary and moving targets. Ground-launch tests in 1982 successfully demonstrated the missile's ability to receive laser guidance signals through the rocket motor plume, and an ability to operate at speeds of more than 1500 m/s in an air-launched role.

In March 1983 an HVM made a successful guided test flight using the laser guidance system after a ground launch at the White Sands Missile Range, New Mexico.

STATUS

Development. Vought was awarded an $11·2 million contract by the Armament Laboratory of the US Air Force Systems Command in September 1981. Major sub-contractors include Hercules Inc for the propellant and polyamide rocket motor case.

CONTRACTOR

LTV Aerospace and Defence Company, Vought Missiles and Advanced Programmes Division, PO Box 225907, Dallas, Texas 75265, USA.

1301.321

HARPOON (AGM-84A) AIR-TO-SURFACE ANTI-SHIP MISSILE

Harpoon is an all-weather anti-ship missile for use against surfaced submarines, patrol craft, destroyers and larger vessels, merchant ships and trawlers.

The missile is capable of being air-launched or, with the addition of a rocket booster, ship or submarine-launched. These latter versions will supplement existing missile systems and will also become operational on those ships which do not currently have a missile capability. Further details of Harpoon in these versions can be found in **2641.221** and **2797.421** in 1976 and earlier editions.

Approximate dimensions are: length 384 cm, body diameter 34 cm, span 91 cm, and weight 522 kg. Ship and submarine-launched versions have an additional booster motor, with four fins, attached to the rear of the missile. Mid-course guidance is performed by a system utilising a digital processor, and a strap-down sensor/guidance sub-system. This system uses computer techniques to process the data from the strap-down gyros to sense missile velocity in three axes and derive control signals from this information.

The missile employs an active radar terminal guidance seeker.

STATUS

In October 1972 the first powered flight was conducted at the US Naval Missile Centre at Point Mugu, California. Entry into service began in 1977. The fiscal year 1985 report by the US Secretary of Defense states that it is planned to continue Harpoon production with a total of 1027 missiles budgeted in the 1984-86 fiscal years programme. It is planned to deploy this missile on S-3 maritime patrol aircraft in addition to the P-3 and A-6 aircraft, and compatibility tests with US Air Force B-52G heavy bombers have been initiated. In early 1984 it was revealed that the US Navy plans to extend Harpoon deployment to F/A-18 strike-fighter aircraft also. Projected cost of the planned 1984-86 Harpoon procurement is $987·7 million.

It was announced in April 1983 that three anti-ship Harpoon missiles had been launched successfully from US Air Force B-52 bombers against a surface target in the Pacific. Two B-52 squadrons are being equipped to deploy Harpoons. Each aircraft can carry 12 Harpoon missiles on external wing mountings.

Royal Air Force Nimrod maritime aircraft having carried Harpoon missiles as an emergency measure during the Falklands conflict, are to retain the Harpoon capability and additional missiles valued at $248 million have been ordered.

CONTRACTOR

McDonnell Douglas Astronautics Company, PO Box 516, St Louis, Missouri 63166, USA.

1123.311

STANDARD ARM (AGM-78) ANTI-RADIATION MISSILE

This is an air-to-ground passive radar homing missile for the destruction of surface-to-air missile battery radars. The system consists of a modified Standard (RIM-66A) medium-range missile for delivery by current high-performance aircraft equipped for the detection, identification, and acquisition of the radar target. It is intended to augment Shrike missiles (**1102.311**) in operation and is used where greater performance is required.

More recently, this weapon has been adapted to two further roles: to provide Standard-equipped ships, and those previously without a missile capability, with a surface-to-surface weapon system. These programmes are described in **2808.221** in 1972-73 and earlier editions and **2669.221** in 1976 and earlier editions.

CHARACTERISTICS

Length: 4·5 m
Diameter: 34 cm
Weight: 635 kg
Speed: Supersonic
Guidance: Passive RF homing
Warhead: HE
Propulsion: Solid, dual thrust
Range: >25 km, estimated

OPERATION

System operation is initiated by reception of hostile radar transmission by the aircraft. The received signal is processed to extract target location, identification, and threat data. A missile is then launched and homes on to the source of radar transmission. The dual-thrust motor of the missile enables it to follow a variety of pursuit courses to the target.

US Air Force aircraft are reported to be using an advanced version of the Wild Weasel radar warning and homing system for target identification and acquisition purposes.

DEVELOPMENT

Design studies for the Standard ARM, and the first development contracts, were initiated in 1966. Flight tests took place in 1967 and were completed in the following year. Full production began in 1968.

Hangar display of Standard ARM (foreground) with AGM-45 Shrike anti-radar missile. Note Shrike seeker mounted on nose of US Navy aircraft in background, presumably a test installation (USN Photo)

Contracts awarded to the main contractor, General Dynamics, total over $300 million. The first production model was the AGM-78B. Subsequent models were the AGM-78C (1969), AGM-78D (1971), and the AGM-78D-2(1975).

STATUS

The AGM-78B Standard ARM entered operational service in 1967 with F-105F and A-6A aircraft. Deployment with F-4 aircraft followed production of the AGM-78D.

Procurement has ceased and the fiscal year 1979 request of $2 million allowed for support of the existing Standard ARM inventory only.

CONTRACTORS

Prime Contractor: General Dynamics Corporation, Pomona Division, 1675 West Mission Boulevard, Pomona, California 91766, USA.

AGM-78B seeker: Maxson Electronics Corporation, Sunrise Highway, Great River, Long Island, New York 11739, USA.

1769.311

HARM (AGM-88A) HIGH-SPEED ANTI-RADIATION MISSILE

The high-speed anti-radiation missile (HARM) is entering service as a replacement for the existing Shrike (**1102.311**) and Standard ARM (**1123.311**). It is between these two missiles in terms of overall size but has a number of operational advantages, including higher speed, faster reaction, longer range and a more destructive warhead. In addition, unlike the Shrike which is configured individually to specific frequency bands, HARM has a broad-band capability, thus enabling a single missile to engage any anticipated air defence-associated surface radar (ship- or land-based). HARM also has software-controlled processing which enables new threats to be addressed by reprogramming instead of hardware modifications as enemy weapons develop. This will enable HARM to be used for the suppression or destruction of emitters other than those associated with surface-to-air systems, including early warning radars, ATC radars and weather radars whose elimination might offer tactical dividends.

The missile seeker, control section, wings and fins are produced by Texas Instruments, and the warhead, rocket motor and fuzing are being produced by other contractors. Technical direction is by the US Naval Weapons Centre, China Lake. The single seeker head employs a fixed antenna, thereby eliminating the complication and cost of gimbals and steering controls, and all pneumatic and hydraulic systems have been eliminated. It comprises the antenna array, ten microwave circuit boards and a video processor. This assembly provides direction finding facilities without requiring a moving antenna array, the latter consisting of a planar spiral-helix associated with other elements housed within a radome which itself forms an integral part of the overall RF antenna sub-system.

A 66 kg prefragmented HE warhead is carried which is triggered by a laser fuze that senses missile height above the terrain and detonates the warhead at one of two settings, depending on whether an overshoot or an undershoot is sensed. These two values are established so that maximum effect of the known dispersion pattern of the warhead fragments is utilised. It is likely that in future there will be more than two settings, which may be inserted automatically prior to launch in accordance with the target detected and engaged. Tests of fragment dispersion and damage characteristics for various typical threat radars will be established by further tests.

The other major part of the HARM weapon system consists of the aircraft avionics and controls; the US Navy will use the AN/AWG-25 equipment installed in the A-7 aircraft, and the US Air Force will utilise the avionics and displays of the Wild Weasel system to interface with HARM.

The command launch computer interfaces with the existing radar warning system and other aircraft avionics, while the cockpit control panel entails simple modifications to the existing panel to adapt it for operation of the anti-radiation missile function. The computer has efficient memory capacity to include all land- and sea-based emitters that US Navy task forces are expected to encounter. The US Air Force has a similar capability in the Wild Weasel system.

OPERATION

Three basic modes of operation for the HARM system are to be provided for the tactical air crew:

(1) *self-protect mode:* this is the most fundamental mode, and uses the aircraft radar warning receiver to detect threatening emitters. The HARM launch control computer then sorts and assigns priorities to these emissions and provides in digital language a complete set of instructions for the missile. This is achieved in a very short space of time and the pilot can fire the HARM almost immediately

(2) *target of opportunity mode:* in this mode the very high sensitivity of the missile seeker head to detect certain parameters of radar operation and also those transmissions associated with other parts of a radar installation, is utilised. It permits the engagement of targets by homing onto emissions that could not be detected and handled by Shrike or Standard ARMs

(3) *pre-briefed mode:* this employs the long range of HARM to engage targets whose signals can be detected but are not adequate for missile lock-on, or it may be used to fire HARM on a pre-computed trajectory into the vicinity of known targets. If these targets emit while HARM is in flight, they are attacked immediately; if the target does not radiate, the HARM destroys itself.

CHARACTERISTICS

Length: 4·16 m
Diameter: 25 cm
Wing span: 1·13 m
Max launch weight: 360 kg
Guidance: Anti-radiation, radar seeking, broad-band
Warhead: 66 kg prefragmented HE
Fuze: Laser proximity
Range: 20 km + (provisional)

DEVELOPMENT

First contracts in support of HARM research and development were awarded during 1972. Among them were the following: Texas Instruments, guidance and avionics; Hughes Aircraft, systems analysis and guidance support; Itek, AN/ALR-45 radar warning receiver modifications; Lockheed, system studies; Dalmo-Victor, modification of DSA-20N signal analyser; Stanford Research Institute, analysis.

In the latter part of 1974 Texas Instruments was selected as the weapon system integration contractor for HARM. If procurement is decided upon the primary US Navy vehicles to carry HARM will be the A-7E, A-18 and A-6E aircraft, and in the case of the US Air Force, the F-4G, AFR-38 fitted Wild Weasel II aircraft.

STATUS

The first production HARM was delivered to the US Navy on December 2, 1983 and another six a few days later. The remainder of this order for 80 missiles was

AGM-88A HARM is certified for flight on A-7E, F-4G Wild Weasel Phantom and F/A-18 aircraft, and has been evaluated for use on A-6E, F-16 and Tornado

delivered over the period ending October 1983. From the following month, Texas Instruments began delivery of 236 more missiles at a rate of 25 per month.

Planned procurement shown in the fiscal year 1985 DoD budget allocates roughly equal quantities for the US Navy and US Air Force, with the actual/projected procurement for the fiscal years 1983/84/85/86 making combined totals of 289 ($161·7 million), 722

($379·2 million), 1674 ($656·4 million) and 2461 ($803·2 million), respectively.

Operational deployment was due to commence in 1984-85.

CONTRACTOR

System integration contractor: Texas Instruments Incorporated, PO Box 405, Lewisville, Texas 75067, USA.

2831.311

TOW AIR-TO-SURFACE APPLICATION

As noted in the main description of the TOW anti-tank weapon system (**2830.111**), this weapon, like several other anti-tank weapons, can be used as armament for fighting helicopters.

Both the gunner's sight and the optical sensor are mounted on a specially developed gyrostabilised platform, which gives the tracking and control system a constant reference surface. The sight is pointed at the target by means of a joystick.

The anti-armour version of the Bell Cobra is equipped with the M65 airborne TOW system, and up to four two-round modular TOW launch pods can be carried, while still leaving the inboard pylons free for rocket or 20 mm minigun pods. The M28 turret with a 7·62 mm minigun and 40 mm grenade launcher is

Filmed sequence showing firing of TOW missile during qualification tests of the system mounted on Hughes 500MD Defender helicopter equipped with mast-mounted sight

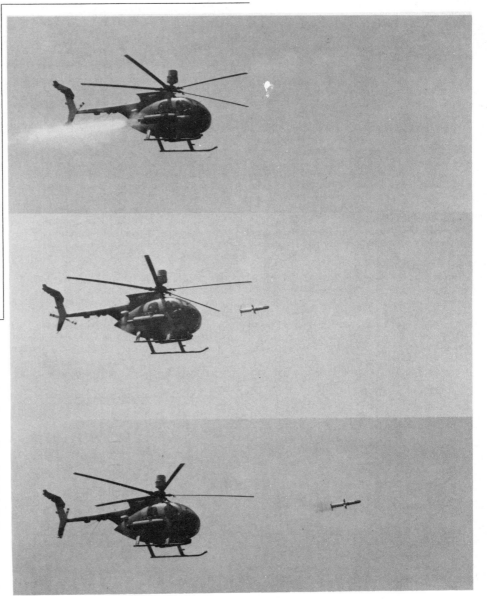

retained. In addition to stabilised optics and a missile tracker, the modified M65 sight has provisions for a laser rangefinder. Helmet sights allow the crew to control the turret directly or provide target acquisition for the stabilised optics.

As a private venture, Bell has developed the TexasRanger, a multi-role Bell 206L helicopter capable of rapid, in-the-field conversion to the anti-tank configuration. The Hughes lightweight roof sight version of the airborne TOW is used, and the system permits a variety of armament configurations, including: four TOW missiles, in two launchers; 2·75 inch rockets in dual pods; or dual pods each with two 7·62 mm machine guns and a total of 2000 rounds. The TOW roof sight incorporates a dual magnification optical telescopic sight, and has provision for later inclusion of FLIR and a laser

rangefinder/designator. Four TOW reloads are carried internally. The Bell TexasRanger was designed for export sales.

In the air-launched role, TOW has a maximum direct range of 3750 metres.

STATUS

Planned and proposed procurement and funding for TOW missiles included in the 1985 Report by the US Secretary for Defense for fiscal years 1984/85/86 was 20 200 ($217·2 million), 21 822 ($297·5 million) and 22 014 ($255·8 million), respectively. These totals refer to both surface-launched and air-launched TOW missiles.

Nine nations of the 33 operating TOW are using the airborne version, including Italy and the UK, the latter producing a special roof-mounted optical sight for Army Lynx helicopters under licence in the UK.

Contracts were awarded to four British companies in September 1978: Pilkington PE Ltd, HML, Rank Optical, and MEL, while British Aerospace as main contractor and licensee for the UK TOW placed a contract for electronic sub-systems with Ferranti in January 1979.

In addition to US forces and British Lynx helicopters, the TOW system has been installed on the Hughes helicopters 500MD, the Italian Agusta A-109, MBB BO-105, Bell 206-L-1 and is planned for Agusta A129 and Sikorsky S-76, TOW can be installed on Aérospatiale Gazelle, Ecureuil and Dauphin.

CONTRACTOR

Hughes Aircraft Company, El Segundo, California 90045, USA.

1391.311

HELLFIRE (AGM-114A) TACTICAL AIR-TO-SURFACE MISSILE

The Hellfire Modular Missile System (HMMS) is the US Army's latest anti-armour weapon system. Hellfire is an acronym derived from 'heliborne-launched fire and forget'. From 1976, when the US Army selected the Missile Systems Division of the Defence Electronics Operations of Rockwell International to undertake engineering development (ED), numerous Hellfire 'prototype' missiles were launched in army concept feasibility tests. Flight and ground tests were conducted during that period at the US Army Missile Command (MICOM). Operational tests were conducted in 1974, 1980 and 1981 by the US Army at Fort Hunter Liggett, California. Hellfire missiles have also been fired by the US Marine Corps. The system achieved high accuracies and hit probability in tests.

For its initial application, Hellfire has been designated as the point target weapon system for the AH-64 Advanced Attack helicopter. The AH-64 carries up to 16 missiles. These are distributed equally on four wing-mounted launchers, two inboard and two outboard. The launchers are modular in design so that the two lower rails may be removed.

Maximum length and weight of the laser missile is 1779 mm and 43 kg respectively, while the diameter is 177·8 mm with wing span of 330 mm. The Hellfire missile is also modular and will accept a variety of mission-tailored guidance modules, but the production version is the laser homing model. The tactical prototype flight test phase was conducted using the Hellfire laser seeker developed by Martin Marietta, Orlando, Florida.

Other guidance modules studied for Hellfire are the Air Defence Suppression Missile (ADSM) seeker and the imaging infra-red (IIR) seeker. Experimental ADSM seekers were successfully launched by Rockwell on prototype Hellfire missiles in 1973. All seekers will allow Hellfire to engage moving targets. The first moving target launch took place in January 1972.

Hellfire is not limited to direct line-of-sight attack. Numerous indirect flights have been performed. In the indirect mode, the laser Hellfire missile is launched without seeker lock-on. It climbs over obstacles, searches for its target, then locks on automatically and impacts with no degradation in terminal accuracy. A factor in reducing helicopter exposure time during direct fire launches and in minimising total engagement time for all missions is laser Hellfire's broad launch window. This means that

US Army AH-64 Apache attack helicopter with eight Hellfire missiles loaded (US Army photo)

the launch heading of the helicopter and the azimuth to the target may differ considerably. Thereby, precision attitude alignment criteria, common to many other systems, are essentially eliminated.

In May 1974, laser Hellfire missiles demonstrated the 'ripple fire' technique of target engagement. With this technique, missiles are launched only fractions of a second apart, at different targets, designated by laser designators on separate codes. If only one designator is used, multiple targets can still be engaged; however, time between launches increases to a few seconds. This technique is called 'rapid fire' and was first successfully demonstrated in November 1974.

STATUS

In full production for US Army and Marine Corps applications. It was anticipated that entry into operational service would begin with US Army AH-64 Apache helicopters in 1984.

A contract awarded to Martin Marietta in late 1983 and valued at $96·6 million called for production of 947 missiles and more than 2000 laser seekers, plus 18 training missiles. This contract effectively made Martin Marietta a second source producer of the

Hellfire weapon, the original source being Rockwell International.

The US Marine Corps is to equip 44 new AH-1T helicopters with hellfire and work on the same modifications to 48 AH-1Ts of the US Fleet Marine Force began in 1984.

Combined procurement and funding for Hellfire for Army and Marine requirements listed in the US Secretary of Defence's fiscal year 1985 report, for the years 1983/84/85/86 (with funding in millions of dollars shown in brackets) was 3971 ($247·4m), 4870 ($235·5m), 6464 ($262·9m) and 7880 ($298m), respectively.

In 1983 firing trials of Hellfire installed in a British Lynx helicopter, and using a Ferranti 306 laser target designator were carried out in Norway. This aircraft can carry up to eight Hellfire missiles.

CONTRACTORS

Rockwell International Missile Systems Division, Defence Electronics Operations, 1800 Satellite Boulevard, Duluth, Georgia 30136, USA.

Martin Marietta Orlando Aerospace, PO Box 5837, Orlando, Florida 32855, USA.

AIR-TO-AIR MISSILES

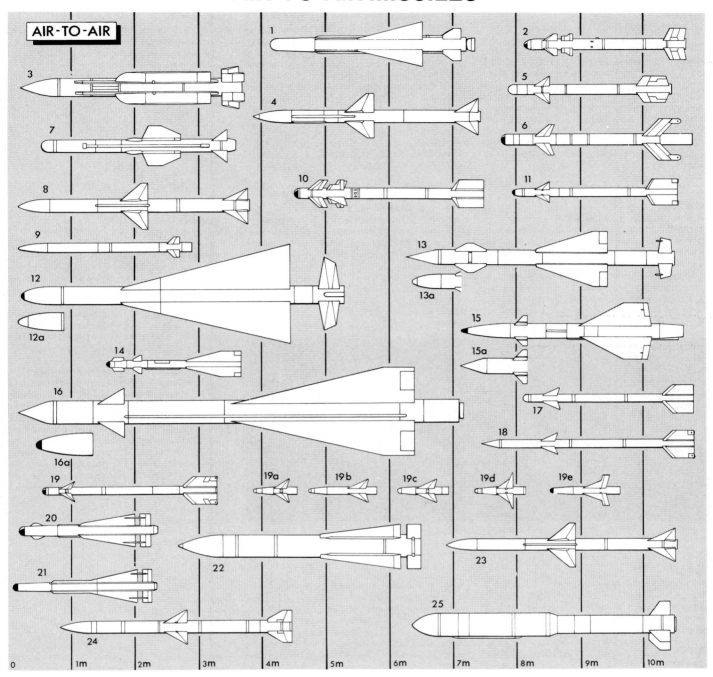

AIR-TO-AIR

1	R 530	12a	Ash Radar	19b	AIM-9E
2	R 550 Magic	13	AA-7 Apex Radar	19c	AIM-9H
3	Super 530	13a	Apex IR	19d	AIM-9L
4	Aspide	14	AA-8 Aphid	19e	AIM-9N/P
5	Shafrir	15	AA-3 Anab IR	20	AIM-4 Falcon
6	Python III	15a	Anab Radar	21	AIM-4G Falcon
7	Red Top	16	AA-6 Acrid Radar	22	Phoenix
8	Sky Flash	16a	Acrid IR	23	Sparrow III
9	ASRAAM (provisional)	17	AA-2 Atoll	24	AMRAAM
10	Kukri	18	Advanced Atoll	25	ASAT
11	AAM-1	19	AIM-9B Sidewinder		
12	AA-5 Ash IR	19a	AIM-9D		

BRAZIL

4192.331

PIRANHA (MAA-1) AIR-TO-AIR MISSILE

MAA-1 Piranha is the designation given to a Brazilian project to develop an indigenous air-to-air missile. The programme has been active for several years, the work being carried out by the Divisão de Sistemas Bélicos (Weapons Systems Division) of the IEA (Instituto de Atividades Espaciais – Space Activities Institute), a branch of the Brazilian Ministry of Aeronautics CTA (Centro Técnico Aeroespacial).

Piranha is intended to be an IR homing weapon with a range of about 10 km at a maximum speed of more than Mach 2 carrying a 12 kg warhead. No information concerning the configuration of the missile has been disclosed for publication, but the general characteristics and the assumed date of its origination suggest that features of contemporary missiles, such as the canard control surfaces of the Sidewinder, R550 Magic, and Shafrir, are likely to be incorporated. Land- and ship-launched versions of the Piranha are envisaged.

CHARACTERISTICS

Length: 2·72 m

Fuselage diameter: 15 cm

Launch weight: 85 kg

Guidance: IR homing

Warhead: 12 kg HE

Speed: Over Mach 2

Range: 10 km (approx)

STATUS

Development began in 1977, but no production decision has been announced. Reports in early 1983 suggested that economic problems could delay production further.

CONTRACTOR

Instituto de Atividades Espaciais, 12200 Sao Jose dos Campos, SP, Brazil.

FRANCE

1176.331
R.530 AIR-TO-AIR MISSILE

This is an all-weather all-aspect air-to-air missile system produced with alternative semi-active radar homing or IR guidance heads. Principal characteristics are: length 328 cm, diameter 26 cm, wing span 110 cm, weight 195 kg. Maximum speed is Mach 3 and range 18 km. Apart from the homing heads the two versions of the R.530 are identical. Propulsion is by a two-stage solid-propellant Hotkiss Brandt motor of 8500 kg static thrust. Either of two types of high explosive warhead produced by the same concern, and weighing 27 kg, can be fitted.

The IR homing version is stated to be capable of successful interceptions from any aspect, relying upon heat from either the jet engine and its exhaust from the rear quarters and local airframe hot-spots by aerodynamic heating when attacking from the front.

The semi-active radar homing head is produced by Electronique Marcel Dassault under the designation AD26 and this is for use with an I-band target illuminating radar.

STATUS

Production ceased in 1980, when deliveries ammounted to at least 2400 missiles, of which 45 per cent are stated to have been exported to 12 countries. Many of these weapons are likely to remain in service.

CONTRACTORS

Matra SA, 2 avenue Louis-Bréguet, 78140 Velizy-Villacoublay, France.

AD26 homing head: Electronique Marcel Dassault, 55 quai Carnot, 92 Saint-Cloud, France.

IR homing head: Société Anonyme de Télécommunications, 41 rue Cantagrel, 75013 Paris, France.

1348.331
R550 MAGIC AIR-TO-AIR MISSILE

The Matra R550 Magic is designed for 'close-combat' operations (from less than 500 metres to more than 6 km), with consequent emphasis upon the ability to withstand high load factors imposed by the severe manoeuvre demands required. The general configuration of the weapon is shown in the accompanying photograph. Propulsion is by a Hotchkiss Brandt solid rocket motor, and operational range is reported to cover from 200 metres, or less, to

as much as 10 km. Twist and steer control of this missile is effected by the canard arrangement of fins at the forward end of the weapon. A SAT IR homing head provides guidance, and the missile launcher houses a liquid nitrogen container to provide cooling for the IR sensor.

CHARACTERISTICS
Type: R550 Magic
Length: 275 cm
Wing span: 66 cm
Diameter: 16 cm

Mirage 2000 fires one of its R550 Magic air-to-air missiles

Weight: 90·7 kg
Guidance: IR homing
Magic Mk 2

In mid-1983 it was revealed that an improved version known as Magic Mk 2 was under development to go into production in 1984. This model employs a new solid-propellant rocket motor, a new IR homing head using the latest technology for high sensitivity, and a new electromagnetic proximity fuze.

The main operating characteristics remain very similar to those of the R550 Magic but with the important addition of a front quadrant attack capability to give an all-aspect engagement facility.

STATUS

Both the French Air Force and Navy have the R550 in their inventories and Magic has been operational since 1975. By April 1983 more than 7000 missiles had been ordered, with some 75 per cent being for export to 15 countries, including: Abu Dhabi, Ecuador, Egypt, Greece, India, Iraq, Kuwait, Libya, Oman, Pakistan, Saudi-Arabia, Spain, South Africa, and Syria. Among the aircraft types that have been fitted are: Mirage III, V and F1, Crusader, Jaguar, Sea Harrier, Super Etendard, Macchi 326K, and Alpha Jet. It is planned to use the R550 Magic on the Mirage 2000.

CONTRACTOR

Matra SA, 2 avenue Louis-Bréguet, 78140 Velizy-Villacoublay, France.

1349.331
SUPER 530 AIR-TO-AIR MISSILE

This is a successor to the Matra R.530 weapon, intended to meet the higher speed and altitude performance requirements of the latest generation of interceptor aircraft.

Two versions have been produced: the Super 530F, which has been operated with the Mirage F1 since 1979; and the Super 530D. The latter is actually a new missile, though with some common items of equipment with the Super F and the same apparent configuration. However, digital processing, a new doppler mode homing head, and increased rocket power lead to increased performance (roughly double in terms of range as that of the Super F, it is claimed).

With a design concept for reaching targets flying at

very high altitude and at high Mach numbers, it comprises: a 'long-wing' of low width, which gives it exceptional aerodynamic qualities, in particular in the area of load factors at altitudes greater than 70 000 feet (21 330 metres); a motor with a very high acceleration rate, which allows the interceptor aircraft to fire with vertical separations of more than 25 000 feet (7620 metres).

The Super 530 is equipped with an electro-magnetic homing head developed by Electronique Marcel Dassault (EMD) and a Matra autopilot, and the missile employs proportional navigation. Steel and steel honeycomb is used for the structures, and this with a ceramic radome allows the Super 530 to withstand speeds of about Mach 4 and manoeuvres of up to 25 g.

CHARACTERISTICS
Length: 354 cm
Tail-fin span: 64 cm (fore), 90 cm (aft)
Body diameter: 26 cm
Wing: Long-chord, small area type, approx 50 cm span
Weight: 245 kg
Homing head: ESD electromagnetic, semi-active
Proximity fuze: Thomson-CSF radar
Propulsion motor: Thomson-Brandt, solid composite
Warhead: Thomson-Brandt, 30 kg, fragmenting
Range: Compatible with Cyrano 4 radar/F1 system
Performance: Shoot-up, shoot-down capability permits engagement of targets more than 7000 m above or below launch aircraft, ECM incorporated
Speed: Mach 4 – 5

STATUS

The French Air Force awarded contracts for the start of series production at the end of 1977, and French squadrons were equipped from January 1980 onward, this model being designated Super 530F. In April 1983 Matra reported outstanding orders for 1200 Super 530 missiles. Following service with the Mirage F1, it is intended for use with the Mirage 2000 in a new version with greater range and snap-up engagement capability, advanced technology, and enhanced ECCM. This is under development as the Matra Super 530D and will be operational in 1986.

A successor project, named MICA (missile d'interception et de combat aérien), is devoted to the development of an advanced interceptor/air combat weapon of the 'fire-and-forget' type to meet anticipated threats of the 1990s.

CONTRACTOR

Matra SA, 2 avenue Louis-Bréguet, 78140 Velizy-Villacoublay, France.

Launch of Matra Super 530 from Mirage 2000

INTERNATIONAL

3340.331
AMRAAM (AIM-120A)

The AIM-120A advanced medium range air-to-air missile (AMRAAM) programme originated in the United States as a joint US Air Force/US Navy study and development project for a new beyond-visual-range air-to-air weapon to replace the AIM-7 Sparrow missile, The AMRAAM programme subsequently evolved into an international project with NATO participation and, with the advanced short-range air-to-air missile (ASRAAM) project (**3622.331** below), it forms an important NATO 'family of weapons' programme. Under this arrangement covering future air-to-air missile requirements, the US is responsible for development of AMRAAM while European NATO members are free to undertake development of a new generation of advanced short-range air-to-air missiles.

The Memorandum of Understanding (MoU) covering the AMRAAM development was initiated in April 1978; progress of the project up to that date, when it was pursued as a joint US Air Force/US Navy programme, is described under the above entry in the US pages of this section in previous editions of *Jane's Weapon Systems*. The air-to-air family of weapons MoU negotiations were completed in February 1980.

AMRAAM will be compatible with F-14, F-15, F-16 and F-18 aircraft as well as Tornado and other air defence and air superiority interceptor aircraft operated by NATO in the late 1980s. It will satisfy the NATO staff requirement for medium-range air-to-air missiles, and the AMRAAM staff target was written by NATO Air Forces Armaments Group SG/13 and is approved by all participating states (with the exception of France). The design calls for an all-weather, all-aspect, radar-guided missile capable of engaging numerically superior aircraft forces before they come within visual range, and there will be a capability for multiple launches at ranges greater than this and for these launches to become autonomous soon after launch to enable the launching aircraft to manoeuvre and/or engage more targets quickly. It is being developed as a successor to the AIM-7F/M Sparrow. Experimental models were built competitively by Hughes and Raytheon and after a fly-off competition, the Hughes design was chosen by the US Air Force in December 1981.

It is anticipated that production AMRAAMs will have about 60 per cent of the weight of the current AIM-7 Sparrow, with the following characteristics which have been issued provisionally by the US Air Force.

CHARACTERISTICS
Length: 3·65 m
Diameter: 178 mm
Wing span: 526 mm
Tail span: 627 mm
Weight: 148 kg
Guidance: Inertial to target area, active radar homing
Speed: Supersonic

The guidance system will employ digital techniques based on a microprocessor and other engineering details include a TWT transmitter, an integrated RF processor on the seeker gimbal, and a steel fuselage structure requiring no thermal protection. It is planned to use semi-custom and standard production LSI chips extensively. The multifunction microprocessor combines navigation, autopilot, data link, radar, fuzing, missile sequencing and self-test in one data processor.

Information given to the US Congress contains details of how AMRAAM is likely to be used with the F-16 aircraft, and this is summarised here. The aircraft

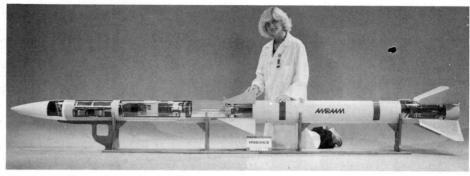

Full-scale cut-away model of AIM-120A reveals internal arrangement details, l to r: antenna/seeker, transmitter and batteries, electronics, warhead (immediately forward of wings), rocket motor and control section

radar will be modified to provide a track-while-scan (TWS) facility and includes a programmable signal processor. The latter will allow multiple target discrimination and tracking, provide software control of radar signal processing to improve responses to ECM, and provide improved air-to-ground features. The TWS mode will be capable of simultaneously tracking multiple targets while continuing to search a large airspace volume for other potential targets. Simultaneous launches of up to eight missiles at multiple targets will also be possible with AMRAAM, and its active radar seeker permits the aircraft to follow a launch-and-manoeuvre pattern, which in the case of a single target engagement follows the following sequence:

(1) in the pre-launch phase the aircraft radar acquires and tracks the target, and an on-board computer calculates the launch acceptability zones and displays the information to the pilot

(2) during the launch phase the pilot first makes his decision to launch the AMRAAM, and inertial reference data on the target and the launch aircraft are fed into the missile computer to provide the necessary initial information

(3) the AMRAAM leaves the aircraft

(4) the inertial mid-course phase is carried out using inertial data provided by the aircraft's avionics system prior to launch and guidance laws stored in the missile computer to navigate the missile to a calculated point in space where the missile seeker will go into the active mode. The aircraft avionics system will display to the pilot the time-to-go to initiation of the active mode, and he continues to track the target on his radar until that point is reached

(5) the terminal phase begins when, at the calculated point, the seeker transmitter is turned on, and the target is detected. The seeker then tracks the target and the missile completes the intercept.

DEVELOPMENT
In 1983 Hughes embarked on a six-month feasibility study into the use of the AIM-120 missile as the basis of a new point defence weapon for ships. Sea AMRAAM, as the project was dubbed was the subject of a contract awarded by US Navy Sea Systems Command, and announced in August 1983.

STATUS
A four-power air-to-air family of weapons MoU was signed by the Federal Republic of Germany, France, the UK and USA in August 1980, under which the US will develop AMRAAM and Britain and Germany will develop the next short-range missile. France adopted 'special observer' status and is not committed to full participation. In June 1984 British Aerospace was chosen as lead contractor in a European consortium

AIM-120A AMRAAM test vehicle on US Navy F-14 Tomcat at Point Mugu Pacific Missile Test Centre

of four companies (BAe, MSDS, MBB and AEG-Telefunken) to study European manufacture of AMRAAM.

The AMRAAM programme completed the initial concept phase in February 1979 when the US Air Force selected Hughes and Raytheon from five bids for validation phase contracts. During this 33-month phase both contractors built and demonstrated their respective models of the AMRAAM, and in December 1981 the Hughes design was selected for full-scale development. This will last for a period of 50 months and a total of 87 guided test vehicles will be launched during this period, with flight testing at Eglin AFB, White Sands Missile Range, and Point Mugu. Production is scheduled to begin in October 1984 and continue into the 1990s, during which time it is planned to manufacture seven lots. A projected total of about 20 000 missiles are expected to be in US Air Force and US Navy inventories by the mid-1990s.

Under the $421 million full-scale development contract awarded to Hughes in December 1981, the company is expected to produce 94 test missiles altogether. This contract contained pre-priced options for 1145 operational missiles and provisions for establishing a US second source for production. The US Air Force selected Raytheon to fulfil the latter function and the international MoU allows for a European production line to be established.

The 1985 US Defence Budget contained sums of $207, $186·7 and $217·7 million in fiscal years 1983/84/85, respectively, and proposed $413 million to fund procurement of 174 missiles in 1985.

CONTRACTOR
Hughes Aircraft Company, Culver City, California 90230, USA.

3622.331
ASRAAM PROGRAMME

The advanced short-range air-to-air missile (ASRAAM) programme began as a joint US Air Force/US Navy project but following the signing of a NATO 'family of weapons' Memorandum of Understanding (MoU) between the USA and certain European nations responsibility for this new generation weapon now rests with the latter countries (see **3340.331**, above). The ASRAAM requirement is for a successor to the AIM-9 Sidewinder missile in the early 1990s and the plan is for European and

American needs for these weapons to be met by production on both sides of the Atlantic.

The European signatories to the air-to-air family of weapons MoU were France, the Federal Republic of Germany and the UK, but with the first of these having only 'special observer' status in respect of both AMRAAM and ASRAAM studies. This however apparently provides France with the option of entering into collaborative production arrangements at a later date. The nominated lead contractors in Britain and Germany are British Aerospace Dynamics Group and Bodenseewerk Gerätetechnik,

collaborated in a feasibility study completed in 1983. Both concerns are applying experience gained in a variety of previous experimental and developmental work, for example the UK short-range air-to-air missile (SRAAM) programme carried out by British Aerospace in the late 1970s. A late model arising from this project was successfully fired in August 1980, when it intercepted an airborne target over the Aberporth range in Wales. The missile was without wings and was steered by swivel nozzle thrust vector control, using an IR seeker. The launch was from a Hunter aircraft and the trial was set up to demonstrate performance under severe intercept conditions. The motor and actuation system were developed by IMI Summerfield and Sperry Gyroscope, Bracknell, and the missile is controlled in roll by a Sperry motor bleed actuation system that vents exhaust gases through four tangential thrusters.

In the Federal Republic of Germany, Bodenseewerke developed in the late 1960s and early 1970s the Viper air-to-air missile as a successor to the AIM-9B/FGW Mod 2 Sidewinder. Viper was equipped with a unique Bodenseewerke two-axis platform IR seeker head of advanced design, giving the high performance missile an all aspect attack capability. After termination of the Viper development in 1974

and selection of the US Navy's AIM-9L Sidewinder, a joint US/FRG back-up programme combining the Viper guidance section and the AIM-9L aft section was launched in 1975. Under this programme, called ALASCA (all aspect capability), two test firings of ALASCA missiles took place in 1980.

In the UK, Marconi Space and Defence Systems are known to be working on a number of missile seeker concepts and designs suitable for small diameter missiles capable of short-range air interception missions.
STATUS
Feasibility studies completed in 1983 were followed by project definition, with production contract to be

awarded after satisfactory completion of trials. A new company, BBG (Bodenseewerk British Aerospace GmbH) was formed in November 1983 to carry out the development and production of ASRAAM. BBG is jointly owned by BAe and Bodenseewerk.
CONTRACTORS
British Aerospace Dynamics Group, Hatfield Division, Manor Road, Hatfield, Hertfordshire AL10 9LL, England.

Bodenseewerk Gerätetechnik GmbH, 7770 Uberlingen/Bodensee, Federal Republic of Germany.

ISRAEL

4185.331
PYTHON 3 AIR-TO-AIR MISSILE
Python 3 is the name given to the third-generation successor developed to follow the Israeli Shafrir II air-to-air missile. It was first revealed publicly at the Paris Air Show in June 1981, and bears a close resemblance to the Shafrir, which in turn reveals much of the influence exerted by the US Sidewinder on its design. Python 3 is IR homing also, and a solid-propellant rocket motor can be reasonably assumed. The rear aerodynamic control surfaces exhibit the same gyroscopically-actuated stabilising tabs that are found on Shafrir, the Soviet Atoll and certain Sidewinders. The canard control surfaces are of similar triangular planform as those of Shafrir but it is not known if they are actuated by the same (pneumatic) technique.

It is almost certain that improvements have been made to the seeker system and its cooling arrangements, as well as to other sub-systems such as the fuze and propulsion. Israeli sources report that the guidance system is much more sophisticated than that of the earlier Shafrir missile, and the acquisition

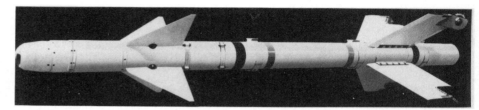
Python 3 air-to-air missile

envelope has been expanded so that engagements can be undertaken from all target aspects. Maximum and minimum engagement ranges are quoted as 15 km and 500 metres, respectively. The warhead charge consists of about 11 kg of high explosive.
CHARACTERISTICS
Length: 3 m (approx)
Weight: 120 kg
Warhead: HE, 11 kg
Max range: 15 km
Minimum effective range: 500 m

STATUS
Official information on when Python 3 became operational has not been forthcoming, but there have been reports of its use in air battles over the Lebanon in Mid-1982. It was confirmed at the time of the Paris Air Show that this missile has now completed its development phase.
CONTRACTOR
Rafael Armament Development Authority, Ministry of Defence, PO Box 2082, 31021 Haifa, Israel.

1659.331
SHAFRIR AIR-TO-AIR MISSILE
Shafrir is an air-to-air, IR homing missile for use against high performance aircraft at heights up to 18 000 metres (60 000 ft). It is a relatively small missile, 16 cm diameter and 260 cm long, with pneumatically-operated control fins at the fore-end and stabilising surfaces at the rear. The latter are fitted with the gyroscopically-actuated tabs found on the Sidewinder and Soviet Atoll missiles, for roll stabilisation. Approximate launch weight is 93 kg, of which the warhead accounts for 11 kg. Contact and proximity firing of the warhead are provided.

Simplicity was a major design objective, and both missile and aircraft-fitted elements of the Shafrir weapon system have been kept to the minimum. Electronics are solid-state. Apart from the firing circuit, no aircraft-installed equipment is needed.

The missile and its launcher are mounted under the wing of the aircraft and attached to a specially-designed adaptor.

The current version is the Mk 2, the Mk 1 model is understood to have been the first pre-production version. The rumoured Shafrir Mk 3 is thought to have become the Python 3 (**4185.331**).
OPERATION
Firing of Shafrir is on a 'see-and-shoot' basis. When a target is detected within the firing range, the audio signal is heard and an indicator light in the cockpit is automatically operated. This indicates that the missile launch button can be used. From this point, the guidance system is completely independent of the launching aircraft.
STATUS
Shafrir has been launched in air combat with a high kill ratio (75 per cent) on numerous occasions, according to official Israeli sources and more than

Shafrir air-to-air missile on Israeli aircraft

200 kills were credited to Shafrir during the October 1973 conflict. Details of export sales have not been released officially but among countries believed to have been supplied are: Chile, South Africa and Taiwan.

The successor is the Python 3 (**4185.331** above).

CONTRACTOR
Rafael Armament Development Authority, Ministry of Defence, PO Box 2082, 31021 Haifa, Israel.

ITALY

1656.331
ASPIDE MULTIROLE MISSILE
Aspide is a high performance multirole missile, optimised for air-to-air and surface-to-air missions. It is based on the use of a semi-active radar, with monopulse receiver, guidance system which ensures all-weather and all-aspect operation.

Principal characteristics are length 3·7 m, body diameter 20·3 cm, wing span 100 cm (air-to-air) or 80 cm (surface-to-air), fin span 80 cm (air-to-air) or 64 cm (surface-to-air), launch weight 220 kg. Propulsion is by means of a single-stage solid-propellant rocket motor which will give speeds of more than Mach 2·5 in the surface-to-air role.

Aspide can be employed on most modern high performance interceptor aircraft, for which this missile constitutes an all-aspect, all-weather air-to-air weapon that is very effective from very high altitudes to very low level engagements, and in the presence of intense ECM activity. In the surface-to-air role, Aspide is now operational in the Albatros naval point defence weapon system (**1551.281**), and in the 'Spada' ground-based low altitude air defence system (**2250.131**).

Technical areas in which major objectives have been achieved are seeker range, sub-clutter visibility, fuzing system, multiple target effectiveness, ECCM capabilities, functional modularity of construction, reliability, and ease of maintenance. Thin-film microwave circuitry developed by Selenia is incorporated in the design.
DEVELOPMENT
Development was started in late 1969 and concluded

Captive missile tests of air-to-air Aspide on Italian F-104S Starfighter

in 1977. The contracting agency is the Italian Ministry of Defence with direction of the programme under the Costarmaereo.
STATUS
Flight tests began in July 1974. The first contractual missile firing took place in May 1975 at the Italian Missile Test Range at Salto di Quirra, Sardinia, where a prototype was launched from a ground platform. In the meantime, captive tests by an Italian Air Force aircraft had proved the main radar seeker functioning and performance. The first phase of firing tests was concluded in December 1975. Both test programmes were regarded as highly successful and proved the full realisation of design objectives.

Full operational firings from the vessels of different navies were successfully carried out in 1979. Some of them were made from a ship equipped with the NATO Sea Sparrow weapon system, and this was made

possible by a modification carried out under an Italian Navy contract. The modification is understood to be readily reversible in either direction, and can be carried out at sea. No details of airborne deployments have been released for publication.

The first batch of production missiles was delivered in 1977 for use in the Albatros system, and production is continuing at full rate at the manufacturer's plant on behalf of various customers.
CONTRACTORS
Prime contractor: Selenia, Industrie Elettroniche Associate SpA, Via Tiburtina, Km 12400, 00130 Rome, Italy.

Main sub-contractors: SNIA-Viscosa SpA, Rome, Italy.

Microtecnica SpA, Turin, Italy.

JAPAN

1187.331
MITSUBISHI AAM-1 AIR-TO-AIR MISSILE
Few details have been disclosed of the air-to-air missile which is replacing the Sidewinder on F-86F and F-104J interceptors of the Japanese Air Self Defence Force. Unofficial data include a missile length of about 2·6 metres and a launch weight of 70 kg. Range is in the region of 7 km. Guidance is by IR homing.
STATUS
It has been reported that the AAM-1 had already entered operational services by 1969, and a total planned production of 330 units had been delivered by late 1971.
CONTRACTOR
Mitsubishi Heavy Industries Ltd, 5-1, Marunouchi 2-chome, Chiyoda-ku, Tokyo 100, Japan.

Mitsubishi AAM-1 air-to-air missile

1188.331
MITSUBISHI AAM-2 AIR-TO-AIR MISSILE
The AAM-2 is under development as a successor to the AAM-1 air-to-air interception missile. The new weapon is understood to have started as a dogfight missile research project in the late 1970s. It has been reported that IR guidance will be employed but the AAM-2 will have improved manoeuvrability and an

enlarged engagement envelope. The new missile will probably have the double-canard control fin configuration of the type employed on the French R550 Magic (**1348.331**) and it is known that this system was under study in Japan during 1980.
STATUS
Development. Basic research was intially carried out by the Japanese Self Defence Agency's Technical

Research Institute. The weapon is understood to be intended for use with Japanese F-4 and F-15 aircraft.
CONTRACTOR
Mitsubishi Heavy Industries Ltd, 5-1, Marunouchi 2-chome, Chiyoda-ku, Tokyo 100, Japan.

SOUTH AFRICA

4526.331
KUKRI AIR-TO-AIR MISSILE
Kukri is the export version of the South African Air Force's (SAAF) V3B IR-guided dogfight missile and like V3B, it is used with a helmet-mounted sight. Compatibility with existing aircraft and weapon systems was maintained by conforming to the Sidewinder Aero 3B and M550 Magic launcher mechanical and electrical interfaces. Development of the earlier V3A system started at the end of 1971 and it went into production in 1975. It was the first air-to-air missile to be coupled to a helmet sight and is still operational. The SAAF operational requirements evolved over the years and work on V3B, an upgraded version of V3A, was started in 1975. System improvements included an IR-head with a bigger look

angle and high sensitivity, an increased helmet sight designation angle and an upgraded motor. V3B went into production in 1979. The export version, Kukri, is now available to selected customers, and the system is cleared for use on the Dassault-Breguet Mirage III and Mirage F1 types. Trial installations have been made on other aircraft types. Both V3A and V3B are currently operational with the SAAF.

Kukri is a highly manoeuvrable dogfight missile with an asymmetric double-canard aerodynamic configuration. In one plane there are two fixed canards in front with two double-delta moveable canards aft and in the other plane there are two simple delta movable canards. The canards are actuated by a hot gas servo and twist and steer control is employed. The triangular canards give roll control and the

double-delta canards control pitch acceleration. The tail fins rotate freely around the rear end of the rocket motor. A double base solid-propellant rocket motor and a conventional fragmentation warhead are used.

The missile is delivered in two sections, the first being the motor and warhead assembly and the second the guidance, control and fuzing assembly (GCF). Assembly of the two sections can be effected in a few minutes using standard tools and a simple alignment jig.

A helmet sight is coupled to the missile, thereby giving the pilot an off-boresight target acquisition capability. The helmet sight consists of an IR diode array attitude measurement system and interface electronics to the missile.

The launcher contains the clean air cooling system

for the missile IR detector as well as the necessary power supplies and helmet sight interface electronics. It is mounted on the wingtip in the case of the Mirage F1 and on an underwing strong-point in the case of the Mirage III.

OPERATION

Besides the special flying helmet and consequent modifications to the personnel connector on the ejection seat, installation of the Kukri missile system requires some minor aircraft wiring modifications and the addition of three black boxes – the reference unit, the pre-amplifier and the data processing unit. The first two of these must be mounted in the cockpit while the data processing unit can be installed in any suitable location.

This system was designed to be as simple as possible in operational usage and all the controls related to mode switching, target designation and missile firing are situated on the joystick and the throttle. The pilot simply has to look at the enemy aircraft and when target acquisition is signalled by an audio tone in his headset, he designates the target, thereby putting his missile in the tracking mode. Once the missile is tracking the target the pilot can move his head at will. The missile can be fired while tracking or even in the aiming mode, provided that the audio tone is present.

The pilot's decision making is further simplified by the aiming reticle extinguishing automatically when the target is outside the helmet sight designation limits.

The missile can be fired over the entire flight envelope of the clean aircraft (any speed, altitude and load factor). Minimum operational range is 300 m and the maximum varies between 2 km at low altitudes to in excess of 4 km at high altitudes.

CHARACTERISTICS

Missile
Length: 2944 mm
Diameter: 127 mm
Tail fin span: 530 mm
Fixed canard span: 420 mm
Weight: 73·4 kg
Launcher
Length: 2495 mm

South African V3 Kukri air-to-air missile

Weight: 32 kg
Data processing unit
Dimensions: 238 × 226 × 82 mm
Weight: 3·8 kg
Reference unit
Dimensions: 85 × 31 × 57 mm
Weight: 0·17 kg
Preamplifier
Dimensions: 132 × 102 × 36 mm
Weight: 0·34 kg
Pilot's helmet
Weight: 2·3 kg
Minimum range: 300 m
Max range: 2 km at sea level; 4 km + at high altitudes
Manoeuvrability: 25 g sustained; 35 g peak
Max speed: Launch velocity + 500 m/s
Launch limitations
Max load factor: 7 g
Max altitude: 50 000 ft (15 240 m)
Max speed: Mach 1·8

STATUS
The V3A went into production in 1975 and both it and the later V3B are operational with the SAAF.

Indigenously developed V3 Kukri missile on SAAF aircraft

Production of the V3B began in 1979. The export version of the V3B, Kukri, has been available since 1982.

CONTRACTOR
Armscor Corporation of South Africa Ltd, Pretoria 0001, Republic of South Africa.

UNION OF SOVIET SOCIALIST REPUBLICS

3337.331
ACRID (AA-6) AIR-TO-AIR MISSILE
The AA-6, NATO code-name Acrid, was the first of a new family of Soviet air-to-air missiles to be seen by the West, when the first picture of it on a MiG-25 Foxbat aircraft was published in Western magazines in the closing months of 1975.

The resemblance to the earlier AA-3 Anab (**1144.331**) is quite clear, but AA-6 is appreciably larger, having an estimated length of 6·29 metres. This dimension refers to the radar-guided version of the missile there being also an IR homing model which has a length of about 5·8 metres. Two of each type are

carried on the Foxbat, the latter type of missile carried on the inner pylons. The launch weight is likely to be in the region of 750 kg, with the radar version somewhat heavier than the IR model. This weight includes a warhead of up to 100 kg, probably high-explosive fragmentation type.

The AA-6 is thought to be the Soviet approximation to the American Phoenix long-range air-to-air missile, although it is doubted if it has that weapon's multiple target capability. However it is possible that the IR homing version is launched very shortly after the initial radar-guided Acrid missile to a similar point in space where it is anticipated that the IR seeker will

detect and lock-on to its own target. Such a mode of operation would be feasible and useful against multiple targets approaching together. For maximum efficacy, the AA-6 would require an inertial- or autopilot-controlled mid-course phase, and it would enable the radar-guided version to fly to the target area without requiring target illumination by the aircraft's radar if an active homing head is incorporated. The size and weight of the AA-6 tend to support this suggestion.

Estimates of range for the radar version have varied between sources but generally seem agreed on figures in the neighbourhood of 40 to 50 km. These may prove to be on the conservative side as may the estimates of about 20 km for the IR homing model. However, the latter case is subject to greater variations due to the operational and environmental circumstances, eg day or night, altitude, weather, aspect of target and sun, etc.

The wings of the Acrid missile plainly have control surfaces and it is conjectured that the canards are also used for control purposes. Solid propulsion is

Foxbat interceptors armed with AA-6 Acrid missiles

Libyan MiG-25 Foxbat A armed with two AA-6 Acrid air-to-air missiles (USN)

assumed, and most estimates credit the AA-6 with a speed of about Mach 2·2.

STATUS
Acrid is the standard armament of the MiG-25 Foxbat, which can carry four such missiles. In addition to the Soviet air forces, other possible users include the Libyan Air Force and perhaps Algeria and Iraq. The AA-6 has been reported more recently on Su-15 Flagon D and E aircraft.

1145.331
ASH (AA-5) AIR-TO-AIR MISSILE

Ash is the NATO code-name assigned to large missiles carried beneath the wings of Soviet Tupolev Fiddler long-range interceptor aircraft. Four such missiles, which are assumed by Western observers to be air-to-air weapons, can be carried by each aircraft. Both I-band radar-guided and IR homing versions are in use, two radar homing missiles generally being carried on the wing outer pylons and two IR homing missiles on the inner pylons of the Fiddler interceptor.

Estimated dimensions are: length 530 cm, wing span 130 cm, diameter 30 cm. Cruciform wing and tail surfaces, in-line, are fitted, the former having a sharply swept delta planform. The tail fins have little sweep on either leading or trailing edges and are mounted close behing the wing trailing edges.

The size of the missiles, parent aircraft, and the large nose radome of the latter, suggests that they are intended for long-range interception. A British MoD report of April 1979 gave a figure of about 30 km as the range. It was also stated that some thousands had been produced.

STATUS
Ash has been reported in service with the forces of Bulgaria, Czechoslovakia, East Germany, Poland and Romania, in addition to the Soviet Union.

Radar and IR guided Ash air-to-air missiles on Soviet Fiddler aircraft

3338.331
APEX (AA-7) AIR-TO-AIR MISSILE

Apex, AA-7, is one of three new-generation Soviet air-to-air missiles which became known in the West in 1976. Preceded slightly by the AA-6, Acrid, (**3337.331**) which was revealed in late 1975, Apex is comparable to the American Sparrow and is thought to be a successor to AA-3, Anab, (**1144.331**) to which there is some resemblance. However, Apex is clearly of superior performance and somewhat larger. In particular, the provision of a supplementary set of control surfaces at the rear of the missile, in addition to the canard fins ahead of the wings, indicates high manoeuvrability.

Both radar-guided and IR homing models have been reported, and the US Defence Intelligence Agency refers to AA-7a and AA-7b versions. One of each type comprises the standard armament of the interceptor version of the MiG-23 aircraft.

Estimated length of the radar version is about 4·3 metres, with the IR homing model slightly shorter. Weight is probably between 300 and 350 kg, of which the warhead could account for up to 40 kg. Solid

Soviet MiG-23 Flogger B all-weather interceptor carries varied armament of air-to-air missiles with AA-7 Apex radar homing weapons on outer weapon pylons and smaller, IR guided AA-8 Aphid missiles on inboard stations

propulsion is assumed, and ranges for the radar and IR versions are probably in the region of 35 km and 15 km, respectively.

STATUS
Apex is used on MiG-21 and MiG-23 aircraft and is thought to be carried on the MiG-25 Foxbat-E also.

3339.331
APHID (AA-8) AIR-TO-AIR MISSILE

Aphid, AA-8, is thought to be a small close combat air-to-air missile, possibly derived from the AA-2 Atoll (**1146.331**) although almost certainly a replacement for that weapon. It may be deployed with the MiG-23 Flogger aircraft, but if it is indeed an Atoll replacement, the list of aircraft types with which it can operate will be considerably longer.

Radar and IR homing models are reported to exist, but to date the only photographs seen are of what is assumed to be an IR guided version. Estimated length is about 2·1 metres for the radar version and slightly less for the IR model. Launch weight is about 54 kg, with a warhead of some 7 to 9 kg of the high explosive type. Probable range is about 8 km for the IR Aphid and rather more for the radar version.

STATUS
In use with MiG-23 Flogger and MiG-21 Fishbed aircraft. Soviet Navy carrier-borne Yak-36 Flogger aircraft have been noted carrying AA-8 Aphid missiles.

MiG-21 Fishbed interceptor carries AA-8 Aphid IR homing missiles on inner weapon stations, and outer stations have AA-2 Advanced Atoll radar homing missiles

4768.331
AA-9 AIR-TO-AIR MISSILE

AA-9 is the numerical designation assigned by the US authorities to the air-to-air missile deployed with a recently sighted MiG-31, Foxhound interceptor aircraft entering Soviet service. This aircraft is reported to have a capacity of eight AA-9s. No NATO reporting name has been associated with the AA-9 missile at the time of publication, and neither have there been any official or unofficial details of the weapon's performance or physical characteristics published. The main function of the missile is understood to be long-range interception with, it is claimed, a 'snap-down' capability for engagement of low-flying targets which may or may not be cruise missiles. Until there is more information and some idea of the weapon's configuration and size, further conjecture at this stage is of dubious value.

4820.331
AA-X-10 AIR-TO-AIR MISSILE

The new missile designed for use with the recently introduced Soviet MiG-29, Fulcrum, and Su-27, Flanker combat aircraft has been assigned the number AA-X-10 in the US sequence; the 'X' denoting the fact that the missile was not then (early 1984) thought to be operational. Very few details of the AA-X-10 have been made public, and no photographs have been obtained, but the official US view is that the weapon is a medium range air-to-air missile with similar capabilities to the AA-9 (**4768.331** above).

A DoD assessment of Soviet military resources states that the MiG-29 Fulcrum aircraft can carry six AA-X-10 missiles, while the larger Su-27 Flanker carries a load of eight missiles. A more detailed appraisal of the AA-X-10 must await more information and, ideally, photographic evidence.

1144.331
ANAB (AA-3) AIR-TO-AIR MISSILE

Anab is the NATO code-name assigned to the Soviet air-to-air missile first seen carried by the Yak-28 (Firebar) in 1961. It was subsequently seen on the Su-9 (Fishpot) interceptor, and is known to have been adopted as a standard weapon by the Soviet forces.

The existence of both I-band radar and IR homing versions has been reported. A radar system with which the AA-3 Anab has been employed is known within NATO by the code-name Skip Scan. Length of both versions is estimated at approximately 360 cm, diameter 28 cm, wing span 130 cm. Anab has a cylindrical body with a large cruciform wing assembly at the rear of the missile, and a set of four in-line fins ahead of the wings, and about one-quarter of the missile length from the nose end.

Solid fuel propulsion is assumed, and the range has been quoted by the UK MoD as in excess of 16 km. The same source also estimated total production as certainly in the thousands.

This weapon has been in operational use for a considerable time and it is reasonable to assume that it has been the subject of periodic improvements and updates in the same way as some long-life western counterparts have been modified.
STATUS
Believed to be in the process of withdrawal from Soviet forces, but this could take a considerable time to complete. In addition to the USSR, other nations supplied include Bulgaria, Czechoslovakia, East Germany, Hungary, Poland and Romania. Aircraft types which are, or have been associated with either or both versions of the AA-3 Anab include: Su-9 Fishpot, Su-15 Flagon, and Yak-28 Firebar.

Yak-28P Firebar armed with AA-3 Anab air-to-air missile

1146.331
ATOLL (AA-2) AIR-TO-AIR MISSILE

Atoll is the NATO code-name assigned to a Soviet air-to-air missile, believed to bear the USSR designation SB06 and/or K13A. American Defence Intelligence Agency reports refer to AA-2a, AA-2b, AA-2c and AA-2d versions of Atoll, lending support to the claim that a semi-active radar homing model has been produced. In any case, it denotes that at least four identifiable models have been deployed during the long operational life of this weapon. UK sources identify two versions as the AA-2 Atoll and the AA-2·2 Advanced Atoll, respectively, the latter being the radar-guided model.

This missile closely resembles the American AIM-9B, IR homing Sidewinder and is of similar dimensions and (estimated) weight. Atoll dimensions are: length 280 cm, diameter 12 cm, forward control surfaces span 45 cm, tail plane span 53 cm. The so-called Advanced Atoll, ie the semi-active radar homing model, is an estimated 30 cm longer than the IR guided versions, the extra length consisting of an extended nose section which is presumed to house the radar receiver and antenna package. Solid-propellant and conventional high explosive warhead are assumed.

Diametrically opposed pairs of the forward control surfaces are linked and work in unison for missile steering. The rear surfaces incorporate small tabs in which are inserted gyroscopic wheels driven by the

MiG-21 Fishbed interceptor is armed with both standard IR homing AA-2 Atoll air-to-air missile and radar guided Advanced Atoll (on outer wing weapon stations)

airstream. It has been deduced that these are locked until after missile launch, and that their subsequent purpose is to provide additional stabilisation and/or a measure of control augmentation for missile steering.
STATUS
Atoll has been widely deployed with MiG-21 (Fishbed) interceptors of the Soviet home forces and on export versions of this aircraft. Known foreign users include Egypt and India. The latter country, which has over 50 MiG-21s, has facilities for Atoll production under licence.

In addition to the Warsaw Pact countries, there is an impressive list of foreign users which includes: Afghanistan, Algeria, China, Cuba, Egypt, Finland, India, Iraq, North Korea, Syria, and Viet-Nam, and the full list of non-Soviet operators of Atoll is thought to number 20 or more countries. In addition to the Indian licence-built version, there is also an indigenous Chinese model.

It is now thought to be obsolescent with Soviet air forces, probably to be replaced by the AA-8 Aphid (**3339.331**).

Libyan MiG-23 Flogger E armed with four standard AA-2 Atoll IR homing air-to-air missiles (USN)

UNITED KINGDOM

1774.331
SKY FLASH AIR-TO-AIR MISSILE

Sky Flash, formerly known as Project XJ521, is a new medium range all-weather air-to-air missile based on the Raytheon Sparrow missile but with a completely new electronics suite and of considerably improved performance. It is a semi-active radar guided missile capable of attacking both subsonic and supersonic targets from very low to high altitudes and has an all-round attack capability. It employs a new advanced guidance system developed by Marconi Space and Defence Systems at Stanmore, Middlesex, and a new advanced fuze system developed by EMI Electronics Ltd, at Hayes, Middlesex. The MSDS seeker employs the monopulse technique which provides very high resistance to ECM. The missile has a snap-up capability which allows launches from low levels (100 metres or less) to intercept high altitude targets; a complementary snap-down facility enables targets to be engaged from above against a background of ground clutter. The autopilot and power systems have been updated by British Aerospace Dynamics Group to include solid-state electronics and thermal batteries. British Aerospace Dynamics Group also manufactures the missile structure and carries out final assembly and testing of the complete weapon.

CHARACTERISTICS
Length: 3·7 m
Wing span: 1·02 m
Diameter: 203 mm
Weight: 192 kg
Range: 40 km
Guidance: Semi-active radar, monopulse
Warhead: 30 kg
Fuze: Radar proximity
Propulsion: Solid Aerojet Mk 52 Mod 2
STATUS
Project definition was completed in 1973 with the development programme following immediately. A contract for full production was awarded by the MoD in 1975.

R & D and RAF evaluation trials were completed in 1977. These trials entailed a variety of attack situations and were completed successfully. Several firings of the non-warheaded missiles produced direct hits and others passed within lethal miss distance of targets.

Targets were representative of a range of hostile aircraft and some were enhanced to produce severe glint and thus pose a severe test of the accuracy of the missile's guidance. Firings were also made against targets with only a small echoing area, and others in exacting ECM and target manoeuvring conditions

Sky Flash firing from Tornado F2

and against multiple targets. Targets were engaged successfully at near sea level and also at high altitude in snap down, snap up, level and manoeuvring attacks.

In December 1978 a £60 million contract with the Swedish Forsvarets Materielverk (FFV) for the supply of Sky Flash missiles to arm RSAF JA37 Viggen all-weather fighter aircraft was confirmed. This follows a two-year integration programme and deliveries of the Sky Flash (Swedish designation, RB71) began in the third quarter of 1980. In the course of the JA37 integration programme, and during routine RAF squadron practice firing, the weapon's high performance obtained in evaluation trials was confirmed.

In December 1983 BAe announced the successful conclusion of a reliability verification and firing programme for the Swedish authorities. At the same time it was revealed that the BAe Lostock plant had completed the 1000th Sky Flash missile.

Sky Flash is in service with RAF Phantoms and will be used with the Tornado F2, from which it has been fired. It has also been fired successfully from the F-16.

In May 1981 Aerojet Tactical Systems received a contract valued at over $1 million for production of Mk 52 Mod 2 rocket motors. The contract called for production to run from July to December 1982, and included an option for a further similar quantity.
CONTRACTORS
Prime contractor: British Aerospace Dynamics Group, Manor Road, Hatfield, Hertfordshire AL10 9LL, England.

Homing head: Marconi Space and Defence Systems Ltd, The Grove, Warren Lane, Stanmore, Middlesex HA7 4LY, England.

Fuze: Thorn EMI Electronics Ltd, Springfield Road, Hayes, Middlesex UB4 OLJ, England.

Main sub-contractor: Raytheon Company, Missile Systems Division, Bedford, Massachusetts 01730, USA.

1080.331
RED TOP AIR-TO-AIR MISSILE

IR homing air-to-air weapon for use against sub- and supersonic aircraft. All-altitude operation is possible against manoeuvring targets and all-aspect attack capability is provided by the Red Top homing and guidance system.

At one time referred to as Firestreak Mk IV (**1079.331** in 1980-81 and earlier editions), Red Top has a similar configuration and dimensions of the same order, but performance is considerably higher as a result of the application of advances in technology.

Red Top retains the configuration of four fixed wings and four moving rear control surfaces. Wing and control surface planforms and sections differ from those of Firestreak, and match the unofficially quoted speed of Mach 3. The IR guidance system has been further developed to allow target interception from virtually any direction, and a hemispherical nose houses the IR sensor.

Internally, the warhead (31 kg) has been moved forward next to the fuzing system, and the control actuators have been located nearer to the surfaces they operate.

The power of the internal solid propellant booster rocket motor provides a range of at least 12 km.

Missile dimensions are length 3·27 metres, diameter 22·2 cm, wing span 90·8 cm. Up to four missiles can be carried without significant detriment to aircraft performance.
STATUS
Red Top is still available for service with RAF

RAF Lightning interceptors carrying Firestreak (upper) and Red Top (lower) air-to-air missile

Lightnings and with aircraft of this type flown by the Kuwaiti and Saudi Arabian Air Forces, but should be regarded as obsolescent.

CONTRACTOR
British Aerospace Dynamics Group, Manor Road, Hatfield, Hertfordshire AL10 9LL, England.

UNITED STATES OF AMERICA

4186.331
ASAT ANTI-SATELLITE WEAPON

Funded under the heading of Space Defence Operations (PE12450F), the US Air Force is developing a prototype miniature air-launched system (PMALS) to meet a need foreseen for an aircraft-launched anti-satellite (ASAT) capability. This need is justified in the DoD Fiscal Year 1982 Report of January 1981 as being necessary in the absence of agreements limiting the use of space to peaceful purposes but while facing a previously tested Soviet ASAT system. Under these circumstances, it was stated, the US President (Carter) directed that vigorous efforts to develop a US ASAT should be undertaken.

Despite this, it is understood that the three main contractors now engaged on this task were already working on this problem, and had been for a considerable period. Boeing for instance is believed to have been occupied in this way since 1975, or earlier, part of the time under contract to Vought. Both these concerns are collaborating with a third, McDonnell Aircraft, in the development and testing of an advanced technology interceptor missile capable of being launched from an F-15 fighter aircraft. The latter is required to be capable of preparation for the ASAT mission from the standard 'line' configuration in six hours or less.

The weapon envisaged for the PMALS tests comprises a first stage based on the Boeing SRAM (**1107.311**) short-range attack missile, an Altair III second stage provided by Vought and a miniature vehicle warhead terminal stage, also a Vought responsibility. McDonnell is modifying the F-15 for the ASAT role, including provisions for housing the 'carrier aircraft equipment' (CAE) package in the F-15's weapons bay. Guidance algorithms for the aircraft, launch and missile initiating procedure will be stored in the F-15 aircraft computer, and the F-15's head-up display will be employed to provide steering cues to the pilot for launching the ASAT weapon. The SRAM-based first stage is being modified by Boeing to carry the Altair III second stage, the basic SRAM having a range of between 60 and 160 km depending on the flight profile etc, at speeds of Mach 3 or more, under inertial guidance and carrying a very respectable payload. No details have been released on the Vought Altair III second stage vehicle beyond the fact that it is the fourth stage propulsion unit of the Vought-built Scout space launch vehicle.

The prototype vehicle resembles a conventional tactical missile about 5·4 metres long and between 40 and 50 cm in diameter. Weight has been estimated at about 1200 kg, of which the miniature homing vehicle payload is believed to account for some 16 kg.

The satellite 'kill' mechanism has not been disclosed but the possibility of the ASAT terminal stage making a direct hit on the target has been reported; this is one aspect that may be assumed to be a major aspect of the experimental development programme for ASAT.

F-15 Eagle aircraft carrying ASAT missile

Cut-away drawing of ASAT Miniature Vehicle

STATUS
Preliminary work by ASAT contractors is thought to have started in the 1970s. Vought was awarded a four-year $268 million contract in late 1980 for ASAT development, and Boeing reported its work during 1980 to be worth $6·7 million.

A Space Defence Operations Centre (SPADOC) was established at the NORAD Cheyenne Mountain Complex in 1979/80 to provide command, control and communications to manage space defence operations. This is being modified to handle ASAT operations and these changes are being carried out with hardware and software developments on a schedule to suit ASAT tests.

In June 1983 it was reported that the US Air Force 318th fighter/interceptor squadron, based at McChord AFB, Washington, was being re-equipped with F-15 aircraft (replacing F-106s) to operate ASAT weapons. The first F-15 was handed over in June 1983. The first test flight launch took place in January 1984.

In February 1984 it was stated that the ASAT programme test and evaluation phase was continuing, and funds are being sought in fiscal year 1985 to start procurement of the system.
CONTRACTORS
LTV Aerospace and Defence Company, Vought Missiles and Advanced Programmes Division, PO Box 225907, Dallas, Texas 75265, USA.

Boeing Aerospace Company, PO Box 3999, Seattle, Washington 98124, USA.

McDonnell Aircraft Company, PO Box 516, St Louis, Missouri 63166, USA.

1085.331
FALCON (AIM-4D) AIR-TO-AIR MISSILE

This is a lightweight air-to-air missile similar in size and configuration to the AIM-4C but equipped with the improved IR homing head of the larger AIM-4G Super Falcon. This gives better performance against high-speed manoeuvring targets and confers all-aspect attack capability. Principal characteristics are: length 198 cm, diameter 16·25 cm, wing span 50·8 cm, weight about 60 kg, solid fuel motor, high-explosive warhead, speed Mach 4.
DEVELOPMENT
Chronologically, development of the AIM-4D took place after that of other members of the Falcon series, such as AIM-4E, F, and G (which see) and its former designation was GAR-2B. As air defence missiles, earlier Falcon versions were designed for the interception of bomber aircraft. AIM-4D development was undertaken to improve performance sufficiently for the engagement of enemy fighter aircraft. This was undertaken under a joint US Air Force/Hughes programme.
STATUS
AIM-4D was used by the US Air Force Tactical Air Command and Air Defence Command, and was carried by F-4, F-101 and F-102 aircraft types. Thousands of AIM-4B and C Falcons were converted to AIM-4D standard.

It is currently carried by CF-101 interceptors of the Royal Canadian Air Force and on Japanese Air Self-Defence F-4J tactical aircraft.

A similar version, known as the HM-58 is built under licence in Sweden, where it bears the designation RB28.
CONTRACTOR
Hughes Aircraft Company, Canoga Park, California 91304, USA.

1086.331
SUPER FALCON (AIM-4E/F) AIR-TO-AIR MISSILE

This missile represents an interim stage in the development of the Falcon series, coming between the AIM-4A and C and the AIM-4F and AIM-4G models. In general configuration the AIM-4E more closely resembles the AIM-4F.

This was equipped with an improved radar guidance system providing increased accuracy and greater resistance to ECM. A new solid fuel, two-level thrust rocket motor was installed to provide a high launching thrust followed by a lower level thrust to sustain missile velocity.

Guidance is by semi-active radar homing as in the AIM-4A. The AIM-4E was powered by a longer burning solid fuel rocket motor to provide longer range, a higher launching speed, and a higher combat ceiling than earlier models. A more powerful high explosive warhead was also fitted. Only about 300 models of this version were produced before being succeeded by the later variant, the AIM-4F. The wings are extended forward by fillets, and weight and dimensions are slightly increased to: length 218·4 cm, diameter 16·5 cm, wing span 60·9 cm, weight about

63·5 kg, in the case of the AIM-4E, and length 218·4 cm, diameter 16·7 cm, wing span 60·9 cm, weight 68 kg, for the AIM-4F. Speed of the AIM-4F is in excess of Mach 3.

DEVELOPMENT

The AIM-4E was originally developed as the GAR-3 and was introduced in 1958. It was succeeded two years later, after 300 units had been produced, by the AIM-4F (formerly GAR-3A).

STATUS

Aircraft equipped include the F-106 Delta Dart interceptor.

CONTRACTOR

Hughes Aircraft Company, Canoga Park, California 91304, USA.

California Air National Guard F-106 fires a radar-guided AIM-4F Falcon missile during firing practice

---

1087.331
SUPER FALCON (AIM-4G) AIR-TO-AIR MISSILE

The AIM-4G Super Falcon is the IR seeking counterpart of the AIM-4F missile. It is equipped with an IR detector system which enables it to lock-on to smaller targets at greater ranges than earlier Hughes IR missiles. The same seeker is used in the AIM-4D Falcon. Compared with the AIM-4F Super Falcon, the

AIM-4G is shorter (105·7 cm) and weighs slightly less (65·7 kg). A high-explosive warhead is fitted. Unofficial weight is 128 kg, and speed Mach 3.

DEVELOPMENT

The AIM-4G was developed under the original designation GAR-4A, in parallel with the GAR-3A (AIM-4F). It was introduced in 1959-60.

STATUS

The AIM-4G is carried in mixed loads with the AIM-4F in the US Air Force and US Air National Guard F-106s.

CONTRACTOR

Hughes Aircraft Company, Canoga Park, California 91304, USA.

1099.331
PHOENIX (AIM-54A) AIR-TO-AIR MISSILE

This is a long-range, high performance air-to-air weapon, now in use with US Navy F-14 Tomcat interceptor aircraft. Officially issued characteristics include: length 396 cm, diameter 38 cm, wing span 91·4 cm, weight 380 kg, radar homing, and a Mk 47 Mod 0 solid-propellant rocket motor by North American Rockwell Rocketdyne Division. Estimated range is between 60 and 90 nautical miles (110 to 165 km).

The complete Phoenix weapon system consists of the Hughes AWG-9 fire control and armament system – also referred to as WCS (weapon control system) – and the AIM-54, AIM-7 and AIM-9 missiles, together with the M61 Vulcan 20 mm cannon. The following paragraphs are concerned with the AIM-54 Phoenix missile, details of the other missiles (Sparrow and Sidewinder) will be found elsewhere in this section of *Jane's Weapon Systems*.

OPERATION

During the cruise phase of missile flight, Phoenix guidance is by sample data, semi-active radar homing, the AWG-9 serving as target illuminator.

The Phoenix missile incorporates a small doppler radar transmitter which is switched on to provide target illumination during the terminal guidance phase and in short-range engagements.

The AWG-9 can launch up to six missiles simultaneously against six separate targets, and the

AIM-54's principal operational role is to attack enemy bombers at long range before they are able to launch cruise missiles against ship targets.

DEVELOPMENT

The Phoenix concept was initiated in 1960 and Hughes was selected as prime contractor by the US Navy in 1962. Flight testing began in 1965, and the first successful intercept was in September 1966. The simultaneous attack capability was demonstrated in March 1969 when two drones were successfully engaged.

Phoenix procurement was initiated during fiscal year 1971. F-14 flight trials started in April 1972, and in December of that year four jet drone targets were successfully engaged by four Phoenix missiles launched and directed by the AWG-9 system of an F-14 Tomcat.

The current and projected threat for the 1980-90 period includes platforms and weapons not originally considered, all of which may be encountered in a severe ECM environment. To meet these threats the US Navy initiated development of an improved Phoenix (AIM-54C) and the first of 15 engineering development models was delivered to the US Navy Pacific Missile Test Centre at Point Mugu, California, in August 1979.

The Phoenix improvement programme involves a new programmable digital signal processor, a digital autopilot with a strap-down inertial reference for the missile, and a solid-state transmitter/receiver for the

active radar terminal guidance mode. The digital signal processor will perform many autopilot functions, offering expanded high-altitude performance capacity for increased ECCM logic, flexibility for the future, and an increase in reliability by using fewer parts. The mechanical flipper actuators and servo amplifier functions are not changed. The Naval Weapons Centre at China Lake, California, also developed a new target detecting device, and the US Navy is finding out the possibility of fitting the AIM-54C with a new warhead and fuze.

STATUS

The first Phoenix units were operational by spring 1974.

In the course of fiscal year 1977, the Phoenix Improvement Programme was started to improve the reliability and performance capability of the missile to cope with the projected threats of the 1990s.

In 1978, under a $41 million contract, Hughes developed a new digital electronics unit, a solid-state transmitter/receiver, and a digital autopilot for the improved Phoenix. In addition, the US Naval Weapons Centre at China Lake has developed a new target detection device for the AIM-54C.

The first AIM-54C engineering development model was delivered in August 1979, one of 15 ordered. Between mid-1981 and early 1982, 30 pilot production AIM-54C missiles were delivered to the US Navy for captive flight, technical evaluation and operational testing.

Fifteen engineering model AIM-54C missiles were delivered between August 1979 and June 1981, and delivery of the first production model was made on schedule in October 1981. The missile has successfully completed the contractor development and US Navy Technical Evaluation Launch programmes, and in 1984 was undergoing a US Navy Operational Evaluation. The US Secretary of Defense, in his 1985 Report to Congress revealed procurement plans for Phoenix missiles for fiscal years 1983-86, as follows, with quantities in brackets and funding in millions of dollars: 1983 – (108) $243·8; 1984 – (265) $333·2; 1985 – (400) $472; 1986 – (567) $508·3.

CONTRACTORS

Prime contractor, missile, AN/AWG-9, and LAU-48 launcher: Hughes Aircraft Company, El Segundo, California 90245, USA.

   Motor: North American Rockwell.

   Motor, second source: Aerojet General Corporation.

   Mk 334 proximity fuze: Downey Plant.

   AWG-9 computer: Control Data Corporation.

Third engineering model of improved AIM-54C Phoenix air-to-air missile after launch from US Navy F-14 Tomcat over Pacific Missile Range

4767.331

SIDEWINDER (AIM-9) AIR-TO-AIR MISSILE FAMILY

The family of air-to-air missiles that evolved from the original AIM-9B weapon developed by the US Navy in the 1950s is now an extensive one comprising numerous versions, with the latest model having the designation AIM-9P. Most of the earlier variants have been described and/or illustrated individually in previous editions of this book under various entry numbers from **1103.331** to **3812.331**. (All previous entries for Sidewinder are included in the Numerical List of Entries at the back of this volume.) The entry that follows is an attempt to summarise the main elements of the evolution of this successful and widely used missile.

The principal Sidewinder models that have been produced in significant quantities are:

AIM-9B

First model to be extensively deployed by US Navy and Air Force. More than 40 000 examples produced by Ford Aerospace, who also upgraded more than 10 000 Sidewinder guidance and control sections.

AIM-9D

Almost 1000 produced for the US Navy. Has guidance and control section improvements to allow expanded engagement envelope.

AIM-9E

Designation of modified AIM-9Bs with new seeker for US Air Force. About 5000 produced.

AIM-9H

Solid state electronics in guidance and control section for higher performance and manoeuvrability. More than 3000 supplied to US Navy.

AIM-9J

Major modifications to AIM-9E seeker servo and electronics for increased performance. About 7600 produced using kits supplied by Ford Aerospace.

AIM-9L

Used by US Navy and Air Force and extensively exported. Has all aspect engagement capability. 5500 guidance and control sections produced by Ford Aerospace for US programme.

AIM-9M

Most advanced model in production for US Navy and US Air Force. Improved guidance performance in the tactical combat environment.

AIM-9B Sidewinder air-to-air missile mounted on wing of F-104A Starfighter

Test firing of Sidewinder from Northrop F-20 Tigershark tactical fighter aircraft at China Lake, California

AIM-9N

Formerly the AIM-9J1, which was the result of a major change in the AIM-9J electronics. Approximately 7000 produced.

AIM-9P

More than 21 000 examples produced for US forces and export, either as reworked AIM-9B/E/J models or as new manufacture. Incorporates improved guidance, an active optical fuze and an improved rocket motor. Ford Aerospace is engaged on a further improvement programme and this is currently known as the Improved AIM-9P, which has increased IR acquisition and guidance performance and optimised fuze design.

DEVELOPMENT

The AIM-9A was the prototype of the Sidewinder and was first fired successfully in September 1953. The first production version (AIM-9B) joined the US Air Force in 1956, but has some limitations in use (inability to engage targets close to the ground or head on, for example). Subsequent versions eliminated these shortcomings, and most 'B' models were later upgraded to the 'E' or AIM-9P status. Some AIM-9Bs were equipped with reduced smoke rocket motors and used for special missions or training roles, these being designated AIM-9B-2.

The AIM-9E has an improved guidance and control system and the rounded nose of the AIM-9B is replaced with a more sharply tapered nose cone. Some of these were given the reduced smoke rocket motor and were designated AIM-9E-2. This model has been in the US Air Force inventory since 1967.

The AIM-9J modification of the AIM-9B/E, with greater manoeuvring capability, higher speed and increased range, was first issued in 1977 to equip the F-15 and other Sidewinder compatible aircraft.

Production of the AIM-9L began in 1976. This has a more powerful motor, improved tracking and manoeuvring ability. A more advanced active optical fuze increases missile lethality and resistance to ECM. An FM-AM conical scan pattern increases seeker sensitivity and gives better tracking stability.

This is the first model Sidewinder with the ability to attack from all angles, including head on. The AIM-9M was also in production in 1982, and this model has the all round capability of the AIM-9L, plus higher performance and increased resistance to IR countermeasures.

The AIM-9P is an upgraded version of the AIM-9J which enable targets to be engaged at longer ranges, and deliveries of this model began in 1978. The AIM-9P-1 has an active optical target detector instead of the IR influence fuze; the AIM-9P-2 has a reduced smoke rocket motor; and the latest version AIM-9P-3 has both the above modifications.

The characteristics in the following table apply to the AIM-9L model.

CHARACTERISTICS

Length: 2·87 m

Diameter: 12·7 cm

Fin span: 619 mm

Launch weight: 86·1 kg

Guidance: IR homing

Warhead: Annular blast fragmentation HE

Power plant: Mk 36 Mod 7/8 solid propellant rocket

STATUS

The 1985 report of the US Secretary of Defense indicated funding (in $millions) for the following quantities of Sidewinder missiles in fiscal years 1983 to 86: 83-2420 ($141·2); 84-2050 ($135·6); 85-1000 ($71·2); and 86-1220 ($92·6). In addition to US production for US forces and certain export contracts, a European consortium led by the Federal Republic of Germany and including Italy, Norway and the UK has been created to manufacture the AIM-9L for their own use.

CONTRACTORS

Raytheon Company, Missile Systems Division, Bedford, Massachusetts 01730, USA.

Bodenseewerk Gerätetechnik GmbH, D-7770 Uberlingen/Bodensee, Federal Republic of Germany.

Ford Aerospace & Communications Corporation, Ford Road, Newport Beach, California 92660, USA.

1106.331

SPARROW III (AIM-7E/F and AIM/RIM-7M) AIR-TO-AIR AND SURFACE-TO-AIR MISSILE

The Sparrow missile is one of the most widely-used US weapons. Its versatility has been demonstrated in surface-to-air applications in addition to its original role as an air-to-air missile. The present production version, the AIM/RIM-7M is the fifth model of the Sparrow III family which includes the AIM-7C, E and F models.

The AIM-7E and F are still in the operational inventory of the US Air Force, US Navy and several allied nations. A variant of the AIM-7E designated RIM-7E-5 is used in the surface-to-air role in the US Navy's Basic Point Defence System. Another AIM-7E variant, the RIM-7H-5, is used in the NATO Sea Sparrow Surface Missile System. The RIM-7H-5 has folding wings and clipped fins to reduce the size and weight of the deck launcher/containers.

The Sparrow AIM-7F is a medium-range, all-weather, all-aspect, semi-active guided missile that is compatible with both CW and pulse doppler illumination. The AIM-7F is similar in external appearance to earlier Sparrow missiles. It is 3·6 metres long and 0·2 metre in diameter. The AIM-7F has a wingspan of 1 metre, a tailspan of 0·8 metre and a total weight of 228 kg.

It features a more powerful rocket motor that provides both extended range and faster speed to intercept, an improved 40 kg continuous rod warhead that is triggered by either contact or proximity fuzes, and greatly increased lethality. An all solid-state seeker provides greater sensitivity and reliability and permits snap starting the missile in less than two seconds.

After a competitive flyoff with General Dynamics, Raytheon was awarded a contract in 1978 for the full-scale development of the AIM/RIM-7M Sparrow missile. This development, now complete, has provided an inverse monopulse seeker that includes a digital signal processor, a new autopilot and a new fuze. The results are performance improvements in seeker sensitivity that permit picking out targets from the heavy clutter in look-down, shoot-down environments. It also provides greater immunity to the growing and changing countermeasures threat.

US Navy F-18A Hornet fighter armed with Sparrow radar guided missiles on fuselage and IR homing Sidewinder on wing-tip (US Navy Photo)

The design features isolation mounting, reduced parts count and built-in test, which contribute to improvements in reliability and maintainability. The AIM/RIM-7M is a common missile with all-weather, all-aspect capability in both air-to-air and surface-to-air applications.

The AIM-7M has the same outside dimensions as the AIM-7F but features a monopulse seeker head which provides improved performance in natural clutter or ECM. The RIM-7M version, by adding the folding wings and clipped tail fins will be compatible with the NATO Sea Sparrow launcher.

The digital processor which controls the AIM/RIM-7M is reprogrammable as the ECM threat changes and offers potential for further growth in missile capability.

STATUS

The AIM/RIM-7M is in full rate production and began entry into active US Air Force and US Navy service inventories in 1983. Current US procurement plans call for the US Air Force and US Navy to be equipped with more than 14 000 AIM/RIM-7M missiles. Initial deliveries began in 1982.

CONTRACTORS

Raytheon Company, Missile Systems Division, Bedford, Massachusetts, 01730, USA.

General Dynamics Corporation, Pomona Division, Pomona, California 91766, USA.

UNDERWATER WARFARE SYSTEMS

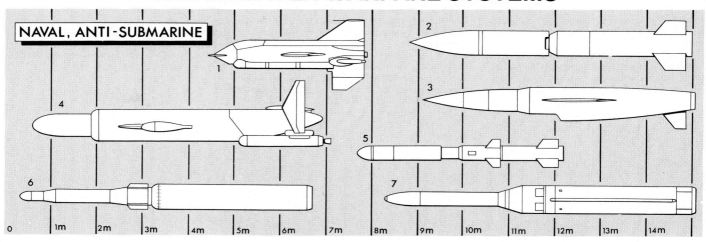

NAVAL, ANTI-SUBMARINE

1 Ikara
2 FRAS-1
3 SS-N-14 (provisional)
4 Malafon

5 Asroc
6 Subroc
7 ASW-SOW

3196.441
UNDERWATER WARFARE SYSTEMS

In this section will be found information on those weapons concerned primarily with underwater targets (submarines) or which operate in the underwater environment for the major portion of their functional life (torpedoes). Under the US heading details will also be found of undersea surveillance projects.

Related entries will be found later in the Systems Section (Naval Fire Control Systems) and in the Equipment Section (Sonar and Underwater Detection).

Anti-submarine Torpedoes

The torpedo is a major anti-submarine weapon. It may be launched directly from a torpedo tube on a surface vessel or submarine, from a drone or missile launched from a ship, or from a manned aircraft or helicopter. All available information on torpedoes will be found in this section, and torpedo fire control systems will be found elsewhere in the Systems Section.

Drones and Missiles

Drone torpedo-launchers and torpedo-carrying missiles are also dealt with in the Systems Section. Their names and reference data are listed below.

Name	Entry No	Country
Asroc	6001.241	USA
ASW-SOW	4181.441	USA
FRAS-1	3968.241	USSR
Ikara	6002.241	Australia
Malafon	1179.241	France
SS-N-14	3969.241	USSR
SS-N-15	3970.441	USSR
SS-N-16	3970.441	USSR
Subroc	1128.441	USA

Of these it should be noted that Asroc has a dual role – as a carrier of either an A/S torpedo or a depth charge. The submarine-launched missile Subroc (1128.441) is not at present a torpedo carrier but implementation of the new US ASW-SOW (combined anti-submarine warfare standoff weapon programme) (4181.441) will remedy this deficiency as

a homing torpedo is under consideration as one of the probable payloads planned for this new weapon.

The details of the Soviet weapons, because of the usual lack of direct evidence, should be regarded as provisional although the information given is considered to be accurate within these constraints.

Depth Charges

Relatively simple cylindrical depth charges that can be rolled or catapulted into the sea are the longest-established anti-submarine weapons: they were first used by the RN in the First World War. They are generally depth-fuzed and have a low sinking rate, thus giving the launching vessel time to get clear. They are still used extensively by many navies: a typical weight of the depth charge is 150 kg and a launcher can project the charge up to about 150 m.

Depth Charge Mortars

Towards the end of the Second World War a more streamlined type of depth charge with a higher rate of sinking was introduced by the RN and subsequently other navies. The intention was to project charges ahead of an attacking ship so that they could be fired more accurately while still in sonar contact, otherwise lost when the attacking ship ran over the submarine to deliver conventional depth charges. Such mortars have been developed in several countries, Squid (6007.241) and Limbo (6008.241) in the UK being two examples and the Italian Menon being a third. The Menon launcher, which exists in three- and six-barrelled forms, is notable for the length of its tubes and has a range of about 1500 m compared with 350 to 1000 m for the two British devices. A single-barrel mortar is fitted on some Italian frigates and corvettes. This is said to have a range of about 1000 m and a rate of fire of 15 DCs/minute.

Another weapon in this category is the French four-barrelled mortar. This is mounted in a turret and is automatically loaded. It fires a heavier projectile and has a longer range (about 2750 m) than any of the others. All these mortars fire 12 inch (305 mm) depth charges.

It is believed that the Soviet Navy has not adopted the streamlined form of depth charge. They do,

however, use depth charge mortars, but it is thought possible that they use compressed air to propel the charge whereas other countries use an explosive cartridge.

Nuclear Depth Charges

Also introduced by the USN is the nuclear depth charge. To take this clear of the launch vessel a rocket is required, and these depth charges have so far been associated only with Asroc (6001.241) and Subroc (1128.441), but the ASW-SOW (4181.441) now being developed is expected to include nuclear depth charges as an optional payload.

Multiple Short-range Rocket Launchers

Another British innovation of the Second World War was the multiple launcher for small (about 25 kg) rockets with impact fuzes. Devices of this nature are widely used by many navies and are commonly known by the name Hedgehog, which was applied to the first US 24-rocket launcher, even though they may not be of identical design. The modern American Hedgehog (which has been considerably elaborated since it was first introduced) has a range of about 350 m; a smaller eight-rocket device known as Mousetrap has a range of about 200 m.

Medium-range Rocket Launchers

One of the most widely adopted developments of the years since the Second World War has been the medium-range (300 to 3600 m) anti-submarine rocket launcher. Brief details of the French system (2057.241) and the Swedish system (6021.241), on which the French system is based, are given, and although it differs in some important respects from these systems, the Norwegian Terne system (6022.241) is in this general weapon category. The USN has also developed systems of this kind, the current one being known as Weapon Alfa, successor to Weapon Able. Many such developments have also taken place in recent years in the Soviet Union.

Other entries give details of the widely used Swedish Bofors four-tube launcher and the more recent two-tube launcher.

AUSTRALIA

2018.241
ANTI-SUBMARINE MORTAR SYSTEM

An improved version of the AS Mk 10 (Limbo) anti-submarine mortar system (6008.241) has been developed in Australia. The design of the Limbo system dates from about 1955 and technological advances since then made it possible to overcome certain disadvantages of the system. In particular, the new development eliminates the use of rotating electric machinery in the pitch and roll servo loops – with consequent saving in power, deck-level weight, and noise – to reduce the weight and noise level of the loading mechanisms (pneumatic for Limbo) and to

eliminate the mechanical problems that can arise from the use of uniselectors in the fuze-setting system.

In the new design the metadyne servo control system for pitch and roll has been replaced by an electric system using silicon-controlled rectifiers to control the launcher drive motors; the pneumatic rammer has been replaced by a smaller and lighter electrical device, and the fuze setting system has been redesigned to use solid-state logic circuits with which have been incorporated additional supervisory circuits that permit checking of the setting before launching.

One effect of all these changes, apart from reduction in cost, weight, and noise, is a manning reduction from seven to three.
STATUS
All production equipments have been delivered to the Royal Australian Navy.
CONTRACTORS
Sponsoring Organisation: Department of Defence – Advanced Engineering Laboratory, Salisbury, South Australia, Australia.

Contractor: Hawker Siddeley Electronics Ltd, Brookvale, New South Wales, Australia.

6002.241

IKARA ANTI-SUBMARINE WEAPON SYSTEM
The concept of Ikara is the employment of a guided missile to deliver an anti-submarine homing torpedo to the target submarine. The missile is launched from a surface ship which uses a computer to calculate the torpedo dropping position. Target information from the firing ship's own sonar, or via a remote radio linked source, together with information regarding the in-flight position of the missile and other data such as ship's position, wind, etc are processed by the computer to maximise kill potential.

The guidance system ensures that the missile flies to the continuously updated optimum dropping position.

After release from the Ikara vehicle, a lightweight anti-submarine torpedo such as the Mk 44 or Mk 46 descends by parachute. When the torpedo reaches the sea the parachute is discarded and the torpedo carries out a homing attack on the target submarine.

In 1982 a number of additional optional torpedo payloads was announced; these included the British Stingray, Swedish TP42, Italian A244/S and Japanese Type 73.

The Ikara vehicle is 3·42 m long, has a wing span of 1·52 m and an overall height of 1·57 m, and the main structural strength is provided by the two-stage Murawa combined boost and sustainer rocket motor that powers it. Flight speed is high subsonic and maximum range is estimated to be about 20 km. In all versions of the system Ikara is launched at a fixed elevation of 55°, generally from a trainable launcher, but in 1982 a 'boxed' version of the system was revealed in which Ikara vehicles are carried in individual container/launchers which are bolted to the ship's deck.

OPERATION
Ikara is capable of attacking enemy submarines out to the maximum range of the ship's sonar regardless of the weather conditions.

Target information from the ship's long-range sonar is fed into a computer which calculates the dropping position, taking into account such factors as ship's own course and speed, wind effect and target movement during time of flight. The outputs from the computer are passed to the missile via the guidance system, a ship-mounted radio/radar system enabling the missile to be tracked and guided accurately to the drop zone where command signals initiate the torpedo release sequence.

The Ikara launcher ensures that the missile takes up its correct flight path as quickly as possible, while the automatic handling system ensures rapid reloading from the magazine, where the missiles are stowed with their torpedoes attached.

The layout of the magazine and handling area varies considerably between the classes of ships already fitted with Ikara, and designs are available to cater for the differing requirements of ships ranging from 1500 tons upwards.

DEVELOPMENT
Initial design was undertaken by the Australian Government. The version to meet RN requirements was subsequently developed in a joint Australian/British programme.

Ikara being launched from Royal Australian Navy destroyer. This system is in service with RAN and RN and a variant (BRANIK) has been installed in four Vosper Mk 10 frigates of the Brazilian Navy

BRANIK
The requirement to fit Ikara to the Brazilian 'Niteroi' class Mk 10 frigates gave rise to the development of a third version of the system. Known as BRANIK, this version again differs from the Australian and RN versions in the way in which the launcher and missile obtain computer service. In the 'Niteroi' weapon control system two fire control computers (Ferranti FM 1600B) are used to control all the ship's weapons. The BRANIK system employs a special-purpose missile tracking and guidance system which is fully integrated with one of these computers. A lightweight semi-automated missile handling outfit is also incorporated in the new version.

BRANIK was the subject of a joint development programme by the Australian Government, Vosper Thornycroft, British Aerospace Dynamics Group (BAeDG), and Ferranti.

In April 1982 the Australian Minister of Defence announced a programme to improve the system and extend its operational life by reducing size and weight and improving reliability and performance. Current Australian plans are thought to relate to development of a system in which Ikara may be used in a containerised form (possibly modified to have folding wings) together with SSMs such as Otomat to comprise a ship's weapons fit.

Work is well advanced on a new version of the Ikara system that incorporates the Italian Otomat anti-ship missile guidance system and a modified Ikara vehicle with a new launcher. The project is essentially a joint Australian and Italian venture with UK participation by BAe, but there are hopes that the system will become the successor to existing NATO ASW weapons. France, for example is understood to be seeking a replacement for the ageing Malafon system.

Oto Melara presented details of the new combination of Otomat and Ikara, in which a new design of 'box' launcher is used to house an Ikara missile modified with folding wings and equipped with the Otomat guidance system. The PRT 406 Ikara missile transponder is a single LRU comprising a power supply unit, logic unit, IF/RF and transmitting RF head unit, and receiving RF head and antenna unit, all integrated into the upper tail fin of the Ikara.

The modified Ikara can carry as its payload any one of the US Mk 44 or 46, Swedish Type 42, Italian A244/S or UK Stingray lightweight torpedoes, and probably the new Italian lightweight torpedo (A-290) believed to be under development, when this is ready. By providing the Ikara with the Otomat guidance system, the former weapon can employ over-the-horizon attack facilities available to the anti-ship missile, with consequent tactical and operational benefits.

Similarly, a ship fitted with boxed Ikara and Otomat has significant advantages in being able to deploy both categories of weapon at the same time, without requiring separate guidance and control systems for each type of missile. The anti-submarine Ikara system enjoys considerably extended range with improved accuracy potential.

Prototypes were expected to be ready for trials during 1984.

STATUS
In service with the Royal Australian Navy and the RN, and in four ships of the Brazilian Navy. The combined value of orders for the Australian, Brazilian, and British navies is in excess of £100 million. The thousandth Ikara missile from the production line was delivered to the RAN in July 1977.

PRODUCTION
Department of Defence Support, Canberra, Australian Capital Territory, Australia.

CONTRACTORS
British Aerospace Dynamics Group, Bristol Division, PO Box 5, Bristol BS12 7QW, England.
Department of Defence Support, Canberra, Australian Capital Territory, Australia.

CHILE

4423.441

AS-228 DEPTH CHARGE
The AS-228 depth charge is an anti-submarine weapon with a hydrostatic pressure activated fuze that permits its use against targets at depths from 100 to 1600 feet (30 to 490 m) and the detonation depth can be preset to any one of 19 depths between these limits. The detonator also incorporates three safety measures for handling and transportation, inertia, and submarine action. The charge itself can be launched by conventional methods from naval vessels or from aircraft, including helicopters. The fuze, manufactured by Cardoen Explosivos, is also supplied as a separate unit as a replacement for outdated fuzes in depth charges and bombs of other manufacture.

This company also manufactures underwater hand grenades for use as an anti-diver weapon for the protection of ships moored or anchored in insecure

Cardoen anti-frogman underwater grenades

Bangalore Torpedo demolition charge

Cardoen AS-228 anti-submarine depth charge

waters. These are operated by hydrostatic fuzes and can be set to explode at depths between 4 and 12 m. Thrown overboard at intervals alongside warships they offer a defence against the attentions of frogmen.

Another product is the Bangalore Torpedo demolition charge, consisting of four pipe charges of light aluminium or steel containing 5 kg of Pentolyte and Mexal explosive.

STATUS
Production.
CONTRACTOR
Cardoen Explosivos, Providencia 2237, 6° Piso, Santiago, Chile.

FRANCE

2057.241
ANTI-SUBMARINE WEAPON SYSTEM
This system comprises an anti-submarine rocket launcher associated with a sonar and a computer. The rocket launcher is remotely controlled, aiming and rocket fuzing being determined by the computer, which in turn receives input data from the sonar.

The launcher is made by Creusot-Loire under licence from Bofors and is a six-tube device with automatic reloading from a magazine. It fires single rockets or salvoes as required, and will accept any of the range of Bofors 375 mm rockets, thereby giving a choice of ranges from about 655 m to about 3625 m. Rate of fire can be up to one round per second.

The most recent version is that equipping the Aviso 69 class of the French Navy and E71 class escorts of the Belgian Navy.

The computer calculates ballistic data for initial velocities of 100, 130, 165, and 205 m/s for the different rockets that may be used with the systems.

Input data from the sonar comprise the location and rate of change of position of the target.

Creusot-Loire is licensed by Bofors for the manufacture of the twin-tube rocket launcher (**2368.241**) and the corresponding munitions. Nine equipments have been installed or are in the course of fabrication.

CONTRACTORS
Launcher: Creusot-Loire, Division de la Mécanique Specialisée, 15 rue Pasquier, 75383 Paris Cedex 08, France.

Computer and sonar (for French Navy): Thomson-CSF.

Creusot-Loire six-tube anti-submarine rocket launcher

1179.241
MALAFON SURFACE TO SUB-SURFACE MISSILE
Malafon is a shipborne weapon consisting of a radio command guided winged vehicle carrying a homing acoustic torpedo. It is intended primarily for use from surface vessels against submarines, but may also be used to attack surface targets.

The Malafon missile has the appearance of a small conventional aircraft with short, unswept tapered wings, and a tailplane fitted with endplate fins. Principal dimensions are: length 6·15 m, diameter 0·65 m, wing span 3·3 m, and the launch weight is 1500 kg. Maximum range is about 13 km.

OPERATION
The missile is ramp launched and propelled by two solid-fuel boosters for the first few seconds of flight. Subsequent flight is unpowered. A radio altimeter is fitted to the missile to maintain a flat trajectory at low level. On reaching the target area, approximately 800 m from the target's estimated position, a tail parachute is deployed to decelerate the missile. The homing torpedo is thus ejected from the remainder of the vehicle and enters the water to complete the terminal guidance phase of the attack by acoustic homing.

Target detection and designation in the case of submerged targets is by means of sonar and by radar in the case of surface targets. These sensors, as appropriate, are used during the flight of the missile to provide data on the target for the generation of command guidance signals which are sent via radio command link to guide the missile. Missile tracking is aided by flares attached to the wing tips.

DEVELOPMENT
Development started in 1956 and by 1959 a total of 21 test launches had been made, 15 from the ground and six from an aircraft. The first sea launch and guidance test took place in 1962. Evaluation of the complete weapon system took place in 1964, during which time over 20 launches were made. Operational trials were carried out the following year.

STATUS
It is understood that Malafon was deployed in an interim form on French Navy vessels, while full development trials were still in progress, these installations probably being updated as development continued. These fittings have been referred to as Malafon Mk 1 systems. Deployment of the latest versions includes installations in the guided weapons frigate *Suffren*, five modified T47 class destroyers and five corvettes.

CONTRACTOR
Société Industrielle d'Aviation Latecoere, 79 avenue Marceau, Paris (16e), France.

Malafon anti-submarine missile on its mount on the French destroyer Aconit *(Stefan Terzibaschitsch)*

3771.441
CI-1 SUBMARINE TARGET
The CI-1 is used for training torpedo launching crews in anti-submarine warfare and for the evaluation of new operational techniques and tactics. It can also be employed in the testing and evaluation of new torpedoes or other underwater weapons. It simulates in a very realistic fashion the characteristics of a submarine and permits effective training under ideal conditions and at a reasonable cost.

The target itself has the appearance of a large electrically powered torpedo (see photograph). It carries acoustic equipment that allows for the generation of the same acoustic responses as a submarine illuminated in the same conditions as those produced by the active sonar of a homing torpedo. It can equally function as the transmitter of a torpedo, with passive detection and localisation being carried out by surface vessels. The CI-1 also has low frequency devices used for target localisation purposes.

It has ample power storage capacity and can be navigated for up to eight hours in the course of an exercise, or the period prior to an exercise, at its minimum speed.

STATUS
In production and operational.
CONTRACTOR
Direction Technique des Constructions Navales, 2 rue Royale, 75200 Paris Naval, France.

DTCN CI-1 submarine target

7501.441

ACOUSTIC TORPEDOES L3, E14, and E15

These torpedoes, which are further described individually in the entries that follow, have been designed with as many common parts as possible.

The weapon systems use part of the equipment pertaining to the submarine weapons of frigates and submarines. The sonar equipment detects, identifies, and gives the position, route and speed of the target and, depending on the type of sonar, the depth of submergence. From these data, the fire control system determines the straight path leading the torpedo near the target and conveys the relevant information to the torpedo tube stations and to the torpedoes. The torpedo follows this route until its homing equipment picks up the target. This then guides the torpedo either to impact or sufficiently close to the target to cause the proximity firing mechanism to operate.

Speed and range performances are selected to match the ranges of the sonar equipment carried by current French vessels.

The effective area of the explosive charge is consistent with the accuracy of self-guidance and with the operating requirements of the proximity fuze.

Propulsion is provided by a high-speed electric motor in series which drives, via a differential inverter-reducer, two contra-rotating propellers. The motor is rated from 40 kW (L3 and E14) to 50 kW (E15). Energy is provided by a storage battery comprising 76 A/h (L3 and E14) or 120 A/h (E15) Ni-Cd cells. The propulsion motor, operating as a rotary converter, powers the acoustic self-guidance system, and supplies the magnetic firing system and its ancillaries (50 V, 400 Hz, single-phase).

An automatic pilot guides the torpedo during the approach phase: it consists of an electric gyroscope which is started by air pressure within 0·4 seconds, and operates in conjunction with a depth regulator that controls the rudders via two pneumatic servo-motors. A 250-barye air tank starts the gyroscope briskly and supplies the servo-motors and the operating gear that sequences the various components.

OPERATION

The L3 torpedo, which is strictly an anti-submarine weapon, incorporates the AS-3 active acoustic self-guidance system. Ultrasonic pulses are transmitted from and received by a bank of magnetostrictive transducers pendular-mounted in the torpedo nose, the arrangement being such as to enable range, bearing and elevation to be measured.

Location in azimuth and elevation is used to guide the torpedo according to a pursuit curve: the self-guidance system sends to the servo-motors, via electric valves that bypass the automatic pilot, the commands providing diving, rising, and lateral control. These commands are applied for about the duration of the interval between successive pulses and cease as soon as the self-guidance system no longer confirms them.

Triple 21 inch (550 mm) anti-submarine torpedo tube mount of French pattern (Stefan Terzibaschitsch)

A pendular system restricts the angle of pitch of the torpedo from +10 to –40°.

As the torpedo nears the target, the pulse rate increases to improve the accuracy of pursuit and of the acoustic exploder mechanism.

On reception of a first distance echo less than 20 m away, the exploder mechanism is triggered, bringing about explosion of the charge 3·5 seconds later. (If used for range practice, an adjuster stops the torpedo when 150 m from the target.) If the torpedo overshoots the target beyond its assumed position, it proceeds with a specific search run.

If after a computed time the torpedo has not detected the target at the previous position it starts a circular search (if in shallow water) or a helical search (if in deep water).

The E14 and E15 torpedoes can be used only against surface ships or against noisy submarines when close to the surface.

The E14 torpedo has the same geometry and mechanical features as the L3 but the self-guidance system is passive. A bank of four transducers, in conjunction with a phase detector detects the target-radiated noise within a 1 kHz bandwidth. This unit supplies two voltages whose difference enables it to locate the target in azimuth. After amplification and when these voltages have reached a given value, the self-guidance system sends lateral control commands by means of electric valves whereby the servo-motors abut against a limit switch (on/off control).

On nearing the target, the self-guidance system initiates the counter-command. The torpedo rotates in the same direction until it receives the counter-command. This avoids 'break-off' of the torpedo when nearing the bows of the target, or permits resumption of an attack that aborted owing to the proximity fuze.

The magnetic proximity fuze system (M-7) is passive. Two probes detect the space variation of the magnetic field. When the torpedo passes under the target a signal of significant form develops which triggers the exploder mechanism of the charge. The range is about 4 m under the hull of a frigate.

The protective system is designed so that arming the exploder system and the authorisation to transmit the self-guidance system commands cannot take place until a 350 m run from emergence from the torpedo tube has been accomplished.

The E15 torpedo has the same self-guidance system as the E14 but the geometry, range, and explosive charge are different.

CONTRACTORS

Programme direction: Direction Technique des Constructions Navales, 2 rue Royale, 75200 Paris Naval, France.

Manufacturer: Sintra-Alcatel, Division Marine, 1 avenue Aristide-Briand, 94117 Arcueil Cedex, France.

1163.441

E14 ACOUSTIC TORPEDO

This is a conventionally-shaped, submarine-launched, anti-ship (or anti-submarine in certain circumstances) torpedo with a strong body in light alloy and a laminated nose cone, with the following five compartments:

(1) acoustic passive self-guidance and electro-magnetic firing device
(2) explosive charge and impact fuze
(3) secondary battery
(4) air tank and automatic pilot
(5) electric motor for propulsion.

CHARACTERISTICS

Length: 4191 mm
Diameter: 550 mm
Weight: 900 kg
Speed: 25 knots
Range: 5500 m
Explosive charge: 200 kg
Submersion: Can be set between 6-18 m (continuously variable)
Guidance: Acoustic, passive, average range 500 m
Firing: Contact (inertial) and influence (magnetic)
Target: Surface vessel from 0-20 knots and submarine at shallow depth

STATUS

Quantity production. The equipment is in service with the French forces and supplied for export.

CONTRACTORS

Programme direction: Direction Technique des Constructions Navales, 2 rue Royale, 75200 Paris Naval, France.

Manufacturer: Sintra-Alcatel, Division Marine, 1 avenue Aristide-Briand, 94117 Arcueil Cedex, France.

1164.441

E15 ACOUSTIC TORPEDO

A conventionally-shaped, submarine-launched, anti-ship (or anti-submarine in certain circumstances) torpedo with a strong body in light alloy and a laminated nose cone, the E15 is a lengthened version of the E14 model 1 torpedo. It has the following five compartments:

(1) acoustic passive self-guidance and electro-magnetic firing device
(2) explosive charge and impact fuze
(3) secondary battery
(4) air tank and automatic pilot
(5) electric motor for propulsion.

CHARACTERISTICS

Length: 6000 mm
Diameter: 550 mm
Weight: 1350 kg
Speed: 25 knots
Range: 12 000 m
Submersion: Can be set between 6-18 m (continuously variable)
Guidance: Acoustic, passive, medium range
Explosive charge: 300 kg
Firing: Contact (inertial) and influence (magnetic)
Target: Surface vessel from 0-20 knots and submarine at shallow depth

STATUS

Quantity production. The equipment is in service with the French forces and supplied for export.

CONTRACTORS

Programme direction: Direction Technique des Constructions Navales, 2 rue Royale, 75200 Paris Naval, France.

Manufacturer: Sintra-Alcatel, Division Marine, 1 avenue Aristide-Briand, 94117 Arcueil Cedex, France.

3623.441
F17 TORPEDO

The F17 is a new electric torpedo designed principally for submarine launched attacks on surface ships. It can be employed in a wire-guided mode of operation or in an automatic homing mode and changing between modes can be effected instantly from the control panel aboard the launching vessel. Normally the final attack phase is under automatic control.

There is a multi-mode version, the F17P, which is equipped with an automatic homing head that provides active/passive target seeking. The F17P can be launched by either surface ships or submarines against surface or underwater targets.

The torpedo is electrically powered by silver-zinc batteries which are activated automatically at launch.

CHARACTERISTICS
Length: 5914 mm
Diameter: 533 mm
Weight: 1410 kg
Guidance: Wire and automatic homing
Target: Surface vessels and submarines
STATUS
Production.

Loading an F17 torpedo in its protective container in 'Agosta' class submarine.

CONTRACTOR
Direction Technique des Constructions Navales, 2 rue Royale, 75200 Paris Naval, France.

1165.441
L3 ACOUSTIC TORPEDO

This is a conventionally-shaped, ship-launched or submarine-launched, anti-submarine (to 300 m) torpedo with a strong body in light alloy and a laminated nose cone, with the following five compartments:
(1) acoustic active self-guidance and electromagnetic firing device
(2) explosive charge and impact fuze
(3) secondary battery
(4) air tank and automatic pilot
(5) electric motor for propulsion.
CHARACTERISTICS
Length: 4300 mm
Diameter: 550 mm
Weight: 910 kg
Speed: 25 knots
Range: 5500 m
Max submersion: 300 m
Explosive charge: 200 kg
Guidance: Acoustic, active, range approx 600 m with favourable inclination of the target submarine. Type AS3T
Firing: Contact (inertial) and proximity (acoustic)
Target: Submarine from 0-20 knots and up to 300 m depth
STATUS
Quantity production. The 550 mm diameter version of

the weapon is in service with the French forces. A 21 inch (533 mm) version has also been designed and is available for manufacture but not in production. Its performance is the same as that of the 550 mm version, but its length is 4318 mm (170 inches), its weight 900 kg, and its diameter, of course, 21 inches.
CONTRACTORS
Programme direction: Direction Technique des

Constructions Navales, 2 rue Royale, 75200 Paris Naval, France.

Manufacturer: Sintra-Alcatel, Division Marine, 1 avenue Aristide-Briand, 94117 Arcueil Cedex, France.

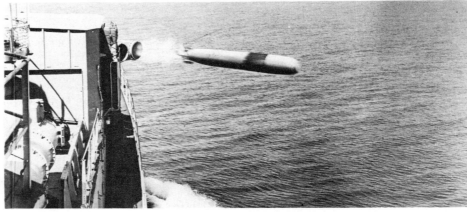

L3 acoustic torpedo launch

2096.441
L4 AIRBORNE ACOUSTIC TORPEDO

This torpedo is designed to be launched from aircraft or from the ASW missile Malafon (**1179.241**). It is suitable for attacking submarines navigating under water at speeds below 20 knots.

It is a conventionally-shaped torpedo having a body made of removable sections of moulded magnesium alloy and comprising the following main compartments:
(1) head section containing the guidance system, the acoustic firing circuits, and the warhead (which is contained in a removable canister) with its inertial percussive firing mechanism
(2) centre section containing the battery and priming elements
(3) tail section containing the air reservoir, the propulsion unit (electric motor driving two contra-rotating propellers through a reduction gear), and the steering mechanisms.
In addition there are the launching devices

designed to insert the torpedo smoothly into the water. These comprise a parachute stabiliser and release mechanism aft and an ejection cap forward.
OPERATION
Once in the water the torpedo describes a circular path until its detection mechanisms locate the target, after which it changes course and homes on the target. On reaching its target the warhead is detonated either by the acoustic proximity mechanism or by an impact fuze.
CHARACTERISTICS
Length: 3.13 m including parachute stabiliser
Diameter: 533 mm
Weight: 525 kg
Warhead: 100 kg
Speed: 30 knots
Guidance: Active acoustic homing
Target: Submerged submarine at up to 20 knots
STATUS
In service with the French Navy. The L4 now exists in a modernised version, capable of operating in shallow

French L4 air-launched torpedo

water and attacking submarines at depths from periscope depth to very deep cruising. A version suitable for launching from torpedo tubes of surface vessels has also been developed. This differs from its predecessor principally only in length (3·30 m) and mass (570 kg).
CONTRACTOR
Direction Technique des Constructions Navales, 2 rue Royale, 75200 Paris Naval, France.

2128.441
L5 MULTIPURPOSE TORPEDO

Most recent of the 'L' series of torpedoes, the L5 is powered by silver-zinc batteries which are activated at launch.

There are four models:
    L5 Mod 1
    L5 Mod 3

    L5 Mod 4
    L5 Mod 4P
The lighter L5 Mod 1 (1000 kg) is intended for use by surface vessels, the heavier L5 Mod 3 (1300 kg) being for submarine launch. Both models are of 533 mm calibre and have a speed of 35 knots. The L5 Mod 4 is solely for anti-submarine use, and the L5 Mod 4P is a multipurpose version.

All models are fitted with a Thomson-CSF active/passive homing head. This has various operating modes, such as direct attack or programmed search with either of the two homing techniques.
STATUS
All versions of the L5 are operational. The Mod 4 models are derived from the Mod 1 and have the same

weight and dimensions. The Mod 4 versions are in production for the French Navy and for export. Belgium is among the foreign users of the L5.

CONTRACTOR
Programme direction: Direction Techniques des Constructions Navales, 2 rue Royale, 75200 Paris Naval, France.

L5 torpedo about to enter the water (DTCN photo)

2146.441
Z16 SUBMARINE-LAUNCHED TORPEDO

This is a large submarine-launched anti-ship torpedo. Electrically propelled and free-running, with gyro angle and running depth preset, for target interception, before discharge, it maintains course for a predetermined distance. If no target is encountered the torpedo switches to a zig-zag pattern.

CHARACTERISTICS
Length: 7·2 m
Diameter: 550 mm
Weight: 1700 kg
Speed: 30 knots
Guidance: Preset plus pattern
Range: 10 km
Submersion: To 18 m

Explosive charge: 300 kg
Firing: Magnetic proximity or contact
STATUS
Obsolescent.

3626.441
THOMSON-CSF SEA MINES

Thomson-CSF is responsible for the production of a variety of sea mines, both war types and for training purposes. Brief details of some current models are given in the following paragraphs.

TSM 3510 (MCC 23)
This is an operational seabed mine designed to be deployed from submarines, and its shape and dimensions are appropriate to its discharge from submarine torpedo tubes (see illustration). Full details of the type of operation employed have not been revealed, but the TSM 3510 probably is of the multiple sensor variety relying upon magnetic, pressure, and acoustic sensors for detection of the target vessel. The sensitivity can be adjusted to suit the depth of the mine and the type of ship(s) intended

as targets. The mine is maintained in a passive condition during storage by a locking bar, and is armed prior to insertion into the torpedo tube by the withdrawal of two safety pins.
CHARACTERISTICS
Length: 2368 mm
Diameter: 530 mm
Weight: 850 kg (loaded)

TSM 3530 (MCT 15)
This mine is a seabed defensive mine for deployment from surface ships. It is launched from rails and settles on the bottom after a parachute-retarded descent. The TSM 3530 is armed by clockwork activated time delay, the elapsed time between sowing and arming being preset.
CHARACTERISTICS
Length: 1100 mm
Diameter: 1200 mm
Weight: 1500 kg (loaded)

TSM 3500 (ED 28B)
This is a recoverable exercise mine for training purposes, such as crew training for minesweeping operations. It is equipped with a magnetic and acoustic detection system, and other items include a float with firing devices and logic circuits that process detected signals. A smoke grenade is fixed to the float, simulating a mine explosion after the mine counter has reached the preset selected number of runs. A ferro-concrete sinker, to which the mine is tethered by a cable, is launched with the mine. The cable is sheared when the clock reaches the time for the mine to ascend and the float rises to the surface to enable the mine to be recovered.
CHARACTERISTICS
Length: 1550 mm
Diameter: 550 mm
Weight: 210 kg in air; 175 kg in water
Sinker: 950 × 800 × 400 mm, 420 kg in air

TSM 3515 (MCED 23)
This is a recoverable exercise mine for minesweeper crew training, and it has the same basic functions as the TSM 3500. It is launched from submarine torpedo tubes.

TSM 3517 (MCEM 23)
This model is intended for training submarine crews in mine-launching tube loading and in minelaying. It is identical with MCED 23, but without magnetic and acoustic sensor system.
STATUS
In service with the French and other navies.
CONTRACTOR
Thomson-CSF, Divisions Activités Sous-Marines, BP 53, 06802 Cagnes-sur-Mer, France.

TSM 3500 (ED 28B) exercise mine with sinker attached

TSM 3510 (MCC 23) submarine-launched sea mine

4415.441
ECA 38 (PAP 104) MINE DISPOSAL SYSTEM

The ECA 38 (PAP 104) system has been developed as a means of remotely placing a mine disposal charge alongside a mine which has previously been located by a minehunting sonar and identified by the PAP 104 vehicle. The ship equipment consists basically of four main parts: a wire-guided submersible vehicle which carries the destruction charge and is equipped with a TV camera (two vehicles per ship), a control console, a TV monitor, and a remote control box. An optional device for moored mines is now entering service. An identification sonar is now proposed as an option on the vehicle to allow positive identification in turbid waters. A new set of equipment permits partially used wire bobbins to be reconditioned.

Overall dimensions of the submersible vehicle are: length 2·7 m, width 1·2 m, height 1·3 m, weight 700 kg

(including the explosive charge). Operating range is 500 m at depths of 100 m or less with standard motors (300 m or less with optional special motors) and battery life is sufficient for five sorties. The maximum speed is 5·5 knots. Two standard versions of the PAP are proposed:
(1) Mk III for depths to 100 m with TV sensor
(2) Mk IV for depths to 300 m, with TV or near-field sonar, and new motors with reduced magnetic field.

A new Mk V version, with re-designed electronics and improved performance was planned for introduction in late 1984. A piloting simulator, known as SIMPAP, is available for training personnel. The ECA 38 (PAP 104) system also includes spares, technical assistance, maintenance equipment, maintenance and operational training and documentation.

DEVELOPMENT
Development of the ECA 38 (PAP 104) system was carried out by Direction Technique des Constructions Navales, Groupe d'Etudes Sous-Marines de l'Atlantique in collaboration with Société ECA.
STATUS
More than 250 vehicles have been built or ordered for the navies of Australia, Belgium, France, West Germany, Malaysia, Netherlands, Norway, United Kingdom and Yugoslavia, and for the European Tripartite Minehunter. Negotiations with other navies are in progress.
CONTRACTOR
Société ECA, 17 avenue du Chateau, BP 16, 92190 Meudon, France.

GERMANY (FEDERAL REPUBLIC)

2570.441

SURFACE AND UNDERWATER TARGET (SUT) TORPEDO

The SUT torpedo is the latest and most versatile member of the Seal, Seechlange and SST 4 family of torpedoes (**2178.441** and **2000.441**). It is a dual-purpose wire-guided torpedo for engaging both surface and submarine targets. The SUT can be launched from submarines and surface vessels, from fixed locations or mobile shore stations. Its electrical propulsion permits variable speed in accordance with tactical requirements, silent running and wakelessness. The wire guidance gives immunity to interference with a two-way data link between vessel and torpedo. The acoustic homing head has long acquisition ranges and a wide search sector for active and passive operation. After termination of guidance wire, SUT continues operation as a highly intelligent homing torpedo, ie with internal guidance programs for target search, target loss etc. The large payload with combined fuze systems ensures the optimum effect of explosive power. The SUT operates at great depths as well as in very shallow waters. Consort operation permits exploitation of the full over-the-horizon range of the SUT.

CHARACTERISTICS
Length: 615 cm (662 cm with guidance wire casket)
Diameter: 533 mm
STATUS
In service and in production.
CONTRACTOR
AEG-Telefunken, Naval Technology Division, Wedel/Holst, Federal Republic of Germany.

AEG-Telefunken Surface and Underwater Target (SUT) torpedo

2178.441

SEAL/SEESCHLANGE TORPEDOES

These two wire-guided, heavyweight 21 inch (533 mm) torpedoes were developed especially for use in the Federal German Navy; Seal for use against surface ships, and the smaller Seeschlange against submarines. There is a high degree of equipment commonality between the two weapons. Major differences are that the anti-submarine model has half the propulsion battery capacity of the Seal, but is fitted with three-dimensional sonar. The following main features apply to both types.

It is possible to transmit all essential data to the torpedo throughout its run via a dual-core guidance wire. Similarly, actual torpedo running data are simultaneously transmitted to the ship. An active/passive homing head is fitted with a steerable transducer array. Attack options following acquisition are either by manual or computer control from the launch ship, or by self-homing by the torpedo.

Provision is made for a programmed run after guidance-wire pay out or loss of signals from the on-board fire control system. Different programs adapted to various tactical situations are available and can be selected via the guidance wire.

Launch arrangements include compressed air firing from surface ships and swim-out from submarines. There are no limitations on ship movements during the launch and guidance phase. The electric propulsion system employed provides long running distances, permitting launch from beyond target defence area. Torpedo speed is selectable.

Other features are: combined impact and proximity fuze; full performance in shallow or deep water; three-dimensional internal stabilisation; identification of different targets and high hit probability; automatic system check before firing.

CHARACTERISTICS
Seal
Length: 608 cm (655 cm with guidance wire casket)

Diameter: 533 mm
Weight: 1370 kg
Warhead: 260 kg
Firing: Magnetic proximity or impact
Seeschlange
Length: 415 cm (462 cm with guidance wire casket)
Diameter: 533 mm
Warhead: 100 kg
Firing: Magnetic proximity or impact
STATUS
Both torpedoes are in service with the West German Navy aboard Class 206 submarines. Seal is also deployed on surface ships, in particular on the Type 142 and 143 fast patrol boats. Seal has been modified to form the special-surface target torpedo SST 4 (**2000.441**) and the dual-purpose surface and underwater target torpedo SUT (**2570.441**).
CONTRACTOR
AEG-Telefunken, Naval Technology Division, Wedel/Holst, Federal Republic of Germany.

4421.441

PINGUIN MINE COUNTERMEASURES VEHICLE

Under a long-term development programme for the Federal German Navy a series of remotely controlled underwater vehicles for mine countermeasures operations has been developed by MBB. Two of these craft have played a significant part in this programme: the first, known as Pinguin A1 was designed by MBB under a pre-development contract awarded by the Government and led to a second prototype in the shape of the present Pinguin B3. The Pinguin B3 is a remotely controlled, unmanned underwater craft which is a very important element in the complete minehunting system. The input of target information (derived from minehunting sonars) will enable it to travel at any selected distance from the seabed and to be guided almost automatically towards a mine-like object. The Pinguin B3 can then identify the mine, and if necessary, release a mine disposal charge to destroy it. A second charge is carried and the Pinguin craft is intended to continue its mission and proceed to destroy a second mine.

The Pinguin B3 is designed to be capable of an improved performance over that of the PAP 104 mine

disposal vehicle, now used by a number of navies to identify and destroy mines which have been detected by a surface minehunting vessel.
CHARACTERISTICS
Vehicle: Pinguin B3
Length: 3·5 m
Hull diameter: 70 cm
Wing span: 1·5 m
Height: 1·4 m
Mass: 1350 kg
Propulsion: 2 variable propulsion electric motors, 1 controllable lift motor
Power supply: Internal nickel-cadmium battery
Diving depth: 100 m
Speed: (Standard) 6 knots, (max) 8 knots
Endurance: 60/120 minutes
Payload: 240 kg, 2 × mine disposal charges, cutter
Sensors: TV camera; sonar

Pinguin B3 remotely-controlled underwater minehunting craft carries two mine destruction charges and sensors for navigation and identification

STATUS
Transition to series production.
CONTRACTORS
MBB, Marine and Special Products Division, Hünefeldstrasse 1-5, 2800 Bremen, Federal Republic of Germany.

Messerschmitt-Bolkow-Blohm GmbH (MBB), PO Box 801109, 8000 Munich 80, Federal Republic of Germany.

2000.441
SST 4 SPECIAL SURFACE TARGET TORPEDO

The SST 4 torpedo is comparable in its dimensions, construction, and capabilities to the Seal weapon (**2178.441**) except for those features which can only be applied within the operational area of the West German Navy. In this respect the SST 4 has been adapted to a standard international version.
CHARACTERISTICS
Length: 608 cm (655 cm with guidance wire casket)
Diameter: 533 mm
Guidance: Wire-guided, dual core with two dispensing systems; active/passive homing sonar
Propulsion: Electric
Submersion: To 100 m
Warhead: 260 kg
Fuze: Impact and proximity
STATUS
In service on Class 209 submarines, fast patrol boats of the 'Combattante I and II' and 'Jaguar II' classes, introduced into various NATO and South American navies.
CONTRACTOR
AEG-Telefunken, Naval Technology Division, Wedel/Holst, Federal Republic of Germany.

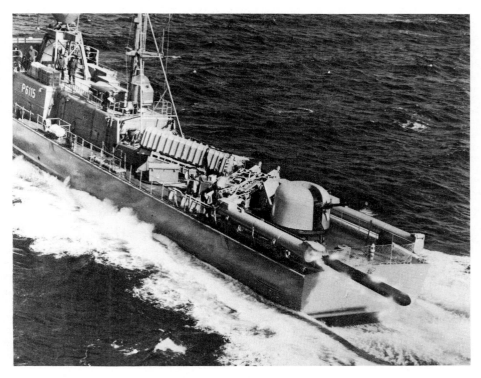

Federal German class 143 fast patrol boat launches AEG-Telefunken torpedo from stern tube

3628.241
TROIKA MCM SYSTEM

The problem of sweeping mines without endangering men and material has been solved by the new Troika system. The concept is based on using three unmanned minesweepers which are radar tracked and remotely controlled from a ship-based operations centre, in order to clear specified laps from acoustic and magnetic influence mines.

The self-propelled minesweepers, designated HFG-F1, are equipped with minesweeping facilities which are accommodated in hollow steel cylinders

encased by a ship-like hull. The overall design of the minesweepers is characterised by extremely high shock resistance. Its propulsion system consists of a diesel-driven hydraulic power transmission and a combined rudder propeller. For optimum operation, even in rough seas, an autopilot is provided.

The magnetic sweeping field is generated by two coils, mounted forward and aft on the cylinder. For acoustic minesweeping two medium frequency acoustic hammers and one towed low frequency acoustic displacer are provided.

The Troika system as used in the Federal Republic of Germany under the navy designation HL 351 uses a converted coastal minesweeper as carrier for the minesweeping operations centre. The system was defined by AEG-Telefunken which also developed the remote control equipment. The latter comprises a horizon-stabilised X/C-band precision navigation radar, a digital target extractor, a master console and three control displays. Each of the latter is associated with one unmanned minesweeper, on the one hand, and with a remote action system operator console, on the other. The control displays allow the radar image of the swept channel to be greatly magnified so that a high degree of precision is achieved in guiding the unmanned minesweepers along the specified tracks electronically inserted into the radar image.

Control commands are sent to the minesweepers in the form of multiplexed data messages, using a UHF link, which provides high reliability. Their responses and functions are monitored automatically by an integrated monitoring system. The last main feature is the reference buoy which provides a geographically stabilised radar image and constitutes a vital component in this Troika configuration.
STATUS
Delivery since mid-1979.
CONTRACTOR
AEG-Telefunken, Geschaeftsbereich Hochfrequenztechnik, Postfach 1730, 7900 Ulm, Federal Republic of Germany.

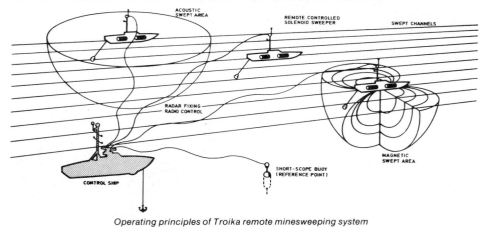

Operating principles of Troika remote minesweeping system

4766.441
FG 1 SEA MINE

The FG 1 is a so-called ground mine, designed to damage or destroy either surface shipping or enemy submarines and warships.

The mine casing is cylindrical configuration, constructed mostly of non-magnetic material, and the mine itself consists of two sections which are combined by means of a clamping ring. The first (smaller) section is the control section which contains the firing mechanism and the safety and arming unit with its ancillary items. The other section contains the explosive charge.

An interface section, located at the bottom of the control section, houses the firing system, which is an electro-pyrotechnic link between the fuze system and the charge. The FG 1 mine is equipped with a proximity fuze. Sensors in the fuze system detect physical fields generated by the hull of a vessel which are then evaluated by the fuze system. If their vessel is within the effective range of the mine, (ie if the signals reach a predetermined level) the charge is detonated.

Depending upon the version, the mine is equipped with various sensors and fuzes. These differences can be established from the external modifications to the

mine and the different equipment and sensors attached to it.

Laying can be performed by submarines or surface ships. Prior to laying, the power circuit is connected by inserting a plug into the carrier system. In a live launch, arming of the safety and arming section and water pressure switch is by means of a rope attachment. For surface vessel laying, this function can be performed manually.
CHARACTERISTICS
Length: 2310 mm; 710 mm (control section); 1600 mm (charge section)

Diameter: 534 mm
Total weight: 770·5 kg; 143·5 kg (control); 627 kg (charge)
Charge: 535 Kg HE
Service depth: 60 m (max)
Negative buoyancy in water: 291·5 kg

STATUS
Production. For training a recoverable mine, FG 1-Ex, is available.
CONTRACTOR
Faun-Werke, PO Box 8, D-8560 Lauuf a.d. Pegnitz, Federal Republic of Germany.

ITALY

3625.441
VS SM600 SEA MINE

The VS SM600 is a multi-sensor influence seabed mine intended for use against medium-tonnage and large surface ships and submarines. This mine is an influence device fitted with a set of sensors coupled to sophisticated processing electronics. Features include a capability for remotely sensing and accurately recognising the magnetic, acoustic and pressure signatures of a wide range of ships and submarines.

Thanks to its extreme flexibility, the mine can be accurately tuned both by a local setting or by a remote control facility so that it can be triggered by the passage of a selected type of vessel. At the same time, the mine possesses good immunity to sweeping operations. The size of the explosive charge is adequate for the destruction of the largest vessels. It can be laid from surface ships, by submarines through a torpedo tube, or parachuted from an aircraft.

CHARACTERISTICS
Length: 2750 mm
Diameter: 533 mm
Weight: Approx 780 kg
Charge weight: 600 kg, TNT
Sensors: 4 – magnetic, pressure, acoustic (LF), acoustic (AF)

Laying depth: 10 – 150 m
Arming time: 1-32 h, adjustable
Safety devices: 5, redundant (safety pin, soluble disc, and pressure device)
Targets: Surface ships, submarines – conventional or nuclear
Additional features: Long-time arming delay; auto-neutralisation; ship counter; anti-removal device
STATUS
Production complete.
CONTRACTOR
Valsella Meccanotecnica SpA, 25018 Montichiari, Brescia, Italy.

3624.441
MISAR MR-80 SEA MINE

The MR-80 seabed mine is actuated by a combination of influence effects from the target and is able to damage or sink surface vessels and submarines of all types, either conventional or nuclear-powered. Its shape is cylindrical, with the body made of epoxy resin and fibreglass; this renders the mine very resistant to sea corrosion and makes it lighter than previous generation mines. The fore-part contains the explosive charge, while the tail section contains all the actuation, priming and operating devices and it is closed by means of a cover, within which the hydrophone, the extender, the entrance membrane of the pressure sensor and the hydrostatic starter are placed.

All influence devices are connected to a central unit (the 'Final Logic'), where all delay functions, safety intervals, sterilisation, influence combinations, ship counting, anti-removal and firing control are located. By means of a remote control device it is possible to control the mine from a control box linked to the mine by a cable. It is possible to dispense with the latter, in which case the control box is connected to a special acoustic transmitter. A special receiver-decoder is located in the mine, with the other influence devices.

The hydraulic compensator for the pressure sensor, the sole plate supporting all the electronic modules and the magnetic sensor are linked to the cover by telescopic slides that run inside the tail section. By unscrewing the bolts of the crown, the tail cover is easily removed with all the devices linked to it; in this way every part of the mine is accessible for assembly and adjustment operations.

CHARACTERISTICS
Type: Seabed mine, actuated by a combination of influence sensors: magnetic, pressure, low-frequency acoustic, audio frequency acoustic

Diameter: 533 mm
Length: Mod A 2750 mm; Mod B 2096 mm; Mod C 1646 mm
Weight: 600 – 1130 kg according to model and type of explosive
Explosive charge: (Type) tritolital, HBX-3 or similar HE; (quantity) 400 – 920 kg according to model
Laying: Surface vessels; submarines through torpedo launching tubes; by aircraft
Depth of use: 8 – 300 m for surface targets and for submerged submarines
Power supply: Dry lithium or alkaline-manganese batteries
Selectivity and range: Obtained by adjustments of the discrimination of the signals coming from the sensors
Remote control: By cable; cableless on request
Firing system: Pressure, magnetic, acoustic signals in any combination; modular
Arming and sterilisation delay: Infinitely variable up to 999 days. Electronic (quartz) clock
Targets: All surface vessels and submarines
Working temperature: –2·5 to +35° C
Storage life: 30 years with a maintenance mean time of 5 years
Operational life: 500-1000 days
Versions: Warhead; inert with data transmission device or smoke signal for exercises
STATUS
In production and in service.
CONTRACTOR
MISAR SpA, Via Brescia 39, 25014 Castenedolo, (Brescia), Italy.

MR-80 seabed mine

MISAR MR-80 mines at depot

4414.441
MISAR MR-80/I EXERCISE MINE

The MR-80/I ground influence mine is the inert version of the MR-80 mine and has an identical configuration but is designed for exercises, training and trials. Mines are equipped before laying with the appropriate devices for the particular intended use. The GP Mk-1 device on the tail contains a flare to simulate actuation of a mine, and a buoy which enables a mine to be recovered by rope at the end of an exercise.

A complete range of accessories and auxiliary instruments are available for mine warfare research and development activities and investigations concerning the capability of minehunters and sweepers against any type of influence mine; target signatures (acoustic, magnetic and pressure); the best mine settings for maximum effectiveness; and the development of new MCM techniques.

CHARACTERISTICS
Type: Exercise, recoverable, influence mine
Diameter: 533 mm
Length: 2096 mm (or according to the model in war stock)
Weight: 750 kg (or according to the model in war stock)
Method of laying: Surface vessels, submarines and aircraft
STATUS
In production and in service. In May 1984 MISAR announced the signing of a five year contract with the Royal Norwegian Navy Materiel Command for the supply of a system of exercise ground mines. Norway is the latest of a number of NATO navies using MISAR systems.
CONTRACTOR
MISAR SpA, Via Brescia 39, 25014 Castenedolo, (Brescia), Italy.

MR-80/I exercise version of MR-80 general purpose mine

4005.441
MISAR MANTA MINE

The Manta mine can damage, sink or destroy amphibious and landing craft, small and medium-sized surface vessels, and submarines. It operates at depths between 2·5 and 100 m. The mine remains effective underwater for more than one year. Its weight and shape are such that it rests firmly on the sea bottom even in running or tidal waters. The mine is about 370 mm high and has a diameter of about 980 mm. Total weight is about 220 or 240 kg depending on the explosive. The mine consists of two units: the body containing the explosive, and the igniter which comprises all the safety, target detection and firing devices. The mine is equipped with all the safety devices needed for handling and transport. The priming device keeps the detonator away from the explosive until the maximum operating depth is reached so as to prevent any explosion due to a casual ignition.

Electronic circuits include:

(1) Delay circuit: started by the priming device, this enables an actuation delay from 0 to 63 days adjustable by steps of one day to be set
(2) Pre-alarm device: this detects the noises caused by the passage of the targets and energises the sensing circuit
(3) Sensing circuit: activated by the pre-alarm circuit, this enables the firing circuit
(4) Sterilising circuit: this sterilises the mine after an adjustable preset time.

The mine can be equipped with an anti-lift circuit.
CHARACTERISTICS
Targets: Landing craft, small and medium-sized surface vessels, submarines
Explosive: 140 kg TNT or other explosives
Laying depth: 2·5-100 m
Laying craft: Surface vessels, underwater operators
Diameter: 980 mm
Height: 380 mm
Weight: About 220 kg
Firing system: Pre-alarm and influence firing circuit

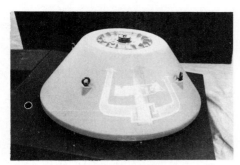

MISAR Manta mine

STATUS
In production and in service.
CONTRACTOR
MISAR SpA, Via Brescia 39, 25014 Castenedolo, (Brescia), Italy.

4006.441
CAM COUNTER-MINE CHARGE

MISAR manufactures this charge for use with automatic mine-clearing systems during minehunting missions. The charge comprises:
(1) explosive charge
(2) igniting device
(3) priming device

These parts are easily and quickly put together; the charge, with its safety devices, can be positioned fully-assembled aboard the minehunter.
CHARACTERISTICS
Max diameter: 360 mm
Length: About 815 mm
Total weight: 110 kg
Main charge weight: 80 kg
Max working depth: 150 m

CAM-T Counter-mine Charge

This charge, also produced by MISAR, is similar to the CAM charge, but with some changes to make it more suitable for mine clearance operations carried out by a diving team.
CHARACTERISTICS
Max diameter: 360 mm
Length: 815 mm
Total weight: 110 kg
Main charge weight: 80 kg
Max working depth: 150 m
STATUS
In production.
CONTRACTOR
MISAR SpA, Via Brescia 39, 25014 Castenedolo, (Brescia), Italy.

MISAR CAM counter-mine charge

2003.441
SUBMARINE- OR SURFACE-LAUNCHED TORPEDO TYPE A 184

The A 184 is a compact dual-purpose, wire-guided, electrically propelled torpedo equipped with an AG 67 panoramic homing head, controlling both course and depth. It is suitable for use against both submarines and surface vessels. It is a dual-speed weapon, carrying a high explosive charge and capable of operating to considerable depths. The fire control system used is the CCRG (console for computation, representation and guidance), which exists in different versions for submarines and surface vessels. The former is described in **3252.481** later in this volume. The launchers are B 512 and B 516 for submarines and surface ships, respectively, although the A 184 may also be used with other launchers for 533 mm torpedoes.

Commands carried by the guidance wires include:

course, depth, acoustic mode (active/passive/combined), enabling point, stratum, speed, impact and influence fuze setting, torpedo stop. Replies from the weapon include: course, distance, depth, acoustic mode, speed, other data on interrogation. The fire control system displays the targets, processes their parameters, and computes the torpedo data during its run. This enables the weapon to be wire-guided up to the stage where the target can be spotted acoustically and intercepted.
CHARACTERISTICS
Diameter: 538 mm
Length: 6 m
Weight: 1300 kg
Propulsion: Electric, silver-zinc battery
Output: 125 bhp
Warhead: HE
Range: >14 km using 2 guidance wires

Type A 184 dual-purpose torpedo

STATUS
Production.
CONTRACTOR
Whitehead Moto Fides, Divisione della Gilardini SpA, Via S Orlando 10, 57100 Leghorn, Italy.

2004.441
SURFACE- OR AIR-LAUNCHED LIGHTWEIGHT TORPEDO TYPE A 244/S

The A 244 is an electrically propelled lightweight torpedo, suitable for use in normal depth or shallow waters. It is intended for anti-submarine operations carried out by surface vessels, helicopters or fixed-wing aircraft.

Type A 244 lightweight torpedo on helicopter

The original version was equipped with a Selenia AG70 homing head but the latest model (A 244/S) is fitted with an advanced guidance system known as the CIACIO-S manufactured by Elsag. This incorporates a torpedo homing head which is capable of both active and passive modes to close on its target. It is able to discriminate between decoys and real targets in the presence of heavy reverberation by special signal modulations and signal processing. The head has a large search volume which is covered by multiple preformed beams which follow a number of self-adaptive search patterns. Other features of the CIACIO-S system are: provision of presettable or programmed combinations of signal processing, spatial filtering and tactical manoeuvres to automatically match the torpedo performance to the current tactical situation; and a wide range of search, attack and re-attack courses that can be implemented in the programmer to suit other operational requirements.

CHARACTERISTICS
Diameter: 324 mm
Length: 2·7 m
Propulsion: Electric
Guidance: Active/passive sonar, self-adaptive programmed patterns

In May 1982 it was revealed that the A 244/S can be used as the payload of the Ikara anti-submarine weapon system (**6002.241**) and there is an Italian programme involving Whitehead Motofides, British Aerospace, CNR and Oto Melara to study such a system.
STATUS
In production for various overseas navies.
CONTRACTOR
Whitehead Moto Fides, Divisione della Gilardini SpA, Via S Orlando 10, 57100 Leghorn, Italy.

3872.281
ILAS-3 TORPEDO LAUNCHING SYSTEM

The ILAS-3 torpedo launching system is designed for the operation of lightweight anti-submarine torpedoes such as the A 244/S, Mk 44, and Mk 46. The system employs two triple-barrel launchers which are pedestal mounted and equipped with thermostatically controlled heaters, and compressed air is used for discharge of the torpedoes from the launch tubes. Launch interlock switches are provided. The system is remotely controlled from a shipborne torpedo control system, also made by the same company, which allows the launcher operator to:

(1) select both the launcher and the individual tube designated for discharge
(2) select the preset data for the torpedo based on information from the combat information centre
(3) initiate the launch command for the designated torpedo.

DEVELOPMENT
The ILAS-3 system was jointly developed by Elsag and Whitehead Motofides.

STATUS
Production. Numerous systems are on order for several navies.

CONTRACTORS
Elsag-Elettronica San Giorgio SpA, Via Hermada 6, 16154 Genoa, Italy.

Whitehead Moto Fides SpA, Via S Orlando 10, 57100 Leghorn, Italy.

Triple-tube launcher of ILAS-3 anti-submarine torpedo system

4412.341
APS SERIES AIRBORNE TORPEDO CONTROL SYSTEMS

These systems are designed to allow remote selection, presetting and launch of the A 244/S torpedo, and other existing types of lightweight torpedo, from any type of helicopter or fixed-wing aircraft. The systems are normally supplied in one of two configurations.

Configuration 1: For helicopters fitted with dunking sonar. The torpedo control can be carried out either in the hover or in forward flight. In the former case, data from the dunking sonar is processed by the control panel computer to determine the target course and speed, and the computer then determines the optimum torpedo presetting values which are sent automatically to the selected torpedo. The hit probability is also calculated and displayed on the control panel to assist in decision taking.

Configuration 2: For fixed-wing aircraft and helicopters not fitted with dunking sonars. This configuration is intended for torpedo launch in forward flight rather than in the hover.

STATUS
In production.

CONTRACTOR
Whitehead Moto Fides, Divisione della Gilardini SpA, Via S Orlando 10, 57100 Leghorn, Italy.

Panel of APS 102 airborne torpedo control system for A 244/S torpedoes

4413.241
SPS SERIES SHIPBORNE TORPEDO CONTROL SYSTEMS

This covers a range of modular integrated torpedo control systems produced by Whitehead Moto Fides. The SPS systems allow remote selection, presetting and launch of lightweight anti-submarine torpedoes and can be supplied in different configurations as follows:

Basic configuration: The torpedo remote control is manually performed by the operator using a control panel installed in the ship's action information room.

Option 1: The control panel is interfaced with the AIO. In this case the optimum torpedo presetting values, which vary with the tactical and kinematic situation, are determined and updated by the AIO computer and automatically sent to the selected torpedo through the control panel. When Option 1 is adopted Whitehead supplies suitable software to give the AIO the capability of displaying information on the ship's recommended launching areas which respectively correspond to given values of the hit probability.

Option 3: This option is intended for light vessels not fitted with AIO. The remote control panel is directly interfaced with the sonar. It determines and updates the target's course and speed and computes the optimum presetting data which are sent to the selected torpedo. A display is incorporated in the control panel to show the tactical situation and the ship's recommended attack manoeuvre.

STATUS
Production.

CONTRACTOR
Whitehead Moto Fides, Divisione della Gilardini SpA, Via S Orlando 10, 57100 Leghorn, Italy.

SPS 104 shipborne torpedo control system console (basic configuration)

3965.441
TAR 6 AND TAR 16 MINES

TAR 6 and TAR 16 (Torpedini A Rosario) are contact moored mines designed to provide a defensive screen of explosive charges at depths from 5 to 300 m, against submarines and ships. Each mine consists of several charges spaced in a vertical line between the sinker and the mine case. In this way a 25 m vertical coverage is obtained from a TAR 6 and about 80 m from TAR 16. The maximum depth for the explosive charge is 300 m and the maximum practicable mooring depth for the complete mine is 500 m.

Spreading the total explosive charge between a number of charges yields a greater coverage than would be obtained with a single charge of the same total weight. In addition, detonation of any one of the charges causes the entire curtain of charges to explode, making the curtain mine more effective than conventional or influence mines of similar weight. Launching is normally effected with the aid of a trolley.

Type	TAR 6	TAR 16
Weight	1456 kg	1500 kg
Number of charges	6+1*	16
Operational depth	45-500 m	120-500 m

*In the TAR 6, the mine case is also filled with explosive, for anti-ship purposes.

STATUS
Production.
CONTRACTOR
Whitehead Moto Fides, Divisione della Gilardini SpA,
Via S Orlando 10, 57100 Leghorn, Italy.

*TAR 6 and TAR 16 curtain mines at Whitehead Moto
Fides works*

4184.441

WP-900 GROUND MINE

The WP-900 naval mine can be laid from surface
vessels or submarines using 534 mm diameter launch
tubes. Detonation is activated by means of magnetic,
directional acoustic, or pressure sensors, in
accordance with a selectable programme. The WP-
900 is produced in several sizes, these depending on
whether one, two, or three high explosive charges are
incorporated. The overall weight consequently varies
between 700 and 1700 kg. The exercise version of this
mine is known as the WPE-900.
STATUS
Early production.
CONTRACTOR
Whitehead Moto Fides, Divisione della Gilardini SpA,
Via S Orlando 10, 57100 Leghorn, Italy.

WPE-900 practice mine

WP-900 ground mine with double explosive charge

3873.491

MIN MINE COUNTERMEASURES SYSTEM

The MIN (Mine Identification and Neutralisation)
system developed and produced for the Italian Navy
by Elettronica San Giorgio (ELSAG) and Riva
Calzoni, has the capability of identifying and
neutralising both bottom and moored mines. The
system consists of:

(1) one self-contained, hydraulically powered, wire-
    guided submarine vehicle mounting a TV camera
    and a high definition sonar transceiver
(2) a main console in the minehunter operations
    room for vehicle guidance and control
(3) one portable auxiliary console for guidance and
    visual control of the vehicle during launching and
    recovery operations
(4) operational accessories, such as auxiliary battery
    charging station, oleo-pneumatic power pack
    recharging, support system for the vehicle etc.

The vehicle is guided from the ship, via a coaxial
cable stored on a reel, through two pairs of thrusters,
each consisting of a propeller driven by a hydraulic
motor, and a main propeller, fixed to a shaft orientable
in the two planes. In the centre of the vehicle there is
an oleo-pneumatic power pack to energise all the
hydraulic equipment. Below the power pack there is a
stowage for the bottom mine destruction charge.

When used against moored mines the vehicle must
be equipped with a cutting device carrying an
explosive cutter. The vehicle is also provided with a
flashing light and an acoustic marker for localisation
and recovery; an acoustic transponder to aid

MIN system underwater vehicle

manoeuvring of the vehicle from the ship's sonar display; a compass, echo sounder, depth gauge and attitude indication device for supplying information to the main console. This latter is fitted with control levers and a joystick for speed and direction control of the vehicle during the search and approach to the mine.

The TV and the sonar monitors, with their associated control devices on the console, provide the operator with information regarding the underwater scenario.

STATUS
Series production. No contract details received.
CONTRACTORS
Consortium for Naval Systems, Via Panama 52, 00198 Rome, Italy.
Elsag-Elettronica San Giorgio SpA, Via Hermada 6, 16154 Genoa, Italy.
Selenia Industrie Elettroniche SpA, Via Tiburtina KM 12 400, 00131 Rome, Italy.

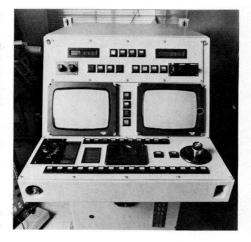

Operator's console for MIN system

NORWAY

6022.241
TERNE III SURFACE TO SUB-SURFACE MISSILE
This is a shipborne medium/short-range anti-submarine unguided multiple missile system.
OPERATION
Ship's sonar provides submarine position for prediction of the Terne launcher elevation and bearing data. The six-barrelled launcher can be used for firing single or multiple salvoes of solid fuelled rockets on an unguided trajectory. A hydro-acoustic

(proximity) fuze detonates the warhead. A six-missile salvo can be fired in five seconds. Reload time is 40 seconds, and is automatic.
CHARACTERISTICS
Range: Probably about 3 km
Firing sector: 360°
Launcher: Sextuple remote-power-controlled. Automatic loading from manually loaded magazine hopper. Special launcher protection against ice and arctic conditions

Missiles: Length 2 m; diameter 20 cm; Fuzing: proximity, time, and impact
DEVELOPMENT
Development, by Kongsberg Vapenfabrikk, started about 1960.
STATUS
Fitted in Royal Norwegian Navy ships.
CONTRACTOR
Kongsberg Vapenfabrikk, Postbox 25, 3601 Kongsberg, Norway.

SWEDEN

6021.241
TYPE 375 ANTI-SUBMARINE WEAPON SYSTEM
This is a shipborne surface to sub-surface medium-range anti-submarine unguided missile system.
OPERATION
Ship's sonar provides submarine position for prediction of Bofors 375 launcher elevation and bearing data. The launcher has either two or four tubes and can fire single- or multiple-shot salvoes. A special design of missile nose ensures a predictable and accurate underwater trajectory. The launcher is reloaded by automatic means from the magazine which is disposed directly below the launcher.

Missiles have three types of rocket motor giving differing range brackets. The missile trajectory is flat thus giving a short time of flight to minimise target evasive action. Fuzes are fitted with proximity, time, and DA devices.

DEVELOPMENT
The initial version of the system, comprising the four-tube launcher and the M/50 rocket, was developed in the early 1950s, and became operational about 1956. The two-tube launcher was developed in 1969-72 and the Nelli rocket in 1969-73. A version made in France by Creusot-Loire under licence from Bofors is described in **2057.241** above.
STATUS
The twin-tube launcher (**2368.241**) and anti-submarine rockets are in production for a number of navies.
CONTRACTORS
Launcher and missile: AB Bofors, 691 80 Bofors, Sweden.
Predictor system: Various: (eg Philips Elektronik AB, Sweden; Ferranti Ltd, England; and NV Hollandse Signaalapparaten, Netherlands).

375 mm anti-submarine rocket

CHARACTERISTICS

375mm ASW	Weight (kg) with fuze	w/out fuze	Length (mm) time fuze	proximity fuze	Charge	Max velocity (m/s) 1 motor	2 motors	Final sinking speed (m/s)	Range to 30 m depth (m)
M/50	250	236	2000	2050	100 kg TNT	70	90	10·9	355 – 850
Erika	250	236	2000	2050	107 kg hexotonal	100	130	10·7	655 – 1635
Nelli	230	216	2000	2050	80 kg hexotonal	165	205	9·2	1580 – 3625
Practice									
M/53	100	86·5	2000	1900	—	93	—	Can be used at least ten times by renewing motor	500 – 820
Type H	100	86·5	2000	1900	—	135	—		980 – 1570

Fuzes for live rockets
Stidar: Length 405 mm, weight 14 kg, time and impact for M/50 and Erika
Zambo: Length 445 mm, weight 14 kg, proximity and impact for all ASW types, working radius 15 m
Type SGF: Length 400 mm, weight 14 kg, smoke and illumination for all practice 375 mm types, reusable

2369.241

SHIPBORNE FOUR-TUBE ANTI-SUBMARINE ROCKET LAUNCHER

The Bofors 375 mm four-tube anti-submarine rocket launcher is electro-hydraulically driven, has an integral fixed-structure loading hoist with a rotatable rocket table, and is remotely controlled.

In an emergency the launcher can be hand laid using a follow-the-pointer device and the hoist can be hand operated. Otherwise remotely controlled electro-hydraulic laying machinery is used. Fuze setting is with the rocket in the tube. The rocket table holds eight rounds. Reload time for four rockets is three minutes, and the minimum interval between firings is one second. The manning complement for continuous firing is four men.

CHARACTERISTICS

Weight, excluding rockets and flame guard: 7·3 t

Traversing speed: 18°/s

Elevating speed: 10°/s

Traverse limits: +130°

Elevation limits: +15 to +90°

Power supplies: 440 V, 60 Hz, 3-phase

Power consumption: Loading 11 kW (mean); tracking 3·2 kW (mean)

'Mogami'-class Japanese frigate with Bofors four-tube A/S rocket launcher before bridge. Launcher is built under licence in Japan by Mitsubishi HI

STATUS

Design was started in 1948 and the launcher first went into service with the Royal Netherlands Navy, which had inititated the work, in 1954. Since then it has been supplied to Argentina, Colombia, France, Federal Republic of Germany, Japan, Portugal and Sweden.

No longer in production. Superseded by the two-tube launcher.

CONTRACTOR

AB Bofors, 691 80 Bofors, Sweden.

2368.241

SHIPBORNE TWO-TUBE ANTI-SUBMARINE ROCKET LAUNCHER

The Bofors ASW rocket launcher is used for firing anti-submarine rockets at close and medium ranges. The launcher has an integral motor-driven twin hoist for loading both tubes at once, and a rotating loading table. The laying mechanism is electro-hydraulic with choice of local or remote operation. Fuze setting is with the rocket in the tube. The rocket table holds four rounds and the total number of rockets in the operating room is 24. The shortest time between successive firings is one second; the time for firing six ready rockets (four on the table and two in the tubes) is one minute and the firing rate for continuous fire is two rockets every 45 seconds. The manning complement during continuous firing is three men.

CHARACTERISTICS

Weight, excluding rockets but including flame guard and deck plate: 3·8 t

Traversing speed: 30°/s

Elevating speed: 27°/s

Traverse limits: Unlimited

Elevation limits: (Mechanical) 0 to +90°; (for firing) 0 to +60°

Power supplies: 440 V, 60 Hz, 3-phase

Power consumption: Tracking 6 kW (mean)

STATUS

In production.

CONTRACTOR

AB Bofors, 691 80 Bofors, Sweden.

Bofors twin-tube ASW rocket launcher

2474.441

TORPEDO TYPE 42 (TP 42)

This 400 mm diameter torpedo was originally intended as a successor to the Royal Swedish Navy's TP41 and was designed for use against submarines and surface targets. The Type 42 (TP 42) torpedo is

Swedish TP427, a developed version of the TP42 torpedo

the base model for several derivatives, among them the TP 422/423 operated by Swedish forces, and a recent derivative designated TP 427.

The TP 42 model can be launched from ships or helicopters and offers combined wire guidance plus a passive homing capability. The TP 427 offers these facilities together with improved data transmission and signal processing techniques. The self-adaptive homing device employs correlation principles to assist sonar operation under adverse conditions. It can be preset to attack surface or submarine targets, and can be launched from submarines, surface vessels, helicopters, fixed-wing subsonic aircraft, or other vehicles such as the Ikara ASW missile. It may be wire-guided from a cruising or hovering helicopter

after launch without a parachute. Torpedo speed changes can be effected under computer control, via the wire-guidance link, or preset control.

CHARACTERISTICS

Length: 260 cm including wire guidance section

Diameter: 400 mm

Weight: 298 kg

Weight of explosive payload: 50 kg (approx)

Weight of wire section: 27 kg

Propulsion: Electric, 2-speed, silver-zinc battery

Fuze: Impact and proximity

STATUS

In production for the Royal Swedish Navy.

CONTRACTOR

FFV, Ordnance, 631 87 Eskilstuna, Sweden.

2367.441

TORPEDO TYPE 61 (TP61)

Torpedo Type 61 is a long-range, high-speed 21 inch (533 mm) wire-guided weapon carrying a 250 kg explosive charge. Designed for use against surface targets, it can be launched from surface vessels, submarines or coastal defence and can be adapted readily to fit a variety of launch tubes and fire control systems.

A thermal propulsion system is used which operates with hydrogen peroxide as an oxidiser. This results in an almost invisible wake, and also gives the TP61 an extremely long range, generally three to five times that of a modern electrically-propelled torpedo at the same speed.

Maintenance requirements are low; storage time without overhaul is ten years with only routine checks each year, and the torpedo will remain operational in its tube for up to four months without overhaul.

Special techniques employed in the handling of hydrogen peroxide have proved to provide a high level of safety.

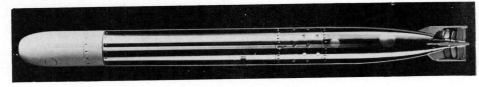

TP·617, latest version of Swedish Type 61 long-range torpedo

CHARACTERISTICS

Length: 702·5 cm

Diameter: 533 mm

Launch weight: 1796 kg

Propulsion: Thermal, wakeless

Warhead: 250 kg HE

Fuze: Impact and proximity

Course lateral dispersion: <0·003

Speed keeping dispersion: Approx 0·003

STATUS

The torpedo is in production and has been delivered

in large numbers for the Royal Swedish Navy (where it is designated TP 613) and is in operational service with some NATO countries, including, it is believed, Denmark and Norway. A developed version of this torpedo, designated TP 617 and including an on-board digital computer, digital data transmission and final acoustic homing, with longer range performance, went into production in 1983.

CONTRACTOR

FFV, Ordnance, 631 87 Eskilstuna, Sweden.

UNION OF SOVIET SOCIALIST REPUBLICS

3968.241
FRAS-1 ANTI-SUBMARINE WEAPON

FRAS-1 (free-rocket anti-submarine) is the designation that has been assigned to the anti-submarine missile associated with the forward twin launcher (SUW-N-1) in 'Moskva' class helicopter carriers and 'Kiev' class aircraft carriers. FRAS-1 is reported to have a maximum range of up to 30 km and to consist of an Asroc-type weapon (**6001.241**) in which a rocket is used to project a nuclear depth charge to the neighbourhood of the suspected target, as determined by sonar and other means, after which the rocket separates from the charge which sinks to a suitable depth before being detonated by either a straightforward pressure/depth fuze or some type of proximity fuze. It has been conjectured that the probable yield of the nuclear payload is in the region of five kilotons.

Provisional dimensions are: length 6·2 m and diameter 55 cm.

Armament of Kiev class carriers includes RBU-6000 ASW rocket launchers, SUW-N-1 twin launch ramp for long-range ASW weapons, eight SS-N-12 SSMs, twin launch ramp for SA-N-3 air-to-surface missiles, 76 mm DP guns and numerous gatling-type air defence guns (Mitsuo Shibata)

3969.241
SS-N-14 ANTI-SUBMARINE WEAPON (SILEX)

The SS-N-14 (Silex) is thought to be somewhat similar in concept to the French Malafon (**1179.241**) or the Australian Ikara (**6002.241**) anti-submarine weapons in which a subsonic winged vehicle carries a homing torpedo to the position of the target submarine and can have its course corrected during flight so as to allow for submarine movements and make an accurate drop. In the Soviet case, however, it is believed that a nuclear warhead can be carried instead of the torpedo and has a weight of about 100 kg and a yield in the low kiloton range. No confirmed photographs of the SS-N-14 have been released for general publication, and indeed, for many years, it was thought to be an anti-ship missile system rather than an anti-submarine system. The evidence which has caused this change of assessment has not been released but is believed to be conclusive.

It is also believed possible that the SS-N-14 has an anti-ship capability and may be able to drop a homing torpedo outside a ship's normal defensive cover. No confirmation of this possibility has ever been seen.

CHARACTERISTICS
Length: 7·6 m
Max range: 55 km
Payload: Nuclear warhead or homing torpedo
Trajectory: Programmed/radio command flight to target area under autopilot control with command override capability. Speed is about Mach 0·95 at 750 m above sea

STATUS
Operational since 1968 and fitted in 'Kirov', 'Krivak', 'Kresta II' and 'Kara' class ships. Later Soviet classes noted with this weapon system include the 'Udaloy' class of anti-submarine destroyers which are fitted with two quadruple launchers, and possibly the new 'Krasina' cruisers.

Powerful armament of the Kara class of Soviet 'large anti-submarine ships' includes 8 containers for SS-N-14 Silex ASW missiles, two 12-barrelled RBU 6000 rocket launchers, two 6-barrelled RBU-1000 rocket launchers, and ten deck-mounted torpedo tubes. Ship carries its own helicopter and has ample missile and guns for air defence also. (Mitsuo Shibata)

3970.441
SS-N-15/16 ANTI-SUBMARINE WEAPON

The SS-N-15 is reported to be an anti-submarine weapon of the same general type as the American Subroc (**1128.441**), a system in which a submarine-launched missile follows a short underwater path before broaching the surface to follow an airborne trajectory for the major part of the distance to the target area. On reaching the latter, a depth charge bomb is released to continue on a ballistic trajectory until it enters the water near the target, sinking to the optimum depth before detonation. This type of weapon relies upon accurate localisation of the target in the first instance, followed by rapid launch and flight to the target area before the target has time to travel far from its last known position. Maximum range was originally estimated as about 35 km but later official US figures suggest between 45 and 50 km. The same source also confirms the torpedo-tipped version of this weapon which carries a homing torpedo payload instead of the depth charge. In the homing torpedo carrying version the weapon is designated SS-N-16.

Part of the threat posed to the ASW forces of the West by Soviet attack submarines

STATUS
The SS-N-15 is probably in 'Papa', 'Alfa', 'Victor III', and 'Tango' class Soviet submarines. Other classes of submarine which may be equipped to operate this weapon include some 'Charlie II' class and 'Victor I or II' boats.

Part of the threat posed to the ASW forces of the West by Soviet attack submarines

---

4422.241
SOVIET ANTI-SUBMARINE ROCKET LAUNCHERS
There is a wide variety of anti-submarine rocket launchers in the Soviet fleet although all appear to operate on much the same principle of firing charges in a pattern ahead of an attacking ship from a mounting which can be trained and elevated under remote control. Two different calibres of 250 mm and 300 mm have been reported and the weight of the bombs in the 250 mm versions has been estimated as 180 to 200 kg. Few details are available of the many different systems but such as are known are given below. The systems may be designated as either RBU or MBU and the associated number is understood to mean the maximum range possible in metres.
MBU 1800: A five-barrelled 250 mm calibre system fitted in some of the smaller and older ships and now probably obsolescent. The launching tubes are in two horizontal rows with three in the top row and two in the bottom row.
MBU 2500: A sixteen-barrelled 250 mm calibre system of much the same vintage and design as the MBU 1800 with two horizontal rows each of eight launching tubes about 1·6 m long. Depth bombs are loaded by hand. The system is fitted in the older cruisers and destroyers although also in the more modern but smaller 'Petya I'.
MBU 4500A: A six-barrelled version hitherto seen only in the one major fleet support ship 'Berezina'. It is thought to be of 300 mm calibre with a launching tube 1·5 m long and to use automatic reloading.
MBU 6000: The most modern system, probably of 300 mm calibre, and fitted very widely. Launch tubes are arranged in circular fashion and it is believed that they are reloaded automatically by bringing them to the vertical and then indexing one by one while depth bombs are loaded from below. Range is 6000 m and the launch barrel length has been extended to about 1·8 m.
MBU 1200: A six-barrelled system which is fitted normally on the quarters of larger ships such as the 'Kirov', 'Kara' and 'Kresta'. Almost certainly it has a range of no more than 1200 m and is probably intended to deal with torpedoes if they can be detected in the closing stages of an attacking run.
STATUS
The MBU 6000 and 1200 are in widespread use throughout the Soviet fleet with the MBU 1200 being reserved for the larger ships.

Six-barrel rocket launcher (USN photo)

USSR Attack Submarines

TANGO CLASS SS

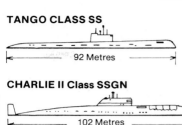

|← 92 Metres →|

Armament: Torpedoes, possible ASW missile
Propulsion: Diesel
Submerged Displacement: 3900 MT

CHARLIE II Class SSGN

|← 102 Metres →|

Armament: Torpedoes, SS-N-9 antiship cruise missile
Propulsion: Nuclear
Submerged Displacement: 5400 MT

VICTOR III Class SSN

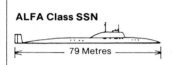

|← 104 Metres →|

Armament: Torpedoes, SS-N-16 ASW missile
Propulsion: Nuclear
Submerged Displacement: 6300 MT

ALFA Class SSN

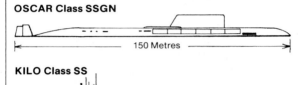

|← 79 Metres →|

Armament: Torpedoes, SS-N-15 ASW missile
Propulsion: Nuclear
Submerged Displacement: 3700 MT

OSCAR Class SSGN

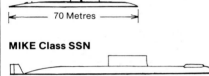

|← 150 Metres →|

Armament: Torpedoes, SS-N-19 antiship cruise missile
Propulsion: Nuclear
Submerged Displacement: 14 000 MT

KILO Class SS

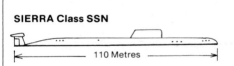

|← 70 Metres →|

Armament: Torpedoes
Propulsion: Diesel
Submerged Displacement: 3000 MT

MIKE Class SSN

|← 110 Metres →|

Armament: Torpedoes, ASW missile
Propulsion: Nuclear
Submerged Displacement: 9700 MT

SIERRA Class SSN

|← 110 Metres →|

Armament: Torpedoes, ASW missile
Propulsion: Nuclear
Submerged Displacement: 8000 MT

'Kresta II' cruiser carries Kamov Ka25 Hormone ASW helicopter, and two MBU 1200 rocket launchers are located on either side of the hangar as well as two MBU 6000 forward (HMS Ark Royal)

2995.441
533 mm TORPEDO
Certainly until recently, and possibly on a continuing basis, the standard calibre of torpedo in service in the Soviet Navy has been 533 mm. A torpedo of smaller calibre was in use on torpedo boats and escort vessels before the Second World War, but this is now to be found only on P-4 patrol boats.
It may confidently be assumed that torpedo development in the USSR has generally proceeded

along lines similar to those of developments in Britain, France, and the USA and has probably taken the form of development from wartime German pattern-running and homing torpedoes.
It is, however, worth noting that somewhere around the late 1950s a version of this torpedo with a nuclear warhead was deployed in some submarines, and this was confirmed in 1981 when a Soviet 'Whiskey' class submarine ran aground in Swedish waters. The Soviets would regard it as normal practice to fit

alternative nuclear warheads to their torpedoes. Swedish sources estimate a warhead yield of about 15 kilotons.
Two distinct stages have been distinguished in the development of surface vessel launchers for torpedoes of this calibre, and the fact that the launchers are of slightly different lengths at these two stages may indicate that the corresponding torpedoes are also different – but it does not necessarily do so. One 533 mm torpedo believed to

be the 1957 pattern, is said to be 825 cm long – which is as large as torpedoes go. It is carried by submarines and torpedo boats. Both surface target and ASW models exist in the Soviet range of 533 mm diameter torpedoes.

The dates of introduction of these two launcher groups appear to have been about 1948/49 and 1957/58. Apart from the difference in length just mentioned the principal change appears to be from manual local training to remote power training. One-, three-, and five-tube launchers are found in the earlier series; two-, three-, four- and five-tube launchers in the later.

STATUS

All the above types of launcher seem still to be in service, as also, presumably are the torpedoes. 533 mm torpedoes are also a standard weapon on Soviet submarines, and the 'Foxtrot' and 'Whiskey' class boats are equipped with four and two 533 mm stern torpedo tubes, respectively.

Other countries operating Soviet 533 mm torpedoes include: Albania, Bulgaria, Chinese People's Republic, Egypt, Finland, German Democratic Republic, India, Indonesia, Iraq, North Korea, Libya, Poland, Romania, Somalia, Syria, Viet-Nam and Yugoslavia.

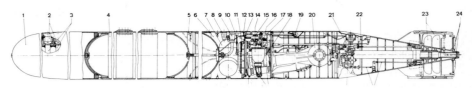

Sectional drawing of Soviet 533 mm torpedo

Key:-
1. Warhead
2. Fuze carriers
3. Detonators
4. Air vessel
5. Water chamber
6. Evaporator compartment
7. Fuel tank
8. Filler valve
9. Boiler shut-off and return valves
10. Depth setting
11. Depth sensor
12. Depth sensor bulkhead
13. Four-way valve
14. Evaporator
15. Pressure regulator
16. Controller
17. Control valve
18. Lubrication oil distributor and cold water pump
19. Priming level
20. Main motor
21. Oil bath
22. Control rod for depth vanes
23. Screws
24. Rudders
25. Rudder rods
26. Steering control box
27. Cylinder block
28. Starter

2997.441
LIGHT TORPEDO

Of comparatively recent development, a 406 mm torpedo is now in service with some submarine chasers and light destroyers of the Soviet Navy. This is launched from trainable tubes that are only about five metres long, so the torpedo must be quite a small

one. These torpedoes are believed to be similar in concept to the American Mk 44 and Mk 46 torpedoes (see later in this section) and are principally anti-submarine weapons. They are deployed aboard 'Hotel II and III' class ballistic missile submarines, 'Echo I' class nuclear attack submarines, 'Echo II' class missile submarines, and 'November' class

boats, and are fired from special stern countermeasures tubes, similar to those found in British 'Oberon' and 'Porpoise' class submarines. Quintuple mounts are fitted in 'Petya 1' class frigates, and 'Mirka' class frigates. Fixed mounts exist on a number of small patrol classes. Bulgaria is known to operate Soviet 406 mm torpedoes.

3627.441
SOVIET SEA MINES

Soviet sea mines in current use fall into four major categories: moored, seabed, floating, and nuclear, and brief notes on each category appear in the following paragraphs.

Defensive moored mines: The main type is the basic contact moored mine that uses an inertia-type firing mechanism which can either be galvano-contact, contact-mechanical or contact-electrical. The mines come in three sizes: small, medium and large according to the explosive charge carried. The two smallest mines are designated YaRM and YaM. The former has an explosive charge of 3 kg and is used in rivers and lakes; the latter has an explosive charge of 20 kg and is used in lakes and shallow coastal areas. Both have the conventional spherical shape with horns and small sinker units. The medium-sized moored contact mine is believed to be confined to the large stocks of the elderly M08/39 series used for coastal defence barriers. This also is spherical with horns and sinker unit but has an explosive charge of about 120 kg. The largest moored contact mine types are cylindrical with explosive charges in excess of 200 kg. These mines are matched by large stocks of an antenna mine variant for defensive ASW barriers and an acoustic influence activated variant for use in areas of strong tidal or current action. The antenna mine is believed to have a 30 m antenna above and below the mine casing and the acoustic mine has a 30 m target location distance. All three types of moored mine have apparently been exported to Soviet client states and the Warsaw Pact nations.

Offensive bottom mines: There are two basic types of conventional ground influence mines used by the USSR: the AMD-500 and AMD-1000 series. The number refers to their weight in kilograms. The AMD-1000 is reported to be the only one capable of laying by submarine, whereas both the AMD-1000 and AMD-500 can be laid by ship and aircraft. In the last case the designation is reported by Middle Eastern sources to change to KMD-1000 and KMD-500,

respectively. The two series are produced in four variants:
(1) magnetic influence that relies on either the intensity of the horizontal or vertical component of the target's magnetic field or the rate of change of the target's field
(2) acoustic influence using either or both low frequency and high frequency noise generated by the target
(3) pressure influence in which the passage of the target over or near the mine causes a reduction in pressure within the water column adjacent to the mine
(4) combination influence in which two or all three of the above influences are combined in a single sensor unit.

For greatest selectivity in target and to maximise sweeping difficulties the combination systems most likely to be used are magnetic-pressure and acoustic-pressure; although the presence of mines with all three influences would be logical for specialist targets such as NATO MCMV forces.

Normal laying depth would be between 4 and 70 m, although the larger AMD-1000 would be effective against submarines down to 200 m. It is assumed that both types can be fitted with ship-counter units, anti-handling devices and self-timed neutralisation devices. Both types have been exported widely to Soviet client states and the Warsaw Pact countries. However the pressure influence variants are likely to be restricted to the Soviet Navy and Pact states that are considered trustworthy.

Offensive moored ASW mines: There are three basic types, two of which for delivery by submarine, ship or aircraft are classed as rising mines and the third assessed for delivery by submarine or ship is known as the underwater electrical potential (UEP) mine. All three have their origins as strategic ASW barrier mine types for use in areas adjacent to NATO submarine bases. The rising mines can also be expected to be encountered on transit and choke point zones frequented by NATO submarine and surface units, as

they have a secondary anti-ship capability. Of the two rising mine types one is designed for use on the continental shelf (believed to have the NATO code-name Cluster Bay) and the other is an improved version for use on the deeper continental ledge region (believed to be code-named Cluster Gulf). Both are thought to be tethered torpedo-shaped devices fitted with a rocket propulsion unit and an active/passive acoustic sensor device. The target is initially detected by the passive component of the detection system and located by transmissions from the active part. If the target is confirmed as being within the vertical attack zone, the tether is cut and the rocket ignited. The very fast upward speed will allow very little time for the target to evade the device if its launch has been detected. Nothing much is known about the UEP mine other than that it relies on the target's electrical field for detection. It is the presence of these three mines in the Soviet Navy inventory that has prompted the RN to introduce the deep sweeping capability into its MCMV forces to protect the UK's submarine bases.

Nuclear mines: The Soviet Union is believed to have a small stockpile of nuclear mines with yields varying between 5 and 20 kilotons for use against high value surface units, and base targets. Laying of these mines is almost certainly assigned to specially selected SSK/SSN units.

The primary Soviet offensive minelaying platform is the 'Foxtrot', 'Whiskey', 'Tango' and 'Kilo' SSK force because of their covert laying capability. Offensive ASW and ground influence mines would be laid by these boats round European NATO bases and at choke points, while overseas bases, SLOCs and deep water choke points would be assigned to the SSN force. Reactive minelaying and renewal of the fields once laid could be accomplished by the Soviet Naval Air Force with Badger A/G, Blinder A and Backfire B aircraft. Defensive minelaying and selective offensive laying in areas contiguous to the Soviet homeland would be undertaken by the surface fleet and the maritime patrol aircraft.

UNITED KINGDOM

6008.241
LIMBO ANTI-SUBMARINE MORTAR SYSTEM (AS Mk 10)

This is a shipborne surface-to-sub-surface medium-range anti-submarine mortar system. Mortars are stabilised in pitch and roll by a metadyne system referenced to the ship's stable platform.

OPERATION

Ship's sonar provides submarine position data to a predictor which computes mortar elevation and lateral tilt. The triple-barrelled mortar fires a pattern of three mortar bombs which are programmed to give a three dimensional explosive pattern ahead of the firing ship. The bombs can be set to explode at variable depths down to 375 m using hydrostatic fuzes and are also fitted with DA fuzes: the fuze setting is by remote control through relays and uniselectors. Loading is accomplished by pneumatic power horizontal ramming from a magazine which is located alongside the mortar.

Weight of the projectile is about 175 kg with a 92 kg HE warhead and range is about 900 m.

DEVELOPMENT

Developed by Admiralty Underwater Weapons Establishment during the 1950s. Ship fitted in the early 1960s.

STATUS

Operational in British and Commonwealth destroyers and frigates and in many other vessels. See also **2018.241** for modified Australian version.

CONTRACTORS

Manufactured to MoD (Navy) designs by several contractors.

2552.441
TORPEDO Mk 8

Quite possibly the longest-lived of all torpedo designs and certainly a remarkable survival in an otherwise reasonably sophisticated navy, the Mk 8 torpedo, which was designed in the early to mid-1930s, was certainly in service in the RN, including nuclear-powered submarines, until 1973, and, may possibly still be in service with some minor vessels and is almost certain to be found in some other navies.

Although it can scarcely be regarded as reasonable that so unsophisticated a device should continue to be the primary armament of the principal attack submarines of the RN it should perhaps in justice be said that, within its limitations, it has performed well and given service which is honourable as well as long. The latest known versions are the Mods 2, 3 and 4, all for surface ship targets.

CHARACTERISTICS

Length: 670 cm
Diameter: 21 inches (533 mm)
Weight: 1521 kg
Propulsion: Compressed air
Speed: 40 – 45·5 knots

Range: 6400 – 4570 m
Warhead: HE 340 kg
Submersion: To 18 m
Guidance: Preset course angle and depth

STATUS

Obsolescent. Being replaced in RN service by the Tigerfish torpedo (**2440.441**).

2440.441
TORPEDO TIGERFISH (Mk 24)

Tigerfish is the name given to the production weapon derived from a redevelopment of the Mk 24 torpedo (**2472.441** *1971-72*). The weapon is a 21 inch wire-guided/acoustic homing torpedo fitted with impact and proximity fuzes and is designed for submarine launch against submarine and surface targets.

Wire guidance is used in the initial stages of an engagement up to the point where the torpedo's automatic three-dimensional active/passive acoustic homing system can control the run into the target. Wire is dispensed from both torpedo and submarine so as to avoid any wire stress due to their relative motion. The torpedo is roll-stabilised by controlling ailerons on retractable mid-body stub wings and is steered by hydraulically powered cruciform control surfaces mounted at the tail.

The torpedo carries its own computer which is connected through the guidance wires to the computer of the submarine's torpedo fire control system. During the wire guidance phase the on-board computer responds to the demands of the submarine computer, and on the homing run it interprets the data from the homing system sensors and calculates and commands the appropriate course, subject to a priority overriding steer-off azimuth control from the submarine.

During a homing run using the torpedo's active sonar the interrogation rate is progressively increased, as the torpedo nears the target, so as to improve system accuracy. The interrogation rate is controlled by the on-board computer, which is thus performing several functions during this phase: interrogation control, sonar data computation, torpedo steering control, and data transmission to the submarine to update its own computer memory.

Both the Mod 0 and Mod 1 Tigerfish have similar external profiles and are propelled by a powerful two-speed electric motor driving a pair of high efficiency, low noise, contra-rotating propellers.

CHARACTERISTICS

Length: 6·464 m
Diameter: 21 inch (533 mm)
Weight: 1550 kg (in air)
Speed: Dual high/low selectable at all times, max 50 knots (estimated)

Tigerfish long-range torpedoes awaiting loading

Range: 21 km (estimated)
Fuze: Impact and proximity
Propulsion: Electrically driven contra-rotating propellers; 2 speeds

DEVELOPMENT

Among the various improvements being examined in the continuing development programme are ways of enabling the weapon to complete successfully fully automatic terminal homing engagements when climbing from depth towards the most difficult types of surface target. A modification kit has been developed which enables Mod 0 torpedoes to be upgraded to Mod 1 standard.

STATUS

In production for the RN. The Mod 0 version has been in service for some years and the Mod 1, higher performance model, was becoming available in mid-1978. Data given above relate to the warshot torpedo; there are also exercise and dummy (handling) versions. The exercise version is similar to the warshot but has rechargeable batteries, becomes buoyant at the end of the run, and has an instrumentation pack for data analysis in place of the warhead.

Tigerfish has been released for export to some foreign navies. The first of these to be identified being Brazil, which in 1982 ordered the Mk 24 Tigerfish for a new generation of Brazilian submarines designed and built in West Germany.

CONTRACTORS

Main contractor: Marconi Underwater Systems Ltd, Elettra Avenue, Waterlooville, Hampshire PO7 7XS, England.

Major sub-contractor: The Plessey Company Ltd, Ilford, Essex IG2 6BB, England.

4559.441
SPEARFISH TORPEDO

Spearfish is the name given to the heavyweight torpedo designed to meet the RN Naval Staff Requirement (NSR) 7525, and currently at an advanced stage of development. Like the existing Mk 24 Tigerfish it is a wire-guided torpedo about 6 m long and with a diameter of 533 mm and an in-air weight of approximately 1850 kg. It is capable of being launched from all types of submarine at their normal operating speeds and depths. Although externally very similar in appearance to the Tigerfish, Spearfish is very different internally and has more in common with the TVX underwater test vehicle (**4416.441**) and the lightweight Stingray torpedo (**2448.441**). Like the latter, Spearfish includes an on-board digital computer which permits sophisticated adaptive operation of the torpedo's guidance system in response to changing environmental, tactical and operational circumstances, as well as being a major element in the functioning of the weapon's homing sonar sub-system.

This capability is enhanced by the ability of the guidance wire cables to exchange data between torpedo and launch submarine in addition to the guidance commands transmitted from the submarine. Thus it is theoretically possible to enjoy the full benefits of a 'programmable' software guidance package in the weapon until, for reasons of choice or necessity, the link is severed and the torpedo is free to complete the attack autonomously. The wire dispensing system is the subject of a £4 million development contract awarded to STC's Defence Systems Division and is said to be able to carry about 70 data messages per second in each direction. The on-board computer, probably a 1412AL, acts as an operational control and is responsible for adjustment of speed, attitude, direction and depth of attack.

The sonar transducer array in the nose of the vehicle is capable of both passive and active modes of operation, the former being the favoured one for the intitial stages of an attack, and the option of changing to active homing remains if target behaviour indicates awareness of the attack. Digital signal processing techniques are employed to ensure maximum freedom from acoustic jamming and other sources of unwanted noise (eg self-noise, natural noises etc).

A major difference between Spearfish and its predecessors is the propulsion system used. Both Tigerfish and Stingray employ electric motors, but for the new weapon this method lacks the power density demanded by the Spearfish performance range and speed specifications and a Sundstrand type 21TP01 gas turbine engine working with a pumpjet is used to achieve long ranges and high speeds (about 60 knots). This engine burns OTTO fuel to which are added sea water and hydroxyl ammonium percholate, increasing the energy content by 40 per cent by weight, or 70 per cent in terms of volume.

The warhead is believed to consist of a newly developed and highly classified directed energy high explosive device capable of penetrating modern advanced separated skin outer and pressure hulls used in the latest submarines. Fuzing, detonation and initiation arrangements of comparable sophistication would also clearly be needed to complement the advanced warhead.

DEVELOPMENT

Based on similar considerations to those which led the USN to embark on the ADCAP (advanced capabilities) improvement programme for the Mk 48 heavyweight torpedo (**2823.441**) (improvements in submarine threats in general, and the Soviet 'Alfa' class submarines in particular). The RN foresaw the need for an eventual replacement for the Mk 24 Mod 1

Early development model of Spearfish heavyweight torpedo during in-water trials

Tigerfish with appreciably higher performance characteristics. This was initially conceived as a combination of the new homing technology then being embodied in the Stingray lightweight torpedo (**2448.441**) and thermal propulsion to field a heavy torpedo capable of high speed and deep submersion coupled with sophisticated target seeking. At that stage (1976-77) the project was known as Naval Staff Target 7525, but subsequently became an NSR (with the same number). A feasibility study covering the original scheme for incorporating the advanced Stingray homing and guidance system in a heavyweight torpedo was the subject of a contract awarded to Marconi Space and Defence Systems in 1977.

This was followed in 1979 by a competition between the projected Spearfish, and procurement of the US Mk 48, which after much lobbying at many levels eventually resulted in a UK MoD contract worth about £500 million for development and initial

procurement of Spearfish as well as including a sum for completion of the Stingray programme. Much related experimental and trials work was carried out in these periods by government agencies using the AUWE TV1 and TVX test vehicles, leading to many valuable inputs to the Spearfish design and development effort.

STATUS

Work on Spearfish development models began early in 1982 and examples were available for in-water trials in the first quarter of 1983. New, purpose-built facilities have been constructed for production of Spearfish as well as for other torpedoes such as Tigerfish and Stingray. No in-service date for Spearfish has been officially disclosed but it is believed to lie between 1987 and 1989.

CONTRACTOR

Marconi Underwater Systems Ltd, Elettra Avenue, Waterlooville, Hampshire PO7 7XS, England.

2448.441

STINGRAY TORPEDO

Stingray is an autonomous acoustic homing lightweight torpedo now entering service with the RN and RAF, and claimed to be the most advanced anti-submarine torpedo in the world with a capability for countering submarine threats effectively until well into the 1990s. It is designed for launching from helicopters, fixed-wing aircraft, and surface ships

over a wide range of speeds and sea states. It is claimed to be unique in that its multi-mode multi-beam sonar, quiet high-speed propulsion system, and fully programmable on-board digital computer enable high performance both in shallow water where sonar conditions are notoriously difficult, and also in deep water. Stingray's computer enables it to make its own tactical decisions during an engagement to optimise the various homing modes to suit the

underwater environment and the behaviour of the target. Both trials and simulation show that the single shot kill probability is very high indeed. The on-board computer enables the torpedo to be tuned to meet a nation's particular requirements by varying the software programs.

Vehicle hydrodynamics are accomplished by an electro-hydraulically driven proportional control system developed by BAe Dynamics Group, Bracknell (formerly Sperry Gyroscope Ltd). The four control surfaces are mounted aft of the propulsor. The new sea-water battery gives extended endurance and no performance degradation with depth.

No official performance details of Stingray have been cleared for publication, but informed comments which have been published enable a few deductions to be made. One such comment, in an indirect comparison with the US Mk 46 torpedo, claimed that it and Stingray had very similar speed, diving depth and endurance characteristics; from known performance of the Mk 46, this implies a maximum depth capability of as much as 750 m, a maximum speed of at least 45 knots and an endurance of about eight minutes at that speed. It was also hinted that anticipated propulsion improvements might enhance Stingray's speed appreciably, and hence its range. Elsewhere, it was claimed that the conventional blast type warhead of the Mk 46 is limited in effect against the deeper-diving submarines with extensive outer hulls that are now entering service, but Stingray is expected to be effective in this respect against the strongest pressure hulls going to sea with the Soviet fleet. Other sources believe that in place of blast type torpedo warheads, some form of directed-energy payload is required to counter modern submarines.

Stingray lightweight torpedo

Such devices require highly accurate guidance to ensure that the torpedo strikes its target in the most vulnerable place at the right angle. This suggests that Stingray therefore incorporates both very precise guidance and an enhanced warhead, but this cannot be categorically confirmed as yet.

STATUS
Marconi was appointed main contractor in October 1977. A £215 million contract from the UK MoD was signed in November 1979. The first production acceptance vehicle produced at the Neston plant was delivered early in August 1981. Contract acceptance trials began April 1982 and the design certificate was issued in December 1982. The torpedo was deployed during the Falkland Islands conflict in 1982.
CONTRACTOR
Marconi Underwater Systems Ltd, Elettra Avenue, Waterlooville, Hampshire PO7 7XS, England.

4765.441
KINGFISHER LAUNCH SYSTEM

To enable the Stingray lightweight torpedo (2448.441) to be operated from a variety of surface vessels, in addition to its primary role of air launch, Marconi Underwater Systems has designed a modular torpedo launch system called Kingfisher. By its adoption it is possible to equip small sea craft for ASW duties, and once used the empty launch assemblies can be rapidly removed and replaced with new, complete units when the ship is back in harbour. Turn-around and reloading time could be as little as 30 minutes.

The basic Kingfisher system consists of a single launch command console (LCC) linked to the multiple launcher tube array. The operator at the LCC can select any tube for launch, preset the torpedo attack pattern and pre-launch data, and fire the weapon. Launcher and torpedo status signals are recorded and interlocked at the LCC to give complete control. In addition to firing in earnest, there is provision for the operator to order safe jettison of the weapon if the circumstances warrant this.

The launcher array consists of a series of individual self-contained launcher modules, fitted in support ramps mounted on the after deck of the vessel. The link to the command operator at the LCC is via a single cable running throughout the ship. Signal distribution and switching between launcher modules is by a unit delivered and mounted as an integral part of the launcher array.

Launch of the torpedo is by means of a single command from the LCC, and this initiates the automatic launch sequence; opening the muzzle door, removing tube/interfaces and ejecting the weapon using stored energy. Once the torpedo is in the water, its stability 'back-pack' ensures that the initial plunge is controlled whilst the sea water battery is energised. After the first few seconds of immersion the propulsion and control system is activated, automatically releasing the back-pack. The attack then commences in the normal manner.
STATUS
No contract details have been disclosed.
CONTRACTOR
Marconi Underwater Systems Ltd, Elletra Avenue, Waterlooville, Hampshire PO7 7XS, England.

4416.441
TVX UNDERWATER TEST VEHICLE

TVX has been developed to provide a payload carrier to explore new ideas in anti-submarine weapons and warfare, and will be used to assist the development of both lightweight air-dropped and heavyweight submarine-launched torpedoes. It is similar in size and shape to a heavyweight torpedo but, instead of the normal torpedo payload, has a compartment in the nose in which experimental equipment can be accommodated. This enables almost any aspect of torpedo research to be carried out and new propulsion systems can also be tested by replacing the appropriate section of the basic TVX assembly.

The vehicle has a 1412AL digital computer based control system and an SGP 500 three-axis gyro reference unit. The computer controls speed, depth, and safety factors. Control is almost entirely through software which can be adapted quickly to particular payloads so that TVX can simulate all types of modern torpedo.

The vehicle is normally launched from a ship. It is capable of rates of turn of 40° per second and pitch angles of ±28° with speeds varying between 28 and 60 knots. Range is 7·5 km with operating depths of 3 to 300 m.
STATUS
Five-year design and development of three vehicles completed with successful sea trials in 1980.
CONTRACTOR
British Aerospace Dynamics Group, Bracknell Division, Downshire Way, Bracknell, Berkshire RG12 1QL, England.

Preparing for tests with TVX developmental vehicle

4482.441
SEA URCHIN MINE

Sea Urchin is a multi-influence ground mine which may be deployed in water depths to 90 m by minelayer or other surface vessels, submarines or transport aircraft. It is effective against submarines, warships, merchant ships, patrol craft and landing craft. The mine consists of a warhead section, available in three sizes, to which is attached a sensing and processing unit (SAP) containing the sensors, batteries, safety and arming unit, microprocessor and electronics. The SAP is common to all three warhead sizes to provide maximum flexibility at minimum cost.

Other salient features include: programmable mission parameters for acoustic, magnetic and pressure sensors with individual or multi-influence actuation; selectable activation delay; multiple target count; and selectable sterilisation delay. Sea Urchin is computer-controlled with a simple setting procedure. There are interlocking safety and arming mechanisms with radiation protection. A self-test facility includes automatic sterilisation if a malfunction is detected.

The mine can be activated and triggered by the acoustic signature of a passing ship, a ship's magnetic signature, the change in water pressure caused by a ship, or a combination of all three. The acoustic, magnetic and pressure sensors are selectable before deployment. In addition, an adjustable ship counting device will enable the mine to be triggered after a predetermined number of ships have passed overhead. The microprocessor ensures that the mine will not detonate until the ship target is at optimum range. Delayed activation is provided and a further device enables the mine to become sterile or inoperative after a predetermined period.
CHARACTERISTICS
Diameter: 533 mm (21 inches)
Lengths (approx): 1·4 m (250 kg warhead); 2·5 m (500 kg warhead); 3·6 m (750 kg warhead)
Weights: 500 kg (250 kg warhead); 900 kg (500 kg warhead); 1300 kg (750 kg warhead)

STATUS
Development. Construction of a new facility for underwater weapon production and testing was announced by BAe in 1983.
CONTRACTOR
British Aerospace Dynamics Group, Bracknell Division, Downshire Way, Bracknell, Berkshire RG12 1QL, England.

250 kg warhead model of Sea Urchin naval ground mine

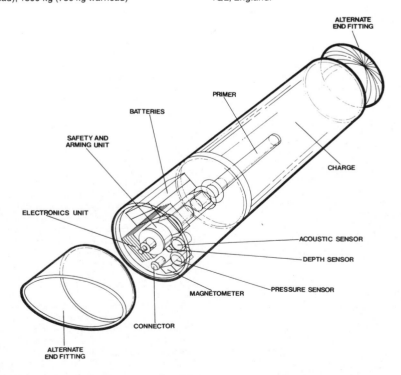

ALTERNATE END FITTING

PRIMER

BATTERIES

SAFETY AND ARMING UNIT

CHARGE

ELECTRONICS UNIT

ACOUSTIC SENSOR

DEPTH SENSOR

PRESSURE SENSOR

MAGNETOMETER

CONNECTOR

ALTERNATE END FITTING

Diagram of internal arrangement of Sea Urchin mine's component parts

4558.441
STONEFISH MINES

Marconi Underwater Systems in conjunction with the Royal Ordnance Factories has developed a new family of mines comprising operational, exercise and training versions. Stonefish, as this family is known, is designed on the modular concept enabling mines to be made up to meet any tactical, exercise or training requirement. All variants may be deployed from surface ships, submarines and aircraft.

The operational variants are provided with a range of warhead sizes designed to optimise the effectiveness of the mine in various depths of water. If required, the warheads can be combined and, together with the appropriate launch kit and a standard tail unit containing the sensors, signal conditioning and processor package, can be configured to cover the range of launch vehicles, depths and targets applicable. The basic sensor pack comprises acoustic, magnetic and pressure sensors. The signal processing includes analogue signal conditioning and digital information processing, the setting of thresholds, and sterilisation delay times. The mine also self-adjusts to its environmental background to achieve optimum performance. The executive program can be modified by means of a portable pre-setter to suit changing threat and operational conditions before the mine is deployed.

The Stonefish warshot versions have a storage life of over 20 years and an in-water or layed life of over 400 days. They are intended to be laid at depths of between 10 and 90 m for surface targets and down to depths of 200 m for submarine targets. To provide training in mine countermeasures Stonefish is available as an exercise variant in several versions. To achieve commonality between components and reduce overall costs these versions are also based on the modular principle. Where appropriate, warshot modules are utilised enabling realistic vehicles fully representative in size and weight of the operational mines to be built-up. In addition to providing a highly accurate recorded assessment of MCM equipment, state of training and efficacy of tactics, the exercise mine can be readily recovered, refurbished and re-deployed.

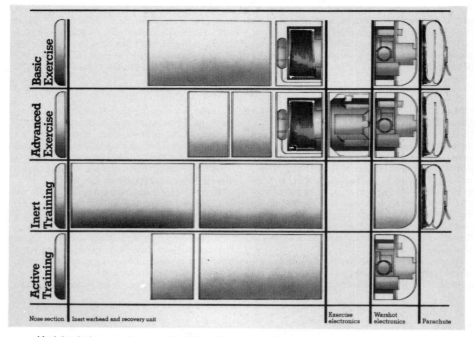

Modular design permits assembly of Stonefish versions for a variety of warshot and exercise roles

The training variant is completely inert but can accept all the available equipment options to facilitate classroom instruction, handling, programming and testing drills. Support spares are essentially those required to refurbish the exercise variant or to replace life-expired items. The refurbishment life for stored warshot weapons is six years.

Stonefish may also be made available as a control mine for the defence of harbours, sea lanes, oil installations and other sensitive offshore areas. Remote control may be by cable from a shore-based defence headquarters or by acoustic transmitter. Mines of the Stonefish family range from 2·6 to 1 m in length, depending on the specific water depth requirement, with a diameter of 533 mm. All-up weight varies between 900 and 205 kg depending on the size of warhead and launch kit employed.

A Stonefish pre-setter designed as a self-contained unit has been produced by the Royal Ordnance Factory, Blackburn, for programming mines. it employs an RCA 1802 micro processor and incorporates built-in data checking during input, and automatic test facilities.

STATUS
Development.
CONTRACTOR
Marconi Underwater Systems Ltd, Elettra Avenue, Waterlooville, Hampshire PO7 7XS, England.

4483.441
TOWED UNMANNED SUBMERSIBLE (TUMS)

TUMS is capable of operating at full ocean depths, performing search, identification, classification and recovery of objects on the seabed. It provides for illumination, photographing and tele-viewing of underwater objects. The system comprises a deep tethered submersible (DTS), a depressor and the associated tether and cabling. The DTS, which contains all the necessary sensors, instruments and manipulators, is tethered to the depressor but operates independently, either on the seabed or in the hovering mode.

The depressor is attached to the surface vessel by a heavy cable and serves as a passive decoupler, isolating the DTS from ship motion and cable instabilities. It also serves as a stores carrier and a recovery vehicle for small objects retrieved from the seabed.

STATUS
Entering service with the RN.
CONTRACTOR
British Aerospace Dynamics Group, Bracknell Division, Downshire Way, Bracknell, Berkshire RG12 1QL, England.

4763.441
TRANSPORTABLE ACOUSTIC RANGE

The transportable acoustic range (TAR) developed by British Aerospace provides portable ranging facilities, where fixed facilities are not available, to determine a ship's susceptibility to acoustic mines.

Developed initially for the Royal Navy this system enables simple and rapid 'go/no go' checks for mine hunting and mine countermeasures vessels prior to deployment on mine warfare activities. The range is simple to operate with visual indication being presented on an electronics unit. No special underwater acoustic experience is required of the personnel using the system.

The TAR equipment consists of an underwater unit, containing a hydrophone which is laid on the seabed in the desired location, an associated shore-based electronics unit and a cable drum carrying a 900 metre cable and a strain relief block. The cable carries signals from the underwater unit via the cable drum and a 30 metre link cable to the electronics unit.

The underwater unit can be deployed in depths between 10 and 50 metres, and within this range automatic gain compensation adjusts all signals to a depth of 10 metres. The unit measures 990 × 990 × 610 mm, and weighs 50 kg. With its cable the cable drum weighs approximately ½ tonne. The electronics unit separates the received broad-band noise into seven octaves covering the mine sweeping range (8 – 500 Hz). Each channel is monitored and compared with a preset reference level and visual indication of the noise level is provided on one of three lamps; amber for levels equal to the preset standard, green for lower levels, or red for levels higher than the standard. Settings for the preset levels may be derived from previous rangings of each ship or the class of ship.

The electronics unit measures 610 × 610 × 610 mm and weighs 15 kg.

Systems with different frequency coverage, to embrace the complete sonics range used for acoustic mines to the torpedo homing bands, for instance, the contractor can deliver a suitable TAR. By using the tape amplifier in the electronics unit it is possible to take recordings of noise signatures for more detailed analysis at a later stage. By the addition of frequency analysis equipment it is also possible to employ the system to provide more elaborate and permanent noise ranging facilities.

STATUS
In production and supplied to the Royal Navy.
CONTRACTOR
British Aerospace Dynamics Group, Bracknell Division, Downshire Way, Bracknell, Berkshire RG12 1QL, England.

4417.441
DEEP MOBILE TARGET

The Deep Mobile Target (DMT) is a fully instrumented self-contained, unmanned, boat-launched, vehicle for use on ASW trials and training exercises designed to simulate the dynamic and acoustic characteristics of submarines and carry out pre-programmed manoeuvres. It was originally conceived as a deep diving mobile torpedo target to obviate the costs, risks, and delays associated with weapons trials versus a submarine and its functions were later expanded to provide a trials and ASW training facility with torpedoes, sonars, sonobuoys and acoustic tracking facilities.

DMT is supplied to meet the customer's requirements for sonar frequencies. It normally carries two sonar/sonics outfits which are interchangeable at base. When used in conjunction with a three-dimensional underwater tracking system, it is fitted with a Thorn EMI synchronised acoustic transmitter (SAT) Type 5 for compatibility with US, UK, German, Italian and Japanese tracking ranges. A miss distance indicator is incorporated.

DMT is claimed to be easy to handle and recover with high availability and reliability. The recovery system is initiated by command, failure of the propulsion battery, by being outside the preset depth limits, or by program tape breakage. The design is modular and repairs are effected by replacing modules.

CHARACTERISTICS

Length: 3·28 m
Diameter: 0·324 m (12·75 inches)
Weight: 236 kg
Speeds: Stop, 8 knots, 14 knots, and 22 knots
Endurance: From 100 minutes at 8 knots to 8 minutes at 22 knots
Depth: 366 m max
Rates: 10°/s turn rate; 45° climb/dive angle; 9·5 m/s climb/dive rate

STATUS

DMT was developed in collaboration with the UK MoD at the Admiralty Underwater Weapons Establishment and has been supplied to the British MoD and several other naval authories.

CONTRACTOR

Thorn EMI Electronics Ltd, Defence Systems Division, Albert Drive, Sheerwater, Woking, Surrey, England.

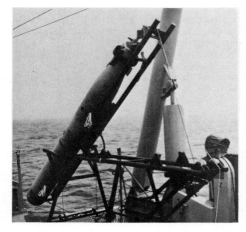

DMT with locally manufactured launch chute before a run

4418.441

THORN EMI UNDERWATER ACOUSTIC RANGES, SYSTEMS AND TARGETS

Thorn EMI Electronics Designs Laboratories has a range of underwater acoustic systems ranging from simple location transmitters and receivers, through acoustic altimeters, to complete three dimensional tracking and navigation systems. In order to make a proper evaluation of system performance, it is essential to track accurately the course of both the weapon and its target, and systems have been developed to measure the performance of underwater vehicles in three dimensions using active sonar techniques. Permanent, semi-permanent, and portable installations are available.

In permanent installations, sea-bed mounted hydrophones are connected by cable to a shore-based control station and tracking is accurately referred to local geography. Where such permanent installations are not possible, generally because of shallow water conditions, a semi-permanent system may be used in which the hydrophones may be deployed from a small surface vessel and data is telemetered by radio to a permanent or portable shore station. In the fully portable system, hydrophone assemblies are suspended from flotation units on the surface which are tethered to moored buoys and data is telemetered by radio from this battery powered seaborne equipment to the control station which is housed in a transportable cabin and can be either ship or shore based. The mooring buoys are semi-permanent and all that is needed to operate the range is to deploy the flotation units and hydrophone assemblies from a small boat. Such a system enables the location to be changed with the minimum of inconvenience and expense.

The principal items of control equipment are radio, signal processors, X-Y plotter, magnetic tape recorder, depth display, teleprinter, and electronics to generate the synchronising pulses to the range. System functions are controlled from a control console. The real-time plot produces symbols denoting the positions of underwater vehicles being tracked and their depth is shown on a digital read-out. All data is recorded and the teleprinter gives a printout of the X, Y, and Z co-ordinates.

All systems can be used in conjunction with Thorn EMI's deep mobile target (DMT) (**4417.441**) or with static targets. Several vehicles can be plotted simultaneously and the whole system gives a record of the target and the performance of each weapon or ship involved in the exercise.

Diagram of arrangement of Thorn EMI portable acoustic tracking system with hydrophones suspended from surface buoys

Target Centred Tracker: The target centred tracker (TCT) is a short base line system which can be used to obtain accurate positional information in three-dimensions on high speed rapidly manoeuvring vehicles. It evaluates the performance of exercise torpedoes against submarine targets during the final attack phase of the weapon. Two four-hydrophone arrays are mounted on the submarine's hull, and received signals are cabled in-board to the TCT processing equipment. Signals are processed to yield positional information on the weapon, which is digitally logged for subsequent track generation and analysis.

Fuze Actuating Static Target: The fuze actuating static target (FAST) deploys tracking hydrophones in an array similar to TCT, and consists of a framework which provides a suitable magnetic signature to actuate weapon fuzes at close range and on acoustic target for homing. The FAST system and associated equipment enable the track of an attacking weapon and its exact position at the time of fuze actuation to be determined.

Distance Measuring Equipment: distance measuring equipment (DME) forms the basis of many of the available tracking systems and enables the slant range between a mobile or static acoustic transmitter and a receiving hydrophone to be measured with great precision. The equipment is automatic in operation requiring minimal operator attention. Modular design enables tracking systems to be configured to meet the user's immediate needs whilst allowing expansion later to a more complex tracking system if needed.

Acoustic Transmitters: Various acoustic transmitters are available for operation in a variety of underwater tracking applications.

DME Pinger is an acoustic pulse transmitter with a 2-wire arrangement for power supply and trigger signal which simplifies hull penetration problems for submarine installations. The body is aluminium bronze and the acoustic head element is encapsulated and profiled to minimise drag. Various frequencies are available to suit the majority of tracking range standards.

A dual-frequency version of the DME Pinger, offering operational versatility between range, has been developed. The unit is 90 mm in diameter with an overall length of 470 mm including cable gland.

A synchronised acoustic transmitter (SAT) is available for weapon tracking and is configured as a torpedo hull section. It is self-contained and has its own power supplies. Mounted on the hull section is an array of acoustic transducers which produces an optimised beam pattern. Various repetition rates and depth telemetry facilities have been incorporated.

STATUS

TCT and FAST were designed and developed for the UK MoD and several equipments have been supplied. Negotiations are underway with other navies. The portable acoustic tracking system has been supplied to UK MoD and sold to the Japanese Defence Agency, and the Italian Navy. DME processing units were designed and developed for the UK MoD and are incorporated in UK range systems. DME type acoustic transmitters have been sold to UK MoD, and SAT has been sold to Italy, Germany and Japan, as well as being supplied to UK MoD.

CONTRACTOR

Thorn EMI Electronics Ltd, Defence Systems Division, Albert Drive, Sheerwater, Woking, Surrey, England.

4420.441

VERSATILE EXERCISE MINE SYSTEM

The Versatile Exercise Mine System (VEMS) provides facilities for the assessment of the effectiveness of ground minesweeping systems and the tactics employed for the clearance of such weapons. It may also be used in mine warfare research and development programmes. A VEM simulates the actuation system of any magnetic, acoustic, pressure or combination influence ground mine and is programmed to record exercise data for subsequent detailed analysis. Provision is made for two-way communication via a transponder fitted to the mine

between the exercise vessel and the mine itself. Data transmitted includes a mine sensor actuation signal and mine-to-ship ranges. The mine remains on the sea-bed for up to six months before recovery and servicing is necessary.

Recovery is initiated by triggering the mine's recovery mechanism using a coded acoustic signal. The mechanism frees the mine of mud and silt by compressed air from the air bottle in the ballast section and then automatically releases the buoyant section which floats to the surface to serve as a buoy to mark the position of the heavier ballast section, which is subsequently recovered by using the 200 m

long recovery rope that tethers the two sections to each other. The mine is normally laid from a mine countermeasures vessel, either by a special laying trolley that forms part of the system or by slipping from a davit. It may also be laid by a helicopter at speeds of less than ten knots and flying below a height of 6 m.

CHARACTERISTICS

Weight: 560 kg
Length: 2·71 m
Diameter: 533 mm
Simulated mine types: Magnetic, acoustic, pressure, combination

STATUS

In production and in service. An order from the USN for two complete VEM systems was disclosed in March 1983.

CONTRACTOR

British Aerospace Dynamics Group, Bracknell Division, Downshire Way, Bracknell, Berkshire RG12 1QL, England.

Versatile Exercise Mine (VEMS) is realistically shaped to provide the correct type of sonar return for mine hunting and is also equipped to simulate a combined influence ground mine.

After use for mine sweeping and mine hunting training, a signal is sent from the surface which causes the mine to separate into two. The smaller portion containing the computer and sensor unit floats to the surface and a rope is used to haul the remainder of the mine to the recovery vessel.

4764.441

DEPTH CHARGE MK 11 (MOD 3)

The Mk 11 Mod 3 depth charge is a new version of the depth charge Mk 11 series with fuzing mechanisms and safety features that are designed specifically to allow its deployment from helicopters and maritime patrol aircraft. It can be used against surface vessels and submarines in shallow water.

The depth charge consists of a 4 mm mild steel outer case which contains the explosive filling, fuzing and arming devices. The tail section is designed to break off on impact with the water and this facilitates hydropneumatic arming and detonation. The depth charge is fuzed by a unit that comprises a valve, a pistol unit, a detonator placer assembly and a primer assembly. Arming is only possible if the safety wire fitted to the tail section is withdrawn on release.

Two realistic exercise versions of the Mk 11 depth charge are produced for training: one is intended for basic drill procedures in weapon preparation and handling, and the other is for use by aircrews in carriage and release practice.

CHARACTERISTICS

Length: 97 cm (body section); 1·39 m (with tail)
Diameter: 279 mm
HE filling: 80 kg
Weight: 145 kg (fully prepared)

STATUS

Production. In November 1983 the contractor was awarded a US contract for a quantity of Mk 11 Mod 3 depth charges for competitive evaluation by the US Navy in a two-year programme.

Inserting fuze in Mk 11 depth charge

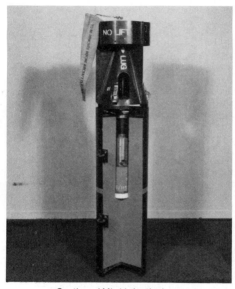

Sectioned Mk 11 depth charge

CONTRACTOR

British Aerospace Dynamics Group, Bracknell Division, Downshire Way, Bracknell, Berkshire RG12 1QL, England

---

UNITED STATES OF AMERICA

3195.441

AMERICAN UNDERWATER SURVEILLANCE

A recent US analysis credited the Soviet underwater combat fleet with more than 260 attack submarines, adding the opinion that quality had improved greatly in recent years. It went on to add that there are several indications that the Soviet submarine fleet will continue to grow in quality during the next decade. In 1984 the USSR was building five different classes of attack submarine, one diesel powered, and four nuclear powered. These are significantly larger and better than their predecessors, and they are also quieter which makes them more difficult for defenders to detect. The improvements are being introduced rapidly into the active fleet as a result of the high rate of production sustained by Soviet shipyards in the past ten years.

There are signs that this threat is diversifying, and in 1984 it was expected that the most modern Soviet submarines would be armed with long-range, land attack cruise missiles broadly comparable to the American Tomahawk, fitted with nuclear warheads. To meet this complex of underwater warfare potential, the USA dedicates a considerable proportion of the total defence effort into systems and

programmes designed to detect, classify and monitor underwater activities on a world-wide basis. The following paragraphs summarise the most important of these programmes.

SOSUS

SOSUS (Sound Surveillance System) consists of fixed undersea acoustic networks of passive hydrophone detector arrays deployed in the Atlantic and Pacific Oceans, and this is stated to provide significant detection capabilities. However, over the years (SOSUS was conceived in the 1950s) it was inevitable that the network gradually expanded as increments were added to enlarge the coverage. Most of these additions were the subject of various classified programmes, of which most details remain secret apart from isolated programme code-names. Among the latter are 'Caesar' and 'Collosus' referring to the US Atlantic and Pacific segments of the SOSUS network. Hydrophones designated AN/FQQ-10(V) are located at intervals of 5-15/miles along a linking cable connected to the shore station(s). Similar shore stations are said to exist beyond the USA (eg the Aleutian Islands, Canada, Denmark, Iceland, Italy, Japan, Korea, Philippines, Spain, Turkey, UK) these

being included in programmes code-named 'Barrier' and 'Bronco'. Constantly changing threat characteristics call for significant system improvements and the USN embarked on a two-phase SOSUS improvement programme. The specific aims of this programme remain classified in detail but are known to include improvements to the communications elements of the system and complementary improvements to the signal and data processing segments, thereby facilitating greater operational utilisation of the data obtained by the undersea sensor arrays.

The ultimate objective for the SOSUS system is the complete integration of all undersea surveillance sensor systems into a fully co-ordinated and centrally controlled network, IUSS.

SURTASS

SURTASS (Surveillance Towed Array Sensor System) is a successor system, due to become operational in late 1984, to the AN/BQR-15 Towed Array Surveillance System (TASS) which is already operational with the US fleet (see **1984.453**). This mobile surveillance system complements fixed networks by providing the essential flexibility to respond to changes in Soviet submarine deployment patterns and by extending coverage to remote ocean areas not monitored by fixed systems. They could also serve as emergency reserve facilities if fixed networks were disabled. There are two shore-based data processing centres (one on the East Coast of America, and one on the West Coast) to which acoustic target information gathered by the towed arrays is relayed. After processing, target information is transmitted back to operational ships at sea. Five or more ships are planned for each of the two processing centres, operating in waters to the east and west of the American continent, respectively. Whereas the BQR-15 is towed by submarines, slow, small surface ships will tow the long SURTASS arrays back and forth over designated patrol lines. Funds have been set aside for a special type of platform to operate SURTASS, designated T-AGOS.

SURTASS commenced full-scale development in fiscal year 1976. Testing was carried out at sea during 1977. Technical evaluation of SURTASS was completed in March 1978 and operational evaluation took place from May to June 1978. The first full tests of the SURTASS system, including the satellite link and data processing, took place in July 1979, and the system was declared ready for operational evaluation, which began in March 1980. Introduction to US Fleet service was expected by late 1984.

Congress has appropriated funds for the first 12 T-AGOS SURTASS ships and funding was sought in the 1985 budget for three more ships in fiscal year 1985 ($200·2 million), and another three in the following year ($192·6 million).

RDSS

RDSS (Rapidly Deployable Surveillance System) is designed to use air-deployable, bottom moored, long-life passive acoustic buoys as the main sensor system in a new mobile monitoring system. It will be emplaced by aircraft to provide undersea surveillance coverage on an urgent basis if required in areas of special interest. It could be used to replace or augment existing systems for long periods. RDSS buoys are capable of use in shallow water and areas unsuitable for either SOSUS or SURTASS techniques. The basic design allows for the transmission of data from the RDSS buoy to existing maritime patrol aircraft for either real-time readout or recording for later replay and analysis. Two versions of RDSS buoys have been identified, as Mod 0 and Mod 1, respectively. The former transmits its data to P-3 or S-3 maritime aircraft for analysis and presentation on the aircraft (it is also recorded for later processing), while the Mod 1 design is intended to send information direct to an ASW processing centre which will utilise the data without delay. The Mod 0 buoy is regarded as a 'near-term' item, and the Mod 1 is thought likely to take longer to reach operation. The approval for full-scale development of the system was given in August 1981, after a lengthy study and research programme. Development funding budgeted for fiscal years 1983/84/85/86 was $19·1 million, $18·2 million, $11·8 million and $26·5 million, respectively. In 1984 it was hoped to deploy RDSS by the end of the decade.

TACTAS

TACTAS (Tactical Towed Array Sonar) is intended to remedy the deficiency of current ASW surface ships in passive detection and classification capabilities against submarines. A long-range (direct path, first and second convergence zone) is required which can be used with other systems (LAMPS Mk III). The TACTAS programme will provide a number of different towed array systems for surface ship use. The AN/SQR-18A is a successor development of a towed array tested under a previous (classified) programme, and operational evaluation was completed in February 1976. The array is designed to be towed at high speed and is being installed on all 46 FF 1052 class ships. The AN/SQR-18A will be followed by the AN/SQR-19 system which will give FFG-7, DD-963, DDG-51 and CG-47 classes of ship a passive detection capability. The SQR-19 is in full-scale development with delivery of the first production system planned for 1984. The first system was installed on the destroyer *Moosbinggen* late in 1981 for technical and operational evaluation. Excellent results were reported and deployment of the SQR-19 is expected in the late 1980s. Present funding plans call for five sets to be procured in fiscal year 1983 at a cost of $71·1 million, 12 in 1984 costing $110 million, 10 in 1985 costing $125·6 million, and 15 proposed for 1986 at a cost of $162·4 million.

3966.241
LAMPS MK III

The USN LAMPS (Light Airborne Multipurpose System) has been designed to extend and enhance the capabilities of surface ships, particularly in anti-submarine warfare (ASW) and increased effective operational range for the weapon systems fitted in surface vessels of the US fleet. This system extends the electronic and acoustic sensors and provides a reactive weapon delivery capability for destroyers and frigate class ships by operating manned helicopters from them. Sensors, processors, and display capabilities aboard the helicopter enable the three-man crew to extend the ship's tactical, decision-making, and weapons delivery capabilities. Classic line-of-sight limitations for surface ships and limitations to underwater acoustic detection, classification, and localisation are thus mitigated through the use of the manned LAMPS aircraft.

LAMPS is being acquired in two phases. The first, Mk I, involved installation of shipboard equipment and conversion of H-2 helicopters already in the inventory to an SH-2 configuration. Mk I became operational in 1972. The Mk III includes the integration of improved avionics and shipboard systems to be used with the SH-60B Seahawk, a modified version of the Army UH-60A Blackhawk helicopter.

In 1974 the USN selected IBM as the system prime contractor to work with the Naval Air Systems Command in developing LAMPS Mk III. By late 1976, after extensive developmental testing, system capabilities were demonstrated in deep water using two modified helicopters with representative avionic and shipboard electronics. Two open-ocean tests concluded the validation of the LAMPS Mk III mission performance. The first was conducted jointly by the Naval Air Systems Command and IBM. After the data reduction was completed and the technical performance was assessed, the test was judged highly successful. The second test was conducted under the direction of the commander of the operational test and evaluation force to verify the operational suitability and performance of the LAMPS Mk III concept. The Navy was given permission to continue with full-scale development by the Department of Defense in 1978 with IBM as system prime contractor, Sikorsky Aircraft as the air vehicle contractor, and General Electric as the engine manufacturer for the new Mk III air vehicle.

The LAMPS Mk III weapon system embodies the integration of the parent ship (frigate, destroyer, cruiser) and the manned aircraft (SH-60B Seahawk) operating from that ship for both ASW and anti-ship surveillance and targeting (ASST) missions. As an adjunct of the sensor and attack systems of the parent or similarly equipped ships, the aircraft extends the detection, classification, localisation, and attack capabilities where needed to increase line-of-sight and range capabilities of the parent ship. Radar and ESM sensors extend the ship's line-of-sight against surface threats, whereas sensors that operate relative to the ocean medium (eg sonobuoys and magnetic anomaly detectors) enable the ship to engage the underwater target.

The primary control of aircraft tactics and selection of sensor and weapon modes remain with the parent ship for both the ASW and ASST missions, with an equally important, independent mode of LAMPS aircraft control provided as a backup.

In an ASW mission, the LAMPS aircraft is deployed from the parent ship when a suspected threat has been detected by the ship's towed array sonar, hull-mounted sonar, or by other forces. It proceeds to the estimated target area, where sonobuoys are dropped into the water in a pattern designed to entrap the target. The sounds (acoustic signatures) detected by the buoys are transmitted over a radio frequency link to the aircraft where they are analysed, codified, and retransmitted to the ship for interpretation and analysis. When the location of the threat has been determined with adequate precision, the aircraft descends near the ocean's surface for final confirmation. This may be accomplished using active sonobuoys, passive directional sonobuoys or by trailing a magnetic anomaly detector behind the aircraft. On final confirmation by any of these methods, a torpedo attack can be initiated. The extension of the ship's sensor, tactical control, and attack capabilities is achieved by using a duplex data link that transfers acoustic, electromagnetic, command data, and voice from the Seahawk, and command data and voice to the aircraft. Data is processed and evaluated aboard the parent ship where tactical and command decisions are made, and tactical instructions, weapon delivery information, and transmission of processed data are linked back to the SH-60B Seahawk.

Data transmitted to the parent ship (or other LAMPS-equipped ship) is processed by digital computers and specialised processors, distributed, and evaluated by the parent ship's operators: the LAMPS air tactical control officer, acoustic sensor operator, remote radar operator, and ESM operator. The combat information centre evaluator uses the data in context of the overall tactical situation to determine what actions to take in attacking. Operation of the LAMPS Mk III system was described in detail in previous editions of *Jane's Weapon Systems*.

LAMPS helicopter flying over USS McInerney

STATUS

Introduction to the US Fleet of the SH-60B LAMPS Mk III began in 1984, when there were plans to deploy such helicopters aboard about 100 US Navy surface vessels, including DD-963 and DDG-993 destroyers, CG-47 cruisers, and FFG-7 frigates. The earlier LAMPS Mk 1 Seasprite will continue to serve in some older FFG-7s. A stable production rate of 18 SH-60B helicopters per year is planned, 90 being requested in the next five years.

Procurement of 84 SH-60B helicopters between fiscal years 1983-1986 is expected to cost $1820 million.

CONTRACTORS

System prime contractor: International Business Machines Corporation, Federal Systems Division, 10215 Fernwood Road, Bethesda, Maryland 20034, USA.

SH-60B Seahawk helicopter: Sikorsky Aircraft.

General Electric Company: Engine contractor.

6001.241
ASROC ANTI-SUBMARINE SYSTEM

ASROC (RUR-5A) is an all-weather, day or night, ship-launched ballistic missile carried as the primary anti-submarine warfare (ASW) weapon aboard USN destroyers as well as some cruisers and frigates. The weapon consists of a Honeywell Mk 46 acoustic homing torpedo (**2822.441**) or a nuclear depth charge (estimated yield one kiloton) attached to a solid-propellant rocket motor. It can be fired from an eight-cell launcher Mk 112, the Mk 26 launching system, or from the Mk 10 Terrier missile launcher (ASROC/Terrier system).

Other major components include a fire control computer and an underwater sonar detector.

OPERATION

After launch the weapon follows a ballistic trajectory. The rocket motor is jettisoned at a predetermined point and the payload continues toward the target. If the payload is a torpedo, it is lowered to the water by a parachute, where its homing mechanism is activated upon submersion. Depth charge payloads sink to a predetermined depth before detonating.

Range of the weapon is classified but has been estimated to be from 2 to 10 km. The missile is 4·6 m long, has a diameter of 32·5 cm, and a span of 84·5 cm. Launch weight is about 435 kg.

DEVELOPMENT

ASROC has been in development since 1955 and

8-round ASROC Mk 112 launcher aboard USS Conolly (Stefan Terzibaschitsch)

entered service with the USN in 1961, becoming widely fitted in anti-submarine vessels of various classes. Plans to develop the ASROC system to utilise a vertical launch system (VLS), initially for some surface ships but later in attack submarines, were at first suspended on grounds of cost and/or a need to merge the project with the ASW stand-off weapon programme (**4181.441**). However, changing circumstances in the USN's overall ASW requirement and its inventory of weapons in this category led to a reversal of the original cancellation of vertical launch ASROC (VLA), and it is intended that the new version will ultimately replace the original ASROC deployed on surface ships.

STATUS

Users of the ASROC system include: USA (27 cruisers, 87 destroyers, 65 frigates), Japan (15 destroyers, 11 frigates), Spain (five each destroyers and frigates), Greece and Taiwan (four destroyers each), Canada (four frigates), Federal Republic of Germany (three destroyers), Turkey (three destroyers), Brazil, South Korea and Pakistan (two destroyers each), and Italy (one missile cruiser). In the 1985 fiscal year report by the US Secretary of Defense funding for ASROC (VLA) was included for development with $29·8m assigned for 1984, $28·6m in 1985, and $27·1m in 1986. Following a request for proposals issued in 1982/83, Goodyear Aerospace was awarded a VLA development contract in November 1983.

The conventional launch ASROC will continue to be supported by Honeywell as prime contractor to the US Naval Ocean Systems Centre, San Diego..

CONTRACTORS

Honeywell Inc, Training and Control Systems Operations, 1200 West San Bernadino Road, West Covina, California 91790, USA (Prime Contractor).

Goodyear Aerospace Corporation, 1210 Massillon Road, Akron, Ohio 44311, USA (VLA development).

1128.441
SUBROC (UUM-44A) ANTI-SUBMARINE MISSILE

This is a submarine launched missile which follows a short underwater path before transferring to an air trajectory for the major portion of its journey to the target area. When this is reached a nuclear depth bomb is separated from the remainder of the missile and then follows a ballistic trajectory to the point where it re-enters the water. The W55 nuclear charge then sinks to a predetermined depth before detonation. Estimated yield of the warhead is about one kiloton.

Principal characteristics of SUBROC are: length 625 cm, diameter 53·3 cm, weight 1853 kg (approximately), range 56 km (approximately), and speed is supersonic. It has a solid-fuel motor.

OPERATION

The UUM-44A missile forms part of an advanced anti-submarine system designed for deployment in nuclear-powered attack submarines operating against submerged vessels armed with strategic missiles. This system includes the AN/BQQ-2 Raytheon integrated sonar system and the Mk 113

SUBROC anti-submarine missile after leaving launch submarine and taking to the air, but before separation of its nuclear depth charge and rocket motor

SUBROC fire control system produced by the Librascope division of Singer-General Precision Inc.

After detection and location of a target submarine, co-ordinate data are fed into the attack submarine weapon system which programmes an optimum mission profile for the SUBROC missile. It is assumed that this can be accomplished in virtually real-time.

The SUBROC missile is launched horizontally from a standard 21 inch (53·3 cm) torpedo tube, by conventional means. At a safe distance from the launch vessel (which need not be directed towards the target area for firing) the solid-fuel missile motor is ignited and the missile follows a short level path before being directed upward and clear of the water. Missile stability and steering is effected by four jet deflectors, which function in both water- and airborne sectors of the trajectory. Guidance is by means of an inertial system (SD-510) produced by Kearfott.

When free of the water, SUBROC is accelerated to a supersonic speed and guided toward the target area. At a predetermined point separation of the nuclear depth bomb is initiated by explosive bolts and a thrust-reversal deceleration system which enables the warhead to continue to the re-entry point on a ballistic trajectory controlled by vanes on the depth bomb.

Impact with the water is cushioned to protect the arming and detonation devices. A preset depth sensor detonates the nuclear charge when the bomb is in the vicinity of the target. It is probable that the target position will need to be established with an accuracy that will permit the warhead to detonate within its estimated lethal radius of 5 to 8 km from the target.

SUBROC missiles can be carried in torpedo tubes without attention for long periods, and launched with minimal preparation time.

DEVELOPMENT

Development of the UUM-44 began in June 1958 at the US Naval Ordnance Laboratory, White Oak, Maryland, under the management direction of the Bureau of Naval Weapons, with Goodyear Aerospace Corporation as the prime contractor. Technical evaluation was completed in 1964, and production and operational deployment began in 1965.

STATUS

SUBROC is operational on nuclear-powered attack submarines and in 1982 there were about 64 USN attack submarines equipped to use the system. Each ship carries four to six SUBROC missiles. An improvement programme to sustain the effectiveness of this weapon against new threats was initiated in 1976/77.

This would have entailed replacement of the SUBROC analogue guidance sub-system by a digital one and regraining of the weapon's rocket motors, and it was estimated that to extend the operational life of the system by five years would have cost about $41 million. A Congressional decision was taken in 1979 not to update the system along these lines, and as a consequence the USN turned to the ASW-SOW (anti-submarine warfare-standoff weapon) programme (**4181.441**) to meet existing and anticipated operational requirements. The SUBROC system is now considered obsolescent and it is proposed to withdraw the system from the USN inventory during the 1980s. It will be replaced by the ASW-SOW.

CONTRACTORS

Prime contractor: Goodyear Aerospace Corporation, 1210 Massillon Road, Akron, Ohio 44311, USA.

Mk 113 fire control system: Singer-General Precision Inc, Librascope Division, 808 Western Avenue, Glendale, California 91210, USA.

SD-510 inertial guidance system: Singer-General Precision Inc, Kearfott Division, 1150 McBride Avenue, Little Falls, New Jersey 07424, USA.

Nuclear warhead: Sandia Corporation, Livermore Radiation Labs, Livermore, California, USA.

Solid-fuel motor: Thiokol Chemical Corporation, Elkton Division, Elkton, Maryland, USA.

4181.441
ASW-SOW ANTI-SUBMARINE WARFARE STAND-OFF WEAPON

The USN ASW-SOW programme was approved by the US Secretary of Defense in 1980 and is intended to develop a long-range anti-submarine weapon by the late 1980s. The ASW-SOW is required to replace the technologically obsolete SUBROC (**1128.441**) which it is planned to withdraw from the USN inventory during the 1980s. The new weapon is also intended to meet the challenge of new threats such as the latest Soviet 'Alfa' class of submarine, and it will be designed for launching from US nuclear attack submarines, and surface fighting ship vertical launch systems. Specific platform applications of ASW-SOW have not been defined more precisely to date.

In USN attack submarines the weapon will be used with existing torpedo tubes and the Mk 117 digital fire control system. (The latter is planned to be the first type of existing shipboard hardware to incorporate Outlaw Shark capabilities, now in research and development to provide a correlated, computer-formated, all-source data handling facility for forces at sea. A major objective of this project is over-the-horizon targeting.) US attack submarines cannot at present launch a weapon against a target unless it closes to within reach of the Mk 48 torpedo. The ASW-SOW will extend this range appreciably, as well as permitting further attacks on submarines which successfully evade a torpedo attack.

Four separate designs for ASW-SOW were proposed but they have in common a combined underwater/air-flight/underwater path from submarine launch platform to target, similar to that of the SUBROC predecessor system, but variations include the method(s) of propulsion employed. The system as defined so far calls for alternative payloads consisting of either a nuclear depth bomb or a homing torpedo. The former has the advantage of a larger kill radius, thus making lesser demands in terms of accuracy and range performance, but it is hoped that development of the ALWT will prove adequate as a basis for a more precise (non-nuclear) ASW-SOW payload.

As already stated, the proposals made by the various contractors selected to submit concept formulation plans in response to the ASW-SOW requirement differed in a number of respects and all four were described in *Jane's Weapon Systems 1981-2*. The team selected to continue development of the project was that linking Boeing, Gould and Hercules Aerospace. Boeing as the leader with responsibility for the vehicle; Gould for the payload, acoustics and signal processing, and guidance; and Hercules for the single solid-propellant rocket motor. The latter is apparently designed to propel the weapon during its initial underwater trajectory (after clearing the launcher torpedo tube) and during the air flight. On clearing the surface of the water, four small wrap-around fins at the rear of the rocket motor casing deploy automatically to aid stability. After booster burnout, the motor is probably jettisoned, leaving the payload section to follow a ballistic path to the target area, where after deceleration it re-enters the water for the payload/warhead section (nuclear or torpedo) to come into action.

It will be possible to fire the ASW-SOW from surface ships or submarines and rounds will be stored in canisters ready to fire from the vertical launch systems of destroyers (DD 963 class), guided missile cruisers (CG 47 class), and guided missile destroyers

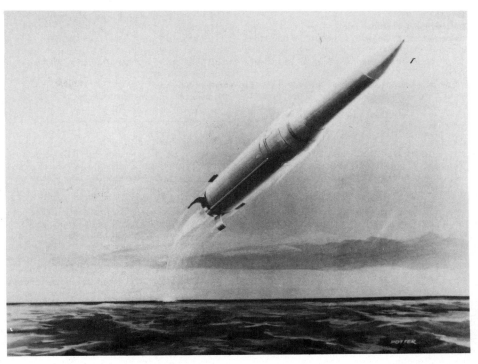

Drawing of the Anti-Submarine Warfare Stand-off Weapon under development for the US Navy by Boeing

(DDG 51 class). From SSN 637/688 class attack submarines, the missile will be carried by capsule to the surface before the solid-propellant rocket motor ignites to propel it to the target area.

Both the surface-launched and submarine ASW-SOW missiles will be able to carry either the US Department of Energy-developed nuclear depth bomb or the advanced lightweight torpedo. Surface ships will have a third payload option in the existing Mk 46 Mod 5 torpedo.

STATUS
The ASW-SOW programme was initiated in 1980 and it was then estimated that the research, development, test and engineering cost would amount to a total of about $550 million. Funding is under Programme Element 63367N of the US DoD budget and the actual funding for fiscal year 1982 was $35·4 million, with $20·2 million in 1983. Proposed development funding in fiscal years 1984/5 is $28 million and $63·4 million, respectively. The 1984 fiscal year report by the US

Secretary of Defense stated that ASW-SOW will be developed to replace SUBROC aboard USN attack submarines, with provisional entry into service during the late 1980s. One of the first classes to be fitted will be the 688 class of nuclear attack submarines, although the weapon will be compatible with surface vessels equipped with vertical launch facilities.

A second static test firing of the Hercules Aerospace rocket motor for ASW-SOW took place successfully in July 1983. In May 1984 Boeing announced a $95·9 million contract to prepare the demonstration and validation phase of the programme which is due for completion by the end of 1985. A submarine launch of the weapon was expected to take place by the end of 1984.

CONTRACTORS
The Boeing Company, Box 3707, Seattle, Washington 98124, USA; with Gould Inc, Government Systems Division, and Hercules Aerospace.

3629.441
TORPEDO Mk 32

The Mk 32 is an acoustic anti-submarine torpedo which is still in use aboard a number of former USN ships now transferred to other navies in various parts of the world, mostly aboard escort types. They are launched by the Mk 4 rack-type launcher unit in most cases, in which a single torpedo is carried in the ready-to-launch position with two more torpedoes stored nearby on deck. The current version is the Mk 32 Mod 2, which is equipped with an active acoustic homing head. It is also capable of air drop launch.

Propulsion is by electric motor, powered by a silver/zinc-oxide battery which is activated by sea water. After launch, the torpedo descends to a depth of 6 m and the active sonar begins to operate, transmitting 50 kHz pulses while the torpedo follows a spiral search pattern, circling to left or right as selected. The search pattern is maintained until the sonar obtains a target response and the homing sequence commences. In the event of failure to obtain a target contact, the circular search pattern continues until the battery is exhausted, after which the torpedo dives deeper prior to self-destruction.

CHARACTERISTICS
Length: 2080 mm
Diameter: 483 mm
Weight: 350 kg
Warhead: HE 49 kg
Propulsion: Electric motor
Range: Approx 8600 yards (7864 m) at 12 knots
Max acoustic range: 560 m
STATUS
Operational but obsolescent.

2817.441
TORPEDO Mk 37 Mods 0 and 3

Designed primarily as a submarine-launched anti-submarine torpedo, but suitable for deck launching by the Mk 23 and Mk 25 torpedo launchers, the Mk 37 torpedo is a 19 inch (482·6 mm) weapon that has been described as the first successful high-performance anti-submarine torpedo. The 19 inch diameter of all versions of this torpedo was chosen to enable the torpedo to swim out from a standard 21 inch (533 mm) launch tube, an arrangement with obvious operational advantages.

Mods 0 and 3 are free-running torpedoes. After one has been launched on a target interception course it

maintains it until, at a preset range, it 'enables' a process involving arming the warhead and switching in the attack logic circuits. The latter include various preselectable options such as depth limits, search pattern, and type of homing. The final attack is by sonar auto-homing which can be active, passive, or both combined.

Mod 3 is an updated version of Mod 0, the updating consisting of the incorporation of a large number of minor modifications based on operational experience.

DEVELOPMENT
Developed by Westinghouse the Mk 37 Mod 0 torpedo first went into service in 1957. Mk 37

torpedoes have been produced in large quantities by the Naval Ordnance Plant, Forest Park, Illinois, and are still in widespread use in the US fleet.

CHARACTERISTICS
Length: 352 cm
Diameter: 483 mm with guides to fit 533 mm tubes
Weight: 645 kg (warshot); 540 kg (practice)
Warhead: 150 kg HE
Speed: 24 knots (Mod 3)
Submersion: To 270 m (Mod 3)
STATUS
Operational, but replacement by the Mk 48 torpedo (**2823.441**) has now begun.

2818.441

TORPEDO Mk 37 Mods 1 and 2

These versions of the Mk 37 torpedo differ from Mods 0 and 3 (**2817.441**) in their size and method of guidance; in other respects they are substantially similar.

Both versions are wire-guided, whereas the Mk 37 Mods 0 and 3 are free-running torpedoes. Both are

4·09 m long and weigh 766 kg (warshot) or 657 kg (practice).

Just as Mod 3 is an updated version of Mod 0 so is Mod 2 a version of Mod 1 updated by the incorporation of a number of minor modifications.

CHARACTERISTICS

Length: 409 cm
Diameter: 483 mm with guides to fit 533 mm tubes

Weight: 766 kg (warshot); 657 kg (practice)
Warhead: 150 kg HE
Speed: 24 knots (Mod 2)
Submersion: To 270 m (Mod 2)
STATUS
Operational.

4762.441

TORPEDO NT 37E MODERNISATION

The NT 37E torpedo is a modernised, improved version of the standard, battery-electric propulsion Mk 37 heavyweight torpedo (**2817.441**, **2818.441**). This dual purpose ASW and anti-ship torpedo can be fired from both submarines and surface ships. Incorporating a standard RS 232 digital fire control interface, the torpedo is compatible with the following platforms and fire control systems: West German 205/206/MSI-70U; West German 209/HSA-SINBADS (later version); RNLN Swordfish/HSA-M8; British Oberon/TCSS-5, TIOS; US Guppy/US Mk 106; US Mk 32 surface launch tubes; or any class equipped to fire Mk 37 torpedoes.

The NT 37E performance improvement kit and hardware, largely installed in the field, upgrades existing Mk 37 torpedo inventories. It consists of three major subsystems:

(1) An Otto-fueled thermo-chemical propulsion system. When compared to the performance of an unmodified Mk 37 silver-zinc battery and electric motor, the new propulsion system demonstrates a 40 per cent increase in speed, a 150 per cent increase in range, and an 80 per cent increase in

endurance. The propulsion system utilises existing Mk 37 motor mounting provisions and is compatible with existing Mk 46 fuelling and engine maintenance facilities, engine tools, and engine refurbishment kits.

(2) A solid-state acoustic system and a noise-reduction laminar-flow nose assembly replaces the Mk 37's vacuum-tube acoustic panel and hemispherical nose. The new sonar substantially improves the passive detection range against high-speed surface targets and active detection range against small silhouette submarine targets; in most cases, target acquisition range has been doubled. The new SUBTIP self-noise reduction nose assembly increases transducer isolation while reducing flow noise effects, reducing the likelihood of self-decoying at all depths.

(3) A solid-state computer-based guidance and control system with inertial navigation capability replaces the Mk 37's vacuum-tube analogue system, resulting in greater system stability, reliability and accuracy. The new system utilises a Honeywell H-478 inertial sensor assembly and a MIL SPEC 8002 microprocessor, allowing fully programmmable tactics and inertial navigation.

Should future naval tactics require modified torpedo command and control, changes can be easily implemented by revision of software and replacement of programmable read-only memory units (PROMs).

Two-speed propulsion and 2-way wire guide telemetry, providing full exchange of data and commands between torpedo and submarine, are also available for the NT 37E as options.

CHARACTERISTICS

Type: NT 37E, wire-guided, Mod 2, non wire-guided, Mod 3
Length: 4505 mm (Mod 2); 3846 mm (Mod 3)
Diameter: 485 mm
Weight: 750 kg (Mod 2); 642 kg (Mod 3)
Run modes: (1) Straight run/salvo-anti-ship; (2) straight run with acoustic miss indicator to initiate acoustic re-attack; (3) active snake and circle – ASW; passive snake and circle – anti-ship
Warshot explosive weight: 150 kg HE
Propulsion: Thermochemical rotary piston cam engine with Otto-fuel; 2-speed option
STATUS
The first major performance upgrading kit for the standard torpedo Mk 37 was developed and produced by the Northrop Corporation in the mid-1970s. This upgraded version was called the NT 37C and included the thermo-chemical propulsion system and anti-ship kit.

Honeywell acquired the rights to the NT 37C in 1979 and, at the request of principal NATO NT 37C user navies, instituted a development programme to improve the logistic support capability and the acoustic and guidance performance of the torpedo. This effort resulted in the new, supportable, solid state acoustic and guidance system and nose assembly.

Advanced development of the solid-state guidance and control system was completed in 1982. Performance of the NT 37E model was demonstrated on a three-dimensional instrumented range and during sea trials with user navies during the period 1981-1983. The tests demonstrated the following improvements: increased dynamic control and accuracy, complete wire guidance capability, ease of changing tactical software, low sonar background noise levels, low acoustic false alarm rate, active and passive acoustic attacks on acoustic targets, increased torpedo reliability and reduced maintainance. The Mk 37 family of torpedoes is used by at least 16 navies.

CONTRACTOR

Honeywell Marine Systems Division, 5303 Shilshole Avenue NW, Seattle, Washington 98107, USA.

Sea trials of NT37E heavyweight torpedo

2820.441

TORPEDO Mk 44

This is a lightweight torpedo designed for launching from aircraft or helicopters, from surface vessels (using Mk 32 tubes), or by the ASROC rocket system (**6001.241**).

Two models have so far been produced but the differences in dimensions are trivial. Both torpedoes are electrically propelled and their calibre is 12·75 inches (324 mm). Approximate length is 2·56 m and the torpedoes weigh about 233 kg with a 34 kg warhead. Active acoustic homing is used. Depth and course settings are entered by umbilical cable. Estimated maximum submersion depth is approximately 300 m. A range of about 5000 m at a speed of 30 knots has been reported. Arming is by seawater scoop.

STATUS

Obsolescent. Licence production was initiated in a number of foreign countries. Replaced by Mk 46 (**2822.441**) in USA and UK service. Some other states

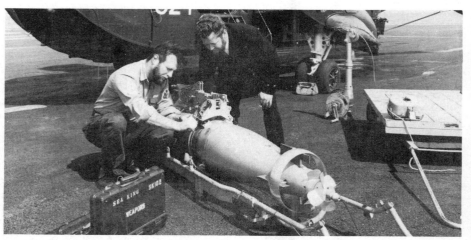

Mk 44 torpedo being prepared for loading on Sea King helicopter

are adopting the Mk 46 but the navies equipped with the Mk 44 are those of Argentina, Australia, Brazil, Canada, Chile, Columbia, Federal Republic of Germany, Greece, Indonesia, Iran, Italy, Japan, Netherlands, New Zealand, Norway, Pakistan, Philippines, Portugal, South Africa, South Korea, Spain, Thailand, Tunisia, Turkey, Uruguay and Venezuela.

2822.441
TORPEDO Mk 46

Torpedo Mk 46 is a lightweight, 324 mm calibre weapon designed as a successor to the Mk 44 (2820.441) for use with several ASW systems. It can be launched from surface vessels, fixed-wing aircraft, or helicopters and can be carried by the ASROC rocket (6001.241). Mk 32 tubes are used for surface launching.

The Mk 46 is a deep-diving, high-speed torpedo fitted with an active/passive acoustic homing system and intended for use against submarines. After water entry it searches for, acquires, and attacks its target; if it misses the target it is capable of multiple re-attacks.

Two models of the Mk 46 have been produced. Mod 0 was the first US torpedo to be powered by a solid-fuel motor: it is 2·67 m long and weighs about 258 kg. Immediately it enters the water it starts a helical search pattern. Mod 1 is slightly lighter and is powered by a five-cylinder liquid mono-propellant (Otto) motor. The Mk 46 torpedo also forms the active element of the Captor mine system (2541.441, below) in which role it has the designation Mk 46 Mod 4.

CHARACTERISTICS
Type: Mk 46 Mod 1
Length: 2·59 m
Diameter: 32·4 cm
Weight: 230 kg
Max speed: 40 knots
Range: 11 000 m (max)
Acquisition range: 460 m (estimated)
Max depth: Classified

Search patterns: Multiple
Warshot explosive weight: 44 kg
Propulsion: Monopropellant
STATUS
Mod 1 is operational: the first delivery to the USN was made in October 1965. Following the cancellation of the Mk 31 torpedo a quantity of Mk 46 torpedoes was purchased as an interim measure by the UK MoD for RN use.

The Mod 0 was produced in limited quantities because the Otto fuel was found to be a more practical propellant. It is used in the US fleet only, for aircraft launch applications.

The Mk 46 Mod 1 was introduced in the US fleet in April 1967 and was followed by the Mod 2 in 1972. Production of the former was completed in February 1971 and conversion of 600 Mod 2 units was completed by early 1975.

Present efforts are directed to the NEARTIP (Near-Term Improvement Programme) to improve the acoustic performance and countermeasure resistance of the Mk 46 torpedo.

In particular, this programme is designed to restore the acquisition range of the Mk 46 torpedo which was reduced by an estimated 33 per cent by the adoption of an anechoic coating for some of their submarines by the USSR. Code-named Clusterguard, this paint reduces the effectiveness of the standard Mk 46's acoustic homing head and NEARTIP is meant to restore this aspect of performance to at least the same as the pre-Clusterguard status. Other improvements are to the guidance and control and associated fire

Mk 46 torpedo deployed on Sea King ASW helicopter (USN photo)

control system to achieve improved performance against the more sophisticated threats envisaged. NEARTIP implementation is in the form of modification kits applied on a retrofit basis to existing Mods 1 and 2 Mk 46 torpedoes. Captor Mk 46 torpedoes (Mod 4) will not be fitted with NEARTIP kits; instead there is a different modification kit for this programme (see 2541.441, below).

As prime contractor for the Mk 46 since 1965, Honeywell has produced more than 9000 torpedoes for the USN and other navies. The fiscal year 1984 report by the US Secretary of Defense included funding for both new Mk 46 (NEARTIP) torpedoes and conversion kits to upgrade older Mk 46s, an estimated 500 of which will be used in the Captor role. Actual, planned and proposed funding and acquisition quantites for the fiscal years 1983/84/85/86 are 440 ($117·2 m); 1200 ($212·9 m); 1565 ($256 m); and 1521 ($313·2 m) respectively. Note: these figures include both conversions and new production quantities.

A successor to the Mk 46 Mod 5 NEARTIP torpedo is being developed under the Advanced Lightweight Torpedo (ALWT) programme (4182.441).

Users of the Mk 46 torpedo include: Australia, Brazil, Canada, France, Greece, Indonesia, Iran, Israel, Italy, Japan, Morocco, Netherlands, New Zealand, Norway, Pakistan, Portugal, Saudi Arabia, South Korea, Spain, Taiwan, Thailand, Turkey, UK and USA.

CONTRACTORS
Aerojet Electro Systems Company, Azusa, California, USA, was responsible for the development and early production of both Mod 0 and Mod 1.

Honeywell Inc and Gould Ocean Systems Division have also been involved in manufacture and the former is now prime contractor for the Mk 46 NEARTIP.

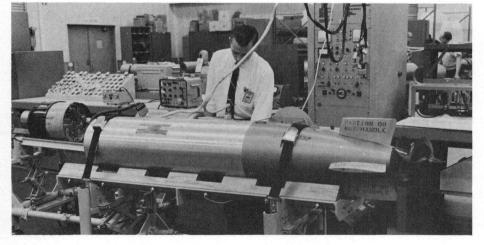

Mk 46 Mod 1 torpedo under test at a USN laboratory (USN photo)

4182.441
MK 50 ADVANCED LIGHTWEIGHT TORPEDO (ALWT)

The Advanced Lightweight Torpedo (ALWT), (once designated EX-50, but now the Mk 50) is being developed for use from ships, submarines and aircraft in order to meet the advancing and sophisticated Soviet submarine threat as a successor to the Mk 46 Mod 5 (NEARTIP) lightweight torpedo (2822.441). The design objectives include an enlarged target detection envelope embracing faster submarines operating at greater depths, and other desired features are increased speed and endurance, terminal homing, signal processing, and greater destructive effect. The last objective will be attained by a new design of directed energy warhead which it will be necessary to place on its target with high precision to ensure that the directed energy blast penetrates the hull and does not glance off. It will also be advantageous to hit the target submarine amidships. The ALWT is expected to have similar dimensions and weight to those of the Mk 46 and have a speed of

about 40 knots with a maximum submersion of some 600 m.

In addition to the ability to operate against fast, deep diving submarines, there is a requirement for capabilities against shallow, slow-moving submarines and surface ships. The most difficult objective to be met, according to the US DoD, is the realisation of reliable terminal homing which is essential if a directed energy warhead is to be used.

Initially two sets of contractors competed under the A-109 procedure whereby each contractor had broad latitude to develop their own unique torpedo so long as it conformed with the Navy's operational requirements. The combination of Honeywell as prime contractor, with Garrett Pneumatic Systems for the propulsion, was selected as sole contractor during 1981. Exhaustive test and evaluation has begun with an engineering development phase to follow. Production torpedoes are likely to come into service in the mid- to late 1980s.

A propulsion test vehicle version of the Honeywell/Garrett torpedo was test launched in the

latter half of 1981. It used a closed cycle steam turbine engine in a stored chemical energy propulsion system (SCEPS) with the energy being supplied by a chemical reaction. The command/control system was computer based and software controlled and given reference information by an autopilot on which to base its decisions for steering and engine control.

Seven modified Mk 45 torpedoes are being built as high speed mobile torpedo targets (ADMATT) for ALWT testing by Rockwell International. These run at up to 41 knots and tow a hydrophone/echo repeater array that simulates the spatial extent of a real submarine, and this method was chosen as the only feasible way of developing and testing the ALWT terminal homing system. A three-dimensional instrumented shallow water range has also been developed for ALWT evaluation.
STATUS
Now in full-scale development, the actual and planned funding for RDT&E in fiscal years 1983/84/85/86 in $millions was 104·2, 115·1, 143·3 and 147·3 respectively.

CONTRACTOR
Honeywell Inc, Defense Systems Division, Hopkins,
Minnesota, USA.

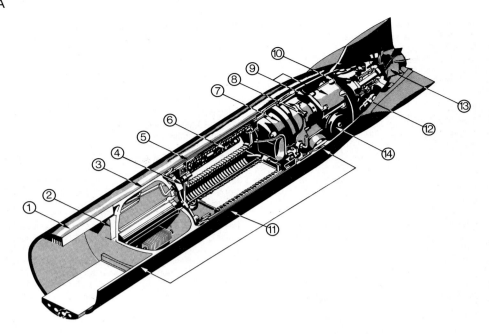

Cut-away diagram of ALWT advanced development model showing SCEPS afterbody. (1) guidance and command section hull (2) full-authority electronic powerplant controller (3) pressure-storage oxidant tank (4) electric-powered oxidant control system (5) high efficiency, hull-integrated condenser (6) high energy, lithium-fuelled boiler/reactor (7) high efficiency, supersonic impulse turbine (8) quiet, lightweight reduction and accessory drive gearbox (9) high speed, rare-earth pm alternators (10) fast start feedwater injector (11) high-strength, lightweight hull structures (12) high-response, electric steering fin actuators (13) pump-jet propulsor (14) vibration isolation engine mounts

2541.441
CAPTOR – ENCAPSULATED TORPEDO

Captor, a contraction of 'encapsulated torpedo', is the name given to an anti-submarine system comprising a Mk 46 torpedo (**2822.441**) inserted into a mine casing.

Deployment is in deep water, generally in the vicinity of strategic routes travelled by enemy submarines, and submarines are the intended targets. US officials have stated that Captor has the ability to detect and classify submarine targets while surface ships are able to pass over a Captor field without triggering the Mk 46 Mod 4 torpedo which carries the warhead (43·5 kg PBXN103 explosive). This capability is reported to have been tested.

The detection and control unit (DCU) that performs these functions is the most costly sub-assembly of the complete Captor weapon and accounts for about 45 per cent of the total unit cost – approximately $130 000. DoD statements imply that the DCU incorporates facilities for turning itself on and off, in addition to its principal operational functions of detecting possible targets, classifying them by their sound signatures, and initiating release of the Mk 46 torpedo when the target is within range of its homing head. It is probable that the turn-on/turn-off system is quite sophisticated in the interests of power conservation to ensure the maximum operational life for deployed Captor mines. Factors which are likely to be taken into account include the levels of traffic (surface and submarine), ambient conditions, sea-state, etc.

Both active and passive sensor modes are employed and the system first operates in a listening (passive) mode which continues for a certain length of time sufficient to identify the target as a submarine and not a surface vessel. The system then switches to an active mode during which it is assumed target ranging is carried out to determine the optimum release time for the homing torpedo.

The detection and control unit is gated to ignore surface traffic and has an estimated range of about 1000 m on submarine targets. There is no IFF capability and friendly units must be warned of Captor minelaying and positions of deployed mines.

There are presumably provisions for some method of self-deactivation or self-destruct for those Captors which are life-expired and which are not capable of retrieval, and other measures to prevent unauthorised salvage or interference may be expected.

The current deployed life of a Captor mine is thought to be in the neighbourhood of six months, but it is not known if this is the USN's target, although it is a fact that considerable effort has been placed on ensuring maximum shelf and operational life.

Captor mines can be sown by surface ships, submarines, and by aircraft. In the former delivery mode, mine rails or other delivery systems are not required, the chosen technique being by means of an over-the-side boom (or yard and stay) with a capacity of 1045 kg. The Captor is brought to a point about 10 m above the surface before release, which has to be at an angle to ensure proper entry into the water. Any submarine equipped with standard 21 inch (533 mm) torpedo tubes can lay Captor mines, these having the advantage of being capable of covert minelaying. Aircraft employ a parachute technique for delivery of Captor.

According to USN statements, there are two main options for Captor delivery: one utilises P-3 maritime aircraft, nuclear strike submarines and surface ships; the other envisages a combination of USAF B-52 bombers and P-3 aircraft, plus surface ships and nuclear strike submarines. Captor has been tested for delivery on P-3C, A-6, A-7 and B-52 aircraft, LKA and other cargo ships, and aboard ten different classes of submarine, including conventionally powered boats.

Most Captor minefields will be barriers located at some distance from possible enemy defences, and in the more highly defended areas Captor mines would be delivered by aircraft or submarines. The unique capability of submarines to plant mines covertly and under ice would be employed selectively.

CHARACTERISTICS
Length: 3·7 m (overall)
Diameter: 533 mm
Weight: 908 kg (with torpedo and mooring)
STATUS

Initial production was started in March 1976, although the US Secretary of Defense's report of January 1981 said the procurement had been at a low level while development and testing were conducted to correct performance deficiencies. In December 1978 reduced performance against shallow water targets had been indicated. Nevertheless initial operational capability was achieved in September 1979. Further procurement was cancelled after fiscal year 1980 by a decision taken in December 1980, and in January 1980 a Captor improvement programme was approved. The weapon was granted approval for service use in February 1980, but no procurement funds were sought in the fiscal year 1981 budget "because Captor failed to provide the high level of effectiveness we had sought. Subsequent testing has demonstrated that recent modifications have corrected its performance deficiencies. The 1982 fiscal year budget requests funds to continue production."

Despite this somewhat chequered history, in spring 1980 Admiral Rowden was able to disclose that about 630 Captors had been procured. The 1985 Report by the US Secretary of Defense, indicated the following procurement and funding for Captor (in millions of dollars and quantities in brackets):

Fiscal year:	**1983**	**1984**	**1985**
Quantity/amounts:	(450)	(300)	(300)
	108·2	111·2	135·2

CONTRACTOR
Goodyear Aerospace Corporation, 1210 Massillon Road, Akron, Ohio 44311, USA.

2823.441
TORPEDO Mk 48

The Mk 48 torpedo is carried by all US attack and fleet ballistic missile submarines. The weapon can be adapted to launch from surface ships. Currently it is operational only on submarines. The torpedo is wire-guided through a two-way communications link in the current Mod 3 version.

The Mk 48 torpedo is propelled with an axial flow pump-jet propulsor driven by an external combustion gas piston engine. This engine, like that in the Mk 46 torpedo (**2822.441**), is a Gould design. The fuel for the engine is a monopropellant, Otto Fuel II.

The Mk 48 torpedo is capable of operation in wire-guided active or passive acoustic and non-acoustic modes. The acoustic modes of operation allow active or passive target detection capabilities.

In the description of the Mk 48 torpedo which follows, the weapon is treated in five distinct sections, known as 'groups', which are from front to back of the torpedo: nose, warhead/exercise, control, fuel tank, and afterbody/tailcone.

The nose group contains units known as functional item replacement (FIR) units which are the transducer Mk 72, transmitter Mk 83, receiver Mk 68, and homing control logic (HCL) Mk 1. The transducer unit occupies the forward portion of the nose shell and transmits and receives acoustic signals to and from the ocean environment. These signals are generated by the transmitter located directly behind the transducer. The receiver, located in the lower half of the nose shell, processes acoustic signals received from the transducer and determines target position relative to the transducer for the development of steering orders during torpedo homing.

The HCL is located in the aft end of the nose shell directly above the receiver. The HCL contains a computer that directs torpedo manoeuvres in search, homing, and re-attack modes. Other circuits within the HCL unit analyse all acoustic signals for valid target returns.

The warhead group is located immediately aft of the nose group and contains the warhead Mk 107, exploder Mk 21, arming device Mk 2, and electronic assembly Mk 12. The explosive charge is loaded into the warhead shell at an explosives loading facility. The loaded warhead shell, with source and sensor assemblies installed, constitutes the warhead. Arming device Mk 2 and exploder mechanism Mk 21 insert into a cavity in the main explosive charge. The arming device and exploder mechanism are accessible from outside the warhead shell. The torpedo is issued with the exploder and arming device installed. Electronic assembly Mk 12 is a FIR item located in the aft warhead compartment. This unit contains target detection electronics which trigger the explosive.

The control group, located between the warhead and the fuel tank group, houses the command control unit Mk 154 or Mk 168, gyro control unit Mk 155, and power control unit (PCU) Mk 156. The command control unit is mounted in the lower third of the control shell. The command control implements fire control instructions, maintains the torpedo at the commanded speed, and monitors depth to ensure that the torpedo stays between the commanded maximum and minimum depth limits. The gyro control unit is mounted in the centre of the control shell. This unit converts steering commands into fin deflection signals to maintain the torpedo on the commanded course. The PCU is mounted in the upper third of the control group.

The warshot fuel tank group is located between the control group and the afterbody/tailcone group. There are no FIR items in the fuel tank group. The fuel tank group stores fuel for the propulsion system and houses the wire dispenser used for command guidance after launch. At launch, the fuel shut-off solenoid valve in the fuel tank is opened, allowing fuel flow to the engine in the afterbody/tailcone group. The warshot fuel tank group carries a full fuel load.

The afterbody/tailcone unit contains the engine, steering control surfaces, and engine accessories, less alternator and chamber and valve assembly. This unit becomes the afterbody/tailcone group when the combustion chamber (grain loaded) and alternator are mounted on the forward bulkhead of the unit. The alternator assembly, mounted on the forward bulkhead of the afterbody/tailcone group, is driven by a power take-off shaft from the engine and provides electrical power required by the torpedo after launch. The chamber and valve assembly is mounted within the water jacket on the forward bulkhead of the afterbody/tailcone group. Fuel is burned in the combustion chamber to provide hot gas to operate the engine.

DEVELOPMENT

Anticipation by the US authorities of impending advances in submarine technology by the USSR noted in the 1960s and 1970s led to studies of the Mk 48's capabilities against likely threats, and in 1975 resulted in an Operational Requirement issued by the Chief of Naval Operations for a programme to develop appropriate modifications to the Mk 48 torpedo to keep pace with anticipated submarine threat developments. The origins of the Mk 48 ADCAP (advanced capabilities) programme lay in this requirement, but the extent and rate of Soviet submarine technology advance hastened both ADCAP progress and another Mk 48 improvement programme.

Recognition (by the USA) of the impressive

Data processor cards which are part of digital guidance and control system being developed by Hughes for Mk 48 torpedo ADCAP programme

operational characteristics of the Soviet 'Alfa' class submarine in late spring 1979 resulted in a decision taken in September 1979 to accelerate the ADCAP programme. It was also responsible for an intensive test and analysis programme to determine the true limits of the then current Mk 48 in terms of depth, speed, and acoustic capabilities. This was known as the expanded operating envelope programme, and showed that the Mk 48 was structurally reliable at the depth needed to engage 'Alfa' class submarines; the target speed recognition capability required could be achieved; the vertical coverage was adequate, as was the self-noise at higher speeds wth the existing nose and array; and additional speed could be achieved. Laboratory modifications were made to a few torpedoes for tests, and these changes were implemented in the form of a programme to update fleet Mk 48 torpedoes to what is now the Mk 48 Mod 4 standard.

Of the performance requirements demanded by the ADCAP programme, the most important are:
(1) sustained long acquisition range
(2) minimised adverse environment and counter-measure effects
(3) minimised shipboard tactical constraints
(4) enhanced surface target engagement capabilities.

Hardware changes involved in ADCAP entail replacing the entire nose of the weapon housing the

acoustics and beam forming circuits and replacement of the signal processing by the latest electronics. The latter will also incorporate the current command and control electronics. Warhead sensor electronics will be improved.

Application of the expanded operating envelope programme findings (see above) to ADCAP has resulted in the upgraded ADCAP, which incorporates: upgraded acoustics and electronics; an expanded operating envelope (depth, target speed, weapon speed options); increased fuel delivery rate and capacity for optimum speed and endurance; improved surface target capabilities.

CHARACTERISTICS
Length: 5·8 m
Diameter: 21 inch (533 mm)
Weight: About 1600 kg
Max speed: 55 knots
Max range: 38 km
Max depth: 500 fathoms (914 m)

STATUS

The Mk 48 has been in production since 1972 and is used aboard USN attack submarines, and strategic submarines for self defence. By early 1980 more than 1900 torpedoes of this type had been delivered to the USN and an estimated 800 plus were in the production and procurement line. It was then estimated that another 1050 might be required to meet inventory objectives and to allow for peacetime training and testing.

In August 1979, Hughes Aircraft Company received a contract for development of digital guidance and control electronics for the Mk 48 ADCAP programme.

The first test run was carried out by the USN at Nonoose Bay in early 1982, using the inertial guidance system developed for the ADCAP programme. About 240 more runs were programmed before completion of this phase of the programme after which it was expected that entry into service will take place in 1983/84. However, the 1985 report by the US Secretary of Defence amended this to indicate anticipated deployment of the system in the mid- to late-1980s.

The fiscal year 1985 report by the US Secretary of Defense stated that production of the Mk 48 would continue at a rate of about 144 Mod 4 torpedoes per annum in fiscal years 1983/84/85/86 and costing $119·9m, $124·5m, $130·4m and $158·2m, respectively. In the same period ADCAP development costs were planned at $159·9m, $180·9m, $127·6m and $64·4m, while ADCAP modification kit production in the fiscal years 1984/85/86 is planned at 25 ($77·7m), 36 ($116·9m) and 96 ($285m).

The only known foreign users are Australia and the Netherlands.

CONTRACTOR

Gould Inc, Ocean Systems Division, 18901 Euclid Avenue, Cleveland, Ohio 44117, USA.

3342.441
AMERICAN MINE WARFARE PROGRAMMES
The American mine warfare programme comprises two main elements, mines and mine-counter-measures. The application of mines in weapons against submarines and surface ships has the objective of denying access to and use of ports and to provide offensive and defensive barriers. The current stock of sea mines consists of the Mks 52, 55, 56 and 57 types.

CHARACTERISTICS
Type: Mk 52, aircraft laid bottom mine
Length: 2·25 m
Diameter: 844 mm
Weight: Mod 1, 542 kg; Mod 2, 567 kg; Mod 3, 572 kg; Mod 5, 570 kg; Mod 6, 563 kg
Charge: 270 kg HBX-1
Max depth: 45·7 m (Mod 2, 183 m)
Actuation: Mod 1 acoustic; Mod 2 magnetic; Mod 3 pressure/magnetic; Mod 5 acoustic/magnetic; Mod 6 pressure/acoustic/magnetic

Type: Mk 55, aircraft laid bottom mine
Length: 2·89 m
Diameter: 1·03 m
Weight: Mod 2, 580 kg; Mod 3, 992 kg; Mod 5, 992 kg; Mod 6, 996 kg; Mod 7, 995 kg
Charge: 576 kg HBX-1
Max depth: 45·7 m (Mods 2/7, 183 m)

Actuation: Mod 2 magnetic; Mod 3 pressure/magnetic; Mod 5 acoustic/magnetic; Mod 6 pressure/acoustic/magnetic; Mod 7 dual channel magnetic

Type: Mk 56 Mod 0, aircraft laid moored mine
Length: 3·5 m
Diameter: 1·06 m
Weight: 1010 kg
Charge: 159 kg HBX-3
Max depth: 366 m
Actuation: Total field, magnetic dual channel

Type: Mk 57 Mod 0, submarine or ship laid moored mine
Length: 3 m
Diameter: 510 mm
Weight: 934 kg
Charge: 154 kg HBX-3
Max depth: 350 m
Actuation: total field, magnetic dual channel

Also employed by the USN is a range of air deployed munitions based on modified general purpose low drag bombs and which can be released without requiring a parachute. The modification involves the use of a Mk 75 Mod 0 Destructor Modification Kit which can be added to 500 lb, 1000 lb and 2000 lb Mk 80 series bombs to form the Service

Destructors (DST) Mks 36, 40 and 41, respectively. These are mostly intended for use in shallow waters such as estuaries etc, against typical coastal targets. There is also the DST 115A, which can be employed with either aircraft or surface craft for use against surface targets.

CHARACTERISTICS
Type: Mk 36, aircraft laid bottom mine
Length: 2·25 m
Diameter: 400 mm
Weight: 240 kg (with fixed conical fin) 261 kg (with tail retarding device)
Charge: 87 kg H-6
Max depth: 91·4 m
Actuation: Mods 0/3 magnetometer; Mods 4/5 magnetic/seismic

Type: Mk 40, aircraft laid bottom mine
Length: 2·86 m
Diameter: 570 mm
Weight: 447 kg (with fixed conical fin) 481 kg (with tail retarding device)
Charge: 204 kg H-6
Max depth: 91·4 m
Actuation: Mods 0/3 magnetometer; Mod 4/5 magnetic/seismic

Type: Mk 41, aircraft laid bottom mine
Length: 3·83 m

Mk 36 mines on A-7E Corsair (USN photo)

Internal stowage of Mk 53 mines on USN aircraft (USN photo)

Diameter: 630 mm
Weight: Mods 0/3, 926 kg; Mods 4/5, 921 kg
Charge: H-6
Actuation: Mods 0/3, magnetometer; Mods 4/5, magnetic/seismic

Type: 115A, aircraft laid surface mine
Length: 0·45 m
Diameter: 620 m
Weight: 61 kg
Charge: 24 kg HBX-3
Actuation: Magnetic/seismic

Quickstrike

The Quickstrike bottom mine development programme is funded under PE 64601N and embraces a family of mines using different size cases but with common target detection and classification mechanisms. The four members of the Quickstrike family are the Mks 62, 63, 64 and 65. The last of these (Mk 65 Mod 0) is in the 2000 lb (900 kg) class and was expected to go into production in 1981. The Mk 64 will probably be the next to enter production and this also is in the 2000 lb (900 kg) class, based on a Mk 84 2000 lb bomb and measuring 3·8 m long and 633 mm diameter.

Quickstrike mines are for shallow water deployment (to approximately 100 m) and targets will have to approach to within a few hundred feet for it to act. It will use existing Mk 80 series GP bomb cases as well as a new mine case. Quickstrike mines will be deployed by aircraft, surface ships, or submarines, but principally from the former.

This family of mines is based primarily on conversion of existing ordnance (bombs and torpedoes). An exception is the Mk 65 mine which is

not a bomb conversion. It has a thinner case than the equivalent bomb and contains the effective underwater PBX explosive. It is 3·3 m long and 734 mm in diameter. In fiscal year 1982, a procurement of 307 out of the total inventory objective of mines is planned. Also, the target detection device, TDD 57, employing influence mechanisms, will convert Mk 80 series bombs to mines, and procurement of an additional 1701 TDD 57s was planned in 1982. The TDD 58 combination sensor for the Mk 65 mine was due to complete development in fiscal year 1982 and enter production in fiscal year 1983.

The fiscal year 1984 report by the US Secretary of Defense stated that ways were being studied to provide Quickstrike and Mk 67 SLMM mines (below) with a wider variety of target detection devices. Quickstrike funding in the 1985 budget was $32·2, $34·9, $35·7 and $56·5 million, in fiscal years 1983/84/85/86, respectively.

Captor

Captor is a deep anti-submarine mine (Mk 60) intended for use in barriers against enemy strategic submarines. It can be emplaced by submarines, surface ships and aircraft. The kill mechanism consists of a Mk 46 Mod 4 homing torpedo (**2822.441**) which is released by a fire control system contained within the detection and control unit of the main Captor unit. Further details of Captor will be found in **2541.441**, above.

SLMM

The submarine-launched mobile mine (SLMM) Mk 67 is intended to provide the US fleet with a capability for planting mines in shallow water (to approximately

100 m) by submarine, using a self-propelled mine to reach water inaccessible to other vehicles. It is also meant for use in locations where covert mining would be particularly desirable from a tactical standpoint. It measures 4·09 m long × 485 mm diameter and weighs 754 kg.

The Mk 67 SLMM consists essentially of a modified Mk 37 torpedo (**2818.441**); alterations involved include some reworking of the Mk 37 torpedo bodies and replacement of the torpedo warhead with the applicable mine components. Tooling and other plant facilities were installed in fiscal year 1978 for production of Mk 67 sub-launched mobile mines in 1979.

Procurement plans for the Mk 67 SLMM in the 1983-86 period budget were for 266 mines costing $22·9 million in fiscal year 1983, and 242 ($23·3 million) 280 ($24·5 million) and 280 ($25·8 million) in the following years of the period.

Mine Countermeasures

In 1983 construction began of the first in a new class of mine countermeasures ships, the MCM-1 Avenger. Ships of this class are intended to match increasing Soviet mine warfare capabilities and to enhance US minesweeping facilities. Five of these ships have been authorised to fiscal year 1984, and nine ships included in the 1985 – 89 shipbuilding plan complete the programme. A second new class of mine countermeasure ship, the MSH-1 will augment the MCM class ships. The MSH-1 minehunters will be equipped with advanced combat systems similar to those in the MCM-1 ships, but will be smaller and less costly. Congress authorised the lead ship of the class in 1984. To complete the 17-ship programme, the five-year building plan contains another 16 vessels.

4425.441

HONEYWELL MNS

The Honeywell mine neutralisation system (MNS) has been developed by the company's Marine Systems Operations and the US Naval Sea Systems Command, and is the result of more than ten years work to provide a system that surpasses the conventional towed mechanical, magnetic and acoustic sweep techniques. It is designed to detect, locate, classify and neutralise moored and bottom mines, using high-resolution sonar, low light-level TV, cable cutters and mine destruction charges. A special underwater vehicle carries these sensors and countermeasures and is remotely controlled from the parent vessel.

Initial target detection and vehicle guidance information is provided by the ship's sonar and vehicle tracking is aided by a Honeywell RS/900 acoustic position indicator. Vehicle sonar is used

during the mid-course search and final homing phases, and high resolution enables operations in poor visibility by sonar guidance alone. Low light TV is used in conjunction with sonar during the precision guidance phase near the target. Underwater launch and recovery of the MNS vehicle assists operations in high sea states.

Vehicle power is provided via a neutrally buoyant umbilical cable which also carries signal and control links between the vessel and the MNS vehicle. Aboard the parent vessel a sonar screen on the control console displays sensor and vehicle status information in digital form. The monitor and control consoles are the focal point for operation and management of the complete system. Display facilities include: sonar, TV, secondary sonar and TV, vehicle control, cutter and dropped-charge actuation.

CHARACTERISTICS
Vehicle endurance: Unlimited
Speed: 6 knots
Weight (in air): 1135 kg
Length: 3·8 m
Propulsion: Hydraulic, twin 15 hp
Thrusters: Horizontal/vertical
Cable length: 1000 m
Total system weight: 11·7 t
Power requirements: 60 kW (peak)
STATUS
A prototype system was successfully tested by the USN aboard USS *Fidelity* during spring and summer 1982. Approval for service use is expected to follow.
CONTRACTOR
Honeywell Marine Systems Division, 5303 Shilshole Avenue NW, Seattle, Washington 98107, USA.

LAND-BASED AIR DEFENCE SYSTEMS

3215.181
AIR DEFENCE SYSTEMS NOTE

This section is concerned principally with national air defence systems, and systems for the command and control of air defence forces comprising a mixture of weapons (eg guns, missiles, and aircraft) intended for deployment in a mobile or semi-permanent fashion in support of an expeditionary force abroad. Within the constraints imposed by what is, by nature, one of the more sensitive areas of defence technology, the aim is to concentrate upon the infra-structure of such systems and the hardware associated with this aspect of air defence. Sensors and weapons are covered elsewhere in this volume. Land radars are also treated in the Equipment section.

The distinction between 'air defence command and control systems' above, and certain army fire control systems is clearly a fine one in some instances: the reader is therefore directed also to that sub-section, which follows this one.

As already observed air defence is a particularly sensitive subject and consequently information on some nations' systems and equipment is often severely limited. Political, as well as military reasons frequently are the cause of manufacturers' reluctance to divulge the destination of equipment such as radars or computers, which might otherwise enable assessments of particular countries' air defence provisions. There is an increasing tendency for long- and medium-range radars to be employed for both air defence purposes and air traffic control (ATC) functions. Up to a point, the demands of both services are almost identical and there is much to be said for combining the requirements in terms of sensors, data handling and display equipment, as far as is possible. Where it seems appropriate, therefore, we are giving some details of certain examples of this practice in this section. Such instances will be clearly identified in the text. In other cases air defences are being freshly constructed and may as yet be incompletely defined. In the following paragraphs brief details are given of what is known of some of these programmes.

Argentina

In the early 1970s Argentina was known to have expressed an interest in a new national network, and later the French Thomson-CSF concern undertook a similar programme to that completed for Brazil, namely an integrated ATC/defence network.

In 1978 an $8·79 million US contract for the supply of three AN/TPS-43 air defence radars to Argentina was announced, and later it was reported that a number of Cardion-built AN/TPS-44 radars had been supplied. No status details of either sale was obtained subsequently and no official information has been disclosed, but it is probable that these radars were sited to afford cover for the main naval and air bases near Buenos Aires, Puerto Belgrano, Commodoro Rivadavia, Santa Cruz, Rio Gallegos, and Rio Grande and Ushuaia. In 1982 one of the AN/TPS-43 radars was deployed to the Falkland Islands in support of Argentinian forces landed there. This equipment is understood to have been captured by British forces when the Islands were reclaimed and subsequently returned to the UK. No information been obtained concerning any possible replacement for use on the Argentinian mainland.

Egypt

Egypt is unusual in that it has four armed services, one of which is dedicated to air defence. To what extent this peculiarity is a result of the period when Egypt relied mostly on the USSR for her defence equipment and consequently absorbed much of the military thinking of that state is not known. However, the fact remains that much of the essential hardware for air defence, particularly anti-aircraft artillery, and surface-to-air missiles, was initially of Soviet origin despite the severance of the Egyptian-Soviet link in successive stages in 1972 and 1975. Since that time military equipment procurement has tended to reflect the various phases of Egypt's evolving relationship with differing friendly nations willing (or anxious) to provide arms or to avail themselves of one or other aspect of Egypt's resources or situation. Examples of such countries which have a capacity in the air defence sphere are Italy, France, UK, China, and the USA.

As a consequence of this somewhat chequered background, it is understood that the present inventory comprises an extremely varied total of hardware. There are almost certainly still examples of Soviet radars associated with missile systems previously supplied, such as the SA-2 Guideline, SA-3 Goa and SA-6 Gainful, various French types and Egypt has also consistently been reported as one of the unidentified Middle Eastern states said to have been supplied with Plessey's AR-3D three-dimensional radar although this cannot be confirmed.

In 1980 four General Electric AN/TPS-59 3-D radars and, later, eight Westinghouse AN/TPS-63 air defence radars were ordered for Egyptian use at a combined cost of about $154 million. In the same period 12 AN/TSQ-143 mobile automated operations centres, which interface with the TPS-59 and TPS-63 radars, were ordered from Westinghouse, for operation of Hawk missile batteries. Each operations centre has four OJ-560 display consoles, two main computers, 12 high-density micro-processors and an audio/video recorder that files all track data, displays and operator actions. The first of these centres had been completed by May 1984.

Hughes received a $210 million contract in December 1983 for the first phase of a new Egyptian national air defence system, and this calls for integration of all existing radars, missile batteries, air bases, and command centres into an automated command and control system. Also to be integrated are E-2C Hawkeye airborne early warning aircraft, four of which are expected to be delivered in the next two or three years.

India

In early 1974 an Indian Air Defence Ground Environment System (ADGES) programme was revealed when it was announced that indigenous production of equipment was to start in January 1974 at the Bharat Electronics Ltd plant at Ghaziabad, east of Delhi. The system is being installed along the Indian northern and western borders (with Pakistan and China) and a communications system for use in the air defence of a limited area along the northern borders was built with American equipment.

The current air defence system is understood to rely on a miscellaneous assembly of radars of varying origin, reflecting India's changing international associations and allegiances since gaining independence. This includes British, French, Soviet and possibly other types of equipment.

Between 1962 and 1978 at least 24 long- and medium-range radars of Italian design were installed ostensibly for ATC use, but clearly so that target data from some of them at least would be useful for air defence/surveillance. Most of these radars are D-band equipments, eight of them ATCR-2 systems and the remainder ATCR-4Ts (**2248.153**). Licensed production of the latter type was undertaken in India from 1971 onward, more than 10 being provided in this way. It is very probable that the Soviet-built SA-2 Guideline air-defence missiles used by the Indian Air Force rely on a number of Soviet radars.

In 1978/79 the second high-power radar of the ADGES plan was installed and installation of the remainder was in progress. The first phase of the associated communications network had been completed, and development of a computer-based ADP system had been completed by the Tata Institute of Fundamental Research. Evaluation under simulated environmental conditions preceded its removal to radar sites for integration and user trials.

Thomson-CSF revealed in February 1984 a contract to supply four 3-D military radar stations to India, and the construction under licence of five more stations.

Indonesia

Following the earlier updating of the previous air defence/ATC network (largely provided by Decca in the late 1950s and early 1960s) by the French Thomson-CSF concern, it was revealed in late 1978 that a further modernisation was in progress. At the same time the ordering of two three-dimensional air surveillance radars was announced. These are TRS 2215 equipments (**3272.153**), the transportable version of the TRS 2230 static E/F-band system.

More recently, certain equipment of Dutch origin is thought to have been acquired for short-range air defence purposes.

On completion of a contract, announced in June 1984, to provide four new ATC centres, Thomson-CSF will have installed over a period of ten years coverage for most of the Indonesian archipelago with TA 10 or TA 23 primary radars, RS 770 or RS 870 secondary radars, and 10 regional control centres.

Jordan

Jordanian air defence is based on F-5 and F-104 aircraft and Improved Hawk SAMs (**2640.131**), supported by AA guns. The main command and control element is the AN/TSQ-73 air defence missile control and co-ordination system (**2835.181**, later in this section). It can now be expected that the radars of western origin (probably including Westinghouse TPS-43 equipments) associated with these systems will have been joined by some Soviet equipment following Jordanian procurement of the SA-8 Gecko SAM and ZSU-23/4 air defence systems from the USSR.

Kuwait

In recent years Kuwait has significantly increased its air defence forces with acquisitions of Mirage F1 interceptors and Hawk surface-to-air missiles, of which seven or eight battalions have been ordered. Recently acquired sensors include the ITT-Gilfillan TPS-32 mobile three-dimensional radar (**2516.153**). Kuwait is also reported to have been the recipient of one or more Plessey AR-3D air defence radars (**2484.153**) although this has not been confirmed. For command and control of the Hawk missiles two TSQ-73 systems (**2835.181**) were ordered and are thought to have been operational since 1982.

In June 1982, ITT Gilfillan was paid more than $5·3 million by the US Army Missile Command for support of two AN/TPS-32 radars in Kuwait. In November 1983 Thomson-CSF was awarded a contract to modernise the low-altitude air defences of Kuwait and to set up an integrated command system for the entire air defence infrastructure. Gradual implementation over the next three years may involve the supply of TRS 2230 3-D radars.

Libya

For several years plans to expand and modernise the Libyan air defence network have been hampered by political obstacles. US, UK, Italian and French companies and consortia competed for the task, but it is now thought that Libyan air defence is modelled on Soviet principles and heavily reliant on equipment from the same source.

Malaysia

After declining to take over the former RAF air defence radar installations following the British withdrawal from the Far East in 1971, the Malaysian Government purchased two Marconi S600 mobile radar units (**2426.181** and **1168.153**) to meet the country's immediate air defence needs and to support the two RAAF Mirage squadrons based in Malaysia. About a year later a third S600 system was procured. A period of uncertainty ensued during which the intentions of the Malaysian authorites were unclear, until in early 1983 it was learned that a Hughes air defence radar, HADR (**3721.153**), had been ordered for MADGE (Malaysian Air Defence Ground Environment) for which Hughes Ground Systems Group is the nominated prime contractor.

Morocco

A series of contracts, collectively assessed as worth about $100 million, for the provision of an air defence network was announced in June 1977. The principal contractors named were Westinghouse, Burroughs and Ford Aerospace. Westinghouse provided the primary radars and integrated the entire system, while Burroughs supplied large-scale B-6700 series computers for processing tracks, ATC data, identification, plot extraction, etc. Ford Aerospace provided microwave communications links under a contract worth about $8 million. Value of the Burroughs contribution was approximately $30 million.

The complete system is based on 16 AN/TPS-43 radars at early warning and coastal sites. A centralised control facility directs Moroccan air defence aircraft.

Philippines

Although independent since 1946, the Philippines has relied almost entirely on the USA for its defence, and this is reflected in the inventory of the Philippine forces. Under the terms of the treaty between the two countries, the USA enjoys important base facilities in the Philippines, notably the Subic Bay naval base and Clark AFB, and over the years there have been appreciable supplies of equipment of US origin. The Philippine forces operate Hawk surface-to-air missile batteries, and F-5 fighter aircraft are also available for air defence. In addition to the target detection and designation radars associated with the Hawk missile batteries, two Italian-built ATCR-3T radars supplied for ATC purposes at Manila and Mactan in 1972 could also serve a supplementary surveillance role. In 1980 the first of four ITT-Gilfillan Series 320 three-dimensional air defence radars was delivered under the terms of a $13 million contract given to the US company by a Dutch contractor.

Saudi Arabia

On to an original air defence network based on radars of American and British origin dating from the 1960s, a succession of improvements have been grafted, either for their overall system enhancement potential or as adjuncts or essential elements of a new weapon system acquired for the Saudi Arabian defences. Examples of the latter process might be the radars associated with US Hawk surface-to-air missile batteries, or with French air defence weapons such as Crotale, and Shahine. In the case of the Hawk system, a contract covering the supply of an AN/TSQ-73 air defence control system (**2835.181**) for Hawk batteries, and to be integrated with the existing air defence network was revealed by the US in 1978. At a time of unrest in the Middle East, America rapidly supplied one AN/TPS-43 3-D radar (**2517.153**) to strengthen the region's defences, and at the same time deployed AWACS aircraft to serve as an airborne control post based in Saudi Arabia. Four of these aircraft were used in this way, and at that time there were already two AN/TPS-43 radars in the country in addition to the one flown out from the USA in October 1980. A fourth radar of the same type was understood to be wanted by Saudi Arabia.

The first of five E-3A AWACS aircraft for the Royal Saudi Arabian Air Force is expected to arrive in 1986, the navigation systems for them being the subject of a $5·3 million contract awarded to Northrop Corporation in early 1983. Deliveries under this contract commence in July 1984 and continue until May 1986. The equipment consists of AN/ARN-129 Omega navigation set, dual Carousel IV AN/ASM-119

inertial platforms and a Ryan AN/ADN-213 doppler navigator.

Defence ministers from six Arab states in the Gulf area have agreed in principle to establish a joint air defence system based on the Saudi Arabian airborne warning and control system aircraft to be supplied by the US under an $8500 million arms deal. The states concerned are Saudi Arabia, Kuwait, United Arab Emirates, Bahrain, Qatar and Oman. Reports indicate that the complete system is likely to comprise an air umbrella, a joint military strike force, a joint military command and a collective air defence system.

The Royal Saudi Arabian Air Force is also seeking a command, control and communications (C³) complex to be supplied by the US. The US Air Force Electronic System Division is requesting information from interested electronic companies. The system will consist primarily of a command operations centre (COC); five sector command centres (SCC), co-located with sector operations centres (SEC) at the main operating bases; two base operations centres, one co-located with an SCC/SEC; 17 combined long-range radar and remote-controlled air/ground radio sites; and associated communications for an operational command and control system. The procurement will be in two stages, a programme definition with two or more possible contractors and a second phase with the main contractor having been selected for implementation of the system. The complete system will consist primarily of off-the-shelf equipment and is due to be installed and tested during 1985/87.

In February 1984 an agreement was reached between the French and Saudi Arabian Governments to integrate new versions of the Shahine missile system with the national air defence network. Estimated value was $4 000 million. Westinghouse also received contracts in 1984 for improvements to TPS-43 radars, communications and troposcatter links.

Singapore

During 1980 a joint civil/military integrated ATC system based on Signaal LAR II long-range surveillance radar and data handling equipment by the same manufacturer, under the name LORADS (long range radar and display system) was commissioned. Most of the hardware, including the radar antenna, is located at the new Changi International Airport, and the data stored in this computer-based system is available to both civil and military authorities. In a move, in late 1982, that was seen in some quarters as a preliminary to the formation of a regional air defence system embracing five ASEAN states (Indonesia, Malaysia, the Philippines, Singapore and Thailand), Singapore requested approval for the purchase of two E-2C airborne early warning aircraft from America and contracts were awarded to Grumman in 1984. In

addition to these machines, the USA has reportedly agreed to supply improved Hawk air defence missiles, and there is a possibility that Singapore may acquire the Mirage 2000 fighter aircraft or the American F-16A.

South Korea

South Korea is being supplied with Improved Hawk surface-to-air missile systems and will probably procure the related TSQ-73 system (**2835.181**) for command and control. A new overall air defence system to provide for target assignment, early warning, and co-ordination of other air defence forces such as interceptors will probably be developed. One aspect of this is the likely procurement of E-2C Hawkeye airborne early warning aircraft, possibly in 1988.

Sudan

The basis of an air defence network for the Sudan is expected to rest on six AN/TPS-43E three-dimensional air surveillance radars (**2517.153**), supported by associated communications links and equipment. The intention of the US Government to supply this equipment to the Sudan was revealed in May 1978, when it was stated that the total value was expected to be $71 million.

Taiwan

It is believed that Taiwan is engaged in the development and implementation of an automated air defence network similar to those provided by Hughes for Japan, Switzerland, Spain, and Israel. In February 1981 the US Government indicated an offer to supply five Hawk missile batteries, with a total of 280 Improved Hawk missiles. Taiwanese plans then envisaged four Improved Hawk battalions, of which three had already been purchased. These are almost certainly operated by AN/TSQ-73 automated air defence systems supplied by Westinghouse who may also have provided TPS-43 radars.

Venezuela

The Venezuelan forces include a number of weapons specifically intended for anti-aircraft applications, and although no details of a dedicated air defence network have been received, two Italian-built ATC long-range radars supplied in 1973 do have the useful advantage of being sited at virtually the western and eastern extremities of the country. A Selenia ATCR-2 with computer-based display system is located at Maracaibo, while in the east there is a Selenia ATCR-3. Westinghouse is known to have supplied air defence equipment, which probably includes the TPS-43 air defence radar. A tri-service evaluation committee was set up in 1980 to consider the development of a national air defence system.

AUSTRALIA

3521.181
AUSTRALIAN AIR DEFENCE
Australia's sparse population in conjunction with its continental size combine to make a conventional static air defence organisation along the lines of that of the USA an unrealistic proposition. Instead, an effective compromise is achieved by the combination of Hub Cap air defence systems (two) (**2016.181**) with the search radars and part of the infra-structure needed for the control of civil and military air traffic serving the main population centres of Australia. In this way the costs of fixed installations are minimised while operational flexibility is maintained.

Hub Cap was described in detail in this section of *Jane's Weapon Systems 1979-80* and in previous editions, but a short summary of the salient features is retained in this entry for convenience. The main air defence forces available consist of Mirage III-O fighter aircraft, Rapier surface-to-air missiles (some equipped with the DN181 Blindfire radar), and AA guns, but the Bloodhound long-range surface-to-air missiles originally deployed with Hub Cap have since been withdrawn from service.

The Hub Cap system provides three-dimensional airspace surveillance and control of fighters to intercept hostile targets over a wide area from fully

mobile air-conditioned shelters designed for deployment by C-130 aircraft.

The use of digital computing permits automatic tracking of targets from the primary radar while plot extraction from the secondary radar returns is used to reinforce the primary radar auto-tracking. For the RAF requirements, the computer is programmed to take account of the Mirage III characteristics, perform an assessment of an interception situation when supplied with the relevant data on weapon availability, and provide a number of alternative intercept solutions for selection by a controller. The computer can be re-programmed to enable the system to operate equally effectively with other types of fighter. Comprehensive communication facilities are provided with Hub Cap enabling operational personnel to communicate with each other, with aircraft under control, and with units external to the system.

The Australian Defence White Paper of November 1976 revealed that the radars of the two Hub Cap systems were to be replaced, and at the same time it was confirmed that obsolescent air traffic control radars at RAAF and RAN bases were being replaced. Tactical radars capable of being carried in C-130 transport aircraft entered service in 1979. These

radars are Westinghouse AN/TPS-43 equipments (**2517.153**) of American origin and both systems are thought to have been commissioned in 1982. This programme was known as Project Recap. At the time of completion (mid-1982) a further contract award to Westinghouse Corporation was announced for the provision of a tactical air defence system. The system to be delivered in late 1983 allows for radar-directed control of defensive fighter aircraft operations wherever the system is deployed.

Construction of a back-scatter over-the-horizon (OTH) radar for the detection of both aircraft and ballistic missiles was first revealed in 1974. Code name for the project is Jindalee and the site is near Alice Springs, close to the US satellite facilities there.

Promising results from the experimental narrow-beam Jindalee OTH radar indicate that future surveillance of the Australian coast and surrounding offshore regions will be undertaken by this technique. By 1978, about $A6 million had been spent on Jindalee research and development. Ranges of more than 1000 miles (1600 km) against civil airliner targets had been obtained with the Jindalee installation, and in late 1978 approval was given for a larger and more powerful version to have a much wider coverage arc (Stage B). Construction started at

Alice Springs, with an anticipated total cost of $A24 million. This installation has greater transmitter power and a larger receiving antenna, and will provide for surveillance cover of airspace to the north of Australia. The new Stage B receiving station was constructed at Alice Springs, next to the original Stage A site on Bond Springs Station. The new reception antenna array is 2·8 km long. Much of the large transmitter complex at Harts Range, about 160 km from Alice Springs, had been completed by early 1982 and it was necessary to build a new 3 MW power house and building to house the additional transmitter equipment. A number of advanced items of new equipment developed at the Australian Electronics Research Laboratory, South Australia, was moved to the Stage B sites in 1981. When the new computer equipment becomes available, it is hoped that it will be possible to track targets while the beam continues to scan the whole surveillance area.

At a later date additional OTH radars might be needed to provide all-round surveillance. It is also hoped that OTH radar will provide a surface target detection capability for the oceanic areas around the Australian coast.

AUSTRIA

3326.181
AUSTRIAN AIR DEFENCE (MRCS-403)
Under contracts awarded to Selenia in 1976 and 1977 by the Austrian Ministry of Defence, the Italian company is supplying a number of mobile and fixed air defence systems for incorporation in the nation's overall defence network. The systems being supplied by Selenia are designated MRCS-403 mobile automatic reporting and control system, and are based on static and transportable versions of the RAT-31S three-dimensional radar (**1953.153**) in conjunction with a data processing and display sub-system.

The radar's main characteristics are simultaneous range, azimuth and elevation measurements of targets at all altitudes, sophisticated ECCM performance, and high resistance to ground and/or weather clutter.

The MRCS-403 produces an air situation picture which is transmitted back to superior command centres via a narrow-band data link. This is performed together with functions such as automatic track initiation, automatic tracking, automatic and/or manual height measurement and automatic track reporting. The system can process three-dimensional low- and medium-altitude air situations, and is also able to perform autonomous control functions such as identification, interceptor and air defence missile control. In its basic configuration it comprises a shelter-housed RAT-31S radar and data processing and display shelter. For expanded operational capabilities, additional shelters are used on a modular basis to provide more operator and communications facilities.

The operations shelter contains a dual NDC-160 computer complex, three display consoles, a communications control unit, and ground-to-air facilities. The computer is integrated locally with the three-dimensional surveillance radar, and for remote IFF/SSR inputs the system is equipped with a data link interface for receiving plots. The computer processed information is fed to the display sub-system as synthetic/alert track information and to remote centres as track information via a data link.

Typically there are five operator positions: master controller, track controller positions (2), manual input operator, and the radar supervisor. Track capacity is 60 (expansible) and three intercepts can be handled simultaneously. The displays employ synthetic video presentation and there are two video maps for each unit.

The Austrian MRCS-403 systems probably interface with other Austrian air surveillance facilities, including the national civil ATC network, and there is known to be a requirement for a number of low-level radars for gap-filling purposes. The Selenia Pluto equipment (**3277.153**) is probably under consideration for this function.
STATUS
The first systems have been delivered and are now operational.
CONTRACTOR
Selenia, Industrie Elettroniche Associate SpA, Via Tiburtina 12 400 Km,00130, Rome, Italy.

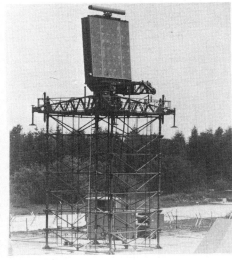

The first Austrian site to be equipped with Selenia's MRCS-403/RAT-31S air defence radar. Operational test and evaluation was completed in 1979

Internal view of a Selenia MRCS-403 system operational shelter supplied to the Austrian MoD

BRAZIL

2166.181
DACTA ATC/AIR DEFENCE SYSTEM
In October 1972 a $70 million contract was concluded between the Brazilian Ministry of Aeronautics and Thomson-CSF, France. The agreement related to the construction of an air traffic control/air defence radar system in Brazil.

Details of the agreement are not known but it is known that the number of sites involved was at least 47 (of which a number are for communications and navigation aid installations) and that the area covered by radar surveillance is the zone bounded by Brasilia, Rio de Janeiro, and São Paulo. There are radar sites at Brazilia, Tres Marias, Rio, and São Paulo, connected by microwave links and providing cover for most of the Brazilia Flight Information Region. All four sites have LP23 long-range surveillance radars (**3099.153**), and all but Tres Marias also have Volex three-dimensional radars (**3271.153**). The main centre is at Brazilia (CINDACTA). Other equipment includes troposcatter microwave communications links, HF and VHF radio, computers, displays, etc. Within two

One of the mountain-top radar sites of the Brazilian DACTA air defence system. Note troposcatter antennas to right of tower

years of signing the original contract much of the hardware had been delivered and the complete system has been tested on site. It is now fully operational.

An extension of this system to provide control/surveillance to the borders of Rio Grande do Sul, and known as DACTA 2, was the subject of international competition which Thomson-CSF won in 1981.

In mid-1981 the Brazilian authorities concluded a contract with the Italian company, Selenia, for a number of mobile radar stations, as part of a modernisation programme for Brazilian airspace control. Valued at about $60 million the contract included MRCS-403 (**3326.181**) mobile reporting and control systems and RAT-31S three-dimensional radars.

Further contracts awarded to Thomson-CSF in 1982 and 1983 provide for another expansion of Brazilian air control facilities. This involves the installation of control and other facilities in Northeast Brazil and Amazonia and new radar stations will be connected to the national airspace surveillance system. At the same time, hardware and software of the first phase of the system which has been operating since 1976 will be updated.

The extension of the system to the north east also entails construction of a new regional air operations centre (CIN-DACTA III). When the fourth phase of the Franco-Brazilian programme is complete, the French company will have supplied and installed more than 40 radars.

CHINA (PEOPLE'S REPUBLIC)

2052.181
CHINESE AIR DEFENCES
No detailed information on Chinese air defences is available, but there are some known statistics on their magnitude.

Until comparatively recently the Chinese were reported to have in service about 50 surface-to-air missile sites and some 4500 anti-aircraft guns of various types. An interceptor aircraft force of over 4000 aircraft is maintained, consisting of MIG-15, MIG-17, MIG-19, and MIG-21 types. A new all-weather fighter of Chinese design recently entered service. Associated with all of these were about 1500 air defence radars, but little is known of the detailed

deployment of these systems or their organisational structure beyond the general information that the radars constitute a network for air surveillance and control and a missile early warning system for the detection of ICBM launches against China. More recent information, while still leaving much open to question, suggests that the country's defences are being substantially modernised; new radars, it seems, have been designed, and improved versions of the SA-2 Guideline missiles (**2942.131**) which the Chinese originally acquired from the Soviet Union are being produced. However a recent American assessment still considers the Chinese air defence system to be subject to major weaknesses, such as an

outmoded command and control system.

In February 1984 it was reported that a French company has, or will have, supplied six long-range radars, three terminal area radars, and control centres for airspace management of the Shanghai/Peking region.

It should also be noted that at least one very large phased-array radar has been constructed in Western China, presumably as part of the missile warning system. However there is still no indication of any Chinese effort to develop an ABM system. Instead there are fairly widely publicised and comprehensive civil defence precautions, which include large air raid shelters, grain storage, and similar measures.

FRANCE

4571.181
T.ACCS
Thomson-CSF Air Command and Control Systems (T.ACCS) is the designation of the improved MIDAS (**2106.181**) range of systems that the company designed and developed for such purposes. There are three basic types of station.

All these stations are implemented using the same line of versatile modular equipments, based on the latest data processing and display techniques. In addition to the radar and telecommunications equipment not described below, these equipments include radar plot extractors, data processing systems, and display systems. Compared with the original MIDAS systems, increased computer facilities make possible significantly greater track capacity and data handling capabilities with little if any increase in manning requirements.

The company range of radar plot extractors includes models matched to 2- or 3-D radars, taking into account the importance of low-altitude surveillance and the possibility of enemy ECM actions. They may be specific sub-assemblies incorporated with the radars in new equipments, or programmable assemblies which can be matched to previously installed radars.

Thomson-CSF air defence systems use general-purpose computers belonging to the MITRA range. This range includes computers and peripherals designed and packaged for various environments: standard environment, aboard transportable cabins or aboard armoured vehicles. This computer family is fully compatible from a software point of view, and all models use the same basic software (assemblers, compilers, real-time operating systems). For the specific air defence software, Thomson-CSF has developed a full set of packages devoted to the various functions: automatic and rate-aided manual tracking, threat evaluation, weapons allocation, automatic interception, missile designation, simulation. Operational software for each station is then built up by linking these various modules.

Visual display systems now used by Thomson-CSF for air defence centres are of the autonomous type; each display console includes its own refreshing memory and a programmable processor, which digitally performs various functions connected with the display, such as scaling and off-centring, synthetic information selection, etc or gives tactical assistance to the operators. These local functions performed by the console processor can be adapted to various requirements, for example for rate-aided manual tracking and to remote these tracks, without having a local data-processing system. These autonomous consoles are also used for displaying mixed raw and synthetic video signals.

The range of autonomous consoles now in production includes two basic models:
(1) the TVT 3540 display console is specially designed for minimum volume and can therefore be installed in small-size cabins.
(2) the AMC 800 and AMC 900 consoles feature an important modularity: besides the 41 cm (or 53 cm) PPI, they can be fitted with TV monitors driven by the console processor for displaying alpha-numeric information. Moreover, by using removable function keys which are interpreted by software, the consoles are standardised; their operational use (for tracking, identification, weapons selection, interception etc) can be modified at any time, giving a multi-console system the possibility of creating a configuration adapted to the current situation.

Three types of station developed by Thomson-CSF using these families of equipments differ mainly in their operational assignments, sizes, and their fitness for mobility.

These three types of station are classified as:
(1) Fixed Operations Centre: air defence operations centre, sector operations centre and control and reporting centre

(2) MCRC: mobile control and reporting centre
(3) LARP/FACP: mobile low altitude reporting post/forward air control post.
FIXED OPERATIONS CENTRE
Functions of a fixed operations centre include:
(1) automatic establishment and updating of the general air situation
(2) identification of detected aircraft
(3) evaluation of the threat
(4) allocation of targets
(5) assignment of weapons
(6) activation and automatic guidance of interceptors
(7) co-ordination between fighters and surface-air missile units
(8) control of military air traffic
(9) complete simulation for the training of military staff.

A typical centre will include MITRA computers with peripherals (typewriter with cassette reader, mobile-head magnetic disc, card reader, printer), for:
(1) local tracking (automatic)
(2) conversion of co-ordinates
(3) track correlation with automatic transmission to other stations
(4) trial intercept identification

T.ACCS AMC 900 operations console

(5) automatic interception computations

(6) simulation for the training of controllers.

Other items are AMC 800 and AMC 900 consoles, and possibly a large screen display, for general air situation presentation.

A centre can be easily adapted to each specific need, by varying the number of autonomous consoles and the central memory size of the computers. If necessary, a second similar computer complex can be added to the system, allowing various degraded modes in case of a computer's failure.

MCRC

This configuration is inherently capable of operating in various roles, either on an autonomous basis, or linked to a fixed operations centre and to other mobile centres. Its operational capacity is less than that of a fixed centre, but it nevertheless affords wide possibilities which make it usable as an addition to an operation centre in territory air defence for an army corps to provide aerial protection. The MCRC is used to complement the fixed air defence organisation and to carry out the control of tactical air defence missions and battle corps cover missions.

It allows the following functions: automatic initiation and automatic following of tracks from local radar data. Both functions can also be performed in rate-aided manual mode; transmission and automatic

or manual correlation of tracks in connection with higher and subordinate levels; identification of tracks; automatic control of up to six simultaneous interceptions; recovery of fighter aircraft; co-ordination with surface-to-air missile units; simulation of eight moving targets, of which four are piloted fighter aircraft.

Typical operational capacities are: 90 tracks; automatic two-way communications with six air defence centres; up to six simultaneous automatic interceptions; eight simulated moving targets of which four can be piloted in real time from pilot consoles.

The MCRC includes MITRA computers, adapted for use in a cabin, with a mini-tape for program loading and data recording, and a teletype. There are three AMC 800 consoles, also adapted for use in a cabin by a master controller and two interception controllers.

This typical configuration, which can easily be extended with additional modules, meets the requirements of the operations centre normally associated with the Thomson-CSF mobile 3D radar TRS 2215 (**3272.153**).

LARP/FACP STATION

This configuration has a dual operational role: it allows an additional radar coverage, in particular at

very low altitude, with minimum personnel and material; and it is designed to carry out control of tactical missions, mainly in aerial support and to aid aerial penetration operations. To fulfil these missions the LARP/FACP makes use of data from a radar adapted to low altitude detection, such as a TIGER radar (**2156.153**), the associated secondary IFF radar, and possibly, visual observation posts. Additionally, it is connected through automatic data link with a fixed or mobile centre.

The LARP/FACP is equipped, for processing and display, with two autonomous consoles TVT 3540.

The main functions are detection of targets; building up of tracks by rate-aided manual tracking of targets; identification (IFF/SIF); introduction of visual observation data into the system; transmission of tracks to the higher level; reception of tracks from the higher level; control of tactical missions.

STATUS

In production and in service with several overseas countries probably including Saudi Arabia and other gulf states.

CONTRACTOR

Thomson-CSF, Division Systèmes Défense et Contrôle, 40, rue Grange Dame Rose, BP34, 92360 Meudon-La-Florêt, France.

2161.181

STRIDA AIR DEFENCE SYSTEM

STRIDA (Système de Traitement et de Representation des Informations de Défense Aérienne) is the French air defence data handling system. The system consists of a network of stations covering French territory with the following main functions:

(1) detection and identification of aircraft moving in French airspace

(2) threat evaluation and dissemination of early warnings. The air situation is centralised and synthesised in the air defence operational centre (ADOC)

(3) updating of active means (aircraft and missiles) status in every sector operational centre (SOC)

(4) weapons selection, engagement and automatic intercept guidance

(5) aircraft recovery to air bases

(6) control of military operational and training flights

(7) co-ordination with the air traffic control system to ensure identification and spacing of operational military flights with respect to general air traffic

(8) progressive integration of the information reported by air base radars for improving the low altitude coverage.

STRIDA consists of different types of operational centres (ADOC, SOC/CRC, CRC, ARP) which exchange digital messages by a special telecommunication network, the Air 70, associated with electronic switching stations.

At ARP and CRC levels, signals coming from 2-D and 3-D long range radars (Palmier) and height-finding radars (SATRAPE with phased-array antenna) are used for providing the labelled air situations needed at SOC/CRC and ADOC levels. All information and orders to be exchanged between these different centres for command and control purposes are transmitted through the Air 70 network.

The STRIDA network is connected to the NADGE

network (**1181.181**), to the 412L (**2533.181**) system and to Combat Grande (**2322.181**) to provide total coverage of western continental Europe. It is also connected to the French ATC CAUTRA system for co-ordination of military and civil air traffic control.

The data handling equipment of a typical latest generation CDCS station mainly consists of:

(1) an EMIR radar data extractor using a programmed extraction concept

(2) a high power processing system using IBM 370 series computers

(3) a display sub-system including from 20 to 30 operational positions (see below).

In some centres, special equipment is found: in the air defence operational centre, a large screen display and in a centre for intercept controller training a piloted aircraft simulator (SACHA) generates a video signal corresponding to up to 12 simulated aircraft. This signal can be mixed with the live video of the radar for a transparent simulation.

Each operator position or console designed for one controller and his assistant is composed of:

(1) a plan view display for presenting raw video (local radar raw video) and data generated by the processing system (synthetic view of the air picture – mainly tracks). A 40 cm diameter screen is used

(2) one or several monochrome or colour screen(s) (diagonal from 13 to 35 cm and capacity up to 4000 characters) for presenting detailed information on certain subjects (tracks, intercepts) or data received in alpha-numeric form (operational status, flight schedules)

(3) several keyboards and a rolling ball (or a joystick) for selecting the data presented and entering functions and data

(4) control keyboards and panels for communications (radio, telephone, interphone) and secondary radar.

STATUS

The research and development programme for the STRIDA system began in 1956 under the responsibility of Service Technique des Télécommunications de l'Air (STTA). The first stations were fitted with specialised IBM/CAPAC real-time computers and SINTRA VISU II display sub-system. They became operational in 1963. Since this date, there has been a continuous programme of improvements for software and hardware during the implementation of the whole military programme, every new centre having to be interoperable with the others. The medium and high level coverage main centres are now near completion. The last ones are equipped with IBM 370/158 computers and SINTRA VISU IV display sub-systems. The next step, which is now being implemented, entails the extension of the low-level coverage of the system by the integration of recovery and tactical operations radars. In 1978, SINTRA was chosen to supply the STRAPP (STRida-APProach) limited to the low-altitude radar at each approach centre. Data to and from STRIDA main centres are automatically processed and transmitted by the STRAPP. The SINTRA S 160 computer is used in STRAPP.

SINTRA has been working continuously on this national programme for 25 years, and has been put in charge by the French Ministry of Defence to promote the marketing of custom-designed air defence command and control systems derived from STRIDA concept/hardware/software. In order to undertake full responsibility for such systems SINTRA has created a team which includes the new French company ISR, bringing with it software expertise acquired over two decades of air defence activities. Negotiations are in progress in several countries.

CONTRACTOR

SINTRA-ALCATEL, 26 rue Malakoff, 92600 Asnières, France.

STRIDA air defence system operations room of the latest (fourth) generation

GERMANY (FEDERAL REPUBLIC)

4275.181
SILLACS LOW-LEVEL AIR DEFENCE SYSTEM

The Siemens low-level air defence control system (SILLACS) evolved from the West German TMLD system (**3607.181**). The latter system was enhanced by adding more functions and improving its effectiveness. In the new system, SILLACS, extensive use is made of automatic data processing for the support of control operations and multiple radar target tracking. SILLACS therefore forms a mobile autonomous low-level air defence control system for sensitive areas that can be interfaced with any nation-wide air defence system for the upper airspace.

Low-level radars are available with ranges of 45, 60 and 90 km for optimum coverage configurations. They combine very high clutter suppression with high ECM-resistance. Two versions of the Siemens pulse doppler radar family are specially designed for use in SILLACS:

(1) the fully mobile MPDR 45/E and MPDR 60/E with detection ranges of 45 and 60 km, respectively, consisting of one vehicle with a mast erectable up to 18 m

(2) the transportable SASR with a detection range of 90 km, consisting of two shelters: an antenna unit and an operator shelter. The radar vehicles can contain one or two operator positions, as required. The Siemens IFF interrogator MSR 400 is integrated in the primary radars. Up to 120 air targets per antenna rotation can be detected, evaluated, and transmitted to the air control and reporting centre. Up to eight of these radars may be connected to a Control and Reporting Centre (CRC) which contains the data processing and display equipment as well as the communication facilities for interceptor guidance and data exchange to higher ranking command centres.

The CRC consists of one equipment shelter, up to two display shelters and separate power generators mounted on trailers. The equipment shelter houses all sub-systems for automatic data processing, data and voice transmission and switching. Each display

SILLACS CRC operator's position

shelter contains two to four operator work stations for air situation display and control and one assistant's position. This equipment is connected to the CRC equipment shelter via cable link.

Incoming target reports from the radars first undergo a validity check. They are then fed into the multiple radar tracker, which generates a consistent unambiguous picture of the air situation. New tracks are initiated automatically. Non-automatic initiation areas can be defined by the operator. Processing and display of target reports can be performed independent of track processing. Thus even in case of computer failure an air situation picture can be

obtained from the system. Mission data, eg speed, heading, bearing, distance are provided by the computer for the support of intercept control operations. The operator work stations consist of:

(1) a 22-inch (56 cm) diameter air situation display for target reports and tracks, symbols and vectors

(2) an alpha-numeric readout for status information and track data

(3) function keyboard

(4) alpha-numeric keyboard

(5) rolling ball.

The display control panel incorporates the facilities to select the displayed area, ie to adjust its centre or to off-centre it by means of the rolling ball, to choose the proper scale for switching the output channel of interest to the connected air situation display and to connect the display unit to any input channel. By means of additional push-buttons the operator can combine and adjust the display of video maps, grid lines, plots and tracks as required. Each operator position in the CRC display shelter is supplied with an IFF remote-control panel to specify mode and expected reply code of IFF interrogations. At this panel the actual, remotely-controlled status of the IFF interrogators of up to eight associated radar sites can be indicated simultaneously. The operational program system and the video map are stored on tape cartridges.

Exchange of information between the four operators and two assistants in the CRC and several subscribers is provided. By means of a communication system containing radio link and multiplex equipment, external communication paths are set up. Furthermore, connections to the operators in the associated radar sites and remote-controlled ground-to-air radio link facilities are installed.

STATUS

The system is in full operation for one customer and is at present being delivered to another country.

CONTRACTOR

Siemens AG, Postfach 70074, 8000 Munich, Federal Republic of Germany.

3607.181
TMLD LOW-LEVEL REPORTING AND CONTROL SYSTEM

The air defence of the Federal Republic of Germany is intimately bound up with the overall NATO air defence ground environment (NADGE) system of radars, communications and data processing and control centres (**1181.181**), and to varying degrees with systems employed by allied nations present in Europe, such as the American 407L air weapons control system (**2533.181**). However, because of limitations in the low-level cover of parts of the former systems and because the AFCENT sector of the Central European NATO area is particularly subject to the threat of low-flying surprise attacks, the Luftwaffe has set up the TMLD (Tiefflieger-Melde-und-Leitdienst) low-level reporting service, additional and supplementary to the other radars.

This is part of the combat operational system of air defence and is designed particularly for the monitoring of low-level airspace. The TMLD radars are located in the area near the border, the individual sites being chosen to ensure continuous surveillance. When the radar detects a target, the information is converted into data messages and immediately transmitted to the low-level reporting centres TMLZ (Tiefflieger-Melde-und-Leitzentralen) and on to the user. The whole TMLD is completely mobile so that changing tactical and operational circumstances can be accommodated. The main tasks of the TMLD are:

(1) monitoring the lower levels of airspace in selected areas

(2) processing the low-level air situation in the control centres and passing the information on to the air defence control centres

(3) preliminary warning and target forecasting for Hawk SAM units

(4) exchange of air target information with the West German Army's air defence and command and control system

(5) assistance to flying units.

The TMLD units are combined into two sections, and are employed in the 2 ATAF and 4 ATAF areas. In

each case they come under the command of the commander of a Type B signals regiment. It is planned to assign them as a NATO command force. The main elements of such a unit are:

(1) a radar crew to operate the radar equipment

(2) an evaluation crew to man the control centre

(3) a radio relay crew for setting up communications links

(4) a maintenance crew for the maintenance and repair of equipment.

In peacetime the TMLD mainly limits its activities to monitoring the area in the immediate vicinity of the border, in a quasi-static role. At other times, however, monitoring of airspace must be extended to a greater area, making use of the system's mobility and flexibility. In this it will be supported by the Army's AAD command and control systems, which will be

employed in monitoring the airspace over the combat area.

The principal hardware used in the TMLD system comprises: MRDR 30/1 mobile pulse doppler radars (**3286.153**); TM control centre; CRC TM display unit; radio link set. The radar consists of two 5-ton trucks, each with a 1½-ton trailer containing a generator, with one truck serving as an equipment carrier and the other as the antenna carrier. In the TM centre all the information provided by all the radar equipment within one sector is processed and displayed. Linked users include: the air defence control centres, Hawk SAM batteries, Army AAD units.

OPERATION

Information on air targets supplied by the TM radar is converted into messages for transmission to the control centre and then sent to the TMLZ. The data

A Siemens MPDR-30 radar of the Federal German Republic's low-level air defence system deployed in the field

transmitted contains the positions of the target as X/Y co-ordinates and the target identification. Two operating modes are planned for the preparation of this information: automatic, and semi-automatic.

Automatic Operation: This is regarded as the normal mode for peace time. Targets detected are automatically evaluated on the basis of whether or not they emit a valid IFF/SIF code, and they are reported accordingly. In addition, the operator in the radar truck (acting on instructions from the control centre) can insert further symbols manually in order to give prominence to certain targets of particular significance.

Semi-automatic Operation: This mode is of special importance when automatic operation with the radar signal processor is not possible for techincal or tactical reasons. In this mode the operator can mark targets identified on the radar display with the aid of a rolling ball, using symbols that he can superimpose on the target blip. Transmission of targets to the TMLZ or the user is again performed automatically. For this purpose various types of symbol are available, to each of which a particular meaning is assigned to assist the responsible air defence officer in reaching decisions.

STATUS

The system has been fully operational since 1977.

In the meantime work has begun on a successor system for the 1990s, HFlaA FiiSys, the German Army Air Defence surveillance and Command and Control System. Following the design and definition phase, development started in early 1983 with Siemens acting as prime contractor and AEG-Telefunken, ESG, IDAS and SEL as sub-contractors.

Development will be carried out in two phases. Phase 1 comprises the radar together with radar data processing and broadcast, the fire co-ordination tank and the adaptation of the AA gun tank Gepard and the surface-to-air missile system Roland. In Phase 2 the units for on-line radar and combat vehicle deployment and frequency planning will be added.

CONTRACTOR

Siemens AG, Postfach 70074, 8000 Munich, Federal Republic of Germany – MPDR 30/1 radars.

3945.181

GEADGE

GEADGE is the acronymic title of a programme to develop and install a new air defence network for the southern part of the Federal Republic of Germany, and is derived from 'German Air Defence Ground Environment', The new system, for which Hughes Aircraft Company was nominated the prime contractor in 1979 under a contract worth more than $150 million, will replace the 20-year old 412L radar network (**2533.181**) operated by the West German Air Force. The new system integrates new and existing long-range surveillance radars into a single network based on four centralised command centres, and it will embrace manned and unmanned fixed and transportable radar systems. Eventually GEADGE will receive radar data directly from E-3A AWACS early warning aircraft. The southern portion of West Germany was not included in the original NADGE system (**1181.181**), but GEADGE fills the gap left in that system and connects directly with it. In addition to fixed and transportable gap-filler radars, the new system will utilise four new permanently located radars known by the manufacturer's name of HADR (Hughes air defence radar) (**3721.153**), which is an advanced three-dimensional, multi-role radar that will automatically detect, classify, and report on targets intruding into their coverage area.

In the GEADGE system, Hughes is also supplying HMP-1116 minicomputers, H-5118M central computers, and HMD-22 display and control consoles, as well as being responsible for software, installation and integration.

STATUS

The first of two sites became operational in 1983 and the final two centres were expected to become operational in 1984.

Control positions with Hughes displays at a GEADGE air defence station

CONTRACTOR

Hughes Aircraft Company, Ground Systems Group, Fullerton, California 92634, USA.

4276.181

SIEMENS BATTERY CO-ORDINATION POST (BCP)

Site defence against low flying aircraft is generally dependent on the use of more or less autonomous short-range AA weapons such as machine guns and surface-to-air missiles. This new system by Siemens is meant to increase the effectiveness of such existing weapon systems. Depending on the topographical features of the site to be defended, on the available defensive weapons, and particularly the anticipated threat, the battery co-ordination post (BCP) optimises air defence.

Equipped with an acquisition radar and command and control equipment, the commander is able to control up to 12 fire units deployed around the site. An integrated digital computer evaluates threat and status information. Data link and weapon terminals are provided to connect the BCP with the fire units for the transmission of aiming and firing instructions and for the exchange of data.

STATUS

Siemens have conducted system tests which have demonstrated increased weapons effectiveness. This system is integrated in the Artemis 30 AA gun air defence system being produced for the Greek armed forces, and in the CORAD (Co-ordinated Roland Air Defense) system.

CONTRACTOR

Siemens AG, Postfach 70074, 8000 Munich, Federal Republic of Germany.

Radar shelter of Siemens BCP system

ISRAEL

2226.181

ISRAEL AIR DEFENCE SYSTEM

A computer-controlled air defence system has been installed in Israel. No official details of the equipment are available, and it is believed that no public statement regarding the existence of the system has been made by either the Israeli authorities or the prime contractor, but it appears to be generally accepted that Hughes Aircraft Company were awarded the contract after completing a study for the new system and it is also understood that the system is based on main control centres situated near Tel Aviv and in the Western Negev in the southern part of the country. There are possibly subsidiary centres elsewhere, and the existence of a tactical operations centre with a PPI display of the entire Israeli airspace for viewing by the Cabinet has been claimed.

There are thought to be many similarities with the USAF 407L tactical command and control system (**2824.181**), and Hughes 4118 digital computers as employed in this system are reported as providing the data processing facilities for the Israeli air defence system. Sensors are understood to include two Westinghouse AN/TPS-43 three-dimensional radars

(2517.153), several FPS-100 radars, and there are almost certainly other radars of British, French, and Israeli origin which have been incorporated into the system.

In January 1976 the sale of four Grumman E-2C early warning aircraft to Israel was reported and these were delivered between November 1977 and mid-1978.

The E-2Cs have either APS-120 or APS-125 long-range airborne early warning radar (**1783.353** and

1965.353) and Grumman had a study contract to make the E-2C data link compatible with the Israeli air defence network to enable the exchange of data between ground and air sensors, as well as integrating the AEW element into the overall system.

The original Israeli defence network is thought to have been completed and handed over by Hughes some time during 1973.

In 1981-82 a major communication control system for air defence sites was supplied to the Israel

Defence Forces by the Electronics Corporation of Israel Ltd (ECI) in co-operation with Elbit Computers Ltd. The multi-function communication control system (MCCS-800) is a computer-controlled system that provides a large number of operators with access to remotely located equipment and it includes a secure switching matrix and associated radio and crypto equipment. The system is operational and a mobile version is under development; an airborne system is planned.

ITALY

3324.181
MARS AIR DEFENCE SYSTEM

Current air defence concepts call for an integrated system with a primary centralised mode of operation and a back-up decentralised secondary mode whereby each peripheral sub-system is provided with a limited autonomous capability. Therefore, by introducing a cost-effective redundancy criterion, the vulnerability factor of the total system is notably reduced, resulting in an overall reliable and responsive air defence network.

A peripheral sub-system, such as a reporting post of a total air defence network as mentioned, requires a certain level of additional capabilities over and above the normal reporting role. These are mainly in the control area, meaning identification and interceptor control functions.

Selenia is offering such a system known as the Automatic Reporting System (ARS), in a mobile (MARS) configuration, which amply fulfils the requirement of a low cost system performing a considerable level of autonomous control as well as the main reporting functions. It is basically capable of producing an air situation and transmitting this situation to superior command centres via narrow band data links. This is performed with the aid of functions such as automatic initiation, automatic tracking, automatic and/or manual height measurement and automatic track reporting.

The identification and the airborne interceptor support-functions are also available for the back-up autonomous mode of operation. The system is able to process low and medium-high coverage air situations and can be easily upgraded to a multi-radar configuration. It can also be upgraded to a reporting and control system (ARCS) which performs the full-scale autonomous control functions such as identification, interceptor and SAM control.

MARS can be integrated with a variety of 2-D plus heightfinders and 3-D radars. It is provided with auxiliary functions such as data recording and data collection.

In the mobile version the system is most suitable for tactical use in forward battle areas, performing in the low cover surveillance and close air support role, or in

a more extensive air defence system, where it performs a high/low cover gap-filling and back-up interceptor/SAM control role.

In this basic configuration it can be housed in one data processing and display shelter. For expanded operational capabilities, additional shelters can be added in modular form to satisfy requirements for increased operator and communications facilities. The system is transportable by helicopter, C-130/C-160 aircraft, road and rail.

The automatic reporting system consists of an extractor/combiner unit, a GP-160 computer, a display sub-system consisting of a central unit and three display consoles, peripherals consisting of a magnetic tape cassette unit integrated with the computer, paper tape reader, teletype and line printer units and a communications unit.

The system may be integrated locally either with 2-D surveillance radar, secondary surveillance radar and associated heightfinder, or a 3-D surveillance radar and secondary surveillance radar. For surveillance radars integrated at video level, the system is equipped with a SR/SSR extractor and combiner unit. For surveillance radar integrated at SR plot message level, the system is equipped with a SSR extractor and combiner unit. For remote SR/SSR radar inputs, the system is equipped with a data link interface for receiving plots.

The heart of the system is the GP-160 computer or NDC-160 for the mobile version, which processes various inputs coming from the local or remote radar via the extractor/combiner unit, operator orders via the display sub-system and cross-tell information from remote centres. The computer process information is then sent to the display sub-system as synthetic/alert information and to remote centres as track information via data link.

The digital cassette is utilised for operational program loading and for data recording, the line printer for data reduction, the teletype unit for data introduction and the paper tape reader for back-up loading. Communications facilities are provided for intercom, ground to ground and ground to air functions and are tailored according to the customer's requirements.

The system includes three operational areas

(surveillance, command and fire co-ordination) each requiring different types of equipment.

OPERATION

Operational roles are:
(1) 2-D/3-D high and low gap filler with single or multiple radar input
(2) early warning surveillance with single or multiple radar input
(3) airborne interceptor support
(4) mobile or static applications
(5) local or remote radar input.

Specific functions include:
(1) 2-D/3-D skin/SSR automatic target detection and initiation
(2) 2-D/3-D skin/SSR automatic tracking
(3) multi-radar processing (with optional multiple radar configuration)
(4) rate-aided manual tracking
(5) height measurement, by 3-D radar automatic tracking, separate heightfinder radars, heightfinder radar sector blanking facilities, and manual height data entry
(6) data link for exchange of track data, command messages, etc with automatic and manual facilities
(7) identification by computer assisted SIF active/passive decoding, automatic data link, or manual input
(8) search radar/IFF video display
(9) synthetic video display.

CHARACTERISTICS
Track capacity: 40 (expansible)
Simultaneous intercept vectoring: 2 (expansible)
Data link: Up to 4 sites
Video maps displayed: 2
Operator orders: 42
Computer: GP-160, static; NDC-160, mobile
Core store: Up to 18-bit. 32 K words, with 4 K increments
Instruction set: 84 (121)
Cycle time: 0·8 μs
I/O channels: 62
Displays: IDM-7, static; MDU-03, mobile
CONTRACTOR
Selenia, Industrie Elettroniche Associate SpA, Via Tiburtina 12 400 Km, 00130 Rome, Italy.

JAPAN

2254.181
BADGE AIR DEFENCE SYSTEM

BADGE (Base Air Defence Ground Environment) is a computerised air defence system designed to provide the information gathering data processing and display functions required for umbrella protection against aerial attack on Japan. The system comprises radars that will automatically detect, track, and identify airborne targets over Japan and a large area of the surrounding ocean, computers to process the radar data and evaluate threats, and other computers to process and furnish data on weapon availability, intercept geometry and related measures, all of which is displayed, together with the processed radar data on complex displays to the appropriate interceptor or missile controllers.

The $56 million system was largely built in Japan for the Japan Self Defence Force. The prime contractor was the Hughes Aircraft Company of the USA and they supplied much of the equipment of the first installation as well as being responsible for system and equipment design. Most of the subsequent manufacture, however, was carried out by Japanese manufacturers.

BADGE sites extend from the northernmost tip of Hokkaido to the southern extremity of Okinawa Island and there are believed to be at least 28 surveillance radar locations. The computers belong to the Hughes H330 series. Japanese airspace is divided into four air defence sectors with a direction centre for each: Western Air Defence Force Control Centre (ADFCC); Central ADFCC, Iruma; Northern ADFCC, Misawa and Okinawa ADFCC. The system became operational in 1969.

BADGE is similar in many respects to ADGE (**2211.181**) and Florida (**2373.181**) and reference may be made to the latter for more detailed information.

Some time ago it was reported that the Japanese authorities were considering an extension to the BADGE system (since officially designated BADGE-X) which would both increase its coverage and provide for the integration of the Japanese Hawk surface-to-air missile batteries with the existing defence systems.

It was then understood that there were likely to be five phases to this operation, although the precise order was not known. The phases were:
(1) updating and expanding BADGE to improve

coverage of the main Japanese islands
(2) linking BADGE to the Nike/Hawk batteries via the JAN/TSQ-51B distribution systems then being built by NEC Corporation under licence from Hughes
(3) developing an airborne early warning system
(4) further extending BADGE to cover other key areas such as Okinawa
(5) introducing improved (three-dimensional) radars for BADGE to replace the FPS-20 surveillance radar (**2528.153**) and FPS-6 heightfinders (see **2523.153**) then used.

STATUS
We first reported this programme in the 1972-73 edition of this book, and late in 1972 an official of Hughes Aircraft estimated that there was a potential of $20 million of business in computerised air defence radar systems for Okinawa. Since then it has been learned that the BADGE system's computers have all been duplicated, thereby greatly enhancing reliability, ease of maintenance and repair, and improving training facilities. Prime contractor for this work was Nippon Avionics Company Ltd. Additional computers and peripheral equipment, designed to

work in parallel with the original hardware were added, and another feature was the addition of a number of magnetic drum memories upon which all operational data are stored automatically. In the event of a malfunction demanding a computer change-over, the drums have all operational data that were contained in the failed system and they will be available for use in the standby system.

In its fiscal year 1979 budget the Japan Defence Agency announced that after evaluating eight possible airborne early warning aircraft types, it was decided to procure four E-2C AEW aircraft to provide the low-flying target capability and extended range facilities not possible with the existing ground-based air defence radars. The first patrol area designated for coverage by the E-2C is expected to be operational in 1983. The Defence White Paper also alluded to other measures to renew and modernise BADGE equipment as well as research and evaluation in support of this.

Although it is not known under which particular segment of the improvement plans outlined above present efforts are being conducted, certain details of progress in the modernisation of the Japanese air defence arrangements are summarised below:

Older early warning and fighter control radars are in the process of being replaced by modern three-dimensional radars. The equipment selected has the JASDF designation J/FPS-2 but is also known as the F3D. Produced by NEC Corporation it is probably either one of the equipments described in entries **2298.153** and **3701.153** or a near derivative. It is understood to have been based on a mobile radar known as the M3D (J/TDS-100) and the first example of the new radar was installed at the Oominata radar site in 1979. The FPS-2 is an electronically scanned array radar which uses mechanical rotation for azimuth scan, other features including dual transmitter/receiver, MTI, digital processing and SIF. The display arrangements employ the same symbols that are used in the BADGE semi-automatic air defence system and six bearing lines and two targets can be displayed simultaneously for GCI. Special ECCM facilities are incorporated.

The contract for development of the J/FPS-2 was awarded in 1977 and manufacture started in May 1978. Tests were commenced in November 1978 and the first radar was installed at Oominata, 42nd Warning Group of the Northern Air Warning/Control Force. The JASDF is believed to have at least seven F3D radars installed and the second modernised J/FPS-2 was installed at the Sado radar site, off the coast of Niigata in the Japanese Sea during 1980. Two mobile J/TDS-100 3-D radars were installed in the North and Centre Air Warning Control Force regions, and it was planned to install an improved TDS-100 in the Western Air Defence District.

In March 1982 it was reported that the air defences of Chitose air base and the Tobetsa radar site were to be upgraded and the 1982 budget allowed for three Toshiba Type 81 air defence missile systems. It was also decided to start development of a new long-range air defence radar system to replace the FPS-20, the new equipment to be an active phased array system with a longer range than the 300 km of the FPS-20.

In early 1983 it was learned that the Japanese NEC concern had been selected as prime contractor to undertake the BADGE-X expansion programme, although formal acknowlegement of this was expected to be delayed, possibly until late 1983 or early 1984. It was also likely that confirmation of Hughes Aircraft Company participation as a major sub-contractor (for systems design, management and licensing of hardware) would be similarly embargoed.

It was revealed in early 1984 that funds for the second phase of the XJ/FPS-3 air warning and control radar development will be allocated in the 1984 Defence Budget. This new equipment will be the main air defence/interceptor control radar of the BADGE system. Bids are expected from Mitsubishi, Japan Electric and Tokyo Shibaura.
CONTRACTORS
Hughes Aircraft Co, Fullerton, California, 92634, USA.

Nippon Avionics, NEC Corporation.

NATO

1181.181
NADGE – NATO AIR DEFENCE GROUND ENVIRONMENT
This is a multi-national programme involving 14 NATO countries (so far as funding and contracts are concerned) in the updating and co-ordination of the air defence systems of nine European members of NATO. They are Norway, Denmark, West Germany, Netherlands, Belgium, France, Italy, Greece, and Turkey. The British air defence network interfaces with NADGE. French participation is limited to use of, and contribution to the reporting and control functions, and that country's defence forces will not be directed against hostile targets by NATO.

NADGE, which is now fully operational, was conceived not as an entirely new air defence installation, but rather as an overall plan for the improvement of some existing hardware and the provision of new equipment in certain areas either to fill gaps in the pre-existing systems or to improve their performance. The original cost was an estimated £120 million. The history of the programme and details of the system and elements of the equipment have been described under this entry number in previous editions of *Jane's Weapon Systems*. The following notes summarise the most significant of the latest detail improvements and system enhancements.
STATUS
Improvements to individual national air defence networks are in train in several NATO countries (or are planned) and these will all be engineered to complement and enhance the overall NADGE capability. In April 1984 it was announced that Portugal is building a new NATO radar station on the Algarve coast. Transportable or mobile three-dimensional radars, are being added to the NADGE network. Norway is to acquire HADRs to enhance the NADGE facilities in that country and by the end of 1984 two of the three radars ordered in 1981 will have been delivered to Norway. The third will follow in early 1985.

In February 1984 a contract was awarded to Hughes and Kongsberg for 18 TPQ-36 radars to form a low-level acquisition radar and control system (ARCS) of air defence. The computer-based ARCS will be used with the Hawk missile system where it will replace three radars and multiple control centres. The ARCS radar is a mechanically rotated derivative of the phase-scanning mortar locating radar. Norway has also agreed to allow NATO AWACS aircraft to operate from its Orland Base on Trondheim Fjord. A new NATO AWACS base at Konya in Turkey was opened in October 1983. This is a part of a network of AEW bases.

During the next few years the Nimrod AEW will join forces with NATO AWACS E-3A aircraft, and special

The three Hughes air defence radars (HADR) being installed in Norway will be housed on elevating platforms that allow the antenna to retract inside mountain shelters for maintenance and/or protection from the weather or enemy action

communications equipment will enable Nimrod aircraft to exchange data with ground stations, ships and other aircraft. The combined NATO airborne early warning aircraft force will consist of 11 Nimrod AEWs and 18 E-3As. The first E-3A aircraft was delivered to the main operating base at Geilenkirchen, West Germany in February 1982 and the Nimrod AEW-3 enters service in 1985. In 1982 Boeing delivered three AWACS aircraft to NATO, the last of the 18 being due mid-1985. As noted elsewhere Saudi Arabia will receive the first of five AWACS in that year, and the USAF has ordered 34, with an eventual total AWACS fleet of 46.

The Airborne Early Warning/Ground Environment Integration Segment (AEGIS) programme provides for the controlled exchange of air surveillance data between the NADGE system and the NATO AEW aircraft by augmenting existing ground facilities. This will enable NATO commanders to direct air defence weapons against enemy aircraft intruding into Western European airspace at any altitude. When fully implemented AEGIS will process in-flight AWACS radar data for dissemination to command and control installations throughout Europe from Scandinavia to Turkey. The award of a $285 million contract in October 1982 for installation of AEGIS equipment at 36 NADGE sites brings the total AEGIS contract value to about $400 million, and the number of equipped sites to 42. Hardware includes the improved terminal version of JTIDS and the HM1116 computer. With this facility, ground controllers will be able to watch targets detected and tracked by AEW radars, thus extending the former's operational range. The first two AEGIS ground stations (in Denmark and West Germany) became operational in October and November 1983, and the complete system is expected to be operational by the mid-1990s.

Denmark awarded contracts to Hughes Aircraft Systems International, the Belgium-based subsidiary of Hughes Aircraft Company, to provide an automated command and control information system (CCIS) for NATO's northern Europe command. The system is designed to give NATO commanders current information on the disposition and readiness of their forces in the field and provide information on enemy air activities through the use of high speed computers. Commanders will also be able to use the CCIS to plan deployment of their forces and to speed transmission of order. Four Scandinavian subcontractors will be used by Hughes and the system is due to be fully operational by the mid-1980s. In a similar programme, in April 1981, Britain embarked on the project definition phase of UKAIR CCIS to meet ASR 1300, which has as a major function linking the C-in-C UKAIR (as local NATO air forces commander) with UK-based air commanders. In late 1982 the UK MoD announced development contracts for JTIDS for British air defence requirements. The CCIS will be connected to the existing NADGE system.

To improve detection of low-flying intruders Denmark instituted, in March 1984, the Coastal Radar Integration System (CRIS) which links data from Danish coastal radars that survey the Kattegat and the western Baltic, a corridor that intruders might seek to use. A £2 million contract was awarded to Thorn EMI and completion is due by 1986. Data from CRIS will be passed to NADGE.

CONTRACTORS

The members of the original six-nation consortium and their main equipment contributions to NADGE are listed below. There are also numerous other subcontractors from the other participating countries which are receiving orders in relation to their own country's contribution to the funding of the project.

Hughes Aircraft Company, Fullerton, California,

In January 1983 the USAF had a force of 28 E-3 AWACS aircraft and the NATO operating component had four. NATO was due to receive five in 1983, with a total of 18 by mid-1985

USA: Computers and specialised software.

GEC-Marconi Electronics, Chelmsford, Essex, England: Heightfinder radars, improvements to existing radars, height-strength measuring consoles, manual tracking posts, and reporting posts.

AEG-Telefunken, Ulm, Federal Republic of Germany: Video link equipment for Norway, Denmark, and Turkey, part of the medium-power

radars under sub-contract from Thomson-CSF.

Thomson-CSF, Paris, France: Medium-power radars.

Selenia, SpA, Rome, Italy: Data displays and video link equipment for Italy.

NV Hollandse-Signaalapparaten, Hengelo, Netherlands: Gap-filler radars, two-dimensional extractors, display system modifications.

OMAN

3325.181

OMAN AIR DEFENCE

The air defences of the Sultanate of Oman have undergone a major modernisation and improvement programme instituted in the early 1970s. The ruler, Sultan Qaboos-bin-Said, engaged BAC, now part of British Aerospace, to undertake the task, with advice and assistance from the British Government. The basic requirement was for a highly mobile and accurate integrated air defence system capable of defending civil or military installations from ground or air attack and able to intercept any intruders anywhere within the Sultanate or its surrounding waters. The hardware selected for these tasks comprised two and one-third batteries of Rapier low-level surface-to-air missiles (**2424.131**) and 12 Jaguar tactical strike and fighter aircraft. To make the most effective use of these forces, a master communication and control network was required urgently to provide the necessary early warning and tactical control and command link to the defence force. Marconi provided the bulk of the radar and communications equipment needed.

The communications system has two main centres, connected by strategically-sited terminal and repeater stations. These link the air defence operations centre with the two sector operations centres, each of which has its own surveillance radar station.

Defence centres in the vicinity of Muscat in the north and along the border with Yemen in the south are linked by a tropospheric scatter system running

Marconi Radar S600 series search and heightfinder radars deployed in the desert

the length of the country and fed by short haul line-of-sight radio links. This network is used to convey processed data and high priority communications from radar sites and sector operations centre to the main operations centre. One of the Rapier squadrons and the Jaguar aircraft are based at Thumrait, a military airfield 700 km south of Muscat and where there is also a radar and communications installation. There are also other units, including the Rapier Squadron HQ at Seeb on the coast to the west of Muscat.

STATUS

Operational. Since the system was originally established it has undoubtedly undergone various embellishments, such as the addition of extra radars either to enlarge coverage or to provide facilities for a new air defence weapon.

CONTRACTORS

British Aerospace, Dynamics Group, Six Hills Way, Stevenage, Hertfordshire SG1 2DA, England.

Marconi Radar Limited, Writtle Road, Chelmsford, Essex CM1 3BN, England.

SPAIN

2322.181

COMBAT GRANDE AIR DEFENCE SYSTEM

Combat Grande is the name of the programme of automation of the Spanish air defence system by the USAF for the Spanish Government and supplied by a jointly owned Spanish-American company registered in California.

The new programme (coded 451D) was designed to automate Spain's manual air defence system by providing a computerised capability for aircraft

surveillance and tracking. It includes the development of a combat operations centre and a sector operations centre and modernisation of seven existing long-range radar and ground-to-air transmitter radio sites located throughout the Spanish peninsula. The programme also calls for the improvement and enlargement of an existing microwave system to tie in to the new defence system.

Included in the radar enhancements were the provision of new IFF/SIF facilities, video extractors, and modems. A capability for remote operation of the radar site ground/air communications from sector operations centres for aircraft control was also provided. The existing microwave links between the various stations forming the network will have their capacity increased and redundant routes will be added where alternatives do not exist at present to ensure reliability and security of communications.

The system employs the Hughes H5118M computer, and the Radex system – developed by Hughes in an earlier air defence programme – provides video extraction and signal processing facilities.

The H5118M is a medium-scale, militarised computer specifically designed for command and control systems. It is smaller, less costly, and more reliable, says the manufacturer, than its predecessors. It has the same maximum capacity as the H3118M, developed 10 years earlier, yet is only one-fifth the size. Software packages developed for a number of other computers may be used interchangeably with the new H5118M, including the H3118M of NATO's air defence ground environment (NADGE) system (**1181.181**), the H4118M used in the USAF 407L system (**2824.18**), and the Mk 158 employed in the USN improved point defence target acquisition system (IPD/TAS) (**1928.281**).

In its basic configuration, the H5118M consists of a processor, buffered input-output channels, and 16 384 words of core memory, housed in a refrigerator-size cabinet, along with power supplies, maintenance-control panels, and cooling mechanism. It is categorised as a modular, 18-bit, binary, parallel, synchronous system with a 2 microsecond add time and a 4·6 microsecond multiply time. A building-block design enables the H5118M to be expanded to a dual-processor system and a maximum of 131 072 words of core memory, with no increase in cabinet size.

The Radex equipment provides automatic tracking of target returns from primary radars. When other modifications are added, tracking performance will be improved by increasing the number of tracks that can be handled by an individual console operator; track accuracy on non-co-operative tracks; the operator's ability to detect valid targets by providing better recognition than with current narrow pulse video display. Radex was recently bought by the USAF for integration into the 407L system.

One of the seven long-range radar sites in the Combat Grande Spanish air defence system. Also known as SADA, Sistem Semi-Automatico de Defensa Area, it was produced by a jointly-owned Spanish-American company, COMCO

It is expected that the modernisation techniques will resemble those applied to some of the older systems which were updated during the NADGE development programme (**1181.181**) and although, so far as is known, there is no definite intention to link the Combat Grande system with NADGE at present, it is a near-certainty that the new system will be so designed as to make such a linking-up operation a simple matter if and when the need is established.

STATUS

Under a new programme, unofficially known as Combat Grande II, additions are being made to the radar facilities and new microwave communications are being installed to improve air defence network data exchange services. In June 1980 the first delivery

of Collins data transmission equipment was made. This was to replace outdated hardware at five of 44 sites being modernised under the programme to improve data transmission from radar sites to Torrejon Air Base, near Madrid, for use in the combat operation centre. Completion of this part of the programme is due by mid-1982. The contract awarded to Rockwell International Collins Transmission Systems Division was worth $15 million.

In an award of $2·37 million announced in July 1980, General Dynamics Corporation was given the task of modification, test and installation of a search radar at Barbanza in the north-west of the country. The equipment will include an antenna array measuring about 12 × 5·4 m and dual transmitter/receivers. A US-built heightfinder radar will also be installed at the site. The new Barbanza Mountain radar station was handed over to the Spanish Air Force by USAF Electronic Systems Division in April 1984, making a total of eight Spanish air defence radar sites modernised by ESD.

With the formal entry of Spain to NATO, the closer linking of the Combat Grande system with the NADGE air defence system (**1181.181**, above) can be expected. There may also be certain new installations as a result of this development also but at this stage details of Spain's admission to NATO and the operational and hardware implications of this event have not been specified.

CONTRACTORS

Prime contractor is COMCO Electronics Corporation, a company jointly owned by Hughes Aircraft and the Compañia de Electronica y Comunicaciones SA (CECSA). Each of the two parent companies has a 50 per cent holding in COMCO.

Hughes built the computers and designed the communications equipment for the new system. CECSA manufactured the communications subsystems and managed the civil engineering construction.

SWEDEN

2358.181
STRIL AIR DEFENCE SYSTEM
STRIL is a fully automatic air surveillance and operations control system operated by the Swedish Air Force.

Inputs to the system come mainly from high and low level air surveillance radars, but a back-up visual reporting service is included to supplement the radar data and to replace it if the radar input is blocked. Information from all these sources is fed into a central data store whence it is extracted for selective presentation to controllers having specific territorial assignments.

OPERATION

When a threat is detected the STRIL controllers, who also have available to them state-of-readiness information on available forces and weapons, decide with what kind of available weapon the threat can best be countered and assign that weapon to the task. In appropriate cases, eg surface-to-air missiles, they will also control the operation. Currently the forces controlled by the system are the SAAB Draken and Viggen interceptor aircraft, AA guns, and a diminishing number of Bloodhound surface-to-air missiles (**2406.131**). Most of the control and reporting centres, and the display and computing equipment at the local operations rooms at radar sites have been delivered by Datasaab, which also participated in the overall system development of STRIL.

The STRIL centre is also linked up to the civil defence organisation, and can both alert them and warn industry or the civilian population.

If the threat cannot be countered by the forces under the control of one centre but can be countered by those of another centre, the system provides both voice and transmission links for giving information to other centres. Both narrow- and broad-band microwave links are employed for the exchange of data between centres.

Although primarily an air defence system STRIL is linked to coastal as well as to anti-aircraft artillery.

The original STRIL-60 system has been the subject of sustained development and improvement

Operational console in a TADOC 311 air defence control cabin

throughout its operational life. The most recent, and so far as is known, the most extensive modernisation programme is now in progress. Recently Datasaab supplied new advanced computerised display systems with such facilities as automatic tracking, etc, and in late 1975 it was confirmed that 16 three-dimensional primary radars are to be installed to supplement and/or replace existing older radars. The radars selected after an international competition were an improved version of the ITT/Gilfillan AN/TPS-32 (**2516.153**) which will be installed in rock shelters and with 'pop-up' antennas. The display equipment, including ECCM control and display processing, will be developed and manufactured in Sweden by Datasaab.

A contract worth SKr35 million has been placed by Svenska Radio AB for a quantity of Marconi multiprocessors and display sub-systems. These will

be installed in cabins for use as transportable operations rooms by the Swedish Air Force.

The two main examples of the Datasaab family of transportable air defence operations centres (TADOC) are the TADOC 311 and TADOC 431. The latter is the more sophisticated with regard to operational functions, computing power etc. These transportable centres can be moved to new locations easily if strategic plans are changed or if it becomes necessary to replace other centres which have been destroyed by enemy action. Another advantage of this technique is that buildings or bunkers in stationary centres can be simplified or even eliminated by housing equipment in TADOC cabins. The general configuration of TADOC units employed in the air surveillance and combat control system is shown diagrammatically nearby. Up to three TADOC 311s can be collocated, and up to four TADOC 431s. Each cabin can contain from two to four operational consoles, and it is possible to exchange data between cabins within a collocated group.

TADOC 311
Normally, the TADOC 311 interacts with radars in the ASCC system. Data from the radars is sent automatically to the CRC without any operator intervention. The primary radar can be of the 2-D or 3-D type and automatic transmission ensures fast target detection within the entire ASCC system and

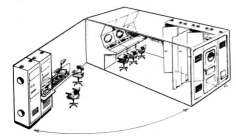

Typical internal arrangement of a TADOC 431 operations centre cabin

thus a short system response time (essential in modern air defence systems). However, since systems that may have to be used in wartime must have fall-back modes of operation, the TADOC 311 can exercise a certain amount of control in addition to its normal reporting role. This permits independent operation, should the CRC or its ground-to-ground communication fail. In addition to its 'own' local radar, the TADOC 311 can make use of a remote radar (either a military gap-filler radar or a civil radar). This remote radar delivers extracted radar data via a narrow-band, telephone-type channel such as a radio link.

The TADOC 311 can also serve as a centre for visual reporting posts (VRP). Their data can be filtered by the centre and transmitted to the CRC.

Main operational tasks of the TADOC 311 include:

(1) Producing target information and transmitting it to the CRC. This is normally automated for radar data (transmission of extracted radar data or plot messages). There is, however, a manual back-up function that can be used if the radar or extractor function is degraded. The manual back-up function can also be used to filter and transmit target information obtained from VRPs

(2) ECCM control, which entails evaluation of the ECM situation and the taking of appropriate countermeasures to eliminate or alleviate the consequences of jamming

Secondary operational tasks include:

(3) Autonomous airspace surveillance, which is carried out within the area covered by the connected radar station(s) in the event that ground communication to the CRC or the CRC itself is out of action

(4) Weapons control, primarily, control of fighter aircraft in the situations cited above

(5) Producing target information and transmitting it

to nearby SAM/AAA units. This can be performed using the manual back-up function mentioned earlier.

TADOC 431

Normally the TADOC 431 serves as a tactical operations centre such as a CRC in the ASCC system. The TADOC 431 is responsible for all tactical operations within an air defence sector. Sensor information from radars and control and reporting posts (CRP) is transferred automatically to the TADOC 431 which can also receive information from visual reporting posts (VRPs) either directly or via a CRP (in which the information is filtered to some extent). The received airspace information forms the basis for weapons control. The TADOC 431 also reports the airspace situation to a co-ordination centre (CC). This reporting is automatic so that the CC will receive an accurate and up-to-date airspace situation picture of the sector in question. However, since systems that may have to be used in wartime must have fall-back modes of operation, the TADOC 431 can take over some CC functions should the CC or its ground-to-ground communication fail.

The main operational tasks of the TADOC 431 include:

(1) Airspace surveillance: this is carried out utilising information obtained from connected sensors of different kinds and from subordinate centres. An airspace situation picture of the air defence sector is compiled and presented in the TADOC 431 itself and can be reported to a superior centre such as a CC

(2) Weapon control, which involves: evaluation of the threat situation; assignment of the appropriate weapon system (fighter, SAM or AAA); allocation of specific fighter aircraft or SAM/AAA unit and weapon controller; interception and recovery control of fighter aircraft or allocation of targets to

SAM/AAA units. Weapons control is exercised throughout the air defence sector and is based upon the airspace situation picture

(3) Civil defence telling and base alerting. This is carried out by issuing warnings to threatened civil targets, such as highly populated areas, industrial areas etc. Warnings are also issued to threatened air bases. Moreover, general airspace situation information is distributed to different 'customers'

(4) Co-ordination of military and civil air traffic control by co-ordinating military and civil air traffic activities in the air defence sector to ensure safety and facilitate identification of civil flights

Secondary tasks include:

(5) Close air support and reconnaissance supervision: for the most part, this entails supervision of reconnaissance flights and supervision and/or direction of close air support aircraft. The objectives are to keep track of these aircraft and be ready to warn them of hostile aircraft

(6) Naval support and co-ordination by co-ordination of naval and air force activities in the air defence sector to minimise the risk of inadvertent firing on friendly units. This can also include the exchange of selected target information between the TADOC 431 and a naval command centre.

Bloodhound SAMs being phased out by the RSAF are being returned to the UK where they will be used to strengthen the British air defences. In Sweden Bloodhound is to be replaced by the American Hawk SAM system.

CONTRACTORS

Prime contractor for the STRIL system is Datasaab AB (formerly Stansaab Elektronik AB), 175 86 Järfälla, Sweden. Datasaab is also responsible for the creation of similar systems in Denmark and elsewhere.

SWITZERLAND

2373.181
FLORIDA AIR DEFENCE COMMAND CONTROL SYSTEM

FLORIDA is the name given to a computerised air defence command and control system that was accepted and declared operational by the Swiss military authorities in April 1970. General contractor for the system was the Hughes Aircraft Company.

DEVELOPMENT

The system consists of several military radar stations with 3-D radar and air defence direction centres, including computers, display consoles, and associated equipment. Information from the radar station is fed into conversion equipment in underground air defence direction centres and processed in turn by a high-speed general-purpose computer.

This computer automatically establishes speed, heading, and altitude of an unidentified intruder. Display consoles present a constantly updated picture of the aircraft's flight track as well as information on the various weapons available, their launch ranges, velocities, armament, restrictions, and time-to-kill.

Should the target be identified as an immediate threat, the air defence commander can electronically request all-weather interceptor aircraft or surface-to-air missiles to intercept and destroy, and can alert the civil defence organisation.

SYSTEM COMPONENTS:

The radar used is a long-range three-dimensional radar, with a planar array antenna using the Hughes elevation frequency scanning technique. This provides simultaneous range, bearing, and altitude data. An IFF system is associated with the radar.

The system includes video extractors that analyse radar returns, with the help of a real-time computer,

and extract actual aircraft tracks from spurious returns such as clouds and ground returns. Track acquisition and updating is automatic.

This processed information is fed to air defence direction centres where it is accepted by a computer. This takes in information from the missile sites, airfields, and other military installations and stores it for use in selecting defensive measures.

It can also simulate air battles for training and instruction, and can be used as a general-purpose data processing centre.

The computer may be required to provide information on weapons available, their launch ranges, velocities, armament, restrictions, and time-to-kill. Numerals and symbols are used to provide this intelligence to the controller and to depict the battle area, the threat and the defences, the problems, and their solutions. The computer, the Hughes H-3324, is of the same type as those associated with the radars but has a much larger storage capacity. Typically it might be called upon to execute between 50 000 and 550 000 instructions in a second.

In the direction centre the display consoles are arranged to display only that information which is pertinent to the tasks of the operator concerned. The principal functions are:

Identification officer – responsible for designating radar tracks as friendly or hostile aircraft.

Interceptor director – interested in his own controlled interceptor and the assigned hostile aircraft. To him, specific data about this intercept is presented including attack geometry, altitude, speed, time to intercept, etc.

Air traffic co-ordinator – concerned with military aircraft requesting clearance to cross civilian airways.

Missile officer – (surface-to-air) in close contact

with the missile batteries and assigns targets to the appropriate site.

Chief of air defence – concentrates on deployment and the threat. Total composite air situation and threat boundaries are important to him.

Aircraft and missile forces currently under control are two Mirage IIIS interceptor squadrons and two Bloodhound 2 surface-to-air missile battalions (**2406.131**). There are also 22 battalions armed with 20 mm and 35 mm AA guns. The first batch of Contraves Skyguard fire control systems (**2377.181**) for the 35 mm AA gun defences was being procured in 1979, and a second quantity of Skyguard systems was due to be requested in the 1979 ordnance procurement programme. It was also expected that approval would be sought for further Skyguard and mobile air defence systems incorporating missiles under the air defence bill.

STATUS

The system officially became operational in April 1970. In the 1979-80 period the Swiss authorities studied competing equipment as a means of providing air surveillance and ground control of interceptor aircraft in the lower airspace. Field tests and evaluations were held of competing systems, among them the Hughes VSTAR (**4080.153**), and the Selenia MRCS-403 mobile air defence system (**3326.181**) and its 3-D radar RAT-31S (**1953.153**). In early 1982 it was announced that under a Swiss air defence programme called Taflir a prototype Westinghouse AN/TPS-70(V)2 radar (**4319.153**) was ordered for delivery in late 1983. If tests are satisfactory further examples are expected to be procured.

CONTRACTOR

System contractor: Hughes Aircraft Company, Fullerton, California 92634, USA.

UNION OF SOVIET SOCIALIST REPUBLICS

3214.181
SOVIET AIR DEFENCE

The Soviet Union maintains and operates an elaborate and extensive air and space defence network consisting of a variety of organisational

levels equipped with a multiplicity of sensors, systems and control and command levels which are frequently interdependent and overlap to provide operational redundancy. This ensures maximum protection from equipment failures or other

interruptions in service due to hostile action or accident.

Early Warning. What is claimed as the world's most comprehensive early warning system provides separately for detection and alerting to both ballistic missile attack and conventional air attack by missiles and aircraft within the atmosphere. The current ballistic missile early warning system consists of a launch detection satellite network, over-the-horizon (OTH) radars, and a series of large phased array radars on the periphery of the Soviet Union.

The launch detection satellite system can give a warning of any American ICBM launch, as well as determining the area from where it was launched. Two large OTH radars, which have been set up to face the US ICBM fields, could provide up to 30 minutes warning of an ICBM attack from the USA. The two systems combine to give more reliable warning facilities than would either on its own.

The next layer of ballistic missile early warning facilities consists of 11 Hen House large detection and tracking radars located at six sites on the Soviet periphery, and these can confirm the warning of an attack given by the satellite and OTH radar systems and give an indication of its scale. The Hen House radars are also able to provide certain target tracking data in support of ABM deployments.

Since 1983, an additional large new phased array radar, claimed to be for ballistic missile early warning purposes, has been detected under construction in Siberia, at Abalakova. This would bring the total of radars of this type in use or being built to six. This new radar closes the gap in the combined Hen House and new phased array radar early warning and tracking radar. Together, this radar and the five others like it form an arc of coverage extending from the Kola Peninsular in the northwest, around Siberia, to the Caucasus in the southwest. Hen House radar coverage completes the circle. In the US viewpoint, the new phased array radar probably violates the 1972 ABM Treaty in that it is not located on the Soviet periphery nor does it point outward from Soviet territory, as required by the Treaty. The complete network provided by these radars, which could provide target tracking data for ABM deployments beyond Moscow, are expected to be operational by the late 1980s.

It should be noted, however, that the Abalakova radar is in the region of the Soviet Baikonour space centre and the Plesetsk missile test range, and that its single face is oriented to provide an arc of cover that embraces the missile down-range area. Other observers have advanced the alternative theory that the new radar may be related to Soviet ASAT researches, rather than forming part of the USSR national defence network.

Ballistic Missile Defence. Throughout the 1980s the Soviet Union has been working to upgrade the Moscow ABM system, which is intended to give a measure of protection for the city itself and for the significant civil and military command installations that exist in and around Moscow. The original single-layer ABM system included 64 reloadable launchers above ground at four complexes for the Galosh ABM-1B, six Try Add guidance and engagement radars at each complex, and the Dog House and Cat House target tracking radars to the south of Moscow. The Soviet authorities are now thought to be upgrading this system to the 100 launchers permitted by the 1972 Treaty. When complete it will be a two-layer system consisting of silo-based long-range modified Galosh interceptors designed to engage targets outside the atmosphere; silo-housed high-acceleration interceptor missiles designed to engage incoming targets within the atmosphere; associated engagement and guidance radars; and a new large radar at Pushkino designed to control ABM engagements. It is believed the ABM silos may be reloadable. Full operational status is predicted for the late 1980s.

Air Surveillance. There are an estimated 7000 or more air surveillance radars deployed in the USSR at about 1200 sites. These provide virtually complete coverage at medium to high altitudes of the airspace over the USSR, and in some areas extending hundreds of kilometres beyond Soviet borders. Limited cover against low-altitude targets is concentrated in the west of the Soviet Union and certain high-priority areas elsewhere. From 1983 onward the Soviet authorities have begun to deploy two new air surveillance radars which will aid the early warning of cruise missile and/or bomber attacks, and will enhance air defence electronic warfare capabilities.

Existing air surveillance radars are also being improved and US officials estimate that more than 20 types are under development. Additionally, the programme to deploy improved air surveillance data networks is continuing, to enhance the exchange of target data throughout the surveillance network to radar outstations to surface-to-air missile sites, and various levels of control posts. This is one aspect of a major overhaul that is thought to be under way, which involves provision of improved capability against low-level threats such as cruise missiles. The programme is understood to embrace the partial integration of

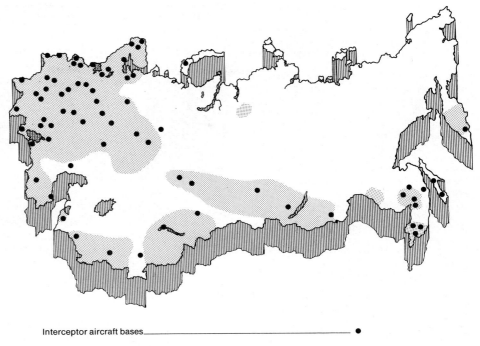

Interceptor aircraft bases _____ ●

Strategic SAM concentrations _____ ▒

Soviet territorial air defence

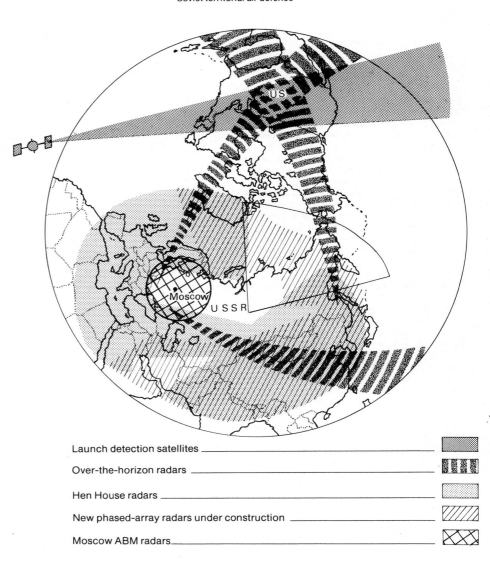

Launch detection satellites _____ ▓

Over-the-horizon radars _____ ▓

Hen House radars _____ ▒

New phased-array radars under construction _____ ▨

Moscow ABM radars _____ ▨

Coverage of ballistic missile detection and tracking systems

strategic and tactical air defences, upgrading of early warning and surveillance facilities, and the installation of the improved data network mentioned above. Other facets are new aircraft and air-to-air missiles, surface-to-air missiles and a Soviet Union AWACS.

The estimated present strength is in the region of 1200 air defence interceptors and approaching 10 000 missile launchers at about 900 sites, dedicated to strategic defence. There are believed to be another 2000 interceptors within the USSR that could be drawn upon, plus 1800 tactical SAMs.

PVO Strany (*Voiska Protivovzdushnoy Strany*) is the national air defence command of the Soviet Union, with an underground headquarters on the outskirts of Moscow. There are four operations/systems commands:

(1) RV-PVO (*Radio teknicheski Voisk-PVO*) radio-technical troops
(2) ZA-PVO (*Zenitnaya Artilleriya-PVO*) anti-aircraft artillery
(3) ZRV-PVO (*Zenitnaya Raketmye Voiska-PVO*) anti-aircraft missile troops
(4) IA-PVO (*Istrebitel 'naya Aviatsiya-PVO*) ·fighter aviation forces.

The 7000 or so air defence radars are the responsibility of the RV-PVO, while missile systems and AA guns are in the hands of the ZA-PVO and ZRV-PVO commands. Fighter aircraft are managed by IA-PVO.

Operationally the Soviet air defence network is divided into four levels of command responsibility: Air Defence (AD) Districts or Rayons, AD Zones, AD Sectors, and 'frontal' AD sub-units defending specific point targets. The rayons are sub-divided into at least two AD zones and these are in turn divided into SAM defence sectors. Each level has a particular command function and operational mission. At rayon level these include search and entry, long-range target identification, designating air threats to lower command echelons, and authorisation of fighter intercepts or missile engagements. Twenty two rayons cover the USSR from the eastern border with China to the Warsaw Pact states of Eastern Europe.

The AD districts are divided into AD zones, some districts having as many as four zones and these are under IA-PVO operational command. The command responsibilities at this level embrace target identification friend or foe (IFF), GCI radar operation, and fighter intercept of hostile/unknown aircraft.

The Moscow Air Defence District is an example of an ADD with four zones, and in keeping with its importance it has recently undergone a number of changes to keep abreast of equipment improvements and availability. The status in mid-1982 was as below:

Yaroslav ADZ: Yaroslav-Tunoshnoye: 36 MiG-23 Flogger G; Bezhetsk: 34 Su-15 Flagon; Kotlas South: 32 MiG-25 Foxbat A.

Brayansk ADZ: Kursk East: 36 MiG-23 Flogger G; Yefremov: 36 MiG-23 Flogger G.

Rzhev ADZ: Andreapol: 30 Su-15 Flagon A/D; Borisovsky: 36 MiG-25 Foxbat; Smolensk: 36 MiG-23 Flogger B; Krichev: 36 MiG-25 Foxbat.

Gor'kiy ADZ: Pravdinsk: 20 MiG-25 Foxbat, 12 MiG-25M Foxhound A; Morshansk: 36 Su-15 Flagon.

An AD sector is a specific, relatively small scale section of airspace under the control of Air Defence Launch Command Centres, and their defence is based on SAMs and their associated target tracking and guidance radars.

Passive defence: The Soviet Ministry of Defence controls the nation-wide civil defence programmes of the USSR. The Chief of Civil Defence is a Deputy Minister of Defence and General of the Army. Full-time civil defence staffs exist at each echelon of the Soviet administrative structure. Civil defence staffs also exist at significant industrial, utility and other installations. In wartime, the civil defence

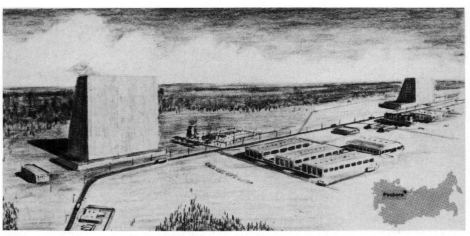

US artist's impression of the receiver and transmitter of a new large phased array early warning and tracking radar at Pechora. Another at Abalakova in Siberia is under construction

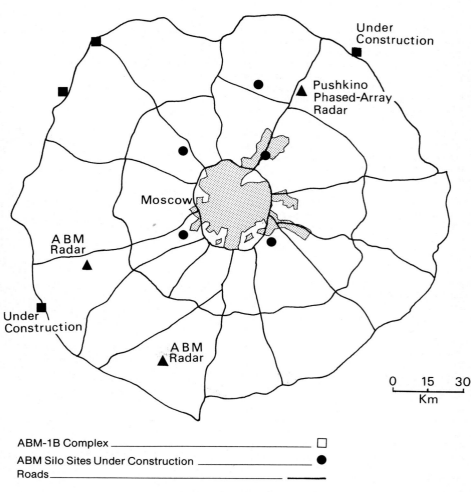

ABM-1B Complex _____ □
ABM Silo Sites Under Construction _____ ●
Roads_____ ▬

Moscow ballistic missile defence

administrative structure, assimilated into an integrated command system, would play a significant role in maintenance of the government and the economy. This goal is supported by the protection provided for the leadership through deep, hard, urban sheltering and an extensive network of hardened

relocation sites outside the cities, with redundant communications systems. The programme also provides for continuity of support for the economy in wartime through the protection of the essential workforce by sheltering at work and by the dispersal of off-shift workers to areas away from work sites.

UNITED KINGDOM

2444.181
UK AIR DEFENCE SYSTEM
The United Kingdom Air Defence Region (UKADR) forms one of four regional commands of the NATO Integrated Air Defence System and stretches for about 1000 nautical miles in an arc from north of the Faeroe Islands to the western flanks of continental

Europe. The systems for warning of attack on the UK are BMEWS (**2525.181**), one station of which is sited in the UK, and the UK Air Defence Ground Environment (UKADGE), the former being concerned with missiles (ballistic) and the latter with aircraft. UKADGE is also linked with NADGE (**1181.181**).

The UK air defence system is coupled into the continental air defence systems by its links with six NADGE stations. The UK data terminal for these links is the West Drayton complex which was originally intended as the heart of Linesman. Incoming data is relayed from West Drayton to the Air Defence Operations Centre (ADOC) at High Wycombe and thence to the sector operations/control reporting centres (SOC) at Buchan, Bulmer, and Neatishead.

Each SOC consists of a radar system and a control and reporting centre, and each is capable of operating independently of other elements of UKADGE.

The 1984 Statement on Defence Estimates revealed that a programme of qualitative and quantitative improvements to UK air defences was under way, and this involves the replacement or modernisation of virtually all the RAF's air defence assets. The UKADGE network of ground radars and command and control and communications systems are being totally modernised. In the 1983 Statement it had been confirmed that as part of the programme, 12 transportable three-dimensional radars had been ordered, and the first of the RAF's 11 Nimrod Mk 3 AEW aircraft is due to enter operational service in 1984.

The first of the new ground radar contracts to be awarded was for two D-band American General Electric AN/TPS-592 variants (see below) to meet ASR 887. This requirement called for transportable sets capable of setting up at a pre-surveyed site and going into operation within six hours of arrival. ASR 1585, met soon afterwards, called for E/F-band radars for the UK East Coast chain and this requirement was met by three Plessey-ITT Gilfillan AR-320 equipments, and also included two Marconi Martello D-band radars. A later requirement, ASR 1586 calls for another two Martellos and three more AR-320s. The original contracts are reported to have also included certain decoy equipment to divert, confuse or frustrate any Soviet anti-radiation weapons that might be deployed against the radars.

A chain of passive sensors is to be established to meet ASR 1584, and in July 1984 a contract was announced by Thorn EMI Electronics who were awarded a £5 million contract for the development of a short range air defence alerting device (ADAD). It has not been confirmed at this stage that the Thorn EMI contract relates to ASR 1584, but the relevance will be clear to readers of this book.

Both E/F-band and D-band systems are required for the UKADGE radar updating programme and four radars, all D-band, have been ordered to date. The first two systems, for installation at Buchan and Benbecula in Scotland, are GE592 radars which are a variation of the US AN/TPS-59 (**3282.153**), a powerful solid-state 3-D equipment, a version of which has been selected for the USAF Seek Igloo programme (**2567.181**) in Alaska. This radar has also been supplied, in GE592 form, to Belgium for incorporation in the NATO air defence network of that nation. For the UK, the GE592 is being supplied as two air defence systems, each mounted on five trailers. The antenna is carried on one of these, the other four being for the radar electronics, IFF, simulation, communications and support equipment. This purchase was funded by NATO.

The next two systems to be ordered, this time under UK funding, were the Marconi Martello

RAF fighter control team at work with new Ferranti large screen colour display in centre

(**3491.153**) long-range, transportable, 3-D radars.

Initially RAF AEW Nimrods will employ Link 11 communications for the exchange of early warning data, while existing NATO AWACS aircraft will at first use Interim JTIDS before all European AEW aircraft use the full JTIDS format. To enable the UKADGE to play its part in this programme, construction and installation of a network of UK data link stations has been started, comprising five receiver stations stretching from the Faeroes in the North to Norfolk. The first of these is for AWACS operations only, to collect information gathered by US AWACS aircraft based in Iceland, while three other stations at Scottish locations will be for use with Nimrods only and will operate Link 11. The fifth station in Norfolk will be able to handle data from both AWACS and Nimrod sources. Thorn EMI Electronics is producing and integrating data link terminals, known as data link buffers (DLB) at these five sites under a programme called Project Cheek.

The DLBs will enable local Command Reporting Centres (CRC), which use a standard NADGE message format, to communicate with the two (later three) message standards of the various types of AEW aircraft and other units.

The withdrawal of Bloodhound from West Germany enabled the number of Bloodhound sites in

the UK to be increased so that there are now seven: Barkstone Heath, Bawdsey, Coltishall, North Coates, Wattisham, West Raynham and Wyton. This weapon is expected to remain viable until well into the 1990s, and an update programme is to be carried out to improve serviceability.

The Improved UKADGE system will provide a significant increase in the capabilities of the UK Air Defence Ground Environment. Automated data processing and display facilities will be installed at a number of underground operational centres and maintenance/training facilities. Airspace surveillance data will cover an area of four million square miles, using data from land, sea and air-based sensors. An air defence operations centre (ADOC) will provide the facilities for the command of a network of control centres and reporting posts. A high capacity flexible digital data network with redundant information paths, employing packet switching techniques, will permit the rapid exchange of information between the operational centres and a large number of external agencies. The design of this network will also ensure that the system will be highly resistant to direct attack, having the flexibility to allow instant reconfiguration to ensure that the command and control functions will not be interrupted.

UNITED STATES OF AMERICA

2525.181
BALLISTIC MISSILE EARLY WARNING SYSTEM (BMEWS)
THE BMEWS (system 474N) comprises a small chain of very large radars for the detection of a ballistic missile attack on North America from the general direction of the USSR. There are three operational sites: Site I in Thule, Greenland, Site II in Clear, Alaska, and Site III on Fylingdales Moor in England.

Three types of radar are used. At Sites I and II there are AN/FPS-50 radars (**2511.153**) which are described in the Equipment Section but it may briefly be noted that they use large static arrays that are scanned by an organ-pipe scanner. At Sites I and III there are AN/FPS-49 radars (**2509.153**) which are large tracking radars with parabolic reflectors. At Site II there is an AN/FPS-92 which is similar to the FPS-49 but is a more modern version.

Information on BMEWS targets is transferred by a communications network to the North American Air Defense (NORAD) Combat Operations Center.
STATUS
The BMEWS sites in Alaska, Greenland, and England have been in operation since 1962, and are reported to have proved extremely reliable. In conjunction with two early warning satellites in the western hemisphere and one in the eastern hemisphere, the BMEWS radars comprise the principal means of warning of a ballistic missile attack. Improvements are planned for both types of warning system, ie the BMEWS radars and satellite infra-red sensors. Additional warning of SLBM attack was provided by six System 474N coastal radar stations (**2810.181**), all but one of which have been replaced by the two Pave Paws phased array radars (Project 2059). (The AN/FSS-7 SLBM detection radar site in Florida has

been retained to provide additional cover for the south-eastern approaches to the USA.) The SLBM detection system will be further expanded by two additional Pave Paws radars in the south east and south west United States, at Robbins AFB Georgia and at or near Goodfellow AFB Texas.

In early 1978 RCA was awarded a $4 million contract for upgrading of BMEWS Sites I and II by replacing the 15-year-old tactical operations rooms installed there. An option to carry out the same modification at Site III was included in the contract. The work was expected to take two years. A $1·9 million contract in respect of Site III, Fylingdales Moor, tactical operations room modernisation was awarded to RCA in June 1979. In November 1980 the USAF announced plans to update the Site I, Thule, BMEWS radar to improve its resolution and data processing capability. A $2·5 million contract was awarded to Raytheon in May 1982 for a definition and design study to improve the tactical warning and assessment capabilities of the Thule site. By early 1983 the updating programmes for the BMEWS stations at Thule and Fylingdales were officially expected to be completed in 1986.

CONTRACTORS
Main contractors for the BMEWS radar systems were RCA, General Electric, and Western Electric.

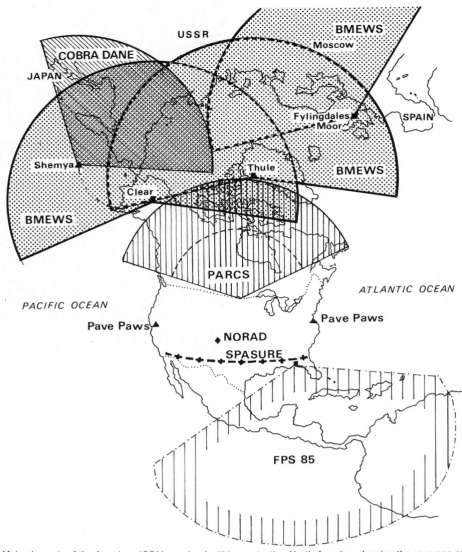

Main elements of the American ICBM warning facilities protecting North America, showing the coverage of BMEWS stations, PARCS (Perimeter Acquisition Radar Attack Characterisation System), and the FPS-85 phased array radar and SPASUR network in the south

2750.181
OVER-THE-HORIZON (OTH) RADAR SYSTEMS

Under Programme 414L the USAF Electronic Systems Division is planning to deploy an over-the-horizon backscatter radar suitable for defence of the continental USA against bomber attack (CONUS OTH-B). Such a system will increase the warning of attack by air-breathing air threats by extending US surveillance coverage by more than 1000 nautical miles (1850 km) from the American coasts, and will provide all-altitude detection capability.

Development is continuing of a prototype OTH radar in Maine and test transmissions by this radar began in December 1979. This limited coverage radar has been used to establish the magnitude of some of the technical risks known to be associated with the OTH programme. These are primarily related to the data handling capacity required to deal with the large volume of air traffic in the North Atlantic airways, and the problems associated with the adverse effects on OTH radar of ionospheric disturbances such as auroral effects.

Results with the prototype installation were evidently sufficiently promising for the US Secretary of Defence to state in February 1984 that it is planned to deploy eight 60° sectors of OTH-B radars for all-altitude surveillance of the eastern, western and southern approaches to the continental USA (see illustration). Funds requested for fiscal year 1985 will permit the procurement to complete the east coast segment and buy the first of three radars needed for the west coast segment.

An original interest in OTH radar to provide long-range surveillance in a northerly direction to replace the DEW Line radar chain (**2567.181** above) has now

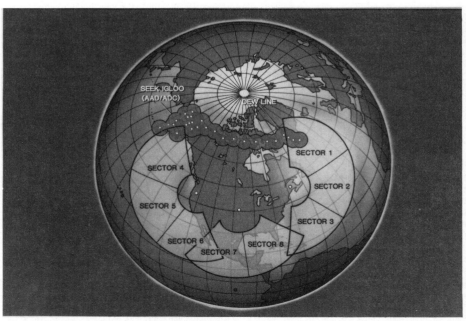

North American air surveillance systems, showing OTH-B sectors for east, west and southern cover and improved DEW Line to north. Pine Tree Line is to be phased out

virtually disappeared following the experimental programmes in Canada described in the 1976 edition of *Jane's Weapon Systems*. However, the deployment of a south-looking OTH radar to complete North American surveillance coverage is now proposed.

The prototype CONUS OTH-B was built by General Electric under a $39 million contract awarded in March 1975. The transmitting antenna includes four arrays covering a total aperture of 690 metres, and the receiver antenna array aperture is 1190 metres. The experimental OTH-B radar uses FM/CW transmissions on frequencies between 6·75 and 21·85 MHz. The transmitting array is at Moscow/Caratunk in Maine, and the receiver antenna site is near Columbia Falls, Maine. An expanded operations centre and support facility will be located in Bangor, Maine. Testing began in early 1980 and all testing and validation of system concepts were due to be completed by 1981, by which time total cost could have amounted to about $50 million.

The $66·7 million contract awarded to General Electric in June 1982 to continue trials with the experimental East Coast OTH-B radar was progressing toward an initial operating capability (IOC) with a 60° sector planned for mid-1986. The remaining two East Coast sectors were expected to follow after that date, funding for sectors having been approved in 1983 and planned for 1985, respectively.

In July 1984 it was reported that tentative advanced planning was in hand for northern (?) and southern OTH-B installations to complement the eastern and western sites previously funded. The new Operations Centre building at Bangor, Maine, was virtually complete at that time and hardware installation was expected to be completed by the summer of 1985. The west coast OTH-B transmitter is to be located at Christmas Valley, California, with an Ops Centre at Mountain Home AFB, Idaho. Funding provides for a start on the first west coast sector in fiscal year 1986.

CONTRACTOR

General Electric Company, Electronic Systems Division, Syracuse, New York 13201, USA.

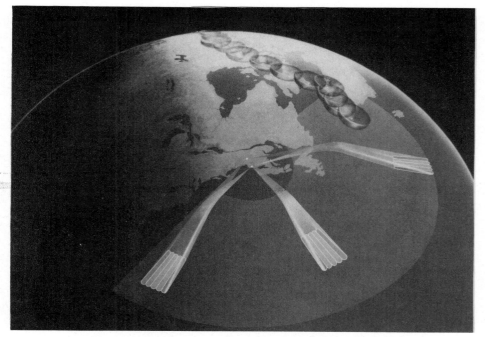

Diagrammatic illustration of OTH-B operation, and DEW Line radar coverage

2567.181

DISTANT EARLY WARNING SYSTEM (DEW LINE)

One of the earlier parts of the complex of radar systems designed to warn the US military authorities of the approach of enemy aircraft or missiles, the DEW Line, is an array of radars that stretches across the northern areas of North America from Alaska to Greenland. The project was implemented as Programme 413L.

Main radars of the line are the AN/FPS-19 and AN/FPS-30. The number of radars in the DEW Line has been reduced in recent years and is now 31 and by fiscal year 1982 the number will be reduced further to a total of 13. This figure will be maintained until a decision on the best method of improving north-facing detection facilities is taken. Information from these radars is conveyed by way of a communications network to the North American Air Defense (NORAD) Combat Operations Center, together with data from the other warning networks described in this section.

STATUS

It is planned to improve the existing DEW Line chain of radars and to fill some of the gaps in it. This new approach is one result of an American re-appraisal of its continental US air defence requirements, a Canadian review, and the newly defined Joint Surveillance System (see **3213.181** below), being implemented under Programme 968H. New radar signal processing techniques developed for the FAA (Federal Aviation Administration) and which offer considerable performance improvements, are under consideration for addition to existing DEW Line radars.

The USAF is testing one of two General Electric AN/FPS-117 pre-production radars, initially at its test range and subsequently at King Salmon Air Force Base, Alaska, for the Seek Igloo programme. If successful a further 12 may be obtained to replace radars in Alaska, where they will be operated as MARS (Minimally Attended Radar System) under control of a new regional centre at Elmendorf AFB, Alaska.

In February 1984, the US Secretary of Defence stated that funds requested in fiscal year 1985 will complete procurement of the long-range radars needed to replace the old DEW Line radars, and will allow continued development of the gap-filler radars. The budget also sought funds for communications systems to link radar stations with command centres, and to achieve further savings the obsolete Pine Tree radar network in southern Canada is to be phased out.

CONTRACTORS

Many manufacturers were involved in the supply of equipment for and the construction of the radar chain. Prime system contractor was Western Electric. Radar main contractors were Raytheon, Budd and Sperry.

3213.181

JOINT SURVEILLANCE SYSTEM

Under USAF Programme 968H the Joint Surveillance System (JSS) has been developed as a successor to the SAGE/BUIC (semi-automatic ground environment/back-up interceptor control) system (**2803.181**) which had been the mainstay of the North American air defence surveillance and warning complex for some 25 years. The expression 'joint' in the title stems from Canadian participation and also by virtue of the fact that in the USA there is joint provision of sensors and data on the parts of the civil and military air authorities (Federal Aviation Administration and the USAF).

Some hardware from SAGE/BUIC is incorporated in JSS but the latter will essentially replace the former system in performing the peacetime air sovereignty mission.

Under the SAGE system, 34 radar sites in the USA were operated exclusively by the USAF, and ten were operated jointly with the FAA. The number of joint USAF/FAA sites will increase to 36 in JSS and the number of exclusive USAF sites will decrease to nine. JSS centres (ROCCs) are located at Griffiss, March, McChord and Tyndall AFBs, and they receive data from 46 radar sites. Fourteen more sites feed data to another ROCC in Alaska at Elmendorf AFB, and two radar sites supply data for another ROCC in Hawaii. Twenty-four air surveillance radar networks in

Military radar console operators at work in a new ROCC where shared civil and military facilities are used for both ATC and air defence purposes, in the JSS

Canada feed data to two ROCCs located at North Bay, Ontario.

The function of the ROCCs is to accept data from multiple sensors, automatically process this data, and display data for detection, tracking, and identification of air targets, and the assignment and direction of interceptor aircraft to ensure peacetime air sovereignty. In time of war or emergency, JSS ROCCs serve as the means of transferring the command and control functions to E-3A AWACS aircraft (**1585.353**), and would continue as a back-up to AWACS. In peacetime, six of these aircraft will be assigned to co-operate with the JSS.

The North American Air Defense Command (NORAD) Combat Operations Center (COC), to which ROCC information is passed, is also undergoing modification under PE 12311F, which provides for command control and communications support to HQ NORAD. Within this PE is the NORAD Cheyenne Mountain Complex Improvement Programme (427M), and acquisition programme to update the data processing, display, and communications elements of the NORAD COC (former 425L system), and the Space Defense Center

part of the Aerospace Defense Command (ADCOM) Spacetrack system (**2825.181**), the old 496L system.
STATUS
The first region of the JSS to enter operation under the USAF Tactical Air Command was in March/April 1983 and the remaining regions were due to become operational at intervals of a few months until by March 1984 all seven continental US ROCCs were operational. Hawaii, the eighth, was expected to become operational by mid-1984 making the whole JSS operational.

2810.181
SLBM DETECTION SYSTEM – SYSTEM 474N

This system, which became operational in 1971, is designed to detect missiles launched by submarines operating either in the Atlantic or in the Pacific Ocean. It consisted of seven radars located three on each coast of the USA and one in Texas. The main radar used was the AN/FSS-7 (**2538.153**), made by Avco; in 1972, however, it was decided to supplement these radars with about 20 per cent of the surveillance capacity of the AN/FPS-85 radar (**2546.153**) which is otherwise assigned to the Spacetrack programme (**2825.181**) and which can provide coverage over most of Central America and the Caribbean.

With the entry into service of the East and West Coast Pave Paws phased array radars in 1980 it was possible to shut down all but the Florida AN/FSS-7 radars.
STATUS
Operational with AN/FSS-7 radars since 1971. Operational with the AN/FPS-85 from mid-1974.

In April 1976 Raytheon was awarded a contract to build the East and West Coast Pave Paws SLBM warning radars (AN/FPS-115) (**3174.153**) which now replace the 474N system. The two selected sites are Otis AFB, and Beale AFB, on the East and West Coasts, respectively. Each includes a dual-faced array about 30 metres high. The SLBM detection and warning system now comprises these two Pave Paws radars, the FPS-85 radar in Florida, and one FSS-7. In response to a growing SLBM threat, two additional Pave Paws radars will be provided, one in the south east and one in the south west United States, one in Georgia and one in Texas. These four, with the PARCS radar in North Dakota will complete a planned five-site phased-array radar SLBM warning network, and will allow removal of the aging FPS-85 and FSS-7 radars.

A $61·2 million contract was awarded to Raytheon in early 1984 for further Pave Paws work. On 13 January 1984, the USAF allocated $57·7 million for construction of the fourth Pave Paws site, at Schleicher County, Texas, and later that month Raytheon received an $11·2 million contract for the power generators for the third and fourth Pave Paws sites.

The four Pave Paws sites are Beale AFB, California; Otis Air Guard Base, Massachusetts; Robins AFB, Georgia; and Schleicher County, Texas. Site three (Robins AFB) is expected to be operational by late 1986, and the fourth a year later.

Warning data is passed to the NORAD Cheyenne Mountain Complex, SAC, and the National Command Authorities. Software is being developed by IBM. The

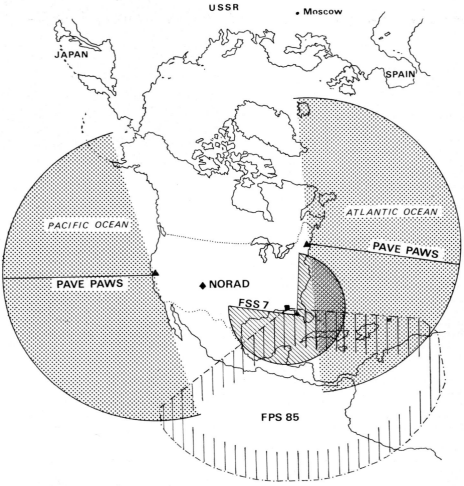

Only one AN/FSS-7 SLBM detection radar needed to be retained after the Pave Paws phased arrays on the East and West Coasts of the USA entered service. Previously there were three FSS-7s on each coast. As two additional Pave Paws radars become operational in the late 1980s, the last FSS-7 and the FPS-85 may be phased out

Otis AFB Pave Paws radar officially became operational in April 1980 and the second of these radars, at Beale AFB, entered service later that year. The Otis installation is operated by the 6th Missile Warning Squadron of SAC and as it became active

two older radar stations manned by detachments of the 14th Missile Warning Squadron, at Fort Fisher and Charleston Air Force Stations were de-activated. The latter, close by Fort Fisher, remains in use as the home of Tactical Air Command's No 701 Radar Squadron.

2825.181
SPACETRACK

Spacetrack is the system code-name for System 496L, the USAF world-wide system for the detection, tracking, and identification of all objects in space. It is composed of large radar optical and radio-metric sensors located around the globe and its control centre maintains a catalogue of all objects in space.

Main sensors of the system are the AN/FPS-85 radar (**2546.153**), Cobra Dane (**1949.153**) and the AN/FSR-2 passive optical sensor. The FPS-85, of which the FPS-46 was the prototype, is an electronically steerable array radar (ESAR) operating in the UHF band and giving three-dimensional information on all satellites and similar objects passing over it. FSR-2 is a passive optical surveillance system.

The complete network of four Spacetrack radar

sites, in addition to the FPS-85 at Elgin AFB in the USA, and the Cobra Dane at Shemya AFB, includes the BMEWS sites at Thule, Greeland; Clear, Alaska; and Fylingdales, England.

The current Spacetrack optical system is a four-site, Baker-Nunn camera system with sites at San Vito, Italy; Sand Island in the Pacific; Mount John, New Zealand and Edwards AFB, California. It is capable of tracking and identifying satellites out to synchronous orbit altitudes of 22 300 miles. A USAF spokesman has stated that communications, research and development, and other types of satellite have been observed by this system. Spacetrack data form part of the input to SPADATS – the NORAD space object detection system.

NAVSPASUR
This system, with the USAF Spacetrack system, forms the NORAD space detection and tracking

system (SPADATS) and is the USN contribution to the latter. The NAVSPASUR detects and tracks satellites which pass through a detection 'fence' consisting of a fan-shaped radar beam extending in an east-west direction from San Diego, California, to Fort Stewart, Georgia. A central transmitter is located at Lake Kickapoo, Texas. There are a total of nine stations, six receiving and three transmitting. The beam cannot be steered and detections are made when a satellite passes through a stationary beam. There is a single Baker-Nunn camera at Cold Lake in Canada. The NAVSPASUR HQ and Computation Center is at Dahlgren, Virginia and nine field stations extend across the southern part of the US along a great circle inclined at about 33° to the Equator. The largest transmitter is at Lake Kickapoo, and the two smaller ones at Gila River, Arizona, and Lake Jordon, Atlanta. The six receiver stations are situated at San

Diego, California; Elephant Butte, New Mexico; Red River, Arkansas; Silver Lake, Missouri; Hawkinsville, Georgia and Fort Stewart. Other sensors feeding into the system are all three BMEWS radar stations, the USAF Eastern Test Range radar on Ascension Island, the Space and Missile Test and Evaluation Center radar at Vandenberg, and the UK's Malvern radar.

STATUS
Under PE 12424F, funding of $4·2 million for fiscal year 1978 was allocated for several projects concerned with providing improved sensors for the 496L Spacetrack system. One, code-named Seek Sail, is a radar development intended to fill a critical gap in the present low altitude (low elevation, rather than height) surveillance coverage. One or more of these radars may be built, possibly at overseas sites. If implemented, Seek Sail radar(s) would be able to provide data on new satellites during their initial orbit.

Another project of the Spacetrack Augmentation programme is GEODSS (ground electro-optical deep space surveillance system). An experimental prototype developed by Lincoln Laboratory has been in operation at White Sands Missile Range since August 1975. It consists of two sophisticated telescopes, a 31 in surveillance and a 14 in tracker, operating in tandem; associated electro-optics; a digital computer; and ancillary electronics and communications equipment. Five sites are planned, with procurement starting in fiscal year 1977. Full operational capability will be achieved in the early 1980s. Algorithms to aid in providing satellite attack warning and software are under development for incorporation in the NORAD Cheyenne Mountain Complex.

The computer provides for on-line analysis and initial presentation, and it also activates an automatic alarm upon detecting unknown space objects. The telescope can detect objects in space which are 10 000 times below the detection threshold of the human eye. A form of MTI is used to control the movement of the telescopes, this being arranged to correspond with either the motion of the target or the star field. The net effect in either case is to isolate the desired target. Five GEODSS sites are planned, of which three have been nominated: Hawaii, Korea and White Sands. The other two will probably include Middle East and Eastern Atlantic locations.

The fiscal year 1984 DoD budget stated that efforts were continuing to complete the required world-wide network of five GEODSS sites, and plans were in hand to modify several existing radars to provide additional high- and low-altitude surveillance coverage. Work is in progress on data processing improvements to track and target enemy satellites more accurately, presumably to assist in designating targets for the developing US anti-satellite (ASAT) capability.

CONTRACTORS
Numerous. Some of the principal ones have been Bendix, Cutler-Hammer, General Electric, Philco-Ford, RCA and SDC.

3073.181

TACTICAL AIR DEFENCE SYSTEM – TADS

The Westinghouse Tactical Air Defense System (TADS) is an integrated, flexible air surveillance and control system for mobile, semi-permanent, or fixed installation. Irrespective of the type of installation, the electronic equipment is identical. TADS can operate autonomously in a manual, semi-automatic, or completely automatic mode, and it can also provide inputs for higher level operations/command centres. Various combinations of equipment can be configured to meet a range of operational requirements in a cost-effective way.

A typical TADS deployment might comprise:
(1) An AN/TPS-43 long-range three-dimensional radar (**2517.153**) complemented by a medium-range 2-D radar such as the AN/TPS-63 (**3475.153**)
(2) One or more operations centres
(3) A communications centre
(4) Cable pallet
(5) Maintenance and storage shelter
(6) Primary power sources
(7) Troposcatter or line-of-sight microwave communications equipment.

A TADS unit can be deployed and fully operational in two hours, and to achieve this mobility, generators, radar antenna, and cable reels are mounted on transportable pallets. All other major units are housed in S-280 shelters. All items can be moved by helicopter, cargo aircraft, or the various land transport techniques.

The communications centre can be adapted to suit a wide variety of air operations and requires only primary electrical power and interfacing with the operation centre to provide ground-air-ground and point-to-point transmission and reception facilities. It typically includes two 28 000-channel HF/SSB transmitter/receivers, interface with line-of-sight microwave equipment, and 24-channel troposcatter interface equipment.

Each operations centre is housed in a standard S-280 shelter, and two or more of these units can be linked to the radar to provide increased operational capability. Equipment in the operations centre includes a radar/IFF signal distribution unit, plotting boards, a video map generator, IFF defruiter, air-conditioning/heater units (operated externally), and associated furnishings and is able to handle up to 100 tracks in a fully automated mode.

STATUS
The configuration was conceived in the early 1970s, and the manufacturers state that TADS is being acquired and deployed by countries in all parts of the world.

Operations centres and communications centres have been custom-manufactured for 13 countries world-wide. They vary in complexity to provide manual, semi-automatic, or fully automatic capabilities. TADS, or related Westinghouse systems, have been ordered for the following countries: Argentina, Australia, Egypt, Federal Republic of Germany, Greece, Iran, Israel, South Korea, Morocco, Singapore, Spain, Taiwan, Thailand and Venezuela.

CONTRACTOR
Westinghouse Defense and Electronic Systems Center, Baltimore, Maryland 21203, USA.

Westinghouse TPS-43 three-dimensional radar used in TADS

4214.181

TAOC-85 TACTICAL AIR OPERATIONS CENTRAL 1985

The TAOC-85 modular control equipment (MCE) is a transportable automated air command and control system for controlling and co-ordinating the employment of a full range of air defence weapons, interceptors, and surface-to-air missiles.

The basic system element is the operations module (OM). A single OM housed in a standard 20 ft ANSI ISO shelter, contains all the air command and control equipment with the exception of search radar, IFF and prime power requirements needed to perform the air defence function. Four operator consoles are located in each OM. Each console is fitted with a multicolour display with radar/IFF video, graphics and alpha-numerics, and a monochrome alpha-numeric display. Full system functional capability is provided by a single shelter which weighs approximately 4500 kg with all the OM equipment, including signal and power cables, installed for transport.

Operations modules are used at the Marine Corps Tactical Air Operations Center (TAOC) and within the USAF Tactical Air Control System, and provide facilities for:
(1) accepting inputs from search radar and IFF systems
(2) performing automatic track correlation, acquisition, identification, classification, tracking, threat evaluation, and weapon selection, assignment and control
(3) receiving and processing track information, orders, commands and status data received via digital data links from other command and control systems and from controlled weapons systems with digital data link capabilities. These data links are TADIL A, TADIL B, TADIL C (one- and two-way), ATDL-1, NATO LINK 1, MTACCS, and JTIDS
(4) processing inputs from operator consoles for the entry, deletion or modification of stored information and initiating the appropriate action both within the operations module and for transmission external to the OM

Operator's console unit of the TAOC-85 MCE system

(5) displaying, on operator consoles, the real-time tactical air situation based on all system inputs, manual and automatic.

The required system capacity of a particular centre is determined by its operational employment. Tailoring a centre to a particular requirement is achieved through the use of one or more operations modules within the TAOC. The present system design permits the interconnection of up to five OMs through the use of fibre optic cables. Cables of 500 metres lengths allow the dispersion of OMs for tactical considerations or because of terrain constraints. Interfacing radars may be located up to 2 km from the OM when connected by fibre optic cables. Radar/OM separation of up to 40 km is achieved through the use of a narrow-band secure radio link.

In addition to the use of wide-band inter-shelter communications via fibre optics, advanced technology is used throughout the system implementation and includes features such as multicolour, touch-entry consoles and a high degree of distributed processing which provides automatic reconfiguration when equipment failures occur. The system is software intensive and can easily be modified to perform additional functions.

STATUS

Under joint development for the US Marine Corps and USAF, the TAOC-85 programme will replace equipment developed under the Marine Tactical Data System (MTDS) programme. MCE will replace equipments developed under the USAF 407L

TAOC using five operations modules

programme. The TAOC-85 equipment is scheduled to be introduced into service in mid-1985 with USAF deliveries six months later.

CONTRACTOR
Litton Data Systems, 8000 Woodley Avenue, Van Nuys, California 91409, USA.

2835.181

AN/TSQ-73 AIR DEFENCE MISSILE CONTROL AND CO-ORDINATION SYSTEM

The AN/TSQ-73 is a command and control system for the fire co-ordination of Nike Hercules, Hawk, and Improved Hawk missiles. Developed and produced by Litton Data Systems under contract to the US Army, this 'Missile Minder' system incorporates a dual-processor AN/GYK-12 computer tailored to real-time control and co-ordination requirements. Two multipurpose display consoles provide PPI formats for the presentation of radar, track, fire unit, map, and other real-time data. Auxiliary tubular display readouts on the same display surface provide amplifying data on tracks, fire units, operator alerts, and other items. In addition, a light emitting diode (LED) status panel presents fire unit, mission, and system status data.

Radar interface equipment simultaneously and automatically extracts airborne targets from 2-D or 3-D radar and IFF and validates the IFF codes. The integral communications equipment provides for digital communications over missile battery, intra-Army, and TADIL-B data links. Facilities for multiple net voice communications are also provided. Built-in simulation equipment provides realistic training of operators through the simulation of complete air defence scenarios. The AN/TSQ-73 utilises a proven 'repair-by-replacement' maintenance concept consisting of automatic fault detection, semi-automatic fault isolation, and self-contained spares to provide greater system availability and reduced maintenance cost.

In its mobile configuration, the AN/TSQ-73 is housed in a single S-280 type shelter 467 cm long, 203 cm wide and 186 cm high. The system is transportable by cargo aircraft, helicopter, or truck, and is powered by either a 400 Hz diesel generator or a local 50/60 Hz supply.

Processing sensor data provided by a wide variety of currently operational local radars and IFF sets, the two-channel radar interface sub-system automatically detects and acquires the targets sending position reports to the automatic data processor. Special features of the radar interface include an integral IFF beacon decoder and an automatic clutter-mapping function by which extraneous radar returns are removed from consideration as targets.

Each multipurpose console presents situation (PPI) and auxiliary readout (ARO) data on a single cathode ray tube (CRT). Situation information occupies a 37cm diameter circle at the top of the CRT, while auxiliary data is presented in a rectangular area near the bottom. The former

AN/TSQ-73 system (left foreground) operating in field test deployment with radar and communications equipment

includes track symbols position and identification, track number, raid size, height, velocity, extended vectors, and source code. Two area maps, selectable from a list of ten, may be displayed simultaneously, with up to three air-defence-safe corridors. Defence weapons status is also presented for total operational control and includes site position, engagement positions, site number, status, commands, and pairing lines. Using computer-generated alpha-numeric data, the ARO presents more detailed track and fire unit information and permits the console operator to edit the displayed data.

The arrangement of display console controls optimises operator effectiveness and minimises operator training. Operator entry is made by action switches, a full 36-character alpha-numeric keyboard, and a control stick for entering position co-ordinates.

Much of the AN/TSQ-73 equipment is the same as that used by the US Army's TACFIRE artillery command and control system so that there will be significant savings in training, support, and procurement costs. The general-purpose nature of these systems also makes many of them readily

adaptable to other electronic command and control systems. The AN/GYK-12 computer is also used in Tactical Operations System Operable Segment (TOS-OS) and the Tri-Service Tactical Switch (TRI-TAC TTC-39). The general-purpose nature of the display console controls takes full advantage of an alterable processor which can be easily programmed to meet the specific requirements of other applications. Both of these systems are suitable for application to requirements like those of the Air Traffic Management System, control of SHORAD, and SAM-D command and control group.

STATUS

Type classified 'Standard'. In full-scale production for the US Army. Deliveries include systems for numerous other countries. In 1981 a co-production agreement covering the manufacture of 11 AN/TSQ-73 systems for NATO was established. Under this agreement a contract valued at $103 million was awarded to Litton, with co-production in France by SINTRA and in Italy by Litton Italia.

CONTRACTOR
Litton Data Systems, 8000 Woodley Avenue, Van Nuys, California, USA.

ARMY FIRE CONTROL SYSTEMS

2642.181
INTRODUCTION
This section deals with a number of more or less elaborate assemblages of equipment whose functions are primarily concerned with the control of guns or gun-missile combinations for the engagement of surface or airborne targets.

There are some systems described here that are always associated with the same weapon, simply because they have never been used with any other. The section does not include systems designed specifically for use with a particular weapon. In such instances the control arrangement is generally covered in the relevant entry for the complete weapon system.

However, this section does include some items which are not complete fire control systems but are major adjuncts to such systems – a good example being the British AMETS system (**2400.161**).

Comprehensive control and reporting and similar systems are dealt with in the section on Land-based Air Defence Systems. The main distinction between systems described in that section and anti-aircraft systems described in this section is essentially one of size; the air defence systems cover sensors and weapons deployed over a wide area extending upwards to sub-continental size; those described below are in general associated with only a few weapons – from a single tank gun to an anti-aircraft battery – although major field artillery systems such as TACFIRE (**2827.161**) and BATES (**2644.161**), while providing a service at battery or regimental level, can cover a wider field.

Readers may find it helpful to consult the companion reference book, *Jane's Military Communications*, which deals with closely related topics to those in the following pages of this section.

BELGIUM

2598.181
SABCA TANK FIRE CONTROL SYSTEMS
SABCA has designed and manufactured over a thousand Laser Tank Fire Control Systems (LTFCS) for Leopard 1, Centurion, Vijayanta, M48, M60 and Belgian JPK tanks.

Leopard
The Leopard LTFCS is fully integrated and uses high accuracy computation techniques in the ballistic computer and automatic sensors. The reticle of the laser/optical sight is always centred by a gimballed mirror drive and the laser and optical axes are perfectly aligned.

Centurion/M48/M60
The Centurion LTFCS and M48/M60 LTFCS are basically identical. They consist of two main groups:
(1) an integrated day/night laser sight group including a laser visual unit and a second-generation image intensifier equipment (a) (see illustration) or an all weather day-and-night thermal imaging system (b) (see illustration)
(2) a ballistic computer group including controls and ammunition selection units, automatic or manual corrections for standard and non-standard environmental conditions (see illustration). An extensive built-in-test system controls at all times the performance of the system and identifies faults through line replaceable units, thus doing away with the need for tank level test equipment.

UTFCS
The new Universal Tank Fire Control System is a full solution fire control system designed to meet current threats and operational requirements as well as those of the next decade (see illustration). The system is equipped with a fully stabilised sight (director system). This approach provides a greater scene stability and continuous tracking of targets. It thus provides a full shoot-on-the-move capability and

Ballistic computer sub-system for Centurion, M48 or M60

minimum reaction time. The integrated day/night sight is associated to a muzzle reference mirror to compensate gun droop.

The fire control computer, besides ballistic computation, includes interfaces to gun/turret

Universal Laser Tank Fire Control System

Integrated day/night laser sight sub-system for Centurion, M48 or M60 MBT

stabilisation system and the sight head electronics; an extensive built-in-test capability; a gunner training mode whereby the gunner can aim and track simulated targets while his performance is monitored permanently.

The major components of the Universal LTFCS are:
(1) an integrated gunner's sight including a stabilised head mirror unit, a laser visual unit and a passive night sight (image intensifier or thermal imager)
(2) a digital micro-computer based on a high performance 16-bit microprocessor
(3) a vertical sensor unit
(4) a gun position sensor
(5) a wind sensor
(6) gunner and commander control units
(7) a muzzle reference unit
(8) a commander's stabilised sight.
CONTRACTOR
SABCA, Chaussée de Haecht 1470, 1130 Brussels, Belgium.

CANADA

3937.161
MILIPAC ARTILLERY COMPUTER
The MiliPAC is a portable artillery computer initially designed for the Canadian Department of National Defence to carry out the calculation of firing data for a battery of six guns of 105 mm or 155 mm calibre, as well as a number of related functions such as field and unit survey and fire control.

Since the original development in 1976-79 MiliPAC has been expanded to the battalion level where it is used as a Tactical Fire Control Computer System. This includes the expansion of the data communication capability for the units used at both the battalion and battery Fire Direction Centres and expansion of the capability to receive digital information from the Forward Observers.

The MiliPAC is built as a single unit which is light enough to be carried easily by one man but is meant for installation in a vehicle or other transportable shelter used as the battalion or battery fire control post. The processor used in MiliPAC is the Intel 8086 microprocessor. The memory is a combination of CMOS RAM and EPROM with battery back-up for the RAM memory. The battery can maintain the contents of the RAM for three months with no recharging. The EPROM memory contains all of the program code and is non-volatile. The combination of memory used is 12 K words of CMOS RAM and 128 K words of EPROM, expandable to 448 K words. The light emitting diode display used on the Canadian configuration has the capacity of 8 × 48 character lines and provides input and output data, as well as cue messages to assist the operator. An alternative 512 by 256 dot matrix electro-luminescent (EL) panel has been developed to display the Arabic script. In addition to data entry input from the keyboard, provision is made for teleprinter input and output, and gun display system.

The standard software package includes routines for calculation of firing data for up to six guns at up to three positions, a combination of 120 target and observer records, each observer being a protected safety zone, an additional five independent safety zones, five fire support lines, five crest clearance zones, two air corridors, minimum firing elevation for each of the firing positions, 12 non-standard muzzle velocities for each gun/projectile combination, 27 lines of meteorological data, ten sets of registration corrections, and ballistic data for four weapons.
CHARACTERISTICS
Computer: Intel 8086 microprocessor

Memory: 12 K words CMOS RAM and 128 K words of EPROM; expandable to 448 K words
Display: 380 character LED (512 × 256 dot matrix EL panel optional)
Weight: 20 kg
Power supply: 20 to 33 V DC or 10 to 16 V DC
Consumption: 50 W

MiliPAC artillery fire direction computer

STATUS
Three prototypes were delivered to the Canadian Department of National Defence in 1979 for evaluation and a production order was placed in 1982

for 66 systems. Deliveries against this order started in August 1983. Several other countries are studying this system and a major export order for battalion level MiliPAC systems is expected in 1984.

CONTRACTOR
Computing Devices Company, a Control Data Company, PO Box 8508, Ottawa, Ontario, Canada K1G 3M9.

FRANCE

4147.181
COTAC FCS
Tank fire control systems for French vehicles are produced in several versions forming the COTAC (Conduite de Tir Automatique) family of systems. The principal known examples are outlined in the following paragraphs.

COTAC APX M401
COTAC M401 is the automatic fire control equipment developed for the AMX-10RC tank. It permits daylight engagement of fixed or moving targets. The equipment comprises the APX M504-04 gunner's sight for observation, fire correction data display by M421 optical compensator, laser rangefinding by APX M550 rangefinder, automatic harmonisation of sight and weapon, and emergency firing using a stadiametric ranging scale. Other items are tachometers on both axes; an automatic cant sensor; automatic displays of wind, temperature and altitude; and a computer for calculating fire corrections.
CHARACTERISTICS
Range measurement: 400 – 10 000 m
Target speed measurement: 0 – 25 mils/s (azimuth); 0 – 5 mils/s (elevation)
Cant measurement: +0·2 to –0·2 rad
Crosswind setting: +10 to –10 m/s

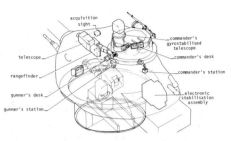

Main components of COTAC APX M581

Outside temperature range: –15 to +45° C
Altitude setting: 0 – 1500 m
Firing correction computation
Bearing: –30 to +30 mils
Elevation: 0 – 50 mils

COTAC APX M581
The COTAC APX M581 is an integrated automatic fire control equipment consisting of day/night optical sight units, a laser rangefinder and associated items for installation in the turrets of AMX-30B2 or AMX-32

tanks equipped with 105 mm or 120 mm guns. The sight tube is a 110 mm diameter unit with ×10 magnification, and is equipped to allow harmonisation of the visible and IR beams. There is also an electro-optical unit and computer for fire corrections and aiming calculations. The laser rangefinder is an APX M550.
CHARACTERISTICS
Range measurement: 400 – 10 000 m
Target speed measurement: 0 – 30 mils/s (both planes)
Slant measurement: +200 to –200 mils
Crosswind setting: +10 to –10 m/s
Outside temperature setting: –15 to +45° C
Altitude setting: 0 – 1500 m
STATUS
The APX M401 COTAC has been in series production since 1979 and the APX M581 COTAC since 1981.
CONTRACTORS
GIAT (Groupement Industriel des Armements Terrestres), 10 place Georges Clemenceau, 92211 Saint-Cloud, France.
Laser rangefinder: CILAS.
Stabilisation: SFIM.
Sights: SOPELEM.
Night vision: SINTRA.

4268.181
SOPTAA FCS
The SOPTAA anti-aircraft fire control system is designed for the direction of weapons in the defence of ground targets against attack from aircraft or helicopters. The operating principle of the system can be applied to a variety of AA weapons, but the SOPTAA 19 version has been designed for use with vehicle-mounted turrets armed with 20 mm cannons. Operation requires two men: an observer/fire director who detects and designates the target; and a gunner who subsequently tracks it and operates the gun.

The observer is equipped with a designator 'gun', such as the CSEE ELDO (**4248.193**), which automatically calculates the necessary parallax corrections for the distance between observer and weapon, and provides for automatic alignment of the turret onto the target. The turret is provided with a periscopic gunner's sight, derived from the M 371 and with the elevation aiming prism mechanically linked

to the gun; an electronic control unit incorporating the computer; and angular transducers or tachogenerators mounted on the cannon. Power is derived from the vehicle's 24 V supply.

The turret sight has a projected aiming graticule, and separate optical channels for ground targets (×6 magnification and 10° field), and for anti-aircraft fire (×1 magnification and a field of 26° vertical × 71° horizontal). The elevation aiming range is from –15 to +55°.

An engagement sequence time of five to six seconds makes it possible to intercept an aircraft designated at 2000 metres at a range of 1000 metres with an accuracy of ±5 mil.
STATUS
Prototypes have been produced.
CONTRACTOR
SOPELEM, 102 rue Chaptal, 92306 Levallois-Perret, France.

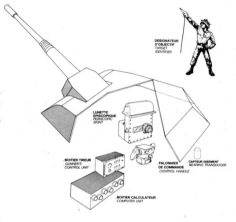

Principal elements of SOPTAA anti-aircraft FCS

3979.181
SOPTAC FCS
SOPTAC is a modular range of day/night fire control systems designed for application to AFV gun turrets such as the various 90 mm turrets (by Hispano, SAMM or GIAT) or the FL 12 by Fives-Cail Babcock. The system provides aiming parameters automatically in accordance with the main ballistic parameters: range, traverse speed of moving targets, ammunition type, meteorological conditions, tank slope, cant angle etc. Various configurations to suit specific turret types have been designed employing different equipment combinations, but mostly based on use of a version of the TJN2 day/night sight (**3754.193**) and the TCV-107 laser rangefinder. The SOPTAC systems applicable to specific turrets are listed below, and main equipment complements and characteristics of each are summarised individually in the paragraphs which follow.

Turret Type	FCS
FL 12 (Five-Cail Babcock)	SOPTAC 18-01, SOPTAC 18-02, SOPTAC 18-03, SOPTAC 18-04, SOPTAC 18-05
TS 90 (GIAT)	SOPTAC 10-A, SOPTAC 11-A, SOPTAC 13-A, SOPTAC 21-A, SOPTAC 22-A
Lynx 90	SOPTAC 10-B, SOPTAC
(Hispano-Suiza)	11-B, SOPTAC 13-B, SOPTAC 21-B, SOPTAC 22-B
AR 90 (SAMM) (equivalent to TS 90)	SOPTAC 10-A, SOPTAC 11-A, SOPTAC 13-A

The base model for the FL 12 turret is the SOPTAC 18-04 day/night system comprising the current M213 aiming sight, a module which projects the graticule of the automatic elevation display (with associated electronic unit), a TCV-107 laser rangefinder fitted with a device projecting the sight graticule, and a TJN2 night sight. Without the night sight, the system is designated SOPTAC 18-03. Both these versions may be used in conjunction with the SOPTAC 18-05 sight which has a moving graticule which permits automatic engagement of moving targets and slope compensation up to ±10°. An aiming accuracy of ±2 mils on a moving target is claimed and the system can handle transverse target speeds of up to 100 km/h. A turret rotation sensor is needed for this version. The SOPTAC 18-02 version is similar to the SOPTAC 18-04 but without the automatic elevation display, and SOPTAC 18-01 is the day-only version of the SOPTAC 18-02.

There is a wider range of versions available for the GIAT TS90 turret, offering four day/night models and four day-only types. The SOPTAC 11-A day/night version comprises a TJN2-90-A2 sight fitted with

automatic elevation presentation (linked to a TCV-107 laser rangefinder located behind a window in the turret), and with slope compensation and moving target capability. A tacho-generator measures turret rotation, and other data is inserted manually on the commander's control panel. With the TJN2-90-A1 sight and without the slope compensation and target speed measurement facility this system is designated SOPTAC 10-A. The SOPTAC 22-A is a simplified version consisting of the TJN2-90-A sight (without slope compensation, automatic elevation display, or tachometry) and an unlinked TCV-107 laser rangefinder. Day-only SOPTAC systems for the TS 90 turret are the SOPTAC 13-A, SOPTAC 06-A, and SOPTAC 21-A which correspond to the SOPTAC 11-A, 10-A and 22-A except that the sights incorporated are the daylight equipment M563-A2 (with automatic elevation presentation, slope compensation and tachometry), M563-A1 (with automatic elevation only), or the APX M563 with manual elevation control.

There are four day/night and four day-only SOPTAC versions for the Hispano-Suiza Lynx 90 turret also. The most comprehensive day/night model is the SOPTAC 11-B which comprises a TJN2-90-B2 sight, a TCV-107 laser rangefinder mounted on the gunshield, and in other respects very similar to the SOPTAC 11-A for the TS 90 turret. By replacing the TJN2-90-B2 sight with the TJN-90-B1, which does

Elements of SOPTAC tank fire control system showing TJN2-90 day/night sight, commander's control unit, computer and CILAS laser rangefinder

Panhard ERC 90 F4 fitted with prototype SOPTAC 36 fire control system for its Mars 90 CNMP turret

not have slope compensation or tachometry facilities, the SOPTAC 10-B fire control system is produced. A simplified version is the SOPTAC 22-B which incorporates the TJN-90-B sight and does not include linking of the TCV-107 laser rangefinder. Day-only equivalents of the SOPTAC 11-B, 10-B and 22-B models are available as the SOPTAC 13-B, 06-B and 21-B versions, in which the M198/1-A2, M198/1-A1 or APX M198/1 day sights are substituted for the day/night sights.

SOPTAC 36
The latest version of the SOPTAC series of FCS is the SOPTAC 36 which is a universal day/night periscopic system designed for incorporation in all types of AFV. Like the similar SOPTAC 11, it is a modular system.
The main elements are:
(1) sight module with a third-generation light intensifier tube with day magnification of ×8 (night ×6) and a day field of 7° (night 6°)
(2) an eyepiece arm adaptable to different turret configurations

(3) laser rangefinder, TCV 186, derived from the TCV 107
(4) fire control mobile graticule giving a set of projected graticules with automatic elevation selection and lateral deviation with deflection correction
(5) electronic units used to control the graticules on acquisition of target range, speed, vehicle deflection, atmospheric temperature and pressure, crosswind, ammunition type
(6) automatic muzzle reference module.

STATUS
Prototypes have been built of the FL 12 and TS 90 turret SOPTAC systems, and some Lynx 90 turret systems have reached the production stage. A prototype Panhard ERC 90 F4 vehicle equipped with the Mars 90 CNMP turret and SOPTAC 36 fire control system has been completed.
CONTRACTOR
SOPELEM, 102 rue Chaptal, 92306 Levallois-Perret, France.

4267.181
SOPTAM FCS
SOPTAM fire control systems have been designed for the operation of mortars from armoured fighting vehicles. Two versions of the system have been identified; the SOPTAM 30 intended for use with turrets equipped with the French DE 81 mm mortar, and the SOPTAM 26 for the Hispano-Suiza Serval mortar turret.
SOPTAM 26
This system is for the operation of mortars from vehicles operating on sloping ground, and the gunner can make the appropriate corrections to bearing aim, resulting from the attitude of the vehicle, according to the horizontal. The system comprises: the Type M 447-03 sight (derived from the APX M371); an electronics unit measuring 212 × 58 × 250 mm and weighing 2·5 kg; an inclinometer weighing 1 kg; and a 24 V power supply. Its performance characteristics are tabulated below:
CHARACTERISTICS
Elevation angle measurement: Up to 70°
Accuracy: 0·8 mil
Deflection and slope correction: Up to 10°
Max error in bearing correction: 5 mil for a level angle of 1100 mils
SOPTAM 30
This was designed for incorporation in lightweight turrets equipped with the DE 81 mortar, and it provides the following functions:

(1) storage of mortar elevation tables
(2) turret attitude correction
(3) acquisition of aiming corrections between rounds
(4) acquisition of data from a remote observer (high-angle trajectory indirect firing), for the various alternative firing configurations (flat or high-angle trajectory, direct or indirect fire).
The system comprises: a monocular periscopic observation sight with a slaved head prism; TPV 89 binocular rangefinder, integrated in the sight and providing a laser rangefinder function, and the binocular sight channel also being used for aiming; the gunner's electronic control unit; tank commander's control unit incorporating the computer; all these being powered from the vehicle's 24 V supply.
CHARACTERISTICS
Observation sight
Magnification: ×1
Instantaneous field: 10° (vertical) × 17° (horizontal)
Total field: 26° (vertical) × 60° (horizontal), with displacement of both eyes
Elevation aiming range: −15 to +45°
Mortar/sight servo accuracy: ±0·3 mil
Rangefinder/aiming sight
Magnification: ×6
Field of view: 7°
Laser wavelength: 1·06 micron
Measurement field: 15° at 9990 m, accuracy ±5 m
Max calculation time: <3 s

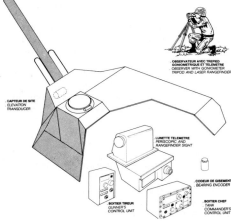

Layout of major components of SOPTAM mortar FCS

System accuracy: ±0·3 mil (flat trajectory modes); ±1 mil (other modes)
STATUS
The SOPTAM 26 has been produced in small batches and prototypes have been manufactured of the SOPTAM 30 system.
CONTRACTOR
SOPELEM, 102 rue Chaptal, 92306 Levallois-Perret, France.

3843.181
APX M586 TANK FCS UPDATE
The APX M586 is a tank fire control improvement equipment intended for the updating of earlier MBTs such as the M48, AMX-13 etc. The equipment comprises an external unit positioned in front of the original firing sight tube, and a control console for use by the tank commander. There is also a TCV-107 laser rangefinder and an electro-inertial sensor unit which contains all the necessary elements for parameter measurement and fire correction calculations.
By the addition of Thomson-CSF Canasta low light-level television equipment a complete day/night capability can be obtained.

CHARACTERISTICS
Range measurement: 300 – 10 000 m
Target speed measurement: 0 – 30 mil/s (both planes)
Cant measurement: +200 to –200 mils
Crosswind setting: ±10 m/s
Altitude setting: 0 – 2000 m
Automatic setting of firing corrections: ±30 mils (azimuth); 0 – 60 mils (elevation)
The afocal module is adaptable to the gunner's sight of T 54, T 55, T 59 battle tanks and is fitted at the forepart of the daylight aiming sight. It enables both daylight and night aiming without any mechanical modification on the turret. Night aiming is performed by using a second-generation micro-channel light

intensifier tube whereas daylight aiming requires the retraction of a swivel mirror. The module is housed in a sealed water-tight casing and can be removed and reset without having to be boresighted again.
CHARACTERISTICS
Magnification: ×1
Field: ⩾70°
Resolution: >0·5 mrad at 10⁻¹ lux
Operating temperature: −40 to +50° C
Performance
Daylight aiming: unchanged
Night aiming: 1000 to 2000 m according to atmospheric conditions
The afocal module incorporates an optical plate for

combining the images from the visible light and infra-red beams, a deviation display collimator and a laser rangefinder.

STATUS

Prototype.

CONTRACTORS

GIAT (Groupement Industriel des Armements Terrestres), 10 place Georges Clémenceau, 92211 Saint-Cloud, France.

Sight: SOPELEM.

Laser rangefinder: CILAS.

3935.161

CAC 101 FIELD ARTILLERY COMPUTER

The Brandt Armements CAC 101 field artillery computer was designed principally for the preparation of firing data for 105 mm and 155 mm guns and howitzers and for heavy mortars. The main operational characteristics of the CAC 101 include storage in the computer memory of six gun positions, 10 targets, 10 observation posts, and 10 protected areas in addition to meteorological data (standard STANAG 4082 message up to line 21). Protected memories are provided. Ballistic data are carried on plug-in modules, each module carrying the data relating to one type of projectile and the weapon firing it. Using this information, the computer calculates the firing data for the main reference piece as well as the subordinate pieces. A built-in test program carries out self-checking of the system.

Data are entered into the computer by means of a keyboard in accordance with the dialogue between the machine and the operator, assisted by an alpha-numeric display panel. In addition to the standard computational routines, there are possibilities for

Brandt Armements CAC 101 field artillery computer

optional calculations, such as the ballistic co-ordinates of a given round during fire adjustment, computation of the residual correction at the end of a registration, and calculation of the correction for

muzzle velocity. Others are topographical computations such as conversion of rectangular co-ordinates to polar co-ordinates and vice versa, direct and inverse bearings, direct and inverse intersections, triangulations, change of grid system, or goniometric network.

Various peripheral equipments may be connected to the computer, including a teleprinter, telex reader, remote data display etc. The CAC 101 can be rapidly changed from one weapon type to another by the simple expedient of exchanging the plug-in ballistic module.

CHARACTERISTICS

Dimensions: 370 × 355 × 313 mm

Weight: 15 kg

Power supply: 19 – 32 V DC (24 V nominal)

Consumption: 60 W

STATUS

Series production. Believed to have been supplied for export.

CONTRACTOR

Brandt Armements, 52 avenue des Champs-Elysées, 75008 Paris, France.

4580.161

ATAC ARTILLERY COMPUTER

A field artillery firing aid (ATAC) is under development by Brandt Armements, and is expected to be available for delivery in 1985. The system comprises a small hand-held digital computer and a console. The computer will perform all calculations for the firing operations of mortars, howitzers and cannon, and is particularly designed for use in autonomous operations where centralised control facilities are not available.

When the lightweight computer unit is fitted to the console, it becomes a system capable of integration into an automated artillery network. The ATAC system can be adapted to any particular weapon (and ammunition type) in the above categories by means of appropriate plug-in modules. Each of these modules carries eight ballistics. The computer has a semi-permanent data memory that can store nine gun

ATAC portable field artillery computer

positions, 99 target locations, 20 observer locations, ten datum positions, safety data, meteorological information (sounding data Stanag. 4082) and prevailing conditions, and other data such as powder temperature and muzzle velocity.

The main functions performed include firing preparation using the arc method, fire control, fire for effect, special firing missions (eg moving targets), and survey. ATAC can be linked to other ATAC computers by cable or radio links, as can the gun remote data display equipment and observers' terminals. Built-in test facilities are incorporated.

CHARACTERISTICS

Dimensions: 230 × 165 × 85 mm (with batteries)

Weight: 3 kg (approx) with batteries

Display: LCD 160-character screen

Power supply: 24 V DC

Endurance: 1 week normal use

Environmental: Military –25 to +55° C

STATUS

Development.

CONTRACTOR

Brandt Armements, 52 avenue des Champs-Elysées, 75008 Paris, France.

3187.161

SIROCCO METEOROLOGICAL RADAR STATION (QR-MX-2)

The Sirocco system comprises an I-band tracking radar for tracking meteorological sounding balloons, and associated telemetry system, processing equipment, and provisions for the transmission of meteorological data for use by artillery units. The last of these may or may not be equipped with an Atila computing system (**3188.161**).

The complete system is built as a self-contained land-mobile unit, the tracking radar being mounted on a two-wheeled trailer, and an air conditioned SH 17 shelter is carried on the towing vehicle. The latter houses the operating crew, the radar and telemetry operating console, a radio-telegraphy system with built-in modem, and stowage for the sondes and radar reflectors. In addition to the radar, the trailer carries the telemetry receiver and two electric generators.

The Sirocco system produces standard met messages, on-line, for transmission by teleprinter or via a radio-telegraphy link for use by artillery units. The messages provide wind speed and direction, and air temperatures at a series of standard altitudes. Maximum range is in excess of 130 km and angular accuracy is better than 0·05° SD. Range can be measured to within 5 m and windspeed can be determined with an accuracy of better than one knot (0·5 m/s).

CHARACTERISTICS

Radar: I-band

Peak power: 80 kW

Sirocco mobile meteorological station deployed

Receiver: 2-axis monopulse

Ranging: Digital in 5 m increments

Angular tracking limits: –8 to +160° elevation; unlimited azimuth

Max range: >130 km

Angular accuracy: Better than 1 mil

Range accuracy: Better than 5 m

Windspeed accuracy: Better than 1 knot (0·5 m/s)

STATUS

In series production and ordered for French and foreign forces.

CONTRACTOR

Electronique Serge Dassault, 55 quai Carnot, 92214 Saint-Cloud, France.

3934.161

ATIBA ARTILLERY FIRE CONTROL SYSTEM

The ATIBA system has been derived from the French Atila (**3188.161**) artillery automation system and is designed to provide fire calculations for artillery formations of lesser scale, ie at battery level. However there are provisions for integrating ATIBA systems into a larger overall system such as Atila when appropriate and if required.

The ATIBA artillery fire control system provides for control of a battery of up to eight guns of any calibre, performs firing calculations for each gun using data provided by up to ten observation posts, ballistic data for any calibre, charge, shell and fuze, and standard STANAG 4061 meteorological message inputs. Trajectory calculation time is less than five seconds for six guns. The system also performs related functions such as survey calculations and various operator option tasks.

The equipment consists of the   ntral processor and control unit which can be fitted in any type of vehicle, such as a Jeep or truck, a number (up to eight) of gun display units (GDUs) located at each gun position, and a 1200 baud radio link (wire or radio) connecting the central battery unit to the GDUs and observer positions. The observer posts are equipped with radio sets and modems permitting the exchange of data in digital form. The battery unit and the GDUs are provided with display panels for the presentation of firing data, command orders and other relevant data. At the central battery unit these facilities extend to man/machine interface facilities such as a plasma display screen, keyboard and printer. The plasma display screen capacity is 256 characters.

The central processor is based on a CIMSA military computer of the 15M series and it performs the following functions:

(1) calculation of the firing data for each gun

(2) determination of the charge with respect to the battery target-range

CIMSA gun display unit (GDU) is used at individual gun positions in ATIBA and ATILA artillery automation systems

(3) processing of any targets, including point and linear targets, in regard to the best distribution of rounds on the target, and the number of rounds per type of shell required

(4) possible mixes of ammunition types to achieve engagement objectives

(5) fire adjustment

(6) determination of registration firing corrections for each charge

(7) dividing the battery into two sections to engage two different targets.

All the programs needed for the various survey functions exist in the standard software package.

The input data at the battery unit is aided by grids displayed on the screen which list the parameters required appropriate to the function selected. A check is made to indicate to the operator any errors he may have made. By means of the keyboard he is able to insert meteorological data, ballistic data, logistic information, gun co-ordinates, observer and target co-ordinates. Fire requests are entered in a similar fashion. Computed firing data is transmitted to individual guns where the GDUs present data on type of shell and fuze, number of rounds, the charge, bearing(s), elevation(s), fuze time, and triggering mode. Status of guns is returned to the battery unit over the same data link.

A group of ATIBAs can be combined to form one regiment or division Atila without modification other than the addition of a fire co-ordination centre. The latter facility enables the following additional functions to be performed:

(1) centralisation of fire requests at a higher level (regiment or division)

(2) evaluation of the tactical situation and the threat

(3) management of six ATIBA systems from a single co-ordination centre

(4) division of targets among batteries to achieve better concentration of fire on a given target

(5) improved management of ammunition.

STATUS

Under evaluation by French Army and on order for at least one foreign country, with others pending. Series production had started by the latter part of 1982.

CONTRACTOR

CIMSA – Compagnie d'Informatique Militaire Spatiale et Aéronautique, 10-12 avenue de l'Europe, 78140 Vélizy, France.

3188.161

ATILA ARTILLERY AUTOMATION SYSTEM

The Atila (artillery automation) system is a data processing system designed to fulfil three major operational requirements of artillery regiments:

(1) computing: this is concerned with the rapid and automatic calculation of ballistic data taking into account such parameters as topography, meteorological conditions, sizes and locations of targets, and locations of gun batteries

(2) transmission: the communication of calls for fire by individual forward observers to the command post, and the transmission of firing data to guns is performed by the system. Automatic inter-command post links provide for the mutual exchange of information

(3) management: decision making is speeded and enhanced by storage of the tactical situation in the computer memory, and by virtue of the facilities provided for man/machine dialogue.

Developed by the French Army (DTAT) in collaboration with CIMSA, an affiliate of Thomson-CSF, the system automates repetitive tasks and provides fire direction control officers with the means for optimised utilisation of available fire power.

To meet the needs of different organisational structures, ie from the autonomous battery to the artillery group which combines the fire from 18 batteries, CIMSA has organised automation of these units around two types of vehicle both of which are based on the AMX-10 in the French Army system;

(1) fire centre vehicle (fire control post) containing the computer which essentially executes fire calculation functions: this is a technical centre. (AMX-10 PCH SAF)

(2) a command vehicle for the relevant fire unit commander (battery commander, regiment commander, or the group commander): this is a tactical centre. (AMX-10 PCH SAL).

The following elements are linked to these two vehicles:

(A) artillery observers who have a terminal to send their message coded for fire requests, fire adjustments, intelligence messages. This information is automatically sent to the fire centre vehicle via radio link

ATILA system chain of command extends to individual batteries or guns. Fire direction centre vehicle (right) seen with GCT-155 SP howitzer

(B) the guns receive the fire centre computer-generated fire data on a remote display unit.

Automatic digital data links ensure the reliable and rapid exchange of data between these various elements of the system, using modems and standard radio sets.

Other fire elements involved in the overall system are the various gun sub-units, and other units which provide input data required for the system. In the latter category are sources of meteorological information; field artillery radar; enemy battery locating radar; and sound ranging system. Gun sub-units (eg batteries within a regimental formation) are linked to the fire centre vehicle and receive fire commands and other information via the automatic data transmission network, They are equipped with either the same sort of vehicle (fire control post and/or commander's vehicle) which permit autonomous operation of these sub-units, or simply terminals that provide two-way communications with other elements. All the information gathered from the system input sources mentioned above is centralised at the technical fire centre which produces appropriate synopses and forwards them to the command centre via the automatic data transmission networks.

The Atila system designed for the French Army is organised around a hardened IRIS 35M or 15M computer located at regimental HQ (duplicated for the back-up mode or for transfer purposes). This computer fulfils the following functions: ballistic and related calculations (including selection of firing units); communications management; and tactical management in support of the command staff.

The IRIS 35M computer has a 64 K-byte memory, and a memory access coupler produced by Sagem provides for connecting the computer to: one to four Sagem MS 200 disc stores of 256 K-byte capacity; one to four Schlumberger PS 6020 mag-tape units; and four to eight additional peripheral devices such as displays. The PS 6020 unit is eight-track equipment capable of storage densities of 800 bits/in, rates of 20 000 bit/s, and a recording speed of 25 in/s. Tape length is 120 m. The alpha-numeric display console is by Sintra, having a capacity of 24 lines of 80 characters on a screen of 19 × 14 cm.

Other peripherals include a Sagem AI 28 teleprinter, and 1200 baud modems by CIT. The link equipment for transmission of communications from observers to the command post is provided by TRT and is capable of transmitting 32-bit messages at a rate of 200 bauds. Firing data are sent from the centre to the guns at a rate of 1200 bauds.

CHARACTERISTICS

Organisation: Battery – regiment (3 batteries) – group (3 regiments)

Basic fire unit: 6 – 8-gun battery

Observers: Up to 36 positions

ATILA system battalion fire direction centre computer

Recorded targets: 150

Simultaneously handled targets: 3

Recorded topographical points: 150

Safety zones: 20 per regiment

Masks: 10 per battery

Trajectory calculation accuracy: 1/2000 in range; 0·5 m in deflection

Transmission time between two posts: 2 s

System reaction time: 1 regiment on 1 target = 1 minute

ATILA II:

In the latter half of 1983 CIMSA revealed a new version of the Atila system configured for use with different artillery organisational structures to those of the original system. Atila II is also believed to incorporate certain design improvements made possible by experience with operation of Atila I, but the basic objectives of both systems are essentially the same.

STATUS

A prototype regimental structure system underwent French Army trials during 1977. Series production of the Atila system for the French Army began in 1978. In the same year, serial production of a regimental Atila system for export was started. The latter system includes five computers: two at the active regimental command post, two at the passive regimental command post, and one at each battery.

Issue of Atila hardware to French Army artillery units began in 1980 and deployment is expected to continue progressively until 1986. Work is in progress on a later version which will be known as Atila II.

A version of Atila has been sold to Saudi Arabia for direction of French-built GCT-155 self-propelled guns, and the designation of this export version is Palmier.

CONTRACTOR

CIMSA – Compagnie d'Informatique Militaire Spatiale et Aéronautique, 10-12 avenue de l'Europe, 78140 Velizy, France.

GERMANY (FEDERAL REPUBLIC)

4231.181

COMBAT MONITORING SYSTEM

The Combat Monitoring System (CMS) is designed as a tactical command system for target acquisition and identification, threat analysis and target assignment in battlefield combat situations. The equipment can be divided into two functional packages, the weapon system data acquisition unit (WSDA) and the central control and command station (CCS). The data input and output to each participating fire unit is made via a WSDA. These are integrated in each fire unit. The weapon carriers attached to the CMS are monitored and controlled by a central station. This may be installed in a shelter, standard cabin or any armoured vehicle.

The system can be used to monitor or control weapons on the ground or in the air. Data relevant to combat action is transmitted from each weapon system either by FM radio or by cable link, to a central control. After the threat is analysed and the target interrogated by IFF, a target assignment is given to the appropriate weapon system. The tactical situation is presented to the command controller on a colour display unit. A printout of the action is available for analysis.

The CMS can be operated as a tactical training system. Alternatively, it can be used as a range instrumentation system for assessing weapon systems.

CONTRACTOR

Dornier GmbH, PO Box 1420, 8990 Friedrichshafen 1, Federal Republic of Germany.

4144.161

HEROS COMPUTER-ASSISTED COMMAND SYSTEM

Studies were initiated in the late 1970s by the Federal German Army into the development of a computer-based command, control and information system, known from its German title (Heeres-Fuhrungs-informationssystem fur die Rechnergestutzte Operationsfuhrung in Staben) as HEROS. Background and some details of the system appeared under the above entry number in the 1982-83 edition of *Jane's Weapon Systems*. The following paragraphs summarise information obtained since then.

HEROS is intended to integrate all primary and special staff areas with the German Army. It is designed to:
(1) support army operations
(2) enhance command and control of own forces and deployment of joint reconnaissance systems
(3) provide a fast flow of information to the Joint Staff, to air force and navy staffs, as well as to NATO and Allied Headquarters.

The planned implementation of the programme envisages the following phased system evolution:

Mobile Systems:
(1) HEROS-2/1 Corps, Division and Brigade Staffs
(2) HEROS-4 Home Defence Brigades

Static Systems:
(1) HEROS-3 Army Staff/Army HQ
(2) HEROS-5 Territorial Army Staffs/Traffic Routing
(3) HEROS-6 Additional tasks in case of crisis, tension and mobilisation
(4) HEROS-7 Additional peacetime tasks.

Currently two of the above versions are under development, a testbed version of HEROS-2/1 designated HEROS-2/1-X, and the first phase of HEROS-3 which is known as HEROS-3-1. Brief descriptions of each version follow.

HEROS-2/1-X

This provides for operational testing by the German Army with the following objectives:

(1) test and validation of operational requirements for the final system to support operational command in corps, division and brigade command posts
(2) checking of critical technical elements such as data communications and program-controlled display of tactical situation
(3) collection of decision criteria regarding the lowest data entry level (brigade or battalion)
(4) test facilities for military peripheral equipment or comparable experimental models.

Software was developed initially on a large computer to implement all functions of the system and was then transferred to mini-computers of the testbed system. This comprises the following command post cells at division and brigade level:
(1) Information Cell
(2) Tactical Operations Cell (G2/G3 and S2/G3, respectively)
(3) Support Cell (artillery).

Facilities are provided for simulation of other staff areas of main command posts. Each command post cell is equipped with a computer, disc storage, two alpha-numeric consoles, printer, the command post network interface, and communications equipment. Other hardware and facilities are: a plotter for three-colour hard-copies on paper or foil and interfaces for AutoKo and combat net radio in the Information Cell; a two-colour graphic display unit with laser projection onto maps (1 m × 1 m) in the Tactical Operations Cell GG2/G3 (division level); and a graphic plasma display unit with slide projection of maps in the Tactical Operations Cell S2/G3 (brigade level). The battalion level command posts are equipped with input/output devices interconnected with the brigade command post via combat net radio.

Information exchanged between command posts is encrypted and formatted according to NATO standards so that interoperability with other national or NATO systems is possible. During 1983 West Germany and the USA completed a memorandum of understanding to the effect that HEROS and the US Army command and control system SIGMA should be interoperable, and bilateral working groups have been established to implement this agreement. The first task of the SIGMA/HEROS working groups is to develop the necessary interface equipment and procedures, and later to demonstrate interoperability in technical and tactical tests.

As now configured, HEROS-2/1-X provides these functions:
(1) editing of formatted and free text messages
(2) redundant storage of information in a data base
(3) display of command and control information as maps and tabular data
(4) system control
(5) command post internal and external communications.

HEROS-3-1

This represents the first phase of development of the principal static version of the HEROS system and it was decided to gain practical experience by operational use of this evolutionary version in Wintex/Cimex 81 NATO exercise for staff. Feasibility had been demonstrated during Wintex/Cimex 79 with a testbed system.

The hardware configuration consists of a central computer and input/output devices capable of direct dialogue intercommunication via data transmission facilities. The central computer complex (DVA HEROS-3-1) is based on a Siemens 7541 machine together with appropriate storage devices (such as discs or drum memories) and central input/output devices. Separate work stations remote from the Army Staff HQ are equipped with data displays with hard copy and/or punched tape input/output devices, and these are interconnected by a secure data link.

For the graphic display of the situation at the main operations centre, staff are provided with a large-screen (3 m × 3 m, or 2 m × 2 m) four-colour BM 8501 display. Selected parts of the map are projected from a diapositive/slide onto the screen, while tactical information is positioned there directly by the processing system itself. The displayed tactical information can be plotted by an operator as a hard copy either on paper or on foil. The large-screen display and plotter are both linked to a control computer (PDP 11/34) which is connected with the central DVA HEROS-3-1 processor by data link.

For analysis by means of tabular information, there are operator positions with displays having a capacity of 24 lines of 80 characters each, and each display is combined with a printer that can print the screen information as a hard copy. Input/output of messages on paper tape takes place at the Staff centre, in the information centre, the army intelligence centre, and at the corps/territorial commands/divisions by intelligent terminals. These terminals are combined with tape reader/punch units and the hard copy devices.

The HEROS-3-1 central computer complex is based on a Siemens 7541 machine which employs the BS 2000 time-sharing operating system. The BS 2000 supports the time-sharing mode as well as local and remote batch processing, so there is a uniform command language for all classes of operation. The software of the Siemens 9687 data transmission preprocessor performs all tasks such as transmission procedures, and information processing.

Peripheral hardware consists of seven discs with a total storage capacity of 882 Mbyte, four magnetic tape units with a speed of 780 Kbyte a second, a high-speed printer, a central console with control screen, keyboard and printer, and the Siemens 9687 data transmission pre-processor which is linked to the distributed peripheral equipment.

The last hardware category comprises the large-screen display and the plotter which are controlled by a PDP 11/34 mini-computer connected to the central processor by a data link, and three PDP 11/03 microprocessors for the processing of data transmission, control of the plotter and of the large-screen display. The PDP 11/34 operates with the RSX 11M (multi-user) real-time operating system, and the PDP 11/03s use the RSX 11S (single-user) operating system. Other distributed hardware consists of two disc units with a total capacity of five Mbyte, a display and a printer connected to the PDP 11/34 and a number of Siemens 8160 displays with report printers as alpha-numeric terminals, Siemens 6610 intelligent terminals with printers and paper tape input/output facilities.

The system manages and supervises a supply file which contains all unchecked input information; a message file containing all formally checked information; the situation file which contains all information checked as far as format and content are concerned; a symbol file with all information available for the graphic display; and a symbol file containing all tactical symbols currently being displayed on the large-screen display.

STATUS
Development of both HEROS-2/1-X and HEROS-3-1 is continuing, with Siemens AG as the main contractor, together with GFS-MIDAS and INFODAS.

CONTRACTORS
Siemens AG, Hofmannstrasse 51, D-8000 Munich 70, Federal Republic of Germany.

GFS-MIDAS Gesellschaft fur Fuhrungssysteme mbH, Siegburgerstrasse 215, D-5000 Cologne, Federal Republic of Germany.

INFODAS Gesellschaft fur Informations-verarbeitung mbH, Rhonestrasse 2, D-5000 Cologne, Federal Republic of Germany.

1626.161

FALKE ARTILLERY COMPUTER SYSTEM

Falke is a computerised artillery fire direction system for use at battalion or battery level. The system was developed by AEG-Telefunken for the Federal German Ministry of Defence in close co-operation with the military user. The result of this co-operation is a system which meets the present and most of the future military requirements.

The central unit of the Falke system is the universal military computer AEG 80-20 MARS. This computer is fully militarised, especially designed for mobile operation under rough operating conditions and available in three versions, differing in computing power and memory capacity. It can be run on a 24 V DC power supply. The word-length is 16 bits and the maximum main memory capacity is 1 Mbyte. Many standardised interfaces for different military peripherals are provided. Special peripherals include a hermetically sealed magnetic tape cassette unit (PLG 38) for program loading (soon to be replaced by a magnetic bubble cassette unit) and a data display and transmission unit (radio and wire transmission) for use by the fire direction officer, the forward observers and as gun display (OAZ 794).

The application programs are: fire direction for various calibres; simultaneous fire control for different firing units; surveying and reconnaissance procedures; and evaluation of meteorological data.

For operating the computer a flexible dialogue principle is used. This means that the computer itself calls for all necessary input data and performs various

Display and transmission unit OAZ 794

Military computer AEG 80-20 MARS

on a 120 km balloon tracking radar, a one-, two- or three-channel radiosonde system and a computerised evaluation system, is available. Radar, radiosonde system and evaluation system (also using the military computer AEG 80-20 MARS) together are installed in a single standard two-wheel trailer, so avoiding any external connections.

STATUS
The Falke system is in production and systems have been delivered to the German Bundeswehr in quantity, as well as to different customers abroad.

CONTRACTOR
AEG-Telefunken, Anlagentechnik, Geschäftsbereich Hochfrequenztechnik, Postfach 1730, 7900 Ulm, Federal Republic of Germany.

plausibility checks. Thus the operation of the Falke system is very easy to learn and to execute. Furthermore, since operation is fully programmable, all specific requirements and procedures can easily be realised.

For the acquisition of meteorological data, a fully mobile and militarised meteorological system, based

---

3797.161

LEMSTAR TANK FIRE CONTROL SYSTEM

The LEMSTAR integrated fire control system has been designed to meet the demand for a fire capability on the move. The basic concept and the philosophy of LEMSTAR is equivalent to the fire control systems of the latest Western tanks, for instance the German Leopard 2 and the American XM1. Most of the system components of LEMSTAR are field proven hardware and already produced in series for various tank applications.

The original intention in proposing the LEMSTAR was not only to equip the West German tank Leopard 1, it was also the intention to make it available for various retro-fitting programmes of, for example, the M48, M60, Centurion etc. Firing on the move will be possible by means of a primarily stabilised gunner's sight with integrated laser rangefinder, a ballistic computer, and a slaved main weapon. In order to meet fully these requirements even on the move, the system comprises the following main components:

(1) combined laser rangefinder aiming sight, primarily stabilised (LV/2 Stab or RZG Stab)
(2) standard fire control computer (FLER-H or FLER-M)
(3) weapon stabilisation system which is slaved to the primarily stabilised gunner's sight

(4) position data transmission between sight and weapon by synchros of high accuracy.

A simple block diagram is shown in the diagram. The most essential asset of the system philosophy is the combination of a primarily stabilised line of sight (LOS) with the slaved weapon. This is an essential prerequisite for achieving high overall performance. Further, this is the most important feature, which is claimed to distinguish LEMSTAR from other fire control systems for tanks.

By use of a primarily stabilised gunner's sight with an integrated laser rangefinder, the aiming and tracking of the target is more precise, even on the move. The stabilisation accuracy of the LOS is essentially higher against that of the gun due to the lower mass, the smaller size and mechanical tolerances of the sight. In order to achieve highest hit probability, the computer receives various inputs by special sensors such as air pressure, air temperature, crosswind, powder temperature, and cant angle; further input signals are: gunwear, jump and droop, target range, vehicle velocity, target angular velocity, terrain slope, ammunition selection, and turret position.

All these inputs are automatically processed for computing the super-elevation and lead angle which are affecting (again automatically and directly) the gun without influencing the LOS. This means that the gunner keeps the LOS continuously on the target. The gun will be kept in the exact fire position via the synchro chain. After pushing the fire button firing will be released when coincidence between LOS and gun bore sight occurs. Because of the high coincidence frequency, the time gap is very low.

Thus, a high first round hit probability, even on the move and against moving targets is achieved. The functions described above belong to the gunner. The tasks of the commander depend on the tactical requirements of the user. Therefore, the possible equipment starts with a simple panoramic periscope up to a primarily stabilised one which is able to take similar functions as the proposed gunner's sight. If night fighting capability is required, AEG-Telefunken recommends the LLL-TV night sight type PZB 200. This is a rugged proven unit for gunshield mounting with separate monitors for gunner and commander. Both sights can be easily incorporated into the LEMSTAR system.

The stabilised rangefinder aiming sight (3580.193) serves the gunner as his main sight for observation, aiming and tracking, and ranging the target. It contains the optical periscope with two magnification steps, the integrated Nd-glass laser rangefinder and the stabilisation equipment. The moving range of the stabilised LOS is ±4° in azimuth and in elevation in accordance with the main weapon allowing for the correction angle of super-elevation. The three optical paths, laser-transmitter, low power and high power sight channel combined with laser receiver are deflected by one common mirror, which is fully stabilised to ensure the constant optical alignment under all dynamic conditions. The sight is monocular. The range is digitally displayed in the eyepiece and in case of multiple echoes there are indication lamps for one, two and more echoes. In total, three different ranges can be detected and stored from one laser transmitter pulse.

The Type FLER-H fire control computer (**1619.161**) consists of the following sub-assemblies: sensors;

vertical gyro; control panel; central computer unit; 400 Hz inverter. The computer sensors can be extended to maximum performance by adding a complete line of sensor units such as crosswind, ammunition temperature etc. Later versions of LEMSTAR may incorporate the FLER-M fire control computer.

The objective of the computer as a part of an integrated fire control system is to improve the firing capacity by increased hit probability, increased effective range, and reduction of the time between target acquisition and firing.

The computer calculates the super-elevation and

the lead angle in azimuth (due to the curved trajectory) from the ammunition selected, the target range, internal and external ballistic data, trunnion cant and the terrain slope. Correction angles in azimuth and elevation are calculated taking into account the laying speed during target tracking. The computer controls the setting of these angles at the sights and weapon. The inputs are measured automatically and fed into the computer, and alignment of weapon and sight is corrected automatically.

The weapon stabilisation system (WSS) is slaved to the gunner's stabilised sight and its task is to slave the gun to the LOS allowing for the correction angles generated by the computer. The LOS is guided by the gunner's handle. Furthermore, the WSS compensates for the disturbance of the gun caused by the moving hull in such a way that the gun is kept stabilised during travel.

The WSS contains the two sub-system components: hydraulic weapon drive pack, and WSS-electronics including the sensors.

The hydraulic weapon drive pack is a field proven hardware with respect to performance and reliability and has been produced in several thousands of units (eg for the West German Leopard 1).

The position of the gun in elevation and azimuth is sensed by gyro units. The electrical synchro chain links the stabilised gunner's sight with the gun. It contains precision resolvers as input elements at the sight and as reception elements at the weapon and both elements are selected as a pair to ensure the high accuracy required.

STATUS

LEMSTAR is proposed for refit applications in MBTs such as the M48, M60 and Centurion. No specific programmes have yet been identified officially.

In early 1981, LEMSTAR had been tested by the West German Army in a Leopard 1 tank and the possibility of refitting all Federal Republic Leopard 1s with the system was under consideration. It is understood that LEMSTAR has also been proposed for Italian Leopard 1 tanks and the system was being fitted to an Austrian Steyr-Daimler-Puch Panzerjaeger, an M48 and an AMX-30 tank for trials. A total of four pre-production systems had been completed.

CONTRACTOR

AEG-Telefunken, Anlagentechnik, Fachbereich Flugwesen und Sondertechnik Steuerungs und Regelungssysteme, Industriestrasse 29, 2000 Wedel (Holst), Federal Republic of Germany.

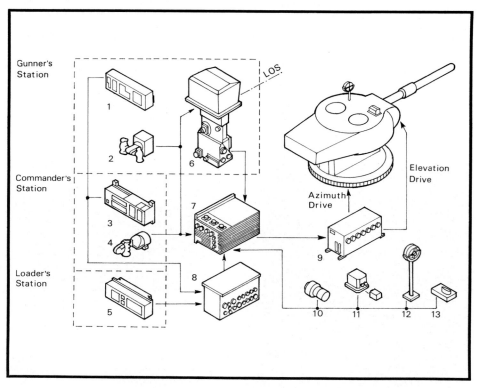

LEMSTAR integrated tank fire control system
(**1**) *gunner's control panel* (**2**) *gunner's handle* (**3**) *commander's control panel* (**4**) *commander's handle* (**5**) *loader's control panel* (**6**) *gunner's sight primarily stabilised with laser range finder* (**7**) *computer and stabilisation electronics* (**8**) *operation mode logic* (**9**) *weapon stabilisation and slave electronics* (**10**) *vertical gyro* (**11**) *powder temperature sensor* (**12**) *crosswind sensor* (**13**) *air data electronics*

1619.161
FLER-H TANK FIRE CONTROL COMPUTER

The FLER-H is a hybrid computer of modular construction, principally designed and developed for use in tank fire control systems, but capable of other military applications such as anti-aircraft and artillery systems. The main elements of the computer are the computer core store and the computer control unit, plus a number of peripheral units. These include a vertical sensor for trunnion cant and terrain slope, an air data sensor, and a powder temperature measurement unit. The store is largely composed of integrated circuits, and the processing of non-linear data such as elevation angle and correction data is effected by hybrid multipliers and using polynomial approximation. Modular ballistic units provide for the known parameters of the various types of ammunition used. Other input data apart from that previously mentioned consists of range, target tracking in azimuth and elevation, crosswind component, gun tube wear, departure error, and parallax. Outputs of the FLER-H cover the correction angles in the form of AC electrical signals to control the sights and the weapon to within 0·5 mrad. These correction angles are inserted into the commander's and gunner's sights and into the weapon system so as to create an independent line of sight without disturbing elevation and azimuth.

The improvement in weapon accuracy resulting from the use of the computer system depends on the

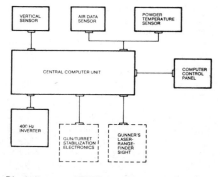

Block diagram of FLER-H tank fire control system

weapon and ammunition used and the range of the target. A factor of improvement in first-round hit probability of three or four is by no means an impossibility.

The modern successor of FLER-H employs current digital technology. Various types are stated to be available of differing performance, but no details have been received.

CHARACTERISTICS

Ammunition types: Choice of 4 ballistics
Distance range: 400 – 3000 m
Calculation accuracy: ≤0·1 mrad

Target velocity: Azimuth 40 mrad/s; elevation 15 mrad/s
Air pressure: 810 – 1215 mbar
Air temperature: –35 to +65°C
Crosswind: –20 to +20 m/s
Powder temperature: –30 to +45°C
Trunnion cant: –12 to +12°
Terrain slope: –20 to +20°
Test circuits: BITE
Power supply: 28 V DC, 90 W
  26 V DC, 400 Hz, 10 W
Weight and dimensions
Core: 21 kg, 360 × 272 × 240 mm
Vertical sensor: 4·5 kg, 250 × 190 × 190 mm
Air data sensor: 6·8 kg, 345 × 220 × 178 mm
Powder temperature sensor: 4·1 kg, 205 × 130 × 160 mm + (125 × 65 × 75 mm)
Control unit: 3·2 kg, 180 × 215 × 105 mm
STATUS

The FLER-H computer is in series production for use in Leopard 1 A4 tanks. It also forms part of the LEMSTAR tank fire control system proposed for modernising programmes for other types such as the M48, M60 and Centurion (see **3797.161** in this section).

CONTRACTOR

AEG-Telefunken, Anlagentechnik, Fachbereich Flugwesen und Sondertechnik Steuerungs und Regelungssysteme, Industriestrasse 29, 2000 Wedel (Holst), Federal Republic of Germany.

INTERNATIONAL

3939.161
BC81 (Re 83/FARGO) ARTILLERY COMPUTER

The BC81 artillery computer is a battery level digital computer for calculating firing data for guns of various calibres, taking into account the usual meteorological, ballistic and other parameters. In service with the Swiss Army, for which it was developed, the system is designated Re 83, FARGO. The processor is a version of the British Aerospace 1412A (formerly Sperry 1412A), which is used in a variety of other military applications, among them co-ordinate conversion for the Exocet MM38 anti-ship missile system (**1156.221**). The standard software package provides for firing calculations for nine different types of guns and ammunition, as well as a number of targets and observer positions, and has a full survey capability. Input data includes meteorological information, target co-ordinates (including altitude), and ballistic characteristics. In

view of the system's intended operating environment (the Swiss Alpine region) elaborate provisions have been made for insertion of crest clearance zones and other restrictions due to the nature of the terrain.
DEVELOPMENT
Began in 1977 at Bracknell, in co-operation with the Swiss company Zallweger Uster AG. Extensive Swiss Army trials and evaluation preceded production decision in 1982/83.
STATUS
Production for Swiss Army confirmed in 1983; large order placed with estimated total value £14 million. Production deliveries due to start 1985.
CONTRACTOR
British Aerospace Dynamics Group, Bracknell Division, Downshire Way, Bracknell, Berkshire RG12 1HL, England. (Formerly Sperry Gyroscope).

BC81 artillery computer incorporates 1412A digital processor. The Swiss Re 83 version differs in minor details

4755.181
KOLLMORGEN CVFCS

The Kollmorgen combat vehicle fire control system (CVFCS) is an advanced computer-based fire control system for fitting in existing MBTs, such as the M41, M47 and M48, without major vehicle modification. Development was carried out jointly by the Electro-optical division of Kollmorgen of the USA and Ferranti Computer Systems Ltd in the UK.

Although primarily designed for American M-series tanks, compact dimensions, low cost and ease of operation make the system suitable for use in a wide range of AFVs, including fire support and infantry combat vehicles. The system is modular in concept and consists of a small number of compact units which are located in various parts of the vehicle.

Data from external sensors is fed to the fire control computer which calculates the correct lead and super-elevation angles required to hit the designated target during the gun-laying sequence. The system generates an aiming mark which is automatically injected into the gunner's sight. Parameters inserted into the computer also include: charge temperature, barrel wear, wind speed, and air temperature and pressure. There is automatic compensation for certain variable factors.

Inputs to the FCS computer which performs ballistic calculations, are accepted from the gunner's control panel, a laser sub-system, and other system sensors. All computations are performed under program control. The gunner's control panel combines the functions of a system control module, data entry terminal, and visual display, and this is the main interface between the vehicle crew and the

system. The gunner uses the controls to conduct system tests, insert crosswind values, and also to select the back-up mode in the event of a malfunction. An ammunition selector panel is used by the loader to inject the ammunition type into the computer so that appropriate ballistics are employed in calculation.

A turret displacement unit and a trunnion tilt sensor also form part of the FCS. The former provides basic data for the lead angle correction, and the trunnion tilt sensor measures deviations from the horizontal directly and inputs the data to the computer automatically, allowing the system to compensate for vehicle attitude during the firing sequence.

The primary sensor of the complete FCS is the sight, a modular monocular day/night instrument equipped with a laser rangefinder and unity vision periscope. Sight modules include the optics block, head module, laser, electronics junction box and vehicle mount. The head module incorporates a 2:1 motion reduction transmission which links the gun elevation position arm to the sight upper mirror. The optics module comprises the main body of the sight, and boresight adjustment is by means of fine azimuth/elevation rotation within the head module.

The laser module is made up of four replaceable units, including a sealed optics unit containing the laser resonator and receiver telescope, a ×2·5 beam expander telescope, a receiver unit with an avalanche photodiode and preamplifier, and a power supply unit.
CHARACTERISTICS
Range: 400 – 9995 m
Trunnion tilt: ± 30°
Crosswind: ± 25 m/s

Charge temperature: –40° to +65° C
Air temperature: –40° to +65° C
Air pressure: 700 – 800 mm Hg
Gun jump correction: ± 5 mil
Ammunition types: 6
MV correction: ± 100 m/s
Computation accuracy: 0·2 mil
Sight
Magnification: ×8
Field of view: 8° (day); 7° (night)
Exit pupil diameter: 6 mm (min)
Boresight adjustment range: ±8 mils
Direct vision FOV: 8·5° (elevation) × 18° (azimuth)
Elevation LOS rotation: +22/–18
Image intensifier tube: 25 mm
Laser rangefinder
Wavelength: 1·064 μm
Range accuracy: ±5 m
Pulse rate: 1/s (cont)
Output energy: 20 mJ (min)
Pulse width: 12 ns
Laser divergence: 0·45 mrad
Receiver FOV: 0·56 mrad
DEVELOPMENT
Development was undertaken jointly by Kollmorgen and Ferranti Computer Systems Ltd.
STATUS
Production. No contract details have been disclosed.
CONTRACTORS
Kollmorgen Corporation, Electro-optical Division, 374 King Street, Northampton, Massachusetts 01060, USA.

Ferranti Computer Systems Ltd, Cwmbran, Gwent NP44 7XX, Wales.

ISRAEL

4492.161
COMBAT ARTILLERY C³ SYSTEM

Combat is the name given by Elbit Computers Ltd to the artillery command, control and communications (C³) system they have designed to meet the needs of artillery formations at battery and battalion levels. The basic configuration is of a modular design which allows the addition of more units to increase the performance and range of facilities. The basic version of Combat provides for C³ functions necessary for operation at battery level. It consists of a battery C³ unit, a section chief display and communication unit for each gun, and a sight display unit for each sight. By the addition of an artillery computer the system will perform functions such as storing up to 30 positions, 100 targets, 15 simultaneous fire missions

and handling of two meteorological telegrams. By adding modems various additional functions can be incorporated to bring the above facilities to forward observers and enable forward observers to undertake tasks such as re-positioning of sights etc.

Combat hardware at the fire direction centre (FDC) is based on an artillery tactical command (ATC) unit, and this includes the ballistic computer and a measurement remote terminal (MRT). The FDC sub-system performs simultaneously on three networks (guns, battalion level, fire control) and displays updated status data on the battery in real-time. It carries the requested artillery computations itself or receives them from the artillery computer when incorporated in a larger system. Messages received or

transmitted are printed automatically. At the gun level, the hardware consists of the gun central unit (GCU), sight control monitor (SCM), the elevation sight monitor (ESM) and various other sensors and actuators. The gun sub-system receives and displays firing data and other command information sent by the FDC. Elevation and bearing sights are automatically set to the requested firing data. Data from sensors is reported via the gun sub-system to the FDC; for example, the gun sub-system receives measured muzzle velocities and transmits the mean values back to the FDC. Forward observers are equipped with a Mini-SACU (**4278.161**) which interfaces with a digital goniometer, a laser rangefinder, and a gyro north-seeker.

Conventional cable, or digital burst transmission radio links, can be used to interconnect the various elements of the complete Combat artillery C3 system.
STATUS
Production.
CONTRACTOR
Elbit Computers Ltd, PO Box 5390, Haifa 31053, Israel.

Artillery tactical command unit of Elbit Combat artillery C3 system

4278.161
SACU COMMAND AND CONTROL
The Israeli electronics concern, Elbit, produces a range of stand-alone digital communications units (SACU) for the transmission and management of most kinds of battlefield communications via line (twin conductor) or radio channels. The latter may employ FM and AM in the VHF, UHF or HF bands.

The basic SACU provides simplified, two-way high-speed burst data transmission in standard message format or as free text. The display incorporated in the unit leads the operator through the message entry sequence. Entries are made via the keyboard in accordance with a pre-stored list. Received messages are stored in a memory and displayed on operator request. The system provides for automatic message acknowledgment, and special purpose computations, such as ballistic or navigation calculations are optional. SACU interfaces with standard communications equipment. Optional interfaces include: printer, central processor, tape cassette, and teleprinter. A microprocessor controls the SACU operation and performs data processing functions. The keyboard is a sealed, flat surface, pressure activated device which is self-luminescent for night operation. Characters are formed by 5 × 7 dot arrays in the display which can present up to 256 characters.
CHARACTERISTICS
Data transmission: FSK at 300 or 1200 bits/s; DPSK at 2400 bits/s
Height: 355 mm
Width: 406 mm
Depth: 355 mm
Weight: 24·9 kg

Mini-SACU
This is another member of the SACU family which provides similar facilities to those of SACU (above) but which is packaged for use by forward observers and at observation posts. A touch-panel keyboard is provided for operator access to the system, and the unit has message coding facilities as well as error detection and correction. Other features include: high-speed burst mode transmission; radio network

SACU family with Mini-SACU on left and Micro-SACU on right

management; automatic message acknowledgement; microprocessor control; long- and short-term memory.

Micro-SACU
This small, hand-held version of Elbit's SACU serves the isolated soldier. It interacts with other components of the SACU family and central computers for integral C3 capability. Powered by an internal battery, power consumption is very low and a touch-panel keyboard operates in conjunction with a 96-character display.
CHARACTERISTICS
Data transmission: FSK at 75, 150, 300 or 1200 bits/s
Height: 220 mm
Width: 105 mm
Depth: 85 mm

Weight: 1·5 kg
Other members of the SACU family of equipment are:
TI-100: an interface unit for linking a teleprinter to SACU
GI-100: an interface for linking special-purpose equipment to SACU
LRCS 100: a long range communication SACU-based system for complex HF networks
PDI 100: a plasma display interface for major command and control centres
STATUS
In production and thought to be employed by the Israeli Defence Forces.
CONTRACTOR
Elbit Computers Ltd, PO Box 5390, Haifa 31053, Israel.

3192.161
DAVID ARTILLERY BATTERY COMPUTER
The DAVID artillery computer was developed to be used by the technical assistant at the battery level. Using LSI technology, a small and low-cost unit has been designed which performs all the calculations

required at this level: firing data, adjustments, fire for effect, corrections, survey, etc, as well as functional checks of data and procedures to prevent operator errors.

By using functional keys, the operating procedures are those in which the technical assistants are trained.

The calculations are, however, performed faster and without errors, all relevant factors being taken into account automatically. No tools or tables are required. The calculator stores the data necessary for handling all combinations of projectile, fuze, propellant type, and charge number for a specific type of gun. This data is stored in a plug-in memory. DAVID may be adapted to different types of gun by using the appropriate plug-in memory.

CHARACTERISTICS

Up to six guns can be handled (larger numbers optional)

Up to 28 targets may be stored

Fire data calculated within 5 s

Mounted on standard VRC adaptor in vehicle

Operates from vehicle battery (24 V), with internal battery for back-up

Environmental: –10 to +52° C ambient temperature 10 – 55 Hz, 0·03 in vibrations. Rain, sand, dust, humidity, and shock to IDF specifications

Size: 470 × 380 × 270 mm

Weight: 23 kg

STATUS

Field tests of the DAVID artillery computer system were performed in 1975, and entry into Israeli service was planned for 1977.

CONTRACTORS

RAFAEL, Armament Development Authority, Israel. Ministry of Defence, Haifa, PO Box 2082, Israel.

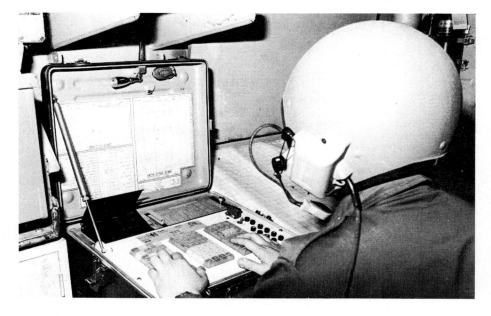

DAVID artillery computer equipment in use

3524.161
GUN DISPLAY SYSTEM

The Gun Display System (GDS) is designed to transfer essential data between the DAVID artillery battery computer (**3192.161**) at the fire direction centre (FDC) and individual guns of a battery. The system addresses each gun separately so that the pertinent information is passed only to the relevant gun, with the single exception that in the registration process, all the guns receive the firing data of the ranging gun. Each new command displayed at the gun activates an audio warning to draw the gun crew's attention to the new orders.

The GDS consists of three main sub-systems:
(1) the display units located at the guns
(2) the message centre for generating and receiving messages in the DAVID artillery computer
(3) a communication system.

A main display unit is mounted in front of each gun crew commander, and an additional display unit can be located near the gun sights. This slave unit will display only the relevant information for the particular

gun layer. The GDU receives firing commands issued by the message centre and displays them to the crew commander and individual gun layers. It receives and displays the following data:
(1) preparation for engagement: projectile and fuze types
(2) firing data: deflection, elevation, fuze setting, propellant and charge number
(3) range adjustment data: ranging gun and ammunition type for range adjustment (the ammunition type is displayed only to the ranging gun)
(4) fire for effect data: number of projectiles, firing mode and fire interval.

GDU transmits the following reports back to the message centre:
(1) acknowledgement of a new command (push-button)
(2) transmission error (by means of error detection techniques in the data transfer system)
(3) READY signal (push-button)
(4) FIRED signal (push-button). This also operates

the count of rounds fired
(5) MISFIRE signal (push-button)
(6) number of rounds remaining for completion of the mission (automatic)
(7) last round fired signal (operates automatically when round remaining reaches zero).

The numeric data, the projectiles and firing mode data appear on seven-segment indicators. The unit is also provided with a test button and an ON-OFF switch.

The message centre is packaged in the DAVID computer container, and uses spare keys of the DAVID keyboard, and no hardware or software changes are required in the DAVID system to add the gun display system. The communication system is based on normal telephone line communications techniques.

STATUS

Production.

CONTRACTORS

RAFAEL, Armament Development Authority, Israel.
Ministry of Defence, Haifa, PO Box 2082, Israel.

3870.161
ELBIT FIRE CONTROL SYSTEM

After a two-year development effort, Elbit Computers Ltd began production of a digital tank fire control system based on a microprocessor central processing unit (CPU) in 1979. Although designed primarily for the Merkava tank, Elbit's concept was to produce a modular system that was flexible enough to permit expansion to meet future requirements and advances, and at the same time to be basically suitable for use in all existing types of tank. Currently Elbit is manufacturing systems (known as the Matador FCS) for M-60, Centurion and other MBTs, based on its successful programme for the Merkava. In addition, the company has designed a low-cost system for retro-fitting in light tanks as well as for use on new AFVs.

In addition to the CPU, the system consists of three operation units (gunner, commander, and loader), control and feedback servo loops, and sensors. The system is capable of operation without power in an emergency. The gunner's unit is the main operation unit and it provides all manual inputs necessary for the ballistic computation. This unit also incorporates a logistics panel which enables bore-sighting and system built-in test as well as display of pre-selected inputs and computed outputs. The gunner's unit also includes controls for the selection of ammunition (any one of six types), and jump compensation for each type of ammunition in elevation and deflection. The commander's unit provides readout of the system's display, range and ammunition inputs and the loader's unit provides ammunition inputs. An

Elbit Matador FCS installed in Centurion MBT

integral facility for firing the gun at night is provided, based on the use of a second generation image intensifier.

The Matador system includes the following automatic sensors: laser rangefinder, turret cant angle sensor, target velocity sensor and a meteorological mast with crosswind velocity, air temperature and pressure sensors. The control loop transfers the computed super-elevation information to the hydraulic gun elevation servo and to the ballistic drive. In addition, deflection data is transferred to the moving reticle. The feedback loop ensures that the actual gun super-elevation and reticle deflection data are identical to the computed

data and will correct any error accordingly. Thus, the gunner's aiming reticle remains on target (full autolay capability) throughout the entire firing preparation process.

Parameters taken into the elevation and deflection compensation calculation typically include range, type of ammunition, cant angle, parallax, ammunition drift, gun jump, gun wear, moving target angular velocity, crosswind, barometric pressure, air temperature, charge temperature, and options such as muzzle reference system, line-of-sight angle, and gun resolver.

CHARACTERISTICS

Operating range: 400 – 5000 m

Elevation compensation: –1 to +99 mils

Deflection compensation: +25 mils

Cant angle range: ±15°

Jump compensation: ±5 mils (for all ammunition types)

Bore-sighting range: 400 – 5000 m

Ammunition selection: 6 types

Electrically inserted range: 300 – 5000 m

Computer memory: EPROM; 16 K total, 5 K utilised

Dimensions

Gunner's unit: 210 × 220 × 220 mm

Commander's unit: 85 × 115 × 134 mm

Loader's unit: 80 × 72 × 134 mm

Cant angle indicator: 100 × 160 × 190 mm

STATUS

Production and operational.

CONTRACTOR

Elbit Computers Ltd, Advanced Technology Centre, POB 5390, Haifa 31053, Israel.

ITALY

4490.161
SEDA AND SEDAB FIELD ARTILLERY FIRE CONTROL SYSTEMS

Galileo's field artillery control systems provide for the complete automation of communication, command and control for battery (SEDAB) up to battalion (SEDA). Both systems use the same main computer (CMP 32 **4233.161**) and the same terminals (DMT and GCD). Firing data computation is performed by numerical integration of the projectile equations, taking into account step by step all meteorological and ballistical conditions.

The SEDAB system manages tactical information and fire requests from three forward observers equipped with DMT terminals, computes firing data for six and eight guns, displays data and orders to the GCD gun terminals. The system can work on three independent missions and record up to 100 targets; the communication networks (radios and cable links) used by the system can be those normally in service.

The SEDA system is built with three or four SEDABs, linked to a CMP 32 computer at the battalion command post.

The systems inter-operate with several devices like muzzle velocity radars, goniometric rangefinder lasers, meteorological stations, land navigators etc.

CHARACTERISTICS

Main computers (battery and battalion): CMP 32 type, 32-bits, 128 K bytes memory, with tactical consoles

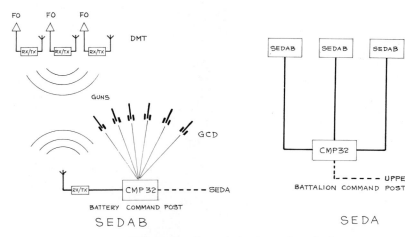

Galileo artillery fire control systems schematic diagram

Portable terminals for forward observers: DMT, 8-bit computer, 16 K bytes memory, with tactical console built-in modem
Power: 24 V DC
Environmental: FINABEL 2.C.10 (equivalent to MIL-STD-810); small sizes and low weights for easy man and vehicle transport

STATUS
Production
CONTRACTOR
Officine Galileo, Divisione Sistemi, 50013 Campi Bisenzio, Florence, Italy.

3932.161
C12 FIELD ARTILLERY COMPUTER

The Galileo Model C12 field artillery computer provides automation of all aspects of firing data computation for units up to field artillery group level. The computer employed is a general-purpose digital machine with a stored program and parallel operation. The man-machine interface consists of a special purpose control panel, which is provided with indicators and push-buttons etc marked with standard artillery terminology. Firing data is displayed for each gun of a battery. In addition to gun firing calculations, the C12 can carry out meteorological and survey computations.

Software packages have been compiled for a number of types of guns, and the C12 can be programmed for any gun or surface-to-surface rocket or missile firing data computation.
CHARACTERISTICS
Type: C12

Storage: 43 K, 32-bit memory; internally and/or externally expansible
Memory cycle time: 1·2 μs
Up to 64 addressable peripheral units.
STATUS
Production, believed operational with Italian Army.
CONTRACTOR
Officine Galileo, Divisione Sistemi, 50013 Campi Bisenzio, Florence, Italy.

4233.161
CMP 32 FIELD ARTILLERY COMPUTER

The CMP 32 field artillery computer provides automation of firing data computation for units up to field artillery group level. It is a developed version of the C 12 (**3932.161**). The software of the C 12 is compatible and can be incorporated in the CMP 32 system. The equipment provides trajectory computation, as in the C12, and field artillery data management including the position data of 99 objectives and 20 observers. An improved control panel enables firing data to be displayed for the reference guns of up to four batteries. Alternatively, the data for six guns in a single battery can be presented. In addition to gun firing computations, the CMP 32 can carry out meteorological and survey computations. The system computer can store firing data for a maximum of six different types of field artillery weapons.

CHARACTERISTICS
Type: CMP 32
Microprogram memory capacity: 1024 × 48 bits
Storage capacity: 28K 32-bit memory
Cycle time: 250 ns
Power consumption: 120 W
Operating temperature range: –40 to +60° C
CONTRACTOR
Officine Galileo, Divisione Sistemi, 50013 Campi Bisenzio, Florence, Italy.

4232.161
OG 14 L2B TANK FIRE CONTROL SYSTEM

The OG 14 L2B modular fire control system is designed for use in the new Italian OF 40 and Leopard medium tanks. It comprises an optical sight with a laser rangefinder, a digital ballistic computer, control panels for the gunner, commander and loader. With the additional sensors the ballistic computer can carry out lead angle computation with the tank and target in motion and integrate data for meteorological conditions, powder temperature and gun wear. The computer is designed also, to accept 120 mm gun ballistic data.

Optional dedicated software permits crew training. In the OG 14 L3 configuration, the standard gunner's optical sight is replaced by a stabilised optical system with an integral laser rangefinder and 8-14 micron infra-red thermal vision system.
CHARACTERISTICS
Laser rangefinder
Max range: 10 000 m
Max pulse rate: 1 pulse/s
Ballistics computer
Max computation distance: 4000 m
Max elevation correction: ±80°
Max traverse correction: ±30°
STATUS
In production.
CONTRACTOR
Officine Galileo, Divisione Sistemi, 50013 Campi Bisenzio, Florence, Italy.

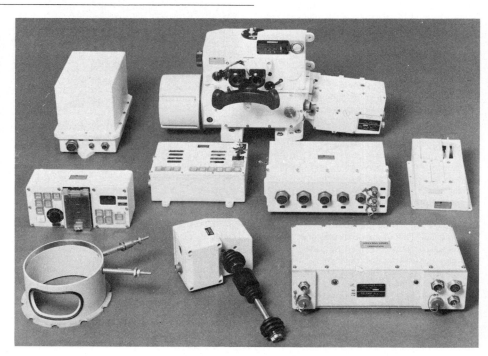

OG 14 L2B laser tank fire control system component units

4532.181
CATRIN
CATRIN (Sistema Campale Trasmissioni Integrato) is an automatic communication system intended for Corps area operations. It functions in the same way as other field communication systems being developed in Europe, such as the British Ptarmigan.

The CATRIN project is based on a feasibility study prepared between 1970 and 1975 by a consortium made up of Marconi Italiana, Selenia, IBM and Telettra. Technical and operational specifications in line with EUROCOM recommendations were established by the Italian Staff in 1978 and the project is presently carried out by the Italian Army with a consortium of Italian industries. The consortium, composed by Italtel, Face Standard, Telettra, GTE, Fatme and Marconi Italiana, is now working on various components of the system, in particular the central software and hardware. By 1983 the Army expects to have completed the study of the central software, of the supervision sub-system and of the single-channel radio access control, and procured a pre-prototype of the main switch.

The CATRIN network consists of trunk-nodes, whose equipment is mounted on shelters for maximum mobility, connected to one another by 32-channel UHF radio-links. Each trunk node may be linked by 16-channel radio relays to Corps and Division access nodes. More mobile users have a radio-access sub-system connected to a radio central.

The grid configuration of CATRIN gives the redundancy necessary to ensure continued operation in the event of damage or failures. A central supervision sub-system continuously checks the operativity of the entire system and gives the Corps signal commanding officer relevant information on the status of the network and instructions for redeployment.

Channels selected for CATRIN are 16 kb/s and 32 ko/s with speech digitally encoded by Delta modulation. Traffic security is obtained through integral ciphering of all communications. A super-cipher is provided to the most sensitive subscribers.

Each user is identified by a seven-digit number which is retained anywhere in the Corps area, no matter how many times he moves.

More mobile users, such as battlegroups or brigade HQs, can use the single-channel radio access (SCRA) sub-system. It gives a subscriber on the move the same local and trunk communication facilities as static users.

The SCRA equipment will be compatible with the new single-channel radio-net family being developed by the Italian Army. This will allow a radio-net user to become a CATRIN subscriber simply by coupling its radio to an SCRA adapter.

A typical Corps network manages 1276 speech users, 248 telegraph and 204 radio users.

The whole system is installed on class 1 and 2 UEO shelters, while terminal equipment is normally mounted on armoured vehicles.

CATRIN network can directly communicate with EUROCOM compatible systems, like the British Ptarmigan. It can also be connected to NICS, national civil and military networks and integrated with the combat-net radio use on the field by lower echelons units.
STATUS
Operational tests of the full system should start in 1986 and series production of the whole range of sub-systems will be possible by 1988, although many elements of CATRIN will be put into production much earlier.

Radio links and Delta multiplexer, for example, are already in production by Marconi Italiana for use in the Hawk anti-aircraft missile regiments.

KOREA (REPUBLIC OF)

4751.181
PYK-80 FIELD ARTILLERY COMPUTER
The PYK-80 field artillery computer is a digital microprocessor-based system which performs ballistic calculations and related computational tasks for the direction of various field artillery weapons. It is produced in a number of versions appropriate to specific types of weapons, as denoted in the following list:

PYK-80(V)1 – 105 mm howitzer
PYK-80(V)2 – 155 mm howitzer
PYK-80(V)3 – 8 inch howitzer
PYK-80(V)4 – 4·2 inch mortar
PYK-80(V)5 – multiple rocket launchers

The configuration of the computer can be seen from the illustration which shows the operator keyboard hinged from the front of the unit and the LED display. The unit is adaptable to any type of gun by means of interchangeable plug-in units which carry the necessary program and parameter changes. Calculations performed include firing data, firing adjustment, target data storage and checking, error checks and built-in test. Optional functions include

PYK-80 field artillery computer unit

firing data transmission and display using a gun display unit, and target data transmission by means of a data message device.

Input data to the system consists of target information, artillery data, and observer positions, FO information such as target position and adjustment data, meteorological data, and battery information including centre of arc bearing, gun position(s), and minimum elevation. Output data includes: firing data, quadrant elevation, charge number and fuze time.

The PYK-80 computer is connected to the FOs, higher command, a survey team for survey data, a met team and the gun batteries.
CHARACTERISTICS
Type: PYK-80 (V)
Width: 390 mm
Depth: 210 mm
Height: 360 mm
Weight: 16 kg
ROM: 16K bytes
RAM: 4K bytes
Cycle time (instruction): 1·2 microsec
STATUS
Production.
CONTRACTOR
Gold Star Electric Co Ltd, 27-2, Yeoeuido-dong, Yongdunpo-ku, Seoul 150, Republic of Korea.

4752.181
GSQ-250K REMOTELY MONITORED SENSOR SYSTEM
The GSQ-250K remotely monitored sensor system consists of a radio frequency monitor (RFM), miniaturised seismic detector (Minisid), audio add-on unit (AAU), and magnetic intrusion detector (Magid). The Minisid, AAU and Magid are implanted in the area to be observed, where they detect vibration, sounds and magnetic disturbances that might indicate human and/or vehicular activity. This information is sent back to the monitoring site in the form of VHF radio signals. The RFM, which can be installed in a monitoring station, a mobile unit or used as a portable unit, receives, analyses and displays the data gathered.

The main elements of the system are:
(1) USQ-46A radio frequency monitor
(2) GSQ-154 miniaturised seismic intrusion detector
(3) DJ-382 audio add-on unit
(4) DT-509 magnetic intrusion detector
(5) geophone, microphone and auxiliary equipment.

This equipment is combined in various ways to suit the environment and the specific operational requirements of the system. Possible configurations include:
(1) using the Minisid alone, with its built-in transmitter, to monitor vibration
(2) using the Minisid with the AAU to monitor vibration and sound
(3) using the Minisid with the Magid main solenoid only to detect seismic vibration and magnetic field changes

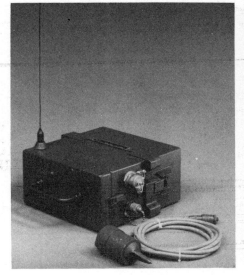
USQ-154 Minisid

DJ-509 Magid

(4) using the Minisid with the Magid's main and auxiliary solenoids to detect magnetic field changes only.

USQ-46A
The USQ-46A RFM consists of a main unit, an antenna and a headset, and is supplied complete with

power supply and mounting base. It may be operated in a man-pack, vehicle-mounted, or fixed station configuration. It receives signals on any one of 840 channels. When a signal from a Minisid is received, the RF monitor displays the remote sensor's identity number on its front panel and relays the received audio to the headset.

CHARACTERISTICS
Frequency range: 160 – 176 MHz
Number of channels: 840
Modulation: FM/FSK
Channel spacing: 18·75 kHz
Identity codes: 64 (max)
IF: 21·4 MHz
LO frequency: 3·75 MHz
Dimensions: 333 × 263 × 103 mm
Weight: 8 kg (approx)

USQ-154

The USQ-154 Minisid consists of a main unit, antenna, and a geophone. When the geophone detects vibrations in the ground, such as those caused by troops or vehicles passing within range, it transmits an alarm signal on a frequency suitable for reception by the RFM. The AAU or Magid can be connected to the Minisid for use as supplementary sensors.

CHARACTERISTICS
Transmitter Power: 2 W (min); 4 W (nominal)
Frequency range: 162 – 174 MHz
Transmission: Digital FSK
Spurious emission: 40 dB minimum
Frequency response: 40 – 2000 kHz
Detection range: 50 m dia (troops); 300 m dia (vehicles)
Dimensions: 210 × 210 × 105 mm
Weight: 5 kg (approx)

DJ-382

The DJ-382 audio add-on unit consists of a main assembly containing a microphone and is used as an ancillary device connected to the Minisid, from which it draws its power. The AAU is activated by three successive occurrences of ground vibrations and

USQ-46A radio frequency monitor unit

sends out audio signals within its range of audibility via the Minisid. An optional daylight sensor permits operation at night only if desired.

CHARACTERISTICS
Audio output: 0·3 to 1·0 V rms
Voltage gain: 80 dB
AGC range: 50 dB (keyed AGC)
Detection range: 3 – 4 m dia(troops); 10 – 20 m dia (vehicles)

DJ-382 audio add-on unit

Dimensions: 135 × 76 mm (dia)
Weight: 1 kg (approx)

DJ-509

The DJ-509 Magid consists of a main solenoid and is used as an ancillary device attached to the Minisid to detect disturbances to the Earth's magnetic field associated with the passage of magnetic material through the area being observed.

CHARACTERISTICS
Voltage gain: 138 to 141 dB
Detection range: 3 m dia (troops); 10 m dia (vehicles)
Dimensions: 310 × 65 mm (dia)
Weight: 1·4 kg (approx)
STATUS
Production.
CONTRACTOR
Gold Star Electric Co Ltd, 27-2, Yeoeuido-dong, Yongdunpo-ku, Seoul, Republic of Korea.

NETHERLANDS

2301.181
FLYCATCHER (VL4/41) AA WEAPON CONTROL SYSTEM

Flycatcher is a versatile AA radar weapon control system designed to detect, identify, and automatically track aircraft flying at low to medium altitudes. It can be used to control either guns or missiles, or any combination of both.

Main elements of the system are a dual retractable search and track antenna system, two radar transmitter/receivers, a radar display and control assembly, a fire control assembly, and a digital computer. The whole system is housed in a transportable military container. Power consumption is about 11 kVA. Up to three different weapons can be controlled independently by the computer.

The radar operates in the I-band, and features track-while-scan, a high data-renewal rate, and a multiplicity of ECCM and anti-interference facilities. An additional K-band facility provides high tracking accuracy with anti-image performance. The search antenna is a slotted waveguide; the tracking antenna is parabolic with a cassegrain reflector and a monopulse feed horn. TV tracking is incorporated as a complementary system.

The general-purpose computer, which can handle targets with speeds up to Mach 2 performs the ballistic computations for medium calibre guns and data processing for missile guidance and a number of other functions.

Signaal Flycatcher radar installation

CHARACTERISTICS
Function: All-weather point and area defence with AA guns and S/A missiles against medium- to low-level air attacks

Sensors: I-band search and track radar, K-band anti-image tracking radar, TV, IFF
Weapons: Up to 3 weapons, being either all guns (30, 35, 40 mm) or any combination of guns and short-range surface-to-air missiles; parallax distance up to 1000 m
Search coverage: Up to 20 km (1 m² target) track-while-scan
Display: PPI, north-oriented, clutter- and interference-free, scales 10/20 km
Target engagement: Joystick indication, automatic acquisition and tracking, automated weapon control
System design: Container construction, retractable antennas, self-contained diesel or petrol-driven power supply, removable wheel-train, micro-miniaturised solid-state electronics
Dimensions: Length 2·73 m; width 2·12 m; height (antenna in) 2·13 m, (antenna out) 3·65 m
System weight: 3000 kg (approx)
Environmental: Operating temperature –40 to +52° C, storage temperature –55 to +71° C, others according to MIL-STD-201A, ground equipment, world-wide, vibration and shock capabilities based on MIL-S-52059A
STATUS
The equipment is in service for the defence of Netherlands air bases and in several other countries.
CONTRACTOR
Hollandse Signaalapparaten BV, Hengelo, Netherlands.

4469.181
REPORTER AIR DEFENCE SYSTEM

The Reporter (radar equipment providing omni-directional reporting of targets at extended ranges) is designed to provide early warning of unknown air targets, flying at altitudes of 15 to 4000 m and ranges of up to 40 km. An integrated IFF system enables the target to be identified by the operator, and after target indication by the operator, target parameters are automatically transmitted in broadcast fashion via VHF/FM radio or by line communications to the terminal equipment. An unlimited number of firing units lacking early warning/alerting systems, eg light AA guns and weapons with target tracking devices

may use this information if they are equipped with the appropriate portable terminal equipment. Weapons with associated surveillance radars are able to maintain radar silence by utilising information from the Reporter system. Each terminal equipment displays the data of the highest priority target, with reference to their own position. The firing units are free to change location at short notice without the need to inform the Reporter unit, as the latter does not need to know weapon positions. Every fire unit is equipped with a terminal equipment set. This set consists of an FM radio, a target data receiver (TDR) and as an option an interface for automatic aiming. The TDR can be programmed to various criteria such

as the allocated defence sector and the position of the firing units.

Reporter consists of the following main items of equipment:

(1) an I-band search radar with integrated IFF
(2) equipment for the control, data handling, transmission (one-way data link) and power supplies
(3) any number of lightweight portable terminal equipment sets for use by the fire units in the field. This equipment receives data on all targets but displays only targets which are significant to each fire unit. The TDRs receive data via a voice channel of a VHF/FM radio, and interface units

Reporter terminal equipment (from top): radio set, TDR, and optional interface for automatic aiming

Reporter radar trailer and operator's shelter on light military truck

are available to convert the information into control signals for automatic aiming of weapons.

The system's main features are: immediate detection of pop-up targets due to a fast scanning rate; simultaneous high quality clutter and ECM suppression; automatic range and bearing tracking of up to 12 targets; one-man operation.

The radar is carried on a two-wheel trailer which carries a mast-mounted antenna. The operator's

console and the associated communications, computer and electronics equipment are housed in a standard shelter.

CONTRACTOR
Hollandse Signaalapparaten BV, Hengelo, Netherlands.

NORWAY

3126.161
BODIL COAST ARTILLERY FCS

BODIL is an electro-optical fire control system for coastal artillery applications developed for the Norwegian Coast Artillery by Kongsberg.

Few details have been revealed but the BODIL FCS includes mini-computers, electro-optical sensors, data transmission links, and gun displays. The system requirements are based on reliability and ease of operation. Only one sensor operator and one system operator are required.

The system is flexible, and can easily be expanded to cater for larger batteries and fortifications, for example, by adding more sensors and tactical and tracking displays. The design allows for the transmission and reception of data from other batteries.

STATUS
Operational.

CONTRACTOR
A/S Kongsberg Vapenfabrikk, PO Box 25, 3601 Kongsberg, Norway.

BODIL fire control system in operation with a Norwegian coast defence battery

2645.161
ODIN ARTILLERY FCS

Odin is the name given to a computer-based battalion-level artillery fire control system which is currently in service with the Norwegian Army.

The basis of the system is the Kongsberg NM90 – a special fire-control version of a general-purpose computer. One of these is located at each battery command post, and there is a further computer of identical pattern at battalion command post. Each computer has a field artillery panel, a combined control and display panel for entering information and displaying data. The important feature of this arrangement is that, in association with programs stored in the computer, the panel not only accepts and displays data but also instructs the operator, by various display devices, leading him through the sequence of actions required by the fire control procedure. Firing data are presented at each gun by means of the gun-display unit NO/VGG-20.

Target data inputs will in general be provided by forward observation posts, each of which is equipped with a Simrad LP3 laser rangefinder (**1804.193**) and the NO/VGC-30 data transmission system produced

by Siemens A/S in Norway. Other inputs accepted by the system are meteorological data, muzzle velocity measured by, for example, the Nera Bergen doppler radar chronograph, and survey data from standard survey equipment. In addition the computer can store gun ballistic data (up to three types of gun simultaneously) and ammunition calibration data.

The computer comprises a central processing unit, a memory unit, the field artillery panel referred to above, and a power supply unit, all contained in one cabinet. General specification details of the computer are set out below.

CHARACTERISTICS
Type: General purpose, digital, 16-bit word
Organisation: Parallel, negative numbers in two's complement. Floating point arithmetic performed in hardware
Instructions: 96 total (32 basic)
Addressing: Any combination of relative, register modified, and indirect
Main memory: 16 K. Asynchronous operation with CPU. Power failure memory protection. Expansible to 64 K

Memory cycle time: 1·5 μs
Input/output: 16 bits in parallel under program control to/from 256 devices. 1 channel for direct memory access
Data words: Single word 16 bits
Double word 32 bits
Floating point number 48 bits
(33 mantissa 15 exponent)
Interrupt: Standard single-level interrupt system
Power requirements: 24 V DC (18 – 32 V)
Power consumption: Approx 400 W (16 K memory)
Dimensions: 630 × 410 × 470 mm
Weight: 70 kg
Environment: DEF-133 Table L-3
Temperature: –40 to +55° C (operating); –55 to +80° C (non-operating)
Vibration: 1g
Shock: 50g – 10 ms
Humidity: 0 – 100% (with condensation)
RFI: MIL-STD-461A
Peripherals: Interface for paper tape reader digitronics 2540 EP. Other peripherals may be connected via the general I/O channel. There is spare

space for introduction of special interfaces according to specifications

DATA CAPACITY

Grid co-ordinates: 9 battery points

18 guns organised in 3 batteries with 6 guns in each battery

36 forward observer locations

100 targets or survey reference points

10 safety zones

2 obstacle points for each of 5 obstacle sectors

Calibration data: 18 guns; 8 ammunition lots

Ballistic data: 3 types of gun at the same time.

Programs are available for the following artillery pieces:

US 105 mm M2A1 or M2A2 howitzer

US 155 mm M1 howitzer

US 155 mm M109G SP howitzer

Other programs are being developed and can be produced for any gun, subject to the availability of ballistic data

STATUS

In production and in service with Norwegian forces and under consideration by several others.

CONTRACTOR

A/S Kongsberg Vapenfabrikk, 3600 Kongsberg, Norway.

NO/VGG-20 gun intercommunication unit and gun display unit used with the Kongsberg Odin artillery FCS to provide automatic data transmission from computer to individual guns

SOUTH AFRICA

4493.161

AS80 ARTILLERY FIRE CONTROL SYSTEM

The AS80 fire control system has been developed to fulfil the need for a decentralised autonomous system which requires minimal operator training while maintaining fast, reliable and accurate fire control computations.

The system consists of a digital computer; a terminal unit with keyboard, visual display keyboard and visual display facilities; a printer and a gun display system. All units have been fully militarised to ensure survival of the system in vehicles. Low power consumption is achieved by automatically reverting to a standby state during inactive periods. All programs and data are non-volatile, and are retained even when the power is switched off. Communication between the user and the system is achieved by means of an interactive dialogue, using menu selections, which guide the user through the correct sequence of operation. The procedures implemented in the dialogue correspond to the manual artillery procedures for the gun. These procedures may be adapted for other weapons or procedures. Approval for the entry of data into the system may be controlled by the officer in charge by use of the confirmation switch.

Currently available software caters for four simultaneous engagements using fire units of up to eight guns. However, with limitations, a total of up to 32 guns can be accommodated. The main facilities offered by the system are:

(1) entry of data

(2) handling of engagements

(3) performing survey calculations

(4) printing of data

(5) hardware check-out.

On having entered the necessary data for the deployment, engagements may be undertaken using the four phases which are provided. These are:

(1) initial orders for the definition of the fire mission

(2) adjustment of fire on the target

(3) fire for effect

(4) end of mission and registration of targets.

During the adjustment and fire for effect phases gun data is calculated and is immediately available for transmission by either radio or landline to the gun display units, which may be either tripod or gun mounted. In addition to the ability to compute ballistic firing data, the system offers several additional features which include: retention of records; ability to perform survey calculations at battery level; warnings of infringements in 'no fire' areas and crest violations; preparation of fire plans; derivation of meteorological conditions (eg from an S700 met system, **4494.161**);

Inside a fire control post container of the South African AS80 system showing the terminal (with keyboard lowered), digital computer and interface unit on lower shelf

AS80 printer unit in its protective case

maintenance of target, weapon and ammunition records.

The principal hardware items of the AS80 system are shown in adjacent illustrations, and most are generally housed in a standard transportable container which also serves as accommodation for the fire control officer and staff. They include a 16-bit minicomputer, a customised terminal offering

protection of the CRT during transportation, a printer using standard teleprinter paper, a gun display unit interface with associated line distribution box and interface to data entry terminals. Up to 32 gun display units may be driven by one interface unit. Communication with the self-contained gun display units may be achieved either by the internal radio or by a landline.

CHARACTERISTICS

Computer: 16-bit; 64 K words, expansible to 256 K words; programs and data non-volatile

Terminal keyboard: 56 characters (36 alpha-numeric, 4 symbols, 11 specific function keys, 5 unspecified function keys); remote 'confirm' switch for FCO

Printer

Line length: 80 characters/6 lines/in

Speed: 30 cps (max)

Character set: 58 characters from ASCII standard code

Interfacing: 20 mA single current loop

STATUS

Operational and in production.

CONTRACTOR

ESD (Pty) Ltd, PO Box 35, Halfway House, 1685, Republic of South Africa.

4494.161
S700 METEOROLOGICAL STATION

The S700 meteorological system provides a simple method of gathering meteorological data for ballistic computations and related battlefield applications. The system is completely mobile, being fitted in a standard military shelter, and offers automatic tracking of a radiosonde from the launch until termination of a flight. The data received from the radiosonde, together with its position, is fed to the digital computer which calculates wind speed and direction, at the various altitudes, together with a pressure, temperature and humidity profile. The results may be presented in formats suitable for direct use in artillery fire prediction calculations. The deployment of the system is simple, requiring only a single vehicle for transportation and a crew of two for operation.

The man-machine interface is by means of a dialogue, the first operation undertaken being the calibration of the radiosonde in a ground check chamber included in the system. Calibration is performed for temperature, pressure and humidity. On completion of the calibration process, the radiosonde is attached to a balloon and the antenna is aligned for tracking by means of a CCTV monitor. Ground meteorological conditions obtained from the monitor unit are fed into the computer system. On releasing the balloon, the antenna automatically tracks and data containing temperature, barometric pressure and humidity are received and recorded,

Tracking and reception unit of S700

being used in conjunction with the tracking antenna position to produce the required meteorological data as a hard copy print-out. The ground receiver antenna automatically tracks the sonde, using the latter's transmissions, thereby eliminating any need for radar tracking of the balloon/sonde. This has the operational benefit of making the ground station passive in use and thus immune to counter-measures.

The hardware consists of a monitor unit, a receiver unit, a tracking unit and a processor unit which offer the following:
MONITOR UNIT
System power conditions, flight clock, CCTV for initial antenna alignment and ground weather conditions.

RECEIVER, TRACKING AND PROCESSOR UNITS
Receiver frequency range: 1680 MHz ± 20 MHz
Tuning: Manual + AFC
IF: 30 MHz
Sensitivity: 100 dBm
Noise figure: 9 dB max
COMPUTER
The digital processor used is a 16-bit mini-computer, understood to be of South African design and manufacture. The system operates from standard lead acid batteries, the supply voltage being 24 V DC. Power consumption is nominally 170 W with a peak requirement of 320 W. Fully militarised, the system conforms to DEF 133 Table L2 (as applicable) and can operate in the temperature range of –10 to +50°C.
DIMENSIONS AND WEIGHTS
Shelter: 419 × 227 × 228 mm (without wheels or legs)
Operating console: 825 × 510 × 400 mm (excluding computer terminal)
Radiosonde ground check chamber: 406 × 400 × 360 mm
Antenna unit: Height (max) 1·7 m (excluding raising mechanism); turning radius 0·96 m; disc diameter 1·2 m
STATUS
The system has been extensively deployed under operational conditions and is in regular service.
CONTRACTOR
DIEL (Pty) Ltd, PO Box 228, Plumstead, 7800, Republic of South Africa.

4495.161
EMVA MK 10B MUZZLE VELOCITY ANALYSER

The EMVA Mk 10B muzzle velocity analyser is a doppler radar measuring instrument capable of measuring projectile velocities over the range 30 to 3000 m/s. Results are presented in metres per second for direct application in fire control calculations. It is suitable for use with gun calibres of 20 mm and above. The instrument consists of an antenna head suitable for mounting on the gun, or on a tripod adjacent to the gun, and a processor unit. The processor unit contains a liquid crystal display and printer for data recording. A single 50 m or optional 100 m shielded cable connects the antenna head to the processor. Power can be obtained from standard lead acid batteries. No warm-up time is required and the equipment is ready to operate immediately after the brief automatic self-test sequence has been completed.

Provision of interactive operator dialogue minimises incorrect data entry, and informs the operator of incorrect procedures. It also enables potential operators to be trained in a matter of hours. The dialogue is currently available in two languages.
OPERATION
The operator enters the expected velocity range, and any other relevant data that may be required to be recorded in hard copy form, into the processor via the keyboard. The measurement process is entirely automatic from the time the system commences measurement until the final hard copy print-out. The antenna head ceases to radiate the moment the projectile is beyond instrument range. The instrument is self triggered by the doppler signal. However, an external trigger unit which operates on gun flash or projectile shadow is also provided. When plugged into the antenna head it automatically over-rides the self-trigger circuit.

From the instant the measurement commences until the projectile leaves the range of the instrument approximately 100 individual velocity samples are taken and stored. The exact number depends on the velocity and cross sectional size of the projectile. These samples are then evaluated, processed and

Doppler radar head for EMVA Mk 10B muzzle velocity measuring analyser

used to calculate to two decimal places, the velocity of the projectile as it left the muzzle of the gun.

This velocity value, which is presented on the liquid crystal display, and printed out within seconds of the round being fired, is the non-standard instrumental velocity. Readout of the standard instrumental velocity may also be obtained provided that the gun tables for any particular gun or guns are known and are pre-programmed by the factory into the processor memory. Similarly the effect of gun wear, elevation and meteorological conditions may also be taken into account. In the rapid fire mode the operator need only press a single key to instruct the processor to assume that all the data entered for the previous round will be the same for the next and to automatically increment the round number.

The complete system consists of an antenna head, processor and tripod as well as a transport box for the antenna head, cables, external trigger unit and

EMVA Mk 10B processor cabinet contains microprocessor, operating controls for system and printer for analysis results

optional charge temperature thermometer. This box also doubles as a field operating bench for the processor. The processor is in its own fully ruggedised box.
CHARACTERISTICS
Velocity range: 30 – 3000 m/s
Accuracy: ±0·05%
Power requirements: 24 V DC: 2 A average
Dimensions
Antenna head: 305 × 145 × 165 mm
Processor unit: 650 × 380 × 290 mm
Accessory box: 720 × 520 × 270 mm
Tripod: Adjustable height from 600 – 1500 mm
Weight
Antenna head: 9 kg
Processor unit: 30 kg
Accessory box: 20 kg
Tripod: 25 kg
DEVELOPMENT
Developed in the Republic of South Africa.
STATUS
In production.
CONTRACTOR
Global Chemicals (Pty) Ltd, PO Box 5008, Cape Town, 8000, Republic of South Africa.

SWEDEN

2378.181
BOFI ANTI-AIRCRAFT FIRE CONTROL SYSTEM

BOFI is an all-weather fire control instrument of multi-sensor type developed by Bofors for their 40 mm L/70 gun (**5528.103**) of which large numbers have been produced. The equipment is fully integrated with the gun and each gun will become an

autonomous firing unit that can combat its targets individually.

The equipment consists of a computer, an operator's panel with joystick, sights for day and night use, laser rangefinder and a tracking radar. The major portion of the equipment is installed in the operator's cab. The main sensor of the multi-sensor fire control

is the Ku-band (J-band) radar, using the MTI function during acquisition and frequency agility during automatic tracking to increase the accuracy. Tracking observation can be done on an A-scope or by using the sights. The optronic sensors consist of a 10 Hz neodymium laser rangefinder, a day sight and a night sight with a three-stage light amplifier. The sensors can be used redundantly to give maximum performance and resistance to jamming.

The computer is of hybrid type which calculates the target co-ordinates continuously as well as the target's future position in a cartesian co-ordinate system. External ballistic corrections are set on the operator's panel and are compensated for in the computer's calculation of super-elevation and wind drift etc.

4307.161

FIELD ARTILLERY FIRE CONTROL COMPUTER 9FA 302

The 9FA 302 is a design development of the 9FA 301 already in quantity service with the Swedish Army for use with the new FH 77 155 mm field howitzer. The design of the new 9FA 302 incorporates experience derived from field trials of the 9FA 301 as well as up-rated performance specifications requested by other customers. The most important changes, apart from software improvements, are: improved temperature range, extending from tropical conditions to arctic environment; higher capacity solid-state memory application for greater target range and increased number of projectiles and propellant charges.

The 9FA 302 is a field artillery computer designed for battery-level operations. Its main application involves the computation of azimuth, elevation, fuze settings and propellant charge for a battery emplacement of up to eight guns.

Discrete firing parameters are computed for each gun and normally transmitted directly via a data link to the RIA gun sight (**3144.193**). Firing parameters can also be transmitted directly to a gun display unit (GDU) placed on or in the immediate vicinity of the gun. All guns receive firing parameters less than five seconds after input of the complete set of target condition data.

The computer can also operate as a back-up system for two additional batteries. There are three basic operational modes for the computer, one for each battery. It is possible to switch between these three modes and always to return to the original operational status. Thus firing data can be computed in sequence for three batteries while a return to the battery which has highest priority is possible at a given instant. Calculation of firing data is performed by solving differential equations. This method gives high accuracy while requiring only a small amount of data to characterise the ballistic behaviour of the

A central search radar is used acting as a combat control centre for a battery of BOFI guns. An optical target indicator is incorporated in the system for designation of targets visually detected at the gun site. The BOFI equipment is designed in such a way that it can also be used on existing 40 mm L/70 field guns.

DEVELOPMENT

Development work and system tests of the all-

PEAB 9FA 302 fire control computer

projectile. Ballistic data for numerous different projectiles can be stored simultaneously.

Besides calculating firing data, the computer is also capable of:
(1) storing 100 target/registration systems
(2) storing five safety zone limits
(3) storing, automatically counting and displaying current ammunition stock
(4) store and display of current corrections
(5) automatic/manual selection of propellant charges
(6) selection of high or low angle trajectory
(7) selection of calibres, shells, charge system and charges

weather equipment were completed in 1979 and further details will be found in **2349.131** in the Mobile Gun and Rocket Systems section of this volume.

STATUS

The basic version without tracking radar was tested during 1972-73 and put into series production in 1976. The system has been exported to several customers.

CONTRACTOR

AB Bofors, 691 80 Bofors, Sweden.

(8) continuous systems diagnostic program
(9) artillery survey routine
(10) final protective fire target; firing data for this target is automatically transmitted to guns in End of Mission mode
(11) UTM Co-ordinates Handler mode can be used worldwide, using current spheroid and zone cross-overs.

The 9FA 302 is housed in a single enclosure consisting of the following modular units: a general-purpose digital computer with a CPU micro-processor, input/output stations, a 80 Kword solid-state memory, and ergonomically designed control and display panels.

Normally the 9FA 302 is mounted in a vehicle but it can be set up separately. Only one man is needed to operate the equipment. The computer has a built-in, continuous self-test program. A special diagnostics program quickly localises faults. The modular system configuration promotes ease of service and maintenance.

CHARACTERISTICS
Width: 580 mm
Height: 420 mm
Depth: 750 mm
Weight: 45 kg
Power: 21 – 30 V DC approx 200 W
Operating temperature range: –30 to +60° C
Operational data
Battery emplacements: 3
Guns per battery: 8 (max)
Projectile types: 8 (max)
Charges: 10 (max)
Target memory: 100
Firing zone limits: 5 areas
STATUS
In production.
CONTRACTOR
Philips Elektronikindustrier AB, 175 88 Järfälla, Sweden.

3313.181

9AA/100 FIRE CONTROL SYSTEM

The 9AA/100, formerly KALLE (**2468.181**), is a light anti-aircraft gun control system developed by Philips Elektronikindustrier AB, as main contractor, in partnership with the Aerospace Division of Saab-Scania who are responsible for the optronic technology. It is intended for fixed or mobile installations controlling typically, two guns of 30 to 40 mm calibre.

The basic system comprises a combined TV director and laser rangefinder assembly, a computer, a display and control unit, and data transmission circuits and adaptors for the guns. The TV director is manually laid for target acquisition, after which it tracks automatically by contrast tracking and with the laser rangefinder provides full target co-ordinates for the computer. The computer is a general-purpose mini-computer and is the same as that used in other

PEAB fire control systems, 9 LV 200 Mk 2, 9KA 400 etc.

Controls on the display and control unit include director controls for acquisition and tracking modes and provision for gun supervision and control. Displays include a TV monitor for presentation of the picture and target data in alpha-numeric form. System options include an IR-camera and associated tracking circuits to give night-time capability. It is also produced in a shipboard version, called 9 LV 100 (**3185.281**).

STATUS
In service.
CONTRACTOR
Philips Elektronikindustrier AB, 175 88 Järfälla, Sweden.

In co-operation with:
Saab Missiles AB, 581 88 Linköping, Sweden.

9AA/100 control and display console

4274.181

BOFORS AFV FIRE CONTROL SYSTEM

The latest Bofors Aerotronics fire control system for armoured fighting vehicles originates from the first computer-controlled FCS developed for the Swedish Ikv-91 tank destroyer, described in **2399.181** in earlier editions of *Jane's Weapons Systems*, and evolved through the Type E tank FCS which succeeded it (**3318.181**).

The current system comprises a day/night optical sight with a passive image intensifier and a laser rangefinder; and an independent line-of-sight for the

gunner and an accurate ballistic and lead-angle digital computer give the system the necessary high technical and performance characteristics needed for the engagement of moving targets from a moving vehicle. This version is suitable for retro-fitting to existing AFVs and can be modified for use in updating many tanks. As an alternative, the gunner's sight can be specified as a day laser sight.

The system has been developed to include a stabilised commander's sight and provisions for the commander to align the gunner's line-of-sight with his cupola position.

Computer/control panel of Bofors Aerotronics tank FCS

CHARACTERISTICS
Gunner's sight (day/night model)
Magnification: ×8·5° (night); ×7 or ×3 (day)
Field of view: 5·3° (night); 9 or 20° (day)
Input pupil diameter: 150 mm (night); 50 mm (day)
Exit pupil: 7 mm
Gunner's sight (day model)
Magnification: ×9
Field of view: 8°
Input pupil: 80 mm
Computer
Range: 200 – 6000 m
Number of ballistics: 5
Air pressure range: –300 to +100 mm Hg
MV range: ±50 m/s
Air temperature: –50 to +30° C
Powder temperature: ±40° C
Crosswind: ±30 m/s
Head wind: ±30 m/s
Cant angle: ±15°
Gun control
Max target speed: 80 m/s (azimuth); 40 m/s (elevation)
STATUS
In series production.
CONTRACTOR
Bofors Aerotronics AB, 181 81 Lidingo, Sweden.

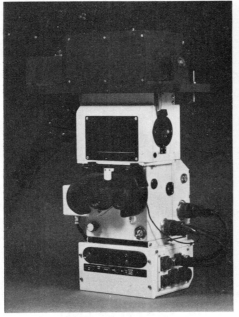

Daylight/laser rangefinder sight   *One version of Bofors tank FCS day/night sight*

1548.181
9KA 400 COAST FIRE CONTROL SYSTEM KASTELL

The 9KA 400 is the modern, digital version of the well-proven coast artillery fire control unit MARELD. It is primarily intended for fixed coast artillery or missile batteries. It can also be used as a sensor in the 9CSI 600 STINA naval command system (**4027.281** and **4028.281**).

Sensors are an I/J-band frequency agility radar with a continuously scanning antenna, and a combination TV-camera/laser rangefinder on a separate pedestal. The radar antenna has a very narrow horizontal beam, 0·6°, to give high resolution in azimuth for fall-of-shot observation, and high jamming resistance. Multiple targets are tracked by track-while-scan methods using digital extractor and Kalman filter techniques.

The TV/laser sensor is remotely controlled by the operator and the information is displayed on a TV-monitor and a digital read-out for the rangefinder. The digital computer is of the same basic type as in the 9 LV 200 Mk 2 (**3127.281**) naval fire control system.

Target data, position, and speed vector are

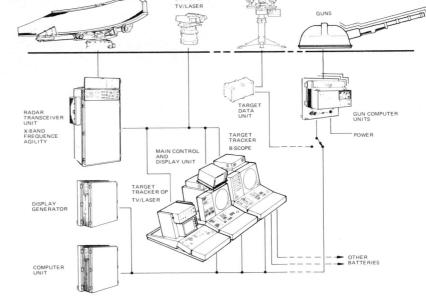

Coast artillery system 9KA 400 Mk 2

generated and fed to ballistic computer units for calculation of gun-laying data. The guns can be dispersed over a large area remote from the fire control unit, and can also receive target data from other fire control units in the vicinity.

The 9KA 400 Kastell can be supplemented with a self-contained electro-optical fire control director using telescopes and a laser for high accuracy computer-aided tracking of one target. Infra-red or image intensifier sensors can be added to obtain all-weather capability.

PEAB 9KA 400 Kastell radar antenna

STATUS
The original 9KA 400 has been operational in large numbers in Sweden, and other countries, since the mid-1960s. The new version entered service in late 1976 and is now in operation and a newer generation Mk 2 version is now in production. At least 70 systems have been ordered for use in Sweden and several other countries.
CONTRACTOR
Philips Elektronikindustrier AB, 175 88 Järfälla, Sweden.

4318.281
9KA 500 COASTAL FIRE CONTROL SYSTEM KARDINAL

The 9KA 500 Kardinal mobile coastal artillery fire control system is derived from the well-proven 9KA 400 (**1548.181**) which has been operational in Sweden and other countries since the mid-1960s. All operational functions of the 9KA 400 are retained and many operational and technical features are added. The major new ones are:

(1) higher mobility through reduced weight
(2) greater deployment flexibility through separation into a sensor unit and an operations unit
(3) additional combat control functions, ie improved

presentation of the tactical situation and automatic tracking of multiple targets
(4) the 9KA 500 Kardinal can easily be supplemented with functions for engagement with missiles and some of those functions are already implemented.

The sensor unit is a single-axle trailer with a hydraulically-operated mast. The top of the mast houses the radar antenna and, below the antenna, an optronics unit. The optronic sensors are: a TV-camera and a laser rangefinder. The turning gear for the optronics is an 'around the mast' design giving both the radar and the optronic sensor a full 360° field of view. Also mounted on the sensor trailer is the radar T/R unit, a hydraulic pump, and a motor-generator,

making the trailer a self-contained unit, remotely controlled from the operations unit. The mechanical design of the trailer is very rigid in order to achieve the stability necessary for fire control purposes, ie fractions of a milliradian even in strong winds.

Two versions of the radar, transmitting in the X- and the Ku-band respectively, are available. In both versions the well-known spin-tuned magnetron is used, giving wide-band frequency agility with the same benefits as in the 9KA 400. The Ku-band version gives the high angular resolution as in the 9KA 400, ie 0·6°, and yet is lightweight and highly mobile. This particularly high resolution is valuable in applications where separation of targets and fall-of-shot observations ('splash-spotting') is required.

The transmitter power at Ku-band (65 kW) is lower than the power at X-band (200 kW) but the shorter wavelength at Ku-band suffers less from the 'beam-lift' due to multipath effects. Thus the detection and tracking ranges against ship targets are the same for the two radars when deployed at such altitudes, and they are both effectively limited by the curvature of the earth.

The sensor unit and the operations unit can be separated by a distance of some kilometres. Transmission of radar and TV video, data, commands, and logic signals between the two units takes place over a lightweight fibre optical link, which greatly facilitates cable laying compared to conventional cables. Furthermore, the fibre can be used in full duplex in both directions by the use of dual wavelength transmission with dichroic prisms in the terminal equipment.

The set-up of displays and control consoles in the operations unit is similar to the 9KA 400. Like that, the number of consoles and their functions can be easily tailored to suit various operational doctrines and functions, and the weapons to be controlled, either guns and/or missiles.

STATUS
In production.
CONTRACTOR
Philips Elektronikindustrier AB, 175 88 Järfälla, Sweden.

9KA 500 Kardinal coastal artillery fire control system deployed

SWITZERLAND

3314.181
FIELDGUARD ARTILLERY FCS

Fieldguard is a near real-time all-weather fire control system for tube and rocket artillery which does not need meteorological information.

The system consists of integral power supply unit, tracking radar, computer and operator desk for man-machine dialogue. Fieldguard can control up to 24 guns or rocket launchers.

Target information is received from forward observers (FOs), battlefield surveillance radars, survey aircraft and other troops and is stored in the fire control centre (FCC) computer with either display on TV monitor or printer. After target selection by the FCC commander, target data is transmitted on line to Fieldguard, where the system's own computer can store up to 50 different targets which are then available at fingertip control.

FO teams are equipped with portable target locating equipment (TLE) which has to be connected to a radio set. Its main task is to find, identify and locate moving targets, transmitting information to the FCC or directly to Fieldguard. Engagement of

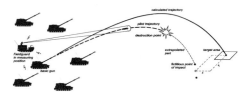

Pilot shot procedure based on Fieldguard

Fieldguard operator's position

stationary targets does not require a forward observer. The TLE consists of laser rangefinder, goniometer and electronic angle transmitter mounted on a tripod. These units are connected to the artillery tactical terminal (ATT) by cable. The ATT is connected to radio for information exchange.

Instead of relying on separate artillery met sounding system(s) for atmospheric data, radar is used to track the pilot shot on its own trajectory, fired by the basic gun/launcher. Out of the difference between the calculated and the measured fictitious point of impact, Fieldguard computes the new and weather-corrected firing command individually for all weapons in a battery/Battalion and transmits them automatically to each gun/launcher.

Data displayed on rocket launchers comprises: bearing, elevation, fuze time, pilot firing command, countdown, effective firing command. Data displayed

Fieldguard system deployed operationally

at guns consists of: type of shell, fuze information, charge, firing mode, rounds, fire density, countdown, azimuth, elevation, elevation jump, timing and timing leap.

Fieldguard can also take over other duties such as ammunition control, evaluation of emplacement area, optimum fire distribution for given targets, test programme for fault localisation, and training programmes.

STATUS
Fieldguard has proved its reliability, accuracy etc in extensive tests and field trials and is now in series production. It is employed by several countries and the armed forces of NATO.
CONTRACTOR
Contraves AG, Dept VMA, Schaffhauserstrasse 590, CH-8052 Zurich, Switzerland.

2377.181
SKYGUARD ANTI-AIRCRAFT FIRE CONTROL SYSTEM

Skyguard is the name now given to the miniaturised fire control system that Contraves have been developing for some time as the successor to the Super Fledermaus (**2376.151**) system that they have marketed so successfully in various versions for many years.

Major differences between Skyguard and its predecessors – apart from a general modernisation of design techniques – are the provision of two radars (one for search and one for track) in place of one and the use of a digital instead of an analogue computer. Another important difference is the use of pulse-doppler type radars in place of pulse radars.

Main system components are a pulse-doppler search radar, a pulse-doppler tracking radar, a TV tracking system, a digital computer, a control console, and a power supply system. The whole is contained in a fire resistant reinforced fibreglass-polyester cabin that can be mounted on a trailer or a wheeled or tracked prime mover, and is air transportable. The power supply system is built into the main equipment but can be removed for external operation and is automatically refuelled directly from cans.

The search radar is a fully coherent pulse-doppler system, the transmitter of which is common to the tracking radar. Working in X-band with a mean power of 200 W it offers fast frequency change and fast PRF change facilities and a choice of 1 and 0.3 microsecond pulses. A cosecant-squared antenna with integrated IFF antenna gives a horizontal beamwidth of 1·7° and a 55° beam in elevation. Scanner rotation rate is 60 rpm. The receiver has range-gated doppler filters and offers an MTI improvement factor better than 50 dB. The PPI display has switched ranges from 0·3 to 20 km and can present simultaneously processed MTI video and raw video. Radar search range is 20 km and range resolution 160 m. The system is IFF-compatible and special features include automatic target alarm, automatic lock-on, and computer-controlled symbol markers on the PPI.

The tracking radar is a fully coherent monopulse-

Skyguard with Ka-band radar in tracking position

doppler system with a cassegrain paraboloidal antenna having a 24° beamwidth. Signal processing circuits provide 80 m acquisition gates around the tracking gate, all gates having doppler filters, and the total acquisition range is 1120 m. The MTI improvement factor is better than 50 dB. The display is an R-trace, displayed on the TV monitor, for tracking supervision and ECM monitoring but target acquisition and tracking is automatic and includes memory tracking and automatic alarm facilities. Special features include fast target exchange and automatic noise jammer tracking.

A closed-circuit TV system provides for optical tracking and automatic TV tracking. An optical sight on a rotating chair is provided for visual target acquisition with provision for target indication by means of a flashing strobe on the PPI.

As part of the program to augment the combat value of the Skyguard, Contraves has designed various technical innovations and developed accessory equipment. These primarily assure optimal acquisition, tracking, and combat of low-flying aircraft under extreme topographical conditions. Besides X-band radar and TV-tracking, Skyguard is now equipped with Ka-band radar. This ensures improved target resolution in terrain where the use of radar is very difficult. At the same time it increases the redundancy of the automatic tracking possibilities. With the additional Ka-band radar Skyguard remains easy to operate. The Ka-data also appears on the Combat Display. The Ka-band radar can be easily and quickly retrofitted to all existing Skyguard fire control units.

The Cora II M computer is third generation equipment working in real time to perform threat evaluation functions, calculate ballistic data for guns and command signals for missiles, aid the target tracking operation and monitor, and check-out the entire system.

In addition to the PPI and R-trace displays already mentioned, the control console incorporates a tactical display with numerical read-out, the TV tracking monitor, rolling-ball control for PPI markers, joystick control for manual tracking, and a matrix panel for data input and output.

OPERATION

A search radar data extractor (SRDE) by Contraves AG in Zurich is available and the system can be integrated into Skyguard's fire-control unit. It enhances the degree of automation and the time required for target acquisition and tracking is shortened and threat evaluation automated.

The SRDE system is used for the following main tasks:

(1) Automatic first-target alert coupled with automatic target acquisition.

As soon as the first-target alert is acquired by the search radar, operators are automatically alerted. Thereupon, the target is automatically

Skyguard with X-band search radar and Ka-band tracker with TV camera

passed on to the tracking radar which keeps on tracking it. Despite very high clutter suppression of the Skyguard's pulse doppler search radar, alerts will unavoidably be triggered also by false targets in the shape of moving objects (motor cars, ventilating fans, etc). Such false targets are specifically marked and can at any time be wholly or partially erased at operator's discretion.

(2) Automatic threat evaluation regarding targets in the combat area or those already acquired by the search radar.

By the track-while-scan system it is possible to simultaneously track several targets as well as to evaluate automatically the respective degree of threat. Skyguard's digital system computes, among other things, the threat degree for each individual target, based on the angle of the approaching target, velocity, range, etc. Targets are shown simultaneously on the PPI in the order of priority corresponding to threat involved.

As a matter of course, the data supplied by Skyguard's integrated IFF unit are also included in the threat evaluation.

Skyguard is able to control medium calibre guns and/or guided missiles. The Contraves-designed

missile launcher uses the proven undercarriage of the Oerlikon 35 mm gun and carries four Sparrow or Aspide missiles in containers, as well as the target tracking and illuminator radar antenna. The launcher is directed either remotely from the Skyguard system or locally by the launcher operator.

For crew training, there are two different simulators available: one is integrated in the system, while the larger one is an additional unit connected to it. (Training Simulator 2)

STATUS

Skyguard was developed by Contraves as a private venture project and, after evaluation, it has been adopted by the armed forces of more than seven countries. More than 300 units have been ordered, and the system is understood to be under evaluation by certain other countries.

In April 1979 the Swiss Federal Military Department stated that the first batch of Skyguard systems for control of 35 mm AA gun air defences in Switzerland was being procured and that a second batch of these systems would be requested.

CONTRACTOR

System and Computer: Contraves AG, Zurich, Switzerland.

2376.181
SUPER-FLEDERMAUS

A member of the series of anti-aircraft fire control systems produced by Contraves in Switzerland, the Super-Fledermaus Type D IX with MTI is an advanced radar optical tracking and computing system suitable for use with medium calibre anti-aircraft guns. Extreme operational versatility coupled with compact and rugged design make it suitable for use in a wide variety of combat situations and it, and its forerunners, are used by more than 20 nations.

The main equipment is compactly mounted on a four-wheel cross-country trailer and comprises a radar/visual tracker for target acquisition and determining the firing data for up to three separate gun emplacements, and a muzzle velocity indicator for measuring the muzzle velocities of up to three guns. A separate power supply unit, mounted on a two-wheel trailer, generates power for the fire control unit. Auxiliary equipment are a signal box for use by the fire control officer and an optical putter-on for rapid visual acquisition of unexpected targets.

A detailed description of the system was published in the 1970 – 71 edition of *Jane's Weapon Systems*, but systems in use may vary since in recent years Contraves has offered various improvements as modification kits for retrospective fitting.

Brazilian Army Super-Fledermaus fire control system showing tracker's position to left of radar and the controller position under shelter at extreme left of unit

CHARACTERISTICS

Type: Combined radar/visual tracker and computer for remote control of medium calibre anti-aircraft guns or missiles
Target detection: Up to a range of 50 km
Target acquisition: All-weather operation with 5 options:
(a) by selectable programmed scanning motion
(b) by optical putter-on
(c) by optical tracker
(d) by tactical radar
(e) by radar/visual combination
Target tracking: Up to a range of 40 km with 5 options:
(a) automatically by radar
(b) automatically by regenerative control
(c) automatically by memory

(d) visually by tracker operation
(e) automatically in range, visually in angle
Firing data computation: Continuous computation individually for 3 gun emplacements
Muzzle velocity and meteorological corrections included
Special modes selectable for driving or curved flights
Muzzle velocity measurement: Separate measurement by built-in equipment for each gun
ECCM: High transmitting power; narrow main beam; high sidelobe attenuation; 2 independent transmitting channels; jump changes of frequency over wide band; IAGC; STC; FTC
Clutter suppression: MTI data processor
Mobility: Cross-country trailer

Maintenance: Built-in test and calibration equipment. Use of modular plug-in units
CONTRACTORS
Complete system: Contraves AG, Zurich, Switzerland.

The system is also manufactured by Contraves Italiana SpA, Rome, Italy, and under licence in India and Japan.

4586.181
GUN KING SIGHTING SYSTEM
Gun King is an autonomous sighting system for use with automatic anti-aircraft guns, such as the Oerlikon Diana twin 25 mm AA gun GBF-AOB (4525.131) or Oerlikon twin 35 mm AA field guns GDF (4537.131) although the system is equally well suited for naval applications or operation of other gun types.

Of modular design, Gun King is based on the use of a new Contraves digital computer coupled with an optical system that incorporates a periscopic sight, laser rangefinder, and includes provision for a TV camera for operator training or for use as a tracking module. There is a common optical path in the sight periscope for the laser beam and the aiming sight-line, and these beams are deflected with high accuracy by a gimballed mirror, thus permitting the use of a fixed eyepiece. The periscope has a multispectral optical system and night operation is possible.

The rangefinding function is performed by the laser rangefinder, which uses a multi-divergence neodymium laser. A novel switch-over device enables the laser beamwidth to be reduced for use against ground targets, eliminating ground clutter.

The digital computer calculates all fire control data at high speed with optimum control and accuracy, using filter and ballistic algorithms. In addition it controls the periscope, laser triggering during the

tracking phase and the drive electronics. At the instant of optimum hit probability, the operator is given an audio signal to open fire. Target changes can be effected very rapidly because target data is stored in the computer memory. All data relating to weather conditions and weapon parameters is entered into the computer so that the operator is free to concentrate on precise target tracking. Sight and gun are commanded entirely by the operator's control yoke which provides full hands-on control.

Modern DC power electronics and servo-drives are used for gun control, and the battery capacity alone ensures full operational readiness of the entire system from a passive, silent standby status. Up to five combat cycles can be carried out before the engine of the power supply has to be started to provide electrical power.

When employed in a naval role, the Gun King system can be gyro-stabilised and may also be used as a stand-alone fire control facility for several weapons. It can be slaved to other target designation facilities, such as radar or other fire control systems, in both naval and land-based applications.
STATUS
Early production. No contract details have been disclosed.
CONTRACTOR
Contraves AG, Schaffhauserstrasse 580, CH-8052 Zurich, Switzerland.

Contraves Gun King laser/computer controlled sighting system

UNION OF SOVIET SOCIALIST REPUBLICS

3323.181
SOVIET ARMY FIRE CONTROL
Very little reliable information is available for publication concerning the systems and equipment used by the Soviet Army for such purposes as artillery fire direction, survey, meteorological data acquisition and distribution, tank fire control, tactical data automation, command and control etc. However it is clear from the scale of the USSR's land forces and the level of sophistication displayed by Soviet equipment in general that such aspects of land warfare have not been neglected. Some of the items of hardware known to have entered service are listed briefly below:
(1) reconnaissance theodolite, RT-2: probably used

for survey in support of both offensive (eg artillery) and engineering operations
(2) periscope artillery compass, PAB-2: suitable for observer/fire director applications and similar uses
(3) battery commander's telescope, AST
(4) stereoscopic rangefinder, DS-0·9
(5) radar meteorological station, RMS-1: for meteorological data (upper winds and temperatures etc) for use in artillery ballistics computations
(6) topographic survey system: consists of a gyro-compass, transformer, sight, a course plotter

incorporating a map display, and radio, mounted in the rear of a GAZ-69TD vehicle
(7) SNAR-2 radar: mounted on AT-L tractor
(8) Arsom: radar for both artillery and mortar locating roles. Dish type equipment.

Laser rangefinders are understood to be added on a retrofitting basis to some earlier types of Soviet tanks, while the latest models include a ballistic computer as well. The T-62s 115 mm gun is reported to be stablised, as is the D-10T2S 100 mm gun which arms the T-54B. The gunner's sight for the latter tank is the TSh 2B-22 or TSh 2-32 and the gun is stablised in both planes.

UNITED KINGDOM

3320.161
WAVELL ADP SYSTEM
Wavell is the British Army's automatic data processing system designed and manufactured to assist commanders and their staffs with the conduct of general operations and intelligence work at Corps, Division and Brigade levels. It is designed to use any suitable communications link and to operate as required with the Battlefield Artillery Target Engagement System (BATES), a semi-automatic data processing and fire control system being developed for the British Army by Marconi Space and Defence Systems. Wavell Stage I uses data links provided on the Army's Bruin trunk communications network. Wavell Stage II enters service during 1985 and will use the new Ptarmigan Tactical Trunk Network.

At each headquarters, conceptually-simple automatic data processing (ADP) facilities will be

provided comprising a central processor, bubble memory backing store, and floppy disc drives for loading programs and data. All these will be located in a Wavell vehicle which will connect to the communications system and the remotely-located visual display units and hard copy printers. Two types of installation are to be provided. At Corps and Divisional headquarters levels the system will be installed in a standard one-tonne container mounted on a Bedford four-ton flatbed prime mover, along with a 20 KW generator. The generator will provide power for the air conditioning and lighting system and, through a power conditioning unit, a 28-volt dc source for the ADP system and back-up batteries. The ADP equipment will be located in a rack based on the Air Transportable Racking (ATR) system. A similar installation is to be provided for use at Brigade HQ but this will be mounted in an FV430 series armoured vehicle with power and environmental

control equipment on the roof.

The heart of the system in both types of vehicle will be the ADP equipment rack. The rack will accommodate the central processor unit and associated fast store in two full-ATR units each holding 0·5 Mbytes of semi-conductor memory. Next to the processor will be the interface unit for the communications and terminals, which will be driven at distances of up to 1 km by balanced line drivers accommodated in two half-ATR units each capable of driving 16 channels. Along the top of the rack, the necessary controls and warning lights will be provided as well as two floppy diskette drive units for loading programs and data into the system.

The bottom row of the rack will accommodate up to three units of bubble memory backing store, each having a capacity of 24 Mbytes. The bubble memory offers a number of advantages over the disc. Apart from its low volume and low power dissipation, the bubble is non-volatile if there is power loss and yet can be easily and quickly erased. The data base capacity of each system will be about 72 Mbytes but it is expected that during the life of the system, advances in bubble-memory technology will enable this capacity to be increased by a factor of four.

In operation, raw data will be collated with data entered into the system prior to deployment and with other data generated by the machine itself. It will then be displayed as meaningful subsets of data (or formats) on the staff visual display unit. These formats will be used by the staff to assist with formulating plans and orders and in the preparation of briefs for higher command. General-purpose free-text facilities will also be provided for messages and orders. All formats can be printed out on a hard copy printer for briefing or fall-back and for staff cells not equipped with Wavell.

STATUS

Project Wavell began in the early 1970s as a study of staff functions in the field with the aim of identifying those time-consuming tasks which might be automated. A wealth of detailed information was accumulated, but with senior officers at that time sceptical of the use of computers in matters of command and control, the British Army in general was not clear how to proceed.

In 1976 a decision was made to field a limited system which would use commercial equipment with minimum ruggedisation and from which staff reaction could be obtained. For this trial phase it was decided

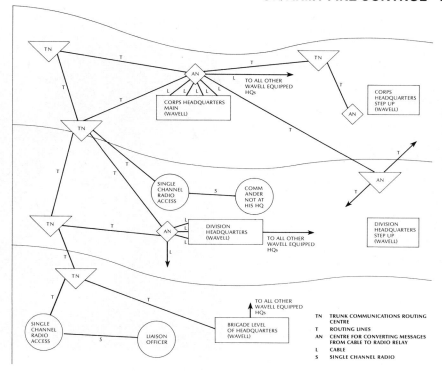

Integration of Wavell system with typical communications network

TN	TRUNK COMMUNICATIONS ROUTING CENTRE
T	ROUTING LINES
AN	CENTRE FOR CONVERTING MESSAGES FROM CABLE TO RADIO RELAY
L	CABLE
S	SINGLE CHANNEL RADIO

MDP 1000 system of Wavell battlefield C² automation system can be accommodated in a wide range of military vehicles (tracked, wheeled, ships or aircraft) or used free standing as shown here

not to attempt automatic signal message handling in headquarters, to provide ADP only for operations and intelligence functions, and to base the system on existing staff procedures.

Stage I equipment was fielded in 1978 with the 2nd Armoured Division in the Hanover area. The system was designed to help collect, collate, evaluate and disseminate information to provide commanders with an overall picture of the state of own forces, to make information about own and enemy forces available to supporting arms, to process information from electronic warfare and other intelligence agencies and to build up a picture of enemy deployment and strengths. As the trial proceeded, such was its success that the system was extended beyond this original concept to become widely used by artillery, engineers and logisticians.

In 1979, the Ministry of Defence gave the go-ahead for a Stage II production with the planned introduction of the system in the mid 1980s to the whole of the 1st (British) Corps in the Federal

Republic of Germany. A contract valued at £25 million was placed with Plessey Defence Systems for the production of 33 Wavell systems following the £6 million phase-one trial.

Full operation is expected in 1985 giving the British Army a clear lead in the use of ADP on the battlefield. Both the US and the Federal Republic of Germany have similar systems under development but not to the advanced stage of Wavell. When deployed with 1(BR) Corps in 1985, Wavell Stage II will provide the Corps with a unique, highly sophisticated and flexible C² system, endorsed by the military user after five years' Stage I experience and well ahead of any operational system available to other armies. The Secure Information Management System (SIMS) at the heart of Stage II will form the core of future applications.

CONTRACTOR

Plessey Defence Systems, Christchurch, Dorset, England.

4753.161

QUICKFIRE ARTILLERY FCS

The Marconi Quickfire artillery fire control system, introduced at the 1984 British Army Equipment Exhibition, is designed for use at battery and battalion level with all types and calibres of indirect fire weapons. It was a private venture development by Marconi Command and Control Systems, and is a successor to the earlier FACE system (**2415.161**).

While many of the FACE features, such as the tactile colour-coded keyboard and customer-language matrix, have been retained in Quickfire, use of later technology (eg CMOS devices) has permitted significant reductions in weight and volume of the equipment. The result is a unit weighing six per cent that of its predecessor, with three per cent of its volume, at less cost than comparable previous generation equipment.

Quickfire uses full ballistic modelling to provide fire control data and the system can be configured as a Battery (serving up to eight guns) or a single gun system. It is based on a common hardware unit that can be configured for use by a forward observer (FO) as a data module, as battery or battery command post modules, and as individual gun display modules. A plug-in software module stores ballistic data to adapt the unit for operation with specific types of weapon. This basic data is available from a library of FACE programs which currently cover most weapons in general use throughout the world.

Entry of mission data into Quickfire units is by

means of a menu-led formats of the matrix whereby visual prompts are given at each stage of the operation. Battery fire control data is computed in less than one third of the time of flight, and the solution is presented in the form of a back-lit LCD which is easily visible in all lighting conditions likely to be encountered. There is storage for up to 100 target locations, ten firing zones, and ten friendly force areas. The system provides for two concurrent fire missions.

Data is conveyed between FOs, command post and gun positions by either radio or cable links, and Quickfire modules have three communications channels which allow for burst transmission of digital data.

As used by a forward observer, the Quickfire module matrix provides preformatted messages to allow the FO to send complete orders for target engagement and to report his own position and friendly locations directly to the command post module. It also receives and displays messages in response.

At individual gun positions, or rocket launchers, Quickfire units are operated as display modules to present all incoming data, while providing answer-back facilities. Individual gun firing data such as, ammunition, charge, fuze, bearing elevation, method of fire and number of rounds are presented.

As a battery or battalion computer module, Quickfire carries out all the necessary survey and ballistic calculations and aids command and control

Quickfire artillery FCS uses common hardware. Same basic module can be used for FO, command post positions as well as ground display module, as here.

of the guns. Each input from FOs is automatically entered and displayed as required, and command post staff have full authority over the input of data and checking of computations. Under operator control, outgoing messages are automatically transferred and transmitted over the radio network.

CHARACTERISTICS

Dimensions: 316 × 290 × 71 mm
Weight: 7 kg; 6·5 kg FO and gun display module
Power consumption: 6·6 W; 2/7 W FO and gun display module
Met data message: Up to 26 lines (any standard)
Target records: Up to 100
Communication channels: 3
Facilities: Printer interface, real-time clock, touch keyboard, 10 firing zones, 2 concurrent missions, survey, etc

STATUS
Ready for production.

CONTRACTOR
Marconi Command and Control Systems Ltd, Chobham Road, Frimley, Camberley, Surrey GU16 5PE, England.

Quickfire module used in the forward observer module role

4754.181

MARCAL GUN CALIBRATION SYSTEM/MOGUL

The Marconi Marcal gun calibration system is an on-gun system that measures the velocity of every round fired, stores this data and produces a statistical basis for gun calibration, offering a more rapid and accurate way of continuously correcting for variables such as bore wear, met conditions, muzzle velocity etc, that affect the accuracy of fire.

Typically, shell velocity, or a corrected quadrant elevation and fuze setting, where applicable are displayed after each round fired, so that effectively the gun performance is continuously monitored. At the same time the gun data base is automatically updated, enabling calculation of gun laying adjustments on a round by round basis. The equipment is designed for permanent fitting on all categories of field guns of 30 mm or above, and consists of two small units: a doppler radar head, and a control unit containing a microprocessor.

The doppler radar head incorporates a microprocessor and provides accurate velocity measurement with low transmitted power. The control unit includes a data analysis and storage system, an operator display, and an automatic data interface for system expansion. A non-volatile store holds the firing data of the last 50 rounds fired and this

information can be retrieved on a simple portable recorder.

CHARACTERISTICS
Radar: 5 mW spread spectrum technique
Transmission duration: 1s (max per round)
Beam: 5° (horizontal) × 10° (vertical)
Velocity measurement error: 0·2% (max)
Projectile speed range: 100 – 1000 m/s
Processing speed: 30 rounds/minute
Min projectile calibre: 30 mm

MOGUL

The Marcal muzzle velocity measuring radar is also employed in the Company's Mogul modular gun laying system which is a derivative of the Marcal system with additional items to suit it for use with SP and towed field guns. In the Mogul system the central unit is the display and processor unit (DPU) which is provided with a fast two-way data bus for on-board operations. A data link compatible with a variety of artillery fire control systems allows for inputs from:
(1) an electronically enhanced indirect and direct fire sighting system
(2) gun safety instrumentation
(3) an inertial gun reference unit
(4) gun control electronics.

Mogul automates the gun laying procedure using the on-board sensors and the microprocessor based control system. The indirect fire sight is rigidly mounted on to the turret and encoders feed traverse and elevation data to the DPU. Correction for sight and turret cant and tilt are provided by precision inclinometers carried on the gun mounting. A shell position sensor confirms that the shell is correctly rammed to avoid fall back, and gun tube temperature is sensed to monitor the approach of cook-off conditions.

A gun attitude reference unit employing a microprocessor and strapdown inertial technology is fixed to the gun mounting to provide direct measurement of gun elevation and azimuth values. A control unit interfaces with the gun laying system and provides rapid autonomous gun laying from the DPU.

STATUS
When the Marcal and Mogul systems were announced in mid-1984 the contractor stated that both were ready for production, although no contract details were available at that time.

CONTRACTOR
Marconi Command and Control Systems Ltd, Chobham Road, Frimley, Camberley, Surrey GU16 5PE, England.

3523.161

MORCOS MORTAR COMPUTING SYSTEM

The Marconi Morcos mortar computing system computes firing data for all types of mortar and is intended to replace the existing manual methods of fire prediction calculation which are slow, prone to inaccuracy and wasteful of ammunition.

Morcos is a single self-contained unit incorporating a computer, keyboard for data entry, display and batteries. The case is built of durable polycarbonate and profiled to fit comfortably in the hand. It is built to full military specifications to withstand adverse climatic, environmental and nuclear effects.

A wide range of drills is available and, as an example, the program for the British Army's L16 81 mm light mortar, includes drills which produce data for HE (high explosive) smoke and illuminating missions, survey problems, target reduction and three concurrent fire missions. It incorporates inputs which take into account variables such as meteorological conditions, charge temperature, difference in altitude between mortar and target, position of own troops, observers' corrections (including laser rangefinders) and individual mortar locations. It has the capacity to accommodate ten mortar positions, fifty targets, ten observer locations

and nine positions of own troops (for warning when own troops are in the danger area).

The computer in Morcos is a microprocessor with access to a semi-conductor backing store. Each ballistic program can predict for one type of mortar and its attendant ammunition. The program can be changed in seconds by removing a plug-in memory unit (called a ballistic module) and by replacing it by another for a different ammunition system. This can be done, in the field, in all weather conditions because the moisture seal in the equipment is not broken.

The elastomeric type keyboard is both waterproof and reliable and is illuminated for night operation by a variable brightness electroluminescent panel. The keyboard has twenty-four keys, ten of which are for digits 0 to 9. The display has a capacity for eight alpha-numeric characters and uses high efficiency, extra bright, light-emitting diodes, which have a variable lighting control.

Morcos is powered by batteries, which can be either throwaway or rechargeable, or from an external power source. It weighs, including batteries, less than 1·35 kg and measures 23 × 10·1 × 5·4 cm. It is a highly reliable system based on the use of large scale integration and hybrid techniques. Faults can be quickly repaired by easily replaceable sub-

Morcos mortar computer system

assemblies, and no special first line test equipment is needed.

STATUS
Full production and supplied to seven countries.

CONTRACTOR
Marconi Command and Control Systems Ltd, Chobham Road, Frimley, Camberley, Surrey GU16 5PE, England.

2400.161
AMETS – ARTILLERY METEOROLOGICAL SYSTEM

AMETS is the name given to a self-contained, computer-based, mobile meteorological system developed for the British Army by Marconi Space and Defence Systems Ltd and Plessey Radar, for obtaining and processing information on atmospheric conditions automatically. It is capable of processing data from a wind-finding radar and radio sonde complex to an altitude of 20 km every hour, and incorporates a facility to output partial messages within seconds of the radio sonde passing through the relevant height band. A single AMETS will normally provide all meteorological data needed in the area of one army division.

AMETS uses a specially-developed radio sonde with a very accurate temperature sensor. The outputs from radio sonde and radar are fed into a computer which can then calculate the required meteorological information. Measurement of surface pressure, and the average humidity figures which can be provided for the particular zone of operation are stored in the computer memory. The loss of accuracy resulting from this simplification of the radio sonde is negligible for artillery purposes, yet it offers appreciable gains in terms of operational simplicity and reliability in military field conditions.

CONSTRUCTION
The data processing part of the system is based on an MC1800 computer, produced by Marconi-Elliot Computer Systems, and already in use in a wide variety of military applications including FACE. The Plessey WF3M radar is built to full military standards, and is derived from the Plessey WF3 wind-finding

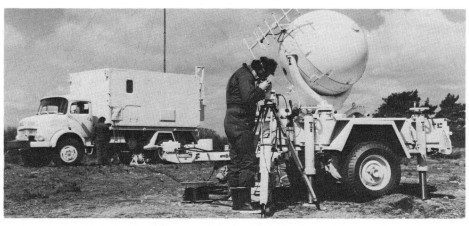

Plessey WF3M mobile wind-finding radar is primary sensor of upper air winds for AMETS. In early 1981 contracts from the Middle East brought the total of these radars sold to 40

radar used for civil meteorology.

AMETS is mounted in a single instrumentation vehicle with a small trailer carrying the radar. In addition there will normally be a command post vehicle, and reconnaissance and stores vehicles to carry hydrogen and other troop stores. The instrumentation vehicle will carry all the data processing equipment, the radar and radio sonde monitoring and display units and a full range of diagnostic test equipment.

STATUS
In service. A more compact version, called

MILIMETS, was introduced in June 1976. This equipment offers sondes as an option and is mounted in Land-Rover vehicles. AMETS is in service with at least three countries (including the UK), and MILIMETS with one.

CONTRACTORS
Marconi Command and Control Systems Ltd, Chobham Road, Frimley, Camberley, Surrey GU16 5PE, England.

The Plessey Radar Ltd, Addlestone, Weybridge, Surrey KT15 2PW, England.

2644.161
BATES – BATTLEFIELD ARTILLERY TARGET ENGAGEMENT SYSTEM

BATES is the acronym for battlefield artillery target engagement system which in turn describes a semi-automatic data-processing and fire control system being developed for the British Army. A major feature is the use of distributed data processing, with each command level having computing power appropriate to its function and information on call from other parts of the system using digital communications.

The function of the system is to accept inputs from observers and artillery staffs using radar, sound ranging systems, reconnaissance devices, and other sensors, and store, analyse, and display them –

including both new and old target information – in such a way as to enable the artillery commander to make decisions. In this aspect the system differs conceptually from that of TACFIRE (**2827.161**): in the latter all possible functions are performed automatically, whereas the British approach is to retain the commander's brain in the control loop.

In-service net and trunk communications systems will link observers and target acquisition equipment with artillery headquarters and fire units; and this, coupled with the automatic data processor, will enable observers to feed target data to the command posts. This will both speed up the engagement of targets and, by reducing the number of human links in the chain, reduce the probability of human error

relative to that of earlier systems. At every level of command all relevant data will be presented clearly to the artillery commander – again with the objective of saving time. Included in the system will be equipment to replace FACE – field artillery computer equipment (**2415.161**), the artillery weapon data transmission system (**3215.161**), and the data processing elements of AMETS (**2400.161**).

STATUS
In full scale development. The projected introduction of operational service is in 1987.

CONTRACTOR
Marconi Command and Control Systems Ltd, Chobham Road, Frimley, Camberley, Surrey GU16 5PE, England.

2415.161
FACE – FIELD ARTILLERY COMPUTER EQUIPMENT

FACE is a field gunnery computer system specifically designed to perform quickly and accurately the lengthy calculations which are involved in producing artillery firing data.

FACE undertakes two specific roles. First, as an artillery survey computer it carries out all the calculations necessary in this task. Second, and more importantly, as a gun data computer it processes all the information required to place a shell accurately on the target and displays this information on a console.

FACE has been modernised by replacing the 920B computer by the MC 1800, which uses the latest LSI sliced technology. This has greatly increased the speed of operation and the memory capacity. This improved capability has resulted in a system that can control the fire of up to 32 weapons, deployed as four batteries, each of up to eight weapons. For greater tactical flexibility, FACE can still be deployed at each battery.

OPERATION
While the guns are deploying for action, the console operator in the command-post vehicle begins to receive setting-up data. This is added to the information already in the computer's store which includes a latitude function allowing for earth rotational effects and the muzzle velocity for each gun for each charge. The first input is the geographical reference of the centre of the battery position – the 'battery grid'; next the position of each gun in relation to battery centre, and the temperature of the

FACE installed in a Land-Rover

ammunition charges. Then meteorological information is received by radio and is also entered into the computer. The equipment is now ready to receive data for shooting in the form of target position and height, the type of ammunition to be used, etc. Once all the relevant information has been fed into the computer, it produces answers which are passed to the guns via the AWDATS (**3215.161**).

The forward observer, noting the fall of shot, radios corrections, determined visually or by the use of a laser rangefinder, back to the command-post. The console operator feeds these straight into FACE which computes updated gun data for relay to the guns.

Frequently gunners are required to deliver fire in support of a pre-arranged battle plan. In practice, battle conditions often call for changes to this fire plan and because FACE has great speed and flexibility, these changes can be easily accommodated.

Modern weapons tend to be multi-charge in nature and to have both high- and low-angle fire capability, employing several types of projectile to give a wide choice of performance. Their versatility could not be fully exploited without the assistance of FACE. A wide variety of gun and rocket programs are available for use with FACE.

STATUS

In service with the armed forces of 18 countries.

CONTRACTOR

Marconi Command and Control Systems Ltd, Chobham Road, Frimley, Camberley, Surrey GU16 5PE, England.

4142.161

EPCS ELECTRONIC PLANE CONVERSION SYSTEM

Designed initially for the SP70 self-propelled howitzer (**2196.103**) project, the electronic plane conversion (EPC) system is a microprocessor-based system which eliminates the necessity for mechanically cross-levelled sights by converting the earth-plane target co-ordinates automatically into individual gun data. The accuracy achieved is stated to be far greater than that possible using opto-mechanical systems and less prone to human error.

Used with a simple optical sight, the EPC enables indirect fire weapon systems to be laid swiftly and with an accuracy and repeatability difficult to achieve using current mechanical methods. Target information in earth co-ordinates is relayed from the central fire direction computer to the weapon using an automatic data transfer unit such as AWDATS (**3125.161**). Taking the inputs from the rugged weapon platform tilt sensors and the sight and gun/launcher attitude encoders, the microprocessor converts this earth-plane target information into corrected weapon-plane data, which is displayed on a control panel adjacent to the sight at the layer's position. LED displays instruct the layer to realign the

Accuracy trials of EPC prototype have been run with FH70 howitzer seen here engaging target at a range of 12 km

weapon and sight, following a simple drill, in the directions indicated by illuminated arrows. When the correct lay is achieved the control panel shows a clear null display.

Laying the weapon on receipt of initial fire orders or between rounds of adjustment or fire-for-effect is accomplished more swiftly and accurately with much less chance of human error than when using conventional mechanical systems. The EPC system is based on established equipment design and because

of its compact and modular packaging can be readily adapted to any indirect-fire weapon system under consideration. It is a flexible system with potential for active development to embrace semi-automatic laying systems in the future.

The predicted reliability of EPC is very high and in-built test programs enable the operator to check the system quickly. A power-down facility ensures no loss of data during temporary fault conditions and a simple optical back-up is provided in case of total system failure.

DEVELOPMENT

Development was undertaken jointly by Marconi Radar Systems Ltd and the Royal Armament Research and Development Establishment for the SP70 self-propelled 155 mm howitzer.

STATUS

Equipment is in production for the SP70. It has been checked for accuracy by firing trials mounted on the FH 70 towed howitzer (**2195.103**). EPC is suitable for use with M109, M109A1 and other guns, and trials are planned with an M109.

CONTRACTOR

Marconi Command and Control Systems Ltd, Chobham Road, Frimley, Camberley, Surrey GU16 5PE, England.

4157.181

PADS POSITION AND AZIMUTH DETERMINING SYSTEM

The Ferranti position and azimuth determining system (PADS Mk II) has evolved from PADS Mk I, now in service with the British Army, and FILS the commercial inertial land surveyor system. It is designed to meet an extended military requirement for a compact vehicle- or helicopter-mounted, accurate survey and navigation system, capable of on-board mission processing in near real-time. The equipment displays continuously its position in geographical or UTM grid co-ordinates, together with orientation relative to true or grid north. Alternatively given the co-ordinates of a destination point, the equipment will display continuously the range and bearing to that point, to assist navigation. The system permits the storage of up to 62 waypoints, which may be a combination of established control and new points being fixed, enabling the accuracy of computed values to be improved as new control data is provided during the traverse. Position information is accurate to within three metres and azimuth to within 0·3 mil after mission processing of an open traverse. For traverses of up 15 km between established control, points may be fixed to a relative accuracy of better than one metre. The equipment is entirely self-contained and is powered from a vehicle 24 V DC supply.

Control and display unit for PADS Mk II

Main unit of Ferranti PADS Mk II

The main application for PADS is to provide artillery units with position and orientation data for guns, launchers, observation posts and to carry out surveys for target acquisition devices. This greatly improves the effectiveness and flexibility of artillery on the battlefield and provides a saving in survey personnel. PADS Mk II is a single box system in a mounting tray with overall dimensions of 540 × 470 × 500 mm and 51 kg weight, together with a control and display unit which may be mounted in any convenient

position in the vehicle. Azimuth is transferred by auto collimation on the systems mirrors or by fixing two bearing pickets.

STATUS

PADS Mk I is in service and quantity production for the British Army overseas. PADS Mk II has been developed to meet overseas orders.

CONTRACTOR

Ferranti plc, Navigation Systems Department, Silverknowes, Edinburgh EH4 4AD, Scotland.

3125.161

AWDATS - ARTILLERY WEAPON DATA TRANSMISSION SYSTEM

AWDATS is an artillery weapon data transmission system which displays the firing data calculated by the field artillery computer equipment (FACE) (**2415.161**) at the individual guns of a battery. Due to the different geographical location of each gun within the battery and variations in muzzle velocity between guns, there is a small but significant difference between the data for each gun in the battery.

The guns are provided with a data display unit which receives the data from a coding and distribution unit in the command post. The display units can either be installed in the vehicle for self-propelled guns or mounted on a frame for towed guns. Data transmission is by a frequency shift modulation audio frequency signal over existing radio or line channels which are also used for voice communications. Transmissions are audible and take less than three seconds for a complete battery of six guns. AWDATS makes a valuable contribution to the

speed of reaction and efficiency of guns within the battery by eliminating the necessity for verbal transmission, checking of gun data and greatly reducing the probability of errors being made.

STATUS

Currently in service with the armed forces of the United Kingdom and a number of other countries.

CONTRACTOR

Marconi Command and Control Systems Ltd, Chobham Road, Frimley, Camberley, Surrey GU16 5PE, England.

4583.181

MARCONI AFCS

The Marconi advanced fire control system (AFCS) has been developed for advanced main battle tanks and is standard fit on the Vickers Valiant. Used in

conjunction with an advanced gun control such as GCE 628 (**4582.181**), and modern sighting systems such as stabilised panoramic sights and thermal imagers, AFCS provides for extremely accurate shooting both static and on the move. The system

comprises a computer using a 16-bit microprocessor to which information is fed from a tilt sensor and meteorological sensor. Rate signals are taken from the gyroscopes and additional information such as ammunition type, wear and ammunition temperature are manually selected on the control panel. This contains its own 8-bit microprocessor and a 36-character alpha-numeric display for ease of operation. The computer calculates the required ballistic offsets which are used to inject an aiming

mark into the sight, and simultaneously the gun is automatically offset by signals fed to the gun control system. Continual updating of information passed to the computer ensures total system accuracy under all conditions.

STATUS
Production.
CONTRACTOR
Marconi Command and Control Systems Ltd, Chobham Road, Frimley, Camberley, Surrey GU16 5PE, England.

3321.181
SFCS 600 TANK FIRE CONTROL SYSTEM

The SFCS 600 fire control system is designed specifically for fitting into existing battle tanks such as the Centurion, M47, M48, M60, T54/55, T62, Vickers Mk 3 MBT, and Vijayanta.

The basic SFCS 600 system uses an all microprocessor-based computer to store ballistic and other information, compute corrections and output these corrections to the system. Target range is obtained from a laser rangefinder, which is usually integral with the gunner's sight. If a moving target is engaged, target rate in both elevation and traverse is obtained from pickoffs on the turret and gun, as the gunner tracks the target.

The type of ammunition, barrel wear, crosswind strength, charge temperature, etc are set in manually, while the tilt of the gun trunnion axis is obtained from a sensor on the gun.

The computed traverse and elevation aim-offs necessary to engage either a stationary or moving target are presented as a spot of light (aiming point), injected into the eyepiece of the gunner's laser sight. When the gunner has acquired the target and commenced the tracking sequence using the laser aiming mark on his sight graticule, he presses the laser range button, which informs the computer that the sight is on-target. After a short tracking period, which is at the discretion of the gunner, the laser button is released. The laser then fires and ranges the target. When range information is received by the computer, all other data is scanned (eg ammunition type, barrel wear, crosswind, average target speed) and the ballistic calculation routine is carried out. The aiming point is then injected into the gunner's sight. By realignment of the target and aiming point, correct aim-off is achieved.

The computer is pre-programmed for the particular gun and types of ammunition used. Read-only memories (ROMs) are used to store the ballistic co-efficients for the various shell trajectories. It is therefore an easy matter to convert to another type of gun or ammunition by changing the program ROMs in the computer.

Schematic diagram of SFCS 600

Equipment supplied with the system includes microprocessor computer unit, control panel, spot injection unit, tilt sensor and target rate units. Any suitable laser rangefinder can be used. The equipment is constructed to UK MoD standards and uses NATO-approved components. External sensors to inject other data (such as the automatic measurement of crosswind) can also be supplied as additional items.

A recent proposal is the use of the SFCS 600 in conjunction with the L7 105 mm tank gun in a naval mount for use aboard patrol boats. (See **3659.203** in Naval Ordnance section.) Additional details can be found in *Jane's Armour and Artillery*.

STATUS
In full production with over 1000 rounds of ammunition having been fired in trials carried out in the UK and overseas. Analysis of firing trials results show that against both stationary and moving targets the hit probability achieved is better than the calculated HITPRO curves derived from theoretical analysis.
CONTRACTOR
Marconi Command and Control Systems Ltd, Chobham Road, Frimley, Camberley, Surrey GU16 5PE, England.

4582.181
EFCS 600

EFCS 600 has been developed from the SFCS 600 (**3321.181**), a system that has fired over 2000 rounds in trials and is now in service in a number of countries. EFCS has been specifically designed for ease of retrofit into any MBT including M41, M48, Centurion, Chieftain, T55 and Vickers MK1 and MK3, and trials have proved the system to be simple to operate providing greatly improved hit probabilities and considerably decreased engagement times.

An 8-bit microprocessor-based computer cubicle is used to store ballistic information and carry out the calculations required to produce the offsets. A simple to operate commander's control panel incorporates switches to manually input ammunition type, barrel wear and if required, range and meteorological data. An alpha-numeric display provides the user with full function information, and a further switch operates a complete system built-in test routine. Sensors supply azimuth and elevation rates, wind speed/direction and air density, and gun trunnion tilt. A sight mounted laser rangefinder supplies target range.

To engage a moving target, ammunition type is selected then the target tracked with the laser button depressed. On releasing the button, the laser is fired, feeding the range and sensor information to the computer, which calculates the offsets required. The resultant aiming mark can then be laid onto the centre of the target ready for firing. When used with a CRT aiming mark system, an Aiming Mark Drive Unit controls the CRT and provides a dot enclosed by an expanding/contracting circle in the sight's FOV.

The computer is programmed for the particular gun and ammunition natures used, however by simply changing the ROMs the system can be converted for

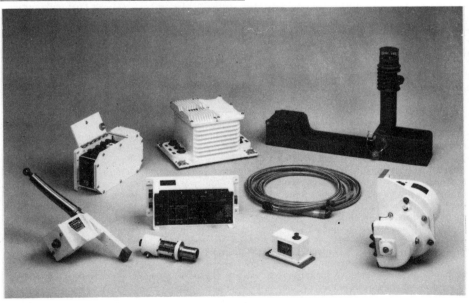

Group photo of EFCS 600 equipment

a different gun or ammunition. Enhancements incorporated into EFCS 600 include the ability to interface with thermal sights, a semi-indirect engagement facility, and a new more compact control panel offering simpler operator control. Other compatible items of gun control equipment are listed in the following paragraphs.

STATUS
Currently in service with two armies and in quantity production, the EFCS 600 is fitted as standard equipment to the Vickers MK3 main battle tank.

Associated gun control equipment for main battle tanks includes the following:

GCE 620

The GCE 620 gun control and stabilisation system is standard equipment on the Vickers Mark 3 main battle tank. Its solid-state modular design also allows the system to be fitted to a number of other tanks including Chieftain and Centurion to provide the improved stabilised performance required for accurate shooting on the move. The system can be interfaced with a fire control system such as the Marconi EFCS 600 to provide a fully integrated weapon control system.

GCE 628

GCE 628 has been designed for advanced main battle tanks and is standard equipment on the Vickers Valiant, although it can be simply retrofitted to su' vehicles as Chieftain or Challenger. It uses advanced solid-state technology to provide a very high performance from a compact design. The system incorporates a solid-state power amplifier which gives a significant increase in performance over the rotary metadyne with a considerable reduction in battery drain. A recent trial has proved the system's capability to complete a full day's static firing without the need to charge the batteries. Additional advantages offered by GCE 628 over previous systems include a considerable space saving, the facility for further expansion, instant warm up enabling the vehicle to be quickly operational, and considerable improvements in low speed tracking accuracy and high slew rates. GCE 628 has been designed to interface with stabilised panoramic sights and a fire control system such as the Marconi AFCS to provide an advanced and fully integrated weapon control system.

GCE 650

GCE 650 has been developed to provide gun control equipment on T-Tanks such as the T59, T55 and T62, with the advantages of solid-state technology. The thermionic amplifier, gyros and vibrating relay are all replaced by solid-state electronics combined in a single cubicle that can be mounted under the breech. The elevation control valve and the gunner's duplex controls are both modified. GCE 650 offers 2-axes stabilisation, improved accuracy of lay, excellent reliability, low drift, ease of maintenance and, if the

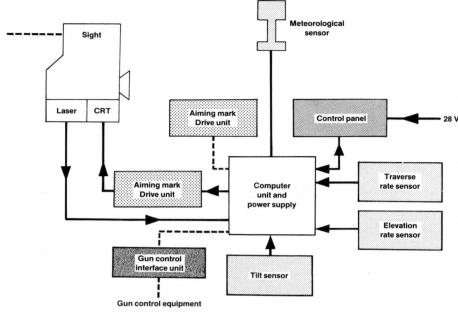

EFCS 600 block diagram

servo motors are modified, improved performance. GCE 650 can also be used as part of a modification package to provide stabilisation for tanks using non-stabilised hydraulic gun control such as M48.

PD700 Power Drive

Experience gained by Marconi in MBT gun control has led to the development of a compact lightweight power drive capable of providing light armoured vehicles, such as Scorpion, with considerably improved performance. The system gives the crew complete control of the turret and gun and provides continuous control from low tracking speeds to slew speed with high acceleration thus allowing the gunner or commander to lay quickly onto a target. Its main advantages over hydraulic systems are

reliability, safety from fire risk, size, ease of installation and maintenance. Items of equipment provided include an electronic cubicle, traverse and elevation gearboxes, thumb controllers and other miscellaneous items such as cable harness and safety switches. It can be interfaced with a fire control system such as EFCS 600 to provide a complete weapon control system.

CONTRACTOR

Marconi Command and Control Systems Ltd, Chobham Road, Frimley, Camberley, Surrey GU16 5PE, England.

2647.181

IFCS - IMPROVED (TANK) FIRE CONTROL SYSTEM

Designed primarily for use in the Chieftain main battle tank (**5006.102**) as a replacement for the FV/GCE No 7 Mk 4 equipment, IFCS is a computer-based integrated digital tank fire control system. Based on the Marconi 12-12P general-purpose digital computer and the Barr and Stroud TLS – 2 tank laser sight (No 1 Mk II), it is a compact system intended for retrofitting in existing vehicles with minimum reduction in the quantity of ammunition carried.

The computer, which can accurately simulate ballistic trajectories out to the longest ranges likely to be used in tank engagements, accepts data for the trajectory calculation from various sensors, which provide continuous information on such parameters as wind speed and direction, air pressure, air temperature, trunnion tilt and angle of sight. Muzzle velocity is derived from ammunition to be fired, charge temperature and barrel wear, which is predicted from a count of equivalent full charges fired. All this information may be readily monitored by the tank commander and can, if required, be overridden by means of a manual input. The equipment is suitable for engaging fixed or moving targets from a stationary or moving vehicle.

OPERATION

When the commander has slewed the turret to the approximate azimuth and elevation of the target, and the gunner has confirmed that it is in his sight, the main armament and ammunition are selected on the

Chieftain tank equipped with the IFCS during trials of the system

firing handle – an operation that automatically charges the laser. The gun is then loaded and simultaneously the gunner lays the sight aiming mark on the target, flashes the laser, and continues to track the target. Range is displayed instantly, both as a digital display in the sights and as an elliptical aiming mark surrounding the target in the sight graticule.

Within about one second (depending on the target and the ammunition to be used) after the laser is flashed, the computer calculates the ballistic trajectory and aim-off for target movement. Then, as soon as the gunner presses the autolay switch, the computer offsets the elliptical aiming mark in the sight to give a new point of aim for target range and speed. Using these corrections, the computer also automatically re-lays the gun, and the gunner fires when the target and aiming mark again coincide.

The controls for all the operator-selected functions are mounted on a single firing handle, which is operated by the gunner's left hand: his right hand is free to lay the gun in azimuth and elevation, using a thumb controller. All system tell-back displays used during an engagement are projected in the sight, so that the operator need never take his eyes off the target nor change his hand positions. Firing handles, thumb controllers, and sights are provided for both the commander and the gunner, but with the difference that the former can override the latter.

STATUS

It was announced in April 1975 that the development of IFCS for Chieftain had entered its final development and production engineering phase with the award of a £1 million contract to Marconi Space and Defence Systems. The same announcement gave the local development cost as £2·5 million. Development trials have been completed successfully and the system is now in quantity production for the UK armed forces. This system is being adapted for fitting to other tanks and fittings have been made in the FV4030/2 (Khalid) MBT for Jordan and the Challenger. The IFCS has also been proposed for retrofitting in Italian Leopard Is by Marconi Italiana who have made arrangements with the British manufacturers for licence production of the system as SICAT.

CONTRACTOR

Marconi Command and Control Systems Ltd, Chobham Road, Frimley, Camberley, Surrey GU16 5PE, England.

4581.181

MARCONI DFCS

The Marconi digital fire control system (DFCS) was originally designed to cater for both new vehicle and retrofit/modernisation markets where improved fire control facilities are required to meet modern AFV specifications. Use of the DFCS enables light and medium armoured fighting vehicles to be equipped with sophisticated gunnery facilities, giving better hit potential and survivability.

The modular design and compact size of DFCS enables it to be fitted into the small turrets of light armoured vehicles and into the restricted space in tanks such as M41, M48 and T series requiring modernisation. Particular attention in the design of DFCS to manufacturing, quality and testing methods has ensured that production costs are compatible with the weapons fit budget of these vehicles. DFCS offers the full capabilities essential to a modern fire control system including moving target capability,

automatic gun laying (Autolay) and a built-in gunnery training simulator. It also has a fire on the move capability for MBT applications.

The DFCS 16-bit digital computer unit calculates a ballistic solution including inputs for meteorological data, relative target motion, barrel wear and trunnion tilt. Its performance is compatible with the accuracy of 76, 90, 105 and 120 mm calibre guns even at extended ranges using low velocity HEAT and HESH rounds. Simple engagement procedures are designed to reduce the dependence on human judgement and skill under stressful battlefield conditions. System ergonomics are such that the gunner maintains visual contact with the target over the entire engagement sequence with all relevant information displayed in the gunner's sight. All necessary controls are mounted on the gunner's handles. A feature of DFCS is that it offers an automatic servo-controlled final lay of the gun in readiness to fire which enables DFCS to achieve faster and more accurate engagements than manual fire control systems. The combination of high first round hit probability, extended range and fast engagement ensures a high probability of battlefield survival.

The main elements of the DFCS are described in the following paragraphs.

COMPUTER

The computer incorporates self-test software and permanently retains data such as barrel wear and 'shooting-in' adjustments. The main programme is held on a plug-in module.

CONTROL PANEL

This provides the following Commander's facilities and displays in any language or script:

(1) system and calibration confidence checks
(2) designation and display of ammunition type
(3) entry of ballistic information such as charge temperature, air density, barrel wear and static offset corrections
(4) monitor of sensor inputs
(5) entry of add/drop corrections
(6) manual override of automatic sensors.

CRT CONTROLLER

This produces computer controlled display images in the sight including aiming mark, alpha-numeric range and ammunition type. It also provides simulated target shape, and tracer trajectories in the training mode.

BALLISTIC SENSORS

To increase system accuracy further sensors for trunnion tilt (cant) and meteorological conditions are fitted, plus optical encoders for Traverse and Elevation to provide high quality target tracking and to ensure accurate automatic gun laying.

CONTROLS

For a power driver turret servo the firing handle and thumb controller provide the gunner with all the controls necessary to conduct an engagement ie weapon selection, ammunition designation, lasing, autolaying and firing on the firing handle, and target

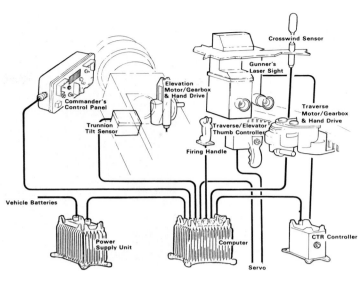

Schematic diagram of Marconi DFCS

DFCS trials were carried out in Cadillac Gage V-150 Commando light AFV with a 90 mm gun

Main DFCS modules (left to right): CRT controller, computer unit, and commander's panel

tracking on the thumb controller. Controls are available for both electric and hydraulic driven turret servo systems.

STATUS

Preliminary firing trials took place in the summer of 1983 in a Cadillac Gage Commando V-150 wheeled

AFV, reportedly with promising results, and DFCS was publicly disclosed for the first time at the Association of the United States Army exhibition in Washington in October 1983. No contract details have been revealed.

CONTRACTOR

Marconi Command and Control Systems Ltd, Chobham Road, Frimley, Camberley, Surrey GU16 5PE, England.

4143.161

DF1-5 FIRE CONTROL SYSTEMS

This series of fire control systems for tanks and other AFVs includes versions for use with tank laser day sights and for use in conjunction with a thermal scanner. The DF1 model was designed principally for vehicles such as the Scorpion light tank and comprises a laser tank sight and DF1 ballistic range calculator, the latter incorporating a number of microprocessors and circuit cards carrying the ballistic characteristics of different ammunition types. The tank sight's Nd-YAG laser rangefinder provides true target range data, which is used in the DF1 processor with ballistic data to generate gun laying information which is injected into the gunner's eyepieces. The gunner can insert range corrections by the use of 'add' or 'drop' buttons which increase or decrease the ballistic range value by 10 m

increments. Such adjustments are meant to combine compensation for such factors as variations from standard ambient conditions within a single correction.

The DF3 is a more comprehensive development of the DF1 intended to equip main battle tanks, and in both cases the preferred tank laser sight is the Barr and Stroud TLS. Addition of a thermal imager, such as the Barr and Stroud IR18 (**3834.093**), to the DF1 or DF3 to provide a night channel results in the DF4 and DF5 fire control systems. The TLS is retained in both cases.

STATUS

The DF1 has been evaluated in Scorpion light tanks, and the DF5 in main battle tanks in the UK and overseas. No production contract details have been disclosed.

Control box of Type DF5 FCS

CONTRACTOR

Barr & Stroud Ltd, Caxton Street, Anniesland, Glasgow G13 1HZ, Scotland.

4148.161

FERRANTI FCS1-3 FIRE CONTROL SYSTEMS (FALCON)

Ferranti Computer Systems has designed a range of fire control systems for fitting in tanks and other AFVs based on the F100-L microprocessor digital computer and intended to be used with a variety of sensors and sighting equipment. The system is designed for retrofitting in existing vehicles and for incorporation in new ones as original equipment. The system offers improved first-round hit capability by providing accurate computation of the correct gun lay with compensation for operational and environmental conditions that most graticule systems do not take into account. These are mostly target motion, trunnion tilt, crosswind, ammunition charge

temperature and barrel wear. Variations in these parameters are fed into the computer by means of automatic and semi-automatic sensors to give the gunner accurate aiming information. With the use of a modern day/night sight which makes possible early identification of the target at long ranges under adverse conditions, the speed of acquisition and engagement can be improved. The sight superimposes the computer-generated aiming point into the gunner's field of view. Accurate range determination by means of a laser rangefinder effectively increases the armament range.

The Ferranti FCS provides the operator with a minimum number of simple controls, with all relevant data being presented in a clear, unambiguous manner. The system has been designed around the

latest microprocessor technology to achieve operational capability in the most cost effective manner. The heart of the system is the F100-L 16-bit military microprocessor, designed to withstand the rigours of a battlefield environment. In addition, F100-L is radiation hardened and has been exposed to a variety of radiations, demonstrating inherent immunity to latchup and satisfactory resistance to degradation from neutron and ionisation doses.

Ferranti FCS1, 2 and 3 are built to full military specifications, offering a range of computerised, laser-assisted fire control systems with modern, integrated day/night sights, which can be readily installed without major engineering to armour or existing AFV systems.

FCS 1

The benefits of automated fire control systems hitherto have been almost entirely restricted to main battle tanks, using systems that are often bulky and costly. The Ferranti FCS provides digital fire control in a system combining small size and low initial cost with simplicity of operation. The basic system comprises the central processor unit, the sealed multi-card F100 module, and associated power supply units. Four automatic sensors including a laser rangefinder are combined with manual data entry to provide system inputs, with up to two control and display panels providing system output.

FCS 2

The inherent flexibility of the microprocessor-based system allows the addition of a wide variety of automatic sensors and interfaces to produce custom-built packages for individual vehicle types. The scope of these enhancements can range from the provision of automatic environmental sensors to complex interfaces with gun control equipments, producing a system to enhance fire-on-the-move capabilities.

FCS 3

Second only to the performance of individual vehicles in the successful conduct of an armoured engagement is the problem of tactical co-ordination. As the speed and momentum of engagement increases, so the need to distribute up-to-date information also increases. The advent of the fully

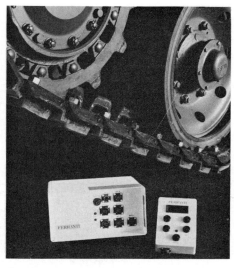

Fire control computer (left) and operator's control panel for Ferranti Falcon. Tank tracks belong to Scorpion

militarised microprocessor has created the opportunity to revolutionise information transfer to battlefield conditions. This possibility was fully

considered during the development of FCS and resulted in the definition of FCS 3. This system further exploits the computing power available from the F100 module to add a battlefield command facility to the basic fire control function. The addition of a VDU to the system means that previously cost-restricted facilities can now be available to junior command levels. When combined with a suitable data transfer system these provide:

(1) tactical information display
(2) tactical map display
(3) tactical *aide memoire*
(4) signal instructions

The system can also be coupled to a navigation equipment providing a moving-map display, effectively co-ordinating with other ground and air forces.

STATUS

The Ferranti F100-L FCS series was introduced in late 1980 and no details of fittings or production contracts have been received to date. The F100-L microprocessor was originally selected as the standard computer for the projected MBT80 tank.

In mid-1982 it was revealed that this range of tank FCS had been refined and is now being offered as the Falcon system. Overseas trials had been conducted at that time and more were planned.

CONTRACTOR

Ferranti Computer Systems Ltd, Western Road, Bracknell, Berkshire RG12 1RA, England.

4531.181
CLASSIC (RGS 2740)

RGS 2740 CLASSIC (Covert Local Area Sensor System for Intrusion Classification) is an extension of the local area sensor system (Project LASS) carried out by the Royal Signals Research Establishment and Racal-SES Ltd to evolve a system that detects, classifies and remotely displays 'target' information on personnel, wheeled and tracked vehicles by means of a variety of remote ground sensors.

The basic system consists of two main units; the sensor and the monitor. Up to eight sensors can be used with each monitor, and the former are designed to be hand emplaced in suitable tactical locations. Each sensor is coupled to a transducer, either a geophone or an infra-red detector. The unit contains signal processing circuitry which classifies the input and broadcasts a tone-coded message by means of a built-in VHF/FM transmitter. The monitor unit receives this signal, decodes the data and presents the information on an LED display to show sensor identification, type and frequency of intrusion. To extend the range of the sensor transmission, a relay unit is available.

CLASSIC is a modular system with a range of optional accessories, which includes alternative antennas and battery units, transducer/pressure pad switches and a hard copy printer to meet a wide range of ground sensor applications. Standard sensors are the TA 2741 used with the MA 2743 seismic

transducer, or the MA 2744 infra-red transducer. The MA 2743 has a switch to select High, Medium or Low Personnel seismic sensitivity, and another switch to select the classification code.

The RTA 2746 monitor comprises a VHF receiver, a tone decoder and an LED display. On receipt of a transmission from a sensor unit, an audible alarm alerts the operator. The sensor's identification and alarm mode setting is displayed on a matrix of three LEDs for each of the eight possible sensors. The display is inhibited after about eight seconds to avoid excessive battery drain, and a pushbutton is provided to enable viewing on demand if required. A user's map panel provides for drawing of a diagram of a tactical deployment.

STATUS

In April 1984 orders for CLASSIC worth £1·5 million were announced: £1 million from the UK MoD, and £500 000 from more than 10 unnamed overseas countries.

CONTRACTOR

Racal-SES Limited, Duke Street, Windsor, Berkshire SL4 1SB, England.

CLASSIC monitor unit gives audio warning and indicates activated sensor and amount of movement

---

UNITED STATES OF AMERICA

3943.161
MIFASS

The US Marine Integrated Fire and Air Support System (MIFASS) is designed for the command and control of forces involved in a marine amphibious assault, and is intended for the control/management of all the supporting assets such as naval gun fire, artillery, mortars, close air support, material evacuation support, and forward air defence. It is a combined data gathering and processing system with extensive display provisions and based on a modular philosophy to meet the varying needs of different units within an overall Marine force. When deployed at divisional level, MIFASS includes 18 computer centres. At the heart of each is a plasma display of the combat area which overlays a standard military map with a schematic diagram depicting the positions of all friendly forces and the locations of reported enemy units.

Plasma panels are display devices used on several of Norden's military electronics systems, including the Battery Computer System (BCS). Flat glass panels contain row and column electrodes in a neon-

xenon gas mixture. At the intersection of each set of electrodes (750 000 in a MIFASS panel) it is possible to apply voltage and light the panel at that spot.

In a battlefield situation, a map is placed behind the display panel and an operator positions computer-generated alpha-numerics and graphics over it, revealing information about the tactical situation. Two sizes are produced for MIFASS.

Sited at each infantry and artillery command post at the battalion level and above, the centre is part of an organisation that is in contact with dozens of forward observers, and each centre can operate independently. The plasma screen is continuously updated as new data is received. Each commander is part of the integrated control network that brings him commands, delivers requests for fire support, performs computations and transmits orders.

Input data is derived from forward observers, patrols, air reconnaissance, intelligence, and from adjacent MIFASS centres. While still aboard ship, prior to a landing, a MIFASS can receive data from NTDS, and while it remains on board ship after a

landing has begun it can exercise control of the landing operations. Air strikes are directed through MIFASS, and for this function the system shows aircraft position and targets; in return the aircraft transmit mission status and fresh intelligence to the system. A regimental level MIFASS goes ashore in one of the landing craft, with its functions taken over during disembarkation by division or shore-based units, so that the overall system remains effective throughout an advance. The battalion level MIFASS receives intelligence and commands from higher levels, calls for fire from forward observers, and target information for input to the system. Remote users, such as forward observers, patrols, and platoon commanders, communicate with MIFASS by means of handheld digital communications terminals (see **3942.161**).

Modular design enables the requirements of these differing operational levels to be met with various combinations of less than 12 basic units, the only difference being the number of these modules required at each centre. At divisional level they occupy a shelter six metres long, while the regimental shelter is half that size. These two types of shelter are air transportable, but at the battalion level the MIFASS elements are not sheltered but are housed in foxholes or other easily relocated centres, and the equipment is designed to be suitable for deployment of this kind.

MIFASS will probably embody a portion of the technology of the US Army BCS produced by Norden

(**3510.161**) and is designed to be compatible with all other US Marine Corps systems such as the Marine Air-Ground Intelligence System (MAGIS), and Position Locating and Reporting System (PLRS). In addition, an interface has been designed and certain hardware and software commonality has been identified with Tactical Air Operations Central – 85 (TAOC-85), the air defence and traffic control elements of MTACCS.

STATUS
Field testing of MIFASS was planned for the third quarter of 1984 prior to taking a decision on full production.
CONTRACTOR
Norden Systems Inc, Norwalk, Connecticut 06856, USA.

3510.161
BATTERY COMPUTER SYSTEM

The Battery Computer System (BCS), an advanced fire control system developed for the US Army, has been designed to replace the current field artillery digital automatic computer (FADAC) (**1125.161**) and extend the capability of TACFIRE (**2827.161**), the tactical fire direction system. It provides computerised control of artillery fire at the battery level. A real-time command, control and communications system, it is capable of providing simultaneous computations for up to 12 howitzers or guns and handling three concurrent fire missions.

It is a portable, single unit system containing 128 K of memory capacity. By providing direct digital access for forward observers and to battalion TACFIRE, it extends that system's capability to the firing battery level. It also operates in an autonomous mode and can be used for fire planning and the engagement of moving targets.

The BCS is composed of the battery computer unit (BCU) located at the battery fire direction centre and one gun display unit (GDU) for each weapon in the battery. The BCU is the electronic centre for fire control. It maintains a digital communication link with fire direction officers, fire support officers, forward observers, and weapon section chiefs. It performs all required computations for first-round accuracy, with results appearing on a 1728-character plasma display. The BCU contains a data management system which maintains target, fire unit, ammunition, meteorological, map, target, forward observers, and other system information to simplify the FDC tasks. The central processor within the BCU contains 128 K × 24-bit words of memory, with error detection and correction circuitry for fail-safe reliability. The time taken to compute a fire mission with individual data for 12 weapons is two per cent of the time of flight to the target.

The BCU houses a magnetic tape cartridge for software program and data storage, the former permitting central processor programming in under one minute. It interfaces with existing US Army COMSEC equipment and printers. Data are transmitted to the guns in one second. The BCU communicates on the battlefield with WD-1 wire and AM/FM radio.

The communications control device is driven by a microprocessor controller and offers high-speed direct access to the memory module. The BCU contains the main power switches and self-test status panel, so that faults in individual elements can be easily isolated and corrected.

The GDU is the final link in the BCS communications chain. Its place is with each weapon in the firing battery. The GDU consists of three assemblies, a section chief assembly (SCA) and two

The battery computer unit, one of two elements of the BCS, acting on the information from the forward observer, automatically computes the firing data and displays it on the unit's screen. Also displayed is the status of the battery's howitzers. The soldier will select a gun for the mission and transmit the firing data to the gun display unit located at the howitzer

gun assemblies (GA), plus a signal and power distribution unit. All elements are of solid-state sealed construction.

The SCA is a personal tool for the section chief (weapon commander), the man who commands the weapon crew. Slightly larger than a commercial hand-held calculator, the SCA is connected by cable to the signal and power distribution unit, giving instant access to all gun-related data and commands. The device contains its own memory bank for sequential or direct access to stored fire mission information. It is equipped with audible alarms and visual cueing to alert the section chief to fire missions and check fires. An eight-digit display shows positive indication of gun commands under all ambient conditions. A single button sequences the display of gun orders.

The two identical GAs on the weapon show the gunner and assistant gunner separate elevation and deflection display. They are connected by wire to the signal and power distribution unit and receive the commands directly.
DEVELOPMENT
Norden Systems of Norwalk, Connecticut, USA, was awarded a multi-million dollar contract for

development of the Battery Computer System in September 1976. Marconi Space and Defence Systems Limited of England was Norden's principal sub-contractor, and has incorporated much of the experience gained in the design and development of the British FACE (**2415.161**) field artillery computer equipment.
STATUS
A production contract was awarded to Norden in April 1980. Deliveries began in November 1981. The multi-year contract is valued at about $97 million and in June 1980 Norden awarded MSDS Ltd a $20 million contract for the supply of BCS GDUs. These units are based on the MSDS MC1800 microprocessor which is also employed in the latest version of the FACE field artillery computer equipment (**2415.161**). By early 1984 issue of BCS equipment to US Army units had reached 20 per cent of the planned level and deployment was continuing on schedule. The 1985 fiscal year budget included $30·1 million for 1983 procurement (146 sets) with a similar number in 1984 costing $28·7 million. Proposed procurement in 1985-86 is 182 sets costing $39·7 million and $18·1 million for 80 sets.
CONTRACTORS
Norden Systems Inc, Norwalk, Connecticut 06856, USA – Prime contractor.
Marconi Space and Defence Systems Ltd, Warren Lane, Stanmore, Middlesex HA7 4LY, England.

Mission assignments for the BCS are received from forward observers who digitally transmit target information to a battalion TACFIRE or directly to the battery computer unit located at the field artillery level

2643.181
INTEGRATED TANK FIRE CONTROL SYSTEM

Intended primarily for installation in the M60 MBT, in Phase 2 of the product improvement programme, this modern integrated tank fire control system can also be used for the control of different guns in other tanks.

The system is based on the Hughes M21 solid-state ballistic computer. With this are associated a laser rangefinder and sensors to detect and measure trunnion cant, crosswind, ambient temperature, powder temperature, barrel wear and departure error, the automatic sensors being for cant, wind, and rate, while manual inputs include air temperature, air pressure, and barrel wear. The computer can be pre-programmed with the parameters of the different types of ammunition that may be used.

A typical version is intended for the M60A3 tank,

and this is composed of two sub-systems, laser/sight and computer.

The laser/sight sub-system is composed of two main units:
(1) a commander's integrated laser/sight with control unit and
(2) a laser electronics unit. Range may be fed automatically to the computer or, if more than one return is received, the commander may select the range return based on his assessment of the situation. Since the gunner's sight is boresighted with the laser rangefinder, either the commander or the gunner can fire the laser and/or the gun.

The computer sub-system includes the ammunition selection sensors. The commander or gunner may select one of the four basic types of ammunition to be used. Actually, the computer stores solutions for six ammunitions within the four basic

types to accommodate ammunitions stored in different geographical locations. The switch at the bottom of the ammunition selection unit is used to set up either tank moving or stationary conditions.

The computer is a solid-state hybrid. It processes all the input data and commands the sight lines for laying the gun.

The top half of the gunner's control unit panel contains three manual inputs: air temperature, pressure altitude (slowly varying inputs, not required to be very accurate), and manual range in the event of laser failure. All other sensors are automatic. The row of lights at the top of the unit is for self-test. Either a green "System OK" light is lit, or a light comes on indicating which unit is faulty. A red light indicates failure of the system. An orange light indicates that the system will continue to function, but with degraded accuracy. This self-test system removes the trouble-shooting burden from the tank crew, and replacement of system units in the field is easily accomplished. The bottom half of the panel (normally covered) is used for boresighting, zeroing, manual crosswind input (if desired) and a switch to select the ammunition within the four basic types.

Automatic sensors feed data directly into the computer. They are:

(1) the rate unit – used against moving targets from a stationary tank. When the tank is moving, this unit (which is most accurate when the tank is stationary) is switched out and replaced by input from the gun stabilisation system gyros, since inertial tracking rates are required

(2) the crosswind sensor – can be stowed horizontally and is spring mounted to prevent damage when the tank encounters low branches. Since this is the only unit not under armour, a circuit in the computer continuously monitors the crosswind sensor output and can be switched to manual input in the event of failure

(3) the cant unit – senses gun trunnion roll.

There is also a gunner's reticle projector that mates with his periscope and provides azimuth deflection of the reticle, and the output unit which drives the periscope head mirror, and the commander's sight in elevation and super-elevation.

CHARACTERISTICS

Operational range: 200 – 5000 m
Range resolution: 2 targets can be resolved at a minimum of 20 m apart
Range accuracy: ±10 m
Target angular velocity: 0 – 50 mils/s
Max target speed: 0 – 20 m/s
Cant angle: 0 to ±15°
Crosswind (auto): 0 – 18 m/s
Crosswind (manual): 0 – 23 m/s
Air temperature: –54 to +52° C
Altitude: –200 to +3000 m

STATUS

During 1977 Hughes, and later Kollsman were awarded quantity production contracts for systems for fitting in M60A3 MBTs.

Hughes' European licensees have built and tested

M60A3 MBT fire control system in use; crewman is using laser rangefinder

laser fire control systems for the Leopard 1 and M47 tanks operated by the Belgian, Italian and Australian Armies. SABCA (Belgium) has begun deliveries to the Belgian and Australian armies, in the latter case Selenia is providing the laser under licence to SABCA. The UK licensee, Barr and Stroud, has been delivering laser rangefinders for a number of years for the Chieftain tank in the UK and overseas.

In April 1983, Spain selected a laser tank fire control system based on the M60A3 to modernise its M48

tanks. About 70 per cent of M60A3 components are used in the Spanish Army system and many will be produced in Spain by ENOSA/EISA of Madrid, under licence.

CONTRACTORS

Hughes Aircraft Company, Culver City, California 90230, USA.

Kollsman Instrument Company, Daniel Webster Highway South, Merrimack, New Hampshire 03054, USA.

4156.181

VARO MODULAR TANK FCS

Varo Incorporated produces a range of laser rangefinder computerised tank fire control systems which can be fitted internally to most existing tanks in the world without modification to the vehicle. The systems differ in the level of sophistication provided and they are offered in the Arrowhead I and II series and the Spearhead I and II configurations.

All Varo tank fire control systems incorporate the modular component approach for maximum commonality regardless of tank application. For example, the Varo Model 9897 gunner's laser rangefinder/day sight (**4151.193**) and the Model 9880 passive night sight (**4155.193**) are identical (except for reticles) for each system and for almost all tanks. The original gunner's periscope head assembly is used in most Arrowhead installations by incorporating a bolt-on adaptor kit to which the laser rangefinder and passive night sight are mounted. In the Spearhead series, the stabilised periscope head mirror feature uses a replacement periscope head assembly that directly replaces the existing unit; thus permitting a no-modification bolt-on installation. Similarly, the gunner's and commander's control modules, sensors, computer units and emergency power supplies are essentially the same compact units for all systems; differences being only in the mounting brackets and cable lengths for each type tank. This concept reduces cost and eases logistics and training problems; particularly for those armoured forces which possess a mix of armoured vehicles. Furthermore, it permits a 'building block' upgrade approach as time and budget permit.

All systems are designed and tested to achieve a very high (90 per cent or better) first round hit probability at the usual battle ranges of between 800 to 2000 m. The design concept is based on fast, precise measurements of the three most dynamic battlefield variables: range, trunnion tilt (cant) and azimuth rate (moving target 'aim off' or 'lead').

Other less dynamic variables, such as crosswind, barrel wear, air temperature, air density, shell grain

Varo Inc Arrowhead II tank FCS units. Arrowhead I version does not have ballistic controller or azimuth rate sensor units

Spearhead II tank FCS. Spearhead I system uses digital computer instead of ballistic controller unit and has no wind sensor; otherwise same modules are used

temperature etc are corrected in the Arrowhead and Spearhead I series by applying the proper zero for the gun and in the Spearhead II system by continuous sensor measurement and digital computer automatic corrections for any given firing situation. In the Arrowhead series, the gunner applies elevation and deflection values (which appear in his field of view) directly to a simple mil scale reticle, aligns the aim point upon the target and fires. In the Spearhead systems, the gunner's sight picture automatically moves downward the precise number of mils for elevation. The gunner merely aligns this displacement by raising the gun until the centre aim point of the reticle is superimposed upon the target and fires. For moving targets, in the Spearhead I system, the gunner applies a mil readout value to a

simple horizontal mil scale reticle. In the Spearhead II configuration a red dot illuminates, is placed upon the centre of mass of the target and the gun is ready to fire.

The Spearhead series incorporates a gyro-stabilised periscope head mirror which affords a steady view regardless of the undulations of the tank and permits accurate laser ranging while the tank is moving.

CHARACTERISTICS

Laser rangefinder
Range: 0 – 9995 m
Accuracy: ±5 m
Resolution: 5 m
Cant angle
Range: 0 to ±15°

Accuracy: ±30 minutes of arc
Crosswind
Range: ±25 m/s
Accuracy: 1 m/s
Azimuth slew rate
Range: 0 to ±50 mils/s
Accuracy: 1 mil/s
Gun elevation
Range: –10 to +20°
Air temperature
Range: –50 to +70°C
Accuracy: ±1°C

Air pressure
Range: 630 – 1080 mb
Accuracy: ±1%
The Model 9895 ballistic computer will accept up to seven input parameters of this sort, and this digital equipment provides automatic lead angle correction for moving targets. Any type of ammunition ballistics can be used in the computation and up to four ballistics can be employed simultaneously. The computer uses all-TTL logic and the 16-bit, 4-bit slice architecture is stated to yield faster computation. A 'battle ready' mode provides preset super-elevation for faster start-to-stop engagements.

STATUS
Varo tank fire control systems have been installed in the following tanks: M-41, M-47, M-48, M-60, T-54, T-55, T-59, T-62, AMX-30 and Centurion; as well as prototype development for new vehicles such as the US Army light armoured vehicle (LAV).
Varo fire control systems are tested at the US Army Aberdeen Proving Ground.
CONTRACTOR
Varo Incorporated, Integrated Systems Division, 2201 W Walnut St, PO Box 401267, Garland, Texas 75040, USA.

3942.161
PORTABLE INTELLIGENT FIELD TERMINALS
Litton Data Systems has developed a family of terminals to provide digital communication and computational capabilities to suit various users' needs. Extensive use of MSI, LSI and hybrid circuits permit the microprocessor-based units to have a substantial functional capability, low cost and high reliability while maintaining a small size and low

weight. The terminal family consists of the fire control calculator being developed for the US Army, the interactive display terminal built for the US Marine Corps and the US Air Force, the digital communications terminal which is in production for the US Marine Corps, and the lightweight digital command terminal which is being developed under a company funded research programme.
All four equipments have been illustrated and

described with details of facilities and specifications under the above entry number in the 1983-84 and earlier editions of this book.
STATUS
Production.
CONTRACTOR
Litton Data Systems, 8000 Woodley Avenue, Van Nuys, California 91409, USA.

2827.161
TACFIRE TACTICAL FIRE DIRECTION SYSTEM (AN/GSG-10)
TACFIRE is a computer-based automated command and control information system for planning and directing artillery fire. It consists of central fire direction centres (FDC) at division artillery and at battalions with a remote device at batteries, the battery display unit (BDU), and another remote device, the variable format message entry device (VFMED) with fire support officers (FSO), fire support elements (FSE). Digital communications between FDCs and remote devices are by tactical radio or wire and can be clear or encrypted. There are provisions for voice back-up.
The battalion level TACFIRE is housed in a single S-280 shelter and consists of the following major sub-systems:
(1) computer (AN/GYK-12) comprising central processor unit (CPU); input output unit (IOU)
(2) mass core memory unit (MCMU)
(3) power convertor group (PCG)
(4) data terminal unit (DTU)
(5) module test set (MTS)
(6) communications control unit (CCU)
(7) removable media memory unit (RMMU)
(8) artillery control console (ACC)
(9) digital plotter map (DPM)
(10) electronic line printer (ELP)
(11) remote control monitor unit (RCMU).
The division artillery level TACFIRE is housed in two S-280 shelters and consists of the same major sub-systems as shown in the battalion plus one additional MCMU, a dual RMMU, an electronic tactical display (ETD), and an auxillary DTU.
The two remote equipments are:
(1) Variable format message entry device (VFMED) consisting of:
Remote data terminal (RDT)
Display editor (DE)
Keyboard
Electronic line printer (ELP).
(2) Battery display unit (BDU) consisting of:
Electronic line printer (ELP)
Remote data terminal (RDT).
The AN/GYK-12 computer, CPU, IOU, memory, is the heart of the TACFIRE system. It is a general-

TACFIRE artillery control console. Located at battalion and divisional artillery fire direction centres, the ACC is the primary device to control data into and from the computer manually. This control and display device provides a visual presentation on two CRTs of both incoming messages and computer mission solutions. It also provides for control and initiate action on those data by use of an alpha-numeric keyboard which permits real-time entry and interrogation of the computer in normal user language

purpose micro-electronic computer specifically programmed to facilitate solution of the real-time command and control system problems required in TACFIRE.
The divisional artillery and battalion computers are identical, except for one additional memory at the former. The other major items of hardware were described in some detail in 1983-84 and earlier editions.

STATUS
In 1981, the US Army procured its fifth option for AN/GSG-10 TACFIRE systems, and production was expected to continue to 1984.
CONTRACTOR
Litton Data Systems, 8000 Woodley Avenue, Van Nuys, California 91409, USA.

3316.161
TACTICAL COMPUTER SYSTEM (TCS)
AN/UYQ-19(V)
The TCS is a militarised compact general purpose data processing, display and communication system. It is intended for army field use at all echelons in a variety of highly mobile tactical applications. Operationally, TCS is capable of transmitting and receiving addressed data from digital message devices, other TCS or similar computer terminals, or other army standard tactical communication circuits.
Modular design of the TCS allows for setting up in a

field environment, and M577 armoured command vehicle, S-250 or S-280 shelters, vans or fixed bases.
The TCS consists of eight major modules:
(1) *Processor:* AN/UYK-19, a fully militarised version of the Rolm 1666 Ruggednova computer which possesses an MTBF in excess of 3200 hours and a MTTR of 12 minutes.
(2) *WORAM:* The word oriented random access memory has 131 072-word capacity for program and data storage. WORAMs can be linked to give each processor access to 589 824 words on a shared basis.

(3) *Display/Keyboard:* For operator/machine interface, message reception and control, and tactical display in both message text and graphics mode.
The display is an 8½ inch square plasma panel, which can superimpose the computer-generated information over a paper map or diagram. The keyboard uses elastomeric construction and folds upwards to protect the display face in transit. It features a standard ASCII character set, cursor control and other control switches, and a joystick for graphics interaction.

(4) *Communications Interface:* Provides interface to standard tactical communications circuits from 45·5 to 32 000 BPS. Digital data and voice can be transmitted on any of the 16 channels. Radio wire capability is up to eight nets of 1 to 16 channels each. The communication netting is programmable by the operator.

(5) *Printer/Plotter:* Produces hard copy printout of data and messages, diagnostic data/errors, and accomplishes system logs. The printer is an 80-column, noiseless, non-impact type capable of 1200 lines/minute. It also produces graphical plots of 8400 lines/minute.

(6) *Input/Output:* This module interfaces all others in the basic TCS system and distributes DC power to other TCS modules. Provision for growth allows for the implementation of 64 tactical radio communication channels.

(7) *Memory Loading:* Two memory loading modules plug into the I/O module to store system programs.

(8) *Power Convertor:* Accepts inputs of 50, 60 or 400 Hz power and converts it to 28 V DC. Output capacity is 50 to 2500 watts.

A communications termination unit provides through-shelter or wall connections for field wire, telephone and remote TCS modules, such as additional display/keyboards and printers.

DEVELOPMENT

The AN/UYQ-19(V) development was initiated in 1973 by Singer's Librascope Division for the US Army Communications Research and Development Command at Fort Monmouth, New Jersey. Computer programs and a software support centre have also been developed by the contractor.

STATUS

US Army deployment in progress.

CONTRACTOR

The Singer Company, Librascope Division, Glendale, California 91201, USA.

The US Army's tactical computer system (TCS), AN/UYQ-19(V)

3317.161
TACTICAL COMPUTER TERMINAL (TCT)
AN/UYQ-30

The TCT is a fully militarised tactical computer terminal compatible with existing military communication equipments. The TCT was developed as an intelligent stand-alone terminal capable of communicating digital messages (text and graphics) with other TCTs, tactical computer systems AN/UYQ-19 (TCSs) **(3316.161)**, and with forward observer equipments, and will be interfaced with the World-wide Military Communication System (WWMCS).

The tactical computer terminal consists of a plasma display panel microprocessor, a keyboard, communications modems, controllers for external peripheral devices such as a printer, and a bulk memory. The microprocessor provides complete functional flexibility with capabilities determined by the software resident in the TCT. Read only memory (ROM) and random access memory (RAM) totalling 208 K-bytes are packaged in the unit. The latest software packages include higher-level languages.

All of these elements, including the required power supplies, are packaged in a single combination case 38 cm high, 43 cm wide and 59 cm deep. The keyboard is an integral part of the case and folds up to form a watertight cover in the transport configuration. In this configuration, the unit is fully immersible to a depth of 1 metre. Cooling is accomplished entirely without the use of fans, either internal or external. The unit operates directly from 24 ±6 V DC vehicular power.

The TCT communicates over two independent full or half duplex ports. It also has provisions for controlling a militarised printer/plotter which is a

Tactical computer terminal (TCT) is compatible with existing US Army communications equipment

component of the AN/UYQ-19(V) system. By simple change of the controller circuitry, other hard copy devices can also be accommodated. An additional port is provided through which the TCT may interface with a bulk memory device such as a magnetic tape, magnetic disk, large scale semiconductor memory or bubble memory modules. An automatic dialling capability is incoporated.

The display consists of a 22 cm square plasma panel which is utilised in both the message text mode and the graphics mode. When used in the graphics mode, tactical information is superimposed over a paper map positioned behind the transparent plasma panel. Larger displays, such as large-screen multi-colour displays at higher command echelons, will interface with the current equipment.

In the graphics mode, the display has the capability of overlaying standard topographic map segments using lines, alpha-numerics and standard or special symbols. It also has the capability of storing these overlays in memory and recalling them at some later time for modification or update. The overlays may be transmitted by wire or radio and hard copies may be obtained by use of an external printer.

The TCT has been packaged to give the maximum mobility possible to operate in the field environment. It meets all appropriate military specifications, including TEMPEST and nuclear survivability requirement.

CHARACTERISTICS

Display medium: Plasma panel

Element resolution: 60 elements per inch 512 × 512 matrix

Character size: 5 elements wide, 7 elements high

Character capacity: 46 lines of 85 characters each

Writing rate: 20 μs per element

Character writing period: 700 μs max

Vector writing rate: 35 μs per element average (computation time included)

Display intensity: 50 ft-lamberts max adjustable to 12·5 ft-lamberts

Refresh: No refresh required

STATUS

During 1976, the TCT was developed from the display/keyboard module of the AN/UYQ-19 tactical computer system, produced for the US Army Communications Research and Development Command. The manufacturer is under contract for the first ten production units.

CONTRACTOR

The Singer Company, Librascope Division, Glendale, California 91201, USA.

3944.161
PLRS (AN/TSQ-129)

The PLRS AN/TSQ-129 is a portable position location and navigation system which uses frequency and time division multiple access (FTDMA) techniques to provide real-time multiple position tracks on several hundred ground and air user units. The information can be used for such purposes as the direction of artillery fire, naval gun fire, air support, navigation of ground mobile forces and rendezvous, guiding a helicopter through safe corridors when flying 'nap of the earth' missions, etc. Positions can be established with an accuracy of 10 metres or less with slow-moving users, and high-speed airborne users can be located to within 25 metres. The system will provide these facilities for any combination of up to 370 manpack, vehicle or airborne user units within the area of one master station network. A typical area covered by one master station is 90 000 km² from ground level to an altitude of 15 000 metres. For an army corps deployment of four divisions in the forward area and one division in reserve, all five PLRS-equipped divisions can operate on a non-interfering basis and handle some 2000 users over an entire battle area, with the command knowing the position of each user on a continuous basis.

The PLRS network operates in the UHF frequency band, and each user unit automatically transmits a self-identification signal burst on a precise time-ordered schedule, measures time-of-arrival of other user unit transmissions, and automatically relays these measurements when commanded by the master unit to do so. The master unit computes and continuously updates the position of each user unit. The position of every PLRS-equipped unit may be:

(1) remoted and displayed at command and control centres for decision taking

(2) sent to PLRS user units, either automatically or on request

(3) displayed in the master unit for network management and technology control.

Position location information exchanged between the master station and any specified user unit is performed by means of PLRS-formated digital messages, with a limited free text capability. All PLRS transmissions are cryptographically secure, and identical in their spectral signature regardless of their content. This, and the fact that the system utilises composite frequency-hop/direct sequence spread spectrum techniques, give PLRS extremely high electronic security and high jam-resistance.

The master station is housed in a standard US

military S-280 shelter, which is air transportable. This contains the network communications facilities, computers, data displays and related equipment required to support a single independent PLRS network, or to co-operate with other master stations in a multi-PLRS network.

The basic user unit consists of a multi-function transmitter/receiver and processor packaged in a 1-ATR short, low case, and equipped with either of two interchangeable input/output devices. In the manpack configuration the hand-held user readout module is employed, together with a battery pack giving 24-hour service. The complete manpack weighs 6·8 kg. The other input/output device is the pilot control display panel for use in fixed- and rotary-wing aircraft, tanks, amphibious assault vehicles, APCs or similar mobile units. This is mounted in a suitable place on the panel and is driven by a remotely mounted user unit elsewhere in the vehicle.

PJH

The US Army has a programme known as the PLRS/JTIDS Hybrid (PJH) that is intended to modify, combine and integrate components of PLRS and JTIDS (Joint Tactical Information Distribution System) to provide a system that will support Army data distribution requirements at divisional level.

Three main elements are employed: enhanced PLRS user units (EPUU), JTIDS Class 2 terminals, and net control stations (NCS). The first of these will be issued to almost all Division units concerned with data communications, identification and position/location, and between 750 and 1000 EPUUs will be allocated to each Division. About 50 to 70 JTIDS terminals will be assigned to major users within the Division.

PJH had reached the advanced development phase by early 1984 and deployment was planned for 1988.

STATUS
The PLRS has been developed for the US Army and US Marine Corps. A $260 million multi-year contract for 11½ systems including 23 master stations and 3500 user units was awarded to Hughes in July 1983.

CONTRACTOR
Hughes Aircraft Company, Ground Systems Group, Fullerton, California 92634, USA.

3936.151
REMBASS

The Remotely Monitored Battlefield Sensor System (REMBASS) is an unattended ground sensor system evolved from Remote Sensors (REMS), which is already in service with the US forces. REMBASS will detect and classify both men and vehicles and it is intended to provide forward units and formations with detailed information on the happenings in the zone immediately to their front. It can also be useful in rear areas for the detection of intruders.

The system works by using remotely monitored sensors placed along likely approaches. These sensors respond to a wide variety of influences, infrared, acoustic, seismic, mechanical energy, magnetic field changes and others. Each sensor produces a signal giving a detection and sends this signal by FM radio incorporated in the body of the sensor. The sensor remains passive when it is not transmitting a detection signal, so it is virtually impossible to locate. The signal may pass direct to the monitor unit, or it may be repeated by emplaced repeaters. With the use of relays/repeaters for ground application, REMBASS is designed to provide targeting data at up to 100 km range. Once at the monitor the signal is

REMBASS sensor monitoring set in use. It incorporates a built-in printer to record data as well as serving as a field operations centre

demodulated, decoded, displayed and recorded. The system provides up-to-date information over a wide area and, due to the variety of sensors, it is largely self-checking, ie the information from one type of sensor is checked against that from another, virtually eliminating false alarms.

The sensors can be emplaced by hand, artillery shell or dropped from aircraft. Once in position they remain passive until some activity alerts their detection system. They then detect and identify the target and transmit that information before relapsing into passivity, waiting for the next movement near them. The range over which the information radios work is limited and the repeaters are themselves emplaced by the same means. All sensors and repeaters contain their own batteries and have an operational life of weeks rather than days. They are not re-charged when the batteries run down; another sensor is dropped into place.

The monitors display information as it comes in, but they also store it and can produce it as a hard copy for analysis.

STATUS
The development phase ended in 1983 and procurement was planned for 1984 with the initial operational capability (IOC) expected in 1986.

CONTRACTOR
RCA Automated Systems Division, PO Box 588, Burlington, Massachusetts 01803, USA.

3940.161
US TACTICAL DATA HANDLING PROJECTS

The US Army and Air Force and the Defense Advanced Research Projects Agency (DARPA) are responsible for a number of projects and programmes, all of which are intended to support one or other aspect of ground forces data collection, processing, dissemination and presentation facilities. The following paragraphs of this entry summarise the main examples of this series of projects.

ACS
Development of the Artillery Computer System (ACS) for the US Marine Corps is continuing. This will be a lightweight, battery-operated computer that will provide rapid, accurate gun-pointing data for individual batteries.

ADDS
The US Army Data Distribution System (ADDS) is under development as a secure, jam-resistant digital communications system that will be used to transmit data among command and control, intelligence, air defence, fire support, electronic warfare, and other computer systems. It is planned to deploy the system in fiscal year 1988. Development funding proposed for 1985 and 1986 is $23·2 million and $39·2 million respectively, with a further $59·7 million for procurement in 1986.

AFATDS
The US Army is continuing development of the Advanced Field Artillery Tactical Data System (AFATDS), a new generation automated fire control system, which may prove to be a successor to the Tacfire system (**2827.161**) and will increase the efficiency and targeting capacity of its artillery batteries. Development funding budgeted for AFATDS in the fiscal year 1985 DoD report is $21·5 million (1984), $33·1 million (1985), and $36·2 million (1986).

LFATDS
In early 1984 the US Army Communications and Electronics Command awarded a $6·7 million contract to Litton Data Systems for the supply of its Lightweight Artillery Tactical Data System (LFATDS) to the US Army 9th Infantry Division. This unit has the task of using off-the-shelf hardware in a test bed operation designed to establish likely procurement for all Army light divisions.

The LFATDS offers all the capabilities of the Tacfire system, but by using the latest hardware and more modern software, the system is much lighter while providing faster, simpler secure operation. The equipment will be employed in areas where weight and portability are major factors and it will replace the Tacfire Battalion Fire Direction Centre and its related variable format message entry device system. LFATDS can perform all the tactical functions of the current Tacfire but is lighter and smaller, and adds graphics to each of the 39 terminals in the system.

This contract award is probably related to the AFATDS programme described above.

PLSS
The precision location/strike system (PLSS) will provide a 24-hour all-weather capability for USAF aircraft to attack a variety of ground targets. In particular it is intended for tactical use against air defence systems that depend on very accurate guidance and detection radars to control anti-aircraft artillery and surface-to-air missiles. The system has been described in detail (**3228.351**) in previous editions of *Jane's Weapon Systems* (1978 and earlier), but in brief, it relies on the use of specialised distance measuring equipment and other equipment on highly instrumented aircraft to detect electronic emissions from enemy radars and relay that information to a ground-based central processor facility. The computers analyse the data, comparing inputs from multiple aircraft to pinpoint the type and location of a radar. This information is then available for use in mounting a strike against the radar. Using photogrammatic techniques, a form of aerial reconnaissance photography, PLSS will also be able to establish the locations of targets that emit no electronic radiations. Strikes on such targets as airfields, bridges, command and control posts etc would be controlled in a similar fashion to those against radar targets.

Lockheed was awarded a contract for full-scale development of PLSS. Funding of this USAF programme, actual and planned in recent years and for the immediate future is (with fiscal year in brackets): $80·5 million (1983), $77·8 million (1984),

GTE's Western Division has developed and produced a number of remote tactical data relay sub-stations, similar to this one, and a centralised processing centre for the US Army

$281·2 million (1985), and $209·5 million (1986). The marked increase in fiscal year 1985 reflects procurement costs, while RDT&E is steady at around $70 million for each of the five years listed. This suggests that the plan to implement the system operationally in the mid-1980s is going ahead despite the reported General Accounting Office recommendation of cancellation of the project in 1980.

Joint STARS

Joint Surveillance and Target Attack Radar System (Joint STARS) is a combined US Army/USAF development programme formed by the merging of USAF's Pave Mover project with the Army's Battlefield Data System (BDS), which, in turn, supplanted SOTAS. (See this entry number in 1983-84 and earlier editions of *Jane's Weapon Systems*). The Joint STARS radar system will locate and track moving targets at extended ranges in the land battle areas of the 2000s. It will give target position information for indirect artillery fire and use of other weapons such as the projected Joint Tactical Missile System (JTACMS). It also provides the ground commander with real-time moving target data from both Army and USAF platforms via a common secure data link.

Airborne tests of the General Electric multimode surveillance radar (MSR) proposed by the Boeing/GE team competing in the JSTARS programme have demonstrated detection and location of ground targets in real-time. The ability to perform MTI and synthetic aperture radar (SAR) from an airborne platform has provided essential data on typical tank column manoeuvres. An unprocessed airborne MTI image showed a column of tanks beyond visual range, and viewed against a map overlay this showed the tanks in relation to the road. A time integration display shows ground processed MTI and map underlay with the dots denoting moving targets. Each sweep of the radar cumulatively adds new detections to the displays and in this way high traffic areas can be detected and additional intelligence data derived from it.

Target ranges contemplated extend to more than 100 km into hostile territory, and the Army plans to employ the OV-1D Mohawk aircraft as the carrier platform. The radar contractor is expected to be selected in late summer 1984. The fiscal year 1985 budget indicated funding over the next four years as follows: $53·2 million (1983), $120·8 million (1984), $232 million (1985) and $335·2 million (1986) for procurement inclusive of RDT&E.

BETA

In early 1982 there were two BETA (battlefield exploitation and target acquisition) test bed installations undergoing user trials, at Hurlbert Field, Florida, and Fort Hood in Texas. These test beds were created to determine techniques that would overcome difficulties encountered in the earlier attempts at large-scale management of battlefield tactical and related information in such programmes as the tactical operations system (TOS) which was denied funding by Congress in 1980 because of its shortcomings. The BETA operator terminal incorporates two CRT-based displays, on the left an alpha-numeric tabular display and on the right an eight-colour unit for map or other diagrammatic information presentation. The terminal incorporates four microprocessors: two 8085s for alpha-numerics, one 8086 for display processing, and an 8086 terminal processor. This work is now regarded as the probable foundation of the Joint Tactical Fusion Programme (below) which is meant to lead to the implementation of a US Army All-Source Analysis System (ASAS) and an Enemy Situation Correlation Element (ESCE) for the USAF.

BETA-LOCE

By 1983 BETA had been deployed with US Forces in NATO in Europe, as the Joint Tactical Fusion –

Battlefield data will be handled automatically by the US Army in centres similar to this RCA mockup of an ASAS/SEWS signals intelligence control and analysis centre

Limited Operational Capability Europe (JTF-LOCE), using a computer system developed by TRW under DoD direction. Two more testbed installations for demonstration and evaluation of ASAS (see below) data correlation were also deployed at USAF and Army sites in the USA. In Europe, the LOCE deployment consists of a central automated data processing centre, interface units at sensor ground stations, and local/remote user display terminals. Sensor inputs to the system include: Sigint, imagery intelligence, and human intelligence (Humint).

The European configuration (BETA-LOCE) employs computer software architecture designed to detect, identify and locate target and significant battlefield threat activities by the simultaneous processing of numerous sensor reports through self-correlation, cross-correlation, and aggregation. The last of these is the computer aided process of identification of parent units based on 'sensed' or known data concerning subordinate entities. This process is operator initiated.

In exercises carried out in Europe during 1983 using BETA-LOCE, which was installed in late 1982, it is reported that analysts were able to predict battlefield events significantly earlier than was previously possible. NATO interest is said to be encouraging and the system capabilities are being demonstrated to major US and allied commanders.

JTF

The Joint Tactical Fusion (JTF) system programme is part of a broad US programme of development in the area of new technologies for defeating large scale armoured attacks by means of deep interdiction tactics. JTF is intended to provide automated facilities to process, analyse,and distribute intelligence reports obtained from a wide range of sources. This information will assist battlefield commanders in assessing the status of opposing forces and their dispositions. In the longer term, the authorities are considering a more advanced version that will permit access to direct real-time intelligence.

Development funding allocations contained in the 1985 budget for JTF were $59·3 million planned for 1984, $124·4 million for 1985 and $162·6 million in 1986.

MCS

The Manoeuvre Control System (MCS) is a command and control system being developed by the US Army to provide an automated information network to assist battle staffs in operational control of the mobile units under their command. Development began in September 1980 with the introduction in the European theatre of a prototype system using microprocessors and minicomputers. From an initial introduction of three systems, the prototype has

grown to some 20 systems which are being used in the field. The eventual system will consist of a network of small computers that will enable tactical commanders to have access to information on the status and disposition of their forces and those of their opponent. The European prototype version is being used for additional development.

Funding in fiscal year 1984 is planned at $9·3 million for development and $16·4 production. The figures proposed for the two succeeding years are: $25·7 million and $9·5 million (development), and $27·9 million and $62·4 million, respectively. Contractors involved include Singer Librascope, General Dynamics, Datametrics and INSGROUP.

ASAS/SEWS

ASAS/SEWS (all sources analysis system/SIGINT electronic warfare sub-system) is a US Army shelter-housed command, control, communications and intelligence system designed to collect and evaluate battlefield data obtained from forward observers, aircraft, foot patrols and intelligence networks. In July 1979 RCA received a $13 million contract to build a prototype signals intelligence control and analysis centre for the US Army Electronics Research and Development Command (ERADCOM), and the following November it was revealed that five advanced development prototypes were being constructed.

RCA is responsible for integrating the communication, data processing and operator work station equipment into tactical shelters. In addition, RCA will perform software qualification tests and train operators. HRB-Singer is the major sub-contractor for software development. Norden Systems is supplying a PDP-11/70M computer as the central processor, working with a C2-RMO3 disc drive mass memory. Norden LS1-11M micro-processors will be used at each work station.

In March 1980 it was announced that RCA had been awarded a $16·8 million contract by the US Army for the production of five transportable special intelligence control and analysis centres. The award by (ERADCOM) is the second part of the ASAS/SEWS programme, the earlier award of $13 million for research and development having been announced in July 1979. Under the new contract five US Army divisions will be equipped with tactical intelligence processing and analysis centres and they will assist division level combat forces in the management of diverse intelligence data received from battlefield sensors as well as the control of tactical EW systems. It is also proposed to employ similar centres at corps levels.

CONTRACTORS
Boeing
Control Data Corporation
E-Systems
General Dynamics
General Electric
Grumman
GTE Sylvania
Harris Corporation
Honeywell
HRB-Singer
Hughes Aircraft Company
IBM
Litton Data Systems
Lockheed Missiles and Space Company
Motorola
Norden Systems
RCA
Rockwell International
Singer Kearfott
Sperry Univac
TRW

YUGOSLAVIA

4584.161

ARS FIELD ARTILLERY COMPUTER SYSTEM

The ARS field artillery computer system is a digital computer-based system designed to provide user-oriented fire control facilities for the direction of artillery fire at the artillery battalion level. Facilities include automated computation, transmission and display of firing data and commands within the battalion.

The basic configuration of the system comprises:

(1) the main equipment within a computer control sub-system (CCS), and consisting of the artillery computer unit, tape reader, three VHF transmitter/receivers, one radio receiver, a telephone switchboard and power supplies

(2) three battery display sub-systems (BDS). Each BDS is a compact two-man portable equipment designed for use at firing battery command posts. The main items of equipment are carried in a rugged frame and comprise a firing data display, VHF transmitter/receiver, telephone set and battery pack.

The CCS is generally housed in a military shelter carried on a 4 × 4 cross-country vehicle such as the TAM 110 T7 BV.

The main operational features of the ARS system include:

(1) integrated fire control of an artillery division consisting of up to three firing batteries equipped with guns, howitzers or rocket launchers

(2) engagement of stationary or moving targets

(3) 200 target locations, 30 of which can be correction points and 10 forward observer positions

(4) fire control of one, two or all three batteries

(5) three separate fire missions at any given time

(6) firing data and commands for each battery separately

(7) division fire, where simultaneous hits on a single target from all three batteries are required

(8) voice communications between CCS, BDS and other sub-systems such as meteorological stations, forward observers, higher command etc

(9) data transmission from CCS to BDS and facilities for data reception from forward observers via cable or radio link

(10) simultaneous data transmission and voice communication over the same channel.

The ARS computer itself is a single unit that incorporates a dual Čajavec-52 micro-processor, power supply and an operator's console that carries controls and displays for the operation of the system. Input data includes battery information such as: grid co-ordinates; base direction, deflection and site; muzzle velocity changes or measured value by MV radar; projectile weight variations; powder temperature (for each battery). Ammunition data inserted into the computer includes: shell type, fuze type, low/high trajectory, charge number (manual or automatic selection). Three different types of standard met messages up to 30 lines can be accepted, and target data consists of grid co-ordinates, polar co-ordinates relative to the forward observer, and grid-shift from known point. Additionally, for moving target engagement there is provision for insertion of time intervals between firings, target speed and direction, or polar co-ordinates relative to FO (artillery radar measurements), or selected impact point co-ordinates. All input data parameter values are automatically checked against acceptable standard limits as a validity test and checked data can be accepted, rejected or left to the operator's decision.

The following principal computational functions are performed:

(1) initial calculations of technical data based on topographical information, met data, weapon data for a particular battery and chosen combination of shell, fuze and charge

(2) firing data such as deflection, angle of elevation, site, fuze setting, range, time of firing, charge, shell and fuze type

(3) adjustment of fire, based on information from FOs

(4) calculation of fire correction points

(5) fire transfer calculations from correction point to designated new target

(6) use of data from one battery to provide firing data

computations for adjustments of other batteries in the battalion

(7) calculation of firing data and commands for moving target engagement.

ARS formats firing data output messages and transmits them to the selected battery, and this includes all fire control data computations, the selected shell/charge/fuze combination, as well as the fire command. An input/output display presents input data as well as computer messages. There is software supported guidance for the operator in entering data and to ensure the correct operating sequence. Other software facilities include a target file manager, test module, input/output data conversion module, ballistic calculation module, fire transfer/correction module, and a dual processor executive system.

System enhancements available as options are: FO direct data entry facilities; on-line laser rangefinder operation; on-line sound ranging equipment; land navigation sub-system; and an advanced command display unit.

CHARACTERISTICS

Accuracy: 0·001 of range (in metres) in bearing and elevation

Fuze setting: 0·1 s

Firing data computation time: 0·5 to 5 s

Data link speed: 1200 bit/s

Correction code: BCH

False alarm probability: Less than 10

Modem: DPSK

Firing data display unit: 300 × 200 × 150 mm

Weight: 12 kg

Power supply: 21 – 29 V DC, 15 W

Computer unit: 680 × 420 × 550 mm

Weight: 60 kg

Power supply: 21 – 29 V DC, <200 W

STATUS

In production and believed operational with Yugoslav Forces.

CONTRACTOR

SPDR, Federal Directorate of Supply and Procurement, 9 Nemanjina Street, 1101 Belgrade, Yugoslavia.

4585.161

SUVOA FIRE CONTROL SYSTEM

Suvoa is a Yugoslav coastal artillery fire control system for the direction and control of coast defence gun batteries. Target data is principally obtained from an M70 optical director, supplemented by radar in certain conditions.

Target information from the M70 optical director is fed to a battery distribution unit from where firing data is passed to individual gun batteries. The data is automatically read off and transmitted in a synchronised way. The necessary corrections are set on the rangefinder which calculates them and passes them on to the guns. Transmission is by means of cable data links. Gun crews have only to bring gun traverse and elevation settings into coincidence with the values sent from the director.

In poor visibility or darkness radar range and bearing data may be substituted for the optical target data, but for safety reasons it is recommended that the radar should be separated from the gun battery by a distance of about 1000 metres. The range and bearing information derived from radar must be

corrected for parallax before being sent to weapons from the rangefinder.

CHARACTERISTICS

Traverse: 360° unlimited

Range: 1000 – 50 000 m

Vertical base variation: 5 – 600 m

Total reading error: 50 m to 10 km range; 200 m to 20 km range; approx 3% to 50 km range

Measuring telescope

Magnification: ×18

Field of view: 4°

Inlet pupil diameter: 54 mm

Exit pupil diameter: 3 mm

Exit pupil distance: 14·8 mm

Adjustment: ±5 dioptres

Reticle: 0 – 35 mils L/R

Periscope: 356 mm

Observation telescope

Magnification: Variable ×3 – ×10

Field of view: Variable 20°, 6°

Inlet pupil diameter: 15 mm – 50 mm

Exit pupil diameter: 5 mm

Exit pupil distance: 15·8 mm

Adjustment: ±5 dioptres

Reticle: 0 – 35 mils L/R

Periscope: 256 mm

DEVELOPMENT

The system has been developed in both stationary and mobile versions. Equipment at each gun comprises a section commander's control box, range data receiver, siting device and bearing indicator. Electrical power for all units (including radar and M70 optical director) is derived from two mobile engine-driven generators, each of which is connected to the system via a transformer unit. The radar is housed in a transportable shelter with the necessary parallax computer.

STATUS

In production and believed operational with Yugoslav Forces.

CONTRACTOR

SPDR, Federal Directorate of Supply and Procurement, PO Box 308, Knez Mihailova 6, Belgrade, Yugoslavia.

NAVAL FIRE CONTROL AND ACTION DATA AUTOMATION SYSTEMS

AUSTRALIA

3220.481

SUBMARINE FIRE CONTROL SYSTEM Mk 1 Mod 0

The SFCS Mk 1 Mod 0 all-digital system was produced initially for the Royal Australian Navy (RAN) as part of a modernisation programme for the 'Oberon' class submarines. The system is also being procured by the Canadian forces for installation in 'Oberon' class submarines. It provides integrated torpedo fire control functions which include the selection and processing of sonar and other sensor data, analysis of contact motion, generation of weapon orders, and the control of weapon selection, setting, firing and guidance.

The SFCS Mk 1 Mod 0 is designed to control conventional and wire guided torpedoes. Conventional torpedoes may be fired singly or in salvo. The system consists of the following equipment:

(1) the fire control consoles are two identical units installed in the control room. Each serves as a tactical analysis console or as a weapon control in a dual-capacity arrangement which enhances operational flexibility

(2) a command display console is installed adjacent to the fire control consoles. This moving paper (hard copy) recorder produces a continuous display of contact bearing information, while providing the means to monitor all sensors and control the assignment of sonars to contact tracks and designates these tracks for contact motion analysis. It monitors the overall status of the SFCS. The command display console has two other major sub-systems: a record/reproduce

unit in the form of a compact digital magnetic tape, and a sensor data converter to convert sonar and other ship sensor data into a digital format suitable for entry into the central processor

(3) sonar assignment units are installed near each of the sonar operator positions. Each provides a display of bearings for investigation, and droptrack assignments for the sonar operators

(4) the central processor (AN/UYK-20) is installed in the control room for SFCS automatic control and computation functions

(5) the mass memory unit is a self-contained Librascope model CL107 MA head-per-track disc memory. This 7M-bit memory is used by the computer for access and storage of sensor data history tables, programs, and other digital information as required by the computations

(6) a weapon data converter is located in the forward torpedo compartment. This equipment performs all data conversion and switching functions between the fire control console and the weapons, including tube selection switching, digital-analogue-digital conversions of weapon orders, readback data, and the generation of signals for weapon presetting, firing, and guidance

(7) a tube order and alarm device is located in the forward torpedo compartment. This device displays tube orders from the fire control console, with a means of response to the control room. It also provides for the entry of weapon loaded status for each of the six tubes for distribution within the fire control system. In addition, it incorporates the functions of battery alarm

monitoring and monitoring of torpedo tube flooding.

The Mk 1 Mod 0 SFCS is organised on a modular basis, particularly in its interfaces with the sensors and with weapons. Since almost all internal functions and logic of the system are embodied in modular computer software, the functions of sensor data processing, contact motion analysis, display, and weapon control functions may be easily adapted to meet a large variety of sensors, weapons, and tactical requirements. Microprocessors are incorporated throughout the major equipment.

STATUS

The RAN awarded a $14 million contract for the development and production of eight systems in October 1975. The initial system was completed in 1977, with production deliveries following in 1978 and 1979.

In 1980 Canada purchased three SFCS Mk 1 Mod 0 systems for 'Oberon' class submarines and a fourth system was procured for shore training purposes. These systems are essentially the same as those built for Australia except for modifications to accommodate a different weapons suite.

In 1982 India purchased four SFCS Mk 1 Mod 0 systems through Howaldtswerke-Deutsche Werft (HDW) of West Germany for its new 1500-ton submarines. The Indian systems are also the same as those built for Australia and Canada except for modifications for different sensor and weapon suites.

CONTRACTOR

The Singer Company, Librascope Division, 833 Sonora Avenue, Glendale, California 91201, USA.

CANADA

4046.261

ADLIPS

ADLIPS (Automatic Data Link Plotting System) is a modular low-cost, command, control and tactical data communication system designed to replace electro-mechanical plotting tables and associated radar displays in non-TDS (tactical data system) equipped ships. The system provides transmission, reception, filtering and display of target track data from Link 11 and Link 14 data communication networks. ADLIPS also collects and processes own-ship sensor data to compile rapidly a composite tactical display and interchanges target track, weapon assignment and status data with own ship's weapon systems. When operating in a TDS environment, ships fitted with ADLIPS can share tactical data with each other as well as aircraft and other ships that are data link equipped.

The main presentation is on the situation information display (SID) console, which has a 20-inch (51 cm) diameter CRT for displaying synthetic and radar tactical data presentation. Three operator stations, each with quick action controls, a tracker ball and an alpha-numeric keyboard enable the SID to serve as an efficient man/machine interface. The plasma displays are suitable for use in high ambient light conditions and the display area measures 22 × 22 cm. They each have an operator station which has the same functional layout as the display console operator stations.

An HF Link 11 radio transmitter/receiver provides for communications over this data link, and a Link 11 modem (AN/USQ-76) allows operation in either picket or net controlled modes. This unit generates and recognises Link 11 control codes, preambles and data formats and provides error detection and

correction. For Link 14 a CV-2757/SGC interface converts the low-level signals from the computer to the high-level signals required by the cryptographic equipment and the inverse conversion.

The complete ADLIPS has a capacity of up to 140 air, surface and sub-surface tracks, and has a full NTDS repertoire.

STATUS

Litton has contracts for and is building 16 ADLIPS sets for the Royal Canadian Navy, and the first was installed in HMCS *Skeena* in October 1981.

CONTRACTOR

Litton Systems Canada Limited, 25 Cityview Drive, Rexdale, Ontario M9W 5A7, Canada.

2046.261

CCS-280 COMMAND AND CONTROL SYSTEMS (DDH-280) CLASS

This equipment is a shipborne automatic data handling and display system based on the Litton L-304 single processor version digital computer. Designated AN/USQ-501(V) data processing set, it comprises one digital computer, eight multi-function displays, and other peripherals.

The computer is fitted with a 40K 32-bit word memory capable of expansion to 80K words by addition of plug-in modules to the existing processor mainframe. Increased I/O capability can be achieved by adding units to the existing data bus using available minor channels in the I/O modules. The system includes radar signal simulation, which provides superimposed or separate radar targets that

are variable in size and brightness for training. Displays are multi-purpose and identical. Quick action buttons provide mode selection and independent selection of up to seven separate radar videos with independent offset and range scales of 1 to 152 miles (1·6 to 244·6 km) in binary increments. Category selection of symbology is programmable on-line, independently, at each display.

Basic operating software has been provided by the manufacturer. In the case of the CCS-280 the Canadian armed forces chose to write all the operational software in a program generation facility provided by the contractor. The overall system provides real-time co-ordination of sensors and weapons by the command at the unit and force level to:

(1) collect, process, and display tactical information from all sensors

(2) control aircraft and other remote surface units

(3) direct own ship's and force weapons

(4) control own ship manoeuvres

(5) exchange information and orders within own ship and force.

STATUS

The system is currently operational at sea in HMC ships *Iroquois, Athabaskan, Huron,* and *Algonquin.* A shore installation for training and program maintenance and generation is fitted in the Combined Support Divisions, Halifax.

CONTRACTORS

Litton Systems (Canada) Limited.

Collins Radio (Automatic Link Equipment).

2047.261
UNDERWATER COMBAT SYSTEM (UCS)
257/280
The UCS 257 and/or UCS 280 comprises two AN/SQS-505 sonar sets (**1792.453**), an anti-submarine warfare data system (ASWDS), and ancillary equipment for both hull-mounted (HMS) and variable depth sets (VDS). Both AN/SQS-505 sonars are electronically identical and comprise a transmitter group, a receiver group, a control indicator group, and a transducer. The ancillary equipment for the hull-mounted set consists of a retractable hull outfit with dome. The ancillary

equipment for the variable depth set consists of the AN/SQA-502 hoist group (including tow cable) and a variable depth body (including gyro compass).

The ASWDS is an action data system designed to accept primary target information from hull-mounted and/or variable depth sonars and secondary target information from radars. This information is processed by a high speed general purpose computer to provide action information to the command, computation of fire control solutions, and a weapon control.

A prototype of the system has been installed and evaluated in HMCS *Terra Nova*. Production models

are fitted in HMC ships *Terra Nova*, *Gatineau*, *Kootenay*, and *Restigouche*, all of which are anti-submarine DDE 'Restigouche' class destroyers commissioned to take ASROC. The AN/SQS-505 sonar system is installed in the four new DDH 280 class anti-submarine destroyers which have two helicopters, and Mk 32 torpedo tubes are fitted instead of ASROC.
CONTRACTORS
Westinghouse Canada Ltd, Hamilton, Ontario, Canada – Prime contractor, AN/SQS-505.

Hollandse Signaalapparaten BV, Hengelo, Netherlands – Prime contractor, ASWDS.

FRANCE

4049.261
RADOP SERIES NAVAL FCS
The MAM (Maritime Aerospatiale et Militaire) department of CSEE offers a range of naval fire control systems suitable for the smallest patrol craft to vessels of more than 200 t, for directing guns against air and surface targets. In addition, these systems provide for surface and low altitude radar surveillance, optical surveillance, and target identification. The range of systems consists of differing combinations of CSEE optical or electro-optical directors, and one or other of the Racal/Decca marine radars.

Four basic systems have been developed in this way:
(1) RADOP 10 series with the CSEE Lynx (**3426.293**) director
(2) RADOP 20 series with the CSEE Panda Mk 2 (**3425.293**) director
(3) RADOP 30 series with the CSEE Naja (**3561.293**) director
(4) RADOP 40 series with the CSEE Najir (**4255.293**) director

Essentially, all four have the same optical surveillance capability, but they differ in their weapon control performance. For each RADOP series, all the Racal/Decca marine radars of group 12 (1226, 1229, 1230 and 2459) are suitable, so that it is possible to select between 3 or 10 cm wavelength radar, 12- or

16-inch (30 or 40 cm) diameter CRT display, and relative motion, true motion or anti-collision presentation.

Each RADOP version can be optionally complemented by an automatic plotter, radio navigation aids, and an air surveillance radar.

Additional details of the CSEE E-O directors are given in the appropriate pages of the Equipment Section of this volume, under the reference numbers listed above, and in the following paragraphs the characteristics of individual systems of the RADOP series are summarised. (The Racal/Decca 1229 radar has been employed as an example in all cases, and obviously use of a different model would modify weights and/or dimensions.)
RADOP 10
This comprises a Racal/Decca radar, CSEE Lynx optical sight, and a control panel. It provides for radar and optical surveillance, optical target tracking and control of a small calibre gun. It is crewed by two men: the radar operator who is in charge of radar surveillance and target designation, and the Lynx operator who is responsible for optical surveillance and weapon control. RADOP 10 is suitable for patrol boats weighing up to 100 t. System weight is approximately 400 kg.
RADOP 20
This system consists of Racal/Decca radar, a CSEE Panda Mk 2 optical director, and a control panel.

Services provided include radar and optical surveillance, optical target tracking, and control of one or two guns. The division of responsibilities between the two-man crew is the same as for RADOP 10. This version is suitable for patrol craft of more than 100 t and weight is about 560 kg.
RADOP 30
The equipment is as for the previous two systems, but with a CSEE Naja director in place of the Lynx or Panda Mk 2 director. This adds the possibility of remote control facilities from the Naja console to those provided by the RADOP 10 or 20 systems. The system weighs approximately 700 kg.
RADOP 40
This system incorporates a Racal/Decca radar and a CSEE Najir director. It is manned by two operators: the radar operator in charge of radar surveillance and target designation, and the Najir operator responsible for optical surveillance and weapon control. System weight is approximately 850 kg.
STATUS
No details of ship fittings received.
CONTRACTOR
CSEE (Compagnie de Signaux et d'Entreprises Electriques) Départment MAM, 17 place Etienne-Pernet, 75738 Paris Cedex 15, France.

3102.281
CANOPUS NAVAL WEAPON CONTROL SYSTEM
Canopus is a lightweight naval tracking system capable of directing and controlling anti-air and anti-surface weapons and also providing optical target designation facilities. The system is designed for all-weather operation and is therefore able to deal with a wider range of operational requirements than an entirely optical or electro-optical tracking unit. Included in the system is an operational fire control console with its associated gun fire computer.

The Canopus system performs the following functions:
(1) autonomous optical surveillance over the full horizon
(2) automatic or semi-automatic target acquisition on radar target designations
(3) tracking of air targets including sea-skimming missiles and surface targets with the Ka-band radar, the TV tracker in bearing, elevation and radar range, and, optionally, the infra-red tracker
(4) target designation to or from other fire control systems

Target data is sent to the artillery computer which performs ballistic computations for gun fire control.

Thomson-CSF lightweight E-O director (TRS 906) for Canopus naval FCS

Association of the Canopus tracker unit with an artillery computer constitutes the Vega Canopus fire control system.
STATUS
In production and delivered to several foreign navies.

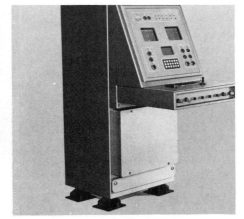

Typical Canopus console

CONTRACTOR
Thomson-CSF, Division Systèmes Défense et Contrôle, 40 rue Grange Dame Rose, BP 34, 92360 Meudon-La-Forêt, France.

4572.281
THOMSEA NAVAL COMBAT SYSTEMS
Thomson-CSF now produces the former VEGA series in their latest versions as the Thomsea naval combat systems, a range of modular integrated naval systems. The basic components of a Thomsea NCS are as follows:
(1) a combined (air and surface) surveillance and target designation radar (Triton G, Triton II MTI, Triton S or Sea Tiger)
(2) one or more fire control radars, Castor II fitted with television tracking

(3) one or more E-O directors fitted with television tracking, infra-red tracking, laser rangefinder or K-band radar
(4) a computer, or several co-operating computers
(5) tactical information unit: console and tactical table
(6) a track-while-scan (TWS) system, incorporated with the tactical table or the console; it allows simultaneous tracking of 16 to 64 air or surface targets detected by the surveillance radar.

Various other equipments may be associated with the system to augment the ship's capabilities in

performing the following functions: designation and tracking (optical sights and directors), radar identification and analyses (IFF, ESM), electronic countermeasures (jammers, chaff-launcher), submarine detection (sonar), navigation (radar, log, heading and vertical reference system). The following weapons are controlled or are fed target co-ordinates:
(1) guns of any calibre
(2) surface-to-surface missiles
(3) surface-to-air missiles
(4) surface torpedoes, conventional or wire-guided
(5) ASW weapons (torpedoes or rockets).

Castor II tracking radar fitted with television camera

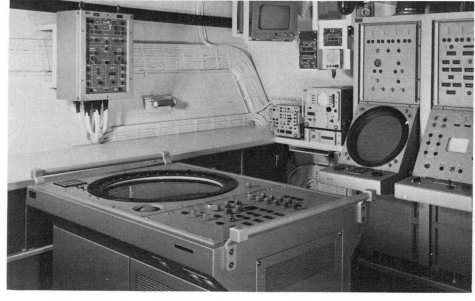

Inside a typical CIC showing Vega FCS console on right (with ESM/EW units to the left)

The number and type of fire control systems as well as computer capacity are essentially dependent on the ship's armament. The choice of surveillance and ASW equipment is more dependent on ship's tonnage and missions.

Tactical information units are designed to take into account diverse operational criteria defined by users. The basic unit is constituted of the operational consoles for surveillance and fire control radars, to which is added the tactical table. On the surveillance console and tactical table PPIs, analogue video is complemented with synthetic marks, alpha numeric labels relating to followed tracks, vectors, symbols and track plotting. The data fed by associated equipments – fire control and navigation radars, radar analyser (ESM), optical devices, sonar – are displayed on the PPIs. Complementary devices added to the display unit allow for: fire correction for surface targets, from splash plotting; data display; inter-ship exchange of track data, from stations equipped with a data link (received tracks are displayed on the PPIs); and recording of simulation or tracks for exploitation or operator training.

Tactical problems are solved by calculations inside the system providing: true-motion presentation on PPI; display of relative bearing and range between two tracks, one of which may be the radar carrier (RBL); display of the collision course and of the time required to intercept a track (CTS); the closest point of approach (CPA); extrapolation of tracks for a given time (time to go); generation of fixed points and measurement of the time elapsed since their initiation (datum).

The operator communicates with the system easily and rapidly through a keyboard. This easy reading of decision-making elements by the operator and technical problem solving reduces to a minimum the reaction time between detection and fire command.

The fire control radar console, which includes the computer, provides the operator with:
(1) acquisition of the designated air or surface target
(2) choice of the operating mode
(3) monitoring of the quality of tracking, using radar or television screens
(4) gun control and fire correction.

Interfacing with associated equipments, whether analogue or digital is achieved with specific couplers. In the tactical table and in the console, digital data flow over a bus-type line. A microprocessor controls display and operational functions. The following concepts are embodied in all Thomsea systems:
(1) modularity, which allows a great variety of configurations as well as adaptation to the most diverse needs
(2) physical separation of the surveillance and fire control platforms and antennas
(3) choice of several different frequency bands. This makes it possible to optimise each function to reduce the system's vulnerability to ensure basic protection against jamming
(4) operational redundancies such as using the fire-control radar for surveillance and the surveillance radar for the guidance of some weapons.

Another significant advantage gained by separating the antennas is greater detection range at the surface of the sea or at low altitudes, obtained by installing at the greatest possible height the surveillance antenna which is not required to meet the same platform rigidity constraints as the fire-control directors.

STATUS

Development of these naval combat systems started in 1967. The first system manufactured, a Vega type I-43, controls two guns, Exocet missiles and AEG SSI4 torpedoes. It has been operational since the end of 1971. From the early systems, mostly adapted to small tonnage ships, to the systems currently available, the evolution has been towards an enlargement in the choice of basic equipment to meet the requirements of a broad range of tonnage and missions, with a particular emphasis on the self defence capability against sea-skimmer missiles. By 1982 more than 140 Thomsea/Vega systems were either operational or in production. More than 15 countries are reported to have acquired Vega systems.

CONTRACTOR

Thomson-CSF, Division Systèmes Défense et Contrôle, 40 rue Grange Dame Rose, BP 34, 92360 Meudon-La-Forêt, France.

4053.261

TAVITAC TACTICAL DATA HANDLING SYSTEMS
The former Vega 3C tactical data handling systems, now designated TAVITAC (Traitement Automatique et Visualisation Tactique) are of modular design for both hardware and software. This makes them highly flexible, fit for any type of ship, and capable of meeting any particular operational need. The display consoles are vertical and horizontal. They can be fitted with different types of screen: monochrome or colour, circular or rectangular. Consoles can receive raw video from several radars, superimposed on synthetic video. Display capacity can be adapted to needs by means of a video compression device associated with optimised processing for picture generation. The consoles can be associated with various data processing computers which can be integral with the consoles or set in separate cabinets.

Software can be adapted to associated sensors and operational requirements, and can be produced on civilian computers which are compatible with the Thomson-CSF computers employed in TAVITAC systems. Standard functions are:
(1) automatic tracking of air and surface tracks, associated with an extractor (TWS), with manual or automatic initialisation, allowing anti-surface gunfire
(2) rate-aided manual tracking
(3) manual entry of tracks and special points

TAVITAC horizontal operator table

(4) track identification
(5) threat evaluation
(6) display of local and external tracks received via data link, with associated symbols, speed vectors and alpha-numeric data
(7) display of optical and ESM bearings, of positions of targets tracked by fire-control directors, of circles, vectors, launching figures
(8) transmission of local tracks via data link

(9) dispatch of target designations to weapons
(10) aids to tactical navigation.
Extended capabilities are:
(11) fully automatic process of engagement of air targets, including track initialisation, threat evaluation, timely target designation, weapons coupling, fire orders, optimised management of directors and weapons in case of simultaneous attacks
(12) tactical situation recording and replay in real- or accelerated-time
(13) training facilities in association with a video simulator
(14) coastline storage and display on PPIs on request
(15) tracking of submarine positions, processing of ASW weapon parameters, guidance of attacks by ASW helicopters or other aircraft.

The display system configurations can be adapted to suit particular ships and their weapon systems. Typical systems might include one console only for the smaller systems, with automatic tracking of 16 air or surface tracks, two to four consoles for larger systems, suitable for modern medium-tonnage ships, with automatic tracking for 16 to 32 air or surface tracks, or up to ten consoles, or more, for larger systems designed for heavy tonnage ships, allowing automatic tracking of up to 200 tracks, with vectors, circles, circle sectors, coastlines, etc.

For all proposed structures, the number of computers devoted to processing of tactical information is defined according to the needs and to the degree of redundancy required.

Different types of console are available: vertical consoles for incorporation with a fire control console, modular vertical consoles, tactical tables with one or two operator positions, and large horizontal consoles with two or three operator positions.

A console is made up of the following modules: a combined radar-synthetic image generator module including a renewal memory of the associated computer, a PPI display module, input devices (order keyboard(s), video control panel, rolling-ball control unit(s)), and alpha-numeric display on a TV or a plasma screen (alpha-numeric information can also be displayed on the PPI edges). Display capabilities are adjustable to customer requirements up to 200 tracks and 100 different symbols.

In the French Navy such systems are known under the name SENIT (Systeme d'Exploitation Navale des Informations Tactiques). Four F2000 T class frigates that France is to supply to Saudi Arabia will be fitted with SENIT naval tactical display systems produced by Thomson-CSF.

STATUS
Production.
CONTRACTOR
Thomson-CSF, Division Systèmes Défense et Contrôle, 40 rue Grange Dame Rose, BP 34, 92360 Meudon-La-Forêt, France.

New vertical display for Thomson-CSF tactical data handling systems

3743.481
DLA ANTI-SUBMARINE FIRE CONTROL SYSTEM

The DLA anti-submarine fire control system is designed on a modular basis to provide the necessary flexibility to permit its use aboard various classes of surface ships, to accommodate various types of weapons, and to enable it to be completely integrated within a ship's combat system. This is achieved by assembling the DLA system from two basic modules: a 'target' module and a 'weapon' module.

The former is built around a large CRT for the display of tactical information, and a microprocessor. The microprocessor is of similar or identical technology to that employed in the weapon module and its function is to accept target data from sonar systems (eg bearing, range, and doppler), and from these to compute the target parameters required by the weapon module (course and speed).

Weapon modules are specific to the weapon(s) fitted in the ship (eg torpedo, A/S missile, rockets, or depth-charges), and current 'standard' weapon modules are available for all French torpedoes as well as the Mk 44, Mk 46 and A 244 types, and for the Creusot Loire/Bofors 375 A/S rocket launcher. Other types of weapon can be accommodated by the designers on request. The weapon module computer accepts data on target bearing, range, course and speed, and processes this information to produce the necessary parameters for the sequencing, setting, and launching or firing of the A/S weapon.

The DLA is supplied either as a completely self-contained system, with both types of module, or as a weapon module (appropriate to the ship's weapon fit) with a suitable interface for integration into a vessel's combat system performing target designation and computation.

STATUS
In series production for the French Navy and one foreign navy.
CONTRACTOR
SINTRA-ALCATEL, Département DSM, 1 avenue Aristide Briand, 94117 Arcueil Cedex, France.

Tactical weapon control console

1522.261
SENIT NAVAL TACTICAL DATA HANDLING SYSTEMS

The French Navy's naval tactical information systems for surface vessels are identified under the acronymic designation SENIT (Systéme d'Exploitation Navale des Informations Tactiques), and five systems of this kind have been identified. All five have the broad functions of gathering, co-ordinating, and distributing sensor data and other information, presentation of information on appropriate displays, and certain weapon system control functions. A digital computer, or computers, provides the central processing facilities. The five systems differ in accordance with the nature and operational role of the vessel fitted and the sensors and armament installed. Details of the five versions identified to date appeared in the 1979-80 edition of *Jane's Weapon Systems*, and in preceding editions. No information has been received concerning any successor systems that may be employed aboard new generation French warships.

STATUS
In addition to the SENIT systems produced for French Navy vessels, a certain number of systems have been supplied to foreign ships according to the manufacturers, but no details have been obtained. Four frigates for Saudi Arabia are to be equipped, as noted in **4053.261**.
CONTRACTOR
Thomson-CSF, Division Systèmes Défense et Contrôle, 40 rue Grange Dame Rose, BP 34, 92360 Meudon-La-Forêt, France.

1739.461
DLT-D3 SUBMARINE TORPEDO FIRE CONTROL SYSTEM

The DLT-D3 torpedo fire control system is used in French Navy submarines. All types of torpedo employed by the French Navy can be launched, including wire-guided. The system may also be expanded for anti-surface missile applications.

Target data is fed to the system from on-board sensors, which comprise fore and aft sonars, acoustic rangefinder and attack and surveillance periscopes.

The system employs a general purpose digital computer, associated with a CRT display terminal. The following functions are performed by the system:
(1) updating of the tactical situation from the data delivered by the various sensor systems fitted and the navigation equipment

(2) assistance in calculating target components by the use of special recorded programs
(3) weapon control, ie computation of the firing path, remote setting of torpedoes, and firing sequence control. The system is designed for launching any type of torpedo
(4) maintaining a chronological record
(5) maintenance assistance by means of test programs.

The DLT-D3 operating programs have been compiled to permit tracking of eight targets, simultaneous guidance of two wire-guided torpedoes and preparation of a third for launching. Each of the three displays of the terminal is dedicated to the presentation of the following data, in accordance with the program implemented: tactical situation, firing path, and alpha-numeric display of parameters (tote)

and decoding of the designations and functions of the two common keyboards. Conversation between the operator(s) and the computer are by means of these keyboards. Emergency launch of torpedoes is possible from either bow or stern station.

The system is designed to be served by one or two operators at the operations centre, and one operator at the bow station with possibly another at the stern station. The equipment arrangement, typically, is one CIMSA 15M125 digital computer (QTD), a monitoring and control console (VIC), an azimuth relay (RZ), a true-bearing diagram (GZ) in the operations centre, a tube selection panel (PAT), and tube servicing station (PST) in the bow and/or aft torpedo tube compartments.

STATUS
This system is in service in 'Daphné', 'Agosta' and 'SNA' class submarines of the French Navy, and is in production for all French and foreign 1200-ton class submarines.
CONTRACTOR
SINTRA-ALCATEL, Département DSM, 1 avenue Aristide Briand, 94117 Arcueil Cedex, France.

DLT-D3 submarine torpedo fire control system

4501.481
UX 37 SUBMARINE WEAPON CONTROL SYSTEM
The UX 37 system studied by SINTRA-ALCATEL provides the following functions: detection, sonar data correlation, display of tactical data generated by internal or external sensors, and weapon fire control. The major element of the system comprises the three multi-colour (three colours) multiple function large-screen display consoles. The essential purposes include:

(1) to increase the bearing measurement and accuracy of passive sonars, to make the detection uniform for medium- and long-range weapons by target integration techniques

(2) to minimise manning demands while still utilising all information at watch and action stations.

The system is capable of:

(1) automatic tracking of 20 noise generators (targets)

(2) tracking of 30 tracks (using all sensors)

(3) tracking four smoothed tracks in true motion with 20 mm history

(4) weapon control for engaging the four smoothed tracks

(5) simultaneous launch and control of two wire-guided torpedoes.

The acoustic sensors are comprised of eight identical hydrophones located along the hull of the vessel; these are similar to those used in the UX 27 system (see Fenelon DUUX 5, **3498.453**).
STATUS
Development.
CONTRACTOR
SINTRA-ALCATEL, Département DSM, 1 avenue Aristide Briand, 94117 Arcueil Cedex, France.

Three-colour large-screen display console of UX 37 submarine weapon control system

---

GERMANY (FEDERAL REPUBLIC)

1824.281
AGIS COMBAT INFORMATION SYSTEM
AGIS (Automatisiertes Gefechts- und Informations-system für Schnellboote) is a fully integrated command and fire control system which has been developed for the West German Bundesmarine's Type 143 fast patrol boats.

AGIS includes the areas of command and fire control system WM 27 (HSA) (**1259.281**), the optical auxiliary fire control system OG.TR 7/3 (Officine Galileo), weapons, data transmission system LINK 11 (Collins), log system SAL 59 (Jungner), gyro compass system PL-41 (LITEF), IFF system (Siemens) and ESM system. The weapons associated with the system are two 76/62 OTO C guns (OTO Melara) both against air and surface targets (**5533.203**), two wire-guided torpedoes Seal (AEG-Telefunken) (**2178.441**) and four surface target missiles MM 38 Exocet on two double launchers (**1156.221**).

In addition to AGIS, the RF, VHF and UHF transceiver units and their associated communications operator stations serve for external communication in the radio-telephone, radio teletyping and radio keying modes – unencrypted and encrypted. Internally, communication is ensured via the simplex/duplex system (Philips). Furthermore, navigation and direction finding aids include an echo sounder, magnetic compass, Decca navigator and navigation radar.

The AGIS mission centre is the combat information centre with the two control units for torpedo direction, the artillery control system for guns and missiles, the horizontal tactical display and the vertical plot. From here, the S143 can operate as lead boat for other units (eg S142 or S148). The system is controlled by two freely programmable digital computers processing the sensor data for displaying on the different displays or for weapon control. One of the computers is for generation and utilisation of the tactical situation and for target assignment to the command units, and the other one operates as fire control computer for target tracking, determination of firing parameters as well as for control of weapons and weapon consoles.

In addition to own ship information acquisition, the automatic data transmission system, LINK 11, permits the display of data on targets outside own ship detection range and to transmit tactical information to other units.

The AGIS is also employed on the new class 143A fast patrol boats. A successor to the class 143 combat system, it mainly differs in having the ASMD (RAM) system in place of the stern gun and the torpedo system is replaced by a mine launcher. The class 143A is equipped with an FL1800 ESM/ECM system.
STATUS
Fitted in Type 143/143A fast attack craft.
CONTRACTOR
AEG-Telefunken, 7900 Ulm, Elisabethenstrasse 3, Federal Republic of Germany – Main contractor.

1825.281
SATIR ACTION INFORMATION SYSTEM
SATIR (System zur Auswertung Taktischer Informationen auf Raketenzerstören) is the tactical data automation and display system fitted in the three 'Lütjens' class guided missile destroyers of the West German Bundesmarine. These ships are a modified version of the American 'Charles F Adams' type and are fitted with US radars such as the SPS-52 three-dimensional search and target designator, SPS-10 surface warning set, SPS-40 air surveillance, and SPG-51 fire control radars for the Tartar surface-to-air missiles. Weight and space considerations decided the Bundesmarine against the installation of the US NTDS (Naval Tactical Data System) and SATIR was developed in its stead to meet the German requirement and in general compliance with the B-2 Concept, a NATO standardised system for destroyers and above. Beyond the participation of Univac, no other reliable details have been obtained.

A version of the SATIR system is fitted in the six vessels of the Type 122 'Bremen' class; this is described in detail in 1982-83 and earlier editions (**3504.281**).

3504.281
CLASS 122 FRIGATE COMBAT SYSTEM

The combat system of the new Class 122 frigates for the German Federal Navy permits the repulsion, engagement, deception and destruction of air, surface and underwater targets as well as communication with other units at sea, in the air and ashore. For the performance of these tasks the combat system consists of a central computer system for processing and correlation of the incoming information which is acquired by means of sensors and data transmission, as well as of display consoles with the synthetic scenario for dialogue during decision-making, and for any resultant missions.

All major functions can be monitored from the combat information centre with the aid of an optimised number of personnel in a reliable, co-ordinated and effective manner and can be controlled directly or indirectly. The high processing speed and the large storage capacity of the computers as well as the very fast peripheral equipment and a considerable redundancy permit measures for equipment maintenance and repair in parallel with the major tasks outlined above. A suitable computer set-up, special system instructions as well as a modular software structure permit effective real-time processing. As far as software programs are concerned, a distinction is made between the mission

software, maintenance software, support software and general software for administrative and other purposes.

This system, which is now being progressively deployed with the West German fleet, is described in detail in 1982-83 and earlier editions of *Jane's Weapon Systems*, together with a list of sensor equipment and weapons fitted in these ships.
CONTRACTORS
AEG-Telefunken, 7900 Ulm, Elisabethenstrasse 3, Federal Republic of Germany – Main contractor for weapon system and integrated logistic support.
Bremer Vulkan – Prime contractor.

INTERNATIONAL

3509.281
SEAGUARD NAVAL WEAPON CONTROL SYSTEM

Seaguard has been developed as a naval close-in weapon system (CIWS) for defence against anti-ship missiles, and comprises a new 25 mm four-barrelled gun on a special mount integrated with a suitably configured modular fire control system. This entry is concerned with the Seaguard fire control system and its constituent command and control, search, tracking, and other sensor modules; the CIWS aspects of the Seaguard system and the special Sea Zenith gun mount are described in the Shipborne Surface-to-Air Weapons section of this volume (**4016.231**).

In addition to the Sea Zenith gun mount module (GM), the other main modules consist of:

(1) command and control module (CCM) console
(2) a Plessey Dolphin C-band search radar (**4004.253**) module (SRM)
(3) Elettronica electronic warfare module (EWM)
(4) an X-band general purpose tracking radar module (GPTM)
(5) a Ku-band close-in weapon system tracking radar module (CIWS-TM)
(6) an electro-optical tracker module (EOTM).

These modules can be configured in various ways to suit the type of ship fitted. The main CCM consists of a large-scale horizontal PPI display which provides a tactical situation presentation for search radar data with target designation facilities by means of a keyboard. It is designed for two operators but there is provision for a third man as either an operator or an observer, if required. Console functions include the

collection of data from all system sensors on the common tactical plot; elaboration of threat data using track-while-scan techniques on several targets and allocation of target priorities; assignment of tracks to tracker and weapon modules on the basis of threat evaluation; and fully automatic control of two modes of engagement.

A typical Seaguard CIWS consists of an above deck sensor mount, a gun mount with below deck ammunition feeding, below deck operator console and associated below-deck electronic cabinets. The fire control element of the CIWS, the tracker module (CIWS-TM), utilises a three-axis tracker mount having Ku-band radar, forward looking infra-red (FLIR) and laser sensors for the acquisition and tracking of missile targets.

Both the CIWS-TM and CIWS-GM have dedicated mini-computers linked by a data bus. Use of distributed and dedicated powerful mini-computers as opposed to a centralised computer has produced a significant advance in accuracy and reaction times. Operationally the CIWS is controlled from the operator console normally located in the operations room. The operator task is principally to monitor the CIWS, since from designation to open fire the main mode is automatic. Should operator intervention be necessary then full facilities at the console are available and operator control is normally exercised through a computer dialogue mode using a keyboard.
STATUS
Certain evaluation trials of Seaguard modules have been completed and, although not officially confirmed, it is expected that first fittings will be in Turkish Navy ships constructed in West Germany.
CONTRACTORS
Contraves Italiana SpA, Via Affile (Km 13150 Via Tiburtina), 00131 Rome, Italy.
Contraves AG, Schaffhausterstrasse 580, 8050 Zurich, Switzerland.
Machine Tool Works Oerlikon-Bührle, Birchstrasse 155, 8050 Zurich, Switzerland.

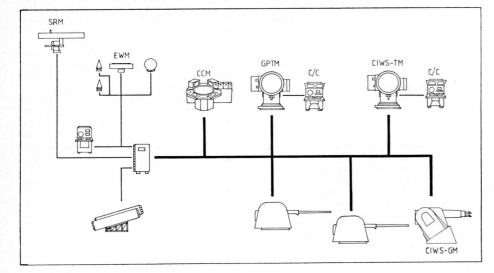

Simplified schematic diagram showing how Seaguard FCS modules might be integrated in a comprehensive ship's weapon system

---

4489.281
SEA TIGER

Sea Tiger is a derivative of the naval electro-optical fire director system originally developed for the US Navy as the Seafire project (**3727.281**) by two of the participants in that programme, Texas Instruments and Ferranti. The Sea Tiger system is designed to provide passive surveillance using high resolution daylight television and high resolution forward looking infra-red (FLIR) for night surveillance, and typical applications include navigation, search and rescue, aircraft and missile detection, and detection of surface craft (ships etc) at the horizon. For fire control purposes three-dimensional tracking is provided by an automatic video tracker used with a laser rangefinder. The system processor carries out calculation of gun or missile orders using three-dimensional track information, ship's sensor inputs and stored ballistic data. Other facilities include

handing-off of targets and line-of-sight designation from other ship systems and there is spare computer capacity for distributed processing. Laser target illumination facilities are provided for guidance of laser seeking ordnance such as the US Navy's 5-inch laser guided shell and air-launched weapons such as LGBs. Laser target designation is frequency codeable to facilitate multiple attacks/targets, and to aid protection from countermeasures.

The Sea Tiger equipment comprises an E-O director mounted above deck and incorporating a daylight TV camera, thermal imaging IR sensor, and a Ferranti Type 905 multi-role laser for designation and laser rangefinding. The E-O director is connected by a data link and video link with a below-deck console that contains the computer for the automatic video tracker and fire control calculations. Provisions are included for interfacing the Sea Tiger system with other ship's sensors and data processing facilities.

Operational applications of the system include passive surveillance by day and night, target detection and designation for defensive and attack purposes, close-in point defence capability, and laser target marking for laser guided weapons such as naval ordnance or air-launched bombs.
STATUS
Joint marketing programme by Texas Instruments and Ferranti world-wide, excluding the USA where it is understood that the Seafire system (which contains a number of system elements common to the Sea Tiger system). It is understood that a US Navy contract for the Seafire system was awarded to Texas Insutruments in November 1983.
CONTRACTORS
Texas Instruments Inc, PO Box 226015, Dallas, Texas 75266, USA.
Ferranti plc, Robertson Avenue, Edinburgh EH11 1PX, Scotland.

ISREAL

3460.281
ELBIT ISRAELI NTCCS

The Elbit Israeli Naval Tactical Command and Control System (NTCCS) is a computer-based system to provide the commanders of ships with real-time tactical information on their area of activity. Using data from own ship sensors and other task force participants, the system processes the data and presents a tactical situation picture. In addition, the NTCCS provides navigational computations, message exchange services between task force units and shore-based headquarters, and recording of tactical data for future debriefing and off-line analysis.

Input data are provided by sensors such as search and fire control radars, EW and ESM systems, sonar, automatic navigation system, ship's log and gyro-compass, and manual inputs including optical sight information and the various communications channels. Additionally, information from other units can be inserted via data link or underwater communications links.

Items of equipment incorporated in a typical NTCCS include: digital computer(s); input/output controllers and interfaces for ship's sensors; radar plot extractors; tactical alpha-numeric tote displays;

Elbit NTCCS colour tactical display console

alpha-numeric terminals for the command team and sensor operators; numeric display generators for plotting tables; display generators for tactical display

consoles (PPIs); and tape recorders. The tactical situation will be displayed on a coloured raster display.

Depending upon the particular ship and its sensor and weapons fit, specific functions performed by the NTCCS include the following:

(1) compilation and presentation of tactical situation pictures
(2) management of the exchange of tactical data between task force units (including submarines and aircraft)
(3) detection, tracking and processing of target data
(4) correlation of EW/ESM and radar data
(5) computation of navigation and manoeuvre data
(6) computation of intercept locations
(7) computation of EW countermeasures area
(8) presentation of correlation charts from the computer
(9) data recording.

The system was especially designed for small patrol craft (missiles/guns) but is suitable for larger ships with additional displays as desired.
STATUS
Operational with the Israeli armed forces.
CONTRACTOR
Elbit Computers Ltd, POB 5390, Haifa 31051, Israel.

4579.281
RESHET NAVAL COMMAND AND CONTROL SYSTEM

Reshet is a shipborne tactical command and control system for vessels of all sizes. It provides the command with an updated and comprehensive picture of the overall tactical situation, based on data from own ship's sensors and information derived from consorts and/or shore-based facilities, via data links.

Several versions have been designed (**3800.261** in 1983-84 and earlier editions), but all are composed of one or more tactical display consoles (TDCs), a central data processing unit, and in certain cases a data management terminal, as well as the essential interface equipment needed to connect the system with sensors and weapon systems.

Operational requirements met by a typical Reshet system include: real-time assembly, assessment, display and application of all available data; co-ordination of task force actions; over-the-horizon targeting; prevention of 'data saturation'; and modernisation of existing CIC facilities.

To fulfil these functions the following facilities are required:
(1) automatic tracking of multiple targets from search and fire control radars' video data
(2) exchange of tactical information and messages within data link network stations
(3) threat evaluation by classification, correlation,

execution of triangulations and selective data display according to operator-defined categories
(4) navigational calculations and other computations for operational purposes
(5) tactical display in colour, with maps, grid, targets and bearing lines, datum points, danger zones, future positions, track histories and other tactical data
(6) comprehensive display, editing and data manipulation facilities such as zoom, off-centring, true/relative motion display, declutter, etc
(7) anti-submarine warfare calculations and display
(8) alpha-numeric presentation of target data, cursor position, system, messages and other information
(9) designation of tracked target to weapon systems and other units
(10) hard copying of tactical scenario for analysis.

All these facilities are provided by a typical Reshet multi-functional system, which might consist of a central processor unit, a number of consoles used as the target acquisition and designation (TAD) position, tactical editor console, commander's tactical console, and data link equipment. The Reshet system's modularity allows two alternative simplified versions to be configured for smaller ships. These

differ from the complete system mainly in the display capabilities. The single console configuration replaces the tactical editor console with a data management terminal that provides the tactical editor with data in tabular form, and supplies the commander with a full picture on the tactical console. The minimal system configuration, Reshet TADS/Data Link includes the target acquisition and designation system console and data management terminal, with the central processor unit. This configuration is sufficient to provide: display of data from ship's own radar(s), automatic tracking, synthetic symbols, data link management and display, and target designation capability.

The tactical display console (TDC) component of the Reshet system can be used as an independent fully computerised multi-function unit. In such a role it can provide: local data processing, display of maps grids and zones, navigational solutions and display, automatic updating of own position, local processing of operator requests, definition of targets and bearing lines, computation and presentation of targets and their track histories, etc.
STATUS
In production and operational with Israeli and other naval forces.
CONTRACTOR
IAI, Israel Aircraft Industries Ltd, Ben Gurion International Airport, 70100, Israel.

4057.261
DG NAVAL FIRE CONTROL SYSTEM

The DG (Dvora/Gabriel) weapon control system is based on the FCS developed for the Gabriel anti-ship missile system (**6019.221**) as fitted in the 'Dvora' fast missile boat. It is especially adapted for smaller naval craft like 'Dvora' class vessels, enabling boats equipped with this system to enjoy a fire power normally available only on larger ships.

A variant of the basic Gabriel integrated fire control system, the DG system has been designed for missile control and guidance only. The system handles search, acquisition and tracking of surface targets,

target designation from one unit to another and Gabriel missile trajectory precision guidance.

The main sub-units of the DG system are: fire control tracking radar (FCR) components, comprised of antenna (FCRA), transmitter (FCRT), and receiver (FCRR); a standard search and navigation radar (adapted by the Electronics Division of MBT Weapon Systems to designate targets to the weapon system); a stabilised periscopic optical sight (OS); a display control and processing unit (DCPU); a vertical reference unit (VRU); and Gabriel missile fixed single launchers.

Only two operators are required to operate the

system. One, the optical sight operator, handles search and tracking by means of the periscopic OS from the closed bridge, while the other, the DCPU operator, handles FCR operation and missile control and guidance.
STATUS
No information released.
CONTRACTOR
MBT, Israel Aircraft Industries Ltd, Yehud Industrial Zone 56000, Israel.

ITALY

4058.281
NA 18 FIRE CONTROL SYSTEM

The NA 18 is an electro-optical fire control system (FCS) belonging to the latest Elsag series of naval fire control systems. It was developed to serve as either a lightweight autonomous system for use aboard small and medium tonnage vessels, or as an alternative to a radar FCS in ships which lack the space to fit a radar system. In larger ships, the NA 18 can be operated as a back-up to the existing radar fire control lines-of-sight, especially in the presence of heavy ECM or when a low-flying target is to be engaged and tracked.

The electro-optical director consists of an Elsag servoed pedestal which carries a television camera and a laser rangefinder. As an option an infra-red sensor capable of passive surveillance duties can be readily integrated with the system. A wide range of sensors can be embodied at the customer's choice to provide a variety of operational facilities.

The operational console contains TV display monitors, all operating controls and a digital multi-processor based on the Elsag-designed ESA 24 microprocessor. This last component provides high speed, high resolution tracking, ballistic data and gun calculations for aiming up to two different calibre guns.

Apart from the laser (which provides target range data) the NA 18 is a completely passive system that provides for:
(1) acquisition of targets, designated by external sensors or self-designated when the surveillance mode is adopted, by automatic scanning patterns

NA 18 E-O director equipped with TV camera, laser and infra-red thermal camera

(2) inter-director designation from/to other weapon control systems
(3) automatic tracking of missile, aircraft, ship and shore targets.

As the operator's console is capable of presenting search or navigation radar video on the same TV display monitor, this console can perform the command and control function on small ships.

STATUS

In series production and in service with several navies.

NA 18 operator's console with radar and TV image presentation

CONTRACTOR
Selenia-Elsag Consortium for Naval Systems, Via Panama 52, 00198 Rome, Italy.

4059.281
NA 21 FIRE CONTROL SYSTEM

The NA 21 Mod 0 is a digital system embodying Elsag ESA 24 microprocessors and is the natural development of the NA 10 series of fire control systems (**1550.281**). The system employs the Orion 10X tracker radar, in a frequency-agile version and with associated television camera, for the direction of guns of two calibres, surface-to-surface and surface-to-air missiles against air and surface targets. A TV tracking system is associated with the radar line-of-sight. For SAM control, the NA 21 is linked with the Albatros missile launcher system and the system is connected to the ship's main CIC network also. There is a single operator console below deck.

The system can carry out:
(1) programmed search, at low elevation if necessary, with the system's own radar

(2) surveillance using the ship's search radar
(3) automatic target acquisition by external or self-designation
(4) inter-director designation to other weapon systems
(5) tracking of missile, aircraft or surface targets by fire control radar and TV
(6) optical back-up by television to radar tracking
(7) weapon control with automatic fire capability.
STATUS

In series production and in service with several navies.
CONTRACTORS
Elettronica San Giorgio (Elsag), Via Hermada 6, 16154 Genoa, Italy.

Selenia-Elsag Consortium for Naval Systems, Via Panama 52, 00198 Rome, Italy.

NA 21 FC radars as installed aboard a corvette. Search radar is the RAN-10S

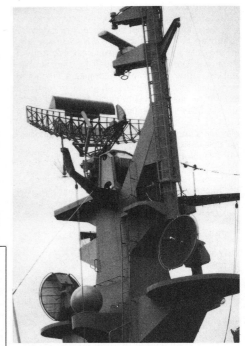

3861.281
NA 30 SERIES FIRE CONTROL SYSTEM

The NA 30 series of fire control systems represents the most complete and advanced example of the new generation equipment designed by the Selenia-Elsag Consortium for Naval Systems to cope with the present and future operational requirements of modern navies. The NA 30 FCS is available in two configurations, NA 30 A and NA 30 B, the main difference being the number of lines-of-sight available. The NA 30 A, as adopted by the Italian Navy for installation in the new ASW frigates of 'Maestrale' class, employs two independent directors for target tracking, one supporting the Selenia Orion 30X radar (**1936.253**) and two FIAR TV cameras (daylight and low-light) and the other equipped with optronic sensors such as a Galileo infra-red thermal camera, a FIAR laser rangefinder and a twilight TV camera. The optronic director can also be the same used in the Elsag NA 18 FCS (**4058.281**) with a wide range of sensors.

Two operator consoles, one for FCR and S/A missile control and the other for electro-optical sensor control are associated with the NA 30 A.

From the weapon control point of view, the NA 30 system can provide up to four independent gun outputs and proper ballistic calculation for up to three different calibres; additionally, it supplies launching data to surface-to-air missile systems like the Albatross (**2228.231**), and target data to those

Operator console of NA 30 A FCS in 'Maestrale' frigate

surface-to-surface missile systems requiring such inputs.

NA 30 B
The NA 30 B, as adopted by the Italian Navy for the new helicopter carrier *Garibaldi*, is provided with a single director, where the same Orion 30 X radar is combined with an infra-red sensor and a daylight TV camera. One operator console is associated with the NA 30 B.

The system can provide up to three independent gun outputs, with one fuze setting computation for the main calibre, proper ballistic calculation for up to two different calibres, as well as supplying launching data to surface-to-air missile systems and target data to surface-to-surface missile systems.

In its basic configuration, the NA 30 B is a general purpose FCS, capable of handling various environments and targets in automatic and manual modes.

CIWS KIT FOR NA 30 B
The basic and successful concept of Dardo CIWS (**4497.231** and **1920.281**), updated to incorporate the latest technical improvements and matched to the increased threat and ECM parameters, can be easily implemented in the NA 30 B FCS, giving extended flexibility and comprehensive operating modes. This is possible because of the main features of the NA 30 B: the characteristics and performance of the

Orion 30 X and its MTI function, the large capability of the ESA 24 multiprocessor and the easy adaptability of the software.

Furthermore, implementing the CIWS functions in the NA 30 B, facilitates the new concept of automatic reaction, combining the SAM and the gun weapons to counteract the close-in threat. The FCS can be operated in three ways:

(1) medium range automatic reaction, with automatic engagement, automatic SAM launch, automatic gun firing
(2) short range automatic reaction, with automatic engagement, automatic gun firing
(3) non-automatic reaction, as a conventional FCS (designation, operator controlled launch and firing).

STATUS
In series production. The NA 30 B with CIWS kit has been adopted by the Italian Navy for its new corvettes.
CONTRACTOR
Selenia-Elsag Consortium for Naval Systems, Via Panama 52, 00198 Rome, Italy.

Orion RTN-30X radar/TV director for NA 30 aboard a 'Maestrale' frigate

Electro-optical director for NA 30 A

1920.281

DARDO FIRE CONTROL SYSTEM

The Dardo close-in weapon system was designed and developed for the Italian Navy's 'Lupo' and 'Maestrale' class frigates and the helicopter carrier, *Garibaldi*, for their defence against sea-skimming and diving missiles. The system in described in an earlier entry (**4497.231**) in this volume. Several other navies have adopted the system also.

Fire control for the Breda compact twin 40 mm L/70 naval gun used in Dardo is provided by a system based on an Elsag data processing and interfacing unit working in conjunction with a Selenia servo-controlled fire control director carrying radar and electro-optical sensors, and an operator's console. In addition to target data provided by Dardo's own sensors, other operational information is derived from other ship's systems such as search radar(s), ESM/ECM, and manual optical target indication sights. Specific operational functions of Dardo include:

(1) defence against sea skimming anti-ship missiles
(2) defence against diving missiles
(3) defence against manned aircraft
(4) effective ranges 300 to 3500 m.

In Dardo a radar of advanced design and optimised for tracking low-flying targets is employed. The system is designed for fully automatic operation by means of:

Dardo supervision consoles

(1) direct use of search radar information, with automatic data evaluation and target selection
(2) automatic target acquisition
(3) target tracking, automatically and with high performance in the presence of noise/ECM
(4) automatic gun fire control.

Sensors include the RAN 10S search radar (**1699.253**), Orion 20X tracking radar (**1935.253**), optical sights, ship's log, compass, attitude references, wing velocity etc.

Orion 20X tracking radar with TV camera used in Dardo system

STATUS
In series production for the Italian and other navies.
CONTRACTOR
Selenia-Elsag Consortium for Naval Systems, Via Panama 52, 00198 Rome, Italy.

4047.281

LINCE FCS

The LINCE system has been designed by OTO Melara as a self-contained naval fire control director, principally for light and medium calibre guns. The system is designed for tracking and firing against low

LINCE electro-optical director head

altitude attacking aircraft, fast patrol boats, and S/S sea skimmer missiles. It is especially effective in tracking and combatting targets moving at low elevation angles (when sea clutter might obscure the target and nodding might strongly affect automatic aiming) in the face of ECM or under radar silence.

The LINCE system, operating as an autonomous firing director, is able to perform the following functions:

(1) surveillance for surface and low air targets
(2) target designation acceptance from an external designation source
(3) target acquisition and tracking by CCTV camera system (or IR camera)
(4) automatic tracking (angular and range) of the target by means of TV tracker system and laser rangefinder
(5) manual rate-aided tracking (angular and range) of the target by means of a joystick or a tracking ball
(6) gun prediction calculation for air or surface target
(7) introduction of range and lateral spotting corrections
(8) kill and damage assessment.

All these operations need only one operator at the LINCE system console.

The director is in the form of a pedestal in which both a TV camera or IR camera and a laser rangefinder can move in elevation; the pedestal has 360° continuous training. The firing computer gives the elevation and bearing lead angles in the form of synchro signals for directing the gun.

The LINCE system is capable of operating in two main modes: completely automatic and semi-automatic or manual. In the fully automatic mode, the target is tracked by the tracker system which, processing the video signal, keeps the line of sight continuously on the target; the range data are automatically provided by the laser rangefinder. Kinematic lead angles and ballistic functions are provided by the firing computer; the introduction of the meteo data is entrusted to the operator, who is provided with suitable hand controls.

In the semi-automatic or manual mode (back-up mode), manual tracking is performed by means of a joystick or a tracking ball; the manual introduction of the range with the relevant spotting corrections is possible through suitable hand controls, while the introduction of the lead angles and of the ballistic corrections is performed through pedals. In both modes of operation, firing is carried out by operating the firing pedal.

Acquisition and angular tracking (manual or automatic) are by the contrast technique applied to the image of the target against its background, as viewed by a high resolution camera (TV or IR). Range information is gathered by means of a high repetition frequency laser rangefinder.

Both the image camera and the laser rangefinder are mounted on the director head, provided with high precision servos, stabilisation unit (including a triad of integrating gyros) and a suitable protective dome with transparent elevating windows. Calculation of automatic kinematic lead angles and ballistic functions is achieved through the use of a hybrid computer, employing microcomputing techniques, operating on the target geometrical and kinematic data, and on the projectile and meteorological data.

Range and lateral spotting correction introduction (only when firing against surface or shore targets) is by operator intervention. The computer, the video and the laser processing unit, servos, supply and logics electronics, monitoring, displaying, and ancillary units are included in an operator console.

CHARACTERISTICS

Traverse: Unlimited
Elevation: –15 to +72°
Angular velocity: >60°/s
Acceleration: >100°/s²
Range: >15 km (ship target); >8 km (aircraft target)

Weight
Optronic head: 220 kg (approx)
Operator console: 300 kg (approx)
STATUS
The prototype phase was completed by early 1984.
CONTRACTOR
OTO Melara SpA, 15 Via Valdilocchi, 19100 La Spezia, Italy.

4263.281
OG 30 NAVAL FIRE CONTROL SYSTEM

The OG 30 is the latest of the Officine Galileo series of optical and electro-optical naval fire control systems. It is designed to provide by E-O means, surveillance acquisition and tracking facilities for weapon control, while avoiding the need for use of 'nodding' techniques against sea-skimmer targets and ECM. Sensors mounted on a stabilised platform include equipments for television search and target tracking, laser rangefinding, and passive infra-red tracking and search. The last of these is the function of the Officine Galileo NCS/2 thermal imaging equipment (**4262.293**) which operates in the eight to fourteen micron band of the IR spectrum. Other sensors include the FIAR P 0700 laser rangefinder and P 4670 television tracker equipments. Target data and other information (eg from reference gyros, controller inputs etc) are processed digitally to produce target designation facilities for other ship's systems and, via the ballistics computer, firing orders for weapons.

The OG 30 is suitable for replacement of existing earlier fire control systems. Target information is presented on displays located in the fire control console below deck together with operator controls for the OG 30 system and for associated weapons.

CHARACTERISTICS
Field of view: 3° × 6°
Image format: 1:2
Instantaneous field of view: 0 – 25 mrad
Frame rate: 25 Hz
Lines per frame: 200
IR detector type: CMT linear array
Working wavelength: 8 – 14 microns
Operating temperature: 77° K
Laser rangefinder: P 0700
Output: 20 – 25 MW

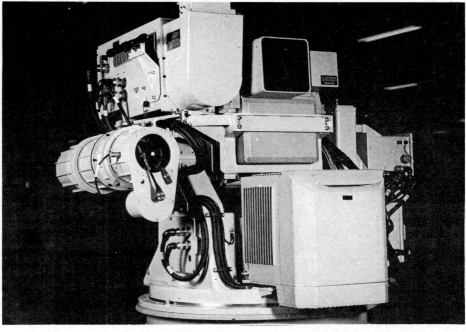
Officine Galileo OG 30 naval fire control multiple sensor head

PRF: 15 Hz
Range: 300 m – 15 km
TV tracker: P 4670
Typical range: 16 km (aircraft); 18 km (frigate); 6 km (sea-skimmer missile)

STATUS
In service with the Italian Navy.
CONTRACTOR
Officine Galileo, 50013 Campi Bisenzio, Florence, Italy.

4498.461
SACTIS COMBAT INFORMATION SYSTEM

SACTIS is the abbreviated title given to the submarine action information system being developed for Italian Navy submarines of the Sauro class by SMA in collaboration with Datamat and other contractors. The former concern was selected as prime contractor for this project in 1981 when it was decided to equip this class of submarine with a new AIO system. Two versions are to be produced known as SACTIS 1 and 2, or by the Italian Navy designations MM/BSN-716(V)1 and MM/BSN-716(V)2, respectively. The two versions are intended for fitting in the second and projected third batches of Sauro class boats. In both cases the principal functions include:

(1) automatic data acquisition from all sensors (eg hydrophone, sonar, passive ranging system, search and attack periscopes, radar ESM, navigation system, depth sounder etc)
(2) manual data input
(3) real-time computation of ship's position and target position (from bearing data only)

(4) data display (raw and processed) with four different presentations: unfiltered situation; tactical situation; time/bearing display; tactical operation tabular evaluation
(5) calculation and display of data for typical manoeuvres such as screen or barrage penetration, evasion, target interception or collision course, approach and divergence routes, CPA
(6) data and event recording
(7) playback for training and analysis.

The hardware comprises two display groups which have vertical CRT displays and keyboards for data input and system management, with separate alpha-numeric 'tote' displays above the situation display CRTs; a central processor unit based on a Rolm MSE 14 digital computer; disk memories; a printer; a specially designed interface unit for input/output between SACTIS and the various sensors. The two displays are arranged side-by-side to form a two-man operating console and up to 30 separate targets can be displayed, from which individual track histories

can be selected for examination and ten of them presented as filtered targets. Main sensors connected to the system include the BPS-704 radar, IPD-70 sonar system, and the Thetis electronic warfare system.

The later SACTIS 2 version includes provision for connection with the submarine's A184 torpedo fire control system (**3252.481**), and inclusion of the ELT/810 sonar prediction system. There is also extended computer capacity and a third operator position at the SACTIS console.

STATUS
The first production installation was ready for fitting in a 'Sauro' class submarine completing a refit in mid-1984. When complete, acceptance tests of the MM/BSN-716 system are planned for this submarine.
CONTRACTORS
SMA – Segnalamento Marittimo ed Aereo SpA, Via del Ferrone-Soffiano, 50100 Florence, Italy. (Main)
Datamat Ingegneria dei Sistemi SpA, Via Simone Martini 126, 00143 Rome, Italy. (Software)

3252.481
A184 SUBMARINE TORPEDO FCS

The A184 system is the fire control system for submarines equipped with Whitehead A184 wire-guided homing torpedoes. The system comprises a computation, display and control station (CCRG), which uses a SEPA ULP12/M mini-computer, the local control and switching box for the torpedoes, and the torpedo electronics. Sensor inputs to the system include radar, navigation and attitude information, periscope, and acoustic data from the integrated active/passive IPD70 sonar system (**3233.453**).

Target and ship's own data from these sources are used to calculate and display target positions and target vectors, impact point predictions, tactical situation, a launch and guidance display, and wire guidance signals. These functions are grouped in the CCRG. The local control and switching box connects

the signals from the CCRG to the selected torpedo, provides launching tube control, and feeds electric power to torpedoes in the tubes. Within the torpedo, the electronic control unit carries out wire signal interfacing, torpedo steering in accordance with CCRG commands, computation of target data from the torpedo acoustic head, and torpedo homing.

STATUS
Entering service.
CONTRACTOR
SEPA-Società di Elettronica per l'Automazione SpA,
Corso Giulio Cesare 294, 10154 Turin, Italy.

Fire control system console (CCRG) of A184 weapon system

4499.261

MM/SSN-714 MINESWEEPER DATA PROCESSING SYSTEM

Under the designation MM/SSN-714, SMA and Datamat have developed a digital navigation and plotting system for the Italian Navy's new Lerici class of mine countermeasures ships. The main functions of the SSN-714 MACTIS (mine-hunting action information sub-system) are:
(1) automatic computation and presentation of the ship's current position
(2) display of the tactical situation
(3) analysis and presentation of target characteristics

(4) location of surface targets
(5) event recording
(6) operations planning
(7) guidance of surface and underwater craft.

The system is based on a computer of the same or similar type to that employed in the SACTIS submarine AIO system (**4498.461**), namely a Rolm MSE 14 machine. In the SSN-714 system this is interfaced with recording units, display units, controls, printer and ship's sensors. The principal items in the last of these categories are radar, sonar, compass, log and various navigation aids. The operator's display has a vertical screen CRT and a

keyboard for communications with the system, and there are supplementary data readout display units and associated input controls on the bridge and in the operations room.
STATUS
Production.
CONTRACTORS
SMA – Segnalamento Marittimo ed Aereo SpA, Via del Ferrone-Soffiano, 50100 Florence, Italy. (Main)
Datamat Ingegneria dei Sistemi SpA, Via Simone Martini 126, 00143 Rome, Italy. (Software)

4500.261

MM/SSN-715 NAVIGATION AND TRACKING SYSTEM

This system was developed for the Italian Navy's Sparviero class of military hydrofoils and it performs the following functions:
(1) mission planning
(2) navigation and tactical plotting
(3) navigational calculations for own ship and various categories of other targets
(4) vector computation and presentation.

The system is based on the use of a Rolm microcomputer which is interfaced with a hand-held input/output terminal device, a video extractor unit, and an X/Y plotter display unit. Inputs to the system include ship's radar, gyro and log.

The SSN-715 is used as an auxiliary system for navigation purposes to provide tracking of own ship's position as well as that of a target tracked by the navigation radar, presented on a chart by means of the X/Y plotter. Use of the latter means of presentation ensures rapid interpretation of the data

and removes possible ambiguities, and the provision of a portable hand-held input/ouput control for operation of the system materially assists the tasks of the ship's command team personnel.
STATUS
Production.
CONTRACTORS
SMA – Segnalamento Marittimo ed Aereo SpA, Via del Ferrone-Soffiano, 50100 Florence, Italy. (Main)
Datamat Ingegneria dei Sistemi SpA, Via Simone Martini 126, 00143 Rome, Italy. (Software)

1551.281

ALBATROS WEAPON SYSTEM

Albatros is a naval all-weather missile and gun weapon system. The missile used is the Aspide (**1656.331**), a new multi-role weapon developed by Selenia under an Italian MoD contract. Missile control is provided by the Albatros Missile Section (**2228.231**), which is integrated with the gun fire control system to achieve a total weapon system. The naval guns can be of any type, provided the required performance matching with the relevant gun fire control system is ensured.

The original development, referred to as Albatros Mk1 Mod 1, was a system for integration with an Elsag gun fire control system and it evolved in various production configurations with the common designation of Albatros Mk2. These configurations comprise:
(1) Albatros Mk2 Mod 3, associated with Elsag type NA10 gun fire control sytems (**1550.281**)
(2) Albatros Mk2 Mod 5, with Elsag type NA21 gun fire control system
(3) Albatros Mk2 Mod 7, with Elsag type NA30 gun fire control systems
(4) Albatros Mk2 Mod 8, with Ferranti WSA-4 gun fire control systems (**1524.281**)
(5) Albatros Mk2 Mod 9, with Hollandse Signaal-apparaten WM 25 fire control systems

Albatros dual-channel tracking and illumination radar

(6) Albatros Mk 2 Mod 11, with PEAB 9LV 200 fire control systems
(7) Albatros Mk 2 Mod 12, with Thomson-CSF Vega/castor fire control systems.

For each configuration the system is available in single or double headed version (type 1/1 or 2/1), the latter having the ability to engage two targets simultaneously. Missile guidance is provided by radar illumination of the tracked target through the director

Albatros Mod 3 operator's control console

antenna. Pre-flight information and launching orders are produced by the Albatros Missile Section and the relevant consoles are contained in a panel fitted in the weapon control console so as to enable full fire control by a single operator, both for missile and guns. The two weapons can be employed simultaneously; however missile engagements are normally performed at long ranges (out to 15 km), permitting target shifting or reiteration of firing, while anti-air gunfire actions are intiated at shorter ranges or the guns are used in the surface fire or shore bombardment roles. Engagement of surface targets can also be accomplished by means of the Aspide missile.

STATUS
At the end of 1983 the orders received for naval installations included the following: Cantieri Navali Riuniti (CNR) 'Lupo' class frigates (10); Blohm & Voss frigates (7); Bazan frigates (5); CNR frigate refitting (1); CNR light aircraft carrier (1); Tacoma corvettes (2).

CONTRACTOR
Selenia-Elsag Consortium for Naval Systems, Via Panama 52, 00198 Rome, Italy.

3184.261
IPN-10/20 TACTICAL DATA DISPLAY SYSTEM

The IPN-10 is a display system tailored for small and medium tonnage ships, such as corvettes, frigates, and destroyers, where a simple system for control of the tactical situation and weapon co-ordination is generally requested. The system is suitable for both installation on new vessels and for retrofitting of older vessels; in the second case it is possible (with this minor change) drastically to improve the tactical capabilities of the ship, starting with its reaction times.

The main tasks of the system are presentation of the tactical situation, by display in a clear, self explanatory mode, and automation of some of the functions normally performed manually by the operators (such as tracking, vectoring, etc). The IPN-10 is composed of a number of display consoles, variable, in the standard configuration, from one to six. All the consoles are of common type and are interchangeable; their operational role (such as surveillance and tracking, weapon control, ASW control, tactical evaluation, etc) can also be changed during the operation of the system, so that the CIC can comply with the changeable requirements of the tactical situation. A central unit interfaces the sensors (radars, sonars, interceptors, etc), the weapon systems (fire control systems, surface-to-surface missile systems, anti-submarine torpedoes), medium or low speed data links, and the display consoles.

From a technical point of view, the IPN-10 is a fully digital system using all solid-state components (except the CRTs). The consoles (SVC-16) use a 16-inch (406 mm) CRT and can be used as independent radar repeaters. A 22-inch (559 mm) version (MHC-22) is also available for the conference or evaluation role. The processing capability is distributed throughout the system and resides in a number of NDC 160/E mini-computers, housed in each display console and in most of the system attachment units (which include all interface circuits, D/A and A/D converters, video extractors, power supplies, etc).

Multiple operator horizontal console for IPN-10 system

(1) single console system for fast patrol boats
(2) with two consoles for corvette-size vessels
(3) with five consoles for use aboard frigates
(4) a six-console system with enlarged data processing capabilities based on two CP-7010 computers (Selenia type CDG 3032). With the denomination SADOC-2, this configuration has been adopted for Italian Navy 'Lupo' and 'Maestrale' classes of frigates.

Most system configurations are provided with multiple serial data bus connection which allows complete interoperation with co-operating processors enabling a 10 Mbit/s data rate on each bus with data flow control distributed and transparent to the application software.

From the early 1980s IPN series systems usually incorporated a number of standard NDC-160/E mini-computers employed as embedded processors in the display consoles as well as being distributed in many

Single operator vertical console of IPN-10 command and control system

basic units of the system. The NDC-160/E is a general-purpose, micro-programmed 16-bit machine which normally has 64 K words core store and/or solid-state memory.

STATUS
IPN-10 systems are in production and are installed on CNR 2400 t and 3200 t fast frigates and on CNR 600 t corvettes. In 1982 a new order from the Spanish Navy was reported.

IPN-20 systems are in production and are being installed on the Italian Navy 'Lupo' class frigates.

CONTRACTOR
Selenia-Industrie Elettroniche Associate SpA, Via Tiburtina Km 12400, 00131 Rome, Italy.

NETHERLANDS

4271.281
GEMINI NAVAL FIRE CONTROL SYSTEM

The Gemini weapon control system has been designed for use aboard smaller naval vessels to provide one-man fire control facilities for guns and/or missile armament for low-level self-defence purposes. It is engineered on a modular basis so that extended versions can be configured to meet differing operational requirements and to enable its use on various classes of ship from corvette to frigate size.

The system consists of a two-axis stabilised I-band search antenna mounted coaxially with a K-band tracking antenna. The most important benefits of the two antennas in one assembly are: all round unobscured coverage for both search and track; both antennas can be located in the most favourable position, ie on the masthead (important for small craft); extremely accurate target designation as errors due to search-track antenna misalignment caused by ship deformation are eliminated.

The use of I-band for search ensures reliable target detection. The K-band tracker permits accurate, pinpoint tracking down to sea-skimmer levels and avoids the problems of surface reflections and multiple imaging. The narrow K-band pencil beam is also very difficult to jam.

Gemini is designed for one-man operation from below deck but two-man operation is possible during operationally tight situations. A labelled position

display presents the search radar video and pertinent synthetic data for surveillance and target indication. A monitor and control display shows the tracking information (A-scope) and alpha-numerics and also displays the lightpen operated controls. Lightpen operation with associated microprocessing minimises the number of hardware controls. Functional changes can easily be carried out since, in most cases, only software is affected.

While the basic configuration will serve the needs of numerous vessels, a number of options are available to expand the system and adapt it to special requirements. These include:
(1) radar: more powerful transmitters, travelling wave tube, larger search antenna, combined I- and K-band tracking; transmitters/receivers (and display) for navigation, circular polarisation, lin/log/MTI/DF
(2) vertical reference platform
(3) optronics: TV camera/IR camera (combined with autotrack), laser rangefinder
(4) target tracking facilities: track-while-scan; video extractor
(5) IFF
(6) shock absorbing mounting for director
(7) radar data handling.

STATUS
In production.

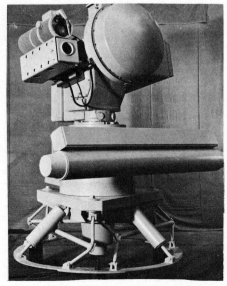
Gemini naval FCS sensor assembly on shock mounts, integrated radar and E-O sensors

CONTRACTOR
Hollandse Signaalapparaten BV, PO Box 42, Hengelo, Netherlands.

3767.281

LIROD 8 NAVAL DIRECTOR

LIROD 8 is a lightweight combined eight-millimetre wavelength pulse doppler radar/electro-optical director designed primarily for use as an autonomous target tracking and observation system aboard naval vessels of all sizes. It is particularly suited to all-weather applications where high accuracy combined with low-level capability and high resistance to jamming are required. Its light weight makes the system appropriate for gun direction on small ships, while it may also be used as an additional tracking and monitoring channel within a WM20 Series weapon control system (**1259.281**).

The LIROD 8 system comprises the following main elements:

(1) a director sensor head very similar to that employed in the LIOD lightweight optical director (**3143.293**), but which carries a complete K-band monopulse doppler tracking radar and a television camera instead of the original sensors employed in LIOD. Alternative EW trackers can be fitted (eg laser-tracker)

(2) a control unit containing electronics for performing the target acquisition and data processing functions

(3) a control console which permits one-man operation below decks and incorporates a display with light-pen controls and computer facilities for tracking and gun control

(4) one or more target designation sights for indication of visually-detected targets, whether intended for subsequent radar or electro-optical tracking, or not. These are also used for track monitoring and correction

(5) an interface cabinet to match the ship's weapon fit.

Operational functions that the system can perform autonomously include: optical and radar surveillance for air and surface targets; target designation for anti-air and anti-surface engagements; air or surface fire control; automatic radar/E-O tracking or rate-aided tracking of one air or surface target; air or surface target gun prediction calculation; simultaneous control of two dual-purpose guns of the same or different calibre; engagement monitoring, kill assessment and gunfire correction; and system status monitoring.

STATUS

Both standard and extended versions were in production in 1983.

Signaal's LIROD lightweight TV and radar tracker. A further development carries a package containing a K-band radar, a TV camera, an IR camera and a laser rangefinder

CONTRACTOR

Hollandse Signaalapparaten BV, PO Box 42, Hengelo, Netherlands.

1259.281

M20 SERIES FIRE CONTROL SYSTEMS

The M20 Series comprises a range of integrated ships' fire control systems for use with guns, missiles and torpedoes, and designed for fitting in vessels ranging in size from fast patrol boats to destroyers. Principal applications are medium/close-range air defence and close-range surface defence. Simultaneous engagement of several targets is possible. A further use is for shore bombardment.

Computation and control is based upon a central digital computer, and the range of available sensors includes separate search and tracking radars, and

optical trackers. The use of TV trackers is a further option.

The search and target tracking radar sub-system comprises separate search and track antennas, mounted on a common stabilised platform, the whole being enclosed in a weather-proof radome. Both antennas are fed from a common I-band transmitter. During search 100 per cent of the output power of the transmitter is supplied to the search antenna. After target detection and designation to the track radar, the output power is divided, by means of the waveguide switching, so that a certain percentage is supplied to the track antenna for target tracking. A

dual arrangement is available with separate search and tracking radars.

In one version of the system (the M26), only the search antenna is fitted. In this case it is mounted on top of the stabilised platform, and enclosed in a hemispherical radome. In all other versions the track antenna is fitted above and the search antenna below. The M20 series of systems, with the advance of electronic technology, have evolved to embody the latest available hardware, especially in the area of data processing, and the current range is the WM series of systems listed in the following paragraphs. The computers employed can be summarised: M20 computers are hard-wired program types; WM20 computers are re-programmable, while in order of miniaturisation these general-purpose machines are as follows: SMR, SMR-S, and SMR-MU, denoted by the suffixes /31, /41 and /61, respectively. Successive SMR generations of computer are upwards software-compatible.

Individual 'M' and 'WM' series versions of this system have been described in greater detail in previous editions (**1259.281** 1983-84 and earlier).

STATUS

The total number of delivered or contracted M20 Series systems of all versions exceeds 300. Many versions of the system are fitted in numerous classes of vessel.

CONTRACTOR

Hollandse Signaalapparaten BV, PO Box 42, Hengelo, Netherlands.

West German Type 143 class of fast patrol boats are fitted with WM20 Series FCS

1663.261

CIDIS – COMBAT INFORMATION DISPLAY SYSTEM

CIDIS is a modular display system designed for use in ships' combat information centres, where data from a number of external sources such as search radars, IFF and data link have to be processed by digital computer and organised and presented for use by the command team. The normal computer is a Signaal SMR family machine, but other types may be employed. The combination of CIDIS and digital computer constitutes DAISY, a digital action information system (**4496.261**).

The equipment comprising a CIDIS installation consists of a display central unit and a number of display consoles appropriate to the operational functions of the system. The former unit can contain a sensor data distribution unit which acts as the interface between the various sensors and the displays, a video extractor which converts the sensor

signals into digital form used in the computer for target detection and tracking, and a computer data distribution unit which interfaces the displays to the computer.

There are two types of display console, vertical and horizontal or 'conference' type. The former is produced in two versions, one for the presentation of radar video and one for sonar video; in each case the console has two indicators, a 40 cm labelled position display (LPD) and a 7-inch (178 mm) TV-type alpha-numeric display (tote). The horizontal console, with a 40 cm LPD for radar presentation, has two operator positions and a third supervisory position. One or two 7- or 15-inch (178 or 381 mm) TV-type totes can be associated with each horizontal display for the presentation of either supplementary alpha-numeric information or TV video.

Instead of the 40 cm LPD unit, a 40/50 cm PVD unit can be provided for bright synthetic presentation.

Functions of the CIDIS include:

Display of raw video from ship's sensors on the LPD.

Display of synthetic data from the computer in two forms: (1) as synthetic data consisting of symbols superimposed on raw radar video on the LPD, with or without track labels, at the operator's discretion or (2) as alpha-numeric information on the tote display.

Communication with the computer by means of manual input keyboards. Quick-entry keyboards, handwheels and a rolling ball, and as special options a light-pen and touch-input device, can be connected.

STATUS

CIDIS and DAISY systems have been delivered for the navies of: Argentina, Belgium, India, Malaysia, Netherlands, Nigeria and Thailand.

CONTRACTOR

Hollandse Signaalapparaten BV, PO Box 42, Hengelo, Netherlands.

4496.261

DAISY AND FORESEE (C⁴) SYSTEMS

DAISY is a modular digital action information system designed to be used in combat information centres on board ships, where data received from several sources, such as search radars, secondary radars, sonar, data links etc must be processed and presented to the command and control team. DAISY forms the heart of a sensor, weapon control and command (SEWACO) system (**1664.281**).

A DAISY system consists of a data handling cabinet and a number of display consoles appropriate to the operational functions of the system. The data handling cabinet contains the data handling computer, a sensor data distribution unit and one or more video extractors. The data handling computer normally used is a Signaal SMR family machine, but other types may be employed. The sensor data distribution unit performs the interface between the various sensors and the displays, while a video extractor converts the video from either a primary or secondary radar into a digital form used in the computer for target detection and tracking. The combination of DAISY hardware and system software constitutes the Foresee C⁴ action information system for comand, control, communication and co-ordination.

For the display sub-system of either the DAISY or

Foresee system two multi-purpose types of display console are available: a vertical display console (VDC) and a horizontal display console (HDC). The VDC is a single operator display console, while the HDC is a conference-type display console provided with two operator positions and a supervisory position. Both VDC and HDC are provided with a 40 cm labelled position display (LPD) as the main display unit. For the presentatlion of either alpha-numeric data in a tabular format or TV video the VDC is equipped with one 7-inch (178 mm) alpha-numeric display and the HDC with one or two 7- or 15-inch (178 or 381 mm) alpha-numeric displays. Instead of the 40 cm LPD unit each type of display console can be provided with a 40/50 cm display unit of the plan view display (PVD) family. This display family is formed by three different PVD units: the PVD, the plan view display mixed (PVDM) and the colour plan view display (CPVD).

The PVD unit is a random-scan graphic display used for a bright presentation of a large amount of computer generated synthetic data. The PVDM is used for a time-shared presentation of time-compressed raw video and computer generated synthetic data. The CPVD is a penetron type display used for a four-colour presentation of computer generated synthetic data. VDCs and HDCs provided with a display unit of the PVD family are also provided

with a display processor which performs display-related processing functions.

The DAISY/Foresee tasks include:
(1) presentation of raw sensor information from primary and secondary radars
(2) compilation and presentation of tactical air, surface and sub-surface pictures
(3) data link operation
(4) designation of targets to weapon systems
(5) assistance in operations, including ASW helicopter direction and tactical navigation.

Communication with the data handling computer is performed by means of manual input keyboards, programmable quick-entry keyboards, a rolling ball and handwheels. Other special input and designation devices such as a light-pen and touch input device can be integrated optionally.

STATUS

DAISY and Foresee systems have been delivered for the navies of: Argentina, Belgium, Canada, Greece, India, Indonesia, Malaysia, Netherlands, Nigeria and Thailand.

DAISY is a designation of the Royal Netherlands Navy.

CONTRACTOR

Hollandse Signaalapparaten BV, PO Box 42, Hengelo, Netherlands.

1664.281

SEWACO – SENSOR, WEAPON AND COMMAND SYSTEM

Under the SEWACO designation Hollandse Signaalapparaten produces integrated sensor, weapon and command systems of varying configurations intended for corvettes, frigates and higher-level combat ships. The same designation is now used also for integrated submarine systems. Full advantage is taken of the integration of the various sub-systems. System functions can be carried out using centralised or decentralised data processing, depending on the operational status of the combat system components.

A SEWACO system in general comprises primary radar sensors for long, medium and short range air and surface warning such as the types ZW08, SMART-S, Goalkeeper search etc, and the search part of the combined search and tracking radar of the WM20 Series weapon control system, secondary radar sensors such as IFF and helicopter transponders, sonar, ESM, and IR sensors. Furthermore, the system includes an action information system of the DAISY or Foresee type, a weapon control system of the WM20 Series optionally extended with one or more separate tracking and illumination radars (STIR), radar/optronic (LIROD) systems, electro-optical (LIOD) system and optical target designation sights. Communication equipment

including automatic data links, one or more primary and secondary video extractors and/or plot history generators for automatic initiation and tracking of air and surface targets, an ECM system and a newly developed sophisticated very short range air defence system against sea-skimmers completes the system. As the system components are of modular concept, the SEWACO system's configuration can be matched to specific requirements.

In some configurations not all the above system components will be of Signaal manufacture. In these cases, however, Signaal takes the responsibility for system integration.

The first integrated SEWACO system was developed for the Royal Netherlands Navy frigates of the 'Tromp' class. This system has been followed by new generations of SEWACO systems in which new technologies have ben incorporated, eg for the sensors, computers and displays.

In defining the DAISY or Foresee action information system (**4496.261**), the nerve centre of the ship's combat system, a configuration is created guaranteeing at any time a rapid and efficient counter-attack with the ship's complete potential against air, surface and sub-surface threats, even with reduced manpower 'on watch'. This is achieved by rapid and where possible automatic collection of all the necessary data from sensors and automatic data links, the processing and display of these data,

computer-assisted threat evaluation and recommended weapon assignment and target designations to appropriate weapon systems. The displays of DAISY are generally mixed displays, ie they present radar and/or synthetic information. Depending on the requirements, various types of display are available. Normally the displays will be of the labelled position display (LPD) type. In cases where no radar data loss is permissible, displays are available based on time compression video. Other types are displays based on the digital scan conversion principle and synthetic-only random access bright (graphic) displays. If required the mixed displays can be provided with multi-persistence penetron-type CRTs, while synthetic-only displays can be equipped for multi-colour presentation.

The displays which are used for picture compilation and command and control functions are available as one-operator vertical display consoles and as horizontal tactical display consoles for two operators and a supervisor. Each display is provided with one or two alpha-numeric display units (totes).

Although each display is intended for a specific function, the displays have multi-function capabilities. By means of operator controls including touch-input devices, light-pen and rolling ball, the operator communicates with the display processor or directly with the central DAISY computer. The processors and computers used in DAISY, as well as in all other Signaal-made computerised system components, are of the SMR family, the fourth generation of which is now in production.

Note: SEWACO sequence numbers are used only for the Royal Netherlands Navy. All other SEWACO systems are assigned a specific customer-related number. Software for most SEWACO systems and sub-systems is also produced by Signaal.

SEWACO I

The principal sensors of the SEWACO I system in the new Royal Netherlands Navy guided missile frigates are the Signaal 3D multi-target tracking search and target designation radar (**1589.253**) and the combined search and tracking radars of the WM25 fire control system (**1359.281**) which is integrated into SEWACO I and the Signaal ESM system. The 3D radar incorporates a slotted wave-guide antenna for IFF/SIF facilities also. Navigation and helicopter control functions will be provided by a dual Decca Transar radar system, with port and starboard scanners to ensure gapless 360° coverage. There is also a secondary radar system as a further aid to helicopter operations. Long-range sonar is fitted. In addition the two SPG-51 fire control radar groups for the ship's Tartar surface-to-air missiles will also be linked with the system. Among the weapons associated with SEWACO I will be Tartar, Standard SM2 MR, the Harpoon SSM, the NATO Sea Sparrow point defence system, and a twin 4·7 inch (109 mm) gun turret.

Vertical display consoles for Signaal SEWACO system

SEWACO II

This system is for ten Royal Netherlands Navy standard frigates and for two Hellenic Navy S frigates. Sensors include the Signaal LW.08, and ZW.06 radars, the combined search and tracking radar of the WM25 weapon control system and ESM system, two optical target designation sights and an automatic data link. Non-Signaal sensors include IFF, a helicopter transponder system and the AN/SQS-505 sonar set. The SEWACO system consists of Signaal's DAISY action information system, WM25 weapon control system, including a separate tracking and illumination radar (STIR) on which a TV-camera is mounted, while the weapons fit comprises the OTO Melara 76/62 dual-purpose gun, Harpoon SSM, Nato Sea Sparrow, ASW torpedoes and a Lynx ASW helicopter. A very short range air defence system specifically for defence against sea-skimmers is to be installed on these ships in the future. For typical action information purposes, DAISY includes five vertical one-operator consoles, two conference-type command displays for two independent operators and a supervisor, and one sonar display console. For weapon control purposes a WM25 weapon control console and a STIR control console are supplied. An ESM console completes the summary but the last four ships are fitted with a Signaal ECM system.

SEWACO III

Discontinued programme.

SEWACO IV

This is the designation of the SEWACO system supplied for the new 'Westhinder' class of escorts for the Belgian Navy. No official details have been revealed but the following data derived from published sources correspond with what is known of these new vessels and their weapons and equipment fits. Functions of the SEWACO system include:

Air, surface, and sub-surface warning;
Compilation and display of tactical air, surface and sub-surface situations;
Threat evaluation and automatic air target selection for engagement by the appropriate weapon system;
Weapon assignment and fire control by the WM 25 FCS against air, surface, sub-surface, and shore targets;

Anti-submarine warfare;
Electronic warfare;
Data link operation;
Assistance in tactical operations, including ASW-helicopter direction and navigation;
Target simulation for training purposes.

Sensors comprise a DA.05 air and surface warning and target indication radar, WM25 combined search and tracking radars, a commercial Raytheon surface search/navigation/helicopter control radar, IFF/SIF, helicopter transponder, a French-made ESM system, data link, optical director, and sonar. Weapons controlled by the SEWACO system include NATO Sea Sparrow surface-to-air missiles, Exocet surface-to-surface missiles, dual-purpose gun, anti-submarine rocket launcher, ASW torpedoes, and ECM systems. The weapon control and combat information equipment consists of the WM25 FCS for missiles, gun, and A/S rockets, three horizontal displays for combat information functions and each with its own separate alpha-numeric 'tote' display, a sonar display console, radar plotting table with true-motion computer, and one video extractor for automatic air and surface tracking.

SEWACO V

This designation is given to the SEWACO system for the mid-life conversion of the six 'Van Speyk' class frigates. Sensors include an LW.02 air warning radar, a DA.05 air and surface warning and target indication radar, a Decca navigation radar with two displays, IFF and helicopter transponder system, two optical target designation sights, two sonar sets, an ESM system and an automatic data link. The action information system is of the DAISY type and includes four horizontal tactical display consoles with alpha-numeric displays and a plotting table. The weapons fit comprises an OTO Melara 76/62 dual-purpose gun, controlled by an M45 weapon control system, Seacat launchers controlled by an M44 system, a Harpoon SSM system, ASW torpedoes and ECM equipment. The ship will be equipped with an ASW helicopter.

SEWACO VI

Now under construction are two Royal Netherlands Navy L frigates (air defence frigates). The SEWACO system for these vessels comprises: Signaal LW.08 extended range and elevation cover version, a

stabilised DA.05, ZW06 and Goalkeeper search radar sensors; a Sphinx ESM system; Ramses ECM system; and weapon control system consisting of three STIRs (one 1·8 m and two 2·4 m scanners) with high power coherent transmitter chains. CW illumination for Standard SM1 MR is provided by each STIR. The Goalkeeper close-in weapon system will be installed. The DAISY system includes six vertical consoles, two horizontal consoles and a sonar display console, primary and secondary video extractors. In addition to the normal DAISY functions it has extensive air defence software facilities. IFF, VESTA and data link are also integrated in the SEWACO system.

The weapons are the SM1 MR to be launched by Mk 13/4 launcher, Sea Sparrow from eight-cell launcher, Harpoon surface-to-surface missiles, RBOC countermeasures, Mk 46 torpedoes and the EX 83 30 mm gun portion of the Goalkeeper CWIS.

SEWACO VII

This version has been nominated for the Royal Netherlands Navy's M frigate SEWACO system which as well as including all normal sensors and weapon systems will incorporate an integrated communications system.

STATUS

Ships fitted or to be fitted with SEWACO systems include: two guided missile frigates, ten Standard frigates and six 'Van Speyk' class frigates of the Royal Netherlands Navy; four Belgian escorts; two Royal Netherlands Navy Air Defence frigates; four Indonesian corvettes; South Korean and Nigerian frigates; the Greek 'S' frigates; Spanish escorts; Argentinian frigates and corvettes; Malaysian corvettes; Thai corvettes and Turkish frigates. Currently more than 70 systems have been delivered or are under contract.

CONTRACTOR

Hollandse Signaalapparaten BV, PO Box 42, Hengelo, Netherlands.

3516.261

GOALKEEPER SGE-30 NAVAL FCS

The Goalkeeper SGE-30 system is based on an integration of the American General Electric Company GAU-8/A 30 mm multi-barrel Gatling gun (4042.203) and new Signaal fire control equipment to form an autonomous, rapid-reaction close-in weapon system (CIWS) for ship defence (3616.231). The design is especially directed toward the anti-ship missile threat as well as low-flying aircraft targets.

Rapid target detection is achieved by the I-band search radar with its horizontally stabilised antenna rotating at high speed. Threat evaluation is accomplished through an integrated video processor and threat evaluation program. Target designation and acquisition are rapidly effected because of the close integration of all the system elements on a single mount. A combined I-band and K-band tracking radar enables the system to track accurately

all types of target, including sea-skimmers, under all sea states. Anti-clutter and ECCM features are included to maintain this capability in adverse conditions.

Prediction calculations are performed by a digital computer, and firing accuracy is achieved through the use of a low-dispersion gun coupled with appropriate ammunition and a rigid, stable mount. Residual bias errors in the system can be eliminated by a closed-loop spotting procedure in the tracking-to-firing cycle.

The chosen kill mechanism is warhead detonation (assured kill); although a few 'control kills' may be expected these are considered unpredictable, and therefore to be regarded as a bonus if they occur. Intercept range is approximately 500 m.

The main operational tasks of the Goalkeeper system are to counter the following threats:

(1) priority 1 threats such as anti-ship missiles like Exocet (1156.221) characterised by a more or less constant low-level trajectory and speeds of about Mach 1

(2) priority 2 threats from sea-skimming anti-ship missiles which include in the final attack phase a pull up manoeuvre followed by a dive onto the target at supersonic speeds of up to Mach 2.

Additionally, Goalkeeper can engage manned aircraft, or small patrol craft.

STATUS

By early 1984 ten Goalkeeper systems had been ordered for the Royal Netherlands Navy, and shortly afterwards the UK placed an order for eight systems for the RN.

CONTRACTOR

Hollandse Signaalapparaten BV, PO Box 42, Hengelo, Netherlands.

1261.281

M40 SERIES FIRE CONTROL SYSTEMS

The M40 Series of fire control systems comprises a range of combined radar and optical directors for the control of short-range missiles and gunfire against air and surface targets. Target designation is performed by one of the ship's search radars. The M44 is used with the Seacat missile and the M45 is for the control of medium and light calibre guns.

The M44 is a fire control system for ships of frigate or destroyer size. The radar/visual director allows radar-automatic target tracking and visual detection and tracking in bearing and elevation. The stabilisation equipment is embodied in the director, so that no axis conversion is needed and the system is lightweight. The computer is of the digital type and fully transistorised; it is provided with a display panel.

It supplies accurate fire control data to the short-range Seacat.

The computer is programmed for: tracking of an air target, tracking of a surface target, firing bracket computation, launcher control.

After the Seacat has been launched, it is gathered by the director operator by means of a flight controller. This is fitted on the aiming bar, which is used for visual target acquisition and tracking. The guidance process is also visual, but provision is made for blind guidance by means of a second range gate and an F-scope on the computer display panel.

For target indication the system can be connected to a TI unit, thus providing target bearing and range to the M44 director and the radar. The lock-on and tracking procedure is fully automatic.

The radar is a conventional I/J-band fire control

radar and includes various ECCM devices and special provisions so that it can operate under adverse weather conditions. For training purposes the computer can be provided with a special program to control an electronic marker in the field of view of the binoculars, thus simulating a Seacat flight.

STATUS

M40 Series FCS have been fitted or specified for: Netherlands 'Van Speyk' class frigates; Indian 'Leander' class frigates; the Malaysian frigate *Hang Jebat*; the Thai frigate *Makut Rajakumara*; Australian 'River' class anti-submarine frigates. Licence production in India for 'Leander' class frigates.

CONTRACTOR

Hollandse Signaalapparaten BV, PO Box 42, Hengelo, Netherlands.

3766.481
GIPSY SUBMARINE DATA HANDLING AND WEAPON CONTROL SYSTEM
Gipsy is an automated data handling and weapon control system designed for the Walrus II class submarines of the Royal Netherlands Navy. The system forms the link between the submarine's sensors and its weapons. The system consists of seven identical display and computer consoles (DaCCs). The built-in computer is of the SMR-MU type; the 16-inch (406 mm) plan view display (PVD) provies a high-load-synthetic picture together with compressed radar video or sonar video and the control panel is a multi-purpose unit. The use of identical DaCCs offers maximum flexibility.

A central control unit (CCU) is used to regulate the mutual data transfer between the DaCCs and the sensors and weapons. For this function two SMR-MU computers are provided, one active and the other a hot standby machine. The large amount of data from the sonars is handled by two extra SMR-MUs, also housed in the CCU. Three types of sonar are fitted (long-range, medium-range and passive), and other sensors and data sources include a noise analyser,

ESM facilities, radar, periscopes, and position finding equipment.

The weapon control system can control a mixed load of weapons for sub-surface and surface engagements, and the ship's launching system consists of two mutually independent sections, each of which is controlled from a launching system control panel (LSCP). The interface with the weapons (modern sub-surface missile) is formed by two identical distribution cabinets. All hardware necessary for the integration of these weapons is included in the distribution cabinet, avoiding the necessity for additional equipment.

The main functions of Gipsy are:
(1) sonar display and control. This makes it possible to omit the original sonar displays and controls
(2) contact evaluation. This entails displaying information obtained from all sensors in a time/bearing format
(3) classification. Where ESM, ASM and noise information is compared with cassette tape stored libraries to provide a rapid classification of the target

(4) contact motion analysis. Modern tracking filters are used for the automatic determination of target movements
(5) tactical plot and general plot functions giving an up-to-date survey of the tactical and/or navigational situation or an historical situation survey
(6) weapon control. Whereby the weapon systems are provided with the requisite aiming data
(7) simulation and test to verify the system's operability and to aid in operator training for the functions (1) to (6).
Additional functions can be inserted easily due to the fact that the system is highly software-oriented.
STATUS
Two systems have been delivered for fitting in the first two boats of the 'Walrus II' class for the Royal Netherlands Navy, together with a reduced system for shore-based training.
CONTRACTOR
Hollandse Signaalapparaten BV, PO Box 42, Hengelo, Netherlands.

1662.481
SINBADS – SUBMARINE INTEGRATED BATTLE AND DATA SYSTEM
SINBADS is a compact data handling and weapon control system suitable for use in submarines of the small coastal type and up to the larger, ocean-going type. It succeeds the Signaal M8 Series of torpedo FCS (**1375.481**) for submarines. The computer used is the Signaal fourth-generation general purpose machine SMR-MU, and the complete system combines the weapon control and data handling functions.

The data handling function covers sensor display and sensor selection for track initiation. The raw sensor data of all sensors can be displayed. Each individual sensor is indicated with a unique label. The development of SINBADS is based on the application of modern passive sonars, capable of automatic tracking of targets. The tracking algorithm is based

on modern filtering techniques and the tracking system basically includes as its main mode of operation a 'bearing-only' analysis which, however, also accepts other inputs of target information. The complete tracking system functions as an interactive system in which the command can intervene in the tracking process. For this purpose there are four display formats available.

SINBADS can handle five targets and three torpedoes simultaneously. These can be guided, unguided or a mixture thereof. The system also includes data recording from on- and off-line use, weapon simulation for training, on-line failure monitoring, and an emergency mode for which hand controls are provided to enable torpedoes to be set, fired and controlled in case of a computer or display failure.
SINBADS DUO
Under this title a successor to SINBADS has been

designed which broadly fulfils the same functions but the design is based on the same philosophy as the Gipsy system (**3766.481**) offering very high availability and more flexibility in control.
STATUS
SINBADS deliveries began in late 1977 and in early 1980 at least 18 systems were in hand. Known contracts include: Argentina, six; Greece, four; Indonesia, seven; Peru, four; Turkey, four.

Following the basic Gipsy philosophy, SINBADS-M systems are in production as fully integrated sensor/weapon/command systems, incorporating sonar (SIASS, **5636.453**), Rapids ESM (**4056.293**), ZW07 radar (**4051.253**) and communications.
CONTRACTOR
Hollandse Signaalapparaten BV, PO Box 42, Hengelo, Netherlands.

1375.481
M8 SUBMARINE TORPEDO FIRE CONTROL SYSTEM
The M8 is a digital computer-based fire control system for use in submarines for the direction of torpedoes against either surface shipping or submerged targets. It was produced in several versions with designations ranging from the M8/0 of the mid-1950s prototype to the latest. M8 is now out of production and succeeded by SINBADS (**1662.481**), Gipsy (**3766.481**) and Submarine SEWACO (**4587.481**). The basic system comprises a torpedo display control and computer console, a sound path display unit, amplifier and supply unit, distribution box, local control panel(s), and gyro angle setting units. Complete system weight is about 900 kg. The system may be operated by one man, or two men if the submarine is operating with consorts.

The system will accept target data inputs from a range of sensors which includes radar, sonar, passive sound detection systems, periscope observation and consort reports. Ship's own navigational data is also fed into the M8 computer. The display, which has range scale settings for 20, 10, and 5 km, presents the positions of all contacts from all sensors,

simultaneously. One or more sensors may be connected to the computer for torpedo engagement, and up to three targets may be attacked simultaneously. The computer is programmed to provide firing data for wire-guided, programmed, conventional, and other types of torpedo, and performs automatic calculation of target position, course, and speed. The CRT display can give true motion, relative motion, or off-centred presentation of the tactical situation.
DEVELOPMENT
The M8 Series originated in a Royal Netherlands Navy contract awarded in 1955 for the development of a torpedo FCS for the 'Dolfijn' class submarines. West German interest in the system gave additional impetus to subsequent development and led to the successful development of systems for use in both submarines and surface ships. Two types of torpedo were involved, the AEG Seal and Seeschlange, for use against surface vessels and submarines respectively. This successful collaboration with the West German industry continued and M8 Series systems are standard fitting on all submarines produced by Howaldswerke Deutsche Werft in Kiel. The ultimate development is the SINBADS system described in

1662.481, but other related developments are the M9 systems in the West German 'Köln' and 'Thetis' class vessels, and the M11 systems for two new Argentinian fast patrol boats.
STATUS
The following list is believed to record accurately the known installations.

Argentina	Type 209 (2)
Colombia	Type 209 (2)
Equador	Type 209 (2)
Germany (Federal)	Type 205 (5)
	Type 206 (18)
Greece	Type 209 (4)
Netherlands	'Dolfijn' class (2)
	'Potvis' class (2)
	'Zwaardvis' class (2)
Norway	Modified Type 205 (15)
Peru	Type 209 (2)
Turkey	Type 209 (2)
Venezuela	Type 209 (2)

CONTRACTOR
Hollandse Signaalapparaten BV, PO Box 42, Hengelo, Netherlands.

4587.481
SUBMARINE SEWACO SYSTEM
Submarine SEWACO (Sensor Weapon Command and Control) is a fully integrated combat system designed to carry out all tactical functions from contact search to target engagement. It is suited for small displacement and larger patrol submarines.

In its full configuration Submarine SEWACO includes a multiple array broad and narrow-band sonar suite (SIASS), a command system including interchangeable multi-purpose display and control consoles and a weapon control system compatible with modern wire-guided torpedoes and air-flight

weapons. ESM (RAPIDS-S) and radar (ZW07) also form part of the complete system configuration. SEWACO subsystems are fully integrated and incorporate a software-based, multiprocessor modular design. Internal and external communications systems are also available in SEWACO.

Data collected by SEWACO's sonar suite and other external sensors (eg ISM and radar) is processed to localise and identify contacts. The search results from the multiple sensor fit are correlated and displayed on the interchangeable consoles to generate a concise tactical picture. From this information decisions are made about target

designation and prioritisation, threat assessment, weapon assignment and tactical manoeuvring of own ship. Weapon employment from warm-up, presets through launch and post-launch guidance are accomplished by the weapon control function. SEWACO also incorporates functions for navigation, data logging and crew and operator training and is capable of integration with electro-optical sensors (periscopes) and electronic navaids.

The full sonar suite consists of passive bow-mounted, flank and wavefront curvature ranging sonars which can detect, track and analyse multiple narrow and broadband contacts. An acoustic intercept sonar provides torpedo and acoustic threat warning. Contacts in automatic track are automatically subjected to passive bearings-only contact motion analysis (CMA). A new generation CMA algorithm is employed which has demonstrated speed and accuracy in at-sea trials. An electronic classification library is included with a capacity of up to 300 specific platforms.

SEWACO's weapon control function is compatible with various submarine launching systems and submarine-launched weapons. To ensure maximum reliability for weapon launch and control three firing modes are provided. The system is capable of simultaneous launch and control of four modern acoustic wire-guided torpedoes and four submarine-launched missiles.

SEWACO employs a distributed data processing system incorporating multiple general purpose SMR-MU computers and microprocessors. The system includes multi-function operator consoles with interchangeable functions, two functionally redundant passive sonar systems, a duplicate set of common and two fully independent and separate weapon electronic units. Any point of failure that would render the system incapable of launching and controlling weapons is avoided. Moreover, the federated software in which each processor is self-supporting and capable of operating autonomously in combination with any multipurpose operator console is fault-tolerant and provides for graceful degradation of system functions in the event of a malfunction.

STATUS

Submarine SEWACO is in production for installation on board new generation diesel-electric patrol submarines.

CONTRACTOR

Hollandse Signaalapparaten BV, PO Box 42, Hengelo, Netherlands.

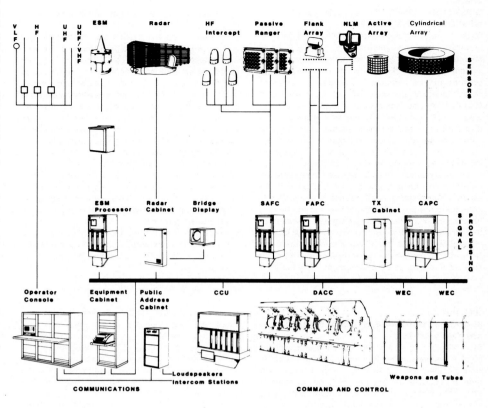

Submarine SEWACO main elements and sensor systems

NORWAY

3744.281

NAVKIS

NAVKIS is the navigation, command, control and information system designed and developed for 2800-ton coast guard vessels in service with the Royal Norwegian Navy. When the development and production contract was awarded in 1978, three main priorities for the NAVKIS system were established: navigation, command and control, and air surveillance and gun control. To satisfy these priorities, while meeting a requirement for the use of equipment of differing levels of sophistication, it was decided to base the design on a number of autonomous sub-systems. Data transfer between the sub-systems and most of the sensors is provided by an autonomous multiplex data transmission system known as BUDOS.

Sensors providing navigation or target information to the system include a Plessey AWS-4 air and surface surveillance radar (**3171.253**), two Decca I-band navigation radars (**3127.281**), a PEAB 9LV 200 Mk 2 autonomous fire control system (which incorporates tracking radar and low light-level television), two optical target designation sights, and navigational inputs such as Decca Navigator, Loran C, navigation satellite receiver, echo-sounder, compasses, gyros, ship's log etc.

A navigation computer, KS-500 with a 64K store, continuously monitors the radio navigation receivers and ship's reference sensors to calculate 'own' position and velocity through Kalman filters. All relevant material is recorded on a cassette. In addition, the computer calculates factors such as sea currents, log errors, gyro drifts etc. Display/operator consoles for the navigation facilities are provided in the operations room and on the bridge.

The command, control and information system (CCIS) is the main operational unit within the overall NAVKIS system, and its main functions are those of surveillance and tracking of all targets. It is also employed for control of the ship's helicopter. This part of the system has much in common with the Kongsberg MSI-80S naval AIO system (**2975.281**) and the main operating console is situated in the operations room, together with the AS/GC (air

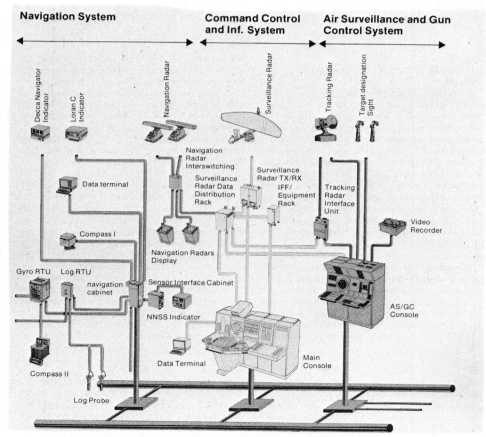

Diagram of Kongsberg NAVKIS system for Norwegian Coast Guard ships

surveillance and gun control) console.

Functions of the CCIS in addition to target tracking and surveillance include: presentation of radar data from any of the ship's radars on the main tactical situation display; identification and continuous automatic tracking of 16 targets; identification and automatic plotting of up to 64 other targets; display of targets from the air surveillance console; video map display of geographical features and/or reference grids etc.

The radar sub-system provides distribution of radar data and integrates information from the two Decca navigation radars and the Plessey AWS-4 (which has digital MTI), as well as providing an interface with the 9LV 200 Mk 2 tracker radar.

STATUS
In production and operational.

CONTRACTOR
Kongsberg Vapenfabrikk, Defence Products Division, PO Box 25, 3601 Kongsberg, Norway.

1975.281
MSI-80S FIRE CONTROL SYSTEM

The MSI-80S is a weapon control system for small ships and was initially specified and developed for the Royal Norwegian Navy's new 'Hawk' class fast patrol boats. The system is equally suitable for tactical data handling and fire control functions in larger ships such as corvettes or frigates. The system provides a multi-target capability using low-cost conventional navigational radars, stabilised electro-optical sensors for night/passive operations, and target filtering/tracking techniques. Homing surface-to-surface missiles, wire-guided torpedoes, and an AA gun can be controlled individually or simultaneously.

Typically, the armament consists of six Penguin SSMs, four torpedoes, and a 40 mm gun. Inputs to the MSI-80S include the twin Decca TM1226 radars, an electro-optical tracker system which incorporates a TV tracker and laser rangefinder, infra-red scanner, optical sights, and electronic warfare sensors. The low-light television camera channels and displays supplied by Marconi-Elliott Avionic Systems Ltd comprise a Marconi low-light camera, incorporating an automatic light control system enabling both daylight and low-light operation. Line-of-sight stability is assured by mounting the camera on a stabilised sensor platform. This platform, manufactured by A/S Kongsberg Vapenfabrikk, also carries the other sensors, both active and passive, which are collimated with the television camera. To preserve the advantages of concealment and surprise attack, the basic philosophy is to employ the various passive sensors. The efficacy of this method rests largely upon the tracking and other software of the fire control computer. In the MSI-80S reliance is placed upon programs which have already been proved in the MSI-70U submarine system, described above. The tracking and guidance problems are solved either automatically or semi-manually by man/machine integration and in the latter case the computer serves as a data bank. Data from all available sensors can be used at any time and in any order.

A three-man operating console is provided, this being crewed by:
(1) tactical operator, who initiates and controls target data calculations and the overall tactical situation plot
(2) weapon control operator, who selects, controls, and designates the guidance mode(s) of the relevant weapons
(3) passive sensor operator, who operates the passive sensors and feeds relevant data to the target tracking system.

A fourth position is provided at the console for the commanding officer.

A horizontal 23-inch (584 mm) CRT is used for the presentation of raw radar and computer-generated data, and a 12-inch (305 mm) CRT is provided for the display of alpha-numeric data. The latter can also serve as a back-up for the main tactical display (23-inch).

STATUS
Development and technical evaluation were completed by early 1978 and series production for the 'Hawk' class ships is now completed. Variants of the system are also in production for foreign navies.

CONTRACTOR
A/S Kongsberg Vapenfabrikk, Postbox 25, 3601 Kongsberg, Norway.

4573.481
MSI-90U SUBMARINE AND WEAPON CONTROL SYSTEM

In 1982 A/S Kongsberg Vapenfabrikk conducted a Basic Command and Weapons Control Study in response to the concept and definition phase of a programme connected with the new West German (211-class) and Norwegian (P-6071 or ULA-Class) submarine projects. The system, MSI-90U, is a modern software-based system which uses distributed processing, high-capacity serial data transmission, and multi-function common consoles. It forms a common core of identical hardware and software for both projects (Norway and Germany), covering the following areas:
(1) data transmission system
(2) central computing complex
(3) display and operating controls related to situation processing and weapons control
(4) the torpedo/ship interface.

Consequently the two national integrated combat systems will consist of the MSI-90U basic command and weapons control system, the actual sensor systems selected by the respective navies and the weapons fitted.

The MSI-90U is modular with a minimum number of different building blocks (consistent with the operational requirement) and the system consists of the following main hardware components:
(1) a micro-processor based computer system, KS-900F, developed by Kongsberg for these projects
(2) standardised multi-purpose operator consoles, KMC 9000 developed by Kongsberg
(3) the BUDOS data bus, a standard Kongsberg product designed primarily for interfacing digital shipboard systems and meeting NATO Stanag 4156
(4) a torpedo board interface developed by AEG-Telefunken under contract to Kongsberg.

Main tasks accommodated by the software tools provided with the multi-processor computer complex

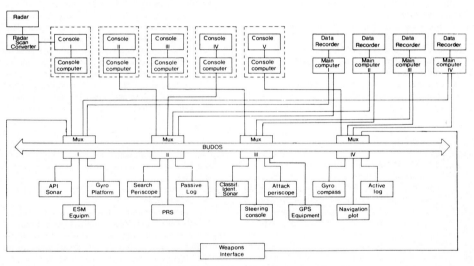

Block diagram of a typical MSI-90U configuration

are: sensor integration functions such as target motion analysis (TMA), classification and identification, threat evaluation and weapon assignment/operation. There are also a number of supplementary facilities such as tactical evaluation and navigation, threat evaluation, engageability analysis, pre-programming of movements, sound trajectory calculations and display, input and presentation of geographical fixed points and areas, data recording, simulation and training.

Operator/system communication is by means of the multi-purpose consoles which are flexibly configured for the main operational tasks required. Each console is equipped with a console computer for operator input handling, picture/data presentation, local computations and data exchange communications. Picture and data are presented on two equivalent colour raster scan displays on each console. Data is exchanged within the system and between the system and other ship's systems by the BUDOS data bus system which is a set of bus-connected multiplexers. This is the core of the MSI-90U system.

STATUS
Development of the main system components and special software modules began around 1980, and a full-scale development contract was awarded and signed in 1982. Prototype multi-purpose operator consoles were demonstrated in mid-1983. A complete prototype will be ready for testing in a factory-based test stand in early 1986. The MSI-90U is expected to succeed the MSI-70U (**1929.481**) in the Royal Norwegian Navy.

CONTRACTOR
A/S Kongsberg Vapenfabrikk, Postbox 25, 3601 Kongsberg, Norway.

SWEDEN

3512.281
DATASAAB COMMAND AND CONTROL INFORMATION SYSTEM (CCIS)

The Datasaab CCIS is a multi-display, computer-controlled system for the collection, storage, evaluation and transmission of naval tactical data, commands and messages. Although specially adapted to the handling of action data on modern frigates and corvettes, the basic principle of the system also applies to smaller or larger vessels.

Typical configuration of the modular equipment includes four horizontal and two vertical displays. Horizontal displays include a local air plot to present the tactical air space situation within the ship's operating area, a surface plot depicting all surface movements within a given area, a sub-surface plot for ASW purposes, and a weapon co-ordination and control station. Operational and tactical area situation is displayed vertically on two large screens.

A horizontal control position consists of a console for three operators with a 16-inch (406 mm) PPI and, for each operator, identical input devices (rolling ball and alpha-numeric keyboard). The PPI presents true-motion raw radar picture, track information, target designation and tell-back symbols, vector lines and intercept solutions. Using the input devices on the console, the operators have control of radar selection, tracking, data link communication, weapon co-ordination display selection and recording.

Significant operational features of the system include the following:
- (1) presentation of data from ship's sensors – radar, ESM, sonar etc
- (2) automatic and rate-aided tracking
- (3) presentation of geographical reference information
- (4) weapon co-ordination and control
- (5) data link communication
- (6) on-line recording of tactical information

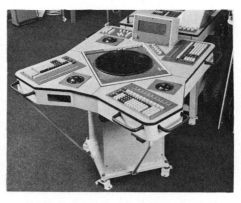

Datasaab CCIS horizontal display with PPI designed for three operators with alpha-numeric keyboard and rolling ball for target designation

- (7) tactical navigation
- (8) intercept calculation
- (9) ship data library
- (10) simulation and training.

COMMAND DISPLAY

Vertical situation displays with 24-inch (610 mm) screens enable the command team to perform evaluation and control functions. Additional information is provided on alpha-numeric displays underneath the large screens. Any information which is relevant to the tactical situation can be extracted by and displayed for, the command team. The screens display: charts, reference grids, operator-generated charts, track information with history marks, target designation and tell-back symbols, alignment and pointer symbols and vector lines. Data tables, system reference information and operator tell-back and warning are presented on the alpha-numeric display.

Tracking, by PPI operators, is initiated by the selection of a target from the raw radar picture using keyboard and rolling ball. A number of symbols and track numbers are available for track labelling. Track location, heading and speed updating is by any one of three methods: automatic tracking using extracted radar data; rate-aided tracking controlled by rolling ball; external updating based on received track data via data link.

The entire equipment complex is assembled from components of the Datasaab Censor 900 display and data processing hardware range, which was developed and produced specifically for defence and ATC systems and for naval applications. For the naval part of the system's range of possible applications, a number of modifications taking into account the specific requirements of a naval environment were necessary.

The central computer complex consists of two Datasaab Censor 900 processor systems operating in parallel. Each contains a full operational program and is capable of taking over all system functions if the other unit fails. In case of failure, immediate switchover is assured with no loss of information. Information input to, and output from, the ship's sensors is interfaced with a set of fast microprocessor units. A number of peripherals such as console teletypewriters and cassette tape recorders are available for specific customer needs.

STATUS

A version of this system is being delivered to the Danish Navy for installation in frigates and corvettes. The first system entered service in 1977.

CONTRACTOR

Datasaab AB, 17586 Järfälla, Sweden.

3186.261
EPLO TACTICAL DATA SYSTEM

EPLO (Electronic Plotting System) is designed to overcome the inherent shortcomings of manual techniques for handling tactical information on board small ships such as fast patrol boats and corvettes. It is an automated system in which the level of sophistication has been governed by cost-effectiveness and space restrictions. The system compiles a tactical picture of an area of operations, and allows data exchange with other ships and with naval radar control centres equipped with a compatible system.

Operational features include the following:
- (1) target selection and semi-automatic tracking by means of track symbols on a true motion stabilised raw radar picture
- (2) exchange of tactical data via a data link with other ships and shore radar stations
- (3) target assignment to on-board fire control system by special assignment symbols
- (4) synthetic presentation of the plotted tactical situation, including reference information such as maps, geographical grids, and fixed points

- (5) calculation and numerical presentation of range and bearing to target as well as speed and course of target
- (6) continuous recording on magnetic tape of the tactical situation.

Targets are selected from the raw radar information displayed on a 16-inch (406 mm) PPI by positioning a free target symbol over the echo. There is a repertoire of 13 different symbols and 24 selectable numbers are available for the labelling of tracks. The symbol co-ordinates are stored on the radar PPI and is presented on the radar PPI and the 24-inch (610 mm) plot indicator. Updating of target position is achieved in cyclic fashion, with either a slow cycle time of two minutes for updating 24 tracks or a faster 30-second cycle time for updating six tracks. Selection of a particular mode is made from the keyboard and depends upon the number of tracks involved.

To correct deviations when tracking in the semi-automatic mode, the target may be moved to the new echo position by means of a rolling ball tracker control. The PPI displays only the new position together with the track history consisting of up to 15 symbols in reduced size. All selected targets in either

cycle-time mode are described by their course and speed as well as range and bearing.

The EPLO operating console is arranged as follows. A vertical display is used for the presentation of synthetic data which include video maps, target tracks, alignment symbols, pointer symbols, and vectors. A horizontal display presents the true motion stabilised raw radar picture on which are superimposed target symbols, markers, vectors, and pointers etc. Tabular displays are provided for readouts of target data and other information and keyboards allow for data insertion, control of symbols, and exchange of information.

STATUS

The system has been supplied to the Royal Swedish Navy and to the Danish Navy. No other fitting details have been released.

CONTRACTOR

Datasaab AB, 17586 Järfälla, Sweden.

1541.281
TORCI TORPEDO FIRE CONTROL SYSTEM

The TORCI torpedo fire control system is produced in several versions by Philips Elektronikindustrier AB (PEAB) for the operation of guided torpedoes against surface targets from fast patrol boats. It is normally supplied with a PEAB I-band frequency-agile surface search radar, but can be used with other radars. The principal tactical functions of the systems are:
- (1) presentation of search radar information
- (2) presentation of the combat situation for the direction of surface engagements
- (3) rapid designation of surface targets
- (4) automatic or manual target tracking
- (5) guidance of two simultaneous torpedo salvoes

The equipment comprises three units: the main display console, target tracker console, and an electronics/power supply unit. The last of these can be located remote from the two manned consoles.

The main display console is provided with a PPI for the presentation of search radar data, synthetic symbols for tactical data, and relative or true motion presentation can be selected by the operator. The console also carries controls for operation of the system and for target designation and houses the torpedo computer and the program selector.

Either manual or automatic target tracking is possible, and the torpedoes can be fired in salvo with chosen dispersion as well as one by one.

STATUS

Swedish vessels equipped with TORCI systems include the 'Spica I' class of fast torpedo boats, in which TORCI is used with an HSA M22 radar/fire control system (**1259.281**), and the new 'Spica II' class. In the latter class, TORCI is used in conjunction with another PEAB fire control system, RAKEL (the Swedish Navy's version of 9 LV 200), which provides gun fire control against surface and air targets. A number of foreign navies also use TORCI. Similar equipment, the TCI family, is in use on board submarines in the Swedish and other navies.

CONTRACTOR

Philips Elektronikindustrier AB, 17588 Järfälla, Sweden.

3248.281
9 LV 100 FIRE CONTROL SYSTEM

The 9 LV 100 is a lightweight, inexpensive ship-board system derived from the 9 AA 100 (**2648.181**) land-based system. It is intended to control one, or possibly two, 30 to 76 mm guns against air and surface targets, and surface-to-surface missiles. Because of its light weight, it can be used on very small boats, from 50 tons up, but it is also well suited for larger ships, eg 300 to 400 tons, with a limited armament. It is also seen as a secondary, independent director-computer sub-system to supplement more comprehensive weapon control systems on board heavily armed ships, when employed with a 9 LV 200 Mk 2, for example. This combination is designated 9 LV 300 (**4026.281**).

The main units of a 9 LV 100 are:
(1) a lightweight radar, operating in the E/F band

(2) an optronic director with TV and laser, with provision for the addition of an IR-tracker
(3) a 41 cm PPI display
(4) a control and display console, with TV-monitor and gun and director controls
(5) computer and associated units.
  The 9 LV 100 systems allow for:
(1) search for surface and air targets
(2) tracking of one air or surface target with the director in fair weather and daylight; and with IR at night
(3) tracking of one surface target with radar track-while-scan (TWS) under all weather conditions
(4) gun, or missile, fire control using director or TWS data.

CONTRACTOR
Philips Elektronikindustrier AB, 17588 Järfälla, Sweden.

9 LV 100 optronic director equipped with IR camera, TV camera, and laser

---

1542.281
9 LV 200 FIRE CONTROL SYSTEM

The 9 LV 200 has been developed as a fire control system for use on small ships from 80 tonnes and upward, for the direction of dual-purpose guns (40 to 120 mm) and other weapons such as anti-ship missiles (Exocet, Penguin, Otomat, etc) or wire-guided torpedoes. In its basic form the system has the capability for directing one or several guns against one or more targets simultaneously.

Target data are obtained from an I-band search radar and a J-band tracking radar, and there is provision for D-band air warning radar with IFF to be incorporated also. The I-band equipment in the 9 LV 200 is used for both search and tracking of surface targets and for air search. If the D-band pulse-doppler radar is included, a combined antenna system for I-band, D-band, and IFF Mk 10 is used. The J-band tracking radar can also be modified with a pulse-doppler function to improve performance in adverse clutter conditions against small low-flying targets.

The search radar is of the frequency-agile type, incorporates comprehensive ECCM facilities, and is provided with a stabilised mounting. A helical scan pattern is used. The director radar is a monopulse equipment, with frequency agility, and the pedestal also carries a TV camera.

Danish Navy 'Wilemoes' class fast patrol boat fitted with 9 LV 200 weapon control system which incorporates television tracker based on JAI 771 low light-level TV camera by JAI

A full description of operational functions appeared in the 1976 edition of *Jane's Weapon Systems*.

STATUS
The 9 LV 200 has been operational with the Swedish Navy since 1973 and has been delivered to foreign navies as well. The original 9 LV 200 is now being followed by the 9 LV 200 Mk 2, see below (**3127.281**).

CONTRACTOR
Philips Elektronikindustrier AB, 17588 Järfälla, Sweden.

3127.281
9 LV 200 Mk 2 WEAPON CONTROL SYSTEM

The 9LV 200 Mk 2 combat information and weapon control system is suitable for use in all types of naval and offshore patrol vessels of 100 tons and upwards. It is optimised for data gathering, compilation and tactical evaluation for the control of one dual-purpose gun (57, 76 mm or larger), one anti-air threat gun (single or twin-mounted 20-40 mm), and surface-to-surface missiles. There are also options for torpedo control. Simultaneous engagement of separate targets is possible, one of which can be an air target. Modular design enables the system to operate independently or as part of a Philips C³I system aboard larger ships.

A typical 9LV 200 Mk 2 installation consists of:

(1) an X-band search and surveillance radar with frequency agility or MTI, with or without on-mounted IFF
(2) a combined Ku-band electro-optical director for gun fire control (with or without TV tracker)
(3) tactical and missile control console for overall viewing, threat evaluation and analysis, data link control and target designation to guns, missiles, or torpedoes
(4) a gun control console, mainly for air surveillance and target designation to the director and fall of shot observation; this console can also be used for fire control against surface targets
(5) a surface gun console primarily for gun fire control against surface targets tracked by the surveillance radar; this may also be used as an air surveillance back-up console

(6) two 'bridge pointer' target designators for use by look outs for direct optical target designation, typically against surface-to-surface missiles
(7) wind sensor.

OPERATION
Surface targets: a three position console with 16-inch tactical display provides for presentation of search and surveillance data from the I/J-band frequency agile search radar to the Plotter, Combat Information Officer and Missile Officer. Automatic TWS plotting of up to 16 multiple targets is possible, with presentation as numbered symbols and with full interchange of designated target data with weapon systems. Target data can also be exchanged with other ships via a VHF/UHF voice channel and short burst transmission.

Air targets: search radar video is presented on a 12-inch PPI on the AA gun control console. Pulse doppler processing for MTI is available. Target designation to the director for automatic acquisition of air or surface targets is provided and TWS facilities for air targets can be provided. The Ku-band monopulse tracking radar is mounted on the director and has automatic acquisition with CFAR control. Facilities include switchable frequency agility. Electro-optical sensors can include TV, infra-red camera and laser with automatic tracking capability. CW illumination for operation of semi-active radar guided missiles is also available.

Computation: this is by means of a digital processor, rather than the analogue techniques used in the earlier version, and simultaneous engagements of air or surface targets are possible. An additional console is provided if the torpedo fire control is exercised.

STATUS
In production.

CONTRACTOR
Philips Elektronikindustrier AB, 17588 Järfälla, Sweden.

KD Handalan of the Royal Malaysian Navy, armed with Bofors 57 mm and 40 mm guns and Exocet MM 38, all controlled by a version of 9 LV 200 Mk 2

3747.281
EOS-400 FIRE DIRECTOR SYSTEM

The Saab EOS-400 is a TV tracker and laser rangefinder fire director system. Accurate target position is obtained using the well-known Saab television tracker for automatic tracking in conjunction with a laser rangefinder, both these units being mounted on a common training and elevating stabilised platform. This unit is the only above-deck item of equipment, apart from the weapon being controlled (usually a gun or guns). Below deck, the control/display unit is usually located in the operations room. The only other major item, the electronics cabinet, can be sited in any convenient position in the ship.

The control/display unit contains a TV monitor and a joystick for sensor platform operation, a mode selector, and target data displays. The electronics cabinet houses the video tracking electronics and other control electronics. The video output is connected to the platform and the video output to the control/display unit.

The system is capable of tracking one target among several in close formation, tracking when radar tracking is not possible, and either surface or air targets may be tracked. Inputs from other systems include those from a ship's surveillance radar, and reference data from ship's compass. The system calculates ballistics for several guns and gives gun-laying data.

CHARACTERISTICS
Tracking parameters
Training: Unlimited
Elevation: –30° to +85°
Platform
Angular speed: ±175°/s in azimuth and elevation
Angular transducers: Multi-speed synchros
Stabilisation: Rate gyros in 2 axes

Tracking: Digital correlation
Contrast selection: Automatic black/white
Lock-on area: Whole field
Daylight camera
Scanning standard: 625 lines
Camera tube: Si-vidicon
Night camera: IR camera optional
Laser rangefinder
Wavelength: 1·06 μm
Repetition rate: 10 Hz
Beamwidth: 1·5 mrad
STATUS
Introduced in September 1979. A new version entered the market in 1983, and this has been ordered for fitting in Finnish Navy corvettes.
CONTRACTOR
Saab Missiles AB, 58188 Linköping, Sweden.

4025.281
9 LV 400 SERIES C³I SYSTEM

The 9 LV 400 Command, Control, Communication and Intelligence (C³I) system is designed for tactical command from flotilla leaders of frigate size and upwards. It has greater surveillance capabilities than the 9LV 300 providing a separate air search radar and integrated ESM/ECM which permits automatic tracking and threat evaluation of a large number of air and surface targets.

The command and control functions are also an improvement on the 9LV 300. The 23-inch tactical electronic plot is included as standard. Separate consoles are used for air and surface surveillance.

The command capability is further augmented by a high capacity data link using the time division multiple access principle. This data link allows for exchange of target data and commands between ships and also between ships and command centres ashore. All transmissions are encrypted to a very high degree of security.

In its standard configuration the 9LV 400 WCS provides simultaneous control of four separate guns of different calibres, SSM and various kinds of ECM. Optional control of a SAM system is also available.
STATUS
In service.
CONTRACTOR
Philips Elektronikindustrier AB, 17588 Järfälla, Sweden.

Swedish mine warfare vessel Carlskrona *is fitted with a 9 LV 400 series command, control, communications and intelligence (C³I) system*

4026.281
9 LV 300 NAVAL C³ SYSTEM

The 9 LV 300 is an extended C³ and WCS suited for larger FPBs or squadron leaders up to corvette size.

The system contains extensive command, control and communication functions including tactical navigation, scenario predictions and weapon simulations. The command sub-system consists of a horizontal PPI for display of radar video and synthetics and an optional vertical 23-inch multi-colour electronic plot for situation display.

The 9LV 300 contains two autonomous AA channels, normally a 9LV 200 radar and a 9LV 100 optronic sub-system. All the capabilities of these two systems are inherent in the 9LV 300 enabling simultaneous engagement of two air targets, surface target engagement using TWS and firing of SSMs.
STATUS
In service.
CONTRACTOR
Philips Elektronikindustrier AB, 17588 Järfälla, Sweden.

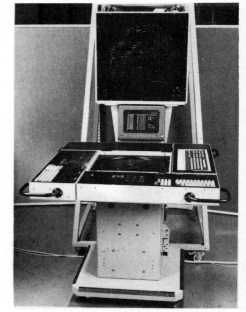

9LV 300 C³I system module

4568.281
9LV+50 ASW SYSTEM

For surface anti-submarine vessels the 9LV+50 ASW sub-system may be added to the 9LV fire control systems raising the designation to 9LV 350 and 9LV 450 respectively. The ASW sub-system contains its own computer hardware and software. The ASW plot contains one PPI, an alpha-numeric display, officers' and operators' panels. The same computer and display techniques are employed as in the 9LV systems (**4025/6.281**).

The main tactical functions of the system are:
(1) search and target tracking in association with the ship's sonar system
(2) presentation of sound path propagation on a sound path indicator presentation, integrated with the ASW plot (ie on the same CRT display as the PPI)
(3) continuous presentation of the combat situation

(4) evaluation of target data and prediction of future target position
(5) calculation of control signals for A/S rocket launcher
(6) calculation of own ship's course and time to fire charges for depth charge attack. The last facility is optional. The basic system is designed for control of the Bofors 375 mm twin A/S rocket system with all available types of A/S rockets including Erika and Nelli. Any type of A/S homing torpedo can be accommodated if this option is specified. Sonar is the principal sensor and various models of different manufacture may be employed. Other inputs to the system are the ship's gyro reference system, and the ship's log
(7) Calculation of control data for A/S homing torpedoes.
STATUS
Production believed to be in progress.

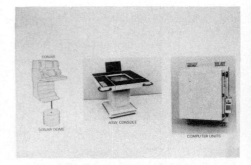

Main elements of typical 9LV+50 ASW FCS

CONTRACTOR
Philips Elektronikindustrier AB, 17588 Järfälla, Sweden.

4027.281

9CSI 500 STINA

The 9CSI 500 STINA (coastal/offshore surveillance and information system) is primarily designed to support a number of peacetime duties, including, but not limited to: maritime traffic control; monitoring of ships with dangerous cargoes; supervision of warships; surveillance of territorial limits for illegal immigration, smuggling etc; surveillance of economic zones, eg for the prevention of illegal fishing; and command of sea rescue operations.

A complete system, eg for nation-wide coverage, normally comprises more than one centre. The concept is modular. A complete system furthermore comprises sensors of various kinds, mainly coastal radars, and communication equipment for data and voice.

Although primarily a peacetime system, the 9CSI 500 can also be used as a naval headquarters in wartime. For mainly wartime use, however, the more comprehensive 9CSI 600 is available (see **4028.281**, below).

A 9CSI 500 centre normally comprises:

(1) computers for data processing, file handling, and generation of graphic pictures

(2) up to three operators' consoles, each consisting of a 41 cm vectorial graphic display, PPI, monochrome or multi-colour, with a control panel, an alpha-numeric display terminal with a keyboard, and a communications panel

(3) one or more colour graphic displays of the raster-scan type, mainly for remote presentation

(4) a printer for logging of events and actions

(5) data transmission equipment.

Radars of different types and radio communication equipment constitute complete systems to fulfil the operational requirement.

A 9CSI 500 centre receives inputs from a variety of sources including: coastal and shipboard radars, observers and look-outs, pilots, harbour authorities, and radio traffic monitoring by 9CSI 500 operators.

Various degrees of input automation are possible. Radar inputs can be fully automatic, from extractor equipped radars, semi-automatic or manual. Radar inputs are displayed continuously on a PPI. Data and standardised telex messages are entered directly. Other inputs are entered by the operators using the keyboard of the alpha-numeric terminal.

The input data is processed to form target tracks. When more data about a target becomes available, eg identity, type of cargo etc, the operator enters it using the text terminal while associating the data to the target number. In this way, the operators compile a comprehensive picture of the situation in the supervised area.

The situation is displayed against a background of coastlines and other references on the PPIs and the graphic displays. The latter show different categories of targets in different colours. If the situation is very complex, selected categories of targets can be shown one at a time, eg all unidentified vessels. Track data are stored in the computer memory for at least 24 hours, and can be recorded at selected intervals on paper by means of a printer. If a situation requires a close study, the operator can order play-back of a target 'history'. Such a play-back is 30 or 300 times faster than real time.

Commands are given either as data messages or by voice. A number of data links of variable complexity are available. These range from a standard telex to high speed automatic links. Data exchange will normally follow standardised formats, but the data link also accepts free text. Messages exchanged by voice can be recorded on a tape cassette recorder, which is an integral part of each communications panel.

Operational functions provide the following:

(1) automatic input from up to six radars

(2) automatic tracking of up to 200 targets, using radar data

(3) automatic plotting of the targets on graphic display

(4) inputs via data links, radio/telephone or telex networks

(5) display of maps and other reference data, at different scales. Continuous positioning of the centre of the displayed area. Total geographical area covered is 2048 km²

(6) logging of selected events and actions.

STATUS

In service with the Swedish Navy.

CONTRACTOR

Philips Elektronikindustrier AB, 17588 Järfälla, Sweden.

4028.281

9CSI 600 STINA

The 9CSI 600 STINA (naval command, control, communication and intelligence system) is designed to automate many of the functions involved in information gathering, filtering and compilation of data, presentation, and transmission of orders and commands with high speed and accuracy. These systems are designed as general purpose equipment but in particular as supplements to the extensive 9 LV family (above) of shipboard combat information and weapon control systems. Like 9 LV systems, 9CSI systems are highly modular using standardised building blocks.

A 9CSI 600 STINA system comprises not only one or more command centres, but also sensors, mainly radars, for gathering input data, and data link communication equipment for exchange of data ship-to-shore and vice versa and for exchange of orders and commands. The 9CSI 600 is primarily designed as a military system for use during a general alert and in wartime. However, many of the functions implemented are equally useful in peacetime for maritime traffic control, coast guard prevention of smuggling and illegal immigration, co-ordination of sea rescue operations etc. For mainly peacetime use, the 9CSI 500 STINA is available (**4027.281**).

Designed as a modern military system, the 9CSI 600 incorporates fast, secure communication with anti-jamming capability and ECCM features in the radars; all in order to enhance survivability of the functions. Speed of communication is achieved in the 9CSI 600 by using a mesh of point-to-point links and the time division multiple access (TDMA) principle over radio links to exchange data and command messages. Security is obtained by encryption of all messages. Anti-jamming and low probability of intercept are inherent in the TDMA principle and can be further enhanced by using spread-spectrum or frequency-hopping techniques.

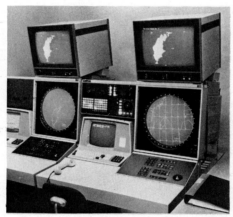

A typical 9CSI 600 STINA operator's console

Other features of 9CSI 600 communications are a high degree of automation and routeing of messages adapted to a changing network with priorities and error correction. The speed of transmission is adapted to the medium used for different routes.

Provisions have been made in the 9CSI 600 centres for storage of intelligence in a data base, which can also contain information about own forces, their status etc. In order to assure proper secrecy for such information, a part of the data base is intended to be 'user programmed'.

A major sensor in 9CSI 600 systems is the 9KR 400 coastal surveillance radar (**1549.153**). This is available for fixed or mobile installations and normally provided with an automatic plot and/or target extractor to permit unattended operation and data transfer over narrow band channels to the centres. The plot and target extractors can work not only with the 9KR 400 but also with other radars to allow upgrading and automatic inputs. The centres will also accept semi-automatic and manual inputs.

9CSI 600 design is highly modular, which permits the building of command centres of various sizes for different tasks, eg central and regional headquarters. The number of operators' consoles and commanders' consoles is variable, as are computer capacity and the exact display configuration. A standard building block is the operator's console shown in the photograph. It consists of a 41 or 51 cm monochrome or colour display (PPI), an alpha-numeric display terminal with a keyboard, and a communications panel. The latter permits fast access to radio channels and telephone lines. Also shown is a raster-scan colour display.

The computers for storage and processing of data receive inputs in different ways. Inputs from extractor equipped radars are entered automatically, as are data link reports. Other inputs can also be entered automatically if received in standardised formats. Non-standardised messages, eg verbal reports over radio or telephone, are entered by the operators using the keyboard of the alpha-numeric terminal. The operators compile a picture of a situation which is continuously updated. The commander and his assistants can now be assisted by the computer to assess the situation and plan the tactics by using prediction and simulation of alternatives. After decisions, commands are transmitted over the data link using a library of standard orders. A situation picture compiled in one centre can be transferred in full or in selected parts to other centres and to ships. In this way, commanders at all levels have continuous access to up-to-date, accurate information, including relevant parts of the intelligence data base.

STATUS

In production.

CONTRACTOR

Philips Elektronikindustrier AB, 17588 Järfälla, Sweden.

3511.481

DATASAAB SUBMARINE ACTION INFORMATION AND FIRE CONTROL SYSTEM

This system, or a specific version of it, is also known by the initials NEDPS, from Näcken Electronic Data Processing System, because of its use in the 'Näcken' class of submarines of the Swedish Navy.

The Datasaab AB action information and fire control system is a fully integrated system to acquire, process and display information for tactical evaluation and to form a basis for decisions regarding selected targets and torpedo guidance. The system includes complete hardware and software for controlling wire-guided homing torpedoes. Also included is computer control and monitoring of ship's function, such as propulsion, steering, depth keeping, trim, storage battery condition, etc.

The system has a dual computer configuration, the information being gathered through an extensive data collecting system from the different surveillance and weapon systems as well as from the navigation system. The information is presented to two operators on two separate displays, each of which is equipped with input facilities in the form of special keyboards and rolling balls. After target acquisition the tracking is carried out automatically and relevant fire control data are calculated continuously. Upon firing, the torpedoes are normally controlled fully automatically with graphic and alpha-numeric presentation of all relevant information. The operators at the tactical and fire control displays can at any time take over or adjust the procedure.

ACTION INFORMATION SYSTEM

One of the display consoles is intended for the tactical display operator. Target data and additional information are displayed for him on the tactical display console. Information is collected from the various sensors in the submarine such as sonars, periscopes, radar, ESM, gyro, log. Most data from the sensors are supplied automatically to the computer by suitable transmitters and interface units. Target data, ie bearing, range, course and speed, are calculated from the data supplied. It is possible to obtain the relevant target data from passive bearing information only.

The tactical display shows target data, own ship's course and speed, torpedo status, etc, thus providing the tactical display operator with a clear picture of the tactical situation. Target data are displayed alphanumerically on the screen, eg target designation, type, range bearing, course, speed, etc, as well as an input data table for computing new data. The latter is intended as a 'tell-back' indicator in connection with data input.

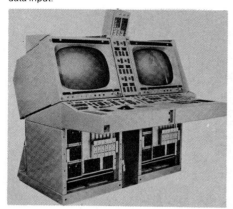

Block diagram of Datasaab submarine action information and fire control system

FIRE CONTROL SYSTEM
The fire control operator uses the second display console in the system. The display presents target data and torpedo data to form a basis for decisions regarding selected targets and torpedo guidance. The equipment enables the fire control operator to carry out an attack on several targets and with several salvoes simultaneously. Tube preparations which have to be made immediately prior to launching, ie pressure equalising and opening of bow caps and hull fairing doors, are actuated from the keyboard associated with the fire control display console.

The torpedo fire control system hardware consists of a display console with keyboard and rolling ball which is connected to the computer. The torpedo fire control display shows the torpedo firing situation as well as data regarding selected targets and torpedo attacks in plan and tabulated forms. The tabular part of the display covers target data for selected targets, supplied from the action information system, and torpedo data for a torpedo attack. Torpedo data consists of input data, instructions and computed data.

The computer system utilises standard modules from the Datasaab AB computer Censor 932. It comprises two central processors each equipped with primary memory and bus system. The total capacity of the primary memory is 64 K words, expansible to 128 K words. Each central processor is capable of taking the full system load, thus giving complete redundancy. Normally, however, when both are active, they are used for separate tasks.

The display system utilises standard modules from the Datasaab AB Display System 800. It comprises two complete display units with display generators. Each operator has a special keyboard and a rolling ball for communication with the computer system. Each display generator can drive both display units,

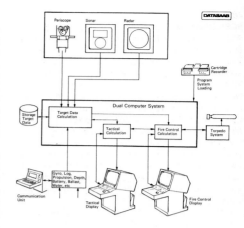

Datasaab submarine action information and fire control system operators' consoles

and the operator can choose which one to use by means of a switch on his display panel. The display generator equipment is housed in a cabinet under the respective display console.

The interface equipment is modular, the modules containing standardised channels for digital and analogue input and output signals.
STATUS
Datasaab has delivered four sets of the NEDPS version to the Swedish Navy, one for each boat of the 'Näcken' class of submarines and one for a training simulator at the Bergas Naval College.
CONTRACTOR
Datasaab AB, 17586 Järfälla, Sweden.

UNITED KINGDOM

4045.261
CACS 1
Ferranti Computer Systems Limited (FCSL), Bracknell Division, has received a multi-million pound contract from the Ministry of Defence for nine new operational systems for the Royal Navy. Known as CACS 1 (Computer Assisted Command System 1), the systems have been designed for fitting in new construction Type 22 frigates. CACS 1 will incorporate two FM1600E computers, 12 Argus M700 miniprocessors and several F100-L microprocessors.

CACS 1 is the first of a family of new command systems for the Royal Navy, incorporating modern computers and a new operator interface. It will provide a substantial increase in system capability which can be directly employed to enhance the command functions necessary in a modern warship. Both the hardware and software will be constructed in modular fashion so that further system development and expansion can be implemented after installation on board and experience at sea, enabling the system performance to keep pace with changing and increasing requirements.

The CACS system architecture is based on a powerful computing facility consisting of two FM1600E computers, the latest and most powerful in the very successful Ferranti FM1600 series. These are connected by a distributed highway to several display positions, each of which contains its own Argus M700/20 microprocessor system to optimise operator effectiveness.

The consoles are based on the new Plessey Series 9 display system which, with greatly increased quality and capacity, supersedes the Mk 8 display technology used in ADAWS. There is extensive use of video re-timing and scan compression techniques. The principal input device is the light pen, which replaces most of the rolling ball and keyboard functions.

CACS employs an all-vertical display concept which, besides offering the operator a more

CACS operator's console

comfortable and efficient working position, overcomes severe shipfitting constraints and the problems associated with conventional horizontal dual-operator displays.

The most significant advance from the user's viewpoint will be the implementation of the 'prompt' interface for operator communication with the system. For CACS 1 the interface has been further developed to include the use of light pens and two TV monitors, one for tote data and one for handling operator inputs. With this interface the tote displays information relevant to the current task in hand and indicates 'prompts' or choices, which when used in conjunction with the light pen and/or keyboard allows the operator to input data and control the system in a logical sequence. The need to remember complicated manual injection sequences has been eliminated with a consequential reduction of operator training requirements.
DEVELOPMENT
The origin of CACS 1 can be traced back to 1977 when Ferranti was responsible for a study on behalf of

the Director, Surface Weapons Projects (Naval) of proposed improvements to the AIO system of the Type 21 frigates at half-life refit. It had been appreciated by the Naval staff that the operational environment and the projected weapon and sensor fits of those ships had outgrown the capabilities of their present system as established in the late 1960s.

Towards the end of this study MoD(N) extended the scope of the work to encompass the Type 22 frigates, as it had become clear that these new construction ships would need an enhanced AIO capability also. A number of design concepts were presented to DSWP(N) who decided that, despite the extra development and production costs involved, the design that involved the greatest changes to system hardware architecture was the one that would best meet their requirements. The resulting development contract was placed on Ferranti in 1979 and detailed work on the design of CACS 1 was initiated, with Ferranti nominated as design authority for the first time for equipment of this type. The development work has been carried out in close co-operation with the MoD at ASWE.
STATUS
A Royal Navy contract has been placed for the CACS system for installation in the Type 22 frigates. The first CACS 1 system, for fitting in the frigate HMS *Boxer*, was delivered by Ferranti in mid-1983. Ferranti supply the FM1600E, Argus M700, and F100-L computers as well as acting as prime contractor and design authority. Plessey Displays is the main display contractor. Further feasibility studies have been carried out for the Royal Navy, in which the application of the CACS family to other ships has been assessed. A version designated CACS 4 has been nominated for the new Type 23 frigates.
CONTRACTORS
Ferranti Computer Systems Ltd, Western Road, Bracknell, Berkshire RG12 1RA, England.

Plessey Displays, Station Road, Addlestone, Weybridge, Surrey KT15 2PW, England.

1524.281

WSA-400 SERIES NAVAL WEAPON CONTROL SYSTEMS

Derivatives of the RN Type 21 frigate Weapon System Automation 4, (WSA-4) (**1496.281**) intended for other classes of vessel carry designations in the WSA-400 Series. There is considerable commonality of both hardware and software between WSA-4 and the WSA-400 Series versions, the principal differences being those necessary to accommodate varying combinations of sensor equipment and the weapon systems fitted for specific operational roles.

Three versions of the WSA-400 Series were fitted in the Vosper Thornycroft Mk 10 frigates for the Brazilian Navy. These ships form the 'Niteroi' class and comprise two types; one specialised anti-

submarine type, whose armament includes Ikara missiles, and a general-purpose type fitted with Exocet surface-to-surface missiles. In addition, both types carry Seacat surface-to-air missiles, 4·5-inch (114 mm) Mk 8 guns, anti-submarine weapons, and a torpedo armed helicopter.

Each type of vessel is equipped with three digital systems based on Ferranti FM 1600B computers, and comprising one tactical and display system, and two fire control systems.

The first of these is a development of the Computer Assisted Action Information System (CAAIS) (**1046.261**), also being fitted to a large number of RN ships, and in the case of the Brazilian vessels, designated CAAIS-400. This system provides target indication to the fire control systems and Exocet

missile system and assists in controlling the torpedo-carrying helicopter. Sonar data, which may be derived from the hull-mounted sonars or the variable depth sonar are transferred in parallel to CAAIS and the two fire control systems in each ship.

STATUS
In service. Successor systems belong to the WSA-420/CAAIS 450 series (**3505.281**), in which the former are principally for weapon control and management while the latter systems are for action information organisation generally.

CONTRACTOR
Ferranti Computer Systems Ltd, Western Road, Bracknell, Berkshire RG12 1RA, England.

3505.281

WSA-420 AND CAAIS 450 SERIES FIRE CONTROL AND ACTION INFORMATION SYSTEMS

These systems are based on and incorporate many of the proven features of WSA-4 (**1496.281**), WSA-400 Series (**1524.281**) and CAAIS (**1046.261**) now in service with the Royal Navy and other navies.

The first main differences between these new systems and their proven predecessors is the computer and associated hardware architecture, where the latest generation of computer and display technology is used. This enables a more compact system to be provided at a cost-effective price without the need for separate computer cabinets. The equipment is housed mainly in the operator's console. Secondly, operation has been optimised to meet the requirements of small ships where reduced manning levels are desirable. It utilises conversational techniques in conjunction with a keyboard and tabular display tote on a TV monitor. This provides a simple means of system control whereby the operator is guided through the process of injecting relevant information to the computer, thus reducing both operator errors and training time.

Bearing in mind the operational requirements, Ferranti has designed a range of new systems which embody a combination of the latest technology and proven techniques, to operate with modern sensors and weapons. These include:
(1) WSA-421 – fire control system with tracker radar (receiving target indication from an external source)
(2) WSA-422 – fire control system with tracker radar and limited AIO facilities
(3) WSA-423 – integrated fire control and AIO system
(4) CAAIS 450 Series – AIO systems.

All systems can include on-board training aids, such as radar echo generators, simulated weapon tellbacks etc.

WSA-421 Fire Control System with Tracker Radar

This is designed primarily for frigates and corvettes fitted with an independent, but linked, AIO/CIC system such as CAAIS 450. For such vessels the main armament would be a 76 mm-calibre gun or a heavier weapon such as a 4·5- or 5-inch (114 or 127 mm) gun. The secondary armament could be a similar or smaller calibre weapon, or a surface-to-air missile. Two tracking heads provide the WSA-421 with two independent channels of fire. The fire control prediction is performed by a Ferranti FM1600E computer. The system accepts target indication from the ship's AIO system.

Ferranti combat system WSA-422 system console

WSA-422 Fire Control System with Tracker Radar with Limited AIO

Designed primarily for vessels of patrol craft size to provide weapon control and surveillance tracking for deployment of 35 mm to 127 mm-calibre guns and/or surface-to-air missiles and optionally, surface-to-surface missiles, the system uses the FM1600E computer.

The main sensor is the ship's surveillance and/or navigation radar. A tracker radar and OFD which can mount a laser rangefinder in addition to the E-O or CCTV is also fitted, thus providing two independent channels of fire and enabling two gun mountings to be controlled. Although the tracker radar will normally be paired with the main gun, the flexibility of the system enables any sensor-target pairing to be achieved. The composite weapon system console is manned normally by a single operator with provision for up to three operators in active conditions, and houses all displays, indicators and controls for surveillance tracking, target designation, control of weapon sensors and of the armament. Manual rate-aided tracking, with computer-generated symbology, is available on up to 60 targets. The power of the FM1600E computer is such that additional facilities may be provided if required, such as a remote-controlled, stabilised video tracker, comprising CCTV and laser rangefinder, to assist tracking in poor ECM environments.

WSA-423 Integrated Fire Control and AIO System

This system is designed for vessels of patrol craft and corvette size to provide weapon control and AIO/CIC facilities for the deployment of guns (35 mm to

130 mm), surface-to-air and surface-to-surface missiles.

WSA-423 is an extension of the WSA-422 system with added AIO facilities to provide an integrated system. These facilities will enable a tactical picture to be compiled on a labelled radar display from one or two surveillance radars for the purpose of command appreciation, using a sub-set of CAAIS programs, including the solution of simple command and navigation problems. In this system, a separate command console is provided, which houses a 16-inch (406 mm) LRD and the necessary hardware to provide auto-tracking of targets on one surveillance radar and an inter-ship digital data link, if fitted. The power of the FM1600E computer is such that additional AIO functions and equipment can be incorporated, if required.

CAAIS 450 Series AIO Systems

This series is designed to provide AIO facilities for a range of vessels of FPB size or larger. Provision is made for passing target indication data to associated fire control systems, which could be a sub-set of WSA-422.

CAAIS 450 can accept tactical data from two surveillance radars, from sonar and ESM equipments. Auto-tracking of targets is provided on both radars. Although the FM1600E computer's capability includes driving up to eight 12- or 16-inch (305 or 406 mm) LRDs, the exact display fit will depend upon the particular application. A basic configuration would have three displays: two for picture compilation and one for command appreciation. Additional display requirements can be envisaged for such functions as ASW, helicopter control, ESM/ECM management or data link management. The software provided is generally derived from the CAAIS programs. However, due to the versatility of this configuration, which results from the use of a powerful computer, specific applications may require that some special software is needed so that the full capability of associated weapons and sensors can be realised.

STATUS
Production began in 1980. Implementation of the first fittings of systems of this series are now in progress. WSA-421 has been selected by the Royal Navy for firing systems. WSA-421 and CAAIS 450 are in production for a number of overseas navies (including Brazil).

CONTRACTOR
Ferranti Computer Systems Ltd, Western Road, Bracknell, Berkshire RG12 1RA, England.

3746.481

SUBMARINE TDHS (DCC)

The submarine Tactical Data Handling System (TDHS) is the action information organisation (AIO) and fire control system designed for the new class of SSK submarine, known as the Royal Navy Type 2400. It has been given the type designation DCC and is derived from DCA/DCB systems in use in British nuclear submarines.

The weapons fit for Type 2400 includes dual-purpose wire-guided torpedoes (anti-submarine/anti-ship), anti-ship air-flight missiles, and submarine mines. The fire control for weapons is integrated in the tactical system, which comprises the following: long-range passive sonar, a medium-range passive/active sonar with a cylindrical array located in

the bow, sonar intercept, analysis and classification facilities, passive ranging using three aligned arrays on each side of the vessel, underwater communications, bathythermograph, and a sound speed-measuring system.

Other sensors include search and attack periscopes, and both are provided with facilities for fitting a variety of electronic and electro-optical devices. A Type 1006 surface surveillance and navigation radar, and omni-directional and directional warning antennas for the boat's ESM system are carried on a separate mast or incorporated in the search periscope.

Digital data transmission and processing is employed and the sensors and DCC are closely integrated; target bearing and range and velocity data

are processed to provide accurate target motion analysis. The tactical system consists of a three-position console with electronics in the lower compartments and six 12-inch (305 mm) circular cursive displays, light-pen units, fire control order and status units in the upper positions. DCC receives tactical and environmental data from the submarine's sensors via a digital data bus. The data is collated, processed, evaluated and presented on the circular displays for final assessment and decision.

The system also provides all necessary weapon control functions. The system computer is the Ferranti FM 1600E: a second fully redundant computer is provided to allow for 'fall-back' modes and future software expansion. Light pens provide the main man/machine interface, and all selection and switching facilities are provided at the operator console positions.

STATUS

First production orders placed.

CONTRACTORS

Gresham Lion Ltd, Twickenham Road, Feltham, Middlesex TW13 6HA, England.

Ferranti Computer Systems Ltd, Western Road, Bracknell, Berkshire RG12 1RA, England. (Prime)

4272.481

KAFS SUBMARINE AIO AND FCS

KAFS is suitable for conventional submarines of all sizes. The system uses the advanced computer technology, latest processing techniques and software algorithms incorporated in similar systems in RN nuclear submarines and the new 2400 tonne class 'SSK'; these provide operational facilities such as picture compilation, target motion analysis and fire control so that the commanding officer may carry out the wide variety of tasks on which such a submarine can be employed. These include area surveillance, attacks on surface and underwater targets, operations in inshore waters (such as minelaying or periscope reconnaissance), intelligence gathering and participation in ASW exercises.

The system hardware and software has been specifically designed in a compact, modular manner

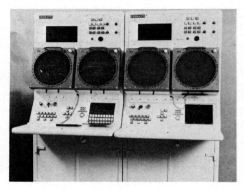

Double KAFS console

to provide a wide range of operator facilities which can be adapted or expanded as necessary to meet individual system requirements.

A high level of automation minimises the requirement for operator intervention so that one operator can control the total system and carry out an urgent attack. However provision is made for two operators who may be necessary in a multi-target situation. Automatic multi-contact association is carried out on all data received from on-board sensors together with simultaneous and automatic target motion analysis (TMA) on 35 or more tracks. The tactical picture is then presented to the command in labelled plan or time/bearing format, as required, on software displays. Two different types of weapon may be prepared for discharge and all weapon discharge functions can be by remote control if required. Two or more wire-guided weapons may be guided automatically at two or more separate targets, or a combination of guided and salvo weapons may be fired. Integration with the navigation system provides the accurate conduct and data recording of such activities as minelaying and periscope reconnaissance.

The main elements of the KAFS system configuration are shown in the photograph. The operator console is located in the control room and is linked by a MIL-STD-1553 data bus to the weapon control equipment in the torpedo room. The base of the operator console houses the FM1600E central processor, the input/output control unit, 256 K semiconductor store, display drive unit, magnetic cartridge unit and PCU, interface units and power supply units. The processor is the latest in the series of 24-bit F1600 computers designed by Ferranti and supplied for RN surface ship and submarine systems and a wide variety of overseas systems.

The top half of the console has two identical

operator positions each having two display areas, a light pen, control panel and a command data panel. Either operator position can control the whole system thereby allowing one position to be shut down in patrol states. The display areas provide the operator with a labelled plan or time/bearing display according to his selection, and a tote providing pages of data and instructions to enable the operator to interact with system control, picture compilation, navigation modes, target motion analysis and weapon fire control.

Training can be carried out on AIO, fire control and weapon control procedures while the system is in the operational mode. Facilities are provided for emergency control of weapon discharge and guidance independent of the central processor. Tube status, weapon status and system status are displayed on a local control panel which also provides weapon discharge and control facilities in fallback mode; maintenance and fault-finding facilities; and training facilities. Microprocessor-based port and starboard weapon interface and tube switching units are provided on a modular basis according to the number of tubes and weapon types. Facilities are provided for weapon pre-heating in stowage and battery/gas monitoring to detect hazardous conditions.

DEVELOPMENT

Studies of an AIO and FCS for RN nuclear submarines carried out by Ferranti in the 1960s led to the Tactical Data Handling System (**3746.418**) which was built under MoD contract for the 'Swiftsure' class of SSNs. A production order has been placed for the first two RN 2400 tonne SSK systems and an unspecified foreign navy has ordered three systems.

CONTRACTOR

Ferranti Computer Systems Ltd, Western Road, Bracknell, Berkshire RG12 1RA, England.

3508.281

CONTROL FOR SURFACE-LAUNCHED TORPEDOES (CSLT)

CSLT is an independent miniaturised torpedo fire control developed by Vickers for operation on any ship having Mk 32 torpedo tubes armed with either MK 44, Mk 46 or other tube-compatible torpedoes. The main features of the system are: small size (control room equipment about 0·1 m³); microprocessor computation; sensor smoothing and target prediction software derived from proven in-service systems; modular construction; flexible interfaces. The equipment is of rugged construction designed for operation in severe naval environments and comprises:

(1) calculator and display module
(2) torpedo selection and setting module
(3) shipboard indicators
(4) local control and display modules (port and starboard)
(5) power supply and switching unit.

The calculator and display module is supplied either as a bulkhead-mounted unit or as a VCS module for incorporation into a user console. Its interfaces accept data from the ship's sensors and a manual keyboard input, and send processed information on relative target motion to the torpedo selection setting module, shipboard indicators and the AIO.

Vickers CSLT control for surface-launched torpedoes

The torpedo selection and setting module performs these functions in either a semi-automatic or a manual override mode. For certain torpedoes, an ancillary setting module is required. The shipboard indicators display course-to-steer and up to six in number may be sited as appropriate. Two local control and display modules are situated above decks, one each in the vicinty of the port and

starboard mountings, to provide monitoring, local control and override facilities.

STATUS

In development.

CONTRACTOR

Vickers Shipbuilding and Engineering Ltd, Barrow Shipbuilding Works, PO Box 6, Barrow-in-Furness, Cumbria LA14 1AB, England.

4576.481

SUBMARINE TACTICAL COMMAND AND WEAPON CONTROL SYSTEM

This is the latest in a series of submarine tactical information organisation and weapon control systems from Vickers Shipbuilding and Engineering Ltd (VSEL), Weapons Department. It is designed for close integration with ship sensors, using the latest technology to reduce size and minimise maintenance

and logistic costs. Functions are partitioned and adaptable to any tube configuration or weapon type. The software concepts from previous systems have been improved and repackaged into smaller units using techniques based on distributed microprocessors.

Well-developed and proven algorithms provide the command with accurate target motion analysis allowing early decisions and initiatives to be taken

against potential targets. Raster scan colour displays provide AIO and fire control operating positions and a command surveillance display. Light-pen control and a user-friendly man/machine interface optimise operator performance within the system.

Processing is carried out by a number of microprocessors and processing electronics and displays are linked via a digital data bus. The design anticipates that data will be distributed within the weapon system by a ship-wide data bus which gives the flexibility to cope with the requirements of each sensor and weapons fit.

STATUS

No contract details have been released.

CONTRACTORS

Vickers Shipbuilding and Engineering Ltd, Weapons Department, Barrow Shipbuilding Works, PO Box 6, Barrow-in-Furness, Cumbria LA14 1AB, England.

Ferranti Computer Systems Limited, Cheadle Heath Division, Bird Hall Lane, Cheadle Heath, Stockport, Cheshire SK3 0XQ, England.

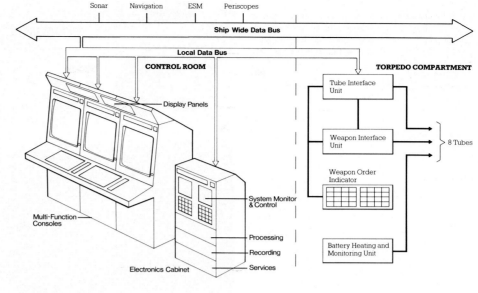

Schematic diagram of VSEL/Ferranti submarine command and weapons control system

4577.481
VSEL COMBAT SYSTEM DATA BUS

The VSEL combat system data bus (CSDB) is for use in warships and provides a flexible self-contained communications medium to which various user equipments can be connected via any type of digital interface. It will be fitted in RN submarines and is applicable to new or existing systems.

The CSDB converts all interfaces to a common format and controls data exchange on a single highway, allowing the advantages of bussed data to be exploited in new or existing systems. Remote terminals are used for interface conversion and data is exchanged on dual redundant serial, single 'twisted pair' highways under the control of one or more bus controllers (BC). The electrical and protocol characteristics of the bus connecting RTs and BCs is based on the communications standard defined in Mil Std 1553 B (Def Stan 00-18 Part 2).

For a particular application the CSDB can be configured by selection of interface equipment to match the weapon system requirements. RTs can be embedded in the user equipment or free-standing. The preferred method of connection is determined by overall system design, balancing data rate, total number of bus links and availability demands. Embedded terminals generally comprise an interface unit between the data bus and the internal computer highway of the user equipment and may contain any level of redundancy up to the complete duplication of the interface.

Free-standing RTs are autonomous units containing a fully duplicated bus interface and are otherwise designed to communicate with any number of users over a wide variety of serial or parallel links. The bus controllers are independent of RTs and users and provide the basis for control of the combat system. The number of bus controllers is determined by the system requirements for availability of data communication. Their main functions are to control the transfer of messages between RTs, monitor the system, diagnose faults and provide guidance instructions to the maintainer. They can also be used to monitor individual messages and extract data as determined by the system designer.

STATUS

Prototype.

CONTRACTOR

Vickers Shipbuilding and Engineering Ltd, Weapons Department, Barrow Shipbuilding Works, PO Box 6, Barrow-in-Furness, Cumbria LA14 1AB, England.

Remote terminal of VSEL CSDB

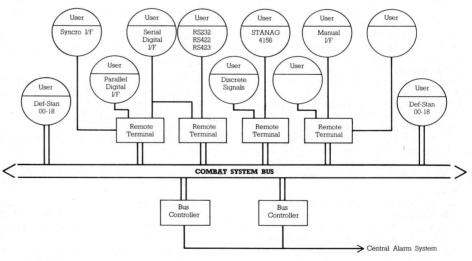

Block diagram of VSEL combat system data bus (CSDB)

3103.481
STWS-1 SHIPBORNE TORPEDO WEAPON SYSTEM MK 1

The STWS-1 is a lightweight torpedo system developed for the RN and designed as a self-contained system to help position a ship for weapon launch and control. The equipment is suitable for fitting in all classes of vessel. Main features of the system include:

(1) launchers for lightweight 12·75-inch (324 mm) diameter homing torpedoes
(2) optimised for ASW roles
(3) minimum manning requirement
(4) port and starboard triple torpedo tube mountings

(5) integration with ship's AIO/CIC system
(6) automatic arming and battery priming of torpedo during the launch phase
(7) jettison facilities for safe emergency disposal of torpedoes
(8) tube muzzle doors for torpedo protection
(9) simulator facilities for outboard training.

The total system consists of two sub-systems, the information sub-system, and the action sub-system, linked by the anti-submarine warfare director (ASWD), who is in control of the complete system.

The information sub-system provides the ASWD with sufficient continuously updated information from the ship's sensors and other sources to enable him to advise the command on the tactical requirements for torpedo engagements. Target information, together with ship's heading and speed is applied to the SWTS-1. The processed target information is passed through the ship's AIO/CIC system and displayed for the ASWD.

The action sub-system contains a series of interlocks which requires a correct sequence of operations to release the torpedo. Faulty operation automatically inhibits release.

STATUS
Fitted to RN frigates and destroyers, and to various ships of other navies. When a contract for five ship-sets of STWS-1 systems was ordered for the RN in January 1979, this raised the total number ordered to over 25.

CONTRACTOR
Plessey Marine, Templecombe, Somerset BA8 0DH, England.

RN frigate operations room showing STWS control position

3742.481
STWS-2 SHIPBORNE TORPEDO WEAPON SYSTEM MK 2

STWS-2 is a second-generation system developed from STWS-1 (**3103.481**) and is suitable for use against any sub-surface target held by the AIO/CIC of the ship. It is a quick-reaction anti-submarine weapon system, capable of pre-setting and firing the new Stingray and Mk 46 torpedoes.

The system consists basically of triple torpedo tubes fitted to port and starboard of the ship and a microprocessor-based tracker and predictor working in non-real time. The system accepts target track data on its information channel simultaneously from either:

(1) the AIO/CIC either automatically or manually – as the primary mode of operation
(2) the ship's sonars – as the secondary mode
(3) manual injection – as the back-up mode.

Target track data is passed to the tracker, which computes the target's current position and the fire control problem is then displayed. This information is also passed to the predictor, which computes the target's future course, and the fire control solution is generated and displayed. The fire control solution chosen optimises the probability of acquisition of the weapon in use. The action channel enables the A/S warfare director to select and pre-set the most appropriate weapon.

The system has an in-built diagnostic monitor which also uses the microprocessor to continually monitor the system functions.

STATUS
STWS 2 is fitted in certain Leander frigates and all the Type 22 class ships, some Type 42 destroyers, and a follow-on production order is in progress at the Newport, South Wales factory for other RN vessels.

CONTRACTOR
Plessey Marine, Templecombe, Somerset BA8 0DH, England.

STWS 2 launcher discharging a Stingray torpedo

1044.261
ADAWS 2 ACTION DATA AUTOMATION WEAPONS SYSTEM

This was the first of a new series of action data automation systems developed for the RN and based upon Ferranti FM1600 series digital computers, and using Plessey display equipment, to provide improved performance and facilities over those of the ADAWS 1 which used Poseidon computers. The important operational difference is that ADAWS 2 and later systems provide, in addition to the action data automation functions, fire control facilities for the various weapons carried by the vessel.

The ADAWS 2 was designed for the Type 82 guided missile destroyer HMS *Bristol*, and accepts inputs from multiple sensors including radars, sonar, passive devices, and data link. The FM1600 micro-circuit computer suite performs the co-ordination, processing, distribution, and display of tactical information derived from these sources. Fire control calculations and co-ordination are also performed by the computers for the armament of Sea Dart surface-to-air missiles, the Ikara ASW weapon, 4·5-inch (114 mm) gun and other weapons fitted.

Inputs to the system comprise the search radars Types 965, 992 and 1006, two fire control/director radars Type 909 for the Sea Dart missile systems, data links, sonars Types 170 and 184, unspecified EW and passive direction finding equipment, and various manual input facilities.

Among the conventional weapons linked to the ADAWS 2 are included facilities for the direction of various categories of co-operating aircraft such as fighters and ASW helicopters.

Auto-tracking of targets is available (using the Ferranti LFX limited area/full extraction and LAX limited area auto extraction) with or without auto initiation of tracks. More details of these facilities will be found in the entry for CAAIS (**1046.261**) which appeared in earlier editions.

Two Ferranti FM1600 computers are employed with a total of 2 × 192 K words of core store. In this system, in the event of one computer failing, various reduced modes of operation are available using the surviving machine. Programs are included for threat evaluation for the Sea Dart missile system, as in ADAWS 4 fitted in Type 42 GMDs (**1234.261**).

In comparison with the earlier ADA systems, still more comprehensive processing is performed on sensor data, and the Plessey Mk 8 digital autonomous displays provide improved facilities for the presentation of operational data in the form of a combined radar and synthetic picture.

The ADAWS 2 display system comprises a number of labelled plan displays (LPD) and electronic data displays (totes) both of which use 305 mm CRTs, and two three-man tactical displays (using a 560 mm CRT). The LPDs are used for picture compilation and weapon control, the tactical displays which replace the traditional projection type plotting tables are used by the command for tactical appreciation and the totes provide alpha-numeric readouts of information in response to the operators' inputs to the computer system through their individual keyboards.

STATUS
The ADAWS 2 equipment for HMS *Bristol* was installed in 1970; further ships of this class were cancelled for economy reasons and Type 82 remains a 'class of one ship'.

CONTRACTORS
Ferranti Computer Systems Ltd, Western Road, Bracknell, Berkshire RG12 1RA, England – main contractors, digital equipment, and software.

Plessey Radar Ltd, Station Road, Addlestone, Weybridge, Surrey KT15 2PW, England – displays, interface, and drive equipment.

1235.261

ADAWS 5 ACTION DATA AUTOMATION WEAPON SYSTEM

This system is essentially a further version of the ADAWS 2 system that is fitted to the Type 82 guided missile destroyer, HMS *Bristol*, and uses the same basic hardware and a large proportion of the software of that system, but configured to meet the requirements of vessels of the 'Leander' class of frigates equipped with the Ikara ASW weapon system. A major difference is that only a single computer is employed. The requisite software for all the ADAWS family of systems is generated and maintained by a Ferranti program team working in collaboration with the Admiralty Surface Weapons Establishment. The sensor, computer programming, and display arrangements for the ADAWS 5 are optimised for the principal role of this class of vessel (ASW) and the Ikara anti-submarine weapon which is the main armament.

The system receives inputs from the search radars Types 994 and 1006, and provides auto-tracking of targets by LAX (limited area auto-extraction), including the special processing of transponder returns from helicopters engaged in anti-submarine warfare operation and Vectas. The IFF associated with the Type 994 radar is also controlled by the computer in association with its integral auto-decoder. On the sonar side, the system receives inputs from Type 184 (main search sonar), Type 199

(variable depth sonar) and Type 170 (attack sonar) which also controls the A/S Mortar Mk 10. Target data are processed, correlated and formed into tracks by the computer, which also controls the firing of the Ikara weapon and provides assistance to the helicopter controller during Vectas. The AS 1077 sonar trainer is also fitted to provide on-board training, both for the sonar operators and the AIO team. Other facilities include data banks and Seacat missiles.

The system hardware is similar to that used in other ADAWS but on a reduced scale, namely, one FM1600 computer, one display central equipment, two tactical displays and six LPDs/totes.

DEVELOPMENT

Development has been carried out in conjunction with the other ADAWS programmes by the same companies and government agencies, and originated in 1967.

STATUS

Eight systems have been manufactured by Ferranti for HMS *Leander* and other ships of the first batch of 'Leander' class frigates.

Software and hardware modifications, including increasing the core store to 128 K words, have been carried out in order to keep the system up-to-date with the latest operational requirements.

CONTRACTORS

Ferranti Computer Systems Ltd, Western Road, Bracknell, Berkshire RG12 1RA, England.

Part of the digital display system supplied by Plessey for ADAWS 5 on HMS Leander

Plessey Radar Ltd, Station Road, Addlestone, Weybridge, Surrey KT15 2PW, England.

1234.261

ADAWS 4 ACTION DATA AUTOMATION WEAPON SYSTEM

This system is essentially a smaller version of the ADAWS 2 (**1044.261**), using the same hardware, but with variations to accommodate the requirements of the Type 42 guided missile destroyer class of vessels and the differences in armament compared with the Type 82 GMD with which the current ADAWS series originated. ADAWS 3 was designed for the CVA 01 carrier which was subsequently cancelled.

The ADAWS 4 is produced in two slightly different versions for the RN Type 42 GMDs and the Type 42s supplied to the Argentinian Navy. The systems fitted in the Batch II and Batch III Type 42 GMDs again have minor differences to reflect the changes to weapon and sensor fits and are thus designated ADAWS 7 and 8, respectively.

The ADAWS family of systems also includes ADAWS 5 (**1235.261**) and ADAWS 6 (**1830.281**). Specific benefits of the modular nature of these systems are reductions in the development effort required and in the time necessary for system proving.

The central data processing complex includes two Ferranti FM1600 micro-circuit digital computers, with a Plessey Mk 8 digital display system for the

presentation of tactical and other information. The computers provide up to a total of 2 × 192 K words of core store, and they will gather data from all the ship's sensors, assemble and correlate this information and that from other vessels obtained via data link, and present it to the command teams on appropriate display consoles.

All information from 'own ship' and consorts in data link contact will be accessible at any console, and on a selective basis, eg either air situation or underwater situation. The computers also include programs to assist in the evaluation of the relative threat posed by different targets, thus assisting the command in the selection of targets and assigning weapons, particularly the twin-headed Sea Dart missile system. When action is joined, the computers also provide control of ship's weapons. In addition to providing all the aiming and fire control computations for the Type 42's Sea Dart missiles, the ADAWS 4 also includes fire control for the 4·5-inch (114 mm) automatic gun mounting, and the calculation of intercept instructions to be passed by radio to fighter aircraft or anti-submarine helicopters.

DEVELOPMENT

Development of the ADAWS 4 was a continuation of the ADAWS 2 work, and began in 1967. Ferranti and Plessey Radar worked as major sub-contractors to

the UK MoD (Navy) in respect of the RN Type 42 destroyers. In the case of the Argentinian Navy, Ferranti worked as main contractor with Plessey Radar as a major sub-contractor.

STATUS

A total of 12 ships of this class was planned originally (two for the Argentinian Navy and ten for the RN). Subsequent changes in the RN fleet, due to the loss of HMS *Sheffield* and *Coventry* in the Falkland Islands campaign of 1982, and the addition of Batch III comprising four ships launched between 1980 and 1982, led to a British complement of 12 ships. Because of the elapse of some ten years between laying down the first of class and launch of the latest, and because of design changes affecting both size, armament and sensor fit, individual ADAWS fitted in Type 42 ships can be expected to differ appreciably in detail.

Ferranti is responsible for implementation of modifications to the system which arise because of changes in operational requirements and to weapons/sensor fits.

CONTRACTORS

Ferranti Computer Systems Ltd, Western Road, Bracknell, Berkshire RG12 1RA, England.

Plessey Radar Ltd, Station Road, Addlestone, Weybridge, Surrey KT15 2PW, England.

1830.281

ADAWS 6 ACTION DATA AUTOMATION WEAPON SYSTEM

ADAWS 6 is the designation of the new system for the RN anti-submarine cruisers HMS *Invincible* and HMS *Illustrious*. A slightly different version, designated ADAWS 10 will be fitted in HMS *Ark Royal*. Ferranti and Plessey, who in partnership have produced ADAWS for preceding RN ships, were contractors for the computer complex and display systems for this class of ships.

HMS *Invincible*, the largest ship to be built for the RN since the Second World War, is claimed to have a more comprehensive automated AIO than any previous vessel, and its functions include deployment and control of the ship's own weapons and aircraft as well as command and control of co-operating forces.

Invincible's armament includes the Sea Dart missile (twin launcher), Sea King helicopters, and Harrier V/STOL strike aircraft. Sensors include a Type 1022 long-range surveillance radar, IFF/SIF, Type 992Q search and target indication radar, two Type 909 radars for the Sea Dart system, Type 1006 navigation radar, data links, EW and sonar.

There is a significant area of commonality in both armament and sensors with other RN ships (Type 42 and Type 82) that have Ferranti/Plessey ADAWS, and as would be expected the new ADAWS for HMS *Invincible* embodies parts of the systems developed for these classes. In ADAWS 6 the two computers are employed in a very similar fashion to those in the ADAWS 2, including the ability to operate in a range

of reduced modes in the event of malfunctions. Additional software to meet the special requirements of the *Invincible*'s new operational role were generated by a Ferranti team in collaboration with the Admiralty Surface Weapons Establishment.

STATUS

The first ADAWS 6 system was delivered to *Invincible* in 1977 and the system for *Illustrious*, the second ship of the class, in 1980. ADAWS 10 for *Ark Royal* was delivered in 1983.

CONTRACTORS

Ferranti Computer Systems Ltd, Western Road, Bracknell, Berkshire RG12 1RA, England.

Plessey Radar Ltd, Station Road, Addlestone, Weybridge, Surrey KT15 2PW, England.

4578.281

NAUTIS COMMAND AND CONTROL SYSTEMS

The naval autonomous information systems (NAUTIS) series of modular naval command and control systems developed by Plessey Displays is based on the company's range of autonomous intelligent consoles. This is itself based on the well-

proven Series 9 display hardware, and now known as the Nautic Intelligent Display system.

Use of Nautic consoles permits systems to be configured for a wide range of applications calling from one console workstation to a full combat display system which would comprise several consoles in a configuration linked by a local area network or a data

highway. The Nautis system uses distributed processing rather than a single central computer or computer complex, offering flexibility and a high degree of survivability. The embedded processors interface with an international standard data bus, and a dual-redundant system data highway complying with Mil Std 1553 B simplifies ship installation.

The full range of available information within the Nautis system is presented on a single screen and the large Nautic display is partitioned into a number of areas: labelled radar picture with computer graphics superimposed and totes giving summaries of sensor, weapon and system status, threat tables and general information. Control procedures are simplified by an interactive menu with prompts on the same screen.

System configurations have been defined for fitting in a variety of ship types. The Nautis system for each application is denoted by an alphabetical suffix:

Nautis-A: assault ships and auxiliaries
   -C: cruisers
   -D: destroyers
   -F: frigates
   -K: helicopter support ships
   -L: assault and logistic landing ships
   -M: minehunters and minesweepers
   -N: minelayers
   -P: corvettes, patrol craft and light forces
   -R: aircraft carriers

Typical configurations range upward from the single Nautic console of a Nautis-P which provides command, control and navigation facilities for a patrol craft or small vessel. In this configuration a labelled radar display permits tactical information to be presented graphically on the radar picture and automatic tracking of up to 20 surface and air targets.

Nautis-F is a multi-console system where individual workstations have the facilities provided by the Nautis-P consoles, but improved by the more powerful multi-processor architecture permitted by the distributed database of the Mil Std 1553 B system highway. Such a configuration has increased system capacity for the wider range of sensor interfaces, and more complex applications software. Nautis-D is configured for larger warships requiring comprehensive command and control facilities, and eight or more Nautic consoles may be employed. A system of this sort can be expanded to operate with a centralised database.

Nautis-M, the version for minehunters and minesweepers, provides all command and control and navigation facilities for naval mine countermeasures operations and typically is a three-console configuration. A variant of Nautis-M has been configured by Plessey Displays in association with CAP Scientific for a new class of Royal Navy single-role minehunters. This version is known as Minesearch and the RN contract award was announced in March 1984.

The Minesearch system comprises three Nautic consoles linked by a high-speed digital data highway, and, using data from radar, sonar, communications and navigation sensors it provides integrated operational control; a continuous, accurate record of own ship's position; updated underwater and surface pictures; navigation and safety facilities; and planning

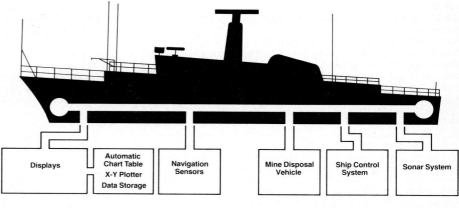

Minesearch minehunting command system

Plessey Nautic autonomous intelligent console

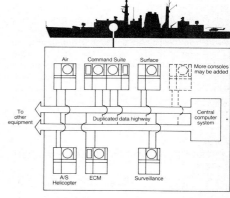

Typical of a larger Nautis complex is the Nautis-D system

and control of ship's track. The consoles will be used to co-ordinate the detection, classification and disposal of mines. Autonomous intelligent consoles eliminate the need for a separate data processing cabinet. A high-speed digital highway provides for future expansion and diversification in equipment and applications, such as the inclusion of surface weapon control and ESM information.

A task-oriented keyboard gives operators ready access to the database that provides aids in manoeuvring the ship at all times. A Nautic console on the bridge for use by the Officer of the Watch is capable of presenting the MCM picture if required. The operational console can be supplied with colour raster viewing units capable of dealing with radar and

synthetic presentation. Console operation is by means of an interactive prompt facility controlled by a keyboard and rolling ball.

STATUS

In production. In March 1984 a £2·5 million UK MoD contract award to Plessey Displays for Minesearch to be fitted in a new class of RN Single Role Minehunters was announced, with Plessey as the prime contractor and CAP Scientific as sub-contractor. CAP is primarily concerned with software.

CONTRACTORS

Plessey Displays, Addlestone, Weybridge, Surrey KT15 2PW, England.

CAP Scientific Ltd, 233 High Holborn, London WC1V 7DJ, England.

3104.481

MCS10M MORTAR Mk 10 CONTROL SYSTEM

The MCS10M is a modernised version of the well-known MCS10 anti-submarine-attack fire control system which combines a Type 170 sonar, a computer with displays, and mortar interface equipment with the ASW Mortar Mk 10 system (**6008.241**).

The modifications undertaken by Plessey Marine on behalf of the UK MoD (Navy) applied to both the

Type 170M sonar and the mortar interface equipment.

In the former equipment one new MC70 cabinet replaces the three originally required, and entirely new electronics are employed which incorporate built-in monitoring. In the sonar control room, existing vacuum-tube equipment in the centre display unit, computer, and SCU tester have been modified to solid-state and the CDU has a new CRT. Additional control facilities have been provided and there are minor modifications to recorders and power supplies.

The stabiliser and plane converter units of the interface with the mortar and transducer have similarly been converted to solid-state circuitry and other modifications have been made to electrical and servo elements of board control, tilt train unit, and remote repeaters.

STATUS

In service with Royal Navy.

4306.261

CANE

The Racal Command and Navigation Equipment (CANE) series is a family of low-cost integrated systems providing comprehensive command, control and navigation facilities for smaller warships and marine policing vessels. It is designed to integrate information from a variety of shipboard radar, sonar and navigation sensors and present a constantly updated display to the command. Computer-generated plots and records are produced. The system is modular and supplied in various forms to meet differing operational requirements: computer-based navigation, comprehensive tactical display, command and control facilities, and target indication to fire control systems may be included.

The original RN CANE 1 system has been improved to produce CANE 2 for the latest RN requirements. It includes high-resolution radar auto-tracking, video mapping on radar displays and inputs from Satnav, Omega, Decca Navigator and Hi-Fix 6 radio positioning systems and can also be integrated with the ship's weapon system.

The CANE 100 and 200 series have since been developed to meet the need for integrated command, control and navigation in smaller vessels based on experience gained with CANE 2 to provide relatively low-cost integrated systems.

CANE 100 is aimed primarily at fast attack craft, patrol boats and submarines. The basic element is a table-mounted control and display unit with a large capacity alpha-numeric display, control panel and

integral KS 590 computer. By itself it forms a comprehensive integrated navigation system operating with various combinations of log, compass, and radio navaids, such as Satnav, Omega, Decca, and Loran C. It also provides an effective command and control capability and can be extended to add an automatic chart table, an operations display unit giving high-performance automatic radar tracking, target indication to multiple fire control systems and the capability to position own ship automatically by radar. An automatic plotter will produce geographically true hard copies of the tactical situation including own ship's track and the positions and movements of radar targets, and a data printer may also be added.

The CANE 200 is designed for the more complex

needs of larger ships such as corvettes and is also based on CANE 2. It provides all the facilities of CANE 100 with additional display consoles to meet increased requirements for surveillance, target tracking, and command and control of air, surface, and sub-surface operations.

STATUS

CANE has been in service with the RN since 1977. CANE 100 and 200 were announced in September 1981 and are in producton to meet the requirements for smaller warships, including missile and gun armed

fast attack craft and fast patrol boats, up to and including corvette size.

CONTRACTOR

Racal-SMS Ltd, Cox Lane, Chessington, Surrey KT9 1SB, England.

1831.281
MINE COUNTERMEASURE CAAIS

Development of this special version of computer-assisted action information system (CAAIS) (see **1046.261**) was entrusted to Ferranti. The new class of MCMVs have reinforced plastic hulls and one of the engineering tasks undertaken by Ferranti was to reduce the magnetic signature of the computer equipment. At the heart of the system is an FM1600B computer driving two Deccascan displays equipped with Ferranti manual input assemblies which enable operators to communicate with the computer by means of alpha-numeric keyboards and tracker balls.

The CAAIS system for MCMVs fulfils a triple role: it compiles and displays information with the speed and precision required for successful MCM operations; it makes the detailed calculations necessary for the accurate navigation and control of the ship; and, as in

all CAAIS systems, it provides a comprehensive display of the tactical situation, such as would be required when the ship is on patrol duties.

The ability of CAAIS to accept automatically and process sensor information presents the command with the ability to reduce errors and action-time operator fatigue, and generally to increase the MCMV's ability to meet its designated task. Peripheral interfaces include the high definition surface surveillance radar, radio fixing aids, the minehunting sonar and the ship's auto-pilot.

The principal advantage that CAAIS for the MCMV offers over other systems is a hardware and software package that provides an automatic and accurate navigation and ship-handling system with good repeatability (the ability to relocate previously detected objects on the sea bed), that places the control of the sonar with the command and enables

comprehensive records to be taken and to be transferred to relieving ships.

STATUS

HMS *Brecon*, the first of the new class of MCMV is operational and nine of the twelve systems ordered originally had been delivered by late 1983. Ferranti has developed a mine countermeasures control system to meet the requirements of smaller MCM vessels; this is described in entry **3506.281**.

In 1982 the RN commissioned an MCMV shore-based training complex (AS1076 Arcturus) which embodies an MCM CAAIS and sonar simulator system supplied by Ferranti Computer Systems Ltd.

CONTRACTORS

Ferranti Computer Systems Ltd, Western Road, Bracknell, Berkshire RG12 1RA, England.

Decca Radar Ltd, Decca House, 9 Albert Embankment, London SE1 7SW, England.

3506.281
MINE COUNTERMEASURES CONTROL SYSTEM

Development of mine countermeasures CAAIS (**1831.281**) for the UK MoD (Navy) enabled Ferranti to design a mine countermeasures control system (MCCS) which meets the requirements of MCM vessels of 35 to 50 m overall length, while incorporating much of the software programs already written for the RN. In these vessels, it is anticipated that the primary role will be minehunting but that a capability of minesweeping, at least with wire sweeps, will be included. Many of the functions will be common to both systems, but the severe constraints on availability of space in the smaller vessels have led to the design of a compact two-man console for MCCS which contains the majority of the electronics directly associated with this system. MCCS is one of the WSA 420/CAAIS 450 family of modular combat systems (**3505.281**).

The main functions of the system are accurate navigation of the ship, including assistance in maintaining the ship on the desired track, a comprehensive and flexible presentation of the operational picture, computer control of the mine-hunting sonar and extensive data recording facilities. Of these functions, accurate navigation is the most important, and here the emphasis is on processing the inputs from navigational aids rather than use of radar fixing, where greater errors can be expected. The Ferranti system can interface with a number of

different navaids with performance parameters which are likely to suit most operational scenarios.

At the heart of the system is an FM1600E computer which is more powerful and of more modern architecture than the FM1600B used in the RN's MCM vessels. This computer and the majority of the associated peripheral control units are housed in the base of a console, which includes a labelled plan display and keyboard and tracker ball. An improvement to the operator interface has been provided by the inclusion of the 'prompt' system first introduced in CAAIS 450 (**3505.281**), whereby the computer leads the operator through his manual injection sequences by showing him the available options on the lower half of his television tote display. The minehunting control officer (MHCO) is presented with a tactical plot comprising computer-generated symbols and, by utilising the wide choice of display range scales available, he can have access to the entire operational picture without moving from his chair. The two-man console also enables the commanding officer to have full access to the operational picture. In the same way as for navaids, the MCCS can accommodate a wide range of mine-hunting sonars. By means of a two-way interface with these sonars, the system brings the control of searches to the MHCO, thus leaving the operators to concentrate all their effort on detection of mine-like objects, while detections are cut in to the computer which then organises their display to the MHCO

without any loss of accuracy. Furthermore, assistance is given in relocating objects already held in the computer store by directing the sonar to the appropriate bearing and range.

A large amount of current operational data is stored and is immediately available to the MHCO. This data includes sea bottom type sonar information, seabed obstructions and environmental data; as well as results of previous minehunting/sweeping activity in the area of interest. A summary of the tasks carried out and the results achieved is recorded on magnetic tape, which can then be passed to a relieving vessel and fed into its computer, enabling it to continue the work without unnecessary delay and wasted effort. For longer-term records, the same data is output to a line printer as a permanent hard copy and an X/Y plotter can also be incorporated.

Another important feature of the design of MCCS is the use throughout of materials which have a reduced magnetic signature. Utilisation of proven hardware modules that are already in naval service and built into the operator's console make installation on board much easier and reduces the setting-to-work time considerably.

STATUS

In production for an overseas navy.

CONTRACTOR

Ferranti Computer Systems Ltd, Western Road, Bracknell, Berkshire RG12 1RA, England.

1496.281
WSA-4 FIRE CONTROL SYSTEM

Weapon System Automation Mk 4 (WSA-4) is the digital weapon control system designed for Type 21 ('Amazon' class) RN frigates. In these ships WSA-4 interfaces with the computer-assisted action information system (CAAIS **1046.261**) and, like that system, is based on the Ferranti FM1600B digital computer. The system has been designed to provide accurate fire control in anti-aircraft, surface, and naval support gunfire modes, to react rapidly to a threat, and be operated by a minimal crew. Weapon direction and target designation is usually performed at a CAAIS display position. Target data are passed to

WSA-4 and the relevant tracker radars and visual sights are automatically controlled to acquire the target. The WSA-4 may operate independently from CAAIS however, using the tracker radars in surveillance mode, or accepting target indication from the visual sights. A key operational feature is the use of electronic data displays (EDDs) and light-pens in a 'conversational' mode. The EDDs provide the operator with information and sets of valid choices from which he selects to control the system. This simplifies control and reduces the training requirement.

Weapons controlled are the Seacat missile and a 4·5-inch (114 mm) gun. Sensors controlled are two

RTN-10X tracker radars (**1368.253**), which are equipped with closed circuit TV, and two visual sights – a lookout and aiming sight and a pedestal sight. System capability is for two simultaneous air engagements, or one air and two surface engagements, and there is provision for emergency control of weapons.

STATUS

In service.

CONTRACTOR

Ferranti Computer Systems Ltd, Western Road, Bracknell, Berkshire RG12 1RA, England.

4273.281
F100-L FIRE CONTROL PREDICTOR

Ferranti Computer Systems Ltd are offering a gun predictor for the Rarden 30 mm naval gun (**3658.203**) based on the F100-L microprocessor. It calculates the required aim-off angles which are presented as an illuminated cross-hair using a dot matrix in a head-up display within the sighting binoculars. The initial application was with the Laurence, Scott (Defence Systems) Ltd stabilised naval mount LS 30R Mk III.

Programs exist for both surface and air engagements.

The principle sensor is an optical sight but the system can accept other inputs such as range data from a laser rangefinder or radar. Manual override and reversionary modes of operation are provided. In the basic system, range information is inserted manually, eg from a surveillance radar display, and may be updated during an engagement. As the operator tracks the target the computer monitors the tracking rate from rate transducers within the gun

mount and calculates the necessary aim-off angles. The operator's sight line is then corrected by the calculated aim-off, enabling the gun to be accurately repointed.

The Mk I version of the LS 30R mounting is controlled locally by a standing operator using a joy-stick to control the training and elevation servos, both velocity and rate-aided modes of control being provided. Line-of-sight stabilisation is provided by two rate-integrated gyros. The Mk II version is

Ferranti F100-L microprocessor-based predictor for naval fire control

LS 30R stabilised gun mounting with Rarden 30 mm gun undergoing sea trials aboard HMS Londonderry

provided additionally with remote control and firing facilities, increased on-mount ammunition capacity and dual optical director. The Mk III mount has all these facilities and the Ferranti digital predictor which enables an aiming point to be predicted and corrections made to the gun point of aim.

STATUS

Land and sea trials of the LS 30R have been carried out by the RN and deliveries are thought to have commenced in 1982 or 1983.

Successful results from the trials of the Rarden gun predictor led to Ferranti offering the F100-L predictor

separately for use as either a primary optical fire director, or as a secondary predictor for back-up applications. In early 1983 Ferranti confirmed that production had begun for a number of navies, including that of Brazil.

CONTRACTORS

Laurence, Scott (Defence Systems) Ltd, PO Box 25, Norwich NR1 1JD, England.

Ferranti Computer Systems Ltd, Western Road, Bracknell, Berkshire RG12 1RA, England.

1828.261

MARCONI/BAe LIGHTWEIGHT GUN FIRE CONTROL SYSTEM (SAPPHIRE)

The Bracknell Division of British Aerospace Dynamics Group (formerly Sperry Gyroscope) and Marconi Radar Systems have collaborated to create a cost effective lightweight gun fire control system. Designed for any size of warship from fast patrol boats upwards, the system is capable of maintaining rapid and accurate control over small and medium calibre guns against air, surface, and shore targets. The system is fully automatic, thus keeping manning requirements to a minimum: only one man, in an essentially supervisory role, is required to operate the system.

The main components of the system are:
(1) the Marconi 800 series autonomous tracking radar, ST802 (**1508.253**)
(2) the BAe Digital Weapon Controller (DWC 100) consisting of the 1412 computer (**1443.063**), associated interfaces and power unit
(3) the control console, incorporating the display and control units for one man to supervise the radar, predictor, and gun.

The total package is designed to be compact and lightweight, thus being suitable for installation in FPBs, corvettes, frigates etc. The predictor uses a dedicated computer leading to operational simplicity and autonomous operation. The radar uses monopulse processing giving a significant advantage in that it is free from fade noise when compared with a conical scan radar. The system will control servo-operated guns with calibres from 20 mm upwards.

In order to make full use of the possible roles of naval guns the system offers three main modes of operation:
(1) anti-aircraft (AA) for defence against high- and low-level air targets:
  (i) AA direct is the normal mode against fast moving air targets. The predictor automatically points the gun and indicates when target is within firing range
  (ii) AA free generation (coasting) mode is entered automatically if the target fades, and the predictor provides extrapolated target flight path data from last known target position and velocity data

(2) surface (SU) for use against surface vessels moving at speeds up to 60 knots:
  (i) SU direct is the normal mode. Splash spotting corrections may be applied for range and bearing using radar data. The predictor provides extrapolated target position data if the target is obscured. Where appropriate, 'throw off' facilities are provided for practice against surface targets
  (ii) SU blind. In this mode target bearing and range are input from the ship's AIO or radar display
(3) naval gunfire support (NGS) including:
  (i) direct bombardment. This mode of operation is used for bombardment of a shore target visible from the ship
  (ii) indirect bombardment. In this mode of operation the gun is trained on to a shore target using spotting corrections from a shore observer
  (iii) blind bombardment. This is used to bombard a point defined by present range, bearing and height from map co-ordinates
  (iv) 'radar assisted' bombardment. This is used when a discrete radar echo ashore can be tracked. Offsets are then added using map co-ordinates to take account of the separation between the radar echo and the required target.

In SU and NGS modes, fuze computation is provided for use with star-shell and window. The system can also be used to give surveillance information by means of horizon search or sector scan.

OPERATION

The system is intended to be integrated with a ship's surveillance and action information organisation and it is this that normally provides initial detection of an aircraft. The Sapphire search facility, however, gives the FCS autonomous operation against the low-level threat. In this, the pencil beam is programmed to search and detect low-flying aircraft, anti-ship missiles and surface craft. Because of the narrow concentrated beam shape and the digital MTI processing, detection is enhanced.

True horizon search mode gives detection of an anti-ship missile with a target area of 0.1 m^2 at 12 to 15 km. Automatic or manual target acquisition may be selected to provide detection of 4 m^2 strike aircraft at 25 km. Detection of surface targets is horizon limited.

Sapphire has the fast reaction time necessary to deal with the low-level threat, whether aircraft or sea-skimming missiles, typically seven seconds, including time to slew to the target bearing.

An 'October' class FPB of the Egyptian Navy on trials in the Solent after major modernisation and re-equipment by Vosper Thornycroft. The work apparently entailed fitting of a Marconi/Sperry Sapphire FCS and Marconi ST802 tracker and S810 search radars can be seen

The television control mode may be used to switch to a second attacker in a stream attack. In this case during the closing stages of an engagement the pointing of the director is manually moved to the second target, after which control is switched back from TV to radar. An electro-optical fire detector can provide an alternative fire channel or can be used in conditions of radar silence, and a laser rangefinder may also be incorporated.

Threat assessment is carried out either on central AIO or on the radar display when in autonomous mode. Digital MTI largely eliminates sea and land clutter and enables low-level targets to be seen through the clutter. Auto acquisition circuitry enables the FCS to slew, search in elevation and acquire the target without manual intervention. Target designation is from either a target vector given to the FCS by ship's surveillance radar AIO, or from the radar display in autonomous mode. Target tracking is carried out normally by radar, either actively or in the case of a jammer, in passive mode. Switching between the two is automatic. In conditions of radar silence the operator may use the television to track the target which again is accomplished automatically after manual acquisition. If an optical sight forms part of the system, tracking may be carried out from this also.

Against very low-level targets, for example less than 1°, the tracker automatically enters the low angle television mode to overcome the effects of multi-path signals. If the aircraft rises above a line of sight of 1·5°, the low angle mode is automatically terminated and full radar tracking is resumed.

A very wide range of ECCM facilities are built into the radar tracker to counter enemy use of jamming techniques. The equipment uses monopulse angle sensing, has continuously variable frequency control and has MTI which enables the radar to see through chaff. Automatic passive/active switching, automatic TV tracking and many other facilities deal with virtually every jamming situation.

CHARACTERISTICS

Radar

Radar beamwidth: 2·4°

Frequency: Band 8·6 – 9·5 GHz

Peak power: 200 kW (typical)

Mean power: 160 W (typical) Non-MTI

Pulse length: 0·3 µs

PRF: Non-MTI 3000 Hz; MTI 4400 Hz

Receiver noise figure: 10 dB

MTI: Coherent on receive improvement factor: better than 25 dB

Computer

Type: 1412A

Capacity: 16 K words

Storage: Semi-conductor, fixed program store

Gun order calculation: 64 times/s

Output refresh rate: 512 times/s

STATUS

First orders were taken in 1976, among them fittings in a number of Egyptian fast patrol boats.

CONTRACTORS

British Aerospace Dynamics Group, Bracknell Division, Downshire Way, Bracknell, Berkshire RG12 1QL, England.

Marconi Radar Systems, Writtle Road, Chelmsford, Essex CM1 3BN, England.

3246.281

SPERRY SEA ARCHER FCS

The Sperry Sea Archer series of naval fire control systems now embraces several versions, ranging from the purely optical Sea Archer 1 to models with multiple sensor capability and correspondingly greater operational facilities. The various versions which have been identified so far are described in the following paragraphs.

Sea Archer 1

The Sea Archer 1 optical fire control system (OFCS) has been designed to provide the advantages of computer-controlled gunnery within a simple system. The predictor itself is similar to that used in the Marconi/Sperry Sapphire system (**1828.261**), a full blind fire radar system. Sea Archer controls servo-operated guns with calibres from 30 mm upwards against aircraft, missiles and surface vessels. While designed as the prime gun controller for FPBs, the system is equally suitable as a secondary weapon controller for larger ships.

The system is comprised of two basic modules, an optical fire director (OFD) incorporating tracking sensors including a range-only-radar or laser rangefinder, and a gun control console containing a digital weapon controller, operator control panels and system communications. In the simplest configuration, an aimer uses binoculars fitted to a line-of-sight, stabilised director to acquire and track the target. To assist in target acquisition the system can accept information derived from the vessel's surveillance radar to slew the OFD on to the target bearing. Optronic sensors such as a television tracking camera may be fitted to give below-decks operation. A TV auto-tracking unit is available if required.

Information regarding the target range, training and elevation is automatically transmitted back to the weapon control console. The computer, utilising ballistic and meteorological data already entered into the system, then calculates gun aiming orders. The gun is controlled from the control console. To reduce reaction time to a minimum, gun slew occurs as soon as the target is acquired and offset adjustments are then made when a valid prediction solution is computed. Typically this process takes two seconds. The gun is fired by means of the console foot push when a valid prediction is achieved and the future range display indicates that the target is within effective gun range.

The system uses a Laurence, Scott line-of-sight, stabilised director operated by an aimer in a standing position. The director provides target training and elevation information in a synchro format to the control console. Provisions are made for voice and signal communication from the director to the control console. The system can accept target bearing from action information systems and the director will slew into line with this data, thus assisting the aimer to acquire the target. To provide accurate range data, the customer is offered the choice of two types of rangefinder. These are a laser rangefinder or a range-only-radar. The laser interrogation unit or the radar transmitter/receiver are mounted on the OFD. They may be energised by the director aimer at the OFD or by the console operator seated at the weapon control console. Range data from the rangefinder is accepted and processed by a Sperry digital weapon controller.

The weapon control console contains the operator's control panel and the digital weapon controller. Its two main roles are to provide a manual interface to the digital weapon controller, and to calculate and control system functions. The control panel provides the manual interface to the system and enables the operator to select the desired engagement mode and to enter ballistic and environmental data. The panel has a numeric display to enable the operator to examine required parameters and push-buttons to provide the necessary operational control signals. The digital weapon controller incorporates the necessary electronic interfaces and the latest Sperry 1412 series mini-computer. The computation techniques and electronic interfaces have been successfully proven with 30 mm, 40 mm, 76 mm and Vickers 4·5-inch (114 mm) Mk 8 guns.

The system is capable of three modes of gun fire control as follows:

(1) AA

In this mode the system is designed to achieve minimum reaction time against fast moving air targets. The director aimer acquires the target and activates the rangefinder. Target data are fed to the control console where the digital weapon controller calculates gun aiming signals. The gun slews onto line with the computed data and when the target is within gun range the digital weapon controller indicates that the system is ready to engage the target. Firing can be achieved from the director or the control console.

(2) Surface

In the surface mode the optical director is aimed at the target and the rangefinder is activated to establish the target range. Gun aiming orders are then computed from the target data transmitted by the director. Splash spotting corrections, observed by the director aimer, are applied via the control console.

(3) Naval Gunfire Support

In this mode the gun is used to bombard shore targets. The target co-ordinates are inserted manually at the control console and gun orders calculated and corrected for ship movement by dead reckoning. Spotting corrections, observed by a shore or ship based observer, are applied at the control console.

Sea Archer 1A (GSA7)

This version is an enhancement of Sea Archer 1 which provides complete integration of a TV sub-system with below-decks control by joystick giving an improved surveillance capability and the option of manned or unmanned director on deck. It also has provision for controlling two different types of gun-mounting (alternately). The ballistics for both gun types can be carried in the 1412A computer. Infra-red sensors may also be integrated in the Sea Archer 1A system.

Sea Archer 2

The blind-fire version of the system is designated Sea Archer 2. In this model the manned optical director mounted on deck is replaced by an unmanned weapon control director, thereby enabling the control of weapons to be performed entirely from below deck. The weapon control director is a mounting on which a variety of sensors may be fitted: laser rangefinder, TV tracker, infra-red tracker, and M-band precision radar tracker. The director may be automatically positioned using target designation data from other ship sources.

The narrow-beam M-band (millimetric wavelength) monopulse radar tracker provides good angle and range resolution for precision low-angle tracking

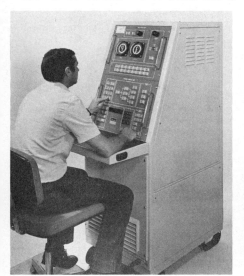

Sea Archer 1 weapon control console

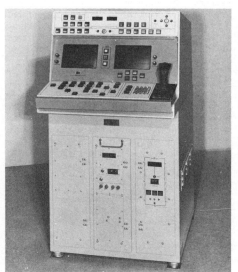

Sea Archer 2 weapon control console

because specular multi-path reflections and sea clutter returns are minimised. Also M-band operation reduces the effects of fog, haze and smoke. An air-cooled transceiver houses a 1·06 micron high repetition-rate laser for rangefinding. The TV tracker employs charge-coupled device sensors, and this equipment is entirely solid-state. It processes angle data based on centroid, edge, or correlation tracking. The IR tracker is thermo-electrically cooled, and is an infra-red imaging and tracking sensor operating in the 3·4 to 4·2 micron spectral region. It processes angle data based on centroid edge, or correlation tracking. All four of these sensors can be mounted on the weapon control director tracking head, which can be trained through 360° and has an elevation angle coverage of −20 to +85°. Installation weight is about 300 kg.

A one-man weapon control console is provided below deck for operation of the ship's weapon system, and computer assistance to the operator is provided at all times for search, acquisition, and tracking phases. A full range of engagement modes is available, as outlined for the Sapphire FCS (above). Sea Archer 2 is also marketed in the USA by the American Sperry Corporation (**4270.281**).

STATUS

The first contract to be announced for the Sperry Sea Archer 1 naval fire control system was for eight systems to be installed in vessels of the Sultan of Oman's Navy. Three types of ship are involved, all of Brook Marine construction. Three of the vessels are equipped with Exocet anti-ship missiles (**1156.221**), probably the 37·5 m class *Al Bushra*, *Al Mansur* and *Al Nejah*, and the Sea Archer systems will control these weapons, and either OTO Melara OTO 76 Compact or Breda Meccanica 40 mm gun mountings. In the case of the Exocet fitted ships, Sperry provides target designation systems consisting of a surveillance radar feeding data to a display used for target detection, threat assessment and target designation to the Exocet system and to the Sea Archer. One of these Sea Archer installations is for a logistic command and landing craft built by Brook Marine.

Equipment supplied by other manufacturers for these systems includes radar by Decca Radar Ltd, Plessey displays, an optical director by Laurence, Scott Electromotors Ltd, and an LM Ericsson laser rangefinder.

Other contracts have been placed by countries in the Far East and Sea Archer 1A (GSA7) has been ordered by the RN for their new Hong Kong patrol vessels.

Sperry Gyroscope is now the Bracknell Division of British Aerospace Dynamics Group, and at the time of printing the future of the Sea Archer systems had not been clarified.

CONTRACTOR

British Aerospace Dynamics Group, Bracknell Division, Downshire Way, Bracknell, Berkshire RG12 1QL, England.

UNITED STATES OF AMERICA

1928.281
TARGET ACQUISITION SYSTEM (TAS)

The Improved Point Defense Surface Missile System (IPDSMS) is a surface-to-air system that will provide self-defence for a variety of ships against the anti-ship missile threat through the 1990s. It can react automatically in seconds to threats in any type of weather. It is a highly reliable system that can be maintained through the use of on-line monitoring, built-in tests and equipment, daily system operability tests, and computer-aided fault isolation. It also has been designed to withstand the adverse effects of physical environment and electro-magnetic interference.

IPDSMS is formed by the integration of a target acquisition system (TAS) and a fire control and launcher system, the NATO Sea Sparrow Missile System (NSSMS). These two systems are under two separate projects, with TAS under contract from the USN with Hughes Aircraft Company in Fullerton, California. Installation of TAS in DD-963 'Spruance' class destroyers and in high-value auxiliary ships began in early 1980.

Although developed as a sub-system to IPDSMS, TAS is designed to designate targets to other weapon systems, such as guns. It is an automatic system composed of a radar, an identification friend or foe (IFF) system, an AN/UYA-4 console, and an AN/UYK-20 digital computer. The system is designed so that the functions of threat detection, track, IFF, evaluation, and designation can be carried out automatically with the operator only monitoring system operation.

As originally conceived, TAS comprised a family of five versions, of varying complexity, and these were designated from Mk 20 to Mk 24 inclusive. The differences between the various TAS configurations were described under this entry number (**1928.281**) in earlier editions of *Jane's Weapon Systems*. The model currently being produced is that known as Mk 23, this being the Radar Automatic version, and as such represents the most sophisticated model except that the infra-red search system has been deleted.

USS John Young *(DD-973) is one of the 'Spruance' class destroyers fitted with TAS. The antenna group is located just behind the aft mast*

The lightweight TAS Mk 23 antenna sits on a roll-stabilised pedestal and rotates at a rapid two-second scan rate. It searches in two regions: in excess of 20 nautical miles for point defence target designation; and more than 90 miles for surveillance and air control. A third, mixed, mode is a combination of normal and long-range modes.

TAS provides optimum radar performance against close-in and distant targets in detecting moving targets in clutter, and discriminating targets in jamming environments.

NSSMS automatically accepts target designation from TAS and assigns a tracking illuminator radar to the target. The illuminator slews to the location designated by TAS, acquires the target, and locks on. The computer assesses engageability, assigns the launcher, and transmits the firing order to one or more of the missiles. When more than one target is designated, a second tracking illuminator is assigned to the second target and the procedure repeated.

Additional targets may be sequentially engaged as each tracking illuminator becomes available.

The firing officer's console contains the controls and indicators for assignment of the launcher system, missile frequency assignment, missile run-up, firing orders, and status monitoring. The controls and indicators provide him with the means to override the automatic operation throughout the engagement sequence.

The main IPDSMS configuration, as on the DD-963s, will consist of a TAS and an NSSMS fire control radar set. However, IPDSMS may be installed in larger or high-value ships with several NSSMSs interfaced with one TAS.

STATUS

The Mk 23 has completed all operational tests and is now in its sixth year of production.

CONTRACTOR

Hughes Aircraft Company, Fullerton, California 92634, USA.

3748.281
R-76 FIRE CONTROL SYSTEM

The R-76 fire control system is a naval director system which operates on both surveillance and tracking modes. It is based on a very low weight multi-mode radar which can be mounted high on a ship's mast, thereby assisting overall performance, particularly early target detection. Gyro-stabilisation is provided, and dual monopulse tracking permits simultaneous missile and target tracking, displayed on the dual A-scope. There is also provision for instantaneous action data entry for weapon system control.

In addition to the radar, there is an alternative director configuration having a TV contrast tracker unit mounted on the radar sensor platform for low-level target tracking and operation in the face of countermeasures.

Operational functions performed by the R-76 include search for air and surface targets, automatic detection, precision tracking, and direction of weapons which may include guns and missiles. The radar is capable of operating in several modes, among them 'track on jam'; simultaneous target tracking, illumination and intercept of air targets; surface target tracking and illumination; detection of enemy missile launch; continuous surface search. In addition to control of fire against surface and air targets, the system provides direct and indirect naval gun fire support and illumination fire. All data processing is accomplished by distributed dedicated micro-computers.

The below-deck operator console has two A-scope displays for simultaneous tracking of two targets, with independent control handles for each and instantaneous action entry for weapon system control. Using this system it is possible to track one target on one display and control a missile on the other. There is also a tactical console with a normal PPI display and operator controls for management of the overall system.

STATUS

The HR-76 made its first appearance as a major element of the H-930 combat control system marketed by Honeywell (**3749.281**), and among the foreign sales of this equipment, South Korea is thought to have fitted the H-930 under the designation Mk 93 fire control system. In September 1979, the manufacturers of the HR-76 announced that this system is to be available on its own with the designation R-76, for fitting aboard all classes of vessel from patrol boat size craft upward, and also for shore coastal defence applications. In late 1982 it was disclosed that the R-76 system will be installed in a Royal New Zealand Navy 'Leander' class frigate. The R-76C5 version of the system has been selected to modernise this class of RNZN ships.

CONTRACTOR

RCA, Government Systems Division, Missile and Surface Radar, Moorestown, New Jersey 08057, USA.

2633.281
GUN FIRE CONTROL SYSTEM Mk 56

Gun fire control system (GFCS) Mk 56 is a shipboard, intermediate range anti-aircraft gunfire control system designed for use against subsonic aircraft and surface targets.

Its primary functions are first to track aircraft targets and secondly to compute train, elevation, parallax, and fuze orders for shipboard guns. The system can also be used to control gunfire against surface targets.

To accomplish its purpose, the system uses a radar sub-system for automatic tracking of either visible or obscured targets, an optical sub-system for tracking visible targets, an electromechanical computer sub-system for computing gun orders, and servo-mechanisms for operating the director power drives.

GFCS Mk 56 may be used against different types of target under different operational modes. The computing sub-system is designed for optimum performance against the types of target most dangerous to own ship, which are incoming high-speed torpedo planes, dive bombers, and medium altitude bombers. Slightly less effectively, the system can also be used against all types of surface vessels.

SYSTEM FUNCTION

The Mk 35 I/J-band radar is of conventional auto-follow design, the elevation and traverse error signals derived from the radar receiver when the target moves away from the radar line-of-sight being used to servo the radar antenna back on target. Inserted in the servo loop are the tracking control circuits which accept the error signal inputs and process them to produce, on the one hand, tracking signals for the line-of-sight gyroscope and, on the other hand, elevation and traverse rate outputs to the fire control computer.

The tracking signals are passed to a gyro unit which is processed to point at the target. The antenna power drive, in driving the antenna to line up with the gyro, automatically compensates for ship's motion due to roll and pitch. The gyro and power drive units form part of the gun director, and from this sub-system are taken two sets of outputs to the computer, one set defining the target line of sight relative to the ship and the other set defining it relative to the gyro platform.

Other inputs to the computer are own ship's speed and course taken from the log and gyro compass and target range from the radar. In addition values are set in for gun dead time and initial velocity, true wind speed and direction. From this information and the fixed displacements between the guns and the radar antenna the computer generates train elevation and fuze orders for the guns.

DEVELOPMENT

Development of the system was initiated by the USN at Massachusetts Institute of Technology in 1942 with industrial support furnished by the General Electric Company and the system went into service in the USA in 1947. More than 700 systems were delivered, and although production ceased in 1955 the system is still widely deployed, particularly in US forces but also in 11 other countries.

STATUS

This classic GFCS is still maintained as operational equipment aboard many USN vessels. Other navies known to have Mk 56 are those of Argentina, Brazil, Chile, Colombia, Germany (Federal Republic), Greece, Japan, Peru, Spain, Taiwan, and Turkey.

CONTRACTORS

Complete system: General Electric Company, Ordnance Systems Division, 100 Plastics Avenue, Pittsfield, Massachusetts 01201, USA.

Computers: Librascope Inc; Reeves Instrument Co; Ford Instrument Co; Bosch-Avma Co.

Telescope: Kollmorgen Optical Co.

Radar: General Electric Co, Syracuse, New York.

Wind Transmitter and Parallax Corrector: Reeves Instrument Co; Belock Co.

Mk 56 fire control director on USS Edward McDonnell *(Stefan Terzibaschitsch)*

2632.281
GUN AND GUIDED MISSILE DIRECTOR Mk 73

This equipment is a major component of the gun and guided missile fire control system Mk 74, one application of which is to the Tartar surface-to-air guided weapon system, and in later models, the Standard naval air defence missile.

Gun and guided missile director Mk 73 is an unmanned, direct-drive motor-driven two-axis unit. It serves as a mount for the antenna of another major component of the system – radar set AN/SPG-51. Three gyroscopes with on-mount electronics provide rate stabilisation. It also provides a platform for the low light-level TV camera Mk 15. The radar line of sight can be rotated continuously in train and can be elevated from –30 to +83° relative to the deck plane. The Mk 73 director mount motors are controlled by the Mk 26 controller developed by General Electric as a more modern, solid-state power drive system, of lighter weight and more compact dimensions than earlier amplidyne systems. The Mk 26 controller contains the controls, servo electronics, and power conversion amplifiers to power the direct-drive motors in the Mk 73 director's elevation and train axes.

DEVELOPMENT

In common with other Tartar sub-systems, development of the director began in 1956. The first prototype was completed in 1958 and the equipment went into service in 1960. Currently in production, 150 systems have been delivered to date for use in USN and foreign ships. While the basic Mk 73 configuration has remained virtually unchanged, the design has been in a continual state of 'Mod' refinement so that the latest servo-mechanical techniques could be incorporated. The Mod 2 version has been produced since 1969. The Mod 1, an earlier producton version, incorporated amplidyne motor-generators and non-solid-state electronics. The even older Mod 0 is still in use after more than 20 years, and a Mod 3 version never progressed beyond the design stage. The Mod 4 became the basis for the Mk 80 director (**1921.281**) for the Aegis system. The first Mod 5 (now designated Mod 6), a complete factory conversion of Mod 1 units that have been operational for some years, has been accepted by the USN. User nations include: Australia, France, Germany (Federal Republic), Italy, Japan, Netherlands, Spain, and USA.

STATUS

Three USN ships of the DDG-15 ('Berkeley') class were the subject of a modernisation programme which entailed refurbishment and modernisation of the Mk 73 gun and guided missile directors. General Electric was awarded a major contract for this work in late 1979 and the first hardware for shore tests was delivered in September 1979, followed by a second refurbished Mk 73 in December of the same year. The modernised equipment is designated Mk 73 Mod 6. General Electric is also under contract to produce two Mk 73 directors and associated hardware for a Japanese guided missile destroyer and to supply Mk 73 kits and parts for the Federal Republic of Germany. Under 1984 funding, three Australian ships are being modernised with two Mod 6 directors each.

Since the late 1950s General Electric has supplied more than 150 Mk 73 directors.

CONTRACTOR

General Electric Company, Ordnance Systems Division, 100 Plastics Avenue, Pittsfield, Massachusetts 01201, USA.

New Mk 73 Mod 6 director prior to delivery for USN DDG-15 modernisation programme

4014.281
Mk 82 (AEGIS) GUN & MISSILE DIRECTOR

The director Mk 82 and the associated director control Mk 200 are components of the Director Group Mk 81 used aboard new Aegis-fitted ships of the USN. The Mk 82 evolved from the Mk 73 family of directors (**2632.281**) employed for Tartar (**6006.231**) and Standard (**1122.231**) naval surface-to-air missile guidance and control. It incorporates the best features of the earlier system but with enhanced search and slew capabilities and a considerable reduction in weight. Other improvements are a new DC torquer gyro and the elimination of hydraulic brakes. These and other improvements are stated to bring a reduction of about 50 per cent in peak power requirement, a calculated MTBF of 2000 hours, and a reduction in weight from approximately 3450 kg to 1217 kg. Improved search and slew capabilities were required to match the SM-2 version of Standard employed in the Aegis weapon system, the quoted characteristics being a horizon search rate of 72°/s, with a rate accuracy of 0·5 mrad/s and an acceleration of 2·5 rad/s².

The Mk 82 director carries the AS-3156/SPG antenna assembly for the Raytheon Mk 99 Mod 1 FCS missile guidance radar (**1247.253**) on an elevation-over-train pedestal and provides stabilisation for the radar line-of-sight. The director provides search pattern and tracking by responding to rate commands from the fire control system. There are no limitations in train or elevation and the system provides train and elevation data and radar line-of-sight rates in traverse, elevation, and cross-traverse for the fire control system computer.

Compared with the Mk 73 director, the Mk 82 has a much lower profile, in addition to being much lighter.

DEVELOPMENT

The Mk 82 director was designed and developed by General Electric Company, Ordnance Systems for the USN Aegis fleet air defence system (**2507.231**). It is developed from the Mk 73 director, also produced by General Electric, and some of the Mk 82 modifications and improvements have been incorporated in the Mod 2 and Mod 5 versions of the earlier system.

STATUS

In production for the USN Aegis air defence system, under contract to Raytheon Equipment Division, who produce the Mk 99 Mod 1 FCS guidance radar for Aegis under contract to RCA. General Electric is building Aegis directors for the USS *Ticonderoga* (CG-47) class of ships. Ten ships (40 directors) are included under present funding. Twelve more directors are included in the 1984 budget (for three ships, CG 57/58/59, with four directors each). At least 24 ships of this class are planned for construction in the next five years.

CONTRACTOR

General Electric Company, Ordnance Systems Division, 100 Plastics Avenue, Pittsfield, Massachusetts 01201, USA.

Aegis Mk 82 directors in final assembly and testing. Mk 200 control is partially visible (right centre) in system test area

1241.281
GUN FIRE CONTROL SYSTEM Mk 86

The Mk 86 GFCS was designed as the major fire control system for the gun batteries being installed in the five most recent classes of USN ships: the new CG-47 guided missile cruiser class (with Aegis combat suite); the nuclear powered cruisers (CGN-36 and -38), which have both the new Mk 45 5-inch (127 mm)/54-calibre lightweight automatic gun mount and Standard missiles; the DD-963 'Spruance' class destroyers (also with the Mk 45 and Sea Sparrow missiles); the DDG-993 'Kidd' class guided missile destroyer; and the amphibious assault ships (LHA). In addition, the Mk 86 is being used in the DDG-19 upgrading programme. The Mk 86 also provides the third Standard missile tracking/ illumination channel on the CGN-38, DDG-993 and DDG-19 (upgrade) classes. The main elements of the system are a high data-rate I-band surface search radar (AN/SPQ-9), an I-band air target tracking and horizon search radar (AN/SPG-60), an optical sensor system, a computing system based on the Mk 152 and AN/UYK-7 machine, and the operator display consoles. Surface, shore, and air targets can be engaged, and the computer is stated to be capable of programming to track automatically up to 120 targets using a track-while-scan routine.

The Mod 8 system selected for the DDG-19 class is essentially the same as that used aboard CGN-38 cruisers except for a redesigned operator's console. This incorporates improved ergonomics and provisions for advanced electro-optical sensor systems.

Expanded operational capability is provided by the integration of the USN's new 5-inch (127 mm) guided projectile and the Seafire (infra-red, laser, TV) electro-optical system (**3727.281**).

OPERATION

The Mk 86 system handles multiple radar sensor inputs, with each radar operating independently and linked via the computer. The SPQ-9 provides surface search as well as low-level air coverage for defence against low-flying threats and for helicopter tracking. The SPG-60 is an automatic scan-to-acquire and tracking radar that also operates in a horizon search mode. The optical sensor system can range from a simple CCTV camera chain to a comprehensive electro-optical sensor system such as Seafire. The complete Mk 86 can be interfaced with other ship's systems (NTDS etc) and can receive data from other sensors or from any one of four target designation transmitters for target acquisition.

The entire Mk 86 operation is controlled and monitored by a control officer and weapon controllers. The control officer's console displays all search radar returns on a PPI presentation. This is used for threat evaluation and selection of targets to be automatically tracked. When a target track has been established, the control officer assigns a specific target and weapon, or combination of weapons, to a weapon control console.

A B-scan and TV display are provided on the weapon control console, and laser and IR displays may be added if the appropriate sensors are fitted. The B-scan gives the weapon controller an expanded radar presentation of his assigned target area, and by examining the display gate around the target on the B-scan he can assess the quality of the track. During an air engagement, the B-scan monitor displays an SPG-60 train and elevation error, enabling the weapon controller to assess track quality. The TV monitor can be used for splash spotting and other functions. Each weapon control console provides a digital readout of target parameters such as bearing, range, course, speed and elevation, and a keyboard is provided for inserting ballistic, target and other data into the computer.

Several operational modes are available:

Radar Surface Fire

Upon target acquisition, a track-while-scan routine is used to track simultaneously multiple designated targets. Smoothed radar data, with appropriate ballistics data, are used to compute weapon orders.

Air Action

The computer automatically and adaptively controls search patterns to acquire and track air targets. Target data, plus a TV view along the SPG-60 boresight axis, are displayed on a weapon control console. The engagement with SM-1 missiles by ships so fitted is facilitated by virtue of continuous wave illumination injection to the SPG-60 tracking radar.

An air pre-action calibration of gun weapons can be initiated from the weapon control consoles.

Anti-Ship Missile Defence (ASMD)

The track-while-scan acquisition gate is expanded to a range sufficient for threat detection. (Full 360° coverage, or over a number of segments to provide surveillance of selected areas, can be chosen.) All targets passing through the acquisition gate are then automatically detected by the system. After target detection, the folowing functions are performed automatically:

(1) threat evaluation

(2) weapon assignment

(3) assignment of targets to tracking channels

(4) slewing of AA director and a weapon to the target

(5) scan of AA director and 3-D track of targets

(6) initiation of firing; transfer of fire to second target.

Visual Surface Fire

A future facility (Seafire **3727.281**) will allow the weapon controller to track the target visually with the TV system and fire the laser to obtain range data. Target range and angle data are entered into the system automatically, and ballistics are computed.

Indirect Shore Bombardment

For shore fire support missions or engagement of targets that are not within view of either radar or optical sensors, target and own-ship co-ordinates are entered at a weapon control console. The system automatically updates these inputs from the ship's compass and log, or by means of other navigational aids. Spotting data is entered at the keyboard. Automatic compensation for orientation of the target line by an on-shore observer is provided.

DEVELOPMENT

Initial in-house studies were started by Lockheed in 1961, and the first prototype was completed in 1966.

STATUS

Deliveries by December 1983 totalled 64 systems. The Mk 86 is used aboard the USN's new fleet of amphibious assault ships (LHA), 'Spruance' class destroyers (DD-963), the 'Kidd' class guided missile destroyers (DDG-993), and guided missile cruisers, CGN-36 and -38 classes. The Mk 86 is also scheduled for the DDG-19 modernisation programme, and is fitted aboard the new CG-47 class Aegis ships.

The Mk 86 constitutes an important element in the modernisation of the USN's DDG-15 class of destroyers; three similar ships for the West German Navy are also being fitted.

CONTRACTOR

Lockheed Electronics Company Inc, US Highway 22, Plainfield, New Jersey 07061, USA.

4538.261
AN/USQ-81(V) COMMAND CONTROL SYSTEM

The AN/USQ-81(V) is a computer driven real-time tactical data display system which receives, processes, correlates, displays and prepares surveillance reports for transmission to similarly equipped units. Display systems are installed in submarines, surface ships, aircraft and command centres ashore and are designed for the requirements of each site.

The AN/USQ-81(V) collects and processes surveillance data from a variety of sensors and sources and converts this into near real-time information which is continuously updated. The information is designed to give the overall commander the maximum amount of information on the tactical situation on land, sea and air, as well as up-to-date data on the location and operational disposition of both his own forces and those that he is opposing.

The system operates in interactive real-time mode with an established data base that can be searched both forward and back in time. Manual data control is achieved by programme function and alpha-numeric keyboards in the operator's console. The operator can select a variety of reports, graphics and calculations to be displayed for briefing, editing, comparing documentation and transmitting. The information can be displayed in great detail or it can be filtered to display the specific data a commander wants to see.

A typical AN/USQ-81(V) configuration includes a central processing unit, an operator interface terminal containing the keyboards and display, the computer control panel, graphic display unit, fixed head memory disc, tape unit, paper-tape reader and a hard-copy unit.

CONTRACTOR
Lockheed Missiles and Space Company, 1111 Lockheed Way, Sunnyvale, California 94086, USA.

1835.281
FIRE CONTROL SYSTEM Mk 92

The Mk 92 FCS has been developed for fitting in two new classes of USN ships, the guided missile frigate (FFG) and patrol combatants missile (hydrofoil) (PHM), and for the US Coast Guard medium endurance cutter (WMEC). The PHM is also known as the NATO hydrofoil, since the overall programme of development and construction is being carried out in collaboration with West Germany and Italy, who planned to have essentially the same craft but differing in some aspects of weapon and sensor fits. One such variation is in respect of the fire control system: the Italian Navy will employ an Argo FCS, while the USN and German Bundesmarine will have virtually the same system, namely the Hollandse Signaalapparaten M28 which has been given the American designation Mk 92 Mod 1, produced under licence in the USA by the Sperry Division. Details of the M20 Series of HSA fire control systems will be found in **1259.281**, earlier in this section.

The Mk 92 is very similar to the M25 and M27 systems built by HSA for the Belgian, West German, and the Netherlands Navies, the former providing for control of air and surface engagements by guns and missiles, while the M27 additionally has provision for torpedo control. The Mk 92 is used for air and surface actions using guns and missiles, and there are a number of other changes from the basic M25/M27 configuration to suit USN requirements. In compliance with the differing sensor arrangements and armament in the three classes of US vessels fitted with the Mk 92 this system is produced in different versions, the Mk 92 Mod 1 for the PHM and WMEC, and the Mk 92 Mod 2 for the FFG. A further version, Mk 92 Mod 5 is in production for ships of the Saudi Arabian Navy. All versions have been built, tested and are in serial production.

Patrol Hydrofoil Missile

The USN variant of the PHM which employs a Mk 92 Mod 1, has as its armament eight Harpoon anti-ship missiles (**2641.221**), and a US-built OTO-Melara 76 mm dual-purpose gun (Mk 75). In addition to the co-mounted search and tracking radars which are a feature of the M20 Series fire control system, other

Mk 92 FCS radar unit (US Navy)

sensors include an I/J-band navigation radar, inertial navigation system, and an electronic warfare suite.

Guided Missile Frigate

The new class of guided missile frigate (FFG) for the USN has as its principal operational roles anti-submarine warfare, anti-air warfare including both anti-aircraft and anti-missile capability, and anti-ship missions. These ships have a dual-purpose launcher able to launch either Harpoon surface-to-surface or Standard surface-to-air missiles. Other armaments include a US-built OTO-Melara 76 mm dual-purpose gun (Mk 75).

The Mk 92 Mod 2 FCS for this class of vessel will operate within a more elaborate environment than the Mod 1 version. In addition to its own search and tracking radars (with integral IFF), other sensor equipment includes an AN/SPS-49 search radar, AN/SPS-55 I/J-band navigation radar, and an AN/SPG-60 STIR (standard target illuminating radar). The complete Mk 92 Mod 2 is integrated with the ship's digital rapid reaction command and control system, Sperry Univac AN/UYK-7 computers being used for this and the Mk 92.

Medium Endurance Cutter

The WMEC employs a Mk 92 Mod 1 FCS which controls a US-built OTO-Melara 76 mm dual-purpose gun (Mk 75) and an optical sight. The ship also contains a Sperry collision avoidance system and command display and control system (COMDAC). This is a shipboard command display and control system which combines both weapons control and ship control. The COMDAC utilises the ship's radar and other sensors to detect and create a display of airborne and seaborne objects and land coastlines. The displays are used by operators to perform navigation/collision avoidance and mission require-ments including search and rescue, enforcement of law and treaties, and military operations.

Hazeltine Corporation will supply three types of electronic equipments in various quantities for the COMDAC system: cue generators, digital scan converters, and a video sync generator for each installation. The cue generator and digital scan converter will generate composite, television-compatible data for display of radar and computer-generated information; the third unit provides the timing and synchronisation for all the electronic equipments in the COMDAC system.

STATUS
In 1982 American procurement plans called for a total of 114 systems, with production extending to 1987. Within this total are Mk 92 Mod 2 systems for three Royal Australian Navy FFGs and three Spanish FFGs, 25 systems for US Coast Guard cutters, six systems for the PHM programme, and 16 Mk 92 Mod 5 systems. The 1985 fiscal year defence budget showed allocations of $24·6, $70·4 and $19·3 millions for Mk 92 programme RDT&E in fiscal years 1983/84/85.

CONTRACTOR
Sperry Corporation, Electronic Systems, Great Neck, New York 11020, USA.

4491.281
H-930 SERIES COMBAT/WEAPON CONTROL SYSTEMS

The H-930 Series of combat weapon control systems is designed to accept inputs from a wide variety of available and future surveillance and tracking sensors and provide outputs to a similar variety of weapon sub-systems for ships ranging from fast patrol boats to destroyers. Significant operational features of the H-930 Series include:

(1) automatic detection, tracking, threat analysis and display of targets from an air search radar (ASR)

(2) semi-automatic detection, and automatic tracking and display of targets from a surface search radar (TWS)

(3) precision tracking from up to two track radars (TR) and an optronic device (OD)

(4) split mode tracking utilising best combination of range and range data from any pair of track data sources from the same target

(5) assignment of any of a ship's guns to any system track data sources simultaneously or all guns on a single track data source or any combination thereof

(6) assignment of a tracking and illuminating radar (TIR) to Standard missile (SM-1)

(7) assignment of a tracking radar to a surface-to-surface missile (SSM) system

(8) integration with IFF, EW and data link in various levels of intimacy

(9) integration with Mk 114 UBFC system (sonar, ASROC and OTS) (**3222.281**)

(10) tactical navigation aids such as intercept/manoeuvre calculations, CPA and time to CPA calculations, true or relative motion display, maintenance on earth grid, and manual or automatic compensation for set and drift

(11) manual, semi-automatic or automatic setting of shell splash spotting data

(12) automatic recommendation of tracker desig-nations and weapon assignments including a means of quick operator acceptance of same

(13) automatic sequencing of tracker designation and weapon assignment as preset by the operator. Such sequences are triggered by an event pre-selected by the operator

(14) demonstrable gun pointing accuracy under realistic test conditions.

The various models within the H-930 Series include all or combinations of the above features. To achieve flexibility and still retain ease of operation, the H-930 operator interface features a common command and control syntax and, in most models, employs a plasma panel that is programmed to accommodate many operator actions and displays, yet preclude illegal actions.

The H-930 Series began with the production of the EX-93 gun fire control system for the USN's Coastal Patrol Interdiction Craft (CPIC) programme. This system was successfully evaluated by the USN and subsequently transferred to South Korea in 1974. Since then the H-930 Series has evolved and con-tinually been improved over the years.

During the development of the Mod 0 system, it became apparent that the H-930 Series must be truly modular in order to be compatible with future technology developments as well as future applications. Accordingly, in the mid-1970s, Honeywell merged the benefits of a distributed computing development programme that had progressed for several years for the USAF into the H-930 Series. As a result, the Mod 1, 2, and 3 systems are the first operational modular ship-board control systems based on a distributed computing architecture for fast patrol boats, destroyer modernisation, and land-based coastal defense installations.

These systems are functionally modular and physically distributed. They have been installed, checked out, and formally accepted by a foreign navy after extensive, rigorous live firing and operational test exercises at sea. The H-930 programme has involved the integration of a wide variety of new and existing weapons and sensors from US and world-wide suppliers.

The most recent modular combat system (H-930 MCS) incorporates the latest technological improvements to realise the full potential of total physical and functional modularity for both new ship classes and modernisation programmes. This new system draws on Honeywell's experience in systems for foreign navies, as well as on research conducted and demonstrated for the USN.

Under the MCS concept, modularity is achieved through a module that is defined as a distributed computing unit (DCU) and the attached system devices that it serves, combined with an equally modular software architecture. The DCU consists of a set of circuit card assemblies, including processors and memory, that perform all of the processing, data routeing, signal conditioning, and protocol functions to allow the attached device(s) to perform effectively as a unit of the total system. These circuit cards, along with special power supplies and cabling connectors, are either mounted in a stand-alone, drip-proof, air-cooled module or are embedded in the cabinets of system control display consoles.

System data is routed as digital messages via the combination of a powerful operating system, local input output control (IOC) processors, and a multiple redundant data bus system. All addressing and local data transfers are accomplished by the IOC and the executive function of the resource processor. All inter-modular tranfers on the data bus system are effected by the global bus interfaces (GBI). The total data routeing system is not dependent on a central master control point that can fail and bring down the entire system. It is this degree of controlled autonomy that allows the system to tolerate the addition or deletion of a given module with the only immediate effect being the presence or absence of that module's function. Access to the global bus is allocated on a rotating basis such that addition of a module will require a slight adjustment, but the inherent intelligence of the bus system can recognise and recover from a non-responding module. Normally, the designed removal of a module will be accompanied by a compensatory change to the allocation sequence.

An area of significance to the shipbuilder is that of long-run cabling. In a recent study for the US Navy, it was determined that the implementation of a data bus in an FFG-7 class ship could eliminate almost 12 000 m of complex signal cables, or more than half of the total cable length. The weight saving was determined to be five tons.

STATUS
H-930 Series system fittings in service and projected and equipment configurations as at early 1983 are summarised in the following table:

CONTRACTOR
Honeywell Inc, Training and Control Systems Operations, 1200 East San Bernardino Road, West Covina, California 91790, USA.

APPLICATION/SYSTEM	EQUIPMENT	ORIGIN
Coastal Patrol and Interdiction Craft	Weapons	
	(2) 30 mm twin gun mount sensors	US[1]
EX-93	(2) Mk 35 OD	US[1]
	LN-66 SSR	Canada
(Fleet introduction 1974)	Mk 16 gyro	US[1]
	speed log/anemometer	US[1]
Fast Patrol Boat	Weapons	
H-930 Mod 0	76 mm 62 gun mount	Italy[1]
	30 mm twin gun mount	US[1]
(Fleet introduction)	Harpoon SSM	US[1]
	Sensors	
	AN/SPS-58 ASR	US
	HC-75 SSR	Canada
	Mk 35 OD	US
	HW 120 TR	US
	Mk 29 gyro	US
	speed log/anemometer	US[1]
Destroyer Modernisation	Weapons	
	(1 or 2) 5 in/38 twin gun mount	US[1]
H-930 Mod 1	(2) 40 mm gun mount	Sweden[1]
	76 mm/62 gun mount	Italy or US[1]
(Fleet introduction 1981)	SSM	Local[1]
	SAM	US[1]
	Sensors	
	AN/SPS-58 ASR (with IFF)	US[1]
	AN/SPS-10	US[1]
	Long-range air search	US[1] [2]
	(2) HR-76 TR	US
	Mk 35 OD (with TV)	US
	Mk 29 gyro	US
	speed log/anemometer	US[1]
Fast Patrol Boat	Weapons	
H-930 Mod 2	76 mm/62 gun mount	Italy or US[1]
	40 mm gun mount	Sweden[1]
(Fleet introduction 1981)	SSM	Local[1]
	Sensors	
	AN/SPS-58 ASR (with IFF)	US
	HC-76 SSR	Canada
	HR-76 TR	US
	Mk 35 OD (with TV)	US
	Mk 29 gyro	US
	speed/log anemometer	US[1]
Coastal Defence Modernisation	Weapons	
	SSM	Local[1]
	Sensors	
H-930 Mod 3	SSR	Japan[1]
(Operational 1980)	Optical sight	Japan[1]
	HR-76 TR (with TV)	US
Destroyer Modernisation	Weapons	
	5 in/38 gun mount	US[1]
H-930 MCS[3]	76 mm/62 gun mount	Italy or US[1]
(Scheduled delivery 1984)	(2) 40 mm gun mount	Sweden[1]
	SSM	Local[1]
	SAM (SM1)	US[1]
	ASROC	US[1]
	OTS torpedo	US[1]
	Sensors	
	DA.08	Netherlands
	ASR (with IFF)	
	AN/SPS-10 SSR	US[1]
	STIR	Netherlands
	HW-160 TR	US
	E-O platform	Honeywell
	AN/SQS-23 sonar	US[1]
	Mk 29 gyro	US[1]
	speed log/anemometer	US[1]
	EW system	US[1]

[1] Customer furnished or specified
[2] Various retained radars (display only)
[3] Under development. Final configuration not firm

4270.281
CHALLENGER SA-2

This electro-optronic fire control system primarily designed for fast patrol boat installation provides precise gun orders or missile guidance functions for a large inventory of weapons. (It was originally introduced as Sea Archer 2 and re-named in late 1982.) Gun calibres accommodated range in size from 20 mm to 76 mm and surface-to-surface missile control includes both inertial and laser guided types. Having both surface and air target capability, SA-2 utilises infra-red (three to five micron and eight to twelve micron common module), TV, and laser sensors mounted on a remotely controlled director. An optional M-band (95 GHz) radar tracker module is

also available for mounting on the director. Associated with the one-man total system operational concept is a below-deck control console which contains TV/IR radar and alpha-numeric displays as well as system control functions including weapon designation information and tellback information. Automatic operation is provided through an AN/UYK-502 militarised 16-bit computer utilising standard USN CMS-2 software compilation.

Since the line-of-sight stabilised director can support over 150 kg of payload and is trainable through 360° with elevation angle coverage of –30 to +85°, a wide variety of target sensors can be accommodated. Currently in use are a 3·4 to 4·2 micron thermo-electrically cooled imaging and

tracking sensor, 7·75 to 11·75 micron common module IR with a new long-life Stirling cycle cooler, a low light-level TV with 10:1 zoom lens elements, and a 1·06 micron high repetition rate rangefinder laser. When laser illumination is required for missile guidance functions a high power coded laser with variable beam divergence is employed. In addition the 95 GHz radar tracker, which is mounted integrally with the E-O director, uses a narrow 0·5° beamwidth to minimise specular multi-path reflections and sea clutter returns. A power output in excess of 1 kW peak provides range and angle information compatible with the detection ranges and performance of the IR and TV sensors.

Processing of data from the available sensors

utilises algorithms for edge, centroid, and correlation target tracking to generate angle error data for servo control. Automatically adjusted gate size corresponding to target size and dynamics reduces track jitter and aids the many signal enhancement techniques used to reduce background clutter effects. Images from the TV and IR sensors as well as the radar module can be displayed simultaneously on the control console for operator interpretation.

Target designation for SA-2 can be accomplished from any of the ship sources such as search radar, other FCS equipment, CIC, or optical director. When initial designation is received, the FCS is programmed in automatic acquisition patterns dependent upon accuracy of the input data. Multiple input/output data channels provide the interchange of information between SA-2 and the controlled weapons.

The SA-2 above-deck equipment weighs 305 kg and below-deck equipment totals 422 kg. Other ship inputs required, dependent upon weapon order generation, include heading, roll, pitch and speed in either synchro or digital format.

STATUS

Land-based testing was carried out contractually by US Naval Surface Weapons Center, Dahlgren, Virginia in April 1981. Demonstrations of high-speed aircraft tracking by production-type equipment were conducted at the Paris Air Show in 1981. Reliability proved to be in excess of 600 hours MTBF over an operational period of 2500 hours. It was also marketed by the associated Sperry, UK Company (but now a division of British Aerospace Dynamics Group).

CONTRACTOR

Sperry Corporation, Electronic Systems, Great Neck, New York 11020, USA.

3727.281
SEAFIRE NAVAL FIRE CONTROL SYSTEM

Seafire is a projected development of a passive electro-optical naval fire control system for fitting and use aboard ships for directing gunfire against surface targets at sea or on shore. Employed aboard ships equipped with the Mk 86 gun fire control system (**1241.281**), the Seafire system will provide all-weather, day/night target acquisition and tracking facilities. Sensors will include a forward looking infra-red (FLIR) sensor, and the electro-optical package will also include a daylight television system for long-range target detection, digital video tracker and processor for automatic tracking, and a laser rangefinder and target marker. The latter will enable Seafire-equipped ships to employ laser-guided munitions against targets. Fine stabilisation of the system for precision fire control computations is incorporated.

STATUS

Honeywell was selected as prime contractor for the Seafire system by the USN in March 1980 when a contract for $17·2 million covering three full-scale engineering models was awarded. Most of the work was carried out at Honeywell's West Covina, California plant and at its Systems and Research Center in Minneapolis. Major sub-contractors were Northrop Corporation for platform stabilisation and certain E-O sensors, and Texas Instruments for the IR sensor package. A laser sub-system produced by Ferranti Ltd was also incorporated.

Originally a four-year development was envisaged, to be followed by a production facility but in 1982-83 the programme was thought to have been cancelled after which a fresh contract was awarded to Texas Instruments in November 1983 following a new Request for Proposals issued by the USN. At one stage it was expected that 12 classes of USN ships would be fitted with Seafire.

In April 1983 it was learned that Texas Instruments and Ferranti had decided to embark on a joint programme to market a system derived from Seafire to be known as Sea Tiger in international markets (**4489.281**).

CONTRACTOR

Texas Instruments Incorporated, PO Box 226015, Dallas, Texas 75266, USA.

1922.481
TRIDENT FIRE CONTROL SYSTEM Mk 98

General Electric Ordnance Systems has received a contract award for the development of US Navy fire control systems and guidance support equipment. The contract covers work extending over a four-year period for design and initial manufacture of fire control systems for the new Trident submarine and for the modifications required for Poseidon fire control systems currently deployed in order to accommodate a larger C-4 missile (**2840.411**).

As a key sub-system of the Trident strategic weapons system, the GE fire control technology will serve the primary purpose of preparing the missile guidance system for flight and controlling the missile launch sequence.

Support equipment will consist of: guidance system test equipment for shore-based activities and nuclear submarine strategic weapons facilities; guidance system containers and handling equipment; and equipment to support fire control and guidance operations at all maintenance levels.

Deliveries of fire control systems and support equipment under this contract will continue into the 1980s. No further details were available at the time of publication.

CONTRACTOR

General Electric Company, Ordnance Systems Division, 100 Plastics Avenue, Pittsfield, Massachusetts 01201, USA.

1925.281
PASSIVE FIRE CONTROL SYSTEM Mk 105 (TAC)

The Mk 105 target acquisition console is a passive fire control system for the detection of targets radiating anywhere in the microwave spectrum and the direction of appropriate ship's weapons against those which are identified as threats. The main elements of the system are a broadband microwave antenna array with direction finding facilities, a countermeasures receiver, signal data processor, and an indicator control unit.

The antenna array consists of eight cavity-backed planar spiral elements with broadband balun feeds, these being disposed on a masthead mounting to permit direction finding by the monopulse amplitude technique.

The countermeasures receiver, derived from the AN/ALR-47 radar homing and warning system developed by IBM for the S-3A, Viking ASW aircraft (**1862.353**), is a four-channel, digitally tuned superheterodyne receiver with a fast-acting diode matrix switching head.

The signal data processor measures the characteristics of the video outputs of the receiver and converts the video pulses to digitised, monopulse, parametric data. All signal processing and system controls are handled by software that can be modified by the operator or by selection in advance of a mission. The processor performs all input/output signal conversions and storage, processes and filters the data, and transmits information to the display for use by the operator. All communication with external displays or interfaces with other of the ship's systems are handled by the signal data processor, which has two memories, the combined capacity of which may be as much as 24 K words. The computers are machines of IBM's System/4 Pi range, model SP-OA.

The indicator control unit is provided with an advanced CRT display for the presentation of emitter bearings, and the associated emitter signal characteristics in alpha-numeric form. Its operation and character generation functions are controlled by the signal processor computer. The operator is provided with a control panel on which are push-buttons and thumb-wheels that serve as data insertion devices. The buttons are illuminated internally and also act as indicators. System software can revise the function of each of the 28 push-buttons without affecting the hardware.

OPERATION

The Mk 105 is a programmable passive fire control system which automatically detects, sorts, identifies, and locates emitters. Multiple digital channels permit two-way communication with weapons direction systems, tactical data systems, and missiles. Several emitters can be processed at the same time, and the system has a large capacity emitter file, which permits operation in dense electromagnetic environments.

The system automatically scans the microwave frequency band, processes the emitter data gathered, displays the emitter signatures, priorities, identification data, and bearing. The operator's controls allow him to set receiver frequency scan limits and select emitter signals for further processing or designation as targets. Emitter data are used by the weapons system, under operator control, for target acquisition. Data can also be supplied to other surveillance systems to enhance target detection and identification.

As programmed at present, the Mk 105 TAC concentrates on short-duration radar transmissions, such as those associated with ship, submarine, and missile guidance radars, but other priorities may be assigned by software changes.

DEVELOPMENT

At the time of adaptation to the Standard anti-radiation missile for the surface-to-surface anti-ship role, in early 1972, the US Navy selected the IBM Mk 105 system to provide passive target acquisition, location, and identification, and weapon initialisation. In November 1972 two systems were delivered for installation aboard the USS *Grand Rapids* (PGM-98) and USS *Douglas* (PGM-100). The first successful launch of a Standard SSM was made from the former vessel in April 1973. In November 1973 IBM was awarded a production contract for 12 improved Mk 105 TAC systems for fitting in DDG and DEG class ships.

STATUS

The first of the production systems was delivered in spring 1974 and in 1976 delivery was completed for guided missile destroyers.

CONTRACTOR

IBM Federal Systems Division, Owego, New York 13827, USA.

3221.481
FIRE CONTROL SYSTEM Mk 113
The FCS Mk 113 is used in SSN 594 class submarines of the US Fleet. Target bearings from the BQQ-5 sonar suite are pre-filtered, and together with own ship motion data, are processed in the Mk 130 digital computer, the first electronic digital computer to be used aboard attack class submarines. With input of own ship state vector information, the target range, course and speed can be computed from passive bearings only. The operator interacts with the target motion analysis (TMA) function at the analyser console Mk 51.

The FCS Mk 113 consists of the following equipments:
(1) the attack director Mk 75 receives own-ship and target information to compute torpedo ballistics and wire-guide controls, and performs position keeping on both target and torpedo. The Mk 75 also supplies necessary data to levelling computer Mk 129 for Subroc ballistic computations
(2) the attack control console Mk 50 is the system firing panel, tactical display, and torpedo room status panel

(3) the levelling computer Mk 129 performs Subroc ballistic computations, and in conjunction with the reference sensing element Mk 1, provides signals for levelling the Subroc inertial platform.
Addition of two torpedo control panels Mk 66, two tone signal generators Mk 47, together with major modifications to existing Mod 2 equipments, results in FCS Mk 113 Mod 6 and Mod 8 which accommodate the Mk 48 torpedo. Torpedo control panel Mk 66 (which represents the first application of MSI/LSI circuit technology on submarines) acts as a preset panel while TSG Mk 47 generates the signals for transmission of data to the torpedo. The Mod 6 is a field-modified Mod 2 while the Mod 8 comes directly from the factory with the modifications built in.
STATUS
The FCS Mk 113 has been operational since 1962. It is the weapon control system deployed aboard the USN's nuclear attack class and fleet ballistic missile submarines. In the late 1960s the additional equipments required for the torpedo Mk 48 were developed.
CONTRACTOR
The Singer Company, Librascope Division, 833 Sonora Avenue, Glendale, California 91201, USA.

Attack control console of Mk 113 fire control system

3222.281
ASROC Mk 114 FIRE CONTROL SYSTEM
Fire control system Mk 114 provides the means of solving the shipboard anti-submarine attack problem, generates launching orders, prepares the weapons for firing, and generates designation data for Asroc (**6001.241**) missile tracking by ship's radar. The ASW weapons controlled by FCS Mk 114 range from Hedgehog projectiles and older Mk 44 torpedoes to the newer Mk 46 torpedoes as well as the Asroc missile.

The FCS Mk 114 consists of the following equipments:
(1) the attack console Mk 53 consisting of an attack plotter and a ballistic computer
(2) a stabilisation computer Mk 134 which generates

stabilised azimuth and depression orders for the ship's sonar
(3) the position indicator Mk 78 provides a continuous display of own ship's target and weapon tactical information including firing control to the commanding officer
(4) the relay transmitter Mk 43 tests Asroc readiness, and programmes and monitors the ignition and separation assembly of the selected Asroc missiles
(5) a relay transmitter Mk 44 which transmits train and elevation orders to the selected gun or missile fire control system for radar tracking of the Asroc missile.

These equipments employ a firing panel and transistorised, electromechanical analogue

computer modules which combine automatic computation with graphic plotting on the Mk 53 console for target motion analysis, and ballistic computations.
STATUS
The Mk 114 FCS, and its predecessor the Mk 111 fire control group have been installed on US Navy destroyers and frigates, and on ASW ships in service with navies of Brazil, Germany (FR), Greece, Italy, Japan, Korea (S), Pakistan, Spain, Taiwan, and Turkey. Originally developed in the early 1960s, the USN maintains a refurbishment and repair facility for the Mk 114 at NTS, Keyport, Washington.
CONTRACTOR
The Singer Company, Librascope Division, 833 Sonora Avenue, Glendale, California 91201, USA.

3223.281
Mk 116 FIRE CONTROL SYSTEM
The Mk 116 Mod 4 is the latest version of this underwater fire control system (UFCS) to be fitted in USN anti-submarine warfare ships. The system has evolved during the period it has been in operation and the Mod 4 uses an AN/UYK-7 computer as the system central processor. It interfaces with the Mk 26 guided missile launch system to launch Asroc missiles against submerged targets at stand-off ranges, and with trainable Mk 32 torpedo tubes to launch the Mk 46 torpedo against submarines at close range.

The principal sensor is the AN/SQS-53 sonar set, with environmental inputs from the electro-magnetic log, wind indicator Type F, advanced design stabilised gyro, AN/SQQ-61 bathythermograph, AN/UQN-4 fathometer, and data from ship's command and decision system. The Mk 116 Mod 4 UFCS includes standard NTDS computers, displays, and interface equipment. It consists of two major sub-

systems, the computer processing sub-system and the weapon control and setting sub-system (WCSS).
(1) computer processing sub-system: AN/UYK-7 digital computer with advanced ASW operational program; RD-358 magnetic tape unit; OA-7984 input/output console (paper tape and teletype)
(2) WCSS: weapon control panel Mk 329, which is normally the only manned unit; missile setting panel Mk 330, one for each launch system; torpedo setting panel Mk 331; weapon status and approved panel Mk 332, installed at the bridge and combat information centre; bridge display panel Mk 333; and interface control panel Mk 377, which provides power distribution and signal routeing for missile/torpedo functions.
OPERATION
The underwater battery supervisor, stationed in the combat information centre, operates the UFCS from the weapon control panel and an adjacent display console. ASW team members are also located at the

torpedo setting panel to facilitate local operations if required, and at the weapon status and approval panels to provide Asroc launch approval.
DEVELOPMENT
The WCSS was developed and produced by Singer-Librascope under contract to the Naval Ocean Systems Center, San Diego.
STATUS
The Mk 116 Mod 4 and its predecessor systems Mk 116 Mods 1, 2 and 3 have been installed in several classes of surface ships: Mod 1 on CGN-38 class cruisers, Mod 2 on DDG-993 class destroyers, Mod 3 on CG-26 with a single launcher, as part of its modernisation programme. Mk 116 Mod 4 is currently being installed on CG-47 'Aegis' class cruisers.
CONTRACTOR
The Singer Company, Librascope Division, 833 Sonora Avenue, Glendale, California 91201, USA. (WCSS)

1923.281
LOCKHEED SHARPSHOOTER
Lockheed Electronics Company's Sharpshooter is a family of digital fire control systems for the control of small calibre rapid-fire guns in the 20 to 40 mm class. The systems can be provided in on-mount or off-mount configurations for a variety of platforms, including fixed emplacements, self-propelled vehicles, towed ground vehicles, and shipboard applications. Sharpshooter directs rapid-fire guns against high-speed aircraft and missiles in both high and low angle attack profiles, as well as surface targets. The system's speed, accuracy, flexibility and ease of operation are achieved through the use of a central GP digital computer or microprocessor, as applicable, monopulse radar, precision optics, advanced tracking sensor rate-aiding servo techniques, solid-state design, and modular software.

Sharpshooter is the natural outgrowth and extension of two LEC programmes: Mk 86 GFCS,

developed and produced for the USN, and the AN/VPS-2 radar set (**2547.153** and **2850.131**), developed and produced for the US Army. It became apparent that mini-versions of the Mk 86 GFCS capability and the excellent sub-clutter visibility characteristics of the AN/VPS-2 pulse doppler radar were needed for control of land-based and shipborne small calibre rapid-fire weapons. During the period of its development, Sharpshooter was proposed in a number of different versions (described in earlier editions) but current designs consist of the two models which follow.

Sharpshooter Mk 1
This version of the Sharpshooter was designed for on-mount installation for the control of 20 to 40 mm calibre guns. The AN/VPS-2 has been upgraded to a full solution tracking radar and is used in conjunction with a general-purpose digital computer and an optical sight. The reaction time (target designation to ready-to-fire) is 3·7 seconds. Target acquisition is

simplified in that the turret can accept target designation from external sources and slew the sensor to the designated position.
OPERATION
Functions of the individual elements of the system are as follows:
Radar: The AN/VPS-2 is modified to a monopulse/pulse doppler full solution tracking radar which automatically searches (on pre-programmed patterns), acquires, and tracks. The monopulse feature provides azimuth and elevation tracking and the pulse doppler provides the target range information.
Stable platform: The system is provided with a stable platform which is capable of accommodating an electro-optical sensor.
Control panel: The gunner controls the operation of the system from this unit. Controls used during an engagement are located on two handgrips, and other controls on the panel are used before an engagement

to set in ballistics and environmental data. During optical or manual tracking, target range and speed are also inserted at the control panel. A TV or IR monitor provides the operator with a visual display of the situation as viewed by the stable platform's sensor. This enables the operator to offset any residual tracking errors or misalignment and is also used in the optical and manual mode for angle tracking.

Data processor: The computer solves the fire control problem by developing the correct lead angles and super elevation based on angular tracking rates and range. These computations are based on target position and rates derived from the stable platform sensors, the radar and environmental inputs

from the gunner. Either electrically or hydraulically operated weapons can be controlled.

Sharpshooter Mk 2
The Mk 2 is essentially the same as the Mk 1 except that it is modified for off-mount operation. The radar pedestal is capable of 360° freedom and a below-decks operator's control console is added. Equipped with a computer generated alpha-numeric display, the TV/IR monitor presents target range, antenna bearing, system status (search, track, coast), ready-to-fire indication and operator entered ballistic data plus environmental data.
DEVELOPMENT
Development was undertaken as a private venture by

Lockheed Electronics Company to exploit the experience accumulated in the design and development of the Mk 86 GFCS (**1241.281**) and the AN/VPS-2 radar system for the US Army Vulcan air defence system.
STATUS
Lockheed Electronics is currently producing 20 Sharpshooter Mk 1 Mod 2 gun fire control systems for the Spanish Navy, to be used with the Meroka multi-barrel gun (**3176.203**).
CONTRACTOR
Lockheed Electronics Company Inc, 1501 US Highway 22, Plainfield, New Jersey 07061, USA.

1493.261
US NAVAL TACTICAL DATA SYSTEM
NTDS (naval tactical data system) is the designation given to the combinations of digital computers, displays of various types, and data links which are installed on USN ships for the on-line collection, processing, storage, and presentation of information from sensors such as sonar, radar, optical, and aircraft or ship consorts, via data link. NTDS also is engineered to interface with ATDS (airborne tactical data system) and MTDS (marine tactical data system). All three systems have the prime function of providing automated organisation and display of information for command and control teams for such purposes as threat detection and assessment, and weapon-target allocation.

Although designed to a common concept, NTDS exists in a number of versions, varying in size and equipment complement according to the age of installation and the size of vessel fitted. The overall system has also been subject to a continuous process of updating since its introduction into service in the late 1950s. By 1969, for instance, three generations of display devices had been employed. The basic digital computer for the system, the AN/UYK-20, was preceded in some installations by other types, and later NTDS employ the Univac AN/UYK-7.
STATUS
In addition to USN fleet fittings of NTDS, installations aboard ships of the Australian, French, Italian, Japanese and West German navies now total more than 100.

In the early 1980s the USN selected the AN/UYK-43 and AN/UYK-44 computers to replace the AN/UYK-7 and AN/UYK-20 as 'standard' digital computers. It was also decided to replace the older machines progressively by UYK-43 and UYK-44 processors as requirements expand beyond the capabilities of the former processors, or other circumstances make appropriate. It was also decided to adopt the

Combat information centre of the USS Spruance, *DD-963, showing part of the ship's NTDS*

'embedded' computer philosophy which provides distributed processing facilities with benefits in survivability, maintainability, flexibility etc. The NTDS has been the object of a programme of up-dating involving replacement of obsolete computers, displays and other equipment, and software modifications to reflect the integration of new sensors and weapon systems into the Fleet.

Hughes has delivered about 2500 displays (UYA-4 and UYQ-21) for these systems. As examples, in the USN, the AN/UYA-4 standard NTDS display system

in an FFG-7 class ship includes seven consoles, while in CG-47 class vessels 17 consoles and the AN/UYQ-21 large screen are fitted. From 1973 to 1982, 87 UYA-4 systems were procured for the USN at costs that varied from $3·5 million for an FFG-7 to $9 million for the CG-47, with 42 AN/UYQ-21 systems procured in the period 1979 to 1982.

The total amount budgeted in fiscal year 1984 is $160 million: $50 million for UYA-4 systems and $110 million for the UYQ-21.

1834.281
AEGIS COMMAND AND CONTROL SYSTEM
Aegis, formerly designated the Advanced Surface Missile System (ASMS), is a surface-to-air weapons system primarily designed to defend against anti-ship missiles. Major components of the Aegis system are the missile, its launching system, the fire control and weapons control systems, the multi-function array radar system with its computer control, the system command and decision, and the operational readiness test system.

The missile to be used is the SM-2 modularised Standard missile (**1122.231**). This is a semi-active radar terminal homing weapon with mid-course command guidance. It is launched from the Mk 26 fully automatic dual-purpose launcher which can also launch Asroc (**6001.241**) anti-submarine missiles.

This launcher has a digital interface with the Mk 1 weapons control system. One of the three computerised systems of Aegis, all of which use the AN/UYK-7 digital computer (**1467.063**), the Mk 1 system accepts weapon assignment commands and special threat criteria from the Mk 1 command and decision system and tracking data from the multi-function radar system. These inputs are processed to determine the possibility of engaging the target and then to generate commands for the Mk 26 launcher and pre-launch orders for the missile, commands for the Mk 99 fire control system for target illumination,

commands to the multi-function radar if mid-course guidance is required, and reports to the Mk 1 command and decision system.

The function of the Mk 99 fire control system is to illuminate the target. To do this it uses the AN/SPG-62 (slaved) radar. Inputs to the system come from the Mk 1 weapons control system which, in the case of slaved radar operation is passing on data from the multi-function radar system.

The multi-function phased array radar, the AN/SPY-1A (described in **1570.253**), is capable of surveillance and the simultaneous detection and tracking of multiple targets. Associated with it is a four-bay AN/UYK-7 computer, and this equipment with ancillaries makes up the radar control system. The primary function is, evidently, to search for and acquire targets and track them to whatever extent may be necessary. Beam scheduling for this and other tasks is organised by the computer. The system also handles the two-way link with the missile for mid-course guidance when requested by the Mk 1 weapons control system. Certain special facilities can be provided such as a 'burn-through' facility for use in ECM conditions or passive angle tracking. The system accepts general operational commands from the Mk 1 Aegis command and decision system and mid-course guidance commands from the Mk 1 control system; and its operational outputs are processed signals giving target detection data to the

Mk 1 command system and target and missile track data to the Mk 1 control plus mid-course guidance commands to one or more missiles.

Together with the AN/SPY-1A radar system and the Mk 1 control, the Mk 1 command and decision system make up the detection and decision loops of the Aegis system. The Mk 1 system is the ship's command and control centre and targets enter the detection and decision loop from the AN/SPY-1A radar, from other ship's own sensors or from data supplied by other ships or aircraft. What happens next depends on which of the four Aegis operating modes has been selected. The modes are automatic special, automatic, semi-automatic, and casualty; in the automatic special mode targets meeting certain predetermined threat criteria are automatically fired upon unless manual override is invoked; in all other modes positive human action to initiate firing is needed.

In these three modes the Mk 1 weapons control system inserts targets into the engagement queue and schedules equipment for launching and terminal illumination. Trial intercepts are computed and a time to fire predicted. Resulting data are fed back to the Mk 1 command and decision centre which is also receiving target detection data from the radar control system, operational readiness data from the Mk 1 operational readiness test system and electronic warfare and other data from the command and decision centre. Incorporated in the Mk 1 system is another four-bay AN/UYK-7 computer and a comprehensive display system, the AN/UYA-4. On the basis of all this data, threat evaluation and weapon assignment processes are carried out so that the engagement decision can be taken.

STATUS

The lead Aegis cruiser *Ticonderoga*, CG-47, joined the fleet in January 1983 and *Yorktown*, CG-48, was to be commissioned in July 1984. CGs -49, *Vincennes*, has Aegis hardware installed, and CGs-50 to -56 Aegis systems are at various stages of manufacture and construction. In May 1984 RCA was authorised produce Aegis weapon systems for CGs-57, -58 and -59.

CONTRACTORS

Prime Contractor: RCA Government Systems, Moorestown (three major RCA divisions are engaged in the project).

FCS Mk 99, radar SPG-62 and SPY-1 high power transmitter: Raytheon Co.

AN/UYK-7 computers: Univac Divison of Sperry Rand.

Mk 26 launcher: Northern Ordnance Division, FMC Corporation.

SM-2 missile: General Dynamics Corporation, Pomona Division.

Computer software: Computer Sciences Corporation.

Technical advice to USN: The Johns Hopkins University, Applied Physics Laboratory.

Also more than 600 other suppliers.

3514.261

W-1200 SERIES FIRE CONTROL SYSTEMS

The W-1200 Series fire control systems are designed to control guns, missiles and defensive measures for fast patrol boats (FPBs) ranging in size from 60 tons up to 400 tons or more. Additional capability can be added to handle fire control requirements up to destroyer size ships.

The W-1200 Series systems have been optimised for FPB's offensive and defensive missions against air, surface and shore targets. Each system of the series is an integration of matched sensors, a versatile fire control computer and a display control console that has been organised for FPB operators. The elements of these systems are fully developed, off-the-shelf hardware. Each hardware element has been selected and integrated with interfacing to provide fire control based on boat size and requirements, enhanced target detection and acquisition, accurate tracking, and weapons direction. Each system provides operators with full and relevant target information. The systems feature quality performance, rapid data processing, high reliability, ease of maintenance, lightweight and rugged construction. Operation is straightforward, minimising the number of dedicated crew members required while sharply reducing the complexity and load of duties or tasks performed by operators. The W-1200 and W-1210 systems for FPBs up to 100 plus tons require one operator while the W-1220, -1230 and -1240 systems only require two operators.

STATUS

All components of the systems are currently operational on FPBs.

In late 1982, the W-160 pulse doppler monopulse radar replaced the W-120 as the principal tracking radar in the W-1200 Series of fire control systems.

CONTRACTOR

Westinghouse Electric Corporation, PO Box 1897, Baltimore, Maryland 21203, USA.

Systems of the Westinghouse W-1200 Fire Control Series

System	Sensors	Weapon Control	Application
W-1200	Navigation/search radar Optical director	One or more weapons, under computer-supported optical director or radar control, against an air, surface, or shore target.	FPBs from 30 to 60 tons with one or two powered gun mounts. Optical director is the primary fire control director.
W-1210	Navigation/search radar W-120 fire control radar	One or more weapons controlled by the W-120 against an air, surface, or shore target. One or more weapons controlled by search radar against a surface or shore target. System also directs chaff/flare launch.	Applies to FPBs from 60 to 100 plus tons with one to three powered gun mounts, and chaff-flare launchers. W-120 can direct weapons against a target of any type, particularly effective against small, fast, low fliers.
W-1220	Navigation/search radar W-120 fire control radar Optical director	One or more weapons under W-120 control, and one or two weapons under optical director control, thereby engaging two targets – air, surface, or shore. One or more weapons controlled by the search radar against surface or shore target. System also directs chaff/flare launch.	Applies to FPBs from 100 to 180 tons with one to three powered gun mounts and chaff-flare launchers. W-120 is the primary fire control director. Optical director supplements W-120 or enables divided fire.
W-1230	Navigation/search radar SPS-58 or W-611 air search radar W-120 fire control radar Optical director	One or more weapons under W-120 or W-160 control, and one or two weapons under optical director control, thereby engaging two targets – air, surface, or shore. One or more weapons controlled by the search radar against surface or shore target. System also directs chaff flare launch, and missile launch.	FPBs from 180 tons upward with one or more powered gun mounts, chaff flare launchers, and missile launchers. W-120 or W-160 and optical director split the fire control responsibility. SPS-58 or W-611 in MTI mode enables point defence against quick appearing, fast closing hostiles (pop-up threats).
W-1240	Navigation/search radar SPS-58 or W-611 air search radar W-120 fire control radar Optical director ESM equipment ECM equipment IFF	Same as W-1230 above, plus gun cueing during radar silence using ESM bearings, plus ECM jamming capability, plus IFF.	Same as W-1230 above.

NOTE: Later versions employ the pulse doppler monopulse W-160 tracking radar instead of the W-120.

DRONES AND RPVs

AUSTRALIA

2017.391
JINDIVIK

The Jindivik continues to be a standard weapons target in Australia and the United Kingdom. The total value of orders, including associated equipment, exceeds $A 81 million, of which export orders exceed $A 52 million.

CHARACTERISTICS
Mk 4A Version
Power plant: 1 Rolls Royce Viper Mk 201 turbojet engine
Systems: Non-regenerative pneumatic system using air stored in accumulator. Engine driven 9 kW 30 V generator, 24 V battery

Remote control: Aircraft controlled from ground station, aircraft performance telemetered to ground constantly
Take-off and landing: Take-off from trolley, landing on retractable skid. 1800 m runway required
Max payload: 250 kg
Max speed: 981 km/h (Mach 0·86) short or intermediate span. Mach 0·82 full extended span
Manoeuvre capability: 70° bank turn, 7 g pull-up
Rate of climb: 4570 m/minute at sea level
Service ceiling: 16 500 m (short span), 18 500 m (intermediate span), 19 500 m (full span)
Range with allowances: 1500 km (short span), 2000 km (intermediate span)

Typical endurance: 2 h
Auxiliary flight equipment: Tracking transponders, optical scoring system, radar or infra-red augmentation, radar or infra-red augmented recoverable towed targets, radar altimeter for low-level (16 m) operations
CONTRACTOR
Department of Defence Support, Canberra, Australia.

BRAZIL

4593.391
CBT BQM-1 BR RPV

The first indigenous remotely piloted vehicle to be produced by Brazilian industry, the BQM-1 BR, has been designed and built by the Aeronautical Division of CBT (Companhia Brasileira de Tratores). Flight trials began in late 1983.

The general configuration of the vehicle can be gathered from the accompanying three-view drawing. Other physical characteristics are tabulated below. The cantilever low wing monoplane RPV is of conventional all-metal construction. It is powered by a small centrifugal flow turbojet engine developed by the PMO Mechanics Division of the Brazilian Ministry of Aeronautics and built by CBT. The power plant is housed in a small nacelle above the fuselage, at the base of the fin.

The BQM-1 BR takes off under its own power using a tricycle undercarriage which is jettisoned when the RPV is airborne. Details of vehicle recovery have not been specified but possibilities may include a parachute descent after engine shut-down. Operational uses foreseen include aerial target for weapons training and tactical reconnaissance by means of sensors such as TV and IR imaging payloads. A civil role of crop dusting has also been suggested. A six-channel VHF FM radio command link with an operating range of about 20 km is provided for guidance and control.
CHARACTERISTICS
Length overall: 3·89 m
Fuselage length: 3·5 m
Wing span: 3·18 m

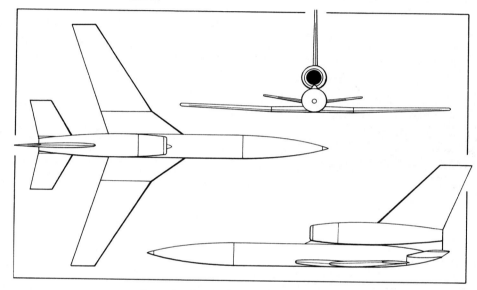

Three-view drawing Brazilian CBT BQM-1 BR RPV

Height overall: 1·28 m
Tailplane span: 1·1 m
Power plant: 300 N PMO/CBT Tietê turbojet
Max launch weight: 93 kg
Max speed: Mach 0·7 at 6100 m
Endurance: 45 minutes

STATUS
Development. Prototype flight trials timed for late 1983.
CONTRACTOR
CBT – Companhia Brasileira de Tratores, Caixa Postal 376, 13560, Sao Carlos, Sao Paulo, Brazil.

CANADA

2034.351
CANADAIR AN/USD-501 RECONNAISSANCE DRONE

This is a short-range battlefield reconnaissance drone for day and night surveillance and artillery target acquisition purposes. It is known as the Midge in British Army service. Configuration of the vehicle is apparent from the illustration and its dimensions are: length 260 cm (plus 113 cm launch booster), diameter 33 cm, and wing-span 94 cm. Straight and level speed is 400 knots (740 km/h) and range is up to 160 km.

The reconnaissance sensor equipment is carried in a sensor pack located midway between the wings and the forward control fins. The sensor pack is capable of rapid removal and replacement. Two versions are in use at present, the Carl Zeiss KRG 8/24 camera and the British Aerospace Dynamics IR linescan Type 201.

The AN/USD-501 is powered by a Williams WR2-6 single-stage turbojet which also drives an alternator giving electrical power during flight. Launching from a vehicle-mounted zero length launcher is assisted by a Bristol Aerojet Wagtail booster.

AN/USD-501 reconnaissance drone launch

OPERATION

After launch, the drone's subsequent flight path is pre-programmed and is maintained by DR navigation, aided by a propeller driven air-distance measuring unit, a directional gyro, and a vertical gyro. Height is controlled by reference to a barometric sensor. Operation of the reconnaissance sensor equipment is also pre-programmed, the results being recorded on film for rapid processing after the return of the drone. To the rear of the sensor pack, and on the upper side of the fuselage, is a flare pack containing 12 flares which are discharged under the control of a stepper switch. Normal operating height of the AN/USD-501 is between 300 and 1200 m above ground.

Recovery is assisted by a homing receiver working in conjunction with a beacon located at the recovery site. The drone may be equipped with a transponder of the user's choice to enable radar tracking for training flights during peace-time operations. Shutdown of the motor initiates parachute deployment and the drone is inverted to come to rest on a pair of air-inflated bags carried in containers in the upper part of the fuselage.

DEVELOPMENT

Development was initiated in 1959 by Canadair under the designation CL-89. In 1963 development contracts were awarded by Canada and the UK and the official designation of AN/USD-501 was allocated. In 1965 West Germany joined the programme, costs being shared equally between the three partners.

STATUS

The system is in service with the armies of Britain and West Germany, and will shortly enter service with the armies of France and Italy. A total of over 2200 flights have been made to date from the 600-plus drones supplied. User states see the system remaining in service through the 1990s. A product improvement programme is being developed by Canadair in conjunction with user countries.

A developed version designated AN/USD-502, and also known by the manufacturer's number CL-289, is the subject of a joint Canadian, French and West German programme (see **3238.351**).

CONTRACTOR

Canadair Ltd, PO Box 6087, Montreal, Quebec H3C 3G9, Canada.

3010.351

CL-227 (SENTINEL) RECONNAISSANCE AND TARGET ACQUISITION RPV

This is a medium-range remotely piloted vehicle (RPV) designed by Canadair Ltd to acquire surveillance and target acquisition data for army

Canadair CL-227 RPV undergoing test flight

brigade and division formations. It is also intended for use at sea from ships that are unable to carry conventional helicopters and can be operated tethered or untethered. It has a vertical take-off and landing capability and can provide real-time information from various types of electro-optical sensors such as TV, low-light level TV and thermal imaging systems. The range of interchangeable payload packages would include laser target designators. According to mission, it is possible that various electronic warfare sensor packages could be carried. It has a very low noise level and a low radar signature. The RPV, which flies itself, is directed from a mobile ground station manned by a flight controller and a sensor data observer/interpreter.

The configuration of the CL-227 is somewhat unusual and the vehicle resembles a dumb-bell, with its axis vertical. It consists of four sections, the upper and lower ones being of near spherical profile, while from each of the two inner sections a three-bladed rotor protrudes. These are contra-rotating and all aerodynamic control over the vehicle is by means of these rotors which can be actuated to provide lift, hover, and transit modes of flight. The upper end section houses the propulsion motor and fuel, while the lower unit contains the sensor package and other vehicle electronic systems.

CHARACTERISTICS

Height: 1·64 m

Max diameter: 64 cm

Weight: 154 kg

Payload: 37 kg (fuel); 31 kg (disposable)

Operating radius: Typically 50 km, but LOS limited

Mission endurance: 3 h

Flight speed: Hover to 130 km/h

Flight altitude: Sea level to 3000 m

STATUS

Full-scale development. First free flight in 1980, more than 400 flights performed by early 1983.

CONTRACTOR

Canadair Ltd, PO Box 6087, Montreal, Quebec H3C 3G9, Canada.

CHINA

4591.391

CHANGCHENG B-2 TARGET DRONE

The B-2 radio-controlled target drone produced by the Changcheng Scientific Instrumentation Factory was first revealed in public at the Guangchou Fair in 1982.

Constructed of lightweight glass-fibre reinforced plastic/honeycomb sandwich material, the B-2 has a rigid airframe of conventional configuration, as shown in the illustration. It can be launched from various surfaces using a zero-length launcher and rocket-assisted take-off.

Principal uses of the B-2 target drone are weapon system training and gunnery practice. For the second role two towed targets can be attached to the drone. Other devices which can be used include items that produce a realistic representation of descending paratroops. Additional roles can be accommodated to meet specific requirements.

The standard drone is equipped with a radio command guidance system and telemetry facilities operating in the HF and VHF bands respectively. The radio command guidance system operates in conjunction with the drone autopilot. The power plant is flat-four, two-stroke engine driving a two-bladed fixed pitch propellor.

CHARACTERISTICS

Length overall: 2·55 m

Wing span: 2·7 m

Height overall: 0·6 m

Power plant: 16 hp Huosai flat-four two stroke engine

Max launch weight: 56 kg

Fuel weight: 6 kg

Max level speed: 220 – 240 km/h at 1000 m

Endurance: 1 h

Max control range: 20 km

STATUS

In service.

Changcheng B-2 target drone on zero-length launcher

CONTRACTOR

Changcheng Scientific Instrumentation Factory, PO Box 2351, Beijing, People's Republic of China.

FRANCE

CT 20 target drone on zero length launcher

2125.391
AÉROSPATIALE CT 20

The CT 20 is a turbojet-powered radio-controlled target of medium performance, which can also be used as a tug for a towed target. It is standard equipment for training military units in the use of air-to-air and surface-to-air missiles, notably the Hawk, and over 1500 have been sold to French, Italian, Swedish, and other armed forces.

Three versions have been developed. TBA version: this model is capable of flight at an altitude of 30 m over water to simulate very low level attacks. Version IV: this variant can be flown between 150 and 14 000 m. Version XX: with about 20 per cent greater endurance than the IV type, this version takes off with its towed target initially stowed beneath its wings. The target is released in flight by a command from the ground and is then towed at a distance of 1200 m.

Derivatives of the CT 20 are the R 20 (**2127.351** in 1979–80 and earlier editions), and the M-20. The latter is an offensive missile specifically designed for ship launching. This was built for the Swedish Navy and was produced in Sweden as the RB-08 (**2366.221**).

CHARACTERISTICS
Length: 5·4 or 5·5 m
Wing span: 3·6 m
Take-off weight: 700 kg
Power plant: 1 Turboméca Marboré II or VI turbojet engine
Remote control: From ground or airborne station. Automatic descent in case of radio control failure

Take-off: From launching carriage powered by powder rockets on a zero length launcher. 7·4 g acceleration
Max speed: At 10 000 m, 900 km/h with Marboré II or 950 km/h with Marboré VI
Rate of climb: Time to 10 000 m, 6 minutes
Service ceiling: 12 000 or 15 000 m with Marboré II or VI
Endurance: Mean 60 minutes
Special features: Low altitude flight can be programmed down to about 100 m. A very low altitude version, the CT 20/TBA, has been developed with height control by a TRT AVH-6 radio altimeter. This permits operating heights down to 30 m. This model also incorporates different control and telemetry sub-systems. Drone can be used to tow various secondary targets with no more than 15% loss of performance.

The last-mentioned feature is important because of the difficulty of using piloted aircraft to tow targets for some modern weapons. It is the result of a joint development by Nord-Aviation and Dornier System GmbH.

STATUS
By the end of 1983 total CT 20 orders amounted to 1549, of which 306 were for export. Production continued in 1982. The successor to the CT 20, the C.22, is operational (**3239.351**).

CONTRACTOR
Aérospatiale, Division des Engins Tactiques, 2 rue Béranger, 92320-Chatillon Cedex, France.

3239.351
C.22 TARGET DRONE

The C.22 is a high-performance, subsonic aerial target, powered by a nacelle-mounted turbojet engine. It is designed for the testing of anti-aircraft weapons and for training air defence units armed with guns, surface-to-air missiles, or air-to-air missile systems. Sizeable dimensions, coupled with an extensive flight envelope and high manoeuvrability make it a realistic target capable of representing a sea-skimming anti-ship missile or a bomber at more than 12 000 m.

Generous compartments and external load hardpoints are provided in the C.22 to house up to 135 kg of special equipment for radar/IR enhancement, active or passive countermeasures, and recording equipment for the assessment of weapon effectiveness during training. It can be equipped for towing one or two tow targets, weighing up to 30 kg each.

Aérospatiale C.22 target drone

Plastic materials and lightweight aircraft techniques are extensively employed in construction of the C.22, which can be launched from the ground or ships by two jettisonable solid propellant rockets. Sustained flight is powered by a Microturbo TRI 60 turbojet of 350 kg thrust. Recovery, on land or sea, is by parachute. An integrated system, called TTL, provides tracking, remote control and telemetry transmission. This system is developed by LCT.

CHARACTERISTICS
Length: 5·25 m
Wing span: 2·5 m
Diameter: 40 cm (fuselage); 34 cm (engine nacelle)
Launch weight: 610 kg (max)
Weight, empty: 300 kg
Service ceiling: 14 000 m
Rate of climb: 5 minutes to 12 000 m
Endurance at 12 000 m: 2 h 30 minutes
Max speed: Mach 0·95
Minimum altitude: <15 m
Manoeuvrability: Over 6 g
STATUS
In development. 14 orders for production units have been signed by the French MoD for deliveries in 1984.
CONTRACTOR
Aérospatiale, Division des Engins Tactiques, 2 rue Béranger, 92320-Chatillon Cedex, France.

GERMANY (FEDERAL REPUBLIC)

3779.351
TUCAN MINI-RPV

The experimental mini-RPV system Tucan RT-900 is under development for the Federal Republic of Germany MoD for use in the evaluation of various payloads on board a safe, small aircraft for battlefield tasks such as reconnaissance, target location and other similar operational roles. The system has been designed with these requirements in mind and is characterised by the following features:

A flying wing configuration has been adopted, with a medium to high aspect ratio. A rear-mounted engine drives a pusher propeller and the fuselage is of modular glass-fibre construction for maximum payload flexibility and minimum radar cross-section. The Tucan mini-RPV carries an on-board autonomous navigation system, which in conjunction with a ground control station equipped with command facilities permits the vehicle to be guided to its target area which it then systematically covers in an autonomous search mode. The payload can comprise TV and/or IR camera/tracker sensors mounted on a stabilised platform, LTDS/rangefinder etc, as well as the command, telemetry and video data link equipment. The integrated high-resolution FLIR camera with remotely changeable optics and stabilised platform ensures accurate location of targets. This part of the payload is housed in the nose of the mini-RPV and is capable of forward, rearward, downward and side-looking operation.

Launch is by means of a booster rocket and Tucan takes to the air direct from a short ramp within its container/launcher unit, which also provides environmental protection and storage facilities. The drones are stored and transported in pairs in these containers which can be mounted on any type of vehicle. Recovery is by means of a parachute, assisted by an inflatable airbag to cushion the shock of landing.

In addition to the container/launch system and the maintenance/overhaul truck, there is a ground control and guidance station and a ground data

Tucan mini-RPV reconnaissance drone immediately after launch

KZO programme target acquisition RPV based on Tucan

terminal forming the overall Tucan system. Here the mini-RPV acquired data transmitted in real-time via a jamming-resistant data link are displayed on a TV screen. Information may also be transmitted from the battlefield for presentation to other centres or simultaneously to artillery batteries.

CHARACTERISTICS
Wing span: 3·3 m
Overall length: 2·055 m
Launch weight: 100–140 kg
Payload: 30–50 kg
Fuel: 15 litres
Operating altitude: 3000 m

STATUS

Development was started in 1978 and the first flight took place in November 1979. The experimental Tucan RT-900 is under development for the German Federal Government and the hardware forms a basis for an operational target acquisition and location RPV proposal to meet the KZO (Kleinfluggerat fur Zielortung) requirement.

MBB and Matra have agreed on a common system concept known as 'Brevel' with similar system characteristics and they have signed a memorandum of understanding with the objective of carrying out a co-operative programme in the event of a Franco/West German government contract.

Sensor testing for the Tucan programme began in 1983, and by early 1984 250 test flights had been made without loss (some with two-thirds scale models).

The Swedish MoD has selected MBB, with certain other companies, as the only European competitors for definition studies of an army reconnaissance RPV, 'UAV' (Unmanned Air Vehicle).

CONTRACTOR

MBB Marine and Special Products Division, Hünefeldstrasse 1-5, 2800 Bremen, Federal Republic of Germany.

4570.391

MBB-UM ATTACK DRONE (PAD)

MBB-UM (formerly VFW) continues the previous Locust mini-drone activities (see **3779.351** and **3166.351**, **3604.391**, **4037.391** and **4038.391** in 1983-84 and earlier editions) by directing them, and concentrating them towards a Combat Weapon System having as its two main tasks: anti-emitter (MHz and GHz bands), and anti-tank and similar battlefield roles.

The combat mini-drone was developed as a tailless, cruciform wing vehicle suitable for direct engagement of targets and consequently having high terminal phase accuracy at a high dive speed approach and broadly similar to a missile in design concept. A pre-requisite for such attacks is survival of the drone until the target is reached, and this is maximised in a number of ways; small size with low radar cross-section, minimal silhouette and small damage-sensitive surfaces; low-power engine with low IR and noise signatures; and a search phase flight altitude above the effective range of AA fire.

Launch of PAD expendable attack drone from experimental container

The attack drone dives at a steep angle on to its target. An integrated terminal guidance sensor directs the weapon with high accuracy, and the warhead is designed to destroy hardened targets. No details of the sensors available have been released but they can be expected to include passive IR homing and radar seeking types appropriate to the classes of target planned for PAD attack drones.

The anti-tank drones are operated in groups, 20 drones in a container can be made ready at one time. Such a container serves as a storage, transport, preparation and launch unit, it can be carried on any suitable truck, military or civil. Only a crew of two men are needed to launch 60 attack drones. A high launch rate is achieved through use of automatic launch sequence control, and only minimal prelaunch reconnaissance data input is required. Autonomous target acquisition and attack capability is complemented by a long-duration search phase and deep penetration features.

Launch is effected by a booster (zero length) which automatically detaches from the vehicle after burnout when the wings of the drone have unfolded after leaving the container. The container launch and vehicle flight characteristics, in particular the un-banked turns and steep dive, have been demonstrated in flight tests.

CHARACTERISTICS

Wing span: 2·26 m
Overall length: 1·81 m
Height: 1·03 m
Fuselage cross section: 0·26 m^2
Weight: 100 kg
Payload and fuel: 50 kg
Speed: 140 – 250 km/h

Locust mini-drone vehicle used in the MBB-UM attack drone (PAD) development programme

Cruise altitude: Up to 3000 m
Duration: Several hours

STATUS

Development project. This work apparently represents a continuation of the joint West German/US Locust programme of expendable combat mini-drone development (**4037.391** 1983-84 and earlier editions) which has now been suspended. The status of the various joint agreements between the West German and American concerns engaged in the original Locust programme has not been stated officially since its termination.

CONTRACTOR

MBB Marine and Special Products Division, Hünefeldstrasse 1-5, 2800 Bremen, Federal Republic of Germany.

3602.351

DORNIER MINI-DRONE/RPV

This is one of two designs competing under Federal Republic of Germany Defence Ministry contracts for a mini-RPV for use in a variety of roles which include: reconnaissance, target location, fire control, target simulation, and point target engagement. Tests have been in progress at the Meppen test establishment since October 1978, the first phase of flights being concerned with the concept of anti-radar mini-drone vehicle development. The Dornier Mini-Drone was also the basis of the joint Texas Instruments/Dornier proposal for the Locust harassment weapon system to be developed jointly by the Federal Republic of Germany and the USA. For test operations, the drones are launched from a catapult designed and built by Dornier and are remotely controlled in flight by a ground-based pilot. Landing is by means of a parachute and built-in shock absorption bags.

The airframe consists essentially of two fibreglass half-shells. The wing unit, integral with the fuselage, has elevons. The vertical tail unit carries the drogue parachute at the top. The keel protects the propeller during landing and also acts as a vertical tail surface. The payload compartment is of modular design and measures 600 mm in length and 200 mm in diameter. In the version with recovery system, the parachute container is in the fuselage centre, with the two fuel tanks to left and right of it. For one-way missions the parachute container can be replaced by an extra fuel tank to extend range, or by other equipment.

The propulsion system is a two-cylinder, two-stroke opposed cylinder engine with a power of 22 hp, fitted at the rear end and driving a pusher propeller.

For the reconnaissance and target acquisition and

Dornier mini-drone (Locust configuration)

Dornier mini-drone experimental vehicle

fire control missions the integration of a sensor package consisting of either a stabilised TV camera or a FLIR with autotrack facility coupled with a laser illuminator is under investigation.

Anti-radar missions and attacks on tanks/point targets are 'kamikaze' missions on which the vehicle homes on to and attacks the target out of a search flight, for example, using passive or active radar and/or IR seeker heads. For target demonstration missions, augmentation aids (such as smoke cartridges, flares or Luneberg lenses) can be integrated.

CHARACTERISTICS

Length: 2 m
Wing span: 2·1 m
Power plant: 22 hp 2-cylinder 2-stroke piston engine
Max launch weight: 70 kg

Payload: 15 kg
Max speed: 250 km/h (sea level)
Max operating height: 3000 m
Max endurance: 3 h

STATUS

Development. Flight tests were carried out at the Meppen Test Establishment in 1978. A proposal for the Locust harassment weapon system programme has been prepared jointly with Texas Instruments of the USA. Current concept-study and design activities are concentrating upon target location, anti-radar, and anti-tank (army combat) applications, taking advantage of available system analysis and flight testing results.

CONTRACTOR

Dornier GmbH, Postfach 1420, 7990 Friedrichshafen 1, Federal Republic of Germany.

3601.351

DORNIER EXPERIMENTAL SPÄHPLATTFORM

The Spähplattform is a small tethered rotor platform which needs no drive system. Its rotor is surrounded by a solid ring which, accelerated to a high speed on the ground, acts as an energy store and as a gyroscopic stabiliser. The stored energy is sufficient for a flight time of just over one minute, in which operating heights of 50 to 100 metres are reached. The Spähplattform was designed as a carrier system for optical and electro-optical reconnaissance sensors. The low range of these sensors requires their use close to the FEBA (forward edge of battle area), and their low weight permits a small, hard to detect carrier system which can be used in this area with good survivability.

The limited range of such a stand-off system is equalised by the advantage of low vulnerability, rapid availability, and low costs in comparison to penetrative reconnaissance systems.

As it is a small uncomplicated system the Spähplattform is suitable as a facility for overcoming the restricted visibility of the crews of armoured vehicles, whose sight in the immediate area is reduced mainly by vegetation and buildings.

The Spähplattform system consists of the flight unit with optical or electro-optical sensors, the tether-cable and the ground system with control and information processing devices. The ground system can be matched to the installation conditions of various vehicles.

The flight unit is characterised by very simple contruction. The momentum ring not only replaces a drive motor on the rotor platform, but also an attitude control for stabilisation in the roll and pitch axes, as it acts as a gyroscope.

Above the rotor plane, there is a platform for the sensor payload.

The tethering cable contains, in addition to signal lines, a coaxial cable for video transmission from the sensor to the ground station.

The ground equipment includes the rotor drive

Experimental Dornier Spähplattform flight unit

motor, the cable winch with winch motor, and the control, monitoring and analysis equipment. The first three components are installed in a container which also holds the flight unit during transport and which acts as start and landing platform during use of the Spähplattform. The drive power is supplied by the vehicle engine.

CHARACTERISTICS
(Experimental Flight Unit)
Rotor diameter: 1·2 m
Max rotor speed: 4000 rpm
Momentum ring mass: 20 kg
Empty mass: 30 kg
Payload: 5 kg
Total mass: 35 kg
Climb/descent speed: 5 m/s
Flight altitude: 50 – 1000 m

Flight time: 1 minute
Required drive output: 25 kW
Note: Operational systems may differ in data according to user specifications.
STATUS
Development undertaken by Dornier under private funding. Under government contract, the prototype is being integrated into a DB-Unimog vehicle, towing a two-wheel trailer. The Spähplattform has already been sucessfully flight tested in more than 400 flights.

In addition to stand-off reconnaissance, an untethered version of the Spähplattform is being examined as a sea-skimmer defence system which will operate from ship decks.
CONTRACTOR
Dornier GmbH, Postfach 1420, 7990 Friedrichs-hafen 1, Federal Republic of Germany.

3733.391

DORNIER Do 34 KIEBITZ

Dornier GmbH developed the tethered rotor platform Do 34 Kiebitz under a contract from the Federal German MoD as a carrier system for raising various sensors or transmitters up to 350 metres above the surface.

The rotor's twin blades are suspended on straps and driven by cold air expanded through the blade-tip nozzles. No torque which could act on the platform is produced with this drive principle.

The Kiebitz uses an Allison 250-C20B shaft engine, and air for the rotor blade drive system is supplied by a radial compressor. The turbine is installed on the slant, which makes for good positioning of the intake.

Dornier Kiebitz tethered rotor platform ascending from its parent vehicle at night

The payload compartment is located on the underside of the airframe, this arrangement enabling sensors to be changed quickly and affording space for a large volume radome. A cone-shaped airframe has been selected to reduce radar reflection.

The complete system is vehicle housed and consists of a landing platform, winch system, guidance and control post, flight vehicle and sensor, check-out system, fuel tank for 12 hour/operation, and auxiliary equipment. After arrival on site, the drone can be in position at an operational height of 350 metres in 25 minutes.

In the guidance and control system the determining factors here are the required wind speed of 14 m/s + 8 m/s, the available thrust reserves, and the requirements of the various sensors. These different factors led to a control system which aligns the Kiebitz according to airframe attitude and position in relation to the ground, a drift control system with the drift from the desired position being measured by an electromagnetic sensor. The flight vehicle's control and guidance system and the display and operating equipment in the ground station enable the Kiebitz to meet a wide variety of requirements as a sensor carrier.
SENSORS
A tethered rotor platform is basically suited for the following land and sea missions:
(1) reconnaissance and surveillance
(2) electronic warfare
(3) fire control
(4) telecommunications and data-transmission.

Within this wide spectrum of applications a number of specific sensors are under consideration and are being examined:
Battlefield Reconnaissance Radar: A bilateral agreement between West Germany and France has been signed to define, integrate, and test the battlefield reconnaissance system Argus (**1809.351**) which consists of the Kiebitz rotor-platform and an advanced version of the LCT Orphée Radar. In the meantime, the French Government has abandoned its participation in the Argus programme.

Passive Electronic Warfare Equipment: Operational trials have been carried out with the Dornier experimental Kiebitz and the Decca RDL-2 at Löwental airfield. The Decca RDL-2 consists of a high probability of interception display, automatic and visual pulse analysis, band and frequency measurement. During the trial a wide variety of radiating targets were detected and identified.

Naval Strike and Surveillance System – Sea-Kiebitz: The performance of current onboard missile guidance or target detection equipment on ships is severely limited by the height of masthead antennas. The strike range of medium range missile systems is therefore limited. This can be avoided by the use of Sea-Kiebitz, a combination of the Kiebitz rotor platform and the Ferranti Sea Spray Radar (**1342.353**), as a missile guidance and surveillance aid for FPBs and ships.

Low Flying Aircraft Detection Radar: Aircraft flying in the shadow of hills are detected too late by ground-based low-flying aircraft detection radars. The reaction time is too short to guarantee an effective defence. Due to its mission height of 350 metres the Kiebitz equipped with a suitable radar extends the range considerably.
CHARACTERISTICS
Dimensions, external
Diameter of rotor: 8·6 m
Height overall: 2·7 m
Body diameter of bottom edge: 1·05 m
Weight without tether and payload: 370 kg
Max payload to 300 m, ISA: 160 kg
Performance
Reel-in/reel-out speed: 3 m/s
Operational ceiling: 350 m
STATUS
After a test programme with the smaller Kiebitz test vehicle in the early 1970s, the first flights with prototypes of the operational Kiebitz started in February 1978. In March 1978, one of the two prototypes of the Do 34 Kiebitz rotor platform rose to a maximum flight altitude of over 300 m.

Integration of the Kiebitz carrier system and the

Orphée radar into the Argus battlefield reconnaissance system (**1809.351**) followed. Flight tests of Argus started in May 1979. By October 1981 170 flight hours with approximately 500 flight tests had been performed.

Current study activities are concentrated on an untethered version of Argus with a higher payload capability and a much higher operational ceiling.

CONTRACTOR

Dornier GmbH, Postfach 1420, 7990 Friedrichshafen 1, Federal Republic of Germany.

3734.391

DORNIER AERIAL TARGET SYSTEM (DATS III)

DATS III is a training system especially designed for air-to-air gunnery in the high subsonic speed range. DATS III consists of an expendable tow target, special aircraft equipment and ground support equipment. Major components include:

(1) Dornier tow target Do-SK10 A1 consisting of:
  (a) target body of three sandwich-constructed plastic fins attached to a central Y-beam also of plastic. The dart-shaped target is 5 metres long and has a span of 1·5 metres
  (b) radar reflector to improve the acquisition characteristics of the target
  (c) scoring sensor DS-SETA 1 which detects projectiles as they pass the target. The sensor signals are telemetered to a scoring unit in the towing aircraft. The sensor is part of the Dornier radar scoring system TASYLL
(2) aircraft equipment consisting of:
  (a) target launcher and reel assembly Do-TLU 3 which attaches the target to the aircraft and provides the functions necessary to deploy the target
  (b) scoring indicator unit DS-SUIT 1 which receives and processes the sensor signals and displays the results
(3) ground support equipment consisting of:
  (a) tow cable winding stand Do-WM 3 for winding the removable spools of the tow reel with tow cable

(b) scoring system test and ground station DS-BDPG 1 which is used primarily for testing the sensor and indicator unit but can also be used as a ground station for receiving and processing scoring results.

The airborne equipment of DATS III is compatible with, and the target can be towed by, several operational aircraft. The performance limits of DATS III when towed by the F-4 aircraft, for example, are altitudes of from sea level to 10 000 metres at speeds to Mach 0·9 (successful test flights indicate an upper limit of Mach 1·1) and g-loadings of +1g while attached to the launch unit and +5g in the towing configuration.

In addition to high speed and high g-loading capabilities, the DATS III airborne system meets all the requirements for modern air-to-air gunnery training such as: high visual and radar acquisition probability of the target; reliable and accurate scoring for high firing rates under severe environmental conditions; low foreign object damage danger to the firing aircraft in the event of target destruction. All target system components are of simple construction and can be handled easily and operated without the need for skilled personnel.

STATUS

Production.

CONTRACTOR

Dornier GmbH, Postfach 1420, 7990 Friedrichshafen 1, Federal Republic of Germany.

Tow target SK10 in towing configuration on an F-4 aircraft

4294.351

DORNIER EXPERIMENTAL MINI-TELECOPTER

Based on the experience with the unmanned mini-helicopter MTC 1, a more powerful prototype, the MTC II, has been developed by Dornier and, after integration of an appropriate payload, can be used for battlefield reconnaissance, target acquisition and fire control, mine detection, detection of NBC contaminated areas, communication link jamming and decoying anti-ship missiles. Unmanned mini-helicopters are particularly effective for many of these types of mission because of their hover, vertical take-off and landing capabilities.

The MTC was designed as a helicopter with coaxial contra-rotating rotors of identical basic torque. This means that a tail rotor can be omitted and the total engine power serves the rotor drive. Each rotor is of three-blade design to decrease vibration. The rotor blades are rectangular and made of a wood/glass-fibre composite. They are connected to the rotor hub by flapping hinges. Lag hinges are not necessary.

The rotors are driven by a two-cylinder, two-stroke engine producing 29·5 kW power via a single-stage coaxial angle gearbox. The connection between the gearbox and engine is a centrifugal clutch ensuring a no-delay separation in the event of engine failure and giving an auto-rotation capability. The MTC II is fully stabilised and also equipped with a yaw damping control. A spider landing skid supports the flight vehicle on the ground and when landing.

In the operational role the MTC II can be equipped with a mission payload of up to 60 kg. Maximum take-off weight is 190 kg and endurance is two hours. For battlefield reconnaissance and target acquisition missions a sensor package consisting of a stabilised TV camera (or FLIR) with autotrack capability coupled with a laser designator is the probable payload. Mine detection missions and missions for detecting contaminated areas require high resolution thermal imagers or special detectors. Appropriate jammers and decoy transmitters can be fitted for ECM flights.

CHARACTERISTICS

(Prototype MTC II)

Width: 0·8 m

Length: 1·5 m

Height: 1·15 m

Rotor diameter: 3·2 m

No. of blades: 2 × 3

Max take-off weight: 190 kg

Max payload: 60 kg

Power plant: 1 Hirth 028 276 RO3 E 40 hp

Max speed: 140 km/h

Note: Operational systems may differ in data according to user specifications.

STATUS

Flight testing of the MTC II commenced in March 1981 followed by mission-oriented concept studies.

CONTRACTOR

Dornier GmbH, Postfach 1420, 7990 Friedrichshafen 1, Federal Republic of Germany.

Dornier experimental mini-telecopter in flight

INTERNATIONAL

3238.351

AN/USD-502 (CL-289) RECONNAISSANCE DRONE

The AN/USD-502 surveillance drone is a follow-on project to the Canadair AN/USD-501 (**2034.351**) adopted by Canada, France, West Germany, Italy and the UK. The designers of the latter, Canadair, several years ago planned an improved performance version of the CL-89 (AN/USD-501), which was designated CL-289. Based on this concept, the AN/USD-502 emerged in July 1976 as a formal international project between Canada and West Germany when Canadair was awarded a $68·3 million contract for the design, development and test of an AN/USD-502 prototype, with Dornier of FRG as the main sub-contractor.

The CL-289 is equipped with a Zeiss reconnaissance camera and a SAT IR linescan sensor with real-time data transmission. The navigation/control system comprises a Canadian Marconi doppler sensor and a Dornier system airborne digital computer in which is stored the mission program which generates the command signals required for navigation, altitude control and sensor activation. A KHD turbojet engine gives the drone a high subsonic cruise speed; a solid-fuel booster is used to accelerate the drone off the launcher.

In March 1977 France joined the programme, with Société Anonyme de Télécommunications (SAT) as the French sub-contractor. The three governments are sharing the funding of the project. Successful flight trials by the contractor were completed in April 1981. Customer evaluation and troop trials began at the beginning of 1982 and were completed early in 1983. Production is expected to commence in 1986.

STATUS
The first successful test flight took place in March 1980. Development is continuing.

CONTRACTORS
Canadair Ltd, PO Box 6087, Montreal, Quebec H3C 3G9, Canada.

Dornier GmbH, Postfach 1420, 7990 Friedrichshafen 1, Federal Republic of Germany.

Société Anonyme de Télécommunications, 41 rue Cantagrel, 75624 Paris, France.

Launch sequence of Canadair CL-289 reconnaissance drone

1809.351
ARGUS SURVEILLANCE SYSTEM
In March 1974 the governments of the Federal Republic of Germany and France signed an agreement covering the joint production of a prototype of the Argus battlefield surveillance system. This system consists of a Kiebitz (**3733.391**) tethered rotor platform from Dornier GmbH, of Friedrichshafen, and the Orphée radar sensor from LCT (Laboratoire Central de Télécommunications), of Vélizy-Villacoublay.

Kiebitz experimental units have flown more than 100 hours on 900 flights at altitudes up to 200 metres. The continued development of the Kiebitz initiated by Dornier in August 1972 under a preliminary contract from the Federal German MoD forms the basis for the German share in the Argus system. The radar sensor installed on the Kiebitz rotor platform will be an advanced version of the Orphée radar developed and successfully tested by LCT in France over the past years under contract to the Délégation Ministérielle à

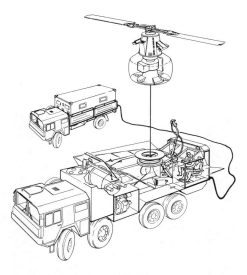

Arrangement of a typical Argus battlefield reconnaissance drone unit

l'Armement (Section d'Etudes et Fabrications des Télécommunications). A modernised version of Orphée (*observatoire radar porté par hélicoptère*) will be used. The original model was for installation in a Nord 510 helicopter but the project was allowed to lapse.

Apart from the tethered and remote-controlled Kiebitz rotor platform and the Orphée radar system, the complete Argus system consists of a mobile ground station and a tethering cable.

The ground station is housed in a container mounted on a ten-ton cross-country truck. The container is furnished with all the equipment required for transport purposes and for a 12-hour operation of the system (eg a measuring system for exact determination of the Kiebitz position and monitoring instruments).

If the radar sensor is raised to an altitude of at least 300 metres above ground, the Argus system can be used to detect, identify, and track vehicles over considerable distances. The Argus system thus makes a substantial contribution to surveillance of the battlefield in depth.

STATUS
The prime contract for the integration of this system and its testing was awarded to Dornier. Since the French government withdrew from the programme in September 1981, it is anticipated that Argus development will continue for the Federal German Army as a national programme.

Development work on Argus is running in parallel with Kiebitz development. Following completion of the system definition in December 1974, the LCT Orphée radar to be integrated with the Dornier platform is being developed under a French national development phase. On conclusion of Kiebitz flight tests, a functional mock-up of the radar was installed in the operational prototype of the rotor platform. Kiebitz, with a simulated radar payload, reached the specified operational height of 300 metres in March 1978, for the first time. During the following 12 months, the radar was integrated with the support system and tests were carried out on the ground and at low altitudes.

The first prototype of the Argus autonomous radar battlefield surveillance system reached the operational height of 300 metres in May 1979 when

Argus integration in progress with French Orphée II radar installed on Dornier Kiebitz Do 34 drone

radar data was transmitted to the ground station via the tethering cable. The LCT radar produces reconnaissance results, both static and moving targets, within the specified range. Successful test flights by the Argus prototype have shown in principle the operational feasibility of the overall systems, as a necessary requirement for the demonstration programme concluded in July 1979. Flight testing of the second, more advanced, prototype system started in September 1979.

Since 1980 the two prototype systems have been tested and troop-demonstrated on two different test ranges in West Germany. By October 1981 500 flights totalling 170 flight hours had been made.

CONTRACTORS
Dornier GmbH, Postfach 1420, 7990 Friedrichshafen 1, Federal Republic of Germany.

LCT (Laboratoire Central de Télécommunications), Vélizy-Villacoublay, France.

ISRAEL

3603.351
TADIRAN MASTIFF MINI-RPV Mk III
The Tadiran Mastiff Mk III is a mini-RPV of conventional miniature aircraft configuration, intended for use in reconnaissance, surveillance, target designation, artillery spotting roles and EW and communications relay missions. The 30 kg payload capacity permits a variety of sensors to be carried, including (in addition to other payloads) still or TV cameras mounted on gyro-stabilised gimbals.

High survivability is ensured by the small radar cross-section, negligible IR signature, low visibility and noise levels of the mini-RPV. All these factors make its detection by opposing forces extremely difficult. The mini-RPV generates 1 kW of electrical power, of which some 400 W are available for various payloads such as:
(1) a TV camera carried on stabilised gimbals operable in yaw (360°) and pitch (−88 to +5°) with remote control of both camera lens viewing angle and 1:10 zoom
(2) a TV camera on gimbals and miniature panoramic (mini-pan) film camera for detail photography
(3) various EW and ECM, or ESM packages
(4) certain other electro-optical (eg laser designator, mini-FLIR etc) payloads to suit specific missions.

The ground control station is housed in a standard S-280 type shelter which is normally carried on a

Interior view of ground control station showing operating consoles

Stabilised platform payload with TV camera

Ground control station for Mastiff Mk III is housed in standard S-280 shelter

2·5-ton military vehicle. The functions of this unit are mainly those of vehicle and payload control, RPV tracking, video and telemetry data reception, with mini-computer processing of received data and display for real-time or subsequent analysis. There is a portable control station that permits RPV take-off and landing at a site remote from the ground control station, and this is used when the latter is located in terrain unsuitable for launch and recovery and/or when extended mission range is required. A vehicle-mounted hydraulic launcher is available for assisted launch when a take-off strip cannot be found. A tail-hook and arrester wire are used for landing and retrieval.

CHARACTERISTICS
Length: 3·3 m
Wing span: 4·25 m
Wing area: 2·16 m²
Height: 80 cm

Power plant: 22 hp 2-cylinder 2-stroke piston engine
Max take-off weight: 115 kg
Mission payload: 30 kg
Fuel: 33 litres
Max level speed: 180 km/h (sea level)
Cruising speed: 90 – 130 km/h (typical)
Max rate of climb: 305 m/minute (sea level)
Max altitude: 3660 m
Range: 100 km
Endurance: >7 h
STATUS
Operational. Several hundred hours of flight have been conducted successfully since the Mastiff system was first offered on a commerical basis in 1978.

Mastiff Mk III mini-RPV

CONTRACTOR
Tadiran Ltd, 11 Ben-Gurion Street, Givat-Shmuel, POB 648, Tel Aviv 61006, Israel.

3736.391
SCOUT MINI-RPV
The IAI Scout is a miniature RPV designed to enable ground troops to control it for reconnaissance or surveillance missions, with minimum training requirements. To ensure this, the control system is organised so that the operator has merely to transmit flight-path demands to the RPV, such as changes in altitude or new headings, rather than using the link between RPV and ground station to convey signals for direct operation of the air vehicle's aerodynamic control surfaces. Instead, the demands transmitted to the air vehicle are fed to the autopilot which contains the necessary control logic to translate the demands into appropriate movements of the control surfaces. This method has an advantage over systems that rely on the ground operator being responsible for 'flying' the air vehicle by remote control; the latter technique requires almost continuous transmission from

ground to air via the command link, whereas the alternative employed in the Scout system requires transmission only when a fresh flight demand has to be passed to the air vehicle. This is clearly less vulnerable to countermeasures actions and offers the possibility of a single operator controlling more than one air vehicle.

The configuration of the Scout can be seen from the accompanying illustration. The Scout fuselage is constructed of composite materials and aluminium with a small radar signature. Launching is assisted by a catapult from a truck-mounted ramp. A transparent dome on the underside of the fuselage houses a gyro-stabilised TV camera equipped with a 1:15 ratio zoom lens and a panoramic camera. The pictures obtained are relayed back to the ground station by data link for real-time display, and it is assumed that the operator has some remote control over the camera. For

recovery the Scout is flown into a net set up at the ground station.
CHARACTERISTICS
Engine: 2-cylinder 22 hp
Wing span: 4·96 m (with wing extension)
Length: 3·68 m
Launch weight: 139 kg (fuel: 24 kg, payload: up to 30 kg)
Max speed: 157 km/h
Economical cruise speed: 100 km/h
Max altitude: 3000 m
Endurance: 7 h (approx at economical cruise speed)
STATUS
Operational with the Israeli Armed Services, and delivered to a number of foreign customers.
CONTRACTOR
Israel Aircraft Industries Ltd, Ben Gurion International Airport, Israel.

Scout RPV on truck-mounted launch ramp. Note also control vehicle on right and relay antennas near tents in background

Internal arrangement of Scout RPV control vehicle showing operator postions

ITALY

3199.391
ANDROMEDA RPV SYSTEM
The Andromeda RPV system is the result of considerable study and developmental work carried out by Meteor in relation to evolving a multi-role system capable of meeting most battlefield and training functions for land, sea and air forces. This is achieved by means of a range of unmanned aircraft which can be operated in conjunction with a self-contained mobile ground support and control system. The latter was described in some detail in the 1977 edition of *Jane's Weapon Systems*.

The overall Andromeda system is composed of the following sub-systems:
(1) the ground station for control of the RPV mission by the crew
(2) equipments for launch, recovery and maintenance of the RPV aircraft
(3) equipments for the preparation, recovery and maintenance, and operation and/or checkout of the payload and/or the data collected
(4) the RPV aircraft. This sub-system comprises a range of five vehicle types (see table) configured to specific operational roles.

The Meteor range of vehicles is known by the name Mirach and a suffix number to denote model/role. The manufacturers state that the Andromeda system may be used with other vehicles.
CONTRACTOR
Meteor, Costruzioni Aeronautiche ed Elettroniche SpA, 146 Via Nomentana, 00612 Rome, Italy.

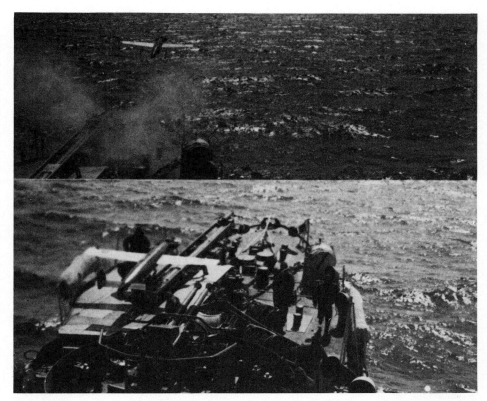

Launch at sea of Mirach 70 RPV

Recently Meteor has given special attention to weapons-related applications of the Mirach range of RPVs. The Mirach 100 in particular has been flown in a variety of air-launched roles which include reconnaissance, with the RPV carried on both fixed-wing aircraft and helicopters. Agusta 109 helicopter carries two Mirach 100 RPVs as shown here

ANDROMEDA SYSTEM FLIGHT VEHICLES

Designation	Mission	Agency	Overall length (m) less booster	Overall span (m) wings or fins	Body diameter (cm)	Launch weight (kg) less booster	Powerplant	Guidance Type	Performance Max speed	Endurance	Remarks
MIRACH 20	RPV: target acquisition, location, designation, surveillance, saturation enemy defences	Italian Army and export	3·6	3·8	35	150	1 × DYAD 26 hp	R/C	200 km/h	240 minutes	Real-time TV, photo and IR reconnaissance, laser designator
MIRACH 70	Target/RPV: surveillance, target acquisition, EW, decoy saturation	Italian Navy and export	3·55	3·53	39	237	1 × McCulloch 70 hp	R/C	310 km/h	60 minutes	Various training payloads, war mission: int payload 20 kg ext payload 10 kg
MIRACH 100	Target/RPV: surveillance, reconnaissance, acquisition, location, designation, EW, strike, saturation	Italian Air Force and export	4·32	1·8	38	280	1 × TRS 18 115 kg	R/C P/P	860 km/h	60 minutes	Various training payloads, war mission: int payload 40 kg ext payload 14 kg
MIRACH 300	Target/RPV: surveillance, reconnaissance, acquisition, location, designation, EW, strike, saturation	Export	6	2·80	52	390	1 × TRS 60 340 kg	R/C P/P	Mach 0·9	60 minutes	Various training payloads, war mission: int payload 80 kg ext payload 70 kg
MIRACH 600	RPV: area reconnaissance, EW, strike, defence suppression	Development	7·81	4·1	77	120	2 × TRS 60 680 kg total	R/C P/P	Mach 0·9	80 minutes	int payload 500 kg ext payload 100 kg

R/C Radio command
P/P Programmed with real-time updating

JAPAN

4295.351
MINI-RPV RESEARCH TEST VEHICLE

A recent development by Fuji Heavy Industries is a mini-RPV research test vehicle. Very little information is currently available but the vehicle appears to be designed to carry out various missions such as battlefield surveillance and carries a pre-programmed TV camera.

CHARACTERISTICS
Length: 2·2 m
Span: 3·8 m
Weight: 89·8 kg
Engine: 18 hp (13·5 kW) DH Enterprises Dyad 220
Speed: 222 km/h
Endurance: 1 h

STATUS
A vehicle was delivered to the Japanese Defence Agency in December 1980.
CONTRACTOR
Fuji Heavy Industries Ltd, Japan.

SOUTH AFRICA

4595.391
EYRIE MINI-RPV

The Eyrie is a multi-purpose mini-RPV designed to fulfil a variety of potential battlefield roles such as reconnaissance, surveillance, electronic warfare and artillery adjustment as well as fleet surveillance and communications relay. The vehicle is a South African project carried out by National Dynamics as a private venture.

The Eyrie is of modular design and the rather unusual Warren-Young rhomboidal wing configuration has been adopted, among other reasons, for its non-stalling and spinning flying characteristics. It is also rugged and has low observable signatures (radar, IR, noise). Construction is from precision moulds, the wing being of composite structure with a Kevlar skin and rigid PVC foam core. The main fuselage is integral with the wing, and the nose-cone houses the video and other electronic equipment.

The Eyrie is powered by a four-cylinder two-stroke engine that drives a four-bladed pusher propellor mounted in an annular duct. A zero-length pneumatic launcher is used with recovery by means of a catch net/cage that incorporates an impact pad in a single unit. The main part of flight control is under the management of the ground 'pilot'/flight controller using a console in the mobile ground control station (MGCS), assisted by an autopilot in the RPV that provides automatic stabilisation in the vehicle's lateral plane. The autopilot function can be overridden at the flight controller's discretion.

The payload includes two TV cameras, one fixed forward looking for navigation and strike applications, and one side-looking with pan and tilt facilities for target identification. The mobile ground station complete with two flight vehicles, MGCS container, launch and recovery sub-systems, power and maintenance supplies can be loaded into four military trucks and may be air-lifted in two Transall C-160 aircraft.

CHARACTERISTICS
Length overall: 3·43 m
Wing span: 4·27 m
Height overall: 1·09 m
Fuselage diameter: 0·63 m (max)
Power plant: 570 cc Konig four-cylinder two-stroke engine
Weights: 66 kg (empty); 159 kg (max launch)
Max level speed: 222 km/h
Endurance: Over 6 hours
STATUS
Several prototypes have been produced but no contract details have been disclosed.
CONTRACTOR
National Dynamics (Pty) Ltd, 813 Permanent Buildings, Smith Street, Durban 4000, Republic of South Africa.

Operational version of National Dynamics Eyrie mini-RPV

UNITED KINGDOM

3645.351
STABILEYE MINI-RPV

Stabileye was designed as a mini-RPV for use in research programmes into a variety of battlefield roles such as reconnaissance and target location etc. A number of experimental payloads have been carried, including a BAe Dynamics IR linescan system. The prototype Stabileye (serial number 30) first flew in September 1980, and nine more vehicles were ordered by the UK MoD for use in a flight trials programme to evaluate the potential of RPVs and various payload/sensor combinations in a battlefield context.

These nine RPVs, ordered in December 1981, and later vehicles were known as Mk 1 and Mk 2 models, and the current version is the Mk 3, but Mk numbers have now been discontinued and the latest version is known as the BAe Stabileye.

The vehicle is configured as a high wing monoplane with constant chord wings supporting a rectangular cross-section fuselage and a twin-boom mounted tail assembly consisting of a tailplane, single fin and rudder. A hinged top to the fuselage provides access to the payload space, and the power plant is mounted at the rear end of the fuselage, driving a pusher propeller. The wings are of foam core

BAe Stabileye mini-RPV in flight

construction and are equipped with conventional ailerons. The power plant is a 25 hp two-cylinder, two-stroke Weslake Type 342 engine with a two-bladed airscrew.
OPERATION
Stabileye is launched from a pneumatic catapault, and recovery is by means of a parachute assisted by an air bag inflated beneath the fuselage to cushion the vehicle against impact with the ground on landing. In the event of contact with the RPV being lost, the parachute and airbag are deployed automatically as a safety precaution to terminate the flight. Parachute release automatically switches off the engine and initiates air bag inflation.

Guidance and control from the ground is by means of a radio telecommand link. The RPV is tracked by radar and other ground equipment includes a plotter unit that shows the position of the vehicle relative to a map of the area of interest and a TV screen on which the view from the Stabileye is displayed in real-time. The on-board flight control system interfaces with the pulse code modulation (PCM) telecommand system, and includes flight control electronics, vertical and yaw rate gyros, magnetometer, telemetry encoder and command receiver/decoder.

CHARACTERISTICS
Length: 2·87 m
Wing span: 3·65 m
Weight: 82 kg
Payload: 25 kg
Cruising speed: 96 – 180 km/h
Duration: 4 h
STATUS
The prototype Stabileye first flew in September 1980. Nine more RPVs were ordered for the UK MoD in December 1981. These are still used for flight trials and a further order for eight more vehicles was announced in May 1983. Another vehicle was later added to this order. In January 1984 construction of a new batch for an unnamed customer had commenced.
British Aerospace Dynamics Group, Filton House, Bristol BS99 7AR, England.

4476.391
THORN-EMI ARGUS UMA

THORN-EMI Electronics Ltd has designed a series of unmanned aircraft known as Argus which are intended for such battlefield applications as covert surveillance and target designation. Features emphasised by the manufacturer as being particularly appropriate for these types of role are the use of electrical propulsion and a number of supplementary benefits associated with propeller(s) driven by electric motor(s). The configuration is that of a conventional small high-wing monoplane aircraft with single tail fin and rudder assembly and a lightweight tricycle undercarriage. A high energy lithium/sulphur-dioxide battery is carried aboard the unmanned aircraft to drive one or two electric motors which power either a single propeller or contra-rotating twin propellers. This form of propulsion it is claimed makes Argus drones virtually inaudible at altitudes of more than 300 m, and low vibration levels make the vehicle an ideal platform for sensors such as cameras or laser target markers. Other characteristics are listed in the nearby table, which also gives performance details and the various sizes of payload compartments provided. It should be noted that Argus II parameters are provisional only.

Specific operational functions envisaged for Argus vehicles disclosed by the manufacturer include: target designation, use as a harassment drone, covert surveillance, illumination, decoy roles, ELINT, store delivery, anti-armour missions, and scanning by IR and/or UV sensors.

STATUS
Project.
CONTRACTOR
THORN-EMI Electronics Ltd, Victoria Road, Feltham, Middx TW13 7DZ, England.

CHARACTERISTICS

	Argus I Mk III	Argus II Mk II
Payload	5 kg	10 kg
Range (max payload)	35 km	51 km
Duration (max payload)	40 minutes	55 minutes
Speed (max payload)	20 m/s (72 km/h)	20 m/s (72 km/h)
Power plant	single electric motor and propeller	2 electric motors contra-rotating propeller
Payload bay dimensions	480 × 120 × 80 mm (amidships)	165 × 165 mm (nose-mounted)

3315.391
FLIGHT REFUELLING TARGETS

Flight Refuelling Ltd has produced pilotless drones and target systems of a wide variety for many years. Its Rushton targets provide an airborne system which, in terms of altitude, air speed and tow length (up to 7·5 miles/12 km) cater for the needs of all types of modern air-to-air and surface-to-air weapons. Sleeve type targets for use with the older conventional weapons are also available. The Rushton target can be towed supersonically and incorporates radar, visual and IR enhancement devices together with facilities for miss-distance measurement. It is made up of easily put together sections and thus by selecting the appropriate modules can be quickly assembled to meet a variety of weapons requirements.

Rushton low-level height-keeping target

To augment this proven system, the Rushton LL height-keeping target has been introduced to simulate sea-skimming missiles' attacks to provide training for a variety of weapon systems. The target provides a facility to 'fly' over a range of pre-set heights from 500 feet (150 metres) down to 15 feet (4·5 metres) above sea level and is designed to give a height keeping accuracy of within ±7 feet (2·1 metres). It is equipped with radar and visual augmentation, an infra-red output and MDI.

Seaflash

The Seaflash radio-controlled surface target has been manufactured to enable the Royal Navy and other services to carry out practice firings against high-speed surface targets and to simulate fast patrol boat attacks.

Seaflash has been in service with the Royal Navy since 1973 and provides a realistic target for surface-to-surface and air-to-surface practice with conventional or guided weapons. The hull is a deep V design, constructed in glass-reinforced plastics and fitted out to withstand hard usage under service trials

Rushton Height Keeping Towed Target maintains stable level flight at heights between 150 and 4·5 metres to simulate anti-ship missiles

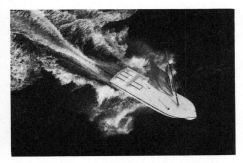

Seaflash radio controlled marine target is designed for training with ships' guns, coastal artillery and air-to-surface weapons

conditions. The size of the boat enables it to be carried aboard fighting ships during exercises.

Seaflash has many features which render it efficient and economical as a surface target-training system. The following features have been found to be especially advantageous:

(1) facilities are provided to enable the boat to be fully tested with a crew aboard, in preparation for unmanned operation

(2) built-in buoyancy is provided to prevent the boat from sinking in the event of minor shrapnel damage, during firing trials

(3) reserve electrical power and adequate stowage space is available for specialised instrumentation and equipment, as required for weapon evaluation trials

(4) the control equipment is on a modular basis for ease of maintenance at sea

(5) an attack by a flotilla of fast patrol boats can be simulated by operating several Seaflash targets simultaneously

(6) visual enhancement of a Seaflash is achieved by fitting a large target flag. The targets can be controlled either from an accompanying vessel or from a helicopter.

CHARACTERISTICS
Length overall: 8·99 m
Max beam: 2·21 m
Height from waterline to command antenna (erected): 5·79 m
Weight (approx): 1800 kg
Engine: Mercruiser Type 470 or Volvo Penta
Speed, max: In excess of 30 knots
Operational endurance: 8 h
Control range: 20 000 m (dependent on height of transmitting antenna)
CONTRACTOR
Flight Refuelling Limited, Wimborne, Dorset BH21 2BJ, England.

4569.391
RAVEN MINI-RPV

The Flight Refuelling Ltd Raven system is designed to provide at low cost an RPV surveillance system capable of producing real-time TV imagery and a collection of still photographs in daylight, and also offer a means of evaluating alternative payloads and operational roles. Although not designed initially as a hardened military tactical system, it includes the primary elements of such a system (eg launcher, air vehicle, navigation system, payload management, telecommand etc), and could form the basis of military systems in the future.

The Raven air vehicle configuration can be seen from the nearby illustration. It is a small mini-RPV with an all-up weight of about 15 kg (see table for detailed characteristics), with a standard payload that comprises a video camera and a down-link transmitter for the return of reconnaissance/target data. Constant chord wings constructed of foam cored glass-fibre and obeche support a glass-fibre fuselage. This contains the payload compartment, which has a transparent camera window in the nose and downward-viewing panels for the still camera; the autopilot and radio equipment; fuel tank; and has a Webra 91 15 cc two-stroke engine driving a pusher propeller mounted at the rear. The high-T tail assembly is carried on a tubular boom structure extending from the underside of the fuselage.

The air vehicle is launched from a special trailer equipped with a folding launch rail and compartments for transporting two mini-drones in partially dismantled form. The launch is powered by elastic cord in which energy is stored by means of an irreversible hand-operated winch. Recovery is effected by an arrester net which can also be dismantled for transport. A recovery video camera is mounted behind the recovery net and aligned with the glide-slope so that the vehicle can be manually controlled into the net.

In addition to the Raven air vehicle and its launch and transportation trailer, the complete system comprises: a ground control module capable of controlling and guiding two Raven mini-RPVs, displaying and recording TV imagery and other data telemetered from air to ground; two generators (1 kW and 2 kW) to provide electrical power for all ground units; and a tracking radar unit. The radar unit, normally a Plessey WF3 equipment, provides range, bearing and elevation data for interfacing with the ground station computer. The latter generates automated commands for transmission to the air vehicle. The control module may be a separate module carried on a suitable flat bed truck, or integrated within another suitable vehicle. The radar antenna would normally be transported from site to site in a second vehicle.

OPERATION

A typical mission is illustrated in diagrammatic form nearby, and the following description should be read in conjunction with the illustration. With the ground station set up and the computer initialised with the datum co-ordinates of the radar tracker, requests for RPV missions are received via normal military communications links. While the air vehicle(s) are unpacked from the transport trailer and prepared for launch, the mission requests are assembled into a flight plan and inserted into the computer as a series of waypoints. These are presented on the VDU so that the operator may assess and amend the complete mission, aided by a full simulation if necessary or desired. Alternatively, it is possible to proceed direct to the planned mission on receipt of instructions from the mission controller.

Launch is generally into wind with the first waypoint up wind from the launcher, thus enabling the vehicle to climb to a suitable height before turning onto course. During flight, the ground computer continuously compares the radar position of the air vehicle with the required track and issues the

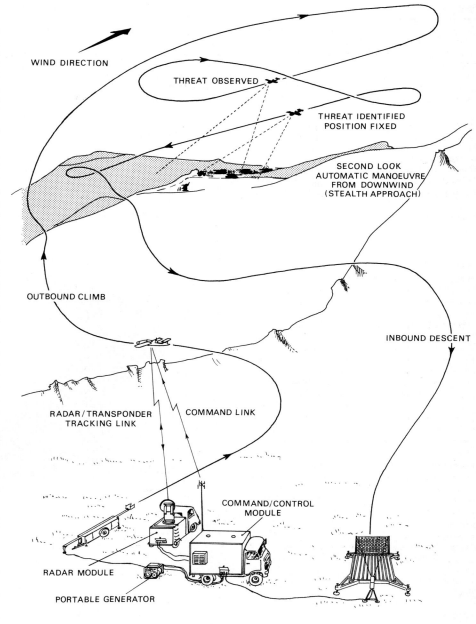

Typical Raven mission

Designed as a mini-RPV for target and surveillance roles, Raven is the latest in the FR family of RPVs

necessary commands to reduce cross-track errors to zero. Demanded rates of turn are proportional to cross-track error so that the Raven will be stabilised on track, heading into wind by the amount needed to offset the cross-wind vector. Aerodynamic trim errors which could result in angular accelerations, and hence constant cross-track errors, are compensated for. The track made good is continuously displayed on the ground station map plotter. The on-board TV system can be switched on or off on command from the ground and imagery displayed in real-time on the ground control module monitor and/or recorded on the video recorder as required.

Normally the still film camera is triggered automatically when a pre-designated point is reached, but film can be exposed at will, either semi-automatically with the operator inserting the location as a map reference, or by directing the vehicle under manual control by reference to the TV monitor display. A 'Return' command automatically modifies the program, by inserting additional waypoints to allow re-examination of a location that has just been overflown. The program data may be changed during flight and new waypoints entered or old ones deleted as necessary. At any time the vehicle can be commanded to descend automatically into wind towards a waypoint, to maximise the TV viewing time and to improve image resolution. This approach also minimises the acoustic signature. Several guidance options are available to the controller in the event of

equipment failure during a mission: if, for instance, the radar tracker or any part of that system should fail, the air vehicle can be commanded to turn onto a homing course calculated by the computer. In this event, progress can be monitored by the TV link and when within visual range manual control can be resumed to recovery.

CHARACTERISTICS
Wing span: 2·7 m
Length: 2·1 m
Height: 0·5 m (over prop)
Launch weight: 15 kg (typical)
Max fuel: 1·5 litres
Endurance: 80 mins at 88 km/h TAS
Max operating altitude: 2500 m
Speed range: 74 – 126 km/h
Stall speed: 46 km/h
Range: Over 100 km
Typical payload: 2·5 kg
Power plant: Webra 91 15 cc two-stroke engine
Autopilot: Skyleader, with Skyleader SRC-4 servos
Telecommand: PCM digital
Radar transponder: Plessey WF3 (X-band)
Computer: HP.86 or equivalent
Tracking radar: Plessey WF3
STATUS
Development project.
CONTRACTOR
Flight Refuelling Limited, Wimborne, Dorset BH21 2BJ, England.

4296.391
AEL SNIPE TARGET DRONES
AEL 4111 Snipe Mk II

Snipe Mk II is a development of the earlier Mk I and differs from Streek (**4297.391**) in that it is intended for use with large calibre weapon systems and ammunition (20 to 40 mm), and man-portable surface-to-air missiles.

The ground support equipment comprises a self-contained trailer unit which carries the launcher, special tools, first and second line spares back-up and is designed to be towed by a Land-Rover or similar vehicle. The launcher is a catapult powered by powerful rubber bungees, requiring no maintenance, and is highly reliable.

Snipe can be flown empty or with a variety of payloads such as radar enhancement, autopilot or smoke/IR enhancement to suit training needs.

CHARACTERISTICS
Wing span: 2·44 m
Length: 2·1 m
Weight: 19 kg
Engine: 100 cc 2-stroke with electronic ignition
Fuel: 20:1 petrol/oil mixture
Duration: 35 minutes
Max level speed: 209 km/h
Max range: Up to 15 km with autopilot and radar. Depending upon visibility – 2 km by eye, 3·5 km with binoculars
Construction: Wood veneer over polystyrene foam core

AEL 4700 Snipe Mk III

The latest addition to the AEL family is now available and has been developed using the experience gained from operating the Mk II target which is in service with 12 armed forces world-wide. The Mk III has been designed to be used with and to meet the target requirements for large calibre air defence and medium range missiles. The Mk III is considerably larger, faster and more representative in physical shape to a modern fighter than the Mk II.

The add-on capability of the autopilot gives the Snipe Mk III an out-of-sight capability up to 15 km, thus satisfying the range requirements of the medium range weapon system. When fitted with the standard low-cost command link, the target still provides an acceptable and economical target for 20 to 57 mm calibre guns and man-portable missiles and is compatible with the Mk II target ground equipment.

System reaction time is very short. A target can be prepared and launched within 15 minutes of the crew arriving and the average turn-round time between sorties is less than ten minutes. Target recovery is by normal belly-landing, if sufficient space is available (a clear area of 600 m diameter), or by parachute.

The built-in fail-safe mechanism ensures that under conditions of lost command signal, severe interference, loss of main power or destruction of the receiver, the engine will be stopped and the parachute deployed automatically.

CHARACTERISTICS
Wing span: 3·14 m
Length: 2·5 m
Engine: 342 cc 2-stroke with electronic ignition
Fuel: 25:1 petrol/oil mixture
Average duration: 1 h
Max service speed: >150 knots
Construction: GRP fuselage, foam core with marine quality ply covering wing

The following points are common to both the Snipe Mk II and Mk III.
Command link: Rugged VHF or UHF transmitter/receiver crystalled to customer requirements. Transmitter power 9·6 V at 1·2 Ah rechargeable. RF output 1 W. Receiver power 6 V at 1·2 Ah rechargeable. High power system available for long range operations
Fail-safe: Receiver has 2 built-in fail-safe devices. If transmitter fails engine will shut down after 1½ s and emergency parachute will be deployed. If there is a power failure or receiver malfunction an independent

auxiliary power supply automatically operates the same fail-safe sequence
Ground support trailer/launcher
Length: 5·18 m including draw-bar
Width: 1·79 m
Height: 1·75 m
Body cube size: 3·048 × 1·79 × 1·07 m
Weight: Approx 1 ton (1000 kg)
The trailer will carry 2 aircraft, all control equipment, spares and tools for extended operation. Construction is on a steel chassis with Avon-ride suspension units matched to Land-Rover track
45 second smoke
Method of attachment: 4 in wing-tip pods
Colour: Red, orange, blue
Firing method: Individually on command from operator
Ignition system: Electrical
25 second IR flares
Attachment: 2 in wing-tip pods (Mk II); rear-mounted cluster (Mk III)
Wavelength: To customer requirement
Bandwidth: To customer requirement
Method of firing: Individually on command from operator
Ignition system: Electrical

A variety of corner reflectors and/or Luneberg lens are available according to requirements. Both Snipe versions are suitable for use with the SAAB-Scania BT39 or Weston Simflak training simulator systems, if required.
STATUS
Both versions of the AEL Snipe are in current production.
CONTRACTOR
AEL (RPV) Limited, Gatwick House, Horley, Surrey RH6 9SU, England.

4297.391
AEL STREEK TARGET DRONE

The AEL Streek was developed to meet a requirement for a low-cost, rugged aerial target for use with small arms and machine guns used in air defence roles. It is highly manoeuvrable and simulates accurately attack profiles flown by ground attack aircraft, giving scale speed, range and angular rates of change.

The 10 cc Glo-fuel engine needs little attention and is easy to start. The target drone is hand-launched by the operator and once airborne is relatively easy to fly, even for a novice. Radio control equipment is rugged and temperature stable. Recovery is by belly-landing on any reasonably level terrain.

AEL Streek, apart from being an all-arms air defence target, is also used as the basic training

aircraft for students working with the larger and faster AEL Snipe Mk II target drone (**4296.391**). Flying characteristics for both drones are similar and after graduating on Streek students change easily to Snipe. All radio equipment is interchangeable between Streek and Snipe.
CHARACTERISTICS
Wing span: 1·7 m
Length: 1·385 m
Weight: 2·7 kg
Engine: Glo-fuel 10 cc
Power: 1·2 bhp
Duration: 20 minutes
Max speed: 140 km/h
Construction: GRP fuselage, veneered polystyrene wing
Fuel: Methanol/castor oil 4:1
Command link: Rugged VHF or UHF transmitter, crystallised to customer specification. Transmitter power 9·6 V at 1·2 Ah, rechargeable. RF output 1 W. Receiver power 6 V at 1·2 Ah rechargeable
The ground support equipment comprises a GRP box, incorporating a fuel container (2·5 litre), electric fuel pump, electric engine starter, ammeter, 12 V battery to power equipment and a selection of hand tools.
STATUS
In current production.
CONTRACTOR
AEL (RPV) Limited, Gatwick House, Horley, Surrey RH6 9SU, England.

AEL Streek target drone on launcher

3730.391
SKEET TARGET DRONE

Skeet is a compact, highly-manoeuvrable, radio-controlled aerial target for use in both target tracking and practice firings of close-range missiles and guns. The drone's 2·7 m long square-section fuselage is constructed of metal and glass-fibre and contains compartments for engine, recovery parachute, fuel, batteries and electronics. Its wings, fin and tailplane are constructed of fibreglass filled with polyurethane foam. Wing span is 3·35 m. Sixteen smoke flares for visual enhancement are carried in the landing skid

and underwing pods may be fitted for customer's optional equipment. The radar returns are enhanced by a reflector mounted in the fuselage.

The aircraft is launched from a simple pneumatically-operated launcher which has an integral two-wheel running gear for easy handling and towing, and carries compressed air storage capacity for eight launches. Launching and flight can be carried out in crosswinds of up to 25 knots.

Operation is by radio-command in the 68 MHz band, using four information channels to control

pitch, roll, throttle, stabilisation trim, height-hold and visual enhancement. Height-hold uses a simple barometric device to maintain the aircraft at the desired altitude. A visual control sight with binoculars is provided to assist the pilot in visually flying the drone over 5 km range and to enable repeat flight-paths to be flown. Recovery is by parachute or by conventional landing, utilising the fuselage underbody fairing as a skid. The parachute is deployed either by pilot demand or automatically in the event of engine, power supply or radio failure.

The target drone can be operated from land or on board ship and maintenance is minimal, being limited normally to refuelling, replacement of batteries, parachute and flares, and checks of the various control and ground equipment. Skeet is powered by a twin-cylinder 274 cc engine and has an endurance of 75 minutes at its maximum speed of 130 knots.

CHARACTERISTICS
Length: 2·72 m (including miss-distance antenna system)
Span: 3·35 m
Weight: 63 kg
Max speed: 130 knots
Endurance: 75 minutes

STATUS
Skeet is now in service with the British Army as well as with overseas customers.
CONTRACTOR
Short Brothers Ltd, Montgomery Road, Belfast BT6 9HN, Northern Ireland.

Skeet target drone on towed pneumatic launcher

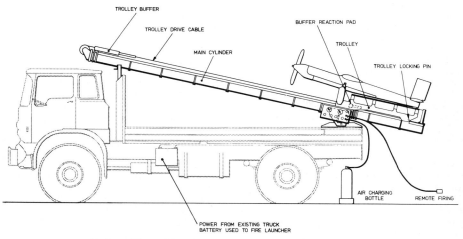

Variant of Shorts Skeet for vehicle mounting is under development

---

3792.391
FALCONET ASAT

Flight Refuelling's Falconet target drone, known as ASAT (Advanced Subsonic Aerial Target), was designed in response to a UK MoD requirement. The development contract provides for the construction of eight flight vehicles, the first of which was flown in February 1982. Seven of the eight development vehicles had flown by the end of 1983, with the lead vehicle still serviceable after 10 flights. Trials have included launch and recovery in wind speeds up to 28 knots and flight speeds in excess of 350 knots have been achieved, with non-visual control throughout. Operation of the system's 'Carousel' circular runway launch system, and the stability and control of the vehicle have been established. A zero-length launch system is also under development to provide added mobility including deployment in ships. Work is well advanced on an initial production batch of RPVs to enter service in 1984.

A maximum fuel load of 60 kg permits sortie times in excess of one hour. Approach and intercept legs of a typical target mission total about 10 km over the whole of which the target vehicle may be flown at more than 400 knots (740 km/h) at sea level. Ten such circuits can be repeated at 4½ minute intervals, but during less demanding operations, or where more time is required between presentations, the rate of fuel usage can be reduced by loiter at 3000 metres altitude. Maximum endurance with full allowances for take-off, climb, descent and recovery, is in excess of 90 minutes.

CONSTRUCTION
The ASAT subsonic target drone is configured as a cantilever low/mid-wing monoplane. The wings, tailplane and elevators are formed in folded flat aluminium sheet, without compound forming. The wings are interchangeable (left/right), have plain ailerons, and are attached to the fuselage by four bolts each. The tailplane is held in place by a GRP fin and two studs. A circular cross-section stressed skin fuselage of aluminium alloy has a frangible, expendable nose that is designed to absorb any nose-down ground impact. A cylindrical canister in the rear fuselage houses the recovery parachute, and there is a large equipment bay in the forward fuselage, aft of

Flight Refuelling Falconet ASAT on new zero length launch stand

the nose cone. The engine pod is attached to the underside of the fuselage by two bolts.

The Ames Industrial Ltd 108 kg static thrust turbojet engine is supplied with fuel from an integral tank in the centre fuselage between the wings. Aft of the fuel tank is a smaller tank for oil which can be injected into the jet pipe by command from the ground, to produce smoke for visual enhancement. The fuel tank is pressurised to 1 bar (15 lb PSI) and has a capacity of 75 litres. Pressurisation for oil and fuel tanks is by engine compressor bleed air. The equipment compartment in the front of the fuselage houses avionics and optional target equipment such as miss-distance indicator and radio altimeter. The guidance and control system includes a radio command PCM sub-system with Skyleader receiver and Marconi Avionics autopilot, the latter effecting aerodynamic control by ailerons and elevators which have actuators located in the rear fuselage between the tanks and the parachute compartment. Control from the ground is by means of a microprocessor-based control station which utilises radar data for vehicle navigation and direction functions. The station is equipped with an operator's control console and there is a programmable ground-based control option using the microprocessor. The RPV has provisions for pylon mounting of optical or IR flares, radar enhancement devices, sub-targets, banners, or other external stores.

The ASAT vehicle takes off under its own power from a three-wheeled trolley tethered to a pylon in the centre of a 115 metre diameter circular track, running clockwise round the track for a distance of about three laps (equivalent to a straight line take-off run of

1000 metres). With this technique the launch can always be into wind. An alternative zero length launch stand was revealed by Flight Refuelling in late 1983 (see picture) which employs booster rockets to accelerate the vehicle, enabling a more rapid launch and/or eliminating the need for a take-off track. A phased-release Irvin parachute recovery system consisting of a drogue and single cruciform main canopy is pre-loaded into a cylindrical pack and deployed by tail-cone release.

CHARACTERISTICS
Wing span: 3·05 m
Gross wing area: 1·4 m²
Aspect ratio: 6
Length: 3·5 m
Fuselage diameter: 387 mm (max)
Tail span: 1·32 m
Height: 1·32 m
Max launch weight: 205 kg
Power plant: Ames TRS 18-075 108 kg st turbojet
Max level speed: 834 km/h
Minimum loitering speed: 278 km/h
Max rate of climb (at sea level): 2600 m/minute
Endurance: 1 h (typical); 1·5 h (max)
Manoeuvring limit: ±6 g

STATUS
Design and development carried out under UK MoD contract awarded in 1978/79. First of eight flight vehicles delivered and flown in 1982 and production of an initial batch started for entry into service in 1984.
CONTRACTOR
Flight Refuelling Limited, Wimborne, Dorset BH21 2BJ, England.

Falconet advanced subsonic aerial target in free flight

3737.391
SHRIKE TARGET RPV

The Intergard Electronics Shrike RPV is a small radio-controlled aircraft designed for gunnery practice using both small arms and larger-calibre weapons. It can be flown in a variety of modes to simulate either direct attacks on the gunner's position or as a target towing system for live weapon practice. The configuration of the air vehicle is that of a conventional aircraft, and construction is of balsa and plywood, with expanded foam and glass-fibre. The radio-control system provided allows for operation on any one of 12 spot frequencies in the 27 MHz band, and it is possible to fly more than one target simultaneously provided suitable channels are selected for each aircraft.

CHARACTERISTICS
Wing span: 305 cm
Length: 232 cm
Weight: 14 kg
Engine: 56 cc
Cruising speed: 110 km/h
Endurance: Up to 50 minutes
Height: Limited by operator's visual range
Range: Limited by operator's visual range
CONTRACTOR
Intergard Electronics Ltd, 34 Frognal, Hampstead, London NW3, England.

1885.391
PETREL TARGET

The Petrel is a non-recoverable supersonic ballistic target developed from the well-known and extensively used Petrel research rocket. It is designed to simulate a missile threat and is used for defence weapon system development and evaluation, and for crew training. A variety of passive radar augmentation systems are provided, depending upon the nature of the trials being carried out. The high initial ejection velocity, about 135 m/s from the tubular launcher, given by four Chick boosters results in a very low impact dispersion; the 2 sigma line error observed in recent trials is about 0·95°. Thus the Petrel is particularly suitable for target applications where a high degree of confidence in the impact point is required.

CHARACTERISTICS
Length: 3·35 m
Diameter: 19 cm
Main motor: Lapwing
Boost motor: 4 × Chicks
Range: Variable with launch angle – 22 500 m at 30°; 130 000 m at 60°
Altitude: Variable with launch angle – 30 km at 60°; 150 km at 85°
Speed: Variable with launch angle – near Mach 3 at low angles, can be reduced with drag devices
Time of flight: Approx 30 s at low launch angles
DEVELOPMENT
Developed as a research rocket, but now additionally used for target applications. The Bristol Aerojet Skua research rocket also is available for use as a supersonic ballistic target.

Launch of BAJ Vickers Ltd Petrel target

CONTRACTOR
BAJ Vickers Ltd, Banwell, Weston-Super-Mare, Avon BS24 8PD, England.

3738.391
SKY-EYE MINI-RPV

Sky-eye has been developed as a close-support information relay vehicle for forward units providing information directly to a command HQ or forward artillery control centre relating to enemy troops or armour deployment and movements. The air vehicle is a small radio-controlled aircraft employed as a RPV equipped to carry a variety of payloads appropriate to different operational roles. For surveillance, a remotely-controlled TV camera would be fitted, while by replacing this unit and the associated data relay transmitter, a chaff dispenser or radar jammer could be carried for use against radar sites. A LTDS is another alternative payload.

Sky-eye is equipped with an electrostatic stabilisation system consisting of elements in each wing tip that are capable of measuring the potential of the Earth's electrostatic field. Comparison of the two values measured (each being proportional to the height of the respective sensor) enables the aircraft's lateral attitude to be determined and appropriate corrective signals generated to maintain the wings horizontal.

Digital proportional radio-control is used for operator control of the vehicle.

CHARACTERISTICS
Wing span: 244 cm
Length: 203 cm
Weight: 12 kg
Engine: 32 or 56 cc
Cruising speed: 55 km/h
Duration: Up to 45 minutes
Range: Limited by operator's visual range
CONTRACTOR
Intergard Electronics Ltd, 34 Frognal, Hampstead, London NW3, England.

4298.391
MACHAN RESEARCH RPV

The Machan unmanned aircraft has been developed by Marconi Avionics, in collaboration with the Cranfield Institute of Technology, as a research vehicle. It is designed to carry specialised, miniature electronics payloads, including surveillance systems, over battlefields and other areas of interest.

The complete system includes the vehicle itself, a ground control station and the various electronic payloads, and is currently undergoing flight evaluation trials after having made its first flight in February 1981. A number of lightweight surveillance payloads such as TV and the associated control and data links have been developed as payload packages. While Marconi has been responsible for these, the Cranfield Institute has designed the airframe, powerplant and the flight control system.

The Machan RPV is a fixed-wing monoplane with a ducted pusher propeller powered by a Weslake twin-cylinder 18 hp (13·5 kW) two-stroke petrol engine. Launch is by means of a pneumatic catapult and recovery by parachute.

CHARACTERISTICS
Length: 2·13 m
Wing span: 3·66 m
Max speed: 115 knots (59 m/s)
Cruising speed: 64 knots (33 m/s)
Gross TOW: 73 kg
Payload: 15 kg
Endurance: 2 h at cruising speed
STATUS
Currently engaged on trials of naval autopilot techniques.
CONTRACTOR
Marconi Avionics Ltd, Flight Automation Research Laboratory, Airport Works, Rochester, Kent ME1 2XX, England.

4592.351
PHOENIX RPV

The Phoenix RPV programme is concerned with the development of a surveillance and target detection/designation remotely piloted vehicle for use principally by the British Army in West Germany. A major function will be the location and acquisition of targets for medium- to long-range battlefield support weapons such as MLRS (**4060.111**) and heavy artillery.

Two teams drawn from British industry are taking part in the Phoenix competition which was in the CED (competitive engineering definition) phase from 1983 until late 1984. One team is headed by Marconi Avionics with Flight Refuelling as the major subcontractor, and the other team is led by Ferranti in partnership with Slingsby. The Ferranti team also includes Smiths Industries which will provide a navigation system comprising a low-cost strap-down attitude and heading reference using the latest gyroscopes and accelerometer technology, together with air data and navigation computation.

The programme evolved from the earlier Supervisor project that was cancelled in 1979, and the system envisaged will probably have an effective target detection/location range of about 50 km and an endurance of at least four hours. Designs are expected to embody a parachute recoverable, fixed wing RPV of conventional configuration. The Ferranti submission for the Phoenix programme is expected to be based on the Slingsby T68 light aircraft, which is a glass-fibre reinforced plastic development of the Slingsby T67 Firefly which made its first flight in 1983.

The RPV payload is likely to include a thermal imaging camera as the main sensor, with an appropriate telemetry system and command link. The

complete system also includes a comprehensive ground control station incorporating a data terminal.

STATUS
CED (competitive engineering definition) contracts were due to expire on September 1, 1984, after which selection of contractor(s) for development and

production was expected to be completed by March 1985. Entry into service is provisionally planned for 1988-89 and several hundred RPVs could be procured.

4480.391
SPRITE RPH
A new remotely piloted helicopter (RPH) design was revealed at the 1982 SBAC Exhibition at Farnborough under the name SPRITE, this being derived from the initial letters of the principal roles for which the vehicle is intended: surveillance, patrol, reconnaissance, intelligence gathering, target designation, and electronic warfare. As the adjacent photograph reveals, the helicopter configuration closely resembles the earlier Westland Wisp vehicle (**3243.351** in 1980-81 and earlier editions), but although the dimensions of Wisp and the later SPRITE are similar the latter is slightly larger in certain respects and has a significantly enhanced payload/range capability.

The general configuration can be seen from the nearby illustration, which shows a main body of oblate spheroid shape supported by a quadruped undercarriage constructed of radar-transparent materials and with counter-rotating twin helicopter rotor blades. There is a rotor head fairing made of similar composite materials as the undercarriage and the main body of the vehicle. The two-stroke petrol driven motor that powers SPRITE is housed within the body as are the sensor packages and four plastic fuel tanks. Other internal compartments house the guidance, autopilot and data link sub-systems.

Typical sensor payloads might include: a stabilised TV camera, thermal imaging equipment, LTDS, ELINT and electronic warfare equipment.
CHARACTERISTICS
Body diameter: 0·65 m
Rotor diameter: 1·6 m
Power plant: 2-stroke flat twin engine; US Kolbo D-238M or UK Piper P.80/2
Fuel capacity: 6 kg
Sensor payload: 6 kg
Take-off weight: 36 kg
Endurance: Up to 150 minutes
Cruising speed: 110 km/h
Operating height: 250 – 500 m (typical)
An engine-driven 28 V 500 W alternator provides electrical power for sensors and autopilot, and SPRITE can be pre-programmed or operated under direct ground control via a data link. A typical mission radius of 32 km has been estimated.
STATUS
Developed as a private venture by ML Aviation, SPRITE made its first flight in February 1983. It was revealed publicly in September 1982. The manufacturers state that both military and civil applications have been considered and there is understood to be close UK MoD interest in the project, possibly in connection with the project Phoenix (see **4479.391**) programme.

The shape and use of composite materials in construction of the SPRITE RPH result in minimal radar signature, and internal location of the power plant gives a very low IR signature. Battlefield surveillance roles are envisaged

CONTRACTOR
ML Aviation Company Ltd, White Waltham Aerodrome, Maidenhead, Berkshire SL6 3JG, England.

UNITED STATES OF AMERICA

2522.391
BEECH MODEL 1107 (AQM-37A)
This is a non-recoverable, supersonic, air-launched missile target system designed to simulate aircraft and missile threats for defence weapon system evaluation and crew training. The target provides both active and passive radar augmentation for radar acquisition and tracking, and a chemical flare is provided for IR homing. Two optical miss-distance systems are available.
CHARACTERISTICS
Power plant: 1 Rocketdyne/AMF LR64 P-4 dual-chamber liquid-propellant rocket-engine
Guidance: Programmed
Launching: Air-launched
Recovery: Non-recoverable. Automatic destruct system operates at end of flight or in case of major failure. Command destruct standby system for added range safety.
Operating speed: Mach 0·4 – 3
Operating height: 300 – 21 337 m
Endurance: 8 minutes (powered)
Special features: Approx 0·4 m³ of space in nose section for optional scoring and augmentation systems. Target compatible with non-co-operative scoring systems.
Model 1107 is the basic version of the AQM-37A target. More than 4000 of these vehicles have been built. Other versions built for the US services are:
Model 1019A: The US Navy contracted in 1975 with Beech to provide 20 AQM-37As capable of flying at 10 to 300 metres altitude for weapon system evaluation. These vehicles used an autopilot that incorporated a homing device for longitudinal guidance and radar altimeter for altitude control.

US Navy Beechcraft AQM-37C target drone. AQM-37C is distinguished from earlier AQM-37A by nose-mounted pitot head and increased fin area

Model 1100, Model 1101: The US Army contracted with Beech to provide 48 AQM-37As for weapon system evaluation in 1975. These vehicles were the first production units to incorporate a two-stage parachute recovery system. Under the Army contract Beech produced two versions of the AQM-37A. One (the model 1101) is a supersonic, high-altitude target capable of operation to 2188 km/h and 21 340 metres altitude, the other (the Model 1100) a low altitude modification which can be flown to within 15 metres of the terrain. Both the 1100 and 1101 models are equipped with a radio-controlled guidance system enabling both longitudinal and vertical positioning. Smoke canisters were provided for visual acquisition.
Model 1104: This is an improved version of the Model 1107 series for Mach 3, 24 380 metre missions. It was ordered by the US Navy after a demonstration programme of ten vehicles in 1981. The Model 1104 (AQM-37C) incorporates a digital autopilot with improved flight control features, and greater range/endurance performance is obtained by an optimum energy management program. The command control facility permits dual launch and in-flight heading control. Initiation of dives of 15 to 65° and pull-out on ground command are available. Radar augmentation in several bands has been improved and a new nose incorporates a new radome and a nose-mounted pitot.

Apart from increased length due to the nose pitot, and an increase of about 40 per cent in the vertical stabiliser fin area, other details are as for the AQM-37A. By early 1984 54 units had been delivered to the US Navy.
Model 1105: This is the Beech designation of a Mach 3·5, 27 430 metre version of the AQM-37C, which has aerodynamic control surfaces protected with thermal insulation. Beech Aircraft is under US Navy contract to provide eight units for development and demonstration.

In addition to the AQM-37A models built for the US services, five other versions have been built.
Model 1072 (Short SD.2 Stiletto): This is a version for the UK and is modified by Short Brothers to meet British requirements, including incorporation of telemetry and radar systems and control system changes. The vehicle is fitted by Beech with a single-chamber rocket motor to give Mach 2 performance at 18 300 metres. The Stiletto is launched from a

Canberra PR Mk-3 aircraft. In the successful first test flight at Llanbedr in August 1968, the drone was released at 16 750 metres and flew for more than 28 nautical miles (52 km) at an average speed of Mach 1·4 before the flight was terminated by a commanded explosive destruct.

The principal modifications made by Shorts were the incorporation of a British EMI T44/1 telemetry system, provision of additional 15 V flight break-up system (WREBUS), installation of radio-active miss-distance indicator (RAMD) with associated radio link, introduction of Plessey IR 112A IR 310 tele-command system with heading and turns command circuitry and changes in the radar augmentation system. The current Stiletto system consists of the basic target vehicle plus a number of optional mission kits which can be either installed by Shorts or delivered separately for customer installation. To date 150 Model 1072 AQM-37As have been delivered to the UK.
Model 1088: This is the manufacturer's designation of 11 targets supplied to Italy. Primarily used for weapon systems evaluation, vehicles had pre-programmed dive manoeuvre to give supersonic presentation at medium altitudes and were equipped with radio-controlled lateral manoeuvring capability to accurately position the target.
Model 1094: This is the manufacturer's designation of 50 targets supplied to the French Air Force. Primarily used for air-to-air weapon system evaluation they were modified by Matra to be compatible with weapon systems. Modifications include addition of scoring, radar augmentation, telemetry, and tracking beacon systems. Primary missions are Mach 1·6 at 16 750 metres and Mach 2 at 21 340 metres.
Model 1095: This is the manufacturer's designation of 40 targets delivered to the UK MoD. This version has been modified to the specifications of the MoD and will be used for crew training exercises on the Hebrides Range.
STATUS
The AQM-37A is in service with the US Navy (1962), US Air Force (1968), US Army (1973), UK (1966), Italian Air Force (1969) and French Air Force (1974), with year of introduction shown in brackets.
CONTRACTOR
Beech Aircraft Corporation, Wichita, Kansas 67201, USA.

3240.391
VANDAL INTERIM ANTI-SHIP MISSILE TARGET (MQM-8G)

Vandal (MQM-8G) is the US Navy's interim supersonic target for ship defence against cruise missiles. It is a modification of RIM-8G Talos naval missiles to serve as a low cost target into the 1990s. The modifications to the normal Talos round include the provision of a tracking beacon, a radar altimeter, a destruct system, an on-board command receiver and telemetry, plus airframe and fuel system modifications to simulate a variety of threat altitudes and speeds. A simulated radar emitter and a scorer are also included. The basic configuration and dimensions are as for the Talos anti-aircraft missile, described in an earlier entry (**1030.231**) in this volume.

A simpler version, Fleet Vandal, has also been developed for use in fleet training exercises. In this version, the altimeter, scorer, telemetry, and simulated radar emitter are not provided.

DEVELOPMENT

The development contract was started in July 1976 and completed in May 1978; it included six flight tests. All test objectives were achieved. Fleet Vandal development took place between May 1981 and July 1982, and programmes are in progress to provide a higher altitude, higher speed Vandal, and a lower altitude, longer range Vandal version. Comparative performance figures of the various models are given in the following table:

	Altitude (m)	Speed (Mach)	Range (km)
Vandal/Fleet Vandal	18 280	2·54	270
Vandal	91	2·1	40
High altitude Vandal	21 330	2·8	304
ER Vandal	15	2·1	74

STATUS

By January 1983, 65 Vandals and 12 Fleet Vandals had been delivered to the US Navy, and 26 more Vandals and 23 Fleet Vandals were in production. The run is expected to continue throughout the 1980s. First demonstration flights of the high altitude Vandal and the ER version were planned for Spring 1983 and 1984, respectively.

CONTRACTOR

Bendix Corporation, Guidance Systems Division, 400 South Beiger Street, Mishawaka, Indiana 46544, USA.

1814.391
BEECH MODEL 1089 ARMY MQM-107A VSTT

Beech Aircraft Corporation was awarded a multi-year production contract in 1975 by the US Army for the Model 1089 variable speed training target (VSTT). The target was designated the MQM-107A Streaker.

The principal function of the Streaker is to provide a variety of threat situations for training of missile and automatic weapons crews. It is the primary subsonic missile training target for the US Army. It is also used for the research and development testing of weapon systems. The standard vehicle is a 4·87 metres long, swept wing, turbojet-powered 430 kg aerial target that operates at altitudes from sea level up to 12 200 metres and at speeds of up to 500 knots (927 km/h). It tows gunnery banners and tow targets out to 2438 metres. With wingtip augmentation and scoring devices the MQM-107A itself also serves as an aerial target for air defence systems such as Stinger, Chaparral, Redeye, Hawk, and Improved Hawk. It is a re-usable target with recovery by command using a two-stage parachute system.

The standard Beech Model 1089 is powered by a Teledyne CAE J402-CA-700 engine. With the pod-mounted engine configuration other engines are easily adapted and are being considered for the MQM-107. The fuel capacity is 65 US gallons (246 litres) with an additional capacity of 4 US gallons (15 litres) for a smoke oil visual identification system. Optional wing insert fuel tanks, supplied in kit form, add 30 US gallons (113 litres) to the total fuel capacity. The target may be surface-launched from a zero-length launcher using a JATO booster, or air-launched from manned aircraft. Thiokol has developed the TX-632 booster for launching MQM-107 vehicles.

The modular design employed throughout the system provides for ease of fabrication and for economy in operation and maintenance. The fuselage is cylindrical. One unique design feature is the flat aerofoil section of the wing and tail surfaces. Low-cost bonded honeycomb is used for the fixed aero surfaces while the aero control surfaces are constructed of aluminium skins and filled with

Beech MQM-107B VSTT drone

poured-in-place foam. Support equipment is both minimal and lightweight providing for transportability and deployment of the system. Launch and checkout equipment is packaged in suitcase-sized containers.

Guidance and control systems, either analogue or digital, provide for both ground control and for pre-programmed flight. The flight controller is provided with all pertinent flight information by radio link from sensors located in the vehicle and the operator can command vehicle manoeuvres as well as recovery. In flight, the guidance and control system automatically stabilises around the roll, yaw, and pitch attitudes and provides an altitude-hold mode. A recently developed and tested autopilot extends the manoeuvring and high-*g* envelope of the vehicle. Either constant airspeed or constant altitude high-*g* manoeuvres can be selected by the flight controller. Another flight control development is a terrain following guidance capability which has demonstrated extremely low altitude flight profiles. To provide a greater internal payload carrying capacity an extended section is now available. This section also provides ease of access to the payload and vehicle electronics and has specialised waterproofing provisions for seawater recoveries.

The 999H version of this target incorporates the extended payload section and improved electronics, but retains the J402-CA-700 engine. This target has been designated MQM-107C.

CHARACTERISTICS

Guidance: Radio command
Wing span: 3 m
Length: 5·13 m (extended version 5·51 m)
Height: 1·47 m
Body diameter: 0·38 m
Wing area: (total projected) 2·52 m²
Horizontal tail surface: 0·55 m²
Vertical tail surface: 0·43 m²
Launch weight: 460 kg (including booster)
Useable fuel: 173 kg
Endurance: >3 h
Beech Model 999E, 999H (Army and Air Force MQM-107B/C)

This new model reflects the incorporation of the various system improvements which had been tested and proven on the MQM-107A. The primary reason for redesignation is the incorporation of the French Microturbo TRI 60-2 Model 074 turbojet engine. The increased thrust of the TRI 60-2 results in speeds up to 530 knots (982 km/h). This model incorporates the increased length electronic payload section (38·1 cm added), along with improved electronic packaging, improved waterproofing, increased smoke oil tank capacity and provisions for the high-*g* manoeuvring autopilot.

STATUS

In addition to the use by the US Army and other Department of Defence agencies, the Army has supplied the MQM-107A system to Sweden (999A), Jordan and Iran (MQM-107A) under the Foreign Military Sales (FMS) programme. Taiwan (999F), Republic of Korea (999D) and the United Arab Emirates (999L) have purchased this system and are now operating the MQM-107. Egypt (999M) has contracted to buy the system and deliveries have been scheduled for mid-1984. Following successful evaluations by the US Army and Air Force, production orders have been placed, deliveries commenced in August 1984. The US Navy has also conducted evaluations of the MQM-107A.

CONTRACTOR

Beech Aircraft Corporation, Wichita, Kansas 67201, USA.

2615.391
FIREBEE I (BQM-34A/BQM-34S/MQM-34D)

Firebee is a turbojet-powered remotely controlled drone used mainly for target purposes but with the capability of being used in a reconnaissance role (see following entries). Designation of the current standard version is BQM-34A by the US Air Force and BQM-34S by the US Navy, and there is also a version known as MQM-34D used by the US Army. Recent incorporation of the J85-GE-7 turbojet engine and the A/A37G-14 three-axis flight control system have enabled the target to execute flight manoeuvres at higher speeds and greater load factors than before.

CHARACTERISTICS

Power plant: 771 kg thrust Continental J-69-T-29 turbojet or the 1112 kg thrust General Electric J85-GE-7 turbojet

Guidance: Coded radar command control and tracking. US Navy BQM-34S version is fitted with Motorola integrated tracking and control system equipment. BQM-34A is equipped with the Vega drone tracking control system. BQM-34S versions have A/A37G-8A flight control system whereas current BQM-34A versions have A/A37G-14 three-axis system.
Launch: Air launch or ground launch with JATO rocket
Recovery: Parachute system deployed by remote command or in the event of loss of power, or guidance signal for a predetermined time
Max level speed: 1124 km/h at 2286 m
Max diving speed: Mach 0·95
Max cruising speed: 1015 km/h at 15 240 m at 816 kg AUW

Rate of climb: 5080 m/minute at sea level
Operating height range: 15-18 300 m
Endurance: 75 minutes 30 s at 15 240 m
Flotation time: 24 h with 25% fuel
Special features: Adjustable TWT amplifiers for D, E, F, G, H, I-band radar signal enhancement. Continuous infra-red wing-tip propane pods for IR augmentation. Built-in 5-6 *g* turn capability
RALACS – Radar Altimeter Low Altitude Control System – available for precision low altitude flights at 5 m altitude over water or 30 m over land
CONTRACTOR
Teledyne Ryan Aeronautical, 2701 Harbor Drive, San Diego, California 92138, USA.

2616.391
FIREBEE II (BQM-34E/F/T)

The Teledyne Ryan Model 166 Firebee II is a supersonic target drone developed for the US Navy and Air Force as an advanced version of the subsonic BQM-34A drone described above. The US Navy designations are BQM-34E and BQM-34T, while it is the BQM-34F in the US Air Force. The Firebee II is designed to provide aerial target presentations above 18 300 metres altitude at supersonic dash speeds up to Mach 1·5 for a period of 18 minutes. With full fuel load, range time may be extended to 74 minutes. Among other improvements the drone is designed to carry much more in the way of radar enhancement and tracking aids than its predecessor.

CHARACTERISTICS
Power plant: 873 kg thrust Continental YJ69-T-406 turbojet engine
Guidance: Drone carried AN/DRW-29 radio control receiver DKW-1 ITCS (BQM-34T) or DTCS (BQM-34F) command guidance package and A/A37G-9A flight control system
Launch: Ground launch with JATO bottle, or air-launched from DP-2E Neptune or DC-130A or E Hercules.

BQM-34F Firebee II supersonic target drone

Recovery: Similar to BQM-34A, or MARS for BQM-34F
Max speed: Mach 1·8 at 13 715 m
Operating height range: 15-18 300 m
Endurance: 74 minutes total
Flotation time: 24 h
Special equipment: AN/DLQ-1, -2, and -3 ECM equipment
AN/DRQ-4 or AN/DSQ-24 (in BQM-34F) missile scoring system

RALACS
I-band and G/H-band tracking beacons
TWT radar augmentation for E/F, G/H, and I-band
Solid-state radar augmentation for B-band
Passive radar reflectors
CONTRACTOR
Teledyne Ryan Aeronautical, 2701 Harbor Drive, San Diego, California 92138, USA.

4036.391
FIREBOLT MODEL 305 HAHST (AQM-81A)

The Teledyne Ryan Firebolt high altitude high speed target (HAHST) is being developed for the US Air Force Armament Division under a contract awarded in December 1979 following a competition with Beech Aircraft Corporation. This supersonic target drone is the outcome of development of the High Altitude Supersonic Target (HAST) programme to meet US requirements for highly advanced threat simulation, particularly at high altitudes and speeds. Flying at altitudes of around 30 000 metres at speeds of up to Mach 4, Firebolt vehicles will be used to

Teledyne Model 305 high altitude high speed target drone (AQM-81A)

authenticate the performance of new weapon systems.

In addition to the guidance and control equipment, the payload can include a point source radar augmentation system and a miss-distance indicator system. Flight manoeuvres can be remotely controlled via a radio link from the ground, or may be pre-programmed before flight utilising a digital control system. The vehicle is capable of between 5 g at 10 000 metres and 1·15 g at 27 400 metres, with an endurance of three minutes at Mach 3.

The target is powered by a hybrid rocket engine using solid fuel and liquid (nitric acid) oxidizer. This engine provides thrust from under 200 lb to over 1200 lb. Electrical power and oxidizer pumping is provided by a ram-air driven turbine in the mid-fuselage section.

Launching is normally from an aircraft flying at between Mach 1·2 and 2·5, with recovery from land or sea following a parachute-controlled descent, or the vehicle can be retrieved in mid-air during its parachute descent.

CHARACTERISTICS
Type: AQM-81A

Length: 5·18 m
Wing span: 1·02 m
Diameter: 33 cm
Launch weight: 558 kg
Performance: Mach 1·2 at 12 200 m to Mach 4 at 30 500 m
Propulsion: Variable thrust rocket motor
Guidance: Radio command
Endurance: 5 minutes at Mach 3
STATUS
Teledyne was awarded a contract for nine test vehicles in December 1979, following a competitive procurement bid against Beech. An option for 12 additional vehicles was taken up in December 1980. A contract modification for development of two configurations for the US Navy was awarded in August 1982, six for delivery in US Air Force configuration and six US Navy configuration. Air Force flight testing began at Eglin AFB in June 1983, and US Navy testing in October 1983 at Point Mugu, California.
CONTRACTOR
Teledyne Ryan Aeronautical, 2701 Harbor Drive, San Diego, California 92138, USA.

4477.391
NV-144 AERIAL TARGET

Northrop reached the flight test stages of a new target drone to serve as a high performance supplement to the BQM-74C (**3731.391**) in early 1984. This private venture target has been designed to meet the US Navy's BQM-126A requirements for a large, low-cost, subsonic vehicle that is capable of both air and surface launches. The new vehicle is designated the NV-144 and it will be able to carry large payloads at lower costs than current targets of comparable performance. It has been designed to take advantage of many new developments incorporated into the BQM-74C and will use the same avionics. The latter include the Northrop-developed digital avionic processor computer system that performs on-board guidance and control functions as well as being compatible with programmed missions. NV-144 will also have common ground support and other sub-systems with the current BQM-74C aerial target. However, more composite materials are being used in the NV-144 construction than in earlier Northrop targets, both the wings and the tail surfaces being made of low-cost plastics.

Air launches will be made from tactical aircraft such as the US Navy A-6 Intruder and the target is expected

to be used for weapon system testing and evaluation of air-to-air and surface-to-air missiles as well as acting as a cruise missile simulator.

CHARACTERISTICS (provisional)
Length: 5·95 m
Wing span: 3·29 m
Fuselage diameter: 51 cm
Power plant: 440 kg st turbojet
Gross weight: 635 kg (approx)
Fuel capacity: 180 kg
Max speed: 1100 km/h (approx)
Range: 1450 km (approx)
Altitude range: 15 – 16 800 m
STATUS
Private venture development. First flight completed successfully on 24 February 1984 after air launch from US Navy A-6 aircraft. Production phase due in late 1984.
CONTRACTOR
Northrop Corporation, Ventura Division, Newbury Park, California 91320, USA.

Production of NV-144 aerial target drones at the Northrop-Ventura plant

---

3731.391
BQM-74C AERIAL TARGET

Northrop's BQM-74C air-launchable aerial target is an improved version of the company's successful MQM-74C Chukar II (**2732.391**) target aircraft, used by the US Navy and 11 allied nations, that can also be used as a cruise missile simulator. The Navy plans to

use the target for various missions, such as the training of pilots in air-to-air missile use. It is capable of air or surface launching from beyond the horizon of the target ship.

The BQM-74C target system also includes pylon adaptors for air launch from A-6 and A-4 aircraft and payload kits for the Mobile Sea Range Operations.

The BQM-74C target was derived mainly through changes in the fuselage and avionics section of the MQM-74C. The fuselage is 8 cm longer and the shape is modified to provide additional space for mission payload. Air launch capability was achieved through modification of the centre fuselage section.

The equipment area incorporates a Northrop-developed digital avionics processor, a microprocessor-based digital autopilot which has significantly more capability and system reliability than analogue autopilots now used in most aerial targets. The device also simplifies both maintenance and checkout tasks associated with the operation of aerial targets.

The BQM-74C is equipped with a radar altimeter for low-altitude flights, a seeker simulator to duplicate cruise missile emissions, a radar transponder for IFF, a miss-distance indicator for weapons system scoring, and/or command over-ride system to assure target ship safety during simulated attack. The target's mission profile can be pre-programmed, including recovery via parachute. It is a mid-wing monoplane with detachable aluminium wings. Flight equipment, powerplant and fuel tanks are housed in the fuselage.

CHARACTERISTICS
Length: 3·95 m
Body diameter: 0·35 m
Wing span: 1·76 m
Engine: Williams International WR24-7B turbojet rated at 86·2 kg thrust
Speed: 300 – 926 km/h
Altitude: Over 7656 m
Flight time (average): >1 h
Max range: 833 km
Max launch weight: 205 kg
Guidance: Radio command or pre-programmed
STATUS
The BQM-74C completed US Navy technical and operational evaluation tests successfully in 1980. The target is now in full production and in early 1984 more than 700 were on order.

BQM-74C Chukar III loading under wing of US Navy A-6 Intruder

CONTRACTOR
Northrop Corporation, Ventura Division, Newbury Park, California 91320, USA.

2732.391
NORTHROP CHUKAR II
The Chukar II (MQM-74C) is a lightweight target drone designed for anti-aircraft gunnery, surface-to-air missile, and air-to-air missile training and weapon systems evaluation. Radio-controlled, it is turbojet powered and is recoverable by parachute. It is readily deployed and operated from aboard naval vessels.
CHARACTERISTICS
Wing span: 1·76 m
Length: 3·87 m
Height: 0·71 m
Launch weight: 233 kg
Service ceiling: 12 200 m
Power plant: Williams International WR24-7B turbojet, two JATO rockets for launching
Guidance: Radio control, automatic stabilisation, and altitude hold
Launch: Rocket-assisted from zero-length launcher
Recovery: Parachute system operating on ground command or automatically on loss of power or radio guidance failure
Max level speed: 886 km/h at sea level; 926 km/h at 6000 m

MQM-74 Chukar II after launch

Economic cruising speed: 463 km/h at sea level
Rate of climb: 1780 m/minute at sea level with full fuel
Endurance: 59 minutes at sea level to 102 minutes at 9200 m (at max endurance speed); 30 minutes at sea level to 60 minutes at 9200 m (at max speed)
Range: 370 – 750 km according to speed and height

The Chukar II employs a selection of passive and active augmentation devices fitted to the target or deployed as a tow to enhance the infra-red and varied

radar cross-section spectrum signatures. In operation, the tow targets are attached to the wing tips and sequentially released for the firing presentations. The tows are deployed from 15 to 150 metres behind the Chukar II dependent upon the weapon system operational characteristics.
STATUS
The internationally deployed Chukar II target system is used extensively within NATO for missile training evaluation exercises at the NAMFI range, Crete, Greece and at the Salto di Querre Range, Sardinia, Italy, and is the standard target for various European, Middle-East and Far-East nations for both land-based and shipborne air defence weapons training. The production of the Chukar series target began in 1968 with more than 4000 targets manufactured for international users, the US Navy and Northrop operated target flight service operations. Production of the Chukar II will continue in addition to the air launchable BQM-74C (**3731.391**) known internationally as the Chukar III.
CONTRACTOR
Northrop Corporation, Ventura Division, Newbury Park, California 91320, USA.

1819.391
PQM-102 TARGET DRONE
In March 1974 it was announced that the US Air Force was about to make its first purchase of 22 F-102 Delta Dagger interceptor aircraft converted for use as unmanned target drones, in which form they bear the designation PQM-102. One of the main functions of this class of target drone was for the testing and evaluation under realistic conditions of the latest types of air-to-air weapons and the new generation of fighter aircraft. F-102s have been withdrawn from reserve service and deep storage and the PQM-102 inventory was established from this source.

The US Air Force had planned to build up a force of up to 128 of these drones at an annual rate of 22. Although classified as drones, the PQM-102 qualifies for the US Air Force RPV definition. A pilot sitting in a van at the end of the runway carries out the preflight checks remotely and then flies the aircraft off the

ground and clear of the airfield area for handing over to the range radar mission controllers. If the drone survives the mission, the procedure is carried out in reverse to recover the target vehicle.
DEVELOPMENT
Sperry was awarded a $5·5 million contract in spring 1973 for the conversion of an initial batch of eight Convair F-102 aircraft for the target drone mission. Of the eight, two retained the manual pilot facilities and were designated OF-102; the other six were configured for full unmanned operation.
STATUS
The first PQM-102 was flown in August 1974 and 530 'Nullos' (un-manned flights) had been made by November 1981. These included the firing of 900 missiles of both air-to-air and air-to-surface types. In the period 1980-1982 a total of 180 PQM-102s were expended.

PQM-102B targets continue to be used for weapon

system development testing and also for ADC and TAC WSEP activities. The most recent contract for 66 PQM-102Bs was valued at $15·9 million and contained options for additional lots of 33 and 46. These additional 79 drones were contracted, with a specified delivery rate of four per month. The last delivery was made in November 1981. The available stock of F-102 airframes for conversion to PQM-102 targets having been used, future US Air Force requirements will be met by QF-100 drones (**3652.391**). Between 30 and 40 PQM-102s remained in service in late 1982.
CONTRACTOR
Sperry Flight Systems Division, Sperry Corporation, PO Box 21111, Phoenix, Arizona 85036, USA.

3652.391
QF-100 FULL-SCALE AERIAL TARGET (FSAT)
In August 1979 the US Air Force issued a $6·7 million contract to Sperry Flight Systems for full-scale engineering development of the QF-100 full-scale

aerial target (FSAT) based on the North American F-100 fighter-bomber airframe. Airframes are drawn from storage at Davis-Monthan AFB, Arizona.

The QF-100 is a multi-service target for air-to-air and ground-to-air missile evaluation and combat crew training. It uses current PQM-102 ground control and test equipments as well as many PQM-102 airborne sub-systems. A digital flight control computer replaces four analogue computers used in the PQM-102 system, offering ease of testing and operational mode growth capability.

Having a versatile performance and manoeuvring capability, the QF-100 can attain Mach 1·3 and fly at altitudes from 200 feet (60 metres) above ground level to 50 000 feet (15 240 metres) above mean sea level. It can perform -2 to +8 g manoeuvres. Drone formation flight capability for flying up to six QF-100s at one time has been developed with the US Army. Each QF-100 has a life expectancy of ten missions before a 'kill' occurs.

The QF-100 aerial target is designed to be remotely

controlled and is equipped with a destruct system in event of control loss. Take-offs and landings are controlled by a mobile control station located next to the FSAT runway. After the QF-100 reaches the 'handover box' a 3 × 5 mile (5 × 8 km) area seven miles (11 km) from the runway, control of the aerial target is switched to a drone tracking control station.

Both the mobile and ground fixed control station require two skilled controllers for a QF-100 mission. Each mission is a highly co-ordinated effort between the ground controllers.
STATUS
QF-100 drones are replacing PQM-102s in US Air Force service, the supply of airframes for the latter having been used. The US Air Force has funded production of 81 QF-100 drones with first units of a batch of 21 were delivered to Tyndall AFB, Florida in May 1983.
CONTRACTOR
Sperry Flight Systems, Sperry Corporation, PO Box 9200, Albuquerque, New Mexico 87119, USA.

QF-100 target drone aircraft in flight

3168.351
AQUILA (YMQM-105) MINI-RPV

The Lockheed Aquila mini-RPV is the successful contender for the US Army's requirement for a small battlefield RPV to undertake reconnaissance, laser target marking, ranging, and similar high-risk operations. The objective was to achieve a unit cost low enough to permit use of the mini-RPV as expendable items where the mission priorities justified, but measures are incorporated for recovery. Simplicity and ease of operation are additional requirements of the system which was formerly known as 'Little R' and is a development of the US Army RPAODS programme.

The aircraft is a flying-wing craft powered by a rear-mounted, two-cylinder engine driving a pusher propeller and the vehicle can fly a pre-programmed flight profile, entirely controlled by an on-board computer. The latter can be overridden by the ground operator who can modify the computer programmed profile as well as being able to select loiter or search modes as required.

The payload is provided by Honeywell and contains a stabilised TV camera and an International Laser Systems laser. The Aquila can also carry a Perkin Elmer mini-panoramic camera. Real-time TV pictures are relayed by a data link to three operators in a distant ground control van. The Aquila system is designed to acquire and locate targets for artillery and also provides laser designation for precision-guided missiles and shells.

Steady development of the US Army requirement and the Aquila payload package has led to a sophisticated tactical application known as the TRAAMS mini-RPV C³/CM sensor concept. This relies upon the time reference angle-of-arrival measurement system (TRAAMS) anti-radiation

Launch (above) and recovery (lower) of Lockheed Aquila tactical drone, using truck-mounted catapult rail and a vertical ribbon barrier for retrieval

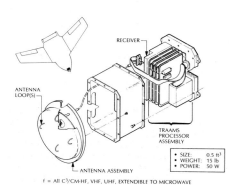

Combination of Aquila mini-RPV and TRAAMS sensor will enable location and engagement, or jamming of battlefield emitters such as enemy C³ centres

sensor used in conjunction with the Aquila vehicle to form a flexible and effective command, control and communications (C³) countermeasure system. TRAAMS is a signal processing device that can measure extremely small delays between the times of arrival of two signals at a single frequency. A combination of surface acoustic wave resonators and a microprocessor, together with simple broadband antennas and an RF receiver, it forms the basis of an interferometer which will provide very accurate directional information about emitters.

TRAAMS is not restricted in frequency and is not dependent on antenna radiation patterns, and the system has the potential of giving accurate emitter location data when used in platforms (such as surveillance drones) which have limited antenna base lines. In the TRAAMS mini-RPV concept the former system is used to 'set on' the drone's TV system to the emitter's line-of-sight to permit remote visual identification of the target. On confirmation of the target, the RPV illuminates it or uses a laser target marker for the use of co-operative weapons such as laser-guided bombs or laser homing missiles. TRAAMS could also be employed for the initiation

and direction of ECM against certain categories of target.

CHARACTERISTICS
Wing span: 3·89 m
Length: 2 m
Wing chord: 1·21 m (approx)
Leading edge sweep: 28°
Take-off weight: 54·4 kg
Payload weight: 16·3 kg
Max speed: 222 km/h (approx)
Endurance: 3 h (max)
Ceiling: 3600 m, plus
Power plant: Two-cylinder air-cooled piston engine developing 26 hp at 8000 rpm
Fuel: 6·8 kg
STATUS

The fiscal year 1985 budget contained a total of $161.3 million for US Army RPV system procurement and $103.1 million for RDT&E. The former figure would provide 32 air vehicles and nine ground control stations.

CONTRACTOR
Lockheed Missiles and Space Company, 1111 Lockheed Way, Sunnyvale, California 94088, USA.

4040.391
E-SYSTEMS MULTIPLE MISSION RPVS

E-Systems, Melpar Division has developed miniature RPVs for multiple missions both expendable and recoverable. Manufacturing capabilities currently exist for three weight configurations of the same basic airframe, 90, 175 and 260 lb (40·9, 79·3 and 117·9 kg respectively). The design features shoulder wing, single tail boom, fuselage and a pusher engine. The wings, horizontal stabiliser, payload nose pod and engine are removable for transportation and maintenance, mission flexibility is achieved by allowing interchangeable payload pods. The main characteristics of the respective models are summarised further on in this entry.

A lightweight and simple autopilot not requiring a

vertical gyro has been developed for flight path control. It is capable of real-time data link update by a ground operator or can be pre-programmed to carry out an autonomous mission. The autopilot has three independent feedback loops that are used to stabilise the aircraft and uses a barometric pressure transducer, angle-of-attack vane, magnetometer, rate gyros and velocity transducer as sensor inputs. The autopilot controls throttle, elevator and ailerons or rudder.

OPERATION
Omega (VLF) or Navstar/GPS (Global Positioning System) are the two recommended means of navigation for the RPVs, although other techniques such as Loran, inertial, area correlation, or beacons may be considered. RPV launch is accomplished

Launch of E.175 for strike application

from the top of a moving vehicle, by a catapult or with a boost rocket. Recovery methods include autopilot-assisted skid landing and recovery net which can stop the aircraft without damage within a distance of 12 metres. Recoverable RPV missions cover roles such as real-time TV reconnaissance, communications relay, and intelligence collection while expendable missions include radar strike, decoys, jamming, radio relay, and false target generation. Payloads appropriate to these missions have been developed.

For remote real-time reconnaissance Melpar has designed and produced a low cost TV camera system in a gimballed mount. Remotely controlled camera

CHARACTERISTICS

Model	E-90	E-175	E-260
Wing span	3·04 m	3·65 m	4·41 m
Length	2·31 m	2·52 m	3·23m
Launch weight	40·8 kg	79·3 kg	117·9 kg
Payload	9·0 kg	18·1 kg	22·6 kg
Fuel	6·8 kg	13·6 kg	24·0 kg
Engine capacity	13 hp	18 hp	24 hp
Cruise speed	177 km/h	193 km/h	160 km/h
Range	338 km	482 km	482 km
Endurance	3 h	4 h	5-6 h

functions are from horizon to –45°, ±90° in yaw, and camera ON/OFF. The camera is illustrated nearby and can be used for numerous remote control applications. For higher resolution a stabilised TV camera or FLIR may be installed in the RPV using an interchangeable nose cone technique.

An RPV jammer also has both height and power advantages over ground-based systems under certain circumstances and at Fort Huachuca, Arizona, Melpar has demonstrated the effectiveness of a 25 W jammer operating against a typical enemy VHF communications net. Three types of jammers are available as RPV payload packages: (1) barrage; wide-band noise and tone, (2) spot; narrow-band noise and tones with remote running or on-board look-through, (3) DART (delay and repeat transmitter); which combines the best features of barrage and spot jamming at low cost.

E-90
The E-90 is an upgraded version of the original low

Remotely controlled gimballed TV camera

E-90 RPV

E-260 RPV in flight

cost expendable RPV which was first flown in October 1977. The power plant is a 13 hp 2-cycle, 2-cylinder piston engine. The E-90 has been designed for light payload expendable applications. It is a very low cost airframe to be used by a two- or three-man launch team where high quantities are required.

E-175
The E-175 is an upgraded version of the earlier E-130. This was accomplished by enlarging the wing surface area and utilising a slightly larger 18 hp engine.

Expendable strike and EW are the principal applications. The E-175 is adaptable to other applications and payloads which are also expendable.

The E-175 has been fully wind tunnel tested at the University of Washington, Seattle, Washington. A photo shows the E-175 configured for radar strike.

E-260
The E-260 is the latest model of E-Systems family of RPVs. The design allows for interchangeable payload nose cones allowing a basic E-260 airframe to accommodate a number of different reconnaissance

missions all of which are recoverable. Endurance versus payload capacity tradeoffs can be accomplished with a typical payload configuration of 54 lb (24·5 kg) having over five hours' endurance. The electrical power generation system provides over 1500 W.

Launching can be accomplished by pneumatic catapult. The E-260 is designed for a minimum radar, IR, acoustic and visual signature. Recovery is accomplished using the autopilot and shock absorbing skids.

The E-260 is a cost effective vehicle for low-level reconnaissance without risk to aircrew.

Melpar also provides the total ground system support equipment including mission planning, mission operations, exploitation, and system maintenance.
CONTRACTOR
E-Systems Incorporated, Melpar Division, 7700 Arlington Boulevard, Falls Church, Virginia 22046, USA.

3740.391
FQM-117A TARGET (RCMAT)
The AN/FQM-117A radio-controlled miniature aerial target (RCMAT) is designed mainly for use in training of ground troops in air defence using light anti-aircraft weapons. It may be used with guns and with guided missiles, and can also be employed as an air-to-air target. The vehicle has a 'flying wing' tailless configuration, and operation is very simple: one

man usually hand-launches the target with another operating the remote radio control.
CHARACTERISTICS
Wing span: 160 cm
Length: 81 cm
Height: 19 cm
Weight: 2·27 kg (empty)
Fuel: 0·45 kg
Payload: 1·63 kg

Max speed: 148 km/h
Max altitude: 3000 m
Endurance: 10 minutes (minimum at full speed)
STATUS
Regularly employed by US forces since 1975, and more than 30 000 targets have been supplied.
CONTRACTOR
RS Systems, 5301 Holland Drive, Beltsville, Maryland 20705, USA.

4298.391
AUGMENTED RCMAT
A method for augmenting the FQM-117A radio-controlled miniature aerial target (RCMAT) (3740.391) has been developed by RS Systems to improve its value for range training for gun systems, as well as AA missiles such as Stinger, Redeye, etc. The method is based upon installing a number of additional components on the standard FQM-117A to simulate the appearance of a threat aircraft. These components include a fuselage element and a vertical stabiliser.

In the augmented RCMAT, realistic profiles are added to the FQM-117A to improve the relationship between the FQM-117A scale dimensional ratio and speed ratio. These profiles are added to the FQM-117A by replacing the present nose crutch with a three-dimensional nose section and adding a two-dimensional fuselage and tail section. If desired, a kit can be provided to allow field modification of the FQM-117A wing in about 20 minutes, retaining the standard engine, fuel system and guidance system. The augmented RCMAT then becomes a threat

aircraft in visual appearance with realistic scale flight profiles. Versions are available representing aircraft types such as Soviet MiG-27 and MiG-21, and US A-7 and F-16.

The added fuselage components improve the visual fidelity of the target in the incoming/outgoing, diagonal incoming/outgoing, and crossing flight profiles. The augmented RCMAT has an authentic scale ratio of width, length, height and speed compared with the real aircraft in these profiles.

The augmented RCMAT can be equipped with a variety of IR devices to widen the target's training role to include IR tracking. These devices include both flares and electronic IR sources. The augmented RCMAT can carry up to two 1 lb (0·45 kg) flares and still maintain its hand-launch characteristics. The flares are mounted under the leading edge of the wing in steel tubes. These flares are a special limited production configuration by RS Systems, and tests have indicated very few problems with the flares being extinguished because of the target's higher speed. Flare duration is 15 minutes. The electronic IR source is a repackaged ITP-2 unit previously

Augmented RCMAT drone in MiG-27 configuration

demonstrated against Stinger, Redeye and Chaparral systems. The ITP-2 is fitted with the batteries mounted in the nose section of the augmented RCMAT and the IR source mounted at the exhaust point of the scale profile used.
STATUS
More than 4500 supplied to the US Army, Marine Corps and one foreign operator.
CONTRACTOR
RS Systems, 5301 Holland Drive, Beltsvillle, Maryland 20705, USA.

4475.391
HEAT DRONE
The hostile expendable aerial target (HEAT) is a further enhancement of the AN/FQM-117A radio-controlled miniature aerial target produced by RS Systems (3740.391 and 4298.391) for training AA gunners and missile operators. The latest version of this system features a larger scale MiG-27 aircraft model and other improvements such as an electrostatic stabiliser, an improved command link and an IR source to allow the target to be used against heat-seeking weapon systems.

The HEAT electrostatic stabiliser is a two-axis system that senses the target's flight attitude and

automatically maintains straight and level flight. The pilot controls the aircraft by overriding the stabiliser to bank the aircraft or change the pitch attitude to climb or descend. This facility and an improved guidance system now enables HEAT targets to be flown in formation for greater realism in simulated air attacks on ground forces. The provision of a specially developed IR source allows the target to be used for training operators of heat-seeking missile systems such as Stinger or Redeye as well as AA guns like Vulcan Phalanx. The characteristics of the various AN/FQM-117A derivatives can be seen in the comparative specification table.

RS HEAT 3D drone in F-16 configuration. Note pusher propulsion arrangement for scale IR signature in this new version. Soviet MiG-27 configuration also produced

CHARACTERISTICS

	FQM-117A	ARCAT	HEAT
Scale	n/a	1/9	1/7
Wing span	1·6 m	1·6 m	2·03 m
Length	81 cm	1·86 m	2·33 m
Height	2·9 cm	6·8 cm	10·6 cm
Max speed	148 km/h	128 km/h	102 km/h
Weight (dry)	24·9 kg	34 kg	29·7 kg
Endurance	10 minutes	10 minutes	10 – 20 minutes

STATUS

More than 200 supplied to US Army by early 1984. A new version, HEAT 3D, has been developed under US Army contract and flew at White Sands Missile Range in December 1983.

CONTRACTOR

RS Systems, 5301 Holland Drive, Beltsville, Maryland 20705, USA.

4481.391
PAVE TIGER MINI-DRONE (YCGM-121A)

Under a $14 million contract awarded in late 1982 by the US Air Force, a low-cost expendable mini-drone for use by tactical air forces is being developed for the Pave Tiger programme. Planned payloads for the YCGM-121A include various types of sensor for electronic warfare roles, and warheads for use in anti-radiation missions for the destruction and/or disabling of enemy radars in battlefield areas or those protecting high-value targets.

Vehicle configuration is based on a stubby fuselage supported by a swept wing which has vertical stabiliser fins at its tips and a canard horizontal control surface towards the nose. A four-bladed pusher propeller driven by a two-cylinder piston engine powers the mini-drone which is constructed of injection moulded composite materials. Launch methods have not been disclosed but there is provision for use of a booster motor. Guidance is by means of a simple autopilot under the control of an on-board microprocessor which is also connected to the mini-drone's sensor package, and probably also has provisions for pre-programming prior to launch.

CHARACTERISTICS

Wing span: 2·56 m
Length: 2·12 m
Fuselage diameter: 0·6 m
Launch weight: 127 kg (excl booster)
Power plant: 28 hp Cuyuna piston engine
Cruise speed: 185 km/h

STATUS

Flight tests of YCGM-121A Pave Tiger mini-drones planned for Spring of 1984 have been preceded by company private venture test flights of similar vehicles which took place in mid-1979. Pave Tiger is funded as a US Air Force quick reaction capability programme and the current $14 million development contract which covers the period up to September 1983 was awarded by the US Air Force Aeronautical Systems Division at Wright-Patterson AFB, Ohio. A total of 14 mini-drones were called for under this contract, 12 for flight tests and two spare machines.

CONTRACTOR

Boeing Military Airplane Company, 3801 South Oliver, Wichita, Kansas 67210, USA.

3164.391
HAYES TARGET SYSTEMS

The Hayes International Corporation produces a wide range of air target systems and aircraft drone augmentation systems for air-to-air and surface-to-air missile and gunnery testing and training. Augmentation devices include both IR and radar types. The main Hayes systems are listed in the following paragraphs.

Model TA-7E (USAF TDU-22B/USN TDU-37B)

This is the standard supersonic tow target used by US forces for simulating threat aircraft for semi-active radar guided missiles. Four Luneberg lenses provide I/J-band radar augmentation for tracking, lock-on, and fuzing. Towing speeds between 150 knots and Mach 1·5 can be employed. The USN TDU-37B incorporates structural changes which strengthen the body and fins for aircraft carrier use.

Model TA-7 CIR (USAF TDU-25B)

The TA-7 CIR (continuous infra-red) provides a continuous heated stainless steel IR source of about one hour duration. Passive radar augmentation in the I/J- and D-bands is provided by means of Luneberg lenses. Towing is possible at speeds between 250 and 500 knots. Recent modifications provide a DIGIDOPS scoring capability instead of the older BIDOPS system.

HUTTS

The Hayes Universal Tow Target System (HUTTS) consists of the Universal Target Launcher, Model LTC-2 with Hayes radar, IR, smoke, or visual tow target. The launcher fits any aircraft pylon with standard NATO 14 or 30 inch (35·56 or 76·2 cm) lugs and is compatible with all Hayes towbodies.

The modular LTC-2 launcher can be mounted on any aircraft equipped with bomb shackles, and allows utilisation of the target system on all aircraft without modification of airframe or wiring system, thereby precluding any requirement for a dedicated tow aircraft. Adaptation to aircraft without pylons is also possible. Multiple target carriage is possible when mission requirements so dictate.

The LTC-2 launcher is constructed of glass-fibre and steel and is aerodynamically shaped. Weight of the launcher varies from approximately 31·5 to 39·25 kg depending on the configuration in use. Because of its simple modular mechanical construction and minimum electrical parts, maintenance of the launcher can be expected to be minor, easily accomplished and completely compatible with current field maintenance shop capabilities.

Major assemblies of the LTC-2 launcher are the pylon unit, the ignition module, the suspension and release unit, the remote control module and the nose cone units.

The pylon unit which interfaces with the aircraft pylon is designed so that it will accommodate a 35·56

HUTTS TRX-3 radar augmented and TGX-1 light augmented targets mounted on the -35A Learjet

or 76·2 cm spacing and the configuration may be varied in such a manner that the 35·56 cm lug spacing may be from the forward lug position or from the aft lug position by rotation of the hardback assembly and centre lug receptacle. This unit employs standard 450 kg class bomb lugs and no electrical interface is required between the pylon unit and the aircraft bomb rack. The pylon unit houses the battery for electrical operation of the launch and release bellows actuators carried in the suspension and release unit.

Immediately forward of the extension unit or pylon, in those cases where the extension unit is not used, an ignition unit may be placed as required for ignition of the propane CIR augmentation sources carried in the TIX series of IR targets. The ignition unit contains a solid-state, 20 kV spark generator operating at a PRF of approximately 1 kHz. The ignition unit operates from the pylon unit battery.

Ahead of the ignition unit or pylon unit, is the suspension and release unit which provides for a two-point suspension of the HUTTS family of targets and for the towing of these targets. Suspension is accomplished by a scissor type mechanism which grasps the suspension lugs of the HUTTS target. A similar arrangement is employed to grasp the towing end of the towline. Four individually operated sway braces are employed to make the launcher/target interface rigid. The release of the target from the launcher is accomplished by detonation of a pyrotechnic bellows actuator. Actuation of the bellows actuator unlocks a four-ball lock and moves a tapered rod aft between the scissor arm allowing the scissor arm to open and release the target. Release of the towline is accomplished by a second pyrotechnic bellows actuator and a similar release mechanism. The two functions of the suspension and release unit require one electrical command for each function.

Immediately forward of the suspension and release unit is the remote control unit which receives the coded commands from the command transmitter carried in the aircraft cockpit and operated by the pilot. Each remote control unit is equipped to receive either left- or right-hand launch and release commands from the command transmitter. These commands close the appropriate relays which connect the pylon unit battery to the appropriate actuator. The command receiver of the remote control unit operates on a separate battery contained within the remote control unit and is a flush-mounted receiving antenna for reception of the command frequency.

The LTC-2 command transmitter is a small solid-state, hand-held RF unit which the pilot carries in the cockpit of the tow aircraft. Switches on the transmitter allow the pilot to select the functions of launch and jettison of either right or left targets. Transmitter commands are controlled by a separate switch to prevent inadvertent operation. Weight of the transmitter is less than 1 kg.

The command transmitter operates on a frequency of 72·9 MHz. Each transmitter contains eight channel encoders. Two channels are dedicated to each of four command functions enabling the launch and jettison of the targets from two launchers on the same aircraft should dual carriage be a mission requirement.

Five types of targets have been developed to date for the HUTTS concept: radar, IR, plume, visual and smoke augmented targets. The radar augmented targets, designated TRX series, feature different arrays of passive radar lens and reflectors which provide the desired augmentation for the needed purpose. IR augmented targets feature propane fired burners/emitters and are designated TIX. Plume augmented targets, designated TPT, provide an all-aspect IR target capability. Two configurations of visual/radar targets have been developed. One is light augmented, the other is smoke augmented and are designated TGX and TVX, respectively.

Each of the five series of targets has or is capable of being configured in several ways depending on mission requirements and the desired payload. Having scoring provisions changes model nomenclatures.

TRX Radar Augmented Targets

The basic fuselage and tail fins of the TRX are constructed of impact resistant thermoplastic. Nose and tail cones adapt to the fuselage with aluminium/steel bulkheads to support mounting of fore and aft lenses. Additional lenses or metallised

F-4 aircraft with TRX and TGX targets

reflectors can be mounted in the tow body to provide beam coverage for radar augmentation. A tow reel with pre-wound towline is located at the centre of gravity of the target. Variable towline lengths from 100 to 6000 metres of either constant- or stepped-diameter cable is wound on the reel during target assembly at the factory depending upon mission requirements. The braking system of the reel controls target reel-out rate. Depending upon the number, type and location of the radar lens, radar cross-section varies from 17 m² monostatic to 5 m² bistatic. Weight of the target, which is approximately 25 kg, will vary depending upon the number of radar lenses.

When required, a low-cost scorer/counter is mounted in the middle section of the TRX fuselage with the antenna located in a specially designed boom protruding through the nose cone. Scorer power is provided for by a battery pack located adjacent to the scorer. Scoring information is telemetered to a telemetry pod where it is re-transmitted to a ground receiving station where display and/or recording is accomplished.

TIX IR Augmented Target
The TIX series of targets are the IR augmented targets of the HUTTS family. Like the TRX series, they are constructed of thermoplastic and are augmented with an IR emitting, propane-fired burner which operates at approximately 1135°C. The IR emitting surface is 21·59 cm in diameter and 22·86 cm long. The approximate output of the IR augmenter is 400 W per steradian in the 1·8 to 2·8 micron band and 250 W per steradian in the 3 to 5 micron band. Liquid propane fuel is carried in a stainless steel cylindrical tank of such capacity to provide for at least 30 minutes of CIR output. The duration of burning is dependent upon altitude of operation.

The nose cone has a 6 cm diameter opening to allow ram air to flow through the target to provide air for the proper fuel-air mixture needed to support fuel combustion. Ignition is attained through electrical spark that is controlled by an ignition module in the LTC-2 launcher.

Tow line provisions for the TIX target are similar to the TRX targets. Towlines up to 6000 metres in length can be provided with TIX targets. TIX targets are 232·41 cm long and the standard 22·86 cm in diameter. All HUTTS targets are stabilised with six fins that give the targets a maximum fin span of 60·32 cm. Weight of TIX targets is a nominal 25 kg but varies depending on length of towline.

TGX Series Targets
The TGX series of targets and the visual/radar augmented targets of the HUTTS family are used primarily in point defence weapons systems training. Coaxial visual/radar augmentation is provided forward along the flight axis by a trihedral radar reflector constructed of extremely fine mesh wire cloth through which the beam of the visual augmentation lamp passes. Visual augmentation is accomplished by use of incandescent lamps with an

Dual-carriage, radar augmented TRX-3 targets with passive lens and reflectors for basic air gunnery training

input of approximately 600 W at 31 V dc. Various beamwidths can be selected from the available augmentation lamps providing naked eye visual contact ranges up to 9 km. Electrical power for operating the on-board electrical system is provided by a generator unit which is turned by a ram air driven turbine wheel at the rear of the target tail cone. Additional radar augmentation may be provided in the beam areas if required, and the target is capable of carrying optional scoring equipment which will provide a missile scoring capability of approximately 15 metre radius and bullet counting for the 20 mm class bullets to approximately five metres. The TGX series of targets are equipped with deployment reels for self-deployment on towlines up to 6000 metres in length. These targets are 22·85 cm in diameter, cylindrical in shape and 223·52 cm in length. They are stabilised with six fins with a maximum fin span of 60·3 cm.

TVX Series Targets
The TVX series of tow targets are visual/radar targets designed for employment where visual/optical tracking of a target is required. Visual augmentation is provided by five smoke generators internally mounted which discharge smoke through a 10·16 cm discharge tube coaxial with the tail cone. Each flare will burn for approximately two minutes. Ignition of the smoke generators is accomplished by radio command. Each generator is ignited by a separate coded command from the command transmitter. A command transmitter operating at a frequency of 72·4 MHz radiates 15 W minimum thus enabling reliable command at all ranges to ten nautical miles at low altitude, and slightly longer range as the target altitude increases.

Radar augmentation is provided by a 17·78 cm monostatic radar reflecting lens which provides approximately 4 m² J-band, over a conical angle of 160° coaxial with the longitudinal axis of the target. A command receiver and battery are mounted on a tray accessible through the nose cone of the target and equipped with flagged safety plug. The TVX targets may also be equipped with the capability of scoring surface-to-air and air-to-air missiles. The TVX target is deployable from either droned or manned aircraft utilising its own internally mounted tow reel which has towlines to 6000 metres in length.

Beech MQM-107 with TRX-4 radar augmented targets for Hawk SAM test and training

Bullet counting provisions are available for each series of HUTTS targets. Antenna and sensor installation varies for the different types of configuration so as to provide the optimum and desired scoring area. The sensitivity of the system can be varied for scoring out to approximately 15 metres. Scoring is achieved when a projectile such as a bullet or missile passes through an RF field which is produced by the sensor transceiver. The frequency shift (doppler effect) created when the projectile transgresses the RF field is detected by the sensor and electronically transmitted through a telemetry link to the tow aircraft then to a ground receiving station. The bullet count is digitally displayed at the ground station. For record purposes the bullet count may be recorded at the ground station. All features of the scoring system for HUTTS can be provided without modification to the towing vehicle. Power for the target scorer and LTC-2 launcher is supplied by the battery packs. Standard telemetry frequencies for the scoring sensor and relay pod are 1775 and 235 Hz, respectively.

STATUS
Earlier target systems, such as the TA-8A/B, TJT-1, TDU-30/B, and TGT-1C MiniMiG, although no longer in production are still widely used; they are described in previous editions of *Jane's Weapon Systems*.

The HUTTS is currently the company's main programme and contracts are in force for supplies to Brazil, UAE and Yugoslavia. The US Army and Navy are using versions of HUTTS and Egypt, Saudi Arabia, Italy, Taiwan, Korea and Japan are considering adoption of HUTTS for sea, air and ground applications. In addition to aircraft types listed in previous editions, the following have been flown with HUTTS: A-4, A-7, Gates-Learjet 35A, MiG-21, T-33/T-34, Mirage 5, MB326, F-100 and MQM-107 drones.

IR plume augmentation for the MQM-107 and BQM-34A drones is under development and test.
CONTRACTOR
Hayes International Corporation, Targets Division, PO Box 707, Leeds, Alabama 35094, USA.

EQUIPMENT

NAVAL GUNS AND BOMBARDMENT ROCKETS

CANADA

6053.203
TWIN 3 inch AA MOUNTING
Certain of the frigates of the Canadian Navy are fitted with twin 3 inch (76 mm) Vickers Mk 6 AA guns (**6016.203**) manufactured in Canada. This is a 70-calibre weapon in a light turret and it replaced the forward 3 inch/50 calibre American mount (**6030.203**), the aft mount being left unaltered.
STATUS
Fitted in the 'Mackenzie' and 'Restigouche' class frigates. The latter class are in reserve.

Twin 3 inch 70-calibre guns on the destroyer escort Chaudière (Canadian Maritime Command)

CHILE

6054.203
SINGLE 5 inch MK 27 DUAL-PURPOSE GUN MOUNTING
Eight of these guns are fitted to the ex-US 'Brooklyn' class cruiser *O'Higgins*. They are believed to be of US manufacture but 5 inch guns of this calibre are no longer in service in the US Navy.

The cruiser O'Higgins. Four of the eight 5 inch dual-purpose guns can be seen in single mountings abreast of the superstructure (Chilean Navy)

CHINA (PEOPLE'S REPUBLIC)

6055.203
CHINESE NAVAL ORDNANCE
Much of the Chinese Navy is made up of vessels originally designed and constructed in the Soviet Union and subsequently transferred to China. A further section – but one of diminishing importance – consists of ex-Japanese and Second World War ships inherited by the present regime from that of Chiang Kai Shek. Most of these latter vessels are now at least obsolescent if not obsolete.

Since the mid-1950s, however, the Chinese have been building many of their own fighting ships. At first these were mainly built from parts supplied by the Soviet Union, but since the two countries have become estranged the Chinese have had to rely increasingly on their own resources.

Because of this overlapping supply it is not possible to say exactly for which vessels the guns have been built in China, or which of those have been entirely manufactured in China. It seems probable, however, that there are Chinese-built guns of at least the following types currently in service: 100 mm dual-purpose (twin and single mounts), 57 mm (twin), 37 mm AA (twin mounts), and 25 mm AA (twin mounts). It is also certain that 130 mm guns (in twin mountings) are being built in China for incorporation in the new 'Luda' class destroyers. 100 mm single mountings too continue to be installed in new Chinese ships. Guns of several other calibres are in service with the fleet, and must therefore be being serviced in Chinese yards, but it cannot be said with certainty that they have been built in China.

14·5 mm calibre AA (twin) mount on P4 Class torpedo boat of Chinese Navy

4513.203
TWIN 130 mm DUAL-PURPOSE GUN MOUNTING
This gun mounting is a copy of the original gun system and mounting used on the Soviet 'Kotlin' class destroyers. Blueprints for the system were probably received prior to 1960, but the Chinese were unable to effect production of the mounting until ten years later when the first of the 'Luda' class destroyers was laid down. The gun houses differ slightly in having rounded edges and do not include the fitting of a ranging radar as installed on Soviet units.
CHARACTERISTICS
Calibre: 130 mm
Barrel length: 58 calibres
Elevation: 85° max
Projectile weight: 33·4 kg
Muzzle velocity: 945 m/s
Max range: 29 300 m
Rate of fire: 15-17 rounds/minute

Twin 130 mm gun mount on Chinese 'Luda' class destroyer. Note open rear to turret and basket on back (G Jacobs)

4514.203
SINGLE 130 mm GUN MOUNTING

This is an old gun mounting originally received with the Soviet 'Gordy' class destroyers transferred to China in 1954-55. Two mountings are also installed in the ex-British 'Castle' class patrol frigate still in Chinese naval use and may possibly have come from spares provided for the 'Gordy' class as it seems unlikely that they were ever built in China. Although

very elderly and relying on the equally elderly Soviet Post Lamp fire control radar for ranging information, the mountings may remain in service for some years since the 'Gordy' class have been fitted with SSMs and this may indicate an extension of their lives beyond the normal length.

CHARACTERISTICS
Soviet designation: Model B-13-2C

Calibre: 130 mm
Length of barrel: 50 calibres
Elevation: 45° max
Projectile weight: 33·4 kg
Muzzle velocity: 875 m/s
Max range: 25 000 m
Rate of fire: 12 rounds/minute

4515.203
SINGLE 100 mm DUAL-PURPOSE GUN MOUNTING

This single mounting was introduced into Chinese naval service in 1956-57 during the assembly of four Soviet 'Riga' class frigates at Hudong shipyard, Shanghai. It was extensively used in the 1960s in rebuilding ex-British and ex-Japanese frigates where all, except for the 'Castle' class, were re-armed with this gun system manufactured in China from blueprints originally sold by the Soviet Union in the late 1950s. It has also been installed in the locally designed 'Jiangnan' class frigates, and also appears to continue to be fitted in the more modern 'Jiangdong' and 'Jianghu' class frigates.

CHARACTERISTICS
Soviet designation: Bu-34
Calibre: 100 mm
Length of barrel: 56 calibres
Elevation: 85° max
Projectile weight: 15·9 kg
Muzzle velocity: 875 m/s
Max range: 21 900 m
Rate of fire: 15-18 rounds/minute

100 mm single dual-purpose mount on stern of a Chinese 'Jianghu' class frigate. Note small size of twin 37 mm mountings where twin 57 mm mounting may have been intended (G Jacobs)

4516.203
SINGLE 85 mm DUAL-PURPOSE GUN MOUNTING

This single 85 mm mounting was first placed in Soviet naval service in 1948 and is controlled by optical directors only. It can be considered obsolescent despite its use in a number of Communist countries. It is fitted to China's 20 'Kronstadt' class patrol vessels.

CHARACTERISTICS
Soviet designation: Model 90K
Calibre: 85 mm
Length of barrel: 52 calibres
Elevation: –5 to +85°
Elevation rate: 8°/s
Projectile weight: 9·6 kg

Muzzle velocity: 760 m/s
Max range: 15 000 m
Rate of fire: 15-18 rounds/minute

4517.203
SINGLE 75 mm DUAL-PURPOSE GUN MOUNTING

The 75 mm dual-purpose gun mounting first became available from captured Nationalist escorts and landing craft after the Civil War. It may subsequently have been manufactured locally from captured blueprints as quantities continue to be seen on refitted American LSTs.

CHARACTERISTICS
US designation: Mark 22 Mods 2 and 17
Calibre: 75 mm
Length of barrel: 50 calibres
Elevation: –13 to +85°
Projectile weight: 13·05 lb (5·92 kg) (AA); 13·07 lb (5·93 kg) (AP)
Muzzle velocity: 2650 ft/s (808 m/s)

Max range: 14 000 yards (12 800 m)
Rate of fire: 18 rounds/minute
Total mounting weight: 7500 lb (3400 kg) (Mod 17); 8310 lb (3769 kg) (Mod 2)

4518.203
TWIN 57 mm AA GUN MOUNTING

This is a water-cooled adaptation of the Soviet 57 mm SIF-31B model. Some 'Luda' class destroyers were initially armed with it as the AA defence system intended for all units of the class. It is, however, now only standard on the 'Hainan' class patrol craft, four of which have been exported to Pakistan. A lead computing optical sight is used for fire control. The magazine on an escort holds about 1600 rounds. The Chinese indicate that they have high explosive, fragmenting, and tracer rounds available.

CHARACTERISTICS
Calibre: 57 mm
Length of barrel: 70 calibres
Elevation: –10 to +85°
Weight of projectile: 6·31 kg
Muzzle velocity: 1000 m/s
Max range: 12 000 m
Rate of fire: 2 × 105-120 rounds/minute

Twin 57 mm AA mount on 'Hainan' class escort. Note twin 25 mm 'over-and-under' mounting amidships (G Jacobs)

4519.203
TWIN 37 mm AA GUN MOUNTING
Both single and twin mountings are standard throughout the Chinese Navy and are currently used by all destroyers, frigates and fleet minesweepers, and some landing ships. Both mounting and ammunition are available for export and equip a number of vessels sold to Bangladesh, Pakistan and Sri Lanka. Only local fire control is available.
CHARACTERISTICS
Soviet designation: B-11-M (twin); Model 70K (single)
Calibre: 37 mm
Length of barrel: 63 calibres
Elevation: –10 to +85°
Weight of projectiles: 1·416 kg
Muzzle velocity: 875 m/s
Max range: 8500 m
Rate of fire: 2 × 160-180 rounds/minute

Twin 37 mm and twin 25 mm 'over-and-under' mounts on Chinese 'Shanghai' class gunboat (G Jacobs)

4520.203
TWIN 14·5 mm GUN MOUNTING
A light AA mounting fitted in the 'Chengdu' class frigates, the 'Kronstadt' class patrol vessels, the 'Huchuan' torpedo-armed fast attack craft, and the T-43 minesweepers. It is not certain that it is still in production although 'Huchuan' class vessels continue to be built. The ammunition however is available for export. Local fire control only is available.
CHARACTERISTICS
Soviet designation: 2M-7
Calibre: 14·5 mm
Length of barrel: 93 calibres
Elevation: –5 to +85°
Weight of projectile: 0·06 kg
Muzzle velocity: 1000 m/s
Max range: 7000 m
Rate of fire: 2 × 600 rounds/minute

FRANCE

6064.203
SINGLE 100 mm DUAL-PURPOSE GUN MOUNTING MODEL 1968-II
The gun mounting Model 1968-II represents the latest version of French 100 mm turret and is a lightened and completely automatic version derived from the Models 1953, 64 and 68-I. This calibre is considered optimum by the French authorities for engaging air targets and surface vessels, as well as shore bombardment. Among the intended targets are missiles, including sea-skimming types.

Prototype Creusot 100 mm Compact

Features of the Model 1968-II 100 mm gun which suit it for multipurpose roles include: fully automatic remote operation, with the option of autonomous operation with a crew of two; high rate of continuous fire; replenishment of magazine when firing is in progress for long engagements; a container-based munition re-supply system; long bore life due to air purging and water cooling after each round is fired. Both a multipurpose and a prefragmented shell can be used. The multipurpose shell uses either a time or a proximity fuze while the prefragmented shell was primarily designed for proximity fuzing.
CHARACTERISTICS
Calibre: 100 mm
Barrel length: 55 calibres
Elevation: –15 to +80°
Max speed in elevation: 25°/s
Max acceleration (elevation): 80°/s²
Max slewing speed: 40°/s
Max acceleration (slew): 50°/s²
Projectile weight: 13·5 kg (1·05 kg charge)
Round weight: 23·6 kg
Rate of fire: 60 rounds/minute (80 rounds/minute on recent models)
Muzzle velocity: 870 m/s
Max range: 17 000 m (9 nautical miles)
Max practical range against air target: 6000–8000 m
STATUS
Operational with the French Navy since 1960, this equipment has subsequently undergone several modernisation programmes. It also serves in the navies of the Federal Republic of Germany, Belgium, Portugal, Argentina and Greece.
Creusot-Loire is developing a 100 mm Compact, derived from the 100 mm French Navy version, which is entirely automatic and which has essentially the same performance characteristics. Its weight of 17 tons allows installation aboard small ships. A

Model 1968-II 100 mm dual-purpose turret

reversible ammunition feed system is provided which also permits the use of several types of ammunition with instantaneous selection. Rate of fire is variable between 10 and 90 rounds/minute. Other significant characteristics include maximum speed and acceleration in elevation of 33°/s and 95°/s² respectively, and maximum slewing speed and acceleration of 50°/s and 57°/s². It has been ordered by Saudi Arabia and Malaysia.
CONTRACTORS
Overall responsibility for the 100 mm Model 1968-II guns and mounts rests with the Direction Technique des Constructions Navales (DTCN), 2 rue Royale, 75200 Paris Navale, France, with manufacture undertaken by:
Turret: Société Creusot-Loire, 15 rue Pasquier, 75383 Paris Cedex 08, France; and ECAN Ruelle, 16600 Ruelle, France (a DTCN establishment).
Control gear: CSEE, 2-8 rue Caroline, 75850 Paris Cedex 17, France.

6065.203
TWIN 57 mm AA GUN MOUNTING
This 57 mm gun is now only fitted in the French Navy in the old cruiser *Colbert*. It consists of twin Bofors guns carried on a mount of French design. Each gun is provided with an ammunition reserve of 80 rounds, which can be replenished from a transfer chamber located below the mount. The gun and mount are normally operated under remote control but autonomous operation is also possible.
CHARACTERISTICS
Calibre: 57 mm
Barrel length: 60 calibres
Elevation: –8 to +93°
Projectile weight: 2·96 kg
Muzzle velocity: 865 m/s
Max range: 13 km (7 nautical miles)
Practical range (air targets): 5000 m (3 nautical miles)
Rate of fire: 2 × 120 rounds/minute
Weight: 16 tons
CONTRACTOR
Direction Technique des Constructions Navales (DTCN), 2 rue Royale, 75200 Paris Navale, France.

French version of the Bofors 57 mm mount
(Stefan Terzibaschitsch)

2135.203
RAP 14 NAVAL BOMBARDMENT ROCKETS
The multiple unguided rocket bombardment system known as RAP 14 is now firmly proposed for naval applications.

The land-based version, which is at a much more advanced stage, was described in detail in **2024.103**, in *Jane's Weapon Systems 1982-83*, so that it is necessary here to draw attention only to those features that are peculiar to the naval version.

The naval version will have a 2 × 9 rocket launcher on a remotely controlled mounting with provision for automatic reloading from below deck with the

launcher in the vertical position. Each of the two magazine drums will contain 36 rockets, giving a total capacity, with a full launcher and full magazine, of 90 rockets.
CHARACTERISTICS
Weight: Complete launcher assembly, less rockets: 10·4 tons. Complete assembly with rockets: 15·09 tons
Magazine dimensions: 5·9 × 2·5 × 2·5 m
Launch combinations: Any number from 1 to 18
Range: Max for standard rocket: 16 km
Rate of fire: 9 s for 18-round salvo
CEP: 90 m

Rocket calibre: 140 mm
Weight: 54 kg
Warhead: 19 kg HE standard. Special warheads possible
Speed: Max Mach 2
CONTRACTORS
System: CNIM (Constructions Navales et Industrielles de la Méditerranée), 50 avenue des Champs-Elysées, 75008 Paris, France.
Mounting: in co-operation with Creusot-Loire, Groupes Marine Schneider, 15 rue Pasquier, 75008 Paris, France.

3655.203
TYPE A NAVAL MOUNTING FOR 20 mm F2 GUN
This naval mounting is installed in small, lightweight ships, and carries the French F2 20 mm automatic cannon which is also employed in land-based and airborne roles. It is designed for one-man operation, and elevation and slewing motions are manually powered. Two types of ammunition can be employed, carried in a pair of magazines on the mount with a combined capacity of 300 rounds. Continuous, limited burst and single-shot firing can be selected, and the mount can be used for both air or surface target engagement.
CHARACTERISTICS
Calibre: 20 mm
Elevation: –15 to +60°

Rate of fire: 720 rounds/minute
Muzzle velocity: 1050 or 1250 m/s*
Effective range: 2000 or 1200 m*
Max range: 10 020 or 6770 m*
Power requirement: 26 V, 7 A
Weight: 470 kg (360 kg without ammunition)
*Depending upon type of ammunition: explosive or armour-piercing.
STATUS
In series production for 'Tripartite' mine-hunter vessels of the Belgian, Dutch and French Navies. This gun also exists on a mobile land mounting for army use (**5599.103**).
CONTRACTOR
Direction Technique des Constructions Navales (DTCN), 2 rue Royale, 75200 Paris Navale, France.

Type A naval mounting for 20 mm F2 gun

GERMANY (FEDERAL REPUBLIC)

3177.203
SINGLE 20 mm NAVAL GUN S20
This is the naval mount version of the Rheinmetall Mk 20 Rh 202 20 mm automatic cannon described in **5600.103**. S20 naval guns are primarily intended for installation on small and fast ships and as secondary armament on larger vessels as well as for static applications ashore. Low weight and one-man body aimed actuation of the mount assure rapid response for the effective engagement of surface and air targets, whereby the gunner always remains in an upright position.

The weapon itself is the Rheinmetall 20 mm automatic cannon Mk 20 Rh 202 which is particularly suited for these purposes because of its low recoil forces. The Mk 20 Rh 202 is also renowned for its functional safety and reliability in spite of restricted lubrication, sea water contamination, heavy fouling and other extreme environmental conditions. Mount and weapon can be dismantled into their major components without the use of any tools.

Rheinmetall single 20 mm gun mount S20

CHARACTERISTICS
Type: Mk 20 Rh 202
Calibre: 20 mm
Rate of fire: 1000 rounds/minute
Muzzle velocities: HEI-T, TP-T 1050 m/s; API-T 1100 m/s; APDS-T 1150 m/s
Recoil force: 550 – 750 kgf
Tactical range: 2000 m
Firing: Mechanical

Type of fire: Single or sustained fire
Ammunition supply: 200 rounds belted in exchangeable ammo box
Traverse: Unlimited
Elevation: –10 to +55°
Sight: Mechanical AA sight with parallelogram linkage and shoulder rest. Night vision device and telescope sight are optional
Weight: Mount complete: 334 kg; ammunition: 74 kg

Length: 3070 mm
Width: 1230 mm
Height: 1570 – 1785 mm
STATUS
In production.
CONTRACTOR
Rheinmetall International, Deutschland GmbH, Ulmenstrasse 125, D 4000 Düsseldorf 30, Federal Republic of Germany.

ISRAEL

3729.203
TCM 30 TWIN 30 mm NAVAL GUN
The TCM 30 naval air defence weapon consists of two automatic 30 mm cannons and their feed systems mounted on a high angular acceleration, electrically-driven stabilised turret. The guns are Oerlikon 30 mm automatic cannons which with their respective 125-

TCM 30 twin 30 mm mount used for naval air defence

round ammunition feed boxes, are carried on a unique barrel-support system which reduces shot dispersion to a minimum. The cradle is carried on an electrically-driven mount which is fitted with rate gyros that provide signals to stabilise the guns against ship's motion. The turret has an elevation angle of –20 to +85°, and both positioning and velocity can be controlled from the ship's fire control system, which in Israeli vessels is generally based on the EL/M-2221 naval fire control radar (**3709.253**).

Five different types of ammunition provide flexibility against various classes of target. Two 125-linked round ammunition boxes are mounted on the gun cradle so that they move with the guns in elevation and traverse. Semi-rigid chutes guide the linked rounds from the boxes to the gun's bolt feed mechanisms, thus ensuring smooth feed paths which do not strain the belt's flexibility. Two back-up magazines provide a 40-round reserve.

The TCM 30 is also adaptable to towed carriage mounts and armoured vehicles, as well as both large and small classes of warship. The same twin gun, on mountings suitable for land-mobile applications, is employed also in the Spider II air defence artillery system (**4508.131**).
CHARACTERISTICS
Main armament: 2 × Oerlikon 30 mm automatic cannon
Traverse: ±160°
Elevation: –20 to +85°
Acceleration (azimuth and elevation): 10 rad/s^2
Max speed (azimuth and elevation): 1·5 rad/s
Rate of fire: 2 × 650 rounds/minute
MV: 1080 m/s
Overall length: 3550 mm
CONTRACTOR
MBT Weapon Systems, Israel Aircraft Industries, Industrial Zone, Yahud, Israel.

ITALY

5534.203
SINGLE 127/54 GUN MOUNTING
The 127/54 is a dual-purpose gun mount of an intermediate calibre which has been designed for use as the main armament for frigates and destroyers.

Design work started in October 1965 as a joint venture with the Italian government. The first prototype was completed in May 1969.

Ready use ammunition is held in three drums just below the turret. A central elevator hoists the ammunition, chosen from one drum, and delivers it to the turret where two oscillating arms perform the final movement to the loading trays. The three drums are automatically reloaded through two hoists manually loaded in the magazine.

This three drum layout makes it possible to stow three different types of ammunition in the ready use magazine from which ammunition can be selected appropriate for the type of action. Remote-controlled fuze setters are provided in the oscillating arms.

The reloading, feeding, loading, and firing sequence is controlled by a control console operated by a single man.

The electrically-operated remote control servo-system is of modular construction using silicon controlled rectifiers. The modules are the same as

those used on other modern OTO Melara weapon systems.

The main technical features are the light alloy construction, the compact installation, and the lightweight control mechanism.

The barrel is fitted with a muzzle brake. The shield is of fibreglass and is watertight.
CHARACTERISTICS
Calibre: 127 mm
Weight: 34 tons
Rate of fire: 45 rounds/minute
Ready ammunition: 69 rounds (3 × 22 + 3)
Trunnion thrust: 24 000 kg
Elevation: –15 to +85°
Traverse: 350°
Elevating speed: 30°/s
Elevating acceleration: 40°/s^2
Traverse speed: 40°/s
Traverse acceleration: 45°/s^2
STATUS
In production and in service with Canada on four DD 280 class destroyers (1 turret); Italy on two 'Audace' class destroyers (2 turrets), eight 'Maestrale' class frigates (1 turret), and four 'Lupo' class frigates (1 turret); Argentina on four Blohm and Voss frigates (1 turret); Nigeria on one Blohm and Voss frigate

127/54 OTO single barrel naval mount

(1 turret); Peru on four 'Lupo' class frigates (1 turret) and Venezuela on six 'Lupo' class frigates (1 turret). Note: this includes ships currently on order or building.
CONTRACTOR
OTO Melara, Via Valdilocchi 15, La Spezia, Italy.

5532.203
SINGLE 76/62 OTO MMI GUN MOUNTING
The 76/72 OTO MMI single barrel automatic gun was developed to a government contract for ships of the frigate and corvette types as a dual-purpose anti-ship weapon. It was the forerunner of the successful 76/62 OTO Compact (**5533.203**) described below, which has superseded it.

The gun is a single barrel, water-spray cooled, on a powered mounting. It is protected by a watertight splinterproof shield, which also houses the one man required to direct the gun. Great efforts have been made to reduce the crew, and all operations are performed automatically.

Ammunition is fed from the magazine up to the loading trays, from where it is rammed into the breech. This feed system can vary in length from a minimum of 2·5 m to a maximum of 11 m, and will therefore accommodate a wide range of alternative deck and magazine locations.

The gun has a high rate of fire for its calibre, the maximum being about 60 rounds/minute.

OTO 76/62 MMI single gun mountings

Ammunition is fixed, and the empty cases are ejected automatically.

Elevation and traverse is by electric and hydraulic control, with an emergency manual operation. The whole system can be controlled remotely or the fire director can exercise local control from his position beside the gun.

CHARACTERISTICS

Calibre: 76 mm

Overall weight: 12 tons
Rate of fire: 55 – 65 rounds/minute
Ready to fire rounds: 59
Elevation: –15 to +85°
Traverse: 360°
Elevation speed: 40°/s
Traversing speed: 70°/s
Elevation acceleration: 70°/s²
Traversing acceleration: 100°/s²

STATUS
There are many in service with the Italian Navy.
CONTRACTOR
OTO Melara, Via Valdilocchi 15, La Spezia, Italy.

5533.203

SINGLE 76/62 COMPACT GUN MOUNTING

The 76/62 OTO compact is a light, small calibre gun mount intended for installation in ships of any type and class down to motor gun boats and hydrofoils as a dual purpose anti-aircraft and anti-ship weapon system.

The gun and mounting were developed from the 76/62 OTO MMI mounting (**5532.203**), the design study being started in 1964, and the first production units came into service in March 1969.

The mounting may be considered in two parts; the shank which is below the weather deck, and the turret which is installed on deck. The shank contains the ammunition feed system, which consists of a rotating platform and a hoist.

It can fire 80 rounds without reloading, and the rate

OTO 76/62 compact gun mount

of fire is adjustable from 10 to 85 rounds per minute. A version is available with a rate of fire up to 100 rounds per minute. Existing guns can be modified with a special kit.

Generally, the system is controlled remotely; optionally it can also be fitted with a stabilised line of sight local control system. A reaction time of 2·8 seconds is quoted.

The shield is made of fibreglass, and is watertight. It offers complete protection against nuclear fall-out. The gun barrel has a small multi-hole muzzle brake and a fume extractor.

CHARACTERISTICS

Calibre: 76 mm
Overall weight: 7·5 tons
Rate of fire: 85 rounds/minute
Max trunnion thrust: 7000 kg
Elevation: –15 to +85°
Traverse: Unlimited
Elevation speed: Max 35°/s
Elevation acceleration: 72°/s²
Traverse speed: Max 60°/s
Traverse acceleration: 72°/s²

DEVELOPMENT
In mid-1980 OTO Melara began work on a version known as the 76/62 OTO compact extended proficiency. The main features are the addition of the LINCE autonomous fire director (**4047.281**, in the Systems section of this volume) to the turret, and provision of a new prefragmented shell with a special

proximity fuze developed for use against sea skimmer or diving missiles. The shell was developed by OTO Melara and SNIA and while retaining the same ballistic performance and weight of conventional HE shells, it has greater lethality due to the greater number of splinters (approx 8000) and their penetration capabilities. The shell is made of special high grade steel, filled with 630 grams of cast Compound 3 and containing about 4660 tungsten 0·2 gram spheres, fitted in the wall of the mid-section of the shell body. The proximity fuze uses the doppler principle and is effective at distances of up to eight metres from the target. The antenna is of the dipole type, with the shell acting as one half of the dipole; this does not radiate in the direction of the shell axis, thus rendering the fuze insensitive in the forward direction so that maximum sensitivity is encountered as the shell passes the target. ECCM devices are incorporated.

STATUS
In service with, or being delivered to, 35 navies. In the USA this gun is produced under licence by FMC Corporation for the US Navy with which service it has designation 76 mm/62 calibre gun mount Mk 75 (**3175.203**), and is also being manufactured in Japan for the Japanese Navy. Production under licence is also undertaken in Spain for 'Lazaga' and 'Descubierta' classes of ship.

CONTRACTOR
OTO Melara, Via Valdilocchi 15, La Spezia, Italy.

2258.203

BREDA COMPACT TWIN 40 mm L/70 NAVAL MOUNTING TYPE 70

This twin 40 mm L/70 naval mounting has been developed by Breda Meccanica Bresciana in close co-operation with Bofors in Sweden as part of the Breda/Bofors System 75 (see also **2349.131**) which is particularly intended for point defence against aircraft and anti-ship missiles.

Claimed to be the lightest and smallest 40 mm mounting currently available, the compact mount is fully automatic in operation, employs new remote controlled servo-systems of high performance to improve accuracy – which is also improved by the

reductions in weight, inertia, and recoil disturbance resulting from the exceptionally small separation between the two barrels – and features a high rate of fire and a substantial supply of ready-use ammunition.

The weapon is available in two versions, Type A and Type B, the difference residing in the quantity of ready-use ammunition contained in the magazine (736 or 444 rounds) and in some consequential weight and dimension changes which are indicated below. In each type the magazine is divided into two halves each with a hoist serving one barrel. Without manual intervention the two hoists operate in synchronism.

Horizontally, the mounting is also divided into two parts. The upper part contains the cradle, the elevating mass, the automatic feeders, the servo-motors, and associated electronics and the firing, aiming, and limiting devices. The lower structure mainly comprises the magazine and hoists. The magazine is made up of several horizontal layers, there being seven of these in Type A and four in Type B. Before firing and during firing intervals these layers are packed with ammunition in four-round clips.

CHARACTERISTICS

Calibre: 40 mm/70
Rate of fire: 2 × 300 rounds/minute
Muzzle velocity: 1000 m/s
Ammunition type: AP tracer, HE direct action, HE proximity fuze
Ready-to-use ammunition: 736 or 444
Traverse
Arc: Unlimited
Speed: 90°/s
Acceleration: 120°/s²
Elevation
Arc: –13 to +85°
Speed: 60°/s
Acceleration: 120°/s²
Swept radius: 3 m
Weight
Mounting without ammunition: Type A 5500 kg; Type B 5300 kg
Mounting with ammunition: Type A 7300 kg; Type B 6300 kg
Power supplies: 440 V 60 Hz 3-phase; 115 V 400 Hz single-phase; Peak demand 13 kW; Mean demand 4·5 – 8 kW

STATUS
The mounting is in mass production and entering service with more than 20 navies.

CONTRACTOR
Breda Meccanica Bresciana SpA, Via Lunga 2, 25100 Brescia, Italy.

Breda 40 mm L/70 twin mountings

2558.203
TWIN 40 mm NAVAL MOUNTING TYPE 106
This Breda/Bofors 40 mm L/70 mounting comprises two guns and two 32-round magazines. It can be controlled remotely, locally by means of the 'cloche' on the left of the mount, or manually. Ammunition feed may be either automatic by means of the Breda 32-round feeder or manually by inserting a four-round charger into the auto-loader of the elevating mass. The aiming device is either the NIFE type SRS-5 or the Mirasole line-of-sight type.
CHARACTERISTICS
Generally as for other 40 mm L/70 mountings
Gun weight: With feeder and battery, less ammunition 6510 + 100 kg
Training speed: 95°/s
Elevation speed: 95°/s
Acceleration: 125°/s²
Power required: Elevation and training 4 kW each
Recoil force: 2 × 2700 kg
STATUS
In service but no longer in production.
CONTRACTOR
Breda Meccanica Bresciana SpA, Via Lunga 2, 25100 Brescia, Italy.

Breda Type 106 twin 40 mm AA mount aboard the West German 'Hamburg' class ship Bayern *(Stefan Terzibaschitsch)*

2557.203
BREDA/BOFORS NAVAL MOUNTINGS
Breda Meccanica Bresciana make a range of single and twin naval anti-aircraft gun mountings incorporating a variety of different automatic feed systems and Bofors elevating mass. Breda also manufacture a 40 mm field mounting, details of which will be found in entry **2603.103**.

Set out in the following entries are brief details of current mountings. All use the 40 mm L/70 increased rate of fire pattern of Bofors gun (**2360.203**) which has the following general characteristics (which are not repeated in the individual entries below).
CHARACTERISTICS
Calibre: 40 mm
Barrel length: 70 calibres
Weight of shell: 0·96 kg
MV: 1005 m/s (range 12·5 km max)

Rate of fire: 300 rounds/minute (per barrel)
Train: Unlimited
Elevation: –10 to +85°
STATUS
In service.
CONTRACTOR
Breda Meccanica Bresciana SpA, Via Lunga 2, 25100 Brescia, Italy.

2556.203
TWIN 40 mm NAVAL MOUNTING TYPE 64
This is a sophisticated Breda/Bofors mounting comprising two 40 mm L/70 guns and twin 100-round automatic magazines. It can be controlled remotely or locally. A graticule, Mirasole, or NIFE reflection sight can be fitted. Special features of this mounting include barrel cooling arrangements and an automatic fuze-setting device.
CHARACTERISTICS
Generally as other 40 mm L/70 mountings
Total weight: Excluding ammunition 7900 + 150 kg
Training speed: 85°/s minimum
Elevation speed: 95°/s minimum
Training acceleration: 110°/s² minimum
Elevation acceleration: 125°/s² minimum
Rate of fire: 2 × 300 rounds/minute
Power requirement: 6 kW each for training and elevation motors plus 1·6 kW for the feeder motor
STATUS
In service but no longer in production.
CONTRACTOR
Breda Meccanica Bresciana SpA, Via Lunga 2, 25100 Brescia, Italy.

Breda/Bofors twin mounting Type 64

2554.203
SINGLE 40 mm NAVAL MOUNTING TYPE 564
This mounting differs from earlier Breda versions of the Bofors L/70 gun in being equipped with a Model 1971 144-round automatic feed of compact design. This permits a more effective use of the gun's high rate of fire and reduces the number of men required on the mount to two, with a third on standby near the mount to reload the automatic feed. A version requiring only one man on the gun is also available. The feed reloading operation can obviously be carried out during lulls in the firing, but with a little practice it is possible to reload while the gun is firing.

A further advantage of this feed system is that it can be fitted retrospectively to gun mountings which incorporate earlier types of feed. Complete modification kits are available to enable a purchaser having access to reasonable engineering facilities to arrange for the modification to be carried out, under Breda supervision, at any convenient location.

It is also known under the designation Breda/Bofors 350P.
CHARACTERISTICS
Generally as for other 40 mm L/70 gun mountings
Gun weight: With automatic feeder and with battery but excluding ammunition 3300 + 100 kg
Training speed: Local or remote control 80°/s

Elevation speed: Local or remote control 45°/s
Training acceleration: 120°/s²
Elevation acceleration: 130°/s²
Power consumption: 6 + 8 kW
STATUS
In service and in production.

Manufacture of the automatic feed device has been licensed by Breda to Bazan for Spanish naval production, incorporated with the Bofors SAK 350.
CONTRACTOR
Breda Meccanica Bresciana SpA, Via Lunga 2, 25100 Brescia, Italy.

Breda/Bofors 40 mm L/70 naval mounting with 144-round automatic feed

2555.203

SINGLE 40 mm NAVAL MOUNTING TYPE 107

This Breda/Bofors mounting comprises a single 40 mm L/70 gun and a 32-round magazine feed. It can be controlled remotely, locally by means of the 'cloche' on the left of the mount, or manually. Ammunition feed may be either automatic by means of the Breda 32-round feeder or manually by inserting a four-round charger into the auto-loader of the elevating mass. The aiming device is either the NIFE type SRS-5 or the Mirasole.
CHARACTERISTICS
Generally as for other 40 mm L/70 mountings
Gun weight: With feeder and battery, less ammunition 3610 + 100 kg
Training speed: 95°/s
Elevation speed: 95°/s
Acceleration: 125°/s²

Power required: Elevation and training 4 kW each
Recoil force: 2700 kg
STATUS
In production and service.
CONTRACTOR
Breda Meccanica Bresciana SpA, Via Lunga 2, 25100 Brescia, Italy.

40 mm Breda/Bofors mounting Type 107

5535.203

TWIN 35 mm OE/OTO MOUNTING

The 35 mm OE/OTO mounting has been produced as a private venture and is intended for use in any type of ship down to motor gun boats and hydrofoils, or as local defence for merchant ships in time of war. It is primarily for close anti-aircraft defence, with a secondary anti-ship and anti-shore role.

The mounting utilises a high proportion of light alloys in its construction. The shield is made of fibreglass and is watertight.

The mounting is remotely controlled without local aiming and is fitted with modular servo-systems of very light weight using electric motors with controlled rectifiers developed by OTO Melara.

The Oerlikon KDA 35 mm gun has a high rate of fire and is belt fed. An interesting feature is that two belts are fed to each gun, and either may be selected in about two seconds. Thus the mounting can switch very rapidly from firing, for example, anti-aircraft ammunition to armour-piercing. Each gun is provided with EVA at the muzzle to measure muzzle velocity, and this information is fed back into the computer to permit corrections in laying to be applied.

The Oerlikon guns used are similar to the KDC 35 mm cannons employed in the Oerlikon GDM-A twin 35 mm naval mount described in entry **6036.203** in the Swiss pages of this section. The GDM-A mount carries KDC cannons while the slightly lighter KDA guns are fitted in the Oerlikon/OTO mount, which has the Swiss designation GDM-C. The two versions of the gun have the same muzzle velocity, rate of fire, barrel length, and gas pressure. The KDA has twin belt feed, selectable left-hand or right-hand; the KDC has automatic clip ammunition feed, independent of the cannon.

OE/OTO 35 mm naval twin mount

Other details will be found in **6036.203** later in this section.
CHARACTERISTICS
Calibre: 35 mm
Barrel length: 90 calibres (3·15 m)
Max recoil: 55 mm
Max range: 6000 m (surface targets); 5000 m (aerial targets)
Elevation: –15 to +85°
Traverse: Unlimited

Elevating speed: Max 75°/s
Traversing speed: Max 115°/s
Elevating acceleration: 140°/s²
Traversing acceleration: 130°/s²
STATUS
This turret is fitted in Libyan 670 ton corvettes built in Italy.
CONTRACTOR
OTO Melara, Via Valdilocchi 15, La Spezia, Italy.

3994.203

BREDA TWIN 30 mm COMPACT NAVAL MOUNTING

Breda has designed and developed this mounting, using two Mauser MK 30 mm × 173 guns, set in a Breda twin cradle. Advanced design features of the twin 40 mm L/70 find their place in the new twin 30 mm, features not hitherto evolved in this calibre.

Reaction time is cut to the minimum through complete automation, and both training and elevation velocities and accelerations are high (see characteristics). There are large ammunition reserves to meet saturation and successive attacks without human intervention in replenishment. Maximum accuracy is assisted by barrel proximity and mounting rigidity. The mounting is protected against the environment by a fibreglass dome, with one access hatch at the rear, and special attention has been given to sealing the mantlet plate and bearing assembly for watertightness.

The Breda patented magazine structure, containing an exceptionally large number of rounds, trains with the mounting, maintaining a constant relation to the feeders, and is divided into two halves,

one half supplying each gun independently. The belted rounds are suspended in vertical folds, each fold being advanced as its predecessor is fired off. Replenishment can take place without firing off all the ammunition.

The mounting is supplied in four versions, designed for siting arrangement in various classes of ship. Dimensions are reduced to the minimum possible, aided by barrel proximity, and weight is contained by employing light alloys to the greatest practicable extent. The gun fires GAU-8 ammunition: HE(I), or armour piercing discarding sabot (APDS), with depleted uranium or swaged tungsten penetrator for missile warhead penetration and detonation. Also a frangible round for anti-aircraft fire.

CHARACTERISTICS
Rate of fire (combined): 1600 rounds/minute
Muzzle velocity: 1040 m/s (APDS M50)
Elevation limits: –13 to +85°
Training limits: Unlimited
Elevation velocity: 75°/s
Elevation acceleration: 100°/s²
Training velocity: 120°/s
Training acceleration: 150°/s²
Ready-to-fire rounds: 2000 (1000/gun)
Distance between barrels: 260 mm
STATUS
Development complete. Production line being set up.
CONTRACTOR
Breda Meccanica Bresciana SpA, Via Lunga 2, 25100 Brescia, Italy.

Breda twin 30 mm compact naval mounting with 2000-round magazine and shown with and without the glass-fibre gunhouse

---

4575.203

BREDA SINGLE 30 MM MOUNTING

This completely new single mounting was exhibited for the first time at the 1984 Genoa Naval Exhibition, and uses one Mauser Model Mk 30 mm × 173 gun, set in a Breda cradle.

The mounting has been designed to provide the lightest vessels with a modern and effective gun, or to give a good auxiliary armament to larger major ships. Its main attributes are: remote control; rate of fire up to 800 rounds per minute; double ammunition feed system; capability for remote control in case of interruption in the power supply; complete protection against environmental conditions; lightweight (1200 kg) due to the extensive use of aluminium alloys; small dimensions and compact design.

The on board installation is simple because it is completely above deck. The ready to fire rounds are contained in two boxes that may be easily reached through two replenishing doors placed on the two sides of the shield. Ammunition of GAU-8 type includes: practice rounds (TP), high explosive incendiary (HEI), armour piercing incendiary (API), high explosive incendiary with self destruction device (HEI-SD), frangible rounds and armour piercing discharging sabot rounds (APDS).

CHARACTERISTICS
Muzzle velocity: 1040 m/s (1150 m/s ROF APDS)
Rate of fire: 800 rounds/minute
Training arc: Unlimited
Training acceleration: 300°/s²
Training velocity: 140°/s
Elevation arc: –13 to +85°
Elevation acceleration: 300°/s²

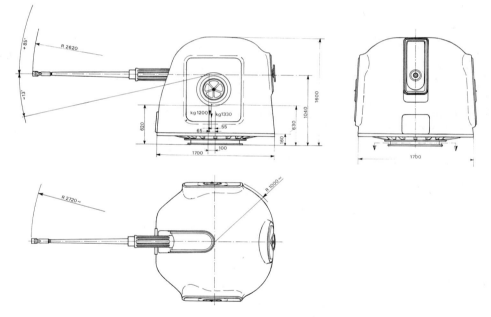

Breda single 30 mm Mounting

Elevation velocity: 80°/s
Weight (without ammunition): 1200 kg
Weight (fully loaded): 1330 kg
Deck ring (outer diameter): 800 mm
Swept radius: 2720 mm

STATUS
Development complete. Ready for production.
CONTRACTOR
Breda Meccanica Bresciana SpA, Via Lunga 2, 25100 Brescia, Italy.

3995.203

BREDA MULTIPURPOSE NAVAL ROCKET LAUNCHER

The Breda multipurpose naval rocket launcher system normally consists of two Breda rocket launchers for 105 mm countermeasures or assault rockets, an Elsag control unit, and a supply of SNIA rockets. The 20-tube launchers are mounted on each side of the ship and they can be trained and elevated by remote control from the control unit. The latter is connected to the ship's radar and a control panel in the ECM compartment from whence it receives the necessary operating signals. The data needed to stabilise the two launchers against pitch and roll are provided by the ship's gyro-compass. The Elsag control system is described in greater detail in the Systems section of this book (entry **1823.281** of Naval Fire Control and Action Data Automation Systems).

The SCLAR 105 mm rocket launcher system is intended to provide passive defence against radar and IR homing missiles, confuse enemy radars, and provide illumination for visual fire control at night. To meet these requirements provision is made for loading different types of rockets in mixed arrangements (long range chaff, medium range chaff, illuminating) to permit mixed salvoes. Automatic selection of the rockets to be fired is possible from the remote fire control unit and the time fuzes and launch sequence may be similarly controlled.

A 105 mm rocket, designed and developed by SNIA Defence and Aeronautical Division, is used by the Italian Navy and the various types are listed in the table of characteristics below.

CHARACTERISTICS
Firing rate: 1 round/s (approx)
Max ready-to-fire rounds: 20/launcher
Training arc: ±150°
Elevation arc: –5 to +60°
Training velocity: 60°/s
Training acceleration: 60°/s²
Elevation velocity: 30°/s
Elevation acceleration: 50°/s²
Launcher weight: 1150 kg (empty); 1750 kg (with 20 rockets)
Trunnion height: 1170 mm
Tubular guide length: 1460 mm
Main power supply: 3 kW
Ammunition
Chaff distraction: 105LR-C (max range 12 000 m)
Chaff seduction: 105MR-C (max range 5000 m)
Illumination: 105LR-I (max range 4000 m)

Breda 105 mm rocket launcher

Close-up view of Breda 105 mm rocket launcher

STATUS

Production. About 100 mountings have been installed in ships of the following navies: Argentina, Ecuador, Federal Republic of Germany, Italy, Nigeria, Peru and Venezuela.

CONTRACTORS

Launcher: Breda Meccanica Bresciana SpA, Via Lunga 2, 25100 Brescia, Italy.

Rockets: SNIA Viscosa, Defence and Space Division, Via Sicilia 162, 00187 Rome, Italy.

3996.203

BREDA MULTI-CALIBRE ASSAULT LAUNCHER

The Breda assault launcher is a special and improved version of the Breda multipurpose rocket launcher (**3995.203**) of which all the main characteristics are retained. It is specifically designed for conducting coastal bombardment.

This launcher is intended more particularly for installation in landing craft providing these ships with the capability for bombarding longer range targets with 105 mm rockets and those at closer range with 51 mm rockets. The assault launcher differs from the standard multipurpose rocket launcher in the following details: the launching tubes are longer in order to provide guidance necessary for the 51 mm rockets, and there is protective covering of the servo

system to improve reliability and maintainability in adverse sea conditions. The ECM and illumination capability remains available with the 105 mm rockets.

STATUS

In production.

CONTRACTORS

Launcher: Breda Meccanica Bresciana SpA, Via Lunga 2, 25100 Brescia, Italy.

Rockets: SNIA Viscosa, Defence and Space Division, Via Sicilia 162, 00187 Rome, Italy.

Breda assault launcher showing 105 mm and 51 mm tubes

4574.203

BREDA 81 mm BOMBARDMENT LAUNCHER

A new Breda Naval Rocket Launcher was presented for the first time at the 1984 Genoa Naval Exhibition. This launcher is equipped with a launching pad consisting of 36 stainless steel tubes for 81 mm bombardment rockets of the Oerlikon SNORA type. The launcher is remote controlled and its servo system is installed in a box-shaped light alloy structure for better protection and reliability.

The ammunition (see **1995.303**) is available in different types (PT, PT with mark charge, HE in three different versions and HEAT).

CHARACTERISTICS

Range: up to 10 km
Ready-to-fire rounds: 36
Training arc: ± 150°
Elevation arc: –2 to +55°
Training velocity: 60°/s
Training acceleration: 60°/s²
Elevation velocity: 30°/s
Elevation acceleration: 50°/s²
Launcher weight: 1270 kg (empty)
Trunnion height: 1170 mm
Swept radius: 1490 mm

STATUS

Ready for production.

CONTRACTOR

Breda Meccanica Bresciana SpA, Via Lunga 2, 25100 Brescia, Italy.

Breda 81 mm bombardment rocket general arrangement

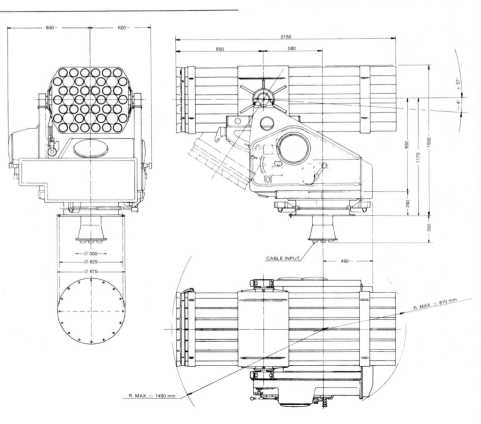

NORWAY

4041.203
KV-SK/20 DUAL-PURPOSE 20 mm NAVAL MOUNTING
To meet the need for a light anti-aircraft and surface target gun for use aboard ships or shore bases, A/S Kongsberg Våpenfabrikk has developed a naval mounting for the Rh 202 gun (**3177.203**). Development was carried out in co-operation with the Ordnance Section of the Norwegian Naval Logistic Command.

The basic concept was to use the Mk 20 × 139 DM 5 gun (Rh 202) in a slightly modified version of the cradle used in the FK20-2 field gun, and to assemble these on a simple pedestal mount, thereby producing a gun which has approximately the same effect as the present field version, FK20-2. It is very reliable since it extensively uses previously developed and proven components and is quickly available because of its

use of standard components. The gun is intended mainly for installation aboard naval vessels such as MTBs and mine-sweepers, fishing boats, and in the defence of coastal forts. The gun can engage fast approaching and slower crossing aircraft and can be used against both land and sea targets.

The pedestal mount consists of the cradle with ammunition feed, the pedestal itself with a fixed base and a rotatable upper part, bowed shoulder-supports and sights. The cradle is basically similar to the existing FK20-2 field gun but where necessary certain components are redesigned, especially those concerned with loading, handling, and servicing. The cradle is supported in bearings at the centre of gravity of the elevating part of the gun and may be locked in four elevation settings (minimum, max, 0° and +30°) for loading and servicing. The elevation locking control is located on the right-hand side of the

rotating part of the pedestal. The adjustable shoulder supports are placed at the rear of the cradle. The trigger is located on the left cradle handle and the selector for single shot/automatic fire is located on the right-hand side of the cradle. The complete cradle can be demounted from the pedestal without special tools.

The pedestal is made of aluminium alloy castings comprising a fixed lower part and rotating U-shaped upper part. The lower part consists of a simple hollow pillar fixed to a baseplate. The baseplate is designed for existing mountings with a diameter between 515 and 670 mm, but can be supplied for larger diameters on request. The baseplate is encircled with protruding footrests for use during aiming. The pedestal's upper part can be locked, by means of a lever, parallel to the ship's longitudinal axis and is also equipped with adjustable rotational stops. The upper part also carries an armoured shield and a box for collection of spent rounds and clips. Both box and shield can easily be removed and replaced.

The sights are of the cross hair and ring type and are fitted to the shoulder supports so that they follow the supports when they are adjusted in height. The sight can be adjusted sideways and in height with respect to the supports, and can also be raised up during servicing of the gun and locked in place again in its previous setting. Other types of sights may be adapted if required.
CHARACTERISTICS
Elevation range: –15 to +70°
Bearing range: 360°
Ammunition capacity (cradle): 2 boxes 100 rounds each
Spent round capacity: approx 200 rounds
Total length: 2870 mm
Max radius: 1730 mm (from end of barrel to axis of rotation)
Weight: 400 kg (with gun, without ammunition)
STATUS
The series produced version is in service on a large number of Norwegian vessels and shore establishments.
CONTRACTOR
Kongsberg Våpenfabrikk AS, 3601 Kongsberg, Norway.

Kongsberg KV-SK/20 20 mm naval mounting

SPAIN

3230.203
OTO 76/62 COMPACT AUTOMATIC GUN
This is a version of the OTO 76/62 compact automatic gun (**5532.203**), built under licence in Spain.
CHARACTERISTICS
Calibre: 76 mm
Barrel length: 62 calibres
Number of rifles: 24

Rate of fire: 80 rounds/minute (adjustable)
Muzzle velocity: 925 m/s
Range: 16·3 km
Elevation: –15 to +85°
Elevation speed: 40°/s
Elevation acceleration: 60°/s²
Traverse: 360°
Traverse speed: 70°/s

Traverse acceleration: 100°/s²
Weight of round: 12·358 kg (complete)
Weight of gun: 8520 kg
Power consumption: 440 V, 60 Hz, 3-phase, 27 kW; 115 V, 60 Hz, 1·5 A; 115 V 400 Hz, 3-phase, 0·6 A
CONTRACTOR
Empresa Nacional Bazán, San Fernando, Spain.

2304.203
40 mm AUTOMATIC GUN SAK L/70 BOFORS-BREDA 144 MOD 76
This is a version of the Bofors L/70 gun (**2360.203**) with Breda automatic feeder, built under licence in Spain.
CHARACTERISTICS
Calibre: 40 mm

Barrel length: 70 calibres
Elevation: –10 to +85°
Elevation speed: 45°/s
Traverse speed: 85°/s unlimited
Range: 12 km max
Rate of fire: 300 rounds/minute
Weight: 3·3 tons

Power consumption: 440 V, 60 Hz, 3-phase; 115 V, 60 Hz
STATUS
Operational in ships of the Spanish Navy.
CONTRACTOR
Empresa Nacional Bazán, San Fernando, Spain.

3176.203
MEROKA NAVAL AIR DEFENCE SYSTEM
The Meroka system is a multi-barrelled 20 mm gun system of Spanish design for close-in air defence of ships and like its US counterpart, Vulcan-Phalanx (**2858.203** and **2543.231**), Meroka features a high rate of fire, comprehensive autonomous fire control provisions and rapid reaction. It is understood that the Spanish specification calls for similar performance characteristics to those of Vulcan-Phalanx.

The naval Meroka is derived from an experimental Spanish Army system (Meroka 12-203). Both consist

of a multi-barrelled non-rotating machine gun with 12 barrels arranged in two horizontal rows of six. All three versions of the standard Oerlikon 20 mm round can be fired with salvoes in four groups of three in a way which minimises the effects of the recoil on aiming. A sub-calibre kinetic energy round is also under development. In the Spanish Navy, Meroka is associated with the Selenia RAN-12L surveillance radar intended to detect 0·1 square metre targets, flying at 300 metres per second at heights of 10 metres or less. Fire control is provided by a Lockheed Electronics AN/VPS-2 I-band monopulse doppler radar (**2547.153**) with the antenna mounted on the

gun turret. Multi-path effects in tracking are minimised by using an offset tracking technique which places the target in the lower part of the radar beam. A secondary low light television tracking system is also provided.

System reaction is entirely automatic and takes under four seconds in normal conditions. Theoretically, ten to twelve salvoes are needed for each incoming missile target, so a single Meroka system can deal with at least five or six engagements without reloading. Considerable attention has been paid to avoiding flexing and resonance in the design with a mean salvo dispersion of less than 2 milliradians. This is claimed to give a 90% chance of a hit from a 12 round salvo.

CHARACTERISTICS

Calibre: 20 mm
Barrel length: 120 calibres
Number of barrels: 12
Max rate of fire: 2700 – 3600 rounds/minute
Re-aiming time (12 barrels): 0·2 s
Time to fire 12-round salvo: 0–60 s
Ready use ammunition: 720 rounds
Ammunition type: HE, AP and incendiary. Sub-calibre KE under development
Reloading time: 3 minutes approx
Weight: 4·5 tons
Dimensions: 3·2 m high, 2·2 m wide at deck, 2·9 m swept radius
Muzzle velocity: 1215 m/s
Range: 2000 m+
Elevation arc: –20 to +85°
Elevation speed: 1·5 rads/s
Training arc: 360°
Training speed: 2 rads/s

DEVELOPMENT

Development was carried out by CETME.

STATUS

In addition to the two prototypes, it is probable that the system will be fitted in the new aircraft carrier *Principe de Asturias*, the 'Roger de Lauria' class destroyer, and 'FFG7', 'Descubierta', and 'Baleares' class frigates.

CONTRACTOR

Empresa Nacional Bazán, San Fernando, Spain.

Meroka multi-barrelled naval air defence weapon at test site in Spain

SWEDEN

6070.203

TRIPLE 6 inch GUN MOUNTING

These 6 inch (152 mm) Bofors guns were first introduced in 1942 and are now to be found as a triple mounting only in the cruiser *Latorre* of the Chilean Navy (formerly the *Göta Lejon* of the Royal Swedish Navy). This ship is the survivor of two cruisers programmed in 1941, laid down in 1943, launched in 1945, and completed in 1947.

CHARACTERISTICS

Calibre: 152 mm
Barrel length: 53 calibres
Projectile weight: 46 kg
Muzzle velocity: 900 m/s
Rate of fire: 10 rounds/barrel/minute

CONTRACTOR

AB Bofors, Ordnance Division, Box 500, 691 80 Bofors, Sweden.

The cruiser Göta Lejon *(now transferred to the Chilean Navy and renamed* Latorre*). The triple 6 inch gun mounting forward can be seen clearly in this picture; less clearly seen are the two twin mountings aft (Royal Swedish Navy)*

6085.203

TWIN 6 inch GUN MOUNTING

The Bofors 6 inch (152 mm) guns described in **6070.203** are to be seen as twin mountings in the *Latorre* (two twin mountings aft) and in the cruisers *Almirante Grau* and *Aguirre* of the Peruvian Navy (formerly the Royal Netherlands Navy cruisers *De Ruyter* and *De Zeven Provincien*).

The guns are fully automatic and radar controlled.

CONTRACTOR

AB Bofors, Ordnance Division, Box 500, 691 80 Bofors, Sweden.

6 inch guns at firing practice (Royal Netherlands Navy)

6086.203

TWIN 120 mm DUAL-PURPOSE AUTOMATIC GUN MOUNTING

These 50-calibre Bofors 120 mm guns are mounted in twin mounts in the 'Halland' class destroyers of the Royal Swedish Navy (2 ships), 'Tromp' class destroyers (2 ships) of the Royal Netherlands Navy, 'Holland' class destroyer (1 ship) and 'Friesland' class destroyers (7 ships) of the Peruvian Navy and modified 'Halland' class (2 ships) of the Columbian Navy.

Introduced in 1950, the guns are fully automatic and radar controlled. The complete twin mounting weighs 67 tons.

CHARACTERISTICS

Calibre: 120 mm
Barrel length: 50 calibres
Elevation: To 85°
Projectile weight: 23·5 kg
Muzzle velocity: 850 m/s
Rate of fire: 40 rounds/barrel/minute
Max range: 20·5 km (11 nautical miles)
Max altitude: 12 500 m

CONTRACTOR

AB Bofors, Ordnance Division, Box 500, 691 80 Bofors, Sweden.

Twin 120 mm gun mounting (Royal Netherlands Navy)

6073.203

SINGLE 120 mm/46 AUTOMATIC GUN MOUNTING
The Bofors L/46 120 mm automatic gun is designed for use against both surface and airborne targets and has a very high rate of fire.

Housed in a 4 mm steel turret mount the gun has two magazines, mounted on the elevating cradle, which are manually filled from a fixed-structure motor-driven rod hoist. Electro-hydraulic remote control is standard with the alternative of gyro-stabilised one-man local control. Telescope sights are also fitted and the hoist and the elevation and traverse mechanisms can be operated by hand. The gun barrel is liquid cooled and has an exchangeable liner.

CHARACTERISTICS
Weight excluding ammunition: 28·5 tons
Traversing speed: 40°/s

Elevating speed: 32°/s
Traverse limits: Unlimited
Elevation limits: −10 to +80°
Power supplies: 440 V, 3-phase, 60 Hz
Power consumption: (mean when firing) 60 kW
Number of rounds in magazine: 52
Rate of fire: 80 rounds/minute
Weight of round: 35 kg
Weight of shell (HE): 21 kg
Weight of charge: 3·15 kg
Muzzle velocity: 800 m/s
Time of flight to 10 km: 21·7 s
Range: 18·5 km
STATUS
Installed on Finnish and Indonesian corvettes.
CONTRACTOR
AB Bofors, Ordnance Division, Box 500, 691 80 Bofors, Sweden.

Bofors 120 mm/46 automatic gun mounting

2362.203

SINGLE 3 inch AUTOMATIC GUN MOUNTING
The Bofors L/50 3 inch (76 mm) automatic gun is designed for surface fire.

This is a sturdy, simple, remotely-controlled single gun. Weighing only 6500 kg and requiring only two loaders in the ammunition room, it is suitable for

installation in small ships and is currently in service on 'Storm' class fast patrol boats of the Norwegian Navy.

Electro-hydraulic remote control is used. The gun is mounted in a 6 mm steel gun house and has a fixed motor-driven hoist with lifting link levers and a five-round feed device. The gun has a monoblock barrel.

CHARACTERISTICS
Weight, excluding ammunition: 6·5 tons
Traversing speed: 25°/s
Elevating speed: 25°/s
Traverse limits: ±175°
Elevation limits: −10 to +30°
Power supplies: 440 V 3-phase 60 Hz
Power consumption: (mean when firing) 60 kW
Number of rounds in hoist and ammunition room: 100
Rate of fire: 30 rounds/minute
Weight of round: 11 kg
Weight of shell: (HS, Mk 27) 5·9 kg
Weight of charge: 0·54 kg
Muzzle velocity: 825 m/s
Time of flight: (to 6 km) 13 s
Range: (30° elevation) 12·6 km
Minimum operating crew: 2
STATUS
Designed and developed as a private venture by Bofors, this gun was first conceived in 1962 and went into service with the Norwegian Navy in 1965. It is no longer in production.
CONTRACTOR
AB Bofors, Ordnance Division, Box 500, 691 80 Bofors, Sweden.

Bofors 76 mm mounting aboard the Sovereignty (Singapore Navy)

6087.203

TWIN 57 mm AA GUN MOUNTING
Introduced in 1950 these 60-calibre guns were at one time widely fitted. Now, however, they are to be found in the cruiser *Latorre* (formerly *Göta Lejon*) of the Chilean Navy and the 'Halland' class destroyers of the Royal Swedish Navy. The same gun in a slightly different twin mounting is still in service in the French Navy (**6065.203**).

The complete turret of the Swedish installations weighs some 24 tons.
CHARACTERISTICS
Calibre: 57 mm
Barrel length: 60 calibres
Elevation: −10 to +90°
Projectile weight: 2·6 kg
Muzzle velocity: 900 m/s
Rate of fire: 130 rounds/barrel/minute

Max range: 14·5 km
Max altitude: 10 300 m
STATUS
No longer in production.
CONTRACTOR
AB Bofors, Ordnance Division, Box 500, 691 80 Bofors, Sweden.

2361.203

SINGLE 57 mm L/70 AUTOMATIC GUN MOUNTING
This 57 mm Bofors single gun in a plastic cupola is designed for both surface and anti-aircraft fire.

Alternatives of electro-hydraulic remote control or gyro-stabilised one-man local control are available. The gun feed system contains 40 rounds of ready-use ammunition with 128 rounds stowed in racks within the cupola, and there are dual step-by-step fixed supply hoists. The barrel is liquid-cooled. The Mk 2 version incorporates a new servo system giving a dispersion of less than 0·5 mrad and high accuracy even in rough seas.

Two types of ammunition are available: one is a proximity-fuzed prefragmented shell for use against aerial targets; the other is a special surface target shell which penetrates the target and is detonated after a short delay.

The gun can be equipped with rocket-launching rails for two-inch (57 mm) rockets.

Bofors 57 mm L/70 automatic gun mounting on board 'Spica T-131' fast attack craft

CHARACTERISTICS
Weight, excluding ammunition: 6 tons
Traversing speed: 55°/s
Elevation speed: 40°/s
Traverse limits: Unlimited
Elevation limits: –10 to +75°
Power supplies: 440 V 3-phase 60 Hz
Power consumption: (mean, when firing) 8 kW

Rate of fire: 200 rounds/minute
Weight of round: 5·9 kg
Weight of shell: (HE: DA or proximity fuze) 2·4 kg
Muzzle velocity: 1025 m/s
Time of flight: (3 km) 3·8 s
Range: 17 km
STATUS
In production, and in service on the Swedish Navy

'Spica T 131' (12 boats), 'Hugin' class (17 boats) fast attack craft, the new 3000-ton Norwegian coast guard vessels, and with several other navies.
CONTRACTOR
AB Bofors, Ordnance Division, Box 500, 691 80 Bofors, Sweden.

2360.203
SINGLE 40 mm L/70 AUTOMATIC GUN MOUNTING
Bofors make a number of different mountings for their shipborne 40 mm L/70 gun for use against both surface and airborne targets.

Three guns are shown here. All of these have

Hand-operated 40 mm Bofors gun

electro-hydraulic laying machinery, and can be supplied with both remote and local control. In local control the guns are gyro-stabilised, and reflex sights with speed rings are used for aiming.

The manually loaded gun can be provided with a light plastic cupola for weather protection. A fully automatic gun with the Breda 144-round feeding device is also available. This gun can also be operated with local control. Breda/Bofors guns are described in more detail in **2557.203** et seq.

The new proximity-fuzed ammunition can be used in all Bofors 40 mm L/70 guns.
CHARACTERISTICS
Weight, excluding ammunition: 2·8, 3, or 3·3 tons
Traversing speed: 85°/s (powered mounts)
Elevating speed: 45°/s (powered mounts)
Traverse limits: Unlimited
Elevation limits: –10 to +90°

Automatic gun with Breda 144 round feed

Power supplies: 440 V 3-phase 60 Hz
Power consumption: 5 kW
Rate of fire: 300 rounds/minute
Weight of round: 2·4 kg
Weight of shell: (HE) 0·96 kg
Muzzle velocity: 1000 m/s approx
Range: Tactical range 4000 m (12 km max)
STATUS
Operational with more than 30 navies, including the Swedish Navy.
CONTRACTOR
AB Bofors, Ordnance Division, Box 500, 691 80 Bofors, Sweden.

Power-operated 40 mm Bofors gun with plastic cupola

4031.203
ALL-PURPOSE 57 mm Mk 2 NAVAL GUN
This unmanned 57 mm all-purpose gun in a compact plastic cupola and with low radar signature is designed for combating both surface and aerial targets. The gun comprises an improved, extremely accurate, electro-hydraulic remote control system with microprocessor-controlled aiming and firing limitations. The new, completely automatic, reloading system allows for 120 rounds available in the cupola, and there are dual step-by-step fixed supply hoists.

Two types of ammunition are available: one is a proximity-fuzed and prefragmented shell for use against aerial targets; the other is a special surface target shell which penetrates the target and is detonated after a short delay.
CHARACTERISTICS
Weight: 6 tons (excluding ammunition)
Traverse speed: 55°/s
Elevation speed: 40°/s
Traverse: Unlimited
Elevation: –10 to +75°
Power supply: 440 V 3-phase 60 Hz
Power consumption: 8 kW (mean when firing)
Rate of fire: 220 rounds/minute
Weight of round: 6·1 kg
Weight of shell: 2·4 kg (HE:DA or proximity fuze)

Muzzle velocity: 1025 m/s
Time of flight: (3 km) 3·8 s
Range: 17 km
STATUS
Prototype and full-scale engineering model tests are completed. In series production.
CONTRACTOR
AB Bofors, Ordnance Division, Box 500, 691 80 Bofors, Sweden.

Artist's impression of Bofors 57 mm Mk 2 naval gun on board Swedish 'Hugin' class fast attack craft

---

6088.203
SINGLE 40/60 AA GUN MOUNTING
This 60-calibre version of the well-known Bofors 40 mm AA gun was introduced in 1942 and is still in service in many places. Its performance is, as one would expect, somewhat inferior to that of the modern 70-calibre weapon.

CHARACTERISTICS
Calibre: 40 mm
Barrel length: 60 calibres
Elevation: To 80°
Projectile weight: 0·9 kg
Muzzle velocity: 830 m/s
Rate of fire: 120 rounds/minute
Max range: 10 km
Tactical range: 3 km

STATUS
In service and still fitted in reconditioned form but no longer in production.
CONTRACTOR
AB Bofors, Ordnance Division, Box 500, 691 80 Bofors, Sweden.

SWITZERLAND

6036.203
35 mm TWIN ANTI-AIRCRAFT GUN TYPE GDM-A
This gun is similar in concept and design to the successful Oerlikon field gun. It is primarily intended for convoy or self-protection against air attack, but can also be used to engage sea and land targets.

It is an all-weather weapon system with a bi-axial stabilised mount on deck, and its electronic control-unit below deck. High laying accelerations and speeds are an important feature of the design.

Oerlikon 35 mm twin naval AA gun type GDM-A

Both 35 mm cannons type KDC are completely interchangeable without the use of additional parts as are the hand cocking devices and the barrels.

Three modes of operation are possible:
(1) Automatic operation, electrically controlled from fire control equipment or an optical aiming mechanism with auxiliary computer.
(2) Local operation, electrically controlled from the gun with joystick and the gyro-stabilised gunsight.
(3) Emergency operation, mechanically controlled from the gun with two hand wheels and the gunsight.

CHARACTERISTICS
Gun type GDM-A
Ready-to-use ammunition: 2 × 56 = 112 rounds
Reserve container: 2 × 112 = 224 rounds
Traverse
Arc: Unlimited
Speed: 120°/s
Acceleration: 130°/s²
Elevation
Arc: −15 to +85°
Speed: 100°/s
Acceleration: 120°/s²
Weight
Gun without ammunition: 5950 kg (approx)
Ammunition (336 rounds): 570 kg (approx)

Servo amplifier cabinet: 272 kg (approx)
Thyristor control unit: 130 kg (approx)
Power supply
Drive voltage: 440 V, 60 Hz, 3-phase
Stabilisation: Bi-axial by gyroscopes
Cannons type KDC
Calibre: 35 mm
Barrel length: 90 calibres
Weight
Barrel: 120 kg
Cannon complete: 430 kg (approx)
Rate of fire: 2 × 550 = 1100 rounds/minute
Muzzle velocity: 1175 m/s
STATUS
In production. The GDM-A mount is known to be in service with the following countries: Ecuador, Greece, Iran, Libya and Turkey. In collaboration with OTO Melara of Italy, Oerlikon also supplies the OE/OTO 35 mm twin naval mount, the Swiss designation being GDM-C. Additional information can be found in entry **5535.203** in the pages of this section covering Italian naval guns. The gun employed varies slightly and is the slightly heavier type KDA, but the main performance characteristics of both types (KDA and KDC) are the same.
CONTRACTOR
Machine Tool Works Oerlikon-Bührle Ltd, 8050 Zurich, Switzerland.

2395.203
30 mm TWIN NAVAL ANTI-AIRCRAFT GUN TYPE GCM-A
Because of its low weight, this modern 30 mm twin gun can be used to provide small fighting ships with an effective weapon of the type whose fire power and ammunition effectiveness were previously reserved for larger ships only. Fast patrol boats, for example, can be equipped fore and aft with this gun. The limitation of weapon use at sea due to environmental effects (sea movement) is considerably reduced since the gun is gyro-stabilised. In addition to its use on fast patrol boats etc, the gun can also be used effectively on large ships for short-range anti-aircraft defence.

Three modes of operation are possible:
(1) Automatic operation, electrically controlled from a fire control system or an optical aiming mechanism with auxiliary computer.
(2) Local operation, electrically controlled from the gun with joystick and gyro stabilised gunsight.
(3) Emergency operation, mechanically controlled from the gun with two hand wheels and the gunsight.

Oerlikon twin 30 mm mounting GCM-AO3-3

The GCM-A is also manufactured in the United Kingdom by the British Manufacture and Research Company Limited and this model is fitted with Ferranti gyroscopic lead angle computing sight.

The gun is produced in three different versions:
AO3-1 with enclosed cabin for remote and local control and with 320 or 500 rounds
AO3-2 with open gunner's station for remote and local control and 500 rounds
AO3-3 without gunner's cabin and with remote control only and 640 rounds of ammunition.
CHARACTERISTICS
Ready-use ammunition (rounds)
GCM-AO3-1, GCM-AO3-2: 2 × 250
GCM-AO3-3: 2 × 320
Traverse
Arc: Unlimited
Speed (max): 75°/s
Acceleration (max)
GCM-AO3-1: 80°/s²
GCM-AO3-2: 85°/s²
GCM-AO3-3: 75°/s²
Elevation
Arc: −10 to +75°
Speed (max): 50°/s
Acceleration (max): 90°/s²
Weight (complete)
GCM-AO3-1: 2910 kg
GCM-AO3-2: 2560 kg
GCM-AO3-3: 2560 kg
Less ammunition
GCM-AO3-1: 2400 kg
GCM-AO3-2: 2050 kg
GCM-AO3-3: 1900 kg
Ammunition
GCM-AO3-1, GCM-AO3-2: 510 kg
GCM-AO3-3: 660 kg
Cannon barrel: 61 kg
Cannon complete: 157 kg
Power supply
Drive: 440 V, 60 Hz, 3-phase AC
Control: 115 V, 400 Hz, single-phase AC
Stabilisation: Gyroscope
Cannons: Type KCB
Calibre: 30 mm
Barrel length: 75 calibres
Rate of fire: 2 × 650 = 1300 rounds/minute
Muzzle velocity: Max 1080 m/s

Oerlikon twin 30 mm mounting GCM-AO3-2

Oerlikon twin 30 mm mounting GCM-AO3-1

CONTRACTOR
Machine Tool Works Oerlikon-Bührle Ltd, 8050 Zurich, Switzerland.

3657.203

25 mm NAVAL GUN TYPE GBM-AO1

This Oerlikon multipurpose naval mount carries a type KBA-CO2 25 mm automatic cannon and its low weight with simple installation make it suitable for use aboard ships of all tonnages. It can be used against land, sea, or air targets, and is designed for one-man operation. Sighting is by simple ring and bead and night sights are available. No electrical power is required and the gun is laid by the gunner using a shoulder harness. Two different ammunition types can be fired at the same time.

CHARACTERISTICS

Gun type GBM-AO1

Ready-to-use ammunition: 200 rounds

Traverse arc: Unlimited

Elevation: –15 to +50°

Weight: 585 kg (ready to fire)

Cannon type KBA-CO2

Calibre: 25 mm

Barrel length: 80 calibres (2173 mm with muzzle brake)

Rate of fire: 570 rounds/minute

Muzzle velocity: 1100-1360 m/s, depending on ammunition

STATUS

Production.

CONTRACTOR

Machine Tool Works Oerlikon-Bührle Ltd, 8050 Zurich, Switzerland. This weapon is also manufactured in the United Kingdom by the British Manufacture and Research Company.

25 mm Oerlikon naval gun type GBM-AO1

4017.203

SEA ZENITH 25 mm MOUNT TYPE GBM-B1Z

Sea Zenith is the name of the four-barrelled 25 mm gun mounting employed in the Contraves/Oerlikon Seaguard close-in weapon system (**4016.231**). It is named from its ability to bear on targets at the zenith by virtue of a slewing axis which is inclined at 55° to the horizontal. Its function is the close-in destruction

Prototype Seaguard CIWS gun module (Sea Zenith) during test firings

of anti-ship missiles using special APDS ammunition with a forged tungsten core designed to ensure that a single hit will be sufficient to destroy a missile target by exploding its warhead. It also has a performance against aircraft using more conventional ammunition.

The four 25 mm guns have a combined rate of fire of 3200 rounds/minute with a barrel life of 2500 rounds. Each gun is independently fed from

ammunition drums which may either be mounted below decks or by the side of the gun with a total mounting ready-use supply of 1500 rounds which is calculated to be sufficient for 14 normal engagements of missile targets. Reloading can be achieved during the firing cycle.

The KBB-RO3/LO3 gun is a positively locked gas operated weapon with two breech locking catches and is ruggedly built to ensure operational reliability under extremely adverse environmental conditions.

CHARACTERISTICS

Gun type: Sea Zenith KBB-RO3/LO3

Calibre: 25 mm

Barrel length: 2300 m

Muzzle velocity: 1400 m/s

Ready-to-use ammunition: 1500 rounds (375 per gun)

Traverse

Arc: ±180°

Speed and acceleration: 2·5 rad/s, 10 rads/s²

Elevation

Arc: –15 to +127°

Speed and acceleration: 2·5 rad/s, 10 rad/s²

Weight

Mounting without ammunition: approx 4500 kg

Ammunition (1500 rounds): approx 1050 kg

STATUS

In initial production for the first customer with an in-service date of 1985.

CONTRACTOR

Machine Tool Works Oerlikon-Bührle Ltd, 8050 Zurich, Switzerland.

2397.203

20 mm NAVAL GUN TYPE GAM-BO1

The Oerlikon GAM-BO1 is a simple, modern, and efficient 20 mm naval mounting, embodying the well-proven KAA cannon.

All-up weight is low enough to permit installation on any type of naval vessel. The gun can be used for either surface- or AA-fire. No electrical power is needed. The gun is laid by the gunner using a shoulder harness. Sighting is by simple ring and bead and a night sight is available.

CHARACTERISTICS

Gun type GAM-BO1

Ready-use ammunition: 200 rounds

Traverse

Arc: Unlimited

Speed and acceleration: Manual

Elevation

Arc: –15 to +60°

Speed and acceleration: Manual

Weight

Gun without ammunition: 410 kg (approx)

Ammunition (200 rounds): 90 kg (approx)

Gun complete: 500 kg (approx)

Cannon type KAA (former design: 204 GK)

Calibre: 20 mm

Barrel length: 85 calibres

Rate of fire: 1000 rounds/minute

Muzzle velocity: Approx 1050 m/s

Weight

Barrel: 26 kg approx

Cannon complete: 92 kg approx

STATUS

Known fittings include Spanish 'Lazaga' and 'Barceló'

20 mm Oerlikon naval mounting type GAM-BO1

classes, a number of British ships, and ships of several other navies.

CONTRACTOR

Machine Tool Works Oerlikon-Bührle Ltd, 8050 Zurich, Switzerland. This weapon is also manufactured in the United Kingdom by the British Manufacture and Research Company.

2396.203
20 mm NAVAL MOUNTING TYPE A41/804
This widely used Oerlikon mounting incorporates the type 804 drum-fed cannon. Suitable for small and very small naval vessels it is operated entirely by one man and can be used for either AA or surface fire. Sighting is by ring and bead.
CHARACTERISTICS
Calibre: 20 mm
MV: 835 m/s
Rate of fire: 800 rounds/minute
Ready rounds: 60 in drum magazine
Weight: Including ammunition 240 kg

STATUS
In production and widely used.
CONTRACTOR
Machine Tool Works Oerlikon-Bührle Ltd, 8050 Zurich, Switzerland.

20 mm Oerlikon naval mounting type A41/804

3656.203
20 mm NAVAL GUN TYPE GAM-CO1
The Oerlikon GAM-CO1 is very similar to the type GAM-BO1 (**2397.203**), employing the same kind of sighting with the addition of an optional night sight, and gun laying by means of a shoulder harness. However, in place of the GAM-BO1's KAA 20 mm cannon, the GAM-CO1 uses the 20 mm automatic cannon type KAD-B13-3 (formerly designated HS820).
CHARACTERISTICS
Gun type GAM-CO1
Ready-to-use ammunition: 200 rounds
Traverse arc: Unlimited

Elevation arc: −15 to +60°
Speed and acceleration: Manual
Weight: 510 kg (ready to fire)
Cannon type KAD-B13-3 (formerly HS820)
Calibre: 20 mm
Barrel length: 1906 mm
Rate of fire: 900 rounds/minute
Muzzle velocity: 1050-1150 m/s, depending on ammunition
CONTRACTOR
Machine Tool Works Oerlikon-Bührle Ltd, 8050 Zurich, Switzerland. This weapon is also manufactured in the United Kingdom by the British Manufacture and Research Company.

20 mm Oerlikon naval gun type GAM-CO1

UNION OF SOVIET SOCIALIST REPUBLICS

6038.203
TRIPLE 152 mm GUN MOUNTING
These guns are in service with several of the older cruisers of the Soviet fleet. The 'Sverdlov' class cruisers each carry 12 guns in four triple mountings, except for the *Dzerzhinski* which has had one of its turrets replaced by a launcher for the SA-N-2 Guideline missile (**2943.231**).

Guns in the turrets are mounted in separate sleeves, thus permitting individual elevation to at least 50°. Projectile weight is believed to be about 50 kg and muzzle velocity 915 m/s so that maximum range is probably in the region of 27 km. The gun is 50 calibres long, semi-automatic, and can fire ten rounds/minute. An eight-metre rangefinder is incorporated in each turret.

The triple 152 mm gun mounting is often described as a 150 mm triple mount.

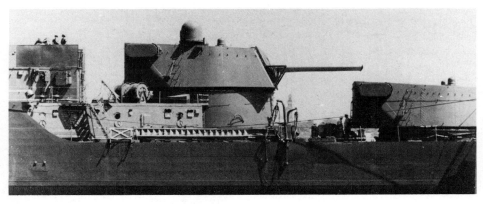

Triple 152 mm gun turrets of Soviet 'Sverdlov' class cruiser

6039.203
TWIN 130 mm GUN MOUNTING
There appear to be two types of twin 130 mm mounting in service in the older destroyers of the Soviet and associated navies. One type is to be found in the older (unmodified) 'Skory' class destroyers, including those supplied to Egypt.

It is believed that the gun is 50 calibres long and fires a 27 kg shell with a muzzle velocity of 875 m/s. The mountings are semi-automatic and a rate of fire of ten rounds/minute can be achieved. Range is about 25 km.

Twin 130 mm guns mounted on the 'Skory' class destroyer Svobodnyi

6040.203
TWIN 130 mm DUAL-PURPOSE GUN MOUNTING
It is believed that this mounting is common to the modified 'Skory' class and the 'Kotlin' class destroyers.

On these vessels, assuming that all the installations are indeed similar, the 130 mm guns, in two twin turrets including firing directors are fully stabilised. The guns are dual-purpose, semi-automatic, and are believed to be 58 calibres long and to fire a 27 kg projectile at ten rounds per minute with a muzzle velocity of 875 m/s. The two guns in the mounting can be independently laid and can be elevated to 70°. They are used with 'Wasphead' stabilised directors with radar.

Twin 130 mm gun mounting, two RBU 2500 ASW launchers, and quadruple 45 mm AA mounting on 'SAM Kotlin' class Vozbuzhdenny (G Jacobs)

4522.203
TWIN 130 mm DUAL-PURPOSE GUN MOUNTING
A new design of automatic, water-cooled, twin 130 mm mounting was first seen on the 7500-ton cruiser *Sovremenny* and is probably controlled by the

Kite Screech director radar. The rate of fire is 30 to 35 rounds per minute. Guns of this large calibre have not been fitted in the Soviet fleet since the 'Kotlin' class destroyers were built in the mid-1950s.

6042.203
TWIN 100 mm DUAL-PURPOSE GUN MOUNTING
Guns of this type are in service with the Soviet Navy on the 'Sverdlov' class cruisers (including the *Dzerzhinski*), on which they are associated with Egg Cup and Sun Visor fire control systems.

These guns are of more modern type than the single 100 mm gun fitted on the 'Riga' class destroyers (**6041.203**). They are reported as being

capable of firing their 16 kg projectile with a muzzle velocity of 900 m/s at 20 rounds/minute. Maximum surface range is understood to be 18 km and maximum AA engagement height 12 000 m (at 80° elevation). Barrel length is 60 calibres. The turret is stabilised and has been said to weigh 35 tons. It is believed that the trunk of the turret extends downwards for at least one deck and contains the ammunition hoist.

Stabilised twin mountings for 100 mm dual-purpose guns on a cruiser. The top of the fire director can be seen to the rear of the gun mounting

6041.203
SINGLE 100 mm DUAL-PURPOSE GUN MOUNTING
This gun mounting is found on the many 'Riga' class destroyers in the navies of the Soviet Union and its client countries, the 'Don' class support ships and one 'Purga' class patrol ship.

These guns are all believed to be the 1947 model, to be 56 calibres in length, and to fire a 13·5 kg projectile with a muzzle velocity of 850 m/s. Surface range is believed to be some 16 km and maximum AA engagement height 6000 m. They are manually operated and obsolescent.

Anti-submarine rockets being fired from a 'Riga' class destroyer. Two single 100 mm dual-purpose gun mountings can be seen. Note the elevation angle of the gun nearer to the rocket launcher (Novosti)

4521.203
SINGLE 100 mm DUAL-PURPOSE GUN MOUNTING (AUTOMATIC)
A new type of single 100 mm dual-purpose mounting, of which little is known, is fitted in the 'Krivak II' frigates, the large destroyer *Udaloy*, and the battle cruiser *Kirov*. It is totally enclosed and is almost certainly automatic unlike the earlier guns of this calibre described in **6041.203**. Control is from Kite Screech radar.

Single automatic 100 mm mountings on the cruiser Udaloy (Federal German Navy)

6043.203

SINGLE 85 mm DUAL-PURPOSE GUN MOUNTING
Fitted on 'Kronstadt' class coastal patrol vessels which are now only in full service in foreign navies and are being converted to torpedo recovery vessels in the Soviet Navy. This gun is presumed to be obsolescent.

CHARACTERISTICS
Soviet designation: 90-K
Calibre: 85 mm
Length of barrel: 4435 mm
Elevation: –5 to +85°
Elevation rate: 8°/s
Traverse rate: 12°/s

Weight of round: 16·17 kg
MV: 800 m/s
Firing rate: 15 to 18 rounds/minute
Horizontal range: 15·5 km

2865.203

TWIN 85 mm AA GUN MOUNTING
This is an elderly semi-automatic heavy AA weapon believed to be installed now only in the unmodified 'Skory' class destroyers. Barrel length is about 52 calibres, muzzle velocity about 800 m/s, maximum range and height about 10 000 and 5000 metres respectively. Maximum barrel elevation is 75°. Rate of fire is about 15 rounds per minute.

6044.203

TWIN 76 mm DUAL-PURPOSE GUN MOUNTING
This mounting seems to have first appeared on the 'Kynda' class cruisers in 1962 and is now widely fitted in the Soviet fleet in 'Kiev' class aircraft carriers, 'Kara' and 'Kynda' class cruisers, 'Kashin' and modified 'Kildin' class destroyers, 'Krivak I', 'Koni', 'Mirka' and 'Petya' class frigates and 'Ivan Rogov' amphibious ships as well as in a number of foreign navies. Doubtless it has been updated during this long period.

The 60-calibre gun can be elevated to about 85°, and this, with a muzzle velocity of about 900 m/s, means that air targets can be engaged at slant ranges up to 14 000 metres. Maximum range is 15 km. Rate of fire is said to be 60 rounds per minute. It is normally associated with Owl Screech or Hawk Screech fire control.

Twin 76 mm dual-purpose gun turret on the 'Kashin' class missile destroyer Odarenny *(G Jacobs)*

4315.203

SINGLE 76 mm DUAL-PURPOSE GUN MOUNTING
This new mounting has appeared recently in the 'Nanuchka III' and 'Tarantul' classes of corvette and the 'Matka' class of missile hydrofoil. It is totally enclosed and therefore most probably automatic, can clearly achieve high elevations, and is suitable for fitting in small craft since 'Matka' displaces no more than 215 tons fully loaded.

6047.203

QUADRUPLE 57 mm AA GUN MOUNTINGS
Quadruple 57 mm mountings are installed in the 'Kanin' and 'Kildin' class destroyers and the 'Lama' class supply ships. The guns are arranged as two pairs mounted vertically one above the other and it is believed that the pairs are essentially similar to the twin 57 mm guns described below (**6046.203**), except that the barrels of the quadmounted guns do not have muzzle brakes. Fire control is by Hawk Screech.

Two of four quadruple 57 mm AA gun mounts aboard a now obsolete Soviet 'Krupny' class destroyer

2869.203

TWIN 57 mm AUTOMATIC AA GUN MOUNTING
Several of the most modern classes of Soviet ships are equipped with fully-enclosed, fully-automatic 57 mm guns in twin mountings. With 80-calibre barrels and muzzle velocities around 1000 m/s, these guns have maximum horizontal and vertical ranges of 12 000 and 5000 metres respectively. Rate of fire is believed to be 120 rounds per minute per barrel. Maximum elevation is around 85°.

Guns of this type are found in at least ten different classes of ship including the 'Moskva', 'Kresta', 'Grisha', 'Nanuchka', 'Poti', 'Ugra', and 'Chilikin' classes. Radar control is normally by Muff Cob (**1611.253**).

Twin 57 mm automatic guns on the submarine tender Ivan Vakrhrameev *(G Jacobs)*

6045.203

SINGLE 57 mm DUAL-PURPOSE GUN MOUNTING
This 57 mm gun is fitted only to the 'Sasha' class coastal minesweepers and the modified 'Skory' class destroyers. It is believed that the gun performance is the same as that of the twin-mounted 57 mm gun described in **6046.203** but the gun barrel is not fitted with a muzzle brake.

6046.203

TWIN 57 mm AA GUN MOUNTINGS
Twin 57 mm AA guns are fitted to many of the more modern or recently modernised Soviet ships. The guns have 70-calibre barrels with muzzle brakes and a rate of fire of some 120 rounds per minute per barrel is believed to be possible. Muzzle velocity is about 1000 m/s, vertical range is believed to be about 6000 metres, and horizontal range about 9000 metres; the weight of the shell is about 2·8 kg.

Guns of this type are installed in 'T-58', 'Don', 'Oskol', and 'Alligator' classes of ship. Although primarily AA weapons, the 57 mm guns are in some cases the sole armament of a ship and must therefore be intended for use in a dual-purpose role.

CHARACTERISTICS
Soviet designation: SIF-31B
Elevation: –10 to +85°
Elevation rate: 25°/s
Traverse rate: 30°/s
Weight of round: 6·6 kg
MV: 1020 m/s
Rate of fire: 100 – 120 rounds/minute
Range: 8·4 km
Range of fuze: 6950 m

Twin 57 mm AA guns (Novosti)

6048.203
QUADRUPLE 45 mm AA GUN MOUNTS
These mounts are very similar in appearance to the quadruple 57 mm AA gun mounts described above.

The only remaining mountings are in the 'Kotlin' class destroyers.

Semi-automatic and with an 85-calibre barrel, each gun can fire about 160 rounds per minute with a muzzle velocity of about 1000 m/s, and vertical and horizontal ranges of some 7000 and 9000 metres.

2870.203
TWIN 37 mm AA GUN MOUNTINGS
Twin 63-calibre AA mountings of various types are found on many of the older cruisers, destroyers, and auxiliaries of the Soviet Navy. The 37 mm AA calibre was first introduced for naval use, adapted from the army weapon, in 1943, but the twin mountings date from some five years later. Fitted in 'Sverdlov', 'Skory' (modified), 'Riga' and 'T43' class.

CHARACTERISTICS
Soviet designation: W-11-M
Elevation: –10 to +85°
Elevation rate: 13°/s
Traverse rate: 17°/s
Weight of round: 1·5 kg
Weight of shell: 732 g
MV: 880 m/s
Rate of fire: 2 × 160 to 180 rounds/minute
Range: 4000 m (horizontal), 3000 m (vertical)

Twin 37 mm AA guns (Tass)

2883.203
SINGLE 37 mm AA GUN MOUNTING 70-K
Derived from an army weapon of the same calibre this gun was introduced for naval use in 1943 and is to be found in open mountings on the older 'Skory' class destroyers, and on 'Kronshtadt' class submarine chasers and in turret mountings on 'T-301' class coastal minesweepers which are now only in service in other navies.

It is also in use in ships of other Warsaw Pact navies.

CHARACTERISTICS
Calibre: 37 mm
Weight: 1750 kg
Max range: 4000 m
Muzzle velocity: 880 m/s
Firing rate: 160 – 180 rounds/minute
Traverse arc: 360°
Elevation arc: –10 to +85°
Traverse rate: 20°/s
Elevation rate: 15°/s
Crew: 6

Single 37 mm AA mountings

2896.203
TWIN 30 mm AA GUN MOUNTING
Widely fitted in many classes of ship including missile boats and other small craft, this is a fully automatic remote-controlled weapon. Barrel length is 65 calibres, muzzle velocity around 1000 m/s, range about 3000 to 4000 metres, and rate of fire around 500 rounds per minute per barrel. Maximum elevation is about 85°.

The gun was first introduced in 1960. It is most commonly associated with the Drum Tilt fire control radar (**1330.253**) or more rarely with Muff Cob (**1611.253**).

Twin fully-automatic 30 mm AA mounting as mounted on missile boats and other small vessels

2897.203
TWIN 25 mm AA GUN MOUNTINGS
LAA guns of this type are mounted in many of the smaller ships of the Soviet Navy and other friendly navies. At least three versions of mounting exist, the

Later twin 25 mm gun mounting, probably aboard a riverine gunboat

simplest being the open type 2-M-3 110PM. This is essentially for local control with visual sighting, although hydraulic power is provided for training and elevation. Later versions, however, may provide for varying levels of remote control.

CHARACTERISTICS
Calibre: 25 mm
Barrel length: 80 calibres
Overall length: 2·845 m
Overall weight: 1500 kg
Muzzle velocity: 900 m/s
Firing rate: 270 – 300 rounds/minute (theoretical)
Traverse: 360°
Elevation: –10 to +85°

Rates:	Hydraulic	Manual
Traverse	2 – 70°/s	25°/s
Elevation	2 – 40°/s	15°/s

Crew: 2

This data refers to the open mounting type 2-M-3 110PM; the performance of the alternative versions is likely to be broadly similar.

Twin 25 mm AA guns in 2-M-3 110PM open mounting

2899.203
122 mm and 140 mm ROCKET LAUNCHERS
For the past 30 years and more the Soviet Army has been using and arranging for the development of a wide range of unguided barrage rockets (**5555.111**). It

is not surprising, therefore, that the Soviet Navy should also use these weapons, indeed it is surprising that they have not made greater use of them.

Systems are fitted in some amphibious ships. The 'Ivan Rogov' class has two 122 mm 20-barrelled

launchers, the Type 3 and 4 'Alligator' class have two launchers each and the 'Polnochny' class have two 18-barrelled 140 mm launchers with a range of about 9 km.

2973.203
30 mm CLOSE-IN WEAPON SYSTEM
This 30 mm six-barrel Gatling type weapon is the new close-in weapon system for the Soviet Navy for defence against cruise missiles and 'smart' weapons. In concept it is similar to the American Vulcan-Phalanx system (**2543.231**). This weapon is controlled by a Bass Tilt radar and is mounted on at least 18 different classes of ship ranging from the battlecruiser *Kirov* to the 210-ton fast attack craft *Slepen*. It is probable that this weapon has a cyclic rate of fire of at least 3000 rounds per minute.

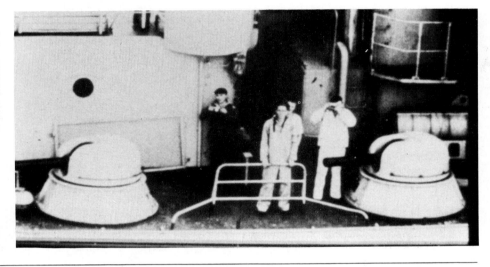

Barbette mountings on 'Kresta II' cruiser

UNITED KINGDOM

6012.203
TWIN 4·5 inch GUN MOUNTING Mk 6
This twin-barrelled remotely controlled power operated 4·5 inch (113 mm) naval gun mount was introduced shortly after the Second World War. Electro-hydraulic power control is normally remotely controlled, but can be locally controlled by a joystick. The loading cycle is semi-automatic, shell and cartridge being separately hoisted and then manually

loaded into the loading tray. The complete turret weighs about 45 tons.

CHARACTERISTICS
Calibre: 113 mm
Barrel length: About 45 calibres
Elevation: To 80°
Projectile weight: About 25 kg
Muzzle velocity: About 750 m/s
Rate of fire: 20 rounds/barrel/minute

Max range: About 19 km (10 nautical miles)
STATUS
Operational in British and Commonwealth navies.
CONTRACTOR
Vickers Shipbuilding and Engineering Ltd (a subsidiary of British Shipbuilders), Barrow Engineering Works, PO Box 12, Barrow-in-Furness, Cumbria LA14 1AF, England.

6011.203
SINGLE 4·5 inch GUN MOUNTING Mk 8
This fully-automatic single-barrelled 4·5 inch (113 mm) gun has been designed for the RN by the Royal Armament Research and Development Establishment (RARDE). It is modelled on the British Army's Abbot gun (**5503.103**) and is fitted with muzzle brake and fume extractor. A range of fixed ammunition has also been developed for use with this mounting.

The gun mounting, designed by Vickers at Barrow, features a simple ammunition feed system with the minimum number of transfer points, and a remote power control system with large stability margins that requires a stiff mounting structure with low inertia. To this end the revolving structure has been kept as light as possible and a sandwich construction glass-reinforced plastic gun-shield fitted. To keep the trunnion height as low as possible the gun is mounted

front heavy, balance being restored by an oil spring. To reduce inertia the training gear is fitted to the fixed structure, the training motors are fitted inside the mounting pedestal, and the driving motors are secured vertically to the ring bulkhead which is part of the ship's structure.

The loading system is hydraulically operated from one power plant sited below decks. The system employs only four transfer points between the gunbay (ready use magazine) and the gun, and is designed so that the nature of ammunition may be changed without unloading or firing off a large number of rounds. A stockpile of ammunition may be accommodated at the mounting and fired remotely from the operations room with no crew closed up at the mounting.

A conventional coarse/fine system is used in both elevation and training for remote power control of the mounting. Processing of the error signal is carried out

in transistor modules. The main feature of the remote power control system is the use of a static direct armature control thyristor system.

Fail-to-safe interlocks are included in all major operations to safeguard equipment and ammunition, and facilities are arranged for manual control of the power drives for maintenance purposes.

CHARACTERISTICS
Performance data for the gun has not been published, but the following suggestions are offered by way of general guidance.
Calibre: 4·5 inch (113 mm)
Barrel length: 55 calibres
Muzzle velocity: 870 m/s
Rate of fire: 25 rounds/minute
Max range: 22 km
Elevation arc: –10 to +55°
Training arc: ±340°

STATUS

The equipment is currently in service with several navies. It is the standard medium calibre gun in the Royal Navy and is fitted to the Type 82 destroyer HMS *Bristol*, the Type 21 and later Type 22 frigates, and the Type 42 destroyers. It will also be fitted in the Type 23 frigate. The Mk 8 is also in service with Argentina on the Type 42 destroyers (1 turret), Brazil on the six 'Niteroi' class frigates (1 or 2 turrets depending on ship), Iran on the four 'Saam' class frigates (1 turret), Libya on the single Vosper Thornycroft Mk 7 frigate (1 turret) and Thailand on the single 'Yarrow' frigate (2 turrets). During the South Atlantic conflict in 1982, the 4·5 inch Mk 8 gun was used to advantage, particularly for naval gunfire support and earned the confidence and commendation of British naval and land forces for its accuracy and effectiveness.

CONTRACTOR

Designed and manufactured by Vickers Shipbuilding and Engineering Ltd (a subsidiary of British Shipbuilders), Barrow Engineering Works, PO Box 12, Barrow-in-Furness, Cumbria LA14 1AF, England.

Vickers 4·5 inch Mk 8 gun mounting on the Brazilian Mark 10 frigate Liberal

---

6014.203

TWIN 4 inch GUN MOUNTING Mk 19

Designed by Vickers, this is a twin-barrelled, hand loaded, remotely controlled naval gun mount which is electrically trained and elevated. Normally laid by remote control it can also be locally controlled using joysticks. Fuze setting devices are located alongside each trunnion support. A good gun crew can achieve a rate of fire of up to about 16 rounds per barrel per minute.

CHARACTERISTICS

Calibre: 102 mm
Elevation: To 80°
Projectile weight: 15·9 kg
Muzzle velocity: 760 m/s
Rate of fire: Up to 16 rounds/barrel/minute
Max range: 19·5 km (10·5 nautical miles)
Max altitude: 13 500 m
Date introduced: 1935

STATUS

Operational in Commonwealth and other navies. No longer in production.

Twin 4 inch Mk 19 gun mounting

6016.203

TWIN 3 inch GUN MOUNTING Mk 6

This is a twin-barrelled 3 inch (70 calibre) automatic dual-purpose, remotely controlled naval gun mount. Local control arrangements are provided but the mounting can be operated unmanned. The rate of fire is about 90 rounds per gun per minute and the barrels are water cooled to allow sustained fire. Turret weight is about 38 tons.

CHARACTERISTICS

Calibre: 76 mm
Barrel length: 70 calibres
Elevation: To 90°
Projectile weight: Probably about 7 kg
Muzzle velocity: 1000 m/s
Rate of fire: 90 rounds/barrel/minute
Max range: Approx 17 km (9 nautical miles)

STATUS

Operational in Canadian Navy. British ships which were fitted have been disposed of.

CONTRACTOR

Vickers Shipbuilding and Engineering Ltd (a subsidiary of British Shipbuilders), Barrow Engineering Works, PO Box 12, Barrow-in-Furness, Cumbria LA14 1AF, England.

Twin 3 inch Mk 6 gun mounting on HMS Tiger *(Stefan Terzibaschitsch)*

6010.203

SINGLE 4·5 inch GUN MOUNTING Mk 5

This single-barrelled, remotely controlled, and manually loaded gun mounting is to be found in the 'Tribal' class frigates of the RN and in similar vessels elsewhere. As an alternative to remote control, local control by joystick is possible. Charge and shell are separate and automatically rammed.

CHARACTERISTICS

Calibre: 113 mm
Barrel length: 45 calibres
Elevation: To about 50°

Projectile weight: About 25 kg
Muzzle velocity: About 750 m/s
Rate of fire: 14 rounds/minute with a good crew
Max range: About 19 km (10 nautical miles)
Date introduced: 1937

STATUS
Operational in British and certain other navies.
CONTRACTOR
Vickers Shipbuilding and Engineering Ltd (a

subsidiary of British Shipbuilders), Barrow Engineering Works, PO Box 12, Barrow-in-Furness, Cumbria LA14 1AF, England.

4·5 inch Mk 5 gun mount in the frigate HMS Ashanti

6015.203
TWIN 40 mm (BOFORS) GUN MOUNTING Mk 5

This is a remotely or locally controlled twin Bofors 40 mm 60-calibre close-range naval gun mount. A splinter protection shield to the front of the mounting is installed. It requires one 'on mounting' loader per gun and one operator to lay and train the gun in 'local control' operation. Separate emergency manual laying and training arrangements using two men are provided. Rate of fire is about 120 rounds per minute per barrel.

CHARACTERISTICS
Weight: Approx 3000 kg
Rate of fire: 2 × 120 rounds/minute
Tactical range: 3000 m
STATUS
Operational in many British and Commonwealth naval vessels.

40 mm Bofors twin mount, British pattern (Stefan Terzibaschitsch)

6013.203
SINGLE 40 mm (BOFORS) Mk 7 GUN MOUNTING

This is a single-barrelled Bofors 40 mm power operated ship's gun mounting. It is a lightweight mounting suitable for fitting in FPBs as well as larger vessels. One-man control is by joystick and uses a gyro sight for aiming. One man is necessary 'on mounting' for loading and rate of fire is about 300 rounds per minute.

For details of the gun in this mounting see **2360.203**.
STATUS
No longer in production but widely fitted in British and Commonwealth naval vessels.

Bofors 40 mm gun on Mk 7 mounting

3658.203
LS30R 30 mm (RARDEN) NAVAL GUN MOUNTING

Laurence, Scott (Defence Systems) Ltd (KSDS) have developed a lightweight naval mounting for use aboard small vessels, based upon the technology employed in the company's optical fire director (OFD) (**3055.293**) described in the Electro-Optical

Laurence, Scott LS30R stabilised 30 mm gun mount

section of this volume. The electronic and servo system package is similar to that used in the OFD, and the LS30R mounting is both power-driven and line-of-sight stabilised. It is designed to accommodate the Rarden 30 mm gun, and all subsequent description refers to this version, although guns of other types can be fitted.

The Rarden 30 mm gun was conceived by the Royal Armament Research and Development Establishment (RARDE) and is a lightweight cannon featuring low trunnion loads and good power and accuracy. It is in use on armoured fighting vehicles such as the Fox and Scimitar, and notes on its land-based uses will be found in entry **5504.103**, in earlier editions of *Jane's Weapon Systems*.

CHARACTERISTICS
Mounting type: LS30R
Elevation arc: –20 to +70°
Training arc: ±160° standard
Elevation speed and acceleration: 35°/s; 120°/s²
Training speed and acceleration: 30°/s; 120°/s²

Weight: 800 kg (complete)
Gun type: Rarden 30
Calibre: 30 mm
Barrel length: 2440 mm
Rate of fire: 90 rounds/minute (max)
Max continuous burst: 6 rounds (22 rounds with extra magazine)
Muzzle velocity: 1100 m/s (HE); 1080 m/s (APSE); 1200 m/s (APDS)
Optional extras: Predictor; image intensifier; IR camera and/or TV camera for remote control
STATUS
A private venture development introduced in September 1979. Extensive trials have successfully been carried out by the Royal Navy. The gun mounting is in production but no ship fit details have been released.
CONTRACTOR
Laurence, Scott (Defence Systems) Ltd, PO Box 25, Kerrison Road, Norwich, Norfolk NR1 1JD, England.

4567.203
LS30 SERIES SEATED OPERATOR GUN MOUNTS

The LS30 series is a family of powered and stabilized naval gun mountings for seated operator control, and is designed to suit weapons of high accuracy and rates of fire. They are compact and lightweight and readily adaptable to different installation requirements. In action, they are easily controlled, convenient for wash-down in NBC conditions, and both the structure and ammunition have a low magnetic signature. The LS30 series can thus provide a credible air defence and surface engagement capability for a wide range of warships and patrol craft.

A further advantage of the LS30 series is that, although intended primarily for local manning, they can readily be used in remotely directed and emergency hand powered modes. When locally manned the seated operator controls the mounting with a thumb joystick while following the target through a sight attached to the mounting. Local control sighting is by a binocular and disturbed sight line arrangement with the sight being offset to provide tangent elevation and lead angle correction. On-mount prediction facilities can be fitted.

CHARACTERISTICS
Operational elevation arc: −20 to +65°
Operational training arc: −155 to +155°
Trunnion height: 1·075 m
Slew velocity (training and elevation): 60°/s
Acceleration (training and elevation): 120°/s²
STATUS
Advanced development.
CONTRACTOR
Laurence, Scott (Defence Systems) Ltd, PO Box 25, Kerrison Road, Norwich, Norfolk NR1 1JD, England.

Seated operator version of LS30 gun mount

UNITED STATES OF AMERICA

4523.203
TRIPLE 16 inch GUN TURRET Mk 7

With the US Navy decision to re-activate and modernise four 'Iowa' class battleships in 1982, the US fleet re-introduced the powerful 16 inch calibre naval gun to the world's navies. *Iowa, New Jersey, Missouri* and *Wisconsin* (BB61/2/3/4) all saw action in the Second World War and later during the Korean conflict, and in the case of USS *New Jersey* also in the course of the Viet-Nam war. The latter ship is the first of the four to be re-activated, this process involving the changing of some lighter armament, the addition of some new weapons (eg Tomahawk cruise missiles and Phalanx close-in weapon systems), but the nine Mk 7 16 inch guns remain the main conventional armament, arranged in three triple turrets.

These major calibre gun turrets are constructed with armour plate which is 43 cm thick at the sides and front, 30 cm at the rear, and with 18 cm tops. The gun was designed to be removed without dismantling the turret; barrel length is 50 calibres, weighing (without breech block) approximately 108 480 kg. A range of about 40 km has been achieved with a shell weighing 1225 kg with a barrel elevation angle of 45°, and for use against surface shipping, 'Iowa' class 16 inch guns are seen as complementing the Harpoon anti-shipping missiles being fitted in these ships with their typical maximum range of about 60 nautical miles.

In mid-1981 it was estimated that there were over 21 000 projectiles for Mk 7 16 inch guns in store, of which about 13 000 were then probably still serviceable. Their number includes: 15 400 high capacity (HC) projectiles, 3200 armour piercing (AP),

The two forward triple 16 inch guns aboard USS New Jersey which was recently re-activated (again), retaining the largest naval guns in service together with new missile armament and other improvements for a new commission (US Navy)

2300 target projectiles, and 138 Mk 19 projectiles. All of the last listed are thought to be unserviceable, while all of the target projectiles and some 90 per cent

of the AP rounds are fit for use. Slightly over half the HC projectiles are regarded as serviceable. In the case of charges for these rounds, about 80 per cent of exisiting stocks of 12 400 full charges and almost 12 600 reduced charges are thought to be fit for use. Each ship of the 'Iowa' class has a magazine load of 1220 projectiles, and the combined weight of round and full charge is approximately 1525 kg. The HC projectile has a payload of 70 kg of explosive 'D' and the AP round has about 18 kg of the same explosive. US assessments calculate that existing ammunition stocks will be adequate for training and structural test purposes until the end of 1991, after which procurement of target projectiles will be required. There are considered to be about 18 000 war rounds available without any need for refurbishing, and it will take about six months to start up the 16 inch/50 calibre projectile loading facility in the USA.

CHARACTERISTICS
Calibre: 16 inch (406 mm)
Barrel length: 50 calibres
Weight: 108 480 kg (without breech block)
Mount: Triple, Mk 7
Max range: Approx 40 km
Rate of fire: 2 rounds/minute
Projectile weights: 1016 kg; 862 kg (service/HC); 1225 kg (AP/target)
MV: 820 m/s (max, full charge)
STATUS
Current plans call for four USN ships of the 'Iowa' class fitted with three triple Mk 7 16 inch gun turrets to be re-activated. The first of these, USS *New Jersey*, was recommissioned in December 1982 and work had started on USS *Iowa*.

6094.203
SINGLE 8 inch MAJOR CALIBRE LIGHTWEIGHT GUN MOUNT Mk 71

The major calibre lightweight gun (MCLWG) development programme is intended to provide US Navy ships of destroyer size with a high-performance 8 inch (203 mm) gun capable of fitting where a gun of

FMC Mk 71 8 inch major calibre lightweight gun mount aboard USS Hull

5 inch (127 mm) calibre would be more usual. Operational roles are anti-ship engagements and shore bombardment in support of amphibious operations. A single operator (below deck) can fire the gun, single shot or at rates up to 10 to 12 rounds per minute, and there is a ready-use capacity of 75 rounds on the prototype 8 inch/55 calibre Mk 71 Mod O. This can be increased by use of specially designed ready-to-use magazines for selected classes of ships. A centre-line ammunition hoist may be used to replenish the ready-use magazine from a lower deck magazine. In that case an additional crew of four loaders is required.

The loading, aiming and firing operation is fully automatic and there is automatic selection of any of six different types of round. All 8 inch/55 calibre semi-fixed ammunition with projectile weights up to 260 lb (118 kg) maximum can be used and two different lengths of projectile are automatically accommodated. Misfire removal, also, is automatic. In addition to standard Mk 25 projectiles, the Mk 71 Mod O gun is capable of firing guided projectiles, and extended range projectiles with a rocket motor.

Control of the gun can be effected by either the existing analogue fire control systems such as the Mk 68 as fitted in the USS *Hull* used for sea firing trials

of the Mk 71 Mod O, or the digital Mk 86 GFCS being fitted to new constructions.

CHARACTERISTICS
Calibre: 8 inch (203 mm)
Barrel length: 55 calibres
Projectile weight: 118 kg (max)
Firing rate: 12 rounds/minute
Ready use: 75 rounds
Mount weight: 78 425 kg
Barrel weight (tube and liner): 9008 kg
Traverse: 300° at 30°/s
Elevation: −5 to +65° at 20°/s
Acceleration: 60°/s² in traverse; 40°/s² in elevation
DEVELOPMENT
The concept of providing ships of destroyer size with a major calibre gun capability originated in the US Navy during the early and mid-1960s, and at one time it was proposed to develop a gun able to use ammunition in common with US Army 175 mm rounds. The latter project was dropped however, and the US Navy then decided to convert the prototype 175 mm gun to use existing 8 inch ammunition. The resultant weapon was the 8 inch/55 calibre gun mount Mk 71 Mod O.
STATUS
The Mk 71 Mod O was delivered to the US Navy

Surface Weapons Center Dahlgren Laboratory for shore testing in 1969, following tests at the manufacturer's (Northern Ordnance Division, FMC) plant. Evaluation at Dahlgren was completed by March 1971, followed by a limited scope operational evaluation from November 1971 to January 1972.

Installation in USS *Hull* for sea trials took place between April 1974 and April 1975 and sea firing tests began later that year. In December 1975 favourable results were reported but the Mk 71 was dropped from DoD procurement plans in 1979. The evaluation mount in USS *Hull* was removed and returned to the

US Naval Surface Weapons Center Dahlgren Laboratory for use as a test and demonstration mount.
CONTRACTOR
FMC Corporation, Northern Ordnance Division, Minneapolis, Minnesota 55421, USA.

6026.203
TWIN 5 inch/38 CALIBRE GUN MOUNTING Mk 32
This is the oldest design of the 5 inch mounting still in service with the USN, but it is also one of the most widely used. The 5 inch/38 calibre gun has indeed been described as 'the prototype of the conventional US naval gun'.

The Mk 32 mounting contains two Mk 12 5 inch/38 calibre guns and an enclosed mounting with ammunition-handling room beneath. It requires a crew of 13 on the mounting and 26 in all. Remotely-controlled, semi-automatic, and dual-purpose, it also has local laying facilities on the mounting. Normal rate of fire is 15 rounds per barrel per minute but the gun's capacity for sustained fire is in excess of this and a good crew can achieve 22 rounds per minute over short periods. Train limits are 300° apart and elevation limits from −15 to +85° but train and elevation velocity and acceleration are significantly lower than those of the later 5 inch mountings.

Semi-fixed ammunition is used, consisting of a projectile weighing about 25 kg (varying according to type) and a case assembly weighing about 13 kg including a full powder charge of 6·8 kg. With a full charge the muzzle velocity is 792·5 m/s giving a maximum horizontal range of 16·5 km (9 nautical miles) and a ceiling of 11 400 m. The ammunition is raised to the gun house by hydraulically powered hoists. The complete mounting weighs about 53 tons.
CHARACTERISTICS
Calibre: 127 mm
Barrel length: 38 calibres

Twin 5 inch/38 calibre gun mounting Mk 32 aboard USS Zellers (Stefan Terzibaschitsch)

Traverse: +150°
Elevation: −15 to +85°
Projectile weight: About 25 kg
Muzzle velocity: 792·5 m/s
Rate of fire: 15 – 22 rounds/minute
Max range: 16·5 km (9 nautical miles)
Max altitude: 11 400 m
Date introduced: 1935

STATUS
Twin mountings were installed in the 'Iowa' class battleships, many heavy cruisers, and a great many destroyers. Some of these are still in service in both the active and reserve fleets of the USN as well as in ex-US ships of other navies. They are also in service with one Spanish-built ship, and aboard certain Italian-built destroyers and Danish frigates.

6093.203
SINGLE 5 inch/54 CALIBRE GUN MOUNTING Mk 39
This gun mounting is an intermediate stage between the 5 inch/38 mountings (**6026.203** and **6092.203**) and the 5 inch/54 Mk 42 mountings (**6027.203**, **6028.203**, and **6029.203**). It can be regarded as a 5 inch/38

calibre single enclosed mounting Mk 30 with the Mk 12 38 calibre gun replaced by a Mk 16 54 calibre gun. This gun fires a heavier shell (about 32 kg instead of about 25 kg) with a slightly higher muzzle velocity and thus a longer range.

It may be noted that in this mounting an amplidyne all-electric power drive is used, whereas in both the

5 inch/38 mountings and the 5 inch/54 Mk 42 mountings the drive is electro-hydraulic.
STATUS
Operational as a single enclosed mounting in 'Midway' class aircraft carriers and also known to be fitted in seven ships of the Japanese 'Murasame' and 'Harukaze' classes.

6092.203
SINGLE 5 inch/38 CALIBRE GUN MOUNTINGS
In addition to the enclosed twin mounting of the 5 inch/38 calibre gun (**6026.203**) there have been three other general types of mounting for this gun. They are:
(a) Enclosed single mount with ammunition-handling room below. Originally on destroyers, destroyer escorts, and auxiliaries. Now mainly found on auxiliary vessels of the USN, these single mounts are also the main surface armament of the ex-US 'Fletcher' class destroyers which are still in service in some navies.
(b) Open single mount with ammunition-handling room below. Auxiliary vessels. Probable designation: Mk 30 Mod 24.
(c) Open single mount without ammunition hoists or handling room. Converted merchant vessels. Probable description: Mk 37.

In performance there is essentially no difference between the first two of these and one gun of the enclosed twin mounting. The third arrangement is necessarily less efficient in terms of ammunition

Single 5 inch/38 calibre gun aboard the Spanish Navy ship Legazpi (J I Taibo)

handling but otherwise the gun characteristics are the same.

The most widespread model is the Mk 30 which carries a single Mk 12 barrel. There are numerous

versions, and those of 'Fletcher' class destroyers are referred to as Mods 19, 30 and 31, depending upon the position of the mount aboard ship.

4468.203
155 mm VERTICAL LOAD GUN SYSTEM (VLGS)
This concept is aimed at developing a gun specifically designed for guided projectiles but also capable of using the wide range of 155 mm ammunition available throughout NATO and which includes high explosive ballistic projectiles and nuclear shells. It is designed for air and surface engagements in a mounting that is lighter, less complex, and more effective than existing 5 inch guns.

The basic concept is of a single barrel which is always brought to the vertical before being loaded by a powered vertical hoist. Similarly after firing the gun is brought to a fixed elevation to align with an empty case door before extracting the used cartridge case. Complex machinery is thus avoided and the simple design is intended to give maximum reliability, ease of maintenance, availability and reduced life cycle costs. The system therefore has 40 per cent fewer parts than the 5 inch/54 calibre gun mount Mk 45 and a

predicted mean rounds between failures of 2100 rounds. Installation on board ship is also intended to be simple and achieved, together with the check-out, in a week with mounting replacement, when needed in three days.
CHARACTERISTICS
Ammunition types: Conventional high explosive, illuminating, smoke, and incendiary. Existing nuclear rounds. Guided projectiles
Traverse: Unlimited

Elevation: –10 to +75°
Rate of fire: 10 rounds/minute (sustained)
Projectile weight: Conventional 46·7 kg, guided 102 kg
Mounting weight: 22 680 kg total

Power requirements: 440 V, 60 Hz, 3-phase. 40 kW stand-by load, 120 kW average firing load
STATUS
The concept has been developed under the direction of Naval Sea Systems Command.

CONTRACTOR
FMC Corporation, Northern Ordnance Division, Minneapolis, Minnesota 55421, USA.

6027.203
SINGLE 5 inch/54 CALIBRE GUN MOUNTING Mk 42

This widely adopted gun mounting has several advantages over both the 5 inch/38 calibre mountings and the 5 inch/54 calibre Mk 39 mounting (**6093.203**). It uses the Mk 18 54 calibre gun, and it is capable of a much higher rate of fire of 35 rounds per minute. The following description applies largely to Mod 7.

Mk 42 Mod 7 is a dual-purpose single enclosed

mounting of the base-ring type fitted with automatic ammunition feed mechanisms. Driven by electric-hydraulic power units, it can be operated in local or automatic control.

The gun housing slide and breech mechanism are quite different from those of the semi-automatic 5 inch/54 calibre and 5 inch/38 calibre designs, as also is the ammunition feed system. The latter involves manual operations only in loading the cylindrical, power-driven loading drums that store

complete rounds of ammunition and use them to feed the hoists. All subsequent operations are performed mechanically and as a result the single gun can achieve a continuous firing rate equal to that achieved only in short bursts by an expert crew on the two guns of the 5 inch/38 calibre Mk 32 mounting. A further obvious advantage is the reduction in the number of men required to man the gun. Crew for the Mk 42 is 14, of whom four are on the mounting.

Projectile weight is about 32 kg, muzzle velocity about 810 m/s, range against surface targets about 24 km (about 13 nautical miles), and ceiling (at 85° elevation) about 13 600 m. Weight of complete turret is some 60 tons.

The Mk 42 Mod 10 is an improved version of the Mod 7 gun mount and over 100 are at sea. A modernisation and overhaul programme substitutes updated control and operating components to incorporate the improved reliability and maintenance features of the Mk 42 Mod 9 gun mount (**6028.203**) into the earlier Mod 7 and 8 gun mounts. The full gun crew complement is reduced to 12 men. Ready-to-use ammunition capacity is 40 rounds and firing rates of 20 or 40 rounds per minute are possible. The associated fire control system is the Mk 68 Mod 11.
STATUS
Operational in ships of the US Navy and elsewhere. Foreign users of the Mk 42 gun include the Royal Australian, Federal German, Japanese and Spanish navies.

5 inch/54 calibre Mk 42 gun on USS Thomas C Hart *(Stefan Terzibaschitsch)*

6028.203
SINGLE 5 inch/54 CALIBRE GUN MOUNTING Mk 42 (Lightweight Mod 9)

Functionally similar to the Mk 42 Mod 7 gun mount described above, the Mk 42 Mod 9 is an improved design featuring lower mount weight (58 700 kg), nearly ten per cent lower power consumption and a smaller crew requirement. State-of-the-art improvements incorporated include replacement of all electronic components of the earlier mount by solid-state devices. Only two men are needed on the mount as against four for the Mod 7, and the total crew requirement is 12 men instead of 14. The only respect in which the Mod 7 performance is known to

be superior is that of elevation acceleration (60°/s² against 40°/s²).
STATUS
Fifty-one units of the above-decks portion of the mount were manufactured by Northern Ordnance and supplied for use on DE-1052 class ships. The below-decks portion was produced by the US Navy Naval Ordnance Station, Louisville.
CONTRACTOR
FMC Corporation, Northern Ordnance Division, Minneapolis, Minnesota 55421, USA.

Lightweight (Mod 9) version of the 5 inch/54 calibre gun mounting Mk 42 in production

6029.203
SINGLE 5 inch/54 CALIBRE LIGHTWEIGHT AUTOMATIC GUN MOUNTING Mk 45

This gun mounting represents a major step forward in medium calibre ordnance for the US Navy. It has been designed primarily for installation in new ships and was required to embody all relevant improvements developed over some 30 years since the 5 inch/38 was first introduced (**6026.203**). It was also required to be light, easily maintained, and exceptionally reliable. The result is a weapon which requires only one-third of the crew of a 5 inch/38 and with which a single man in a control centre can fire a drum load of 20 shells without help. It is also certainly the lightest naval gun mount of its size in the West and probably the lightest in the world.

Specifically, the major differences in characteristics between the Mk 42 (**6027.203**) and Mk 45 mountings are:
Mount weight: Reduced from 60 t to 25 t
Crew: Reduced from 14 to 6
Crew on mounting: Reduced from 2 to 0
Max elevation: Reduced from 85° to 65°
Rate of fire: Reduced from 40 rounds/minute to 20
Ready service rounds: Reduced from 40 to 20

The gun will be used with the lightweight Mk 86 GFCS (**1241.281**).
DEVELOPMENT
Development of the new weapon started in 1964 on a contract placed with the Northern Ordnance Division

5 inch/54 calibre Mk 45 gun aboard USS Briscoe

of the FMC Corporation. Initial production was by Northern Ordnance, who continue to make the mounting, and General Electric Company Ordnance Systems were brought in as a second source although now understood to be no longer producing this mount.

Northern Ordnance were also the developers and the sole manufacturers of the Mk 6 ammunition hoist, which is an integral part of the Mk 45 installations on CGN-41, CGN-36, DD-963, LHA, DD-993 and CG-47 ships. Gun barrels are produced by US Government ordnance factories.
STATUS
Initially Northern Ordnance produced 33 Mk 45 mounts, and later General Electric produced 56 additional mounts. In September 1975 Northern Ordnance was awarded contracts for two gun mounts per ship for (initially) six Iranian DD-993 class ships and one American CGN. By October 1977 FMC had delivered 45 Mk 45 gun mounts to the US Navy and was under contract for eight more for fitting in CG-47 AEGIS cruisers. The four remaining DD-993 class ships ordered by Iran were cancelled but completed and delivered to the US Navy; they contain two Mk 45 gun mounts each.

Gun system changes are currently under development at Northern Ordnance to increase the capabilities of the Mk 45. The new Mod 1 system will include round selectivity, guided projectile firing capability and remote round type selection.
CONTRACTORS
FMC Corporation, Northern Ordnance Division, Minneapolis, Minnesota 55421, USA.

General Electric Company, Ordnance Systems of the Electronic Systems Division, 100 Plastics Avenue, Pittsfield, Massachusetts 01201, USA.

6031.203

40 mm ANTI-AIRCRAFT GUN MOUNTINGS

There are single, twin, and quadruple barrelled versions of the 40 mm automatic recoil operated gun in service in the US Navy. The twin model is the Mk 1, the quadruple version is the Mk 2, and both types are water-cooled. The single barrel Mk 3 is air-cooled. Most mounts can be either locally or remotely controlled, and are power operated, with emergency hand operation. The gun is derived from the Bofors

design and the accompanying photograph shows a single barrel mount.

CHARACTERISTICS

Calibre: 40 mm
Barrel length: 56 calibres
Projectile weight: About 0·9 kg
Muzzle velocity: About 820 m/s
Rate of fire: 140 to 160 rounds/barrel/minute
Max range: About 11 km but tactical range much less

40 mm Bofors single mount US pattern

6030.203

3 inch/50 CALIBRE GUN MOUNTING

These 3 inch (76 mm)/50 calibre gun mounts are primarily intended for air defence but can be used also against surface targets. Planned during the Second World War but not completed in time for combat use in that conflict, the mounts have since proved themselves so effective that they have virtually displaced their predecessors – 40 mm twin and quadruple mounts – on combat vessels.

Mks 27 and 33 are twin mounts and Mk 34 a single. Mks 27 and 33 are identical in almost all respects, the main difference being in the slide. All marks use the same gun and similar backing mechanisms, except that in the twin mounts the assemblies are of opposite hand. Some models of the Mk 33 are enclosed twin mounts with an aluminium or fibreglass reinforced

plastic (FRP) shield, and others again are twins with modifications for installation of a fire control radar antenna. The Mk 34 mount is an open single with a right-hand slide and loader assembly. Some models of the Mk 34 are also FRP shielded. Mount weights are in the region of 32 000 lb (14 500 kg) for the twins and 17 000 lb (7700 kg) for the Mk 34.

CHARACTERISTICS

Calibre: 76 mm
Barrel length: 50 calibres
Elevation: To 85°
Projectile weight: 6 kg approx
Muzzle velocity: About 825 m/s
Rate of fire: 45 – 50 rounds/minute
Max range: About 13 km (7 nautical miles)
Max altitude: About 9000 m

STATUS

Operational. Twin mounts of an earlier 70 calibre 3 inch gun were installed in some ships in or shortly after 1945 but it is believed that none are now in service. An even earlier (circa 1936) three inch gun Mk 22 is, however, still to be found in some US auxiliary vessels and foreign navies.

3 inch/50 calibre twin mounting (US Navy)

Single mounting of 3 inch/50 calibre gun (US Navy)

3175.203

76 mm/62 CALIBRE GUN MOUNT Mk 75

This gun mount is being produced by FMC Corporation, Northern Ordnance Division, for the United States Government under licence from OTO Melara SpA of La Spezia, Italy and is identical to the single 76/62 compact gun mounting described in entry **5533.203**.

It is a single barrel, lightweight, rapid fire, remote controlled, dual-purpose gun and has been selected by the United States authorities for installation on US PHM hydrofoils, FFG-7 frigates and Coast Guard cutters, and patrol craft of the Royal Saudi Navy.

STATUS

Five mounts (of which only one was used) were delivered by OTO Melara for comprehensive tests on USS *Talbot* and technical evaluation on board this ship was completed in early 1975 with favourable results. The 76 mm/62 calibre gun mount Mk 75 is now in production at FMC Corporation, Northern Ordnance Division, and by December 1983 Northern Ordnance had delivered 75 guns for FFG-7, Coast Guard and Saudi Arabian vessels.

CONTRACTOR

FMC Corporation, Northern Ordnance Division, Minneapolis, Minnesota 55421, USA.

Mk 75 after 400-round acceptance firing test

2584.203

EMERLEC-30 TWIN 30 mm MOUNTING

Emerlec-30 is a twin 30 mm naval ordnance system currently in production at Emerson Electric Co, St Louis, USA. The Emerlec-30 was originally developed as the EX-74 MOD 0 for the coastal patrol and interdiction craft under a USN programme. The system incorporates design improvements that have resulted from land-based and sea testing of the EX-74.

Designed for anti-missile, anti-aircraft and surface fire the system comprises two Oerlikon 30 mm cannon, daylight reflex or night image intensifier sight with gyroscopically-assisted hand grip assembly, an integral below-deck magazine with substantial ready-use ammunition and an enclosed environmentally-controlled cabin for the operator. The mount can be operated by remote control and will interface with standard fire control systems.

Ship's power supplies are used in normal operation, but an on-mount battery provides sufficient power to operate the guns and fire a full complement of ammunition in an emergency. Traditional hand crank mechanisms provide further back-up.

CHARACTERISTICS

Calibre: 30 mm
Elevation: –15 to +80°
Traverse: 360°

Rate of fire: 600 rounds/barrel/minute
Ready rounds: 985 rounds/gun
Projectile weight: 0·35 kg
Max range: 8 km
Total weight of system (less ammunition): 1905 kg
STATUS
In series production since 1976 and known to be in service with or on order, for Ecuador, Greece, Malaysia, Nigeria, Philippines and South Korea.

CONTRACTOR
Government & Defense Group, Emerson Electric Company, 8100 W Florissant, St Louis, Missouri 63136, USA.

Emerlec-30 twin mounting aboard 105 ft (32 m) 'Swiftships' fast patrol boat

---

4042.203
EX-83 LIGHTWEIGHT 30 mm NAVAL GUN MOUNT
The EX-83 lightweight 30 mm naval gun mount designed and developed by the General Electric Company, USA, is a high performance mount embodying the seven-barrel GAU-8/A Gatling gun. It

General Electric EX-83 lightweight 30 mm naval gun mount set up for shore firing tests

has been designed to provide naval craft with an effective close-in defence against air and anti-ship missile threats.

The production ammunition consists of a ballistically matched set of 30 mm HEI, API, and target practice rounds. The ammunition feed/storage drum is mounted vertically and rotates in the train axis. This configuration minimises unbalanced loads and inertia changes as the ammunition is expended and the total amount varies, reduces the above-deck profile of the mount, and minimises the swept radius required below deck. The below deck location of the feed drum also provides a protected environment for reloading and maintenance of the ammunition replenishment and feed system.

Particular design emphasis was placed on the positioning of the GAU-8/A relative to the mount's train and elevation axes, to ensure reliable ammunition feed to the gun's transfer unit. The elevation axis of the gun passes through the centre of the transfer unit, which minimises chute distortion as the gun is elevated or depressed. Gun firing torque about the elevation axis is eliminated by having the centroid of the firing pressure pulse coincident with the centre-line of the elevation trunnion bearings. The longitudinal axis of the gun assembly is displaced 102 mm from the centre of the train bearing, which positions the firing barrel coincident with the mount's train axis.
CHARACTERISTICS
Gun type: 7-barrel Gatling GAU-8/A
Calibre: 30 mm

MV: 1021 m/s
Drive: Electric
Rate of fire: 2100/4200 rounds/minute
Ammunition types: HEI, API, TP, APDS
Capacity: 1350 rounds
Feed: Linkless
Mount
Weight (loaded): 5399 kg
Height above deck: 1646 mm
Depth below deck: 2011 mm
Max diameter: 2529 mm
STATUS
The EX-83 was test fired in late 1979 in Den Helder, and used with the Signaal Flycatcher all-weather fire control system (**2301.181**) for a demonstration programme code-named Shortstop. This combination is the basis of the autonomous naval air defence system called Goalkeeper (SGE-30) (**3516.261**). In early 1983 demonstrations were given to representatives of ten countries in the course of trials at Burlington of the Goalkeeper system which is to be fitted in ships of the Royal Netherlands Navy. Simulated engagements included a replica missile of the same size as the Exocet anti-ship weapon, and various attack profiles.

The EX-83 is also planned to undergo USN at-sea evaluation integrated with an ASMD-capable Mk 86 GFCS aboard a DD-963 class destroyer.
CONTRACTOR
General Electric Company, Armament Systems Department, Lakeside Avenue, Burlington, Vermont 05302, USA.

4043.203
EX-84 20 mm NAVAL MOUNT
The EX-84 is a lightweight, low profile mount developed to provide firepower for small naval craft. It is designed to accept and fire the 20 mm M197 gun, the XM188E1 gun, the M134 7·62 mm gun, the M19 40 mm grenade machine gun, the Stinger AA missile and other selected weapons. An engineering model of the EX-84 with an M-197 was constructed and tested under a US Navy prototype programme.

The EX-84 mount has many components that are common with the UTS turret as used on the AH-1 Cobra helicopter, and the system is a remotely controlled flexible gun mount with five main elements: a microprocessor-based gun corrector module, mount electronics, ammunition storage and feed system, the mount structure and a pantograph sight.

The gun corrector is a fire control computer which makes the EX-84 mount self-sufficient, and in addition to the microprocessor it has the necessary components to provide memory and analogue and digital input/output facilities. The corrector compensates for velocity jump, gravity drop, parallax, target motion, and provides self-testing for the whole system.

The ammunition feed and storage system comprises a box assembly and a cover assembly with booster. The box has a capacity of 750 20 mm rounds or 500 rounds of 30 mm ammunition. This electrically primed ammunition can be handled and stored in a

Components of EX-84 universal naval mount, shown with M197 20 mm gun mounted in turret

RADHAZ environment. The gun feeder is designed to remove the ammunition from regular links or links with radiation tabs. Flexible chuting provides for transfer of ammunition from the container to the feeder assembly.

The structural components of the mount are the lower support, upper support, and the saddle assembly. The lower support provides the ship interface and mounting. The upper support is mounted to the lower support through a train bearing and drive, and contains an integral gear drive for the

elevation axis. The saddle is a frame that supports the weapon which is mounted through the recoil system. The EX-84 is arranged to accept a ring sight, a reflex sight, night vision sight, or a dual-mode gunsight (currently under development).
CHARACTERISTICS
Mount: EX-84 (with M197 gun)
Gun type: 3-barrel Gatling
Calibre: 20 mm
MV: 1030 m/s
Recoil force: 545 kg
Weight: 363 kg (empty); 613 kg (loaded with 750 rounds)
Height above deck: 609 mm
Turret diameter: 609 mm
Swept radius: 1676 mm
Position accuracy: 3 mils (static in either axis)
Dispersion: 12 mils max (80% rounds fired)
Rate of fire: 750/1500 rounds/minute
Ammunition: 20 mm M50 series
Capacity: 750 rounds
Training: ±110°
Training rate: 80°/s
Elevation: −10 to +55°
Elevation rate: 60°/s
STATUS
Development and test.
CONTRACTOR
General Electric Company, Armament Systems Department, Lakeside Avenue, Burlington, Vermont 05302, USA.

2836.203

20 mm THREE-BARREL DECK MOUNT Mk 10

Designed for installation on a wide range of sea-going and riverine craft, this three-barrel 20 mm gun can provide a small vessel with very substantial fire-power.

The system comprises an M197 three-barrel 20 mm gun and ancillary equipment mounted on a USN Mk 10 stand. The gun and its associated delinking feeder (M89) are currently in use by the USMC in helicopters and in US naval aircraft.

The M197 weapon is electrically operated and power for this is supplied by a battery mounted on the gun stand. Twenty complements of ammunition can be fired without battery recharging; the battery can conveniently be connected to a main power source to provide a 28 V trickle feed, thus maintaining the battery in a charged condition.

The three-barrel gun is derived from the six-barrel M61 (Vulcan) gun (**5547.103**) and has alternative rates of fire of 600 and 1200 rounds/minute. The M89 delinking feeder includes a declutching arrangement which, when the trigger is released, automatically stops the supply of ammunition to the gun but permits the gun to continue firing long enough to clear the barrels.

The Mk 10 gun mount provides convenient room for the installation of the 300-round ammunition can behind the right-hand shield, the battery and control box being mounted behind the other half.

CHARACTERISTICS

Deck-mounted on Mk 10 mount

Weapon: M197 20 mm 3 barrels

Elevation: –15 to +75°

Traverse: Unlimited

MV: 1030 m/s

Dispersion: 80% in 8 mil circle

Rate of fire: 600 or 1200 rounds/minute

Ammunition: M50 series

Feed: XM89

Ready rounds: 300

Battery fire out capability: 6000 rounds

Weight: (Without ammunition) 500 kg approx

CONTRACTOR

General Electric Company, Aircraft Equipment Division, Burlington, Vermont, USA.

AIRCRAFT ARMAMENT

ARGENTINA

3806.303
CBAS-1 ALBATROS AIRCRAFT ROCKET
The Argentinian CBAS-1 Albatros is an unguided aircraft rocket used for typical air-to-surface tactical roles but primarily in naval applications for which it was originally designed. The rocket is of 70 mm calibre and the solid rocket motor case is constructed of aluminium. A peripherically inhibited double-base extruded propellant weighing 5·5 kg is used in the rocket motor, and the wrap-around forged steel tail fins are provided with a mechanical opening device which operates after launch.

CHARACTERISTICS
Calibre: 2·75 inch (70 mm)
Propulsion: Solid rocket motor
Launch weight: 8·7 kg
Warhead
Training (smoke): 2·9 kg
Anti-tank/anti-personnel (ATAP): 4·45 kg
Fragmentation: 4·65 kg
Anti-personnel/anti-light material: 4·8 kg
(Production of a submunition warhead was due to begin in March 1984)
Range: 8000 m

DEVELOPMENT
The CBAS-1 was designed by the Argentinian Scientific and Technical Research Institute of the Armed Forces (CITEFA) and produced by EDESA.
STATUS
Operational with the Argentinian Navy since 1973. More than 78 000 rockets have been exported. The contractor (EDESA) also produces integrated weapon systems which employ this 2·75 inch rocket.
CONTRACTOR
Empresa de Desarrollo Especiales Sociedad Anonima (EDESA), Corrientes 1642, Buenos Aires, Argentina.

BRAZIL

4145.303
AIRCRAFT ARMAMENT
A number of aircraft armament systems have been developed in Brazil, and are currently in production and in local service and abroad. Brief details follow:
37 mm SBAT-37 rocket
This spin-stabilised air-to-ground rocket is fired from the seven-round LM-37/7 launcher, and can be fitted to light aircraft and helicopters.
70 mm SBAT-70 rocket
This solid-propellant air-to-ground folding-fin rocket is similar to the US-made 2·75 inch FFAR, and can be used with re-usable multiple launchers of two (LM-70/2), four (LM-70/4), seven (LM-70/7) or nineteen (LM-70/19) rounds. A disposable 19-round launcher is also available.

SBAT-70 rockets are produced in two main versions: the SBAT-70 M1 non-spinning type generally used with high-speed aircraft: and the SBAT-70 M2 spinning model for low-speed aircraft and helicopters, but also providing greater accuracy and longer stand-off ranges for fighter-bombers etc. The current range of warheads for these rockets is as follows:

Warhead	Type
AVC-70/AC	HEAT anti-tank
AVC-70/AP	HE fragmentation anti-personnel
AVC-70/AC/AP	Combined anti-armour/anti-personnel
AVC-70/F	Flechette anti-personnel/anti-material
AVC-70/FB	Smoke WP (white phosphorus)
AVC-70/EF	Smoke practice
AVC-70/E	Inert practice (dummy)

The double base motor weighs 4·98 kg, has a thrust of 470 kg, a burn time of 1·2 seconds and uses BD-108 propellant: the alternative composite motor weighs 5·15 kg, has a thrust of 525 kg, a burn time of 1·2 seconds and uses CV-7 propellant.
127 mm SBAT-127 rocket
In the same class as the US-built five inch (127 mm) HVAR and Zuni Mk 16, this air-to-ground rocket has a 20 kg warhead and cruciform fins at the tail. It may use two- or four-rocket launchers.
Helicopter armament system
This consists of a flexible mounting for a 7·62 mm FN MAG machine gun and rack for an LM-70/7 launcher for seven SBAT-70 70 mm FFARs. In Brazilian use

this system has been fitted to Air Force Bell UH-1D/Hs and to Navy Helibrás Esquilos (locally-built Aérospatiale Écureil), Westland Wasps and Westland Lynx. It has been exported to several countries.
7·62 mm machine gun pods
Pods for two 7·62 mm machine guns for aircraft use are operational and in production for local use and export.
Aircraft bombs
Five types of aircraft bomb are known to be in production in Brazil for its air forces and for export:
CHARACTERISTICS
AV-BAFG-120
Length: 1·8 m
Body diameter: 230 mm
Total weight: 120 kg (equivalent to US Mk 81)
AV-BAFG-250
Length: 2·2 m
Body diameter: 270 mm
Total weight: 250 kg
(equivalent to US Mk 82)
AV-BI-200
Length: 1·81 m
Body diameter: 420 mm

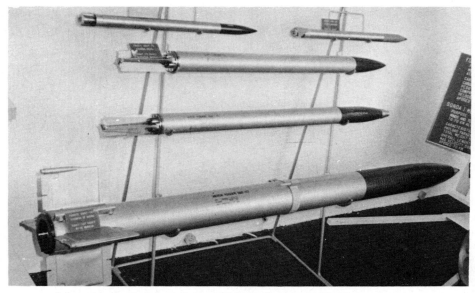

Avibras aircraft rockets (top to bottom) SBAT-37, SBAT-70, SBAT-127 (Ronaldo S Olive)

Avibras LM-70/19 multiple launcher on Brazilian Air Force F-5E (Ronaldo S Olive)

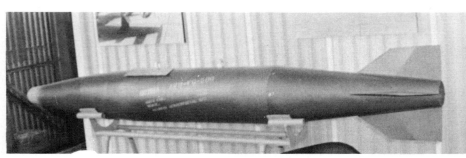

Avibras 500 lb general-purpose bomb (Ronaldo S Olive)

Avibras LM-70/7 multiple launcher on Brazilian Navy Wasp helicopter (Ronaldo S Olive)

Total weight: 177 kg
(equivalent to US 400 lb fire bomb)
AV-BI-250
Length: 3·46 m
Body diameter: 400 mm
Total weight: 271 kg
(equivalent to US BLU-32)
AV-BI-375
Length: 3·63 m
Body diameter: 480 mm
Total weight: 362 kg
(equivalent to US BLU-27)
CONTRACTOR
Avibrás – Indústria Aeroespacial SA, Caixa Postal
229, 12200 São José dos Campos, SP, Brazil.

Avibras twin machine-gun pod for 7·62 mm machine guns (Ronaldo S Olive)

Avibras helicopter armament system combining 7·62 mm machine gun mounting and 7-round rocket launcher pod (Ronaldo S Olive)

AV-BAFG-120 250 lb low-drag general-purpose bomb (Ronaldo S Olive)

CANADA

4539.303
CRV7 AIRCRAFT ROCKET

Designed and developed by the Canadian Department of National Defence, the CRV7 2·75 inch (70 mm) wrap-around fin aircraft rocket operated by Canadian Forces aircraft is claimed to possess a number of advantages compared with similar rockets such as the Mk 4/40 series. These include: higher velocity, giving a flatter trajectory and three times the impact energy; greater stand-off range; more precise control of rocket motor ignition timing, giving reduced dispersion and enhanced accuracy; and improved aerodynamic stability through decreased deployment time for deployment of the wrap-around fins.

The CRV7 rocket weapon system has two motors: the RLU-5001/B (C14) and RLU-5002/B (C15). The C14 consists of a case-bonded high energy composite propellant which uses a hydroxyl-terminated polybutadiene (HTPB) binder with an 88 per cent solids content of ammonium perchlorate, aluminium and ferric oxide. This is primarily for fixed-wing use. The C15 motor is the same as the C14 with the exception that the aluminium powder is omitted. Consequently the production of primary smoke has been virtually eliminated. This is intended primarily for helicopter use. Weight of the assembled motor is 14½ pounds (6·6 kg). The propellant for both motors is an internal burning cylinder 83·8 cm long with a bore diameter of 20·5 mm.

The fibreglass/phenolic moulded nozzle has metallic inserts to provide strength, electrical contacts and a shear pin release system. Integrally moulded vanes induce spin prior to exit from the launcher. Aluminium wrap-around fins are fully deployed within 36 cm of exit from the launcher and further stabilise the rocket in flight.

Operationally the CRV7 is fired from the 19-tube LAU-5003 A/A launcher. In training roles the CRV7 is fired from the six-tube LAU-5002 A/A. The SUU-20 bomb/rocket dispenser has been modified so that it is compatible with the CRV7.

The launchers are compatible with the standard 14-inch (35·6 cm) suspension systems, use standard

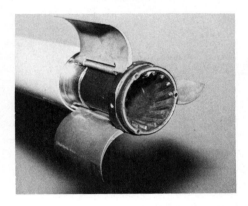

Deployed wrap-around tail fins of CRV7 aircraft rocket and integrally moulded vanes in motor exit cone to induce spin

intervalometers and the standard five-pin electrical connections all of which conform to STANAG 3763AA.
CHARACTERISTICS
Calibre: 70 mm
Length: 104·2 cm (without warhead)
Rocket weight: 6·6 kg (without warhead)
Action time: 2·2 s
Max thrust: 7 KN
Spin: 40 cycles/s (with 4·5 kg warhead)
Max velocity: 1250 m/s (a/c speed 540 KTAS, 4·5 kg warhead); 1500 m/s (a/c speed 540 KTAS, 3 kg warhead)
Effective range: Air-to-ground 6500 m; ground-to-ground 18 km
Launchers
LAU 5002A/A 6-tube re-useable training/operational launcher
LAU 5003A/A 19-tube disposable combat launcher
SUU 5003A/B 4-tube training dispenser
Warhead weights: 3, 4·5, 7 kg

Loading CRV7 rockets into LAU 5002A/A launcher on BO-105 helicopter

Complete CRV7 rocket fitted with practice warhead

A practice warhead, WTU 5001/B, has been developed specially for spinning 2·75 inch rockets. The design eliminates dynamic instability problems. It weighs about 4·25 kg and is also able to penetrate light and medium armour.
DEVELOPMENT
Development and flight proving was carried out by the Canadian Department of National Defence. Primary research was performed by the Valcartier Defence Research Establishment in association with Bristol Aerospace Ltd.
STATUS
The Canadian Forces have chosen the CRV7 as a replacement for earlier versions of the 2·75 inch rocket. In full production.
CONTRACTOR
Bristol Aerospace Limited, PO Box 874, Winnipeg, Manitoba R3C 2S4, Canada.

CHILE

4426.303
PJ-1 MANUALLY OPERATED BOMB

The PJ-1 is a manually dropped bomb which can be used from almost any type of aircraft or helicopter and also allows civil aircraft to be used in an emergency. It measures 500 mm long by 85 mm in diameter and weighs 3 kg including 800 grammes of high explosive. The main explosive charge is surrounded by 110 steel fragments which are projected to an effective operating range of 35 metres.

The bomb is of simple construction and safety is ensured through safety locks which do not allow the fuze to activate until three seconds after leaving the aircraft. The head may be copper covered to allow perforation of armoured vehicles or installations, or alternatively fitted with a hollow charge device to give considerable anti-armour effect.

CONTRACTOR
Cardoen Explosivos, Providencia 2237, Santiago, Chile.

Cardoen PJ-1 bomb with storage and transportation container

4598.303
CB 130 & CB 500 CLUSTER BOMBS

Promising experience with the earlier Cardoen 100 lb and 500 lb cluster bombs (**4427.303** and **4487.303** in the *1983-84* edition) led the company to embark on development of improved models, the CB 130 and CB 500 which are 130 lb and 500 lb cluster bombs respectively. Both feature bomblets of a new indigenous design and a new programmable fuze designed by Cardoen.

Using these bombs, low or high altitude attacks can be made at high aircraft speeds against targets dispersed over wide areas without the need for extreme delivery accuracy. After release, the bombs are opened in mid-air by an electronically programmed fuze, and a number of armour-piercing bomblets has an elliptical shape of between 15 000 from the CB 500. The surface area covered by the bomblets has an elliptical shape of between 15 000 and 50 000 square metres, depending on the size and operational use of the bomb. Release height also has a considerable effect. The altitude at which the bomb opens after release is controlled by the programmable electronic fuze which provides a variety of opening delay times.

The Cardoen bomblet is intended for use against tanks and armoured vehicles, troop concentrations etc. It is stated armour plate of more than 203 mm can be penetrated. Used against troop concentrations, shrapnel spreads over an area of up to 50 000 square metres. The complete cluster bomb is intended to withstand sustained forces of 6 g encountered by combat manoeuvres of a high speed attack aircraft. The CB 130 and CB 500 are fitted with lugs for the standard NATO 14 inch, Warsaw Pact 250 mm spaced suspensions and the single point bomb lug.

CHARACTERISTICS

Type	CB 500	CB 130
Length	2·64 m	2·05 m
Diameter	446 mm	253 mm

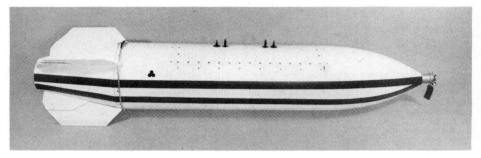

CB 500 cluster bomb

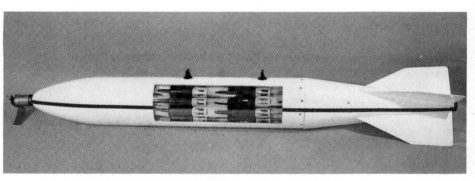

CB 130 cluster bomb with cutaway skin

Fin span	650 mm (closed)	-
	1140 (open)	400 mm (open)
Weight	245 kg	60 kg

Fuze: Nose mounted, adjustable delay 3 – 18 s
Bomblet (for both versions)
Weight: 740 g
Length: 360 mm
Diameter: 48 mm
Tail diameter: 48 mm
STATUS
Production.
CONTRACTOR
Cardoen Explosivos, Providencia 2237, Santiago, Chile.

4488.303
CARDOEN GENERAL-PURPOSE BOMBS

Cardoen manufactures a standard range of general-purpose aircraft bombs suitable for use with bomber or fighter aircraft. Various sizes are produced, standard items being the 250 lb (113 kg) Mk 81, 500 lb (227 kg) Mk 82, and the 1000 lb (454 kg) Mk 83. All are constructed of forged seamless steel bodies with a tempered steel nose section and cruciform tail assembly for flight stabilisation. Standard explosive fillings are employed and mechanical time fuzes are fitted normally. Bombs are provided with NATO standard coupling eyebolts at 14-inch (35·6 cm) centres.

STATUS
Production.
CONTRACTOR
Cardoen Explosivos, Providencia 2237, Santiago, Chile.

CHINA (PEOPLE'S REPUBLIC)

4437.303
57 mm AIRCRAFT ROCKET

Among the range of aircraft armament indigenously produced in the People's Republic of China, the 57 mm aircraft rocket is employed on Chinese-built F6 fighter/ground attack aircraft for use against either aircraft targets or surface targets such as naval craft or battlefield strong points, tanks, personnel concentrations, fuel dumps etc. On the F6 aircraft the 57 mm rockets are carried in underwing pods, each of which contains eight rounds. These may be fired (electrically) separately or in salvo. The rocket is stabilised in flight by a set of folding tail-fins.

CHARACTERISTICS
Calibre: 57 mm
Length: 915 mm (overall)
Span: 230 mm

Weight: 3·992 kg (complete)
Warhead weight: 1·372 kg (HE)
Operating temperature range: +50 to –60° C
STATUS
Production.

AERO-AMMUNITION 30-1

The F6 fighter aircraft mentioned above has as its normal armament three 30 mm cannon and weapons of this calibre are found on other aircraft of the Republic's air forces. A range of ammunition is manufactured for use in 30 mm cannon against air and surface targets; standard types include: high explosive incendiary tracer (HEIT), high explosive incendiary (HEI), armour piercing explosive (APE), and practice. All types are supplied with cartridge cases of 70/30 brass.

CHARACTERISTICS

Type	HEIT	HEI	APE
Calibre	30 mm	30 mm	30 mm
Weight of round	840 g	840 g	828 g
Total length	266 mm	266 mm	266 mm
Projectile weight	418 g	418 g	407 g
MV	795 m/s	795 m/s	800 m/s
Pmax (kg/cm²)	3050	3050	3050
Penetration	—	—	10 mm*

*Penetration means the depth of penetration of the shell when encountering a uniform steel target at a distance of 50 to 75 m with a velocity of 360 m/s and an angular incidence of 30°.

STATUS
Production.
CONTRACTOR
China North Industries Corporation, PO Box 30X, 2137 Beijing, People's Republic of China.

FRANCE

1274.303
68 mm SNEB ROCKET

The 68 mm SNEB rocket has been developed as an air-to-ground and air-to-air weapon for subsonic and supersonic interceptor and ground attack aircraft.

The rocket is unguided and is stabilised in flight by eight folding fins. It is carried and fired from a conventional multi-tube launcher. The rocket motor gas is used to actuate the fin opening as the rocket leaves the launcher tube. In flight the fins are locked in the extended position. The types used for helicopter firing incorporate a special design of fin assembly which yields a smaller dispersion.

The 68 mm rockets can be fired from various types of rocket-launcher containing 6 to 36 rockets and suitable for any aircraft or helicopter attack.

The production range of rockets allows the following missions to be carried out:
(1) practice firing with rockets fitted with practice inert or practice smoke heads allowing the spotting of impacts
(2) intervention and combat fire missions in any circumstances such as air-to-air with rockets with HE warhead EAA; air-to-ground with rockets with HE anti-personnel warhead EAA: air-to-ground with rockets with hollow charge anti-personnel warhead ECC which can penetrate 40 cm thick armour plate.

All the active warheads are provided with a piezo-electric fuze, an initiator box with interruption of the explosive train, an accelerometer-actuated clockwork delay and a bore-riding pin for alignment of the explosive train.

These various rockets are fitted with the F.1 motor with all-weather propellant, but a more powerful F.2 motor is being developed.

Rockets fired from aircraft equipped with a modified fire control unit are normally launched at ranges of 4000 metres or more. The dispersion of the rockets depends on firing conditions and aircraft stability. The standard deviation in air-to-ground firing is normally close to two mils and has nearly the same value either in distance or laterally.

In addition to the various 68 mm aircraft rockets above, since 1983 the Brandt range has included rockets of this calibre that are equipped with sub-munition warheads. Two such warheads are produced: AMV for use against aircraft, vehicles and military material; and the ABL for attacking APCs and lightly armoured vehicles. Both are particularly appropriate for use against anti-aircraft batteries and SAMs.

Sub-munition warhead 68 mm rockets can be launched from Brandt Types 68-12, 68-22 and 68-36 helicopter launchers (**4542.303**), or Matra Types 150 and 155 aircraft launchers. Conventional 68 mm

68 mm AMV warhead with cutaway showing anti-armour darts and typical effect on steel plate

68 mm AMV aircraft rocket

CHARACTERISTICS

Type	Length mm	Weight kg	Warhead kg		Warhead type	Velocity **m/s	Role
250	911	5·05	1·8	FUM	Smoke	600	Practice
251P	847	4·3	1·05	EAA	Blast	800	Air-to-air
252	924	5·06	1·8	IN	Inert*	–	Air-to-ground practice
253	924	5·06	1·8	ECC	Hollow charge and fragmentation	600	Air-to-ground against armoured vehicles and personnel
256P	924	6·25	3	EAP	Fragmentation	450	Air-to-ground
259	1165	6·15		LEM	Chaff		Decoy, self defence
—	1165	6·4	3·15	ECL	—		Illuminating

*Inert warheads are available to simulate all types of operational warhead.
**Maximum velocity increment reached by rocket to be added to launching aircraft speed.

CHARACTERISTICS

Warhead type	AMV	ABL
Weight	6·2 kg	6·2 kg
Length	1165 mm	1165 mm
Warhead weight	3 kg	3 kg
Number of sub-projectiles	36	8
S/projectile length	132 mm	270 mm
S/projectile weight	37 g	190 g
S/projectile diameter	9 mm	13·5 mm
Ejection time	1·7 s	1·7 s
Ejection range	1000 m	1000 m
Target range	1500-2200 m	1500-2200 m
S/projectile velocity/range	400 m/s (1800 m)	500 m/s (1800 m)

SNEB aircraft rockets are suitable for use with a wide variety of helicopter and fixed-wing aircraft launchers and numerous examples will be found in this section of *Jane's Weapon Systems*.

STATUS
In production and widely employed with French and other air forces. The newer sub-munition warhead rockets have completed French qualification tests and are entering service.

CONTRACTOR
Brandt Armements, 52 avenue des Champs-Elysées, 75008 Paris, France.

4542.303
BRANDT HELICOPTER ROCKET LAUNCHERS

Several sizes of launcher have been developed for the use of 68 mm SNEB aircraft rockets from helicopters for ground attack roles. Similar construction methods are used for the three current sizes, which are capable of firing 12, 22 or 36 rockets. The tubes are grouped together to form a single unit which can be mounted on the helicopter by standard NATO 14-inch (356 mm) suspension lugs, or saddle suspensions. The principal features of the existing range are given in the following table.

Brandt Armements 12-round helicopter rocket launcher unit

CHARACTERISTICS

Type	68-12	68-22	68-36
Number of tubes	12	22	36
Length	120 cm	120 cm	140 cm
Width	31 cm	45 cm	70 cm
Height	26 cm	34 cm	37 cm
Weight empty	25 kg	43 kg	81 kg
Weight loaded	86-100 kg	155-181 kg	263-306 (F1 motor) kg
			335-378 (F2 motor) kg
Power supply			22-30 VDC

STATUS
Production.
CONTRACTOR
Brandt Armements, 52 avenue des Champs-Elysées, 75008 Paris, France.

5212.303

BRANDT 68 mm ROCKET LAUNCHERS

Brandt manufactures two under-wing rocket launchers for the 68 mm SNEB rocket (**1274.303**) and brief details of these are given below; both use standard 14-inch (356 mm) NATO suspension hooks. They are also suitable for use with chaff, IR and multiple-projectile type rockets of 68 mm calibre, and facilities exist for pilot setting from the cockpit while in flight. Two sizes of launcher are produced, with capacities of seven and 18 rockets respectively, as indicated in the table below.

CHARACTERISTICS

Type	68-7	68-18
Length	1·3 m	1·5 m
Diameter	240 mm	394 mm
Weight empty	31 kg	75 kg
Weight loaded	66-73 kg	166-188 kg
Launch speed	100-600 knots	

CONTRACTOR
Brandt Armements, 52 avenue des Champs-Elysées, 75008 Paris, France.

68 mm rocket launcher Type 68-18

3867.303

HELICOPTER GUN MOUNTING 19A001

The 19A001 mounting is designed for use in SA 330 Puma helicopters to carry a 20 mm automatic gun Type 621 which is located in the right-hand fuselage door of the helicopter, enabling the machine to be used for attacking ground troops, armed reconnaissance, and similar air support actions. The Type 621 automatic gun is equipped with the left-hand flat feed mechanism, and a muzzle brake with two vent ports. The gun is supported in a monobloc cradle with air suspension assemblies. The ammunition supply consists of four boxes of 240

rounds and the gun is fitted with an SFOM optical sight. Firing is under the pilot's overriding authority and an ADS CPL8 control box is provided which enables firing in a free mode, or in eight-shot limited bursts at a rate of 740 rounds/minute. There is compensation for aerodynamic forces acting on the gun by means of an adjustable device which is electrically and mechanically controlled. There is electro-mechanical locking of the fork after azimuth setting.

CHARACTERISTICS

Calibre: 20 mm
Elevation: +5 to –40°, relative to aircraft floor

Azimuth: ±45° from axis of aircraft R/H door port
Ammunition: 4 × 240 rounds
Weight of mounting with gun: 165 kg
Overall weight: 632 kg (with 960 rounds)
STATUS
Series production. Operational with the French Army.
CONTRACTOR
GIAT (Groupement Industriel des Armements Terrestres), 10 place Georges Clémenceau, 92211 Saint-Cloud, France.

1271.303

30 mm AIRCRAFT GUN DEFA 552A

The 30 mm DEFA gun is the French development of the German Mauser revolver gun principle and is similar to, and virtually interchangeable with the British ADEN Mk 4. Over 10 000 units have been manufactured and the gun has been proved in combat in a number of theatres. Since 1971 a long-life version has been developed, called Canon Automatique de 30 mm, 550-F2A (DEFA 552A) which replaces the gun type 552 and with which it is directly interchangeable.

The principal characteristics of the DEFA 552 and the DEFA 552A are light weight, a rate of fire of 1200 rounds per minute, and provision for automatic recocking in the event of a stoppage. The gun uses

30 mm ammunition developed for the DEFA/ADEN weapons which is available in the usual variety of types: armour piercing, HE incendiary, etc. Belted ammunition may be fed to either side of the gun. Spent cases are ejected from the same side of the weapon as accepts the feed. Links are ejected on the opposite side. The ammunition is electrically ignited.

The DEFA 552 revolver gun incorporates safety devices to ensure that firing is impossible unless the cartridge is in the firing position and the control slide, which carries the round firing contact, is in the forward position. In operation the whole gun recoils about 12 mm. On the ground a special device is used to cock the gun by hand. A single pyrotechnic cartridge is provided for automatic recocking during firing if a stoppage should occur.

CHARACTERISTICS

Calibre: 30 mm
Gun weight: 81 kg
Rate of fire: 1300 rounds/minute
Chrome barrel life: 5000 rounds
STATUS
The DEFA 552 and DEFA 552A cannon are in service with the French Air Force, the Israeli Air Force and others throughout the world. Two 552s are standard equipment on all Mirage III and Mirage Vs, and other aircraft types fitted include the Jaguar, Etendard IV M, Fiat G91 and Super-Etendard.
CONTRACTOR
Groupement Industriel des Armements Terrestres (GIAT), 10 place Georges Clémenceau, 92211 Saint-Cloud, France.

1273.303

30 mm AIRCRAFT GUN DEFA 553

The DEFA 553 30 mm aircraft cannon is a direct development of the DEFA 552. Its performance is similar to the 552 but design modifications have been made to improve service life and facilitate installation. A new barrel in nitro-chrome steel is used with a muzzle device to reduce muzzle pressure. Other changes have been made to simplify installation and the DEFA 553 weapon will now accept ammunition feed from either side without modification.

Other features, including in-flight recocking, correspond to the DEFA 552 model, and the same ammunition is used.

The electric control for the DEFA 553 provides the following facilities:

'OFF' – firing of the gun completely inhibited.

'Continuous fire' – not normally used in action.

'0·5 s' – maximum continuous burst length 0·5 s.

'1 s' – maximum continuous burst length 1 s.

In twin installations a unit is needed for each gun and an additional control and junction box providing:

Position 1 – both guns inhibited.

Position 2 – continuous fire, both guns.

Position 3 – both guns in burst lengths (which may be different) set into each individual control unit.

Position 4 – gun camera switched on.

CHARACTERISTICS

Calibre: 30 mm
Gun weight: 81 kg
Rate of fire: 1300 rounds/minute
Chrome barrel life: 5000 rounds
STATUS
The DEFA 553 cannon is in production and is fitted in Mirage F1, Jaguar, Alpha-Jet, Macchi 339K, Casa 101, and Puccara aircraft.
CONTRACTOR
Groupement Industriel des Armements Terrestres (GIAT), 10 place Georges Clémenceau, 92211 Saint-Cloud, France.

5246.303

30 mm AIRCRAFT GUN DEFA 554

The new DEFA 554 lightweight aircraft gun is a further development of the DEFA 553 (**1273.303**) gun and has been designed for installation on high performance aircraft. It has already been selected for the Mirage

2000 fighter and each of these will have two fuselage mounted guns. The gun, which can also be pod mounted, weighs only 85 kg and has two rates of fire, 1800 rounds a minute for use in the air-to-air role and 1100 rounds a minute for the air-to-ground role. Muzzle velocity is about 820 m/s.

CHARACTERISTICS

Calibre: 30 mm
Gun weight: 80 kg (approx)
Rate of fire: 1800 rounds/minute
STATUS
Development.

CONTRACTOR
Groupement Industriel des Armements Terrestres
(GIAT), 10 place Georges Clémenceau, 92211 Saint-
Cloud, France.

30 mm aircraft gun DEFA 554

1275.303
AIRCRAFT GUN 20 mm M.621

The M.621 20 mm cannon is a versatile weapon
developed in France by Manufacture Nationale
d'Armes de Tulle, the national armaments factory.
The weapon is particularly suitable for helicopter and
light aircraft mounting because of its light weight and
low recoil forces.

The M.621 utilises 20 mm ammunition which is
interchangeable with the US M56 series used in the
Vulcan cannon. It is electrically ignited and a full
range of types is available: armour piercing,
incendiary and fragmentation. Steel and brass
cartridge case versions are manufactured. On firing,
cases and links are ejected from the gun either
downward or to the side according to installation.

Provision is made for left- or right-hand belt feed,
and for special application, ammunition of different
types can be fed to each side of the gun and selected
at will by the gunner. The rate of fire is either 300 or
740 rounds per minute. Provisions can also be made
for firing single shots.

Initial cocking of the gun is by cable, but provision
is made for automatic recocking by pyrotechnic
cartridge. This is available once only and is
automatically triggered after a 0·3 s delay in firing.
While firing, the whole gun mechanism including the
barrel recoils, sliding on guide rails which are part of
the mount cradle.

A variety of mountings and accessories are
available to adapt the M.621 to different applications.
One such is a gun pod which is under development
and designed for installation on helicopters and light
aircraft for attacking enemy ground forces, lightly
armoured vehicles and helicopters. It contains 150
rounds of belted ammunition and has a rate of fire of
740 rounds per minute. Attachment is by standard
NATO 14-inch (356 mm) pylons, overall length is
2810 mm and weight with ammunition is 140 kg.
Other applications are a pintle mount for use in
helicopters with shields for the gunner, chutes for
spent cases and links, and a reflector sight mounted
above the breech mechanism. In applications where
minimum recoil force is essential a muzzle brake can
be fitted in place of the flash eliminator. By this
means, and using a shock absorbing mounting, the
average recoil force can be reduced from 400 to
250 kg.

CHARACTERISTICS
Calibre: 20 mm
Gun weight: 47 kg
Muzzle velocity: 980 – 1030 m/s
Rate of fire: 740 or 340 rounds/minute
Accuracy: 80% rounds inside 2 mils (hard gun mount)
Length: 2207 mm
Round weight: 0·32 kg
Projectile weight: 0·1 kg
Range*: Over 1500 m
Average recoil force: 400 kg
*Gun stationary
STATUS
In production, and using specific mountings it has
been fitted on Alouette III, Puma and Gazelle
helicopters. A pod containing the M.621 gun and 140
rounds is also available for light aircraft and
helicopters. The 20 mm M.621 is also used in ground
applications.
CONTRACTOR
Groupement Industriel des Armements Terrestres
(GIAT), 10 place Georges Clémenceau, 92211 Saint-
Cloud, France.

3865.303
BRANDT MODULE BOMB

The BRANDT module bomb is produced in the 400 kg
version. It is designed as a low altitude air-to-ground
saturation weapon for the destruction of targets such
as armoured vehicles, road or rail convoys,
ammunition dumps, radars, missile launchers and
similar high value equipments. This is achieved by
successively ejecting three modules from the bomb
body after its release, at preset times. Each module
consists of a pre-fragmented warhead. The tail
parachute, attached to each bomb module, slows it
and ensures that its final descent onto the target is
almost vertical.

On impact with the ground, each module ejects a
horizontal sheet of high velocity calibrated fragments.
Two fragment generators are available comprising
respectively about:
(1) 800 main fragments, able to perforate 17 mm of
    steel at 50 metres from the explosion point
    (12 mm at 100 metres)
(2) 1500 main fragments, able to perforate 12 mm at
    50 metres from the explosion point (7 mm at 100
    metres).

An area of 600 metres long by 100 metres wide (or
more depending on the perforation power and
fragment density needed) can be covered using only
two 400-kg modular bombs with suitable module
spacing. Launching can be effected either by
releasing the bomb(s) from an aircraft flying over the
target area, or by the "toss-bombing" method. The
range of the bomb varies from 500 metres to more
than 5 km. To increase this stand-off capability, a

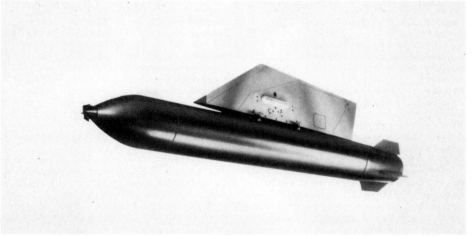

BM 400 modular bomb and pylon

rocket booster can be fixed at the rear part of the
bomb. Ranges of 10 km have been achieved in this
way.
CHARACTERISTICS
Length: 3·2 m
Diameter: 0·32 m
Weight: 390 kg
Weight of single module: 100 kg
Number of modules: 3 (a 250-kg modular bomb could
be produced with only 2 modules)

Attack altitude: 30 m
Launching speed: 350 – 600 knots
STATUS
Production. Qualification completed in 1982.
CONTRACTOR
Brandt Armements, 52 avenue des Champs-Elysées,
75008 Paris, France.

3864.303
BRANDT IMPACT FUZE/RETARDER PACKAGE

Brandt has designed an impact fuze/retarder package
for use with standard 125 kg fragmentation bombs to
enhance their tactical performance and versatility.
The 125 kg model derives from the fragmentation
bomb type 81A thick wall ammunition, designed to
scatter numerous fragments and manufactured by
Brandt for the French Air Force.

The complete package comprises two distinct
parts: the fuze which is inserted into the bomb, and
the retarder tail that is attached to the rear of the bomb
body.
FP 78 Fuze. This is a high sensitivity super-rapid
impact type, which can also be used with standard
250 kg bombs. It ensures that the bomb will explode
at optimum height by means of a rod which extends
from the nose of the weapon. Arming of the fuze is
achieved at a safe distance by means of a faired air-
driven motor and an acclerometer-based locking
device after removal of the mechanical safety
actuated by a pylon sensor.

CHARACTERISTICS
Length: 450 mm (350 mm clear of bomb body)
Weight: 2·6 kg
Safety arming delay: 7 s for 125 kg bomb at 500 knots

Retarder Unit. Specially designed by Brandt for the 125 kg bomb, the retarder tail unit appreciably improves the aerodynamic efficiency of the bomb. A near-vertical final trajectory is achieved by use of a parachute retarder, which is locked into the bomb body only after appropriate safety measures have been completed. The parachute opens after a preset delay, which is selected on the ground before take-off, according to mission requirements.

CHARACTERISTICS
Length: 770 mm (outside bomb body)
Span: 310 mm (packed); 640 mm (deployed)
Weight: 12 kg
Parachute delay: 13 – 17 s (preset on ground)

STATUS
The complete fuze/retarder package is in production.
CONTRACTOR
Brandt Armements, 52 avenue des Champs-Elysées, 75008 Paris, France.

4486.303
ALKAN GROUND ATTACK CARTRIDGE LAUNCHERS
Alkan ground attack cartridge launchers are designed as simple, low-cost ground attack weapons for use on various categories of aircraft, ranging from light machines such as the SIAI-Marchetti SF260 to higher performance types like the Super-Etendard and the Mirage. As an external pod, the launcher system is fitted on any pylon equipped with standard 14-inch (356 mm) spaced ejector hooks and it is also compatible with rocket launchers. In operation a ground attack is made at the aircraft's upper speed limit in horizontal flight and at very low altitude over the target to minimise exposure to defensive fire. A wide range of cartridges to suit roles such as illumination, anti-armour, anti-personnel, countermeasures etc are produced. The anti-tank grenades are hollow charge munitions which can be parachute-retarded to ensure that they drop onto the target nearly vertically. They have a penetration potential of 200 mm of armour. The anti-light vehicle cartridges have an effective range of about 15 metres.

Launchers also are produced in a variety of sizes and configurations: the 500 model with 20 74 mm cartridges weighs 74 kg fully loaded and is designed for light aircraft (eg SIAI-Marchetti SF260); the 530 model has a capacity of 40 cartridges of the same size, weighs 135 kg fully loaded and is already used with the Alpha-Jet, Mirage III, Super Etendard and F-5.
STATUS
In production and service.
CONTRACTOR
R Alkan et Cie, rue du 8 mai 1945, 94460 Valenton, France.

Model 430 ground attack cartridge launcher on an Alkan pylon of a Super Etendard (launcher open for loading)

1510.303
BRANDT 100 mm AIRCRAFT ROCKET
The 100 mm Brandt aircraft rocket has been designed as a larger calibre, longer range, and more lethal alternative to the well known 68 mm SNEB rocket (**1274.303**). The principles of the 68 mm design including the stabilising system and warhead have been followed in this later design. Brandt has designed and produces its own range of launchers (**3151.303**). The French Air Force is operating the four-tube (F3) launcher. Various versions of the 100 mm rocket have been developed, the only difference between them being the warhead type. All versions have similar ballistic properties.
CHARACTERISTICS
Length: 2525 mm (715 mm for w/head)
Weight: 38 – 42 kg
Velocity: 760 m/s gain over launch velocity
Typical firing range: 2000 – 3000 m
Standard deviation: 2 mrad
Warhead
EEG: General purpose, fragments lethal to 200 m
ECC: Hollow charge armour piercing – penetration 600 mm armour
DEM: Demolition, delayed action fuze, 3 m earth plus 0·3 m reinforced concrete penetration
LUM: Flare, about 2 million candelas for 1·5 minutes
IN: Inert

In addition, sub-projectile warheads are now available in three versions: AMV for use against material and soft-skinned vehicles; ABL for targets such as lightly armoured vehicles and APCs; and the AB24 which is intended for use against tanks and armoured targets. The AMV and ABL types are

Brandt 100mm aircraft rocket

CHARACTERISTICS

Type	AMV	ABL	AB24
Length	2·7 m	2·7 m	2·7 m
Warhead length	885 mm	885 mm	885 mm
Warhead weight	14 kg	14·5 kg	15·5 kg
Total weight	39 kg	39·5 kg	40·5 kg
Number of s-projectiles	192	36	6
Sub-projectile length	132 mm	270 mm	548 mm
Sub-projectile weight	35 g	190 g	1650 g
Sub-projectile calibre	9 mm	13·5 mm	24 mm

particularly suited for attacks on ground AA batteries and SAM installations.
STATUS
The EEG, ECC, DEM, AMV and ABL warhead types are in production. Development of the LUM and AB24 models continues.
CONTRACTOR
Brandt Armements, 52 avenue des Champs-Elysées, 75008 Paris, France.

Cutaway ABL 100 mm rocket warhead

3151.303
BRANDT 100 mm ROCKET LAUNCHERS
In addition to supplying 100 mm rockets to the producers of a variety of rocket pods and launchers the Brandt Armements organisation also manufactures its own launcher pods. The Type 100-4 (F3) is intended for use with any of the Brandt 100 mm diameter aircraft rockets described in **1510.303** and is available in both four- and six-tube versions. Both are suitable for mounting on all aircraft fitted with standard NATO 14-inch (356 mm) attachment points. The four-tube model has been selected by the French Air Force in which service it is known as the F3.

Brandt 100-6 rocket launcher

CHARACTERISTICS
Type 100-4 (F3)
Length: 290 cm
Width: 23 cm

Brandt 100 mm rocket launcher 100-4 (F3)

Height: 24 cm
Weight: 70 kg (empty); 240 kg (loaded)
Rate of fire: 400 rounds/minute
Number of tubes: 4

Type 100-6
Length: 300 cm
Width: 34 cm
Height: 34 cm
Weight: 115 kg (empty); 370 kg (loaded)
Rate of fire: 400 rounds/minute
Number of tubes: 6

STATUS
Production.
CONTRACTOR
Brandt Armements, 52 avenue des Champs-Elysées,
75008 Paris, France.

3863.303
BAT 120 RETARDED BOMB

The Brandt BAT 120 is a 120 mm calibre parachute retarded bomb for tactical applications (Bombe d'Appui Tactique) which is designed to engage various surface targets such as convoys of vehicles, parked aircraft and missile sites. With an incidence nearly vertical on impact with the ground, the BAT 120 bomb meets this requirement by scattering a horizontal sheet of calibrated fragments. Two different versions are available:

(1) AMV anti vehicle and equipment. This delivers more than 2600 main fragments regularly distributed and designed to perforate four millimetres of steel at a distance of 20 metres from detonation point

(2) ABL anti lightly armoured vehicle. This version ejects about 800 main fragments, each capable of penetrating eight millimetres of steel 20 metres from impact point.

In both cases, the explosion produces numerous secondary fragments which may be effective against many targets.

BAT 120 bombs are released in sticks, from the same Brandt adaptors as BAP 100 cratering bombs (**3152.303** below). For example, 72 BAT 120 bombs could be released using only four store stations on a single aircraft. An accurate intervalometer integrated in each adaptor ensures correct sequencing of bomb release.

CHARACTERISTICS
Bomb length: 1·5 m
Weight: 34 kg
(This equates to about 125 kg for a 3-bomb load, with

BAT 120 tactical retarded bombs loaded on BAe Hawk aircraft

adaptor; 330 kg for a 9-bomb load, with adaptor; 740 kg for an 18-bomb load, with adaptor.
Release speed: 350 – 600 knots; 150 – 350 knots light aircraft versions.
Nominal release height: 80 m

STATUS
Series production.
CONTRACTOR
Brandt Armements, 52 avenue des Champs-Elysées, 75008 Paris, France.

3152.303
BRANDT BAP 100 mm CRATERING BOMB

The Brandt BAP 100 cratering bomb is specially designed to neutralise airfield runways and taxiways. It can be used against other hard targets such as highroads, concrete buildings and shelters.

A stick of bombs is released to provide a very high hit probability despite low level altitude aiming difficulties. In order to achieve one cut, it has been calculated and demonstrated that 12 to 18 bombs are needed depending on the aircraft sighting system and the size of the target. After a parachute braking phase, a rocket assisted acceleration phase ensures concrete penetration. The bomb explodes under the concrete slab thanks to an optimised delay. A long delay fuze bomb is also available.

Up to 18 bombs can be carried on one attachment point by means of special Brandt adaptors fitting with all pylons and used also for BAT 120 bombs (**3863.303**). A quick hooking system allows the loading of 18 bombs in less than ten minutes without any special training.

CHARACTERISTICS
Length of bomb: 1·8 m
Weight: 32·5 kg
HE weight: 3·5 kg
Release speed: 350 – 600 knots
Nominal release height: 65 m
A similar version (37 kg), released at a nominal height of 80 metres against standard runways, is also available.

The main adaptors designed for the Brandt BAP 100/BAT 120 system are:

French Air Force Jaguar aircraft with 18 BAP 100 runway cratering bombs mounted on the under-fuselage attachment point

	Lug spacing	Maximum load	Total weight (kg)
14-3-M2	14 inches	9 bombs	320
14-10-3-M2	250 mm	9 bombs	320
30-6-M2	30 inches	18 bombs	710

Two special adaptors (14-4-M2) are also used to carry and release 16 bombs on Alkan PM3 pylons (2 × 323 kg) for Mirage III and V aircraft.
STATUS
In series production and operated by five countries.

CONTRACTOR
Brandt Armements, 52 avenue des Champs-Elysées, 75008 Paris, France.

F-5 releases BAP 100 bombs

4597.303
BRANDT 74 mm GROUND ATTACK CARTRIDGE

Brandt produces a 74 mm cartridge that can be fired from all 74 mm diameter launchers (eg. Alkan types 501, 530 and 5120 associated with a multistore carrier CEM 1 or AMD-BA). It is a saturation weapon which can equip aircraft to attack armoured and ancillary vehicles, using a shaped charge grenade which has a significant secondary fragmentation effect. A chaff type grenade for other purposes is under development.

CHARACTERISTICS
Calibre: 74 mm (cartridge); 70 mm (grenade)
Length: 214 mm (cartridge); 190 mm (grenade)
Weight: 2 kg (cartridge); 1·6 kg (grenade)
Release speed: 350 – 600 knots
Release height: 50 m
Main effect: >200 mm armour steel perforation
Secondary effect: lethal fragments up to more than 10 m
STATUS
Production.
CONTRACTOR
Brandt Armements, 52 avenue des Champs Elysées, 75008 Paris, France.

Brandt 74 mm anti-armour cartridge showing parachute deployed form

1600.393
ALKAN STORE EJECTORS

Alkan pyrotechnic ejector release units (ERUs) meet the requirements of most kinds of stores whether fitted with the NATO 14 inch and 30 inch lug suspension system, with 250 mm-spaced lugs, or with some other suspension system.

The locking/unlocking of the hooks is obtained through toggle device with no overcentre system; the mechanism operation is therefore totally safe and independent of the hook-applied loads. The ejector's structure is generally made up of two half-shells, the one which positions and retains the mechanism, the other which serves as the cover and can be easily removed for inspection and maintenance. All components of the pyrotechnic subassembly are designed with a view to facilitating their maintenance and removal. The pistons can be retractable and telescopic (2 or 3 stages). These new generation ERUs can perform up to 50 firings between two cleanings.

The type 165 and type 176/178 ERUs are designed conventionally, ie they are fitted with swaybraces and chocking screws. The 165 model has a very low height and is therefore particularly adapted for multiple store carriers and low pylons. The three-hook 176/178 models provide for both the 14 inch and the 250 mm lug suspension as well as the single lug store carriage.

The series of saddle system bomb racks includes a heavy duty unit, the type 1405, and an automatic unit, the type 1005. The chocking system, eliminating the crutch arms, ensures significant aerodynamic reduction and excellent boresight retention.

A new generation of ERUs, the hook lifting series, is designed to equip modern combat aircraft with an improved store suspension system; the aerodynamic drag is greatly reduced by eliminating the chocking screws and having very small fixed swaybraces. The store is lifted up through its hooks by an appropriate mechanism ensuring the chocking with the necessary preload balanced between the fore and the aft hook on ground and in-flight. The new series of hooks lifting ejectors is mainly composed of the 1216 (for Mirage 2000) and its derivatives the 1218, the 1259 (meeting the USAF/USN joint requirements) and the heavy duty 1459 model. A light aircraft release unit also uses the same concept.

ERU 1216

This very low height ejector release unit is used in the Alkan twin store carrier TSC 4035 and is being series produced to equip all the light duty pylons of Mirage 2000.
Ultimate load: 16 000 daN per hook; 12 000 daN per swaybrace
Weight: 10 kg
The derived model, type 1218, equips the TSC 4036, flight tested on the F-16 aircraft.

ERU 1259

This model complies with the US Air Force/US Navy

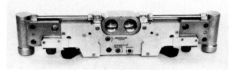

Alkan semi-automatic crutchless ERU Type 1005

Articulated swaybrace heavy duty ERU Type 1405 for Mirage 2000

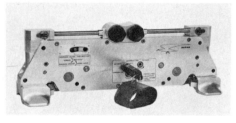

Hook lifting ejector of the 1200 Series

Alkan triple-hook ejector Type 176

specifications: automatic and independent hook-latching, practice bomb carrying capability, integrated safety handle, secondary release. Three integrated fuze arming units are mechanically connected to the unlatch mechanism. A store presence indicator is connected to the hook-lifting mechanism.
Ultimate load: 16 000 daN per hook; 15 000 daN per swaybrace
Weight: 9·57 kg
The 1259 ERU has been ground qualified and in-flight tested (carriage and firing) with the F-16 and F-16 XL (using a twin store carrier 4037).

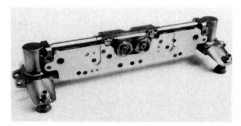

Low height light duty ERU Type 165

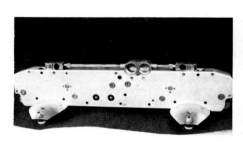

Alkan Type 105 ejector

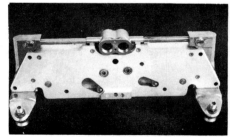

Alkan Type 115 ejector

ERU 1405

The 1405 ERU has been specially designed to equip the heavy duty centreline and inboard pylons of Mirage 2000, for which it is now manufactured in series.
Ultimate load: 18 000 daN per 14 inch hook; 32 000 daN per 30 inch hook; 15 000 daN per swaybrace
This ejector is fitted with semi-automatic, single point controlled articulated swaybraces.

ERU 1459

This semi-automatic 14/30 inch heavy duty ERU is designed to be installed in the place of the MAU 12 or 40. Store chocking is ensured by the centrally

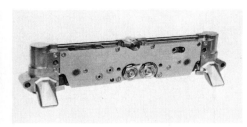

Alkan Type 1216 hook lifting ejector

controlled hook lifting system. The ERU 1459 has the same general features as the above-described 1259 model.

Ultimate load: 25 600 lb per 14 inch hook; 61 200 lb per 30 inch hook

ERU 1240
The ultra-light type 1240 ERU has been designed essentially for aircraft where pyrotechnic ejection is only required for emergency jettison. The store is chocked by two independent hook-lifting devices, a simple solution for lower load factors.

Weight: 4·99 kg

TYPE 6091 MAST
The Alkan type 6091 suspension mast has been designed to equip light planes and helicopters. It is mainly made up of an electromechanical release unit with an automatic hook latching mechanism and a lifting hook chocking system. For boresight harmonisation, the mast's support can be adjusted laterally (±1 degree). After harmonisation, the weapon's boresight position is constant and repeatable, even after store removal and re-installation.

Carriage capacity: 500 lbs under 8591 MIL STD load factors

Weight: 10 kg

STATUS
Series production is in progress of the ERUs 1216, 1405 and the Type 6091 mast; series pre-production has begun of the 1259; and prototypes have been constructed of 1240 and 1459 equipment.

CONTRACTOR
R Alkan et Cie, rue du 8 mai 1945, 94460 Valenton, France.

3866.393
ALKAN TWIN-STORE CARRIERS
A new generation of twin-store carriers has been developed by Alkan, based on their small lightweight, semi-automatic ejector release units (ERUs). Their main feature is the small frontal area resulting from the ERU's reduced volume which gives optimum drag characteristics and carrying capacity/weight and dimensions ratio. They are designed for the carriage of any NATO-standard bombs and more particularly the laser-guided bombs which require special structure arrangements for their nose and tail guidance surfaces.

TSC 4010
The type 4010 twin store carrier can carry two 500 lb bombs fitted with either 14 inch or 250 mm spaced lugs. Specially designed for the BAe Hawk aircraft, with which it has been successfully flight tested, it is in series production and can be adapted to various training and light ground attack aircraft types.

TSC 4035
Fitted with 1216 ERUs, this model has a carrying capacity of up to two 500 lb bombs and is suitable for the Hunter aircraft and similar types. Pre-production has started.

Alkan TSC 4010

Alkan TSC 4037 can carry up to 2 × Mk 81 bombs

TSC 4036/7
These meet the requirements of the MSER-2 programme. Respectively equipped with type 1218 and type 1259 ERUs, with a carrying capacity of two 1000 lb bombs, aircraft types for which they are suited include: the A-4 Skyhawk, the F-16 (on which flight tests have been carried out, see photo), the F-111, Jaguar, Mirage 2000 and others. Pre-production has started.

CONTRACTOR
R Alkan et Cie, rue du 8 mai 1945, 94460 Valenton, France.

1514.393
MATRA TYPE 200 BOMB RETARDING SYSTEM
The Matra Type 200 bomb retarding system was approved for use by the French Air Force in 1964. It can be used with SAMP-made 250 and 400 kg GP bombs (**5214.303**). The equipment consists of a cruciform nylon parachute packed into a container within the tail of the bomb, together with the appropriate fuzing equipment according to the mission being flown and the characteristics of the retarding system. In typical operations the bomb is released at an altitude of about 30 m (100 ft) at a forward speed of between 400 and 600 knots. The bomb will then hit its target, exploding on impact, at a time when the attacking aircraft is about 480 m (1500 ft) ahead of the explosion. This ensures complete safety for the attacker. Provision can be made before loading the weapon on to the aircraft to adjust the fuze operation for different release conditions.

Comprehensive safety provisions are made in the Matra 200 system. The parachute is locked to the bomb body only after release has taken place, so that should the parachute deploy while the weapon is still being carried by the aircraft it will pull away before dangerous turning moments are built up by the drag of the 'chute'. Similarly the parachute does not open until it is well clear of the aircraft. Provision is also

Release of Matra Type 200 retarded bombs by Mirage aircraft

Type 200 retarded bomb

made for the parachute to rotate with respect to the bomb while it is in flight eliminating the possibility of parachute twist.

Nose and tail fuzes are fitted with the retarding mechanism. These normally operate in the 'instantaneous' mode unless safety requirements are not met, ie when parachute functioning, release altitude, and release speed are all correct. If safety requirements are not met then there is a danger that the attacking aircraft will be damaged by the bomb explosion, and the fuze is automatically set to operate after a delay of 15 s. Provision is made within the fuze to prevent inadvertent instantaneous explosion in the case of a ricochet when conditions required for normal operation have not been met and the system is operating within 15 s delay.

STATUS
In production and in service with the French and other Air Forces. By March 1983, 30 000 had been ordered, 95 per cent for export. In 1975 Matra introduced a new weapon, Durandal (**1999.303**), for this role.

CONTRACTOR
Matra SA, BP No 1, 37 avenue Louis Breguet, Velizy-Villacoublay Cedex 78146, France.

4596.393
MATRA SFA BOMB RETARDING SYSTEM

The Matra 2000 bomb retarding system (1514.393) has been in use since 1965 with a variety of 250 and 400 kg 'conventional' bombs of French and other manufacture. In order to extend the release envelope of such weapons to fit smaller bombs and also to permit air burst detonations, Matra has developed a new system, SFA, which consists of a new retarding and arming system.

SFA is designed to fit on SAMP 125 or 250 kg general purpose or reinforced splinter effect bombs and allows bombing from heights half those of earlier systems and over a much wider speed range (in particular low speeds). The SFA system permits bombing from a distance by delaying the retarding function.

The system is delivered as a single rear-end unit to be connected onto the bomb frame as any conventional tail unit would be. There is a choice of operating mode; a proximity fuze for initiating detonation above ground level, or an impact fuze for detonation on contact. Performance characteristics are adequate for release heights ranging from 20 to 30 metres, and permit diving bombing approaches. It is also possible to employ 'toss-bombing' stand-off attack techniques using the ability to vary the

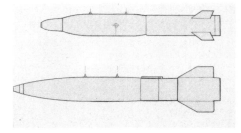

General arrangement drawing of Matra SFA retarding system fitting to SAMP 125 and 250 kg bombs

retardation delay from zero (ie at release) to 24 seconds.

Other adjustable parameters include: release speed, 350 – 650 knots; release height, down to 24 metres; and proximity or impact fuzing. Safety features ensure that detonation is inhibited if any of the following conditions are encountered: insufficient altitude, inadequate speed, parachute failure etc.

DEVELOPMENT
Development was undertaken by Matra as a private venture using company funding, and by early 1984 was virtually complete.

SFA 250 retarded bombs on Mirage 2000 aircraft

STATUS
The in-flight qualification and firing programme was due for completion in October 1983, and the first operational systems are expected to be ready in 1985.
CONTRACTOR
Matra SA, BP No 1, 37 avenue Louis Bregeut, Velizy-Villacoublay Cedex 78146, France.

1999.303
DURANDAL PENETRATION BOMB

The Matra Durandal penetration bomb, developed in co-operation with Thomson-Brandt and SAMP, has been designed particularly for the disablement of airfields by low-level bombing attacks in which the objective is to render the runways unusable for a long period. Naturally it can also be employed against other targets of a similar nature. The technique of Durandal consists of an initial rapid retardation of the bomb after release until it adopts the optimum non-ricochet angle, followed by prompt acceleration to a very high impact velocity to ensure penetration of the runway. It is stated that concrete slabs up to 40 cm thick can be penetrated in this way. The ensuing explosion of the warhead from beneath the runway surface results in extensive damage over a wide area because of the heave effect, according to the makers.

Durandal system qualification has already been carried out for the Mirage III, Mirage 5, Mirage 2000 and Jaguar aircraft and adaptation and qualification testing under other aircraft are continuing. The Mirage III or 5 can carry between six and ten

Durandal while the Jaguar can carry between six and eleven Durandal.
CHARACTERISTICS
Length: 270 cm
Max diameter: 22·3 cm
Max wingspan: 43 cm
Weight: 195 kg
Max carrying speed: Mach 1·8 at 10 000 m
Release conditions: Minimum launching altitude 60 m, launching speed 350 – 550 knots
Effectiveness: Destruction of 150 – 200 m² of concrete runway
STATUS
Series production began in summer 1975 and over 7000 units have so far been ordered for use by six countries. The first operational Durandals were delivered in 1978. Operational on Mirage III, 5, and Jaguar aircraft types. A USAF evaluation took place in the early 1980s.
CONTRACTOR
Matra SA, BP No 1, 37 avenue Louis Breguet, Velizy-Villacoublay Cedex 78146, France.

Multiple load of Matra Durandal penetration bombs carried by Mirage aircraft

3150.303
BELOUGA DISPENSER WEAPONS (BLG 66)

The Belouga is a ground attack dispersion weapon of the 'cluster-bomb' type which satisfies the requirement for a low-drag air-to-ground weapon producing a regular and homogenous pattern of grenades which reach the ground almost vertically for maximum effect. It is suitable for attacking stationary or mobile area targets and can be released from low-flying high-speed aircraft.

Three types of grenade have been developed for the following attack missions:
(1) general purpose (fragmentation) for vehicle convoys, equipment, and fuel stores, parked aircraft etc
(2) anti-tank (armour-piercing) for tanks, AFVs, APCs etc
(3) area interdiction for use against airfields, harbour areas, shunting yards, highway junctions, etc.

After release the Belouga bomb is braked to enable the aircraft to clear the area before the grenades are ejected. The grenades are dispensed at a regular rate and these are also braked. The weapon is supplied as a complete round, armed and ready for use, in a special packing, and a standard NATO 14-inch (356 mm) attachment is used. The pilot can select either of two pattern configurations prior to release.
CHARACTERISTICS
Overall length: 3300 mm
Diameter: 360 mm
Span: 580 mm
Number of grenades. 151
Grenade calibre: 66 mm
Grenade weight: 1·2 kg each

Belouga submunition dispensing weapons on Jaguar

Total weight: 290 kg
Release conditions: 60 m minimum height, 550 knots max speed
Area coverage: 40 – 60 m wide, 120 or 240 m long
STATUS
Mass production began in 1979, and in mid-1983 at least 3000 units had been ordered for French and other air forces.

CONTRACTOR
Matra SA, BP No 1, 37 avenue Louis Breguet, Velizy-Villacoublay Cedex 78146, France.
  Thomson-Brandt, 52 avenue des Champs-Elysées, 75008 Paris, France.

1511.393
MATRA UNGUIDED AIRCRAFT ROCKET LAUNCHERS

The Matra company in France have specialised in the design and manufacture of unguided aircraft rocket launchers. All calibres, including the British two-inch rocket, are catered for and Matra launchers are in widespread use. They have been adopted by NATO and are manufactured under licence in a number of countries.

Although the range of the launchers is wide they all embody similar design principles. The construction is in the form of a faired tube which, when charged with rockets, forms an aerodynamically smooth pod for external carriage under the wings or fuselage of fighter aircraft at high and low altitudes. Provision is made to insulate the rocket propulsion motors from thermal effects. Comprehensive safety provisions are built into the electrical rocket firing systems.

Recent developments include a series of expendable launchers which are used once only and then jettisoned. Further flexibility is provided by launchers combined with an external fuel tank.

Around the three calibres, 37 mm (less used today), 68 mm, and 100 mm and offering many variants for each of them, Matra produces a complete range:
(1) RL F2 6 (68 mm) training rockets
(2) RL F4 MA 18 (68 mm) rockets
(3) RL F1 36 (68 mm) rockets
(4) RL 100 mm 4 or 6 Th-Brandt 100 mm rockets
(5) RL HALMA 10/68 mm rockets

The new 100 mm rocket, tipped with a large warhead, permits effective firing at long range.
STATUS
Orders at mid-1983 amounted to 5000 for France and 60 per cent export.

Alpha Jet armed with two Matra Model F1 rocket launchers for 68 mm rockets

Firing 68 mm rockets from Type F4 Matra rocket launchers beneath Mirage F1 aircraft

CONTRACTOR
Matra SA, BP No 1, 37 avenue Louis Breguet, Velizy-Villacoublay Cedex 78146, France.

5213.303
SAMP PRACTICE BOMBS

All these bombs can be provided with a spotting charge of either the visual or acoustic type, and can be used with any type of bomb rack. The type 2 is used to simulate anti-personnel and anti-material bombs, type 6 is used to simulate retarded bombs and types 7 and 8 are used to simulate low altitude and dive bombing attacks.

CHARACTERISTICS

Type	Weight	Length	Diameter
2	2·2 kg	489 mm	98·5 mm
6	6·1 kg	489 mm	98·5 mm
7	5·3 kg	610 mm	98·5 mm
8	12·2 kg	610 mm	98·5 mm

CONTRACTOR
Société des Ateliers Mécaniques de Pont-sur-Sambre, 37 Grande Rue, 59138 Pont Sur Sambre, France.

5214.303
SAMP GENERAL-PURPOSE BOMBS

50 to 120 kg bombs. These are intended for use on light attack aircraft and are carried on underwing pylons, and in addition they can be carried on multiple ejector racks of fighter-bombers. They all have NATO suspension lugs and a standard two-inch well for the fuze.
250 to 500 kg bombs. These can be carried under any NATO bomb rack and can also be provided with a retarding device for low altitude bombing and an integrated arming control device.
1000 kg bomb. This can be carried by any aircraft with 30-inch (762 mm) suspension lugs and can also be provided with a retarding system or a guidance system, such as that developed by Matra.

Type 25 (250 kg) general-purpose bomb

CHARACTERISTICS

Nominal weight	Type	Weight	Explosive content	Length	Body diameter
50 kg	BL 5	50 kg	40%	1·32 m	176 mm
120 kg	BL 6	118 kg	45%	1·778 m	228 mm
120 kg	BL 7*	115 kg	50%	1·66 m	228 mm
250 kg	EU 2	250 kg	40%	2·253 m	273 mm
250 kg	25	247 kg	50%	2·121 m	324 mm
400 kg	T 200	345 kg	50%	2·195 m	403 mm
500 kg	EU 3	452 kg	45%	2·855 m	356 mm
1000 kg	BL 4	1000 kg	55%	3·5 m	457 mm

*Only for use with SF 260 aircraft.

CONTRACTOR
Société des Ateliers Mécaniques de Pont-sur-Sambre, 37 Grande Rue, 59138 Pont Sur Sambre, France.

5215.303
SAMP FRAGMENTATION BOMBS

These bombs have been designed for delivery against light vehicles, light structural framed buildings and un-sheltered personnel. All have a standard two-inch well for a nose fuze. The BL 9 can be used only with the Italian SM 260 aircraft and T 15 bombs are normally dropped in a cluster of four. The BL 18 125 kg fragmentation bomb can be provided with a French proximity fuze to give an airburst capability.

CHARACTERISTICS

Type	Weight	Explosive content	Length	Body diameter
T 15	15 kg	20%	752 mm	119 mm
BL 8	120 kg	17%	1584 mm	195 mm
BL 9	120 kg	17%	1380 mm	195 mm
BL 18	125 kg	20%	1805 mm	195 mm

CONTRACTOR
Société des Ateliers Mécaniques de Pont-sur-Sambre, 37 Grande Rue, 59138 Pont Sur Sambre, France.

GERMANY (FEDERAL REPUBLIC)

3805.303
HBS 202 HELICOPTER ARMAMENT SYSTEM

The helicopter armament system HBS 202 has been specifically designed for installation on the MBB helicopter BO 105. It is a rigid mounted system which is aimed by helicopter manoeuvring. It consists of a frame fixed underneath the fuselage between the skids, a cradle for gun installation, an electro-hydraulic cocking and triggering device and the control panel. The ammunition is stored in an in-board container with a flexible connecting chute to the gun. A reflex sight is employed.

The weapon itself is the Rheinmetall 20 mm automatic cannon Mk 20 Rh202 (**5600.103**) which is particularly suited to these purposes because of its low recoil forces and its high reliability under extreme service conditions.

CHARACTERISTICS
Weapon
Type: Mk 20 Rh202
Calibre: 20 mm × 139 NATO
Rate of fire: 1000 rounds/minute
Muzzle velocity: HEI-T, TP-T 1050 m/s; API-T 1100 m/s; APDS-T 1150 m/s
Recoil force: 550 – 750 kgf
Tactical range: 2000 m
Type of fire: Single fire; or controlled burst
Cocking: Electro-hydraulic
Triggering: Electro-hydraulic
Ammo storage capacity: 525 rounds
Sight: Reflex
Weight
Gun mount: 96 kg (without gun and ammo)
Mk 20 Rh202: 75 kg (approx)
525 linked cartridges: 175 kg
Combat weight: 346 kg
STATUS
Production.
CONTRACTOR
Rheinmetall GmbH, Ulmenstrasse 125, 4000 Dusseldorf 30, Federal Republic of Germany.

Helicopter armament system HBS 202 with Mk 20 Rh202 mounted below fuselage. Note flexible ammunition feed from inside aircraft

---

5186.303
27 mm MAUSER CANNON

Mauser in participation with Diehl and Dynamit Nobel (combat ammunition, propellant and primer cap) developed the Mauser 27 mm weapon system under contract with NAMMO (NATO MRCA Development and Production Management Organisation).

The main characteristics of this cannon are high muzzle velocity, high rate of fire from the first round, high degree of accuracy and reliability, favourable installation parameters such as low weight, small volume envelope, low reaction forces and for all types of ammunition identical exterior ballistics (permit mixed belts) and fuze response at extreme angle of impact (HE). The five types of ammunition are: AP, APHE, HE, TP and TP-F.

The MRCA Tornado aircraft is armed with two of these installed cannons and the German version of the Alpha-Jet with a single cannon in a pod. The new Swedish multi-role combat aircraft (JAS-39 Gripen) now under development will also be equipped with one internally installed cannon.

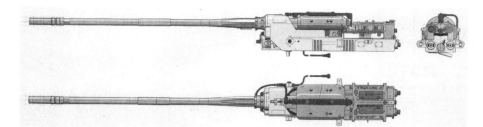

General arrangement drawings of the 27 mm Mauser cannon showing the main components of the weapon

CHARACTERISTICS
Calibre: 27 mm
Length with barrel: 2·3 m
Length of barrel: 1·7 m
Weight of gun (incl barrel): 100 kg
Power supply: 24 – 28 V DC

STATUS
In production.
CONTRACTOR
Mauser-Werke Oberndorf GmbH, Postfach 1349+1360, 7238 Oberndorf, Federal Republic of Germany.

INTERNATIONAL

4541.303
LU250 EG-FT BOMB

The LU250 EG-FT bomb is a general-purpose low-drag explosive bomb complying with American Mk 82 bomb specifications (MIL-B-82548). The bomb is designed to meet the requirements of the largest possible majority of bombing missions using both the blast and fragmentation effects along with the concussion effect produced in the ground and buildings.

The fuzes used for 'smooth' bombs with conical fins are generally mechanical. The bomb bodies are equipped to receive either mechanical or electrical fuzes. The first type is assembled using booster adaptors.

A BSU 49/B retarder is also fitted to use the LU250 EG-FT in low-altitude attacks. Two versions are offered:
(1) bomb body with conical fin
(2) bomb body with retarder.

The BSU 49/B inflatable retarder is a cruciform tail stabiliser that can be used in either the 'low-drag' configuration without inflating the retarder, or in the 'high-drag' configuration with the retarder deployed.

The inflatable retarder is used in low-altitude bombing with a high drag to allow the bombing aircraft to escape the blast and fragmentation effects of the bomb. This high drag is achieved by opening a balloon-parachute, called ballute, enclosed in the container fin.

When the bomb is dropped, the spring which holds the arming wire stretched, unwinds. When completely unwound, it frees two pin safeties and opens the cover. The ballute assembly is then freed under the effect of the external springs on the cover and of the internal ejection spring, and is immediately inflated by the external airflow, which comes in through four symmetrical inlets. The cover remains integral with the ballute, thus avoiding any risk of projection to the rear which might strike the bombing aircraft.

CHARACTERISTICS

Type LU250 EG-FT	(conical fin)	(with retarder)
Length	2·154 m	2·162 m
Diameter	273 mm	273 mm
Fin span	380 mm	385 mm
Weight	240 kg	254 kg

The retarder is a Goodyear Aerospace design which is also employed with US Mk 82 500 lb general-purpose bombs, and the American company also produces a larger version (BSU-50/B) for use with the 2000 lb Mk 84 bomb. Retarder characteristics are as follows.

CHARACTERISTICS

Retarder type	BSU-49/B	BSU-50/B
Diameter	222 mm	403 mm
Span	381 mm	940 mm
Length	660 mm	775 mm
Weight	25·4 kg	43·5 kg

STATUS

Production. In 1983 a licence arrangement covering marketing of the Luchaire-produced LU250 EG-FT bomb with BSU-49/B retarder and Borletti fuzes was revealed by an Italian consortium called Consor.

CONTRACTORS

Luchaire SA, 180 Boulevard Haussman, 75008 Paris, France.

Goodyear Aerospace Corporation, Defense Systems Division, 1210 Massillon Road, Akron, Ohio 44315, USA.

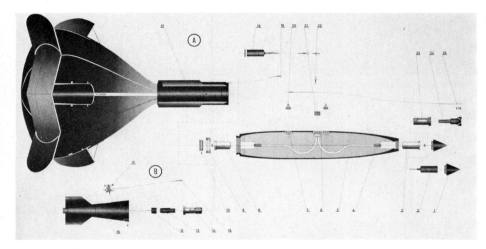

LU 250 EG-FT bomb with retarder or conical fin, electrical or mechanical fuzes

(A) LU250 EG-FT bomb with retarder (B) LU250 EG-FT bomb with conical fin (1) nose cap (2) nose electrical fuze (3) nose adaptor bushing (4) explosive charge (5) bomb body (6) NATO lug and arming wells for electrical fuzes (7) NATO suspension lug insert (8) tail adaptor bushing (9) rear blanking plate (10) sleeve coupling (11) wind vane (12) coupling regulator (13) fin mechanical fuze (14) priming relay (15) fin mechanical fuze arming wire (16) conical fin (17) retarder (18) electrical fuze (19) retarder opening control wire (20) NATO suspension lug (21) electrical circuit wells closure (22) fuze arming swivel hook (23) priming relay (24) nose mechanical fuze (25) nose mechanical fuze arming wire

ISRAEL

4428.303
TAL CLUSTER BOMBS

The TAL-1 cluster bomb is designed to achieve a high spin rate when dropped so that, when the fuze is activated after a preset time delay, sub-munition bomblets will be scattered evenly over a wide area in a circular pattern. The pattern size is governed by the point of fuze activation and can be a maximum of 53 000 m². 279 bomblets are carried, each with a weight of 500 grammes containing 160 grammes of high explosive and with a kill radius of eight metres.

TAL-1 is designed for external carriage by tactical ground support aircraft. It may be carried singly on a standard bomb rack pylon or in multiple mounting on tandem, TER, or MER type bomb rack. Safe carriage is ensured by a single arming wire which locks the time fuze and, after separation from the aircraft, a safety and arming mechanism allows a safe distance

between the cluster and the aircraft. Each bomblet also has its own arming wire which is withdrawn by aerodynamic forces produced by the free air-stream when the cluster is activated.

CHARACTERISTICS

Weight: 250 kg
Length: 2159 mm without fuze, 2345 mm with fuze
Diameter: 406 mm
Fin span: 560 mm
Suspension: 356 mm (14-inch) twin lug
Payload: 279 bomblets (500 g each)

A new model, TAL-2, was revealed publicly in 1983. This is believed to be very similar in design to the AL-1. Between 270 and 315 bomblets are released when the bomb splits open, and these are armed by aero-dynamic forces produced by the airstream and they explode on impact.

TAL-2 cluster bomb, after pre-set delay, splits open and its spin scatters between 270 and 315 bomblets

STATUS

First revealed in 1981 and believed to be operational. The TAL-2 model was revealed in 1983.

CONTRACTOR

Rafael, Ministry of Defence, PO Box 2082, Haifa, Israel.

ITALY

4074.303
AEREA TWIN GUN POD 7·62

The Aerea twin gun pod P/N 781 586 is designed to carry two 7·62 mm FN machine guns with a total ammunition supply of 1000 rounds (500 rounds per gun). The pod may be carried as an external store on any aircraft pylon equipped with two standard NATO 14-inch (356 mm) lugs. Each gun is supported by a damping cradle to minimise recoil effects, and can be easily collimated using a double-axis front support. Cartridge cases and coupling links are normally ejected through special ducts, but an improved pod with retained cases and links can be provided. The normal bomb jettison feature may be used to jettison the pod in an emergency.

Aerea twin gun pod on light trainer aircraft

CHARACTERISTICS
Length: 1750 mm
Height: 290 mm
Width: 395 mm
Weight: 55 kg (empty, with guns); 84 kg (loaded)
Rate of fire: 650 – 1000 rounds/minute

STATUS
Production.
CONTRACTOR
Aerea SpA, Via Sapri 42-44, 20156 Milan, Italy.

4071.303
AEREA ROCKET PODS

The current Aerea production programme includes an extensive range of rocket pods for use on fixed-wing tactical aircraft, helicopters and training aircraft. Built in glass reinforced fibre plastics or light metal alloy, according to their purpose or the rocket calibre, all the launchers are of the non-expendable type. The firing tubes are of light alloy and can be replaced if necessary. All pods have a frangible protective nose fairing which protects the rockets during flight but permits the rockets to leave the launcher when fired, whether fired singly or in ripple or salvo.

The launcher pods are attached to the aircraft by standard NATO 14-inch (356 mm) lugs. The main characteristics of the various models are listed in the paragraphs below, which follow a table of the principal types (the manufacturer's identifications conform to the following code):

Prefix letters	Purpose	No of tubes	Calibre (mm)
HL	Helicopter launcher	eg 7	eg 80
AL	Aircraft launcher	eg 18	eg 68
SAL	Supersonic aircraft launcher	eg 12	eg 80

Current Aerea rocket pods:
HL-14-50: Helicopter launcher, 14 tubes for 50 mm rockets
HL-18-50: Helicopter launcher, 18 tubes for 50 mm rockets
HL-28-50: Helicopter launcher, 28 tubes for 50 mm rockets
AL-18-50: Aircraft launcher, 18 tubes for 50 mm rockets
AL-25-50: Aircraft launcher, 25 tubes for 50 mm rockets
AL-8-68: Aircraft launcher, 8 tubes for 68 mm rockets
AL-18-68: Aircraft launcher, 18 tubes for 68 mm rockets
AL-6-70: Aircraft launcher, 6 tubes for 2·75 inch rockets
AL-18-70: Aircraft launcher, 18 tubes for 2·75 inch rockets
HL-7-70: Helicopter launcher, 7 tubes for 2·75 inch rockets
HL-12-70: Helicopter launcher, 12 tubes for 2·75 inch rockets
HL-19-70: Helicopter launcher, 19 tubes for 2·75 inch rockets
HL-7-80: Helicopter launcher, 7 tubes for 81 mm rockets
AL-6-80: Aircraft launcher, 6 tubes for 81 mm rockets
SAL-6-80: Supersonic aircraft launcher, 6 tubes for 81 mm rockets
SAL-12-80: Supersonic aircraft launcher, 12 tubes for 81 mm rockets
STATUS
Production.
CONTRACTOR
Aerea SpA, Via Sapri 42-44, 20156 Milan, Italy.

Ground firing tests of Aerea SAL-12-80 supersonic aircraft rocket launcher pod for 81 mm SNORA rockets

Aerea AL-18-50 aircraft rocket launcher pod

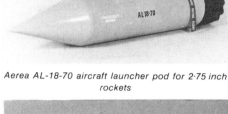
Aerea AL-18-70 aircraft launcher pod for 2·75 inch rockets

Aerea HL-28-50 helicopter rocket launcher pod

Aerea HL-7-70 helicopter rocket launcher pod for 2·75 inch rockets

Aerea AL-6-80 aircraft rocket launcher pod

CHARACTERISTICS

Type	Rockets	Weight	Rate of fire	Length	Diameter
HL-14-50	14 × 2 inch SNIA-BPD	15 kg (empty); 76 kg (loaded)	10/s	1123 mm	270 mm
HL-18-50	18 × 2 inch SNIA-BPD	27 kg (empty); 96 kg (loaded)	10/s	1400 mm	305 mm
HL-28-50	28 × 2 inch SNIA-BPD	40 kg (empty); 147 kg (loaded)	10/s	1400 mm	380 mm
AL-18-50	18 × 2 inch SNIA-BPD	30 kg (empty); 99 kg (loaded)	10/s	1740 mm	305 mm
AL-25-50	25 × 2 inch SNIA-BPD	47 kg (empty); 155 kg (loaded)	10/s	2000 mm	392 mm
AL-6-70	6 × 2·75 inch FFAR	30 kg (empty); 121 kg (loaded)	10/s	1900 mm	284 mm
AL-18-70	18 × 2·75 inch FFAR	62 kg (empty); 242 kg (loaded)	10/s	2100 mm	410 mm
HL-7-70	7 × 2·75 inch	23·9 kg (empty); 79 to 96·9 kg (loaded)		1550 mm	262 mm
HL-12-70	12 × 2·75 inch	33·6 kg (empty); 128 to 148 kg (loaded)		1550 mm	330 mm
HL-19-70	19 × 2·75 inch	51·2 kg (empty); 201 to 249 kg (loaded)		1550 mm	422 mm
HL-7-80	7 × 81 mm SNORA	33 kg (empty); 123 to 143 kg (loaded)	10/s	1800 mm	296 mm
AL-6-80	6 × 81 mm SNORA	38 kg (empty); 114 kg (loaded)	10/s	2214 mm	296 mm
SAL-6-80	6 × 81 mm SNORA	48 kg (empty); 124 to 163 kg (loaded)	10/s	2600 mm	296 mm
SAL-12-80	12 × 81 mm SNORA	66 kg (empty); 218 to 297 kg (loaded)	10/s	2600 mm	396 mm

4073.303
BRD-4-250 and BRD-4-450 BOMB AND ROCKET DISPENSERS

The BRD-4-250 bomb and rocket dispenser is used for training pilots, and this model can be loaded with four practice bombs mixed with 2 inch, 2·75 inch or 68 mm SNEB rockets. It is constructed of light alloy metal and its weight makes it suitable for use with light aircraft and helicopters as well as other tactical aircraft. A newer version, the BRD-4-450, can carry four practice bombs and four rockets of the same calibre as the BRD-4-250. Suspension is by means of standard NATO 14-inch (356 mm) lugs.

9BRD-4-250 bomb and rocket dispenser with typical load

CHARACTERISTICS
Length: 2400 mm
Width: 432 mm
Weight: 73 kg (empty)

Payload: 4 × Mk 76 practice bombs, and/or Mk 106 bombs, 2 × 2 or 2·75 inch rockets or 68 mm SNEB rockets

STATUS
Production.
CONTRACTOR
Aerea SpA, Via Sapri 42-44, 20156 Milan, Italy.

1696.393
TWO-INCH ARF/8M2 ROCKET

The two-inch ARF/8M2 air-to-ground rocket is a weapon system developed to provide efficient action from fixed-wing aircraft and helicopters against defence posts, scattered troops, surface transportation, and general hard targets.

The main characteristics of this system are: low weight, such that the total number of the rounds per aircraft is substantially increased; excellent accuracy, especially due to a patented free rotating folding fin assembly; several types of warhead, weighing 2·2 kg: HEI (high explosive incendiary), PFF (pre-formed fragmentation), AT-AP (anti-tank anti-personnel), SM (smoke), SP (spotting), illuminating, practice (smoke, flash and inert), which assure firing efficiency against varied ground targets, whether protected or otherwise, and the most convenient training of pilots.

Six different launchers are used at present: 14, 18 or 28 tubes for helicopter; 18 or 25 tubes for subsonic craft; 28 tubes expendable, for supersonic aircraft.
CHARACTERISTICS
Diameter: 51 mm
Length: 1048 mm
Weight: 4804 g
Combustion time: (−30 to +50°C) 1·1 s
Total impulse: (−30 to +50°C) 202 kg/s
Max pressure: 120 kg/cm²
Burn out velocity: 515 m/s

Weight of the loaded launchers
for helicopter:
  14 tubes: 83 kg
  18 tubes: 115 kg
  28 tubes: 176 kg
for subsonic aircraft:
  18 tubes: 118 kg
  25 tubes: 168 kg
for supersonic aircraft:
  28 tubes: 183 kg
STATUS
In production and in service with the Italian Air Force and other air forces.
CONTRACTOR
SNIA BPD, Settore Difesa e Spazio, Via Sicilia, 162-00187 Rome, Italy.

4429.303
DOOR GUNNER POST

The Door Gunner Post (DGP) is a device used to mount 12·7 mm (0·5 inch) machine guns in helicopters and capable of rapid fitting or removal in either single or double installations. DGP can fire at up to 70° downwards with the gunner always seated. A wide variety of helicopters including the very smallest can be fitted and the system includes a rotating support which incorporates a damping cradle to minimise recoil effects; a gas shock absorber to balance the gun for better aiming; a gunner's seat with inertia belts; and a base fitting sliding on rails with a locking device. An ammunition box is mounted on the gun with other boxes being located within easy reach of the gunner. A flexible chute is provided for case ejection and a net box collects the ammunition links.
CHARACTERISTICS
Gun: FN Browning 0·5 inch or equivalent
Ammunition: 100 rounds on mounting with stowage for 400 – 1000 rounds off mounting
Weight (with gun): 70 kg
STATUS
Production.
CONTRACTOR
Aerea SpA, Via Sapri 42-44, 20156 Milan, Italy.

Aerea Door Gunner Post installation for mounting in ground attack helicopters

3868.303
81 mm SNORA ROCKETS (ITALY)

The 81 mm SNORA is a modern and versatile rocket system suitable for different launching platforms, such as subsonic and supersonic aircraft, helicopters, tracked and wheeled vehicles and ships.

The SNORA is a high-performance solid-propellant rocket applicable to air-to-ground and ground-to-ground engagements. It is used with pods for supersonic and subsonic aircraft and is capable of engagements on area and point targets. It has high target effectiveness and carries warheads for every purpose, uses simple tube launchers, and is highly reliable.
CHARACTERISTICS
Calibre: 81 mm

Length: 1417 – 1783 mm (depending on warhead)
Launch weight: 13·2 – 19·7 kg (depending on warhead)
Range: 10 km (ground-to-ground)
Weight of motor: 8·7 kg
Mean thrust: 1342 kg (+18°C)
Action time: 0·7 s (+18°C)
Max speed: 520 – 820 m/s (ground launch)
Warheads: Practice (TP), 4·5 kg, 7 kg, 11 kg; high explosive (HE-PFF), 4·5 kg, 7 kg, 11 kg; hollow charge (HEAT), 4·5 kg
STATUS
In production.
CONTRACTOR
SNIA BPD, Settore Difesa e Spazio, Via Sicilia, 162-00187 Rome, Italy.

Typical airborne SNORA installation

SOUTH AFRICA

4540.303
SA AIRCRAFT BOMBS

Various types of free-fall bombs and special to purpose fuzes of indigenous design and manufacture, meeting NATO standards, are produced for use by aircraft of the South African forces. Current production includes the following:

Mk II Fragmentation Weapon System

Believed to be known also as 'Alpha' this is a 6 kg anti-personnel and anti soft-skinned vehicle aircraft bomblet. It was designed to produce a high-density uniform fragmentation pattern over a large ground area. It is normally used with Canberra aircraft, which release large numbers from sealed boxes containing 25 bomblets. Each bomblet is constructed of a thin-walled, approximately spherical, steel casing and a thick-walled inner steel casing containing an HE charge detonated by an SA222 inertial fuze having a 0·65 second delay. With most types of terrain except mud or water, good bounce characteristics ensure an air burst for maximum effects. Lethality decreases from 100 per cent within 1 metre radius of the detonation point to 30 per cent at a radius of 20 metres.

120 kg Aircraft Bomb

This is a conventional free-fall bomb consisting of a cast or forged body filled with RDX/TNT or TNT in the HE model, or filled with HE substitute in the practice model. The body can be fitted with a penetration nose cone and cup support, a charging tube (front and rear) for electronic fuzing, and an arming wire assembly for mechanical fuzing. The filling is either RDX/TNT 60/40 or TNT and the standard fuze is the SA771 mechanical nose fuze. The latter is a selective arming delay time point detonating or delay action fuze with back-up from the SA772 tail fuze. This tail fuze is impact firing and also arming delay time selective, with either non-delay or various delayed firing options in the millisecond range.

A tail assembly weighing 8 kg completes the bomb. The empty bomb case weighs approximately 60 kg, or 107 kg assembled and filled.

250 kg Aircraft Bomb

This is of similar construction and configuration to the 120 kg bomb, but has an empty weight of about 116 kg, 219 kg assembled and filled, with a tail assembly weighing 9 kg.

460 kg Aircraft Bomb

This bomb is made as either the HE version with a filling of Torpex 4B for the cast steel body, or HE substitute for the practice version. Other components are a penetration nose and cup support, front and rear charging tubes for electronic fuzing, and an arming wire assembly for mechanical fuzing. The same fuzing arrangements as for the 250 kg bomb are available for the heavier weapon. Weights are: empty bomb, approximately 225 kg; bomb body assembled and filled, approximately 438 kg; tail assembly 28 kg.

The 120, 250 and 460 kg bombs are all fitted with NATO 500 suspension lugs for carriage on aircraft.
STATUS
In production and believed available for export to approved customers.
CONTRACTOR
Armscor, 224 Visagie Street, Pretoria, Republic of South Africa.

SPAIN

1839.303
CASA TYPE 06.070 ROCKET LAUNCHER

This re-usable rocket launcher is designed to carry and launch six FFAR 2·75 inch 178 mm rockets, or six INTA S-11 rockets. It can be installed in any pylon type with standard NATO 14-inch (356 mm) suspension system. Basic and low-drag versions are produced.
OPERATION
Rocket firing is by means of an electronic intervalometer incorporated in the rocket launcher. Single rocket firing or ripple firing is selected by the pilot in the cockpit or by adjusting the mode selector incorporated in the launcher. Rate of fire is according to a firing interval of 30 ms (the intervalometer can be adjusted for a different firing rate upon request).

CHARACTERISTICS
Basic model
Length: 1·24 m
Diameter: 25 cm
Weight (empty): 14·8 kg
Weight (loaded): 63·6 kg
Low drag model
Length: 1·9 m
Diameter: 25 cm
Weight (empty): 17·8 kg
Weight (loaded): 66·6 kg
CONTRACTOR
Construcciones Aeronauticas SA, Rey Francisco 4, Madrid-8, Spain.

CASA 06.070 launcher

1840.303
CASA TYPE 18.037 ROCKET LAUNCHER

This re-usable rocket launcher is designed to carry and launch 18 INTA S9 37 mm rockets. It can be installed in any pylon type provided with the standard NATO 14-inch (356 mm) suspension system. Basic and low-drag models are produced.
OPERATION
Rocket firing is by means of an electronic intervalometer incorporated in the rocket launcher. Single rocket firing or ripple firing is selected by the pilot in the cockpit or can be adjusted by the mode selector incorporated in the launcher. Rate of fire is according to a firing interval of 30 ms (the intervalometer can be adjusted for a different firing rate upon request)

CHARACTERISTICS
Basic model
Length: 1·24 m
Diameter: 25 cm
Weight (empty): 15·7 kg
Weight (loaded): 35 kg
Low drag model
Length: 1·9 m
Diameter: 25 cm
Weight (empty): 19·3 kg
Weight (loaded): 38·6 kg
CONTRACTOR
Construcciones Aeronauticas SA, Rey Francisco 4, Madrid-8, Spain.

CASA 18.037 rocket launcher

1841.303
CASA TYPE 18.070 ROCKET LAUNCHER

This re-usable rocket launcher is designed to carry and launch 18 FFAR 2·75 inch (70 mm) rockets, or 18 INTA S-11 rockets. It can be installed in any pylon type provided with the standard NATO 14-inch (356 mm) suspension system. Basic and low drag versions are produced.
OPERATION
Rocket firing is by means of an electronic intervalometer incorporated in the rocket launcher. Single rocket firing or ripple firing can be selected by the pilot in the cockpit or by adjusting the mode selector incorporated in the launcher. Rate of fire is according to a firing interval of 30 ms (the intervalometer can be adjusted for a different firing rate upon request).

CHARACTERISTICS
Basic model
Length: 1·24 m
Diameter: 40 cm
Weight (empty): 37·3 kg
Weight (loaded): 183·8 kg
Low drag model
Length: 2·27 m
Diameter: 40 cm
Weight (empty): 46·8 kg
Weight (loaded): 193·3 kg
CONTRACTOR
Construcciones Aeronauticas SA, Rey Francisco 4, Madrid-8, Spain.

CASA 18.070 launcher

1842.303
CASA TYPE 54.037 ROCKET LAUNCHER
This re-usable rocket launcher is designed to carry and launch 54 INTA S9 37 mm rockets. It can be installed in any pylon type with standard NATO 14-inch (356 mm) suspension system. Basic and low-drag versions are produced.

OPERATION

Rocket firing is by means of an electronic intervalometer incorporated in the rocket launcher. Single rocket firing or ripple firing can be selected either by the pilot in the cockpit or by adjusting the mode selector incorporated in the launcher. Rate of fire is according to a firing interval of 20 ms (the intervalometer can be adjusted for a different firing rate upon request).

CHARACTERISTICS
Basic model
Length: 1·24 m
Diameter: 40 cm
Weight (empty): 39·5 kg
Weight (loaded): 97·5 kg
Low drag model
Length: 2·27 m
Diameter: 40 cm
Weight (empty): 49 kg
Weight (loaded): 107 kg
CONTRACTOR
Construcciones Aeronauticas SA, Rey Francisco 4, Madrid-8, Spain.

CASA 54.037 launcher

1843.303
LANCO RC-06-100
This re-usable unit is designed to carry and fire six heavy 100 mm INTA S12 rockets. It can be fitted to any aircraft with 14- and 30-inch (356 and 762 mm) NATO attachments. The conversion from 14 to 30 inches is carried out by changing the position of the rear attachment.

OPERATION

Rocket firing is controlled by an electronic intervalometer incorporated in the launcher. Single rocket firing or continuous ripple firing can be selected by the pilot or set in on the ground if this unit is not available. The firing sequence can be controlled between 20 and 70 ms by adjusting the intervalometer without removing it from the rocket launcher.

CHARACTERISTICS
Length: 3·4 m approx
Weight (empty): 100 kg
Weight (loaded): 460 kg
CONTRACTOR
Construcciones Aeronauticas SA, Rey Francisco 4, Madrid-8, Spain.

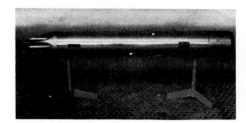

LANCO RC-06-100

1601.393
CASA 04.080 ROCKET RACK LAUNCHER
The CASA 04.080 rack launcher carries four 80 mm Oerlikon rockets and is designed for light aircraft and helicopters. It may be pylon mounted, either using the AH 039220 pylon or others with NATO attachments. The firing rate is controlled electrically and can be adjusted from 20 to 50 ms. The launcher is also available in the CASA 04057/080 version to carry and fire either four 57 mm (2·25 inch) rockets or four 80 mm Oerlikon rockets.

CONTRACTOR
Construcciones Aeronauticas SA, Rey Francisco 4, Madrid-8, Spain.

CASA 04.080 rocket rack launcher

1603.393
CASA AH 039220 UNIVERSAL PYLON
The universal pylon produced by CASA can be used to attach honeycomb or rack launchers, or machine-gun or bomb pods. The body has a main section attached to the aircraft by four screws, and a forward fairing mounted by one screw. The forward fairing contains accessible electrical ejector and firing circuits. A detachable yoke at the trailing end provides for long weapons which might otherwise meet the trailing edge of the aircraft wing. Ejector hooks are located at the standard NATO distance of 14 inches (356 mm).

CONTRACTOR
Construcciones Aeronauticas SA, Rey Francisco 4, Madrid-8, Spain.

5207.303
BRFA BOMB
The BRFA bomb has been designed specifically for attacking aircraft runways and can be carried by high performance aircraft such as the F-4 Phantom. Once released from the aircraft a parachute is deployed which retards the bomb and ensures that it is in the vertical position. A rocket motor is then ignited and propels the bomb to the target. The bomb penetrates the runway to a depth of some 600 mm before it explodes. Area of damage is quoted as 180 m.

CHARACTERISTICS
Length: 3·2 m
Diameter of bomb: 300 mm
Diameter over fins: 600 mm
Weight of bomb: 330 kg
Weight of explosive: 75 kg
CONTRACTOR
Explosivos Alaveses SA, Apartado 198 Vitoria, Spain.

5245.303
EXPAL BRP RETARDED BOMBS
The BRP range of low drag parachute retarded bombs have been designed specifically for fast low-level bombing by aircraft such as the F-4 Phantom. When the bomb is released, the arming wires activate the parachute system, braking the bomb while the aircraft pulls away. The bombs have safety devices which prevent explosion of the bomb in the event of any failure in any of its components, or if launching altitude does not guarantee a minimum safety distance. All EXPAL general-purpose low drag bombs (**5244.303**) can be transformed into BRP retarded bomb configuration by replacing the standard tail unit by the BRP tail and fitting a KAPPA nose fuze.

STATUS
In production. In service with the Spanish Air Force.
CONTRACTOR
Explosivos Alaveses SA, Apartado 198 Vitoria, Spain.

CHARACTERISTICS

Type of bomb (kg)	500	375	250	50
Diameter of body (mm)	360	330	290	180
Length (m)	3	2·855	2·285	1·425
Diameter over fins (mm)	510	470	404	250
Distance between lugs (mm)	355·6	355·6	355·6	355·6
Weight of explosive (kg)	206	170	112	20

5244.303
EXPAL GENERAL-PURPOSE LOW DRAG BOMBS
The EXPAL range of general-purpose low drag bombs have been designed to be carried by high performance aircraft such as the F-4 Phantom used by the Spanish Air Force. The bombs can be delivered with either a nose or tail fuze of either the instantaneous or delayed action type. The bombs can be fitted with a variety of lugs including a single central lug or two lugs. The tail of the bomb is detachable and can be replaced by a braking kit as fitted to the EXPAL BRP retarded bomb (**5245.303**).

CHARACTERISTICS

Type of bomb (kg)	1000	500	375	250	125	50
Diameter of bomb (mm)	460	360	330	290	240	180
Length (m)	3·82	2·94	2·805	2·15	1·82	1·395
Diameter over fins (mm)	538	500	500	440	360	275
Distance between lugs (mm)	762	355·6	355·6	355·6	355·6	355·6
Weight of explosive (kg)	475	210	170	115	55	20

STATUS
In production. In service with the Spanish Air Force.
CONTRACTOR
Explosivos Alaveses SA, Apartado 198 Vitoria, Spain.

SWEDEN

5224.303
SWEDISH AIRCRAFT ARMAMENT
Listed below is a resumé of Swedish aircraft armament.
Bombs
75 kg M62 Flash
80 kg M60 LYSB (HE-fragmentation)
100 kg (Flash)
120 kg M51 SB (HE)
120 kg M63 FFV Virgo (para-fragmentation) **(7514.393)**

250 kg M50 SB (HE)
500 kg M56 MB (HE)
600 kg M50 MB (HE)
Cannon
20 mm – four 20 mm in Saab-32 Lansen
30 mm – two 30 mm in Saab-35 Draken
30 mm – one Swiss 30 mm KCA cannon **(1269.303)** mounted in pod under Saab-JA-37
Rockets
75 mm M57AC anti-tank (single or in pods of 19 rockets)

75 mm M57B fragmentation (single or in pods of 19 rockets)
75 mm M57 7 kg (single or in pods of 19 rockets)
135 mm M56 42 kg HE (single or in pods of 6 rockets)
135 mm M56B fragmentation (single or in pods of 6 rockets)
135 mm M60 42 kg HE (single or in pods of 6 rockets)
135 mm M70AP fragmentation (single or in pods of 6 rockets) **(1513.303)**
145 mm M49 PSRAK anti-tank (single)
150 mm and 180 mm (no details available)

5216.303
FFV UNI-POD 0127
The FFV Uni-Pod 0127 has been designed for installation on jet trainers, light aircraft and helicopters. The pod is fitted with a single 0·5 inch (12·7 mm) Browning AN-M3 machine gun which has a rate of fire of up to 1250 rounds per minute. A total of 220 rounds of belted ammunition are carried and the spent cartridge cases and links are ejected or, as an option, may be collected in the pod. The machine gun can fire a variety of ammunition including ball, AP, API, APIT, and the API (HC); the latter will penetrate 13 to 19 mm armour plates at a range of 800 m at impact angles between 40 and 90°. A special damper on the upper part of the pod attenuates the recoil

forces and the strain on the suspension lugs is less than 2000 N (204 kg).
The latest version of the pod is equipped with a remotely controlled gun charger which makes it possible to charge the gun, recharge it after a jam, make it safe, and count the rounds fired while airborne.
CHARACTERISTICS
Length: 1916 mm
Diameter: 360 mm
Suspension: 14-inch (356 mm) MIL-A-8591E
Weight loaded: 118 kg
Weight empty: 90 kg
Power supply: 28 V DC

FFV Uni-Pod 0127

STATUS
Certified for various aircraft and helicopters.
CONTRACTOR
FFV Maintenance Division, 581 82 Linköping, Sweden.

4430.303
FFV 30 mm ADEN GUN POD
The FFV 30 mm Aden gun pod has been designed for installation on jet aircraft for air-to-air and air-to-ground use. It is of the so called self-contained type and houses the 30 mm Aden gun, a magazine with 150 rounds and an option for 200 rounds, an electrical power unit, and a relay box. The gun is cocked pneumatically on the ground and a safety device prevents firing until the aircraft is airborne. The suspension system may be either 30- or 14-inch (762 or 356 mm) NATO standard lugs, MIL-A8591E, or Douglas T-shape lugs.

CHARACTERISTICS
Length: 3850 mm
Diameter: 500 mm
Weight loaded: 364 kg
Weight empty: 290 kg
Power supply: 28 V DC and 400 V AC, 400 Hz, 0·5 A 3-phase
STATUS
Produced in large numbers to arm the Saab-Scania AJ 37 Viggen and 105 aircraft.
CONTRACTOR
FFV Maintenance Division, 581 82 Linköping, Sweden.

FFV 30 mm Aden gun pod on AJ 37 Viggen

7514.393
VIRGO 120 kg FRAGMENTATION BOMB M/71
The M/71 120 kg fragmentation bomb has been developed for use against diverse targets such as landing craft, aircraft on the ground, anti-aircraft weapons, field artillery, light armoured, and unarmoured vehicles etc. Designed to disperse a large number of fragments of a predetermined size and weight at high striking velocity, the bomb is designed for one-point suspension in ejector release units.
To meet the demands of tactical requirements of being used at low altitudes the bomb is equipped with a built-in brake parachute which retards the bomb sufficiently to give the aircraft enough lead distance to be safe at the moment of burst. The bomb can be dropped from higher tactical altitudes with or without the brake parachute. As the bomb is designed for supersonic speeds it is equipped with protection against aerodynamic heating. A proximity fuze is fitted in the nose of the bomb, and this is based on the capacitance principle. The fuze system causes the bomb to detonate a few metres above the target or the ground vegetation.
The bomb body consists of three main external parts which are retained together by the central tube. The central unit features the lug and contains the electrical connector. The lug contains a sliding

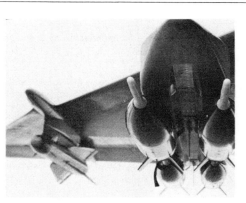

Virgo retarded bombs beneath Swedish Viggen attack aircraft. Note also Swedish-built Falcon air-to-air missile

plunger which comprises a safety device blocking the arming of the proximity fuze. Another safety device to which the brake parachute is attached is installed in the rear part of the central tube. The front part of the tube houses the main components of the proximity fuze.
The bomb tail, which is permanently attached to the bomb, is made of glass-fibre-reinforced plastic. It

houses the brake parachute with its electronic release device.
CHARACTERISTICS
Bomb: M/71
Length with fuze and parachute fitted: 1895 mm
Diameter of body: 214 mm max
Fin span: 368 mm
Total weight of bomb (ready to drop): 121 kg max
Charge: RDX/TNT
Weight of charge: 30 kg
Position of lug from the front of the fuze: 1098 mm
Centre of gravity from the front of the fuze: 1094 mm
Proximity fuze
Length overall: 945 mm
Diameter: 64 mm max
Weight: 1·7 kg
Brake parachute
Length of container: 290 mm
Diameter of container: 89 mm
Weight of container: 1·2 kg
Diameter of open parachute: 530 mm
Release delay: 0·7 s
STATUS
Designed for A32 Lansen and adaptable for A35 Draken and AJ 37 Viggen attack aircraft. The Royal Swedish Air Force is the only known user.
CONTRACTOR
FFV Ordnance, 631 87 Eskilstuna, Sweden.

1513.303
135 mm BOFORS AIR-TO-GROUND ROCKET SYSTEM M70
The 135 mm air-to-ground rocket system manufactured by AB Bofors is intended as part of a range of armament developed for the Saab AJ 37 Viggen. It consists of a launcher carrying six rockets

and a pulse distributor of electronic type, which can be set for single or ripple firing. The launcher has a low-drag design. The rockets are protected against thermal heating during high and low altitude flight at supersonic speeds. Standard NATO-type suspension lugs can be provided so that the system is compatible with a wide range of tactical aircraft.

The rockets can be provided with either a general-purpose or an armour-piercing fragmentation warhead. A practice head is also available. Two fuzes can be used: a direct-action fuze with post-impact delay, or a highly sensitive direct-action fuze.
The rocket motors give high velocity and low dispersion, which gives a time of flight of

approximately 3·5 s to 2000 m slant range in typical launching conditions.

CHARACTERISTICS

Total weight with six rockets: 400 kg
Weight (empty): 125 kg
Length: 3226 mm
Diameter: 486 mm
Pulse distributor for single or ripple firing
Firing interval in ripple firing: 0·1 s
135 mm rocket
Weight of rocket motor: 25 kg
Burning time: 2 s
Velocity at burn-out: 600 m/s
Weight
GP warhead with fuze: 21 kg
AP fragmentation warhead with fuze: 20 kg
GP warhead charge: 3·7 kg
AP fragmentation warhead charge: 5 kg
Practice head: 21 kg

STATUS

In service with the Swedish Air Force on the Viggen aircraft. Successful installations have also been made on the F-4 Phantom, A-7 Corsair, A-4 Skyhawk and Hunter.

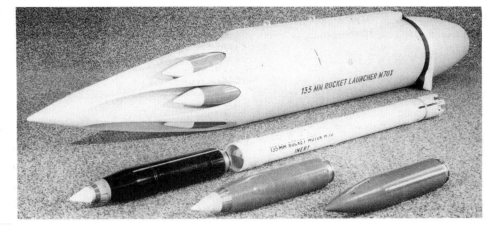

Bofors 135 mm rocket system M70X showing launcher and rockets

CONTRACTOR

AB Bofors, Box 500, 691 80 Bofors, Sweden.

SWITZERLAND

4134.303

OERLIKON 81 mm AIRCRAFT ROCKET

The Oerlikon 81 mm SURA-D aircraft rocket is an upgraded version of the SURA-FL. This unguided solid fuel rocket with sliding fins is intended for air-to-ground use by fighter aircraft, and has proved effective when fired from helicopters and light reconnaissance aircraft. It can be used to engage point or area targets.

The fin assembly is a sliding fit on the rocket body and has a dual function; before firing the assembly acts as the front suspension, engaging with the front suspension lugs on the aircraft underwing rail. Lower rockets in the same cluster can also be engaged by means of the fin slots and by an additional integral suspension ring located forward of the main fin ring. The rockets are fired electrically, and on firing the sliding fin ring acts as a guide until it is met by the rear cone of the motor. It is then carried on with the rocket, stabilising it in flight.

Based on a standard propulsion element, the TWK 007, a variety of rocket types is produced by the use of differing fuze arrangements and warheads. These are summarised in tabular form.

Calibre: 81 mm
Length: 1077 – 1212 mm (depending on type of shell)
Initial mass: 12·7 – 14·2 kg (depending on type of shell)
Max velocity at +18° C: Approx 530 – 595 m/s
Ignition voltage: 24 – 28 V
Propulsion unit mass: 8·4 kg
Mean thrust at +18° C: 7300 N
Burning time: 0·9 s

Rocket launchers for fighter aircraft with standard suspension

Type RAK 052 rocket launchers with NATO 14 inch 1000 lb class suspension for helicopters

SURA-D CONFIGURATIONS

SURA-D-rocket with:	**Rocket type**	**Shell type**	**Propulsion unit**
Practice shell	3 kg RAK 051	USE-3	
	4·5 kg RAK 048	UGK 033	
Marker shell	4·5 kg RAK 049	USK 035	
Fragmentation explosive shell	3 kg RAK 053	US-3	TWK 007
	4·5 kg RAK 050	SSK 031	
Incendiary blast shell	3 kg RAK 052	UIS-3	
Hollow charge warhead	3 kg RAK 047	PI-3	

STATUS

In production. SURA rockets are in service with numerous air forces. Installations have been made on many aircraft and helicopter types.

CONTRACTOR

Machine Tool Works Oerlikon-Bührle Ltd, 8050 Zurich, Switzerland.

1995.303

OERLIKON SNORA 81 mm ROCKET

The Oerlikon 81 mm SNORA rocket is an unguided solid fuel rocket with folding fins. It has a pure internal burning propulsive element. This rocket can be fired from multi-tube launchers both in subsonic air-to-ground engagements and ground-to-ground roles. Pods are used for supersonic air-to-ground missions. The design has been carried out with the needs of fighter aircraft, helicopter, tracked and wheeled vehicle installation in mind. The SNORA rocket is provided with the necessary safety devices for storage, transportation, handling, and firing. Correct functioning is ensured over a temperature range of –45 to +65°C. Based on a standard propulsion element, the TWK 006, a variety of types of rocket are produced by the use of differing fuze arrangements and warheads. These are summarised in the following paragraphs.

CHARACTERISTICS

Propulsion element type TWK 006
Weight: 8·7 kg
Mean thrust at +18° C: 11 000 N
Total impulse at +18° C: 910 kg/s
Action time at +18° C: 0·85 s
Length: 1033 mm

Rocket type RAK 022
Length: 1548 mm
Weight: 15·7 kg
V max from ground at +18° C: Approx 670 m/s
Range ground-to-ground at +18° C: Approx 10 km
Flight time over 10 km at +18° C: 50 s
Shell type UGK 028: Practice
Weight: 7 kg

Rocket type RAK 023
Length: 1416 mm
Weight: 13·2 kg
V max from ground at +18° C: Approx 820 m/s
Range ground-to-ground at +18° C: Approx 10 km
Flight time over 10 km at +18° C: Approx 50 s
Shell type SSK 031: Fragmentation explosive
Weight: Trotyl explosive: 1 kg
**   Shell ready to fire:** 4·5 kg
Number of spherical fragments: 702
Fragment weight: 2 g
Nose fuze type RKX332: Mechanical impact
Length of fuze: 46 mm
Muzzle safety: Minimum 30 m
Armed after: Max 100 m
Weight: Explosive: 9·5 g
**   Fuze ready to fire:** 320 g

Response angle: 15°
Response sensitivity on 2 mm aluminium: 100 m
Detonator safety
Rain safety

Rocket type RAK 024
Length: 1548 mm
V max from ground at +18° C: Approx 670 m/s
Range ground to ground at +18° C: Approx 10 km
Flight time over 12 km at +18°: Approx 50 s
Shell type SSK 029: Fragmentation explosive
Weight: Trotyl explosive: 1·7 kg
**   Shell ready to fire:** 7 kg
Number of spherical fragments: 1215
Fragment weight: 2 g
Nose fuze type RKX 332: Mechanical impact

Rocket type RAK 025
Length: 1783 mm
Weight: 19·7 kg
V max from ground at +18° C: Approx 520 m/s
Range ground to ground at +18° C: Approx 10 km
Flight time over 12 km at +18° C: Approx 50 s
Shell type SSK 032: Fragmentation explosive
Weight: Explosive: 2·8 kg
**   Shell ready to fire:** 11 kg

Number of spherical fragments: 2133
Fragment weight: 2 g
Nose fuze type RKX 332: Mechanical impact

Rocket type RAK 026/RAK 054
Length: 1510 mm
Weight: 13·2 kg
V max from ground at +18° C: Approx 820 m/s
Flight time over 2 km at +18° C: Approx 3·2 s
Warhead type PHK 030: Hollow charge
Weight: **Explosive:** Approx 1 kg
      Warhead ready to fire: 4·5 kg

Warhead with fragmentation effect
Penetration in steel: Minimum 350 mm
Response angle: 15°
Ignition via contact cap
Base fuze type RBK 331: Electro-mechanical, with mechanical and electronic time element
Detonator safety : to 30 m
Armed after: 100 m
Rain safety
Ignition energy from propulsion element
  A range of rocket launchers suitable for fitting to fighter aircraft and helicopters is produced by

Oerlikon, and these are detailed in entry **4135.303** which follows.
STATUS
In production. SNORA rockets have been successfully tested on various aircraft types including the following: SF260 W, Hawk, MB326K, MB339, Venom, Hunter, Mirage, Skyhawk A4.
CONTRACTOR
Machine Tools Works Oerlikon-Bührle Ltd, 8050 Zurich, Switzerland.

4135.303
OERLIKON ROCKET PODS
A range of rocket pods for firing Oerlikon SNORA aircraft rockets is produced for fitting in various fighter aircraft and helicopters. The main characteristics of these are listed in the following tables.
Rocket Launcher Type SAL-12-80 (RWK 020)
Suitable for use on all types of sub- and supersonic aircraft, the SAL-12-80 pod is of lightweight metal construction with a replaceable frangible nose fairing to close the 12 firing tubes during flight. It is fitted with a standard NATO and centre lugs suspension system.
CHARACTERISTICS
Calibre: 81 mm
Number of tubes: 12
Length: 2550 mm (approx)
Diameter: 396 mm (approx)
Weight: 69 kg (empty); 227 – 305 kg (with rockets, depending on type of shell)
Firing: Single, or salvoes of 2, 6, or 12 rockets
Rate of fire: 12 rounds/s

Rocket Launcher Type SAL-6-80 (RWK 021)
This is a six-tube launcher for use on supersonic aircraft.
CHARACTERISTICS
Calibre: 81 mm
Number of tubes: 6
Length: 2600 mm
Diameter: 296 mm
Weight: 48 kg (empty); 127 – 166 kg (with rockets, depending on type of shell)
Firing: Single, or salvoes of 2, 3, or 6 rockets
Rate of fire: 10 rounds/s

Rocket Launcher Type AL-6-80 (RWK 024)
This is a six-tube launcher for use on subsonic and light aircraft.
CHARACTERISTICS
Calibre: 81 mm
Number of tubes: 6
Length: 2214 mm
Diameter: 296 mm
Weight: 38 kg (empty); 117 – 132 kg (with rockets, depending on type of shell)
Firing: Single, or salvoes of 2, 3, or 6 rockets
Rate of fire: 10 rounds/s

Rocket Launcher Type HL-7-80 (RWK 022)
This launcher is designed for use on helicopters.
CHARACTERISTICS
Calibre: 81 mm
Number of tubes: 7
Length: 1800 mm
Diameter: 296 mm
Weight: 33 kg (empty); 125 – 143 kg (with rockets, depending on type of shell)
Firing: Single, or salvoes of 2, 3, or 7 rockets
Rate of fire: 10 rounds/s
STATUS
In production.
CONTRACTOR
Machine Tools Works Oerlikon-Bührle Ltd, 8050 Zurich, Switzerland.

Type HL-7-80 rocket launcher installed on a helicopter

Type SAL-12-80 rocket launcher installed on a fighter aircraft

Type SAL-6-80 rocket launcher for supersonic aircraft

Type AL-6-80 rocket launcher for subsonic and light aircraft

Type SAL-12-80 rocket launcher (RWK 020)

Type HL-7-80 helicopter rocket launcher

1269.303

OERLIKON 30 mm GUN TYPE KCA

The aircraft gun type KCA is of 30 mm calibre and has been developed by Oerlikon, Switzerland. The weapon is a further example of the development of the Mauser revolver principle which has been almost universally adopted for single barrel aircraft cannon since the end of the Second World War.

Oerlikon Type 30 mm KCA cannon

The KCA differs, however, from almost all comparable guns in the present generation in using a new design of ammunition in which the ratio of propellant charge to projectile weight is over 2:1 whereas in most other guns, the ratio is likely to be 3:2. In addition, the KCA ammunition has a higher projectile weight than other 30 mm types.

As a result of these factors and lightweight design of the moving parts of the weapon, a firing rate of 1350 rounds per minute is obtained and a muzzle velocity of over 1030 m/s. The weapon is therefore well suited to ground attack as well as air-to-air engagements, and for the former role a long gun range is required to give the attacker a wide firing bracket.

The Oerlikon KCA has a four chamber revolver mechanism so that before firing the gun mechanism has to be cycled three times to charge all chambers. This can be done in the air by a pneumatic re-loading system.

Ammunition for the KCA is available in a range of types: TP, HEI, SAPHEI, and AP.

CHARACTERISTICS

Calibre: 30 mm
Length of barrel: 1976 mm
Length of gun overall: 2691 mm
Width of gun: 242·5 mm
Height of gun: 249·5 mm
Gun weight: 136 kg
Muzzle velocity: 1030 m/s
Rate of fire: 1350 rounds/minute
Accuracy: 50% rounds inside 2·5 mils
Round weight: 0·89 kg with steel cartridge
Projectile weight: 0·360 kg
Range: Over 2000 m gun stationary
STATUS
The Oerlikon KCA is in series production, and has been selected by the Swedish Air Force for installation under the Saab Viggen attack aircraft.
CONTRACTOR
Machine Tool Works Oerlikon-Bührle Ltd, 8050 Zurich, Switzerland.

4070.303

OERLIKON HELICOPTER ARMAMENT

To meet the growing need for armament on helicopters for both transport and combat duties, Oerlikon has developed and tested a number of cannon installations for the engagement of enemy helicopters and various ground targets. This work has been carried out in close collaboration with helicopter manufacturers such as Agusta, CASA and Westland. The most suitable cannons are the Oerlikon 20 mm KAA, KAD and the 25 mm KBA types. Details of each are given in the table.

The cannons with their cradle are rigidly fixed to the helicopter structure. Depending on the size of the aircraft, the configuration may consist of either a cannon on each side or of a single cannon on the fuselage centre-line or pintle-mounted in the cabin. Belted ammunition is fed to the cannons from containers inside the helicopter through specially designed chutes. Ammunition types available cover the range of TP, AP, APDS-T, SAPHEI and HEI, all of which can be supplied with or without tracer

STATUS
The fixed forward firing installation has been tested and proved on the Westland Lynx helicopter.
CONTRACTOR
Machine Tool Works Oerlikon-Bührle Ltd, 8050 Zurich, Switzerland.

CHARACTERISTICS

Type	KAA	KAD	KBA
Calibre	20 mm	20 mm	25 mm
Muzzle velocity	1040-1100 m/s	1040 m/s (approx)	1100-1360 m/s (approx)
Rate of fire (rounds/min)	1100	850 (approx)	570
Total length	2690 mm	2744 mm (approx)	3105 mm
Mass of cannon	88 kg	68 kg	112 kg
Mass of cradle	45 kg	49 kg	33 kg
Firing system		Electro-mechanical	
Projectile mass	110-125 g	125-144 g	180 g*
Mass of comp round	322-337 g	306-337 g	500 g*
Length of comp round	203·5 mm	213 mm	223 mm

*25 mm APDS-T projectile mass 150 g, complete round mass 475 g.

Helicopter installation of twin-belt feed Oerlikon KBA 25 mm cannon

Oerlikon 20 mm helicopter armament installed on Westland Lynx

1272.303

HISPANO OERLIKON 20 mm TACTICAL AIR ARMAMENT

Two types of 20 mm calibre aircraft cannon were manufactured by Hispano Suiza in Switzerland and by their UK company, British Manufacture and Research Co Ltd of Grantham, Lincolnshire. Both types, the 20 mm Mk 5 and 20 mm Mk 2* are similar and are derived from the original Hispano type 404 weapon. The Mk 5 model is lighter in weight than the Mk 2* and has a higher rate of fire. Although no longer part of the company's programme, this weapon remains in extensive service in many parts of the world.

A wide range of 20 mm ammunition types is available, including armour piercing, tracer, ball, and HE incendiary. Different types of fuze are also available. The round has a brass case and is percussion fired. Ammunition is normally supplied in 60-round belts or as individually packed rounds.

A wide variety of tools and accessories are available for 20 mm Mk 2* and Mk 5 guns.

CHARACTERISTICS

20 mm Mk 5 gun
Calibre: 20 mm
Gun weight with feed: 42 kg
Muzzle velocity: 850 m/s
Rate of fire: 580 – 640 rounds/minute

Length of gun: 2052 mm
Round weight: 1367 g
Projectile weight: 138 g
Range: 1600 m, to velocity 300 m/s, gun stationary
STATUS

Hispano 20 mm aircraft cannon are in service with over 30 air forces. Over 98 000 20 mm guns of all types have been made in the UK alone. It is now regarded as obsolete though many examples can be expected to remain in service for a considerable period to come.

UNION OF SOVIET SOCIALIST REPUBLICS

3181.303

SOVIET AIRCRAFT ARMAMENT NOTE

Unclassified information on Soviet aircraft armament tends to be limited in both quantity and precision but the increasing emphasis on this aspect which has been detected by observers of Soviet military activities calls for a summary of the known characteristics of Soviet equipment of this nature.

Bombs

The following types of free-fall bomb are known to have entered service with Soviet forces and those of some allied nations:

(1) HE – High explosive bombs are issued in 100, 250, 500, 750 and 1000 kg sizes

(2) Incendiary – Incendiary bombs are issued in 100, 250 and 1000 kg sizes

(3) AP – Armour piercing bombs are issued in 250 and 500 kg sizes

(4) Concrete dibbers are known to be used in both 250 and 500 kg sizes, the latter being designated the M62

(5) Cluster bombs have been in service for a number of years and the following varieties are known to exist: HE, incendiary, HEI, fragmentation, and anti-tank (shaped charge)

(6) Napalm bombs are available.

Categories (4) and (5) probably include one or more types of retarded bomb mechanism.

Unguided Rockets

Unguided rockets are employed in both air-to-air and air-to-ground roles and are carried by fixed-wing aircraft and helicopters. In the case of the heavier rockets, use is restricted to ground attack (or anti-ship) roles. The following types have been identified:

57 mm: The rocket itself is designated S-5 and is of 55 mm diameter for use with 57 mm launcher tubes. A variety of warheads is available including: chaff, anti-tank, HE, and fragmentation. Applications have been noted on such types as the Fitter and Fishbed fighter aircraft and the Hind helicopter. A range of launcher pods has been observed of 8, 16, 19 and 32 round capacities and designated: UV-8-57; UV-16-57; UV-19-57; UV-32-57.

137 mm: This rocket is known as the M-100 and has a launch weight of 15·6 kg.

160 mm: No information is available on this rocket apart from its designation (S-16) and the fact that it can be launched from the Hind-A helicopter.

190 mm: Of 190 mm calibre, and designated TRS 190, this rocket has a launch weight of 46 kg and can be launched by the MiG-19.

212 mm: Little is known apart from the designation, ARS 212, launch weight of 116 kg and use with the MiG-19.

220 mm: No information is available, but some sources report the existence of a 210 mm rocket known as the S-21 which is used with the Hind-A.

240 mm: Known as the S-24 and associated with the MiG-17 and Mig-21 (one rocket per pylon) and the Hind helicopter.

325 mm: No details available.

Cannon and Machine Guns

The following types are known to be in service:

12·7 mm: UBK machine gun has been used in the MiG-15UTI trainer aircraft and more recently in the MI-24 helicopter. The latter is probably the most important application of this calibre of machine gun in aircraft, beginning with the single chin mounting in the Hind. This was followed by a multi-barrelled,

Mi-24 Hind ground attack helicopter is armed with four UV-32-57 rocket launcher pods, rails for anti-tank guided missiles, and a four-barrel Gatling-type 12·7 mm machine gun in a remotely aimed chin turret

Reloading UV-32-57 rocket launcher pods on Mi-24 Hind ground attack helicopter with 57 mm unguided rockets

Badger bomber's twin NR-23 23 mm guns in remotely controlled ventral turret

Nose-mounted 12·7 mm machine gun on Mi-6 (Hook) helicopter

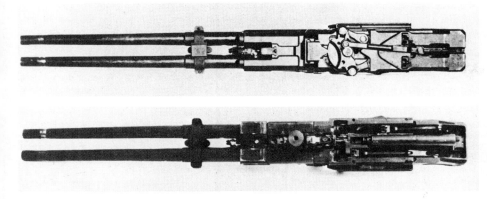

Top and bottom views of the Soviet GSh-23 23 mm twin-barrel gun

Gatling-type gun with four 12·7 mm barrels mounted in a turret that provided coverage of 70° left and right of the aircraft datum in azimuth, and elevation movement from –60 to +15°. The estimated range of this weapon is about 1500 m. It has been suggested that the four-barrel 12·7 mm gun may be succeeded on the Hind helicopter by the GSh-23 (see below) as used on the MiG-21.

23 mm: Two 23 mm single-barrel cannon have been identified, the NS-23KM (Nudelman-Suranov) and the NR-23 (Nudelman-Rikter). In many installations the two are probably interchangeable. The NS-23 is understood to be of earlier design and to have a lower rate of fire, ie 550 rounds/minute compared with about 850 rounds/minute for the NR-23. Widely used in fighter, bomber, and certain transport aircraft.

23 mm GSh-23: This is a twin-barrel 23 mm gun employed both as an internal weapon and in the GP-9 gun pack for belly mounting. In the latter case, as used on the Fishbed 'E', the pack has a capacity of 200 rounds. Cyclic rate of fire is about 3000 rounds/minute and effective range 3000 m. A version of this weapon has been noted that is designed for mounting within a pod for carriage on an aircraft underwing attachment point. This variant has been seen on some Yak-36 Forger carrier aircraft.

23 mm: A 23 mm six-barrelled cannon is known to be in use on some recent Soviet aircraft but the only known installation of this is on MiG-27 aircraft.

30 mm: The NR-30 cannon is used on the Su-7, Su-20, Yak-28, and MiG-19S, and has a rate of fire of 850 rounds/minute with normal, HE, and HEI

Close-up of Badger tail gun installation with two NR-23 23 mm cannon

ammunition. A capacity of 70 rounds is typical.

30 mm: The 2NR cannon is used in Fitter A and Fitter C aircraft.

37 mm: The N-37 (or NS-37) cannon has a cyclic rate of fire of 400 rounds/minute and is used in such aircraft as the MiG-15, MiG-17, MiG-19, Yak-25, and Yak-27R.

UNITED KINGDOM

5185.303
30 mm ADEN CANNON

The 30 mm Aden cannon was developed shortly after the end of the Second World War by the ADE (now the Royal Armament Research and Development Establishment at Fort Halstead), and the Royal Small Arms Factory (RSAF) at Enfield Lock. The first production model was known as the Mk 1 and the current production cannon is the Mk 4. An improved Mk 5 version was also developed, known as the Straden, which had a higher rate of fire (see below).

The design of the weapon is simple with the whole assembly contained within the cradle unit; installation mounting points are at the rear and front barrel entry position of the cradle. Mounting of the cannon is possible at any angle on the longitudinal axis to suit the specific aircraft requirement, and both left- or right-hand feed versions are available. Cocking is pneumatic with provision for manual operation, and the ammunition, which is belt fed (disintegrating link), is electrically fired.

The Aden operates in the following manner. A cylinder (revolving drum) has five cartridge chambers, into which the cartridges are loaded in two stages, indexed by the movement of a gas operated slide. Firing takes place when a round is in line with the barrel, the whole mechanism being safely locked at the moment of firing; a round cannot be fired if the barrel/cylinder is not correctly locked in position, and with a round in line with the barrel. When a round is fired, the gas pressure passing through the barrel gas port acts via a piston onto a slide mechanism, which, travelling rearward within the cradle unit revolves the breech cylinder and feed sprockets, bringing a round into position for feeding into a chamber. The slide mechanism is then moved forward by the action of return springs, further indexing the cylinder and feeding into a chamber. The Aden cannon can be mounted internally in an aircraft, in a pod for installation under a pylon, or in a blister pod which is mounted under the fuselage of the aircraft.

TYPICAL INSTALLATIONS

Harrier with two cannon, each with 130 rounds of ammunition.

Hawk trainer with a blister pod with one 30 mm cannon.

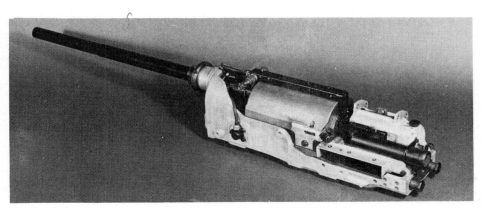

30 mm Aden cannon

HAL Gnat with two cannon, each with 115 rounds of ammunition.

HF-24 Maut with four Mk 4 guns, each with 120 rounds of ammunition.

Hunter with four cannon, each with 150 rounds of ammunition.

Jaguar (RAF) two cannon with 150 rounds of ammunition per cannon.

CHARACTERISTICS

Type: Aden Mk 4
Calibre: 30 mm
Gun length: 1590 mm
Total gun weight: 87 kg
Barrel length: 1080 mm
Barrel weight: 12·25 kg
Muzzle velocity: 790 m/s
Rate of fire: 1200/1400 rounds/minute
Recoil load: 31·4 kN
Cocking: Pneumatic
Firing: Electric (26 V DC)
Ammunition
Practice round (Mk 4*Z)
High explosive round (Mk 6*Z)
Armour piercing (Mk 1*Z)
Armour piercing incendiary (under development)
Typical system weight: 196 kg (gun + 200 rounds)

DEVELOPMENT

RSAF Enfield have now completed the development programme designed to increase the effectiveness of the Aden Mk 5 cannon by increasing its rate of fire from 1200/1400 rounds/minute to 1500/1700 rounds/minute combined with improved reliability. Guns modified to this standard are termed Aden Mk 5 (Straden) cannon. One requirement for the Mk 5 was for it to retain its capability to fit into existing installations without modifications to aircraft structures; this requirement has been achieved, Aden Mk 5 being externally no different from the Mk 4. Mounting points are identical, with recoil and run-out loads being no higher than on the original gun.

The gas piston, which has been redesigned to make more efficient use of the available gas pressure so as to achieve higher rates of fire, also purges the gas back through the barrel more effectively. Consequently gas loss is less in the new model.

Increased rate of fire correspondingly increases case ejection speed and slight modifications to case exit points may be necessary.

CONTRACTOR

Royal Small Arms Factory, Enfield Lock, Middlesex. Enquiries to Director of Sales, Ministry of Defence, Stuart House, 23-25 Soho Square, London W1V 5FJ, England.

1277.303

CLUSTER BOMB No 1 Mks 1, 2, 3, and 4 (BL 755)

BL 755 has been developed to meet a requirement for a weapon that will yield a high kill probability against a range of small hard and soft targets encountered in the battlefield and immediate tactical area. Because of the efficiency of modern surface-to-air weapon systems it is operationally necessary for air-to-ground attacks, in support of ground forces, to be carried out at very low level. Any other form of attack necessitates prolonged exposure to the enemy ground defences and negates any element of surprise. This will result in unacceptable losses to the attacking aircraft.

To compensate for the aiming errors inherent in low-level attack, BL 755 covers the target area with a pattern of bomblets the dimensions of which are proportional to the aiming errors. The dual function bomblets are effective against armoured and soft-skinned vehicles, parked aircraft and personnel, and are distributed evenly within the pattern.

Before take-off, one of four time delays is set to ensure a safe weapon/aircraft separation distance. When the bomb is released, its primary striker is armed and, on completion of the selected timer interval, the striker operates and fires the primary cartridge. The gas pressure generated by this cartridge releases the two-part bomb body skins before activating the main gas cartridge to eject the bomblets. 147 bomblets are carried in seven bays with 21 bomblets in each bay of the bomb body. The bomblet ejection velocity is varied between the bays to ensure an even ground pattern. Each bomblet is armed after a short period of flight and, on impact, uses a shaped-charge effect to give a penetration of armour of at least 250 mm. In addition to its armour penetration capability, each bomblet casing explodes into over 2000 fragments which have an effective penetration against non-armoured vehicles and other targets.

BL 755 is compatible with current and future strike aircraft. It can be carried in a bomb bay or externally with twin 14-inch (356 mm) or single suspension. It can be delivered using a simple or sophisticated sighting system; it is immune from electronic countermeasures and incorporates a safety mechanism which provides protection for the aircraft during carriage and release and the deployment of bomblets.

CHARACTERISTICS

Weight: 277 kg
Weapon payload: 147 bomblets
Length: 2451 mm
Diameter: 419 mm
Fin span: 566 mm
Suspension: Twin lug at 14-inch (356 mm) spacing or single lug

Main variations from Mk 1
Mk 2, shorter time delays
Mk 3, addition of 250 mm twin lug suspension
Mk 4, incorporates same time delays as Mk 2

IMPROVED BL 755

The interim RAF requirement to increase its anti-armour capability against MBTs with improved armour that are entering service is to be met by an Improved BL 755.

The Improved BL 755 system retains the shot-gun principle of compensating for aiming errors but takes advantage of the higher weapon aiming accuracy of modern aircraft by modifying the pattern of bomblets.

The submunition is retarded to increase angle of attack thus permitting later target acquisition and better target penetration whilst the warhead incorporates advances made in shaped charge technology and explosives since the introduction into service of the original BL 755.

Other BL 755 design features are unaltered so that full aircraft compatibility and flexibility of operation of the current weapon are retained.

STATUS

BL 755 has been in service with the Royal Air Force since the early 1970s and has been supplied to six primary NATO air forces and those of other nations. It is used on numerous aircraft types. In Swiss service the BL 755 is designated Fl Bb 79. Improved BL 755 will enter RAF service shortly and is available for export to approved clients.

CONTRACTOR

Hunting Engineering Ltd, Reddings Wood, Ampthill, Bedfordshire MK45 2HD, England.

Improved BL 755 bomblet

Tornado GR1 with BL 755 anti-armour weapons

1267.393

BRITISH BOMB RETARDING SYSTEM

The British bomb retarding system was developed in the UK by Hunting Engineering Ltd. The retarder is incorporated in a special bomb-tail assembly which can be readily applied to a wide range of existing ballistic bombs.

The retarding tail with its associated fuze has been designed to overcome the problem of low altitude attack. If a conventional bomb is used from low altitudes it is likely that the separation of the attacking aircraft from the bursting of the bomb will be small enough to endanger the attacking aircraft. The purpose of the retarding tail is to decelerate or retard the bomb after release, and allow the aircraft to reach a safe separation distance before the bomb impacts and explodes. Conventional delayed action bombs, if used in this way, are liable to ricochet and to miss their targets.

The retarding tail utilises a combination of a ribbon parachute and air-brakes (retarder arms) formed from the structure of the tail. This technique has the advantages of providing very high drag after a closely predictable time delay, essential for accurate control of bomb stick spacing leading to improved probability of target destruction.

The basic structure of the retarder tail consists of a base ring made in forged steel in which are incorporated eight securing pads for attaching the tail to the bomb. The steel inner cone is welded to the base ring and at the aft end carries the one-piece fin casting in light alloy. This casting is riveted to the steel inner cone. The four retarder arms consist of spines carrying the outer skin sections. The spines pivot at the root of the fins and when extended form four airbrakes. When closed the skin sections form the tail cone enclosing the folded ribbon fabric.

The design incorporates various safety measures which ensure that at no time does the bomb constitute an unacceptable hazard to the aircraft during carriage or after release.

A timer mechanism which controls the operation of the unit is housed within the inner cone. As the bomb is released from the aircraft this timer is initiated by a lanyard. After a short interval to allow the bomb to fall clear of the aircraft the timer triggers the release of the retarder arms. These arms are forced into the

Multiple release of retarded bombs from Phantom aircraft

airstream by a spring and then aerodynamic forces extend them to the fully open position. The energy released in this operation is absorbed by a tear-webbing shock absorbing device.

At the base of the tail, couplings are provided to connect with the tail fuze of the bomb, so that the arming of the latter is controlled by the action of the retarding tail mechanism.

While being carried aboard the aircraft, retarding tail bombs resemble conventional fixed fin types. The fins are provided to stabilise the bomb aerodynamically immediately after release. In the event of the bomb being jettisoned the retarding tail is not operated and neither is the fuze armed. Retarded bombs can be carried externally or internally in subsonic or supersonic aircraft.

CHARACTERISTICS

Bomb Retarder Tail Type 117

This tail is 1035 mm long and 584 mm span. It was developed initially for use with British 1000 lb HE medium capacity Mk 6 and 9-19 series bombs. Two types of tail, Mk 3 and Mk 4, are available. The Mk 3 with a tail fin span of 584 mm is suitable for external carriage while the Mk 4 with a tail fin span of 419 mm

is suitable for both external and internal bomb carriage.

Bomb Retarder Tail Type 118

This tail is 970 mm long and 463 mm span. It was originally designed for use with the British 540 lb HE medium capacity bomb.

Adaptors are available to couple type 117 and 118 retarding tails to many other types of HE bombs, including the principal US types such as Mk 82 and 83, Mk 64, Mk 65, and Mk 117.

Both types of retarder are designed for a shelf life of at least five years without attention.

STATUS

The retarding system is in service with the Royal Air Force and is being supplied to air forces overseas.

CONTRACTOR

Hunting Engineering Ltd, Reddings Wood, Ampthill, Bedfordshire MK45 2HD, England.

5218.303

JP233 LOW ALTITUDE AIRFIELD ATTACK SYSTEM

The JP233 airfield attack weapon system has been developed for the Royal Air Force for use in counter air operations. The operational concept of the weapon is the suppression of an enemy's ability to mount aircraft sorties by damaging the aircraft operating surface of his airfields and then preventing its repair, to an extent that prevents take-off and landing for prolonged periods.

The weapon is designed for the high speed, low level, simultaneous delivery of two complementary weapons - a cratering weapon to attack and render unuseable, runways, taxiways and grass operating strip, and an area denial weapon to pose a continuing threat to vehicles and crew engaged in airfield repair. The JP233 weapon comprises a cratering weapon designated SG357 and an area denial weapon designated HB876. Each of the weapons consists of a dispenser loaded with submunitions, 30 for the SG357 and 215 for HB876. A Tornado carries two JP233 systems mounted in tandem on the port and starboard shoulder pylons with the forward positions occupied by the two HB876 dispensers and with two SG357 dispensers aft.

To ensure effective ground cover both types of submunitions are dispensed simultaneously in a co-ordinated sequence. The SG357 submunitions disrupt the operating surfaces by causing craters, heave and fractures over a large area whilst the HB876 mines overlay the cratered area to delay runway repair operations for some considerable time. The submunitions also cause a considerable amount of consequential damage to secondary targets such as aircraft, vehicles or buildings adjacent to the area being attacked.

The system can be configured for carriage by a range of advanced aircraft including Tornado, F-111 and F-16 where multiple dispensers are employed on either fuselage or wing mountings.

Apart from denying the enemy the use of his airfields, JP233 can equally well be employed against other important targets such as railway marshalling yards, transport and tactical vehicle concentrations, road networks, supply support depots, areas to which the enemy requires freedom of access and use.

It is claimed that typically, JP233 is five times more effective per aircraft load than other systems.

JP 233 full load release from Tornado GR1 aircraft

HB876 area denial sub-munition for JP233 airfield attack weapon

SG357 runway cratering sub-munition for JP233 airfield attack weapon

STATUS

The JP233 Weapon System is in the production phase and will be introduced to the RAF inventory by the mid 1980's.

CONTRACTOR

Hunting Engineering Ltd, Reddings Wood, Ampthill, Bedfordshire MK45 2HD, England.

1845.393

WESTLAND-FRAZER NASH HIGH STRENGTH MACE

The ejector release unit (ERU) is in the form of a beam with the operating mechanism, breech etc, sandwiched between a pair of sideplates, one a baseplate, and the other a closure plate. The sideplates terminate in two identical gas operated ejector ram assemblies which also carry the store retaining jaws and incorporate integral wedge systems conforming to the crutchless form of store retention.

The jaws are designed to suit the recommended STANAG saddle lugs which are mounted on the store at 14-inch (356 mm) centres. The jaws are connected to the locking wedges by spring loaded links so that when the jaws are engaged with the saddles the wedges are forced into the clearance between the abutments on the ram cases and the surface of the saddle lugs. This effectively 'locks' the store to the ERU preventing any sway or pitch. Spigots are incorporated in the base of both ram case forgings to control yaw and fore and aft movement of the store.

The jaws are linked by connecting rods to a central operating toggle which, when turned on its axis,

High-strength 14-inch (356 mm) MACE ejector release units for the Tornado

withdraws or engages the jaws. The linkage forms a geometric lock comprising an 'over-centre' system which is maintained in both locked and unlocked positions by a compression spring coaxial with a rod suspended between a projection on the breech and one arm of the linkage. In the locked position this rod is at the limit of its travel and so maintains the over-centre attitude, thus preventing the toggle turning. The release is achieved by a gas operated plunger which drives the toggle round so that the line of action

of the spring on its rod now swings above the toggle pivot, reversing the sense of the geometric lock and maintaining it in the unlocked position with the jaws retracted from the bomb lugs. The design of the mechanism is such that the weight of the store tends to intensify the geometric lock in the loaded position, and, when released, to contribute a positive force to open the mechanism and prevent any possible 'hang-up'.

The plunger which operates the mechanism is housed in the breech block which forms the central unit of the gas system. The plunger is held in position by a screw cap and a spring. In operation the gases enter the cylinder at the upper end, via internal porting leading from the combustion chambers, and forces the plunger down against the spring, tripping the geometric lock, and retracting the jaws. The combustion chambers are twin receptacles bored in the breech block and threaded to receive the cartridge holders. These are inter-connected internally so that they both feed the gas system to ensure that if only one cartridge fires from electrical initiation the other will ignite sympathetically.

Internal ports lead from the combustion chambers fore and aft to the gas tubes which conduct the gases, on firing, to the ejector ram assemblies via interchangeable throttles housed in the inlets to the ram cylinders. These throttles are 'plug-in' units drilled with a gas port of some pre-determined diameter to govern the amount of gas entering the ram. By interchanging throttles with different orifice diameters the thrust of the rams can be adjusted to suit a limiting aircraft reaction, or by installing throttles of differing bore sizes at the forward and aft rams a differential thrust can be obtained to vary the attitude of launching of the store. These throttles can

also be supplied with ports drilled to exhaust the gas directly to atmosphere so that the rams are inoperative when a free-fall gravity drop is required.
STATUS
Following the Panavia 'Intent to Purchase' notification issued in March 1973, development testing continued through 1973 to qualification of units in early 1974. Design was in accordance with a Panavia specification to meet the requirements of the multi-role combat aircraft for which the unit will be produced. Subsequent design improvements include

an increase in overall strength and the option of quickly converting the unit to conventional sway braces in order to carry stores with the standard bail lug.
CONTRACTORS
Normalair-Garrett Ltd, Ordnance Division, Blacknell Lane, Crewkerne, Somerset, England.
Frazer-Nash Ltd, Lower Teddington Road, Hampton Wick, Surrey, England – design consultants.

1604.393
ML CARRIER BOMB LIGHT STORES NO 200

The ML Aviation carrier bomb light stores No 200 (CBLS 200) is an aerodynamically faired carrier combining maximum strength and stiffness with minimum weight. It was developed from world-wide experience gained with the earlier ML CBLS 100, several hundred examples of which were supplied to many air forces before production ceased.

Standard carrier-to-aircraft suspension is via lug pockets for single suspension, NATO twin 14-inch (356 mm) and NATO twin 30-inch (762 mm) suspension. Lug pockets for twin 250 mm and other suspensions are also provided as required.

CBLS 200 is fitted with four ML ejector release units

(ERUs) permitting the carriage and ejection, with standard ERU jaws, of four stores each up to 103 mm diameter and 750 mm long. Jaws for larger diameter stores are provided as required. Electrical and/or mechanical fuzing devices are fitted as and when called for by the particular types of stores to be carried. Stores up to an individual weight of 35 kg can be fitted at each ERU station. All stores are ejected vertically.

A comprehensive range of optional extra role change kits permits CBLS 200 to be converted rapidly from one type of light bomb to another with normal first line servicing tools. A simple modification allows two five-inch flares to be carried to provide a night illuminating capability.

CBLS 200 incorporates a continuously re-cycling autoselector thus requiring only the simplest of electrical connections to the parent aircraft.

As an optional extra, rocket panniers to accept either four FFAR 2·75 inch or four SNEB 68 mm or four SNIA-VISCOSA 50 mm rockets can be provided to clip to the sides of CBLS 200 (two rockets in each side panel). In such cases, suitable electrical wiring systems, including a further continuously recycling autoselector, are added to the CBLS 200 itself.
CHARACTERISTICS
Overall length: 2464 mm
Diameter: 423 mm
Weight (less stores and rocket panniers): 53·5 kg
Weight with rocket panniers (less stores and rockets): 78 kg
STATUS
CBLS 200 is in production for air forces world-wide for use on a large number of aircraft types including Hawk, Alpha Jet, Jaguar and Tornado. It has also been adopted for aircraft currently in development.
CONTRACTOR
ML Aviation Co Ltd, White Waltham Aerodrome, Maidenhead, Berkshire, SL6 3JG England.

Four CBLS 200 on inner wing pylons and beneath fuselage of Tornado

ML carrier bomb light stores No 200 with rocket pannier

1264.393
ML AVIATION LIGHTWEIGHT LOW-DRAG TWIN STORE CARRIER

This carrier increases the capacity of a normal single external weapon station so that two stores can be carried. It is designed for use on wing or fuselage stations and incorporates two ML ejector release units, (ERUs) of the No 119 Series. These may be either ERU 119 Mk 1 providing for NATO twin 14-inch (356 mm) suspension or, alternatively, ERU 119 TH – a three hook variant combining within itself NATO twin 14-inch, twin 250 mm and single suspension. All the necessary fuzing services for a full range of modern conventional stores are incorporated in the carrier which can be supplied with electrical wiring for pilot or auto-selection according to requirements. Typical weapons used with this carrier are 250 kg HE bombs or rocket launchers.

The carrier consists basically of a main spar and baseplate machined from stretched light alloy plate. Raised lugs on the sides of the main spar form the attachment points for the two ERUs. Lightweight

ML Aviation lightweight low-drag twin store carrier

fairings are fitted over the main structure to minimise the aerodynamic drag of the carrier.

Twin lugs at the standard 14-inch (356 mm) centres are provided for mounting the carrier on any standard weapon pylon. If desired the carrier suspension can

be offset from the centre line by 57 mm to either side, to adjust rolling moments or to increase store-to-aircraft clearance. Adaptors are available to use this carrier with single lug type store suspension or the 30-inch (762 mm) centres type.
CHARACTERISTICS
Carrier weight, including 2 × ERU 119: 37 kg
Length overall: 1638 mm
Width overall: 655 mm
Depth overall: 146 mm
Max store diameter: 420 mm
Max store weight: 550 kg
Max aircraft speed: Mach 0·95 loaded; supersonic empty
STATUS
The ML lightweight low-drag twin store carrier is in service with, or in production for, Alpha Jet, Harrier, Hawk, F-104 and Hunter aircraft. Flight trials with other aircraft types are also in progress.
CONTRACTOR
ML Aviation Co Ltd, White Waltham Aerodrome, Maidenhead, Berkshire SL6 3JG, England.

4484.393
ML AVIATION CARRIER BOMB TWIN STORE 30°

This carrier increases the capacity of a normal single external weapon station so that two 1000 lb class stores can be carried. It was designed primarily for the Harrier GR3 but is equally suitable for the wing and fuselage stations of most modern high performance aircraft and incorporates two ML ejector release units (ERUs) of the 119 Series (**7513.393**).

Arming connector assemblies are mounted on swivelling brackets which rotate from the vertical to horizontal position allowing free access for the operator to connect lanyards after stores are loaded to the carrier; each arming bracket assembly is then swivelled back to the vertical position for flight.

The ERUs are mounted 30° from the vertical to provide increased horizontal distance between adjacent weapons thus reducing mutual aerodynamic interference and giving a subsequent reduction in release disturbance.

Each carrier has a Port/Stbd (Left/Right) selector switch to provide ground presetting if required and an auto selector which sequences the release pulses.
CHARACTERISTICS
Carrier weight: 48 kg (including 2 × ERU 119)
Length overall: 1498 mm
Width: 407 mm (less sway braces)
Depth: 194·5 mm
STATUS
Production.

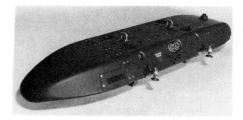

ML carrier bomb twin store 30°

CONTRACTOR
ML Aviation Co Ltd, White Waltham Aerodrome, Maidenhead, Berkshire SL6 3JG, England.

4485.393
ML AVIATION TWIN STORE INTEGRATED CARRIER

This carrier increases the capacity of a normal single external weapon station so that two 1000 lb class, or three lighter stores, can be carried.

The carrier introduces a new philosophy where the ejection system and operating linkage of a production ERU 126 (BRU 36A) (**4431.393**) is embodied in the structure of the carrier. This significantly reduces the carrier weight in relation to the strength provided. Logistic advantages accrue where the parent aircraft uses the ERU 126 (BRU 36A). Provision of electrics and store arming facilities for the central (third station) are built in as standard, however the third station is an optional extra.

Maintenance and ground handling functions are greatly facilitated by hinged side access panels which open to expose the complete ERU and arming

ML twin store integrated carrier

connectors. These arming connectors can be rotated to the horizontal position, to allow connection of arming lanyards and cables after the weapon has been satisfactorily loaded to the ERU. The connector assembly is then rotated to the vertical position for flight.

The two shoulder stations are 22½ degrees from the vertical. This provides the optimum store body separation and minimum release disturbance for the AV8B pylon installation for which it was initially designed. The TSIC is, however, totally suited to all known high performance aircraft pylon installations embodying NATO standard suspension and is capable of adaptation to other suspension standards if required.

CHARACTERISTICS
Carrier weight: 45 kg (two-store configuration)
Length overall: 1422 mm
Width overall: 433 mm (less sway braces)
STATUS
Production.
CONTRACTOR
ML Aviation Co Ltd, White Waltham Aerodrome, Maidenhead, Berkshire SL6 3JG, England.

7513.393
ML EJECTOR RELEASE UNITS No 119 SERIES

The basic ML Aviation ejector release unit (ERU) No 119 accepts a very wide variety of stores with NATO twin 14-inch (356 mm) suspension. The two hooks are connected by a linkage forming a geometric lock via an over centre toggle mechanism thus ensuring complete integrity of carriage. All 119 Series ERUs are operated by two NATO standard

ML ejector release unit No 119

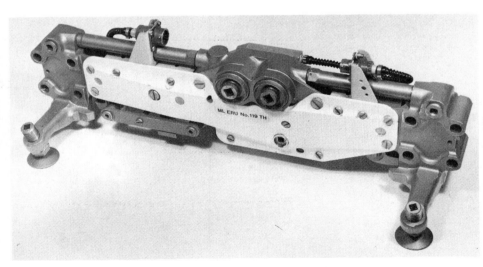

ML Aviation ejector release unit No 119TH

cartridges housed in a central breech. The gas system incorporates provision for the control of the debris of cartridge combustion thus ensuring a considerable number of firings before the ERU requires servicing (up to 30 firings in 30 days).

When the cartridges are fired the gases so generated operate a release piston which positively opens both hooks simultaneously and, also, after passing through the throttles, extend the two ejector

rams against the store, thus imparting ejection velocity to the store. By fitting differing throttle sizes ejection velocity against a given store can be increased or diminished within the total capacity of the ERU. Reaction loads against aircraft or carrier structure can also be adjusted as desired in the same way. By fitting differential throttles variable thrust can be obtained on the ejector rams thus enabling adverse release characteristics in pitch to be corrected so that a clean and stable release may be obtained. The ejector rams are housed in the two forged steel ejector ram barrels at the ends of the ERU which also incorporate the crutching arms (sway braces) and the holes for the mounting bolts.

The ERU is exceptionally light and is suitable for installation in aircraft pylons and in multi-store weapon carriers. It can be mounted between side-plates (as in a pylon) or side-mounted on a carrier beam or structure.

Several variants of ERU No 119 have been developed to meet the specific requirements of many customers throughout the world and the basic design permits such variations to be quickly and readily introduced. Among the latest designs is ERU 119TH incorporating a third suspension hook with the result that the particular variant will accept stores with either NATO twin 14-inch (356 mm) suspension, twin 250 mm suspension or single suspension.

CHARACTERISTICS
Overall length: 495 mm
Overall height: 143 mm
Overall width: 44·5 mm – mounting width, sway braces etc protruding
Typical performance
Store weight 952 kg: Ejection velocity 2·4 m/s
Store weight 454 kg: Ejection velocity 3 m/s
Store weight 66 kg: Ejection velocity 8 m/s
Temperature range (without cartridge):
–60 to +150°C
Strength data
ERU 119: (Two-hook variants) depending on type selected
Ultimate hook load: Up to 13 608 kg
Ultimate crutch arm load: Up to 8618 kg
Ultimate yaw movement: Up to 2560 kg/m
Weight: 7·5 – 8·2 kg (with cartridge holders and throttles)
STATUS
Aircraft using the ERUs of the No 119 Series include Alpha Jet, Canberra, CF104, Casa 101, Draken, F104G, FST-2, Gnat, Harrier, Hawk, Hunter, Jaguar, Lightning, Phantom F4F, F4K, and F4M, Strikemaster aircraft, and Lynx and Sea King Commando helicopters. ERU 119 is now in service with over 20 nations.
CONTRACTOR
ML Aviation Co Ltd, White Waltham Aerodrome, Maidenhead, Berkshire SL6 3JG, England.

1993.393
ML EJECTOR RELEASE UNIT No 120

This ERU is provided with two sets of suspension hooks to accommodate stores fitted with bomb lugs at either 14- or 30-inch (35·6 or 76·2 cm) centres. Therefore it can, if necessary, carry the larger stores or multi-weapon carriers. It is suitable for installation in a wing pylon or bomb bay. The positive lock and

release mechanism for both pairs of hooks is mounted between two forged steel ejector ram barrels incorporating crutching arms and mounting holes.

The unit is operated by gas pressure from a central breech containing two cartridges. When fired the rapidly expanding gases are transmitted to an actuator piston which first unlocks the hook

mechanism and thence, via a variable throttle system, to each of the ejector rams which thrust the store off. Readily interchangeable throttles enable the ram characteristics to be adapted to the role.
CHARACTERISTICS
Linear velocity: 15 ft/s on 1000 lb store (4·6 m/s on 454 kg store) with a reaction of 19 000 lb/ft (860 kg)

Temperature range: –60 to +150°C (without cartridge)
Strength data
Max reaction load at 120°C: 22 000 lb/ft (9980 kg)
Ultimate crutch arm load: 50 000 lb/ft (22 700 kg). Normal to 16·5 inches/diameter store (42 cm)

Ultimate hook load 14-inch (35·6 cm) centres: 47 000 lb/ft per hook (21 300 kg)
Ultimate hook load 30-inch (76·2 cm) centres: 58 000 lb/ft per hook (26 300 kg)
Weight: 67½ lb (30·6 kg)

STATUS
In service with, or in production for, Buccaneer and Jaguar aircraft.
CONTRACTOR
ML Aviation Co Ltd, White Waltham Aerodrome, Maidenhead, Berkshire SL6 3JG, England.

4431.393
ML BOMB EJECTOR RACK BRU-36/A AND EJECTOR RELEASE UNIT No 126

The ML BRU-36A has been developed for installation at all seven weapon pylon stations on the McDonnell-Douglas AV-8B development of the V/STOL Harrier. With minor modifications to meet RAF requirements, the BRU is given the British designation of Ejector Release Unit No 126 and will be installed on the British version of the AV-8B known as the Harrier GR Mk 5. The design is based on the proven principles of the ML ERU No 119 (**7513.393**) with a central geometric lock coupling two bomb hooks, but provides a greatly enhanced load carrying capability within stringent weight limits. It will accept a range of stores up to 1045 kg with NATO twin 14-inch (356 mm) suspension manually crutched at four points by fore and aft crutch arms (sway braces). Variable store pitch control is effected by fore and aft self retracting ejector pistons each of which is controlled by the setting of a three-position throttle selected on the ground on-aircraft. An integral ground safety lock is incorporated to eliminate the need for separate safety pins and warning flags. Fuzing units are fitted to provide a store nose and/or tail mechanical arming facility.

A number of design features are included to minimise maintenance and turn round operating costs and allow the BRU to be operated for 180 days before it becomes necessary to remove it from the aircraft for routine maintenance. The most significant of these is the ability to remove all gas-affected moving components for cleaning at 50-shot or 30-day intervals with the BRU remaining fitted to the aircraft. Off-aircraft maintenance times are themselves reduced by the ability to remove and refit the gas system as a complete assembly for routine cleaning without dismantling or disturbance of the mechanical linkages. Likewise the complete electrical assembly including bomb-on-station microswitches can be removed and replaced without linkage disturbance and with no switch adjustment necessary after replacement.

CHARACTERISTICS
Length: 612 mm
Height: 160 mm (from store line)
Width: 215 mm (at crutch arms)
Weight: 12·7 kg
Cartridges: 2 CCU-44B or CERU No 201
Ultimate hook load: 21 795 kg
Ultimate crutch arm load: 16 044 kg
Ultimate yaw movement: 14 445 Nm
Carriage capability
Max store weight: 1045 kg
Max store diameter: 711 mm
Minimum store diameter: 229 mm

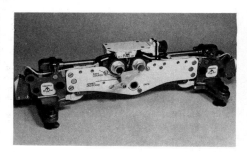

ML Aviation bomb rack unit BRU-36/A, UK designation ERU No 126

Operational temperature range: –40 to +70°C
Typical ejection velocity: 3·05 m/s for 500 kg store with up to 5670 kg reaction and BRU throttle settings of 100%/100%
STATUS
Qualification testing complete and in production for the AV-8B and Harrier GR Mk 5.
CONTRACTOR
ML Aviation Company Limited, White Waltham Aerodrome, Maidenhead, Berkshire SL6 3JG, England.

1681.393
HUNTING HIVOLT CARRIER BOMB LIGHT STORES

The crutchless principle for carriage and release of stores is the basis of a new generation of light stores carriers produced by Hunting Hivolt. The basis is a free fall modular release unit, EMRU No 21, which is so designed that by combining units together three-store carriers, CBLS No 105, and four-store carriers, CBLS No 104, or other combinations can be built up. Provision is made for unit selection, fuzing, and store-on-station indication.

The units are designed for current and future flares, markers, and other light stores of up to 22·7 kg in weight, 914 mm in length, and diameter varying between 77 and 127 mm. They will carry and release, or jettison, stores at all heights up to 4570 metres, at speeds of 0 to 250 knots and function within the temperature range –60 to +90°C.

The EMRU is operated electrically by the same stored energy actuator (SEA) which is used on the

Carrier bomb light stores No 105

EMRU No 22. Stores, for carriage on this unit, need a special lug which is simply attached to existing stores by bands. Four hooks engage with this lug and a spring loaded wedge system provides automatic and progressive take-up of any tolerance in attachment of the store without inhibiting its release.

Loading of stores onto the carrier is quick and simple. The unit is cocked by means of a cocking lever at the rear of the unit; the store is raised against the unit and pressed against a small platform between the hooks which then close over the lug. A safety pin and manual release are provided for use on the ground.

CHARACTERISTICS
EMRU No 21 Mk 1
Length: 290 mm
Width: 168 mm
Depth: 105 mm
Weight: 3·9 kg
Operating voltage: 18 – 28·5 V DC continuous or pulsed (14 ms minimum)
Max store weight: 22·7 kg
Max store size: Length 914 mm, diameter 77 – 127 mm
Operating temperature range: –60 to +90°C
STATUS
In production for UK MoD.
CONTRACTOR
Hunting Hivolt Ltd, Riverbank Works, Old Shoreham Road, Shoreham-by-Sea, Sussex BN4 5FL, England.

1266.393
HUNTING HIVOLT WEAPON RELEASE EQUIPMENT EMRU No 20 Mks 1 to 5

The Hunting Hivolt electromagnetic release units (EMRU) No 20 were designed basically for free fall release and electro-mechanical operation. They are twin hook types with suspension centres at the NATO Standard of 14 inches (356 mm). The normal method of release is through an electrically operated spring stored energy unit, solenoid unit Type 1000, but a cartridge unit Type 2000 can be fitted in its place if cartridge operation is desired.

The system is intrinsically safe and reliable but for some applications an independent bomb release safety lock (BRSL) may be called for. The requirement is met by fitting a Hunting Hivolt actuator MAL 19. When these are fitted, a store-on-station switch is also used to indicate when a weapon is in place.

Two basic types of EMRU No 20 are manufactured; one type having a stainless steel body and the other, a lightweight version, with aluminium alloy body. All units are similar in appearance and have the same dimensions.

In operation, each suspension hook is independently latched thus meeting NATO

CHARACTERISTICS

Release unit designation	EMRU No 20 Mks 1, 2 & 5	EMRU No 20 Mks 3 & 4
Normal store weight	680 kg	454 kg
Ultimate load	22 700 kg	11 350 kg
Body material	Stainless steel	Aluminium alloy
Weight	8 kg (Mk 2)	4·7 kg (Mk 4)
Bomb release safety lock	MAL 19 (Mk 1 only)	MAL 19 (Mk 3 only)
Length		524 mm
Width		71 mm (no BRSL)
Depth	All types	138 mm (no BRSL)
Stores suspension centres		356 mm (14 inch)
Operating voltage range		18 – 28·5 V DC continuous or pulsed (14 ms minimum)
Operating temperature range		–60 to +150°C

requirements. When the unit is cocked the hooks are closed and held so by a linkage mechanism consisting of a system of jointed struts maintained by a sear in a near straight condition. The sear is released by the action of the solenoid or cartridge, the strut system collapses and the hooks open. The possibility of a hang-up is eliminated by positive displacement of a strut joint when the sear is released.

EMRU No 20 Mk 3 fitted with MAL 19 actuator and store-on-station switch

Although basically free fall units, a bolt-on ejector pack has been developed.

STATUS

EMRU No 20 is in production. The Mk 1 and Mk 2 units are used on Nimrod aircraft, while the Mks 3 and 4 are in service on Wessex, Wasp, and Sea King naval helicopters. The Mk 5 is fitted to some Lynx helicopters.

CONTRACTOR

Hunting Hivolt Ltd, Riverbank Works, Old Shoreham Road, Shoreham-by-Sea, Sussex BN4 5FL, England.

1844.393
EMRU No 22

The EMRU No 22 is the first of the new generation of free-fall crutchless release units for the carriage and release of weapons and other stores from aircraft. The unit requires a new type of lug on the weapon and, by providing what is effectively self-adjusting four point suspension, the need for conventional crutches (sway braces) is eliminated. There is an overall weight saving in installation and the loading of stores is easier and quicker.

The EMRU is operated electrically by a well proven spring stored energy actuator (SEA). This is a hermetically sealed device consisting of a spring loaded plunger held, when cocked, in a compressed state by a rotary solenoid operated lock unaffected by mechanical forces and responding only to a specific voltage. Duplication is provided to meet service requirements.

The EMRU No 22 consists of two dual (two tongued) pivoted hooks in a frame controlled by a simple linkage mechanism. The mechanism and SEA

EMRU No 22

are hand-cocked by the use of a simple cocking tool, the weapon is raised to the unit and locked in place, again by simple hand tool. The mechanism is held mechanically in place by a release lever and a safety pin is provided to meet ground safety requirements. Spring loaded wedges in the base of the unit provide automatic and progressive take-up of any tolerance in

the attachment of the store without inhibiting store release in any way.

A bomb release safety lock (BRSL) can be provided within the overall envelope of the unit, if required. This is the Hunting Hivolt actuator MAL 19. The complete equipment has been designed to meet the very difficult environment of naval helicopter operations.

CHARACTERISTICS

Length: 426 mm
Width: 81 mm
Depth: 338 mm
Total weight: 7·75 kg without BRSL; 8·63 kg with BRSL
Operating voltage range: 18 – 28·5 V DC continuous or pulsed (14 ms minimum)
Max store weight: >450 kg
Ambient temperature range: –60 to +90° C

STATUS

In production for UK MoD.

CONTRACTOR

Hunting Hivolt Ltd, Riverbank Works, Old Shoreham Road, Shoreham-by-Sea, Sussex BN4 5FL, England.

1679.393
ML TRIPLE STORE CARRIER

This carrier is mechanically and electrically interchangeable with the American triple ejector rack (TER) currently used on many aircraft throughout the world.

The ML triple store carrier (TSC) is fitted with three ML ERU 119s thus giving improved ejection velocity, pitch control of stores at release, twin cartridge reliability, and increased bomb release speeds. An international range of stores can be carried and released: flares, rocket launchers, and bombs (including the Matra type retarded bombs for which reaction points are provided). Full fuzing is available

for all stores and modern electrical systems are installed.

The MLTSC can either be supplied new or, if desired, be produced by conversion of customer's existing US TERs.

CHARACTERISTICS

Overall length: 1697 mm (66⅘ inches)
Overall height: 383·5 mm (15⅖ inches)
Weight (less stores): 68 kg (150 lb)

STATUS

In production for Phantom and other aircraft.

CONTRACTOR

ML Aviation Co Ltd, White Waltham Aerodrome, Maidenhead, Berkshire SL6 3JG, England.

ML triple stores carrier fitted with three ML ERU 119s

UNITED STATES OF AMERICA

5225.303
UNITED STATES AIRCRAFT ARMAMENT

The range of American aircraft armament is without doubt the most extensive of any nation in the world, and probably the most varied. It includes well over 200 types of bomb, among them conventional free-fall bombs of many weights and sizes, as well as 'cluster' bombs containing sub-munitions of all types. In the following paragraphs certain specific types are described in greater detail, eg Mk 20 cluster bomb (**1998.303**), while in the Analysis section of this volume will be found a comprehensive table (**1850.314**) listing more than 300 types of air-deliverable munitions produced in the USA. Elsewhere in this book there are other entries dealing with related aspects such as the use of add-on guidance packages to convert conventional 'iron' or 'dumb' bombs into guided weapons, or 'smart' bombs (**1597.311**), HOBO (EO) and laser-guided smart bombs, Paveway laser-guided bombs (**1534.311**), and Paveway air-to-ground weapon delivery systems (**1533.311**) in the Systems section.

The American inventory of air-deliverable weapons includes free-fall nuclear bombs which may be capable of both tactical and strategic use, and these also are listed in the table. Additional details of these and other payloads in the strategic context will be found in appropriate entries in the Systems section dealing with US strategic weapon systems.

Another type of aircraft-carried munitions dealt with in other parts of *Jane's Weapon Systems* are those used for anti-submarine warfare, eg mines and depth charges.

US airborne munitions have been widely supplied to foreign nations, and therefore can be found in the inventories of many countries; for this reason, and because of the long period over which such supplies

General Dynamics F-16 with Mk 82 (500 lb) bombs

General Dynamics F-111 with B-61 nuclear weapons

may have been delivered, no attempt has been made to compile extensive lists of users.

1847.303
FUEL-AIR EXPLOSIVE WEAPONS

Each of the arms of the US forces, Army, Air Force, Navy, and Marine Corps, is pursuing its own programme of research and development of fuel-air explosive (FAE) munitions of varying types and sizes for differing operational roles. The basic principle consists of creating an aerosol cloud of a fuel-air mixture which is then detonated to achieve an explosive effect as compared with the fire effect of napalm. Specific areas of R and D are concerned with such aspects as ensuring consistency in the size and mixture of the aerosol, means of delivery, and precise control of detonation.

The operation of weapons of this category, and various ingredients employed to form the explosive mixtures, were described in greater detail under this entry number in earlier editions of *Jane's Weapon Systems*.

Both helicopter launched and high-speed aircraft compatible weapons are being studied, and surface-launched FAE weapons also have been tested.

CBU-55B

This weapon was used to a relatively limited extent in Viet-Nam by the USN, mostly for defoliation and mine clearance, and is a free-fall cluster-bomb munition. It was deployed on both helicopters and low speed range fixed-wing aircraft. The CBU-55B is in the 500 lb (226 kg) class and each bomb has three 100 lb (45 kg) canisters 53 cm long and 35 cm in diameter. Each canister contains about 72 lb (33 kg) of fuel, and after release from the aircraft the individual canisters separate and are retarded by drogue parachutes as they approach the target. The cloud of fuel/air mixture produced is about 15 m in diameter and 2·4 m thick, and blast overpressures of up to 300 psi (210 kg/cm²) are reported.

The US Army is interested in adapting one of the CBU-55B bomblets, the Blue 73 FAE warhead, as the basis of a surface-to-surface FAE weapon for clearing minefields. The vehicle used is the Zuni rocket, a number of which are ripple-fired from a truck-mounted launcher rack. A modified FAU-83 standard mechanical fuze is used to produce varying delays in deployment of the warhead parachutes to achieve an area coverage pattern of FAE detonations.

CBU-72

The CBU-72 resulted from USN modifications to the CBU-55B to suit it for dropping from high-speed jet aircraft. Specific types with which the CBU-72 was used successfully were the A-4 and A-7. Drogue parachutes to retard the individual canisters were retained and the development of FAE weapons for use with high-speed aircraft, and without parachutes, is a separate project.

OV-10 Bronco aircraft armed with four Marceye bombs (FMU 56 A/B fuze in nose of each is protected during ground handling with removable cover) and two 0·30 inch M60 machine-guns in each 'sponson' (US Navy)

FAESHED

FAESHED (fuel air explosive helicopter delivered) is a mine (land) neutralisation system designed for low intensity conflicts where air superiority is maintained. The technique uses the standard USN CBU-55 FAE munition and standard Army helicopter stores racks and bomb racks. The only non-standard item is the fire control box. This is a US Army project, and another carried by the same agency was **SLUFAE** (surface launched unit FAE). This consists of a mobile platform carrying an array of 30 launch tubes which can be ripple-fired to produce a path through a minefield by the detonation effects of the FAE warheads. It can be fired from a 600 m stand-off position behind the forward edge of battle area.

Tests of 155 FAE warheads against over 4000 mines of US, British, French, Soviet, Italian, and North Vietnamese origin produced 100 per cent kill radii of 8·8 m for pressure-fuzed mines and 25·9 m for pull-fuzed trip-wired mines. The latest types of American and other land mines with complex, long impulse and double impulse fuzes, including hydraulic long impulse fuzes, seismic/infra-red, electronic and magnetic influence fuzes have been detonated successfully or neutralised by FAE blast effects.

MAD FAE

The USMC has its own programme for the development of a helicopter-deployed fuel/air explosion system, known as Mass Air Delivery FAE. Aluminium dispenser racks, each holding 12 FAE warheads weighing 136 lb (61·7 kg) each, are hooked to a helicopter's freight hook. Stabilising surfaces are provided to prevent twisting or oscillation of the racks. Single or salvo release of the FAE bombs is possible. Tests have been carried out with CH-46, CH-53, and UH-1 helicopters.

DEVELOPMENT

USN design work on FAE weapons under a government Research, Development, Test, and Evaluation programme began in 1966 at China Lake, but this was pre-dated by some six years when the USN exploded its first FAE device at the same site. Navy interest continued from then until the formal programme of 1966. By 1967 there was also USAF and USMC activity, the former service carrying out tests of a 2500 lb (1134 kg) weapon developed under the **Pave Pat** programme. Two versions evolved, Blue 72 and Blue 76 for dropping by A-1 and F-4 aircraft types, respectively. However, parachute retarding techniques prevented attainment of the required accuracy. The Blue 73 canister used in the CBU-55B had its origins as a ground deployment weapon, when in 1976 they were placed at the edges of minefields and then detonated by remote control for mine clearance. The first USN air-dropped operational FAE weapons (500 lb/226 kg class) were ready in October 1970 and were deployed in Viet-Nam.

4599.303
ROCKEYE II MK 20 CLUSTER BOMB

The Rockeye Mk 20 cluster bomb is an unguided free fall weapon, delivered in the same manner as a conventional bomb, for use with all bomb rack configurations. Rockeye dispenses 247 dual-purpose armour-piercing shaped charge bomblets, which are distributed over a variable attack area. Since precise aiming is not required, the pilot need maintain delivery attitude for only a short duration prior to release of the bomb, thereby reducing the aircraft's vulnerability to ground defences and improving pilot safety.

The MK 339 dispenser opening fuze provides pilot options for dispenser opening delay, provides safe separation from the aircraft prior to arming, and initiates a linear shaped charge which splits open the container. The bomblet fuze discriminates between soft and hard targets, detonates the bomblet, and provides additional safety for pilot and aircraft.

Rockeye is smaller and lighter but contains more net explosives than similar cluster bombs, and its smaller size and weight permit as much as 800 lbs more fuel per mission according to the weapon's manufacturer, thus considerably increasing aircraft range and endurance.

No special storage facilities of handling equipment are required, and no periodic maintenance is necessary. The store is delivered ready to fly and service life exceeds 20 years it is claimed. Only visual inspection is needed before flight.

OPERATION

Delivery is literally the same as that for a conventional

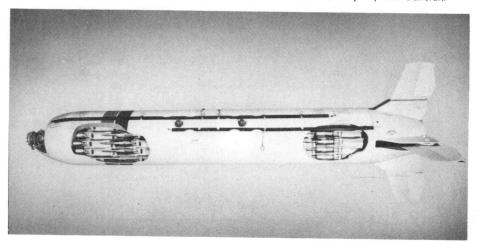

Cutaway Rockeye II cluster bomb, showing internally stowed bomblets

Rockeye II Mk 20 cluster bomb loaded onto aircraft

500 lb bomb. The sizes and shapes of impact areas can be changed according to aircraft speed, altitude, dive angle and the dispenser opening delay time. In heavily defended target areas, Rockeye can be delivered at high speeds and at altitudes as low as 30 metres pitch up or 76 metres in level flight.

CHARACTERISTICS
Length: 2·33 m (without fuze cover); 2·4 m (with fuze cover)
Diameter: 335 mm
Fin span: 437 mm (closed)
Lug spacing: 355 mm
Centre of balance: 165 mm (fwd of aft lug)
Weight: 222 kg (assembled)

Explosive payload of bomb cluster: 45·3 kg
Bomblet weight: 151·5 kg (total)
Release altitude: 76 m (minimum in level pitch); 30 m (minimum pitch up)
Typical bomblet impact pattern: 2700 m² (released from 152 m)
STATUS
Operational, entered service in early 1970s. In use by US forces and more than ten other countries throughout the world. Modern tactical aircraft that have carried Rockeye include: A-4, A-6, A-7, A-10, F-4, F-5, F-8, F-15, F-16, Mirage, Jaguar, and Hawk.

ISC is the main international contractor for Rockeye, and assumes total responsibility for the supply of all contracted goods and services.

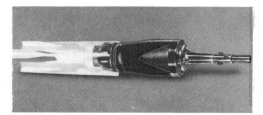

Single dual-purpose Rockeye II bomblet

CONTRACTOR
ISC Technologies Inc, Lancaster, Pennsylvania, USA.

1996.303
GAU-8/A 30 mm GUN SYSTEM

The GAU-8/A 30 mm gun system is designed to provide a cost-effective weapon to engage the full array of ground targets encountered in the close air support role. The system has an ammunition capacity of 1174 rounds and weighs 1723 kg when fully loaded. Aluminium cased ammunition with either armour piercing incendiary, HE incendiary, or target practice projectiles can be fired at either 2000 or 4000 shots per minute. Ammunition for the GAU-8 weapon is manufactured by the Aerojet Ordnance and Manufacturing Company of Downey, California and Honeywell Inc of Hopkins, Minnesota. The family consists of the following rounds: armour piercing incendiary (API), high explosive incendiary (HEI) and training practice (TP). The API round has a lightweight body which contains a sub-calibre high-density penetrator of depleted uranium. In addition to its penetration capability, depleted uranium is a naturally pyrophoric material which enhances incendiary effects. The HEI round employs a standard M505 fuze and explosive mixture with a body of naturally fragmenting material that is effective against lighter vehicle and material targets. The TP projectile simulates the exterior ballistics and provides a ballistic match to the HEI and is used for pilot training and gunnery practice. Development of the aluminium

alloy case material instead of the conventional brass or steel resulted in a 272 kg reduction in weight of a fully loaded system. The GAU-8/A gun system is composed of three major sub-systems: gun, feed system, and drive system.

The gun is an externally-powered, Gatling-type mechanism. Each of the gun's seven barrels fires only once during each revolution of the barrel cluster. Barrels are attached to the gun rotor by quick release interrupted lugs. The gun rotor is journalled within a stationary housing and contains the seven gun bolts. The bolts slide fore and aft on tracks and provide the ram, lock, fire, unlock, and extracting functions. The stationary outer housing contains a cam which drives the bolts through their respective functions. The GAU-8/A uses a rotary-lock bolt which provides ample locking area and support for the high pressure, aluminium cased 30 mm ammunition. The gun design features a three-shaft transfer unit which transfers rounds coming from the feed system into the gun rotor.

A new reverse clearing technique is used to clear ammunition from the gun after each burst. An electro/hydraulic drive system controls the clearing function and assures consistent positioning of the first live round on the feed side of the gun. Live rounds which have cycled into the weapon but have not yet fired at trigger release are returned to the feed side of

the gun in less than one second ready to fire at the next trigger application.

The GAU-8/A gun system is driven by hydraulic drives operating off the aircraft hydraulic system. Dual motors are employed operating from independent hydraulic systems. Only one motor is energised to fire the system at half rate. The hydraulic drive units include controls for the two firing rates and the reverse clearing function.

A linkless ammunition feed system is used to store and feed ammunition. Spent cartridge cases and any unfired rounds are returned to the storage drum after passing through the gun.

The major components are the cylindrical drum unit in which the ammunition is stored; the exit unit which removes rounds from the drum unit and inserts them into an endless conveyor belt; the conveyor system comprising the conveyor belt and the chuting through which it moves; the transfer unit which removes rounds from the gun end of the conveyor belt, feeds them into the gun, and re-inserts the spent cartridge cases into the belt for return to the storage drum; and the entrance unit which transfers cases from the conveyor system back into the drum unit. Each round and case is in smooth, continuous motion when the system is feeding and the gun is firing.

CHARACTERISTICS
Firing rate: 2100/4200 rounds/minute
Length: 6400 mm
Weight: 1723 kg
Ammunition capacity: 1174 rounds
Power requirements: 77 hp
Muzzle velocity: 1066 m/s
Barrel life: 20 000 rounds (minimum)
Time to rate: 0·55 s
Dispersion: 5 mil
STATUS
Operational testing at Nellis AFB has verified its ability to defeat medium tanks. Over eight million rounds have been fired. The General Electric Company has delivered more than 600 for the A-10 close air support aircraft.
CONTRACTOR
General Electric Company, Armament and Electrical Systems Department, Lakeside Avenue, Burlington, Vermont 05402, USA.

General Electric GAU-8/A 30 mm gun system

4061.303
GAU-12/U EQUALISER 25 mm AUTOMATIC GUN

General Electric's 25 mm five-barrel Gatling gun (GAU-12/U Equaliser) was designed making full use of the technology developed and proved on the GAU-8/A 30 mm gun programme. High rate of fire, combined with high muzzle velocity and excellent ballistics of the 25 mm round, make it a candidate for numerous applications in either air-to-air, air-to-ground, or ground-to-air roles.

The outstanding terminal ballistics are attributable to the standard 25 mm round of ammunition. This round produces a muzzle velocity of 1097 metres per second which, when combined with the rate of fire of up to 4200 rounds/minute, makes the GAU-12/U Equaliser extremely effective for a variety of combat missions.

The lightweight (122 kg) externally powered weapon features reverse clearing, a 20 000-round maintenance cycle, and an MRBF of 15 000 rounds. Although providing much more effective firepower than the 20 mm Vulcan, the GAU-12/U Equaliser is similar in size and power requirements to the 20 mm.

The standard 25 mm round family includes TP, HEI and APDS rounds with steel cases and percussion primers. In addition, a full-bore API round has been developed for use in high performance aircraft.

CHARACTERISTICS
Type: 5-barrel Gatling, 25 mm
Length: 2134 mm
Max diameter: 279 mm
Weight: 122 kg
Power to drive: 10·4 kW
Ammunition: Standard 25 mm (TP, HEI, APDS)
Muzzle velocity: 1097 m/s HEI
Dispersion: 6 mil (80% of rounds fired)
Rate of fire: Variable up to 4200 rounds/minute
Time to rate: 0·4 s
Drive type: Externally powered
Feed system: Linkless or linked
Clearing: Gun reversal
Recoil force
Peak max: 9000 lb (40 kN)
Peak recurrent: 8000 lb (36 kN)
Average at 3600 rounds/minute: 4000 lb (18 kN)

General Electric GAU-12/U Equaliser 25 mm automatic gun and ammunition

STATUS
In production and in US Marine Corps service.
CONTRACTOR
General Electric Company, Armament and Electrical Systems Department, Lakeside Avenue, Burlington, Vermont 05402, USA.

3891.303

GAU-13/A 30 mm LIGHTWEIGHT GUN

The GAU-13/A 30 mm lightweight aircraft gun is a four-barrel, Gatling design, which although based on the General Electric GAU-8/A seven-barrel gun (**1996.303**), incorporates a number of innovations to improve serviceability and reduce overall weight while retaining comparable ballistic performance. With a firing rate of 2400 rounds/minute, the GAU-13/A employs the same reverse clearing operation as the GAU-8/A. The gun is suitable for internal or external mounting on an aircraft, and GE has developed a special pod to house the GAU-13/A.

GPU-5/A

The GPU-5/A is a compact external store incorporating the GAU-13/A 30 mm four-barrel gun to provide a significant anti-armour capability for attack or fighter aircraft. The pod can be used with a wide variety of aircraft types such as the F-4, F-5, A-7, F-15, F-16, A-4, A-10 and F-18. The main components are the GAU-13/A gun, a helical ammunition feed system which surrounds the gun, a self-contained pneumatic drive, and a supporting structural assembly. The ammunition feed has space for 350 rounds, enough air capacity to fire two full complements of ammunition, and the only power required from the aircraft is 7·5 A of 28 V DC or 115 V AC, 400 Hz, 300 W. The support structure can be configured for use as either a standard 30-inch (762 mm) rack fitting or as an adaptor for direct mounting on specific aircraft.

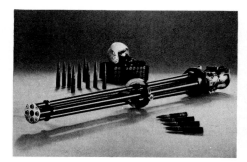

New four-barrel GAU-13/A Gatling 30 mm lightweight gun with GAU-8/A range of ammunition

GPU-5/A lightweight 30 mm gun pod on wing station of USAF A-7 aircraft.

CHARACTERISTICS
Gun: GAU-13/A (4-barrel)
Calibre: 30 mm
Length: 2794 mm
Max diameter: 304 mm
Ammunition: GAU-8/A TP, HEI, API
Rate of fire: Up to 3000 rounds/minute
MV: 1037 m/s TP/HEI; 987 m/s API
Gun life: 250 000 rounds
Pod: GPU-5/A
Length: 4320 mm
Diameter: 610 mm
Weight: 862 kg (loaded); 621 kg (empty)
Ammunition capacity: 353 rounds

STATUS
In production and in USAF service.

GPU-5/A has been successfully flight-tested against ground targets on the Northrop F-5, the Vought A-7, and the McDonnell Douglas F-4E and F-15.

CONTRACTOR
General Electric Company, Armament and Electrical Systems Department, Lakeside Avenue, Burlington, Vermont 05402, USA.

1678.303

GPU-2/A 20 mm LIGHTWEIGHT GUN POD

The GPU-2/A 20 mm pod is a lightweight self-contained gun system requiring only a trigger signal from the aircraft. This pod can be mounted on a wide variety of existing helicopters and fixed-wing aircraft by using standard suspension racks. The total system weight when loaded with 300 rounds is less than 600 lb (272 kg).

General Electric Company has designed and produced a quantity of GPU-2/A pods for the USN. These systems use the three-barrel M197, 20 mm gun which has been in military inventory since 1969. The firing rate for the GPU-2/A is selected at either 750 or 1500 shots per minute. Rounds are fed to the gun through a linkless ammunition storage and feed system. This system maintains positive round control throughout all storage and feed operations.

The design concept of this system has been proven by combat experience with the SUU-11/A mini-gun pods. Power for the system is provided by a 32 V DC rechargeable nickel-cadmium battery located in the aft section. This battery will fire up to three ammunition complements without a recharge. If the aircraft has sufficient power available, provision is made to trickle charge during operation of the aircraft.

The pod can be loaded with ammunition while suspended from the aircraft. The storage drum is made accessible by simply removing the aft fairing. A belt of ammunition is attached to a loader mechanism which strips the links and feeds rounds into the storage drum in the proper attitude.

The first maintenance required for the GPU-2/A is at 15 000 rounds. At this time the front track bolts on the gun rotor are re-torqued. Barrel life is 15 000 rounds; however, the barrels can be changed within two minutes while the pod is still suspended from the

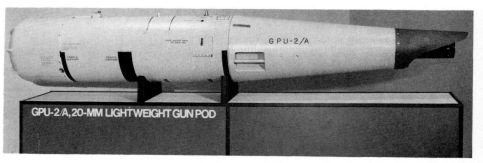

GPU-2/A 20 mm lightweight gun pod

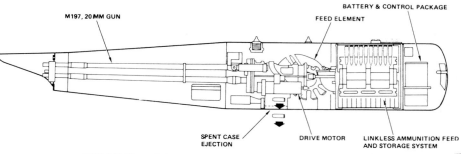

GPU-2/A 20 mm lightweight gun pod mechanical arrangement diagram

aircraft. No special tools are required for maintenance.

CHARACTERISTICS
Weight: Approx 270 kg
Length: 304 cm
Diameter: 48 cm
Ammunition capacity: 300 rounds

Rate(s) of fire: 750 or 1500 rounds/minute
Gun: 20 mm M197

CONTRACTOR
General Electric Company, Armament and Electrical Systems Department, Lakeside Avenue, Burlington, Vermont 05402, USA.

4434.303

GPU-5/A LIGHTWEIGHT 30 mm GUN POD

The GPU-5/A is a lightweight 30 mm gun pod with a high rate of fire developed to destroy heavy armour and a wide variety of mobile and fixed targets at extended ranges. It is adaptable to many fighter and attack aircraft, weighs about 862 kg when loaded, and is completely self-contained.

The system comprises the newly developed GAU-13/A 30 mm four-barrel Gatling gun (**3891.303**), a helical closed loop ammunition feed system, a self-contained pneumatic drive with microprocessor controls, and a strongback and structural assembly. The linkless ammunition feed system holds 353 rounds in two helical layers of ammunition carriers surrounding the gun and extensive use is made of

fibre reinforced plastics to save further weight. The pneumatic drive uses a reversible turbine capable of generating 60 hp at 9000 rpm and sufficient air is stored for two outfits of ammunition to be fired in one-second bursts.

The primary structural component is the strongback which is a one-piece aluminium housing used to mount the pod to the aircraft with the recoil adaptors mounted inside it and connected by linkage to the gun. The skin of the pod is made of aircraft-type structural aluminium honeycomb and the entire pod is designed to be capable of withstanding supersonic flight speeds.

CHARACTERISTICS
Gun: GAU-13/U 4-barrel Gatling
Calibre: 30 mm

GPU-5/A lightweight 30 mm gun pod

Rate of fire: 2400 rounds/minute
Ammunition capacity: 353 rounds
Length: 4·3 m
Height: Approx 610 mm
Weight (loaded): 862 kg
Weight (empty): 621 kg
Power requirements: 115 V, 400 Hz, 300 W, 3-phase
or 28 V DC, 210 W

STATUS
In production and in service with USAF. Can be
installed on wing or centre body stations of a variety
of tactical aircraft including the A-4, A-7, AV-8B, F-4,
F-5, F-15, F-16, F-18, A-10, and OV-10.

CONTRACTOR
General Electric Company, Armament and Electrical
Systems Department, Lakeside Avenue, Burlington,
Vermont 05402, USA.

4433.303
AV-8 HARRIER 25 mm ARMAMENT SYSTEM
The AV-8 armament system is a lightweight 25 mm
gun system with a high rate of fire designed to provide
an effective air-to-air and air-to-ground attack
capability. It was developed for the USN and is based
on the GAU-12/U gun.

The GAU-12/U gun is a five-barrel Gatling type
which is similar in overall dimensions to the M61A1
Vulcan gun (**5547.103**) and fires the Bushmaster
family of ammunition which includes practice, HE
incendiary and armour piercing discarding sabot
ammunition and is also compatible with European-
made 25 mm ammunition. A full-bore armour

piercing incendiary round has been developed as a
part of the AV-8 armament contract.

The system consists of two pod-like structures
bolted to the bottom of the left and right of the aircraft.
The pod on the left contains the GAU-12/U gun, blast
deflector and drive mechanism. That on the right
contains a compact 300-round linear linkless feed
system. A cross-over fairing connects the two pods
and contains the ammunition chuting and drive shaft.
The pneumatic drive employs a rotary drive motor
turning at 9000 rpm and developing 35 hp. The
production version uses bleed-air from the aircraft
engine. Gun recoil forces are transferred directly to
the left forward aircraft mounting points.
CHARACTERISTICS
Gun: GAU-12/U
Calibre: 25 mm
Muzzle velocity: 1036 – 1065 m/s depending on
ammunition used
Rate of fire: 3600 rounds/minute
Ammunition capacity: 300 rounds
Weight
Gun: 125 kg
System (loaded): 558· 4 kg
System (empty): 408·6 kg
Power requirements: 28 V DC 15 A max
STATUS
In production for the USN.
CONTRACTOR
General Electric Company, Armament and Electrical
Systems Department, Lakeside Avenue, Burlington,
Vermont 05402, USA.

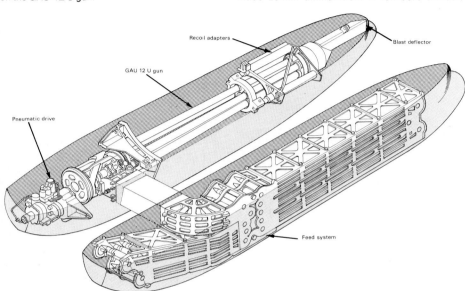

Internal arrangement of AV-8 Harrier armament system

1287.303
VULCAN GUN PODS SUU 16/A AND SUU 23/A
These gun pods are of identical size and weight and
both incorporate six-barrel Vulcan 20 mm cannon
and ammunition. Designed for installation on
standard external store pylons, these pods provide a
ready means of greatly increasing the cannon fire
power of subsonic and supersonic fighter and ground
attack aircraft. The pod mounted Vulcan gun is
particularly well suited to the engagement of ground
targets from ranges of 700 m or more. The pods are of
aerodynamic shape and attachment to the aircraft is
by bomb lugs at standard 760 mm (30-inch) centres.

Both pods are of similar internal layout, a
cylindrical ammunition drum containing 1200 rounds
occupying the rear portion of the pod. A linkless feed
system couples this to the gun.

The pods differ in the type of Vulcan gun fitted but

their performance and hitting power are identical. In
the earlier SUU 16/A design the cannon is the
standard M61A1 mechanically driven by a ram air
turbine. This turbine is mounted on a hinged skin
panel of the pod and is lowered into the airstream
prior to firing. The use of a ram air turbine restricts the
rate of fire at aircraft speeds below 350 knots
(650 km/h). A further consequence of the turbine is
that pod drag is somewhat greater than for the
SUU 23/A pod in which a self-powered GAU-4 model
Vulcan is used. For initial rotation of the GAU-4 gun in
the SUU 23/A pod an electric inertia starter is
provided.

In operation Vulcan gun pods are aimed using a
gunsight or fire control system. During firing spent
cartridge cases are ejected overboard and not
retained. The gun is cleared automatically after the
firing button has been released so that 'cook-off' is

eliminated. During the clearing process a small
number of live rounds are ejected.

A number of accessories are available to simplify
loading, maintenance, and testing of the pods.
CHARACTERISTICS

	SUU 16/A	SUU 23/A
Length	5·05 m	
Diameter	560 mm	
Weight with 1200 rounds	780 kg	785 kg
Weight empty	484 kg	489 kg
Boresight adjustment elevation	±1°	±1°
Azimuth	±0·5°	±1°
Accuracy	80% shots inside 8 mil	
Rate of fire	6000 rounds/minute	
Ammunition	20 mm M 50 series	
Power input from aircraft at 208 V 400 Hz 3 phase	7 A	10 A
at 28 V DC	—	3 A

STATUS
Both SUU 16/A and 23/A pods are in service with US
forces. They are compatible with a wide range of
tactical aircraft including F-100, F-105, F-4, A-4D, and
F-111. The SUU 23/A pod is in service on Royal Air
Force McDonnell Douglas Phantoms.
CONTRACTOR
General Electric Company, Armament and Electrical
Systems Department, Lakeside Avenue, Burlington,
Vermont 05402, USA.

SUU 23/A Vulcan 20 mm gun pod

1270.303
**GENERAL ELECTRIC VULCAN 20 mm AIRCRAFT
GUN AND LINKLESS FEED SYSTEM**
The General Electric M61A1 Vulcan aircraft cannon is
of 20 mm calibre and employs the multi-barrel
principle first used by Dr Gatling. The Vulcan is the
standard USAF aircraft gun and is increasingly being
used by the USN.

The gun has a rotary action and in the M61A1 is
externally powered from the aircraft hydraulic or

electric supply. A self-powered version, the GAU 4 is
similar in all respects except that barrel rotation and
operation of the action is derived from gun gas bled
from four of the six barrels.

The outstanding features of the Vulcan are its high
rate of fire, normally 6000 rounds per minute, the high
muzzle velocity of about 1036 m/s and its exceptional
reliability in comparison with more conventional
weapons.

Ammunition linked into belts has been used with

Vulcan guns but feed reliability was poor at the high
rates of fire characteristic of the weapon. There are
also problems of link disposal. For these reasons in
the majority of applications Vulcan cannon are
associated with a linkless feed system. There are
considerable variations in the detailed layout of gun
and feed systems in service as each is tailored to the
particular requirements of the aircraft installation.
The essential elements are the M61A1 or GAU 4 gun,
the linkless feed ammunition chutes which contain

the ammunition conveyor, the cylindrical ammunition canister, and the drive power coupling between the gun and the ammunition drum.

The Vulcan gun has six rifled barrels and is externally powered. All barrels are rigidly clamped together and attached to the forward end of the breech rotor which rotates in a stationary housing. The rotor revolves anti-clockwise looking in the direction of fire. Cam followers operate the bolt for each barrel successively chambering, firing, and extracting the rounds as the gun rotates. The linear actions needed for these operations are imparted to the followers by an elliptical slot machined in the rotor housing.

The multi-barrel design gives long weapon life by reducing heat dissipation and barrel erosion. A variety of barrel muzzle clamps are available to give different shot dispersion patterns. When the minimum dispersion clamp is in use 80 per cent of shots are within an eight mil cone.

Standard M50 series electrically primed ammunition is used which is available in a variety of types: incendiary, armour piercing with and without tracer etc.

In the self-powered variant, the GAU 4, gun gas is bled from four of the six barrels to operate the mechanism by means of a gas piston and drive which is mounted between the barrels ahead of the gun action. The GAU 4 develops sufficient power to operate the feed system. The gun is initiated by an electrically operated inertia starter.

Linkless Feed System

The linkless feed ammunition drum may be tailored to meet specific ammunition capacity requirements or to fit a specific envelope. Linking the drum to the gun is a single or twin ammunition conveyor belt contained in flexible chuting. With a single conveyor belt the spent cases are ejected overboard, but in many installations a return conveyor for spent cartridge cases is provided.

The ammunition drum carries the rounds stored between radial partitions. A central rotor in the form of a helical archimedean screw then moves the rounds from the drum into the conveyor in a multistage operation.

Many accessories are available for loading and maintaining Vulcan cannon and their feed systems.

CHARACTERISTICS

The self-powered GAU 4 variant of the basic M61A1 Vulcan cannon has virtually identical performance and characteristics, except that it is approximately 5 kg heavier.

Calibre: 20 mm
Weight: 120 kg
Length: 1875 mm

Linkless ammunition feed system and 20 mm M61A1 Vulcan gun for F-4E aircraft

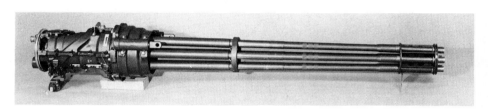

20 mm M61A1 Vulcan gun

Recoil travel: +6 mm
Average recoil force: 1810 kg
Max rate of fire: 6600 rounds/minute
Time to max rate: 0·3 s
Stopping time: 0·5 s
Ammunition: M53, M55AZ, M56A3 etc
Muzzle velocity: 1036 m/s
Round weight: 0·25 kg
Projectile weight: 0·1 kg
20 mm Linkless Feed System

The exact specification for the 20 mm linkless feed depends upon aircraft design considerations. The data below relate to the installation on the LTV A-7D aircraft which is typical:

Ammunition capacity: 1020 rounds
Firing rate: 6000 or 4000 rounds/minute
Ammunition weight: 114 kg

Feed system weight (less ammunition): 190 kg
Drive system: Shaft coupling to gun hydraulic motor
System type: Double ended – cases retained in drum
Total ammunition chuting length: 4·57 m
STATUS

The M61A1 and GAU 4 20 mm Vulcan guns with their associated linkless feed systems are in service with the USAF, the Royal Air Force, and with other air forces operating F-104 and F-4 aircraft. The weapon and its associated feed are in service on A-7, F-104, F-111, F-105, F-14, F-15, F-16, F-18 and other aircraft. Podded installations are also available and are in service.

CONTRACTOR

General Electric Company, Armament and Electrical Systems Department, Lakeside Avenue, Burlington, Vermont 05402, USA.

1118.303

M35 ARMAMENT SUB-SYSTEM

The XM35 is a fixed mounted armament sub-system located under the left weapon sponson on an AH-1G helicopter. The system carries one 20 mm automatic gun XM195, a Vulcan type with six barrels. This is a modified M61A1 gun with blast deflectors on the end of 102·6 cm barrels. The 20 mm ammunition is linkfed to the right side of the gun from ammunition containers mounted on the left and right sides of the

helicopter outside the aircraft. The weight of the system with ammunition is 530 kg; without ammunition 245 kg. The system carries approximately 950 rounds of ammunition with a firing rate of 750 ± 100 rounds/minute. The 30 mm cannon has a maximum effective range of 3500 m. The sight used is an XM73 reflex type.

DEVELOPMENT

The XM35 system was developed by the US Army Weapons Command and the General Electric

Company. A production contract was awarded to the General Electric Company in 1968.

STATUS

US forces.

CONTRACTOR

General Electric Company, Armament and Electrical Systems Department, Lakeside Avenue, Burlington, Vermont 05402, USA.

1182.303

Mk 4 MOD 0 GUN POD

The Mk 4 Mod 0 pod is a self-contained and self-powered 20 mm gun system. The pod contains a twin-barrelled 20 mm Mk 11 Mod 5 gun. The container is a low-drag cylindrical shape with detachable nose and tail cones, designed for supersonic flight in fighter and attack type jet and propeller aircraft. Belted ammunition is carried forward from the rotary magazine through dual feed chutes. Expended cases and links are ejected downward from the bottom of the pod at a velocity of 23 m. A salient feature of the gun pod is the instantaneous full rate-of-fire. The pod is equipped with mounting provisions for both 30- and 14-inch (762 and 356 mm) suspension systems and is normally attached to the aircraft on a standard ejector rack such as the Aero 7A, Aero 27, MAU 9A/A etc.

CHARACTERISTICS

Primary kill mechanism: Blast fragments, or

Hughes Mk 4 gun pod

penetration (depending on whether HEI or API ammunition is used)

Weapon type: Anti-material and anti-personnel
Payload fuzing: Contact
Range: 950 m
Firing rate: 700 or 4200 rounds/minute
Delivery: Strafe
Weight
Total, loaded: 630 kg
Total, empty: 357 kg
Payload (750 rounds): 269 kg
OPERATION

The Mk 4 gun pod is aimed with either a fixed sight or a fire control system. It is fired by pressing the control stick trigger. Gun reaction time is instantaneous.

Delivery is normally made in a shallow dive of 5 to 30°. Slant range for a 'point' target should be 900 m or less. Area targets may be profitably attacked from a longer range because accuracy is not of primary importance. Normally delivery speed is 400 knots but may be at any speed within the performance limits of the aircraft.
STATUS

The Mk 4 gun pod has been flown and fired from the following aircraft: A-4 (1, 2, and 3 pods), F-4 (1 and 3 pods), A-7 (1 and 2 pods), A-6 (1, 2, 3, and 4 pods), OV-10A (1 pod), F-100 (1 and 2 pods), H-34 (1 pod).

The first production pod was delivered in August 1965, and by that time more than $12 million had been expended on development at Hughes and about one

million rounds of 20 mm TP ammunition had been fired. The first USN production contract was for 347 pods and this was closely followed in June 1965 by another for a further 482 pods. The last deliveries were made in October 1967 but Hughes continued active in-service development and support under later USN contracts.

Active service on USN and USMC A-4, F-4, and OV-10 aircraft took place in SE Asia, and a number of pods were transferred to the Israeli Air Force with which service they were used on A-4 aircraft.
CONTRACTOR

Hughes Helicopters Inc, Culver City, California 90230, USA.

1183.303
Mk 11 MOD 5 GUN

This weapon is intended for aircraft air-to-ground, air-to-air and ground vehicle installation. Each installation consists of a 20 mm Mk 11 Mod 5 gun mechanism and a Mk 2 Mod 1 loader. The gun mechanism consists of the following major components: receiver assembly, breech assembly, revolver cylinder assembly, and one Mk 19 Mod 3 and Mk 20 Mod 3 barrel.

The Mk 11 Mod 5 gun is a twin-barrel, air-cooled, belt-fed, combination gun-gas and recoil-operated automatic weapon firing electrically primed ammunition from an eight-chamber revolver cylinder. The gun is fed by two belts of Mk 6 links which enter the mechanism on opposite sides of the loader. Belts are simultaneously advanced by a single sprocket within the loader which is driven by the revolver cylinder shaft. The mechanism simultaneously rams two cartridges, fires two cartridges, and ejects two cases which are relinked and ejected from the gun at approximately 30 m/s.
CHARACTERISTICS

Gun length: 199 cm (with loader); 179 cm (without loader)
Gun weight
Gun mechanism: 65·3 kg
Barrels: 23·1 kg
Loader: 20·4 kg
Rate of fire: 4200 or 700 rounds/minute (other rates available)
Time to rate: Instantaneous (0·003 s)
Chamber pressure: 4·077 kg/cm²

Mk 11 Mod 5 20 mm gun

System of operation: Recoil gun-gas boosted
System of locking: Fixed breech revolver principle
System of feeding: Self-feeding through gun-driven sprockets
Method of loading: Gun-gas powered dual rammers
Location of feed opening: Left and right side of loader, 2 belts (top and bottom feed optional)
Location of ejection opening: Rear of loader, 2 openings
Method of charging: Integral, air operated valve
Method of cooling: Air
Recoil distance: 28·5 mm
Distance between barrels: 104·7 mm
Number of chambers in revolver: 8
Belt velocity, average: 1·5 m/s (each belt)
Ignition system: 120 V, 400 Hz
Barrel length: 143·5 cm
Actual length: 143·5 cm
Effective length: 161·3 cm (including revolver)
Barrel removal: Quick disconnect lever, 60° interrupted threads

Rifling
Barrel: None (smoothbore system)
Revolver: 8 rifled, replaceable inserts
Number of grooves: 9
Twist: 26°, right hand
Recoil
Average: 1134 kg
Peak: Recoil 3628 kg; counter-recoil 2268 kg
Ammunition: 20 mm Mk 100 series; 20 mm Mk 50 series
STATUS

Developed for USN as part of the Mk 4 gun pod programme (see **1182.303**, above). Although demonstrated successfully as an internally fitted aircraft gun in the F-8, the Mk 1 gun has only seen active service in the podded application. Details of these roles with the USN, USMC, and Israeli Air Force are noted in the Mk 4 pod entry.
CONTRACTOR

Hughes Helicopters Inc, Culver City, California 90230, USA.

1119.303
M156 ARMAMENT MOUNT

The M156 multipurpose armament mount consists of two separate mountings, one fitted to each side of the UH-1 helicopter. Each mount is capable of carrying and firing the M158A1 and M200A1 2·75-inch rocket

launchers or carrying external stores suspended from standard 14-inch (356 mm) bomb racks, MA-4A. External stores must not exceed 245 kg per mount. A product improvement proposal to enable the M156 to carry a fully loaded 19-tube rocket launcher using the later heavy warhead rocket has been evaluated.

Both mounts are fixed in elevation and traverse, and sighting is by means of an XM60 reflex fixed sight. Total empty weight is 37 kg.
STATUS
US forces.

4432.303
XM188E1 30 mm THREE-BARREL AIRCRAFT GUN

The XM188E1 is a lightweight 30 mm three-barrel variant of the basic General Electric 20 mm M61A1 Vulcan design (**5547.103**) and succeeds the earlier XM188 (**1285.303**). It is designed to fire the XM-788/789/799 ADEN/DEFA ammunition at rates of fire variable up to 2000 rounds/minute. Its low recoil force attenuation system and lightweight design make it suitable for air-to-air and air-to-ground applications on small fixed-wing aircraft and helicopters as well as for surface-to-surface and surface-to-air applications on small naval craft. The gun is completely interchangeable with the 20 mm M197 weapon (**2856.103**) with no modifications to the vehicle. Its variable rate of fire allows the optimum rate to be selected to avoid resonance effects of the vehicle.

CHARACTERISTICS
Type: Externally powered 3-barrel Gatling
Calibre: 30 mm
Muzzle velocity: 792 m/s
Rate of fire: Variable up to 2000 rounds/minute
Recoil force: From 696 kg max at 730 rounds/minute to 1814 kg max at 2000 rounds/minute
Length: 1440 mm
Max diameter: 234 mm
Weight: 50 kg
STATUS

Prototype weapons were built and tested by the US Army, but no production plans have been revealed to date.
CONTRACTOR

General Electric Company, Armament and Electrical Systems Department, Lakeside Avenue, Burlington, Vermont 05402, USA.

XM188E1 30 mm three-barrel aircraft gun

4435.303

UNIVERSAL TURRET FOR HELICOPTER GUNSHIPS

This is essentially the same turret as that now in production for the US Army's AH-1J and AH-1T helicopters but in production for the AH-1S Cobra helicopter. It is a fourth-generation system incorporating numerous improvements over the initial production version.

The basic components consist of the turret, linked feed system, and three electronics boxes containing the turret, gun, and logic controls. The turret aim is controlled by the pilot or co-pilot through helmet sights or by the co-pilot through a dedicated pantograph sight or a companion missile sub-system sighting station such as the TOW sight unit. The turret is electrically driven by two servo motors which receive position commands from the sighting system and give quick response and safe reliable operation.

The turret can operate the 7·62 mm Minigun, the 20 mm M197 Vulcan, the 30 mm XM188E1, and the 30 mm XM230E2 Chain Gun and all can be interchanged without using special tools in less than 30 minutes. 750 rounds of 20 mm ammunition or 500 rounds of 30 mm ammunition can be carried. The prime armament to date has been the M197 Vulcan 20 mm gun and the following characteristics apply to this installation.

CHARACTERISTICS
Gun: M197
Calibre: 20 mm
Rate of fire: 750 or 1500 rounds/minute
Ammunition capacity: 750 rounds
Elevation
Limits: +21 to –50°
Slewing rate: 60°/s
Training
Limits: ±110°
Slewing rate: Over 80°/s
Pointing accuracy: <3 mil in each axis

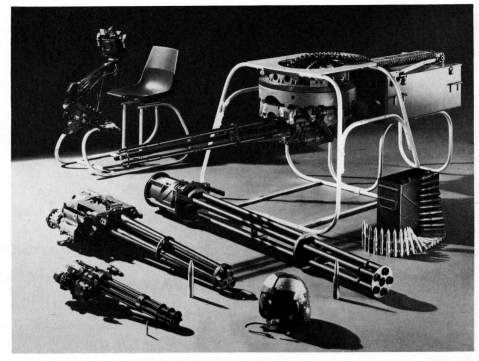

General Electric universal turret for helicopters, with selection of various guns which can be fitted, and gunner's station in background

STATUS
In production for the US Army AH-1S Cobra helicopter.

CONTRACTOR
General Electric Company, Armament and Electrical Systems Department, Lakeside Avenue, Burlington, Vermont 05402, USA.

1286.303

M197 20 mm THREE-BARREL AIRCRAFT GUN

The M197 aircraft gun is a three-barrel, fully automatic gun. It is a lightweight derivation of the 20 mm Vulcan M61A1 six-barrelled weapon. The M197 utilises many of the M61A1 components and has a rate of fire variable to 3000 shots per minute.

Like other guns in the Vulcan series the M197 needs external power – about 3 hp – for its operation.

The M197 fires standard US 20 mm ammunition of the M.50 series. Ammunition can be fed to the gun as a standard linked belt or by a linkless feed system.

CHARACTERISTICS
Calibre: 20 mm
Rate of fire: 400 – 3000 rounds/minute

Muzzle velocity: 1036 m/s
Number of barrels: 3
Weight: 66 kg
Length: 1892 mm
Average recoil force: 68 kg (at 1500 rounds/minute)
STATUS
In production since October 1969 and in service on the USMC, Iranian Sea Cobra attack helicopter AH-1J, and the OV-10A aircraft. The M197 forms part of the GE flexible weapon system and is used in the GE lightweight gun pod.
CONTRACTOR
General Electric Company, Armament and Electrical Systems Department, Lakeside Avenue, Burlington, Vermont 05402, USA.

20 mm M197 aircraft gun

1112.303

M21 MAMEE HELICOPTER ARMAMENT SYSTEM

The M21 aircraft armament system is made up of two 7·62 mm M134 machine guns (miniguns) and two M158 pods with seven 2·75 inch folding fin rockets each. MAMEE comprises a pair of novel ammunition storage and feed containers which provide a capacity of 3000 rounds of 7·62 mm ammunition in each of the two 11-inch (30 cm) diameter cylindrical containers. The system can fire six pairs of rockets in one second or 4000 rounds of 7·62 mm ammunition a minute. The rocket pods are aimed by manoeuvring the aircraft to which they are fixed. The machine guns, however, traverse 12° inboard to 70° outboard and +15 to –90° in elevation and depression. When the guns traverse

inboard to 12° they operate a limit switch that stops the firing on the inboard pointing gun. The gun on the opposite side then increases its rate of fire from 2400 to 4000 rounds/minute, compensating for the non-firing gun. This allows a heavy volume of fire to be placed on the target.

A complete M21/MAMEE installation consists of the following major components:
(1)   two 2·75 inch rocket launchers (M158A1)
(2)   two 7·62 mm six-barrelled machine guns (M134)
(3)   two MAMEE ammunition storage and feed systems
(4)   one pilot's rocket launcher reflex sight and intervalometer
(5)   one gunner's sighting station for machine guns

(6)   one gunner's control panel for guns
(7)   control box assembly for 7·62 mm guns
(8)   two gun mount assemblies
(9)   two rocket rack assemblies.
STATUS
American and Italian Forces. Over 600 M21 systems and about 1000 MAMEE installations have been produced.
CONTRACTOR
Emerson Electric Company, Government & Defense Group, 8100 West Florissant Ave, St Louis, Missouri 63136, USA.

1116.303

M28 ARMAMENT SYSTEM

The M28A1 armament sub-system is an electrically controlled, hydraulically operated, dual weapon that provides wide angle coverage and rapid fire for the AH-1G Hueycobra. The M28A1 consists of a power operated chin turret, mounting the 7·62 mm machine gun M134 on the right and the 40 mm grenade launcher M129 on the left. Ammunition is stored in the ammunition bay and moved to the turret through fixed and flexible chuting. Fire control equipment is located at the gunner/co-pilot station and allows the gunner to train the weapons in azimuth and elevation. Provisions are made for the pilot to fire the weapons in

the stow position. The system provides the AH-1G Hueycobra with area and point fire for attack on personnel and lightly armoured and unarmoured material targets during escort and armed reconnaissance missions.
CHARACTERISTICS
Max effective range: 1500 m (7·62 mm gun); 1500 m (40 mm grenade launcher)
Elevation/depression: +12 to +17·5/–50°
Muzzle velocity: 838 m/s (MG); 240 m/s (grenade launcher)
Rate of fire: 2000 or 4000 SPM (MG); 420 SPM (grenades)
Traverse: 114° l or r of aircraft datum

Weight: 203 kg (empty); 407 kg (loaded)
Ammunition
Capacity: 4000 (M134), 300 (M129) rounds
Type: Linked 7·62 and 40 mm
Sighting: M73 pilot's reflex with lighted reticle and manual range adjustment; gunner's flexible reflex sight with automatic airspeed compensation
STATUS
US Forces.

1117.303
XM28E1 ARMAMENT SUB-SYSTEM
The armament sub-system XM28E1 is similar to the M28 (**1116.303**) except for minor changes in the drive

motor, which is a motor with two distinct speeds as opposed to a motor which produces two speeds through use of a control resistor.

STATUS
US forces.

1836.303
XM30 AIRCRAFT ARMAMENT SUB-SYSTEM
The XM30 sub-system is a two-gun installation of XM/140 30 mm guns, one on each side of the UH-1B

helicopter. Ammunition is stored inside the aircraft. The sub-system weighs approximately 1800 lb (816 kg) when fully loaded. It is capable of firing at a combined rate of approximately 850 rounds per

minute. The guns are remotely controlled and may be fired by the co-pilot. The pilot can also fire the guns when they are in the fixed forward (stow) position.

1268.303
MINIGUN POD TYPE SUU 11B/A
The General Electric M134/GAU 2B/A Minigun is a 7·62 calibre development of the 20 mm M61 series of 'Vulcan' cannons. It has outstanding firepower and the SUU 11B/A pod provides a convenient means of giving its power to any tactical aircraft. The pod is light in weight and small in size and is equipped with standard bomb lugs for attachment to the weapon pylon. The pod can be carried on a wide range of fixed-and-rotary wing aircraft up to a maximum speed of Mach 1·2.

The gun is mounted in the forward half of the pod and fires through the stainless steel nosecap. The centre section of the pod contains the linkless ammunition feed system. A drum magazine is employed containing 1500 rounds of standard NATO 7·62 mm ammunition Type M59, M80, or M60. In the rear of the pod is the electrical control package. The linkless feed system is essentially the same as the larger scale one already developed for the Vulcan. In the Minigun pods the feed is single-ended and spent cartridge cases are ejected overboard through a port on the bottom of the pod. The ammunition is conveniently loaded from standard belted ammunition using a hand operated de-linking loader.

Provision for gun harmonisation is built into the gun mounting. A screw adjustment provides movement of the gun line through approximately ±¾°. Shot dispersion can be varied to suit operating conditions and target characteristics. At minimum dispersion 80 per cent of shots are within a 6·5 mil included angle.

SUU 11B/A Minigun pod

CHARACTERISTICS
Designation: USAF Minigun pod SUU 11B/A; US Army Minigun pod M18A1
Gun: 7·62 Minigun M134/GAU 2/A
Feed: Linkless type MAU 7
Drive: SUU 11B/A electric. AC or DC: 28 V at 15 A or 208 V AC 400 Hz 3-phase 2 A per phase. XM 18 E1 electric, 28 V DC 15 A only
Length: 2159 mm
Diameter: 305 mm
Weight: 147 kg (loaded); 111 kg (empty)

Ammunition capacity: 1500 rounds
Rate of fire: SUU 11B/A 3000 or 6000 rounds/minute; M18A1 2000 or 4000 rounds/minute
Average recoil force: 136 kg at 6000 rounds/minute
STATUS
In service with US and other forces.
CONTRACTOR
General Electric Company, Armament and Electrical Systems Department, Lakeside Avenue, Burlington, Vermont 05402, USA.

3890.303
HUGHES LIGHTWEIGHT ROCKET LAUNCHER XM260
Hughes Aircraft Company, under US Army contract, has developed a lightweight launcher for the 2·75 inch rocket system to be used on Army attack helicopters. It will be fitted to both the AH-1 Cobra, and the AH-64 Apache attack helicopter. The lightweight rocket launcher (LRL) is produced in two models, with capacities of seven and 19 rounds respectively and both are lighter than their predecessors. With a combat ordnance load of four 19-tube launchers, the LRLs provide a gross weight saving of about 120 kg per aircraft. This reduction is effected by the inclusion of the stores management, fuzing and fire control system, thus allowing an increase in fuel load. Fuze-timing selection is possible from the cockpit and the LRL is capable of launching 2·75 inch rockets powered by either the standard Mk 40 or its replacement higher thrust, Navy-developed, Mk 66 motor.
CHARACTERISTICS

Type: M260	7-tube	19-tube
Length	1651 mm	1651 mm
Diameter	254 mm	406 mm
Weight (empty)	15·5 kg	35·9 kg
Rocket capacity	7	19
Suspension	NATO 14 inch	NATO 14 inch
Firing interval	0·06 s	0·06 s

DEVELOPMENT
Development was carried out by Hughes Aircraft's Missile Systems Group for the US Army Missile Command, Redstone Arsenal, Alabama.
STATUS
The initial production contract awarded in late 1979 called for delivery of 1500 M-260 (7-tube) and 1200 M-261 (19-tube) models. Production was completed six months ahead of schedule in October 1981. A second production contract for nearly 4000 M-261 and 600 M-260 models was placed in May 1983, with deliveries to be completed in 1986.
CONTRACTOR
Hughes Aircraft Company, Missile Systems Group, Canoga Park, California 91304, USA.

US Army AH-64 Apache attack helicopter fires a pair of 2·75 in rockets from launchers on outboard wing pylons

---

1592.303
EMERSON FLEXIBLE TURRET SYSTEM (FTS)
Designed specifically as a 'strap-on' system for light observation and reconnaissance helicopters, Emerson's lightweight, flexible FTS (previously named MINI-TAT) has been extensively evaluated by the US Army Weapons Command, Project MASSTER, and the Canadian Defense Forces. It is claimed to be the only 'off-the-shelf' proven flexible armament system that will fit several light helicopters without structural modification. Customers include the Iranian Army Aviation (for Agusta 206B

helicopters – see accompanying illustration), the Canadian Defense Forces (for CH-136s), and the French Army (for the SA-341 Gazelle).

Offering a field of fire of 360° azimuth, +10° elevation, and –70° depression, the FTS is easily adaptable to a variety of helicopters and can be rapidly installed in the field. System weight is 62·6 kg exclusive of weapon and ammunition.

After initial adaptor kit installation, the FTS can be re-installed or removed in 30 minutes. In most configurations the FTS is mounted to the existing helicopter skid mounts. Versatility is one of its most

attractive features. The system is compatible with a wide variety of helicopters including the military UH-1 series, the international AB-205, AB-206, British Westland Lynx, Scout, and Wessex V, West German Bo-105, Japanese OH-6J, Canadian CH-136, French SA-341 Gazelle.

Electrically powered, the FTS can be slewed at rates of 80°/s in azimuth, elevation, and depression. Design of the FTS provides for easy access to the system for simplified maintenance. Additionally, in the event of the loss of aircraft power, the FTS can be quickly jettisoned.

CONTRACTOR
Emerson Electric Company, Government & Defense Group, 8100 West Florissant Ave, St Louis, Missouri 63136, USA.

Emerson Flexible Turret System installation on Agusta 206B helicopter

1115.303
XM27E1 7·62 mm ARMAMENT SUB-SYSTEM HELICOPTER

The XM27E1 was developed by Hughes under contract from the US Army Weapons Command for use with the OH-6A/OH-58A Scout helicopters. The basic concept was an outgrowth of the Hughes XM7 system which was proposed as a part of the original US Army Scout helicopter competition. The XM7, with similar characteristics, mounted two 7·62 mm M60 machine guns. The XM27E1 system, on the other hand, mounted a GFE General Electric M134 7·62 mm Minigun which was modified by Hughes to incorporate a dual speed drive assembly consisting of an electric motor, speed control unit, and a gear reduction assembly.

The XM27E1 is a compact, self-contained unit which is positioned on the left floor of the rear compartment. The unit can be mounted or demounted in less than ten minutes by two men and attachment is accomplished through use of three quick-release pins. The gun is flexible in elevation only (+10°, –24°) and fired at a 'two-step trigger' selectable rate of 2000 or 4000 rounds/minute. System capacity is 2000 rounds of belted 7·62 mm NATO ammunition. The Hughes-developed XM70E1 reflex sight was provided with the system for fire control purposes. This sight is an optical beam splitter type which is mechanically linked to the system.

CHARACTERISTICS
Armament sub-system
Weight (without ammunition): 48·5 kg (107 lb)
Weight (with ammunition): 106·6 kg (235 lb)
Effective range: 1100 m
Ammunition capacity: 2000 rounds
Elevation limits: +10°, –20°

Hughes XM27E1 7·62 mm armament sub-system

Elevation rate: 30°/s
Operating voltage: 22 – 30 V DC

Automatic gun M134 (Minigun)
Calibre: 7·62 mm
Rate of fire: 2000/4000 rounds/minute
Weight: 30·4 kg (67 lb)
Muzzle velocity: 869 m/s
Cooling: Air

Feed: Gun-driven de-linking feeder Mau 56/A
Links: M-13
Power: Electric, dual-speed drive motor

Helicopter reflex sight XM70E1
Type: Collimated, illuminated reticle
Weight: 2·2 kg (4·8 lb)
Width (extended/stowed): 254/356 mm (10/14 in)
Height: 228 mm (9 in)
Range: Adjustable, 250 – 1500 m
Drive: Mechanically coupled to gun
Lamp power requirements: 0·68 A (each filament)
Range compensating for 7·62 or 40 mm ammunition

STATUS
In April 1966, an initial contract was awarded to Hughes by the US Army Weapons Command, Rock Island Arsenal, Rock Island, Illinois for the development and subsequent production of 268 XM27E1 kits plus spares. Further contracts for the production of 606 additional kits plus spares were awarded in 1967 and 1968. Total value of all contracts was over $27 million.

Over 10 000 000 rounds were fired from XM27E1 kits mounted on OH-6A helicopters during the Viet-Nam conflict. To our knowledge, the XM27E1 was never utilised on the OH-58A in combat, although it was checked out and cleared for use in US testing. The XM27E1 earned a reputation as one of the Army's most reliable helicopter weapon systems. This same weapon system, under Hughes Helicopters Inc's designation of HGS-5, is now in limited production for sales world-wide for use on the Hughes 500MD light attack helicopter.

CONTRACTOR
Hughes Helicopters Inc, Culver City, California 90230, USA.

4436.303
HGS-55 7·62 mm ARMAMENT SUB-SYSTEM

Capitalising on the XM27E1 technology (**1115.303**), Hughes Helicopters Inc has developed and built a light combat helicopter armament sub-system designated the HGS-55 which mounts the Hughes 7·62 mm EX-34 Chain Gun weapon. As adapted to the Hughes 500MD Defender helicopter, the extraordinarily reliable EX-34 provides accurate point target suppressive firepower at ranges out to 900 metres. In concert with the highly manoeuvrable 500MD, the EX-34 is extremely effective against non-armoured soft targets such as general material and transportation systems.

In the HGS-55 system, the EX-34 fires 570 shots a minute of NATO standard 7·62 mm ammunition. Over 500 000 rounds have been fired through a series of EX-34 prototypes and all firings confirm the exceptional reliability of this weapon. The contractor claims the potential for combat availability several orders of magnitude better than any comparable weapon of this calibre.

Hughes 500MD helicopter equipped with HGS-55 armament sub-system

CHARACTERISTICS
Gun: EX-34
Calibre: 7·62 mm
Rate of fire: 570 rounds/minute
Muzzle velocity: 856 m/s
Ammunition: 2000 rounds NATO standard
Weight (with ammunition): 98·9 kg
Weight (without ammunition): 40·8 kg
Power supplies: 26·5 V DC at 0·22 kW
STATUS
Following extensive tests in 1978-79 by the British Royal Small Arms Factory, a number of these guns were purchased by the British Army. Subsequently the EX-34 was adopted by the UK MoD for use on the MCV-80 vehicle and future AFVs, and licence production of the weapon at Royal Small Arms Factory was due to begin in late 1984. The Canadian Forces are also evaluating the EX-34 for various applications.
CONTRACTOR
Hughes Helicopters Inc, Culver City, California 90230, USA.

7·62 mm EX-34 Chain Gun in HGS-55 configuration

HGS-55 helicopter armament system equipment

1108.303

M5 AIRCRAFT ARMAMENT SYSTEM

The M5 is used on the UH-1B/M helicopters. It consists of a flexible remote controlled, servo-power driven gun turret mounted in the nose of the UH-1B/M. The turret incorporates one M75 40 mm grenade launcher. Linked ammunition is stored in a rotary ammunition drum in the cargo hook hole, pulled through a flexible chute by an ammunition booster, and fed to the grenade launcher. The system also has a box feed system in addition to the rotary ammunition drum. A master armament control panel is located in the instrument console and is accessible to both the pilot and co-pilot gunner. A flexible hand control sight assembly mounts above the co-pilot's seat from which the co-pilot can sight and fire the system. The sub-system can also be fired in the stow position by either the pilot or co-pilot by means of a trigger switch on both cyclic stick grips. In this mode, the turret is flexible in elevation. An MWO has been applied to the sub-system to give the sight lead angle compensation. A dual-range reticle has been applied for more accuracy at long range.

CHARACTERISTICS
Effective range: 1500 m
Elevation/depression: +15°, –35°
Muzzle velocity: 240 m/s
Rate of fire: 230 SPM
Traverse: 60° right and left
Ammunition
Type: Linked 40 mm
Capacity: 150 rounds; 300 rounds
Sighting: Reflex type: gunner/co-pilot operated in elevation and deflection

Weights	Box fed	Drum fed
Empty	106 kg	101 kg
Loaded	152 kg	208 kg

STATUS
US forces.

1109.303

XM8 40 mm ARMAMENT SUB-SYSTEM HELICOPTER

The XM8 was developed by Hughes Helicopters Inc under contract from the US Army Weapons Command for potential use with the OH-6A/OH-58A Scout helicopters. The present concept is based on a prototype effort performed by this contractor in support of the original US Army Scout helicopter competition eventually won by Hughes. This prototype system mounted on an M75 high velocity grenade launcher and its characteristics were very similar to the XM8 system mounting an M129 grenade launcher later sponsored by the Army.

The XM8 is a compact, self-contained unit which is positioned on the left floor of the aft compartment. The unit can be mounted or demounted in less than ten minutes by two men and attachment is accomplished through the use of three quick-release pins. The XM8 uses the same mounting points and is interchangeable with the XM27E1 helicopter armament sub-system (**1115.303**). The XM8 utilises a simple integrated feed system with a compact, quickly detachable ammunition container. Linked ammunition is spiral wound in this container to provide reliable, positive control of each round. Ammunition boost is not required.

The XM8 mounts an M129 grenade launcher which fires 40 mm rounds with a muzzle velocity of 240 m/s (790 ft/s). System capacity is 150 rounds of belted M384 ammunition. The gun is flexible in elevation only and fires at a rate of 400 rounds per minute. The XM8 incorporates a proven hydrospring recoil system which reduces peak recoil loads of the M129 by over 60 per cent. The Hughes-developed XM70E1 reflex sight is provided with the system for fire control purposes. This sight is an optical beam splitter type which is mechanically linked to the system and is used interchangeably with the XM27E1 armament sub-system.

Hughes XM8 40 mm armament sub-system

CHARACTERISTICS
Armament sub-system
Weight (without ammunition): 54·4 kg (120 lb)
Weight (with ammunition): 107·9 kg (238 lb)
Ammunition capacity: 150 rounds
Elevation limits: +10°, –24°
Elevation rate: 25°/s
Operating voltage: 22-30 V DC
High velocity grenade launcher 40 mm M129
Rate of fire: 400 rounds/minute
Weight: 20·4 kg (45 lb)
Muzzle velocity: 240 m/s (790 ft/s)
Range: 2200 m
Method of operation: Electric motor
Links: M16, M16A1
Ammunition: M384 (HE), M430 (HEDP)
DEVELOPMENT
In June 1967, a contract was awarded to Hughes by the US Army Weapons Command, Rock Island, Illinois for the development and testing of eight XM8 helicopter armament sub-systems. This programme included a firing test fixture, two development models, two service test models and four prototype systems. Extensive flight tests were conducted on the OH-6A helicopter at Fort Irwin, California, and Apalachicola, Florida, and all hardware was subsequently delivered to the Army.
STATUS
Inactive.
CONTRACTOR
Hughes Helicopters Inc, Culver City, California 90230, USA.

1284.303

XM214 5·56 mm AUTOMATIC GUN

The General Electric Company has designed and developed a 5·56 mm automatic gun. The gun design is based on the proven principles of the operational M61A1, 20 mm Vulcan gun, and the GAU-2B/A, 7·62 mm Minigun. Selectable firing rates are available within the range of 400 to 6000 rounds per minute, permitting optimum engagement of a variety of targets. As few as three rounds to as many as 1500 rounds can be fired in single bursts. The weapon is a multi-barrelled machine gun externally powered and suitable for aircraft, helicopter, or ground vehicle installation. The 5·56 mm M193 (M196 Tracer) round weight is approximately half that of the 7·62 mm round and is the same as is used on the M-16 rifle.

A single, rugged main spring is used for actuation of the firing pins. Elimination of the springs from the individual bolts allows the bolts and entire gun to be simpler, smaller, and lighter. A de-linking feeder provides a declutching action which, when the trigger is released, immediately stops the feeding of rounds. The gun continues to fire for a fraction of a second, firing out remaining rounds. This operation automatically clears and 'safes' the gun at the end of each burst. A combination access handle and safing lever separates the main spring from the six gun bolts and provides a positive visual verification of the safe position.

A side-stripping feeder strips and disposes the ammunition links and feeds rounds to the gun. This feeder permits rapid installation of flexible ammunition belts or ammunition cans. The gun's access cover, bolts, and feeder can be removed and installed without tools or timing procedures. Reliability and maintainability of the 5·56 mm gun are expected to be equal to or better than that of the 7·62 mm Minigun.

The power input needed by the gun varies between

0·75 and 3·2 hp according to rate of fire selected. Electric or hydraulic motor drives are available for this purpose. A self-powered propellant gas-driven variant of the Minigun has also been developed. For the electric drive a range of nickel-cadmium batteries is available giving a duration of fire up to 80 000 rounds at 1000 rounds per minute.

CHARACTERISTICS
Calibre: 5·56 mm
Muzzle velocity: 990 m/s
Rate of fire: Up to 10 000 rounds/minute
Dispersion: 80% shots within 4 mils
Length: 686 mm
Weight (gun and drive): 15 kg
Recoil force, average: 110 kg (at 10 000 rounds/minute)
STATUS
Prototype weapons have been assembled and tested.

XM214 5·56 mm automatic gun

CONTRACTOR
Aircraft Equipment Division, General Electric, Burlington, Vermont 05402, USA.

1846.303
M230 30 mm CHAIN GUN WEAPON
Developed by Hughes Helicopters Inc, the 30 mm M230 chain gun is a single-barrel, externally powered weapon which incorporates a rotating bolt mechanism driven by a simple and reliable chain drive. The entire gun weighs 123 lb (55·9 kg) and will achieve firing rates from single round to 625 rounds per minute. The chain drive principle permits a simplified gun cycle which operates safely from an open bolt without requirement for chargers, declutching feeders, or other special devices. Since the M230 is motor driven, it provides inherent high belt pull, thereby eliminating the need for a powered booster. Long bolt-lock time insures an essentially gasless action and the resultant long dwell following firing provides for hangfire safe weapons.

As all the moving parts are totally keyed together, each and every motion within the chain gun is precisely timed and fully controlled. Further, 100 per cent positive round control within the M230's ballistically independent system eliminates those malfunctions due to conventional ammunition problems. These factors, coupled with the smooth power flow from its drive motor, ensure the highest reliability at all rates of fire.
DEVELOPMENT
Hughes Helicopters Inc initiated development of a

Hughes M230 cannon

30 mm chain gun weapon in December 1972 and after an accelerated engineering and fabrication effort, the weapon was first fired in April 1973 and burst fired in May of that year. A 2500-round feasibility trial sponsored by the US Army was successfully completed in September 1973 and by December 1973, 4000 rounds had been fired. Subsequent models of XM230s were built and tested and a quarter of a million rounds of XM552/XM639 ammunition were fired through these several chain guns. Early in 1976, the DoD directed that the XM230 be rechambered to fire ADEN/DEFA type ammunition for purposes of NATO interoperability. To ensure

interoperability, Hughes Helicopters Inc was given the responsibility for development of a family of US 30 mm rounds: M788 (TP), M789 (HEDP) and M799 (HE). The modified XM230 – designated the M230 – was first fired in March 1978. While the basic M230 gun can fire either linked or linkless ammunition through the use of a lightweight interchangeable transfer unit, the AH-64 will employ a linear linkless conveyor system.

Another member of the chain gun family, the M242, is in production for the US Army as the primary weapon for installation in the M2 and M3 Bradley fighting vehicles and the Light Armoured Vehicle (LAV-25) for the US Marine Corps. This weapon (**5237.103**) fires both European and US 25 mm ammunition.
CHARACTERISTICS
Calibre: 30 mm
Combat ammunition: ADEN/DEFA/M789/M799
Practice ammunition: M788
Weight of receiver: 28·6 kg
Weight of barrel: 15·9 kg
Weight of recoil adaptor: 5·5 kg
Weight of linked or linkless transfer unit: 5·9 kg
Total gun system weight: 55·9 kg
Length: 1·638 mm
Width: 0·254 m
Height: 0·292 m
Barrel life: To 10 000 rounds
Rate of fire: 625 ±25 rounds/minute
Time to fire: 0·2 s
Time to stop: 0·1 s
Clearing method: Open bolt
Effective impulse (with muzzle brake): 20·42 kg
Power required: 6·5 hp
Reliability predicted: 15 000 MRBF
STATUS
In production.
CONTRACTOR
Hughes Helicopters Inc, Culver City, California 90230, USA.

Hughes AH-64 Apache attack helicopter armed with 30 mm Hughes M230 chain gun/cannon and 16 Hellfire missiles

---

1110.303
M16 ARMAMENT SUB-SYSTEM
Armament sub-system M16 contains two 7·62 mm M60CAL machine rocket launchers mounted on a UH-1B/C helicopter. Each set of guns is flexible in both elevation and azimuth. Capacity for the machine guns is 6000 rounds which is link-fed to the left side of

each gun. The machine guns shoot 2000 to 2600 rounds/minute with a maximum effective range of 1000 m. Elevation of the guns is from +11 to –63° while traverse ranges from 12° inboard to 70° outboard. Machine gun firing cuts off electrically or mechanically when guns on a given side of helicopter are in danger of firing into the aircraft.

The rocket launchers M158 have an effective range of 3000 m. The pilot aims through a manual reflex sight for both machine guns and rockets. The co-pilot uses a flexible reflex sight for machine guns only. Machine guns cut off while rockets fire.
STATUS
US forces.

1113.303
M23 ARMAMENT SUB-SYSTEM

The M23 armament sub-system consists of two M60D 7·62 mm machine guns and two mounts, one on each side of the aircraft in the doorways. The pintle post assembly is attached to a base tube assembly which is attached to hard points on the helicopter fuselage. The machine gun, which is a belt fed, gas operated, air-cooled automatic weapon, is attached to a pivot cradle on top of the pintle post. The base can be employed at either the right or left side, and the pedestal is designed for right or left installation. The machine gun installs on either right or left pintle mounts without adaptation, and is a modified machine gun, M60, with aircraft ring type sights, spade grips and an improved feed system. A rapid reloading capability is provided by a 550-round ammunition box attached to the weapon by a flexible chute. A canvas bag attaches to the right side of the receiver to catch links and ejected cartridges. Free traverse and elevation is allowed within fixed stop limits to prevent self-inflicted damage to the helicopter. The sub-system utilises all standard 7·62 mm ammunition.

CHARACTERISTICS
Max effective range: 1100 m
Elevation forward: +3·5°, Aft +6·5° depression −80°
Muzzle velocity: 838 m/s
Rate of fire: 550 SPM
Traverse: 2 – 178° in azimuth
Ammunition
Capacity: 550 rounds per gun
Type: Linked 7·62 mm
Weight: 78 kg (empty); 95 kg (loaded)
STATUS
US forces.

1114.303
M24 ARMAMENT SUB-SYSTEM

The armament sub-system M24 is similar to armament sub-system M23 except that it is mounted on the CH-47A helicopter and carries 200-round ammunition boxes. One machine gun mounts in the left forward escape hatch, the other across the right forward door.

STATUS
US forces.

5220.303
M41 ARMAMENT SYSTEM

The M41 armament system consists of a pintle mount, a 7·62 mm M60D machine gun, link and brass retainer, ammunition box and a gunner's safety harness, and the complete system is mounted on the rear ramp of the Boeing CH-47 helicopter used by the United States Army. The M60D is provided with positive mechanical stops to limit the elevation and traverse of the weapon.

CHARACTERISTICS
Ammunition capacity: 200 rounds
Weight without ammunition: 19 kg
Maximum effective range: 1100 m
Muzzle velocity: 838 m/s
Rate of fire: 550 rounds/minute
Elevation: +12·5 to −69°
Traverse: 47° left and right
Sight: Aircraft ring and post type
STATUS
In service with the United States Army.

5221.303
XM94 ARMAMENT SUB-SYSTEM

Each sub-system provides two identical pintle installations which can be interchangeably mounted on either the right or left doorway compartment of a helicopter. These weapons can be utilised as a flexible pintle installation, or fixed in a forward attitude and remotely fired by the pilot. The grenade launcher used in the XM94 sub-system is the M75.

CHARACTERISTICS
Ammunition capacity: 800 rounds
Weight without ammunition: 540 kg
Effective range: 1500 m
Muzzle velocity: 240 m/s
Rate of fire: 400 rounds/minute
Elevation: +3·5 to −60°
Traverse: From fixed forwards to 135° aft

5222.303
XM59 ARMAMENT SUB-SYSTEM

The XM59 sub-system is an exterior mount sub-system for mounting one 7·62 mm M60D and one 0·50 XM213 (modified AN-M2) machine gun, in each side door of the UH-1D or UH-1H helicopter. The XM59 is basically an M23 system adapted for use with the 0·50 machine gun. The 0·50 kit pintle post assembly is attached to the M23 sub-system base tube assembly. A link receptacle and an expended brass deflector are provided to eliminate any hazard to the aircraft as expended cases and links are ejected from the weapon. Mechanical stops are provided to prevent any self-inflicted damage to the aircraft.

CHARACTERISTICS
Ammunition capacity: 100 rounds of 0·50 ammunition; 550 rounds of 7·62 mm ammunition
Weight: 126 kg with ammunition; 98 kg without ammunition
Range: 0·50 weapons 3000 m; 7·62 mm weapons 1100 m
Muzzle velocity: 0·50 – 857 m/s; 7·62 mm – 838 m/s
Elevation: +6·5 to −80°
Traverse: 2 – 178° in azimuth

YUGOSLAVIA

5223.303
YUGOSLAV AIRCRAFT ARMAMENT

Listed below is a resumé of aircraft armament used by the Yugoslav Air Force. It should be noted that the Soviet designations for bombs are very similar to those of Yugoslavia, for example Soviet HE general-purpose bombs are the FAB-100, FAB-250 and FAB-500 etc, Soviet incendiary bombs are the ZAB-100 etc, Soviet HC anti-tank bomblets are the PTAB-5 etc and the Soviet chemical bombs are the VAP and ZAP series.

BOMBS:
1·5 kg PTAB-1·5 HC anti-tank bomblets
2·5 kg PTAB-2·5 HC anti-tank bomblets
2·5 kg RAB-2·5 fragmentation bombs
3·5 kg RAP-3·5 fragmentation bombs
16 kg RAP-16 fragmentation bombs (normally used in clusters of eight)
45 kg ZAB-45 incendiary bomb
50 kg SAB-50 parachute flare
50 kg FOTAB-50 photo-flash
120 kg RAB fragmentation cluster bombs

250 kg FAB-250 HE general-purpose bombs
500 kg FAB-500 HE general-purpose bombs
DPT-150 cluster bomb unit with 54 PTAB 1·5 kg or 44 RAB 2·5 kg or 34 RAP 3·5 kg
150 litre PLAB-150L napalm

ROCKETS:
57 mm VRZ-57 high explosive (or anti-tank) in pods of 12 (pod is Lanser L57)
127 mm VRZ-127 high explosive (or anti-tank)

GROUND RADAR

BRAZIL

Note: Indigenous radar development in Brazil began in 1970, at the instigation of the PEA (Divisão de Eletrônica (Electronics Division) of the IPD – Instituto de Pesquisa e Desenvolvimento (Research and Development Institute)) a branch of the Brazilian Ministry of Aeronautics, the Centro Técnico Aerospacial – CTA (Aerospace Technical Centre). Following preliminary studies and programmes related to the acquisition of basic microwave expertise, and the formation of a nucleus of qualified personnel, two programmes were initiated. As reference to the brief descriptions which follow show, both these Brazilian radar initiatives employ S-band equipments, but future developments can be expected to embrace the other radar bands eventually to include certain more specifically military applications.

4132.153
S-BAND METEOROLOGICAL RADAR

This radar operates in the 2700 MHz frequency band and has preset ranges of 25, 50, 100, 200 and 400 km. The configuration of the equipment can be seen from the adjacent photograph, from which it will be noted that the large circular reflector can be steered in azimuth and elevation on its tower-mounted pedestal. This presumably allows the radar to be employed for both radiosonde tracking or weather/precipitation surveillance purposes.

Digital techniques are employed in signal processing with presentation as raw radar video. Other facilities include azimuth and range integration, iso-echo and iso-contour presentation with height density levels, colour TV screen display, and remote facsimile presentation. The normal display arrangements provide for sectorial coverage, PPI and RHI displays, and the antenna can be adjusted in elevation from the operating console.

STATUS

The PEA-built prototype has been fully tested and approved, and transferred to private industry for commercial production. Full-scale production was due to commence in mid-1983. Companies involved include Tecnasa for system integration and electronics, Motoradio for the microwave elements, and Jamy for tower, pedestal and antenna. Thirty-two of these radars were due to be procured, initially as part of the Brazilian Ministry of Aeronautics' Plano de

Antenna assembly of the Brazilian S-band met radar (Ronaldo S Olive)

Desenvolvimento do Sistema de Proteção ao Vôo (Flight Protection System Development Plan).

CONTRACTOR

IPD/PEA – Divisão de Eletrônica, 12200 São José dos Campos, SP, Brazil.

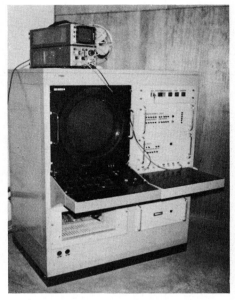

Brazilian met radar console (Ronaldo S Olive)

4133.153
ASR-BR1 AIRPORT SURVEILLANCE RADAR

This S-band airfield surveillance radar is the result of PEA's 'Meta 2' project, and the equipment is being procured in quantity for the Brazilian ATC system although it is equally suitable for military tactical applications.

The ASR-BR1 has a conventional transmitter with a magnetron modulator and delay line pulse generation. Apart from the magnetron and a thyratron switching tube, the transmitter is an all solid-state system providing adjustment of the PRF within ±10 per cent of its normal value. All transmitter components have automatic protection circuits against malfunctions. Receiver characteristics include: low noise figure due to a parametric input amplifier; self-radiation protection; synthesiser local oscillator with automatic frequency control; IF preamplifier with time-variable gain. The last feature equalises the returns from identical targets at different ranges, as well as protecting the IF amplifier against saturation caused by excessively strong re-run echoes from short range targets.

Signal processing is based on the use of a digital MTI which rejects fixed echoes, and the PRF can be varied to eliminate blind speeds. A conventional PPI CRT display is provided, and there is a video map facility which generates synthetic video representing the local geography of the airfield including such features as towers, tall buildings, mountains, etc.

CHARACTERISTICS

Frequency: 2700 – 2900 MHz
Peak power: 450 kW (typical)
Pulse width: 0·75 μs
PRF: 1000/s (variable ±10%)
Antenna beamwidth: 1·5° azimuth; Cos^2 5·5 – 40° elevation
Antenna gain: 32 dB (max)
Sidelobe attenuation: 25 dB
Rotation rate: 15 rpm

Receiver noise: 2 dB (at parametric amplifier input)
IF: 30 MHz
Max range: 110 km (2 m² target)
Detection probability: 0·9
False alarm probability: 10^{-5}
Sub-clutter visibility: 25 dB
First blind speed: 3500 km/h

STATUS

A prototype has been completed and has undergone certification testing preparatory to production by private industry. Twenty-four sets have been ordered for the Brazilian ATC network, and the first two installations are at the Porto Alagre (Rio Grande do Sul State) Airport and the São Pedro da Amdeia (Rio de Janeiro State) Naval Air Force Base.

CONTRACTOR

IPD/PEA – Divisão de Eletrônica, 12200 São José dos Campos, SP, Brazil.

ASR-BR1 display mounted in an ATC console (Ronaldo S Olive)

ASR-BR1 transmitter/receiver cabinets (Ronaldo S Olive)

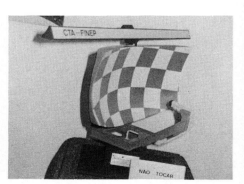

Model of Brazilian ASR-BR1 airfield surveillance radar (Ronaldo S Olive)

CANADA

5678.153
CMR-3 COASTAL SURVEILLANCE RADAR
The CMR-3 Coastal surveillance radar is derived from the AN/SPS-503 naval radar (**5677.253**), and is designed for long range surveillance under severe weather and ECM conditions. The system operates in the E/F frequency band for optimum performance and uses a driven transmitter with pulse-to-pulse frequency agility over a wide bandwidth. The antenna is a tower-mounted, high gain, narrow-beam unit and the system is able to operate unattended in remote sites.

The transmitter uses a TWT amplifier fed by a frequency synthesiser and the low-noise, high dynamic range receiver employs pulse compression. This combination of frequency agility and pulse compression is designed to give excellent clutter and jamming suppression. The digital signal processing unit contains independent MTI (optional) and non-MTI channels. Each channel has its own CFAR circuits, and PRF discrimination is applied to both channels. Adaptive velocity compensation can be supplied with the MTI channel.

The tactical display used with the CMR-3 is a development of a marine collision avoidance system. It is capable of simultaneously tracking of up to 20 targets out to a range of 64 nautical miles.

Although the CMR-3 system is configured primarily for the surface surveillance role, it is also available in a combined air/surface search radar version. A version of the antenna with a cosec^2 beam shape would be used in this instance, and a digital MTI processing system can be added. Since the equipment is designed with dual, independent MTI and non-MTI channels, air and surface search can be carried out simultaneously.
CONTRACTOR
Canadian Marconi Company, 415 Legget Drive, PO Box 13330, Kanata, Ontario K2K 2B2, Canada.

CHINA (PEOPLE'S REPUBLIC)

2019.153
CHINESE MILITARY RADAR
Little is known of Chinese activities in the military field. As with many other military systems the Chinese were almost certainly for many years largely dependent on Soviet radar equipment and with Soviet equipment fairly readily available – obsolescent though the available equipment very probably was – it would have been only reasonable for the Chinese to have concentrated their attention on other problems.

Although there is probably still a good deal of operational Soviet radar in China, it is apparent that they have a substantial radar development programme in hand. It is known that they have constructed a missile early warning system (**2052.181**), and with respect to these and other radar developments some code names are beginning to emerge from American sources. One of these is the name Cross Legs given to a surveillance radar working in the 1250 MHz band with PRFs of 300 and 600 Hz – suggesting a maximum range capability of something under 500 km. Another name is Thick Skin which is applied to a heightfinder working in the 6500 MHz band. (H-band in the American military frequency band scale.) Apparently other radars are known to be operating in the American military I-band – ie around 9 GHz.

Recent reporting names for Chinese radars to emerge include the following:
Chop Rest
This is stated to be of Chinese origin and is an early warning radar. In general configuration it is similar to the Soviet Spoon Rest (**2889.153**) VHF equipment, with an array of multiple Yagi antennas, but having a distinctly larger number of elements. Operating frequencies are 162 to 169 MHz and 175 to 189 MHz. Range performance should reach about 250 km.
Cross Legs
Cross Legs is another early warning radar claimed to be deployed throughout China, often in company with heightfinder radar(s), which indicates CGI/air-defence reporting centre installations. The antenna is an elliptical paraboloid with horn feed, supported on a four-legged base.
Cross Slot
Primarily employed for coastal defence, Cross Slot is also an early warning radar, located at fixed sites and often with heightfinder radar(s). Operating frequency is in the E/F-band and the probable range is about 80 km. In addition to installations in China, Cross Slot has been reported in North Korea and Viet-Nam.
Gin Sling
Fan Song type radars (**2866.153, 2867.153, 2868.153**) for surface-to-air missile guidance used by the Chinese armed forces are known by the designation Gin Sling.

Moon Cone
Reported to have been developed in China, Moon Cone is an early warning radar consisting of multiple stacked dipole arrays, located one above the other on a vertical mast. The arrays diminish in area from bottom to top, there being three in a typical installation. VHF operation is almost certain and ranges of 250 km or more should be obtained.
Moon Face
Similar to Moon Cone, but having only one stacked dipole array.
Moon Mat
Similar to Moon Cone, but having only one stacked dipole array.
Moon Plate
Stacked dipole VHF array on trailer mounting.
Slot Rest
Reported to have been developed in China for early warning and target acquisition, Slot Rest is similar to the Soviet Spoon Rest (**2889.153**) radars. Operation is in the A-band (VHF). It is truck-mounted and has been observed in Viet-Nam as well as China.
Team Work
Team Work is a fire control radar deployed at anti-aircraft artillery sites in China and possibly elsewhere. It was first seen in Viet-Nam in 1972. Operating frequencies are believed to be in E-band.

CZECHOSLOVAKIA

4331.153
RL-42 SURVEILLANCE RADAR
The RL-42 operates at 10 cm wavelength and is designed to control traffic inside controlled airspace and in the terminal area. The range of surveillance is 120 km and its specifications meet CMEA standards for Group V 2 airport radars and also those given in ICAO Annex 10. It is the successor to the older OR-1, OR-2 and RL-41 models. Information on characteristics and features is sparse but includes operation in the diversity mode on two frequencies with auxiliary antenna lobe, digital MTI, digital target detector and plot extraction.
CONTRACTOR
Tesla, Pardubice, Czechoslovakia.

RL-42 surveillance radar

4332.153
RP-4G PRECISION APPROACH RADAR
The RP-4G system is for use on medium and large airports for conventional landings and also for V/STOL and STOL traffic. It is a normal type of PAR radar and is used for aircraft guidance and the final approach from 30 km away to touchdown. Information provided to the controller includes the flight altitude inside the approach sector, deviation from the glide path and cloud pattern and cloudbase in the vicinity of the approach sector. The equipment can be integrated into an automated air traffic control system without any modification.

STATUS
Probably in operation in civil and military airfields.
CONTRACTOR
Tesla, Pardubice, Czechoslovakia.

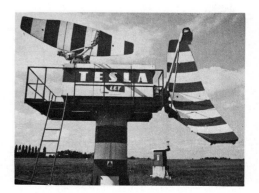

RP-4G precision approach radar

DENMARK

5629.153
TERMA DOPPLER RADAR SYSTEMS
These equipments are a series of doppler radar systems designed for the continuous velocity measurement of rockets, missiles, mortars and projectiles ranging from the smallest to the largest calibre. They are based on a number of antenna/transmitter units which can be varied to some degree to carry out specific functions. Seven basic antenna units are available in either X- or S-band. Presentation of data is by desk-top calculators or desk-top computer.

There are four main systems, brief details being as follows:
DR552
This uses a 3·2° X-band antenna and is primarily for the measurement of small projectiles. It has been developed for use at low elevations and is suitable for measurement at indoor ranges.
DR564
An S-band antenna unit system for both projectile and rocket measurement.
DR570
This system is basically a combination of DR552 and

DR564 since it uses two antennas, the 12° S-band for projectiles and rockets and the 3·2° X-band for low elevation and indoor range measurement.
DR580
This features a 1·6° antenna unit for long range measurement and a 15 × 7° antenna unit for accurate measurement of initial velocities.
CONTRACTOR
Terma Elektronik AS, Hovmarken 4, 8520 Lystrup, Denmark.

FRANCE

2056.153
ADOUR INSTRUMENTATION TRACKING RADAR
Adour (TRS 2504) is a G-band tracking radar using the conical scanning principle. It is intended for acquisition and automatic tracking and is specifically designed for making measurements in:
(1) Flight test centres, for the calibration and evaluation of prototype aircraft, of airborne equipment such as altimeters and autopilots, and of ground equipment such as surveillance radar.
(2) Rocket and missile test centres and launching centres for measurements relating to missile, sounding rockets, and satellite launchers.
In addition, the radar is used at such centres for windfinding and similar measurements.
STATUS
Adour is installed on Australian, Brazilian, French, Swiss and other firing test ranges. It is still in production to meet French and export needs.

CONTRACTOR
Thomson-CSF, Division Systèmes, Défense et Contrôle, 40 rue Grange Dame Rose, BP34, 92360 Meudon-la-Foret, France.

Note: Adour is a member of an extensive range of French instrumentation tracking radars, other members of this family being:
Artois   **(2063.153)**
Atlas   **(1943.153)**
Bearn   **(2065.153)**
Savoie   **(1944.153)**
Details of these radars will be found on this and succeeding pages of this section of *Jane's Weapon Systems*. More detailed information on Adour is given in previous editions and details of the earlier Aquitaine tracking radar, will be found under entry number **2062.153** in the 1974-75 and previous editions of *Jane's Weapon Systems*.

Adour tracking radar TRS 2504 installed at the Brazilian Army's Marambala Proving Grounds near Rio de Janeiro (Ronaldo S Olive)

2060.153
ANTARES HEIGHTFINDING RADAR
Under the code name ANTARES (for antenna tracking altitude, azimuth, and range by electronic scan) Thomson-CSF has developed a heightfinding radar operating in E/F-band that can be used for air defence and civil air traffic control purposes. This system is designed mainly to measure the altitude of targets tracked by a 2-D search radar which is associated with it, with a very high accuracy and a high data renewal rate. ANTARES is an automated system, and all its input or output data are controlled or generated by an automatic digital processing unit. This feature, together with the utilisation of electronic scanning in elevation, enables the system to satisfy a practically unlimited number of altitude requests.

The ANTARES system consists of a heightfinding radar and a processing unit. Principal units of the radar are an antenna under a radome, a servo system for slaving the rotation of the antenna to that of the associated plan radar antenna, transmitter, receiver, and one angular error measuring receiver. More detailed information is given under this entry number in previous editions of *Jane's Weapon Systems*.
STATUS
No longer in production.
CONTRACTOR
Thomson-CSF, Division Systèmes, Défense et Contrôle, 40 rue Grange Dame Rose, BP34, 92360 Meudon-la-Foret, France.

ANTARES heightfinding radar antenna. It is normally enclosed within a protective radome

2063.153
ARTOIS INSTRUMENTATION TRACKING RADAR
Artois is an electronic-scan multi-target tracking radar designed to perform highly accurate differential trajectory measurements.
The principal features of this radar are electronic scanning in a cone having a vertex angle of 10° minimum, instantaneous deflection from pulse-to-

pulse, and multi-target tracking with controlled variable interlace.
More detailed information is given under this entry number in previous editions of *Jane's Weapon Systems*.
STATUS
No longer in production. One installed at Centre

d'Essais des Landes on the French Atlantic coast for ballistic and tactical missile trials and training.
CONTRACTOR
Thomson-CSF, Division Systèmes, Défense et Contrôle, 40 rue Grange Dame Rose, BP34, 92360 Meudon-la-Foret, France.

2121.153
ATC APPROACH RADAR TRS 2060
The TRS 2060 radar station is an improved version of the THD 1098 (described under this entry number in previous editions while it was still in development), which can be supplied with an integrated IFF antenna and is now available as either a mobile or a static

installation. It has been designed for easy transport and setting up, and can be used in a variety of operational conditions. Both its mobility and its performance make it well suited for use as an autonomous surveillance station, or for complementing or locally enlarging the coverage of a long-range

radar (gap-filler) role, for example in an air defence system.
CHARACTERISTICS
Antenna
Type: AC316
Polarisation: Linear/circular

Reflector dimensions: 5 × 2·3 m
Horizontal beamwidth (3 dB): 1·4° ± 10%
Cosecanted pattern: In excess of 40°
Gain: 34 dB
Rotation speed: 7·5/15 rpm
Transmitter/receiver
Type: TH.D.047
Frequency range: (covered with 2 tunable magnetrons) 2900 – 3200 MHz
Peak power: 1 MW
Average power: 2 kW
Pulse duration: 4 or 2 μs
PRF: 500 Hz; 1000 Hz
Receiver: Parametric amplifier incorporated
Noise figure: <5 dB
Reception chains: Log with differentiation/expansion and CFAR chain

Digital MTI (phase-coding): Double canceller loop 3 PRFs; sub-clutter visibility 25 dB
Power supply: 220/380 V, 50 Hz, 20 kVA
Detection range: 130 km on modern fighter, for a detection probability of 80% with single T/R unit
STATUS
No longer in production.
CONTRACTOR
Thomson-CSF, Division Systèmes, Défense et Contrôle, 40 rue Grange Dame Rose, BP34, 92360 Meudon-la-Foret, France.

TRS 2060 approach radar

2065.153
BÉARN INSTRUMENTATION TRACKING RADAR
Béarn is a high-precision G-band automatic tracking radar designed for the trajectory of high-speed missiles at long range.

Facilities offered by the radar include manual or automatic acquisition of a target dynamically or statically designated by the rendezvous method; automatic tracking of radar echoes or transponder signals up to 4000 km; elevation, azimuth, and range

co-ordinate read-out as numerical data in real time; automatic change-over to memory tracking in case of signal loss; polarisation switching without interruption of tracking; synchronisation of a chain of radars interrogating the same transponder; and, for shipborne installations, autonomous and automatic stabilisation of the pointing axis.

More detailed information is given under this entry number in previous editions of *Jane's Weapon Systems*.

STATUS
In operational use in France and a number of other countries.
CONTRACTOR
Thomson-CSF, Division Systèmes, Défense et Contrôle, 40 rue Grange Dame Rose, BP34, 92360 Meudon-la-Foret, France.

1943.153
ATLAS INSTRUMENTATION TRACKING RADAR
Atlas is a very high precision tracking radar designed for trajectography and satellite tracking. A monopulse G-band radar, Atlas automatically tracks radar echoes or transponder signals at distances up to about 4000 km. The equipment comprises an antenna turret with which are associated the RF and IF receiver circuits, a 1 MW peak transmitter codable and tunable from 5450 to 5825 MHz, an operating console, an interconnection cabinet, and a mains supply cabinet. The rangefinding unit, in the console, is fitted with a synchronising device that allows the radar to be used in series with other tracking radars of the same or different types.

The Atlas radar is available in fixed or transportable form. Operational optional facilities include TV monitoring, TV tracking and IR tracking.

CHARACTERISTICS
Antenna
Cassegrain feed system:
Diameter: 4 m
Polarisation: Vertical/circular
Gain: 44 dB
Beamwidth (3 dB): 0·9°
Transmitter
1 MW magnetron, codable and tunable: 5450 – 5825 MHz
Pulse length: 0·25 – 1·7 μs
Transmitter frequency controlled by a high-precision standard cavity
STATUS
In production.
CONTRACTOR
Thomson-CSF, Division Systèmes, Défense et Contrôle, 40 rue Grange Dame Rose, BP34, 92360 Meudon-la-Foret, France.

Atlas tracking radar antenna

3275.153
LOUXOR AIR DEFENCE RADAR
Louxor is an experimental prototype electronically scanned radar for short-range air defence applications. It was built as a research and development instrument in the definition and design of a production equipment suitable for use in such systems as Systèmes d'Armes sol-air à Courte Portée (SACP) planned for future close-in air defence applications.

Gun and surface-to-air missile systems will be directed and both fixed and mobile versions are likely to be developed.

The experimental prototype is mounted on a wheeled truck, and the rectangular planar array antenna can be folded flat for transport, erection being by hydraulic jacks. Operating frequency is in the G/H-band and the antenna consists of 2500 radiating elements containing dipole phase-shifters under the control of a microprocessor computer. Front illumination of the array is employed, with multiple horns for monopulse operation. This arrangement provides search over a sector of –5 to +45° in elevation and ±45° in azimuth without physical movement of the array. An operational system might have several arrays in a back-to-back

configuration to provide all-round or sectorial cover greater than 90°. Alternatively, a single array could be directed in azimuth to provide cover over a 90° sector centred on any required bearing.

Transmitter power has not been disclosed, but the detection range against a nominal 1 m² target is quoted as 23 km, and the Louxor system has a target capacity of 32 targets of which any three can be automatically tracked with outputs for the direction of three guns or other weapons simultaneously. Digital signal processing is employed using microprocessors, and a digital MTI facility is incorporated. Tracking and search operations can be conducted simultaneously. Tracking accuracy is 1 mrad at 12 km.
STATUS
Prototype.
CONTRACTOR
Thomson-CSF, Division Systèmes, Défense et Contrôle, 40 rue Grange Dame Rose, BP34, 92360 Meudon-la-Foret, France.

Thomson-CSF Louxor experimental air defence radar prototype

3274.153
RAMSA LOW-ALTITUDE SURVEILLANCE RADAR TRS 2140

In mid-1977 a new mobile short-range, low-altitude surveillance radar was introduced under the name Ramsa, with the manufacturer's designation TRS 2140. The radar is of the pulse-doppler type and is installed in a cabin. Operational roles are associated with its use in an air defence system for warning and target designation for gun or missile air defence batteries.

Few details are available for publication other than those main characteristics listed below. An extending tower mounting for the antenna head is an alternative option for the Ramsa system.

CHARACTERISTICS
Frequency: D-band (former L-band)
Peak power: 150 W
Average power: 20 W
PRF: Dual with matching pulse-lengths
Antenna rotation rate: 60 rpm
Detection range: 15 km (fighter aircraft target); 20 km as an option
Associated IFF
STATUS
In production for an unspecified customer.
CONTRACTOR
Thomson-CSF, Division Systèmes, Défense et Contrôle, 40 rue Grange Dame Rose, BP34, 92360 Meudon-la-Foret, France.

TRS 2140 Ramsa low-altitude surveillance radar mounted on container carried by flat-bed truck

1944.153
SAVOIE INSTRUMENTATION TRACKING RADAR

Savoie is a multi-tracking radar, intended for automatic tracking at long ranges. The equipment is designed to be shipborne or ground based.
CHARACTERISTICS
Type: Monopulse tracking radar
Antenna
Diameter: 8 m
Gain: 28 dB
Beamwidth (3 dB): 6°
Polarisation: Vertical (transmission); vertical and horizontal (reception)
Turret
Weight: 12 t
Azimuth rotation: +110°
Elevation rotation: 0 - 90°
Speed: 0·25 rad/s
Acceleration: 0·5 rad/s²
Accuracy of analysis axis: 5×10^{-4} rad
Transmitter
Peak power: 150 kW

Mean power: 22 kW
Pulse duration: 500 µs (pulse compression ratio 100)
Receiver
Pulse compression: Receiver controlled by computer
Noise figure: 2·5 dB
STATUS
One installed on the trials research ship *Henri Poincaré*.
CONTRACTOR
Thomson-CSF, Division Systèmes, Défense et Contrôle, 40 rue Grange Dame Rose, BP34, 92360 Meudon-la-Foret, France.

Savoie tracking radar antenna

2157.153
LMT GROUND-BASED IFF INTERROGATORS

The equipment described below can be used to make any of three types of IFF ground interrogation equipment.

Heart of the system is the transmitter/receiver (interrogator-responsor) ER-116-A/B which, but for one tube, is a fully solid-state unit making extensive use of digital integrated circuits. The sub-assemblies of this unit are pluggable and are common with the airborne and shipborne versions and also with other specialised systems such as that for the Crotale, Roland, and Hawk Helip weapon systems.

By itself the ER-116-A constitutes a single locally controlled interrogator-responsor. If this is added to a BC-361-A control box it becomes the NRS1-1A locally or remotely controlled single interrogator-responsor. Addition of a further ER-116-A/B and a switching unit TK-256-A converts the system to the NRSI-1B dual interrogator with local or remote control.

LMT ground-based IFF interrogators have been and are produced under a variety of other designations and a brief summary of the most important of these follows:
NRSI-1A
This is the designation of the first interrogator to be produced by LMT following prototype development in response to a French Government contract awarded in 1967. Under the same contract, a mobile version for use aboard aircraft was developed as the NRAI-3A. The two equipments were virtually identical

electrically, differing only in packaging and in environmental aspects.
NRSI-1B
This comprises dual NRSI-1A interrogators to make the equipment suitable for continuous, unattended operation. In October 1967 the French Government ordered a total of 90 equipments for use at French Air Force airfields and air defence stations, and for the French Fleet Air Arm.
NRAI-5A
This interrogator was designed for use with the Crotale air defence missile system (**2074.131**) and is based on the use of similar technology to that employed in the NRSI-1B and NRAI-3A above. At least 50 equipments have been delivered.
NRAI-6A
This version has been developed specifically for the French Roland anti-aircraft missile system (**2218.131**). Unlike the NRAI-5A, it is a solid-state design. At least 30 sets have been delivered.

A new version has been developed for use with the Shahine missile system (**2074.131**). In 1975 LMT was chosen to supply interrogators for French Improved Hawk anti-aircraft batteries, and the prototype was tested in 1976. A total of 26 sets have been supplied, the last of them in October 1977.
CHARACTERISTICS
Transmitter/receiver ER-116-A
Incorporates coder, transmitter, and 1 or 2 receivers. The ER-116-B transmitter is the same but has an integrated antenna switch
Peak radiated power: Selectable; 0·5, 1 or 2 kW

Transmission frequency: 1030 ± 0·5 MHz (0·2 MHz optional)
Receiver sensitivity: -83 dBm
Receiver frequency: 1090 MHz
Double receiver: For sidelobe suppression (optional)
Possible modes: 1, 2, 3/A, and C; mode 4 with associated equipment
Interlacing facilities: 3 modes out of 4, with changing selections each rotation of the antenna. Permanent self-monitoring of all operational characteristics. Antenna switch for sidelobe suppression at the interrogator (optional)
Size: 3 units of standard 19 inch (483 mm) rack
Power supply: 220 V, 50 Hz, 120 W
Switching supply TK-256-A
Enables ground based installations to operate with 2 transmitter/receivers ER-116-A with automatic switchover in the event of failure of 1 of the systems
Size: 3 units of standard 19 inch (483 mm) rack
Control box BC-361-A
Allows the remote control of a single ER-116-A, or of 2 of them associated with a switching unit TK-256-A
CONTRACTOR
LMT Radio Professionelle, 46-47 quai Alphonse Le Gallo, 92103 Boulogne-Billancourt, France.

3099.153
D-BAND EARLY WARNING RADAR
TRS 2052/TRS 2053/TRS 2056

The TRS 2052 is a D-band early warning radar which has been developed as a successor to the TRS 2050 (**2100.153**). Externally, and in other general characteristics, the later radar is very similar to the TRS 2050. The double-curvature antenna is of the same dimensions (9 × 13 m) and independent high- and low-cover beams are radiated. Cosecant beam shaping in elevation extends to over 40° and sharp ground cut-off of the high-cover lobe produces a strong contrast between air target echoes and ground returns. High-grade circular polarisation ensures rejection of weather returns.

An IFF antenna of the sum/difference type is mounted on the primary radar reflector, as is the side-lobe suppression antenna.

Further development of this successful equipment has led to two more models, the TRS 2053 and TRS 2056. The TRS 2052 air-defence long-range surveillance radar, the medium-range and SRE radars TRS 2053 and TRS 2056, use different antennas with the same electronics. A fully equipped cabin transportable by air, rail and road, houses a transmitter/receiver unit which comprises mainly: two high-stability transmitter/receivers of the 2 MW 2 kW class, equipped with long-life magnetrons, tunable by single-knob control, operating in dual diversity; an associated IF interrogator; two reception and processing units comprising a logarithmic receiver and a digital linear MTI filtering assembly.

Optionally, an SLS reception box to get rid of sidelobes can be included.

In this fashion, a set suitable for both fixed and mobile installations is available to associate with different antennas to constitute the TRS 2052, TRS 2053 and TRS 2056 stations.

With a large antenna (13 × 9 m) featuring high gain and dual coverage, a highly jam-resistant air-defence master station, the TRS 2052, is obtained. This has a detection range capability in excess of 350 km for modern fighter aircraft. With a smaller antenna (9 × 5 m), it becomes the TRS 2053, designed for equipping military airfields as recovery station or as gap-filler radar in an air defence network. These radars are widely distributed around the world. The third one of this family, the TRS 2056, developed for the French Air Force as a movable recovery station, uses an 8·5 × 3·5 m antenna which can be dismounted without special tools. It is known also as Centaure.

Simultaneous use of operationally variable frequency, frequency diversity, constant-false-alarm-rate receivers, of high-performance, compatible MTI, and of sidelobe suppression, endows the radar with excellent anti-jamming capabilities.

All three sets are compatible with fully automatic operational use, and feature built-in test equipment.

CHARACTERISTICS
Type: TRS 2052
Operating frequency range: 100 MHz in D-band
Antenna
Reflector dimensions: 13 × 9 m
Gain (low cover): 36 dB ± 0·5 dB
Gain (high cover): 35·5 dB ± 0·5 dB
Beamwidth in azimuth (3 dB): 1·2°
Cosecant: >40°
Polarisation: Circular, fixed
Rotation speed: 6 rpm
Transmitter
Frequency-tunable magnetron
Peak power: ≥2·2 MW
Pulse duration: 3 μs
PRF: 350 Hz (3-period staggered)
Receiver
Noise figure of RF amplifier: 3 dB
Noise figure at input to reception chain: 4 dB
Intermediate frequency: 30 MHz
Sub-clutter visibility: ≥25 dB
Digital post-detection integration
Power supply: 3-phase, 220/380 V, 50 Hz
Consumption: 40 kVA (55 kVA for diversity operation)
Performance
Detection range for fluctuating 2 m² target: >180 nm (330 km)
Detection in altitude: >60 000 ft (18 300 m)
DEVELOPMENT
The TRS 2052 was developed in the mid-1970s as a successor to the TRS 2050 air defence early warning radar and the other derivatives followed shortly thereafter. The TRS 2053 and TRS 2056, developed for the French Air Force under the name Centaure, use the same transmitter/receiver as the TRS 2052 but have different antennas (see photographs).
STATUS
Numerous radars of this family have been supplied in France and to overseas customers. The TRS 2056, developed for the French Air Force as the Centaure, has been supplied in some quantity, and the TRS 2052 is known to be employed in the DACTA civil/military ATC and surveillance system supplied by Thomson-CSF to Brazil. The TRS 2053, also, is known to have been installed in France and other countries but details are lacking.
CONTRACTOR
Thomson-CSF, Division Systèmes, Défense et Contrôle, 40 rue Grange Dame Rose, BP34, 92360 Meudon-la-Foret, France.

TRS 2052 D-band early warning radar

TRS 2056 (Centaure) D-band early warning radar

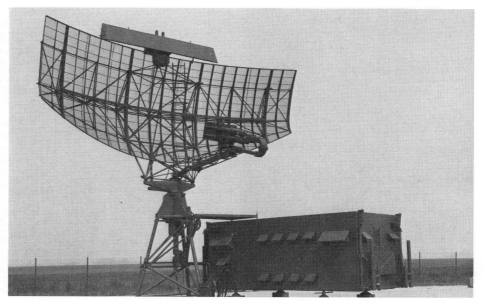

TRS 2053 air surveillance and approach radar

3683.153
LP 23K SERIES LONG-RANGE SURVEILLANCE RADAR

The LP 23K is a coherent, klystron-powered, long-range surveillance radar operating in the D-band of the radar spectrum. It has been evolved for air traffic surveillance roles and similar applications, and is thought to have been based upon experience gained with the TRS 2052 series of radars (**3099.153**). It embodies the latest concepts in steerable pattern null, coherent double-pulse operation and auto-regulating signal processing. This dual-channel 23 cm radar is claimed to be able to detect small aircraft at ranges of up to 200 nautical miles (370 km), and superior clutter see-through capabilities permit detection down to low levels. An integral plot extractor enables the radar to be connected to a data processing system.

The dual beam antenna uses offset feeds for reduced masking of the energy radiated by the reflector, thereby reducing sidelobes, and there is an elongated lower edge to the reflector to intercept radiation from the primary sources so that back lobes are reduced. The feeds are designed to ensure that the reflector edges are only illuminated by low-energy radiation, thus reducing spillover to a level comparable to the background level. A cosecant-squared radiation pattern, boosted at high elevation angles is employed, providing good contrast between short range targets and ground clutter. There is a sharp roll-off at low elevation angles, which also improves the signal-to-clutter contrast, and this is obtained by employing a reflector with a larger-than-usual vertical dimension. Compact stacking of the main and auxiliary feeds, gives good focusing for the high beam and reduced boresight separation between the two beams, while still maintaining a target-to-clutter enhancement of 16 to 18 dB. Programmable range/azimuth gated beam mixing (steerable pattern null) further improves clutter rejection.

The transmitter uses a TH 2068 klystron which is stated to have a saturation gain of over 50 dB. It is a pulse-driven tube with five cavities giving a peak output of 5 MW, although in the present application it is deliberately under-driven to increase its service life. It is operated at 3·5 MW peak power and 4·7 kW mean power. The transmitter is crystal-controlled. At each pulse repetition interval, the transmitter generates a coherent pulse train consisting of a long duration pulse followed immediately by a short pulse. This provides a means of obtaining simultaneously in a single radar the benefits of both long- and short-pulse operation. The latter gives a precise radar cell and so improves both target resolution and signal-to-clutter contrast, these characteristics being especially valuable at short and medium ranges. At greater ranges, the longer pulse results in an increased useful detection range.

Signal processing and remoting is provided by a TPL 800 processor with enhanced capability thanks to the coherent signals received. Video processing includes log/FTC/anti-log conversion to suppress slow-moving clutter patches. In the UHF spectrum, STC is controlled through digital programming with a matrix of 64 × 64 cells. The receiver input stage is a low-noise solid-state, wide-band amplifier, and the linear amplifier which drives the MTI processor prevents clutter spectrum spreading. IF gain is automatically controlled by a dynamic clutter memory having a capacity of 128 × 128 azimuth/range cells (3° × 2 or 1 nautical miles), and ten-bit phase-coding of in-phase and quadrature channels eliminates MTI blind speeds. The MTI filter can be either a three-pulse filter or a three-stage recursive filter with programmable negative feedback. Video diversity summing is performed digitally.

Other members of the family include the TR 23K which uses the same transmitter/receiver as the LP 23K and the same antenna as the TRS 2053. The TR 23M is a magnetron-powered alternative to the TR 23K.

STATUS

In production and sold to France and other countries.

CONTRACTOR

Thomson-CSF, Division Systèmes, Défense et Contrôle, 40 rue Grange Dame Rose, BP34, 92360 Meudon-la-Foret, France.

LP 23K long-range surveillance radar

3272.153
TRS 2230/TRS 2215 3-D RADARS

This family of E/F-band air-defence three-dimensional radars, employing electronic phase scanning in elevation, is directly derived from the very high precision heightfinding radar SATRAPE which has equipped the French Air Force (see **2060.153** ANTARES).

The TRS 2230 is the fixed or relocatable version in this family. The TRS 2215 and TRS 2215D are the mobile versions, transportable by road, rail or aircraft (Transall, C-130, or equivalent), and can be deployed in less than one hour. Both radars employ the same space scanning techniques, the same transmitter, the same reception and processing circuits, and the same antenna components. They use two types of antenna; either a cylindro-parabolic reflector (TRS 2215 only) or a planar phased-array reflector (TRS 2215D and 2230D). This commonality, which has particular relevance to maintenance, logistics and training, allows in addition a high flexibility of deployment of the facilities in a system incorporating both versions (eg backing up of a fixed-station antenna by a mobile-station antenna).

In the antenna with a cylindro-parabolic reflector, azimuth scanning is obtained by rotating the antenna continuously about a vertical axis. The primary feed is a linear array of elementary feeds, radiating circularly polarised waves, coupled with two waveguides through directive couplers. In the planar array antenna the two-waveguide feeder is linked to a set of horizontal rows of elementary feeds radiating circularly polarised waves. The two waveguides allow monopulse operation to perform the heightfinding function. Digital electronic phase-shift networks inserted between the elementary feeds and the corresponding directive couplers control the pointing of the beams.

The transmitter is an amplifying chain transmitter using a high-efficiency crossed-field amplifier as its final tube. It permits the use of the pulse-compression technique and that of pulse-to-pulse frequency agility. It is characterised by high efficiency (greater than 70 per cent) and a modular modulator allows repair operations, if required, to be carried out without shutting down the station.

The receiving section groups the receivers, the MTI unit, the extractor, the plot processing and altitude computing equipment, the control device for the tilting of the antenna according to the mode of operation imposed, and the monitoring desk.

The receiver circuits comprise the anti-jamming chains and three angle error chains. The MTI device processes the signals received from any one of the three lower beams by programming. The extractor performs the extraction of primary and secondary plots and allows them to be associated together. It is followed by a plot processing system which computes altitude, and filters plots so as to transmit only useful data. The device generates the data in a digital form permitting the transmission of plots to a remote centre. The monitoring desk groups the monitor controls of the station's operation.

CHARACTERISTICS

Detection range (fluctuating 2 m² target): 510 km

Ceiling: >30 500 m

Elevation coverage: –3 to +30°; programmed operating multimode

Altitude accuracy:

TRS 2230: ±300 m at 300 km

TRS 2215: ±450 m at 200 km

Data renewal rate: 10 s

Antenna: TRS 2215

Gain: 40 dB

Beamwidths (3 dB): Azimuth 1·5°; elevation 1·9 – 4°

Polarisation: Circular, fixed

Rotation speed: 6 rpm

Transmission

Peak power: 700 kW

Average power: 10 kW

PRF (average): 380 Hz

Reception: CFAR

MTI improvement factor: 40 dB

STATUS

In production for French and other forces. The TRS 2215D is a later development which was shown for the first time at the 1983 Paris Air Show. An electronic scanning radar, the TRS 22XX which belongs to the same family, has been developed, and offered for the NATO E/F-band update programme.

CONTRACTOR

Thomson-CSF, Division Systèmes, Défense et Contrôle, 40 rue Grange Dame Rose, BP34, 92360 Meudon-la-Foret, France.

TRS 2215 air defence station

Planar array antenna TRS 2215/2230

3197.153
OEIL VERT RADAR

The Oeil Vert radar is a D-band equipment used in the AMX-30 SA self-propelled 30 mm twin gun anti-aircraft system (**2138.131**) for surveillance and target detection. It is a pulse doppler system and is mounted on the turret of the AMX-30 carrier vehicle, the indicator and control units being inside and the transmitter/receiver, signal processor, antenna erection mechanism, and junction box being housed in a protective container attached to the rear of the turret.

Two surveillance modes are provided: (a) distant, with a range of 15 km intended for normal use, and (b) close-in, with a range of 6·5 km which is available at the operator's discretion to suit operating conditions. Each mode has several range gates. MTI and track-while-scan facilities are provided and good sub-clutter visibility also is claimed.

CHARACTERISTICS

Type: Pulse doppler

Frequency: 1710 – 1750 MHz

Power: 120 W (peak)

Max range: 15 km and 20 km as an option

Azimuth accuracy: ±2° (approx)

MTI radial speed range: 30 – 160 m/s (slow targets); 160 – 300 m/s (fast targets)

Tracking range: 13 km to almost 0 km

STATUS

In production. Used in the AMX-30 SA tracked AA gun system (**2138.131**) and the Dragon AA tank project (**3679.131**).

CONTRACTOR

Thomson-CSF, Division Systèmes, Défense et Contrôle, 40 rue Grange Dame Rose, BP34, 92360 Meudon-la-Foret, France.

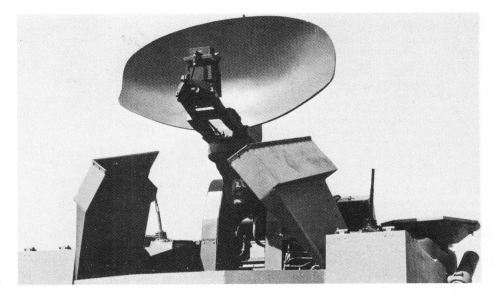

Oeil Vert scanner erected and ready for use

5601.153

RA 20S FIRE CONTROL RADAR

RA 20S is a coherent pulse doppler radar used for the detection and tracking of fixed and rotary wing aircraft flying at low and very low altitudes and is

TA20/RA20S fire control radar mounted on an anti-aircraft defence vehicle

presumably the successor to the RA 20 and RA 21 systems described under **3717.153** and **3718.153** in previous editions of *Jane's Weapon Systems*. It has been specially developed for integration in anti-aircraft defence systems fitted with 20 or 25 mm twin-gun turrets or carriages, such as the TA20 turret designed by ESD. It can be used as the 'leader' of an anti-aircraft defence unit and operated to serve four vehicles or carriages with automatically slewed weapons.

The radar is discreet, lightweight and small, employing a solid-state transmitter, track-while-scan techniques and incorporating a built-in test system. It can be easily operated after a simple training course.

The RA 20S is IFF compatible and consists of two main sub-assemblies:

(1) an antenna unit comprising a retractable antenna, transmitter/receiver and processing circuits

(2) a control console fitted with the controls and a display module.

CHARACTERISTICS

Acquisition envelope

Azimuth: 360°

Elevation: –5 to +45°

Range: 1 – 12 km

Tracking type: TWS

Number of tracks: 2 (with possible extension)

Range: (to combat aircraft) 12 km; (to tactical helicopter) 12 km

Weight

Antenna unit: 60 kg

Console: 25 kg

STATUS

In full production and more than 50 systems have been delivered to several defence forces.

CONTRACTOR

Electronique Serge Dassault, 55 quai Carnot, 92214 St Cloud, France.

5602.153

RODEO 2 FIRE CONTROL RADAR

RODEO 2 (radar d'observation et de designation d'objectifs) is a coherent pulse doppler radar used for the detection, tracking and identification of aircraft flying at low and very low altitudes and is particularly suitable for use against hovering helicopters on watch or at firing position. Identification of the latter is possible from an analysis of its blade flash and comparison with the signature of rotor blades held in a library bank. The basic concept of this equipment is very similar to that of the RA 20S (**5601.153**), and it is presumably the successor to the RODEO 20 system described under **3719.153** in previous editions of *Jane's Weapon Systems*.

RODEO 2 can be used as the 'leader' of an anti-aircraft defence unit and operated to serve four defence vehicles, fitted with guns or missiles, the weapons of which are automatically slewed. It is IFF

compatible and uses frequency agility against electronic countermeasures.

The system consists of two main sub-assemblies:

(1) an antenna unit comprising an antenna (in a radome), a transmitter/receiver, and data extraction and processing circuits

(2) a control console fitted with the controls and display module.

The equipment is a discreet, lightweight and small radar employing a solid-state transmitter, track-while-scan techniques and incorporating a built-in test system.

CHARACTERISTICS

Acquisition envelope

Azimuth: 360°

Elevation: –5 to +35°

Beamwidth: 6·5°

Range: 1 – 10·5 km

Tracking

Type: TWS

Number of tracks: 2 (with possible extension)

Range: On aircraft or moving helicopter >10 km; hovering helicopter at firing position >7 km; helicopter on watch (rotor motion) >5 km

Output: 40W

Weight

Antenna unit: 60 kg

Console: 25 kg

STATUS

RODEO 2 is a prototype equipment which belongs to the RA 20S series of fire control radars (**5601.153**). It is a candidate for the French Army vehicle-mounted fire control radar. A decision was expected by mid-1984.

CONTRACTOR

Electronique Serge Dassault, 55 quai Carnot, 92214 St Cloud, France.

3276.153
WEATHER RADAR TRS 2730

This radar makes conventional meteorological measurements; detects precipitation (rain, hail and snow) within a radius of 400 km; and manually tracks meteorological balloons (automatic tracking available as an optional feature).

The station comprises:
(1) a parabolic antenna, 3·05 m in diameter, mounted on a turret which provides mobility in both elevation and azimuth
(2) a servo cabinet
(3) a transmitter/receiver cabinet
(4) switchable display (PPI/RHI) on colour TV screen.

CHARACTERISTICS
Transmission frequency: Tunable, 5·6 – 5·8 GHz
Peak power: 250 kW
Pulse duration: 2 µs
Noise figure: 7·5 dB

Video: High degree of automation, allowing the set to be manned by one operator. Optional features include: picture transmission by synchronous line coupler or facsimile coupler; short range remoting.
STATUS
In production.
CONTRACTOR
Thomson-CSF, Division Systèmes, Défense et Contrôle, 40 rue Grange Dame Rose, BP34, 92360 Meudon-la-Foret, France.

TRS 2730 weather radar

2120.153
PERCEVAL/SPARTIATE RECOVERY RADAR TRS 2300

Perceval is a highly mobile helicopter and aircraft recovery radar station developed for the French forces. Its functions include early warning (secondary radar), approach and recovery (primary radar), and landing. All these functions can be carried out simultaneously.

The station comprises a lightweight trailer supporting the radar transmitter/receiver unit, MTI unit, the IFF interrogator and the antennas, a cabin housing two displays, associated means of telecommunication, and a trailer carrying a power generating set.

The antenna system comprises an azimuth antenna which can rotate continuously and an elevation antenna which scans in the vertical plane. The IFF antenna is integrated with the primary radar antenna.

The transmitter and the receiver operate in I/J-band and are transistorised and miniaturised.

The designation Perceval is that given to the export version of a system developed for the air elements of the French Army, to which service it is known as SPARTIATE (système polyvalent d'atterrissage, recueil, télécommunications, identification de l'Armée de Terre).

Additional details will be found under this entry number (**2120.153**) in earlier editions of *Jane's Weapon Systems*. No longer in production.
CONTRACTOR
Thomson-CSF, Division Systèmes, Défense et Contrôle, 40 rue Grange Dame Rose, BP34, 92360 Meudon-la-Foret, France.

TRS 2300 Perceval/SPARTIATE recovery radar

3492.153
PRECISION APPROACH RADAR TRS 2310

This J-band equipment replaces the TH.D 1012 (**2133.153**), a PAR which is used all over the world. Specific improvements are:
(1) the equipment's total mobility
(2) performance in the presence of heavy rainfall greatly improved by the use of velocity filters in the processing chain
(3) possibility of controlling several approaches simultaneously by optimisation of antenna radiation patterns.

The equipment can be delivered for static installation with the same constituent elements. Approach control room equipment also is available in a static and in mobile versions, with a remoting capability of up to 3000 m. The PAR TRS 2310 meets ICAO recommendations. Fully solid-state design ensures very high reliability and ease of maintenance. The operation detection range is 20 nautical miles for Mirage aircraft with 90 per cent detection probability.

CHARACTERISTICS
Frequency band: 9000-9200 MHz
Antennas: Mounted on orientable turret allowing angular displacement of 200 or 270° (at least 2 QFUs)
Beamwidths (3 dB): 0·6° (elevation antenna); 1·1° (azimuth antenna)
Gain (high-resolution plane): 39·5 dB (elevation antenna); 38·5 dB (azimuth antenna)
Attenuation of first sidelobes: < –25 dB
Polarisation: Circular
Transmitter: High-gain TWT stage fed by high-stability pilot
Average power: 100 W (bad-weather mode); 50 W (clear-weather mode)

PRF: 3 PRF values in mode 2; 2 PRF values in mode 1
Receiver: Digital doppler processing
Noise figure: 3·5 dB
PERFORMANCE
Operating modes: Bad and clear weather
Ranges: 10 and 20 nm
Scanning ranges: Elevation from –1 to +9°; azimuth 20°
Data rate: 1 azimuth and elevation picture every half second

Improvement factor: 40 dB (fixed echoes); 30 dB (heavy rain echoes)
Precision: According to ICAO standards
STATUS
In production for several countries.
CONTRACTOR
Thomson-CSF, Division Systèmes, Défense et Contrôle, 40 rue Grange Dame Rose, BP34, 92360 Meudon-la-Foret, France.

TRS 2310 precision approach radar

2119.153
PICADOR MOBILE 3-D RADAR

Picador TRS 2200 is a mobile air defence radar station operating in E/F-band. This station combines in a single system the radar functions of 3-D surveillance, heightfinding, and low-altitude surveillance. Designed to be transportable and capable of being deployed rapidly, it can be used for surveillance and interception control either as an autonomous station

or as a gapfiller integrated into a large air defence system.

The complete station comprises an equipment cabin, an operations cabin, and power generators.
Equipment Cabin
On the reinforced roof of this cabin is fixed the antenna system which comprises a single reflector and three primary feeds. One of these is for 3-D search and heightfinding coverage and is an electro-

mechanical rapid scan feed; a second is for low-altitude plan coverage; and the third is for IFF coverage (with a supplementary omnidirectional antenna for the ISLS function).
STATUS
No longer in production. More detailed information is given under this entry number in previous editions of *Jane's Weapon Systems*.

CONTRACTOR
Thomson-CSF, Division Systèmes, Défense et Contrôle, 40 rue Grange Dame Rose, BP34, 92360 Meudon-la-Foret, France.

Picador mobile air defence radar station, with operations cabin

3100.153
COASTAL SURFACE SURVEILLANCE RADAR TRS 3405

This equipment is an I-band radar specially intended for the surveillance of maritime traffic in straits, harbour approaches, access channels, and harbours.

It is designed to provide high performance in range, resolution, accuracy, and protection against the various detection impairments encountered in sea surface surveillance, namely sea and rain clutter, and propagation loss in rain and heavy fog. High resolution is achieved by the use of an antenna with a narrow azimuth beamwidth, and a very short transmission pulse, which results in a very small radar cell. The use of frequency diversity allows decorrelation of sea clutter peaks, reducing the false alarm rate and improving the detection of small ships or buoys.

The radar operates in the I-band (former X-band). To achieve a high gain and avoid unwanted rain echoes which would result from the illumination of clouds at high altitude, the antenna elevation beamwidth is also narrow, and radiation polarisation can be switched from linear to circular. Detection at very close range is ensured by an elevation pattern of the inverted cosecant-squared type down to an angle of –25°.

Round-the-clock operating requirements demand two transmitter/receivers for each radar station. In this equipment, they are connected to the antenna through a passive diplexer rather than through a switching device, which enables both units to be operated simultaneously on a frequency diversity basis. As this mode of simultaneous operation is necessary only in heavy weather, the operating cost is not increased significantly. In addition, each reception channel is fitted with an automatic false-alarm regulation control slaved to the mean level of sea clutter.

This equipment is fully compatible with extractors and data remoting.

CHARACTERISTICS
Antenna
Gain: 44 dB
Resolution: 0·24°
Low sidelobes: 25 dB
Inverted cosecant: Squared pattern in elevation down to –25°
Linear and circular polarisation
Rotation rate: 5 or 10 rpm
Transmitter/receiver
Frequency: I-band (formerly X-band)
Peak power: 200 kW
High resolution pulse: 0·05 μs
PRF: 1080-570 Hz
Advanced anti-clutter and anti-jamming processing.
STATUS
In production.

TRS 3405 coastal surface surveillance radar

CONTRACTOR
Thomson-CSF, Division Systèmes, Défense et Contrôle, 40 rue Grange Dame Rose, BP34, 92360 Meudon-la-Foret, France.

4224.153
TRS 2600 RADAR

The TRS 2600 radar combines the functions of surveillance and target designation. It is intended to pin-point targets flying at low and very low altitudes for very short range weapon systems. An E/F-band coherent pulse doppler radar with a digital processing system, the equipment consists of two solid-state sub-assemblies, one for transmission and reception, the other for data processing and display. The antenna is located inside a radome. The transmitter is wide-band with frequency agility in the search mode. Thirty-two vertical channels are used to obtain the radial rate of the target.

The equipment, which is capable of tracking four targets automatically, is being developed to detect helicopters, partly hidden, while hovering. It is possible to identify the type of helicopter by analysis of the rotor blade flash. Velocity filters are incorporated to enable the system to operate in an ECM environment.

CHARACTERISTICS
Frequency: E/F-band
Antenna: Radiating pattern, 40 rpm
Coverage: Azimuth 360°
Range: Aircraft ≥10 km; concealed hovering helicopter ≥6 km
Accuracy: Aircraft ≤1° azimuth, ≤60 m range; Helicopter ≤0·6° azimuth, ≤60 m range
Weight: 80 kg

STATUS
Under development for the French Army. Originally conceived for use with a Matra missile system, can be fitted to any very short range AA weapon system (missiles and/or guns). It is a competitor for the French Army vehicle-mounted SAM radar. A decision was expected in mid-1984.
CONTRACTOR
Thomson-CSF, Division Systèmes, Défense et Contrôle, 40 rue Grange Dame Rose, BP34, 92360 Meudon-la-Foret, France.

3273.153
MOBILE COASTAL SURFACE SURVEILLANCE RADAR TRS 3410

This mobile, cabin-installed station utilises the I-band transmitter/receiver of the TRS 3405 radar (**3100.153**) operating in frequency diversity for decorrelation of sea clutter peaks, coupled with a 4·4 m antenna located on a trailer. Installed at 40 to 50 m above sea level, this station detects small boats up to 25 km away, whereas for larger ships with superstructures at a height of 10 m or more, the detection range reaches 40 km.

The TRS 3410 radar is fitted with a track-while-scan (TWS) device which refines and maintains the data from a surface track, starting from a target designation made by the operator. These data are processed through a computer for the control of various types of anti-ship missiles whose batteries can be located next to the radar station or remotely sited. The compounding of its own accuracy and of the data refinement by the TWS device gives an overall target parameters accuracy which is sufficient for the control of coastal artillery fire against surface targets.
CHARACTERISTICS
Antenna: 4·4 m parabolic reflector
Gain: 39·5 dB
Azimuth beamwidth (3 dB): 0·55°
Elevation beamwidth (3 dB): 4°
Polarisation: Circular

Rotation rate: 11 rpm
Transmitter/receiver
Frequency: I-band
Peak power: 200 kW
High resolution pulse: 0·05 µs
PRF: 1080-570 Hz
Advanced anti-clutter and anti-jamming processing
STATUS
In production.
CONTRACTOR
Thomson-CSF, Division Systèmes, Défense et
Contrôle, 40 rue Grange Dame Rose, BP34, 92360
Meudon-la-Foret, France.

*Thomson-CSF TRS 3410 mobile coast defence radar
includes tracking of the co-operating helicopter to
provide over-the-horizon target data*

2141.153
RASIT 3190B BATTLEFIELD SURVEILLANCE RADAR

Rasit 3190B is a long range (30 km) battlefield surveillance radar, for the detection, acquisition, localisation, and recognition of moving targets, either on or near the ground in all weathers. The Rasit 3190B is available in three versions: man-portable and broken down into four 30 kg sections, shelter-mounted and vehicle-mounted.

The equipment is a pulse doppler radar. It operates in I/J-band and uses a coherent receiver and multiple range gates and filters designed for a high probability of detection.

Echoes detected over the surveyed zone are displayed on a B-scope daylight display, connected to an electronic memory.

For each target acquired, the polar and UTM co-ordinates are displayed on the B-scope and the doppler tone is transmitted to the operator either by loudspeaker or by earphone. The operator is thus able to recognise pedestrians, wheeled and tracked vehicles, aircraft, and helicopters.

An automatic system can be arranged to trigger an acoustic alarm as soon as a target enters the surveyed zone. The operator can select the width of the surveyed zone from 30 to 120° and can choose the length surveyed by operating in either of two modes:
(a) Normal: overall radar range of 20 km
(b) Magnifier: any zone 2·5 km long within the total range.

The equipment can be operated by a single inexperienced operator in a variety of conditions. Typical operating times are ten seconds to survey a zone 100° wide and 20 km long, and 30 seconds to acquire a target.

The antenna beam can automatically sweep a sector or can be stopped and then oriented towards a target. The antenna is equipped with a polariser making the radar insensitive to atmospheric perturbations. The radar also has very effective ECCM capabilities.

The RF unit can be mounted on a tripod with the control cabinet 50 m away. Alternatively it can be mounted on any of a variety of military vehicles, such as the APC Steyr, the APC Mowag, the Alvis-British

Leyland Spartan, the Panhard M3 or the APC VAB, with the control cabinet inside the vehicle.

In addition to built-in tests, a tactical test bench can be supplied for third and fourth echelon maintenance. A tactical simulator designed for an efficient and comprehensive training of one or several operators is available.

CHARACTERISTICS
Operating frequency: I-band (200 MHz range)
Peak power: 2 kW
Polarisation: Linear or circular
Range (90% probability of detection)
Pedestrian: 18 km
Vehicle: >30 km
Helicopter: 15-25 km
Low-flying aircraft: 28 km
Range reduction: (4 mm/h rain) <10%
Accuracy: Azimuth ±10 mrd, range ±10 m
Sub-clutter visibility: More than 43 dB
Display: B-type daylight oscilloscope, numerical display of polar and UTM co-ordinates, doppler tone, automatic acoustic alarm
Power drain: 150 W (28 V)
Temperature range: –40 to +55° C
Reliability: Field tested MTBF >900 h
Overall weight: 90 kg
Number of loads: 4
Weight of the heaviest load: 28 kg
Distance between radar head and operator unit: 80 m max
Provision for target data transmission
Built-in tests
Options: Remote slave TV monitor; plotting table; compatible with Siclamen IFF (**3173.153**).
STATUS
In production. Rasit has been adopted by 12 armies and is under consideration by others. The French Army designation is DDMT-1-A. LMT signed an agreement with LCT and SEL (West Germany) whereby LMT supplies a third of the sub-systems for Rasit systems built by SEL for the West German Army.

By mid-1983 more than 350 radars had been ordered, of which over 300 had been delivered, including the first shelter housed models (see illustration) for the French Army.
CONTRACTOR
LMT Radio Professionelle, 46-47 quai Alphonse Le Gallo, 92103 Boulogne-Billancourt, France.

Shelter mounted version of Rasit DDMT-1-A battlefield surveillance radar

3173.153
SICLAMEN IFF SYSTEM
Siclamen is the name given to a D-band IFF compatible system designed to meet all the identification requirements of mobile units operating in a combat zone. It is known as BIFF, battlefield IFF, by the French originators. The main operational conditions satisfied are:
(1) Ground-to-ground identification of friendly vehicles

(2) The ability to provide an integrated system in conjunction with RATAC (**1528.153**), Rasit 3190B (**2141.153**) or any other type of battlefield radar or other sensor
(3) Compatibility with existing ground-to-air system of IFF for the identification of helicopters and aircraft operating over the combat zone
(4) An ability to operate in conjunction with a cryptographic system, thereby enhancing reliability and facilitating anti-tank operations.

The decoder has three main functions:
(a) Location of friendly units
(b) Searching for a particular vehicle by means of its discrete code
(c) Identification of a return from a friendly unit and display of its range.

The Siclamen system consists of a network of Type 3565A interrogators, each associated with a Type 3565B control box. Vehicles are fitted with Type 3565C transponders, and directional and omni-directional antennas are employed. Full code selection facilities are available.

A directional BIFF antenna is used to transmit interrogator signals and this is normally co-mounted with the primary sensor, such as the Rasit radar scanner, or optical or laser rangefinder/sight. An omni-directional antenna is standard for reception of replies, and in some versions a rotating antenna may be fitted for transmission of replies.

Twelve versions of Siclamen are possible, these depending principally upon the primary sensor with which it is associated. These include the RATAC battlefield radar, the Rasit radar, and a laser rangefinder for use on helicopters.

CHARACTERISTICS
Frequency: 1030 MHz interrogation; 1090 MHz reply
Peak power: 10 W
Receiver sensitivity: –75 dBm
Modes: 3 in IFF (1, 2 and 3/A), 1 in BIFF. Mode 4 (Mk XII) or other secure mode used in both IFF and BIFF

Codes: 1 in BIFF, 2 in IFF
Passive decoder: 1 in BIFF, 2 in IFF
Active decoder: 1 each in BIFF and IFF
Range display: Metres × 10 up to 20 km in BIFF; metres × 100 up to 20 km in IFF
Range discrimination between two BIFF-equipped vehicles: 100 m
DEVELOPMENT
The Siclamen project was initiated in 1968 and by 1972 the first prototype equipment was presented to SEFT (Section d'Études et de Fabrications des Télécommunications) which had carried out a separate programme. SEFT requested LMT to make a certain number of modifications to improve such aspects as the coding facilities (limited then to 16), discrimination, and security. As a result the Yagi type antenna used initially was dropped at this time and a plate substituted.

In 1975, LMT was able to demonstrate a new facility of the BIFF system, based on the use of a rotating antenna for transmission of responder replies. These

Siclamen IFF equipment

resulted in each vehicle interrogated having its own doppler characteristic, and with the other data provided by the Siclamen system this enabled the locations of all friendly vehicles equipped with it to be automatically determined by a battlefield surveillance radar such as RATAC.
STATUS
In production and in service with the French Army.
CONTRACTOR
LMT Radio Professionelle, 46-47 quai Alphonse Le Gallo, 92103 Boulogne-Billancourt, France.

3287.153
STENTOR BATTLEFIELD RADAR
Stentor is a doppler radar used for ground surveillance of critical areas, such as battlefields and frontiers. It is claimed to have the longest range for ground surface surveillance radars, making possible surveillance of remoter areas and, as a medium-range radar, it provides a significant increase in warning time to aid the interception of hostile units. At shorter ranges the benefits of a powerful signal are evident for high detection probability against very small or

intermittent targets, or for minimising the absorption effects of adverse weather conditions. The Stentor ranges are: 30 to 40 km for pedestrian targets; 50 to 60 km for targets such as a Jeep, tank, truck; and 20 to 60 km for boats (depending on sea conditions) and helicopters (a major threat when flying low at low speeds since they are not detectable by classical air defence or low flying aircraft detection radars).

It is a transportable system comprising the radar head and an operator's console which can be remotely sited several hundred metres from the radar

head. The radar head can be located on a tower, or on a naturally elevated site, to increase the surveyed area and, thus, distant detection.

The operating frequency is in the X-band (US I-band), tunable over 200 MHz with pulse transmission, ground clutter cancellation being by coherent detection and doppler filtering; rain cancellation circuits provide for all-weather operation. Moving targets are displayed on a daylight CRT with a digital memory. The surveyed sector can be instantaneously adjusted in aperture and in azimuth.

A tactical data communication system which enables a command post to simultaneously receive and process the data issued from one to ten Stentor radar stations is also optionally available, as are operator training simulators and third echelon bench test units.

Stentor is simple to operate (even by a single inexperienced operator) and to maintain, with high mobility, fast deployment and effective ECCM capability.
CHARACTERISTICS
Frequency: I/J-band, tunable
Peak power: 60 kW
Polarisation: Vertical or circular
Antenna span: 1·6 m
Range: 0-60 km, according to target
Accuracy: 20 m (range); 4·4 mrad (0·25°) (azimuth)
Weight: 370 kg (radar head and operator's unit)
Power: 1·5 kVA, 220 V, 50/60 Hz
MTBF: >1000 h
STATUS
In production and operational with various armies.
CONTRACTOR
LCT (Laboratoire Central de Télécommunications), 18-20 rue Grange Dame Rose, 78141 Vélizy-Villacoublay, France.

Stentor deployed in typical surroundings

2155.153
THREE-DIMENSIONAL RADAR TRS 2201
The TRS 2201 is a long-range three-dimensional E/F-band air defence radar. A modern technology version of the ARES radar used in NATO's NADGE network, it ranks among the most powerful radars of its type in the world.

Major features of this radar are its high-power (20 MW peak) transmitter, its elaborate antenna structure, and its range of ECCM facilities that enable it to function satisfactorily in an ECM environment. The equipment is solid-state to the maximum extent possible, is of modular construction, and has built-in test facilities. More detailed information is given under this entry number in previous editions of *Jane's Weapon Systems*.
PERFORMANCE
Range capability of the TRS 2201 is more than 250 nautical miles (460 km) on fighter aircraft, there being no practical altitude limitation. Height measurement accuracy is ±1500 ft (457 m) up to 150 nautical miles (280 km). The data renewal rate is six per minute.

TRS 2201 long-range 3-D air surveillance radar

STATUS

More than 30 sets have been constructed but the equipment is no longer in production. Besides France several countries have been equipped with TRS 2201 stations and the equipment was selected by NATO as the main feature of its radar coverage (NADGE plan – see **1181.181**).

CONTRACTOR

Thomson-CSF, Division Systèmes, Défense et Contrôle, 40 rue Grange Dame Rose, BP34, 92360 Meudon-la-Foret, France.

3271.153

VOLEX IV 3-D SURVEILLANCE RADAR TRS 2206

Volex is a fixed, E/F-band, 3-D surveillance radar providing continuously and simultaneously the azimuth, range, and altitude of any target within its cover volume; it may be used either as a 3-D air defence station or as a heightfinder.

The equipment consists, in the main, of an antenna system and dual transmitter/receivers. The antenna system comprises two antennas mounted side-by-side on a common turntable. Both are equipped with a Robinson elevation rapid-scan primary feed. The electronics are cabin-mounted and include two transmitter/receivers operating at a single-knob-controlled variable frequency, and equipped with constant-false-alarm-rate anti-jamming receivers. These solid-state equipments are fully interchangeable. Other features are sidelobe blanking and new-generation technology processing and data extraction facilities which result in high precision and resistance to ECM.

The Volex IV radar is intended to feed an automatic exploitation system housed in the same cabin as the transmitter/receiver. Heightfinding accuracy is ±460 m at a range of 240 km.

The earlier Volex III radar (**2160.153**) was described in previous editions of *Jane's Weapon Systems*, and certain successful features of this design are retained in the Volex IV which is also more fully described in previous editions.

Volex IV 3-D radar TRS 2206 in its fixed site configuration

STATUS

No longer in production.

CONTRACTOR

Thomson-CSF, Division Systèmes, Défense et Contrôle, 40 rue Grange Dame Rose, BP34, 92360 Meudon-la-Foret, France.

2156.153

TIGER RADAR TRS 2100 SERIES

Under the code name TIGER (terrifically insensitive to ground effect radar), Thomson-CSF has developed a family of lightweight high-performance radars, the first being the TRS 2100 for the detection of low-flying aircraft. A special version is produced for the French Air Force, designated Aladin. High performance in severe clutter is achieved by the simultaneous use of MTI circuits based on doppler frequency filtering and of pulse compression to limit the volume in which clutter echoes can mix with useful echoes. The radar can be used either as an autonomous detection centre, with local exploitation of radar data, or as a gap-filler station linked to an air defence network. Specific operational functions listed by the manufacturer include: control of tactical operations; low-altitude gap-filler; coastal and maritime surveillance; alert and target designation for SAM batteries; surveillance radar equipment role; and similar mobile or air-transportable applications.

The use of E/F-band makes it possible to have an antenna with a high gain and high angular resolution but with a relatively small reflector (5 × 2·3 m). The reflector profile is C-shaped with a double curvature and the vertical pattern has a steep slope at low elevations and is super-cosecanted at high elevations. An IFF sub-system is incorporated (IFF antenna integral with primary radar antenna) and a BITE facility monitors the main parameters and locates any faulty functions.

The transmitter uses a coherent amplifier chain. The transmission frequency is obtained from a highly stabilised crystal oscillator, and for frequency agility purposes transmission is carried out at different frequencies distributed at random over 200 MHz. The output power is provided by three successive amplifier stages (one transistor stage, one TWT stage, and one CFA stage). The phase stability of this chain is such as to ensure good clutter rejection performance. Pulse compression is achieved by incorporating crystal dispersive networks, the propagation time of which varies with the frequency in the transmit and receive circuits.

The receiver is preceded by a wide-band, low noise RF amplifier. Rejection of fixed echoes is obtained by a digital linear MTI. A constant-false-alarm-rate chain operates with the MTI processing chain.

TRS 2105 mobile radar

Tiger mobile radar

The radar head can be linked by either a single coaxial cable or microwave link to a remotely sited operations unit. Utilisation can be manual, semi-automatic or fully automatic.

Other members of the TIGER family are the C-band TRS 2105 and TRS 2106 which are intended respectively for the detection of low-flying aircraft and target designation to SAM systems.

TRS 2100 Tiger radar on tower

OPERATION

The radar is transportable by helicopter or by conventional truck or cargo aircraft. The transmitter/receiver and antenna are mounted on a trailer. The antenna can also be mounted on a mast (14 or 54 m).

CHARACTERISTICS

Operational performance: On 2 m² (fluctuating target) with Pd = 80%

Detection range: 120 km

Altitude detection: >6000 m

Elevation pattern: Cosecanted up to 45°

Sub-clutter visibility: >40 dB

First blind speed: >1500 knots

Antenna characteristics

Size: 5 × 2·3 m. IFF antenna integrated with primary radar antenna

Gain: 34 dB

Polarisation: Circular, fixed

Rotation speed: 12 rpm

Transmitter/receiver characteristics

Frequency range: 550 MHz in E/F-band

Mean power: 800 W

Overall receiver noise figure: <3·5 dB

Frequency-agile using synthesiser; dual-PRF operating mode; linear 3-memory digital MTI filter; CFAR; post-detection integration circuits.

STATUS

In production for French Air Force (Aladin) and a number of other governments including Egypt and Zaire.

CONTRACTOR

Thomson-CSF, Division Systèmes, Défense et Contrôle, 40 rue Grange Dame Rose, BP34, 92360 Meudon-la-Foret, France.

GERMANY (FEDERAL REPUBLIC)

3286.153

SIEMENS MILITARY RADARS

Siemens-Albis Fire Control Radar

This J-band tracking radar was developed by Siemens-Albis Ltd for use in the Oerlikon-Contraves Type B2 version of the 35 mm AA Gepard tank (**2370.131**). A monopulse pulse-doppler equipment, it has an operating range of 15 km and permanent echo rejection of better than 23 dB. In this application it is used in conjunction with the MPDR 12.

MPDR 12

The MPDR 12 is the acquisition radar of the Gepard AA tank Mk3. It is an E-band pulse-doppler radar with high sub-clutter visibility and high data rate (60 rpm). The system is integrated with the MSR 400 interrogator for IFF.

MPDR 16

This is the search radar used in the Roland mobile surface-to-air missile system (**2218.131**) and is a pulse doppler equipment operating in the D-band. The minimum and maximum target acquisition ranges are 1·5 and 16·5 km respectively. The 2 × 1 m antenna rotates at a rate of 60 rpm and is of cosec²-type. An integrated IFF facility is provided, using an MSR 400 interrogator.

The doppler processor eliminates ground clutter.

The extractor generates radar and feeds the computer of the associated tracking radar with azimuth, range and IFF response.

DR 621/641

These pulse doppler search radars are multiple application radars for the detection of low and very low flying aircraft and helicopters. Due to their construction, the systems can be installed in shelters, vehicles, tanks (eg Wildcat) and ships. The systems can be used as acquisition and target designation radars in automatic weapon systems, and as radar sensors, in site defence systems. They can also be expanded to form command and control centres by adding data processing equipment and display.

MPDR 30

The MPDR 30 is a short-range D-band air surveillance radar with a range of some 30 km and operating in a pulse-doppler mode for use in mobile air defence networks. The West German Air Force employs these radars, in the TMLD system to provide a sophisticated gap-filler capability in support of the national air defence system. The radar is mounted on a five-ton truck chassis, the antenna being supported by a folding extensible mast which gives an effective increase in operating height of up to 15 m. The associated displays, electronics, and control facilities are housed within other vehicles which combine with the radar truck to form a mobile radar belt.

DR 151

The DR 151 is an improved version of the MPDR 30 radar, in which the range is extended to 45 km. It is basically intended for export. The system can be mounted on one truck or in one shelter with the antenna mounted on the shelter roof. Shipboard installation is also feasible by adding a velocity compensation facility. The DR 153 is another version of this radar.

DR 171

Using a larger reflector and improved input sensitivity in addition to a number of other modifications the range of the DR 151 can be extended to 90 km. This radar can be stowed in two wheeled and air-mobile shelters and is particularly suitable for airspace surveillance on islands and in coastal areas. The DR 173 is another version of this radar.

B2 version of 35 mm Flakpanzer Gepard showing Siemens-Albis fire control radar and MPDR 12 acquisition radar

DR 171 radar with control centre

Siemens DR 151 on a truck

MPDR 3002 S

This is a medium-range E-band radar for air surveillance, used by the West German Army. It is equipped with a folding antenna mast mounted on a Marder tank chassis. Range is approximately 30 km.

MSR 400

The MSR 400 is an IFF-interrogator for use in mobile short- and medium-range radar systems. The equipment employs passive decoding and can be equipped for active decoding. It is compatible with Mk X SIF and Mk XII techniques. Known applications include the Gepard AA tank mentioned above. The MSR 400 is compatible with all radars of the MPDR series, MPDR 30/1, MPDR 16 (Roland), MPDR 3002 S, DR 151 and DR 171.

MSR 200/MSR 2000

The MSR 200 and MSR 2000 are parts of a new lightweight IFF-equipment family. They comprise a modern, fully solid-state technology.

The MSR 200 is a compact mobile IFF-interrogator for use in short- and medium-range radar systems. The interrogator employs passive decoding (including civil and military emergency decoding as options) in compliance with STANAG 5017, ie it is compatible with Mk X-A and, if applicable, with Mk XII techniques. Applications thus far are in Wildcat (with

Siemens MPDR 3002 S air surveillance radar used by West German Army

Siemens DR 621 radar in shelter-housed configuration

radar MPDR 18/30X) and in the mobile radar system Reporter (produced by Hollandse Signaalapparaten BV).

The IFF/SSR-interrogator MSR 2000 is suitable for all applications in civil and military air traffic control systems. The MSR 2000 is a more powerful IFF-interrogator for use with larger, long-range radar and weapon systems (ground- or ship-borne).

CONTRACTOR
Siemens AG, Postfach 70074, 8000 Munich, Federal Republic of Germany.

3706.153

OREST MOBILE AIR DEFENCE RADAR

OREST is the name of a fully-phased array mobile radar under study by Siemens intended to be the prototype of a family of air defence radars. The principal requirements to be met are the detection, identification, and tracking of high-speed, low-flying targets in a high target-density environment under

Orest phased array antenna

severe ECM conditions, to recognise threats and to control defence activities.

These requirements are met by the OREST experimental prototype, which is designed for three-dimensional detection, acquisition and tracking of low-level targets. The main feature of OREST is its antenna, a fully-phased array which allows the beam to be steered in any desired direction for any period of time and any desired number of times. Mounted on the roof of a wheeled vehicle, this antenna provides a radar system which can combine the functions of four separate types of conventional radar: ie search, tracking, target illumination, and secondary surveillance. Operation is in the I/J-band of the radar spectrum.

Electronic stabilisation against vehicle motion not only eliminates disturbances to the antenna plane (in three axes), but also enables compensation to be made for changes in the vehicle's location. This permits three-dimensional operation even with a moving vehicle. The signal processing technique is adaptable to the mode of operation employed, and the data outputs are in digital form. For the purpose of accurate co-ordinate determination, incoming target information is evaluated by monopulse techniques, and clutter signals are handled coherently with any remaining interference being eliminated by means of the clutter map being constantly renewed.

Reliable identification, threat analysis and

engagement of multiple air targets in a clutter environment, ECM, low-level attacks, and extreme evasive manoeuvres are ensured by effective co-ordination between the radar and the signal processing sub-systems. In OREST these tasks are handled by flexible software in conjunction with a functionally structured multi-computer system.

Azimuth and elevation monopulse evaluation of target echoes in combination with simultaneous adaptive sidelobe cancellation ensures high accuracy target detection. Provision of mechanical antenna rotation through 360°, in addition to electronic beam steering, gives all-round coverage from a single antenna with high target detection probability. Blind speeds of up to 900 m/s are eliminated by changing the frequency between pulses and by varying the PRF. OREST eliminates powerful noise jammers by such measures as the provision of nulls in the antenna radiation pattern in the direction from which jammer noise arrives (sidelobe cancellation). Pulse jammers are also eliminated in the antenna sidelobes by sidelobe blanking.

STATUS
Experimental models of critical components were built and tested in 1977-78. No production plans have been revealed.

CONTRACTOR
Siemens AG, Postfach 70074, 8000 Munich, Federal Republic of Germany.

3016.153

TRMS RADAR

The designation TRMS refers to the Telefunken radar, mobile search, a 5 cm wavelength system being manufactured by AEG-Telefunken under contract to the West German Ministry of Defence. The objective underlying the TRMS project was to develop a radar system providing the capacity for detecting and identifying targets independently of interference factors and rapidly changing air situations. TRMS is characterised by combined surveillance and heightfinding capabilities. Combining the surveillance and heightfinding characteristics renders the system especially suitable for coverage of

TRMS operator's position and displays

low-flying aircraft and for use in topographically difficult terrain. The radar is capable of automatic tracking and identification in a rigorous environment with natural and intentional interference factors. The system reliably accomplishes practically continuous coverage of all aircraft movements. Moreover, if used as a coastal radar it detects sea targets also in the presence of strong sea clutter. Maximum range is stated to be 110 nautical miles (200 km) for a 3 m^2 target, with altitude coverage up to 20 000 m (65 000 ft).

The TRMS incorporates facilities for digital data processing to the extent that it is appropriate to carry out data processing at the radar site. These facilities include special filtering processes which condense and reduce the incoming data volume to such an extent that the entire situation in the air and, if applicable, at sea can be transmitted to the operations centre via one single telephone line. The production of tracks represents an essential filtering process which serves to exclude undesirable and insignificant target information from further processing and transmission.

The TRMS is also suitable for employment as an autonomous centre, being highly mobile, usable in widely spaced locations, ready for operation within the shortest time, and capable of operating rapidly under camouflage and cover. The IFF and SLS

antennas are integrated into the array forming one unit.

TRMS is designed to be highly mobile and to allow its antenna to be raised above medium height vegetation. The antenna unit, the shelters with all the electronic equipment as well as the vehicles are designed for heavy-duty military use. Two trucks of the new Bundeswehr vehicle generation with cross-country capability serve as the carriers. One truck accommodates the sensor (radar assembly with antenna, transmitter, receiver, and signal processor), the other truck carries the operations equipment (target extractor, PR/IFF correlator, data and communications buffer, display unit and control panels). Both groups of equipment may be taken off the trucks. Up to a distance of 300 m they are connected by cable: over longer distances wide-band radio links may be installed.

A phased-array antenna is used for the TRMS which rotates mechanically in azimuth while simultaneously providing for step-scanning in elevation with a highly focused beam of circular or elliptic cross-section. The angular width of the beam varies according to the angle of elevation. To achieve a sufficiently high data rate, the pulse repetition frequency, the scanning rate and the beamwidth are adjusted to the search volume. Another feature contributing toward achieving the required data rate is the step-scanning in elevation with moving target indication. In other words, a step-scan MTI is used which, with a few hits, achieves a high improvement factor. Consequently, despite the consecutive 3-D scanning, it was possible with relatively little effort to find a solution which allows normal data rates to be achieved but is not liable to undesirable saturation phenomena.

The principal measure taken against interference of any kind is the selection of a small resolution cell, achieved by means of strong beam focusing and pulse compression. Furthermore, an MTI operating with optional single or double cancellation is available. Also provided is the frequency de-correlation of clutter echoes in the case of sea clutter, and circular polarisation in the case of weather clutter. Mutual interference of two TRMS installations is statistically very unlikely since this would require a common azimuth and elevation angle as well as identical frequency and polarisation. When the antenna was designed importance was attached to obtaining only very small sidelobes in the azimuth and elevation. As regards interference, the first countermeasure is again a high resolution characteristic in conjunction with frequency agility and high average transmitter power. Various operating modes of different data rates allow for further adjustments with regard to electronic threats. This variety of measures enables the TRMS to eliminate both natural interference and clutter and ECM to a large extent.

The operator's position is designed for one to three radar operators. From here the entire system including the offset sensor assembly is controlled. The functioning of the equipment is monitored at the indicator panel of the automatic self-test feature and through the performance monitor. This allows the operators to be easily and directly informed as to the state and efficiency of the equipment. For supervision within the area of coverage of the TRMS installation, a synthetic video display is available at which the ECM situation and the countermeasures selected in each case may be observed.

Targets are displayed on a computer-controlled 16-inch (406 mm) radar indicator in either analogue or digital form. The following information may be shown simultaneously on the analogue display: PR video, IFF video, PR and IFF jamming markers and five concentric range rings. The synthetic display comprises various geometric target and marking symbols. As a maximum the following functions may be displayed simultaneously: six height layers distinguished by symbol shape, target track with maximum five history position dots, IFF and code designation by five-digit labels (alpha-numeric), and target identity by symbol shape. The synthetic display may be supplemented by an analogue video background. A rolling ball is used for various purposes as, for example, the control of a measuring

TRMS unit demonstrating its antenna elevation

marker or the de-centring of the radar display up to the coverage limit.

In order to comply with the different requirements of different users, great importance was attached to making the TRMS flexible and expansible. This has been achieved on the one hand by the modular structure of the system, on the other hand by the provision of a freely programmable digital control system and adaptable software on the evaluation side. It is thus possible not only to program the antenna for different beamwidths at freely selectable angles of radiation, but also the synchronising pulse generator in respect of frequency and polarisation, pulse repetition and staggering times, pulse lengths and STC pattern. The digital MTI can be switched from single to double cancellation. For naval applications a special addition to the digital target extractor allows for automatic detection of sea targets as a result of the reduction of undesirable echoes due to sea clutter.

STATUS

Evaluation and field testing of TRMS prototype by the German Procurement Agency (BWB) was finished

TRMS antenna unit in transit configuration

successfully in 1980, but orders have not yet been received. AEG is understood to have permission to market this radar to other countries.

CONTRACTOR

AEG-Telefunken, Geschaftsbereich Hochfrequenz-technik, Postfach 1730, 7900 Ulm, Federal Republic of Germany.

4140.153
WIMERA TRACKING RADAR

The Wimera tracking radar is a mobile balloon tracking radar currently in use with various armed forces. Wimera's wide operational scope necessitated modular construction and high mobility. It provides all the meteorological data necessary to compile complete weather reports, eg for field artillery, air forces and tactical staffs. The Wimera equipment has three components: radar, radiosonde system and computer.

All modules are housed in a compact shelter which enables operation in any terrain independent of the weather. The system requires only one operator. After a change of location, the Wimera can be fully operational again in only 15 minutes, and only two men are required to set up and level the radar units.

Target acquisition incorporates pre-selection facilities for various functions:
(1) optical target assignment
(2) spiral scanning
(3) sector scanning
(4) manual target assignment
After the target has been acquired, the Wimera system self-switches to automatic target tracking. The radar data are indicated in digital form and printed out. Together with the data received from the

radiosonde, (eg temperature, air pressure, humidity), a complete weather report can be transmitted by wire or radio.

A drone tracking version integrates two Wimera units into one system in order to guarantee exact control and recording of drone flight paths.

CHARACTERISTICS

Frequency: fixed, 9375 MHz
Peak power: 140 kW
Pulse length: 0·1/1 μs selectable
PRF: 1000/2000 Hz
IF: 60 MHz
Antenna diameter: 1200 mm
Antenna gain: 38·5 dB
Beamwidth: 1·8°
Polarisation: Linear
Range: 120 km
Acquisition range: ≥40 m minimum
Tracking accuracy: ±10 m (range); ±1·5 mils (angle)
Scan frequency: 30 Hz

STATUS

In production.

CONTRACTOR

Elektro Spezial, Unternehmensbereich der Philips GmbH, Hans-Bredowstrasse 20, 2800 Bremen 44, Federal Republic of Germany.

Wimera tracking radar trailer

5613.153
METEOR 300 WEATHER RADAR SYSTEM
Meteor 300 is a weather radar system suitable for both military and civil applications, as an analysis radar or a fully automated balloon tracking system for measurement of wind.

Transportable version of Meteor 300

The analysis mode, provided by Meteor 300A, detects and evaluates precipitation areas in the atmosphere and also measures and presents their extent, position, height, intensity, direction of movement, speed and distance up to 400 km. The balloon tracking mode, provided by Meteor 300W, tracks and calculates elevation, azimuth and slant range. This data is then processed by a computer to obtain a profile of the upper wind structure in terms of speed and direction.

Meteor 300 systems are available for X-, C- or S-bands. The assemblies are designed with modular components for ease of servicing. No radome is required for the antenna. As an option, antennas may be equipped with different sized parabolic reflectors for diverse applications.

The systems are available in a mobile configuration (mounted on a vehicle or trailer), transportable version (installed in a shelter) or as a fixed installation.

The equipment can also be modified to a fully computer-controlled digital windfinding system, including computer-stabilised antenna for pitch, roll and yaw, for shipborne applications.

CHARACTERISTICS
X-band system
Antenna
Reflector: Parabolic 2 m diameter
Beamwidth: 1·2° ±10%
Sidelobe attenuation: 22 dB
Gain: 42 dB
Transmitter/receiver
Frequency: 9375 MHz
Peak power: 180 kW
Pulse width: 0·5 and 3 μs
PRF: 1200 and 200 Hz
CONTRACTOR
Gematronik GmbH, Raiffeisenstrasse 10, 4040 Neuss 21, Federal Republic of Germany.

INTERNATIONAL

1528.153
RATAC BATTLEFIELD RADAR
RATAC (*radar de tir pour l'artillerie de campagne*) is a lightweight (eight cabinets of 35 kg, or less, each) battlefield radar providing for detection, acquisition, identification, location, and tracking of surface targets such as troops, tanks, vehicles, low-flying helicopters and light aircraft. Other operational functions include artillery direction, surveillance of own forces, and helicopter control. It is comprised of six units and is designed for vehicle mounting. Pulse-doppler and monopulse techniques are employed and the operating frequency is in the 5 cm wavelength region. A highly effective fixed target cancellation system is said to make it possible to locate very slow moving targets with a small radar cross-section, such as a single man. Detection ranges are reported to be better than 15 km against vehicles and 8 km against troops, with an accuracy of 10 and 20 m in surveillance. Good all-weather performance is claimed.

The system incorporates its own computer, and target data can be presented in terms of either polar or grid co-ordinates. An optional plotting board unit permits target positions and movements to be recorded. A loudspeaker is provided to aid target identification by listening to the doppler characteristics of targets. Automatic target tracking facilities are included, and there are provisions for the transmission of data to own artillery. Operation with vehicle installed IFF is a possible option.
DEVELOPMENT
Development of RATAC was undertaken by LCT (Laboratoire Central de Télécommunications) under the direction of the French military authority, in 1966. A subsequent agreement between the French and West German governments provided for joint procurement and production for the armies of both countries. Tests were later carried out by the US Army at Fort Sill.
STATUS
RATAC is in service in France, West Germany, the USA and several other countries. Production in the USA was undertaken by ITT-Gilfillan under the nomenclature AN/TPS-58.

RATAC radar on VT 13 vehicle

CONTRACTORS
LMT Radio Professionelle, 46-47 quai Alphonse Le Gallo, 92103 Boulogne-Billancourt, France.

Standard Elektrik Lorenz AG, Hellmuth-Hirthstrasse 42, 7 Stuttgart 40, Federal Republic of Germany.

ISRAEL

4330.153
EL/M-2121 BATTLEFIELD SURVEILLANCE RADAR
The EL/M-2121 intelligence battlefield surveillance radar has been developed by Elta as an all-weather, mobile, very long range ground surveillance radar capable of detecting, locating and classifying targets moving on or near the ground in any type of weather or time of day/night.

One of the principal uses of the EL/M-2121 is for reconnaissance troops at ground observation posts to provide continuous surveillance and real-time information on activities of enemy forces deep behind the front line.

The complete system can be used as a transportable equipment with the radar and control equipment in a military centre, or divided with a fixed control centre operating a remote radar head. The antenna normally rotates continuously through 360° but can also carry out sector scans, or be pointed at designated targets.

The equipment is of modular construction and employs quadrature (I/Q) digital processing. A strong ECCM capability has been incorporated. It is microprocessor controlled and provides the operator with an eight-colour TV multi-mode display on a 19-inch screen. Built-in expansion options include the ability to be interfaced with other computers to process signals and data.
CHARACTERISTICS
Detection ranges
Pedestrian: 20 km (0·1 m² target)
Small vehicle: 40 km (1 m² target)
Medium size truck: 70 km (10 m² target)
Large truck: 120 km (100 m² target)
Accuracy: Range 15 m; azimuth 0·1°
Resolution: Range 15 m; azimuth 0·3°

EL/M-2121 control cabin

STATUS
In production.

CONTRACTOR
Elta Electronics Industries Ltd (a subsidiary of Israel Aircraft Industries Ltd), Ashdod, Israel.

3708.153
EL/M-2215 SURVEILLANCE RADAR

The Elta EL/M-2215 is a general-purpose surveillance radar, evolved from the successful EL/M-2205 search radar (**1958.153**), and many of the engineering features of the latter radar have been retained in its successor. Improvements made possible by advances in the state-of-the-art have been incorporated, such as more elaborate signal processing facilities and increased transmitter output power. The transmitter/receiver is a redesigned and repackaged version of the former EL/M-2205. Modular design allows the second-generation EL/M-2215 to be configured in either single or dual transmitter/receiver versions, the latter offering a further choice between a dual-channel arrangement for redundancy or dual-channel with diversity operation. Other features include high resolution; a dual high/low-beam antenna; high clutter suppression; quadrature (I/Q) digital MTI; and fast frequency tuning.

The EL/M-2215 employs the AT-103 single beam antenna (as used in the EL/M-2205) or the AT-104 dual high/low-beam antenna. It may also be used with the AT-102 antenna to form the EL/M-2216 coastal radar for surface and low air cover search applications.

CHARACTERISTICS
Transmitter
Frequency: 3·1 – 3·3 GHz (2·7 – 2·9 GHz optional)
Output power: 425 kW peak
Pulse width: 0·95 μs (selectable 0·95 or 0·4 μs for EL/M-2216)
PRF: Fixed 1 of 4, or 4 staggered 900 – 1050 pps (1340 – 1560 pps for EL/M-2216 short pulse)

Receiver
Type: Superheterodyne
IF frequency: 60 MHz
Noise figure: 2·5 dB (at transistorised amplifier input)
Sensitivity
Normal, –107 dBm;
MTI, –104 dBm
Processing
Digital MTI: Quadrature (I/Q) 3-pulse canceller with or without feedback
Improvement factor: 33 dB
Blind speeds: None below Mach 3
Antenna AT-104
Gain: 34 dB low beam; 33 dB high beam
Azimuth beamwidth: 1·4°

TABLE OF ELTA EL/M-2200 RADARS

Model	EL/M-2207 Shipborne	EL/M-2208 Shipborne	EL/M-2215/D Air Traffic Control	EL/M-2216 Coastal
Range	30 nm	30 nm	80 nm	50 nm
Range accuracy	50 m	50 m	50 m	50 m
Range resolution	80 m	50 m	200 m	80 m
Azimuth accuracy	1°	1°	1°	1°
Azimuth resolution	3°	1°	1·5°	1·5°
Power (peak)	425 kW	425 kW (F) 25 kW (I)	425 kW	425 kW
Pulse width	1·4 μs or 0·4 μs	1·4 μs (F) or 0·4 μs (F) 0·25 μs (I)	0·95 μs	0·95 μs or 0·4 μs
PRF (pps)	1000 – 1500 or 500 – 750	1000 – 1500 or 500 – 750	900 – 1050	900 – 1050 or 1340 – 1560
Digital MTI improvement factor	27 dB	27 dB	33 dB	33 dB

Vertical beamwidth: 5°
Cosec squared up to: 42° low beam; 45° high beam
Sidelobes: Better than –24 dB
Polarisation: Linear horizontal or circular, selectable
Rotation rate: 12·5 or 6 rpm, selectable
Reflector dimensions: 5·46 × 3·20 m
Weight: 500 kg
Rotary joints: Dual E/F and D (for IFF)

STATUS
Production.
CONTRACTOR
Elta Electronics Industries Ltd (a subsidiary of Israel Aircraft Industries Ltd), Ashdod, Israel.

4606.153
EL/M-2220 MOBILE SURVEILLANCE RADAR

Another variant of the EL/M-2215 (**3708.153**) is the EL/M-2220, a 2-D mobile air search and surveillance radar designed for tactical aircraft control, AA defence, or as a gap-filler. It features high clutter suppression, quadrature digital MTI, redundancy or dual-channel with diversity and improved signal processing.

Three versions of the system are available:
(a) EL/M-2220F for mobile fast deployment, comprising a S-280 shelter containing an EL/M-2215 transceiver, a 16-inch operator display console, and a small lightweight radar and IFF antenna mounted on top of the shelter. The EL/M-2220F can be deployed within 30 minutes
(b) EL/M-2220S for mobile air surveillance comprising an S-280 shelter containing an EL/M-2215 transceiver and a 16-inch display console, with an AT-103 large antenna on a towable platform
(c) EL/M-2220D for long-range mobile surveillance which consists of two shelters, one containing two EL/M-2215 transceivers (dual-channel), the other housing two consoles; plus an AT-103 antenna on a towable platform.

CHARACTERISTICS
Frequency: 3·1 – 3·3 GHz (2·7 – 2·9 GHz optional)
Output power: 425 kW, peak
Pulse width: 0·95/1·4 μs
PRF: 1000/750 Hz, 4 staggered or random variable

Operation	EL/M-2220D	EL/M-2220S	EL/M-2220F
Detection range	80 nm	60 nm	30 nm
Azimuth resolution	1·4°	1·4°	3°
Range resolution	220 m	150 m	150 m
Height coverage	30 000 ft	25 000 ft	18 000 ft

EL/M-2220 mobile air surveillance radar

CONTRACTOR
Elta Electronics Industries Ltd (a subsidiary of Israel Aircraft Industries Ltd), Ashdod, Israel.

3646.153
EL/M-2106 POINT DEFENCE ALERT RADAR

The Elta EL/M-2106 point defence alert radar is designed to provide an early warning capability for anti-aircraft emplacements and forward installations. The EL/M-2106 is a portable battlefield radar that can also be used in such applications as target acquisition for surface-to-air missile systems and AA guns, as well as gap-filling roles.

The operating frequency is in the D-band (former L-band) of the spectrum, and typical detection range performance is about 16 km for fixed-wing aircraft and 10 km for helicopters (2 m² targets). Aural and visual warning of aircraft approach is given to the operator, and conventional scanning through 360° is normally provided, but a programmed sector scan with sweep-to-sweep memory is also available. The radar may also be remotely controlled from distances up to 100 metres.

The system is comprised of a transmitter, receiver, antenna assembly and display unit, and the entire installation breaks down into easily carried man-portable units. It can be set up in less than ten minutes and can be operated by one man with only minimal training.

The EL/M-2106H version is able to detect helicopters in movement or hovering. A processing channel analyses the signal reflected from the rotor blades while the helicopter is hovering and can differentiate between fixed-wing aircraft and helicopters in flight.

The EL/M-2106H is also designed to be fully operational in a moving vehicle such as an armoured car. A special mast mounted on the vehicle enables different deployment heights according to the geographical and tactical environment.

CHARACTERISTICS
(EL/M-2106H)
Transmitter/receiver frequency: D-band
Peak power: 150 W
Average power: 10 W
Pulsewidth: 6·6 or 13·3 μs

PRF: 8 or 16 kHz
Range gates: 10
MTI improvement factor: 50 dB
Dimensions: 40 × 26 × 33 cm
Weight: 26 kg
Antenna dimensions: 200 × 80 cm
Weight: 55 kg (including stand and pedestal)
Gain: 23 dB
Horizontal beamwidth: 5°
Vertical beamwidth: 17°
Display: Synthetic with sweep memory. For each range gate, concentric circle of 36 LEDs. Indication of antenna position
Azimuth presentation: LED at 10° intervals
Range presentation: LED range circles spaced at 1 or 2 km intervals, giving max range of 10 or 20 km, selectable
STATUS
Production. A licenced version, known as Sentry, is being produced by the Astronics Division of Lear Siegler, USA.
CONTRACTOR
Elta Electronics Industries Ltd (a subsidiary of Israel Aircraft Industries Ltd), Ashdod, Israel.

EL/M-2106H radar mounted in an armoured car

1958.153
ELTA SURFACE RADARS
Elta Electronics Ltd produces a range of surface radars for ATC, search and acquisition, and similar applications, with fixed and land-mobile systems for surveillance roles, coastal protection etc.

The base model for most of this equipment, which is built on a modular design concept, is the EL/M-2205, and unless otherwise stated the following text relates to this model. (The current range is now based on the EL/M-2215 (**3708.153**) a modernised and improved version of the EL/M-2205.) Other models are the surface and low air cover search radar, EL/M-2206 and the coastal surveillance radar EL/M-2216XH which both employ the AT-102 antenna in place of the AT-103 used in the EL/M-2205, the EL/M-2220 mobile air surveillance radar (**4606.153**), and the naval version EL/M-2207 (**3264.253**) and EL/M-2208. All versions are constructed to conform to the MIL-E-16400 specification and are provided with BITE. Conventional PPI displays or synthetic (raster-type) displays are available for use with all models. Integrated IFF is available as an option and is used in military models. A high performance, compact, and lightweight E/F-band transceiver forms the basic building block, and two of these units may be operated together in dual diversity. Receiver models available include: linear with switchable STC, FTC, IAGC, Log-FTC-Antilog, CFAR. There is single-knob tuning of the transmitter frequency between 3·1 and 3·3 GHz, and a stable synthesiser enabling the whole equipment to cover this band in less than 20 seconds, in the EL/M-2206 version.

More details of the characteristics of this radar are given in previous editions of *Jane's Weapon Systems*.
STATUS
Unspecified models of the EL/M-2200 series are stated to be in service in Israel and elsewhere.
CONTRACTOR
Elta Electronics Industries Ltd (a subsidiary of Israel Aircraft Industries Ltd), Ashdod, Israel.

Elta EL/M-2205 search radar scanner AT-103 with on-mounted IFF

4611.153
HELICAPTURE TACTICAL RADAR SYSTEM
HELICAPTURE is a tactical ground radar system designed to automatically detect and classify hovering and moving helicopters. The system uses the distinctive radar signature generated by each helicopter's rotor blades to classify the target, with a high detection probability and low false alarm rate. The radar has 360° or selected scan capability, a range of up to 15 km, providing the target is within the line-of-sight, and an accuracy of approximately 300 metres.

HELICAPTURE consists of a solid-state transmitter, signal processor, display and control unit and antenna unit. It is completely self-contained and incorporates ECCM capabilities and built-in test equipment. The data display includes target range and azimuth, target position in grid co-ordinates, and helicopter type. The unit also includes a sound indicator and data communication output.

The system can be either tripod or vehicle mounted and includes a remote control mode so that it can be readily integrated in ground forces. The modular design makes it convenient to deploy, operate and maintain.

CHARACTERISTICS
Range: Up to 15 km from zero altitude
Resolution: ±300 m (range); ±2·5° (azimuth)
Sector scan: 360° or selected scan
Height (tripod mounted): 2·6 m (including antenna)
System weight: 130 kg
STATUS
The system was said to be due to enter production in February 1984.
CONTRACTOR
Rafael Armament Development Authority, PO Box 2082, Haifa 31021, Israel.

ITALY

3278.153
MM/SPQ-3 COASTAL RADARS
The SPQ-3 series of radars comprises a variety of equipment conbinations, centred on co-mounted I/J-band and E/F-band radars, configured to produce sets appropriate to coastal surveillance and harbour surveillance functions and related applications. The system is transportable by trucks or helicopters, and is generally intended to be integrated in larger defence control networks. The complete equipment is housed within two cabins, plus a trailer motor-generated power supply unit. The first cabin contains the two radar transmitter/receivers, and the associated antennas which are mounted on top can be folded inside for transport. The second cabin contains the operational part of the system, such as displays, processing unit, video recorder, and plotting table. The electronic recording system can be independently connected to the I/J-band or to the E/F-band radar, and is based on processing radar data (range scale, antenna speed, bearing etc) by means of a TV scan converter and connecting these to a magnetic recorder. Restitution of stored data is obtained by connecting the magnetic recorder output data to a TV-type display. Remote and local control facilities are provided.

The principal operational roles are medium to long

range detection of air attack or of combined air/seaborne assaults by means of the E/F-band radar; and close to medium range surface surveillance by means of the I/J-band radar to assist defence against surface craft attack, landings etc. In the SPQ-3B version, a special feature is the detection and location of the splashes caused by air-dropped mines in harbours or confined waters.

Features of the E/F-band radar include: variable-frequency transmission; random PRF; high directivity antenna pattern; Dicke-fix IF receiver; and linear-logarithmic IF receiver. The I/J-band equipment has most of these features with the exception of the Dicke-fix, and two back-to-back antennas as compared with the single horn-fed parabolic reflector of the E/F-band unit. Both are essentially very high image resolution systems with low average emitting power, particularly suitable for operation (by means of frequency and polarisation decorrelation) in high traffic density environments. Sector transmission is possible.

Scan converter displays are provided and there are facilities for video recording and replay. Digital and analogue format remote data transmission outputs are available.

STATUS
Production. Italian forces and foreign governments are believed to have been supplied.
CONTRACTOR
SMA (Segnalamento Marittimo ed Aereo), PO Box 200, Via del Ferone Soffiano, 50100 Florence, Italy.

Internal view of SPQ-3 radar control cabin, showing the two identical PPI consoles, each of which can be switched independently to either of the system's two radars

CHARACTERISTICS

Transmitter	E/F-band	I/J-band
Peak power	1 MW+	180 kW+
Pulse-length/PRF	1·5 µs/450 Hz	0·15 µs/2500 Hz
		1·5 µs/450 Hz
Receiver	Superhet	Superhet
RF noise factor	<6·5 dB	<7 dB
IF	60 MHz	60 MHz
IF bandwidth	1 MHz	10 MHz
Antenna	Horn-fed parabolic	2 back-to-back with end-fed slotted wave-guide feeders. 1 antenna can vary inclination −2 to +15°
Polarisation	Horizontal/circular	Horizontal
Beamwidth	1·5° horizontal × 7° vertical Cosec² to 28° ±2 dB	0·5° horizontal × 3·5° vertical Cosec² to 45° ±2 dB
Rotation speed	4, 8, or 16 rpm	15, 30, or 60 rpm
Dimensions	450 × 180 cm	440 × 108 cm

Main radar cabin of SPQ-3 system, showing back-to-back scanners for I/J-band spotting and tracking radar and upper early warning E/F-band search radar scanner

---

1529.153
LPD-20 SEARCH RADAR
The LPD-20 is a search and acquisition radar developed to counter air threats from low- and very low-level targets in the region below the useful coverage of other radars. Two basic versions have been designed:
(1) Integrated version: The radar can easily be fitted into the Contraves Super Fledermaus family of fire control systems. This simplest arrangement employs the PPI display as the fire control system, so that the search radar is unattended and a single operator is able to control the complete radar system for both search and tracking of targets
(2) Autonomous version: The LPD-20 used as an autonomous radar set is equipped with a separate PPI display, for alerting light AA weapons (guns or very short-range SAM) for different purposes (target designation to light unslaved AA artillery emplacements, low and very low altitude surveillance, etc).

To provide additional operator safety, the PPI display (where remote control of the radar set also takes place) may be sited in a protected and defiladed position, at a distance up to 100 m from the radar site.

IFF facilities are also integrated into the radar system. Contraves Italiana SpA in September 1974 concluded an agreement with Cossor Electronics Ltd by which integrated IFF facilities produced by the UK firm can be provided as a customer option for LPD-20 systems.

The main parts of the radar are:
(1) a rotating section, comprising antenna, transmitter/receiver, signal processor, and modulator

(2) turning gear
(3) a cabin containing power supplies and operational controls
(4) trailer chassis.

System weight (trailer version) is 2500 kg.

The LPD-20 is a fully coherent pulse-doppler radar. An MTI improvement factor of better than 50 dB is claimed, together with a detection range of about 20 km on targets travelling at speeds between 20 and 410 m/s at heights up to 4000 m. Angular resolution is of the order of 1·4° and range resolution about 500 m. Rapid reaction to sudden low-level threats is aided by a high data rate, the use of a common PPI for search and fire control, accurate target range and azimuth designation data and transfer from search radar to fire control radar in two to three seconds. Provision is made for the incorporation of IFF Mk 10/SIF facilities into the basic LPD-20 radar. Furthermore, as an optional alternative to the autonomous version, an automatic data transmission system can be provided, which allows forwarding of target data information to other users. This system consists of a data transmission unit (DTU) built into the display unit and a data receiver unit (DRU), which is associated with the user's weapon or weapons.

Numerical data corresponding to target position and identification (polar or cartesian co-ordinates and IFF) is transmitted by the DTU (FSK modulator and buffer amplifier) through a two-wire field telephone line or radio link to the user's DRU (filter and demodulator), where it is displayed in numerical form. A maximum of three targets can be handled simultaneously by the system. Maximum range of

telephone transmission amounts to about 5 km. The DRU is provided with autonomous supply (rechargeable DC battery). Data transmission is uni-directional (from display unit to weapons).
STATUS
The radar has undergone rigorous field tests in Italy and elsewhere and is now in series production. Although detailed information has not been released, this system is known to be widely used in many parts of the world. Over 150 units have been produced.

Current production of the Super Fledermaus fire control system (**2376.151**) incorporates modifications to enable it to be associated with the LPD-20.
CONTRACTOR
Contraves Italiana SpA, Via Affile 102, Via Tirburtina Km 13150, 00131 Rome, Italy.

Contraves LPD-20 search and acquisition radar with Cossor IFF unit (LPD-20, autonomous version)

Data receiver unit for LPD-20 radar

Typical deployment of Super Fledermaus fire control system with LPD-20 radar (integrated version)

4018.153
ALERTER RADAR

The Alerter pulse doppler search/acquisition radar and command post system was developed by Contraves for air surveillance at low altitude and the co-ordination and control of associated weapon systems.

The following specific tasks are performed:

Automatic detection of targets at low and very low altitude either in a fixed position or on the move

Target identification

Threat evaluation

Automatic assignment of targets to a maximum of 12 targets

Simultaneous engagement of 12 targets

Control and co-ordination of the operational status of the weapon systems

Exchange of data with other battlefield radars and easy integration into a higher level air defence system.

Alerter comprises the following basic units: shelter cabin and operational console with computer radar indicator; cradle with telescopic antenna mast; and power generator.

The system is installed on the M548/6 carrier vehicle; all parts are mounted on a unified mechanical interface structure which makes it possible to install the system easily on other available vehicles.

The antenna can be elevated up to ten metres through its telescopic mast in order to help conceal the vehicle, giving greater flexibility in selecting operational locations.

Alerter radar unit ready to move

The shelter is detachable from the carrier vehicle and can be placed in a defiladed position up to 100 metres away, thereby achieving protection against defence suppression systems.

Alerter can be combined as a surveillance and detection radar with any AA guns and SAM systems which do not have their own electronic surveillance sensor. It can also be used as a command and co-ordination post for AA weapon systems connected directly to a higher level air defence centre.

CHARACTERISTICS

Frequency: X-band, frequency agile

Type: Coherent, pulse-doppler, pulse compression

Detection range: Up to 23 km

Processing: TWS, threat evaluation

Presentation: CRI (computer radar indicator)

Transport: Train or helicopter

Alerter radar with antenna mast extended

STATUS

Extensive trials performed successfully with Oerlikon 35 mm self-propelled twin AA gun type GDF-CO2.

CONTRACTOR

Contraves Italiana SpA, Via Affile 102, Via Tiburtina Km 13150, 00131 Rome, Italy.

5618.153
SHORAR SEARCH RADAR

The short range and acquisition radar (SHORAR) is a search, acquisition and target designation system which has been developed from the Alerter radar (**4018.153**). It is designed for use against medium, low and very low airborne targets and can be installed on a variety of vehicles, such as the M113, M548 etc.

To allow for installation on different types of vehicle, the equipment is designed in three modules: an antenna and transceiver assembly mounted on top of the carrier vehicle, an operations console assembly and an electronic cabinet, the latter two being accommodated inside the vehicle. The radar has been specifically designed as a low power consumption and lightweight system to enable it to be used in a variety of situations.

SHORAR is a fully-coherent X-band pulse-doppler system for high clutter rejection, very low target detection and high azimuth angular discrimination. Doppler filtering and data processing are performed by a digital computer system for flexibility in different scenarios. Track-while-scan and automatic threat evaluation are incorporated, as are multiple target handling and a search-on-move capability.

CHARACTERISTICS

Frequency: X-band

Azimuth accuracy: 0·5° rms

Range discrimination: better than 100 m

Antenna scan: 60 rpm

Radial speed range: 16 – 400 m/s

Max range: 17 – 25 km

Overall system weight: 530 kg (1226 lb)

STATUS

Development has been completed successfully. All qualification tests have been passed and the radar is shortly entering series production.

CONTRACTOR

Contraves Italiana SpA, Via Affile 102, Via Tiburtina Km 13150, 00131 Rome, Italy.

SHORAR antenna and transceiver assembly

3277.153
PLUTO LOW-COVERAGE SURVEILLANCE RADAR

Pluto is a low-coverage surveillance radar for air and coastal defence, designed to detect medium- low- and very low-flying aircraft and small surface vessels under the most adverse environmental conditions

Pluto low-coverage radar deployed

(ECM, atmospheric and sea clutter etc). The radar is suitable for fixed and/or mobile installations and can operate either independently or be integrated into a complete defence system. Design features include the following:

Capability to detect and measure the range and azimuth of surface and air targets at medium and low altitudes up to a maximum range of 110 km.

High accuracy and resolution, integral target designation capability and flexibility to interface computer-assisted display and defence systems.

Pulse compression of the radiated waveform with a resultant small scale radar cell size, ie resultant visibility even of very slow moving targets such as small ships (FPB).

Sophisticated ECCM processing with visibility maintained even in presence of heavy active and passive jamming.

Good adaptability and CFAR characteristics under various environmental conditions, ie capability to detect targets and reject interference by automatic evaluation and selection of the best transmisssion and processing configurations.

Capability of operating in frequency-agility from sweep to sweep, with clutter rejection and sub-clutter visibility of moving targets outgoing or incoming at

speeds up to Mach 3 by means of sophisticated MTI processing techniques.

Antenna pattern with high directivity and very low sidelobe levels.

Large transmission bandwidth.

High MTBF and reduced MTTR.

High reliability, maintainability and supportability.

BITE facilities.

CHARACTERISTICS

Antenna

Type: Reflector, feed

Frequency: E/F-band

Polarisation: Horizontal or circular, selectable

Beamwidth: Horizontal 1·5°; vertical 4°

Beam shape: Horizontal – pencil beam; vertical – super-cosec^2 matched to a very high clutter environment

Scan rate: 15 rpm

Tilt: –2 to +5° adjustable

IFF antenna: Integrated

Transmitter

Type: Coherent chain

Final stage: TWT

Frequency: E/F-band

Bandwidth: 10%

Peak power: 135 kW minimum

Transmitted waveform: Phase coded (code agility)
PRF: Prefixed or random stagger
Operating modes: Fixed frequency; random/pre-programmed frequency agility; adaptive frequency selection (option)
Receiver
Type: Superheterodyne/Dual conversion; RF adaptive clutter attenuator
Noise figure: <3 dB
MTI channel: Linear amplifier
Normal channel: Dicke-fix

Signal processor
Detectors: I & Q phase detectors A/D converters
Anti-clutter filters: MTI processor
MTI velocity response: >Mach 3
Matched filter: Digital
Amplitude detectors: Digital modulus extractor
Azimuth correlator: Moving window and pattern recognition
Jam strobe: Unambiguous azimuth information (option)
Plot extractor

Rate: Compatible with narrow-band transmission
Message format: Programmable
Information: Azimuth, range, quality, decoded
Configuration: 1 shelter plus antenna
Transport: C-130/160, road, rail and helicopter
STATUS
In production.
CONTRACTOR
Selenia-Industrie Elettroniche Associate SpA, Via Tiburtina Km 12400, 00131 Rome, Italy.

1953.153
RAT-31S TRANSPORTABLE 3-D RADAR
The RAT-31S has been designed as a highly mobile three-dimensional radar capable of performing a wide range of operational functions associated with air defence, tactical air applications, and civil/military air traffic control. The construction method employed makes the system equally suitable for air- or land-mobile applications. The system comprises an antenna group, a transmitter shelter, a receiver and signal processing shelter and a primary power supply. The antenna group can be moved by a trailer or by a demountable running gear, which is the preferred method when using C-130 aircraft for transportation. The shelters may be moved by any of the methods complying with NATO STANAG standards.

The operating frequency is in the E/F-band and the RAT-31S is intended for aircraft detection and range, elevation and azimuth target measurements at high, medium, and low altitudes. Comprehensive ECCM facilities include the ability to operate in frequency agility from pulse-to-pulse, and/or within pulse-groups, with an automatic adaptive transmission frequency selection. Height measurement of detected aircraft is compatible with frequency agility, and the sub-clutter visibility is sustained even when operating in pulse-to-pulse frequency agility.

The RAT-31S uses a novel antenna system that employs a system of three stacked beams with a phased array control of the elevation of each beam. The configuration is that of a rear-fed planar array, which avoids aperture blocking, minimises sidelobes, and provides good mutual screening characteristics. A coherent chain transmitter, with a TWT final amplification stage is used, which facilitates the frequency agile features of the radar. A staggered position and phase code is used in the transmitted pulse. Features of the receiver include: monopulse operation with Dicke-fix processing; anti-clutter filtering by means of a double canceller; adaptive clutter attenuator; coherent limiter; and moving window azimuth correlator.
CHARACTERISTICS
Antenna
Type: Rear-fed planar array

Polarisation: Linear horizontal
Beamwidth: 1·5° (azimuth and low elevation beams)
Azimuth scan mode: Mechanical rotation over 360°
Scan rate: 5 – 10 rpm
Elevation scan mode: Electronic by phase control from 0 – 21°
Number of beams: 3 different groups of beams are radiated on 3 separate bandwidths
Pattern: Multiple pencil beams
Transmitter
Type: Coherent amplifier chain
Final stage: TWT
Overall bandwidth: 400 MHz (E/F-band)
Peak power: 135 kW minimum
Average power: 3·78 kW minimum
Duty ratio: 2·8%
Average PRF: 450 Hz
Max unambiguous range: >300 km
Stagger sequence: Variable
Transmitted waveform: 3 separate coded waveforms
Receiver
Type: Dual conversion
Receiving channels: 3, sum and difference
Noise figure: <3 dB
MTI/receiver: Adaptive to clutter level
Normal receiver: Dicke-fix, all beams; log for jam strobe; log for AFS; and lin for raw video
Range gating: The ACA adaptive switching is controlled by a clutter mapper. The normal/MTI channel selection is controlled by an adaptive channel selection mapper
Signal processor
Detectors: I and Q phase detectors
A/D converter: 8-bit
Normaliser: Digital, coherent limiter
Matched filters: Digital matched filters
Final detector: Modulus extractor
Azimuth correlator: Moving window
Height computation: Monopulse processing and azimuth averaging by means of a microprocessor
Plot extractor
Rate: Compatible with narrow-band transmission
Message format: Programmable
False alarm rate: 10^{-6}
Mechanical
Configuration: 2 S-280 type shelters plus antenna
Deployment time: 55 minutes with 6-man team
MTBF: 450 h
MTTR: 35 minutes
STATUS
The RAT-31S is in full production. It is operational in the mobile air defence system, MRCS-403, delivered to Austria (see **3326.181**). Two MRCS-403 systems were ordered by the Italian Air Force in early 1984 and systems have also been sold to other countries. Negotiations are in progress for the sale of a significant quantity of additional systems to an undisclosed state.

In March 1983 an agreement between Selenia and the Sperry Corporation (USA) was revealed that covers the joint development of a long-range version designated RAT-31SL. This radar has been submitted for the NADGE South Flank radar network updating programme competition.
CONTRACTOR
Selenia-Industrie Elettroniche Associate SpA, Via Tiburtina Km12400, 00131 Rome, Italy.

Selenia RAT-31S transportable 3-D radar deployed with an MRCS-403 mobile reporting and control system station

1959.153

ARGOS-10 EARLY WARNING RADAR

The Argos-10 is a high-power, modern early warning search radar, with an effective range in excess of 250 nautical miles (460 km). It incorporates a transmitter designed and manufactured by the Heavy Military Electronics Systems Division of the General Electric Company. The salient features include: a high-power coherent transmitter chain; full adaptability to fixed and/or moving clutter; environmental pattern recognition; high resistance to ECM; reception status matched to the actual environment; fully digital signal processing; integrated primary/secondary video extractor; and modular construction.

The antenna is a large lattice construction with a lattice boom projecting from the lower edge to support the dual horn feeds which provide for dual beam operation. This element of the Argos-10 radar has a marked resemblance to the antenna and feed of the Canadian Raytheon ASR-803 D-band airport surveillance radar, and may be the same design. Provision is made for enclosing the antenna assembly in a protective radome. An auxiliary antenna can be added if required for multiple stand-off jammer cancellation and to provide for unambiguous jam-strobe indication.

The transmitter is water cooled and operates in the D-band. The output has not been stated but is probably several megawatts. A codified output pulse is produced and there is a code agility facility. In accordance with the jamming situation encountered, adaptive frequency selection is available, other operating options being MTI-compatible frequency agility and random frequency agility. The receiver incorporates dual-beam coherent combination; a low-noise RF amplifier; parallel channels for multiple jammer coherent cancellation; and linear with adaptive clutter attenuator facilities.

The digital signal processor has phase and quadrature channels, a three-pulse digital MTI double canceller, and clutter map storage for adaptive clutter cancellation. There is a low velocity clutter filter for reducing or eliminating the effects of rain or chaff. Real-time sensors are provided for moving clutter cancellation and rain contour mapping. Automatic optimum channel selection is incorporated. Measures employed to eliminate second and third time around echoes comprise a pattern recognition technique and multiple stagger codes. There is also a time on target dual threshold integrator in the signal processor section.

Plot extraction with a 10^{-6} false alarm rate in a combined clutter/jamming environment is performed by the video extractor, which also includes a primary/secondary plot combiner, and an interface-buffer to a central computer for narrow-band transmission.

STATUS

Prototype evaluation tests began in late 1977, these running concurrently with series production against NATO and Italian Government contracts placed in 1976/77. At least ten sets are being produced and commissioning of the first Argos-10 station began in March 1978. Among these orders are one system to

Argos-10 high-power early warning radar in protective radome

be installed on the island of Sicily under NATO project 130, and a number to be used for updating the Italian air defence network. It is understood that in some instances the Argos-10 will be used in conjunction with fixed or semi-permanent RAT-31S 3-D radars.

CONTRACTORS

Selenia-Industrie Elettroniche Associate SpA, Via Tiburtina Km12400, 00131 Rome, Italy.

General Electric Company, Heavy Military Electronic Systems Division, USA – Transmitter.

2248.153

SELENIA CIVIL/MILITARY RADARS

The Selenia series of air traffic control radars consists of three types of equipment:

(a) D-band high power long range radar ATCR-22

(b) E-Band medium power terminal area radar ATCR-33

(c) D-band medium power terminal area radar ATCR-44.

The equipment is designed to be used in both civil and military applications.

ATCR-22 Primary En-route Radar

The ATCR-22 is a high power 23 cm wavelength, fully solid-state (except for the magnetron and thyratron), search radar for use in both military and civil environments. In an air traffic control configuration the radar consists normally of an antenna group, two transmitter units, two receiver units and the common wave-guide system. In the dual channel version, a dual frequency diplexer allows the radar to work in frequency diversity. A third single channel can be used as a hot stand-by to any of the two main channels. Two antenna systems are available, the G-14 high gain, extra long range antenna and the smaller G-7 antenna, both equipped with a dual feed.

A clutter mapper is also provided: this device automatically defines areas in which MTI video is desired because of clutter, but in other areas normal raw video is displayed. A video correlator eliminates 'second time round' echoes and rejects non-synchronous returns and noise. It can be automatically introduced, checking on the level of residues. Log-FTC is introduced when needed in both MTI and normal operation. A special output displays rain contours. A FAN circuit guarantees a constant false alarm rate of 10^{-6}. Provision for on-mounting SSR is standard and the antenna has a triple channel rotating point.

The ATCR-22 can be controlled and checked out remotely. A performance monitor continuously monitors noise figure, transmitted and received power. Alarms are initiated (remotely, if required) when these pass a preset threshold.

A built-in extractor performs a very sophisticated pattern analysis of each returned echo. A micro-computer keeps tab on all processing done to the individual echoes, controls the returned signal for multiple targets, defines the plot position with an unsurpassed accuracy, and provides feedback loops to the entire system in order to protect subsequent tracking system or transmission lines against overload.

The accuracy obtained by this method equals or surpasses the accuracy of raw video.

CHARACTERISTICS

G-14 antenna group

Operating frequency: 1250 – 1350 MHz

Polarisation: Horizontal and circular (switchable)

Turning rate: 5, 6, or 7·5 rpm (other rates available upon request)

Feed type: Dual horn

G-7 antenna group

Operating frequency: 1250 – 1350 MHz

Polarisation: Horizontal through elliptical to circular

Turning rate: 5 – 10, 6 – 12 or 7·5 – 15 rpm, other dual rates available upon request

Feed type: Integrated 8 horns

Transmitter

Magnetron: M5051 (1250 – 1310 MHz) or M5052 (1350 – 1355 MHz)

Peak power: 1·8 MW minimum

Average power: 2250 W (minimum output of magnetron)

PRF (average): 300 – 800 pps, staggered in 6 different repetition periods

Adaptive MTI, MTD and ECCM facilities are available as options

STATUS

In current production.

ATCR-33 Primary Terminal Area Radar

This equipment is an E-band 10 cm medium power radar suitable for approach or GCA surveillance. It employs the same receiver as the ATCR-22 and is equipped with the G-33 antenna. This turns at 15 rpm and with the transmitter operating at 1000 pps, the coverage achieved on a small jet aircraft with the single channel ATCR-33 is about 45 nautical miles (83·4 km) in range and over 6000 metres in height. Short-range low cover properties make the system very suitable for aircraft recovery.

CHARACTERISTICS

Transmitter

Peak power: 0·5 MW minimum

Average power: 500 W (minimum output of magnetron)

Frequency: 2·7 – 2·9 GHz

PRF: Staggered in 6 different repetition periods

G-33 antenna group

Operating frequency: 2·7 – 2·9 GHz

Polarisation: Variable from linear to circular through all degrees of ellipticity

Coverage: Modified cosec[2] with improved high elevation angle cover

Turning speed: 15 rpm (other speeds available on request)

Main beam

Horizontal beamwidth (3 dB): 1·45° ±0·05°

Gain: 33·5 dB

Main sidelobes: Better than –25 dB

ATCR-22 installation in Mexico

ATCR-33 installation in Nigeria

Auxiliary beam

Horizontal beamwidth (3 dB): 1·45° ±0·05°

Gain: 32 dB

Main sidelobes: Better than –25 dB

Operating temperature range: (indoor units) 0 – 50° C; (outdoor units) –40 to +70° C

Adaptive MTI, MTD and ECCM facilities are available as options

STATUS

In production.

ATCR-44 Primary Radar

This radar is a medium powered version of the ATCR-22 employing a peak power of 500 kW and is especially suitable as an approach radar or for GCA surveillance. Either the G-21 or the G-14 antenna can be used according to operational requirements. With the antenna rotating at 15 rpm, the range coverage on a small jet aircraft is over 60 nautical miles (111 km) in single channel, with a height coverage of over 9000 metres. In dual diversity the range coverage on the same aircraft is over 75 nautical miles (139 km) with height cover over 12 000 metres. In its normal version, the radar has a PRF of 1000 pps with a pulse width of 1 μs giving an average power output of 500 W. The pulsed magnetron is tunable over the frequency band 1280 to 1350 MHz. The receiver/MTI chain is identical to that of the ATCR-22 and features the same digital processor resulting in a system that is flexible, reliable and easier to maintain. As with the ATCR-22, a clutter map is provided to delineate segments in which MTI video is desired; in all other segments the video is normal. Video correlator, video integrator and plot extractor are also identical to those of the higher-powered radar.

CHARACTERISTICS
Transmitter
Magnetron: 5J26 (air cooled)
Tuning range: 1280 – 1350 MHz
Peak power: 0·5 MW
Average power: 500 W
PRF: Up to 1000 Hz
Antenna: As for ATCR-22
Operating temperature range: (indoor units) 0 – 50° C; (outdoor units) –40 to +70° C
Adaptive MTI, MTD and ECCM facilities are available as options
STATUS
In production.

SELENIA SIR Secondary Surveillance Radar

The SIR secondary surveillance radar is the latest development from Selenia. A fully solid-state D-band radar, SIR can be operated on a single or dual channel configuration.

The radar is equipped with power programming which reduces the incidence of confusing reflections by ensuring that a smaller amount of power is radiated in the critical direction. Therefore the reflected energy is much lower and does not trigger the transponder, thereby eliminating any erroneous reply. In this way the effects of site-related phenomena such as reflections and interference between adjacent stations can be minimised.

SIR includes ten-mode interlace selector thumb-wheel switches which allow a wide range of interlace patterns, including different triple interlace in three azimuths, varying interlace on successive antenna revolutions and also external interlace. The transmitter consists of four to eight power modules (each module has a 500 W drive capability) all in parallel. The power transistors in each module are also in parallel, so that in the event of failure only a small power reduction occurs.

CHARACTERISTICS
Transmitter
Frequency: 1030 ± 0·1 MHz
Peak power: 1·8 kW; 3·4 kW (option)
Power regulation: 3, 6 and 12 dB steps
Pulse duration: 0·8 μs
Modes: 1, 2, 3/A, B, C, D, test, external
Interlace types: Circular, azimuth, scan/scan, test
Interlace modes: 3 groups of 3 thumb-wheels select any modes
Azimuth gates: 4 sectors covering 360° with 0·08° boundary definition
Receiver
Frequency: 1090 MHz

Selenia ATC radar installation in Zimbabwe

Bandwidth: 8 MHz
Tangential sensitivity: ⩾ –87 dBm
Gain time control: 8 range gates with ±10 dB attenuation
Antenna
Length
8·2 m; beamwidth 7°; gain 21 dB
4·1 m; beamwidth 4·5°; gain 19 dB
2·8 m; beamwidth 2·35°; gain 19 dB
Operating temperature range: (indoor units) 0 – 50° C; (outdoor units) –40 to +50° C
STATUS
In production. The unit is compliant with ICAO and STANAG recommendations
CONTRACTOR
Selenia-Industrie Elettroniche Associate SpA, Via Tiburtina, Km12400, 00131 Rome, Italy.

2249.153
SENTINEL RQT-9X PORTABLE INFANTRY RADAR

The Sentinel RQT-9X is a lightweight, man-portable battlefield surveillance radar. It provides instantaneous detection and location of any moving target at ranges from 0 up to 3·8 km.

The radar design, with the exception of the transmitting tube, is all solid-state and is based upon the technique of transmitting a continuous wave radio frequency signal for search in azimuth (surveillance mode) and a continuous wave with 0 to 180° phase modulation according to a pseudo-random code for ranging (ranging mode). In both cases frequency modulation of the transmitted signal is added to

achieve better performance. Change over from surveillance to ranging mode is obtained simply by operating a switch.

CHARACTERISTICS
Antenna system
Polarisation: Vertical
Azimuth beamwidth (3 dB): 4°
Elevation beamwidth (3 dB): 12°
Gain: 26 dB
Transmitter
Klystron: VA210 B modified
Power output: 40 mW
Type of emission: CW-FM with 0 – 180° phase modulation by a pseudo-random code

Code element width: 0·4 μs
Receiver
Noise figure: 16 dB
Display: Aural
Detection frequency bandwidth: 50 – 1530 Hz
STATUS
The equipment was type approved by the Italian Army in 1970. It is in service with the Italian infantry and has been supplied to the armies of other countries. No longer produced.
CONTRACTOR
Selenia-Industrie Elettroniche Associate SpA, Via Tiburtina Km 12400, 00131 Rome, Italy.

3279.153
SIT 431 (AN/TPX-54) IFF INTERROGATOR

The system consists of an interrogator unit, a sum-and-difference antenna and up to six AN/UPA-59A decoders. In SIF operation the primary controls are provided on the UPA-59As. In Mode 4 operation the interrogator is used with an external KIR-1A/TSEC computer. The Mode 4 controls and the secondary SIF controls are contained in a master control box remoted to the display area. An IFF system fault indicator is also included in this unit.

The receiver/transmitter module contains a 1500 W transmitter, a dual-channel receiver and RF interface module. The transmitter module is a completely solid-

SIT 431 (AN/TPX-54) IFF interrogator

state unit. A dual-channel receiver provides the receiver sidelobe suppression (RSLS) function when operated with either a sum-and-difference antenna or a sum-and-omni antenna. The use of RSLS provides a means of artificially sharpening and controlling the antenna beamwidth for received signals. One of the unique features of the receiver is the six-stage logarithmic IF amplifier. The output of each stage varies linearly as a logarithmic function of the input. Thus a large dynamic range is obtained without appreciable distortion even at very large signal levels.

An ISLS control gate diplexed into transmitter sum channel controls RF switching action. An omni antenna (AS 177) may be connected to the difference antenna connector for RLS operation or, alternatively, the dual-channel receiver may be operated on sum channel only (single-channel operation). In order to provide flexibility for any variation in antenna systems the interrogator is designed to allow removal of the diplexer module and replacement with an integral RF switch. This RF switch module is used in those applications where a dual IFF RF rotary joint is available. Modifications are not required, selection of the applicable modules is all that is necessary to satisfy various antenna arrangements.

The signal processor consists of a coder, defruiter, evaluator and video interface module. As an option a computer interface can be provided. The coder

module provides SIF modes 1, 2, 3/A, C and Mk XII Mode 4 challenge pulse to the transmitter. The SIF challenge pulses are generated by the coder, and the Mode 4 challenge pulses are supplied by the KIR computer. ISLS pulses are generated by the coder for both SIF and Mode 4. The coder is programmable to accept an interface pattern of up to five modes. Mode 4 can be used either interlaced or on an over-ride basis. The coder initiates challenges either from manual commands via switches located on a challenge gate or from an associated computer.

The defruiter module accepts receiver video and applies it to shift register memory. On successive PRPs the incoming video is compared to the video received from the memory. When pulse-to-pulse correlation is obtained, video is supplied to the associated UPA-59A decoding units.

The Mode 4 reply evaluator accepts receiver video and detects Mode 4 triple-pulse video. The triple-pulse decoded video is provided to the KIR-1A/TSEC for time decoding. The evaluator utilises real-time processing for target detection and microprocessor technology for the reply evaluation.
STATUS
In production.
CONTRACTOR
ITALTEL (Società Italiana Telecomunicazioni), 12 Piazzale Zavattari, 20149 Milan, Italy.

JAPAN

4081.153
JAN/MPQ-N1 (TYPE 92) MORTAR LOCATING RADAR

The Type 92 mortar locating radar is apparently a Japanese licence-built version of the American AN/MPQ-4 equipment which is produced by the General Electric Company. The Japanese model, designated JAN/MPQ-N1, is thought to have essentially the same performance as the US-built radar which is described in entry **2497.153**, later in this section of *Jane's Weapon Systems*.

The purpose of these radars is to detect and locate enemy mortar positions so that counter-battery action can be carried out. The two-beam intercept principle is employed, first-shell acquisition is possible and the system can handle multiple targets.
STATUS
Operational with the Japanese Ground Self-Defence Force.

It is usual for the reflector to be folded down when the Type 92 mortar locating radar is being towed (K Ebata)

Japanese Type 92 (JAN/MPQ-N1) mortar locating radar on the move with its reflector erected (K Ebata)

4141.153
J/MPQ-P7 ARTILLERY LOCATING RADAR

This artillery locating radar is apparently of Japanese design, but it is not known if there has been any technical collaboration from America or elsewhere, although there is an obvious similarity with the recent Hughes AN/TPQ-36 and AN/TPQ-37 mortar and artillery locating radars (**2848.153** and **1976.153**). Like the US-designed radars, the J/MPQ-P7 employs electronic scanning of a planar array antenna to generate the multiple beams necessary for detection and trajectory analysis of incoming projectiles. In this respect the Japanese equipment is so far the only known comparable radar to appear from beyond the American defence industry for operational service. The moderately large antenna array is transported on a wheeled trailer towed by a tracked vehicle which houses items of equipment and the radar crew. The antenna is erected when deployed, but folds flat for transit. Electronic beam steering probably obviates any need for the array to rotate in use. It is likely that a sufficiently broad azimuth coverage arc can be achieved by electronic scanning to provide surveillance of the designated threat direction(s).

Few technical details have been obtained but it is reported that the equipment has a peak output power of 250 kW, operates in the I/J-band (former X-band), and is capable of ranges of more than 30 km.
STATUS
In service with the Japanese Self-Defence Forces.
CONTRACTOR
Toshiba Electric Company, 1-6 Uchisaiwaicho, 1-chome, Chiyoda-ku, Tokyo 100, Japan.

J/MPQ-P7 artillery locating radar equipment in transit configuration (K Ebata)

J/MPQ-P7 artillery locating radar set up for operation

2298.153
NPM-510 MOBILE 3-D RADAR

The NEC NPM-510 3-D radar is a highly mobile system with several novel features. Among these are the antenna system, which is rotated in azimuth but electronically scanned in elevation and which consists of a planar array that can be folded for transport, and a rapidly erected inflatable equipment shelter.

A compact and lightweight system relying extensively on solid-state technology the radar is claimed to be highly reliable. Salient features of the circuitry are a CFA transmitter chain, chirp pulse compression, digital MTI and automatic target detection, tracking, and altitude computation.
STATUS
The radar has been supplied to the Japan Defence Agency.

Inflatable operations centre for the NEC radar

CONTRACTOR
NEC Corporation, 33-1, Shiba 5-chome, Minato-ku, Tokyo 108, Japan.

Planar antenna of the NEC mobile 3-D radar NPM-510

3702.153

NPG-880 3-D AIR DEFENCE RADAR

The NPG-880 is a static three-dimensional air defence radar developed by NEC in Japan; a mobile version, NPM-510, is also produced (**2298.153**, above). Both equipments employ an antenna that embodies a unique phase/frequency scanning technique of a planar phased array in elevation, with mechanical rotation in azimuth. A combination of serpentine feed and ferrite phase shifters is used for scanning a pencil beam in elevation.

The radar embodies energy management concepts and signal processing techniques giving high detection and stable accuracy, with a TWT and CFA transmitter chain, chirp pulse compression and amplitude comparison for height measurement. The advanced digital signal processing techniques used for clutter reduction and rejection (and ECCM) significantly enhance performance for automatic detection and tracking under severe clutter and jamming environments.

The NPG-880 is capable of direct interfacing with any automated air defence network, and it is linked with air defence ground environment and air defence command post systems. The system has dual channel configuration with high reliability design features and substantial built-in-test equipment to minimise system down-time.

The general configuration of the NPG-880 can be seen from the nearby photograph. The associated transmitter/receiver, display, and other electronics can be housed either in permament or temporary buildings.

Planar array of the NPG-880 static 3-D air defence radar

STATUS
Supplied to the Japanese Air Self-Defence Force.

CONTRACTOR
NEC Corporation, 33-1, Shiba 5-chome, Minato-ku, Tokyo 108, Japan.

2297.153

AIR TRAFFIC CONTROL RADARS

Numerous radars covering most aspects of civil aircraft movement are made by the NEC Corporation. These radars are made primarily to comply with ICAO and other civil aviation specifications: some of them have been supplied to the Japan Defence Agency (JDA) and these are briefly described below.

Air Route Surveillance Radar (ARSR)

D-band long-range surveillance radar intended for en route air traffic control.

NEC provides two types of ARSRs, the NPG-434 (magnetron transmitter version) and the NPG-630 (klystron transmitter version), which are used with the NPG-905A secondary surveillance radar (SSR), radar data transmission systems such as the NPG-359 radar microwave link (RML) or the NZG-594 radar video bandwidth compression (VBC) system and associated equipment.

The NPG-434/NPG-630 ARSR employs modern computer-aided design, a dual beam antenna, solid-state circuits and advanced digital signal processing

techniques providing extended coverage of more than 200 nautical miles and 70 000 feet. The NPG-359 all solid-state RML (which is operated in the 7 GHz band and has a standard transmission range of 50 km) is based on the high reliability and perfected system design techniques of NEC's microwave equipment.

NEC has developed the NZG-594 VBC system which makes it possible to transmit ARSR raw radar video and SSR digitised radar data utilising narrow-band 12 voice telephone channels (48 kHz) and one channel of the telecommunication network as a transmission means.

Fourteen of these systems have been supplied to the Japan Civil Aviation Bureau (JCAB).

Airport Surveillance Radar (ASR)

NEC manufactures an E/F-band surveillance radar for use in terminal area air traffic control. Three versions exist: the NPG-360 and NPG-1240 which have a range of 64 nautical miles and 40 000 feet on small commercial aircraft and the NPG-460 which has a range of 80 nautical miles and 50 000 feet on a jet

fighter. Many radars in various combinations have been supplied to JDA, JCAB and foreign customers. These versions have beamwidths of 1·2°, data renewal rates of 15 rpm and digital MTI. NPG-360 has a 500 kW magnetron transmitter and a transistor RF amplifier giving an overall noise figure of 3·5 dB; the NPG-1240 is a klystron version of the NPG-360 and the NPG-460 has a 3·5 MW transmitter with a transistor RF amplifier, as in the NPG-360.

Precision Approach Radar (PAR)

The NPG-435 is a PAR which has been designed to a standard above the ICAO requirement making it suitable for fighter airfields. Detection range is more than 15 nautical miles.

Secondary Surveillance Radar (SSR/SIF)

The NPG-905A is a complete ICAO-specification SSR system with interrogator/responsor decoder and defruiter and SIF capability. A large number of systems have been supplied to the Japanese military and civil aviation authorities.

Ground Controlled Approach Radar (GCA)

The NPM-554 is an integrated system comprising ASR, PAR, and SSR/SIF elements together with communications sub-systems. These sub-systems are essentially those described above but slightly reconfigured to suit the integrated installation. The secondary radar antenna is in a linear array mounted on the primary radar antenna. These systems have been supplied to the JDA.

Fixed Type GCA

The NPG-864 is a system featuring a high performance alpha-numeric radar display that automatically detects and tracks aircraft equipped with a beacon transponder, then correlates them with flight plans previously registered at a terminal ATC. In addition to conventional GCA component elements such as NPG-460 ASR, NPG-435 PAR, NPG-905A SIF, CCU and associated equipment, it features a data processing system to conduct the above functions. These equipments are installed in shelters at the ASR, PAR and ACC operational areas. The radar has been supplied to the JDA.

Automated ATC System

NEC has developed a sophisticated ATC automation system for the JCAB and semi-automated air warning and control systems for the JDA.

STATUS

All the above are believed to be operational with the JDA. Three other radars developed by NEC are the high-power NPG-434 ARSR magnetron version, NPG-630 ARSR klystron version, which have been bought by the JCAB and the NPM-510 mobile 3-D radar described in **2298.153**.

Surveillance radar display, PAR display and associated equipment of NEC GCA NPG-864

NPG-630 ARSR

CONTRACTOR
NEC Corporation, 33-1, Shiba 5-chome, Minato-ku,
Tokyo 108, Japan.

NPM-554 mobile GCA system

4605.153
XJ/FPS-3 AIR DEFENCE RADAR
The XJ/FPS-3 air defence radar is a next generation phased array radar project which is intended to be the main air defence/interceptor control radar of the Japanese Base Air Defence Ground Environment (BADGE) air defence system. Current plans are for eight XJ/FPS-3 sites, each with a long- and short-range radar antenna.
STATUS
Three Japanese companies, Mitsubishi Electric, Japan Electric and Tokyo Shibaura Electric are tendering for the project, development of which should be complete by early 1987. The second development phase has been allocated 4500 million yen (£13 million) in the 1984 defence budget. Technical and operational tests will follow the end of the development phase and a purchase decision is expected in 1990.

NETHERLANDS

3283.153
FLYCATCHER RADAR
The radar employed in the Signaal Flycatcher low-level anti-aircraft weapon control system (**2301.181**) is essentially a repackaged version of that developed for the Leopard 35 mm AA tank CA1 (**2302.153** below), allied to an SMR digital computer.

The computer is also used to generate track data for a second target, of particular importance for fast target change in a multi-target environment and when the radar is connected to a mix of weapons, such as medium calibre guns and surface-to-air missiles. In addition to this computer-assisted track-while-scan capability, provision is made for the display of targets acquired by other systems.

The general arrangement of the Flycatcher radar employs coaxial mounting of the search and tracking antenna as compared with the separate positions used in the 35 mm AA tank installation. The main characteristics are otherwise similar for both versions of the radar.

STATUS
Deliveries to the Netherlands forces for defence of air bases and missile batteries began in 1978. The system has also been ordered by Thailand and the first equipments were delivered in early 1983.
CONTRACTOR
Hollandse Signaalapparaten BV, Zuidelijke Havenweg 40, PO Box 42, Hengelo, Netherlands.

2302.153
INTEGRATED RADAR SYSTEM FOR 35 mm AA TANK
One version of the 35 mm AA tank systems described in the Systems section (**2370.131**) is equipped with an integrated radar system designed and manufactured by NV Hollandse Signaalapparaten. This fire control system is mounted on a Leopard tank chassis armed with twin, rapid-firing 35 mm Oerlikon AA cannon. The Signaal system is based upon the well-proven advanced integrated radar technology in which the same I-band transmitter is used for both search and tracking purposes. A dual-band tracking radar operating in both I- and Ka-bands, with a broad beamwidth compared with that of the search antenna and a very small beamwidth for tracking the extremely low flying targets, reduces reaction time to the barest minimum and allows the tracking of the lowest, tree-top level aircraft. Simultaneous search transmissions are continued through the entire tracking phase, permitting complete coverage against further airborne threats to be maintained. Rapid automatic or manual switching facilities allow the system to cope with a multi-target environment.

The radar system has been designed to detect and identify aircraft at very low to medium altitudes and to track them automatically. It has the following important features:
(1) integrating all-weather search and tracking systems with a very short reaction time
(2) search while tracking through 360°
(3) search on the move, with compensation for vehicle's speed
(4) good performance in clutter and ECM environment
(5) compact rugged design and module concept to facilitate maintenance
(6) dual frequency tracking radar
(7) integral IFF.
CHARACTERISTICS
Antenna system
Search antenna: Slotted waveguide type
Length: 1·5 m
Horizontal beamwidth: 1·4°
Vertical beamwidth: 30°
Polarisation: Horizontal or circular

Rotational speed: 60 rpm
Range: 15 km
MTI improvement factor: 30 dB
Tracking antenna: Parabolic with cassegrain reflector and monopulse feedhorn
Diameter: 0·6 m
Beamwidth: 4·2°
Transmitter/receiver
Transmitter power: 160 W average
Frequency: I-band
Search channel: MTI with double canceller (digital)
Tracking channel: Pulse doppler and built-in anti-image radar
ECCM: Digital video correlator (ISU), pulse-length discriminator (PLD). Passive tracking in I-band, PRF stagger
Noise figures: Search receiver 7 dB, tracking receiver 9 dB
Radar display and control panels
PPI: Diameter 25 cm, north orientated clutter-free picture, compensated for vehicle's speed. Arrangement of controls to high standard of human engineering. IFF completely integrated with the search system
Power consumption: 200 V 380 Hz approx 2 kVA
STATUS
A pre-production series of five and a main series of 95 units are now in service with the Royal Netherlands Army.
CONTRACTOR
Hollandse Signaalapparaten BV, Zuidelijke Havenweg 40, PO Box 42, Hengelo, Netherlands.

Signaal integrated radar system for 35 mm AA tank

POLAND

2340.153
POLISH RADAR
Little information is available on Polish radar developments. It is known, however, that the Industrial Institute of Telecommunications in Warsaw has for many years been working on radar developments and some definite information has been made available on the radars that have been developed for civil ATC purposes.

As an illustration of radar capability, therefore, it may be of interest to note a few details concerning one of these radars, the Avia B D-band airways surveillance radar.

Avia B is a 23 cm wavelength radar using high-power magnetron transmitters and a low-noise parametric amplifier in the receiver. Operating in frequency diversity it has two 1·5 MW peak power transmitters. The parametric amplifier used in the receiver is an original Polish development. The radar has an MTI system, and staggered PRF is used to eliminate blind speeds in the practical range of aircraft performance. The polarisation of the transmitted radiation may be varied from linear to circular.

Maximum range on a 15 m² target with 90 per cent detection probability is 240 km with a ceiling of 26 000 m.

CHARACTERISTICS
Avia B
Operating frequency: 1310 and 1346·2 MHz
Peak power output: 2 × 1·5 MW (frequency diversity)
PRF: 400 Hz mean (recurrence 7:8)
Pulse length: 3 μs
Noise factor: 3·5 dB
Fixed echo suppression: 30 dB
Antenna rotation speeds: 5 or 10 rpm
Antenna gain: 32 dB
Horizontal beamwidth: 1·3°
Vertical beamwidth: 40°
Polarisation: Variable from linear to circular

SOUTH AFRICA

4601.153
EMVA MK10B MUZZLE VELOCITY RADAR
The EMVA Mk10B is a doppler radar analyser designed to measure muzzle velocity over the range 30 to 3000 m/s. The equipment can be used for guns of 20 mm calibre or larger. The instrument consists of an antenna which can be mounted on the gun or tripod, plus a processor with a liquid crystal display and a hard copy printer. Power is by standard 24 V dc batteries.

The equipment is triggered automatically by the radar echo from the shell when the gun is fired. An external trigger unit is also provided which operates on the muzzle flash or projectile shadow and when connected to the antenna head, overrides the automatic radar echo trigger. Up to 100 readings are taken before the shell is out of range and are then analysed to give muzzle velocity.
CHARACTERISTICS
Range: 30 – 3000 m/s

Accuracy: ±0·05%
Dimensions
Antenna head: 30·5 × 14·5 × 16·5 cm
Processor: 65 × 38 × 29 cm
Weights
Antenna head: 9 kg
Processor: 30 kg
CONTRACTOR
Armscor, Pretoria, Republic of South Africa.

SWEDEN

1957.153
GIRAFFE SEARCH RADAR
Giraffe is the family designation of a mobile search pulse doppler radar system developed by Ericsson in Sweden. The basic version, PS-70/R, is designed for use with the new Swedish Army/Bofors short-range surface-to-air missile system RBS 70 (**2348.131**) or any short-range missile or AA gun system. The complete radar together with radio communication equipment, tactical control facility and power supply is linked with a number of firing units for precision target designation and combat control.

A prominent feature of this installation is the use of a folding mast for the antenna, giving an effective operating height of 12 m. Together with excellent clutter suppression characteristics (MTI improvement factor is better than 50 dB) this gives the Giraffe very low altitude coverage. The range coverage is 40 km in the surveillance mode and 20 km in the target designation mode.

The radar employs a broadband TWT final amplifier which delivers 15 kW peak, 300 W average, over the G/H-band. The high gain, low sidelobes antenna generates a cosecant-squared beam up to 60° with an azimuth beamwidth of 2°. Digital doppler processing and constant false alarm circuitry are used to automatically extract, detect and present the target of interest. A digital plan position indicator presents video signals and target tracking symbols. The target data link constitutes the interface between the search radar and the firing sites. Information about target geographical co-ordinates, speed and course is derived and transmitted from the target data transmitter, which is located in the search radar. The target data receiver, located at the firing site, performs certain calculations, generates signals for slewing the gun or missile sight towards the target and displays information as to whether the target is engageable or not.

The Giraffe search radar is offered with comprehensive ECCM options and an IFF equipment can be installed. Training equipment, available as an optional accessory, can easily be installed in the cabin without requiring any connections to external units.

The basic Giraffe radar parameters provide for more than adequate range and altitude coverage required by any AA artillery or short-range surface-to-air missile system. The adaptation to different short-range systems is achieved mainly by modifying the interfacing target data receiver. To extend the range coverage required for medium-range surface-to-air missile systems, a more powerful transmitter can be installed. This constitutes the only major modification of the basic design. The Giraffe concept in general and its MTI performance in particular, suit the system for handling the low altitude air surveillance task in early warning and air command systems.

Naval versions (**4299.253**) for installation on board fast patrol boats and up to frigate size ships are available. They combine air surveillance with superior MTI performance, surface surveillance and surface fire control with high resolution capability in one radar only. The MTI improvement factor gives naval versions excellent sea skimmer detection capability.
CHARACTERISTICS
Radar
Frequency: G/H-band (former C-band)
Output power: 15 kW (peak), 300 W (average)
MTI improvement factor: 50 dB
Pulse length: 3 or 6 μs
Range coverage: 20 or 40 km
Target velocity range: 30 – 375 m/s
Antenna revolution rate: 60 rpm
Antenna gain: 29 dB
Beamwidth azimuth: 2°
Elevation pattern: Cosec² to 60°
PRF: Either staggered or switched every antenna revolution
Mechanical
Total weight: 6500 kg (excluding vehicle)
Transport width: 2·5 m
Transport height (on vehicle): 3·4 m
Antenna operating height: 12 m
Interior volume: 12 m³
Interior height: 1·7 m
STATUS
The PS-70/R model has been ordered by the Swedish Defence Materiel Administration for use with the RBS 70 AA missile system and deliveries have commenced. In addition, the Swedish Defence Materiel Administration has ordered the more powerful version of the Giraffe, PS-707/R, for a

Ericsson Giraffe tactical radar deployed and ready for use

medium-range surface-to-air missile system, and this is now in production. An AA artillery version has also been ordered and is in production for a number of foreign governments. Yet another version for a different short-range surface-to-air missile has also been ordered and is in production. A shipborne version of the Giraffe radar (**4299.253**) has been ordered by the Swedish Government for fitting in 'Spica II' fast patrol boats and by Canada for fitment in the new Canadian Patrol Frigate. A contract worth $9·5 million has been received from the Norwegian Army for the basic Giraffe. The radar is already in service in Norway under previous contracts. More than 200 Giraffe systems have been ordered since 1978 and the radar is in service in seven countries outside Sweden.
CONTRACTOR
Ericsson Radio Systems AB, Defence and Space Systems Division, 431 26 Mölndal, Sweden.

4029.153
9KR 400 COASTAL RADAR

The 9KR 400 consists of a 9GR 600 I-band frequency-agile transceiver (**1546.253**), a 9GA 205 antenna and a variable number of displays and/or automatic plot extractors, permitting narrow-band transmissions. It forms the main sensors element of the 9KA 400 Mareld coastal artillery fire control system (**1548.181**) and the 9CSI 600 STINA naval command system (**4028.281**).

The transceiver is completely solid-state with the exception of the magnetrons. The wide-band frequency agility capability offers very high jamming resistance, very long range, and good tracking accuracy. Alternatively, the radar can be run in a fixed-frequency mode for MTI operation.

Other applications are shipborne or ground-based, and further entries can be found in the appropriate sections of this volume.

CHARACTERISTICS

Operating modes: Frequency agility/fixed frequency/MTI
Transmitter tubes (2 off): Magnetron VJ1180/YJ1181
Frequency agility range: Minimum 400 MHz, typically 450 MHz within 8700 – 9500 MHz

Frequency shift: Randomly within frequency agility range from pulse-to-pulse
Pulse peak power: 200 kW
Pulse width/PRF: Typically 1 μs/1000Hz and 0·25 μs/3000 Hz
Receiver
Frequency range: 8500 – 9600 MHz
IF: 30 MHz
Noise figure: Typically 5·5 dB, max 7 dB with low-noise preamplifier
Receiver characteristics: Lin and log, log/lin, STC
Operational features: Image rejection mixer, Dicke-fix receiver, PLD, IAGC, narrow band jamming suppression, passive ECM mode
Transceiver dimensions: 1200 × 635 × 510 mm
Weight: Approx 225 kg
Antenna 9GA 205
Reflector type: Parabolic
Frequency range: 8·5 – 9·6 GHz
Rotation speed: Up to 40 rpm
Beamwidths
Horizontal: 0·6°
Vertical: 4°
Gain: 40 dB

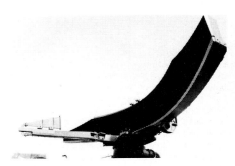

PEAB 9GA 205 antenna

Sidelobes
Within ± 10° of main lobe: –26 dB
Otherwise: –33 dB
Aperture: 4500 × 625 mm
Weight (including turntable): 260 kg
STATUS
In service.
CONTRACTOR
Philips Elektronikindustrier AB, 17588 Järfälla, Sweden.

2357.153
UAR 1021 COMBINED SEARCH AND TRACK PULSE-DOPPLER RADAR

This combined fully coherent search and track pulse-doppler radar is a successor to the earlier ECSTRA I equipment. It employs a single I-band transmitter which feeds the independent search and track antenna by way of a power splitter. The tracking sub-system uses a monopulse technique with a cassegrain antenna; the search system uses a cheese antenna or a cosec^2 antenna with integrated IFF dipoles.

Important features of the equipment are the high clutter attenuation resulting from the coherent pulse-doppler system; the ECCM capability resulting from the broad-band system (900 MHz), and the possibility of operating either on a fixed frequency (chosen from five with a change time of less than ten milliseconds) in the pulse-doppler mode or with random pulse-to-pulse frequency agility within 900 MHz in the non-doppler mode; the monopulse angular tracking system; and the digital range tracking system.

CHARACTERISTICS
Frequency: 8·6 – 9·5 GHz

MTI improvement factor: 45 dB
Peak power: 26 kW
Noise factor: 12 dB
PRF: 3 different triplets in 4·8 – 8·1 kHz interval with rapid cyclic switching
Pulse width: 1·5/0·5 μs selectable
Tracking antenna gain: 36 dB
Tracking antenna diameter: 1 m
Range coverage: PD-mode 0·3 – 18 km; FA-mode 0·3 – 25 km
Acquisition interval: 1120 m
Velocity window: 22 – 385 m/s
Angle tracking accuracy: 1 mrad
STATUS
In production for the Contraves Skyguard system (**2377.151**). The related UAR 1302 equipment, a coherent-on-receive system, is an integral part of the Marconi S800 series of anti-aircraft radars (**2464.153** and **2466.153**) and has been in production since early 1975.
CONTRACTOR
Ericsson Radio Systems AB, Defence and Space Systems Division, 431 26 Mölndal, Sweden.

UAR 1021 combined search and track radar in Contraves Skyguard system

UNION OF SOVIET SOCIALIST REPUBLICS

2860.153
BACK NET GCI RADAR

An early Soviet ground control interception (GCI) radar and a predecessor of Barlock (**2861.153**), the radar known to NATO as Back Net has a six-feed antenna system similar to that of Barlock.

Multiple feeds are widely used in Soviet surveillance and GCI radars. Part of the reason for this is the possibility of increasing the total radiated power within the confines of component limitations; but another reason is the possibility of using such antenna systems to provide some form of height information.

Other predecessors of Barlock include Big Bar A (**2862.153**) and Big Mesh (**2863.153**) both of which also have six-feed antenna systems.

2861.153
BARLOCK GCI RADAR

This large ground control interception and search radar is trailer mounted equipment that has two large truncated paraboloid reflectors with clipped corners.

Operating frequencies of the radar are in the E/F-band. Each of the reflectors is fed by three feeds so that six stacked beams result, each beam having a power output in the region of 1 MW. These beams may enable the radar to be used as a height indicator, but it is also likely that they are part of a system for providing surveillance cover over different altitude bands. Both the reflectors can be adjusted in elevaion angle by the operator while the radar is operating to permit manual variations of vertical cover. Individual frequency bands for the stacked beams are:

2695 – 2715 MHz
2715 – 2750 MHz
2815 – 2835 MHz
2900 – 2990 MHz
2990 – 3025 MHz
3080 – 3125 MHz

Inside view of Barlock operations vehicle, showing one of the plotting positions

Known to the Soviet forces as P-50 this radar has a PRF of 375 pps and pulse widths of 1·83 to 3·1 microseconds for the E/F-band transmission and 2·4 microseconds for a D-band identification (IFF-type) secondary radar transmitter that is often found in association with Barlock.

Range capability of Barlock is about 300 km, range accuracy is about 90 m, and angular accuracy about 0·5°. The entire trailer body rotates for azimuth scanning at rates up to about 12 rpm.

STATUS
Known to have been in operational use since at least the mid-1960s and widely deployed in the USSR and friendly nations.

Barlock GCI radar deployed

2862.153
BIG BAR A GCI RADAR
A ground control interception radar with a six-feed antenna system similar to that of Barlock (**2861.153**). See also entry for Back Net (**2860.153**) above.

A significant difference is that the two antennas are arranged to provide V-beams in elevation, thereby making possible heightfinding by means of this technique. The rear, upper antenna is displaced so that the major axis of the elliptical reflector is tilted about 25 to 30° from the horizontal.

2864.153
DOG HOUSE ABM RADAR
One of several large fixed phased-array radars deployed by the Soviet authorities for missile detection. Dog House is the NATO name given to a radar with a very large array antenna.

Complicated signal processing is used in the installations to which these large antenna arrays belong. It is believed that this is an area where Soviet technology is somewhat weaker than, say, that of the USA; and in support of this view it has been pointed out that such signal processing techniques are not much used in smaller Soviet radar installations and that this may be because they have decided to apply limited resources first and foremost to the solution of such critical problems as strategic missile defence.

The principal known use of the Dog House radar is as the intermediate range radar of the Moscow ABM complex. It accepts targets from the long-range Hen House radar (**2879.153**) and hands them on to the Try Adds radars. Dog House operates in the VHF band at around 100 MHz – hence the need for the very large phased array to achieve a sensible beamwidth. It is said to be capable of radiating a peak power up to 20 MW and to have a PRF of 50 pps – which is broadly consistent with its reported range of some 1500 nautical miles (about 2800 km).
STATUS
Operational in the Moscow ABM network.

4329.153
BIG FRED ARTILLERY/MORTAR LOCATING RADAR
The Soviet Union artillery/mortar locating radar (NATO reporting name Big Fred) is a mobile system normally fitted to armoured vehicles. Information on the equipment is scanty but it is believed to be similar to the Cymbeline system manufactured by EMI of the United Kingdom (**1018.153**). The radar is believed to operate in J-band. The antenna folds flat in the forward position for travelling.
OPERATION
The system enables the operator to plot two points in the shell or mortar bomb trajectory and measure the slant range and bearing to each of these positions. The time taken for the projectile to travel between the two points is also measured and the on-board computer uses this information, together with the pre-set elevation angles, to determine the position of the enemy mortar or howitzer. This information is then passed to the field artillery for counter-action.
STATUS
Big Fred is fitted to the multipurpose armoured vehicle MT-LB and the ACRV-2 (armoured command and reconnaissance vehicle) of the Soviet Army. The Yugoslav Army has recently taken delivery of a number of the former vehicles fitted with Big Fred.

The Soviet forces also use a BMP MICV fitted with the Small Fred radar. Small Fred is believed to operate in J-band with a detection range of 39 km and a tracking range of 7 km.

Soviet 'Big Fred' radar is used by Warsaw Pact and other friendly states as well as the USSR

2863.153
BIG MESH GCI RADAR
A ground control interception radar with a six-feed antenna system similar to that of Barlock (**2861.153**). See also entry for Back Net (**2860.153**). Like Big Bar A (**2862.153**), Big Mesh has the rear, upper antenna array tilted to one side to permit heightfinding by the V-beam method.

2866.153
FAN SONG MISSILE CONTROL RADARS
Fan Song is the NATO code-name given to a family of compound radar installations that have been developed for use with the Guideline (SA-2) surface-to-air missile (**2942.131**).

Seven of these radars have so far been identified (by suffix letters A to G) and common to all of them are the detection and tracking of the target, the command guidance of the missile and the tracking of the missile. It is said that these radars can handle up to six targets at once and guide three missiles at a time. It appears, however, that the missile must pass through the guidance beam within a few seconds (reportedly six) of launch if it is to be acquired and steered towards the selected target. A further problem appears to be a limitation in the amount of steering information that the missile is capable of receiving from the ground station. Nevertheless, Soviet forces have kept Guideline (in various versions) in service for many years and it has been used in action successfully by the North Vietnamese: although

Operational deployment of Fan Song C

possibly expensive in operation, therefore, the system as a whole would appear to be effective.

Details of some of the Fan Song series are given below. All members of the series contain as a major element a track-while-scan radar which scans a designated sector with two flapping fan beams radiated from two orthogonal antenna systems. The flapping motion has a sawtooth profile and uses the electromechanical system known as the Lewis scanner. The 'fan' in the code-name refers to these fan beams and the 'song' to the bird-like sound of the demodulated radiation from these radars.

STATUS
Fan Songs of various kinds are in service with Guideline missiles in the USSR, satellite and client countries and are also deployed at Soviet air bases in Afghanistan.

Rear view of Fan Song radar group showing details of antenna feed arrangements

---

2867.153
FAN SONG B MISSILE CONTROL RADAR
Fan Song B is an E/F-band member of the Fan Song series (see **2866.153** above). Radiation from its two Lewis scanners is at 2965 to 2990 MHz for one and 3025 to 3050 MHz for the other: peak power output is in the region of 600 kW and the equipment has a

first-time-round range capability of between 60 and 120 km.

The equipment is trailer-mounted and the scanned sector can be changed by rotating the trailer and tilting the whole superstructure. The sector scanned is about 10° high and 10° wide, these dimensions being the approximate fan beam width, the beam

width in the scanning direction being only about 2° for each beam.

A small parabolic antenna, mounted at one end of the horizontal Lewis scanner is used to transmit UHF command guidance signals to the missile.

2868.153
FAN SONG E MISSILE CONTROL RADAR
Fan Song E is a G-band member of the Fan Song radar series (see **2866.153** above). Similar in many respects to Fan Song B (**2867.153**) its main differences are the frequency of the radiation from the Lewis scanners and the fan beam (and hence the sector) dimensions. The beams in Fan Song E are about 7·5° wide in the fan and about 1·5° wide in the scanning direction, carrier frequencies are 4910 to 4990 MHz and 5010 to 5090 MHz and peak power is about 1·5 MW. Unambiguous range is 70 to 145 km.

In addition to the antenna for the command guidance signals, which is similar to that of Fan Song B, Fan Song E has two further parabolic dishes

mounted on top of the horizontal Lewis scanner. One of these is horizontally and the other vertically polarised and their purpose is to provide a lobe on receive only (LORO) feature. This is an ECCM technique in which the scanning action of the Lewis scanner is restricted to the receive channel by diverting the transmitted signal, which otherwise would be radiated from the scanner, into a dummy load. This signal is then replaced by a signal from one of the parabolic dishes (the other being for use with the other Lewis scanner) of sufficient power to operate the whole system.

The reason for adding the LORO facility is that by monitoring the Lewis scanner radiation an enemy pilot can tell roughly whether or not he is the prime

focus of the attention of the ground forces. If he is, he can employ deceptive electronic countermeasures (DECM) to confuse the radar – such countermeasures typically involving an apparent shift of target angle.
STATUS
G-band Fan Song radars are in widespread use with Guideline missiles. A version that has been dubbed Fan Song F has been reported, identified by a box-like housing on top of the radar shelter. This is said to contain a visual observer's position (with or without optical aids is not known) to assist target and/or missile acquisition. The extent of operational deployment of this modification is not known.

2871.153
FIRE CAN FIRE CONTROL RADAR
This E-band trailer-mounted radar appears to have been derived from the American SCR-584 radar that was extensively used during the latter years of the Second World War and which was supplied to the Soviet forces by the USA. A typical war-time application of the SCR-584 radar was its use on the 'Diver' gun sites that were set up on the east coast of Britain to combat the V1 attack. The radars then were used with a 3·7 inch (94 mm) AA gun and the electronic predictor. The Soviet radar appears to be used with smaller 57 mm and 85 mm guns.

Fire Can operates at a frequency of 2700 to

2900 MHz, has a pulse width of 0·3 to 0·8 microseconds and a PRF of 1840 to 1900 pps. Peak operating power is believed to be about 300 kW.

Like the SCR-584, the Fire Can antenna is a parabolic dish, perforated to reduce weight and windage, that is mounted on a pedestal on top of the flat roof of the radar trailer. Power is radiated from a rotating dipole feed driven from the rear of the dish and signals from the common T/R system are used, in the tracking mode, to operate a lock-follow system that produces tracking accuracies of about 1·6 minutes of arc in azimuth and 2 minutes in elevation.

The radar can also be operated in a search mode with the antenna rotating continuously in azimuth

and nodding in elevation. In this mode the antenna, which has a diameter of about 150 cm, produces a pencil beam with an effective beamwidth of about 5°. In this mode all received signals are displayed on a PPI but the dipole feed is driven all the time so that the operator can switch rapidly from search to track.

It is believed that Fire Can can acquire targets (search mode) at a maximum range of about 80 km and track them from about 35 km. Tracking accuracy in range is said to be about 13 to 15 m.
STATUS
In service. It is reported that some 75 of these radars were at one time deployed for use in North Viet-Nam.

2872.153
FIRE WHEEL FIRE CONTROL RADAR
Fire Wheel is the NATO code-name for another SCR-584-derived fire control radar similar to Fire Can and Whiff (**2871.153** and **2893.153**).

2873.153
FLAP WHEEL FIRE CONTROL RADAR
Flap Wheel is the NATO code-name for a conical scan radar that is believed to have much the same range of

operating frequencies as Gun Dish (**2876.153**). It is used to provide fire control data for 57 mm and 130 mm AA guns.

2874.153
FLAT FACE TARGET ACQUISITION RADAR
Flat Face is the NATO code-name of a radar known in the USSR as the P-15. It is a vehicle mounted acquisition radar that is used in conjunction with the Low Blow missile control radar (**2884.153**) and the Goa surface-to-air missile (**2938.131**).

This radar operates in the UHF C-band and radiates its signals from two elliptical paraboloid reflectors each measuring about 11 × 5·5 m. The radar has a range capability of about 250 km with a range accuracy of about 90 m and an angular accuracy of about 0·5°. Frequency bands are about 810 to 850 MHz and 880 to 950 MHz, PRFs are 200 to 800 pps

and 600 to 680 pps. Vertical beamwidth is about 5° and horizontal about 2°. Peak power is about 500 kW.
STATUS
Operational in Egypt and Viet-Nam, where 40 Flat Face radars have been reported. Deployed generally with Goa missiles but also reported with tank and motorised infantry divisions. May also be in use with SA-8 Gecko missiles.

Soviet Flat Face mobile radar unit

2875.153
GAGE ACQUISITION RADARS
Gage is the NATO code-name for an acquisition radar that is used in conjunction with the Yo-Yo missile

control radar (**2895.153**) which in turn is used with the early Soviet surface-to-air missile Guild (**2944.131**). Operating frequency is believed to be about 3 GHz and peak power about 2 MW.

2876.153
GUN DISH FIRE CONTROL RADAR
This broad-band fire control radar is used in conjunction with the quadruple 23 mm AA gun mounting on the ZSU-23-4 SP AA vehicle (**5548.103**). This vehicle is used by the AA battalions of the armoured and mechanised divisions of the Red Army and of other Warsaw Pact armies. The NATO code-name Gun Dish is obviously prompted by the appearance of the ZSU-23-4 vehicle.

Designed as it is to oppose low-level aircraft attacks the system of which Gun Dish is a part has to have a short reaction time. The guns can be slaved to the radar in elevation and are mounted, in the ZSU-23-4, in a rotatable turret on which the radar is mounted also and which contains a fire-control computer. A more recent application of this radar that has been reported is its installation on BRDM-2A AFVs mounting SA-9, Gaskin surface-to-air missiles (**3072.131**).

Gun Dish fire control radar with 23 mm AA guns on ZSU-23-4 SP AA vehicle (Novosti)

The Gun Dish radar operates in J-band with a frequency range of 14·6 to 15·6 GHz. The panoramic search radius extends up to 50 kilometres and the target tracking range up to eight kilometres. Antenna diameter is one metre.

2878.153
HEIGHTFINDING RADARS
Several basically similar nodding heightfinder radars have been identified and named by NATO. The generic code-name is Cake, and variants on this basic concept are known by such names as Patty Cake, Rock Cake, and Sponge Cake.

These radars, with their large, peel-shaped nodding antennas typically radiate beams with a width of some 3·5° in the vertical plane. Nodding frequency is typically about 30 to 40 cycles/minute and range is upwards of 200 km. One such radar, Sponge Cake, has a range in the region of 300 km, with a range accuracy of about 2·5 km at 200 km.

All appear to operate at frequencies somewhat above 2 GHz and to have peak powers around 3 MW.
STATUS
Operational.

2877.153
HEN SERIES EARLY WARNING RADARS
Several exceptionally large early warning radars observed by American reconnaissance have been given a series of names containing the word 'Hen'. First to be so named was Hen House (**2879.153**): others whose names have been reported are Hen Egg, Hen Nest and Hen Roost. Few details have been received concerning these radars: the notes below summarise the available information.
Hen Egg
Operating frequency around 2 GHz. Peak power

around 3 MW. Pulse width 5 to 15 microseconds and PRF up to 300 pps. These figures suggest the high mean power of about 5 kW per beam.
Hen House
Measures 300 × 20 m high. Thought to have an early warning and tracking role in the Soviet ABM system. Probable detection range 3200 nautical miles. (See **2879.153**, below.)
Hen Nest
Operating frequency about 800 MHz. Peak power about 3·5 MW.

Hen Roost
Operating frequency not definitely known but thought not to be less than 500 MHz. Peak power similarly believed to be about 5 MW. 2 × 2° beam.
STATUS
All these Hen radars – and probably several others – are believed to be operational although it is quite possible that some of them are only experimental designs (albeit used operationally) that may well not be repeated.

2879.153
HEN HOUSE ABM RADAR
This is the name given by the US authorities to a very large Soviet array that was first detected in the late 1950s and was at that time thought – if indeed it was a radar – to be part of a detection tracking and control network for satellites.

Subsequently, however, it was discovered that these enormous radars perform an important early warning and tracking function in the Soviet ABM weapons system, providing radar coverage comparable with that planned for the US Safeguard

(**2798.131**) system. No details of the radar are known other than that the antenna array is exceptionally large – perhaps as much as 300 m long and 20 m high. This billboard array is said to be inclined at about 45° from the vertical.

It is reported, however, that the performance of Hen House is comparable to that of the FPS-50 detection radars (**2511.153**) of the American BMEWS system (**2525.181**) – ie a detection range in the region of 3200 nautical miles (about 6000 km) and a track-while-scan capability. It is believed to operate on about 150 MHz and has been reported as having a variety of

PRFs from 25 to 100 pps, variable pulse widths, a complicated beam scan pattern with two beams scanning in azimuth, two scanning in elevation and one scanning in a circular pattern. Peak power is believed to exceed 10 MW.
STATUS
Hen House radars have been reported as being operationally deployed near Irkutsk, near the Barents Sea and in Latvia not far from the Baltic. See also general notes on the 'Hen' series (**2877.153**).

2880.153
KNIFE REST A EARLY WARNING RADAR
Knife Rest radars, as they are known to NATO, have the Soviet designation P-10. They were the forerunners of the Spoon Rest radars (**2889.153**). The array consists of four Yagi antennas in two crossed-brace supported pairs one above the other, each pair

mounted on each side of a single tubular support carried on the turning gear. The whole unit is fixed to the top of a tubular mast, braced by guy-ropes.

Knife Rest A has an operating frequency band of 70 to 73 MHz, radiates about 100 kW peak power, has a pulse width somewhere between 4 and 12 microseconds and horizontal and vertical

beamwidths in the region of 20 to 25°. Range capability is somewhere around 350 km.
STATUS
Operational – certainly in Viet-Nam – although the more modern Spoon Rest was deployed in the same theatres.

2881.153
KNIFE REST B AND C EARLY WARNING RADARS
General characteristics of these early warning radars are similar to those of Knife Rest A (**2880.153**) except

that the range capability is lower at only about 90 km. Knife Rest B is shown to operate in the frequency band 83 to 93 MHz. Another difference is that Knife Rest B is a vehicle-mounted system, with the antenna

array carried on a rectangular cross-braced sectional mast instead of the tubular pole used in Knife Rest A.
STATUS
Knife Rest B was certainly operational in Viet-Nam.

2937.153
LONG TRACK SURVEILLANCE RADAR

Long Track is the NATO code-name for a tactical surveillance radar used with surface-to-air weapon systems as an early warning/putter-on.

Long Track is commonly associated with the Ganef missile system (SA-4 – **2934.131**). It is also associated with the Gainful, SA-6 (**2930.131**) and Gecko SA-8 (**3209.131**) systems. In all cases the radar is mounted on a tracked carrier vehicle. It operates in E-band with a range and altitude in excess of 150 km and 30 000 metres respectively.

STATUS

Operational, certainly with SA-4 missile and possibly elsewhere. Used for SA-4, in conjunction with the Pat Hand fire control radar (**2936.153**).

Soviet 'Long Track' radar is used by client states as well as USSR, this one serves with Yugoslav forces

3294.153
LONG TALK RECOVERY RADAR

Long Talk is the air search and surveillance radar element of the Soviet standard ground controlled approach and aircraft recovery system used at Soviet air bases. The other elements of the system are the precision azimuth and elevation tracking radars known to NATO as Two Spot (**3295.153**) that form the precision approach radar portion. In some installations all three radars are mounted on one long four-wheeled trailer vehicle, which may also house the two- or three-man operating crew, but the Two Spot installation has been observed mounted on a platform above the driving cab of a standard military truck.

The Long Talk antenna has a moderately large elliptical paraboloid reflector, illuminated by radiating elements carried on a pyramid-shaped strut built up of four tubes. At the horizontal extremities of the reflector, one or two vertically positioned supplementary antennas which could be IFF units are located. Some installations have one such item on each end of the primary radar reflector, others have one only. A radar similar in general appearance to Long Talk and with one vertical supplementary attached to it is reported under the code-name One Eye.

Checking siting of Long Talk air search radar at a Soviet installation. Note associated heightfinder and approach radars

A number of Long Talk radars have been deployed at Soviet air bases in Afghanistan, associated with Two Spot precision approach radar (**3295.153**).

2884.153
LOW BLOW TRACKING AND MISSILE CONTROL RADAR

Low Blow is the NATO code-name given to a family of I-band radars used with land-based Goa (SA-3) missiles (**2938.131**). These radars are not the same as those used with shipborne Goa missiles which are known as Peel Group radars (**1323.253**). The name Low Blow reflects the ability of the radar to guide the missile towards low-flying targets through heavy clutter.

Like the Fan Song series (**2866.153**) the Low Blow radars use pairs of electromechanically scanning trough antennas mounted orthogonally, but to improve low-angle performance the troughs are mounted at 45° from the horizontal. It appears, too, that the troughs are not Lewis scanners but a form of organ-pipe scanner.

Carrier frequencies of the Low Blow family lie in the 9000 to 9400 MHz band, PRF between 1750 and 3500 pps with unambiguous range correspondingly lying between 40 and 85 km. Radiated beamwidth is

in the region of 12° in the fan and 1·5° in the direction of scan. Pulses are between 0·25 and 0·5 microseconds in duration and peak power output is around 250 kW.

STATUS

Operational with Goa missiles. Commonly associated with Flat Face (**2874.153**) or Squint Eye (**2891.153**) acquisition radars.

3296.153
NYSA C LONG-RANGE RADAR

Nysa C is a long-range, early warning air defence radar, according to East German sources, being used in Warsaw Pact states as a part of the overall air defence system to provide target information for interceptor aircraft and surface-to-air missiles.

The antenna array consists of two large parabolic cylinder reflectors mounted one above the other, both

facing the same way, carried on a large trailer cabin. The two reflectors are presumably to provide separate high and low cover radiation patterns, and each is fed by a horizontal row of 26 dipole elements. The operating frequency may be in the VHF or UHF band and high power levels are probably employed.

Nysa C long-range early warning radar operated by the Polish air defence forces

2936.153
PAT HAND FIRE CONTROL RADAR

Little information is available on this radar which is used in conjunction with the SA-4 (Ganef – **2934.131**) surface-to-air missile system. Pat Hand is, of course, a NATO code-name.

In normal operation the Pat Hand radar is put on by the Long Track surveillance radar (**2937.153**). It

acquires and tracks the target, provides command signals to guide the missile, and tracks the missile by a secondary radar process using a missile-borne beacon transponder. Pat Hand works in the H-band and is mounted on a tracked carrier vehicle.

STATUS

Operational with SA-4 missiles.

2974.153
SCORE BOARD IFF RADAR
Score board is the NATO code-name for an IFF-type ground interrogator used by Soviet forces. Presumably very early equipment, it has an antenna array consisting of two horizontal rows of two radiators per element, the two double rows being mounted one above the other to give a four-array of what appears (in some poorly reproduced pictures) to be a total of 32 dipole radiators. The whole is mounted on a rectangular rotatable framework.

STATUS
Apparently operational.

4328.153
PORK TROUGH (SNAR-2) COUNTER-BATTERY RADAR
Pork Trough (SNAR-2) is a counter-battery radar designed to locate enemy artillery in order to provide position information to its own guns for counteraction. It operates in J-band and uses a small parabolic cylinder antenna. The antenna and operations cabin are mounted on an AT-LM light tracked artillery tractor. No other information is currently available.

Soviet Pork Trough weapon locator radar is a highly mobile self-contained unit

3289.153
SIDE NET HEIGHTFINDER
Side Net is a large transportable nodding heightfinder radar, usually employed in conjunction with early warning surveillance radars such as Barlock, Back Net, and Tall King to provide GCI facilities. Operating frequency is in the range 2560 to 2710 MHz with an effective range of about 180 km at heights up to 32 000 m. The large (8·5 × 3·5 m) elliptical paraboloid antenna is mounted on a pair of lattice trunnions cantilevered from the sides of the cabin containing the associated electronics. The cabin can be rotated in azimuth.

Developed in the early 1960s, Side Net has been exported to countries outside the Soviet Union that have been supplied with Goa and Guideline surface-to-air missile systems.

3290.153
SQUARE PAIR GUIDANCE RADAR
Square Pair is the NATO code-name of a target-tracking and missile guidance radar associated with the SA-5 Gammon long-range air defence missile system (**2940.131**). It is understood to be normally co-located with Back Net (**2860.153**) heightfinder radars, and to be widely deployed within the Soviet Union. No technical or physical characteristics have been obtained to date, but Square Pair is thought to have been operational since 1964.

3291.153
SQUAT EYE ACQUISITION RADAR
Squat Eye is an air search and target acquisition radar, sometimes used instead of Flat Face (**2874.153**), and with Low Blow (**2884.153**) for Goa SA-3 (**2938.131**) air defence missile batteries. Such applications appear to be those where low altitude coverage is of particular importance.

The antenna is of relatively large dimensions and of elliptical paraboloid configuration. It is usually mounted on top of a slender rectangular lattice tower of sectional construction to increase the effective operating height. About 500 kW transmitter power is likely and the radar's role may be essentially that of a gap-filler. A maximum range of about 200 km has been estimated. Squat Eye is reported to employ the same electronics as the Flat Face radar (**2874.153**).

Squat Eye acquisition radar

2891.153
SQUINT EYE ACQUISITION RADAR
This air target acquisition radar is used in place of Flat Face (**2874.153**) and in conjunction with the Low Blow missile control radar (**2884.153**) and the Goa surface-to-air missile (**2938.131**) in circumstances in which good altitude cover is required.
STATUS
Operational.

2889.153
SPOON REST A EARLY WARNING RADAR
Known in the USSR as the P-12, the radar known to NATO as Spoon Rest A is an early warning radar that is used sometimes in conjunction with the Fan Song radars (**2866.153**) and the Guideline surface-to-air missile (**2942.131**).

This is a VHF radar working in the 147 to 161 MHz, A-band and radiating at about 350 kW peak from a Yagi array. Range capability is up to about 275 km and antenna beamwidths are around 2·5° in the vertical and something over 1° in the horizontal plane.

The radar is a heavy one and is mobile in two vehicles, one carrying the generator and the other the antenna array and the radar cabinets.

STATUS
Operational, certainly in Viet-Nam, where 34 sets are believed to have been used operationally, and in Egypt where one was captured by the Israeli forces.

Deployment of Spoon Rest A (P-12) early warning radar

2885.153
STRAIGHT FLUSH FIRE CONTROL RADAR
Straight Flush is the NATO name given to the radar and command guidance system used with the SA-6 Gainful (**2930.131**) surface-to-air missile system and possibly with the SA-11 (**4470.131**). It is believed that the system performs the following functions –
Limited search
Low-altitude detection/acquisition
Target tracking and illumination
Missile radar command guidance
Secondary radar missile tracking
Reports of the frequencies used for these functions have not been entirely consistent. It seems, however, that the first three functions are performed in G/H-band, the low altitude function being performed at about 5 GHz and the high-altitude functions at about 6 GHz. Target tracking (and probably illumination) is an I-band function at around 8 GHz and so probably is the command link, while the secondary radar response for missile tracking is probably at a rather lower frequency. Range is believed to be 60 to 90 km, with a maximum altitude coverage of 1000 metres.

The arrangement of the system can be seen in the accompanying picture. The upper, tracking, radar antenna assembly is assumed to be able to rotate independently of the lower antenna and it is further assumed that the two antennas and associated apparatus can be rotated relative to the carrying vehicle on a turntable which is presumably located at the top of the circular turret on which the whole assembly is mounted. Examination of the original photographs suggests that the lower antenna may be pivoted so as to execute a sector scan of some kind

and there is some indication that it can be tilted up or down, presumably to compensate for vehicle attitude. These observations are consistent with the assumed functions listed above; the combined radar superstructure is probably too massive for any kind of continuous circular search process and the arrangement probably provides for a slow circular search into an associated sector scan, the circular motion being halted when a target is located and resumed only if the target starts to move out of the sector.

The feed arrangements of both antennas are interesting. The lower antenna appears to have two feeds (which can be seen more clearly in the original picture) the upper one consisting of a single horn, which presumably produces a low angle pencil beam, and the lower feed comprising two or possibly three horns which may well produce a slightly shaped high-cover beam. There could be more sophistication to it than this but if so it is not obvious or obviously likely. The use of two separate feeds, however, is consistent

with the suggestion that the low- and high-altitude patterns are radiated at different frequencies.

There is, however, some additional waveguide in this feed which is not explained by what has been said above. It appears to be for a higher radiation frequency (than G/H-band) and could be for one of the other functions (command link or secondary radar – more probably the former). Finally it looks as though both parts of the main feed have a quarter-wave-plate circulariser in front of them. If this is a correct reading of the photographs it tends to date the technology of the equipment: a radar of this sort built in the West in the late 1960s would have used waveguide circularisers. It also looks as though the third (higher-frequency) feed bypasses the plate – which makes sense.

Turning now to the upper antenna, the function of the tripod-mounted device projecting in front of the dish is not clear. The remainder of the assembly is fairly evidently a conical scanning system using a rotating feed driven by a motor in the housing at the rear of the dish. This housing also almost certainly contains the microwave transmitter/receiver stages to avoid the need for multiple rotating waveguide joints.

Two of the struts supporting the projecting device appear to be simple metal rods or tubes secured to the face of the dish: the third (bottom) strut, however, is different, fairly certainly passing through a hole in the dish, and could be a waveguide. The way in which the upper struts meet the 'device' seems a little clumsy if they are no more than supports however, and while it may be that the 'device' is yet another antenna of some sort, we incline to the view that it is either another quarter-wave plate or a beam-spoiler for some operational purpose and that the bottom strut is merely a kind of push rod (hence the need to go through a hole – a waveguide would not) for moving the 'device' into and out of the way.

Apart from the microwave stages of the tracking radar it seems probable that the bulk of the radar electronics is housed in the bin-shaped structure beneath the tracking radar pedestal. The turret may be assumed to house the displays and control gear.
STATUS
Operational. Radars of this type were used with Gainful missiles in the 1973 Arab-Israeli War.

Straight Flush fire control radar. Note pairs of AFV-mounted SA-3 (Goa) missiles in the background
(Sava Haery/SIPA Press)

3293.153
TALL KING EARLY WARNING RADAR

Tall King is the name given by NATO to a large early warning radar P-14 for air defence of the Soviet Union and Warsaw Pact states. The origin of this name can be guessed quite easily from the impressive appearance of the structure which incorporates a reflector estimated to measure about 15 m high by 25 to 30 m wide, surmounted by a pylon of perhaps another five metres or so to which are attached the guy-ropes needed to steady this large array.

The method of illuminating the antenna is not clear but operation at metric wavelengths, probably between 150 MHz and 180 MHz, is almost certain.

The effective range is probably at least 500 km or 600 km. Tall King is reported to have been introduced in the 1950s to provide early warning against high-altitude intruding aircraft. Although obviously a fixed-site radar, sectional construction is employed so that, although a lengthy undertaking, Tall King is capable of transportation and re-siting without undue difficulties.

It is believed that Tall King radars have been deployed in Afghanistan to survey activities on the borders with China and Iran.

Side Net (**3289.153**) transportable heightfinder radars have been associated with Tall King installations.

Soviet Tall King early warning radar

Close-up of Tall King early warning radar showing technicians carrying out either final stages of erection or routine maintenance

2892.153
TOKEN EARLY WARNING AND GCI RADAR

This E/F-band early warning and ground control interception (GCI) radar is similar to the US CPS-6B radar (the first V-beam radar). Like Barlock (**2861.153**) it has twin truncated parabolic mesh reflectors. Five beams are produced and in the GCI role it has a range of about 150 km and can measure to within 0·5° in azimuth and 300 to 1500 m in elevation. In the early warning role it has a range of 250 to 300 km and a range accuracy of about 1 km.

3292.153
THIN SKIN HEIGHTFINDER RADAR

Thin Skin is the NATO name for an H-band nodding heightfinder radar, generally deployed as part of a ground control interception formation. Both trailer and track-mounted versions have been observed and its operational role is probably in support of tactical air defence units. In all cases it will be associated with air search and surveillance radars to provide them with complementary height information on targets detected. This radar is reported to be associated with Soviet Ganef, Gainful and Gecko surface-to-air missile regiments. Range is approximately 240 km.
STATUS
First reported in 1965, Thin Skin has since been supplied to nations outside the USSR, both within and beyond the Warsaw Pact states.

Thin Skin heightfinder radar

3295.153
TWO SPOT PAR

Two Spot is the NATO code-name of the radar group employed by Soviet air forces for use in precision approach radar (PAR) aircraft recovery and landing guidance. It is usually associated with the Long Talk air search radar (**3294.153**) which provides aircraft with ATC and homing directions to the airfield, and positioning for the PAR 'talk-down' landing itself. In some installations the Two Spot and Long Talk systems are both mounted on the same trailer vehicle, but Two Spot has also been observed mounted on a platform above the driving cab of a truck.

There are two antennas, both of parabolic section, one for elevation tracking and the other for azimuth. They are carried on a combined mounting, which permits limited rotation of the whole assembly to enable the system to be aligned to the bearing of the runway in use. The antennas and other items can be folded for transit. The operating frequency is in the I/J-band.

Two prominent discone VHF or UHF communications antennas for the ground/air link used for talk-down are carried on a tubular mast, and these may be the origin of the NATO code-name.

Several Two Spot PAR systems have been deployed at Soviet air bases in Afghanistan, associated with Long Talk radars (**3294.153**).

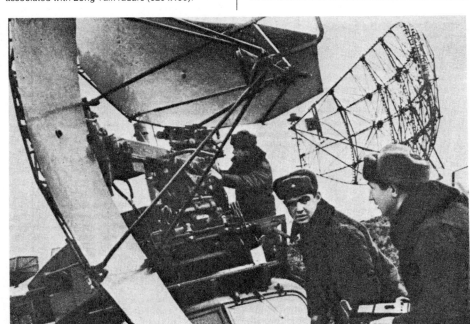

Vehicle-mounted version of Two Spot PAR

2893.153

WHIFF FIRE CONTROL RADAR

This is a van-mounted E/F-band gun fire control radar. Like Fire Can (**2871.153**) it is derived from the American SCR-584 equipment that was supplied to the USSR during the Second World War.

Construction and performance are generally similar to those of Fire Can. The antenna gain of Whiff, however, is somewhat greater.

2895.153

YO-YO MISSILE CONTROL RADAR

An early missile control radar, Yo-Yo is used to control the Guild (**2944.131**) surface-to-air missile (SA-1).

It is reported that this radar can track more than 30 targets at a time. Flapping beam techniques are used for target tracking and the radar uses six rotating antennas to cover a scanning area of some 70° both in azimuth and in elevation. Operating frequency is around 3 GHz and peak power around 2 MW.

4602.153

PSNR-1 BATTLEFIELD RADAR

The PSNR-1 is a portable battlefield radar used in reconnaissance companies of Soviet tank and motorised rifle regiments. It operates in the 9·6 GHz band with a maximum range against vehicles of 10 km and 5 km for personnel. The equipment is tripod mounted, can be carried by three men and takes approximately 15 minutes to prepare for operation. Divisional anti-tank battalions are believed each to have three systems for target acquisition purposes.

UNITED KINGDOM

1018.153

CYMBELINE MORTAR LOCATING RADAR

Cymbeline (British Army nomenclature: Radar FA No 15) is an extremely rugged self-contained radar (including power supply) with a detachable display unit. The radar is mounted on a four-legged structure supported on screw jacks fitted with hydraulic absorbers. It is produced in two versions: Mk 1, which is the towed version and Mk 2 which is the self-propelled variant.

The equipment is transported either on a two-wheeled trailer or on an FV432 armoured personnel carrier (**5007.102**). In the latter mode the screw jacks are replaced by an automatic hydraulic levelling system.

The antenna system consists of a Foster Scanner which illuminates a parabolic cylinder reflector and produces a pencil beam scanning in azimuth. The complete radar head can be rapidly rotated to cover any required sector; for example, 180° rotation in 15 seconds. When in transit the reflector folds down.

Below the antenna is an equipment box which houses the main electronics unit, the power unit, and the display unit during transit.

The main electronics unit contains the transmitter/receiver and the radar timing and computer modules.

The display and co-ordinate indicator units can be removed from the equipment box for remote operation for distances up to 15 metres. The display unit consists of a short-persistence 'B' scope on which the radar returns are displayed. It also carries all the controls necessary for the operation of the radar. The mortar co-ordinates are displayed on the co-ordinate indicator which can be used at distances up to two metres from the display.

OPERATION

The radar enables the operator to plot two points in the bomb trajectory, and to measure the slant range and bearing to each of these positions. The time taken for the bomb to travel between the two points is also measured and the computer uses this information together with the pre-set elevation angles to determine the firing position of the mortar. This entire process takes place in about half a minute.

Additional facilities have been provided to ensure the maximum accuracy of location and ease of operation over a wide range of operational conditions. For maximum range performance a switched single beam is used, and an additional beam position is available to alert the operator for making

Cymbeline mortar locating radar

the first interception. For short range work a double-beam mode of operation may be selected to obviate operator reaction time errors. This facility also improves the multiple target capability.

Provision has also been made for the internal fitting of an optional digital data storage module. This enables the radar returns to be stored to provide a long-persistence display so that operator concentration can be reduced while improving the marking accuracy. Data storage also improves multiple handling capability.

CHARACTERISTICS

Frequency: I/J-band

Peak power: 100 kW

Antenna: Foster Scanner with reflector

Sector scan: 720 mils

Bearing limits: 12 000 mils total rotation

Speed of rotation: 200 mils/s

Presentation: 'B' type display with displayed 0 – 20 000 m and selected 4000 m and 8000 m zones

Minimum range: 1000 m

Max displayed range: 20 000 m

Radar reliability: 200 h MTBF (excluding power source)

STATUS

Deliveries to the British Army commenced in mid-1973 and the first delivery of the self-propelled version was made in January 1975. Total deliveries to the British Army and 16 overseas countries had reached 300 sets by January 1984 and are continuing.

With the cancellation of the Cervantes mortar and rocket locating radar project (**5631.153** *Jane's Weapon Systems 1983/84*) it seems likely that Cymbeline will be updated.

CONTRACTOR

Thorn EMI Electronics Ltd, Hayes Division, Dawley Road, Hayes, Middlesex UB3 1HN, England.

3490.153

RADAR GS20 HOSTILE FIRE LOCATOR CLARIBEL

The Claribel hostile fire locator radar GS20 is designed to provide vehicles of any type or fixed locations with an automatic warning of sniper fire and an indication of the direction of the source of such fire. It is intended to eliminate the problems and disadvantages of locating snipers by traditional methods based on such techniques as the 'crack and thump' acoustic method.

The radar is a CW equipment based on an I/J-band Gunn diode microwave transmitter, and is all solid-state. No mechanical scanning is involved and a number of sensors are arranged around the vehicle (or fixed position) to provide all-round coverage. A circular display unit indicates the direction of hostile fire sources within 30° sectors, the appropriate sector(s) normally being illuminated before the sound of the shot reaches the vehicle. Usually one display is mounted in front of the commander of the vehicle with a second display located in a convenient position for viewing by the other members of the patrol. The GS20 incorporates a second shot capability, so that the location of two snipers firing

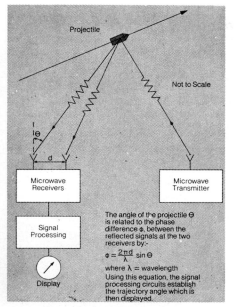

Radar GS20 in use with the British Army

from different sites can be identified simultaneously. Another useful feature in vehicle installations is an orientation facility which ensures that the information displayed is continuously updated to compensate for

Projectile

Not to Scale

θ

d

Microwave Receivers

Microwave Transmitter

Signal Processing

Display

The angle of the projectile Θ is related to the phase difference ϕ, between the reflected signals at the two receivers by:-

$$\phi = \frac{2\pi d}{\lambda} \sin \Theta$$

where λ = wavelength
Using this equation, the signal processing circuits establish the trajectory angle which is then displayed.

Operating principle of the GS20 hostile fire locating radar

any evasive action that the vehicle driver may take after sniper's shot(s).

A recent development now enables GS20 to transmit the displayed information, plus an alarm and vehicle identification code, to follow-up vehicles and/or command operation posts.

A typical vehicle GS20 installation would consist of four radar heads, commander's display unit, crew display unit, orientation unit, central processor and power unit.

OPERATION

The direction of source of any shot detected is derived from calculation of the trajectory of the projectile and extrapolation back to infinity. Computation is performed by a digital machine. The instantaneous angle of the projectile relative to the radar is obtained by the use of multiple receiver antennas and comparing the phase of the signals received simultaneously in each antenna. The doppler shift of the returns is measured and used to determine the projectile speed, so that signals from slow moving objects such as stones can be ignored.

DEVELOPMENT

The radar GS20 was developed for the British Army jointly by the UK MoD and MESL.

STATUS

In service with the British Army.

CONTRACTOR

Racal-MESL Radar Ltd, Preston Road, Linlithgow, West Lothian EH49 6EU, Scotland.

3715.153

FALCONER PRECISION APPROACH RADAR

In 1979 Cossor Electronics was awarded a contract to provide new precision approach radars (PARs) for MoD airfields in the UK and abroad. The new radar, designated the Cossor Falconer, will replace the SLA-3 generation of equipment currently in service, which will progressively reach the end of its useful life by 1985. It carries out the same essential functions of providing runway approach and landing guidance to aircraft equipped with two-way communication in either VHF or UHF.

The Falconer consists of radar-head equipment installed in a transportable cabin together with ATC display consoles and associated remote control equipment in the operations room. In addition, the radar head cabin is fitted with a display console for engineering use or, with the addition of suitable communications equipment, for use as a stand-alone or fall-back control position. The radar head installation is transportable by road or air and can be quickly and easily reassembled at another site.

The radar-head is a dual-channel system employing solid-state circuit elements, except for the main modulator thyratron and coaxial magnetron. Modular construction is used wherever possible; moreover, the widespread use of small easily replaceable modules ensures relatively inexpensive replacement costs. The use of digital circuitry also maintains drift and significantly reduces warm-up time.

The clear air range of the system on a 1 m² target has been calculated as 33 km; in operation this has reached 42 km so that the operational requirement of 28 km is comfortably exceeded. To enhance target detection in range and in adverse weather conditions, the radar incorporates selectable linear/circular polarisation, a digital MTI and a video correlator to reject uncorrelated clutter returns. A second-time-around rejection circuit and FTC and GTC circuits are also included. In addition, a five-stagger PRF is used to eliminate blind speeds between 20 and 600 knots.

Significant cost savings are being achieved by the use of customers' existing antennas; Cossor being able to refurbish and modify these to interface with the new radar. A modern simplified drive is fitted, together with a direct digital angle data take-off for improved stability.

Each system comprises an azimuth and elevation antenna installed in a robust module mounted directly onto the cabin exterior. Each antenna has a beamwidth of 0·5°, in its principal plane with a scanning rate of approximately one second. The

Falconer display in control tower at RAF Wyton

elevation antenna scans vertically from –1 to +6°, while the azimuth antenna scans from –10 to +10°. Resolution is such that two targets at the same range can be distinguished at 0·6° separation in elevation and 0·8° separation in azimuth. In range, two targets can be distinguished with a separation of 60 m.

Two display consoles are provided for fitting in the operations room. Each has a 16 inch (41 cm) azimuth/elevation display, an electronic map generator with associated controls and a removable desk unit. Each display shows both azimuth and elevation information from maximum range to touchdown. The displays also contain an operator control which can slew to tilt the antenna to optimise radar returns; the relative position of each beam being indicated on the radar display by an area of intensified or de-intensified range markers. Remote control facilities are provided to transfer data between the radar head and the operations room over distances in excess of 3000 m. The control facilities permit selection of either of the two radar channels virtually

Cossor Falconer installed at RAF Wyton

instantaneously and control the performance of the selected channel while providing continuous status information on both channels. The system also provides remote control of the antenna and cabin turntable positioning to any one of four preset positions with return status indication.

While employing cross-site coaxial cabling as the normal link between the radar head and the operations room, provision is made for housing extra units for the remote control system to be operated over a microwave link for any special site or operational reasons.

STATUS

Cossor is supplying a total of 43 static and 2 mobile Falconer systems for RAF and MoD airfields in the UK and elsewhere. The four-year delivery programme started in 1981, with full flight testing completed by mid-1982 and systems are in full operational service with the Royal Air Force.

CONTRACTOR

Cossor Electronics Ltd, The Pinnacles, Harlow, Essex CM19 5BB, England.

2413.153

FIRELIGHT TARGET ILLUMINATING RADAR

Firelight is a target illuminating radar for use with the Bloodhound and Thunderbird surface-to-air guided missile systems. The equipment is land mobile and air-transportable and the complete radar is housed in a single trailer.

Basically an I/J-band CW doppler auto-follow radar, the equipment also performs the function of illuminating the target and thereby providing the reflected radiation to activate the semi-active homing system of the Bloodhound and Thunderbird missiles. In addition it has a limited target search facility and is equipped for target identification. Firelight went into service in December 1962 and has been progressively updated to incorporate later techniques.

Further information is given under this entry number in previous editions of *Jane's Weapon Systems*.

CONTRACTOR

Ferranti Plc, Radar Systems Department, Ferry Road, Edinburgh EH5 2XS, Scotland.

2458.153

MARCONI HIGH-POWER STATIC SURVEILLANCE RADARS (LINEAR FED)

Included among the range of Marconi high-power static radars is a family of surveillance radars using single curvature reflectors illuminated by linear feeds. The antenna system may comprise single or back-to-back dual reflectors operating in E/F- or D-band. The later antennas feature a squintless feed (see **1168.153**). A range of transmitter/receivers can be operated singly or in diversity.

Members of this family believed still to be operational are:

Types S247, S266: EF- and D-band back-to-back antennas Type SA116, 45 ft (13·72 m) aperture. Transmitter/receivers SR1000 2·5 MW E/F-band; SR1030 2·25 MW D-band.

Type S647: E/F- and D-band back-to-back antennas Type SA116, 45 ft (13·72 m) aperture. Transmitter/receivers S2012 2·25 MW E/F-band; S2011 2 MW D-band.

Type S631: E/F- and D-band back-to-back antennas Type S1011 and S1014 with squintless feeds, 45 ft (13·72 m) aperture. Transmitter/receivers in diversity 2 × S2012 2·25 MW E/F-band; 2 × S2011 2 MW D-band.

Type S690: E/F- and D-band back-to-back antennas Type S1011 and S1014 with squintless feeds, 45 ft (13·72 m) aperture. Wide-band coherent transmitter/receiver S2018 3·3 MW E/F-band, S2019 3·3 MW D-band.

E/F-band antennas for all the above have a parabolic section while the D-band antennas are cosecanted.

Back-to-back D-band (front) and E/F-band antennas with squintless linear feeds on S631 surveillance radar

Other radars in the earlier series which were specified but are not known to be operational were:

S255: Single 45 ft (13·72 m) D-band cosecanted antenna.

S265: Back-to-back 45 ft (13·72 m) E/F-band parabolic and cosecanted antenna.

S320: Back-to-back 45 ft (13·72 m) D-band parabolic and cosecanted antennas.

CONTRACTOR

Marconi Radar Systems Ltd, Writtle Road, Chelmsford, Essex CM1 3BN, England.

2463.153

MARCONI MOBILE AND TRANSPORTABLE TACTICAL CONTROL RADARS

This entry relates to a pair of radars, Types S330 and S404, developed on a British defence contract for use with the Thunderbird guided weapon system (**2460.131**).

Little information concerning these radars is available for publication. The S330 is a surveillance radar with back-to-back antennas working in E/F-band and D-band; the S404 is a heightfinder working in G/H-band. In operation these radars are used for tactical control in association with a sophisticated display and data processing system such as Nomad (**2421.181**). Both radars are fully mobile and air-transportable. They are not, however, the only mobile and transportable Marconi radars and attention is drawn to **1168.153** which deals with the S600 series.

STATUS

In service.

CONTRACTOR

Marconi Radar Systems Ltd, Writtle Road, Chelmsford, Essex CM1 3BN, England.

2462.153

MARCONI LONG-RANGE HEIGHTFINDING RADAR TYPE 669

This is a long-range E/F-band heightfinder radar capable of providing at least 17 heights per minute with an overall accuracy of ±1500 ft (457 m) at 150 nautical miles (280 km). Discrimination at this range is better than 900 ft (247 m). Modes of operation are single shot, automatic, or manual searchlight, burn-through, volumetric, and sector scan. The single curvature linear fed antenna has very low sidelobes and is hydraulically driven for minimum response times. Either manual or automatic height extraction is available.

The radar is a derivation from the S269 radar, 14 of which are used in the NADGE chain stretching 3000 miles (4828 km) from Norway to Turkey, itself a derivation from the S244.

In June 1977, the award of a contract worth over £1 million by Selenia for a Type S669 radar was announced. The Italian company will install the heightfinder at a new automated air defence site in Italy, probably the one in Sicily (see the Argos-10 entry in the Italian section, **1959.153**), to form part of the programme for the expansion of the NATO network's southern flank.

The total number of Marconi heightfinders supplied to NATO has now reached 40.

Heightfinding radar Type 669

CHARACTERISTICS
Antenna
Gain: 40·5 dB
Vertical beamwidth: 0·6°
Sidelobes: –20 dB
Nod duration: 2 s
Slew rate: 90° in 2·5 s

Transmitter
Peak power: 2·25 MW
Pulse length: 2·5/5 μs
PRF: 300/600
Receiver
Noise figure: 3·8 dB

STATUS
No longer in production.
CONTRACTOR
Marconi Radar Systems Ltd, Writtle Road, Chelmsford, Essex CM1 3BN, England.

3491.153
MARTELLO 3-D SURVEILLANCE RADAR

The Marconi Martello three-dimensional surveillance radar is a mobile D-band long-range equipment designed to provide complete air defence coverage throughout the 1980s and 1990s.

The system consists of the antenna, a radar container, a cooling/air conditioning unit and a power generation unit which are all based on the ISO freight container concept so that they can be transported by standard prime movers or carried in transport aircraft such as the C-130. The radar can be ready for action within six hours of arrival at its operational site. The antenna consists of 60 identical horizontal linear array elements, vertically stacked, each with its own receiver. The antenna rotates at six revolutions per minute and each array receives returns which are assembled into a passive IF beam-forming network. This forms eight beam patterns to achieve the required vertical cover and heightfinding accuracy. Cover is provided from the radar horizon up to 30°, with height measurement up to 24° elevation. The array is tilted back at an angle of about 14°, the bottom beam being flat along the ground and all beams being fixed in elevation. The array can be operated in winds of up to 70 knots, and is designed to withstand gusts up to 120 knots.

Range and bearing information is obtained by conventional scanning with elevation data being derived by monopulse processing of the signals in adjacent beams. Since this processing is carried out on a common radiated frequency, accurate height measurements are achieved even when the transmitter is in the frequency agile mode. The three-dimensional data is then processed to deal with clutter, chaff and ECM conditions and correlated with extracted SSR/IFF information before onward transmission to either a local or remote operations centre.

Marconi Martello mobile 3-D surveillance radar

Pulse compression and doppler filtering are also employed to give moving target detection in conditions of clutter and heavy chaff accompanied by significant wind shear.
STATUS
In production. Seven Martello radars have been ordered. Of these, five were ordered for the Royal Air Force, three in March 1982 and a further two in September 1982. These last two plus two more

ordered at the same time by the UK MoD for Denmark were purchased using NATO infrastructure funds at a cost of over £20 million.

A new version of the Martello radar is known to be in the late development stage. No details of this version are available.
CONTRACTOR
Marconi Radar Systems Ltd, Writtle Road, Chelmsford, Essex CM1 3BN, England.

2464.153
MARCONI 800 SERIES RADARS (LAND-BASED)

The Marconi 800 series of surveillance and tracking radars was introduced in 1972. The early members of the series (type numbers in the range 801-839) are all naval radars and are described in the next section of the book. Type numbers in the ranges 840-849 and 850 onwards have been allocated to coastal defence radars and land-based weapon radars respectively.

ST860 surveillance radar on transportable cabin

Several radars of these types have so far been announced and are briefly described below.

Type S841 is a coastal defence surveillance radar which provides and continuously updates accurate range and bearing co-ordinates on surface targets for weapon fire control systems.

The radar operates at a fixed frequency, selected in the band 9·3 to 9·5 GHz; it incorporates track-while-scan, digital range, and bearing data extraction and has an autonomous fixed coil display. Several sizes of antenna are employed.

The ST850/M target tracking radar and television system has been designed, in co-operation with Short Brothers and Harland, as an integral part of the Tigercat weapon system (**2465.131**) to improve its performance in conditions of poor visibility by giving a dark fire capability.

The ST850/M is contained in a mobile air

ST850 transportable tracking radar

conditioned cabin with the radar director on its roof. The system is simple to use, is flexible in operation, and can be speedily deployed. This radar is more fully described in **2466.153**. The ST850/G target tracking radar is a derivative of the ST850 which incorporates a Sperry general-purpose digital computer for the prediction of aim-off to give blind fire gun control. Without the TV system, this unit will control small calibre rapid fire AA guns and the complete equipment gives maximum flexibility to a combined missile/gun point defence system.

The ST855/856 are range instrumentation radars incorporating full facilities for data recording and analysis. The ST857/858 is similar equipment designed to interface with customers' own instrumentation. A major feature of the ST858 is its ability, when locked on to an aircraft target, to instantaneously change over to track a small object leaving the aircraft. Tracking of projectiles with calibres down to 20 mm is possible.

The S860 is a mobile surveillance radar designed to support the ST850 radars through the provision of target positional data. The S860 is an I/J-band, 200 kW (peak), surveillance radar with a typical range of 60 km against high level targets. Digital MTI is incorporated and there is provision for IFF. The radar is mounted on top of a manned cabin with a dual operator position feeding target co-ordinate data to up to three fire control units. Two PPI displays are fitted, each capable of rate-aided tracking on four targets. Allocation of target data to the selected fire control unit is fully automatic on operation of the appropriate key. Co-ordinate data are parallax corrected to ensure speedy target acquisition and to reduce reaction time.
STATUS
Land-based 800 series radars are in production for the UK MoD and other customers. S860 and ST850

units have been supplied overseas as part of the Short Brothers Radar Enhanced Tigercat 2 air defence missile system. The Royal Aircraft Establishment employs an ST858 as a precision tracker for range instrumentation.

2479.153
MARCONI S613 HEIGHTFINDING RADAR

This is a mobile/transportable heightfinder radar working in the G/H-band. It integrates with any of the surveillance radars in the S600 to S605 range, utilising the same form of construction. The digitally controlled antenna is capable of providing 22 heights a minute and the height is automatically extracted, a unique facility in mobile systems. Modes of operation are normal, sector scan, and volumetric scan.

CHARACTERISTICS

Antenna
Gain: 39·5 dB
Vertical beamwidth: 0·9°
Sidelobes: −25 dB
Nod duration: 2 s
Slew rate: 180° in 2 s
Transmitter
Peak power: 1 MW
Pulse length: 2/5 µs
Receiver
Noise figure: 4·5 dB

STATUS

This radar has been supplied to the UK MoD, NATO, and a number of other nations.

CONTRACTOR

Marconi Radar Systems Ltd, Writtle Road, Chelmsford, Essex CM1 3BN, England.

Marconi S613 heightfinder radar

5615.153
MARCONI S500 SERIES STATIC AND TACTICAL AIRFIELD SURVEILLANCE RADARS

The S500 series of radars is designed primarily for static and tactical airfield surveillance. It is also suitable for low cover and gap filling with its good sub-clutter visibility in fixed and moving clutter and its excellent ECCM capability. The series comprises six systems: S511, S512, S513, S525, S531 and S532, operating in the 10 cm or 23 cm frequency band.

In the E/F band there are four systems: the S511 and S512 static equipments and the S531 and S532 tactical systems. All use the same antenna, signal processing and display systems and differ only in their transmitter/receivers.

The high performance antenna consists of a double curvature cosecant squared carbon fibre reflector and a double horn system to provide dual beam operation. Variable polarisation between linear (vertical) and circular is provided on the lower beam and fixed circular polarisation on the upper beam. In the static versions the antenna is mounted on a modular tower, with a choice of height.

The S511 and S531 use a transmitter/receiver Type S2022 which incorporates a tunable magnetron driven by a highly stable, modular, solid-state modulator with a fail-soft capability, and a high stability Coho-Stalo receiver. Frequency diversity using two transmitter/receivers is available.

The S512 and S532 use a rugged, wide-bandwidth, cathode modulated TWT transmitter/receiver S2062.

S511 airfield surveillance radar

This coherent transmitter/receiver uses pulse compression techniques and provides full frequency flexibility (block by block and pulse by pulse frequency agility).

A signal processor, S7113, with adaptive beamswitching, eliminates moving and fixed clutter and reduces tangential fading. Temporal thresholds (clutter maps) ensure constant false alarm rates under all conditions. A plot extractor, S7204, provides the necessary interface between the signal processing and the data handling system. The Marconi Astrid display system, which permits remote operation up to two miles (3·2 km), is available for use with these radars.

The tactical radars S531 and S532 are transportable by road, rail and C-130 type aircraft with a time-in-service on a new site of three and a half hours using a team of four people.

In the D-band there are two static radar systems: S513 and S525. The S513 is for military and civil approach/departure and terminal area control. It employs a rugged dual beam antenna based on the S1020 and a stable transmitter/receiver S2027, with the S7113 signal processor. Good sub-clutter visibility with clutter mapping and adaptive beam switching is provided on all types of clutter.

Longer range performance is available with the S525 which uses the S2019 wideband, high power transmitter/receiver. An adaptive signal processor, S7128, with pulse compression and full frequency flexibility gives good ECCM performance as well as good sub-clutter visibility.

Both systems use the Plot Extractor S7204 to give the necessary output for data handling, either locally or at a remote control centre.

CONTRACTOR

Marconi Radar Systems Limited, Writtle Road, Chelmsford, Essex CM1 3BN, England.

4630.153
MARCONI S700 SERIES MOBILE RADAR SYSTEMS

The S700 series of radars is intended primarily for mobile military use. The series comprises five systems: S704, S705, S706, S711 and S712.

The S704 and S705 are long range radars in D and E/F band respectively, having 25 foot (7·6 metre) single curvature antennas with linear squintless feeds giving cosecant squared cover. The intrinsic sidelobe performance of these antennas is ideal for military operation. Both systems use high power (3·3 MW) wideband transmitter/receivers with pulse compression techniques and full frequency flexibility which, with the S7128 adaptive signal processor and S7204 plot extractor, give good clutter and ECCM performance. The S704 operates with antenna S1061 and transmitter/receiver S2109, and the S705 with antenna S1062 and transmitter/receiver S2018.

The S706 is a medium range equipment operating in E/F band using the same antenna, S1062, as the S705. The transmitter/receiver uses the rugged wide-bandwidth cathode modulated TWT system S2062. Pulse compression and full frequency flexibility is an essential part of the design and with a signal processor and plot extractor provides high quality performance in clutter and ECCM.

The S711 is a short-to-medium range radar for low-level and gap-filling roles. It operates in E/F band and uses a high performance double curvature, cosecant squared, carbon fibre reflector, horn-fed antenna, S1074. This antenna can be hydraulically elevated up to 65 feet (20 metres) for visibility over local obstructions. The S2062 transmitter/receiver, S7113 signal processor and S7204 plot extractor provide the necessary high performance.

The S712 is a short-to-medium range radar for low level defence. It operates in the E/F band and has a linear antenna with a parabolic cover profile mounted on the equipment container. The same transmitter/receiver, signal processor and plot extractor are used as with the S711.

CONTRACTOR

Marconi Radar Systems Limited, Writtle Road, Chelmsford, Essex CM1 3BN, England.

3280.153
PLESSEY TYPE 431 and TYPE 431M COASTAL DEFENCE RADARS

The Plessey Type 431 coastal defence radar has been developed specifically for detection of intruders in a coastal area. The antenna is fed by a transmitter/receiver providing a pencil beam for the detection of helicopters and small surface craft out to a maximum range of 32 nautical miles. The use of I-band provides excellent discrimination and performance from a small antenna system which can be tilted as required from the operator position for optimum radar coverage.

The basic 431 coastal defence radar consists of only two equipment groups, the antenna assembly and the display group, which leads to extremely simple and rapid installation. The display group can be located remotely from the antenna installation by up to 1000 m. The basic system can be extended to provide specific command and control facilities designed for particular operational needs. The displays supplied in the basic system employ an electronic cursor to display in digital form a readout of target position.

The antenna reflector is approximately four metres wide, curved in two planes and fed by two microwave horns. The 50 kW transmitter/receiver with its power unit is located in the housing at the back of the antenna. There is a choice of data rates and the antenna is tiltable for optimum radar coverage. Anti-jamming facilities are provided to the same standards as those in current use on board ship. The control and display equipment comprises two Plessey 16-A2 autonomous 504 mm free-standing display units and a control unit. The operator's facilities available at the displays include range rings, electronic cursor and off-centring as well as standard brilliance and gain controls. Control facilities are remoted from the radar to the display position, which enable the operator to select antenna rotation rate, anti-jamming mode, PRF etc.

Both static and mobile versions can be provided with a compact display providing both PPI and B-scope facilities. This enables a single operator to carry out both search and weapon direction functions. The CDR 431M is the mobile version of CDR 431 and comprises two groups, namely display cabin and a single trailer for the antenna assembly, diesel generator and cables. Thus a single prime-mover with trailer provides a completely self-contained coastal defence package. See also the Guardsman defence radar.

STATUS
In service.
CONTRACTOR
Plessey Radar Ltd, Oakcroft Road, Chessington, Surrey KT9 1QZ, England.

Plessey CDR 431 coastal defence radar mobile unit

2484.153
PLESSEY AR-3D THREE-DIMENSIONAL AIR DEFENCE RADAR

AR-3D is an E/F-band air defence surveillance radar giving three-dimensional information on targets by mechanically rotating the radar beam in azimuth and electronically scanning in elevation. All elements of the system are trailer-mounted for transport by land, sea or air.

The AR-3D antenna, which combines mechanical scanning in azimuth with electronic scanning in elevation, consists of a compact circular polarised linear array positioned at the focus of a simple parabolic cylinder reflector. The reflector has a height of 4·9 m and a width of 7·1 m. The azimuth sidelobes of the antenna are –36 dB in the 5 to 15° sector and –48 dB in the 15 to 90° sector. An alternative 5·5 m planar array antenna is also available which combines lower sidelobes and accurate beam formation for improved ECCM performance. This latest antenna folds in half for transportation by C-130 aircraft. The electrical characteristics of both antennas are identical to allow retrofit of the new antenna, if required. The transmitter consists of a coherent two-stage E/F-band transmitter. Each of the two stages uses a linear beam pulse microwave tube. Both tubes are designed for excellent phase, noise, and amplitude performance commensurate with the pulse compression and MTI requirements. The transmitter has a peak pulse of 1·11 MW (mean power 10 kW) and a bandwidth of 200 MHz.

The signals received from the antenna are amplified in a wideband (200 MHz) amplifier. After amplification the signals are separated into channels representing elevation bands of approximately 2° (bandwidth 20 MHz per channel). The signals are then time-compressed to 0·1 microsecond and their frequencies measured to enable the fine elevation within each beam to be obtained.

The function of the plot extractor is to detect targets which meet prescribed criteria. This target information is then fed to tracking and display equipment in the form of digital words containing three-dimensional positional information as polar co-ordinates. The on-line processor stores the positional data, carries out azimuth and height calculation, and takes into account various corrections. Plot and track data are then transmitted to the local displays and modems as required.

The varying demands of air defence are met by supplying AR-3D in different operational configurations, as a radar reporting post, control and reporting post, or command and control post. The different requirements are met by variants of the processing and control cabin, with hardware and software organised in modular packages appropriate to the specific function.

As a reporting post the AR-3D provides two

Plessey AR-3D radar being deployed with reflector

operational consoles with automatic plot extraction and reporting to a remote centre of up to 40 combined primary radar and IFF/SSR plots. As a control and reporting post with five operational consoles, automatic initiation and tracking of up to 40 aircraft is provided with automatic reporting of data to a remote operations centre, while up to eight simultaneous computer-aided interceptions can be controlled. The command and control post additionally varies in providing for autonomous computer-aided control of own aircraft and missiles.

CHARACTERISTICS
Coverage: Adjustable. Typically 180 nm on 2 m² target
Radiation: Frequency selective within E/F-band. The operating bandwith is 200 MHz. Independent frequency selective filters for each of 13 elevation channels, each having a bandwidth of approximately 20 MHz. The data below refer to linear polarisation
Antenna 'A'
Type: Linear array and parabolic cylinder
Polarisation: Circular
Beamwidth (azimuth): 1°
Beamwidth (elevation) 2°
Peak sidelobe (azimuth): 25 dB
Peak sidelobe (elevation): 23 dB
Scanning angle: 30°
Gain: 41·3 dB
Adjustment: +4, –2°
Rotation rate: 6 rpm
Antenna 'B'
Type: Planar array, horizontal slotted waveguide radiator and serpentine slow wave feed
Polarisation: Linear

AR-3D planar array antenna

Beamwidth (azimuth): 1·5°
Beamwidth (elevation): 1·5°
Peak sidelobe (azimuth): 35 dB typical
Peak sidelobe (elevation): 25 dB
Scanning angle: 20°
Rotation rate: 6 rpm
Transmitter
Peak pulse power: 1·11 MW
Mean power: 10 kW
PRF: 250 pps
Frequency band: E/F-band
Bandwidth (to 1 dB): 200 MHz
Pulse length: 36 μs
PA tube: High power klystron grid modulated
Transmit modes: Continuous or fast on/off
Receiver
Bandwidth: 20 MHz/channel
Compression ratio: 130:1 (lower channels)
Accuracy
Elevation: 0·15°
Range: 15 m
Range resolution: 40 m
STATUS
In production and in service with the UK MoD and a number of overseas countries. Two AR-3D systems have been deployed in the Falkland Islands.
CONTRACTOR
Plessey Radar Ltd, Oakcroft Road, Chessington, Surrey KT9 1QZ, England.

1141.153
PLESSEY AR-15M MOBILE SURVEILLANCE RADAR

The AR-15-M is a mobile radar system for air defence and ATC medium range surveillance and approach roles. In its air defence role it optimises coverage against low flying targets and operates as a manual reporting post

The system, providing both primary and secondary radar/IFF facilities, is a mobile unit with a cross country capability which includes the possibility of deployment in desert conditions: the equipment is installed in containers which can be loaded into C-130 transport aircraft when detached from the trailers. The configuration of equipment is as follows:

Antenna Trailer
A special-purpose trailer carries the primary radar reflector antenna, turning gear and IFF/SSR antenna. Facilities are provided to hoist the antenna on to the cabin.

Radar Cabin
The cabin, which is trailer mounted for transportation, contains a dual magnetron transmitter/receiver, the IFF/SSR interrogator/receiver, signal processing and displays. The equipment is of solid-state design and incorporates an ECCM receiver and an advanced digital target indicator. The cabin also contains two operational displays and ground/air communications equipments. It is air conditioned and provides storage for carried spares, test equipment and ancillaries. Jacking gear is fitted to facilitate loading and unloading from the trailer as well as for levelling for operation.

Diesel Generators
Two mobile diesel generators are used for supplying power to the system. One of these is for stand-by purposes. In addition, further cabins can be provided to house the crew and to provide mess facilities if required. The two diesel generators have adequate

AR-15M mobile surveillance radar

power to provide the local domestic supply for the crew.
STATUS
In production.
CONTRACTOR
Plessey Radar Ltd, Oakcroft Road, Chessington, Surrey KT9 1QZ, England.

2456.153
PLESSEY AR-15/2C SURVEILLANCE RADAR

The AR-15/2C is a medium-range primary air surveillance radar for use in both military and civil ATC. The main units consist of the antenna, two solid-state transmitter/receivers (working in frequency diversity), control rack, digital MTI equipment and radar control unit. A standard variant of the system uses only one transmitter/receiver.

The system uses a two-beam antenna and sophisticated digital signal processing equipment. The second or auxiliary beam is used at short range to reduce returns from ground clutter, sea clutter and 'angels' when compared with signals from the main beam. The signals from both beams are presented on a standard PPI display. The antenna system includes a variable linear to circular polarisation facility which is adjustable from the radar control panel.

In operation, the RF power is transmitted from the main horn and the return signals are received both by the main horn and the auxiliary horn. The auxiliary horn and antenna reflector together form a small beam tilted up compared with the main beam. Clutter normally occurs at low angles of elevation and hence should not be detected by the auxiliary horn. The changeover from main to auxiliary beam is carried out at a range chosen to suit the terrain and the operational requirements. Typically a changeover range of up to 15 nautical miles (28 km) is suitable for most applications.

CHARACTERISTICS
Frequency: Dual operation 2700 – 2900 and 3000 – 3040 MHz (spot frequency in both bands); single transmitter 2700 – 2900 or 2900 – 3100 MHz (spot frequency in either band)
Polarisation (main beam): Variable from linear through elliptical to circular
Polarisation (auxiliary beam): Fixed, circular
Transmitter
Peak power: 600 kW at 1 μs; 700 kW at 0·6 μs
PRF: 700/1000 pps with 7-period stagger
Receiver
Noise factor: Not worse than 3 dB
Intermediate frequency: 30 MHz
Overall bandwidth: 1·2 MHz
Antenna
Gain: 33 dB relative to isotropic radiator (nominal)
Horizontal aperture: 4·6 m
Horizontal beamwidth: 1·5° to half power points
Vertical aperture: 2·2 m
Horizontal sidelobes: 27 dB ±5°
Rotation speed: 15 rpm
STATUS
The AR-15/2C is a development of the AR-15/2B which is operational in the United Kingdom and a number of other countries. The AR-15/2C entered production in 1981.
CONTRACTOR
Plessey Radar Ltd, Oakcroft Road, Chessington, Surrey KT9 1QZ, England.

AR-15/2C surveillance radar installed at Seeb International Airport, Oman

5608.153
WATCHMAN AIR SURVEILLANCE RADAR

Watchman is the latest addition to Plessey's S-band medium-range surveillance radar series. It is designed to offer high performance in terminal area and approach surveillance, fighter recovery, GCA surveillance, approach control, radar sequencing control, outbound control and helicopter surveillance.

New technology in microwave generation and signal processing and the use of a TWT in the transmitter has permitted advanced capabilities and considerable flexibility in the frequency and pattern of transmitted pulses. A dual pulse train is used consisting of a very short pulse (0·4 μs) giving high discrimination at short ranges, and a much longer pulse (20 μs) for detecting aircraft which have small echoing areas at long ranges. The long pulse is compressed in the receiver using a surface acoustic wave equaliser. Signal separation is achieved by using different radio frequencies for the long and short pulses. Target detection is further enhanced by interchanging these frequencies every nine pulse repetition intervals.

Watchman thus provides frequency diversity operation with a single transmitter, and the overall stability of the latter contributes significantly to the anti-clutter performance of the system. High receiver sensitivity is provided by low noise field effect transistor (FET) radio frequency amplifiers, one for each beam. A beam switching system ensures that only the selected beam output is passed to the main receiver as required.

In the signal processor, the adaptive moving target

detector provides maximum target detection against clutter. Radar returns are processed in parallel through normal radar, ground clutter filter and moving clutter filter channels each of which uses both in-phase and quadrature processing. Target detections from all three processing channels are automatically integrated and passed on for transmission to the display system. This ensures that the operator views a clean video picture, and also provides considerable 'fail-soft' capability. Compatibility with staggered PRF operation ensures good velocity response free from blind speeds and immunity to second-time-around clutter returns.

Transmission of the control and signal data between the radar head and display sites is via a two-core fibre-optic cable link. In addition to the advantages of lightweight and low cost, the complete electrical isolation of the optical link provides absolute immunity to any form of electro-magnetic interference.

An autonomous display is also available to complement the flexibility of Watchman. Designed for high reliability and ease of both operation and installation, each display console incorporates all the requisite hardware and software facilities associated with the accurate display of primary radar signals. A selection of high resolution digital maps may be generated from internally stored data. Supporting ATC data and, where required, SSR plot data and labels, can be selectively displayed with or without primary radar video.

The Watchman system can be used in both civil and military applications. For the military requirement, the equipment is likely to have to operate in a jamming

environment in addition to providing a basic control service. Desirable ECCM characteristics such as low antenna sidelobe level, PRF stagger, pulse compression and moving clutter filter, have already been included as standard items in the system but improved ECCM facilities may be required. To further improve the system's resistance to ECM, extensive frequency agility modes can be made available by simple replacement of the driver source by a variant with selected multi-frequency capability.

A number of additional options are also available, these include primary plot extraction, IFF and secondary surveillance radar.

The Watchman display system is a self-contained, intelligent equipment which allows it to be configured for military and civil uses and for static and tactical air defence.

CHARACTERISTICS
Frequency: 2750 – 3050 MHz
Antenna: Two-beam, horn fed, double curvature reflector
Beamwidth (azimuth): 1·45°
Rotation rate: 15 rpm
Transmitter
Type: Solid-state driver with TWT output power amplifier
Mean power: 1·1 kW
Pulse pattern: Short pulse (0·4 μs) followed by long pulse (20 μs)
Receiver
Type: Low noise FET RF amplifier, double superheterodyne IF with pulse compression
Noise factor: 2 dB
Pulse compression ratio: 50:1 (long pulse only)

Signal processor
Type: Adaptive moving target detector
MTI improvement factor: 46 dB
STATUS
In production. On 1 June 1983, Plessey announced an order from the UK MoD for a number of Watchman systems to be installed at MoD airfields. The initial order is for at least 30 systems with a probable total of 39 for the UK. The value of this order is believed to be about £25 million. In August 1983 three systems were ordered by the Finnish Air Force for delivery commencing in 1985. The value of this order, which

includes spares, training, documentation, etc, is in excess of £4 million. An option on four further systems was also placed. Civil airfield orders have also been placed and an order has been received from an unnamed African country for joint military/civil applications. By February 1984 £29 million worth of Watchman radars had been ordered. More than 200 display consoles have been ordered by the UK MoD and a number of other countries.
CONTRACTOR
Plessey Radar Ltd, Oakcroft Road, Chessington, Surrey KT9 1QZ, England.

Watchman air surveillance radar

4631.153
TRANSPORTABLE WATCHMAN DEFENCE RADAR

Transportable Watchman is a mobile S-band radar designed to meet a wide range of tactical requirements. Roles include gap-filling, forward area alert, coastal surveillance, missile and gun acquisition, surveillance for a ground approach control system and automatic plot reporting. The basic configuration allows operation as a manual reporting post and can be extended to operate as an automatic post with fall-back for limited control. The system can function autonomously, with its own communications and power supplies, or it can be integrated as a gap filler into a larger air defence system.

Two equipment cabin configurations are available. The first is a single equipment cabin and antenna; both units are transportable by road trailers, heavy lift helicopters or C-130 type aircraft and can be deployed in less than one hour. The antenna is

mounted on the cabin during operation. The cabin contains an IFF interrogator/receiver and interference blanker, two operational displays and VHF/UHF communication equipment.

The second configuration consists of two smaller equipment cabins and an antenna mounted on a pallet. All three units are mounted on mobilisers for transport, providing cross-country mobility. The system can be transported by medium lift helicopters or C-130 type aircraft for tactical deployment. During operation the antenna is mounted on the cabin holding the primary radar, IFF interrogator/receiver and monitor display, while the other cabin contains two (optionally three) autonomous displays and VHF/UHF communications equipment. The radar cabin and operational display cabin can be separated by up to 4 km, with transmission of control and signal data between them via a two-core fibre-optic cable link.

Two antenna configurations are available, a horn-fed low sidelobe reflector incorporating an integral

IFF feed or a high gain horn-fed reflector which provides low sidelobes, with additional high angle enhancement.

The transmitter is the same system as used in the Watchman series (**5608.153**) and uses a solid-state driven, high power TWT amplifier providing wide bandwidth for frequency agile operation.

Options include primary and secondary plot extraction, plot combination, two autonomous displays based on the latest microprocessor technology and data communications to allow operation as an autonomous reporting post.
CHARACTERISTICS
Frequency: S-band

Antenna	A	B
Beamwidth	1·5° azimuth	1·5° azimuth
Gain	30 dB	33·8 dB
Polarisation	Variable, linear/ circular	Circular
Rotation speed	10/20 rpm	12/15 rpm

Transmitter: Solid-state, air-cooled
Peak power: 60 kW
Mean power: 1·1 kW
Pulse pattern: Fixed frequency, pulse-to-pulse agile, burst-to-burst agile
Receiver: Low noise FET amplifier, double superheterodyne IF with pulse compression
Noise factor: 2 dB
Pulse width: 0·4 μs (compressed)
Signal processor: Adaptive moving target detector I & Q processing
STATUS
In production for the UK MoD and other countries
CONTRACTOR
Plessey Radar Ltd, Oakcroft Road, Chessington, Surrey KT9 1QZ, England

Transportable Watchman radar

4607.153
GUARDSMAN DEFENCE RADAR

Guardsman is a two-dimensional mobile radar system designed to meet the requirements of low level surveillance and anti-aircraft artillery alerting. It will also act as a coastal surveillance radar where reliable detection has to be achieved in the presence of heavy sea clutter.

The system is contained within a single cabin for vehicle mounting which gives cross-country mobility for rapid tactical deployment. An antenna mast allows the antenna to be elevated rapidly to a height of 9·5 metres. The system contains its own prime power generators and is transportable in aircraft of the C-130 type. With a trained crew of two, the system has an in-action time of less than 15 minutes. System 'march-order' action time is less than 5 minutes.

Guardsman features a low sidelobe antenna, a high power wide-bandwidth transmitter and advanced

digital signal processing. These provide optimum detection in all forms of ECM and severe clutter likely to be encountered in the forward battle area or in coastal surveillance. At the same time they yield a low constant false alarm rate for maintenance of target tracks.

An associated on-mounted IFF antenna and interrogator/receiver provides secondary plots which can be extracted and combined with primary plots. The combined plots can be transmitted to a track extractor for generation of sensor tracks to an operations centre.

The Guardsman radar can be configured to a variety of uses, for example an autonomous plot/track reporting post or an alerting radar for gun or missile batteries via a command post. It can also be integrated into a long range surveillance air defence system. Alternative communication sub-systems are available for each tactical role.

Guardsman is the C-band variant of the Watchman radar system (**5608.153**) and the two systems are similar in many respects.
CHARACTERISTICS
Frequency: C-band
Antenna: Low sidelobe, line fed parabolic cylindrical reflector with integrated IFF
Azimuth beamwidth: 1·5°
Polarisation: Linear (circular/linear selectable optional)
Rotation rate: 1, 30 or 60 rpm (depending on instrumented range)
Transmitter: Solid-state driven TWT amplifier, fixed frequency, multi-mode operation
Receiver: Low noise FET RF amplifier, pulse compression
CONTRACTOR
Plessey Radar Ltd, Oakcroft Road, Chessington, Surrey KT9 1QZ, England

3649.153

AR-320 THREE-DIMENSIONAL AIR DEFENCE RADAR

The AR-320 is an advanced three-dimensional radar system produced jointly by Plessey Radar and ITT-Gilfillan. It meets all aspects of performance stipulated by the NATO Air Defence requirements for radars in the E/F-band.

The system is self-contained in a number of vehicles and is suitable for transport by land, sea or air. It is designed to provide the optimum combination of long range, fine resolution, good performance in ECM and clutter, high reliability, ease of maintenance, and system survivability. The state-of-the-art digital processing and low sidelobe antenna provide immunity to active and passive jamming, inter-jammer visibility, detection probability in the presence of clutter, and constant low false-alarm rate.

The associated radar-mounted SSR/IFF interrogator/receiver provides secondary plots which are extracted and correlated with primary plots. The combined plots are then transmitted to an operations centre for use in the tracking process. These capabilities, and the common module concept of the radar, ensure that it can be configured to meet a variety of tactical or strategic operational needs, and can be used either independently or integrated with a national defence system.

Field Deployment

For tactical operations, the various system elements are installed in cabins mounted on trailers and self-powered vehicles for transport by land, sea or air. The system is designed for rapid deployment and, with a trained crew, can be dismantled, set up, and brought into service again within six hours, transportation time excluded. Typically, the vehicle group will consist of:

(1) an antenna assembly transported on a flat-bed trailer or rail car. In transit the radar antenna is folded down by means of a hydraulically operated mechanism; an attached IFF antenna can be easily removed and stowed

(2) a trailer-installed transmitter cabin containing primary and secondary radar transmitters

(3) a trailer-mounted processing and display cabin containing signal processing equipment, the radar management suite, operations consoles, and the radar environment simulator

(4) transportable diesel-electric generator(s) able to provide power for the complete system

AR-320 3-D air defence radar antenna

(5) a trailer-installed cabin containing workshop, human support and storage facilities.

The entire vehicle group can be transported to a prepared or unprepared site and operated as a field group with radio link communications to a reporting post or sector operations centre.

Radome Installation

Where environmental conditions require, the vehicle group can be housed under cover with the radar antenna protected by a rigid radome. In this configuration the antenna is hoisted into the radome and supported on structural cross-members.

Silo Installation

An alternative arrangement allows for installation of the antenna and associated electronic sub-systems within a below-ground shelter or silo. The antenna is permanently mounted on an elevator and, for operational deployment, is raised and unfolded hydraulically. The antenna is capable of rapid retraction into the silo when required. The radar hardware in this configuration is arranged in equipment rooms in conjunction with associated power supplies, heating and ventilation equipment.

CHARACTERISTICS

Long-range high-cover performance within E/F-band

High gain, narrow pencil beam with ultra-low azimuth and elevation sidelobes

Planar phased array utilising within pulse, phase/frequency elevation scan

Wideband frequency agility

SSR/IFF antenna

Wideband transmitter with mean power greater than 24 kW

Variable pulse length and PRF

Multi-channel, pulse compressed signal processing

Digital MTI processing with velocity compensation for good anti-clutter and ECCM performance

Small resolution cell to resolve multiple targets and maximise signal to clutter detectability

Fully automatic, 3-D plot extractor

Accurate 3-D co-ordinates from every plot

High performance Series 9 display system with digital display drive

Bright, synthetic presentation with high quality characters and excellent registration accuracy

Radar environment simulation for operator training

High reliability and availability

Wide environmental tolerance

Transportable configuration for rapid field deployment

DEVELOPMENT

The AR-320 air defence radar is the result of collaboration between Plessey Radar Ltd and ITT-Gilfillan, combining the ITT-Gilfillan Series 320 3-D antenna and transmitter with Plessey AR-3D receiver, signal processor, displays and software. The Series 320 radars represent a family of defence radars based on three-dimensional radars developed for the American Services by Gilfillan, such as the AN/SPS-48 (**1252.253**) and AN/TPS-32 (**2516.153**) which have since been supplied to a number of other countries.

The Plessey AR-3D is a 'within-pulse' frequency scanning radar, in quantity production. The combination of techniques provide an inertialess elevation scan of a single pencil beam which can be accomplished by either frequency or phase control to steer the beam in space. This technique maintains high resolution throughout the coverage volume, high data rate and accurate target location.

STATUS

The AR-320 is in production and six systems were ordered by the UK MoD in early 1983. These are the last major radars in the current improvement programme for the UK air defence network. Three will be NATO funded and three will be funded by the UK government. The AR-320 has also been offered for the NATO E/F-band bulk buy to update the NADGE air defence network on NATO's southern border. The bids were due to be submitted by the end of 1983 with a decision in the Spring of 1984.

CONTRACTORS

Plessey Radar Ltd, Oakcroft Road, Chessington, Surrey KT9 1QZ, England.

ITT-Gilfillan Inc, 7821 Orion Avenue, PO Box 7713, Van Nuys, California 91409, USA.

2425.153

RAPIER SEARCH AND ACQUISITION RADAR

This system is an integral part of the Rapier anti-aircraft guided weapon system (**2424.131**). Little information has been officially released on this part of the system, and the following is an assessment based on available data.

This equipment comprises a primary surveillance radar working in conjunction with a computer and a secondary radar (IFF) interrogator to locate, identify and, where appropriate, initiate the tracking of enemy targets. The whole equipment is located in the fire unit of the Rapier system.

In the search mode the radar (coherent pulsed doppler equipment) scans continuously through 360° in azimuth. When a target is detected its azimuth range and velocity are measured, and on the same scan it is interrogated by the IFF whose antenna is combined with that of the primary radar. If a 'friendly' response is received the information on that target is cancelled from the system and the search continues without interruption.

If the target is adjudged hostile an alarm signal is

sent to the remainder of the equipment and the measured co-ordinates are used to direct the tracker (see description of Rapier) and the launcher towards the target.

It is, of course, possible that a friendly target might fail to respond to the IFF interrogation on a single pass of the surveillance system (eg because of an unfavourable aspect of the airborne antenna) but the system allows for a 'friendly' response to be accepted before the engagement has gone too far.

STATUS

Since the complete equipment forms an integral part of the Rapier system, deployment and similar details given in the description of the weapons system apply equally to the search and acquisition radars.

An autonomous version of this radar, known as Possum, has been developed by Racal for battlefield surveillance against aircraft.

CONTRACTORS

Primary radar and antennas

Racal Radar Defence Systems Ltd, Davis Road, Chessington, Surrey KT9 1TB, England.

Microminiature IFF equipment

Cossor IFF transmitter/receiver on the Rapier

Cossor Electronics Ltd, The Pinnacles, Elizabeth Way, Harlow, Essex CM19 5BB, England.

2428.153

SCORPION TARGET ILLUMINATING RADAR

Scorpion is a target illuminating radar used with the Bloodhound surface-to-air guided missile system. Intended primarily for use with static installations of this system, the equipment can nevertheless be dismantled into transportable units.

Basically an I/J-band CW doppler auto-follow radar, the equipment also performs the functions of illuminating the target and thereby providing the

reflected radiation to activate the semi-active homing system of the Bloodhound missile. In addition it has a limited target search facility and is equipped for target identification.

More detailed information is given under this entry number in previous editions of *Jane's Weapon Systems*.

CHARACTERISTICS

Type: Static CW doppler auto-follow radar

Frequency: I/J-band

Main antenna: 4·2 m diameter

Facilities: Search and follow. Target identification

Associated system: Bloodhound SAGW system

CONTRACTOR

Marconi Radar Systems Ltd, Writtle Road, Chelmsford, Essex CM1 3BN, England.

2439.153
RAPIER BLINDFIRE TRACKING RADAR

The DN 181 Blindfire radar was developed by Marconi Space and Defence Systems, with Marconi Avionics as a major sub-contractor. This development was carried out on a UK MoD funded programme with BAe as prime system contractor. The radar tracker, with the Rapier SAM (**2424.131**) is designed to meet the threat posed by low-level strike aircraft which can operate at night and in low visibility. Addition of the Blindfire radar gives the system an all-weather/night capability to extend the original 'clear-weather' Rapier devised by BAe with optical tracking to meet this threat. With the radar tracker in the system, the operator has a choice, until the moment of launch, of which system will be the most efficient for the engagement.

The radar uses differential tracking for simultaneous target and missile tracking. An electronic angle tracking receiver incorporated within the tracker detects boresight errors for accurate positioning of its own antenna and the angular difference between the missile and target sightlines for the generation of command guidance signals. The extremely narrow beamwidth, coupled with precisely positioned individual range gates for target and missile, is the key to the accuracy and very low-level

capability of the system, and also reduces the chances of background clutter, such as ground echoes or rainfall, obscuring the target echo. A number of other electronic measures are also designed into the system to minimise the effect of clutter and other unwanted signals, both spurious and deliberate.

The tracking radar is initially alerted to a hostile aircraft by the system surveillance radar, which indicates the approximate direction of the threat. The tracking radar will immediately swing on to this bearing, and rapidly establish the exact bearing, range, and height of the target. When the radar is locked on to the target, the missile is launched and this, too, is tracked by the radar. The difference between the target and missile angles is instantly derived within the system and commands are automatically transmitted to the missile to guide it on to the target.

The radar tracker is a self-contained, 'plug-in' unit, and requires no extra personnel to operate it.
STATUS
The initial UK MoD production contract was awarded in early 1973 and the equipment is now in service. Full production is continuing for the British Army, Royal Air Force and various foreign operators of Rapier.

The DN 181 tracking radar also forms part of the RN

Marconi Blindfire tracker radar

Type 911 system (**5630.253**) ordered by the UK MoD for the lightweight Seawolf programme.
CONTRACTOR
Marconi Space and Defence Systems Ltd, Warren Lane, Stanmore, Middlesex HA7 4LY, England.

2466.153
ST850 TIGERCAT RADAR

Designed for use with the Tigercat surface-to-air missile system (**2465.131**) the ST850/M radar with its associated television equipment gives the missile system an all-weather capability as well as enhancing the clear-weather performance through the provision of a television auto-gather facility. In conditions where the missile is visible, it is automatically gathered within a few seconds of launch after which the engagement is completed automatically or manually using the television monitor.

The radar is housed in a mobile cabin and can be integrated with the S860 mobile surveillance radar.

The radar may assume control of either of two Tigercat fire units, providing fully automatic control of the channel whilst the second channel reverts to optical control.

The ST850 is fully autonomous and can carry out its own low-level search in which the antenna is rotated at 40 rpm in a spiral scan. A PPI display unit is provided.

The cabin contains the equipment cabinets: one bay houses the tracker servo drive circuits and the I-band transmitter, a second houses the receiver and signal processing equipment and the last the ARCU.

System controls and monitoring/indicating equipment are located in a separate control console sited at one end of the cabin. Two operator positions

are provided at the console, one for the unit commander and the other for system control.

The cabin is fully air conditioned and its dimensions are approximately 3·7 m long by 2 m high by 2 m wide. It is fitted with attachment points for mobilisers, screw jacks for levelling, and lifting eyes for transportation.

The director is mounted on the roof of the cabin. It carries a one-metre diameter antenna and the TV camera. It is capable of continuous rotation in azimuth, being mounted clear of the cabin roof so that radar and TV visibility extends from an elevation of 85° to a depression of 5°. When the equipment is sited higher than the surrounding terrain, targets flying below 0° elevation level can be tracked.

Facilities are incorporated in the director support framework on the cabin, so that the director can be lowered from its operational position into the cabin for stowage during transportation, when its overall height is 2·4 m.

The antenna is of the twist-cassegrain type. A four-horn monopulse feed and comparator provide three separate RF outputs (viz sum, elevation difference, and azimuth difference signals) for processing in the IF receivers to produce acquisition and auto-follow data. High accuracy of angular data results from the combination of a narrow pencil beam and the monopulse signal processing.

The TV camera is aligned to the radar boresight and

provides optical information on the target being tracked by the radar. This system consists not only of a conventional camera and display, but also a data processing system which permits guidance of the Tigercat missile on to the TV line-of-sight.

The pulse modulated transmitter employs an I-band magnetron to deliver a typical power of 160 W mean and 180 kW peak. The magnetron is motor tunable over the frequency band 8·6 to 9·5 GHz, being manually controlled from the radar console.

The local oscillator is a solid-state microwave source with voltage tuning to permit automatic frequency control, which controls the oscillator frequency to follow the tuning of the magnetron and maintains the correct intermediate frequency in the receiver.

The RF portion of the receiver system is housed on the elevation assembly behind the antenna. The IF outputs are connected via coaxial cables and the azimuth slip-ring unit to the IF portion of the receiver, which is housed in one of the equipment cabinets in the cabin.

The signal processing equipment has two channels: the main one for acquisition and tracking of the wanted target; the subsidiary one for acquisition and tracking of the missile. All functions are carried out automatically using digital techniques under control of the master programming unit.

The master programming unit organises the operational sequence of the radar in response to commands from the operator at the control console, and signals from the radar sub-system.

In a mixed defence environment employing both missiles and guns, the ST850/M fire control unit is extended by the addition of a general-purpose digital computer, to form the ST850/MG. This latter unit provides prediction of aim-off and automatic system control, thus allowing blind-fire gun control, as in the Marconi/Sperry Sapphire lightweight gun fire control system (**1828.261**).

In support of the ST850 Series tracking radars, the mobile surveillance radar type S860 is available. The S860 is fully autonomous with its own operators and provides a control designation facility for the larger site. Target data, parallax-corrected, are automatically passed to the selected fire control unit.
STATUS
800 Series radars are in production for the UK MoD and other customers. ST850 units have been supplied overseas as part of the Short Brothers Radar Enhanced Tigercat 2 air defence missile system.
CONTRACTOR
Marconi Radar Systems Ltd, Writtle Road, Chelmsford, Essex CM1 3BN, England.

Tigercat deployed showing ST850 radar on right

2490.153
ZB 298 SHORT-RANGE GROUND SURVEILLANCE RADAR

The ZB 298 battlefield surveillance radar was developed by Marconi Avionics Ltd to meet a British General Staff requirement (which in turn conformed to the NATO basic military requirement) for a portable battlefield radar, and has since been supplied to overseas customers. The radar can be transported by two soldiers and operated by one man to give an all-weather, day and night facility to detect any significant movement on the battlefield. This includes the location and recognition of men singly or in groups, single or multiple vehicles and low-flying helicopters. ZB 298 can also be used in a counter-insurgency role in keeping watch on sensitive areas such as an airfield.

Targets can be detected on land or over water at ranges from 50 metres to 20 km and the radar can be used for observing ground or sea bursts of artillery or mortar fire and for fire correction.

The original 6 km version of ZB 298 is designated by the British Army as Radar GS no 14 Mk 1. The range of the radar has twice been extended and it is now available in a 20 km version. The opportunity was taken while incorporating the 20 km modification, to introduce major engineering changes in the display unit and tripod which utilise the most up-to-date component technology. Supporting equipment for the ZB 298 includes a training simulator, to give realistic training in the classroom, special test equipment for rapid check-out and fault-finding and a telescopic mast to elevate the radar head thereby improving surveillance coverage.

More detailed information on ZB 298 can be found under this entry number in previous editions of *Jane's Weapon Systems*.

ZB 298 mounted on a Spartan combat reconnaissance vehicle (Alvis Ltd)

CHARACTERISTICS
Operating frequency: I-band
Range: Max 20 000 m; minimum 50 m
Range resolution: 35 m
Range accuracy: 25 m
Antenna beamwidth: 90 mils vertical; 90 mils horizontal
Bearing resolution: 100 mils
Bearing accuracy: 15 mils
Elevation limits: ±350 mils

STATUS
In service with British, Danish, Dutch, and certain other armies.
CONTRACTOR
Marconi Avionics Ltd, Applied Physics Division, Elstree Way, Borehamwood, Hertfordshire WD6 1RX, England.

5627.153
PACER MK 2 MUZZLE VELOCITY RADAR

Pacer Mk 2 is a private venture equipment which has been developed to measure muzzle velocities of artillery guns, naval guns and mortars during operational firing missions. It uses doppler radar techniques to measure the velocity in the range from 100 to 1400 metres per second to an accuracy of 0·1 per cent.

The system consists of only two units; a sensor unit containing all the electronics which can be mounted either on a non-recoiling part of the gun or on a free-standing mount, and a small hand-held terminal display and control unit which is connected by a cable. The radar transmitter is switched on automatically at the moment of firing, by a flash detector, and is automatically switched off after the measurement is complete. This takes between 0·1 and 1 second, depending on muzzle velocity, and the very short measurement period brings detection and ECM risk to a minimum.

The measured muzzle velocity is shown directly in metres per second on the alpha-numeric liquid crystal display, to two decimal places, and the data on

up to 16 rounds can be stored in memory. These can be recalled as necessary and any number can be averaged.

Pacer Mk 2 can be connected directly to a fire control computer via its internal interfaces.
CHARACTERISTICS
Frequency: 10·5 GHz
Output power: 500 mW
Transmission time: 0·1 – 1 s
Velocity range: 100 – 1400 m/s
Accuracy: 0·1%
Beamwidth: 10° vertical; 15° horizontal
Calibre: 75 mm and above
STATUS
One Pacer Mk 2 equipment was ordered by the Sultanate of Oman in late 1983. The British Army is known to be interested and was due to make a decision in 1984.
CONTRACTOR
Ferranti Computer Systems Ltd, Cheadle Heath Division, Bird Hall Lane, Cheadle Heath, Stockport SK3 0XQ, England.

Pacer Mk 2 mounted on an FH 70 howitzer

3692.153
CEL 850 IFF INTERROGATOR

The Cossor CEL 850 IFF interrogator system is based on the CRS 390 transmitter/receiver which is the standard unit employed in a wide variety of IFF/SSR applications where identification facilities are required in association with long- or medium-range primary radars. These may be fixed or mobile, and one of four standard antennas will normally be employed, either on-mounted with the primary radar scanner, or with its own turning gear. Characteristics of these antennas are given below.

Apart from specially-designed IFF equipments for applications such as the Rapier (**2424.131**) and Bofors RBS 70 missile systems, the Cossor CEL 850 IFF system using the CRS 390 transmitter/receiver is normally used. Its compatibility with a wide variety of primary radars, coupled with features that permit ready interfacing, suit it for either slaved, on-mounted or autonomous operation. Small size, lightweight and rugged construction make it suitable for mobile applications, and it is also used at sea. Operating features include: wide range of acceptable trigger

pulses; external computer control facility; external modulation facility; flexible mode programme; video outputs to match processing system needs. A logarithmic receiver coupled to special video processing circuits make the equipment particularly resistant to ECM interference.
CHARACTERISTICS
Antenna CRS 320
Length: 9·65 m
Weight: 305 kg
Gain: 23 dB (minimum)
Half-power beamwidth: 2·2°
Antenna CRS 389
Length: 4·35 m
Weight: 79 kg
Gain: 17·5 dB (minimum)
Half-power beamwidth: 4·5°
Antenna CRS 381
Length: 3·35 m
Weight: 57 kg
Gain: 16·5 dB (minimum)
Half-power beamwidth: 6°

CRS 381 3 m SSR/IFF antenna on-mounted at the upper edge of an AR-1 airfield radar

Antenna CRS 379
Length: 1·16 m
Weight: 13·8 kg
Gain: 16 dB (minimum)
Half-power beamwidth: 12·5°
Transmitter/receiver CRS 390
Transmitter section
Frequency: 1030 MHz
Power output: 33 dBW
Modes: 1, 2, 3/A, B, and C; external modulation
PRF: 150 – 1000 Hz
Mode interlace: Single, dual or triple

Receiver section
Centre frequency: 1090 MHz
Tangential sensitivity: Not less than –85 dBm
Bandwidth: 10 MHz, at –3 dB points
Video outputs: 2 – 5 V, adjustable into 75Ω
Identification pulses: Pre-trigger; mode pulse pairs
Display trigger pulses: +5 V into 75Ω between P3 and
P3 + 60μs
STATUS
More than 90 complete systems have been ordered.
CONTRACTOR
Cossor Electronics Ltd, The Pinnacles, Harlow, Essex
CM19 5BB, England.

*Cossor CVP 190 modular multi-role video processor
system in use with a CEL 850 IFF system (control
panel to left of right-hand display)*

3693.153
870 SERIES IFF INTERROGATORS
This series of Cossor IFF interrogators is intended to
equip short- and medium-range primary radar
systems, where there is often a requirement for the
hardware to be relatively compact. For example, in
land-mobile units, there is a need for rapid and
positive target identification because speed of
response is essential, but space considerations may
also be critical. For these reasons, IFF 870
equipments interrogate on one mode at a time and
process up to two reply codes at a time. For ease of
integration the hardware has been constructed as two
units: a transmitter/receiver and a defruiter/decoder.
Various packaging arrangements have been
developed for specific applications. In some cases
there are also special antenna arrangements but

otherwise one of the four standard Cossor units, CRS
320/379/381/389 described in **3692.153**, is employed.
Specific models of the IFF 870 series that have been
identified include:
IFF 875 for Contraves LPD-20 radar (**1529.153**)
IFF 877 for Selenia RAN-11L/X naval radar
(**1365.253**)
IFF 878 for LM Ericsson Giraffe mobile radar
(**1957.153**)
IFF 879 for Signaal Flycatcher mobile radar
(**3283.153**)
STATUS
All the above versions are in production.
CONTRACTOR
Cossor Electronics Ltd, The Pinnacles, Harlow, Essex
CM19 5BB, England.

*Cossor IFF 875 interrogator equipment as configured
for use with Contraves LPD-20 primary radar*

3694.153
880 SERIES IFF INTERROGATORS
The Cossor IFF 880 series of equipments were
designed for use in forward battle areas in which there
may be a multiplicity of air defence weapons and
probable targets. Because of the highly effective
nature of many of these weapons, lack of an
identification facility with each weapon could lead to
the inadvertent destruction of valuable friendly
aircraft engaged on strike, interdiction or air defence
operations. It was to meet this need that the IFF 880
range of interrogators was introduced with the aim of
providing equipments suitable for application to
weapons as a stand-alone, self-contained IFF system.
Interfaces for integration with towed air defence
guns, turret-mounted AA guns, man-portable air
defence missiles, and vehicle-mounted air defence
missiles have been developed. Outputs from the IFF
can be used to inhibit firing, or to provide visual or
aural status indications. Integration with primary
radars is also possible where required.

Packaging of the transmitter and receiver units is
configured to suit the weapon system being
equipped. Usually there are requirements for
minimum dimensions and weight together with
special mounting arrangments. The requirements are
easily met by the small size of the equipment.
Similarly, a special-to-type antenna is provided in
most cases. A typical IFF 880 application is the
Swedish RBS 70 air defence missile system (**2348.131**
and **3617.131**). Variants of the IFF 880 are available for
man-portable, Land-Rover mounted and armoured
vehicle installations of RBS 70.

IFF 880/1 Free-standing IFF System
This derivative of the IFF 880 series has been
designed for operation by an air-defence weapon
detachment commander and requires no
modification of in-service weapons. The system
comprises a transmitter/receiver/processor unit,
which is normally carried in a haversack, an antenna
which is hand-held and an interconnecting cable

*IFF 880 interrogator equipment integrated in Bofors
RBS 70 man-portable surface-to-air missile system*

fitted with quick release connectors. Incorporated in
the open array is an optical aiming system.

In operation, the commander sights the target
through the antenna and interrogates the target,
using the trigger fitted by the hand grip. The status of
the IFF system and whether the target is friendly or
hostile is indicated by a light emitting diode
incorporated in the antenna unit.

Typical applications are provision of IFF facilities to
Blowpipe, SA-7 and other short-range air defence
systems. The characteristics of the system are similar
to those of the IFF 880 series. Weight of the system is
5 kg for the interrogator and 1·5 kg for the antenna.

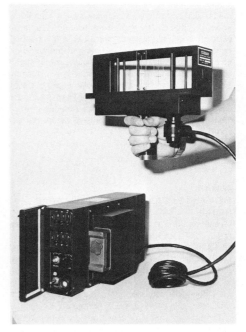

IFF 880/1 free-standing IFF system

CHARACTERISTICS
Transmitter frequency: 1030 MHz
Power output: 13 dBW (P1, P3), 18 dBW (P2)
Modes: 1, 2, 3/A
PRF: Presettable
Receiver frequency: 1090 MHz
Tangential sensitivity: –76 dBm
Bandwidth: 8 MHz at –3 dB points

Antenna gain: 10 dB
Antenna beamwidth: 20° + 11° – 8° at 3 dB points in azimuth depending upon transponder performance
Dimensions: 355 × 180 × 152 mm, interrogator and antenna but less bracket
Weight: 5·3 kg (less bracket)

STATUS
IFF 880 is in production for several users. IFF 880/1 is in advanced development.
CONTRACTOR
Cossor Electronics Ltd, The Pinnacles, Harlow, Essex CM19 5BB, England.

4604.153
COSSOR MONOPULSE SECONDARY SURVEILLANCE RADAR

The Cossor monopulse secondary surveillance radar (SSR) provides accurate and reliable track data in environments which cause errors in conventional SSR systems. It has been designed to take advantage of the advances in code extraction techniques which enable garbled transponder replies to be decoded successfully. Unlike conventional SSR, a monopulse system measures the bearing of an aircraft from each received frame and code pulse of its transponder reply. An average of these measurements gives consistent, high accuracy azimuth data even in areas where normal sliding window extractors would output track errors caused by 'fruit' and 'missed replies'. The Cossor system consists of the CRS 512 antenna (**5622.153**) the SSR 950 interrogator and the CVP 250 plot extractor.

The CRS 512 large vertical aperture antenna, combined with low sidelobe levels, is designed to provide a considerable improvement in SSR system performance. It reduces the incidence of ground reflections and false targets caused by local buildings, parked aircraft, etc. The SSR 950 interrogator has been designed to meet the requirements of ICAO Annex 10 and was developed specifically for monopulse operation. It includes two matched logarithmic receivers for monopulse operation plus a third receiver for receiver sidelobe suppression. Other main features of the SSR 950 are improved sidelobe suppression (site selectable),

programmable gain time control in range and azimuth, digital plot extractor interface and computerised management system interface. The interrogator has been designed to be readily extendable for Mode S operation when this comes into operation. The CVP 250 plot extractor, which is built into the same cabinet as the SSR 950, uses advanced microprocessor technology and incorporates extensive self-test and fail-soft features. Target reports are compiled using monopulse data from the SSR 950.

STATUS
The Cossor monopulse SSR system has been selected by the UK MoD to equip its military airfields throughout UK and West Germany. Installation is due to commence in 1986. The SSR 950 and the CVP 250 are essentially the same as those currently being installed throughout the UK on behalf of the Civil Aviation Authority (CAA) as part of the new civil radar network. The CRS 512 LVA antenna is also being supplied to both the MoD and the CAA; one of these units is undergoing evaluation trials by the CAA during 1984.

Monopulse SSR systems are being supplied to Saudi Arabia and Switzerland. Cossor is also carrying out a contract definition phase of the major Canadian radar replacement programme for 41 monopulse SSR sites.

CONTRACTOR
Cossor Electronics Ltd, The Pinnacles, Harlow, Essex CM19 5BB, England.

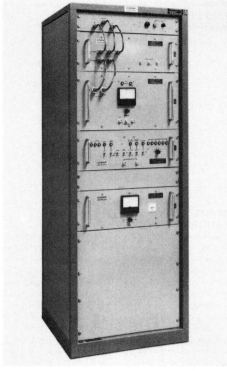

SSR 950/CVP 250 monopulse interrogator

5622.153
CRS 512 SSR ANTENNA

The CRS 512 is a large aperture secondary surveillance antenna designed as a replacement for the familiar linear array which has been the standard antenna since SSR was first introduced. The large vertical aperture, which measures 5 ft (1·53 m), contains a vertical array of radiating elements which give more flexibility in the control of the transmit and receive patterns and provides improved performance. This system overcomes the disadvantages of linear array antennas, which can cause gaps in radar coverage and false replies due to reflections from local terrain and buildings, caused by its narrow aperture.

New constructional techniques have been

employed for the radiating elements to minimise weight while retaining strength. This has resulted in keeping the weight to approximately 500 lb (227 kg) for an antenna length of 28 ft (8·25 m). The open array construction also reduces wind resistance and has been designed to withstand a wide range of environmental conditions. The CRS 512 is available for use at airfields, where reflection problems can be most severe, and also for long range surveillance with good coverage at low angles of elevation.

STATUS
In development.
CONTRACTOR
Cossor Electronics Ltd, The Pinnacles, Harlow, Essex CM19 5BB, England.

Cossor large vertical aperture antenna of CRS 512 SSR

4603.153
MESSENGER SECONDARY SURVEILLANCE RADAR

Messenger is a monopulse secondary surveillance radar (SSR) designed for future requirements of select addressable systems, such as implied by the US/UK current Mode S plans. Messenger consists of a large vertical aperture (LVA) antenna, an interrogator/responder and a decoder/plot extractor, the electronics being mounted in a standard 19-inch rack housed in a transportable container.

The LVA antenna produces three azimuth patterns at the SSR transmit and receive frequencies of 1030 and 1090 MHz, symmetrically disposed about the boresight and forming the means of effecting interrogation sidelobe suppression (ISLS), improved interrogation sidelobe suppression (IISLS), received sidelobe suppression (RSLS) and monopulse direction finding (MDF). The antenna is manufactured to a computer-optimized electrical design giving a high forward gain of better than 29 dB and a robust mechanical construction to ensure operation and survival in severe environmental conditions. The LVA antenna reduces the incidence of ground reflections and false targets caused by local buildings, parked aircraft, etc.

Marconi Messenger LVA antenna

The interrogator/responder consists of three associated units; interrogator, monopulse multiple receiver and a performance monitor. It is completely solid-state, including the final output power stage ranging from 500 W to 2 kW, and is capable of being upgraded to include operation to Mode S standards at a much higher duty cycle than standard SSR. This will enable full SSR data link facilities to be established when international agreement on signal

formats and protocols have been ratified. Much of the technology involved in Messenger is derived directly from the Marconi Martello air defence radar (**3491.153**). The monopulse receivers are housed in a separate unit; their balanced outputs allowing accurate direction finding of targets on single inputs (monopulse DF) over the full antenna beamwidth and suppression or flagging of replies not received by the main beam (RSLS). Off-boresight azimuth processing employs the module developed for the Marconi GWS 25 tracking radar (**1562.253**).

The decoder/plot extractor uses monopulse decoding equipment having special logic included to ensure retention of wanted data in poor or ambiguous signal conditions. The circuits are constructed on printed circuit boards interconnected by a fast multi-highway system. Outputs to companion circuit boards in the same unit are used to form data plots expressing the range, azimuth identity and altitude code of all SSR targets in the radar cover. Decoding and plot extraction modules are combined to provide a high speed data bus and unlimited capability for system configuration and reconfiguration.

Data can be outputted in a number of different formats including that specified by the UK MoD. Standard modems are used to interface the decoder/extractor output, via telephone cable, to the local display and data handling equipment.

STATUS
In development. System trials were due to take place during 1984 with production units available from mid-1985.

CONTRACTOR
Marconi Radar Systems Ltd, Writtle Road, Chelmsford, Essex CM1 3BN, England.

UNITED STATES OF AMERICA

1949.153
COBRA DANE RADAR

Cobra Dane is the code-name of a large phased array radar at Shemya Air Force Base in the Aleutian Islands under USAF Program 633A. Its purpose is the detection and tracking of ICBMs, SLBMs and satellites. It is a new type of radar which has replaced two existing radars of the old intelligence variety (AN/FPS-17 and AN/FPS-80), which were themselves pressed into service to undertake Spacetrack duties. They had a limited real-time tracking capability and the new Cobra Dane installation is intended to remedy this shortcoming.

The large fixed phased array of this radar measures about 30 m in diameter and is composed of about 35 000 elements of which some 15 000 are active elements. The system will survey a 2000-mile (3220 km) corridor to collect data on Soviet missile

development flights, provide early warning of ICBM launches, detect new satellites, and update known satellite parameters.

The array provides coverage over a 120° sector of the Soviet missile test range, and in its space tracking role the Cobra Dane installation has a range of 25 000 nautical miles (46 000 km). In its data collection role on Soviet missile flights, Cobra Dane has the ability to track up to 100 objects simultaneously with precise data on up to 20 targets. These data are processed at the Shemya site and transmitted to the USAF Foreign Technology Division.

Employed as an early warning system, Cobra Dane has the capacity to track 200 targets and provide detailed information on these to NORAD Headquarters. Among the latter data will be predicted impact locations in the USA.

The installation comprises a total of 12 transmitting

groups, each incorporating eight TWTs, with a peak power of 16 MW and an average level of 1 MW.
DEVELOPMENT
The responsible agency is the USAF Electronic Systems Division. The project was authorised in 1971 and Requests for Proposals were issued in 1972, funding being approved in that year also. A contract for $39·6 million was awarded to Raytheon in July 1973. Construction was well advanced at the close of 1974 and the system testing was completed in late 1976.
STATUS
Cobra Dane achieved First Operational Capability in 1977. Total cost is estimated at $68 million.

Eventually it was planned to close down the BMEWS radar at Clear, Alaska, when the ability of Cobra Dane and the new West Coast SLBM phased array radar (Pave Paws) to take over Clear's warning functions have been determined. Currently Cobra Dane augments the BMEWS system in early warning.

However, in the meantime, plans have been implemented for a 'three-element' BMEWS improvement programme to provide more precise data on the character and size of a missile attack. These modifications will ensure the continued usefulness of BMEWS well into the 1980s.

A similar project named Cobra Judy, a shipborne phased array radar for endo-atmospheric tracking to complement Cobra Dane is now in operation in the Pacific (**4301.253**).
CONTRACTOR
Raytheon Company, Equipment Division, Wayland, Massachusetts 01178, USA.

Giant radar at Shemya Air Force Base, near western tip of the Aleutian island chain off Alaska, is a phased array system. Known as Cobra Dane, it is used for tracking Soviet ballistic missile flights. Cobra Dane was constructed by Raytheon Company under contract to USAF Electronic Systems Division

3714.153
AN/FPN-62 PRECISION APPROACH RADAR

The AN/FPN-62 is an updated version of earlier equipment in which new electronics have been substituted for older, more difficult to maintain hardware. The original azimuth and elevation antennas are retained, these being electronically scanned elements providing separate beams for tracking of an approaching aircraft in azimuth and elevation. Guidance signals are normally passed back to the aircraft voice radio link. Operation is in the radar I-band.
STATUS
The AN/FPN-62 was developed by Raytheon in a competitive programme sponsored by the USAF for the updating of fixed PAR facilities based on the

AN/CPN-4, AN/MPN-13 and AN/FPN-16 equipments. This resulted in a contract for the upgrading and supply of 40 systems for the USAF, and the prototype was produced in 1976. By mid-1979 more than 20 systems had to be delivered.

In 1979, Cossor Electronics, the Raytheon UK subsidiary, won a similar contract for the upgrading of RAF SLA-3 PARs, and is engaged on the production of an Anglicised version of the FPN-62 which is designated the 'Falconer' by Cossor. The UK concern will supply 43 static and two mobile systems for use at home and overseas RAF bases.
CONTRACTOR
Raytheon Company, Equipment Division, Wayland, Massachusetts 01178, USA.

AN/FPN-62 upgraded PAR

4125.153
QUADRADAR Mk V ATC RADAR

The Quadradar Mk V is a multi-function ATC radar providing four functions: air surveillance, precision approach, heightfinding and airfield taxi control. The radar equipment is tripod mounted for siting adjacent to the airfield runway and normally operates unattended via remote control. The system includes cable remoting (up to 3000 m, or 10 000 feet).

The system has two mechanically operated antennas, scanning in azimuth and elevation on a time-shared basis, as required by the four modes of operation. The arrangement can be seen from the nearby photograph.

Further information is given under this entry number in previous editions of *Jane's Weapon Systems*.

CHARACTERISTICS
Transmitter
Frequency: 9000 – 9160 MHz, tunable
STATUS
More than 350 systems have been produced and are in operation throughout the world. Since its introduction in the late 1950s, the Quadradar has been continuously updated and today the Mk V constitutes a modern, completely solid-state ground control approach radar.
CONTRACTOR
ITT-Gilfillan, 7821 Orion Avenue, Van Nuys, California 91409, USA.

Gilfillan Quadradar Mk V ATC radar

4328.153
QUADRADAR MK VI ATC RADAR

Quadradar Mk VI was developed from the Quadradar Mk V and incorporates a high performance digital MTI feature. As with the Mk V, the equipment is a multi-function ATC radar providing air surveillance, precision approach, heightfinding and airfield taxi control.

The receiver/transmitter unit is a later development but the antennas and mechanical drive unit are the same as the Mk V. The indicator display unit is housed in a new design slanted face display unit but otherwise uses the same electronic components as the Mk V with some modifications for DMTI compatibility. The mechanically operated scanners perform in the same way as the Mk V.

CHARACTERISTICS
Transmitter
Frequency: 9100 – 9200 MHz, tunable
Pulse width: 0·26 or 0·5 μs selectable
PRF rates: 3300 pps; 3300 average with 7:8:9 stagger
1925 pps; 1925 average with 7:8:9 stagger
Peak power: 180 kW (nominal)
Beamwidth: Azimuth 0·95° × 3·5°, csc² to 30°; elevation 0·85° × 2·5°
Receiver
MDS: –108 dBm
IF: (1st): 290 MHz, (2nd): 60 MHz
Bandwidth: 2·5 MHz
Range scales: ASR: 1·5 nm (taxi) 5, 7·5, 15 and 30 nm (surveillance)
PAR: 3, 7, 15 and 30 nm
CONTRACTOR
ITT-Gilfillan, 7821 Orion Avenue, Van Nuys, California 91409, USA.

ITT-Gilfillan Quadradar with MTI

4076.153
SERIES 52 PRECISION APPROACH RADAR

The ITT-Gilfillan Series 52 is a turntable-mounted, precision approach radar (PAR). The radar data is remotely fed to control centres or control towers. Air traffic controllers provide precise approach guidance to aircraft down to the runway threshold through voice communications with the pilot.

The turntable is remotely controlled for aligning to cover multiple runway approaches. Up to six radar displays may be remotely controlled a maximum 3636 m from the equipment shelter. Radar ranges of 10, 15, and 20 nautical miles provide coverage for all types of aircraft and all traffic pattern variations. For transportation, the Series 52 is packaged into two major sub-assemblies: the shelter and turntable pallet.

Radar scan angles of 20° in azimuth and 8° in elevation are developed by the delta-A scanning antennas. These antennas feature minimum sidelobe performance and circular polarisation, coupled with a digital moving target indicator and integrated video. Dual channel radar transmitters and receivers, and high-gain, low-sidelobe antennas, remote control of PAR landing direction, and four sets of preset course and glideslope cursors are operational features of the Series 52 PAR.

CHARACTERISTICS
Frequency: 9000 – 9160 MHz
Peak power: 80 kW
Azimuth antenna gain: 39·7 dB
Elevation antenna gain: 40·3 dB
Max range: 20 nm
Resolution: 0·55° elevation; 0·85° azimuth; 48 m range
STATUS
Production.
CONTRACTOR
ITT-Gilfillan, 7821 Orion Avenue, Van Nuys, California 91409, USA.

ITT-Gilfillan Series 52 PAR

3174.153
AN/FPS-115 PAVE PAWS RADAR

Pave Paws is the name given to a system of large phased array AN/FPS-115 radars to replace the 474N SLBM detection and warning system radars, AN/FSS – 7 (**2538.153**). Raytheon was named as contractor to the USAF Electronic Systems Command in April 1976, when a contract valued at $46·6 million was awarded. This covered the first Pave Paws radar at Otis AFB, Massachusetts. A second site at Beale AFB, California has been built and both sites are operational. Two further sites at Robins AFB and near Goodfellow AFB are planned.

Raytheon was expected to draw upon the experience gained with the Cobra Dane radar described above (**1949.153**), but it is understood that there are important technical differences between the two types of radar.

Pave Paws is an important addition to the World Wide Military Command and Control System (WWMCCS), and will be operated and maintained by the USAF Strategic Air Command. The radar's primary mission of detection and warning of SLBM attack also involves the provision of attack characterisation to the NORAD Cheyenne Mountain Complex, the Strategic Air Command and the National Command Authorities. The system's secondary role in support of the USAF Spacetrack system feeds in positional and velocity data for the display of all Earth satellites in orbit. Capable of multi-target tracking, it simultaneously detects and discriminates many objects, while providing early warning data, launch, impact, position and velocity information as required.

Automated features of the system include detection, track initiation, and mission decisions. Two standard computers, CYBER 174-12s, generally serve as the CPU, programmed for beam steering, the storage and display of data, as well as performing post-mission data reduction and analysis.

Pave Paws operates at UHF frequencies and employs solid-state technology more extensively than Cobra Dane, with transistors driving transistors to produce radiation. In Cobra Dane TWTs are employed.

Pave Paws consists of a pair of circular planar arrays about 30 m in diameter, each consisting of 5400 elements. The arrays are inclined from the vertical and mounted in adjacent sides of a building measuring about 32 m high, forming sloping walls on the seaward facing side of the structure. Combined coverage of the electronically steered beams from the two arrays is 85° in elevation and 240° in azimuth. Range is estimated as about 3000 miles (4800 km).

The Otis AFB Pave Paws was declared operational officially in April 1980, with the Beale AFB entering service the following summer.

In mid-1978 it was disclosed that concern over the possibilities of improved Soviet SLBM capabilities require the construction of two more Pave Paws radars to cover additional south-east and south-west facing arcs. These have now been designated as Robins AFB and a site 17 miles south of Goodfellow AFB. Raytheon received a $77 million contract in late-1983 to build the former. The contract included an option for the Goodfellow site which is also scheduled to support NORAD tracking of space objects. The Robins site is to be fully operational by 1986.

CHARACTERISTICS
Frequency: 420 – 450 MHz
Transmitter: Solid-state
Module peak power: 322 W
No. of active elements/modules (67% filled): 1792

Pave Paws phased array radar installation at Beale AFB, California

Array type: Corporate feed, density tapered
No. of sub-arrays: 56
Antenna gain: 38·4 dB directive gain
Beamwidth: (transmit/receive): 2·0°/2·2° at boresight
Polarisation (transmit/receive): Right hand/left hand circular

Array diameter: 72·5 feet (utilised)
Face tilt: 20°
Azimuth: ±60°, 240° with two faces
Elevation: 3·85°

CONTRACTOR
Raytheon Company, Equipment Division, Wayland, Massachusetts 01178, USA.

Other contractors include CDC, and United Engineers.

3149.153
BPS-1000 SURVEILLANCE RADAR

The BPS-1000 is a long-range D-band surveillance radar for air defence and ATC applications, introduced by Bendix in 1976.

The dual diversity transmitter is a coherent type using a long-life L3035 power klystron, and can be operated in either simplex or duplex modes. In the former mode, the second channel provides full

Bendix BPS-1000 surveillance radar

redundancy except for the common antenna system. Predicted MTBF in this mode is better than 19 000 h. Solid-state receivers and processors contribute to the high overall reliability.

The coherent transmitter design eliminates second-time-around returns and permits the linear digital receiving system to achieve an MTI improvement factor of 45 dB. The receiver processor provides five basic receivers:

(1) normal
(2) Dicke-fix
(3) log
(4) MTI
(5) LINAR

With the exception of the Normal mode, all provide a constant false alarm rate (CFAR) output. Anti-jamming and weather countermeasures include: automatic clutter gating, delay-line blanking, leading edge blanking, wide dynamic range CFAR receivers. MTI anti-weather system. The LINAR and log receivers are also effective against weather interference and further rejection of rain clutter is provided by circular polarisation.

The log and Dicke-Fix receivers provide effective rejection of wideband noise jamming interference, and the Bendix LINAR receiver is effective against wideband and narrow-band noise jamming, as well as CW and swept-frequency.

The receiver processor provides outputs for manual and automatic systems, simultaneously. Computer driven displays may be used, in which case the Bendix radar data processor is added to facilitate the target and IFF/SSR data transmissions to the display sub-system. The computer-driven graphic

displays employed operate in a distributed system without a central data processor. Consoles use identical hardware, and operation is determined by the program loaded and operator keyboard commands. Radar and IFF/SSR input data and data exchanges between consoles use a common bus. The displays track targets, store flight plans, calculate intercepts and transmit interceptor commands.

The antenna is a large aperture, dual-curvature structure of lattice construction with dual horn feed. There are provisions for SLC, SLS, and direction IFF/SSR antennas.

CHARACTERISTICS
Frequency: 1250 – 1350 MHz
RF output: 2 – 2·75 MW peak
4·3 – 6·0 kW average
Range (1 m² target): Over 200 nm (370 km)
Range accuracy: 0·12 nm (0·22 km)
Range resolution: 0·6 nm (0·11 km)
Pulse length: 6 µs
PRF: Selectable 350, 355, 360, 365, or 370 pps
MTI cancellation ratio: 40 dB, minimum
Azimuth accuracy: 0·135°
Azimuth resolution: 1·5°
Beam shaping (vertical): Cosec² to 50°
Beamwidth (horizontal): 1·3°
Sidelobe level: –25 dB max
Antenna rotation: 6 rpm

STATUS
No details of operational installations have been obtained.

CONTRACTOR
Bendix Corporation, Communications Division, East Joppa Road, Baltimore, Maryland 21204, USA.

2846.153
AN/FPQ-6 AND AN/TPQ-18 PRECISION INSTRUMENTATION RADARS

AN/FPQ-6 and its transportable version AN/TPQ-18 are high-accuracy, amplitude comparison monopulse, C-band instrumentation radars designed primarily for tracking long-range high-velocity targets such as missiles and re-entry vehicles. They can function either in skin-tracking (single-pulse) or beacon tracking (pulse train) modes. The only difference between the two radars relate to the arrangement of their constituent units.

Physically the radars are large, five transmitter cabinets and 60 cabinet racks being required to house the basic electronics. The antenna is 885 cm in diameter, uses a five-horn cassegrain feed and can be rotated continuously in azimuth, and from –2 to +182° in elevation. The transmitter has a peak power of 2·8 MW.

Targets can be tracked out to some 60 000 km and at target speeds up to 18 km/s. Several systems have differing configurations and performance including

MW transmitters, pulse compression, 0·03 m/s rms accuracy pulse doppler, 'on-axis' computer aided tracking and low noise high gain feeds. Polarisation is console selectable. The antenna can track targets or be slewed at rates between 0·0006 and 28°/s. One unit was modified recently to track two in-beam targets simultaneously. It incorporates new integrated circuit design which greatly reduces size, power and air conditioning requirements. It is known as the AN/FPQ-19.

CHARACTERISTICS
Azimuth, elevation tracking precision: 0·05 mils rms at 20 dB S/N
Range tracking precision: 4·7 m rms at 20 dB S/N
Antenna beamwidth: 8 mils
Ro, IM², 0 dB S/N: 1000 km

STATUS
Eleven of these units are in operation at various USAF, US Army and NASA ranges.

CONTRACTOR
RCA, Government Systems Division, Missile and Surface Radar, Moorestown, New Jersey 08057, USA.

AN/FPQ-6 precision instrumentation radar

2492.153
AN/FPS-6 HEIGHTFINDING RADAR

For many years the AN/FPS-6 radar has been the principal heightfinder used by US armed forces and many allied nations. At least 450 of these systems have been delivered, including the mobile version, the AN/MPS-14 (**2496.153**).

A high-power E/F-band nodding-beam radar, the AN/FPS-6 is noted for extreme accuracy at long range, and three available versions give it wide versatility under a variety of environmental conditions.

The arctic tower installation consists of a 50 ft (15·25 m) radome (either air-supported or rigid) mounted on a 25 ft (7·6 m), two-storey enclosed tower structure. De-icing is provided by a battery of infra-red lights inside the radome. Radome

pressurising (when required), RF, and other electronic equipment is housed in the tower structure.

The temperate tower installation is designed for moderate or tropical climates. The 25 ft (7·6 m) supporting structure for the antenna includes an enclosure for RF equipment.

The mobile version (AN/MPS-14) is a six-truck, three-trailer system designed for transport on short notice to new strategic or tactical sites.

The reliability and capability of the basic AN/FPS-6 system has benefited from a continuous improvement programme. Sets with various improvements have been designated as AN/FPS-6A,

AN/FPS-6 heightfinder radar, temperate tower and arctic tower versions

AN/FPS-6B, AN/FPS-6C, AN/FPS-6D, AN/FPS-89 (**2513.153**) and AN/FPS-90. All these improvements are available in field conversion kit form for the updating of radar sets from earlier production.

CHARACTERISTICS
Peak power: 4·5 MW
Average power: 3·6 kW

Frequency: 2700 – 2900 MHz
PRF: 300 – 405 pps
Pulse width: 2 μs
Receiver sensitivity: NF <9·3 dB; MDS –108 dBm
Beam characteristics: Pencil beam
Beamwidth: Azimuth 3·2°; elevation 0·9°
Antenna azimuth rate: 180° in 4 s

Elevation rate: 20 or 30 nods/minute
Antenna gain: 38·5 dB
STATUS
Operational.
CONTRACTOR
General Electric Company, Electronic Systems Division, Syracuse, New York 13201, USA.

2526.153
AN/FPS-7 3-D SEARCH AND GCI RADAR
AN/FPS-7 is a very high power D-band (1250 to 1350 MHz) monopulse 3-D search radar. The equipment uses a stacked-beam heightfinding technique, the stack consisting of seven channels.

Search range is approximately 500 km and height coverage is up to 45 000 m. The transmitter output stage is a high power klystron which delivers 10 MW at any of up to ten preset transmitter frequencies and with a pulse width of six microseconds. A dual-channel transmitting system is provided. When channel A is connected to the antenna through the waveguide switch, channel B is fed to a dummy load. This feature permits full preventive maintenance to be performed without having the equipment off the air.

The basic radar uses several separate but identical receiving systems. Spare receiving channels are available, and may be switched in place of some of the active receivers. The receiver incorporates MTI and anti-jamming circuits.

CHARACTERISTICS
Peak power: 10 MW
Average power: 14·5 kW
Frequency: 1250 – 1350 MHz
PRF: 244 pps
Pulse width: 6 μs
Receiver sensitivity: NF = 9·5 dB
Beam characteristics: Stacked beam, cosec²
Beamwidth: Azimuth 1·4°; elevation 18°
Antenna azimuth rate: 3·3, 5, 6·6, and 10 rpm
STATUS
Operational. About 30 units produced.
CONTRACTOR
General Electric Company, Electronic Systems Division, Syracuse, New York 13201, USA.

AN/FPS-7 3-D search radar

2493.153
AN/FPS-8 SEARCH RADAR
The AN/FPS-8 is a medium-power D-band search radar designed for aircraft control and early warning and is installed at commercial airports and military bases both in the United States and overseas.

In most installations the antenna is exposed, being mounted on a temperate tower. For severe environmental conditions, the AN/FPS-8 is self-contained in an arctic tower with a protective radome.

Over the years improvements have been made to the basic AN/FPS-8, culminating in the present version whose nomenclature is AN/FPS-88 (V) (**2512.153**).

The AN/FPS-8 also has two mobile versions, the AN/MPS-11 and the AN/MPS-11A (**2495.153**).
CHARACTERISTICS
Peak power: 1 MW peak
Average power: 1·1 kW
Frequency: 1280 – 1380 MHz
PRF: 360 pps
Pulse width: 3 μs
Receiver sensitivity: FPS-8: NF 9 dB; FPS-88: NF ≤2·5 dB with parametric amp

Beam characteristics: Cosec²
Beamwith: FPS-88: azimuth 1·3°, elevation 58°; FPS-8: azimuth 2·5°, elevation 30°
Antenna azimuth rate: FPS-8: 0 – 10 rpm variable; FPS-88: 5, 10 rpm
STATUS
Operational. Over 200 produced.
CONTRACTOR
General Electric Company, Electronic Systems Division, Syracuse, New York 13201, USA.

AN/FPS-8 search radar

4327.153
AN/FPS-16 INSTRUMENTATION RADAR
The AN/FPS-16 tracking radar is designed specifically for range instrumentation purposes and is claimed to be the first to be so designed. Its transportable version is the AN/MPS-25. Both systems are C-band units. The antenna pedestal can be rotated continuously in azimuth and from –10 to +190° in elevation. First introduced in the mid-1950s, these units have been extensively modified in the intervening years; almost all now use integrated circuit electronics. Most of the 60 AN/FPS-16 and seven AN/MPS-25 radars have additional modifications including larger diameter antennas,

AN/FPS-16 instrumentation radar

3 MW transmitters, low noise receivers and pulse dopplers.

CHARACTERISTICS

Angle tracking precision (20 dB S/N): 0·1 mils rms
Range tracking precision (20 dB S/N): 4·7 m rms
Azimuth tracking rate: 750 mils/s
Azimuth tracking acceleration: 1020 mils/s²

Elevation tracking rate: 400 mils/s
Elevation tracking acceleration: 1020 mils/s²
Ro, IM², 0 dB S/N: 235 km

STATUS

In current use. Units are in operation at United States and United Kingdom ranges.

CONTRACTOR

RCA, Government Systems Division, Missile and Surface Radar, Moorestown, New Jersey 08057, USA.

2528.153

AN/FPS-20 – AN/FPS-100 FAMILY OF LONG-RANGE SEARCH AND GCI RADARS

AN/FPS-20 is one of a family of very long-range dual-channel search and GCI radars. It is widely used partly because it was one of the systems supplied under the MAP programme.

A D-band system, FPS-20 has a search range of some 350 km. The transmitter uses a power klystron with a 2 MW output. Pulse width is six microseconds and the PRF is 360 Hz. The antenna gain is 35 dB and the receiver noise figure 9 dB.

MTI is fitted and the radar has anti-jamming circuits. Data transmission facilities are included.

STATUS

In service in many countries. AN/FPS-20 and subsequent members of the family are used in the SAGE (**2803.181**) and AWCS (**2533.181**) systems. Other static radars in the family are AN/FPS-20A, -20B, -64, -65, -66, -67, and -100. AN/GPS-4 and AN/MPS-7 are the mobile versions.

CONTRACTOR

The Bendix Corporation, Communications Division, Baltimore, Maryland 21204, USA.

2494.153

AN/FPS-24 SEARCH RADAR

The AN/FPS-24 is a high-power low-frequency search radar. Each channel consists of 26 major cabinets, with an additional 11 cabinets that are common to both channels. It has very highly sophisticated anti-jamming features that make it extremely valuable in hostile environments.

The radar is usually installed in a six-storey building with the antenna on top. In severe climatic conditions the antenna is enclosed in a radome which is designed to withstand winds up to 150 knots. The overall antenna system weighs 92·5 tons.

CHARACTERISTICS

Peak power: 5 MW per channel
Average power: 25 kW with 278 pps, 18 μs pulse width
Frequency: 214 – 236 MHz
PRF: 278 pps
Pulse width: 6 μs without pulse compression; 18 μs with pulse compression
Receiver sensitivity: 4·5 dB NF; –113 dBm MDS
Beam characteristics: Cosec²
Beamwidth: Azimuth 2·9°; elevation 30°
Antenna azimuth rate: ¼ rpm CW or CCW; 5 rpm CW only

STATUS

Operational. Eleven systems have been built and are installed at USAF sites in the United States.

CONTRACTOR

General Electric Company, Electronic Systems Division, Syracuse, New York 13201, USA.

AN/FPS-24 search radar

2509.153

AN/FPS-49 EARLY WARNING AND TRACKING RADAR

One of the two basic types of radar used in the ballistic missile early warning system (BMEWS – **2525.181**), the AN/FPS-49 is a very large tracking radar that can also be used in a surveillance mode. It is installed at two of the three BMEWS sites, Thule (Greenland) and Fylingdales Moor (England). At the third site, Clear (Alaska), a slightly different radar, the AN/FPS-92 – which is an improved version of the AN/FPS-49 – is in use. Thus, the tracking radars at each of the three BMEWS stations have different designations, although they are essentially the same: Thule – AN/FPS-49A; Fylingdales Moor – AN/FPS-49; Clear – AN/FPS-92. The description that follows relates in the main to the AN/FPS-49 radars at Fylingdales Moor.

The main reception and transmission element is a 25 m diameter parabolic reflector mounted on a conical pedestal and capable of being rotated in azimuth and elevated and depressed so as either to track a detected target or to search for one continuously. A variety of possible scanning patterns provides for a number of search modes as well as for target acquisition and tracking. Scan rates of at least 10° per second are attainable and the powerful hydraulic drive system employed is said to eliminate backlash.

Dish illumination is, by four horns, to provide monopulse operation in both planes, with separate horns for reception. The system radio frequency is in the UHF band and the radar operates on several

FPS-49 radar dome at Fylingdales Moor (UK Ministry of Defence (Air))

frequencies in that band. Having regard to this and the dish diameter it is probably reasonable to suppose that the beamwidth, between half-power points, is in the region of 1 to 2°.

Output power is in the megawatt region, PRF is 27 pps (pulse duration unknown) and maximum range is about 5000 km. Each radar has three power amplifiers and in normal operation two of these are on-line at a time while the third is a 'hot spare' feeding into a dummy load. The receivers incorporate low-noise parametric amplifiers.

The antenna structure is protected from the elements by a 43 m diameter radome. This is of honeycomb-sandwich construction and consists of two high-density skins 1 mm thick with a Kraft-paper honeycomb core 15 cm thick. The honeycomb is made up in hexagonal and pentagonal blocks and 1646 of these blocks make up the radome. The transmission efficiency of the radome is 98 per cent; the average boresight error is 0·1 mil and the maximum error 0·3 mil; the boresight error rate is 0·005 mil.

STATUS

Operational. There was an FPS-49 installation in use at Moorestown, New Jersey, which filled a role in the 474N SLBM detection and warning system (see **2538.153** – FSS-7 radar – in *Jane's Weapon Systems 1980/81*) but this was phased out in December 1974. See note on FPS-50 status (**2511.153**) below.

In early 1976 the US DoD revealed proposals for a 'three-element' BMEWS improvement programme which would consist of upgrading the tactical operations room, replacing the original computers which are becoming increasingly difficult and costly to maintain, and improving the radar resolution. These modifications will ensure the continued usefulness of the system well into the 1980s. In February 1978, RCA received a $4 million contract for the modernisation of the tactical operations rooms at the Clear and Thule stations. An option to carry out similar work at Fylingdales was exercised in February 1979.

CONTRACTOR

RCA, Government Systems Division, Missile and Surface Radar, Moorestown, New Jersey 08057, USA.

2511.153

AN/FPS-50 EARLY WARNING RADAR

AN/FPS-50 is the big static radar of the ballistic missile early warning system (BMEWS). It is installed at two of the three BMEWS sites at Thule (Greenland) and Clear (Alaska); there are three radars at one site, and four at the other.

The radar uses a fixed antenna system comprising a 122 m wide and 50 m high parabolic-torus reflector which is fed by an organpipe scanner. Two narrow beams at two different angles of elevation are produced by this antenna and these two beams are caused to scan simultaneously over a sector in the near-horizontal plane so as to produce two horizontal direction fans, one above the other. As a missile passes through these beams its position and velocity co-ordinates are measured, from which can be calculated the trajectory, impact point, impact time and launch point.

A parabolic-torus reflector was chosen for this radar because it provides an economical measure of scanning the beam from a physically large antenna over a wide scan angle without deterioration of pattern over this arc. The disadvantages of the arrangement are the large size of the total assembly and the large sidelobes that appear in intermediate planes.

Scanning such a reflector can be achieved in various ways, but in the AN/FPS-50 it is accomplished by arranging a series of feeds on the focal points of the torus and switching the transmitter power from one point to the next with an organpipe scanner.

At Clear and Thule the AN/FPS-50 radar is used in conjunction with the AN/FPS-49A or AN/FPS-92 tracking radar. At the third station (Fylingdales Moor, England) only AN/FPS-49 or equivalent radars are used for early warning and tracking.

CHARACTERISTICS

Peak power: 5 MW
Average power: 300 kW
Frequency: 425 MHz range
PRF: 27
Pulse width: 2 ms

AN/FPS-50 early warning radar

STATUS

Operational, but see **1949.153** (Cobra Dane) and **1948.153** (Over-The-Horizon Radar) for probable changes in status of the BMEWS radars.

In early 1976 it was revealed that the DoD is proposing a three-element BMEWS improvement programme consisting of upgrading the tactical operations room, replacing the original computers which are becoming increasingly difficult and costly to maintain, and improving the radar resolution. These modifications will ensure BMEWS a useful life extending well into the 1980s.

CONTRACTOR

General Electric Company, Electronic Systems Division, Syracuse, New York 13201, USA.

AN/FPS-50 early warning radar

2546.153

AN/FPS-85 LONG-RANGE PHASED ARRAY RADAR

This is a very large fixed-array radar located in Florida with its principal axis aligned due south across the Gulf of Mexico and capable of transmitting and receiving over an arc extending 60° on either side of this axis.

A UHF system with a nominal frequency of 442 MHz, the radar uses separate transmit and receive arrays located side by side and both inclined at approximately 45° to the horizontal. Exact dimensions of the arrays are not known but the transmitter array is square, contains 5184 transmitter modules and has a side of something over 30 m. The receiver array is octagonal, contains some 39 000 antennas feeding 4660 receivers, and has a width of some 60 m.

Peak radiated power has been reported as 32 MW with a nominal transmitter beamwidth of 1·4°. Effective receiver beamwidth is said to be 0·8°. As already noted the radar beams are steerable over 120° arc in azimuth: in elevation the coverage is about 105°

– from the radar horizon to 15° beyond the zenith. The radar is thus able to track objects northwards at high elevation angles. In the normal tracking mode the receiver complex uses a 3 × 3 matrix of 'beams' (ie receiving directions) in a monopulse mode for optimum resolution. Radiated energy can be varied, by using different modulations, to suit target requirements. In the original design only two energy levels could be selected but additional modulators are being provided to extend the range of choice and hence improve the efficiency of the radar.

This power level selection, together with all other control functions, is performed by IBM 360/65 computers, there being two of these in main and standby roles in the radar complex. These computers are programmed with both routine surveillance and routine and special tracking requirements, they carry in their memory orbital details of space objects for routine tracking so that the radar beam can, at an appropriate time dependent both on its position and the relative priority of the observation, be pointed in the direction in which the target would lie if its orbit had not been perturbed: since both intentional and

accidental perturbation are common, the radar will normally have to execute a small search to locate and lock on the target.

Originally designed as the main US-based active sensor of the Spacetrack system (**2825.181**) the FPS-85 is now to be used also to supplement the FSS-7 radars of the SLBM detection system (**2810.181**) and to operate as an alternative space defence centre (ASDC). The FPS-85 receives its Spacetrack directions from NORAD space defence centre (SDC) which also has as its SPADATS inputs the BMEWS (**2525.181**) and the US Navy SPASUR sensors. At this centre all known data on space objects near the earth are filed in the computer memories and incoming data on a space object can be checked against these memories to determine whether or not it is a known object in approximately two seconds. To guard against computer or other failure at the SDC the same data are to be held on file at ASDC, which has an IBM 360/40 as well as its two IBM 360/65 computers, but in a form requiring more human intervention for a full search than is required at SDC. It is said that a full search at the ASDC may take one minute.

Similarly the SDC processes data from all SPADATS sensors fast enough to issue new orbital data for all stations three times a day, whereas the ASDC will be able to do this only once a day.

DEVELOPMENT

The FPS-85 was developed by Bendix, starting in 1962, and was the first large phased-array project in the USA. The first model was destroyed by fire in 1965 but was rebuilt and put into operation in 1969. It is currently operational in its Spacetrack role, dedication approximately one-third of its time to space surveillance and the remaining two-thirds to routine and special tracking assignments from NORAD. It is also now operational as an ASDC.

It was modified, by the addition of the new modulators referred to above and of suitable software, to perform the SLBM detection function.

CONTRACTORS

Prime contractor for the radar: The Bendix Corporation, Communications Division, East Joppa Road, Baltimore, Maryland 21204, USA.

Computers: IBM.

AN/FPS-85 phased array early warning radar

2512.153
AN/FPS-88 SURVEILLANCE RADAR
AN/FPS-88 is a medium-size D-band static surveillance radar. It is an improved version of the long-established AN/FPS-8 (**2493.153**), the improvements relating to range performance and to signal processing facilities.

The radar features a high-gain antenna, circular polarisation, dual-channel operation, a parametric amplifier receiver, and a radar signal processor with some ECCM capability. There is also provision for using the main antenna as an IFF radiator.
STATUS
Operational.
CONTRACTOR
General Electric Company, Electronic Systems Division, Syracuse, New York 13201, USA.

AN/FPS-88 surveillance radar

2513.153
AN/FPS-89 HEIGHTFINDING RADAR
The AN/FPS-89 is a high-power (4·5 MW, peak) E/F-band nodding-beam radar. Accuracy of heightfinding is ±1000 ft (300 m) at 110 nautical miles (203 km) range. It is an improved version of the AN/FPS-6 radar (**2492.153**), and like the AN/FPS-6 it is available in an

arctic tower installation, a temperate tower installation and a mobile version

An Italian licence-built version, AN/FPS-89S, is produced by GE, and among a number of improvements incorporated is a reduction in the receiver noise figure from 9 to 4·5 dB.

STATUS
Operational.
CONTRACTOR
General Electric Company, Electronic Systems Division, Syracuse, New York 13201, USA.

2847.153
AN/FPS-105(V) RANGE INSTRUMENTATION RADAR (CAPRI)
AN/FPS-105(V) is designed for range use to make accurate measurements of target position and velocity for performance evaluation. It can be installed either in a permanent ground station or be packaged for transportable use.

Its standard antenna is a 366 cm diameter solid-surface parabolic dish fed by a monopulse four-horn feed. Polarisation is vertical. The antenna can rotate continuously in azimuth and can be rotated through 200° (–10 to +190°) in elevation, a cable being used to avoid the need for a rotating joint. Microwave circuits are mounted on the rotating section of the antenna mounting. Larger antenna pedestals, 488 or 885 cm, are fitted to some systems. The transmitter will radiate single pulses, pairs, or triplets as required. Peak power is 1 MW and recurrence frequencies and pulse widths can be chosen for 160 and 640 pps and from 0·25, 0·5 and 1 microseconds respectively. Transmitter frequency is in the G/H-band.

The digital range tracker contains a precise

frequency standard and 'nth time round' circuits to enable a relatively high recurrence frequency to be used despite the long measuring ranges. Automatic search and lock-on are provided during target acquisition. Twenty-five bits of range data are supplied by the system at data rates up to 40 times per second.
CHARACTERISTICS
Azimuth tracking rate: 850 mils/s
Azimuth elevation tracking acceleration: 800 mils/s^2
Azimuth elevation tracking precision: 0·2 mils rms at 20 dB S/N
Elevation tracking rate: 500 mils/s
Range tracking precision: 4·7 m rms at 20 dB S/N
Unambiguous tracking range: 60 000 km
Ro, IM^2, 0 dB S/N: 200 km
STATUS
Five units of this configuration are in use at several US ranges.
CONTRACTOR
RCA, Government Systems Division, Missile and Surface Radar, Moorestown, New Jersey 08057, USA.

AN/FPS-105 (V) range instrumentation radar

4326.153
AN/FPS-117 AIR DEFENCE RADAR
The AN/FPS-117 solid-state radar system is an L-band, three-dimensional air defence radar designed to provide long-range accurate aircraft identification and position data for air defence, navigational assistance and tactical control for both close air support and counter air operations.

The system provides automatic adaptation to, and rejection of, land, sea and weather clutter by using clutter rejection processing. Adaptability in siting the radar is achieved by low-beam coverage enhanced by MTI processing, with doppler filtering for look-down beam positions on elevated sites. Sidelobe nulling is used to eliminate ground clutter for high beam positions.

The planar array measures 7·3 × 7·3 metres and produces a series of pencil beams phase-positioned

to scan in elevation up to 20° while the complete antenna rotates in azimuth. The elevation scan consists of 5 to 100 nautical miles short-range beams, and 100 to 250 nautical miles long-range beams. The use of pencil beams is designed to obtain elevation coverage while eliminating clutter problems associated with large transit beamwidths. The transmitter/receiver system consists of 44 row transmitters, each containing eight 100 W RF solid-state power modules, and 44 receiver modules, all mounted on the rear of the array.
CHARACTERISTICS
Range: 200 nm
Accuracy: 0·25 nm
Altitude: 100 000 ft (30 480 m)
Elevation angle: –6 to +20°
Transmitter power: 24·75 kW peak
Frequency: 1215 – 1400 MHz

Bandwidth: 185 MHz
Agility: 20 frequencies (quasi-random selection, beam-to-beam)
STATUS
Successful trials of the AN/FPS-117 to replace older search and heightfinding radars in Alaska have been completed. In April 1983, General Electric announced a $77 million contract for eight systems with an option for four more, and in July 1983 the company received a $16·4 million contract to obtain long-lead items for the latter. In January 1983 Hazeltine Corporation announced a $3·5 million contract for the supply of eight Seek Igloo IFF systems as an integral part of the AN/FPS-117.
CONTRACTOR
General Electric Company, Electronic Systems Division, Syracuse, New York 13201, USA.

3713 153
AN/GPN-22 PRECISION APPROACH RADAR
The AN/GPN-22 precision approach radar (PAR) is intended specifically for use in fixed base high-density ATC system operations under all weather conditions. It operates in X-band and is a development of the high-performance AN/TPN-25 PAR (**3712.153**) used in the USAF AN/TPN-19 landing control system (**2537.153**). Both these radars employ phased array antennas to perform simultaneous scanning and tracking modes over the full radar coverage volume without any mechanical motion of the antenna. In the case of the TPN-25, up to six aircraft targets can be monopulse tracked simultaneously; in the case of GPN-22, the same number of targets can be handled but the coverage pattern measures 20 × 8° compared with the 20 × 15° of the earlier equipment. The range is about 35 km in both cases. Provisions are made for the display of landing aircraft position data in the operations centre up to 3500 m from the radar head.

The only significant difference between the GPN-22 and the TPN-25 is in the physical arrangements of the antenna. The GPN-22 feed assembly is supported by a boom structure projecting over the upper edge of the main reflector, whereas in the TPN-25 it is mounted beside the reflector.

STATUS
Deliveries have been made of 39 sets to the USAF, 2 sets to Austria and 11 sets to the Netherlands.
CONTRACTOR
Raytheon Company, Equipment Division, Wayland, Massachusetts 01178, USA.

2497.153
AN/MPQ-4 MORTAR LOCATING RADAR
The AN/MPQ-4 provides quick identification to pinpoint enemy mortar positions in map co-ordinates, enabling artillery units to launch counter-attacks. It uses a two-beam intercept principle of location with positive first-shell acquisition and has the capability for handling multiple targets.

All the equipment is mounted on two two-wheel trailers, each designed for its specific purpose. One trailer carries the primary radar equipment, while the other carries the primary power supply (a petrol engine generator set) and auxiliary equipment such as cable and spare parts.

The AN/MPQ-4 can be operated from virtually any site and can be set up in 15 minutes. Once set up it can be operated by one man. The operating and control console may be used on the equipment trailer or in a remote location.

CHARACTERISTICS
Frequency: 16 GHz
Peak power: 50 kW (minimum)
PRF: 8·6 kHz
Pulse width: 0·25 μs
Detection range: 10 000 m (max); 170 m (minimum)
Sector scan: 25°
Elevation coverage: 6 to +12°
Accuracy: Within 50 m at 10 000 m
Presentation: B scope, 140 mm CRT
Weight: 2268 kg
Mounting: 2-wheel trailer
Antenna: Reflector with Foster dual scanner feed
STATUS
Operational. It is produced under licence in Japan as

AN/MPQ-4 mortar locating radar

the Type 92 mortar locating radar JAN/MPQ-N1.
CONTRACTOR
General Electric Company, Electronic Systems Division, Syracuse, New York 13201, USA.

2500.153
AN/MPQ-10A MORTAR LOCATING RADAR
The AN/MPQ-10A radar was initially developed in August 1950 by the US Army Electronics Command and was the first American mortar locating radar system. A total of 485 radar sets were delivered to the US Army between September 1951 and September 1954. Radar AN/MPQ-10A is a mobile radar designed to locate and track mortar and artillery shells. It can be used with associated recording equipment to locate the point of origin and point of impact of the projectile. Further information is given under this entry number in previous editions of *Jane's Weapon Systems*.

CONTRACTOR
Sperry Corporation, Electronic Systems, Great Neck, New York, USA.

4478.153
AN/MPQ-53 GUIDANCE RADAR
The AN/MPQ-53 is a multi-function radar group which performs all the surveillance, IFF, tracking and guidance functions entailed in the Patriot (XMIM-104) tactical air defence missile system (**2800.131**). The antenna array is a multi-element phased-array planar configuration carried on a semi-trailer chassis. The antenna unit has separate arrays for target detection and tracking, missile guidance and IFF functions. The last of these tasks is carried out by an AN/TPX-46(V)7 interrogator, using supplementary arrays adjacent to the main circular search and track array on the antenna unit. Other supplementary arrays are for command and guidance signal transmission and reception.

STATUS
Entering service with US forces, planned for NATO use in Europe.
CONTRACTORS
Prime contractor: Raytheon Company, Andover, Massachusetts, USA.
    IFF interrogator: Hazeltine Corporation, Commack, New York 11725, USA.

Side view of AN/MPQ-53 missile guidance and control radar group for Patriot air defence missile system reveals main planar array and supplementary antennas for other functions on single unit which folds down for transit

---

5628.153
REAL-TIME VELOCIMETER RADAR (RTVS)
This system is a transportable X-band CW artillery tracking radar designed to measure and record target radial range, velocity, acceleration and angular position. The equipment is carried in two mobile elements; an antenna trailer which contains the transmitter and receiver plus the steerable antenna system and a control cabin which carries the operator control console and data processing units. The RTVS is intended to allow tracking of targets from 100 to 10 000 ft/s and will acquire and track targets down to 0·0032 m² at ranges up to 20 km. Accuracy at 20 km is stated to be 1 ft/s for velocity, 1 ft/s² for acceleration and 6 m in range. Operating frequency of the radar is pre-tunable between 10 and 10·26 GHz.
CONTRACTOR
Datron Systems Inc, 20700 Plummer Street, Chatsworth, California 91311, USA.

2495.153
AN/MPS-11 AND AN/MPS-11A SEARCH RADARS
The AN/MPS-11 and AN/MPS-11A are mobile versions of the AN/FPS-8 medium-power D-band search radar (**2493.153**). The difference between the two mobile versions is that the AN/MPS-11 antenna is mounted after arrival at site on a manually erected tower, while the AN/MPS-11A antenna is permanently installed for transport and operation on a 40 mm gun carriage, permitting more rapid initial operating capability.

The AN/MPS-11 may be transported by aircraft or by two trailers and nine M35 trucks. Set-up time, with 15 men, is two hours.
STATUS
Operational.

AN/MPS-11A search radar
CONTRACTOR
General Electric Company, Electronic Systems Division, Syracuse, New York 13201, USA.

AN/MPS-11 search radar

2496.153
AN/MPS-14 HEIGHTFINDING RADAR

The AN/MPS-14 radar is the mobile version of the AN/FPS-6 high-power E/F-band nodding-beam radar (2492.153). It is designed for transport by six trucks and three trailers to temporary strategic or tactical sites. Trailers are functionally designed for quick loading and unloading, and assembly and disassembly may be accomplished in rapid and efficient fashion.

The trailers serve the dual purpose of transporting the equipment and supporting certain electronic components during operation. For example, the RF

equipment need not be removed from the trailer for operation, and the entire unit is protected by a prefabricated shelter assembled at the site. The shelter is equipped with space heaters and lighting fixtures.

The AN/MPS-14 system's electronic components are identical to and interchangeable with those of the AN/FPS-6.

STATUS
Operational.

CONTRACTOR
General Electric Company, Electronic Systems Division, Syracuse, New York 13201, USA.

AN/MPS-14 heightfinder radar

2514.153
AN/MPS-36 INSTRUMENTATION TRACKING RADAR

AN/MPS-36 is a C-band mobile instrumentation radar built originally in 1970 for the US Army testing grounds at White Sands Missile Range.

The radar can accurately track targets travelling up to 36 000 knots at ranges up to 60 000 km. Data accuracy has been measured at one metre in range and target velocities within 5 cm/s on trajectories of missiles and missile re-entry vehicles.

Advanced integrated circuits are extensively designed into the equipment and pulse doppler capability is integral. A general-purpose computer has been integrated into the radar to provide pulse doppler signal processing. Polarisations are console selectable.

The radar is housed in a 12·4 m electronics trailer and a 366 cm diameter antenna is mounted on an 11 m pedestal trailer. With this arrangement, the radar can be moved from site to site by road, air, or sea and be operational within eight hours after arrival.

CHARACTERISTICS
Transmitter power: 1 MW minimum
Antenna gain: 43 dB minimum
Antenna beamwidth: 1·2° max
Antenna sidelobes: 20 dB minimum
Pedestal coverage (elevation): −5 to −185°
Pedestal coverage (azimuth): Continuous
Azimuth tracking rate: 890 mils/s
Elevation tracking rate: 500 mils/s
Azimuth acceleration rate: 400 mils/s^2
Elevation acceleration rate: 400 mils/s^2
Azimuth tracking precision at 20 dB S/N: 0·2 mils, rms
Elevation tracking precision at 20 dB S/N: 0·2 mils, rms
Range tracking precision at 20 dB S/N: 2·7 m rms
Range rate tracking precision at 20 dB S/N: <0·03 m/s rms accuracy
Unambiguous range tracking: 60 000 km
Installation time to power on: 8 h max
Receiver noise figure: 4 dB max
Ro, IM^2, 0 dB S/N: 350 km
Reliability (design goal): MTBF 100 h

STATUS
The first equipment was delivered in 1970 and met or exceeded all design specifications. Fourteen radars are now operational at US test ranges and three have been provided to the Federal Republic of Germany. The radars are used for studies of weapons systems and space programmes.

CONTRACTOR
RCA, Government Systems Division, Missile and Surface Radar, Moorestown, New Jersey 08057, USA.

AN/MPS-36 missile tracking radar

2540.153
AN/PPS-5 COMBAT SURVEILLANCE RADAR

AN/PPS-5 is a portable battlefield radar designed to detect and locate individual men up to 5000 m and groups of men or small vehicles up to 10 000 m. A later model, the AN/PPS-5B, which incorporates advanced technology, is now the standard equipment.

The AN/PPS-5 solves the major problems of personnel detection radars by providing automatic sector azimuth scanning and range coverage with visual display of moving targets over the sectors under line-of-sight surveillance. The radar can be switched from MTI operation to normal operation, permitting the operator to locate fixed targets.

A range-gated filter MTI processor is especially suitable for detecting targets moving as slowly as 1·6 km/h. Operation while scanning is silent.

The control/indicator unit provides remote control of the radar set with the appropriate readout and control devices as well as visual displays of 10 000 m range in 5000 m increments on both MTI and normal displays (A-scope and B-scope). Target range is measured by a manually controlled magnetostrictive

delay line coupled to a counter; this system was selected instead of the more conventional pulse-delay system because it permits table calibration without having to add calibrators and to make slope, zero, and other adjustments. Target range is measured by a manual range control knob coupled to a direct-reading range counter. A range mark on the display scope shows the position of the range gate. An aural doppler processor consisting of a clutter filter and audio amplifier drives the headphones.

A 50-channel range-gated filter system is used to provide MTI over a 5000 m range. Each range-gated filter channel in the system sequentially covers a 100 m range increment. Each channel is identical in design. The outputs from the 50 filters are added to provide MTI video for the displays.

The selectable scan speeds are held relatively constant by a feedback motor-speed control circuit that supplies only enough power to meet the demand in the presence of varying wind loads; this conserves power. Azimuth co-ordinate readout is obtained remotely from a follow-up servo that repeats the antenna position data. To minimise power consumption, this control is used on demand by the

operator only when fine azimuth data are desired.

One version of the radar set has been equipped with a 360° scan and a PPI display kit for the US Army Special Forces. Another version of the radar set has been installed in a vehicle and used for perimeter protection of air bases.

The equipment works in the 16 to 16·5 GHz band (tunable) and has a peak power of 1 kW and a PRF of 4000 pps. An accuracy of ±20 m in range and ±10 mils in azimuth can be achieved.

Physically the equipment consists of three rugged packages weighing about 40 kg. Power consumption is about 57 W.

STATUS
Quantity deliveries of the PPS-5 have continued over a period of some years. The PPS-5B is now the standard issue in the US Army. In addition to the USA, other unspecified governments have been using the AN/PPS-5A since 1967 and are procuring the AN/PPS-5B.

CONTRACTOR
Eaton Corporation, AIL Division, Deer Park, Long Island, New York 11729, USA.

5604.153
AN/PPS-6 BATTLEFIELD SURVEILLANCE RADAR

AN/PPS-6 is a man-portable tripod-mounted X-band non-coherent pulse-doppler radar capable of automatic scanning and giving an audible indication of the presence of moving targets. The transmitter/receiver and small parabolic antenna form a single unit which, with the angular control

assembly, is mounted on a folding tripod, and the user has the option of manual control of the pointing direction or any of three azimuth sector scans.

There is also a choice of range sectors. A range gate enables the user to search an area of 45 m depth in range beyond a chosen range; in the automatic modes the equipment will either scan continuously an area extending in range for 315 m beyond a chosen

range, or search, in alternate sweeps, this area and a further area extending from the 315 m range to 630 m beyond the chosen range. When a target is located its co-ordinates can be determined by manually adjusting the antenna and range control for maximum signal, and reading off the required angle and range.

CHARACTERISTICS
Frequency: 9 – 9·5 GHz
Range: Personnel 1500 m; vehicles 3000 m
Accuracy: Azimuth ±18 mils; range ±25 m
Sector scans: 600, 900 or 1200 mils
Weight: 20 kg
Power supply: Battery

STATUS
In current production and in service with US forces.
CONTRACTOR
General Instrument Corporation, Government Systems Division, 600 West John Street, Hicksville, New York 11802, USA.

5616.153
AN/PPS-11/12 BATTLEFIELD SURVEILLANCE RADARS

The AN/PPS-11 is a hand-held battlefield surveillance radar which weighs only 4·5 kg. It is a modulated CW doppler correlation equipment, operating in Z-band with a range of approximately 1 km against vehicles and an accuracy of 8 m. The operation of the system is extremely simple in that once the equipment has detected a target in the 1 km range, the operator can narrow the options by selecting various range gates until the target is fixed and the range and bearing are available. An audio signal is also available for identification of the type of target.

An improved and expanded version of this equipment, known as the AN/PPS-12, weighs about 7 kg and has an increased range of up to 3 km. A number of refinements, such as automatic scanning, automatic target warning and simultaneous scan and search have also been provided.
CONTRACTOR
RCA, Government Systems Division, Missile and Surface Radar, Moorestown, New Jersey 08057, USA.

1947.153
AN/PPS-15A INFANTRY RADAR

The AN/PPS-15A is a J-band (former X-band), lightweight ground surveillance radar for the detection and location of moving targets such as men, vehicles, or boats. Range and azimuth of a moving target are read directly from solid-state LED displays, and the nature of the target is deduced from its aural signature. The radar set consists of the antenna assembly, control indicator, an antenna drive, a headset, a tripod, remote cable and an internal disposable battery which provides power for 12 hours continuous operation. The AN/PPS-15A can be hand-held, pintle or tripod mounted and remotely controlled. The control indicator and antenna assembly are integral for most operations but may be separated for remote operation at distances up to nine metres. Automatic sector scan can be centred on a selectable bearing, and the scan width also is selectable. Elevation control is manual.

Target returns are fed to an 'all-range' channel and a 'discrete-range' channel. During search, the all-range channel automatically discriminates against clutter and produces both aural and visual alarms when a moving target is detected. During ranging, the discrete-range channel produces a light display and an increased doppler tone when a moving target enters a range gate positioned by an operator-control. Both channels are active during the search-range mode, enabling an operator to monitor detected targets on the all-range channel as he ranges a selected target by means of the discrete-range gate control.
CHARACTERISTICS
Frequency: Low J-band
Peak power: 50 mW
Antenna: 20 × 30 cm
Mode: Homodyne
Weight: 10·7 kg (remote operation)
Detection ranges: Personnel 1·5 km; vehicles 3 km
Battery: BA4386/PRC-25
STATUS
The AN/PPS-15A radar equipment has been US Army 'type classified' for use to the armed services, and the following have been delivered: 167 to Argentina, 213 to Canada, 25 to Norway, 150 to Spain, 40 to the UN and 1000 to various US military units. Additional sales have recently been made to the UN and Norway, and both Israel and Taiwan have taken delivery of an unspecified number. Advanced versions are being developed and tested.
CONTRACTOR
General Dynamics, Electronics Division, PO Box 81127, San Diego, California 92138, USA.

AN/PPS-15A lightweight ground surveillance radar

4324.153
AN/PPS-15B BASE SECURITY RADAR

The AN/PPS-15B is a development of the AN/PPS-15A and provides additional surveillance capability in a 350 m range segment, divided into seven 50 m range gates. The system is designed to detect and locate moving targets, eg vehicles and personnel, to provide perimeter surveillance for virtually any type of installation.

The 350 m segment may be positioned by the operator anywhere within the detection range of the system to provide surveillance without interference from, or alarms caused by, traffic moving inside the base perimeter itself. The seven range gates are individually displayed to provide automatic detection. Sector scan width is variable, by the operator, between limits of 22 and 180°. Five transmitter frequencies are available for selection by the operator. Power sources are supplied with the radar which can be operated from either AC (115 or 230 V) or DC (12 or 24 V).

The AN/PPS-15B can be hand-held, pintle or tripod mounted and remotely controlled. Both aural and visual alarms are produced when a moving target is detected, and the LED type display is identical to that of the AN/PPS-15A.
CHARACTERISTICS
Frequency: Low J-band
Detection range: 3000 m
Remoting: 35 m
Power source (external): 115/230 V AC, 12/24 V DC
Weight
Radar: 15 kg (including DC power source and cable)
DC power source: 7 kg
AC power source/battery charger: 9·5 kg
Remote cable and reel: 7 kg
STATUS
In service with the US armed forces.
CONTRACTOR
General Dynamics, Electronics Division, PO Box 81127, San Diego, California 92138, USA.

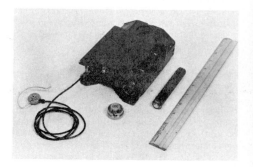

AN/PPS-15B base security radar

5605.153
AN/PSS-10 BATTLEFIELD RADAR RECEIVER

The AN/PSS-10 is a miniature battlefield radar receiver, weighing only 680 grammes, which is capable of detecting battlefield radars at distances well beyond their effective detection range. It is designed for hand carrying and indicates direction and the type of radar being detected.

The unit comes with special cold weather kit which allows it to be operated in temperatures down to −48°C.
STATUS
The equipment has been developed under a US Army Electronics Command contract.
CONTRACTOR
General Instrument Corporation, Government Systems Division, 600 West John Street, Hicksville, New York 11802, USA.

AN/PSS-10 miniature battlefield radar receiver

4325.153
TYPE 386 GROUND SURVEILLANCE RADAR

The model 386 radar is the latest in a range of ground surveillance radars produced by General Dynamics. The equipment is currently in the late development phase and is a lightweight system with a detection range of 6 km. A number of advanced features have been incorporated, including a hand-held remote control/indicator unit with keyboard push-button controls and a 32 × 16 LED matrix synthetic B-scope display for visual presentation of moving target information. Target detection tracking and alarm warning is automatic and a radar netting capability is incorporated. Remote operation is available out to approximately 1·5 km using a standard military single pair field wire.

Both visual and aural warning is provided, target doppler being fed to the operator's headset for identification. Sector scan width is variable by the operator from 22·5 to 90°.

CHARACTERISTICS
Frequency: Low J-band (previously X-band)
Detection range: To 6 km
Modulation: CW pseudo-random code (PRN)
Power output: 100 mW
Sector scan width: Adjustable 22·5° to 90°
Weight: Basic radar (9 m remote) 12·6 kg; extended remote (optional to 1·5 km) 16 kg
STATUS
The radar has been demonstrated in US Army and US Air Force tests using RF and field wire links for remote operation.
CONTRACTOR
General Dynamics, Electronics Division, PO Box 81127, San Diego, California 92138, USA.

Model 386 lightweight ground surveillance radar

3129.153
AN/TPN-18A RADAR

The AN/TPN-18A ground controlled approach radar system, developed for the US Army, is a lightweight, tactical ground-based radar which provides precise three-function information to airport/heliport controllers. These functions consist of terminal area surveillance, precision approach for control of landings, and heightfinding for aircraft monitoring. This versatile system is readily transported by helicopter, cargo aircraft, or truck, and is suitable for truck/trailer mounting for full mobility in combat-related operations. The earlier TPN-8 version, designed for the US Marine Corps' military all-weather tactical operations, has since been adapted by other military services. Radar set AN/TPN-18A is a component of landing control central AN/TSQ-71A and AN/TSQ-72.

CHARACTERISTICS
Type: Pulse modulated
Frequency: 9 – 9·6 GHz
Peak power: 200 kW nominal
PRF: 1200 pps
Pulse width: 0·2 or 0·8 µs
Range: 8, 16, 32, and 64 km (128 km for IFF). 5, 10, 20, and 40 miles (80 miles for IFF)
Displays: Surveillance – PPI
Approach – B-scope
Elevation beam: 1·1° vertical, and 3·4° horizontal, vertical or circular polarisation
Azimuth beam: 3·5° vertical, cosec^2 to 2·7°, and 1·3° horizontal, horizontal or circular polarisation
STATUS
In US Army service. In February 1978, a contract was placed for 46 product improved TPN-18A radars. These incorporate new solid-state modules and built-in test equipment.
CONTRACTOR
ITT-Gilfillan, 7821 Orion Avenue, Van Nuys, California 91409, USA.

ITT-Gilfillan AN/TPN-18A precision approach radar

2537.153
AN/TPN-19 LANDING CONTROL CENTRAL

AN/TPN-19 is a terminal ATC system comprising an airport surveillance radar (ASR), a precision approach radar (PAR) (AN/TPN-24 and AN/TPN-25 respectively), and an operations centre. The radar systems are linked to the operations centre by microwave links (10 nautical miles). The system is designed for rapid world-wide deployment as well as fixed base installations. Packaging techniques make the system completely transportable by aircraft, helicopter or road vehicle.

The AN/TPN-24 ASR (**3711.153**) is a dual-channel, 2 × 500 kW E/F-band, MTI radar. Its most noteworthy features are a multiple (12) horn antenna feed which produces lobe-free coverage up to 12 000 metres and 60 nautical miles on a 1 m² target; a low-angle pattern which is electrically variable and programmable in

range and azimuth to reduce clutter returns; a digital coherent and non-coherent MTI system to eliminate weather returns, and a staggered PRF to eliminate blind speeds below 1100 knots.

The AN/TPN-25 PAR (**3712.153**) is said to represent a significant advance in the state-of-the-art. Operating in I/J-band, it has a range of 20 nautical miles even with precipitation at 5 cm/hour. This results from the use of the narrow pencil beam (0·75 × 1·4°) produced by the 824-element phased-array antenna of 320 kW. A monopulse system, it can track up to six targets simultaneously. For multiple runway coverage the antenna assembly can be slewed through 270°.

In the GCA configuration there are three displays but through simple modular extension the system provides seven displays for a full RAPCON configuration. All displays are dual mode and can be

changed to display either an ASR or PAR presentation simultaneously.
STATUS
Both the complete TPN-19 and separate examples of the two radar sets incorporated in it have been supplied or ordered for US and foreign forces. The US Air Force has 11 TPN-19s; Australia has one TPN-19, six TPN-25 PARs and one TPN-24 ASR; the Netherlands has fixed installations for six TPN-24 ASRs and 11 GPN-22 PARs (the latter being an improved TPN-25); Austria has one GPN-22 with options on more; the US Air Force is taking delivery of 39 GPN-22s; and West Germany is being supplied with 44 TPN-24s for fixed base installation.
CONTRACTOR
Raytheon Company, Equipment Division, Wayland, Massachussets 01178, USA.

4075.153
AN/TPN-22 PRECISION APPROACH AND LANDING RADAR

The AN/TPN-22 is a precision track-while-search radar that uses phase/frequency scanning to provide high data rates for automatic detection and tracking while simultaneously searching a 46 × 8° sector. The radar consists of antenna, transmitter, receiver, digital processor and sub-systems.

The AN/TPN-22 planar array antenna operates at I-band (former X-band) and radiates a computer-controlled pencil beam using phase/frequency scanning. The antenna consists of 94 electronic digitally controlled diode phase shifters feeding 94

serpentine arrays and incorporates circular polarisation for improved performance in bad weather.

The transmitter final stage consists of an air-cooled, high-power TWT using a solid-state regulated high voltage power supply and line-type modulator. The transmitter first stage is also a TWT amplifier.

The receiver, a double conversion superheterodyne configuration, uses a GaAsFET amplifier and provides flexible operation through the incorporation of STC, AGC, GAGC and CFAR features. A three-pulse (track mode) digital moving target indicator is provided for rain discrimination.

The data processor consists of an AN/UYK-20 general-purpose computer and a hard-wired special-purpose digital processor. The data processor controls and operates the radar under the local direction of the radar system operator or the remote command and control segment. The special-purpose digital processor provides major support to the general-purpose UYK-20 by performing general radar system control and communication functions. The digital processor also provides an interface with the general-purpose computer and the display, receiver, transmitter and antenna sub-systems.

The AN/TPN-22 precision approach and landing radar is an integral part of the Marine Air Traffic

Control and All-weather Landing System (MATCALS) under production by the Naval Electronic Systems Command to upgrade air traffic control and all-weather landing control capabilities at Marine Corps' expeditionary airfields. The system is transportable by truck or helicopter.

The AN/TPN-22 provides three landing modes:
Mode I: automatic control via the aircraft flight control system from acquisition to touchdown
Mode II: control of cockpit landing display including

pseudo-ILS flight path error presentation for pilot controlled approach and Mode I monitoring. Pseudo-MLS capability is planned
Mode III: ground controlled approach using voice communications between controller and pilot 'talkdown'.

CHARACTERISTICS
Frequency: 9 – 9·2 GHz
Peak power: 120 kW
Average power: 180 W

Pulse duration: 0·25 μs
PRF: 6000 – 4200 pps
Antenna
Azimuth scan: 46, 30 and 20° (30 and 20° steerable)
Elevation scan: 8°
Azimuth beamwidth: 0·98° at beam normal
Elevation beamwidth: 0·67° at beam normal
Track data rate: Variable, approx 5/s (minimum) to 10/s (max)
MTI: 2-pulse canceller (search); 3-pulse canceller (track)
Track capacity: 6 targets simultaneously
Search data rate: 4 s max for 46° when tracking 6 targets
Detection: 10 nm on 2 m² target in 1-inch/h, 5 mile rain cell
Minimum range: 228 m from radar
Detection probability: 95% cumulative in acquisition gate
False alarm probability: 10⁻⁴ (false track)
Droptrack probability: 10⁻⁶ (false track)
Accuracy
Azimuth: ±0·086°
Elevation: ±0·057°
Range: ±3 m or 1% of range whichever is greater
System weight: 3628 kg (equipment group); 2494 kg (antenna group)
Set-up time: 1 h (4-man crew)
STATUS
A production system has been in operation at NATC Patuxent River, Maryland since 1981. Production is now completed. The first full-automatic (hands-off) landings to touchdown were conducted in April 1979 at Patuxent River.
CONTRACTOR
ITT-Gilfillan, 7821 Orion Avenue, Van Nuys, California 91409, USA.

ITT-Gilfillan AN/TPN-22 precision approach and landing radar developed for the US Marine Corps

4077.153
PAR-80 PRECISION APPROACH RADAR
The ITT-Gilfillan PAR-80 is a fixed site, turntable-mounted, precision approach radar (PAR) set that features a pencil-beam planar array antenna employing ferrite phase shifters for azimuth beam displacement and mechanical actuator for vertical beam positioning. Radar scan angles of 30° in azimuth and 7° in elevation when combined with the 10 or 20 nautical mile radar range provide large service volume coverage for all aircraft types and traffic pattern variations. The PAR-80 utilises circular polarisation for operation in adverse weather, with optional constant false alarm rate (CFAR) circuitry.

The radar set group (antenna, scan programmer, and the dual receiver/transmitters) are pallet-mounted on a turntable that is remotely controlled for coverage of multiple runway approaches. Control/indicators with an accompanying video processor may be remotely controlled from operations centres or control towers up to 3048 m distant.

The PAR-80 incorporates solid-state design, digital clutter-reduction sub-systems, dual-channel radar transmitters and receivers, high-gain low-sidelobe antenna, remote control of PAR landing direction with four sets of preset course and glideslope cursors and other features.

This equipment is related to the AN/TPN-22 (4075.153) and there are a number of common design features. The PAR-80 produces a greater RF output though, and the antenna and its mounting arrangements differ somewhat from those of the TPN-22.
CHARACTERISTICS
Frequency: 9000 – 9160 MHz
Pulse width: 0·2 μs
PRF: 3450 Hz
Peak power: 150 kW
Beamwidth: 1·1° horizontal × 0·6° vertical
Antenna gain: 45 dB
Sidelobes: –22 dB max
Max range: 30 nm
Resolution: 1·1° azimuth; 0·6° elevation; 70 m range
Receiver noise: 11 dB max
Signal processing: Lin/log FTC and linear; log CFAR (optional)
STATUS
ITT-Gilfillan was awarded a $41 million contract in 1979 for the producton and support of PAR-80 equipments to the Federal Republic of Germany. The radars are being installed at West German Air Force and Navy bases. A further contract for $11 million was awarded in 1981 for the supply of six systems to Belgian Air Force bases.

ITT-Gilfillan PAR-80 precision approach radar

CONTRACTOR
ITT-Gilfillan, 7821 Orion Avenue, Van Nuys, California 91409, USA.

5623.153
ARSR-3/ASR-30 SURVEILLANCE RADARS
The ARSR-3 and the ASR-30 are minimally attended D-band surveillance radars which are suitable for both civil and military requirements. The systems meet both FAA and military specifications and use the latest technology.

The ARSR-3 provides cover up to 200 nautical miles (370 km) in range and 100 000 feet (30 km) in elevation against a 2 m² target. A number of refinements are used to detect small targets against

heavy clutter. These include dual beam elevation pattern to enhance short range detection, an antenna pattern which produces a sharp cut-off underside to reduce ground returns, and RF sensitivity time control to eliminate close-in ground reflections.

The ARSR-3 has complete redundancy in electronics with extensive built-in test equipment, and a demonstrated MTBF of 3000 hours. The system also has a very high weather clutter cancellation feature by the use of circular polarisation.

The ASR-30 is based on the ARSR-3 and is a dual

channel D-band surveillance radar that will detect small aircraft (2 m²) out to 120 nautical miles (220 km). Using the circular polarisation mode, targets can be detected throughout severe weather conditions and it is claimed to reject weather with over 40 times the efficiency of S-band surveillance radars.
CONTRACTOR
Westinghouse Electric Corporation, PO Box 746, Baltimore, Maryland, USA.

3711.153
AN/TPN-24 AIRPORT SURVEILLANCE RADAR
The AN/TPN-24 is the airfield surveillance radar employed in the AN/TPN-19 landing control central system (2537.153), and was orginally designed for that system although it has subsequently been widely

delivered separately for use on its own or with other equipment. The original version was designed and packaged for use as a highly mobile, tactical radar equipment, but other versions have been configured for different applications, including a fixed site variant, a tower-mounted model (ASR-910), and a

semi-static version designated the ASR-909. The antenna and transmitter/receiver units are the same in each version as those of the basic AN/TPN-24 (see nearby photograph).

CHARACTERISTICS

Radar: Dual channel, dual frequency, diversity. Redundant or single channel and spectrum filter options

Frequency: 2700 – 2900 MHz

Transmitter type: Magnetron

Peak power: 500 kW (per channel)

Pulse length: 1 μs

Pulse rate: 1050 pps, average

PRF: 12 staggers

Antenna size: 4·26 × 2·43 m

Azimuth beamwidth: 1·6°

Elevation beamwidth: 4°

Rotation speed: 13 rpm

Beam elevation tilt: +15 to –2°

Detection range: 110 km (clear weather, 1 m² target)

STATUS

In addition to those supplied for use in AN/TPN-19 systems (a total of about 12) more than 50 separate AN/TPN-24 sets have been supplied or ordered, including: 44 fixed base installations for West Germany and six similar installations for the Netherlands. The AN/TPN-24 has also been supplied to Australia and Austria.

CONTRACTOR

Raytheon Company, Equipment Division, Wayland, Massachusetts 01178, USA.

AN/TPN-24 landing control central

3712.153

AN/TPN-25 PRECISION APPROACH RADAR

The Raytheon AN/TPN-25 is the high-performance precision approach radar (PAR) developed for the AN/TPN-19 landing control central tactical airfield control system (**2537.153**). Designed to fulfil a requirement for a highly mobile system capable of assisting the landing of fixed-wing aircraft and helicopters in adverse weather conditions, the

AN/TPN-25 can also be deployed at fixed bases. It employs a unique phased-array antenna that constantly scans the entire service volume of 20 × 15° and 35 km in range, as well as tracking up to six approaching aircraft in elevation and azimuth. No antenna movement is required except when it is necessary to re-orientate it to allow a different runway direction to be used. This can be performed under remote control to permit any one of four runways on

an airfield to be served. The TPN-25 is capable of automatic remote feeding of guidance information to the landing aircraft via a data link.

Operation is in the radar I-band and no mechanical scanning is necesary. A four-lobe monopulse feed horn is directed at the main antenna reflector, radiation having to pass through a digitally-controlled microwave 'lens' consisting of an array of 824 phase-shifting elements. The latter are controlled to produce sharp, digitally-steered, step-scanned pencil beams.

CHARACTERISTICS

Radar: Single-channel, dual function (scan/track)

Frequency: 9000 – 9200 MHz

Transmitter type: Solid-state oscillator with TWT and CFA amplifiers

Peak power: 320 kW

Pulse length: 1 μs

PRF: 3500 pps (average)

Stagger ratio: 3:2

Antenna beamwidth: 1·4° azimuth; 0·75° elevation

Detection range: 37 km (clear weather, trainer aircraft target)

STATUS

Production. Apart from about 12 sets supplied as part of complete US Air Force AN/TPN-19 systems, another eight equipments have been supplied to Australia, both as fixed-base systems and in the tactical mobile mode. A development of the AN/TPN-25, with higher performance characteristics, has been developed as the AN/GPN-22 and this has been ordered and supplied in quantity both to the US Air Force and to foreign customers (**3713.153**).

CONTRACTOR

Raytheon Company, Equipment Division, Wayland, Massachusetts 01178, USA.

AN/TPN-25 PAR

2498.153

AN/TPQ-10 RADAR COURSE DIRECTING CENTRAL

The AN/TPQ-10 radar course directing central is designed to provide accurate all-weather guidance to aircraft for performance of close air support missions.

The equipment consists of a tracking radar and an operational shelter containing the radar controls, a computer, displays and communication equipment.

Designed specifically for tactical air operations, it is easily transported by helicopter, cargo aircraft or truck.

Further information is given under this entry number in previous editions of *Jane's Weapon Systems.*

STATUS

Twenty-three production systems were built and delivered to the US Marine Corps from 1960 onward.

The system saw extensive use in Viet-Nam, and is still in operational use in US Marine Corps air support squadrons.

CONTRACTOR

General Electric Company, Electronic Systems Division, Syracuse, New York 13201, USA.

1526.153

FORWARD AREA ALERTING RADAR AN/TPQ-32/MPQ-49/MPQ-54

The forward area alerting radar (FAAR) has been designed to meet a US Army requirement for a lightweight early warning air surveillance radar to increase the effectiveness of air defence weapons,

such as Chaparral and Redeye missiles and the Vulcan 20 mm gun system, against low-level aircraft attacks. It has been developed in both transportable and mobile versions, these being designated TPQ-32, MPQ-49 and MPQ-54, the latter two being the mobile versions. The principal system elements and operation are identical or similar in both.

The complete system comprises a 25 cm primary radar with an on-mounted secondary (IFF) horn antenna, shelter- or truck-mounted radar data extraction and processing units, operator's console, VHF data link and a number of remote target indicators for use at individual missile or gun sites. The weight of the system is given at 1865 kg.

The primary radar is a pulse-doppler system using a low-noise stable master oscillator, a grid-modulated TWT transmitter and an all solid-state homodyne (zero IF) receiver. The receiver translates target information to video frequencies which are range gated, doppler filtered, and compared with an alarm threshold. Target data are then transmitted via the VHF data link to remote sites, and presented on the operator's console CRT. The antenna measures 183 × 107 cm and is carried on a telescopic mast. The latter is of four sections, pneumatically operated, and capable of extension to a height of about 11 m. 360° coverage is provided. A horn antenna for the IFF is mounted on the upper edge of the main reflector. The IFF system used is the TPX-50, and this provides for either automatic or manual target interrogation.

The operator's console has a 25 cm diameter PPI display which normally presents only processed video which is time-shared with the PPI generator and the symbol generator to show targets, a 7 × 7

FAAR AN/MPQ-49

rectangular grid matrix, and target designation symbols for transmission to remote indicators via the data link. Controls are provided for selection of 'black-scope' or processed video display, sector blanking, threshold adjustment, automatic or manual IFF interrogation, IFF mode selection, radar transmitter/receiver control and self-test functions and data link operation. The console can be removed from the truck or shelter to enable the complete system to be operated from a position up to 50 metres from the radar site.

The VHF data link VRC-46 had three operating modes: data, voice, and rapid alerting and identification display (RAID). This link carries target information from the central operator's console to up to 12 remote target alert data display sets (TADDS) at weapon sites.

Each TADDS (GSQ-137) consists of a single 6 kg unit comprising a display, audio warning, and VHF receiver. The display consists of a replica of the 7 × 7 matrix appearing on the operator's PPI display with each square representing a specific area of the total radar coverage. The presence of a target in any one square, as determined by the central operator, is denoted by the appearance of a coloured disc in the appropriate square of the TADDS. Green discs denote friendly aircraft and red hostile. Plotting of target tracks is by means of a wax pencil. Controls on the TADDS unit provide for test functions, data link address code selection, and data link receiver frequency selection between 30 and 76 MHz. The lid of the unit carries a magnetic compass for orientation purposes.

One mobile version of FAAR, MPQ-49, is housed in a transportable S-250 shelter, utilising the six-wheel drive M561 vehicle as prime mover. The other mobile version is the MPQ-54 which is mounted on a trailer towed by an M35 truck. The system can also be carried by C-130 transport aircraft, or air positioned in a battlefield environment by a CH-47 helicopter. The TPQ-34 is a modified version of FAAR, in non-mobile form, which provides all-weather target detection and location against personnel and vehicles in densely foliated environments. This version is also known as GSR, ground surveillance radar, TPQ-34.

Other applications ascribed to the system include 360° detection of first round mortar and rocket fire, and use as a tactical ATC centre. Although designed for essentially manual operation, FAAR is capable of integration with automatic air defence systems.

DEVELOPMENT

Development was undertaken by Sanders Associates Inc for the US Army Missile Command under a series of contracts. Prototypes were delivered to the US Army in late 1968 and early 1969, and initial production was ordered under a $7·1 million contract in March 1969. In addition to tests at US home bases and engineering establishments, FAAR has been deployed in south-east Asia in the TPQ-34 ground surveillance radar configuration. In this role, the IFF antenna is apparently deleted. Automated versions have been tested successfully.

An export version, LAADS, is described in **3123.153**. The most obvious external difference is the scanner which in LAADS is of less rectangular appearance.

STATUS

The first production model MPQ-49 was delivered to the US Army in January 1972, when it was stated that contracts amounting to $30 million had been awarded.

A second production award was made in May 1974 to Gyroscope, an operating unit of Sperry Division. Sperry Corporation has produced 86 MPQ-49s and associated assemblies (ie 1621 TADDS, 25 organisational maintenance test sets, and ten support maintenance test sets). A total of 180 has been produced.

CONTRACTORS

Sperry Corporation, Electronic Systems, Great Neck, New York 11020, USA.

Sanders Associates Inc, Defensive Systems Division, 95 Canal Street, Nashua, New Hampshire 03060, USA.

3123.153

LAADS LOW ALTITUDE AIRCRAFT DETECTION SYSTEM

LAADS (an improved version of FAAR) is a transportable air defence radar system designed for the detection and identification of low-flying targets and for the co-ordination of defensive weapons directed against such targets.

The radar employed is a coherent, pulsed doppler D-band system using a TWT transmitter. The 12 operating frequencies are generated by highly stable master oscillators. A zero IF receiver detects moving targets, rejects fixed clutter, and presents analogue data to the digital data processor which drives the local PPI and generates digital data messages for broadcast. The radar location is fed into the processor and the target locations are then computed in map co-ordinates. Target data are corrected on each antenna rotation and transmitted to all associated weapons via the data link. Target track capacity is 64. Instrumented range is 60 km with a 30 km range for hovering helicopters.

The weapon display unit (WDU) receives digital data messages and displays targets with respect to the weapon location (centre of display). Targets within 16 km from the weapon are displayed in near real-time with 1 km resolution. Flashing red dots show hostile targets (steady dot for friend). Previous positions are scanned to show target direction and to facilitate threat evaluation. The display mounts directly in front of the gunner, with a cursor showing direction of the gun. A hand-held version of the display is available for the unit commander or platoon leader.

The complete radar equipment, with positions for a crew of three, is housed in a standard US S-280 shelter. This is helicopter transportable or land-mobile on an M36 or similar 2½-ton truck. The system is also available for housing in an H-281 shelter for use on M548 tracked vehicles. The weight of the complete system is 3100 kg.

The 188 × 300 cm scanner is mounted on the shelter and is automatically raised and levelled from its folded stowed position. On-mounted antenna facilities are provided for the integrated IFF which is a

LAADS radar deployed

modified AN/TPX-50. The LAADS scanner differs slightly from that of the related US Army FAAR (**1526.153**) in having a less rectangular profile, but in general the two equipments are essentially the same apart from the mode of mounting. The FAAR is, of course, a US Army system whereas LAADS is mostly exported.

OPERATION

The general concept of operation is similar to that of the earlier FAAR (**1526.153**) described above. A single radar is used to provide search, IFF and associated facilities for remote weapons positions. Each of the latter is provided with the necessary data link reception equipment and WDU to permit individual target engagement. The WDUs are LED matrix type displays and the VHF data link provides for an unlimited number of weapon sites within line-of-sight radio range (normally in excess of 15 km).

Provisions are made for linking other LAADS radars to form networks to give improved protection against 'nap-of-the-earth' attacks.

LAADS is able to serve and provide target acquisition data to an unlimited variety of weapon types, gun and missile systems, and it embodies the latest signal processing and ECCM techniques.

STATUS
The system has been delivered to an overseas government and negotiations have been opened with other undisclosed countries.

CONTRACTOR
Sanders Associates Inc, Defensive Systems Division, 95 Canal Street, Nashua, New Hampshire 03060, USA.

4323.153
HUGHES LOW ALTITUDE SURVEILLANCE RADAR

The Hughes Low Altitude Surveillance Radar (LASR) is designed as a three-dimensional air defence surveillance radar system for the detection and tracking of hovering helicopters and fast, low-flying aircraft. It is a later development of the AN/TPQ-36 system (**2848.153**) and has evolved from this system using 90 per cent common hardware.

LASR is an advanced short-range battlefield radar that automatically detects and tracks modern low-flying threats, such as heavily-armed pop-up helicopters and low-flying fixed-wing aircraft unmasking at low altitudes and short ranges. It provides very high three-dimensional accuracy in severe clutter and severe ECM environments.

The equipment features three-dimensional pencil beams and frequency agile phase beam scanning and provides accurate weapons cueing data. High-speed and hovering targets are detected as they appear at extremely low altitudes. LASR target reports are automatic and compatible with current and projected automatic digital data netting systems. Emission control techniques (blinking) and air space management functions are enhanced by the equipment's capabilities which enable radar-to-radar track correlation.

A low sidelobe, electronically phase-scan (elevation), pencil-beam antenna minimises clutter illumination for nap-of-the-earth detection, and reduces enemy ECM effectiveness and vulnerability to anti-radiation missiles. The antenna rotates mechanically in azimuth to provide 360° coverage with a variable rate azimuth scan. Beam scheduling is computer-controlled and adaptive to mission requirements.

LASR is transportable by light vehicles and aircraft and is available with antenna elevator mechanism. Logistics and support are simplified by extensive built-in-test equipment and automatic fault isolation. There are obvious benefits in the area of maintenance and repair because of its commonality with AN/TPQ-36.

STATUS
Still in the development phase. The system has been selected for the Norwegian Adapted Hawk (NOAH) programme. The contract, awarded in January 1984, calls for 18 systems to be delivered by a joint company (HKV), established by Hughes and Kongsberg Vaapenfabrikk. LASR has been demonstrated successfully against fixed-wing and helicopter targets from 10 to 6000 feet (3 to 1800 m) and from hovering to over 450 mph (724 km/h).

CONTRACTOR
Hughes Aircraft Company, Ground Systems Group, Fullerton, California 92634, USA.

Hughes LASR low-level air defence radar

2848.153
AN/TPQ-36 WEAPON LOCATING RADAR

The AN/TPQ-36 is an artillery, rocket and mortar-locating radar designed as a replacement for the AN/MPQ-4 and older technology weapon locating radars. Although designed to replace the AN/MPQ-4, the AN/TPQ-36 is more than a mortar locating radar and has proven to be very effective in locating artillery and rockets. Location of artillery at ranges beyond the capability of the AN/TPQ-36 is provided by the AN/TPQ-37 (**1976.153**), the other radar that makes up the Firefinder system. Using only a different computer software program, the same operations shelter can be used for either Firefinder radar.

Location of hostile artillery and mortars by the AN/TPQ-36 is completely automatic. The system electronically scans the horizon over a 90° sector several times a second, intercepting and automatically tracking hostile projectiles, then computing back along the trajectory to the origin. The co-ordinates and altitude of the weapon are then presented to the operator. Automatic location is so rapid that the co-ordinates of the weapon are normally with the operator before the enemy round lands.

In addition to its ability to locate artillery, a number of other modifications have been incorporated. The normal 90° sector can be expanded to as much as 360° for use in insurgency operations. The radar can also provide information on the hostile weapon's target by extrapolating the trajectory to the impact point, allowing the information to be used in the priority of return fire.

AN/TPQ-36 weapon locating radar

A very important feature for the modern hostile battlefield is the capability to track and locate weapons firing simultaneously from different locations. Using separate track channels, the radar can track several projectiles at once while continuing to scan for other projectiles in its 90° sector. A further feature allows the radar to ignore subsequent firings from weapon positions already located. As many as 39 different weapon positions simulating an artillery preparation for attack have been used in tests to demonstrate the capability of the system to provide numerous locations in a short period of time.

High mobility allows the system to be used as close as 2 km to the front line. Emplacement takes 15 minutes and displacement five minutes or less. The system can be mounted in a single vehicle plus trailer. Since the operations shelter weighs only 2500 lb (1136 kg), vehicles as small as 1½ tons can carry the shelter and pull the trailer.

The AN/TPQ-36 is a coherent, electronically-scanned, range-gated pulse doppler radar. Beams are moved electronically in the horizontal dimension by phase shifts and in the vertical dimension by frequency shift. Ground, sky and electronic clutter are filtered by a signal processing software system which discriminates hostile projectiles from aircraft, birds, insects or other interference. The three-dimensional radar then tracks the projectiles, computing the firing point and providing the information to the operator within seconds of the firing. The extent of automation allows a single operator to perform all functions necessary to locate the hostile weapon and inform the counterfire systems.

Fault detection sensors constantly monitor performance of each sub-system and provide status information. Should a failure occur, built-in test equipment isolates the problem and informs the operator of the location of the problem, frequently the specific card that must be replaced. These corrective actions should reveal up to 90 per cent of all problems and can normally be accomplished in 15 minutes.

The AN/TPQ-36 has proven to be a reliable system. To date each radar is subjected to not only the normal 'burn-in' at +125°F (+52°C) but is screened for performance at –25°F (–32°C). The result is a reliability of in excess of 125 hours, validating an early field test MTBF of 93 hours. In addition to the high and low temperature screening, the performance of each radar is checked using live artillery and mortar firings.

STATUS

A full-scale three-year production contract was awarded by the US Army to Hughes in August 1978 for $166 million, with two additional option years; and nearly 200 AN/TPQ-36 systems are currently in

production with a delivery rate of one per week. The US Army and Marines will receive 154 systems. In October 1980, to satisfy a requirement for the Netherlands, seven systems were added to the initial 154 ordered. By the end of 1983, all of the Netherlands systems and over half of the remaining ordered had been received by the US Army.

Additional orders were received during 1982 and 1983 from the US Army for 37 radars for Jordan, Saudi Arabia, Pakistan and two members of the Association of Southeast Asia Nations. In December 1982 Hughes signed a $US44 million contract with Australia for seven AN/TPQ-36 radars, spares, training devices and support equipment for delivery beginning in 1986. An $11·2 million contract was awarded by Hughes to BAe (Australia) to provide the operations control centre for each system. At least 10 other nations have indicated intention of ordering systems.

In 1983 press reports stated that two radars were deployed to support the US Marine contingent to the Multi-national Peacekeeping Force in Beirut. Initial crews were provided by the US Army.

Deployment of the AN/TPQ-36 to US Army operational forces continued in 1983, with completion of deployment scheduled for 1984. Initial

deliveries to the US Marines are also scheduled for 1984. Deliveries of the second foreign batch are scheduled for 1985.

Originally configured using the then standard Gamma Goat articulated vehicle, the AN/TPQ-36 now uses a 2½-ton truck to carry the operations shelter and pull the antenna/transceiver trailer. With its versatility of design, the shelter has been configured on the militarised 1½-ton pick-up truck, and will use the Mercedes Unimog for Australia.

An air defence variant, the Low Altitude Surveillance Radar (**4323.153**), has been successfully demonstrated to have the capability to track such different targets as pop-up helicopters and high speed fixed wing aircraft in high clutter environments. The first contract for production of this variant was awarded in January 1984. The high percentage of logistic commonality between the two systems should provide benefits in logistic support and life cycle cost effectiveness.

CONTRACTOR

Hughes Aircraft Company, Ground Systems Group, Fullerton, California 92634, USA.

1976.153

AN/TPQ-37 WEAPON LOCATING RADAR

The AN/TPQ-37 radar provides the US Army's first capability to locate hostile artillery and rocket launchers at their normal firing ranges. It is believed to be the only system with this capability anywhere in the world. Additionally, it is the first tactical radar in large scale production to use phased array techniques for scanning in both azimuth and elevation, by using miniaturised diode phase shifters distributed throughout the antenna.

The AN/TPQ-37 radar programme was initiated in response to the threat of massive concentrations of artillery and rockets in support of both offensive and defensive operations. Prior to this, there had been no effective means to locate and counter indirect fire, with combat troops having to analyse craters to estimate direction and range as a last resort.

The AN/TPQ-37 uses a combination of radar techniques and computer-controlled signal processing for detection, verification, tracking of projectiles, and extrapolating the track-data points to the location from which the projectile was fired. Once the origin of a projectile has been identified, that location can be provided by voice or digital data link to the fire direction centre for initiation of counterfire. These techniques are very similar to those applying to the AN/TPQ-36 weapon locating radar (**2848.153**) described above.

Like the AN/TPQ-36, the AN/TPQ-37 is a coherent, electronic-scanned, range-gated pulse doppler radar. The AN/TPQ-37 incorporates monopulse and its beams are moved in both azimuth and elevation by shifting the inter-element phase using diode phase shifters, the first such application in a tactical system. Significant improvements were incorporated into the AN/TPQ-37 before entering production, ensuring state-of-the-art technology, particularly in the antenna, signal processor and computer. Since then, lightweight kevlar armour plating has been added to protect the antenna.

Operationally the AN/TPQ-36 and AN/TPQ-37 will be complementary, the former between 1 and 4 km from the FLOT to provide for artillery counter-fire

AN/TPQ-37 weapon locating radar

against mortars and close-in artillery. Three AN/TPQ-36 radars will be deployed in each division sector. The AN/TPQ-37 will be sited further behind the front line to locate opposing long-range artillery, with two AN/TPQ-37s to each division sector.

Together, the AN/TPQ-36 and AN/TPQ-37 are referred to as the Firefinder System. The modification of the programme to incorporate an operations shelter that can be coupled to and operate either the AN/TPQ-36 antenna or the AN/TPQ-37 antenna provides unique operational and maintenance advantages.

The AN/TPQ-37 consists of two vehicles and an antenna trailer. A five-ton vehicle carries the 60 kW generator and pulls the antenna trailer. The operations shelter is mounted on a 2½-ton vehicle. All components are air transportable in C-130 aircraft and are helicopter transportable. Crew size is between 8 and 12, though once emplaced normal operation can be carried out by a single operator.

STATUS

Since 1977 the US Army has ordered 72 systems. Full-scale production was started in 1981 and will

reach a rate of three systems every two months. By the end of 1983 more than half the total quantity for the US Army had been delivered and deployed in the US and overseas. Deployment is scheduled for completion in 1984. Production reliability tests have demonstrated a mean-time-between-failure of over 120 hours.

A moratorium on international sales was imposed in 1981 after concern regarding transfer and potential compromise of high technology. After a study of this issue the moratorium was lifted in late 1983 and sales to US allies was authorised. The sale of 10 systems to Saudi Arabia and Jordan was expected to be the first implemented. At least seven other countries have indicated an intention to procure the AN/TPQ-37.

Improvements in mobility have received high priority among the evolutionary changes incorporated during production. In addition to placing the operations shelter on a 2½-ton truck in place of the 1½-ton pick-up, the US Army is replacing the mobilisers initially used for the antenna/transceiver with a tandem-wheel trailer which promises much better stability. Mobility and field tests have shown that the antenna/transceiver can be easily mounted on the FVS carrier, the tracked vehicle chassis used for the Multiple Launch Rocket System in production for the US and several NATO nations.

Since the shelters for the AN/TPQ-36 and AN/TPQ-37 are identical, and operational procedures are similar, those countries that have procured the former will find the transition to the AN/TPQ-37 facilitated.

An air defence radar based on the hardware of the AN/TPQ-37, had been demonstrated in several locations both in the US and overseas. The VSTAR (variable search and track air defence radar) (**4080.153**) has demonstrated a capability to track small aircraft flying through heavy ground clutter and has tracked small sea-going vessels in sea state 4. Most of the VSTAR is common with the AN/TPQ-37 providing considerable logistic and support advantages.

CONTRACTOR

Hughes Aircraft Company, Ground Systems Group, Fullerton, California 92634, USA.

2849.153

AN/TPQ-39(V) INSTRUMENTATION RADAR

AN/TPQ-39(V) is a one-man instrumentation radar of modular design which is available in fixed building and transportable versions. It is intended for range applications involving system evaluation, range safety, vehicle control or other target tracking uses.

Several variants are in use, including the digital instrumentation range (DIR) and Nike digital instrumentation radar (NIDIR). DIR operates at C-band while current units of NIDIR are at X-band. Other variants are also available.

As the equipments names suggest, solid-state

digital techniques are used extensively in the system. A digital computer is used as the basis of the system, with many radar functions (angle and range servos, AFC, AGC, target acquisition and detection, input/output and display control) provided by the radar computer programming.

Many optional extras have been selected for individual range requirements, such as parametric amplifiers, higher power transmitters, data recording facility, plotting boards adjacent to the operator's position, timing equipment and star calibration.

The following characteristics describe the basic DIR variant.

CHARACTERISTICS (DIR Variant)

Azimuth, elevation tracking rates: 500 mils/s

Azimuth, elevation acceleration: 300 mils/s²

Azimuth, elevation tracking precisions: 0.3 mils, rms

Range tracking: 235 km at 640 Hz PRF

Ro, IM², 0 dB S/N: 93 km

Range tracking precision: 4·7 m

STATUS

Units are operational at US Army, Navy and Air Forces sites in the USA, and at the West German Aerospace Research Establishment (DFVLR) at Braunschweig. NIDIR variants are operated in the Far East, in the UK and at US Navy sites in the USA.

CONTRACTOR
RCA, Government Systems Division, Missile and Surface Radar, Moorestown, New Jersey 08057, USA.

NIDIR variant of the AN/TPQ-39(V) radar

2529.153
AN/TPS-21 AND AN/TPS-33 PULSE DOPPLER BATTLEFIELD RADARS

These two radars are I/J-band portable manpack systems used to detect persons or vehicles in motion on the ground. Targets are detected at ranges lying between approximate limits of 100 and 18 000 m with a range measurement accuracy of ±23 m or ±1 per cent of range, whichever is the greater. Angular accuracy is ±25 mils.

Scanning is either manual or automatic in range with sector scan. For the TPS-21 radar detection is solely by audible tone in the operator's headphones; in the TPS-33 equipment there is also an A-scope display.

STATUS
Operational in US armed forces.
CONTRACTOR
Admiral Corporation, USA, now incorporated in: La Pointe Industries, 155 West Main Street, Rockville, Connecticut 06066, USA.

2516.153
AN/TPS-32 3-D LONG-RANGE SURVEILLANCE RADAR

AN/TPS-32 is a ground-based, long-range, tactical, lightweight radar which automatically provides precise, three-dimensional position data on multiple targets. The equipment has been designed to operate as the primary 3-D radar sensor for the marine tactical data system. It also provides two positions for operators to vector interceptor aircraft to assigned targets. It is easily transportable by helicopter, cargo aircraft, or by conventional M35 truck. Automatic target detection, clutter elimination, and IFF are included.

Air search coverage of the radar extends to 300 nautical miles (556 km) in range to a ceiling of 100 000 ft (approximately 30 500 m). The search volume is obtained by continuous rotation of the antenna (at six rpm) in the azimuth plane and electronic frequency scanning, –1 to +18° in the elevation plane. The elevation scan is accomplished by changing the frequency of the E/F-band RF energy applied to the planar array, frequency-sensitive antenna. The antenna radiation appears as a series of pencil beams; each beam is 0·84° high and 2·15° wide.

The AN/TPS-32 radar consists of an antenna assembly and three shelters. Two of the shelters contain transmitter stages and the third contains receiver, data processing, including radar and IFF plot extractors, displays and system control equipment. In the transport condition, the radar set consists of two antenna array pallets, one tripod pallet, and three shelters. The complete system is helicopter transportable in six pallets and can be made operational in less than two hours.

To make the most efficient use of transmitter power, the peak power level and inter-pulse period are changed during the complete elevation scan to fit the coverage volume more precisely. This allows more energy to be spent in the longer range portions of the coverage volume at the lower angles of operation.

CHARACTERISTICS
Coverage
Elevation: 19° within interval –1 to +18° (electronically scanned)
Height: 100 000 ft (30·5 km)
Azimuth: 360° (mechanically scanned)
Displayed range: 2·5 nm (4·6 km) – 300 nm (556 km)
Data rate: 10 s
Probability of detection/range (1 m² target): 90% to 200 nm (371 km), 50% at 300 nm (556 km)
False alarm rate: <10 false target messages per azimuth scan
Accuracy (standard deviation)
Range: 750 ft (229 m)
Azimuth: 0·5°
Height: 1200 ft (336 m) at 100 nm (185 km), 3000 ft (914 m) at 300 nm (463 km)
Resolution
Range: 1500 ft (457 m) (manual), 2625 ft (800 m) (automatic)
Azimuth: 2·15°
Elevation: 0·85°
Transmitter
Operating frequency: 2905 – 3080MHz
Pulsewidth: 30 μs
Interpulse period: 1090 – 3772 μs

AN/TPS-32 long-range surveillance radar

Peak power output
Three-stage RF amplifier: 60 kW peak (high elevation, short range and MTI)
Driver RF amplifier: 665 kW peak (medium elevation, medium range)
Final RF amplifier: 2·2 MW peak (low elevation, long range)
Radar antenna
Elevation beamwidth: 0·84° (nominal)
Azimuth beamwidth: 2·15° (nominal)
Gain: 41 dB (minimum)
Sidelobes (azimuth and elevation): –25 dB (minimum) referenced to peak of main beam
Polarisation: Horizontal
Rotational speeds: 6 rpm

4078.153
SERIES 320 3-D AIR DEFENCE RADARS
The Series 320 3-D air defence radar utilises highly stable, modern state-of-the-art signal processing techniques to maintain target detection and a low false alarm rate in high clutter areas. Its operation is highly automatic and under computer control with extensive on-line monitoring of radar performance. Fault isolation is accomplished using computer diagnostic programs. The radar operates at E/F-band (former S-band) and is available in 150, 200 and 300 nautical mile range versions. Fixed site and transportable configuration of Series 320 modules have been specified, with frequency control and phase/frequency versions available.

This series of radars combine inertialess elevation scanning with groups of multiple pencil beams. Elevation scanning is accomplished by using either frequency or phase/frequency control to steer the pencil beam in space. This technique provides time on target for multiple pulse processing required for clutter suppression, while maintaining high resolution, high data rate and accurate target location. Phase/frequency control versions of the system provide frequency agility and clear channel operation.

The Series 320 planar array antenna with frequency-steered pencil beams subdivides the full elevation profile into elevation segments. Each segment is searched by five vertically positioned narrow beams each derived from five distinct RF frequencies until the full elevation sector is covered. The antenna is rotated in azimuth achieving full volumetric coverage extending to 300 nautical miles in range and up to 30 000 metres in altitude. A 2 m² target is detectable within this volume with a 99·5 percent probability or greater. Out to a range of 100 nautical miles, the accuracy of the radar is less than 450 metres in azimuth and 760 metres in height. The range accuracy is 18 metres.

MTI is employed in areas where ground clutter is present. ECCM capabilities include jammer-frequency analysers, jammer-strobe reports and radar silence.

This radar system was developed by ITT-Gilfillan for the international market and has been ordered in a joint submission for a European air defence requirement. It is related in certain respects to the AN/TPS-32 (**2516.153**) above.
CHARACTERISTICS
Frequency: 2·9 – 3·1 GHz
Peak power: 150 kW/1·1 MW
PRF: Variable
Receiver noise figure: 2·5 dB
Antenna: 6·4 × 5·18 m

4079.153
ARBAT INSTRUMENTATION RADAR
The ARBAT (application of radar to ballistic acceptance testing of ammunition) equipment is an X-band pulse doppler range instrumentation radar under development by the US Army. It is designed for ballistic testing of a wide variety of projectiles including new sophisticated ammunitions. The radar employs a pencil beam planar array antenna for pointing accuracy and provides test results in both real-time on a CRT display and as hard copy. Data provided on test rounds fired includes position in space (X, Y and Z co-ordinates), velocity (X, Y and Z), event detection and impact data. A magnetic tape records target position, rate acceleration, drag

STATUS
In 1975 this radar was selected as the basis of a new model of three-dimensional surveillance ordered for the Swedish Air Force. Sixteen of these will be used as part of a modernisation programme for the Swedish air defence system. The standard TPS-32 has been supplied to the US Marine Corps, Kuwait and Turkey.

In 1980, ITT-Gilfillan received a contract from the US Marine Corps to supply three fibre-optic data links to be used with the AN/TPS-32 air surveillance radar system. Each data link consists of a fibre-optic cable with modulator and demodulator equipment. The cable is 2 km long, and carries signals from the AN/TPS-32 radar system to the Marine Corps tactical data system (MTDS), part of the tactical air operations center (TAOC).

This is ITT-Gilfillan's second contract from the US Marine Corps for a fibre-optic data link to remotely feed signals from the AN/TPS-32 radar system. The first contract, awarded in early 1978, was delivered to the Marine Corps at Camp Pendleton in May 1979. This was transferred to the east coast in December 1979 and was later deployed with the Marine Corps for NATO exercises in Norway.
CONTRACTOR
ITT-Gilfillan, 7821 Orion Avenue, Van Nuys, California 91409, USA.

Typical deployment of ITT-Gilfillan Series 320 3-D transportable air defence radar system

Gain: 41·2 dB
Azimuth beamwidth: 1·4° (0·84° optional)
Elevation beamwidth: 1·6° (2·2° optional)
Scan rate: 6 rpm
Polarisation: Horizontal
Signal processor: Digital
Improvement factor: 40 dB
Detection performance (2 m² target): 200/300 nm (PD = 0·5)
Number of false alarms: 5/scan
Azimuth coverage: 360°
Elevation coverage: 0 – 20°
Height coverage: 0 – 30 000 m
Resolution at 100 nm: Range 125 m; azimuth 2·8°; elevation 3·5°

Accuracy (1 sigma at 100 nm): Range 18 m; azimuth 460 m; height 760 m (400 m with option)
STATUS
Gilfillan is known to have received contracts for four radars of this series from International Technical Products NV, these equipments being intended for the Philippines. An agreement with Plessey, UK, has resulted in a combination of the 320 3-D and the Plessey AR-3D being ordered by the UK MoD from Plessey as the E/F-band radar in the current improvement programme for the UK air defence network. (**3649.153**).
CONTRACTOR
ITT-Gilfillan, 7821 Orion Avenue, Van Nuys, California 91409, USA.

Mobile phase-scanned antenna array of the ITT-Gilfillan ARBAT instrumentation radar showing an obvious family resemblance to the 3-D air defence radars produced by this concern

vectors and radar cross-section at a 20 Hz rate for post firing analysis. The ARBAT system is packaged in two major equipment groups: the antenna/transceiver group and instrumentation van. It is capable of covering multiple firing positions from a single location or it may be sited down range to analyse terminal performance of long range projectiles.

Specified system accuracy requirements include 2 mils in azimuth and elevation, 0·05% in range and 1 m/s velocity.

STATUS
The ARBAT system is currently completing retrofit to upgrade elements of hardware and software, and to improve performance, at the Yuma Proving Grounds under the direction of the US Army's Armament, Munitions and Chemical Command (AMCCOM).

CONTRACTOR
ITT-Gilfillan, 7821 Orion Avenue, Van Nuys, Caifornia 91409, USA.

4322.153
FALCON SERIES GPS-100 SURVEILLANCE RADAR

The Falcon (frequency agile low coverage netted) radar is a two-dimensional air/sea surveillance radar providing search, acquisition and tracking of low altitude aircraft and the simultaneous coastal surveillance and tracking of ships, small boats and low-flying helicopters. The automatic tracking of large numbers of aircraft and ship targets can be monitored by operators within the radar control cabin, and transmitted in digital format to air and surface control centres at a distant location to provide an overall command and control display from a number of Falcon radars.

The radar equipment can be installed in a protected bunker configuration, in a shelter, or in a mobile configuration, and is designed for unattended operation. Integrated IFF and radar tracks data can be transmitted by digital data link to air and surface operations centres.

The antenna is a dual beam reflector with a cosec² coverage to 25° elevation, and integral IFF. The transceiver is crystal controlled and uses a single-stage high-gain TWT.

The entire system is designed to incorporate strong ECCM capabilities and includes automatic built-in-test equipment to minimise maintenance requirements.

CHARACTERISTICS
Operating frequency: C-band
Antenna type: Reflector, high gain, dual-beam with very low sidelobes
Polarisation is circular, horizontal, operator selectable
Beamwidths: 2·4° (azimuth), cosec² to 25° (elevation)
Search scan: 360° at 6 or 12 rpm
Instrumented range: 100 or 160 km
Peak power: 60 kW
Mean power: 1500 W
Altitude coverage: 0 – 3000 m
Simultaneous tracks: Up to 100, air or surface
Availability: 99·6%
STATUS
In current quantity production. A number of foreign governments have expressed interest in Falcon-based coastal surveillance systems. An order for more than 24 systems has been received from Sweden and the first system was due for delivery at the end of 1983. Two other countries have also

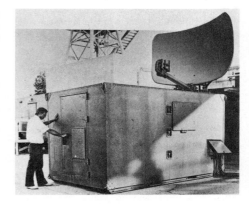

Falcon surveillance radar

selected the Falcon system. Up to mid-1983, $50 million of orders had been received for the system.
CONTRACTOR
ITT-Gilfillan, 7821 Orion Avenue, Van Nuys, California 91409, USA.

2530.153
AN/TPS-34 TRANSPORTABLE AIR DEFENCE RADAR

AN/TPS-34 is a tactical early-warning radar for use in forward air defence systems. It is said to be the first tactical radar to utilise the V-beam 3-D technique.

The radar provides long-range 3-D data on high-speed aircraft and missiles from battlefield sites. It can be transported by helicopter in units averaging less than 200 kg in weight and can be assembled and operating in less than eight hours from touchdown.

STATUS
In service in the British armed forces.
CONTRACTOR
Sperry Corporation, Electronic Systems, Great Neck, New York 11020, USA.

2517.153
AN/TPS-43E TACTICAL 3-D RADAR

AN/TPS-43E is a lightweight air transportable radar designed for use with manned aircraft or SAM batteries in a wide variety of tactical environments. It provides solid 3-D cover to 240 nautical miles on a fighter or fighter-bomber aircraft and measures heights over the full range by signal amplitude comparisons in six channels. Extensive clutter rejection and ECCM features are incorporated in the design, including a digital coherent MTI system, pulse-to-pulse frequency agility, jamming analysis and transmission selection (JATS), coded pulse anti-clutter system (CPACS) and sidelobe blanking. This latest model of the AN/TPS-43 includes extensive equipment refinements and increased operational capability.

For ease of air shipment the equipment divides simply into two pallet loads each of less than 3400 kg. One load comprises the shelter unit, transmitter/receiver and displays; the other consists of the antenna assembly, the feed and ancillary equipment. The entire equipment can be packed into two M35 trucks for road transport.

To minimise weight, light alloys are used wherever possible in the main mechanical structures and micro-miniaturisation techniques are used in the electronics circuits. The transmitter uses a completely solid-state modular modulator to pulse a linear beam twystron.

The feed array features the use of a stripline matrix to form the heightfinding beams. The IFF antenna is a sum and difference type providing an interrogator sidelobe suppression (ISLS) capability. A small printed circuit reference antenna is mounted on the back of the radar feed to act as the radar sidelobe reference antenna; use of this latter antenna during the dead time between transmitter pulses is available for the JATS function.

CHARACTERISTICS
Range: Solid 3-D coverage on fighter-bomber aircraft to 408 km
Data rate: 10 s (6 rpm antenna)
Elevation coverage: 0 – 20°
Height accuracy: ±305 m at 100 nm
Electrical characteristics
Power output: 4 MW peak, 6·7 kW average
Frequency: 2900 – 3100 MHz in 16 discrete steps (with pulse-to-pulse agility)
Pulse duration: 6·5 µs
Antenna gain: Transmit, 36 dB; receive, 40 dB
Azimuth beamwidth: 1·1°
IFF azimuth beamwidth: 4° (or sum/difference ISLS antenna)
Noise figure: 4·5 dB
Prime power: 400 Hz 3-phase 120/208 V
Mechanical characteristics
Weight: Shelter module 3310 kg; antenna module 2050 kg
Transport: Single C-130 aircraft, 2 M35 trucks, 2 sets of transporters, or 2 helicopter loads
Road speeds: Up to 96 km/h
Air lift altitudes: Up to 15 000 m
Siting requirements: 6 × 10·5 m clear area on slope of 10% or less
Reaction time: 50 minutes with a 6-man team
Wind resistance: Operate to 52 knots, survive 92 knots (tied down)
Operating temperature: –40 to +125° F (–40 to +52° C)
Other
MTBF: 400 h

AN/TPS-43 search radar

MTTR: 30 minutes
Outputs to: 3 120 m cables with storage reels
Operations centres PPI: 2 operational positions featuring AN/UPA-62 (40 cm) CRT, digital height readouts, and AN/UPA-59A active/passive IFF decoders. Each position also has access to built-in UHF ground/air communications and HF point-to-point communications facilities.
IFF/SIF equipment: AN/UPX-23 interrogator set and AN/UPA-59A active/passive decoder
Transmitter tube: Linear beam twystron
STATUS
The TPS-43 series of radars (the latest versions are the E, F and G models) have been extensively deployed by the armed forces of the USA and up to 20 other countries. In 1981 the US Air Force placed another repeat order for the TPS-43E version and at that time there were 23 units in production with the latest solid-state modulator and IFF system. The latest versions also include a built-in programmable post processor for target extraction, target tracking and forward tell of data to automated command centres.

Among the known foreign users of this radar are Somalia, Morocco and Saudi Arabia, and civil derivatives have been supplied to several countries.

One system was deployed by Argentina in the Falklands and was taken by British forces. It is believed to have been refurbished and updated in the UK.

Planned evolution of the series continues with the ultra-low sidelobe antenna (ULSA) which has a planar array and is under test. It is planned for service in the mid-1980s with two antennas already delivered.
CONTRACTOR
Westinghouse Defense and Electronic Systems Center, Baltimore, Maryland 21203, USA.

2518.153

AN/TPS-44 TACTICAL SURVEILLANCE RADAR (ALERT Mk II A/O)

Alert Mk II (AN/TPS-44) is a lightweight, solid-state, transportable D-band air surveillance radar. It was designed for use anywhere in the world as the sensor for the forward air-control post of the US 407L system (TACS).

Alert Mk II is the latest version of the Alert radar series. Information of airborne targets is presented in the form of synchronised radar and IFF video on a 16-inch PPI display console. It also has optional provisions for supplying range and azimuth information to additional tactical operations centres.

The equipment consists of the Alert IIA radar set, a complete IFF/SSR system and the operator display console. All components are housed in two major packages; an equipment shelter houses the electronic components and display console and an antenna pallet carries the folding antenna and feed system, together with the pedestal and antenna drive system. The entire system can be transported by M35 trucks, C-130 aircraft, helicopters or towed on transporters. It can be converted from transport to operational configuration by a team of four people in less than 40 minutes.
DEVELOPMENT
Prototypes of the equipment were submitted to the US Air Force and successfully passed all tests. Following this the equipment was put into production, and by February 1983 deliveries were known to include 26 systems to the US Air Force, and 13 modified systems to other countries.
CHARACTERISTICS
Antenna
Type
Search: Modified parabolic
IFF: Integral with search radar feed system and reflector
Aperture, search
Horizontal: >45 m
Vertical: >2·7 m
Beamwidth (one-way), search and IFF
Horizontal: 3·8°
Vertical: 8° with cosecant squaring 7 – 27°
Polarisation
Search: Horizontal
IFF: Vertical
Type of feed: Search and IFF: horn
Beam pattern search and IFF
Horizontal: Conventional fan beam (cosine between 3 dB points), sidelobes 25 dB down, back lobes 30 dB down

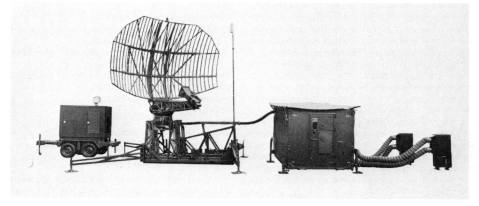
AN/TPS-44 tactical surveillance radar deployed

Vertical: Conventional fan beam with cosecant squaring
Scan
Azimuth: 0 – 15 rpm, clockwise in automatic, or manually searchlighting, clockwise or counter-clockwise. Also available with 6 rpm clockwise fixed-speed option
Elevation: Manually adjustable, –3 to +6°
Transmitter
Power
Peak: 1 MW, or greater
Average: 1·12 kW at 800, 0·745 kW at 533, 1·12 kW at 267
PRF
Manually selectable: 800, 533, 400
Momentary selectable: ±10 μs stagger on 800 PRF. Also available with 4-pulse stagger to eliminate MTI blind-speeds
Frequency: 1·25 – 1·35 GHz, continuously tunable – over full range by local or remote tuning control
Tuning rate: 1 MHz/s
Pulse: Width automatically selected when PRF is selected:
   1·4 μs for 800 PRF
   1·4 μs for 533 PRF
   4·2 μs for 267 PRF
   2·8 μs for 400 PRF
Rise time: 100 ns, max
Receiver
Noise figure: Typically 3 dB, overall
Dynamic range: 65 dB
Choice of IF: Logarithmic, linear, or wideband limiting

Signal processing
MTI:
   (a) Digital type
   (b) Double (3-pulse) canceller
   (c) Cancellation ratio – typical 40 dB
   (d) Sub-clutter visibility –30 dB searchlighting, 20 dB scanning (6 rpm)
   (e) Staggered PRF eliminates blind speeds
VSI:
   (a) Digital type
   (b) Feedback factor –0·875
   (c) 2-channel: MTI and normal
   (d) Railing suppression 12 dB minimum
Accuracy
Range: 0·5 nm on 400 PRF; 0·1 nm on 800 and 533 PRF
Azimuth: ±1°
Type of information displays:
   (a) PPI
   (b) A-scope
   (c) Output jacks and cabling provided for remote displays
STATUS
In 1980 it was reported that a number of the latest version of this radar, Alert IIA, were being supplied to Argentina for air defence use.
CONTRACTOR
Cardion Electronics, Long Island Expressway, Woodbury, New York 11797, USA.

3282.153

AN/TPS-59 3-D TACTICAL RADAR

The AN/TPS-59 is a D-band, long-range 3-D air surveillance phased array radar. The export version is known as the GE 592. Claimed to be unique as a tactical radar, its transmitter is totally solid-state and power is generated by direct amplification at the transmission frequency using D-band power transistors. The antenna is a 9·1 m high by 4·9 m rotating planar array located about two metres above ground level. The three trailer assemblies used as the antenna support structure also carry the array sections during transport. The display and processing equipment, including an AN/UYK-7 general-purpose digital computer, are housed in two air-conditioned cabins (S-280), and these and three 45 kW diesel generators complete the TPS-59 system.

The antenna array is made up of 54 identical row-feed networks and associated row-level transceivers, comprising power supplies, transmitters, pre-amplifiers, phase shifters, duplexers and logic controls. Each set is housed in a single package directly behind the row feed. The vertical, or row-to-row distribution, is accomplished by three column feeds. The antenna rotates mechanically in azimuth, and a pencil beam electronically scans in elevation from 0 to 19° to cover the specified surveillance volume in a raster-scan pattern.

Two basic waveforms are used for the surveillance function: one throughout the short-range interval from 5·5 to 185 km, and the other over the long-range interval from 185 km to the limits of coverage. Eight pencil beams are used to scan the long-range interval in elevation, and 11 are used to cover the short-range. Provisions are made in the lower long-range and

short-range beams to counter the effects of multi-path propagation, and a special low-angle heightfinding technique is employed. There is also a special weather mode of operation which automatically optimises energy management and MTI processing according to prevailing weather conditions. This is performed at intervals of five minutes to adjust to weather changes.

In addition to its various functions in beam steering, energy management, and signal processing, the AN/UYK-7 computer stores the position of all detected targets (in three co-ordinates) and correlates the stored positions with fresh data on a scan-to-scan basis. It also performs the special range correlation processing associated with second-time-around returns concerned with MTI operation, and correlates the data from targets in closely spaced beams to avoid the reporting problems associated with multiple detections. All monopulse calculations are performed in the computer.

All controls and indicators for the operation of the TPS-59 are located at the display console, at which there are two operators' positions with three CRTs. Two of these are PPIs and the other is used as either an RHI display or for the presentation of alphanumeric data. Other facilities include IFF controls, a performance monitoring status display, a clutter gating panel and communications controls.

The AN/TPS-59 is designed primarily to provide long-range surveillance of a tactical airspace to the tactical air operations central (TAOC). Its detection capabilities (500 targets per ten-second scan), 3-D positional accuracy, and console readouts and controls meet the requirements of an autonomous build-up or back-up ground control intercept role. The system's high data rate capability supports the additional ATC mission. The design specification

AN/TPS-59 3-D phased array tactical radar

includes threat criteria such as 1 m² scan-to-scan fluctuating targets flying at speeds up to Mach 4.

CHARACTERISTICS
Radiated peak power: 34·9 kW
Average duty cycle: 18%
Transmit gain: 38·9 dB
Effective receive area: 14·5 dBm²
Antenna sidelobe levels: –25 dB
System noise temperature: 540° K
Signal processing losses: 2·4 dB
Frequency: 1215 – 1400 MHz
Surveillance coverage: 360° azimuth; 5·5-560 km range; 0 – 19° elevation; 30 500 m altitude
Frame time: 10 or 5 s
Detectability-in-the-clear: PD: 0·7 beyond 200 nm; 0·9 within 200 nm; FAR: 5 per scan
Accuracy: Range 24 m; azimuth 3 mrad; elevation 1·7 mrad
Resolution: Range 60 m; azimuth 3·2°; elevation 1·6°
Reliability: MTBF 1400 h
Maintainability: MTTR 40 minutes
Weight: System 12 700 kg; max package 2360 kg
Prime power: 89 kW (nominal)
Mobility: Assembly in 1 h; disassembly in ½ h
DEVELOPMENT
General Electric was awarded a contract for the development of the TPS-59 for the US Marine Corps by the Naval Electronic Systems Command in 1972. It began US Marine Corps acceptance testing in 1976-77.

Based upon the modular nature of the antenna array and its 54 identical row/feed networks, and flexibility inherent in the digital signal processor coupled with extensive use of software control

techniques, GE has produced designs for other derivatives of the TPS-59 for a variety of applications. Brief details follow:

Fixed 3-D long-range radar: This has an antenna array measuring 7·3 × 7·3 m (the row/feeds are 50 per cent longer than the TPS-59) and a range capability of about 450 km.
Medium-range transportable 3-D radar: Antenna size 4·3 × 4·9 m, range 225 km, 50-track capabilty.
Long-range 2-D fixed radar: Antenna size 3·7 × 6·1 m with row/feeds disposed vertically instead of horizontally, range 370 km, track-while-scan processing.
Medium-range limited-sector 2-D radar: Antenna size 3·7 × 1·5 m with row/feeds disposed vertically, range 55 km, inertialess azimuth scan of 120°, track-while-scan processing.

A shipboard long-range 2-D radar using an array measuring 4·6 × 2·3 m contained within a 9·2 m diameter radome and with a range of 370 km has also been publicised.
STATUS
In 1980 GE received a \$134 million contract for AN/TPS-59 radars for use by the US Marine Corps. This award followed a successful four-year test and evaluation programme. The 15 radars ordered under this contract are being delivered. A transportable version, the GE 592, is described below (**4321.153**).
CONTRACTOR
General Electric Company, Electronic Systems Division, Syracuse, New York 13201, USA.

4321.153
GE 592 TRANSPORTABLE AIR DEFENCE RADAR
The transportable GE 592 air defence radar system is the export version of the AN/TPS-59 system (**3282.153**). It is a completely mobile equipment and is totally solid-state computer controlled. Operating in L-band and comprising a complete air defence system with IFF or secondary radar for target identification, the equipment is housed in four enclosures and transported on four trailers.

The GE 592 is a versatile system and in its normal transportable configuration is moved by four vehicles which carry the antenna array, data and signal processing units, radar and control management and the power generation equipment. A fifth vehicle is needed to carry the microwave communication equipment, if required. The entire system can also be air-lifted by fixed-wing aircraft or helicopter.

The planar array measures 7·3 × 7·3 metres and phase positions a series of pencil beams to scan in elevation up to 20° while it rotates in azimuth. The transmitter/receiver group is located on the antenna and comprises 44 transmitters, each containing eight 100-watt RF solid-state power modules and 44 receiver modules. The IFF secondary radar antenna is mounted on top of the main array.

The data processor controller provides all radar operational management as well as on-line, automatic performance monitoring to detect possible system failures. The controller provides plot extraction data output and performs sweep-to-sweep and scan-to-scan correlations to reduce false alarms and multiple reports. It also provides automatic radar/IFF correlations as well as monitoring the system for adverse environmental and ECM effects.

Although the GE 592 is completely automatic in operation, it can also be controlled by manual override from operations consoles in the operations and control group trailer.

The secondary radar sub-system (SRS) provides identification, altitude, azimuth and range information on transponder equipped aircraft. The SRS radar coverage is 360° in azimuth, 400 km in

Composite impression of GE 592 transportable air defence radar systems to be supplied for UK air defence network in Scotland

range and up to 100 000 feet (30 480 metres) in height.

The complete radar system can be housed in a radome/shelter complex, if required. The equipment trailers can be dispersed in any location within 300 metres of the radome. If field dispersal is chosen, the array operates without a radome.
CHARACTERISTICS
Frequency: 1215 – 1400 MHz
Range: Up to 400 km
Azimuth: 360°
Elevation: –4 to +20°
Height: 100 000 ft (30 480 m)
Range accuracy: 100 m rms (5 – 150 nm); 200 m rms (150 – 250 nm)

Height accuracy: 1200 ft (366 m) at 135 nm
Azimuth accuracy: 0·17°
Peak power: 25 kW
Beamwidth: Azimuth 2·2°, elevation 2°
STATUS
In 1980 two transportable GE 592 systems were ordered for installation in Scotland as part of the NATO air defence modernisation programme. These were due to be in operational use in 1983. A fixed-site system was delivered to Belgium in 1979 and the US Air Force is procuring two systems for the Seek Igloo air defence updating programme.
CONTRACTOR
General Electric Company, Electronic Systems Division, Syracuse, New York 13201, USA.

3475.153
AN/TPS-63 TACTICAL SURVEILLANCE RADAR
The AN/TPS-63 is a D-band air surveillance radar used to provide low altitude coverage for tactical air defence operations. This radar, with the companion equipment, AN/TPS-65 (**3476.153**), was built to meet US Marine Corps requirements, and both these

radars feature extensive use of micro-electronic and solid-state techniques. An advanced MTI facility is claimed to provide a 90 per cent probability of detecting a 1 m² target out to the full instrumented range of 80 nautical miles (approx 150 km). The digital MTI uses a four-pulse canceller with variable time intervals between pulses to distinguish moving

aircraft from ground returns while eliminating MTI radar blind speeds. There is an additional digital three-pulse MTI weather canceller and digital CFAR processing. Dual diversity operation is normal and there are built-in test facilities.

The AN/TPS-63 is designed for transportable or mobile applications, but fixed installations are also possible. The 4·9 × 5·5 m antenna is constructed of sections and the system can be operational within one hour of arrival at a new site.

CHARACTERISTICS

Frequency: D-band, dual diversity, 51 selectable frequencies between 1250 – 1350 MHz
Range: 80, 120 and 160 nm (operation selectable)
Data rate: 6, 12, 15 rpm (10, 5, 4 s)
Elevation coverage: 12 000 m shaped coverage to 45°
Power output: 100 kW peak; average 3 kW
Antenna gain: 32·5 dB
Angular resolution: 2·7°
Range resolution: 152 m
ECCM: Coded-pulse anti-clutter, frequency agility, PRF stagger
MTBF: 500 h
MTTR: 20 minutes
Weight: 3400 kg
MTI improvement factor: 60 dB

DEVELOPMENT

The AN/TPS-63 was designed and developed under US Navy contracts for use by the US Marine Corps in the latter's Tactical Operations Center to facilitate detection, automatic acquisition and target tracking of aircraft targets. The AN/TPS-65 version serves as the primary airfield surveillance radar sensor for the US Marine Air Traffic Control and Landing System.

STATUS

Series production of the AN/TPS-63 was announced in February 1978, and at that time 15 equipments had been ordered for the US Marine Corps. By summer 1980, these had been delivered and an additional five radars had been ordered for the US Marine Corps. Through 1982, over 60 TPS-63/65 radars have been ordered by the US Marine Corps and six international customers. A version of the TPS-63 has been designed for airship installation to give increased coverage. Entry **3162.353** under the Airborne Radar section gives more details.

CONTRACTOR

Westinghouse Defense and Electronic Systems Center, Baltimore, Maryland 21203, USA.

AN/TPS-63 tactical air surveillance radar, set up and ready for operation. A four-man team can erect and prepare the radar within an hour

3476.153
AN/TPS-65 TACTICAL SURVEILLANCE RADAR

The AN/TPS-65 is a member of the Westinghouse family of two-dimensional D-band air search radars which includes the AN/TPS-63 (**3475.153**) radars. The TPS-65 has similar performance characteristics which suit it for its principal role as the primary airfield surveillance radar sensor for the US Marine Air Traffic Control and Landing System. This system provides automated and manual control information for aircraft landings at expeditionary airfields.

Essential details of the AN/TPS-65 are as shown for the AN/TPS-63, and the reader is referred to entry **3475.153** for the main characteristics.

STATUS

Initial production completed.

CONTRACTOR

Westinghouse Defense and Electronic Systems Center, Baltimore, Maryland 21203, USA.

4319.153
AN/TPS-70(V)-1 TACTICAL RADAR

The TPS-70(V)-1 is a mobile tactical radar designed to detect and track hostile aircraft in a variety of environments at ranges out to 450 km. It incorporates clutter rejection and ECCM features, with an ultra low sidelobe antenna making it very difficult for enemy countermeasures to detect and jam the system. Also incorporated are advanced signal analysis and processing and a digital coherent MTI system.

The antenna, a flat-slotted array measuring 18 feet wide by 11 feet high (502 × 335 cm), is combined with programmable doppler signal processing and an automated target extraction/tracking computer to provide the total operational scenario capability for automated and manual command centres.

The complete system consists of the main antenna, with a secondary radar mounted on top and an operations/electronics cabin shelter unit. For ease of transport the TPS-70(V)-1 is deployed as two modules which can be carried to a forward position by either truck or helicopter.

The TPS-70(V)-1 is modular in design, the software being flexible to permit fast reprogramming to meet specific operational requirements. The system can be remotely controlled and can be operated either autonomously or as part of a larger network. Several versions are under development, including a medium range gap filler as well as a long range surveillance version.

CHARACTERISTICS

Frequency: 2900 – 3100 MHz
Peak power: 3 MW (mean power 4·9 kW)
Range: 450 km
Height accuracy: 220 m minimal
Elevation coverage: 0 – 20° with option to –3°
Antenna type: Flat-slotted array
Antenna rotation speed: 6 rpm
Azimuth beamwidth: 1·6°

STATUS

In production for several overseas customers. Another version of the TPS-70, known as the TPS-70(V)-2, is under development and was due for delivery in late 1983 for evaluation by Switzerland. This programme, known as TAFLIR, will lead to additional units after successful field trials. Two other variants, the TPS-70(V)-3 and (V)-4 will also be available for production by 1984.

AN/TPS-70 tactical radar

CONTRACTOR

Westinghouse Defense and Electronic Systems Center, Baltimore, Maryland 21203, USA.

4320.153
TWS-QR TRACKING RADAR

The TWS-QR (track-while-scan-quiet-radar) system is a tracking radar designed by Hughes Aircraft Company and intended for use with a variety of ground-to-air defence missile systems. It has been designed specifically to operate under severe ECM and to present the minimum possible 'target' to anti-radiation devices and artillery threats. A number of potential uses are envisaged, including that of the surveillance and control radar for advanced SHORAD weapon systems or air defence versions of the AMRAAM air-to-air missile systems.

TWS-QR is a three-dimensional X-band radar and employs a 45 rpm rotating antenna with multiple electronically scanned elevation beams which provide continuous 360° azimuth search surveillance and multiple target track functions with a high update rate. The antenna has been designed to ensure ultra-low sidelobe performance as a protection against ECM, and this, plus a low power waveform, is used to counter anti-radiation homing and artillery threats from passive position locating radars. A number of features are used to provide the essential high tracking accuracy, including single-dwell, unambiguous range and doppler measurement, a pencil-beam antenna, elevation monopulse, a high update rate, doppler processing and high resolution coded waveform.

Operationally there are number of possible uses for the TWS-QR system. These include use as a new sensor for SHORAD C² and as a sensor for a new generation LOMADS weapon system where the high data rate could be combined with a weapon system having inertial or other self-contained guidance, eg an advanced Chaparral or an air defence version of AMRAAM.

In a tactical configuration, the entire system can be mounted on a single-axle trailer or a tracked vehicle for rapid mobility and positioning.

DEVELOPMENT

The TWS-QR was designed and built under contract to the US Army Missile Command. The prototype model delivered in 1982 uses a specially designed antenna. The US Army has also proposed a large scale integrated circuit programme to reduce size, weight and power, and to upgrade processing.

STATUS

The first prototype model (Exploratory Development Model) was delivered in early 1982 and field tests began in mid-1982. The EDM system is mounted in two mobile vehicles. The antenna, transmitter and receiver are mounted on a standard HAWK trailer while the signal processor, displays, control and data recording/reduction equipment are based in a standard van.

CONTRACTOR

Hughes Aircraft Company, Ground Systems Group, Fullerton, California 92634, USA.

2535.153
AN/TPX-42 PIDP IFF-ATCRBS EQUIPMENT

The PIDP (programmable indicator data processor) is an advanced sophisticated version of the AN/TPX-42 secondary radar system which was built for US Air Force, Navy, civil ATC and military air defence purposes. This latest state-of-the-art version nomenclatured AN/TPX-42A(V)10 is a secondary radar system comprising interrogator/receiver, data processor and display equipment which will be installed in over 100 AN/FPN-47, AN/GPN-12, AN/GPN-20 and AN/FPS-67D airport surveillance radars. The heart of the PIDP, which provides a significant automated extension of existing ATC capabilities, is a newly-developed programmable digital processing system that will provide the controller with more useful information consisting of flight identification, aircraft type, altitude, and ground speed. The PIDP system utilises a NOVA 3 mini-computer (utilising only 26 000 words of programmed storage), new vertical displays (OD-153/T) and/or indicator modification kits (OD-152/T or OD-152A/T) to upgrade existing OD58 and OD58A indicators to accept programmable features. Each system is capable of driving 16 indicators and provides the following salient features:

(1) directly compatible with the existing TPX-42 systems
(2) modular system concept facilitates system interface with other existing ATC facilities
(3) on-line diagnostic displays for routine and system tests
(4) operational software includes advanced tracking algorithms
(5) full NAS interface
(6) reflection identification and filtering
(7) minimum safe altitude monitoring and warning (MSAW)
(8) altitude deviation monitoring and warning.

Keyboards at each display are used for message entry and control of the display formats. Additional expansion features available include provisions for digitising primary radar, BRITE interface equipment for converting PIDP data into high-resolution TV video for presentation on BRITE indicators in the daylight ambient or tower cab environment, generation of digital maps and ATC simulators that permit mixing of live and synthetic targets at the facilities consoles.

Main units of the system are the SSR interrogator/receiver, the synchroniser/coder, the interference blanker (defruiter), the video signal processor (VSP), the indicator data processor (hard-wired for the original TPX-42 and a NOVA 3 computer for the PIDP) and the display consoles. The displays feature simultaneous display of PPI radar video and stroke written synthetic alpha-numeric data. Coded pulse trains appropriate either to the Mk X IFF/SIF or to the ATCRBS system are transmitted by the interrogator which is triggered by the synchroniser/coder; the latter providing either internally generated pulse or pulses counted down from associated primary radar. The defruiter accepts incoming signals from the receiver and applies automatic three-mode interlace defruiting. It can operate over a wide PRF range of from 150 to 450 Hz. The defruiter output is applied to the VSP which standardises and decodes all replies in the interrogator coverage area (active decoding). The VSP also identifies potential garble situations, detects true target position for range and azimuth, correlates and validates identity and altitude codes, and combines all this information into a single message for each aircraft once per antenna revolution.

These messages are received by the display processor computer which in addition to performing the functions of tracking, keyboard command processing, MSAW, reflection filtering, etc, also converts and corrects the altitude according to the prevailing conditions, converts the polar radar co-ordinates into Cartesian co-ordinates, and provides the converted data to the displays. Display refresh is locally provided at 30 times per second via a micro-processor located in each display.
STATUS
322 basic AN/TPX-42 military and civil systems were built by AIL and are presently in place at various sites in the United States and overseas bases. Basic and programmable versions of the AN/TPX-42 have been supplied to the civil/military authorities of Brazil, Bulgaria, Canada, Czechoslovakia, Iran, the Netherlands, Norway, Philippines, Poland, Spain and Taiwan. The PIDP production contract, calling for over 100 systems, was awarded to the AIL Division in August 1966 and was due to be completed in 1983.
CONTRACTOR
Eaton Corporation, AIL Division, Deer Park, Long Island, New York 11729, USA.

3703.153
AN/TPX-46(V) IFF INTERROGATOR
The Hazeltine interrogator set AN/TPX-46(V) is compatible with a wide range of missile systems and associated radars, including the Hawk and Nike-Hercules configurations and most versions of the AN/FPS and AN/TPS radar sets. Interface capabilities for other radar systems are incorporated. An easily transportable ground IFF (secondary surveillance radar) interrogator, the AN/TPX-46(V) interrogates radar targets and, when the aircraft replies correctly, provides indications of aircraft identity for display on the associated radar PPI. The interrogator also has the ability, when its associated radar has been disabled – except for the PPI and its power supplies – to generate its own main trigger, to rotate its own antenna producing antenna synchronising signals, and to display on the radar indicator IFF replies from suitably equipped aircraft. Even when subjected to environmental extremes, the interrogator antenna can synchronise with the radar antenna at speeds up to 25 rpm. In addition, the interrogator transmitter power can be reduced, making it suitable for use with ground control approach radar systems.

The interrogator consists of four basic operating units: the receiver/transmitter, the coder-decoder group, the control box and the antenna group. The antenna consists of an array capable of a beamwidth of 5·5° (nominal). This is achieved by means of sum and difference antenna pattern techniques providing interrogator sidelobe suppression and receiver sidelobe suppression. Until now, production of so narrow a beamwidth has required the use of arrays approximately twice as long.

The AN/TPX-46(V) provides a clean display by means of the defruiting action of its processor unit. Other circuits make possible the automatic countdown of the repetition rate of the radar trigger, when necessary, to a frequency suitable for use by the interrogator set. Also provided is a gain time control circuit.

A solid-state transmitter module is now available as a direct replacement for the original electron tube version, resulting in reduced maintenance costs of labour. The AN/TPX-46(V) operates in Modes 1, 2, 3/A and C or in the Mk XII configuration on Mode 4 in conjunction with a KIR-1A/TSEC computer, and if additional circuits are installed, the AIMS mode also can be provided.
CHARACTERISTICS
Receiver frequency: 1090 MHz
Sensitivity: 80 dBm
Transmitting frequency: 1030 MHz
Peak power: 1000 or 2000 W, selectable; lower power model available
Antenna: 2·23 m long; 22·7 kg weight
STATUS
In service with US Army Improved Hawk and Nike-Hercules missile systems, AN/TSQ-38 radars, and AN/TSQ-51 AADCPs; US Marine Corps Improved Hawk missile batteries. Also in service with a number of foreign states. The AN/TPX-46(V)7 configuration is now in production for the US Army Patriot air defence system (**2800.131**). In January 1983, Hazeltine received a $2·5 million contract for component modernisation and technical improvements to the system.
CONTRACTOR
Hazeltine Corporation, Greenlawn, New York 11740, USA.

3704.153
AN/TPX-50 IFF INTERROGATOR
The AN/TPX-50 interrogator is designed for integration with radars. The compact AN/TPX-50 has a nominal range of 24 km (expansible to 32 km). It can be used for aircraft identification in forward areas, for shipboard defence, for military and civil ATC, including ground control approach radar systems, and for other low-power applications.

The AN/TPX-50 operates in Modes 1, 2 and 3/A and also recognises identification-of-position and emergency replies. The interrogator decoders provide for 32 reply codes in Mode 1, as well as 4096 reply codes in Modes 2 and 3/A. If desired, it is also possible to process all Mk X (SIF) replies in the bracket decode mode. Bracket decode replies contain the characteristics common to all Mk X (SIF) replies and are therefore displayed on the radar PPI regardless of the specific code being used. In addition, upon inclusion of the required equipment, the interrogator can also operate in the additional AIMS mode.

More detailed information is given under this entry number in previous editions of *Jane's Weapons Systems*.
STATUS
Employed in some Improved Hawk, Nike-Hercules, and forward area alerting radar air defence systems used by the forces of Belgium, the Netherlands, Saudi Arabia and possibly other countries.
CONTRACTOR
Hazeltine Corporation, Greenlawn, New York 11740, USA.

3705.153
AN/TPX-54 IFF/SSR INTERROGATOR
Using a modular building block approach, the AN/TPX-54(V) provides an interrogator which meets military and civil needs of secondary surveillance radar users in ground and shipborne applications. The modular system provides sufficient flexibility for a single compact interrogator to meet a diverse range of mission requirements, including those of ground and shipborne air defence and military and civil ATC. The AN/TPX-54 is designed to military specifications and operates in up to four SIF modes from Modes 1 or B, 2 or D, 3A and C and also in Mode 4. The unit is capable of operating with up to a five mode interlace when used with a KIR-1A/TSEC computer in Mode 4. The mode selection may be made remotely at an external decoder or at a remote control box. The interrogator front panel also provides mode selection for maintenance purposes.

The AN/TPX-54(V) includes a number of options to make it suitable for a variety of applications. The basic system consists of five plug-in printed circuit boards in addition to the modular power supply and the receiver/transmitter. It has a predicted MTBF given as 3800 hours. Space in the unit allows the addition of up to 11 more circuit boards for various standard options or special requirements.

More detailed information is given under this entry number in previous editions of *Jane's Weapons Systems*.
STATUS
The AN/TPX-54(V) is in use in the United States as well as other countries. It is being supplied for use in a standard 19 inch (48 cm) rack and meets DoD-AIMS 65-1000, NATO STANAG 5017 and ICAO Annex 10 requirements.
CONTRACTOR
Hazeltine Corporation, Greenlawn, New York 11740, USA.

4317.153
OX-60/FPS-117 IFF INTERROGATOR

The Hazeltine IFF interrogator OX-60/FPS-117 is the beacon processor group for the FPS-117 minimally attended radar. The OX-60 is a 200 nautical miles system with sidelobe suppression and interrogator sidelobe suppression. It is capable of interlacing Modes 2, 3, C and 4 and parallel processing the replies. The system is all solid-state and to meet the requirements of a minimally attended site, it is designed in a redundant, automatic switch-over configuration. The configuration consists of a control processor, two processors, signal data and two receiver/transmitters which provide an MTBF given as 118 765 hours. The automatic fault test and isolation is extensive and under the control of an 8086 microprocessor. Self-test of the beacon system is carried out on a continuous basis and consists of both a local circuits self-check as well as a full test accomplished by the generation of simulated targets. This function occurs in parallel to normal operation and is completely transparent to it.

Once a fault has been detected the microprocessor goes into a fault-isolation function to isolate automatically the fault to a single or group line replaceable unit. A status message is then passed to the computer indicating which module is at fault and needs to be replaced. This automatic fault isolation reduces MTTR and simplifies maintenance procedures.

CHARACTERISTICS
Receiver frequency: 1090 ±3 MHz
Sensitivity: –83 dBm decoding

Transmitter frequency: 1030 ±0·2 MHz
Peak transmitter power: 2 MW
Duty cycle: 1%
Range: 200 nm
Effective beamwidth: 2·75 – 0·5°
Power input: 115/200 V AC 50 – 400 Hz, 3-phase. Single channel 350 W, dual channel 700 W
Specification: Designed to MIL-E-4158
STATUS
Being procured by the US Air Force under the Seek Igloo programme for the Alaskan Air Command. Meets DoD-AIMS 65-1000 and FAA 101051A requirements.
CONTRACTOR
Hazeltine Corporation, Greenlawn, New York 11740, USA.

4632.053
MODEL 2679 IFF INTERROGATOR

Model 2679 IFF interrogator is a compact, rugged equipment designed to operate and survive in the battlefield. It provides weapon systems with an all-weather fire capability permitting rapid engagement of enemy aircraft at maximum system range. It is particularly suitable for land mobile systems, helicopters and small ships, where the need is for short range identification, smallness, lightness and low power consumption. The equipment includes both interrogator side lobe suppression and receiver side lobe suppression capability for good azimuth accuracy while using small antennas. The model 2679 interrogator can be controlled directly from an associated fire control system computer or an associated control box.

The system consists of a receiver/transmitter, video processor, reply processor (sequential observer), timing and control, self-test, memory module and power supply. It has operator controls that allow mode selection, initiation of challenges and target identification.

CHARACTERISTICS
Transmitting frequency: 1030±0·2 MHz
Receiver frequency: 1090±0·2 MHz
Peak power output: 200 W
Sensitivity: –76 dBm
Weight: 28 lb (12·7 kg)
CONTRACTOR
Hazeltine Corporation, Greenlawn, New York 11740, USA

2547.153
AN/VPS-2 RANGING RADAR

This coherent pulse-doppler MTI radar is the range sensor of the Vulcan forward area air defence system (**2850.131**). Targets are acquired and tracked optically in this system but high-speed range and range rate data are required as inputs to the lead computing sub-system.

The axis of the radar antenna is servoed to the optical line of sight. The sight case and gun bore are physically fixed in alignment, but the sight reticle, which defines the optical line of sight, can move relative to the sight cage and is controlled by the gunner (see PIVADS **4015.131**). As the gunner tracks the target, the angular tracking rate and the radar-measured range and range rate are computed to predict future target position and then to control the gun position, introducing between the optical and firing axes the lead angle and super elevation required for successful target engagement.

Although primarily directed by optical means, the AN/VPS-2 radar has an automatic search and lock-on characteristic so that it tracks the target accurately.

CHARACTERISTICS
Frequency: 9200 – 9250 MHz, 6 crystal-controlled channels
Peak power: 1·4 kW
Average power: 10 W
Antenna: 4° conical beam ±20° in azimuth and elevation
Search range: 5000 m
Tracking capability: 15 – 310 m/s
Sub-clutter visibility: 40 dB or better

AN/VPS-2 range-only radar on a self-propelled multi-barrel gun

STATUS
Operational. The radar was developed under a US Government contract placed in 1966. The first prototype was completed in the same year and the equipment entered US Army service in 1969. In 1973, General Electric was awarded a product reliability improvement programme (PRIP) contract to study ways of increasing performance and the MTBF of the AN/VPS-2 radar, and as a result the latter characteristic rose from 37 to 122 hours. This led to the award of a further contract in 1975 for the production of modification kits for 2600 radars at US Army bases throughout the world. All sets have now been modified.
CONTRACTOR
Lockheed Electronics Company, US Highway 22, Plainfield, New Jersey 07061, USA.

2499.153
HIPAR (HIGH POWER ACQUISITION RADAR)

HIPAR (high power acquisition radar) is designed specifically for use with the United States Army's improved Nike Hercules surface-to-air missile system. The improved Nike Hercules system is deployed in key areas in the United States and overseas as a defence against high-performance aircraft, air-to-ground missiles, and tactical ballistic missiles. HIPAR was developed as an integral part of the system to provide significantly increased detection capabilities. It supplies long-range coverage and extremely precise azimuth data on small supersonic targets.

In addition to long range, the high-gain narrow-beam antenna used by HIPAR provides high-angle coverage. Its high-altitude coverage is said to be appreciably better than that of most present-day acquisition or surveillance radars.

To permit the full detection capabilities of the high-gain antenna to be realised despite the presence of enemy jamming, what are said to be unique MTI and receiver circuits have been developed for use with HIPAR. These circuits employ anti-jamming techniques that are said to provide capabilities not previously possible with conventional MTI techniques.

Both static and mobile HIPAR systems have been produced for the Army's use in both the United States and Europe. The mobile version (AN/MPQ-43), which uses the same electronics and components as the static version, is said to be the highest-powered mobile radar of its kind in the West. An important

HIPAR

feature of the antenna for the mobile version is its ability to be changed quickly from cosec² coverage to fan-beam coverage.

Mobile HIPAR is transported on five flat-bed trailers and can be emplaced by field army personnel after minimum training.

CHARACTERISTICS

Peak power: Classified
Average power: Classified
Frequency: 1350 – 1450 MHz
PRF: 417 – 438 pps
Pulse width: 6 μs
Receiver sensitivity: –113 dBm
Beam characteristics: Cosec² or fan
Beamwidth: Azimuth 1·2°; elevation 0 – 60°
Antenna azimuth rate: 6 or 10 rpm

STATUS

Operational. A total of 91 fixed HIPAR systems and 23 mobile HIPAR systems have been completed.

CONTRACTOR

General Electric Company, Electronic Systems Division, Syracuse, New York 13201, USA.

Mobile HIPAR

3721.153
HUGHES AIR DEFENCE RADAR (HADR)

HADR is the acronym by which Hughes refers to an advanced three-dimensional multi-mode radar designed for use in national air defence networks, either to replace ageing equipment, to enhance system performance or to fill gaps in the existing system. It is understood that many of the advanced features of this radar are a result of experience gained within the AN/TPQ-36 and AN/TPQ-37 mortar and artillery locating radars (**2848.153** and **1976.153**). Designed to meet new NATO ACE (Allied Command Europe) standard radar specifications, HADR will automatically detect, classify and report on all targets in its area of coverage. Operation is in the E/F-band (former S-band) of the spectrum and a 4·8 × 6 m planar array antenna is used, generally protected within a radome.

The HADR is a member of the same family as the VSTAR (**4080.153**) and there may be commonality of certain parts of equipment as well as operating principles.

The HADR primary radar operates over a bandwidth greater than 12 per cent. The radar achieves a detection range of at least 320 km for a 1 m² target. The instrumented range coverage is 500 km. Versatile computer control enables radar coverage to 30 000 m altitude and up to 24° elevation. False target reports are controlled to prevent ADGE system computer overloads.

Target positional data is provided in three dimensions. Target range is measured to the nearest range cell while target azimuth and elevation are obtained by beam splitting. Performance in clutter is achieved by a digital mean velocity clutter tracker in conjunction with a single or double delay MTI canceller. A range gated pulse doppler waveform and associated processing implementation also is provided. An antenna rotation period of 10 or 12 seconds is consistent with ADGE system data rate requirements. Primary or secondary radar target report rates can exceed 400 per scan at the radar output. However, transmission rates to the remote command and control site may be limited by data link capacity.

The HADR antenna sub-system scans a single pencil beam in the elevation plane under computer control by controlling the phase shifters of the antenna. By properly positioning this beam in sequential steps, complete elevation coverage is provided. The elevation scan is completed before the antenna moves one beamwidth in azimuth, providing complete coverage of the surveillance volume with no holes. Antenna beamwidth and the transmitted waveform are controlled at each beam position to optimise management of the radar time and energy resources. Beamwidth is 1·1° in elevation and 1·7° in azimuth.

The operational modes in the HADR system are

HADR antenna

defined by tables stored in the computer memory. The computer controls the following elements for each beam in the search raster:

(1) Instrumented range
(2) Peak power
(3) Pulse length
(4) Elevation beamwidth
(5) Waveform
(6) Elevation angle
(7) Frequency
(8) Detection criteria
(9) Plot extraction criteria
(10) Operation changed by software

The secondary surveillance radar (SSR) sub-system incorporates an IFF interrogator and antenna. The HADR antenna makes provisions for mounting the primary IFF antenna as well as the sidelobe blanking IFF antenna and for routeing the RF signals through the rotary joint. The beacon video processor which is part of the multi-function processor provides extraction of IFF video and provides active and passive decoding. It also provides SSR target report outputs to the radar controller. The radar controller provides a correlation of these plot reports with primary radar plot reports for a consolidated output to the command control site.

The HADR primary radar utilises several techniques to reduce the effectiveness of ECM. Sophisticated jammers are thwarted by the radar operational characteristics including frequency agility, coded pulses, multiple pulsewidths and multiple PRFs. The primary radar design has low susceptibility to jamming through the use of pencil

beams, a low sidelobe level antenna design, high receiver dynamic range and sharp channel selectivity. Automatic threshold control, target detection correlation and sidelobe blanking are techniques provided to handle any residual jamming which does get into the system. The burn-through mode and automatic frequency selection are special modes available for use in an ECM environment. Single pulse MTI is provided out to 60 nautical miles and two-pulse MTI out to 100 nautical miles. Seven-pulse range-gated pulse doppler is used to suppress rain or chaff clutter.

The system is capable of selecting operating frequency under computer control, and each frequency can be selected in about 40 μs, and may be changed on pulse-to-pulse or dwell-to-dwell basis. When selected by the operator, the system will automatically measure the interference level in each of the available operational channels and select that which is least affected.

The normal surveillance mode can be interrupted, at the operator's discretion, by a special mode which will intensify the energy on a specific target location. Normal surveillance volume is interrupted and all of the energy available is concentrated in a high energy waveform with a long dwell time in a sector automatically centred around the jam strobe which has been measured by the system and which indicates jammer direction. At high elevation angles, full antenna gain will be employed on the target even through the normal surveillance volume might call for a broadened beam.

STATUS

Hughes is building four HADR equipments for use by the Federal Republic of Germany, two to be used in conjunction with the NATO Air Defence Ground Environment (NADGE), and known as GEADGE (German ADGE), where they will replace AN/FPS-7 radars of the 412L radar network now in use. The first system went on-line at an unnamed site in the Federal Republic of Germany in October 1982. Two more systems became operational in 1983 and the fourth should be in service in 1984. HADR is also a contender for the NATO bulk buy of 10 cm radars to update the organisation's air defence system on the southern flank.

In January 1981 Hughes announced a contract for the supply of radars for Norwegian air defence. All three of these are to be used in shelters built into the tops of mountains. The antennas will be on elevators so that they can be retracted into environmentally controlled areas for routine maintenance.

One HADR system has been sold to Malaysia as part of the Malaysian Air Defense Ground Environment (MADGE) programme. Hughes is prime contractor on this programme.

CONTRACTOR

Hughes Aircraft Company, Ground Systems Group, Fullerton, California 92634, USA.

4080.153
VSTAR/VSTAR-PT AIR DEFENCE RADAR

Hughes has introduced a new air defence radar based on the operating principle of the company's AN/TPQ-36 and AN/TPQ-37 weapon locating radars (**2848.153** and **1976.153**) and incorporating some elements of the hardware of the latter, thus achieving common logistic support between the two radars. The new radar, VSTAR (variable search and track air defence radar), is an E/F-band (former S-band) equipment designed for rapid deployment and is configured in a variety of transportable forms and is primarily intended as a mobile system and secondly for static use in a gap-filler role. VSTAR has a wide instantaneous field of view (90°) and a 30° elevation field of view. The precision tracking (PT) variant has 90° elevation and 30° azimuthal field of view.

The planar antenna array measures approximately 7 × 11 metres and employs a combination of electronic scanning and mechanical rotation for target search and detection, although multiple targets can be tracked by electronic beam steering with the antenna array stationary. While rapidly rotating, the radar scan covers the entire aircraft penetration envelope, and a precision radar beam searches to a range of 250 km and up to 30 000 metres in altitude. Simultaneously, a beam also scans medium range at a faster rate to provide a quick reaction to low-flying or pop-up targets. The electronically scanned beam can search and track any point within the large azimuth-elevation sector while the antenna is being rotated. This allows electronic back and forward scan for immediate target verification and track initiation, multiple target tracking in high traffic density, variable track update rates, long dwell for non-cooperative identification, and ECM burn-through.

STATUS

VSTAR was demonstrated in three nations in 1980-82 and it is understood that this radar has been submitted for a number of other air defence

VSTAR air defence radar mounted on a tracked vehicle

requirements in NATO and elsewhere. Production contracts have been received but no details are available.

CONTRACTOR

Hughes Aircraft Company, Ground Systems Group, Fullerton, California 92634, USA.

5607.153
MULTI-FUNCTION RADAR (MFR)

The Multi-Function Radar (MFR) is a next generation land-based weapon control system that has been developed from the naval FLEXAR programme (**3258.253**). It uses technology derived from this programme and is intended for use with existing I-HAWK and other short-to-medium range missiles to provide a significant reduction in manpower and equipment, improved mobility and transportability, improved operation in ECM conditions and reduced life cycle costs. Further information is given under the FLEXAR entry in the naval radar section.

STATUS

Development is proceeding in parallel with FLEXAR. During 1983, the system successfully completed testing with the Improved Hawk missile and US Navy Standard.

CONTRACTOR

Hughes Aircraft Company, El Segundo, California 90245, USA.

5617.153
CONUS OTH-B OVER-THE-HORIZON RADAR

A new generation radar system, known as CONUS OTH-B (Continental United States over-the-horizon-backscatter) has been developed to provide electronic surveillance of aircraft at extended ranges of 500 to 1800 nautical miles (800 to 2880 km). Operating in the high frequency band, where the radar energy is reflected by the ionosphere, this ground-based radar is capable of over-the-horizon detection and tracking of aircraft and cruise missiles at any altitude. The system operates between 6·7 and 22·3 MHz, although this frequency range will be extended to 5 to 28 MHz later, and has two separate (bistatic) transmit and receive sites. On the United States eastern seaboard a prototype system has been in operation, the transmitter being located at Moscow US Air Force Station, Maine, with the receive site at Columbus Falls US Air Force Station, Maine, 110 miles (177 km) away. The latter also houses the operations centre although it is eventually due to be transferred to Bangor International Airport. Southward-looking and western seaboard systems are also planned. To adapt continuously in real-time to the prevailing ionospheric conditions, both the transmit and receive functions are completely computer controlled. Operation of the transmit and receive sites is synchronised in absolute time to better than one microsecond accuracy by Loran-C. The experimental transmissions from the Maine site covered an arc from 016·5 to 076·5° and 500 to 1800 nautical miles (800 to 2880 km) in range. This region was selected to evaluate the radar performance in an area where propagation will be most likely affected by the aurora, and to provide surveillance of the busy North Atlantic routes where aircraft targets are readily available at all times. Full-scale development is now taking place and the eastern seaboard system will become operational in three 60° phases. The first, covering the north-eastern sector, will be ready by mid-1986, and the second by the end of 1986. The entire OTH-B project is due for completion by 1989 and will consist of a three-sector eastern seaboard system covering 180°, a similar western seaboard system and a two-sector southward-looking coverage of 120°.

The transmit antenna array consists of four separate side-by-side 12-element sub-arrays, each optimised to cover a different portion of the total operating range. Together they provide the capability to operate anywhere between 6·7 and 22·3 MHz and present low voltage-standing-wave-ratios to the transmitters at all scan angles. The highest frequency sub-array (Band E) uses vertical dipole elements, the other three sub-arrays use canted dipoles. This arrangement provides elevation patterns which match that required for propagation to the desired ranges via ionospheric reflections. The elements are

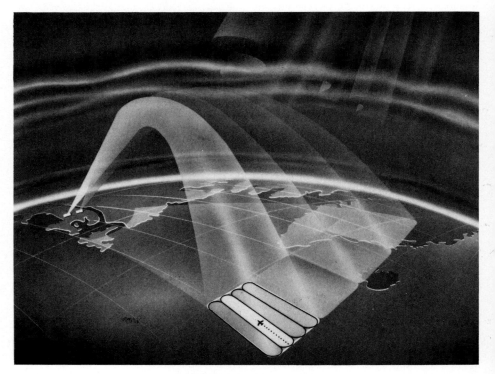

OTH-B range/azimuth sectors

mounted in front of a common backscreen ranging from 45 to 100 feet (14 to 30·5 m) high and approximately 2265 feet (690 m) long. This will be extended to 3630 feet (1106 m). A common groundscreen extends 750 feet (230 m) in front of the arrays.

Twelve transmitters operate simultaneously into the 12 elements of a selected sub-array. Each transmitter contains four band-tuned tank circuits which respectively match the four antenna sub-arrays. Each transmitter produces up to 100 kW average power, with very high spectral purity at any operating frequency between 6·7 and 22·3 MHz. A 100 kW water-cooled tetrode is used in the final high-power amplifier stage of each transmitter. The 12 transmitters are driven by a beamformer at low power level which causes the transmitter/array combination to collimate the desired 7·5° beam and steer it to the selected positions. In operation the transmit site generates up to 100 MW of effective radiated power.

The receive antenna is a broadside array of 137 fan monopole elements mounted in front of a backscreen which is 3906 feet (1190 m) long and 50 feet (15 m) high. In an operational antenna, the length will be increased to 5230 feet (1594 m). As in the transmit array, a groundscreen extends 750 feet (230 m) in front of the entire receive array. Two bands are used to cover the 6·7 to 22·3 MHz range, a low band covering 6·7 to 11·2 MHz and a high band from 11·2 to 22·3 MHz. On the low band, every other element is used across the array giving a total of 68 active elements. Dividing the array in this fashion and using variable aperture weights in beamforming results in virtually constant receive beamwidths of 2·75° with no grating lobes over the full 60° azimuth coverage.

The active receive elements are fed via buried coaxial lines to elemental receivers, one for each active element, for a total of 82. Each elemental receiver employs 16 RF preselectors to cover the frequency range. In each receiver, the received signals are amplified, filtered and digitised before being passed to the beamformer/signal processor group. The beamformer combines the outputs to form four simultaneous receive beams spatially coincident with the range/azimuth sector. This four-beam cluster scans synchronously with the transmit beam. Beamwidth, beam spacing, pointing angle correction for frequency and real-time measured receive sub-system errors are controlled by the receive control computer. The signal processor processes the four receive beams virtually simultaneously. Functions include MTI, interference suppression, range and doppler resolution processing, non-coherent integration, peak detection and parameter estimation.

At the heart of the system are very high speed computer, data processing and display systems which are used to control the radar, process the returned signals, monitor the HF propagation environment and display the information in a variety of formats to the operator. These displays are both alpha-numeric and graphic types to provide the operator with the maximum amount of information on target speed, track, position, altitude and other special characteristics, and also to adjust the transmission frequency to suit the prevailing HF environmental conditions. When the system is fully operational it is designed to give advanced warning of at least 1 to 1½ hours, even for supersonic aircraft, and, since it uses skywave propagation techniques, it can track very low-flying aircraft and cruise missiles at the same ranges as those flying at higher altitudes.

CONUS OTH-B has three modes of operation:

Normal mode
In this mode a surveillance barrier is established up to 30° wide, anywhere within the 60° azimuth sector, and up to 500 nautical miles (800 km) deep. A step-scan technique is used to illuminate this barrier on a regular, periodic basis by sequential illumination of four contiguous range azimuth sectors. Each sector normally covers a 7·5° by 500 nautical miles (800 km) area, thus four sectors form the 30° wide barrier. Four parallel receive beams, with 2·5° centre spacings, are formed to be coincident with each range azimuth sector and collect the signals reflected from targets in the coverage area. The starting range for each sector in the barrier can be chosen independently.

Interrogate mode
The interrogate mode illuminates one particular range azimuth sector and can be positioned anywhere within the 60° azimuth by 500 to 1800 nautical miles (800 to 2880 km) range capability of the radar. The interrogate range azimuth sector is illuminated by contiguous coherent dwells. As with the normal mode, four parallel receive beams, spaced

CONUS OTH-B E-band transmit antenna section

on 2·5° fixed centres, collect the reflected target energy. The interrogate mode is a special mode intended to provide extra detection energy, contiguous illumination, and high range, velocity and azimuth resolution. It is used in circumstances to enhance the characterisation of particular targets.

Interleaved mode
This combines the interrogate and normal modes. One interrogate mode dwell is provided after each full scan of the normal mode barrier. Separate radar operating parameters can be selected independently for the interrogate and normal mode portions of the scan. This mode allows the barrier surveillance to be retained while focusing on special target situations anywhere in the coverage region.

DEVELOPMENT
A contract for the prototype system was awarded to General Electric in 1975 and, after the contract was restructured in 1977, an experimental system was developed to demonstrate technical feasibility. Initial testing took place from June 1980 to June 1981 and about one year later General Electric received a contract from the US Air Force to begin full-scale development of the project. The first part of this, the initial operating sector (IOS), was approximately 30 per cent complete in January 1984 and is scheduled to be fully operational by mid-1986. The IOS is a 60° wide sector, located in Maine, and is orientated north-east to illuminate the same geographic region as that used for testing of the experimental system. Funding for the second 60° sector was approved in 1983 but that for Sector 3 was delayed until 1985. When the

complete system is operational it will cover 180° of the United States eastern seaboard.

For the proposed western seaboard system, sites have been chosen at Mountain Home Air Force Base, Idaho, Klamath Falls, Oregon, and Rimrock Lake near Alturas, California. The first west coast sector will be commenced in 1986. Long-term planning for the southward-looking system has been implemented. Consideration was also given to a northwards looking sector but the wider irregularities of the ionosphere and the effects of the aurora preclude a reliable system. This region is already covered by the DEW line and the Seek Igloo chain. The cost of the complete OTH-B system has been estimated at $1300 million with a completion date of 1989.

As well as the static OTH-B systems a tactical system known as ROTHR (relocatable over-the-horizon radar) is being investigated. The system would be transportable and could be used in such areas as rapid deployment forces or carrier battle groups. Because of the requirement for deployment, it would be a great deal smaller and lighter than OTH-B and, consequently, less capable. The US Navy is investigating a number of competitive proposals for detection of aircraft and ships over a 64° sector from 500 to 1600 nautical mile range.

STATUS
In full scale development. The first 60° sector, looking north-east, is due to be operational in 1986.

CONTRACTOR
General Electric Company, Electronic Systems Division, Syracuse, New York 13201, USA.

4082.153
DANISH COAST RADAR
Cardion is developing and producing a new E/F-band (former S-band) coastal defence radar under a contract awarded in 1979 by NATO with the code-name Baltic Approach. A number of these radars will be installed around the Danish coast and the system is also known by the initials DCR, for Danish coast

radar. Very little has been revealed of the radar itself, apart from the operating frequency band and the fact that it is thought to be a modestly priced equipment.

Other European companies believed to have submitted proposals for the Baltic Approach project include Plessey, AEG-Telefunken, Selenia and SMA. It is thought likely that similar requirements in other

NATO countries will be met in the future with radars of this type.

STATUS
Development and installation.

CONTRACTOR
Cardion Electronics, Long Island Expressway, Woodbury, New York 11797, USA.

3648.153
STARTLE
STARTLE is a prototype surveillance and target acquisition radar for tank location and engagement, under development by Martin Marietta for the US Army Night Vision and Electro-Optics Laboratories, the Combat Surveillance and Target Acquisition Laboratory and the Defense Advanced Research Projects Agency. Martin Marietta is applying advances made in 94 GHz radar technology to demonstrate its ability to enhance target acquisition, location, and engagement under conditions of rain, snow, dense fog, or smoke which characteristically reduce visibility and limit these capabilities both by day and night.

The system has been installed and tested on an M60A3 tank, and it avoids undue complexity and increased tank gunner workload by integrating radar information with the thermal sight display. The gunner can therefore locate and fire on targets using radar acquisition as easily as he can using the thermal sight. The integrated display also avoids the need for additional space for displays in the tank interior.

STARTLE operates with low power consumption in either of two modes: coherent MTI is used to detect radially-moving targets; area MTI permits acquisition of creeping and tangential targets. The spread spectrum waveform, used with area MTI processing, also provides smoothing of clutter, glint, and multi-

path effects. The solid-state transmitter operates with a mirror-scanned paraboloid antenna located on the left of the tank turret. A rotating closure and armoured housing protects this component from indirect artillery fire, and accidental damage from trees or other obstructions. With the lid open the antenna can scan 3·75° up or down and 20° left or right independent of the movement of the gun.

STATUS
Development programme is now completed. No further activity at present.

CONTRACTOR
Martin Marietta Orlando Aerospace, Orlando, Florida 32855, USA.

NAVAL RADAR

CANADA

5677.253
AN/SPS-503 SURVEILLANCE RADAR

The AN/SPS-503 is a high performance, lightweight surveillance and target indicating radar operating in the E/F-band. In its standard configuration it is suitable for naval ships with displacement of 500 tons upwards. It is of rugged construction and has been designed to operate in very hostile electronic environments.

The main features of this radar are a coherent E/F-band transmitter with broadband frequency agility; pulse compression; a narrow beam, low sidelobe cosecant^2 antenna; and digital MTI with adaptive velocity compensation. The transmitter employs a TWT amplifier fed by a frequency synthesiser with high stability giving very good MTI performance. The low noise, high dynamic range receiver compresses target returns to provide high jamming resistance and range resolution. This pulse compression system has been optimised to ensure very low range sidelobes, even in the presence of large doppler shifts.

The signal processor is an all-digital unit providing MTI, CFAR and PRF discrimination facilities. Two independent signal channels are provided, one for MTI data and one for non-MTI data. The MTI system embodies adaptive velocity compensation which

AN/SPS-503 transmitter/receiver/signal processor assembly

shifts the notch of the MTI filter to compensate for the average clutter velocity. This is done independently for each area cell within the scan coverage to compensate for gross clutter motion. In addition a fast response loop is used to compensate for antenna movements due to the ship's motion. The optional plot extractor outputs digital reports of the range and azimuth of target centroids. The thresholding system

employed gives maximal detection probability for targets and minimal probability of clutter-induced false alarms.

The SPS-503 uses a double curvature reflector antenna with horn feed. The reflector is configured to give a cosec^2 pattern in the elevation plane. Polarisation is variable from linear to circular and dual rotation rates of 10 and 20 rpm are provided. Antenna stabilisation is available and an IFF antenna is integral with the main antenna. A smaller, lightweight antenna is also available for applications where masthead weight is critical.

STATUS

This system has been ordered by the Canadian Armed Forces for fitment during the Destroyer Life Extension Programme (DELEX). Initial deliveries will take place in 1984. Both this radar and the CMR-3 (**5678.153**) were developed in co-operation with the Marconi Company, England, where they are known under the nomenclature S1800 series (**3687.253**). Other company products include C-band naval air search radar and land-based mobile low-level air defence systems.

CONTRACTOR

Canadian Marconi Company, 415 Legget Drive, PO Box 13330, Kanata, Ontario, Canada K2K 2B2.

DENMARK

1575.253
TERMA SCANTER MIL NAVIGATION AND SURVEILLANCE RADARS

The Terma navigational radar systems are designed to form an integral part of the total radar system on board naval vessels. They operate in S- and X-bands and are suitable for both navigation and surveillance. A multi-display system capable of operating in various master/slave combinations is available. The operational mode is selected on either display by illuminated push-buttons.

All units are autonomous, ie containing their own power conditioning circuits, and are built up as a modular system using accessible plug-in modules for ease of servicing. The system can be single X-band, single S-band, combined S- and X-bands, double X- and S-bands, or synchronised twin X-band. The modular technique also facilitates system extension. The following features can be supplied as options: electronic bearing line, sector transmission, reflection plotter, and true motion.

Terma Scanter Mil display

Scanner Unit

The antenna is a horizontally-polarised slotted waveguide antenna with narrow beam and low sidelobe level. The antenna feed system (including a waveguide rotary joint) offers a low standing wave ratio at the input flange. Two scan rates may be selected by electronic switching of the drive system. The scanner position information is given through synchro transmitters and heading marker signal. The unit is driving-rain proof and a de-icing system is included.

Receiver/Transmitter Unit

The transmitter tube is a pulsed magnetron which is controlled from a solid-state magnetic modulator. Two pulse repetition rates and two pulsewidths may be selected individually. The modulator is divided into two separate assemblies with common input and output circuits, one for long and one for short pulse. The trigger assembly synchronises the total system and selects automatically internal or external synchronising mode. A trigger-pulse shaper and delay assembly perform compensation for transit times in the waveguide and receiver system. The RF system is integrated in one assembly and includes the waveguide duplexer, the T-R switch, the IF mixer, the AFC mixer and the solid-state local oscillator.

Display Unit

A whole range of displays is available all of which have the same physical size and common basic circuitry. The 16-inch tiltable display is flat-faced with all controls and readouts available from the front.

Deflection is based on the fixed coil principle. Presentation of radar video and synthetic video presentation such as vectors, target number, electronic bearing lines, etc are performed simultaneously. A series of displays ranging from navigational to complex tactical with automatic target tracking and target assignment to weapon systems of medium complexity is available.

All displays are fitted for operation from three independent radar sources of virtually any kind.

CHARACTERISTICS

Antenna: 2·1 m slotted waveguide (X-band), 4 m (S-band)

Terma Scanter Mil X-band antenna

Scanner rotation: Switchable between 24 and 48 rpm ± 10% at 60 Hz or 20 and 40 rpm ± 10% at 50 Hz input frequency

Horizontal beamwidth: <1° within 3 dB points (X-band), 2° (S-band)

Vertical beamwidth: 20° within 3 dB points

Polarisation: Horizontal

Gain: >30 dB (X-band), >28·5 dB (S-band)

Receiver/Transmitter unit

Transmitter frequency: 9 GHz (X-band), 3 GHz (S-band)

PRF

Short pulse: Nom. 4000 Hz ± 200 Hz

Long pulse: Nom. 2000 Hz ± 200 Hz

Pulse length: 0·06 ± 0·01/µs, or 0·6 ± 0·1/µs

Peak power: 20 kW ± 1 dB measured at the output flange

STATUS

In service with the Danish and Swedish Navies.

CONTRACTOR

Terma Elektronik AS, Hovmarken 4, 8520 Lystrup, Denmark.

4633.253
TERMA SCANTER MIL PLOT DATA SYSTEM

The Plot Data System (PDS) is a modular Command, Control, Communications and Information system (C³I) designed to replace electro-mechanical plotting tables and to provide data link communication capability in naval vessels not equipped with Tactical Data Systems (TDS).

The system enables NATO data link communication but can also be supplied for customer specified data link. Naval vessels fitted with PDS are able to exchange tactical data as well as with other TDS with compatible data link capability.

The system provides high speed plot correlation and tactical situation assessment and displays simultaneously raw radar video, synthetic video, IFF and computer generated colour graphics on two special purpose display systems.

PDS consists of the following basic modules:

(1) a central system processor which contains all interfaces to navigation instrumentation, ships sensors, communication systems and weapon systems in addition to all PDS system units. It also serves as the main PDS co-ordination unit
(2) a local operation plot (LOP) display which is a 16-inch plan position indicator with its own tracking and display processors. The LOP will display raw radar video and IFF video as well as synthetic video such as target symbols, measurement vectors, alpha-numeric characters, small maps and index lines
(3) a general operational plot (GOP) display consisting of a high resolution 19-inch raster scan colour monitor and a graphic processor which compiles and controls the picture complete with maps, tracks, plots, target vectors, target symbols and measurement vectors
(4) a system terminal forming the operator's interface

and consisting of a keyboard with a high precision rollerball and dual alpha-numeric displays. Each display provides 12 lines of 40 alpha-numeric characters. One display is used for PDS command menus, the other for own ship data, track information, pointer position and measurement vector information, as well as for high priority messages
(5) peripheral equipment which includes a dual tape station for instant dumping of the GOP picture, a printer and a graphic colour printer.

STATUS

In production and sold to a number of NATO and non-NATO countries for installation on small and medium naval and surveillance vessels.

CONTRACTOR

Terma Elektronik AS, Hovmarken 4, 8520 Lystrup, Denmark.

FRANCE

1894.253
DRBC 32 NAVAL RADAR

The DRBC 32 designation embraces a family of I/J-band fire control radars, of which there are at least five variants (denoted by suffix letters running from A to E) in use in French Navy ships, and which are associated with a variety of director units. The latter may or may not include optical direction facilities. Weapons associated with these directors normally are either 100 mm or 57 mm guns.

A stabilised mount is usual for DRBC 32 installations and, in all but the DRBC 32 A the radar dish is protected by a radome attached to the antenna assembly itself. The 'A' model, as seen on the

helicopter-cruiser, *Jeanne d'Arc*, has exposed circular reflector and feed assemblies. However, the DRBC 32 A as seen on anti-submarine 'T 47' class escorts do have a protective radome for the antenna. The *Aconit* anti-submarine corvette is fitted with the DRBC 32 B. The 'C 70' class corvettes, the *Colbert* and the *Duperré* have the DRBC 32 C, and the DRBC 32 D installation is aboard the 'F 67' class frigates. The 'A 69' class of Avisos are fitted with the DRBC 32 E.

DRBC 32 D fire control radar

1593.253
DRBI 10 3-D NAVAL RADAR

The DRBI 10 is a three-dimensional, E/F-band naval air surveillance radar for search and interceptor control functions. It is believed to be a naval version of the land-mobile radar Picador (TH.D 2200) (**2119.153**), which in turn evolved from the TH.D 1940.

More detailed information is given under this entry number in *Jane's Weapon Systems 1982-83*.

STATUS

The only known fittings are aboard French vessels. These include the carriers *Clémenceau* and *Foch*, which each have two; the helicopter carrier *Jeanne*

d'Arc; the guided missile cruiser *Colbert* and the trials ship *Ile d'Oléron*.

CONTRACTOR

Thomson-CSF, Division Systèmes, Défense et Contrôle, 40 rue Grange Dame Rose – BP 34, 92360 Meudon-la-Foret, France.

1889.253
DRBI 23 3-D NAVAL RADAR

The DRBI 23 naval radar is a D-band (23 cm) three-dimensional air search and target designation radar forming the main detection element of the French Navy Masurca surface-to-air missile system (**1177.231**). Transmitter peak power is quoted as several MW, and it incorporates a carcinotron oscillator. Six amplification stages are provided, these being capable of virtually identical gain at any frequency within the range of the carcinotron oscillator.

The antenna, which is protected by a large radome, is of the inverse cassegrain type. An array of feed horns directs radiation to a semi-reflective parabolic mirror which in turn returns the energy to a flat plate reflector. This imparts a 45° polarisation change which permits the formed beams to pass through the semi-reflector. Vertical angular information is

obtained by the use of monopulse techniques, these data being processed to provide corrected height information on aircraft targets. This information, together with plan position data, is available for use in the ship's action data system and weapon systems. Stabilisation against ship's motion is incorporated, and the antenna assembly includes an IFF antenna unit. The system provides for auto plot extraction and the DRBI 23 is interfaced with a digital computer. Associated with it are the Masurca missile tracking and guidance radar groups DRBR 51.

STATUS

In service with the French Navy missile frigates *Suffren* and *Duquesne*.

CONTRACTOR

Thomson-CSF, Division Systèmes, Défense et Contrôle, 40 rue Grange Dame Rose – BP 34, 92360 Meudon-la-Foret, France.

DRBI 23 radome on the Suffren *(Stefan Terzibaschitsch)*

3741.253
DRBJ 11 NAVAL RADAR

The DRBJ 11 is a new shipboard electronic phase scanned radar being developed by Thomson-CSF for the French Navy. Few technical details have been released for publication, but some indications can be gathered from the company's previous extensive work in this area of radar technology, and from a picture of the experimental antenna unit of the new radar. From the latter it will be seen that the array is composed of numerous separate radiating elements arranged concentrically on a disc surface. The active elements are connected in lines to be fed; in-situ computers determine their phases.

Thomson-CSF has revealed a preference for the use of diode phase-shifters for beam steering in electronically scanned arrays, and in this technique each source element (or reflector) has an associated

module which offers the microwaves several alternative paths corresponding to different propagation times. Diodes controlled by DC voltages perform the switching needed to select required phase shifts. In addition, each source contains its own control logic which receives instructions from the beam steering computer circuitry. From the photograph, the individual elements appear to consist of spirals, supported by ceramic bases, but in the absence of anything from which to obtain an indication of scale it is not possible to deduce the likely frequency employed with any certainty.

STATUS

The prototype is undergoing operational testing.

CONTRACTOR

Thomson-CSF, Division Systèmes, Défense et Contrôle, 40 rue Grange Dame Rose – BP 34, 92360 Meudon-la-Foret, France.

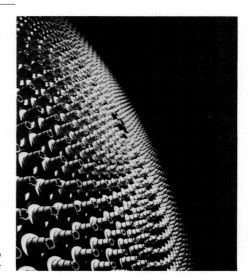

Close-up of Thomson-CSF electronic phase scanning naval radar

1890.253

DRBR 51 NAVAL RADAR

The DRBR 51 radar group provides for the tracking and missile guidance functions of the French Navy's Masurca surface-to-air missile system (**1177.253**). Search and target designation facilities are provided by the DRBI 23 three-dimensional air search radar (**1889.253**). The DRBR 51 is a multi-mode equipment and associated with the antenna assembly is a TV camera for optical tracking of low-flying targets. The complete system provides for the control of the Masurca missile.

Command signals are transmitted at frequencies in the 7 cm-band, and two missiles may be simultaneously controlled. There are two 5 cm radar tracking channels, 'blue' and 'yellow', one for each missile, and each radio command Masurca round is equipped with a 5 cm transponder to facilitate missile tracking.

When firing the Mk 2 Mod 3 radar homing version of Masurca, the main dish of the DRBR 51 operates as target tracker and I-band illuminator.

STATUS

The missile cruiser, *Colbert*, and the two missile frigates, *Suffren* and *Duquesne*, each have two DRBR 51 systems.

DRBR 51 radar group on the Suffren *(Stefan Terzibaschitsch)*

CONTRACTOR

Thomson-CSF, Division Systèmes, Défense et Contrôle, 40 rue Grange Dame Rose – BP 34, 92360 Meudon-la-Foret, France.

1893.253

DRBV 13 NAVAL RADAR

The DRBV 13 naval radar is pulse-doppler equipment, believed to operate in the E/F-band. It is stated to be a multi-mode radar providing both search and tracking facilities for the SENIT action data automation system installed in the *Aconit* corvette, which is the only vessel known to be fitted with the DRBV 13. The antenna array and turning gear are completely enclosed by a large plastic radome, itself mounted atop a prominent structure which is presumed to house the associated electronics, in an almost amidships location. No technical or performance data have been obtained.

1892.253

DRBV 20 NAVAL RADAR

The DRBV 20 is a long-range search radar operating in the metric waveband. Two antenna outfits are employed. The smaller, DRBV 20 A, version is installed in a variety of French Navy vessels and can be identified by its large open lattice antenna, of rectangular outline, slightly curved, and with a horizontal array of dipole feed elements. The larger, DRBV 20 C, is fitted on French aircraft carriers and has a flat, rectangular antenna array comprising three horizontal rows of dipole feed elements. No performance or other details of technical characteristics have been obtained.

STATUS

The DRBV 20 A is installed in the Tartar-armed 'T 47' escorts. The DRBV 20 C is fitted in the aircraft carriers *Clémenceau* and *Foch* and on the missile cruiser *Colbert*.

CONTRACTOR

Thomson-CSF, Division Systèmes, Défense et Contrôle, 40 rue Grange Dame Rose – BP 34, 92360 Meudon-la-Foret, France.

1891.253

DRBV 22 NAVAL RADAR

The DRBV 22 is a conventional naval search radar, having a L-band operating frequency and possibly incorporating dual-beam (high- and low-cover) facilities in some cases. It is widely fitted, both in French Navy vessels and in the ships of other countries. Different versions that have been identified are the DRBV 22 'A', 'C' and 'D' models.

The antenna assembly is very similar in appearance to the American SPS-6 and SPS-12 radars (**1744.253** and **1566.253**, respectively) but the French equipment can be readily distinguished from both US radars by the two supporting stays for the feed horn that are attached to the upper edge of the reflector of the DRBV radar.

STATUS

Known fittings in French Navy vessels include:
DRBV 22 A: five 'T 47' anti-submarine escorts; nine 'A 69' Aviso escorts; and the 'C 65' corvette *Aconit*.
DRBV 22 C: the trials ship *Ile d'Oléron*
DRBV 22 D: the helicopter-cruiser *Jeanne d'Arc*; the missile tracker ship *Henri Poincaré*.

Ships of several other nations have been fitted with the DRBV 22, in most, if not all, cases the 'A' version.

CONTRACTOR

Thomson-CSF, Division Systèmes, Défense et Contrôle, 40 rue Grange Dame Rose – BP 34, 92360 Meudon-la-Foret, France.

DRBV 22 A radar antenna on Aconit *(X I Taibo)*

1594.253

DRBV 23 NAVAL SURVEILLANCE RADAR

The DRBV 23 is a L-band (23 cm) long-range naval air search and surveillance radar, similar in appearance to the Jupiter naval radar (**1236.253**). The most readily discerned external difference is the prominent tubular horizontal supports for the DRBV 23 scanner, compared with the lighter structure of the Jupiter.

Two versions have been identified, the DRBV 23 B and DRBV 23 C, the former being that fitted in aircraft carriers of the French Navy, and the latter being a solid-state version fitted in the missile cruiser *Colbert*.

STATUS

The only known fittings are on the following French Navy ships: the aircraft carriers *Clémenceau* and *Foch*, the missile cruiser *Colbert* and the command cruiser *De Grasse*.

CONTRACTOR

Thomson-CSF, Division Systèmes, Défense et Contrôle, 40 rue Grange Dame Rose – BP 34, 92360 Meudon-la-Foret, France.

DRBV 23 L-band air surveillance radar

1062.253
TRITON II SURVEILLANCE RADAR
TRS 3030/TRS 3035

This is a C-band, 5 cm, air and surface surveillance radar for shipboard mounting, and is used for surveillance and target designation functions in the Thomson-CSF Thomsea naval combat systems (**1053.281**). In these systems, Triton can be used for target designation to the fire control units (Castor or Pollux) and with a TWS for surface-to-surface missiles and/or torpedo launching. It may also be used alone as a surveillance and navigation radar. Triton is produced in an MTI version (TRS 3035).

More detailed information is given under this entry number in *Jane's Weapon Systems 1982-83*.
STATUS
The Triton radar is in production for use in systems being supplied to French and other navies.
CONTRACTOR
Thomson-CSF, Division Systèmes, Défense et Contrôle, 40 rue Grange Dame Rose – BP 34, 92360 Meudon-la-Foret, France.

Triton naval surveillance radar

3685.253
TRITON C DOPPLER SURVEILLANCE RADAR
TRS 3050

TRS 3050 is designed for ships of 150 tons upwards to perform air and surface surveillance, low altitude missile detection, target designation to weapon systems, and emergency navigation under adverse conditions. It is suitable for either original fitting in new ships, or for use during refits.

It is a C-band radar, fully coherent synthesiser driven, with two receiver channels:
(1) air: with digital doppler processing, burst-to-burst frequency agility, automatic tracking and initialisation of targets
(2) surface: with pulse compression, pulse-to-pulse frequency agility, and advanced anti-clutter and anti-jamming processing.

As the adjacent photograph shows, Triton C employs the normal radar reflector of the Triton series

Triton C radar antenna

of radars but can be fitted with a new antenna allowing detection of modern threats such as diving and sea-skimming missiles. Most of the operational advantages are apparently the result of advances in transmitter/receiver and processor design and/or the antenna feed arrangements.

CHARACTERISTICS
Frequency: C-band
Max detection range: 30 km (Pd = 0·5, 2 m² aircraft target, doppler operation) or 60 km
SCV: At least 45 dB
First blind speed: Over 800 m/s
Antenna gain: At least 27·5 dB
Elevation pattern: 22°
STATUS
No details of development state or sales of the Triton C have been released for publication.
CONTRACTOR
Thomson-CSF, Division Systèmes, Défense et Contrôle, 40 rue Grange Dame Rose – BP 34, 92360 Meudon-la-Foret, France.

3254.253
TRITON S SURVEILLANCE RADAR TRS 3033

Triton S is an S-band air and surface surveillance radar for shipboard mounting, used for surveillance and target designation functions in the Thomson-CSF Vega II series of ships' fire control systems.

Specially developed for detection of small air targets (aircraft and missiles) in a heavy clutter environment, Triton S is a fully coherent, digital processing, pulse doppler radar which includes an independent pulse compression, frequency-agile receiver for detection of surface targets.

The antenna is of the non-stabilised type with a broad elevation lobe to counteract the effects of ship motion. The transmitter comprises a travelling wave power tube and the average power is quoted as 250 W. The radar provides two video signals; an air surveillance video and a surface video, which can be used for display, target designation and track while scan processing.

CHARACTERISTICS
Frequency: S-band – frequency agile
Average power: 250 W
Two receivers: Pulse doppler (processed range 1·5 – 26·5 km); pulse compression
Antenna rotation: 24 rpm
Detection range: Air target (fighter), 33 km; surface target, radar horizon
SCV: At least 50 dB
STATUS
In production. Ordered by Nigeria, Tunisia and other navies.
CONTRACTOR
Thomson-CSF, Division Systèmes, Défense et

Triton S radar antenna

Contrôle, 40 rue Grange Dame Rose – BP 34, 92360 Meudon-la-Foret, France.

3481.253
TRITON X NAVAL RADAR TRS 3040

This is an X-band air and surface surveillance radar for shipboard mounting, used for navigation, surveillance and target designation functions in the Thomson-CSF Vega-Canopus series of ships' fire control units (Pollux or Optronic directors) and with a TWS for surface-to-surface missiles and/or torpedo launching.

CHARACTERISTICS
Frequency: 300 MHz in X-band
Peak power: 200 kW with 0·3 µs pulse
PRF: 1500 Hz
Noise ratio: 9 dB

Antenna
Dimensions: 2·3 × 1·4 m
Weight: 175 kg
Azimuth beamwidth (3 dB): 1·2°
Rotation: 24 rpm
Transmitter/receiver: 1 × 0·6 × 0·4 m; weight 80 kg
Detection range: Air target (fighter), 20 km; surface target, radar horizon
STATUS
In production for foreign navies.
CONTRACTOR
Thomson-CSF, Division Systèmes, Défense et Contrôle, 40 rue Grange Dame Rose – BP 34, 92360 Meudon-la-Foret, France.

Thomson-CSF Triton X antenna

1063.253
CASTOR II FIRE CONTROL RADARS

Two versions of Castor II are available, Castor IIB and Castor IIC. Both versions are compact, lightweight and suitable for installation on both small and large vessels.

Castor IIB is an X-band monopulse and MTI tracking radar for weapons control. The radar is managed by a microprocessor which ensures high performance, even in severe environmental conditions against low altitude targets and jamming, by the use of monopulse techniques, broadband operation, high efficiency anti-clutter filters and an integrated TV tracker.

Operationally Castor IIB performs the following functions:
(1) fully automatic acquisition enabling very short reaction times
(2) accurate tracking of targets in the radar mode, TV mode and a combined radar/TV mode
(3) passive tracking of a jammer with range information sent from a tracking device linked to a surveillance radar
(4) display of splashes in the case of anti-surface firing
(5) autonomous surveillance, both continuous and by sector, with set absolute elevation.

Castor IIC is an X-band doppler filtering tracking radar for weapons control which is able to acquire and track targets in conditions of active jamming, chaff and heavy clutter. The high performance of the system is achieved by the use of fully coherent transmission, frequency agility, analysis of received jamming signals within all the useful bandwidth, auto-adaptive doppler filtering and central management by computer which matches the radar to the environmental conditions at all times.

Operationally Castor IIC provides:
(1) fully automatic acquisition enabling very short reaction times
(2) short bursts operation (1·5 ms) with simultaneous frequency agility and doppler processing

(3) pulse-to-pulse operation giving true frequency agility
(4) TV tracking or combined TV/radar tracking
(5) passive tracking of a jammer with range information sent from a tracking device linked to a surveillance radar
(6) display of the angular error between the shells and the target
(7) display of the angular tracking error on a jammer
(8) autonomous surveillance, both continuous and by sector.

CHARACTERISTICS
Frequency: X-band
Peak power: More than 30 kW

Range: 0 – 30 km
Acquisition mode: Fully automatic
Dimensions
Antenna: 1 m diameter
Transmitter: 1 × 0·6 × 0·42 m
Receiver and servo: 1·92 × 0·6 × 0·75 m
Weight: 620 kg
STATUS
In production. Supplied to a number of foreign navies.
CONTRACTOR
Thomson-CSF, Division Systèmes, Défense et Contrôle, 40 rue Grange Dame Rose – BP 34, 92360 Meudon-la-Foret, France.

Castor II tracker radar head

1064.253
POLLUX TRACKER RADAR TRS 3220
This is a shipborne tracker radar used in the Thomson-CSF Vega series of naval fire control

Pollux tracking radar, with opto-electronic sensor

systems and usually operated in conjunction with a Triton 5 cm surveillance and target designation radar. It is mainly for gun control operations.

The Pollux radar operates on a frequency in the X-band, 3 cm region, and is a fast conical scan tracker radar. Circular polarisation and solid-state circuitry, using silicon semi-conductors, are employed, and peak transmitter power is quoted as 200 kW. Range finding capability extends to 30 km, and target acquisition is stated to remain reliable to 20 km under the most adverse weather conditions.

CHARACTERISTICS
Frequency: X-band
Circular polarisation
Peak power: 200 kW
Rangefinder: 0 – 30 km
Precision
Range: 20 m
Azimuth: 0·5 mrd

Display: Type A/R, A/B or A/E
TV tracking: Optional
Dimensions and weight
Antenna: 450 kg
Transmitter and servo cabinet: 1850 × 600 × 600 mm
Receiver cabinet: 1850 × 600 × 600 mm
Fire control console: 1850 × 600 × 600 mm (computer included)
STATUS
Details of users have not been revealed but contracts for Vega fire control systems have been placed by both French and foreign navies. Known fittings include four Portuguese corvettes of the 'João Roby' class and West German, Greek, and Malaysian fast missile patrol boats. No longer in production.
CONTRACTOR
Thomson-CSF, Division Systèmes, Défense et Contrôle, 40 rue Grange Dame Rose – BP 34, 92360 Meudon-la-Foret, France.

1687.253
SEA TIGER II SURVEILLANCE RADAR TRS 3001
Sea Tiger II is a shipborne S-band combined surveillance radar, which can be used in the Thomson-CSF Thomsea naval combat systems. It has been developed to provide detection and tracking of missiles, including sea-skimming anti-ship weapons. By virtue of modular design and operating flexibility, Sea Tiger II can be supplied with either of two antenna types, thus allowing fitting aboard medium or large tonnage ships, or small fast patrol boats. It is designed to perform the following functions in a very severe clutter and jamming environment:
(1) air surveillance
(2) surface surveillance
(3) anti-missile surveillance
(4) target designation for weapon systems (guns; missiles)
Visibility in clutter is achieved through the use of complementary techniques such as circular polarisation, pulse compression, doppler filtering, and an anti-clutter reception chain.

A typical Sea Tiger II installation comprises:
(1) a transmitter with coherent amplifier chain emitting frequency-modulated pulses (pulse compression) over a wide frequency range
(2) a receiver with multiple reception chains: MTI,

Sea Tiger stabilised radar antenna head

lin/log, CFAR. The MTI is a digital linear device whose characteristics, associated with the stability of the amplifier chain, make it possible to detect a missile in the most severe clutter environment
(3) an antenna appropriate to the class of ship, either:
(A) stabilised double-curvature antenna with switchable circular/linear polariser and integrated IFF for medium tonnage ships and above
(B) non-stabilised lightweight antenna with a

broad elevation lobe to counteract the effects of ship's motion (FPBs).
CHARACTERISTICS
Operational performance
Detection range: 60 nm on 2 m² (fluctuation) target with Pd = 50%
Altitude detection: 50 000 ft (15 240 m)
Elevation pattern: Cosecant up to 50°
Sub-clutter visibility: >42 dB
First blind speed: Mach 2
Antenna
Gain: 30 dB
Polarisation: Circular/linear, switchable
Rotation speed: 15 and 30 rpm
Stabilisation: Better than ± 1·5%
Transmitter: Frequency agility, pulse compression, average power 1 kW, 66 kW peak
Receiver: Noise figure better than 5·5 dB, 4 different reception chains – MTI, lin, log, CFAR anti-clutter
STATUS
Derived from the Tiger radar (**2156.153**). In production. Ordered by the French Navy (DRBV 15), installed in Colombian F1500 frigates built in West Germany, and the Saudi Arabian F 2000 frigates.
CONTRACTOR
Thomson-CSF, Division Systèmes, Défense et Contrôle, 40 rue Grange Dame Rose – BP 34, 92360 Meudon-la-Foret, France.

1236.253
JUPITER NAVAL AIR SURVEILLANCE RADAR TRS 3010
The Jupiter is a L-band (23 cm), long-range air surveillance radar with a peak transmitter output power of 2 MW with a 2·5 microsecond pulse and a prf of 450 pulses/second. The antenna measures 7·5 × 3 m and has two rotation speeds: 7·5 and 15 rpm. Weight is approximately 1000 kg. Both primary and secondary (IFF) radar functions are provided by the one antenna system. Beamwidth at half power points

of the primary radar pattern is 2·5° or less. The elevation pattern is cosecant² up to 50°.

Range performance figures quoted give detection out to at least 200 km on a fluctuating target of two m² cross-section with a detection probability of 50 per cent, and under the same conditions a target with ten metres cross-section can be observed out to 275 km.

Solid-state circuitry is used throughout, with the exception of the microwave stages, and a fixed-frequency, water-cooled magnetron is used in the transmitter. Comprehensive signal processing

facilities are incorporated to provide maximum protection from natural interference (such as sea clutter) and ECM.

The receiver section provides multiple reception chains, wide dynamic range receiver and anti-clutter circuits for surface surveillance and detection of low-speed targets. Jupiter is produced in both non-MTI and MTI versions. The latter is equipped with a linear digital MTI receiver for operation in clutter environment.

The Jupiter is in use with medium and large vessels of the French Navy, as the DBRV 26 with different antenna, and on South African frigates. A solid-state transmitter version is in late development for the French Navy (DRBV 27).

CONTRACTOR
Thomson-CSF, Division Systèmes, Défense et Contrôle, 40 rue Grange Dame Rose – BP 34, 92360 Meudon-la-Foret, France.

Jupiter long-range surveillance radar antenna

3255.253
IFF INTERROGATOR ANTENNA 3973-A

The IFF antenna 3973-A is designed for transmission and reception of IFF signals. It provides for dual pattern capability (sum and difference). Part of the signal applied to the difference pattern is directed toward a rear radiating plane which provides an additional cover needed for completing the rear lobe of the difference pattern.

The 3973-A antenna also has provisions for mounting an RF switch and associated SLS switch driver, if required.

The equipment consists of a radiation plane, a distributor and a rear radiating plane, supported by an antenna base and covered by a radome.

CHARACTERISTICS
Frequencies: 1030 and 1090 MHz
Polarisation: Vertical
VSWR: 1·5:1 max
Input impedance: 50Ω
Power capability: 3 kW (peak)
Gain: ⩾17 dB
Effective horizontal beamwidth: 6°
Vertical beamwidth: 45°
Dimensions: 2 × 0·3 × 0·355 m
Weight: 21 kg
Complies with French Navy specifications E.591 and CA 203 for shipborne equipment installed in the upper works.
STATUS
In production.

IFF radar antenna 3973-A

CONTRACTOR
LMT Radio Professionnelle, 46-47 quai Alphonse Le Gallo, 92103 Boulogne-Billancourt, France.

1688.253
ELI 4 IFF SSR INTERROGATOR

The LMT ELI 4 is a shipboard secondary surveillance radar interrogator for IFF functions in association with transponders carried by friendly aircraft and ships. The equipment is designed for either rack mounting or independent installation. Apart from one tube, the ELI 4 is of solid-state design and extensive use of digital ICs is made. A number of the sub-assemblies are pluggable and are common to other interrogator versions such as the ground-based ER-116-A, the airborne ER-115-A and the NR-AI-3-A, NR-AI-6-A, NRJC-1-A for weapon systems.

CHARACTERISTICS
The ELI 4 incorporates a coder, a transmitter, and a receiver and, optionally, an RF antenna switch.
Peak radiated power: Selectable: 0·5, or 2 kW
Transmission frequency: 1030 ± 0·5 MHz
(± 0·2 MHz optional)
Receiver sensitivity: –83 dBM
Receiver frequency: 1090 MHz
Possible modes: 1, 2, 3/A and C, Mode 4 with suitable coder and decoder
Interlacing facilities: Up to 4 SIF modes. Permanent self-monitoring of all operational characteristics
Dimensions: 200 × 510 × 600 mm
Weight: 25 kg
Power supply: 115 V 400 Hz 3-phase 120 W

LMT IFF ELI 4 interrogator

CONTRACTOR
LMT Radio Professionnelle, 46-47 quai Alphonse Le Gallo, 92103 Boulogne-Billancourt, France.

1933.453
CALYPSO III SUBMARINE RADAR TRS 3100

Calypso III is a higher performance radar than Calypso II (**1240.453** in 1979-80 and earlier editions), but with the same general characteristics and same functions (navigation, surveillance, target designation) with a greater detection range and the additional capability of accurate range measurement. It is also of compact design and well fitted to the severe environment characteristics of a submarine.

Calypso III results from the joint studies of a submarine mast specialist (IKL – Ingenieur Kontor Lubeck) and a radar specialist (Thomson-CSF).

Its main features are as follows:

The periscope mast does not rotate, the antenna rotation being achieved by a pressure-tight drive mechanism fitted at the top of the mast. The upper part of the mast is streamlined. The transmitter/receiver is integral with the mast, which allows:
(1) simpler connection and reduced RF losses between T/R and antenna
(2) simpler connection with the fixed part of equipment (flexible cables).

Scanner of the TH.D 1030 Calypso II submarine radar. Span is 1 metre

Calypso III comprises four main parts: an antenna (the Calypso II antenna); a non-rotating periscopic mast (hoisting is achieved using the ship's hydraulic system pressure); a transmitter/receiver cabinet (secured at the foot of the mast); and an operational console.

The transmitter is a conventional magnetron transmitter with a frequency adjustable magnetron and the same I/J-band transmitter as Calypso II is employed. The receiver is fitted with RF elements of long service life, a modern mixer and a logarithmic anti-clutter chain. The operational console comprises: the control panel for radar and antenna; the display (16 inch (406 mm) CRT) with an accurate digital rangefinding device; and an operational panel. The optical-periscope direction and the ESM and sonar data can be displayed on the PPI. The accurate range measurement of a detected target can be made during short-time transmission.

The detection range capability of Calypso III for a typical ASW aircraft at 2500 metres altitude is 18 nautical miles, and for a surface vessel depends on the radar horizon.

STATUS
In production and supplied to three foreign navies. The earlier Calypso II radar was supplied to at least 13 foreign navies.

CONTRACTOR
Thomson-CSF, Division Systèmes, Défense et Contrôle, 40 rue Grange Dame Rose – BP 34, 92360 Meudon-la-Foret, France.

1934.253
ELR 3 IFF TRANSPONDER

The ELR 3 is the shipboard element of the Mk 10 IFF, and is compatible with the IFF Mk 12 system. It includes selective identification feature (SIF) and sidelobe suppression (SLS) on Modes 1, 2, 3/A and with provision for operation on Mode 4. Codes are set manually. The position identification (I/P) function is used for selecting friendly moving targets on the radar PPI. The ELR 3 is derived from the NR-AI-2A transponder produced by LMT for airborne applications, and it comprises two units: a remote box weighing 2 kg, and the main unit which contains receiver, decoder, encoder, and transmitter. The latter weighs 20 kg.

STATUS
In production. Considerable numbers have been procured by the French Navy.

CONTRACTOR
LMT Radio Professionnelle, 46-47 quai Alphonse Le Gallo, 92103 Boulogne-Billancourt, France.

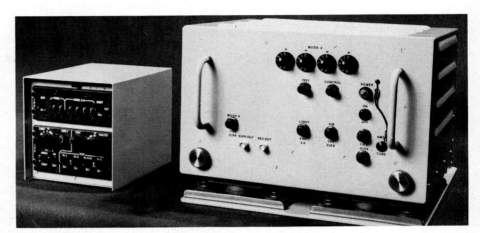

LMT ELR 3 IFF transponder

3684.453
CALYPSO IV SUBMARINE RADAR TRS 3110

The TRS 3110 Calypso IV radar is an I/J-band equipment designed to provide surveillance and navigation facilities for submarines. It is comprised of three units: an antenna, a transmitter/receiver cabinet and an operating console. Antenna and operating console are similar to Calypso III. To fulfil its functions, the Calypso IV is built around a simple navigation radar equipment, and modular design enables it to carry out additional functions merely by the addition of appropriate functional circuit cards, without changing the basic equipment.

Using a 1 ms pulse, it has a good detection range, limited only by the radar horizon (at least 10 nautical miles in free space), and using the narrow (50 ns) pulse, it has very high resolution over shorter detection ranges (down to about 15 metres). The receiver design has been developed to give good capabilities and performance in the presence of clutter.

The transmitter is a 25 kW (peak) klystron-driven unit providing several transmission options (continuous, sectoral, burst, or receive only – radar silence) giving maximum operational flexibility to meet specific requirements. The overall radar transmission parameters have been chosen to enhance the submarine's security by arranging for them to be similar to those of merchant ship radars, frequency and pulse length, in particular.

The operating console and its data processor permit the presentation, in either raw radar or synthetic form, of information such as target echoes, range and bearing labels, transmission sectors etc, as well as providing for operational control of the radar equipment itself.

STATUS
Development of the TRS 3110 Calypso IV was carried out by Thomson-CSF in 1978, and the first production deliveries were made in 1980 for various foreign navies.

CONTRACTOR
Thomson-CSF, Division Systèmes, Défense et Contrôle, 40 rue Grange Dame Rose – BP 34, 92360 Meudon-la-Foret, France.

INTERNATIONAL

3312.253
Mk 95 MOD 0 RADAR SET

This radar set provides search, acquisition, tracking and illumination for the NATO Sea Sparrow point defence missile system Mk57 developed by Denmark, Italy, Norway and the USA (**2770.231**). As such, the radar forms part of the Mk91 guided missile fire control system; Mk91 Mod 0 has a single director group, and the Mk91 Mod 1 has dual directors. Each radar has separate antennas for transmission and reception, the dishes of which are protected by radome covers. The radar receiver is carried on the antenna unit. The antennas share a common mounting on the Mk78 Mod 0 missile director. An on-mount TV camera is also provided.

Operation is probably in the I/J-band part of the spectrum.

The receiver is the responsibility of the Danish Radartronics Company, and this unit's functions include clutter filtering, ECM channel, signal conversion and amplification. The Mk83 Mod 0 radar set console has search and tracking displays, status and fault indicators, radar operating controls and built-in test equipment. Operating controls provide for such functions as scan pattern selection, ECM facility selection, check-out etc. The transmitter group Mk73 Mod 0 provides RF power for search acquisition, and tracking in air and surface modes,

target illumination and modulation for the Sea Sparrow missile; a reference signal for missile tuning; local oscillator for the receiver; range reference for the radar target data processor which provides target detection, doppler tracking, range tracking and angle track signals; visual and aural indications to the radar set console; ECCM; and test functions.

DEVELOPMENT
Development was initially undertaken in the late 1960s by Raytheon, and subsequently on a joint basis by companies in four of the seven nations which form the NATO Sea Sparrow group. The four were Denmark, Italy, Norway and the USA.

STATUS
In production.

CONTRACTORS
Raytheon, USA – Main contractor.
  MBLE Société Anonyme – Printed circuit boards.
  Radartronics, Denmark – Radar receiver.
  NEA-Lindbert, Denmark – Static frequency converter.
  Selenia, Italy – Firing officers console.
  Bronswerk-Amersfoort, Netherlands – Liquid cooler group.
  Fokker VFW BV, Netherlands – Director controller and launcher rails.
  Kongsberg Vapenfabrikk, Norway – Radar pedestal and fire control computer.

Mk 91 FCS for NATO Sea Sparrow system aboard Spruance, *showing the Mk 95 radar. Antenna on left is for satellite communications*
(Stefan Terzibaschitsch)

ISRAEL

3709.253
EL/M-2221 NAVAL FIRE CONTROL RADAR

The Elta EL/M-2221 is an I/J-band monopulse tracking radar for naval fire control applications. Its operational roles include: surface and air search and acquisition; surface-to-surface missile fire control; surface-to-air missile fire control; gun fire control against surface targets; and gun fire control against air targets. Low weight and compact dimensions make it suitable for installation aboard ships of all sizes, including small patrol craft and missile boats. In addition to its ability to control the Israeli Gabriel anti-ship missile (**6019.221**), both active and semi-active homing missiles can be controlled.

Dvora fast missile boat uses Elta EL/M-2221 fire control radar to control Gabriel SSMs and guns

Target acquisition can be initiated by designation from a search radar, other sensors (eg optical, ESM etc), or can occur automatically within a given sector. In the tracking mode there is automatic lock-on, and the radar is TV/optical tracker compatible. In the search mode, the radar performs track-while-scan, and miss-evaluation and ranging facilities are available.

CHARACTERISTICS
Frequency: I/J-band
Antenna: Monopulse
Diameter: 1 m
Height: 1·5 m
Weight: 230 kg
Radar cabinet
Height: 1·2 m
Width: 70 cm
Depth: 50 cm
Weight: 120 kg
STATUS
Production and in service.
CONTRACTOR
Elta Electronics Industries Ltd, (a subsidiary of Israel Aircraft Industries Ltd), Ashdod, Israel.

5696.253
AUTOMATIC MISSILE DETECTION RADAR

The Automatic Missile Detection Radar (AMDR) has been developed by Elta as a shipborne radar designed to automatically detect incoming sea skimming missiles in addition to normal air surveillance with automatic detection and TWS capability. It is designed for installation on ships from 450-tons upwards.

AMDR is a coherent pulse doppler radar operating in S-band to give fast alarm warning at ranges of over 30 km with a very high probability of detection. The system will detect and warn of an approaching 0·1 m² missile at 15 km with 90 per cent probability of detection. Velocity coverage is 0·3 to 3 Mach. The antenna is a lightweight, stabilised cosecant² unit with a total weight of 220 kg at the masthead. Coherent pulse doppler technique, combined with discrete Fourier Transform, doppler filtering processing and programmable data processing enable apriori filtering out of slow moving targets (below Mach 0·2) and target radial velocity measurement during a single antenna scan. Display options include a 16-inch PPI, digital scan converter colour TV display and an alpha-numeric tabulated data display.

The AMDR may be installed as a stand-alone system or added to the EL/M-2207, EL/M-2208, or other naval search radars.
CONTRACTOR
Elta Electronics Industries Ltd (a subsidiary of Israel Aircraft Industries Ltd), Ashdod, Israel.

3264.253
ELTA EL/M-2207 NAVAL RADAR

Elta Electronics Industries Ltd produces a number of military radars, details of most of which are classified. However some particulars have been released concerning the EL/M-2207 F-band general purpose naval radar, which is one of the EL/M-2200 range of shore and shipboard radars. The same basic transmitter/receiver unit (either singly or duplicated for diversity operation) is assumed to be used throughout the range, with differences in the antenna employed and the extent of additional facilities incorporated accounting for the main variations between models.

The EL/M-2207 is a medium power equipment offering high performance in both air and surface search roles. A lightweight stabilised antenna is used, the AT-101, which is claimed to require a reflector area only 66 per cent of that required by a conventionally designed antenna to achieve the same performance characteristics.

Operational roles include air early warning surface surveillance, target indication, and navigation. Other features are operator selection of transmitter pulse width, single knob frequency tuning, true motion display, and integrated IFF.

One or two IP-33 41 cm diameter PPI display consoles are normally fitted. Antenna polarisation is switchable linear/circular and there is remote control of antenna elevation angle.
CHARACTERISTICS
Transmitter
Peak power: 425 kW typical
Average power: 425 W typical
Frequency: 3·1 – 3·3 GHz tunable
PRF: 500 – 700 pps, long pulse; 1000 – 1500 pps, short pulse
Pulse length: 1·4 or 0·4 μs
Receiver
Type: Linear, with switchable STC, FTC, IAGC, Log-FTC-A Log, CFAR
Noise: 2 dB
IF frequency: 60 MHz
IF bandwidth: 1·4 MHz, long pulse; 3 MHz, short pulse
Antenna
Polarisation: Vertical/circular
Gain: 28 dB (F-band); 17 dB (IFF)
Beamwidth (3 dB): 3·3° azimuth; 10° elevation, cosec² to 30°
Rotation rate: 12 or 24 rpm, selectable
Stabilisation: ±15°
Dimensions: 2·4 × 1 m (reflector)

AT-101 antenna used in EL/M-2207 naval radar system

Performance
Detection range: 55 km, against fighter aircraft size target
Resolution: <75 m, short pulse; <230 m, long pulse
STATUS
No details of ship fittings have been released for publication.
CONTRACTOR
Elta Electronics Industries Ltd (a subsidiary of Israel Aircraft Industries Ltd), Ashdod, Israel.

4610.253
EL/M-2208 SHIPBORNE SEARCH RADAR

The EL/M-2208 is another member of the EL/M-2200 family and is a dual band shipborne radar, with integral IFF, for simultaneous air and surface surveillance. Two transceivers (S- and X-band) use a common lightweight, small size antenna mounted at masthead. Full automatic stabilisation provides complete coverage even in adverse sea states.

Long pulse and DMTI are provided for long range and air surveillance functions. A navigation facility is included by selection of a short pulse. Either separate or combined S- and X-band presentation, plus IFF, can be selected on a 16 inch display.

CHARACTERISTICS
Antenna
Stabilisation: ±15°
Polarisation: Linear/circular
Detection range: 32 nm (59 km)
Resolution: 1° (azimuth); 50 m (range)

Technical specification	S-band	X-band
Frequency	3·1 – 3·3 GHz (tunable)	9·345 – 9·405 GHz (fixed)
Peak power	425 kW	25 kW
Pulse length	1·4 or 0·4 μs	0·25 μs
PRF	500 – 750 pps (long pulse)	1000 – 1500 pps
	1000 – 1500 pps (short pulse)	

CONTRACTOR
Elta Electronic Industries Ltd (a subsidiary of Israel Aircraft Industries Ltd), Ashdod, Israel.

ITALY

1364.253
RAN-3L NAVAL RADAR (MM/SPS-768)

The Selenia RAN-3L (Italian Navy MM/SPS-768) is a long range, early warning radar, specifically designed for service in naval vessels in the frigate/destroyer/cruiser class.

The radar is of advanced design and provides air/surface warning and target identification for a modern shipborne defence system. A double curvature reflector with double channel IFF/radar feed is used. A new concept in radar design is the use of a composite coded waveform. This offers the following main advantages:

(1) ability to obtain great range accuracy and discrimination together with long range detection and a good overall reliability

(2) ability to maintain an adequate target visibility in the presence of either deliberate or natural interference, through the codification of information

(3) ability to take advantage of the diversified information contained in each packet of RF energy in order to extract the doppler components within a single repetition period. This provides the improved capability for cancelling clutter echoes while performing an RF agile transmission

(4) ability to ensure a CFAR condition and SCV in a clutter environment (also against clutter received through antenna sidelobes when the ship is underway).

Digital techniques are used extensively and

Antenna complex (large antenna on lattice structure) of the early warning search radar MM/SPS-768 (Selenia type RAN-3L) installed on board the Italian Navy cruiser Doria. *The same equipment is installed on* Veneto *and* Audace/Ardito, *and will be fitted on the* Garibaldi *and the new DDGs*

applications of this include: transfer of functions, coping with weather and clutter returns, verifying false alarms, mode change-over etc. The RF generation and amplification process is entirely

compatible because of a fully coherent transmitter/receiver chain. Therefore, changes in radar waveform, repetition interval, transmission frequency, pulse phase, and gain level are accomplished in real-time thereby giving greatly enhanced performance. A multi-pulse coded radiation in frequency agile operation is used in transmission. Code-matched filtering and pulse compression is performed in reception together with doppler discrimination to enhance echoes from genuine targets relative to noise or jamming.

CHARACTERISTICS
Frequency: D-band
Antenna: 3·6 × 7·6 m
Rotation: 6 rpm
Polarisation: Linear
Range: Approx 280 km
Range accuracy: 70 m
Angular accuracy: 0·4°
Outputs: Main video to air plots; normal video to surface plots; synthetic video to computer

DEVELOPMENT
Development was started in 1968 under Italian Navy contract.

STATUS
In current production, a number of systems are in service with the Italian Navy. An upgrade modification was developed in 1982 and is currently being introduced to achieve improved performance.

CONTRACTOR
SELENIA-ELSAG Consortium for Naval Systems, Via Panama, 52, 00198 Rome, Italy.

1699.253
RAN-10S NAVAL RADAR (MM/SPS-774)

The RAN-10S (Italian Navy designation, MM/SPS-774) is an advanced E/F-band coded radar for combined air and surface surveillance. The radar design philosophy is the same as that of the RAN-3L early warning radar (**1364.253**), and a number of items are common to both systems. Basic characteristics that the two radars share include:

(1) improved accuracy and resolution due to time compression of the radiated waveform

(2) excellent sub-clutter visibility in natural or deliberate interference

(3) clutter cancellation simultaneous with RF agility

(4) advanced CFAR under varying environmental conditions.

The antenna assembly is a pitch and roll stabilised reflector with double channel radar/IFF feed. The transmitter is medium powered coherent equipment, and the receiver incorporates a parametric amplifier, frequency programmer, quadrature IF channels, and digital processing.

The MM/SPS-774 is intended for fitting in vessels of medium tonnage such as corvettes, frigates, or fast destroyers. Typical operational roles include air warning, tactical air control, helicopter direction,

surface surveillance, navigation, and anti-ship missile direction.

The radar is optimised for target designation to gun and/or missile weapon control systems and for interfacing with automatic or semi-automatic command and control systems. Use of a coded waveform and digital processing of returns gives excellent clutter and jamming rejection performance. Frequency agility operation is available.

CHARACTERISTICS
Frequency: E/F-band
Antenna: 3·2 × 4·5 m
Rotation: 15 and 30 rpm
Polarisation: Linear and circular
Range: Approx 75 km
Range accuracy: 20 m
Angular accuracy: 0·35°

STATUS
In current production on behalf of several navies, and various systems are in service in 'Lupo' and 'Maestrale' class frigates as well as in CNR 600-ton corvettes.

CONTRACTOR
SELENIA-ELSAG Consortium for Naval Systems, Via Panama, 52, 00198 Rome, Italy.

RAN-10S antenna installation aboard a 'Lupo' class frigate

1365.253
RAN-11 L/X AND RAN-12 L/X INTEGRATED NAVAL RADAR SYSTEM

The Selenia/SMA RAN-11 L/X and RAN-12 L/X are combined naval search radar systems for fitment to ships ranging from fast patrol boats to multi-purpose corvettes as the primary search radar, or on larger ships as complementary close-range radar.

The system consists of two radar sets, one operating in D-band (formerly L-band) and the other in I-band (formerly X-band), mutually synchronised and radiating through a common stabilised antenna. The antenna can also accommodate IFF. The D-band equipment is a pulse-doppler radar based on fully digitised techniques and utilising a coherent transmitter/receiver chain with final transistor power amplifier stage. The I-band equipment is a well proven, ruggedised system in the family of pulsed oscillator radars, employing a reliable magnetron as the power source and fitted with completely updated signal processing facilities.

The video signals from the two radars are comprehensively processed through an interface unit

providing selectable output radar channels to feed the display system. The output channels comprise the I-band video for surface surveillance, the MTI video from the D-band radar and the combined D/I-bands video for air surveillance.

The system can be supplied in the RAN-11 L/X basic configuration or RAN-12 L/X extended range configuration. The former employs the D-band transceiver RTM-11 L; and uses an add-on solid-state power amplifier to provide a power output three times greater for the extended range version. The I-band radar, as well as the antenna group, remains unchanged in both configurations.

STATUS
In production. Operational with the Royal Danish Navy 260-ton fast attack craft, and on the CNR 2400-ton frigates and CNR 600-ton corvettes.

CONTRACTORS
SELENIA-ELSAG Consortium for Naval Systems, Via Panama, 52, 00198 Rome, Italy.
SMA – Segnalamento Marittimo ed Aereo, Via del Ferrone Soffiano, PO Box 200, 50100 Florence, Italy.

Roll and pitch stabilised antenna complex of the RAN-11 L/X search radar produced by Selenia-Elsag and SMA. The upper portion of the reflector operates only for the D-band

1368.253
ORION RTN-10X NAVAL TRACKING RADAR

The Orion RTN-10X is a conical-scan pulse radar operating in the I/J-band. It has been especially developed for one man operation, and installation with gun or missile fire control systems in naval vessels. Specifically, the Orion is used in conjunction with Selenia equipment (see Albatros system) or with other equipment (El San Giorgio, Ferranti, Galileo etc). Operational range is about 40 km.

The antenna system consists of a slatted parabolic reflector and feed, with integral trunnion box, mounted on an elevation over train director. Elevation coverage is +90 to –30°. The trunnion box contains the feed drive motor for high-speed conical scanning, and the assembly which performs the target acquisition scanning mode. The unit is fitted to accept a CCTV camera and camera control unit.

Acquisition of a target is initiated by external designating input sources. The radar then switches to the acquisition phase and upon detection of the target, automatic tracking is started. As an alternative, the radar can perform an autonomous search programme, in this way further complementing the surveillance system with the low altitude detection capability inherent to the Orion equipment.

More detailed information is given under this entry number in *Jane's Weapon Systems 1982-83*.
DEVELOPMENT
The development of the Orion series started in the early 1960s on behalf of the Italian Navy. Significant improvement in technology and design has been successfully introduced into the original project. The last series, which is named Orion-10X, was developed in 1970 and series production began in 1972. A further design upgrade was introduced in 1982.
STATUS
The radar has been extensively supplied to the Italian Navy and to many other navies. In series production. Orders by Ferranti Limited for the Royal Navy and Brazilian Navy were revealed in 1982.
CONTRACTOR
SELENIA-ELSAG Consortium for Naval Systems, Via Panama, 52, 00198 Rome, Italy.

Orion RTN-10X radar antenna director

1935.253
ORION RTN-20X NAVAL RADAR

The Orion RTN-20X is another of the family of I/J-band tracking radars that has evolved from the Orion-10X. It has been developed particularly for use in the Dardo ships' close-in weapon system (**1920.281**). In this application it is used for the automatic acquisition of air targets and spotting of rounds. It is a digital coherent monopulse radar, featuring high ECCM, sub-clutter visibility, and tracking performance.

Autonomous, automatic acquisition occurs at ranges from 5 to 12 km depending on target size and relative altitude of the radar antenna and target. Fully automatic, self-adaptive target tracking takes place thereafter, using monopulse techniques. Among its main features are:

(1) nodding free operation during tracking
(2) automatic spotting of the rounds
(3) automatic acquisition and tracking of a missile launched by the tracked platform.

Much consideration has been given in design to the reliability of the radar and to the rapid location of faults.
DEVELOPMENT
Development was started in 1973 as a private venture.
STATUS
Operational. The equipment is in production for installation on board 'Lupo' class frigates of the Italian, Peruvian and Venezuelan Navies.
CONTRACTOR
SELENIA-ELSAG Consortium for Naval Systems, Via Panama, 52, 00198 Rome, Italy.

Orion RTN-20X tracking radar

1936.253
ORION RTN-30X NAVAL RADAR

The Orion RTN-30X is a monopulse acquisition and tracking radar operating in the I/J-band. Its performance specifications have been dictated by the requirement of integration with advanced weapon systems having an intercept capability up to 15 km and particularly optimised to counter the low and very low altitude threat in an environment characterised by rain, sea, and land clutter, and dense electronic countermeasures. The RTN-30X antenna is implemented with a cassegrain type twisted polarisation reflector, which avoids aperture blocking, thereby optimising antenna gain while reducing the sidelobe level.

The RTN-30X employs a coherent chain for RF generation and operates in frequency agility with simultaneous MTI processing. This gives the radar an excellent anti-clutter capability, denying the jamming threat and improving the tracking accuracy. Independent search and acquisition patterns are automatically performed according to computer programs. After radar lock-on, the radar switches to automatic tracking, in which regeneration is provided by the computer.

This radar is particularly designed for integration with the Albatros Mk 2 missile and gun fire control system.
DEVELOPMENT
Its research and development programme was commissioned by the Italian Defence Technical Scientific Committee within a wider development programme for a new GFCS. Now in production.
CONTRACTOR
SELENIA-ELSAG Consortium for Naval Systems, Via Panama, 52, 00198 Rome, Italy.

3483.453
MM/BPS-704 SUBMARINE RADAR

The MM/BPS-704 is a naval search and navigation radar for use aboard submarines, and is a version of the 3RM series of naval radars (**1702.253**). The general characteristics are similar to the MM/SPN-703 surface ship version (**3482.253**), using the same 20 kW transmitter and with the same pulse length/PRF combinations. The principal differences are indicated in the following table.
CHARACTERISTICS
Antenna span: 1 m
Beamwidth: 2·2° horizontal; 11° vertical
Gain: At least 27 dB
Noise figure: Better than 11 dB
STATUS
Italian Navy 'Sauro' class submarines are fitted with the BPS-704.
CONTRACTOR
SMA-Segnalamento Marittimo ed Aereo, Via del Ferrone Soffiano, PO Box 200, 50100 Florence, Italy.

1702.253
3RM SERIES NAVAL RADARS

The 3RM Series are I-band navigation and surface warning radars, with some air target capability. The equipment has been tested and qualified in full accordance with MIL-E-16400F specifications. The antennas used are of the slotted waveguide type and provide horizontal beamwidths from 0·8 to 2°, depending upon the antenna length, and a vertical beam pattern of 26°, shaped to 40°. Scanner rotation rate is 25 rpm. Two transmitters are available, with outputs of 7 or 20 kW. The display unit has a nine inch (23 cm) diameter PPI.
CHARACTERISTICS
Frequency: 9375 MHz
Peak power: 7 or 20 kW
Antenna: Slotted waveguide
Rotation rate: 25 rpm
Pulse length/PRF: 0·05 μs/6000 Hz; 0·15 μs/3000 Hz; 0·5 μs/1500 Hz; 1·5 μs/750 Hz
Receiver: Linear, lin-log
Display: 9 inch (23 cm) PPI; 8 ranges 0·25 – 40 nm
True motion unit: On request
STATUS
In production and fitted to ships of a number of navies, and notably those of the Italian Navy, and on the West German fast patrol boats of the '143' and '148' classes. The 3TM20-H version of the 3RM radar is the selected standard navigation radar for the PHM NATO hydrofoil. The US Navy has officially approved introduction of this equipment into its inventory under the military nomenclature AN/SPS-63. The Italian Navy missile hydrofoil, 'Sparviero' class, is fitted with the 3RM 7-250 version, which has a

3RM antenna group

different antenna and a second 250 kW transmitter. A submarine version (MM/BPS-704) is a standard production item.

Other variants include the 3RM20-B (MM/SPN-703) for the Italian Navy; the helicopter models MM/APS-705 and MM/APS-707; and the Marte system radar MM/APQ-706.

CONTRACTOR
SMA-Segnalamento Marittimo ed Aereo, Via del Ferrone Soffiano, PO Box 200, 50100 Florence, Italy.

3482.253

MM/SPN-703 NAVIGATION RADAR

The Italian Navy MM/SPN-703 is the latest version of the 3RM navigation radar (**1702.253**), incorporating the latest state-of-the-art developments in electronic design. Most characteristics are similar or identical to those of the 3RM, above; known differences are listed in the following table.

CHARACTERISTICS

Peak power: 20 kW

Antenna: Low profile slotted waveguide with cylindrical-paraboloid depolarising reflector

Beamwidth: 1·2° azimuth; 25° vertical

Pulse length/PRF: 0·05 µs/5200 Hz; 0·15 µs/2600 Hz; 0·5 µs/1300 Hz; 1·5 µs/650 Hz

Noise figure: 9 dB

DEVELOPMENT
Evolved from the 3RM series as the 3RM20-B for the Italian Navy.

STATUS
Adopted by Italian Navy and probably others.

CONTRACTOR
SMA – Segnalamento Marittimo ed Aereo, Via del Ferrone Soffiano, PO Box 200, 50100 Florence, Italy.

SMA MM/SPN-703 radar antenna

1703.253

SPQ-2D/F NAVAL RADAR

The SPQ-2D/F is a medium power I/J-band radar the principle operation of which is based on time shared transmission of long and short pulses to achieve simultaneous video signals with high sensitivity for surface search and short-range air search, or with high resolution for navigation and close-in control. The last feature is particularly appropriate for rescue operations and the direction of ASW helicopters.

The SPQ-2D equipment is currently integrated as the target designation radar in various electronic combat systems. A later model is the SPQ-2F.

Two control units which include all the operational controls of the radar permit use of remote or local controlling facilities by either CIC or EW operators. The SPQ-2D/F is designed for IFF compatibility and there is provision for 'Beacon' operation in conjunction with an I/J-band transponder. Among the optional additional facilities which are available are: TWS operation at an antenna rotation rate of 40 rpm; frequency agility; MTI D-band transceiving section integrated with the I/J-band (and with a common SPQ-2 type antenna group) for low-flying target detection; and varying modes of operation.

The antenna assembly is produced in both roll and pitch stabilised and non-stabilised forms. The reflector is a double-curvature lattice and mesh structure of about three metres span, and is illuminated by a feed horn carried by an underslung support boom.

The sensor's output signals can be processed for different types of plot extraction and displayed on SMA-designed and manufactured weapons management consoles.

STATUS
The SPQ-2D/F has been in production for several years and is fitted on ships of several navies including the Italian Navy ('Lupo' and 'Alpino' class frigates), Canadian Navy (DDH 280 frigates), and the Venezuelan Navy ('Lupo' class frigates).

CONTRACTOR
SMA – Segnalamento Marittimo ed Aereo, Via del Ferrone Soffiano, PO Box 200, 50100 Florence, Italy.

SPQ-2D/F antenna group with stabilised mount

3262.253

MM/SPQ-701 NAVAL RADAR

The SMA MM/SPQ-701 naval radar is an I-band equipment designed for surface and air target detection and primarily intended for fitting in small vessels such as hydrofoils and fast patrol boats. It is essentially a combined system that includes navigational and search components, and the roll-stabilised mount carries both antennas.

Reportedly of advanced design, the MM/SPQ-701 employs frequency agility and is provided with digital MTI. Good performance is claimed, including long and short range target detection in ECM. Provisions include an antenna and appropriate rotary joints etc.

STATUS
No details obtained.

CONTRACTOR
SMA – Segnalamento Marittimo ed Aereo, Via del Ferrone Soffiano, PO Box 200, 50100 Florence, Italy.

3263.253

MM/SPS-702 NAVAL RADAR

The SMA MM/SPS-702 naval radar is derived from the MM/SPQ-701 described above (**3262.253**), and is essentially comprised of the search components of that equipment. An I-band system, it provides assistance in missile guidance, supplying data for TWS processing and also providing a mount for the command guidance antenna. IFF facilities are incorporated.

STATUS
No details obtained.

CONTRACTOR
SMA – Segnalamento Marittimo ed Aereo, Via del Ferrone Soffiano, PO Box 200, 50100 Florence, Italy.

NETHERLANDS

1973.253

LW.08 NAVAL EARLY WARNING AND WEAPON DIRECTION RADAR

The LW.08 is a high-power D-band frequency synthesiser-driven travelling-wave tube (TWT) radar with pulse-to-pulse coherence, designed to fulfil the following functions:

(1) long-range air warning with high definition
(2) long-range surface surveillance
(3) target designation for weapon control radars and systems.

It is used in both naval and land-based applications.

Long-range performance is aided by use of a high mean-power TWT in the transmitter. A pulse-compression receiver with MTI provides for good performance in rain and in the presence of ground clutter. For naval use, the antenna is mounted on a platform which is stabilised in roll and pitch against ship's motion. As is general practice with Signaal radars, a stainless steel antenna reflector is used to counteract the effects of the salt atmosphere and corrosive exhaust gases. The electronics are solid-state. Other technical features include: frequency agility over a wide band; linear and circular polarisation; frequency synthesiser-controlled coherent transmitter; MTI with digital quadrature canceller; digital video processor, and provision for integration of IFF. Range performance against a 2 m² air target is 145 nautical miles. Peak power is 150 kW and mean power is 5·2 kW.

STATUS
LW.08 systems have been delivered for fitting in Royal Netherlands Navy S-type frigates and for the RN anti-submarine cruisers and 'Type 42' frigates as well as the Argentinian aircraft carrier *Veinticinco de Mayo*. In the RN installation a Marconi antenna is employed, and the radar is designated Type 1022 (**3486.253**).

LW.08/3 systems (land-based) are employed in the Netherlands and Portugal, at Changi Airport in Singapore and at two airfields in Paraguay.

An extended range version of the LW.08 has been designated for the command-and-control air-defence version of the S-type frigate for the RNN.

LW.08/2S early warning and weapon direction radar

CONTRACTOR
Hollandse Signaalapparaten BV, PO Box 42, Hengelo, Netherlands.

3484.253
SIGNAAL STIR

The Signaal STIR tracking radar is a lightweight two-axis tracker capable of rapid and accurate target tracking down to sea-skimmer missile heights, without the aid of TV. The initials STIR denote Signaal track and illuminating radar. The modular tracker system with its electric servo drives was originally developed as a short/medium-range I-band monopulse tracker with J-band illumination for the Seasparrow missile. A later version has a concentric I/K-band monopulse radar for improved tracking, as well as J-band illumination. Another variant is a long-range I-band monopulse tracker with J-band illumination and a larger antenna dish. A variety of MTI and ESM/ECCM features are incorporated.

The antenna feed assembly is weather protected by a polyamide radome, with all the electronics equipment for transmission, reception, control and power supply housed in a container. A containerised version is available for fitment to merchant ships, etc.
STATUS
By the end of 1983 more than 30 sets had been ordered for fitment to the ships of the Netherlands, the Federal Republic of Germany, Argentina and other unspecified navies. The Royal Netherlands Navy has fitted STIR systems to its 'Kortenaer' class frigates and has ordered units for the 'Jacob van Heemskerck' class frigates. The West German navy has fitted STIR to its 'F122' class frigates and the equipment is also installed on the 'Meko 360' destroyers of the Argentinian Navy.
CONTRACTOR
Hollandse Signaalapparaten BV, PO Box 42, Hengelo, Netherlands.

Signaal STIR, VM40 naval tracking and illumination radar

1554.253
DA.05 NAVAL SURVEILLANCE RADAR

The DA.05 is an E/F-band surveillance radar transmitter/receiver for shipboard and land-based applications. Various antenna types are available, both stabilised and unstabilised. It provides for air surveillance, surface warning, target designation for fire control radars, and weapon director systems. A solid-state transmitter/receiver is used, a tunable magnetron providing for operation on any one of a number of pre-set frequencies with a peak power of 1·2 MW. Facilities are provided for an on-mounted or integrated secondary radar (IFF) antenna on the main radar scanner. The latter is constructed of stainless steel to permit operation in adverse salt and exhaust environments.

Range performance for the naval DA.05/4 is typically 135 km against a 2 m² target. Operational features include high discrimination; medium-range air cover and good surface detection; two rates of antenna rotation; linear and circular polarisation; low-noise receiver; video processing, including MTI with digital cancellation and digital interference suppression; automatic test facilities. The naval DA.05/5 includes a lightweight antenna and is designed for FPBs and refit programmes.
STATUS
Signaal has reported that over 50 DA.05 systems are in use with, or ordered for, the navies of Belgium, Malaysia, Netherlands, Finland, Indonesia, South Korea, Ireland, Morocco, Spain, Thailand and Argentina. Five land-based DA.05/3 versions have been ordered by the Netherlands, Chile, Ghana and Zaire.
CONTRACTOR
Hollandse Signaalapparaten BV, PO Box 42, Hengelo, Netherlands.

Scanner and turning gear of the Signaal DA.05/4 radar

3479.253
DA.08 NAVAL WARNING AND WEAPON DIRECTION RADAR

The DA.08 is a high-power F-band frequency synthesiser-driven TWT radar with pulse-to-pulse coherence, designed to fulfil the following functions:
(1) medium-range air warning with high definition and high elevation coverage
(2) medium-range surface surveillance
(3) target designation for weapon control
(4) en route and terminal area control.
The combination of functions depends on the antenna version employed.

The design is a derivative of the LW.08 D-band radar (**1973.253**). Consequently, the main characteristics of the DA.08 are the same as for the LW.08. The range performance against a 2 m² air target is approximately 200 km for the DA.08/1S model. Peak power is 145 kW and mean power 5 kW.

A variant, known as the DA.08/5S, with lightweight stabilised antenna is available for FPBs and small corvettes.
STATUS
The DA.08/2S system has been fitted to the type 'F122' class frigates of the Federal Republic of Germany. The DA.08/1S is being fitted to the Argentinian Navy type 'Meko 360' frigates, the aircraft carrier *Veinticinco de Mayo* and also to Royal Malaysian frigates. The frigate *Aradu*, flagship of the Nigerian Navy, is also fitted with a DA.08 system.
CONTRACTOR
Hollandse Signaalapparaten BV, PO Box 42, Hengelo, Netherlands.

Signaal DA.08 antenna on stabilised mount

1555.253
ZW.06/1 SURFACE SEARCH AND NAVIGATION RADAR

The ZW.06 is an I-band naval surface search and navigation radar providing surveillance, navigation, helicopter control, and limited air surveillance facilities. Of compact and lightweight construction, it is suitable for installation on very small vessels. The transmitter/receiver is of solid-state design, and the scanner is of stainless steel construction to permit siting in adverse environments.

Operational features include: surface coverage to radar horizon; air coverage sufficient for helicopter

guidance; high resolution for navigation, provision for integration of helicopter transponder systems; digital video processor. Anti-clutter measures and ECCM provisions include: circular polarisation; logarithmic receiver with pulse length discrimination; sensitivity time control; suppression of non-correlated pulses; tunable transmitter.

CHARACTERISTICS
ZW.06
Antenna: Parabolic reflector 2·7 m wide, 1·2 m high, with off-set feed horn
Polarisation: Horizontal or circular, selectable
Vertical beamwidth (at –3 dB): 19°

Horizontal beamwidth (at –3 dB): 0·9°
Sidelobe level: –25 dB
Gain: 31 dB
Rotation speed: 24 rpm
Max windspeed: 185 km/h
Transmitter
Type: Tunable magnetron
Frequency band: 8600 – 9500 MHz
Receiver
Overall noise: 9 dB
Intermediate frequency: 60 MHz
Receiver channels: Linear, or logarithmic with PLD. Pulse interference suppression on both channels. Digital video processor
DEVELOPMENT
A ZW.06/1 version was announced in 1975. This model embodies improvements resulting from the application of value engineering, and is stated to be of lower cost.

ZW.06/1 fittings include: Brazilian 'Niteroi' class frigates and 'Aratu' class minesweepers; Netherlands 'Kortenaer' class frigates; Spanish 'F 30' class frigates; Indian Navy 'Leander' class frigates; Moroccan Navy 'Lazaga' class missile patrol boats and one F 30 class corvette and the South Korean frigate 'Ulsan'. The ZW.06/1 has also been ordered for the Thailand Navy, the 'Meko 360' class frigates of the Argentinian Navy, and for the LST of the Indonesian Navy.
CONTRACTOR
Hollandse Signaalapparaten BV, PO Box 42, Hengelo, Netherlands.

Signaal ZW.06 surface search and navigation radar antenna

1256.253
LW.02 NAVAL AIR SURVEILLANCE RADAR

The LW.02 is a D-band (23 cm), high-power long-range air surveillance radar for use on vessels of frigate size or above. Peak transmitter power is 500 kW and maximum detection range about 100 nautical miles. Vertical cover extends to 18 000 metres.

A double curvature reflector measuring 7 m by 2·9 m is used and a distinguishing feature of this radar is the large 'trunk' at the rear of the centre section of the scanner. There is also an LW.03 version of this radar, the only known difference between the two

models being in the scanner rotation rates. The LW.02 rate is between one and ten rpm, and the LW.03 five or ten rpm.
STATUS
The LW.02 has been fitted to a large number of vessels in several countries. These include the navies of the Netherlands, Peru, West Germany, Sweden, Colombia, Malaysia, Australia and Argentina.

Production has ceased, the replacement model being the LW.08 (**1973.253**).
CONTRACTOR
Hollandse Signaalapparaten BV, PO Box 42, Hengelo, Netherlands.

LW.02 antenna

4051.253
ZW SERIES NAVAL RADARS

This range of general-purpose search radars, the so-called ZW series, has been extended with three new types, these being:
ZW07: submarine radar for navigation, distance measuring, surface search and limited air warning. The ZW07 is specially suited for use on board submarines. A single shot mode has been adapted for ranging of surface targets. Other operational features are: surface coverage up to radar horizon; limited air warning and high resolution for navigation. Anti-clutter measures and ECCM provisions include: sector scan facilities, logarithmic receiver with pulse length discriminator, suppression of non-correlated pulses and a tunable transmitter.
ZW08: low-level air warning and sea skimmer

detection radar. The ZW08 is a newly developed radar system with the special capability of detecting accurately small, fast, low and very low-flying targets at such ranges that successful engagement and combatting of these targets is possible. The basic configuration of the radar system consists of a stabilised antenna fed by a high power TWT transmitter and a full coherent chain receiver. The system operates in the I-band.

Operational features include: surface search to the radar horizon, limited air warning and excellent sea-skimmer detection capability. Anti-clutter measures and ECCM provisions include: fully coherent receiver/transmitter system, pulse compression, adaptive waveform transmission, interpulse frequency diversity, pseudo-jumping frequency over bursts, FFT doppler processing, high average output

power, and automatic selection of radar parameters.
ZW09: surface search and low-level air warning radar. The configuration comprises a stabilised antenna fed by a magnetron transmitter with matching receiver channels. Its application is on board small ships, giving the following operational features: surface search to the radar horizon, limited air warning and detection capability against low-flying targets. Anti-clutter measures and ECCM provisions are: circular polarisation, DMTI, pseudo jumping frequency, video correlator, linear, logarithmic, Dicke Fix and MTI receivers, pulse length discrimination and suppression of non-correlated pulses.
CONTRACTOR
Hollandse Signaalapparaten BV, PO Box 42, Hengelo, Netherlands.

1590.253
SIGNAAL WM20 SERIES FIRE CONTROL RADAR

This radar is the principal sub-system of the Signaal WM20 series of naval fire control systems, and in its full form consists of two radars sharing a common stabilised mount and housed in a near-spherical radome. In the double installation, the tracker/illuminator is carried above the search radar, with the

gimbal and stabilising assembly in between. The general arrangement can be seen from the accompanying illustration.

Both antennas are fed from a common I/J-band transmitter. During search, the entire transmitter output is applied to the search antenna. After target detection and designation to the tracking radar, the output power is divided (by waveguide switching) so

that a certain proportion is supplied to the tracking antenna for target tracking.

The search radar carries out the surface and air search functions, and automatic tracking of surface targets for weapon control purposes. The tracking radar performs tracking functions for weapon control against air targets.

One version of the WM20 series, the WM26,

employs only the search antenna, this being mounted on top of the stabilised platform and enclosed in a hemispherical radome. In all other versions the tracking antenna is fitted in the upper position with the search antenna below.

STATUS

The WM20 series of fire control radars is widely fitted and details of known installations are given in the M20 series fire control systems entry (**1259.281**) in the Systems Section of this edition of *Jane's Weapon Systems*.

CONTRACTOR

Hollandse Signaalapparaten BV, PO Box 42, Hengelo, Netherlands.

Signaal WM20 radars aboard Singapore patrol boats

1589.253

SIGNAAL 3D MULTI-TARGET TRACKING RADAR

The Signaal 3D multi-target tracking radar (MTTR) is an advanced air search and target tracking radar capable of handling more than 100 aircraft tracks. A very high data rate is achieved by the use of an antenna array consisting of back-to-back pairs of parabolic reflectors and planar electronically scanned antennas, all four of which have common turning gear. IFF/SIF secondary radar are integrated with the MTTR. The parabolic dishes are used for search and the electronic-scan antennas for target tracking. High and low cover is provided. Beam steering and data extraction are performed by an SMR series digital computer.

Operational functions include: long range search; search information with high data rate for low-flying aircraft; search information with high resolution of close-in air targets; automatic position and height information; simultaneous tracking of over 100 aircraft targets; target designation facilities for other systems. No performance or other technical details have been obtained. Estimated diameter of the parabolic dishes is in the region of six metres. Both land and naval uses are likely, and the latter is understood to incorporate full stabilisation.

DEVELOPMENT

Development has been in progress since the late 1960s under sponsorship of the Netherlands Ministry of Defence. At one stage a radar of this description was the subject of a joint UK/Netherlands project, and the radar was to have been fitted to RN Type 82 class vessels, but the UK subsequently withdrew from the programme.

STATUS

The 3D MTTR forms one of the major sensors of the SEWACO action information and fire control system for the 'Tromp' class of Royal Netherlands Navy guided weapon frigates. There are no other known fittings at this stage.

CONTRACTOR

Hollandse Signaalapparaten BV, PO Box 42, Hengelo, Netherlands.

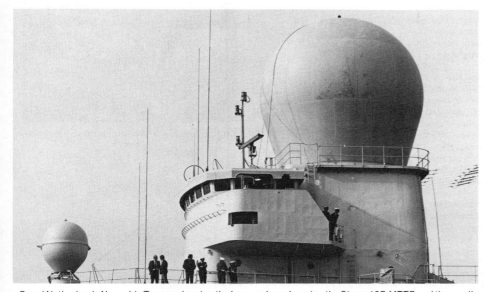

Royal Netherlands Navy ship Tromp, *showing the large radome housing the Signaal 3D MTTR and the smaller one for the WM25 fire control system radar*

5626.253

SMART NAVAL SURVEILLANCE RADAR

SMART (Signaal Multibeam Acquisition Radar for Targeting) is an all-weather three-dimensional naval surveillance radar system intended for all types of naval vessel from corvettes upwards. Its prime application is as the main sensor for data handling and weapon system control and it has a very high performance in the presence of heavy clutter and electronic countermeasures. The equipment has been designed to cope with small high-speed anti-ship missiles, with radar cross sections down to 0·1 m² and approach speeds of Mach 3+, which can be either sea skimmers or arriving from high angles of 60° or more.

The SMART system operates in F-band (formerly S-band) where it offers an optimum balance between range, clutter rejection and antenna dimensions. An alternative version operating in I-band is also available. It provides an uninterrupted search envelope from 0 to 70° in elevation with single scan detection followed by automatic initiation and target tracking. It incorporates anti-clutter and ECCM features such as multiple reception beams with ultra low side lobes in elevation and azimuth, a clutter analysis sensor, broadband transmission, PRF and RF agility per burst and a jamming analysis sensor which automatically changes PRF and transmit frequency.

The system comprises an antenna and four below-decks units. The antenna unit consists of a single horn transmitter array combined with a linear array of 16 strip line receiving antennas. To ensure high sensitivity, pre-processing of the received signals takes place in the antenna unit itself. The output of the 16 antennas is fed to a digital beam forming network in which eight independent elevation beams are produced. The transmitter is based on a high power, pulse-to-pulse coherent TWT. For the complete integration of any type of IFF, an IFF antenna, rotary joint and an IFF extractor are incorporated.

CHARACTERISTICS

Antenna unit

Rotation speed: 30 rpm

Stabilisation: ±30° in roll; ±10° in pitch

Polarisation: Horizontal

Transmitting antenna

Type: Single horn antenna array

Beamwidth: 2° horizontal; up to 70° vertical

Receiving antenna

Type: 16 strip line radiators

Signaal SMART naval surveillance antenna

Beamwidth: 2° horizontal; 70° vertical (after beam forming)
Transmitter
Type: TWT with pulse compression
Peak power: 150 kW
Frequency: F-band
PRF: 3800 Hz average
Transmission modes: Fixed frequency; frequency agility over scan, burst-to-burst frequency jump

Weight
Antenna: 1900 or 850 kg
Below-deck units: 2960 kg
Antenna dimensions: 360 × 250 or 400 × 320 cm
STATUS
In development. The basic version has an antenna weighing 1900 kg with dimensions some 360 cm wide by 250 cm high with the stabilisation gearing mounted underneath the turning gear. An additional

version with hydraulic stabilisation is also available. This lightweight (850 kg) version offers the same performance as the heavier unit.
CONTRACTOR
Hollandse Signaalapparaten BV, Zuidelijke Havenweg 40, 7550 GD Hengelo, Netherlands.

SWEDEN

1546.253
9GR 600 NAVAL RADAR
The 9GR 600 is an I-band radar transceiver extensively used in naval radar systems both in the Swedish and other navies.

With the 9GA 205 antenna it is used in the Mareld coastal radar system (**1548.181**). It is used in the 9LV 200 fire control system (**1542.281**), the 9LV 200 Mk 2 weapon control system (**3127.281**), the Seafire system (**1543.281**), the Torci torpedo fire control system (**1541.281**), and with the 9GA 300 antenna in the Subfar submarine radar system (**1545.453**).

The radar can be used either in its broadband frequency agility mode, or in a fixed frequency mode for MTI operation.
CHARACTERISTICS
Transmitter
Operating modes: Frequency agility/fixed frequency MTI
Transmitter tubes (2 off): Magnetron YJ 1180/YJ 1181
Frequency agility range: Minimum 400 MHz, typically 450 MHz within 8700 – 9500 MHz
Frequency shift: Randomly within the frequency agility range from pulse to pulse
Pulse peak power: 200 kW
Pulsewidth/prf: Typically 1 μs/1000 Hz and 0·25 μs/3000 Hz

Receiver
Frequency range: 8500 – 9600 MHz

Dual-frequency, I- and D-band, stabilised surveillance antenna 9GA 218, for the 9GR 600 naval radar

PEAB 9GA 209 I-band stabilised surveillance antenna

IF: 30 MHz
Noise figure: Typically 5·5 dB; 7 dB with low-noise preamplifier
Receiver characteristics: Lin and log, log/lin, STC
Operational features: Image rejection mixer, Dicke-Fix receiver, PLD, IAGC, narrow-band jamming suppression, passive ECM mode
Transceiver
Dimensions: 1200 × 635 × 510 mm
Weight: Approx 225 kg

Antenna GA 209
Type: Parabolic, hornfed, stabilised
Reflector material: GRP and metal wires
Frequency range: 8·5 – 9·6 GHz
Rotation speed: Up to 60 rpm
Beamwidths
Horizontal: 1·1°
Vertical: 7°
Gain: 35·5 dB
Sidelobes: –21 dB at ±1·5°; –33 dB beyond ±15°
Spiral scan coverage: Up to 40°
Stabilisation: Direct driving hydraulic motors
Stabilisation limits: Roll ±32°, pitch ±12°
Aperture: 2100 × 300 mm
Weight (including turntable): 260 kg

Antenna 9GA 218
Type: Parabolic, dual frequency, stabilised
Reflector type: GRP and metal wires
Frequency range
I-band: 8·5 – 9·6
D-band: 1·01 – 1·11 and 1·25 – 1·35 GHz
Beamwidths
Horizontal: 1° at I-band, 6/8° at D-band

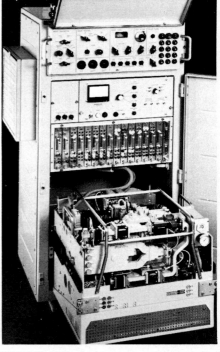

PEAB 9GR 600 radar frequency-agility transmitter/receiver

Vertical: 3° at I-band, 20/25° at D-band
Gain
8·5 – 9·6 GHz: 38 dB
1·25 – 1·35 GHz: >20 dB
1·01 – 1·11 GHz: >17 dB
Stabilisation: Direct driving hydraulic motors
Stabilisation limits: Roll ±30°, pitch ±10°
Aperture: 2700 × 700 mm
Weight (including turntable): 260 kg
STATUS
In service.
CONTRACTOR
Philips Elektronikindustrier AB, 17588 Järfälla, Sweden.

1547.253
9LV 200 Mk 2 TRACKING RADAR
This is a J-band frequency-agile naval fire control radar forming part of the 9LV 200 fire control system (**3127.281**) in which it is used with an I-band search radar. The main role is that of target tracking for gun fire control, and the radar is monopulse equipment with stabilised antenna and a cassegrain scanner system. The radar mounting can also carry TV, IR camera and laser rangefinder for autonomous electro-optical (optronic) tracking. A feature of the mounting is a new type of direct drive hydraulic motor capable of a slewing speed of 85°/s, and an initial acceleration of 500°/s².
CHARACTERISTICS
Type: J-band frequency-agile MTI monopulse

Frequency range: Random pulse-to-pulse in J-band
Magnetron type: Philips YJ 1321
Pulse peak power: 65 kW
PRF: About 2000 Hz
Pulse width: About 0·2 μs
Receiver noise: 11 dB
Antenna
Diameter: 1 m
Beamwidth (at 3 dB): 1·3°
Gain: 40 dB
Sidelobes: 22 dB
STATUS
In service.
CONTRACTOR
Philips Elektronikindustrier AB, 17588 Järfälla, Sweden.

PEAB 9LV 200 Mk 2 tracking radar antenna assembly with TV camera, IR camera and laser rangefinder

4299.253
SEA GIRAFFE NAVAL SEARCH RADAR
The Giraffe family of air defence search radars is based on the fully coherent TWT transmitter concept featuring an extremely good sub-clutter visibility of moving targets. Various versions of the Giraffe radar are in operation in different system configurations in seven countries. The latest version, Sea Giraffe, is a multi-purpose naval search radar designed to meet the operational requirements of a variety of warships from small fast patrol boats to frigate sized ships. There are five different versions (HC denotes extra height coverage versions):

(1) Sea Giraffe 50 and 50HC for small and medium-sized patrol boats and fast attack craft
(2) Sea Giraffe 150HC for large fast attack craft, corvettes and frigates

Modified Spica II class fast attack boat of the Swedish Navy fitted with Sea Giraffe

1545.453
SUBFAR 100 SUBMARINE RADAR
The Subfar 100 equipment is an air and surface search radar for submarines and comprises the 9GA 300 antenna, a 9GR 600 I-band frequency-agile transceiver, and a display system.

The 9GA 300 antenna is designed for mounting with its hydraulic turntable on top of the submarine radar mast. This way of mounting eliminates bearing error sources from torsion effects in the radar mast. The hydraulic turntable gives a very low noise level as well as flexible control of antenna rotation speed. The antenna direction can be manually set or slaved to external sources such as the periscope.

Sector transmission as well as short time transmission down to emitting a single pulse can be selected. Automatic target detection can be incorporated, which facilitates automatic target tracking by an external fire control computer.

CHARACTERISTICS
9GA 300 antenna
Frequency range: 8·5 – 9·6 GHz
Rotation speed: 0·5 – 24 rpm, and pos. control

(3) Sea Giraffe 50 and 100 for off-shore patrol vessels.

All versions of the Sea Giraffe are essentially repackaged versions of the Giraffe family to satisfy a variety of requirements in the area defence and point defence roles. They provide all-weather anti-ship missile detection to enable successful defence, long range aircraft detection in severe environmental conditions and ECM, and surface target detection up to the radar horizon. For area defence, Sea Giraffe supplies air and surface data to the ship's fire control system, target information to own surface-to-surface missiles and surface gun fire control with accurate fall-of-shot observations. Ancillary uses for the system include long range navigation and helicopter guidance.

Low altitude coverage is obtained at a considerable range with obvious benefits in the detection of low-flying aircraft and sea skimming missiles.

The radar uses a broadband fully coherent TWT transmitter giving 15 kW output power for Sea Giraffe 50 and 100, and 60 kW for Sea Giraffe 150. The antenna for the Sea Giraffe 50 is the standard Giraffe family version while a special antenna has been developed for the 100 and 150. The HC versions of the 50 and 150 have an optional antenna for extra high cover to detect steep diving missiles (60 to 80° dive angle). A high MTI improvement factor ensures excellent low-level detection capability, and frequency agility in both MTI and non-MTI operation is used for high ECCM performance. Agility is on a pulse-to-pulse basis in non-MTI mode and on a pulse burst basis in MTI mode. The adaptive computer based coherent MTI is used to give optimised suppression of mixed clutter from sea, land, rain and chaff. Digital pulse compression is used for high range resolution and improved clutter performance. G/H-band operation enables optimum detection of

Subfar 100 submarine antenna 9GA 300

Beamwidths
Horizontal: 2·4°
Vertical: 16°
Gain: 26 dB
Sidelobes: 18 dB
Antenna aperture: 1000 × 140 mm
Height above mast tube: 600 mm

both air and surface targets.
(1) Sea Giraffe 50 and 50HC to 15 km for missiles and 35 km for aircraft
(2) Sea Giraffe 150HC to 25 and 55 km respectively.

All versions are normally supplied with a stabilised platform and for operation in extreme winds the antenna should be enclosed in a radome.
CHARACTERISTICS
Frequency: 5·4 – 5·9 GHz
MTI improvement factor: 45 – 50 dB
Antenna rotation rate: 30/60 rpm
Output power (peak): 15 kW (50 & 100 versions); 60 kW (150 version)
Output power (mean): 300 W (50 & 100 versions); 1200 W (150 version)
Antenna size: 2·3 × 0·7 m (50 version); 2·4 × 0·8 m (50HC and 150HC); 2·4 × 1·8 m (100 and 150)
Masthead weight: 250 kg (50 version); 700 kg (100 and 150 versions, radome included)
STATUS
Sea Giraffe was first ordered in 1980 by the Swedish Navy for the mid-life refit of the Spica II attack craft, and has been subsequently ordered for the new Spica III 'Stockholm' class fast missile vessels, as well as for the minelayer/training ship *HMS Carlskrona*. Sea Giraffe has been in full operational use with the Swedish Navy since early 1983 in the modified Spica IIs.

At the end of 1983, Sea Giraffe 150HC was ordered for the new Canadian patrol frigate programme. On this vessel, Sea Giraffe will be used as the medium range surveillance radar and as target indication radar to the fire control system.

Negotiations are also being conducted with a number of other customers for various applications of Sea Giraffe.
CONTRACTOR
Ericsson Radio Systems AB, 431 26 Mölndal, Sweden.

Rotating circle diameter: 1040 mm
Antenna system weight: 95 kg
9GR 600 transceiver
See **1546.253**, above, for full characteristics.
Display system
CRT diameter: 300 mm (12 inch)
Deflection: Magnetic, fixed coils
Scale factors: 1:20 000
1:50 000
1:100 000
1:200 000
True motion: Selectable
Range readout: Digital
Bearing readout: Digital
Dimensions
Height: 1100 mm
Width: 665 mm
Depth: 600 mm plus desk 250 mm
Weight: 135 kg
STATUS
In service.
CONTRACTOR
Philips Elektronikindustrier AB, 17588 Järfälla, Sweden.

UNION OF SOVIET SOCIALIST REPUBLICS

4090.253
BAND STAND NAVAL RADAR
Band Stand is the name given to the radar identified by its large dome shaped radome, and considered to be associated with the ship's overall air surveillance requirements, although there may be some connection with the vessel's main armament.

The latter is thought to be less likely in the light of the continued fitting of the Band Stand radar (or its radome, at least) in the 'Nanuchka' class missile corvettes supplied by the USSR to India, although the latter ships are armed with SS-N-2B anti-ship missiles instead of the six SS-N-9 missiles which arm the Soviet vessels of this class. However, it is possible that in the Soviet ships the Band Stand radar may be employed in a complementary fashion in the SS-N-9 system in addition to having air surveillance as its

The Soviet ship Sovremenny includes a Band Stand radar in its radar fit. Other items seen here include a Kite Screech fire control radar and Top Steer group

main role. This might include tracking of the out-going SS-N-9 missiles, with guidance signals being transmitted via the two Fish Bowl equipments (which smaller radomes are missing from Indian examples of 'Nanuchka' ships).

Both Indian and Soviet ships of the class are fitted with SAN-4 anti-aircraft missile systems and an air surveillance function of the Band Stand radar, with a fairly high data rate, would be a valuable complement to this system.

4085.253

BASS TILT FIRE CONTROL RADAR

Bass Tilt is a Soviet naval fire control radar which resembles Drum Tilt (**1330.253**) and Muff Cob (**1611.253**) in both general appearance and broad functional purpose. Of these three radars, Bass Tilt is the most modern, having entered service in the mid-1970s; it is also decidedly larger than the oldest of the three types, Drum Tilt. They all share a common main operational function of radar direction of small or medium calibre anti-aircraft guns, with Muff Cob generally being associated with Soviet twin 57 mm gun mounts. Both Drum Tilt and Bass Tilt are usually used with smaller calibre weapons, particularly multiple turret twin or single Gatling-type installations. Drum Tilt fittings are mostly confined to smaller ships with a single gun turret such as the common-place 'Osa' class missile boats.

The Sovremenny *presents a radar identification challenge with multiple fittings of both Muff Cob and Bass Tilt fire control radars (plus one other radome of similar size which is neither of these types but more probably a communications satellite terminal). Other radars are Top Steer air search radar pair, Kite Screech fire control radar, and Band Stand missile director radar*

Bass Tilt fittings have been noted on one ship of the 'Kresta I' class (which underwent modernisation in 1975), 'Kresta II' class and 'Kara' class cruisers, some 'Kashin' class destroyers, 'Nanuchka II' and 'Grisha III' class corvettes, and various miscellaneous types of vessel such as the 'Ivan Rogov' class of amphibious assault ship and the *Berezina* fleet replenishment ship. 'Kresta II' class ships present one of the best opportunities to make direct visual comparisons between the most difficult pair of these three types of fire control radar to identify accurately, Muff Cob and Bass Tilt, as two of each type are fitted in these ships; two Bass Tilt forward for control of four Gatling-gun AA turrets, and two Muff Cob athwart the funnel for the aft twin 57 mm gun turrets. More recent examples of Bass Tilt fittings are the new *Kirov* cruiser and the Sovremenny class destroyers, the first of which emerged into the Baltic briefly in the summer of 1980. The latter ship has both Muff Cob and Bass Tilt radars fitted in some profusion, offering something of a challenge to radar 'spotters'. The 'Kiev' class of aircraft carriers each have four Bass Tilt radars for their eight Gatling-gun AA mounts.

1608.253

BIG NET SEARCH RADAR

Big Net is a very large, long-range air surveillance radar operating in either the E/F- or D-band, probably the latter although even C-band operation has been suggested. The open lattice reflector is of elliptical parabolic form, illuminated by an underslung horn feed, carried on a solid boom. Behind the reflector are two balance vanes. Range performance is estimated as more than 100 nautical miles (185 km) against an aircraft at medium altitude, and up to 200 nautical miles (370 km) at higher altitudes.

According to the latest information, all four of the 'Kresta I' class of guided missile cruisers carry Big Net, on which ships it is mounted over the funnel. Some of the 'Kashin' class of guided missile destroyers are fitted with this radar, in which cases it is mounted on a pylon type mast aft of the forward funnel. The cruiser *Dzerzhinsky* has also been seen with Big Net and some of the 'T43/AGR' class of radar picket ships (converted from minesweepers of the 'T43' class) have a Big Net search radar. Other vessels of this class have either a Squat Eye or Knife Rest radar instead of the Big Net.

Big Net long-range search radar

1330.253

DRUM TILT FIRE CONTROL RADAR

This is a pedestal-mounted fire control radar which probably provides acquisition and tracking functions only for AA guns. It is housed in a weather-proof container which is attached to the scanner assembly tilted at about 25°. Maximum acquisition range of aerial targets is approximately 22 nautical miles. Operating frequency is almost certainly in the I-band. It is principally fitted aboard 'Osa' class missile boats, on a platform between the two aft missile launchers, for the direction of four 30 mm AA guns carried by these craft.

Drum Tilt fittings have also been noted on some 'Sverdlov' cruisers, and ships of the 'Kanin', 'Kotlin', 'Shershen', 'Stenka', 'Turya', 'Natya', 'Yurka', 'Senyarin', and 'Polnochniy' classes. The type is gradually being supplanted by later radars such as Muff Cob and Bass Tilt which are fitted in more recent classes of Soviet ship.

This East German 'Koni' class escort vessel, at anchor off the Shetland Islands is equipped with a Drum Tilt and a Hawk Screech fire control radar for gun direction, and a Pop Group for use with the SAN-4 missile system. The air search radar is a Slim Net or Strut Curve (RN photo)

4089.253

EYE BOWL NAVAL RADAR

The Eye Bowl radar is associated with the Soviet SS-N-14 naval missile system fitted aboard 'Krivak' class frigates and the Soviet cruiser *Kirov*, although other classes thought to be fitted with the SS-N-14 system have not yet been noted with the Eye Bowl radar. The precise function of the Eye Bowl radar tends to remain as problematical as that of the SS-N-14 missile with which it is associated. The latter is generally thought to be somewhat similar to the Australian/British Ikara (**6002.241**) in that the payload/warhead is believed to comprise a torpedo, thus making the SS-N-14 principally an anti-submarine weapon although there will also be a certain surface ship target capability. On these assumptions, the main role of the Eye Bowl radar is probably that of tracking and guidance of the outgoing SS-N-14 missile to ensure that it reaches a previously designated target position determined by another of the ship's sensors and the combat information system. This seems to be confirmed by what is discernible from photographs of the Eye Bowl radar. The reflector dish is comparatively small and there appear to be several auxiliary (possibly electro-optical) sensors mounted immediately behind the reflector dish. Command signals to the SS-N-14 missile are probably transmitted as coded information within the radar transmissions, as no separate command antennas can be seen.

The operating frequency is most likely in the I-band of the radar spectrum, although the G/H-band is also feasible. Either would suffice for the estimated range of the SS-N-14 system, which is generally thought to be in the neighbourhood of 30 nautical miles.

Beam view of the two Eye Bowl guidance radars on a Soviet 'Krivak' class destroyer, abaft and above the Pop Group radar for the ship's SA-N-4 anti-aircraft missile system (HMS Londonderry)

1605.253
FAN SONG E NAVAL RADAR

This is a shipboard version of the Guideline (SA-N-2) surface-to-air missile fire control and guidance radar (**2868.153**) which is widely used by Soviet land forces. In place of the mobile housing used on land, the shipboard installation is mounted on a stabilised gun mount.

Fan Song E operates in the G/H-band range of frequencies with a maximum acquisition range of 80 nautical miles. The antenna array consists of horizontal and vertical scan Lewis antennas, and three circular parabolic dishes. Two of the latter are for lobe on receive only (LORO) ECCM, and the third

dish is for command guidance purposes. Operation of Fan Song E is described more fully in **2868.153**.

The only known fitting of this radar is on the Soviet Cruiser *Dzerzhinsky*, on which ship the Fan Song E is mounted on a platform aft of the after funnel and forward of the twin Guideline missile launcher.

1325.253
HAWK/OWL SCREECH FIRE CONTROL RADARS

Hawk Screech and Owl Screech are fire control radars of conventional design, widely used in many classes of Soviet vessels. They are distinguished by a circular dish scanner, behind which are mounted fairly bulky housings which are assumed to contain transmitter and receiver, and probably turning and stabilisation gear. The complete radar is pedestal mounted. The 2·3 metre diameter scanner has a central feed supported by a four-leg structure. Feed arrangements could incorporate a rotating dipole to provide a conical-scan search pattern. Dish diameter

is approximately two metres, with Owl Screech somewhat larger than Hawk Screech, and the operating frequency is probably in the G-band for both types.

The NATO designations, Hawk Screech and Owl Screech, are apparently derived from signal characteristics noted in the course of Elint monitoring. They appear to refer to two versions of the same basic radar, and close examination of photographs of this equipment does reveal external differences to support this. These visible variations do not as yet permit positive identification of either with one of the NATO names although information has been obtained suggesting that Owl Screech is an improved version of Hawk Screech.

The two most obvious physical differences between the two types are in the arrangement of equipment behind the dish and in the mounting of the feed. In Owl Screech, the hardware behind the dish is contained in more numerous housings, giving a less tidy appearance than in the other version. Also, the four legs of the feed support are fixed to the dish at points nearer its centre than in the other radar. The pedestals also differ, Owl Screech being tubular, and that of Hawk Screech being slightly tapered. In the photographs studied by *Jane's Weapon Systems* it has been noticed that the feed housing in the Owl Screech version is at an angle of about 45°, whereas in the other version it is orthogonally mounted. This may be a clue to the signal characteristics of the two types. There is one other feature, which is less obvious, that distinguishes the two types. That believed to be Hawk Screech has a small aperture in the dish, on the centre line and near the upper edge. This could be for a closed-circuit TV camera, and there is a small housing on the rear of the reflector. This could be used for optical target acquisition and/or tracking.

Gun fire control radar believed to carry the NATO designation Owl Screech. Note the angled feed housing, numerous separate equipment housings behind the reflector, tubular pedestal, and feed mounting, which distinguish this radar from that known as Hawk Screech, shown in an adjacent photograph

The principal function is that of gun fire director against aircraft targets, although this type probably also has a certain capability against surface targets, and possibly splash detection.

Hawk Screech is associated with quadruple 45 mm, twin and quadruple 57 mm, and twin 76 mm guns, while Owl Screech is employed with 76 mm twin gun installations. Classes of Soviet Fleet vessels fitted with Hawk Screech include: 'Kanin' (one), 'Kotlin' SAM (one), modified 'Kildin' (two), 'Kotlin' (two), modified 'Skory' (two), 'Lama' (two), 'Koni' (one), 'Don' (one), 'Petya' (one), 'Mirka' (one). Owl Screech fittings include: 'Kiev' (two), 'Kara' (two), 'Kynda' (two), 'Kashin' (two), some 'Kildin' (two), 'Krivak' (two), 'Ivan Rogov' (one).

Fire control radar for main guns, believed to carry NATO designation Hawk Screech. Compare feed arrangements with those of Owl Screech

1328.253
HEAD LIGHT GROUP

This group of radars was first seen on the helicopter cruiser carrier, *Moskva*, but has subsequently made its appearance on its sister ship *Leningrad* and on the 'Kresta II' and 'Kara' classes of guided missile

cruisers. Two of these groups of radars are fitted, fore and aft on the 'Kresta II' and 'Kara' vessels, and two forward on the *Moskva*. In very general configuration, and possibly function to some degree, this group resembles the Peel Group missile control radar group for Goa surface-to-air missiles on other Soviet

vessels. The Head Light group consists of a group of four radars, apparently comprising two identical pairs of equipment combined on a common mounting. There is a fifth, smaller dish, possibly fulfilling a command link or IFF function. Two versions have been identified, designated Head Light A and Head

Light B, respectively. The former is associated with Goblet surface-to-air missiles and the latter with the SS-N-14 missile system.

The four main reflectors of the group are circular dishes, of open mesh construction, one small and one large to each pair, with the smaller in the upper position, and all being disposed symmetrically about the central mounting pillar. Estimated dish sizes are 1·8 and 3·8 m. The electronics for each radar, transmitter/receiver etc, are carried behind the individual reflectors and the whole assembly of four radars is supported from the top of the pedestal turning gear on a yoke of triangulated tube construction.

The whole assembly rotates in azimuth, and can also move in elevation. The two upper radars also appear to have provision for individual movement in both axes, possibly limited, and the dynamic balancing vanes fitted to them could support this suggestion.

The upper dishes have unusually large feed arrangements which may be of the cassegrain type, and the larger dishes appear to be front fed. Operating frequencies are reported to be in the G-band for acquisition and H/I-band for tracking.

On the *Moskva* and *Leningrad* there is one Head Light group to each of two surface-to-air missile launchers, each for two missiles. On 'Kresta II' class ships there is one Head Light group associated with similar launchers fore and aft. The arrangement on 'Kara' class ships is similar.

This photograph of the 'Kara' class cruiser Nikolaev *shows Head Light radar groups for SAM guidance and control, fore and aft. Air surveillance radars are the big Top Sail on the mainmast and a Head Net C back-to-back system (RAF)*

1318.253
HEAD NET A AIR SURVEILLANCE RADAR
This appears to be the most widely fitted of the numerous radars employed by the Soviet Navy, and appears to be of fairly conventional construction. It has a large (about 6 × 1·5 m) elliptical paraboloid reflector of open lattice construction. This is

Head Net A surveillance radar, with Sun Visor radar director below and to right. Note also High Pole IFF and assorted direction-finding and ESM antennas

illuminated by a horn feed carried by a boom projecting from below the lower edge of the scanner. An unusual visual feature, compared with practice outside the USSR, is a pair of prominent 'butterfly' vanes extending behind the scanner which are for dynamic balancing.

The scanner mounting is also quite distinctive and

has a rather 'lighthouse' like appearance, being quite regular and with a domed top. It is possible, though considered unlikely, that this accommodates some form of scanner stabilisation against ship's motion. It is possible that a relatively high rotation rate is employed.

Operating frequency is in either the D- or E/F-band, probably the latter, with a detection range, on aircraft at medium altitude, of 60-70 nautical miles. No details of the radiated power are available.

The principal function of the Head Net A is assumed to be air search and surveillance and it can be expected to provide target designation facilities for other fire control radars for guns and missiles, carried by the vessel.

It is normally mounted on a mast-top location, or other high positions, and both single and double installations have been seen on various classes of Soviet vessel. 'Kynda' and 'Kashin' class guided missile destroyers have one on each of the two masts; the *Bravy* ('Sam Kotlin' class destroyer) has a single installation on the mainmast.

Head Net mountings and scanners are also employed in two types of dual installation. One is a back-to-back configuration (**1319.253**) with one of the scanners at a larger elevation angle (about 15° more than the companion scanner) to provide separate high and lower cover antennas. The second dual configuration (**1320.253**) is also a back-to-back arrangement, but in this case one scanner is tilted laterally from the horizontal with the probable objective of providing a three-dimensional capability.

1319.253
HEAD NET B AIR SURVEILLANCE RADAR
This is a dual installation of the Head Net A radar (**1318.253**) in which two scanners are mounted in a back-to-back configuration. One is tilted at an angle of about 15° elevation in relation to the other scanner to provide separate high and low cover. Operating frequency probably lies within the E/F-band of the spectrum, although D-band is a possibility also.

Functions of the radar are search and surveillance, and target designations for the fire control radars carried for the direction of surface-to-air missiles and guns.

This radar has been seen on a 'Krupny' class destroyer (No 229 – since renumbered), but does not appear to be in widespread use. The general mechanical arrangement is very similar to the Head Net C (**1320.253**), which is also a back-to-back

system using dual Head Net A arrays, and it is possible that individual vessels have been converted from one version to the other. Latest information is that of the five 'Krupny' class ships; *Gnevnyi* now has Head Net C and the others have a Head Net A. The only known remaining Head Net B installations are on two Soviet range instrumentation ships, *Chazma* and *Chumikan*, which entered service in the early 1960s.

1320.253
HEAD NET C AIR SURVEILLANCE RADAR
This radar is apparently a back-to-back combination of two Head Net A scanners (**1318.253**), similar to Head Net B (**1319.253**) but with the significant difference that one of the scanners has its aperture (ie. its 'span' dimension) tilted from the horizontal by approximately 30°. This has the effect of displacing

the resulting fan-shaped elevation beam by the same amount from the vertical. This beam, in combination with the vertical beam produced by the companion scanner, thus provides the means for heightfinding by the so-called 'V-beam' technique, such as is used in the American AN/TPS-34.

There are important differences, however, in the way in which these two radars employ this principle,

apart from other variations between them. The most significant is that the US equipment has both beams (slant and vertical) radiating along a common azimuth, rotating in synchronism, whereas in the Head Net C the beams are separated in azimuth by 180° – as a result of the back-to-back configuration employed.

In practice, the vertical beam fulfils the search

function and the operator selects a target for which height data is required, and by placing a marker on this target (or similar technique) this places a range gate in the second (inclined) beam and excludes other targets. Computation to give a height readout can be performed by analogue or digital methods.

This radar has been seen on both 'Kresta I and II' classes of guided missile cruisers, the *Moskva* and *Leningrad* cruiser helicopter carriers, some 'Kashin', 'Kanin' and 'Krupny' GMDs, and 'Kotlin SAM II' GMDs. The newest class of vessel to carry Head Net C is the 'Krivak' general-purpose leader type.

Head Net back-to-back three-dimensional air-surveillance radar on 'Kresta II'

4084.253
KITE SCREECH FIRE CONTROL RADAR

Kite Screech is a gun fire control radar, probably an evolutionary development of the Hawk Screech and Owl Screech family of fire control radars (**1325.253**). A distinguishing feature that enables the Kite Screech to be identified from the other two types is the antenna illuminating feed support assembly which has a noticeably more 'pointed' appearance compared with the Hawk and Owl Screech radars. The latter types also have a comparatively large dielectric housing protecting the actual radiator element, whereas the equivalent item on the Kite Screech is much less prominent. G- or I-band operation is probable, and possibly this recently introduced radar incorporates monopulse tracking instead of conical scan tracking.

The only fittings noted to date are aboard the new 'Kirov' class cruiser, where the Kite Screech radar is used for the direction of two 100 mm gun turrets mounted aft, the 'Sovremenny' class destroyers and the new guided missile cruiser *Slava*.

Aboard the Soviet cruiser Kirov a single Kite Screech radar is used for direction of two single 100 mm dual-purpose gun turrets

Kite Screech fire control radar on the Soviet ship Sovremenny showing the very pointed appearance of the antenna feed assembly (see text)

1611.253
MUFF COB FIRE CONTROL RADAR

The Muff Cob fire control radar is similar in general appearance to the Drum Tilt fire control radar (**1330.253**), but the former has provision for elevation motion, being supported by a trunnion yoke carried on the traversing mounting. The operating frequency is probably in the G/H- or I-band part of the spectrum. Some drawings of Muff Cob show what appears to be an on-mounted TV or optical tracking sub-system, but this has not been confirmed.

In all the installations of Muff Cob studied, this radar is employed for gun fire control purposes only. On the helicopter carriers *Moskva* and *Leningrad*

there are two Muff Cobs mounted high on each side of the main superstructure for direction of the twin 57 mm guns on either side of these ships. Both 'Kresta I' and 'Kresta II' classes of guided missile cruiser have two Muff Cobs each, carried on platforms on the sides of the funnel. These are for control of twin 57 mm guns on each side. Some of the 'Ugra' and 'Lama' classes of support ships have two Muff Cob installations, and there are single fittings on ships of the 'Poti' class of coastal escorts. The 'T58' class of fleet minesweepers carry a single Muff Cob on top of the bridge house. Some 'Polnochniy' amphibious landing craft (Type IX) carry a Muff Cob for direction of anti-aircraft guns.

Muff Cob fire control radar

1323.253
PEEL GROUP FIRE CONTROL RADAR

This group comprises four distinct radars on a common mounting and is associated with the Goa surface-to-air armament of Soviet vessels. The radars entered operational service in the early 1960s. Within the group are an H/I-band tracking radar for high altitude targets and an E-band guidance radar for lower altitudes. The maximum range is reported as 30 to 40 miles (55 to 75 km). All four scanners are of solid-reflector construction and of elliptical paraboloid shape. There are two large and two small scanners in each group, one of each size being disposed with its major axis horizontal and the other vertical.

The two Peel Group missile control radars stand out, fore and aft, on this modified 'Kashin' class destroyer, at anchor off the Libyan coast. Also prominent are the air search radars Head Net C and Big Net on the two lattice masts, Bass Tilt fire control radars for the Gatling-gun turrets, fore and aft Owl Screech fire control radars for twin dual-purpose gun turrets, and the ship's impressive armament (HMS Intrepid)

The central mounting has noticeably rounded proportions and appears to provide a common axis about which the group rotates in azimuth, and the forward side of this mounting is another large housing providing for rotation of the group in elevation. It cannot positively be ascertained if this provides for separate elevation rotation of the individual elements of the group. Viewed from the front, the large vertically disposed scanner is to the right of the central mounting and the other three scanners are to the left of it.

Although unrestricted rotation of the individual vertical and horizontal elements of the Peel Group is unlikely, sector scanning is probable for the performance of air target tracking. Target designation is probably provided by one of the Head Net series of air surveillance radars, and the Peel Group does not seem to have been designed to give a search capability.

The feed arrangements are a matter of some conjecture. Those of the two smaller scanners are distinguished by large offset boom-mounted illuminator housing boxes the shape of which seems to suggest that they contain multiple horns. One feasible explanation for this is that a monopulse tracking technique is used, with separate radars for each co-ordinate, azimuth and elevation. Operating frequency of the two smaller radars of the group is probably in the I-band.

The feeds of the two larger radars are smaller than those of the other two radars of the group and are not offset. The feed housings are of cylindrical form and may contain devices such as a quarter-wave plate to provide circular polarisation as an aid to higher weather penetration.

Information is too limited to draw firm conclusions concerning the functions of the individual elements of the Peel Group in tracking the target and directing the missile. A likely assessment is that the two larger scanners are employed for the longer range target acquisition and 'coarse' tracking, while the two smaller scanners provide precision tracking.

Between the large vertically oriented scanner and the central mounting a further unit of uncertain function is located. This could be a radiator for guidance signals to the missile until its own homing system comes into operation. It is also a reasonable assumption that some provisions for IFF are made within the system.

The normal deployment arrangements associate one Peel Group unit with one dual Goa surface-to-air missile launcher. 'Kresta I' class guided missile cruisers have two installations, one forward above the bridge and the other aft, atop a short tower, and 'Kashin' class GMDs are similarly fitted. The 'Kynda' class GMDs have a Peel Group installation above the bridge, and on 'Kotlin' class GMDs there is a Peel Group on a square, tapered tower amidships.

1609.253

PLINTH NET SEARCH RADAR

Plinth Net is a medium-range E-band general-purpose search radar with an elliptical lattice reflector illuminated by an underslung boom-mounted feed horn. Functions include air search and target designation. Range against air targets at medium altitudes is about 80 nautical miles (150 km), and 20 nautical miles (37 km) against surface ship targets. There are no balance vanes behind the scanner. The turning gear is housed in a tapered cylindrical mounting, from which the NATO name for this radar is derived. Plinth Net is fitted in certain ships of the 'Kynda' and 'Kresta I' class, 'Talin' class, and 'Sverdlov' class cruisers.

1897.253

POP GROUP FIRE CONTROL RADAR

Pop Group is the NATO code-name for the fire control radar group associated with the Soviet Navy's SAN-4 surface-to-air missile system (**2954.231**). The name has its origin in the fact that the launcher for this missile system pops up from a silo-type housing preparatory to launching.

Few details have been obtained regarding the operation of the Pop Group radar but at least two antennas are used for radar functions, with a third for the transmission of command signals to the missile. The arrangement consists of a cube-shaped container with sides of about 2·2 m in which is probably housed the bulk of the electronics such as

A similar view of the Pop Group radar on a 'Krivak' class destroyer. The Owl Screech gun fire control radar below the Pop Group is facing the opposite way showing the feed arrangements more clearly

transmitter/receiver units, power supplies, and turning gear, and on the top of this is a trainable radar head assembly. The latter unit, so far as can be ascertained from the limited evidence available, has a parabolic antenna of about two metres aperture which is probably for target search and which may rotate independently of the rest of the radar head (which, as noted above, can be trained in azimuth). On the front face of the head are two circular arrays that are assumed to be for target tracking and missile guidance. Operating frequencies are likely to lie in that part of the spectrum contained within the G- to J-band region.

The public display by the Soviet Union in November 1975 of the land-mobile SA-8 missile system, complete with its associated radar group, rapidly led observers to comment upon the similarities between this radar and Pop Group. The theory that the two recent sea and land air-defence missiles are related is an attractive one, but it should be noted that whereas the SA-8's radar group has two antennas which are assumed to be for command link signals, the Pop Group set has only one. The fact that the main tracking array of the land radar has cropped sides is not significant, and this measure was probably adopted to enable the overall dimensions of the radar to be reduced to measurements compatible with those of the carrier vehicle.

Operating frequencies for SA-8 are conjectured to be G- or H-band for search and target acquisition with I-band for tracking.

STATUS

Since Pop Group was first detected on Soviet 'Nanuchka' class missile frigates in the late 1960s, it has been fitted to an increasing number of types of vessel of widely differing sizes.

'Nanuchka' class ships have a single Pop Group installation on top of the bridge housing, and a similar arrangement is employed in the 'Grisha' escorts, the SAN-4 launcher 'bin' being located in the forecastle on both types of vessel. The 'Krivak' missile destroyers have SAN-4 installations fore and aft, with a Pop Group radar for each system, one on top of the bridgehouse and the other on a raised mounting amidships. 'Kara' class missile cruisers have two

Pop Group fire control radar

SAN-4 systems, located one on each side of the mast and with their associated Pop Group radars are two automatic anti-aircraft gun turrets on each side, and these would appear to be directed by the Pop Group radars to form (with the SAN-4 missile launchers) port and starboard integrated close-in autonomous air defence weapon systems.

In the case of the converted 'Sverdlov' cruisers, the largest vessels equipped with SAN-4, various arrangements exist. *Zhdanov* had its SAN-4 silo fitted in place of the original 'X' 152 mm gun turret, and the associated Pop Group radar was installed on a platform attached to the aft mast. The *Admiral Senyavin* has its SAN-4 installation incorporated in the helicopter hangar, with the Pop Group in the same position as on the *Zhdanov*. In the former ship, however, there are four automatic AA gun turrets mounted adjacent to the SAN-4 system.

The 'Nanuchka' class fittings were the first to appear in quantity, but since those early days many classes and individual ships of the Soviet Fleet have appeared armed with the SAN-4 missile system and equipped with Pop Group radar. A single Pop Group is fitted to ships of the 'Koni', 'Grisha I' and 'III', and 'Sarancha' classes, as well as the *Ivan Rogov* landing ship and the fleet replenishment ship *Berezina*. Two Pop Group installations are found on ships of the 'Kara', 'Kiev', 'Kirov', and 'Krivak I' and 'II' classes.

1612.253

POT DRUM NAVAL RADAR

Pot Drum is a small surface search radar, probably operating in H/I-band and protected by a flat, slightly domed, radome from which its NATO code name is derived. The diameter of the radome is about 1·5 m and the unit is typically installed at the masthead of small patrol boats. This radar is probably of conventional design with the possible exception of a rather higher than usual rate of scanner rotation and the inclusion of ECCM and perhaps a passive direction finding mode of operation. The transmitter/receiver is housed below decks. The display unit has a small CRT display (about 15 cm), so that short range operation of the radar is likely. In addition to surface target detection, Pot Drum probably is used for pilotage purposes also and may have a limited air warning capability. The principal operational role is that of surface search and fire control for torpedoes carried by fast MTBs. Range is about 20 nautical miles (37 km).

Coastal escorts of the 'Stenka' and 'Kronstadt' classes are fitted with Pot Drum, as are torpedo boats of the 'Shershen' class, some 'P6' class boats, and the 'Pchela' class of hydrofoil craft.

Soviet 'Shershen' class torpedo boat with Pot Drum surface search radar and Drum Tilt fire control radars for guns

1613.253
POT HEAD NAVAL RADAR

Pot Head is similar in appearance to the Pot Drum surface search radar (**1612.253**) but is slightly smaller with an estimated diameter of 1·2 m. Another distinguishing feature is that the top of Pot Head is flatter than that of Pot Drum. The operating frequency is probably in the I-band but the possibility of E-band

operation has been quoted by certain sources. The main function will be that of surface target detection, with pilotage and limited air warning facilities as supplementary capabilities.

Fittings appear to be confined to torpedo boats of the 'P6', 'P8' and 'P10' classes operated by the Soviet and East German Navies.

Pot Head short-range surface radar with IFF antenna

1324.253
SCOOP PAIR SURFACE TARGET RADARS

This radar system is a feature of Soviet vessels equipped with Shaddock surface-to-surface missile launcher tubes. It consists of two apparently identical radars mounted above and below a spherical housing supported at the end of a sponson. Photographs indicate that these sponsons, which are aligned with the ship's fore-and-aft axis, may include provision for rotating the radar group to provide stabilisation against roll motion, and there may also be pitch stabilisation but this is not known for certain.

The scanners are of open lattice construction and of essentially elliptical paraboloid form, although the contours are rather angular. They have quite a high span/depth ratio and the former dimensions are estimated at approximately 4·2 m. They each have the typical Soviet balance vanes behind the scanners, in this case of almost square outline. Each scanner is illuminated by a double horn assembly carried on a boom, coming from beneath the scanner in the case of the upper radar of the group, and above in the case of the lower radar. The disposition of the horns

suggests that they are arranged to provide maximum elevation coverage from the combined pair of radars. A further possibility for the use of double horns is that they are associated with special signal processing equipment to provide optimum target detection in the presence of sea clutter returns.

It is not known if the two radars comprising the Scoop Pair group are rotated in azimuth independently, although there is no mechanical reason why they should not be.

Operating frequencies are in the E-band. Probable functions include surface search, and target detection to provide range and bearing data for the Shaddock missile fire control system, and tracking of the missile after launch.

All Shaddock-carrying Soviet vessels appear to be equipped with one or two Scoop Pairs, depending upon the Shaddock launching arrangements. 'Kresta I' class guided missile cruisers have a single installation, high on the main 'tower', and this serves two twin launchers below, and on each side of the bridge. 'Kynda' class ships have two groups, fore and aft, each serving a four-tube launcher.

Scoop Pair radars for surface-to-surface Shaddock missiles. The projection above the upper-scanner could be for IFF. The scanners can be seen to employ a solid reflector in front of which is a parallel grid, presumably to improve clutter rejection.

1614.253
SKIN HEAD NAVAL RADAR

The Skin Head radar is principally associated with Soviet torpedo boats and its function is assumed to be surface target detection for use in association with torpedo fire control systems. Its appearance is characterised by a thimble shaped dome from which the NATO code-name is derived, and generally a masthead mounting. Diameter of the radome is estimated to be about 0·8 m. The nature of the scanner assembly inside is not known but a high rotation rate is assumed. Operating frequency is probably in the I-band.

Although Skin Head is mostly associated with torpedo boats of the 'P4' and 'P6' classes, used by the Soviet and friendly navies, the 152 mm gun turrets of Soviet 'Sverdlov' cruisers carry a radome of similar proportions (NATO code-name Egg Cup) which suggests that the same radar may be used for fall-of-shot measurement or other purposes on these ships.

Skin Head radar on masthead of 'P'-type Soviet torpedo boat. The array on top may be an alternative IFF antenna

Skin Head radar used for surface target detection on Soviet torpedo boats. Small antenna is for IFF

1322.253
SLIM NET SURFACE WARNING RADAR
Slim Net is a surface warning, high definition, radar of generally conventional naval design, plus the typical Soviet characteristic of balancing vanes behind the scanner. It also has an air search capability. The scanner is of open lattice construction and approximately 5·5 m span and 1·8 m maximum depth. The general shape is of a tapered rectangle, and the balance vanes also are rectangular. The horn feed is mounted on a boom overhangng the scanner. Operating frequency probably lies within the E/F-band of the spectrum.

Vessels seen with this radar include some ships of the 'Kildin' class of guided missile destroyers (in which it may be associated with the Strela surface-to-surface missile launcher); 'Kotlin' class destroyers; and 'Tallin' class destroyers. In all three cases it is carried on top of the rear tripod mast. It is believed that some 'Riga' class and 'Petya' class escorts have been equipped.

Slim Net scanner assembly, with Yard Rake rotating Yagi array (right)

1595.253
SQUARE HEAD NAVAL RADAR
The antenna of this system consists of a broadside array of dipoles with a rectangular reflector/support frame measuring about 1·4 m high by 2 m wide. It was originally thought to be a long wavelength search radar of modest power, but later evidence confirms that its function is that of an IFF interrogator antenna, or a directional array for the transmission of guidance signals to surface-to-surface missiles. It is most frequently seen on Soviet missile carrying boats of the 'Osa' class (but apparently not on craft of this class of the navies of countries friendly to the USSR), and these generally have two such arrays carried on sponsons fore and aft of the tubular mainmast. Some 'Kotlin' class destroyers of the Soviet fleet carry four, and Square Head has been seen on vessels of the 'Skory' class.

Recent information suggests that the Square Head antenna is associated with an IFF system operating in the G-band.

1329.253
SQUARE TIE NAVAL RADAR
Square Tie is a small lightweight search radar, probably operating in the I-band to provide short range air and surface search facilities. It is extensively fitted on Soviet vessels of the 'Osa' class armed with anti-ship missiles. The scanner is an elliptical paraboloid reflector illuminated by an overhung horn feed. Functions will include target detection and tracking for anti-ship missile direction and possible target designation for the Drum Tilt gun fire control radar carried by 'Osa' class craft. Maximum range is believed to be about 70 nautical miles (130 km).

1331.253
STRUT CURVE SEARCH RADAR
Strut Curve is a medium-range general-purpose air search radar, probably operating in the E/F-band to provide both air and surface search facilities. An elliptical lattice reflector is used, illuminated by a horn feed carried by a boom projecting from the lower edge of the scanner. The boom is supported by two struts which attach to stays at the upper edge of the reflector. Somewhat unusual for Soviet naval radars, the Strut Curve has no balance vanes behind the reflector.

Range performance against an aircraft target at medium altitude is about 60 nautical miles (110 km) with a likely maximum range of 150 nautical miles (280 km).

Strut Curve search radar

Strut Curve antenna profile

Soviet vessels fitted with Strut Curve include the 'Poti' class of escorts and certain support ships.

1326.253
SUN VISOR FIRE CONTROL RADAR
Sun Visor is identified as a solid paraboloid scanner fixed to the front of a spherical shaped gun fire director station. Two types of director have been identified carrying this type of radar. These have the NATO code names Round Top and Wasp Head, and in the former the radar is carried near the top of the unit compared with a lower location on Wasp Head, which is stabilised. Span of the dish is estimated at approximately 2·2 m, and the depth at 1·3 m. Operating frequency is probably I- or G/H-band. The reflector is illuminated by a dielectric-enclosed feed carried on a solid boom structure projecting from over the upper edge of the reflectors. The disposition of these components suggests that surface target detection is the principal role of this radar.

The fire director units on which Sun Visor is mounted are capable of 360° rotation, but since they are manned units incorporating optical rangefinding equipment also, it is unlikely that it is normally used for target search and surveillance on a continuous basis. A more likely mode of operation is for target co-ordinates to be passed to the system by another of the ship's radars and for the former to operate in a target acquisition and lock-on role to provide either range and bearing data for blind firing or to assist the operator in the training of optical sighting systems.

Sun Visor has been seen on certain vessels of the 'Krupny' class of GMDs, the 'Kanin' class, 'Kotlin' class, 'Talin' class, and 'Sverdlov' class cruisers.

Sun Visor gun fire control radar

4088.253
TOP DOME RADAR GROUP

Top Dome is the name of the radar group associated with the SA-N-6 naval area air defence weapon system fitted in the Soviet cruiser *Kirov*. This system is thought likely to be an approximate Soviet equivalent of the American Aegis surface-to-air naval air defence missile system, in which case the Top Dome radar group will embody long-range tracking and guidance functions, probably incorporating multi-mode operating facilities of one sort or another. At this early stage it is possible only to embark on preliminary conjecture concerning the functioning of the Top Dome radar group. The *Kirov* has two such director groups located fore and aft, this being more to achieve an all-round engagement capability rather than by any requirement to associate the individual directors with missile launcher installations in specific parts of the ship. The SA-N-6 is believed to employ a vertical launch technique so that once missiles are launched from the magazine on the foredeck of the ship and are clear of the ship's superstructure, they can be commanded to turn onto any course required to engage the specified target.

Targets are probably detected by either passive means (of which *Kirov* has an ample selection) or the Top Pair radar group, and targets are designated to either of the two Top Dome director groups which are then laid on to the necessary threat direction. When the Top Dome radar (or passive detection subsystem) acquires the target and locks on and when the target has reached an appropriate engagement range one or more SA-N-6 missiles are launched and commanded to the proper direction, after which automatic guidance to interception takes place. The Top Dome radar group is probably capable of tracking both the SA-N-6 missile and the designated target simultaneously, and there is also the possibility of a combined mode of guidance involving target tracking through the SA-N-6 seeker with the command link relaying data back to the ship. In any event, the new system is likely to incorporate several guidance options to cater for changing circumstances and to deal with opposing counter-measures.

The Top Dome group mounting is obviously designed to rotate in azimuth and probably has some horizontal stabilisation against ship's motion also, but continuous rotation of the mount is thought unlikely. Stabilisation gear is possibly housed within the hexagonal portion of the mounting. The 'front' face of the latter carries three antenna housings of hemi-cylindrical shape; these are thought to contain passive sensors or command link elements. A similar purpose is also possible for the small 'thimble' shaped housing carried above the hemi-cylindrical units, at an angle. The contents of the main dome remains uncertain at this stage.

Top Dome radar director group on the Soviet cruiser Kirov *with Kite Screech gun fire control radar to the left*

4087.253
TOP PAIR RADAR GROUP

Top Pair is the name of a back-to-back configuration of two very different naval radar types employed for long-range air surveillance. One is the well-known Top Sail 3-D radar which is associated in this configuration with what appears to be the Big Net long-range search radar (or a derivative of it). All known fittings are aboard recent ships known to have a major air role, such as the aircraft carriers of the 'Kiev' class. The Top Pair group has also been noted more recently fitted in the Soviet guided missile cruiser *Slava*, as well as the cruiser *Kirov*, which in addition to carrying its own helicopters is fitted with the new SA-N-6 surface-to-air missile system and is thought to have an important anti-air escort role in support of the Soviet carrier force. Operating frequencies in the D-band, and possibly E/F-bands, are thought likely for the Top Pair radars. Detection ranges of several hundred kilometres can be expected.

Soviet cruiser Kirov, *showing the Top Pair air surveillance radar group at the very highest position on the ship's superstructure, with another new radar group, Top Steer, to be seen further aft on top of the pyramidal mast. The ship also displays two Top Dome fire control radar groups (fore and aft) for the ship's SA-N-6 vertical launch area defence anti-aircraft missile system. Numerous ESM and EW antennas are clearly visible*

Enlargement of Top Pair radar group on the Soviet cruiser Kirov

1327.253
TOP SAIL THREE-DIMENSIONAL RADAR

Top Sail is a very large air surveillance radar, first seen on the Soviet cruiser helicopter carrier, *Moskva*, and her sister ship *Leningrad*, but later on the new 'Kresta II' and 'Kara' classes of guided missile cruisers. In all installations the radar is mounted at the highest point of the vessel; in the case of the 'Kresta II' class on a large diameter tubular pedestal atop the principal tower, and on the helicopter cruisers supported by a tubular tripod. In the 'Kara' installation the scanner surmounts a typically Soviet pyramid shaped structure amidships.

The scanner is of cylindrical cross-section, the axis of which is tilted from the vertical at an angle of about 20°. It is of lattice construction and has a frontal aspect of rhombic shape (estimated 5·5 m sides), with 'cropped' corners. Illumination of the reflector is by a linear radiating element located parallel to the reflector's cylindrical axis, and supported top and bottom. The feed appears to be from the upper end. It may consist of multiple horns to provide three-dimensional air target data by the 'stacked-beam' method, or some form of electronic scanning in elevation (such as the ridged waveguide) may be used to achieve the same result. Operating frequency is probably in the D-band, although one authority has quoted G-band operation, with high transmitter power. The theoretical maximum range is more than 300 nautical miles (555 km).

The photograph of a 'Kresta II' Top Sail antenna shows what appears to be a second system of waveguide, of smaller dimensions than the main system, apparently feeding a horn at the top of the main illuminator. This might indicate dual band operation facilities for some purposes. There is a subsidiary antenna fixed to the top of the Top Sail scanner which could be for IFF. In addition to the two plates which are the most prominent feature of this secondary antenna there are also three dipoles. Near the bottom of the illuminator of the main Top Sail are what could be a similar group of three dipoles. The function of these elements has not been ascertained.

In all three classes of vessel equipped with Top Sail it is associated with similar radars, a Head Net C back-to-back 'V-beam' set, and Head Light group missile fire control director radars. The Top Sail is probably used for long-range air surveillance and target designation.

The profile of the Soviet aircraft carrier *Kiev* clearly illustrates the ship's comprehensive radar fit. Ahead and abaft of the Top Globe on its mast are Top Sail and Top Steer air surveillance radars, respectively, emphasising their size difference; below these radars are fore and aft Head Light missile control radar groups, Owl Screech gun fire control radars, with a navigation radar between the forward Head Light and Owl Screech

4086.253
TOP STEER RADAR GROUP

Top Steer is the name given to what appears to be a new generation Soviet air search radar group comprising a pair of scanners mounted back-to-back, usually high up on the superstructure of the ship. The two scanners are not the same and one is somewhat similar in appearance to the well-known Top Sail 3-D air surveillance radar fitted to several classes of recent major Soviet ships. However the Top Steer antenna is noticeably smaller, as can be seen on ships such as the new *Kirov* cruiser which has both Top Sail and Top Steer fitted. The other scanner appears to be either a standard Head Net A search radar or a modified derivative of it. It is not known if the two radars are operated together as part of a single complex system of a new type, or if the two scanners are merely co-mounted as a matter of structural convenience with either one of the two radars being capable of independent operation on its own (apart, of course, from having common turning gear and/or stabilisation).

Operating frequencies of both radars are likely to be in the D/E/F-bands of the radar spectrum and it is possible that the larger antenna may incorporate some form of frequency scanning of the beam in elevation to provide a heightfinding capability. The probable function of this radar group is that of air control of the ship's helicopters, or other aircraft operating with the ship.

Top Steer installations have been noted on the cruiser, *Kirov*, on the *Sovremenny*, which is thought to be the lead ship of a new class, on the recent 'Kiev' class aircraft carriers, and the guided missile cruiser *Slava*.

Top Steer radar group on the *Sovremenny*

This view of the Soviet aircraft carrier *Kiev* clearly shows the considerable difference in size between the Top Sail 3-D radar and the Top Steer radar group mounted aft of the Top Sail and the flaired-in mast that carries the Top Dome (RAF)

1610.253
TOP TROUGH SURVEILLANCE RADAR

Top Trough is a C-band long-range air search radar with a probable maximum range of up to 300 nautical miles (555 km). The only known installations are on some ships of the Soviet 'Sverdlov' class of cruisers, in particular Mikhail Kutuzov, Senyavin and Zhdanov.

Soviet 'Sverdlov' class cruiser, Mikhail Kutuzov, showing Top Trough radar on aft mast. Knife Rest (Uda-Yagi) antenna for air warning can just be discerned forward of aft gun turrets

1900.253
OTHER SOVIET NAVAL RADARS

Photographs have been obtained of a number of other radars fitted to ships of the Soviet Fleet additional to those described in the preceding entries. Insufficient information is available to make possible individual entries, but the photographs are reproduced to assist readers with identification.

Don K navigation radar

Top Bow gun fire control radar

Ball Gun

Knife Rest

High Sieve

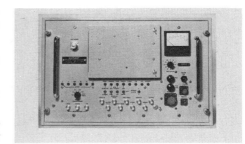

Top Bow is an H/I-band fire control radar for 152 mm guns

UNITED KINGDOM

3699.253
CEL 850 NAVAL INTERROGATOR

The Cossor CEL 850 naval IFF interrogator is the shipboard version of the CEL 850 general-purpose interrogator, and additional details will be found in **3692.153** in the Ground Radar section of this volume. In the naval application it is suitable for use in all classes of ship, down to fast patrol craft in size. The transmitter section has an output of 2 kW (peak), and the equipment can operate on Modes 1, 2, 3/A, C and External. It is designed to accommodate many different interfaces so that integration with numerous types of primary radar presents no problem.

STATUS

In production with deliveries to navies all over the world.

CONTRACTOR

Cossor Electronics Ltd, The Pinnacles, Harlow, Essex CM19 5BB, England.

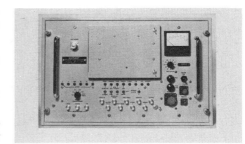

Cossor CEL 850 general-purpose interrogator equipment

3701.253
IFF 2750 (TYPE 1013) NAVAL TRANSPONDER

Under contract to the Royal Navy, Cossor modified their IFF 2720 airborne IFF transponder (**3695.353**) for naval applications. The resulting equipment, IFF 2750, has a low magnetic profile, low weight and low volume, thus making it suitable for fitting in all classes of vessel, including minehunters. In the RN the IFF 2750 is designated the Type 1013. The key features of the IFF 2720, high reliability, ease of access for maintenance, and continuous on-line monitoring, have been retained in the IFF 2750.

CHARACTERISTICS

Modes: 1, 2, 3
Receiver frequency: 1030 MHz
Receiver sensitivity: –76 dBm
Transmitter frequency: 1090 ±3 MHz under all service conditions
Transmitter power output: 750 W (nominal); 500 W (minimum)
Reply coding: 4096 on all modes
Dimensions: 91 × 193 × 381 mm
Weight: 4·6 kg

STATUS

In production and supplied to the Royal Navy and other customers.

CONTRACTOR

Cossor Electronics Ltd, The Pinnacles, Harlow, Essex CM19 5BB, England.

Cossor IFF 2750 naval transponder (Type 1013) and control unit Type IFF 2753

1941.253
RACAL SURVEILLANCE AND NAVIGATION RADARS

Racal navigational radars are now in service with some 90 navies, not only for general navigational purposes, but also as prime sensors for action information systems and weapon control. These standard commercial marine radars, in both the F- and I-bands, are frequently interfaced with a wide variety of fire control systems, surveillance radars, EW systems and computers.

The use of standard commercial equipment with transmitter emission characteristics indistinguishable from those of thousands of commercial users reduces the chances of identification by ESM.

Racal Clearscan video processing provides sea and rain clutter and radar interference suppression and echo stretching. The first anti-collision radar was introduced in 1968 and shows true and relative motion data simultaneously. Markers can be placed on five echoes to show the movement of targets which are being shadowed or attacked.

The Racal Command Tactical Console (CTC) is based on the well-tried all-weather commercial ARPA and autotracks up to 20 targets, air or surface, with

ground stabilisation, true motion storage and target indication facilities.

The Racal 2459 F/I radar with its widely spaced dual frequency capability provides combined air and surface surveillance for warships fitted with guns and sea-to-air or -surface missiles.

CONTRACTOR
Racal Marine Radar Limited, Burlington House, 118 Burlington Road, New Malden, Surrey KT3 4NW, England.

1563.253
MRS3/GWS22 FIRE CONTROL RADARS
TYPES 903/904

The MRS3/GWS22 is standard Royal Navy equipment for the control of guns (MRS3) and Seacat missiles (GWS22). The initial application was gun fire control for quick-firing medium guns of 3, 4·5, and 6 inch calibres. Following application of the system to the Seacat system, the MRS3/GWS22 has been the subject of steady modification and can be seen in several forms.

The radars carried by this director are known as the Types 903 and 904, and both are conventional I/J-band conical scan tracking radars.

More detailed information is given under this entry number in previous editions of *Jane's Weapon Systems*.

STATUS
The MRS3/GWS22 has been extensively fitted in many ships of the Royal Navy. A number of Commonwealth and other navies are equipped with the system, including ships of the Australian, Chilean,

Indian, and New Zealand navies. Production is continuing. The systems have now been updated under a contract awarded to Sperry Gyroscope (now part of British Aerospace).

CONTRACTOR
British Aerospace Dynamics Group, Bracknell Division, Bracknell, Berkshire RG12 1QL, England.

1751.253
AWS-2 NAVAL RADAR

The Plessey AWS-2 naval tactical radar is a versatile E/F-band surveillance radar designed for installation on vessels of the destroyer, frigate, and corvette classes. The AWS-2 will detect small aircraft at a range of the order of 60 nautical miles at a height of

25 000 feet. The equipment can be readily integrated into a ship's gun or missile fire control systems.
STATUS
Numerous fittings of the AWS-2, and its predecessor AWS-1, have been made. There are about 20 of the former aboard the ships of five navies and there are about 30 AWS-1 in vessels of 11 navies. The AWS-2

has now been superseded in production by the AWS-4 and AWS-5.
CONTRACTOR
Plessey Radar Ltd, Oakcroft Road, Chessington, Surrey KT9 1QZ, England.

3171.253
AWS-4 NAVAL RADAR

The Plessey AWS-4 naval search radar meets the operational needs for air and surface search, target indication and weapon control. It can perform effectively in conditions of jamming, sea clutter and precipitation. With a lightweight, compact antenna system the AWS-4 is readily installed in small ships, such as fast strike craft, and is equally suitable as the search radar for corvettes and light frigates, or as the tactical radar for larger vessels in association with a separate long-range air warning radar. The AWS-4 uses a tunable magnetron transmitter with a low-noise parametric amplifier and an ECCM receiver to give an effective anti-jamming performance.

A two-speed antenna, operating with dual pulse lengths and PRFs, optimises the performance of the AWS-4 in the roles of air and surface search and target indication. Variable antenna polarisation enables the operator to minimise the effect of bad weather. IFF facilities are provided by the incorporation of the D-band IFF radiator in the main feed horn. This irradiates the search radar reflector which allows an improved coverage pattern from a lower-power interrogator and reduces masthead weight and windage.

The optional digital moving target indicator (DMTI) provides further protection against clutter caused by sea, land or rain. The DMTI system is self-compensating for clutter velocity, hence also providing good discrimination against chaff. Data from ship's log and gyro is not required.

Radar coverage of the single transmitter version

AWS-4 masthead equipment fitted in Norwegian coastguard patrol ship K/V Nordkapp

against a 4 m² target is 104 km and over 11 500 m free space range with a detection probability of 80 per cent. Against the same target a diversity system will provide increased coverage operationally, enhance anti-jamming performance, increase system reliability and improve availability as one

transmitter/receiver may be closed down for maintenance without loss of radar service.

In addition to the optional features of DMTI and diversity operation mentioned above, a two-axis stabiliser is available to improve overall system performance in cases where AWS-4 is used with a computerised AIO/CIC. A modular data distribution rack is also available to provide optimised interfaces between the radar and the rest of the ship's weapon system.
DEVELOPMENT
The AWS-4 has been derived from extended experience with the preceding AWS-1 and AWS-2 radars in service with 14 navies. Programmes for the progressive up-dating of earlier radars to AWS-4 standards are available.
STATUS
Plessey Radar has supplied AWS-4 radars to a number of overseas customers including the Royal Norwegian Navy and the Sultan of Oman's Navy. Four stabilised diversity systems are being manufactured for the Brazilian Navy.

The AWS-4 below-deck equipment is also extensively employed for modernising obsolescent radars such as the Type 293 and the Type 993 (see **3260.253** and **3261.253**). Conversely, AWS-4 antennas are being used to improve the performance of existing radar systems. Eight antennas are being fitted to Royal Canadian Navy ships as part of the DELEX (Destroyer Life Extension) programme.
CONTRACTOR
Plessey Radar Ltd, Oakcroft Road, Chessington, Surrey KT9 1QZ, England.

3172.253
AWS-5 NAVAL RADAR

The Plessey AWS-5 is an advanced technology E/F-band tactical radar designed to provide comprehensive surveillance facilities for corvettes and frigates in the range 1000 to 4000 ton. It is also suitable as the search and target indication radar in larger ships, in conjunction with a long-range air warning radar. Advanced features of the AWS-5 enable it to combine the following functions:
(1) air and surface warning, with cosecant² coverage for typical air targets to 150 km in range and 20 km in altitude
(2) point-defence search, with enhanced missile detection capability against low level attack and detection beyond 30 km against small high elevation diving targets.
The AWS-5 provides excellent anti-jamming protection and clutter rejection principally through:
(1) high-low beam operation to counter stand-off jamming
(2) circular or linear polarisation by selection to improve rejection against rain

(3) pulse-to-pulse programmable/random frequency agility for ECCM protection and decorrelation of clutter
(4) frequency coded transmissions against deception jamming
(5) high ratio pulse compression for finer resolution and better clutter performance
(6) adaptive coherent DMTI to remove echo responses due to sea and land clutter, bad weather and chaff.
The lightweight masthead equipment of the AWS-5 comprises a compact two-axis stabilised mount on which is fitted a dual-beam antenna system incorporating variable polarisation and integral IFF facilities.

The main below-decks equipment comprises a compact transmitter/receiver cabinet in which are housed the wide-band frequency-modulated transmitter with its drive circuits, power supplies, and a programmable frequency agile source. The receiver chain incorporates pulse compression, CFAR processing, and adaptive MTI. Additional equipment in the AWS-5 outfit includes the stabiliser control

system and a data distribution unit with a high-resolution video extractor and comprehensive interface facilities for supply of video and other data to the ship's operations room and AIO/CIC computer.

Time multiplexing and frequency coding techniques are used in both transmitter and receiver chains in conjunction with the dual-beam antenna. This enables the performance characteristics of two radars to be achieved simultaneously from a single AWS-5 outfit. Radar facilities which could previously be accommodated only in large ships are thus now available for ships of the corvette and light frigate categories.

The various modes of video processing provide good protection against clutter and jamming, enhanced by the programmable frequency agility, the clutter-free high beam, accurately controlled antenna characteristics with good sidelobe performance, and high-ratio equalisers giving an exceptionally short compressed pulse. Integrity of performance under hostile conditions was given priority in the development programme.

The AWS-5 is designed for maximum flexibility in

use. A modular set of control panels gives the operator a wide choice of facilities including:
(1) independent control of main beam and high beam
(2) active or passive mode
(3) DMTI on either or both beams
(4) separate or combined videos
(5) fixed frequency, limited or full agility
(6) variable main beam polarisation
(7) two data rates.

Certain performance characteristics are programmable during manufacture, enabling the AWS-5 to be closely matched to the role of a particular class of ship.

AWS-5D

This is a single beam general-purpose surveillance radar for corvettes and frigates. Using a high gain

horn-fed reflector on a stabilised mounting, the system provides good air target detection to over 100 nautical miles (185 km), and excellent performance against low-flying aircraft and sea-skimming missiles.
STATUS
Equipments are in service with the Royal Danish Navy and a containerised system is in use with the Nigerian Navy.

The AWS-5 is being developed to provide the new 3-D surveillance radar for the Royal Navy Type 996 programme.
CONTRACTOR
Plessey Radar Ltd, Oakcroft Road, Chessington, Surrey KT9 1QZ, England.

Nigerian frigate, NNS Aruda, *fitted with AWS-5 radar*

5620.253
AWS-6 SERIES NAVAL RADAR

The AWS-6 is a range of C-band radars designed for naval surveillance combined with maximum missile detection capability. It is intended to provide the multi-function of surveillance and point defence sensor in fast patrol boats, corvettes and other small ships generally. In larger vessels where multiple radar installations are provided, the AWS-6 will be used in a point defence role only. The equipment is offered in a wide range of configurations and signal processing options and can be profiled to specialised defensive requirements.

The antenna is small and lightweight which allows it to be mounted at masthead with dual-axis stabilisation. The optimum rotational rate is 60 rpm and IFF and navigational functions are integral. Single- or dual-beam configurations are available; the single beam is used for general surveillance operation and target designation while the dual beam mode enables near hemispherical coverage for threat detection at all angles of elevation. Incoming targets

Antenna unit of the Plessey AWS-6/Dolphin surveillance radar

as small as 0·1 m² radar cross-section can be detected, typical of anti-ship missiles. The radar is then used to control the ship's defences – either guns or missiles. One version, the AWS-6/Dolphin missile

detection radar, is the search radar module for Seaguard (**3509.281**), the Contraves close-in weapon system, and employs the dual beam configuration for the detection of high diving and sea-skimming missiles.

The AWS-6 has been designed to operate under severe environmental conditions; and frequency agility, pulse compression and within-pulse coding have minimised the effects of ECM. This has been combined with adaptive MTI to give high performance against clutter, chaff and target glint.

The equipment is also available in containerised form for integration with other weapon systems on ships such as armed merchantmen.
STATUS
The equipment is in full production and trials with the Seaguard system are well advanced. Seven AWS-6 systems are being manufactured for delivery in 1985 for fitment to Danish fishery protection vessels.
CONTRACTOR
Plessey Radar Ltd, Oakcroft Road, Chessington, Surrey KT9 1QZ, England.

1559.253
RN TYPE 909 RADAR

The Royal Navy Type 909 radar provides target tracking and illuminating facilities for the Sea Dart, GWS-30 air defence missile (**6004.231**). This weapon has an anti-ship capability, and the radar is stated to be suitable for gun laying also, so that a surface target capability must be assumed. The antenna is of the cassegrain type and has a diameter of 2·44 m. A small dome mounted near the upper edge probably houses an associated IFF antenna. On board ship, the complete antenna assembly will be protected by a cupola radome. The radar head and the office cabin, containing transmitter/receiver unit and associated electronics, are constructed as a single pre-fabricated assembly to reduce installation and replacement time and to enable functional testing before fitting.

Few technical particulars have been revealed. A G/H-band operating frequency range is likely and a

high transmitter power can be expected. It has been stated that elaborate ECCM are incorporated to counter both active and passive ECM. A photograph appears with the Sea Dart missile entry.
STATUS
The Type 909 is fitted to Type 42 destroyers for the Argentinian and British Navies, and for the RN Type 82 destroyer. Each ship has two radars of this type, mounted in fore and aft radomes. Full production started in 1971.
CONTRACTOR
Marconi Radar Systems Ltd, Writtle Road, Chelmsford, Essex CM1 3BN, England.

Type 42 destroyer, showing the fore and aft Type 909 Sea Dart missile guidance radars in large radomes. Note missiles on forward launcher (Royal Navy)

1752.253
RN TYPE 901 RADAR

The Royal Navy Type 901 radar equipment provides target tracking and missile guidance for the Seaslug shipborne surface-to-air missile system (**6003.231**). Each of the seven RN 'County' class guided missile

destroyers is fitted with a single Type 901 radar, forward of the helicopter deck, for use with the twin Seaslug launcher aft. A stabilised mount is provided and the right-hand side of the director head carries equipment for initial 'gathering' of the beam-riding Seaslug missile. No performance details of the

Type 901 have been released. Operation at G/H-band frequencies is probable.
CONTRACTOR
Marconi Radar Systems Ltd, Writtle Road, Chelmsford, Essex CM1 3BN, England.

1558.253
RN TYPE 912 RADAR

Type 912 is the Royal Navy designation for the Selenia Orion RTN-10X fire control radar fitted to RN ships. It is an I/J-band conical-scan pulse radar, and

the mounting arrangements include facilities for a closed-circuit TV system for acquisition and missile gathering functions. More details will be found in **1368.253** among the Italian entries of this section.

1562.253
RN TYPE 910 RADAR

The Type 910 is the radar tracking element of the GWS 25 Mod 0 Seawolf point defence missile system. It is used with, and receives target designation data from, the Types 967 and 968 air and surface surveillance radars (**1561.253**). It is a monopulse

differential tracker radar, incorporating electronic angle tracking in the tracking loop as a means of correcting the missile guidance line-of-sight for small angles without calling for physical movement of the mount. This benefits both accuracy and the smoothness of tracking. After launch, the Seawolf missile is rapidly acquired by the Type 910 wide-angle

antenna and automatically gathered onto the target line-of-sight. Subsequently, target and missile are tracked together, using the same antenna and receiver by means of time division multiplex techniques. Few technical details have been released but operation in the I/J-band has been confirmed. The Seawolf system uses command to line-of-sight guidance with radar differential tracking and a microwave radio command link, and some of the related antennas can be seen flanking the main Type 910 antenna unit. This is a self-adaptive system and is capable of controlling and directing a number of Seawolf missiles to interception. The system also includes a differential tracking optical TV system which monitors the firing and is capable of taking over missile control during flight should circumstances demand.

Information from this tracker could be used for gun control also, and the TV tracker on the same pedestal could also be employed for gunnery purposes.

STATUS

In production. Fitted to all Type 22 and 'Leander' class frigates of the Royal Navy.

CONTRACTOR

Marconi Radar Systems Ltd, Writtle Road, Chelmsford, Essex CM1 3BN, England.

Type 910 tracking radar with type 967/968 antenna in the background

1560.253
RN TYPE 965 RADAR

The Type 965 long-range air search radar of the Royal Navy is widely used on ships of sizes ranging upwards from frigates. The operating frequency range lies in the metric wavelength band and output powers in the megawatt range are assumed. In addition to air surveillance, the Type 965 fulfils target designation functions for guided weapons systems, and on-mounted IFF Mk 10 facilities are provided.

The antenna array consists of a row of eight dipoles, each at the rear of a 'horn' formed of metal mesh, the whole having a characteristic 'bedstead' appearance. The complete antenna scanner assembly may consist of either one or two such groups, and both versions are extensively employed. An IFF antenna is usually mounted on the upper edge of the primary array.

STATUS

The Type 965 has been in production for several years and is widely deployed in either single or double array form on most ships of the Royal Navy from frigates upwards, including Type 42 and 82 destroyers. It is however being currently replaced in the Type 42 ships by the Type 1022 (**3486.253**).

CONTRACTOR

Marconi Radar Systems Ltd, Writtle Road, Chelmsford, Essex CM1 3BN, England.

Close-up view of Type 965 AKE-1 antenna array, with Cossor IFF antenna on upper edge

1561.253
RN TYPES 967 AND 968 RADARS

The Royal Navy Type 967 is an air surveillance radar which is integrated with the Type 968 surface surveillance radar to form a very compact medium-to-short range defence radar. They provide high performance facilities to fulfil the requirements of air and surface warning, search and target designation, from sea level to high elevation angles. These radars with the Type 910 target tracker and missile guidance radar form the radar group for the Seawolf anti-aircraft and anti-ship missile weapon, GWS 25 (**2442.231**).

The waveguide antennas for both radars are mounted back-to-back in a common housing carried by a single fully stabilised mount protected by a radome. The Type 967 provides air surveillance with cover up to high elevation angles. Operating frequency is in the D-band of the radar spectrum and pulse doppler mode is employed. An enhanced version, known as the Type 967M, is now in production. The Type 968 provides low air cover and surface search, and operates in the E-band. The antenna rotation rate for both is 30 rpm. The Seawolf surveillance radar system is a high-power self-adaptive system, with sophisticated data handling, which resolves both velocity and range ambiguities, initiates track, carries out threat evaluation, takes the engagement decision, and performs attack allocation by assigning a tracker and feeding the track co-ordinates to it. IFF and system ECCM are incorporated. The system has its own digital processor, a Ferranti FM1600 series computer.

STATUS

In production. Fitted to all Type 22 and 'Leander' class frigates of the Royal Navy.

CONTRACTOR

Marconi Radar Systems Ltd, Writtle Road, Chelmsford, Essex CM1 3BN, England.

Scanner and stabilisation arrangements of RN Type 967/968 for Seawolf point defence system. Separate antennas for surface and air search contained in a common housing

1253.253
RN TYPE 975 RADAR

The Type 975 is a lightweight, I/J-band, high definition surface warning radar designed for fitting on frigates, coastal and inshore minesweepers, and other naval craft of similar size. Its primary function is navigation, but in some installations it is specially adapted for minehunting in conjunction with a suitable plot and underwater detection equipment. This version is designated Type 975ZW, and

incorporates true motion displays and provision for marking sonar targets on the display.

Transmitter power is 50 kW (nominal), and either a 182 or 304 cm slotted waveguide scanner is used. Two models of display unit are available, JUC/1 and JUC/2. The former is a watertight unit with magslip range and bearing, and the latter has synchro range and bearing transmission. Seven range scales provide displays of 0·75 to 48 nautical miles. Minimum detection of the radar is less than 32 metres, and

bearing accuracy is within 1°.

STATUS

This radar has been extensively fitted to ships of the RN and other navies, and although now superseded by the Type 1006 (**1394.253**), many Type 975 units are still in use.

CONTRACTOR

Kelvin Hughes Division, Smiths Industries Ltd, New North Road, Hainault, Ilford, Essex IG6 2UR, England.

1753.253
RN TYPE 992Q RADAR
The Royal Navy Type 992Q radar is a fully stabilised 10 cm (E/F-band), high-power pulse radar equipment, fitted in destroyers and frigates. It is a prime source of surface/air target information for the action information organisation system, and provides space-stabilised output data which can be synchronised in pulse and rotation with that of other radars fitted in the ship. It is of solid-state electronic construction apart from certain circuit elements which retain vacuum tube devices.
STATUS
Fitted in RN 'County' class and Type 82 destroyers.
CONTRACTOR
Marconi Radar Systems Ltd, Writtle Road, Chelmsford, Essex CM1 3BN, England.

'County' class destroyer, HMS Glamorgan, *with Type 992Q scanner on foremast. Below is Type 978 navigation radar, and MRS3 radar director over bridge. Mainmast has Type 965 search radar with AKE (2) antenna outfit. Note ECM arrays*

3260.253
RN TYPE 994 RADAR
This new radar incorporates a transmitter/receiver based on the Plessey AWS-4 radar described in **3171.253**. It uses the existing antenna of its predecessor Type 993. The below-decks equipment is the same as for the Plessey AWS-4 radar system, for which Plessey supplies a new high performance lightweight antenna system. The transmitter/receiver is designed to occupy the same space as the original equipment. An interface unit is supplied to simplify the installation work. Widespread use of solid-state technology ensures better reliability and simplifies maintenance procedures.

The radar's performance can be further enhanced by the addition of a digital moving target indicator (DMTI), providing increased protection against clutter caused by sea, land or rain. The DMTI is self-compensating for clutter velocity, hence also providing good discrimination against chaff. Data from ship's log and gyro is not required.

Similar E/F-band tactical radars of various Royal Navy types, both search and heightfinders, are in service with other navies around the world. The introduction of Type 994 means that cost-effective and proven facilities are available for modernising tactical radars on board many different classes of ship, using either the antenna already fitted or the new AWS-4 antenna according to circumstances.

Trials carried out on a typical aircraft target at several different altitudes established clearly that the new equipment not merely matches the improved requirements but exceeds it by a significant margin.
STATUS
In quantity production for fitting aboard Royal Navy frigates and ships of other navies. The RN installation programme commenced in 1978.
CONTRACTOR
Plessey Radar Ltd, Oakcroft Road, Chessington, Surrey KT9 1QZ, England.

HMS Arethusa *fitted with one of the Type 993/994 conversions showing the antenna at the top of the foremast*

4634.253
TYPE 996 NAVAL SURVEILLANCE RADAR
Type 996 is the Royal Navy staff requirement nomenclature for a new S-band, 3-D surveillance and target indication radar which is intended for fitment to the Type 23 frigates, and retrofitted into Type 42 destroyers, Type 21 frigates and the 'Invincible' class carriers.

No technical details of the Type 996 are available currently, other than that it is largely based on the AWS-5 (**3172.253**) with the addition of 3-D technology from the AR-320 system (**3649.153**). It is understood that two variants of the Type 996 are to be produced.
STATUS
Plessey Radar received a contract, valued at approximately £70 million, from the UK MoD in September 1983 to develop the Type 996 radar. No information is available on deliveries for either new ships or retrofits.
CONTRACTOR
Plessey Radar Ltd, Oakcroft Road, Chessington, Surrey KT9 1QZ, England.

3486.253
RN TYPE 1022 NAVAL RADAR
The Type 1022 is a long-range D-band frequency synthesiser-driven travelling wave tube (TWT) radar with pulse-to-pulse coherence. It was developed as a replacement for the Royal Navy's Type 965 surveillance radar. Long-range performance is aided by the use of a high mean-power TWT in the transmitter. A pulse-compression receiver with MTI provides for good performance in rain and in the presence of surface clutter.

The antenna uses a squintless feed to provide tapered illumination of the main reflector. This results in good sidelobe performance across the band. Other technical features include solid-state electronics, frequency agility over a wide band, horizontal and circular polarisation, frequency synthesiser-controlled coherent transmitter, MTI with digital quadrature canceller and digital video processing.

It is understood that the Type 1022 is a joint Anglo/Dutch project in which Signaal is providing the transmitter/receiver and Marconi the antenna. This suggests that the finished equipment will appear on the vessels of both British and Netherlands fleets.

Type 1022 antenna on HMS Nottingham *Type 42 destroyer*

STATUS
In production and fitted to a number of Royal Navy ships.

CONTRACTOR
Marconi Radar Systems Ltd, Writtle Road, Chelmsford, Essex CM1 3BN, England.

1394.253
RN TYPE 1006 RADAR
The Type 1006 is the standard I-band navigational radar of the Royal Navy.
Antenna Outfit AZJ
The surface role antenna outfit consists of a 2·4 m slotted waveguide linear array rotated at 24 rpm by a turning mechanism. The array has a horizontal beamwidth of 1° and low sidelobe levels to give good bearing discrimination. The vertical beamwidth of 18° gives good performance in conditions of roll and pitch. To meet special ship fitting requirements the antenna outfit may be inverted and mounted on the underside of a mast spur.
Antenna Outfit AZK
This antenna outfit consists of a 3·1 m slotted waveguide !inear array rotated by the same type of turning mechanism as outfit AZJ. It is used when the improved bearing discrimination given by the 0·75° beamwidth is required. The increased antenna gain also improves the range performance of the radar system. The remaining details of outfit AZK are similar to those for AZJ.
Transmitter/Receiver (Surface)
The equipment is non-thermionic with the exception of the magnetron, and operates at a frequency of approximately 9445 MHz. The solid-state modulator, which may be externally synchronised, provides three pulse lengths at two repetition frequencies to drive the magnetron which is coupled directly to the RF head. The advanced broadband design of the RF head ensures the best obtainable minimum range under adverse waveguide conditions. The three pulse lengths of 80, 250, and 750 ns ensure good short range discrimination and long range performance. A Gunn diode local oscillator is controlled by an AFC with tuning indication; the IF generated is fed to a combined linear/logarithmic receiving system. The linear video is used for navigational radar displays and the logarithmic video is used for weapon system data extraction. The receiver bandwidth is automatically optimised for the transmitter pulse length in use.
Transmitter/Receiver (Submarine)
In order to be compatible with the existing submarine antenna system a variant of the transmitter/receiver operating at 9650 MHz is available. It is otherwise identical to the surface role equipment. The design of the RF head prevents damage to the equipment from massive waveguide reflections which occur if the antenna is submerged while transmitting.
Display Unit JUD
This unit is non-thermionic with the exception of the cathode ray tube. The display unit uses a rotating scanning coil system to provide range scales from ½ to 96 data miles. The unit uses a 31 cm (12 inch) cathode ray tube. Fixed coils provide off-centring facilities of up to 75 per cent of a radius from either an external true motion unit or from internal sources.
Symbolic Data Display
The facilities of the display have been extended for surface role applications to operate in conjunction with computer systems such as CAAIS (computer assisted action information system). Additional symbol writing coils and amplifiers are provided together with pulsed off-centring amplifiers to enable the display of interscan symbolic data on appropriate range scales from analogue information inputs.
True Motion Outfit QAB
The outfit QAB is a solid-state electro-mechanical computer for the provision of true motion presentation on the radar 1006 JUD display.
The Type 1006 is compatible with the JQ submarine bridge display which is primarily used to assist conning when submarines enter or leave harbour.
STATUS
The Type 1006 radar has been in series production for the Royal Navy and other navies since 1971.
CONTRACTOR
Kelvin Hughes Division, Smiths Industries Ltd, New North Road, Hainault, Ilford, Essex IG6 2UR, England.

5632.253
TYPE S1100 NAVIGATION AND SURVEILLANCE RADAR
The Type S1100 is the nomenclature for a series of radars which comprise a comprehensive range of modular units, and are configured to meet nearly all naval and commercial requirements for navigation, pilotage and short-range surveillance. The major units of the system; antenna, transceiver, scan converter, display and processing systems have been derived from the latest technology and also from current developments within the commercial field.
A range of raster scan displays are available which use digital scan conversion techniques to meet the requirement for daylight viewing.
STATUS
In development.
CONTRACTOR
Marconi Radar Systems Limited, Writtle Road, Chelmsford, Essex CM1 3BN, England.

1508.253
ST 802 NAVAL TRACKING RADAR
The ST 802 is a lightweight I-band monopulse search and tracking radar for the direction of small and medium calibre guns, and for target tracking in guided missile systems. It is intended for use against air or surface targets, and the weight and dimensions of the system are appropriate to installation on all classes of vessel from patrol boats upwards. The ST 802 is designed with facilities for independent operation and control in weapon systems not equipped with a central computer complex, but can also interface with, and be controlled by, the weapon system's own computer.
The radar director head is a two-axis mount carrying a one metre diameter antenna, and optionally, a TV camera. The mount is controlled by electric servos in azimuth and elevation, with stabilisation of the sight line during tracking by means of rate gyros. The antenna is of the twist cassegrain type. A four-horn monopulse feed and comparator provide three separate RF outputs (sum, elevation difference, and training difference signals) for processing in the IF receivers to produce acquisition and auto-follow data. Accurate angular data result from the combination of a 2·4° pencil beam and monopulse signal processing. With TV camera, the director head weighs 532 kg.
The I-band transmitter incorporates a tunable magnetron, and a short pulse length is used in the interests of range resolution and tracking accuracy. The receiver employs monopulse tracking and embodies features such as the tunable magnetron, monopulse signal processing, MTI, passive tracking of targets using ECM, and CFAR, to reduce the effects of countermeasures. MTI (coherent on receive) provides discrimination against sea clutter when tracking small, low-flying targets.
A frequency agile version of this radar, known as the ST 1802 is also available. It includes a fully coherent transmitter to produce true random frequency agility across a wide bandwidth, offering significant performance advantages, particularly in jamming environments.
OPERATION
Weapons which can be associated with the ST 802 include Seacat, Exocet, and medium and small calibre guns of 20 mm upwards. Acquisition of air or surface targets is automatic, following target designation by search radar or other means. After acquisition, the target is automatically tracked and appropriate data supplied to weapon systems. The antenna head is able to rotate continuously in azimuth at 20 rpm, and this feature in conjunction with MTI is of value in providing additional surveillance cover at low elevation.
If the TV sub-system is fitted, it may fulfil either of two distinct roles, depending upon the weapon system employed. With command line-of-sight missiles, the TV system will permit automatic missile guidance after launch, from a below-decks position. Alternatively it may be used as a back-up to radar

ST 802 naval tracking radar with IR camera

tracking in either daylight or low light-level mode. Other electro-optical sensors may also be fitted, such as infra-red or laser rangefinder.
STATUS
The ST 802 is a private development in collaboration with L M Ericsson, and has been proposed to a number of navies with various gun and missile fire control systems. In production, it forms part of the Marconi/Sperry Sapphire gun control system of the Egyptian 'October' and 'Ramadan' fast missile craft.
CONTRACTOR
Marconi Radar Systems Ltd, Writtle Road, Chelmsford, Essex CM1 3BN, England.

1754.253
S810/820 NAVAL SURVEILLANCE RADARS
Lightweight surveillance radars in the S800 series are comprised of various combinations of two sizes of scanner, and two transmitter/receiver equipments. These are summarised in the table of characteristics.
The Marconi Type S810 is a lightweight stabilised I-band surveillance radar suitable for fitting in small warships down to the size of fast patrol boats where there are limitations of space and weight. I-band gives good performance against surface targets, a major requirement for fast patrol craft, while satisfactory coverage is maintained against air targets by the use of a stabilised antenna in a radome, with vertical fan beam shape. A narrow horizontal beamwidth ensures accurate target indication data for pointing weapons and for putting on a tracking radar.
Detection of surface targets such as fast patrol boats is horizon limited and strike aircraft of 5 m² can be detected at ranges in excess of 25 km with the smaller antenna and up to 40 km with the larger one. A DMTI system is provided to enhance the system performance against small high-speed targets in clutter and the magnetron transmitter is tunable to ECCM or other interference.
S810 series radars use a pulse transmitter of the same design as in the lightweight search/tracker radar Type ST 802 (**1508.253**), resulting in a reduction in the on-board spares if both radars are fitted in a ship. In all versions, the receiver provides either logarithmic/linear or integrated video for the operational displays.
The antenna head, stabilised in roll and pitch, rotates at 20 or 40 rpm and is enclosed in a radome for protection and minimum weight. An elliptical reflector is used, which measures 1·2 by 0·45 m or 1·8 by 0·6 m. Both types are constructed of glass-reinforced plastic. A single horn feed is located at the focus of the reflector which is contoured to provide a narrow horizontal beam and a fan-shaped vertical beam. The turntable consists of an aluminium alloy centre tube and outer casing, azimuth bearing and azimuth drive and data units. The complete antenna/turntable assembly is supported on a platform giving stabilisation for roll angles up to 25°

and pitch angles up to 10°, with acceleration up to 30° per second. The 1·8 or 2·7 m diameter radome which encloses the whole antenna assembly is constructed of a 12 mm thick sandwich of glass-reinforced plastic and foam.

The transmitter employs a tunable magnetron operating within the frequency band 8·6 to 9·5 GHz and delivers a typical peak power of 200 kW. All components are solid-state except the magnetron and the hydrogen thyratron in the pulse modulator.

Two receiver channels, one logarithmic, the other linear, are provided. The required channel is selected by a switch located near the PPI display. MTI processing is available, the DMTI filter being a double canceller employing shift-register storage and feedback. The radar operates with a staggered PRF in the MTI mode in order to overcome the disadvantages of 'blind speeds'. Compensation is provided for ship and wind velocity. When clutter cancellation is not required, the MTI can be switched out and the radar then operates with a jittered PRF of 1·5 kHz allowing a maximum displayed range of 80 km.

For the larger FPB, there is the radar Type S820 operating in the E/F-band. This employs a 2·4 m stabilised antenna enclosed in a radome giving a total masthead weight of 550 kg. The transmitter is tunable within one of two frequency bands. The receiver

CHARACTERISTICS

	S810 (MTI)	S820
Antenna size	1·2 × 0·42 m	2·4 × 0·9 m
Beamwidth		
Vertical	Shaped to 25°	Shaped to 30°
Horizontal	2·2°	3°
Rotation rate	24 rpm	24 rpm
Platform	2 axis stabilised	2 axis stabilised
Radome	1·7 m diameter	3·3 m diameter
Base	1·3 m diameter	3 m diameter
Transmitter/receiver	I-band tunable	E/F-band tunable
Frequency	8·6 – 9·5 GHz	2·7 – 2·9 GHz or
		2·9 – 3·1 GHz
PRF	1500/4400 Hz	750/1500 Hz
Pulse length	0·67/0·33 μs	1·2/0·6 μs
Signal processing	Logarithmic linear	Logarithmic linear
	Integrated MTI	and MTI

employs a parametric amplifier and has linear/logarithmic processing and can be supplied with or without MTI.

A recent development is a low cover version of the S810 which has a concentrated low-level beam and a high antenna rotation rate (40 rpm) which is intended for detection of sea-skimming targets.

STATUS
Radars of the S800 series are in production for the UK

MoD and other unspecified customers. The S810 is fitted to the 'October' class and the S820 to the 'Ramadan' class fast missile craft of the Egyptian Navy.

CONTRACTOR
Marconi Radar Systems Ltd, Writtle Road, Chelmsford, Essex CM1 3BN, England.

4302.253
805 SERIES NAVAL TRACKING RADARS
The 805 series has been developed as lightweight naval tracking radars for the control of missiles and guns. They are intended for use primarily against air targets and are suitable for virtually any type of naval vessel from patrol boats upwards. There are five different types: 805SW, 805SD, 805AS, 805SS and 805G.

The 805SW has been designed for the lightweight Seawolf system and is currently being fitted to ships of the Royal Navy. Details are given under entry **5630.253**, RN Type 911 tracking radar.

The 805SD is designed for use with the lightweight Sea Dart system for smaller warships. The system uses standard modules from the 800 series radars (**1754.253**), and the Type 909 (**1559.253**) which is currently in operational use in Royal Navy Type 42 destroyers. The radar director carries a 2·1 metre antenna, which fulfils the functions of target tracking and illumination, plus an optronics package tailored to meet the particular requirement. The system is suitable for ships of 300 tons and above, a containerised fit is available. The 805SD is a private venture equipment intended for the export market.

The 805AS has been developed in co-operation with Selenia as a lightweight tracking radar for use with the surface-to-air version of the Aspide missile. It uses the Selenia 200 watt transmitter and has been designed so that it can take full advantage of the complete missile envelope. The 805AS Aspide system is known as the Albatros Mark 10. The radar can also be used for gun control.

The 805SS has been designed in co-operation with Raytheon for use with the Sea Sparrow missile. It uses the Raytheon illuminating transmitter, is extremely lightweight and can also be used for gun control.

The 805G is a millimetric radar system for controlling fast firing or medium calibre guns. The 805G employs a variant of the DN 181 Blindfire tracking radar (**2439.153**) to give high accuracy

performance against low-level targets such as sea-skimming missiles and low-flying aircraft. The system includes facilities for correcting alignment against both air and surface targets.

STATUS
The 805SW has been selected as the tracking radar for the Royal Navy's lightweight Seawolf system and is being fitted aboard Type 22 frigates. The system is also the subject of considerable interest from a number of foreign countries for smaller types of warship.

The 805SD has been designed for the export market and is currently being studied by a number of defence forces as part of lightweight Sea Dart.

CONTRACTOR
Marconi Radar Systems Limited, Writtle Road, Chelmsford, Essex CM1 3BN, England.

805SD tracking radar for lightweight Sea Dart

5630.253
RN TYPE 911 TRACKING RADAR
The Marconi 805SW is a lightweight tracking radar for use with the Seawolf short-range point defence system. It is designated Type 911 by the Royal Navy and will be fitted on Type 22 and 23 frigates.

The radar is a dual frequency (I-band and millimetric wave) differential tracking system which includes a command link to control the Seawolf missile in flight. The I-band antenna and transmitter form part of the Marconi ST 800 range and the signal processing uses fast Fourier transform techniques to ensure effective operation in severe clutter environments. The millimetric part of the system is a version of the DN 181 Blindfire radar (**2439.153**) used

Marconi lightweight tracking radar 805SW (RN Type 911) for lightweight Seawolf naval SAM system

with the BAe Rapier missile. It provides accurate tracking at low sight angles against targets close to the sea surface, such as sea-skimming missiles and low-flying aircraft. A system of independently illuminating the upper and lower parts of the millimetric antenna ensures that the missile receives good guidance data while flying at low level.

The radar is fully automatic to provide fast reaction time against small targets and is autonomous, requiring only the allocation of the fire control channel to the selected target and information on ship's motion. Excellent clutter rejection is provided on both bands for operation in both open and enclosed waters and ECCM facilities are incorporated to enable use in hostile electronic environments.

STATUS
In production. The system is due to be fitted to all Royal Navy Type 22 and 23 frigates, with deliveries commencing in 1984. Orders from the UK MoD had reached £100 million by January 1984.
CONTRACTOR
Marconi Radar Systems Limited, Writtle Road, Chelmsford, Essex CM1 3BN, England.

3687.253
S1800 SERIES NAVAL SURVEILLANCE RADARS

This range of modular surveillance radars has been developed by Marconi Radar Systems Ltd as a private venture, in association with Canadian Marconi, although some of the technology was developed as part of the RN Type 1030 STIR radar (**3485.253** in 1982-83 and earlier editions). Three of the range have been described to date, the S1820, S1821 and the S1840, although other models have been designated.
S1820
This model has been described as the minimum configuration version within the S1800 series of equipments, the series itself comprising a range of modular elements, such as antennas, transmitter/ receivers, signal processors. The S1820 antenna is a stabilised unit (pitch and roll) of 2·4 m span, very similar to that of the S820 (**1754.253**), housed in a protective radome and associated with a frequency agile transmitter. The latter unit incorporates pulse compression and operates at E/F-band frequencies, and alternative modes of frequency agile working are available. The use of long pulse techniques yields a high mean power which increases range performance while subsequent pulse compression

restores range accuracy. Pulse compression on reception also gives additional noiseless gain to genuine echoes.

The MTI processor, particularly when fitted with adaptive velocity compensation, discriminates against land, sea and rain clutter. Combined frequency agility and MTI processing are provided, and CFAR circuits precede the automatic target tracking circuitry. The optional IFF can be integrated with the main antenna.

The S1820 is suitable for fitting aboard ships of 300 tons or above, and provides for air and surface tactical surveillance in addition to target indication data for ship's weapons.
S1821
The S1821 uses the same transmitter, receiver and processing system as the S1820 but employs a higher gain 4-metre antenna to give higher elevation cover, increased range performance and improved angular resolution.
S1840
This model is a high power, lightweight 3-D naval surveillance radar which operates in the NATO G-band and is designed to give range bearing and height data on all targets within its instrumented

cover. The S1840 design enables early detection of high-speed anti-ship missiles and subsequent fast reaction to counter this type of threat. Good target detection and tracking is achieved under the severe levels of clutter and ECM interference likely to be encountered in naval environments. The radar is designed to provide the facilities required by both medium range area and point defence systems.
CHARACTERISTICS
Type: S1820
Frequency: E/F-band, frequency agile
Transmitter power: 20 kW (peak); 800 W (mean)
Antenna: 2·4 m span stabilised with integral IFF
Antenna weight: 550 kg
Range: Approx 85 km (max)
STATUS
No details of ship fittings are available for publication although the S1820 system is in production for the Canadian Navy, by Canadian Marconi, under the nomenclature AN/SPS-503 (**5677.253**).
CONTRACTOR
Marconi Radar Systems Ltd, Writtle Road, Chelmsford, Essex, CM1 3BN, England.

3487.253
TRANSPONDER REPLY RECEIVER RRB

The reply receiver RRB has been developed to enable ships' radars operating with naval aircraft equipped with transponders (ARI 5983) or airborne radar (ARI 5954) to receive and display the responses from the latter.

The airborne transponders are principally employed to assist in navigation when aircraft are operating beyond visual range of the controlling unit, each aircraft or helicopter carrying an identical transponder which can be interrogated by the ship's ordinary radar system. This mode of operation

considerably enhances range performance of the ship's radar.

The airborne transponder receives over a wide range of frequencies but replies on a single frequency only, and some types of shipboard radar incorporate a reply receiver so that either transponder (beacon) replies or normal radar returns may be displayed. Where this is not available, a separate reply receiver must be attached to the ship's radar to tune it to the transponder's frequency. This is the reply receiver RRB which enables a naval fixed-frequency receiver to receive pulse radar emissions from airborne radar ARI 5954 (**1027.353**) and ARI 5983 (**3310.353**).

An associated video code suppression unit (VCSU) processes the coded video pulse train output from the receiver so that the first framing pulse is passed and the remainder of the pulse train is suppressed. This enables coded replies to be displayed at will on the radar. The VCSU has facilities for three modes: permanent suppression, manual selection of suppression facility, and remote selection.
STATUS
In production for Royal Navy.
CONTRACTOR
Microwave Associates Limited, Dunstable, Bedfordshire LU5 4SX, England.

5676.293
RADAR ANTENNA PEDESTALS

Radamec (formerly Bentley Engineering) is the largest supplier of stabilised and general surveillance antenna pedestals for the Royal Navy and has been a prime naval contractor for over 40 years. The company has full UK MoD approval to DEF STAN 05-21.

The illustration shows a reference model stabilised pedestal maintained by the company for the Royal Navy. In service the unit carries a 6·4 m medium-range surveillance antenna on vessels such as guided missile destroyers. A more recent development is a stabilised pedestal for mounting on top of a pole mast

where low weight is essential. Unstabilised pedestals range from a small unit for 'half-cheese' antennas up to a heavyweight mounting for 1½ tonne arrays. Manufacture of this equipment includes production of RF components (rotating and nutating joints, tuners, attenuators, etc) and bearing data transmission units. Servo amplifier and micro-processor-based control equipment is also available.
STATUS
Radamec equipment is fitted to over 120 ships of frigate size and above in the navies of 14 nations.
CONTRACTOR
Radamec Ltd, Bridge Road, Chertsey, Surrey KT16 8LJ, England.

Radamec stabilised reference pedestal

UNITED STATES OF AMERICA

1932.253
AN/SPG-60 RADAR

The AN/SPG-60 is a monopulse, X-band pulse doppler search and tracking radar forming part of the Mk 86 fire control system (**1241.281**). It is used for acquisition and tracking of air targets to ranges of about 60 nautical miles (110 km), tracking being either automatic or manually aided. The radar's search-to-acquire capability is computer directed, and it accepts two- or three-dimensional target designation co-ordinates in digital or synchro format from either the AN/SPQ-9 radar (**1931.253**), which is also part of the Mk 86 FCS, or other shipboard search radars.

Acquisition for SPG-60 is automatic, the radar performing its programmed scan search pattern about the designated point under computer control.

The computer resolves the problems of blind range and range rates inherent in doppler radars, as well as range ambiguity.

The computer also automatically controls and calibrates receiver gain and monopulse channel balance.

Other features include four-horn monopulse antenna arrangement; continuous azimuth rotation; bore-sighted TV camera; passive angle tracking; adaptive scan patterns for automatic acquisition; adaptive computer control of PRF and pulse-length. The Mk 86 FCS uses the SPG-60 to provide tracking data for the SM-1 SAM system, and it also provides

SPG-60 (STIR) radar aboard USS South Carolina
(Stefan Terzibaschitsch)

target illumination by means of CW injection at the SPG-60 antenna.
DEVELOPMENT
Prototypes of the complete Mk 86 FCS were delivered to the US Navy in March 1970, and by December 1983, 64 production units had been delivered for fitting aboard various US Navy ships. These include the 'Ticonderoga', 'Virginia' and 'California' class guided missile cruisers, 'Spruance' class destroyers, 'Tarawa' class amphibious assault ships, 'Kidd' class guided missile destroyers and three ships of the 'Charles F. Adams' class guided missile destroyers.
STATUS
The system is now at sea with the US Fleet.

Production is continuing for applications related to the DDG 15 class Fleet Modernisation programme for the American and West German Navies, and USN CG 47 Aegis ship class.
CONTRACTOR
Lockheed Electronics Company Inc, US Highway 22, Plainfield, New Jersey 07061, USA.

1247.253
AN/SPG-51 RADAR
The AN/SPG-51 pulse doppler radar forms a major element of the missile and gun fire control system Mk 74, with the Mk 73 gun and missile director system (**2632.281**) being intended mainly for use with the Tartar (**6006.231**) and Standard (**1122.231**) surface-to-air missile systems, for which it fulfils target tracking and missile guidance functions. Operating frequency is probably in the I-band. A circular parabolic dish reflector with offset horn feed is used, mounted on a gearless power drive produced by General Electric.

The radar line-of-sight can be rotated continuously in train, and can be elevated from -30 to +83° relative to the deck plane. Initial pointing information is supplied to the SPG-51 by a search and target designator radar. This information is received via the Raytheon Mk 72 signal data converter and digital fire control computer which generates a search pattern for the SPG-51 until target acquisition is accomplished. Automatic tracking is then initiated and the SPG-51 feeds angle and range information to the computer. The computer generates fire control data for transmission to gun mounts and missile launchers. It also provides missile seeker and angle data.
STATUS
The SPG-51 is widely used on US Navy vessels, and development proceeded through A, B, C, and D versions. The last of these began deployment in 1972.

SPG-51 missile guidance radars. Three-dimensional search radar on left is SPS-52

Among the other navies using this radar are those of Australia, France, Federal Republic of Germany, Italy, Japan, the Netherlands, and Spain.

CONTRACTOR
Raytheon Company, Equipment Divison, Wayland, Massachusetts 01778, USA.

1748.253
AN/SPG-55 RADAR
The AN/SPG-55 radar is the G/H-band guidance radar for the Terrier surface-to-air missile system (**6005.231**) fitted in ships of the US and a number of allied navies. Transmitter power is thought to be of the order of 50 kW and the typical operating range, 50 km. Three versions of this radar have been identified: SPG-55, A and B models. Some references have been found to the use of an associated CW target illuminator system, AN/SPA-44, but no other details have been obtained. Early American Terrier installations employed, instead of the SPG-55, a radar designated AN/SPQ-5, which in appearance is similar to the SPG-49. It is not known how many of these installations remain operational but the SPG-55 remains on three ships of the Italian Navy.

In 1977 Sperry Rand Corporation received US Navy contracts for updating and refurbishing SPG-55B radars, four of which have been brought to a Mod 8 Block 1 configuration for the Mk 86 Terrier fire control system.

SPG-55 Terrier missile guidance radars aboard USS Dahlgren

1564.253
AN/SPS-10 RADAR
The AN/SPS-10 is a surface search radar operating at G-band frequencies. Limited air search and tracking capabilities are available also. The scanner is of open lattice construction and is illuminated by a horn feed supported by a boom projecting from beneath the lower edge of the scanner. The transmitter/receiver is mounted below decks, so that radar head weight is minimised, thus permitting mounting as high as possible on the ship's upper-works. The span is estimated to be about 2·4 m.

The SPS-10 is widely used and now exists in a variety of forms, denoted by suffix letters to the main designation, and five or six manufacturers have produced one or more models.
STATUS
The SPS-10 has been in service since the early 1960s and is extensively fitted on US Navy ships, and vessels which have been passed on to friendly navies by the US Navy.

The SPS-10 antenna has been the subject of a modification in which a new dual feed is substituted for the original unit to permit integrated use of the SPS-10 scanner for both that radar and the SPS-58 (**1359.253**).
CONTRACTORS
ITE Circuit Breaker Company. (AN/SPS-10B).
  Daystrom Incorporated. (AN/SPS-10D).
  Raytheon Company, Equipment Division, Wayland, Massachusetts 01778, USA. (AN/SPS-10E).
  Sylvania Electronic Systems, Needham, Massachusetts 02194, USA. (AN/SPS-10 and AN/SPS-10C).
  Capehart Corporation; Dero Research and Development Corporation. (AN/SPS-10F).

SPS-10 surface search radar antenna

1931.253
AN/SPQ-9 RADAR

The AN/SPQ-9 is a high-resolution, track-while-scan (TWS), pulse compression, X-band naval radar. It forms part of the Lockheed Mk 86 fire control system (**1241.281**) and provides detection and tracking facilities within a range of 20 nautical miles (37 km). The minimum range is 150 yards (137 m). The radar antenna provides surface search and limited air cover (up to 2000 ft, or 610 m). A separate transmitter/receiver interrogates, receives, and decodes replies from transponders such as the AN/TPN-7, AN/TPN-16, or AN/UPN-32. The surface-search-only antenna is mounted on a stabilised platform and protected by a radome. The combined surface-and-air search antenna is deck mounted and also is stabilised.

A high scanner rotation rate is a feature of the SPQ-9 giving a one-second data rate. Real-time signal and data processing permit detection, acquisition, and simultaneous tracking of multiple targets. The basic capacity of the complete Mk 86 system is four targets, and TWS is expansible to 120 targets. The radar operates in any one of five selectable frequency ranges, with pulse-to-pulse frequency agility as an additional countermeasure to jamming and natural clutter. This feature also permits a number of radars to operate without mutual interference. An MTI facility can be added to further enhance sub-clutter visibility.

Other elements of the Mk 86 system are the AN/SPG-60 radar (**1932.253**) and an electro-optical sensor system, connected to an AN/UYK-7 computer complex and consoles for command and weapon control. Both guns and missiles can be controlled by the system.

DEVELOPMENT

Prototypes of the complete Mk 86 FCS were delivered to the US Navy in March 1970. By December 1983, 64 sets had been delivered for installation aboard various US Navy ships. These include the 'Ticonderoga', 'Virginia' and 'California' class guided missile cruisers, 'Spruance' class destroyers, 'Tarawa' class amphibious assault ships, 'Kidd' class guided missile destroyers and three ships of the 'Charles F. Adams' class guided missile destroyers. The Mk 86 is also scheduled for fitting in the DDG 19 modernisation programme and the West German DDG modernisations.

STATUS

The system is now at sea with the US Fleet. Production is continuing, see SPG-60 status, above.

CONTRACTOR

Lockheed Electronics Company Inc, US Highway 22, Plainfield, New Jersey 07061, USA.

Radars aboard the USS South Carolina *include (from top) Tacan beacon, SPS-40 search radar, and SPQ-9 in radome (Stefan Terzibaschitsch)*

1744.253
AN/SPS-6 RADAR

The AN/SPS-6 is a naval air and surface search radar, operating in the D-band of the radar spectrum and having an output of the order of 500 kW. Approximate range of the equipment is 100 to 200 km. The SPS-6 is widely used on ships of the US Navy and numerous other nations and has been in service for many years. During this period various versions, denoted by suffix letters to the designation, have been evolved. These differ in transmitter/receiver and antenna details.

The SPS-6, SPS-6A, and SPS-6B all employ the same below-decks equipment but have different antennas. The SPS-6C has the same antenna as the SPS-6B (on a different pedestal) and with certain differences in the below-decks equipment. The principal effect of the different antennas used is in the vertical beamwidth for each: SPS-6, 10°; SPS-6A, 20°; SPS-6B/C, 30°. The SPS-6C is believed to incorporate more comprehensive receiver video processing.

STATUS

In addition to the various classes of US Navy vessels fitted with the SPS-6, it is used by the navies of Italy, Japan, Spain, Taiwan, Turkey, Venezuela, and West Germany, and all those navies supplied with 'Fletcher' class destroyers are users.

CONTRACTOR

Westinghouse Command and Control Division, PO Box 1897, Baltimore, Maryland 21203, USA.

The larger of the two search antennas is the SPS-6, the higher antenna being the SPS-10. Note also the extensive communications arrays aboard the communication relay ship USS Arlington *(Stefan Terzibaschitsch)*

1745.253
AN/SPS-30 RADAR

The AN/SPS-30 is a long-range three-dimensional radar fitted in certain aircraft carriers and some guided missile ships of the US Navy. Among its features are a high-gain antenna of characteristic configuration (see illustration), broadband frequency operation, and high power output. The antenna is mechanically stabilised against ship's motion, with compensation for roll and pitch. It is stated to provide range, bearing, and height information on multiple airborne targets with 'extreme' accuracy. Although primarily a high-grade heightfinding radar, the SPS-30 is capable of being used for additional tasks such as long-range air search and target designation.

CHARACTERISTICS

Peak power: Classified
Average power: 9 kW

Frequency: E/F-band
PRF: Classified
Pulse width: Classified
Receiver sensitivity: -117 dBm
Beam characteristics: Pencil beam
Beamwidth: 1·5° azimuth; 1·2° elevation
Antenna azimuth rate: 1, 2, 3, 5, 10 rpm plus sector scan
Elevation rate: 240, 480, 720, 1200, 2400 scans/s
Elevation scan sector: Any 12° sector from 0 - 36°
Antenna gain: 41 dB

STATUS

The SPS-30 was introduced into US Navy service in the early 1960s and is carried on many aircraft carriers and some guided missile ships.

CONTRACTOR

General Electric Company, Electronic Systems Division, Syracuse, New York 13201, USA.

SPS-30 3-D radar head

1565.253
AN/SPS-37 RADAR

The AN/SPS-37 is a metric wavelength, long-range air surveillance ship's radar of conventional design. The antenna consists of lattice structure with an open mesh reflector, and supporting an array of 28 dipoles arranged in four horizontal rows of seven. The upper edge of the scanner usually carries an associated IFF antenna. Approximate dimensions of the SPS-37 array are: span 6 m, and height 3·3 m. This is the same item as employed by the earlier SPS-29, thus complicating the identification problems. No performance details have been disclosed.

STATUS

The SPS-37 entered service in 1958 and production ceased in 1962. It is widely fitted on ships of the US Navy and of some friendly navies. In recent years the driver has been replaced by an all-solid-state version.

CONTRACTOR

Westinghouse Defense and Electronic Systems Center, Baltimore, Maryland 21203, USA.

1249.253

AN/SPS-39A (FRESCAN) RADAR

The AN/SPS-39A is a shipborne 3-D radar for air surveillance. It uses mechanical rotation for azimuth coverage and electronic scanning for beam steering in the vertical plane. Vertical scanning is achieved by selection of the transmitted frequency input to the sinuous feed on the side of the AN/SPA-72B antenna. Although still fitted in US Navy guided missile ships and also to ships of France, Italy and Japan, this radar is now out of production. More information is given in *Jane's Weapon Systems 1982-83* and earlier editions.

CONTRACTOR

Hughes Aircraft Company, Fullerton, California, 92634, USA.

1746.253

AN/SPS-40 RADAR

The AN/SPS-40 is a naval search and surveillance radar for the detection of air targets at long and medium ranges and a range of 320 km has been quoted. Official performance data have not been released but operation in the E/F-band is probable and a transmitter power of about 1 MW may be expected. The reflector is of open lattice construction and has somewhat irregular, angular outlines. A prominent characteristic is the use of an overslung, lattice construction boom to support the feed assembly.

STATUS

The SPS-40 was first introduced into US Navy service in the early 1960s and is now seen on numerous classes of ship of all sizes from escorts upward. It has subsequently been fitted in ships of other navies, among them those of Argentina, Australia, Brazil, Chile, Federal Republic of Germany, Greece, Saudi Arabia, Spain and Turkey.

In 1979 Norden Systems was awarded additional contracts to continue the SPS-40 updating programme, among them one contract for 11 modification kits for SPS-40A radars to bring them up to the latest production standard, SPS-40B. Sets modified in this way carry the designation SPS-40D. Similarly, earlier SPS-40 sets previously updated by Norden were re-designated SPS-40C. Altogether, Norden has modified 176 equipments.

The company also designed an automation module for the SPS-40 which allows the radar to interface with the AN/SYS( ) system which automatically computes and compiles a total tactical picture for the ship's commander from several radar inputs.

In mid-1979 Norden Systems was awarded a contract to produce a modified transmitter for US Navy SPS-40B, C and D radars. A total of 86 sets to receive the modified transmitter have been delivered.

In February 1980 Norden Systems was awarded a contract to update the SPS-40 long-range naval radar for the Turkish Navy. This entailed refurbishing an existing SPS-40, installing an SPS-40D modification kit and testing and delivering the completed system to the Turkish Navy.

A contract was awarded to Norden in January 1982 for the conversion of four SPS-40A radars to SPS-40D configuration. The contract, from US Naval Sea Systems Command, also includes the supply of 20 DMTI kits to replace analogue versions.

In 1981 the AN/SPS-40 solid-state transmitter (SSTX), developed by Westinghouse was designed to replace the existing transmitter in the AN/SPS-40 radar series. The SSTX has successfully passed evaluation trials and a $14·4 million contract for eight units plus spares was awarded to Norden in October 1983.

CONTRACTOR

Norden Systems, United Technologies Corporation, Norden Place, Box 5300, Norwalk, Connecticut 06856, USA.

SPS-40 search antenna atop the mainmast. Note also Tacan and other antennas (above), intercept radomes, and Mk 68 gunfire control system (below)

1747.253

AN/SPS-43 RADAR

The AN/SPS-43 is a high-power, very long-range search radar, probably operating at metric wavelength frequencies and using a transmitter output of 1 to 2 MW. The large (about 13 metres span) antenna assembly is of open lattice construction and rectangular aspect, but with a characteristic 'sideways-W' profile in side elevation. The upper edge of the array generally carries an on-mounted IFF antenna.

STATUS

The SPS-43 has been in operational service with the US Navy since the early 1960s and is fitted to many of the larger ships of the US Navy. In recent years the driver has been replaced by an all-solid-state driver.

CONTRACTOR

Westinghouse Electric Corporation, Command and Control Division, PO Box 1897, Baltimore, Maryland 21203, USA.

SPS-43 antenna aboard USS Springfield (Stefan Terzibaschitsch)

1939.253

AN/SPS-49 RADAR

AN/SPS-49 is a very long range two-dimensional air search radar designed for use as the primary detection radar aboard various combatant ships of several countries. The radar antenna is line-of-sight horizon-stabilised to provide acquisition of low altitude targets in all sea states. It has a state-of-the-art ECCM capability and modern adaptive DMTI and CFAR for reliable detection in clutter.

The radar is all solid-state with a klystron final amplifier. Each production system is subjected to a minimum of 150 hours of continuous test in a shipboard simulated environmental chamber thus eliminating failures through this accelerated maturing of each system.

STATUS

The AN/SPS-49 is fitted, or due to be fitted to the US, Australian and Spanish FFG 7 class, the new Canadian patrol frigate, Terrier missile firing cruisers and destroyers, Aegis CG 47 class cruisers, battleships, attack aircraft carriers and LSD class landing ships. By early 1984 130 systems had been procured and it is anticipated that 15 to 20 systems will be procured each year over the next few years.

CONTRACTOR

Raytheon Company, Equipment Division, Wayland, Massachusetts, 01778, USA.

1252.253

AN/SPS-48 AIR SURVEILLANCE RADAR

The AN/SPS-48 is a three-dimensional, long-range air surveillance radar for ship-board applications. It uses a combination of mechanical scanning in azimuth and electronic beam steering in elevation to provide plan position and height information on aircraft targets. Multiple beams can be formed, and elevation scanning is accomplished by changing the frequency under computer control of the E/F-band (10 cm) RF energy to the planar array, frequency-sensitivity antenna, thereby radiating a series of pencil beams. Stabilisation of radiation against ship's motion is achieved electronically. Eight operating modes are available under computer program control, and a range of over 400 km at 30 500 m for target designation and aircraft direction is reported.

In general appearance and in operating principles the SPS-48 is similar to the SPS-52 (which see). Several features enable the two types to be distinguished, however. The SPS-48 is somewhat larger, and there is only one 'end-plate' to the flat antenna array, on the left side when facing the antenna. The scanner is of square proportion, compared with the oblong configuration of the SPS-52. In most installations, the SPS-48 has an on-mounted IFF antenna at its upper edge, whereas with the SPS-52 the IFF is normally mounted at the lower edge.

STATUS

A later development in the SPS-48 radar's evolution is the introduction of the SPS-48(C) model which includes MTI and automatic detection and tracking.

The latter significantly increases the overall effectiveness of the ships' combat systems by providing the capability to detect and track multiple air targets automatically.

The contractor has completed the development of modifications to the radar for the New Threat Upgrade (NTU) programme. Designated the AN/SPS-48E, the radar provides early detection of anti-ship missiles launched from a bomber, such as the TU-26 (backfire), in heavy ECM conditions; it also provides positional data for mid-course guidance to the extended range SM-2 weapons system. The modifications include a lower sidelobe antenna, increased available energy from the transmitter, adaptive energy management, and computer software interface with the ship's automatic detection and tracking modifications. The US Navy plans to provide NTU modifications to 30 SPS-48 systems serving on Terrier and Tartar missile equipped combatants and a $44 million contract was awarded in September 1983 to upgrade SPS-48 radars to meet new threats. A contract worth $14·9 million for final design work prior to production of the AN/SPS-48E was announced at the end of 1982.

The SPS-48 radar is the primary 3-D air search radar and is installed on CVs, CGs/CGNs, DDG-37 and certain DDG-31 class ships. In April 1981 a $10·8 million contract was awarded for the production of an SPS-48C radar for the US Navy's carrier CVN-71. An order for eight AN/SPS-48E systems, and two SPS-48C radars for CVN-72 and -73, was awarded in mid-1983 with a contract value of about $170 million.

CONTRACTOR
ITT-Gilfillan, 7821 Orion Avenue, Van Nuys, California 91409, USA.

ITT-Gilfillan AN/SPS-48 antenna array

1248.253
AN/SPS-52/52A/52B RADAR

This series of shipborne radars evolved from the AN/SPS-39A radar. With the addition of a digital stabilisation computer, and transmitter/receiver modifications, the AN/SPS-39A was upgraded to the AN/SPS-52. Minor modifications subsequently upgraded the latter to the AN/SPS-52A. Further modifications produced the AN/SPS-52B which has a

clutter rejection capability to enable moving targets to be detected in the presence of natural clutter. More detailed information of the AN/SPS-52/52A/52B is given in previous issues of *Jane's Weapon Systems*. The latest version, AN/SPS-52C, is covered under entry **5606.253**.

STATUS
The AN/SPS-52 and 52A will soon be out of service. The AN/SPS-52B is scheduled to be used aboard the

US FFG-1 class ships. Several 52B systems will also remain in use in ships of the Spanish and Japanese navies. The 52, 52A and 52B are now out of production.

CONTRACTOR
Hughes Aircraft Company, Fullerton, California 92634, USA.

5606.253
AN/SPS-52C RADAR

The AN/SPS-52C is a shipborne air surveillance, three-dimensional radar system providing target position in range, bearing and elevation. Three-dimensional coverage from a single antenna is achieved by electronic scanning in elevation and mechanical rotation of the antenna in azimuth. The AN/SPS-52C uses the same AN/SPA-72B antenna as the earlier AN/SPS-52 systems but employs completely different below-decks electronics and incorporates the latest in advanced design and signal processing concepts. As a result, significant improvements have been achieved in the detection performance and in reliability, maintainability and availability.

The antenna assembly is a planar array, tilted back at an angle of 25° from the vertical. This tiltback makes possible coverage to high elevation angles. The array consists of rows of slotted waveguide radiators, fed from a sinuous feed system running the length of one side of the array. Scanning in the vertical plane is achieved by selection of the transmitted frequency. Frequency selection is controlled by a digital computer.

DEVELOPMENT
Development started in 1973 with a study of the system requirements. One of the key requirements resulting from this study was the use of automatic target detection and in 1974 the design of this was commenced. The resulting design was implemented into the pre-production model which underwent extensive testing at a land-based test site and at sea aboard the USS *Towers*. Approval for service use was granted in 1978 and production started that year.

STATUS
The AN/SPS-52C is scheduled to be deployed in the US navy aboard the LHA-1 and LHD-1 class ships and aboard three DDG-15 ships. The system will also be fitted to ships of the Australian, West German, Spanish, Italian and Japanese navies.

AN/SPA-72 antenna for the SPS-52 3-D radar. This antenna replaced the original units fitted in SPS-39 radars aboard US and other ships

CONTRACTOR
Hughes Aircraft Company, Fullerton, California 92634, USA.

1697.253
AN/SPS-55 NAVAL RADAR

The SPS-55 is a modern solid-state surface search and navigation radar developed as a replacement for the SPS-10. It is designed for service on ships of destroyer size or above. Operational uses are: the detection of small surface targets from ranges of less than 50 m to the radar horizon; navigation and pilotage; tracking of low-flying aircraft and helicopters, detection of submarines at schnorkel and periscope depth.

A lightweight antenna (less than 90 kg) has a low profile configuration to minimise installation space requirements and consists of two (selectable) back-to-back, end fed, slotted arrays, one with circular polarisation and the other linear-horizontal polarised. The horizontal beamwidth is 1·5°, and beam squint compensation is used to optimise bearing accuracy over the operating frequency range. Vertical beamwidth is 20°.

The transmitter/receiver sub-system is housed below decks in a single cabinet, and is capable of

operating at any selected frequency in the band from 9·05 to 10 GHz. Two pulse widths (1 and 0·12 μs) are provided. The minimum peak transmitter output is 130 kW. Variable sector radiation is also provided.

The SPS-55 set does not normally include its own display, and a separate control unit is provided to permit remote operation of the transmitter/receiver and scanner sub-systems.

CHARACTERISTICS
Antenna
Rotation rate: 16 rpm
Polarisation: Circular or linear
Horizontal beamwidth (3 dB): 1·5°
Gain: 31 dB
Transmitter
Frequency band: 9·05 – 10 GHz (a version operating in the band 5·45 – 5·825 GHz is also available)
Peak power: 130 kW
PRF/pulse width: 750 pps/1 μs; 2250 pps/0·12 μs
Receiver
Type: Low-noise, image-suppression mixer
IF: 60 MHz
Bandwidth: 1·2 MHz (long pulse); 10 MHz (short pulse)
Receiver processors: Linear logarithmic, FTC, variable sensitivity time control
DEVELOPMENT
Developed as replacement for SPS-10.
STATUS
In production and installed in some US Navy ships including the DD-963, FFG-7, CGN-41, and CGN-47 classes.
CONTRACTOR
Cardion Electronics, Woodbury, New York 11797, USA.

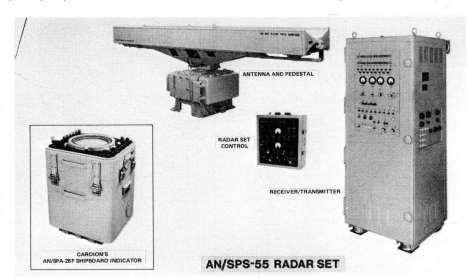

ANTENNA AND PEDESTAL

RADAR SET CONTROL

RECEIVER/TRANSMITTER

CARDION'S AN/SPA-25F SHIPBOARD INDICATOR

AN/SPS-55 RADAR SET

1359.253
AN/SPS-58/SPS-65 NAVAL RADARS

The basic AN/SPS-58 (latest US Navy version, AN/SPS-65(V)) is a D-band, pulse doppler air search and target acquisition radar, designed to operate with the US Navy point defence surface missile system, but capable of use with a variety of other weapons and produced in several versions. A major design consideration has been the achievement of good low elevation angle performance, high data rate, and clutter rejection characteristics to meet the threat of low-flying aircraft or missile attacks.

This is achieved by means of a modular design, AN/SPS-65 (V1) (V2) models being assembled from various combinations of standard units. The transmitter (common to all four) is a self-contained, air cooled, coherent amplifier unit of solid-state design with klystron power amplifier stages. The receiver/processor also is solid-state and includes a low noise superheterodyne RF receiver. A DMTI filter provides a good anti-clutter performance, and built-in test facilities are incorporated. This unit is common to the 58 and 58A while the 65 V1/V2 configurations utilise a high performance variant of the basic receiver/processor. The 58 and 58A also include a console group for display and weapons interface. The

display console provides multiple video display and control functions for manual threat assessment and target designation to weapon systems.

The AN/SPS-65 (V1) configuration, now in production, will be installed on ships with existing tactical display systems. Target data is provided on every detected target (ATD) in digital format by a MIL-STD-1397 ANEWS interface. Automatic detection and tracking (ADT) can be performed using this output and an external computer or the V2 hardware which includes its own computer. The AN/SPS-65 (V2) includes an advanced radar/weapons interface group and is intended for use on non-TDS ships. Both the V1 and V2 include a radar set control for remote operation of the radar.

A variety of antenna arrangements are available. One is a medium size double-curvature open lattice array of approximately elliptical outline, illuminated by a stacked feed arrangement on a stabilised pedestal. This antenna provides extended vertical coverage, and allows dual operation of radar and IFF system. For smaller ships, a dual-feed unit enables the SPS-58 radar to share an existing SPS-10 lightweight antenna, and permits simultaneous SPS-58, SPS-10, and IFF radar operation.

For installations where there is no SPS-10 antenna,

and it is not possible or desirable to mount the larger stabilised antenna unit, a passive planar array is available, this being suitable for back-to-back mounting with almost any existing antenna, or on its own turning gear.

The various configurations of these modules are as follows:

AN/SPS-58: This comprises a stabilised antenna, transmitter, receiver/processor, antenna control unit, signal data converter, and display console.
AN/SPS-58A: This version has the lightweight antenna (SPS-10), transmitter, receiver/processor, signal data converter, and display console.
AN/SPS-65 (V1): This consists of the lightweight, integral antenna, transmitter, high performance receiver/processor, and radar set control unit. Radar data are fed directly to ship's display/action data system.
AN/SPS-65 (V2): This is the same as the V1 version but includes an advanced, radar/weapons interface unit.

The SPS-58/SPS-65 family is fully compatible with Mk 10 and Mk 12 IFF systems, and it provides correlation of IFF and target returns for improved threat reaction time. This latter characteristic is further aided by a high data rate and a low false alarm rate for rapid reaction/threat evaluation and weapon assignment.

Provision has been made in the design for the addition of further facilities such as automatic target designation to weapon systems, or the application of adaptive radar techniques. Modification kits to convert and upgrade AN/SPS-58 units to AN/SPS-65 units are available.

STATUS
The SPS-65 (V) is the latest naval radar of those developed by Westinghouse. The SPS-58 series radar has completed operational evaluation and is service approved by the US Navy. Systems with which various versions of SPS-58 have been integrated successfully include:

Mk 37 gun fire control system 5 in/38
Mk 68 gun fire control system 5 in/54
SPA-50
Mk 5 WDS (Tartar, Standard)
Basic point defence surface missile system
NATO Seasparrow surface missile system
Naval tactical data system
CONTRACTOR
Westinghouse Electric Corporation, 1801K Street NW, Washington, DC 20006, USA.

SPS-58 scanner on third-level platform, beneath SPS-10 scanner and above and to left of SPS-30 dish. Large antenna on left is for SPS-43

4300.253
AN/SPS-58LR NAVAL SURVEILLANCE RADAR

The SPS-58LR is a long-range version of the AN/SPS-58/65 family of radars (1359.253) currently in the US Navy inventory. This radar uses a 25 kW solid-state power amplifier of advanced design to achieve very high reliability, maintainability and performance. The AN/SPS-58LR retains features of the SPS-58/65 family such as the detection of low flying missiles and high performance digital MTI, while at the same time providing long-range surveillance capability.

The SPS-58LR has an instrumented range of 100 nautical miles. It uses a phase-coded, compressed pulse to increase the transmitter average power and to provide good target resolution. Frequency agility on a burst-to-burst basis is provided as an ECCM feature. Advanced DMTI permits operation in severe clutter environments. The radar outputs digital target reports suitable for direct entry into a wide variety of fire control systems.

The solid-state transmitter uses 44 identical power amplifier modules of 650 watts each to achieve the full 35 kW output. It is designed such that the failure of any module will reduce output power by less than three per cent rather than cause a catastrophic failure. Each power module has an MTBF of 56 000 hours. The highest voltage present in the transmitter is 40 V DC.

Although the SPS-58LR has its own lightweight array-type antenna it is also capable of operating with any D-band antenna which has matching frequency and power handling characteristics. It provides a modern replacement for the AN/SPS-6, AN/SPS-12 and other radars still in service around the world and can use the existing antennas of these radars.

CONTRACTOR
Westinghouse Electric Corporation, 1801K Street NW, Washington, DC 20006, USA.

AN/SPS-58LR transmitter

3722.253
AN/SPS-67 RADAR

The AN/SPS-67(V) is a solid-state C-band equipment designed to replace the 30-year old SPS-10 (1564.253) surface search radar, which is very widely fitted in US Navy and other ships. The antenna of the older radar is retained as an interim measure but will be eventually replaced, and the below-deck equipment is replaced by solid-state hardware utilising standard electronic modules that will replace the vacuum tube technology of the SPS-10. In the latter equipment there are 12 below-deck boxes which will be replaced by five SPS-67 units: transmitter/receiver, video processor, radar set control, antenna controller, and antenna safety switch.

Performance of the SPS-67 is improved through the addition of a very narrow pulse mode (0·1 μs) for better navigation and improved resolution of small

targets at short ranges. Long and medium pulse (1 and 0·25 μs) modes will be used in open sea for detection of long and medium range targets. Performance is also improved by a digital noise suppressor. An add-on unit for the SPS-67 will provide DMTI and automatic target detection and will also permit its integration into the AN/SYS shipboard system which automatically correlates data from several ships' radars to present a combined single tactical track.

STATUS
After technical and operational evaluation, a production contract for the US Navy was awarded in late summer 1982. A separate contract was awarded to Norden to design a new antenna system which was tested in autumn 1983. The first production systems were delivered in autumn 1983 for installation on the battleships *Iowa* and the LSD-41 dock landing ship.

CONTRACTOR
Norden Systems, United Technologies Corporation, Norden Place, Box 5300, Norwalk, Connecticut 06856, USA.

1940.253
AN/SPS-63 RADAR

AN/SPS-63 is the American designation given to the 3TM20-H version of the 3RM series of radars

produced by the Italian company Segnalamento Marittimo ed Aereo (SMA) and described in 1702.253. The 3TM20-H model is the selected standard navigation radar for the PHM NATO hydrofoil.

The 3RM series of naval radars are I-band equipments, for which different sizes of scanner and high and lower power transmitters are available.

1570.253
AN/SPY-1 MULTI-FUNCTION ARRAY RADAR

The AN/SPY-1 is the electronically scanned fixed array radar for the US Navy Aegis fleet air defence missile system (2507.231). It operates in the E/F-band, and the output is several megawatts. The Raytheon transmitter serves several parallel channels simultaneously. The phase scanned arrays are mounted in pairs on each ship, two on the forward deck-house and two on the after deck-house, to provide all-round radar cover. Each array has 4100 discrete elements, and measures 3·65 × 3·65 m. These elements are controlled by AN/UYK-7 digital computers to produce and steer multiple radar beams for target search, detection, and tracking. The SPY-1 also tracks own ship's missiles fired against hostile

targets. It also has the function of providing target designation data for the Raytheon target illuminating radars (up to four on a ship) which direct the semi-active homing missiles employed in the Aegis systems.

DEVELOPMENT
The SPY-1 radar was developed by RCA, the prime contractor for the overall Aegis system, under a contract awarded in late 1969. The antenna array began tests in 1972, and by 1973 the transmitter and array were integrated for further tests before embarking on full-scale testing with other elements of the Aegis system.

By early 1974 land-based tests of the radar had been completed and the radar moved from RCA's Moorestown, New Jersey, test site to Long Beach

US Navy Combat Systems Engineering Development site, at Moorestown, New Jersey, showing location of the two SPY-1A planar arrays and AN/SPG-62 slaved radars for target illumination

Artist's impression of the US Navy guided missile cruiser Ticonderoga *equipped with the Aegis air defence missile system and engaging multiple targets*

Assembly of Aegis AN/SPY-1A arrays at the Moorestown, New Jersey plant of RCA

Naval Shipyard, California, for installation in the USS *Norton Sound* in preparation for sea trials. In May 1974 it was announced that while operating in the USS *Norton Sound*, the SPY-1 had detected and automatically gone into the tracking mode to track multiple aircraft flying over the Pacific.

STATUS

The AEGIS system (**1834.281**) is now at sea and RCA have announced advanced versions of the SPY-1A radar system. SPY-1B is to be fitted to AEGIS cruisers

starting with CG-59. It uses a new antenna design to give much lower sidelobes, plus an improved signal processor and a new transmitter tube having double the duty cycle with the same peak power. SPY-1C is a private RCA proposal for use on board aircraft carriers and as yet has no official backing or funding. A fourth version, SPY-1D, has been proposed for the DDG-51 and uses only one transmitter with the antennas mounted on a single deckhouse, as opposed to two for the SPY-1A. Considerable space

savings have been made in the SPY-1D by using VLSI technology. ECCM capabilities have also been improved.

CONTRACTORS

RCA Missile and Surface Radar, Moorestown, New Jersey 08057, USA – SPY-1 antenna array.

The Raytheon Company, Wayland, Massachusetts, USA – SPY-1 high power transmitter.

Computer Sciences Corporation, Moorestown, New Jersey, USA – computer programs.

4301.253

AN/SPQ-11 COBRA JUDY RADAR

The Cobra Judy shipborne phased array radar is a detection and tracking system enabling data to be collected on foreign strategic ballistic missiles tests.

The system is similar to the land-based Cobra Dane radar (**1949.153**) although considerably smaller.

The large octagonal array of this radar measures 22·5 feet (approximately seven metres) in diameter and is composed of 12 288 antenna elements. The

elements are co-ordinated to form transmission patterns by a large scale Control Data CYBER 175-112 computer which allows the radar to detect and track objects at very high rates. After detection and tracking the information is fed to a computer for storage and display as well as post-mission reduction and analysis.

Cobra Judy is installed on the stern of a former merchant vessel, the USNS *Observation Island*, which has been extensively modified. The system weighs 250 tons (approximately 250 000 kg), stands four stories high and is integrated into a steel turret which can be rotated mechanically. The octagonal array makes up one wall of the pyramid-like structure. The complete shipborne sensor is operating in the Pacific Ocean, based at Pearl Harbor, Hawaii.

STATUS

The radar has been acquired and operated by the US Air Force Systems Command, Electronic Systems Division. Test and evaluation trials took place during 1981 and the system is fully operational.

CONTRACTOR

Raytheon Company, Equipment Division, Wayland, Massachusetts 01778, USA.

Cobra Judy radar installed on the USNS Observation Island

3256.253

W-120 SHIPBOARD FIRE CONTROL RADAR

The W-120 is a lightweight I/J-band acquisition and tracking radar especially adapted from the AN/APQ-120 airborne radar design for small ship gun fire control systems and consists of four major elements:

(1) a lightweight compact equipment enclosure containing both the transmitter and receiver for the radar

(2) a lightweight antenna/pedestal assembly enclosed by a radome

(3) a displays/control assembly providing both 'A' and 'C' scope displays and the operating controls for the radar

(4) an antenna control unit which provides manual control of the antenna.

This radar provides both automatic and manual acquisition and tracking. Automatic acquisition is based on a designation received from the fire control system computer. The automatic acquisition is a result of a search using a selected search pattern around the designation. If automatic track is lost, the W-120 automatically seeks to re-acquire the target. In the automatic mode, when the fire control system computer is not designating or the radar is not processing a current track, the W-120 reverts to ready status wherein the system is fully operational except that the full antenna motion and radiation is inhibited.

In the absence of a fire control system designation, a manually designated bearing, elevation position and range gate can be given and the antenna scans a selected search pattern in azimuth and elevation about the designated position. A 4000 yard acquisition window is positioned to the designated range.

The W-120 provides a low flyer detection mode for acquisition and tracking operations. The off-

W-120 antenna/pedestal assembly and radome

boresight mode may be selected for tracks lying within 0·8 beamwidths of the sea surface and provides a significant improvement in rejection of multi-path interference as compared with boresight tracking of the same target.

Detection range of the W-120 is 30 nautical miles (56 km) against a 1 m² target. Range accuracy is ±0·01 to 2·5 nautical miles, then ±2 per cent over that

distance. Tracking accuracy is better than two milliradians in both bearing and elevation.

STATUS

No information on ship fittings is available.

CONTRACTOR

Westinghouse Electric Corporation, Command and Control Division, PO Box 1897, Baltimore, Maryland 21203, USA.

4048.253

W-160 SHIPBOARD FIRE CONTROL RADAR

The W-160 shipboard tracking radar is based on technology used in the AN/APG-66 radar (**3303.353**), built by Westinghouse for the US Air Force F-16 aircraft. The W-160 combines the lightweight and low cost of an airborne system with the capability to track, at all altitudes, small, high speed targets on and over the surface of the sea. A medium-PRF, X-band, multimode, pulse doppler system, the W-160 has two-axis monopulse tracking which provides accurate

position data at ranges necessary to achieve a fire control solution. It can acquire and track targets in rain, heavy clutter, and in smooth or rough seas.

The W-160 utilises coherent pulse doppler MTI for superior sub-clutter visibility and operation in high clutter environments. Doppler processing and circular polarisation greatly improve performance in rain. In low elevation tracking, the boresight of the antenna is maintained above the target. This off-boresight tracking (or low-flyer) mode reduces tracking inaccuracies caused by reflections from the

surface of the sea, an interference problem known as multipath reflection. Interface between the radar and the shipboard fire control system is made possible through the use of modular-digibus techniques.

The W-160 has seven radar modes:

(1) ready mode: Antenna motion and radiation are inhibited but the radar may be instantaneously switched to full operating status. The ready mode prevents enemy detection of radar signals and reduces system overall operating time

(2) automatic acquisition, automatic track: The radar

automatically steps from the ready mode to full operating status when designated by the fire control computer; no operator is required. The system automatically locks-on and tracks targets in the search volume (±4, ±8 or ±12° azimuth by 30 or 60° elevation by 5000-yard (4570 metre) range window) and presents its co-ordinates to the computer

(3) manual acquisition, automatic track: In the presence of multiple targets or certain types of interference, the operator uses the radar displays and controls to select the target and initiate tracking. Following acquisition the radar automatically tracks the target

(4) manual track: The operator uses console controls to position the antenna beam and range gate on the target

(5) general search mode: The W-160 may be used to search 360° in azimuth and can display this video to supplement or replace the coverage of a search radar. This mode may also be used to provide additional coverage in selected, high-risk azimuth sectors

(6) low-flyer mode: Used when the track lies within 0·8° beamwidth of the water's surface, this off-boresight mode results in at least a 10 dB improvement in the rejection of multipath interference over boresight tracking of the same target

(7) self-test mode: Extensive built-in test equipment (BITE) automatically indicates faults and performs fault isolation to a line replaceable unit (LRU).

The W-160 consists of three main elements; the antenna/pedestal unit, a radar electronics assembly, and the controls and displays.

The antenna is a 36-inch (91 cm) effective diameter paraboloid with a six-horn feed. This combination yields a two-axis monopulse capability. The operator can select either linear or circular polarisation, and antenna instruments indicate angular position and rate. Capable of continuous 360° azimuth rotation with elevation coverage from 0 to 90°, the pedestal is an electric, two-axis, elevation-over-azimuth configuration which incorporates gearless torque motor drivers. Full gyrocompass stabilisation is provided during all search and track operations. The antenna assembly is enclosed in a radome to protect it from wind and water damage; it can operate in wind velocities up to 100 knots. A 72-inch (183 cm) antenna is also available with a gain of 43 dB. Use of this antenna extends the radar range to 90 km. Provision is made for missile illumination.

The RF front end of the receiver, a rugged waveguide assembly designed to provide its own stable operating temperature (60° C), is located above deck with the antenna/pedestal assembly. Solid-state devices providing RF sensitivity time control, transmitter/receiver protection, and low noise RF gain are located with the duplexer in an armoured box for protection and also to preserve system low noise temperature. The 227 kg radar electronics assembly, mounted below deck, contains the transmitter (a coherent amplifier with a TWT final power amplifier), IF/video portion of the receiver, antenna servo-drive circuits, range tracker, digital signal processor, computer, and associated sub-systems. The entire assembly is shock mounted and slides from its cabinet for ease of maintenance. A common multiplex bus (DIGIBUS) permits interface between the computer, major radar sub-systems, and other shipboard equipments.

CHARACTERISTICS

Frequency: X-band

Peak power: 16 kW

Pulse widths: 1 and 0·25 μs

PRF: 1800 – 14 000 pps

Detection range: 46·3 km against a 1 m² target with 91 cm antenna; 70 km with 183 cm antenna

Tracking accuracy: 1 mrad in bearing and elevation, 15 m in range

Angle tracking capability: Targets with angular rates up to 60°/s and velocities up to 2500 knots

Tracker type: Kalman estimator

Receiver noise: 4 dB

Antenna type: 2-axis monopulse

Antenna gain: 36 dB

Antenna beamwidth: 2·5°

Antenna polarisation: Linear (vertical), circular (right), circular (left)

Search pattern: ±4, ±8, ±12° azimuth × 30 or 40° elevation; 10° azimuth × 15° elevation; spotlight or fixed beam position; 360° low angle air or surface search

Clutter processing: Coherent pulse doppler

Platform speed: Motion compensation for complete range of ship's velocities

Reliability: 600 h MTBF

Weights

Antenna/pedestal assembly: 136kg

Radar electronics: 227 kg

Display/controls: 38·5 kg

STATUS

The W-160 is used in the W-1200 series of naval fire control systems (**3514.261**) but no details of ship fittings are available.

CONTRACTOR

Westinghouse Electric Corporation, Defense and Electronic Systems Center, Baltimore, Maryland 21203, USA.

W-160 shipboard fire control radar

3257.253
W-611 NAVAL RADAR

The W-611 is a lightweight air search and target acquisition D-band radar that provides ships with self-defence capability against small, high speed incoming threats at ranges to 25 nautical miles (46 km). It is a shipboard version of the land-based range surveillance radar, AN/TPS-61.

The W-611 radar is especially designed to perform in a severe clutter environment by elimination of unwanted returns from slow or stationary targets and from rain or chaff. The transmitter utilises a three-stage coherent amplifier which incorporates highly reliable and tunable klystrons for mid and final power amplification. The remaining transmitter circuitry is solid-state. Peak power is 12 kW.

The receiver/processor utilises all solid-state designs and provides built-in self test. The MTI and signal processing are digital. The antenna is a lightweight passive planar array which incorporates an IFF antenna and provides compatibility with IFF equipment.

Provision is made for a common antenna to be shared with a G/H-band surface search and navigation radar to minimise topside weight and to optimise and simplify antenna positioning. Provision is also made for extended range capability through the modular addition of a crossed-field amplifier. Automatic target detection and automatic detection and tracking are available through the addition of available optional equipment.

W-611 lightweight air search radar antenna

CONTRACTOR
Westinghouse Electric Corporation, Command and
Control Division, PO Box 1897, Baltimore, Maryland
21203, USA.

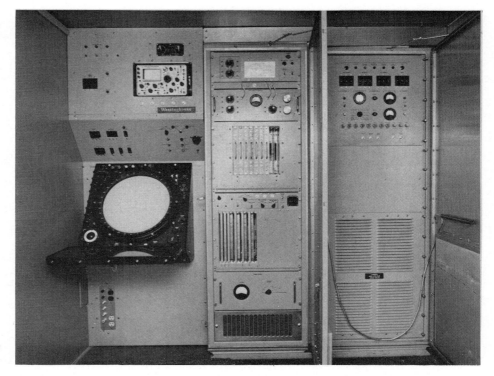

*W-611 radar transmitter, receiver and control
consoles*

3258.253
FLEXAR WEAPON CONTROL SYSTEM

FLEXAR (flexible adaptive radar), is proposed as a
next generation shore or shipboard weapon control
system for short- and medium-range missiles or guns
against ships, aircraft or missiles. The system

FLEXAR display unit

combines fire control functions with surveillance
modes that complement existing air search radars.
Very fast reaction time to short-range, high-speed
targets makes FLEXAR an effective defence against
anti-ship missiles. Target acquisition and track
initiation are completely automatic. The adaptive
radar accepts designation from other active or
passive sensors and provides automatic threat
evaluation, automatic weapon assignment and rapid
kill assessment. It employs multiple waveforms
adaptively selected for high performance in clutter,
rapid resolution of complex targets and optimum
tracking.

The system uses a 40-inch electronically agile dish
antenna that rotates mechanically at 60 rpm to
provide hemispheric coverage, but also operates with
the antenna stationary in sector fire control modes.
The transmitter is capable of handling multiple
waveforms and a programmable signal processor
provides an optimum match for each waveform. The
entire system is under real-time control by a general
purpose digital computer with clutter-free data being
displayed on a symbolic plan position indicator. The
many modes of the system are interleaved by the
general purpose computer to provide effective

simultaneous search, acquisition, multi-target track
and weapon control. The mode of most interest to the
US Navy is that in which FLEXAR would serve as a
positionable multiple target tracker/illuminator for
the latest US Navy ship-launched missiles.

A land-based fire control system, known as Multi-
function Radar (MFR) (**5607.153**) is a new application
that uses technology derived from the FLEXAR
programme. This system, intended for use with
existing I-HAWK and other short-to-medium range
missiles, can provide a significant reduction in
manpower and equipment, greater mobility and
transportability, improved operation in ECM and
reduced life cycle costs.

STATUS
FLEXAR completed first phase proof of principal
search and multi-target track tests in 1981 and
intermediate weapon control testing in 1982.
Evaluation of the system's multi-function roles with
captive I-Hawk and navy standard missiles was
completed successfully during 1983. Other additional
testing was scheduled to continue in 1984.

CONTRACTOR
Hughes Aircraft Company, El Segundo, California
90245, USA.

3768.253
R-76 NAVAL FIRE CONTROL RADAR

The RCA R-76 naval radar is an I-band monopulse fire
control radar with combined search, detection and
tracking capabilities. It is employed as the principal
sensor in the Honeywell H-930 series of naval fire
control systems (**3749.281** in 1982-83 and earlier
editions), in conjunction with other equipments, and
also in the RCA HR-76 naval fire control system
(**3748.281**). Lightweight construction permits
mounting high on a ship's superstructure thereby
aiding early detection, and the gyro-stabilised
antenna provides for continuous 360° search. Dual
monopulse tracking enables simultaneous missile
and target tracking, with the data displayed on the
system's dual A-scope presentation unit, with
facilities for instantaneous entry for weapon system
control.

The main elements of the equipment are the
director, the transmitter, receiver/signal processor,
computer and a servo controller. A complete ship's
installation typically weighs approximately 1200 kg,
of which the above-deck equipment accounts for
about 205 kg. As the illustration shows, the antenna is

a four-horn cassegrain unit, housed in a protective
radome and mounted on a stabilised elevation-over-
azimuth director. The transmitter employs a vacuum
tube modulator allowing multiple waveforms; other
transmitter features include multiple pulse widths,
multiple jittered PRFs, and provision for CW
illumination. Crystal control allows for a narrow-band
missile link. A micro-computer performs such
functions as: angle and range servo controls; CFAR;
AGC; beacon AFC; control; and data correction.

CHARACTERISTICS
Transmitter
Frequency: I-band
Tuning: 12 pre-selected frequencies
Peak power: 250 kW
Pulse width: 0·25, 0·5, 1 µs
PRF: 1000 – 3000 Hz
Receiver: 2-channel monopulse
Antenna
Diameter: 1 m
Beamwidth: 2·7°
Signal processor: Digital
Acquisition range: 40 km (on 1 m² target)
Tracking range: 40 km (on 1 m² target)

RCA R-76 naval fire control radar

Accuracy at 20 km: 10 m range; 1 mrad angular
Search scan period: 4 s
Reaction time: 3·5 s average from designation to
tracking
STATUS
Production.
CONTRACTOR
RCA Government Systems Division, Missile and
Surface Radar, Moorestown, New Jersey 08057, USA.

4223.253
MBAR FIRE CONTROL RADAR

Multiple Beam Acquisition Radar (MBAR) is a new C-band defensive weapon control system designed to provide smaller ships with self defence capability against small high-speed threats approaching at very low angles, as well as targets diving simultaneously from very high angles.

The MBAR employs a fan beam transmit antenna and a 17-beam receive antenna, which are stabilised electronically in pitch and mechanically in roll. The system can acquire targets in range, azimuth, elevation and range rate during a single scan (1·5 s). The equipment analyses the threat and designates the targets in order of priority to available weapon systems. Up to 100 targets can be accommodated by the system. Target threat assessment is performed on every antenna scan and weapon designation on the following scan.

The receive antenna is equipped with ultra low sidelobes of –50 dB rms for operation in a severe ECM environment. The transmitter employs a high reliability TWT and uses high average power coupled with frequency agility to minimise ECM. The digital processor employs a coherent pulse doppler waveform with fast Fourier transform processing. It is capable of automatic target detection in severe weather and clutter, with a sub-clutter visibility of 60 dB. The equipment can also be operated in a long range search mode or in a navigation surface gun mode.

CHARACTERISTICS
Transmitter: TWT
Frequency: C-band
Peak power: 70 kW
PRF: 17·2 kHz nominal
Receiver: 16 beams time-multiplexed into 8 processor channels
Noise figure: 3·5 dB
Antenna
Azimuth: 1·75° beamwidth
Elevation
Transmit – fan beam, peak gain 26 dB
Receive – beam forming lens, peak gain 32 dB
17 beams varying from 5 – 8° in vertical beamwidth; 16 active, 1 reserved for electronic stabilisation

Dimensions: 2·6 × 0·9 m
Scan rate: 40 rpm (less in long range mode)
Detection range: 55 km (1 m² target); 36 km (0·2 m² target) (110 nm instrumented range in long range search)
Target speed: Up to 1189 m/s incoming; up to 366 m/s outgoing
Accuracies: ⩾0·4° azimuth; ⩾1° elevation; ⩾61 m in range; ⩾7 m/s in range rate; ⩾0·15° azimuth in surface gun mode
Angular resolution: 5° elevation beamwidth (low angle); 8° elevation beamwidth (high angle)
Target tracking: 100 targets simultaneously
Weight: 1500 lb (682 kg) at masthead; 4500 lb (2045 kg) below decks

STATUS
In development as a private venture.
CONTRACTOR
Raytheon Company, Equipment Division, Wayland, Massachusetts, 01778, USA.

4608.253
FLANKING-BEAM ARRAY SWITCHING TECHNIQUE RADAR (FAST)

FAST is a shipborne search radar system developed by General Electric, one prototype having been completed in 1982 as a private venture. It employs two phase-scanned antenna faces, mounted back-to-back, which are rotated at either 30 rpm in C-band or 15 rpm in S-band. Each face consists of 5736 elements, scanned only in elevation, and multiple pencil beams (1·4 × 2°) are generated in four different directions at 15 and 45° either side. By the use of eight simultaneous beams, FAST achieves a high data rate to provide precise tracking, mid-course guidance and target illuminator guidance. Peak power is claimed as 1 MW in C-band and 2 MW in S-band, with detection ranges as 143 nautical miles (C-band) and 246 nautical miles (S-band). Pulse compression techniques are used in the signal processor.

STATUS
In development as a private venture.
CONTRACTOR
General Electric Company, PO Box 4840, Syracuse, New York 13221, USA.

4609.253
Mk 23 TARGET ACQUISITION SYSTEM RADAR

The Mk 23 target acquisition system (TAS) radar is a two-dimensional, D-band rotating fan-beam pulse doppler radar intended for use with NATO Sea Sparrow. It is designed to counter both sea-skimming and high-diving anti-ship missiles. The radar antenna is mounted back-to-back with an IFF antenna, the radar giving coverage from zero to over 75° in elevation. Hughes claims that the system will function effectively in dense ECM environments and that the clutter attenuation is more than 50 dB with respect to a moving target radar return. A number of modes are available which include operation on a very narrow sector scan and a 'quiet working' mode.

STATUS
In production for US Navy aircraft carriers, 'Spruance' class destroyers and other support vessels fitted with Sea Sparrow. Development of a 3-D system, providing target elevation, is in progress.
CONTRACTOR
Hughes Aircraft Company, Fullerton, California 92364, USA.

AIRBORNE RADAR

FRANCE

3297.353
MIRAGE 2000 RADARS

New radars have been developed for the multi-role and all-altitude interceptor versions of the Mirage 2000 aircraft. Both the radars are pulse doppler equipments; that for the interceptor aircraft has a high PRF and is designated RDI, while the multi-role version radar has a low PRF and is designated RDM. However, due to programme delays, the first 50 interceptor aircraft for the French Air Force will be equipped with the RDM radar. Both radars are illustrated nearby, enabling both the external differences and similarities to be seen. Few technical details have been cleared for publication but the following paragraphs contain summaries of the salient features of each.

RDM doppler radar for the multi-role version of the Mirage 2000

RDI pulse doppler radar for the air superiority versions of the Mirage 2000

RDI

This version will equip the all-altitude air superiority interceptor variant of the Mirage 2000 for the French Air Force. It uses a TWT I/J-band coherent 4 kW transmitter, and features a flat slotted plate antenna with a diameter of only 67·4 cm. The antenna has an integrated IFF antenna and the overall system incorporates an integrated IFF transmitter/receiver. The equipment is optimised for air superiority in all weather conditions at any height, and range is stated as being in the region of 120 km against a head-on target and 50 km against a tail-aspect target. TWS facilities are available and the RDI radar incorporates an internal digital data bus to facilitate sophisticated radar signal processing. Other facilities include digital doppler filtering circuits and higher resistance to ECM. The available air-to-ground and air-to-air modes will allow the following functions to be performed:

(1) air-to-air search at all altitudes
(2) long-range continuous tracking and missile guidance

Antilope V terrain-following and navigation radar

(3) automatic short-range tracking for missiles or guns
(4) ground mapping
(5) contour mapping
(6) air-to-ground ranging.
STATUS
In development. Flight testing continuing. The first production systems are scheduled for 1986.

RDM

This low PRF pulse doppler radar will be fitted in multi-role variants of the Mirage 2000. It employs a TWT I/J-band coherent transmitter in conjunction with an inverse cassegrain antenna. Features emphasised in the design are operational versatility, extensive options and growth potential. The radar is capable of accommodating a CW illuminator for the guidance of missiles that use a doppler homing head, an IFF interrogator, doppler beam sharpening circuits for high resolution mapping and ground target identification, as well as new high reliability sub-systems for low level penetration and sea surface search and tracking. The basic operational functions provided are:

(1) air-to-air search (all-altitude, all sectors) and interception. Detection range is given as 60 nautical miles in clear air and 20 nautical miles looking down against ground clutter (5 m² cross-section target)
(2) low level strike (mapping, terrain avoidance, blind let-down)
(3) air-to-ground attack
(4) sea surface search and attack.
  TWS facilities are available, and the design

incorporates an internal digital data bus, and built-in test equipment (BITE).
  For both RDI and RDM, radar data are displayed on a HUD and on a trichromatic multi-mode CRT head-down display, linked to an interception and firing computer.
STATUS
The first flight tests of the RDM model began in 1979 and first production deliveries were made in March 1983. By the end of 1983, 15 systems had been delivered. A total of 86 Mirage 2000 aircraft have been ordered by Egypt, India and Peru and will all be equipped with RDM radars.

MIRAGE 2000 N RADAR
Antilope V TC

The Antilope V TC radar has been designed to equip the penetration version of the Mirage 2000 N. Its basic functions are terrain following, air-to-air, air-to-sea, air-to-ground and navigation with mapping and updating. It uses a TWT J-band coherent transmitter and features a flat slotted plate antenna. The radar data are displayed on a HUD and on a trichromatic multi-mode CRT head-down display.
STATUS
Electronique Serge Dassault is the main contractor for this programme and co-operates with Thomson-CSF. Prototype equipments are being flight tested and the 2000 N system is due to enter service in 1986.
CONTRACTORS
Thomson-CSF, Avionics Division, 178 boulevard Gabriel Péri, 92240 Malakoff, France.
  Electronique Serge Dassault, 55 quai Carnot, 92214 St Cloud, France.

3298.353
IGUANE/AGRION/VARAN AIRBORNE RADARS

Under French Government contract, a family of airborne radars has been developed for sea surface surveillance and maritime warfare applications. Three versions have been named:
Iguane: This model is in production to replace the DRAA 2A ASV radar (**1961.353**) fitted in the Breguet Alize carrier-borne maritime and ASW aircraft, and is also being fitted to the Breguet Atlantic ATL2 long-range maritime patrol aircraft.
Varan: This is essentially an Iguane radar with a smaller antenna which makes it suitable for virtually all the present and planned lightweight and ultra lightweight maritime patrol aircraft. This model is in production for the Gardian (Dassault-Breguet Mystère Falcon 20) being delivered to the French Navy and is to be installed on navy helicopters for several customers.
Agrion: This model exists in several versions but is primarily designed for use aboard helicopters or light aircraft forming a part of task forces employed for support at sea or for coastal protection. An important function of the Agrion radar is AS 15TT missile (**3359.311**) guidance in strike missions against small surface vessels and patrol boats, where it is fully integrated via data link, to the ship's weapon system. Agrion is on order for several foreign navies including

Agrion radar antenna on a Dauphin helicopter

that of Saudi Arabia for Dauphin shipborne helicopters, deliveries of which commenced in 1983.

Each member of the Iguane family can perform the following operational missions:
(1) surface and anti-submarine warfare
(2) over-the-horizon targeting for shipborne SSMs
(3) search and rescue
(4) marine environmental protection
(5) maritime law enforcement
(6) navigation
(7) weather avoidance.

All three models operate in the X-band, using pulse compression and frequency agility to ensure high performance on maritime targets in all combinations of weather, sea state, and operating altitude. These same techniques also provide the Iguane family of radars with maximum protection against ESM and ECM. The Iguane and Varan radars are also reported to be capable of providing sideways-looking radar imagery in real-time using the basic antenna as an optional extra facility.

Last design of the family is the ARCANA radar for the French Air Force.

STATUS

The Iguane is in production for the Alize update programme and the Breguet Atlantic ATL2, as noted above. The Varan version is fitted to the sea

surveillance model of the Gardian aircraft. The Agrion radar is in service on Dauphin helicopters of the Saudi Arabian defence force. The Agrion 15 version is also designed for use with OTHT ship-launched surface-to-surface missile.

Antenna assembly of the Varan radar

Iguane airborne radar

CONTRACTOR

Thomson-CSF, Avionics Division, 178 boulevard Gabriel Péri, 92240 Malakoff, France.

1793.353
ORB-31 AIRBORNE RADAR

The ORB-31 designation covers a series of I-band radars for use on helicopters or small aircraft, and the main functions are surface vessel detection, navigation, and also as a weather radar. The range of equipment includes three types of transmitter/receiver and several antenna options, from which installations appropriate to a variety of missions can be assembled.

The main items of equipment and their variations are as follows:

Transmitter/receivers

Type	OEB 312	OEB 315	OEB 314
Frequency	I-band	(9375±40 MHz)	
Pulsewidth	0·25 µs	4 µs	
PRF	1600 Hz	800 Hz	400 Hz
Bandpass (−3dB)	5±1 MHz	2·5 ± 0·5 MHz	1+0·25 MHz −0·5

Receiver noise factor: 9·5 dB
Receiver gain control
Manual: 45 dB minimum
Automatic: 24 dB from 1·5 – 24 nm
Weight
Single transmitter/receiver: 22·6 kg
Dual transmitter/receiver: 42·6 kg

Antenna type	OAB 3110	OAB 3112	OAB 3113
Width	608 mm	728 mm	460 mm
Height	308 mm	368 mm	308 mm
Weight	1·1 kg	1·3 kg	0·8 kg
Gain	29·2 dB	30·5 dB	28 dB
Beamwidth (3 dB)			
Horizontal	4°	3·2°	4·8°
Vertical	7·5°	6°	7·5°

All are elliptic reflector primary source, rear-illuminated units, with horizontal polarisation. There are two types of scanner mechanism, OAB 3102 and OAB 310ID, the latter being a modification of the former with different sensors and mounting arrangements. Both types can accept all three scanner sizes. Pitch and roll stabilisation is provided and manual control of the elevation datum is possible within limits of ±15°

Indicators: Four types are produced:
OSB 315 surveillance PPI display
OSB 316 surveillance PPI with mobile markers, digital azimuth display (designation by marker), digital range display (optional)
OSB 317 target designation PPI
OSB 318 target designation B-scope indicator.

The data display in each is by means of a 5 × 3 inch (127 × 76 mm) rectangular CRT, and the front panel carries the appropriate controls for the type of operation for which each type of indicator is designed.

Telemetry box OTB 310: This is used to generate and transmit the oblique range and bearing of a preset target and provides for automatic target tracking. The position of the target designation window on the OSB 317 display is controlled by means of a small joystick and the area thus defined is displayed on indicator OSB 318. In addition to the joystick, controls are provided for selection of target designation or tracking modes of operation, selection of No 1 or No 2 transmitter, and selection of No 1 or No 2 indicator.

Various permutations of this equipment are described in the Heracles entry (**1960.353**).

STATUS

The ORB-31-W is fitted to French Lynx helicopters. For other details see Heracles (**1960.353**) which follows.

CONTRACTOR

Omera-Segid, 49 rue Ferdinand Berthoud, 95101 Argenteuil, France.

1960.353
HERACLES RADAR SYSTEM

The Heracles I system (*Système héliporté de radar pour le contrôle du lancement d'engins et pour la surveillance de surface* – Airborne radar system for missile launching control and surface surveillance) is a range of airborne radar systems designed to carry out the following missions:
(1) detection of surface ships
(2) target designation
(3) weather mapping
(4) radar navigation
(5) search and rescue at sea.

All the Heracles I system radars operate in the I-band and are especially suited to helicopter-borne uses. The configurations, based on modular units, are calculated according to the mission and the carrier. The different sub-systems available are described in the ORB 31 radar (**1793.353**), which exists in the following configurations:
ORB 31 S1 Alouette III (SNIAS Helicopter Division)
ORB 31 W French Navy WG 13 helicopter
ORB 31 AS anti-submarine
ORB 31 D Super Frelon (Exocet system).

ORB 31 S1

The ORB 31 S1 system is an airborne surveillance radar fitted to the Alouette III helicopter. The choice of the transmitter (0·5 or 4 µs pulsewidth) enables the system to be adapted to the scheduled mission.

ORB 37 airborne weather radar equipment

OPERATIONAL CHARACTERISTICS
Pitch and roll antenna stabilisation
180° azimuth and 30° elevation coverage

Range: 35 nm on naval target of 1000 m² with sea state 4 and 4 mm per hour rain
Weight: 38 kg

ORB 31 W

The ORB 31 W system is an airborne surveillance system fitted to the French Navy's WG 13 helicopter (design undertaken under STTA contract).

The ORB 31 W system uses two transmitter/receivers. The first is intended for long-distance detecton and the second, with its higher resolution, is less sensitive to clutter.

OPERATIONAL CHARACTERISTICS
Pitch and roll antenna stabilisation
180° azimuth and 30° elevation coverage
Range: 50 nm on naval target of 1000 m² with sea state 4 and 4 mm per hour rain
Weight: 61 kg

ORB 31 AS

Anti-submarine warfare model for the detection, identification, location and station-keeping of other helicopters of a tactical ASW group. A continuous and updated display of sonar contact and the tactical situation is provided, and features of the large-display console include time motion, offset, scales up to 100 nautical miles, and all controls positioned on the front panel.

ORB 31 D

The ORB 31 D system is a target designation airborne radar fitted to the Super Frelon helicopter carrying the Exocet system. Its function is to detect, track, and then locate accurately a target on the sea in order to supply the data necessary to the weapon system with which it is integrated.

The system consists of two transmitter/receivers, three indicators (two PPI and one B-scope), and a telemetry box.

OPERATIONAL CHARACTERISTICS
Pitch and roll antenna stabilisation
180° azimuth and 30° elevation coverage
Range: 80 km on naval target of 1000 m² with sea state 4 and 4 mm per hour rain
Automatic target tracking, bearing range or azimuth range data delivered to the weapon system in BCD form with ±50 m precision in range and ±1° in bearing
Weight: 75 kg

HERACLES II

Heracles II is a range of I-band airborne radars, based on the considerable experience acquired by Omera during the development, manufacture and operation of Heracles I, of which it is a logical extension. It is built from modular sub-assemblies compatible with one another, each performing one of the following functions:

(1) maritime patrol
(2) anti-submarine warfare (ASW)
(3) active missile fire control (TD)
(4) search and rescue (SAR)
(5) radar navigation
(6) weather radar.

Reduced weight and dimensions facilitate installation on all types of aircraft.

OPERATIONAL CHARACTERISTICS
Pitch and roll antenna stabilisation
360° azimuth and 30° elevation scanning
Sectoral scans of 60, 120, 180 or 240°
Azimuth, bearing or true motion stabilisation
Peak power: 80 kW, fixed, tunable, frequency agile
Range: 90 km on 500 m target
Special-to-type characteristics appear below.

ORB 32 W

This is a simple, compact and lightweight system, suitable for small aircraft and helicopters, specially designed for surface reconnaissance, search and rescue (SAR), radar navigation, weather radar.

The system comprises:
1 OAB 3118   antenna (60 × 30 cm)
1 OAB 3105   drive mechanism
1 OJB 321   junction box
1 OEB 321   transmitter/receiver (tuned frequency, 0·25 - 2 µs, 80 kW peak)
1 OSB 330   5-inch (127 mm) digital indicator, 120 or 240° scan, daylight viewing type, iso-contour, memory (freeze)
1 OFB 320
and
1 OFB 326   ancillaries for OSB 330
1 OFB 322   control box
Weight: 44 kg

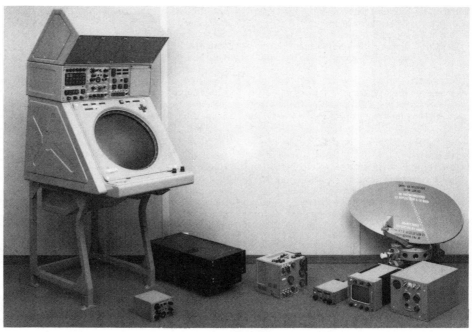

ORB 32 WAS system

ORB 31D airborne maritime surveillance and missile firing radar

ORB 32 WN

This system, which uses one of the larger display consoles, performs all the functions required for maritime patrol missions.

The system comprises:
1 OAB 3124   antenna (85 × 36 cm)
1 OAB 3105   drive mechanism
1 OJB 321   junction box
1 OEB 321   transmitter/receiver
1 OFB 322   control box
1 ODC 327   9-inch (229 mm) indicator, fixed range rings and moving markers, true motion with or without reset, anti-sea-clutter signal processing
or, ODC 323   16-inch (406 mm) indicator
Weight: 58 kg

ORB 32 WAS

This is one of the elements of the anti-submarine warfare weapon system in the SA 321 Super Frelon helicopter. It performs the following functions: helicopter station holding in ASW, tactical situation information, guidance and helicopter attack on a designated target, navigation, weather mapping. The ORB 32 WAS consists essentially of a system performing both primary radar and secondary radar functions. The use of transponders allows the localisation and identification of helicopters flying at low altitudes by eliminating sea-clutter.

The system comprises:
2 OAB 3114   antenna (72 × 36 cm)
1 OAB 3103   drive mechanism
1 OJB 321   junction box
1 OEB 321   transmitter/receiver
1 OSB 330   5-inch (127 mm) indicator
1 ODC 323   display console, 16-inch (406 mm) displays secondary radar data simultaneously with primary radar echoes and displays sonar contact co-ordinates in decimal form
1 switching unit
1 OAB 3115   transponder antenna
1 ODA 312   transponder
1 ODB 312   transponder control box
Weight (moving parts only): 129 kg

ORB 32 WLD

The ORB 32 WLD is an airborne reconnaissance and target designation radar. When integrated in a weapon system, its purpose is to detect, designate and accurately track two sea-targets. Target co-ordinates may be automatically transmitted to the active missile carried by aircraft, or helicopter or to a launch vessel (over the horizon surface-to-surface attack).

The system comprises:
1 OAB 3119   antenna (72 × 36 cm)
1 OAB 3105   drive mechanism

1 OJB 321   junction box
1 OEB 321   transmitter/receiver
1 OFB 322   control box
1 ODC 321   display console (9-inch (229 mm) scope, TWS and telemetry circuits)

ORB 32 ASD

Combination of the WAS and WLD types.

One version of the ORB 32 has been selected by the Swedish Navy for integration into a new anti-surface, anti-submarine and search rescue system for helicopters.

ORB 37

This is a high performance radar for aircraft and helicopters designed for detection and analysis of cloud masses and navigation by radar. It is equipped with a digital indicator in the forward compartment (one sector of 120 or 240°) on which dangerous zones are emphasised by the iso-contour function; a PPI-type analogue indicator at the operator station, (one sector of 240° and mobile alidade) particularly suited to the ground display function; a beacon channel which affords an additional navigation aid.

The ORB 37 is fitted to Transall C-130 aircraft of the French Air Force.

CONTRACTOR
Omera-Segid, 49 rue Ferdinand Berthoud, 95100 Argenteuil, France.

1211.353
AIDA II FIRE CONTROL RADAR

The Aida II fire control radar is a miniaturised system designed for installation in light interceptors and aircraft with restricted accommodation in the nose. It is also suitable for pod mounting. It performs automatic search, acquisition, and range tracking of targets (air or sea) within a cone of 18°. It can also supply the surface range in the boresight axis. Used with a gyroscopic gun sight it will supply all the data necessary for interception and attack by guns, rockets, bombs, or missiles, viz range of the target or ground, angular position of an air or sea target with respect to the boresight axis, gravity drop, and sensitivity corrections for air-to-air firing.

More detailed information on Aida II is given under this entry number in *Jane's Weapon Systems 1982-83* and earlier editions.

CONTRACTOR
Electronique Serge Dassault, 55 quai Carnot, 92214 St Cloud, France.

3131.353
CYRANO RADAR FAMILY

The Avionics Division of Thomson-CSF designed and developed the Cyrano family of airborne fire control radars for the Mirage fighter aircraft. The first one of the family, Cyrano I, was fitted on the Mirage III C. The subsequent versions were:

Cyrano II
Multi-function radar for the Mirage III E.
CHARACTERISTICS
I/J-band; monopulse; cassegrain antenna; peak power 200 kW; liquid cooling; mounted in a pressurised radome. Data are displayed on a CRT and a head-up display. Weight of equipment: 188 kg in nosecone; 29·5 kg in equipment bay and cockpit.
DEVELOPMENT
The first prototype was completed in 1962 and the radar put into service in 1963.
STATUS
Cyrano II is used on the Mirage III E aircraft of the French Air Force and a number of other countries.

Cyrano III
Cyrano III radar has a design which is not specific to a given aircraft. It was developed as a prototype and should be considered merely as a development phase of the Cyrano IV.

Cyrano IV
The Cyrano IV radars constitute a family of multi-role radars designed to meet the requirements of different users.

Cyrano IV M
This is the latest model of the Cyrano IV series and embodies the latest advances in technology to obtain improvements in reliability and maintainability. Cyrano IV M is described in detail under entry **1396.353**.
CONTRACTOR
Thomson-CSF, Avionics Division, 178 boulevard Gabriel Péri, 92240 Malakoff, France.

1051.353
CYRANO II AIRBORNE ATTACK RADAR (RA 537)

This is an airborne AI radar providing search, tracking, and air-to-air interception modes, plus air-to-ground modes and terrain mapping. It is a monopulse, I/J-band set employing a cassegrain scanner and with a transmitter peak power of 200 kW. It is liquid-cooled and housed in a pressurised radome nosecone.

More detailed information on Cyrano II is given under this entry number in *Jane's Weapon Systems 1982-83* and earlier editions.
STATUS
Superseded by later Cyrano models. Over 1000 sets have been delivered and it is fitted to Mirage III aircraft of the French Forces and those of a number of other nations.
CONTRACTOR
Thomson-CSF, Avionics Division, 178 boulevard Gabriel Péri, 92240 Malakoff, France.

1396.353
CYRANO IV/CYRANO IV M ATTACK RADAR

The Cyrano IV is the latest development of the Cyrano series of airborne radars and is a multi-role system. The Cyrano IV M is the newest version of this series. Basic functions performed by the radar are:
(1) air-to-air search
(2) automatic tracking
(3) interception and fire domain computations
(4) dog-fight engagements
(5) home-on-jam mode
(6) ground mapping
    Additional options are:
(7) contour mapping
(8) terrain avoidance
(9) blind let-down
(10) air-to-ground ranging.

The Cyrano IV M model incorporates TWS facilities and is also suitable for air-to-sea search and tracking roles in addition to those listed for the Cyrano IV.

Data can be presented by means of a Type 196 gunsight or CRT HUD, and inputs to weapon systems are available also. Other aircraft systems providing inputs to the radar system include an inertial or gyro platform for altitude reference information, and an air data computer for aircraft performance and ambient parameters.

Operational missions include interception, air superiority or interdiction using guns or missiles; all-weather penetration; air-to-ground attack with guns, bombs and rockets.

The Cyrano IV M, as well as being a multi-function radar, differs from its predecessor in the embodiment of new technology which confers improved reliability and maintainability on the later model.
STATUS
The Cyrano IV was produced in quantity for French Air Force F1 aircraft. All aircraft have been fitted with the Cyrano IV M version. Production of the IV M began in 1980. Two versions of this radar, the Cyrano IV M3 have been developed for adaptation to the Mirage III and Mirage 50.
CONTRACTOR
Thomson-CSF, Avionics Division, 178 boulevard Gabriel Péri, 92240 Malakoff, France.

Cyrano IV and Cyrano IV M attack multi-function radars pictured side-by-side for comparison. The later Cyrano IV M (right) incorporates TWS facilities and improved reliability and maintainability due to new technology

---

1672.353
AGAVE AIRBORNE RADAR

The Agave is a lightweight, multi-role radar, fitted to the Super-Etendard carrier-based aircraft and the Jaguar International strike aircraft. It has been optimised for naval applications, but its air-to-air and air-to-ground functions give it appreciable interception and ground attack capabilities. Basic functions fulfilled are:
(1) search: air-to-surface
         air-to-air
(2) target designation for the homing head of a long-range active missile or to a HUD
(3) automatic tracking: air-to-surface
                 air-to-air
(4) ranging: air-to-air
       air-to-ground
(5) map display.
CHARACTERISTICS
I-band; monopulse; inverse cassegrain antenna stabilised in roll and pitch; PRF and pulsewidths adapted to operating conditions; beam shaping; solid-state construction; integrated circuits; built-in test equipment. Weight of equipment: 48 kg in nosecone, 17 kg in cockpit and fuselage.

OPERATION
In the search mode, the scanned sector is 140° in azimuth and 60° in elevation. After target identification, the pilot switches to automatic tracking. Target data are supplied either to the homing head of an active missile, or to a HUD. In the air-to-air mode, the detection range for a fighter aircraft is within 10 and 15 nautical miles (18 to 28 km). In the air-to-surface mode, the detection range for a patrol boat is within 22 and 30 nautical miles (40 to 55 km).

The angle of search in azimuth as noted above is

±70° forward from the line-of-flight, thus giving 140° sweep coverage ahead from left to right. In elevation, the angle of search can be either 6 or 12° depending on whether a one- or two-bar scan pattern is used. In practice, a one-bar pattern is selected automatically for low level altitudes and, at higher altitudes, a two-bar scan cuts in to improve near coverage. The pilot, however, has the option of moving this scan pattern up or down through 60°.

Agave airborne radar

To keep the pilot's work-load to a minimum, the Agave radar system has been automated as far as possible. For example, the radar is provided with an instantaneous automatic gain control, which uses the echoes received for adjusting the receiver so that extensive and scattered echoes – such as sea, cloud and ground clutter – are considerably reduced in comparison with the pin-point reflections sought, such as aircraft and surface vessels, which are sharply displayed. In another example, when the air-to-ground mode for ground mapping is used, the best possible tracking elevation for maximum ground coverage ahead of the aircraft is automatically set up. The pilot can still, however, override this computed elevation and has the option of fine adjustment when short-range, high power echoes are present.

Once airborne, the pilot must select manually the mode and the range to be scanned from 5 to 80 nautical miles and, to simplify the operation, the radar-pulse repetition frequency and pulse width are automatically and directly related to the scanning range thus selected.

All essential radar controls are positioned on a control stick, the handgrip controlling not only the

antenna elevation, designation marker bearing and range, but also the commencement of lock-on for the automatic tracking sequence which, once the target has been pinpointed, will provide the pilot with continually updated range and bearing information.

In the model for the Jaguar, all radar information will be displayed either on a raster head-up display by means of a scan converter on a combined map/radar head-down display, thus retaining the projected map display in its normal place. The radome is fitted in the nose of the aircraft in place of the laser ranger and marked target facilities of the 'S' version of the aircraft.

STATUS

Agave is fitted to the French Navy Super Etendard aircraft, the international version of Jaguar and the export versions of the Mirage F1 and Mirage 50. Over 150 Agave systems have been ordered.

CONTRACTORS

Thomson-CSF, Avionics Division, 178 boulevard Gabriel Péri, 92240 Malakoff, France.

Electronique Serge Dassault, 55 quai Carnot, 92214 St Cloud, France.

1674.353

NR-AI-3-A AIRBORNE IFF INTERROGATOR

The NR-AI-3-A system is based on the LMT ER-115-A transmitter/receiver unit. This incorporates a coder, one transmitter, and one or two receivers. The respective operating frequencies are 1030 MHz and

1090 MHz. The equipment is designed to provide certain types of aircraft with secondary surveillance radar and IFF interrogation capabilities, and the possible Modes are 1, 2, 3/A, and C, with Mode 4 if the system is equipped with a suitable coder and decoder. Up to four modes may be interlaced.

Transmitter power can be selected at any of the three levels, 0·5, 1 or 2 kW. Apart from the one transmitter tube, the equipment is all solid-state, and weighs 8 kg.

CONTRACTOR

LMT Radio Professionnelle, 46-47 quai Alphonse Le Gallo, 92103 Boulogne-Billancourt, France.

1962.353

ESD 3300/3400 IFF/SIF TRANSPONDERS

The range of type 3000 IFF airborne transponders designed by ESD are used for the identification of any type of fixed or rotary wing aircraft by interrogation from a secondary radar or air traffic control system. These micro-miniaturised equipments represent a new generation of airborne transponders and can be installed easily in the cockpit of any aircraft or helicopter. Their modular design facilitates maintenance and a built-in automatic test system allows permanent monitoring of operation.

The type 3000 range has been designed for association, if required, without any internal modification, with an automatic code switching system, increasing airspace protection. In addition, the ESD 3400 possesses a space diversity system maintaining contact with interrogating stations independently of aircraft manoeuvres, thereby reinforcing mission safety.

The range of transponders meets military specifications: Stanag 5017 (Mk XA/IFF 3300; Mk XII/IFF 3400), Air 7304 and civilian specifications ICAO (Appendix 10) and ARINC 572. They are used as standard equipment by various air forces.

Modular design has permitted the two functionally identical versions to be packaged in either the ESD 3300 single-box model or the ESD 3400 two-box configuration.

CHARACTERISTICS

Reception

Frequency: 1030 MHz

Sensitivity: –77 dBm

IF: 60 MHz

SLS: 3-pulse

Transmission

Frequency: 1090 MHz

Power output: 500 W peak

Power consumption: 28 V DC 50 W

Dimensions

ESD 3300: 133 × 146 × 145 mm

ESD 3400: 133 × 146 × 75 mm (controller)
194 × 90 × 319 mm (transmitter/receiver)
⅜ short ATR

Weight

ESD 3300: 4 kg

ESD 3400: 7·8 kg

MTBF: Given as 1500 h

ESD 3300 IFF/SIF transponder

CONTRACTOR

Electronique Serge Dassault, 55 quai Carnot, 92214 St Cloud, France.

INTERNATIONAL

1784.353

AN/APS-503 and LASR-2 RADARS

The AN/APS-503 airborne search radar is installed in Sea King helicopters of the Canadian Forces (Sea Element) in service with DDH280 class destroyers.

The AN/APS-503 radar is lightweight (45 kg) with high power (50 kW peak) for its size. It comprises five units: a transmitter/receiver, an antenna complete with mounting, an azimuth range indicator (PPI), a radar control unit, and a range bearing unit. The ARI is seven inches (18 cm) P-7 phosphor, designed for use by a radar operator, and possesses three scales each with range markers spaced appropriately.

The range and bearing unit positions a range strobe and an azimuth marker on the PPI, at the same time transmitting this information to ancillary equipment such as navigation systems.

The transmitter operates in the I-band, with a pulse-width and pulse recurrence frequency optimised for maritime reconnaissance, and a 50 kW peak power. The receiver has a solid-state local oscillator with

AN/APS-503 airborne radar system

logarithmic response and sensitivity time control and fast time constant.

The antenna is a 24 × 18 inch (61 × 46 cm) parabola, providing a 4° beam in azimuth and a 5° beam in elevation. The antenna is stabilised for pitch and roll and has a manual tilt control. Top-mounted, belly-mounted, and nose-mounted antenna versions are also available. A pilot's bright display is available as an option.

CHARACTERISTICS
Transmitter
Frequency: 9·2 – 9·4 GHz, fixed
Power output: 50 kW peak
Pulse width: 0·5 μs
PRF: 400 Hz
Antenna: 24 × 18 inch (61 × 46 cm) parabola
Gain: 30 dB
Beamwidth: 4° azimuth; 5° elevation
Sidelobes: –20 dB
Polarisation: Horizontal
Rotation rate: 30 rpm
Stabilisation: Automatic compensation for pitch and roll up to ±20°

Tilt control: ±8°
Receiver
Local oscillator: Solid-state with AFC
Type: Balanced mixer with 60 MHz IF
Noise figure: 8 dB
Bandwidth: Matched to pulse width
Response: Logarithmic
Processing: STC, FTC
Display
Type: 7-inch (18 cm) PPI with P-7 phosphor
Scales: 3 – 20 nm, variable; 50 nm; 100 nm; 250 nm
Markers: Range markers; heading strobe; slewable azimuth cursor and range dot, each with digital readout

LASR-2
A higher-power commercial version is also available. The Litton airborne search radar LASR-2 is a development of the AN/APS-504. Peak power is 100 kW, and it possesses dual pulse widths, four pulse recurrence frequencies and three rotation rates in normal operation. Weight is 170 lb (76 kg) with a pilot's bright display included. A variety of antenna

sizes are available. Sector scan, a delayed sweep, ground stabilisation, and beacon mode are included.

System characteristics are generally similar to the AN/APS-504 (**3473.353**) below.
STATUS
At the 1977 Paris Air Show, the Australian Government Aircraft Factories introduced the Search Master maritime surveillance version of the twin-engined Nomad aircraft. Two models were announced, of which the less sophisticated version is equipped with the Bendix RDR 1400 radar, while the Search Master L uses the LASR-2 with a 36-inch (91 cm) diameter, 360° rotating antenna in a chin-mounted radome.

The system is no longer in production but is still in service.
CONTRACTORS
Litton Systems Canada Ltd, 25 Cityview Drive, Rexdale, Ontario M9W 5A7, Canada.

Eaton Corporation, AIL Division, Deer Park, New York 11729, USA.

3473.353
AN/APS-504(V)3 AIRBORNE RADAR
The APS-504(V) airborne search radar has been designed for tactical transport and maritime surveillance applications. It can be employed in either a fixed or rotary wing type of aircraft. The system is operationally suitable for use in a sea search, ground mapping, navigation, station keeping or weather avoidance role.

The APS-504(V) provides digital signal processing and scan conversion allowing the use of standard RS343A high-resolution 875 line TV displays. This system also allows recording and playback of mission radar data and alpha-numerics on compatible TV systems.

The system consists of six basic units:
(1) receiver/transmitter
(2) antenna/pedestal assembly
(3) digital TV displays
(4) radar control unit with joystick cursor control
(5) radar processor and converter
(6) key pad entry unit.
The antenna is stabilised for pitch and roll and is designed to make use of available radome volume. Features include variable width sector scan, range delay, offset sweep, sweep expansion, true motion display using inputs from the navigation system and an MS-1553B interface to the tactical mission computer.

CHARACTERISTICS
Peak power: 100 kW
Pulse widths: 0·5 μs, 2·4 μs
Receiver noise: 5 dB
Beacon mode/search mode/simultaneous beacon/search
Linear and logarithmic receivers
Digital X-Y displays viewable in high ambient light
Multi-function display
CONTRACTORS
Litton Systems Canada Ltd, 25 Cityview Drive, Rexdale, Ontario M9W 5A7, Canada.

Eaton Corporation, AIL Division, Deer Park, New York 11729, USA.

5621.053
NATO IDENTIFICATION SYSTEM (NIS)
NATO's future IFF system, the NATO Identification system (NIS), was in the early design phase in early 1984 with studies and development being carried out in USA, UK, West Germany and France. Present Mk X and Mk XII IFF systems in use with NATO are becoming outdated. Both use a fixed frequency system which can easily be jammed by hostile action. Another problem is that the current systems can only identify friendlies and the lack of a response leaves the operator uncertain whether he is interrogating a hostile aircraft or a friendly one whose IFF is faulty, turned off or jammed.

The new system being developed, under NATO Standardisation Agreement (Stanag) 4162 will use spread spectrum and additional ECCM techniques to counter jamming, and will have a high level of message security. It is intended to combine the basic

information with other data sources to provide a high accuracy IFF. Two frequency bands are currently being investigated, D-band (1 to 2 GHz) and E/F-band (2 to 4 GHz). The USA and France favour D-band, West Germany E/F-band, while the UK chose D-band with modifications. This last involves the addition of a radar mode whereby a ground radar transmission is modulated with IFF information and a transponder on board the aircraft responds when scanned by the radar beam. With the vast US investment in the current range of IFF operating in D-band, its own national IFF development programme (Mk XV), the US Combat Identification Systems, under development in D-band and also with the Joint Tactical Information Distribution System (JTIDS) using the same frequency region, it seems likely that NIS will be in D-band probably with the added radar mode.

The main companies involved in development are

two teams in the US – Bendix/Raytheon and Texas Instruments/E-Systems/Teledyne; Cossor and Plessey in UK, Siemens in West Germany and Thomson-CSF in France. Agreement has been reached between Cossor and Siemens for a joint development programme. Time scales are difficult to assess, the two teams in the US are being funded by the US Air Force to carry out development work in two phases. Phase 1, which consists of building 'breadboard' models, was due to be reviewed in mid-1984 with Phase 2 lasting a further three years and involving the building of advanced development models. The US Air Force expects to award contracts early in 1988 with production deliveries probably starting around 1990. It is understood that the European companies, which are also being funded by their individual governments, are on a similar time scale.

ISRAEL

3305.353
EL/M-2001B RADAR
The Elta EL/M-2001B dual-mode radar for combat aircraft is a range-only equipment for air-to-air and air-to-ground operations. Of compact dimensions

and weighing less than 50 kg, it is suitable for installation in the nose position of small new combat aircraft or for retrofitting to earlier types.

It is constructed of six line replaceable units: transmitter, receiver, power supply, RF exciter, RTU, and servo unit. These are attached to the radar chassis/mounting unit which also carries the beam directing unit, gear box, RF head and TWT. The last of these items is the only component that is not solid-state.
OPERATION
Modes of operation are air-to-air, all altitudes and all aspects; air-to-ground, manual or computer controlled. Target detection is by visual means and the radar will automatically acquire and track any target viewed in the HUD by the pilot. It operates in heavy ground clutter and remains clutter-free even in very low level air combat, according to Elta.

Target acquisition is also automatic in the air-to-ground mode, although in both modes there is

provision for pilot intervention for selection of targets of interest. Information provided by the EL/M-2001B can either be displayed on the aircraft HUD or fed into the weapons' control computer where it may be used for CCIP and CCRP weapon delivery computation.
CHARACTERISTICS
Frequency: Probably I- or J-band
Form factor: Frustum of a cone
Length: 49 cm (including connectors)
Base diameter: 45 cm
Antenna aperture: 195 mm
Weight: <50 kg
Power requirements: 115 V, 400 Hz, 3-phase, 1 kVA, DC 30 W
STATUS
In production.
CONTRACTOR
Elta Electronics Industries Ltd, (a subsidiary of Israel Aircraft Industries Ltd), Ashdod, Israel.

EL/M-2001B airborne radar

3306.353
EL/M-2021 RADAR

The Elta EL/M-2021 multi-role combat radar was revealed at the 1977 Paris Air Show. Operating in the I/J-band of the radar spectrum, it provides facilities for a variety of air-to-air and air-to-ground missions. These include air interception, close-in combat, air-to-ground bombing and gunnery, terrain following, avoidance and mapping.

In the air-to-air mode it performs search and automatic tracking, and in the air-to-ground mode it supplies ranging information to the bombing computer (both CCIP and CCRP weapon delivery modes are available). Head-up and head-down displays provide the pilot with data for interception of targets and provide fire control for guns. A stabilised radar picture is produced which is of value in the navigation mode using radar mapping.

The equipment is constructed of line replaceable units which include transmitter, processor, modulator, missile illumination unit, RF head, weapon delivery unit, receiver, RF exciter, servo amplifier unit, power supply, interface computer unit, and missile delivery computer. An inverse cassegrain antenna is employed and solid-state circuitry is used.

Coherent processing using digital techniques is used, and both look-up and look-down waveforms are understood to be provided.

CHARACTERISTICS
Transmitter
Frequency: Probably I/J-band
Bandwidth: 500 MHz
Peak power: 3 kW
Average power: 200 W
Receiver noise: –5 dB
Antenna: Inverse cassegrain

Scan	Tracking	Search/AI	Dogfight
Azimuth	±70°	±45°	±10°
Elevation	+80 to –40°	±5°	–0 to +60°

EL/M-2021 multi-role combat radar

Range tracking accuracy: 10 m ± 10%
Processor: CCD processor for signal extraction; digital data processor for avionics interface
Dimensions (excluding antenna)
Max diameter: 74 cm
Minimum diameter: 44 cm
Height: 1·295 m
Weight: 120 kg (including antenna)
STATUS
Development. The EL/M-2021B has been flight tested in an F-4 Phantom. Although designed originally for the F-16 aircraft of the Israeli Air Force, the system is

also destined for the Lavi fighter, due to fly in the mid-1980s.
CONTRACTOR
Elta Electronics Industries Ltd, (a subsidiary of Israel Aircraft Industries Ltd), Ashdod, Israel.

ITALY

3307.353
MM/APS-705 RADAR

The MM/APS-705 is an airborne search and navigation radar designed specifically for naval helicopters, in particular the AB.212 and SH-3D types, providing for ASW, mapping, SAR, and similar operations. The operating frequencies are in the I-band and two transmitter/receivers are used for frequency diversity operation providing clutter decorrelation and enhancing reliability. There are four pulse length/PRF combinations and eight range settings matched to bearing/range discrimination.

Antenna groups for either ventral or dorsal mounting are produced and there are also size variations, that for the SH-3D having a wider aperture

than that for the AB.212 (1·6 m compared with 1·2 m). Line-of-sight stabilisation is provided in both cases, and there are alternative, selectable antenna rotation rates, 20 or 40 rpm. Manually controlled antenna tilt provides for ±20° of movement. An alternative back-to-back antenna is another option for use where higher data rates are required, for instance.

The display unit incorporates a 9-inch (23 cm) diameter CRT PPI with digital true motion presentation facilities, electronic and mechanical cursors, markers, and complemented by a separate digital readout X-Y reference display.

There is an expanded micro-B display for chaff or multi-target detection, and the radar provides outputs for other displays and extractor units. Other facilities

include sector transmissions and blanking; interfaces for Beacon receiver, IFF, ASW and ESM systems; built-in test; data link; TWS and dense-environment tracker. Equipment options, in addition to the back-to-back antenna already mentioned, include a 75 kW frequency-agile transmitter/receiver, a pilot's bright display, and the auto-tracker with ECCM provisions and micro-B display.
CHARACTERISTICS
Transmitter/receiver: Dual, I-band
Peak power: 25 kW each
Pulse length/PRF: 0·05 µs/1600 Hz, 0·15 µs/1300 Hz, 0·5 µs/1300 Hz, 1·5 µs/650 Hz
Noise figure: 8·5 dB
Receiver characteristics: Linear; log up to 80 dB
Anti-clutter: STC, FTC, log-averaging
Antenna: Cylindrical-paraboloid segment. Horn feed
Polarisation: Horizontal
Beamwidth: 2° azimuth × 7° elevation (AB.212, 1·2 m aperture); 1·5° azimuth × 10° elevation (SH-3D, 1·6 m aperture)
Rotation rate: 20 and 40 rpm
Stabilisation: ±20° pitch and roll
Manual tilt: ±20°
Display: P33 phosphor, 9 inch (23 cm)
Range settings: 0·5, 1, 2, 5, 10, 20, 40, 80 nm
System weight: 87 kg
STATUS
Standard equipment in Italian Navy AB.212 and SH-3D helicopters, and procured by other navies.
CONTRACTOR
SMA (Segnalamento Marittimo ed Aereo), PO Box 200, Via del Ferrone Soffiano, 50100 Florence, Italy.

MM/APS-705 airborne radar installation

3308.353
MM/APS-707 RADAR

The MM/APS-707 is essentially a simpler version of the MM/APS-705 (**3307.353**), with a single 20 kW transmitter/receiver for fixed frequency operation (I-band), and suitable for airborne applications where reduced weight, lower power consumption, and cost

considerations call for a less sophisticated equipment.

In most other respects the two systems are the same and the APS-707 is designed to provide for helicopter requirements associated with navigation, surface search, tracking, mapping, rescue, ASW etc. Similar additional options are available, such as 1·2 or

1·6 m aperture antenna and mounting on top or beneath the helicopter fuselage.
CONTRACTOR
SMA (Segnalamento Marittimo ed Aereo), PO Box 200, Via del Ferrone Soffiano, 50100 Florence, Italy.

3309.353
MM/APQ-706 RADAR

The MM/APQ-706 search and attack radar is used in the Italian Navy Marte helicopter-launched anti-ship missile system (**1651.321**). It consists of two I-band transmitter/receiver channels operating in frequency diversity, with frequency agility facilities on one channel, and is provided with a data processing and extraction system and tactical display console. The MM/APQ-706 can fulfil typical naval helicopter roles such as surface search, navigation, ASW etc in addition to providing target detection, acquisition and missile guidance facilities for the Marte system.

The antenna group utilises a pair of back-to-back mounted parabolic antennas, line-of-sight stabilised, housed in a chin radome in the case of Italian Navy SH-3D helicopters. High accuracy and acquisition capability against small surface targets in the presence of severe sea clutter and/or intense EW opposition are among the main features of this radar.

Many details of the MM/APQ-706 are classified but it belongs to the SMA APS/APQ-700 series of airborne radars and is probably closest to the MM/APS-705 version (**3307.353**) with the addition of known enhancements such as the back-to-back antenna, 75 kW frequency-agile transmitter/receiver, auto-tracker/ECCM package, and certain other unspecified additions.

Back-to-back antenna assembly of MM/APQ-706 airborne radar

STATUS
Installed on Italian Navy SH-3D helicopters for Marte anti-ship missile system.

CONTRACTOR
SMA (Segnalamento Marittimo ed Aereo), PO Box 200, Via del Ferrone Soffiano, 50100 Florence, Italy.

3488.353
SIT 432 (AN/APX-104(V)) AIRBORNE INTERROGATOR

The SIT 432 (AN/APX-104(V)) is a lightweight airborne IFF interrogator equipment suitable for installation on helicopters or fixed-wing aircraft to provide air-to-air and air-to-ship identification facilities.

The receiver/transmitter module contains a 1200 W transmitter, a dual-channel receiver and an RF interface module. The receiver operates at 1090 MHz and is of a dual-channel type which, in conjunction with a dual-channel antenna, provides for receiver side lobe suppression.

The design employs surface acoustic wave technology in the local oscillator to obtain a reliable, simple design with good stability and no field alignment requirements. The transmitter is solid-state. It accepts coded video pulse trains from an external source and the internally generated Mode 4 ISLS pulse, converts the coded video pulse trains and Mode 4 ISLS pulse into radio-frequency pulse groups for transmission as IFF interrogation.

CHARACTERISTICS
Frequency: 1090 ±0·2 MHz (receiver); 1030 ±0·2 MHz (transmitter)
Sensitivity: –83 dBm
Output power: Not less than 1200 W
Duty cycle: 1% max
Dynamic range: 50 dB
Weight: 6·5 kg
STATUS
Co-development with Hazeltine USA.
CONTRACTOR
ITALTEL (Società Italiana Telecomunicazioni), 12 Piazzale Zavattari, 20149 Milan, Italy.

SIT 432 (AN/APX-104(V)) airborne interrogator

3489.353
SIT 421 (MM/UPX-709) TRANSPONDER

The SIT 421 (MM/UPX-709) is a 'one-box' airborne IFF transponder, suitable for fitting in fixed-wing aircraft or helicopters. It operates in Modes 1, 2, 3/A, 4 and C. The receiver/transmitter includes a 500 W solid-state transmitter, dual-channel receiver and RF interface module. The first of these comprises a delay line oscillator, modulator, driver and power amplifier.

The controls for operation of the transponder, code and mode selection, etc, are mounted on the front of the equipment (which is designed for cockpit mounting) but versions are produced in which remote control facilities are provided.

CHARACTERISTICS
Frequency: 1030 MHz (receiver); 1090 MHz (transmitter)
Sensitivity: –77 dBm (adjustable 69 – 77)
Dynamic range: 55 dB
Output power: 27 ±3 dBW at 1% duty cycle
Weight: 3·5 kg
STATUS
Production.
CONTRACTOR
ITALTEL (Società Italiana Telecomunicazioni), 12 Piazzale Zavattari, 20149 Milan, Italy.

SIT 421 (MM/UPX-709) IFF transponder

SWEDEN

1210.353
PS-37/A AIRBORNE ATTACK RADAR

This is a multi-mode airborne attack radar, operating in the I/J-band, and using the monopulse technique. High output power is employed to provide long range performance. Cassegrain or parabolic dish scanners with fixed feed have been developed for this radar, but the latter is the preferred antenna system.

The PS-37/A is an important element in the attack system of the Saab Viggen aircraft, and its design provides for considerable integration with the navigation, display, and digital computer-based data processing sub-systems.

The radar is comprised of two main units: the electronics package and the scanner assembly. The former is made up of 13 replaceable units housed in a main assembly which carries the interconnecting cable looms. The division of electronic functions between the individual replaceable units has been arranged so that, as far as possible, related functions are housed within one unit, enabling the replacement of units to be effected without the need for subsequent trimming or adjustment. Each of the replaceable units contains between three and eight sub-units, which provide further facility for servicing.

With the exception of certain high-frequency devices, the PS-37/A is a completely solid-state equipment. The mechanical design incorporates an hydraulic drive for the antenna scanning and stabilisation system, providing accurate and rapid movement over wide angles.

In the interest of high performance and optimum operational flexibility, including conditions of high interference (natural or ECM), elaborate signal processing facilities at both the radio-frequency and video levels are provided in the PS-37/A. Another technique employed to increase accuracy and resolution is lobe-shaping, which synthetically produces the effect of increased antenna aperture and reduced sidelobes.

In the Viggen installation both head-up and head-down display of radar information is provided, the data presented varying in accordance with the operational mode employed.

OPERATION

To comply with the requirements of operation of the Viggen by a single crew member (pilot), the PS-37/A is designed for semi-automatic operation to reduce cockpit work-load. Facilities provided include: search, target acquisition, air target ranging, surface target ranging, obstacle warning, fixed point radar navigation, and terrain mapping. The system is designed to allow for terrain following by the addition of one unit.

Radar information is shown on the head-down display in the form of sector-PPI or B-scope presentation. This unit features a dual persistence CRT in which rapidly changing data (such as a radar map) are presented with a shorter persistence than alpha-numeric characters or other symbols. The latter can be used for the display of flight information or target designation, and are derived from a

waveform generator driven by the aircraft central digital computer.

DEVELOPMENT

The PS-37/A is the third generation of airborne radar equipment developed by Ericsson. Theoretical studies for a radar to meet the requirements of the Viggen were started in 1958, and ground tests on the first prototype took place in 1961. The first system-engineered model was built in 1965 and air tests began in 1966, with the radar fitted in a Lansen test-bed aircraft equipped with Viggen electronics. Verification tests in a Viggen took place in 1968, and production was ordered, starting in 1970. A version for the Swedish fighter version of the Viggen (JA 37) is described under **1964.353**.

STATUS

Operational but no longer in production.

CONTRACTOR

Ericsson Radio Systems AB, Airborne Electronics Division, 431 26 Mölndal, Sweden.

PS-37/A radar in AJ 37 Viggen aircraft

1209.353

UAP 13 SERIES AIRBORNE ATTACK RADARS

This is a range of nose-mounted, forward-looking radars for search and fire control applications in interceptor aircraft. The radars in this series are pulse radars operating in the I/J-band of the spectrum.

The basic model of the range is the UAP 13102, which is also designated PS-01/A. It is fitted to the Saab Draken J35F. The UAP 13103 (PS-011/A) is similar to the UAP 13102 but is designed to be used with the S71N infra-red search and track set. Both these models are intended for use in aircraft having a fire control computer.

OPERATION

The following operating modes are provided: search, acquisition, lock-on and tracking. An additional feature is the provision for slaving of missile radar and infra-red guidance systems to the aircraft radar. A two-bar scanner search pattern is used in the elevation plane for the UAP 13102, and a choice of two- or four-bar in the UAP 13103.

DEVELOPMENT

The UAP 13 series is largely associated with the requirements of the J35F version of the Draken. The project started in 1959.

STATUS

UAP 13102 and 13103 models are fitted to Swedish Air Force Draken aircraft, the latter variant of radar being the one used with the S71N infra-red search and track set. The UAP 13104 model equips Drakens of the Finnish Air Force.

CONTRACTOR

Ericsson Radio Systems AB, Airborne Electronics Division, 431 26 Mölndal, Sweden.

1964.353

PS-46/A MULTI-MODE AI RADAR

PS-46/A is the multi-mode AI radar fitted to the JA 37 fighter version of the Saab-Scania Viggen. The pre-production models of this radar were described in **1741.353** (*Jane's Weapon Systems*, 1974-75) under their developmental designation, DAX-100/200.

To the general operational requirements of all-weather capability, ability to operate effectively in an ECM environment, and high availability, the PS-46/A specification covers the following particular requirements for air-to-air roles:

(1) capability against high-performance aircraft, transports, and helicopters
(2) all hemisphere coverage
(3) look-down capability

Ericsson PS-46/A multi-mode AI radar installed in Viggen

(4) air-to-ground ranging with (optional) mapping.

In considering the transmitter waveform options to meet the above multi-role requirements, a number of techniques are available.

The air-to-ground requirements can be met by the conventional non-coherent pulsed waveform whereas the air-to-air requirement calls for a more sophisticated waveform. Waveforms that provide look-down capability are:

HPD: high PRF pulse doppler
MPD: medium PRF pulse doppler
LPD: low PRF pulse doppler

These waveforms are mainly characterised by their pulse repetition frequencies since this parameter is the determining factor on overall performance.

HPD and MPD require an internal radar frequency reference and subsequently coherent transmission, whereas LPD in addition can use a pseudo-coherent transmission (coherent-on-receiver) or a non-coherent transmission resulting in auto-coherent or non-coherent airborne moving target indicator. A careful review of the pros and cons of these waveforms led to the selection of the two waveforms:

(1) low PRF waveform for look-up modes
(2) medium PRF waveform with doppler filters and signal processing to resolve range ambiguities for look-down modes.

The radar is designed as a 'cartridge' fixed to the forward aircraft bulkhead with four bolts. The aircraft systems supply the necessary electric power, cooling air, and hydraulic power for the hydraulic vane motors that drive the two-axis antenna. The radar consists of ten line replaceable units (LRUs) and these are supported or housed in a lightweight frame

which is in itself an LRU. The construction provides for simple removal and replacement of units.

The main design characteristics of the PS-46/A radar are summarised as:

I/J-band
medium PRF pulse doppler operation
coherent transmitter (TWT)
large antenna with low sidelobes
digital signal and data processing
integrated CW target illumination
built-in test.

Target data extraction and smoothing are carried out by Kalman filtering in stabilised Cartesian co-ordinates.

OPERATION

The PS-46/A radar can be configured to provide the following modes of operation:

(1) target search
(2) target acquisition
    (a) automatic using HUD
    (b) semi-automatic using HUD
(3) target tracking
    (a) TWS mode
    (b) continuous track
(4) target illumination
(5) air-to-ground ranging.

Single- and multi-bar scans, wide or narrow, are provided as well as spiral or raster scans for HUD lock-on in dogfights.

STATUS

In production.

CONTRACTOR

Ericsson Radio Systems AB, Airborne Electronics Division, 431 26 Mölndal, Sweden.

4083.353

ERICSSON SLAR

Ericsson SLAR (side-looking airborne radar) is a lightweight system for maritime surveillance and other reconnaissance purposes. It is an I-band equipment and consists of a three metre long antenna pod which is usually mounted underneath the aircraft, with the other electronics carried in standard 19-inch (483 mm) racks in the aircraft cabin. The total

weight of the equipment, including the antenna housed in the pod, is less than 70 kg.

The radar uses a standard TV display, which gives a true real-time presentation of flicker-free images with 64 grey-tone levels. Digital signal processing is used, and digital recording of radar video is possible on the aircraft for further processing on the ground later. The TV images may also be recorded on a standard tape recorder for replay of sequences of interest on

the ground. All images are annotated with alpha-numeric information, including time, position and heading etc. The TV image display gives a rolling map presentation covering either one or both sides of the aircraft, and medium or large ships can readily be detected at ranges of up to 100 km.

DEVELOPMENT

Development was carried out by Ericsson in co-operation with the Swedish Coast Guard.

STATUS
In production and in service with the Swedish Coast
Guard and several other countries.
CONTRACTOR
Ericsson Radio Systems AB, Airborne Electronics
Division, 431 26 Mölndal, Sweden.

*Ericsson SLAR in use aboard a Swedish Coast Guard
Cessna 337 engaged on maritime surveillance*

5684.353
ERICSSON JAS-39 AIRBORNE RADARS
In addition to the various airborne radars described
under separate entries in this section, Ericsson is
engaged in other development programmes. Two of
these are described briefly below.

JAS-39 Gripen radar
The JAS-39 Gripen is the replacement aircraft for the
Viggen. Prototypes are due to fly in 1987 and the
aircraft is scheduled to enter operational service in
the early 1990s. Ericsson is currently engaged in the
development of an advanced multi-mode, pulse
doppler radar for this aircaft. The system uses the
planar array antenna and employs FM pulse
compression for long-range detection. Ferranti of UK
is a nominated sub-contractor and has recently been
awarded a contract for the antenna pedestal and for

participation in design and development of the signal
processor. In the air-to-air role the new radar will
perform long-range search and multi-target TWS,
short range wide-angle quick scan, and missile and
gunfire control. The air-to-ground functions are sea
and ground target search, ground mapping and
missile fire control.

AEW radar
Ericsson, in co-operation with the Swedish Air Force,
is studying a new air defence, pod-mounted early
warning radar which could be carried under combat
aircraft, including the new JAS-39. No details are
available but synthetic aperture techniques are
believed to be the probable basis. The pod would
probably carry the complete radar and signal
processor, plus air-to-ground communications. It is
unlikely that there would be any control function as in
the more sophisticated AEW systems.

Artist's impression of the JAS-39 Gripen radar

CONTRACTOR
Ericsson Radio Systems AB, Airborne Electronics
Division, 431 26 Mölndal, Sweden.

UNION OF SOVIET SOCIALIST REPUBLICS

3311.353
JAY BIRD AIRBORNE RADAR
Jay Bird is the NATO reporting name of the air-to-air
ranging radar fitted in the intake nosecone of the
MiG-19 Fishbed-J multi-role fighter aircraft. It is not
clear if the NATO designation derives from the 'J' of
the aircraft model name, or from the fact that the radar
operates in the J-band, on frequencies between 12·88
and 13·2 GHz according to one source.
Antenna gain has been calculated at about 33 dB

for an approximate diameter of 40 cm. Three PRF
ranges have been quoted: 2042 to 2048 pps; 1592 to
1792 pps; 2716 to 2724 pps; and the provisional
search and tracking ranges are 30 and 20 km,
respectively.
Raster scanning is used for the search mode and
lobe switching for tracking. A transmitter peak power
in the region of 100 kW is assumed.
The Fishbed-J armament is said to include a radar-
homing version of the Atoll air-to-air missile, in which

case a target illuminating radar mode will be required
of the Jay Bird.
The NATO designation, Jay Bird B, applies to an
alternative version which may be the export version
for MiG-19M Fishbed-Js and/or MiG-19SMT
Fishbed-K used by India and Warsaw Pact states,
respectively. Alternatively, this designation may refer
to a version of Jay Bird said to be fitted to the MiG-25
Foxbat in one of its versions.

1475.353
LOOK TWO AIRBORNE RADAR
Look Two is the NATO designation for an I-band
Soviet bombing and navigation radar system. No
mechanical or technical details are available beyond

1253 pps, and 1871 to 1879 pps. Presumably, pulse
length is also varied, changes being made according
to operating mode and height. Fittings are apparently
limited to certain versions of the Yak-28 Brewer twin-
engined aircraft.

the signal characteristics which have been obtained
by 'Western' Elint (electronic intelligence) operations.
These include operating frequencies in the band 9245
to 9508 MHz, with frequency agility capability and
four PRFs: 320 to 336 pps, 619 to 632 pps, 1247 to

1476.353
PUFF BALL AIRBORNE RADAR
Puff Ball is the NATO designation given to an I-band
Soviet search radar which has been stated to equip
the Bison long-range, four-jet reconnaissance
bomber. It is also probably fitted in certain versions of

the Badger and Bear. Its principal function is long-
range surface mapping, and among its uses may be
the direction of air-launched missiles such as
Kangaroo, Kennel, Kelt, and Kipper.
American reports state that Puff Ball has facilities
for providing friendly surface-to-surface missile

batteries with target designation services, and that
this is accomplished by transmitting via a data link the
relative positions of target and missile battery as
presented on the radar PPI display.
Puff Ball PRFs are 414 to 418 and 621 to 628 pps.

1477.353
SCAN FIX AIRBORNE RADAR
Scan Fix is the NATO designation given to the AI
(airborne intercept) radar fitted to MiG-17 and MiG-
19 interceptors. Like those aircraft, the Scan Fix must

be considered obsolescent. Both I-band and E/F-
band versions are believed to have been produced.
The latter equipped the Frescoe series of MiG-17s,
while the MiG-19 Farmer A, C, and D versions were
given I-band models, these being known by the

NATO designation High Fix. American reports
confusingly state that both versions employ fixed
scans. This may mean that there is no antenna
stabilisation, or that the radars may provide only
target ranging and illumination facilities.

1479.353
SCAN ODD AIRBORNE RADAR
Scan Odd is the NATO designation for the AI
(airborne intercept) radar fitted in MiG-19, Farmer B,

Soviet interceptors. It is an I-band set, operating at
frequencies between 9300 and 9400 MHz. This is
apparently a later system than the Scan Fix AI radar,
and is reputed to have an unusually complex scan

pattern. There are differing PRFs for search and
tracking modes of operation.

1480.353
SCAN THREE AIRBORNE RADAR
Scan Three is the NATO designation for the AI (airborne intercept) radar fitted in the Yak-25, Flashlight, Soviet interceptor aircraft. It operates in the same frequency band, I-band between 9300 and 9400 MHz, as the Scan Odd radar (**1479.353**). Three scan patterns for different operational modes have been detected and Scan Three is reported to employ a very high PRF. The Yak-25 was introduced in 1955 and this radar is presumably obsolete.

1478.353
SHORT HORN AIRBORNE RADAR
Short Horn is the NATO designation given to an airborne bombing and navigation radar, which, from the Elint (electronic intelligence) data available, appears to be an example of some of the latest Soviet radar technology. The operating frequency is in the J-band, between 14 and 15 GHz, and there are frequency agility and frequency diversity facilities. There are four PRF/pulse-width combinations for various operational modes: 313 to 316/1 to 1·8, 496 to 504/0·5 to 1·4, 624 to 626/0·4 to 1·3, and 1249 to 1253/0·01 to 0·9 pps/μs. Both circular and sector scans have been recorded.

No information is available on the physical configuration but the parameters above suggest that its uses include air-to-surface vessel and maritime applications. Aircraft type reported to be equipped with Short Horn include the Brewer Yak-28 in its B, C, D and E variants, the Tu-22 Blinder A, C and G models, and the Tu-16 Badger H.

1481.353
SKIP SPIN AIRBORNE RADAR
Skip Spin is the NATO designation for the AI (airborne intercept) radar installed in Su-11, Flagon-A, and Yak-28P, Firebar interceptors. The Soviet designation is understood to be RP11. Introduction took place in the mid-1960s. The operating frequency is in the I-band, and estimated transmitter power is in the region of 100 kW, giving a reported range of 40 km. The frequency has been quoted as being between 8690 and 8995 MHz, pulse width about 0·5 μs, and PRF 2700 to 3000 pps.

The Flagon-A and Firebar interceptors generally are armed with Anab air-to-air missiles (**1144.331**), (though the IR homing Atoll air-to-air missile (**1146.331**) is also carried) and therefore Skip Spin can be assumed to provide search and tracking modes for both these weapons, and target illumination for the radar homing version of Anab. The Yak-28P has also been observed with a significantly longer nose radome but the reason for this is not known.

1482.353
SPIN SCAN AIRBORNE RADAR
Spin Scan is the NATO designation given to a series of AI (airborne intercept) radars. The Soviet designation is believed to be R1L, and in the export version (eg, India) the R2L. They operate at I-band frequencies, and have a transmitter power in the 100 kW region.

Soviet aircraft fitted with Spin Scan radars are the D and F models of the MiG-21, Fishbed interceptor, and the Su-9, Fishpot B. In all cases, the radar installation is of the type where it is housed in an aerodynamic pod in the nose air intake of the aircraft. These differ in size, that of the Fishbed D being larger than the Fishbed F version. Spin Scan A/B fitted in Fishbed D and Fishpot B, has two PRFs, 825 to 950 pps for search, and 1750 to 1850 pps for the intercept and tracking modes. A rotating scan pattern is employed.

Another version known to NATO as Spin Scan B is designated by Soviet Forces RP9.

4616.353
SUAWACS AIRBORNE AEW RADAR
A second generation SUAWACS (Soviet Union Airborne Warning and Control System) is currently being developed to follow-on to the TU-126 system illustrated below. Very little is known about the radar other than it will probably be carried in an AWACS version of the IL-76 aircraft (known to NATO as 'Mainstay'), and is coupled with the MiG-25M Foxhound aircraft which has a nose radar able to display and track 20 targets simultaneously. Unconfirmed reports have suggested that the antenna is the conventionally located rotating 'saucer' type.

NOTE: Other Soviet airborne radars will be found listed in the Airborne Radar Table (**1194.354**) in the Analysis Section of this volume. Separate entries have not been made for this equipment as it has not been possible to establish reliable data in sufficient quantity to justify such action. However the tabular references contain the salient information that has been obtained.

Spin Scan AI radar installation in MiG-21 interceptor

Kamov Ka-25 Hormone ASW/maritime helicopter with prominent chin radar for surface search. This may be coded Puff Ball by NATO

Another view of Bee Hind installation in Tu-22 Blinder aircraft

Badger-D maritime/electronic reconnaissance aircraft. Large nose radar installation is probably Puff Ball

Hormone helicopter has relatively large radar for surface vessel and submarine detection

Tu-126 Moss Soviet airborne early warning aircraft

Another view of Badger-D showing Puff Ball nose radar. Bee Hind tail radar. Foremost of three ventral radomes may house Short Horn bombing and navigation radar; the other two have not been identified

Close-up of Bee Hind radar in tail of Badger bomber

UNITED KINGDOM

1785.353
FOXHUNTER AIRBORNE INTERCEPTION RADAR
The Foxhunter airborne interception radar was first publicised in early 1974 when Marconi Avionics was awarded a major development contract for the AI (airborne intercept) radar of the RAF air defence version of the Tornado. The Electronic Systems Department of Ferranti is the major sub-contractor. The Foxhunter system made its first flight in a Tornado in June 1981 after extensive proving trials in other types of aircraft.

The design of this AI radar provides a multi-mode system compatible with the size and weight limits of the RAF air defence variants of Tornado and the operational requirements of the next two decades. A substantial part of the signal processing is performed digitally, in addition to digital radar data handling. The equipment anticipates trends in offensive tactics such as low-level penetration, use of ECM, etc, and has the flexibility to operate as part of ground or AEW based control environments while retaining the ability to operate autonomously.

Foxhunter is designed to detect and track subsonic and supersonic targets at ranges in excess of 100 nautical miles at both low and high level. Although it is intended to form part of an overall air defence system, ie in a ground or AEW control environment, the

equipment has been designed to operate independently since either or both of the former may be nullified or degraded by enemy action. In normal circumstances, however, Foxhunter will be integrated within the overall UK air defence system, unified by the JTIDS – ECM resistant data link fitted in the Tornado ADV aircraft.

Foxhunter operates in I-band (3 cm) using a pulse-doppler technique known as frequency modulated interrupted continuous wave (FMICW). At the heart of the radar is a master timing and synchronising unit, employing phase-locked loop techniques, which generates the complex transmission waveforms for amplification by the transmitter, and the accurately related reference signals and sets of precise timing pulses employed within the receiver and signal processing circuits.

High performance microwave integrated circuits are used in the receivers giving benefits in size and weight. Compact and lightweight surface acoustic wave devices, developed by Marconi, provide signal waveforms for the pulse compression modes of the radar. The antenna uses the 'Elliott' twist-reflecting cassegrain principle which combines rigidity and light weight with extremely low levels of spurious radiation lobes, a key feature in the rejection of ground clutter and jamming signals. This type of

antenna has been developed to a very advanced level of performance. The scanner, built by Ferranti, employs a hydraulic drive mechanism and very high grade servos to achieve the speed and precision of beam pointing and stabilisation demanded while the aircraft is manoeuvring under conditions of high *g* and rapid rates of roll.

The transmitter, which is also the responsibility of Ferranti, has been designed with the flexibility to provide the optimum form of transmission for the wide variety of operational tasks. The heart of the signal processing system is a signal processor embodying fast Fourier transform techniques of frequency analysis to filter the signal returns into narrow frequency channels enabling target echoes to be segregated from clutter returns and enabling a particularly uniform detection threshold to be achieved against all target velocities. Digital data processing assembles the various output data in format for clearly displaying on the Tornado TV displays.

OPERATION
With the radar in the main FMICW mode, the targets are detected and their tracks stored in the main computer. The radar must be capable of detecting mass raids at long range, whether terrain following over land or sea or approaching at high supersonic speed at high altitude. Once the targets are detected and tracked the threat is assessed. Foxhunter has the ability to track a number of targets while the radar continues to scan for others, so enabling the crew to evaluate the overall situation and carry out attacks in rapid succession. This has an added advantage since, because the radar continues to scan normally, tracked targets will be unaware that they are being analysed and assessed.

The data on each tracked target is produced on the navigator's tactical electronic display which gives an overall view of the entire tactical area. Weapon selection is then made and the attack can be commenced referring to head-up and/or head-down target data. As the attack develops the navigator continues to process target data and to monitor the overall tactical scene. An IFF interrogator is integrated with the radar and correlated returns are displayed, differentiating between hostile and friendly tracks.

Foxhunter also provides target illumination for the Sky Flash medium range air-to-air missiles which have semi-active homing heads and, since heavy jamming is virtually certain, the system incorporates strong ECCM facilities.
STATUS
The first flight of Foxhunter in a Tornado F.2 took place in June 1981 and trials are continuing. Extensive flight trials have also been carried out in a

Foxhunter radar mounted in the nose of a Tornado

Canberra and a specially modified Buccaneer. Proving and evaluation trials in the latter aircraft are continuing in parallel with those in the Tornado.

Pre-production radars have been delivered to BAe Warton and are flying in the second and third prototype Tornado ADV. The system is now in production and will enter service with the RAF, as AI24, during 1984 as an integrated part of the complete Tornado avionics fit and as an important segment of the overall UK air defence environment.

CONTRACTOR
Marconi Avionics Ltd, Elstree Way, Borehamwood, Hertfordshire WD6 1RX, England.

1971.353
UK AEW RADAR
In March 1977 the British Government announced its intention to proceed with development of the Nimrod AEW equipped with the Marconi airborne early warning radar, following the inability of NATO nations to agree a satisfactory basis for the establishment of a NATO AEW force. The Nimrod AEW radar installation comprises a pair of scanners mounted fore and aft in protective radomes. The general arrangement of this and the crew stations is shown in the illustration.

At the centre of the AEW system is a digital data handling system (DHS), accepting data from the two radar scanners and their associated receiver and integrated IFF systems, and from the ESM equipment. Other inputs are navigation data and information received via tactical data links. Within the DHS, the data from all sensors is analysed to provide automatic initiation and tracking of targets, and the association of tracks from radar, IFF and surface based systems. All these provide a picture in the computer store which will be displayed and monitored by the operators. Other outputs are control signals to the radar and ESM systems and tactical data via the data link(s). Other communications include UHF, VHF, and HF radio with a secure voice link facility in addition to the secure digital data link(s).

The pulse doppler radar system operates at E/F-band frequencies with pulsing of the transmission enabling range measurement while doppler filtering is used for MTI and clutter rejection purposes. The receiver analyses groups of return pulses to detect any doppler shift. At any instant the returning pulse corresponds to a narrow cross-section of the radar beam at a particular range. Areas not at this range return no simultaneous signals. In this way small moving targets can be resolved from strong stationary ground returns. A maritime detection and surveillance capability is also provided and this may be interleaved with the airborne detection mode to provide a combined air and surface surveillance capability. The radar PRF can be varied, as presumably can the pulse width, to maximise detection in different terrain conditions or sea states. The radar passes to the DHS target plots comprising range, bearing, radial velocity, and height. Highly sophisticated ECCM provisions are stated to be incorporated.

The radar antennas have been specially designed to minimise sidelobes, and are of identical shape. Mounted in the nose and tail of the aircraft their respective 180° azimuth scans are synchronised. The antennas are automatically roll and pitch stabilised by a pair of gyro platforms which compensate for structural flexing, and overcome the cyclic error present in other systems. A new airborne IFF interrogator has been designed and developed by Cossor Electronics for AEW Nimrod, under the codename Jubilee Guardsman. The IFF interrogator uses the same antennas as the primary radar to aid correlation of returns.

Internal layout of AEW Nimrod equipment and crew positions. There is a flight crew of four and a tactical crew of six operators

OPERATION
Operation of the AEW Nimrod requires a tactical crew of six and a flight crew of four. The navigator is primarily a member of the flight crew but also supports the tactical crew and is located in that part of the aircraft. The specialist AEW team consists of a tactical air control officer who directs the mission and five air direction officers responsible for track monitoring and reporting and fighter direction as required; one of these acts also as communications control officer and one as ESM officer for the identification and correlation of ESM intercepts. The flight positions for the tactical controller and air direction officers are identical in layout and facilities allowing maximum interchange of roles to meet changing circumstances. The communications and ESM consoles carry additional equipment for their specific functions but have standard multi-function keyboards enabling the operators to have access to the DHS. All positions have access to internal and external communications networks, overall control residing with the communications control officer.

The operators interface with the system through their multi-function display consoles. Each has a tactical situation CRT display to show the tracks selected by the operator, and there is also a tabular display for the selective presentation of detailed track control information. Operator control of the DHS is by tracker-ball and keyboards. Much of the data control is entirely automatic and the following functions require no operator action.
(1) track initiation
(2) tracking
(3) association of radar, IFF and ESM
(4) data storage

Operator functions include:
(1) system control
(2) track classification
(3) fighter control
(4) data link management.
STATUS
Roll-out of the first development aircraft, a modified Comet, carrying a full radar system took place in March 1977. Flight trials began later the same year and have since been successfully completed. Three further Nimrod AEW development aircraft, two having complete nose and tail antennas and equipped with full ECM and ESM facilities, have been built. The first of those aircraft dedicated to aerodynamic trials made its initial flight in July 1980 and was publicly exhibited at the Farnborough Air Show in that year. In addition, a Nimrod equipped with a full communications system was flight-tested throughout 1980 with reportedly highly successful results. The first complete mission system avionics was formally switched on by Controller Aircraft, Air Chief Marshal Sir Douglas Lowe in July 1980 and this equipment is now installed in the development batch aircraft. Trials for RAF training release took place during 1983 as scheduled. The UK force of 11 Nimrod AEW, together with the other new major elements of Tornado ADV and the Improved Ground Environment (UKADGE), will provide a greatly enhanced UK air defence system from the mid-1980s onwards. In addition the UK Nimrod AEW force will form the British contribution to the NATO AEW mixed force and will be inter-operable with the E3 AWACS.
CONTRACTOR
Marconi Avionics Ltd, Elstree Way, Borehamwood, Hertfordshire WD6 1RX, England.

4614.353
SKY GUARDIAN AEW RADAR
Sky Guardian is the name of a family of AEW radars being developed by Marconi Avionics. The systems are based on the comprehensive range of equipments designed for the RAF's Nimrod AEW aircraft (**1971.353**) and are for fitment to a variety of maritime and AEW aircraft to customer requirement. Layout designs for various types of aircraft and configurations are in existence, based on the company's expertise in system integration and preparation of software for Nimrod.

STATUS
Early design.
CONTRACTOR
Marconi Avionics Ltd, Elstree Way, Borehamwood, Hertfordshire WD6 1RX, England.

1740.353
SEARCHWATER SURVEILLANCE RADAR
(ARI 5980)
Searchwater is the commercial name for the long range maritime surveillance radar which, under the designation of ARI 5980, entered service in 1979 as standard equipment on the Nimrod MR Mk 2 aircraft of the Royal Air Force. During 1982 a slightly modified version of Searchwater was fitted to two Sea King helicopters for AEW use, and is being retrofitted to a number of other Sea Kings.

Claimed as the most advanced deployed maritime patrol radar in the Western world, the performance of Searchwater in terms of detection, information extraction, ergonomics and aircraft compatibility has been achieved by several features:
(1) a frequency-agile radar which uses pulse compression techniques and a pitch and roll stabilised scanning antenna with controllable tilt and automatic sector scan. IFF systems are included for the interrogation of surface vessels and helicopters
(2) a signal processing system which enhances the detection of surface targets (including periscopes) in high sea states at long ranges. Plan corrected presentation and classification of targets and transponder returns are eased by an

integrating scan converter. The single radar observer is presented with a selection of bright flicker-free TV-type PPI, B-scope and A-scope displays in a variety of interactive operating modes. Weather radar and navigation facilities are provided within the system

(3) a real-time digital computer which continuously and automatically tracks, stores and analyses classification data on a multiplicity of targets at the same time. Built-in test equipment provides automatic detection and diagnosis of faults

(4) a compact heat extraction system for the radar transmitter, based on the use of fluorocarbon PP3.

These facilities enable patrol aircraft to operate effectively in a 'stand-off' mode out to ranges beyond the surface horizon and avoids the need to overfly the target for visual confirmation. They also provide 'over-the-horizon' targetting data for anti-ship weapons such as Harpoon, Sea Eagle, etc.

All units are designed on a modular basis, with the interface and mechanical construction optimised for ease of fault-location and replacement. Major units are designed to be functionally self-contained as far as possible with a minimum of inter-connections to

A RN Sea King helicopter fitted with the AEW version of Searchwater radar

Radar operator at the Searchwater display console during flying trials with the Nimrod Mk 2 aircraft

other parts of the system. Extensive use is made of hybrid and integrated circuit micro-electronic techniques.

The radar system and its services consist of separate line-replaceable units, most of which contain built-in test equipment which is connected to a central processing and display unit at the operator's position. The radar is controlled by a single operator using separate control panels arranged around the display screen.

The transmitter uses solid-state frequency generators and mixers, followed by two cascaded TWTs. A fluorocarbon liquid cooling system is used.

The scanner, which transmits and receives both radar and IFF signals, uses a reflector of lightweight construction based upon resin-bonded carbon-fibre techniques. Control of the pitch, roll and azimuth axes is effected by hydraulic servo mechanism. Surface acoustic wave technology is employed in the pulse compression system.

DEVELOPMENT

The entire Nimrod fleet is due to complete conversion by the mid-1980s. Further improvements in Searchwater performance are being developed to

counter increasing threats in the maritime scenario. The US Navy has also finished a series of operational trials with Searchwater fitted in a P-3B Orion maritime surveillance aircraft for possible retrofit into a number of these aircraft for long range target surveillance.

As a result of lessons learned during the Falklands campaign in 1982, Searchwater has been fitted to two Sea King helicopters for trials as an AEW system. These trials have proved successful and the RN will operate a flight of three Sea Kings, fitted with Searchwater, on each of its carriers. The equipment is housed in a retractable dome and only minor hardware changes were necessary for its adoption into this new role.

STATUS

In service. Thorn EMI announced at the 1983 Paris Air Show that contracts totalling £35 million had been placed by the UK MoD for Searchwater radars. These contracts cover both the standard reconnaissance radar and the AEW version. Deliveries of the AEW version began in mid-1984.

CONTRACTOR

Thorn EMI Electronics Ltd, Radar Division, Dawley Road, Hayes, Middlesex UB3 1HN, England.

3310.353
ARI 5983 AIRCRAFT TRANSPONDER

The ARI 5983 transponder is used in RN helicopters operating beyond visual range of their parent or co-operating ships to provide a means of enabling interrogation by normal primary radars aboard the ships. This provides navigational assistance, enhances ship's radar range performance and gives an identification facility in the course of patrol, ASW, and sonar operations involving ships and helicopters.

The equipment operates at frequencies in the I-band and consists of two units, transponder and control unit. These operate in conjunction with two antennas mounted on the exterior of the helicopter.

The transponder receives interrogating signals, via the antenna, from pulse radars at any frequency in two bands, 100 MHz wide. On the receipt of such interrogation the transponder will transmit a reply at a

closely controlled fixed frequency in the same region. This will be either a single RF pulse, which provides enhancement of the radar return, or a coded group of up to six pulses which provide identification. Sixteen different reply codes are available. These facilities may be selected by the operator at the transponder control unit.

Reception and transmission can take place via either of two antennas, the required antenna being selected by means of an RF switch in the transponder which in turn is controlled from the control unit. Another switch causes a reduction of the transmitted power of approximately 11 dB. The equipment is arranged so that it will be suppressed during the operation of other 3 cm equipment in the aircraft. Similarly, a suppression pulse is fed to other 3 cm equipments when the transponder is replying.

Each transponder can transmit a choice of

differently coded replies, selected by the operator simply setting a switch on the operator's control unit. A self-test generates an interrogate signal which is fed into the system input and if the transponder is functioning correctly a green acceptance lamp is illuminated.

The same basic transponder design can have several forms. For example, the system can be designed so that it requires double or multiple pulse interrogation to provide a reply selectively where there are many interrogating radars (such as in a harbour or other busy area). Where there are few radar-bearing vessels, a single pulse is usually sufficient.

CHARACTERISTICS

Transponder: I-band
Receiver frequency: 2 bands, centre $F_1 \pm 85$ MHz
Bandwidth: ±50 MHz
Sensitivity: –93 dBW sufficient to trigger reply
Transmitter frequency: $F_2 \pm 7$ MHz
Output power: 135 W minimum to 300 W max peak
Pulse duration: $0.4 \mu s \pm 0.1 \mu s$
Reply code: 6-pulse code, 16 settings, single-pulse reply capability
Pulse spacing: $2.9 \mu s$ nominal
Duty cycle: 0.005 max
Weight: 2.5 kg

STATUS

In production for the RN. Fittings include current types such as the Lynx and the Sea Harrier. Ten sets have been supplied to the Royal Marine helicopter squadron, the system was also fitted in RAF Harriers for the Falklands campaign.

See also transponder reply receiver RRB (**3487.253**) in the Naval Radar section of this volume.

CONTRACTOR

Microwave Associates Ltd, Dunstable, Bedfordshire LU5 4SX, England.

ARI 5983 I-band transponder and control unit

3695.353
IFF 2720 AIRBORNE TRANSPONDER

The Cossor IFF 2720 is a general-purpose secondary surveillance radar transponder which is now in service with all types of aircraft from helicopters to interceptors. The equipment is housed within a ⅜ ATR case size and provides 4096 reply code capability on all modes 1, 2, 3/A, B, and with 2048 codes on mode C. The basic equipment operates, without the need for cooling air or pressurisation, up to an altitude of over 15 000 m. For operation above this altitude a pressurised version is available.

The complete equipment consists of the type 2720 transponder with an IFF 2743 control unit. Single or dual antenna installations can be provided, in the latter case an automatic antenna switch is available. Electronic warfare provisions include resistance to CW, MCW, and pulse jamming, sidelobe rate limiting, short pulse and spurious interference protection, single pulse rejection and long pulse discrimination.

CHARACTERISTICS
Transmitter frequency: 1090 MHz
Transmitter power: 27 dBW (500 W)
Receiver frequency: 1030 MHz
Sensitivity: -76 dBm
Dynamic range: ⩾50 dB
Sidelobe suppression: 3 pulse
Low sensitivity reduction: 14 dBm
Dimensions: 90 × 194 × 314 mm
Weight: 4·6 kg
IFF 2723 control unit: 146 × 95 × 76 mm; 0·91 kg
IFF 2733 control unit: 146 × 57 × 114 mm; 0·56 kg
STATUS
In quantity production and in service with British and other air forces. Nearly 1000 sets have been delivered.
CONTRACTOR
Cossor Electronics Ltd, The Pinnacles, Harlow, Essex CM19 5BB, England.

IFF 2720 airborne transponder showing internal accessibility

5603.353
IFF 2743 ELECTRONIC CONTROL UNIT

The Cossor IFF 2743 is a microprocessor-based digital controller used with IFF 2720 and other transponders. In a panel height of 95 mm, full 4096 code selection on modes 1, 2, 3/A and 3/B, together with height encoding, enables emergency and identification. Position selection facilities are available. Code readout is by means of large easy-to-read LED displays. LED dimming is microprocessor controlled and is provided by a flick switch. Code selection is by flick switches, which offer many advantages over older thumbwheel switches.
STATUS
In production for many customers.
CONTRACTOR
Cossor Electronics Ltd, The Pinnacles, Harlow, Essex CM19 5BB, England.

Cossor IFF 2743 control unit

3696.353
IFF 3100 AIRBORNE TRANSPONDER

The Cossor IFF 3100 transponder was designed initially as a compact single unit for cockpit mounting in the Tornado multi-role combat aircraft. Full 4096 code capability on modes 1, 2, 3/A, and B and 2048 codes on mode C are provided together with space for future expansion. Other features of this equipment include ECM/interference protection measures such as long pulse limitation, short pulse rejection, single pulse rejection, and echo suppression.

A two-unit version, known as IFF 3100B, has now been developed. This equipment is basically similar to the IFF 3100 but has been designed specifically to meet the needs of aircraft requiring a non-cockpit mounted transponder for use with conventional IFF control units.

CHARACTERISTICS
Transmitter frequency: 1090 MHz
Transmitter power output: 27 dBW
Receiver frequency: 1030 MHz
Sensitivity: ⩾-76 dBm
Dynamic range: ⩾50 dB
Sidelobe suppression: 3 pulse; rate limiting provided
Dimensions: 146 × 132 × 165 mm
Weight: 5·3 kg (max)
STATUS
In production for the Tornado IDS and F2 aircraft. The IFF 3100B has been selected for the BAe P110, forerunner of the Agile Combat Aircraft.
CONTRACTOR
Cossor Electronics Ltd, The Pinnacles, Harlow, Essex CM19 5BB, England.

Cossor IFF 3100 transponder for RAF Tornado

3697.353
IFF 3500 AIRBORNE INTERROGATOR

The Cossor IFF 3500 airborne interrogator has been designed for use in any type of aircraft, including high-performance interceptors and helicopters. It has also been specified by the UK MoD for use in the AEW Nimrod aircraft, (**1971.353**). It is regarded as having

Cossor IFF 3500 airborne interrogator designed for use in any class of aircraft and being produced for Tornado (ADV), Phantom and AEW Nimrod for the RAF

previously been impossible to achieve a narrow beamwidth for airborne IFF systems, but in this equipment Cossor claims to have solved the problem. The company says that techniques have been developed that yield extremely high resolution, even when operating within small radomes. Collaboration with radar manufacturers and aircraft constructors ensures that the system achieves the required performance.

Within a 1 ATR case size, the IFF 3500 contains a transmitter, logarithmic receivers, encoder, decoder, defruiter and improved video processing. Automatic code changing is provided to reduce pilot workload, to eliminate incorrect code selection and to improve the security of the IFF Mk 10A system. The automatic code change units are suitable for use, not only with interrogators but also with transponders. Coding information in either serial or parallel format ensures commonality with all in-service transponders.

Special video processing circuits in IFF 3500 provide an indication if incoming signals are garbled, and echo suppression and multipath suppression circuits reduce the effects of reflections from ground and sea surfaces.

After extensive studies, Cossor rejected such previously used methods known as receiver sidelobe suppression, centre beam marking, sliding window

techniques, and others as unsuitable to achieve high bearing resolution. The transmitter employs P2 emphasis to provide antenna beam sharpening. P1 and P3 are transmitted on the antenna sum channel and P2 on the difference channel, and 6 dB of emphasis is available, variable in steps of 3 dB.
CHARACTERISTICS
Transmitter frequency: 1030 ± 0·75 MHz
Power output: P1, P3: 30·5 dBW
P2: 36 +3 -0 dBW selectable -3 and -6 dBW
Receiver frequency: 1090 ± 1·5 MHz
Sensitivity: -80·5 dBm
Dynamic range: 60 dB
Weight: No more than 15·9 kg
STATUS
In production for the UK AEW Nimrod, Phantom and Tornado (ADV) aircraft. Deliveries to the RAF are in progress. In August 1983, Cossor announced a £2·5 million order for a variant, known as IFF 3570, for Sea King AEW helicopters, designed for integration with Searchwater radar. The IFF 3500 has also been selected for the BAe P110, the forerunner of the Agile Combat Aircraft.
CONTRACTOR
Cossor Electronics Ltd, The Pinnacles, Harlow, Essex CM19 5BB, England.

4341.353
MAREC II MARITIME RECONNAISSANCE RADAR

The MAREC II (maritime reconnaissance radar) is based on MEL's helicopter systems. Suitable for both fixed-wing aircraft and helicopters it provides a large true-motion plotting table display with 360° azimuth cover out to a range of 250 nautical miles and a pilot's display. As well as general surveillance, operational roles include:
(1) search and rescue
(2) fishery and oil field patrol
(3) ASV
(4) ASW
(5) weapons control.

CHARACTERISTICS
Scan cover: 360° and sector steerable scanning
Plotting table display ranges: 17 – 219 nm
Plotting table: 43 × 43 cm
Pilot's indicator ranges: 10 – 250 nm
Frequency: I-band, 9345 MHz
Power output: 80 kW

Pulse widths: 0·4 and 2·5 μs
PRF: 200 and 400 Hz
Antenna gain: 33·7 dB
Receiver noise factor: 7 dB

The plotting table display is a development of the ARI 5991 display. Information is presented in three modes, all of which are north stabilised. Centre PPI, ground stabilised or true motion PPI, and ground stabilised with offset. Range and bearing markers are provided for data transfer for weapons control etc. Transparent overlay maps build up a complete record of a sortie with position and movement of targets. The position and track-made-good of the parent aircraft can be displayed even with the radar transmitter OFF. A roller-ball controlled marker gives target range and bearing measurements on LED readouts.

Anti-clutter facilities include a logarithmic receiver, STC and FTC. A colour pilot's display can be provided as a repeat of the main plotting table display or as a weather radar. This display has independent range selection. Built-in test facilities are incorporated.

MAREC II has been selected for various aircraft including the BAe HS748 Coastguarder maritime reconnaissance aircraft. This provides a full 360° scan together with sector scanning which is steerable to any heading and may be controlled in sector width from about 60 to 120°.

The MAREC II system is also included in the proposed BAe HS125 Protector where the antenna is mounted in the droop nose, giving 240° scan coverage.

On the Dornier Do-128-6 the installation design locates the antenna beneath the fuselage to provide full 360° scanning. MAREC II is also suitable for the new Do-228 series of Dornier aircraft and all other makes of patrol aircraft.

CONTRACTOR

MEL, Manor Royal, Crawley, Sussex RH10 2PZ, England.

Dornier Do-128-6 used for coastal surveillance, note MAREC radome beneath fuselage

---

5614.353

ASR 360 AIRBORNE SURVEILLANCE RADAR

The ASR 360 is an X-band radar designed for maritime surveillance in small to medium size low performance fixed-wing aircraft and medium size helicopters. It is based on the Racal standard range of solid-state marine radars which are currently in service with many naval forces and merchant ships throughout the world. The system has now been adapted for airborne use and consists of three main units: antenna and gear box, transmitter/receiver, true motion display.

The antenna unit consists of the antenna itself, which is a centre fed slotted waveguide radiator with an aperture of 30 inches (76 cm), and the necessary gearing and drive. The antenna rotates at 23 rpm around a coaxial feed which runs concentrically through the main gear wheel, and is coupled into the waveguide between the magnetron and the transmitter/receiver. The radiation pattern at the 3 dB (half-power) points has a beamwidth of 3° in the

horizontal plane, and 27° in the vertical plane for a stable picture under pitch and roll conditions.

The transmitter/receiver unit contains the 25 kW transmitter, duplexer and receiver, together with the power supply and the processing circuits. The transmitter consists of a trigger-controlled thyristor modulator driving a magnetron which produces the short bursts of RF energy. The PRF and the pulse lengths are controlled from the display unit.

The true motion display provides a bright, clear, high-definition picture based on the Clearscan video processing system to give high resolution for small targets to be detected against rain and sea clutter. Eight range scales are provided with range rings at fixed intervals; all of these, with the exception of the longest range scale, can be off-centred.

CHARACTERISTICS

Antenna

Type: Centre-fed slotted waveguide contained in fibreglass radome

Aperture: 760 mm

Rotation speed: 23 rpm
Polarisation: Horizontal
Beamwidth: 3° horizontal; 27° vertical
Transmitter
Peak power: 25 kW nominal
Pulse lengths: 0·05, 0·25, 1 μs
Display
Minimum range: 23 m on 10 m² targets
Discrimination: 9 m on the 0·5 nm scale with 10 m² targets
Range scales: 8 ranges covering 0·5 to 95 nm
STATUS
ASR 360 has been sold to the Sultanate of Oman for installation in Short Skyvan aircraft.
CONTRACTOR
Racal Avionics Ltd, Burlington House, Burlington Road, New Malden, Surrey KT3 4NW, England.

3710.353

ARI 5991 SEA SEARCHER AIRBORNE RADAR

Sea Searcher ARI 5991 is an airborne radar with primary and secondary radar capability for ASV, ASW, SAR, and other maritime roles. While it was designed for updating RN Sea King helicopters, it is also applicable to other helicopters and fixed-wing aircraft.

The ARI 5991 is a high-power I-band (3 cm) system with selectable pulse widths, 360° scanning and sector scan, plus a multiple TWS facility and digital readout plot extraction. The indicator is a large 43 cm diameter plotting table, with a stabilised true-motion tactical display. It provides presentation of raw radar data, secondary radar and numerous markers, and generates and displays multiple tactical symbols in response to digital position and identification information from a computer store. Optional features include: I-band IFF compatibility; pilot's repeater display; a weather radar mode of operation.

The Sea Searcher antenna is constructed from metal giving a price claimed to be one-tenth of an equivalent unit in carbon-fibre for a weight penalty of only 2 kg. The antenna scans through 360° with an elevation coverage of ±10°. It is available in 24, 36 or 42 inch (610, 914 or 1067 mm) sizes, and can be operated either upright or inverted. The largest version has been selected for the Sea King and will be

mounted on top of the fuselage. The antenna can be set to cover a desired sector so that a search can be concentrated in that sector while maintaining radar silence over the remainder.

Among the operational features of the Sea Searcher are the following: direct plotting tactical display; rolling-ball target designation marker; target designation interface with ASM systems, via voice or data link; I-band beacon/transponder capability; and raw radar and synthetic data display. The built-in test equipment is operable in flight, in radar silence if necessary.

In operation the rolling ball is used to set the grid datum initially or to change it in flight and for correction of any accumulated dead-reckoning errors. The navigation data is continuously updated despite changes of radar mode. The tracking processor unit provides automatic plot extraction on two targets simultaneously and maintains an output of their positions on LED readouts. Other LED displays give radar contact position, rolling ball marker position and offset distances. Any of this data can be supplied to on-board weapon systems. The two-target TWS facility allows both a missile in flight and its target to be tracked, enabling mid-course guidance to be transmitted to the weapon.

Effective range of the Sea Searcher will be

Display and control section of the MEL Sea Searcher ARI 5991 which is destined to equip RN Sea King helicopters

approximately double that of predecessor equipments.
STATUS
MEL received an initial contract worth £10 million from the UK MoD, for RN Sea Kings, in early 1980. The system is in operational service and deliveries are continuing.
CONTRACTOR
MEL, Manor Royal, Crawley, Sussex RH10 2PZ, England.

5625.353

SUPER SEARCHER AIRBORNE RADAR

Super Searcher airborne radar is a lightweight, high performance I-band system designed specifically for the ultimate C³I facility for single operators in complex multi-threat situations. It is optimised for the maritime surveillance, ASW and ASTT scenario but

high technology signal processing provides also a functional AEW mode.

Antennas are supplied with a standard 42-inch horizontal aperture, with variants between 35 and 48 inches. The antenna can be mounted in either the dorsal or ventral positions on rotary or fixed-wing aircraft. 14-inch colour or monochrome displays are

provided which can be a master/slave configuration or operated singly. They show true motion of centre PPI, and variable sector scan-down to illuminate for missile systems such as Sea Skua.

Super Searcher incorporates three selectable pulses, one of which is stated to be ultra-short providing high definition of small targets in poor weather conditions. Contact recognition is also improved by the use of integrated circuit techniques which clean up the picture. The screen display includes freeze frame and memory storage facilities as well as an MTI. The display operates in either true motion/offset modes or relative motion latitude/ longitude lines, grids, previous mission intelligence, etc. It provides accurate and permanent plotting on 32-plus individually vectored point markers. A TWS capability is integral to the system.

Both primary and secondary radar are available, either separately or combined, providing the operator with an integrated display in real-time. A library of symbols, which can be vectored, is also provided.

STATUS
Super Searcher has been selected by the Indian Navy for its Sea King helicopters. Delivery is scheduled to begin in 1986.

CONTRACTOR
MEL, Manor Royal, Crawley, Sussex RH10 2PZ, England.

Super Searcher airborne radar

4617.353
SKY SEARCHER AIRBORNE AEW RADAR
Sky Searcher is a lightweight airborne early warning radar combined with comprehensive fighter direction capability. The system is designed specifically for maritime aircraft, including helicopters, and is based on the Sea and Super Searcher radars described in **3710.353** and **5625.353**. Commonality with these radars is maintained down to line replaceable units.

The radar provides 360° coverage with selectable scan between 60 and 120°. The configuration allows one man operation during both the search and fighter direction phases for up to three simultaneous intercepts although, should further operators be available the system is capable of providing extra simultaneous intercepts.

STATUS
In development.

CONTRACTOR
MEL, Manor Royal, Crawley, Sussex RH10 2PZ, England.

1032.353
AIRPASS III
Developed between 1957 and 1962, Airpass III (at one stage known as Blue Parrot) was evolved from the highly successful Airpass I radar (**1031.353**) to provide a forward-looking, air-to-surface, attack radar for the BAe Buccaneer aircraft. This radar provides long range search, ground mapping, radar ranging and tracking, terrain warning, and weapon delivery inputs, to give the Buccaneer an all-weather attack/strike capability.

Airpass III uses a two-plane monopulse beam technique, operating in I/J-band. For ground mapping and ranging modes cosecant^2 and pencil beams respectively, can be employed. The system weighs 104 kg, and is mounted in the nose of the aircraft.

Operational functions include: navigation; terrain avoidance; target acquisition; target range and bearing; and weapon delivery profiles, for both conventional and strike attacks over land or sea.

STATUS
Airpass III is still in operational service with the RAF and the South African Air Force. Additional information appeared under this entry number in *Jane's Weapon Systems 1979-80* and earlier editions.

CONTRACTOR
Ferranti plc, Radar Systems Department, Ferry Road, Edinburgh EH5 2XS, Scotland.

1342.353
SEASPRAY HELICOPTER ASV RADAR
Seaspray was specifically developed for, and is fitted to, the RN's Westland Lynx helicopter, in which application it carries the designation ARI 5979. The equipment has been designed to detect and track small high-speed surface craft of the type increasingly used as platforms for anti-shipping missiles. Other possible applications include general maritime surveillance and over-the-horizon targeting.

The system consists of five line replaceable units (LRUs): scanner assembly, transmitter, receiver, processor, and a display and control unit. The system operates at I-band frequencies with a high transmitter power, and employs frequency agility operation. This is employed for reasons of improved detection of targets in sea and weather clutter and ECM conditions, and also improves bearing resolution by reducing the effect of target 'glint'. Built-in test facilities are incorporated.

The scanner LRU is located in a nose radome on the Westland Lynx naval helicopter, and is capable of providing a wide angle search (±90° relative to aircraft heading), or narrow angle search (±30° on selected bearing). The observer is provided with a scan-converted, bright TV-type display unit, on which target range and bearing information are displayed in alpha-numeric form in addition to PPI of radar returns. In addition to the display controls, this unit also carries push-buttons for radar operational mode selection and other functions.

Two new models, designated Mks 2 and 3 are available. The Mk 2 incorporates TWS of multiple targets to permit tracking of these on the observer's display. The processor LRU is replaced to allow TWS processing and a control panel is added. The Mk 3 version incorporates 360° scanning (as well as TWS) for use in the control of the Sea Skua missile (**1530.321**), and can be fitted to a variety of helicopters and fixed-wing aircraft, or to small naval vessels for ship-launched missile control.

OPERATION
Two principal operational modes are provided: search and track, and transponder beacon. In the former mode either wide-angle or limited sector scans may be employed, depending on the phases of the various operations. Either scan might be used for the detection of surface targets while the sector scan would be used for extra performance and to provide a higher data rate prior to target tracking. Four range scales can be selected with automatic switching of the pulse length.

Seaspray naval helicopter radar system

In the tracking phase, the monopulse technique is used in azimuth to provide high angular accuracy.

In the transponder/beacon mode the display of friendly transponder beacons is provided, for tactical purposes and for operations such as station keeping and homing.

STATUS
Seaspray is in full production for the RN and a number of overseas customers. More than 200 sets have been produced to date.

Other countries which are operating, or have ordered Seaspray radars include Argentina, Brazil, Denmark, Federal Republic of Germany and Norway.

CONTRACTOR
Ferranti plc, Radar Systems Department, Ferry Road, Edinburgh EH5 2XS, Scotland.

4615.353
BLUE VIXEN RADAR

Ferranti has been awarded a contract from the UK MoD to develop a new radar system, known as Blue Vixen, for the update programme for Sea Harrier, in conjunction with the fitment of the AMRAAM air-to-air missile, to provide a look-down/shoot-down capability. The design to be developed is a multi-role coherent pulse doppler system which may well be suited to other aircraft in addition to Sea Harrier.

STATUS
Early development. Sea Harriers fitted with AMRAAM are due to be operational by 1988.

CONTRACTOR
Ferranti plc, Radar Systems Department, Ferry Road, Edinburgh EH5 2XS, Scotland.

5612.353
SKYRANGER AIRBORNE RADAR

Skyranger is a new, lightweight airborne weapon control radar developed for light fighter and light attack aircraft and with the retrofit market very much in mind. It consists of three main units: antenna, transmitter/receiver and signal processor/power supply, and since the amount of space available for retrofit programmes can often be limited and irregular in shape, the modularity of Skyranger has been established at printed circuit card level. The individual cards can, therefore, be packaged into housings designed for the space available.

Skyranger accepts discrete digital commands from a cockpit-mounted control panel and provides output data in the form of a digital serial link (ARINC 429) to a HUD and other weapon aiming systems. Range resolution is 150 metres. In the gun mode the equipment has a range of up to 5 km, rising to 15 km in the missile mode. Target relative velocities of from −500 to +1000 metres/second may be handled.

The equipment operates in X-band and has five per cent pulse-to-pulse agility. MTBF is given as 200 hours and the equipment contains built-in test systems. The current version has a fixed antenna but a scanning antenna is planned as an option.

CHARACTERISTICS
Frequency: X-band
Range: 15 km for missiles; 5 km for gun operation
Range resolution: 150 m
Pulse-to-pulse agility: 5%
Power requirements: 27 V DC, <50 W; 115 V 400 Hz single phase, <400 VA
Weight
Antenna: 4 kg
Transmitter/receiver: 25 kg
Signal processor/power supply: 8 kg
Total installed weight: 40 kg

STATUS
In production. No information on orders has been received.

CONTRACTOR
Marconi Avionics Ltd, Elstree Way, Borehamwood, Hertfordshire, England.

1224.353
PTR 820 AIRBORNE IFF

This is a lightweight D-band transmitter/receiver unit, with an associated encoder-decoder and control unit, designed to provide certain aircraft with IFF interrogation facilities in modes 1, 2, 3/A, B, C and D. Interlaced mode operation using any three modes is available. Mode selection is from the control unit, or the modulator can be triggered by an external pulse train. Passive decoding is to customer requirements.

Digital shift registers using silicon integrated circuits are employed in the encode and decode sections, eliminating bulky and temperature-dependent delay lines. Solid-state digital defruiters use pulse-to-pulse validation techniques to ensure reliable operation in the presence of PRF jitter. A modular range store is used which can be matched to SSR range and mode requirements. The PTR 820 includes self-test facilities.

DEVELOPMENT
Development was carried out by Plessey under UK Government contract, and was started in 1967. The first prototype was completed in mid-1969.

STATUS
Nimrod maritime aircraft of RAF Strike Command have been equipped with the PTR 820.

CONTRACTOR
The Plessey Co Ltd, Vicarage Lane, Ilford, Essex IG2 6BB, England.

1972.353
BLUE FOX RADAR

Blue Fox is a lightweight, high-performance, radar designed to fulfil the dual role of airborne interception and air-to-surface search and strike. It has been developed primarily for the RN Sea Harrier V/STOL aircraft in which it forms part of a fully-integrated weapon system.

Blue Fox operates in I-band and uses frequency agility to enhance the radar's immunity to ECM, and improve its ability to detect small targets in bad weather or rough sea states.

For air-to-air interception, Blue Fox can be used for lead-pursuit or chase attacks and incorporates a transponder mode for identifying friendly aircraft or ships.

Using a flat aperture, slotted array antenna stabilised in pitch and roll, Blue Fox fits neatly into the nose of the Sea Harrier. Built on the line replacement unit principle, each component part of the radar (transmitter, receiver, processor, amplifier) can be easily checked or removed for servicing independently.

The radar display provides a bright, digital scan-converted picture, which can be used to display other sensors requiring a TV-type display. Superimposed on the display are the flight symbols showing aircraft attitude, speed, heading etc, so that the pilot can monitor and control the aircraft's manoeuvres while using the radar.

STATUS
Blue Fox is in production for the Sea Harriers of the RN and the Indian Navy. The first aircraft for the latter was delivered in May 1982.

CONTRACTOR
Ferranti plc, Radar Systems Department, Ferry Road, Edinburgh EH5 2XS, Scotland.

Ferranti Blue Fox radar development model for the RN's Sea Harrier. A distinctive feature of the radar is its flat aperture antenna

5685.353
BLUE KESTREL HELICOPTER RADAR

Ferranti is designing and developing a new radar for the Sea King replacement helicopter, the EH-101, for the RN. It is an advanced ASV/ASW system, known as Blue Kestrel, with 360° scan and TWS facilities. No other information is available.

STATUS
Early development.

CONTRACTOR
Ferranti plc, Radar Systems Department, Ferry Road, Edinburgh EH5 2XS, Scotland.

4613.353
CORPS AIRBORNE STAND-OFF RADAR (CASTOR)

The Castor project is a study into the application of airborne radar to long-range battlefield surveillance. It is designed to be operated from a suitable fixed-wing aircraft, probably by the Army Air Corps, to acquire information by flying past the target area at long range. Two solutions are being evaluated; a conventional coherent pulse doppler system, and one using synthetic aperture radar (SAR) techniques. The use of SAR, combined with high power and pulse compression techniques, enables sharply focused images at any range up to the radar horizon. The information gathered will be used for tactical evaluation, as well as other purposes such as direction of RPVs.

When used in the battlefield surveillance role, the short sideways-looking, real antenna of a synthetic aperture radar is flown past the area to be monitored at long range. Radar returns are collected at intervals progressively along the aircraft track and this return data is processed to reconstruct the signals as if they originated from a much longer antenna with consequently much higher resolution. In practice, if in the data collection interval the aircraft has travelled one kilometre then that would be the length of the apparent antenna and the width of its synthetic aperture.

DEVELOPMENT
In April 1984, Ferranti was selected by the UK MoD to carry out an engineering definition study. The Ferranti system uses an advanced coherent pulse doppler radar, based on its Blue Falcon development, mounted in the nose of a specially modified light aircraft. A modified Britten-Norman Islander, fitted with a Ferranti radar was handed over to the UK MoD in May 1984.

Thorn-EMI has been developing SAR techniques since the early 1970s and has been carrying out trials in a Canberra and a Britten-Norman Defender since early 1982. This was privately funded but the company received a £1 million contract from the UK MoD in mid-1983, also to carry out an engineering study and make recommendations.

Engineering studies from both companies were due to be completed by September 1984 and the MoD was scheduled to make a decision by the end of the same year.

UNITED STATES OF AMERICA

1765.353
AN/APG-63 AIRBORNE RADAR

The APG-63 is an advanced multi-mode nose radar installed in the US Air Force F-15 supersonic fighter aircraft. It is a pulse doppler system thought to operate on a number of (selectable) frequencies in the I/J-band. A gridded TWT transmitter is employed, with digital doppler signal processing, and digital mode/data management. These features permit operation over a wide range of PRFs, pulse widths, and processing modes. The I/J-band antenna is a planar array type, carried on a three-axis gimbal system. Mounted on the same gimbal system are three other antennas, a set of dipoles for IFF, a guard horn, and a null-filling antenna. System weight is 224 kg.

Radar information is digitally processed and there are two types of display employed: one is a small CRT located at the upper left-hand corner of the instrument panel and called the vertical situation display (VSD); the other is the HUD. In general, the VSD is employed for the longer-range, initial stages of an interception, while the HUD is for use during actual engagements or close-in encounters.

The VSD presents the pilot with a 'cleaned' synthetic display of computer-processed radar video data, together with alpha-numerics and symbols.

Controls for the APG-63 are located at three positions in the cockpit. The main control panel is on the console on the left side of the pilot. This console also carries the two throttles and key radar operating controls are located on them. The third location for radar controls is the aircraft control stick.

Mounted on the main control panel are switches for power, frequency channel selection, selection of various antenna scan patterns in azimuth and elevation, range, display control, and mode selector switches. The main mode selector has positions for four air-to-air modes, three air-to-ground modes, and 'beacon' for homing and rendezvous use of the radar. A separate selector switch for the SPL mode has OFF, MAN TRK (manual track), SNIFF (passive, open receiver operation), and FLOOD (probably a target illumination mode). A two-position switch provides for manual or automatic mode control. The latter mode is mostly applicable to the air-to-air roles of the APG-63, and this function enables the pilot to operate the radar according to the changing circumstances of an engagement while keeping his hands on the control stick and throttles. Controls on the latter are the antenna elevation adjuster, target designator button, IFF interrogate button, and the weapon selector. The last of these is a three-position switch that enables the pilot to select either medium- or short-range air-to-air missiles (Sparrow or Sidewinder) or guns. Having made his selection, the information displayed on the VSD and HUD is programmed to the appropriate format automatically and radar scan patterns are similarly adjusted automatically to suit the weapon chosen.

Typical alpha-numeric information that can be presented on the VSD are target altitude, ground-speed, heading, range, aspect angle, closure rate, and g-force. Ground-speed and g-force data give valuable indications of the kind of target being tracked. A satisfactory response to an IFF interrogation is indicated by a symbol displayed on the VSD.

An automatic acquisition switch on the aircraft control stick enables the pilot to lock the radar on to targets within the 10 nautical mile range. There are three modes: in the boresight mode, the radar locks on to the first target that enters the aircraft boresight, as designated by the gun reticle on the HUD; the second, called super-search, locks the radar on to the first target that comes within the HUD field of view; the third, vertical scan, locks the radar on to the first target that enters an elevation scan pattern normal to the aircraft's lateral axis.

STATUS

The APG-63 is in production. In February 1978 an APG-63 fitted in an F-15 aircraft was used as a test bed for a study intended to increase the accuracy of aircraft armament by means of on-board radar gun direction. Modifications to the radar software improve accuracy at ranges approaching 1200 metres. New software-controlled programmable signal processors were incorporated in new F-15 APG-63 radars in mid-1980 and retrofitting programmes are being implemented for earlier F-15 aircraft. Features include doppler beam-sharpened ground mapping and the ability to discriminate several close formation targets.

An AN/APG-63 radar, with modifications to incorporate synthetic aperture radar for real-time all-weather high resolution ground mapping and air-to-ground weapons delivery, has been flying in a Hughes/McDonnell Douglas sponsored F-15 advanced fighter capability demonstrator for several years. The modified radar utilises doppler processing to distinguish closely spaced targets within an antenna beamwidth. Aircraft motion provides the doppler spectrum to be processed and the resultant radar picture is synthesised electronically.

Trials of ground mapping have produced results claimed to have a resolution ten times better than that of any previous airborne tactical radar maps. The system produced high resolution ground maps, as if seen from overhead, at ranges in excess of 100 nautical miles and resolution down to 8·5 feet (under three metres).

CONTRACTOR

Hughes Aircraft Company, Radar Systems Group, El Segundo, California 90245, USA.

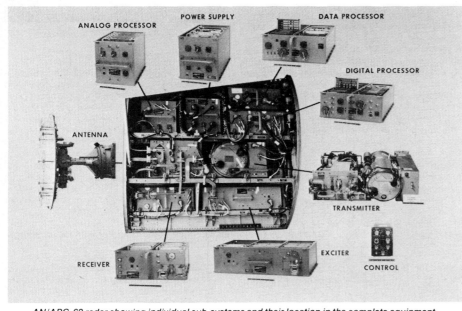

AN/APG-63 radar showing individual sub-systems and their location in the complete equipment

---

3302.353
AN/APG-65 AIRBORNE RADAR

The APG-65 radar was developed by Hughes for use in the US Navy's F/A-18 Hornet strike fighter aircraft. It is an I/J-band equipment designed as an all-digital, multi-mode system suitable for both air-to-air combat and air-to-ground weapon delivery missions.

It provides radar information for the control of the F/A-18's 20 mm gun, Sparrow and Sidewinder missiles in aerial combat, and a full range of conventional and precision guided weapons in the ground attack role.

In its air-to-air role, the APG-65 presents a 'clean-scope', synthetic scan-converted display against airborne targets in all aspects, all altitudes and through all target manoeuvres. It incorporates complete search, track and air combat mode variations.

The radar includes a velocity search mode to provide maximum detection range capability against nose aspect targets; a range-while-search mode to detect all-aspect targets; a TWS mode which, combined with a future autonomous missile such as

AN/APG-65 radar, extended from the nose of an F/A-18 aircraft for inspection at Patuxent River, Maryland, US Naval Air Test Center

AMRAAM, will give the aircraft a launch-and-leave capability; a single target track mode; a gun director mode; and a rapid assessment mode which enables the operator to expand the region centred on a single tracked target, permitting radar separation of closely spaced targets.

Three air combat manoeuvring modes provide automatic target acquisition in various search volumes; the HUD acquisition mode to scan the entire HUD volume and to lock onto the first target located within a specified range; the vertical acquisition mode in which the radar scans vertically in a narrow width volume and automatically acquires the first target found within a specific range; and a boresight acquisition mode to allow the pilot to point the aircraft at the desired target and acquire it automatically. The pilot can step through successive targets until he acquires the one he wants.

Surface attack modes include long range, high resolution surface mapping which, combined with other modes, gives the pilot the ability to detect and track fixed or moving targets on land or sea. The APG-65 radar includes a precision velocity update feature to improve navigational accuracy; a terrain avoidance mode for low-level penetration missions in limited visibility conditions; ground moving target indication/track or fixed target modes which the pilot may select depending on the target tactical situation; air-to-surface ranging; and a sea surface mode which enables the radar to detect ship targets regardless of sea condition.

STATUS

In operational service. The first F/A-18 Hornet squadron was formed at Lemoore Naval Air Station, California on 13 November 1980 to train US Navy and Marine pilots. The first operational squadron to receive the aircraft was at the Marine Corps Air Station, El Toro, California on 7 January 1983. Canada has ordered 137 CF-18 aircraft, and initial deliveries of the AN/APG-65 radars were made in 1982 and are in service. Additional units will be delivered to Canada until 1988. Australia and Spain have also ordered the F/A-18 to serve as their new combat aircraft. Australia has ordered 75 Hornets with delivery commencing in late 1984, and Spain has ordered 72, with an option on 12 more, for delivery beginning in 1986. A $46 million contract was received by Hughes in late 1982 for the production of nine test sets for the AN/APG-65.

CONTRACTOR

Hughes Aircraft Company, Radar Systems Group, El Segundo, California 90245, USA.

3303.353

AN/APG-66 F-16 RADAR

Developed for the US Air Force F-16 multi-role air combat fighter, the F-16 radar is a coherent, I/J-band pulse doppler equipment with low and medium PRFs to permit both look-up and look-down operations. The system comprises six line replaceable units (LRUs): antenna, transmitter, low-power RF unit, digital signal processor, radar computer, and a radar control panel.

The antenna is a slotted-plate planar array on a two-axis gimbal mount, and provides high gain and low sidelobes over all scan angles. An electric drive is used for steering and stabilisation. The entire transmitter is solid-state apart from an air-cooled TWT final output tube. The pilot can select one of four different frequencies, and the transmitter also provides frequency agility for certain air-to-surface modes. The digital signal processor carries out clutter rejection and other radar signal processing.

The radar computer configures the radar system for the various operating modes, directs the signal processor to inject symbols into the video output, performs calculations, routes data to the fire control computer, and interfaces with other aircraft and radar LRUs. It also provides the AIM-9 Sidewinder missile target seeker with a pointing signal.

OPERATION

Air-to-air

In the air-to-air role, the F-16 radar provides all-aspect, all-altitude coverage in four modes of operation.

(1) look-up (up look) for search and tracking above the horizon
(2) look-down (down look) for search and tracking below the horizon

(3) air combat for automatic target acquisition in a dogfight engagement
(4) auto for automatic selection of up look or down look.

The pilot selects the appropriate operating mode and mode parameters by controls on the radar control panel, or the aircraft's fire control computer automatically selects a radar mode appropriate to the tactical situation. In normal operation, up look or down look is automatically selected depending on the radar sensed absence or presence of clutter. Auto-acquisition is always selected manually by a switch on the throttle grip which immediately configures the entire aircraft for a dogfight engagement.

In either up look or down look, the pilot can select antenna scan limits of ±10, ±30, or ±60° about any centre datum within the maximum ±60° scan limits relative to aircraft centre-line. Elevation can be set at one, two, or four bars. Although actual range performance is dependent on search volume and target size, the radar provides range-scale selections of 10, 20, 40, and 80 nautical miles.

Up look is a low-PRF search and tracking mode designed to increase the detection range in a clutter-free environment. Radar operation is the same as in the down look mode except that it provides about 25 per cent greater detection range at medium altitude.

Down look is a medium-PRF pulse doppler search and tracking mode which provides target detection and acquisition in the presence of clutter. In this mode, low-flying aircraft can be distinguished from ground clutter.

For close-in combat, the pilot can initiate an automatic air combat search and tracking mode by pressing the 'Dogfight' switch on the throttle grip. In this mode, the radar scans the HUD field of view

F-16 radar mounted in ground rig

(20 × 20°), automatically acquires the first target it encounters, and then tracks that target. Depending on the geometry of the engagement, the pilot has the option of selecting an alternative search pattern (10 × 40° in elevation) to aid in target acquisition.

When automatic tracking has been initiated, the F-16 radar computer will then provide the AIM-9L Sidewinder missile target seeker with pointing information and will provide the F-16 fire control computer with accurate target data for aircraft envelope calculations. Provisions have been made in the F-16 radar to add, if desired, a missile illuminator signal for the Sparrow (AIM-7) missile.

Air-to-Surface

Eight air-to-surface modes of F-16 radar operation are available:

(1) a real beam mapping mode provides the pilot with an all-weather map of a select ground area ahead of the aircraft. The range scales for the real beam mapping mode are 10, 20, 40 and 80 nautical miles (20, 40, 75 and 150 km)

(2)(3) the pilot can select an expanded real beam map mode for 4:1 expansion of the displayed video centred around the tracking cursors. A doppler beam sharpening mode can be selected for an improvement in the azimuth resolution of the expanded real beam ground map. These mapping modes can be used for navigation fix-taking using recognisable landmarks, for detection and location of ground targets, and for direct and offset weapon delivery

(4) a scan freeze mode can be selected for quasi-silent mapping operation. In this mode, the ground map is frozen on the display while the radar transmitter is in standby. Cursor movement displays aircraft motion relative to the frozen ground map using information from the F-16 inertial navigation system. Periodically a radar scan can be initiated by the pilot to update the ground map

(5) an air-to-ground ranging mode provides real-time measurement to a designated ground point. The command for this mode comes from the F-16 fire control computer which uses the slant range and rate information for accurate surface weapon delivery

(6) the pilot can also select a beacon mode which provides accurate navigation fix-taking and offset weapon delivery relative to a ground beacon. This mode can also be used for rendezvous with aerial tankers

F-16 aircraft with radar receiver and transmitter in lower section for easy accessibility

(7)(8) two sea-surface search modes can be selected by the pilot for detection of ships in a variety of sea states. SEA 1 employs frequency agility techniques to detect stationary and moving ships in conditions up to sea state 4, and in SEA 2 targets can be detected in higher sea states by using a narrow doppler notch filter. This mode can also provide an MTI capability against moving radar-significant ground targets.

Additional radar modes, such as high-resolution synthetic aperture mapping, ground target tracking and terrain following/terrain avoidance, could be added to further increase the radar's existing capability for all-weather strike and reconnaissance.

DEVELOPMENT

General Dynamics Corporation awarded a full-scale development contract to Westinghouse in November 1975. The predecessor to the F-16 radar was the WX-200 model in the WX Series (**1673.353**). A variety of other roles is foreseen.

STATUS

The first full-scale development model was delivered to General Dynamics in June 1977. Peak production is expected to reach betwen 21 and 42 units per month. Co-production contracts have been placed with companies based in European countries procuring the F-16 aircraft. In Belgium, MBLE will build up to 800 radar computers; up to 500 antenna assemblies will be produced in the Netherlands by Signaal; B & W Electronik will manufacture up to 800 radar control panels in Denmark; and Nera of Norway will provide up to 800 radar equipment racks. Total contracts for development and long term production for the improved APG-66 now exceed $150 million. Flight tests of this version of the radar began in late 1981. A designation, AN/APG-68, has been used to describe an uprated version for future derivatives of the F-16 aircraft.

Westinghouse received a $25·2 million US Air Force contract in August 1980 for full scale development of modifications which will enable more effective use of the APG-66 with the Advanced Medium Range Air-to-Air Missile (AMRAAM), and improved ECCM facilities. Deliveries were due to commence in early 1984. This version includes a programmable signal processor and a dual mode transmitter. In January 1982, Westinghouse delivered the 1000th radar system to the US Air Force and in March 1982 the Japanese Air Self-Defence Force selected the AN/APG-66 to replace the AN/APQ-120 in its F-4EJ aircraft. It was announced in January 1982 that the new terrain following and navigation radar for the B-1B bomber, being developed by Westinghouse, would be similar to the AN/APG-66/68. This system, known as AN/APQ-164, is described briefly under entry **4647.353**.

CONTRACTOR

Westinghouse Defense and Electronic Systems Center, Baltimore, Maryland 21203, USA.

5610.353
AN/APG-67 MULTIMODE AIRBORNE RADAR

The AN/APG-67 multimode airborne radar is a coherent X-band pulse doppler system which has been designed for both air-to-air and air-to-surface modes for the F-20 Tigershark aircraft. The system comprises four line replaceable units (LRUs): antenna, transmitter, radar target data processor and a radar data computer containing two central processing units (CPUs).

The antenna is a flat plate slotted array which features low sidelobes and full azimuth and elevation monopulse operation. Scan capability covers ±60° in both azimuth and elevation. Variable sector width scans are selectable and elevation search can be accomplished in either 1, 2 or 4 bar modes. The antenna can be either line-of-sight or rate gyro stabilised. The radar receiver is mounted on the antenna assembly and features a low noise front end which gives additional detection range. The receiver consists of two channels which provide the monopulse sum and multiplexed difference channels (azimuth and elevation).

The transmitter is coherent, containing a TWT operating in X-band, and is programmable providing a high degree of mode flexibility. It operates at low, medium and high PRFs and other features include variable output power and pulse widths.

The radar data computer is the heart of the system and contains two CPUs. One CPU handles radar mode control via the internal radar data bus and interfaces with the F-20 mission computer. This CPU also conducts the built-in-test function to determine operational status without the need for special flight line test equipment. The second CPU performs the radar data processing requirements associated with motion compensation and target tracking, and provides raster scan output of the radar data and symbology to the cockpit display. The radar target data processor receives raw data from the receiver and integrates this to establish firm target reports. To achieve its various capabilities, this unit performs a variety of functions including fast Fourier transformation, MTI, pulse compression, motion compensation, variable waveforms and variable bandwidth operation.

OPERATION

The AN/APG-67 is designed for six main missions: supersonic intercept, combat air patrol and air superiority in the air-to-air mode with interdiction, close air support and sea detection in the air-to-surface mode.

Air-to-air

In the air-to-air role the AN/APG-67 provides all-aspect, all-altitude coverage in three main modes of operation:

(1) search and track in the look-up (up look) (above the horizon)

AN/APG-67 multimode airborne radar installed in an F-20 Tigershark

(2) search and track in the look-down (down look) (below the horizon)

(3) automatic acquisition and tracking for air combat.

The pilot selects the appropriate operating mode and mode parameters by controls on the radar control panel or the fire control computer automatically selects a mode appropriate to the tactical situation. In either look-up or look-down modes the pilot can select antenna scan limits of ±10, ±30 or ±60° and elevation can be set at 1, 2 or 4 bars. Range scales are set at 5, 10, 20, 40 and 80 nautical miles although ranges against a typical fighter are 30 nautical miles in the look-up mode and 22 nautical miles for look-down.

In the air combat mode, the radar scans a 20 × 20° field of view and automatically acquires the target. The pilot can also select an alternative search pattern of 10 × 40° or boresight.

Air-to-surface

Six air-to-surface modes are available:

(1) ground mapping using a real beam mapping mode with azimuth scans of ±10, ±30 or ±60° and range scales of 5, 10, 20, 40 and 80 nautical miles

(2) an expanded map mode using doppler beam sharpening techniques to improve resolution for navigation and/or target location

(3) an air-to-ground ranging mode providing real-time measurement to a designated ground point

(4) a freeze mode whereby the ground map is frozen on the display in a quasi-silent operation, with the transmitter on stand-by. Aircraft movement relative to the map is shown from outside information and the map can be updated periodically by operating a radar scan

(5)(6) two sea surface search modes for surface vessel detection. Sea 1 employs frequency agility techniques to detect stationary and moving targets with a detection range of 35 nautical miles for a 50 m² target in sea state 1. Sea 2 uses a coherent MTI mode with a detection range of 30 nautical miles for the same target in sea state 4.

STATUS

All development and ground testing phases had been completed in November 1982, approximately 18 months after commencing the multimode radar programme. Flight testing on a C-54 aircraft continued until mid-1983 with test flying aboard an F-20 Tigershark later the same year.

CONTRACTOR

General Electric Company, Aircraft Equipment Division, French Road, Utica, New York 13503, USA.

4333.353
TORNADO NOSE RADAR

The nose-mounted radar for the interdictor/strike version of the Tornado aircraft has been developed and manufactured by Texas Instruments under contract to Panavia. The radar is essentially two separate systems which share a common mount, power supply and processor/computer. The two systems are the terrain following radar (TFR) and the ground map radar (GMR). Both systems are designed to operate in severe ECM conditions.

The TFR is an advanced terrain following radar enabling the aircraft to make blind, low-level, high speed terrain following attacks using natural geography masking to avoid radar detection.

The GMR is the primary attack sensor for the Tornado and operates in the air-to-ground and air-to-air modes to provide high resolution mapping for navigation update and target identification, air-to-air fire control and air-to-ground fire control. The system enables the pilot to have accurate fixes that update the navigation system, perform air-to-ground ranging and target tracking for weapon delivery, and air-to-air ranging and tracking for self-defence.

The radar also provides obstacle warning above a zero height clearance plane which is horizontally stabilised. Video signals of all obstacles penetrating this clearance are displayed simultaneously with ground map video. Terrain following can be either automatic or manual.

For air-to-ground attack the GMR automatically acquires, locks-on and tracks designated ground targets. In the air-to-air mode, the radar locks on to designated airborne targets in range and angle for weapon delivery.

Both radars incorporate a high degree of advanced technology and feature broadband frequency agility, monopulse (four-lobe for GMR), wide and narrow antenna scan, fast and slow antenna scan and ECCM features. The system operates in the Ku-band.

STATUS

Currently in production for the Tornado interdictor/strike aircraft being built by Panavia on a tri-national basis for the United Kingdom, West Germany and Italy. In addition to its own production, Texas Instruments has licensed a European manufacturing consortium to produce the radar.

CONTRACTOR

Texas Instruments Inc, PO Box 226015, Dallas, Texas 75266, USA.

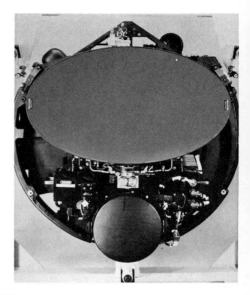

Head-on view of Tornado nose radar installation

1585.353

E-3A (AWACS) RADAR AN/APY-1

The primary radar of the E-3A airborne warning and control system (AWACS) is the Westinghouse AN/APY-1. This radar was specially developed for airborne early warning and control applications and for mounting on a modified Boeing 707-320B airframe. The radar antenna is mounted back-to-back with a complementary IFF/SSR antenna, both of which are contained in a saucer-shaped radome carried above the fuselage of the aircraft. Within the fuselage are radar transmitters, computers, displays and other associated electronics. The radome has a normal rotation rate of six rpm, to give a scan rate of one every ten seconds. Operating frequency of the AN/APY-1 is in the 10 cm wavelength band and there are seven operating modes. On any azimuth scan, the surveillance volume can be divided into as many as 24 sub-sectors, each with its own set of operating modes and conditions. These modes can be accommodated on subsequent scans or re-arranged to vary the type of coverage for any given area of interest, or to accommodate changes in operating conditions. The seven modes are summarised briefly as follows:

(1) pulse doppler non-elevation scan (PDNES): this provides surveillance of aircraft down to the surface using pulse doppler, with narrow doppler filters and a sharp beam, to eliminate ground clutter. Target elevation is not measured

(2) pulse doppler elevation scan (PDES): radar operation in this mode is similar to PDNES, but target elevation is derived by electronic scanning of the beam in the vertical plane

(3) beyond-the-horizon (BTH): the BTH mode uses pulse radar – without doppler – for extended

Two of the multipurpose consoles aboard the US Air Force AWACS aircraft

range surveillance where ground clutter is in the horizon shadow

(4) passive: the radar transmitter can be shut down in selected sub-sectors while the receivers continue to process ECM data. A single strobe line passing through the position of each jamming source is generated on the display console

(5) maritime: this involves use of a very short pulse to decrease the size of the sea clutter patch to enhance the detection of moving or stationary surface ships. An adaptive digital processor adjusts automatically to variations in sea clutter, and blanks land returns by means of computer-stored maps of land areas

(6) test/maintenance: control is delegated to the radar technician for maintenance purposes

(7) standby: radar kept in a warmed operational condition, ready for immediate use. Receivers are shut down.

PDES and BTH can be used simultaneously or alone; either or both can be active or passive, as required. PDNES may be used simultaneously with the maritime mode. Blanking commands in BTH and pulse doppler modes can be used in each of the 24 sub-sectors, thus enabling the maximum potential of the system to be concentrated in those sub-sectors of greatest interest.

The technical functioning of the AN/APY-1 radar and its associated signal processing was described at some length under this entry number in the 1977 edition of *Jane's Weapon Systems* and other details appeared in earlier editions.

Arrangements have been made to reshape the radar pulse in order not to interfere with certain ground radars used in the European network.

There is also a programme called Salty Net designed to enable AWACS to operate with the 412L, NADGE, and other systems. The NATO AWACS will also interface with 407L in the American Tactical Air Control System.

STATUS

AWACS requirements for CONUS air defence depend on the air defence alert condition. In peace time, a total of five AWACS aircraft would be deployed on a rotational basis, one at each of the US Region operations control centres of the Joint Surveillance System (JSS). Four are in the continental USA, and the fifth in Alaska.

The first AWACS aircraft were delivered to the US Air Force in March 1977. The 552nd AWACS Wing at Tinker Air Force Base became operational in the spring of 1978. All 24 aircraft, now designated the E-3A Sentry, have been delivered to the US Air Force.

In December 1978, the NATO Defence Planning Council, made up of the Defence Ministers of the member nations, gave a go-ahead to acquire a fleet of 18 E-3A aircraft for the NATO AEW requirement. This is an $1800 million undertaking. Boeing is the major contractor for the programme.

In addition to the sub-contract team assisting with the E-3A Sentry, a team of West German and Canadian sub-contractors are engaged on the NATO AEW aircraft. These include AEG-Telefunken, Ulm, which co-operates with Westinghouse in the manufacture of the E-3A radar system. First delivery of a NATO system was made on 22 January 1982 and deliveries are due to continue until mid-1985. By mid 1983, Westinghouse had delivered 45 radar systems for USAF and NATO aircraft.

Five E-3A aircraft, also to be fitted with the AN/APY-1 system, have been ordered by the Royal Saudi Air Force, with deliveries due to commence in 1985.

CONTRACTORS

Westinghouse Defense and Electronic Systems Center, Baltimore, Maryland 21203, USA.

Boeing Aerospace Company, PO Box 3999, Seattle, Washington 98124, USA.

E-3A Sentry (AWACS) aircraft take-off showing rotating radome of AN/APY-1 early warning radar

1970.353
APQ-99 RADAR

The AN/APQ-99 is a forward-looking radar developed by Texas Instruments for the RF-4 version of the Phantom aircraft. It is an elevation (two-lobe) monopulse system with ground-mapping and terrain-following capabilities. Operation is at J-band frequencies.

STATUS

The APQ-99 has been supplied to the air arms of the United States, Federal Republic of Germany, Iran, and Japan.

CONTRACTOR

Texas Instruments Inc, PO Box 226015, Dallas, Texas 75222, USA.

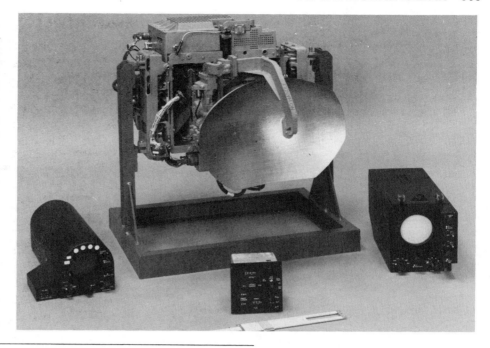

Texas Instruments AN/APQ-99 radar

4340.353
AN/APN-215 AIRBORNE RADAR

The latest in a series of airborne terrain mapping and weather radars, the APN-215 has been developed by Bendix from its successful commercial equipment, the RDR1300. The APN-215 is a digital, full-colour, multi-mode lightweight equipment designed for terrain mapping, surface search and weather information. It is designed specifically for such aircraft as heavy twins, transports, etc and has a range of up to 240 nautical miles.

Weather is shown on the display in three discrete colours and when used with other on-board equipment, pictorial navigation data can be superimposed over the weather map, or over the terrain map when the precision mapping mode is used. The system also enables a pilot-programmable check list display of selected flight data to be used, eg terminal areas, airways, beacons, etc.

The complete system comprises a transmitter/receiver, a 30 cm diameter, fully stabilised antenna and a panel mounted colour display unit.

CHARACTERISTICS

System weight

Receiver/transmitter: 6·8 kg

Antenna: 3·6 kg

Display: 5 kg

Mounts: 1·3 kg

Frequency: 9345 MHz

Power output: 10 kW

Range: 240 nm

STATUS

Fitted in the US Army U-21 and RU-21 aircraft.

CONTRACTOR

Bendix Corporation, Avionics Division, PO Box 9414, Fort Lauderdale, Florida 33310, USA.

1966.353
AN/APQ-113 RADAR

The APQ-113 radar is a multi-mode nose radar system developed in the early 1960s for the F-111A, C, and E aircraft. The radar operates in the J-band frequency range and provides both air-to-ground and air-to-air facilities. In the air-to-ground mode the system is used for navigational position fixing, all-weather weapon delivery, and air-to-ground ranging. The air-to-air mode is compatible with the AIM-9 Sidewinder missile systems and provides automatic range search, target acquisition, and track, while angle tracking in a TWS mode.

The APQ-113 radar is the first of a family of attack radars which includes the AN/APQ-114, the AN/APQ-144, and the B-1 bomber forward-looking radar.

CHARACTERISTICS

Frequency: 16 – 16·4 GHz

Tuning: Frequency agility/manual tuning

PRF: 337/674/2022 pps

Pulse width: 2·4/1·2/0·4 µs

Noise figure: 10 dB

IF: 40 MHz

Scan width: ±10 or ±45°

Scan speeds: 40 or 74°/s

Range scales: 5, 10, 30, 80, 160 nm

Dynamic range: 80 dB

STATUS

In service with the F-111A and F-111E of the US Air Force and the F-111C of the Royal Australian Air Force.

CONTRACTOR

General Electric Company, French Road, Utica, New York 13503, USA.

AN/APQ-113/114 radar installation on the General Dynamics F-111 aircraft

1967.353
AN/APQ-114 RADAR

The AN/APQ-114 is a member of the APQ-113 family (**1966.353**) and was developed in the mid-1960s specifically for use in the FB-111A strategic bomber. In addition to the basic characteristics of the APQ-113, modifications were incorporated to add the following facilities:

(1) a north-oriented display

(2) beacon mode of operation

(3) automatic photo recording.

CONTRACTOR

General Electric Company, French Road, Utica, New York 13503, USA.

1310.353
AN/APQ-120 FIRE CONTROL RADAR

This is the latest in the APQ series of aircraft fire control radars produced by Westinghouse for the various versions of the F-4 Phantom. In 1959/60 the first of this series, the APQ-72, was delivered to the US Navy in the F-4B which remains a fundamental item in the US Fleet's interceptor and tactical aircraft inventory. Participation by the US Air Force in the Phantom aircraft programme from 1962 onwards resulted in three versions of the initial weapons'

control radar – the APQ-100 in the F-4C, APQ-109 in the F-4D, and finally the APQ-120. The various versions which followed the APQ-72 were all the result of advancing performance and air-to-ground operational mode requirements additional to the original air interception functions.

The APQ-120 offers considerable improvements in weight (290 kg), volume, performance, and reliability through the use of solid-state circuitry. It is also designed to operate reliably in close proximity to the nose-gun installation of the F-4E.

STATUS
In production since 1967, nearly 2000 examples of the APQ-120 had been built when production was completed in 1980. It is in the inventory of nine nations. The APQ-120 is now being modified with a new digital computer produced by Westinghouse.
CONTRACTOR
Westinghouse Defense and Electronic Systems Center, Baltimore, Maryland 21203, USA.

1487.353
AN/APQ-122(V) AIRBORNE RADAR

The AN/APQ-122(V) is a dual frequency nose radar developed for use in the US Air Force AWADS (adverse weather aerial delivery system) programme for installation in C-130E transport aircraft. This long range navigation sensor is used for weather avoidance and navigation in supply dropping missions. The equipment provides ground mapping

out to more than 200 nautical miles, weather information up to 150 nautical miles and beacon interrogation up to 240 nautical miles when using the I-band frequency radar. K-band frequencies are used when short range high resolution performance and target location are required. In the K-band role the radar provides a high-resolution ground map display to permit target identification and location for position fixing and aerial delivery missions. In this

situation, the radar detects and displays a target with a radar cross section of 50 m² while operating in a rainfall environment of 4 mm per hour.

In addition to the dual frequency system designed for AWADS (designated APQ-122(V1)), three other configurations have been developed. A single frequency (I-band) radar has been designed under the designation AN/APQ-122(V5) as a direct replacement for the AN/APN-59 radar for use in C-130 and E-4B aircraft. Facilities include long range mapping, weather evaluation and avoidance, and beacon rendezvous. A navigation trainer version of the V5, the AN/APQ-122(V7), has been designed, for use in T-43A aircraft.

Another dual frequency radar, the AN/APQ-122(V8) incorporates a terrain following capabililty in the basic radar for use in C-130 aircraft. In addition to the normal ground mapping, weather information and beacon interrogation modes, this configuration provides terrain following, terrain avoidance and cross-scan. In the terrain following mode the radar supplies commands to fly the aircraft at a fixed distance above the terrain while in the terrain avoidance mode the radar displays all terrain at and above the altitude of the aircraft. The cross-scan mode combines the terrain following and avoidance functions on a time-shared basis. The K-band radar supplies the high resolution map display for target identification and location.

In the terrain following, terrain avoidance and cross-scan modes a smaller circular antenna is connected to the I-band receiver/transmitter. Both antennas are mounted on the forward assembly.
STATUS
The APQ-122(V) is being supplied to the US Air Force as well as Austria, the Philippines, Israel, Egypt, Morocco, Portugal, Ecuador, Bolivia, Zaire, Cameroon, Congo, Denmark, Spain, Nigeria, Greece, Iran, Venezuela, and Saudi Arabia. Installations have been carried out in C-130H, RC-135C, RC-135A, KC-135A, RC-130A, and B747 (AABNCP) aircraft.
CONTRACTOR
Texas Instruments Inc, PO Box 226015, Dallas, Texas 75266, USA.

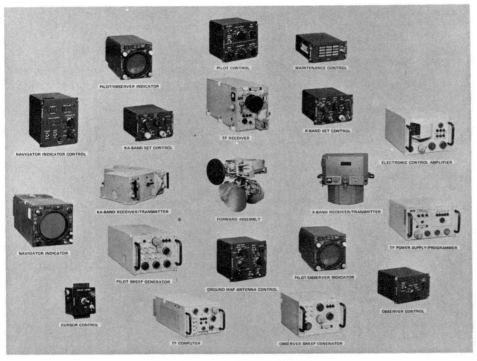

Texas Instruments AN/APQ-122(V)1 radar

1401.353
AN/APQ-137 AIRBORNE RADAR

The APQ-137 is a lightweight K-band high definition radar designed to provide for the detection of ground targets from the air. It has MTI facilities for locating moving targets against background clutter, and the MTI threshold and other parameters can be adjusted during operation.

The APQ-137B is used in pod-mounted form in the US Army SMASH programme (**1400.302**) in which it is used in conjunction with a forward-looking infra-red sensor on board a number of modified AH-1G Huey Cobra helicopters for night operations.

Operating frequency is 34·5 GHz and peak power is 25 kW, giving a maximum range of about 18 km. Pulse-length is 0·25 µs and the PRF is 4000 pps. It is reported to employ an externally coherent doppler technique of signal processing. Detection speed range of the MTI system is 3 to 30 km/h.

Search and target ranging modes of operation are possible, with a cosecant² beam pattern for the former and a pencil beam for the latter. A 40° sector is scanned during search.

A 13 cm diameter direct view storage tube display is provided, with B-scan presentation of data. Three range scale settings are provided.

Emerson AN/APQ-137 radar pods

DEVELOPMENT
Development of the APQ-137 began as a private venture by Emerson Electric, under the designation Motardes which derives from moving target detection system, but was later supported by the US Army.

CONTRACTOR
Emerson Electric Co, Government and Defense Group, 8100 West Florissant Avenue, St Louis, Missouri 63136, USA.

4334.353
AN/APQ-126(V) AIRBORNE NAVIGATION AND ATTACK RADAR

The AN/APQ-126(V) is a forward looking, variable configuration, airborne navigation and attack radar in production for the US Navy A-7E and the US Air Force A-7D aircraft. Operating frequency of the APQ-126(V) is in J-band and its primary functions are ground mapping, air-to-ground ranging and safety of flight (TF/TA). The units of this radar provide the following modes of operation:

(1) ground mapping (GMP/GMS) – pencil-shaped beam
(2) air-to-ground ranging (AGR)
(3) air-to-air boresight ranging
(4) terrain avoidance (TA)
(5) terrain following (TF)
(6) cross-scan terrain following/terrain avoidance (CSTA)
(7) cross-scan terrain following/ground map pencil (CSGMP)
(8) beacon (BCN)
(9) television (TV)
(10) radar homing and warning (RHAW).

The AN/APQ-126(V) also features adverse weather 'look-through' using selectable circular polarisation, slaved antenna pointing in air-to-air ground ranging and variable antenna tilt control which allows the system operator to optimise ground maps displays and highlight targets of interest.
STATUS
The AN/APQ-126(V) has been supplied to the US

AN/APQ-126 airborne radar

Navy and Air Force, as well as Greece and Portugal. A variant, known as the AN/APQ-158, has been developed for the HH-53 helicopter (**4336.353**).

CONTRACTOR
Texas Instruments Inc, PO Box 226015, Dallas, Texas 75266, USA.

1488.353
AN/APQ-140 AIRBORNE RADAR

The AN/APQ-140 is a multi-mode phased array forward-looking radar. In place of a mechanically steered reflector, beam steering and formation is accomplished by electronic scanning. This technique offers the possibility of mechanical simplicity allied to greater flexibility and increased capabilities.

Of the two generic types of airborne phased arrays, the APQ-140 is of the reflective variety in which a matrix of individual elements (3800) which are capable of controlled variation of phase are illuminated from the front. The beam formation and steering functions are effected by computer control of the individual elements so that the combined effect on the energy they reflect is the generation of a beam which is capable of being steered at rates impossible by mechanical means.

The phase shifting elements are ferrite rod devices located within control coils, the driver amplifiers for which are also located within each individual element.

The amplifiers are solid-state units and a single phase-shift element measures about 12 c × 16 mm diameter. The complete array of 3800 elements measures approximately 72 cm diameter. The computer used for phase-shift/beam steering is believed to be the Honeywell Alert.

Illumination of the array is by means of a circular ridged horn supported about 75 cm ahead of the phase-shifter mounting. The horn is fed by six waveguides. Linear or circular polarisation of signals can be employed. Operating frequency is in the J-band and it is believed that there are facilities for frequency-agile operation.
DEVELOPMENT
Development of the APQ-140, and other electronically scanned radars, began in 1965 and continued throughout the 1970s with flight evaluation.
STATUS
Experimental radar; tactical utilisation not designated.

APQ-140 multi-mode phased array radar test installation on Boeing KC-135 aircraft

CONTRACTOR
Raytheon Company, Missile Systems Division, Hartwell Road, Bedford, Massachusetts 01730, USA.

1968.353
AN/APQ-144 RADAR

The APQ-144 is another in the APQ-113 family of forward radars (**1966.353**) and was developed in the late 1960s for use in the F-111F tactical bomber. The basic features of the APQ-113 and APQ-114 (**1967.353**) radars were retained with a number of

performance enhancement features added. The principal among these were the addition of a 0·2 µs pulse width and a 2·5 mile (4 km) display range.
DEVELOPMENT
Programmes for adding DMTI and K-band transmitter facilities have been carried out and successfully flight tested, but these features have not

been incorporated in production units. A modified APQ-144 radar was produced in small numbers for the B-1 bomber prototype programme. This was given the designation AN/APQ-163 (**3682.253**).
CONTRACTOR
General Electric Company, French Road, Utica, New York 13503, USA.

4335.353
AN/APQ-146 AIRBORNE RADAR

The AN/APQ-146 is a dual channel, forward looking, multi-mode radar developed for the F-111F. The radar's primary function is to provide proper commands to automatically control the F-111 aircraft at a pre-selected set clearance (altitude) above the terrain. This allows the F-111 to follow a low altitude contour to the earth's surface, thereby avoiding detection. Each channel of the terrain following radar (TFR) system is identical, providing system flexibility and improving overall system reliability and mission success. The units of this radar provide the following modes of operation:

(1) terrain following
(2) situation (terrain avoidance)
(3) ground map.

AN/APQ-146 airborne radar

There are two F-111 attack radar backup modes which may be selected by equipment external to the APQ-146. One is an air-to-ground ranging mode which uses the elevation monopulse resolution improvement capability of the TFR, and is slaved in elevation to an externally generated position taken from the lead-computing optical sight, the azimuth axis being aligned with the drift angle. The other is a ground map backup mode where the TFR transmitter/receiver is routed through the attack antenna.

DEVELOPMENT

Earlier versions of the APQ-146 were the APQ-110 designed for use on the F-111A, F-111C and F-111E aircraft; the APQ-128 designed for use on the F-111D aircraft and the AQP-134 designed for use on the FB-111. In addition the APQ-146 was modified for installation on the B-1 bomber.

CONTRACTOR

Texas Instruments Inc, PO Box 226015, Dallas, Texas 75266, USA.

1567.353

AN/APQ-148/156 MULTI-MODE RADAR

The AN/APQ-148/156 is a J-band airborne multi-mode radar specially developed to combine the functions of two radars previously required by US Navy A-6A all-weather attack aircraft, in a single radar. These two radars are the APQ-92 (search, and terrain avoidance/following) and the APQ-112 (target tracking and ranging). The APQ-156 system is a modification of the APQ-148 to accommodate the addition of a FLIR/laser target recognition attack multi-sensor system to the A-6E aircraft. Functions performed by the APQ-148/156 include:

(1) search
(2) ground mapping
(3) tracking and ranging of fixed or moving targets
(4) terrain avoidance or terrain following
(5) beacon detection and tracking.

The TWS capability provides simultaneous range, azimuth, and evaluation data for weapon delivery. As in other systems, range and azimuth markers must be placed on the target, but elevation data are available on a continuous basis and are derived from a separate phase interferometer array carried below the main scanner dish. The latter has a width of about one metre and is illuminated by a conventional horn feed, to produce a very narrow beam in azimuth.

The beam has a cosecant^2 profile in elevation and this, with the interferometer elevation data provided, eliminates the need for mechanical scanning in the elevation plane. The interferometer array consists of two adjacent rows of 32 horns and moves with the main dish. Energy reflected from ground targets arrives at the upper and lower rows with a time difference which is measured by phase comparison techniques and translated into angular information.

There are two cockpit displays in the A-6E APQ-148 installation: a 5-inch (127 mm) storage tube unit for the pilot, and a 7-inch (178 mm) direct view radar indicator (DVRI) for the bombardier/navigator. In the case of the APQ-156, only the DVRI is provided.

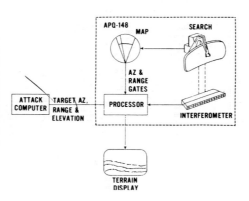

Schematic diagram of the APQ-148/156 radar. The interferometer generates an elevation-versus-range profile of approaching terrain, this information being presented to the pilot on a separate display to permit 'nap-of-the-earth' flight paths. It also gives the precise elevation angle to the target, the point where azimuth and range cursors intersect. This means that while the radar is providing a clear mapping display, it can also track a moving or stationary target to the instant of weapons release

Terrain data from the radar system are also presented on a vertical display for the pilot. The system incorporates comprehensive built-in test facilities. System weight is about 500 lb (230 kg).

STATUS

In 1970 Norden received a $5·946 million contract for the delivery of 13 systems, and the first production equipment was handed over in 1971. Approximately 200 systems had been developed by the end of 1975, some of which are being used to retrofit equipment in A-6A aircraft.

Norden AN/APQ-148/156 multi-mode radar for A-6E aircraft

In 1978 the manufacturer was awarded a $394 000 contract for the first 18 production MX-9736/APQ video processor-airborne moving target indicator (AMTI) units for A-6E aircraft. Six pre-production examples were developed in 1976. The AMTI enables the radar to detect moving surface targets in the presence of clutter.

In June 1980 Norden received a $5·2 million US Navy contract for 295 AMTI units, and in July there was a further award of $3·8 million for six complete radars for new aircraft and 56 units for updating AN/APQ-148 radars of older A-6E aircraft to AN/APQ-156 standard. In April 1981 a $15 million contract was received which included updating 39 AN/APQ-148 radars, and a number of new AN/APQ-156 systems.

CONTRACTOR

Norden Systems, United Technologies Corporation, Norden Place, Box 5300, Norwalk 06856, Connecticut, USA.

1675.353

AN/APQ-153 FIRE CONTROL RADAR

The AN/APQ-153 ASTAR (airborne search target attack radar) is a lightweight search and range tracking radar used aboard F-5E aircraft. This system operates in the I-band frequency range and provides stabilised search, automatic acquisition and target illumination, and automatic target ranging with boresight steering in the missile mode for heads-down launch of the Sidewinder AIM-9 series missiles. In the gunnery modes, the radar automatically provides range and range-rate outputs for targets within the sight lead angle computation envelope.

The system comprises five main units: antenna assembly, receiver/transmitter, radar processor, indicator, and set control. Combined weight is 110 lb (50 kg). The antenna is a parabolic 12 × 16 inch (30 × 40 cm) dish with horizontal polarisation. The indicator uses a 5-inch (127 mm) direct view storage tube and provides a 'B' type search display and a lock-on missile mode display. Built-in test is provided for radar performance verification.

OPERATION

The APQ-153 has the following principal modes of operation:

Search Mode

In search operation, a 7° elevation beamwidth is stepped up 3° at the right azimuth limit and down 3° at the left azimuth limit, providing a two-bar scan coverage of 10° in elevation. This two-bar 10° coverage can be adjusted ±45° in elevation by the pilot. Azimuth search coverage is ±45°. The search pattern is space stabilised for aircraft pitch and roll motion to allow searching a given volume of space and to prevent loss of the target and/or smearing of the display. Range of search coverage extends to 20 nautical miles (37 km).

Boresight Missile Mode

The missile mode enables the pilot to lock-on to targets out to 10 nautical miles (19 km) and provides aircraft steering information to align the acquisition envelope of the AIM-9 missile with the target. Once a target has been acquired a lock-on occurs, and azimuth and elevation steering data are provided on the indicator display in the form of a target steering bar. The aircraft is flown towards the bar to align it within the allowable AIM error circle scribed on the overlay. Missile acquisition occurs when the steering bar is within the allowable AIM error circle and the IN-RANGE indicator is illuminated.

Air-to-Air Gunnery Modes

There are two air-to-air gunnery modes in the APQ-153: dogfight, and AA1/AA2. Both are external commands to the radar. The gunnery modes are heads-up and the radar automatically provides range and range rate information to the sight. Activation of a gunnery mode causes the antenna to align to a boresight in azimuth and a 2·2° down in elevation. The range gate will automatically slew from 500 to 6000 feet at 22 000 feet per second (152 to 1830 m at 6700 m/second). Acquisition is automatic for the first target encountered.

STATUS

Currently in production for use aboard Northrop F-5E aircraft of 14 countries.

CONTRACTOR

Emerson Electronic Co, Government and Defense Group, 8100 West Florissant Avenue, St Louis, Missouri 63136, USA.

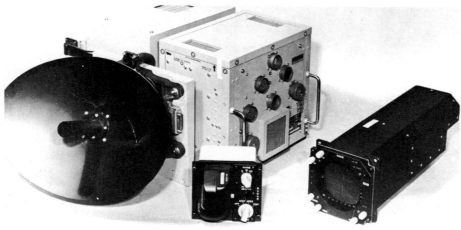

APQ-153 fire control radar

3113.353
AN/APQ-157 FIRE CONTROL RADAR

The AN/APQ-157 is a dual control lightweight search and range tracking radar used aboard F-5F aircraft. This system operates in the I/J-band frequency range and provides stabilised search, automatic acquisition and target illumination, and automatic target ranging with boresight steering in the missile mode for heads-down launch of the Sidewinder AIM-9 series missile. In the gunnery modes, the radar automatically provides range and range-rate outputs for targets within the sight lead angle computation envelope.

The system comprises eight main units: radar processor, antenna assembly, receiver/transmitter, front indicator, rear indicator, coupler power supply, and two set controls. Combined weight is 140 lb (64 kg). The indicators use a 5-inch (127 mm) direct view storage tube and provide a 'B' type search display and a lock-on missile mode display. Video trim is provided for harmonisation of video displays. Each display can be adjusted to suit the individual pilot operational preference and will correlate information within 1°. The set controls are transferable for individual cockpit control. The antenna is a parabolic 12 × 16 inch (30 × 40 cm) dish with horizontal polarisation. Built-in test is provided for radar performance verification.

OPERATION

The APQ-157 has the following principal modes of operation:

Search Mode

In search operation, a 7° elevation beamwidth is stepped up 3° at the right azimuth limit and down 3° at the left azimuth limit, providing a two-bar scan coverage of 10° in elevation. This two-bar 10° coverage can be adjusted ±45° in elevation by the pilot. Azimuth search coverage is ±45°. The search pattern is space stabilised for aircraft pitch and roll motion to allow searching a given volume of space and to prevent loss of the target and/or smearing of the display. Range of search coverage extends to 20 nautical miles (37 km).

Boresight Missile Mode

The missile mode enables the pilot to lock-on to targets out to 10 nautical miles (19 km) and provides

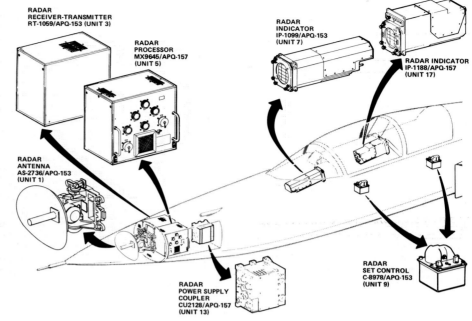

Emerson AN/APQ-157 radar and location of units in F-5F aircraft

aircraft steering information to align the acquisition envelope of the AIM-9 missile with the target. Once a target has been acquired a lock-on occurs, azimuth and elevation steering are provided on the indicator display in the form of a target steering bar. The aircraft is flown toward the bar to align it within the allowable AIM error circle scribed on the overlay. Missile acquisition occurs when the steering bar is within the allowable AIM error circle and the IN-RANGE indicator is illuminated.

Air-to-Air Gunnery Modes

There are two air-to-air gunnery modes in the APQ-157: dogfight, and AA1/AA2. Both are external commands to the radar. The gunnery modes are heads-up and the radar automatically provides range

and range-rate information to the sight. Activation of a gunnery mode causes the antenna to align to a boresight in azimuth and 4·7° down in elevation. The range gate will automatically slew from 500 to 6000 feet at 22 000 feet per second (152 to 1830 m at 6700 m/s). Acquisition is automatic for the first target encountered.

STATUS

Currently in production for use aboard Northrop F-5F aircraft.

CONTRACTOR

Emerson Electric Co, Government and Defense Group, 8100 West Florissant Avenue, St Louis, Missouri 63136, USA.

3114.353
AN/APQ-159 AIRBORNE RADAR

The AN/APQ-159(V)-1 is a lightweight multi-mode forward-looking I/J-band pulse radar used on the F-5E aircraft. This system incorporates a dual PRF frequency agility transmitter and provides stabilised search, automatic and manual acquisition and tracking on and off boresight, and target spotlight with automatic target ranging and tracking for air targets. In the missile mode the radar provides range, range rate and angular position from boresight, for heads-down launch of the Sidewinder AIM-9 series missiles. In the gunnery modes the radar automatically provides range and range-rate outputs for targets within the sight lead angle computation envelope. In the electro-optical (EO) mode the radar displays a normal or expanded image from the AGM-65A Maverick missile, and control is provided for the EO sensor.

The AN/APQ-159(V)-2 is a dual control radar

system with characteristics the same as the (V)-1, and is used on the F-5F aircraft. In addition it provides independently selectable radar/EO presentations with transferable functions on the set controls and video indicators.

The (V)-1 system comprises six main units: antenna assembly, receiver/transmitter, radar processor, signal data converter, set control, and video indicator. Combined weight is 140 lb (64 kg). The antenna is an 11 × 19 inch (28 × 48 cm) planar array with vertical polarisation. The video indicator uses a 5-inch (127 mm) high brightness CRT and provides a radar 'B' type search display, a lock-on missile mode display, and an electro-optic TV image.

The (V)-2 system consists of the (V)-1 units plus the addition of another set control and video indicator. Combined weight is 155 lb (70 kg). Built-in test is provided in both systems for radar performance evaluation and signal data converter and video indicator fault isolation.

There are also (V)-3 and (V)-4 models which have identical performance to the (V)-1 and (V)-2 sets, and which are also configured for single-seat and twin cockpit aircraft types, respectively. The essential difference is in the display arrangements; in place of the 12 × 12 cm rectangular CRTs used for the (V)-1 and (V)-2, the (V)-3 and (V)-4 versions have one or two 8·6 cm circular direct view storage-tube (DVST) displays; and in the absence of EO data presentation facilities, the signal data converter unit is not required in the later two versions of the APQ-159. System weights for the (V)-3 and (V)-4 are 56 kg and 71 kg, respectively.

OPERATION

The APQ-159 has the following principal modes of operation:

Search Mode

In search operation, a 8° elevation beamwidth is stepped up 3° at the right azimuth limit and down 3° at the left azimuth limit providing a two-bar scan coverage of 11° in elevation. In longer range selection a single-bar scan is provided. The antenna elevation coverage is ±45° and is controllable by the pilot.

Azimuth search coverage is ±45°. The search pattern is space stabilised for aircraft pitch and roll motion to allow searching a given volume of space and to prevent loss of target. Range of search coverage extends to 40 nautical miles (74 km) with 20, 10, and 5 nautical miles (37, 19, and 9 km) selectable.

Missile Modes

The off boresight missile mode acquisition enables the pilot to lock-on to targets over the full angular coverage out to 10 nautical miles (19 km) and provides steering information to align the acquisition envelope of the AIM-9 missile with the target. A boresight missile mode acquisition is also provided with acquisition to 5 nautical miles (9 km). Once a target has been acquired and lock-on occurs, azimuth and elevation steering data are provided on the video display in the form of a steering cross. The aircraft is flown toward the cross to align it within the allowable AIM error circle. Missile acquisition occurs when the steering bar is within the allowable AIM error circle and the IN-RANGE indicator is illuminated. There is also an auto-acquisition mode for targets within 5 nautical miles range, in which case the pilot may select on-boresight missile acquisition (dogfight missile).

Planar scanner of Emerson AN/APQ-159

Transmitter/receiver of Emerson AN/APQ-159

Air-to-Air Gunnery Modes

There are two air-to-air gunnery modes in the APQ-159: dogfight guns and AA1/AA2. Both are external commands to the radar. The gunnery modes are heads-up and the radar automatically provides range and range-rate information to the sight. Activation of a gunnery mode causes the antenna to align to boresight and the range gate will automatically slew from 500 to 6000 feet at 22 000 feet per second (152 to 1830 m at 6700 m/s). Acquisition is automatic for the first target encountered. Lock-on is maintained while switching between the gunnery and missile modes.

Electro-Optical Modes

These are available only with (V)-1 and (V)-2 versions. The CRT indicator units enable the pilot to present raster-type images from the EO sensor of missiles such as the Maverick at either normal or expanded (2:1) scale. The latter presentation can be 'frozen' for an indefinite period to permit a detailed examination of the image displayed. Sixteen shades of grey are available in both scales.

STATUS

Currently in production for use aboard the F-5E, F-5F and F-5G aircraft. To provide additional radar growth

for the F-5, Emerson has repacked the EC-153 radar which can retrofit into existing F-5 aircraft with minimum airframe changes.

CONTRACTOR

Emerson Electric Co, Government and Defense Group, 8100 West Florissant Avenue, St Louis, Missouri 63136, USA.

4336.353

AN/APQ-158 AIRBORNE RADAR

The AN/APQ-158 is a multi-mode forward-looking radar used primarily for terrain following/terrain avoidance at low altitudes, in the Pavelow III Night/Adverse Weather Search and Rescue helicopter, HH-53. The equipment is similar to the AN/APQ-126 but is modified for compatibility with unique helicopter characteristics and Pavelow III mission requirements. The radar contains 15 line-replaceable units which provide the same basic ten modes of operation as detailed for the AN/APQ-126 (**4334.353**).

System upgrades provide this radar with the capability to supply updates in all modes except TF and to perform TF missions over very high clutter areas such as cities.

CONTRACTOR

Texas Instruments Inc, PO Box 226015, Dallas, Texas 75266, USA.

AN/APQ-158 airborne multi-mode radar

3301.353

AN/APQ-161 RADAR

The APQ-161 is an update of the APS-144 radar (**1968.353**) for use in the PAVE TACK F-111F tactical

bomber. Modifications to the radar include a digital scan converter and a dual-tube display which enables the operator to display multi-sensor data simultaneously.

CONTRACTOR

General Electric Company, French Road, Utica, New York 13503, USA.

3682.353

AN/APQ-163 RADAR

The AN/APQ-163 radar is a modification of the APQ-144 (**1968.353**) which was specifically designed for the B-1 supersonic bomber prototype programme. Three of these equipments were supplied and a pre-production programme had been established by mid-1977. Among the modifications to the APQ-144 were an increase in the scan angle from 45 to 60° and nuclear hardening of the system electronics.

Subsequently a doppler beam sharpening mode of

synthetic aperture radar operation has been undergoing flight tests since September 1978 on one of the B-1 prototype aircraft. This operating technique is implemented by means of a coherent-on-receive modification to the APQ-163.

STATUS

Experimental flying and development work is continuing.

CONTRACTOR

General Electric Company, French Road, Utica, New York 13503, USA.

One of the APQ-163 forward-looking radars built by General Electric for the B-1 bomber programme

---

4647.353

AN/APQ-164 AIRBORNE RADAR

The AN/APQ-164 is the airborne radar developed for the US Air Force B-1B aircraft. This radar system combines technology from the F-16 aircraft AN/APG-66/68 system (**3303.353**) and the Electronically Agile Radar (EAR) programme of the US Air Force.

The system provides radar information for the four basic capabilities of navigation, penetration, weapon delivery and ancillary functions such as air refuelling. The primary navigation and weapon delivery mode is based on a high resolution synthetic aperture radar which overcomes the physical constraints of antenna

size through software techniques to provide high accuracy target location. The penetration function of the radar includes automatic terrain following and avoidance to enable aircraft to fly at low altitude in all weather conditions.

The AN/APQ-164 consists of a single phased array antenna, two transmitters, two signal processors and a special display for the high resolution imagery. The antenna, which allows the radar to change the shape and position of its beam electronically without mechanical movement of the array, is derived from the EAR programme. This system, plus sophisticated digital signal processing allows simultaneous

presentation of multiple modes to the operators. The APG-66/68 radar has provided the dual mode transmitter, a programmable signal processor and the modular low power RF which provides all the receiver and stable local oscillator functions.

STATUS

The AN/APQ-164 is in production, the first production system having been delivered to the aircraft manufacturer in February 1984.

CONTRACTOR

Westinghouse Defense and Electronic Systems Center, Baltimore, Maryland 21203, USA.

1484.353

AN/APS-94D SIDEWAYS-LOOKING RADAR

The AN/APS-94D is a side-looking airborne radar carried by US Army OV-1 Mohawk aircraft and used for battlefield and forward area reconnaissance and surveillance. The radar also has survey and mapping applications.

The aircraft installation comprises five main sub-assemblies:

(1) antenna
(2) receiver/transmitter
(3) power supply/mount
(4) signal processor
(5) interconnecting box
(6) cockpit complex.

The antenna unit consists of a pod in the case of the Mohawk (other configurations are possible) containing two slotted waveguide arrays mounted

back-to-back on a gyro-stabilised assembly that pivots at the centre. In flight, the antenna arrays are yaw stabilised to preserve the quality of the radar picture.

The receiver/transmitter is tunable within a portion of the radar band. It is located in the Mohawk equipment bay, with the signal processor and the interconnecting box. The antenna and other units can be simply removed and replaced on the aircraft to permit its use for alternative duties at short notice. Apart from high-power microwave devices, and certain display components, the APS-94D is of solid-state design.

The cockpit complex consists of the units necessary for operator control of the radar, recording and presentation of the data gathered. Two radar area maps are available to the operator. One depicts the entire sensed area, including all detected ground targets as though they are stationary; this is called the fixed target map. The other radar map shows detected moving targets and displays them against a suppressed background map of the area resulting in a moving target map. The radar imagery is developed in the air using a dry silver film process.

An area up to 100 km on each side of the aircraft can be mapped when both of the antenna arrays are in use. Either one can be selected if it is desired to map only one side. A range control determines the width of the target area to be mapped and presented on the photo-radar map. This control has three settings corresponding to 25, 50, and 100 km wide scans by each antenna. When used in conjunction with the antenna switch to select either left, right, or both arrays, maps corresponding to four standard scales can be presented on the display: 1:250 000, 1:500 000, 1:1 million and 1:2 million. Provisions are made for the insertion of fiducial markers and other data.

DEVELOPMENT
The AN/APS-94D was developed under contract to the US Army Electronics and Readiness Command.

STATUS
In service on US Army OV-1 Mohawk reconnaissance aircraft. The APS-94D has also been fitted in an Argus of the Canadian Forces and installations have been made in B-26 and P-3 aircraft and the UH-1 helicopter. Other installations have included the P-2V Neptune, SD-2 drone, and C-130 Hercules aircraft. Three Boeing 737-200 aircraft, equipped with Motorola side-looking radar are operated by Indonesia for long range surveillance duties.

CONTRACTOR
Motorola Inc, Government Electronics Division, Group Radar Operations, 2100 East Elliott Road, Tempe, Arizona 85252, USA.

AN/APS-94D sideways-looking radar mounted on a US Army OV-1 Mohawk

---

1969.353
AN/APS-115 AIRBORNE RADAR
The AN/APS-115 is one of the Texas Instruments family of airborne search radars, and is an I-band frequency-agile system of modular design. It is employed principally for ASW and maritime roles. The AN/APS-115 is a dual system to provide 360° coverage for the P-3C 'Orion' land-based ASW aircraft. One antenna is mounted in the nose and the other in the rear. In addition to the underslung, stabilised antenna assemblies, the equipment includes dual receiver/transmitters, an antenna position programmer, dual radar set controls and a common antenna control unit.

STATUS
In operational service.

CONTRACTOR
Texas Instruments Inc, PO Box 226015, Dallas, Texas 75266, USA.

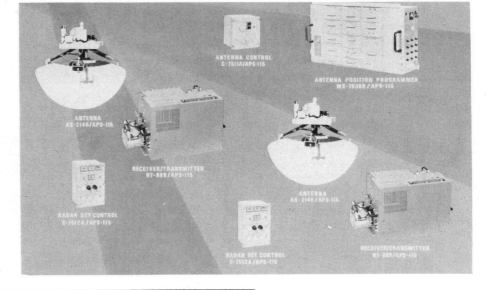

AN/APS-115 radar system

1783.353
AN/APS-120 RADAR
The APS-120 radar was installed in the first 33 E-2C aircraft. It operates in conjunction with the OL-93/AP radar detector processor (RDP) and APA-171 antenna group incorporating many of the techniques proven in the APS-111 (XN-1) flight test programme to detect targets at even longer ranges and in more severe clutter environments than the APS-96. An APS-120 improvement programme, known as advanced radar processing sub-system (ARPS), has resulted in a new US Navy nomenclature, AN/APS-125. This system is described in entry **1965.353**.

STATUS
The last production models of the APS-120 and OL-93/AP RDP were delivered in mid-1976. Subsequent production was then devoted to the APS-125. A programme to retrofit existing APS-120 radars to APS-125 configuration was completed in 1984.

CONTRACTOR
General Electric Company, French Road, Utica, New York 13503, USA.

1485.353
AN/APS-116/AN/APS-137(V)1 AIRBORNE RADAR
The AN/APS-116 is the ASW search radar currently in use in the US Navy's fleet of S-3A 'Viking' carrier borne ASW aircraft. It was specifically designed for detecting periscope-type targets of limited exposure time in high sea states. Its suitability in meeting the design objectives and requirements has been demonstrated in sea trials and fleet operations. It operates in the I-band with the scanner housed in a nose radome. Principal features include high transmitted energy (obtained from a high-power TWT driving a cross-field amplifier), low-noise receiver, linear FM pulse compression, rapid-scan antenna, scan-to-scan integration for sea clutter decorrelation, and multiple display formats (PPI, B scan, scan converter, raw) available to the sensor stations.

The system is integrated with the aircraft's ASW data processing and display system, and in addition to periscope and other small target detection, it

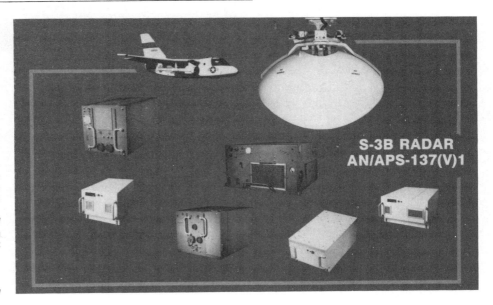

AN/APS-137(V)1 radar system

provides mapping, navigation, and general surface vessel detection.

STATUS

The AN/APS-116 is currently being upgraded to the AN/APS-137(V)1 as part of the weapon system improvement programme to upgrade the 'Viking' to the S-3B configuration. The most significant of the radar improvements is the addition of inverse synthetic aperture radar imaging to provide long-range ship classification capabilities.

CONTRACTOR

Texas Instruments Inc, PO Box 226015, Dallas, Texas 75266, USA.

1965.353
AN/APS-125/138 AIRBORNE RADARS

ARPS (Advanced Radar Processing Sub-system), is an improvement to the AN/APS-120 (**1783.353**) which combines increased sensitivity in noise and clutter conditions with sophisticated false alarm control and significant ECCM advances to provide the E-2 aircraft early warning system with a truly automatic overland capability. It also provides a digital airborne MTI in place of the analogue MTI of the AN/APS-120. Another capability is the suppression of sidelobe jamming. Implementation of ARPS into the APS-120 has occasioned the US Navy nomenclature of APS-125 to denote the improved model. Two sets of ARPS modified APS-120 radars existed in 1974 and, after laboratory testing, underwent flight test at Grumman. Testing continued until early 1978 when US Navy requirements were met completely.

STATUS

A retrofit programme for existing APS-120 radars to bring them up to APS-125 standards started in 1977 and was completed in 1984. Production of the basic radar, now designated APS-138, is expected to continue until the early 1990s. The first APS-138 was delivered to Grumman in December 1982 and a retrofit programme has been started to upgrade all APS-125 systems to the APS-138 configuration. This change is relatively minor when compared to that of the ARPS implementation.

The radars for the E-2 series aircraft have represented an evolutionary programme causing a change in nomenclature when a major change, such as ARPS, occurs, or when a number of small improvements have accumulated as was the case with the APS-138. Further major changes or updates are likely which will provide different nomenclatures before production of complete basic radars ceases. Beyond those, since the E-2C is projected to continue flying until at least the year 2000, other major improvements may well be made in the 1990s.

Four aircraft, fitted with the APS-125, have been purchased and are being operated by Israel, eight purchased by Japan, and four each by Egypt and Singapore. The APS-138 is also a candidate for installation in a Lockheed P-3 as an airborne early warning proposal for the international market, and possibly to the US Customs Service in a drug enforcement role.

General Electric has embarked on a Conformal radar programme (**5609.353**) with Grumman for the US Navy. Use of parts of the conformal radar concept and/or provision of adaptive processing could provide the basis for enhancements beyond those currently underway.

CONTRACTOR

General Electric Company, French Road, Utica, New York 13503, USA.

E-2C Hawkeye aircraft equipped with AN/APS-125 airborne early warning radar

3518.353
AN/APS-124 AIRBORNE RADAR

The AN/APS-124 search radar was designed and developed specifically for use in the US Navy SH-60B Seahawk helicopter (also known as LAMPS Mk III). It is specifically designed for helicopter installation featuring a low-profile antenna and radome. Optimum detection of surface targets in high sea states is accomplished by several unique features including fast scan antenna and interface with the auxiliary OU/103 signal data converter (digital scan converter) to achieve scan-to-scan integration.

The system is integrated with a multipurpose display and with the LAMPS data link for display of airborne radar video on board LAMPS equipped ships.

STATUS

The equipment is currently in main production to support the LAMPS Mk III system production schedule. The first LAMPS Mk III helicopter was due for delivery in late 1983.

CONTRACTOR

Texas Instruments Inc, PO Box 226015, Dallas, Texas 75266, USA.

AN/APS-124 search radar equipment for US Navy LAMPS helicopter

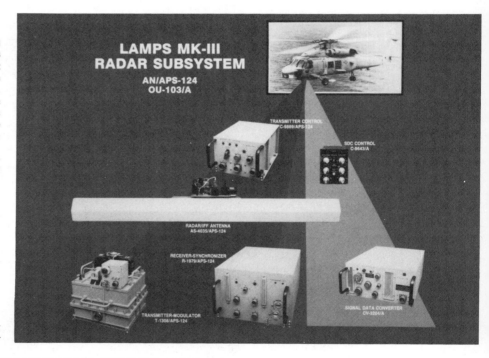

3519.353
AN/APS-127 AIRBORNE RADAR

The AN/APS-127 search radar is produced for the US Coast Guard for use in the Falcon Guardian HU-25A aircraft. The system was developed to support search and rescue missions as well as for enforcement of laws and treaties. A unique feature that characterises the AN/APS-127 is the stabilised, lightweight, high efficiency fast scanning antenna. Scan-to-scan integration is accomplished by interface with separate direct-view storage-tube displays for both the pilot and the surveillance system operator.

STATUS
The equipment is in production for both domestic and international applications.

CONTRACTOR
Texas Instruments Inc, PO Box 226015, Dallas, Texas 75266, USA.

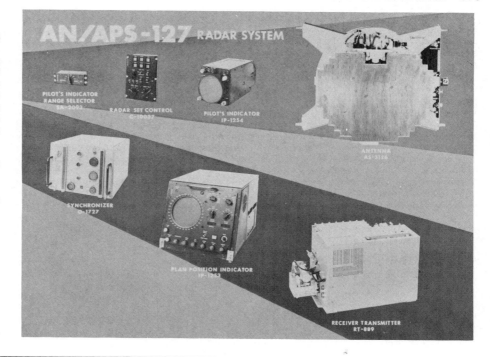

AN/APS-127 radar equipment

3132.353
AN/APS-128 MODEL D SURVEILLANCE RADAR

The AN/APS-128 Model D surveillance radar is an all-digital equipment using a scan converter to present data in TV raster format. It contains target enhancement and clutter reduction circuitry consisting of frequency agility, sensitivity time control, CFAR and scan-to-scan integration.

The system consists of a rectangular flat-plate antenna and pedestal, a transmitter/receiver, a radar control unit, a digital scan converter, a trackball or joystick cursor and a bright display. Dual display for cockpit weather presentation is available as well as add-on cabin displays. The system uses fully programmable microprocessor operational features with alpha-numeric and graphic options to meet varied mission requirements. A number of antenna array sizes are available to suit aircraft and radome configurations. An alternative parabolic antenna features a dual-polarisation capability in one moulded dish to provide pencil beam for sea search and shaped beam for mapping.

Target detection of the system are given as:
(1) 30 nautical miles on a snorkel or fishing vessel (assumed six metres long), 10 m² cross-section, in sea state 3
(2) 60 nautical miles on a trawler (160 metres long), 150 m² cross-section, in sea state 5
(3) 100 nautical miles on a freighter (360 metres long), 500 m² cross-section, in sea state 5
(4) 120 nautical miles on a tanker (600 metres long), 1000 m² cross-section, in sea state 5.

The system also functions as a weather radar with a range of approximately 200 nautical miles.

CHARACTERISTICS
Frequency: 9375 MHz
Frequency agility: 85 MHz peak/peak
Power output: 100 kW peak
Pulse width: 2·4 and 0·5 μs (0·1 μs pulse compression system optional)
PRF: 400, 1200, 1600 Hz
Noise figure: GAS-FET 3·5 dB low noise RF amplifier
Pulse compression: Retrofit transmitter/receiver to provide linear chirp capability for pulse width of 0·1 μs. Provides detection of 1 – 5 m² targets in heavy sea states
Antenna rotation rate: 15 or 60 rpm continuous. 15 rpm sector scan from 30 – 360° selectable
Bright display: High ambient light, 875 line high resolution
System weight: 91·8 kg (202 lbs) with 8 inch display

STATUS
Over 90 AN/APS-128 systems have been sold worldwide and the radar is operational with the Brazilian Air Force, Chilean Navy, Gabon Air Force, Indonesian Air Force, Japanese Maritime Safety Agency, NASA, Royal Malaysian Air Force, Spanish Air Force, Uruguayan Air Force, Uruguayan Navy and the US Customs Service.

CONTRACTOR
Eaton Corporation, AIL Division, Commack Road, Deer Park, Long Island, New York 11729, USA.

AN/APS-128 Model D airborne surveillance radar

4612.353
DIGITAL TACTICAL SYSTEM (DITACS) RADAR

The Digital Tactical System (DITACS) radar is a full AN/APS-128 Model D surveillance radar with added tactical sensor capability for enhanced multi-mission applications.

Tactical navigation and sensor plot data are displayed alternately or in combination on a bright display, together with radar target data. Control and management data are stored, recalled and displayed in operator-oriented formats. Both display and radar are under microprocessor control providing bright presentation with alpha-numeric designations, tailored graphic formats and multi-sensor overlays.

Digital Tactical System (DITACS) radar

Keyset functional firmware is based on specialised mission operational sequences. DITACS requires only the addition of a keyset control panel in hardware, the remaining features being added in software ROM and RAM programming capability.

This provides a stand-alone tactical control and display system.

STATUS

DITACS is installed on the Beech multi-mission 200T aircraft and is under development for the Grumman

S-2E Tracker aircraft as well as several helicopter installations.

CONTRACTOR

Eaton Corporation, AIL Division, Commack Road, Deer Park, Long Island, New York 11729, USA.

3520.353
AN/APS-130 AIRBORNE RADAR

The AN/APS-130 radar is a variation of the Norden Systems AN/APQ-148 radar system (**1567.353**) in the US Navy A-6E Intruder all-weather attack aircraft. The Intruder is an electronic warfare aircraft and carries no offensive weapons, and therefore the APS-130 uses only the navigational features of the APQ-148. It replaces an older radar system, also supplied by Norden Systems, which was used on the EA-6B.

STATUS

A contract for the manufacture of three pre-production models of the APS-130 was announced in July 1978, when it was stated that about 100 sets were expected to be supplied. Total value of the programme is thought to be in the region of $5 million. The prototype was delivered in September 1978, and all three pre-production models the following January.

Production of 103 radars and spares were ordered

for the US Navy. The first production model was delivered in December 1980 and production was completed two years later.

CONTRACTOR

Norden Systems, United Technologies Corporation, Norden Place, Box 5300, Norwalk 06856, Connecticut, USA.

4337.353
AN/APS-133 AIRBORNE RADAR

The airborne full colour, multi-mode radar, AN/APS-133, manufactured by Bendix, is a high performance weather and terrain mapping radar used in military transports and commercial aircraft. Although its main function is en-route weather evaluation, the AN/APS-133 provides high resolution terrain mapping, plus a beacon homing mode.

The display is in full colour with each of three different levels of cloud moisture content, or ground return, being presented as three colours, red, yellow and green. The display may also be used in

conjunction with other systems to display various types of information such as programmable check lists and area navigation information superimposed on the weather or terrain map.

The complete system consists of four units, a receiver/transmitter, display unit, control panel and a 30-inch (76 cm) diameter, fully stabilised antenna.

CHARACTERISTICS

Frequency: 9375 ±5 MHz

Power output: 65 kW

Range: 300 nm

Antenna: 30-inch (76 cm) parabola with CSC²Cos fan beam

Weight

Receiver/transmitter: 24·9 kg + 4 kg mounting

Indicator: 6·3 kg + 0·6 kg mounting

Controller: 0·9 kg

Antenna: 15 kg

DEVELOPMENT

The AN/APS-133 is derived from the commercial RDR-1F radar in widespread use in wide-body aircraft.

CONTRACTOR

Bendix Corporation, Avionics Division, PO Box 9414, Fort Lauderdale, Florida 33310, USA.

4338.353
AN/APS-134(V) MARITIME SURVEILLANCE RADAR

The AN/APS-134(V) ASW and maritime surveillance radar is the successor to the AN/APS-116 system

used in the US Navy for airborne surveillance. It is designed specifically to detect periscopes under high sea conditions and incorporates all the features of the previous generation with improved performance and a unique maritime surveillance mode. The principal

features include a fast scan antenna and associated digital signal processing which form an effective means of eliminating sea clutter. Two other techniques, pulse compression and scan-to-scan processing, are used to combat the inherent problems of detecting small targets in the sea clutter environment.

Three modes of operation are available:

(1) periscope target detection in sea clutter using fast scan (150 rpm), high PRF (2000 pps) and high resolution with display ranges selectable up to 32 nautical miles

(2) maritime surveillance out to 150 nautical miles with high resolution, low PRF (500 pps) and medium scan speed (40 rpm)

(3) long range search and navigation out to 150 nautical miles with medium resolution, low PRF and slow scan (6 rpm).

Long range performance is provided by a high power transmitter (500 kW peak power) coupled with a high antenna gain. A radar control/display gives video presentation on a ten inch square CRT, with the necessary controls and indicators.

CHARACTERISTICS

Transmitter frequency: 9·5 – 10 GHz (modes A & B) 9·6 – 9·9 GHz (mode C)

Power output: 500 kW, peak, average 500 W

Antenna beamwidth: 2·4° azimuth, 4° elevation

Polarisation: Vertical

STATUS

The AN/APS-134(V) is in production to meet several international requirements, including the Federal German Atlantic maritime patrol aircraft and the Royal New Zealand Air Force P-3Bs. A helicopter version is under development.

CONTRACTOR

Texas Instruments Inc, PO Box 226015, Dallas, Texas 75266, USA.

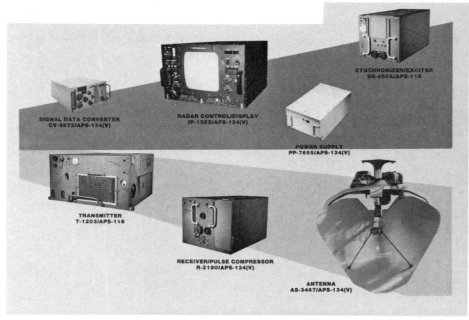

Elements of the AN/APS-134(V)1 radar installed in the Federal German Atlantic maritime aircraft

---

5609.353
CONFORMAL RADAR SYSTEM

General Electric has confirmed that it is engaged on a Conformal Radar programme with Grumman Aerospace, for the US Navy. This concept involves a radar embedded in the wings and sides of an aircraft using solid-state transmit/receive modules. This would eliminate the need for a rotodome antenna for

early warning radar as employed with the APS-125/138 (**1965.353**) in the E-2C aircraft.

DEVELOPMENT

As at early 1984, in the first phase of the development programme, the passive receive only portion of the concept was being pursued in an aircraft wing structure and ground tests were due to take place during the summer of 1984. These were scheduled to

be followed by flight testing. The active capability will be added after these tests are completed.

STATUS

Development in conjunction with Grumman Aerospace.

CONTRACTOR

General Electric Company, French Road, Utica, New York 13503, USA.

3690.353

AN/APX-76 AIRBORNE IFF INTERROGATOR

The AN/APX-76 airborne interrogator exists in two main versions, the original electron tube model having been updated by the introduction of a solid-state transmitter. The earlier model, AN/APX-76A is described first.

AN/APX-76A

The AN/APX-76A is an air-to-air interrogator for all-weather interceptor and other tactical aircraft, and has full AIMS capability in modes 1, 2, 3/A and 4. It achieves a narrow antenna beamwidth, and a reduction in 'fruit' through ISLS and RSLS circuits (interrogation and receiver sidelobe suppression, respectively), in conjunction with special antennas having sum (main-lobe) and difference (sidelobe) suppression patterns. Bracket-decoded video and discrete code-decoded video are displayed on the radar screen to provide unambiguous correlation between IFF and primary radar targets. The equipment is fully IFF Mk XII compatible. The equipment consists of four black boxes with a combined weight of 16·8 kg: the receiver/transmitter, control unit, a switch/amplifier, and an electrical synchroniser. Various antennas have been designed for different aircraft types, but a typical arrangement,

AN/APX-76 IFF interrogator system

on the F-4E Phantom, consists of eight small dipoles mounted in two horizontal rows of four on the reflector for the aircraft primary radar antenna.

AN/APX-76B

Hazeltine has developed an all solid-state transmitter and power supply unit for the APX-76, under a US Navy contract, thus yielding a number of advantages, both operational and in respect of maintenance and reliability; MTBF increased to 400 hours, compared with 225 hours for the AN/APX-76A.

The new version of the AN/APX-76 is directly

interchangeable with its predecessor, and no re-alignment is necessary, the complete operation requiring only 15 minutes. The D-band power output of the tube transmitter is 2 kW with power reduction steps of 2 and 4 dB. As the transmitter tube ages, the power output gradually decreases, the tubes normally being replaced when the output has dropped to 1 kW. The power output of the solid-state transmitter is 1·5 kW with a power reduction step of 3 dB, and there is no decrease in power output with age, nor is periodic maintenance required.

STATUS

The AN/APX-76 entered production in 1967, and it is estimated that more than 4500 of these sets have since been supplied to the air forces of the USA and friendly nations. Orders have been placed for the APX-76B version and the US Navy is retrofitting all APX-76As with solid-state transmitter/power supply assemblies. The APX-76A/B is installed in the F-4B, C, E, J, EC-121, P-3C Orion, CP-140, E-2C, F-111D, F-14, F-15, SH-60B and others. In addition to American forces, the equipment has been supplied to Australia, Canada, Greece and South Korea.

CONTRACTOR

Hazeltine Corporation, Greenlawn, New York 11740, USA.

3688.353

AN/APX-72 AIRBORNE IFF TRANSPONDER

The AN/APX-72 is an airborne IFF transponder which is widely used on US military and certain civil aircraft. It provides automatic radar identification, emergency signals, altitude reporting (when used in conjunction with a suitable altitude digitiser) and responds to interrogations in modes 1, 2, 3/A, C and 4. The last mode requires use of a KIT-1A/TSEC computer. The equipment incorporates the latest IFF Mk XII performance improvements.

CHARACTERISTICS

Frequency: 1090 MHz

Transmitter power output: 27 dBW nominal

Receiver frequency: 1030 MHz

Dynamic range: >50 dB

Sensitivity: –90 dBV nominal

Dimensions: 146 × 162 × 340 mm

Weight: 6·8 kg

STATUS

Operational in US fixed-wing aircraft, helicopters and shipborne installations. Well over 45 000 transponders have now been manufactured.

CONTRACTOR

Hazeltine Corporation, Greenlawn, New York 11740, USA.

AN/APX-72 IFF transponder

1569.353

AN/APX-83 AIRBORNE IFF INTERROGATOR

The AN/APX-83 is an airborne IFF interrogator installed in EC-121 airborne early warning aircraft to upgrade their surveillance capability. Each aircraft is equipped with an interrogator system and control/indicator equipment groups for each operator position in the aircraft. Each group semi-automatically processes and displays IFF responses from aircraft, ships, and ground transponders within the EC-121 interrogation range. There are provisions for expansion to a fully automated processing and display system.

A complete equipment set consists of either a synchroniser/coder or coder, decoder, decoder controls, decode displays, interrogator control, receiver/transmitter, and RF switch.

The coder interfaces with the associated radar, R/T unit, RF switch, decoder, decoder control, and the aircraft's APX-72 transponder. It accepts an external pre-trigger from the associated radar set and generates synchronous pulse-pairs and SLS pulses. These pulses are sent to the R/T unit for modulation of the RF signals. A sync-trigger is sent to the decoder

for range correlation of replies. Mode coding on a per sweep basis is done on two data lines which are also connected to the decoder. Video is steered through the coder to the decoder.

The decoder accepts raw video and mode triggers from the coder and generates bracket decodes, delayed raw video and identity, or altitude data for processing by the decoder control.

The following functions are performed:
(1) reply detection
(2) garble sensing
(3) altitude conversion
(4) emergency detection and alarm
(5) identification of position (I/P or SPI).

The decoder control receives the digital data and sync-triggers, bracket video, and raw video from the decoder. It performs two different types of filtering: passive decoding and active decoding. The former is accomplished by six sets of thumbwheel switches. A target whose mode and code combination is dialled into any one of the thumbwheel sets causes its bracket decode video to be stretched on the PPI. Two degrees of stretching (narrow and wide) are available in order to sort out the six sets.

Active decoding is accomplished by generating an area gate around an unknown IFF target by means of a range 'marker' on the PPI and a hand held switch which is activated just prior to the radar sweep passing through the target of interest. When the target is thus acquired, its coded replies to the interrogation modes are transferred for display by the decode indicator.

The indicator accepts the active decode target code and/or altitude data from the decoder control, and displays them for approximately one scan period (8 to 15 seconds) on a set of numeric readouts. It also displays the current interrogation modes. A military or civil emergency or communication failure causes one of three alarm lights to flash.

The interrogator control is a small box which performs the control functions for the IFF interrogator receiver.

STATUS

In production and fitted to EC-121 early warning aircraft.

CONTRACTOR

Eaton Corporation, AIL Division, Commack Road, Deer Park, Long Island, New York 11729, USA.

4339.353

AN/APX-100(V) AIRBORNE IFF TRANSPONDER

The AN/APX-100(V) transponder is a panel mounted IFF transponder using micro-miniature technology in both digital and RF circuitry, and is currently in production for a number of US military aircraft to enable them to operate in the military ATC surveillance system.

The system is a completely solid-state, modular constructed equipment with a complete dual channel diversity system, comprehensive built-in test, digital coding and encoding and high anti-jamming capability. Two antennas form part of the equipment and the diversity system receives signals from each

AN/APX-100(V) IFF transponder

and switches the transmitter output to the antenna which received the strongest interrogation signal. This system is designed to cure the problems of poor coverage with a single antenna which suffers on occasions from aircraft manoeuvre and antenna 'shadowing'.

The transmitter is all solid-state with its 500 watt peak power output obtained from four parallel microwave transistors. Two additional transistors complete the transmitter oscillator and driver stages. The diversity system provides improved antenna coverage and allows improvement in performance in

overloaded, jamming and multipath environments. Automatic overload control and anti-jamming features are also incorporated.

For retrofit to aircraft that have no cockpit space available, a remote configuration, RT-1157/APX-100(V), is available. In addition, a data bus version, operating in accordance with MIL-STD 1553B, will be available in late 1984.

CHARACTERISTICS
Transmit frequency: 1090 ± 0·5 MHz
Receiver frequency: 1030 ± 0·5 MHz
Peak power output: 500 W ± 3 dB

Dimensions: 13·3 × 12·7 × 17·1 cm
Weight: 3·8 kg
STATUS
Currently in production for all new US tri-service aircraft including the F-18, AV-8B, C-12, EC-130, SH-60B, UH-60, AH-1S, HH-65A, AH-64A, T-46A, SH-65A, C-5B, HH-60A and US Navy 'Sea Fox' surface craft. It is also being retrofitted to several other aircraft, including the OH-58 and CH-47.
CONTRACTOR
Bendix Corporation, Communications Division, 1300 E Joppa Road, Baltimore, Maryland 21204, USA.

3300.353
AN/APX-103 AIRBORNE INTERROGATOR
The AN/APX-103 interrogator set being provided for use in the E-3A airborne warning and control system (AWACS) (**1585.353**) by the Eaton Corporation, AIL Division, under contract to the Boeing Company, is the first airborne IFF interrogator set to offer complete AIMS Mark X SIF air traffic control (ATC) and Mark XII military IFF processing capabilities in one integrated system. Simultaneous Mark X and Mark XII multi-target and multi-mode operations permit an operator to obtain instantaneously the position (range, azimuth and elevation), code identification, and friend/foe status for all targets within the radar surveillance volume. This information can be used in conjunction with the radar to perform ATC, AEW, intercept tracking and escort surveillance missions.
OPERATION
Command words received from the E-3A display

processor functional group initiate processor action and direct the mode of operation. The processor generates interrogations to the active receiver/transmitter (R/T), which modulates interrogations and sends them via an RF switch to sum and difference antenna channels. Target aircraft within the surveillance volume respond with coded RF replies via the antenna and RF switch. Replies are demodulated and detected by the active R/T and are sent as video pulses to the processor.

The processor detects, degarbles, and decodes replies and forms target records for replies which meet certain criteria. Completed target records are sent to the E-3A DPFG as target reports.

Features of the AN/APX-103 include:
(1) simultaneous multi-target, multi-mode, Mark X SIF and Mark XII IFF operation
(2) superior positional accuracy and resolution
(3) unique friend-from-foe evaluator

(4) full compatibility with DOD/AIMS requirements
(5) extended surveillance range
(6) use of jittered PRF
(7) full ISLS, RSLS, and GTC capabilities
(8) dual frequency transmit/receive capability
(9) MTBF exceeds that of present IFF systems
(10) completely redundant R/T and power supply units with automatic failure sensing and switchover
(11) built-in self-test facilities to allow automatic fault detection and isolation of failures in conjunction with the E-3 OBTM&M system.
CONTRACTOR
Eaton Corporation, AIL Division, Commack Road, Deer Park, Long Island, New York 11729, USA.

3689.353
AN/APX-104 AIRBORNE IFF INTERROGATOR
The AN/APX-104 is a lightweight IFF interrogator providing all the functions required for air-to-air and air-to-ship identification and determination of the range and bearing of friendly aircraft and ships under all weather conditions. Typical applications include such operations as flight refuelling rendezvous with tanker aircraft and maintaining contact with other aircraft engaged on a common mission.

The controller unit is separate from the receiver/transmitter, and the combined weight is about 9 kg. The equipment provides for operation in modes 1, 2, 3/A and 4 (when a KIR-1A/TSEC computer is fitted), and operation is on the conventional transmission and reception frequencies of 1030 and 1090 MHz, respectively.

The transmitter is all solid-state, employing high peak power transistor amplifier modules in parallel to obtain the specified maximum output of 1·2 kW; output can be switched to half power where required,

and a 1 per cent duty cycle is specified. Integrated circuits are extensively utilised and Hazeltine employed surface acoustic wave technology in the local oscillator design in the interests of reliability, low cost, and ease of maintenance.
CHARACTERISTICS
Frequency: 1030 MHz transmit; 1090 MHz receive
Decoding sensitivity: –83 dBm
Power output: 1·2 kW, up to 1% duty cycle
Dimensions: 194 × 127 × 445 mm
Weight: 9 kg
STATUS
The APX-104 can be used to modernise existing IFF interrogator capabilities in aircraft originally fitted with the APX-76 (**3690.353**), and a simple retrofit can be made in the KC-130, S-3, P-3, E-2, F-4, F-111 and existing F-14 series aircraft with a slight cable change. The F-15 accepts the APX-104 without modification.

Other fittings foreseen for the APX-104 include the LAMPS Mk 111 helicopter, F-16, F-18, F-18L and F-5E aircraft.

AN/APX-104 IFF interrogator

Licence production of this equipment is also carried out in Italy by Italtel (**3489.353**).
CONTRACTOR
Hazeltine Corporation, Greenlawn, New York 11740, USA.

3691.353
MM/UPX-709 AIRBORNE IFF TRANSPONDER
The MM/UPX-709 is an airborne multiplex diversity IFF transponder providing civil and military air controllers with full aircraft identity information and automatic altitude reporting. The equipment can be fitted in aircraft, helicopters and ships, and coverage is all-round. The diversity features give full spherical coverage, and continuous track data is supplied to automatic processing systems regardless of aircraft attitude: antenna blind spots are virtually eliminated because of the antennas located above and below the aircraft fuselage.
CHARACTERISTICS
Frequency: 1030 MHz receive; 1090 MHz transmit
Sensitivity: Adjustable (–90 dBV matched load); normal –77 dBm

Modes: 1, 2, Test, 3/A, C, AIMS mode 4
Dimensions: 136 × 136 × 213 mm (remote version); 133 × 146 × 160 mm (panel mounted)
Weight: 4·1 kg (remote); 3·2 kg (panel)
STATUS
Production. Licence manufacture is undertaken in Italy by Italtel (**3489.353**).
CONTRACTOR
Hazeltine Corporation, Greenlawn, New York 11740, USA.

MM/UPX-709 IFF transponder – panel mounted version

1100.353
AN/AWG-9 AIRBORNE WEAPON CONTROL SYSTEM
This is the aircraft-fitted element of the Phoenix (AIM-54) weapon control system (which see) developed for the US Navy F-14 aircraft. It comprises a fire control and target illuminating radar, digital computers, and displays. Provision is also included for the automatic exchange of data link information between the AWG-9 and the naval tactical data system (NTDS) and

airborne tactical data system (ATDS) for target designation and other functions.

For on-board target acquisition, the AWCS includes a long range, high-power pulse doppler radar. This system has a look-down capability that enables it to pick moving targets out of the ground clutter that normally obscures targets in a conventional radar.

In addition to its long range, the AWCS introduced into the fleet for the first time in an aircraft, the ability

to track many targets at once, with computer-aided selection of target priority. The system is designed for consecutive launch and for simultaneous guidance of up to six AIM-54 missiles against separate targets.

The radar antenna is a planar, slotted-plate array, and represents a significant step forward in design, with a high aperture efficiency for increased radar range.

The principal weapon is the long-range Phoenix, AIM-54 (**1099.331**) air-to-air missile, but the AWG-9 system can be used also for launching Sparrow (**1106.331**), Sidewinder (**1308.331**), and AMRAAM missiles,and control of an M-61 Vulcan 20 mm cannon.

OPERATION

The AWCS uses the pulse doppler radar as its primary target sensor, a multipurpose digital computer, and associated control and display sub-systems. The pulse doppler radar system represents several years of development in transmitter tubes, crystal filters, and planar array antenna techniques to enable the long range requirements of Phoenix to be met. A low noise parametric amplifier in the receiver section contributes to this long range capability. Advanced doppler techniques make look-down target acquisition possible. A flexible, high capacity computer permits simultaneous track of a large number of targets and aids the radar intercept officer (RIO) in the assignment of kill priorities and in missile firing.

Target detection, tracking, and ranging functions for all F-14 air-to-air weapon configurations (6 ×

Phoenix; 6 × Sparrow; a mixture of these; plus 4 × Sidewinder; and the 20 mm Vulcan cannon) are handled by the AWG-9 radar. It can operate in either pulse doppler or conventional pulse modes. A separate TWT provides CW illuminating energy for the semi-active homing Sparrow (AIM-7E or -7F CW). Time-sharing techniques allow up to six Phoenix missiles to be given pulse doppler mid-course guidance simultaneously.

Data processing in the AWG-9 AWCS is performed by a general-purpose digital computer that features high speed operation and a large memory capacity in an extremely compact package. The central computer keeps track of targets detected by the radar while the radar continues to search. Based on preprogrammed logic the computer evaluates threats, generates steering information for the pilot, and paints a complete tactical situation for the RIO in standard NTDS symbology, all based on data generated either internally or obtained through external data links.

For control of the Phoenix weapon system, the

aircraft's RIO is provided with two CRT display units. One, a 12·7 cm diameter unit, is used as a multi-mode display for the presentation of raw radar derived target information and IFF returns, while a larger (25·4 cm diameter) unit is used for the display of processed data.

The latter includes target track information, alpha-numeric and symbolic data obtained via data link from other units of a naval force. The display is also used as a computer read-out device for the presentation of computer-generated missile/target assignments.

A new digital display (see picture) has been developed for the F-14. It incorporates a computer keyboard with software programmable switches and display symbols essential to the capabilities added to the system by a programmable signal processor (PSP). This new PSP is a high-speed, special purpose computer to extend the AWG-9 mission capability.

DEVELOPMENT

The AWG-9 AWCS is related to the AN/ASG-18 developed by Hughes for the YF-12A Mach 3 interceptor, and it is believed that considerable similarity in concept and technology exists between the two systems.

After cancellation of the US Navy F-111B in 1968, the AWG-9 system was selected for development for the F-14A aircraft. Among changes made were provision for controlling weapons additional to Phoenix (Sparrow, Sidewinder and Vulcan 20 mm cannon), additional operational modes for dogfight missions, and a reduction in overall size and weight. The first test model was delivered to the US Navy in February 1970.

STATUS

US Navy squadrons now operational with the F-14A are embarked on four aircraft carriers in the Pacific and four in the Atlantic. More than 845 F-14s are planned by the US Navy to support its 12 carrier oriented force structure. Currently funded US Navy programmes include doubling the core memory in the central processor and converting the analogue signal processors to programmable digital processing. A passive non-co-operative target recognition mode is also under development. In early 1984, Hughes received a $20 million contract from the US Navy for AN/AWG-9 systems.

CONTRACTOR

Hughes Aircraft Company, Radar Systems Group, El Segundo, California 90245, USA.

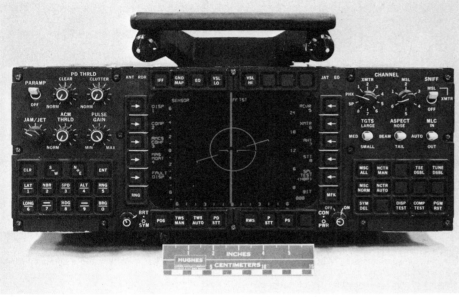

AWG-9 digital display on US Navy F-14

3018.353

AN/AWG-10 MISSILE CONTROL SYSTEM

The AN/AWG-10 is the airborne, multi-mode, missile control system (MCS) which is fitted to the US Navy F-4J aircraft. It provides pulse doppler (down look) and pulse air-to-air search and track modes, high/low map modes and air-to-ground ranging as well as a variety of ECCM. It also provides missile launch computations and semi-active illumination for AIM-7

AWG-10 missile control system radar

radar missiles. This MCS became operational in 1967 and was first deployed in 1968.

In addition to the antenna, the radar nose package includes the transmitter, receiver, RF oscillator, scan pattern generator, trackers, and power supplies. Cockpit units include the pilot's indicator, indicator control, radar set control, antenna control, and built-in test unit. The aircraft equipment bay houses the three remaining AWG-10 units – the computer elements.

AN/AWG-10A Weapons Control System

The AN/AWG-10A weapons control system is an improved version of the AN/AWG-10 MCS. Only three of the 29 line replaceable units (LRUs) of the AN/AWG-10 are utilised, unchanged, in the AN/AWG-10A. Six completely new LRUs are added, seven LRUs are deleted entirely, and 19 LRUs are modified in varying degrees.

The results of two early-1970 development programmes were combined to create the AN/AWG-10A. One effort was a development programme for reliability/maintainability improvement. The second was a demonstration of the improved effectiveness of weapon delivery through the use of modern digital computer techniques and improved displays.

The AN/AWG-10A incorporates a new servoed

optical sight and adds one air-to-air and three air-to-ground modes to the basic AN/AWG-10 system.

An important product of this effort is the improved maintenance capability resulting from the new digital built-in test mode.

AN/AWG-11/12

The AN/AWG-10 was produced as the AN/AWG-11 and AN/AWG-12 for UK Royal Navy and Royal Air Force Phantoms, F-4K and F-4M with Ferranti of Edinburgh as the UK main contractor.

AN/AWG-11A/12A

The reliability/maintainability improvements incorporated into the AN/AWG-10A have been procured by the UK for incorporation into the AN/AWG-11/12 missile control system.

STATUS

Between 1963 and 1971 more than 850 AN/AWG-10/11/12 radars were delivered. About 300 AN/AWG-10A modification sets were delivered between 1975 and the end of 1980.

CONTRACTOR

Westinghouse Electric Corporation, Aerospace Divisions, Baltimore-Washington International Airport, PO Box 746, Baltimore, Maryland 21203, USA.

5611.353

MULTIBEAM MULTIMODE SURVEILLANCE RADAR

The Multibeam Multimode Surveillance Radar (MSR) is an air-to-ground system for battlefield surveillance applications and is being developed by General Electric as a candidate for the new US Air Force/Army Joint Surveillance Target Attack Radar System (J-STARS).

The MSR system consists of a multibeam electronically scanned phased array antenna and a real-time all digital LSI radar signal processor. It is a computer controlled multi-mode radar that operates in the MTI search, MTI area track, synthetic aperture radar spotlight, and doppler beam-sharpened modes, and includes extensive ECCM capabilities.

The MSR uses multiple waveforms and includes a reconfigurable real-time radar signal processor. The

system consists of nine core line replaceable units:
(1) pod-mounted multibeam electronically scanned phased array antenna
(2) coherent transmitter
(3) exciter/synchroniser
(4) multi-channel receiver/converter
(5) preprocessor
(6) digital pulse compressor
(7) spectral analyser

(8) target detect and data report

(9) radar controller.

The preprocessor, spectral analyser, digital pulse compressor, and target detect and data report form the radar signal processor.

The system operates at Ku-band, using linear and non-linear frequency modulation plus binary coded waveform with bandwidths of 5 and 20 MHz. The pod-mounted, side-looking multibeam antenna has a 2·5 metre aperture length and provides ±60° azimuth scan coverage in both the single and multibeam modes. Real-time radar signal processing, especially pulse compression and spectral analysis, is accomplished by using fast Fourier transforms hardware.

The radar controller contains two computers; one controls the operation of all units over a data bus, the other implementing the required motion compensation of the data for the imaging modes.

Except for the antenna, standardised packaging has been used throughout the units with microwave, analogue, digital, LSI and power supply circuitry all packaged in standard ¾ ATR modules, making them applicable in other programmes.

STATUS

The MSR has been under development by General Electric since 1978. The antenna was developed under sponsorship of the Defense Advanced Research Projects Agency (DARPA), with the balance of the radar being designed on a private

venture basis. The system is currently undergoing flight tests on a C-54 aircraft.

The MSR is one of four contenders for the J-STARS programme (**5624.353**) which is a follow-on to the DARPA/US Air Force Pave Mover battlefield surveillance radar (**3940.161**). In July 1982 four contenders were selected to conduct preliminary design studies and the outcome was expected to result in proposals for full-scale development in 1984.

CONTRACTOR

General Electric Company, French Road, Utica, New York 13503, USA.

3304.353
HOWLS EXPERIMENTAL AIRBORNE RADAR

A new experimental airborne radar system for detecting and locating hostile weapons has been developed by General Electric as part of the hostile weapons location systems (HOWLS) programme under the sponsorship of the US Defense Advanced Research Projects Agency (DARPA) and management of MIT's Lincoln Laboratory. The HOWLS radar is an extremely versatile coherent J-band phased-array radar, which is designed to investigate techniques from which solutions may be defined to detect and locate fixed tactical targets in a clutter environment. Particular emphasis is being given to the detection of artillery.

Key to the new radar system is a lightweight, phased-array antenna designed and developed by GE. The antenna system utilises a low cost, highly producible phased array element that combines the radiating element and PIN diode phase shifter in a single integrated structure to minimise weight and cost.

HOWLS has six basic modes of operation. These are: contextual ground map, fixed target detection, ground moving target detection, low level doppler spectrum signature analysis, projectile detection and tracking, and doppler beam sharpening. Through microprocessor control, the radar has mode parameter flexibility and is capable of interleaved multi-mode operation. Selectable parameters include antenna scanning pattern and rate, PRF, data sampling window position, and data sampling pattern. The radar is capable of switching among parameters in an orderly manner so that up to four

HOWLS programme experimental phased-array radar

operating modes can be interleaved. Characteristics of one of the experimental HOWLS radars appeared in *Jane's Weapon Systems 1978*.

Results of the experimental HOWLS programme will provide the technology base from which radars for RPVs, helicopters, and fixed-wing aircraft can be configured to meet a variety of operational missions.

STATUS

The HOWLS radar is undergoing a comprehensive flight test programme.

CONTRACTOR

General Electric Company, French Road, Utica, New York 13503, USA.

1673.353
WESTINGHOUSE WX SERIES FIRE CONTROL RADARS

The Westinghouse WX Series is a private venture project for the development of a range of forward radars for fighter and attack aircraft, based on the use of modular design. The latter feature is intended to enable radars appropriate to varying roles and with differing degrees of sophistication to be constructed from mostly standard units, with consequent cost benefits.

The 'base' model of the range is the WX-200 and this is a pulse doppler system intended for air-to-air combat purposes. Beyond a provisional system weight of about 350 lb (160 kg), without cockpit display, few specific details have been revealed, but the following general design characteristics are known. A TWT will be used in the transmitter to provide wide bandwidth, a high peak-to-average power ratio, and to permit the adoption of frequency agility techniques of ECM.

Wherever possible digital circuitry is used, with

incoming returns being converted to digital format as near the receiver front as convenient. The receiver employs a parametric amplifier. A cassegrain scanner is employed to eliminate the cost, weight, and reliability considerations of a rotary joint. The scanner itself is not stabilised, this function being performed electronically to provide a stabilised cockpit display, the data presumably being derived from the aircraft's own attitude sensors.

The Westinghouse development plan is to evolve other radars from the WX-200 which are both simpler and more sophisticated than the base model. The WX-50, a lightweight air-to-ground system for close-air-support applications, has also been fabricated. The WX-50 is a non-coherent Ka-band radar with a reflector antenna for ground mapping and a receive-only elevation phase monopulse antenna for letdown terrain clearance. Additional growth modes include ground MTI, terrain avoidance, air-to-ground ranging, and EO cueing. The production WX-50 will weigh 64 kg.

The other models of WX radar would be achieved either by the addition of modules to provide extra desired operational features, or by a simplification of the basic WX-200 to satisfy less elaborate requirements. The company has given a number of provisional designations to other models which could be developed in the WX series. The WX-150 is a reduced power version of the WX-200. By adding data processing capacity to provide beam sharpening for high resolution ground mapping, the WX-200 would become the WX-300 for air-to-air and air-to-ground roles. The WX-400 would be a higher power version, without air-to-ground facilities but capable of long-range AI missions. A lightweight , lower cost, non-coherent pulse version would carry the designation WX-60.

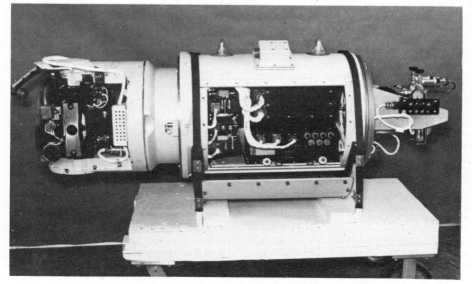
Westinghouse WX-50

STATUS

Two models of the WX-200 have been fabricated and have undergone extensive engineering testing at the Westinghouse facility. A pod-mounted version of the WX-50 has been flight tested by the US Navy on a TA-4J, on OV-10 and a UH-1N helicopter. The 208 kg prototype system demonstrated excellent performance and achieved a field MTBF of 160 hours without any contractor support.

In November 1975, Westinghouse was selected by the General Dynamics Corporation to develop the fire control radar system for the F-16 and an initial contract valued at $36 million was awarded. The F-16 radar is derived from the WX-400 and the WX-200 models. The US Air Force may purchase as many as 650 F-16s and the four-nation consortium (Belgium, Denmark, the Netherlands, and Norway) which chose the F-16 is expected to add another 350 to the total. Co-production of the F-16 radar in Europe is taking place for NATO purchases of this aircraft (see **3303.353**).

In early 1978 a WX-50 model was supplied to Fairchild to be used in flight trials intended to demonstrate the A-10 aircraft's ability to operate at night and in bad weather. The test installation uses a modified M9A pod carried on an aircraft stores pylon, but if production is decided upon, the WX-50 radar could be accommodated in a wheel nacelle. Radar features appropriate to this programme include a terrain avoidance mode and a ground MTI facility.

CONTRACTOR

Westinghouse Defense and Electronics Center, Baltimore, Maryland 21203, USA.

1676.353

AN/UPD-4 SIDE-LOOKING RADAR SYSTEM

The AN/UPD-4 side-looking radar system is an advanced design, all-weather, high-resolution reconnaissance sensor system for airborne collection of tactical and strategic intelligence information. Utilising I/J-band radar energy to illuminate selected terrain swathes, it operates equally as well in darkness as in daylight and in adverse weather.

The AN/UPD-4 consists of an AN/APD-10 synthetic aperture radar set mounted in an RF-4 aircraft, a ground-based correlator/processor set and test consoles for the maintenance of airborne and ground equipment. Airborne data link transmitters and ground receiving and processing systems are optional additions to provide radar-collected information to ground commanders more rapidly than the basic system.

The airborne system includes multi-element, phased, linear waveguide antenna arrays individually gimballed for left or right side operation. Look-angle of the antennas is maintained in flight by a control system that receives error signals from the aircraft inertial navigation system and gimbal-mounted gyroscopes and accelerometers.

The frequency converter/transmitter generates the stable radio frequency used for phase locking the radar signals and contains the transmit/receive and antenna switching components. It also supplies the swept frequency for modulating the transmitted pulses, amplifies the reflected signals and converts the received RF to IF. The amplifier/modulator is a high pulse RF pulse amplifier.

The signal data generator receives information relative to the aircraft velocity and mode, and uses this data to establish the radar PRF and generate the basic timing reference signals required throughout the system.

The radar mapping recorder contains the optical, electronic and electro-mechanical assemblies required to record the radar video data and associated coded data on 241 mm wide photographic film. These data are displayed on two 5-inch CRTs as four intensity modulated traces that are transferred by two mirror assemblies and four recording lenses to focus the images on the film. Mode strips that convey essential operational information and multi-element blocks containing information pertinent to the mission are recorded on the film. For data link operation, an identical recorder is used at the correlator/processor on the ground to establish a continuous recording/correlation path. Film speed is

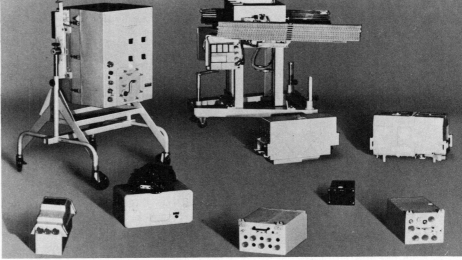

Basic components of the airborne equipment of the AN/UPD-4 radar reconnaissance system with data link equipment

carefully controlled in either application to maintain a fixed relationship to aircraft ground speed.

OPERATION

The equipment has several modes of operation, providing a variety of stand-off distances and altitudes, and the option of recording only fixed target imagery (FTI), or both FTI and MTI. Imaging of the terrain at either side can be obtained at the discretion of the operator. With data link equipped systems, the information may be transmitted to a ground station in real-time for recording and processing. The final imagery is recorded on 241 mm wide film in four channels at a scale of 1:100 000 for all modes. In the azimuth (along track) direction, targets and terrain features are imaged in terms of distance travelled and represent true ground separation. In the range (across) track direction, the imagery is recorded in slant range or the distance from the aircraft to the target.

STATUS

The AN/UPD-4 is in service in several versions with Phantom aircraft of the US Marine Corps and the Japanese Air Force. The system was developed for the US Air Force as a successor to the AN/APD-102A; but have since been enhanced and designated AN/UPD-8 (**5686.353**).

The US Marine Corps UPD-4 programme commenced with a $2·5 million contract in September 1976 for two sets of airborne equipment as part of its SURE (Sensor Update and Refurbishment Effort) programme for RF-4B aircraft. In July 1978 additional contracts amounting to $14 million for procurement of five more sets of airborne equipment, a correlator/processor and AGE. In October 1979, contracts worth more than $20 million were announced for more airborne units, correlators/processors, and AGE containing the 5-year programme for the RF-4B. In November 1982, a contract for $6 million was awarded to give the US Marine Corps a data link capability with several data link transmitters and a ground receiving station. An additional $19 million was awarded in 1983 to complete the addition of data link capability to the RF-4B fleet. Total contract value, including logistic support, exceeds $90 million.

The Japanese Air Self Defence Force has equipped 14 RF-EJ Phantoms with AN/UPD-4 radar systems under contracts amounting to about $30 million since 1972.

CONTRACTOR

Goodyear Aerospace Corporation, Arizona Division, Litchfield Park, Arizona 85340, USA.

5686.353

AN/UPD-8 SIDE-LOOKING RECONNAISSANCE RADAR

The AN/UPD-8 is a side-looking, synthetic aperture airborne reconnaissance radar system for the US Air Force. It is, in fact, an updated and improved version of the AN/UPD-4 equipment (**1676.353**), and gives a much greater range. The system provides an all-weather, day/night, stand-off, tactical and strategic reconnaissance capability, and with its extended range antenna pods and airborne data link electronics is the latest in a sequence of Goodyear airborne reconnaissance radars to have been operational since 1964.

Operating in the I/J band, the system records with equal effectiveness during daylight and darkness, and through periods of adverse weather that would render other types of reconnaissance systems ineffective. The airborne radar system's stand-off capability, which is increased by 60 per cent in the new equipment, allows coverage of border regions, harbours and coastal areas without violating another nation's airspace or national waters.

OPERATION

The airborne sensor part of the overall system, the AN/APD-12, operates in eight modes selectable by the operator according to aircraft altitude and the distance to the target area. The system can record to left or right of the aircraft with the normal antennas or with the extended-range antennas which are mounted in a centre-line pod. Target information can be transmitted to the ground in real-time through a data link, or can be recorded in flight for later processing on the ground. The former facility enables a commander on the ground, perhaps several hundred kilometres away, to evaluate detected targets while the aircraft continues its mission.

STATUS

The US Air Force awarded a $25·9 million contract to Goodyear Aerospace in May 1980 for the manufacture of a number of AN/UPD-8 systems in addition to enhancing predecessor systems currently in operational service. Options in United States FY1981 and FY1982 have brought the contract total to $45·1 million.

CONTRACTOR

Goodyear Aerospace Corporation, Arizona Division, Litchfield Park, Arizona 85340, USA.

4618.353

PROJECT SEEK SKYHOOK BALLOON-BORNE RADAR

Project Seek Skyhook is a tethered balloon-borne radar system in operation in Florida to provide surveillance of the state's coastal regions. The radar system used is an RCA AN/DPS-5 equipment which has a range of 150 nautical miles at an altitude of 12 000 feet. It is designed to detect low-flying unidentified aircraft for the US Air Force and other users. It is the latest in a series of aerostat developments that began in 1969, and four systems are in operation in Florida.

The AN/DPS-5 radar is an S-band equipment using a rotating parabolic dish measuring 22 × 12·5 feet which returns an inverted cosecant signal with two selectable polarisations that can be directed circular and horizontal or vertical and horizontal.

The radar ground sub-system has an RCA digital processor with the capability of simultaneous operation with two aerostats. Normal and MTI radar video are selectable with or without CFAR. Display can be either PPI or digitised video. The radar beacon digitiser includes capabilities for clutter mapping, target sorting and use of target track history.

CHARACTERISTICS
Frequency: 3100 MHz
Range: 150 nm (278 km) at 12 000 feet altitude
Resolution: Range 500 feet, azimuth 1°
Antenna: Rotating parabolic dish
Scan speed: 5 rpm

Weight: 1000 lb (455 kg) including mounting, gimbal, antenna, transmitter, receiver and power supply
Endurance aloft: 120 h normal, 143 h peak
STATUS
Operational.
CONTRACTOR
RCA, Government Systems Division, Missile and Surface Radar, Moorestown, New Jersey 08057, USA.

3162.353
WESTINGHOUSE BALLOON-BORNE RADAR
Under contract to the US Defense Advanced Research Projects Agency (DARPA), Westinghouse has provided radars for use with advanced aerostat or balloon platforms. In the mid-1960s DARPA initiated

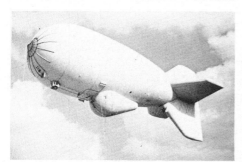

Example of a Westinghouse balloon-borne surveillance radar installation on a DARPA Family II aerostat

an R and D programme to develop a stable balloon platform and to exploit the use of such platforms for sensor and communications applications. Early work was carried out using modified British barrage balloons and these were later superseded by purpose-designed aerostats, of various sizes. Typical dimensions range between 1415 and 16 990 cm; 35 and 8·5 metres in length; and 9 and 30 metres in diameter.

This family of tethered balloons is stated to be capable of operations at altitudes of 3000 and 4500 metres. A powered tether system and low helium leakage allow the aerostat to operate at altitude for extended periods, providing greatly increased radar surveillance or communications coverage due to the increased line-of-sight ranges obtainable. Typical radar applications proposed include surveillance and AEW, location, and tracking of targets, fire control and weapons direction. Communications, EW, and target location/designation by other means, eg electro-optical sensors, are other possibilities.

Radars employed at first were all of the non-coherent variety but Westinghouse later received a contract from the US Air Force Rome Air Development Center to build a coherent system to detect airborne moving targets.

DEVELOPMENT
The following brief details of this programme refer to the Westinghouse balloon-borne radar projects which have been identified.

Low Altitude Surveillance Radar
This is a static tethered balloon-borne system which is able to carry a radar such as the AN/TPS-63. It can carry 1800 kg to a height of several thousand metres for periods of up to 20-30 days.

Small Tethered Aerostat Relocatable Systems (STARS)
A tactical, transportable system built by TACOM Corporation, a subsidiary of Westinghouse. Normal use is for coastal surveillance and at 750 metres altitude a small balloon-borne radar can detect a target with a radar cross-section of 100 m² at ranges of up to 110 km.

CONTRACTOR
Westinghouse Defense and Electronics Center, Baltimore, Maryland 21203, USA.

3299.353
EC-153 AIRBORNE HUNTER RADAR
The EC-153 Airborne Hunter radar is designed for use in lightweight fighter aircraft, and is the latest addition to Emerson's APQ-153 (**1675.353**) and APQ-159 (**3114.353**) family. Unlike those equipments the EC-153 is a coherent system using digital processing techniques, the latter comprising a feature called digital plant control by the manufacturer. By this is meant that a general-purpose mini-computer enables all scan patterns and servo stabilisation loops to be software controlled. In addition to the range, velocity and angle, the computer also controls tracking loops. This technique yields a claimed reduction of 30 per cent in the hardware employed.

The EC-153 is a pulse doppler radar operating in the I/J-band, with a look-down capability in the air-to-air mode. The digital coherent waveform maintains a low false alarm rate, and a set of nine PRFs are used to eliminate range and velocity blind zones, and to resolve range and velocity ambiguities.

The three main functions are search, acquisition and tracking, but additional roles such as air-to-ground ranging, high-resolution mapping, missile illumination, and terrain avoidance are also possible. In the air-to-air look-down search mode, coherent pulse doppler processing is used to detect targets against ground clutter, while in the look-up air search mode, a non-coherent pulse waveform provides long-range detection where background clutter levels are lower. Target tracking can be initiated in the latter

EC-153 radar test installation with radome removed to show scanner

mode. In the look-down search mode, the pilot initiates the acquisition and tracking sequence. The radar locks on and tracks the target in range, velocity and angle, and automatically switches PRFs to keep the targets in a clear region. In an air combat situation, manual or automatic acquisition and tracking sequences are provided for use with guns or dogfight missiles.

The EC-153 comprises the following hardware: a flat plate antenna array; a coherent transmitter/receiver; digital electronic signal conditioner; a radar data controller; scan converter and indicator unit; and control panel. The antenna is a two-axis monopulse planar array of slotted waveguides with a guard horn, digitally controlled with rate gyro track stabilisation.

The transmitter/receiver employs a crystal source coherent exciter with a ring loop TWT. The display unit contains a bright CRT for the presentation of TV format information derived from a digital scan converter.

CHARACTERISTICS
Frequency: I/J-band
Peak power: 10 kW
Waveform: Pulse, low PRF; pulse doppler, medium PRF
Receiver: 2-channel, GaAs FET/microwave ICs
Antenna: Plate
Gain: 29·5 dB
Sidelobes: –40 dB
Search coverage: 90 × 90°

Detection range	Look-up Pulse	Look-down Pulse doppler
Search/track	37 km	24 km
Range tracking accuracy	150 – 300 m	15 m
	300 – 915 km	9 m
	915 m – 150 km	1%

Range rate accuracy: 3 m/s
Range rate limits: –300 to +150 m/s
Max range: 150 km
Minimum range: 150 m
STATUS
Flight tested by US Navy in 1978.
CONTRACTOR
Emerson Electric Co, Electronics and Space Division, 8100 West Florissant Avenue, St Louis, Missouri 63136, USA.

5624.353
JOINT SURVEILLANCE AND TARGET ATTACK RADAR SYSTEM
The Joint Surveillance and Target Attack Radar (J-STARS) project is a joint US Air Force and US Army development which combines the former's Pave Mover programme with the latter's Battlefield Data Systems projects (Assault Breaker programme). J-STARS was scheduled for development commencing in 1983, under the control of a joint US Air Force/US Army team, as an airborne anti-tank radar system for the two services. Various designs were proposed and four of these were flight tested during 1982. Four industry teams are bidding for the contract; Hughes/E-Systems; Grumman/UTC

Norden Systems/TRW Systems Engineering and Development; Westinghouse/Lockheed and Boeing/General Electric.

The radar is primarily intended to detect enemy armour on and behind the battlefield and also to direct attacks against it. The system is designed to direct real-time attacks against moving ground targets by low-flying aircraft and missiles, and also to provide guidance of missiles carrying sub-munitions to the target locale. Installation of the system is proposed on the Lockheed TR-1 or the Boeing C-18 for the US Air Force and the OV-1D for the US Army.

It was originally intended that requests for proposals for full-scale development be issued in early 1983, this date has slipped to 1984, with

contracts likely to be awarded later the same year. The process has been complicated by the integration of the Air Force and Army requirements. The latter wants wide area surveillance and an MTI capability only whilst the US Air Force requires a system that will detect both stationary and moving targets and will employ a data link for weapon guidance.

Although funds for J-STARS itself, the J-STARS ground stations and the associated J-TACMS (Joint Tactical Missile System) have been earmarked for 1984, the only piece of equipment so far selected is the Motorola intelligent raster-scan display system which will be common to both airborne and ground equipment.

4648.353
COVERT STRIKE RADAR
Covert Strike is a bistatic radar system project under development by the USAF Avionics Laboratory at Wright Patterson Air Force Base. The system provides for illumination of a target by a stand-off

radar installed on either a satellite or an aircraft, with only a receiving system required on board the strike aircraft. This allows the latter to approach the target in a passive, or covert, manner, and is also designed to seriously hamper the enemy in his jamming techniques. No technical details have been disclosed

other than that the radar is probably a synthetic aperture system.
STATUS
A long-term project in the design phase with development and trials continuing until about 1990.

ELECTRONIC WARFARE EQUIPMENT

CANADA

1714.253
MODEL 100 NAVAL DF SET

The Model 100 is a shipboard direction finding, intercept, and surveillance system covering the frequency range 10 kHz to 180 MHz.

The Model 100 DF set operates on the principle of resolving the electromagnetic field at the antenna location into a set of orthogonal vectors which are then amplified and applied to the plates of a cathode ray tube (CRT), so as to trace a bearing line indicating the azimuth of arrival of the signal.

Two antennas are used: one for the LF to HF ranges and one for VHF. The LF/HF antenna derives the DF vectors from a pair of multi-turn, switched loops while the sense is obtained from a set of balanced dipoles. The VHF antenna comprises 16 separate monopole elements which can be arranged as crossed-Adcock and parallel dipole arrays in both the horizontal and vertical plane of polarisation. The VHF antenna is constructed around a hollow column which permits the passage of cable to the LF/HF antenna and to an

aircraft warning light, located uppermost.

The DF signal vectors are amplified by two identical receiver channels which are accurately matched in phase and gain under all conditions of tuning and signal strength. A third channel, matched in phase only and equipped with a separate AGC, serves to amplify the omni-directional sense signal which is applied to the grid of the CRT to blank out the unwanted half of the bearing trace.

In addition to the instantaneous single-signal DF mode, the receiver can be operated in a panoramic mode (amplitude/frequency display), or in a wideband sweep mode, allowing the operator to see simultaneously the bearings and frequencies of all the signals present within the search band. This '3-D' display is made possible by using colour modulation as the frequency parameter.

A phantom omni-directional audio output is available at all times for intelligence interception purposes. This monitor channel can be tuned to any of the signals within the sweep band without

disrupting the panoramic bearing display.

Digital, automatic tuning (local or remote) is derived from a phase-locked frequency synthesiser fitted with an oven stabilised frequency standard. The synthesiser is designed for fast access manual tuning, using the 3-DEK decade reed switches which are gear-interlocked to count up or down automatically. The tuning frequency is indicated directly by the decade knobs and in addition there is a projection-type luminous readout which can be duplicated in a remote location.

The equipment is also produced in a land-mobile configuration, under the designation Model 109, to form a complete two-man vehicle-mounted DF and surveillance unit.
CONTRACTOR
General Precision Industries Ltd, PO Box 88, Place Bonaventure, 32 Brome Street, Montreal 114 PQ, Canada.

4161.293
CANEWS

The Canadian Electronic Warfare System (CANEWS) is a fully automatic naval integrated system incorporating ESM, ECM, and chaff counter-measures elements. It is designed to provide threat warning and surveillance facilities and also has the potential for Elint electronic intelligence gathering operations.

The passive, ESM, section provides surveillance over a frequency range of 1 to 18 GHz and an eight-horn antenna assembly gives 360° coverage in azimuth. An instantaneous frequency measuring (IFM) receiver covers the frequency range with frequency determined to an accuracy of about 5 GHz, and bearings to better than 4° rms. A sensitivity of –70 dB provides maximum detection range, which reaches beyond the horizon (depending upon conditions).

A Westinghouse Canada Ltd signal processor based on two Univac AN/UYK-20 digital computers performs system control and signal processing and analysis. Data rates of up to 500 000 pulses per second can be accepted and there is special purpose hardware in the system to carry out pre-processing of

digitised pulse trains. The emitter library store is carried on magnetic tape, with a reported repertoire of 2000 emitter modes arranged in geographical segments. The library is programmable with full operator and access control and a capacity of up to 128 known emitters. Parameters of unidentified emitters that are intercepted can be recorded.

The system is operated from a single full-colour display and control console which incorporates two display units: a tactical PPI presentation showing threat, hostile and friendly sectors, and above it a VDU giving a page-by-page read-out of emitter parameters and other alpha-numeric data.

The receiver employed is an updated version of the MEL UAA-1 (Abbey Hill) equipment and the antenna assembly resembles that company's SUSIE array (**1707.253**) rather than the Abbey Hill antenna. The antenna assembly weight is less than 200 kg, and reliability has been increased by the substitution of solid-state amplifiers for the TWTs formerly employed.
DEVELOPMENT
CANEWS evolved from an experimental project 'Zander', initiated in Canada in the 1960s. A joint Canada/UK successor project called 'Percept' of 1973

involved the mating of the MEL/Royal Navy UAA-1 ESM system with a Canadian signal processor. Trials were carried out in 1973 and these led to the Canadian decision to develop an advanced automated naval ESM system under the project name 'Ogee'.
STATUS
Sea trials of the project Ogee system took place aboard the RCN frigate *Saguenay* in 1976 and the Canadian Government authorised the construction and trials of CANEWS in 1978. A contract was awarded in May 1979.

System integration was carried out in July 1980 and the first set was delivered in October and installed on the frigate *Terra Nova*. A total of 14 sets have been authorised for fitting in DDH 280 class ships and for the Canadian Destroyer Life Extension Programme. Production of these began in 1981 and in late 1983, MEL received a further £10 million contract from the Canadian Department of Defense.
CONTRACTORS
MEL, Manor Royal, Crawley, Sussex, England.

Westinghouse Canada Ltd, Electronics Systems Division, PO Box 510, Hamilton, Ontario L8N 3K2, Canada.

FRANCE

3374.353
TYPE BF RADAR WARNING RECEIVER

The Type BF radar warning receiver is for airborne applications in aircraft of the Mirage and similar types. It provides the pilot with warning of most categories of airborne or surface threat radars and an indication of their direction.

The system consists of four wide-band antennas, a video receiver, and optionally, a synchronisation unit. In aircraft other than the Mirage, in which case the system controls and indicator unit are integrated into the cockpit by the aircraft manufacturer, these items are supplied as separate units.

Each antenna unit contains a photographically etched spiral antenna and microwave circuits such as: RF test oscillator; limiter modulator diodes; high-pass filter; detector circuits; video modulation unit; video preamplifier. Packing of the antenna units is of two types, one having a flush-mounting radome for the left- and right-hand units, and the other having a conical radome and housing suitable for mounting on the aircraft fin to provide fore and aft coverage. Each antenna has a 90° cover, to provide all-round search

capability with the full system.

The BF equipment will detect signals of pulse, CW, ICW, or TWS radars, either fixed frequency or frequency-agile. PRFs between 600 and 12 000 Hz can be accommodated.

An audio alarm is given for each radar threat detected, and the general direction of the threat is given by the illumination of one or more of four signal lamps around the aircraft outline on the indicator. The nature of the threat is shown by illumination of one of three indicator lamps denoting:
(1) conventional pulse radar
(2) CW or ICW radar
(3) TWS ground threat radar.
CHARACTERISTICS
Antenna (L and R) dimensions: 53 × 148 mm diameter
Antenna (F and R) dimensions: 360 × 82 mm diameter
Video receiver dimensions: 322 × 193 × 57 mm
Synchroniser dimensions: 209 × 110 × 45 mm
Indicator dimensions: 68 × 61 × 61 mm
Control box dimensions: 146 × 95 × 40 mm
Combined weight: 9·2 kg

Type BF radar warning receiver equipment

STATUS
Production. Operational in Mirage F1-C and Super Etendard, also Mirage F1-A, Netherlands F-5, and Mirage IIIZ aircraft. A helicopter version is produced as the TMV 008H.
CONTRACTOR
Thomson-CSF, Avionics Division, 178 boulevard Gabriel-Péri, 92240 Malakoff, France.

3377.293
DAGAIE NAVAL COUNTERMEASURES EQUIPMENT

The Dagaie countermeasure equipment is an automatic dispenser for IR decoy flares and chaff grenades to provide naval vessels with passive self-protection against heat-seeking, radar homing and

dual-mode anti-ship missiles. The system will accept threat data from a variety of sources, such as radar, ESM systems, optical, etc, and this information is used with data such as ship's own speed and heading to compute the optimum countermeasures deployment.

The Dagaie launcher comprises ten replaceable

containers, each of which is loaded with either IR or chaff rockets. The containers weigh 40 or 45 kg, according to type.

The firing sequence runs automatically and is triggered on a missile alarm from a variety of sources, such as radar, ESM systems, optical sights, thus providing a very short reaction time. The firing direction is optimised in accordance with the threat bearing, wind speed and direction, ship heading and speed data.

The launching of radar and IR decoys is so arranged that the most advanced mixed-guidance missile cannot discriminate them and thus co-location of both decoys is achieved.

The installation is either a double mounting for ships over 800/1000 tons, or a single mounting for smaller vessels, and comprises:

(1) one trainable mounting (or two) which carries ten replaceable containers (suitcases), each of which is loaded with either IR or chaff projectiles. The range of existing ammunition enables decoys to be adapted to the various types of ships
(2) one or two servo-units
(3) one data-processing unit whose purpose is to compute the firing data
(4) one power-supply unit
(5) one supervision unit used to operate the system and display the loading state of the mounting
(6) one manoeuvre indicator which displays the proposed ship's manoeuvre in order to extend the protection time as long as possible without renewing the decoy.

For either the single or double installation a reduced size mounting carrying six suitcases can be supplied.

CHARACTERISTICS

Resetting time for 90°: <2 s
Medium aiming speed: 1·5 rad/s
Average reaction time: <4 s (reaction time is the time lapse between reception of 'missile alarm' information and the end of IR firing)

STATUS

In production for several navies, including those of France, Argentina, Bahrain, Kuwait, Malaysia, Colombia, the SAWARI programme of the Royal Saudi Navy, the Combattante II in Qatar and the Combattante III in Tunisia.

CONTRACTOR

Compagnie de Signaux et d'Entreprises Electriques, 17 place Etienne Pernet, 75738 Paris Cedex 15, France.

Dagaie countermeasure launcher in operation during tests of a production equipment off Toulon

---

4350.293

MAGAIE NAVAL COUNTERMEASURES DECOY SYSTEM

The MAGAIE decoy launcher has been designed to protect small or medium displacement surface vessels against attacks by missiles fitted with electromagnetic (EM) or infra-red (IR) seekers or a combination of the two. It is derived from the DAGAIE system (**3377.293**), using the same principle, but is more compact and adapted for installation on small patrol boats under construction, or on larger vessels in the course of refits when the lack of space prevents the installation of a larger system.

The missile neutralisation is achieved by deception, using the centroid effect; EM and IR decoys are placed very close to the vessel and then move away under the wind action to decoy the missile away from its intended target. The firing direction is computed in accordance with the threat bearing, wind speed and direction, and ship's heading and speed.

The MAGAIE system is based on the joint use of original ammunition of an EM/IR combined type, fired from mortars pre-orientated in elevation, gathered in only one consumable suitcase, and a trainable mounting capable of accommodating three suitcases.

The operation is fully automatic from the reception of a missile threat alarm by computation of firing data and selection of ammunition suitcase during the resetting of the launcher to firing of the suitcase.

The MAGAIE processing and launching installation includes, according to the ship's capabilities:

(1) one or two mobile launchers, fully trainable, capable of receiving three suitcases
(2) a processing and servo control unit where all firing data is computed and the mounting reset order is generated
(3) a supervision unit controlling the system operation
(4) a manoeuvre indicator showing the recommended manoeuvre for the vessel.

The system with its simple interfaces is easily adapted to the various sensors (radar, ESM, optical).

CHARACTERISTICS

Average reaction delay: <5 s
Launcher
Max training arc: 330°
Reslewing time for 90°: ≤2 s
Reslewing speed: 1·2 rad/s
Sweeping radius: 400 mm
Height: 1200 mm
Weight: 400 kg
Ammunition suitcase weight: 65 kg

STATUS

In production.

CONTRACTOR

Compagnie de Signaux et d'Entreprises Electriques, 17 place Etienne Pernet, 75738 Paris Cedex 15, France.

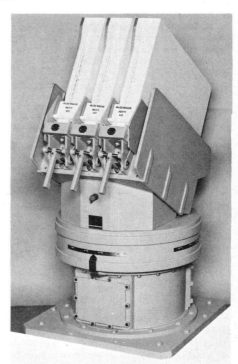

MAGAIE decoy launcher

5656.293

SAGAIE NAVAL COUNTERMEASURES DECOY SYSTEM

SAGAIE is a fully automatic, passive counter-measures system designed to protect medium and large ships from surface-to-surface and air-to-surface missiles. It will provide protection from missiles guided by electromagnetic (EM) or infra-red (IR) seekers, or any combination of these two, even when the missiles are attacking simultaneously over the entire horizon.

The system operates in conjunction with DAGAIE (**3377.293**) and provides long-range defence by confusion and dilution effects against enemy target designating radars, and close-in defence by distraction and seduction against acquisition and tracking systems in missile seekers, in order that DAGAIE can complete its centroid deception effect.

The SAGAIE system is fully automatic from the reception of a missile threat alarm originating from any of the surveillance systems (radar, IR, optical or ESM) and will optimise the use of decoys in a very short reaction time. The equipment can be used alone (confusion and distraction) or jointly with a jammer (dilution, substitution after concealment, substitution

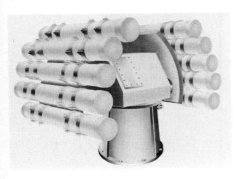

SAGAIE countermeasures system

after deception) by firing of substitution decoys.

The installation comprises:

(1) one or two fully stabilised launchers loaded with ten rockets in containers and trainable in azimuth and elevation

(2) one or two servo units

(3) one or two aiming and maintenance units

(4) a processing unit which computes the rocket launching sequence and provides information for the supervision unit

(5) a supervision unit with controls and status displays

(6) an interface unit which provides for operation with any tactical data or target designation system.

SAGAIE can fire either EM or IR decoy rocket type ammunition. The rocket is packaged in a waterproof launcher container. This container is used for handling, transport and storage, and when secured to the mounting ensures guidance of the rocket at the moment of launch.

CHARACTERISTICS

Height: 2000 mm
Sweeping radius: 1600 mm
Weight(empty): 1900 kg
Number of rockets: 10
Container
Length: 1800 mm
Diameter: 330 mm
Weight: 30 kg
STATUS

The SAGAIE system is under study and development for the French Navy for fitment to larger ships (frigates, destroyers and aircraft carriers).

CONTRACTOR

Compagnie de Signaux et d'Enterprises Electriques, 17 place Etienne Pernet, 75738 Paris Cedex 15, France.

3379.393
DB 3163 (REMORA) JAMMER POD

The DB 3163 jammer pod, known also as Remora, is designed to provide self-protection for tactical aircraft against both air and ground radar threats. Both pulse and CW emitters can be detected, identified and countered automatically by means of the power management system incorporated in the pod.

A superheterodyne receiver performs a frequency scan search on emissions received by antennas located at both ends of the pod, this being carried out simultaneously. Up to three frequency bands can be selected by the pilot from six bands pre-programmed before flight. Threat data are stored digitally and up to

three can be jammed at the same time by means of electronic switching and power management of the TWT transmitter system. A 'boot-strap' system of air cooling is employed.

CHARACTERISTICS

Frequency: Probably I/J-band. Pre-programmed
Pod length: 3·52 m
Diameter: 254 mm
Weight: <160 kg
Power consumption: <1·7 kVA (transmit); <0·7 kVA (receive)

CONTRACTOR

Thomson-CSF, Avionics Division, 178 boulevard Gabriel Péri, 92240 Malakoff, France.

DB 3163 jammer pod

5665.393
ALKAN COUNTERMEASURES DISPENSERS

Alkan designs and supplies a range of airborne countermeasures dispensing equipment for the self protection of both fixed and rotary wing aircraft against IR and radar seeker fitted missiles. This equipment takes cylindrical chaff and/or IR pyrotechnic cartridges and is either mounted on existing stores stations or fitted to the airframe.

The Type 532 countermeasures dispenser pod, currently in production, is appropriate for most aircraft capable of carrying external stores, whether NATO standardised or not. Like other pods it can be easily installed and removed from the aircraft.

The structure-fitted dispensers can be integrated into or conformally fitted to the airframe, in both cases leaving free all external store carrying stations. The dispenser construction is modular and is designed for the use of fully interchangeable IR and EM cartridge magazines. Alkan also designs and supplies the associated electronic systems for the cartridge firing sequence.

STATUS

In development for Jaguar, Mirage and other aircraft.

CONTRACTOR

R Alkan & Cie, rue du 8 Mai 1945, 94460 Valenton, France.

Type 532 zone saturation countermeasures dispenser

3533.293
TMV 433 NAVAL COUNTERMEASURES SET

The TMV 433 countermeasures set is an electronic warfare system designed principally for fast patrol boats to provide them with the fast reaction times needed for success in anti-missile operations. It includes the following items of equipment: DR2000 broadband receiver; warning, analysis and identification unit (DALIA or ARIAL); a noise and deception jammer; and a printer. It can be integrated with any weapons system due to the use of digital processing. Additionally, the TMV 433 system can be configured for use aboard submarines, aircraft, or as a shore-based installation. The set is completed in each case by an appropriate antenna or antennas.

The main characteristics of each item of equipment are as follows:

DR2000 Receiver

(1) six DF antennas and one omni-directional broadband antenna

(2) six reception channels for DF

(3) wide-open crystal video receiver, pulse and CW detection

(4) display of azimuth, signal level, frequency band

(5) signal selection capacity based on frequency band, level, pulse width, bearing.

DALIA/ARIAL

(1) warning of threat radar (locked-on, CW, submarine)

(2) automatic analysis with high accuracy

(3) automatic identification by comparison with stored parameters

(4) digital output for connection with a weapon system.

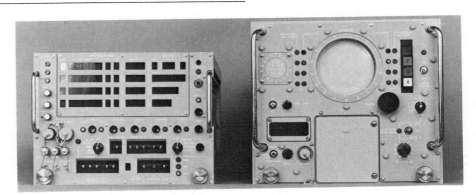

DALIA analyser (left) and associated DR2000 receiver/display (right) used in TMV 433 naval countermeasures set

The following table shows the equipment complements for various TMV 433 applications

	Ships	Submarines	Helicopter surveillance	Patrol aircraft	Ground stations
DR2000	X	X	X	X	X
DALIA	X	X	X	X	X
ARIAL	X	X	X	X	X
Printer	X	X	X	X	X

The DR2000 weighs 43 kg (including display) and for surface ships an antenna weighing 27 kg is fitted; for submarines the antenna weighs 34 kg, while for aircraft installations six one-kilogramme units are employed. The DALIA analyser weighs 33 kg and the alternative ARIAL equipment weighed 30 kg.

Typical antenna for surface ship fitting of DR2000 system, with and without radome cover

3376.353

TMV 026 AIRBORNE ESM SYSTEM

The TMV 026 airborne ESM system consists of a DR2000 radar intercept receiver, an alarm, analysis, and identification equipment (DALIA 500 or ARIAL 15) and a set of six DF antennas and one omni-directional antenna. The equipment is suitable for use in both helicopters or fixed-wing maritime patrol aircraft.

The DR2000 provides all-round passive search, detection of all pulse and CW signals, and gives an instantaneous audible and visual alert.

Additional alarm and analysis capabilities are given by the DALIA 500 (or ARIAL – *analyse radar pour identification et alerte*) equipment. This provides specific threat warning signals; automatic analysis of received signals to yield frequency, PRF, pulse width, RF level, antenna rotation rate, jitter, etc; and automatic identification of emitters by comparison with a library including 500 or 15 radars (DALIA 500 or ARIAL 15)

STATUS

Series production. Limited numbers only were delivered with the ARIAL analyser, most employing the higher capacity DALIA equipment.

CONTRACTOR

Thomson-CSF, Avionics Division, 178 boulevard Gabriel Péri, 92240 Malakoff, France.

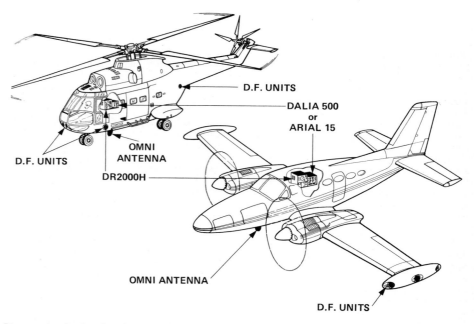

Diagram showing location of equipment in typical helicopter and fixed-wing aircraft installations of TMV 026 airborne ESM system

3534.053

TMV 200 ELISA ELINT RECEIVER

The Elisa ESM/Elint receiver is designed for search and analysis of pulse or CW signals for use in strategic or tactical operations conducted by land, air or naval forces. It can be deployed in airborne, shipborne or ground based configurations. The equipment consists of a rotatable broadband antenna array, frequency converter, receiver and an operator's console.

The Elisa system was developed to ensure detection of radars having a high pulse compression rate and also radars with fixed, random and coded parameters. The system has a high instantaneous probability of intercept and through the use of reprogrammable software, is able to face changes of the threat.

The digitally controlled receiver features fast frequency commutation, a high sweep rate, modular design and includes a microprocessor unit for data processing and automatic system operation. The frequency converters in association with the basic receiver provide operation over the whole radar

spectrum. Automatic measurements are made of the usual parameters, assisted by the use of high accuracy quartz-driven oscillators and low-noise RF amplifiers for high sensitivity. Pulse-by-pulse DF is possible, and the display incorporates a memory device to assist interception of brief signals and frequency-agile radars.

The search pattern is easily programmed by the operator in terms of frequency coverage, disabled frequencies, wide or narrow band selectivity, dwell time, etc, which results in quick adaptation to operational needs. The operator communicates with the system via a keyboard. The console includes a plasma screen showing the panaromic situation, radar parameters and a detailed radar analysis (emission histograms and spectrums).

The system is compatible with peripheral equipments for additional analysis and immediate or delayed operational exploitation.

CONTRACTOR

Thomson-CSF, Avionics Division, 178 boulevard Gabriel Péri, 92240 Malakoff, France.

Thomson-CSF Elisa ESM/Elint receiver control/ display console

5657.293

SAPIENS EW SYSTEM

SAPIENS (Surveillance Alarm and Protection, Intelligence EW Naval System) is an EW system designed for small and medium size vessels. It is a joint system by Thomson-CSF and CSEE and comprises elements of both companies' EW equipment. SAPIENS 1, for small patrol boats and mine countermeasures craft, consists of a DALIA

analyser/identifier with a radar library of at least 1000 possible threats, a DR2000 crystal video ESM receiver and a DAGAIE decoy launcher.

SAPIENS 2, for corvette and frigate sized ships, is basically the same as SAPIENS 1 but uses the DR4000S IFM receiver, instead of the DR2000, to give high sensitivity for longer range surveillance, low frequency radar detection and synthetic data display facilities. A third variant, SAPIENS 3, incorporates a

jammer which additionally provides noise and deception jamming or a combination of both.

CONTRACTOR

Thomson-CSF, Avionics Division, 178 boulevard Gabriel Péri, 92240 Malakoff, France.

Compagnie de Signaux et d'Entreprises Electriques, 17 place Etienne Pernet, 75738 Paris Cedex 15, France.

3913.193
FRENCH LAND-BASED EW SYSTEMS
A number of French military EW systems have been identified which are land-based if not necessarily dedicated to the French Army; most are mainly concerned with communications aspects of EW and while there is insufficient detail to warrant individual entries for each, the following paragraphs give what information can be revealed.
BROMURE
This is believed to be a communications jammer.
BINOC
Probably another jammer, possibly covering a different part of the spectrum to Bromure.
ELEBORE
Elebore operates in the HF part of the telecommunications spectrum and performs several functions (eg detection, location, monitoring, etc). It is computer-based and uses a version of the CISMA 15M digital computer.
ELFA
Elfa is the name of an intercept system. The frequency coverage is not known.
ELODEE
Elodee is the name of a DF, emitter locating system. The frequency coverage is not known in detail but it is known that the system operates in the communications bands so that it is probable that the HF, VHF and UHF parts of the spectrum are covered. A CISMA 15M computer is incorporated.
EMERAUDE
Emeraude operates in the VHF band and is a combination system providing several facilities relating to communications monitoring, surveillance, and emitter location. A CISMA 15M computer is used in the system.
STATUS
All are believed to be operational with the French Armed Forces.
CONTRACTORS
Not identified, but probably most of the major French electronics companies have been involved. The government DGA (Délégation Générale pour l'Armement) establishment SEFT (Section d'Etudes et Fabrications des Télécommunications) was responsible for development of the above systems

3914.153
THOMSON-CSF COMMUNICATIONS INTELLIGENCE EQUIPMENT
The Thomson-CSF concern produces a wide range of special-purpose receivers and associated equipment for communications intelligence gathering, surveillance and monitoring purposes and the main examples of the current range are described briefly in the following paragraphs.

The range is suitable for equipping listening stations (fixed or mobile) for strategic or tactical applications, and frequency bands from 100 kHz to 1 GHz are covered.
TRC 291
The TRC 291 is a VHF intercept receiver covering the 20 to 120 MHz frequency range, or 20 to 500 MHz if the TRC 2919 converter is added, and it has been designed for driving modern communications countermeasures systems. Applications such as listening posts, automatic DF stations, jamming posts etc are typical. The TRC 291 (9) provides for activity detection, display of the received signal within a selected ten MHz sub-band, and selection and analysis of a particular signal. Another unit which can be added to the TRC 291 is the TRC 2913 AM/FM demodulator which permits aural monitoring of appropriate signals of this type that are intercepted.
TRC 294
The TRC 294 is a combined VHF/UHF receiver for radio monitoring and listening in the band 20 to 120 MHz, with the possibility of extending the upper frequency limit to 500 MHz or 1000 MHz. Frequency selection is by either a keyboard or a flywheel fine tuning knob, for reception of known frequencies or for surveillance purposes. The receiver can store up to ten frequencies with transmission mode and band-pass, and it can also be remotely controlled. There is an add-on panoramic receiver, TRC 2941, which can be used in conjunction with the TRC 294 to provide for display of a bandwidth up to 180 MHz and analysis of received signals.
TRC 394
The TRC 394 is the HF monitoring receiver. The TRC 394C uses a high stability synthesiser with 10 Hz steps to cover the 100 kHz to 30 MHz band. The frequency can be selected by either a keyboard or flywheel tuning control with increments of 10 Hz, 100 Hz or 1 kHz, and there is provision for 20 stored frequencies. The TRC 3941 is a panoramic adapter for use with the TRC 394C and provides for the display of signals in a band centred on the frequency tuned on the receiver. The bandwidth of the frequency range displayed on the panoramic display for analysis is selected according to the scanned frequency band. Like the TRC 291 and TRC 294, the TRC 394C is compatible with remote control operation for use in computer-based COMINT or SIGINT systems.

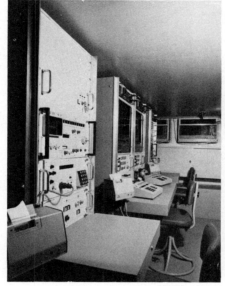
Interior of command station of French communications countermeasures systems. TRC 291 VHF intercept receiver can be seen among other equipment on the left

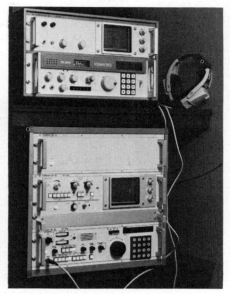
Upper units are TRC 394 HF monitoring receiver and associated TRC 3941 panoramic adapter, while the lower three items are (top to bottom) TRC 2919 transposer unit, TRC 2941 panoramic receiver, and TRC 294 VHF/UHF receiver

STATUS
This equipment is in production and is thought to have been supplied to French and overseas forces.
CONTRACTOR
Thomson-CSF, Division Telecommunications, 66 rue du Fosse-Blanc, BP156, 92231 Gennevilliers, France.

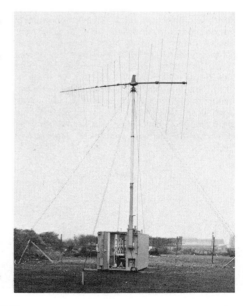
Listening post of Thomson-CSF communications countermeasures system

3535.053
XR100 COMINT RECEIVING SYSTEM
The XR100 V/UHF receiving system has been designed for surveillance and analysis of communications signals (AM, FM, CW or pulse) in the frequency range 20 to 1000 MHz (1500 MHz on request). It can be operated either as a manual, semi-automated or a fully automated system (computer controlled). The basic system consists of: XRP100 panoramic receiver; and XRA100 analysis receiver. Both types are equipped with the XRT100 series of RF voltage-tuned heads.

The modular design allows for additional equipment options:
(1) frequency indicator and repeater for the manual system, used for dialogue between the chief controller and the operators
(2) automatic tuning module for XRA analysis receiver for semi-automatic system working operationally as a manual system but without need for manual tuning.
XR100 SA Automatic Receiving System
The automatic receiving system uses a synthesised local oscillator for XRP panoramic receiver controlled by a data processing equipment in the automatic system. The data processing equipment is composed of a mini-computer with a mass memory and a CRT/keyboard console. The sweeping of the XRP panoramic receiver is controlled according to the inhibited sub-bands and frequencies (permanent or temporary inhibition) and to the already detected transmissions. As soon as a transmission is detected a vacant XRA analysis receiver is looked for, and when found it receives the control messages for automatic tuning to this frequency. Then the XRP receiver sweeping starts again. The CRT/keyboard

console is used for updating the list of sub-bands and frequencies either to be inhibited or more frequently swept.

A system can be equipped with six XRA analysis receivers in a manual configuration, or more (up to 16) if automated. A DF system (manual or automatic) can also be associated with the equipment.

Design features and objectives include: versatility, compactness, ease of operation; frequency automatic digital display on all receivers; modular construction; 2400 bauds multiplexed digital frequency signals between instruments (connections

by a simple coaxial cable, or remote control by modems on telephone line). Provision is made for central operation between several receiving stations (for triangulation), and for coupling with a DF system. The equipment is suitable for use in airborne, shipborne or ground based systems.

CHARACTERISTICS

XRP100 Panoramic Receiver

Dynamic range: 70 dB

Operating modes

PANORAMIC (the whole frequency range of the RF tuning head is displayed on the 8 × 10 cm CRT)

PARTIAL (or sector)
PANORAMIC/PARTIAL (uncalibrated)
PANORAMIC/PARTIAL (calibrated)
ANALYSIS
Digital readout of the centre tuning frequency with:
5 digits during the panoramic sweep,
6 digits in the analysis mode.
Push-button transfer of this tuning frequency to the selected analysis receiver XRA100 for the manual mode.
In the analysis mode: same specifications as for the analysis receiver (except the loudspeaker).

XRA100 Analysis Receiver

Operates with the same voltage tuned heads as the XRP100,
Digital readout of the frequency to be tuned (sent by the chief operator in the manual system),
Digital readout of the tuned frequency (6 digits),
AM, FM, CW and pulse reception.

IF bandwidths: 300, 50, 20 and 10 kHz,
BFO and COR facilities (for magnetic recorder)
Sensitivity: –103 to –109 dB/m for 10 dB (S + N)/N ratio (depends on the RF tuning head)

Spectrum display section

Sweep width: 0 – 3 MHz

Resolution: 10 kHz

Sweep rate: 20 Hz

Marker frequency: at the IF: 30 MHz
Loudspeaker or headphone monitoring

Audio output power: 100 mW (minimum) into 600 Ω load

Audio frequency response: 20 Hz – 20 kHz
Meter: signal strength
Phase lock of the tuned frequency (on the quartz oscillator of the frequency meter),
Push-button link with the chief operator (end of a signal analysis),
Possibility of automatic tuning on the frequency sent by the chief operator (semi-automatic mode) or by the data processing system (automatic mode).

STATUS

In series production.

CONTRACTOR

Sintra-Alcatel, 26 rue Malakoff, 92600 Asnieres, France.

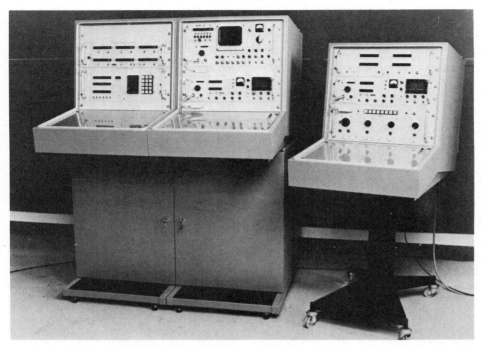

XR100 SA automatic receiving system

4351.053

DR4000 IFM ESM RECEIVER

The DR4000 is a highly sensitive crystal IFM ESM receiver with frequency coverage from C- to J-band, display of graphic and alpha-numeric signals being provided on a three-colour CRT, together with associated data. Symbols, alpha-numeric data and interface comply with NTDS standards. The display shows the tactical situation in the upper part and intercept parameters below.

Very little information is available on this system other than that there are three variants – DR4000S, DR4000A and DR4000U for surface vessels, maritime patrol aircraft or helicopters, and submarines. The system can be interfaced with decoy dispensers or

jammers and automatically controls their operation.

The antenna system of the DR4000S includes two DF arrays (2 × 6 DF channels), one omni antenna (frequency channel) and modules housing RF amplifiers. The installation can be at the masthead, around the mast or on both sides of the bridge or superstructure. The processing unit, either frequency band designation or instantaneous frequency measurement, has reprogramming capabilities with deinterleaving, analysis and identification.

STATUS

In production. Saudi Arabia is buying four systems.

CONTRACTOR

Thomson-CSF, Avionics Division, 178 boulevard Gabriel Péri, 92240 Malakoff, France.

DR4000 IFM ESM system console

4635.393

LACROIX COUNTERMEASURES AMMUNITION

Société E Lacroix manufactures a range of electromagnetic (EM) and infra-red (IR) passive countermeasures ammunition for combat aircraft. These munitions are used in aircraft such as the F-16, Tornado, Viggen, Jaguar, Mirage, Alpha-Jet,

Phantom and a number of helicopters.

The EM cartridges, Types 622, 651 and 888L, are made up of aluminium coated fibre-glass, with the length cut according to the individual customer requirements, and are electrically ejected. The IR munition, Types 407, 587 and 623, consists of one or two IR flares fitted with a pyrotechnic part containing

ignition and safety devices and is ejected electrically from the cartridge.

STATUS

Mass production.

CONTRACTOR

Société E Lacroix, Departement Contre-mesures, Route de Toulouse, 31600 Muret, France.

GERMANY (FEDERAL REPUBLIC)

3643.293
BUCK-WEGMANN DECOY SYSTEM

The Buck-Wegmann Hot Dog/Silver Dog equipment is an IR/chaff dispenser decoy system for use on boats and ships as a countermeasure against anti-ship missiles equipped with active radar and/or IR seeker heads. The rapid deployment of IR and radar decoy materials from the vessel, and the good radar returns provided by the chaff cloud cause an attacking missile to lock on to this instead of the

vessel itself, allowing the target to take evasive escape action.

The system essentially consists of the reloadable 12- or 24-tube launcher, the main and auxiliary control units, the emergency release, the IR decoy grenades (Hot Dog), and the chaff grenades (Silver Dog). Two or four carrier mountings with three launcher tubes each are deck-mounted on the port and starboard sides of the ships. The launcher tubes may be loaded with either IR decoys or chaff

grenades only, or with a combination of both depending on the threat encountered. The grenades can be fired in single shots or in a series of shots. When using the latter mode whereby continuous firing is carried out automatically, the decoy cloud becomes effective after only two seconds, and is sustained over a considerable period. Small dimensions and low weight make the equipment suitable for use aboard vessels of all sizes down to small craft.

CHARACTERISTICS
Type: 76 mm decoy grenade launcher
Number of tubes: 12 or 24 per system
Weight: 115 or 185 kg (approx), complete system excluding grenades
Dimensions: 185 × 710 × 420 mm (w × l × h), 1 group of 3 launch tubes
IR decoy
Grenade type: Hot Dog 76 mm
Weight: 0·74 kg (approx)
Payload weight: 0·41 kg (approx)
Cloud development time: 2 s
Chaff decoy
Grenade type: Silver Dog 76 mm
Weight: 0·95 kg (approx)
Payload weight: 0·45 kg (approx)
Cloud development time: 2 s
STATUS
Current production. In service with West German navy and other NATO navies.
CONTRACTORS
Wegmann & Co GmbH, 3500 Kassel, Federal Republic of Germany – Launch system.
    Buck Chemisch-Technische Werke GmbH & Co, 8230 Bad Reichenhall, Federal Republic of Germany – Grenades.

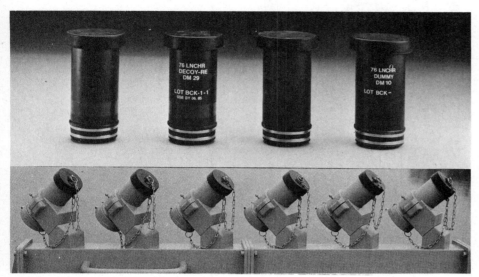

Grenade launcher installation for Buck-Wegmann Hot Dog/Silver Dog naval decoy system

5659.293
SCHALMEI COUNTERMEASURES DECOY SYSTEM

SCHALMEI is an IR/RF countermeasures system designed to provide self-protection for light and medium size naval units against shipborne, aircraft and missile radar and IR sensors by the use of rocket-borne decoy targets. The size and configuration of the targets can be selected either by manually initiated single firing or by an automatic self defence program. The program sequence is controlled by an electronic 'cubicle' which is interfaced with the fire control system. Typical decoy targets are obtainable in the RF range between G and K wavebands and in the IR range of the medium μm bands with maximum radiated power.

The system comprises:
(1) launcher containers and rockets
(2) a CIC control panel
(3) emergency control panel
(4) an electronic 'cubicle'.

The rocket is a 70 mm calibre solid-fuel decoy device, supplied in a standard size of 560 mm long and a weight of approximately 2·5 kg, with an IR flare payload (high radiation power and long position hold by means of a parachute), and high performance RF chaff payload (aluminised fibreglass dipoles). An RF decoy rocket of 800 mm length with double chaff is also available. An alternative possibility is arming of the rocket with IR high performance emitter units in the appropriate frequency bands.

Up to a maximum of four launching containers can be installed on each side of the ship, with ten rockets

in each container. In order to reduce the flight time the rockets are fired from individual closed launching tubes. Fully loaded weight of each container is 40 kg.

Operation and control is effected by means of the CIC control panel which can be installed in an existing control panel or in a separate console. The panel provides for a maximum of 80 rockets, and launching for all operational types can be manual, or automatic with the fire control system. Configuration of the selected program is controlled and displayed,

together with the number of IR and RF decoy rockets ready for launching. The emergency control panel allows the automatic self-defence program to be initiated from the bridge.
STATUS
In production.
CONTRACTOR
AEG-Telefunken, Anlagentechnik Fachbereich Marinetechnik, Hafenstrasse 32, 2000 Wedel (Holst), Federal Republic of Germany.

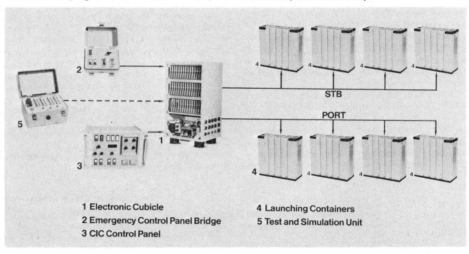

1 Electronic Cubicle
2 Emergency Control Panel Bridge
3 CIC Control Panel
4 Launching Containers
5 Test and Simulation Unit

SCHALMEI IR/RF countermeasures system

1901.053
ROHDE & SCHWARZ DIRECTION FINDING EQUIPMENT

Rohde & Schwarz produces a comprehensive range of radio and electronic DF equipment, embodying a variety of techniques and covering most of the spectrum. Some of this equipment is reviewed in the following paragraphs.

Direction finders operating on the doppler principle are frequently used in the VHF and UHF ranges. In these cases, the DF antenna system consists of a large number of vertical dipoles (16 to 32) arranged in a circle with a diameter of a few wavelengths. To simulate the rotation of a single dipole about a circle, the individual elements are cyclically scanned,

thereby producing a frequency modulation of the incoming signal, which can be automatically evaluated. Triangulation systems with unattended direction finders can be realised by using the accessory remote frequency-control or remote bearing-transmission equipment PU 004 or PU 040.

The doppler-type wide-aperture direction finders PA 007 and PA 008 are available for the VHF range and the PA 009 for the UHF range, and are mainly used for air traffic control. For reconnaissance applications, the broadband doppler direction finder PA 055 (see **3532.093**) is recommended for the VHF/UHF range, and model PA 010 for the shortwave range from 0·5 to 30 MHz.

The PA 003 rotating direction finder covers the

range to 1300 MHz. Two pairs of log-periodic antennas, and active loop antennas, are used for vertical and horizontal polarisation and are suitable for minimum-signal (differentiating circuit) and maximum-signal DF. The bearing diagram is represented on the screen of a CRT, a manually adjustable bearing graticule being used for determining the exact azimuth.

By means of the data multiplexer PU 004 or PU 040, several doppler direction finders can be remotely controlled and the bearings taken transmitted back via CCITT telephone lines. Rohde & Schwarz provides computer-controlled display consoles for such automatic triangulation systems. These display the result of the triangulation process on suitable maps or include it in a synthesised representation. Such a computer-controlled DF system by Rohde & Schwarz receives RF transmissions in the frequency range 0·5 to 1000 MHz and locates the respective transmitter, if necessary, by triangulation. The system is devised such that it can be assembled and extended in stages, particular importance being attached to the possibility of adding equipment without making other equipment redundant. The complete system contains the following main components: one or more monitoring positions as required, a command and evaluation centre, and DF stations depending on the number or the size and nature of the areas being monitored. The individual radio monitoring and DF stations are interconnected by an audio frequency (AF) and data transmission system with the command and evaluation centre.

Tape recording equipment is provided for the storage of the modulation information. The assembly also contains an AF junction panel to which the telephone set can be connected, and a control unit for linking the monitoring position and central station or DF station. The received signals present at the monitoring position can moreover be transmitted from a command centre to the DF stations via this control unit, thereby ensuring that all stations used for the bearing determination take the bearings of the same transmitter. The central station includes evaluation desks, a control centre with interface, the AF distribution network, and the data transmission equipment. The evaluation desks contain a data display unit for indication of the DF frequency, the direction finders in use, the bearings taken, and for monitoring the data input. The individual units include an alpha-numeric keyboard for control command inputting, data stores, an alpha-numeric printer for printing out the screen contents of the data display unit, a telephone set for the monitoring position and for the radio-telephone traffic to the interception and DF operators, and a DF triangulation display which projects the bearings on to a transparent map. A process computer with peripherals controls the data distribution and storage processes centrally as well as the data display units, the DF triangulation system, and the AF switching network.

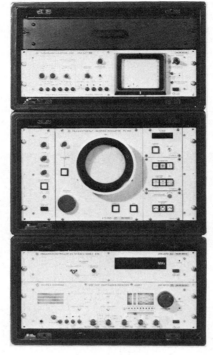

PA 003 DF equipment

CONTRACTOR
Rohde & Schwarz, Mühldorfstrasse 15, 8000 Munich 80, Federal Republic of Germany.

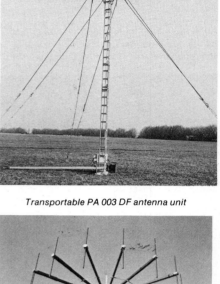

Transportable PA 003 DF antenna unit

PA 008 VHF direction finder equipment and commutated dipole antenna unit

---

5658.153

DIRECTIONAL ANTENNA SYSTEM AC 002

The controllable directional antenna system AC 002 has been designed for radio monitoring tasks in the frequency range 1 to 12 GHz within computer-controlled systems. This antenna system has high gain of 25·5 to 45·7 dB at the output of the driven element and permits simultaneous reception of horizontally and vertically polarised waves as well as small-power transmission.

The highly directive broadband antenna consists of a 2·7 m parabolic reflector and a crossed log-periodic element for horizontal and vertical polarisation. It is set to the desired position by a microprocessor-controlled azimuthal rotator with high angle accuracy. The maximum azimuth run-in speed is 12°/s with a maximum run-in error of 0·1°. The

elevation of the basic antenna system can be set manually within a range of ±6° about the horizontal, using a handwheel. A control unit and a distant motor control unit are used for manual control of the rotating equipment; the control unit can either be operated from a computer or integrated in a computer-controlled radio-monitoring system via a bus interface in line with IEC 625-1 and IEEE 488.

Four-digit, seven-segment displays indicate the actual and desired angles. The control unit has a stop button for search operation and switches for setting north or any other reference and for electronic limiting of the rotating range. A self-test facility is incorporated with an LED display for error indication.
CONTRACTOR
Rohde & Schwarz, Mühldorfstrasse 15, 8000 Munich 80, Federal Republic of Germany.

Directional antenna system AC 002

4352.053

AEG-TELEFUNKEN RECEIVERS AND ANCILLARY SYSTEMS

AEG-Telefunken produces a range of receivers and ancillary equipment for monitoring and surveillance applications. The following paragraphs list the salient features of major examples of this range. All systems listed are in current production.

E 1600 VU VHF/UHF Receiver

The receiver E 1600 VU is designed for radio monitoring in the VHF/UHF range up to 1000 MHz and is used in combination with the WAG 1600 panoramic display. This receiver is designed for operation in both fixed and mobile radio monitoring stations.

The frequency range from 20 to 500 MHz may be extended without increasing equipment dimensions by inserting a module for frequencies up to 1000 MHz. The receiver is characterised by its compact and rugged construction and by simple operation.

For special purposes the receiver is supplied for a frequency resolution of 100 Hz instead of 1 kHz.
CHARACTERISTICS
Frequency range: 20 – 500 MHz, optional to 1000 MHz
Operating modes
Standard: CW, MCW, AM, FM, pulse modulation
Optional: SSB

General Purpose Receiver E 1700

The E 1700 is characterised by high immunity to large signals, easy operation and compact construction. With a high quality input circuit and a very low noise synthesiser, the receiver features large signal characteristics not achieved before. The receiver may be complemented with a passive automatically

E 1600 VU VHF/UHF receiver

E 1700 general purpose receiver

locked preselector which improves its reception properties, particularly for operation on board ships. The equipment is provided with a 30-channel service data memory. Appropriate plug-in modules are supplied for many further types of service, such as ISB, FSK high data rates and diversity operation.

CHARACTERISTICS
Frequency range: 10 kHz – 30 MHz
Operation modes
Standard: A1, A2, A3, A3J, A3A, A3H
Optional: 6A3B, 6A7B, F1, F4, F6

General Purpose Receiver E 1800

The E 1800 is a service monitoring receiver for the frequency range from 10 kHz to 30 MHz. Its technical features include a remote control facility, a microprocessor control and immunity to large signals. Through a serial data interface, the E 1800 may be controlled remotely in all its functions. By means of an addressing system several receivers may be set by one or more central control panels. Depending on the requirement, all types of normal service in the VLF-HF bands may be demodulated by means of integration. In a service data memory with 100 channels all receiver settings may be programmed. The incorporated microprocessor-controlled scanning unit extends the range of uses and allows, for example, the scanning of fixed programmed frequencies or scanning over a programmable frequency range.

A signal detector makes possible reliable automatic detection of busy frequencies by checking the signal-to-noise ratio. For the selection of different receiving antennas, control signals are available at an additional interface for an external antenna switching panel. A microprocessor-controlled BITE allows rapid checks of serviceability.

CHARACTERISTICS
Frequency range: 10 kHz – 30 MHz
Operation modes
Standard: A1, A2, A3, A3J, A3A, A3H
Optional: 6A3B, 6A7B, F1, F4, F6

VHF/UHF Receiver E 1900

The E 1900 is a search and monitoring receiver for the frequency range from 20 MHz to 500 MHz. The frequency coverage may be extended to 1000 MHz by inserting a plug-in module. Its features are a remote control facility, a microprocessor control and compact construction. Through a serial data interface, the E 1900 may be remotely controlled in all its functions. By means of an addressing system, several receivers may be set by one or more central control panels.

The receiver is designed for the reception of A1, A2, A3, F3, pulse-modulated signals and optionally for A3J signals. In a service data memory with 100 channels all receiver settings may be programmed.

Other technical details are identical with the E 1800 above.

CHARACTERISTICS
Frequency range: 20 – 500 MHz. Optional to 1000 MHz
Operating modes
Standard: CW, MCW, AM, FM, pulse modulation
Optional: SSB

Digital Frequency Measuring Equipment DFM 1500/2

The DFM 1500/2 frequency measuring equipment is used for measuring the frequency of modulated, unmodulated and keyed transmitter signals (CCIR) in the frequency range from 10 kHz to 30 MHz. The measured frequencies are indicated digitally, quickly and accurately. On combination with the type E 1600 receiver and a microwave converter, the frequency coverage may be extended to 1 GHz and 10·5 GHz respectively. Further accessories for digital and analogue registration make it possible to record using suitable printers and recorders and the output of data to computers.

The system provides accurate measurement of frequency, microprocessor-controlled automatic measuring cycle, digital display of results, and digital and analogue output of results for record purposes.

Measurement of F1, F4 and F6 demodulation may be made using the type E 1700 receiver, and diversity reception by means of an antenna diversity combining assembly. Setting reception frequencies, modes, bandwidths and measurement control can be remotely controlled by computer. A panoramic display can also form part of the overall system.

CHARACTERISTICS
Frequency range 10 kHz – 30 MHz
With receiver E 1600: 30 – 500 MHz (1000 MHz)
With Microwave converter: 1 – 10·5 GHz
Modes (basic edition): A0, A1, A2, A3, A3A, A3B, A7B, A9B, A3H, F1, F4, F6
Modes on extension above 30 MHz: FM, AM

Direction Finder Telegon 7

The Telegon 7 direction finder consists of the VHF/UHF receiver E 1600 and a single-channel DF unit (EP 1650) with a frequency coverage of 20 to 500 MHz. The equipment operates on the principle of the electronically rotating antenna and automatically evaluates the bearing angle. This angle is displayed non-ambiguously in digital and analogue form. In addition the relative field strength is indicated, an advantage on mobile operations.

For mobile and camouflaged operation, the manual control unit HB 1650 is supplied and carries the most important control elements for the single-channel direction finder, and also indicates the bearing angle in digital and analogue form.

The Telegon 7 may be installed in fixed, semi-mobile and mobile DF systems. Appropriate data interfaces allow the operation of unattended remotely-controlled DF stations.

CHARACTERISTICS
Frequency range: 20 – 500 MHz (1000 MHz)
Frequency display: 7-digit LED display
Evaluation of bearing: Digital by integrating phase measurement

Direction Finder Telegon 8

Telegon 8 is a Watson-Watt direction finder with a frequency range from 10 kHz to 30 MHz. It consists of the DF receiver P 1520, control unit BP 1520 and display unit SH 1520. All information important to the operator, ie frequency, digital and analogue bearing,

are indicated on a single display.

The more important features of Telegon 8 are:
(1) three-channel DF with non-ambiguous sense indication
(2) microprocessor controlled DF procedure
(3) electronic bearing cursor, digital bearing read-out following setting of cursor
(4) HF stability with ten Hz resolution.

An extensive test programme is integrated into the equipment and the operator can test the entire equipment from antenna input to display, step by step. The digital frequency input makes possible the remote control of the direction finder through other equipment, such as receivers. By the use of additional modules, the Telegon 8 may be used in fully automated DF networks.

CHARACTERISTICS
Frequency range: 10 kHz – 30 MHz
Frequency display: 7-digit display on CRT
Resolution: 10 Hz

Active Adcock DF Antenna AK 1205

The mobile basic omni-directional receiving antenna A 1205 was developed to receive vertically polarised waves in the MF and HF bands. Its horizontal pattern is circular and the vertical pattern is cosine-shaped. Active receiving antennas of this type are especially suitable for use in antenna groups and Adcock systems since their mutual coupling is negligibly small and the antennas have excellent amplitude and phase synchronism.

A combination, the Adcock System AK 1205, is particularly suitable for use in conjunction with the AEG-Telefunken receiver system Telegon VI or Telegon 8.

Due to light weight, small stowage space and the low constructional height of the antennas, the equipment is highly mobile and is especially suited for use wherever high mobility is demanded and small terrain space is available.

CHARACTERISTICS
Frequency range: 0·25 – 10 MHz (with 20 m base). 2 – 30 MHz (6 m base)
System error: 1° rms
Construction height: 2 m
Weight of each antenna: 7 kg
CONTRACTOR
AEG-Telefunken, Anlagentechnik, Geschaftsbereich Hochfrequenztechnik, Postfach 1730, 7900 Ulm, Federal Republic of Germany.

E 1800 general purpose receiver

E 1900 VHF/UHF receiver

Telegon 7 direction finder

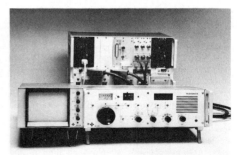

Telegon 8 direction finder

4353.153
HUMMEL VHF JAMMER

The HUMMEL jamming transmitter is an automatically responding VHF jamming transmitter for use against voice and data links. The transmitter works as a multi-channel jamming transmitter in look-through operation in which the frequencies to be

jammed may be distributed throughout the entire frequency range without restriction.

A computer controlled transceiver consisting of modules from the 'Baustein-program' is the basic unit of the jamming transmitter. Operating modes are:
(1) transmission and reception with manual control

(2) automatic single-channel operation as responding jamming transmitter
(3) multi-channel fixed frequency operation
(4) search operation with multi-channel jamming transmissions.

The HUMMEL system is normally installed in an

armoured station vehicle with integrated power supply which ensures high mobility and effective operation in the forward edge of the battle area.

Through a remote command system, the jamming transmitter may be connected directly to an ELINT centre. All settings needed for this operation may be performed directly at this ELINT centre without the operator in the vehicle having to make adjustments. One ELINT centre can control several transmitters at the same time.

STATUS
In development.

CONTRACTOR
AEG-Telefunken, Nachrichten-und Verkehrstechnik, Geschaftsbereich Hochfrequenztechnik, Postfach 1730, 7900 Ulm, Federal Republic of Germany.

4138.093
ESM 500 SERIES VHF/UHF RECEIVERS

The ESM 500 is a family of microprocessor-controlled receivers covering VHF and UHF ranges (20 to 1000 MHz) for applications which are primarily in radio detection, radio monitoring and surveillance. It includes broadband desk-top receivers offering a high degree of operating ease and, for use in computerised radio detection systems, hand-off receivers with receive bands tailored to the frequencies of different radio services.

High sensitivity, high overload capability, low oscillator phase noise and tracking input filters provide a wide dynamic range and the high accuracy of frequency tuning is achieved with a built-in synthesiser. Other major features are fast tuning, non-volatile memory for all the settings associated with up to 99 frequencies, programmed scanning for any of the stored 99 frequencies and BITE for self-testing. The desk-top version, ESM 500A (20 to 1000 MHz), is suitable for use in mobile stations, at manually or remotely controlled observer positions (eg in master-slave operations, one master driving up to ten slaves without a controller), in semi-automatic systems or as a purely remotely controlled receiver in automatically or centrally controlled monitoring and DF systems.

Frequency tuning is either by a keyboard with a buffer memory and check display, by transfer from an internal memory, by a rotary knob with magnetic locking and stepping increments or externally and remotely by a bus or interface. As tuning aids there are two pointer meters for indicating level and offset, plus a built-in panoramic display that makes a signal visible before it is in the IF receiving bandwidth.

For simultaneous monitoring of large numbers of frequencies there are hand-off receivers ESM 508K, ESM 517K and ESM 540K, which, with their facility for centralised control and supply (as many as eight receivers in a group), can be used to form large-scale, multi-channel monitoring systems. The hand-off receivers are driven with sub-addresses, ie only one main address is required for each group. In this way an IEC-bus controller can handle up to 120 receivers.

STATUS
In production and operational.

CONTRACTOR
Rohde & Schwarz, Mühldorfstrasse 15, 8000 Munich 80, Federal Republic of Germany.

ESM 500A VHF/UHF monitoring receiver

Group of eight ESM 508/517/540K remotely controlled receivers

4139.093
ESP SCANNING RECEIVER

The ESP automatic receiver 'intelligently' scans the frequency spectrum at a rate of 1000 channels per second in the range from 10 kHz to 1300 MHz. An optional extension to this frequency range is available and extends the range to 2500 MHz.

The receiver is designed for communications intelligence and radio monitoring and, in conjunction with other equipments such as direction finders, monitoring receivers and printers, general-purpose radio monitoring installations can be established and are suitable for computer-control and provide high detection probability.

STATUS
In production and operational.

CONTRACTOR
Rohde & Schwarz, Mühldorfstrasse 15, 8000 Munich 80, Federal Republic of Germany.

ESP intercept receiver with ESP-T1 and -T2 tuner units

3532.093
PA 055 & PA 010 DOPPLER DIRECTION FINDERS

Rohde & Schwarz has developed the PA 055 broadband doppler direction finder to enable DF and source location as well as detection and signal analysis.

The PA 055 can indicate the direction of a target transmitter to within ±1°. Frequency coverage is from 20 to 1000 MHz, using two antenna systems, one for the band 20 to 200 MHz and the other for the band 200 to 1000 MHz.

The doppler system employed by Rohde & Schwarz is claimed to offer considerable advantages over conventional Adcock systems, including: wide aperture; low bearing error with high angle of incidence or depolarised waves; the possibility of using normal receivers; simple separation of the antenna system from the actual DF instrumentation; digital bearing readout; fully automatic operation; fully remote operation; high sensitivity through the use of an integrating IF summator and a special method of compensating for unwanted frequency modulation in the input signal. In addition to the digital bearing readout, there is an analogue display to permit an assessment of bearing quality. Full remote operation is available. The direction finder can already take bearings of signals as short as 10 milliseconds duration.

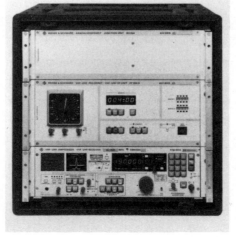

PA 055 DF installation

PA 055 DF antenna

PA 010

Engineering advances by Rohde & Schwarz have resulted in what is claimed as the first HF doppler direction finder, the PA 010 which covers the range from 0·5 to 30 MHz. The proven technology applied to the shortwave range offers several advantages, for example: the possibility of taking bearings using high-angle signals (sky waves) and indicating their angle of elevation. All the other advantages of the doppler principle, such as uncomplicated remote-control capability, automatic transmission of bearing data, and immunity to multipath propagation due to the use of wide-aperture antennas, are retained with the new HF system.

STATUS

Both the PA 055 and the PA 010 are in full production and deliveries are currently in progress.

PA 010 HF direction finder unit

CONTRACTOR

Rohde & Schwarz, Mühldorfstrasse 15, 8000 Munich 80, Federal Republic of Germany.

Rohde & Schwarz circular ground antenna array (HF doppler direction finder PA 010)

4636.193
ROHDE AND SCHWARZ ANTENNA SYSTEMS

In addition to the equipment and systems detailed elsewhere in this section, Rohde and Schwarz design and manufacture a wide range of antenna systems, many of which are used in the ELINT and ESM fields.

VHF/UHF Coaxial Dipole HK 014

This is a vertically polarised broadband omni-directional antenna (100 to 1300 MHz) suitable for transmission and reception. As a transmitting antenna, the dipole is suitable for CW operation of 400 W maximum up to 400 MHz, and of 200 W over the total range. The VSWR of this coaxial dipole is better than 2 dB over the total frequency range, the typical maximum value being 1·8 dB. It is especially suitable for shipboard installation.

Crossed Log-periodic Antenna HL 037

Log-periodic antennas are especially useful for wideband measurements and monitoring of RF signals. For reception and identification of signals with the two most common types of polarisation (horizontal and vertical) in the VHF/UHF range, the HL 037 consists of two orthogonally arranged radiator systems so that both types of polarisation can be received simultaneously. The HL 037 can also be used for low-power transmission (100 W). The antenna is suitable for semi-mobile use, has a wide frequency range from 25 to 1000 MHz and has almost frequency-independent radiation patterns.

Active Rod Antenna HE 010

The HE 010 has excellent receiving characteristics achieved by careful matching of the passive antenna structure to the active circuitry. It has a wide frequency range from 10 kHz to 80 MHz and is optimised for maximum dynamic range (high sensitivity and excellent large-signal characteristics).

Active Receiving Dipole HE 202

This is a high sensitivity, lightweight, small dimension antenna with a dipole length of only 515 mm, and a weight of 1·7 kg. It covers the frequency range 200 to 1000 MHz and has a high immunity to non-linear distortion.

Crossed log-periodic antenna HL 037

Active Antenna Systems HE 003, 004, 005, 006

These antenna systems are a combination of the Active HF Rod Antenna HE 001 and one or two horizontal Active HF Dipole Antennas HE 002. Two dipole antennas can be interconnected via a 90 degree coupler to produce an omni-directional antenna pattern for the reception of horizontally polarised signals. Frequency range coverage is from 1·5 to 30 MHz.

Active Antenna Systems HE 112 and HE 115

The HE 112 and HE 115 are small dimensional, high sensitivity antennas covering the frequency range 20 to 200 MHz. They are combinations of the Active Vertical Dipole HE 109 and one or two crossed Active Receiving Dipoles HE 101.

STATUS

In full production.

CONTRACTOR

Rohde and Schwarz, Mühldorfstrasse 15, 8000 Munich 80, Federal Republic of Germany.

Active HF antenna system HE 003

Active receiving dipole HE 202

4637.193
PA 510 MOBILE DIRECTION FINDING SYSTEM

The PA 510 is a vehicle mounted mobile DF system. Frequency range is from 1 to 30 MHz with a narrow bandwidth of ±75 Hz, and a 3-digit readout of instantaneous value or average value plus standard deviation. Excellent results are claimed up to elevation angles of 30 degrees. The antenna can be set up on a tripod and operated remotely to avoid any adverse effects caused by the vehicle.

The vehicle also contains the VHF/UHF DF system,

PA 555, which is a mobile version of the PA 055 direction finder (**3532.093**) and has similar characteristics. It has a frequency range of 20 to 1000 MHz.

Only 3 antennas are required to cover the complete frequency range from 1 to 1000 MHz.

STATUS

In production.

CONTRACTOR

Rohde and Schwarz, Mühldorfstrasse 15, 8000 Munich 80, Federal Republic of Germany

Vehicle mounted antennas for PA 510 and PA 555

3536.193
EP 1650 AUTOMATIC VHF/UHF RADIO RECONNAISSANCE SYSTEM

The EP 1650 system consists of a central station, at least three remote DF stations and other equipments. The central station incorporates a computer-controlled search receiver consisting of indicator and analysis receiver for the rapid detection and analysis of radio traffic as well as equipment for the direction of the DF stations and for passing instructions to the monitoring receivers and other equipments.

Technical features include:
(1) recognition of signals present in frequency bands
(2) coarse analysis of new transmissions
(3) DF and position fixing
(4) detailed analysis and monitoring reception
(5) ECM
(6) determination of the times relevant transmitters are on the air.

The search receiver sweeps frequency channels sequentially and in cycles, whereby the reporting accessory detects in a very short time the presence of a transmission and reports the fact to the computer.

The computer keeps a file showing the occupancy of the channels and when a new transmission is detected it instructs the analysis receiver to measure the exact frequency. The computer instructs the direction finders in the mobile DF base to take bearings on this frequency. From the bearings determined automatically by at least two DF stations the computer fixes the most likely transmission position.

If the position determined is situated in a definite area then a monitoring receiver is automatically instructed to register or record the contents of the message. The results obtained are available in suitable forms for further processing. The dialogue with the system is performed through a data display station. This dialogue includes both the input of data for the search receivers as well as the printing out of results in formats.

CONTRACTOR
AEG-Telefunken, Nachrichten-und Verkehrstechnik, Geschäftsbereich Hochfrequenztechnik, Postfach 1730, 7900 Ulm, Federal Republic of Germany.

Vehicle of the EP 1650 automatic VHF/UHF radio reconnaissance system deployed

INTERNATIONAL

5683.293
SIBYL EW NAVAL DECOY SYSTEM

Sibyl is a joint Anglo/French comprehensive, fully automatic and 'intelligent' missile decoy system for ships. It is designed to counter the anti-ship missile but not replace any 'hard kill' elements of ship defence.

The main components of the Sibyl system are a multi-tube trainable rocket launcher, seven different rocket-powered munitions to cover all decoy modes and a below-decks display and automatic control console. Using the ship's area defence threat evaluation, the control console integrates this with own ship's information, such as speed and heading, and automatically selects an appropriate combination of decoys. The console initiates arming of decoys, trains the launcher and automatically fires the munitions.

The system is a complete 'soft' weapon system and operates in all decoy modes, seduction, distraction, confusion, location denial and alternative target. The munitions are available in two calibres, 170 mm and 263 mm. There are six main munition types, several of which are of completely new design, plus an exercise round. The munitions, or combination of munitions, operate by preventing the missile head locking on by creating false targets and also by by breaking the missile seeker lock using EW techniques of off-board simulation/jammers and smoke screens. Munitions available have a range capability from 0 to 8·5 km.

The six main types of munition are:
(1) an ARM decoy which operates in the seduction

mode and is a floating device simulating the ship's radar
(2) an off-board jammer which is another floating unit and includes a jammer which can be activated by remote control
(3) an EM decoy with a long-term deployment payload
(4) a combined EM/IR payload
(5) a 'hot balloon' decoy where the payload consists of 'hot balloons' plus chaff
(6) an absorbent decoy effective in all wavelengths (visual to 14 microns).

The specific rocket launcher, which is stabilised in two axes, is unique among decoy systems in that it trains and elevates. Each launch system consists of one or more 12-tube launchers. The console module is the heart of the system containing a ruggedised military computer that provides turret stabilisation, decoy management, initiation of the rockets and real-time control of the complete command and control system.

Sibyl munitions are also offered in containers for installation on all existing trainable launchers and turrets.

STATUS
In development.

CONTRACTORS
British Aerospace Dynamics Group, Bracknell Division, Downshire Way, Bracknell, Berkshire RG12 1QL, England.
BRANDT Armements, 52 avenue des Champs-Elysées, 75008 Paris, France.

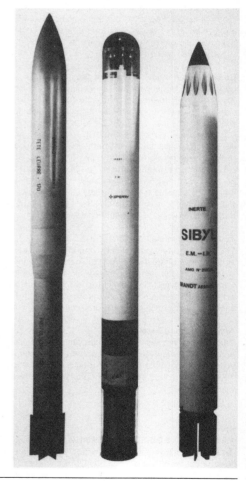

Sibyl decoy system munitions

ISRAEL

4225.093
IAI ELECTRONIC WARFARE SYSTEMS

Israel Aircraft Industries has disclosed an extensive capability in electronic warfare. Few details have been released but it is possible to comment on some of the systems.

For radio monitoring, Elta, the IAI Electronics subsidiary has developed a line of digitally-controlled receivers which include the EL/K-1160 HF receiver, the EL/K-1150 VHF/UHF receiver, and the EL/K-1250 VHF/UHF compact receiver. Among the electronic surveillance systems, Elta has produced the EL/L-8300 family of instantaneous frequency measurement (IFM) receivers and the EL/L-8312

superheterodyne computer-controlled system.

For naval applications, Elta has developed equipments for ESM and ECM with chaff dispensing. Typical suites cover a wide spectrum of frequencies and are designed to counter modern naval weapon systems. The ESM is performed by the EL/L-8300 line of modular IFM receivers and DF antennas. ECM is accomplished by the EL/L-8200 family of noise jammers, the EB series of deception systems and the naval version of the EL/L-7010 system.

EB41 Naval ECM System
The EB41 is designed for protection of ships of all sizes against radar controlled weapon systems. The system features a wide frequency range, automatic or

manual operating modes, high gain antenna and selectable ECM techniques.

EL/L-8303 ESM System
This is a computerised ESM system for shipborne, airborne and ground-based applications. The system is designed to intercept, digitise, identify, display and record radar signals over the frequency range 2 to 18 GHz, with an optional extension down to 0·5 GHz. The processed data of the system can activate ECM or chaff systems manually or automatically.

The system provides computer control and processing, instantaneous direction finding over 360° with high accuracy and high intercept probability. A combined alpha-numeric and graphic display and a built-in emitter library for storage of data are provided.

EL/L-8310 ELINT/ESM System

The EL/L-8310 is an advanced microwave superheterodyne receiving system designed for all ELINT/ESM applications. The normal frequency coverage is from 0·5 to 18 GHz although this range can be extended at both ends to cover from 60 MHz to 40 GHz. It is one-man operated and capable of airborne, shipborne, transportable or fixed deployment.

EL/L-8312 ELINT/ESM System

This is a fully computerised microwave receiving system with a high capability of signal analysis. It is based on Elta units such as the EL/L-8310, EL/L-8320 pulse digitiser, EL/S-8610 computer and the EL/S-8570 display. It provides signal acquisition and analysis, display, emitter classification and identification with a high probability of intercept. Normal frequency coverage is from 0·5 to 18 GHz but this can be extended from 60 MHz to 40 GHz.

EL/K-7001 Communications EW System

The EL/K-7001 is designed to provide close communication intelligence and jamming support at tactical levels. The system consists of two units; the EL/K-7001RC receiving and control unit and the EL/K-7001T transmitter. The EL/K-7001RC incorporates a compact VHF/UHF receiver and microprocessor control circuitry, with a CRT display and keyboard in the front panel permitting convenient data presentation and operation. The EL/K-7001T includes a solid-state wideband transmitter operated by remote control from the EL/K-7001RC. Operating frequency is from 20 to 500 MHz receiving, and 20 to 90 or 100 to 400 MHz for transmission. Normal transmitter output power is 400 W, although up to 1 kW can be provided.

The system is intended for either COMINT operation using only the EL/K-7001RC or both COMINT and COM-JAM activities. A direction finder unit is available to enable more comprehensive

EL/K-7012 jamming exciter

EL/K-7010 communications jammer

COMINT operations. The EL/K-7001 is normally installed in light vehicles, such as jeeps and armoured cars, but is also suitable for installation in light aircraft, helicopters and boats.

EL/K-7010 VHF Communications Jammer

The EL/K-7010 is a VHF communication jammer of modular construction with microprocessor control which is primarily designed for ground-based mobile use. It employs the EL/K-7012 exciter which offers multi-task simultaneous jamming and selectable modular transmit modes to allow communication with friendly forces, free of interference. This system has now been developed for use in naval vessels and small transport aircraft.

EL/K-7012 Communication Jamming Exciters

The EL/K-7012 series of exciters is intended to generate the low level RF signal, further amplified by a power amplifier, for communications jamming purposes. The series consists of three units; EL/K-7012 operating over the frequency range 20 to 100 MHz, EL/K-7012A from 0·5 to 3 MHz, and the EL/K-7012B from 100 to 400 MHz. Each exciter contains two signal generators, a modulation signal generator and an RF synthesiser. Remote control is normally

used since the exciter is designed to operate as a basic element of larger ECM computerised systems.

EL/K-7020 EW System

This is a command and control centre deployed at divisional or higher level. Its capabilities consist of automatic search and acquisition, target location and identification, preset tasks monitoring and interception, and countermeasures management by remote control over several EL/K-7010 or equivalent systems. The system is modular and expandable according to requirements.

CONTRACTOR
Elta Electronics Industries Ltd (a subsidiary of Israel Aircraft Industries Ltd), Ashdod, Israel.

4354.293

RAFAEL SHORT RANGE CHAFF ROCKET

This is a short range chaff rocket (SRCR) developed as a ship perimeter defence system to create decoys against missile attacks. Three rockets are encased together in a triple-barrel launcher serving as a loading unit and two sets are mounted on a standard 12·7 mm machine gun stand. This can be rotated to any desired bearing and is normally set to 45 degrees elevation. A remote firing box will operate two such launchers through a rotary selection switch. A solid, single stage rocket motor boosts the rocket into a

preselected trajectory and the chaff dispersion takes place at a predetermined distance from the ship.
CHARACTERISTICS
Rocket
Weight: 3·2 kg
Length: 640 mm
Diameter: 90 mm
Chaff content: 1·75 kg
Launcher (three rockets)
Weight: 22 kg loaded
Length: 800 mm

Rafael SRCR

CONTRACTOR
Rafael Armament Development Authority, PO Box 2082, Haifa 31021, Israel.

4355.293

RAFAEL LONG RANGE CHAFF ROCKET

This is a long range chaff rocket (LRCR) system which serves as a naval search radar decoy. It is normally fired from launcher tubes mounted on the ship's superstructure. Loading is quick and simple and may be carried out by one man so that four tubes are considered sufficient for any one vessel. Rockets are fired from a remote control box with a launch tube selector switch. A two stage motor gives an initial boost thrust and a subsequent sustainer stage. Chaff dispersion is actuated by an altitude fuze which is energised from the launcher so that no internal power supplies are needed. A compact water-tight design ensures a long life and minimum maintenance.

CHARACTERISTICS
Rocket
Weight: 9·4 kg
Length: 922 mm
Diameter: 89 mm
Chaff content: 1·3 kg
Launcher (double barrelled)
Weight: 12·5 kg
Length: 1250 mm
Diameter: 216 mm
CONTRACTOR
Rafael Armament Development Authority, PO Box 2082, Haifa 31021, Israel.

Rafael LRCR

4638.193

RAJ 101 GROUND RADAR JAMMER

The RAJ 101 is a ground radar jammer covering 180 degrees and ranges of up to 30 km. The system uses a high ERP jammer and wide frequency band, and is capable of dealing with three threats simultaneously. In the acquisition mode, RAJ 101 measures

frequency, direction, PRF, pulse width and amplitude in order to detect, identify and locate hostile radars. The information collected can also be used for battle analysis.

The high power jammer operates in fully automatic or semi-automatic mode. Frequency and direction are set up to prevent hostile radars from detecting and

locating friendly forces. The system is completely self-contained, is vehicle mounted and able to operate and travel in extremely rugged terrain.
CONTRACTOR
Rafael Armament Development Authority, PO Box 2082, Haifa 31021, Israel.

5660.293
AUTOMATIC COUNTERMEASURES DISPENSING SYSTEM

The Automatic Countermeasures Dispensing System (ACDS) has been designed for shipboard anti-missile application to control the launch of dispensable electronic countermeasures such as chaff and flares. The system operates automatically thereby reducing reaction time to a minimum, optimising response and providing effective anti-missile protection.

Operating in full automatic mode, with manual back-up, the ACDS selects the countermeasures rockets appropriate to the threat definition, range and direction and launches them with the correct priority and timing. The system will adapt to existing rocket decoy launch systems with suitable interfacing, and will adapt to any tactical arena by software adjustment.

CONTRACTOR
Elbit Computers Ltd, Military Systems and Products Division, Advanced Technology Center, PO Box 5390, Haifa 31053, Israel.

Automatic countermeasures dispensing system

3461.093
ELBIT MN-53 ESM SYSTEM

The Elbit MN-53 is an ESM system for interception and identification of radar emitters. Modular in design, it can be configured to meet a variety of operational requirements. In one configuration, it uses three different functional receivers. The system provides high sensitivity and detection for high intercept probability.

The MN-53 system detects, displays and records radar emitters. These data, when cross-referenced with Elint information, facilitate accurate and quick tactical decision making. The system is readily adaptable to various military environments. Main operational features are:

(1) manual/automatic DF
(2) manual/automatic frequency search
(3) manual/automatic analysis on PRF, PW, PRF wobbulation
(4) automatic printing and recording of RF, PW, PRF, PRF wobbulation, TOA and direction
(5) connection to external computer.

The system incorporates in its design the extensive experience and lessons gained in sea combat during the Yom Kippur war. Human engineering principles applied to the design of consoles, displays and controls allow for simple and comfortable system operation, even under stress conditions.

System components are slide mounted for ease of maintenance and accessibility. The system includes built-in test facilities for fault-detection.

CONTRACTOR
Elbit Computers Ltd, Military Systems and Products Division, Advanced Technology Center, PO Box 5390, Haifa 31053, Israel.

4356.093
TIMNEX-4CH AUTOMATIC ELINT/ESM SYSTEM

The Timnex-4CH system is an Elint/ESM receiver intended for intercepting radar signals and for operating in land, sea or airborne environments. It covers the frequency range from 2 to 18 GHz and is designed to intercept simple or complex transmissions and to sort and compare them with a preprogrammed radar library.

The system features a channelised IFM receiver, a sophisticated IDF sub-system and real-time computer processing. Tabular display of the signal parameters with instantaneous spectra and gonio displays are presented to the EW operator. Hard copy print out and data logging on magnetic media are additional features.

Timnex-4CH has been designed to intercept radars at a range of several hundred kilometres. By making several measurements during a known path, computations of the radar location are carried out to provide a full tactical picture of the area. The data acquired may be either used in the vehicle or transmitted to ground/shore control stations by data link. Processed information is displayed on a 19-inch (483 mm) colour raster display in several desired cross-sections.

CONTRACTOR
Elbit Computers Ltd, Military Systems and Products Division, Advanced Technology Center, PO Box 5390, Haifa 31053, Israel.

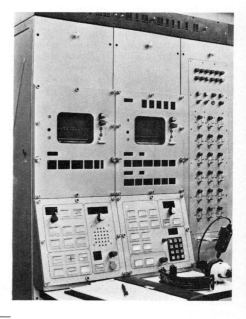

Timnex-4CH automatic Elint system console (submarine version)

4357.393
EL/L-8202 ECM POD

The EL/L-8202 is a compact ECM pod designed to provide self-protection for combat aircraft against both surface and air radar threats. It has a wide frequency coverage and a high broadband output with selectable ECM techniques. A number of optional versions are available which include specified frequency ranges, an enhanced receiver/processor unit and interfaces which are adaptable to a particular aircraft's avionics.

The EL/L-8202 pod comprises the following major units: antennas and radomes, RF unit, RF power amplifier, logic unit, pod shell and cooling unit. The RF unit generates electronic countermeasures, jamming signals according to the required ECM programme. These signals are further amplified by the power amplifier, employing broadband high-power TWTs and transmission is through the antennas which are located at both ends of the pod and features special beam-shape patterns. The logic unit generates the logic and video signals required for the selected ECM programme and provides interface functions to the aircraft radar warning system and to the cockpit control unit.

The pod itself is carried on the normal ordnance station of the aircraft and is designed to have a minor impact on aircraft performance. Cooling is performed in the normal ECM pod method, namely an integral ram/air liquid unit.

CHARACTERISTICS
Frequency range: F – J-bands
Power consumption: 1·7 – 2·3 kVA (0·5 kVA standby)
Dimensions: 26 × 39 × 290 cm
Weight: 200 kg
CONTRACTOR
Elta Electronic Industries Ltd (a subsidiary of Israel Aircraft Industries Ltd), Ashdod, Israel.

5730.393
EL/L-8230 AIRBORNE ECM SYSTEM

The EL/L-8230 is a combined noise and repeater jammer designed to protect combat aircraft against both surface and air radar threats. It is internally mounted and operates over the G to J frequency band with a power output of nearly 1 kW. The system consists of antennas, an RF unit, an RF power amplifier and a logic unit. The latter unit provides logic and video signals for the application of the required ECM programme, and also provides interface functions to the aircraft radar warning receiver. The system contains its own receiver and is capable of automatic or manual operation modes. It can be packaged in different configurations for a variety of aircraft installations.

CONTRACTOR
Elta Electronic Industries Ltd (a subsidiary of Israel Aircraft Industries Ltd), Ashdod, Israel.

4639.193
ELTA COMINT RECEIVERS

The EL/K-1150, -1160 and -1250 receivers are stand-alone or modular units for use in communications intelligence (COMINT) systems. The EL/K-1150 is a VHF/UHF equipment operating over the frequency range 20 to 500 MHz and the EL/K-1160 is an HF system operating over 0·5 to 30 MHz. Both are synthesised receivers incorporating internal microprocessors to enable local or remote control, and a variety of operational roles such as auto-scan and preset tasks according to remotely controlled programmes. Detection modes are AM, USB, LSB, ISB, CW and FM.

The EL/K-1250 is a compact synthesised receiver operating in the 20 to 510 MHz band. Its main use is as a basic building block of larger COMINT or EW systems. The EL/K-1250 demodulates AM, FM, CW and SSB signals, employing four selectable IF filters. Operation is by digital remote control.

Elta COMINT receivers

STATUS
In production

CONTRACTOR
Elta Electronic Industries Ltd (a subsidiary of Israel Aircraft Industries Ltd), Ashdod, Israel.

4640.353
SPS-20 AND SPS-200 AIRBORNE SELF-PROTECTION SYSTEMS
The SPS-20 and 200 are wideband warning systems, the SPS-20 being the current version. The SPS-20 has been designed to fit existing airborne installations while providing improved characteristics and additional capabilities. The system detects and displays pulsed radar threats operating within the 0·7 to 18 GHz frequency range. CW radar threats are

detected by a dedicated high sensitivity receiver. A high sensitivity, three-inch display unit provides an alpha-numeric presentation of the type, coarse angle-of-arrival, relative lethality and status of the analysed radar threats.

The SPS-20 features an advanced digital signal analyser which executes data processing and interfacing tasks. It also provides an extensive emitter library file which can be easily updated for new and changing environments and/or systems. The system

was originally designed for helicopters but is also used in fighter aircraft. Older fighters, such as the F-4 Phantom, have the system coupled to a CRT display, as used with the SPS-200. The smaller, high definition display unit is being fitted to front line fighters.
STATUS
In service.
CONTRACTOR
Elisra Electronic Systems Ltd, 48 Mivtza Kadesh Street, Bene Beraq, 51203 Israel.

4731.153
CR-2740 ELINT SYSTEM
The CR-2740 is a mobile electronic intelligence (ELINT) equipment intended primarily for use in the forward battlefield area. It covers the frequency range from 500 MHz to 18 GHz, and consists of a two-man operations cabin, upon which is mounted a high frequency antenna system, and a trailer carrying a low frequency antenna.

The cabin is a standard S280 shelter, suitable for transport on a variety of vehicles, with two 1·2 metre diameter antennas mounted on top which are used for reception in the 4 to 18 GHz band. A 3 metre diameter antenna for the 500 MHz to 4 GHz range is mounted on the trailer. The two operators, using basically identical equipment, monitor the two bands individually. Most of the data acquired is computer analysed.

Although the system is designed as a mobile forward listening post, the control cabin can be remoted from the antennas, with cable or radio links, for semi-static use.
STATUS
In operational service.
CONTRACTOR
Elisra Electronic Systems Ltd, 48 Mivtza Kadesh Street, Bene Beraq, 51203 Israel.

4732.253
ELISRA NAVAL EW SYSTEMS
For use in the naval EW scenario, Elisra has developed a range of self-defence systems for use in small strike and patrol vessels. Each consists basically of a mast-mounted antenna, control and processing units and a display console, covering the frequency band from 2 to 18 GHz.

The antenna weighs less than 70 kg and consists of 60 static horns, 36 of these covering the Ku band and 12 each covering X and C bands with a 1° accuracy in

Ku band and 3° in X and C. Two horns in each band can be selected for feeding into high-sensitivity receivers and processors for detailed analysis. An omni-directional antenna is provided to give all-round warning and is co-mounted with the receiver to give added sensitivity at up to twice the normal radar horizon distance.

The operator is provided with a tabular display of the detected emitter's characteristics, together with either an orthogonal frequency/azimuth or a polar amplitude/azimuth display. The characteristics

displayed include frequency, PRF, pulse width, antenna scan rate, and whether the emitter is in search, track or track-while scan mode.

The system is also able to launch countermeasures, such as chaff or missiles, automatically. This decision is normally left to the operator.
STATUS
In operational service
CONTRACTOR
Elisra Electronic Systems Ltd, 48 Mivtza Kadesh Street, Bene Beraq, 51203 Israel.

ITALY

4645.093
ELT/128 COMMUNICATIONS DIRECTION FINDER
The ELT/128 is a direction finder, suitable for airborne, ground and naval applications, operating in the HF, VHF and UHF frequency bands. The equipment automatically measures direction of arrival and technical analysis of any kind of signal modulation in the requisite bands. ELT/128 is currently in use on a stand-alone basis in ships and land vehicles, and in integrated ESM systems.

The system consists of an RF unit, control unit, control panel and antenna assembly, the last being tailored to suit the required band coverage, platform and application (fixed or mobile). For the HF band the

antenna assembly normally consists of half-dipoles for fixed or transportable applications, and crossed-loop ferrites for mobile work. For VHF/UHF an array of active dipoles for naval or ground applications and active half-dipoles when integrated in ESM/COMINT airborne systems.

Outputs are provided for use in a display unit and a printer for sequential printout.
STATUS
In operational service.
CONTRACTOR
Elettronica SpA, Via Tiburtina Valeria, Km 13700, 00131 Rome, Italy.

ELT/128 control panel

4167.193
ELT/132 PORTABLE RADAR WARNING RECEIVER
The need for troops on the battlefield to be able to detect potentially hostile radar transmissions and locate their source, whilst being without total ESM support facilities, led Elettronica to develop the ELT/132 lightweight portable radar warning receiver. The equipment is designed for use by small mobile fighting units (commandos, patrols etc) and can be installed on cross-country vehicles, inflatable boats and other such small platforms and may also be used as a manpack.

The ELT/132 consists of a single unit housing the antenna assembly, circuits and batteries. The equipment's control panel is of the plug-in type, permitting easy disassembly when the equipment is used in the vehicle/boat mounted role. In this latter role the ELT/132 can be mounted on a pole support for increased range advantage. When used in the manpack role, the entire equipment weight does not exceed three kg while the compactness of the design does not inhibit the operator's mobility. Operational features include: detection through 360° of all radar emissions present in the scenario; automatic

identification of pre-programmed priority emissions; precision DF of pre-programmed emissions; coarse DF of all other emissions; good sensitivity giving excellent range advantage factor; low power consumption; high yield rechargeable batteries contained in the equipment; lightweight and compact construction.
STATUS
Production.
CONTRACTOR
Elettronica SpA, Via Tiburtina Valeria Km 13700, 00131 Rome, Italy.

4358.393
ELT/156 RADAR WARNING RECEIVER
The ELT/156 airborne passive warning receiver is designed to provide rapid non-ambiguous warning of illumination by an enemy search or tracking radar transmission. It is intended for use on light fighter/ground attack aircraft and helicopters employed in the low altitude ground support activities.

The ELT/156 provides warning against radar threats through the frequency coverage of the appropriate radar bands, full 360° azimuth and elevation coverage and bearing/range presentation on a cockpit mounted dual mode bright display. An audio warning facility is also provided to alert the pilot of possible danger. Simultaneous warning is given of

multiple threats.

The system is computer-controlled and provides a very high measure of protection and warning for aircraft forced to enter areas protected by radar controlled surface-to-air and air-to-air missiles or anti-aircraft artillery. The software is easily reprogrammable to combat new types of threats.

ELT/156 radar warning receiver display

CHARACTERISTICS
Azimuth coverage: 360°
Weights
Antenna (4 off): 0·15 kg each
RF head (2 off): 1 kg each
Signal processor: 5·2 kg
Display: 1·9 kg
Control panel: 0·6 kg
Total system weight: 10·3 kg

STATUS
The system is currently in production for a number of national air forces.
CONTRACTOR
Elettronica SpA, Via Tiburtina Valeria Km 13700, 00131 Rome, Italy.

4169.293
ELT/211 NAVAL ESM EQUIPMENT

The ELT/211 equipment was designed to fulfil the operational ESM requirements of naval vessels ranging in size from fast patrol boat to destroyer. It is a highly integrated computer-based digital system employing sophisticated software-controlled de-interleaving and data handling techniques. The processor is of Elettronica design and is capable of effective operation in dense electromagnetic (EM) environments. Digital processing also permits maximum automation of the analysis, identification and tracking processes, enabling single-operator facilities with adequate surveillance and supervision capabilities combined with override options. Designed as a self-contained system, the ELT/211 can also be integrated with active ECM elements such as noise or deception jammers and it forms a major

ESM element of the Elettronica Newton EW system (4172.293).

The above-deck equipment consists of a DF antenna unit, service module, and four omni-directional antennas and RF unit. Masthead units weigh about 60 kg. Below deck is the operator console which incorporates the digital processor and display unit.

Surveillance facilities include:
(1) instantaneous automatic warning of pre-programmed threats
(2) continuous azimuth and frequency surveillance of the EM environment with 100% intercept probability even in very dense environments
(3) automatic tracking of selected emitters
(4) tactical evaluation of the radar scenario by means of threat identifications symbols

The associated analysis functions provide the following additional facilities:
(5) automatic measurement and alpha-numeric presentation of a detected emitter's characteristic parameters
(6) recognition of emission modes
(7) automatic emitter identification
(8) automatic indication of appropriate ECM reaction.

The ELT/211 can be interfaced with the ship's command and control system, FCS, or with a larger EW system, as mentioned above.
STATUS
In production for several navies.
CONTRACTOR
Elettronica SpA, Via Tiburtina Valeria Km 13700, 00131 Rome, Italy.

4166.393
ELT/263 AIRBORNE ESM EQUIPMENT

The ELT/263 airborne ESM system is designed principally for use in maritime aircraft such as the Beech 200T but has been configured for other types such as the Guardian, Casa C212, Learjet 36A, F27 Maritime, Bandeirante, Piaggio P166, and Britten Norman Maritime Defender. The surveillance of coastal water is the main function, and detection, analysis and identification of emission in the E to J-bands is performed in addition to bearing measurement, which permits emitter location by using a series of successive bearing measurements.

The ELT/263 equipment, in addition to its surveillance tasks, provides for emitter location by the triangulation method. The information gathered (emission analysis, identification, bearing, etc) can be transferred to external users such as ground stations, naval units and the patrol aircraft's radar operator/tactical navigator, and can also be recorded on an optional printer. The system's coverage is depicted in the diagram and the associated tables.

The main items of equipment comprise: a set of four DF antennas; an omni-directional antenna set; DF receiver; IFM receiver; ESM display and control console; a radar warning processor; and a radar warning display unit.
STATUS
Production and in operational service.
CONTRACTOR
Elettronica SpA, Via Tiburtina Valeria Km 13700, 00131 Rome, Italy.

ELT/263 receiver antennas mounted in wing tip pods and tail cone of a Learjet 35A

Display/control console for the ELT/263 airborne ESM equipment

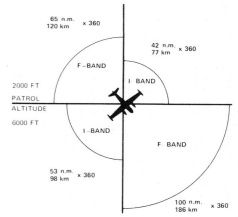

Manufacturer's coverage diagram and performance tables for the ELT/263

Radar type	Flight altitude (feet)	Speed (knots)	Instantaneous surveillance coverage Radius nm/km	Area nm²/km²	Area covered in 1 hour's linear flight nm²/km²	Area covered in 4 hour patrol mission nm²/km²
I-band navigation	2000	180	42/77	5500/18 600	20 600/70 000	66 000/224 000
	6000	200	53/98	8800/30 200	30 000/102 800	93 600/320 300
F-band search	2000	180	65/120	13 300/45 200	36 700/125 300	106 900/365 400
	6000	200	100/186	31 400/108 600	71 400/246 500	191 400/659 900

4170.293
ELT/318 NAVAL JAMMER

The ELT/318 is a naval noise jamming equipment, generally associated with the Elettronica ELT/211 ESM equipment (**4169.293**) and with that equipment forming the major part of the Newton naval EW system (**4172.293**). The ELT/318 is a dual-band continuous wave noise jammer which employs advanced power management techniques to provide protection within the recognised radar threat bands.

Among its facilities are: the ability to inhibit and/or delay weapon system acquisition; jamming of all types of search radar; variable modulation techniques; fast reaction and flexibility to counter new types of threat; full threat frequency band coverage.

The transmitter final output stage incorporates a travelling wave tube amplifier of Elettronica design and manufacture. It is normally employed with one or two ELT/828 stabilised transmit/receive antenna

assemblies, although the ELT/318 equipment is suitable for use with medium or high gain antenna sets, depending on the type of ship. The ELT/828 antenna equipment is steerable and this model is generally employed in Newton systems.

STATUS
In production for several navies.
CONTRACTOR
Elettronica SpA, Via Tiburtina Valeria Km 13700, 00131 Rome, Italy.

4171.293
ELT/521 NAVAL DECEPTION JAMMER

The Elettronica ELT/521 is a naval deception jammer using advanced techniques to ensure the self-protection of naval platforms against all types of radar-supported threat. The transmitter's high peak power, together with the possibility of using omni-directional and/or directional antennas, makes ELT/521 suitable for the protection of ships of any size and tactical role. When associated with omni-directional antennas, the ELT/521 provides completely autonomous operation, while bearing data is required from a DF receiver when operating

with the higher gain directional antennas (eg ELT/828). The ELT/521 deception jammer can be associated with virtually any ESM receiving equipment; when integrated with the Elettronica computerised ELT/211 ESM receiving system (**4169.293**) it constitutes a complete electronic warfare system combining the radar detection, threat warning and tracking facilities of the latter with the fast reaction capabilities of the ELT/521. It can also be incorporated in the Newton naval EW system (**4172.293**).

The ELT/521 equipment comprises the following modules: an air- or water-cooled transceiver, and a

combined circulator and self-test unit. Various deception techniques can be employed and there are programmable deception routines. Multiple target engagement is possible and there is full threat frequency band coverage, providing protection from all types of fire control radars and active and semi-active homing missiles.

STATUS
In production for several navies.
CONTRACTOR
Elettronica SpA, Via Tiburtina Valeria Km 13700, 00131 Rome, Italy.

4168.393
ELT/555 JAMMER POD

The ELT/555 is a pod-housed airborne deception jammer and warning system designed for the self-protection of modern attack and fighter aircraft from enemy anti-aircraft systems (surface-to-air and air-to-air, and anti-aircraft artillery). The system is completely self-sufficient as regards cooling and primary power and makes no demands whatsoever on the carrier aircraft's power supply. The philosophy

ELT/555 supersonic jammer pod on CASA C101 aircraft

adopted for the ELT/555 system ensures that the jammer will automatically tailor its reaction to the type of detected enemy radiation. The system operates against both pulsed and CW radar emissions and presents the following salient operational features: simultaneous multi-threat reaction; very high resistance to ECCM, including any type of frequency agility; full automation; optimised threat deception programs; multi-band frequency coverage (H- to J-band).

The equipment is effective against all types of fire control radars, say the manufacturers, and active or semi-active homing missiles. Various deception techniques are employed, and multiple target engagement is possible.

Air speeds of up to Mach 1·1 at sea level and Mach 1·5 at 40 000 feet were tested during the qualification of the pod. The central main body section and tail module is completely clean, except for the two bottom radomes and stabilising fins. The latter, located toward the rear of the main body section, serve to increase the safety envelope during jettison. The pod can be jettisoned by the pilot and is provided with a self-destruction device. Self-destruction occurs at a presettable interval after the jettison command. The device can be installed or removed at flight-line level.

The pod is provided with a cooling system and self-sufficient power generating system which supplies the electric power necessary to the pod's equipment, independent of the carrier aircraft's supply. The prime mover of the power generating system consists of a ram air turbine (RAT) which drives a four-pole permanent magnet generator. The RAT also drives the compressor of the pod's cooling system, which operates on a closed circuit fluid recycling principle.

There are forward and rear facing CW transmission antennas on the under-surface of the pod body, and nose and tail radomes house antennas for transmission and reception of pulse signals, and reception of CW signals.

The ELT/555 pod measures 300 cm in length, with a body diameter of 27 cm (34 cm RAT maximum) and a weight of 140 kg. Types of aircraft nominated by Elettronica as capable of using the ELT/555 include: F-5, Mirage III, Alpha Jet, MB 326, MB 339, Jaguar, Mig-21, Phantom, Mirage 5, Hawk, Saab 105, etc.

STATUS
In production and operational service. No contractual information is available.
CONTRACTOR
Elettronica SpA, Via Tiburtina Valeria Km 13700, 00131 Rome, Italy.

4359.393
ELT NOISE JAMMER PODS

A range of pod-contained automatic airborne noise jammers, ELT 457, 458, 459 and 460 are designed by Elettronica for installation in high performance ground attack and fighter aircraft. They are intended for operation against ground based air defence radars to mask target infomation on attacking and thereby neutralise anti-aircraft systems. Instantaneous automatic warning is given against pulsed radar emissions, with a very high resistance to ECM, including any type of frequency agility. Multi-threat reaction capability is provided and each jammer contains a large 'library' which can be programmed before flight with a selection of probable radar threat characteristics and relative priority levels.

The systems incorporate power management techniques, by which jamming power and optimised modulation are allocated on a threat priority basis, ie the signals for jamming are radiated in the correct sector, at the correct time and at the appropriate frequency. The power management philosophy therefore ensures that the entire electromagnetic

resources of the system are directed against the most dangerous programmed threat or threats.

Each of the four system variants operates on a different radar frequency band and pod deployment can be optimised in view of the expected threat; simultaneously multi-band frequency coverage can be achieved by deploying more than one pod on one or more aircraft.

The pods can be jettisoned by the pilot and are provided with a self-destruct device. Self-destruction occurs after a presettable interval after the jettison command.

The main unit of the ELT range is the external pod designed for supersonic speeds up to Mach 1·1 at sea level and Mach 1·5 at 40 000 feet. The pod houses the receivers, transmitters and relevant antennas, the warning processor and the cooling and power generators. The antennas, which are protected by radomes, differ for each type of noise jammer pod. A control panel is installed in the cockpit containing the commands for two pods.

The jammer electronics have been designed for easy maintenance with modular construction and

ELT/460 supersonic ECM pod

easy access. The pods are provided with a self-sufficient power system in order to render them independent of the aircraft supply. The prime mover of the power generating system is a ram air turbine (RAT).

CHARACTERISTICS
Length: 312 cm
Diameter: 27 cm (34 cm RAT)
Weight: 145 kg
STATUS
In production and operational service
CONTRACTOR
Elettronica SpA, Via Tiburtina Valeria Km 13700, Rome, Italy.

4172.293
NEWTON NAVAL EW EQUIPMENT

Newton is a family of naval ESM/ECM systems designed by Elettronica to meet the operational requirements of naval forces operating in a dense electromagnetic environment. The systems are configured to suit vessels of various sizes from 100 tons upwards. They provide facilities for complete

passive surveillance, DF, analysis and identification of the radar emitters in the operational area, and electronic means of protection against modern anti-ship weapons.

The Newton system consists of an ESM section and an ECM section, with the related antennas, controlled from an operator console. The former section is designed to provide 100 per cent intercept

probability, passive surveillance, automatic instantaneous warning of pre-programmed threat, automatic analysis of threat parameters, automatic identification and tracking of threats, a synthetic data display, instantaneous DF, and broad frequency coverage. The ECM section provides self-protection by noise and/or deception jamming.

The modular concept is centred on the ELT/211

ESM receiver equipment (**4169.293**) and on several ECM peripheral equipments, in particular the ELT/318 noise jammer (**4170.293**) and/or the ELT/521 deception jammer (**4171.293**) while interface channels are provided to integrate with the ship's command and control as well as other active reaction elements (chaff rocket launchers, FCS etc). The detailed configuration of individual Newton systems are adapted to suit specific ships. Advanced signal processing and handling techniques and software controlled functions, ensure the flexibility necessary to counter the anticipated threat evolution over the next decade. Because of a high level of automation, single-operator control of all ESM and ECM functions from one console is possible, and integration with command system is easily available via computer channels.

The range of Newton configuration possibilities is shown in tabular form nearby, and a typical system for vessels of 250 to 650 tons is shown as Newton B. The principal modular elements of Newton systems are shown in another diagram while additional details of these will be found under the entry numbers mentioned above.

STATUS
In production and in service with several navies.
CONTRACTOR
Elettronica SpA, Via Tiburtina Valeria Km 13700, 00131 Rome, Italy.

Display/control console and processing unit of Newton integrated naval EW system

Newton integrated naval ESM/ECM system antenna

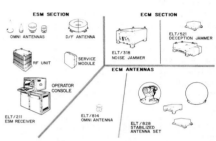

System modules employed in Newton system

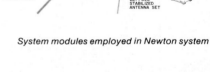

Schematic diagram of Newton naval EW system

Typical Newton system configurations

	Size of craft			
	100–500 tons	250–1500 tons	1000–3000 tons	2500+ tons
ESM (ELT/211)*	1 1	1	1 1	1 1
ECM (ELT/318) noise	1	1	1	1 2
ECM (ELT/521) deception	1	1	2 2	3 2
ECM Antennas (ELT/814)	1	1		
ECM Antennas (ELT/828)	1	1	3 2	4 4

*ELT/211 interfaces up to 4 ECMs

5661.253
FARAD NAVAL EW SYSTEM
Designed for corvettes, fast patrol boats, fast attack craft and other small naval ships, FARAD is a complete EW system which can provide passive detection and identification of targets coupled with self-protection against radar guided weapons.

FARAD is based on four principal units which can be integrated to provide a flexible system adaptable to operational requirements. The principal units are the

ELT/123 basic ESM equipment, the ELT/261 analysis module, the ELT/521 deception jammer and the ELT/361 noise jammer with its associated ELT/828 antenna system. The ELT/123 is the fundamental unit. Other units are added as required according to the type of vessel and its operational role.

The ELT/123 supplies radar warning and DF functions to give instantaneous DF of pulse and CW emissions with automatic warning of pre-programmed threat emissions on a CRT display.

Information can then be passed to the ELT/261 for automatic analysis of intercept signals and automatic tracking, with continuous surveillance of the radar environment on a panoramic display. The ELT/521 is a high-power deception jammer and is described under entry number **4171.293**. The ELT/361 is a dual-band CW noise jammer with spot and barrage jamming capability. It is driven automatically through the FARAD ESM section (ELT/123 plus ELT/261).

The complete FARAD system is able to operate in a

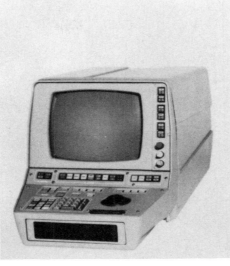

very dense electromagnetic environment and can cope with a large number of simultaneous threats whether by search and acquisition radar or radar homing missiles. In an operational installation, several combinations of the various units described above can be fitted with the ELT/123 either as a stand-alone unit or as the basis upon which the other installations are built.

STATUS
In production and operational service.

CONTRACTOR
Elettronica SpA, Via Tiburtina Valeria Km 13700, 00131 Rome, Italy.

Units of FARAD ESM/ECM system

5662.453
THETIS SUBMARINE ESM SYSTEM

THETIS is a modular ESM system designed to fulfil the EW requirements of a submarine. The system is produced in two configurations. The first and simpler of these, the ELT/124-S, performs high sensitivity threat warning and DF functions, while the second, the ELT/224-S, extends these functions to those of a full ESM system or tactical ELINT. Both variants use the same DF antenna as the sensor and both can be fitted with an additional and separate RF pre-amplified omni-directional antenna as an option. This latter antenna is very small and can be installed on top of the submarine's attack or search periscope for primary warning.

The ELT/124-S variant consists of a threat warning and DF receiver system. The hardware comprises a DF antenna and receiver, a processor unit and a warning display. It provides instantaneous, high sensitivity, automatic warning of threats programmed into the processor and continuous surveillance of the

radar environment with 100 per cent intercept probability. A dedicated operator is not required.

The ELT/224-S consists of the units of the ELT/124-S plus an IFM receiver and an ESM display. It provides instantaneous DF with 100 per cent intercept probability of pulse and CW emissions, display of all intercepted emissions, IFM, automatic technical analysis and identification of emitters and their platforms. It will also provide warning that the vessel is entering an area under hostile radar surveillance. A single operator is required for this system.

The antenna assembly consists of one conical spiral omni-directional antenna plus eight plane spiral DF antennas assembled in single casing. It has a very low radar cross-section and is also covered with microwave absorbing material. It is light and strong enough to be mounted on the search periscope. The small, lightweight optional antenna can be mounted on the attack periscope and will provide the submarine commander with a first alarm facility but without DF facilities.

THETIS submarine ESM system (display/control console and two antennas)

STATUS
In production and operational sevice.

CONTRACTOR
Elettronica SpA, Via Tiburtina Valeria Km 13700, 00131 Rome, Italy.

4360.353
ELT COLIBRI HELICOPTER ESM/ECM SYSTEM

The Colibri system is an integrated ESM/ECM equipment designed for installation on any type of medium sized helicopter operating in the naval surveillance, anti-submarine and anti-ship roles,

thereby extending the ESM/ECM range of the parent ship. The system provides a helicopter with the facilities for passive surveillance, DF analysis, identification and location of radar emitters, even when the system is operating in a dense electromagnetic environment. It also provides for

effective self or mutual protection against radar guided missiles.

Colibri can be configured to meet particular operational roles by combining a variety of basic modules. The basic configuration is represented by the ELT/161 ESM and radar warning system. A helicopter's radar warning function can then be supplemented by the ELT/562 deception jammer to obtain effective self-protection and the configuration can be further expanded by the addition of the ELT/261 for ESM capability and ELINT roles. An additional unit, the ELT/361, can be added to achieve even greater protection capability.

In the basic configuration, Colibri comprises the ELT/161, consisting of a receiver, the antenna system, a warning processor and a radar warning display. The ELT/161 operating in conjunction with the ELT/261 system, gives overall capability in that field and is designed to fulfil the maritime surveillance and EW roles to extend the electronic warfare range of the parent ship. In this role, the system supplies instantaneous direction finding and display of intercepted emissions, frequency measurement of pulse and CW emissions, automatic analysis, identification of source and automatic tracking of selected emissions. The addition of the ELT/562 deception jammer provides the helicopter with self-protection against sea-to-air and air-to-air missiles. The ELT/361 noise jammer is added to suppress enemy surveillance radars.

STATUS
In production and in service with several navies.

CONTRACTOR
Elettronica SpA, Via Tiburtina Valeria Km 13700, 00131 Rome, Italy.

ELT naval Colibri antenna installation on AB-212 helicopter

4173.093

ELETTRONICA EW EQUIPMENT

In addition to those items of electronic warfare equipment described in separate entries in this section, Elettronica produces a comprehensive range of hardware. A list of all Elettronica products so far identified follows:

ELT/116:	naval ESM/ECM system
ELT/123:	naval ESM (FARAD)
ELT/124-S:	ESM system for submarines (THETIS)
ELT/128:	communication direction finder
ELT/132:	hand-held battlefield radar warning receiver
ELT/156:	airborne radar warning receiver
ELT/161:	airborne radar warning system
ELT/211:	computer-based naval ESM system
ELT/214:	naval ESM
ELT/224-S:	ESM system for submarines (THETIS)
ELT/261:	naval ESM analysis module (FARAD)
ELT/263:	ESM/RWR system for maritime aircraft
ELT/311:	jammer
ELT/318:	dual-band CW naval noise jammer
ELT/361:	noise jammer
ELT/457-460:	supersonic noise jammer pods
ELT/511:	naval deception jammer
ELT/521:	naval deception jammer
ELT/555:	supersonic deception jammer pod
ELT/562:	deception jammer
ELT/566:	deception jammer
ELT/711:	naval ESM radar identification module
ELT/712:	naval EW programming unit
ELT/716:	naval EW data interface
ELT/724-S:	omni-directional ESM antenna module for submarines (THETIS)
ELT/814:	naval omni-directional ECM antenna
ELT/828:	stabilised naval ECM transmit/receive directional antenna

A great deal of the detailed information about these equipments and others which have not been identified remains classified, but the following items have been partially analysed and the information concerning them that can be published appears in the following paragraphs.

A typical ship's EW suite might comprise:
(1) ELT/116 radar intercept receiver
(2) ELT/711 radar identification unit
(3) ELT/712 programming unit
(4) ELT/716 data transmission module
(5) ELT/311/511 jammer.

This ELT/156 aircraft radar warning receiver equipment weighs only 10·3 kg with antennas. It provides automatic warning and coarse DF measurements of threats

ELT/457 ECM supersonic pod

ELT/460 ECM supersonic pod

The complete system covers the frequency range 2 to 18 GHz and is based on a four-band instantaneous frequency measuring (IFM) receiver which performs all ESM functions. The four channel outputs are presented to the EW operator on two surveillance CRTs, and it is possible to discriminate between pulse and CW signals. Separate displays are provided for DF and signal analysis and measurements, these two CRTs being positioned below the surveillance CRTs on the EW operator's console; an additional CRT for dealing with the D-band (former L-band) signals is mounted above, if fitted. The former displays are part of the ELT/711 radar identification unit, and the latter is the ELT/214 display unit. There are also threat warning indicator lamps for drawing the operator's attention to about 30 intercepted emissions. These may be selected for individual analysis etc by operation of push-buttons associated with the warning indicators.

The ELT/116 radar intercept receiver system includes omni-directional and DF antennas, an auxiliary DF unit, RF unit and the display and console unit at the EW operator's position. The IFM receiver operates with a crystal video DF receiver in all bands. Frequency measurement accuracy is 0·2%, with a dynamic range of about –70 dBm to zero. Complete digital messages are transmitted to the ship's CIC aboard larger vessels, data transmitted including such items as platform identification, emitter characteristics, lock-on/search warnings and confidence levels etc.

The ELT/311/511 jammers can be used in conjunction with the above passive EW elements to provide a complete EW facility, and jammers can be under operator control or by CIC direction. A wide variety of jamming techniques is employed, including: noise, deception, automatic and semi-automatic. Range blanking with spot noise or amplitude modulation spot jamming is normally used against search radars, tracking systems and either

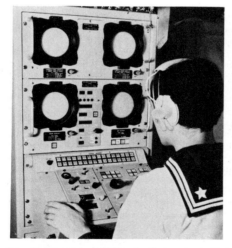

Operator's console of Elettronica 'Gamma' naval EW suite. Two upper CRTs are for surveillance, left lower CRT is main display and lower right CRT is for DF

Elettronica EW antennas aboard an Italian Navy ship; note stabilisation on 2 larger units. Planar array is AN/SPA-72 for SPS-52 3-D search radar

active or lobe-on-receive-only (LORO) conical scan radars. Angle jamming with spot noise is used against sequential lobing and track-while-scan (TWS) radars. Look-through and time-gated circuits are provided to control jammer operation in conjunction with the system receivers. These circuits are generally employed when the system is required to operate against multiple threats.

CONTRACTOR
Elettronica SpA, Via Tiburtina Valeria Km 13700, 00131 Rome, Italy.

4642.353

SMART GUARD HELICOPTER ESM SYSTEM

Developed for helicopter operation, Smart Guard provides continuous and automatic surveillance of VHF/UHF communications bands. In particular, the system can intercept, analyse and DF any signal in these bands, even those of extremely short duration. Smart Guard will automatically correlate successive intercepts of the same emitter for location purposes.

Basic elements of the system are:
(1) a high scan velocity surveillance receiver

(2) an analysis and monitoring receiver with associated IFF display
(3) a very high precision direction finder
(4) a computer and data processing system
(5) a plasma display
(6) a dual-track audio recorder
(7) a digital recorder for mission data.

Smart Guard performs automatic surveillance of one or more frequency ranges, automatic control of

predetermined channels, demodulation of intercepted emissions for operator audio or recording, and display of the data acquired.

STATUS
In production.
CONTRACTOR
Elettronica SpA, Via Tiburtina Valeria, Km 13700, 00131 Rome, Italy.

4643.353
FAST JAM HELICOPTER ECM SYSTEM

Fast Jam is a communications ECM system developed specifically for helicopter installation. The system provides surveillance and automatic jamming of hostile emissions with provisions to safeguard friendly emissions.

System elements consists of:

(1) an analysis and monitoring receiver with associated IFF display. The receiver is computer-controlled and operates in look-through mode during jamming to confirm the continuing presence of the hostile emission

(2) a computer for system management which controls the status of the channels under surveillance, processes and displays the collected data and activates jammers following stored instruction

(3) one or more solid-state jammers

(4) a plasma display.

The system normally operates in an automatic mode under the supervision of the operator who assigns the initial instructions, updates of which can be made even during a mission. In the automatic mode the system has an extremely short reception and transmission time. The system may also be wholly or partially manually controlled. Sophisticated jamming techniques allow surveillance of the hostile emission (look-through) and the simultaneous jamming of more emissions without loss of effectiveness.

STATUS

In production.

CONTRACTOR

Elettronica SpA, Via Tiburtina Valeria, Km 13700, 00131 Rome, Italy.

4644.293
CO-NEWS NAVAL ESM SYSTEM

CO-NEWS (Communications Naval Electronic Warfare System) is a naval ESM system which provides full monitoring and analysis of communications in the VHF/UHF frequency band. The system is completely automated to achieve very high intercept probability and to handle high density traffic. It comprises a lightweight antenna assembly, normally mounted at masthead, consisting of three co-planar dipole arrays and a switching matrix, and an operator console located below decks. The equipment is modular in design to cater for expansion and for additional units.

CO-NEWS automatically carries out continuous surveillance of the communications band, technical analysis and bearing of the intercepted emissions and real-time data processing and presentation. The intercepted signals can also be demodulated for monitoring purposes.

The operator console houses the system modules including:

(1) the surveillance receiver which scans automatically through the frequency bands at a velocity sufficiently high to ensure 100 per cent intercept probability

(2) a direction finder that takes the bearing and performs the technical analysis of intercepted emissions and also serves to monitor these signals

(3) a computer which manages the sensors, and processes and presents the data

(4) displays for the presentation of the measured data, and the operator's command keyboard. Two different displays are provided; a panoramic display dedicated to a synthetic presentation of the search results, and a plasma display for data and situation evaluation.

The system operates automatically under the supervision of an operator who can also over-ride the system's automatic operation to solve ambiguous situations or to monitor the emissions.

STATUS

In operational service.

CONTRACTOR

Elettronica SpA, Via Tiburtina Valeria, Km 13700, 00131 Rome, Italy.

CO-NEWS VHF/UHF antenna assembly

3343.253
RQN-1 RADAR INTERCEPT EQUIPMENT

The RQN-1 radar intercept equipment is a wide-band radar receiver which provides DF, frequency band measurement, video analysis of pulse width and pulse repetition frequency. Being wide open in frequency, it provides high probability of detection of every radar signal within its sensitivity range, which extends well beyond the radar horizon. Its DF accuracy, together with a number of additional features, like pulse length and prf measurement and frequency band determination, lend themselves to use in both limited ELINT (electronic intelligence) missions and as a quick reaction device for self and mutual protection.

The RQN-1 measures on a pulse by pulse basis the bearing, pulse length, pulse repetition rate and frequency band of simultaneous radar signals, allowing the operator to identify each of them and to determine the relative danger. Thus, a very valuable means to analyse the tactical situation is available. Better operational effectiveness is achieved if the PAW-1 warning unit and the RIN-1 identification unit are connected to the radar intercept equipment, as well as a TQN-1X radar jammer.

When installed on very small vessels, it can be used for detection and analysis of enemy radiations, while the carrier remains beyond the enemy radar detection range. The manufacturers state that the sensitivity in this mode is sufficient to give as much as five to ten minutes of advance warning (ie detection before the radar receives a valid target echo) when used against ship or airborne search radars. This equipment is also used as the passive target acquisition sensor for ship-to-ship missile systems, eg Otomat, Exocet, etc. On larger ships, the RQN-1 may be used in conjunction with active jammers to provide a full ECM capability. The signal analysis facilities are adequate for limited ELINT missions, as well as emission identification and optimisation of active ECM signals.

A separate digital module can be connected to the RQN-1 to give automatic warning of up to eight pre-selected radars.

The main features are: instantaneous detection and DF of all radar emissions; omni-directional wide open coverage; built-in video analysis capability; threat frequency band indication and selection; blanking of nearby radars; solid-state (apart from CRTs).

CHARACTERISTICS

Type: RQN-1A/RQN-1B

Frequency coverage: 1 – 12 GHz (RQN-1A)
1 – 18 GHz (RQN-1B)

Sensitivity: –48 dBm (nominal)

DF accuracy: 5° rms (all azimuth, all frequencies 2 – 12 GHz)

PRF measurement: 50 – 10 000 pps, ±10%, on 3-inch (76 mm) PPI

Pulsewidth measurement: 0·3 – 5 μs, ±10% plus 0·05 μs

Frequency band indication: L, S, C, X, Ku-band lamps ±3%

High level RF protection: 30 MHz – 18 GHz; 100 W/1 μs/1000 pps; 1 W CW

Weights and dimensions

Antenna and radome: 30 kg, 38 cm diameter, 76 cm height

Auxiliary unit: 35 kg, 47 × 39 × 35 cm

Display: 45 kg, 47 × 34 × 55 cm

STATUS

In production and operational.

CONTRACTOR

Selenia Industrie Elettroniche Associate SpA, Special Equipment and Systems Division, Via dei Castelli Romani 2, 00040 Pomezia, Rome, Italy.

Antenna array for Selenia RQN-1A radar intercept. Height is approximately 75 cm

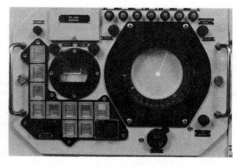

Operator's console of Selenia RQN-1B radar intercept equipment

3528.253
RQN-3 RADAR INTERCEPT EQUIPMENT

The Selenia RQN-3 radar intercept equipment is an advanced version of the RQN-1 system, providing a variety of improved operational facilities. It is based on the use of an instantaneous frequency measuring (IFM) receiver in conjunction with discriminators and solid-state microwave amplifiers in the high frequency coverage bands. The reported system sensitivity is about –65 dBm, and the RQN-3B has a frequency range extending up to 18 GHz.

It is normally used in conjunction with the IPN-10 computerised display system and with the RIN-1 radar and threat library which enables sorting and priority ordering of threats, and allows an operator to confirm threats and initiate jamming or other countermeasures.

STATUS

Stated to be in service with several unspecified navies.

CONTRACTOR

Selenia Industrie Elettroniche Associate SpA, Special Equipment and Systems Division, Via dei Castelli Romani 2, 00040 Pomezia, Rome, Italy.

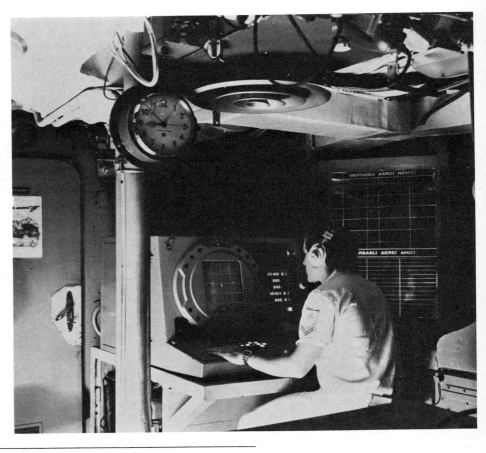

Selenia RQN-3/3B radar intercept equipment operator's console

3382.393
IHS-6 ESM/ECM EQUIPMENT

The IHS-6 is an integrated ESM/ECM system designed for tactical ECM missions in operational roles such as stand-off jamming, support for air strikes against ground targets, fleet protection etc. The system is composed of two main sections: the RQH-5 ESM system, and the TQN-2 modular jamming system.

The former has evolved in at least two versions, denoted by a suffix /1 or /2; the latter is modular and computer based, and is the variant employed in IHS-6 to provide detection, analysis and identification of any radar emission in the 1 to 18 GHz band. The wide open receiver is of the instantaneous frequency measuring (IFM) type with monopulse DF capabilities for automatic emitter analysis, warning and tracking. There is capacity for an automatic emitter library of more than 2000 types and at least 50 targets can be tracked in real-time. A CRT display provides multimode presentation with alpha-numeric and graphic facilities. The ECM jammer section of the system, TQN-2, enables up to four bands to be jammed from one helicopter installation in the full capability model (the system for the Agusta A 109A EW helicopter has two jamming bands only) with a steerable antenna for I- and J-band targets and fixed antennas for the other bands. Jamming modes available include: spot, barrage, and hybrid, and as an option, chaff release for passive countermeasures

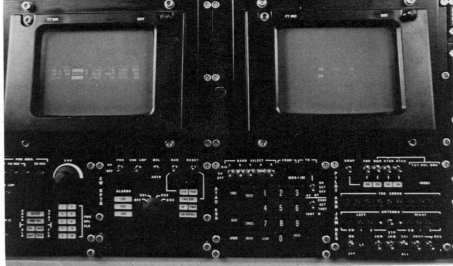

Selenia RQH-5 ESM system console in a helicopter installation

can be incorporated.

The installation on the Agusta A 109A helicopter comprises RQH-5 DF antennas mounted on the underside, rear (2), and nose (2) of the aircraft; two FBR-2 antennas on the rear fuselage; a TQN-2 I/J-band antenna; an FR-2X IFM receiver; RQH-5 ESM transceivers; processing unit; auxiliary unit; and a power supply unit.

CHARACTERISTICS

ESM section (RQH-5 receiver)
Frequency coverage: 1 – 18 GHz
Azimuth coverage: Omni-directional
Receiver type: Wide open, with IFM and monopulse DF
Emitter analysis, warning and tracking: Automatic
Tracking capacity: >50 emitters (real-time)
Automatic identification library: >2000 emitters
ECM section (TQN-2 jammer)
Frequency: Selectable
Antenna: High gain
Polarisation: Random
Jamming modes: Spot, barrage, hybrid
  Precision AFC on selected emitters
STATUS

Among the exports reported for the IHS-6 system are Westland Commando EW helicopters for the Egyptian forces.

CONTRACTOR

Selenia Industrie Elettroniche Associate SpA, Special Equipment and Systems Division, Via dei Castelli Romani 2, 00040 Pomezia, Rome, Italy.

IHS-6 ESM/ECM helicopter equipment mounted on a Westland Commando helicopter

4174.393
SL/ALQ-234 ECM POD

The ALQ-234 is designed to provide protection against AA artillery radar directors and surface-to-air missile systems, and it also provides a radar warning facility for the pilot, to indicate any threat which has locked onto the aircraft. It is self-contained and incorporates its own broad-band ESM section, using a wide-open receiver, and intercepted data are fed to the pod's on-board digital computer for use in threat list compilation and comparison against an existing threat library. Intercepted threats are arranged in order of priority automatically. The computer also performs jamming power management against several threats simultaneously (where necessary) in order of priority. Travelling wave tube (TWT) transmitters are used for jamming, covering a band about 6 GHz wide in the fire control region of the radar spectrum. Closed-loop liquid cooling combined with air cooling allows aircraft speeds and altitudes ranging from low level/speed to supersonic/high altitude to be accommodated.

Each pod contains three jammers, a receiver/processor and antennas at each end. One jammer, at the front, is used to counter doppler and CW threats. Two centrally located jammers are 'smart-noise' transmitters. The rear section houses the superheterodyne radar warning receiver (RWR) with an instantaneous frequency measurement (IFM) system.

CHARACTERISTICS
Pod
Length: 3·825 m
Diameter: 414 mm
Weight: 270 kg
Power generation: RAT, 7·5 kVA
Cooling: Dual circuit with heat exchanger
Pulse countermeasures
Frequency band: I-J
Sector coverage: Fore and aft
Detection: Built-in RWR with automatic designation and reaction management
Jamming: Noise and deception. Multiple threat capability by computer controlled power management
CW countermeasures
Frequency band: H-J
Sector coverage: Fore
Detection: Built-in RWR with automatic designation and reaction management
Jamming: Deception. Multiple threat capability
STATUS
Earlier ALQ-234 pods have been supplied to air forces of other countries and it is still in production. A new

Selenia SL/ALQ-234 self-defence ECM pod for carriage by high performance aircraft

version has completed trials and is now in production for the Italian Air Force. Development is being carried out on versions with a lower frequency capability (eg C, D, E, F-bands) for use against air defence search radars. The Egyptian Air Force has equipped its Mirage 5 and MiG-21 aircraft with ALQ-234 pods.
CONTRACTOR
Selenia Industrie Elettroniche Associate SpA, Special Equipment and Systems Division, Via dei Castelli Romani 2, 00040 Pomezia, Rome, Italy.

3526.193
IGS-1 MOBILE INTEGRATED ECM SYSTEM

The IGS-1 is an ECM system mounted on a trailer, and intended to be part of a major EW system. It is capable of autonomous data collection, analysis and reaction, as well as co-ordinated operation with a command and control centre, where intercepted data are received and orders are generated.

The system is driven through RQN-1B radar intercept equipment (3343.253), which is a wide open receiver with omni-directional coverage, providing direction of arrival, pulse-width, PRF and frequency band measurement. The same parameters are available in digital form on the PAW-1 pulse analyser and warner, where threat radars can be programmed as such for a prompt evaluation and reaction. Digitised data are sent via radio link or telephone cable to the co-ordination centre. Bi-directional voice communication is possible, and orders can be received through the same way.

The TQN-1 jammer provides the active reaction against the threat. A highly directional antenna is tracked on the target and the jamming is deployed to deny the use of airborne or surface radars.

All equipments composing the system are fitted in an operational console, housed inside an air conditioned shelter. A trailer with wheels suitable for rough and soft terrain is supplied.

A reduced configuration of the IGS-1 system is also available, installed in a smaller shelter and carried by a Land-Rover (long wheel base) vehicle. This configuration includes only the ESM section of the system, with the addition of a computer based radar identification facility.

CHARACTERISTICS
ESM section: RQN-1B/PAW-1
Frequency coverage: D – J-band
Azimuth coverage: Omni-directional
Elevation coverage: –10 to +20°
D/F accuracy: 5° RMS
ECM section: TQN-1X
Frequency coverage: I/J-band
Antenna: High gain
Polarisation: Dual
Jamming: Noise
Precision frequency/angle tracking of selected targets
Identification: RIN-P
Library capacity: Up to 3000 radar modes
Identification: Weighted comparison
Processing time: 1 s
Communication: RP-1
Modulation: FSK (1200 bauds), voice, TTY
STATUS
In production and operational in several countries.
CONTRACTOR
Selenia Industrie Elettroniche Associate SpA, Special Equipment and Systems Division, Via dei Castelli Romani 2, 00040 Pomezia, Rome, Italy.

Land-Rover mounted version of Selenia IGS-1P ESM system

Selenia IGS-1 ESM/ECM system in containerised form on trailer platform. Note TQN-1 jammer antenna to left and below conical array for ESM receiver

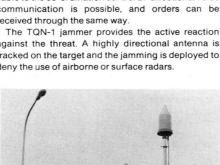

3527.153
SELENIA ELECTRONIC SURVEILLANCE SYSTEM

The Selenia Electronic Surveillance System is an ESM system, carried on a Mercedes Unimog type vehicle, and is mainly designed for coastal and battlefield surveillance, as part of a major EW system. Radar emissions are intercepted by RQN-1B radar intercept equipment (3343.253), which is a wide open receiver with omni-directional coverage, providing direction of arrival, pulse-width, PRF and frequency band measurement. The same parameters are available in digital form on the PAW-1 pulse analyser and warner, where threat radars can be programmed as such for a prompt evaluation and reaction. A monopulse antenna system is slaved to the RQN-1B handwheel, and feeds an FBR-1 fine bearing receiver for azimuth measurement with high accuracy. At the same time the FR-1 frequency receiver performs spot frequency measurement.

The RP-1 remoting panel allows exchange of information between the surveillance system and the co-ordination centre via radio link or telephone cable. Bi-directional voice communication is also possible.

The sub-units are fitted in an operations console, which together with the remaining ancillaries is housed inside a NATO 1 type shelter with air conditioning and provided with suitable lifting and levelling devices.

Selenia Electronic Surveillance System on its Unimog carrier vehicle. Note wheeled container which is air-conditioned and fitted with suitable lifting and levelling devices. Antennas are provided which enable signals in the frequency band 1-18 GHz to be intercepted, measured and their origins located

5663.253
INS-3 NAVAL ESM/ECM SYSTEM

INS-3 is a total system which allows a single operator to perform both ESM and ECM functions, and is composed of a passive section and an active section. The passive section, RQN-3B, provides automatic detection and analysis, and tracking of emissions in a dense electromagnetic environment. It provides warning of emissions in its coverage area and automatic identification of threats based on parameters stored in a dedicated computer library. Information on threat direction, identification parameters, etc is displayed in alpha-numeric and. graphic symbology on a 16-inch CRT display mounted in the INS-3 control console.

The active section, TQN-2, is integrated with the RQN-3B and receives instantaneous data for fast and automatic reaction. It will provide noise and pulse jamming of threat emissions, as well as computer control of passive EW launch systems, eg chaff and flares. It also performs passive tracking in azimuth and elevation of high-speed radar emitters, such as hostile aircraft and anti-ship missiles, and passes this data to other self-defence weapons.

CHARACTERISTICS
ESM operating frequency: 1 – 18 GHz
Receiver: wide open with IFM and monopulse DF
Horizontal coverage: omni-directional
Real-time tracking capacity: over 50 emitters
Automatic identification library: up to 3000 emitters
ECM operating frequency: I/J-band
Jamming modes: FM-AM-Pulse
CONTRACTOR
Selenia Industrie Elettroniche Associate SpA, Special
Equipment and Systems Division, Via dei Castelli
Romani 2, 00040 Pomezia, Rome, Italy.

ECM antenna of INS-3 system

5664.153
ESS-2 ELECTRONIC SURVEILLANCE SYSTEM

ESS-2 is a mobile integrated surveillance and analysis system designed to operate against ground-based radars, and for coastal and battlefield surveillance against shipborne and airborne radars, as part of a major EW network. It provides high detection probability, high accuracy emitter bearing, optional parameter measurement and identification, and gives instantaneous threat warnings. The system can operate on a stand-alone basis, or it may be integrated into a wider ESM/ECM network.

The hardware is installed in a standard NATO air-conditioned shelter which can be mounted on a suitable vehicle for transportation or mobile operation.

CHARACTERISTICS
Frequency coverage: L to Ku-band
Warning channels: 8 or 16
Azimuth coverage: 360°
Maximum displayed identities: 15
Identification library size: 1000, 2000 or 3000
STATUS
In production and operational use in several countries.
CONTRACTOR
Selenia Industrie Elettroniche Associate SpA, Special
Equipment and Systems Division, Via dei Castelli
Romani 2, 00040 Pomezia, Rome, Italy.

4175.093
SELENIA EW EQUIPMENT

In addition to those equipments described individually in this section, Selenia produces a wide range of electronic warfare hardware, much of which is protected by security classification. To assist readers, the following list of the major current items of Selenia EW hardware has been compiled as an aid to identification:

ALQ-X	Series of airborne jammer pods, various models
ALQ-234	ESM/ECM self-protection jammer pod
ESS-2	Mobile ESM system
IGS-1	Mobile integrated ESM/ECM system
IGS-1P	Version of IGS-1
IGS-3	Computerised mobile integrated ESM/ECM system
IHS-6	Integrated helicopter ESM/ECM system
INS-1	Integrated system for FPBs, RQN-1 + PAW-1 + RIN-1
INS-3	Integrated naval ESM/ECM system, computer-aided
PAW-1	Pulse analyser and warner
RIN-1	Naval radar identification unit
RQA-5	Fixed-wing aircraft version of RQH-5
RQH-5	Computer-based helicopter ESM system

One version of Selenia TQN series jammer antenna

RQN-1	Radar intercept set for submarines and small ships
RQN-3	Naval radar intercept and analysis set
TQN-1	Naval jammer
TQN-2	Modular airborne jammer (multi-band)
TQN-3	Jammer
TQN-4	Jammer

Selenia INS-1 naval ESM/ECM antennas

Another Italian Air Force EW project is the Aeritalia G222 VS EW aircraft, the first of which was delivered to the Italian Air Force in March 1983. Both Selenia and Elettronica are believed to be engaged on this project but no details have been announced. The Elettronica RIDE ESM system (**4165.393**) described elsewhere in this section is certainly appropriate to this requirement as would be a fixed-wing version of

the IHS-6 heliborne ESM/ECM system (**3382.393**) by Selenia. Communications for the G222 VS system are understood to be the responsibility of Elmer, while SMA of Florence is providing radar.

CONTRACTOR
Selenia Industrie Elettroniche Associate SpA, Special Equipment and Systems Division, Via dei Castelli Romani 2, 00040 Pomezia, Rome, Italy.

Selenia INS-1 naval ESM system operating position and console

---

4641.281

SCLAR Mk 2 ROCKET LAUNCHING SYSTEM

The SCLAR Mk 2 system is a development of the UCLAR System (**1823.281** *Jane's Weapon Systems* 1982-83 and earlier editions) and has been designed and manufactured for installation in the Italian Navy's 'Maestrale' class ASW frigates and the helicopter carrier 'Garibaldi'. The SCLAR Mk 2 employs the same rocket launcher of the previous system but data is processed by a digital multiprocessing computer based on the Elsag designed ESA 24 microprocessor.

The system is defined as multipurpose since it provides for the execution of various operations, such as decoying incoming missiles, confusion of hostile radars, illumination or HE bombardment, by simply selecting the type of rocket.

A very large set of decoying patterns can be stored in the digital computer and may be recalled and automatically executed as required. Each stored pattern may be substituted easily and rapidly at any time.

The SCLAR Mk 2 consists of one control console which requires a single operator; one data processing

unit; one or two rocket launchers; one or two power supply cabinets; and one or two local control panels. In addition the system requires a set of peripheral panels comprising one alarm loading panel and one acoustic warning device for each launcher. An optional illuminating launching remote control panel is also available.

Two remotely controlled rocket launchers can be driven by the SCLAR Mk 2, which will position them in azimuth and elevation and perform all the necessary logic and computation. This includes rocket pattern programming, azimuth and elevation continuous computation for the accurate launch of each rocket to the programmed burst point and rocket automatic selection and firing.

STATUS
In production.
CONTRACTORS
Selenia-Elsag Consortium for Naval Systems, Via Panama 52, 00198 Rome, Italy.
Breda Meccanica Bresciana SpA, Via Lunga 2, 25100 Brescia, Italy.

SCLAR Mk 2 rocket launcher

3997.293

BREDA LIGHT CHAFF ROCKET LAUNCHING SYSTEM

This system consists of two launchers, installed port and starboard, and a control panel. Each launcher holds six 105 mm short rockets, set in tubes at fixed elevation and bearing (45° and 135° relative to ship's head) so as to launch on each quarter and form a chaff 'cross' pattern over the ship. The control panel monitors the state of the launcher, and commands launching from each launcher independently. Two operational cycles, each consisting of one pattern of four followed by one pair ahead, are performed without reloading. The resulting radar homing missile decoy is accompanied by evasive ship manoeuvres. This launcher is particularly intended for the defence of very light craft. The rockets were designed and developed by BFD Difesa-Spazio.
CHARACTERISTICS
Launcher
Height: 1700 mm

Length: 480 mm
Width: 300 mm
Weight: 85 kg (without rockets); 125 kg (with rockets)
Control panel
Height: 260 mm
Length: 400 mm
Width: 220 mm
Weight: 8 kg
Rocket
Calibre: 105 mm
Weight: 5 kg (without container); 6·5 kg (with container)
Power consumption: 0·2 kW
STATUS
In production.
CONTRACTORS
Launchers: Breda Meccanica Bresciana SpA, Via Lunga 2, 25100 Brescia, Italy.
Rockets: BFD Difesa-Spazio, Via Sicilia 162, 00187 Roma, Italy.

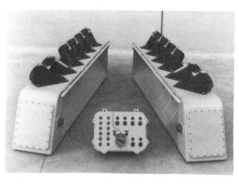

Breda light chaff rocket launcher unit (aft end nearest camera)

JAPAN

4176.093

JAPANESE EW EQUIPMENT

As with many other categories of defence equipment, Japanese requirements for electronic warfare equipment have previously been met mostly from American sources, but with the steady development of advanced technical abilities and facilities in Japan an increasing range of defence hardware is being produced indigenously. This entry summarises the information about such items that has been obtained.
J/APR-1
A radar warning receiver (RWR) for the Japanese F-104J Starfighter. Production has long since been completed and the equipment will be retired from service in the near future.
J/APR-2
This RWR was developed by Tokyo Keiki for the Japanese F-4EJ Phantom. Production has been completed and the equipment is still in service.

J/APR-3
Based on the J/APR-2, this RWR was designed by Tokyo Keiki to update the threat capability for the Japanese F-1 support fighter. The system is still in limited production.
J/APR-4
Based on experience gained in the course of development of the J/APR-2 and -3, Tokyo Keiki has designed an advanced RWR, designated the J/APR-4,

This unidentified item of Japanese equipment is apparently a transportable battlefield ESM system, although the flexible waveguides which can be discerned on the original photograph could equally indicate facilities for transmission at microwave frequencies. This would suggest a possible combined ESM/ECM role for the equipment. (K Ebata)

for the Japanese F-15J Eagle. This is capable of processing multiple inputs simultaneously in a dense electromagnetic environment and has a digital computer with a reprogrammable software package to permit reconfiguration to meet future threats. The indicator provides for daylight viewing and multiple-threat data presentation in alpha-numeric and graphic format. The system is also designed to interface with other on-board aircraft EW equipment such as J/ALQ-8, etc.

AIRBORNE EW

Various other items of airborne EW equipment have been identified and associated with a number of specific Japanese aircraft types. Although detailed information on the hardware remains classified, the following list shows a number of known EW equipment/aircraft associations:

EW Equipment	Aircraft Type
J/ALQ-2	T-33
J/ALQ-3	C-46, YS-11
J/ALQ-4	F-104
J/ALQ-5	C-1
J/ALQ-6	F-4, ET-2 (F-1)
J/ALQ-8	F-4, F-15J
J/APR-1	F-104J
J/APR-2	F-4EJ
J/APR-3	F-1
J/APR-4	F-15J

The J/ALQ-8 countermeasures set is understood to operate in three bands: 1 – 4, 4 – 8, and 7·5 – 18 GHz.

CONTRACTORS
Mitsubishi Electric Corporation, Mitsubishi Denki

The J/APR-4 radar warning receiver system designed by Tokyo Keiki Co for the F-15J Eagle aircraft. Multiple threats can be handled on a simultaneous basis

Building, Marounouchi, Tokyo 100, Japan.
Tokyo Keiki Company Ltd, 16, 2-Chome, Minami-Kamata, Ohta-ku, Tokyo, Japan.

NETHERLANDS

4054.293

RAMSES NAVAL ECM

RAMSES (reprogrammable advanced multi-mode shipborne ECM system) is a versatile, modular naval electronic countermeasures equipment, designed principally to provide protection for ships against I/J-band radar threats. Although few details have been cleared for publication, RAMSES has been described as an integrated responsive noise and deception repeater jammer. It provides for jamming of the target indicating search radars at long range to disable or confuse missile launchers (with emphasis on noise jamming) and deception of any missiles launched at shorter ranges (after they have gone into the active radar homing mode, where jamming relies more heavily on deception). Jamming parameters can be revised and updated in the light of experience and developing tactics by reprogramming.

The basic configuration of RAMSES has provisions for interconnection with other ship's systems, such as ESM equipments like Sphinx (**4055.293**) or RAPIDS (**4056.293**) and a tactical data handling system. If necessary, one operator can handle all the EW functions of a ship by these means. Optionally, the control panel and processing cabinet can be

integrated into a single console with additional frequency/amplitude and alpha-numeric display.

The principal features of the system are as follows, and the physical characteristics of the hardware are listed in the table below. RAMSES operates in I/J-bands and is capable of high pulse and CW effective radiated power (ERP). Multimode jamming operation is possible with multi-target handling capability. The system is reprogrammable and power management is provided. The antennas are fully rotatable and stabilised, and are lightweight.

CHARACTERISTICS

Dimensions	Width (mm)	Height (mm)	Depth (mm)	Weight (kg)
Antenna module (×2)	458	1560	945	100
RF cabinet	938	2058	906	526
Processing cabinet	650	1692	782	250
Control panel	284	321	194	2·5

STATUS

The system was designed and developed by Signaal in co-operation with MEL (UK) Ltd. In production.

CONTRACTOR

Hollandse Signaalapparaten BV, PO Box 42, 7550 Hengelo, Netherlands.

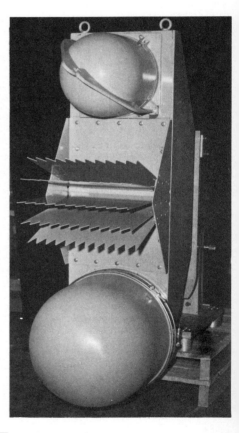

RAMSES antenna assembly

4056.293

RAPIDS NAVAL ESM

RAPIDS (radar passive identification system) is a shipborne electronic support measures (ESM) system for the interception, analysis and identification of all forms of radar emissions. It is entirely passive and operates autonomously. The system features:

(1) high probability of interception by an instantaneous field of view of 360° and a large instantaneous frequency coverage

(2) high sensitivity

(3) high pulse density capability

(4) unattended operation as far as threats are

concerned when integrated with a data handling system

(5) high bearing accuracy.

Operational functions include: interception, threat processing, analysis, identification, tracking, data exchange with ECM and data handling systems, data logging.

The basic configuration of RAPIDS is illustrated.

Signals of linear as well as circular polarisation can be intercepted by the high sensitivity receiver. The Electronic Data Display provides an overview of the situation by presenting: bearing frequency plots of intercepted signals; alarm cursors for tracking radars locked on to own ship; alarm cursors for radars that

trigger the threat warner; symbols to indicate identified interceptions; tell-back data from an ECM when integrated with such a system. Other information displayed includes alpha-numeric data on lock-ons; alpha-numeric data on triggered threat warner channels; alpha-numeric data on identified targets; software keys for the selection of particular system functions.

RAPIDS has provisions for interconnection with a data handling system and an ECM system such as RAMSES (**4054.293**) or Scimitar (**3598.293**). The basic version is illustrated. The frequency range covers 2 to 18 GHz.

CHARACTERISTICS

Dimensions	Width (mm)	Height (mm)	Depth (mm)	Weight (kg)
Antenna, radome and base	536	1554	620	94
Receiver unit	597	835	502	145
Processor unit	650	1570	660	250
Display unit	530	813	440	40
Air cooler	597	1045	505	60

STATUS

Production.

CONTRACTOR

Hollandse Signaalapparaten BV, PO Box 42, 7550 Hengelo, Netherlands.

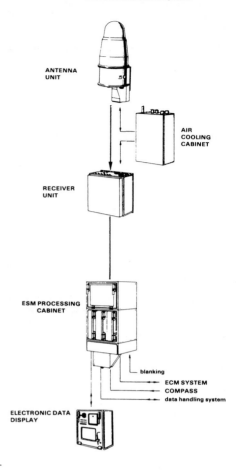

RAPIDS
Radar Passive Identification System

Diagram of typical RAPIDS installation

4055.293
SPHINX NAVAL ESM

Sphinx (system for passive handling of intercepted transmissions) is a shipborne electronic support measures (ESM) system for the interception, analysis and identification of all forms of pulsed radar emissions. It is entirely passive and operates autonomously. The system features: a high probability of interception by an instantaneous field of view of 360° and a continuous coverage of the entire frequency range, high sensitivity, high pulse density capability. It is capable of the following functions:

(1) omni-directional interception of signals in the range 1 to 18 GHz and determination of their frequency, and bearing

(2) lock-on detection, ie automatic detection and warning of any radar locked on to own ship

(3) automatic analysis of selected signals in terms of: level, pulse, duration, frequency (max, minimum), PRF (max, minimum), scan period

(4) automatic tracking in bearing of selected signals

(5) blanking of selected signals tracked in bearing

(6) area blanking

(7) identification of signals by comparison with library

(8) data exchange with ECM and data handling system

(9) data logging on cassette of information acquired.

The basic configuration of Sphinx is illustrated and consists of a frequency receiver and an eight-sector bearing receiver. Both are untuned and wide open in all directions so providing simultaneous coverage of 360° in azimuth and 40° in elevation (nominal). Interception probability approaches 100 per cent. Signals of linear as well as circular polarisation can be intercepted.

The operator's console has three displays:

(1) a situation display for presentation of bearing/frequency plots of detected signals and tell-back data from the ECM system

(2) an alpha-numeric display for analyser results

(3) an alpha-numeric display for identification results.

Sphinx has provisions for interconnection with a data handling system and an ECM system such as RAMSES (**4054.293**). One operator can then take care of both ESM and ECM functions on board the ship. Sphinx has built-in test facilities for checking both before and during operation. The bearing array is designed to form part of the load bearing structure of a mast. A WM20 series combined antenna system can be easily mounted on top.

Optional enhancements include: a K-band reception package (33 to 40 GHz) with alarm; a threat alarm, sets of parameters; and a CW detection package. Detailed characteristics of this equipment appear under the above entry number in *Jane's Weapon Systems 1981-82*.

STATUS

Production.

CONTRACTOR

Hollandse Signaalapparaten BV, PO Box 42, 7550 Hengelo, Netherlands.

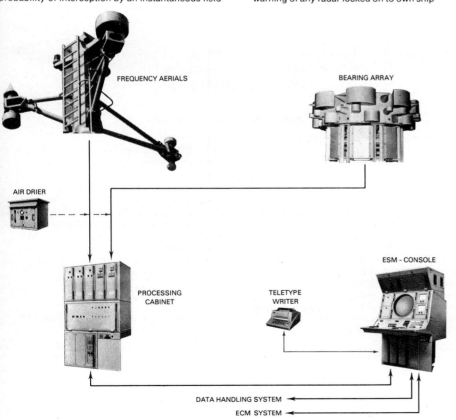

Basic SPHINX naval ESM configuration

4735.193
SPECTRA ELINT SYSTEM
Signaal has developed a communications intercept and monitoring system covering the LF, MF and HF frequency bands, with an option to cover the VHF and UHF bands. The system is normally operated as a net with several modular designed monitoring stations, tailored to individual requirements, each being equipped to perform specific tasks.

Spectra is intended for emission interception, analysis and storage, as well as emitter location using direction finding techniques. It is completely computer-controlled with operator positions for the monitoring and analysis of voice, telegraphy or facsimile messages. All components are controlled via keyboards and displays from the operator positions.
STATUS
In development.
CONTRACTOR
Hollandse Signaalapparaten BV, PO Box 42, 7550 Hengelo, Netherlands.

NORWAY

3344.153
SIMRAD RL1 LASER WARNING DEVICE
The Simrad RL1 laser warning receiver detects radiation from pulsed laser rangefinders and target markers. The instrument can detect pulsed radiation within the 0·66 to 1·1μm near infra-red band, covering the most common types of pulsed lasers (ruby, GaAs, neodymium) currently being used in rangefinders and target markers. The instrument does not detect continuous radiation.

A detector unit mounted on top of the vehicle has a 360° field-of-view and can in addition detect radiation coming from above. An indicator unit is mounted inside the vehicle. It indicates the approximate direction to the radiating source by means of light-emitting diodes mounted in a circle. Eight 45° sectors are indicated. A ninth emitting diode mounted in the centre indicates radiation received from above. Due to the overlapping fields of view, a total of 17 sectors can be indicated.

The receiver will give an acoustic alarm consisting of a pulsed audio signal in the crew's intercom when a laser pulse is detected. The duration of the alarm is two seconds for a single laser pulse. When more than one pulse is being detected the alarm stays on as long as laser pulses are being received.

CHARACTERISTICS
Detector Unit
Number of detectors: Horizontal:4; Vertical:1
Detector field of view: 360°
Type of detector: PIN photodiode
Optical bandwidth: 0·66 – 1·1μm
False alarm rate: <10⁻³/h
Indicator Unit
Resolution: Horizontal: 45°; Vertical: 45°
Number of sectors: Horizontal: 8; Vertical: 1
Display brightness adjustment range: >100 X
Duration, acoustic alarm: 2 s
Duration, display: 8 s
Operating voltage: 20 – 32 V (24 V nom)
STATUS
Production.
CONTRACTOR
Simrad Optronics A/S, PO Box 6114, Etterstad, Oslo 6, Norway.

RL1 laser warning receiver detector unit and indicator unit (front)

4646.293
SR-1A ESM RECEIVER
The SR-1A is a shipborne ESM radar warning receiver, suitable for installation in larger warships, and designed to intercept, analyse and measure incoming radar signals. It consists of two units; an antenna assembly and a display/control console. The antenna assembly comprises a rotating antenna in a protective radome and a fixed omni-directional octagonal horn array. The fixed antenna gives a coarse bearing to ±22·5 degrees while the rotating antenna accuracy is approximately ±3·5 degrees.

Frequency coverage of the system is from 2·5 to 18 GHz with a claimed frequency measurement of better than ±1 per cent. The display systems give visual indication of DF, pulse analysis and frequency measurement functions. A separate indicator giving radar warning and coarse directional information is also provided and can be installed remotely from the main units.
CONTRACTOR
Nera A/S, Bergen, Norway.

SWEDEN

3025.393
AR 753 JAMMER SET-ON RECEIVER
The AR 753 set-on receiver has been designed for use with the AQ 31 range of pod mounted jammers (**3024.393**). As all components employed in the AR 753 have good wide-band characteristics, the operating ranges can readily be varied. Other features claimed include high sensitivity and good selectivity, with digital indications. The cockpit unit, which is common to all pod configurations, contains the displays, the antenna selector switch, and the gain control. Pod dimensions are 1600 mm long, by 140 mm diameter, and the weight is 25 kg. All other

AR 753 jammer set-on receiver pod

information on the AR 753 remains classified.
STATUS
In production and operational.
CONTRACTOR
SATT Electronics AB, PO Box 32006, 126 11 Stockholm, Sweden.

3537.393
AR765 RADAR WARNING RECEIVER
The AR765 is a lightweight radar warning receiver (RWR) specially designed for fitting on the Agusta Bell 206A Jet Ranger helicopter, but also suitable for use with other types of fixed-wing aircraft and helicopters. The AR765 provides visual and aural threat warning and indication against surveillance as well as fire control radars, and specific features include: DF and homing facilities; multi-octave band frequency coverage; built-in test equipment (BITE). In the case of the Jet Ranger, installation is very simple as the main unit is designed as a direct replacement for the battery access panel in the front of the helicopter fuselage, and the RWR is bolted on in place of the normal battery hatch cover plate.
CHARACTERISTICS
Frequency coverage: Multi-octave or narrow-band
Warning sectors: 2 in front ±45° relative to line of flight
Azimuth coverage: ±90°
Elevation coverage: ±45°
Antennas: Broad-band circularly polarised spirals
Receiver: Crystal video, 2 channels
Sensitivity: –40 dBm (TSS)
Dynamic range: >40 dB
Minimum pulsewidth: 0·1 μs
Threshold adjustment range: 35 dB (from cockpit)
Threat indication: Lamps on panel, and headset
Supply voltage: 28 V DC, 40 VA
Options: CW detection, rejection on non-hostile emitters, laser warning
STATUS
In service but no longer in production.
CONTRACTOR
SATT Electronics AB, PO Box 32006, 126 11 Stockholm, Sweden.

3904.393

AR 777 AIRBORNE MICROWAVE RECEIVER

The AR 777 is a rugged, computer-controlled airborne microwave receiver intended for signal acquisition and jammer set-on. The system performs rapid and unambiguous detection and identification of emitters in dense signal environments.

The AR 777 is a superheterodyne receiver with a high performance YIG-tuned RF head. Due to linear YIG oscillators, a special IF processor and a microcomputer-controlled calibration routine, an excellent frequency accuracy and resolution has been obtained over the entire frequency range.

It covers the frequency range 1 to 8 GHz with three RF-heads, each covering one octave. An RF-head includes YIG-filters, YIG-tuned oscillators and drive circuits. By adding or replacing RF-heads the frequency range can be extended or changed. The receiver uses several modes of tuning and sweeping which are controlled by a microprocessor.

In the present design, two sweep widths are selected, 100 and 300 MHz. The YIG-filters are designed so that they overlap each other; in this way switching between the filters while sweeping is avoided. In order to optimise frequency tracking and linearity over environment, the YIG-filters and LOs are matched with their respective drive circuits. The 4-pole YIG-filters have 25 MHz 3 dB bandwidth, spurious depression outside band 70 dB and skirt selectivity of 24 dB per octave. An SP6T switch is used to select any of six inputs to the receiver (see block diagram). A double balanced mixer followed by a preamplifier generates the IF of 160 MHz. Log

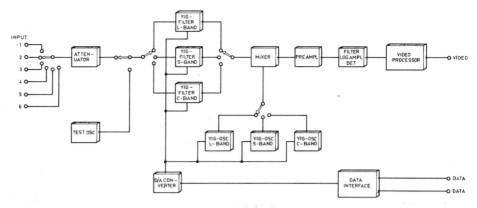

Block diagram of AR 777 receiver

amplifiers and bandpass filters are used together with a video processor using special techniques to get very high selectivity and unambiguous readouts.

The receiver uses a microprocessor to perform control functions and to process, store and display data. All RF circuits are housed in a standard ATR package called the receiver unit. The microprocessor and associated circuitry are housed in a tailor-made unit called the display unit.

The two units communicate through a digital 32-bit serial word data highway which contains information for the tuning (12 bits), control functions and parity check. A D/A converter converts the digital data to

tuning voltages for the YIG components. A keyboard on the display unit is used to communicate with the microprocessor. This is also used to select the centre frequency. The received signals are displayed on a spectrum-type display consisting of two rows of lamp indicators (see figure). The upper row has a memory function and stores the displayed data for a preset time while the lower row gives a momentary indication. Different search patterns can be initiated as well as a fixed tuned mode. In this (identification) mode the PRF is evaluated and the result is displayed on two digital displays. The displays can simultaneoulsy display two PRFs. If more than two PRFs are present at one RF-frequency they are displayed sequentially on one of the displays. A separate display is used to indicate if garbled or jittered PRFs are present. The spectrum analysis mode is used for recording the output spectrum from a co-operating jammer system.

A digital output is provided from the microcomputer. All essential panel settings and all received emitter information can be transmitted in serial form to an external digital recorder. Stored data can be further analysed in a ground based evaluation equipment.

CHARACTERISTICS

Frequency range: 1 – 8 GHz (std)
Sensitivity: –65 dBm
Dynamic range: 65 dB
Sweep width: 100/300 MHz
Sweep rate: 10 sweep/s
Frequency accuracy: 5 MHz
Frequency resolution: 5 MHz
PRF measurement: 200 – 2000 Hz
PRF accuracy: 1 Hz
Power supply: 200 V 3-phase 400 Hz 300 VA
Dimensions
Receiver unit: 497 × 257 × 194 mm
Display unit: 580 × 355 × 173 mm
STATUS
Deployment and production plans have not been released.
CONTRACTOR
SATT Electronics AB, PO Box 32006, 126 11 Stockholm, Sweden.

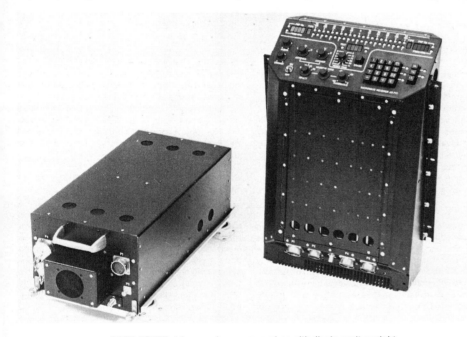

SATT AR 777 airborne microwave receiver with display unit on right

---

4733.393

AR 830 AIRBORNE WARNING SYSTEM

The AR 830 is a fully programmable threat warning system for the detection of radar and laser transmissions. It incorporates a special purpose, high speed signal processor, a general-purpose computer and broadband receivers for both radar and laser signals. It is modular in design to allow updating of

the system to handle new threats and can be interfaced to jammers, chaff dispensers, flare dispensers, recorders and other systems.

The signal processing provides rapid and unambiguous threat identification in dense electromagnetic environments and an extensive emitter library allows comparison and fast analysis of

threats. The library can be easily reprogrammed and updated with new threat information. The incoming threat data is either displayed on a separate CRT or integrated with the aircraft display system.
CONTRACTOR
SATT Electronics AB, PO Box 32006, 126 11 Stockholm, Sweden.

3024.393

AQ 31 JAMMER

The AQ 31 is CW radar jamming equipment designed for aircraft pod mounting and up to full band coverage in the E- to J-bands can be provided. Few specific details have been released but AM, FM noise/sawtooth jamming modes are known to be available and high power output is claimed. Ram-air cooling is employed. Digital control of all major functions is provided and interface facilities are available for use of the AQ 31 with digital signal processing equipment. A single control panel in the

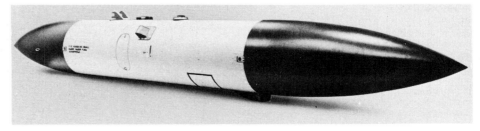

AQ 31 jammer pod

cockpit enables operation of one or two pods, and pre-programmable routines can be employed. The manufacturers also offer a bolt-on companion set-on receiver for use with AQ 31 jamming pods, designated AR 753 (**3025.393**). No other details are available for publication.

STATUS
In production and operational.
CONTRACTOR
SATT Electronics AB, PO Box 32006, 126 11 Stockholm, Sweden.

4361.393
AQ 800 JAMMER
The AQ 800 jammer is intended for use in the training of radar operators and for evaluation of radar station performance. It is pod-mounted and hung from a pylon under the wing or fuselage of an aircraft, the

pod is ram-air cooled and has its own built-in cooling system. The method of mounting is flexible to allow mounting on many different types of aircraft.

The system consists of a pod and a cockpit unit. The pod contains a TWT type transmitter and a sweeping superheterodyne set-on receiver. Each pod

covers one frequency band, ie S-, C-, X-, or Ku-band. The cockpit unit can handle two jammer pods of any frequency combination. The transmitter can generate up to three simultaneous jamming signals. The modulation, centre frequency and bandwidth of each signal are independent of each other. Available modulation types are AM-noise, FM-noise and FM-sawtooth plus noise.

Both the receiver and the transmitter have two antennas, one pointing forward and the other pointing aft. Either direction of operation is selected from the control panel. The system can be operated by a special instructor operator or by the pilot himself.
CHARACTERISTICS
Frequency range: S-band (2-4 GHz), C-band (4-8 GHz), X-band (8-12 GHz), Ku-band (12-18 GHz)
Signal generators: Each pod contains 3 signal generators, each generator covering the following part of the band: S-band 700 MHz, C-band 1200 MHz, X-band 2000 MHz, Ku-band 2000 MHz
Antennas: 2; beamwidth 70° horizontal, 30° vertical. Polarisation is slant linear
Weight: 220 kg
Dimensions: 3·9 m long × 0·43 m wide × 0·52 m high
CONTRACTOR
SATT Electronics AB, PO Box 32006, 126 11 Stockholm, Sweden.

AQ 800 airborne jammer

4734.393
AQ 900 AIRBORNE SELF-PROTECTION SYSTEM
The AQ 900 is a pod-mounted automatic jamming system which is available in different wideband versions covering the frequency range from S-band to Ku-band. The complete system consists of two pods, operated from one cockpit control unit, one pod for jamming search radars in S-band and one for jamming fire control radars in X- or Ku-band. The pods are systemwise interchangeable and are designed for pylon mounting on the aircraft.

The S-band and X/Ku-band versions are essentially

identical in operation and consist of a receiver, a threat analysis unit, a decision and control unit and a transmitter. Each pod has its own ram air turbine generator and cooling system.

The receiver contains all the RF and signal processing circuitry for reception and threat identification. The signal is then passed to the analysis unit where the signals are analysed and compared with data stored in the system library. The decision and control unit includes a microcomputer that gives the system tactical flexibility and allows

threat priority, technique selection, power management, signal generation and control, and cockpit control and indicator interface.

The transmitter contains all the signal generating circuitry and the high power TWT amplifier. The X- and Ku-band version also contains a unit for various deception techniques to counter fire control and tracking radars.
CONTRACTOR
SATT Electronics AB, PO Box 32006, 126 11 Stockholm, Sweden.

4362.393
POD KA NOISE AND DECEPTION JAMMER
This pod is an airborne noise and deception jammer, operating in X-band and offering automatic warning and control of countermeasures. The pod contains three receiving and three transmit antennas, each covering a 120° sector in the horizontal plane. The radar pulses are detected and fed to the radar warning

receiver for analysis as to threat and direction. From information thus derived, the operator can determine the direction in which jamming should take place.

The CW jamming power can also be frequency modulated and is achieved by mixing with noise from a noise generator with an adjustable bandwidth. The resultant noise signal is amplified and finally transmitted. For range deception, the signal is pulse

modulated before transmission. For angle deception the spin modulation of the threat radar is detected and inverted before being fed to the modulator in the pod's transmitter. The pod is approximately four metres long and weighs about 225 kg.
CONTRACTOR
SRA Communications AB (LM Ericsson subsidiary), Spanga, Sweden.

4363.393
LAKE 2000 AIRBORNE JAMMING POD
Lake 2000 is an airborne subsonic jamming pod which has been developed as the successor to a range of jammers designed and manufactured by SRA, such as the Pod KA and the Pod 70, which were both fitted to the Viggen and Draken aircraft, as well as a number of trainers. Lake 2000 operates over any one octave in the 8·5 to 17·5 GHz frequency range.

Transmission is from both ends of the pod and a radar warning receiver is incorporated in the system. The pod uses medium and large scale integration to improve packaging density, and is capable of automatic or manual operation.

The automatic version is designed for tactical aircraft and is completely computer controlled. Jamming routine can be preprogrammed at squadron level. The techniques employed include both

deceptive and continuous wave noise, and pseudo-random noise is also available. The manual version is normally fitted in training aircraft where the aft radome is replaced with control electronics actuated from the pilot's control panel. The pod weighs 225 kg and has an output power between 100 and 150 watts.
CONTRACTOR
SRA Communications AB (LM Ericsson subsidiary), Spanga, Sweden.

5666.393
BO SERIES COUNTERMEASURES DISPENSERS
A range of aircraft countermeasures dispensers is currently in production or development by Philips Elektronikindustrier.
BOZ 100
This is a pod-mounted advanced ECM dispenser originally developed for the Swedish Air Force but also supplied to export customers. It is capable of sophisticated break-lock and corridor operation at subsonic and supersonic speeds and provides self-protection against electromagnetic and heat-seeking missiles. The unit has a comprehensive EW system interface and is suitable for use in deep-penetration strike, reconnaissance and EW roles. It is microprocessor controlled and has a reprogrammable memory.

BOZ 100 pod dispenser

STATUS
In service with the Swedish Air Force (under the nomenclature BOX 9), and also fitted to the Tornado and the French Air Force Jaguar.

BOZ 3
BOZ 3 is a high capacity chaff pod dispenser originally designed to a Swedish Air Force requirement and since adapted for training use. It can be manually or automatically initiated and has both break-lock and corridor chaff modes.
STATUS
In production.
BOP 300
The BOP 300 is designed for the protection of light- to medium-weight fighter aircraft. It is modular in design and can be adapted to various requirements by the addition of one to four dispensing blocks to dispense both chaff and IR flares. The dispensing blocks are designed to give maximum mounting flexibility to

avoid interference with the aircraft stores capability. The unit can be adapted to different types of chaff and flare ammunition.

STATUS
In development.

BOH 300
A chaff/flare dispenser for helicopters and designed to provide protection in hovering and forward flight. It is processor controlled and has reprogrammable operation features. The BOH 300 is suitable for radar, optical and IR deployment. The dispensers can be mounted on the landing gear, fuselage or weapon hard points.

STATUS
In development.

BOH 300 helicopter dispenser

CONTRACTOR
Philips Elektronikindustrier AB, 17588 Järfälla, Sweden.

BOP 300 fighter aircraft dispenser

3538.293
EWS-900 PNEUMATIC CHAFF EQUIPMENT
The EWS-900 shipborne chaff system has been developed by Saab-Scania, principally for use aboard smaller vessels. The main purpose of the system is to establish a chaff radar target, large enough and properly located in space and time, to make the ship and the chaff cloud appear as a single target in the seeker of an approaching missile. Ship manoeuvres, based on wind data, ship's course and line-of-sight to the missile, will cause separation of the false target from the actual ship target. The chaff cloud, having a larger radar target area than the ship, will thus cause the missile to miss the ship.

The main components of the basic EWS-900 system are a pneumatic launcher and similarly pneumatic ammunition. To achieve flexibility in the size of installations, and also to permit mixed salvoes, the launcher is built up in modules and the projectiles are provided with payloads optimised for any seeker frequency band that may be encountered. Not only the launching of the projectiles, but also the ejection of the payload from the projectile is pneumatically operated. The ejection is by means of pressurised air fed into the projectile at launch and hermetically stored in the projectile during its flight. Thus the stored EWS-900 ammunition is non-pyrotechnic, non-pressurised, and so completely harmless and insensitive to severe environments.

To minimise reaction time, the system can be operated from any of several locations on board. In a fully automatic version of the system, introduced in September 1979, (EWS-900 CA) on-board radar warning facilities can be used to feed a minicomputer with all relevant data for automatic launch of chaff and calculation of information for ship's evasive action.

The system consists of an optional number of launchers, control boxes, and an adapter unit. The launcher is connected to either the ordinary compressed air system on board or to separate air bottles. Firing is by means of electro-mechanical valves. The launcher has eight launching tubes for chaff projectiles, an adequate number for the protection of a small vessel. The number of modules fitted depends on how many frequency bands are to be covered and on the endurance required of the ship.

Normally, however, the number of modules will be kept low as reloading at sea can be carried out repeatedly without difficulty. The harmless ammunition can be stored anywhere on board and no powder residue has to be removed from the tubes

The PPI-collar and control/display unit of EWS-900 CA automatic chaff launcher system

before reloading. The control boxes are located in the CIC near the search radar operator, adjacent to the radar warning operator, and accessible to the lookouts eg on the bridge.

STATUS
A similar system has been developed and delivered to the Swedish Navy.

CONTRACTOR
Saab Missiles AB, 58188 Linköping, Sweden.

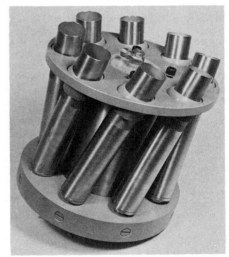

Saab EWS-900 pneumatic launcher unit with high pressure cylinder and eight cartridges

3133.293
PHILAX COUNTERMEASURES LAUNCHER
Philax is a chaff and IR decoy grenade launching system for the protection of small warships against attacking anti-ship missiles. Of very lightweight construction, it requires only a simple installation.

A ship normally carries two launchers, one on each side, but larger ships might carry four launchers. The launchers are of the fixed type, ie they are not required to be trainable, and their elevation is fixed.

Each launcher consists of four easily exchangeable chaff magazines, two of which may be replaced by three IR containers, requiring only a removable interface plate (the electrical interface is unchanged). Each chaff magazine contains four groups of grenades, each of which is fired by a single ejection cartridge. The nine grenades in each group are distributed to provide an effective chaff-cloud in

space in a very short time, typically less than four seconds.

Each IR container is fired with a single ejection cartridge of the same type as for chaff. The IR decoy consists of sequentially-ignited flares, distributed for optimum deflection of IR or multi-sensor seekers. The IR decoy is effective in both the 3 to 5 and the 8 to 14 micron bands.

A range of associated fire control systems are available from simple manual firing panels, to fully automatic systems, which give information on optimum manoeuvring, launcher selection, etc.

Philax chaff and IR decoy launcher

CHARACTERISTICS
Launcher
Number of magazines: 4
Groups per magazine: 4
Grenades per group: 9
Ejection cartridge: 1/group
Launcher weight: 180 kg
Grenade
Grenade manufacturer: Société E Lacroix, France
Calibre: 40 mm

Grenade weight: 0·35 kg
Payload weight: 0·175 kg
Flight time: 1 s
Chaff manufacturer: Chemring Ltd, UK
System data
Grenade flight time: 1 s
Cloud development time: <4 s
IR decoys
Containers per launcher: 3 or 6

Container dimensions: 131 × 468 × 357 mm
Container weight: 28·5 kg
Payload: 4·5 kg (chemicals and flares)
STATUS
In service.
CONTRACTOR
Philips Elektronikindustrier AB, 17588 Järfälla, Sweden.

5731.253
9CM 100 AND 200 NAVAL ECM SYSTEMS
The 9CM 100 and 200 naval ECM systems are designed for integration with the 9LV suite of naval fire-control systems. The 9CM series systems feature an overall concept with ESM and threat warning sensors, ECM dispensers and jammers fully integrated with the ship's fire-control system. They are based on a combination of the Philips Philax system (**3133.293**), and a threat warning system such as Matilda in the case of the 9CM 100 and Rapids, Phoenix II or Cutlass for the 9CM 200.

Data from the ESM/threat warning module and the fire-control system is fed to the 9CM 200 system computer and processed together with the ship's heading and speed, roll angle, wind direction, radar

cross-section, IR signature, etc. The incoming threat can then be classified and the appropriate action taken. The latter will include not only the use of chaff/IR expendables but also the firing of anti-missile and/or manoeuvring of the ship.

The 9CM 200 system consists of a quadruple chaff and IR decoy system launcher with the launch sequence controlled by a microprocessor to optimise decoy effect. The 9CM 100 system is more compact and features two launchers. In all other respects it is identical to the 9CM 200
STATUS
In production.
CONTRACTOR
Philips Elektronikindustrier AB, 17588 Järfälla, Sweden.

9CM 100 system computer unit with integrated operator panel

UNITED KINGDOM

3383.393
ARI 23246/1 ECM POD (SKYSHADOW)
The ARI 23246/1 (Skyshadow) ECM pod was first shown publicly at the 1976 Farnborough Air Show when it was stated that it was being developed as a modern technology ECM pod for RAF strike aircraft. A multi-million pound contract was awarded to a consortium of British companies led by Marconi Space and Defence Systems (now Marconi Defence Systems), which included Racal-Decca Radar (now Racal Radar Defence Systems), Hawker Siddeley Aviation, Marconi Avionics and Plessey. Marconi Defence Systems is the prime contractor with responsibility for overall design and development and subsequent testing.

Unofficial statements suggest that a high-power TWT amplifier is used with a dual-mode capability for deceptive jamming and CW operation. A voltage-controlled oscillator uses a varactor-tuned Gunn diode covering the full frequency band. The set-on receiver is of Racal design and signal processing uses Marconi Avionics hardware and MSDS software.

Few technical or performance details can be published, but the pod is known to incorporate both active and passive EW systems which include an integral transmitter/receiver, processor and cooling system. The pod has radomes at both ends and is stated to be capable of countering multiple ground and air threats, including surveillance, missile and airborne radar types. Automatic power management can be assumed, and modular construction probably allows for variations in the pod's configuration for differing operational missions. Approximate dimensions are: length 3·35 m and diameter 38 cm.

Skyshadow countermeasures pod for UK strike aircraft

STATUS
The system is in full production for the UK MoD.
CONTRACTOR
Marconi Defence Systems Ltd, The Grove, Warren Lane, Stanmore, Middlesex HA7 4LY, England.

ARI 23246 Skyshadow pod mounted beneath wing of RAF Tornado

3038.353
MARCONI RADAR WARNING RECEIVERS
Marconi Defence Systems Ltd has developed and produced in quantity the two types of radar warning receivers (RWR) fitted to the Harrier, Jaguar, Buccaneer and Phantom strike aircraft of the Royal Air Force.

Two versions of the RWR were needed to meet the

separate requirements of the multi-seat and single-seat aircraft. Whilst both types use the same antenna/RF sub-system, the Jaguars and Harriers are fitted with a lamp type display which shows the quadrant in which the priority threat is located, whilst the Buccaneer and Phantom have the multi-threat CRT displays. Both systems indicate frequency band and type of signal being detected. Frequency

coverage is E- to J-band. Audio alarm is also available.

For the Tornado F2, a multi-threat warning system is being developed to provide threat analysed read-outs in alpha-numeric form. Other extensions are planned. Marconi Defence Systems is prime contractor for the design, development and production of this new technology.

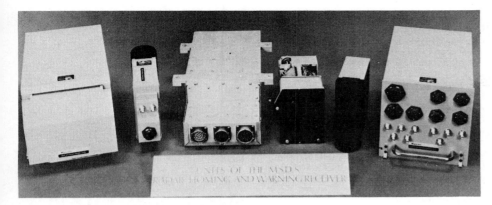

CONTRACTOR
Marconi Defence Systems Ltd, The Grove, Warren Lane, Stanmore, Middlesex HA7 4LY, England.

MSDS radar warning receiver equipment units

5689.353
ZEUS AIRBORNE ECM SYSTEM

Zeus is a compact multi-purpose EW counter-measures system for modern combat aircraft, designed by Marconi Defence Systems and using major components from Northrop Defense Systems Division, USA. It provides a complete defensive system consisting of a radar warning receiver (RWR), and a jammer. These may be fitted as a 'stand-alone' RWR, or as a full ECM system with the RWR also providing the jammer control inputs.

The Zeus RWR is the latest in a series of MSDS passive intercept systems. It is based on the best features of IFM and fast superheterodyne techniques and is able to intercept and measure the characteristics of all radar controlled systems likely to be a threat to the aircraft. These include radar-controlled anti-aircraft guns, surface-to-air missile radars, air-to-air missile radars and airborne intercept radars. Having measured the threat parameters, the receiver passes the signal to the Zeus digital processor which identifies the radar type and causes it to be shown on the display. This digital processor can also be used to control the Zeus jammer and other means of countermeasures (eg chaff, flares and decoys).

The Zeus jamming system is controlled directly by the RWR digital processor and the transmitter chains have alternative configurations to meet specific tasks of each type of aircraft to which it is fitted. Signals from the processor set all the necessary parameters to allow the transmitter chains to jam both pulse and CW radars, while control features ensure that home-on jam weapons are not allowed enough time to acquire the aircraft. A range of different jamming modes is available with each installation tailored to the operational requirements of the individual customer.

Zeus airborne ECM system

Typically, a full Zeus system (RWR and jammer) would weigh approximately 110 kg although the actual weight would depend on the number of transmitter chains and the exact configuration.

STATUS
The system will be fitted to the UK Harrier GR-3s and GR-5s under a £100 million contract received in April 1984, and the two companies are proposing the

equipment for the AV-8B aircraft. Installations have also been designed for the Hawk, F-16, F-18, F-5 series, A-4, Jaguar and Mirage.

CONTRACTORS
Marconi Defence Systems Ltd, The Grove, Warren Lane, Stanmore, Middlesex HA7 4LY, England.

Northrop Corporation, 2301 West 120th St, Hawthorne, California 90250, USA.

5732.053
HERMES ESM SYSTEM

Hermes is a range of ESM surveillance systems which provide the information necessary for planning operations and defence by the interception and analysis of enemy signals. These systems can be part of air defence and coastal defence land-based nets, can be used in the airborne role in many types of aircraft and also have naval applications.

In the airborne role, Hermes can be configured into a range of equipments from a basic radar warning receiver in light strike aircraft and helicopters to a full ESM system for reconnaissance or AEW aircraft. A version can also be fitted to remote piloted vehicles for battlefield surveillance, coupled with a data link to pass vital information to the ground.

In the land-based role, Hermes can be configured to meet a variety of battlefield surveillance roles to provide signal intercept and analysis capability. For naval applications the system would normally be

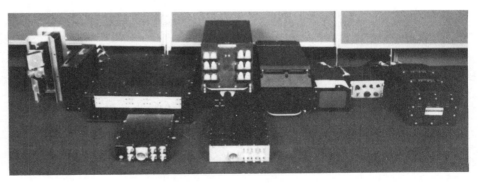

Units of the Hermes ESM system

employed in smaller ships, such as fast patrol boats, to provide interception, analysis and display, and also to activate chaff/flare dispensers if necessary.

CONTRACTOR
Marconi Defence Systems Ltd, The Grove, Warren Lane, Stanmore, Middlesex HA7 4LY, England.

4226.293
BARRICADE NAVAL DECOY EQUIPMENT

Barricade is designed to provide ships with an effective and lightweight means of deploying chaff and infra-red decoys as countermeasures to missile attack. The system gives a layered defence against the various phases and types of anti-ship missile attack, ranging from the long-range confusion mode,

through medium-range distraction and dump modes to the close-in centroid mode.

The complete system consists of port and starboard launchers, safety switches, a control unit, ready-use ammunition lockers and rockets. The launcher consists of six sets of triple barrels, the lower three sets being angled 60° from the next so that a

pair of launchers provide all-round coverage. The upper three sets are pre-set to point to the same bearing, as required. These upper three sets fire short-range Palisade rockets in centroid mode, while the lower barrels fire medium- and long-range Stockade rockets in dump, distraction and confusion modes.

Barricade decoy modes are:
(1) Confusion: Long-range rockets fired to confuse enemy search radar and make target selection difficult
(2) Distraction: Medium-range chaff and/or infra-red rockets fired in a pattern of six around the ship to present alternative targets to missiles during their search phase. This mode affords defence against any number of missiles from different directions
(3) Dump: If a missile is locked on to a ship and its range gate is removed from the ship by the use of a jammer, the gate may be 'dumped' on a suitably placed chaff cloud, allowing the jammer to be re-deployed. Single medium-range rockets are used
(4) Centroid: If a missile is locked on to a ship, a pattern of short-range chaff and/or infra-red rockets is fired quickly to create a large alternative target close to the ship. The ship then manoeuvres away and the missile will home on to the decoy. This is a close-range mode for final defence against single missiles.

The Barricade system is based on a spin-stabilised 57 mm rocket plus infra-red and chaff sources. The rockets are fired by induction ignition and the high-speed spin produces very rapid chaff blooming. Launchers may be used in pairs on fast patrol boats and similar vessels and in larger numbers on bigger ships. Even smaller Stockade and Palisade launcher variants are available for larger ships/auxiliaries and small fast patrol boats/hydrofoils respectively.

A small microprocessor-controlled tactical computer for accurate centroid mode control and manoeuvring is available for siting near the control unit. The complete Barricade system is designed for easy integration with EW/AIO/C² systems.
STATUS
In production with 65 systems sold or in service with seven navies. A Mk II version is now available with microprocessor control and the ability to fire stored decoy sequences.
CONTRACTORS
Wallop Industries Ltd, Arkay House, Weyhill Road, Andover, Hampshire SP10 3NR, England.
Aish and Company Ltd, Fleets House, Fleets Lane, Poole, Dorset BH15 3BU, England.

Barricade Lightweight 18-barrel launcher

4227.193
RAMPART
Rampart is designed to give protection to key military areas such as airfields and missile sites against air attacks and is believed to be the world's first passive defence system for this purpose. It is based on a number of individual firing units which are radio controlled by a compact transmitter from a single central convenient position. Any combination of defensive measures can be activated instantly at any time and up to a range of 4 km.

A complete Rampart system is inexpensive, requires a minimum of personnel and is at immediate readiness for action at all times. It provides protection against manned aircraft, laser and TV guided missiles by the rapid emission of smoke; against heat-seeking missiles by infra-red decoys; and against aircraft and missile radars by chaff decoys. It also offers a unique defence against low-level aircraft attack by the quick release of a mass of 'Skysnare' airborne tethered obstructions which provide a formidable obstruction and which can remain aloft indefinitely. A series of Skysnare balloons is placed around a target area and, because of the kite-like design, will hold station even in the lightest wind. Attacking aircraft will be caused severe weapon aiming and delivery problems and will be forced to climb to an altitude which will expose them to active defence systems.

Firing stations are portable, self-contained, solar-powered units, each capable of firing nine rocket decoys (chaff or infra-red), nine smokes and three 'Skysnare' obstructions. Rapid or slow burning black and white smoke is available to give both immediate area coverage and sustained coverage thereafter. The 'Skysnare' system consists of a balloon, 300 m of strong line, case, ground anchor, a gas cylinder and pyrotechnic inflation and release. It is at continuous readiness and can be fully deployed within two minutes by radio signal.
STATUS
In full production. A £4 million order has been received for the complete system, including Skysnare.
CONTRACTORS
Wallop Industries Ltd, Arkay House, Weyhill Road, Andover, Hampshire SP10 3NR, England.
Aish and Company Ltd, Fleets House, Fleets Lane, Poole, Dorset BH15 3BU, England.

Rampart firing station

5667.393
MASQUERADE AIRBORNE DECOY SYSTEM
Masquerade is a chaff and infra-red decoy defence pod for combat aircraft, and provides self-defence against air-to-air and ground-to-air radar, infra-red guided missiles and anti-aircraft shells. It carries 48 Wallop 'Radashield' chaff decoy cartridges and 42 Wallop 'Infrashield' infra-red decoy cartridges and can dispense any combination at varying time intervals as required. The pod is an adaption of ML Aviation's light stores bomb carrier CBLS 200 already in service with the RAF and other air forces. Masquerade will fit on the stores station of virtually any aircraft and requires little or no aircraft modification.

The pod has a microprocessor-controlled decoy dispensing system which can be initiated manually or by a radar warning receiver. This latter may be mounted in the pod if required. The cartridges are contained in three separate modules, each containing 30 decoys. These are loaded before being inserted into the pod to give an extremely low operational turn-round time.
STATUS
In production. The first export order was obtained in 1982 from a Middle East country.
CONTRACTOR
Wallop Industries Ltd, Arkay House, Weyhill Road, Andover, Hampshire SP10 3NR, England.

Masquerade airborne decoy system

5668.393
CASCADE HELICOPTER DECOY SYSTEM
Cascade is a chaff and infra-red decoy system for helicopters. It fires chaff and/or infra-red decoys to protect the aircraft from surface-to-air and air-to-air missile attacks. The decoys are designed specifically for helicopter protection and burst clear of the aircraft to afford protection without the need to manoeuvre, and are also designed to eliminate the danger of matter being ingested by the engines.

The system consists of a small cockpit unit, a lightweight launcher with a rapid reload facility and an automatic sequencer which can disperse any number or variation of decoys as required. The disposable magazine contains completely encapsulated firing circuits and charges for operation under all environmental conditions. Cascade can be fitted to most types of military helicopter and is also easily integrated with a radar warning receiver to provide automatic or semi-automatic firing.
STATUS
In development.
CONTRACTOR
Wallop Industries Ltd, Arkay House, Weyhill Road, Andover, Hampshire SP10 3NR, England.

4650.393
EVADE AIRBORNE DECOY SYSTEM
Evade is an airborne decoy system which provides a highly effective means of firing chaff and infra-red decoys as false targets against radar-guided and heat-seeking missiles. Although intended primarily for fighter aircraft, the system is suited for any fixed-wing type. It comprises four or more lightweight 'scab-on' dispensers and a cockpit control unit. The system is very easy to install and operate and the dispensers can be fitted on any suitable external surface. Pylon mounting is suitable and does not affect the store carrying capacity of the aircraft. On fighter aircraft better chaff dispersion is achieved by mounting on the fuselage underside as far aft as possible.

The aerodynamically-designed dispenser unit is a two-piece container which comprises a firing unit containing the electronic circuitry, and either a chaff or flare pack (the standard Evade suite being two of each). The firing unit is aircraft mounted and connected to the cockpit control unit. The chaff or flare pack is fixed to the firing unit with quick release bolts for rapid rearming. The chaff pack contains 21 cartridges which fire to the rear of the aircraft where the chaff is dispersed in the surrounding turbulence. Dipole lengths are supplied to individual requirements. The chaff is slip coated to maximise rapid blooming and minimise 'birdsnesting'. The flare pack contains 10 infra-red cartridges which ignite when just clear of the aircraft and burn from 3 to 5 seconds. The cartridges in both packs are ejected by electronically detonated squibs.

A compact lightweight microprocessor in the cockpit gives the pilot complete control of the system. Firing sequences can be preset before flight to give single, burst, salvo or continuous firing modes.

Display lamps indicate the system state. Built-in-test is incorporated and can be interfaced with other on-board systems.
STATUS
In full production
CONTRACTOR
Wallop Industries Ltd, Arkay House, Weyhill Road, Andover, Hampshire SP10 3NR, England.

Evade dispenser unit

4651.293
STOCKADE-SEAFLASH DECOY SYSTEM
The Stockade-Seaflash decoy system is intended to place confusion chaff decoys at distances of up to 20 km from its own forces. This is designed to create ship-like echoes on the enemy's radar screen at a considerable distance from the real force without the

need for rocket or gun-propelled systems. The system consists of a Flight Refuelling 'Seaflash' remotely-controlled boat fitted with two Stockade decoy launching systems. Both Seaflash and Stockade are under positive secure radio control from a single unit on the controlling ship. Confusion chaff can be dispersed as required from 18 barrels disposed

in groups of three at 60 degree bearing intervals.
CONTRACTORS
Wallop Industries Ltd, Arkay House, Weyhill Road, Andover, Hampshire SP10 3NR, England.
Flight Refuelling Ltd, Brook Road, Wimborne, Dorset BH21 2BJ, England.

3145.293
3-IN WINDOW DISPENSING ROCKET SYSTEM (CORVUS)
This is a simple, lightweight, quick reaction system for the self-defence of surface vessels against surface-to-surface and air-to-surface missiles. Window (chaff)- dispensing rockets are fired to form a radar decoy screen around the vessel. The system can be installed in any surface vessel other than patrol boat types and its simplicity of construction makes it particularly suitable for installation in destroyers and frigates down to the smallest size and retrospective fitting offers no problems.

The complete system comprises: two multi-barrelled rocket launchers, launcher control and firing panel, and the 'window' dispensing rockets themselves.

Two modes of operation are available for the system. The modes differ in the azimuth angle at firing and the range at which window is released. The modes of operation are:
(1) Distraction decoy
(2) Centroid decoy.
These are illustrated in the nearby diagrams.

A firing and control panel can be ideally situated in the combat information centre. The maximum loading of 16 'window' rockets provides protection against three missile attacks, before reloading. Any member of the combat information centre crew can control and operate the system.

A cylindrical rotating structure carries eight launching tubes mounted in two sets of three, one

The latest 8-barrel launcher for British Corvus naval radar decoy system

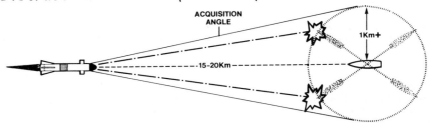

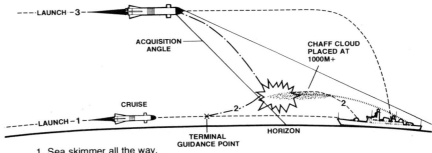

1. Sea skimmer all the way.
2. Sea skimmer final dive.
3. Air launch high dive.

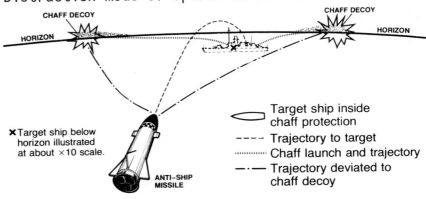

Mode 1, Distraction decoy. This mode provides up to four separate decoy chaff clouds, deployed in a pattern surrounding the ship at a range of about 1 km+, to present alternative targets to hostile missiles during their search phase. This mode of operation is particularly effective against simultaneous attacks from one or several directions. Under such an attack the majority of missiles will lock-on to decoys, leaving the ship to deal with the remaining threats by direct action, active ECM or other modes of operation

above the other, and crossed at 90° in azimuth with two further tubes set above, and aligned midway between the other tubes, all at a fixed elevation of 30°. A deck mounted pedestal supports the rotating structure on its training bearing and also houses a self-contained electrical power conversion unit for the control circuits and the associated electrical equipment. The training drive consists of a gearbox driven by a reversible motor, while braking is achieved by an electro-magnetic brake. A slip-ring positioning unit, located within the pedestal, controls the training of the launcher to pre-selected bearings. The normal limits of the training arc for the launcher are between 60 and 120° but as the lower sets of rocket barrels are angled about the centre line of the rotating structure, the arc covered by the rockets is considerably greater. Within these normal limits, fixed firing bearings for the launcher, at 15° intervals, can be selected by completing the appropriate circuits at the control panel. Training stops and a buffer assembly are incorporated to prevent over-stressing and twisting of the cable bight in the event of an accidental over-run. The launchers can be fitted in any position on No 1 deck or above, providing adequate space is available for slewing and loading, and there is a clear firing arc of approximately 160° in azimuth and 30° elevation.

CHARACTERISTICS

Training
Bearing arc (normal) ie launcher axis: 60 – 120°
Bearing arc (max) ie tube axis: 15 – 165°
Launcher weight: 585 kg
Off-launcher equipment weight: 42 kg
Tube diameter: 195 mm
Tube length: 1·6 m
Weight (empty): 25 kg
No of guides: 4, RH spiral

STATUS
A new broad-band chaff rocket for use with Corvus launchers has been developed by Plessey (**3650.293**) and is in service with the Royal Navy.

CONTRACTOR
Vickers Shipbuilding and Engineering (a British Shipbuilders subsidiary) Ltd, Barrow Engineering Works, Barrow-in-Furness, Cumbria LA14 1AB, England.

Centroid Mode of Operation

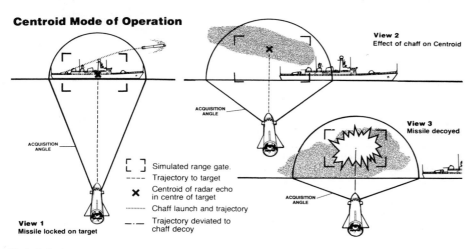

View 2
Effect of chaff on Centroid

View 3
Missile decoyed

[ ] Simulated range gate.
- - - - Trajectory to target
× Centroid of radar echo in centre of target
.... Chaff launch and trajectory
—·— Trajectory deviated to chaff decoy

ACQUISITION ANGLE

View 1
Missile locked on target

Mode 2, Centroid decoy. Regarded as the last form of passive defence available to the ship, this mode requires the deployment of chaff close to the ship so that large chaff radar echoes remain as the ship moves on. The missile is decoyed sufficiently to avoid a direct hit

5737.293
EPO NAVAL ROCKET LAUNCHER
This is a fully trainable naval rocket launcher suitable for launching chaff and infra-red flares. The launcher has two-axis stabilisation and can be target designated from the ship's fire control system. The system is normally mounted in interchangeable pods located midships to port and starboard.

The EPO launcher is of steel frame construction supporting multi-barrel pods at right angles to the elevation trunnion with the barrels pivoting about their centre of gravity. The elevation drive is by a permanent magnet DC servo motor. The launcher base will fit the mounting centres for existing unstabilised launchers.

CONTRACTOR
Evershed Power-Optics Ltd, Bridge Road, Chertsey, Surrey KT16 8LJ, England.

EPO naval rocket launcher

3650.293
CHAFF ROCKET
Plessey Aerospace manufactures chaff dispensing rockets for the UK MoD (Navy). The Royal Navy uses the Corvus 3-inch rocket launching system (**3145.293**) for which a Plessey rocket was developed. One rocket, using the same launcher and without modification to the control system, produces a multi-frequency cloud equivalent to the combined clouds of the three previous service round types it replaces.

Each rocket is in three sections:
(1) an electrically ignited solid fuel motor
(2) the payload head which contains chaff packs and dispensing mechanisms
(3) the nose which carries the fuze and head charge.

At a predetermined time the fuze ignites the head charge which separates the nose, chaff packs and dispensing mechanism from the remainder of the rocket. The dispensing of pairs of chaff packs is then evenly and quickly effected to create an efficiently distributed chaff cloud with a rapid bloom characteristic.

The system will provide Distraction or Seduction decoy clouds simply by fuze time adjustment.

STATUS
In production.

CONTRACTOR
Plessey Aerospace Ltd, Abbey Works, Titchfield, Fareham, Hampshire PO14 4QA, England.

5682.293
SHIELD ANTI-SHIP MISSILE DECOY SYSTEM
Shield is a chaff and infra-red decoy system which is designed for both medium/large warships and fleet support ships. A range of modules enables the system to be built up to suit the differing installation requirements and they can be configured to suit ships with, or without, control to command. Launcher barrel modules can be mounted on simple bases in either parallel or crossed formation to give any combination of barrels from 3 to 12 per launcher. Four parallel barrel launchers are normally specified for large ships to give all round protection. The flexibility offered by the Shield module range is such that a complete system can be containerised for use on merchant ships without the need for external services.

The Shield system is suitable for an inventory of different types of decoy ammunition and studies and development programmes are in progress. The current decoy most appropriate for defence against anti-ship missiles is a chaff rocket equipped with variable fuze for medium- or short-range cloud deployment. Its large multiband payload is particularly suited to both distraction and seduction modes.

Distraction
This provides for a number of separate decoy chaff clouds deployed in a pattern around the ship to present several alternative targets to hostile missiles while they are seeking targets.

Seduction
The Seduction mode is for use against threats that have a short time interval between detection and arrival at the target and which are locked-on at the time of detection. The decoy is deployed at a range and relative bearing such that it and the ship will combine to become a single target within the missile radar cell. As the combined target elongates, due to continuing chaff cloud bloom and ship movement, the missile radar cell remains centred on the mean cloud/ship signature causing sufficient deviation of the missile flight path to miss the ship.

Shield decoy system launcher

Two versions are available: a manually fuzed version for use in simple independent systems or an electronically fuzed type for use with automatic systems interfaced with the ship's own computer. The command module can be situated ideally in the combat information centre and can be interfaced with the ship's EW suite.

DEVELOPMENT
An infra-red rocket for use with the Shield system is in an advanced stage of development. It is designed to give protection against heat seeking missiles in the seduction mode.
STATUS
In production for the Royal Navy and the new

Brazilian corvettes. An order worth $4 million was announced in April 1984 for the Canadian Navy.
CONTRACTOR
Plessey Aerospace Ltd, Abbey Works, Titchfield, Fareham, Hampshire PO14 4QA, England.

3372.193
TYPE 405J MOBILE ECM EQUIPMENT

The ground-to-ground mobile ECM equipment, Type 405J, is a transportable ground jammer which includes an ESM receiving system to detect and analyse the characteristics of a victim radar and an ECM system which provides various types of jamming to combat the victim radar. The equipment is designed to fit into a long-wheelbase Land-Rover which also carries the appropriate receiving and transmitting antennas on a folding mast. The antennas can be adjusted in azimuth and elevation to point towards a chosen victim radar.

The receiver sensitivity, assuming free space propagation conditions and the radiated power output of the jammer, allows the equipment to operate at ranges up to 100 km from a victim radar.

The 405J can be supplied to cover any one of four frequency bands: 1 to 2 GHz, 2 to 4 GHz, 4 to 8 GHz and 8 to 16 GHz. Low jamming-power versions are available to provide a mobile autonomous ECM simulator. The equipment can be located within a few kilometres of an operational radar to give realistic ECM training for radar operators by generating RF signals corresponding to targets and jamming for radiation into the operational radar antenna. High jamming-power versions are available for operational use.

The equipment rack is mounted in the rear of the Land-Rover and there is space for two operators. A portable power supply generator and cables are stored in the rear of the vehicle during transit. Each equipment unit is mounted on slides for easy removal for maintenance. Deployment of the equipment normally takes 10 to 15 minutes and a similar time is taken to dismantle and stow the equipment for transit.

The ESM receiving system, with its processing and display unit, analyses received signals and displays radar parameters in terms of pulse length, PRF, dwell time, radar antenna rotation rate and corrected bearing. The transmitter/receiver control unit receives inputs from the processing unit and generates the selected ECM and target waveforms required by the transmitter. Types of ECM that may be selected include:

(1) CW (spot frequency)
(2) Swept CW (bandwidth controllable)
(3) FM Noise (bandwidth controllable)
(4) Pulse (PRF and pulse length controllable).

The equipment also has the capability to produce false targets in both range and velocity. The Type 405J system is designed on a modular basis and various types of ECM facilities can be included to meet particular customer requirements.

STATUS
In production and supplied to various users.
CONTRACTOR
Plessey Radar, Oakcroft Road, Chessington, Surrey KT9 1QZ, England.

Type 405J ECM equipment deployed on Land-Rover

3373.053
TYPE R505 ECCM RECEIVER

The R505 receiver is designed to be added easily to or included in new design ground radar equipments. It is compatible with all types of pulsed radars having pulse lengths of 0·2 to 1·5 μs and operates at an intermediate frequency of 60 MHz. Converter units can be provided for operation at other intermediate frequencies. The receiver should be used with a preamplifier having an adequate bandwidth (greater than 12 times the optimum for the pulse length of the radar) and good resistance to saturation and paralysis effects.

It is constructed in a single equipment frame which can be rack-mounted or free-standing and provides a compact unit which, including its associated power supply, occupies a single 480 mm wide rack. The front panel of the receiver contains all the required operator control switches and indicators. Processing circuits are contained in either plug-in printed circuit cards or modular box assemblies for ease of

maintenance. The R505 remote control unit is small and compact with height 187 mm, width 120 mm and depth 70 mm. Its weight is 680 g.

Type R505 can be added to radars whether or not they are fitted with MTI, frequency agility or automatic plot extraction. Further features include short radar pulse operation, dual pulse length capability and dual polarity video outputs. The receiver also provides increased sensitivity under practical conditions of clutter, interference and jamming, for short pulse radars together with a high degree of reliability.

The equipment provides ECCM operation and functional circuits can be selected to provide the following modes:

(1) Linear receiver
(2) Optimised logarithmic (narrow band)
(3) Logarithmic (wide band) with pulse length discrimination
(4) Dicke-fix
(5) Quantised Dicke-fix

(6) Combined logical receiver.

Differentiation (FTC) may be selected with linear or optimised logarithmic as further video processes. Anti-logarithmic may also be selected with logarithmic outputs to expand further the video contrast. Pulse length discrimination is selected automatically with logarithmic (wide band). It can also be selected with the combined logical receiver wide band logarithmic, and gated by quantised Dicke-fix.

Comprehensive remote control facilities are built into the R505 receiver and allow separation of up to 1000 metres between the receiver and the operator's remote control unit.
STATUS
In production and supplied to a variety of users around the world for incorporation in radars of both British and foreign manufacture.
CONTRACTOR
Plessey Radar, Oakcroft Road, Chessington, Surrey KT9 1QZ, England.

1712.153
PLESSEY HF MONITORING AND DF SYSTEM

This system is produced in several configurations, appropriate to varying operational requirements, for the reception, monitoring, direction finding, and in some cases, analysis of radio signals in the HF band 1·5 to 30 MHz. In those instances where the full frequency coverage is not required, some items of equipment, such as part of the antenna array, are omitted. The following description relates principally to the complete system.

The main elements of the system are the PVS1120A multiple beam HF receiving antenna system and the PVS860 Series direction finding equipment. Additional equipment is used as required to provide those extra facilities such as analysis and recording to suit specific operational needs.

The PVS1120A antenna array consists of two sets of 24 monopoles equally spaced on 150 and 50 m diameter circles respectively. The outer ring

(PVS890A) covers the band 1·5 to 10 MHz and the inner (PVS880A) the band 8 to 30 MHz, and either may be employed on its own if the other frequency coverage is not required. Sets of electrically equal feeder cables carry antenna signals to beam-forming networks at the centre of the circle, and the net effect of the array is 360° cover in azimuth and 24 simultaneous 15° wide beams. Each of these beams can be fed to a number of monitor receivers.

The addition of the PVS860 Series HF direction finding systems to the multi-beam antenna array provides accurate information on the azimuthal direction of arrival of any given signal. This facility is obtained independently of the 24 beams available from the antenna systems for normal receiver operation. The complete system functions by connecting the 24 outputs from the antenna system to the stator of a goniometer and scanning by a continuously revolving rotor, using capacitative coupling. At any particular instant, outputs from a

group of eight adjacent antennas are coupled to the rotor and are phased and combined to give optimum response in a direction dependent upon the physical position of the eight antennas in the complete system. There are two DF outputs from the rotor, one being the sum of all eight antenna outputs and the other being the difference between two theoretically equal halves of the group. The result is the continuous scanning of the full 360° coverage, yielding at any instant, 'sum' and 'difference' outputs optimised for a direction normal to the sector formed by the coupled group of eight antennas.

The rotor outputs are connected to two receivers and the IF outputs relative to the required RF are displayed on the face of a CRT. This display also shows the amplitude of the sum and difference outputs, back-to-back, over the sector being scanned, the coincidence of maximum 'sum' signal and minimum 'difference' amplitudes indicating the bearing of the signal being examined.

STATUS
Systems of this type have been supplied to a number of unspecified users in Australasia, North America, Scandinavia, the Far East, and in the UK.
CONTRACTOR
Plessey Avionics and Communications, Martin Road, West Leigh, Havant, Hampshire PO9 5DH, England.

PV871 bearing and display console equipped with the new Plessey PR2250 HF receivers in master/slave configuration. These receivers are now in world-wide use

3905.153
PR2250 SURVEILLANCE RECEIVER

The Plessey PR2250 receiver has been designed to meet the most exacting requirements of communication and monitoring system applications with a frequency range of 10 kHz to 30 MHz, synthesised in 10 Hz increments. The tuning system, which consists of a keypad and a tuning knob with rate control, allows tuning to either a specific frequency, or 'searching', and in a manner which is fast, accurate and positive.

Single knob tuning provides a smooth method of covering the entire 0 to 30 MHz range and the fast/slow control provides, in 10 Hz increments, either 20 kHz or 1 kHz per revolution of the control knob. Rapid and precise frequency setting to 10 Hz is obtained and a VFO 'feel' is retained. Frequency read-out is by seven-segment non-flicker LEDs down to 10 Hz with decimal point. AM, CW, SSB and ISB modes are a standard facility and the receiver is equipped with a programmable, synthesised BFO and reconstituted carrier frequency correction.

A 16-channel non-volatile memory provides instant recall of 16 frequencies and their associated modes, bandwidth and AGC characteristics. This recorded information can be updated when required by simple application of front panel controls. Having selected

the channel, the normal tuning can be used to tune around the segment of the band. The memory is also used to retain the front panel setting, if mains interrupt occurs. Instant access to a 'dump' channel is also provided.

The mode selection button 'F' provides a synthesised fixed offset BFO which can be preset to any offset frequency up to 8 kHz in 100 Hz steps. By this means the centre frequency for external demodulations (FSK, facsimile, etc) can be accurate, preset and stability-assured.

The PR2250 is designed for local and/or remote control. An optional internal module containing a microprocessor can be programmed to allow the receiver to interface with any extended remote and computer control available. If only local control is required, this module is replaced by one which provides just the 16-channel memory.

The receiver is entirely of plug-in module design, enabling the signal path modules, synthesiser, power unit or master oscillator to be instantly removed and replaced. The logic-board sub-front-panel and front panel are easily removed and the whole receiver can be dismantled in a few minutes resulting in a very short MTTR with an inherently excellent MTBF. Flexible printed circuit cableforms are used

throughout, aiding maintenance and giving superior reliability.

For diversity operation a PR2250 and PR2251 slave receiver are used together with a PV2272 path selector. Additional equipments include a PF183 FSK converter keyer and a PV2273 channel scanning unit.
STATUS
In production and operational service throughout the world.
CONTRACTOR
Plessey Avionics and Communications, Martin Road, West Leigh, Havant, Hampshire PO9 5DH, England.

Plessey PR2250 surveillance receiver

3370.053
CERES COMMUNICATIONS MONITORING SYSTEM

Developed by Rediffusion Radio Systems Ltd in response to a British Government requirement, CERES (computer enhanced radio emission surveillance) provides for communications monitoring in the frequency range 15 kHz to 30 MHz.

A typical system provides monitoring facilities for a team of six operators, each equipped with a console for remote manual and computer control of four receivers and associated equipment, including antenna selection units and two four-channel special purpose tape recorders. Incorporated in the console is a visual tuning aid for each receiver, and audio selection and control circuits for each receiver and tape recorder. The receivers, antenna switching, receiver memories, minicomputer, tape recorders, time-code generator and a disc store, are located as remote equipment in an optimised environment. Automatic control of the remote equipment by the computer is made by means of a visual display unit, which is also used for the transcription of received information. Hard copy is provided by an associated needle printer sited in the console control room.

The range of operational tasks that can be carried out by the CERES system is wide, and includes

monitoring of a precise frequency, narrow band or wide band search, and other functions. Each operator can control four different tasks simultaneously, transcribing one transmission in real time and, if necessary, recording other transmissions for subsequent replay and transcription.

Serial command data used to control the remote equipment are generated by units in the operator's control console. Dedicated control lines are used, but address recognition is included for system flexibility and to allow for future expansion. Manual control and computer command data use the same format and share the same control lines, with provision for either to take priority. Command data are stored in a dedicated memory for each control unit, the memory being updated when a command is changed. The memory output is a continuous stream of data for onward transmission to the commanded unit and back to the control unit to provide status monitoring.

The control parameters of any of the four dedicated receivers can be changed and monitored at the associated console, and include frequency tuning, with BFO control, and selection of antenna input, AGC time constants and bandwidth. A CRT visual tuning aid enables accurate tuning and precise measurement of frequency to be made. Audio output for headphones is available at the console from any of

the four receivers, and recordings can be made of any or all the receiver outputs for subsequent replay during periods of reduced activity. During recording, the output of a time code generator is also recorded on a separate track to indicate, on replay, the time the recording was made and the amount of recorded tape used.

Using the VDU at the console, the computer can be

Rediffusion CERES communications monitoring system in use

instructed to assign automatically controlled tasks to particular receivers. A typical instruction could be to sweep a receiver frequency between specified points at a specified rate. Facilities to monitor these tasks as they are performed and the capability to interrupt or modify them are provided. The computer can also be instructed to accept transcribed information and store it on the computer disc store. Other functions include editing of transcribed information and printing of data retrieved from the disc store as hard copy for analysis.

The computer employed is a 16-bit minicomputer with 32K of main store. Facilities include high speed input/output, hardware arithmetic, a 1 mega-word disc store, paper tape reader and punch, two line printers, teletype, and appropriate interfaces.

STATUS

Operational.

CONTRACTOR

Rediffusion Radio Systems Limited, Newton Road, Crawley, West Sussex RH10 2PY, England.

3922.153
RA1792 PROGRAMMABLE RECEIVER

The Racal RA1792 is a programmable synthesised communications and surveillance receiver covering the frequency band 100 kHz to 30 MHz in 10 Hz steps. It was designed as a successor to the RA1770 series of HF receivers. There is an American-built version, designated RA 6790, which has considerable commonality with the original UK designed equipment.

The receiver can be controlled directly from its own front panel or remotely using the MA1075 control unit which is visually identical to the RA 1792. All controls operate in exactly the same way as those on the receiver front panel and three methods of connection are available.

(1) a simple extension cable, up to 100 m

(2) Racal serial control system (SCORE)

(3) two voice frequency telephone links (with modems).

Frequency setting over the entire range is available from either a key-pad or a single, variable rate, flywheel tuning knob. Reception of USB, LSB, AM, CW and FM modes is provided as standard, with ISB operation available as an optional extra. FSK reception is possible by the use of an external modem. It is possible to store, for immediate recall, frequency and mode data on up to 100 channels, and up to 10 of these may be scanned automatically.

Two liquid crystal displays on the front panel indicate channel number, frequency, receiver operating conditions and mode, and include indications of audio line or RF signal level.

STATUS

In production and in operational service.

Racal RA1792 HF receiver embodies novel circuit techniques

CONTRACTOR

Racal Communications Ltd, Bracknell, Berkshire RG12 1RG, England.

3919.153
RA1794 TACTICAL EW RECEIVER

The Racal RA1794 tactical receiver was designed as a basic block of the Racal 3000 EW and radio surveillance system (**3918.193**), and related systems, although it is also ideally suited to other communications EW applications.

The receiver incorporates an LSI synthesiser and microprocessor techniques to provide continuous tuning in 10 MHz steps over the entire coverage of 2 to 512 MHz. The synthesiser embodies a new development by Racal, called the Digiphase technique, whereby the synthesiser generates both the phase and frequency of a signal. It is this feature which enables the entire HF/VHF spectrum to be covered with a single phase-locked loop. The RA1794 is normally controlled by a separate operator control unit, although it may be operated as a stand-alone equipment. Traditional receiver front panel controls have largely been replaced by a multi-function key-pad which provides continuous tuning, at various rates, direct frequency entry, selection and setting of up to 100 frequency and mode channels, filter bandwidth, reception mode and other functions including an in-built test program. All display and metering functions are provided by an analogue/digital LED readout on the front panel.

The MA1122 Tactical DF Processing and Display Unit is designed for use with this receiver. Bearing indication is provided by a digital readout to 0·5° resolution and a polar display using LEDs spaced at 10° intervals. A quality factor is computed automatically for each bearing.

STATUS

The RA1794 is in production and operational service.

Racal RA1794 tactical EW receiver

CONTRACTOR

Racal Communications Ltd, Bracknell, Berkshire RG12 1RG, England.

5679.153
RA1795 VHF/UHF RECEIVER

The RA1795 is a programmable synthesised receiver designed primarily for communications intelligence and electronic warfare applications in the frequency range 20 to 1000 MHz, and is suited for use in standard computer-based systems in both fixed and transportable roles. These include the Racal System 3000 Interception and RDF 3200 Series Direction Finding systems. Tuning is in 10 Hz steps across the whole band with reception of AM, LSB, USB, FM, CW and Pulse modes. It is fitted in a standard rack mounting unit or in a bench mounting cabinet.

The receiver uses microprocessor techniques to provide a wide range of operational capabilities combined with a high degree of RF performance. These techniques include automatic scanning of frequencies held in a 100-channel memory, comprehensive display of the receiver operating conditions and provision for external control. A wide selection of filters provides for the interception of all transmissions normally encountered in the VHF/UHF spectrum, including wideband radio relay systems. The 100-channel memory can be loaded with frequencies of interest together with associated receiver control settings ready for immediate access by means of a tuning knob or keypad. Automatic scanning of any of the channels can be carried out, the receiver pausing on each channel for a preset dwell time selected with the keypad.

The receiver can be operated by local, extended or remote control. In local mode, tuning is by means of a multi-purpose tuning knob with fast and slow rates. The fast tune provides an adaptive tuning rate which is varied automatically with the speed of rotation, the slow tune is at a fixed rate in 10 Hz steps. Alternatively, frequency can be entered directly by means of the keypad. The built-in carrier operator relay with adjustable threshold can be set to detect activity in any channel and to activate automatically an external system, eg a tape recorder. All receiver conditions are displayed by either illumination of relevant push-button controls or by an LED display. A compatible signal display unit, type MA 1119C, is available and enables a spectrum of up to 8 MHz to be displayed.

STATUS

In production

CONTRACTOR

Racal Communications Ltd, Bracknell, Berkshire RG12 1RG, England.

RA1795 VHF/UHF receiver

4737.053
RA1796 HF/VHF/UHF RECEIVER

The RA1796 is a rugged compact synthesised receiver intended for communications EW operation covering the frequency range from 2 to 1000 MHz in 10 Hz steps. This gives complete coverage of the HF, VHF and UHF communication bands. It employs microprocessor techniques to provide a wide range of capabilities, including automatic scanning of frequencies held in a 100 channel memory, automatic search across a specified frequency range and provision for external control.

The equipment is designed to operate under exacting environmental conditions and is suitable for deployment in forward combat areas installed in soft-skinned or armoured vehicles, and also in shelters, in ships, submarines, aircraft or fixed ground stations.

The RA1796 incorporates a frequency synthesiser based on a new LSI design of high reliability and performance, with microprocessor control and storage for 100 frequencies and associated control settings. Tuning is in 10 Hz steps across the complete band with reception of AM, LSB, USB, FM, CW and MCW modes.

The receiver can be operated in local, extended or fully remote control. In local mode, tuning is by spin-wheel control in selected step sizes or at selected rates, by direct frequency entry via a keypad or by means of UP/DOWN keys. These keys can be used for continuous scanning or for scanning in selected step sizes at a pre-determined rate. The receiver can also be set to scan automatically across a prescribed frequency band, the frequency limits, step size and scanning rate being selected by means of the keypad. A 100 channel memory can be loaded with frequencies of interest together with associated receiver control settings ready for immediate access by means of the keypad or spin-wheel. Automatic scanning of the selected channels can be carried out, the receiver pausing on each channel for a preset dwell time. The receiver can be set to stop the automatic band scan and channel scan routines when signal activity is detected, and also to activate a recorder or other external system.

A compatible signal display unit, the Type MA1119, is available and enables a spectrum of up to 3 MHz to be displayed centred on the receiver tuned frequency. The MA1122 Tactical DF Processing and Display Unit can also be used with the receiver to provide bearing indication to 0·5° resolution on a digital readout, and a polar display using LEDs spaced at ten degree intervals. A quality factor is computed by the MA1122 for each bearing.

CHARACTERISTICS
Frequency range: 2 to 1000 MHz in 10 Hz steps (2 to 512 MHz optional)
Power consumption: 50 W typical
Dimensions: 205 mm high × 390 mm wide × 400 mm deep
Weight: 21 kg

CONTRACTOR
Racal Communications Ltd, Bracknell, Berkshire RG12 1RG, England.

3920.153
RTA1470 AND RDF3200 SERIES DIRECTION FINDING EQUIPMENT

The Racal RTA1470/RDF3200 series of radio direction finding equipment has been designed principally to meet the needs of EW requirements for emitter location for both tactical and strategic applications. The frequency bands covered include MF/HF/VHF/UHF between 150 kHz and 512 MHz, extending to 1 GHz if required, and fixed, transportable or mobile versions can be supplied.

The system uses electronically commutated four-element antenna arrays to generate a signal which is amplitude modulated with azimuth information. After conversion to digital form, this signal is fed to a microprocessor-based bearing evaluation and display unit (MA1110) which derives the bearing information and presents it directly in numerical form. Seven antenna arrays are available, covering the whole spectrum, two of them being ground-mounted and the others mast-mounted. The four models for the upper segments of the spectrum may be mounted together in pairs on a single mast.

Standard Racal communications/surveillance receivers are employed according to the frequency range(s) of interest, for example:

DF System	Frequency range	Receiver
RTA1472	150 kHz – 30 MHz	RA1792
RTA1471	20 – 512 MHz	RA1794
RTA1474	Suitable channelised receiver	
RDF3205	Suitable channelised receiver	

Bearing evaluation and presentation is performed in all systems by the MA1110 processing and display unit. This has a numeric LED readout which is updated five times per second giving a direct indication of bearing. There is also a polar display which shows the bearing as a radial line, the length of which denotes the signal amplitude. The latter display is provided with an electronic cursor. The same display screen may also be used for an alternative presentation which includes a dual Cartesian display and a histogram presentation. The latter has the horizontal axis representing the bearing angle while the vertical axis shows a continuously accumulating record of bearing data on the selected frequency.

Three or more RTA1470 series DF stations can be linked to form a locating net, which can be manually or semi-automatically controlled. The RTA1470 series of equipments is also fully compatible with the Racal 3000 EW radio surveillance system (**3918.193**) of strategic and tactical intercept and monitoring equipments.

RTA 1470 direction finding equipment in mobile configuration deployed for operation

STATUS
In production and in service in several countries.
CONTRACTOR
Racal Communications Ltd, Bracknell, Berkshire RG12 1RG, England.

3918.193
SYSTEM 3000 EW AND RADIO SURVEILLANCE EQUIPMENT

Racal Communications manufactures a comprehensive range of modular equipment from which a variety of radio surveillance and EW interception and processing systems can be configured to meet widely differing operational requirements. Series 3000 systems have been specified for 'strategic', or fixed-base monitoring applications, and for theatre mobile or semi-mobile roles, but both types are based on a common philosophy centred on what the manufacturer terms the Operator Position. This refers to the combination of control unit provided for the operator and the related interface units and other facilities. Two receivers are normally incorporated in a Series 3000 system at each operator position, although more can be accommodated, and it is

possible to link several operator positions in large fixed systems by data and audio highways.

Any type of receiver can be employed, provided they have a compatible serial data control facility. Generally they will be drawn from the following Racal types, to suit the frequency coverage required:
RA1784: 15 kHz to 30 MHz
RA1792: 100 kHz to 30 MHz
RA1794: 2 to 512 MHz
RA1795: 20 to 1000 MHz
RA1796: 2 to 1000 MHz

There are two types of operator control unit: the MA1113 is a console or rack-mounted item designed for use in fixed or semi-fixed stations: and MA1114 which is a rugged unit with somewhat reduced facilities and intended for use in vehicles or military shelters where space may be limited. One of these units will be employed with the MA1116 audio

switching and operator processor unit to provide for the control and operation of the receivers and to effect the appropriate transfer and exchange of data between other operating positions. These standard modules and sub-systems are based on the use of microprocessor technology and System 3000 embodies the principle of distributed processing.

Racal has defined three levels of complexity for the basic operator positions:
(1) Level 1: This provides for the display of receiver settings, receiver status, antenna in use, intercom calling indicator and procedure prompts for setting the parameters for automatic scanning; selection of any antenna; manual control of the receivers; automatic control of one receiver to search through a list of frequencies (LIST mode) or scan a band of frequencies (SCAN mode) in conjunction with optional automatic signal detection devices; selection of audio outputs for monitoring and recording; control of recorders; intercom with other operators; the exchange of data with other system elements.
(2) Level 2: At this level an interception system processor (ISP) is introduced to serve a number of collocated operator and supervisory positions, together with other operational elements equipped with keyboard devices that can be interfaced to it, such as a DF control position. With VDUs at the operator positions and the addition of a disc store, the ISP provides facilities for: logging and editing of traffic by the operators; routeing (by address) data information between all terminals in the system;

System 3000 operator position type RS3153

RS3152 small station intercept

access to reference data to assist the operators in identifying target networks; management and information displays for the supervisor. The standard software package provides the operators with four different displays: target files, task files, search lists, and log files. The supervisor has access to all the files available to the operators, and two other displays are available to him, a current activity file and the receiver status display. Choice of ISP hardware depends on the number of operator and other positions to be served, but typically a PDP 11/34 serves up to eight fully equipped operator positions, or a Ferranti Argus 700 will serve up to 20 positions.

(3) Level 3: To expand facilities still further, an information processing system (INFOPS) is added, with the main purpose of providing data handling and retrieval capabilities for analysts, voice tape transcribers, reporting staff and managers. It is connected to one or more ISPs so that data can be exchanged between the operator and analyst areas.

Log files compiled by the operators can be displayed at analysis positions (for example), while technical data bases created by the analysts, such as target files, can be made available to the operators. In a strategic station the ISP and the INFOPS are co-located. In an EW system the ISPs at forward intercept (ESM) stations feed information by radio relay to the INFOPS at the EW control centre where it acts as the nerve centre for command and control of the total system.

There are three standard operator positions which, with choice of the appropriate equipment options, suffice for all intercept system applications.
RS3151: This version is designed for use in fixed station installations, with those items of equipment requiring direct operator attention being located in the operator's console and the remainder of the hardware housed in racks in the equipment room.
RS3152: This is designed for installation in more confined accommodation such as small stations,

military field mobile containers or shelters. It includes almost the same facilities as the RS3151 but all the equipment is fitted in twin cabinets provided with desk units and secured to the shelter structure.
RS3153: The third type of operator position is meant for installation in a small shelter or in soft-skinned or armoured vehicles used by forward units employed in EW roles. The same three basic units are included which are common to all operator positions, but in this case the rugged version of the operator control unit (MA1114) is employed. All of the units are frame-mounted so that they can be dispersed in the shelter or vehicle as space allows.
STATUS

In production and in service in several countries.
CONTRACTOR

Racal Communications Ltd, Bracknell, Berkshire RG12 1RG, England.

3917.193
RJS3101 500W RESPONSIVE VHF JAMMER

The RJS3101 responsive VHF jammer has been designed to meet the requirements for an automatic mobile jammer system covering the 20 to 80 MHz band for ECM applications in the forward combat zone. It can automatically detect and jam signal activity on any one of 16 preselected target channels, on a priority basis. Since jamming only takes place when targets are active, it is possible to disrupt several nets simultaneously depending upon the activity of individual target nets. Alternatively, the RJS3101 can be programmed to scan a specified band of frequencies and disrupt any non-friendly transmissions detected above a preset threshold level.

Integral communications are included in the equipment with facilities for a remote ECM control station to call the ECM operator, if necessary, by interrupting the jamming action. The equipment is designed for mounting in either soft-skinned or armoured vehicles and is fully ruggedised.

The system is controlled from an MA1112 control

and display unit which includes a keypad for entering instructions, an internal clock for timing jamming periods and intervals etc, and a comprehensive display for indicating channel information and signal activity. This microprocessor-based unit contains three types of channel store holding data required in the various modes of operation. The jammer channel stores up to 16 target frequencies, each with a priority rating, and a signal level above which jamming is to be initiated; the communications channel stores contain details of up to four frequencies for communications with the control station; and the protected channel stores hold details of up to nine friendly frequencies on which jamming is inhibited when the system is in the 'Band' mode.

Two PRM4090 VHF transceivers are used, for search and jamming, one of them also acting as a communications receiver. In the transmit condition the output of one transceiver is fed into a PA1840 500 W amplifier. The output of the amplifier is then fed via the MA1019 antenna switch unit to a directional antenna which gives a 2 kW ERP signal. An optional whip antenna may be used for receive only.

An MA4280 modem links the jammer system with a printer and keyboard unit, and the MA1017 vehicle interface unit provides for the various interfaces with the other equipments in the system as well as housing the noise generator for modulating the jammer signal.
OPERATION

There are four modes of operation:
(1) Automatic jamming, where both tranceivers initially carry out a search of the 16 target frequencies and four communications channels stored in the memories. Jamming is then automatic on any active channel encountered, on a priority basis. Alternatively, a band of frequencies is searched and any non-friendly signal encountered above a specified threshold level is jammed.
(2) Dedicated single frequency jamming. In this mode the operator can select any individual frequency, including the stored frequencies, for jamming when active.
(3) Passive search. With jamming switched off, the receivers scan the 16 target channels and signal levels are displayed for each active channel. There is also a panoramic display facility in this mode.
(4) Communications. This facility allows the ECM operator to use the equipment for communications with control using either voice (encrypted if secure mode PRM4090 is used) or the MA4270/MA4245 keyboard and MA4333 line printer for data communications.

RJS3100

An alternative to the RJS3101 is provided by the RJS3100 system. This is a 100 W output system which uses whip antennas for both transmit and receive; otherwise operation is the same as for the 500 W system. The RJS3100 is suitable for mounting in small vehicles as a part load and is ideally suited for operations on the move close to the combat zone or for operations in an urban role. It is also useful as a training aid to give personnel experience of radio operating in the face of ECM. This jammer can also be supplied with a directional antenna to produce 400 W ERP.
STATUS

In production and in service in several countries.
CONTRACTOR

Racal Communications Ltd, Bracknell, Berkshire RG12 1RG, England.

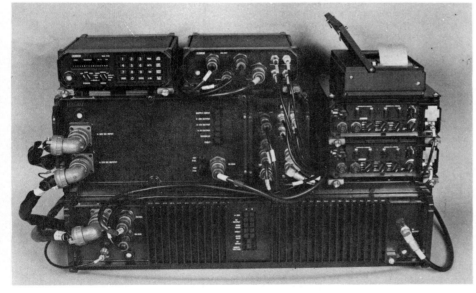

RJS 3101 500 W responsive VHF jammer

4738.193
RJS3105 SERIES COMMUNICATIONS JAMMERS

The RJS3105 series of responsive jammers has been designed to operate in the ground/air communi-cations bands of 110 to 156 MHz and 225 to 400 MHz. They are intended to provide support in the tactical battlefield area by disrupting communications used

for close air support, but can be equally effective as part of air defence systems at fixed installations. Three configurations are available, the RJS3106 which covers the frequency range 110 to 156 MHz, the RJS3107 covering from 2 to 400 MHz and the RJS3105 which is a combination of the first two.

All jammers in the series can be programmed to

search continuously through a preset list of up to 16 frequencies and to jam automatically, within one second, the highest priority target found active at any given time; or they will scan across a selected band of frequencies in 25 KHz steps and attack hostile targets as they find them. In both modes individual threshold levels can be set to avoid false triggering and there is provision for automatic protection of nine programmable bands of friendly frequencies.

An automatic 'look-through' capability ensures that jamming only takes place when a target is active and that jamming is always concentrated on the highest priority target. Other functions provided include single frequency jamming, passive search with panoramic display of signal activity, intrusion into enemy nets, and automatic printing of all jamming carried out.

Both the RJS3106 and the RJS3107 consist of a transceiver section, a power amplifier, an interface unit, a control unit and an optional printer, contained in a single standard bench mounting cabinet. The RJS3105 is supplied in two cabinets for vehicle installation, or a single cabinet for shelter or fixed station installation. The systems are normally supplied with discone antennas where omni-directional coverage is required, or with log periodics for increased radiated power.

CHARACTERISTICS

Frequency: 110 to 156 MHz (RJS3106); 225 to 400 MHz (RJS3107)

Channel spacing: 25 kHz

Jamming modulation: Noise (3 Hz audio bandwidth)

Radiated power (with directional antenna): 3 kW (RJS3106); 1·5 kW (RJS3107). Output level switchable to low power

CONTRACTOR

Racal Communications Ltd, Bracknell, Berkshire RG12 1RG, England.

RJS3105 communications jammer

4736.193

RJS3140 UNATTENDED EXPENDABLE JAMMER

The RJS3140 is a low power barrage jammer intended for remote deployment against communication nets operating between 20 and 90 MHz. It is a small, easily concealed unit for use against important targets which are out of range of stand-off jammers, and is deployed by hand. A number of them can be grouped together to increase the area of coverage as well as making location by DF more difficult. When used at

close range it is claimed to be the simplest available technique for attacking frequency hopping radios.

CHARACTERISTICS

Frequency range: 20 to 90 MHz

Bandwidth: 1 to 31 MHz (set by a programming unit)

Power output: Typically 10W from 14V DC battery

Jamming signal: Pseudo-random continuous noise

Operation time: 2 hrs minimum (−10 to +60° C); 1 hour (−30 to −10° C)

Internal timer delay: 1 minute to 100 hours selectable by programming unit in 1 minute steps

Antenna: Telescope whip adjustable from 1 to 1·8 m

Dimensions: 80 mm high × 133 mm wide × 279 mm deep

Weight: 2·5 kg (including battery)

CONTRACTOR

Racal Communications Ltd, Bracknell, Berkshire RG12 1RG, England.

5680.153

SAT 3311 HF SIGNAL ANALYSIS TERMINAL

The SAT 3311 terminal is a comprehensive aid to search and monitoring operations in the HF spectrum with full provision for technical analysis. It provides the search operator with an ability to detect and examine the structure of unusual or complex signals in addition to the more usual facilities provided by traditional monitor operational terminals. Equally it gives full facilities to the PTT monitor operator for investigating signal usage in conformity with CCIR directives.

The terminal consists of an RA1792 receiver (**3922.153**) covering the frequency range 100 kHz to 30 MHz, an SA3300/2 digital signal processor unit and an SA3300/1 operator console and display unit mounted in a single standard cabinet or console. An instrumentation recorder can be included if off-line processing is required and an ASCII printer can be provided for hard copy production of teleprinter traffic.

The equipment incorporates a CRT which is used

to display up to three traces simultaneously of any intercepted signal, from a selection of time waveforms and instantaneous and averaged spectra. The dual and triple trace displays can also include spectra which are recalled for comparison purposes from a stored library of up to 25 signal patterns relating to known types of signal or to unidentified transmissions still under investigation. In the case of FSK teleprinter transmissions, traffic content is displayed and printed automatically. With these displays the operator can determine target signal parameters including carrier frequency, type of modulation, the nature of the modulating signal and the type of information being transmitted. The spectra or time waveforms are presented together with alpha-numeric notation including calculated signal parameters, message text derived from demodulated FSK signals, data concerning the operational status of the equipment and 'menus' for selecting the various operating functions. The maximum bandwidth displayed is 16 kHz and there is a 'zoom' facility to provide a range of bandwidths

SAT 3311 HF analysis terminal

down to 20 Hz to permit examination of individual transmissions in detail.

STATUS

In production.

CONTRACTOR

Racal Communications Ltd, Bracknell, Berkshire RG12 1RG, England.

5681.153

CCS 3900 COMMAND AND CONTROL SYSTEM

The CCS 3900 is an automatic data processing system for command, control and information handling in communications EW and surveillance operations. It is deployed as a network of nodes,

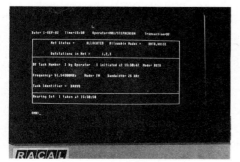

CCS 3900 visual display unit

interconnected over existing communication links, thereby spreading the load between HF, VHF, landline and microwave radio relay and ensuring minimum reorganisation of communications. Major nodes contain data processing equipment and databases, and are normally situated adjacent to field command posts. Visual display terminals are provided to allow staff users to display and change information stored in database and to prepare and receive messages including directives for the control of EW resources such as direction finding and jamming. Minor nodes, some comprising communication terminals with little or no data processing ability, provide access for lower levels of command. Many configurations are available and are tailored to user needs.

Used in a typical communications EW system, the CCS 3900 can provide a range of facilities such as:

(1) database management of information, including enemy identities, organisation, personalities, equipment, movement and other intelligence data

(2) database management of EW targetting information and results, including enemy signal plans, DF results, etc

(3) database management of operational information including deployment and status of own forces

(4) secure and flexible message handling and data transmission network

(5) simple means of entering, retrieving and changing database data

(6) automatic or semi-automatic control of DF and jammer sub-systems.

Data may be displayed on the visual terminals in a wide range of formats tailored to the user requirement. The data may be changed simply by authorised users and the databases at the various CCS 3900 nodes are automatically synchronised. Alerts may be set to warn the user automatically when certain data is changed.

CONTRACTOR

Racal Communications Ltd, Bracknell, Berkshire RG12 1RG, England.

4162.193
TYPE S373 ECM EQUIPMENT

Under government contract, Marconi Radar is working on the Type S373 ECM system which is a mobile multi-band EW system which provides for high power jamming while the S373 vehicle also carries an autonomous surveillance system which will detect, locate and analyse the radiations of enemy emitters. It is anticipated that S373 ECM vehicles will also be employed for such tasks as monitoring the performance of friendly radars under jamming conditions and for training purposes.

The S373 antenna array consists of two horn-fed parabolic dish reflectors which are housed in a double-bubble glass-fibre radome, which is raised to its normal operating elevation by a hydraulic jack system. The two antennas can be turned at rates of up to 200 rpm by means of slab torque motors; these drive the arrays directly, eliminating gear boxes. This arrangement allows scan to be varied from 5 to 180° with positional accuracy of <0·1°, and electrical actuators enable elevation angles of –5 to +8° to be selected remotely. Antenna scan speed and positions in azimuth and elevation are displayed on the operator's console in the cabin. The latter consists of a one-ton container, which houses the electronic equipment and is mounted behind the antenna system on a flat-bed vehicle such as a four-ton Bedford truck.

Each jamming band has an independent high-power TWT (travelling wave tube) transmitter feeding its own antenna, and each transmitter incorporates a digitally controlled variable frequency oscillator (VFO), a driver stage and modulator with an output amplifier stage. A comprehensive range of modulation types and patterns is provided for both transmitters, including AM and wide-band FM, which may be sinusoidal, linear swept or noise, pulse modulation over a wide range of pulse widths and duty cycles, and any reasonable combination of these.

To permit an instantaneous response to known threats or to allow a particular jamming pattern to be memorised for future use, a store is provided to hold preset patterns which can be called up from the operator's keyboard. Other operator controls provide for any pattern to be changed or jammers to be set manually. A source locking counter is also available.

The S373 system includes a scanning superhet receiver with associated frequency counter; a radar signal analyser and displays are provided which allow the equipment to operate in an autonomous role. When employed with an associated ESM system, the built-in receiver enables the ECM operator to identify and acquire any emission to which he is directed and thereafter monitor and report any changes in characteristics that are noticed.

During surveillance the antenna operates in a step scan mode, and in each position the receiver sweeps over a preset frequency band. When a signal is detected above a preset level, the sweep is automatically stopped and the frequency, pulse width and PRF are measured and the data stored. Azimuth bearing of an emitter is obtained by continuous scanning of the antenna with the receiver tuned to the emitter frequency. The bearing is extracted automatically as the antenna scans the emitter and it is then added to the stored data and presented on a VDU display. The output of the receiver during the scan can be displayed on an oscilloscope to permit manual emitter bearing measurement, and the presence of sidelobe reception to be detected. Sidelobe reception in the automatic mode can be eliminated by raising the detection threshold until only main beam signals are accepted.

The S373 cabin also contains radio and teleprinter equipment for communications with EW control centres and HQ units by voice and digital data links. Both VDU and hard copy presentation of messages are provided.

STATUS
No production information or service deployments have been revealed.

CONTRACTOR
Marconi Radar Systems Ltd, Writtle Road, Chelmsford, Essex CM1 3BN, England.

Marconi S373 mobile ECM system on its four-ton truck, showing 'double-bubble' antenna housing in raised position

4163.193
BARBICAN EW SYSTEM

Barbican is a tactical, mobile battlefield automated radar bearing intercept classification and analysis system. The MEL ESM station utilises a configuration very similar to that of the S373 (**4162.193**) in that a one-ton container housing the electronics and operator facilities is carried on a four-ton flat bed truck behind an antenna array which is retracted for mobility. While the Marconi S373 system is intended mainly for active jamming operations, Barbican is a passive ESM system for rapid detection, location and analysis of battlefield threat emitters.

A typical operational deployment of the Barbican system would consist of three or more ESM stations linked by voice and digital data links to one of the control stations which are the responsibility of Ferranti Computer Systems Ltd. An ECM station may also be incorporated. The Ferranti EW tactical control station of Barbican provides facilities for:

(1) system control and co-ordination
(2) communications control
(3) location and classification of emitters
(4) data management
(5) reduction of routine tasks.

The hardware required for these functions includes an FM1600D digital processor, one or more teleprinters, VDUs, communications equipment, and DF facilities for manual or automatic plotting of the bearing data provided by the ESM stations. The FM1600D is the smallest of the powerful 24-bit FM1600 series, which has been adopted by the UK MoD as a standard series of computers for military applications in land, sea and airborne roles. CORAL

Barbican EW system mounted on a 4-ton vehicle

66 real-time high level language is employed for the associated software, and this too is compatible with other FM1600 series systems.

The arrangement of the MEL Barbican ESM vehicle equipment can be seen from the general arrangement drawing. Barbican system facilities include a high gain direction finding antenna; automatic or manual control of DF antenna modes; an automatic signal logger; tunable YIG filters; a digital instantaneous frequency measuring (DIFM) receiver; digital random access display coupled with multiple display options; VDU readout of analysed target parameters; VDU message formatting; compilation and presentation; hard copy printer; microprocessor control of system switching; video and audio outputs for operator signal analysis; and a digital data link. The frequency coverage is from 1 to 18 GHz with a 360° antenna azimuth cover.

Features of the system compatible with FEBA operations include both operating aspects and performance characteristics. The designed performance provides for high system sensitivity; high intercept probability; accurate DF; frequency measurement on a single pulse; and automatic analysis of radar parameters. One man can operate the Barbican ESM unit due to the comprehensive automatic facilities provided and the equipment is

designed for rapid set-up and dismantling for redeployment. The rotating DF antenna, for example, is elevated by a simple scissors mechanism with the turning gear carried on what appears to be a self-levelling platform. Automation ensures rapid processing and interpretation of collected signal data, and system switching is also controlled by the MEL 99 microprocessor, resulting in a compact one-man ESM station providing real-time facilities for the following functions:

(1) signal detection
(2) signal sorting
(3) direction finding
(4) information display
(5) parameter analysis
(6) data formatting
(7) data transmission.

STATUS

The Barbican system is a joint private venture on the parts of MEL and Ferranti Computer Systems Ltd. No contract details have been released.

CONTRACTORS

MEL, Manor Royal, Crawley, Sussex RH10 2PZ, England.

Ferranti Computer Systems Ltd, Western Road, Bracknell, Berkshire RG12 1RA, England.

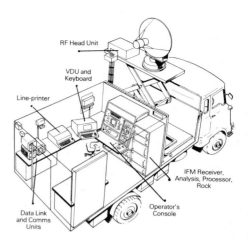

General arrangement drawing of MEL Barbican ESM station vehicle, showing equipment layout

---

3912.193

MIRANDA MICROWAVE INTERCEPT EQUIPMENT

Philips Research Laboratories introduced a mobile microwave interception and analysis equipment in the mid-1970s under the name Miranda. Little has been heard of this development since the original announcement and security has denied any subsequent progress reports. However, an announcement in October 1978 of the award of a multi-million pound contract for the provision of a tactical, 'non-communications' electronic warfare system by the UK MoD may well be related to the Miranda project, and for this reason the known details of the latter are reproduced below.

The Miranda equipment consisted of an antenna array mounted on a mast (possibly telescopic) carried by an enclosed vehicle in which were the other elements of the system. Its function was to receive and process signals from radars and other emitters in the 1·5 to 16·5 GHz band, and it was reported to be able to identify the radar type, provide direction of arrival data, and record information gathered. The microwave receiving system had two wide-open channels, one of them omni-directional for initial detection of all signals, irrespective of direction or frequency, after which the directional channel would be used to provide for signal measurement and analysis.

STATUS

Not accurately known. The work is believed to be on behalf of the British Army and possibly embodies the earlier Miranda work. In October 1979 the UK MoD awarded a major feasibility study contract to a consortium led by Marconi Defence Systems for the investigation of the role of EW in support of the Army in the field. Partners in this activity were Thorn-EMI and Racal. The early warning aspect features in this work, but no details have been released.

CONTRACTOR

MEL, Manor Royal, Crawley, Sussex RH10 2PZ, England.

1707.253

SUSIE ESM RECEIVER SYSTEM

This passive intercept receiver is designed to detect all types of pulsed radar transmission and automatically present the received signals on a tactical display for assessment by the operator. The equipment may be left unattended and will give an alarm when signals of a pre-selected type or on a pre-selected bearing are intercepted.

A situation display gives instantaneously a correlated pulse width/bearing indication together with frequency band simultaneously for all detectable signals. Thus the total radar environment is at all times shown without intervention by the operator. Signals may be selected by a strobe controlled by the operator for automatic readout of signal parameters or for automatic tracking, blanking, or warning. The equipment is all solid state (except CRT and lamps), employs digital techniques, and is of modular construction. It has considerable stretch potential to provide for more sophisticated requirements.

The basic SUSIE equipment provides coverage from 2 to 18 GHz in four bands. Additional coverage in the range 1 to 40 GHz can be provided. The antenna system for SUSIE has no moving parts and can be supplied for mounting either on a platform or integrated into the mast structure.

Two separate versions of this equipment have been identified. These are briefly described in the following paragraphs.

SUSIE 1

Intended for the smaller ship, SUSIE 1 features include:

(1) 100 per cent probability of interception
(2) wide frequency coverage
(3) all received signals appear instantaneously on tactical display with automatic correlation of frequency band, pulse width, and bearing
(4) instantaneous presentation on alpha-numeric display of pulse width, bearing, frequency band, pulse repetition interval (PRI), and signal level of operator selected signal
(5) automatic warner and blanking stores
(6) automatic tracking

(7) built-in test equipment
(8) one man operation.

CHARACTERISTICS

Frequency coverage: E/F band 2 – 4 GHz; G/H band 4 – 8 GHz; I/J1 band 8 – 12 GHz; J2/J8 band 12 – 18 GHz

Sensitivity: Fine mode 30 dBm; coarse mode 40 dBm

Dynamic range: 50 dB

Antenna gain: 5·5 – 7·5 dB

Antenna coverage: 360° static

Bearing accuracy: Fine mode 3½° rms

Pulse width range: 0·1 – 100 μs

PRI range: 10 μs – 10 ms

Display: Frequency band plus pulse width/bearing

Display writing time: 18 μs

Automatic warner stores: 5

Blanking stores: 2

Auto-track stores: 7

Console weight: 270 kg (approx)

SUSIE 1F

SUSIE 1F embodies all the features of SUSIE 1 but with the added capabilities of accurate frequency measurement and improved system sensitivity. Intended for the medium sized ship, SUSIE 1F features include:

(1) 100 per cent probability of interception
(2) wide frequency coverage
(3) the frequency and bearing of all received signals are measured, correlated, and displayed instantaneously on the tactical display
(4) instantaneous presentation on alpha-numeric display of frequency, bearing, pulse width, PRI, and signal level of operator selected signals
(5) automatic warner and blanking facilities
(6) automatic tracking facilities
(7) high system sensitivity
(8) built-in test equipment
(9) computer interface.

CHARACTERISTICS

Frequency coverage: E/F band 2 – 4 GHz; G/H band 4 – 8 GHz; I/J1 band 8·12 GHz; J2/J8 band 12 – 18 GHz

Frequency accuracy: 5 MHz rms

Sensitivity: Frequency receiver 40 – 47 dBm, (optionally) 65 dBm

Operator console of SUSIE

Bearing receiver: Fine mode 30 dBm; coarse mode 40 dBm
Antenna gain: Frequency 1 – 3 dB; bearing 7 – 9 dB
Antenna coverage: 360° static
Dynamic range: 50 dB
Bearing accuracy: Fine mode 3½° rms
Pulse width range: 0·1 – 100 μs
PRI range: 10 μs – 10 ms
Display: Frequency/bearing
Display writing time: Not greater than 18 μs
Automatic warner stores: 5

Typical MEL SUSIE antenna assembly

Automatic blanking stores: 2
Auto-track stores: 7
Audio and video outputs provided
Console weight: 270 kg (approx)

Two basic antenna systems, Types A and B, are available for use with the SUSIE 1 and 1F ESM receivers:
ANTENNA TYPE A1
Type A1 comprises a total of 24 antenna modules contained in single casting. System includes all common processing units and interfaces directly with the SUSIE 1 or SUSIE 1F console.
Antenna weight: 154 kg approx
ANTENNA TYPE A2
Similar to Type A1 but designed to carry fire control/search radar above. Common processing circuits contained in a separate masthead unit ensures direct interface with SUSIE 1 and SUSIE 1F console.
ESM antenna weight: 170 kg approx
Common process unit: 10 kg approx
ANTENNA TYPE B1
Type B1 is designed to accommodate the larger search/tracking radar and permits sharing of the much sought after top mast position. With the ESM

antenna effectively replacing the top section of the mast, the mechanical design permits through access for maintenance of radar and also inner access to ESM electronics. Interfaces with SUSIE 1 and SUSIE 1F via masthead unit.
ESM antenna weight: 315 kg approx
ANTENNA TYPE B2
The Type B2 antenna enables sharing of top mast position between ESM and radar equipment, differing from the Type B1 in that access to ESM antenna modules is from outside. The Type B2 antenna embodies standard Type A antenna modules. Interfaces with SUSIE 1 and SUSIE 1F via masthead unit.
ESM antenna weight: 315 kg approx
Typical dimensions

	Height	Diameter	Weight
2 – 4 GHz	280 mm	500 mm	6 kg
4 – 7·5 GHz	225 mm	350 mm	4·5 kg
7·5 – 12 GHz	200 mm	200 mm	4·5 kg
12 – 18 GHz	100 mm	140 mm	4 kg

STATUS
In production and ordered for several navies.
CONTRACTOR
MEL, Manor Royal, Crawley, Sussex RH10 2PZ, England.

5740.093

MEL ESM RECEIVERS

MEL manufactures a range of IFM receivers for use as frequency measuring devices, with digital readout, for use in ESM and ECM equipment. The receivers operate from 0·7 to 18 GHz and are primarily for application in microwave receiving systems where radar analysis pulse train de-interleaving is required on the basis of the frequency of the received signal.

They measure the frequency on a pulse-by-pulse basis for signal durations of 50 ns to CW. This is achieved without prior knowledge of the time of arrival or frequency of the signal; the receivers monitor the whole of the operating band

simultaneously. There are two families of these receivers, binary and quaternary. Binary receivers provide high measurement integrity where the signal environment is complex and where high data rates are normal. Quaternary receivers are small, lighter and cheaper and are suitable for applications where measurement integrity requirements are less demanding.

Both families can be made to measure and identify CW signals, or to discriminate against them, while looking at pulsed signals. These pulsed signals can be above or below the simultaneous CW signal being received provided that they exceed the threshold of

the receiver.

The receivers are available in various combinations of control functions, data interfaces and frequency range. Sampling facilities cover delayed sample, multi-sample and external sample. A digital coded output is provided with a 10, 11 or 12 bit resolution, the 12 bit versions giving improved frequency resolution and accuracy.

STATUS
In production.
CONTRACTOR
MEL, Manor Royal, Crawley, West Sussex RH10 2PZ, England.

3598.293

SCIMITAR JAMMER

The MEL Scimitar jammer derives its name from 'system for countering interdiction missiles and target acquisition radars', and is designed for use with most types of naval on-board ESM system, although specifically intended as a complementary system to the range of major naval ESM equipments produced by MEL, including RAPIDS and CANEWS.

Full jamming capability is provided over the

frequency range 8 to 16 GHz to give protection both against all types of radar homing missiles and full area defence capability against T.I. radars. Power output is rated at 1·5 kW pulse and 150 W CW. Jamming modes include: CW, programmed band and wide band noise, range-gate pull-off, scan rate and swept scan rate modulation, inverse scan gain and false target generation.

CHARACTERISTICS
Frequency range: 8 – 16 GHz

Output: 1·5 kW pulse; 150 W CW
Frequency channel sensitivity: –60 dBm
Antenna gain: 23 dB
Beamwidth: 7° azimuth; 7° elevation
STATUS
In series production for several navies.
CONTRACTOR
MEL, Manor Royal, Crawley, Sussex RH10 2PZ, England.

3539.253

MATILDA RADAR WARNING RECEIVER SYSTEM

Matilda has been designed by MEL to meet the requirement for an effective, low-cost radar threat warning equipment for smaller ships. It operates on frequencies from 7·5 to 18 GHz, and is intended to act primarily as a trigger for the MEL Protean chaff launching system (**3193.293**). Matilda can also be successfully integrated with most types of short-range chaff systems to provide automatic defensive measures against missile attack. Matilda can detect and recognise the threat, indicate the bearing in which it lies and, if required, can activate the chaff launcher. Compact modular design permits location in the most convenient positions on board. The system comprises three basic elements: a small, lightweight antenna covering 360 degrees in azimuth, a processing unit and a small display. It can be fitted to a vessel, such as a merchant ship, in approximately two hours.

The antenna unit, which is designed to clamp round a mast, consists of four antenna horns with their associated microwave components, circularly polarised for the detection of vertically, horizontally and circularly polarised signals. It is supplied in two matching halves, each comprising a tube of approximately 115 mm diameter; simple brackets are provided to clamp to either a pole mast or a flat faced mast structure. A multi-pair screened cable is routed down the mast to feed the processing unit. Its weight is approximately 7 kg.

The processing unit, which contains the printed circuit cards for signal processing, parameter measurement and the warning unit counter memory, is approximately 320 × 250 × 195 mm in size and weighs 9 kg. The unit is fitted with integral power supplies and may be located in any convenient position. It is able to achieve a processing time of less than 10 μsec and a total warning time of under 1 second.

The warning unit display consists of a small indicator panel designed for location at any convenient position in the operations room, remote from the processing unit if so desired. On detection of a threat, the unit activates an audio warning with the option of a programmable voice module and provides an indication of the threat and bearing sector channel. It may be directly interfaced with the Protean chaff launcher fire control panel. The unit's dimensions are 155 × 155 × 55 mm and it has a weight of 0·45 kg.

CHARACTERISTICS
Frequency range: 7·5 – 18 GHz
Frequency resolution: 1·5 GHz
Pulse width range: 100 ns – 6·4 μs
Pulse width resolution: 200 ns
Bearing coverage: 360°
Bearing resolution: 45°
Sensitivity (referred to isotropic): –30 dBm
Dynamic range: 40 dB

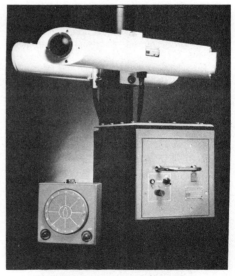

Matilda radar warning receiver system

Antenna gain 7·5 – 18 GHz: 6 – 8 dB
Voice module: Programmable to any warning required in any language

Dimensions

	Weight kg	Width mm	Height mm	Depth mm
Antenna	7	680	114	114
Processor	9	193	257	318
Display unit	0·45	155	155	55

STATUS
In production.
CONTRACTOR
MEL, Manor Royal, Crawley, Sussex RH10 2PZ, England.

5733.153
MATLOCK RADAR WARNING SYSTEM

Matlock is a radar warning receiver system based on the shipborne Matilda system (**3539.253**) and is intended to provide land-based sites with the same degree of early warning as given to ships by Matilda. The principal function of the equipment is to provide indication and warning of low-flying aircraft, using on-board radars such as terrain following or ground mapping systems to fly under defensive radar cover. Should jamming occur, Matlock will provide a clear indication that the main radars are being jammed, and will provide sector bearing on the direction of threat. These functions are carried out within one second of intercepting the threat signal.

The system consists of an antenna assembly, a processor unit and a display unit. The complete equipment has been made as small and light as possible to be easily transportable and, other than the power supply, could be back-packed. It is automatic in operation.

The antenna assembly consists of two four-inch (10 cm) diameter aluminium tubes, each about two feet (61 cm) long and each containing two receiver channels. The antenna receives all the RF pulses over 360°, each receiving channel having approximately 120° of coverage. The assembly can be mounted on a mast or on a vehicle for mobile use. The processor unit houses the video and digital data processing equipment plus the associated power supplies. It incorporates the latest technology to achieve a processing time of less than ten microseconds and a total warning time of less than one second. It also incorporates a voice module which can be programmed to give the alarm in any language. In addition to the aural warning, the display unit provides information on a simple eight-sector arrangement of lamp indicators. If required the display and processor unit can be combined into one unit. Weight of the complete system is approximately 16 kg. Technical characterisitics of the Matlock system are identical to those of Matilda.
STATUS
In development and pre-production.
CONTRACTOR
MEL, Manor Royal, Crawley, Sussex RH10 2PZ, England.

5734.353
KATIE AIRBORNE RADAR WARNING SYSTEM

KATIE is the acronymic name (killer, alert, threat identification and evasion) of a new airborne radar warning system for helicopters and light fixed-wing aircraft. It has been developed jointly by MEL of the UK and Dalmo Victor, USA. The collaborative agreement between the two companies is for Dalmo Victor to further develop the processor and display of its existing Mk III system and for MEL to develop a new receiver and other elements.

The KATIE system provides automatic threat warning and identification, automatic triggering of chaff and IR decoys, and a clear unambiguous display of threats on a 'bright scope' in the cockpit, plus an aural warning to the pilot by a synthetic voice.

Operation of the system covers C- to J-band inclusive and the modular construction of the processor allows extended operation above or below these bands if required. The display unit provides indication of the threat in alpha-numeric symbology, giving bearing and distance and indicating priority of threat in terms of danger. Outputs are provided to chaff dispensers and/or IR decoys.

The complete system consists of a C/D-band blade antenna, an H/M- or E/J-band antenna, two H/M or E/J dual channel receivers, a digital signal processor, a pilot's display and a system control panel. Weight of the entire system is 13⅛ lbs (5·9 kg) and cubic capacity is 355 in³ (5818 cm³).
STATUS
In development. Flight trials were due to commence in 1984. KATIE is presumably the successor to the now defunct experimental airborne Matilda system reported in the 1982/83 edition of *Jane's Weapon Systems*.
CONTRACTOR
MEL, Manor Royal, Crawley, West Sussex RH10 2PZ, England.

Units of the KATIE airborne RWR

3193.293
PROTEAN CHAFF LAUNCHER

The Protean chaff grenade launcher system is designed for naval use as a countermeasure against active radar homing anti-ship missiles. Two or four Protean launchers may be fitted to give forward or fore and aft protection on the port and starboard sides of the ship.

Each launcher is equipped with four reloadable magazines, each containing 36 chaff grenades to give a total ready-use load per launcher of 144 grenades. The launcher is deck mounted and fixed in elevation and azimuth. Firing is in groups of nine grenades and up to four groups can be fired simultaneously. Provision can be made to replace one or more of the chaff grenade magazines by infra-red decoy grenade magazines.

Threat detection and direction can be derived from radar or other sensors, or from an associated ESM warning system.

The Protean launcher appears to be identical to that of the Swedish Philax system (**3133.293**) produced by another member company of the Philips group.
OPERATION
Chaff is one of the primary electronic counter-measures available for use against missiles using active radar seekers for terminal homing, particularly those of the sea-skimming type. With or without the use of active ECM, the deployment of chaff greatly improves the probability of successfully countering the threat, provided that the chaff launching system is capable of reacting quickly, since the flight time from detection to impact of an in-flight missile is normally very short.

For maximum effectiveness, the chaff and own ship's echo must appear simultaneously in the seeker's range resolution cell. Ideally, the chaff cloud should appear at a closer range than the ship and have a larger radar target echoing area. Separation of ship and chaff cloud causes the seeker to lock on to and track the chaff cloud.

The design of the ejection system enables any number of barrels (1 to 9) per group to be loaded without deterioration in performance, thus providing a useful economy feature for training exercises.

Each launcher is provided with thermostatically controlled heaters in order to avoid icing in the pyrotechnic components. Each also has an isolating switch.

The firing panel provides two basic facilities:
(1) selection of groups of grenades (with clear visual indication of selection) including either IR or chaff selection. Indication is also given of salvoes available of each type in each launcher
(2) firing of groups of grenades.
Firing is manually controlled or automatically initiated by remote sensors, eg ESM or radar.
CHARACTERISTICS
Launcher
Type: MEL AA 1067
Magazines: 4
Groups per magazine: 4
Barrels per group: 9
Pressure source: 1 cartridge per group
Firing interval: 0·1 s between groups
Weight (excl grenades): 180 kg
Dimensions: Width 835 mm; length 750 mm; max height from deck 550 mm
Grenade
Calibre: 40 mm
Weight (total): 0·35 kg
Chaff type: Chemring Ltd
Frequency coverage: Manufactured to order
Weight: 0·175 kg
Flight time: 1 s
Cloud development time: <5 s
Cloud height dispersion: 40 – 60 m
STATUS
In production and ordered by several navies.
CONTRACTOR
MEL, Manor Royal, Crawley, Sussex RH10 2PZ, England.

Protean chaff grenade launcher

4652.493

MANTA SUBMARINE ESM SYSTEM

Manta is a submarine-borne, passive, long-range ESM system to analyse, classify and identify enemy radars for defence against threats from surface vessels and aircraft. The system is designed to operate in dense multi-radar environments and can be tailored to any type of submarine.

Manta uses a central management computer controlling 'intelligent peripheral' sub-systems each of which incorporates an advanced microprocessor carrying out local processing. This distributed computer concept is made possible by continuing development of an MEL designed modular system and avoids the possibility of the central processing unit becoming the limiting factor in design flexibility. The system is capable of independent operation or integration with the submarine's data handling system, and can be easily updated with replacement hardware modules and revised software programs. Operator override allows for unassigned emitter identification and display of detailed information on threats and system status.

The simplest Manta system uses a lightweight primary antenna attached to the search periscope to provide detection of enemy radars. A more comprehensive second antenna provides accurate bearing data. A compact unit incorporates the receiver, analysis and processor modules, power supply interface and a real-time display. The system provides 360 degree coverage and 100 per cent intercept probability with automatic threat warning and identification. In addition to its fully automatic mode, Manta can be operated manually using a light pen or keyboard and rollerball. Information obtained can be recorded and printed out for post-mission analysis.

STATUS
In development.
CONTRACTOR
MEL, Manor Royal, Crawley, West Sussex RH10 2PZ, England.

1743.263

SARIE-SELECTIVE AUTOMATIC RADAR IDENTIFICATION EQUIPMENT

Speed and capacity are all-important in the modern identification system, because in the present environment the rate of radar intercepts can be high and the time that can be permitted to elapse between intercept and threat evaluation may be only a matter of seconds. Dependence upon operator reference to known radar parameters is thus unacceptably time-consuming and automatic identification is essential. It is to meet this type of operational requirement that the SARIE system has been produced. This system produces a solution to the problem by providing the results of automatic comparison of intercepted signal characteristics with a flexible dictionary of radar parameters in approximately 350 msecs. The equipment is also a useful tool in extending the existing library of data by analysing and indicating previously unrecorded transmissions, which can be stored by the operator using a built-in scratch pad memory. The new data is then treated as a high priority extension of the library.

The equipment consists of a display unit, control unit, and a data processing unit. The latter houses the dictionary, logic circuitry, magnetic tape reader, and power supply. It can be remotely sited, as access is needed only for maintenance or to modify the dictionary contents. Dimensions are 483 × 355 × 564 mm and the weight 43 kg. The display and control unit carries all the essential controls for operation of the system and the electronic display panel. Separate location of the control and display sections, to suit CIC or EW room requirements, can be accommodated if desired.

SARIE can be used with any EW receiver, accepting the video signal derived from the intercepted transmission. It automatically measures the PRF, pulse width and scan period with high accuracy, and detects the presence of PRF jitter. The equipment also accepts data on frequency, frequency agility modulation type, and scan type for use in identification. This additional data, where available from the EW receiver, can be accepted automatically, or may be entered manually by the operator from the control panel. The operator is able to select intercepts for identification. The library is capable of storing parameter information on 1000 radar types; these will be selected by the user to suit the anticipated operational requirements, and are loaded by means of a magnetic tape cassette.

The display presents data in alpha-numeric form, and typical information displayed includes the parameters of the intercepted signal, the results of the

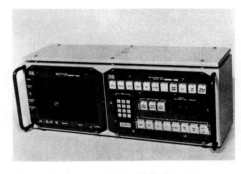

SARIE control unit and display unit

automatic comparison with the stored data to give possible identification(s) of the signal, and the associated platform or hostility index. Each comparative identification is given an automatic confidence level figure.

STATUS
In production for the Royal Navy and NATO.
CONTRACTOR
Thorn-EMI Electronics Ltd, Radar Division, Hayes, Middlesex, England.

4653.293

GUARDIAN NAVAL EW SYSTEM

Guardian is an advanced shipborne active and passive EW system in development for the Royal Navy. The major provisions meet a wide range of operational requirements against threats, particularly those of radar-guided missiles. The system is able to counter and confuse surveillance and missile homing radars by the use of jamming techniques for both area and point defence. Azimuth coverage is 360 degrees with an elevation cover of 50 degrees and a detection range of up to 500 km.

The Guardian system has two antenna mounts to ensure uninterrupted all-round view. The mounts can be installed either port and starboard, or at forward and aft positions. Each antenna mount carries a direction-finding receiving antenna together with transmit antennas, using mechanical steering to give full azimuth and elevation coverage.

Received signals are passed from the antenna to a wide-band receiver. They are then analysed to indicate those which may represent a threat and the selected signals are processed to allow generation of the jamming signal.

High power transmitter sub-systems, matched to the antenna, provide jamming capability against several types of target simultaneously. A comprehensive ECM library stores the appropriate countermeasures to a range of potential threats and on receipt of a warning from the ESM system, the ECM processor selects the appropriate jamming mode to give fast response.

System hardware is controlled at high speed by distributed microprocessors, and overall control is carried out by a micro-computer central processor which also controls the console and interfaces with the ship's systems.

The main equipment cabinets, situated below decks, contain the receivers, signal processing and generation, and fast control processing. They are connected to the RF power amplifiers which are situated close to the antenna. The cabinets are designed in modular form to give ease of installation and maintenance in smaller ships. A plasma panel display is provided.

STATUS
In development under a £28 million contract from the UK MoD.
CONTRACTOR
Thorn-EMI Electronics Ltd, Dawley Road, Hayes, Middlesex UB3 1HN, England.

5738.053

THORN-EMI EW SYSTEMS

In addition to the SARIE and Guardian systems already described, Thorn-EMI are known to be designing and manufacturing a number of EW systems of which very few details have been released.

Airborne Elint pod mounted on wing of trials aircraft

ESM Systems

A family of advanced ESM systems for naval, airborne and land use ranges from threat warners to EW suites with full ESM capability.

Outfit UAA(1) ESM system

Thorn-EMI supplies the complete data processing and antenna systems for this advanced ESM system.

Outfit YAF pulse analyser

This is in service with Royal Navy and other users.

Airborne Elint Pod

This is a 3·5 metre long pod designed to provide tactical information on the location and identification of ground and maritime radars. The company is also developing the associated ground processing, analysis and display equipment.

CALFAC

A contract worth some £8 million was awarded by the UK MoD in mid-1983 for the supply of a number of installations to calibrate and monitor the performance of the EW systems of naval vessels and helicopters. Calibration is performed by interrogating the ship's EW systems with suitable signals generated in the CALFAC.

To calibrate ESM receivers, radar type reference signals are transmitted to the vessel at accurately defined frequencies, pulse widths and PRFs. The overall accuracy of the ship's DF system is checked by comparison with an independent DF reference system based on acoustic, hyperbolic radio or transponder principles. The performance of ECM equipment is assessed by analysing the jamming signals generated by the vessel in response to the interrogating signals. Appropriate signal parameters are measured to check that they come within specified limits. This facility is extended by the provision of check radars at additional sites.

CALFAC will be all UK-based initially but it will be possible to containerise the installations for rapid deployment overseas.

CONTRACTOR
Thorn-EMI Ltd, 135 Blyth Road, Hayes, Middlesex UB3 1BP, England.

4410.393
KESTREL AIRBORNE ESM

The Kestrel airborne ESM system is intended to provide electronic intelligence (ELINT) during all phases from peace to active wartime operations. The system enables staff to gather information on possible hostile threats, their deployment and movements, at long range without the hazards associated with other methods or reconnaissance.

Kestrel receives and processes radar emissions over the frequency range 600 MHz to 18 GHz. A six port amplitude comparison bearing measurement system is used providing instantaneous digital bearing over 360 degrees in azimuth. At the same time a frequency measurement receiver with omni-directional azimuth coverage provides instantaneous digital frequency. The pulse-by-pulse digitised information is then passed to the preprocessor which de-interleaves the overlapping pulse trains from the different radars, deriving their pulse repetition and frequency agility characteristics. The data continues into the main processor which extracts long term information. The most likely identification of the radars is made by comparison of the measured and derived parameters with those stored in the library of known emitters.

Full information about the radar signal environment is presented to the operator on an ordered tabular or tactical display. Alternatively the information can be displayed on remote displays via a standard data highway to allow the use of common avionic displays.
STATUS
Development.
CONTRACTOR
Racal Radar Defence Systems Ltd, Davis Road, Chessington, Surrey KT9 1TB, England.

4411.093
RACAL EW PROGRAMMES

In addition to the various EW systems and equipment described in separate entries in this section, Racal is known to be engaged in a number of other developments in this area. These are mainly the subject of security constraints but the following summaries of certain of these projects can be revealed.
UAF-1
A new ESM system for the Royal Navy is in early development under a UK MoD contract. The system, known as UAF-1, will ultimately succeed the UAA-1 Abbey Hill equipment in Royal Navy ships. No technical details are available.
Auditor
Little has been released beyond the description stating that this ESM equipment is for use in ground-based roles with light surface-to-air missile systems. The programme was under development in 1981.
Full-back
This is a radar warning receiver designed to meet the combat and training requirements of light tactical fighter and advanced training aircraft. It provides a clear, unambiguous quadrantal bearing on threat radars with simultaneous identification of three pre-programmed threats and an audio cue of threats to crew members. It also provides a facility for automatic or manual selection of chaff or flare dispensers. It is a version of the Prophet system (**5673.353**)
Peregrine
This is a pod-mounted warning receiver combined with a chaff and flare dispenser. It is designed for easy installation on high performance aircraft of all kinds.

Pisces
A semi-automatic ESM system for submarines. No other information is available.
ESM/ELINT Systems
Racal is involved in the development of a number of ESM/ELINT systems. These include a ground-based equipment in development for a central European country, the UAF-1 referred to earlier, a version of Cutlass for the Royal Navy's Type 23 frigates (see **3553.293**), and a submarine system for the Royal Navy Type 2400.
CONTRACTOR
Racal Radar Defence Systems Ltd, Davis Road, Chessington, Surrey KT9 1TB, England.

1942.293
RCM SERIES ECM EQUIPMENT

The Racal RCM series of countermeasures equipment covers a range of radar jammers, either ship or land based, and operating in I or J bands to provide both responsive noise and deception jamming. The series is designed to jam early warning and target acquisition radars at long range and to jam and unlock missile guidance radars on launch platforms and missiles.

RCM requires only bearing information to counter a threat but, in addition, the ESM system normally provides warning that action should be taken against a particular radar plus an identification and allocation of priority. Single or dual antenna systems are available to provide 360° cover for small and large platforms. RCM units have their own receivers to provide RF for re-transmission after modulation.

In the responsive noise mode, a frequency measuring unit is used to fast tune a local oscillator to the frequency of the incoming pulse. For deception jamming the same unit can also be used but a frequency memory loop is offered as an option to provide a jamming capability against frequency agile radars. The incoming pulse frequencies are remembered and re-transmitted after modulation to provide a 'range gate pull-off' deception.

RCM-2 is as described above. Types of modulation available include Conscan and 'range gate pull off'.

RCM-3B jammers are improved versions of RCM-2 with a processor and an instantaneous frequency unit giving very efficient processor controlled power management and modulation sequences.

RCM-4B jammers have additional jamming modes such as noise cover pulse and combination jamming and a much higher effective radiated power.
STATUS
In production and in service with various defence forces worldwide.
CONTRACTOR
Racal Radar Defence Systems Ltd, Davis Road, Chessington, Surrey KT9 1TB, England.

1341.253
RDL SERIES ESM EQUIPMENT

The purpose of this equipment is to detect radar transmissions and so provide warning of the approach of surface ships, submarines, or other weapon platforms employing radar controlled weapon systems.

The main RDL systems are: RDL-1, a basic tactical small ship ESM system covering the 2 to 11·25 GHz range, and including an APA-1C pulse analyser; RDL-2 which also provides the frequency of a particular threat; RDL-257 extends the frequency coverage to 1 to 18 GHz; and RDL-268 provides for actual frequency measurement over this extended range. All RDL systems can be enhanced by addition of the SRU-1 signal recognition unit which can store the parameters of up to 500 emitters to permit threat identification. Versions of this equipment are now available for surface ships, submarines, aircraft, or vehicle use.
Surface Ships
A typical system for use on a fast patrol boat is the RDL-1BC, which provides instantaneous bearing, automatic pulse analysis and alarm, together with measurement of frequency band. Frequency coverage is from E to I band. The equipment comprises an antenna, a bearing display, a control unit, a power unit, and a pre-pulse unit, all of which, apart from the display tubes, are solid state. The antenna is light and compact, and has been designed in two halves to wrap around a mast or other mounting and thus avoid the coveted mast head position.

The automatic pulse analyser APA-1C is a self-contained unit which may be used with any suitable EW receiving equipment. Used with the RDL-1BC the unit provides an automatic digital readout of the pulse parameters of all signals or those selected from the switched lower antenna array. The unit is completely automatic and requires minimal operator skill or attention. For Elint purposes a line printer can be used to give a fast permanent record of the measured parameters of the intercepted radar transmissions.

There are also facilities available for the pulse parameters of up to five sets of independent radar transmissions to be set into the unit by plugging in printed circuit cards. When a signal is received which falls within these parameters, the operator is warned by the illumination of a solid state lamp or other remote triggered alarm, that a hostile transmission is present. The unit is completely solid-state and employs LED numerical indicators.

Add-on units are available which convert the RDL-1BC equipment to meet the more exacting requirements of larger ships. The RDL-2ABC equipment has all the facilities of the RDL-1BC and in addition provides frequency measurement, visual pulse analysis, and RF amplification in the analysis channel. The latter increases the range and permits better use of analysis facilities. The equipment consists of the units described previously and in addition contains an RF amplifier unit, a frequency and pulse analyser, and additional power supply units.

The antenna is identical to the RDL-1BC unit but contains additional components to upgrade the performance. The initial simple system can therefore be readily converted to the more comprehensive system.

In the RDL system, frequency is displayed panoramically with signals appearing as vertical deflections on the horizontal frequency scale. The operator must first select the azimuth sector containing the required signal and the band he requires to sweep. Then he may select one of two modes, auto-stop or auto-pause. In the auto-stop mode, the receiver stops sweeping automatically on signal reception and the radio frequency is indicated digitally.

Other facilities permit further expansion of the

RDL Console

frequency bands, fine tuning of the received signal to obtain better frequency accuracy, and the suppression, if required, of up to three specific frequencies. This enables the operator to prevent the receiver from stopping automatically on the friendly signals or those already analysed.

The RDL-2ABC system contains, in addition, a visual pulse analyser with a dual trace display, This enables two ranges of either pulse width or pulse repetition frequency to be measured visually against an illuminated graticule. This display also enables pulse peculiarities to be identified, including jittered PRF.

Elements of the RDL Series, RDL-5 and RDL-6, provide for the addition of a D-band capability. All facilities available for the RDL-2 series are either usable or available as additions for signals in this frequency band. Similarly RDL-7 and RDL-8 equipment extend the system capability up to band J8.

The system RDL-2ABC 6AC 8AC covers the full 1 to 18 GHz band with frequency measurement and automatic pulse analysis over the whole range. This equipment, with the addition of standard peripheral units such as computer injection panels, printers, and recorders, represents a system comprehensive enough to fulfil the most stringent requirements, but is nevertheless only a few steps away from the simplest tactical system in the series.

Submarines

The system RDL-4BC is a compact, instantaneous bearing measurement and pulse analysis equipment covering the frequency range 2·5 to 20 GHz. It is in full production in a submarine version, RDL-4BCS, where it uses the standard RDL Series units inboard. The bearing display uses coded vectors automatically to identify the frequency band of intercepted signals.

RDL-1BCS is a submarine version of the RDL-1BC and is identical operationally. It uses a novel antenna in which each of 16 antenna elements are individually encapsulated rather than using an overall submersible radome. Other submarine systems are produced ranging from a simple warner, RWR-1, for very light submarines to complex systems for NATO.

STATUS

Production. RDL Series in service or on order for 18 navies.

CONTRACTOR

Racal Radar Defence Systems Ltd, Davis Road, Chessington, Surrey KT9 1TB, England.

3553.293

CUTLASS ESM/ECM EQUIPMENT

The Racal Cutlass series of equipment consists of a range of advanced computer-controlled ESM and ECM systems, primarily intended for use aboard ships, but capable of deployment on other land-, sea- or air-based platforms. Designed for operation in very dense signal environments the equipment receives signals in the 1 to 18 GHz frequency range, measures their parameters, compares these with those in a pre-programmed radar library and displays the information within 1-2 seconds. The EW operator is presented with a tabular display for threat identity and threat evaluation and a tactical display giving a pictorial representation of the RF environment. Selected digital outputs can be sent to other local systems, and hard copy printout of the intercepted radar is also available. The tabular display can indicate 300 intercepts, in the order of priority. The Cutlass central processor is very advanced with a library containing the parameters of up to 2000 radars.

Cutlass is wide open in both bearing and frequency, ie it does not employ sweep techniques, giving a very high intercept probability (nearly 100 per cent, degraded by simultaneous pulse arrival in extremely high density environments).

Cutlass is a modular equipment and can be configured to suit fittings in various classes of ships. The two main variants are Cutlass and Cutlass B1; both use the advanced Cutlass processor which can be integrated with a variety of man-machine interfaces and both use an instantaneous frequency measurement (IFM) receiver. Cutlass has a six-port antenna array for bearing measurement using amplitude comparison techniques, and a separate omni-directional antenna to provide RF for the IFM. Cutlass B1 has a 32-element array antenna to provide bearing measurement by phase analysis techniques. This antenna also provides RF for the IFM. In both systems the processor is provided with fast and accurate information on incoming pulses.

For an integrated EW system, Cutlass can be employed either in conjunction with one of the Racal RCM series of jammers (**1942.293**) or with the Racal Cygnus jammer (**5670.293**). Cutlass will readily integrate with other ship's systems, such as a tactical data system.

Cutlass antenna system mounted at masthead

STATUS

In production since 1977 and in service with several overseas navies. In mid-1983, Racal was awarded a £30 million contract for the development and reconfiguration of the Cutlass system for installation on board the Type 23 frigates. In January 1984, a contract valued at £12 million for Cutlass and Cygnus systems was received from the Middle East. It is understood that a version of Cutlass has been offered to the Royal Navy against a requirement for a combined ESM and chaff-triggering system, known as UAG-1.

CONTRACTOR

Racal Radar Defence Systems Ltd, Davis Road, Chessington, Surrey KT9 1TB, England.

Cutlass Console

3554.393

MIR-2 ESM EQUIPMENT

The MIR-2 ESM equipment was originally designed for use in helicopters but is also suitable for use on fixed wing aircraft and small naval craft where lightness and compact dimensions are important. The MIR-2 uses an advanced digital receiver, covering a wide range of frequencies from C- to J-band, around which a fully solid-state wide-band system has been built. It features lightweight antennas and a cockpit display which incorporates a very compact solid-state LED (light emitting diode) presentation of signal intercept data.

Six antenna packages, which can be flush mounted or externally mounted, are fitted on the aircraft with their boresights at 60° intervals in azimuth. Each

MIR-2 control indicator

antenna package consists of two antennas, both cavity-backed spirals. The modules contain all RF components and received signals are transmitted to the main processing unit.

The pulse receiver processes the signals received from the antennas and presents the information on the control indicator unit. Signals are displayed to the operator by frequency band, bearing and amplitude on the solid-state activity display. The total frequency coverage is divided into four frequency ranges with three amplitude levels indicated in each band at each bearing.

STATUS

Developed for the Royal Navy and in operational service with Lynx and Sea King helicopters. A further contract worth over £11 million was received from the UK MoD in April 1984 for these aircraft. Total sales exceed 200 sets and the equipment is in full production.

CONTRACTOR

Racal Radar Defence Systems Ltd, Davis Road, Chessington, Surrey KT9 1TB, England

5695.153

PINEMARTIN GROUND-BASED ESM SYSTEM

Pinemartin is a vehicle-mounted tactical ESM system providing surveillance of the radar environment, over the frequency range 600 MHz to 18 GHz, for special task forces, border patrols or similar missions. It is the latest in an advanced range of Racal ESM equipments and is based on the MIR-2 airborne system (3554.393) used by the Royal Navy in its Lynx and Sea King helicopters.

A compact, lightweight self-contained ESM system, Pinemartin can be installed in a small vehicle such as a ¾-ton Land-Rover, leaving ample room for the crew, essential stores and other equipment. It can be deployed rapidly to monitor the radar environment over a full 360° in azimuth with a high intercept probability.

The control/indicator unit can be fitted in a vehicle dashboard in front of the co-driver. The main display shows the frequency band, signal strength and

bearing information while a separate unit gives the bearing to an accuracy not normally achieved with tactical ESM equipments. The six antenna units are mounted in two housings which are fixed around a mast. The main processing unit can be located at any convenient position in the vehicle.

CONTRACTOR

Racal Radar Defence Systems Ltd, Davis Road, Chessington, Surrey KT9 1TB, England.

1876.053

HWR-2 RADAR WARNING RECEIVER

This is a miniature warning receiver, designed specifically for use in environments such as helicopters and small patrol craft where space and weight are invariably at a premium and the installation of sophisticated electronic warfare equipment is uneconomical. In its basic form the receiver is handheld and operates completely independently of available supplies and mounting arrangements (although it may be hard-mounted in rotary wing aircraft and surface ships).

Held by a pistol-grip handle, it can be used to locate pulsed radar transmissions of any frequency in the range 2 to 11 GHz. The presence of a radar transmission is indicated by listening to the audio note of the transmitted PRF on a headset. The electronic circuits are housed in a cast metal case designed to withstand rugged service conditions.

All controls are grouped on the rear face of the receiver with the single multiway connector for electrical interfaces. Using the handheld receiver, an operator can assess the following characteristics of a radar signal.

(1) Bearing. By scanning the receiver in azimuth and noting the direction of maximum signal volume in the headset, the bearing of a radar can be ascertained to an accuracy of approximately ±10°.

Racal hand-held warning receiver

(2) Polarisation. By twisting the receiver for maximum signal volume, an assessment can be made of the radar polarisation. When the receiver is held normally with the handle pointing downwards the antenna polarisation is linear at 45°, and thus horizontal, vertical, and circular polarisation can be received. The receiver polarisation is indicated by an arrow on the back of the case.

(3) Frequency Band. By operating the Band switch from the All position to the High position, an assessment can be made of the radar frequency band. If the signal is in I/J-band, then it will remain audible, if it is E/F-band, it will be suppressed.

(4) Scan Pattern. The audible sequence gives a very good indication of the type of radar scan, eg continuously rotating, sector scanning etc.

(5) PRF. An experienced operator will be able to discern quite accurate information about the radar PRF from the audible note.

(6) Range and Power. The relative intensity of a received set of signals provides some indication of their range and power. The sensitivity of the receiver can be reduced by 15 dB by operation of the sensitivity control from high to low.

DEVELOPMENT

Newly developed models are available which extend the frequency coverage to 18 GHz and provide for switching over four bands, together with five position sensitivity selection and CW and pulse reception modes. In addition models can be obtained with RF amplification giving greatly increased sensitivity over all bands, or dedicated to a particular 100 MHz bandwidth at customer specified frequencies.

STATUS

In production and delivered to various users.

CONTRACTOR

Racal Radar Defence Systems Ltd, Davis Road, Chessington, Surrey KT9 1TB, England.

5669.153

WEASEL ESM AND ELINT COLLECTION SYSTEM

Weasel is a combined electronic support measures (ESM) and electronic intelligence gathering (ELINT)

Weasel display console

system operating over the frequency range from 2 to 18 GHz with extension capabilities from 0·5 to 2 GHz and from 18 to 40 GHz. It is an advanced automatic system designed to operate in a dense radar environment and to achieve a low workload for a two-man crew operation.

The ESM part of the system acts as a search receiver with an instantaneous bandwidth equal to the full input range, thereby providing a 100 per cent intercept probability. As a stand-alone equipment it can provide accurate direction finding and identification of intercepted emissions. This latter is achieved by measuring the emitter parameters and comparing them with data stored in a library of known emitter characteristics. This is a fully automatic process and the operator is presented with a tabular display of identification and threat significance. Selected digital information can be recorded, hard copied and transmitted to external stations. An operator can select emitters for close attention and hand over this task to the narrow bandwidth, tunable analysis receiver for attention by the analysis

operator. The ESM thereby acts as a filter to reduce the workload on the analysis receiver.

The analysis receiver accepts digital data on any nominated emitter and automatically tunes the receiver to the correct frequency. The higher sensitivity and accuracy of the analysis receiver then permits detailed analysis of the signal. The data obtained can be used to update the library, create new entries and/or be recorded and transmitted to external stations. Both search and analysis receivers are capable of fully independent operation.

The system is designed for installation in a vehicle and for use at both fixed and temporary sites. The equipment is transported and operated in 19 inch special transport housings and is capable of withstanding rough handling and harsh environments.

STATUS

In development.

CONTRACTOR

Racal Radar Defence Systems Ltd, Davis Road, Chessington, Surrey KT9 1TB, England.

5670.293

CYGNUS ECM SYSTEM

The Cygnus radar jammer is a ship- or land-based equipment operating in the I- or J-bands. Originally designed for integration with Cutlass ESM equipment (3553.293), Cygnus uses both responsive noise and deception jamming to provide an effective jamming capability against all types of radar including early warning, target acquisition and missile guidance.

Cygnus has a narrow beamwidth giving very high effective radiated power (300 kW) and is kept on

target by a built-in, interferometer type passive tracking system, in both azimuth and elevation. The tracking system may also be used to relay accurate position data to systems of other ships. RF received by the tracking antennas is also used as the basis of transmitted RF and modulation and power management is under the control of a processor which also controls the tracking procedure. Types of modulation sequence available include range gate pull off and false target generation.

STATUS

In production and in service worldwide. In January 1984 a £12 million contract was received from the Middle East for Cygnus and Cutlass equipment.

CONTRACTOR

Racal Radar Defence Systems Ltd, Davis Road, Chessington, Surrey KT9 1TB, England.

5671.453

PORPOISE SUBMARINE ESM EQUIPMENT

A submarine version of the Cutlass ESM equipment (3553.293), Porpoise is a fully automatic ESM system operating throughout 360° of azimuth. The equipment receives signals in the 2 to 18 GHz frequency range, measures their parameters and compares these with those contained in a pre-

programmed radar threat library. Processing of the radar emitter signals is carried out against the library to give the operator an alpha-numeric or graphic display of identification in threat significance order.

The system is capable of integration with the vessel's fire control and communications systems and may also be integrated with periscope mounted radar warning equipments, eg Sprat (5672.493).

Porpoise also has the ability to give an alert warning when prime threats, such as helicopter or maritime surveillance radars, reach a pre-programmed danger level.

The Porpoise antenna is a compact 6-port system giving adequate bearing accuracy and may be mounted on either hull penetrating or non-hull penetrating masts. It is pressure resistant to 60 bar.

With the exception of the antenna system, the primary sub-assemblies of Porpoise are fully compatible with those of Cutlass and so enable common logistic facilities.

STATUS
In production and has been ordered by an unnamed overseas country.

CONTRACTOR
Racal Radar Defence Systems Ltd, Davis Road, Chessington, Surrey KT9 1TB, England.

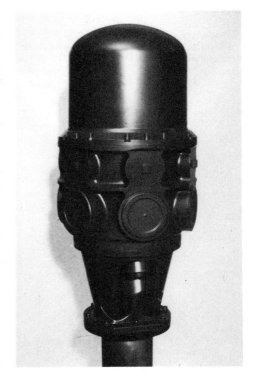

Porpoise antenna unit

5672.493
SPRAT SUBMARINE ESM SYSTEM

Sprat is a compact submarine ESM receiver designed to give radar warning of possible hostile emissions as soon as the periscope is raised. The system consists of an omni-directional antenna and receiver mounted on top of the periscope, and an indicator unit in the control room. The receiver operates over the frequency range 8 to 18 GHz. Detected radar signals are passed to the indicator unit and are displayed as relative signal levels with a corresponding audio output denoting radar activity.

The Sprat antenna/receiver may be integrated with the Porpoise ESM system (**5671.453**), enabling the operator to carry out radar interception prior to raising the main ESM mast. The antenna is pressure resistant to 60 bar. Full built-in-test equipment (BITE) is provided, interlocked to the periscope to prevent BITE signal radiation when the periscope is raised.

STATUS
In development

CONTRACTOR
Racal Radar Defence Systems Ltd, Davis Road, Chessington, Surrey KT9 1TB, England.

5673.353
PROPHET RADAR WARNING RECEIVER

The Prophet system is a radar warning receiver for helicopters and light fixed-wing aircraft designed to reduce vulnerability to radar associated threats on the battlefield by providing the pilot/observer with a real-time and unambiguous threat warning. It is a modular, easily interpreted equipment and system design has taken into account the possible requirement to integrate laser warning, hostile fire indicator and frequency extensions.

The receiver detects radiation in H, I and J bands and, by means of a processor using programmable threat data, warns of the presence of imminent threats. The system can operate in a dense RF environment with a low false alarm rate. A 4-port antenna system is used, bearing being derived by amplitude comparison and a digital IFM is used to provide frequency data. The processor extracts the data necessary to recognise any threat emission when compared with its field reprogrammable threat library. Audible warning of danger is provided and fed to the aircraft internal communication system.

The display uses light emitting diodes to form an array so that up to three threats can be displayed

Prophet radar warning receiver

simultaneously. The information displayed consists of an arrow indicating the direction of the threat relative to the aircraft heading with octantal resolution, together with a two or four character alpha-numeric identifier. The colour and brightness of the display is such that it can be viewed in bright sunlight and through night vision goggles. Display controls are mounted on the display panel, chaff dispensing controls may also be co-located if required. The total equipment weight is 7 kg and power consumption is 70 W.

STATUS
In production.

CONTRACTOR
Racal Radar Defence Systems Ltd, Davis Road, Chessington, Surrey KT9 1TB, England.

5674.193
SAVIOUR WARNING SYSTEM

The Saviour system combines radar and laser sensors to provide an integrated threat warning equipment which can be fitted to any type of armoured vehicle. By sensing the electronic irradiation of the vehicle by laser or radar beams, it gives instantaneous aural warning of impending missile or tank gun attack to the tank crew. In addition to the aural warning, an octantal indication of direction and type of attack is displayed and an optional automatic counter measure ie, emergency smoke screen, can be selected.

The radar frequency band coverage is from 6 to 16 GHz with laser coverage from 0·66 to 1·1 μm. Up to eight threats can be displayed simultaneously.

STATUS
In development.
CONTRACTOR
Racal Radar Defence Systems Ltd, Davis Road, Chessington, Surrey KT9 1TB, England.

Saviour radar warning receiver

5675.293
SEA SAVIOUR EW SYSTEM
Sea Saviour is designed as a radar threat warning system for small warships with a chaff/infra-red decoy trigger capability. It covers the frequency range from 8 to 18 GHz using a 4-port amplitude comparison bearing measurement system to provide bearing over the full 360° in azimuth. The sensor package gives an immediate audible warning when emissions are received indicating that the vessel is being illuminated by a threat radar. An octantal display of the direction of the emission is also provided. Immediate countermeasures to missile or fire control radars can be made by an automatic decoy dispensing system. The Sea Saviour package provides an integrated system which can include sensors, receiver, processor, display and decoy dispensers.

CHARACTERISTICS
Azimuth coverage: 360°
Elevation coverage: –5° to +40° (approximately)
Frequency bands: H, I and J
DF accuracy: to within a 45° sector
Dectection time: within one second
STATUS
In development.
CONTRACTOR
Racal Radar Defence Systems Ltd, Davis Road, Chessington, Surrey KT9 1TB, England.

Sea Saviour display unit

4365.193
RL1 and RL2 LASER WARNING INSTRUMENTS
The RL1 and RL2 are laser warning instruments able to detect radiation from pulsed laser rangefinders and target markers, and designed for mounting on armoured fighting vehicles. They can detect pulsed radiation within the 0·66 to 1·1 μm near infra-red band, covering the most common types of pulsed lasers (ruby, GaNa and neodymium) currently in use with rangefinders and target markers.

The RL1 has a 360° field of view and can also detect radiation coming from above. An indicator unit is mounted outside the vehicle and indicates the approximate direction of the radiating source by means of light emitting diodes mounted in a circle. Eight 45° sectors are indicated. A ninth emitting diode mounted in the centre indicates radiation from above. Due to the overlapping fields of view, a total of 17 sectors can be indicated.

The receiver gives an audible alarm consisting of a pulsed audio signal in the crews' intercom system when a laser pulse is detected. The duration of the alarm is about two seconds for a single laser pulse. When more than one pulse is being detected the alarm stays on for as long as laser pulses are being received.

The RL2 warning device also has a 360° field of view with a detector unit mounted on top of the vehicle and a control unit mounted inside. The control unit gives an acoustic alarm when a laser pulse is detected in a similar way to the RL1.

CHARACTERISTICS
No of detectors: 4 horizontal and 1 vertical (RL1); 1 (RL2)
Detector field of view: 360°
Type of detector: PIN photodiode
Detector active area: 1 mm²
Optical bandwidth: 0·66 – 1·1 μm
CONTRACTOR
Lasergage Limited, Newtown Road, Hove, East Sussex BN3 7DL, England.

RL1 laser warning unit

3369.393

HOFIN HOSTILE FIRE INDICATOR

The MS Instruments Ltd hostile fire indicator (HOFIN) is a passive warning system designed to alert a helicopter pilot that his aircraft is under fire. The first indication is an audible warning which draws the pilot's attention to a visual display which shows the general direction of the threat. This enables evasive action to be taken according to the current operational situation.

Three small units comprise the complete system, which weighs less than 6 kg: sensor array, computer unit, and the indicator unit.

The sensor array is mounted beneath the helicopter, and is aligned to the longitudinal airframe axis. It detects the shock wave front generated by the projectile and converts the impulsive pressure change to electrical signals. The electrical signals are fed to the computer unit for further processing.

The computer unit is housed in a 3/8 ATR short case, and is normally mounted in the equipment bay of the aircraft. This unit processes the signals provided by the sensor array, and computes the general direction of the hostile fire. The computer unit generates the one second audible warning signal, which is fed into the intercom system of the helicopter and also drives the indicator unit.

The indicator unit is housed in a 4 ATI instrument case which is normally located on the instrument panel, and consists of a circular red display which is divided into eight 45° octants. When displaying information to the pilot, four adjacent octants are illuminated for five seconds. The illuminated arc rotates in 45° steps and shows the source of the hostile fire relative to the longitudinal airframe axis. The indicator unit houses the operating controls of the system and consists of the display dimmer control, power on/off switch, system test switch, and the reset switch.

Although the HOFIN system has been designed primarily for helicopter use, it is clear that it can also be used in other situations where the detection of hostile fire is of importance. It should be realised that the detection range can be considerably increased for ground-based applications.

Complete HOFIN hostile fire indicator system with (left to right) detector unit, indicator and computer

CHARACTERISTICS
Power supplies: 22 – 28·5 V DC
Power consumption: 30 W standby, 60 W when display illuminated
Sensitivity: Responsive to supersonic projectiles with miss distances of up to 20 m
Calibration: By means of special-purpose test equipment
Display: 8 45° octants, of which 4 adjacent octants are illuminated. The illuminated 180° arc rotates in 45° steps. The display colour is red, and the brightness can be adjusted by means of a dimmer control
Audio warning: 300 Hz square wave, duration 1 s
Self-test: Built-in test equipment checks computer system

Temperature: Operating conditions –20 to +50° C
Storage conditions –40 to +70° C
Humidity: 95% non-condensing
DIMENSIONS:
Sensor array: 305 × 305 × 195 mm. 1·93 kg
Computer unit: 94 × 418 × 228 mm. 2·72 kg (with tray and cables)
Indicator unit: 106 × 106 × 125 mm. 1 kg
STATUS
Supplied to the British and Canadian Forces and evaluated by a number of other nations.
CONTRACTOR
MS Instruments Limited, Rowden Road, Beckenham, Kent BR3 4NA, England.

5735.393

B.AE INFRA-RED JAMMER

British Aerospace has developed an infra-red jamming system designed to protect helicopters operating in forward battle areas from attack by surface-to-air heat-seeking missiles. The jammer consists of an electrically powered infra-red source, an optical enhancement system, and a mechanical modulation assembly. This assembly modulates the infra-red radiation at a rate which degrades the tracking performance of the missile. Mechanical and electrical complexity has been avoided by the design of the optical enhancement system to provide maximum modulation for increased jammer efficiency.

CHARACTERISTICS
Azimuth cover: 360°
Elevation cover: ±25°
Dimensions: 40 cm × 20 cm diameter
Weight: 15 kg
STATUS
Successful airborne trials carried out by UK MoD. Now in engineering product development stage. A production order has been received from an unspecified customer.
CONTRACTOR
British Aerospace Dynamics Group, Bristol Division, PO Box 5, Filton, Bristol BS12 7QW, England.

B.Ae infra-red jammer

5736.053

B.AE ESM SYSTEM

British Aerospace is designing an analysis radio receiving system covering the frequency band from 1 to 18 GHz. The design and development will include

receiver and system controllers and a demodulator to handle a wide variety of signals. Both manual and automatic operation of the system will be possible.
STATUS
Under development for the UK MoD.

CONTRACTOR
British Aerospace Dynamics Group, Bracknell Division, Downshire Way, Bracknell, Berkshire RG12 1QL, England.

5739.353
VICON 77 ESM POD

Vicon 77 is a passive ESM pod containing a Racal micro-processor controlled radar threat warning system coupled directly to a salvo processing unit for discharging chaff and infra-red flares. The pod can be mounted on a wide variety of fixed- and rotary-wing aircraft and is equipped with four dispensers with a total capacity of 128 chaff cartridges and 64 flares. The dispensers are identical in overall dimensions, allowing them to be interchanged according to operational requirements.

The system is designed to operate automatically or manually. In the automatic mode, the microprocessor controlled radar warning system can detect up to three different radiations simultaneously, identify their directions and compare their characteristics with up to 15 pre-programmed specific threats. The aircrew is alerted by both aural and visual warnings, and the unit can feed information to the salvo processing unit to discharge chaff or infra-red flares. In the manual mode, chaff, flares or a mixture of the two can be discharged in a variety of configurations.

CHARACTERISTICS
Frequency coverage: H, I and J bands
Pod dimensions: 2·6 m long × 0·41 m diameter
CONTRACTOR
W Vinten Ltd, Western Way, Bury St Edmunds, Suffolk IP33 3TB, England.

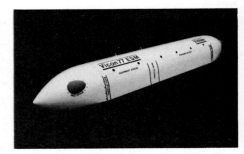
Vicon 77 ESM pod

UNITED STATES OF AMERICA

4662.393
AN/AAR-34 INFRA-RED RECEIVING SET

The AN/AAR-34 is an infra-red receiving set intended for aircraft self-protection against threats from heat seeking missiles. It consists of four units: a scanner and cryogenic converter normally mounted on the tail unit, a processor and a cockpit controller. The system gives automatic pilot warning on a CRT type display, and automatic countermeasures command.

Multiple threat detection and multiple discrimination modes are provided and the equipment is insensitive to clouds, sun and ground clutter.

CONTRACTOR
Cincinnati Electronics Corporation, 2630 Glendale-Milford Road, Cincinnati, Ohio 45241, USA.

AN/AAR-34 infra-red receiving set

3901.393
AN/AAR-44 INFRA-RED WARNING RECEIVER

The AN/AAR-44 airborne infra-red warning receiver was developed under sponsorship of USAF/ASD to provide warning of launched missile attacks. The set continually searches the lower hemisphere while tracking and verifying missile launches. It warns the aircrew of the position of missiles, and automatically controls countermeasures to neutralise threats and enhance survivability.

Design features of the equipment include: automatic pilot warning and countermeasure command; continuous track-while-search processing; multiple missile threat capability; discrimination against solar radiation, terrain and water backgrounds and countermeasures; multiple discrimination modes; lower hemispherical coverage.

CHARACTERISTICS
Control and display unit: 104 × 145 × 79 mm
Weight: 0·64 kg
Processor: 191 × 168 × 259 mm
Weight: 4·22 kg
Sensor: 366 × 376 mm (dia)
Weight: 15·56 kg
Displays: Sector threat indicators; external countermeasures command and audio tone
STATUS
Production.
CONTRACTOR
Cincinnati Electronics Corporation, 2630 Glendale-Milford Road, Cincinnati, Ohio 45241, USA.

AN/AAR-44 infra-red warning system

3109.393
LUNDY COUNTERMEASURES

Lundy Electronics and Systems Inc has been a major supplier of penetration aids and expendable countermeasure systems and equipment for over 30 years, and claims to be the world's largest producer of metallised glass chaff. So far as is known, Lundy concentrates on the passive aspects of EW, and in addition to the Minuteman III, Mk 12 re-entry vehicle penetration aids sub-system for which the company was awarded a contract in 1962, a full range of dispenser systems has been produced for aircraft and drone applications. The full list includes the following, some of which are described in more detail in individual entries, as indicated:

AN/ALE-1 and -2: Dispensing sets, pioneer pod system
AN/ALE-24: Chaff dispensing system for B-52G and H strategic bombers

AN/ALE-27: Chaff dispensing system for B-52C to F model bombers
AN/ALE-29A: Countermeasure dispensing set; deployed on various tactical aircraft (**3360.393**)
AN/ALE-32: Chaff dispensing system for EA-6A aircraft
AN/ALE-33: Chaff dispenser for BQM-34 target drone
AN/ALE-43: Chaff cutter/dispenser pod (**3110.393**)

Mk 12 penetration aids system for Minuteman ICBM

AN/ALE-27 chaff dispenser for B-52 C and F aircraft

AN/ALE-24 chaff dispenser for B-52 G and H aircraft

AN/ALE-44: Chaff and flare dispensing system, housed in supersonic pod (**3111.393**)

AN/ALE-XX: Universal pod for expendable countermeasures for RPV applications.

CONTRACTOR

Lundy Electronics and Systems Inc, 3901 NE 12th Avenue, Pompano Beach, Florida 33064, USA.

High capacity chaff/flare dispenser system on EA-6A

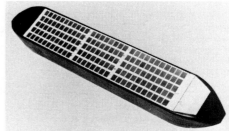

Universal pod for expendable countermeasures RPV

3360.393

AN/ALE-29A COUNTERMEASURES DISPENSER SYSTEM

The AN/ALE-29A countermeasures dispensing equipment is used on tactical aircraft for the controlled pyrotechnic ejection of chaff and IR decoy flares as a means of self-defence against radar directed and IR homing missiles. The equipment is comprised of one programmer; two sequencer switches; two dispensers (each consisting of a block and printed circuit board); two dispenser housings; and inter-connecting cable. The ALE-29A system carries 30 chaff or flare payloads per dispenser, and RR-129 and RR-144 chaff cartridges, and Mk 46 and Mk 47 IR flares are used.

The programmer is normally located in the aircraft cockpit and carries the necessary controls for selection of dispensing patterns, timing sequences, etc. An optional feature is a dual-channel programmer, which allows the simultaneous dispensing of chaff and flares via separate programmes.

The AN/ALE-29A system can be interfaced with threat warning devices.

STATUS

Operational on USN tactical aircraft.

CONTRACTOR

Lundy Electronics & Systems Inc, 3901 NE 12th Avenue, Pompano Beach, Florida 33064, USA. (Lundy is the latest of several manufacturers to build this system.)

AN/ALE-29A dispenser and dispenser housing, showing sequencer mounted on back of housing

---

4657.393

AN/ALE-36 COUNTERMEASURES DISPENSING POD

The AN/ALE-36 (QRC-490) is a modified AN/ALE-38/41 tactical fighter countermeasures dispenser pod adapted to carry RR-136 and RR-137 chaff units. The QRC/TBC-600 version is a modified AN/ALE-38 pod carrying 600 RR-170 chaff units for saturation/corridor chaff applications. Payloads are carried in 10 dispenser blocks of 60 payloads each and include an integral programmer. Each dispenser can be loaded with chaff units or flares. The fully loaded weight is 680 lbs (309 kg).

STATUS

In production.

CONTRACTOR

Tracor Aerospace, 6500 Tracor Lane, Austin, Texas 78721, USA.

1904.393

AN/ALE-37 CHAFF DISPENSER

The AN/ALE-37 is a high-capacity chaff dispenser for large area coverage, and although not officially confirmed, it is assumed to be carried internally by the seeding aircraft. It is capable of dispensing chaff or expendable jammers for anti-radar purposes, or flares. The probable use for this equipment is not so much self defence for the seeding aircraft as an element of full-scale EW support for a large-scale bomber attack or other large formation operation. Although it cannot be confirmed, it is probable that there are provisions in the equipment for programmed shot dispensing of the chaff or other stores, and that a range of radar frequency bands can be handled.

4654.393

AN/ALE-38/41 BULK CHAFF DISPENSER

The AN/ALE-38 (US Air Force) and AN/ALE-41 (US Navy) equipments are similar high capacity bulk chaff dispensers. They employ unique dispensing techniques and provide continuous dipole dispersal and instantaneous bloom for laying chaff corridors. They can also be used for aircraft self-protection and can be turned on automatically by the radar warning receiver. Pre-cut dipoles are sandwiched between two wraps of mylar film; six 50 lb (22·7 kg) rolls are carried in each pod. The AN/ALE-38/41 can be fitted to aircraft such as the F-105F, F-4, A-3, EA-4, A-7 and AQM-34H.

STATUS

In production.

CONTRACTOR

Tracor MBA, Bollinger Canyon Road, PO Box 196, San Ramon, California 94583, USA

1905.393

AN/ALE-39 ECM DISPENSER

The AN/ALE-39 ECM dispenser is a third generation expendable countermeasures dispenser system for protection of tactical aircraft from ground and air launched missile threats and radar directed anti-aircraft guns. It represents the culmination of over 10 years' evolution of dispenser system refinement by the US Navy, and is designed with flexibility of response to meet present and future needs in a changing threat environment.

The system is capable of accommodating up to three types of expendable payloads (chaff, IR flares and expendable jammers), loaded in any combination of multiples of 10. All three types of payload can be dispensed manually (single payload) or automatically in accordance with preset programs. The dispensing function can be initiated by the pilot (or EWO officer in the case of the F-14). The system is also capable of accepting dispense commands from aircraft warning receivers.

The programming flexibility, payload loading versatility, operational modes and wide selection of payload dispensing options and sequences (which includes simultaneous multiple flare ejection, random chaff ejections and rapid dump of flares) combine to make the AN/ALE-39 one of the better first generation analogue programmable countermeasures dispensing systems in the US inventory.

The system is operational on A-4, A-6, A-7, and F-14 aircraft and is planned for use on US Marine Corps Harriers and the F-18.

STATUS

More than 900 systems have been delivered since the initial production release in October 1973.

CONTRACTOR

Tracor MBA, Radcon Operations, 6500 Tracor Lane, Austin, Texas 78721, USA. (Tracor is the latest of several manufacturers to build this system.)

1906.393

AN/ALE-40 COUNTERMEASURES DISPENSER SYSTEM

The AN/ALE-40 countermeasures dispenser system, RR-170 chaff cartridge and MJU-7/B flare cartridge were developed for the F-4 family of aircraft. Each AN/ALE-40 consists of four dispensers, a chaff/flare programmer and a cockpit control unit (CCU). One dispenser is mounted on each side of the inboard armament pylons. A dispenser consists of a mounting plate to provide attachment to pylon structure, an aerodynamic nose fairing for drag reduction, and a detachable magazine for carrying the chaff cartridge. Each dispenser accommodates 30 RR-170 chaff cartridges for a total of 60 cartridges per pylon and 120 per aircraft. The outboard dispensers can carry 15 MJU-7/B IR flares. System drag is comparable to a Sidewinder missile and launcher. No weapons are displaced. Loaded weight is under 60 kg.

The RR-170 cartridge is square in cross section, 23 mm on each side and 184 mm long. The MJU-7/B flare is rectangular in cross-section, 23 × 50 × 184 mm.

Utilising the technology base of the AN/ALE-40 system, various configurations have been developed for adaptation to other aircraft types. With each new configuration, every attempt is made to install the system in such a way as to avoid interference with weapons stores/capabilities. Installation configurations vary from internal, flush mounted, skin mounted or scab-on, to semi-internal mounting.

An example of an internal flush mounted system is the AN/ALE-40(V) 4, 5, 6 installed on F-16 aircraft which consist of CCU, chaff/flare programmer, sequencer switch, EMI filter and two dispensers. The dispensers are mounted internally in the aft fuselage. Each dispenser carriers 30 RR-170 chaff units or 15 MJU-7/B IR flares.

Examples of the semi-internally mounted systems are the AN/ALE-40(V) 7, 8, 9 installed on F-5E/F aircraft. The system consists of CCU, chaff/flare programmer, sequencer switch, EMI filter and one dispenser housing containing two dispenser magazines. Each dispenser magazine carries 30 RR-170 chaff units or 15 MJU-7/B IR flares. The dispenser is mounted in the belly of the aircraft near the left wing root.

The AN/ALE-40(N) is the adaption of AN/ALE-40 for skin mounting on the NF-5 (Royal Netherlands AF) aircraft. A system consists of cockpit controls, chaff/flare programmer and two dispensers. Each dispenser carries 30 RR-170 chaff units or 30 flares. The dispensers are skin mounted onto aft fuselage. Drag is negligible. Loaded weight is less than 30 kg.

A similar AN/ALE-40(N) installation has also been adapted and flight tested on F-104 aircraft. Skin mounting is in the same aft fuselage area with similar controls and dispenser components providing 30 RR-170 chaff units or flares.

Other variants of the AN/ALE-40 are operationally deployed on Hunter and Mirage aircraft.

STATUS

The AN/ALE-40 system is in production and operationally deployed world-wide.

AN/ALE-40 countermeasures dispensers mounted on aircraft stores pylon

CONTRACTOR

Tracor MBA, Radcon Operations, 6500 Tracor Lane, Austin, Texas 78721, USA.

5688.393

AN/ALE-40(V)X COUNTERMEASURES DISPENSER SYSTEM

The advanced generation AN/ALE-40(V)X is an exact mechanical replacement for AN/ALE-40(V) systems (**1906.393**), and uses solid-state technology to incorporate a threat adaptive programmer. The microprocessor controlled programmer accepts information from the aircraft radar warning receiver and tail warning system if available, air data computer and throttle quadrant power setting, and enables the optimum deployment routine for available expendables.

The AN/ALE-40(V)X is capable of the following operating modes:
(1) Off/standby
(2) Manual – in this mode the pilot initiates a preselected dispensing programme
(3) Automatic – this is a fully automatic mode and causes automatic selection of the appropriate expendables as well as automatically selecting

AN/ALE-40(V)X countermeasures dispenser system

the optimum dispensing programme for the threat engagement at hand
(4) Semi-automatic – this requires pilot initiation of the automatically selected optimum dispensing routine.

Mode selection is made by a single switch on the cockpit-mounted control and display unit. An emergency jettison mode is available to dispense all expendables on command.

The AN/ALE-40(V)X is a next generation countermeasures dispensing system fully suited to the latest aircraft. It includes growth capabilities that allow quick updates to programmer decision logic, by modifying microprocessor software for updating threat characteristics or future mission scenarios. The additional mechanical interchangeability feature with conventional AN/ALE-40(V) systems enables inexpensive and rapid retrofit installation in aircraft equipped with the latter system, as well as providing a retrofit for unequipped aircraft requiring sophisticated self-protection.

STATUS

Engineering development of the AN/ALE-40(V)X system is complete. Production deliveries were due to begin in 1984.

CONTRACTOR

Tracor MBA, Radcon Operations, 6500 Tracor Lane, Austin, Texas 78721, USA.

3362.393

FAC COUNTERMEASURES DISPENSER

The Lundy FAC countermeasures dispenser is a compact, lightweight system which fires both chaff and flares. Designed for the US Air Force to dispense the percussion initiated MK-50 flare, the FAC dispenser has been successfully flight tested on the 0-2 and UH-1 aircraft.

To augment its operational usefulness, Lundy developed and flight tested a percussion initiated chaff unit which is compatible with the FAC dispensing mechanism. The chaff unit provides effective protection against known radar controlled threats operating in 3 to 16 GHz frequency range.

The basic FAC system contains a cockpit control/display unit, two payload modules, and two firing mechanisms. A cascade feature in the control circuitry allows any number of dispenser assemblies to be added to the basic system. The payload module holds 20 chaff units or flares interchangeably and is removed from the aircraft during ground operations for loading. The FAC dispenser is configured for both internal and external mounting.

Although primarily developed for use with forward air control aircraft types, this dispenser can be used to fire any 40 mm munitions from air or land vehicles.

CONTRACTOR

Lundy Electronics & Systems Inc, 3901 NE 12th Avenue, Pompano Beach, Florida 33064, USA.

Lundy FAC countermeasures dispenser equipment

3110.393

AN/ALE-43 CHAFF CUTTER DISPENSER POD

The AN/ALE-43 chaff cutter dispensing system is believed to be the first cutter-type dispenser to receive an American 'AN' nomenclature. It provides the EW operator with the option of selecting, while in flight, various tuned dipole lengths to meet changing threats in frequency ranges from A-band to K-band.

The concept of cutting chaff from a continuous supply to various dipole lengths, while in flight, has numerous advantages. The limitations in utilising the 'cutter' concept for chaff countermeasures in the past was the lack of a suitable chaff supply material. Lundy has developed a chaff cutter roving which is now available in a variety of filament counts and package configurations.

The AN/ALE-43 is designed for two types of installation: an external pod or an internal mount. In the external pod installation, the chaff cutter assembly is mounted on a structural bulkhead at the rear of the pod centre section. This assembly consists of a drive motor, clutch/brake unit, cutting mechanism and supporting framework. The cutting mechanism contains a rubber platen roller and three cutter rollers. The cutter rollers are designed with blades that yield three specific combinations of dipole lengths as commanded. In the internal installation the cutter assembly is mounted directly to the aircraft structure.

For either installation, the system consists of a chaff roving supply, chaff cutter assembly and a cockpit programmer. The chaff supply is made of metallised glass roving packages contained within a chaff hopper. The chaff is dispensed when rovings are drawn simultaneously from each of the roving supply packages. Each roving passes through a guide tube and is drawn between the platen roller and the cutter rollers for dipole cutting. The cut dipole lengths of chaff are then discharged at the exit which opens into the airstream.

A control unit allows the pilot to select dispensing programs and to start and stop dispensing sequences. The pod has mounting provisions for standard NATO 14 inch and 30 inch stores suspension hardware and can be mounted conveniently on existing stores stations.

CHARACTERISTICS
Pod length: 337 cm
Pod diameter: 48 cm
Weight: pod 138·5 kg (empty); Internal unit 36 kg
Chaff payload: pod 145 kg (8 roving packages); internal 164 kg (9 packages)
Dispensing rate: pod $7·2 \times 10^6$ dipole inches/s; internal $8·1 \times 10^6$ dipole inches/s
STATUS
In production.
CONTRACTOR
Lundy Electronics and Systems Inc, 3901 NE 12th Avenue, Pompano Beach, Florida 33064, USA.

AN/ALE-43 chaff cutter/dispensing pod

3111.393
AN/ALE-44 DISPENSER POD
The AN/ALE-44 is a dispensing pod for use on tactical, support, and strike aircraft capable of supersonic flight. It is a lightweight unit for use with both chaff and flare countermeasure stores, and meets 'HERO' requirements. A typical system consists of a control unit and two dispenser pods. Each pod houses two dispenser modules and a sequencer.

The pod features single- or dual-channel dispensing and quick turn-around time. A low frontal profile, small size, and central mounting pod provide for pod mounting on a wingtip, stores pylon, or fuselage. Fully laden weight is only 20 kg.

Payloads for the system, the RR-129 chaff package and Mk 46 IR flare, are both US Navy inventory items.

The payload capacity for each pod is 32 chaff and/or flare expendables which are ejected by impulse cartridges. The dispensers (loaded) can be installed in the pod without removal from the aircraft.

A cockpit control unit permits selection of various burst rates, burst intervals, and units per burst, with simultaneous dispensing of flares and chaff.
CHARACTERISTICS
Pod dimensions: $206 \times 10·7 \times 18$ cm
Weights: 13·6 kg (empty); 19·9 kg (chaff loaded); 22·6 kg (flare loaded); 1·1 kg (control unit)
Mode: 1 or 2 units per burst
Program: 1, 2, 4, 8 or continuous bursts per program
Rate: 4, 2, 1, or ½ bursts per s
CONTRACTOR
Lundy Electronics and Systems Inc, 3901 NE 12th Avenue, Pompano Beach, Florida 33064, USA.

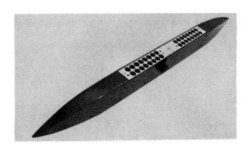

AN/ALE-44 dispenser pod

3345.393
M-130 COUNTERMEASURES DISPENSER
The M-130 aircraft general purpose dispenser is a lightweight countermeasures dispenser system developed using AN/ALE-40 (**1906.393**) technology for the US Army. The system is designed for employment on tactical rotary or fixed wing aircraft, such as the AH-1, CH-47, OH-58, UH-1, RU 21 and OV-1D, to provide self-protection from radar directed weapons by dispensing of chaff, and/or to provide protection from infra-red homing weapons by dispensing flares.

The M-130 system is of a modular design to allow

flexibility of operational configuration. The modules consist of a cockpit control unit, and electronics module, one or more dispensers, cabling, and aircraft adapters. The cabling and adapters are unique to the aircraft type, whereas the other modules are common among all aircraft types.

The M-130 uses the M-1 countermeasures chaff and the M-206 aircraft countermeasures flare as payloads. Each payload module accommodates 30 payloads of a single type. The system configuration may be either a single dispenser of 30 payload capacity, or a double dispenser of 60 payload capacity. The system weight, with 60 payloads, is

21·8 kg.
The M-130 will function with input from the infra-red threat warning device directly to the electronic module, obviating the need for pilot action.

The payloads, the M-1 countermeasures chaff and the M-206 countermeasures flare, have a nominal 25 by 25 mm square configuration, and are 210 mm in length. The payload form factor is identical to the RR-170A/AL chaff used in the AN/ALE-40 and is functionally interchangeable.
CONTRACTOR
Tracor MBA, Radcon Operations, 6500 Tracor Lane, Austin, Texas 78721, USA.

4655.393
MODULAR CHAFF/FLARE DISPENSER
This is a pyrotechnic cartridge type chaff and IR flare dispensing system which has been developed for service with both United States and NATO forces for passive aircraft protection. Because of its modular design, the system can be adapted to a great variety of aircraft and a short cartridge length allows flush mounting to F-16 and other types.

Chaff cartridges developed for use in the MCFD incorporate several advanced features including transverse chaff dipole orientation for rapid bloom and frequency coverage versatility. The flare cartridge which was designed in conjunction with the equipment is twice the size of the chaff cartridge and is replaceable on a two-to-one exchange basis. The flare incorporates improved composition and a rapid ignition system for fast time rise.

STATUS
In production for the F-35 Draken aircraft of the Royal Danish Air Force and under evaluation for the Harrier aircraft of the RAF.
CONTRACTOR
Tracor MBA, Bollinger Canyon Road, PO Box 196, San Ramon, California 94583, USA

3541.393
AN/ALQ-78 COUNTERMEASURES SET
Countermeasures set AN/ALQ-78 is used by the US Navy aboard the P-3C maritime aircraft as the ESM sensor. It automatically detects and measures the characteristics and bearings of intercepted radar signals of ASW and EW interest.

The measured parameters and bearing of the intercepted signals are supplied to the aircraft central data processing system for evaluation, recording and presentation on the aircraft displays.

The system uses a high-speed rotating antenna and a scanning, superheterodyne receiver for acquisition of signals in specific frequency bands of particular interest to the P-3C. Operation is to a great extent automatic, based on parametric data. The countermeasures set normally operates in an omni-directional search mode. When a radar signal of interest is acquired and analysed, the AN/ALQ-78 automatically initiates a direction finding routine. The signal data is processed by the central data computer and formatted for readout on a multipurpose display.
STATUS
Operationally deployed with the US Navy since 1969. The AN/ALQ-78 is currently being upgraded to the 'A' configuration. A new ESM system for the P-3C is currently under development (**5690.393**).

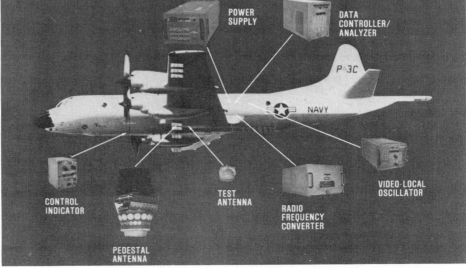

AN/ALQ-78 countermeasures set showing location of units on P-3C Orion maritime aircraft

CONTRACTOR
Loral Electronic Systems, Ridge Hill, Yonkers, New York 10710, USA.

3112.393
LUNDY CHAFF AND FLARES COUNTERMEASURES SYSTEM

Lundy produces a form of unitary design for expendable countermeasures systems. The basic element of the system is the dispenser unit, which contains 14 flares or chaff cartridges.

Positioned in a back-to-back pair, the two dispenser units form an externally mounted dispensing assembly, having a low aerodynamic profile. Dispenser units are attached to the aircraft with a contoured mounting plate. The plate serves as both a mechanical and electrical interface. This allows mounting options at numerous locations on the surface of the aircraft. Only the contour of the mounting plate is altered to accommodate the skin line curvature at any location.

The dispenser unit contains the payload module and sequencer. These components are handled as a single unit during ground operations. As a result the electrical initiators (squibs) are shorted at all times. This design feature provides immunity to HERO environment. In addition, the signal routeing circuits of the dispenser unit conform to the highest level of EMI specifications.

A particular advantage of this system is that it offers a mission-oriented flexibility, wherein any aircraft can be provided with a flare and chaff capability by the simple installation of mounting plates. These aircraft can be flown with or without dispenser units, reducing the quantity of dispenser units required to support a fleet of aircraft.

A cockpit mounted control/display unit allows the pilot to pre-select chaff and flare dispensing programs, initiate and terminate dispensing activity, and monitor the status of the system operation.

The control display unit responds to input commands from warning receivers (automatic mode) and to input commands from the air crew (manual mode).

The performance of the flare (intensity, burn-time) is sufficient for the self-protection of military jet aircraft (F-4, F-16), during maximum cruise conditions. The chaff cartridge responds at threat frequencies in the E, F, G, H, I, and J bands. The radar cross-section (RCS) created by the chaff cartridge immediately after ejection, 'less than 2 seconds', will exceed the average (RCS) of an F-4 aircraft.

CHARACTERISTICS
Dispenser assembly
Dimensions: 71 × 13 × 15 cm
Weights: 5·5 kg (empty)
14·2 kg (flare loaded)
IR flare
Dimensions: 127 × 40 mm (dia)
Weight: 0·32 kg
Output, average: 15 kW, 3 – 5 microns
Burn time: 3 s minimum
Chaff unit
Dimensions: 127 × 40 mm (dia)
Weight: 0·30 kg
RCS, average: 20 m²; 1 – 2 s
Frequency bands: E, F, G, H, I, and J
CONTRACTOR
Lundy Electronics and Systems Inc, 3901 NE 12th Avenue, Pompano Beach, Florida 33064, USA.

1908.393
AN/ALQ-99 ECM EQUIPMENT

The AN/ALQ-99 is a large and sophisticated tactical noise jamming system forming the major portion of the US Navy EA-6B ECM aircraft's operational payload. It comprises five external pods, each capable of housing two very high powered jamming transmitters, a tracking receiver, the requisite antennas and a ram-air turbine to provide electrical power. Other associated equipment is housed in the large fin-top blister of the EA-6B, and in the aircraft itself there is further ALQ-99 equipment which includes a digital computer and display, and control facilities for two operating crew members.

The pods are detachable from the aircraft and are capable of housing various combinations of transmitters to cover any desired frequency bands. These can be arranged to provide an aircraft with any combination of duplicated and different operating bands, within the total capacity of the equipment and as required by operational necessities.

An IBM 4 Pi general purpose digital computer inside the aircraft carries out processing for the tactical jamming system as well as performing a navigational function. The latter facility enables the computer to perform a transmission beam steering (or transmission blanking) function so that jamming radiation can be restricted to a given 30° azimuth sector. The computer also interfaces with the display sub-systems.

In the automatic mode, one of three possible operating modes for the ALQ-99, the computer performs the sorting of detected signals and directs the selection and activation of jamming against threats. In this mode, the two operators monitor system operation. In the semi-automatic mode, the computer identifies and indicates threats and the operators select and indicate ECM actions. In the manual mode the operators each search their apportioned parts of the spectrum, identify threats, and assign jammers to them.

STATUS
In service with USN EA-6B aircraft. An internally located version of the ALQ-99 was selected by the USAF for use in the EF-111A ECM aircraft currently in production. This version, ALQ-99E, incorporates a number of improvements (some of which are already incorporated into the EA-6B), among them: (1) reduced search time for receivers to search the radar bands and identify enemy signals; (2) an increase in the number of radars that can be jammed by each ALQ-99 transmitter by increasing the jamming bandwidth and generating (modulated?) instead of (noise?) jamming signals; (3) increased operational flexibility by permitting several jammers with different frequency coverage to employ the same exciter, or

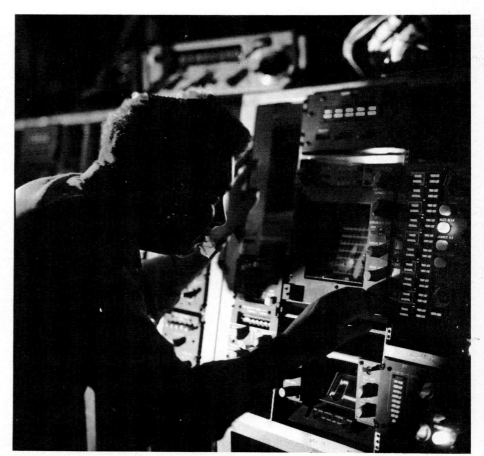

AN/ALQ-99 ECM system used in US Navy EA-6B aircraft seen undergoing final test at the AIL Long Island plant

signal source; and (4) further extra operational flexibility by adding omni-directional antennas to permit selection of either directional or omni-directional transmissions. Note: The words in brackets in the above passage have been substituted for the word 'deleted' which appeared in the original document. It is believed, also, that the EF-111A version of the ALQ-99 employs more transmitters than that used on the EA-6B. A contract worth $35 million for ALQ-99E sets was awarded to Raytheon in December 1981, and other contracts worth $30 million were awarded to AIL Division (Eaton Corporation) for additional sets for EA-6B and EF-111A aircraft in early 1982.

As at January 1982, more than 600 transmitters and 300 exciters for the EA-6B programme had been delivered. Total Raytheon sales for ALQ-99 systems exceeds $330 million. See also **4667.393**
CONTRACTORS
AIL Division – transmitting antennas, receivers, displays, controls, power supplies, encoders, low-band jammer control
Raytheon – transmitters and exciters
AEL – transmitters
Hughes, Microwave Associates, and Teledyne – travelling wave tubes
McDonnell Douglas – pods
IBM – computer
Garrett – ram-air turbines
Astronautics Corporation of America – display

1909.393
AN/ALQ-100 ECM EQUIPMENT
The AN/ALQ-100 is an internally-mounted deception electronic countermeasures (DECM) equipment fitted in US Navy A-4, EA-6B and A-7 aircraft. It is a multiple-band, repeater-type track breaking jammer and operates in conjunction with the aircraft's threat

warning receiver. No official details have been revealed but it is thought that the ALQ-100 responds to detection of a radar signal associated with a known Soviet AA missile threat by high-power, broad-band noise jamming in the same radar band, or in the DECM mode by repeating the threat radar's signals after a delay to deceive the system and break track.

An advanced version of the ALQ-100 was procured by the US Navy under an updating programme called PRIDE.
CONTRACTOR
Sanders Associates Inc, Daniel Webster Highway South, Nashua, New Hampshire 03060, USA.

1910.393
AN/ALQ-101 ECM PODS
The AN/ALQ-101 designation embraces a large family of jamming pods with varying capabilities, which have evolved over a period of about 14 years.

All earlier versions of the ALQ-101 were of circular cross-section and were about 25 cm in diameter, the first model having been approximately 230 cm long and the three succeeding versions about 390 cm in length. The final model of the series, the ALQ-101(V)-10, was the first of the so-called 'gondola' type in which the underside of the pod has throughout its length a trough-shaped compartment which considerably increases the available volume of the pod without serious increase in cross-sectional area. This model enlarged the frequency coverage once again and also incorporated other improvements to provide 'full capability', or the ability to counter all known anti-aircraft threats. Earlier ALQ-101 pods

were updated to (V)-10 standard and a total of more than 400 was procured. This final model of ALQ-101 is approximately equivalent to the ALQ-119 which followed after the USAF awarded a contract in 1970.

The ALQ-101 pod is usually employed on F-4 aircraft and has been supplied to US forces and other operators of this type. One Buccaneer squadron of the Royal Air Force is equipped with this pod (Mk 10 version) and it is believed that the RAF has 22 further sets.

One other derivative of the original pod should be mentioned. This is the ALQ-105 which consisted of a repackaged version that amounted to a longitudinal splitting of the pod, the two halves being grafted on to the sides of the F-105 fighter-bomber aircraft. About 90 were produced.
CONTRACTOR
Electronic Warfare Division, Westinghouse Electric Corporation, Baltimore, Maryland 21203, USA.

AN/ALQ-101(V)-10 countermeasures pod on F-4

1911.393
AN/ALQ-119 ECM POD
The AN/ALQ-119 is a dual-mode jammer pod which was developed for the USAF to provide 'full-capability' protection for strike aircraft. By full-capability is meant a complement of counter-measures against known radar threats. Various types of aircraft can be equipped with the ALQ-119 but the

principal mode is the F-4 Phantom. The system is also fitted to, or specified for, A-7, A-10, F-15 F-16 and F-111 aircraft. It is reported to be a three-band system, and qualifies for dual-mode status by virtue of facilities for both noise jamming and repeater deception jamming.

When initiated as QRC-522 in 1970, the equipment was given extended frequency capabilities and

enhanced modulation performance to become the USAF production version designated ALQ-119. The three frequency bands covered by the equipment have not been disclosed but are probably E/F-, G/H-, and I-bands.
DEVELOPMENT
Development was initiated by QRC-522 and R & D was carried out by Westinghouse. In 1970 a contract for 20 prototype pods was awarded. It entered service in Viet-Nam in 1972.

It is claimed to be the first dual-mode jammer to enter volume production, a claim which is also made for the dual-mode TWT employed.
STATUS
More than 1600 ALQ-119 pods have been produced, at rates from 10 to 30 per month.

In addition to US Forces, the ALQ-119 is in service on aircraft operated by Israel, West Germany, Egypt and Turkey.

An update to the ALQ-119 is planned whereby it will be provided with a computer-controlled power management system, by means of which the power radiated by the pod, in terms of frequency, type of signal etc, will be automatically controlled in accordance with the threat encountered.

The pod has been continually updated to combat new threats. The current model (ALQ-119(V)-15) is physically different from earlier versions in that it has a short radome mounted below the forward end of the gondola. All previous models are being upgraded to (V)-15 configuration. A physically shorter version, designated ALQ-119(V)-17, is also employed by the USAF.
CONTRACTOR
Electronic Warfare Division, Westinghouse Electric Corporation, Baltimore, Maryland 21203, USA.

AN/ALQ-119 ECM pod on a USAF A-10 aircraft

1912.393
AN/ALQ-123 INFRA-RED COUNTERMEASURES
The AN/ALQ-123 is airborne IR jamming equipment, developed to provide aircraft with protection from IR-homing missiles. It is pod-mounted and powered by a ram-air turbine, and was designed for carriage on A-6 and A-7 type attack aircraft. Modification of the system for internal installation in the tail of fighter aircraft has been given some consideration by the US Navy.

The ALQ-123 is not an IRCM of the flare dispensing type (which is a known technique of decoying IR-homing missiles), and it is understood to comprise a

method of generating a train of light pulses appropriately coded to confuse or break the lock-on of an IR seeking missile.
STATUS
In operational service.
CONTRACTOR
Loral Electro-Optical Systems, 300 N Halstead Street, Pasadena, California 91107, USA.

AN/ALQ-123 installed on a US Navy fighter

4366.353
AN/ALQ-125 TACTICAL ELECTRONIC RECONNAISSANCE SENSOR

The AN/ALQ-125 Tactical Electronic Reconnaissance Sensor (TEREC) is an airborne equipment which provides automated threat recognition, direction of arrival and threat location of ground based transmitters, including surface-to-air missiles and AA batteries. The system is fully automatic, except for control provisions which allow the operator to monitor system operation and to designate which threat should be displayed. The primary roles of the system are for rapid threat recognition in the tactical battle area and for dissemination of this information to tactical commanders at all levels of command. TEREC provides two options: a cockpit display for operator readout which provides on-board operators with the ability to pass information to other users and a second option of a data link to transmit data to selected ground sites.

TEREC uses two antennas to provide coverage for both sides of the aircraft. A computer directed frequency search is provided over a broad bandwidth and under computer control the receiving sub-system scans through the pre-programmed RF ranges of interest. Once the data of a threat emission is in the TEREC computer, a direction of arrival is calculated on the basis of quantitised values as measured by the interferometer array. The system general purpose computer enables automatic data collection, data processing and reformatting of the data for display, data linking and magnetic tape recording. Operator controls include the tape recorder, data link, system power and coverage side. In addition a built-in-test function can be performed at the operator's discretion.

STATUS

The US Air Force has ordered 23 production units for outfitting a number of RF-4C aircraft. Work has also begun on a F-15 prototype which can carry the AN/ALQ-125 system internally, as the RF-4C does. Litton has also received a $15 million contract from the USAF for eight systems for tactical electronic surveillance aircraft. The US Marine Corps is also considering the system for installation in RF-4B aircraft to support its reconnaissance requirements.

CONTRACTOR

Litton, Amecom Division, College Park, Maryland, USA.

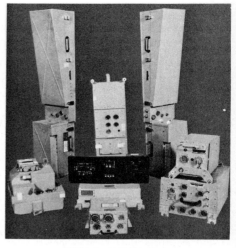

AN/ALQ-125 TEREC system

1913.393
AN/ALQ-126 ECM EQUIPMENT

The AN/ALQ-126 is a deception electronic countermeasures (DECM) system developed under the US Navy's Charger Blue EW updating programme. It provides a wider coverage of radar frequency bands than the ALQ-100, upon which it is based, and was initiated in response to the new threats represented by recently introduced Soviet anti-aircraft missiles and gun systems.

The ALQ-126 is internally fitted in US Navy tactical aircraft such as the A-7, A-6, and RA-5, and is intended to replace progressively the ALQ-100. In addition to increased frequency coverage, the ALQ-126 incorporates improved deception techniques, more modern construction, packaging, and cooling arrangements.

An improved version, the ALQ-126B, has completed a four year development and flight test programme. The ALQ-126B includes a distributed microprocessor control system to enable the system to be reprogrammed to meet changing threats and also provides considerable improvements in signal processing.

STATUS

More than 1100 ALQ-126A systems have been supplied to the US Navy, plus a small number for the Royal Netherlands Air Force F-104 aircraft.

In the latter half of 1982, the US Navy awarded a contract, estimated at more than $75 million for production of the ALQ-126B. First systems have been delivered and production is expected to continue until 1987 under continuing contract awards. The ALQ-126B has also been selected by a number of countries for fitment to F-18 aircraft.

CONTRACTOR

Sanders Associates Inc, Daniel Webster Highway South, Nashua, New Hampshire 03060, USA.

4668.393
AN/ALQ-128 WARNING RECEIVER

The AN/ALQ-128 is a multi-mode threat warning receiver forming part of the Tactical EW System (TEWS) used on the US Air Force F-15 aircraft. It is combined with the AN/ALQ-135 (**3346.393**) and the AN/ALR-56 (**3347.353**). No details have been released regarding this equipment but it is known that recent updating changes have been included to increase the number and type of threats that the equipment can recognise.

STATUS

Most, if not all, units required for the US Air Force F-15 aircraft have now been procured.

CONTRACTOR

Magnavox Electronic Systems, Fort Wayne, Indiana 46808, USA.

1914.393
AN/ALQ-130 ECM EQUIPMENT

The AN/ALQ-130 is tactical communications jamming equipment for use by US Navy fighter and attack aircraft, including A-4, A-6, A-7, and F-4 types. The principal function is probably the disruption of the communications links associated with enemy defence networks and surface-to-air missile formations. The jamming may include broad-band electrical and/or acoustic noise or spot frequency jamming, but the former is probably more likely.

Development of the ALQ-130 was initiated as an updating programme for the ALQ-92 tactical communications jammer, which on the USN EA-6B is internally mounted, suggesting that the ALQ-130 will also be carried this way.

CONTRACTOR

Eaton Corporation, AIL Division, Deer Park, Long Island, New York 11729, USA.

1915.393
AN/ALQ-131 ECM POD

The AN/ALQ-131 is an advanced ECM, jamming pod developed under Programme Element 64739F which covers protective systems for various aircraft types. Dimensions of the ALQ-131 shown here are 285 cm × 63 cm deep × 30 cm wide, and weight is 260 kg. It is modular equipment, described in US defence circles as a full-capability-plus system, and is based on the use of a digital computer contained within the pod. Adoption of the modular technique will allow dual-mode (noise/deception) jamming pods covering from one to five frequency bands to be assembled to meet the specific requirements of varying missions and theatre of operations. Particular targets are the radars and guidance systems associated with anti-aircraft defensive systems. The power-management facility of the ALQ-131 is currently scheduled to be a software re-programmable processor. There are a number of different modules for one version of the pod, providing for jamming of all known anti-aircraft missile system frequency bands. The modular design allows assembly of up to 16 structural configurations to meet various requirements. Smaller or larger pod configurations can be used ranging from 221 to 392 cm long.

The pod is a software re-programmable model which allows a tactical commander to tailor his

AN/ALQ-131 ECM pod mounted on F-16 aircraft

available pod equipment for his mission requirement(s). Another important feature of the ALQ-131 is its ability to be re-programmed, on the flight-line, in response to threat changes by making changes in the pod's digital computer. This will obviate long and expensive hardware modifications when threat techniques or parameters change and can even be made on the flightline. The final capability of this pod is the self-contained power management feature. This is included in a single receiver-processor module which not only detects radar threats but also directs the optimum jamming programme.

DEVELOPMENT

Development was undertaken in response to a USAF RFP, (QRC-559) in the 1971-72 period, when proposals were put up by a number of US industry teams. That headed by Westinghouse was chosen to develop the ALQ-131. Other members of this team were Motorola and Dalmo Victor whose modules did not go into production. Present power management module developments include Loral's improved

receiver/processor to be supplemented in the late 1980s by the W/ITT CPMS module from ASPJ.

In August 1980 the manufacturer was awarded a USAF contract worth $15·6 million to carry out a classified modification to the ALQ-131 under the Have Exit programme. This is understood to embrace the addition of facilities giving protection against new threats.

STATUS

Since 1976 over 600 systems have been ordered, including orders from the Royal Netherlands and Pakistani Air Forces.

In mid-summer 1977, the ALQ-131 was officially designated as being compatible with the F-16 fighter aircraft by the USAF. Other types of aircraft associated with this pod include the F-4, F-111, A-7,

A-10, and F-15.

It is expected that by 1986 the USAF will have ordered over 1000 systems and further sales will be concluded with other air forces bringing the total production to approximately 1500 systems.

CONTRACTOR

Westinghouse Electric Corporation, Electronic Warfare Division, Baltimore, Maryland 21203, USA.

3877.363
AN/ALQ-131 RECEIVER/PROCESSOR

The receiver/processor is a self-contained, single modular package that fits within the AN/ALQ-131 jamming pod (**1915.393**). It enhances the operation of this ECM system by maximising its jamming capability and effectiveness against a multiple radar threat environment. This is accomplished through the concept of power management.

The receiver conducts a signal search within a prescribed frequency range, under control of the processor. When a signal representing a threat is acquired the signal is analysed for parameter values,

formatted, and used to control the operation of the jammers so that jamming energy is applied with optimum timing and is better concentrated within the emitters RF, IF and servo bandwidths. The concept of power management thereby assures that energy waste, normally inevitable in conventional jamming, is minimised. A look-through feature of the receiver/processor permits continuous surveillance of the radar environment while jamming is in process.

CONTRACTOR

Loral Electronic Systems, Ridge Hill, Yonkers, New York 10710, USA.

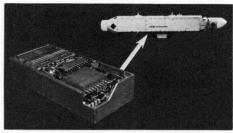

Loral AN/ALQ-131 receiver/processor showing its location in ALQ-131 jamming pod

1916.393
AN/ALQ-133 ELINT EQUIPMENT

The AN/ALQ-133 (Quick Look) is a tactical Elint system deployed in OV-1D Mohawk aircraft for emitter detection and passive surveillance by the US Army. The ALQ-133 has also been proposed for use in a number of A-10 tactical aircraft.

The configuration of the ALQ-133 consists of two pods: one contains Elint receivers needed to cover a frequency range extending probably from VHF or UHF up to 18 GHz, and equipped with the appropriate

broad-band antennas; the other contains data processing equipment housed in the aircraft fuselage. The pod antennas will be phased interferometer elements, capable of providing direction-of-arrival measurements over a 90° sector abeam of the aircraft to a typical accuracy of 0·5°. If some degradation of bearing accuracy is acceptable, the coverage sector can be enlarged to 120°.

The data processor is responsible for control of the search receivers, analysis of intercepted signals, and comparison of these against a file of known hostile

radar characteristics. Other data processing options include housing this part of the equipment in a third pod (this is proposed for the A-10), and locating it on the ground, the raw Elint being passed from the aircraft by data link.

STATUS

In operational service with the US Army.

CONTRACTOR

United Technology Laboratories, 410 Kirby, Garland, Texas 75042, USA.

4368.393
AN/ALQ-134 EXPENDABLE JAMMER

This is an expendable jamming system which includes a microstrip receiver-transmitter occupying a space of approximately 3 cubic inches inside a total package of less than 15 cubic inches. The complete system weighs less than 16 ounces (0·45 kg) and is

installed with a spring-loaded unfurlable antenna that includes a reef-cutter drogue chute plus parawing.

The system is battery powered and uses the latest technology in lithium battery development.

STATUS

In production.

CONTRACTOR

Sanders Associates Incorporated, Microwave Division, Grenier Field, Manchester, New Hampshire 03103, USA.

3346.393
AN/ALQ-135 INTERNAL COUNTERMEASURES SET

The AN/ALQ-135 internal countermeasures set (ICS) has been developed for the F-15 aircraft's tactical electronic warfare system (TEWS) and is the active jamming part of that system, working in conjunction with the ALR-56 radar warning receiver (**3347.353**).

Automatic jamming of threat radars is provided and a dual mode capability enables both CW and pulse radiation threats to be countered. TWTs, integrated circuits and microprocessors are used in construction, and ECM frequency sources are computer managed so that the system can adapt automatically to changing enemy threats.

STATUS

Northrop Corporation's Defense Systems Division

received a contract in September 1975 for production of an initial batch of 44 ALQ-135 ICS sets, costing $25 million, inclusive of spares, data, and production start-up costs. The first of these units were delivered in February 1977. A few weeks earlier, in January 1977, the company had been awarded another contract by the USAF, valued at $15·2 million and calling for a further production batch. In 1978 Northrop was awarded a $19·4 million USAF contract for spares to support ALQ-135 equipment in USAF Tactical Command F-15s and subsequent contracts received in late 1978 and 1979 have brought the contract total to $190 million, with further orders expected.

By January 1980 more than 200 sets had been delivered and contracts under this programme amounted to over $300 million; USAF announced

contract awards in early 1980 totalling $93·8 million. A further contract for $100 million to supply sets for the USAF F-15 aircraft was announced in December 1981.

A follow-on contract for $60 million was awarded in 1983. This contract, for additional ECM systems with enhanced capabilities, could extend production for F-15s into the next decade. Northrop has produced 900 systems for the F-15 under contracts totalling over $800 million and the US Air Force plans to equip over 400 F-15s with the new version. Production of these units is planned to begin in late 1984.

CONTRACTOR

Northrop Corporation, Defence Systems Division, 600 Hicks Road, Rolling Meadows, Illinois 60008, USA.

4369.393
AN/ALQ-136 JAMMER

The AN/ALQ-136 is an airborne jamming system designed for helicopters operating in the tactical role. Its primary role is to protect helicopters against anti-aircraft missile radar systems and operates in the I/J band. It is intended only as a short term jammer to enable the aircraft to carry out a mission from a low-

level approach and to 'pop-up' and complete its operational role before the hostile radar can initiate countermeasures.

The system consists of three units: a control unit, two spiral antennas (one each for transmit and receive) and a transmitter/receiver. The latter analyses received signals and responds with the appropriate deception jamming. When the helicopter

is illuminated by a hostile radar, the jammer automatically operates, analyses the received pulses and provides the necessary electronic counter-measures.

The entire system weighs approximately 18 kg and is a microprocessor-based system, software programmable and designed for future expansion requirements.

STATUS
Approximately 600 systems are being procured by the US Army, and the system has been evaluated by the US Marine Corps for its AH-1T helicopters.

CONTRACTOR
ITT Avionics Division, Nutley, New Jersey, USA.

AN/ALQ-136 receiver/transmitter

4669.393
AN/ALQ-137 AIRBORNE JAMMER
The AN/ALQ-137 is an updated version of the AN/ALQ-94 and fills the self-protection jammer role for the F/FB-111 and EF-111A aircraft of the US Air Force. It is a power-managed deception jammer using a wide-band crystal-video set-on receiver and can be operated in three modes: repeater, CW noise and transponder. The system is broken down into three subsystems covering E/F, G/H and I/J bands. A pulse power of more than 1 kW is provided at 4 to 5 per cent duty cycle, with a power output on CW of 100 watts. Jamming techniques available include RGPO, VGPO, jets mode and selective range jamming. The jammer response time is approximately 100 nanoseconds with a memory duration of about 2·5 microseconds. The AN/ALQ-137 works in conjunction with the AN/ALR-62 radar warning receiver (**4377.393**).
STATUS
In production
CONTRACTOR
Sanders Associates Inc, Daniel Webster Highway South, Nashua, New Hampshire 03060, USA.

3548.393
AN/ALQ-140 IR COUNTERMEASURES SET
The AN/ALQ-140 is an internally mounted IR countermeasures equipment for the protection of F-4 aircraft from attack by heat-seeking missiles. It is generally similar in operation to the ALQ-147, Hot Brick, IR deception jammer equipment (**3545.393**) but in this instance it is carried in the tail of the F-4 aircraft in the tail parachute door position. The IR source is ceramic and it is believed to be electrically heated.
STATUS
Production.
CONTRACTOR
Sanders Associates Inc, 95 Canal Street, Nashua, New Hampshire 03061, USA.

4367.353
AN/ALQ-142 ESM SYSTEM
The AN/ALQ-142 is a lightweight, high performance ESM system which is designed for helicopters, marine patrol aircraft and small vessels (fast patrol boats, etc). The system consists of three variants; ASW operations, surface ship surveillance and missile targetting, and airborne area surveillance and missile targetting. Each system has been designed to fulfil a specific mission role.
The ASW operations variant provides real-time identification and bearing of surveillance radars and their associated platforms. It is the basic helicopter configuration to which modules can be added for increased performance. Sorting techniques are used to detect, identify and analyse all electromagnetic radiation from aircraft and surface vessels in the tactical area.
The surface targetting variant is formed by the addition of receiver modules. This allows surveillance and missile targetting from a small surface ship at ranges beyond the radar horizon, including the detection of long range cruise missiles.
The maritime patrol variant provides additional frequency coverage for assessment of enemy forces from the air. Airborne area surveillance and missile targetting use the receivers in the ALQ-142 to identify emissions at extended ranges, to measure its bearing accurately and provide targetting information for air/sea and surface/surface missile systems.
CONTRACTOR
Raytheon Company, Electromagnetic Systems Division, PO Box 1542, Goleta, California 93017, USA.

3546.393
AN/ALQ-144 IR COUNTERMEASURES SET
The AN/ALQ-144 is an electrically powered infra-red countermeasures set to provide helicopters with protection against heat-seeking missiles. It is an omni-directional system consisting of a cylindrical source surrounded by a highly efficient modulation system to confuse the seeker of the incoming missile. The electrically heated source is ceramic, and the complete equipment weighs less than 14 kg.

CHARACTERISTICS
Weight: 12·7 kg (transmitter)
0·3 kg (control unit)
Size: 24·1 × 24·1 × 33·6 cm (transmitter)
Field of view: 360° azimuth
STATUS
Two production contracts have been awarded: 822 sets for the US Army for use on AH-1S and UH-60 helicopters and 182 sets for the US Marine Corps for use on AH-1J, AH-1T and UH-1N. Deliveries commenced in March 1981.
CONTRACTOR
Sanders Associates Inc, 95 Canal Street, Nashua, New Hampshire 03061, USA.

3550.393
AN/ALQ-146 IR COUNTERMEASURES SET
The AN/ALQ-146 infra-red countermeasures set is a lightweight system for the protection of US Navy CH-46D heavy lift, and other, helicopters. Two IR jamming sources are mounted on the helicopters, one forward above the cockpit and the other aft above the tail door opening of the CH-46D. The IR source is understood to be ceramic, probably electrically heated. The air crew is provided with some measure of control over the modulation employed, as well as over other equipment functions.
STATUS
Produced for US Navy. Now updated and replaced by the AN/ALQ-144 (**3546.393**).
CONTRACTOR
Sanders Associates Inc, 95 Canal Street, Nashua, New Hampshire 03061, USA.

3545.393
AN/ALQ-147A IR COUNTERMEASURES SET
The AN/ALQ-147A(V)2 is one of two IR countermeasures equipments referred to under the code name 'Hot Brick'. It is a directable system that fits the aft end of the 150-gallon external fuel tank of the OV/RV-1D aircraft. Because of limited electrical power resources on these aircraft, the ALQ-147A employs a fuel-fired source, and only 200 W of electrical power is required. The heart of the system is a ceramic IR source which is heated by burning a small amount of JP fuel with ram air. The IR output from the source is then modulated mechanically to provide the jamming signal. The system contains a covert filter to minimise the visible emissions, and it cannot be seen at night.
The system is modular in that the fuel tank or modulator can be removed by means of a single clamp. It is this feature which facilitated the later development of a 'stand-alone' version designated AN/ALQ-147(V)1. This is a podded equipment specifically developed for use on the OV-1D aircraft, which is thereby enabled to carry IR protection without the need for heavy external fuel tanks.

AN/ALQ-147A(V)2 infra-red countermeasures set, Hot Brick, mounted at rear end of 150-gallon fuel tank

STATUS
Production.
CONTRACTOR
Sanders Associates Inc, 95 Canal Street, Nashua,
New Hampshire 03061, USA.

AN/ALQ-147A(V)1 pod mounted version of Red Brick IR countermeasures set

---

4678.393
AN/ALQ-149 JAMMER
The AN/ALQ-149 is a communications jammer intended to replace the AN/ALQ-92 equipment on the US Navy EA-6B Prowler aircraft. The system is still in the early development stage after a competitive evaluation between two teams of contractors. No other details are available.
STATUS
A full scale engineering development was authorised in mid-1983 under a contract worth $43 million to a joint Sanders/ITT team. Development and trials are expected to last for two to three years and a production contract is expected in 1986.
CONTRACTORS
Sanders Associates Inc, 95 Canal Street, Nashua, New Hampshire 03061, USA.
　ITT Avionics Division, Nutley, New Jersey, USA.

4370.353
AN/ALQ-150 ESM RECEIVER
The AN/ALQ-150 is a tactical airborne ESM system used as part of the Cefire Tiger programme of electronic warfare. It is employed against multi-channel communication transmitters and has an electronic support measures capability for integration with jamming systems. The complete system is deployed in four modular units in three US Army RU-21 aircraft and can be used against frequency division multiplexed (FDM), frequency modulated (FM) and time division multiplexed (TDM) emitters.

The Cefire Tiger airborne ESM system interfaces with the Le Fox Grey control processing centre and the forward control and analysis centre to provide overall control of all ECM missions on a real-time basis. The control processing centre has wide-band data links which communicate with up to three Cefire Tiger systems simultaneously. The effective radiated power is from 3 to 10 kW, depending on frequency. Frequency ranges per system are:
(1) Aircraft 1: 60 to 115 and 1500 to 9000 MHz
(2) Aircraft 2: 115 to 480 MHz
(3) Aircraft 3: 450 to 1500 MHz.
STATUS
The first units were due to be deployed by mid-1984.

4371.393
AN/ALQ-151 AIRBORNE EW SYSTEM
The AN/ALQ-151, otherwise known as Quick Fix, is a direction finding, intercept and electronic countermeasures system fitted on standard US Army helicopters. It operates in the frequency range from 2 to 76 MHz and has a jamming output capability of 40 to 150 W. The system can interface with all other tactical army aircraft using a secure communications link, and also interfaces with the operations centre.

Quick Fix is normally deployed in the US Army Blackhawk utility helicopter EH-60B and is operational up to 10 000 feet under nearly all weather conditions. Three units are normally deployed with division support companies and two units with brigade support companies. As a communications jammer, the AN/ALQ-151 has been designed to be interoperable with the US Army Aircraft Survivability Equipment (ASE) and will be mounted on the same platform.

CONTRACTOR
ESL Incorporated, Sunnyvale, California, USA.

3384.393
AN/ALQ-153 TAIL WARNING SET (TWS)
The ALQ-153 tail warning set (TWS) is a rear-looking pulse doppler radar that detects and discriminates approaching missiles and aircraft. It is a range-gated doppler system which automatically ejects chaff and flares against the most dangerous threats.

The system is currently under full-scale production

AN/ALQ-153 tail warning set in B-52 aircraft configuration

for USAF B-52 aircraft with 321 systems scheduled to be delivered up to 1985. The first two systems were delivered in April 1980, and have been installed in B-52 aircraft. System ground tests were completed successfully in 1976. Competitive 'fly-off' testing against the AIL ALQ-154 in a B-52 aircraft began in 1976 and was completed in 1977, after which Westinghouse was selected for full-scale production.

The TWS is also in development for F/FB-111 aircraft. Other aircraft under consideration are USAF F-15 and A-10, and US Navy A-6 and F-14. A slightly modified version is being developed for use in the B-1B.

STATUS
Currently production is six to eight systems per month for the B-52 aircraft.

CONTRACTOR
Westinghouse Defense and Electronics Center, Electronic Warfare Division, Baltimore, Maryland 21203, USA

3552.393
AN/ALQ-155 COUNTERMEASURES SET

The AN/ALQ-155 countermeasures set forms part of the up-grading programme to improve the defence avionics of the USAF B-52 bomber fleet. The system consists of several airborne set-on receivers, a signal processor, and an electronic warfare system control unit. This improved computer-managed system will provide greater protection against defensive weapons by automatically jamming radar signals. It automatically controls and directs the radiated power of improved ECM jamming transmitters, and concentrates all available energy against the most lethal threat.

STATUS
Northrop's Defense Systems Division received a

contract in 1975 for design and development of the B-52's improved ECM system, and the award of a production contract followed flight test evaluation and qualification. In January 1978 a $27·9 million USAF production contract for the ALQ-155(V) was awarded to Northrop and subsequent contracts have brought this total to more than $160 million. Additional upgrades of the system are planned for the 1984-1994 period.

CONTRACTOR
Northrop Corporation, Defence Systems Division, 600 Hicks Road, Rolling Meadows, Illinois 60008, USA.

Dual heat exchanger element of new AN/ALQ-155(V) computer-managed ECM set for USAF B-52 bomber

3547.393
AN/ALQ-156 MISSILE DETECTION SYSTEM

The AN/ALQ-156 missile detection system was developed to provide a means of automatically triggering the ejection of IR decoys from an aircraft (specifically the CH-47C helicopter and RU-21 aircraft) in response to an attack by heat-seeking missile(s).

The ALQ-156 is a pulse doppler radar which effectively creates a continuous protection ring around the aircraft and senses an incoming missile. This results in automatic triggering of an XM-130 dispenser to eject IR decoy flares. The system evaluates the threat by comparison of the closing rates and other parameters, and is stated to be capable of operating in close proximity to the ground without detriment to the performance. The equipment consists of four units: a receiver/transmitter, a control indicator, and two identical antennas. The complete installation weighs about 20 kg.

The use of a microprocessor and a programmable digital signal processor permits rapid adaptation of the ALQ-156 from a helicopter to a fixed-wing aircraft configuration and it can be used in conjunction with other systems such as laser or radar warning receivers.

AN/ALQ-156 missile detection set hardware

DEVELOPMENT
The initial prototype was developed by the Sandia Corporation, but Sanders was subsequently awarded a competitive contract to carry out full-scale engineering development.

CHARACTERISTICS
Weight: 20 kg
Size: 51·8 × 25·9 × 19·3 cm (receiver/transmitter)

MTBF: 300 h
Power: 350 W

STATUS
Production. The system is being considered for installation in A-6E aircraft.

CONTRACTOR
Sanders Associates Inc, 95 Canal Street, Nashua, New Hampshire 03061, USA.

4375.393
AN/ALQ-157 INFRA-RED COUNTERMEASURES SYSTEM

The AN/ALQ-157 is designed to provide military helicopters with protection against enemy infra-red heat-seeking missiles, and is being manufactured for the US Naval Air System Command for use on large troop-carrying helicopters. Installation is simple and straightforward and the system is adaptable to other types of aircraft. The accompanying illustration shows installation on the sail of a helicopter. Two units are installed, one on each side of the sail.

The AN/ALQ-157 installation consists of four basic sub-systems: two transmitters, a control power supply, EMI filter assembly and a pilot's control indicator. A switch on the control power supply allows selection of any one of up to five jamming codes pre-programmed into the microprocessor.

Additional codes can be pre-programmed as new threats are defined. The microprocessor also directs all operational sequences of the system.

The system ensures full-time protection against threats, easy access to all components and employs built-in test circuits to perform operational readiness tests automatically.

STATUS
Operational testing has been completed successfully and production commenced in December 1983 under a $5 million contract to fit the system to US Navy CH-46 helicopters.

CONTRACTOR
Loral Electro-Optical Systems, 300 North Halstead Street, Pasadena, California 91107, USA.

AN/ALQ-157 system installed on sail of heavy-lift helicopter

3034.393
AN/ALQ-161 B-1 RFS/ECM SUB-SYSTEM

The US Air Force announced the selection of AIL Division in late 1973 to develop the defensive avionics sub-system for the B-1 strategic bomber.

The $70 million cost-plus-incentive-free contract award is for the development, fabrication, and testing of the B-1 radio frequency surveillance/electronic countermeasures sub-system. This sub-system is designed to monitor radio frequencies and employ electronic countermeasures. AIL Division is one of

three other Air Force contractors presently working on the B1 development programme. These include Rockwell International Corporation of Los Angeles, system contractor; General Electric Company of Evendale, Ohio, engine contractor, and The Boeing Company of Seattle, avionics sub-systems interface contractor.

The Air Force Systems Command's Aeronautical Systems Division at Wright-Patterson Air Force Base, Ohio, is responsible for overall B-1 system development.

The B-1's defensive avionics system is intended to counter surface-to-air missile, anti-aircraft, and air-to-air missile fire control radars and to degrade by noise jamming early warning and GCI radars.

A single AN/ALQ-161 system contains and controls a large quantity of jamming transmitters and antennas. In addition to the jamming hardware, a sophisticated control system managed by a network of digital computers is employed. This can jam signals from many radars simultaneously. The numerous jamming chains are deployed around the periphery of the B1-B to jam signals in any frequency band coming from any direction.

Integrated with the jamming control system is a network of separate receiving antennas, receivers and processors which act as the 'ears' of the system. By means of this receiving subsystem, new signals can be picked up, identified and then jammed, with optimised jamming techniques, in a fraction of a second. One of the advantages of having the receiving function completely integrated with the jamming function is that it allows the receiving system to detect new signals and continue to monitor old signals while jamming in the same frequency band. A special subsystem allows this to be accomplished by monitoring the output of the jamming transmitters and continuously adjusting the receivers.

The AN/ALQ-161 system is made up of over 100 units which, exclusive of cabling, displays and controls, weighs approximately 5200 lbs (2363 kg) and consumes about 120 kW of power in the 'all-out'

jamming mode.

An operator will have displays and controls by which he can monitor and direct the system. The computer will perform the power management role based on radar threats sensed by the RFS system and pre-stored information about the threats.

Terminal threat jammers, phased-array antennas and other hardware are being provided by sub-contractors.

USAF and AIL Division are relying on two features to extend the life and effectiveness of the ALQ-161 system against changing threats in the future in a way that was technologically impossible with the original B-52 ECM hardware. The equipment uses versatile components capable of being adapted. Because the system is digital, it can be software-controlled, permitting changes to be made more easily. Modulation techniques can be added or modified, for example, by changes in the software or by the addition of plug-in modules. There is also growth

space to accommodate hardware growth if this becomes necessary. A tail warning function is being integrated.

STATUS

The AN/ALQ-161 is in the development stage and two contracts totalling more than $657 million for full-scale development and initial production were awarded to Eaton Corporation in mid-1982. The development contract for $198·8 million includes modifying one of the original B-1A bombers and conducting a flight test programme. The production contract totals $458·9 million for building the initial systems. Delivery of the first line replaceable units began in February 1984. A $9 million contract was awarded to Eaton in September 1983 to incorporate a tail-warning function into the system.

CONTRACTOR

Eaton Corporation, AIL Division, Deer Park, Long Island, New York 11729, USA.

4373.393
AN/ALQ-162(V) ELECTRONIC COUNTERMEASURES SET

The AN/ALQ-162(V) is a new, compact radar jammer for US Navy and Army aircraft being developed by Northrop under a contract to the US Navy. The programme has a total sales potential, including NATO and overseas markets, of $300 million.

This new system makes use of advanced jamming techniques. It is software programmable to meet new threats and includes built-in-test devices to increase maintainability. It can operate autonomously, using its own receiver/processor, in a 'stand-alone' capacity, or in conjunction with a variety of current radar warning receivers. The system is modular for interchangeability of components, and can be configured for internal or pod mounting. Weight of the complete equipment is 35 lb (15·9 kg).

DEVELOPMENT

In January 1980, Northrop won a competition to develop a small, lightweight, receiver/processor controlled radar jamming system to complement the ALQ-126B on US Navy tactical aircraft, and the ALQ-136 on US Army SEMA aircraft. A contract was awarded in December 1979 for 15 engineering development models and production options for 300 systems.

STATUS

US Army testing was completed in 1983 and US Navy operational evaluation was scheduled for completion in May 1984. Production is due to commence in

AN/ALQ-162(V) CW radar jamming equipment

October 1984 with first production units delivered 12 months later. System installation is planned on F-4, F-16, F-18, F-35, A-4, A-7, AV-8, EH-1, EH-60, OV/RV and RC-12 aircraft.

CONTRACTOR

Northrop Corporation, Defense Systems Division, Rolling Meadows, Illinois 60008, USA.

4740.393
AN/ALQ-164 ECM POD

The AN/ALQ-164 is an airborne pod-mounted jamming system for both pulse and CW modes. It is reprogrammable to provide for threat changes and features mid and high band pulse capabilities developed from the AN/ALQ-126 system (**1913.393**). It is also designed to accommodate the AN/ALQ-162 jammer (**4373.393**) in the pod. It is intended for fitment on the centre-line pylon of the AV-8B VTOL aircraft.

CONTRACTOR

Sanders Associates Inc, Daniel Webster Highway South, Nashua, New Hampshire 03060, USA.

3894.393
AN/ALQ-165 AIRBORNE SELF PROTECTION JAMMER

The AN/ALQ-165 Airborne Self Protection Jammer (ASPJ) is the next generation electronic countermeasures system designed for the United States Air Force F-16 and US Navy F-18 tactical aircraft, and also for other fleet aircraft such as the F-14, A-6E/EA-6B and AV-8B. The equipment is being developed jointly by the US Navy and Air Force and will incorporate the latest technology in travelling wave tubes, microwave components and packaging. It can be electrically reprogrammed on the flight line and the built-in-test and modular plug-in design permits rapid replacement of assemblies at the operational level without external test equipment. Weight of the system is between 91 and 123 kg, depending on configuration, and it occupies a space of 2·1 ft³.

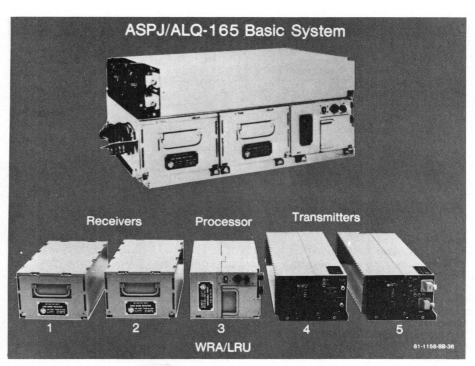

AN/ALQ-165 ASPJ basic system elements

The AN/ALQ-165 has the ability to select automatically the best jamming techniques to use against any given threat, based on the system's own computer data and real-time data of the threat signal from the receiver/processor. The computer software can be modified to accommodate new threats as they arise. The equipment covers the frequency range in only two bands, and is technically expansible to cover a greater frequency range, if required.

The transmitters with the system can jam a large number of threats simultaneously over various ranges and in different modes. The computer selects the power and duty-cycle criteria. An augmented version, with an additional transmitter power-booster is being considered.

It is understood that two configurations are being designed. One of these will be inside the aircraft while the other, a comprehensive power management system, will be installed in a standard AN/ALQ-131 jammer pod. This latter version is for the AV-8B and may be used on other aircraft.

STATUS

An industry team from ITT Avionics Division and Westinghouse Electronic Warfare Division is under contract to the US Navy to develop and build both engineering developments and prototype models for operational testing and evaluation. In March 1982 the two companies received a $22 million contract for engineering and prototype models. Ten engineering development models (EDMs) are due for eventual delivery plus eight comprehensive power management systems. It is understood that eight receiver-processors were ordered from Loral in mid-1983. Extensive reliability and maintenance testing is planned to ensure the readiness of the ASPJ for entry into full production in the mid-1980s, with tests and flight trials scheduled for 1984. Production is due to start in mid-1985 with the first production delivery in late 1986. Potential value of this programme is projected at $3000 million and export licences exist for a number of countries.

CONTRACTORS

Westinghouse Electronic Warfare Division, Baltimore, Maryland 21203, USA.

ITT Avionics Division, Nutley, New Jersey 07110, USA.

4374.353

AN/ALQ-171(V) TACTICAL ECM SYSTEM

The AN/ALQ-171(V) is an electronic countermeasures system developed by Northrop's Defense Systems Division for the US Air Force and friendly nations. The system is available both in a pod version and as a conformal countermeasures system (CCS).

The pod adaptation is mounted on an existing pylon station and is designed for a wide variety of aircraft such as A-7, F-4 and F-16. The CCS is mounted directly on the aircraft fuselage without interfering with any existing weapons or stores stations or hampering the aerodynamic capability of the aircraft. The CCS is designed to fit on existing F-5E/F models as well as the new F-20 Tigershark.

Designed to provide protection against terminal radar threats, the system uses advanced multiple jamming techniques and is fully automatic. The CCS includes a self-contained radar warning receiver, operating over the E to J frequency bands with associated antennas, a programmable system controller, four transmitter groups providing coverage from H to J bands, transmit antennas and a control indicator. It features deception modulation generators and power management.

STATUS

Northrop built and conducted successful laboratory and flight tests of two CCS prototype systems during 1982. In 1983, the conformal countermeasures system prototype programme was completed. Ground tests for the pod-mounted version were also completed in 1983 and flight tests on an F-16 test bed aircraft were due to be completed in early 1984.

CONTRACTOR

Northrop Corporation, Defense Systems Division, Rolling Meadows, Illinois 60008, USA.

AN/ALQ-171(V) pod-mounted on a USAF F-16 aircraft

5693.393

AN/ALQ-172 NOISE DECEPTION JAMMER

This is an advanced ECM system intended for installation in the US Air Force B-52 strategic bomber fleet and is a modified version of the AN/ALQ-117 noise deception jammer currently operational in the B-52G/H fleet. An interim modification of the latter jammer, known as Pave Mint, was due to be flight tested late in 1982.

The improvements incorporated in the AN/ALQ-172 are unknown but are expected to include a threat reprogramming capability (possibly automatic), monopulse deception capability and an improved power management system to enable greater power to be directed against hostile emissions.

STATUS

In development. Flight testing was due to start in early 1984.

CONTRACTOR

ITT Corporation, Avionics Division, Nutley, New Jersey, USA.

4100.393

AN/ALQ-176(V) SUPPORT PAC(V) JAMMER

The Sperry Support Pac(V) is a ten inch (25 cm) diameter, pod-mounted version of lightweight, high powered, affordable jammers designed primarily for tactical ECM support, standoff jamming, and electronic counter-countermeasures training missions. This slim pod is easily mounted on a standard aircraft munitions station and can be powered by either internal aircraft power or self-powered by adding a ram air turbine generator (RAT). The modular design allows the system to be used in either a two- or three-canister configuration. Each canister houses two high-efficiency, high powered voltage tuned magnetron transmitters which were specifically engineered to cover threat radar frequencies from D- to J-bands. Solid-state jammers are available to cover frequencies below 1 GHz. Sperry engineers designed a standard voltage tuned magnetron transmitter to cover different threat frequencies simply by changing the output VTM tube.

Sperry Support Pac (V) in 2-canister configuration with ram air turbine (RAT) electrical supply

This standardised transmitter reduces the quantity of spares necessary to maintain a large number of jammers, thus significantly reducing maintenance and training costs.

CHARACTERISTICS

Frequency coverage: 115·5 GHz
Transmitter power output: 150 – 400 W CW
Modulation: Noise (various)

Weight of transmitter and antenna: 11 kg (each)
Pod input/output power: 2 canister (4 Tx): 3·5 kVA/1·6 kVA; 3 canister (6 Tx): 5 kVA/2·4 kVA
Weights: 2 canister 84 kg (aircraft powered), 89 kg (RAT); 3 canister 114 kg (aircraft powered), 121 kg (RAT)
Diameter: 25 cm
Length: 199 cm (2 canister); 259 cm (3 canister)

STATUS

Support Pac(V) systems have been developed and are currently undergoing tests for US and foreign sales applications. It has now received official US Air Force type designation as the AN/ALQ-176(V)

CONTRACTOR

Sperry Corporation, Electronic Systems, Great Neck, New York 10020, USA.

4009.393
AN/ALQ-178 ECM SYSTEM

The AN/ALQ-178 ECM system is an integrated RWR/ECM suite for the F-16 aircraft. Based upon tested components and techniques, the ALQ-178 provides the F-16 with the automatic countermeasure capability to survive in the increasingly deadly, and sophisticated, hostile air defence environments. The system utilises a central programmable computer for data analysis and system control, with independent microprocessors to direct RWR, display and jamming functions. The wide-band RWR continuously scans the threat radar environment. Detected signals are de-interleaved and identified as to radar type and displayed to the pilot on a daylight viewable CRT, in legible, unambiguous format. The power management algorithm optionally matches the countermeasures to the RWR's constantly changing threat picture. Separate forward and aft jammers are used for maximum spatial coverage. The jammers are accurately set for maximum power output at each victim radar's frequency to maximise ERP and jammer effectiveness. The jammer frequency range provides coverage of the entire threat band while the jammer power is sufficient to counter these radars throughout their lethal area. See **3543.393**.

CONTRACTOR

Loral Electronic Systems, Ridge Hill, Yonkers, New York 10710, USA.

AN/ALQ-178 ECM system units and their location in F-16 aircraft

1917.353
AN/ALR-45 ESM EQUIPMENT

The AN/ALR-45 is an aircraft radar warning receiver which is fitted to most types of US Navy tactical aircraft. It is similar to the earlier APR-25 warning receiver but provides for high-speed, digital processing of threat data as well as having a wider frequency coverage.

Four cavity-backed planar spiral antennas are used, each with its own preamplifier and interface unit linking it to the central receiver and processor.

It is re-programmable in the field, but not in the air.

STATUS

Extensively used by the USN and since by a number of NATO nations, including Denmark and Canada. Production has reached some thousands of sets.

The ALR-45 is due to be replaced by the US Navy with the AN/ALR-67(V) and the ALR-45F. The latter is the processor for the ALR-67(V) and consists of a control indicator and the CP-1293 computer. The first three AN/ALR-45F systems were delivered in April 1983 as part of a $3·6 million contract and an additional 105 sets were due to be delivered by early 1984. An $8·5 million contract was awarded in January 1984 for 55 systems.

CONTRACTOR

Litton Applied Technology, 645 Almanor Avenue, Sunnyvale, California 94088-3478, USA.

AN/ALR-45 digital threat warning receiver system

3035.353
AN/ALR-46 RADAR WARNING SYSTEM

The AN/ALR-46 is a digital threat warning receiver system based on improvements incorporated in the APR-36/37 receiver system. A major conversion in this development was to digital operation by the addition of a Dalmo-Victor DSA-20 processor.

The ALR-46 system is a 2 to 18 GHz, wide-open front-end, crystal video, field programmable system. It detects threats from ground, shipboard, and airborne radar signal sources and provides audio and visual alarms to the aircraft crew. The ALR-46(V)-3 uses a Dalmo Victor processor and an Itek receiver and controller. The ALR-46(V)-6 uses an Itek analyser (analogue processor).

AN/ALR-46 radar warning system

STATUS
In service in US aircraft. Also used by Iran, Korea, Malaysia and Saudi Arabia. The ALR-46(V)-3 has been supplied to Egypt, Portugal, Switzerland, Taiwan, and the USAF.

CONTRACTOR
Litton Applied Technology, 645 Almanor Avenue, Sunnyvale, California 94088-3478, USA.

1862.353

AN/ALR-47 RADAR HOMING AND WARNING SYSTEM

The AN/ALR-47 countermeasures receiving set has been developed for the US Navy's newest ASW aircraft, the S-3A Viking (**1403.302**). In the Viking the ALR-47 obtains emitter signature and directional data which is fed into the aircraft's general-purpose digital computer for display on a multi-function display console. Among new features of the ALR-47 are automatic operation with variable control for frequency band limits, speed of tuning, and signal selection. Fixed antennas are used (four in each wingtip), as are superhet receivers, and a digital processor.

Twin narrow-band receivers are incorporated in each ALR-47, and these incorporate an IF discriminator, out-of-band rejection logic, and voltage controlled oscillators which are tuned directly by computer control. The receiver channels are designed for high sensitivity and there is logarithmic compression of video outputs.

The characteristics of video outputs from four monopulse receiver channels are derived in a signal comparator which converts the data to digital format. All subsequent signal processing is performed digitally under computer control.

The two antenna groups are each comprised of two pairs of cavity-backed planar spiral broad-band antennas, arranged in a near orthogonal disposition for monopulse direction finding.

Control of the ALR-47 system is by means of computer programs which provide for receiver tuning, signal processing, and initiating warnings of significant contacts or known threats identified by stored signal characteristics. Provision is made for human intervention and manipulation of the software in the course of a mission to meet specific operational needs. Examples of this are facilities for filtering out unwanted signals of various types so that the overall processing and display load is reduced. Similarly parameters such as scan speed and frequency scanning limits, PRF, pulse-length, or bearing limits can all be varied at the discretion of the operator.

STATUS
In production for the USN S-3A Viking ASW aircraft.
CONTRACTOR
IBM, Federal Systems Division, 10215 Fernwood Road, Bethesda, Maryland 20034, USA.

1918.353

AN/ALR-50 ECM EQUIPMENT

The AN/ALR-50 is a surface-to-air missile alert and launch warning receiver set. Official details of its frequency coverage range have not been released but the ALR-50's coverage is believed to provide for warning of the radars associated with such Soviet surface-to-air missiles as the latest SA-6 Gainful as well as the earlier SA-2 and SA-3 weapons. It is possible, however, that whereas systems of this type (ALR-50) normally provide the aircrew with some indication of the status of the threat (eg, search, tracking, lock-on, etc), in the case of the SA-6 Gainful the use of as many as five bands for this missile's associated radars may prevent the ALR-50 from providing complete threat status information.

STATUS
In service with various US Navy aircraft types, including A-4, RA-5, A-6, A-7, F-4 and F-8.
CONTRACTOR
Magnavox Government and Industrial Electronics Company, 1313 Production Road, Fort Wayne, Indiana 46808, USA.

1919.353

AN/ALR-52 ECM RECEIVER

The AN/ALR-52 is a multi-band IFM (instantaneous frequency measuring) receiver for airborne or land mobile applications. A naval variant is also produced under the nomenclature AN/WLR-11. Typical systems cover the microwave frequency band from 0·5 to 18 GHz, using receiver modules that cover octave bandwidths. Additional capabilities include provision for selection of a particular signal or frequency band, blanking of signals which are of no further interest, separation of interleaved pulse trains, measurement of radar parameters, analysis of CW as well as pulse signals, and direction-of-arrival (DF) measurement. The complete equipment provides for two operator positions, each equipped with a control unit and a display. The two IFM control units are capable of complete control over any band selected. If the same band is selected by both units, the video processing unit gives priority control to one position only. All intercepted signals, however, are presented on the displays at both positions.

A modified version of the ALR-52 has been developed and deployed, in which one of the operator positions has been replaced by an interface unit to link the IFM receiver with a digital computer. This system also employs a 1 to 18 GHz DF antenna system. The computer uses the data to 'tag' every received pulse with its frequency, pulse width, time of arrival, and azimuth. This information is stored and used to develop an emitter parameter.

STATUS
In operational service.
CONTRACTOR
ARGO Systems, 1069 East Meadow Circle, Palo Alto, California 94303.

3347.353

AN/ALR-56 RADAR WARNING RECEIVER

The AN/ALR-56 radar warning receiver is used with the AN/ALQ-135 internal countermeasures set jamming equipment (**3346.393**) to form the tactical electronic warfare system (TEWS) of the F-15 fighter aircraft.

The main items of equipment comprising the ALR-56 are: processor and low-band receiver (R-1867); high-band receiver (R-1866); countermeasures display (IP-1164); receiver control (C-9428); receiver control (C-9429); power supply (PP-6968); and the antenna system.

The processor and low-band receiver unit contains three major sections; a single-channel low-band superheterodyne receiver, a dual-channel IF section, and a processor.

The low-band receiver is electronically tuned under control of the processor. The dual channel IF section operates with either the high-band dual-channel receiver (R-1866/ALR-56) or the low-band single-channel receiver. Selection of the receiver to operate with the dual-channel IF section is under the control of the processor.

The processor contains a pre-processor and a general purpose digital computer. The pre-processor contains all the video circuits for analysing intercepted signals. It also provides digital outputs to the computer which represent the measured signal parameters. On the basis of these measurements, a digital output is provided to the display and an audio signal generated. The computer also controls all AN/ALR-56 system functions and is software programmable for the expected threat environment.

The solid-state, digitally controlled, dual-channel high-band receiver is capable of scanning an extremely large portion of the electromagnetic spectrum. Its single conversion superheterodyne design provides high sensitivity; the use of dual YIG RF pre-selection affords excellent selectivity and spurious rejection.

High frequency accuracy is obtained through the use of a frequency synthesised local oscillator.

The RF input ports are configured to accept two main antenna inputs to each channel and two additional RF inputs which may be designated to either channel. All switching functions are provided internally.

The receiver is capable of receiving signals over a large dynamic range for analysis and DF measurements. A self-contained precision signal source is provided for calibration and/or BIT over the entire tuning range. Provision is also made for multiplexing out important receiver functions.

All receiver functions are controlled by serially generated NRZ Manchester coded data. The precise data rate also serves as the reference clock for the receiver frequency synthesiser.

On the countermeasures display, rapid threat evaluation for aircraft defensive manoeuvres, at night

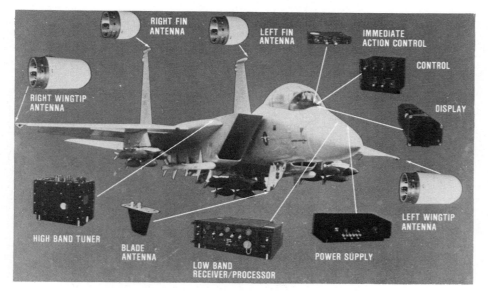

AN/ALR-56 internal countermeasure set equipment, showing positions of main units in F-15 Eagle

or in direct sunlight, is accomplished through automatic intensity control utilising ambient light sensing techniques. Sharp, high contrast, unambiguous alpha-numerics and special symbology allow immediate assessment of the overall tactical threat, without requiring pilot display adjustments as external ambient light fluctuates. Phosphor screen-optical filter matching provides contrast enhancement to overcome direct sunlight contrast degradation.

A range-bearing data presentation is provided with special clutter elimination programs as well as special threat status. Built-in test circuits determine display system malfunction and automatically indicate 'GO' conditions. An integral lighting panel provides control illumination for night time viewing.

The antenna system consists of four circularly polarised spiral antenna assemblies, each within its own radome, and a blade antenna. Collectively this antenna system provides omni-directional acquisition and direction finding over the operating frequency range of the RWR. The four spiral antennas, which cover the high band frequency range, are mounted in a manner that provides 360°

azimuth coverage. DF operation is accomplished under computer control. The blade antenna provides omni-directional coverage of the low-band frequency range.

Of the two receiver control units, one provides for control of the RWR as well as other countermeasure sub-systems. A single switch controls the entire RWR on/off function, and separate switches and relays are provided for the sub-systems under RWR control. Audio tone cues are controlled from this unit also.

The other receiver control panel is for activating in-flight functions that require instant pilot reaction. In addition to countermeasures sub-system mode control, interrogated data readout on this unit can be called up from the sub-systems by means of push-button operation.

CHARACTERISTICS
System functions
(1) programmed frequency search of threat parameters with:
  (a) low-band priority
  (b) look-through capability
  (c) jammer blanking
(2) signal acquisition and sorting

(3) signal analysis
(4) direction finding
(5) establishment of threat priorities
(6) jammer management and look-through
(7) display threat data
Display: CRT, radar type, degree of threat, range readout
Data input rate: 20 Hz
Refresh rate: 66·6 Hz
Contrast ratio: 1:4 (minimum)
High-band receiver: Superhet, dual-channel RF
Low-band receiver/processor: Superhet, dual-channel IF, video processing, GPDC
System weight: 62·6 kg
STATUS
In production and operational on F-15 Eagle aircraft. A major update is under way and is expected to reach the production phase in 1984. Main improvements are reported to be in the processor to cope with threat density and changes. It is believed that prototypes were flight tested in 1982.
CONTRACTOR
Loral Electronic Systems, Ridge Hill, Yonkers, New York 10710, USA.

4376.353

AN/ALR-60 COMMUNICATIONS INTERCEPT AND ANALYSIS SYSTEM

The AN/ALR-60 communications intercept and analysis system is carried on the US Navy EP-3E electronic reconnaissance aircraft and is believed to be used to keep track of the Soviet fleet. It is a huge complex and has multiple operator positions, equipped with video terminals that allow the operator

to randomly access raw audio data and processed text data. Digitally controlled receivers are operated on a priority basis.

Only seven systems have been built, as far as is known. They use the latest advances in computer technology to provide the maximum information to the operators. Computer formatted CRT pages, and overall control by the computer of the receiving, recording, priority and processing functions, are

used to ensure more complete coverage of all signals intercepted.
STATUS
In operational service.
CONTRACTOR
GTE Sylvania, Electronic Systems Group, 100 Ferguson Drive, Mountain View, California 94040, USA.

4377.393

AN/ALR-62(V) RADAR WARNING SYSTEM

The AN/ALR-62(V) is the standard radar warning receiver used in the US Air Force F/FB-111 and EF-111A aircraft. The ALR-62(V)-3 is used in the FB-111 aircraft while the ALR-62(V)-4 is installed in the EF-111A electronic warfare aircraft being produced for the USAF. The ALR-62(V)-4 represents

a major part of the EF-111A terminal threat warning system. It analyses and monitors radar threats and has the capacity to 'look-through' high power jamming from the AN/ALQ-99 transmitters (**1908.393**) carried on the aircraft.

The AN/ALR-62(V) is a third generation equipment which evolved from the AN/APS-109 radar homing and warning system and consists of forward and aft

receivers, an antenna system, a digital signal processor and cockpit-mounted threat indicator and countermeasures control units.
STATUS
In operational service.
CONTRACTOR
Dalmo Victor Operations, Bell Aerospace Textron 1515 Industrial Way, Belmont, California 94002, USA.

4378.393

AN/ALR-64 COMPASS SAIL WARNING SYSTEM

The AN/ALR-64 Compass Sail warning system is fitted to various USAF tactical aircraft, including the F-4, A-10 and F-16. The equipment provides C/D band direction finding capability and consists of a

multiple receiver intercept unit and a direction finding antenna array. The system is designed to provide information on missile guidance systems associated with hostile surface-to-air missiles. As a missile launch alert receiver, the AN/ALR-64 forms part of the USAF Compass Tie radar warning suite. The receiver

also forms part of the AN/ALR-69 radar warning system (**4378.353**).
CONTRACTOR
Dalmo Victor Operations, Bell Aerospace Textron, 1515 Industrial Way, Belmont, California 94002, USA.

3642.353

AN/ALR-66 SERIES RADAR WARNING RECEIVERS

The AN/ALR-66(V)1 is a fully programmable radar warning receiver that incorporates a digital computer specially designed to provide rapid, unambiguous identification of emitters in complex signal environments. Unique identification of all detected emitters, both friendly, non-hostile and hostile, is given by alpha-numeric symbols on a high-brightness CRT display. The system incorporates an extensive emitter library capable of storing more than 100 emitters and over 1000 operating modes. Up to 15 of these emitters can be displayed at one time on the CRT display, and direction-finding accuracy is better than 15°. True or relative bearing display of DF information can be selected, and other features of the system include: an audio alarm under computer control; operator-initiated emitter hand-off; and 64 specialised computer modes under operator control.

Suitable interfaces are available for use of the ALR-66 with other systems such as chaff or flare dispensers, telemetry links, recorders, and serial and parallel input/output for jammers. The processor memory capacity is 8000 words E²PROM/RAM/ROM (68 K words total capacity), and it is able to perform 1·2 million operations per second.

A variety of system assembly configurations are available to satisfy a wide range of installation and mission requirements. These include fighter aircraft, attack aircraft, helicopters and fast patrol boats.

The AN/ALR-66(VE) is the fighter aircraft

AN/ALR-66(V)2 radar warning receiver

configuration of the AN/ALR-66 series and provides enhanced performance and extended versatility due to the introduction of E²PROM devices in its computer memory. It is designed as a 'drop-in' replacement/upgrade of older systems in combat

aircraft. The use of E²PROM devices allows complete memory reprogramming in 90 seconds on the flight line.

The AN/ALR-66(V)2 is a recent development for the US Navy and is an important enhancement in capability for its multimission aircraft. The system forms an integral part of its ocean surveillance systems and can be used on offensive as well as defensive missions. Derived from the AN/ALR-66(V)1, the AN/ALR-66(V)2 provides extremely advanced capabilities in such areas as precision DF accuracy, exceptionally high sensitivity for OTH detection, precise frequency measurement, advanced signal processing concept coupled with expanded data memory, multimode operator-interactive display and controls, precision emitter parameter measurement, capability to integrate with other aircraft primary sensors and E²PROM in-flight reprogramming capability. The ALR-66(V)2 is in production and in worldwide operational service with the US Navy.

CHARACTERISTICS

Receiver type: Crystal video

Frequency coverage: Continuous over E to J bands; CW detection; C & D band detection available

Azimuth coverage: 360°

Emitter types: all pulsed, pulse doppler & CW; known and unknown

DF accuracy: Better than 15°

Shadow time: 2 μs

Emitter storage: More than 100; more than 1000 operating modes

Weight: 27 kg; 29·2 kg (ALR-66(VE))

Power consumption: 400 W

MTBF: Over 500 h

STATUS

In production for the US Navy Lamps Mk1 (SH-2) helicopters, and for other navies on HSS-2 and Sea King helicopters. (VE) version on US and other countries' fighters.

AN/ALR-66 (V)1 radar warning receiver equipment. ALR-66(VE) is similar but employs different processor and antenna coupler units. The same cavity-backed spiral antenna units are used in both versions

CONTRACTOR

General Instrument Corporation, Government Systems Division, 600 West John Street, Hicksville, New York 11802, USA.

4372.393

AN/ALR-67(V) RADAR WARNING SYSTEM

The AN/ALR-67(V) is a countermeasures warning control system which is the United States Navy's front line threat warning system in tactical aircraft. The programme for development of this system began in March 1975 and is currently in the operational evaluation phase by the US Navy. A subset of the AN/ALR-67 is the AN/ALR-45F which consists of the central digital processor and the azimuth indicator. The AN/ALR-45F system is replacing the AN/ALR-45 equipment currently deployed.

STATUS

In production. Designed for installation in the US Navy F/A-18 Hornet aircraft and for the A-6E and AV-8B. Litton has received contracts totalling over $150 million for the AN/ALR-67V from Australia, Canada and Spain as well as the US Navy.

CONTRACTOR

Litton Applied Technology, 645 Almanor Avenue, Sunnyvale, California 94088-3478, USA.

AN/ALR-67(V) developed by Itek for the US Navy

3525.353

AN/ALR-68 ADVANCED RADAR WARNING SYSTEM

The ALR-68 is a digital threat warning receiver system based on improvements incorporated in the ALR-46 receiver system. A major conversion in this development was to digital operation by the addition of the ATAC (Applied Technology Advanced Computer).

The ALR-68 system is a wide-open front-end, crystal video, field programmable system. It detects threats from ground, shipboard, and airborne radar signal sources, and provides audio and visual alarms to the aircraft crew. The ALR-68(V) with the Itek ATAC also provides in-cockpit threat parameter programming; provides for unambiguous identification; incorporates processing for all guidance techniques; and provides hand-off to tactical ECM systems.

The AN/ALR-68 was developed for the West German Air Force.

STATUS

In production.

CONTRACTOR

Litton Applied Technology, 645 Almanor, Sunnyvale, California 94088-3478, USA.

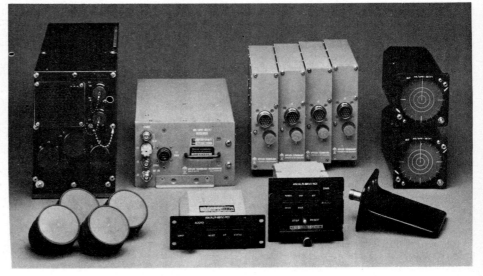

AN/ALR-68 digital threat warning receiver system

4379.353
AN/ALR-69 RADAR WARNING RECEIVER

The AN/ALR-69 radar warning receiver is a development of the earlier versions of the AN/ALR-46 equipment. It is essentially an ALR-46 with a frequency selective receiver system and a low-band missile alert receiver (AN/ALR-64 Compass Sail) (**4378.353**) added to the basic system. The Compass Sail equipment detects and analyses surface-to-air missile guidance emissions and provides a warning to the pilot of the direction and nature of the threat.

The system is designed to activate countermeasures equipment, eg chaff and flare dispensers, automatically and to integrate with on-board jamming systems. A CM-479 signal processor provides control over the system. It accepts video inputs from five receivers and processed information from the frequency selective receiver system, processes all the information and provides the threat warning to the operator. The frequency selective receiver performs warning and direction finding on the incoming signals, resolves ambiguity and manages jamming blanking.

STATUS

The AN/ALR-69 uses Litton Applied Technology receivers and displays, Dalmo Victor signal processor and C/D-band receiver, and Sperry Flight Systems azimuth indicator. It is the basic system for the F-16 aircraft used by Denmark, Israel, Netherlands,

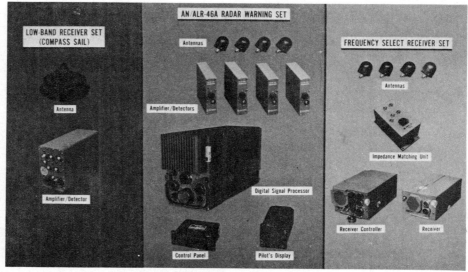

AN/ALR-69 radar warning receiver

Norway and the US Air Force. Litton received a $24 million contract in September 1983 to update the ALR-69 system.

CONTRACTOR

Litton Applied Technology, 645 Almanor Avenue, Sunnyvale, California 94088-3478, USA.

4164.393
AN/ALR-73 PASSIVE DETECTION SYSTEM

The AN/ALR-73 passive detection system (PDS) is an airborne ESM equipment developed for the US Navy's E-2C airborne early warning aircraft. The primary operational roles assigned to the E-2C consist of surveillance of both airborne and surface, hostile and friendly forces; early warning of hostile aircraft in order to protect the fleet; and the exercise of real-time control of the carrier tactical aircraft. The ALR-73 is intended to augment the AEW, and surface, sub-surface, command and control role of the E-2C by enhancing the threat detection and identification performed by the aircraft. It is a completely automatic, computer-controlled, superheterodyne receiver/processing system that communicates directly with the E-2C aircraft command and control central processor. The design of the system was motivated by four major considerations:

(1) very high probability of intercept in dense environments
(2) automatic system operation
(3) high reliability
(4) ease of maintenance.

Features of the ALR-73 which are related to its intercept probability performance include: four quadrant 360° antenna coverage; four independently controlled receivers; dual processor channels; digital closed loop rapid tuned local oscillator. Others concerned with automated system operation are: low false alarm report rate; automatic overload logic; AYK-14 computer adaptively controls hardware; degraded mode operation.

The PDS system can measure DOA, frequency, pulse width and amplitude, and PRI simultaneously. Scan rate information is also available if called for by the central processor. Special emitter tags can also be provided. A functional block diagram of the PDS is shown in Figure 1. The PDS detects and analyses electromagnetic radiations within the microwave spectrum. It sends emitter data reports (pulse width, PRI, DOA, frequency, pulse amplitude and special tags) to the E-2C's central processor via the PDS data processor. The central processor performs the identification function. The PDS immediately reports new emitters to the central processor. It eliminates redundant data on emitters for a programmable period of time, thus significantly reducing the data rate to the central processor. The PDS - a multiband, parallel scan, mission programmable, superheterodyne receiving system - covers the frequency range in four bands through step sweeping. Programmable frequency bands and dwell time permit very rapid surveillance of priority threat bands. Non-priority bands are also monitored, but at a reduced rate. Probability of intercept is increased without sacrificing sensitivity through the detection of both real and image sidebands.

Installation of the ALR-73 on an existing aircraft required a functional and mechanical modularity in

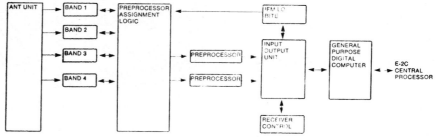

Fig 1 AN/ALR-73 passive detection system block diagram

Antenna
4 quadrant 360° coverage
compact light ground planes
binary beam for accurate DOA

Pre-processors
parallel processing
real-time pulse train de-interleaving
DOA encoding on each pulse
FREQ encoding on each pulse
DOA correlation

Receivers
4 band parallel scan
large dynamic range
rejects sidelobes of high power narrow pulses
logical selection of real or image sideband
no preselection track and slave tuning problem

IFM LO BITE
rapid tuning
self test

Receiver control
INDEP band tuning
INDEP band dwell time control
RCVR sensitivity control

Computer functions
computer operator controlled spectrum surveillance
real-time emitter data processing
new emitter report generation
redundant data removal
BITE.and fault isolation programs
activity-window processing (real image)

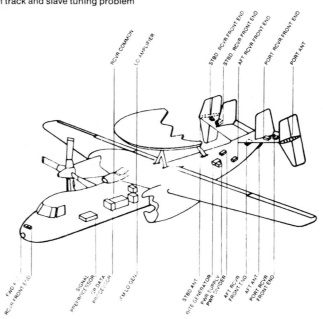

Fig 2 installation of AN/ALR-73 equipment on E-2C aircraft

the system partitioning to facilitate installation on the aircraft (Figure 2). Antenna packages located in the four quadrants of the aircraft provide 360° azimuth coverage. The large phase tolerance of the binary beam minimises the sensitivity of the DOA system to radome distortion and aircraft reflection. All four bands in the normal mode of operation scan through their respective frequency limits independently and simultaneously.

Activity indications may be obtained on any of the four bands. Following an indication of activity, permitted dwell time is increased, and processing of the intercepted signal is started. Dual-signal processing circuits allow intercepted signals in any two of the four bands to be processed simultaneously.

The signal processor is a special-purpose logic processor which performs pulse train separation, DF correlation, band tuning and timing, and built-in test equipment (BITE) logic functions. The signal processor also contains the I/O circuitry necessary for the computer to communicate with both the signal processor and the aircraft central processor. The AYK-14 provides the system control function, data storage, and formatting. Variable frequency coverage, along with variable dwell times and processing times, provide a means for optimising probability to intercept for any given theatre.

The local oscillator system consists of three units: the IFM/LO generator, LO amplifier and LO power divider. The system is unique in that it is extremely fast and accurate. The key unit in the local oscillator system is the instantaneous frequency measurement (IFM) receiver, which samples the LO frequency and converts it to a digital tuning command. This closed loop system permits frequency measurement accuracy, while being largely insensitive to environmental variations. The local oscillator signals from the IFM/LO are amplified by the LO amplifiers to overcome the long LO cable losses, and are then routed, via the power divider, to the various receiver front ends.

STATUS

Production. Litton has received a contract for the update of the EW system on the EA-6B Prowler aircraft of the US Navy. It is expected that this will be based on the AN/ALR-73 system technology. Engineering development models are scheduled for delivery in 1986.

CONTRACTOR

Litton Systems Incorporated, Amecom Division, 5115 Calvert Road, College Park, Maryland 20740, USA.

5694.353
AN/ALR-74 RADAR WARNING SYSTEM

The ALR-74 was formerly known as the AN/ALR-67/69 update and is designed to achieve commonality between US Air Force and Navy radar warning systems. Technologies developed for the AN/ALR-67 system (**4372.393**) are to be used to modify the AN/ALR-69 equipment (**4379.353**). The system consists of five line replaceable units.

STATUS

More than $52 million has been awarded to Litton for this system. Deliveries of prototype models commenced in late 1983 and flight testing in an F-16 began in March 1984. First production contract was due in mid-1984 against a US Air Force requirement for 2600 units.

CONTRACTOR

Litton Applied Technology, 645 Almanor Avenue, Sunnyvale, California 94088-3478, USA.

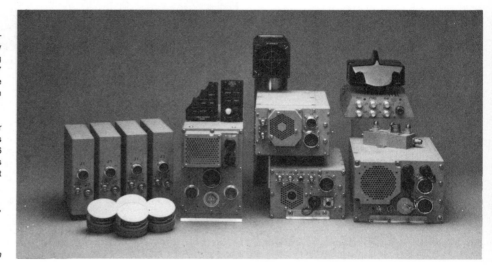

AN/ALR-74 radar warning system

5690.393
AN/ALR-77 ESM SYSTEM

The AN/ALR-77 ESM system for the P-3C Orion anti-submarine warfare aircraft is in the development stage. The antennas are housed in the wing tips of the aircraft. When in operation, the system detects shipborne and airborne radar signals and feeds this information to an on-board computer. The information is then processed and a readout is provided for the crew with such parameters as the signal location and threat potential. The system also provides targetting data for the radar-guided Harpoon missiles.

STATUS

Eight systems are due to be produced during a pre-production period with the first scheduled for delivery in early 1984. Following a successful test period, production schedules call for the manufacture of approximately 275 more systems.

CONTRACTOR

Eaton Corporation, AIL Division, Comac Road, Deer Park, New York 11729, USA.

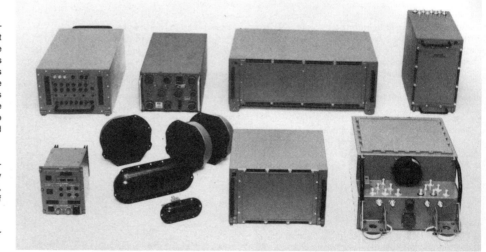

Units of the AN/ALR-77 ESM system

5687.353
ENHANCED RADAR WARNING SYSTEM

This advanced radar warning equipment was developed and manufactured for use by the Federal Republic of Germany Air Force and Navy on the Tornado aircraft. The system uses the Applied Technology Advanced Computer (ATAC) which provides for data collection, sorting, analysis, threat priority and alphanumeric display functions using software algorithms. The emitter library is accessible in the cockpit for user-programming for threat update.

STATUS

In production. Co-production agreements with AEG-Telefunken cover both flight and support systems to include exchange of technical data.

CONTRACTOR

Litton Applied Technology, 645 Almanor Avenue, Sunnyvale, California 94088-3478, USA.

Enhanced radar warning system

3908.353
AN/ALR-606(V)1 AND (VE) RADAR WARNING RECEIVERS

The ALR-606(V)1 and (VE) radar warning receivers are the latest models to be introduced by General Instrument Corporation. They share the same hardware configuration as the ALR-66(V)1 and (VE) respectively (**3642.353**) but software enhancements provide additional facilities. The main items of equipment are a digital signal processor; a high intensity CRT cockpit display; four cavity-backed planar spiral antennas and their associated receivers covering the E to J-bands; a power supply unit; and a control indicator unit. The processor separates and categorises the characteristics of received signals, and unique symbols are presented on the display to indicate the range and bearing of each detected target. Symbol blinking and an audio alarm denote high priority radar types. The operator is able to select standard and special equipment operating modes. Radar data is presented in the form of alpha-numeric symbols which indicate specific parameters such as pulse width, PRF (scale 0 – 9), and frequency band (E, G, I or J).

CHARACTERISTICS
Frequency: E to J-band continuous; C/D band optional
Radar types: All pulse types, CW detection
Receiver type: Crystal video

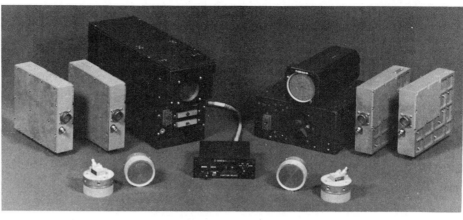
ALR-606(VE) radar warning system

Azimuth coverage: 360°
DF accuracy: Better than 15°
Shadow time: 2 μs
Processor memory: 18 000 words E²PROM/RAM/ROM 68 K total capacity
Radar capacity: 15 symbols can be displayed simultaneously. System signal tracking capacity is 35 radars simultaneously
Weight: 29·22 kg ALV-606(VE); 27 kg ALR-606(V)1

STATUS
The ALR-606(V)1 and –606(VE) were designed specifically for the export market and have been selected by a number of air forces for fighter aircraft fitment.
CONTRACTOR
General Instrument Corporation, Government Systems Division, 600 West John Street, Hicksville, New York 11802, USA.

3544.393
AN/APR-38 WILD WEASEL CIS

The AN/APR-38 control indicator set (CIS), designed to be the "eyes and ears" for the Wild Weasel II aircraft, is composed of seven line replaceable units (LRUs) that receive, display and transmit real-time data, in association with other on-board equipment. It provides the aircraft commander with computer-supplied data that permits him to complete his mission successfully. The system can be operated in either automatic or semi-automatic mode, at the pilot's option. The antenna/receiver systems are installed on the nose and the tail fin.

The CIS receives computer-generated information on detected radar emitters. The digital information is transmitted serially. The highest priority emitters are classified as to threat type, priority of threat, range, magnetic bearing and other pertinent information. A threat library is contained within the central computer.

The CIS can select the types of emitters to be displayed on a PPI display and can be controlled by the computer semi-automatically or manually at the option of the operator.

STATUS
The CIS is currently operational in the F-4G aircraft.
CONTRACTOR
Loral Electronic Systems, Ridge Hill, Yonkers, NY 10710, USA.

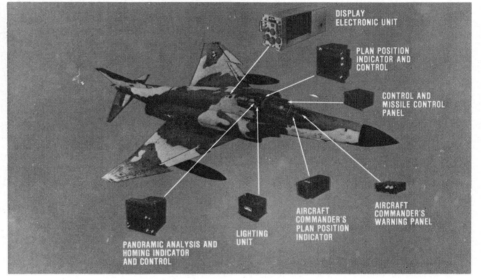
Location of units of APR-38 control indicator set (CIS) in F-4G Wild Weasel aircraft

3542.393
AN/APR-39(V) RADAR WARNING SYSTEM

The AN/APR-39 radar warning receiver equipment provides automatic warning of emitters in the E, F, G, H, I, and most of J radar bands, as well as the appropriate portions of C and D-band radar associated signals. It is intended for use on either fixed-wing or helicopter type aircraft. The equipment provides indications of bearing, identity, and the mode of operation of detected signals, this being displayed on a cockpit indicator. Proportional PRF of displayed signals, and alarm tones, are presented to the aircraft crew via the audio system also.

The equipment of the basic APR-39(V)1 system comprises: two dual video receivers, four spiral cavity-backed antennas, one blade antenna, an indicator unit, a comparator, and a control unit. Without cables and brackets, this weighs about 3·63 kg, and either internal or pod mounting is possible.

An updated version, APR-39(V)2, is in production. In the APR-39(V)2 the comparator is replaced by a Loral CM-480/APR-39(V) digital processor. This performs signal sorting, identification of emitters, bearing computation, and character generation for the presentation of threat details in alpha-numeric

Units of the AN/APR-39(V) system

form on the cockpit display. This unit weighs only 6·5 kg, and incorporates an adaptive noise threshold and angle-gate, programmable pulse repetition interval filters, and coded emitter outputs. A 19 K word programmable read-only memory/random access memory is provided.
DEVELOPMENT
The AN/APR-39(V)1 was designed and developed by

E-Systems. The APR-39(V)2 processor was designed and developed by Loral under contract to the US Army Electronic Command.
STATUS
Both the APR-39(V)1 and APR-39(V)2 are in production. Deliveries of the APR-39(V)1 totalled 5200 systems by January 1984. It has been fitted to 15 aircraft types, as well as fast patrol boats and gun

boats. The West German MoD placed an order in early 1984 for 230 systems for installation on PAH-1 anti-tank helicopters
CONTRACTORS
E-Systems, Memcor Division, PO Box 23500, Tampa, Florida 33630, USA.
    Loral Electronic Systems, Ridge Hill, Yonkers, New York 10710, USA.

5692.353
AN/APR-39A(XE-1) RADAR WARNING SYSTEM
The AN/APR-39A(XE-1) is a new, miniature digital computer-based radar warning system designed to warn helicopter and light fixed-wing aircraft pilots of such threats as surface-to-air missiles, radar controlled anti-aircraft artillery and air-to-air

weapons. It is intended for aircraft operating at very low altitudes and provides both visual and aural warnings when threat radar signals are received and analysed in the computer-based digital processor. The system can be reprogrammed in the field to make it effective against new weapons and changes in existing weapons.

STATUS
Dalmo Victor Operations has been awarded a $7·8 million contract to supply 23 engineering models.
CONTRACTOR
Dalmo Victor Operations, Bell Aerospace Textron, 1515 Industrial Way, Belmont, California 94002, USA.

4010.393
AN/APR-43 TACTICAL RADAR WARNING RECEIVER
The AN/APR-43 is the USN new warning receiver developed under the Compass Sail Clockwise programme to provide operational tactical aircraft with threat warning and identification, direction finding and approximate range information against pulse and CW missile weapon systems. The system consists of two units (weighing approximately 11 kg); a multi-element antenna WRA and multiband receiver WRA containing a crystal video receiver for pulse emitter detection and a superheterodyne receiver for the CW emitters. The APR-43 directly interfaces to the AN/ALR-45 and AN/ALR-45F (ALR-67 processor) warning receivers and defensive jammers AN/ALQ-126 and AN/ALQ-162 to form the USN tactical aircraft ECM protection system. The APR-43 also contains those ALQ-162 antenna output elements required for CW jamming.
STATUS
In production
CONTRACTOR
Loral Electronic Systems, Ridge Hill, Yonkers, New York 10710, USA.

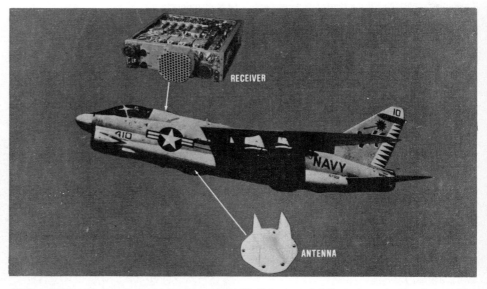

US Navy A-7 Corsair aircraft showing location of AN/APR-43 Compass Sail Clockwise tactical warning receiver and its antenna

---

4381.353
AN/APR-44 RADAR WARNING RECEIVER
This is a series of warning receivers designed to provide warning to the pilot of continuous wave (CW) threats from the SA-6 Gainful missile. The equipment provides a visual and audio alert signal whenever a CW threat emission is received in the 14·5 to 16·5 GHz frequency passband created by an input filter.

The system comprises an omni-directional antenna with vertical polarisation; a receiver containing an RF filter, detector limited switch assembly, video amplifier, processing and output circuitry; and a control panel. The receiver is an RF-chopped, crystal-video unit.
DEVELOPMENT
The system was developed as a result of a crash

programme during the 1973 Middle East war and made use of television chassis, cables and low-cost antennas. The system is to be installed in AH-1J and AH-1T helicopters.
CONTRACTOR
American Electronic Laboratories Incorporated, PO Box 552, Lansdale, Pennysivania 19446, USA.

3365.353
CMR-500B WARNING RECEIVER
The CMR-500B is a small, low-cost warning receiver, designed to detect CW signals. The warning receiver provides a visual and aural output of detected CW RF signals within the frequency range determined by an input filter. The CMR-500B is a modification of the AN/APR-42 (CMR-400) warning receiver (**3364.353**) and is electrically interchangeable and compatible with the AN/APR-42 for full threat detection capability. The system consists of the following three parts: monopole antenna, providing omni-directional vertically polarised coverage; receiver, which contains an RF filter, detector limiter switch, video amplifier, processing and output circuitry; control panel containing alert indicator lamp, ON/OFF volume control, and phone jack.
    The AEL Model AOS-1543 antenna is an omni-directional vertically polarised antenna, designed to mount on any flat, horizontal surface on the underside of an aircraft fuselage. When mounted on the conductive ground plane the antenna provides coverage in the solid angle defined by an elevation sector 50° wide and omni-directional in azimuth. The gain is 3·5 dB at the beam peak which occurs 15 to 25°

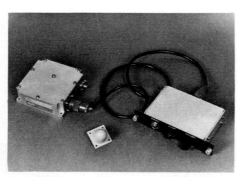

CMR-500B CW radar warning equipment

below the horizon as a function of the ground plane shape.
    The receiver is an RF-chopped, crystal video type with a CW sensitivity of –45 dBm. The receiver consists of a bandpass filter followed by an RF switch/detector module (MIC format), a linear video amplifier and processing circuitry. The output of the video amplifier is routed to a comparator, and then to the processing logic where it is compared to the RF

chopping signal to detect the presence of a CW signal. The processing circuitry provides a 3 kHz audio output, a 1·5 kHz logic output, an alert lamp driver, and a logic blink signal (2 Hz), upon reception of a CW signal. The receiver RF frequency is restricted by the bandpass filter to the frequencies of interest. Special pulse suppression circuitry is incorporated in the receiver to prevent false alarms. A power supply regulator is integral with the receiver for operation from 28 V DC aircraft power.
    The incorporation of a control panel is optional, determined by the mission requirement. The control panel provides an alert light indicator and a phone jack for a headset for alert aural indication. The control panel also provides an ON/OFF switch and two interface cables.
CHARACTERISTICS
Receiver frequency and bandwidth: Selectable
Sensitivity: –45 dBm (minimum)
Max RF input level: 1 W CW (integral limiter)
Receiver dimensions: 91 × 91 × 33 mm
Receiver weight: 354 g
CONTRACTOR
American Electronic Laboratories Inc, PO Box 552, Lansdale, Pennsylvania 19446, USA.

3893.053
DALMO VICTOR MK III MINIATURE DIGITAL RADAR WARNING SYSTEM

The Dalmo Victor Mk III Mini-RW system is specifically designed for helicopter, light aircraft, and fast patrol boat use. It features complete, unambiguous threat warning, with alpha-numeric threat display. It is lightweight, uses little power, is small, and inexpensive.

The DV Mk III consists of a digital signal processor fed by threat signals derived from wideband antennas and receivers. The processor is microprogrammable, with erasable PROM memories that can be reprogrammed for changing threat parameters. The system presents threat data in alpha-numeric symbols on either a liquid-crystal display or a standard CRT. The LCD provides high intensity for undiminished effectiveness even in direct sunlight.

The solid-state processor permits future growth through software reprogrammability. This miniature solid-state package combines high reliability with utmost utility and low cost. There is an integral, continuous self-test function, plus operator-initiated self-test and an audio alarm interface is provided.

STATUS
In production. (Also see KATIE – **5734.353**).

CONTRACTOR
Dalmo Victor Operations, Bell Aerospace Textron, 1515 Industrial Way, Belmont, California 94002, USA.

Dalmo Victor Mk III digital radar warning system equipment

3892.363
ALR-46A DIGITAL SIGNAL PROCESSOR

The ALR-46A is a digital signal processor designed as a direct replacement for the analogue, hardwired type of analyser used in radar homing and warning systems (RHAW) such as the ALR-45, APR-25, APR-36, and APR-107. The ALR-46A is interposed between the existing RHAW receiver(s) and threat display and bearing indicators, and no aircraft modifications are called for. A major benefit claimed for this equipment is the improved presentation of information on the RHAW azimuth indicator. In place of the conventional families of radial lines for each emitter detected, the ALR-46A provides alpha-numeric symbols for each class of contact, and the digital system permits priority allocation by push-button so that overlapping threats may be separated and unwanted signals cleared from the display. The use of digital processing offers another significant advantage in that changes in threat signatures that have been detected by Elint operations can be inserted rapidly into the RHAW, with far less delay than is possible with hardwired, analogue analysers.

STATUS
In production for the USAF.

CONTRACTOR
Dalmo Victor Operations, Bell Aerospace Textron, 1515 Industrial Way, Belmont, California 94002, USA.

4742.393
AN/ASQ-171 AIRBORNE ELINT SYSTEM

The AN/ASQ-171 is an airborne electronic intelligence gathering system fitted to the US Navy's EP-3E ECM aircraft. Very little information has been released on this equipment but it is believed to have the capability of detecting backlobe radiation at long distances. It is understood to operate from A- to J-bands, with a capability of extension to K-band. The system can sort and track signals in a dense ECM environment and can carry out automatic search and analysis over the complete spectrum at the same time that detailed threat analysis of previous signals is taking place.

CONTRACTOR
IBM, Federal Systems Division, 10215 Fernwood Road, Bethesda, Maryland 20034, USA.

3543.393
RAPPORT ECM SYSTEMS

The Rapport II ECM system was developed for the Belgian Air Force Mirage V aircraft. It provides pilot warning and automatic, optimal countermeasures required to survive the present day and future hostile air defences. The system weighs less than 100 kg, and consists of separate RWR and jammer sub-systems. The RWR, which includes a programmable core memory computer, provides power management capability required for optimal use of the jammer sub-system. Functionally, the RWR provides the means to sample and sort the environment. It uses a programmable digital processor for all signal analysis, and provides the pilot with an easily readable, unambiguous warning display. The power management capability, incorporated in the RWR processor, matches the countermeasures response to the constantly changing threat picture, for an optimal jamming response. The jammer sub-system, under RWR control, provides the actual response to the hostile radar environment. To conserve jamming power and maximise ERP, the jammers are accurately set to the exact frequencies of the victim radars. The jammer frequency range provides coverage of all threat radars, while its power output is sufficient to counter these radars at lethal range.

A development of the system, known as Rapport III, is being produced for the F-16 aircraft ordered by the Belgian Air Force. This latest version is an internal integrated EW system having both radar warning and jamming functions controlled by a central processor, and is described under entry **4009.393** (AN/ALQ-178)

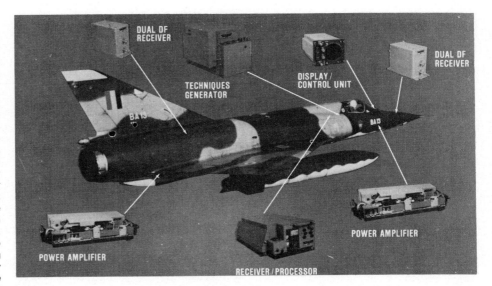

Rapport II ECM equipment and its location in Mirage V aircraft

STATUS
The Rapport II system is operational with Mirage V aircraft of the Belgian Air Force. Loral is developing Rapport III for the Belgian F-16 aircraft under contract, and also received in September 1983 an $88 million contract from an unidentified country to fit Rapport III into its F-16s.

CONTRACTOR
Loral Electronic Systems, Ridge Hill, Yonkers, NY 10710, USA.

4160.393
ARI 18240/1 AEW NIMROD ESM

A new airborne ESM (electronic support measures) equipment has been developed for the AEW3 (airborne early warning) version of the British Nimrod aircraft, under the designation ARI 18240/1. Few details have been cleared for publication but the main items and their approximate locations on the aircraft can be seen from the adjacent photograph.

Special wingtip pods were built by British Aerospace to house the 16 cavity-backed planar spiral antennas and the two front-end receivers (LRU-1). Two other line-replaceable units (LRU-2 and LRU-3) are housed in the fuselage. These probably include the signal processors and comparator circuitry, as well as providing the requisite interfaces with the sensor elements and receivers and the associate control and display facilities. The last of these facilities almost certainly includes provision for integrating ESM data with that from other sources on the aircraft's main tactical display sub-system.

The 16 antenna elements comprise two sets of eight high-band and low-band signal intercept antennas, these being arranged to produce separate fore and aft coverage quadrants on each side of the aircraft in each of the broad frequency bands covered by the equipment. No information has been given of the frequency limits but the upper limit is practically certain to be 18 GHz and may well be higher. Superhet receivers are believed to be used.

STATUS
In production.

CONTRACTOR
Loral Electronics Systems, Ridge Hill, Yonkers, New York 10710, USA.

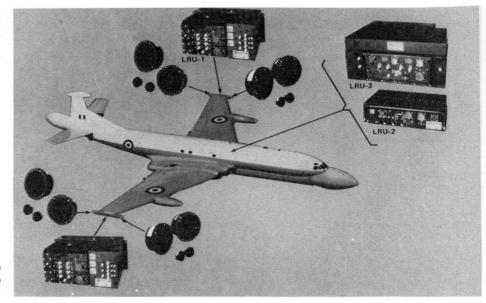

Loral ARI 18240/1 ESM system for RAF's AEW3 airborne early warning Nimrod aircraft showing location of antennas and main equipment

4382.353
EW-1017 ELECTRONIC SURVEILLANCE SYSTEM

As an airborne electronic surveillance the EW-1017 automatically acquires and identifies those emissions over the known frequency band that are liable to provide a threat to the aircraft safety, eg surveillance and tracking radars, both ground-based and airborne. The system is designed to receive and identify all those emissions illuminating the aircraft, including short bursts, in particular when the aircraft is operating in very dense signal environments. The warning of possible danger is given both visually and aurally on a display unit; preferential scan is used to ensure immediate recognition of possible lethal threats.

The system consists of antenna arrays, receiver, a processor system and a cockpit display/control unit. Broadband spiral antennas are used to provide omni-directional coverage and, together with their separate multi-band receivers, are mounted in pods on each wingtip. This location drastically limits aircraft 'shadowing' and the proximity of the receiver cuts signal losses to a minimum. Angular bearing of the emissions is determined by using selected pairs of antennas.

The hybrid superheterodyne receiver combines acquisition probability, high sensitivity, frequency accuracy and a high degree of frequency selection and selectivity to measure emissions. A broad bandwidth is used in the acquisition mode to obtain the initial intercept, and a narrow bandwidth for accurate bearing measurement and analysis. To ensure processing capability in highly dense signal conditions a high speed digital computer performs the data processing functions, supplemented by microprocessors. This enables the receivers to scan the frequency band continuously, on a reprogrammable basis, so that the conventional CW and agile signals are processed for identification.

A control/display unit allows the operator to monitor and control the automatic surveillance function to resolve possible ambiguities and evaluate and use to the best advantage, the data displayed.

CONTRACTOR
Loral Corporation, Loral Electronic Systems Division, 999 Central Avenue, Yonkers, New York 10704, USA.

4099.393
JAM PAC(V) ELECTRONIC COUNTERMEASURES JAMMER SYSTEM

The Jam Pac(V) is a newly developed family of low cost, high powered electronic countermeasure jammers specifically designed for lightweight fighter and helicopter aircraft. These modern, miniaturised radar jammers are tailored for aircraft self-protection and combat systems evaluation. The Jam Pac is a modular, variable configuration, conformal carriage-mounted jamming system. Unlike ECM jamming pods, Jam Pac does not use an aircraft weapon's station. The system is designed to fit into a specially made carriage which can be attached under the wing or to the fuselage. The Jam Pac's aerodynamic shape and light weight have little effect upon aircraft performance. The Jam Pac offers simple retrofit and rapid mounting facilities for mission-adaptable configurations. Through the use of interchangeable modules, engineered to cover frequencies from D- to J-band, the Sperry Jam Pac can provide self-protection against various types of threat radar systems. Each Jam Pac system consists of two voltage tuned magnetron transmitters, which have a combined output power of up to 800 W. Power management receivers are also available to control the tuning of the transmitters automatically to the appropriate jamming frequency.

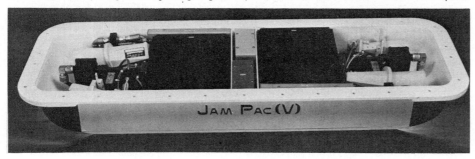

Internal view of Sperry Jam Pac(V), showing the two voltage tuned magnetron transmitters, each with a pair of forward- and rear-facing horn antennas. It is designed for under-fuselage or under-wing mounting on fighter aircraft or helicopters

STATUS
Jam Pac(V) systems are currently under development and test for US and foreign sales applications.

CONTRACTOR
Sperry Corporation, Electronic Systems, Great Neck, New York 10020, USA.

5742.393
NORTHROP INFRA-RED COUNTERMEASURES SYSTEMS

Northrop Defense Systems Division manufactures a number of infra-red countermeasures equipments, both for internal and external mounting on a variety of aircraft. Very few details have ever been released on these equipments although they are known to be deployed on various US aircraft. The AN/AAQ-4 is a full-flight, subsonic, internally-mounted system which has been further developed into the AN/AAQ-4(B). The AN/AAQ-8(V) is designed for supersonic flight and is contained in an externally mounted pod.

The Modularised Infra-Red Transmitting Set (MIRTS) is a version designed for export. Its modular design provides commonality for internal or pod-mounted applications and is suitable for helicopters and fixed-wing aircraft. MIRTS is digitally controlled, has automatic built-in test and can provide all aspect protection against infra-red homing missiles. It is believed to be based technically around a single sapphire lamp with multiple heads, covering the 3-5 μm and 8-14 μm wavelengths.

CONTRACTOR
Northrop Corporation, Defense Systems Division, 600 Hicks Road, Rolling Meadows, Illinois 60008, USA.

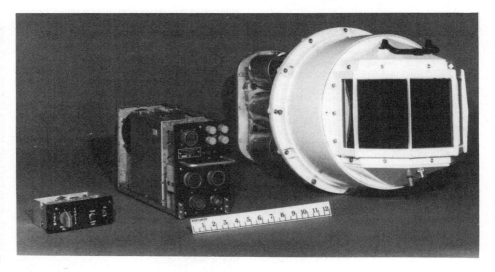

Modularized infra-red transmitting set (MIRTS)

5743.353
ESCORT AIRBORNE ELINT SYSTEM
ESCORT (Electromagnetic Surveillance Collection of Radar Transmissions) is a real-time electromagnetic surveillance and collection system, suitable for installation in a variety of aircraft. The M804 maritime surveillance equipment combines the capabilities of a high probability intercept receiver with a high-speed signal processor to perform real-time signal sorting, direction finding and identification. Full azimuthal coverage is obtained by antenna arrays in each wing tip. The M805 ELINT system provides precise direction finding by using phase interferometer antenna arrays in conjunction with the M804 receiver, processor and display unit. Outputs are displayed on a CRT unit for use by the electronics surveillance operator.

The receiver/processor library of the system is programmed with emitter characteristics of interest and identification; priority, display and alert criteria are programmed into the resource management portion of the processing unit. When an intercepted signal is received, the processor sorts the detected radiation, compares its characteristics with those stored in the library and displays the results. The display format can be changed from situation to tabular and may also be reformatted to the user's need during the mission.

CONTRACTOR
Raytheon Company, Electromagnetic Systems Division, 1578 Route 3, Wayne, New Jersey 07470, USA.

4384.393
AN/ULQ-11 AIRBORNE JAMMING SYSTEM
This airborne jamming system, known as the AN/ULQ-11 Cefirm Leader, is an ECM equipment system operated by the US Army and comprises nine RU-21 aircraft fitted with various types of electronic countermeasures equipment. It is designed to conduct ECM missions, ESM missions, jamming, initiate communications deception and direction finding. Of the nine aircraft, four are designated as 'A' aircraft which carry out airborne direction finding, three are 'B' aircraft conducting intercept and acting as system control, and two are 'C' aircraft which carry out jamming.

The types of communication against which the AN/ULQ-11 operates include amplitude modulation, frequency modulation, frequency shift key, CW, ICW, MCW and single side-band. The system is operated by RU-21 US Army utility aircraft.

CHARACTERISTICS
System frequency: 2 – 80 MHz
Jamming power: 500 W at 2 MHz and 70 W at 80 MHz
STATUS
In operational service.

4385.153
AN/ULQ-14 RADAR COUNTERMEASURES
The AN/ULQ-14 is a ground-based radar countermeasures complex operated by the US Army in the 8·5 to 17 GHz frequency band and is designed to be the ground element of the AN/ALQ-143 airborne multi-target electronic warfare system. The system provides electronic countermeasures capability for all army echelons from division upwards for countering ground and air-based threats from radar systems. The primary targets are counter-mortar/counter-artillery radars, surveillance and target acquisition radars and other radar systems in line-of-sight propagation.

The system is housed in a standard US Army S250 shelter for use with a 1½ ton truck and has a data interface with the AGTELIS control processor (**4408.153**), the AN/ALQ-143 MULTEWS airborne systems, Quick Look II and the AN/MSQ-103 Teampack mobile ESM system (**4404.193**). The capabilities of the system include the jamming of four to six signals over a 15 km range.

4670.353
GUARDRAIL AIRBORNE SIGINT SYSTEM (AN/USD-9(V)2)
Guardrail is an airborne signal intelligence (SIGINT) system that intercepts, locates and classifies target systems and transmits data to ground processors to provide real-time intelligence information. The Guardrail suite consists of a transportable ground-based system and C-12 aircraft carrying remotely controlled mission equipment.

The Guardrail system operates in three frequency bands, 20 to 75 MHz, 100 to 150 MHz and 350 to 450 MHz.

STATUS
Guardrail has been in operational service with the US Army for a number of years. The original Guardrail II was updated to IIA, and later was updated to Guardrail IV. Further updating has provided the latest version, Guardrail V, with better facilities, under the nomenclature AN/USD-9(V)2. A further product improvement programme has been called for but it seems more likely that a completely new system will be developed eventually.

CONTRACTOR
ESL Inc, Sunnyvale, California, USA.

1861.053
SYLVANIA EW ANTENNAS
The Sylvania Systems Group of GTE has developed and produces a comprehensive range of special antennas for various electronic warfare applications. These are described in some detail under the above entry number in previous editions. Illustrations of typical examples, and summarised information, have been retained for the benefit of readers without access to earlier volumes of *Jane's Weapon Systems*.

AN-10 Broadband Horns
This is a range of microwave horn antennas, usually of the ridged type, and which often are provided with a dielectric phase-correcting lens in the flared section. Individual examples from the range have specific frequency coverage.

AN-13 High-gain Omni-directional Antennas
This range of omni-directional antennas has been developed for signal acquisition and sidelobe suppression applications. The basic construction is that of a bi-conical horn, with metal grids or meander lines in the aperture, yielding 45° slant linear or circular polarisation, respectively.

AN-14 Log Periodic Antennas
Log periodic antennas are linearly polarised structures covering very broad frequency bands with constant performance characterstics (ie frequency independent). They are directional antennas with medium gain, and are suitable for use with direction finding and electronic reconnaissance systems.

AN-15 Conical Log Spiral Antennas
These are produced by means of a three-dimensional

Sylvania AN-27 fan-beam horns

printed-circuit technique for generating precision log spirals on dielectric cones. These conical log spirals maintain essentially constant radiation pattern performance with low polarisation axial ratio over several octaves of bandwidth.

AN-16 Cavity-backed Spiral Antenna
The AN-16 is a precision-backed, planar-spiral antenna covering a frequency band of 2 to 18 GHz.

AN-18 Dual-polarised Horn Antenna
A number of broadband, quadruple-ridged horn antennas have been developed covering frequencies in the range 50 MHz to 18 GHz. This series of antennas was designed for use in reconnaissance and surveillance of signals of unknown polarity.

AN-20 Corrugated Horns
Corrugated horns are used as (cassegrainian or prime focus) feeds in reflectors to obtain maximum efficiency and gain. They are ideal as feeds because of their very symmetrical beams and low sidelobes.

The corrugated horn consists of a conical horn with corrugated interior walls. The corrugations act as 'chokes' to cause the current which would exist on the walls of a conventional horn to go to zero. These currents are the cause of high sidelobes and pattern deterioration in conventional antennas.

AN-23 Lindenblad Antennas
GTE Sylvania has developed printed circuit board circularly polarised omni-directional Lindenblad antennas to cover octave frequency bands. Five different units are available in the 0·5 to 12 GHz range. They are produced as complete sealed units, with integral radome, and are suitable for airborne use in intercept/collection and other applications.

AN-27 Fan-beam Horns
The fan-beam horn design allows independent control of broad azimuth beams and narrow elevation beams, while providing low axial ratios over the entire beam. E- and H-plane beamwidth ratios of approximately 7:1 are characteristic of these horns.

AN-33 Septum Horns
The septum horns are pyramidal horns whose E-plane aperture distribution is compensated to provide sidelobe reduction in that plane.

AN-34 Conical Spiral Array
Under this designation a series of conical-spiral antenna arrays for broadband, high-accuracy tracking and direction finding is produced. Features of such arrays include circular polarisation, low polarisation axial ratio, frequency-independent performance, small bore-sight shift and phase and amplitude tracking among antennas.

AN-121 Rotating DF Antenna Systems
The AN-121 series of rotating DF antenna systems has been developed to meet a wide variety of DF and high gain monitor system applications using GTE Sylvania standard antennas, pedestals, radomes, and control units.

CONTRACTOR
GTE Sylvania Systems Group, Western Division, 100 Ferguson Drive, Mountain View, California 94040, USA.

GTE Sylvania has been responsible for the development of numerous broadband antenna systems for reconnaissance and ESM applications. This example consists of four circularly polarised horns operating in the VHF/UHF bands which can be used separately for acquisition or together for more accurate tracking through the process of sequential lobing. A 10-ft (3·04 m) offset-fed reflector centred in the assembly provides high-gain precision tracking from 1 to 11 GHz

This monopulse tracking system has a bandwidth of 25:1 and provides both senses of circular polarisation. It consists of a log-periodic array feeding a 30 ft (9·4 m) parabolic reflector. Intercept capabilities are provided by the dually-polarised log-periodic antenna mounted on the side of the dish. A tracking accuracy of ±0·01 beamwidths is claimed

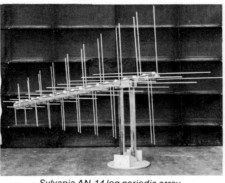

Sylvania AN-14 log periodic array

Sylvania AN-20 corrugated horn antenna

CHARACTERISTICS

	AN-20A	AN-20C	AN-20D	AN-20F	AN-20H
Frequency (GHz)	8 – 12	8 – 18	1·7 – 2·6	3·95 – 5·85	8·2 – 12·4
Beamwidth	30°	30°	28 – 17°	28 – 18°	30 – 18°
VSWR (max)	1·5:1	1·5:1	1·5:1	1·5:1	1·5:1
Gain (dBi)	15·5	15·5	15·2	15·2	15·2
Aperture (in)	4·75	4·75	27	11·8	5·6
Length (in)	2·4	2·4	37·5	16·4	7·6

Other models covering the bands of 12 – 18, 2·6 – 3·95, and 5·85 – 8·2 GHz are also available.

4677.153

J-3400 MOBILE ECM SYSTEM
The J-3400 system is a mobile passive/active equipment designed for both signal intercept and jamming in the VHF frequency band. The complete system consists of transmitters, receivers, computers and an antenna system and is normally mounted on a tracked vehicle for mobility in practically any terrain.

It is designed for one man operation and can be deployed within three minutes.

In the active mode the J-3400 will automatically jam up to four frequencies in a sequential time-shared mode. There is also a priority jamming mode which jams on a single priority signal whenever it is active. 1 kW (4 kW ERP) jamming power is provided.

In the passive mode the J-3400 functions as a signal

intercept system. It continually sweeps all bands, or spot checks preprogrammed frequencies. In either case the receiver pauses on active signals for active analysis.

CONTRACTOR
GTE Sylvania, 100 Ferguson Drive, Mountain View, California 94039, USA.

3032.153

CIRCULARLY DISPOSED ANTENNA ARRAY (CDAA)
A CDAA is an antenna system which consists of a number of monopoles, or dipoles, uniformly spaced in front of a circular reflector that has its axis normal to the earth's surface. The antenna operates as a broadside array and is capable of providing several different types of beams to cover 360° in azimuth.

As the wave front of an emitted radio signal passes over the antenna array, each antenna element is excited at a different time. The output from each element is amplified and distributed by power dividers. The outputs of the element pairs that are symmetrically displaced with respect to the arriving

wave front are combined. Each of the combined outputs is then delayed by an amount required to cause the outputs of those elements that are used to form a beam to be coherent in phase.

The summing of these equal phase outputs results in a highly directive beam. The directivity of the beam is a function of how many elements are combined.

During the past 20 years, GTE Sylvania has designed, developed, and installed many CDAA systems which operate from HF through to the UHF ranges. The physically large antenna systems operate over bandwidths up to 10:1 and achieve DF accuracies that vary between 3 and 5°. These custom-designed systems were developed under government or company-sponsored funding to meet

specific requirements. Delivered fully operational, and based on state-of-the-art information, the systems meet or exceed all performance requirements.

Hardware developments over the years have greatly expanded the capabilities of this antenna system. The development by GTE Sylvania of low NF and high dynamic range preamplifiers led to a large improvement in the system sensitivity. Development of low loss beam forming networks and power combining hybrids provides the capability to form high gain antenna beams simultaneously present over the full 360° azimuth. An arrangement of high dynamic range amplifiers followed by power dividers, patch panels, and selector switches enables the operators to have unrestricted access to each antenna beam.

GTE Sylvania and others have also developed new hardware which permits extension of the frequency range of CDAA systems.

CONTRACTOR
GTE Sylvania, Systems Group, Western Division, 100 Ferguson Drive, Mountain View, California 94048, USA.

Sylvania circularly disposed antenna array

4386.093
SPERRY UNIVAC ANTENNA SYSTEMS EQUIPMENT
Sperry Univac has developed and produces a wide range of special antennas and ancillary equipment for electronic warfare applications. The salient features of major examples are listed below.

Single-axis Antenna Assembly
This is a single-axis antenna designed to operate in severe environmental conditions extending from ocean surface vehicles to high performance aircraft. The primary application is for use as part of an airborne commmand and telemetry link, where maximum gain through beam stabilisation is required to maintain command and control between the aircraft and a ground control station.
Polarisation: Right hand circular
Frequency: 10 - 10·4 GHz
Beamwidth: 18° at 2 dB points

AN/UPQ-3A Steerable Antenna
The AN/UPQ-3A steerable antenna is a versatile directional system designed to operate in severe environments from surface vessels to high altitude airborne vehicles. The primary application is for use as part of an airborne command and telemetry link (as with the single-axis antenna described above).

The antenna is steerable in both azimuth and elevation. Steering is accomplished by the antenna receiving digital pulses, each corresponding to small antenna movements. The antenna will output two three-wire synchro angles representing elevation and azimuth position of the horn relative to its mounting base.

It consists of two basic parts: the antenna assembly containing the horn, drive mechanism and position sensing elements, and the controller assembly containing programmable circuitry for directional control and two-axis stabilisation control.
Frequency range: 9·75 - 10·57 GHz
Beamwidth: 8·5 - 12° (3 dB points)
Polarisation: Circular; right hand or left hand
Azimuth: 360° continuously steerable
Elevation: +45 to –85°
Rate: 30°/s, either axis
Position accuracy: 1·75° at max slew rate in either axis

Two-axis Steerable Antenna
This is a directional antenna system with applications identical to the previous item. It consists of two major units: the antenna assembly containing the horn, drive mechanism and position sensing means, and the controller assembly containing programmable circuitry for directional control and three-axis stabilisation compensation. The antenna assembly is normally installed in radomes 12 inches in diameter or less. The mounting base can be supplied with a pressurisation seal for installation through the airframe structure.

Two-axis Corrugated Horn Antenna
This lightweight compact airborne antenna is designed specifically for use where the antenna is located close to other radars or other microwave systems. The corrugated horn design provides low backlobes and minimises interference with other sensors. It is also ideal for installation in pods or mounted in remote locations on the aircraft. Used in tandem with suitable controller and RF switching, this unit can maintain constant link-up with directional ground trackers even when mounted on high performance aircraft.

The antenna is steerable in both azimuth and elevation. Steering is accomplished by the antenna receiving differential TTL digital pulses corresponding to rates up to 60°/s in azimuth and 30°/s in elevation, each corresponding to small antenna movements. The antenna outputs two three-wire synchro angles representing elevation and azimuth position of the horn relative to its mounting base.
Frequency range: 16·7 - 17·7 GHz
Beamwidth: 20° horizontal; 22° elevation
Polarisation: Linear. Circular, right hand or left hand
Azimuth: 360° steerable continuously
Elevation: +45 to –85°
Rate: 30°/s for either axis
Position accuracy: 1·75° at max slew rate on either axis

Multi-band Tracking Antenna
The multi-band tracking antenna is designed for line-of-sight aircraft tracking and control. It will operate in severe environmental conditions and has been tested to military specifications. Two electronic servo control packages are available to operate the antenna. One requires operator presence within 100 feet of the antenna; the other allows remote antenna control from up to 1320 feet away. The servo motor drive uses high-efficiency, pulse-width modulation techniques. The small power ampifiers require no external cooling.

A single-axis tracking feature provides for tracking in areas where multi-path has a tendency to distort the elevation components of spin modulation. The system design permits mobile, fixed or shipborne installations.

Mobile Ground Tracker Terminal
The mobile ground tracker terminal is a rugged multi-band antenna system designed for operation in severe environments. It employs a servo drive using high-efficiency pulse-width modulation techniques to ensure fast slew tracking. Integrated levelling jacks allow rapid set-up in difficult terrain. It can be located up to 1320 feet away from the ground control system to safeguard operator personnel from attacks. The parabolic antenna dish folds down into a stow position and interconnect cables are stowed in the fixed reels to permit air transport.

The ground mobile tracker terminal consists of three major assemblies: the M-390 trailer with levelling system and stowage equipment, the pedestal antenna system, and the electronics enclosure with the antenna control and RF interface electronics.
Frequency range: C, X or Ku
Beamwidth: 1 - 2·25°
Polarisation: Circular, right hand
Slew rates: 30°/s (azimuth and elevation)

125-watt TWT Amplifier
The 125-watt TWT amplifier assembly is a single-unit TWT and power supply designed to withstand the severe environments associated with military aircraft and tactical ground installations. The primary application is a high power, airborne or ground digital data or imagery transmitter.

The assembly consists of three major units: the TWT amplifier providing 150 W (X-band) of CW output power, a solid-state power supply and a built-in test system.
Frequency: X or Ku band
Output power: 150 W
70-watt TWT Amplifier
This amplifier consists of two major assemblies: the TWTA providing 70 W (X-band) of output power and the solid-state power supply. As an optional feature this unit is also available with 35 or 50 W power output, and in C or Ku band frequencies with the power output varying slightly with frequency.

Spread Spectrum Modem
The Spread Spectrum Modem has applications as an interface compatible with the AN/UPQ-3(A) data link, as part of an airborne command system, as part of ground-to-air/ground-to-ground/air-to-air data link and is also applicable to reconnaissance use in a jamming environment.

The equipment uses a direct sequence modulated FM carrier at the specified signal levels. The received signal is collapsed to an FM modulated IF by code tracking the PN sequence and multiplying the received signals by the code estimate. The resultant FM signal is phase-lock loop detected and the baseband data is provided at two output ports of the receiver.
Frequency: X or Ku band
Modulation type: FM
CONTRACTOR
Sperry Univac Defense Systems, 640 North 2200 West, Salt Lake City, Utah 84116, USA.

4387.153

TACTICAL ELECTRONIC RECONNAISSANCE (TEREC) REMOTE TERMINAL (TRT)

The Tactical Electronic Reconnaissance (TEREC) Remote Terminal (TRT) is a collection of equipment, computers and procedures which forms a simple-to-operate portable terminal for tactical operations centres. The system is able to receive, process and report TEREC radar emitter location reports in near-real-time without reliance on ground communi-

cations. The TRT accepts voice and data information from the TEREC (AN/ALQ-125) equipped airborne sensor platform and consists of a computer, decryption equipment, a data demodulator, HF and UHF receivers, antennas, and a keyboard and printer.

The radio communications, data processing, keyboard and printing equipment are contained in portable containers which can be transported rapidly (via land, sea or air) and deployed quickly into full operational capability at the operational site. The

equipment is fully ruggedised for military use, and can operate from a variety of power sources, including 120 V, 60/400 Hz single phase and 220/240 V, 50 Hz single phase.

STATUS

All units under contract are in the field. Follow-on requirements are not yet funded.

CONTRACTOR

Texas Instruments Incorporated, PO Box 405, M/S 3400, Lewisville, Texas 75067, USA.

3031.053

SYLVANIA COMPUTER CONTROLLED RECEIVING SYSTEMS

During the past decade the traffic in the RF environment encompassing the radar and communication bands has rapidly expanded. This growth coupled with the sophistication of new systems has placed stringent demands on the operations of reconnaissance and electronic warfare communities.

Since mid-1960, GTE Sylvania, California, has been developing receiving systems designed around modern computers to meet these complex challenges; many of these systems are now in field operation. These systems, deployed in ground based, air, naval, and mobile applications, are divided into two areas: radar receiving systems and communication receiving systems.

Radar Receiving Systems

Typical radar receiving systems consist of five sub-systems: antennas, receivers, displays, signal digitisers, and the computer and its peripherals. In operation the system performs five major functions: monitor, signal acquisition, identification, cataloguing, and reaction.

The computer controls the system's antennas and receivers in a programmed pattern as directed by the operator. Incoming signals are digitised and routed to the computer where they are sorted, identified, and catalogued according to their measured parameters.

Depending on the mission of the system, reaction to threat signals can consist of alerting the operator, controlling a weapons or countermeasure system, or direct communications. Under control of the operator the computer will sort, correlate, update, and retrieve selected information for analysis and output data to magnetic tape, disc, paper tape, or provide data in numerical form on a CRT display or high speed printer.

Communication Receiving System

Communication receiving systems are divided into eight major sub-systems including: antennas, receivers, demultiplexers, mode analysers, activity detectors, recorders, distribution equipment, and the computer and its peripherals. Incoming communications signals are separated by the system's demultiplexers. The mode analyser determines signal

Sylvania computer-controlled receiving system

modulation, and passes this information to the computer. The activity detector informs the computer when communications activity takes place. The computer uses this information to control the communications system, routeing signals via the distribution equipment to various recorders and operators, and to maintain activity files.

In summary the availability of today's computer control receiving systems allow five major advantages: (1) rapid identification of signals in high density environments; (2) relief of operators from direct involvement in the repetitive control and logging functions making them available for system

management and signal analysis; (3) increased operator scope and efficiency reducing operating cost; (4) increased system response time, and probability of detection; (5) modular design of both hardware and software providing an economical building block approach to tailoring systems to meet customer needs and future expansion.

STATUS

Operational.

CONTRACTOR

GTE Sylvania, Systems Group, Western Division, 100 Ferguson Drive, Mountain View, California 94042, USA.

3897.053

SYLVANIA BRAGG CELL RECEIVER

A Bragg Cell channelised receiver with wide, instantaneous radio frequency signal bandwidth, excellent spur free range, and simultaneous signal handling capability has been developed by the Western Division of GTE Sylvania, a subsidiary of General Telephone & Electronics Corporation. The receiver is suitable for frequency sorting in radiometer-type radio frequency receiving systems. Applications include spread spectrum signal acquisition, detection and priority ordering. In the new receiver, acoustic and optic techniques are combined with electronics to modulate a laser's light with sound.

Bragg Cell receivers permit rapid analysis of multiple radio frequency signals over wide bandwidths without scanning. Designed to upgrade spread spectrum signal detection systems, the Sylvania unit offers a centre frequency of 2 to 3 GHz and a bandwidth of 1 GHz. This represents the greatest information handling capability of current Bragg Cell units, according to the producers.

Unlike conventional surveillance receivers, Bragg Cell units provide instantaneous, wideband operation over the receiver intermediate frequency bandwidth; simultaneous sorting of in-band frequencies; and 100

per cent signal intercept capability. They also are smaller and have simpler processing. The Sylvania units are projected to be less expensive in quantity manufacture than competing systems.

Acoustic and optic techniques are combined with electronics in the receiver to modulate a laser's light with sound. Heart of the unit is an acousto-optical diffraction cell crystal through which radio frequency signals, transformed into acoustic waves, travel. When the crystal is illuminated by laser light, that light is modulated by the acoustic waves. This modulation, which includes the signal information, is detected by a photo-detector diode array.

A multiple channel optical data processor can function as a monopulse direction finder system. This type of system enables instantaneous frequency channelisation to combine with real-time angle of arrival sorting of signals via amplitude matched receiver channels. Both four- and eight-channel processors have been delivered. Instantaneous two-dimension frequency/direction of arrival signal sorting has been developed at GTE using a multiple-dimensional optical data processor.

Optical representations of signals are permanently recorded on film using photo-optic recording.

The Sylvania channelised receiver has an instantaneous bandwidth of 1 GHz; frequency cell

GTE Sylvania Bragg Cell wideband channelised receiver

resolution of 1 MHz; centre frequency of 2 to 3 GHz; and continuous wave sensitivity of –80 decibels below one milliwatt. Work is progressing on the next generation of the device which is expected to offer a centre frequency capability of 3 to 4 GHz. Integration times are 1, 2, 4, 8 and 16 milliseconds. Dynamic range is 45 decibels spur free and detector range is 30 decibels. The unit weighs 9·5 kg, including power supplies, and measures 279 × 482 × 101 mm.

CONTRACTOR

Sylvania Electro-Optics Organization, 100 Ferguson Drive, Mountain View, California 94042, USA.

3082.253
AN/WLR-8 TACTICAL EW RECEIVER SYSTEM

The AN/WLR-8 is a tactical electronic warfare and surveillance receiver designed for fitting in both surface ships and submarines of the US Navy. The system is of modular construction and provisions are made for operation in conjunction with numerous types of direction finding or omni antennas and a wide range of optional peripheral equipment to provide comprehensive ESM (electronic support mission) facilities. The WLR-8 is compatible with NTDS (navy tactical data system) and similar action information automation systems. The system can be expanded in frequency or signal handling capability by means of simple additions and/or software changes. Four versions are available; V(1) for submarines, V(2) for SSN-688 class submarines, V(4) for aircraft carriers and V(5) for Trident submarines.

Two digital computers are incorporated: a Sylvania PSP-300 for system control, automatic signal acquisition and analysis, and file processing; and a Sylvania PSP-200 microcomputer for hardware level control functions. Digital techniques are employed throughout the WLR-8 system, which is all solid-state.

Operational facilities provided include:
(1) automatic measurement of signal direction of arrival
(2) signal classification and recognition
(3) sequential or simultaneous scanning over a wide frequency range
(4) signal activity detection for threat warning
(5) analysis of signal parameters such as frequency, PRF, modulation, pulsewidth, amplitude, scan rate etc
(6) logging of signal parameters for display to operator(s), and printout of hard copy to teletype or printer
(7) extensive built-in test equipment
(8) directed priority searches of specific frequency segments.

Direct reporting to on-board computers, such as NTDS, permits response times in the millisecond range with minimal operator involvement. A two-trace CRT is provided for display purposes and this can be supplemented by an optional five-trace panoramic display for presentation of signal activity data. Another CRT display is incorporated if the WLR-8 is used with automatic or manual DF antenna systems.
STATUS
Operational with USN and possibly other navies. 21 systems are in use on board SSN-688 class submarines, and the V(5) version is fitted to Trident fleet ballistic missile submarines.
CONTRACTOR
GTE Sylvania, Systems Group, Western Division, 100 Ferguson Drive, Mountain View, California 94042, USA.

Operating console of AN/WLR-8 tactical EW receiver

4665.093
DF-8000 DIRECTION FINDING SYSTEM

A high accuracy, automatic direction finding system, the DF-8000 covers the 20 to 1000 MHz frequency range and is designed for communications monitoring in mobile, fixed, airborne and shipborne applications. The equipment operates on the time-difference-of-arrival principle, providing a range of accuracies from better than one degree to several degrees depending on calibration and installation factors. This accuracy performance is maintained at low signal-to-noise ratios against any typical communication signal modulation and is not sensitive to amplitude change. Instantaneous coverage is 360 degrees.

The DF system consists of an antenna array, standard single channel communications receiver and a DF processor with detachable control and display panel. A range of functions includes storage of 100 signals for automatic search operations. The system can be operated locally or remotely with automatic or manual control. Weight, excluding antenna, is 65 lbs (29·5 kg).
CONTRACTOR
GTE Sylvania, 100 First Avenue, Waltham, Massachusetts 02254, USA.

DF-8000 Direction Finder

3551.293
AN/SLQ-17 NAVAL ELECTRONIC COUNTERMEASURES SUITE

The AN/SLQ-17 naval countermeasures set is a deception jammer for shipboard use. It provides the appropriate threat detection and jamming techniques to counter threats and is equipped with the requisite microwave sources and antennas.

The system is designed to protect carriers and other major ships against cruise missiles and other intruders by developing an electronic "image" of the target ship as it is sensed by the enemy's guidance radar. It then offsets the image so that the weapon guides itself to a false "ghost" target some distance from the real one.

The automated SLQ-17 system is designed to operate in dense electromagnetic environments. It detects and tracks signals of several score missiles of many types, and will track up to several hundred signals from other platforms. The system keeps track of signals used for navigation, search, and tracking in the frequency bands that are in the emission range of present and future hostile platforms. It can intercept and track potential missile launch platforms beyond the ranges at which the attacking missiles lock on to the ship and automatically identify both threat and friendly platforms.

As a signal is received on either of the two antennas, the SLQ-17 automatically measures the radar parameters emitted and the computer searches its memory files to separate friend from foe. If it identifies the signal as a missile radar, it generates the most effective deception for the missile, causing it to strike the ocean safely away from the carrier. Meanwhile, the system automatically keeps track of signals in its area, displaying their platforms for the operator to review on his tactical situation display. Information on all the platforms is displayed for the operator's action in order of their decreasing threat level.

The system is made up of the AN/UYK-20 computer, a disc file memory, the operator's CRT graphic display unit (with a keyboard for data entry and display control), and the two highly accurate roll-stabilised antennas with their antenna control units, high and low power amplifiers, signal processors, and RF oscillators. Aboard carriers and other vessels, an antenna and related equipment are installed on each side of the ship. The mini-computer and control and display equipment are installed in the ship's combat information centre (CIC).
STATUS
In early 1978 the US Naval Electronics Systems Command awarded Hughes Aircraft Company's ground systems group an initial $8·5 million letter contract to build the first production system, called the AN/SLQ-17A(V)2. A total of 14 systems has been procured with six additional systems planned to complete installation requirements.

An AN/SLQ-17 antenna mounted on the superstructure of a US Navy ship

CONTRACTOR
Hughes Aircraft Company, Fullerton, California 92634, USA.

4388.293

AN/SLQ-30 TRUMP

The AN/SLQ-30 is an integrated shipborne defensive electronic countermeasures system designed for the US Navy Electronic Systems Command. The name TRUMP is an acronym of Threat Reactive Update Modernisation Programme and the system is designed to improve effective ECM action and response times while still using existing hardware. It comprises extensively modified ULQ-6B transmitters and SLA-12 antennas, a broadband interception receiver and a processor. The digital processor carries out threat analysis, assigns priority of action, selects the appropriate ECM response and operates overall system command.

CONTRACTOR

Kuras-Alterman Corporation, 1578 Route 234, Wayne, New Jersey 07470, USA.

4389.293

SR-200 SHIPBORNE ESM SYSTEM

The SR-200 is a shipborne instantaneous frequency measuring system used for protection against surface-to-surface missiles. The system performs automatic threat detection and identification and provides alarm signals on a priority basis using emitter profiles stored in the memory of its high-speed digital processor. The system covers the frequency range 500 MHz to 18 GHz with an optional extension up to 40 GHz. Bearing accuracy in the I/J band is better than ± 2° rms.

An omni-directional antenna is used to pass on signals of interest to a rotating direction finding antenna which provides outputs into the equipment. A display unit provides information on the hostile transmissions as well as providing an order of priority on those considered most hostile.

STATUS

The SR-200 is fitted to a number of national naval forces.

CONTRACTOR

Sanders Associates, 95 Canal Street, Nashua, New Hampshire 03061, USA.

4671.353

S-2150 ESM SYSTEMS

The S-2150 ESM systems are shipborne threat warning equipments normally fitted to smaller ships and submarines. They are automatic in operation and provide warning and direction finding facilities.

The S-2150-01 provides instantaneous direction finding cover over the frequency range 2 to 18 GHz, with an accuracy of 10 degrees rms. The system consists of a masthead unit containing the antenna array and receiver, and a processor/display and control panel. An emitter library is referenced with each signal intercepted and an audio alarm is activated if the signal is matched with a possible threat. Information is also displayed in alpha-numeric and graphic form on the display panel.

The S-2150-03 is also an automatic surveillance system that detects and analyses signals in the 2 to 18 MHz band and provides direction finding with a five degree accuracy. The equipment operates independently or as part of an overall EW suite. An operator display provides threat symbology, bearing and approximate range as well as other data.

CONTRACTOR

EM Systems Inc, Sunnyvale, California, USA.

3349.293

AN/SLQ-32 SHIPBOARD EW EQUIPMENT

The AN/SLQ-32 is a naval electronic warfare equipment developed to replace AN/WLR-1 receivers and AN/ULQ-6 deception jammers aboard many USN ships. The equipment is the result of a USN/industry programme lasting three or four years, in the course of which Hughes and Raytheon designed and built competitive models for test and evaluation. The Hughes system was designated AN/SLQ-31, and the successful Raytheon version, the AN/SLQ-32.

The AN/SLQ-32 consists of three modular variants of increasing levels of complexity and cost. The basic version, AN/SLQ-32(V)1, provides for warning, identification and direction finding of incoming radar-guided anti-ship missiles; the (V)2 version provides the facilities of the (V)1 plus early warning, identification and direction finding of those radars associated with the targeting and launch of the missiles; (V)3 includes the (V)2 capability to which is added a jamming capability for the prevention or delay of targeting and launch of missiles, and also for the deflection of any missiles that are launched away from their target. The (V)1 was designed for 'Knox' class frigates and smaller auxilliary ships; the (V)2 with its expanded ESM capability for DDGs, FFGs, and 'Spruance' class destroyers; and the (V)3 version with the active jamming system will be fitted in cruisers and certain other larger vessels.

All of the AN/SLQ-32 systems employ multiple beam antennas for reception in all bands except the lowest frequency band, and the lens-fed multiple beam array is a major feature of the system. The antenna consists of an array of elements fed through coaxial cables by a multiple beam parallel-plate lens which is constructed in stripline form using printed circuit techniques. This array provides a set of individual, contiguous high-gain beams, all existing simultaneously, and with each beam having the full gain of the array aperture. For a single array, more than an octave of frequency coverage is provided.

AN/SLQ-32(V)1 Suite

This version is designed to detect all RF signals in Band 3 at all azimuths, covering all potential enemy radar-guided anti-ship missiles and their associated supporting radars. By this ESM the (V)1 suite provides alert facilities to an attack on the ship and also allows for the control of the Mk 36 chaff rocket system (**3363.293**) carried by the ship. The (V)1 receivers are wide-open in both angle and frequency, and the complete suite consists of two antenna assemblies each having two Band 3 direction finding receiver arrays and lenses covering 90° each. One Band 3 semi-omni antenna covering 180° is located on each antenna assembly. In parallel with the multi-beam antenna and direction finding receivers the system employs a semi-omni antenna to sense the dominant pulse and feed it to the IFM receiver.

AN/SLQ-32 (V)3

AN/SLQ-32 (V)3

A special purpose digital processor, known as the presorter, consists of a direction/frequency correlator and digital tracking unit sections; coarse frequency data from the IFM receiver and amplitude data from the direction finding receiver are correlated in the direction/frequency correlator. Time of arrival data is added to form a pulse descriptor word, which is then stored by frequency and angle cell in the emitter file memory section of the digital tracking unit. If three or more pulses with this angle and frequency signature are received within a programmable time interval (up to 32 milliseconds), the digital tracking unit informs the computer that a new emitter is present. The computer then commands the digital tracking unit to provide enough additional pulses to permit further extensive analysis. The computer calculates from this data the PRF, type of scan, scan period and frequency; these parameters are usually sufficient to characterise an emitter.

Identification is completed by comparing the observed signal characteristics with parameters stored in a library of friendly and threat emitter characteristics within the computer memory. On completion of the identification processs, the computer initiates appropriate alert signals and other actions.

AN/SLQ-32(V)2 Suite
The increased capability of this version is achieved by the addition of two receiving sub-systems. Two Band 2 direction finding receivers and arrays and lenses each covering 90° are added to each of the port and starboard antenna assemblies, and a Band 2 semi-omni antenna covering 180° is added to each assembly. Four small Band 1 spiral antennas are located on a yardarm (port and starboard) to cover 360°. As well as the necessary extra electronics needed to handle the increased input data, the AN/UYK-19 computer remains the same as in the (V)1 version apart from having an additional 16 K of storage capacity.

AN/SLQ-32(V)3 Suite
The ESM capability of the (V)3 suite is the same as that of the (V)2 suite. The active electronic countermeasures (AECM) function of this suite requires two more racks of equipment in the EW room. The main additions are: eight high-voltage power supplies for the TWTs, a transponder, a digital switching unit and a techniques generator. The computer remains the same except for a further increase in memory capacity from 64 K to 80 K. The outboard antenna assemblies are enlarged to accommodate Band 3 transmitter antennas and electronics; two are located in the lower portion of each assembly.

The (V)3 antenna assemblies are hydraulically roll-stabilised.

The AN/SLQ-32(V)3 AECM mode can be operated semi-automatically, where the operator initiates jamming against a given emitter; or automatically, under computer control, where the system initiates countermeasure action as soon as a threat is identified. In each case the actions of the system are essentially the same. The library identifies the

One of the antenna arrays of the AN/SLQ-32 naval EW system (Stefan Terzibaschitsch)

jamming technique most appropriate to the particular threat encountered. The parameters of the technique designated in this way are passed to the technique generator unit (TGU), which synthesises the waveforms and applies them as modulation to voltage controlled oscillators in the transponder and the associated drive unit. The output of the drive unit is switched to the appropriate input of the transmission lens to ensure that the energy of the output tubes is directed in the required beam direction. The computer schedules the transmission of energy associated with a given target so that several hostile emitters can be engaged at one time.

STATUS
The AN/SLQ-27 (Shortstop) naval defensive EW system developed between 1966 and 1971 was too expensive for the US Navy to fit in all ships needing an EW capability, and as a result of a study, a decision was taken in 1972 to design a series of EW suites to match the series of target unit prices allocated to ships of various sizes for this requirement. This led to

the new system becoming known as the Design-To-Price Electronic Warfare Suite (DTPEWS). In January 1973 six contracts were awarded for a four-month definition phase, after which two contractors, Hughes Aircraft and Raytheon, were awarded contracts for engineering development in August 1973. Two competing (V)3 systems were delivered to the US Navy in January 1976 for trials in USS *Leahy*. Tests and evaluation lasted until September 1976, and the following November Raytheon's design was chosen for production and a contract valued at about $180 million was awarded for a total of 284 sets to be delivered over a period of about four years. It is expected that there will be 107 (V)1 equipments, 113 (V)2 versions, and 64 of the full (V)3 model. More than 300 are expected to be produced for different classes of surface ship. The US Navy has announced that it is negotiating for the design of an EHF transmitter for the SLQ-32

CONTRACTOR
Raytheon Company, Goleta, California, USA.

4020.293
SEA SENTRY NAVAL ESM
The Kollmorgen Sea Sentry is a passive electronic surveillance system designed to detect and track the direction of radar threats, with an analysis capability, both integrated into a single compact system. There are several versions of the Sea Sentry system:

Sea Sentry I: An ESM system that can be utilised to enhance the Kollmorgen Sea Serpent fire control system (**4019.281**), or an existing fire control system, or can be used as a stand-alone system for fast patrol boats and other coastal craft.

Sea Sentry II: A complete cost-effective electronic surveillance system for large surface ships. Like the Sea Sentry I, it will detect and track the direction of radar threats in addition to processing, analysing, and displaying all radar threats. Sea Sentry II with its higher sensitivity can also be utilised to enhance ECM jamming systems and reduce the effectiveness of threat countermeasures.

Sea Sentry III: A completely automatic broadband radar threat detection and analysis system that is designed for integration into a submarine surveillance platform. The system comprises four main elements:

(1) a multiple antenna array and microwave receiver integrated into a single housing that mounts on a submarine mast. This incorporates an antenna array of two low frequency antennas and four DF spirals; and the microwave receiver, a four-channel receiver contained in the antenna array fed by the four DF spiral antennas. Each channel of the receiver contains a quadruplexer, a high gain video amplifier and a processor interface assembly. The operation of any functional channel is controlled from the display and control console

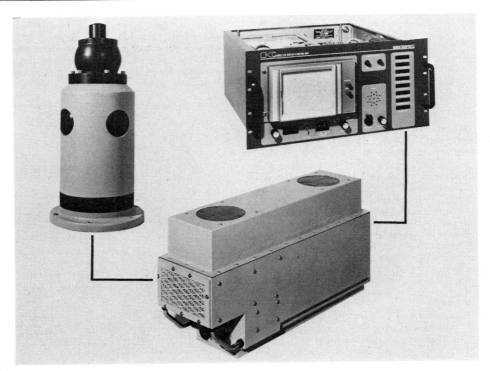

Kollmorgen Sea Sentry ESM set showing broadband antenna/receiver unit, DF/threat-processor, and display and control unit

(2) a display and control unit which includes digital and CRT displays and operational controls and indicators

(3) the DF threat processor that receives pulses from the antenna/receiver sub-system and electronically processes them into digital information and

transmits this information to the display and control unit

(4) an optional low frequency receiver, of the spectrum analyser type, which displays low frequency threat signals received by the omni-directional antennas on its own built-in CRT display.

The principal features of the Sea Sentry are omni-directional coverage; simultaneous automatic direction finding; DF accuracy to better than 10° rms; high system sensitivity; threat analyses; broadband coverage; detection of pulsed or CW signals; 100 per cent probability of detection; CRT display of threat identification, bearing, range and other status information.

CHARACTERISTICS
Model: Sea Sentry I
Frequency coverage: 2 – 18 GHz
Azimuth coverage: 360°
DF accuracy: 10° rms

Sensitivity: –35 dBmi typical
Dynamic range: 40 dB RF
Limiter power protection: 1 W CW; 100 W peak
Signal detection: Pulsed or CW
Signal processing capability: 35 simultaneous signals
Emitter library capacity: 128 emitters
Emitter identification time: 1 s (constant illuminators); 2 scan periods (scanning emitters)
Power requirements: 115 V/400 Hz
System weight: 125 kg (approx)

Sea Sentry V
Sea Sentry V provides wide signal reception bandwidth, high sensitivity, high precision direction finding and rapid emitter detection and identification over a frequency range from 0·5 to 40 MHz. The system is composed of five major subsystems:
(1) a direction finding receiver system integrated into a combination housing assembly that mounts on the ship's existing mast or on one specially provided

(2) a frequency measurement unit which provides the digital pulse to the processing subsystem, in addition to frequency measurement across the complete system range
(3) a processor which is a high speed digital computer optimised for the EW functions it must perform
(4) a display and control unit which is a variation of the standard Sea Sentry unit. Additional display of frequency is provided and provision of extra control features is included
(5) a system power supply.

Sea Sentry V operates over the frequency range 0·5 to 40 MHz with a DF accuracy of ±2 degrees rms. Programmable library capacity is 200.

STATUS
Production.
CONTRACTOR
Kollmorgen Corporation, International Products, 347 King Street, Northampton, MA 01060, USA.

3910.253
SLR-600 SERIES NAVAL ESM EQUIPMENT
This range of naval ESM equipment at present comprises three models, of which the base model is the SLR-600. This is a fully automatic and compact equipment primarily intended for fitting in fast patrol boats and similar classes of naval craft, where limited crew numbers are usual and fully automatic operation is of particular value. The SLR-600 combines a broadband E- to J-band microwave receiving system with a specially designed EW processor to ensure both maximum signal intercept probability and rapid system response. The display facilities present signal activity in range and bearing format, and the operator may also select a display which gives a readout at the bottom of the CRT of the operating parameters of selected emitters.

The normal installation aboard a ship includes four combined antenna/receiver units which can be mounted either as a group of four around a mast to give 360° azimuth coverage, or at the ends of yardarms etc to achieve the same result. The display is available as a single console for fitting in the bridge or wheelhouse, or alternatively the display can be configured for use as a separate unit for shelf or overhead mounting in the bridge or as a stand-up bridge control. Display modes include:
(1) radar identification, which gives specific radar identification based on programmed radar data
(2) unknown characterisation, providing automatic characterisation (pulse width, PRF, frequency, and scan) for unprogrammed radars
(3) radar parameter readout, which provides means for the operator to select any displayed radar for detailed parameter readout on the CRT.

Alarm audio and visual warning indications are given also.

CHARACTERISTICS
Frequency coverage: Continuous E- to J-band in 4 bands, C and D band detection available
Receiver type: Crystal video
Azimuth coverage: 360°
DF accuracy: Better than 15°
Shadow time: 2 μs
Processor memory: 18 000+ words E² PROM/RAM/ROM
Emitter library storage: 100+ emitters; 1000 operational modes
Emitters displayed: Up to 15 simultaneously, with identity, status, range and bearing
Display: CRT with computer-controlled symbology
Weight: 56·7 kg
Power consumption: 465 W

SLR-610
The SLR-610 provides the same performance as the SLR-600 but with extended frequency coverage and an alternative method of data display. This display is similar to the SLR-600 except that the radar parameter readout is provided by a column of multiple digit LED panels which show the parameters of the selected radar. There are also facilities for operator monitoring of intercepted radar audio signals.

SLR-640
The SLR-640 provides the highest level of ESM capability in the SLR-600 series and is designed to provide a complete ESM facility for fast patrol boats, frigates and destroyers. It provides broadband, high sensitivity signal detection and frequency measurements together with precision direction of

SLR-600 stand-up bridge console configuration

arrival information. A dual-mode CRT display combines a polar plot of total signal activity with a detailed radar parameter readout on a selected list of active emitters over C to J band.

STATUS
Production. Selected by an overseas navy.
CONTRACTOR
General Instrument Corporation, Government Systems Division, 600 West John Street, Hicksville, New York 11802, USA.

3363.293
RBOC Mk 33 MOD 0
The Mk 33 Mod 0 Rapid Bloom Off-board Countermeasures (RBOC) launching system comprises a family of mortar launchers, countermeasures cartridges, and appropriate control and support arrangements for the protection of ships of all sizes. The number of launchers per ship, and the number of tubes per launcher, can be tailored to the needs of each particular vessel, as can the cartridge payload. All RBOC installations make use of standardised launch tubes, firing circuits, and cartridges. Mk 33 is the designation for a four-launcher system; there is also a two-launcher system designated Mk 34. The major items of equipment are as follows:
(1) Launcher Mk 135 Mod 0. This is a deck-mounted, fixed tube launcher with six tubes arranged in pairs at quadrant elevation angles of 55, 65, and 75°. The firing circuits employ electromagnetic induction to initiate the propelling charge.
(2) Power supply Mk 160 Mod 0. This converts ship's AC power to DC for operation of the mortar firing circuits and the monitor and indicator lamp circuits. A standby battery and trickle charger are incorporated for emergency use.
(3) Master launcher control Mk 158 Mod 0. This provides the primary firing controls and status

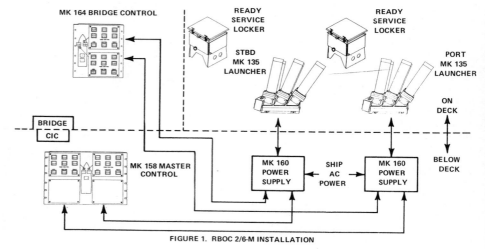

FIGURE 1. RBOC 2/6-M INSTALLATION

SYSTEM OPTIONS AND CODE DEFINITION

RBOC 2/6-M

number of launchers per system: 1, 2, 4 or 8.   *number of tubes per launcher:* 2, 4, or 6.   *type control:*
M = manual only
A = auto programmer
C = computer control

displays for all RBOC launch tubes aboard the ship. It also controls the activation of auxiliary launcher control panels in installations fitted with them.

(4) Bridge launcher control Mk 164 Mod 0. This provides auxiliary firing controls and status displays for the bridge.

(5) Ready use locker Mk 4 Mod 0. These units provide storage adjacent to launchers, and each locker houses 18 cartridges.

A typical arrangement is shown in the nearby block diagram (Figure 1).

The cartridges employed are the Mk 171 Mod 0 chaff payload, the HIRAM infra-red decoy, and the Gemini which combines chaff and infra-red payloads in a single cartridge. There is also a test cartridge (Mk 173 Mod 0) which is equipped with a pick-up coil and indicating meter, and is used to verify complete system functioning of the firing circuit for every launch tube.

When launched from a shipboard mortar (Mk 135 or equivalent) the Mk 171 cartridge rapidly forms a large chaff cloud which confuses radar seekers and fire control systems. Small vessels, such as fast patrol boats, are protected by firing a single Mk 171 cartridge. Ships of arbitrary size are protected by firing an appropriate number of cartridges. The radar cross-section of the Mk 171 chaff cloud is large enough to be effective without any special manoeuvring by the launching ship in most cases.

The Mk 171 Mod 0 chaff cartridge is a cylinder of 112 mm diameter with an overall length of 412 mm. The cylinder is closed at one end by an aluminium cap and at the other by a base plate. A plastic obturating skirt at the base acts as a gas seal to contain the propelling gases. Threaded to the base plate is an assembly containing the firing coil, propelling charge, and pyrotechnic time delay. A burst charge is located along the centreline of the cylinder, with the chaff payload packed around the charge. Inductive initiation is employed to eliminate electric connectors and provide complete HERO and RADHAZ safety.

When loaded into the launch tube, the cartridge firing coil nests within an excitation coil at the bottom of the launch tube. An electric current from the power supply passes through the excitation coil and induces a voltage in the firing coil. This voltage fires a squib, igniting the propelling charge and driving the

Loading chaff cartridge into Super-RBOC six-barrel launcher during system technical evaluation aboard USS Leahy

Loaded Super-RBOC launcher

cartridge from the tube. The gas pressure also impels a firing pin into a primer which initiates the pyrotechnic delay. After 3·4 seconds, the delay ignites the burst charge, driving the chaff payload radially through the cylinder walls at high velocity. The payload is subdivided into a large number of packages which travel great distances before deploying the chaff which can consist of material suitable for any single frequency, or multiple frequencies, or band coverage within the limits 2 to 20 GHz.

The HIRAM (Hycor infra-red anti-missile) decoy cartridge is designed to attract anti-ship missiles that employ IR seekers. When launched from a shipboard

mortar (Mk 135 or equivalent) the HIRAM decoy cartridge quickly deploys an IR flare which is equipped with a parachute and float. The flare presents an attractive alternative target to the missile's IR seeker. The output of a single flare is sufficient to simulate the radiant intensity of even a large ship.

The HIRAM decoy cartridge is a cylinder of 112 mm diameter and overall length of 417 mm. The flare is located within a tube along the centreline of the cylinder. Within the flare are a deployment charge, ignition mix, and the flare fuel mixture. Attached to the flare are a CO_2 cartridge, a rubber float (deflated), a folded parachute, and a folded self-erecting staff.

Within a few seconds after launch, the Gemini decoy cartridge develops a large radar echo and simultaneously generates a highly effective IR decoy signal. A small vessel (eg a fast patrol boat) may be protected from radar guided anti-ship missile by firing a single Gemini cartridge. Larger ships are protected by firing additional cartridges.

The IR flare, similar to the HIRAM unit, presents an attractive alternative target to a missile employing an IR seeker. The output of a single Gemini flare is sufficient to simulate the radiant intensity of even a large ship.

The Gemini cartridge is a cylinder of 112 mm diameter with an overall length of 451 mm. The chaff payload is primarily packaged within the bottom portion of the cartridge, identical to the Mk 171 chaff cartridge. The IR flare, its ignition mechanism and folded parachute occupy most of the upper section of the cartridge.

STATUS

Supplied to the US Navy and the navies of several other countries. Hycor is the sole producer of all components of the MK 33/MK 34 launch system, and HIRAM and Gemini cartridges are proprietory developments by Hycor. The Mk 171 chaff cartridge has been produced by both Hycor and Lundy.

CONTRACTORS

Hycor, Military Systems Division, 10 Gill Street, Woburn, Massachusetts 01801, USA.

Lundy Electronics & Systems Inc, 3901 NE 12th Avenue, Pompano Beach, Florida 33064, USA – Mk 171 cartridges.

Tracor MBA, Radcon Operations, 6500 Tracor Lane, Austin, Texas 78721, USA.

4656.293

MK 36 SUPER RAPID BLOOM OFF-BOARD COUNTERMEASURES

The Mk 36 Super Rapid Bloom Off-board Countermeasures system (SRBOC) provides a deck-launched self-protection against radar or IR guided anti-ship missiles. SRBOC can be activated automatically by the shipborne countermeasures system or by a dedicated microprocessor

programmer with interface to the on-board radar warning receiver, IR warning receiver, ship computer, fire control system or other emitter threat data sensors.

The system has large-size expendable decoys and is designed for ships more than 550 feet long. SRBOC is available in either Mod 1 (two launchers) or Mod 2 (four launchers) configuration. This includes six tube launchers, internal battery power for each launcher,

bridge remote controls, master launcher control and ready storage locker for each launcher. The decoys are identical in size and weight and use an induction firing system.

CONTRACTOR

Tracor MBA, Radcon Operations, 6500 Tracor Lane, Austin, Texas 78721, USA.

4739.293

TRITON THREAT WARNING SYSTEM

Triton is a digital threat warning system for small combat ships, such as fast patrol boats, to provide warning of attack by air-to-surface and surface-to-surface radar-guided weapons, as well as the presence of unknown threats. It features user-programmable synthetic voice alerts and visual presentation of multi-sensor threats, including the type of threat, its direction of arrival and whether it is tracking or still searching for the target. An indication

is also given when the hostile radar lock has been broken.

The system contains a threat library for comparison and analysis which can be reprogrammed on board within minutes to provide for new and updated threats. The display symbols and audio alerts can be adapted quickly to suit user requirements. The system is designed as a direct replacement for older equipments, using the same electrical connections and interfaces.

CONTRACTOR

Dalmo Victor Operations, Bell Aerospace Textron, 1515 Industrial Way, Belmont, California 94002, USA.

3105.093

MPI-5 MINIATURE PULSE ANALYSER

The MPI-5 is designed as a militarised display to allow operator analysis of signals as detected in radar environments. The unit is a reliable, miniaturised, solid-state, modular replacement for the AN/ULA-2 with improved characteristics and additional features. It can be used to perform the following:

(1) pulse width measurement
(2) pulse repetition frequency measurement
(3) pulse risetime measurement
(4) signal envelope analysis
(5) pulse signature analysis
(6) signal sorting

(7) frequency band activity monitor
(8) audio monitoring of video signal.

The MPI-5 is a five-gun CRT display, each successive sweep being 10 times slower than the preceding sweep. The sweeps are triggered when the incoming pulse exceeds a threshold. With the use of delay lines, the entire incoming pulse is displayed. The fifth trace can be switched to a panoramic mode which provides a built-in frequency band monitor. An internal calibrator is provided to permit accurate calibration of the display to its scale. An audio output is also provided for audio monitoring or recording of the video signal.

Operating controls and display of MPI-5 miniature pulse analyser

CONTRACTOR
American Electronic Laboratories, PO Box 552, Lansdale, Philadelphia 19446, USA.

3664.093
WJ-945 RECEIVING/DF SYSTEM

The WJ-945 receiving/DF system is a sophisticated microwave receiving system covering the entire 0·5 to 18 GHz frequency range. The system provides combined control and display functions for a high sensitivity superheterodyne receiver and a servo-controlled rotary DF antenna. The WJ-945 system is configured to minimise the total number of components, offering maximum operator control and display flexibility in the minimum possible equipment rack space.

The system configuration provides each operator with a receiver/DF control unit and two storage type CRT display monitors. Both CRTs in the standard system design are installed directly above the receiver/DF control unit to optimise operation and observation of the system. The microwave tuners used in the WJ-945 system are miniature WJ-940 tuners (described in **3352.053** in earlier editions). These are mounted in groups of three in tuner

enclosure/junction units. Two tuner enclosure/junction units, housing six WJ-940 tuners, allow coverage of the 0·5 to 18 GHz frequency range.

A control/servo drive for the DF antenna is generally located near the antenna pedestal and tuners, and this contains all of the required video processing, digital control and analogue circuitry necessary for antenna control and the DF display generator. This unit also provides digital control outputs for controlling RF switches between the DF and omni antennas and the microwave tuners. The EP-30 antenna pedestal is designed for simplicity, ruggedness, reliability, and ease of maintenance. The pedestal contains a permanent magnet DC torque motor for clock- and counter-clockwise rotation and heavy duty sealed bearings for rotational support.

The L6 spinning DF antenna provides frequency coverage from 0·5 to 18 GHz. The WJ-8535-11 is a very small bi-conical horn broadband omni-directional antenna covering 0·5 to 18 GHz. The polarisation is 45° slant linear.

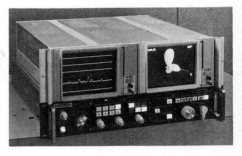

Watkins-Johnson WJ-945 receiving/DF system

STATUS
Production.
CONTRACTOR
Watkins-Johnson Company, 2525 North First Street, San Jose, California 95131, USA.

4391.053
C-204/WJ-1140 ANALYSIS CONTROL UNIT

The C-204/WJ-1140 analysis control unit performs three major receiving system functions: operator interface and system control, automatic signal parameter measurement and automatic signal identification. The ACU is a compact unit that replaces four separate units required in older receiving systems (receiver control, video processing, digital processing and alpha-numeric display units). The ACU's automatic operating modes decrease signal identification time and operator training requirements.

The ACU's electronics contain a high-speed microprocessor that controls the unit and performs signal analysis. Under firmware control, the microprocessor compares received signals to a user provided signal library and outputs an alpha-numeric code representing the signal source. Signal parameters are derived from time of arrival (TOA), amplitude, pulse width, and angle of arrival (AOA) data.

To facilitate real-time operator decision making, the ACU provides six different alpha-numeric analysis display formats. Indicators in the upper-left-hand and upper-right-hand fields of display formats notify the operator of 'page' numbers being presented and number of pages of stored information. As an example of display applications, System Status

C-204/WJ-1140 analysis control unit

Displays give overall information concerning system operations (operating mode, threshold level, frequency range, marker location, IF bandwidth, sweep speed, and IF attenuation for each RF tuner), while Pulse-by-Pulse and average PRI formats give parameters for individual pulses within current pulse trains. Average PRI and Pulse-by-Pulse formats used together (cross-referenced by using a NEXT CHAPT button) are particularly useful in determining n-tuplet and stagger characteristics of multiple pulse train signals.

The ACU can control up to six tuners with a

frequency range of 500 MHz to 18 GHz (ACU generated tuner modes include fixed, band scan, limit scan or sector scan). In typical configurations using six tuners, each tuner can be used to cover one octave band. The ACU generates frequency control commands and transfers them via the tuner junction to each of the tuners. The ACU serially sequences through tuners at a scan rate determined by the ACU under operator control or automatic control. The ACU also controls the parameters for IF bandwidth filtering, IF attenuation, and log-video detection, which are used by an external demodulator to process the RF-to-IF converted signals routed to it from the tuners. The demodulator, in turn, provides the ACU with the IF for its signal-centring circuitry and the log video for the ACU's signal parameter measurements.

In addition, ACU control determines manual or automatic system operating modes, which gives the operator flexibility to operate effectively in the changing environment. When used in automatic modes, the system performs scan lock, scan search and auto search functions. In each of the automatic modes, the ACU halts tuner scan for signal measurement whenever emitters exceed operator controlled threshold levels.
CONTRACTOR
Watkins-Johnson Company, 2525 North First Street, San Jose, California 95131, USA.

4392.093
WJ-1920 MULTIPARAMETER DISTRIBUTED PROCESSING SYSTEM

The WJ-1920 multiparameter distributed processing (MDP) system, combines superhet and wideband technologies in a unique way to build a wide open receiver that provides instantaneous intercept and recognition of signals in the 0·5 to 40 GHz range. The

WJ-1921 pulse interval processor

WJ-1920 system is built upon three functional units: the IFM, the superhet, and the display/filter sub-systems. In the instantaneous frequency measurement unit, signals from an IFM or other broadband receiver channel, are processed through a WJ-1921 pulse interval processor (PIP) and tagged in real-time according to their PRI characteristics. This PIP is central to the entire multiparameter distributed processing concept and uses a newly developed PRI time domain transform algorithm which allows a receiver to function in the PRI domain as a channelised receiver does in the frequency domain.

In addition to signal parameters, the WJ-1920 system can incorporate other parameters into its sorting matrix to enhance monopulse character-isation and measurement capabilities (eg, pulse width, pulse amplitude, pulse direction of arrival) and even more subtle characteristics, such as pulse risetime, or pulse shape characteristics. This additional data can then be screened by the WJ-1234 (ACU) channel, displayed on the multiparameter display, or diverted for further automatic processing.
CHARACTERISTICS
Input waveform: Log or threshold video
Outputs: PRF versus activity display; PRI versus

activity display; option for display cursor and gated video output; residue output
PRI range: 100 μs – 10 ms (100 Hz – 10kHz). Extended ranges available. Jitter tolerance 1 – 256 μs, switch selectable
Pulse density: Up to 250 kpps single-signal, up to 50 kpps for most multiple signal environments
De-interleaving: Unlimited number of simultaneous pulse trains provided total pulse density is within limits
Sub-harmonics: Automatic rejection of sub-harmonic responses
Acquisition: 3 – 8 consecutive pulses depending on mode control setting
Scan rate: Channelised operation: processor is wide open to all PRIs
POI: Probability of intercept equals 100% for qualifying pulse trains
Display: Flicker-free refreshed PRI/PRF spectrum with adjustable decay rate
Size: 177 × 482 × 482 mm
Weight: 18·2 kg
CONTRACTOR
Watkins-Johnson Company, 2525 North First Street, San Jose, California 95131, USA.

3665.093
WJ-1205B VIDEO DIGITISER UNIT (VDU)

The WJ-1205B video digitiser unit (VDU) is a microprocessor-controlled, high-speed pulse train analyser with a pulse sample capacity of up to 512 pulses. These pulses may be digitised for analysis of pulse characteristics – pulse width (PW), pulse repetition interval (PRI), and average pulse amplitude. The WJ-1205B furnishes average pulse repetition interval screening for interpreting complex pulse trains. A visual indication of these pulse rates is provided on the front panel of the video digitiser unit, along with operator controls. A self-test capability for unit checkout is also provided. Auxiliary equipment, such as an external computer, or line printer may be connected through a single rear-panel connector.

The WJ-1205B may be operated with its own internal, temperature-controlled crystal oscillator or phase-locked to a reference frequency provided by an external signal source (video tape recorder). Front end signal sampling may be gated internally by program control or by an external signal source (video disc). The VDU permits precise pulse-by-pulse analysis of modulated signals as well as other complex-grouped signals. To facilitate the de-interleaving of multiple pulse trains, the unit analyses all pulse repetition intervals present in the video input stream and can compute up to eight independent PRIs that might exist. Pulse amplitude measurements permit additional analysis of the received signals.

CHARACTERISTICS

Video input dynamic range: 0·2 – 2 V (other ranges available)
Pulse sample capacity: 511 pulses standard; can be expanded to 767 in increments of 32
Sample interval: 100 ns
Event measurement accuracy: ±100 ns
Pulsewidth measurement: 100 ns (minimum)
Pulse amplitude measurement: Relative value of 0 –255 over video dynamic range
Tape reference tone input: 50, 100, or 200 kHz; amplitude 1 – 18 V rms
External sync input: Positive true range from 5 – 12 V peak, 100 μs minimum pulsewidth
Threshold output: TTL compatible
Digital data output: TTY and RS-232 compatible, serial rates up to 9600 baud. Parallel output also available for computer or line printer output
Internal clock: 10 MHz temperature-controlled crystal

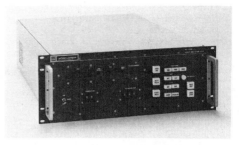

Watkins-Johnson WJ-1205B video digitiser unit (VDU)

Dimensions: 482 × 177 × 457 mm
Mounting: Standard 19 in equipment rack
Weight: 15·8 kg
Displays: 0·5 in LEDs
STATUS
Production.
CONTRACTOR
Watkins-Johnson Company, 2525 North First Street, San Jose, California 95131, USA.

4390.053
WJ-927 ESM EQUIPMENT

The WJ-927 system is a highly versatile microwave DF and signal analysis system which provides carry-on ESM capability for airborne, as well as shipboard, mobile, and fixed-site applications. It is small and lightweight, and consumes little power, while attaining high sensitivity and overall exceptional performance characteristics (5 to 18 GHz; expansible to 40 GHz coverage).

The WJ-1234 analysis control unit (ACU), the heart of the WJ-927 system, provides both flexibility and data handling capability previously available only in larger and more complex units. Highly specialised control and analysis functions are performed automatically by the ACU through the use of its solid state base and microprocessor control technology. Specific parameters of signals of known interest can be programmed into the unit. Used as a basis of comparison, this data provides the operator with quick identification of detected signals that match these parameters. In addition, its automatic signal analysis techniques allow the ACU to perform specific or directed search processes. In this mode of operation, the ACU enables only information on detected signals that constitute a match to be displayed to the operator.

In addition, the ACU offers disc and CRT options which allow on-line modifications of the user's library file. Several other interface options are also available to allow integration of the ACU with other on-board systems or units such as the line printer, magnetic tape recorders, and time code reader interfaces, as well as video and IF outputs for analogue recording of signals of interest.

The antenna sub-system of the WJ-927 consists of a direction-finding antenna, an omni-directional antenna, a control/display unit, and an antenna pedestal.

Watkins-Johnson has developed a DF antenna with a fan-beam pattern that yields narrow azimuth beamwidths for accurate direction-finding and broad elevation beamwidth to enhance the probability of detecting signals independent of aircraft altitude. Antenna DF accuracy is ±1° RMS over the full band and not greater than ±5° absolute at the low end of the band.

The WJ-8535-11 omni-directional antenna which has been chosen for this application gives excellent performance in the 0·5 to 18 GHz frequency range with a deviation from omni-directional of ±3 dB over 90 per cent of the band. The antenna is available with vertical or slant linear polarisation. The antenna itself is 14 cm high with a 14·7 cm diameter base and is mounted inside a low-loss dielectric radome.

The EC-60 control/display unit is the only unit available which provides all control functions (including sector scan) and all display functions, while also containing all of the servo modules necessary for the pedestal.

CONTRACTOR
Watkins-Johnson Company, 2525 North First Street, San Jose, California 95131, USA.

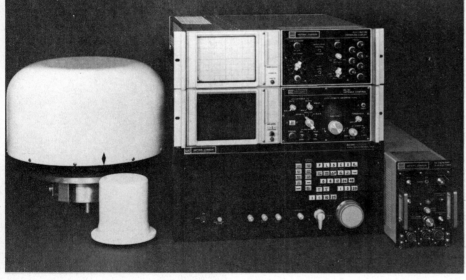

WJ-927 signal analysis equipment

4393.053
WJ-1988 AMPLITUDE MONOPULSE DF PROCESSOR

The WJ-1988 amplitude monopulse DF processor is an economical direction finding sub-system designed to be used with various types of static antenna arrays within tactical and strategic ESM applications. By enabling a single wideband tuner to simultaneously process the DF outputs of each antenna within an array, the WJ-1988 eliminates the need for multiple tuners/receivers.

The WJ-1988 equipment provides processing of five channels of simultaneous RF information (one omni antenna and four sector antennas) over the frequency range of 2 to 18 GHz. It consists of an active multiplexer (a small set of components located directly at the antennas), an MD-200 DF processor unit, and a C-100 control and display unit. Antennas and the receiver are separately required and are dependent on the user requirements. Because the composite signal after encoding is a wideband signal (500 MHz bandwidth), a wideband receiver such as the Watkins-Johnson Company TN-1000 MINCEIVER is recommended.

When used in combination with standard wideband receivers, the WJ-1988 develops a monochannel processing technique, which is made possible by a special bi-phase encoding method which the WJ-1988 uses to 'tag' or encode antenna signals. Bi-phase encoding is accomplished by spreading the original spectral power to produce a null at the original signal frequency. This encoding procedure prevents interferometry effects from occurring in signal processing when signals are combined for RF summation, and it also results in an improvement upon the maintenance of original signal integrity during signal processing.

CHARACTERISTICS

Number of channels: 5 (4 DF and 1 omni-channel)
Frequency range: 2 – 18 GHz
DF sensitivity: –78 dBm (typical antennas)
Omni sensitivity: –83 dBm (typical antenna)
Dynamic range: 60 dB minimum
DF accuracy: 4° rms

WJ-1988 amplitude monopulse DF processor

Instantaneous bandwidth: 5 MHz
Throughput rate: 700 kps
Weight: MD-200 16 kg; C-100 and display 13·6 kg
CONTRACTOR
Watkins-Johnson Company, 2525 North First Street, San Jose, California 95131, USA.

1381.053
L-6/A-WJ-1140 MICROWAVE DIRECTION FINDING SYSTEM

This is an integrated microwave direction-finding (DF) system, produced by the combination of the L-6/A broadband DF antenna system and the WJ-1140 modular microwave receiving system.

The broadband DF antenna system (L-6/A) is designed to function as a component of an electro-mechanical reconnaissance system when used in conjunction with the WJ-1140 receiver system. The L-6/A provides a visual display of the direction of arrival (DOA) of incoming RF signals that have been processed through the receiving portion of the overall DF system.

Lightweight and compact mechanical packaging makes the L-6/A suitable for use in airborne configurations as well as shipboard and fixed/mobile ground installations. The frequency coverage of this antenna system is 500 MHz to 18 GHz in six bands. Variable azimuth rotation sweep from 0 to 2000 rpm is accomplished through a control on the console.

In addition, the antenna can be steered to any desired azimuth point by a manual control knob located on the indicator. The radiation patterns of the antenna are relatively broad, with circular polarisation. This offers an optimum compromise between probability of signal intercept, direction-finding accuracy and gain. The RF output of the L-6/A system is entirely compatible with the WJ-1140 and the interface is accomplished through the use of standard RF coaxial cabling and connectors.

Used in conjunction with the L-6/A, the WJ-1140 would involve RF tuners covering the ranges 500 to 1000, 1000 to 2000, 2000 to 4000, 4000 to 8000, 8000 to 12 000 and 12 000 to 18 000 MHz. Signals acquired by the L-6/A are simultaneously available at all times to the WJ-1140 tuners without the requirement of RF band switching. Incoming signals are then processed through the appropriate tuners and mixed down to an IF frequency of 160 MHz for processing by the demodulator.

By use of another broadband antenna system, the L/5A, frequency coverage is extended from 18 to 40 GHz. This has similar pedestal and turning gear to the L6/A, but instead of rotating horn elements, the L5/A has fixed horns near the centre of rotation, directed up on a spinning reflector plate which is responsible for 360° azimuth coverage. To extend frequency coverage downward a companion antenna/receiver combination (L4/A/RS-160) is available covering the band 40 to 550 MHz.

CONTRACTOR
Watkins-Johnson Company, 2525 North First Street, San Jose, California 95131, USA.

WJ-1140 0·5 to 18 GHz microwave direction-finding receiver system with omni-directional antenna system

1716.053
WJ-1240 RECEIVING SYSTEM

The WJ-1240 is a computer-controlled receiving system for reconnaissance and surveillance applications over the radio frequency band 0·03 to 40 GHz, and it also has independent digital tuner control and parallel video display. The equipment consists of a modular integrated electronics package comprising the computerised WJ-1240 receiver itself, display and controls, and a direction-finding antenna system.

Independent tuner control permits multiple situation surveillance and provides independent video outputs for each tuner. This control operates in the absence of the computer for manual systems or as a standby mode of operation in computer-controlled versions. A digitally refreshed display with adjustable decay time retains single pulse signals for detailed visual observation. Display traces are automatically scaled during sector scan.

Several antenna assemblies may be used with the WJ-1240 depending upon the total frequency coverage demanded. The WJ-8312 provides direction-finding facilities over the range 0·1 to 18 GHz. Other Watkins-Johnson arrays which can be employed are the L4/A (40 to 550 MHz), L/5A (12 to 40 GHz), and the L/6A.

The WJ-8312 consists of a rigid box structure supported on the turning gear pedestal and carrying a series of microwave receiver horns. Intercepted signals are directed into the horns (which are of dimensions appropriate to the frequency bands covered) by a curved plate reflector which rotates with the whole assembly. This reflector carries at its upper edge a log-periodic array for reception of the lower frequencies.

CONTRACTOR
Watkins-Johnson Company, 2525 North First Street, San Jose, California 95131, USA.

WJ-8312 direction finding antenna

3666.193
WJ-1424 MICROWAVE RECEIVER (TLR-31)

The WJ-1424 microwave receiver is a small, rugged, special-purpose system covering the frequency range from 10 to 40 GHz (the lower frequency limit may be extended down to 1 GHz as an option). Its compact, modular design lends itself well to applications requiring minimum weight and space consumption. Many functions normally designed into individual units have been integrated to provide multi-functional control and display units. The system includes all the elements necessary for a completely operational receiver. The system is comprised of a spinning directional antenna with radome, RF distribution, receiver control, and signal analysis units. The prime power requirement is 110 V AC, 9·2 amps, 37 to 400 Hz.

In its vehicle mounted form, it is believed to carry the designation AN/TLR-31. The receiver control unit provides all system operating control functions including antenna scan control. It also contains pulse analysis circuitry to perform fundamental signal analysis. The receiver operates in three modes: Spectrum, Pan and Analysis/DF. A single-frequency amplitude display is presented to the operator in the Pan mode. When the operator selects DF at the control, the CRT presents signal amplitude in a polar format for bearing information. Signal RF frequency and azimuth are displayed to the operator in digital form via LEDs on the control unit front panel. When utilising the pulse analysis function, the same LEDs provide digital readouts of pulse repetition interval or pulse repetition frequency..

The stand-alone system has been integrated with the AN/MLQ-24 countermeasures receiving set to extend the frequency range coverage into the millimeter wave region.

STATUS
In production and operational.

CONTRACTOR
Watkins-Johnson Company, 2525 North First Street, San Jose, California 95131, USA.

WJ-1424 microwave receiver set (TLR-31) with antenna radome and drive unit on right

---

4394.053
WJ-1440 MICROWAVE RECEIVER SYSTEM

Derived from the fully-militarised WJ-1740 microwave receiver system (**3354.053**), the WJ-1440 incorporates added features that allow it to achieve a wider range of application with fewer optional requirements. The microprocessor controlled memory scan, for example, which is an option in the WJ-1740, has been standardised in the WJ-1440 system. This feature permits the operator to store up to 16 scan control blocks for recall. By selecting the memory scan mode, the operator can cause the receiver to automatically scan through any pre-selected number of scan control blocks, causing them to be sequentially displayed on an analysis display, which can be used to display DF and pulse analysis as well as normal receiver functions. Another WJ-1740 option that has been incorporated into the WJ-1440 standard design is a tuner integrated local oscillator synchroniser (TILOS). TILOS increases overall stability and frequency accuracy to 1 part in 10^7 per day standard.

The WJ-1440 also has analysis alternate mode selection and control to enable expansion of a sector within a band without compromising operator contact with a full-band scan display. In alternate mode, the controller alternately sweeps a tuner through a sector and an entire band, which are displayed on analysis display as two distinct traces, with full-band activity displayed above sector activity display.

Another feature, automatic signal acquisition circuitry, alerts an operator whenever signals exceed a variable (operator-set) threshold level within a sector of interest. Automatic signal acquisition has two basic operating modes: in LOCK mode, receivers lock onto signals exceeding a threshold level within a selected sector; AUTO mode, while similar to LOCK mode, enables receivers to also automatically resume sweep operations several seconds after lock-on. The WJ-1440 also has a DWELL mode that is unrelated to signal threshold level. DWELL enables receivers to dwell at a marker frequency once every sweep, thus allowing analysis of a specific frequency while maintaining continuous sector coverage.

The WJ-1440 system also offers optional scanner hardware, which, when used in conjunction with a refreshed display, enhances system capability by providing multiple scan sectors in each tuner and completely independent sweep rates. The scanner

WJ-1440 microwave receiver system

option enhances system capability by allowing each tuner to scan one or more operator-programmed frequency sectors independently from and in parallel with all other system tuners. In essence, the scanner permits each tuner to perform its own memory scan.

CONTRACTOR
Watkins-Johnson Company, 2525 North First Street, San Jose, California 95131, USA.

3354.053
WJ-1740 RECEIVING SYSTEM

The WJ-1740 is a parallel-scanned, digitally controlled superheterodyne receiver system which can include as many as eight tuners (12 for special applications) in any combination of frequency bands. The tuners cover the 0·03 to 40 GHz range in nine frequency bands. Tuners are scanned synchronously, in parallel, although the operator can call any one tuner from the scan for signal analysis.

Selection of a tuner for manual analysis switches the IF output of the tuner to an analysis demodulator channel that provides IF attenuation control, IF bandwidth control, and linear with or without AGC, log, or FM video outputs. The tuner selected can also be phase-locked to a stable crystal-controlled reference in a local oscillator synchroniser to provide frequency accuracy and stability of one part in 10^7 per day.

The analysis video is presented on the analysis display, and the tuner selected for analysis can be operated in manual, sector scan, or band scan modes. In the first of these modes, the analysis display provides an IF pan signal presentation; when the tuner in the analysis channel is in either of the other two modes, the display indicates signal activity versus frequency, with the horizontal frequency scale automatically expanded to cover the full width of the CRT.

The system provides auxiliary IF outputs from each tuner, and auxiliary scan demodulator log video outputs for each tuner. It also provides IF and video outputs from the analysis channel.

Individual tuners can be placed in the Hold mode to provide continuous monitoring of signals, and up to 16 frequencies can be stored in memory for instantaneous push-button controlled recall. In the Hold mode, a tuner is tuned to one frequency and its IF and video outputs can be applied to either a tape recorder or special analysis equipment.

An optional memory scan unit provides 64 memory cells and a memory scan mode permitting a programmed search strategy.

The complete system was designed to permit full manual or computer-assisted operation and control by as many as four different operators through individual receiver control panels.

In a computer-assisted WJ-1740 system, the computer monitors the receiver scan, monitors signal activity, makes tentative signal identifications, and records data, leaving the operator free to identify signals and perform detailed analysis tasks.

DEVELOPMENT
The WJ-1740 receiver system was developed for a USAF airborne application.

CONTRACTOR
Watkins-Johnson Company, 2525 North First Street, San Jose, California 95131, USA.

3355.053
WJ-1840 RECEIVING SYSTEM

The WJ-1840 microwave receiver system is a broadband equipment that covers the frequency range 0·5 to 18 GHz with a single two-segment superheterodyne RF tuner contained within an A1D enclosure. The 0·5 to 8 GHz segment is an up-converting dual superhet, while a standard pre-selected single-conversion superhet is used for the 8 to 18 GHz segment. Digital control circuitry permits band scanning, sector scan, and manual modes of operation as well as special dependent, dwell, and intercept modes.

A two-trace display shows signal activity over the full frequency range, over two sectors, or over one sector and a dependent sub-sector. Frequency data is written directly on the face of the CRT in alpha-numeric form. A five-trace display is available as an option.

An optional analysis display is available for time base analysis of pulses as short as 10 nanoseconds.

Additionally, IF pan analysis with 1 MHz resolution and 200 MHz bandwidth polar display are available within the analysis display. The optional WJ-8535-11 antenna is a slant-linear polarised bi-conical omni-directional antenna covering the whole of the receiver band.

CHARACTERISTICS

Frequency range: 0·5 – 18 GHz
Noise figure: 18 dB typical, 23 dB max
RF IF bandwidth: 200 MHz nominal
Image rejection: 80 dB typical, 60 dB minimum
Local oscillator radiation: 1 – 12 GHz: –80 dBm max; 12 – 18 GHz: –70 dBM max
Frequency accuracy (max): 0·5 – 18 GHz; ±(·00zf + 10) MHz
Incidental FM (rms): 10 kHz typical, 50 kHz max
1 dB compression point: –20 dBm minimum
Sweep rate: 175 GHz/s max
Video: Logarithmic
Input power: 115 ± 10 or 220 ± 20 V AC, 48 – 420 Hz
CONTRACTOR
Watkins-Johnson Company, 2525 North First Street, San Jose, California 95131, USA.

Watkins-Johnson WJ-1840 broadband receiving system

WJ-8535 antenna unit

4395.053
TN-1000/WJ-1840 MINCEIVER

The TN-1000/WJ-1840 is an alternate tuner for the WJ-1840 receiving system. It uses advances in miniaturisation technology which make it highly

Watkins-Johnson TN-1000/WJ-184

suited for applications where small size, weight, and general portability are important.

The TN-1000 MINCEIVER has an RF performance that matches or exceeds that of larger units. It covers 0·5 to 18 GHz frequency range with a 500 MHz instantaneous bandwidth and a noise figure of 19 dB. With this dynamic range, it is excellent for both single signal and two tone intermodulation.

The equipment incorporates its own power supply and synthesiser, and uses isolated microstrip modules within its circuitry to reduce interstage loss, gain variation and signal radiation. The MINCEIVER also has a modular MINPAC low-profile mixer and an amplifier design to simplify repair and replacement of individual RF functional blocks, which can be extremely difficult with conventional MIC design. Modularity also allows for upgrading performance as better mixers and amplifiers are developed.

Preamplifiers are not included as part of the basic MINCEIVER. In many applications, a wide dynamic range is of greater importance than high sensitivity (low noise figure) because the receiver sees an R² signal power advantage over the radar receiver. However in specialised surveillance applications, where high sensitivity is a primary concern, preamplification is available to reduce the overall noise figure. Depending on system constraints and the noise figures required, preamplifiers may be either inside or outside the MINCEIVER.

CHARACTERISTICS

Frequency range: 0·5 – 18 GHz
Noise figure without preamplifiers: 19 dB
Gain (RF to IF): 15 dB
Two-tone dynamic range: 70 dB
1 dB compression dynamic range: 94 dB
Image rejection: 70 dB
Minimum frequency step size: 500 kHz
Output IF: 0·75 – 1·25 GHz
Temperature range: 0 – 50° C
Weight: 7·7 kg
Total power consumption: 60 W max
CONTRACTOR
Watkins-Johnson Company, 2525 North First Street, San Jose, California 95131, USA.

4396.053
QRC-259 RECEIVER SYSTEM

The QRC-259 receiver system is a solid-state, electronically-tuned superheterodyne receiver system providing high frequency accuracy, high stability and high sensitivity. It is qualified to meet severe environmental and EMI specifications, and has been deployed under both field and airborne conditions. The QRC-259 also permits unmanned automatic/semi-automatic or fully-integrated operator computer operations.

Up to ten tuners, in any combination of types, can be connected in any QAR-259 receiver system. This flexibility enhances the system's frequency stretching capability above or below typically used frequency limits. All tuners in the system are connected to a tuner relay, which can select one of the tuners for direct operator control by switching tuning commands to the tuner and by switching the tuner's IF output to an IF processor. Tuners not under direct operator control can be controlled independently, as separate tuners, or by auxiliary digital-control inputs applied to the tuner relay.

The QRC-259 system can be operated manually or by automatic band and limited frequency scanning. It can also be operated in either scan-lock or tuner-hold mode. When the receiver is in scan-lock, it intercepts signals exceeding an operator-set threshold level. If an intercepted signal meets criteria for qualification as a true signal, the receiver locks on to the signal by switching to the manual mode at the signal frequency. In hold mode, the tuner remains tuned to the frequency it was tuned to when the operator put it in hold, and its IF output is made available for processing by peripheral equipment. During this time, the other units of the receiver remain under normal operator control.

Another QRC-259 feature is a pulse coincidence detector function that determines the time coincidence between a received pulsed signal and an

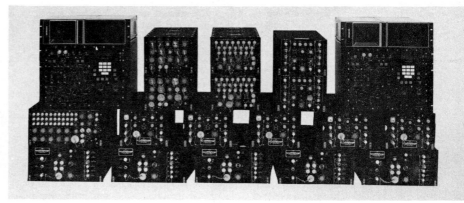

QRC-259 receiver system equipment

externally-applied video pulse. The reference pulse used for this purpose can be derived from another receiver or by local generation. When the system is used in a dual-channel configuration (using two operators), two channels can be connected together to examine the environment for coincident emitters. (Coincidence is defined as existing when two pulses are within five microseconds of each other.)

QRC-259 Available Options

AFC
Provides the operator with the capability of automatically centring the received signal in the passband.

CW
Provides increased sensitivity to CW signals.

Frequency Limit Readout
Allows operator to read out stored upper and lower scan limit frequencies.

Hold Frequency Readout
Allows operator to read out frequency of tuner in hold.

Memory and Memory Gate
Stores up to eight frequencies for instantaneous pushbutton recall, and for frequency gating.

Raster Display
Provides falling raster display for time-history of signal activity and for detection enhancement.

RF Gating and Crystal Video
Provides crystal video outputs of each tuner and permits video to be blanked when tuner's dynamic range is exceeded.

Predetection Conversion
Provides predetection IF conversion for recording.

Product Detector
Provides BFO capability.

STATUS
Production.
CONTRACTOR
Watkins-Johnson Company, 2525 North First Street, San Jose, California 95131, USA.

3875.093
L6-24 DF SYSTEM

The L6-24 DF system is used for radar signal collection and analysis operations and related EW applications. It is a passive ECM equipment consisting of a Watkins-Johnson L6-24 spinning direction-finding antenna and EP-30 pedestal, controlled by an EC-60 control/display unit. The EC-60 is mounted with a companion storage-tube CRT display in a standard 19-in rack. The EC-60 contains a four-decade digital display for bearing read-out and has three modes of antenna operation; scan, slew, and sector scan, which are selectable from the front panel. Available options include true or relative bearing presentation, adjustable video threshold, panel modifications and additional cabling to suit specific installations requirements. The system is capable of use in airborne, shipboard and land-based applications and the control system may be used with other Watkins-Johnson antenna and pedestal installations.

The L6-24 spinning DF antenna is a small unit (203 × 381 mm) and provides a frequency coverage over the range 1 to 18 GHz. There is a wide selection of frequency band breaks and signal polarisation options, as well as a choice of switched or simultaneous radio frequency outputs. The antenna consists of a rotating dish with a foam-filled feed, enclosed within a protective radome. The EP-30

The L6-24 DF system with EP-30 pedestal and L6-24 spinning antenna unit on left, and EC-60 control/display on right

pedestal provides for rotation of the antenna at variable speeds of up to 200 rpm in either direction.
STATUS
The 6-24 system is used by the US Air Force for radar signal collection. In early 1980 Watkins-Johnson was awarded a $3·5 million contract to extend the

capabilities of the system; this probably involves extending the frequency coverage beyond 18 GHz but may also entail additional analysis facilities.
CONTRACTOR
Watkins-Johnson Company, 2525 North First Street, San Jose, California 95131, USA.

4397.053
CMR-610A WIDEBAND DF RECEIVER

The CMR-610A is a wideband DF receiver designed to provide both visual and aural signal indication of microwave and millimetric activity occurring in the 1·5 to 40 GHz frequency range. The CMR-610A will detect, locate and assign direction to CW, AM, FM and pulse-modulated signals. The receiver has the provision for demodulating audio-modulated signals and has an integral recorder output.

The CMR-610A is a miniature, hand-held, solid-state, battery powered, five-band, crystal video

receiver with integral antennas and battery pack. The frequency band to be monitored is selected by the band switch which connects the selected antenna/detector combination to either the video or audio amplifier, according to the mode switch setting in the AM mode of operation. The selected detector output is connected to the video amplifier whose output is routed to the operator's headset, the signal level meter and the recorder output jack. In CW and audio operation the selected detector output is connected to the audio amplifier.

CHARACTERISTICS
Frequency bands:
Band 1: 1·5 – 8 GHz; Band 2: 8 – 12·4 GHz; Band 3: 12·4 – 18 GHz; Band 4: 18 – 26·5 GHz; Band 5: 26·5 – 40 GHz
Dimensions: 89 mm high × 89 mm wide ×197 mm deep
Weight: 1·6 kg
CONTRACTOR
American Electronic Laboratories Incorporated, PO Box 552, Lansdale, Pennsylvania 19446, USA.

4673.093
RG-5202A VHF SCANNING RECEIVER

The RG-5202A is a scanning receiver designed to scan and monitor up to sixteen RF channels in the frequency range 20 to 512 MHz. Each channel can be set to receive either AM or FM signals with a choice of IF bandwidths of 10, 20, 40 or 60 kHz. The receiver

can be operated by the front panel controls or remotely through control lines. A memory bank stores the tuned frequency, the IF bandwidth, the demodulator mode and the manual/automatic gain choice for each of 16 channels. Frequency information to the nearest 10 Hz is entered into memory by a keyboard.

The time devoted to each channel can be set from 0·1 to 10 seconds. The channel being monitored is indicated by a tone encoded output for remote indication.
CONTRACTOR
Racal Communications Inc, 5 Research Place, Rockville, Maryland 20850, USA.

4398.053
RG-5540 VHF/UHF MONITORING RECEIVER

The RG-5540 is a high performance VHF/UHF receiver designed for reception of signals in the 20 to 500 MHz band with 10 Hz tuning resolution. It can detect AM, FM, CW, USB, LSB, and ISB signals. The receiver includes four IF modules with bandwidths from 10 to 500 kHz; 10, 20, 50 and 100 kHz bandwidths are standard.

The RG-5540 has three operating modes; Manual, Remote and Fast Scan. In the manual mode the receiver is a conventional 'hands-off' receiver with operator control of all functions. Tuning is by a large tuning knob or up/down slew key (with three rates), direct numeric key pad entry or an internal scan mode. The scan mode continuously tunes the receiver up and down at nine selectable rates between 10 Hz/second and 1000 MHz/second. Frequency is indicated by an eight-digit LED display; tuning and level meters located under the display aid operator

tuning. LED-illuminated keys select IF bandwidth, detection mode, gain control mode, and internal or external reference. A dual (stereo) headphone level control, remote/local switch, RF gain slew key and power switch complete the front panel operator controls. A non-volatile memory preserves all operating parameters when power is removed.

In the remote mode, the receiver functions are controlled via an IEEE-4888 interface. These functions include tuned frequency, IF bandwidth, detection mode, RF gain mode, RF gain frequency scan and internal/external reference. Commands are provided for full set-up or the setting of individual parameters. The receiver status can also be requested, in either remote or local mode. The receiver front panel displays the operating conditions at all times.

In the fast scan mode, the receiver operates under the control of a spectrum surveillance controller to provide a high-speed spectrum scan with digitally

refreshed display. A discrete scan of up to 15 channels is also provided.

An optional front panel plug-in spectrum display is available. When installed, this unit, the RG-1320A spectrum display unit, provides a visual display of signal activity about the tuned frequency. The sweep width is variable from 0 to 400 kHz, with 1 kHz resolution.
CHARACTERISTICS
Frequency range: 20 – 500 MHz
Frequency resolution: 10 Hz
Demodulation modes: Standard: AM, FM, CW; Optional: USB, LSB, ISB
Dimensions: 48·3 cm wide × 13·3 cm high × 51 cm deep
Weight: 27·3 kg
CONTRACTOR
Racal Communications Inc, 5 Research Place, Rockville, Maryland 20850, USA.

4674.093
RG-5545A VHF/UHF RECEIVER

The RG-5545A is a high-performance VHF/UHF receiver that has been specifically designed to allow versatile configured features by means of performance options to the basic unit and is ideally

suited for monitoring purposes. The basic unit is a 20 to 500 MHz receiver with AM and FM detectors and four selectable IF bandwidths. Tuning is accomplished to 10 HZ resolution by means of a synthesiser. All local oscillators are phase-locked to a single master reference oscillator, either internal or

external, for low phase noise and maximum frequency stability. The RG-5545A has been designed for signal handling in dense electromagnetic environments.

A frequency extension option extends the range to 20 to 1000 MHz, 20 to 1400 MHz or 20 to 1800 MHz.

These options include preselection above 500 MHz for a +50 dBm 2nd order intermodulation intercept point.

CONTRACTOR
Racal Communications Inc, 5 Research Place, Rockville, Maryland 20850, USA.

RG-5545A receiver and RG-1320A display

4676.093
RA6778-C RECEIVER/RA6778-Q CONVERTER

The RA6778-C receiver is a fully synthesised microprocessor based equipment for communication or monitoring over the frequency range from 10 kHz to 30 MHz. The equipment can be controlled manually or by computer and has an interactive man/computer interface. Control capability is hardware adaptable to conform to system requirements.

The RA6778-Q converter is a microprocessor controlled tuneable equipment for communication or monitoring over the band 50 kHz to 30 MHz. It provides a 70 kHz IF signal 100 kHz wide which may be used in applications for wideband spectral analysis or demodulation of HF signal.

Both equipments are of modular construction and have LED tuned frequency indicators. Frequency stability of 1 part in 10 is provided as standard with 1 part in 10 optionally available.

CONTRACTOR
Racal Communications Inc, 5 Research Place, Rockville, Maryland 20850, USA.

RA6778-C receiver

4675.093
RA-6793A HF RECEIVER

The RA-6793A is an HF receiver covering the range 0·5 to 30 MHz and used for monitoring purposes in the communications field. Two of the features of this system are its ability to provide full scan and sweep facilities under both local and remote control. The standard scan provides a means to scan up to 100 channels actively with a fixed but selectable dwell between channels for operation interaction. A secondary scan mode allows the operator to set different activity recognition thresholds to each scanned channel, whereupon the receiver will halt on activity.

Sweep provides the capability to set start and stop frequencies and step increment. After sweep initiation, the operator can control the incremental speed and halt the sweep if required. The equipment operates in AM, FM, CW, USB and LSB reception modes. Frequency display is by easy-to-read illuminated liquid crystal display on the front panel.

CONTRACTOR
Racal Communications Inc, 5 Research Place, Rockville, Maryland 20850, USA.

RA-6793A HF receiver

4399.093
RG-1340 SPECTRUM SURVEILLANCE CONTROLLER

The RG-1340 spectrum surveillance controller is designed to work in conjunction with the RG-5540 (4398.053) receiver and an external cathode ray tube display forming a surveillance group for monitoring any segment of, or 15 discrete frequencies in, the 20 to 500 MHz band. The RG-1340 provides external scan control to the RG-5540 receiver and X, Y and Z axis information to the display. The spectrum surveillance group may be controlled locally using its own RG-1340 controls or remotely using an IEEE-4888 interface. Alpha-numeric information on the display provides status and operator prompting, and the display is refreshed 50 times per second.

The controller has three operating modes: band scan, discrete scan and manual.

In band scan mode, the controller steps the receiver between two programmed frequency limits. The controller also controls the receiver bandwidth. A signal averaging feature enables an operator to integrate noise and make signals more visible. The operator-controlled cursor can be positioned on a signal of interest; alpha-numerics display the cursor frequency.

In the discrete scan mode, up to 15 different frequencies can be monitored. Frequency, IF bandwidth, dwell time, threshold level and actual level for each channel are displayed in alpha-numeric form on the display. Channel set-ups are automatically arranged from top to bottom in order of ascending frequency, and any channel can be skipped during the scan.

In manual mode, the controller returns control of the system to the receiver front panel. At this time, the display indicates an IF panoramic scan identical to that of an RG-1320A spectrum display unit installed in the left side of the receiver.

The controller front panel consists of two keyboards (functional and numeric), a cursor control, a display brightness control, and local/remote and power switches. To set parameters, the operator selects the operating mode, the PROMPT function and four keys which can position the prompted parameter. The numeric keyboard is then used to update the parameter.

CONTRACTOR
Racal Communications Inc, 5 Research Place, Rockville, Maryland 20850, USA.

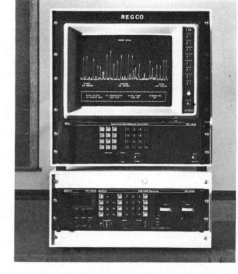

Spectrum surveillance system comprising RG-5540 receiver, RG-1340 controller and display

4400.093
RG-1320A SPECTRUM DISPLAY UNIT

The RG-1320A spectrum display unit provides a visual display of the signal activity present around the tuned frquency of an associated receiver. The display is most useful in tuning and analysing signals intercepted by the receiver. The unit plugs into an RG-5540 or similar receiver and derives its power from that source.

The equipment presents a 60 dB logarithmetic display of a band up to 400 kHz wide. A 1 kHz bandwidth Gaussian filter provides high resolution and the sweep rate is adjustable from 2·5 to 25 Hz to allow full resolution at maximum sweep widths.

The one- by three-inch cathode ray tube display uses a bright P31 green phosphor with grey contrast and EMI screen. The X and Y deflection signals are available for an external display.

CONTRACTOR
Racal Communications Inc, 5 Research Place, Rockville, Maryland 20850, USA.

4672.093
RG SERIES SPECTRUM MONITORS
Racal Communications Inc manufactures a range of spectrum monitors designed to provide a visual display of the signal activity present and around the tuned frequency of an associated ESM monitoring receiver. Data is displayed on a CRT display forming part of the monitor.

The RG-1307A features a sweep width of 0 to 40 MHz, manual gain control and an accurate frequency marker. Resolution bandwidth is 250 kHz nominal. The RG-1308A provides a variable sweep width of 0 to 8 MHz, a variable sweep rate of 5 to 25 Hz and a resolution bandwidth of 10 kHz.

In group monitor equipments the RG-1309A and RG-1309A2 provide visual displays of the individual voice frequency channels in the telephone basic group 'B' of 60 to 108 kHz. The RG-1317A and RG-1317A-1 give four independent visual displays of the individual voice frequency channels in the telephone basic group 'B' and also have provision for displaying channels in basic group 'A' (12 to 60 kHz).
CONTRACTOR
Racal Communications Inc, 5 Research Place, Rockville, Maryland 20850, USA.

4401.193
AN/GLQ-3A HF/VHF COMMUNICATIONS JAMMER
The AN/GLQ-3A is designed to disrupt voice and data communications over the frequency range from 20 to 230 MHz. The system incorporates all-solid-state transmitters and microprocessor controls for look-through jamming, initiated jamming and continuous jamming. It is capable of operating with amplitude modulation, frequency shift keying, continuous wave and frequency modulated continuous wave signals.

The system is housed in a 239 cubic foot shelter and is carried by a ¾- or 1¼-ton truck. System weight is approximately 7500 lb (3400 kg) and is powered by a standard US Army generator supplying 10 kW, 400 Hz power.

The AN/GLQ-3A incorporates a HF/VHF broadband co-planar, log-periodic antenna which can be erected rapidly. The antenna is in three sections which can be used for each of three segments of the frequency coverage, with spot jamming available on any single frequency.
STATUS
In current service with the US Army.
CONTRACTOR
Fairchild Weston Systems Inc, 300 Robbins Lane, Syosset, New York 11791, USA.

3037.053
SR SERIES SURVEILLANCE RECEIVERS
Norlin Communications Inc produces a wide range of surveillance and monitoring receivers covering the frequency bands of interest for Comint and Sigint operations. The major units of this range are described in the following paragraphs.
SR-209
The type SR-209 solid-state, modular receiving system is capable of reception of AM, FM, CW, and pulse signals in the frequency range of 20 MHz to 12 GHz. It will accommodate a signal display unit to provide a visual display of signals in a band around the received signal.

Three IF amplifier FM demodulator boards may be used at one time with operational selection by front panel switch. For VHF/UHF, selection of IF bandwidths from 10 kHz to 8 MHz are available. In HF there are three bandwidths.

The wide frequency range of 20 MHz to 12 GHz for a manually tuned receiver is provided through the use of ten plug-in RF tuning heads.

To make the receiver completely self-sufficient for field use a battery pack plug-in unit may be used in lieu of one tuner. No adjustments or changes in the receiver are necessary when this nickel cadmium battery pack is installed. A built-in charger is provided in the battery back unit.

The front ends employ at least two section pre-selectors at the RF input to provide maximum reduction of cross modulation and intermodulation interferences.

The SR-209 basic receiver contains a carrier operated relay to control accessory equipment such as recorders. All operating controls are located on the front panel of the SR-209 and except for the phone jack, all inputs and outputs are located on the rear panel. An exception to this is the optional first local oscillator output which is provided on the plug-in tuning head panel. Two meters, one for tuning and one for signal strength, are on the receiver front panel.

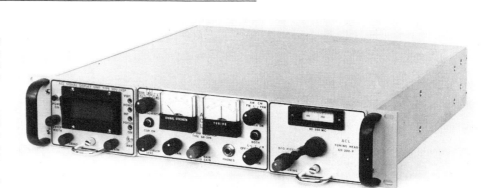
SR-209 modular receiver system

STATUS
Versions of the SR-209 have been supplied for signal intercept, search and DF applications at fixed sites, mobile monitoring stations, airborne, shipborne and submarine collection systems.
CONTRACTOR
Applied Communications (a division of Amstar Technical Products Company Inc), 9125 Gaither Road, Gaithersburg, Maryland 20877, USA.

3903.053
SERIES 2000 RECEIVER SYSTEM
The Norlin Communications Series 2000 range of equipment comprises a number of VHF/UHF receivers, several display units, and a variety of peripheral units from which can be assembled systems for radio surveillance and communications. Modular design permits the combination of units to form equipments appropriate to typical ESM, Elint, Sigint and related functions in both fixed and mobile installations. The basic standard receiver frequency range is 20 to 500 MHz, with a 1200 MHz upper limit as an option.
Six receiver models have been identified:
SR 2080: Directly controlled 20 – 1200 MHz
SR 2082: Slave version of SR 2080
SR 2090: Directly controlled 20 – 500 MHz (option to 1200 MHz) with liquid crystal display status indicator (see below)
SR 2091: As SR 2090 with 8 memory slots
SR 2092: Slave version of SR 2090
SR 2100: Directly controlled version of SR 2090 plus solid-state IF/RF panoramic facility
A three-model series, SR 2070/1/2, with a frequency coverage of 0·05 to 30 MHz has been designed but is not in production.
There are three display units:
DU 2081: RF/IF panoramic facility, autoscan mode
DU 2090: RF/IF panoramic facility, 8 memory slots; hand-off to 8 receivers
DU 2091: RF/IF panoramic facility
Typical specimens from this range are the SR 2090 and DU 2090 receiver and display units, and these are described more fully in the following paragraphs.

Norlin Series 2000 VHF/UHF surveillance receiver (above) with a DU 2090 display unit

SR 2090
The basic receiver tunes the 20 to 500 MHz frequency range, expansible to 1200 MHz. The microprocessor control enables single knob tuning and a single direct-reading display of tuned frequency, even with the frequency expansion option installed. The microprocessor also enables the selection of a wide range of IF bandwidths and detection modes. The receiver is prewired to accept modules meeting all standard digital remote control interface specifications. A liquid crystal display (LCD) presents complete receiver tuning information at one focal point and improves the shock and vibration resistance by elimination of conventional signal strength and tuning meters. The LCD is uniformly backlit with an electro-luminescent panel for display under all ambient lighting conditions.

All tuning commands to the receiver can be applied from a remote location through a digital data interface. The interface translates the remote control data format to digital commands that are accepted by the receiver's microprocessor. A wide variety of digital interface format specifications are accommodated by a selection of the proper interface module. The receiver is prewired to accept all interface modules. Within the command the tuned frequency is in BCD format and the IF bandwidths and detection modes have pre-assigned digital codes. A total of 64 receivers can be addressed by the remote controller. Special command formats and functions can be developed upon request.
DU 2090
The DU 2090 display unit is designed to complement Series 2000 VHF/UHF electronic controlled receivers. The DU 2090 enables the system to provide master/slave operation of up to eight receivers from a central control point. An additional eight signals can be stored in memory for operator convenience. The DU 2090 features a dual trace, digitally refreshed, flicker free, panoramic display of the spectrum in scan operation. Scanning is accomplished by rapidly stepping the synthesiser receiver LO. When Receiver 1 is not swept the CRT becomes an IF Pan display for that receiver. Memory update can be inhibited to freeze the display for elusive push-to-talk targets, because the display is digitally refreshed. Since the stepped synthesiser sweep provides extreme linearity, the marker on the display can be exactly placed over the desired signal on the frozen display.

Then, returning the receiver to the manual mode, a 100 per cent intercept probability results on the next target transmission.
STATUS
Production.

CONTRACTOR
Applied Communications (a division of Amstar Technical Products Company Inc), 9125 Gaither Road, Gaithersburg, Maryland 20877, USA.

4659.093
SR-2020 TACTICAL ESM SYSTEM

The SR-2020 is a digitally remote controlled ESM receiver covering the 0·5 to 500 MHz frequency range in a single package. It meets the need for effective, reliable and maintainable mobile tactical EW systems to satisfy COMINT, SIGINT, ESM and direction finding requirements. It is designed for independent operation or as an integral part of a larger system where a companion power supply will service groups of four receivers. Specifically designed to meet the needs of mobile, airborne or shipboard applications, the equipment is suited for tactical deployment in either wheeled or tracked vehicles under extreme environmental conditions.

The receiver control unit, RCU-2020, provides comprehensive control and status display for up to eight SR-2020 tactical receivers. All receiver functions are controlled by the internal microprocessor and a variety of proven hardware routines. In addition to receiver control, the unit forms the nucleus of a collection system by providing control and data interface ports for system ancillary equipments.
STATUS
In development and undergoing various acceptance trials in a variety of operational vehicles.
CONTRACTOR
Applied Communications (a division of Amstar Technical Products Company Inc), 9125 Gaither Road, Gaithersburg, Maryland 20877, USA.

SR-2020 ESM system

4660.193
SRS-2500 VHF/UHF RECEIVING SYSTEM

The SRS-2500 VHF/UHF receiving system is an adaptive and comprehensive collection of units for strategic signal intercept, acquisition, direction finding and analysis applications. It is designed for independent or computer-controlled operation for the reception of AM, FM, CW, SSB and pulse signals over the frequency range 20 to 500 MHz. The coverage may be extended down to 0·5 MHz and up to 1200 MHz if required. System architecture enables additional subsystem groups to be added where each group communicates via a serial multi-address data bus.

The system group consists of a control address unit CA-2100, a digital distribution unit, and IF switch and from one to sixteen SR-2154 surveillance receivers. The heart of the system is the CA-2100 which carries out all the selection, tuning and control functions. It also alters and lists receiver memory content as well as displaying signal parameters of the addressed receiver to be handed off to another receiver. A built-in gas plasma IF spectrum display and alpha-numeric readout panel provides the operator with a read-out of parameters.

The SR-2154 receiver covers the range 20 to 500 MHz with optional down and up converter units to extend this range to 0·5 to 20 and 500 to 1200 MHz.

Each receiver in the system has audio and carrier operator relays outputs for recorder interface or separate operator monitoring.

Fibre optic data links are used so that the receivers, digital distribution unit and the IF switch unit can be remotely controlled by the control address unit.
CONTRACTOR
Applied Communications (a division of Amstar Technical Products Company Inc), 9125 Gaither Road, Gaithersburg, Maryland 20877, USA.

4661.093
SR-2152 VHF/UHF RECEIVER

The SR-2152 receiver is a high-speed, low-phase noise synthesiser applicable to real world COMINT requirements. The receiver tunes the 20 to 500 MHz frequency range and is expandable to 1200 MHz. It is fully microprocessor controlled and has a large screen gas-plasma display for IF pan and scanning presentations. The display also presents frequency readout, signal strength, f1 – f2 frequency band and BFO offset alphanumeric data. The receiver is designed for signal, intercept, search and DF applications. The system may be deployed for use in fixed station sites, mobile monitoring systems, airborne, shipboard and submarine systems.

The receiver accepts a wide variety of standard modules that enable growth and adaptability. Due to this modularity, the receiver is easily configured and specifically designed to form the nucleus of computer controlled and master/slave hand-off systems. AM, FM, CW, LSB, USB and pulse modulation capability is provided. Up to six IF bandwidths can be installed.
CONTRACTOR
Applied Communications (a division of Amstar Technical Products Company Inc), 9125 Gaither Road, Gaithersburg, Maryland 20877, USA.

4664.193
AN/MLQ-T6 COMMUNICATIONS DATA LINK JAMMER

The AN/MLQ-T6 is a mobile, general purpose, ground-based communications and data link jammer, operating in the frequency band of 960 to 1850 MHz, at a power level of 1 kW CW or 2 kW peak. It is capable of simulating the projected threat jammers in the 1980 to 1990 period and is employed during the development, test and evaluation of future communications and data link systems. Major subsystems are a transmitter, receiver, antennas/ pedestal, processor/controller, automatic tracker, control and display console and the shelter.
CONTRACTOR
Cincinnati Electronics, 2630 Glendale-Milford Road, Cincinnati, Ohio 45241, USA.

AN/MLQ-T6 communications data link jammer

4741.193
AN/MLQ-33 ECM SYSTEM

The AN/MLQ-33 is a ground-based search and jamming system operating over the frequency band 100 to 450 MHz, and is designed primarily to detect and jam air-to-ground communications. The system scans the complete frequency band automatically in approximately 0·5 second and on detecting a high priority communications signal will jam automatically. It is housed in a standard US Army S-250 shelter and has an effective radiated power output of approximately 4 kW.

STATUS

The AN/MLQ-33 has been developed under a contract from the US Army. The first systems were due for delivery in mid-1984.

CONTRACTOR

GTE Sylvania, Electronic Systems Group, 100 Ferguson Drive, Mountain View, California 94042, USA.

3895.193
AN/MLQ-34 TACJAM

The AN/MLQ-34 TACJAM is a highly mobile tactical communication countermeasures system produced for the US Army Signals Warfare Laboratory by GTE Sylvania. TACJAM can disrupt and deceive communication links over a broad, multi-octave frequency range at multi-kilowatt effective radiated power (ERP) levels. The AN/MLQ-34 has multiple receivers, exciters, and high power transmitters to provide simultaneous multiple threat capability.

The TACJAM equipment operates under computer control to permit quick reaction to changes in the electromagnetic environment. A wide range of modulation formats permit effective jamming of virtually any threat emitter present in the equipment's frequency range.

Each multi-kilowatt solid-state broadband transmitter is constructed of basic power modules (BPMs). These are interchangeable and replaceable in the field. All system electronics are programmed for automatic checkout and fault isolation by the AN/USM-410 EQUATE automatic test equipment.

The complete system is mounted on a tracked cargo carrier which is highly mobile. Rapid deployment is achieved by using an automatic ground rod driver and an unfolding log-periodic antenna mounted on a pneumatically operated telescopic mast.

All TACJAM electronic and cooling equipments are enclosed in an S-595 shelter which has ballistic protection.

STATUS

Production of 17 systems was completed by 1984. A contract worth over $44 million was awarded to American Electronic Laboratories in June 1983 for 31 TACJAM systems plus spares and engineering support.

CONTRACTORS

GTE Sylvania, Systems Group, Western Division, 100 Ferguson Drive, Mountain View, California 94042, USA.

American Electronic Laboratories, PO Box 552, Lansdale, Pennsylvania 19446, USA.

GTE Sylvania TACJAM (AN/MLQ-34) mobile tactical jammer unit deployed in field

4405.193
AN/MSQ-103 TEAMPACK ESM SYSTEM

The AN/MSQ-103 ESM system is a ground-based transportable equipment designed to collect, identify and provide the direction of signals from ground-based transmitters. It operates in the 500 MHz to 40 GHz frequency range and is intended for use in the field at division level. The system is housed in a ballistically protected shelter and then mounted on an XM-1015 tracked vehicle. It can also be mounted on an M-35 utility truck, a light armoured vehicle, jeep and other types of combat vehicles. It will replace the US Army AN/MLQ-24 as the basic countermeasures receiving equipment and includes built-in computer processing from a ruggedised mini-computer installed in the vehicle.

The system is also known under the name of TEAMPACK and contains secure voice and wideband data link to a forward control and analysis centre. The equipment is also designed to operate with the ULQ-14 ground element of MULTEWS and the TSQ-109 AGTELIS system (4408.153).

STATUS

In current service with the US Army. A contract for engineering development and enhancement has been awarded to Emerson by the US Army. Among other improvements the system will be networked.

CONTRACTOR

Emerson Electric Corporation, St Louis, Missouri, USA.

4403.093
AEL TYPE 6040 UNIVERSAL JAMMER

The Type 6040 ECM universal jammer is a signal source for use in testing system jamming vulnerability. Three classes of jamming signals are generated: barrage noise jamming, spot noise jamming and deception jamming.

Operation is controlled from a digital control unit. The 'dial-a-jam' capabilities of the control unit allow complete operation of the system in a simple and straightforward manner. The system includes a receiver section, a modulation source section and a transmitter.

Depending upon the operator selected mode of operation, the receiver section affects the operation in three different ways. In the transponder modes, the output of the receiver triggers the AEM signal transmissions for which internal RF carrier sources are used; in repeater modes the receiver performs as the front end of the repeater/transmitter configuration; and in the manually actuated modes, the receiver is a passive indicator of the signals which are present in the band of interest. A multi-frequency determining unit and an automatic signal recognition unit are included as part of the receiver section. These signal sorting units identify the class of signal being received, display the information on the control panel, and programme ECM response in transponder modes of operation.

The transmitter section accepts the undetected receiver output for use in repeater modes and the detected receiver output for use in the transponder modes as a trigger. The transmitter applies the modulation source signals to either the received RF or to the RF sources, which are internal to the transmitter. Two types of RF sources are included in the transmitter; voltage controlled oscillators and a multi-output frequency synthesiser.

The jammer is controlled by the digital control unit which selects the jamming modes of operation, varies the parameters, controls system gains, and displays this information in simplified form so that an unskilled operator can operate and control the system. When a given type of jamming is required the operator simply dials in the required mode. This establishes an initial set of conditions which can be altered, if necessary by the front-panel controls.

BITE signals are injected into the system by the use of a front-panel control on the controller. System parameters are displayed to the operator. Actual control is easily accomplished and allows fully automatic operation.

A spectrum analyser and preselector are provided to monitor samples of the received input signal, the drive to the high-power amplifier and the transmitted output signal.

A remote control panel for the high power amplifier is provided to allow the operator to monitor amplifier performance.

CONTRACTOR

American Electronics Laboratories Inc, PO Box 552, Lansdale, Pennsylvania 19446, USA.

3367.193
AN/TLQ-15 COMMUNICATIONS AND COUNTERMEASURES SET

The AN/TLQ-15 communications and countermeasures equipment is a transportable system for tactical use either as a truck-mounted installation or as a deck-mounted unit aboard ship. Fixed or semi-permanent ground-based applications also exist, and the TLQ-15 is capable of airborne use by means of a trailing wire antenna. All units of the equipment are air transportable by fixed- or rotary-winged aircraft.

At the centre of the system is an HF communications transmitter/receiver covering the 1·5 to 20 MHz range. Associated with this unit are: a panoramic indicator unit; frequency counter; modulation generator; RF amplifier; low-pass filter assembly; and an antenna coupler. In addition to the main antenna (a 35-foot telescopic whip, with counterpoise) provisions are made for feeding into a dummy load and for connection to an auxiliary antenna.

The transmitter/receiver is a solid-state design with synthesised receiver/transmitter tracking, and providing the following operational facilities:

(1) continuous transmission
(2) look-through transmission (90 per cent transmit/10 per cent receive)
(3) signal-initiated transmission (signals of 5 μV or above put system into look-through mode)
(4) receive/transmit, AM, FM, or DSB voice.

In the first three of these modes, modulation available includes: CW, AM, DSB, FM, AM and FM, and FSK.

Automatic frequency control (AFC) tracking of received signals is provided, and there are facilities for signal analysis, various modulations are available for countermeasures operation, and an auxiliary communications link using the AN/VRC-47 can be provided as an option. Additional system potential includes the possibility of using a phased array of two TLQ-15 systems to produce 8 kW of RF power in any desired direction, and continuous reception in the pattern null for a monitoring receiver. The basic power output is 2 kW CW.

STATUS
Operational with US Forces and possibly used by other countries.
CONTRACTOR
American Electronic Laboratories Inc, PO Box 552, Lansdale, Philadelphia 19446, USA.

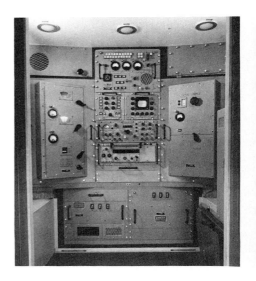

AEL AN/TLQ-15 communications and counter-measures set

4406.093
AN/TLQ-17A COUNTERMEASURES SET

The AN/TLQ-17A countermeasures jamming and monitoring set has been designed to cover the HF/VHF portion of the frequency band. The system is an updated version of the original AN/TLQ-17 using a modular packaging concept and can be fitted into both aircraft and ground vehicles.

The equipment utilises a microprocessor controlled receiver, with programmable sector scans, and can be programmed to search the HF and VHF portions of the frequency spectrum for signal intercepts. It employs a fully synthesised, digitally tuned, high stability receiver to allow the operator to monitor and record both voice and digital communication links.

The wideband solid-state transmitter uses a high power amplifier capable of producing 550 watts of radiated power over the entire frequency range to interrupt tactical communication links.

CHARACTERISTICS
Frequency range: Band 1: 1·5 – 20 MHz; Band 2: 20 – 80 MHz
Effective radiated power: 550 W
Receiver tuning time: 1 s
Preselected frequencies: 256
MTBF: In excess of 400 h
STATUS
In production.
CONTRACTOR
Fairchild Weston Systems Inc, 300 Robbins Lane, Syosset, New York, USA.

AN/TLQ-17A system mounted in cross-country vehicles

4408.153
AN/TSQ-109 AGTELIS SIGINT SYSTEM

This is an automatic ground transportable emitter location and identification system (AGTELIS) which is designed to locate transmitters in the 500 MHz to 18 GHz frequency band. The AN/TSQ-109 uses both time of arrival and direction of arrival of emissions to provide the necessary information to an accuracy in direction finding of one degree rms with a 30-metre circular error probability at a range of 30 kilometres.

The complete system consists of remote sensor outstations and a two-vehicle control processor set-

up. The outstations provide measurements of frequency, pulse width, pulse repetition frequency and various other parameters to identify and locate hostile emitters. One control processor controls the outstations by sending search and tuning commands, and receives data while the second processor integrates this data with that of airborne systems and transmits the result to a forward control and analysis centre. The outstations can, however, be operated independently of the control processors.

Three AGTELIS systems are normally deployed with each operational company and consist of three

outstations and one control processor, all of which are contained in 2½-ton trucks. The individual units each have a different nomenclature; the outstations are AN/GSQ-189, the first control processor is AN/TYQ-17 and the second processor is AN/TSQ-11.
STATUS
In operational service. Frequency extension to 40 GHz is being studied.
CONTRACTOR
Bunker Ramo, Westlake Village, California, USA.

4409.153
AN/TSQ-112 TACELIS ESM SYSTEM

The AN/TSQ-112 is a location and identification ECM system operating in the frequency range 500 kHz to 500 MHz. The system is fully automatic and performs communication collection, transmitter location and processing functions. It is designed to combat hostile tactical communications radio by generating early warning, target and decision information, and jamming.

TACELIS (tactical automated communications emitter location and identification system) is a major

component of the TACOM early warning system and consists of two remote master stations and four slave stations. It is deployed with each operations company forward in one ten-ton truck and three six-ton vans plus a truck tractor. Remote master stations are deployed in three five-ton trucks and each remote slave station is carried by one M113 truck. The component elements of TACELIS include the various stations plus one AN/UYK-7 computer, 13 AN/UYK-19 minicomputers and AN/ULR-17 receivers. The remote slave stations have a direction finding capability only while each master station has 14

receivers and two search/acquisition receivers. The TACELIS system is inter-operable with forward control and analysis centres, the AN/MLQ-34 TACJAM (**3895.193**) via the AN/GRC-103 communications link directly out of the remote master stations, and the Cefly Lancer aircraft.
CONTRACTOR
GTE Sylvania, Electronic Warfare Organization, 100 Ferguson Drive, Mountain View, California 94042, USA.

4008.193

CP-1380/VRC STEERABLE NULL ANTENNA PROCESSOR (SNAP)

SNAP was developed for the US Army to provide the receiver of a standard VHF-FM communications set with the capability of recovering a desired signal which is masked by a stronger interfering signal. SNAP automatically recognises a desired signal to prevent nulling it, and tracks moving interference sources. This equipment reduces a strong interfering signal to a level below a weaker desired signal by electronically pointing a spatial null in the direction of the interference. SNAP requires two antennas (eg AS-1729, AS-2731, or other). To achieve a spatial null, SNAP inserts an appropriate phase shift and amplitude adjustment in series with one antenna signal so that subtraction between the two antenna signals occurs at the angle of interference. During transmission, SNAP is automatically bypassed and only one antenna is used.

SNAP does not require modification to the radio set to be protected, and operates with any standard VHF antenna (two required). It is a low-cost, rugged, self-contained unit housed in a standard R-442/VRC case.

The unit is suitable for direct installation on a standard MT-1898/VRC mount. SNAP provides for the recovery of VHF signal from high level interference; processes both analogue and digital signals; requires no modification to radio set to be protected; automatically tracks moving interference source; is fully interoperable with non-equipped radios and is a passive ECM device with no electronic signature.

CHARACTERISTICS

Frequency range: 30 – 88 MHz
Dynamic range: 0 to –114 dBm
Insertion loss: 1 dB max
Power: 50 W max; 22 – 32 V DC
Operating modes: Bypass; automatic; manual
Dimensions: R-442/VRC case 30·5 × 14 × 16·9 cm
Weight: 7·7 kg

STATUS

Completed full-scale engineering development (pre-production) for the US Army. Production was due to commence in 1983 but no details have been released.

CONTRACTOR

Hazeltine Corporation, Greenlawn, New York 11740, USA.

CP 1380/VRC (SNAP) system

4407.293

AN/KAS-1 CHEMICAL WARFARE DIRECTIONAL DETECTOR

The AN/KAS-1 is a passive infra-red imaging sensor capable of detecting certain chemical agents. It consists of a sensor mounted on a two-axis pivot and a power conversion unit, and can operate over extended periods by the use of a miniature Stirling-cycle cooler.

The detector sensor unit is based on the man-portable thermal imager (3823.093) developed for the US Army. This system is well-proven in the field, is lightweight and rugged, and is in volume production.

The AN/KAS-1 has been designed for use on ships, and to complete the system for shipborne chemical warfare roles, the original man-portable imager has been modified to include a spectral filter wheel, a power conversion unit and a two-axis mount.

In addition to its primary role in chemical warfare detection, the AN/KAS-1 can also be utilised for other operational roles, such as reconnaissance, base defence, surveillance, threat detection, pilotage, and search and rescue.

STATUS

The AN/KAS-1 is in service with the US Navy.

CONTRACTOR

Texas Instruments Incorporated, PO Box 226015, Dallas, Texas 75266, USA.

3368.193

COMBAT VEHICLE SACS

The US Army is working on the development of a semi-automatic counterfire system (SACS) for combat vehicles and a production prototype model has been built by LTV Aerospace and Defense Company and tested by the Army in an M60 tank.

SACS uses microprocessor electronics to detect and counter laser and helicopter threats. Integration of electro-optical and acoustic sensors with the fire control system allows timely response to threats and improves vehicle survival. In addition to providing a warning to the whole crew, the system simultaneously displays the threat information to the commander and semi-automatically initiates a response. Manual override can be activated when required.

In addition to counterfire and evasive manoeuvres, flare, smoke and jammer countermeasures can be used. Current development work is on the integration of alternate passive warning sensors, information transfer through secure data links and unit cost reduction measures to make system costs attractive for potential high volume production.

STATUS

Experimental. Under development by US Army.

CONTRACTOR

LTV Aerospace and Defense Company, PO Box 225907, Dallas 75265, Texas, USA.

5741.193

HAND-EMPLACED EXPENDABLE JAMMER

The hand-emplaced expendable jammer (HEXJAM) is a solid-state device designed for use against communication links in the HF and VHF bands. It uses wide-band frequency barrage jamming that operates continuously against threat signals. It can be used for screening and protecting friendly communications and for supporting countermobility operations by disrupting enemy communications. It is small and lightweight, easily man-portable, and the rugged design allows assured operation. Panel switches allow the user to select the desired function modes and delay times. A self-disable feature will render the unit inoperable.

HEXJAM is re-usable and capable of multimission operational and training use. It is claimed to be effective against both spot jammers and frequency-hopping radios. It has a selectable activation time delay and can be turned on from a remote location using ordinary bell wire.

STATUS

In production and ordered by the US Army.

CONTRACTOR

Fairchild Weston Systems Inc, 300 Robbins Lane, Syosset, New York 11791, USA.

4663.193

LQ-102 HAND-EMPLACED EXPENDABLE JAMMER

The LQ-102 is a low-power continuous FM-by-noise jammer intended for hand-emplacement near the intended target's receiver. Two VHF bands are selectable for 'threat' and 'training' functions. The unit is of small size and can be easily transported and deployed.

The jammer features ON/OFF remote control, via a wire pair, up to at least 10 km. Delay of jamming operation is operator selectable in 6 minute increments up to 30 hours. Continuous jamming in excess of five hours is claimed. An electrical destruct mechanism is fitted to the unit.

CHARACTERISTICS

Dimensions: 27·3 × 11·4 × 6·4 cm
Weight: 2·3 kg with battery
Antenna: Folding vertical monopole
Output: 10 watts minimum ERP

CONTRACTOR

Cincinnati Electronics, 2630 Glendale-Milford Road, Cincinnati, Ohio 45241, USA.

LQ-102 expendable jammer

4658.053

MULTIPLE RADAR EMITTER SYSTEM

The Multiple Radar Emitter System (MRES) is a flexible set of ECM and C³CM threat generators that support personnel training and equipment tests and evaluations in dense electronic operational environments. HF, VHF and UHF communications jammers are available with either high power or moderate power transmitters. Radar, navigation and IFF jammers are also available over the frequency range from 500 MHz to 18 GHz. The jammers can be in either manned or unmanned airborne or field deployable configurations. These threat generators simulate threat signal electromagnetic radiation patterns, modulation techniques and tactics of known or possible threats.

STATUS

In production.

CONTRACTOR

Flight Systems Inc (Tracor), PO Box 2400, Newport Beach, California 92660, USA.

4666.393
SMALL PLATFORM EW SYSTEM
A tactical jamming system to be carried by a remotely piloted vehicle is being developed by Motorola under contract from the US Air Force. This system is known as the Small Platform EW (SPEW) and is intended for use against ground-based radars in support of the US Air Force EF-111A aircraft. The proposed vehicle is the Pave Tiger RPV. Although no details have been released the system appears to consist of a combined transmitter/receiver/processor and a four quadrant antenna.

STATUS
In early development. Laboratory testing was due to take place during 1984.
CONTRACTOR
Motorola Inc, Government Electronics Group, Scottsdale, Arizona, USA.

4667.393
AIRBORNE RADAR JAMMING SYSTEM
The Airborne Radar Jamming System (ARJS) is a new high-power standoff jammer intended to be used against air defence, surveillance and target acquisition radars. It is designed to be helicopter mounted, probably in a UH-60 Apache attack aircraft, and would be deployed behind the forward troop positions.

The technology employed would be based on the AN/ALQ-99 jamming system used by the US Navy in its EA-6B aircraft and the US Air Force in its EF-111As. This would provide detection of a threat signal, location of the emitter, comparison against a threat library held in the system's computer and transmission of a jamming signal.

STATUS
In development.
CONTRACTOR
Grumman Aerospace, South Oyster Bay Road, Bethpage, New York 11714, USA.

SONAR AND UNDERWATER DETECTION EQUIPMENT

AUSTRALIA

1790.453
MULLOKA SONAR

Mulloka is a lightweight active hull-mounted scanning sonar for installation in Royal Australian Navy anti-submarine escorts. It is a solid-state forced air-cooled equipment of high reliability which has been designed using a standardised packaging approach to aid maintainability and keep production simple.

The equipment includes a dedicated on-line computer which is used to control transmission parameters, perform automatic signal processing functions, and conduct checkout procedures. All signal interface equipment with other ship's systems has been grouped at a single location so that modifications necessary to interface Mulloka with other ship equipment configurations are confined to one unit.

The sonar beam-forming process involves the development of a large cylindrical transducer array consisting of 96 staves with 25 transducers per stave, driven in differing combinations and phases under computer control to form the required sonar beams electronically. The hydrophone elements of the array are driven by 480 power amplifiers during the transmit period, the length of which is a function of the pulse-

length of the transmitted signal. The transmit period is selectable over the range of approximately one to four seconds. The transmitter beams are formed sequentially during this period and cover the ocean for 360° in azimuth. The formation of the beam transmit pattern is random in nature from one transmission to the next in order to prevent the submarine commander having any indication of detection. Immediately following the transmission, the sonar reverts to the listening mode for a period determined by the range scale selected by the operator.

DEVELOPMENT

Both Australian and foreign companies participated in the production of the pilot model sonar. Production engineering for electronics equipment is being undertaken in Australia by EMI (Australia). Production of the transducers is by Honeywell in the USA.

STATUS

In 1979 a prototype Mulloka sonar was formally handed over to the RAN after undergoing trials in HMAS Yarra since 1975. A production programme to build systems to equip six RAN 'River' class destroyer escorts is in progress.

In April 1980 it was announced by the Australian Ministry of Defence that an initial contract worth US$1·1 million had been awarded to Honeywell Inc in America to provide a transducer array for the Mulloka sonar. Two Australian companies, Plessey Australia Pty Ltd and Dunlop Industrial and Aviation, are also participating. A contract for the electronics of the system was let to EMI (Australia) Ltd in 1979.

In early 1982, two production contracts were awarded to the 'River' class ships to be fitted with Mulloka sonars. One contract for A$16·1 million was awarded to EMI (Australia) Ltd and the other to Honeywell, USA for A$9·4 million. The EMI contract was for six systems for delivery in the period 1983-85 and the Honeywell contract for five transducer arrays to be delivered in 1983/84. This latter contract also provided for the transfer of all technology to Australian industry for future production of transducers in Australia. Plessey Australia has put the transducer design into production and has tendered for the first Australian built array as a result of this transfer of technology.

1791.453
PROJECT BARRA

Project Barra concerns the development and production of an advanced submarine detection system for use by long range maritime patrol aircraft.

The project evolved from successful development work under Project Nangana, a research and development programme, undertaken by the Weapons Research Establishment in close collaboration with the RAN and RAAF for the development of improved methods of submarine detection.

Following successful completion of an engineering study, initial development and the establishment of production facilities, together with the first production contract, Amalgamated Wireless

(Australasia) Limited was appointed prime contractor, and completed the production of this initial Barra sonobuoy contract by the end of 1981. A further A$55 million contract was let in early 1982 for full production against RAF and RAAF requirements. This contract is being fulfilled and further orders have been received.

The project is a collaborative programme with the UK; Australia developed the SSQ-801 Barra sonobuoy and the airborne processing equipment was developed in the UK under the direction of the UK Ministry of Defence. (See **1981.363**, AQS901 acoustic data processing and display system, in the UK sub-section of this section.) The platform equipment is suitable for installation in a range of aircraft, and has

been fitted in RAF Nimrod MR2 and RAAF P-3C Orion maritime aircraft.

Development of the Barra system generated the need for a ground support facility for the associated aircraft. AWA has designed and built for the RAAF a compilation, mission support, integration and training facility (CMI). This is a self-contained modular cabin complex which was initially transported by road to the RAAF Orion base at Edinburgh in South Australia. This computer-based facility provides training, briefing and analysis facilities.

CONTRACTOR

Amalgamated Wireless (Australia) Limited, PO Box 96, North Ryde, NSW 2113, Australia.

RAAF P-3C Orion maritime patrol aircraft equipped with Barra ASW system

The advanced sonobuoy communication link receiver for Barra sonobuoy data exchange

3998.453
SSQ-801 BARRA SONOBUOY

The SSQ-801 sonobuoy was developed specifically for the Australian Project Barra anti-submarine programme (**1791.453**, above) and is a passive directional sensor which may be used either singly or deployed in patterns to detect and locate submarine targets. It provides both range and directional information. Within a standard A size buoy, two parts separate on reaching the water, the upper portion containing radio transmission equipment rises to the surface while the other part housing the acoustic

sensor array sinks to a predetermined depth. A cable links the two parts.

The lower portion contains a compass and booms fitted with specially developed hydrophones. Arrays are sequentially switched to give the required directional beaming. Multiplexed signals from the lower section are fed to the floating portion of the buoy for transmission by radio to patrol aircraft, where data are analysed by the Barra system AQS-901 sonics processor (**1981.363**). Each sonobuoy transmits information on a pre-selected VHF radio channel so that the aircraft crew can select a

particular buoy's data for analysis. Digital techniques are used in the SSQ-801 to convert the combined sonar and compass information into signals to modulate the buoy's VHF transmissions.

The SSQ-801 is suitable for release from fixed-wing aircraft such as the P-3C Orion or Nimrod, and from helicopters of various types.

CHARACTERISTICS

Type: Passive directional array
Size: A
Length: 914 mm
Diameter: 124 mm

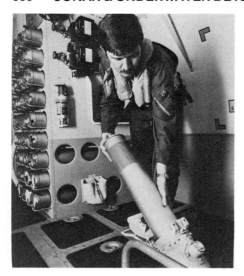

Weight: 13 kg
Operating life: Selectable up to 9 h
RF transmitter frequencies: 136 – 173·5 MHz
RF modulation: Narrow-band FSK
DEVELOPMENT
Development of the SSQ-801 sonobuoy was undertaken as part of the Australian Barra project (see above).
STATUS
Adopted by both the Royal Air Force and the Royal Australian Air Force, a contract valued at A$55 million was placed in early 1982, for the production of SSQ-801 sonobuoys for both air forces. A number of other countries are reported to be interested in the Barra

system, including France, Japan, the Netherlands and the USA. Amalgamated Wireless (Australasia) Limited is the prime contractor with Plessey Australia, Commonwealth Aircraft Corporation, Tube Makers and Cable Makers Australia, as major subcontractors.

In mid-1983 the RAAF ordered a further $48 million worth of Barra sonobuoys from AWA for delivery over the period 1984-86, bringing the total value of RAAF orders for Barra sonobuoys to more than $120 million.
CONTRACTOR
Amalgamated Wireless (Australasia) Limited, North Ryde Division, PO Box 96, North Ryde, NSW 2113, Australia.

SSQ-801 (Barra) sonobuoy about to be launched from an RAAF Orion ASW aircraft

CANADA

1636.453
HS-1000 SERIES SONAR
The HS-1000 series of sonars is a family of lightweight omni-directional ASW sonars which have been developed to give small naval vessels a modern sonar capability in search, detection, and attack. The numbering of each sonar designates transducer mounting and/or sonar power.
(1) HS-1001: lightweight variable depth sonar (VDS)
(2) HS-1002: lightweight hull-mounted (HM) sonar
(3) HS-1001/2: lightweight combined VDS/HM sonar with single electronics and a transfer switch
(4) HS-1007: medium-sized sonar available in either the HM or VDS configuration featuring higher power
(5) HS-1007/7: medium-sized combined VDS/HM sonar with single electronics and a transfer switch.
The HS-1001 and HS-1002 sonars are intended for use on patrol craft and corvettes. The HS-1007s are intended for use on corvettes, frigates, and destroyers.

HS-1001 and HS-1002 Sonars
The HS-1001 and HS-1002 feature:
(1) single cabinet containing receiver, transmitter, display and controls, power supplies, and energy storage
(2) simultaneous search and attack
(3) R-θ ball tracker for cursor control
(4) digital readout of range and bearing
(5) selectable true or relative bearing
(6) VOSIW setting 1400 – 1550 m/s steps
(7) three transmission modes: CW; wideband; alternate CW/WB
(8) integrated test equipment (ITE): tests down to replaceable module resulting in a MTTR of 3·5 minutes as proven under tests witnessed by Canadian Department of National Defence inspectors
(9) ten-second overall test for quick check of receiver

inputs/outputs, digital or analogue. Interface unit offers flexibility in interfacing with ship's systems.
Hull-mounted transducer sub-system
The double-walled, stainless steel dome is matched to the transmission frequency and acoustically isolated from the ship. It may be either fixed or retractable. Retracting mechanisms of either the vertical lifting type or the rotating type are available. The rotating type presents less drag, with the lifting mechanisms outboard of the sea chest to prevent corrosion of the working parts.

Variable depth transducer sub-system
The acoustic window of the low drag towed body is fabricated from stretch formed stainless steel. The body contains both heading and depth sensors. The 2 cm diameter armoured tow cable is faired over its 100 metre (or longer if required) length. With 100 metres out, the tow bar pull on the ship is approximately 2700 kg at a speed of 30 knots. Normal launch and recovery speeds are 8 to 10 knots with a maximum towing speed of about 36 knots. The system bolts flush to the ship's deck and transom, permitting ease of installation and removal. After the initial fitment, outfitting of a multipurpose ship to the VDS role will take less than 24 hours.

HS-1007 Sonars
The HS-1007 sonars are medium-sized sonars which utilise the receiver, display transducer, HM sub-system, and VDS sub-system of the HS-1001 and HS-1002 but with the transmitter and transmitter power supply of the AN/SQS-505 series design so that four times (omni mode) and 20 times (TRDT mode) more sonar energy can be transmitted into the medium. Dimensions of the two additional cabinets are:
Transmitter: Width 63 cm; depth 63 cm; height 173 cm; weight 386 kg
Transmitter power supply: Width 63 cm; depth 63 cm; height 173 cm; weight 600 kg

HS-1001 VDS showing the body in the launch position

STATUS
The HS-1000 series sonar is available on a current production status and has been delivered in the VDS configuration and in the combined VDS/HM configuration.
CONTRACTOR
Westinghouse Canada Limited, Electronic Systems Division, PO Box 510, Hamilton, Ontario L8N 3K2, Canada.

1792.453
AN/SQS-505 SONAR
The AN/SQS-505 is a medium-size search and attack sonar intended for use on vessels of 1000 tons and above. It may be used in a hull-mounted and/or variable depth application.

In the Canadian ships, each vessel has two separate but identical SQS-505s on board. One system is variable depth, the other is hull-mounted retractable. Other navies have used the SQS-505 in hull-mounted only applications, with and without hull outfit retracting mechanisms. It is possible to use the 505 in direct communication with a digital computer either for the transfer of range and bearing information or for assistance to the operator in detection and tracking (see **2047.261** underwater combat system).

The essential SQS-505 system features are:
(1) Continuous 360 degree long range search

(2) Capability of tracking several targets while maintaining search
(3) A five 'ping' history to enhance initial detection through visual integration
(4) Classification system using target history, hydrophone effects, doppler, aspect, and audio techniques
(5) 360 degree passive surveillance during active operation
(6) Single operator control
(7) Facilities for computer-aided tracking plus two-way command and control and ASW data systems interchange
(8) Built-in semi-automatic test equipment
(9) Ease of operation through quick entry button and symbology
Transducer
The transducer for the SQS-505 is identical for the

VDS or hull-mounted application. The array is approximately 1·2 metres in diameter and 1·2 metres high. It consists of 360 individual elements, each of which can be removed while the array is still in water.
Transmitter Group
The main units of a transmitter group consist of a power supply and a transmitter. The power supply converts the ship's prime AC power to DC, required for the operation of the transmitter. The power supply is contained in one standard SQS-505 size cabinet.

The transmitter consists of 36 power output modules, each driving one stave of the transducer. The transmitter is completely solid-state and contains its own integrated test equipment unit. The principal transmission modes are OMNI and TRDT. In addition, the transmitter can be operated in either CW or wideband.

Receiver Group

The receiver is contained in three cabinets of the standard 505 size. The group is completely solid-state with its own automatic built-in test equipment which will enable the operator to determine the location of a fault down to the replaceable module level.

Control and Indicator Group

The operator's control and indicator console consists of a cluster of displays and controls which will enable one operator to have complete control over the operation of the sonar plus the ability to detect, classify, and track targets. In addition, via separate displays in the console, he is able to maintain continuous independent surveillance of the sonar's passive mode.

VDS Mechanical Equipment

The VDS hoist group for the SQS-505 has been designated the AN/SQA-502, which is manufactured by Fleet Industries Division, Ronyx Corporation, Fort Erie, Canada. This mechanical equipment is located in a cutaway situated on the stern of the Canadian ships. The total weight of the mechanical equipment, hoist auxilaries, VDS body, and cable is approximately 20 tons.

Hull-mounted Hull Outfits

The 505 hull-mounted transducer can be used in any one of the following five applications:

(1) Fixed transducer and dome
(2) Fixed dome/retractable transducer
(3) Bow dome
(4) Retractable dome and transducer using a vertical retracting mechanism
(5) Retractable dome and transducer using a rotating mechanism.

The requirement for these various alternatives would depend upon the configuration of the ship and the location available for the mounting of the transducer.

STATUS

The SQS-505 is currently in production. Several advancements in the sonar's capability have been incorporated since the system was first installed in ships in the early 1970s.

AN/SQS-505 sonar control and indicator group manned by a single operator

In addition to the seven Canadian ships outfitted with dual SQS-505 sonars (VDS/HM), four hull-mounted systems have been installed on the latest Belgian frigates. The Royal Netherlands Navy has fitted systems to its 'Kortenaer' class frigates.

CONTRACTOR

Westinghouse Canada Limited, Electronic Systems Division, PO Box 510, Hamilton, Ontario L8N 3K2, Canada.

3999.353

AN/ASQ-502 SUBMARINE DETECTING SET (MAD)

The AN/ASQ-502 magnetic anomaly detector (MAD) is a sensitive magnetometer system developed for airborne submarine detection roles. A basic sensitivity of 0·01 gamma is claimed for this equipment, which has a total system weight of less than 15·6 kg (34·5 lb).

In place of the multiple cell detection method, the AN/ASQ-502 employs a single orientated caesium cell as the principal element. It is an optically pumped system, but the unwanted dead zones and heading error effects which are normally minimised by the multi-cell technique, are counteracted in the AN/ASQ-502 by orientating the single caesium cell on a mechanical gimbal system. This, combined with an inherently stable self-oscillator caesium sensor loop and a low-noise, infinite dynamic range, frequency-to-voltage converter, is claimed to yield the most sensitive airborne magnetometer available.

CHARACTERISTICS

Sensitivity: 0·01 γ (10^{-7} oersteds)

Detecting head figure of merit (FOM)
Uncompensated: 1·50 γ or less
Compensated: 0·30 γ or less

AN/ASQ-502 submarine detecting set (MAD)

Detector: Single orientated caesium cell, optically-pumped self-oscillator Larmor frequency 3·5 Hz/γ
Operating range: 0·20 – 0·75 oersteds
Larmor output (total field): 14 Hz/γ
Analogue output No 1 (minimally filtered): 105 mV/γ uncompensated and 30 mV/γ compensated
Analogue output No 2: 15·0 V p-p fsd
FSD sensitivities: 20, 10, 4, 2, 1, 0·4, 0·2 γ

HP filter: 0·04, 0·06, 0·1, 0·15, 0·3 Hz
LP filter: 0·4, 0·8, 1·2, 1·6 Hz
Military specification: MIL-E-5400
Operating temperature range: -54 to +71°C
Storage temperature range: -62 to +85°C
Power requirements: 115 V AC 400 Hz, 3-phase, 120 VA and 5 V AC/DC 10 VA for panel illumination
Specified reliability: MTBF 1000 h

STATUS

Service test models have been delivered and successfully evaluated by the Royal Navy for use on the Lynx helicopter. Successful evaluation has also been completed by the RAF on the Nimrod, and by the Canadian Forces on the National Aeronautical Establishment MAD aircraft. Production quantities have been delivered for the Canadian Forces CP-140 Aurora. Several other countries have expressed interest in the equipment for use in their ASW aircraft.

CONTRACTOR

CAE Electronics Ltd, PO Box 1800, St Laurent, Montreal, Quebec H4L 4X4, Canada.

4621.353

AN/ASQ-504(V) MAD SYSTEM

The AN/ASQ-504(V) Advanced Integrated MAD System (AIMS) is designed to provide optimum performance when used on helicopters, fixed wing aircraft and lighter-than-air platforms. AIMS is a fully automatic magnetic anomaly detection (MAD) system which improves detection efficiency while significantly reducing operator work load. For helicopter installation, the detecting head is fixed to the aircraft body. This provides true 'on top' contact when over a target by eliminating the delay inherent in a towed detecting system.

The AN/ASQ-504(V) system combines sensitivity and accuracy with ease of operation, eliminates aircraft generated interference fields and delivers continuous, automated feature recognition. Contact alert, both visual and audible, is provided. Slant range via an LED display allows the operator to determine if he is within target acquisition range.

AIMS eliminates hazards associated with towed systems and permits high speed surveillance and manoeuvrability, thereby increasing patrol range, improving detectability and substantially reducing false alarms. When used with dipping sonar, transition from one system to the other can be performed quickly and effectively.

The AIMS package weighs 50 lb (22·7 kg) and consists of a 0·005 nano tesla optically pumped magnetometer, a vector magnetometer, amplifier computer and a control indicator. The system operates from a single phase, 115 V, 400 Hz power source and requires less than 200 VA power. AIMS has the flexibility either to perform independently or

Units of AN/ASQ-504(V) MAD system

to accept and execute commands from common control/display units via a 1553 data bus.

CHARACTERISTICS

Sensitivity: 0·01 gamma (in-flight)

Features: Automatic target detection. Operator alert, visual and audible. Slant range estimate to 2800 feet (854 m)

Outputs

Visual: Contact alert and estimated slant range

Analogue: Adaptive MAD signal

Digital: Display interface to MIL-STD-1553

Audio: ICS alert

STATUS

Fully developed and ready for production.

CONTRACTOR

CAE Electronics Ltd, PO Box 1800, Saint Laurent, Quebec H4L 4X4, Canada

---

4000.453

AN/SQS-509 SONAR

The AN/SQS-509 is a lower frequency version of the SQS-505 (**1792.453**) intended for use on vessels of 2500 tons and above. It has been derived from the SQS-505 by changing the frequency-dependent items, such as the transducer, and consequently there is considerable logistic commonality with the SQS-505. Apart from a lower operating frequency (5·4 kHz) and a higher source level, the SQS-509 has the same operational features as the SQS-505 described above.

The transducer is approximately 1·6 m in diameter and 1·6 m high. It consists of 360 individual elements, each of which can be removed while the array is under water. The transmitter group consists of two cabinets, the power supply cabinet and the transmitter cabinet. The power supply converts the ship's prime AC power to DC, required for the operation of the transmitter. The transmitter contains 36 power output modules, each driving one stave of the transducer. It is completely solid-state and contains its own integrated test equipment. The principal transmission modes are OMNI and TRDT.

The receiver is contained in three cabinets of the standard SQS-505 size. It is completely solid-state with its own automatic built-in test equipment which enables the operator to determine the location of a fault down to the replaceable module level.

The control and indicator console consists of a cluster of displays and controls which enables one operator to have complete control over the operation of the sonar and the ability to detect, classify and track targets. In addition, via separate displays in the console, he is able to maintain continuous independent surveillance of the passive mode. Because of the larger transducer size, the preferred mounting for the transducer is in a bow-dome.

STATUS

The SQS-509 is in production for the Royal Netherlands Navy.

CONTRACTOR

Westinghouse Canada Limited, Electronic Systems Division, PO Box 510, Hamilton, Ontario L8N 3K2, Canada.

4222.353

AN/ASA-64 SUBMARINE ANOMALY DETECTOR

The AN/ASA-64 is a primary signal processor designed to identify and mark submarine-produced local distortions in the earth's magnetic field. When such an event occurs, the operator is alerted by visual and audio alarms, thereby eliminating the requirement for constant signal monitoring.

CHARACTERISTICS

Dimensions	Length (mm)	Width (mm)	Height (mm)	Weight (kg)
Control unit	102	146	90	0·68
ID-1559	229	150	153	2·95

Operating temperature range: –54 to +71° C

Military specification: MIL-E-5400

Power requirement: 115 V AC, 400 Hz, 20 VA

STATUS

Production quantities have been manufactured and delivered for the USN P3C Orion. CAE has completed a product improvement programme with more processing power. This design improvement is being evaluated by the Royal Navy, Royal Air Force, and the United States Navy. A variant for helicopters is proposed.

CONTRACTOR

CAE Electronics Ltd, PO Box 1800, St Laurent, Montreal, Quebec H4L 4X4, Canada.

AN/ASA-64 submarine magnetic anomaly detector equipment

3231.393

AN/ASA-65 COMPENSATION GROUP ADAPTOR

The compensation group adaptor (CGA) has been developed to increase operational efficiency in existing installations of the AN/ASA-65 magnetic compensator group (**1388.393**). By the incorporation of *total system* built-in test features and automatic data gathering, preflight, troubleshooting and compensation update requirements are significantly reduced with a corresponding improvement in performance.

The CGA consists of a small indicator, magnetic field and a computer, magnetic field containing signal conditioning circuits and a special-purpose micro-computer. Installation does not require any modifications to the existing AN/ASA-65 equipment. Input data from the AN/ASA-65 and the detector magnetometer are used by the micro-computer to calculate the numerical values which indicate changes required for each of the nine terms to produce optimum compensation.

No stringent manoeuvre requirements are necessary. Data to update compensation terms

AN/ASA-65 compensator group adaptor

require a simple flight programme that involves low amplitude manoeuvres on four headings. The total time required for this programme is no more than six minutes after which the operator is required to adjust the AN/ASA-65 terms as indicated on the CGA control.

CHARACTERISTICS

Figure of merit: Equal or better than best performance obtainable from standard AN/ASA-65 (generally 1 *y* or less)

Standard update compensation

Terms compensated: 9

Time: 8 minutes

Manoeuvres required: Small random type on 4 headings

Weapon drop compensation

Terms compensated: 4

Time: 2 minutes

Manoeuvres required: Small manoeuvres on four headings

Dimensions (CGA only)

	Height (cm)	Width (cm)	Depth (cm)	Weight (kg)
Control unit	9·5	14·6	12·7	1·35
Amplifier converter	22·1	22·9	41·8	10·0

STATUS

Fitted to RAF Nimrod, USN P-3C Orion and S-3A Viking maritime aircraft.

CONTRACTOR

CAE Electronics Ltd, PO Box 1800, St Laurent, Montreal, Quebec H4L 4X4, Canada.

1388.393

AN/ASA-65(V) NINE-TERM COMPENSATOR

The CAE nine-term compensator (AN/ASA-65(V)) provides semi-automatic compensation for aircraft-generated manoeuvre interference signals. By minimising unwanted interference signals, it substantially improves MAD detection capability, especially during tactical and turbulent flight conditions. This equipment compensates all significant permanent, induced and eddy-current interference fields in approximately 30 to 45 minutes. Permanent terms can be trimmed up on each flight in about five minutes compared to close to one hour for manual compensation systems.

The AN/ASA-65(V) is compatible with all existing magnetometer systems in present use. Accommo-dation for the varying compensation requirements of different aircraft types is conveniently accomplished by means of internal patch connectors. The equipment satisfies the requirements of applicable military specifications, and using state-of-the-art techniques has a demonstrated MTBF of more than 1800 hours. The use of completely solid-state circuitry has resulted in a total system weight of less than 13·6 kg.

The compensation figure of merit is stated to be consistently less than 1 gamma, and the equipment is capable of accommodating maximum compensation fields of 50 gamma on each aircraft axis.

AN/ASA-65(V) 2 nine-term compensator

CHARACTERISTICS

Dimensions	Height (mm)	Width (mm)	Depth (mm)	Weight (kg)
Control indicator	229	146	165	3·85
Electronic control				
amplifier	197	149	346	7·94
Magnetometer				
assembly	152	152	152	0·68
Coil assembly (V)1	89	89	89	0·90

STATUS
Production quantities have been manufactured and delivered to the RAF for the Nimrod maritime aircraft, and the AN/ASA-65(V) has also been delivered for USN P-3C Orion aircraft and S-3A Viking.

CONTRACTOR
CAE Electronics Ltd, PO Box 1800, St Laurent, Montreal, Quebec H4L 4X4, Canada.

1980.393
OA-5154/ASQ AUTOMATIC MAD COMPENSATION SYSTEM

The OA-5154/ASQ is the latest and most advanced version in a series of CAE compensator systems. This system was developed for use with boom-mounted magnetometers to minimise manoeuvre-related noise caused by the effect of magnetic fields inherent in the aircraft structure from interfering with underwater submarine detection or geological surveying. Excellent compensation combined with the ability to update minor variations rapidly and efficiently increases detection sensitivity to the limits of the magnetometer equipment.

The system is completely self-contained providing signal compensation by means of a micro-computer. The uncompensated 'raw' magnetometer input signal is conditioned and produced in a compensated state. This approach eliminates the requirement for output coils which were necessary to generate opposing fields in previous systems. Other than the 'raw' detector magnetometer signal, input requirements are limited to orthogonal vector magnetometer signals that provide heading, manoeuvre and total Earth's field information. The micro-computer is programmed to process this input data and both generate compensation requirements and update any changes on operator command.

No stringent manoeuvre requirements such as purity or accuracy of aircraft heading are necessary.

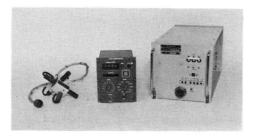

OA-5154/ASQ automatic MAD compensation system

Data to update all 16 independent compensation terms are simultaneously evaluated during a simple flight programme which involves performing small aircraft manoeuvres on four headings. The total time required for this is no more than eight minutes. The equipment requires no operator involvement other than to initiate the recompensation procedure and update request. Incorporation of built-in test functions and fault indicators allows the operator or technician to perform a systematic checkout of the equipment to the WRA and SRA level.

CHARACTERISTICS
Figure of merit: <0·4 γ
Residual interference signals: <0·03 γ average
Terms compensated: 16
Compensation time: 8 minutes

Aircraft manoeuvre requirements: 1 minute of manoeuvres on each of 4 approximate orthogonal headings. If desired, other manoeuvres, such as trapping circles, or clover-leafs can be used
Military specification: MIL-E-5400
External input requirements: Minimally filtered analogue output from detector magnetometer
Power requirements: 115 V AC, 400 Hz, and 28 V AC/DC, 10 VA for panel illumination
Specified reliability: 1000 h MTBF
Dimensions

	Height (cm)	Width (cm)	Depth (cm)	Weight (kg)
Control indicator	18·2	14·7	16·6	2·2
Electronic				
amplifier	22·9	22·9	54·6	11·3
Vector				
magnetometer	15·2	15·2	15·2	0·7

STATUS
Production quantities have been delivered for the Canadian CP-140 Aurora and the Breguet Atlantic for the Netherlands and West German navies. Several other countries have expressed interest for use in their ASW aircraft.

CONTRACTOR
CAE Electronics Ltd, PO Box 1800, St Laurent, Montreal, Quebec H4L 4X4, Canada.

3086.453
AN/SSQ-522 SONOBUOY

The AN/SSQ-522 is an active sonobuoy developed specially from the AN/SSQ-47B to meet the requirements of the Canadian Forces. The SSQ-47B is produced by both Sparton of Canada and the parent Sparton company in the USA and is described in **1988.453**.

CHARACTERISTICS
Type: Active
Sonar modes: Automatic keyed CW
Transducer depth: 60 or 800 ft (18 or 244 m)
Weight: 24 lb (10·9 kg)
Sonar channels: 6 (HF)
RF channels: 12
Operation of the SSQ-522 is identical to that of the

SSQ-47B, except that up to 12 buoys can be launched and operated simultaneously. Two different CW sonar modes are selectable by choice of VHF channel; even channel buoys have sonar modes the same as the SSQ-47B, and odd channel buoys have longer pulse-lengths and intervals.

CONTRACTOR
Sparton of Canada Ltd, London, Ontario, Canada.

3087.453
AN/SSQ-523 (CANCASS) SONOBUOY

The AN/SSQ-523 is the commandable active sonobuoy of the Canadian Command-Active Sonobuoy System (CANCASS), the other main elements being the airborne command signal monitor and active sonar processor.

The SSQ-523 provides ASW aircraft with remotely selectable and controllable sonar capability, and is used to detect, locate and track underwater targets. Proper channel command is achieved by the employment of UHF command channels paired with VHF output channels. The sonar output power level and frequencies are identical to those of the AN/SSQ-

47B (**1988.453**); however, sonar mode capability is enhanced to include short, medium, and long CW sonar pulse and linear FM sonar sweeps, thus providing detection and tracking capabilities that exceed those of the AN/SSQ-47B.

CHARACTERISTICS
Type: Commandable active
Sonar modes: Pulsed CW or linear FM
Transducer depth: 60 or 800 ft (18 or 244 m) commandable
Weight: 32 lb (14·5 kg)
Sonar channels: 6 (HF)
RF channels: 12

Auxiliary command functions permit remote deep-depth selection and remote scuttle. The digital technique employed for these facilities is capable of expansion to provide extra functions with very little additional circuitry.

DEVELOPMENT
This was undertaken by Sparton under a Canadian Government contract awarded in 1973, which also included associated CANCASS avionics.

CONTRACTOR
Sparton of Canada Ltd, London, Ontario, Canada.

3780.453
AN/SSQ-527B SONOBUOY

The AN/SSQ-527B is an omni-directional, passive sonobuoy which enables fixed wing maritime patrol aircraft, helicopters and surface ships to conduct underwater search and surveillance using low frequency analysis and recording (LOFAR) techniques.

The AN/SSQ-527B is identical in function to the US Navy AN/SSQ-41B but incorporates features which improve detectability of low level, low frequency signals in a noisy sea environment. These features include a sub-surface assembly suspension system which maintains hydrophone depth within specified limits in shear currents up to 2·5 knots and an acceleration noise cancelling hydrophone.

The sonobuoy can be launched at airspeeds between 30 and 300 knots from altitudes of 30 to 7600 metres. Descent is controlled and stabilised by a

parachute. Immediately after entry the sea water activated battery energises a mechanism which deploys the sonobuoy. A flotation bag is inflated and carries the upper electronics assembly, containing a VHF transmitter, to the surface while the hydrophone descends to a pre-selected operating depth. Three depths are available: 30, 100 or 300 metres. The sonobuoy becomes operative within 60 seconds of impact at the minimum depth and within 100 seconds at the maximum depth. It remains in operation for a minimum of 1, 3 or 8 hours, according to the preselected operating life.

The AN/SSQ-527B can be launched by hand from a ship moving at up to 30 knots without it being necessary to activate mechanical or electrical devices before launch. The electrically activated deployment mechanism functions regardless of attitude on entry since it is not dependent on impact forces acting on the bottom plate.

CHARACTERISTICS
Type: Passive omni-directional
Audio Frequencies: 10 – 5000 Hz
Depth: 30, 100 or 300 m
Size: A
Weight: 7·5 kg
Operating life: 1, 3 or 8 h
Launch altitude: 30 – 7600 m
Launch speed: 30 – 300 knots
RF channels: 31 (162·25 – 173·5 MHz band)
RF power: 1 W
STATUS
AN/SSQ-527A (two-depth): 35000 units produced 1979-82.
AN/SSQ-527B: in production.
CONTRACTOR
Sparton of Canada Ltd, London, Ontario, Canada.

4619.453

AN/SSQ-529 (DICANCAS) SONOBUOY

The AN/SSQ-529 is a directional version of the AN/SSQ-523 CANCASS commandable active sonobuoy (**3087.453**), which in turn is derived from the AN/SSQ-47B/522 range-only sonobuoy (**1988.453**).

Energy from target echoes received by the transducer is converted into a directional command active sonobuoy system (DICASS) compatible composite signal containing directional information. This composite signal modulates the output of a VHF transmitter in the floating surface unit. Launch platforms equipped with DICASS-capable electronic

equipment can employ the AN/SSQ-529 to determine the range and direction of a target relative to the position of the sonobuoy.

Command functions are identical to DICASS except that three transducer operating depths are provided (20, 100 and 250 metres).

The AN/SSQ-529 provides a cost-effective alternative to the DICASS sonobuoy for tactical training and for improved performance in shallow water.

CHARACTERISTICS

Type: Commandable, directional active
Sonar modes: Pulsed CW or linear FM

Transducer depth: 20, 100 or 250 m (intermediate and greatest depths are command selectable after deployment)
Weight: 14·5 kg
Sonar channels: 6 (HF)
RF channels: 12
DEVELOPMENT
The development was initiated under Canadian government contract awarded in March 1981.
STATUS
Production is scheduled to commence in early 1986.
CONTRACTOR
Sparton of Canada Ltd, London, Ontario, Canada.

4620.453

AN/SSQ-530 DIFAR SONOBUOY

The AN/SSQ-530 is a directional, passive sonobuoy which provides ships and fixed and rotary wing maritime aircraft with the dual capability of detecting and determining the source direction of underwater acoustic energy radiated by submarines. VHF transmissions containing this information are received by the launch vehicle and are analysed and processed to find the true bearing of the source using directional low frequency analysis and recording (DIFAR) techniques.

The AN/SSQ-530 is an improved version of the AN/SSQ-53A DIFAR sonobuoy (**1990.453**) and is able to select a third intermediate hydrophone operating depth of 100 metres. Depths below the minimum

depth setting of 30 metres can be adjusted to suit operating environments. Storage life has been increased from 5 to 7 years.

Launch is possible from aircraft at airspeeds between 30 and 300 knots from altitudes of 30 to 7600 metres. Descent is controlled by parachute. On entry, a sea water activated battery starts deployment of the buoy which becomes operative for one or four hours according to the preselected operating life. Ship launch is helped by the electrical activation which ensures reliable deployment regardless of attitude on entry since it is not dependent on water forces acting on the bottom plate.

The sonobuoy is compatible with the AQA-7, OL-82(AYS) and AQS-901 processors. The Sparton TD-1135A demultiplexer/processor/display can

provide a self-contained stand-alone DIFAR capability for ships, helicopters and aircraft.
CHARACTERISTICS
Type: Passive, directional LOFAR (DIFAR)
Function: Search and localisation
Hydrophone depth: 30, 100 or 300 m
Weight: 10·2 kg
RF channels: 31
RF power: 1 W
Launch altitude: 0 – 7600 m
Operating life: 1 or 4 h
STATUS
Developed under Canadian government contract. In production.
CONTRACTOR
Sparton of Canada Ltd, London, Ontario, Canada.

4649.363

SBP 1-1 (AN/UYS-503) SONOBUOY PROCESSOR

The SBP 1-1 sonobuoy processor is a small, lightweight, low cost multi-sonobuoy equipment designed for a variety of ASW platforms. It employs a new concept in processor architecture and uses a Computing Devices proprietary universal demultiplexer to assure future growth capability. The

equipment is capable of handling eight Jezebel omni-sonobuoys, four DIFAR, four DICASS, four range only active and BT buoys. It is the fourth sonobuoy processor developed by Computing Devices since the early 1970s.
STATUS
In production. An order worth C$1 million was received from the Swedish Navy in early 1984, and

additional orders have been received from Canada for ASW helicopter ASW application.
CONTRACTOR
Computing Devices Company (a division of Control Data Canada Ltd), PO Box 8508, Ottawa, Ontario K1G 3M9, Canada.

FRANCE

3791.363

TSM 8200 AIRBORNE SONOBUOY PROCESSING EQUIPMENT

Installed aboard fixed- or rotary-wing aircraft, this equipment processes and displays signals received from various types of sonobuoy. Modular design permits optimum system configuration to suit all sonobuoy types and the specific number to be processed simultaneously. All signals received are permanently recorded before being processed to allow more extensive utilisation of data at shore-based processing stations. Categories of sonobuoy whose data can be processed include: passive buoys (directional and omni-directional); active buoys (directional and omni-directional); environmental buoys such as bathythermographic, sea noise measuring, etc; and numerous buoys of the same or several different types can be handled simultaneously.

Three main elements comprise the TSM 8200 equipment:

(1) Communications unit, in which will be found a 99-channel VHF receiver, a UHF transmitter/receiver for active sonobuoy remote control, and ASSG overall test systems. Each set is associated with a control box for the system operators.

(2) Signal processing and display unit. This carries out analogue pre-processing and full processing functions in the active and passive modes using digital processors and appropriate software. Information is presented by a high density graphic recorder and a CRT display. The latter is associated with a high-capacity bulk storage unit and numerous image formats are available by means of elaborate software appropriate to the specific types of buoy and signal processing. The dual processor configuration is normally operated by two operators using an alpha-numeric keyboard and tracker ball. A digital data bus permits dialogue between the operators and

TSM 8200 airborne acoustic system installed on French Navy 'Atlantic' maritime patrol aircraft

the tactical co-ordinator, via the tactical computer. Several signal processing and display units can be associated aboard the same aircraft so that system performance can be enhanced by increasing the number and types of buoys which can be processed simultaneously. An on-top-position indicator is used in conjunction with a radio compass for homing towards the sonobuoy.

(3) Magnetic recording unit. This multi-track recorder records all the sonobuoy data at the analogue processing level for subsequent analysis ashore

(4) Other optional equipment includes an acoustic signal generator simulator for test purposes, and remote control of active sonobuoys.
STATUS
In production.
CONTRACTOR
Thomson-CSF, Division Activités Sous-Marines, Chemin des Travails, BP 53, 06801 Cagnes-sur-Mer, France.

4347.363

TSM 8210/8220 (LAMPARO) LIGHTWEIGHT AIRBORNE SONOBUOY PROCESSING EQUIPMENT

Derived from the TSM 8200 (**3791.363**), these airborne sonar signal processing and display systems are designed as modern digital equipments for ASW fixed or rotary wing aircraft.

The processing capabilities of the TSM 8210 are essentially identical to those of the TSM 8200, but the configuration is based on a single processing unit in a lighter and more compact packaging. It is manned by a single ASW operator. The same wide panel of facilities and processing modes is available.

The TSM 8220 is orientated towards the processing of omni-directional passive and active buoys.

The signals are displayed on a CRT in TV format and hard copy can be connected for permanent recording. An on-top-position indicator is used in conjunction with a radio compass for homing on the sonobuoy. Weight of the complete system is 140 kg for the TSM 8210 and 70 kg for the TSM 8220.
STATUS
The TSM 8210 and TSM 8220 are currently in the pre-production phase.
CONTRACTOR
Thomson-CSF, Division Activités Sous-Marines, Chemin des Travails, BP 53, 06801 Cagnes-sur-Mer, France.

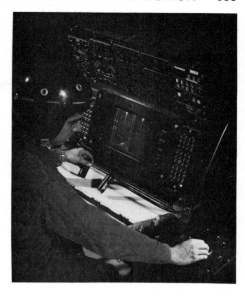

TSM 8210 processing and display system

1159.253

DUBV-23D SURFACE VESSEL SONAR

The DUBV-23D is a bow-mounted, low-frequency, panoramic sonar for anti-submarine operations. The 48-column transducer array is housed in a bulb at the forepart of the ship, the bulb being of streamlined design to reduce parasitic noises to permit listening at high speeds. The panoramic sonar is intended for both search and attack roles.

In addition to the transducer array, the equipment includes the transmitter/receiver unit, a computer section for the processing of data being fed to weapons, and control and display consoles at the anti-submarine attack station.

The DUBV-23 is of identical design to the towed sonar DUBV-43 (**1334.453**) and in French vessels the two sonars are used together for anti-submarine warfare.
OPERATION
Operating modes provide for: panoramic surveillance, sector surveillance, step surveillance, passive surveillance at sonar frequency, panoramic attack transmission, or 'searchlight' attack transmission. In addition to the system's own display devices, the DUBV-23D provides for target data outputs to other ship's systems and repeater PPIs.

The following notes refer to combined use of the DUBV-23 and DUBV-43 sonars. Advantages claimed for this method are:
(1) The attack and target data processing section of the DUBV-23 can be connected to the towed sonar by remote control, which provides for control of weapons by the sonar giving best results
(2) The simultaneous use of a hull transducer and a towed transducer, whose depth can be selected within the limits of 10 to about 200 m, considerably increases the sound volume and correspondingly limits the chances of attack by conventional submarines
(3) The use of a towed transducer array offers a significant measure of protection against performance degradation due to sea-state effects
(4) It is possible to attack a target whilst continuing surveillance
(5) Deep submersion of the DUBV-43 sonar permits a doubling of transmitter power, with an appropriate increase in detection range.

DUBV-43 sonar control console

Four modes of operation are possible:
(1) INDEPENDENT. The two sonars are independent except for reciprocal connections for audio and video sensitivity control during transmission. This mode is normally employed only when one sonar is defective.
(2) 23 SYN. In this mode the transmissions of the two sonars are synchronised, using the same or different frequencies, with the DUBV-23 as the master. The hull sonar is for attack, and the towed sonar for surveillance.
(3) 43 SYN. This mode is identical to the preceding mode, but with the towed sonar as master.
(4) 43 ATT. This mode is divided into two phases: the first, Delayed 43 ATT, is a preparatory stage for effecting certain remote switching operations, and the second, Standby 43 ATT, permits processing of data from the towed sonar and its transmission to the weapons via the attack section of the DUBV-23 sonar. In this mode the attack section of the DUBV-23 and the DUBV-43 must use the same frequency. However, the surveillance section of the DUBV-23 can, if necessary, be operated on a frequency different from that assigned to the DUBV-43.

CHARACTERISTICS
Transmitter
Frequencies: 4 operating frequencies in the neighbourhood of 5 kHz, of which 2 are operational
Power: 96 kW (2 × 48 kW)
Type: FF (fixed frequency), FM (linear frequency modulation with non-coherent data processing at reception)
Duration: 4, 30, 150 or 700 ms
Scatter echo: With or without rejection
Doppler effect correction: On all 48 channels
Cadence: Adjustable step by step from 1500 to 48 000 yards
Receiver: Panoramic, directional, passive listening in sonar band
STATUS
The DUBV-23D is in service in converted anti-submarine escorts Types T47 and T56, frigates of the 'Suffren' class and Type C67, and corvettes Type C70 of the French Navy.
CONTRACTOR
SINTRA-ALCATEL, Département DSM, 1 avenue Aristide Briand, 94117 Arcueil Cedex, France.

1786.453

PAP 104 MINE DISPOSAL WEAPON

The PAP 104 system has been developed as a means of remotely placing a mine disposal charge alongside a mine which has previously been located by means of a minehunting sonar. It consists basically of four main parts: a wire-guided submersible vehicle which carries the destruction charge and is equipped with a TV camera, a control console, TV monitor, and remote control box, the last three items being located on the carrier vessel. An optional cutting device for

moored mines is entering service. Overall dimensions of the submersible are: length 2·7 m, width 1·2 m, height 1·3 m, and weight 700 kg (inclusive of explosive charge). Operating range is 500 m at depths of 100 m or less with standard motors (300 m or less with optional special motors) and battery life is sufficient for five sorties. The maximum speed is 5·5 knots. A piloting simulator, known as SIMPAP is available for the training of personnel.
DEVELOPMENT
Development of the PAP system was carried out by

Direction Techniques des Constructions Navales, Groupe d'Etudes Sous-Marines de l'Atlantique in collaboration with Société ECA.
STATUS
More than 180 have been built for the navies of France, Belgium, Netherlands, Norway, the United Kingdom and West Germany and for the European Tripartite minehunter. Orders have been placed by Australia and Malaysia, and negotiations with other navies are in progress.

CONTRACTOR
Société ECA, 17 avenue du Chateau, BP 16, 92190
Meudon, France.

PAP 104 mine disposal system submersibles at the
ECA factory

1334.453
DUBV-43B VARIABLE DEPTH SONAR
The DUBV-43B variable depth sonar consists of a
streamlined towed body called the 'fish', containing
the sonar transducer array. This is towed from the
rear of the parent vessel at distances of up to 250
metres and can be set to run at depths between 10 and
200 metres. It is equipped with stabilisers providing
for control in roll, pitch, and depth. An attack version
of the system is also provided with a gyro-compass.
Dimensions of the 'fish' are: length 550 cm, width
170 cm, and submerged weight 7·75 tonnes. The
towing cable also incorporates 48 pairs of signal
conductors. The range of towing speeds is 4 to 24
knots, and detection ranges of up to 25 km are
quoted. The DUBV-43B is identical to the DUBV-24C
sonar (**1217.253** *1982-83* and earlier editions) except
for the transducer array, which in the DUBV-24C is in
a hull-mounted sonar dome, while the DUBV-43B
array is towed. The increased operating depth of the
latter permits an increase in radiated power to 96 kW.

The transducer array is 1 metre in diameter and 1·2
metres high. It consists of 24 vertical 'staves' of eight
transducers to give a total of 192 elements.

DUBV-43 VDS towed transducer and towing gear
aboard the French corvette Georges Leyghes

STATUS
The DUBV-43B is in service in converted anti-
submarine escorts Types T47 and T56, frigates of the
'Suffren' class and Type C67, and corvettes Type C70
of the French Navy.

CONTRACTORS
Direction Technique des Constructions Navales,
2 rue Royale, Paris 8, France.
    SINTRA-ALCATEL, Départment DSM, 1 avenue
Aristide Briand, 94117 Arcueil Cedex, France.

1356.453
ELEDONE SUBMARINE SONAR
ELEDONE is a family of submarine sonars, the most
comprehensive of which combine the main
submarine sonar functions within a single integrated
system. The system may be fitted to any size of
submarine or operational requirement by the simple
addition of standard cabinets and the appropriate
transducer arrays. Simultaneous use of these various
functions is achieved by the use of a colour display
which integrates all relevant data. Built-in
redundancy and built-in test facilities maintain
availability. The system provides:

Passive listening
This facility gives high sensitivity, fine bearing
accuracy and great flexibility of installation in all
types of submarines. The number of hydrophone
staves can be selected, either 32 staves for small
diameters down to 1·2 metres, 64 staves for large
diameters up to 3·5 metres or 96 staves for the largest.
Specific processing channels can provide from four
to twelve automatic tracks. Accurate target data are
sent continuously to the tactical system to allow
effective target motion analysis.

Passive adaptive processing
The adaptive processing function is based upon
optimal array processing theory which minimises the
effect of jamming by strong signals, when listening to
low level signals. It is a very useful facility in the
discrimination between two targets when both are
within a common limited sector.

Interception
Interception of all active sonar pulses from low
frequency surface ship sonars to high frequency
torpedo acoustic heads. Very early warning against
enemy sonars, with a very low false alarm rate, is
provided. Interception warnings are integrated on the
passive listening scope with specific colour (visual
correlation). Accurate parameters of pulses are

ELEDONE submarine sonar acoustic arrays

presented on digital read-outs and systematically transmitted to the tactical system.

Active capability

Although initial bearings are provided by the passive detection, the operator can also initiate a low frequency wide sector transmission on the same bearing to determine accurate range. In this mode, reception is performed by the passive listening array and associated with high detection sensitivity.

Spectral analysis

The spectrum analysis facility complements the audio function by providing the operator with specific data in target identification. This analysis can be performed in real-time or played back from memory store. Paper recorders, tape recorders, cavitation warnings, additional mass memory data and other facilities can be provided.

Tactical display

The tactical display system is the operational heart of the submarine and provides a continuous tactical situation review. It provides navigation information, storage and display of sensor data, target parameters analysis, geographical and tactical presentation, target motion analysis and weapons control.

STATUS
In operational service and in serial production for several navies.
CONTRACTOR
Thomson-CSF, Division Activités Sous-Marines, Chemin des Travails, BP 53, 06801 Cagnes-sur-Mer, France.

1634.453

DUUA-2A ACTIVE/PASSIVE SONAR

The DUUA-2A sonar is fitted to modernised 'Daphne' class submarines and 1200 tonne submarines, and provides for simultaneous surveillance and attack. It can be used:

(1) For active detection in single (FP), or frequency modulation (FM) modes
(2) For passive detection
(3) As an interceptor, ie location of a sonar source.

The DUUA-2A may also be used for ultrasonic communications purposes and for depth sounding in very deep water.

CHARACTERISTICS

Transmitter: Frequency 8·4 kHz

Power: 20 kW in nominal operation, and 1 kW in reduced operation, SGF and IC. Each emission is manually triggered. Emission duration 30 ms in SFG; 300 ms in FP; 500 ms in FM

Receiver

Pass band: ±170 Hz in FP; ±350 Hz in FM in the neighbourhood of 8·4 kHz; ±500 Hz in EBM in the neighbourhood of a selected frequency between 2·5 and 15 kHz

Range scale in active mode: 3, 6, 12, and 24 km

Transducer: Directional, Type B 88T 8·5, driven by servo mechanism MSS 5 directivity on site and bearing 2 θ_3 = 10° at 8·5 kHz. Manual orientation by crank on azimuth or automatic orientation at 4 or 8°/s from −175 to +175° on bearing. Reset between stops at 60°/s. Site positioning from +15 to −30°

STATUS
In service in the French 'Daphne', 'Agosta' and 'Narval' classes of submarines.
CONTRACTOR
SINTRA-ALCATEL, Département DSM, 1 avenue Aristide Briand, 94117 Arcueil Cedex, France.

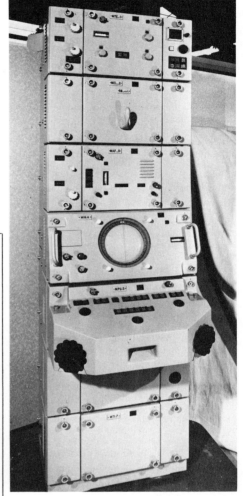

DUUA-2 sonar operator console

3232.453

DUUA-2B ACTIVE/PASSIVE SONAR

The DUUA-2B sonar can be fitted in all types of submarine and it provides for simultaneous search, attack, sonar interception, and depth sounding in deep water.

Two versions exist:
  Model I: Active sonar
  Model II: Passive sonar

Either one or two sonars can be fitted in each submarine, but if two active sonars are fitted only one transmitter need be employed.

CHARACTERISTICS

Transducer: Directional. Manual or automatic search in continuous rotation

Transmitter

Frequency: 8 kHz

Power: 3 kW

Pulse: FP or FM mode

Receiver: In passive mode, from 2·5 to 15 kHz

STATUS
In series production and ordered for the French Navy Type SNA72 fleet submarines.
CONTRACTOR
SINTRA-ALCATEL, Département DSM, 1 avenue Aristide Briand, 94117 Arcueil Cedex, France.

Control console of DUUA-2B active/passive sonar

3498.453

FENELON - DUUX-5 PASSIVE SONAR AND ACOUSTIC RANGEFINDER

Fenelon is the name given to a panoramic sonar capable of automatic and simultaneous tracking of three targets. The equipment incorporates a passive acoustic rangefinder for measuring the range of three targets within 120° sectors, and a panoramic sonar interceptor measuring the true bearing of all sonar transmissions received within the 2 to 15 kHz band.

The DUUX-5 equipment was developed by Alcatel as a successor to the DUUX-2 series (**1162.453** *1979-80* and earlier editions), of which at least 120 equipments were built and supplied to 14 navies for fitting in eight types of submarine. The Fenelon equipment enables range and bearing information on targets to be obtained by the submarine without the need for any transmissions and with minimum delay. Speed of operation permits target course and speed to be computed rapidly, also allowing any changes in either speed or course to be detected without delay. Four targets can be tracked simultaneously (three on radiated self-noise, one on sonar pulses), and there is a continuous panoramic bearing display over 360°. Range information is provided over arcs of 120° on each side of the submarine. There are facilities for transmission of target data automatically to the ship's weapon control system and plotting table.

Performance characteristics include high accuracy and discrimination, immunity against sonar pulse interference, simplified calibration, and integrated test facilities. Two types of hydrophones are available. The hydrophonic unit is composed of two bases with three hydrophones each on the starboard and port side of the submarine. All other technical details remain classified.

The UX27 is an improvement of the basic DUUX-5, through the use of heterogeneous hydrophones with ten staves, and the addition of preprocessing (filtering, multiplexing, beam forming) to improve the detection threshold and protect against interference.

STATUS
In series production. Replaces DUUX-2 passive acoustic rangefinder.
CONTRACTOR
SINTRA-ALCATEL, Département DSM, 1 avenue Aristide Briand, 94117 Arcueil Cedex, France.

Fenelon – DUUX-5 control and display console

1631.353
HS/DUAV-4 HELICOPTER SONAR

The HS is an active/passive directive sonar designed for submarine surveillance and location (azimuth, distance, and radial speed). It is specially designed for use on board light, versatile, ship-based helicopters of which the WG13 Lynx is a typical example. It may also be fitted aboard small surface vessels as either a hull sonar or as a VDS system.

The HS differs from conventional sonar in its signal processing system which is designed to give improved detection, especially in severe reverberation conditions such as shallow waters. The sonar can be operated in either the active or passive mode, true bearing, range, and radial speed are measured in the former mode, true bearing only in the passive mode.

A combined display unit permits surveillance display (initial detection) or plotting display (precise azimuth determination). Total weight (including electronic rack, cable, and dome) is 250 kg.

STATUS
The HS is used by the French Navy under the designation DUAV-4. In series production for the French and several other navies.

HS/DUAV-4 helicopter sonar installation in WG 13 Lynx

CONTRACTOR
SINTRA-ALCATEL, Département DSM, 1 avenue Aristide Briand, 94117 Arcueil Cedex, France.

4097.453
SS 48 SONAR

The SS 48 sonar is a high performance search and attack equipment designed for large ASW ships. It is comprised of two low frequency (LF) panoramic sonars with preformed beams. The first of these sonars is equipped with a cylindrical hull-mounted transducer having 48 vertical staves. The array is housed in a bow sonar dome and suspended to permit freedom in the roll axis. Dimensions are: 1864 mm diameter, 1643 mm height and nine tons weight. The second sonar is a variable depth equipment (VDS) consisting of a cylindrical 24-stave transducer housed in a 'fish' which is towed behind the ship. A mechanical handling equipment located on the after-

deck is fitted for stowage, and deployment and towing of the fish.

Both sonars provide for coherent processing in CW and FM in all beams, doppler measurement in both modes, classification, extraction and multi-sweep correlation (using synthetic video). The microprocessors employed also permit rapid fault location and self-test. The equipment (additional to the transducers and gear) comprises four electronics cabinets, two junction boxes, and one operational console with two three-colour displays and interactive dialogue facilities.

The latter item enables a single operator to handle detection, location, classification and situation evaluation. The facilities provided include:

(1) Panoramic active search with multiple correlation
(2) Sector active search (raw video)
(3) Time analysis of echoes
(4) Doppler analysis
(5) Range and bearing measurements
(6) Continuous presentation of tactical situation
(7) Target and firing elements (12 tracked targets)
(8) Continuous torpedo search
(9) Panoramic passive search (96 beams for hull sonar and 48 beams for VDS).

STATUS
The SS 48 is involved in an updating programme for French Navy DUBV-23/DUBV-43 sonar systems (**1159.253** and **1334.453**) which equip all major ASW ships of the French Navy.

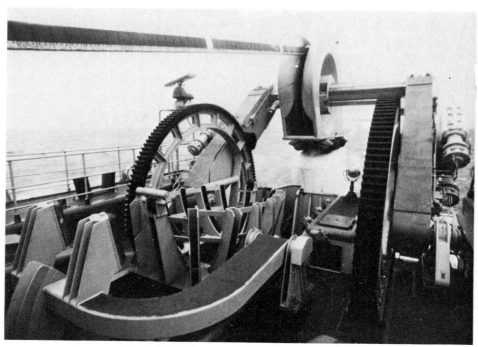

Close-up of SS 48 VDS deck handling gear and tow cable

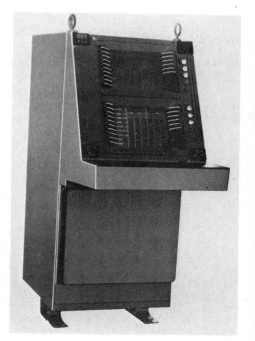

Console of SS 48 sonar equipment

CHARACTERISTICS

Transducer	Hull	VDS (LF)
Frequencies	3 in 5 kHz band	3 in 5 kHz band
Panoramic transmission level (dB)	230	228
Directional transmission level (dB)	241	237
Modes	CW – FM	Crossed codes FM
Handling system and weight		MSR2D (90 t) ECAN Ruelle

CONTRACTOR
SINTRA-ALCATEL, Département DSM, 1 avenue Aristide Briand, 94117 Arcueil Cedex, France.

4096.453
SS 24 LF SONAR

The SS 24 LF is a high performance surface ship sonar for vessels of more than 1000 tons, and is designed primarily for ASW use. The system is based on a panoramic sonar with 24 preformed beams operating in the low frequency band around 5 kHz. A hull-mounted transducer in a sonar dome is employed and the system may or may not be associated with a towed variable depth sonar (VDS). The VDS is a medium frequency sonar with 12 performed beams and is carried on deck handling equipment (Mini-Ulis) produced by Ateliers et Chantiers du Havre (ACH), fitted on the after deck and weighing four tons (**4094.453**).

A single operator can assume responsibility for search and attack, and a situation history display is provided for his use. After coherent processing of CW and FM signals for each beam, the operator has available stored information for:
(1) Panoramic active search; true bearing and range in rectangular co-ordinates with synthetic video
(2) Passive search (24 preformed beams for the hull-mounted sonar and 12 for the VDS)
(3) Active sector search using raw video
(4) Echo analysis
(5) Torpedo alarm
(6) Sonar interception
(7) Situation history.
The sonar can be linked to a weapon control system (DLA) and to all combat systems. A three-colour display unit is provided and provisions are included

CHARACTERISTICS

Transducer	Hull (LF)	VDS (MF)
Diameter (mm)	1060	200
Frequencies	3 in 5 kHz band	3 in 13 kHz band
Transmission level (dB)	Panoramic 223 Directional 232	212
Transmission modes	CW or FM	CW or FM

for interactive dialogue between the SS 24 LF and its operator. These are mounted in the operational console and there are three other electronic/electrical equipment cabinets. The inclusion of microprocessors facilitates self-test and rapid fault-finding.
STATUS
The SS 24 LF is involved in a major refit programme relating to the French Navy DUBV-24C sonar (**1217.253** *1982-83* and earlier editions) associated with experience gained with the DUBV-43 (**1334.453**) and VDS.
CONTRACTOR
SINTRA-ALCATEL, Département DSM, 1 avenue Aristide Briand, 94117 Arcueil Cedex, France.

Three-colour operating console of SS 24 LF sonar

4094.453
SS 12 SMALL SHIP SONAR (HULL AND VDS)

The SS 12 is a panoramic sonar operating at medium frequencies and with preformed beams for fitting in small ships and medium tonnage vessels. It has also been developed in a version suitable for helicopter use (**4095.453**). The use of the same electronics on helicopters and aboard ships yields common training procedures and maintenance facilities.

For surface ships the SS 12 can be supplied as a hull-mounted sonar in either fixed dome or retractable dome configuration, and/or as a variable depth sonar (VDS). In the latter configuration the Mini-Ulis handling system developed and produced by La Société Nouvelle des Ateliers et Chantiers du Havre (ACH) is usually employed, and this has a deck weight of less than four tons. A dipping sonar version can a!so be provided; in this configuration the complete electronics are housed in a container fitted to the after-deck of the ship.

ALCATEL's considerable experience of shallow water sonars has been applied to enable optimisation of the SS 12 for small, noisy ships. Special display provisions for the coherent signal processing of CW and FM data enables the operator to carry out panoramic search without the strain of conventional PPI presentation, and by preserving all modes the sonar realises the maximum figure of merit. Availability of all data permits rapid and reliable classification of targets.
CHARACTERISTICS
Frequencies: 3 in 13 kHz band
Operating modes: CW, rectangular or cos² pulse; FM, hyperbolic modulation
Transmission level: 212 dB (ref 1 pascal/yard)
Scales: 2, 4, 8, 16 km or ky
Passive listening: Noise or pinger. Automatic tracking of two echoes and data transmission to the control system (DLA) of the weapon system.

Mini-Ulis
Mechanical System
Fish stabilisation: Servo-control system (fish amplitude about ±2 m)
Towing speed: 16 knots
Max speed on brakes: 30 knots
Hoisting and lowering time: 6 minutes
Max cable speed: 3 m/s
Cable length: approx 200 m
Diameter: 14 mm
Breaking load: 7 tons
STATUS
In production.
CONTRACTOR
SINTRA-ALCATEL, Département DSM, 1 avenue Aristide Briand, 94117 Arcueil Cedex, France.

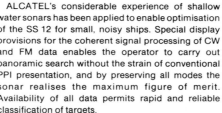

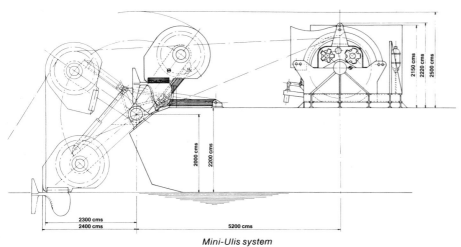

Mini-Ulis system

Operating console of SS 12 sonar

5633.453
SS 24A LF SONAR
The SS 24A LF sonar is a panoramic sonar equipment of 24 beams operating at low frequencies and designed for fitting to medium tonnage vessels. This sonar is derived from the SS 12 (**4094.453**) and uses similar electronics, although with better performances due to a higher power level and a lower frequency. The SS 24A LF will also be available in a fixed dome version.

A medium frequency version (three frequencies in the 12 kHz band) can also be provided under the name of SS 24 MF.

CHARACTERISTICS
Frequencies: 3 in 5 kHz band
Operating modes: CW, rectangular or cos² pulse; FM, hyperbolic modulation
Transmission level (dB)
Panoramic: base line 218; option 221
RDT and DIR: base line 223; option 229

Scales: 2,4,8,16 km or Ky (32 in option)
Passive listening: Noise or pinger. Automatic tracking of two echoes and data transmission to the control system (DLA) of the weapon system.
CONTRACTOR
SINTRA-ALCATEL, Département DSM, 1 avenue Aristide Briand, 94117 Arcueil Cedex, France.

4095.453
HS 12 ACTIVE/PASSIVE HELICOPTER SONAR
The HS 12 is an active/passive panoramic helicopter version of the SS 12 small ship sonar (**4094.453**) and uses the same electronics as the surface vessels version. It has similar capabilities for operation in shallow/noisy waters, and has a system weight of less than 240 kg, thus suiting it for installation on light naval helicopters such as the Lynx. The HS 12 transducer is raised and lowered by a hydraulic winch and this has a capacity for a 300 metre long cable; the winching cable speed is about five metres/second.

Operation in CW and FM modes is possible and digital signal processing is employed by the system's microprocessor. Automatic tracking of two targets and transmission of elements to an external equipment, such as a plotting table, are provided.
CHARACTERISTICS
Frequencies: 3 in 13 kHz band
Transmission level: 212 dB (ref 1 pascal/yard)
Passive search: Noise or pinger. Display of 12 preformed beams, each subject to adaptive signal processing. Other characteristics as for the SS 12.
STATUS
In series production.
CONTRACTOR
SINTRA-ALCATEL, Département DSM, 1 avenue Aristide Briand, 94117 Arcueil Cedex, France.

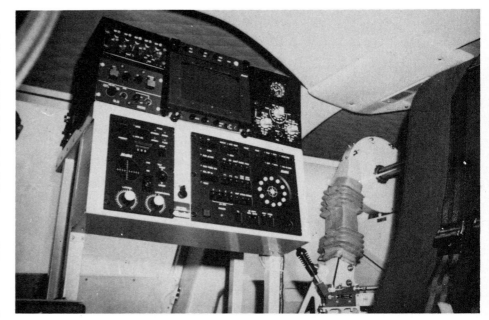

Typical helicopter installation of the HS 12 sonar on Dauphin naval helicopter

---

4461.453
DSRX 61X EXPERIMENTAL TOWED LINEAR ARRAY SONAR
In May 1980 a simplified processing system was delivered to the French Navy for an experimental linear towed array sonar designated DSRX 61X. Following successful trials carried out on the research ship *L'Agenais* since January 1981, the Departement de Detection Sous-Marine of SINTRA-ALCATEL has obtained a contract from the French Navy to develop a new generation of passive sonars, reflecting a significant evolution in submarine warfare by surface ships and submarines.
CONTRACTOR
SINTRA-ALCATEL, Département DSM, 1 avenue Aristide Briand, 94117 Arcueil Cedex, France.

Experimental linear towed array sonar aboard trials ship L'Agenais

---

5634.293
SINTRA-ALCATEL ANCILLARY SONAR EQUIPMENT
For the majority of the SINTRA-ALCATEL sonar systems the following ancillary equipment is available:
Sonar Maintenance Simulators
These include a transmission dummy load as well as a simulation unit giving a number of synthetic echoes corresponding to the various sonar operational modes.
Training Simulator
The training simulator consists of a maintenance

simulator and a second unit which controls the synthetic echoes. Each target can be modified in terms of course, speed and immersion, and eventual contact losses due to bathythermic conditions can also be simulated, based on conditions previously put into the memory of the simulator.
Sonar Target Transponders
These sonar target transponders are for active sonars and simulate the reflection of a sonar wave on the submarine hull. Transmission and transducer immersion can be manually adjusted before target lowering. The target transponder pass band covers widely the various sonar transmission frequencies.

Calibration Equipment for Passive and Active Sonars – SEB
This equipment has three operational modes:
(1) Transmission mode in CW (from 1·8 to 12 kHz)
(2) Noise transmission mode; permanent or by pulses (from 1·2 to 12 kHz)
(3) Transponder mode; fixed or real.
The calibration equipment can be either towed up to 5 knots or dunked. The maximum depth for the system is 200 metres.
CONTRACTOR
SINTRA-ALCATEL, Département DSM, 1 avenue Aristide Briand, 94117 Arcueil Cedex, France.

3501.453
DSTV-4M/DSTV-7Y SONOBUOYS

These sonobuoys are passive omni-directional types for the detection and location of submarines by aircraft. The DSTV-4M is A size (914 mm length) and the DSTV-7Y is F size (305 mm). Both have standard diameters of 123 mm. The DSTV-7Y is equipped with a synthesiser enabling in-flight selection of the VHF channel among 31 channels.

CHARACTERISTICS

Hydrophone depth: 20 m, 100 m (possibly 300 m also)

Frequency: 10 Hz to 20 000 Hz
Operating life: 1, 3, or 8 h
RF channels: 31 (or 99)
RF output: 1 W minimum
Antenna: ¼-wave whip

STATUS

The DSTV-4M is in production and delivered to the French Navy. The DSTV-7Y is in the pre-production phase.

CONTRACTOR

Thomson-CSF, Division Activités Sous-Marines, Chemin des Travails, BP 53, 06801 Cagnes-sur-Mer, France.

DSTV-7Y passive sonobuoy

3095.263
SOUND RAY TRACER (TSM9310)

Derived from the earlier TSM9300, this equipment uses both a DDA special-purpose processor for sound field computation and a mini-computer for improved data input facilities. Design is to French Navy specifications. The purpose of the equipment is to compute and display the sound rays transmitted or received by an acoustic source, according to a given sound velocity profile. The latter depends upon bathythermic conditions, and can be obtained directly with a sound velocimeter or derived from a bathythermograph profile. On a ship or aircraft, the equipment's ray diagram display shows the actual limitations of sonar equipment and enables ASW personnel to decide upon the best tactics in a given situation.

The TSM9310 is a single unit on the front face of which are the 150 × 200 mm CRT display and all necessary input and operating controls. The high rate of calculation (1000 km/s) of the TSM9310 permits real-time display of a large number of rays (over 20), which is essential for effective analysis of the ray diagram. Provision is made for use of a polaroid camera to provide a hard copy record of sound field displays.

Thomson-CSF TSM9310 sound ray tracer

The displayed ray diagrams depend upon the data input and parameters:

(1) Source data: depth, vertical beamwidth, vertical inclination of beam axis
(2) Sound velocity profile: couples depth/sound velocity determining layers with a constant sound velocity gradient (maximum 12 layers), bottom depth
(3) Ray diagram parameters: scales, angle step between computed rays, number of bottom and surface bounces permitted, and possibly magnified zone range.

CHARACTERISTICS

Input data
Max source depth: 10 000 m
Vertical beamwidth: 0 – 180°
Beam elevation: –90 to +90°
Sound velocity profile
Bottom depth: 10 000 m max
Dimensions: 57 × 44 × 55 cm
Weight: 80 kg

STATUS

In operational service but no longer in production.

CONTRACTOR

Thomson-CSF, Division Activités Sous-Marines, Chemin des Travails, BP 53, 06801 Cagnes-sur-Mer, France.

1724.253
DUBA 25 (TSM 2400) SONAR

The Tarpon TSM 2400 (service designation DUBA 25) is a powerful attack sonar fitted in the French 'Aviso' class ships and similar anti-submarine vessels. It is an active sonar with a panoramic transducer array and assembly with sonar dome supplied by the French Navy. Although the sonar is suitable for use as towed VDS equipment, in the DUBA 25 configuration it is hull-mounted, and provides 'Aviso' class ships with all-round surveillance, acquisition and attack facilities for ASW operations. The power employed is sufficient for operating ranges of several kilometres. The transducer array consists of 36 staves arranged to form a cylinder 110 cm in diameter and provided

Thomson-CSF (TSM 2400) sonar in DUBA 25 configuration

with roll stabilisation.

The electronics assemblies comprise a transmitter cabinet housing 12 identical units, each driving three groups of transmitter transducer elements. Thyratron modular transmitters are employed. An inverter provides the necessary DC electrical power for the transmitters from the ship's mains. Three receiver cabinets of identical dimensions contain:

(1) Received signal amplifiers and circuits for achieving the 36 preformed channels
(2) Data processing circuits for frequency changing, filtering, and rejection, AGC and detection-integration
(3) Interface units for connections to and from other ship's systems, and including the target data memory computer.

The display unit is equipped with all the controls and indicators needed for control of the sonar and its operational use. These include:

(1) Panoramic target acquisition scope
(2) Fine aiming scope
(3) Target doppler measuring CRT indicator
(4) Audio channel
(5) Digital readouts of target azimuth and range parameters
(6) Controls for target data memory circuits
(7) Transmission frequency and mode controls
(8) Reception mode controls.

A test box is provided which permits the injection of calibrated signals into the sonar to simulate an echo to enable circuit tests, performance measurements, or operator training to be undertaken. A target box enables the manual input to the computer of estimated target speed and course.

CHARACTERISTICS

Transmission: Panoramic, pure or modulated, on 3 frequencies

Time: 30 or 90 ms at normal or reduced power

Reception: Panoramic on 36 preformed channels, with or without rejection; one directional channel with magnifier doppler measurement and audio.

	Height (cm)	Width (cm)	Depth (cm)	Weight (kg)
Reception units (3)	194	60	67	430
Display	194	60	113	410
Test box	42	60	45	57
Target box	27	21	71	23
Repeater boxes (2)	17	21	22	3
Inverter	136	135	278	3800
Starting cabinet	143	73	55	310
Transmitter	199	60	78	700

STATUS

Operational since 1975. No longer in production.

CONTRACTOR

Thomson-CSF, Division Activités Sous-Marines, Chemin des Travails, BP 53, 06801 Cagnes-sur-Mer, France.

1725.253
DIODON SONAR

The Diodon sonar is an advanced equipment for fitting in ASW ships of small or medium tonnage. It is an active, all round system employing digital techniques and advanced signal processing facilities. It performs all round submarine detection, target tracking, and attack operations. It is supplied with automatic integrated test facilities and on-board training equipment. The acoustic transducer array for fitting on board smaller ships is provided with an active roll stabilisation system. It can be fitted within a fixed dome, retractable dome, or supplied as a variable depth (towed) sonar (VDS). Among the optional additional facilities that can be provided with the Diodon system are underwater telephonic equipment, sound ray path indicator, shore training equipment, and maintenance equipment.

The transducer array is cylindrical in shape and consists of 24 identical and interchangeable vertical staves of transducer elements, each stave being capable of radiating 600 watts of acoustic power. The array is pivoted in roll and active stabilisation is effected by means of an hydraulic actuating ram. The sensor is a pendulum-type device. Three (selectable) transmission frequencies are provided, 11, 12, and 13 kHz, and there are several modes of operation.

Transmission facilities include:

(1) Normal panoramic transmission
(2) Sector or panoramic transmission by the electronic scanning of directional beams (sector beamwidth and sector axis can be controlled throughout 360° in 15° increments)
(3) Normal or reduced power
(4) Pure or modulated frequency
(5) 20, 80, or 200 ms pulses.

The display unit provides the operator with all the necessary controls and indicators, such as:

(1) Panoramic CRT display for active or passive mode acquisition
(2) Target-axis error scope for fine aiming and tracking
(3) Doppler CRT indicator for measurement of target speed
(4) Digital read-out of target data
(5) Audio channel
(6) Controls for the active tracking circuits
(7) Transmission mode controls
(8) Remote control of transducer array assembly
(9) Integrated test system indicator
(10) Control of operational test.

Reception is achieved simultaneously on 24 preformed beams in either of two alternative modes:

(1) Standard filtering (with or without reception), detection and integration
(2) Coherent signal processing.

Diodon sonar system, showing (left to right) display console, receiver, and power supply

The sonar can be linked by either synchro or in digital form with other ship's systems, such as ship's log, gyro compass, plotting table, ASW fire control system, tactical displays, etc.

CHARACTERISTICS

Frequency: 11, 12, or 13 kHz, selectable

Beamwidth transmission (3 dB): 15° elevation, 15° azimuth

Panoramic reception: 24 preformed beams

Passive: In band 10 – 14 kHz

Active: Pure frequency with or without rejection (30 Hz). Modulated frequency with coherent signal processing. BT products = 50 on each beam

Range: Fine bearing and range on one target. Semi-automatic or automatic tracking on one target

Dimensions

Display: 180 × 60 × 50 cm, weight 450 kg

Transmitter: 180 × 60 × 50 cm, weight 600 kg

Power supply: 1100 × 60 × 50 cm, weight 500 kg

Transducer: Weight 580 kg

Hydraulic unit: 160 × 55 × 121 cm, weight 470 kg

STATUS

In production for several navies and operational aboard a number of ships.

CONTRACTOR

Thomson-CSF, Division Activités Sous-Marines, Chemin des Travails, BP 53, 06801 Cagnes-sur-Mer, France.

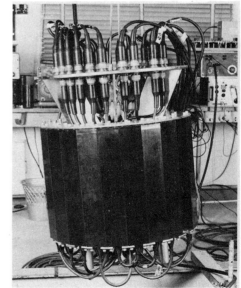

Diodon sonar transducer array

5646.253
TSM 2630 DIODON SONAR

The TSM 2630 Diodon sonar is a compact panoramic, active sonar for surface ships. The acoustic array may be either hull-mounted or towed (VDS).

The main features of the TSM 2630 are sophisticated signal processing, both in CW (optional FFT) and FM modes (pulse compression), for detection of slow and fast moving targets; comprehensive data processing with computer aided detection and tracking facilities; advanced multi-colour displays; integrated sound-ray tracing and prediction of detection range; and digital interfaces to international standards.

The basic version of the sonar includes:

(1) Hull-mounted acoustic assembly (dome and array)
(2) Matching unit
(3) Power supply cabinet
(4) Cabinet housing the transmitting, receiving and video processing circuits

(5) Display console incorporating two identical high-resolution multi-colour TV screens.

Optional equipment includes a panoramic passive capability, a video cassette recorder for play-back training and debriefing, and a torpedo or rocket launching control.

CHARACTERISTICS

Acoustic array: 24 staves; source level 230 dB (μPa/1 yard); weight 340 kg

Transmitter: Omnidirectional transmission in CW or FM

Receiver: 48 preformed beams with true bearing stabilisation; conventional and coherent processing (BxT up to 300); directive and steerable audio

Video processing: Data processing in FM and CW (normalisation, interpolation, correlation, automatic tracking of up to 5 targets); conversational procedure for sonar operation; target analysis (apparent length and aspect angle, doppler measurement)

Display console: 2 identical flicker free, high resolution colour TV monitors

Weight: 1750 kg

STATUS

In production. Over 23 units of the Diodon family are in operation with various navies.

CONTRACTOR

Thomson-CSF, Division Activités Sous-Marines, Chemin des Travails, BP 53, 06801 Cagnes-sur-Mer, France.

TSM 2630 acoustic array

5648.253

TSM 2640 SALMON SONAR

The TSM 2640 is a compact, medium range, variable depth sonar system for anti-submarine warfare on board light surface patrol craft operating in shallow waters. It provides a high detection capability even against severe background noise and reverberation. The system provides sophisticated signal processing with pulse compression in FM and spectral analysis (FFT) in CW, comprehensive data processing and computer aided facilities, and advanced multicolour display with high resolution TV monitor.

The basic version consists of an acoustic array of 24 staves in a streamlined fish, a towing winch, an operator console equipped with a multicolour screen, and a receiver unit and a transmitter unit contained in small cabinets. Optional facilities include automatic extraction, passive listening, sound ray tracer, an additional colour TV screen, video tape recording system and an integrated on-board simulator.

CHARACTERISTICS

Acoustic array: 24 identical staves; source level 217 dB/uPA/1 yard; weight 120 kg

Transmitter: Omni-directional transmission in CW or FM

Receiver: 48 preformed beams in FM (24 in CW); conventional processing; filtering, detection, integration in FM, FFT in CW; coherent signal processing (pulse compression) with BxT up to 200; noise listening in active band

Video processing: Data processing in FM and CW (normalisation, interpolation, correlation, automatic target tracking of up to 3 tracks simultaneously); conversational procedure for sonar operation; target analysis (apparent length and aspect angle, doppler measurement)

Display: High resolution, flicker-free colour TV monitor

Total weight: 750 kg (additional 5 tonnes for winch)

STATUS

In production. Two TSM 2642 systems have been

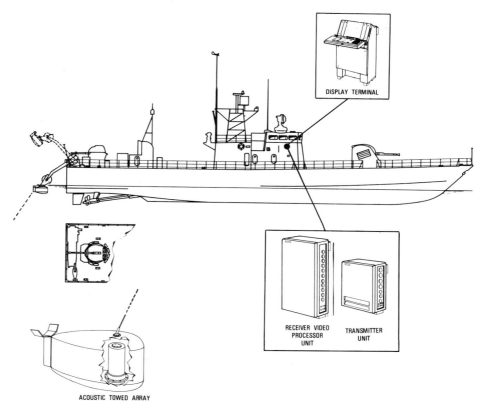

Diagram of TSM 2640 system on a patrol craft

ordered by the Swedish Navy for installation on SPICA III Stockholm class surface attack ships and were due for delivery in early 1984.

CONTRACTOR

Thomson-CSF, Division Activités Sous-Marines, Chemin des Travails, BP 53, 06801 Cagnes-sur-Mer, France.

5649.253

TSM 2820 TARPON SONAR

The TSM 2820 is a long-detection range sonar for surface ships. It is a single operator, low-frequency hull-mounted system (HMS) which can be combined with a medium or a low frequency variable depth sonar (VDS). The HMS and VDS can operate simultaneously in alternate modes.

The main facilities of the TSM 2820 are:

(1) Combined HMS/VDS, medium/low frequency capabilities

(2) Sophisticated signal processing, with pulse compression in FM and spectral analysis (FFT) in CW. The TSM 2820 can operate alternatively in

FM and CW for optional detection of slow and fast targets

(3) Comprehensive data processing and computer aided facilities with automatic track extraction

(4) Multi-colour display with high resolution TV monitors

(5) Integrated sound ray trace and prediction of detection range

(6) Digital interfaces to international standards.

The basic version of the hull-mounted Tarpon sonar consists of:

(1) Hull-mounted acoustic assembly (dome and acoustic array)

(2) Matching unit and power transformer unit

(3) Energy storage unit

(4) Transmitter unit, active receiver unit and video processing unit, all working in either HMS or VDS

(5) Display console with two identical multi-colour screens. Optional facilities include panoramic passive receiver for torpedo warning and short-range self protection; 1000 × 1000 colour TV display; and video cassette recorder for training or de-briefing.

CHARACTERISTICS

Acoustic array: 32 identical staves of transducers, high efficiency piezo-electric ceramics, source level 222 dB/uPa/1yard

Transmitter: Omni-directional transmission in CW or FM

Receiver: 32 preformed beams; simultaneous signal processing on all beams; spectral analysis (CW); 96 (FFT) doppler channels; pulse compression (FM) with BxT 80 – 240 according to range scale; directive and steerable audio

Video processing: Data processing in FM and CW (normalisation, interpolation, correlation, track extraction of up to 25 tracks simultaneously); conversational procedure for sonar operation; target analysis (apparent length and aspect angle, doppler measurement)

Display: 2 identical high resolution colour TV monitors

Weight: 6000 kg

CONTRACTOR

Thomson-CSF, Division Activités Sous-Marines, Chemin des Travails, BP 53, 06801 Cagnes-sur-Mer, France.

TSM 2820 Tarpon Sonar Console

1726.453
DUBM 41B SIDE-LOOKING SONAR

The Thomson-CSF TSM2050 (service designation DUBM 41B) system is a high-resolution side-looking sonar system designed for the location and classification of objects, such as mines, lying on the sea bed. The system consists of three towed sonar vehicles, two consoles, and the necessary cables and shipboard hoists and handling gear. In normal operation two of the three sonar bodies are used, with the third kept as a ready spare. A permanent record of the sonar data gathered is made on a facsimile type recorder and a tape recorder. The information also is presented simultaneously on two CRT storage tubes, these console-mounted displays providing an image of the sea bed. The system is designed for use by low tonnage vessels, and in waters 100 m or deeper. The towed sonars operate at about 5·5 to 7·5 m above the sea bed at speeds of two to six knots. The tow cables are provided with deflector vanes which ensure that the sonar bodies are towed at a distance to left and right of the ship's track, and marker floats are provided to indicate the line of travel for each sonar.

The sonar body is a streamlined vehicle fitted with the side-looking sonars, plus additional sonar transducers for determining height above sea bed and for obstacle detection. Servo-controlled fins are provided for depth control and roll stabilisation is incorporated by means of a separate set of four fins. Dimensions of each sonar vehicle are: length 3·725 m, diameter 36 cm, in-air weight 340 kg. An acoustic pinger is installed as an aid to recovery should the sonar body break its tow. Manual controls are provided at the operating console to permit manual piloting, either to override automatic control or as a standby mode.

Each of the two sonar bodies operates on its own

frequency, the two being separated by 50 kHz, with the area of sea bed between the two bodies being scanned by both sonars. A typical scanned area covered by the two bodies amounts to a total width of about 200 m, with maximum sonar range selected. There are two other range settings, 50 and 25 m. At the latter setting, resolution is stated to be better than 5 × 10 cm in the lateral (scan) direction and in the line of travel.

DEVELOPMENT

Development of the DUBM 41B was conducted in collaboration by the French Navy Mine Warfare DTCN (GESMA) and Thomson-CSF.

STATUS

In service.

CONTRACTOR

Thomson-CSF, Division Activités Sous-Marines, Route du Conquet, 29283 Brest, Cedex-France.

Towed sonar DUBM 41B on manoeuvres

4348.453
IBIS MINEHUNTING SONAR SYSTEMS

IBIS 3 and 5 are fully integrated minehunting systems using a high performance sonar and a tactical display system which integrates and displays all critical information.

The system consists of:

(1) A minehunting sonar, TSM2021 (**1977.253**) or TSM 2022 (**4349.453**)

(2) A tactical display console, TSM 2060 NAVIPLOT

(3) A doppler sonar log, TSM 5730 or TSM 5722

(4) Navigations systems, autopilot, windspeed sensors, etc.

Mine detection and classification is the function of the sonar (TSM 2021 or TSM 2022). Detection is performed at distances up to 600 m (2000 m in the case of submarines). Classification is possible in two modes, echo mode and shadow mode, allowing identification of moored and bottom mines.

The action/information data display and storage is performed by the tactical display system which provides ship's track monitoring, location of contacts and records of operational data. Positions of classified mines, possible contacts and non-mine objects are recorded and displayed simultaneously.

STATUS
See under separate TSM 2021 and TSM 2022 entries.
CONTRACTOR
Thomson-CSF, Division Activités Sous-Marines, Chemin des Travails, BP 53, 06801 Cagnes-sur-Mer, France.

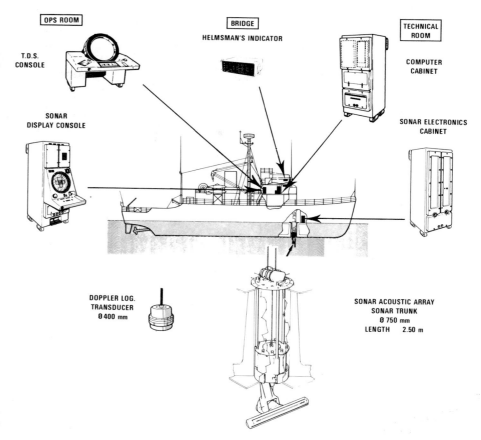

System installation drawing of IBIS minehunting sonar

1977.253

TSM 2021B MINEHUNTING SONAR

The Thomson-CSF TSM 2021B (service designation, DUBM 21B) is a modern minehunting sonar, the design of which applies experience with the DUBM 20A, also developed by Thomson-CSF (**1357.253 1974-75** and earlier editions). It is a hull-mounted equipment intended for use in conjunction with precision navigation equipment and a mine countermeasure (destruction) system such as the PAP 104 (**1786.453**). A former version is the 2021A with different array housings and minor display variations. TSM 2021 functions are:

(1) The detection of mines at distances up to 600 metres

(2) The classification of such targets by the study of the shape of their echo and acoustic shadow, at distances up to 250 metres.

Each detection and classification sonar chain consists of an acoustic transmitter/receiver transducer; the associated transmission and reception electronics; and a display console. The STH sub-assembly performs the stabilisation, steering, and retraction of the detector and classifier arrays. This part of the system is the result of studies and development by ECAN at Ruelle.

The electro-acoustic assembly (ELA) includes:

(1) The classification sonar transmitter/receiver chain cabinet

(2) A display console which controls the transmission and reception functions and has CRT presentation of mine detection and location by the detector sonar chain

(3) A display console with CRT displays for presentation of mine locations within the classification chain

(4) Bridge repeater display, showing range and bearing of designated targets.

CHARACTERISTICS

Coverage: ±175° in sectors of 30, 60, and 90° for the detector chain; 3, 5 or 10° for the classification chain

Elevation: Variable, between –5 and –40°

Stabilisation (roll): ±15°

Stabilisation (pitch): ±5°

Detection sonar

Frequency: 100 kHz (modulated ± 10 kHz)

Pulse duration: 0·2 or 0·5 m/s

Range scales: 400, 600, or 900 m

Max sound level: 120 dB

Channels: 20

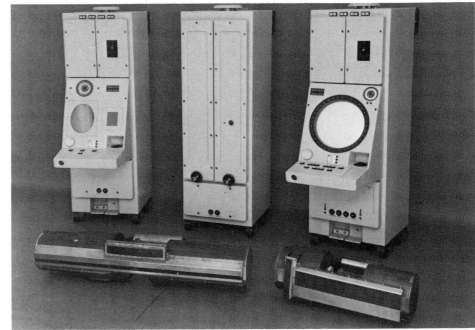

TSM 2021B minehunting sonar, showing the main electronics cabinet flanked by the classification and detection display consoles (left and right), with the transducer arrays in the foreground

Beam aperture: 1·5°

Display: PPI

Classification sonar

Range scales: 200 or 300 m

Max sound level: 122 dB

Channels: 80

Beam aperture: 0·17°

Display: CRT and storage magnifier tube

STATUS

In service. Five TSM 2021A sets were ordered by the French Navy in late 1974 for fitting in former ocean-going minesweepers to be refitted as minehunters. The TSM 2021B is being fitted on 40 GRP minehunter being built jointly for the Belgian, Netherlands, and French Navies' Tripartite Programme.

The TSM 2021 is in service with navies other than the French navy. Altogether some 60 systems have been ordered.

CONTRACTOR

Thomson-CSF, Division Activités Sous-Marines, Route du Conquet, 29283 Brest, Cedex-France.

4349.453
TSM 2022 MINEHUNTING SONAR

The TSM 2022 is a modern lightweight minehunting sonar designed specifically for small and medium sized mine countermeasures vessels. The sonar can also be used for mine avoidance on minesweepers, or in civil applications such as bottom profiling and side-scan surveys.

The TSM 2022 is based largely on experience gained with the DUBM 21B in the field of high resolution beam forming techniques. It is a hull mounted equipment intended also for use in conjunction with precision display and navigation equipment and a mine countermeasures system.

The main feature of the TSM 2022 is its small-size retractable array assembly which enables easy installation and maintenance. The high resolution features of the DUBM 21 are maintained and improvements are mainly in the field of digital processing technology.

The main functions of the sonar are: detection and

Thomson-CSF minehunting sonar operation room

classification of moored and bottom mines, detection at distances up to 600 metres (2000 metres for submarines), classification of targets by analysis of the shape of their echo or shadow at distances up to 250 metres.

The main assemblies are:
(1) The hoisting and stabilisation system together with the retractable array, which is installed in the sonar trunk (0·75 metres diameter). The total weight does not exceed 1500 kg
(2) Electronic cabinet
(3) Operator's console.

The operator console provides display of sonar images in the various modes, memory and display of former sonar contacts, and includes interfaces with current mine disposal and navigation equipments.

STATUS
12 equipments have been ordered by three foreign navies, including the Swedish Navy which has six systems on order for new minehunting vessels. Initial deliveries were made at the end of 1983.

CONTRACTOR
Thomson-CSF, Division Activités Sous-Marines, Chemin des Travails, BP 53, 06801 Cagnes-sur-Mer, France.

1389.353
DHAX-1 MAGNETIC ANOMALY DETECTOR

The type DHAX-1 MAD is designed for use in aircraft for the detection of submerged submarines by detection of the disturbance to the local natural magnetic field caused by their large ferrous bulk. The system comprises three units: a probe containing two caesium vapour paramagnetic resonance cells (this is usually tail-mounted on the aircraft, and weighs 15 kg), an electronics unit weighing 18 kg, and a control unit (3 kg).

The last of these units incorporates a manual test facility for checking correct operation and calibration of the system in flight. Data from the MAD are fed to the aircraft's ASW tactical data system. No performance details other than a sensitivity of less than one gamma, have been revealed.

STATUS
The DHAX-1 is fitted in French Atlantic ASW aircraft, and in those of a number of other nations. Production has now ended.

1390.353
DHAX-3 MAGNETIC ANOMALY DETECTOR

The DHAX-3 is an improved and more modern version of the DHAX-1 MAD equipment (1389.353), and primarily designed for deployment at the end of a cable from ASW helicopters. In place of the four-cell detector unit used in the DHAX-1, the DHAX-3 employs six caesium vapour paramagnetic cells, and is stated to have a very low susceptibility to rotational and heading effect.

Weights of the three units which comprise the equipment are: probe 6·2 kg, electronics unit 7·5 kg, and control unit 0·8 kg. These figures suggest that the use of solid-state electronics has permitted a system weight of less than half that of the DHAX-1 to be achieved. No performance details have been released.

STATUS
In service with French forces, but no longer in production.

5650.453
ARGONAUTE SONAR SYSTEM

Argonaute is the name of a new sonar system ordered by the Royal Navy for use in its forthcoming Type 2400 class submarines.

Argonaute consists of elements of the ELEDONE sonar which have been modified to interface with Royal Navy equipment and operational requirements. The ELEDONE system operates in both the active and passive modes, full details are given in the entry **1356.453**. No other details are available.

STATUS
In serial production.

CONTRACTOR
Thomson-CSF, Division Activités Sous-Marines, Chemin des Travails, BP 53, 06801 Cagnes-sur-Mer, France.

GERMANY (FEDERAL REPUBLIC)

4228.453
DSQS 21 SERIES SONARS

The DSQS 21 series sonars are designed for operation in surface ships as part of an anti-submarine weapon system. For operations against submarines below the layer, the sonar can be supplemented with a towing system providing a variable depth sonar (VDS) capability.

Computer aided detection techniques are used for classification and tracking and the information is presented on colour CRT displays to permit doppler coding and the discrimination of data on the integrated displays. The 'Z' indicates variants equipped with electronic stabilisation to minimise the effects of ship's motion.

The variable depth sonar (VDS) is designed to alternate with the hull mounted sonar, and the displays of the two sonars are integrated. Fitted with automatic depth control and heave compensation for stability of the 'fish', the VDS can be handled automatically or manually.

CHARACTERISTICS

Sonar		Diameter of Transducer Arrays		No of Pre-formed Beams		Class of Ship
		VDS	hull-mounted	VDS	hull-mounted	
DSQS-21	B	1·8 m		64		Corvettes frigates
	BZ	1·8 m		64		Corvettes frigates
	B/VDS	1·8 m	1 m	64	32	Corvettes frigates
	BZ/VDS	1·8 m	1 m	64	32	Corvettes frigates
DSQS-21	C	1 m		32		Corvettes frigates
	CZ	1 m		32		Corvettes frigates
	C/VDS	1 m	1 m	32	32	Corvettes frigates
	CZ/VDS	1 m	1 m	32	32	Corvettes frigates
DSQS-21	D	1 m		32		Up to corvettes
	DZ	1 m		32		Up to corvettes
	D/VDS	1 m	1 m	32	32	Up to corvettes
	DZ/VDS	1 m	1 m	32	32	Up to corvettes

CONTRACTOR
Fried Krupp GmbH, Krupp Atlas-Elektronik Bremen, Sebaldsbrücker Heerstr 235, POB 448545, D 2800 Bremen 44, Federal Republic of Germany.

4229.453
KRUPP ATLAS-ELEKTRONIK SUBMARINE SONARS

Krupp Atlas-Elektronik has developed a range of submarine sonar equipment. Little information has been disclosed but it is possible to give brief summaries of some of the systems.

CSU 3 Sonar
The CSU 3 is a conventional submarine sonar designed for a single operator. It is a fast-scanning medium range active sonar which can be used as a long range passive device, an intercept sonar and as an underwater telephone. In its active mode, the sonar operates using a single beam. The equipment has a cylindrical transducer array with electronic beam steering. The display is a magnified PPI presenting a 20° sector with continuous memory-refreshed display of target echoes. Target information is transferred digitally to the fire control equipment. In the passive mode, the sonar has 360° azimuth coverage with automatic tracking of up to four targets simultaneously. The target information is presented on a CRT display in true or ship's relative bearing and target elevation angle can be determined for estimation of distance and optimum sound raypath. The sonar is equipped with automatic interference suppression against acoustic countermeasures.

PSU 1-2 Sonar
The PSU 1-2 is a passive sonar for use in small conventional submarines. The equipment has the capability for detection, classification, and bearing determination of noise radiating targets with simultaneous azimuth coverage over 360°. It can be used also to receive underwater telephone signals. The target noise information received by the cylindrical hydrophone array (CHA) is processed into 32 pre-formed beams and presented on a CRT display in true or ship's relative bearing. Four targets can be

automatically tracked using the ATT equipment and the respective target bearing is transferred to the weapon control systems.

PRS-3 Passive Ranging Sonar

The PRS-3 is a passive submarine sonar designed to be operated in conjunction with the CSU-3. It has two principal operating modes. In the normal mode, the sonar can detect target noise and determine bearing and distance as well as computation of course and speed for a maximum of four targets. A level of confidence in the range measurement is indicated by the equipment. In the automatic mode, the target information is tracked automatically using the ATT channels of the CSU-3 sonar.

OSID Sonar System

OSID is an integrated sonar system developed for use

in small submarines. It comprises a passive sonar, data distribution with a tactical display and a torpedo guidance system. The sonar has a broad-band channel for bearing determination and classification, and utilises minimum correlation techniques for the location of weak targets. It features a 360° panoramic presentation of targets on a CRT display, according to azimuth. The processing computer calculates the position and vectors of the target, own submarine, and the torpedo and the information is presented on a tactical display. The torpedo control is a replaceable module designed for each type of torpedo.

SIP 3 Sonar Signal Processor

The SIP 3 is a sonar information processor developed for use with fast-scanning multi-target tracking sonars of the CSU series. The prime function of the

equipment is to provide passive classification of targets using low frequency detection and analysis, spectrum survey and comparison, high target resolution and demon analysis. Doppler analysis of target echoes received by the active sonar of the own submarine is used to determine the target's speed. Sound raypath analysis produces an estimate of the conditions for sound propagation. The system has the capability to determine and present specific sonar signal characteristics, comparing them to sound signatures of selected targets held in a data bank.

CONTRACTOR

Fried Krupp GmbH, Krupp Atlas-Elektronik Bremen, Sebaldsbrücker Heerstr 235, POB 448545, D 2800 Bremen 44, Federal Republic of Germany.

4230.453

KRUPP ATLAS-ELEKTRONIK/MCM SYSTEMS

Krupp Atlas-Elektronik has developed equipment for use in mine countermeasures (MCM). Few details are available but the following are brief summaries of the equipment.

DSQS-IIA Sonar

The DSQS-IIA is a mine avoidance sonar designed for the location of underwater objects, in particular moored mines. It can be used as a navigational aid in mined areas, for surface ships and submarines. When an object is located, the distance, bearing and depth are presented to the operator on a PPI display, with the bearing referenced to the ship, North, or shown in a true motion mode.

DSQS-IIH Sonar

The DSQS-IIH is a mine countermeasures sonar suitable for the detection and classification of surface, moored and ground mines. The equipment features independent operation of detection and classification modes through 360° of azimuth, with simultaneous azimuth coverage of 90° in the detection mode. Target images are stored in the system to facilitate recognition. Electronic beam stabilisation is fitted for both modes and the sonar can be operated at speeds up to ten knots with minimal degradation of performance.

MWS 80 Mine Countermeasures

MWS 80 is a fully integrated mine countermeasures

weapons system developed for the operations rooms of MCM vessels. It comprises the DSQS-IIH sonar; the command and navigation equipment (NCE) for navigation, co-ordination of the MCM operation, and recording and plotting of the surveyed area; and a remote-controlled mine disposal vehicle which is used for the identification and destruction of mines. The MWS 80 is manned by two operators.

CONTRACTOR

Fried Krupp GmbH, Krupp Atlas-Elektronik Bremen, Sebaldsbrücker Heerstr 235, POB 448545, D 2800 Bremen 44, Federal Republic of Germany.

ITALY

3233.453

IPD70/S INTEGRATED SONAR

The IPD70/S sonar is an improved version of the IPD70 currently installed on the Sauro class submarines and, like the former equipment, it is the result of co-operation between USEA and ELSAG.

The main components of the system are a passive sonar and an active sonar, with three optional equipments: a high precision intercepting equipment, a long-range directional and omni-directional underwater telephone and a spectral analysis sub-system. An additional option, the MD100 passive rangefinder, is also available. This latter option can, however, stand alone and is therefore described in entry **3773.453**.

The LPD70/S uses three transducer arrays to serve the various functions:

(1) a passive low-frequency conformal array disposed along the hull and working from a few hundred Hz up to several kHz.

(2) a cylindrical array, common to the active sensor, the high-frequency passive component, the interceptor and the underwater telephone. This transducer is housed in a suitable hull cavity and protected by a high-resistance low flow-noise GRP dome

(3) an optional linear array for the passive rangefinder set.

The equipment can track up to four targets. In the

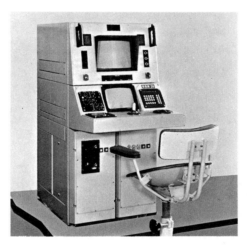

Control console for IPD 70 integrated sonar

passive operation mode, very long detection ranges can be achieved with the high-directivity characteristics of the conformal array and the signal processing techniques employed. In the active mode bearing, range and doppler data are obtained from a single sonar pulse to minimise the probability of

interception by the target. The intercept facilities provide measurement of bearing, pulse length and frequency by enemy sonars within several tens of kilometres.

Long range communication capabilities are given by the underwater telephone which can be operated on either an omni-directional or directional basis. The narrow band spectral analysis sub-system enables the operator to classify a target based on its radiated noise distribution.

The most important change from the earlier IPD70 equipment is the display and control console which has been completely redesigned. The operator's panel now features two high-resolution raster screens on which all relevant data collected and processed by the system can be displayed in an easy-to-read, graphic and alpha-numeric format. The operator controls have been simplified.

DEVELOPMENT

The equipment has been developed directly from the IPD sonar system, the design of which began in the early 1970s following some years of research in the field of electro-acoustic submarine technology.

STATUS

The first IPD70/S equipments were installed on the Sauro III series submarines in 1983.

CONTRACTOR

SELENIA-ELSAG Consortium for Naval Systems, Via Panama 52, 00198 Rome, Italy.

3773.453

MD100/S PASSIVE RANGEFINDER SET

The MD100/S is an upgraded version of the MD100 and is the result of co-operation between the companies USEA and ELSAG. The system has been designed for installation on small or medium size submarines and can be supplied either as a stand-alone device or as an optional component of the integrated sonar set IPD70/S (**3233.453**). In the latter case, all necessary space allocation, as well as command and display facilities, are shared on a common basis with the host system.

Though the system has been redesigned, many of the technical solutions employed in the earlier MD100 have been retained. Like its predecessor, the MD100/S is equipped with an independent set of acoustic sensors arranged as two linear arrays, each

composed of three equally spaced transducers and steered towards the port and starboard sectors.

The signals collected by the transducers, after initial processing, are fed to the main unit for all the relevant stages of signal processing. Handling of signals entails the evaluation of correlation and coherence relationships existing among the various couples of waveforms involved, so as to obtain bearing and distance estimates of a noise source with high accuracy within the sector coverage of ±60° athwartships.

The MD100/S features simultaneous tracking in bearing and range of up to four targets; bearing initiation data can be either collected by the equipment itself or from a surveillance sonar.

The display unit, both in the stand-alone and in the integrated version, is based on a high-resolution

raster-scan type screen, which allows constant monitoring of trajectories and all relevant data (both in graphic and alpha-numeric form) pertaining to the targets being tracked. In addition, continuous indication is given of special parameters, eg reliability coefficients of processed data, tracking losses, etc, which could be valuable in deciding the operator's course of action.

STATUS

The integrated version has been installed in the Sauro III submarines.

CONTRACTOR

SELENIA-ELSAG Consortium for Naval Systems, Via Panama 52, 00198 Rome, Italy.

5754.293

MULTI-APPLICATION SONAR SYSTEM (MAST)

A trainer for sonar operators, known as MAST, is being developed by ELSAG, in co-operation with Raytheon, USA, for installation at the Italian Navy's training centre. The MAST system consists of the following units:

(1) Trainee equipment consisting of a set of units identical to those used on board
(2) An instructor control station

(3) A computer system
(4) Simulation hardware producing signals relevant to 'own ship's signals' and those of simulated craft. These include all possible variations due to motion, mutual interference, propagation and environmental conditions simulated.

The MAST system will be used for the training of operators and maintenance personnel on the DE 1160 and DE 1164 sonar systems. Further improvements

will allow training facilities for other passive sonar systems produced by ELSAG and also for the DE 1167 being manufactured under license from Raytheon.

STATUS
In production.
CONTRACTOR
SELENIA-ELSAG Consortium for Naval Systems, Via Panama 52, 00198 Rome, Italy.

1723.453

SERVOMECCANISMI SONOBUOY EQUIPMENT

The Servomeccanismi organisation produces three types of passive sonobuoy:

BIT-3: This is an A-size omni-directional passive sonobuoy for use at depths between 20 and 100 m, with a selectable life of one to three hours, and

transmitting data over a 31-channel, IW link.

BIT-8: This is similar to the BIT-3 but has different frequency/sensitivity characteristics.

BIR: This is a miniature (500 mm long × 100 mm diameter, three kg) sonobuoy for use with helicopters. It is omni-directional and can be deployed at depths to 20 m. Life is one hour.

Receivers for use with these sonobuoys are the REA-16 and REA-31, having 16 and 31 reception channels, respectively.
CONTRACTOR
Servomeccanismi Ing E Olivetti, Via Mediana Km 29.3, 00040 Pomezia, Italy.

3234.453

FIAR MINE DETECTION AND CLASSIFICATION SONAR

The FIAR AN/SQQ-14 is an improved version of the original General Electric AN/SQQ-14 minehunting sonar and is produced under licence from that company.

The equipment is a dual frequency system having two modes of operation: search mode to detect probable targets up to 900 yards and a classify mode so that a trained operator, who can discriminate between mines and mine-like objects, can classify these after detection. The equipment provides range and bearing information which, related to the wide scanned field of view and narrow resolution in both range and bearing, are used to observe and direct a manned or unmanned neutralisation vehicle to mark or destroy the target.

The FIAR AN/SSQ-14 is operational either as a

hull-mounted or variable depth sonar. The variable depth feature provides for lowering the towed body, including the transducers, to a maximum depth of 150 feet (46 metres). This gives increased depth for minehunting, optimum positioning of transducers in adverse water conditions and favourable acquisition angles. In the variable depth mode the system can function effectively in sea state 5 when the towed body is lowered beneath the ocean surface effects.

In search mode the equipment uses a PPI display and electronically scans a 90° azimuth sector with a narrow beam (1·5 to 2°). In addition, the field may be automatically slewed through 180°, centred as selected on the bow, port bow or starboard bow, at a continuous rate of 15°/second at manually selected ranges of 300, 600 and 900 yards. An azimuth resolution of 1·5° and range resolution of 2·4 feet (0·7 metres) is obtained.

In classify mode the equipment uses a B-scope display associated with a memory display and electronically scans an azimuth sector of 18° with a 0·3° beam. An azimuth resolution of 0·3° and range resolution of approximately seven centimetres is obtained.

Additional details of the AN/SQQ-14 appear in entry **1789.453** in the USA pages of this section.
STATUS
The AN/SQQ-14 is used by the US, Belgian and Spanish navies aboard 'MSO' class minesweepers; the Italian and Saudi Arabian navies have installed it on 'MSC' class ships.
CONTRACTOR
FIAR-Fabbrica Italiana Apparecchiature Radioelettriche SpA, Via Montefeltro 8, 20156 Milan, Italy.

1720.453

IP64-MD64 SONARS

The USEA IP64 sonar set is designed for installation aboard small or medium-size submarines, and it combines passive sonar equipment operating in the band 175 to 5000 Hz, and an active echo-ranging sonar operating at a frequency of 4000 Hz. It is also designed for integration with the MD64 sonar set for range measurement of noise sources by passive means. The receiving transducer elements, which are common to the passive and active mode, are arranged in the bow of the vessel in a long conformal array to enhance the directional capabilities. The transmitting transducer elements are arranged in a circular array located on deck.

Two linear arrays are provided for range measurement by passive means. Each array has a total length of 30 m and is formed by three transducers. The arrays are located on deck, port and starboard.

Search and detection are carried out primarily by means of the passive listening set, which incorporates advanced correlation techniques and records the received signals on a graph plotter. After target detection, a single transmission pulse in the direction

of the target by the echo-ranging sonar is sufficient to provide range and relative speed target data.

The MD64 equipment measures the range of a detected noise source and direction is determined by the measurement of the relative time delay of sound waves detected by three hydrophones. Two groups of three hydrophones each are provided, for port and starboard measurements. Each hydrophone uses a number of elements arranged in five vertical staves and phased in the horizontal plane to produce a reception beam, directed toward the source. Main lobe beamwidth is ±15°.

The audio frequency band employed is 1000 Hz wide, centred on any frequency between 4 and 20 kHz. Operation is automatic and after acquisition of the noise source, the equipment locks on and continuous bearing data is produced. Range is measured continuously and is recorded graphically.
CONTRACTOR
USEA, Via G Matteotti 63, 19030 Pugliola di Lerici, La Spezia, Italy.

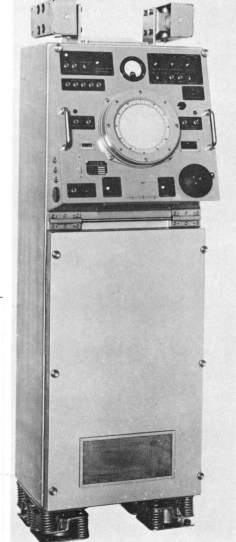

IP64-MD64 sonar display console

3235.453

SELENIA SONAR ACTIVITIES

Few details have been revealed of the sonar and underwater systems activities of the Selenia-Elsag Consortium for Naval Systems which was set up in 1983 by merging the Naval Systems Divisions of the two companies. The following paragraphs record briefly a summary of some of the most significant of the known programmes.

MLS-1A

This sonar was the company's first major underwater product, having been developed at the Fusaro laboratories, and production continued from 1956 to 1959. More than 30 equipments were made for supply to several navies. Licence production of the DE102 echo sounder sonar followed.

Mk 44 Torpedo

Between 1962 and 1966, more than 400 acoustic homing heads for the Mk 44 torpedo were produced under a joint programme carried out by the Italian Navy and Whitehead-Moto Fides.

CIACIO

In 1964, design work was started on the CIACIO system. This is a self-homing system for torpedoes to be fitted on lightweight and wire-guided torpedoes for both anti-submarine and surface target operations. Design features include good counter-countermeasures performance, and reliability in shallow water and anomalous propagation conditions. There are provisions for presettable or programmed combinations of signal processing, optical filtering and tactical manoeuvring, to match the operating performance to the current tactical situation automatically. It is possible to insert a wide range of search, attack and re-attack torpedo tracks into the programmer to suit any operational circumstances.

The system uses active and passive homing modes to approach its target, and torpedoes equipped with CIACIO are able to deal with current conventional and nuclear-powered submarines.

Dynamic sea trials were carried out using Mk 44 torpedoes equipped with the CIACIO system, although it is suitable for fitting on all types of 12·75 inch (388 mm) torpedoes. A lightweight CIACIO is being mass produced for fitting in A244 torpedoes manufactured by Whitehead-Moto Fides of Livorno.

Production of several hundred sets is in progress.

SFM-A
Between 1968 and 1970 the SFM-A underwater target

identification system equipment was produced for the Italian Navy. This system is an active sonar for the detection and classification of underwater targets, and digital processing involving the use of cross-correlation techniques is employed.

FALCO and GIARDA
These form a system for the detection and localisation of submarines by submarines, helicopters and ASW aircraft. Production began in 1972.

P MICCA
Work on this integrated system for remote control of deep sea mines by means of secure acoustic and radio links began in 1976.

CONTRACTOR
SELENIA-ELSAG Consortium for Naval Systems, Via Panama 52, 00198 Rome, Italy.

1722.353
FALCO SUBMARINE LOCATING SYSTEM
The FALCO system is airborne equipment designed to increase the capability for helicopters and fixed-wing aircraft to detect, classify, and locate submarines. The system operates on the low-frequency noise radiated by targets and gathered by

directional low frequency passive sonobuoys.

Noise spectral analysis, target data processing and display are performed by a real-time digital computer. It is claimed that the FALCO system is able to determine target position with an accuracy sufficient to carry out an attack with automatic homing

torpedoes, and with errors due to sonobuoys drifting automatically cancelled out. The equipment is produced in several versions.

CONTRACTOR
Selenia Industrie Elettroniche Associate SpA, Via Tiburtina Km 12400, 00131 Rome, Italy.

4007.453
MISAR MSR-810 SONOBUOY
The MSR-810 passive sonobuoy for detecting and locating submarines from aircraft is manufactured by MISAR under Thomson-CSF licence for the Italian market. It is very similar to the Thomson-CSF DSTV-4L (**3501.453**). The sonobuoy transmits, by VHF/FM radio, the underwater acoustic AF signals received from the hydrophone. The MSR-810 complies with NATO and Italian Navy specifications.

CHARACTERISTICS
Type: Passive
Frequency: Low
Weight: 8 kg
Operating life: 1·3 or 8 h
RF channels: 31
RF output: 500 mW (at antenna)
Antenna: 1/4 wave
STATUS
Production and in service.
CONTRACTOR
MISAR SpA, Via Brescia 39, 25014 Castenedolo (Brescia), Italy.

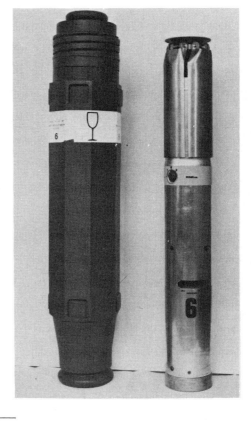

MSR-810 passive sonobuoy and transit case

5653.263
ELT/810 SONAR PREDICTION SYSTEM
The ELT/810 is designed to supply accurate prediction of both active and passive sonar range and propagation characteristics in various environmental conditions. Inputs of depth, temperature, salinity, sea state, sonar parameters, target characteristics and other information is obtained from various sensors and inserted into the system by means of a keyboard. The data is processed by the system computer and displayed on the CRT. Basic information, in real-time, is depth/temperature and depth/velocity curves, acoustic ray propagation diagrams, sonar detection range prediction.

The system can be used in surface ships,

submarines or ASW aircraft. In the surface ship role, the ELT/810 supplies data which allows the maximum exploitation of the sonar's duct propagation characteristics, the establishment of optimum VDS depth and the efficient deployment of an ASW screen. For submarines the system will enable the commander to establish the best attack and/or evasion paths and depths without using his own active sonar. In an ASW helicopter, the system will work in conjunction with the aircraft dipping sonar.

STATUS
In production and in operational service.
CONTRACTOR
Elettronica SpA, Via Tiburtina Km 13700, Rome, Italy.

ELT/810 operator console

NETHERLANDS

4464.453
HSS-15 COMPACT SURVEILLANCE SONAR
The HSS-15 is a compact panoramic sonar system for use on fairly small ships in the range of 100 to 800 tons. It fills the gap between commercial fishing sonars and more advanced professional sonar systems and is most useful in ships which need a limited anti-submarine capability, such as small patrol boats on coastal defence work and corvettes or

coastguard ships which hitherto could not be fitted with sonar because of size, weight, and cost.

The HSS-15 operates in the 9·3 to 11·7 kHz range with a detection range of four to six km. The design is based on the assumption that the ship in which it is installed will produce fairly high noise levels. The system's main features are: multi-beam panoramic surveillance; relatively low operating frequencies to avoid high transmission loss; three different pulse

lengths (25, 50, and 100 ms); three operating frequencies; active or passive operation; ease of operation with light pen control; and small transducer and cabinet dimensions. The overall system weight is about 600 kg.

CONTRACTOR
Hollandse Signaalapparaten BV, PO Box 42, 7550 GD Hengelo, Netherlands.

3142.253
PHS-32 SONAR

The PHS-32 is a medium-range high performance search and attack sonar in which the newest technological developments for signal processing and operation are employed, and helped by the use of a general purpose computer. The computer yields a compact, lightweight sonar for corvettes from 500 tons up to frigate-size ships.

The signal processing facilities provided include Fast Fourier Transformation processing of all preformed beam receiving channels. All data is presented on a single TV-type display, while operation has been much simplified by the use of light pen control. These features combined with a high accuracy make this sonar very useful in an attack.

A circular transducer permits all round coverage in various modes of transmission such as: OMNI, TRDT, MCC (wide vertical beam), LISTEN (passive with time/bearing recorder presentation). An audio beam is also available. The system can be delivered in a fixed, retractable or VDS-dome outfit.

CHARACTERISTICS

Features: single operator control; display data processing for continuous presentation and memory

mode (ping history); four-target automatic tracking; built-in energy storage for lower peak power demands on ships mains; integrated on-line and off-line test system.

Frequencies: 3
Pulse lengths: 12·5, 25, 50, 100 m/s and 400 m/s long pulse (CW or FM)
Notch filtering: Selectable rejection bandwidth
Own doppler correction: On all 60 channels
Roll and pitch performance: Automatic co-ordination of transmitting pulse and vertical beamwidth in rough weather
Weights
Electronic cabinets: (Sonar console, duplexer and amplifier cabinet, transmitter cabinet) 1041 kg
Retractable hull-outfit including transducers: 7900 kg
Fixed hull-outfit including transducer: 2500 kg
Variable depth system: 5000 – 8000 kg

STATUS

In series production. Entered operational service in 1978.

CONTRACTOR

Hollandse Signaalapparaten BV, PO Box 42, 7550 GD Hengelo, Netherlands.

PHS-32 sonar console

5635.453
PHS-34 SONAR

The PHS-34 is a long-range high performance panoramic sonar designed for the export market. The equipment employs fully coherent digital signal processing of FM, CW or combined FM-CW signals using Fast Fourier Transformation techniques and pulse compression to enable simultaneous high and low doppler detection, independent of target behaviour, under reverberation as well as noise limited conditions.

The equipment consists of five units: a transmitter cabinet, an energy store cabinet, a processor unit, a transducer with junction box and a sonar console. Total weight of the system is 2700 kg. Optional equipment includes an on-line launcher for XBT or XSV expendable probes, a simulator, glass-fibre domes to suit different ship sizes from corvettes to frigates, and variable depth sonar hoist and fish.

The system operates on four frequencies in the 7 kHz region and has OMNI, MCC, RDT, SDT and DT modes of operation. Automatic co-ordination of

transmission pulse and vertical beamwidth under rough weather conditions is another characteristic of the equipment.

Targets are presented with clear track history and up to 12 contacts can be autotracked simultaneously. Integrated support functions are ray trace, passive time/bearing plot (simultaneous with active), range prediction and underwater telephone.

CONTRACTOR

Hollandse Signaalapparaten BV, PO Box 42, 7550 GD Hengelo, Netherlands.

5636.453
SUBMARINE INTEGRATED ATTACK AND SURVEILLANCE SONAR SYSTEM (SIASS)

The submarine integrated attack and surveillance sonar, developed by Signaal, is available in two versions: SIASS-1 and SIASS-2. The former is a stand-alone system with its own sonar consoles, and interfaces with a submarine data handling and fire control system. SIASS-2 is a sonar system as an integrated part of the Signaal Submarine Sensor Weapon and Command System (SEWACO).

Both SIASS-1 and SIASS-2 perform and integrate the following tasks:
(1) Low (long range) and medium (medium range) surveillance of noise radiating targets through the use of broadband and multi-channel narrowband signal processing for surveillance, analysis and

tracking (LOFARGRAMS, ZOOM-FFT, Demon, ALI displays)
(2) Passive range detection
(3) Automatic target tracking for a multitude of targets, including automatic line tracking
(4) Contact motion analysis (position determination on bearings-only information)
(5) Active sonar
(6) LF, MF and HF intercept
(7) Classification
(8) Noise level monitoring and cavitation indication.

The SIASS signal processing is entirely digital and high resolution FFTs are used throughout the system for detection and analysis. Distributed computer architecture and extensive database facilities allow high flexibility, reconfigurability and availability. Analysis and classification aids are provided with

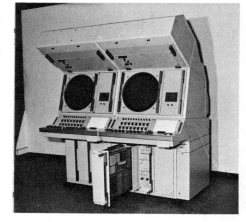

SIASS display and computer consoles

electronic libraries and ample history of spectral analysis results (LOFAR) is retained from all preformed beams simultaneously for immediate review. Integrated support functions are sound velocity measuring, ray path indication and performance prediction.

Latest-design acceleration-cancelling hydrophones form the basis of the multi-array configuration which may consist of:
(1) Two low frequency arrays
(2) A medium frequency circular array
(3) A high frequency intercept array
(4) Two sets of medium frequency passive ranging arrays
(5) An active transducer array
(6) Noise and cavitation monitoring hydrophones.

Control is exercised from multi-purpose consoles which may be integrated parts of a total SEWACO system (SIASS-2). These display and computer consoles are equipped with a multi-function control panel, a high resolution raster-scan display and an alpha-numeric display. Because of the built-in computer each console is virtually autonomous.

STATUS

In production.

CONTRACTOR

Hollandse Signaalapparaten BV, PO Box 42, 7550 GD Hengelo, Netherlands.

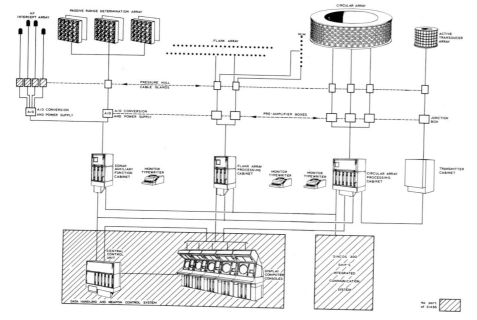

SIASS-2 sonar system

4001.453
PHS-36 SONAR
The PHS-36 is an active panoramic sonar designed for the Royal Netherlands Navy. The sonar provides various active modes (OMNI, TRDT, RDT, MCC) with both single-channel and combined CW and FM type pulse transmission. A passive mode operates simultaneously with the active modes. The signal processing is fully digital.

The plan view display (PVD) displays a high-resolution colour coded graphic picture of the active sonar information. A TV-monitor presents the time-bearing plot for passive sonar, the sound velocity profile as measured by on-line XSV or XBT probes and the sound ray path prediction, as required. Each page displays the necessary function keys which are controlled by lightpen for quick operation.

The computer employed is an SMR-Mu and its software allows computer-aided detection and interactive operating procedures. The PH-36 has a high flexibility to suit present and future requirements. Built-in test equipment ensures a high availability and also allows for integration of a simulation function.
STATUS
Entering production stage after successful sea trials conducted in September 1980. When produced for export this system can be manufactured to suit different classes of ships by varying the transducer arrays and operating frequencies.
CONTRACTOR
Hollandse Signaalapparaten BV, PO Box 42, 7550 GD Hengelo, Netherlands.

3493.453
XSV-01 EXPENDABLE SOUND VELOCIMETER
Complete knowledge of the sound velocity/depth profile is provided by this equipment which comprises the XSV processor and display units used with XBT expendable probes.

The XSV 01 probe contains a sound velocimeter sensor, a battery power supply and an integrated

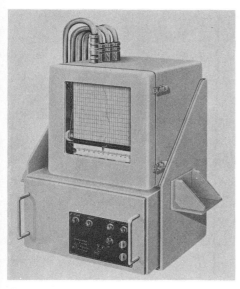

Processor and recorder units of the XSV-01 sounding equipment

circuit. The probe falls free from the ship with the aid of a launcher and is activated upon water impact. Its ballistic shape provides a known rate of descent while sound velocity data is continuously relayed to an onboard processor and recorder via a wire link. The system is also able to launch XBT probes (type T4, T5, T7) which have the same well-known dual spooling technique.

The system is easily operated, in virtually any sea-state requiring only a few minutes per measurement during which the ship need not reduce speed or change heading. It provides the input data required for sound ray path calculations (see **1525.263**, SPI-04).
CHARACTERISTICS
XSV measuring ranges: 1410 – 1510 m/s; 1440 – 1540 m/s; 1460 – 1560 m/s
XBT temperature range: –2·2 to +35·5° C
XSV depth range: 850 m (XSV-01 probe); 2000 m (XSV-02 probe)
XSV system accuracy: Better than 0·3 m/s
XSV depth accuracy: ±2% or 5 m, whichever is greater
XBT depth ranges: 460 m (T4); 760 m (T7); 1830 m (T5)
Launcher types: Deck launcher, through-hull launcher, hand-held launcher
Option: Magnetic digital recorder for high density data registration
Weights: Deck launcher, XSV processor and recorder: 95 kg; probe in canister: 1·25 kg
STATUS
Entered production phase in 1978 and now in series production for various navies. The XSV is a result of co-operation between Sippican Ocean System Division and Van Der Heem Electronics (the latter

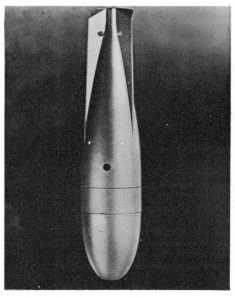

XBT expendable sound velocity probe for XSV-01 system

initially developed the system with Philips Scientific Research Laboratories).
CONTRACTORS
Van der Heem Electronics, Regulusweg 15, PO Box 16060, 2500 AB, The Hague, Netherlands, in co-operation with Sippican Corporation, Marion, Massachusetts 02738, USA.

1525.263
SPI-04 SOUND RAY PATH ANALYSER
The SPI-04 is a small special-purpose computer-based equipment providing instantaneous prediction of sound ray paths calculated directly from sound velocity over long, medium, and short ranges. All electronics, including power supply, are housed in a single cabinet weighing 70 kg. An eight inch (20·3 cm) diameter CRT display is provided, and sound ray paths are displayed with a spacing of 0·5°, the number depending upon beamwidth selection. The SPI-04 is suitable for both anti-submarine operations and oceanography applications. Sound velocity/depth information is provided by equipment such as the Van der Heem/Sippican expendable sound velocimeter (XSV) or similar equipment.

Main features include: use of microprocessors for high speed and reliability; stable presentation due to high display repetition rate; seven adjustable layers with sound velocity settings; variable bottom depth with reflections ON/OFF switch; profile setting display on LED numerical indicators.

Operational applications include:
(1) On surface ships to provide a clear picture of the sonar conditions to enable the best depth for VDS to be established, and to evaluate the possible submarine tactics

Sound ray path analyser SPI-04

(2) In submarines for the determination of optimum listening and escape depths, and defensive tactics against helicopter sonars and sonobuoys.
(3) In ASW aircraft and helicopters to establish the best depth for deploying sonobuoy hydrophones and transducers
(4) Minehunting in shallow waters
(5) Instant presentation of sonar coverage.
CHARACTERISTICS
Angular ray spacing: 0·5°
Function switch: Fixed, 4·5 m depth; variable, 0 – 600 m depth

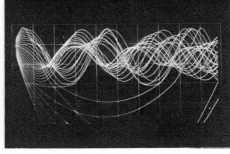

SPI-04 ray path analyser presentation

Range/depth scales: 5; 9 km/375 m – 72 km/6000 m
Bottom depth setting accuracy: Better than 2 m
DEVELOPMENT
Development was undertaken by Van der Heem BV in the Netherlands.
STATUS
The SPI-04 is in operational service with the Royal Netherlands Navy and various other navies.
CONTRACTOR
Van der Heem Electronics, Regulusweg 15, PO Box 16060, 2500 AB, The Hague, Netherlands.

NORWAY

4128.453
SS 105 SCANNING SONAR
This sonar is intended to fulfil the sonar requirements of modern ocean going coast guard vessels. It is a 360° scanning sonar with 48 preformed receiving beams with 11° beamwidth and 'split beam' processing in each beam. The working frequency is 14 kHz. The sonar system consists of an operator's console, transmitter unit, receiver unit, hydraulic power unit and hull unit.

The transmitter consists of 48 switching type amplifiers, 600 W each. Total output power is approximately 15 kW. Both OMNI, Single RDT and Triple RDT are available transmission modes. The main display has a CRT PPI, 280 mm in diameter, with scale ranges from 2 to 16 km. Markers provided are target cursor, stern cursor, transmitting and receiving sectors. An LED display shows target range, relative/true target bearing and ship's speed. Target data is transmitted digitally to other systems on board as required.

The 48 stave transducer is installed in a streamlined retractable sonar dome which will take ship's speed up to 25 knots. A fixed dome-arrangement is also possible.

CHARACTERISTICS

Transmitter

Type: Class S amplifier
Number of channels: 48
Max power output per channel: 600 W
Pulse lengths: 10, 30 and 60 ms
Frequency: 14 kHz
Transducer
Number of staves: 48, circular mounted
Active face per stave: 225 cm^2
Beamwidth vertical plane: 12 ± 1°
Resonance frequency: 14 kHz
Tilt: 6° mechanical
Transmitting modes and performance
OMNI
Beamwidth vertical plane: 12 ± 1°
Beamwidth horizontal plane: 360°
Max output level: 219 dB rel. 1 μPa at 1 m
Directivity index: 9·5 dB

SRDT
Beamwidth vertical plane: 12 ± 1°, one beam
Beamwidth horizontal plane: 8·5 ± 1°, scanning a sector variable from 10 – 115°
Directivity index: 25 dB
Max output level: 230 dB rel. 1 μPa at 1 m
TRDT
Beamwidth vertical plane: 12 ± 1°
Beamwidth horizontal plane: 8·5 × 1°, 3 beams each scanning a sector of 120°
Max output level: 230 dB rel. 1 μPa at 1 m
Directivity index: 25 dB
Receiving performance
Number of simultaneous beams: 48
Bandwidths: 400 and 800 Hz
Beamwidth vertical plane: 12 ± 1°
Beamwidth horizontal plane: 11 ± 1°
Directivity index: 26 dB
STATUS
The Norwegian Navy has ordered the SS105 scanning sonar for new coast guard vessels.
CONTRACTOR
Simrad Marine AS, PO Box 111, 3191 Horten, Norway.

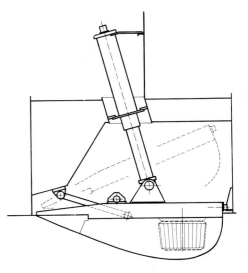

5645.253
SS304 SCANNING SONAR
The SS304 is a high resolution scanning sonar suitable for installation in small ships down to 150 tons. It is designed for detection and tracking of submarines and submersibles, as well as for minehunting.

The system consists of a hull-mounted sensor, a transmitter unit, a receiver unit, and a control/display which provides the operator with a six-colour, memory refresh, true motion 14-inch picture of the underwater situation. The fixed streamlined fibreglass sonar dome is capable of withstanding ship speed up to 40 knots.

The sonar system consists of 17 simultaneous receiving beams which in a single ping cover 85°. The 85° fan-shaped beam can be trained and tilted in any direction, for quick searches 360° around the vessel, tiltable down to 90°. The vertical beam width is only 7° which eliminates nearly all interfering noises from the sea bottom.

CHARACTERISTICS
Frequency: 34 kHz
Range: 3000 m
Source level: 232 dB rel 1 Pa, ref 1 m
Transducer beamwidths: 9° horizontal; 7° vertical
Dome: Fibreglass (GRP) max speed 40 knots
Tilt: Upper limit 15° up; lower limit 105° down; speed 10°/s
Transmitter: Output power to transducer – 4 kW
Display: 14-inch colour monitor; 3 colours for symbols, 3 colours for echoes, 50 Hz refresh, 512 lines raster scan
STATUS
In production.
CONTRACTOR
Simrad Marine AS, PO Box 111, 3191 Horten, Norway.

Control console of the SS304 scanning sonar

UNION OF SOVIET SOCIALIST REPUBLICS

3236.453
SOVIET SONAR
Because of Soviet security constraints and the generally inaccesible location of sonar equipment it is not possible to treat this aspect of Soviet underwater equipment in the same manner as has been adopted for that of other nations. Instead, the following notes summarise what little has been gathered, and which is free of Western security restrictions. While this inevitably falls well short of the ideal treatment, it is

hoped that readers will find the ensuing paragraphs of some help.

Underwater acoustic experiments, initially in relation to communications applications, by the Soviet Union are widely agreed to date back to the years immediately prior to the First World War, but the earliest references to anything resembling what is now known as sonar occur in the 1930s when research into hydrophones for submarines is mentioned. At this general time, the possibilities of

'Foxtrot' class submarine bow sonars

thermal detection devices for both aircraft and surface shipping were pursued. In the same period, the Soviet Union is credited with the production of passive sea bed acoustic detector equipment. Soviet claims record that the Soviet Union's naval forces at the start of the Second World War had available a variety of sonar equipments for shore and ship installations.

Most, if not all, of those reported were apparently passive devices, those for submarine fitting consisting of an elliptical array made of 8, 12 or 16 hydrophone elements. There were also passive sonar

Large sonar arrays feature prominently on the bows of these Soviet submarines

'Juliet' class submarine bow sonars

vessels have hull-mounted sonars and some of the earlier 'Petya' class have been retro-fitted with a variable depth sonar which replaces the after torpedo tubes. The 'Kresta I' ASW cruisers have hull-mounted sonar and can carry Hormone helicopters which have been equipped with dipping sonar and a magnetic anomaly detector, and can deploy sonobuoys. A bow-mounted sonar is fitted in the later 'Kresta II' class, and the still more recent 'Kara' class ships have a variable depth towed sonar. The 'Krivak' class ships, which appeared at sea in 1971, have both bow sonar and a variable depth sonar.

In addition to the Hormone helicopters, the earlier Hound is believed to be capable of operating a dipping sonar, or possibly a towed magnetic anomaly detector (MAD). The MI-14 Haze shore-based helicopter also carries MAD. Other fixed-wing maritime aircraft, such as the Be-12 Mail and the Il-38 May are equipped with MAD, and the latter type also can deploy sonobuoys and process data obtained by this means. Mail has been followed into service by an ASW version of the Tu-20 Bear F which is understood to employ sonobuoys for submarine target detection.

Many submarines of the Soviet fleet prominently feature large sonar arrays and it has been estimated that between 30 and 40 nuclear attack submarines have been commissioned, supported by perhaps as many as 150 diesel attack submarines. These are in addition to the large classes of nuclear and diesel ballistic and cruise missile submarines, all of which have sonar installations.

sets for surface ships, one of these being named Tamir and which began sea trials in 1940. This equipment is stated by the Soviet Union to have become the standard Soviet sonar employed in the anti-submarine campaign of that time. Neither the

Soviet Union's then allies, nor her enemies, appeared to have been unduly impressed by the results achieved, according to historians, official and unofficial. By the post Second World War period, the USSR had gained access to sonar technology originating in America, Britain, and Germany, either by gift or as booty.

Since then, there has been steady and impressive growth of Soviet interest in all aspects of submarine warfare and it is reasonable to suppose that sonar equipment is accorded a priority within these activities at least as great as that given it by the Western navies. The advent of the Soviet ASW helicopter and aircraft carriers, such as the *Moskva*, *Leningrad* and *Kiev*, in advance of comparable ships being commissioned in Western navies, might imply a higher priority.

The appearance of these ships was preceded by smaller vessels designed for ASW operations and special-purpose aircraft and helicopters for naval duties, the latter being deployed in both land-based and embarked formations. These developments occurred in the mid-1950s to mid-1960s period.

Among the ASW ships, 'Petya' and 'Mirka' class

'Foxtrot' class submarine bow sonars seen from abeam

'Golf' class submarine bow sonars

UNITED KINGDOM

Note: A range of new sonar systems is under design and/or review by the Royal Navy for surface and underwater vessels. This range includes the Type 2050 hull-mounted sonar for surface ships, in particular the Type 23 frigates, and the Type 2054 hull-mounted for submarines which is a Trident submarine version of the Type 2050. For towed arrays the RN requirement is for two passive systems, a

surface ship version, the Type 2031, and a submarine equipment, Type 2046. An interim version of the Type 2031 is being manufactured by Waverley Electronics, under contract to the Admiralty Underwater Establishment, using technology developed by the latter. Companies competing for this business include Plessey Marine, Ferranti Computer Systems, Marconi Avionics, Marconi Underwater Systems and

Waverley Electronics. In addition to the surveillance sonars, a new minehunting system, Type 2093, is also under consideration, and is intended for the single-role minehunter to be ordered by the RN in the near future. A decision regarding the hull-mounted sonar was due in mid-1984.

1981.363
AQS 901 ACOUSTIC DATA PROCESSING AND DISPLAY SYSTEM

AQS 901 is the designation of the sonics system developed for the Mk 2 version of the RAF's Nimrod and the RAAF P-3 Orion long-range maritime patrol (LRMP) aircraft.

The ASQ 901, comprising on-board receivers, advanced digital processors, and electronic displays, enables submarines to be detected and located for attack using a wide range of sonobuoys. Additionally the system can accept inputs from fixed arrays and dipping sonar, and provisions have been made for any projected new type of sonobuoy to be employed as well as those in current service. Examples of specific types of sonobuoy with which AQS 901 can operate include the Australian Barra, British CAMBS and Jezebel, plus the US-designated Dicass, Difar, and Ranger buoys. It is the only system in squadron service which can process the data from the Barra buoy.

In Mk 2 Nimrod aircraft, receivers supplied by McMichael Ltd receive signals from sonobuoys as part of the AQS 901 system. These receivers each provide 99 channels in the 140 to 176 MHz band.

The processor is based on a Marconi Avionics 920

ATC digital computer used in conjunction with a Fast Fourier Transform (FFT) analyser for spectrum analysis. Associated with the AQS 901 is an advanced eight-channel receiver and command system, and it also interfaces with a new central tactical system (CTS) developed for the Nimrod. This last system is also based on the 920 ATC processor which has an expandable memory capacity up to 256 k words of directly addressable memory. An important feature of AQS 901 is the FFT analyser which is capable of performing a 2048 complex transform in 11·25 milliseconds. Micro-programs in the FFT are initiated by the 920 ATC, thus providing flexibility and adaptability.

Interpretation of received data in the various modes from active and passive sonobuoys and other sensors is provided by both CRT displays and chart recorders. They have provision for presenting a wide variety of types of information, control of this being under direction of the operator who uses his keyboard to effect the necessary changes in computer operation to vary the display formats.

DEVELOPMENT
By virtue of its flexible computer-based processor and powerful FFT analyser, the AQS 901 system is applicable to other vehicles intended for anti-

submarine warfare. Versions have been configured for other types of aircraft.

Development of the Mk 2 Nimrod system was initiated in 1971 with the award to Marconi Avionics Ltd of a UK contract for a feasibility study, followed closely by a larger design, development, and manufacture contract.

STATUS
The AQS 901 has now successfully entered squadron service with both the RAF Nimrod MR Mk 2 fleet and the RAAF P3-C Orion aircraft.

Update of the present RAF fleet of Mk 1 Nimrods is almost complete to the Mk 2 standard. This programme involves the installation of the Searchwater computer-assisted radar, a new inertial navigation system, the AQS 901, a new tactical computer which increases computing speed and power about 50 times, and a new communications system which includes radio teletype and on-line encryption.

The first complete aircraft installation of the AQS 901 sonobuoy data processing equipment for the RAF was formally handed over in March 1979. Each aircraft installation comprises two complete AQS 901 systems; these operate independently, but can inter-communicate for mission management purposes.

Each system is operated by one crew member. There is a fifth display for system management on which data from either of the two AQS 901 systems can be presented.

The installation of AQS 901 into the RAAF's P-3C fleet and operational development of the complete system is carried out in Australia entirely by Australian industry. Major contracts were placed with Commonwealth Aircraft Corporation, EMI Electronics, and Amalgamated Wireless Australasia supported by Computer Sciences Australia.

An order worth £25 million was placed with Marconi Avionics in April 1983 to equip the fleet of Lockheed P-3C Orion maritime aircraft recently purchased by the RAAF. This order also included more systems for the RAF's Nimrods.

CONTRACTORS

Design authority: Marconi Avionics Ltd, Airport Works, Rochester, Kent ME1 2XX, England.

Sub-contractors: Rank Pullin Controls Ltd, Computing Devices of Canada, McMichael Ltd.

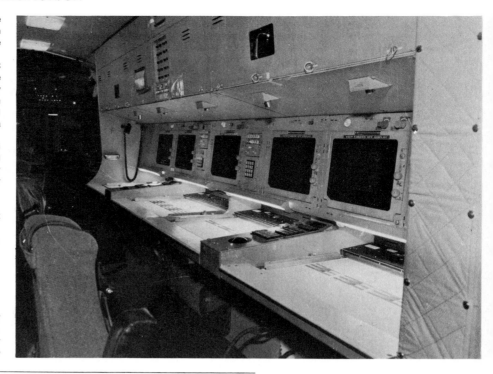

Complete aircraft installation consists of two full AQS 901 acoustic processing and display systems. Deliveries for RAF Nimrods and RAAF Orions are now being made

---

3497.363

AQS 902 LIGHTWEIGHT ACOUSTIC PROCESSING AND DISPLAY SYSTEM (LAPADS)

LAPADS is the designation of a lightweight acoustic processing and display system designed and developed by Marconi Avionics Ltd, principally for use in ASW helicopters and shorter range maritime patrol aircraft. A version has been adopted by the UK government for installation on RN Sea King helicopters. The system is also known as AQS 902.

It is a modular system which enables various configurations to be assembled appropriate to the type of aircraft to be fitted, its operational role(s), and the number and types of sonobuoys required to be employed. Depending on the configuration selected, any or all of the current NATO sonobuoy inventory can be processed. The system will interface with any approved type of sonobuoy receiver, British or American, using either a 31 RF frequency-channel or 99 RF frequency-channel capability, as required.

Three basic units comprise the LAPADS installation in the helicopter or aircraft. Each of these units contains dedicated modules which permit the selected system configuration to be constructed at minimum cost and weight. This also permits subsequent expansion or modification to operational facilities with minimum hardware changes. One unit is the processor unit which converts the received sonobuoy signals into digital form, carries out the necessary filtering and analysis, and processes the data into a form suitable for display. It is packaged in a Short 1 ATR case and carries on its front panel the push buttons by means of which a crew member controls the complete operation. The receiver unit is housed in a ¾ ATR case, and with its associated

antenna preamplifier and small panel-mounted controller, is produced by McMichael Ltd. The third unit is a display which may be the hard copy recorder, and is a standard unit produced by Rank Pullin Ltd for the AQS 901 acoustic processing and display system (**1981.363**). If desired, LAPADS can operate with a hard copy chart recorder or a CRT display, either separately or in any chosen combination. If a CRT is installed, an extra unit will be a post processor which includes a waveform generator to prepare data for CRT presentation as well as providing additional system facilities.

All hard copy and CRT formats are fully annotated, and the CRT displays have a rolling ball and cursor with which the operator may designate data for subsequent action. Associated with this facility are frequency dividers, markers, and data read-out by interrogation. Fixing aids are provided for correlation and detection and recording (CODAR), manual doppler fix, manual Hyfix, and Lloyds mirror depth analysis. Range and bearing data are available on the CRT display, and in some configurations on the hard copy recorder, from the directional buoys, and operator control is exercised via a dedicated key set to specify processing modes and parameters.

DEVELOPMENT

LAPADS development began in late 1976 as a private venture programme and it is now in service. Current developments include the integration of dipping sonar sensors to provide a compact and simultaneous sonobuoy and dipping sonar processing and display capability, together with a fully integrated tactical processing and display system.

Lightweight acoustic processing and display system in an RN Sea King

STATUS

LAPADS is in squadron service with the RN's fleet of Sea King Mk 5 ASW helicopters, has been supplied to the Royal Swedish Navy and ordered by another overseas customer.

CONTRACTOR

Marconi Avionics, Airport Works, Rochester, Kent ME21 2XX, England.

5655.363

AQS 903 ACOUSTIC PROCESSING AND DISPLAY SYSTEM

The AQS 903 is a lightweight acoustic processing and display system primarily designed for use in helicopters but equally well suited for fixed-wing aircraft. It has been selected by the Royal Navy to equip the Sea King replacement helicopter, the EH101, which is due to enter service in the late 1980s.

The AQS 903 is a modular system and draws heavily on the experience gained in operating the AQS 902 (LAPADS) system (**3497.363**) in the Royal Navy Sea Kings. The modular concept allows various configurations to be assembled appropriate to the type of aircraft to be fitted, its operational role and the number and type of sonobuoys required to be employed. In the basic configuration for the Royal Navy, the processor is designed to handle the complete range of NATO sonobuoys, particularly BARRA and DIFAR. It has an eight-buoy capability

and allows the operator to transit smoothly from one mission phase to another, irrespective of the buoy types in use.

For the primary application, a single acoustic operator is required in the aircraft, with twin CRT displays to the normal TV raster standards, as the output medium. Hard copy facilities are also available as an option. The operator interfaces to the processor via a CRT based control panel with multifunction associated keys and a menu-driven option selection mechanism. The analysis and display cues provided for the operator are in plain language which allows system control with a lower level of training than would otherwise be needed. The system will also interface to other on-board systems responsible for sonobuoy launching, navigation, tactical tracking and weapon release.

The processor can handle up to eight buoys simultaneously and provides 360° surveillance on all underwater submersibles. It also provides sector

coverage for additional classification and/or tracking analysis. Extensive use is made of distributed processing, with the system incorporating the latest component technology, to provide the operator with very large amounts of data. Auto-alert is incorporated into both the passive and active modes to assist the operator to monitor the necessary sonobuoys and to make the important analysis decisions.

The display system uses current high-level technology to provide the operator with the information necessary to implement decisions, and sonar data can be called up in a variety of formats to assist him.

STATUS

In development.

CONTRACTOR

Marconi Avionics Limited, Airport Works, Rochester, Kent ME21 2XX, England.

3268.493

G 738 TOWED DECOY

The G 738 is an improved and re-engineered version of the Royal Navy Type 182 towed torpedo decoy, now being manufactured for several other navies. Known features of the equipment are modern solid-state signal generation equipment and compact, lightweight, deck machinery.

The equipment is designed to decoy both active and passive homing torpedoes from a ship fitted with the G 738/Type 182. Decoy signals are electronically generated within the ship and fed via the towing cable to electro-acoustic transducers within the towed body; the signals thus produced divert passive homing torpedoes astern and confuse or jam the steering mechanisms of active homing torpedoes.

A variety of deck-handling arrangements is produced, and dual systems may be fitted. Remote control of selection of signal characteristics provides for instantaneous changes from operations room or bridge. Parameters include noise, frequency and amplitude, modulated as well as unmodulated CW random and pre-programmed output beam formations.

The operating characteristics remain confidential between the manufacturer and the purchaser.
STATUS
In production. 14 systems sold overseas.
CONTRACTOR
Graseby Dynamics Ltd, Park Avenue, Bushey, Watford, Hertfordshire WD2 2BW, England.

3266.453

G 750 SONAR

The G 750 is a search and attack all-round sonar for ships of frigate size and above. It is a modernised and improved version of the Type 184M (**3265.453**), providing accurate fire control data from two independent automatic tracking systems whilst simultaneously maintaining all-round surveillance, independent doppler search, and classification and continuous torpedo warning.

Three separate processing and display systems are incorporated for:
(1) all-round search and tracking (PPI)
(2) doppler
(3) passive search.

Digital readout displays are used extensively and visual displays are supplemented by audio in all three systems. Nine cabinets are required for the complete electronics. Three are display consoles, three contain transmitter and control equipment, two house receivers, and one is for monitoring purposes. For installation in smaller ships or submarines, single passive or PPI display systems, with smaller transducers, are produced. In the standard G 750 system, an improved version of the Type 184M 32-stave transducer is used to form a large number of beams. Range and bearing measurement is by in-beam scanning, obviating the need for separate expanded displays.

Target range and bearing are measured by either of two methods:

Type G 750 sonar control console

(1) by means of a manually positioned marker technique in which the circular markers are placed over the target echo and it is the marker position that is measured; or

(2) by echo gating where the echo range and bearing are measured directly. This form of tracking is normally on acquisition of a possible target and is available on either computer-assisted or non-computer-assisted basis. Marker boxes representing the gated area replace the circles. In both methods the targets are individually identified by dotted or full markers.

Provisions are made for interfacing the G 750 sonar with computer-based ASW and tactical information systems to provide a source of range, bearing, and target doppler data. Operational capabilities of the equipment include active detection of submarines throughout 360° and the ability to track two targets simultaneously. Similar detection coverage and tracking capabilities are available in respect of torpedo targets, with suitable outputs to torpedo warning and avoidance systems. There is also an active search capability over a 45° arc with facilities for determining target doppler. The system is designed for operation in adverse reverberation conditions, with ripple or omni-direction dual-frequency modulated and doppler CW transmission modes.
STATUS
In production. Three systems sold to Royal New Zealand Navy.
CONTRACTOR
Graseby Dynamics Ltd, Park Avenue, Bushey, Watford, Hertfordshire WD2 2BW, England.

3269.453

GRASEBY SONAR PROJECTS

In addition to the sonar and underwater equipments described in individual entries within this volume, Graseby Dynamics is known to be engaged on a number of other projects of this nature. Brief summaries of some are given below.

800 Series Sonar

A new generation of sonars incorporating the latest in sonar concepts and technology. This development programme is designed to provide a whole range of underwater electro-acoustic equipment for large, medium, and small ships thereby minimising logistic support maintenance and training expenditure. The programme also includes sonars primarily for small submarines.

SACACS

A transportable long range Sonar Accuracy Check and Calibration System (SACACS) is in service with the Royal Navy. Known as the G 740, about 12 of these systems are now in use for sonar and anti-submarine weapon system acceptance trials and periodic calibration.

SLUTT

The G 733 SLUTT (Ship Launched Underwater Transponder Target) simulates an underwater target to permit functional tests of sonar equipment and operator training. This equipment is produced in various sizes and a large number has been sold.
CONTRACTOR
Graseby Dynamics Ltd, Park Avenue, Bushey, Watford, Hertfordshire WD2 2BW, England.

7002.253

PMS26 and PMS27 SURFACE SHIP SONARS

Hull-mounted ship sonars designed for single operator control in both the surveillance and attack roles, the PMS26 and PMS27 are also used as 'dunking' sonars in certain helicopters, under the designation Type 195.
OPERATION
The PMS26 is a self-contained system for ships and patrol craft down to 150 tons. It provides full 360° coverage in four steps of 90° and may be manually controlled to cover a particular sector, or set to carry out automatic search procedure. It incorporates a 'maintenance of close contact' facility for tracking close or deep targets. The single operator controls the sonar through a special console. He is provided with three sources of sonar information – audio, visual doppler, and visual sector.

The doppler facility provides increased initial detection range and improved classification capabilities compared with conventional small ship sonars. The PMS26 transducer array is mounted within a hull outfit with a glass-reinforced plastic dome.

The PMS27 differs from the PMS26 only in its associated hull outfit. The PMS27 transducer array is mounted in a Royal Navy hull outfit 19 or similar,

CHARACTERISTICS				
PMS26 and PMS27	Width (mm)	Height (mm)	Depth (mm)	Weight (kg)
Operator's console	530	430	300	26·5
Doppler receiver	400	292	520	20·7
Sector receiver	400	292	380	10·8
Transmitter	292	190	520	13·7
Auxiliaries unit	400	292	510	27·1
Sonar power supply	432	380	500	73
Transducer assembly	445	996	530	100
PMS26 hull outfit	800	1373	1400	1015
PMS26 sonar dome	483	725	1320	1015

which makes the equipment suitable for installation in small escorts down to about 650 tons displacement. The PMS27 can be used as a surveillance sonar in association with a separate fire control sonar within the same hull outfit. This enables the ship to continue surveillance for new threats whilst engaging a target already detected.

Both systems use fully transistorised circuits to ensure high reliability, while modular construction techniques permit rapid maintenance and minimise loss of operational time. They also offer a means of economically providing secondary sonar capability in multi-role vessels. Under slow speed operation, when the background noise is that caused by breaking and pounding of waves, equivalent to, say, sea state 4, the theoretical initial detection range can be calculated at about 7000 m. A practical working range of detection under most conditions is approximately 4500 m.

The equipment is sub-divided into small units which may be sited in convenient areas not necessarily adjacent to the control console.
ADDITIONAL EQUIPMENT
Various other ancillary units are available which will measure transmitter output power and receiver sensitivity; indicate figure of merit under prevailing noise conditions; provide at points remote to the

control console tactical information on target movement; provide *in situ* system checking which locates any system fault or performance deterioration; and provide a controlled simulated display for training purposes.

STATUS

Now in quantity production. The PMS26/27 has been adopted by nine navies, including two NATO member countries.

CONTRACTOR

Plessey Marine, Templecombe, Somerset BA8 0DH, England.

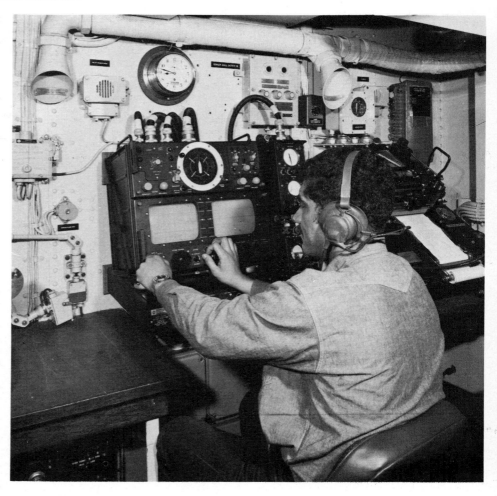

PMS26 sonar operator's console

1024.353

TYPE 195 HELICOPTER SONAR

This is a helicopter-mounted 'dipping' sonar, from which the Plessey PMS26/27 range of surface vessel sonars are derived. The principal difference is the use of a winch-controlled transducer for detection and location in place of the hull-mounted units employed in the PMS26/27. Other essential details are the same and will be found in the entry for the PMS26/27 sonars (**7002.253**).

The facilities available to the sonar operator are as follows:

(1) controlling the physical movements of the submersible unit

(2) provision of data on temperature profiles from the bathythermograph

(3) selection of the most appropriate operating procedure in terms of transducer depths, search technique, pulse length, and a range setting in relation to sea conditions and tactical requirements

(4) a doppler display which shows the initial detection of any target-like echoes in the area under examination, thus alerting the helicopter (and possibly other units) to the presence of potential targets

(5) to provide elementary classification of 'contacts' to establish whether further action is appropriate

(6) maintenance of sonar contact with recognised targets during any subsequent manoeuvres, which may include moving and 're-dunking' the submersible unit as well as target movements

(7) provision of co-ordination information (range and geographical bearing relative to helicopter) when required for attack procedures or enemy reporting.

STATUS

The Type 195 sonar is part of the equipment forming the Westland Sea King ASW helicopter system. In squadron service with the Royal Navy and sold in substantial numbers to other countries.

CHARACTERISTICS	Width	Height	Depth	Weight
	(mm)	(mm)	(mm)	(kg)
Transmitter (2)	290	190	510	15·54
Receiver-doppler	390	290	510	19·28
Receiver-sector	390	290	510	19·28
Power supply	300	290	510	12·92
Submersible unit, upper	580	1670		43·4
Submersible unit, lower	580	1670		55·97
Control indicator	510	520	320	25·63
Winch	680	840	710	69·4
Monitor	140	250	140	1·93
Bathythermograph recorder	190	320	220	5·84

Type 195 sonar under a Sea King helicopter

CONTRACTOR

Plessey Marine, Templecombe, Somerset BA8 0DH, England.

1755.453

TYPE 162M SIDEWAYS-LOOKING SONAR

Sonar Type 162M, which is fitted as standard in ships of the Royal Navy, detects and classifies both mid-water and sea bed targets. It displays port and starboard recordings simultaneously on a single straight-line recorder, which has a maximum range scale of 1200 yards. Operation is simplified by entirely automatic gain control. Reliability is enhanced with solid-state technology and maintenance is facilitated by ease of access and comprehensive built-in testing and monitoring features.

The three transducers are all similar and employ 49·8 kHz barium titanate elements. Their beam pattern is fan-shaped, about 3° wide and 40° vertical angle; the side-looking elements have their axes 25° below the horizontal.

The recorder design uses a double helix (left and right hand) so that there are two points of contact with the moist electro-sensitive paper. As the helix rotates, the two points of contact move outwards from the centre. Port and starboard signals are fed respectively to the left- and right-hand points of contact so that they are recorded simultaneously. There are two zero lines near the middle of the paper, and the 18 mm gap between them is used for time marks every five minutes. The paper width is 286 mm, and each trace occupies 133 mm.

An electronic oscillator provides a controlled frequency supply for the driving motor and interval marks. Motor speed changes, for the three range scales, are made by frequency division so as to avoid the use of change speed gearbox, and a stroboscopic arrangement is included so that the helix speed may be easily checked.

A loudspeaker and a socket for headphones enable signals to be monitored aurally if required.

The three range scales are 0 to 300, 0 to 600, and 0 to 1200 yards, and accuracy is better than 2 per cent assuming a sound velocity of 4920 ft/second. The paper speed changes automatically when the range scale is selected, and the speeds are 6, 3, and 1·5 inches/minute (152, 76 and 38 mm/minute) respectively. At a ship speed of 10·8 knots the display scales are the same across the paper and vertically. A take-up spool is fitted but its use is optional. A fix marker draws a line across the width of the paper when a button is pressed, and it can be operated in conjunction with a Type 778 echo sounder or other equipment.

The receiver/transmitter contains:
(1) the transmission system in which a crystal oscillator supplies the correct energising frequency, which is gated to form pulses of 0·75 m/s duration at intervals commanded by the recorder; the pulses are amplified to deliver 80 W to each of the sideways-looking transducers and 40 W to the centre (downward-looking) transducer. There is a switch to cut out either the port or starboard transducer when not required, and the centre transducer is automatically disconnected on the longest range scale
(2) the reception system, which includes signal amplifiers, mixers, transmit/receive switches, initial reverberation suppression and automatic gain control. By careful selection of time constants, it has been found possible to preserve a sufficient level of sea bed reverberation to display target shadows, and yet to permit weak echoes from distant targets to be seen in the presence of the reverberation. This system is so effective that the operator has no need of a manual gain control
(3) the monitoring and test facilities, which enable all supply voltages and the functioning of the transmitter and receiver to be checked and test signals to be injected.
STATUS
In production.
CONTRACTOR
Kelvin Hughes, New North Road, Hainault, Ilford, Essex IG6 2UR, England.

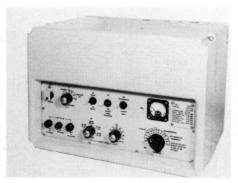

Type 162M sonar transmitter/receiver unit

Type 162M sonar recorder

3265.453
SONAR TYPE 184M
The Type 184M is one of the Royal Navy's primary surface ship anti-submarine search and attack sonars.

It is a 360° scanning sonar incorporating both active and passive modes of operation; it provides range, bearing and target doppler data to the fire control computer. The Type 184 was designed in association with the Admiralty Underwater Warfare Establishment (AUWE), and is fitted in the majority of RN surface ships. The equipment has also been supplied to a number of other navies.

Few technical details have been cleared for publication, but it can be stated that the equipment provides a dual frequency transmission and three receiver systems. The latter comprise:
(1) an all-round search and tracking PPI system
(2) a doppler system with B-scan display
(3) a continuous torpedo warning system with its own display.
A circular 32-stave transducer array is employed.
STATUS
Operational with RN and other navies. RN fittings include Type 21 frigates, Type 42 destroyers and 'Leander' class ships. The G 750 medium-range sonar (**3266.453**) is a solid-state, improved version.

Type 184 sonar control console

CONTRACTOR
Graseby Dynamics Ltd, Park Avenue, Bushey, Watford, Hertfordshire WD2 2BW, England.

1374.253
MINEHUNTING SONAR 193M/193M MOD 1
The 193M is a short-range, high definition sector scanning sonar, operating at two frequencies, providing detection and classification of mines. It has been developed from the Type 193 minehunting sonar; the adoption of solid-state electronics and other advances in technology have resulted in a reduction in installed weight to about 860 kg, which compares with a figure of some 2100 kg for the older Type 193. Among the operational improvements are extensive use of digital displays and facilities for interfacing with computer systems.

The basic concept is to employ high-definition sonar to locate and classify mines which are then destroyed by explosive charges. Other elements of the complete system include a surface warning radar which fixes the ship's position relative to short-scope buoys, and a Mk 20 plotting table into which data is fed from radar and sonar to provide an automatic and continuous display for ship and target position.

The sonar provides both bearing and range data; the fine range and bearing resolution enables the operator to assess accurately the shape of a target and hence its nature. Since the resolution depends both on operating frequency and pulse length, two selectable frequencies are provided, each with a choice of pulse length.

Range and bearing data appear on two displays: in the search mode one display shows the total range covered; in the classification mode, a 27 m (30 yards) section of the search display is expanded to fill the second display screen and permit close examination of the target.

Two frequencies are employed by the 193M sonar, 100 kHz for long range search and 300 kHz for short-range search and classification. The transducers for these signals are carried beneath the ship on a stabilised, steerable mounting, the whole assembly contained within an inflated fabric dome. The receiver uses a modulation scanning technique with 15 beams, 1° wide in LF and 0·5° wide at HF giving azimuth coverage of 15° and 6° respectively. The searching of wider areas of the sea bottom is achieved by means of an automatic search sequence selected in accordance with the type of sea bottom. The returned echoes are presented to the operators on separate CRTs at the control console. One of these displays range and bearing of targets within the sector being scanned by the search transducer, while

Type 193M sonar operators' console

the other is used for the presentation of the classification channel data. The controls for adjusting the transducer position, signal parameters such as frequency and pulse length and for co-operating with the rest of the minehunting and destruction team, are also provided at the console. Type 193M data can also be fed into other ships' systems.

The Plessey Speedscan system can be fitted to the

Type 193M to allow it to be operated in the side-scan mode and to generate a hard copy print-out of the sea-bed.

DEVELOPMENT

Development of the Type 193M was undertaken by Plessey in 1968. Since then a continuous programme of development and operational trials in conjunction with the UK MoD has resulted in further system improvements defined as the Type 193M Mod 1.

The system offers greatly improved performance in detection and classification by the use of digitally-processed video and display systems, together with computer-aided target classification.

STATUS

In service with the Royal Navy and Federal German Navy, the Type 193M can also be used with the Racal minehunting system and can operate in the Vosper 47 m glass fibre re-inforced minehunter vessel. It is suitable for use with the Sperry Cat mine-disposal weapon (**3161.253** 1983-84 and earlier editions) or the French PAP 104 system (**1786.453**) and can interface with any digital plotting and action information system such as Ferranti CAAIS, Racal CANE and other plotting tables in current use.

Type 193M is fitted in the Royal Navy's 'Hunt' class MCMVs. Twelve navies have now purchased some 50 Plessey minehunting sonar equipments, including both the 193M and the earlier version 193. A continuing programme of enhancement will ensure that the efficiency of the equipment is kept continually under review.

The Type 193M Mod 1 enhancements will be retrofitted as a modification to RN ships fitted with 193M, while complete Type 193M Mod 1 sets are available for export.

CONTRACTOR

Plessey Marine, Templecombe, Somerset BA8 0DH, England.

3787.453

TYPE 2016 FLEET ESCORT SONAR

The Royal Navy's Type 2016 fleet escort sonar is a replacement for the existing RN sonars Types 177 and 184. It employs computer-aided techniques which are operator interactive, have automatic detection and tracking, enhanced signal processing and displays complemented by an information storage facility.

The Type 2016 is a hull-mounted panoramic surveillance and attack equipment with facilities for classification and multiple target tracking. Interference between nearby vessels using the Type 2016 sonar is largely eliminated by the use of a new type of broad band transducer. The sonar display console is designed for manning by a single operator under normal cruise conditions, this crew member being able to initiate the preparatory actions necessary for urgent action.

Digital data processing facilities are based on use of Ferranti computer equipment, with other sub-contractors including Marconi Radar.

The Type 2016 system comprises the following main elements: four active receiver cabinets, one passive and control cabinet and one T/R switch and beamformer cabinet, all housed in Plessey MC70 type cabinets. The Ferranti computer suite consists of three of their D.811A cabinets and a separate cabinet for computer spares. The two transmitters are housed in two standard RN/AUWE cabinets. The solid-state electronics are based on a modular system approach using medium scale integrated devices, printed circuit back planes with wire wrap connections and standard line-drive receivers for all inter-cabinet signal connections. Extensive use is made of hybrid circuit techniques to reduce volume.

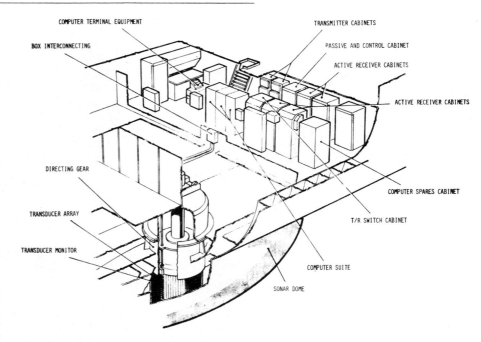

Arrangement of Type 2016 fleet escort sonar equipment and the hull outfit compartment

The Type 2016 array system, which is roll stabilised, is fitted in a ribless monocoque glass reinforced plastic sonar dome within a fixed hull outfit. The current Royal Navy practice employs a keel dome but the array could equally be mounted in a suitable bow dome.

The display console contains three main displays and a top-mounted versatile console system (VCS) unit. The surveillance display incorporates a special simple keyboard for transmission of information to the command/AIO and for the selection of the appropriate display. The surveillance display also displays monitoring information about the performance of the equipment. When a fault is indicated, the maintainer on stand-by is alerted and proceeds direct to the sonar instrument space where further sub-unit monitoring systems enable him to pinpoint the fault down to board level. The classification display provides expanded presentation of part of the surveillance display in both B-scan and A-scan modes to permit the operator to examine the target structure more closely.

The passive and auxiliary data display with two different integration times enables both torpedoes and more distant targets to be tracked. The auxiliary data display is used for data logging and system information which includes the display of such items as course, speed, weather, sea bottom conditions, and bathymetric information.

DEVELOPMENT

Design was initiated in the late 1960s and an experimental equipment underwent tests in HMS Matapan. A development contract was awarded in 1973 and the first prototype was completed in 1978.

In April 1980 Plessey Marine announced that it had received UK Ministry of Defence contracts amounting to more than £50 million, including initial research and development contracts which added up to £10 million. Type 2016 fleet escort sonars have been supplied for the Royal Navy Type 22 frigates HMS *Broadsword* and *Battleaxe*.

STATUS

In service with the Royal Navy in Type 22 frigates.

CONTRACTORS

Plessey Marine, Templecombe, Somerset BA8 0DH, England – prime contractor, with Ferranti Computer Systems, Marconi Radar Systems and other sub-contractors.

Console of Type 2016 sonar aboard a RN frigate. The three displays (left to right) are for classification, surveillance, and passive presentation

5651.453
TYPE 2020 SUBMARINE SONAR
The Type 2020 is one of the latest systems from Plessey's range of sonar equipments. It is intended for use in the Royal Navy's hunter-killer nuclear submarines and provides both passive and active detection capabilities from its bow-mounted acoustic array. Although considerable emphasis has been placed on passive detection the equipment incorporates a highly effective computer-aided active capability.

Passive detection is sub-divided into low frequency and high frequency bands with information presented on dual-speed multi-pen recorders. The system is intended primarily for operation in a computer-aided mode but can be automatically reconfigured to a fall-back mode of operation, with target information being passed to the action information organiser in both modes. Facilities for expansion are included in the design to allow interfacing with future sonar systems. Solid-state switching is used for the transmit/receive function and electronic beam steering techniques are employed. The design provides high detection sonar performance with a full 360° coverage.

A computer-controlled automatic monitoring sub-system is incorporated in the equipment, with a central monitoring unit driving local monitoring units within each equipment cabinet. Diagnosis of computer faults and programme loading is accelerated by the use of a floppy disc.
STATUS
The Type 2020 is intended as the replacement for the currently installed Type 2001 and is scheduled for fitment in 'Trafalgar' and improved 'Swiftsure' classes of nuclear-powered submarines. Each system costs £6 million.

The first production model was accepted by the Royal Navy in October 1982. Three prototypes had already been manufactured, one of which was installed and commissioned in HMS *Trafalgar*.

Display/console of the Type 2020 submarine sonar

CONTRACTOR
Plessey Marine, Templecombe, Somerset BA8 0DH, England.

5637.353
HISOS 1 (CORMORANT) LIGHTWEIGHT DIPPING SONAR
HISOS 1 is a new helicopter integrated sonar system which incorporates a sensor array unit of advanced design, together with a winch, from Plessey Marine, and a lightweight acoustic processor and display from the Marconi Avionics AQS 902 LAPADS series (**3497.363**). The system, known as Cormorant, can be supplied as a 'stand-alone' dipping sonar, for active or passive use, or as an integrated system in which both free sonobuoys and dipping sonar are employed.

HISOS is suitable for installation in medium size helicopters, with an all-up-weight of 4100 kg (9000 lb) and above. The system has a good active detection range against quiet targets in 'inner zone' or noisy environments and its use as a passive detector allows covert surveillance to be maintained.

The sonar array is a wide bandwidth type, probably

dual frequency, and is claimed to have a long-range and high bearing measurement accuracy. Mosaic (**5654.363**) integration techniques developed by Marconi are described as permitting more efficient exploitation of the sensor array.

A more sophisticated version, HISOS 2, is under development, aimed initially at the RN new helicopter, the EH101, and intended for operation with the Marconi AQS 903 processor and display system (**5655.363**).
STATUS
In development.
CONTRACTORS
Plessey Marine, Templecombe, Somerset BA8 0DH, England.

Marconi Avionics Ltd, Maritime Aircraft Systems Division, Airport Works, Rochester, Kent ME1 2XX, England.

HISOS 1 sensor array deployed under water

5639.253
PMS 40 SERIES SONAR SYSTEMS
The PMS 40 series sonar systems use a modular design to ensure that the series suits the majority of applications and warship types, with emphasis on export potential. Three variants are available, each using the same single-operator dual-display console. These are:
(1) PMS 42 with a single electronics cabinet and a 686 mm diameter transducer array for small patrol vessels, corvettes and larger warships with a less demanding ASW role
(2) PMS 44, with two electronics cabinets and a 1200 mm diameter transducer array for corvettes and larger warships

(3) PMS 46, with three electronics cabinets and a 2000 mm diameter transducer array for major ASW vessels.

The PMS sonars are hull-mounted, intended for shallow and deep water anti-submarine detection, classification and tracking. They also provide a passive detection and tracking capability against torpedoes. Surveillance of 360 degrees is provided.

A flexible modular concept has been adopted, permitting common electronics and display console to be employed throughout. Advanced digital signal processing techniques are used and the design approach allows for various options and extensions. The systems provide omni-directional surveillance,

simultaneous active and passive operation, automatic active and passive target tracking, LPM and CW (doppler) modes, operator selectable transmission frequencies and colour displays. They can also be integrated with a towed array.

Each sonar in the series consists of four elements: the transducer array, a sonar dome, operator's console and the electronics cabinets(s). The transducer array for each sonar comprises a fixed cylindrical configuration of transducer elements in vertical staves. The staves are designed for maximum reliability and are independently sealed against water. The sonar dome is of glass reinforced plastic and conforms to an optimum hydronamic shape to provide good flow and cavitation. An acoustic baffle reduces the effects of propellor noise and internal reflections.

Transmit beam steering/widening is provided by multiple transmitters which incorporate an element of system redundancy. The transmitted pulse may be either linear period modulated (LPM) or continuous wave (CW). LPM with a one second duration is the normal mode since it offers a good range resolution and high detection capability over a wide range of sonar conditions. CW can be selected at will in conditions of high reverberation of known low target strength to give improved detection of moving targets. Another important feature of the PMS 40 series is the ability to operate in active and passive modes simultaneously. Echo signals received at the transducer array are, therefore, separated into active and passive processing channels. In both active and passive modes, half beam pairs are formed to allow later extraction of fine bearing information. The system can be modified to allow transmission of a composite LPM/CW pulse plus simultaneous processing of LPM and doppler data. This provides further aid to classification on initial contact without the need to select an alternative mode.

The single-operator dual-display console incorporates raster scan colour viewing units mounted one above the other in an ergonomically designed layout. Three display formats are available, two of which, 'Active LPM' and 'Doppler CW', are presented as alternatives, normally on the lower viewing unit. The 'Passive' format is usually presented on the upper unit. The units are identical and the formats can be interchanged. All display-data is normally north-stabilised but can be stabilised to an alternative operator-selected bearing. Automatic tracking of up to ten active contacts can be made and

PMS 40 console

PMS 42 transducer array

data on these is presented on the 'tote' at the bottom of the display.

All sonars in the PMS 40 series are provided with a digital interface to the ship's AIO or command system.

STATUS
In late development.
CONTRACTOR
Plessey Marine, Templecombe, Somerset BA8 0DH, England.

4127.453
TYPE 2034 SONAR

The Waverley sonar Type 2034 is a short range, high definition, dual side-scan sonar, suitable for establishing the position of ships, aircraft or other objects lost at sea; for charting obstructions in shipping channels or at sea floor engineering sites; and for evaluating underwater topography. Designed for the utmost reliability and to meet exacting military standards, Type 2034 sonars have been in use with the Royal Navy since 1976. The system is now standard equipment on all ocean going and coastal vessels of the survey fleet.

The sideways-looking, left and right, transducers are housed in a towed body, called the 'towfish', the current version of which is the Mk 3. Some of the electronics are contained in the towfish but the majority of this part of the system is housed in the recorder unit which provides for operation and control of the equipment, and display by hard copy, print-out chart recordings. Three models of recorder unit are available:
(1) recorder E1, is operated manually with panel controls for adjusting the quality of recordings
(2) recorder E2, retains all of the manual controls of

the E1 recorder, but with the option of microprocessor control of the signal processing electronics permitting 'hands off' operation
(3) recorder E3, is microprocessor controlled. Manual control is provided only for the initial setting of the threshold of printing. The E3 incorporates a self-test facility.

The sonar operating frequency is 110 kHz with a nominal transmitted pulse length of 100 microseconds. A choice of three range scales, 75, 150 or 300 m and one of three recording paper speeds, 30, 60 or 150 lines/cm can be selected to suit the prevailing operating conditions. The transmission repetition rate depends on the selected range scale, and is 10 pps for 75 m range, 5 pps for 150 m range or 2·5 pps for 300 m range. For all range settings, scale lines are recorded at 15 m range intervals, to aid interpretation of the recordings. Facilities are provided for putting event markers on the recording.
STATUS
In production and operational with the Royal Navy and other services.
CONTRACTOR
Waverley Electronics Ltd, Waverley Road, Weymouth, Dorset, England.

Photograph taken from a recording by a Type 2034 sonar showing the British submarine M2 lying at 18 fathoms in West Bay, off the Dorset coast. The M2 was the first submarine to carry an aircraft and sank in 1932 with the loss of 60 lives

---

4625.253
FMS SERIES SONAR SYSTEMS

The FMS (Ferranti Modular Sonar) family is a range of all-digital processing systems using a modular concept for low cost and high performance. The range consists of four basic systems:
(1) FMS 12 two-octave narrowband passive sonar
(2) FMS 15 five-octave narrowband passive sonar
(3) FMS 20 active sonar
(4) FMS 31 broadband passive sonar.

A major feature of the range is its modular approach which allows the systems to be configured from a number of standard units which simplifies

installation, in-service support and future system enhancement. The equipments can operate with a wide range of new and existing transducer arrays and use advanced digital signal processing and distributed computer processing techniques.

The FMS 12 is the basic set which operates with a two-octave towed array and provides narrowband surveillance and analysis facilities. It provides 360-degree bearing cover, 32-beam resolution, automatic tracking of designated targets, single multiple-beam display for surveillance and high resolution vernier analysis for classification. Dual 1000-line TV displays are normally monochrome but colour displays can be

used and the resolution can be increased to 2048 lines per frame, with 2048 pixels per line. In the processing system distributed Argus M700 computers connected internally by Eurobus and using Coral and Mascot software, are claimed to provide a much greater processing power than current systems.

The FMS 15 is a more sophisticated version for use with a five-octave towed array while the FM 31 is a broadband passive system. The active sonar member of the family is the FMS 20 and a version of it with facilities for the use of a towed array out of the end of the VDS is believed to be in development.

CONTRACTOR
Ferranti Computer Systems Ltd, Cheadle Heath Division, Bird Hall Lane, Cheadle Heath, Stockport, Cheshire SK3 0XQ, England.

FMS series universal console

4452.453
MARCONI MINEHUNTING AND SURVEILLANCE SONAR

The Marconi minehunting and surveillance sonar is a fast scanning system designed for a variety of requirements in minehunting, submersible detection, harbour surveillance and underwater navigation.

The sonar consists of an acoustic projector, a

Marconi small ship minehunting sonar housed in towed submersible body

circular acoustic array of 100 plastic transducer elements (electronically beam formed to sweep rapidly and repeatedly through 360°), processing electronics and a CRT display. The polarised plastic transducers are capable of operation over a very wide range frequency band so that the frequency, and therefore, the range capability, can be changed during operation.

The transducer head of the equipment operates at one of two frequencies selected on the controls. The higher frequency of 250 kHz gives a greater azimuth resolution of 1·1° and is used primarily for high resolution work at ranges out to 150 m. The lower frequency of 83·3 kHz is usable at all ranges out to 1·2 km with a lower azimuth resolution of 3·3°.

In the minehunting role the equipment consists of:
(a) a 'wet end' housing the acoustic projector, receiver amplifiers, multiplexer and power supplies. Full electronic stabilisation is provided
(b) a 'dry end' module containing the controls, decoder, beam-former display electronics and a radar type PPI display.

The wet end may be either hull-mounted or housed in a towed submersible unit depending on individual user requirements. The sonar may be used when the ship is in harbour or at anchor to give warning of underwater saboteurs.

For harbour surveillance purposes up to four sonar heads can be deployed, cabled together to provide

the requisite coverage across a harbour entrance. A mobile control centre, with all the displays and electronics, is normally mounted in a completely self-contained cabin/caravan with its own power supplies and deployment aids. In this role the detection ranges of each sonar head covers up to 1·2 km radius. Divers and chariots can be tracked out to distances of 400 m and mini-submarines up to 1·2 km.

The system produces a high resolution radar type PPI display with a fast refresh rate (typically one second) by means of an entirely solid-state electronic scan.

CHARACTERISTICS
Size: (Towed body) 1·2 m long × 0·32 m diameter; (Static surveillance unit) 1·3 m long × 0·57 m diameter
Weight: (Towed body) 90 kg; (Static unit) 132 kg
Operating frequency: 83·3 kHz and 250 kHz
Range scales: 0 – 9 m, 18 m, 37 m, 75 m, 150 m, 300 m, 600 m, 1200 m
Range resolution: 1·1° azimuth × 90 mm range at 250 kHz; 3·3° azimuth × 90 mm range at 83·3 kHz
Towing speed: Any speed from 0 – 5 knots
Field cover: 360° × 15° elevation
STATUS
One equipment, for underwater surveillance purposes, was delivered to the UK MoD in mid 1983.
CONTRACTOR
Marconi Underwater Systems Ltd, Elettra Avenue, Waterlooville, Hampshire PO7 7XS, England.

4626.453
MARCONI AREA DEFENCE SONAR

Marconi has designed a 360-degree sonar based on the minehunting and surveillance system described under **4452.453**. It has been specifically designed for extended range performance; the longer detection ranges provide much greater surveyed area using a single sonar head.

The system is available in both single and multiple frequency versions. Single fixed frequency versions are factory preset to one of three (high, low or mid) frequencies. The higher frequency version (68 Hz) is optimised for diver and free swimmer detection out to 500 metres from the sonar head, the low frequency (23 Hz) for submarine detection up to 3 km, and the mid-frequency (33 Hz) for well-balanced performance between the two. The multiple frequency

version covers all three ranges and allows the operator to select any one frequency in the field. The sonar head is designed for either bottom mounting or for mid-water flotation using an attachable conformal low drag buoy.

The system produces a high resolution radar type PPI display with a fast refresh rate (typically one second) by means of a solid-state electronic scan. It will also provide a CCTV standard picture for transmission to remote monitors.

CHARACTERISTICS
Azimuth field cover: 360°
Azimuth resolution: 1·6°; 3·4°; 4·6°
Typical detection ranges
High frequency: 500 m (diver); 1 km (submarine)
Mid-frequency: 300 m (diver); 1·5 km (submarine)
Low frequency: 200 m (diver); 3 km (submarine)

Sonar head size: 0·75 m diameter × 0·68 m height
Sonar head weight: 130 kg (in air)
STATUS
In development.
CONTRACTOR
Marconi Underwater Systems Ltd, Elettra Avenue, Waterlooville, Hampshire PO7 7XS, England.

3769.453
DEL RANGER (SSQ-47B) SONOBUOY

The DEL Ranger is an omni-directional active sonobuoy, based on an American design, the AN/SSQ-47B, and intended for use in the detection, classification, tracking, and location of submarines. It is slightly lighter than the US model, but in most other respects the performance and operational characteristics are believed to be very similar. For comparison, see **1988.453**, later in this section.
CHARACTERISTICS
Type: Active
Length: 914 mm
Diameter: 124 mm
Weight: 13·2 kg
Transducer depth: 60 or 800 ft (18 or 244 m)
Sonar channels: 6 in 13-19 kHz band

Sonar power output: 200 W approx
Duration: 0·5 h
RF power output: 0·25 W
RF channels: 12
STATUS
Production against UK MoD contracts commenced in 1980.
CONTRACTOR
Dowty Electronics Ltd, Communications Division, 419 Bridport Road, Greenford Industrial Estate, Greenford, Middlesex UB6 8UA, England.

Current DEL sonobuoy production range showing (rear from left to right) Jezebel, Ranger (SSQ-47B), and CAMBS, with the new miniature bathythermal sonobuoy (left) and the miniature Jezebel sonobuoy (right) in front

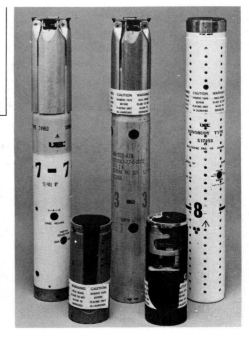

3502.453
JEZEBEL SONOBUOY

Jezebel is the code name for the standard A-size omni-directional passive sonobuoy system used by the Royal Air Force and the Royal Navy for the detection of submerged submarines. Most details remain classified but it has been stated that these sonobuoys have improved frequency response, a

choice of three life settings and a deep hydrophone system which allows various operating depths to be selected.

STATUS
Many thousands of DEL Jezebel sonobuoys have been produced for the British forces over a period of years, and production is continuing, although contracts have been awarded for the newer miniature

passive sonobuoy which is about one-third the length of the standard item (**3503.453**).
CONTRACTOR
Dowty Electronics Ltd, Communications Division, 419 Bridport Road, Greenford Industrial Estate, Greenford, Middlesex UB6 8UA, England.

3503.453
MINIATURE JEZEBEL SONOBUOY TYPE SSQ904

This sonobuoy is designed to be launched from aircraft or helicopters at airspeeds between 60 and 325 knots and at altitudes between about 50 and 3000 m. Once deployed, it detects and amplifies underwater sounds to modulate the self-contained FM transmitter. The FM signals are received by the aircraft processor, which is currently the AN/AQA-5 system, but the sonobuoy is fully compatible with all known processors currently being designed,

including the Marconi AQS 901, AQS 902 and AQS 903.

A significant feature is the fact that this buoy is only about one-third the length of a standard A-size sonobuoy, and half the weight, yet is claimed to have precisely the same performance characteristics.
CHARACTERISTICS
Type: Miniature passive omni-directional
Frequency coverage: 10 Hz – 3 kHz
Hydrophone depth: Selectable from either 60 or 300 ft (18 or 91 m); or 60 or 450 ft (18 or 137 m)

Operating life: 1, 4, or 8 h
RF channels: 99 or 31
RF output: 1 W minimum
Dimensions: 30·5 × 12·5 cm (diameter)
Weight: 4·5 kg
STATUS
Production for UK forces commenced in 1980.
CONTRACTOR
Dowty Electronics Ltd, Communications Division, 419 Bridport Road, Greenford Industrial Estate, Greenford, Middlesex UB6 8UA, England.

3237.453
XI7255 COMMAND ACTIVE MULTI-BEAM SONOBUOY (SSQ 963)

The XI7255 command active multi-beam sonobuoy (CAMBS) is a new A-size sonobuoy developed by Dowty Electronics under contract to the British Ministry of Defence. It was first revealed at the 1976 Farnborough Air Show.

CAMBS is an advanced active directional sonobuoy, which features a high data rate, and directional information is obtained by the use of a transmitting acoustic projector combined with a

directional receiving hydrophone array. Hydrophone depth is adjustable by radio command and there is a 31-channel radio telemetry link operating on standard NATO frequencies for communication with the parent aircraft. The antenna is a monopole with ground plane, erected by and integral with the buoy flotation bag. The design incorporates a flux-gate compass with very rapid stabilisation.
CHARACTERISTICS
Length: 914 mm
Diameter: 124 mm
Weight: 15·9 kg

Transducer depth: Adjustable
RF channels: 31
STATUS
The new sonobuoy is part of the equipment developed for the Mk II version of the Nimrod ASW aircraft. Full production was achieved during 1980.
CONTRACTOR
Dowty Electronics Ltd, Communications Division, 419 Bridport Road, Greenford Industrial Estate, Greenford, Middlesex UB6 8UA, England.

3770.453
DEL MINIATURE BATHYTHERMAL BUOY (SSQ 937)

This miniature bathythermal buoy is the second 'A' size buoy to have been reduced by Dowty to the new 'F' size (A/3). It provides all the facilities of the SSQ-36 but is only one third of its size and half the weight.
CHARACTERISTICS
Length: 305 mm

Diameter: 124 mm
Weight: 5 kg
Operating depth: To 427 m
Descent rate: 1·5 m/s (to 305 m)
Temperature range: –2 to +35° C
Gradient accuracy: ±20%
Modulation frequencies: 1360 – 2700 Hz
Probe time constant: >1 s
RF power output: 0·25 W

STATUS
In full series production against UK MoD contracts.
CONTRACTOR
Dowty Electronics Ltd, Communications Division, 419 Bridport Road, Greenford Industrial Estate, Greenford, Middlesex UB6 8UA, England.

3789.453
PLESSEY-SIPPICAN XBT AND XSV

The Plessey-Sippican expendable bathythermo-graph (XBT) is a surface ship and submarine bathythermograph equipment which uses an expendable probe to obtain accurate and continuous ocean temperature against ocean depth measurements. These can be made in any sea state at ship speeds of up to 56 km/h (30 knots).

The Plessey-Sippican expendable sound velocimeter (XSV) is a new development which reduces the difficulties of direct collection of sound velocity data at sea. This system measures sound velocity directly with the ease and accuracy associated with the well known XBT system.

STATUS
XBT is in service with the Royal Navy and has been sold to over 20 countries. The XSV is now being adopted for service in a number of navies.
CONTRACTOR
Plessey Marine, Templecombe, Somerset BA8 0DH, England, under licence from The Sippican Corporation, Marion, Massachusetts 02738, USA.

XBT/XSV Mk 8 recorder

5638.263
PMS 75 SPEEDSCAN

The PMS 75 Speedscan is a self-contained equipment for ships already fitted with a compatible sonar system. It allows the sonar system to be operated in a sidescan mode and generates a hard copy printout of the sea bed. It can be fitted to all types of mine-hunting sonar.

When the sonar is operating with Speedscan, its transducer is trained 90 degrees to port or starboard of the ship's track. As the ship proceeds along a predetermined track, an area of sea bed, parallel to the track, is interrogated by the sonar. The received sonar data and reference timing signals are fed to the Speedscan processor which forms a sidescan beam and presents the processed data as hard copy on continuous recording paper.

The Speedscan equipment consists of two main assemblies, each contained in a portable case. In use the two cases are stacked and locked together with the end covers removed. The upper case houses the processor and the operator's control panel, the lower case the recorder unit.

Speedscan presents information on light-sensitive paper exposed in the recorder. On the record, the sea bed is represented as a series of parallel narrow strips of selected length, perpendicular to the ship's track. The sonar data from the whole azimuth sector scanned by the sonar is extracted by Speedscan to represent a narrow strip of sea bed along the sonar beam axis. This data is extracted by the beamformer to generate a parallel beam of sufficient width to overlap the strips covered by the two previous transmissions, so providing the 3-ping sample of each point of the sea bed along the range axis. The beamforming system is programmed by ship's speed and sonar range to provide a controlled interrogation of the sea bed. This information is used to intensify and modulate a light source in the recorder which draws a line across the record for each sonar transmission, echoes appearing as dark spots on the recording paper.
CONTRACTOR
Plessey Marine, Templecombe, Somerset BA8 0DH, England.

PMS 75 Speedscan

4681.273
NAUTIS-M SYSTEM

Nautis-M is an integrated navigation and action information system to provide the command, control and navigation facilities required for naval mine countermeasures. The Nautis (Naval Autonomous Information System) family of systems is modular in design and uses distributed processing rather than a central computer. The family consists of 10 versions, with applications in a wide variety of ships from aircraft carriers to small offshore patrol boats. It can be a single console/single operator system in the smaller type of vessel to a comprehensive multi-operator, multi-console equipment for larger ships. It has been developed by Plessey in association with CAP Scientific Ltd, the latter supplying all the software.

Nautis-M can consist of one, two or three consoles to meet the specific operational requirements and provides an effective method of co-ordinating and controlling the detection, classification and disposal of mines. The system takes in data from navigation, radar and sonar sensors, acts on this data and provides a variety of information and control. This includes operational planning, ship control guidance, a continuous record of own ship movements and sonar coverage, updated underwater and surface pictures, command and control facilities for mine countermeasures and comprehensive operational records.

Presentation is on a 'scissored-screen' viewing unit which combines plan-position display and computer data. Information is presented on mine countermeasures route boundaries, mine danger zones, own ship position, planned search path, current sonar coverage, hunted path, mine disposal vehicle position, and sub-surface contact and environmental data. A raster type screen can also be provided to give facilities for the simultaneous display of other information.

STATUS
Nautis-M has been ordered by the UK MoD for fitment to the Royal Navy's new single-role minehunters.
CONTRACTOR
Plessey Displays Ltd, Addlestone, Weybridge, Surrey KT15 2PW.

4453.363
ARR 901 SONAR RECEIVER

The ARR 901 is a multi-channel sonar receiver of modular construction for use in fixed wing maritime patrol aircraft. It simultaneously receives eight VHF channels which are selected by serialised digital commands from a processor or control unit. Advanced filter technology, extensive use of hybrid circuits and wideband techniques ensure high availability. An antenna preamplifier unit gives a low noise figure and the system's high dynamic range and wide bandwidth enables high speed telemetry data to be received.

The receiver provides its full RF performance when installed at up to 50 m from the preamplifier. All interfaces are to ARINC specification 404A. Outputs are compatible with existing aircraft data processing systems and with more advanced systems under development. A built-in test signal generator provides extensive check facilities for the receiver and associated processing equipment and is designed to facilitate servicing by automatic test equipment.
CHARACTERISTICS
Frequency band: 134·5 – 174·625 MHz
Frequency stability: ±3 ppm (at –26° C to +45° C-ambient temperature)

No of channels: 8
Channel coverage: 101 rf channels plus two test channels
Channel spacing: 375 kHz
Input impedance: 50Ω
Modulation: FM/FSK
CONTRACTOR
Marconi Underwater Systems Ltd, Elettra Way, Waterlooville, Hampshire PO7 7XS, England.

5654.363
MOSAIC ASW INTEGRATED SYSTEM

MOSAIC is an ASW mission avionics system designed to integrate the numerous sensors and navigation sub-sensors required in modern maritime and surveillance aircraft. It is intended for both fixed- and rotary-wing aircraft and allows selection of sensor and navigation sub-systems to meet particular requirements, and has the ability to obtain the benefits of an integrated system even when the sub-systems are of varying design standards. A major advantage is that multi-function controls and multi-purpose displays can replace the variety of individual controls and displays which are normally dedicated to each sub-system.

Suitable interfaces, controls and displays and data processors can be supplied together with a wide range of proven software to make the MOSAIC system particularly versatile. Use of a data highway between system elements, to interchange information, reduces hard wiring to a minimum and eases changes or additions to the system once installed. Using this type of integration system the wide choice of sensor options normally only available on larger aircraft can also be applied to smaller aircraft.

STATUS
In production.
CONTRACTOR
Marconi Avionics Ltd, Airport Works, Rochester, Kent ME1 2XX, England.

4624.453
PLESSEY ACOUSTIC INTRUDER DETECTION SYSTEM

The Plessey Acoustic Intruder Detection and Harbour Surveillance system is intended for a variety of safety and security purposes. It provides coverage of jetty and harbour areas against swimmers, surface and subsurface craft by an automatic detection and alarm system. It is a totally intergrated system employing acoustic elements, radar and communications linked to a central command console.

Swimmer detection and craft location form the primary acoustic elements, the frequencies and coverage of these being matched to the environment and mission requirements. The secondary acoustic elements comprise an acoustic fence and VHF system. The fence provides within-harbour security and preliminary warning of possible violation.
STATUS
Early design stage.
CONTRACTOR
Plessey Marine, Wilkinthroop House, Templecombe, Somerset BA8 0DH, England.

4627.463
AMEECO TOWED ARRAYS

Ameeco Hydrospace Ltd has been the main supplier of towed arrays to the defence industry for some years and has supplied all the arrays for the Royal Navy surface ships and submarines. No details are available on technical construction but the company is now concentrating on arrays for the next RN requirement in this field, the Type 2031 and 2046 sonar systems. Although this is the next requirement, Ameeco is also carrying out research into increased performance and improvements that can be brought about by multiplexing, fibre optics, etc.

Ameeco is engaged in a number of other products in the underwater field such as seismic arrays for survey, torpedo firing systems, sound velocity meters and the design and supply of underwater cable assemblies. A subsidiary, Geophysical Systems Ltd, has produced an underwater orientation sensor for use in remote equipment to measure and transmit the heading, pitch and roll angles of the body in which it is positioned.
CONTRACTOR
Ameeco Hydrospace Ltd, Oceanographic and Marine Division, 2 North Way, Andover, Hampshire SP10 5AZ, England.

4628.063
MUSL SONAR PRODUCTS

The Sonar Division of GEC-McMichael, which was taken over by Marconi Underwater Systems Ltd in April 1984, designs and manufactures a wide range of underwater detection products. These include ASW sonobuoy telemetry systems, hydrophones and arrays, advanced signal processing equipment and displays, and an intercept processing system.

Sonobuoy telemetry equipment can be used in fixed and rotary wing aircraft. Sonobuoy receiver systems being supplied are the ARR 901 receiver and command transmitter (**4453.463**), AQS 901 sonic systems for the RAF Nimrod and RAAF P3C aircraft, and Type 843 receivers for the AQS 902 system on the RN Sea King helicopters. A miniaturised derivative is under development for the EH 101 ASW helicopter (Sea King replacement).

An add-on broadband processing system has been produced for the Type 2024 submarine towed array sonar and lightweight processing and display systems for submarine use are in the design stage. The intercept processing system uses a new approach to the problems of random noise and incident wave reflection by automatically storing and comparing all acoustic sources to establish real or false signals compared with noise. The system is automatic until an active sonar is detected when an alarm is activated and a continuous indication of bearing, elevation and range (signal level) is given on a command display.
CONTRACTOR
Marconi Underwater Systems Ltd, Elettra Way, Waterlooville, Hampshire PO7 7XS, England.

4679.453

THORN EMI UNDERWATER ACOUSTIC RANGES AND SYSTEMS

Thorn EMI Electronics has a range of underwater acoustic systems from simple location transmitters and receivers, through acoustic altimeters to complete three dimensional tracking and navigation systems. Permanent, semi-permanent and portable installations are available.

In permanent installations, sea-bed mounted hydrophones are connected by cable to a shore-based control station and tracking is accurately referred to local geography. Where permanent installations are not possible, generally because of shallow water, a semi-permanent system may be used in which the hyrophones are deployed from a surface vessel and data is telemetered by radio to a permanent or portable shore station. In the fully portable system, hydrophone assemblies are suspended from flotation units on the surface, which are tethered to moored buoys, and data is telemetered to the control station housed in a transportable cabin, either ship or shore based. The mooring buoys are semi-permanent, and to operate the range the flotation units and hydrophone assemblies are deployed from a small boat. Such a system enables the location to be changed with the minimum of trouble and expense.

The principal items of control equipment are radio, signal processors, X-Y plotter, magnetic tape recorder, depth display, teleprinter and electronics to generate the synchronising pulses to the range. System functions are controlled from a console and a real-time plot produces symbols denoting the positions of underwater vehicles being tracked, their

Torpedo Centred Tracker

depth being shown on a digital read-out. All data is recorded and the teleprinter gives a printout of the X, Y and Z co-ordinates.

All systems can be used in conjunction with Thorn EMI's deep mobile target (**4680.493**) or with static targets. Several vehicles can be plotted simultaneously and the system gives a record of the target and the performance of each weapon or ship involved in the exercise.

Target Centred Tracker (TCT)

This is a short base line system used to evaluate the performance of exercise torpedoes against submarine targets in the final phase of the attack. Two 4-hydrophone arrays are mounted on the submarine hull and received signals are cabled in-board to the processing equipment.

Fuze Actuating Static Target (FAST)

This equipment deploys tracking hydrophones in an array similar to TCT and consists of a framework

providing a suitable magnetic signature to actuate weapon fuzes at close range and on acoustic targets for homing.

Distance Measuring Equipment (DME)

DME enables the slant range between a static or mobile acoustic transmitter and a receiving hydrophone to be measured with high precision.

Acoustic Transmitters

Various acoustic transmitters can be provided. DME Pinger is an acoustic pulse transmitter with a 2-wire arrangement for power supply and trigger signal which simplifies hull penetration on submarines. Various frequencies are available to suit tracking range standard. A dual-frequency version offering operational versatility between range has been developed.

Synchronised Acoustic Transmitter (SAT) is an equipment configured as a torpedo hull section for weapon tracking. It is self-contained and has an array of acoustic transducers mounted on the hull section to produce an optimised beam pattern.

STATUS

TCT and FAST have been supplied to UK MoD and negotiations with other navies are underway. Portable acoustic ranges have been supplied to the UK MoD, the Japanese Defence Agency and the Italian Navy. DME processing units were designed for the UK MoD and are incorporated in UK range systems. DME type acoustic transmitters and SAT have been supplied to the UK MoD, and SAT has also been supplied to Italy, Germany and Japan.

CONTRACTOR

Thorn EMI Electronics Ltd, Defence Systems Division, Albert Drive, Sheerwater, Woking, Surrey GU21 5RU, England.

4680.493

DEEP MOBILE TARGET

The Deep Mobile Target (DMT) is a fully instrumented self-contained, unmanned ship-launched vehicle for use on ASW trials and training exercises to simulate the dynamic and acoustic characteristics of submarines and carry out pre-programmed manoeuvres. As well as being a trials and training facility, it is intended as a deep diving mobile torpedo target to avoid the costs, risks and delays associated with weapon trials against a submarine.

DMT is supplied to meet individual requirements for frequencies. It normally carries two sonar/sonics outfits which are interchangeable at base. When used in conjunction with a three dimensional underwater tracking system it is fitted with a SAT Type 5 (**4679.493**) acoustic transmitter for compatability with US, German, Italian and Japanese tracking ranges. A miss-distance indicator is incorporated.

DMT is claimed to be easy to handle and recover with high availability and reliability. The recovery system is initiated by command, failure of the propulsion battery, by being outside the preset depth limits or by program tape breakage.

CHARACTERISTICS

Length: 3·28 metres
Diameter: 0·324 metres
Weight: 236 kg
Speeds: Stop, 8, 14 and 22 knots
Endurance: From 100 minutes at 8 knots to 8 minutes at 22 knots
Depth: 355 metres (1165 feet)
STATUS

DMT was developed in conjunction with the United Kingdom Admiralty Underwater Weapons Establishment and has been supplied to the UK MoD and several other naval authorities.

CONTRACTOR

Thorn EMI Electronics Ltd, Defence Systems Division, Albert Drive, Sheerwater, Woking, Surrey GU21 5RU, England.

Deep Mobile Target ready for launch

UNITED STATES OF AMERICA

3777.363

AN/AKT-22(V)4 TELEMETRY DATA TRANSMITTING SET

The AN/AKT-22(V)4 telemetry data transmitting set forms an essential element of an airborne ASW installation for the operation of sonobuoys and the relaying of sonobuoy data to co-operating ASW surface vessels.

Two AN/ARR-75 radio receiving sets are included in the airborne element, providing eight VHF receiving channels. This configuration permits relay of up to eight passive sonobuoy transmissions, up to six channels of R-O, and passive data of which up to four channels may be R-O, or two channels of DIFAR sonobuoy data. An air-to-ship voice channel is available except when the DIFAR mode is used. The AN/AKT-22(V)4 produced by EDMAC consists of the following major units:

(1) transmitter-multiplexer T-1220B

(2) control indicator C-8988A
(3) antenna AS-3033
(4) actuator TG-229.

The multiplexer section of transmitter-multiplexer T-1220B/AKT-22(V)4 uses low-pass filters and VCOs to provide the eight-channel capability. The trigger filter assembly for this set is located in control indicator C-8988A/AKT-22(V)4. Setting any of the trigger-select switches on the control-indicator to the ON position disables data channels 3C and 4C. Composite trigger tones are brought into the multiplexer on a separate line and combined with the sonic and voice channels at the mixer-amplifier to form the composite FM modulation signal. This composite signal FM modulates the transmitter.

In the DIFAR operating mode, the composite FM modulation signal is disconnected from the transmitter input. Two DIFAR sonobuoy transmissions, received on dedicated receiver

channels are demodulated in the receivers and are provided to the transmitter-multiplexer. The receiver output is conditioned in an amplifier-adapter and the DIFAR-A sonic signal is conditioned in a low-pass filter. The DIFAR-B sonic signal is used to drive a VCO centred at 70 kHz and then passes through a bandpass filter. The two filter outputs are linearly combined, and the composite modulation signal is coupled to the transmitter input when the control-indicator mode select switch is in DIFAR position. Composite sonic or composite DIFAR input to the transmitter is selected by a relay in the DIFAR filter controlled by a switch in the control-indicator.

The shipboard receiving equipment required for the eight-channel data link is telemetric data receiving set AN/SKR-( ). The receiver demodulates and demultiplexes the composite sonic or DIFAR transmission, and routes the separate outputs to appropriate processing equipment.

CHARACTERISTICS
Transmitter-multiplexer (T-1220B) and control indicator (C-8988A)
Operating modes
(1) standby mode, which turns on and applies power to multiplexer circuits
(2) operate mode, which applies operational power to transmitter and enables multiplexing and transmitting of active data, passive data and voice signals
(3) DIFAR mode, which enables multiplexing and transmitting of 2 composite DIFAR signals.
Operating stability: Over 100 h (continuous or intermittent operation)
Output frequencies: 2·200 – 2·290 GHz, one of 20 switch-selectable S-band channels.
Frequency accuracy: ±0·003% of specified unmodulated carrier frequency.
Multiplexer inputs
(1) 8 sonic/sonar data channels (7 with 10 – 2000 Hz bandwidth; 1 with 10 – 2800 Hz bandwidth), 0·16 – 16·0 V rms
(2) 4 sonar trigger channels, 26 kHz' – 38 kHz, 1·0 – 3·0 V rms

(3) 1 voice channel, 300 – 2000 Hz bandwidth, 0 – 0·25 V rms
(4) 2 composite DIFAR signal channels, 10 Hz – 20 kHz bandwidth; 3·6 V rms or 10·6 V rms nominal, switch-selectable to interface with AN/ARR-52A through AM-6695/AKT-22(V) or with AN/ARR-75 directly.
Multiplexer scaling: Input scaling is adjusted so that 16 V rms will cause full-scale deviation of VCO channels.
Channel phase correlation: Difference in phase delay between any 2 passive data channels is less than 1° (10 – 500 Hz)
Antenna AS-3033
Polarisation: Vertical
Radiation pattern: Omni-directional in azimuth plane
Transmitting element frequency range: 2200 – 2290 MHz
RF power: 100 W max
Receiving element frequency range: Standard VHF sonobuoy channels
STATUS
In production.

Two main elements of the EDMAC AN/AKT-22(V)4 telemetry data transmitting set: transmitter-multiplexer (T-1220B) left, and control-indicator (C-8988A) right

CONTRACTOR
EDMAC Corporation, 7500 Main Street, PO Box 750, Fishers, New York 14453-0750, USA.

4013.373
AN/ASA-66 TACTICAL DATA DISPLAY
The AN/ASA-66 is a multipurpose cockpit display for the P-3 Orion maritime patrol aircraft. A 9 inch (23 cm) diameter CRT provides pilot and co-pilot with real-time presentation of tactical situations. Graphic and alpha-numeric data are presented on the high brightness and contrast screen for viewing in either high ambient or controlled lighting conditions. The display is designed to be driven from a remote display generator to provide analogue deflection and video drive from computer data or direct from aircraft sensors.
STATUS
In operational service.
CONTRACTOR
Loral Electronic Systems, 999 Central Park Avenue, Yonkers, New York 10704, USA.

AN/ASA-66 tactical data display group

4012.373
AN/ASA-82 TACTICAL DATA DISPLAY SYSTEM
The AN/ASA-82 tactical data display system (TDS) is the primary data display for the US Navy S-3A Viking maritime aircraft. It serves as a real-time link between the four-man crew and the various electronic sensors which the aircraft carries for its task of maritime reconnaissance and anti-submarine warfare. High speed, high density data in the form of alpha-numeric symbols, vectors, conic projections and other appropriate display formats from both acoustic and non-acoustic sensors are presented to the crew. Information is stored, updated and refreshed by the on-board general-purpose digital computer and selectively displayed. Tactical and tabular data, controlled by the computer, are routed to the display via the display generator unit (DGU), which also provides the computer with display fault status information on a priority basis, controls the routing of display information, and generates the system built-in test functions.

The equipment consists of five CRT displays in addition to the DGU. The TACCO and SENSO (tactical co-ordinator and sensor operator) are each provided with identical multipurpose display units in their respective consoles. In addition, the SENSO has a multipurpose display, and the pilot has a display which presents a summary tactical plot. The DGU provides all of the displays with digital computer data except the ARU which receives acoustic data direct from the acoustic data processor.

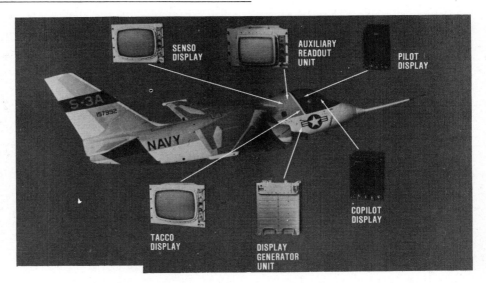

US Navy S-3A Viking ASW/maritime patrol aircraft, showing the location of the various items of equipment comprising the AN/ASA-82 tactical data display system

STATUS
In operational service.
CONTRACTOR
Loral Electronic Systems, 999 Central Park Avenue, Yonkers, New York 10704, USA.

1982.363
AN/AYA-8B ASW DATA PROCESSING SYSTEM
Since 1968, the General Electric Company has been producing the P-3C data processing system (DPS). The DPS equipment constitutes a major portion of the P-3C anti-submarine aircraft avionics.

The purpose of the AN/AYA-8B DPS is to provide an interface between the central computer and other aircraft systems. The main aircraft systems consist of the tactical co-ordinator (TACCO) station, non-acoustical sensor station, navigation communications (NAV/COM) station, acoustical sensor stations, pilot station, radar interface unit, armament/ordnance system, navigation systems, ARR-72 receivers (**3454.263**), submarine anomaly detector, and OMEGA. The DPS consists of four major logic units, as well as a selection of manual keysets and panels.
LOGIC UNIT 1 provides an interface to four types of peripheral information systems:
(1) manual entry
(2) system status

(3) sonobuoy receiver
(4) auxiliary readout display.

The manual entry sub-system provides the communication between the operator stations and the central computer of the man/machine interface. Each operator has a complex of illuminated switches and indicators by which he communicates with the central computer.

System status is received and stored by the status logic sub-unit of logic unit 1 and transmitted to the central computer. The status words are transmitted whenever any status bit changes or upon interrogation by the computer.

The sonobuoy receiver logic provides for the digital tuning of the sonobuoy receiver sub-system by the central computer. Each of the 20 receiver processor channels can be tuned to one of 31 RF cells by the central computer or manually by the operator.

The auxiliary readout display logic provides the digital interface between the computer and the ARO displays located at the TACCO station and the NAV/COM station.

LOGIC UNIT 2 provides digital communications to three major aircraft sub-systems:

(1) navigation
(2) armament/ordnance
(3) magnetic tape transports.

The interface between the central computer and the navigation system is provided by the navigation multiplexer sub-unit, which enables the computer to obtain data from the doppler radar set and two inertial navigation systems. An armament and ordnance interface provides the means for the central computer automatically to launch search and kill stores. The magnetic tape sub-system allows the computer to read and write digital information on magnetic tape transports.

LOGIC UNIT 3 provides the interface between the computer and three display sub-systems:

(1) TACCO multipurpose display
(2) sensor multipurpose display
(3) pilot display.

The TACCO multipurpose display logic sub-unit enables the computer to present characters, vectors, and conics on the TACCO display to assist the TACCO operator. A sensor multipurpose display logic sub-unit provides the same capability as the TACCO except that conics cannot be displayed on the sensor display. The pilot display logic provides the capability to present characters, vectors, and conics on the pilot's display.

LOGIC UNIT 4 provides for the expansion of the computer input/output capability by means of the data multiplexer sub-unit (DMS), furnishes an increased memory capacity by means of the drum auxiliary memory sub-unit (DAMS) and provides an interface between the computer and two aircraft sub-systems:

(1) OMEGA
(2) auxiliary display.

The DMS can service up to eight input and eight output peripherals as selected by the computer. One output channel is used by the auxiliary display logic (ADL) to provide the capability to present characters,

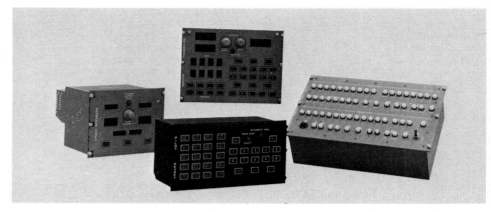

AN/AYA-8B pilot keyset (front) with (left to right) ordnance panel, universal keyset, and armament/ordnance panel

vectors, and conics on the auxiliary display. One input channel services the OMEGA sub-system and one input and output channel is used for diagnostic purposes. The remaining channels are available for future peripherals. The DAMS increases the memory available to the computer by 393 216 words so that the operational program can be expanded to accommodate additional functions and sub-systems.

Keysets and Panels

Three universal keysets provide the navigation/ communication operator and the two acoustic sensor operators with the capability of entering information into and receiving information from the computer program. The pilot keyset is used by the aircraft pilot to control information presented on his CRT display, to enter navigation stabilisation information into the computer, to drop or cause the dropping of smoke floats and weapons, and to enter information on visual contacts.

The ordnance panel is used to display commands from the computer to the ordnance operator concerning search stores, ie bin and chute number, and status information.

The armament/ordnance test panel provides the capability of monitoring each output to the aircraft armament and ordnance systems from the armament output logic unit and ordnance output logic sub-units of logic unit 2.

STATUS

In March 1978 General Electric received a USN contract worth $16·7 million to produce 14 AN/AYA-8B systems for use aboard P-3C aircraft as part of

AN/AYA-8B modernised logic units for the P-3C aircraft

'Update III' which adds new capabilities. Firstly an adaptive controlled phased-array antenna system, consisting of four antennas, is arranged in a diamond pattern on the underside of the aircraft fuselage. An advanced sonobuoy communications link receiver, presumably the AN/ARR-75(), is provided to extract data received from the sonobuoy signals, and also from simulated acoustic data on 99 radio frequencies to check the system on the ground. Finally an IBM Proteus acoustic analyser is added which processes the acoustic signals, and also determines whether the signals are produced by random ocean noise or by a source such as a submarine.

The first 'Update III' P-3C aircraft has been undergoing flight tests and production versions of the system were scheduled for delivery in May 1984.

CONTRACTOR

General Electric Company, Aircraft Equipment Division, French Road, Utica, New York 13503, USA.

3454.363

AN/ARR-72 SONOBUOY RECEIVING SET

The AN/ARR-72 sonobuoy receiver system is currently used on the P-3C patrol aircraft in conjunction with acoustic signal processors and a digital computer. The receiver system receives, amplifies, and demodulates frequency-modulated radio signals in the 162·25 to 173·5 MHz band transmitted by deployed sonobuoys. These radio signals contain information related to the frequency and directional pattern of the sound spectrum received by each sonobuoy hydrophone array. The baseband information from the receiver is demultiplexed and submitted to a special analysis and/or time correlation and doppler analysis by the acoustic signal processing equipment. Bathy-thermograph buoys and equipment enable determination of the seawater temperature for acoustic range measurement.

Monitoring of the RF level signals from the 31 on-line receivers enables the digital computer to perform many tactical functions such as the determination of the channel usage or presence of jamming prior to sonobuoy launching, connections of the proper

channel RF receiver to each processor, and a determination of remaining sonobuoy life. These same RF level monitoring and channel selection functions may also be accomplished manually through the use of the receiver control-indicator boxes located at the individual sensor stations.

The AN/ARR-72 system is compatible with LOFAR, CODAR, BT, RO, CASS, and DICASS equipment currently being deployed. Specific sonobuoy types include: AN/SSQ-36, AN/SSQ-41, AN/SSQ-47, AN/SSQ-50, AN/SSQ-53, and AN/SSQ-62.

The AN/ARR-72 sonobuoy receiver system is a dual conversion superheterodyne VHF receiver system designed for receiving FM signals from deployed sonobuoys. Radio frequency signals are received at the dual aircraft VHF blade antennas, amplified by the system's AM-4966 dual RF preamplifiers, and provided to the CH-619 31-channel receiver assembly. Within this assembly a multi-coupler distributes the preamplified RF to the 31 fixed tuned receivers where it is further amplified and demodulated to provide baseband audio and RF level signals.

The SA-1605 audio assembly accepts the baseband and RF level outputs of the 31 receivers and outputs them to the computer and processing equipment. Each of the 19 audio channels contains a 31 × 1 switching matrix to select the output of a given receiver. This receiver signal is then amplified and provided through two individually buffered outputs to the processing equipment. Selection of a particular receiver channel may be accomplished by the digital computer or the C-7617 dual channel control indicator. An individual 31 × 1 switching matrix is provided within the audio assembly to service the RF level requirements of the digital computer. This switching assembly is controlled by the computer and provides an integrated RF level for the selected receiver in a digital format upon computer interrogation.

STATUS

Operational. An advanced version sonobuoy receiver, probably the AN/ARR-75() is being supplied under the P-3C 'Update III' programme. See **3455.363** and **1982.363**.

3455.363
AN/ARR-75 SONOBUOY RECEIVER

The AN/ARR-75 is compatible with all FM sonobuoys in US Navy inventory or in development. Among the improvements incorporated in this receiver are:

(1) single-conversion, frequency-synthesised local oscillator
(2) extremely high dynamic range
(3) linear phase response over broad spectrum
(4) threshold extension of sensitivity through the use of phase-locked demodulation
(5) true, balanced, floating audio output
(6) extremely high rejection of interfering signals
(7) built-in antenna filter utilising helical resonator techniques.

The AN/ARR-75 receiving set was developed as a replacement for the AN/ARR-52A, but may be used to replace the AN/ARR-72. Four AN/ARR-75 equipments can provide the 16 simultaneous audio output channels required in some patrol aircraft configurations with significant size, weight and cost savings. System reliability is improved since any receiver can be tuned to any sonobuoy channel, thus overcoming the limitations of fixed-tuned receivers for each channel.

As a replacement for the AN/ARR-52A (Y configuration), the AN/ARR-75 provides a reduction in volume of approximately 3:1 and a reduction in weight of approximately 2:1. The solid-state design, the use of high reliability components and the use of fixed-tuned circuits to eliminate tuning adjustments has resulted in a tenfold improvement in reliability according to the manufacturer. Operational adequacy of this receiver has been extensively proven in the S2G aircraft. It is currently installed in SH-3H, SH-2F, and LAMPS Mk III.

The AN/ARR-75 receives, demodulates and amplifies FM sonobuoy transmissions in the VHF band between 162·25 and 173·5 MHz, and provides the demodulated output for analysis and display equipment. The receiver is a general-purpose multi-channel FM equipment suitable for use in fixed- or rotary-wing aircraft.

The equipment consists of two units: the receiver group assembly OR-69/ARR-75, in which are the majority of the necessary electronic modules, and the radio set control C-8658/ARR-75. Their respective weights are 9·75 kg and 1·13 kg.

A 99-channel version, the AN/ARR-75 ( ), is also available and probably forms part of 'Update III' to the P-3C aircraft sonar system (see **1982.365**). Export versions include the model R-75 (31 channels) and the model R-75 ( ) (99 channels).

STATUS
Production.
CONTRACTOR
EDMAC Corporation, 7500 Main Street, PO Box 750, Fishers, New York 14453-0750, USA.

4455.453
AN/WQC-2A SONAR COMMUNICATION SET

The AN/WQC-2A is a sonar underwater communication set for surface ships, submarines and shore installations. The system provides an SSB general voice and CW communication set consisting of a control station, remote control station, receiver/transmitter, and LF and HF transducers.

The system employs voice, audio and low speed telegraphy in two frequency bands: high (8·3 to 11·1 kHz) for close range and low (1·45 to 3·1 kHz) for long range. In addition the system facilitates the use, through separate input and output connectors, of a final transmitter amplifier in a frequency range of 100 kHz to 13 kHz.

The receiver/transmitter contains the main electronic assemblies of the sonar communication system. It consists of a rack-type cabinet with removable drawer assemblies containing the power supply and test panel assembly, the receiver/transmitter assembly and the final amplifier assembly. The primary functions of the receiver/transmitter are to develop the high-powered single sideband transmission from voice, audio and

Control and remote control stations for the AN/WQC-2A system

CW signals to drive the LF or HF transducers and to receive and demodulate signals received from the transducers. The receiver and transmitter outputs are made available to external tape recordings and monitoring equipment. The circuits are also capable of muting, or being muted, by other external equipment.

The control station contains the required controls, indicators, microphones, etc. The remote control station is a secondary operating position, if required.

The two transducers (LF and HF) have a horizontal (radial) omni-directional beam pattern. The electro-mechanical energy conversion is accomplished by piezoelectric ceramic elements which are totally encapsulated and covered by an acoustically transparent neoprene boot.

CHARACTERISTICS
Frequency bands: 1·45 – 3·10 kHz (LF); 8·3 – 11·1 kHz (HF); 100 Hz – 13·0 kHz (auxiliary mode)
Output power: 600 W (LF); 450 W (HF); 1000 VA (auxiliary mode)
Weights
Receiver/transmitter: 223 kg
Control station: 6·8 kg
Remote control: 4·1 kg
Transducers: (with 175 feet of cable) 200 kg (LF) 45·5 kg (HF)
STATUS
In production for US Navy and overseas navies.
CONTRACTOR
General Instrument Corporation, Government Systems Division, 600 W John Street, Hicksville, New York 11802, USA

5640.453
AN/PQS-2A HAND-HELD SONAR

The AN/PQS-2A is a continuous transmission, frequency modulated hand-held non-magnetic sonar set intended for use by divers to locate and close on submerged objects such as mines, lost equipment, downed aircraft and sunken vessels in depths to 300 feet (91 m). Because of its non-magnetic construction, the set can be used safely when working near magnetically-influenced underwater explosive devices.

The equipment has an active (continuous transmission) mode and a passive (listening) mode. In the active mode, one of three range scales is selected (20, 60 or 120 yards (18, 55 or 110 m)) and an acoustic signal is transmitted over a 30 kHz bandwidth, swept from 114 to 145 kHz. When a submerged object is detected a ringing tone, proportional in frequency to the distance of the object, is produced in the earphones. The sonar has a 6° beamwidth and can detect a 12-inch (30·5 cm) diameter air-filled sphere at 120 yards (110 m). In the passive mode, the unit detects active sound sources (pingers) in the 24 to 45 kHz range. The sonar can detect a 39 kHz acoustic beacon at a range of at least 2000 yards (1800 m).

CHARACTERISTICS
Transmission: Continuous transmission frequency modulated (CTFM)
Read-out: Variable audio tone according to range
Active sonar range: Three ranges 18, 55, and 110 m
Passive range: Up to 1800 m
Weight in water: 0·23 kg (positive buoyance collar included in accessories)
Size: 31·75 cm long by 11·43 cm diameter
STATUS
In production.
CONTRACTOR
General Instrument Corporation, Government Systems Division, 600 W John Street, Hicksville, New York 11802,USA.

AN/PQ2-2A hand-held sonar

3788.363
SPARTON AIRBORNE SONAR PROCESSING EQUIPMENT

Sparton's modular airborne processing systems and components are a flexible, lightweight, low-cost means to process and display data from sonobuoys and similar submarine tracking devices. The modular approach allows individual units to be used separately or combined to form a compact system capable of processing and displaying signals from most of the sonobuoy types currently in use or being developed. Typical hardware is described briefly in the following paragraphs although more detailed information is given in earlier editions of *Jane's Weapon Systems*, under this entry number.

Active Processing System
The active processor system consists of five modules: command signal transmitter; command signal generator; active processor; sonar display; power supply. The active processor system is capable of simultaneously processing and displaying two AN/SSQ-47 or AN/SSQ-522 active sonobuoys. The system can also be modified to provide two-channel processing and displaying a single AN/SSQ-50 or AN/SSQ-523 command active sonobuoy. The modifications provide the matched filter processing required for the additional CW pulse lengths and an FM processor utilising replica correlation. The system can be further expanded to process and display the AN/SSQ-62 or proposed DICANCASS directional command-active sonobuoys by the addition of a sixth module. This module contains a digital arc tangent computer that calculates and displays bearing with a direct readout in degrees.

Command Signal Generator
The command generator is the active sonobuoy's information source. It is a dual-channel control unit that generates the sonar pulse information for two sonobuoys. Selected channels from the sonobuoy receiver are routed to the active processor. The command signal generator also provides the active processor with trigger pulses and other digital control information.

Active Processor
The active processor is a lightweight, dual-channel

unit capable of simultaneously processing two command-active sonobuoys. It automatically analyses information for the detection and localisation of submarines. It is completely solid-state, with integrated circuits used extensively in the analyser portion of the unit. The processed signals from two sonobuoys can be displayed in a split-screen mode on the sonar display.

Sonar Display

The sonar display can be used with the active processor to provide target range and doppler information in the CW mode and target detection and range information in the FM mode. The Sparton sonar display utilises a variable-persistence cathode-ray tube that provides bright, high-quality readouts. In use, the screen is divided vertically into two displays where a combination of A scans or B scans can be displayed for either one of two sonobuoys simultaneously. Persistence time is adjustable from zero to full storage. Stored spot resolution is equivalent to 20 lines/cm.

CHARACTERISTICS
Display: 2 channels, A and/or B scan
CW: Target range and doppler
FM: Target detection and range
Display integration: Variable-persistence CRT for time integration.
Controls
Threshold: Provides capability to optimise target detection

TD-1135/A Demultiplexer Processor/Display

The TD-1135/A is a high-quality instrument for testing directional frequency analysis and ranging (DIFAR) and directional command active (DICASS) sonobuoys. The TD-1135/A accepts a composite DIFAR/DICASS signal from any standard sonobuoy receiver, demultiplexes it, and displays the output as a radial vector on a variable-persistence CRT calibrated in degrees from magnetic north. North-south, east-west and omnidirectional outputs are provided for computer analysis if greater accuracy is required.

Designed for use with standard sonobuoy monitoring equipment, the TD-1135/A is compatible with receiver types AR/ARR-52, AR/ARR-72, and AR/ARR-75, and with analyser display group types AN/AQA-3, AN/AQA-4 and AN/AQA-5. Included with the TD-1135/A is a Sparton DFS-101A digital frequency synthesiser, with crystal oscillator reference, which is tunable in discrete steps over the entire DIFAR/DICASS frequency band. If an AN/AQA -3, -4, or -5 is not available, the TD-1135/A and frequency synthesiser can be modified by adding a spectrum analysis capability.

The TD-1135/A demultiplexer is available as a

TD-1135A demultiplexer processor/display

separate unit for operation with DIFAR or DICASS sonobuoys.

CHARACTERISTICS
Frequency range: Broadband DIFAR audio
Input impedance: 10 kΩ minimum
Output impedance: 10 kΩ max
Variable gain: 48 dB manual or remote
Time constants: 0·1, 1 and 10 seconds
Phase pilot bandwidth: 1 Hz max
Processor analysis bandwidth: 1 Hz max
MTBF: 1500 h minimum
Outputs available
Demultiplexer: N-S, E-W, and omni
Processor: N-S, E-W, and omni

Spectrum Analyser

The Sparton spectrum analyser is a low-cost, special-purpose digital processor that performs real-time spectral analysis. The signature of the target being analysed is displayed simultaneously, using both channels of the Sparton sonar display. Discrete Fourier transform technology is used with circuits operating at optimally low bit rates. Features include linear integration of spectral estimates, manual or automatic modes, internal cursor for accurate frequency identification, and total spectrum coverage.

CHARACTERISTICS
Frequency range: 14 – 912 Hz
Frequency bands: 14 – 114 Hz (0·25 Hz resolution); 112 – 912 Hz (2 Hz resolution)
Number of spectral estimates per band: 400
Linear integration of spectral estimates
Manual: 1 – 100 samples
Automatic: 100 samples
Input amplitude dynamic range: 80 dB

OL-5003(-)/ARR Signal Processor Group

The Sparton OL-5003(-)/ARR sonobuoy signal processor is a lightweight, versatile, active processor

and display system. Designed to make data from either the AN/SSQ-47 or AN/SSQ-522 sonobuoys instantly available with minimum operator involvement, the OL-5003(-)/ARR automatically synchronises with sonobuoy range trigger, analyses signal returns for echo level and doppler, and displays the result on a variable-persistence storage cathode-ray tube. The single display tube simultaneously presents, in a split-screen mode, the data from two sonobuoys. The B-scan format displays range on the horizontal axis, doppler on the vertical axis, and echo level on the intensity axis.

The OL-5003(-)/ARR processor is completely solid-state with the exception of the storage CRT. Integrated circuits are used extensively in the analyser portion of the unit. The processor is also compatible with the AN/SSQ-523 sonobuoy system in the short-pulse mode.

CHARACTERISTICS
Analysis bandwidth: 10 Hz
Doppler coverage: Compatible with AN/SSQ-47B or AN/SSQ-522 sonobuoy
Doppler accuracy: ±1 knot
Range scale: Selectable, 3600 or 7200 yards
Power: 120 W (115 V, 50 – 400 Hz, single phase)

DICASS Command Signal Monitor

The Sparton DICASS (directional command active sonobuoy system) command signal monitor is used to monitor valid command signals during testing of the AN/SSQ-50. The unit is self-contained and requires a UHF antenna and 115 V AC for operation. It provides a permanent printed record of the VHF channel command, identification of command function, RF signal level during command, time of signal transmission, length of command, and RF signal level prior to command.

Sea Noise Directionality and Level Indicator (ID-1872/A MOD)

The ID-1872/A MOD adds the ambient sea noise directional estimator (ANODE) function to a standard ambient sea noise indicator. It maintains the capability of the ASNI ID-1872/A, which measures and displays the omni-directional sea noise level sensed and transmitted by an AN/SSQ-57 sonobuoy and adds the ANODE function.

CHARACTERISTICS
Analysis centre frequency: 50, 100, 200, 440, 1000, 1700 Hz
Analysis bandwidth: 25 Hz
Weight: 3·18 kg
CONTRACTOR
Sparton Corporation, 2400 East Ganson Street, Jackson, Michigan 49202, USA.

3778.363
AN/ARR-78(V) ADVANCED SONOBUOY COMMUNICATION LINK (ASCL)

The AN/ARR-78(V) radio receiving set, also known as ASCL (Advanced Sonobuoy Communication Link), is for the operation and management of anti-submarine sonobuoys by the crew of ASW aircraft such as the P-3C Orion (Update III) maritime patrol aircraft, S-3B Viking and LAMPS III helicopter. The equipment comprises five main items (described below) which can be employed with an associated AN/ALQ-158 airborne adaptive controlled phased array antenna system and on-board ASW signal processor. The main units of the AN/ARR-78(V) are:

(1) the AM-6875 RF preamplifier is an optimised high performance, low noise VHF preamplifier which provides amplification and pre-filtering of received RF signals

(2) the R-2033 radio receiver contains 20 fully synthesised high performance receiver modules (16 acoustic and 4 auxiliary), and one each of the following modules: RF/ADF amplifier multi-coupler, reference oscillator, PROTEUS digital channel, I/O processor, clock generator, BITE, and DC power supply module. Each single conversion receiver module includes mixer conversion, frequency synthesised LO, demodulator, and output interface circuits. Each of the acoustic receiver modules processes FM/analogue signals at any of the 99 channels in the extended VHF band. Each of the four auxiliary

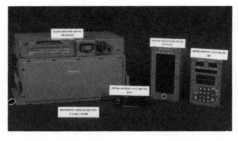

AN/ARR-78(V) sonobuoy communications link equipment

receiver modules processes FM/analogue signals at any of the 99 channels and provides one channel for selection and processing of the on top position indicator (OTPI) signals; two channels for the operator to monitor acoustic information; and one channel to monitor the RF signal level in any of the RF channels. Common receiver modules are interchangeable.

BITE circuits provide comprehensive end-to-end evaluation of each receiver from the VHF preamplifier to the receiver output interface circuits. BITE is initiated automatically by the computer (such as PROTEUS) and/or by the operator through the indicator control unit (ICU). Performance status is displayed on the ICU and routed to the computer

(3) the C-10126 indicator control unit (ICU) provides the operator with a means for manual control of each receiver channel frequency assignment, receiving mode, self test. It also displays status of the receiving set and operator entry information

(4) the ID-2086 receiver status indicator continuously displays the control mode setting, the RF channel number, and the received signal level for each receiver

(5) the C-10127 receiver control unit provides the operator with control over the OTPI channel frequency.

Surface acoustic wave (SAW) IF filters are incorporated to provide high selectivity, coupled with good linear phase characteristics which yield low levels of distortion. Microprocessors are used in the ICU and I/O module to process the commands to, and display status data from the receivers. Versatile programs accommodate changes without requiring aircraft modification.

The auxiliary receivers permit the operator to aurally monitor analogue signals in any of the 99 RF channels without interrupting data processing in that channel.

CHARACTERISTICS
Frequency: Extended VHF
Receivers: 20 (16 acoustic/4 auxiliary) for P-3C/S-3B ASCL configuration; other configurations available
Channels: 99 per receiver
Audio output
Analogue: 2 V or 4%V rms balanced

Power input: 115 V AC ±10%, 380 – 440 Hz, 3 phase 450 W; 18 – 32 V DC, 7 W; 26·5 V AC, ±10%, 400 Hz, 50 W
Dimensions
AM-6875: 7·6 × 14·6 × 10·8 cm; Wt: 0·95 kg
R-2033: 30·9 × 54·1 × 38·9 cm; Wt: 45·9 kg
C-10126: 22·9 × 14·6 × 16·5 cm; Wt: 3 kg

ID-2086: 26·7 × 14·6 × 12·7 cm; Wt: 1·9 kg
C-10127: 5·7 × 14·6 × 8·3 cm; Wt: 0·6 kg
STATUS
Full-scale development was completed in 1980 under US Navy contracts. The first production contract for P-3C systems and S-3B systems was awarded in December 1982. Applications include derivative

configurations for the S-3B maritime aircraft and the LAMPS III helicopter.
CONTRACTOR
Hazeltine Corporation, Greenlawn, New York 11740, USA.

3776.253
RADIO RECEIVER R-1651/ARA SONOBUOY OTPI
The R-1651/ARA is a VHF radio receiver of solid-state construction used in locating sonobuoys. It also acts as a receiving converter when employed with compatible automatic direction finding (ADF) systems; when a command is initiated in the control unit of the ADF, the R-1651/ARA switches the direction finder from a UHF/ADF function to a VHF sonobuoy on-top position indicator/locator (OTPI) mode. The equipment is a replacement for the obsolete R-1047 A/A.

The R-1651/ARA is fitted in ASA patrol aircraft or helicopters and used with the AN/ARA-25 direction finder group. It receives, amplifies, and demodulates RF signals from deployed sonobuoys on any one of 31 RF frequencies within the range 162·25 to 173·50 MHz.
STATUS
Production.
CONTRACTOR
EDMAC Corporation, 7500 Main Street, PO Box 750, Fishers, New York 14453-0750, USA.

EDMAC R-1651/ARA sonobuoy OTPI radio receiver

4622.253
AN/SQR-18A TACTICAL SONAR TOWED ARRAY (TACTAS)
The AN/SQR-18A sonar has been designed to enhance the air/sea warfare capabilities of the US Navy surface fleet. Its long-range, passive detection capability complements the hull-mounted sonar of the US Navy FF 1052 (Knox) class frigates. The 800-foot long array consists of an acoustic section, a vibration isolation module and a rope drogue. It is towed behind the variable depth sonar (VDS) body of the AN/SQS-35(V) (**4179.453**). Preamplifiers are in the VDS body, while signal processing and other electronics are on board the ship.

The AN/SQR-18A is being upgraded to the

AN/SQR-18A(V)1, which will include a "noise canceller" that will remove own-ship radiated noise from the operator's display. Another version, the AN/SQR-18A(V)2, will have its own towing and handling capability, permitting it to be used on ships without a VDS.
STATUS
In use with the US Navy, and with the Netherlands and Japan. Approximately 40 AN/SQR-18A systems have been delivered to the US Navy and are being progressively updated to AN/SQR-18A(V)1 standard.
CONTRACTOR
EDO Corporation, Government Systems Division, 14-04 111th Street, College Point, New York 11356, USA.

AN/SQR-18A console/display

4463.253
AN/SQR-19 TACTICAL SONAR TOWED ARRAY
The AN/SQR-19 is a passive towed sensor array designed to give surface vesels long range detection and tracking of both submarines and surface ships. It includes a towed sensor array with improved ranging ability and reduced self-noise; a handling system which improves system performance by maintaining array position and depth; and a sophisticated signal

processing system providing more sonar information with less operator workload. It is designed for installation on several classes of frigates, destroyers and cruisers including Aegis system ships.
STATUS
The first operational system was installed on board the USS *Moosbrugger* (DD 980) early in 1982 and has completed both technical and operational evaluation. It will be fitted in several classes of frigates, destroyers

and cruisers, including Aegis ships. The US Naval Sea Systems Command has awarded a $23 million contract to Gould for production of 12 AN/SQR-19 systems. Initial deliveries are scheduled for mid-1985.
CONTRACTOR
Gould Inc, Defense Electronics Division, Glen Burnie, Maryland, USA.

2536.253
AN/SQS-53/26 SONARS
Claimed to be the most advanced surface ship ASW sonar in the US Navy inventory, the AN/SQS-53 is a high-power, long-range system evolved from the AN/SQS-26CX. Functions of the system are the detection, tracking, and classification of underwater targets, and also underwater communications, countermeasures against acoustic underwater weapons, and certain oceanographic recording uses. Target data obtained by the sonar is transmitted to the ship's Honeywell Mk 116 digital underwater fire control system. The latter translates target range, bearing, and depth data sent from the sonar to the ship's central computers into signals controlling the launch of ASW weapons (ASROC or torpedoes).

The AN/ASQ-53 can detect, identify, and track multiple targets and is the first USN surface ship sonar designed specifically to interface directly with a vessel's digital computers. The system has a cylindrical array of 576 transducer elements housed in a large bulb dome below the water line of the ship's bow. There are 37 cabinets of signal processing, transmitting, and display equipment. Passive and active operating modes are possible.

There are three active modes:
(1) surface duct
(2) bottom bounce
(3) convergence zone.

The surface duct mode depends upon sound energy being transmitted essentially in the horizontal plane. Because of the high level of noise introduced

into the return signals near the surface, this mode is useful only for relatively short distances. Nevertheless, this method is conventional for many surface ship sonars, and the high transmission power of the AN/SQS-53 is stated to provide longer range capability in the surface duct mode than previous sonars.

In the bottom bounce mode the sound energy is directed obliquely toward the sea bed. The energy is reflected upward from the ocean floor toward the surface at considerable distances from the ship. Submarine echoes are received via a similar return path. This method is useful in waters of more than certain minimum depths and where the sea bed has the requisite favourable characteristics.

Convergence zone mode operation takes

Bow housing of SQS-26 sonar

advantage of the characteristics of very deep water. The sound energy is refracted downward due to the temperature and pressure conditions near the surface, but, as depth increases, these physical effects change and the sound path alters direction to cause the energy to return to the surface in a coarsely focused convergence zone. This zone can form at great distances from the ship, and provides the longest range of coverage for the sonar when the water conditions are favourable for this mode of operation.

Passive detection gives the bearings of targets based on their own noise generation, rather than by echo location. It has proved a valuable method on the currently deployed AN/SQS-26 equipped ships, especially at low speed. The *Spruance* and her successors are expected to have improved passive detection capabilities at higher speeds due to improved noise suppression measures. The passive mode can be operated simultaneously with the active modes.

STATUS

The AN/SQS-26 is fitted in ten FF1040 'Garcia' class frigates; six FFG-1 'Brooke' class missile frigates; and 46 FF1052 'Knox' class frigates. The AN/SQS-53 is being fitted in DD963 'Spruance' class destroyers as they are built and a total of 30 ships is planned. The five CGN-38 'Virginia' class nuclear cruisers are fitted with AN/SQS-26CX or AN/SQS-53A systems. An updated version, known as the AN/SQS-53B, is in service and a $77 million contract was awarded to Hughes Aircraft Company by the US Navy for 23 AN/SQS-53B digital display sub-systems.

A new version of the system, the AN/SQS-53C Battle Group Sonar, has been developed by General Electric. The AN/SQS-53C is a much more advanced system which uses 22 fewer cabinets with a consequent reduction in cabling, etc. The new version uses seven Sperry AN/UYK-44(V) computers linked together in a multiple embedded configuration.

CONTRACTOR

General Electric Company, Electronic Systems Division, Farrell Road, Syracuse, New York 13201, USA.

Bow dome cutaway showing partial view of AN/SQS-53 cylindrical transducer (to right of engineers)

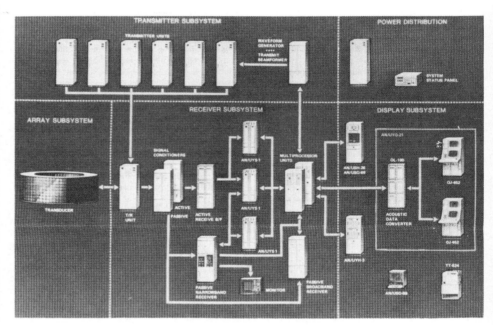

AN/SQS-53C equipment configuration

4179.453

AN/SQS-35 VARIABLE DEPTH SONAR AND AN/SQS-36, AN/SQS-38 HULL-MOUNTED SONARS

These systems have been designed to detect submarines at medium-ranges in both deep and shallow waters. The AN/SQS-35 and the AN/SQS-38 sonars have been in service with the US Navy since the mid 1960s.

The US systems are improved miniaturised solid-state versions of previously developed vacuum-tube equipments manufactured for the Italian, Norwegian and Japanese Navies.

Some versions combine both variable depth capability and hull sonar capability, selectable by the sonar operator at the control console.

Weapons associated with the system are the Mk 44 torpedo and ASROC (USA), Terne (Norway) and Lanciabas (Italy). Over 75 systems have been delivered.

CONTRACTOR

EDO Corporation, Government Systems Division, 14-04 111th Street, College Point, New York 11356, USA.

AN/SQS-35(V) variable depth sonar seen aboard the escort ship USS Francis Hammond

3494.253
RAYTHEON STANDARD SONAR TRANSMITTER (SST)

The Raytheon SST provides sonar systems with the benefits of modern, solid-state technology, for example greatly reduced maintenance costs through increased reliability, plus very significant space savings relative to vacuum tube transmitters. This transmit sub-system is made available for system modernisation or for new system applications.

Configured to meet a specific system's requirements, the SST consists of multiple one kW modules with associated power supplies. As configured for the AN/SQQ-23 and AN/SQS-23 sonars upgrade, the sub-system consists of two cabinets of 24 modules each and a performance monitor/system interface cabinet. It replaces more than 30 units of the previous transmitter, including all of the energy storage motor generators.,

CHARACTERISTICS
Standard 1 kW module (1 per channel)
Power output: 1 kW
Operating frequency: ±1·5 kHz (nominal)
Distortion: 6% max
Load: Nominal ±100%
Duty cycle: 15%
Linearity: ±1 dB from 0 to –12 dB

Gain adjustment: 3 dB
Protection: Short circuit and over-temperature
Mean time to repair: 3 minutes
Weight and size: 1651 kg in 1·2 × 1·8 m of deck space
SST as manufactured for AN/SSQ/SQS-23
Power requirements: 115 V AC 60 Hz 1-ph, 0·37 kVA, 0·92 PF; 440 V AC 60 Hz 3-ph, 128 kW (Max 0·9 PF)
Modes of operation
(1) Transmit: same as any associated system such as omni, sector, FM or CW
(2) Performance monitoring: automatic and manual
(3) Self-test: receiving system not required.
STATUS
Current production includes transmitters for five navies. Similar transmitters are used on the AN/BQS-13, AN/SQS-56, DE1160 series and the AN/SQQ/SQS-23 sonar systems. An air-cooled version of the SST has also been delivered in a programme to upgrade the AN/BQS-4 submarine sonar.
CONTRACTOR
Raytheon Company, Submarine Signal Division, Portsmouth, Rhode Island 02871, USA.

Raytheon standard sonar transmitter

1807.453
AN/SQS-56/DE 1160

The AN/SQS-56 is a modern hull-mounted sonar developed as a company funded product by Raytheon's Submarine Signal Division and now in production for the US Navy's FFG-7 class frigate. The US Navy has provided the AN/SQS-56, via the Foreign Military Sales (FMS) programme, to Saudi Arabia for its PCG ships and to Australia for its FFG-7 class frigates. Turkey is procuring this sonar, via US FMS, for its MEKO 200 programme. Versions commercially exported with the designation DE 1160 are operational on the Italian Navy's 'Lupo' class frigates and the Spanish, Moroccan and Egyptian navies 'Descubierta' class frigates, and are being considered for new ships of several other navies. The DE 1160, when configured with 36 kW transmitters, is identical to the AN/SQS-56. Outfitted with a VDS array and handling subsystem, it becomes Raytheon's DE 1164 sonar (**3115.453**) and is installed in the Italian Navy's 'Maestrale' class ships.

The DE 1160, when equipped with a larger, low-frequency transducer array and three additional transmitter cabinets, is designated DE 1160LF and is capable of convergence zone performance. The DE 1160LF was delivered to the Italian Navy for the helicopter carrier 'Garibaldi' early in 1984.

A VDS version of the DE 1160LF will combine the convergence zone performance of the 'Garibaldi' sonar with the environmental adaptability of the DE 1164 under the denomination DE 1160LF/VDS, a sonar system for major ASW combatants.

The AN/SQS-56 sonar features digital implementation, system control by a built-in mini-computer, and an advanced display system. Digital implementation allows packaging of the complete multi-function active and passive sonar in five medium-size electronic cabinets and one operator's console. Computer controlled functions provide a system that is extremely flexible and easy to operate. The computer is also used to provide automated fault detection and localisation and a built-in training

AN/SQS-56 operator's console

capability. The human engineered display ensures proper interpretation by operators, even by those with relatively low levels of training.

The sonar is an active/passive, preformed beam, digital sonar providing panoramic echo ranging and panoramic (DIMUS) passive surveillance. All signal processing, except transducer received signal amplification and linear transducer transmit drive, is accomplished in digital hardware, most of which is implemented using US Navy SEMP (standard electronic module programme) components in compact water-cooled cabinets small enough to allow installation through standard size hatches. All visual data are presented on flicker-free, digitally refreshed television type raster scan CRT displays. Complete symbol and alpha-numeric facilities are included. System timing, control, and interface communication are accomplished by a general purpose mini-computer which is a component of the basic system. Both 400 Hz synchro and MIL-STD-

1397 Type A or C, category II digital interfaces are available in the basic sonar system. Except for the 400 Hz synchro reference power, the entire sonar operates from 440 to 480 V, three-phase 60 Hz ship's power.

The basic system includes the transducer array, transducer junction box, five electronic cabinets (array interface, transmitter(s), receiver and controller), operator console, sonar dome, and control unit. Options in production include: a loudspeaker/intercom, a water cooling unit, a remote display, and a performance prediction sub-system. Additional functions under development include computer-aided detection and classification, target tracking, attack manoeuvring, and torpedo weapon setting data. A half frequency version, the DE1160 LF with convergence zone capability, will be delivered to the Italian Navy in mid-1984.

A single operator can search, track, classify, and designate multiple targets from the active system while simultaneously maintaining anti-torpedo surveillance on the passive display. Computer assisted system control permits the operator to concentrate on the sonar data being displayed rather than on the system controls.
STATUS
Approval for service use was issued early in 1980 by the US Navy following successful completion of final operational test and evaluation. Systems ordered up to November 1983 totalled 104, including 75 for the US Navy and FMS, 16 for Italy (5-DE1160, 10-DE1164, 1-DE1160LF) and 13 for Spain (8-DE1160, 1-DE1160 for Morocco, 4-SQS 56(SP) for Spanish trainer and FFG-7 ships). Of the 104 systems contracted, 99 were completed as of December 1983. All the Spanish and Moroccan sonars have significant Spanish content. EISA, Aranjuez is the prime contractor to the Spanish Navy for the four SQS-56(SP) systems for the Spanish FFG-7 ships.
CONTRACTOR
Raytheon Company, Submarine Signal Division, Portsmouth, Rhode Island 02871, USA.

1789.453
AN/SQQ-14 MINEHUNTING SONAR

The AN/SQQ-14 system is essentially a variable-depth, dual-frequency sonar for detecting and classifying bottom mines in shallow water. It utilises a towed body in the shape of an elongated sphere towed through a centre well on a US Navy minesweeper.

A unique aspect of the AN/SQQ-14 design is the towing cable. This consists of discrete, 18 inch (457 mm) sections of articulated struts with universal joints at each section, permitting the cable to flex in any vertical plane, but restraining it from torsional motion. This configuration imparts a constant heading to the towed body, thereby eliminating the

need for a gyroscopic heading reference system.

A rubber-jacketed electric cable containing 35 shielded, coaxial, and individual conductors passes through the centre of the strut sections, terminating in a slip ring in the towed body and in a winch with compound winding drum in lieu of a slip ring installed on the 01 deck of a mine countermeasures ship.

The articulated strut type of tow cable posed unique problems related to winching, storage on the winch drum, and ship's tow point construction. Struts, of which there are 117 per system, are stored in a single layer on a cylindrical drum equipped with specially designed pads serving as contact points for the articulated strut knuckles. Since a conventional level wind mechanism could not be used with the

struts, the winch drum itself is designed to traverse axially by means of an Acme lead screw and rotating nut, thereby accomplishing the level wind function and maintaining a fixed fleeting point. All equipment for this application must be non-magnetic. Struts, bearings, and knuckles are fabricated of high strength Inconel alloy. The winch drum is cast aluminium and supporting structure is aluminium and stainless steel.
STATUS
In operational service.

The SQQ-14 sonar is produced under licence in Italy by CGE SpA, who have supplied equipment to the Italian Navy. Other users include the Belgian and Spanish Navies.

CONTRACTOR
General Electric Company, Electronic Systems
Division, Farrell Road, Syracuse, New York 13201,
USA.

AN/SQQ-14 projectors and hydrophone arrays

4623.253
AN/SQQ-30 MINE-HUNTING SONAR

The AN/SSQ-30 is the successor to the AN/SQQ-14 system (**1789.453**) and is a latest technology mine-hunting sonar. The system consists of two sonars, a search sonar for initial detection and a high frequency, high resolution sonar for classification of targets. The two sonars are separated to give the area coverage needed. The two sonars are housed in a hydrodynamically, egg-shaped vehicle and towed at various speeds by the mine-hunter. The towed body is streamed from a well in the foward part of the ship, using a winch driving a 3-metre diameter cable drum on the foredeck. Two display consoles are provided for the search and classification sonars.

STATUS
Scheduled for fitment to the first few US Navy MSM-1 'Avenger' class mine-hunters.
CONTRACTOR
General Electric Company, Electronic Systems Division, Farrell Road, Syracuse, New York 13201, USA.

5652.253
AN/SQQ-32 ADVANCED MINEHUNTING SONAR SYSTEM

A full scale engineering development programme of an advanced minehunting sonar system (AN/SQQ-32) has been undertaken, with a $24·8 million contract from the US Navy, by Raytheon teamed with Thomson-CSF, France. The new system is scheduled to be installed in the US Navy's newly constructed minesweepers designated MCM-1 and MSH-1.

The proposed system consists of two separate sonars, a search sonar for initial detection and a high frequency, high resolution sonar for classification of the targets. The two sonars are partially housed in a hydrodynamically shaped vehicle and towed at various speeds by the minehunting ship. The latest technologies in beamforming, signal processing, modular packaging and displays are used throughout the system.

The detection sonar is being designed and manufactured by Raytheon and will be able to detect mines over a wide range of distances and bottom conditions. This system incorporates a computer-aided detection facility which is designed to help the sonar operator to discard non-mine objects detected by the sonar. Raytheon is also providing the computer facilities and display consoles and is responsible for overall system integration.

The classification sonar is being designed and fabricated by Thomson-CSF and will be based on its experience with the DUBM-21 and TSM-2022 minehunting sonars. The classification sonar will provide very high resolution transmission and reception of underwater signals to enable targets to be identified with near-picture quality.

The 'wet end', consisting of a hydrodynamically shaped vehicle, a deployment/retrieval system, a tow cable and a winch is being designed by Charles Stark Draper Laboratory of Cambridge, Massachusetts.
STATUS
In development. The initial contract calls for design and fabrication of three engineering models with delivery starting before the end of 1984.
CONTRACTORS
Raytheon Company, Submarine Signal Division, Portsmouth, Rhode Island 02871, USA.

AN/SQQ-32 sonar is to be installed on US Navy minesweepers

Thomson-CSF, Division Activités Sous-Marines, Chemin des Travails, BP 53, 06801 Cagnes-sur-Mer, France.

3115.453
DE1164 SONAR

The DE1164 sonar consists of the Raytheon DE1160B hull-mounted sonar (**1807.453**) augmented by a fully integrated variable-depth sonar sub-system. All sonar functions of the DE1164 are identical to those of the DE1160B. However, the DE1164 provides transmission and reception via various combinations of the hull-mounted and/or the towed variable depth sonar (VDS) transducer arrays. Addition of the VDS sub-system improves overall sonar flexibility, and allows the VDS transducer array to operate at acoustically favourable depths and in a much quieter environment.

In addition to the components of the full DE1160B hull-mounted system the DE1164 includes one extra cabinet of electronics, a VDS towed body with associated cable, and the electro-hydraulic mechanism associated with launching, towing, and retrieving the VDS body. The VDS handling equipment provides for one-man operation for launching and retrieving and unattended no-power towing. For reliability, two independent hydraulic power supplies are provided, either of which may support the entire operation. VDS body weight, cable size and length and careful attention to drag provide a VDS depth capability greater than 200 metres at 20 knots of ship's speed.

Both the hull-mounted and VDS arrays use the common set of DE1160B transmitting, receiving, and display electronics. Selection of the particular combination of transmit/receive array functions is ordered by the operator via the sonar console input keyboard; the system computer then sets up the required sequence. Alpha-numeric symbols on the display inform the operator about which particular array is in use during any specific ping-cycle.

During the normal operation the power requirements of the DE1164 are identical to those of the DE1160C. A maximum of 50 kW additional power is required from the 440 V, three-phase, 60 Hz power mains during high speed retrieval or launching. The hull-mounted sonar may be operated during VDS launch/recovery operations.
STATUS
Ten have been ordered by the Italian Navy and nine had been delivered by the end of 1983. Successful initial evaluations of the DE1164 were held by the

Italian Navy in March 1982 aboard a 'Maestrale' class frigate.

CONTRACTOR

Raytheon Company, Submarine Signal Division, Portsmouth, Rhode Island 02871, USA.

VDS configuration of DE 1164 sonar on the Libeccio of the Italian Navy

3116.453
DE1167 MODERNISATION SONARS

Raytheon's DE1167 family of sonars implements the proven features of the SQS-56/DE1160 systems (**1807.453** and **3115.453**) using advanced microprocessor architecture and state-of-the-art display and transmitter technology. The DE1167 series is based on large modules and air-cooled cabinets, which permit the production of smaller, simpler, cheaper sonar systems, and facilitate local manufacturing and repair. The DE1167 family is designed to satisfy the requirements of most ASW platforms and missions. Configurations include hull-mounted, VDS and integrated HM/VDS systems featuring a 12 kHz VDS and either 12 kHz or 7·5 kHz hull-mounted 36-stave transducer arrays. Configurations using 48-stave arrays, or a frequency lower than 7·5 kHz are possible. A DE1167 receiver and display sub-system, when combined with Raytheon's Standard Sonar Transmitter (SST) (**3494.253**), provides a complete inboard update for older SQS-23 sonars. Raytheon states that this SQS-23 modernisation equipment, DE1191, when coupled with the existing SQS-23 transducer array and dome, results in operability, reliability, maintainability and performance exceeding those of most modern medium-range sonars at a fraction of the cost.

Like the Raytheon DE1160B/C and DE1164 sonars, the DE1167 features primarily digital electronics and an advanced control and display system. The standard inboard electronics consist of three cabinets and a single operator console. Outboard units consist of a transducer array and 2·74 m long dome for the hull-mounted 12 kHz installation (4·17 m long dome for 7·5 kHz) and/or the VDS winch, overboarding assembly, control station, hydraulic power supply and towed body for the 12 kHz variable depth sub-system.

The DE1167 HM is an active/passive, preformed beam, omni and directional transmission sonar which uses three non-interfering 600 Hz wide FM transmission bands centred at 12 or 7·5 kHz and a spatial polarity coincidence correlation (PCC) receiver. The passive mode, which is selected automatically when transmissions are stopped, is primarily useful for torpedo detection. Optional items in production include a performance prediction sub-system, an auxiliary half-frequency passive receiver, an auxiliary display, a remote display, and a training/test target remote control unit. Signal reception and beamforming are accomplished by broadband analogue circuitry followed by clipper amplifiers for perfect data normalisation. Detection processing, display processing, system control/timing and waveform generation are done digitally. Two microprocessors perform display ping history, cursor ground stabilisation, and target motion estimation functions for torpedo direction. The modular air-cooled 12 kW transmitter uses highly efficient class A/D power transistor techniques.

Several operational features are unique to a sonar of this size/range. First, the display processing incorporates a ping history mode through which the sonar data obtained in as many as three of the previous ping cycles is retained on the viewing surface, allowing the operator to readily differentiate between randomly spaced noise events and geographically consistent, valid acoustic reflectors. Second, the clipped PCC processing permits accurate thresholding of all signals such that the false alarm rate, or number of random noise indications on the screen, remains relatively low and constant over all variations in background noise and reverberation levels, further facilitating contact detection. Third, ground-stabilised cursors and target motion analysis permit rapid determination of contact motion over the bottom, an excellent clue as to the nature of the contact. These three operational features, combined with extremely accurate tracking displays, a built-in fault detection/localisation sub-system, performance verification software and test/training, result in a high performance system which is easy to operate, maintain and support.

CHARACTERISTICS

Centre frequency: 12 kHz (HM) and (VDS), 7·5 kHz (LF) (HM)

Source level: Triple 227 dB (HM), Omni 217 dB

Pulse type: 600, 2000 Hz FM sweep 100, 200, 50, 25, 6 ms pulse lengths

Receiver type: Spatial polarity coincidence correlator (PCC) between 36 pairs of half beams

Beam characteristics: 36 sets of right and left half beams for active and passive detection. Selectable 10°H × 13°V sum beam for audio listening. 1·25° bearing interpolation for display

Active display: 300 range cells, 288 bearing cells; single and multiple echo history; 4 intensity levels

Operator's display/control console of Raytheon DE1167 sonar

Passive display: Electronic bearing time recorder (EBTR) with medium time averaging. DIMUS-type LTA/STA with optional passive receiver

Track displays: Sector scan indicator (1000 yards × 10°) and target doppler indicator (1000 yards × ±60 kts)

Target data: Range: 8 yd (6·1 m) resolution. Bearing 1·25° resolution plus active search display – 0·1° and 3·3 yards on SSI display. ±60 kts of doppler at 1 kt steps on the TDI

Data format: Standard: NTDS ANEW (digital). Optional: NTDS slow, Fast Serial D/S synchro converters

Power requirements: Passive 800 W. Active 20 kVA (pulse) at 10% (max) duty cycle 440 V, 60 Hz, 3-phase, VDS launch/retrieve 75 kVA (max) 440 V, 60 Hz, 3-phase

Weights: Hull-mounted 1500 kg (nominal); VDS 10 000 kg (nominal)

STATUS

Fifteen systems were under contract in December 1983 to the Korean Navy (8 DE1167 HM), Spanish built corvettes for the Egyptian Navy (2 DE1167 HM/VDS at 7·5/12 kHz), and ELSAG for the Italian Navy (5 DE1167 HM – lower frequency – 7·5 kHz). ELSAG has implemented a licence agreement with

Raytheon for manufacturing DE1167 sonars for the Italian Navy corvette programme. The first ELSAG system and four of the Korean systems were delivered during 1984. ELSAG has also been awarded a contract from the Italian Navy for a multi-application sonar trainer to be built in co-operation with Raytheon (**5754.293**).

CONTRACTOR

Raytheon Company, Submarine Signal Division, Portsmouth, Rhode Island 02871, USA.

1635.453

BATHYTHERMOGRAPH DATA RECORDER RO-308/SSQ-36

The BT recorder is an integral part of US Navy/Lockheed P-3C Orion aircraft ASW system. The equipment converts seawater temperature information provided by the AN/SSQ-36 bathythermograph buoy-transmitter set (**3781.453** *1982-83* and earlier editions) and AN/AAR-72 radio receiving set (**3454.363**) to two output forms:

(1) a permanent record of the vertical temperature profile (temperature v depth) on a paper strip chart
(2) a parallel mode, eight-bit binary coded data word for delivery to the AN/AYA-8 data processing system (**1982.363**).

The BT buoy is dropped from an aircraft in the target area. Seawater is utilised as the activating agent and after an initial, predictable delay, the buoy releases a temperature sensing probe (TS probe). The TS probe is the variable element in a frequency

generation circuit. A radio frequency signal, transmitted by the BT buoy is modulated at a frequency correlated to the temperature of the water. On board the aircraft the ARR-72 radio is tuned to the BT buoy carrier frequency. Water temperature information is converted to an audio frequency signal and delivered to the BT recorder.

CONTRACTOR

Fairchild Weston Schlumberger, Weston Controls, Archbald, Pennsylvania 18403, USA.

2580.253

EDO MODEL 610 LONG RANGE HULL-MOUNTED SCANNING RADAR

Designed for the long-range detection of submarines in deep and shallow water, the EDO Model 610 scanning sonar has two active consoles, enabling it to perform a search-while-track function. Facilities offered include a search capability in three 120° sectors, passive correlation, and reverberation processing. The transmitter and receiver beams are preformed. Output is available for a fire control system. All mode changes and range scale changes are controlled by console push-buttons, and displays include a doppler display on each of the active consoles and a passive sonar bearing-time recorder display.

DEVELOPMENT

Model 610 was developed by the EDO Corporation as a private venture starting in 1965. The first prototype was completed in 1966 and the first production model completed its sea trials in 1969. The Model 610 has been continuously improved, and the current 610E model is of all solid-state construction.

STATUS

Over 25 Model 610 systems have been ordered for use in the Royal Netherlands Navy, the Italian Navy and other navies. Associated weapon systems include the Mk 44 torpedo (US), 375 rocket launcher (Sweden), Lanciabas (Italy), and Ikara (Australia).

CONTRACTOR

EDO Corporation, Government Systems Division, 14-04 111th Street, College Point, New York 11356, USA.

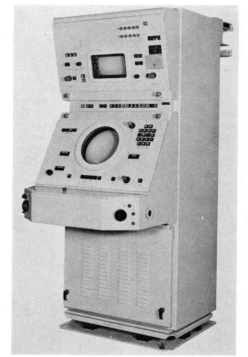

Model 610E sonar control console No 1

2581.253

EDO MODEL 700 SERIES SONARS

Latest equipment of this range of single operator sonars is the model 700E medium-range hull-mounted sonar. The Model 700/702 hull-mounted VDS uses common 700E electronics with a hull-mounted transducer and a lightweight VDS hoist. Selection of hull-mounted or VDS operation is by push-button on the operator's console. The Model 700/701 is a variable depth sonar which provides a capability to detect deep targets when bathythermal conditions are unfavourable for hull-mounted sonars.

The basic equipment has a 254 mm panoramic CRT display and a doppler display. All mode and range-scale changes are made by push-button controls on the operator's console.

DEVELOPMENT

Like the Model 610 (**2580.253**) the Model 700 series has been developed by the EDO Corporation as a private venture for sale on the international market. Over 20 of these items of equipment have so far been ordered, customers include the Brazilian, Royal Netherlands and Japanese Navies, and other sales are pending. Associated weapon systems include the Mk 44 torpedo (US), the Bofors 375 launcher (Sweden), Lanciabas (Italy), and Ikara (Australia).

CONTRACTOR

EDO Corporation, Government Systems Division, 14-04 111th Street, College Point, New York 11356, USA.

EDO 700E VDS in stowed position aboard the Brazilian Mk 10 frigate Niteroi

3495.253
EDO MODEL 780 SERIES SONAR
The EDO Model 780 Series sonar is a family of high performance computer-based sonars designed to maximise the ASW capability of ships ranging from high-speed patrol craft to ASW frigates. Configured as a modular system, the Model 780 Series can be assembled to match ship-size constraints and required ASW capability for hull-mounted or variable depth sonar operation. The following models are available:

780: 13 kHz Variable Depth Sonar (VDS)
786: 13 kHz hull-mounted
795: 5 kHz hull-mounted
796: 7 kHz hull-mounted
7860: Combined 13 kHz hull-mounted with 13 kHz VDS
7950: Combined 5 kHz hull-mounted with 13 kHz VDS
7960: Combined 7 kHz hull-mounted with 13 kHz VDS

Simultaneous active and passive detection capabilities are provided as well as an integral acoustic-intercept receiver. In the VDS configuration its lightweight, compact hoist permits installation on very small ships without sacrifice in performance. The completely solid-state design and integral automatic fault detection and localisation equipment provide for high reliability and ease of maintenance.

In all configurations the Model 780 Series employs the latest state-of-the-art computer-aided control and display equipment. Designed for a single operator, a digital computer, with high speed random access memory, provides direct operator control over every facet of the sonar, and selective display of all target data, system status, and related ship operational information. Centralised communication between the operator and computer is provided by an action entry panel and a track ball. Accuracy figures of the series are ±0·5% of the range scale for active range, ±1° for active bearing and ±0·5° for passive bearing.

The Model 780 Series electronics is comprised of four major units; the control indicator, a transmitter, a receiver, and a data storage and control unit. A preamplifier unit of small dimensions is separately housed for remote location. All units are air cooled.

Model 780 sonar system equipment comprising sonar control console, data storage and control, transmitter/power supply and sonar receiver

The VDS hoist consists of two major units, the winch unit and the towed vehicle. A small operator's console is easily located in close proximity to the handling unit. The simplicity of the system allows towed body depth to be controlled from the bridge as well as the sonar control room. It is light enough for fitting in ships as small as 250 tons.

DEVELOPMENT
The Model 780 Series has been developed by the EDO Corporation for sale on the international market.

STATUS
Systems in the VDS configuration are currently deployed at sea, and the 780 has passed formal technical and operational testing and is fully operational. Two Far Eastern navies are using the hull-mounted configuration which became fully operational in 1983.

CONTRACTOR
EDO Corporation, Government Systems Division, 14-04 111th Street, College Point, New York 11356, USA.

Model 780 VDS hoist under test

5644.453
EDO MODEL 900/910 UNDERWATER DETECTION SYSTEMS
The Model 900 underwater detection set is designed for use on submarines in mine avoidance and underwater obstacle location. It is composed of only three small units; a scanning assembly, a transmitter/receiver and a control indicator. The control indicator contains a 7-inch display which presents target data to the operator in ship-centred plan-position format. The scanning assembly contains the transmitting and receiving transducers, and an electrical drive system to train the transducers over 340° of azimuth. The transmitter/receiver unit incorporates a frequency analyser for high resolution of target data.

The model 910 is a small lightweight system for use on board small surface vessels engaged in minesweeping operations. In all other respects it is basically the same as the type 900 described above.
CONTRACTOR
EDO Corporation, Government Systems Division, 14-04 111th Street, College Point, New York 11356, USA.

4462.353
AN/AQS-14 AIRBORNE MINEHUNTING SONAR
This is a helicopter towed side-looking multibeam sonar, with electronic beam forming, all-range focusing and an adaptive processor, intended for use with the RH-53D Sea Stallion helicopters used by the US Navy for mine clearance. The underwater vehicle is three metres long and has an active control system which enables it to be run at a fixed height above the seabed, or at a fixed depth beneath the water surface, as chosen by the operator in the helicopter. The tow cable is armoured and is non-magnetic.

Controls in the helicopter include: a TV-type moving window sonar display; underwater vehicle controls and status displays; system status indicators; and a magnetic tape recorder for sonar data recording. The system functions include all that is needed to locate, classify, mark, permanently record, and review records of mines, mine-like objects, and underwater features in the search area. Because the sonar employs multibeam techniques, a rapid search speed is possible. The system is adaptable to surface platforms, especially hovercraft, for route survey missions. Non linear parametric array and synthetic aperture sonar technologies are incorporated.
STATUS
The AQS-14 is in production under a contract worth more than $17 million and deliveries commenced in early 1984. It is believed that about 30 units have been ordered.
CONTRACTOR
Westinghouse Electric Corporation, PO Box 1488, Annapolis, Maryland 21404, USA.

3496.453
EDO MODEL 1102/1105 SUBMARINE SONAR
The EDO Model 1102/1105 is a passive and active sonar system designed for use on medium size submarines. The Model 1102 passive system is the primary detection configuration. In the passive mode, the sound horizon is scanned. Also available to the operator is a manual mode for selection of a specified bearing. The data received from the automatic channel is presented to the operator on a bearing/time recorder which provides a permanent record of all targets detected. An automatic tracking (ATF) channel may be assigned to any target detected for accurate tracking and bearing determination simultaneous with continuation of search. Target bearing outputs are provided for external use.

The Model 1105 active sub-system is designed as an integral supplement to the passive Model 1102 and is intended for use after detection in the passive

Model 1102 (passive) sonar control console

Model 1102/1105 submarine sonar equipment

mode. The Model 1105 uses the same array, preamplifiers, and beam formers of the passive system. Active data received by the tracking channel is fed to a FFT (Fast Fourier Transform) processor. Data is presented to the operator in doppler versus range format on a CRT display. Outputs of target range and range data are available for external use. This equipment is available either in the passive Model 1102 or passive/active Model 1102/1105 configuration.

DEVELOPMENT

The Model 1102/1105 was developed by the EDO Corporation as a private venture for sale on the international market. No information is available on any orders received.

CONTRACTOR

EDO Corporation, Government Products Division, 14-04 111th Street, College Point, New York 11356, USA.

1637.353

AN/AQS-13 HELICOPTER SONAR

The AQS-13 is a helicopter dunking system, the AQS-13B model continuing in production. It is one of a series of such equipment which began with the Bendix AN/AQS-10 in 1955.

The B system is a long-range, active scanning sonar which detects and maintains contact with underwater targets through a transducer lowered into the water from a hovering helicopter. Opening or closing rates of moving targets can be accurately determined and the system also provides target classification clues.

The AN/AQS-13B has significant advantages in operation and maintenance over earlier systems. To aid the operator, some electronic functions were automated to eliminate several controls. Maintenance was simplified by eliminating all internal adjustments and adding built-in-test (BITE) circuits.

These advantages were brought about by the use of the latest electronic circuits and packaging techniques which also reduced system size and weight.

To enhance detection capability in shallow water and reverberation-limited conditions while essentially eliminating false alarms from the video display, Bendix developed an adaptive processssor sonar (APS) for the system.

The APS is a completely digital processor employing Fast Fourier Transform (FFT) techniques to provide narrow-band analysis of the uniquely shaped CW pulse transmitted in the APS mode. The display retains the familiar PPI readout of target range and bearing but APS adds precise digital readout of the radial component of target doppler.

With APS, processing gains of greater than 20 dB with zero false alarm rates have been measured for target dopplers under 0·5 knot.

The higher energy transmitted with the longer pulse APS mode, combined with the narrow-band analysis, also substantially improves the figure of merit (FOM) in the non-reverberant conditions more typical of deep water operation. Measured processing gains for APS under ambient, wideband noise limited conditions exceeded 7 dB.

CHARACTERISTICS

Frequencies: 9·25, 10, 10·75 kHz

Sound pressure level: 113 dB ref 1 microbar

Range scales: 1, 3, 5, 8, 12, 20 k yds (0·9, 2·7, 4·6, 7·3, 11, 18·3 km)

Operational modes: Active 3·5 or 35 ms, MTI, APS, passive, voice communications, key communications (13-A only)

Visual outputs: (13-A) range, bearing; (13-B) range, range rate, bearing, operator verification

Audio output: (13-A) single channel with gain control; (13-B) dual channel with gain control plus constant level to aircraft intercom

Recorder operation: Bathythermograph, range, aspect, MAD self-test

System weight: (13-A) 373 kg; (13-B) 282 kg

STATUS

The AQS-13 is widely used by American forces and has been supplied or ordered for naval helicopters of 15 foreign navies in Europe, Asia, Middle East, and South America. The AN/AQS-18 (**4456.353**) an advanced version of the sonar featuring smaller size, lighter weight and increased performance, has been developed and is in production.

CONTRACTOR

The Bendix Corporation, Oceanics Division, 11600 Sherman Way, North Hollywood, California 91605, USA.

4456.353

AN/AQS-18 AIRBORNE SONAR

The AN/AQS-18 is a helicopter-borne, long range active scanning sonar. The system detects and maintains contact with underwater targets through a transducer lowered into the water from a hovering helicopter. Active echo-ranging determines a target's range and bearing, and opening or closing rate relative to the aircraft. Target identification clues are also provided.

The AN/AQS-18 is an advanced version of earlier dunking sonars made by Bendix and includes digital technology, improved signal processing and improved operator displays. The system consists of a small high density transducer with a high sink and retrieval rate, a built-in multiplex system to permit use of a single conductor cable, a 305 m cable and compatible reeling machine and a lightweight transmitter built into the transducer package. Offered as an optional extra is the Adaptive Processor Sonar (APS).

The AN/AQS-18 offers a number of improvements over earlier dipped sonars. These include increased transmitter power output giving longer range, high speed dip cycle time and reductions in weight of all units.

The adaptive Processor Sonar increases detection capability in shallow water and reverberation-limited conditions while essentially eliminating false alarms from the video display. The APS is a micro-programmable processor which uses Fast Fourier Transform (FFT) techniques to provide narrow-band

AN/AQS-18 sonar deployed from West German Navy Westland Lynx Mk 88 helicopter

analysis of the uniquely-shaped CW pulse transmitted in the APS mode. The PPI display retains the normal read-out of target range and bearing.

The APS processing gain improvement over the normal AN/AQS-18 analogue processing is 20 dB for a two knot target and 15 dB for a five knot doppler target. The higher energy transmitted with the longer pulse APS mode, combined with the narrow-band analysis also improves operation in the non-reverberant conditions more typical of deep water. The gain improvement outside the high reverberation zone (ten knots or greater) under wideband noise limited conditions exceeds 7 dB.

CHARACTERISTICS
Operating depth: 305 m
Operating frequencies: 9·23, 10, 10·77 kHz
Sound pressure level: 215 dB ref 1 μPa at 1 yard (0·9 m)
Range scales: 1, 3, 5, 8, 12, 20 Hyd
Operational modes: 3·5 or 35 ms MTI, passive, communicate (voice)
Visual outputs: Range, range rate, bearing, operator verification
Audio output: Dual channel with gain control, plus constant level to aircraft intercom system

Recorder operation: Bathythermograph, range, ASPECT, MAD, BITE
System weight: 252 kg plus 13·3 for APS
STATUS
In production.
CONTRACTOR
The Bendix Corporation, Oceanics Division, 15825 Roxford Street, Sylmar, California 91342, USA.

3772.453
MICROPUFFS PASSIVE RANGING SONAR

The MicroPUFFS system is a high accuracy, long-ranging passive sonar designed for installation aboard submarines. The name suggests that this equipment is a derivative of the original US Navy PUFFS (passive underwater fire control feasibility study) hardware; the PUFFS designation was also applied to USN AN/BQG-1/2/3/4 anti-submarine warfare system. It was developed for the detection and tracking of submarine and surface targets, and provides automatic target tracking of up to four

targets simultaneously, instantaneous and continuous ranging solution, fire control range and bearing output and secure operation. The basic technique is signal enhancement by cross correlation of the signals received at the arrays with conversion of two measured time differentials into bearing and range data.

The system consists of three hydrophonic baffled arrays mounted on each side of the submarine. The arrays are connected to a display control console, which utilises an analogue processor, digital processor and AN/UYK-26 computer. The console

also includes built-in fault localiser equipment. The system is built to US military specifications, and uses standard electronic modules throughout.
STATUS
MicroPUFFS systems are currently installed aboard six 'Oberon' class submarines of the Royal Australian Navy. A subsequent model has been built for the US Navy for test installation on the USS *Barb*.
CONTRACTOR
Sperry Corporation, Electronic Systems, Great Neck, New York 11020, USA.

1983.453
AN/BQQ-5 SONAR

The BQQ-5 sonar system is the principal sensor system of the US Navy's nuclear attack submarines, the SSN-688 class, all of which are to be fitted in addition to retrofitting all 'Permit' and 'Sturgeon' class SSNs during regular refits. The BQQ-5 is a digital, multi-beam system employing both hull-mounted and towed acoustic hydrophone arrays. The latter of the two arrays will be produced in two types; initially a manually detached and attached receiver array connecting to a fixed towing point will be employed, to be replaced later by a towed array that will be retractable and housed along the submarine's hull. Both fixed tow and retractable array versions will have provision for mechanically cutting the array adrift in the event of an emergency, except for the first seven equipped with the fixed tow point. The polyethylene-covered tow cable, which has a maximum length of about 800 m, is 9·5 mm in diameter, and the array at the end of the cable where the hydrophones and electronics are located is 82·5 mm in diameter. The array is tapered fore and aft to minimise flow noise. Drag is stated to account for a maximum reduction in speed of 0·5 knot, with no serious inhibition on submerged manoeuvres and little adverse effect on

surface manoeuvres with the one exception of those entailing going about.

A US defence spokesman has stated that the BQQ-5 will provide for detection of Soviet submarines at significantly greater ranges than are now attainable, and that the advanced beam forming and display features will yield much higher search rates.

The AN/WLR-9A acoustic intercept receiver, produced by Norden, has been successfully evaluated and will form an integral sub-system of the BQQ-5 and BQQ-6 on new attack and Trident missile submarines. The sub-system features a CRT display, a digital readout and a remote unit for the submarine commander. A 'sensitivity improvement' kit for the AN/WLR-9A has been developed by Norden and deliveries to the US Navy are in progress.
STATUS
The AN/BQQ-5 underwent extensive developmental testing during 1972 and 1973, and was approved for production later in 1973. The original initial production appropriation planned for a batch of eight sets but this was subsequently reduced to six as a result of budget cuts. The fiscal year request was for $55.8 million to produce a further quantity of nine sonars, later amended to eight, to be fitted in seven submarines (SSN Nos 606, 612, 637, 638, 661, 663,

and 677) with the eighth equipment being assigned to the training role.

In April 1975 $84·2 million was requested for fiscal year 1976 and $42·6 million in successive years for another nine and five systems, respectively. This request was for equipment to retrofit SSN 594/637 class submarines.

In May 1978, the US Navy Sea Systems Command announced a contract modification by which eight BQQ-5 towed array (hydrophones) handling and stowage equipments would be supplied.

Commencing in October 1979 Raytheon was awarded a series of US Naval Sea Systems Command contracts calling for refurbishment and conversion of AN/BQS-11, 12, and 13 sonar transmission sub-systems to AN/BQQ-5 standards.

Over the period 1980-1982, IBM, Gould, Raytheon and Norden were awarded contracts worth nearly $50 million. Tracor has also been awarded a $45 million contract to provide technical support.
CONTRACTORS
IBM, Federal Systems Division, 10215 Fernwood Road, Bethesda, Maryland 20034, USA.
Raytheon Company, Portsmouth, Rhode Island, USA.

4629.453
AN/BQQ-6 SONAR

The AN/BQQ-6 is an advanced active/passive sonar set developed for the Trident submarine. Forming part of the Trident command and control system it is an integrated complex of command, control, communications and ship defence equipment.

The AN/BQQ-6 is based on the AN/BQQ-5 (**1983.453**) and has many of the same parts. The primary detection group is a digital integrated system

employing spherical array, hull-mounted line array and towed array sensors, with an active emission acoustic intercept receiver and high frequency active short range sonar. In the passive mode the system used is identical to that of the AN/BQQ-5. Support equipment has been added to provide for underwater communications, environmental sensing, magnetic recording and acoustic emergency devices. All other technical details are classified.

STATUS
Installed on Trident class submarines.
CONTRACTORS
IBM, Federal Systems Division, 10215 Fernwood Drive, Bethseda, Maryland 20034, USA.
Gould Inc, Defense Electronics Division, Glen Burnie, Maryland, USA.

1984.453
AN/BQR-15 SONAR

The BQR-15 is a towed array sonar used by US Navy fleet ballistic missile submarines (SSBNs). Because the array is towed behind the submarine, these sonars provide the first long-range passive detection capability astern. In addition, since the sensors are removed from the submarine hull and internal ship's noise, detection of other submarines is possible at greatly increased ranges. As installed, the BQR-15 includes specially designed hydraulically operated handling equipment that permits the cable array to be

partially or completely streamed, retrieved, and adjusted automatically while the SSBN is submerged. The equipment forms part of the SSBN sonar system which also includes the AN/BQR-19 receiving set and the AN/BQR-21 (**1985.453**).
DEVELOPMENT
In May 1972 contracts were awarded for the design and development of SPAD (signal processing and display) systems to exploit more fully the signal gathering potential of the BQR-15 towed array sonar, but difficulties and delays led to the cancellation of this effort in March 1974. Since then funds have been

allocated for procurement of a multiple channel signal processing and display equipment for use on FBM submarines and at FBM training facilities with the BQR-15 sonar system.
STATUS
In operational service. A modified array was due to enter production during 1984.
CONTRACTOR
Western Electric Company, Winston-Salem, North Carolina, USA.

1985.453
AN/BQR-21 DIMUS SONAR

The BQR-21 DIMUS sonar is a hull-mounted preformed beam passive sonar with improved digital signal processing for the detection and tracking of quiet nuclear submarines. It is intended for fitting on all pre-Trident SSBNs and selected SSNs, and will be a direct replacement for the AN/BQR-2. The BQR-21 will incorporate the same array configuration as the earlier equipment but will embody significantly enhanced signal processing capabilities. In addition to improvements in the electronics, performance will be improved through platform noise reductions which are being made in the bow dome of the submarine. These include the addition of an array baffle.

DEVELOPMENT
A contract for AN/BQR-21 development was awarded to Honeywell in June 1972. One engineering model was delivered in early 1974, sea trials were completed in mid-1974, environmental testing and service approval were accomplished in November 1974.

STATUS
Funding of $47·1 million in fiscal years 1975/76/77 allowed for BQR-21 procurement for both SSBN and SSN fittings, and for training installations at New London, Charleston, and Pearl Harbor, and the SSN training facility at San Diego. 42 submarines were scheduled for fitting under this programme.

A total of 56 of this equipment for fitting in fleet ballistic missile submarines and certain attack submarines has now been procured. System delivery began in August 1977 and was completed in December 1979. Two engineering models have been refurbished and delivered for use as trainers. In November 1982 Honeywell was awarded a $5 million contract for engineering support.

CONTRACTOR
Honeywell Inc, Training and Control Systems Operations, 1200 East San Bernardino Road, West Covina, California 91790, USA.

AN/BQR-21 DIMUS sonar display console

1986.453
AN/BQS-13 SONAR

The BQS-13 sonar system is the primary sonar in USN 'Permit Sturgeon' SSN class nuclear attack submarines. The system was service approved in December 1971 and is in operation. A system addition providing new functional capability was service approved in late 1974. This addition, the BQS-13 multipurpose sub-system (BQR-24), is being procured for a limited number of SSNs.

DEVELOPMENT
Acceptance testing of the multipurpose sub-system began in late 1973 and technical and operational testing were conducted aboard the *Archerfish* during 1974. The BQS-13 multipurpose sub-system (BQR-24) was service approved in late 1974. The extended operational test programme delayed procurement to fiscal year 1975/76 when 11 systems plus support were procured for $25·3 million. These sub-systems provide interim improvement in sonar and fire control capability for those submarines not scheduled to receive the BQQ-5 sonar (**1983.453**) until late in that programme. The BQR-24 has been installed only in submarines where it will have a useful life of at least

three years prior to receiving a BQQ-5 sonar system.

Commencing in October 1979, Raytheon was awarded a series of US Naval Sea Systems Command contracts calling for refurbishment and conversion of AN/BQS-11, 12, and 13 sonar transmission sub-systems to AN/BQQ-5 transmission sub-system configuration. These sub-systems are part of the AN/BQQ-5 system.

CONTRACTOR
Raytheon Company, Submarine Signal Division, Portsmouth, Rhode Island 02871, USA.

1987.453
AN/SSQ-41B SONOBUOY

The Sparton AN/SSQ-41B is an omni-directional, passive sonobuoy with a multiple life and depth capability. In volume production since 1963, the series has been the mainstay of US Navy sonobuoy operations but is gradually yielding this role to the newer, directional AN/SSQ-53A.

The AN/SSQ-41B, extensively redesigned from the earlier AN/SSQ-41, provides an audio bandwidth expanded to ten kHz and improved dynamic range capabilities. The depth selection is 60 or 1000 feet and life selection is one, three, or eight hours.

The AN/SSQ-41B may be launched from an aircraft at airspeeds between 30 and 425 knots and from altitudes of 100 to 40 000 feet (30·5 to 12 200 metres).

After a controlled and stabilised descent and upon impact with the water, the termination mass and the hydrophone are released and descend to a

preselected operating depth of either 60 or 1000 feet (18·3 or 305 metres). On contact with seawater, the battery is activated and the sonobuoy becomes fully operative within 60 seconds.

Modulation is accomplished in the crystal oscillator stage by a variable-capacity diode. Two frequency-doubling amplifiers multiply the rf oscillator-doubler frequency to the desired operating frequency of the sonobuoy, which is preset to one of thirty-one channel frequencies within the 162·25 to 173·50 MHz band.

CHARACTERISTICS
Type: Passive
Audio frequencies: 10 – 10 000 Hz
Depth: 18·3 or 305 m
Size: A
Weight: 9 kg
Operating life: 1, 3, or 8 h
Launch altitude: 30·5 – 12 200 m

Launch speed: 30 – 425 knots
RF channels: 31
RF power: 1 W
STATUS
Although large scale production was contracted through 1982, the US Navy has discontinued further development. This unit will continue to be available, however, for the next five to ten years. Sparton had completed the preliminary engineering to add a 99-channel, transmit capability with electronic function selection of channel, life and depth similar to that of the AN/SSQ-53B before the programme was stopped.

CONTRACTORS
Sparton Corporation, Electronics Division, Jackson, Michigan 49202, USA.
Magnavox, Fort Wayne, Indiana 46808, USA.

1988.453
AN/SSQ-47B SONOBUOY

The AN/SSQ-47B is an active sonobuoy. The operational function is that of detection, classification, tracking, and location of submarines.

Sonobuoy AN/SSQ-47B provides an active sonar capability for fixed-wing aircraft. It can be operated from a minimum range of zero to ten nautical miles at an altitude of 500 feet (152 metres) and in sea conditions up to sea state 5. The AN/SSQ-47B permits launching and operation of up to six

sonobuoys, either individually or simultaneously, without encountering rf or sonar interference.

CHARACTERISTICS
Type: Active
Sonar modes: Automatic keyed CW
Depth: 18·3 or 244 m
Size: A
Sonar channels: 6 (HF)
RF channels: 12
RF power: 0·25 W
Weight: 14·5 kg

STATUS
Sparton has received the following US Navy contracts: 139 700 SSQ-47 sonobuoys between 1963 and 1974; a $5·12 million contract for SSQ-47B sonobuoys in 1975 which brought orders for 28 732 buoys in 1975 and 1976; 4900 buoys in 1978 for which some of the work was carried out at the Canadian Sparton plant; and 15 440 buoys in mid-1983.

CONTRACTOR
Sparton Corporation, Electronics Division, Jackson, Michigan 49202, USA.

1990.453
AN/SSQ-53A DIFAR SONOBUOY

The AN/SSQ-53A DIFAR (directional frequency and ranging) sonobuoy is becoming the US Navy's primary sonobuoy sensor. As compared to earlier passive sonobuoy types, the Q-53A provides target bearing information as well as improved acoustical sensitivity, particularly in the low-frequency ranges.

The Q-53A sonobuoy is the result of a US Navy-sponsored development programme to improve the operational capabilities of the earlier Q-53. Changes include a dual-depth capability (90 or 1000 feet (27 or 305 metres)), an extended launch envelope and improved low-frequency performance. The

sonobuoy's electrical and mechanical design was extensively revised to improve reliability and to lower production costs.

Deliveries of the Q-53A began early in 1975. To date, Sparton has delivered or has contracts for a total of 341 702 Q-53A sonobuoys.

The AN/SSQ-53A sonobuoy may be dropped from an aircraft at indicated airspeeds of 30 to 425 knots and from altitudes of 100 to 40 000 feet (30 to 12 200 metres). Descent of the sonobuoy is stabilised and slowed by a parachute assembly.

Immediately after water entry, the seawater-activated battery system is energised. Gas-filled cylinders inflate the sonobuoy float, jettisoning the

parachute assembly and erecting the VHF transmitting antenna. This permits the surface assembly to rise and separate from the sonobuoy housing. The sonobuoy housing serves as a descent vehicle and separates from the sub-surface assembly at the operating depth.

CHARACTERISTICS
Type: Directional LOFAR
Depth: 27 or 305 m
Size: A
Weight: 11·3 kg
Operating life: 1 or 4 h
Launch altitude: 30 – 12 200 m
Launch speed: 30 – 425 knots

RF channels: 31
RF power: 1 W
STATUS
An RFP for up to 100 000 buoys was issued by the US Naval Avionics Center in October 1982. The AN/SSQ-53A is also being manufactured under licence in the UK by Plessey Marine. In January 1983 Sparton

received a US Navy contract, reportedly the final purchase of SSQ-53As, for nearly 50 000 units. Production will continue for 5-10 years.
CONTRACTORS
Sparton Corporation, Electronics Division, Jackson, Michigan 49202, USA.

Magnavox, Fort Wayne, Indiana 46808, USA.
Nippon Electronic, Japan (licence)
Ultra Electronics Ltd, UK (licence)
Plessey Electronics Ltd, UK (licence)

4457.453
AN/SSQ-53B SONOBUOY
In addition to Q-53A production, a successor model, the AN/SSQ-53B is well advanced. Acoustical performance is not significantly changed, but the B model offers electronic selection of RF transmit channels, life, and operating depth. Operating parameters are switch selected and verified by a light-emitting diode display on the sonobuoy. The Q-53B can be programmed to transmit on any one of 99 channels, with three depth and three operating life choices instead of a single, preset transmit frequency and two operating depths and lives. The first deliveries of the Q-53B for fleet use are expected in early 1984.
CHARACTERISTICS
Type: Directional LOFAR
Depth: 27, 122 or 305 m, electronically selected
Size: A

Weight: 11·3 kg
Operating life: 1, 3, or 8 h electronically selected
Launch altitude: 30 – 12 200 m
Launch speed: 30 – 425 knots
RF channels: 99, electronically selected
RF power: 1 W
STATUS
In October 1982 the US Naval Avionics Center issued an RFP for up to 180 300 AN/SSQ-53B sonobuoys. The three major manufacturers, Sparton, Magnavox and Hazeltine each received contracts in November 1981. 273 412 AN/SSQ-53B sonobuoys were ordered by the US Navy in November 1983. Contracts were awarded to Sparton, Magnavox, Hermes and Rockwell International.
CONTRACTOR
Sparton Corporation, Electronics Division, Jackson, Michigan 49202, USA.

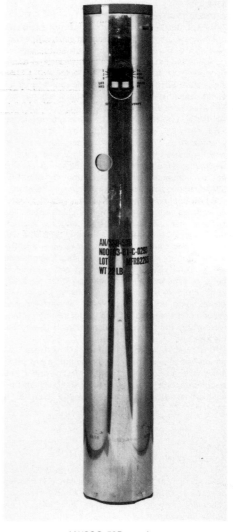

AN/SSQ-53B sonobuoy

3083.453
AN/SSQ-57A SONOBUOY
The AN/SSQ-57A sound reference sonobuoy features a hydrophone that affords exceptional performance stability under temperature and pressure extremes. The hydrophone is a piezoelectric ceramic segmented cylinder with a smooth frequency response to 20 kHz. The sonobuoy is calibrated to allow determination of underwater acoustic sound pressure levels over this wide frequency range.

The AN/SSQ-57A can be air-launched from altitudes between 150 and 10 000 feet (46 and 3048 metres) into sea conditions of up to sea state 5 and is effective at ranges up to ten nautical miles.

Immediately after entering the water the seawater-activated battery system is energised. Gas-filled cylinders inflate the sonobuoy float, jettisoning the parachute assembly and erecting the VHF transmitting antenna. This permits the surface assembly to rise and separate from the sonobuoy housing. The sonobuoy housing serves as a descent vehicle and separates from the sub-surface assembly at the operating depth.

Operating life is one, three or eight hours, selected before launch. At the end of the operating life, the transmitter is shut-off. The watertight sonobuoy housing is equipped with a seawater-soluble plug that dissolves to effect scuttling. The plug's dissolution

rate varies as a function of water temperature but is never less than eight hours (maximum selectable operating life) or more than 20 hours. The AN/SSQ-57A also features an externally selectable attenuator that can decrease the sensitivity by 20 dB for special applications.

The AN/SSQ-57A (XN-5) is a version of the AN/SSQ-57A that has a fixed operating depth of 1000 feet (305 metres).
CHARACTERISTICS
Type: Passive, calibrated audio
Audio frequencies: 10 – 20 000 Hz
Depth: 18 – 91 m
Size: A
Weight: 8·6 kg
Operating life: 1, 3, or 8 h
Launch altitude: 30 – 12 200 m
Launch speed: 30 – 425 knots
RF channels: 31
RF power: 1 W
STATUS
The AN/SSQ-57 has been in production since 1968. A US Navy contract for 9300 buoys was awarded in November 1983.
CONTRACTOR
Sparton Corporation, Electronics Division, Jackson, Michigan 49202, USA.

1991.453
AN/SSQ-62B DICASS SONOBUOY
The AN/SSQ-62B is the sonobuoy component of the Directional Command-Activated Sonobuoy System (DICASS). A high-performance sonobuoy, it detects the presence of submarines using sonar techniques under direct command from ASW aircraft. The AN/SSQ-62B can also determine the range and bearing of the target relative to the sonobuoy's position.

The DICASS sonobuoy is composed of three main sections, an air descent retarder, a surface unit and a sub-surface unit. The air descent retarder consists of a spring-loaded parachute release assembly and a parachute to retard descent immediately after launch. The surface unit receives commands from the controlling aircraft, via a UHF receiver, and sends target information to the aircraft, via a VHF transmitter. The sub-surface unit transmits sonar pulses in the ocean upon command from the aircraft and receives sonar target echoes for transmission to the aircraft.

Command signals are received by the sonobuoy and are accepted if the correct address code is identified by a decoder. The command capability includes depth selection, scuttle, and selection of transducer (sonar) transmission signals. The echoes from the selected activating signal are multiplexed in the sub-surface unit before being transmitted to the receiving station or aircraft.

The AN/SSQ-62B may be launched from fixed- or rotary-wing aircraft within the parameters specified in the launch envelope.

Upon impact with the water, the transducer is released for descent to its shallow operating depth. Immediately after entry, the float is inflated and the VHF-transmitter/UHF-receiver antenna is erected. When the float surfaces, the VHF transmitter begins emitting a continuous FM carrier signal. The sonobuoy is now operating in the passive mode and is ready to receive commands.

The main power source for the sonobuoy comes

from a lithium battery pack instead of the more costly silver chloride batteries commonly used in sonobuoys. The sonobuoy is designed for economical volume production without compromising performance or reliability. Electronic design is exclusively solid state with maximum use of multifunction integrated circuits.
CHARACTERISTICS
Type: Commandable, omni-directional active, directional receive
Sonar modes: Pulse CW or linear FM
Depth: Commandable, 27, 119 and 457 m (89, 396, 1518 ft)
Size: A
Life: 30 minutes
Weight: 15 kg
Sonar channels: 4
RF channels: 31
RF power: 0·25 W

STATUS
Production. The US Navy awarded a contract for a total of 18 600 SSQ-62B units to Sparton and Magnavox in November 1983.

CONTRACTORS
Sparton Corporation, Electronics Division, Jackson, Michigan 49202, USA.
The Magnavox Company, Fort Wayne, Indiana 46804, USA.

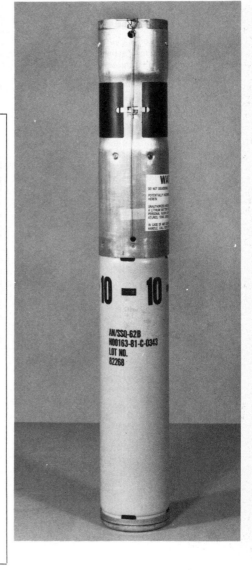

AN/SSQ-62B DICASS sonobuoy

3786.453
AN/SSQ-71 ATAC BUOY

The AN/SSQ-71 air transportable acoustic communication (ATAC) buoy is an expendable two-way sonic RF receive-transmit communications device. It is launched from surface vessels or either fixed-wing or rotary-wing aircraft. Incoming UHF signals are encoded into a multiple-tone format for sonic transmission; incoming sonic signals are likewise processed for VHF transmission. The AN/SSQ-71 borrows heavily from designs developed and refined in other Sparton sonobuoys programmes. The antenna system, for instance, which receives UHF and transmits VHF signals, is derived from the Sparton AN/SSQ-62 sonobuoy. The entire mechanical layout is based upon the AN/SSQ-53A, designed and produced in volume by Sparton.

When deployed, the ATAC comprises two major assemblies with a connecting compliant cable. The surface unit includes the float and its inflation mechanism, the antenna assembly and the RF receiver and transmitter. Both the receiver and the transmitter are miniaturised solid-state designs and are powered by a seawater-activated, non-silver battery. The compliant cable provides separate conductors for the receive and transmit signals. The coiled compliant feature isolates the wave-induced motion of the surface assembly from the sub-surface assembly to provide the desired low-noise background.

The sub-surface assembly includes an encode/decode unit, a sonic transmitter, a projector, a hydrophone, sonic amplifiers, and a line driver. The encode/decode unit uses discrete standard, off-the-shelf logic elements with analogue circuits. It analyses input signals for validity as well as coding them for either sonic or RF retransmission. The sonar transmitter is a linear amplifier whose output is matched to the characteristics of the simple resonant bender projector to provide efficiently the necessary acoustic pressure level over the desired bandwidth. Incoming sonic signals are detached by an omni-directional hydrophone, amplified by the sonic amplifier, decoded, and sent to the surface unit via the line driver for RF transmission. The entire sub-surface unit is powered by an array of lithium batteries.

Deployment of the ATAC buoy is conventional. If air launched, it is slowed and stabilised by a windflap-deployed parachute. If launched from a surface vessel, it is merely thrown over the side. In either case, water entry triggers the water deployment sequence.

Long or short life is selected by a switch before launch. At the end of the period selected, VHF transmission ceases and the buoy automatically scuttles.

CHARACTERISTICS
Type: Communication buoy
Transmitter frequency: 163·75 – 166·75 MHz
Size: A
Weight: 6·8 kg
RF channels: 3
RF power: 1 W
Launch altitude: 46 – 3048 m
Launch speed: 30 – 250 knots
STATUS
Early development.
CONTRACTOR
Sparton Corporation, 2400 E Ganson Street, Jackson, Michigan 49202, USA.

3084.453
AN/SSQ-77 (VLAD) SONOBUOY

The AN/SSQ-77 VLAD (vertical line array DIFAR) is a passive, tactical search and surveillance sonobuoy designed to improve detection and tracking capability for the DIFAR system in a noisy, high-traffic environment.

The AN/SSQ-77 concept utilises a vertical line array of omni-directional hydrophones in place of the single omni-directional hydrophone used in the standard DIFAR unit. A directional DIFAR hydrophone mounted at the array phase centre provides target bearing data.

The signal format for the AN/SSQ-77 sonobuoy is identical to that for the AN/SSQ-53 and is compatible with the AN/AQA-7 processor and the Sparton TD-1135/A demultiplexer/processor/display. All beam-forming functions are accomplished within the sonobuoy, with provisions for sea-noise equalisation and omni-directional phase tracking.

The AN/SSQ-77 may be dropped from an aircraft at indicated airspeeds of 45 to 380 knots and from altitudes of 100 to 30 000 feet (30 to 9144 metres). Descent is stabilised and slowed by a parachute assembly.

An internal microprocessor electronically selects the desired RF channel and sonobuoy life. Verification of these settings is provided by an LED display readable through the SLC.

Lithium batteries are activated upon entry to the water. These detonate a squib, causing gas-filled cylinders to inflate the sonobuoy flotation bag and initiate deployment. Inflation of the flotation bag provides a pressure force, releasing the release plate in the top of the sonobuoy and causing the parachute to be jettisoned. This permits the surface assembly to rise and separate from the sonobuoy housing. The sonobuoy housing serves as a descent vehicle and separates from the sub-surface assembly at the operating depth.

CHARACTERISTICS
Type: DIFAR with VLA omni
Size: A
Weight: 13·1 kg
Operating life: 4 or 8 h
Launch altitude: 30 – 9144 m
Launch speed: 45 – 380 knots
RF channels: 99, electronically selected
RF power: 1 W
STATUS
In quantity production. Contracts to the value of $17 million were placed with Sparton, Hazeltine and Magnavox for AN/SSQ-77A items in July 1981. A requirement for 35 870 sonobuoys was issued by the US Navy in November 1982 and for 59 928 in November 1983.
CONTRACTORS
Sparton Corporation, Electronics Division, Jackson, Michigan 49202, USA.
Sippican Ocean Systems Inc, Marion, Massachussets, USA.

3783.453
TUNED VERTICAL ARRAY OMNI SONOBUOY

The Sparton tuned vertical line array (TVA) sonobuoy is the result of efforts to supply the US Navy with improved target detection capability by means of discrimination against horizontally arriving noise. Externally the design is similar to the Sparton AN/SSQ-53 sonobuoy (**1990.453**). Inside, only the surface unit remains unchanged. The SSQ-53 lower unit has been replaced with a new electronics package and a five-element array. The array is designed to have low drag to maintain verticality and is protected from the flow induced mechanical noise (cable strum). A new suspension system has been incorporated to provide good surface wave isolation while reducing the current flow past the array.

Improved detection is achieved by the use of a tuned line array consisting of five omnidirectional hydrophone elements in a centre-phased configuration yielding two independent three-element arrays tuned to specific frequencies. The array provides a signal-to-noise ratio improvement over a single omnidirectional hydrophone of 6 to 15 dB in the frequency range of interest, depending upon the target range and the specific noise conditions. Each hydrophone assembly includes a low-noise, high-input-impedance preamplifier to minimise cable losses and to ensure that the array shading factors and phase characteristics are not compromised.

Immediately after water entry, sea-water activated batteries are energised. A 1·5 V float inflation battery detonates a squib, causing gas filled cylinders to inflate the sonobuoy flotation bag and erect the VHF transmitting antenna. A 1·5 V life timer battery and a 12 V primary battery are contained in the same pack. The life timer battery operates a circuit that can be set to scuttle the sonobuoy one hour or eight hours after water entry. The 12 V primary battery supplies power to all the electronic circuits and the sonobuoy begins transmitting.

CHARACTERISTICS
Type: Vertical line array
Size: A
Weight: 13·1 kg
Operating life: 8 h minimum

RF channels: 31
RF power: 1 W
CONTRACTOR
Sparton Corporation, 2400 E Ganson Street, Jackson, Michigan 49202, USA.

3782.453
SPARTON DWARF DIFAR SONOBUOYS

The Sparton Dwarf DIFAR sonobuoy is the electrical and acoustical equivalent of a standard AN/SSQ-53B sonobuoy, but occupies only a third of the volume. The Dwarf DIFAR has the 4·87 inch (124 mm) diameter of a conventional A-sized sonobuoy but an overall length of only 12 inches (305 mm). The small size of the Dwarf DIFAR sonobuoy enables a threefold increase in the number of units an ASW aircraft can carry and is particularly valuable with small fixed-wing ASW aircraft and helicopters. Dwarf DIFAR sonobuoys are compatible with existing shipping containers and handling equipment, and the cost saving in shipping and handling is substantial. They can be incorporated into existing fleet operations with minimal changes to associated equipment and deployment philosophy.

The Dwarf DIFAR sonobuoy can be deployed from fixed-wing or rotary-wing aircraft at indicated airspeeds of 0 to 370 knots and from altitudes of 40 to 30 000 feet (12 to 9144 metres). Air descent is stabilised and slowed by a parachute assembly.

The major components of the DWARF DIFAR sonobuoy are the external sonobuoy housing, the

Sparton dwarf DIFAR sonobuoys

antenna/VHF assembly, the suspension assembly (which consists of the cable pack, the stabilising kite, the damper disc, and the compliant cable), and the integrated hydrophone and electronics assembly.

Upon entry to the water, the Dwarf DIFAR lithium-sulphur dioxide battery pack is activated by a seawater switch that detonates a squib, causing gas-filled cylinders to inflate the sonobuoy flotation bag, jettisoning the parachute assembly and erecting the VHF transmitting antenna. Inflation of the flotation bag provides the pressure force that activates the release plate in the top of the sonobuoy. This causes the parachute to be jettisoned and permits the surface assembly to separate from the sonobuoy housing and the surface housing. The sonobuoy housing serves as a descent vehicle and falls away from the sub-surface assembly at the operating depth, either 30 or 300 metres.

CHARACTERISTICS
Type: Passive
Depth: 30 or 300 m
Size: A diameter × 304 mm
Weight: 4·5 kg
Operating life: 1 or 4 h
Launch altitude: 12 – 9144 m
RF channels: Multi-channel
STATUS
Development.
CONTRACTOR
Sparton Corporation, 2400 E Ganson Street, Jackson, Michigan 49202, USA.

4458.453
SPARTON DWARF OMNI SONOBUOY

The Sparton Dwarf Omni is an omni-directional passive sonobuoy that has an A-sized sonobuoy diameter but is only 305 mm long yet offers performance equivalent to a standard AN/SSQ-41B plus 99-channel transmit capability and electronic function selection of channel, life, and depth. Use of dwarf sonobuoys increases the number of sonobuoys that can be carried by an aircraft and is especially valuable for small fixed-wing ASW aircraft and helicopters. The 12 inch (305 mm) sonobuoys are compatible with existing shipping containers, handling equipment, and launching methods. They could be incorporated into existing fleet operations with minimal changes to associated equipment and deployment philosophy.

The Dwarf Omni sonobuoy may be dropped from an aircraft at indicated airspeeds of 30 to 425 knots and from altitudes of 100 to 40 000 feet (30 to 12 200

metres). Descent is stabilised and slowed by a parachute assembly. Operation on entry to the water is identical to the Dwarf DIFAR sonobuoy (**3782.453**).

CHARACTERISTICS
Type: Passive
Depth: 18 or 305 m
Size: A diameter × 305 mm length
Weight: 4·5 kg
Operating life: 1, 3, or 8 h
Launch altitude: 30 – 12 200 m
Launch speed: 30 – 425 knots
RF channels: 31
RF power: 1 W
STATUS
Development.
CONTRACTOR
Sparton Corporation, 2400 E Ganson Street, Jackson, Michigan 49202, USA.

Sparton Dwarf Omni sonobuoy, cut away to show internal components

3784.453
WIDETRAC SONOBUOY

Widetrac is a developmental communications buoy intended to receive, convert and retransmit data. Both RF-to-acoustic and acoustic-to-RF may be received and transmitted simultaneously. Built to a standard A-size format, Widetrac can be launched from any aircraft equipped to handle sonobuoys.

The Widetrac sonobuoy may be dropped at indicated airspeeds of 30 to 425 knots and descent is slowed by a drogue parachute. Upon water impact, the buoy automatically activates in the receive mode. The operating depth is determined by manual selection before deployment. The acoustic transmit mode is activated only when the output of the UHF receiver contains information signals for transmission; scuttle commands or commands

intended for other equipment such as CASS or DICASS sonobuoys do not cause any form of transmission from the Widetrac buoy. Operation is terminated by either a VHF scuttle command, a built-in timer, or a passive backup device. The sonobuoy system includes a floated surface assembly, a long interconnecting cable with mechanical stabilisation provisions, and a sub-surface assembly.

Widetrac consists functionally of an up-link and a down-link. The communication link can be established either as an up-link channel only or as simultaneous up and down channels. Upon receipt of a down-link message, acoustic signals are transmitted. The buoy system continuously maintains an acoustic listening mode so that incoming signals or the acoustic output of the

sonobuoy itself can be detected, processed, and transmitted on a VHF link. The communication system is compatible with the submarine underwater telephone AN/WQC-2.

CHARACTERISTICS
Type: Communications buoy
Transmitter frequency: 162·25 – 173·5 MHz
Size: A
Weight: 15·9 kg
RF channels: 4
RF power: 1 W
STATUS
Development.
CONTRACTOR
Sparton Corporation, 2400 E Ganson Street, Jackson, Michigan 49202, USA.

4459.453
AN/SSQ-86(XN-1) DOWN-LINK COMMUNICATION SONOBUOY

The AN/SSQ-86(XN-1) down-link communication (DLC) sonobuoy is a one-way communication device designed to transmit a pre-programmed message to a submerged submarine. Developed to meet the need for a reliable means of transmitting a message without revealing the receiving submarine's position, the DLC is compatible with existing sonobuoy launch platforms. The unit is packaged in a standard A-sized sonobuoy envelope and can be launched from any

properly equipped fixed-wing aircraft or helicopter or from a surface ship.

The desired message is programmed into the DLC using a single push-button switch and four 7-segment LED displays. Four groups of three digits make up the message. The message can be verified and corrected if necessary with a second push-button provided to ensure proper data insertion. Once programmed, all remaining operational functions are automatic.

When air launched, the DLC is slowed and stabilised by a small parachute. For launches from surface vessels, it is merely thrown overboard. Upon

water entry, the DLC immediately deploys. As soon as the sub-surface unit reaches the shallow operating depth, the message, coded into appropriate tones, is acoustically transmitted. The first transmission is followed by a five-minute pause while the sub-surface unit deploys to the deep depth. The message is repeated at the deep depth; after a second five-minute pause, the message is transmitted a third time. At the end of the final transmission, the DLC automatically scuttles. The nominal life of the DLC from water entry to scuttle is 17 minutes.

For maximum reliability and minimum

development time, extensive use has been made of existing technology and hardware from other Sparton sonobuoy designs. Examples include the lithium battery power supply, the air descent and float inflation hardware, and much of the circuit design. The omni-directional projector is a simple resonant bender element designed to operate efficiently at the desired bandwidth.

CHARACTERISTICS
Depth: Shallow and deep
Size: A (123 × 910 mm)
Weight: 11·4 kg
Operating life: 17 minutes nominal
STATUS
Development.
CONTRACTOR
Sparton Corporation, 2400 E Ganson Street, Jackson, Michigan 49202, USA.

AN/SSQ-86(XN-1) down-link communication sonobuoy

3599.253
AN/ASQ-81(V) AIRBORNE ASW MAGNETOMETER
The AN/ASQ-81(V) magnetic anomaly detector (MAD) system was developed for the USN for use in the detection of submarines from an airborne platform. The system operates on the atomic properties of optically-pumped metastable helium atoms to detect variations in total magnetic field intensity. The Larmor frequency of the sensing elements is converted to an analogue voltage which is processed by bandpass filters before it is displayed to the operator.

Two configurations of the AN/ASQ-81(V) are available; one for installation within an airframe, and one for towing behind an aircraft. The USN uses the AN/ASQ-81(V)-1 inboard installation with carrier-based S-3A aircraft as well as with the land-based P-3C ASW aircraft. For towing, the configuration is the AN/ASQ-81(V)-2, which is employed by USN SH-3H and SH-2D helicopters. The towed version is also fitted in the USN's latest helicopter the SH-60B Seahawk.
STATUS
The AN/ASQ-81(V) is in production for the USN and a variety of international customers on helicopters such as the WG-13, HSS-2 and 500D.
CONTRACTOR
Texas Instruments Inc, PO Box 226015, Dallas, Texas 75266, USA.

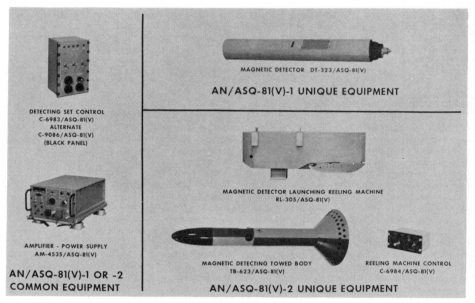

AN/ASQ-81(V) magnetometer family

4460.453
KLEIN HYDROSCAN SYSTEMS
Klein Hydroscan systems map the topography of the sea bed and profile the shallow bottom sediment layers, although they can also be used for underwater detection of objects moored on the sea bed. A side-scan sonar/sub-bottom profiler system consists of a side-scan towfish with a sub-bottom profiler attachment, a towing cable and a graphic recorder.

The side-scan sonar towfish contains transmitting circuitry to energise the transducers which project high frequency bursts of acoustic energy in fan-shaped beams which are narrow in the horizontal plane and wide in the vertical plane. The sub-bottom profiler attachment contains its own electronics and transducer to project a conical beam straight down to the sea floor. Echoes from both side-scan and profiler transducers are received and sent up the tow cable to the graphic recorder for processing and printing.

The standard towfish has a 100 kHz frequency and a horizontal beam angle of one degree which is the

optimum for general purposes. A very high resolution version has a frequency of 500 kHz whilst another variant for long range operates at 50 kHz. They can be towed up to a maximum speed of 16 knots and are rated for a depth of up to 1000 m. Deeper units which are rated to 12 000 m are also available and have been tested by the US Navy.

The sub-bottom profiler is used to give a high resolution vertical profile of shallow sediments on the sea floor. It has an output frequency of 3·5 kHz and a normal depth rating of 300 metres, although a special deep tow attachment can operate down to 12 000 metres. Resolution is approximately 600 mm and the beam angle is 50°, conical and pointed straight down.
STATUS
All versions of both side-scan sonar and sub-bottom profiler attachment are in current production.
CONTRACTOR
Klein Associates Inc, Undersea Search and Survey, Klein Drive, Salem, New Hampshire 03079, USA.

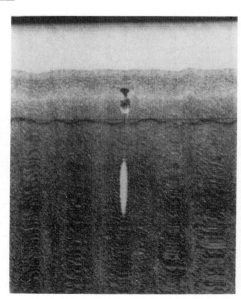

Klein side-scan sonograph of a Mk 17 mine with a Mk 18 base

5643.453

UNDERWATER ORDNANCE LOCATOR MK.24 MOD O

The Mk.24 Mod 0 ordnance locator is a dual-beam side-scan sonar for use in locating mines and other types of underwater ordnance. It is available with modular accessories which adapt the equipment for use in channel conditioning/route survey mine countermeasures operations as well as for use in explosive ordnance disposal operations.

The Mk.24 system consists of a side-scan sonar towfish, weighing approximately 22 kg (48 lb), a lightweight Kevlar towcable, and a combined transceiver and graphic recorder weighing 44 kg (95 lb). The system and its accessories are lightweight and portable, and can be deployed from any available vessel down to 5 m in length. It can also be towed from any available and unmodified helicopter.

The side-scan towfish contains the circuitry to energise the transducers which project high frequency bursts of acoustic energy in fan-shaped beams, narrow in the horizontal plane and broad in the vertical plane. Echoes from both transponders are processed by the combined transceiver and printed by the graphic recorder. Three types of towfish are available; a 50 kHz long range towfish for covering up to 1·2 km swaths of the bottom; a 100 kHz high resolution version for detection operations covering up to 400 m swaths; and a 500 kHz very high resolution towfish for target classification applications with a sweep width of 150 m. A 3·5 kHz sub-bottom profiler is available for assessing bottom hardness to determine potential buried mine hazards.

The towfish can be towed at speeds up to 16 knots,

Components of the Mk 24 mine-hunting sonar

but for optimum operation against small targets the recommended speed is 5 to 6 knots. Standard towfish can operate down to depths of 1000 m (3280 feet) with options permitting operation down to 2270 m (7445 feet). Special units are available for operations down to full ocean depth.

STATUS

All versions of the system are in full production, and are in use by the US Navy Explosive Ordnance Disposal units.

CONTRACTOR

Klein Associates Inc, Klein Drive, Salem, New Hampshire 03079, USA.

ELECTRO-OPTICAL EQUIPMENT

Note: This section contains details of electro-optical (also referred to as opto-electronic and/or optronic) equipments which formerly occupied the Rangefinding and Sighting Equipment section of this book. For the convenience of users of *Jane's Weapon Systems* the contents of the section have been divided into three sub-sections, devoted to land, sea and air applications of these equipments respectively. In those cases where an item may be employed in more than one role, it will be found, as a general rule, within either the sub-section relating to its initial application, or the sub-section appropriate to the most common use of the equipment.

Within the complete section readers will find examples of purely optical devices, such as sights and sighting equipment, as well as others which involve the use of different parts of the spectrum beyond the visible region. As a matter of convenience, a number of items will be found in which the use of optical components is incidental (albeit essential). Such entries are mostly related to equipment which has as its main function some role such as weapon delivery, which is a prime objective of most of the entries in this section.

More specifically, the section contains entries concerned with optical sights for land, sea and air use; laser equipment for rangefinding and target designation or marking purposes; infra-red techniques applied to such functions as passive surveillance and detection, thermal imaging sights, night driving periscopes, and forward looking infra-red for aircraft and other uses. From this brief summary it will be appreciated that most of these applications are related closely with one or more of the other aspects of military technology which are the subject matter of this volume, and that certain of them (elaborated to a greater or lesser degree) could equally well be assigned to another part of the book. For example, many of the newer electro-optical (E-O) naval tracking equipments are capable of being expanded, with little additional equipment, to form a naval fire control system for small vessels. Similarly, many of the infra-red techniques employed in equipment in this section have applications in the fields of reconnaissance and countermeasures. For such reasons as these, users with specific interests in such areas should also consult related sections such as Army and Naval Fire Control Systems, Electronic Warfare, etc.

ELECTRO-OPTICAL EQUIPMENT (LAND)

BELGIUM

4743.193
LRS 4 Mk II FIRE CONTROL SYSTEM

This is a portable battery-operated laser rangefinder with a built-in ballistic computer. It is claimed to be one of the smallest fire control systems available and is intended for day and night operation. It is designed for direct firing on weapons such as small turrets on armoured vehicles, recoilless guns and portable anti-tank weapons. Depending on the application, the system can be operated by the built-in rechargeable battery or by an independent battery, eg the vehicle supply.

The LRS 4 Mk II consists of a ×3·8 day channel, a ×3·8 image intensifier night sight, an Nd:YAG laser rangefinder, a digital ballistic computer programmed for two different types of ammunition, a moving target tracking system, a computer-driven ballistic aiming mark, a ballistic reticle for emergency firing and a rechargeable battery.

The reticle configuration is identical for night and day observation. There are three separate groups of reticles: a laser cross with moving target marks, a red-coloured cross ballistic aiming mark and a ballistic reticle. Most of the controls for the gunner are push-button types, integrated into the keyboard, either on the instrument itself or a remote control unit.

CHARACTERISTICS
Day and night sights
Magnification: ×3·8
Field of view: 8·5°
Dioptre adjustment: −3 to +3 dioptre
Laser
Type: Nd:YAG
Wavelength: 1·064 μm
Resolution: 5 m
Accuracy: ± 10 m
Range: 200 to 5000 m
Minimum range gating: 200 to 3000 m
STATUS
In late development.

LRS 4 Mk II fire control system

CONTRACTOR
OIP Optics, Meersstraat 138, 9000 Ghent, Belgium.

4744.193
LRS 5 FIRE CONTROL SYSTEM

The LRS 5 is a compact day/night laser rangefinder with a built-in ballistic computer. It is designed for use in most types of battle tanks and other armoured vehicles. The LRS 5 is a monobloc, fully integrated system with no separate boxes except for a small overriding control box for the vehicle commander.

The main components of the system are: a unit vision eyepiece, a ×8 power day sight, a ×4 power second generation image intensifier night sight, an Nd:YAG laser rangefinder, a digital ballistic computer able to be programmed for 4 types of ammunition, a moving target tracking system, a computer-driven ballistic aiming mark, a manual range input as the first emergency mode and a ballistic reticle as the second emergency mode. The system provides a firing sequence identical for both day and night modes of operation, a manual correction for secondary parameters such as temperature and humidity and a visual warning to both commander and gunner for every control being operated.

A number of optional items are also available including an automatic computer-controlled correction for cant angles and a slaved commander's sight allowing 100 per cent override facility. In addition, an agreement between OIP and Thorn-EMI (UK) provides for the development and integration of a thermal imager night sight. This is based on the latter company's Multi-Role Thermal Imager (**4260.193**) which is in operational service.

CHARACTERISTICS
Magnification: ×8 (day sight); ×4 (night sight)
Field of view: 7° (day sight); 7·2° (night sight)
Laser
Type: Nd:YAG
Wavelength: 1·064 μm
Radiant energy: 4 mJ (typical)
Ranging resolution: 5 m
Ranging accuracy: ±10 m
Range: 200 to 9995 m
Minimum range gating: 200 to 4000 m
STATUS
Over 500 systems sold to six customers. The thermal imager module is expected to reach prototype stage by the end of 1984.
CONTRACTOR
OIP Optics, Meersstraat 138, 9000 Ghent, Belgium.

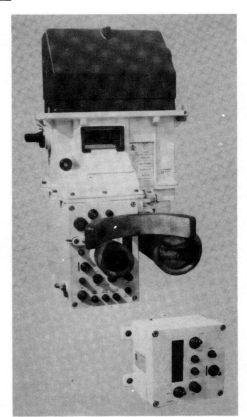
LRS 5 fire control system

4745.193
LRF 104 HAND-HELD LASER RANGEFINDER

The LRF 104 is a rangefinder approximately the size of a pair of 7 × 35 binoculars and weighing only 1 kg. Instant range operation enables the operator to distinguish moving targets up to 10 km distance. Range data and operational indicators displayed in the sighting optics provide the operator with the necessary information without loss of aim to the target.

CHARACTERISTICS
Laser: Nd:YAG
Receiver: Silicon avalanche photodiode
Wavelength: 1·064 μm
Pulse energy: 4 mJ nominal
Magnification: ×5
Field of view: 113 mrad
Range: 50 to 10 000 m
CONTRACTOR
OIP Optics, Meersstraat 138, 9000 Ghent, Belgium.

LRF 104 hand-held laser rangefinder

DENMARK

4237.193
TYPE 772 SIGHTING SYSTEM

This tank sighting system employs the JAI Type 772 low light-level television camera which is similar to the Type 771 produced by the same company for naval applications (3857.293), in this case employed with an automatic ballistic calculator and an input from a laser rangefinder to provide a day/night sighting system for use in main battle tanks. The data generated by the system is presented on a TV monitor screen together with the camera picture of the outside scene. These facilities are available to both the gunner and the tank commander, each having his own monitor display.

CHARACTERISTICS
Field of view: 64 × 48 mrad
Focus: 30 m to infinity
Range: Dependent on guns and ammunition (typically 0–3995 m)
Sensitivity: 2 × 10⁻⁶ lux, fp (100% contrast, 200 lines)
Recognition limit: 1·5 m target at 1000 m with 10⁻⁴ lux illumination (target reflection 30%, contrast 50%)
Automatic fire flash protection
CONTRACTOR
JAI – Jorgen Anderson Ingeniofirma AS, Produktionsvej 1, 2600 Glostrup, Copenhagen, Denmark.

JAI Type 772 low light-level television camera for tank fire control

FRANCE

3039.193
TCV 29 AND TCV 30 TANK LASER RANGEFINDERS

The type TCV 29 laser rangefinder has been designed for installation on existing tanks in order to improve their capabilities without any major modifications, and thus increase their operational efficiency. The TCV 30 is an equipment derived from the TCV 29, and has the same main characteristics as those described in the following paragraphs. It is suitable for installation on the T54 and T55 series of tanks.

The equipment consists of a power-supply transmitter-receiver unit and two display and control boxes. The former includes, in a watertight cast housing, the laser transmitter and the detector together with their associated optical systems, the signal processing electronic circuits and the power supplies for the various parts of the rangefinder. It also includes a removable optical sight for aligning it on the gun bore axis. The equipment can be operated either by the tank commander or by the gunner. The first control box is assigned to the tank commander and includes means for transmitting orders to the gunner. The second one is assigned to the gunner and is identical to the commander's box in its functions.

In use, three operations only are involved:
(1) accurately aim at the target
(2) depress the measurement button
(3) read off the range presented in numerical form.

In the case of two echoes being detected, the second measurement is recorded and a warning light indicates this second echo to the operator. The corresponding distance can be displayed by depressing another button.

TCV 30 tank laser rangefinder

TCV 29 laser rangefinder installed on tank turret

OPERATION
The light pulse is generated by a neodymium-doped glass laser emitting in the near infra-red.

The laser beam goes through a beam expander, the purpose of which is to reduce its divergence. The echo returned by the target is received through an optical system on an avalanche photodiode.

A small fraction of the laser beam is used as a start signal for a pair of counters. The stop signal for the first counter is derived from the first incoming echo; a second echo will act likewise for the second counter.

The receiver gain automatically increases with the time elapsed from the start of the transmitted pulse to compensate for the effects of target remoteness. The information relating to the distance is also available in a digital form for possible transmission to a firing computer.

Laser rangefinding consists basically in measuring the time interval between the emission of a short laser pulse and its reception after reflection on a target. This time interval is automatically converted into distance and the result is numerically displayed. The accuracy is ±5 m with the normal operating range, ie between 400 m and 10 km.

CHARACTERISTICS
Transmitter
Wavelength: 1·06 μm
Peak power: >4 MW
Pulse duration: 25 × 10⁻⁹ s
Energy: over 0·1 J
Repetition rate: 1 measurement every 2 s; 12 per minute
Divergence (at the exit of beam expander): Over 0·5 mrad
Exit pupil (after beam expander): 30 mm Q-switching by rotating prism
Avalanche photodiode detector
Minimum detectable power: 10⁻⁷ W
Receiving pupil: 40 mm
Clock frequency: 29·97 MHz
Accuracy: ±5 m
Measurement range: 400 – 9995 m
Number of counters: 2
Multiple target distance resolution: 50 m
Output to computer: Parallel BCD (1, 2, 4, 8) coded
Removable optical sight
Field: 3°
Magnification: ×5

Ocular ring: 4 mm
Automatic shutter for protection of emission and reception optical parts.
Power supply
Voltage: 24 ± 8 V, DC
Consumption: 50 W between measurements. 200 J per measurement

Power supply/transmitter/receiver unit
Weight: 19·5 kg, cables: 2 kg
Dimensions: 240 × 350 × 120 mm
Control box I
Weight: 2·7 kg + cable
Dimensions: 150 × 72 × 115 mm
Control box II
Weight: 2·7 kg + cable
Dimensions: 210 × 90 × 115 mm

STATUS
In production. Among others, this equipment is fitted to the Austrian Army Kurassier tank (**5032.102**).
CONTRACTORS
CILAS (Compagnie Industrielle des Lasers), Route de Nozay, 91460 Marcoussis, France.
 SOPELEM, 102 rue Chaptal, 92306 Levallois-Perret, France.

3557.193
TCV 107 TANK LASER RANGEFINDER
The TCV 107 is a miniature laser rangefinder for use on any type of tank. Small size and weight permit its

TCV 107 tank laser rangefinder with its associated control box

installation outside the vehicle, or inside where it may be associated with an optical sight. It is of modular construction and consists of two parts:
(1) a sealed transmitter receiver power unit. A removable optical sight is used for aligning this unit with the gun boresight axis, by means of an integrated beam deviator.
(2) a control box for operating the equipment and displaying the results.
 The digital readout of range measurement is displayed on the control box. A warning light indicates when there are several echoes and the distance of the furthest echo is automatically displayed; the range of the nearest one can then be obtained by pressing a button. For installation outside the vehicle, an armoured container with an automatic shutter for the protection of the optics is available.
CHARACTERISTICS
Wavelength: 1·06 μm
Pulse duration: 20 × 10⁻⁹ s

Peak power: 1 MW
Detector: Avalanche photodiode
Output to vehicle computer (option)
Dimensions: 290 × 140 × 100 mm
Mass: 6·3 kg
Measurement range: 150 – 9500 m
Accuracy: ±5 m
Angular resolution: Better than 0·5 mrad
Repetition rate: 1 measurement every 2 s for 3 successive shots; 12 measurements per minute
STATUS
Series production.
CONTRACTORS
CILAS (Compagnie Industrielle des Lasers), Route de Nozay, 91460 Marcoussis, France.
 SOPELEM, 102 rue Chaptal, 92306 Levallois-Perret, France.

3660.193
TCV 109 TANK LASER RANGEFINDER SIGHT
The TCV 109 is a combined optical sight and laser rangefinder designed for installation inside a tank turret. The equipment consists of four items: an optical sight for observation and aiming, adapted to a prismatic head, providing one channel for observation and another for rangefinder operation; a laser rangefinder, incorporating within the same case the emission, reception, timing, display, and power supply functions; a slaved cross-hairs projector located in a casing mounted at the rear of the rangefinder unit, and which allows superimposition on the aiming sight cross-hairs of a set of computer-generated correction cross-hairs; and a remote control and display box. The last item is optional.
 Operating features include: control of the minimum ranging gate; comprehensive display of information within the eyepiece (distance of first and second laser echoes, warning of multiple echoes, warning of an echo within the gated zone, and 'ready-to-fire' gun warning); data output to tank fire control computer; built-in test.
CHARACTERISTICS
Optical sight
Magnification: ×8 and ×1·2, switchable
Field: 7 and 44°

Eyepiece adjustment: –5 to +2 dioptres
Laser rangefinder
Wavelength: 1.06 micron
Pulse duration: 25 × 10⁻⁹ s
Peak power: 1 MW
Detector: Avalanche photodiode
Minimum detectable power: ≤2 × 10⁻⁸ W
Receiver field: 0·5 mrad
Operating voltage: 20 – 32 V DC
Dimensions: 190 × 240 × 380 mm
Weight: 15 kg (complete)
Measurement range: 320 – 9995 m
Accuracy: ±5 m
Minimum ranging gate adjustable: 300 – 3000 m
Repetition rate: One measurement every 2s for 3 successive shots; 12 measurements per minute. Dichroic plate and filter in observation channel protect observer's eye during laser emission; this provides at least 60 dB attenuation at 1·06 micron
CONTRACTORS
CILAS (Compagnie Industrielle des Lasers), Route de Nozay, 91460 Marcoussis, France.
 SOPELEM, 102 rue Chaptal, 92306 Levallois-Perret, France.

TCV 109 combined tank sight and laser rangefinder

3040.193
TM 17 (TM 12) ARTILLERY SIGHT/LASER RANGEFINDER
The TM 17 (formerly designated TM 12) is a portable equipment that combines in a single unit an optical sight and a laser rangefinder. The former provides target elevation and azimuth information, and the latter gives range data. Arrangements are made for this information to be fed into an automatic fire control system.
 It is also possible to use the TM 17 for taking topographic measurements and survey work by provision of a suitable north seeking system.
CHARACTERISTICS
Laser material: Nd-doped glass
Wavelength: 1·06μm
Pulse duration: Approx 25 × 10⁻⁹ s
Energy: Over 100 mJ
Peak power: Over 4 MW
Divergence: 0·5 mrad
Measurement range: 150 – 19 900 m. Simultaneous display of 2 echoes
Range blanking: Adjustable between 150 and 5000 m
Measurement accuracy: ±5 m
Repetition rate: 1 measurement every 2 s for 3 successive shots; 12 measurements/minute

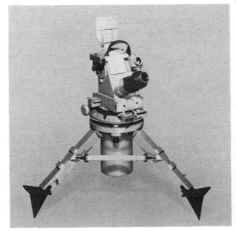

TM 17 tripod mounting

Optical sight
Azimuth range: 360°
Azimuth accuracy: 1 mil

TM 17 for vehicle mounting

Elevation range: –20 to +40°
Elevation accuracy: 2 mils
Orientation: By trough compass
Power supply: 24 V Ni-Cd rechargeable battery allowing over 400 measurements
Weight: <15 kg complete

STATUS
Series production.
CONTRACTORS
CILAS (Compagnie Industrielle des Lasers), Route de Nozay, 91460 Marcoussis, France.
SOPELEM, 102 rue Chaptal, 92306 Levallois-Perret, France.

3416.193
TPV 89 LASER RANGEFINDER
The TPV 89 is a hand-held laser rangefinder, similar in size and appearance to a pair of field binoculars. The instrument was designed for observation and

CILAS TPV 89 laser rangefinder

rapid and accurate range measurement of targets or other items of interest. In use, the operator centres the cross-hairs on the target and triggers the laser by means of a push-button; the distance in metres is displayed immediately in the eyepiece. Accuracy is ±10 m whatever the target distance, within the range limits of the sight. An optical device provides absolute protection of the operator's eyes during laser emission. Other features include a device to prevent accidental triggering of the laser, a multiple echo indicator, a blanking control adjustable between 150 and 2300 m, and an internal power supply. A tripod mounting with elevation and azimuth control, charger for the nickel-cadmium battery, remote trigger, lithium battery and a removable attenuator are also available.
CHARACTERISTICS
Monocular sight
Magnification: ×6
Field of view: 7° (+120 mrad)
Ocular ring: 5 mm

Laser rangefinder
Wavelength: 1·06μm
Beam expansion ratio: 1:4
Energy: 30 mJ
Repetition rate: 12 shots/minute
Time to range: 0·1 s
Detector: PIN photodiode
Measurement range: 150 – 9990 m
Accuracy: ±10 m
Range blanking: Adjustable 150 – 2300 m
Dimensions: 180 × 150 × 75 mm
Weight: 1·9 kg
Power supply: 12 V 0·5 Ah Ni-Cd battery giving 600 shots at 25°C
STATUS
Series production.
CONTRACTORS
CILAS (Compagnie Industrielle des Lasers), Route de Nozay, 91460 Marcoussis, France.
SOPELEM, 102 rue Chaptal, 92306 Levallois-Perret, France.

3146.193
APX M504 OPTICAL SIGHT AND RANGEFINDER
The APX M504 equipment consisting of a laser rangefinder, an aiming optical system, and an optical deflection device, is part of the COTAC fire control system of the AMX-10RC tank. The equipment provides an optical sight for the gunner, with ×10 magnification and a 120 mil field of view (SOPELEM), a laser rangefinder by CILAS, and a line-of-sight deflector by GIAT (Groupement Industriel des

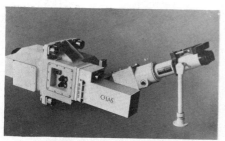

APX M504 sight and rangefinder

Armements Terrestres). The last of these is used to introduce automatically fire corrections into the optical sight.
In addition to its observation and aiming functions, it provides information automatically on the distance of the target to the firing control system. Its accuracy is ±5 m regardless of the distance of the target within the limits of the range. The maximum measurable distance depends on the visibility, and can reach 10 km. The unit comprises a pilot light indicating the possible presence of two echoes, in which case the measurement of the second echo can be selected.
CHARACTERISTICS
Rangefinder
Laser material: Nd-glass
Wavelength: 1·06 μm
Pulse duration: 25 × 10⁻⁹ s
Energy: 100 mJ
Peak power: 4 MW
Divergence: 0·5 mrad
Repetition rate: 1 measurement every 2 s for 3 successive firings, 12 measurements per minute
Receiver
Detector: Avalanche photodiode

Field angle: 0·5 mrad
Dimensions: 250 × 110 × 150 mm. 3·5 kg (rangefinder only)
OPERATION
The gun-layer's function is simply to aim at the target. As soon as this is correctly performed, he triggers the laser rangefinder, and then inserts the corrections which have been computed automatically. A number of sub-systems developed by GIAT enhance the performance of the overall COTAC system: a device for measuring the angular speed of the target in two axes; an automatic cant angle sensor; meteorological sensors; and a computer for producing fire corrections from the measured parameters.
STATUS
The APX M504 was designed under DTAT contract and is now in series production.
CONTRACTORS
CILAS (Compagnie Industrielle des Lasers), Route de Nozay, 91460 Marcoussis, France.
GIAT, 10 place Georges Clémenceau, 92211 Saint Cloud, France.
SOPELEM, 102 rue Chaptal, 92306 Levallois-Perret, France.

1797.193
APX M409 OPTICAL SIGHT AND RANGEFINDER
The APX M409, consisting of a laser rangefinder, a daylight sight, a night-time sight, and a prism head, is intended for the AMX-30S tank.

APX M409 optical sight and laser rangefinder

In addition to its observation and aiming functions, it provides information on target range directly to the tank commander.
Its accuracy is ±5 m regardless of the distance of the target within the limits of the range. The maximum measurable distance depends on the visibility and can reach 10 km. When distances relating to two targets are measured simultaneously, the two readings are displayed at the same time one above the other.
Through a blanking device, it is possible to eliminate any echoes from less than a predetermined distance.
CHARACTERISTICS
Emitter
Laser material: Nd-glass
Wavelength: 1·06 micron
Pulse duration: 25 × 10⁻⁹ s
Energy: 100 mJ
Peak power: 4 MW

Divergence: 0·5 mrad
Measurement range: 400 – 9995 m
Range blanking: Adjustable between 400 and 5000 m
Repetition rate: 1 measurement every 2 s, 12 measurements per minute
Dimensions
Optical sight and rangefinder: 350 × 200 × 150 mm; 10 kg
Supply unit: 320 × 200 × 160 mm; 25 kg
STATUS
The APX M409 was designed and developed under DTAT contract. It is now in series production for AMX-30S tanks ordered by an undisclosed defence force.
CONTRACTORS
CILAS (Compagnie Industrielle des Lasers), Route de Nozay, 91460 Marcoussis, France.
SOPELEM, 102 rue Chaptal, 92306 Levallois-Perret, France.

3415.193
APX M546 OPTICAL SIGHT AND RANGEFINDER
The APX M546 optical day and night sight and rangefinder has been developed for AMX-10 AFVs armed with the HOT anti-tank missile system (**2212.111**). It is used by the vehicle commander for observation and rangefinding purposes in target acquisition in the operation of the HOT missile.
The portion of the equipment protruding from the cupola (M517 for HOT, M605 for SAO) is made of armour steel. It incorporates an elevation prism

transmitting the landscape image to the inside of the cupola, this prism being under manual control.
The lower part of the equipment (M427) inside the vehicle has two functions: as a day telescope, and as a rangefinder. The former portion of the equipment is the responsibility of SOPELEM and the main features are ×8 magnification, an 8° field of view, adjustable eyepiece (–5 to +2 dioptres), infra-red filter, and a

APX M546 optical sight and rangefinder

retractable neutral filter. The rangefinding element is the responsibility of CILAS and the laser rangefinder has the following principal characteristics: 1·06 micron operating wavelength, range capability of 400 m to 10 km with an accuracy of ±5 m, range

blanking continuously variable between 400 and 5000 m, two echoes are displayed, and measurements can be made at a rate of one every two seconds.
STATUS
In series production.

CONTRACTORS
CILAS (Compagnie Industrielle des Lasers), Route de Nozay, 91460 Marcoussis, France.
    SOPELEM, 102 rue Chaptal, 92306 Levallois-Perret, France.

3414.193
APX M550/TCV 80 LASER RANGEFINDER

The APX M550/TCV 80 laser rangefinder was specially designed for mounting on the optical sight of AMX-10RC and AMX-30 tanks, and on some APX gyro-stabilised sights for helicopter applications. A single unit of small dimensions houses the laser emitter, the receiver, power supply and the electronic clock. In addition to the above applications, this rangefinder can be adapted to any fire control system for accurate distance measuring.
CHARACTERISTICS
Laser type: Nd-glass
Wavelength: 1·06 micron
Pulse duration: 25×10^{-9} s
Energy output: 100 mJ

Peak power: 4 MW
Repetition rate: 1 measurement every 2 s for 3 successive shots; 12 shots/minute
Detector: Avalanche photodiode
Minimum detectable power: $\leqslant 2 \times 10^{-8}$ W
Measurement range: 320 – 9995 m. Output to fire control computer
Range accuracy: ±5 m
Dimensions: $260 \times 110 \times 160/110$ mm (height)
Weight: 3·5 kg
Power supply: Vehicle, 19 – 28 V DC
STATUS
Series production.
CONTRACTOR
CILAS (Compagnie Industrielle des Lasers), Route de Nozay, 91460 Marcoussis, France.

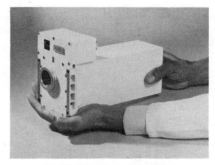

CILAS TCV 80 laser rangefinder

3663.193
TCY 133 LASER RANGEFINDER/ILLUMINATOR

The high repetition rate laser rangefinder TCY 133 was designed for integration into gyro-stabilised sights used with anti-aircraft weapon optical sights. The equipment is provided with a device that projects cross-hairs into the aiming sight of the weapon system, thus aiding alignment of the rangefinder channel, since the rangefinder channel employs the observation optical channel. Rangefinder, electronic clock, and power supply are all contained in the same casing.
CHARACTERISTICS
Laser material: Nd-YAG
Wavelength: 1·06 micron
Pulse duration: 20×10^{-9} s

Peak power: Over 5 MW
Detector: Avalanche photodiode
Detector field: 2 mrad
Dimensions: $470 \times 230 \times 220$ mm
Weight: 15 kg
Power supply: 115 V/400 Hz 3-phase
Measurement accuracy: ±5 m
Repetition rate: 5, 10, or 20 pps (as specified)
STATUS
Series production.
CONTRACTOR
CILAS (Compagnie Industrielle des Lasers), Route de Nozay, 91460 Marcoussis, France.

CILAS TCY 133 laser rangefinder/target illuminator for anti-aircraft weapons

4682.193
TN$_2$1 NIGHT AIMING SYSTEM

The TN$_2$1 consists of a mask-mounted binocular night vision device and a near IR spotlight mounted on the operator's rifle and aligned with the weapon's bore. The mask-mounted image intensifier binocular sight is worn during night operations. In operation, the user detects a target and then switches on the IR spotlight. He can then line up the luminous spot on the target and open fire without shouldering the weapon or otherwise taking aim. Maximum engagement range is about 150 metres.
CHARACTERISTICS
Type: Binocular monotube sight (2nd generation, 18 mm wafer tube, double focus), retractable in quiescent position

Field of view: 40°
Magnification: × 1
Weight: 0·5 kg
Searchlight
Fixed setting: 10 cm spot at 100 m
Weight: 0·25 kg
STATUS
Pre-production.
CONTRACTOR
SOPELEM, 102 rue Chaptal, 92306 Levallois-Perret, France.

TN$_2$1 night aiming system

3418.193
OB-44 NIGHT OBSERVATION BINOCULARS

The OB-44 low light-level binoculars are designed for general night observation purposes and are capable of use from a moving vehicle. The latter feature is assisted by the eyepiece design which requires no inter-pupillary adjustment (between 58 and 72 mm), has no exit pupil and no eyepiece focusing, which enables an observer to retain spectacles (if worn). A special high-performance refractive lens, designed for low light-level applications, is used, and an inverter type micro-channel intensifier tube with manual and automatic gain control is employed.
CHARACTERISTICS
Magnification: ×2·5
Field of view: 11·5°
Resolution: $\geqslant 0·6$ mrad at 10^{-3} lux

Focus: Adjustable 20 m – ∞
Lens: Dioptre 120 mm focal length
Aperture: f1·6
Image tube: 25 mm type S-20ER cathode
Resolution: 30 line pair/mm
Range performance: 600 m for human targets and 1200 m for tank targets at 10^{-1} lux; 450 m and 900 m at 10^{-3} lux
Dimensions: $90 \times 120 \times 330$ mm
Weight: 2 kg
Power: 2·7 V mercury or lithium battery
STATUS
Production. Operational with French and foreign forces.
CONTRACTOR
SOPELEM, 102 rue Chaptal, 92306 Levallois-Perret, France.

Sopelem OB-44 night observation binoculars

3752.193
OB-47 NIGHT SIGHT
The OB-47 night sight is a light intensification monocular sight which enables the gunner of an AMX-30 main battle tank to aim the tank's main armament in darkness. The image intensifier tube employed has automatic gain control and is of the microchannel inverter type. In the AMX-30, the OB-47 is associated with OB-44 observation binoculars, and an M 427-02 laser rangefinder sight. The driver can be provided with a CN2 516 night driving periscope.

CHARACTERISTICS
Magnification: ×5·5
Field of view: 7°
Elevation travel: –8 to +20°
Dioptre adjustment: –5 to +2 dioptre
Range: 1000 m with 10^{-3} lux illumination
STATUS
Production and in service with a foreign army.
CONTRACTOR
SOPELEM, 102 rue Chaptal, 92306 Levallois-Perret, France.

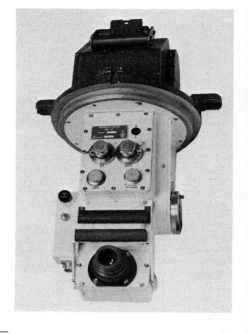

SOPELEM OB-47 night sight

3978.193
OB-49 COMBINED DAY AND NIGHT AIMING SIGHT
This sight comprises two day paths, one with a wide field of view, an image intensification night path, and an eyepiece common to the three paths.
It is connected to the M591 prism head of the AMX-30 tank cupola. For use by the commander, it enables day and night firing of the 20 mm weapon from the turret, as well as firing the cupola light weapon.
CHARACTERISTICS
Day path
Magnifying power: ×1·2 and ×7

Field of view: 30° and 6°
Night path
Magnifying power: ×3·5
Horizontal field of view: 11°
Micro-channel image intensifier tube automatic and manual gain control
Range: 600 m with 10^{-3} lux
Head prism elevation range: –10 to +45°
STATUS
In production.
CONTRACTOR
SOPELEM, 102 rue Chaptal, 92306 Levallois-Perret, France.

OB-49 combined day and night aiming sight

5698.193
OB-50 NIGHT AIMING TELESCOPE
The OB-50 telescope is designed for night observation and aiming without artificial illumination of the target by intensification of the residual light from the night sky. It is cylindrical in form and is equipped with a high definition objective lens, second generation light intensifier tube and a wide adjustment eyepiece. The line of sight is represented by a micrometer with LED illumination, adjustable in two perpendicular directions for alignment with the weapon. It is mounted on the weapon by a mechanical support.

CHARACTERISTICS
Magnification: ×3
Field: 10°
Resolution: 0·6 mrad at 10^{-1} lux; 0·8 mrad at 10^{-3} lux
Range recognition: 400 m at 10^{-1} lux; 150 m at 10^{-3} lux
Weight: 0·9 kg
STATUS
In service with the French Army.
CONTRACTOR
SOPELEM, 102 rue Chaptal, 92306 Levallois-Perret, France.

OB-50 night aiming telescope

3754.193
TJN2-90-A COMBINED DAY/NIGHT SIGHT
The TJN2-90-A combined aiming sight comprises both day and night weapon aiming facilities within a single instrument. It employs a light intensifier tube with automatic gain control to enable sighting in darkness without the need for any artificial illumination.
The TJN2-90-A is specially designed for the GIAT TS90, Hispano Lynx type, and SAMM AR 90 turrets. Incorporating slave micrometers, this sight forms the principal aiming element of the SOPELEM SOPTAC range of fire control systems.
CHARACTERISTICS
Sight
Elevation field: –8 to +15°

Day path
Magnification: ×6
Field of view: 8°
Night path
Magnification: ×6
Field of view: 8°
Range: 800 – 2000 m, depending on light
STATUS
In production and operational with the French Army and foreign forces.
CONTRACTOR
SOPELEM, 102 rue Chaptal, 92306 Levallois-Perret, France.

TJN2-90-A combined day/night sight for TS90 turret

2105.193
TELESCOPE-PERISCOPE M112/3
This combined monocular telescope and binocular periscope is designed for use with the AML-60 and other light armoured cars. By changing the micrometers, however, it can be adapted for use on anti-aircraft cupolas.
Elevation aiming control is linked to the weapon but

provision is made for manual scanning. The micrometers can be illuminated for night firing.
CHARACTERISTICS
Telescope
Magnification: ×1
Field of view: 356 (vertical) × 1132 (horizontal) mils
Elevation range: –20 to +45°
Periscope height: 180 mm

Sight
Magnification: ×5
Field of view: 230 mil
Elevation range: –20 to +45°
Eyepiece adjustment: –2 to +1 dioptres
Weight: 8·6 kg

STATUS
Production.

CONTRACTOR
SOPELEM, 102 rue Chaptal, 92306 Levallois-Perret, France.

4269.183
SOPTAL 29 FIRE CONTROL SYSTEM

The SOPTAL 29 fire control equipment is an optical director designed for use with the ACL-STRIM anti-tank missile weapon (**2055.111**). It is used to generate a line-of-sight based on target range (determined by laser rangefinder), weapon cant (pendular graticule), type of ammunition, crosswind (manually inserted), target lateral velocity (transducer between weapon launcher and tripod), temperature and pressure. A detachable afocal unit for night firing is an optional addition.

The equipment comprises three interchangeable basic sub-assemblies: sight, processing electronics and laser module; sight aiming module (afocal system with light intensifier); and base, comprising weapon support and tacho bearing data encoder.

CHARACTERISTICS
Optical
Magnification: ×4
Eyepiece aperture: 4 mm
Focal length: 40 mm
Field of view: 8°
Aiming
Elevation setting accuracy: 0·3 mil
Bearing offset accuracy: 1 mil
Rangefinder: 150 – 2000 m

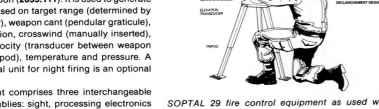

SOPTAL 29 fire control equipment as used with ACL-STRIM anti-tank rocket launcher

Elevation correction: Between 150 and 800 m for two types of ammunition
Lateral target velocity limit: 20 m/s
Autonomy: 1000 rounds
STATUS
Prototype.
CONTRACTOR
SOPELEM, 102 rue Chaptal, 92306 Levallois-Perret, France.

SOPELEM M112/3 vehicle periscope

3751.193
CN2-500 SERIES PASSIVE VEHICLE PERISCOPE

The CN2-500 series is a range of second generation passive driving periscopes which enable AFVs to be driven at night without the aid of any artificial lighting. Daylight driving is possible also with the same equipment. The second generation light intensification tube employed is stated to eliminate the effects of sudden glare resulting from unexpected exposure to light sources when operating in darkness.

The optical module is fitted with a bi-ocular eyepiece enabling simultaneous viewing with both eyes without adjustment. Models have been designed within the CN2-500 series for fitting in a range of vehicles, as follows:

CN2-508: Panhard and AMX-13T
CN2-516: AMX tanks and Saviem vehicles
CN2-548: M48 tanks and derivatives
CN2-555: T55 tanks and derivatives
CHARACTERISTICS
Magnification: ⩾ ×0·9
Resolution: 1·5 mrad at 10^{-1} lux
Objective lens aperture: 1:1
Image tube: TH 1313 with AGC
Tube gain: At least 30 000 FL/FC
Luminance gain: >400
STATUS
Production.
CONTRACTOR
SOPELEM, 102 rue Chaptal, 92306 Levallois-Perret, France.

CN2-508 passive driving periscope for Panhard and AMX-13T vehicles

4245.193
OB-31 NIGHT-DRIVING PERISCOPE

The OB-31 passive periscope is designed to equip AMX-10 and AMX-30 tanks and various other AFVs and may be interchanged with the daylight driving periscope installed in these vehicles to provide combined day/night driving facilities from broad daylight to starlight, without headlights. Two light intensification tubes and suitable optical arrangements provide two separate channels and allow stereoscopic vision. A manually-operated diaphragm permits limiting of image brightness in high ambient light levels and there is a device to protect the tubes from excessive brightness. When the unit is switched off the diaphragm is automatically closed. The use of modern single-stage tubes (XX 1080 type) makes it possible to produce a compact periscope of high performance with simple operation. It can be operated in daylight levels up to about 10 000 lux.

CHARACTERISTICS
Magnification: ×0·9 (approx)
Horizontal field: 48°
Vertical field: 40°
Eyepiece diameter: 20 mm
Lens diameter: 45 mm
Distance between lens axes: 65 mm
Illumination levels: (minimum) classified; (max) 10 000 lux
Dimensions: 327 × 193 × 163 mm
Weight: 11·85 kg (with transport case); 7·85 kg (less case)
STATUS
Production for French and foreign armies. Officially approved by French Army for use in AMX-10, AMX-30 and VAB.
CONTRACTOR
TRT (Télécommunications Radioélectriques et Téléphoniques), 88 rue Brillat-Savarin, 75640 Paris Cedex 13, France.

OB-31 night-driving periscope

4246.193
OB-41 NIGHT-DRIVING BINOCULARS

The OB-41 passive night-driving binoculars have two separate optical paths each consisting of a micro-channel light intensifier tube with double proximity focus. In this way comfortable stereoscopic vision is obtained. Adjustment of the inter-pupillary distance is by rotation of the body elements in the interior of the close-fitting face mask of the instrument. With the aid of a faint additional light source, the OB-41 can be used in very poor ambient lighting conditions (eg less than 10^{-4} lux) up to a distance of about ten metres.

CHARACTERISTICS
Magnification: ×1
Field: 33°

Focus: Adjustable by 4-position switch for each eyepiece
Distance between eyepieces: Continuously adjustable
Weight: <900 g (complete with battery pack)
Typical range: 250 m

STATUS
In series production and in service with the French and other armies.

CONTRACTOR
TRT (Télécommunications Radioélectriques et Téléphoniques), 88 rue Brillat-Savarin, 75640 Paris Cedex 13, France.

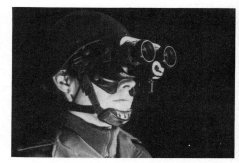
OB-41 night-driving binoculars

4247.193
OB-42 NIGHT OBSERVATION BINOCULARS

The OB-42 light intensifier micro-channel passive binoculars have a magnification of ×4 and are composed of two objectives and two eyepiece lenses. The tubes employed are micro-channel tubes with double proximity focusing. The equipment is designed for observation of military objectives at night and the light intensifier technique enables a tank to be recognised at a distance of 600 metres when lit by only starlight (luminosity 1 millilux). The right-hand optical path is equipped with an illuminated graticule graduated in mils for azimuth and elevation and this graticule has adjustable brightness.

CHARACTERISTICS
Magnification: ×4
Field: 8°
Distance between eyepieces: Continuously adjustable
Focus: Continuous, 20 m – ∞
Light levels: 10^{-4} to 10^2 lux
Typical range: 1000 m

STATUS
Production. In service with the French and other armies, police forces and customs authorities.

CONTRACTOR
TRT (Télécommunications Radioélectriques et Téléphoniques), 88 rue Brillat-Savarin, 75640 Paris Cedex 13, France.

OB-42 night observation binoculars

4683.193
CIRCE PORTABLE NIGHT SIGHT

Circe is a portable night sight which employs a great deal of the thermal imaging technology developed for the Mira sight (**3845.193**). It is a portable, compact and lightweight night observation camera which allows detection at distances greater than 2 km. A number of options are also available, including an eyepiece display, a laser rangefinder and a TV camera for remote display.

STATUS
In development.

CONTRACTOR
TRT (Télécommunications Radioélectriques et Téléphoniques), 88 rue Brillat-Savarin, 75640 Paris, France.

Circe portable night sight

4746.193
CASTOR THERMAL IMAGING SIGHT

The Castor thermal imaging camera is designed for use on armoured vehicles in conjunction with observation and fire control systems. It detects and identifies targets by converting their thermal radiation in the IR spectrum into a visible image which can be displayed on a TV monitor. The system is intended for observation and firing under all conditions of daylight, poor visibility and at night. It can be installed in any armoured vehicle, observation vehicle and various turrets, and can be used with artillery.

CHARACTERISTICS
Wavelength: 8 to 13 microns
Analysis: Series parallel scanning
Detectors: Photovoltaic HgCdTe cooled by Split-Stirling cycle system
Field of view: 6° × 9° (wide); 2·7° × 4° or 2° × 3° (narrow)
Range: Up to 4000 m, depending on lens

STATUS
Prototypes are undergoing trials and evaluation. Trials are scheduled for completion by the end of 1984 with production commencing in 1985.

CONTRACTOR
TRT (Télécommunications Radioélectriques et Téléphoniques), 88 rue Brillat-Savarin, 75640 Paris, France.

Units of the Castor thermal imager

3845.193

MIRA THERMAL IMAGER

The Mira thermal imaging sight was developed for use with the Milan anti-tank missile system (**2215.111**). The equipment projects an IR image of the landscape into the observer's day-sight eyepiece permitting use of the normal eyepiece for both day and night operation. Automatic harmonisation of the sight and localiser axes ensures that no adjustment is required by the operator. The equipment includes the Mira sight itself, to which is attached a removable battery pack and a compressed gas bottle, plus an interface which allows the sight to be mounted on the Milan firing post by a single person in a few seconds.

The Mira imager is a compact, robust, sealed metal instrument comprising the following:

(1) a germanium objective lens
(2) a series/parallel mechanical scanner
(3) a detection/visualisation block consisting of a photoconducting CMT detector array and LED array
(4) associated electronics

(5) a cryogenic cooling sub-system (JT self-regulating minicooler).

CHARACTERISTICS

Wavelength: 8 – 13 μm
Processing: Series-parallel
Display: LED
Target detection range: 4000 m (approx)
Target recognition range: 2000 m (approx)
Target identification range: 1500 m (approx)
Field of view: 6 × 3°
Power and cooling supply: 2 h
Weight: Less than 8 kg

STATUS

Series production, carried out under the general management of TRT and their contractors, started in 1983.

CONTRACTORS

TRT (Télécommunications Radioélectriques et Téléphoniques), 88 rue Brillat-Savarin, 75640 Paris, France.
    Siemens AG (Federal Republic of Germany)
    Marconi Command and Control Systems (UK)

Milan anti-tank weapon with Mira night sight fitted

1737.193

APX M396 STABILISED SIGHT

The APX M396 has been derived from the APX M334 (**7032.393**), and is also referred to as the 'cabin version' of that sight. It is intended for observation, target detection and acquisition, and missile guidance applications in vehicles liable to high amplitude motion over a wide frequency range, such as fast patrol boats, aircraft and helicopters. Stabilisation is by means of gyros, supplemented by elastic suspensions and damping. Detection and

acquisition can be effected at ranges up to 30 km. Magnifications of 2·5 and 10 are provided, the respective fields being 22° and 5·5°. Magnification change is accomplished in less than 0·15 second.

STATUS

Production. In service in Breguet Atlantic maritime patrol aircraft.

CONTRACTOR

SFIM (Société de Fabrication d'Instruments de Mesure), BP 74, 91301 Massy Cedex, France.

APX M396 gyro-stabilised sight and control box

3560.193

VS 580 GYRO-STABILISED VEHICLE SIGHT

The VS 580 sight is intended for the detection, recognition, identification and acquisition of fixed or moving targets from a moving combat vehicle, with accurate line-of-sight stabilisation.

The VS 580 is a family of models which includes:

(1) VS 580 Observation, a panoramic sight for observation and identification
(2) VS 580 Standard, a panoramic sight with a target acquisition aid
(3) VS 580 Multirole, a panoramic sight with complete target processing capability (stabilised laser rangefinder)
(4) VS 580 Gunner, for fire control on the move with an optional night-vision device.

The VS 580 sight can also be used by night, either as a driving aid, for close defence, or to assist night firing of the main gun at a combat firing range. Night vision is through the same eyepieces as daytime vision.

The VS 580 sight is compatible with a large number of existing vehicles and fire control systems.

CHARACTERISTICS

Warm-up time: 6 s
Magnifications: ×3 and ×10·5

Angular freedom: 360° in azimuth and 77° in elevation
Line-of-sight displacement speeds: 0·02 mrad/s to 1 rad/s in azimuth and elevation
Line-of-sight stabilisation: Aiming error < 0·1 mrad in normal conditions of use in combat vehicles in motion
Pointing accuracy error: <0·15 mrad
Night vision
Magnification: ×1·3 or ×6
Angular freedom: 360° in azimuth and 70° in elevation
Laser rangefinder
Range: 400 – 10 000 m
Measurement accuracy: ≤5 m
Angular discrimination: <0·3 mrad
Measurement frequency: 1/s

STATUS

In production. Fitted to 11 different vehicles in various versions.

CONTRACTOR

SFIM (Société de Fabrication d'Instruments de Mesure), BP 74, 91301 Massy Cedex, France.

Three views of the VS 580 gyro-stabilised vehicle sight

4250.193

CDN 13 NORTH SEEKER

The CDN 13 north seeker is a portable instrument designed for tripod mounting and intended for use as a means of determining the azimuth for the autonomous alignment of military systems such as: navigation systems fitted in aircraft, ships, land vehicles or missiles; long range guns; missile launchers; fixed or mobile radars; and for various survey operations. A version for vehicle mounting is available.

CHARACTERISTICS

Accuracy
Measurement: Better than 0·3 mil

Orientation and azimuth measurement resolution: 0·1 mil
Latitude limits: 70° N – 70° S
Run-up and measurement time: 5 minutes
Weights
Electronic unit and battery etc: 13 kg
Carrying case and cable: 31 kg
Tripod: 8 kg
Loader: 9 kg

STATUS

Series production.

CONTRACTOR

SFIM (Société de Fabrication d'Instruments de Mesure), BP 74, 91301 Massy Cedex, France.

SFIM CDN 13 north seeker

4249.193

CDN 22 NORTH SEEKER

The CDN 22 north seeker is an instrument for determining the azimuth for the alignment and orientation of military systems such as: autonomous navigation systems fitted in aircraft, land vehicles or missiles; long range guns; missile launch ramps; and mobile or semi-mobile radars. It is completely automatic in operation and self-contained.

CHARACTERISTICS

Accuracy: Better than 0·5 mrad

Run-up and measurement time: 4 minutes

Overall weight: 34 kg

Digital output.

STATUS

In production.

CONTRACTOR

SFIM (Société de Fabrication d'Instruments de Mesure), BP 74, 91301 Massy Cedex, France.

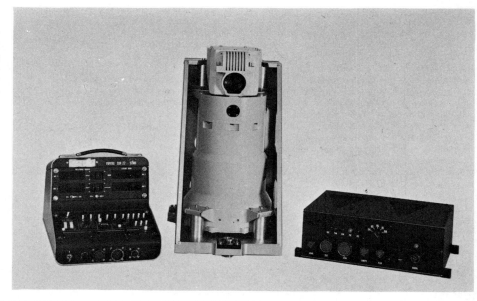

Three units comprising the CDN 22 north seeker equipment

5697.193

CC-35 DIRECTION REFERENCE SYSTEM

The CC-35 is a high accuracy direction reference for self-propelled guns and land vehicles. It is designed to provide continuous indication of the direction, or heading, of the axis of its mounting with an azimuth definition of 0·1 mrad. Elevation indication is also available if required. The system includes a gyroscopic sensor and a control/display unit and is claimed to provide the best cost/efficiency ratio for the realignment of artillery pieces without external aid.

CHARACTERISTICS

Drift: <1 mrad/h

Sensitivity: 0·1 mrad

Output: Digital or analogue

STATUS

In production. Incorporated in the French self-propelled gun 155 mm GCT.

CONTRACTOR

SFIM (Société de Fabrication d'Instruments de Mesure), BP 74, 91301 Massy Cedex, France.

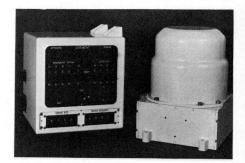

CC-35 direction reference system

3838.193

APX M363 FIRE CONTROL

The APX M363 is the fire control unit for the French 155GCT self-propelled gun, providing day and night engagements with the following facilities:

(1) indirect fire from an external directional reference by the 'bearing firing method'

(2) direct fire

(3) elevation angle measurement of obstacles

(4) transfer of a reference bearing to another unit

The equipment weighs, with vertical sensor plate and computer, 160 kg and has an overall height of 1·28 m.

CHARACTERISTICS

Direction finder

Field: 175 mrad

Magnification: ×5

Eyepiece diameter: 4 mm

Elevation: –90 to +1200 mils

Panoramic observation field

Automatic tilt correction: ±10°

Max tilt: 10°

Aiming accuracy: 0·5 mil

Direct fire sight

Field: 120 mils

Magnification: ×8

Eyepiece diameter: 5 mm

Aiming (elevation): –90 to +360 mils

Observation (elevation): –300 to +600 mils (turret stationary)

Accuracy: 0·5 mil

STATUS

Derived from the APX M589-01, the M363-01 has been adopted by the French Army and is in series production for export.

CONTRACTOR

GIAT (Groupement Industriel des Armements Terrestres), 10 Place Georges Clémenceau, 92211 Saint Cloud, France.

3840.193

APX M520 PANORAMIC SIGHT

The APX M520 is the panoramic sight fitted on the VADAR anti-aircraft vehicle (**3333.131**) turret and is one of the main elements of that system's fire control. For simultaneous use by the tank commander and the gunner (separate eyepieces), the unit provides panoramic search at low magnification, and target acquisition, allocation, tracking and engagement at high magnification, against low-level aircraft. The sight is provided with means of coupling a tracker television camera to allow automatic target tracking.

The sight is rate controlled from the cross-bar of either of the two operators, for the search or tracking modes.

CHARACTERISTICS

Magnification: ×2 (600 mrad field); ×4 (300 mrad field)

Camera field depth: ∞

Magnification: ×1 (100 mrad field)

Sighting range: n × 360° (azimuth); –8 to +73° (elevation)

Overall dimensions: 730 × 676 mm

Weight: 115 kg

STATUS

Prototype.

CONTRACTOR

GIAT (Groupement Industriel des Armements Terrestres), 10 place Georges Clémenceau, 92211 Saint Cloud, France.

3841.193

APX M527 TANK SIGHT

The APX M527 multipurpose tank commander's sight is designed for installation in an appropriate housing for fitting in the AMX-32 MBT. Of modular design, it provides the tank commander with stabilised day vision (two magnifications), night vision (600 metres), and observation on the move at high magnification. It permits target detection and engagement of fixed or moving targets.

CHARACTERISTICS

Day

Magnification: ×8, ×2

Field of view: 100, 400 mils

Exit pupil diameter: 4 mm

Elevation limits: –12 to +24° (×2); –20 to +40° (×8)

Night

Magnification: ×1

Field of view: 580 mils

Elevation limits: –8 to +24°

Range: 600 m (typically)

STATUS

Series production began in 1983.

CONTRACTOR

GIAT (Groupement Industriel des Armements Terrestres), 10 place Georges Clémenceau, 92211 Saint Cloud, France.

4107.093
SMT MODULAR THERMAL IMAGING SYSTEM

The French SMT (modular thermal imaging system) was developed in collaboration by SAT and TRT, the first prototypes being completed in 1980. The equipment will be used with a variety of weapon systems and fitted on various platforms.

For each application, the equipment consists of (a) specific parts such as the housing or package, the optics and presentation, and (b) the standard internal modules. These latter items are:
(1) an opto-mechanical scanning module which relies on the parallel serial scanning principle
(2) a detection module consisting of a dewar, the photovoltaic MCT detector array, sensitive to the 8 to 13 micron region of the infra-red, and the associated preamplifiers

Thermal image obtained with SMT FLIR (black = hot polarity)

(3) a linear electronic module
(4) a signal processing module producing the video signal
(5) cryogenic module, with either the Joule Thomson or closed cycle cooling system
(6) a display module with two options: miniaturised CRT or LEDs
(7) an integrity module for built-in test.

The image format is 2:3 which can be viewed on a TV screen to CCIR standard.

A typical SMT thermal imaging system can have up to three fields of view, from 50 degrees for reconnaissance down to 3 degrees for fire control.

STATUS

Several French weapons systems are scheduled to be equipped with the SMT systems. These include the ANG (new generation Atlantic) maritime aircraft, the VAB vehicle, AMX-30 tank and the HAC helicopter with rangefinder and special night flying equipment.

Prototype cameras built by both companies have already been delivered and are undergoing field and/or flight trials. In December 1983, TRT and SAT were giving official permission to prepare assembly lines for series production modules, scheduled to started in mid-1985. The first of these should be available about six months later.

Among the programmes being investigated using SMT modules are the camera for the VAB Mephisto HOT anti-tank vehicle, the Tango forward-looking-infra-red (FLIR) system for the Atlantic ATL2, the Castor camera for the VOA artillery observation vehicle and the camera on the Guardian coastal patrol aircraft. In addition, a number of other equipments, based on the common modular programme, are in development. Brief details of these are as follows.

Judith

This is the name for a series of thermal imaging goggles weighing less than 3·5 kg and operating in the 3 to 5 μm waveband using a CMT detector. They have been accepted by the French Army for further development.

Dorothée

Dorothée is a simple thermal equipment designed for detection and alarm and has also been accepted by the French Army for further development.

Porthos

This is a thermal sight intended for use by helicopters firing HOT missiles at night. It has an adjustable three-field lens assembly (45° × 30°; 8° × 5°; 3° × 2°), with the thermal image presented on a small CRT in the sighting system.

Visir

An experimental thermal sight for main battle tanks. This is a very long term programme with production not expected until the early 1990s.

Aphrodite

A night flying aid for helicopter use. The system is mounted in a stabilised turret and can be used with either a helmet type sight or displayed on a TV monitor. This is probably another long term programme.

CONTRACTORS

SAT (Société Anonyme de Télécommunications), 41 rue Cantagrel, 75624 Paris Cedex 13, France.

TRT (Télécommunications Radioélectriques et Téléphoniques), 88 rue Brillat Savarin, 75640 Paris Cedex 13, France.

4283.193
VIPERE INFRA-RED SURVEILLANCE EQUIPMENT

The Vipere equipment is an infra-red panoramic surveillance system developed by SAT for the Section d'Etudes et de Fabrications de Telecommunications (SEFT) of the French Army Direction Technique des Armements Terrestres (DTAT). It is designed to detect and locate aircraft at low and medium elevation angles in an entirely passive manner. When employed in an anti-aircraft defence system, Vipere will provide target designation data. A very low false alarm rate is claimed for the specially adapted data processing system manufactured in co-operation with Thomson-CSF.

The optical sensor head can be mounted as a fixed installation on the ground or carried on a vehicle with the electronic data processing system. The former unit incorporates a number of mosaic arrays consisting of multiple elements, cooling being by means of a closed-circuit system built into the head with its own compressor.

CHARACTERISTICS
Weight of optical head: <70 kg
Azimuth coverage: 360°
Elevation coverage: >20°
Detection range: >10 km (aircraft target)
Target designation accuracy: 1 mrad (approx)
STATUS
Development project for French Army.
CONTRACTOR
SAT (Société Anonyme de Télécommunications), 41 rue Cantagrel, 75624 Paris Cedex 13, France.

4248.193
ELDO TARGET DESIGNATOR

The Eldo system has been designed to enable manual designation of targets such as aircraft, tanks or ships to be carried out by a foot soldier (or seaman aboard ship) with a minimum of equipment and with minimum restriction on his ability to carry out visual search functions. Targets designated in this way can be 'handed off' to radars or other tracking systems associated with suitable weapons to engage the target(s) or directly to the weapons themselves. Multiple targets, it is claimed, can be handled in rapid succession by a single operator of Eldo and the equipment can be connected to a number of defensive weapon systems and tracking facilities. The Eldo operator has facilities for selecting which weapon systems or trackers are to be 'laid on' to each target designated.

The pistol-shaped aiming sight contains a three-axis gyro sensor, a target designator trigger and an indicator light to show when a target has been handed over and acquired by an associated weapon or tracker system. The control unit houses a microprocessor, the gyro electronics, an alpha-numeric display, weapon selection switches, stowage for the aiming sight 'gun' and miscellaneous switches and indicators.

By pointing the designator 'gun' at the target the operator aligns a line-of-sight from the location of the unit and the computer automatically calculates the parallax corrections necessary for associated weapons or trackers to be brought to bear on the same target. As each weapon/tracker selected by the operator acquires the target a signal is sent back for display on the designator 'gun', after which the operator can designate any other targets detected. Radio or cable links may be used between the Eldo control panel and associated weapons/trackers for the transmission of designation data and the return of acquisition signals.

STATUS
Development project.
CONTRACTOR
CSEE (Compagnie de Signaux et d'Enterprises Electriques), 17 place Etienne-Pernet, 75738 Paris Cedex 15, France.

Eldo target designator

3134.193
THOMSON-CSF CANASTA DAY/NIGHT AIMING EQUIPMENT (DIVT 13)

Thomson-CSF produces a day/night aiming equipment based on low light-level television, and several versions have been developed. The French Army has adopted the equipment for fitting to its AMX-10RC, AMX-30B2 (modernised) and AMX-32 AFVs where it will be integrated with the tanks' IFCS. In French Army service the equipment is designated DIVT 13, while the name employed by Thomson-CSF for export models is Canasta. Different versions were previously referred to as the TMV560/562, but these designations are no longer employed.

The complete equipment includes a night and day TV camera with its control unit and one or two display units for the gunner and/or the tank commander. Its use permits full passive detection, identification and engagement of static and moving targets by main battle tanks and other classes of AFV. A moving electronic reticule, driven either manually from the control unit in accordance with target distance and selected ammunition, or automatically from a ballistic computer in accordance with firing data, gives the gunner aiming information and firing corrections.

The Canasta system is compatible with any gun ballistic and fire control system and is reported to be capable of installation in any type of MBT without turret modification.

CHARACTERISTICS
Lens assembly: Dioptric
Focal length: 210 mm
Aperture: f 1·5
Angular field: 4·1 × 5·5°
Camera tube: Super nocticon – silicon
Illumination range: 10^{-4} – 10^{5} lux
Alignment accuracy: Better than 0·25 mrad
Video output: ITCC standard
Power supply: 20 – 30 V DC

STATUS
Series production. The Canasta system has been installed in M48, Centurion, Leopard, T55, T62, AMX-13, AML 90, ERC 90 Sagaie, and PAC90 vehicles.
CONTRACTOR
Thomson-CSF, Division des Equipements Avioniques, 178 boulevard Gabriel Peri, 92240 Malakoff, France.

Components of Thomson-CSF Canasta: control unit (top right), TMV 562 camera (centre), TMV 563 monitor (left)

4251.193
MARILU 80 × 240 TELESCOPE
The Marilu 80 × 240 is a high magnification telescope for observation of either land or coastal targets'at long ranges. Its high magnification requires a steady and vibration-free mounting and a fixed pedestal is normal. A laser rangefinder may be associated with the Marilu telescope and is available as an option. A 24 × 36 photographic attachment is available, and the telescope is rust- and water-proof. The mounting can be moved easily on retractable wheels.

CHARACTERISTICS
Focal length: 2·4 m
Magnification: ×80
Resolution: Better than 1″
Exit pupil diameter: 3 mm
Image focusing range: 300 m – ∞
Finder telescope: 8 × 40
Line of sight: Adjustable from 1·5 to 1·7 m high
Total weight: 110 kg
STATUS
Production.
CONTRACTOR
REOSC (Recherches et Etudes d'Optique et de Sciences Connexes – a SFIM subsidiary), 10 rue des Ecoles, Ballanvilliers, 91160 Longjumeau, France.

REOSC Marilu 50 × 240 long-range telescope

5699.193
DALDO TARGET ACQUISITION AID SYSTEM
Daldo is a helmet-mounted target designation aid system designed primarily for anti-aircraft defence applications although it is adaptable to other fire control systems. The basic principle is the slaving of the gun line-of-sight with the observer's line-of-sight, with the direction of the Daldo sightline being referenced in an axis system based on the earth's magnetic and gravitational fields. Data is supplied by a magnetometer which detects the components of the

magnetic field along the helmet reference axis system and therefore along the sightline reference axis system, and two accelerometers which give the vertical reference. The target azimuth and elevation angles are then calculated continuously by the system.

The basic system consists of a helmet cover which contains the sensors and a sight system, a portable control console mounted on the gunner's chest and a processor unit to provide the computation of azimuth and elevation parameters for each gun battery.

CHARACTERISTICS
Accuracy: ± 3° in both azimuth and elevation
Field of use: Azimuth 360°; elevation –5 to +85°
STATUS
Developed for the French Army 76 T2 anti-aircraft twin gun system.
CONTRACTOR
SV2 Crouzet-Sfena, Tour Vendome, 204 Rond-Point du Pont de Sevres, 92516 Boulogne Billancourt, France.

GERMANY (FEDERAL REPUBLIC)

3848.193
B171-II IR AIMING UNIT
The Type B171-II infra-red aiming unit is installed in armoured vehicles where it serves for observation, identification and aiming at night.

Both the security area and the target are illuminated by an IR searchlight. The reflected IR radiation is converted to a visible image by the built-in image converter tube. The B171-II IR-aiming unit is part of the Leopard 1 tank standard equipment.

STATUS
Production.
CONTRACTOR
Eltro GmbH, Postfach 102120, 69 Heidelberg 1, Federal Republic of Germany.

3849.193
CE632 LASER RANGEFINDER
The CE632 laser rangefinder provides accurate rangefinding and operates according to the pulse time-delay method with a repetition frequency of 1 Hz.

Both assemblies, transmitter-receiver and display control with built-in power supply, are of compact and rugged design. The unit is designed to operate self-sufficiently as well as in connection with vehicle-integrated electro-optical fire control systems.

STATUS
In production and in service with West German Army AFVs.
CONTRACTOR
Eltro GmbH, Postfach 102120, 69 Heidelberg 1, Federal Republic of Germany.

Eltro CE632 laser rangefinder

3852.093
CE618 LASER RANGEFINDER
The CE618 laser rangefinder measures accurately the range to moving and fixed targets by transmitting ten pulses per second by the pulse time-delay method. It

consists of a Nd-YAG laser transceiver unit, the power supply with electronics and control box.

Apart from other application fields the unit was designed for use in aircraft for target illumination and rangefinding, in electro-optical fire control systems

on ground and on ships, as well as a redundant rangefinder for radar anti-aircraft tracking systems.
CONTRACTOR
Eltro GmbH, Postfach 102120, 69 Heidelberg 1, Federal Republic of Germany.

3850.193
CE624 LASER RANGEFINDER/SIGHT
When used with gated viewing, this rangefinder is a combined gunner's sight for use in battle tanks. The range to moving or fixed targets is continuously measured by a laser transmitter and a gated receiver

by means of the pulse time-delay method. Range gating enables the observer to determine which target out of several within view was measured by the laser rangefinder. Thus a selection of single targets is provided.

CONTRACTOR
Eltro GmbH, Postfach 102120, 69 Heidelberg 1, Federal Republic of Germany.

3851.193
CE628 LASER RANGEFINDER
This Nd:YAG laser rangefinder is integrated into the fire control system of the Leopard 2 battle tank and is capable of providing three accurate rangefinding values within four seconds. It consists of laser transmitter, receiver and processing electronics with the related supply unit.

Because of its integration into the observation and aiming equipment, the observer may at all times get an exact digital range readout, the computer simultaneously processing the range data for accurate firing.

STATUS
In production for Leopard 2 MBTs.
CONTRACTOR
Eltro GmbH, Postfach 102120, 69 Heidelberg 1, Federal Republic of Germany.

Eltro CE628 laser rangefinder integrated in periscope control unit, seen here with laser electronics unit

3096.193
RZ1001 THERMAL IMAGING EQUIPMENT
The RZ1001 thermal imaging equipment is the successor to the RZ502 (**1802.193**) from which it has been developed. A feature of the RZ1001 is its high geometrical resolution which particularly suits it for the detection of targets at long distances. Operation

is possible in day and night conditions or in adverse weather. Due to the equipment's high temperature resolution, the objects of interest are displayed as a flicker-free image on the monitor and with good contrast against their background.

The equipment is of modular design and is suitable for applications such as target recognition in armoured or 'soft' vehicles, aircraft, helicopters, or ships.
CHARACTERISTICS
Field of view (azimuth): Approx 13° (if desired, variable from 6 – 13°)
Field of view (elevation): Approx 4·5°
Entrance pupil: Approx 130 mm
Focal length: 260 mm
Number of lines: 400
Line interlacing: 4:1
Geometrical resolution: 0·2 mrad
Frame rate: 25 frames/s
Detector: CdHgTe (100 elements, 4 times line displaced)
Waveband: 8·5 – 12·5 μm
Cooling: Joule-Thomson cooler

RZ1002 thermal imaging unit with small monitor unit

RZ1001 thermal imaging equipment

Monitor: screen diagonal
Power supply voltage: 24 ± 6 V
Power consumption: Camera with Joule-Thomson cooler 200 W approx
Monitor 50 W approx
CONTRACTOR
Eltro GmbH, Postfach 102120, 69 Heidelberg 1, Federal Republic of Germany.

3434.093
ELTRO ELECTRO-OPTICAL EQUIPMENT
The Eltro organisation produces a wide range of military electro-optical equipment for use both as independent items or as part of a complete weapon

system in addition to those items described above. Full details are not available but the following paragraphs briefly describe some significant items.
IR-weapon sight Type B8-V
Mounted on small arms the Type B8-V serves for observation and aiming at night. The associated IR-searchlight illuminates the scene. An image converter tube converts the back-scattered IR-radiation, which is imperceptible to the human eye, to a visible image. This unit was was found to be extremely useful for the operations of the West German Border Guards and the Police.
Image intensifier aiming unit Type Orion
This equipment serves for observing the scene and aiming weapons at night. The Orion 80 and Orion 110 are passive night vision equipments which electronically amplify low-level light by means of a

three-stage image intensifier tube to an extent to be perceptible to the human eye. This equipment is being used by the Police, the West German Border Guards and the West German Armed Forces. This is a joint development by Eltro and Zeiss.
HOT tracker
This is part of the anti-tank weapon system HOT (**2212.111**) which is for long-range use. The missile guidance via wire occurs semi-automatically. The system was designed as a high-resolution stabilised periscope. Target acquisition and tracking is accomplished via visual optics designed as a periscope. The determination of the missile position is accomplished by an integrated IR-goniometer, whose deviation values are used for missile guidance.
Milan tracker
This unit is part of the lightweight, semi-automatic anti-tank guidance system Milan (**2215.111**) which is for medium-range use. Target acquisition and tracking is accomplished via the optical sight designed as a periscope. The determination of the missile position is by means of an IR-goniometer, and the combination of the latter with the line of sight gives the guidance function. The Milan anti-aircraft weapon can be fired from vehicles as well as from ground level.
Roland sight
This is part of the low-level air defence system Roland (**2218.131**) which is equipped with guided missiles. The sight serves for target acquisition and tracking. A built-in IR-goniometer supplies the deviation signals of the missile which are used for determining the guidance command signals.

Mini-laser rangefinder

CO_2 laser rangefinder

Thermal pointer WOG 3

This equipment serves for passive reconnaissance and observation of heat-radiating objects. It was designed for use in armoured and non-armoured vehicles. In combination with observation and aiming units the heavy contrast thermal signature is superimposed congruently on the image. Thus searching, observing and aiming processes are considerably reduced and facilitated. This is a joint development by Eltro and Zeiss.

CO₂ laser rangefinder

Eltro is developing a CO_2 laser rangefinder operating in the 10·6 μm waveband. The equipment is in the prototype stage.

Mini-laser rangefinder

This is a device in early development and designed for infantry use. It employs a semi-conductor laser, probably an Nd:YAG, and offers low power transmission and a special measuring system.

CONTRACTOR

Eltro GmbH, Postfach 102120, 69 Heidelberg 1, Federal Republic of Germany.

4685.193
OFRIS TARGET TRACKER

OFRIS (Optronische-Feuerleit-RIcht-Saule) is a target tracker consisting of a day sight, integrated thermal imager, CO₂ laser rangefinder and IR tracking electronics. To ensure flexibility in the design a modular approach has been adopted to provide various expansion stages and operating modes.

In its basic configuration OFRIS includes a viewing optics block, a drive block and an ocular block with day sight (periscope adaptable to 1·5×, 6× and 12× magnification), and a thermal imager composed of US common modules. The path of the light rays in the day sight and night sight is deflected at right angles into a common broadband optical system. This is accomplished through a window and by way of a tilting mirror, prior to separate processing in the ocular block. The IR image is displayed on an array of LEDs and can be injected into the periscope for night operations. This version makes use of range data supplied by existing surveillance sensors, such as radar and laser ranger, for lead angle calculation and tracking. Manual tracking, with the aid of a joystick, can also be provided.

Integration of a CO₂ laser and IR tracker, with external monitor where applicable, will afford various additional modes up to a version constituting an autonomous, passive sensor for automatic target tracking. This sensor allows redundant second target tracking and unrestricted night combat capability even in an ECM environment. An autonomous tracking computer, using distributed digital processing can be incorporated.

DEVELOPMENT

The OFRIS concept has been developed for the West German authorities by Siemens as prime contractor in collaboration with Zeiss (optics and thermal imager) and Texas Instruments (tracking electronics). Possible uses include the Gepard anti-aircraft tank, the Roland air defence system and the proposed battle tank of the 90s.

STATUS

In development. Production is likely to start in the second half of 1987.

CONTRACTOR

Siemens AG, ZVW 144, Hofmannstrasse 51, 8000 Munich 70, Federal Republic of Germany.

1727.193
DRIVER'S PERISCOPE TYPE BM 8005

The BM 8005 has been designed for the Marder personnel carrier, Leopard main battle tank, and other armoured vehicles having a standard vision port or the M113 and vehicles with an adapter. It is fitted extensively in NATO forces.

The driver's passive periscope is a binocular night vision device (one optical path for each eye), operated on the principle of image intensification and particularly developed for armoured vehicles provided with the standard vision block port of 65 by 130 mm.

The periscope serves mainly as a driver's vision device enabling night driving, without the assistance of any artificial light sources, down to a minimum illumination level of about 5 × 10⁻⁵ ft-c.

In addition the periscope can be utilised for surveillance purposes. There is an individual dioptre control for each eye and eyepiece heating prevents the accumulation of moisture.

CHARACTERISTICS

Magnification: ×1

Field of view: 55 × 40° (horizontal × vertical)

Image intensifier tube: Philips XX 1080

Dioptre adjustment: ±4 dioptres

Angular resolution: 0·6 mrad

STATUS

Over 12 000 units have been supplied for armies throughout the world.

CONTRACTOR

Elektro Spezial, Unternehmensbereich der Philips GmbH, Hans-Bredow-Strasse 20, 2800 Bremen 44, Federal Republic of Germany.

BM 8005 driver's passive periscope

3810.193
BM 8025 PASSIVE NIGHT SIGHT

The BM 8025 passive night sight and observation equipment was developed by Elektro Spezial for the West German armoured personnel carrier Marder and the armoured scout car Luchs. Vehicles equipped with the BM 8025 are qualified for night fighting and do not need any searchlight (IR or white).

In the BM 8025 system, the combination of low light-level imaging and thermal radiation detection offers high tactical efficiency; heat-dissipating targets, like tanks and vehicles, even when camouflaged are rapidly located in the battlefield; and the time for observation, recognition and aiming is shortened to a minimum.

The full field of view of the image-intensifying sight is covered by the scanning thermal target locator. The true position of a detected target is indicated to the operator by a red flashing spot within the light-intensified image of the scene.

CHARACTERISTICS

Magnification: ×6

Field of view: 5·6°

Dioptre focusing range: ±5 dioptres

Thermal target locator

Spectral range: 3 – 5 μm

Field of view: 6 × 2° (horizontal × vertical)

Resolution: 2 mrad

STATUS

The BM 8025 is now in service with the West German Army.

CONTRACTOR

Elektro Spezial, Unternehmensbereich der Philips GmbH, Hans-Bredow-Strasse 20, 2800 Bremen 44, Federal Republic of Germany.

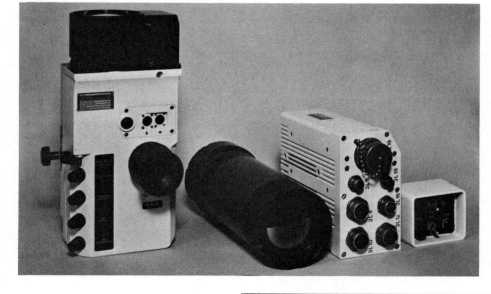

Units of BM 8025 night sight (left to right): image intensifier sight, thermal sensor, power supply unit, and control unit

---

4252.193
BM 8028 IMAGE-INTENSIFIER GOGGLES

The BM 8028 image-intensifier night vision goggles are designed for use by AFV drivers, helicopter pilots, reconnaissance patrols and a wide range of similar applications where the ability to see in darkness is a requirement. The equipment comprises the binocular goggles, a face mask and a harness which allows the goggles to be worn under almost any type of helmet or military headgear. Separate multi-channel image intensifier tubes are provided for each eye and there are provisions for adjustment of the inter-pupillary distance, a synchronous focus control for both optical channels and individual dioptre adjustment. There is a small auxiliary infra-red lamp for illumination at close quarters, if necessary, incorporated in the goggles. An indicator in the eyepiece shows when this is in use.

CHARACTERISTICS
Magnification: ×1
Field of view: 48°
Focus range: 0·25 m – ∞
Depth of focus (at infinity): 15 m – ∞
Dioptre range: ±5 dioptres
Inter-pupillary adjustment: 58 – 72 mm
Length: 120 mm
Width: 130 mm
Height: 80 mm (goggles with housing)

Weight: 1 kg (without balance weight)
Power supply: 2·2 – 3·2 V (2 × Ni-Cd batteries)
Life: 14 h (without IR source)
STATUS
Series production for Federal German armed forces.
CONTRACTOR
Elektro Spezial, Unternehmensbereich der Philips GmbH, Hans-Bredow-Strasse 20, 2800 Bremen 44, Federal Republic of Germany.

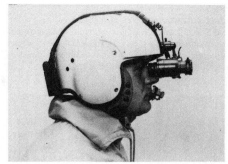

BM 8028 image-intensifier goggles (helicopter use)

4684.193
BM 8042 INFRA-RED TARGET MARKER

The BM 8042 target marker is an IR laser projector used together with the BM 8028 night vision goggles (**4252.193**) for aiming infantry weapons (rifles, sub-machine guns, anti-tank weapons, etc) at night. It consists of a narrow beam projector providing an IR spot, invisible to the naked eye, onto the target.

The BM8042 is a small size, ruggedised unit using a specific adaptor for mounting on each weapon. The mechanism for alignment is integrated.

STATUS
In series production.
CONTRACTOR
Elektro Spezial, Unternehmensbereich der Philips GmbH, Hans-Bredow-Strasse 20, 2800 Bremen 44, Federal Republic of Germany.

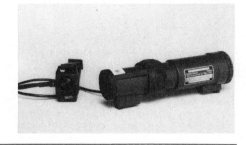

BM 8042 target marker

ISRAEL

4244.193
TD22 THERMAL IMAGING SYSTEM

The Rafael TD22 is a compact high performance thermal imaging system for observation at all ranges. It is built to meet the requirements of a battlefield environment with emphasis on simplicity of operation and maintenance, low cost and long life.

The equipment is based on a parallel scanning mechanism operating in the three to five micron band of the infra-red spectrum and the detectors employed are indium antimonide (In-Sb) devices cooled to 77° K by a Joule-Thompson system which uses pressurised

nitrogen. The TD22 has a standard television-type video output enabling remote observation as well as viewing on a built-in direct monitor. It is man-portable, and both portable and vehicle-mounted versions of the equipment have been developed. Company literature suggests that various telescopes can be coupled to to the infra-red camera for different applications.

CHARACTERISTICS
Waveband: 3 to 5 μm
Detector: 100 element parallel-scan indium antimonide

Detection range: 6·5 km (tanks); 2·5 km (personnel)
Recognition range: 2 km (tanks); 1·5 km (personnel)
Dimensions: 350 × 200 × 150 mm
Weight: 9·5 kg
STATUS
Production.
CONTRACTOR
Rafael, Ministry of Defence, PO Box 2082, 31021 Haifa, Israel.

4686.193
RAINBOW LASER RANGEFINDER

Rainbow is a CO_2 laser rangefinder capable of ranging on targets out to seven km with a 50 metre separation discrimination. The instrument is of modular design, to facilitate maintenance and repair,

and consists of a TEA CO_2 laser and beam expander, a receiver, an optical telescope with ×8 magnification, power supply and an associated display unit. Rainbow weighs approximately 22 kg and measures 200 × 200 × 350 mm. No other details are available.

STATUS
Believed to be still in development.
CONTRACTOR
Rafael, Ministry of Defence, PO Box 2082, 31021 Haifa, Israel.

3802.093
GYRO-STABILISED SIGHTING SYSTEM (GSSS)

Tamam's gyro-stabilised sighting system (GSSS) is an essential aid for observation, identification and tracking during aerial, naval, and ground-based missions. Versions are produced suitable for use in helicopters and light aircraft, ships, and armoured vehicles.

The GSSS neutralises motion-produced disturbances of the vehicle, vibration and environmental conditions affecting visual image and alignment accuracy. The system consists of a dual-magnification periscope/telescope the upper folding element (mirror) of which is gyro-stabilised. The mirror coating is effective over a wide spectral range, from the visual to the near infra-red, and permits optional use of laser or IR tracker in parallel with the visual optical path.

High magnification of the stabilised optics enables the observer to identify and lock on to the target at distances greater than the missile's or gun's range, and to distinguish details sufficiently for weapon guidance to the most vulnerable point.

A TV camera permits bi-ocular conventional sighting. TV enables better sighting conditions, and enhances haze penetration. The recording system allows storage and subsequent retrieval of information received during combat patrols, surveillance sorties and training exercises. It is possible to adapt an automatic contrast lock-on target using the TV option. A CRT and simulator assembly enables the GSSS to function as a training aid during simulated and real field firing conditions.

The high precision goniometer serves as an aiming facility for accurate launching and automatic guidance of missiles against armoured targets. The goniometer is mounted on the gyro-stabilised system optical frame and may be aligned with the optical line-of-sight to within 0·1 mrad or better. Alignment can be checked and adjusted by means of an internal collimator. A laser rangefinding system enables accurate target range information for successful launching.

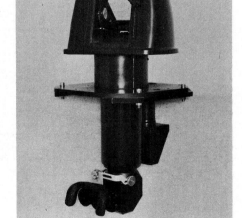

Tamam gyro-stabilised sighting system (GSSS)

STATUS
Production.
CONTRACTOR
Israel Aircraft Industries Ltd, Yehud Industrial Zone 56000, Israel.

CHARACTERISTICS

	Helicopters/ light aircraft	Long range airborne	Ships	Armoured vehicles
Dynamic resolution (mrad)	0·05	0·02	0·06	0·05 – 0·1
Optical resolution (static) (mrad)	0·04	0·01	0·05	0·04
Stabilisation accuracy (vibration) (mrad)	0·02	0·015	0·02 – 0·1	0·02 – 0·1
Surveillance field (*)				
Azimuth	±120 – 360°	360°	360°	360°
Elevation	−40°/+20°	−60°/+30°	−40°/+60°	−30°/+40°

(*) NOTE: Sight surveillance field can be modified to fit customer's specifications.

4286.183
LAND NAVIGATION SYSTEM (LANS)

The Tamam land navigation system (LANS) is a small lightweight inertial navigation equipment which provides complete navigational facilities for military land combat vehicles, wheeled or tracked. It consists of three main sub-systems.

Tamam land navigation system (LANS)

(1) heading reference unit (HRU), based on inertial components and an eight-bit digital microprocessor
(2) control and display unit (CDU), which employs an identical microprocessor
(3) distance transmitter (DT), based on a photo-diode technique.

The HRU contains a two-gimbals platform providing, as the principal output, the vehicle's heading, the associated electronics, the DTU interface, and a microprocessor performing the gyrocompassing, navigation and automatic gyro drift measurements and computation. The CDU transmits control panel information serially to the HRU and receives the information to be displayed on the panel.

Operating modes include: gyrocompass, navigation, and autocalibration (gyro drift measurements). Navigation is possible by co-ordinates, by bearing and distance, or with four different types of 'terrain compensation'. Any co-ordinate system besides UTM (geographic) can be

displayed and other optional facilities include a remote display unit, integration with laser rangefinder, IR etc, or moving map output. It is also possible to report position and azimuth data in real-time via radio links to rear echelons.
CHARACTERISTICS
Position accuracy: ±0·18% of total distance travelled, irrespective of terrain
Heading accuracy: 2 – 3 mrad
Cold start time: 1 minute (stored heading); 15 minutes (full gyrocompassing); 10 minutes (degraded accuracy)
Power supply: 28 V DC 4·5 A
Dimensions: (HRU) 360 × 170 × 27 mm; (CDU) 190 × 130 × 260 mm
Weight: 24 kg
STATUS
Production.
CONTRACTOR
Israel Aircraft Industries Ltd, Yehud Industrial Zone 56000, Israel.

4287.183
TAMAM PADS

The Tamam position and azimuth determining system (PADS) is a precise ground-based inertial digital navigation equipment supplying instant readout of position, elevation and azimuth for artillery units. The equipment provides firepower co-ordination and orientation for mobile artillery units. It can be mounted on APCs, Jeeps, SP guns or other types of vehicle and is a self-contained, autonomous, all-weather, day/night equipment. Continuous display of co-ordinates and track is available on a moving map and remote display facilities are available. The equipment can be integrated with other sub-systems such as a laser rangefinder or an infra-red sensor.

The main items of the PADS equipment (see illustration) are:
(1) the inertial measurement unit (IMU), which is based on the Singer-Kearfott KT-70 unit operated by the USAF, USN, Israeli and other forces, and its associated power unit
(2) a digital computer, which is software compatible with the Data General Nova and Eclipse families
(3) the control and display unit, which enables the operator to communicate with the computer and accommodates entry of data such as initial position and position updates
(4) a display unit that informs the driver of system status, and particularly any need to stop for velocity updates
(5) an azimuth transfer unit (ATU) which provides remote users with accurate azimuth readings generated by the IMU resolver.

Operation of the ATU is based on a rigid linkage between the optical element and the inertial platform. The gun sight is boresighted and rests with the platform on a common base plate, the whole being gimbal-mounted to permit movement in two axes.
CHARACTERISTICS
Position accuracy: 27 m (CEP at 50° lat)

Tamam position and azimuth determining system (PADS)

Elevation error: 10 m (1 sigma); 33 m (max)
Azimuth error: 0·55 mrad (1 sigma at 50° lat)
Mission duration: 6 h
Latitude limits: 75° N – 75° S
Velocity updates: At 10-minute intervals for 20 s stops

STATUS
Production.
CONTRACTOR
Israel Aircraft Industries Ltd, Yehud Industrial Zone 56000, Israel.

4687.193
MATADOR FIRE CONTROL SYSTEM

Matador is a derivative of the enhanced fire control system for the Merkava Mk 2 battle tank. The system is for the export market and has two principal components: a digital ballistics computer, provided by Elbit Computers, and an improved M32 gunner's peritelescope with an integral mini-laser rangefinder

and night viewing channel. The rangefinder is incorporated within the peritelescope and provides an accuracy of 10 metres up to a range of 10 000 metres. The night viewing channel is an image intensifier elbow telescope, with a second generation 25 mm tube, and has a field of view of 7·1 degrees with ×7 magnification.

STATUS
In development.
CONTRACTOR
Electro-Optics Industries Ltd (EL-OP), Advanced Technology Park, Kiryat Weizmann, PO Box 1165, Rehovot 76110, Israel.

5699.193
EL-OP DAY/NIGHT GUNNER PERITELESCOPE

The day and night gunner's Peritelescope is a modular integrated electro-optical system designed to upgrade the ranging and aiming capabilities of tanks and armoured fighting vehicles. Its main features are passive night vision, day and night laser rangefinding and enhanced magnification. The primary role of the Peritelescope is to replace the existing system in the Centurion tank, although due to its small size it can be adapted to other tanks and turrets where space is limited.

Two versions are available. The first consists of a mini-laser rangefinder and a 1x prism, both of which permit observation, aiming and rangefinding during daylight. The 1x prism is fully interchangeable with a passive night elbow so that observation, aiming and rangefinding are possible at night. The elbow contains a standard NATO reticle and a laser for night rangefinding. The reticles are projected and collimated on the image intensifier tube giving accurate aiming and rangefinding in the dark. The second version is designed to function without the mini-laser and consists of an 8x daylight elbow

combined with a passive night elbow for use both day and night. Since the 1x prism is fully interchangeable with the night elbow, a combination of an 8x daylight elbow and a 1x prism enables observation and aiming during daylight.
CONTRACTOR
Electro-Optics Industries Ltd (EL-OP), Advanced Technology Park, Kiryat Weizmann, PO Box 1165, Rehovot 76110, Israel.

4786.193
LANCELOT FIRE CONTROL SYSTEM
Lancelot is a tank fire control system designed for fitment to older tanks such as the AMX-13, M-41 and M-47. It consists of a laser rangefinder operating in the 8 to 13 μm waveband, a second generation image intensifier, a computer with a built-in cant angle sensor, control units for both commander and gunner and a moving target velocity sensor. The system is based on the experience gained in the digital fire control system and laser rangefinder fitted to the Israeli Merkava main battle tank.
CONTRACTOR
Elbit Computers Ltd, Advanced Technology Center, PO Box 5390, Haifa 31053, Israel.

ITALY

4216.193
C 215 ARTICULATED TELESCOPIC SIGHT
The C 215 articulated telescopic sight, designed by Aeritalia, is part of the secondary direct fire control system of the new Italian-designed OF 40 main battle tank. It is mounted coaxially with the weapon and is used in conjunction with the M114 telescope mount. The instrument consists of a head assembly which includes an eyepiece, support arm and adjustable head-rest, an articulated body in which the prisms are located, and an objective tube assembly.
CHARACTERISTICS
Magnification: ×8
Field of view: 7·5°

Objective focal length: 305 mm
Eyepiece focal length: 38 mm
Exit pupil: 5 mm diameter
Eye relief: 24·5 mm
Eyepiece setting: –4 to +4 dioptres
Dimensions: 1200 × 178 mm
Weight: 25 kg
Operating temperature range: –40 to +65° C
Storage temperature range: –60 to +70° C
STATUS
In production for OF 40 main battle tank.
CONTRACTOR
Aeritalia (Società Aerospaziale Italiana), Viale Europe, 20014 Nerviano, Italy.

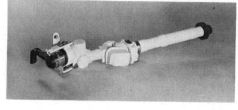

Aeritalia C 215 articulated telescope for new Italian OF 40 tank

3558.193
VAQ-3 TANK LASER RANGEFINDER
The VAQ-3 neodymium-glass laser rangefinder for battle tanks has been designed for integration with a computer fire control system. Long-range firing with a very high first round hit probability is possible, even against moving targets. Furthermore, a much shorter reaction time is achieved. The VAQ-3 is now the standard laser rangefinder fitted in the Leopard main battle tank of several armies. An updated version, the VAQ-33, has been produced.
CHARACTERISTICS
Type: VAQ-3
Laser material: Nd-glass
Mode of operation: Q-switched
Wavelength: 1·06 μm
Peak power: 6 MW
Energy per pulse: 150 mJ
Pulse repetition rate: 12 pulses per minute or bursts of 3 pulses in 4 s with an interval of 11 s between bursts
Detector: Avalanche photodiode
Range capability: 400 m – 10 km
Range accuracy: ±5 m
Distance discrimination: 30 m
Azimuth discrimination: 0·25 mrad
Signal to computer: Digital in BCD code with DC logic level of TTL circuits
System composition
Laser optical head (transmitter/receiver)
Gunner's laser control unit (GLCU)
Commander's laser control unit (CLCU)
Laser power supply unit (LPSU)

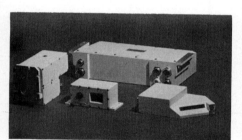

Selenia VAQ-3 tank laser rangefinder

Laser Optical Head
Weight: 6·8 kg
Dimensions: 280 × 116 × 180 mm
GLCU
Weight: 1·9 kg
Dimensions: 280 × 170 × 75 mm
CLCU
Weight: 0·8 kg
Dimensions: 218 × 131 × 91 mm
LPSU
Weight: 13·9 kg
Dimensions: 511 × 126 × 257 mm
Power supply: 24 V DC (vehicle supply)
STATUS
In quantity production. Several hundred units have been produced for the Leopard tank.
CONTRACTOR
Selenia SpA, Special Equipment and Systems Division, Via dei Castelli Romani 2, Pomezia, Rome, Italy.

5700.193
SELENIA LASER UNITS
In addition to the VAQ-3 described above, Selenia have produced a number of other laser rangefinders and visual units of which very few details are available. These include the VAQ-33 which is an updated version on the VAQ-3, and the GAQ-4. This latter equipment is a high repetition rangefinder for naval and ground anti-aircraft fire control systems and has recently been adopted for use with the new Italian Army self-propelled four-barrel 25 mm gun. Another new unit is the MLS-6 laser visual equipment for day and night aiming on tank guns. It can be installed in many types of tank, without modification, and is claimed to provide very high performance at very low cost.
CONTRACTOR
Selenia SpA, Special Equipment and Systems Division, Via dei Castelli Romani 2, Pomezia, Rome, Italy.

3584.193
MR36 AIMING SYSTEM
The MR36 gun aiming system is designed for fitting on light anti-aircraft guns of about 20 or 25 mm calibre. It comprises an optical computing sight, an electrical servo system, and the necessary items for integrating the equipment with a variety of gun/mount combinations.

The optical sight is of a special 'box' reflex type with a large field of view. On the background a luminous red segment is projected which indicates the lead angle for fire against aerial targets. This luminous segment is formed by a series of dots which determine its length. It rotates about its own origin and its extension varies in proportion to the angular speed of the weapon during tracking. The computer is a hybrid analogue/digital machine. The ballistics of the weapon are stored in a semi-conductor read-only memory, which leads to the possibility of simple changes in the ballistics used to cater for different weapons or ammunition.

Servos can be mounted independently of the sight box, and the use of electric direct control motors for the traverse and elevation movements enables the use of either batteries or an external generator as a power supply.
CHARACTERISTICS
Total elevation range: –15 to +80°
Magnification: Reflex vision
True optical field: 60°

Officine Galileo MR36 lightweight aiming system installed

Max lead angle: 16° (inc super elevation)
Crossing range: 100 m (minimum), 700 m (max)
STATUS
Pre-production.

CONTRACTOR
Officine Galileo, 50013 Campi Bisenzio, Florence, Italy.

4253.193
VTG 120 LIGHT THERMAL IMAGER

VTG 120 is a man-portable thermal imaging system for field observation and night operation of anti-tank missile weapon systems. It operates in the 8 to 13 micron band and is provided with an eyepiece for direct viewing on an internal CRT display, where there is an adjustable sighting reticle for fine alignment with the weapon. The equipment is engineered also for mounting on the TOW anti-tank missile system (**2830.111**).

The VTG 120 is completely autonomous in operation and is provided with a 24 V rechargeable battery and a gas bottle for detector cooling by open cycle JT.

CHARACTERISTICS
Detection range: Better than 3000 m (tank target)

Reconnaissance range: 2500 m (tank)
Field of view: 60 × 120 mrad (observation); 20 × 40 mrad (sighting)
Resolution: 0·5 mrad (observation); 0·16 mrad (sighting)
Detector: MTC photoconductor, 8 – 13 micron band, operating at 77° K
Set-up time: 2 – 3 minutes
Autonomy: 2 h
Dimensions: 420 × 290 × 190 mm (overall)
Weight: 12 kg
STATUS
Production.
CONTRACTOR
Officine Galileo SpA, 50013 Campi Bisenzio, Florence, Italy.

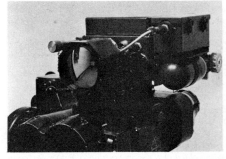

Officine Galileo VTG 120 thermal imaging night sight fitted to TOW anti-tank missile launcher

3588.193
P36 COMPUTING SIGHT AND GUN DRIVE

The P36 equipment is designed for local control of light calibre guns against low- and very low-flying aircraft and ground targets. The sight consists of two individual articulated telescopes with fixed eyepieces for separate aiming at aircraft and ground targets. A simple and reliable mechanical analogue computer is used for the calculation of lead angles, etc. This unit generates amplitude and direction of total lead angle (including super-elevation) according to initial setting of target speed and crossover point range. Accurate lead angle computation is maintained throughout the entire engagement without resetting initial data.

There is a two-degrees-of-freedom control stick for velocity control of the hydraulic drive unit. Tracking assistance is provided by non-linear control characteristics and automatic assessment of traverse and elevation speed ratio. Train and elevation handwheels provide manual drive for maintenance and emergency operation against non-moving targets. The hydraulic drive unit is comprised of an axial piston pump and motor system to allow for very rapid target acquisition and smooth tracking. Standard models are equipped with air-cooled internal combustion engines (two-stroke or Wankel cycle) with recoil starter, centrifugal clutch, and speed governor. Other motors may be fitted to suit special needs.

An indoor training system is produced under the designation S11 for AA gun crews operating the P36 and P56 sighting systems.

CHARACTERISTICS
Air target telescope
Elevation: –7·5 to +85°
Magnification: ×1·1
True field: 45°
Automatically displaced reticle for off-centre aiming; 3 coloured filters

Ground target telescope
Elevation: –7·5 to +45°
Magnification: ×4
True field: 12°
Super-elevation setting by range-graduated dial
Computer
Target speed: 60 – 350 m/s (typical)
Crossover point range: 200 – 1400 m (typical)
Lead angle output: Up to 21·5°
STATUS
About 2000 P36 equipments have been produced and delivered for 20 and 40 mm AA guns of all types for the land forces of a number of countries.
CONTRACTOR
Officine Galileo SpA, 50013 Campi Bisenzio, Florence, Italy.

3589.193
P56 SERIES COMPUTING SIGHT AND GUN DRIVE

The basic P56 equipment is a self-powered computing sight and gun laying equipment for local control of light calibre guns against low- and very low-flying targets. It may also be used for the engagement of ground targets. Suitable for fitting on any existing gun, it has been chosen for use with guns of 20 to 40 mm calibres by several countries.

The sight consists of one panoramic articulated telescope with fixed eyepiece for aiming at both air and ground targets. The computer is a solid-state electronic machine. The gun drive consists of an axial pump and hydraulic motor, with prime power being provided by an internal combustion engine or by an electric motor. This motor also drives a generator to provide electrical power for the computer. Tracker training equipment is also available

Sights of this series are encountered frequently on 20 mm guns produced by Rheinmetall in West Germany, GIAT in France and Swiss Oerlikon weapons. The P56/40 version was specially designed for upgrading the Bofors 40/56 weapon.

CHARACTERISTICS
Sight
Elevation: –7 to +85°
Magnification: ×5
True field: 12°
Target speed: 60 – 350 m/s
Crossover point range: 100 – 600 m
Total lead angle: Up to 21°

P56T

The P56T is a turret computing sight and gun laying equipment based on the standard P56 and specially designed for installation on the turret of any wheeled or tracked vehicle intended for AA defence with light calibre guns.

P56/40

This is a special version of the P56 designed for retrofitting to existing 40 mm AA guns, such as the 40/60, to provide an autonomous capability and to enhance performance.

Specific versions for upgrading other weapons are available.
STATUS
Several thousands of the P56 equipment have been supplied for many types of guns of 20 to 40 mm calibre for European and other armed forces (20, 30, 37 and 40 mm calibre). Over 1500 units are in operation in NATO countries and some hundreds in other countries. A series (P56T version) has been produced for use in turrets manufactured by Electronique Serge Dassault.
CONTRACTOR
Officine Galileo SpA, 50013 Campi Bisenzio, Florence, Italy.

P56 computing sight and gun drive for fitting to AA guns

3590.193
P75 LASER COMPUTING SIGHT AND GUN DRIVE

The P75 is a development of the Officine Galileo P36 and P56 series of computing sights (**3588.193** and **3589.193**) and is based on the same principle, although providing increased performance and having a different configuration. It also differs in incorporating an integral laser rangefinder to provide instantaneous range information to the prediction computer. The equipment is suitable for fitting to AA guns of 20 to 40 mm calibre, and is stated to be easily adapted for remote control and/or shipboard use.

The optical system, gun drive, and computer are thought to be essentially the same as those of the P56 so far as the main characteristics are concerned, and the laser rangefinder is a neodymium unit with a five-metre ranging accuracy. The computer is a programmable digital type, and the optical head can be supplied with night capability. Versions for turrets are available.

STATUS
In production for several types of AA guns.

CONTRACTOR
Officine Galileo SpA, 50013 Campi Bisenzio, Florence, Italy.

P75 computing sight and gun drive with integral laser rangefinder

4220.193
V 200 VISION BLOCK

The V 200 vision block is designed for observation from the inside of the M113 APC and other armoured vehicles, giving the observer protection from small arms fire. The V 200 is capable of withstanding direct hits from 7·62 mm ammunition.

CHARACTERISTICS
Magnification: ×1

Field of view: 90° horizontal; 30° vertical
Transmission: 64%
Dimensions: 291 × 187·5 × 114 mm
Weight: 10 kg
Operating and storage temperature range: –54 to +68° C

CONTRACTOR
Aeritalia (Società Aerospaziale Italiana), Viale Europe, 20014 Nerviano, Italy.

4217.193
P 186 TELESCOPIC SIGHT

The P 186 telescopic sight is designed for use as part of the primary fire control system of the Palmaria 155 mm self-propelled howitzer. Fitted on the Bofors telescopic mount, the device is used for laying the weapon in azimuth for indirect fire control. The instrument consists of a head assembly with a right angle prism, top and bottom body assemblies, and an eyepiece which contains an Amici prism.

CHARACTERISTICS
Magnification: ×4
Field of view: 10° (177 mils)
Objective focal length: 110 mm
Eyepiece focal length: 28 mm

Entrance pupil: 19 mm diameter
Exit pupil: 4·75 mm diameter
Eye relief: 19·5 mm, 435 mm
Azimuth range: 6400 mils
Elevation limits: –645 to +345 mils
Dimensions: 525 × 162 × 240 mm
Weight: 8 kg
Operating temperature range: –25 to +70° C

STATUS
In production for the Italian-built Palmaria 155 mm SP howitzer.

CONTRACTOR
Aeritalia (Società Aerospaziale Italiana), Viale Europe, 20014 Nerviano, Italy.

Aeritalia P 186 telescopic sight for the Palmaria SP howitzer (right), with the P 204 periscope (see below) on the left

4218.193
P 192 NIGHT DRIVING PERISCOPE

The P 192 is a passive night vision device for drivers of AFVs using a second generation light intensifier tube. With this periscope, it is claimed to be possible to drive vehicles at a speed of more than 40 km/h in starlight conditions without any artificial illumination. It consists of a head prism, S 25 micro-channel light intensifier and a bi-ocular eyepiece. A head prism was selected for the instrument instead of a mirror, because of its smaller size for a similar field of view, and greater strength. The light intensifier is fitted with a gain control which is automatically switched off when the photocathode illumination level becomes too high. A filter allows a correct observation within a luminance range from 10^{-3} lux to 10^4 lux. The instrument is equipped with a bi-ocular display which enables the driver to view the scene with both eyes through one large diameter eyepiece. The equipment is designed to be fitted on various types of vehicle including the 6616, M113, VCC 1, Marder, M41, M47, M48, M60, Leopard and the TAM.

CHARACTERISTICS
Magnification: ×0·9
Field of view: 48° horizontal, 40° vertical
Objective lens focus: 25 mm
Relative objective aperture: 1:1·3
Eyepiece lens focus: 43 mm
Eyepiece aperture: 1:0·54
Focus range: 10 m – ∞
Eyepiece pupils distance: 35 mm
Transmission: >75%

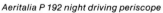

Aeritalia P 192 night driving periscope

Weight: 7 kg
Operating temperature range: –30 to +45° C
STATUS
Production.

CONTRACTOR
Aeritalia, (Società Aerospaziale Italiana), Viale Europe, 20014 Nerviano, Italy.

4219.193
P 204 PERISCOPE

The P 204 periscope is designed for day and night operations as part of the primary fire control system of the BM 6616 armoured car. It can be adapted to

replace M32, M34, and M36 periscopes installed in other vehicles. The instrument consists of the body and either a daylight elbow sighting telescope or a night elbow sight with an image intensifier. The two sights are interchangeable. The body contains the

head prism, a unity power optical system and includes lever linkage to the weapon.

(A photograph of this instrument appears in entry **4217.193** for the P186 telescopic sight, above.)

CHARACTERISTICS:	day	night
Magnification	×8	×8
Field of view	9° (160 mils)	7·9°
Resolution (contrast 1 lux)		0·3 mil
(contrast $10^{-\pi}$ lux)		0·4 mil
Reticle setting	−7 to +7 mil	−7 to +7 mil
Objective focal length	240 mm	145 mm
Eyepiece focal length	30 mm	27 mm
Relative aperture		1·5
Entrance pupil	40 mm	
Exit pupil	5 mm	
Eyepiece setting	−3 to +3	−5 to +5
	dioptres	dioptres
Dimensions	466 × 295 × 202 mm	
Weight	12 kg	
Operating temperature range	−40 to +70°C	

STATUS
Production.
CONTRACTOR
Aeritalia (Società Aerospaziale Italiana), Viale Europe, 20014 Nerviano, Italy.

4689.193
P 233 NIGHT VISION PERISCOPE
This passive night vision device is intended to satisfy the technical requirements of the commander on various types of armoured vehicles (armoured personnel carriers, infantry fighting vehicles, etc). It can also be retrofitted to earlier types of battle tanks. The instrument consists of the head assembly, including the right angle prism, and the body assembly which contains the objective lens, the second generation image intensifier tube, the reticle, the binocular eyepiece and the electronics.

The periscope has an operational illumination range from 10^{-3} to 10 lux. Range in starlight is up to 800 metres. The instrument is interchangeable with all European and US daylight periscopes.

CHARACTERISTICS
Magnification: ×3
Field of view: 16° horizontal, 15° vertical
Weight: 7·5 kg
CONTRACTOR
Aeritalia (Società Aerospaziale Italiana), Viale Europa, 20014 Nerviano, Italy.

4688.193
OG-P20 PERISCOPE
The OG-P20 is an optical periscope designed for use in light armoured vehicles. It is primarily intended to fulfill the technical and operational requirements for observation and aiming in vehicles where the crew accommodation does not rotate in concert with the turret.
CHARACTERISTICS
Magnification: ×1·5 and ×4·5
Field of view: 28° (×1·5) and 10° (×4·5)

Elevation: −10 to +60°
Azimuth training: 360°
Transparence: 42% (×1·5) and 40% (×4·5)
Dimensions: 680 × 320 × 340 mm
STATUS
In production.
CONTRACTOR
Officine Galileo SpA, 50013 Campi Bisenzio, Florence, Italy.

OG-P20 periscope

5701.193
GM 79 GONIOMETER
The GM 79 goniometer has been designed by Officine Galileo to meet a requirement of the Italian Army. It consists of a 45° elbow analytic telescope with a reticle for distance measurement, a reading microscope to provide measurement of horizontal and vertical angles, a built-in tubular compass and an LED system for night illumination. The instrument is equipped with filters, optical plumb, target with built-in illuminator, stave with sighting telescope, tripod and carrying cases.
CHARACTERISTICS
Telescope
Image: Erect
Magnification: ×8 (×16 with focal doubler)

Effective aperture: 20 mm
Field of view: 7° (120 mils)
Focus range: 50 m – ∞
Eye relief: 12 mm
Eyepiece setting: −5 to +5 dioptres
Circles
Diameters: Horizontal 100 mm; vertical 80 mm
Reading accuracy: Direct reading 0·5 mils, estimation to 0·25 mils
Weight
Complete equipment: 40·1 kg
STATUS
In production.
CONTRACTOR
Officine Galileo SpA, 50013 Campi Bisenzio, Florence, Italy.

GM 79 goniometer

4221.193

T178/278 GONIOMETER

The T178/278 goniometer is designed by Aeritalia to meet artillery requirements. It consists of an elbow sighting telescope, reticle for distance measurements, a reading microscope, and a built-in magnetic declinator device. Two graduated circles provide measurement of horizontal and vertical angles. The instrument is equipped with an optical plumb to aid positioning. Two versions are produced with different illumination systems. The T178 uses a tritium self-illumination system. The T278, designed for the Italian Army, is equipped with a diode illumination system.

CONTRACTOR

Aeritalia (Società Aerospaziale Italiana), Viale Europe, 20014 Nerviano, Italy.

CHARACTERISTICS

Magnification: ×8
Field of view: 7° (120 mils)
Objective focal length: 128 mm
Eyepiece focal length: 16 mm
Focusing range: 10 m – ∞
Entrance pupil: 24 mm diameter
Exit pupil: 3 mm diameter
Eye relief: 12·2 mm

Eyepiece setting	–5 to +5 dioptres		
	Horizontal circle	Elevation circle	Declinator
Graduation	6400 mils	–800 to +1200 mils	553 mils E – 553 mils W
Direct reading	0·5 mil	0·5 mil	1 mil
Estimated reading	0·25 mil	–	0·5 mil

Weight: 5 kg
Operating and storage temperature range: –40 to +55°C

Aeritalia T178 artillery goniometer instrument

NETHERLANDS

3432.193

TYPE UA 1116 WEAPON SIGHT

The UA 1116 weapon sight is a second-generation lightweight sight intended mainly for infantry weapons. The micro-channel image intensifier tube employed has its own integrated power supply and automatic brightness control together with protection against flare and highlights.

A fully adjustable graticule is incorporated; both objective and eyepiece lenses are also adjustable.

CHARACTERISTICS

Magnification: ×4
Field of view: 9°

Resolution: 1 mil at 1 mlux (starlight) at a target contrast of 30%
Focusing range: 25 m – ∞
Eyepiece adjustment: –5 to +3 dioptres
Power supply: 2·2 – 3·4 V DC
Weight: 1·6 kg
STATUS
In production and in service or ordered by several forces.
CONTRACTOR
Philips Usfa BV, Meerenakkerweg 1, PO Box 218, 5600 MD Eindhoven, Netherlands.

Weapon sight Type UA 1116

4264.193

MS4GT PASSIVE MINI-WEAPON SIGHT

The MS4GT is a lightweight second-generation night aiming device for use on portable weapons. It is a passive device which requires no lighting other than natural illumination for its use in darkness. Mounting brackets have been designed to enable fitting on a variety of weapons from rifles and machine guns to portable recoilless weapons. It may also be used as a night observation device and infra-red detection system.

CHARACTERISTICS

Total amplification: ×4
Field of view: 11°
Centre resolution: 0·6 mrad at 10⁻³ lux
Input optical system: Mirror

Focal length: 86 mm
Relative aperture: 1:1·4; fixed objective setting, 200 m – optional setting on request between 20 m and infinity
Image intensifier: Micro-channel
Input cathode: S25
Screen: P20 aluminised
Eyepiece focal length: 21 mm
Eye adaptation: fixed at –1 dioptre ±0·5
Weight: 950g (approx)
STATUS
Early production.
CONTRACTOR
Oldelft (NV Optische Industrie De Oude Delft), PO Box 72, 2600 MD Delft, Netherlands.

MS4GT mini-weapon sight

3394.193

TYPE RS4TS INDIVIDUAL WEAPON SIGHT

This is a small, lightweight image-intensifier system for observation and direct firing with weapons at night. Though suitable for mounting on most basic infantry weapons, the sight can also be used as a hand-held viewer. In its modular concept the sight is similar to the crew-served weapon sight type GS6TS (**3395.193**) having the central housing incorporating tube and controls in common.

Design features include automatic brightness control, an adjustable sky light diaphragm to suppress the disturbing effects of night sky illumination, and reticle with adjustable illumination. To prevent tube damage when observing hits on armour special flash-proof image intensifier tubes are incorporated.

CHARACTERISTICS

Magnification: ×4
Field of view: 10°
Focus range: 20 m – ∞
Detection range: Typically 500 m for infantry targets and 1000 m for tanks
Length: 365 mm
Width: 135 mm
Weight: 2 kg
STATUS
In quantity production; deliveries to various military and para-military forces.
CONTRACTOR
Oldelft (NV Optische Industrie De Oude Delft), PO Box 72, 2600 MD Delft, Netherlands.

Type RS4TS individual weapon sight

4747.193

RS4MC SMALL ARMS WEAPON SIGHT

This is a small, lightweight second-generation night vision device for observation and direct firing with weapons at night. It is suitable for mounting on most basic infantry weapons and can also be used as a hand-held sight. It is similar in modular construction to the GS6MC crew-served weapon sight (**4690.193**), as it also has the central housing, which incorporates tube, eyepiece and controls. The reticle can be adjusted to the scene brightness.

CHARACTERISTICS

Magnification: ×4
Field of view: 10°
Focus range: 20 m – ∞
Dimensions: 360 mm (long) × 100 mm (high) × 98 mm (wide)
Weight: 2 kg
CONTRACTOR
Oldelft (NV Optische Industrie De Oude Delft), PO Box 72, 2600 MD Delft, Netherlands.

RS4MC small arms weapon sight

3395.193

TYPE GS6TS CREW-SERVED WEAPON SIGHT

This night vision sight can be attached to all types of crew-served weapons such as heavy machine guns, recoilless rifles and anti-tank guns. The modular design permits the use of either a straight or rectangular eyepiece. Reticles can be fitted matching the ballistics of the weapon concerned. The reticle illumination is adjustable. A sky light diaphragm is incorporated for an optimal adaption to night sky illumination. To prevent tube damage when observing hits on armour special flash-proof image intensifier tubes are incorporated.

CHARACTERISTICS

Magnification: ×6·4
Field of view: 6·6°
Focus range: Adjustable 50 m – ∞
Detection range: Typically up to 800 m for infantry targets and 1500 m for tanks
Length: 430 mm
Diameter: 150 mm
Weight: 3·5 kg
STATUS
In quantity production for various armies.
CONTRACTOR
Oldelft (NV Optische Industrie De Oude Delft), PO Box 72, 2600 MD Delft, Netherlands.

Type GS6TS crew-served weapon sight

3396.193

TYPE HV5X80AT MINI-WEAPON SIGHT

The mini-weapon sight is a small lightweight image intensifier system for observation and aiming with personal weapons at night. Its operation is passive: the light available at the scene is electronically intensified so that targets can be observed and engaged even in the darkest night without any artificial illumination and with a maximum security from detection. The system can be used as a mounted weapon sight on basic infantry weapons, such as rifles, light machine guns and rocket launchers, and as a hand-held observation device. The sight has the capability of detecting enemy use of near infra-red emitters.

CHARACTERISTICS

Magnification: ×5
Field of view: 10°
Focus range: 30 m – ∞
Detection range: Typically 500 m for infantry targets and 1500 m for tanks
Dimensions: 365 × 98 × 125 mm
Weight: 2·2 kg
STATUS
In use with various armies.
CONTRACTOR
Oldelft (NV Optische Industrie De Oude Delft), PO Box 72, 2600 MD Delft, Netherlands.

Type HV5X80AT mini-weapon sight

3397.193

TYPE PG1MS NIGHT VISION GOGGLES

These goggles are primarily intended for use by drivers of armoured vehicles and by helicopter pilots. 'Hands-free' operation also provides paratroops, commandos, reconnaissance patrols, sentries and security forces with a useful aid at night. A snap-on IR light source gives additional illumination for map reading and other short-range tasks.

CHARACTERISTICS

Magnification: ×1
Field of view: 47°
Focus range: Adjustable 30 cm – ∞
Range: Typically up to 150 m
Weight: 1 kg (approx)
STATUS
In quantity production for NATO and other forces.
CONTRACTOR
Oldelft (NV Optische Industrie De Oude Delft), PO Box 72, 2600 MD Delft, Netherlands.

Type PG1MS night vision goggles

4748.193

PC1MC NIGHT VISION GOGGLES

These are known as "Cyclop" goggles and incorporate a single second-generation image intensifier. They can be used for a variety of night tasks, including night driving of all types of vehicles. They are lightweight and the near-face position of the centre of gravity makes them easy to wear, even with a helmet. The special material of the wearing frame allows ventilation of the skin.

CHARACTERISTICS

Magnification: ×1
Field of view: 40°
Focus range: 25 cm – ∞
Dimensions: 142 mm (long) × 131 mm (wide) × 73 mm (high)
Weight: 560 g
CONTRACTOR
Oldelft (NV Optische Industrie De Oude Delft), PO Box 72, 2600 MD Delft, Netherlands.

PC1MC night vision goggles

3578.193
TYPE TS7TS PASSIVE AIMING SIGHT
The passive aiming sight TS7TS has been designed to replace the infra-red sight on various types of tanks. It enables gunners to locate, identify and engage targets at night, without the use of any artificial illumination. The combination of high-speed entrance optics, a 25 mm image-intensifier tube and an optimally shaped eyepiece ensures a clear view of the field of fire. A gun-following mirror links the two parts (gun and sight).

CHARACTERISTICS
Total magnification: ×7
Field of view: 6°
Focus: 100 m – ∞
Eyepiece adjustment: ±5 dioptres
Image-intensifier tube: 3-stage with ABC, DC and FP
Power supply: 21-30 V DC
STATUS
Production.
CONTRACTOR
Oldelft (NV Optische Industrie De Oude Delft), PO Box 72, 2600 MD Delft, Netherlands.

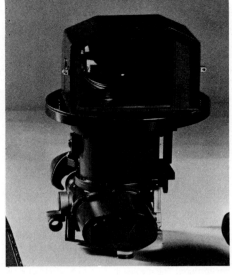

Type TS7TS infra-red tank sight head

3433.193
TYPE UA 1242 NIGHT OBSERVATION SIGHT
The UA 1242 is a lightweight hand-held night observation device with bi-ocular presentation of the image to the eyes. It has a second-generation micro-channel image-intensifier tube with an integrated power supply, automatic brightness control and point highlight suppression.

Both objective and eyepiece lenses are adjustable, as is the inter-ocular distance.
CHARACTERISTICS
Magnification: ×5
Field of view: 7·5°

Resolution: 1 mil at 1 mlux (starlight) at a target contrast of 30%
Focusing range: 25 m – ∞
Eyepiece adjustment: –5 to +3 dioptres
Interocular distance: 58 – 72 mm
Power supply: 2·2 – 3·4 V DC
Weight: 1·9 kg
STATUS
In production.
CONTRACTOR
Philips Usfa BV, Meerenakkerweg 1, PO Box 218, 5600 MD Eindhoven, Netherlands.

Type UA 1242 night observation sight

3400.193
TYPE PB4DS PASSIVE BINOCULARS
These binoculars are designed for general-purpose night surveillance by AFV commanders, outposts, reconnaissance patrols, border guards, security and police forces. A single two-stage fibre-coupled image-intensifier is used to produce a single image which is viewed through a bi-ocular eyepiece.
CHARACTERISTICS
Magnification: ×4
Field of view: 10°

Focus range: Adjustable 4 m – ∞
Detection range: Typically 400 m for infantry targets and 1500 m for tanks
Weight: 2·3 kg
STATUS
In service with several armed forces and police; in series production.
CONTRACTOR
Oldelft (NV Optische Industrie De Oude Delft), PO Box 72, 2600 MD Delft, Netherlands.

Type PB4DS passive binoculars

4749.193
PB4SL NIGHT BINOCULARS
The PB4SL binoculars are a lightweight second-generation device designed for general-purpose night surveillance and reconnaissance by armoured fighting vehicle commanders, outposts, patrols, border guards, security and police forces. A fibreglass-windowed image intensifier is used to produce a single image which is viewed through a binocular eyepiece. The binoculars are similar to the PC1MC goggles (**4748.193**) and, with the exception of the front optics, all parts are interchangeable.

CHARACTERISTICS
Magnification: ×4
Field of view: 10·5°
Focus range: 8 m – ∞
Dimensions: 230 mm (long) × 125 mm (high) × 90 mm (wide)
Weight: 1·1 kg (approx)
CONTRACTOR
Oldelft (NV Optische Industrie De Oude Delft), PO Box 72, 2600 MD Delft, Netherlands.

PB4SL night binoculars

3576.193
MINILASER RANGEFINDER
The Oldelft Minilaser is a small lightweight laser rangefinder suitable for use in either tripod or vehicle-mounted form. Adapters are available for the latter applications. The Minilaser is of modular construction and has the following sub-assemblies: rangefinder, goniometer, tripod, battery unit, and vehicle adapter (if required). The rangefinder and goniometer have separate housings, enabling each unit to be used independently. A north-seeker incorporated in the instrument facilitates orientation of the observer in respect of magnetic north. Instant digital readouts are provided for distance, azimuth, and elevation angles.

CHARACTERISTICS
Transmitter
Type: Nd-YAG
Wavelength: 1·06 micron
Output energy: 40 mJ
Pulse width: 7 μ sec
Power output: 6 MW
Beamwidth: 0·7 mrad
Pulse rate: 10 per minute
Receiver
Field of view: 0·3 mils
Aperture: 45 mm
Range accuracy: ± 10 m
Range (minimum/max): 200/9900 m
Target selection: First or last reply mode

Sight
Magnification: ×7
Field of view: 7°
Eyepiece adjustment: +5 to –5 dioptres
Goniometer
Azimuth: 0 – 6399 mils
Accuracy: ±2 mils
Elevation: ±300 mils
Resolution: ±2 mils
Dimensions
Rangefinder: 184 × 184 × 85 mm
Goniometer: 250 × 225 × 180 mm
Battery: 220 × 110 × 100 mm
Weight: 7·8 kg (rangefinder and goniometer)

CONTRACTOR
Oldelft (NV Optische Industrie De Oude Delft), PO Box 72, 2600 MD Delft, Netherlands.

5702.193
RSI TANK LASER RANGEFINDER

The RSI (Rationalisation, Standardisation, Interoperability) laser rangefinder is specifically designed for easy retrofitting to existing battle tanks provided with the M 35 E1 periscope (eg Centurion, M 48 and M60). Daylight aiming sight and laser rangefinder are combined in one unit to replace the existing daylight elbow in the M35 periscope. For use as part of a fire control system, a projected reticle channel is provided to display reticle offsets in the eyepiece. To minimise volume at the gunner's station, the electronic elements are contained in one unit.

The field of view of the instrument is 7° with a magnification of ×8. A minus blue filter and a neutral density filter are included, and can be actuated with a lever on the housing of the optical unit. The aiming reticle is illuminated to stand out against a dark background. The display in the eyepiece field of view gives measured range, first/last return mode indication, multiple return indication, master failure indication and projected reticle (azimuth offset angle).

RSI tank laser rangefinder

CONTRACTOR
Oldelft (NV Optische Industrie De Oude Delft), PO Box 72, 2600 MD Delft, Netherlands.

Oldelft Minilaser on tripod mount

3429.193
TYPE UA 9120 SERIES DAY/NIGHT PERISCOPE

This periscope system has been designed for both day and night observation and gun-laying. The system is specifically meant for use in one-man turrets such as fitted to the Armoured Infantry Fighting Vehicle (5120.102) and the Oerlikon 25 mm

Type UA 9124/9126 day/night periscope

APC turret (**5586.103**). The modular construction permits independent operational use of the day and night systems. Apart from the day and night periscopes a vision block of unity magnification has been incorporated. The entry optics of both periscopes are coupled to the aiming mechanism of the main armament providing for the elevation of the line-of-sight in collimation with the gun. The vision block has a steady line-of-sight to create a continuous forward observation capability for the gunner, independent of the gun elevation.

The night system is provided with: a second-generation image-intensifier tube with automatic brightness control and point highlight suppression; a built-in and adjustable sky-screen; a reticle for ground targets; and an adjustable iris-diaphragm.

The daylight system is provided with: switchable magnification; a built-in and switchable filter for excessive brightness; and a reticle for ground and air targets.

The reticles of both systems are adjustable for both azimuth and elevation (±5 mrad) and can be illuminated.

The system can be extended with a ballistic compensator proportionally designed to fit within the system dimensions.

CHARACTERISTICS
Night system
Magnification: ×6
Field of view: 125 mrad
Eyepiece adjustment: –3 to +3 dioptres
Elevation: –10 to +20°
Daylight system
Magnification: ×6 or ×2
Field of view: 170 and 510 mils
Eyepiece adjustment: –3 to +3 dioptres
Elevation: –10 to +60°
Vision block
Magnification: ×1
Horizontal field of view: 75°
Vertical field of view: 30°
Power supply: 20 – 30 V DC 20 W
CONTRACTOR
Philips Usfa BV, Meerenakkerweg 1, PO Box 218, 5600 MD Eindhoven, Netherlands.

4235.193
UA 9090 TANK SIGHT

The UA 9090 tank sight is a thermal imaging system designed for target aiming and observation where a target-to-background temperature difference exists in the infra-red wavelength 'window' between 8 and 12 microns. The thermal radiation received from the scene is converted into a CCIR video signal and is presented on video monitors. A controllable aiming mark is added to the video signal for aiming orientation during gun-laying. The system features a stabilised line-of-sight for mobile observation as a search mode. It is supplied ready to interface with a fire control computer and is fitted with BITE. An optional thermal pointer is available for use in a tracking mode. Positioning of the thermal sensor in a vehicle is not restricted by the location of the gunner's or commander's station.

CHARACTERISTICS
Field of view: 5° horizontal; 3° vertical
Spectral range: 8 – 12 microns
Effective object lens aperture: 125 mm
Focal length: 260 mm
Cooling system: Philips Usfa UA 7011 Stirling military mini-cooler
Time to reach camera operational status: 10 minutes
Range of elevation: +23 to –13°
Azimuth: +120 to –120°
STATUS
Pre-production.
CONTRACTOR
Philips Usfa BV, Meerenakkerweg 1, PO Box 218, 5600 MD Eindhoven, Netherlands.

UA 9090 thermal sight and head

3430.193
UA 9630 SERIES UNIVERSAL PASSIVE PERISCOPE

The universal passive periscope has been designed to enable armoured vehicles to be driven at considerable speeds under starlight conditions. Although it has been optimised for driving under starlight conditions it can be employed at higher

illumination levels up to daylight. This leads to uninterrupted operation and avoids disruption of the vehicle's sealing under severe conditions such as an NBC warfare environment. The image brightness can be adjusted to suit the user by means of a manually controlled iris-diaphragm. Automatic brightness control (ABC) has also been incorporated and the periscope is fitted with a device providing point

highlight suppression, automatically reverting to normal use afterwards.

The periscope is of full binocular design and contains two NATO-standard tubes XX 1080 with a long operational life. The required input power is drawn from the vehicle's battery. Built-in electrical heating of the eyepieces can be switched on to prevent misting and condensation. The equipment meets the optical, mechanical and climatic requirements of the relevant military specifications.

The periscope consists of a main instrument, type UA 1624, and an exchangeable top prism. Changing of the top prism does not affect the sealing of the main instrument. A range of top prisms is available facilitating the fitting of the periscope to all types of armoured vehicle. Among others, top prisms are available for main battle tanks such as Leopard, Centurion and M60 and armoured vehicles like M113, AIVF and Scorpion.

CHARACTERISTICS
Magnification: ×0·9
Horizontal field of view: 50°
Vertical field of view: 40°
Illumination range: 10^{-3} to 10^4 lux
Range: 5 m – ∞

Tubes: Philips Type XX 1080
Power supply: 20 – 30 V DC
Weight of main instrument: Approx 6 kg
Weight of top prism: 1·5 – 6 kg depending on type
CONTRACTOR
Philips Usfa BV, Meerenakkerweg 1, PO Box 218, 5600 MD Eindhoven, Netherlands.

Type UA 9630 series universal periscopes, for Leopard (left) and M113 (right)

1800.193
TYPE HV7X200AT NIGHT SIGHT
This is a night observation device consisting of an image intensifier system for medium range forward-edge-of-battle surveillance or in a supplementary role as an aiming sight on crew-served weapons. No artificial illumination of any sort is needed. For general surveillance, the system is either tripod- or vehicle-mounted. The spectral sensitivity characteristics of the tubes employed permits detection of the presence of enemy near infra-red emitters.

Entirely self-contained, the unit comprises a high-speed mirror objective, a three-stage fibre-coupled image intensifier assembly with power supply, an eyepiece system, and graticule projector with

adjustable illumination. Monocular or binocular eyepieces are available. There is an automatic brightness control and a manual gain control.
CHARACTERISTICS
Magnification: ×7
Field of view: 7°
Focus: Adjustable 30 m – ∞
Length: 540 mm
Diameter: 260 mm
Weight: 12·8 kg
STATUS
In series production and used by several armies.
CONTRACTOR
Oldelft (NV Optische Industrie De Oude Delft), PO Box 72, 2600 MD Delft, Netherlands.

Type HV7X200AT night sight

1801.193
TYPE TP1MS NIGHT PERISCOPE
The TP1MS is a passive night periscope for combat vehicles. It is a small, binocular, wide angle, passive night vision image intensifier system for direct visual observation by the driver of the road and terrain in front of the vehicle under ambient night illumination conditions. The system will enable movement of combat vehicles at a speed of approximately 40 km/h under starlight conditions without the aid of artificial illumination, and with maximum security from detection.

The field of view of 55° in the horizontal plane gives the driver a clear view of the roadside.

The high-tension power packs are stabilised and will automatically protect the tube against high photo-cathode illumination, and automatically restore normal use afterwards.
CHARACTERISTICS
Total magnification: ×1
Field of view: Horizontal 55°; vertical 40°

Centre resolution: Under starlight conditions 1 mlux, 2·5 mrad
Weight: Approx 7 kg
Number of tubes: 2
Tube type: Special diode, photocathode S25, phosphor screen P20
Power supply: 20 – 30 V DC
Entrance optics: Focal length 45 mm relative aperture 1:1·1. Fixed focus 15 m
Ocular system: Binocular and adjustable between +5 and –5 dioptres
Operating temperature range: –20 to +50°C
Storage temperature range: –30 to +60°C
STATUS
Series production.
CONTRACTOR
Oldelft (NV Optische Industrie De Oude Delft), PO Box 72, 2600 MD Delft, Netherlands.

Type TP1MS night periscope

4690.193
GS6MC CREW-SERVED WEAPON SIGHT
This passive weapon sight is based on a second generation image intensifier tube and is suitable for medium-range crew-served weapons, such as heavy machine guns, recoilless guns and anti-tank guns. The modular design allows the use of either a straight or rectangular eyepiece. Reticles can be fitted, matching the ballistics of the weapon concerned. Reticle illumination is adjustable to the scene brightness..

CHARACTERISTICS
Magnification: × 6·8
Field of view: 6·6°
Focus setting: 45 m – ∞
Focal length: Entrance optics 150 mm; eye piece 21 mm
Dioptre setting: +5 to –5 dioptres
Tube type: Two-stage 18 mm fibre-glass coupled second generation hybrid
Weight: 3 kg
CONTRACTOR
Oldelft (NV Optische Industrie De Oude Delft), PO Box 72, 2600 MD Delft, Netherlands.

GS6MC crew-served weapon sight

4691.193
TP1MC NIGHT PERISCOPE
The passive driving periscope TP1MC is a small binocular wide-angle night viewing system for direct observation of the road and terrain in front of the vehicle. It consists of two independent viewing channels, each comprising one objective lens system,

one second generation flash-protected image intensifier tube, one high voltage unit and an eye piece. The TP1MC can easily be adapted for use in a great variety of armoured combat and personnel carrying vehicles.
CHARACTERISTICS
Magnification: ×1

Field of view: 50° horizontal; 26° vertical
Centre resolution: 2·3 mrad at $3 × 10^{-2}$ lux; 3·2 mrad at 10^{-3} lux; 4·2 mrad at 10^{-4} lux
Focal length: 20 mm (approx)
Relative aperture: 1:1·1
Focus setting: Fixed 15 m
Dioptre setting: –3 to +3 dioptres

Tube type: Second generation 18 mm microchannel wafer with fibre-optic input and twisted fibre output window
Weight: 6 kg (approx)

CONTRACTOR
Oldelft (NV Optische Industrie De Oude Delft), PO Box 72, 2600 MD Delft, Netherlands.

TP1MC night periscope

NORWAY

1804.193
LP3 LASER RANGEFINDER

The SIMRAD LP3 laser rangefinder is a one-man portable, tripod-mounted combined sight and laser rangefinder. It enables range, bearing, and elevation

SIMRAD LP3 laser rangefinder

data for targets to be rapidly acquired and used directly by weapons or fed into computerised artillery fire control systems. A quick-aiming sight is provided to permit rapid orientation towards targets appearing only briefly, such as shell bursts or gun flashes. A Q-switched neodymium-doped glass laser is used, providing a peak power of 1·5 MW. With a pulse length of 30 nanoseconds this amounts to an equivalent radiated energy of about 45 mJ. A range display shows the ranges to two targets on LED numeric indicators with a resolution of five metres and range discrimination of 30 metres.

CHARACTERISTICS
Transmitter
Laser: Q-switched Nd-doped glass
Wavelength: 1·064 μm
Power (peak): 1·5 MW
Pulse length: 30 × 10^{-9} s
Pulses per minute: 12 continuous; 30 intermittent
Beamwidth: (90% energy) 1 mrad
Receiver
Field of view: 1 mrad
Detector: Photodiode optimised for 1·06 μm
Effective aperture: 70 mm
Sensitivity: 0·5 A/W
Minimum/max range: 200/20 000 m
Resolution: 5 m
Range discrimination: 30 m
Minimum-range setting: 200 – 6000 m continuously adjustable
Sight
Magnification: ×7

Field of view: 7°
Effective aperture: 50 mm
Eye protection: Dichroic beamsplitter and absorption glass in eyepiece
Goniometer
Elevation: ±350 mil
Azimuth: 6400 mil
Resolution: 1 mil
Dimensions and weights
Rangefinder with goniometer: 260 × 280 × 260 mm; 7·9 kg
Battery pack: 65 × 85 × 230 mm; 1·5 kg
Tripod, folded: 370 × 140 mm diameter; 2·2 kg
Weight, total: 11·6 kg
Transit case: 350 × 350 × 350 mm; 7·8 kg
DEVELOPMENT
The SIMRAD LP3 laser rangefinder was developed for the Norwegian Army under government contract. The programme was supported by the Norwegian Defence Research Establishment.
STATUS
In production for the Norwegian Army and the forces of unspecified countries. It is also in production for the British Army, where it is known as the LP6, in this form being supplied without a tripod, goniometer, and battery.
CONTRACTOR
SIMRAD Optronics A/S, PO Box 6114, Etterstad, Oslo 6, Norway.

3155.193
LP7 LASER RANGEFINDER

Intended for use by infantry units in the close support role, the LP7 laser rangefinder weighs only 2·2 kg and is the same size as a standard 7 × 50 binocular. It can be either hand-held or mounted on a support and, when combined with a night observation device, can also be used for ranging at night.

Range is determined by laying the telescope reticle on to the target and pressing the fire button on top of the unit. Range is then immediately displayed in the eyepiece. Indication is given if echoes from more than one target have been detected and unwanted echoes may be gated out by a minimum range control. Indication is also given if one or more targets have been gated out.

The transmitter is a miniaturised Q-switched Nd:YAG laser. The sighting telescope, with a performance comparable with that of a standard observation monocular, is combined with the optical receiver by a beam-splitting technique.

The receiver uses a silicon avalanche-photodiode giving a range capability up to 10 km with a resolution of 5 metres. The four-digit LED display is observed through the left eyepiece and superimposed on the picture seen in the right eyepiece. Display intensity may be adjusted by rotating the eyepiece housing.

After three seconds the display is automatically switched off to preserve battery power. Indication is given if the voltage is too low.

Options are digital setting of minimum range, built-in test and data output from the range counter. A rugged lightweight tripod with angulation head is available. This unit provides azimuth and elevation readouts with a resolution of 5 mils.

CHARACTERISTICS
Dimensions: 215 × 202 × 93 mm
Weight: 2·2 kg (including battery)
Minimum/maximum range: 150 – 9995 m
Transmitter
Laser: Nd:YAG; 1·064 μm wavelength
Output energy: 5 mJ (nominal)
Repetition frequency: 12 pulses/m (30 intermittent)
Beamwidth: 2 mrad
Receiver
Field of view: 1·3 mrad
Aperture: 45 mm
Range resolution: 5 m
Minimum setting: 150 – 4000 m (continuously adjustable)
Telescope
Magnification: ×7
Field of view: 120 mils (nominal)
Aperture: 45 mils

SIMRAD LP7 laser rangefinder

STATUS
In production. In service with the Norwegian, Swedish and British armies, and the forces of a number of other countries. A contract from the New Zealand MoD, worth N. Kr. 6 million, was received in mid-1984.
CONTRACTOR
SIMRAD Optronics A/S, PO Box 6114, Etterstad, Oslo 6, Norway.

3579.193
LP8 LASER RANGEFINDER

The SIMRAD LP8 laser rangefinder is a very small lightweight unit primarily intended for mounting directly on weapons, night observation devices,

theodolites and anti-tank weapon systems. The rangefinder contains all electronic and optical units required to enable the operator to lay the instrument on to a target, make measurements and read the range to the target from a digital display.

The transmitter is a miniaturised Q-switched Nd:YAG laser. The receiver uses an avalanche photodiode giving an operational range to typical targets of about 5 to 6 km when optical visibility is 10 km. Unwanted nearby echoes may be gated out from the display by a minimum range control on the operator's side of the instrument.

The range display shows range to the target to the nearest five metres. In addition there are two indicators to warn the operator either that more than one target has been detected or that one or more targets have been gated out.

The 7-segment LED display lights up when a range has been measured and switches off after three seconds. The rangefinder has been designed on modular principles to simplify repair and maintenance and is contained in a sturdy waterproof housing. Mechanical interfaces suitable for weapons, theodolites and night observation devices are available.

CHARACTERISTICS

Transmitter
Laser type: Nd-YAG
Wavelength: 1·064 micron
Output energy: 5 mJ

Pulse width: 10×10^{-9} s
Pulse rate: 12/minute (30 intermittent)
Beamwidth: 1·5 mrad (90% energy)
Receiver
Field of view: 1·3 mrad
Detector: Avalanche diode
Aperture: 45 mm
Clock frequency: 29·97 MHz
Range resolution: 5 m
Display: 7-segment LED
Minimum/max range: 150/10 000 m
Telescope
Magnification: ×7
Field of view: Approx 120 mils
Aperture: 45 mm
Eye protection: Dichroic beamsplitter and absorption glass in eyepiece
STATUS
Production.

SIMRAD LP8 laser rangefinder (with battery and control unit)

CONTRACTOR
SIMRAD Optronics A/S, PO Box 6114, Etterstad, Oslo 6, Norway.

3755.193
LV5 LASER RANGEFINDER
The SIMRAD LV5 laser rangefinder is designed for external mounting on armoured fighting vehicles to improve their combat effectiveness by providing them

SIMRAD LV5 laser rangefinder outfit for AFV installation, showing (left to right) control/display unit, transmitter/receiver, and optional range display unit

with accurate range information for weapon aiming. The compact and low profile laser transmitter/receiver unit is mounted on the gun and accurately boresighted to it. The control/display unit is located inside the vehicle in a position where it may be seen and used by the gunner or commander; an LED range display shows the ranges to two targets with a resolution of 5 metres. An auxiliary output provides range information either to an external fire control computer or to an optional range display unit.

CHARACTERISTICS
Transmitter
Laser: Nd-YAG
Wavelength: 1·064 micron
Pulse length: 10×10^{-9} s
Output energy: 10 mJ
Firing rate: 12 continuous; 30 intermittent pulses/minute
Beamwidth: 2 mrad

Receiver
Field of view: 1·3 mrad
Detector: Avalanche photodiode
Effective aperture: 45 mm
Minimum/max range: 150 m/10 000 m
Range resolution: 5 m
Range discrimination: 30 m
Minimum range setting: 150 – 400 m continuously variable
Sight
Magnification: ×7
Weight: 2·2 kg (transmitter/receiver); 2 kg (control unit)
STATUS
In production. Manufactured under licence in UK by Lasergage Ltd.
CONTRACTOR
SIMRAD Optronics A/S, PO Box 6114, Etterstad, Oslo 6, Norway.

4285.193
KN150 NIGHT OBSERVATION DEVICE
The KN150 hand-held passive night observation sight combines high performance with simple operation and low weight. Extensive tests show that tanks can be detected at ranges up to 1500 metres. Military applications include general surveillance, battlefield night observation and target location.

The use of binocular rather than monocular eyepieces minimises operator fatigue and makes it possible to maintain continuous surveillance for long periods. To ease handling, only two controls are fitted, an ON-switch and a twist grip focusing. Focusing range is from 25 metres to infinity. An electronic OFF-switch turns the instrument off after approximately one minute of action.

An automatic brightness control reduces the amplification of sudden bright lights. Normal operation is restored less than one second after a sudden light flash.

The KN150 incorporates a large aperture

catadioptric lens and a second generation, high resolution microchannel image intensifier tube. Two standard 1·5V dry cells provide more than 40 hours of observation. The KN1150 can be combined with a Simrad laser rangefinder for night observation and localisation of targets.

CHARACTERISTICS
Magnification: × 8
Field of view: 8°
Maximum detection range: 500 m (target 2·3 × 2·3 m, contrast 30%, reflectivity 50%)
Illuminance level: 3×10^{-3} lux
Focusing range: 25 m – ∞
Resolution: 0·65 mrad (target contrast 30%)
Objective lens: Catadioptric, EFL/135 mm, F No/1·3, T No/1·9
Eyepiece exit pupil: Two; 9 mm
Dioptre setting: 1 dioptre (fixed)
Image intensifier tube: Second generation, microchannel tube with ×1·5 magnification
Weight: 2·6 kg

KN150 night observation device

STATUS
In production for the Norwegian Army.
CONTRACTOR
SIMRAD Optronics A/S, PO Box 6114, Etterstad, Oslo 6, Norway.

5703.193
LP160 LASER RANGEFINDER
The LP160 lightweight, one-man portable laser rangefinder is for use by artillery and mortar forward observers. It measures range, azimuth and elevation angles to targets and may be used for fixing own position, target position and for adjustment of fire. Azimuth and elevation angles to the target are measured within 1 mil.

The transmitter is a miniaturised Q-switched Nd:YAG laser with an output energy of typically 10 mJoules. The receiver uses a silicon avalanche photodiode giving a range of up to 20 km. Unwanted echoes can be gated out from the display by a minimum range control which can be set at any range from 150 to 6000 metres.

The operator can select between measuring the range to the first target detected beyond the minimum range setting or the last target within the maximum range. The range display shows the range to the nearest 5 metres. In addition there are indicators to warn the operator if more than one target has been detected, one or more targets have been gated out, battery voltage is too low, laser output is too low or the

receiver electronics have failed. Display time is limited to three seconds to save the batteries.

CHARACTERISTICS
Dimensions and weights
Rangefinder and goniometer: 270 × 240 × 230 mm; 5·8 kg
Battery and control unit: 45 × 80 × 220 mm; 0·5 kg
Tripod, folded: 370 × 140 (dia) mm; 1·6 kg
Minimum/max range: 150 – 20 000 m
Transmitter
Laser: Nd:YAG
Wavelength: 1·064 μm
Output energy: 10 mJ (nominal)
Pulse width: 8 ns
Pulse rate: 12 pulses/m (30 intermittent)
Beamwidth: 2 mrad (90% energy)
Receiver
Field of view: 1·3 mrad (nominal)
Aperture: 45 mm

LP160 laser rangefinder

Range resolution: 5 m
Discrimination between close targets: 50 m
Display: 5-digit LED
Telescope
Magnification: ×7

Field of view: 120 mils
Goniometer
Elevation: ± 350 mils
Azimuth: 640 mils
Resolution: 1 mil

STATUS
In production.
CONTRACTOR
SIMRAD Optronics A/S, PO Box 6114, Etterstad, Oslo 6, Norway.

4692.193
LP100 LASER RANGEFINDER

The LP100 is a miniaturised combined weapon sight and laser rangefinder for mounting on various types of anti-tank and other direct firing weapons. It replaces the traditional sights and provides instant target range and aiming information. A built-in ballistic computer, pre-programmed for the type of weapon and ammunition used, calculates the elevation angle and the time of flight for the projectile.

LP100 laser rangefinder mounted on a 88mm Carl Gustav

The transmitter is a miniaturised Q-switched Nd:YAG laser with a nominal output energy of 3mJoules. The receiver uses an avalanche photodiode giving an operational range of up to 500 metres.

Unwanted nearby echoes may be gated out by a minimum range control which can be set to any range between 50 and 2000 metres. First/last target logic is also included.

The operation of the LP100 has been made as simple as possible with the number of controls reduced to a minimum. For ergonomic reasons the laser trigger button is mounted on the weapon. During operation of the rangefinder, all information is displayed in the sighting eyepiece. The range display shows the range to the target to the nearest five metres and there are other indicators to warn the operator if more than one target is detected, battery voltage is too low, start pulse is not present and no target is detected.

The reticle pattern can be designed to comply with various types of weapons and ammunition. Triggering the laser yields a range reading to the target. Simultaneously this range information is fed to the ballistic computer which controls an array of 36 LEDs along the vertical axis. The correct superelevation angle corresponding to this range is indicated by lighting up one of the diodes. This diode is then used for aiming when the weapon is fired. The

ballistic computer also activates an indicator when the calculated time of flight for the projectile has elapsed. This information is used to estimate the lead angle applied when firing.
CHARACTERISTICS
Dimensions and weight: 75 × 105 × 240 mm; 1·2 kg
Minimum/max range: 50 – 5000 m
Transmitter: Nd:YAG
Wavelength: 1·064 μm
Output energy: 3 mJ (nominal)
Pulse rate: 12 pulses/m (30 intermittent)
Beam divergence: <2·0 mrad w/6x beam expander (90% energy)
Receiver
Field of view: 1 mrad
Aperture: 21 mm
Range resolution: 5 m
Telescope
Magnification: ×3
Field of view: 200 mils
Aperture: 21 mm
Reticle pattern: As required
Eye protection: Dichroic beamsplitter and absorption glass in eyepiece
STATUS
Pre-production.
CONTRACTOR
SIMRAD Optronics A/S, PO Box 6114, Etterstad, Oslo 6, Norway.

4693.193
TC10 THERMAL IMAGER

The TC10 thermal imager is intended specifically for naval and coastal artillery use to provide high penetration of smoke, haze and camouflage. It is a passive system giving high resolution with a minimum resolvable temperature difference of 0·08° C for long-range detection and identification. Detection is independent of ambient light and the system operates by day and night. The thermal picture is displayed on a TV monitor.

The equipment consists of a thermal camera, signal processing unit and a TV monitor. In a typical shipborne application the thermal camera is mounted on a stabilised platform.
CHARACTERISTICS
Field of view: 1° horizontal, 3° vertical
Resolution: 0·22 mrad
Focusing range: 25 m – ∞
Detector: Cadmium Mercury Telluride
Spectral band: 8 – 12 μm
Detector cooling: Compressed gas

Mission time: 20 h with a 5 litre cooling bottle at 300 atmospheres
Weight: 8 kg (camera); 7·5 kg (signal processor)
CONTRACTOR
SIMRAD Optronics A/S, PO Box 6114, Etterstad, Oslo 6, Norway.

SOUTH AFRICA

5704.193
E4020 MINIATURE COMBAT NIGHT SIGHT (MNV)

Equipped with an 18 mm second-generation image intensifier, the MNV night sight is optimised for small arms application in a variety of military operations.

The instrument has been evolved from extensive combat experience and features a fixed focus objective, and is instantly ready for aiming when switched on. The only adjustments required, prior to action, are boresight and eyepiece diopter setting.

Power supply is by means of two readily available

penlight-type batteries. Boresight adjustment is incorporated in an integral quick-release type mounting bracket. Breech cover mounts for a variety of rifles are available.
CHARACTERISTICS
Length: 200 mm (excluding eyecup)
Magnification: ×2·6
Field of view: 16°
Entrance pupil: 40 mm
Exit pupil: 7 mm
Eye relief: 18 mm

Eyepiece adjustment: –4 to +4 diopters
Boresight range: 20 mils continuous, azimuth and elevation
Night vision range: 110 m – 8 line pairs 1·8 m at 30% contrast and reflectivity at 10^{-3} lux
Weight: 960g (without mount and batteries)
CONTRACTOR
Armscor, 224 Visagie Street, Pretoria, Republic of South Africa.

5705.193
E5010 LASER RANGEFINDER

The E5010 is a ruggedised laser rangefinder with up to 8 km ranging capability. Its low mass and small size make the instrument ideal for hand-held and support mounted ranging applications such as:
(1) fire control for mortars, artillery and armour
(2) target ranging for missiles and light anti-tank weapons
(3) air-to-ground ranging.

The design is based on a combined transmitter/

receiver and sighting telescope optics. This ensures a compact and convenient-to-use instrument. Range is displayed instantaneously in the eypiece on pressing the firing button with the telescope reticle laid on the target. A continuously adjustable minimum range gate is provided to gate out unwanted echoes. Multiple echo with range-to-first echo, and no-echo indications are also provided.
CHARACTERISTICS
Transmitter: Nd-YAG, beam divergence 0·7 mrad
Monocular sight: ×6 magnification, 6° field of view

Ocular adjustment: –4 to +4 diopters
Accuracy: ± 5 m
Minimum range adjustment: 200 – 3200 m continuous
Pulse energy: 8 mJ nominal
Dimensions: 125 × 160 × 70 mm nominal
Weight: 1·5 kg
CONTRACTOR
Armscor, 224 Visagie Street, Pretoria, Republic of South Africa.

5706.193
E2030 NIGHT DRIVERSCOPE

The E2030 passive night driverscope is a bi-ocular viewing wide-angle night periscope employing a second-generation image intensifier tube. The instrument enables vehicles to be driven by night at normal speed, without artificial lighting.

The special fixed focus bi-ocular eyepiece enables

simultaneous viewing with both eyes to provide ease of observation and free head movement for instrument viewing. A fixed focus objective lens is used and adjustable gain setting of the image intensifier tube provides brightness control for high light levels.

The head prism is designed to be removed easily and fits into a standard NATO driver's day periscope

mount, thereby making the periscope adaptable to a wide variety of armoured vehicles. A horizontal scanning mechanism provides manual scanning capability of 30° total in the horizontal plane. Instantaneous field of view is > 40° in both horizontal and vertical planes.

CHARACTERISTICS
Magnification: ×0·92 ± 0·05
Field of view: > 40° horizontal and vertical
Horizontal scanning: ± 15°
Focus: Fixed 15 m
Periscopic height: 227 mm max
Exit pupil: >78 mm

Eye relief: 55 mm
Dioptre setting: –2 ±0·5 dioptres
Dimensions: 360 × 200 × 220 mm
Weight: 6·95 kg; 18 kg with case and accessories
CONTRACTOR
Armscor, 224 Visagie Street, Pretoria, Republic of
South Africa.

E2030 night driverscope

SPAIN

5707.193
ENOSA ELECTRO-OPTICAL SYSTEMS
A range of aiming sights and periscopes is
manufactured by Empresa Nacional de Optica SA
(ENOSA) of Madrid. These electro-optical
instruments are intended primarily for the Spanish
armed forces. In addition, as a result of a Franco-
Spanish agreement, ENOSA manufactures the
optical equipment for those AMX-30 tanks produced
in Spain.

Brief details of the equipment range are as follows.
PP-01 Aiming Periscope
The PP-01 has been designed and developed to equip
CETME TC-3 turrets mounted in armoured vehicles
such as the BMR and M-113. It consists of a prism
head and sight on a mounting stand. A reticle with
cross-hairs in the display sight facilitates accurate
aiming. Field of view is 43° horizontal and 11° vertical.
PP-02 Observation and Aiming Periscope
This sight consists of a prism head, binocular
observation sight and a monocular telescope with a
magnifying power of ×2 and ×6 respectively for land
and air aiming. It has been designed for the BMR

armoured vehicle turret but can be adapted to other
automatic gun or machine-gun mounts.
M-92D Elbow Telescope
The M-92D is an optical aiming telescope for the CSR
106 mm gun. It has a ×3 magnifying power and can be
used both by day and by night. Aiming by night can be
carried out with illumination by either a dry battery or
by photoluminiscence using tritium-phosphorus gas
capsules.

106 mm Gun Night Aiming Sight
This is an elbow night sight using image intensifier
techniques. Magnifying power is ×2·5 with a real field
of view of 9·5°.

Grenade Night Aiming Sight
Designed for grenade launching at night, this image
intensifier type sight is based on the 106 mm night
aiming sight with broadly similar characteristics.

Grenade Launcher Sight
A standard optical sight for day and night use. Night
illumination is provided by either a dry battery or by
using tritium-phosphorus gas capsules.

AA 40/70 Bofors Gun Collimator Sight
A manually operated bi-ocular sight to cater for fire
prediction against low-level aircraft attack.
Goniometric Aiming Devices
Goniometric aiming devices are available for 60, 81-
105 and 120 mm mortars. They are based on a 'plumb-
line' system whereby the aiming device, freely
suspended from a tilted axle and on an assembly of
high sensitivity balls, automatically and accurately
guarantees the alignment in the vertical plane with the
mortar bore., The optical system is an elbow
telescope, and reticle lighting is provided by means of
a dry battery.
AMX-30E Tank Optics
As a result of agreements with a number of French
companies, ENOSA manufactures the optical
systems for the AMX-30E tanks being built in Spain.
These systems include telescopes, rangefinders,
periscopes and night driving equipment for aiming
and observation under both day and night conditions.
CONTRACTOR
Empresa Nacional de Optica SA, Avenida de San Luis
91, Madrid 33, Spain.

SWEDEN

3144.193
RIA GUNSIGHT
For modern guns and howitzers Philips
Elektronikindustrier AB has developed an automatic
electronic gunsight called RIA, which can be used
both for indirect and direct firing. It has a very simple
interface to the gun and can therefore easily be
mounted on various types of guns.

RIA comprises the following main units:
Control and Display Unit: The panel has displays for
presentation of firing data received from a fire control
computer, knobs for different operating modes, and

preset values. The unit also comprises electronics for
necessary computations including compensation for
tilt of the gun and servo-control circuitry for the sight.
Sighting Unit: This unit comprises a panoramic sight
and an automatic levelling device. It includes a zero
setting instrument for laying the gun in elevation, and
also includes, as a reserve mode, mechanics and
bubble levels for manual laying. The panoramic sight
has a servo-driven setting of bearing.
Direct Sight: For laying the gun by direct firing.

The equipment receives firing data (bearing,
elevation, fuze setting, and charge) from a fire control

computer via a data link. Based on these data and the
tilt of the gun, etc, RIA automatically calculates
relative bearing and elevation.

In azimuth this information controls a servo-driven
top-prism in the panoramic sight and thereby the line
of sight. The reference for aiming in traverse can be
sticks, plates, or a collimator. Gun laying in elevation
is done with the aid of a zero-setting instrument.
Setting in traverse and elevation can take place
simultaneously.

RIA has the following tactical functions:
(1) automatic reception of firing data
(2) presentation of firing data on the control and
    display unit
(3) settings of gun corrections in azimuth and
    elevation
(4) automatic computation of relative bearing and
    elevation, including automatic correction for the
    tilt of the gun
(5) automatic levelling of the sighting unit
(6) automatic control of the sight in azimuth
    including automatic setting of bearing
(7) reserve modes for use when the data transmission
    or the computation is out of order
(8) supervision of tactical and electrical functions by
    built-in test circuits.
STATUS
In service with the FH 77A in Sweden and in
production for the FH 77B gun.
CONTRACTOR
Philips Elektronikindustrier AB, 175 88 Järfälla,
Sweden.

RIA automatic gun sight for field artillery, and associated control and display unit

3042.193
ERICSSON ANTI-AIRCRAFT LASER RANGEFINDER

The Ericsson high repetition rate anti-aircraft laser rangefinder is designed to be the ranging sensor in electro-optical fire control systems where the tracking is performed either automatically, by a TV or infra-red sensor, or manually. It can also be used in radar fire control systems to give range information under jamming conditions.

The laser rangefinder consists of a transceiver unit, a power module and a range counter, which can easily be integrated into existing systems. The transceiver unit contains the YAG-laser transmitter with its air-cooling system and the optical receiver.

The YAG-transmitter of a high repetition rate laser rangefinder dissipates a considerable amount of heat and must be effectively cooled. The Ericsson anti-aircraft laser rangefinder uses forced air cooling, which is a simple and effective method. The transceiver unit is completely sealed. Via the fan, the air in the unit is circulated through the transmitter. The heated air is then cooled on the case by the cooling fins. This forced air cooling gives simplicity of construction, high reliability and easy maintenance.

CHARACTERISTICS

Range capability: 8-14 km depending on target size. Extinction value 50 dB

Coverage: 280-20 475 m (12-bit parallel form, TTL-level)
Accuracy: 4 m
Adjustable minimum range: 280 – 20 440 m (9-bit parallel form, TTL-level)
Range gate: Length 500 m (other values optional) or to the end of the range coverage
Transmitter
Laser: Nd-YAG
Wavelength: 1·06μm
Beamwidth: 1·2 – 1·5 mrad
Repetition rate: 10 pulses/s
Receiver
Detector: Silicon avalanche diode
Area of optics: 80 cm²
Field of view: 1·5 mrad
Power
Supply: 3-phase 220/380V, 50 Hz
Max consumption: 250 VA during transmitting interval
Weights
Transceiver unit: 13 kg
Power module and range counter: 12 kg

STATUS

In production. The Ericsson anti-aircraft laser rangefinder has been ordered by a large number of system manufacturers both in and outside Sweden.

Ericsson AA laser rangefinder (left) mounted on director with Saab-Scania TV camera

The total number of lasers ordered exceeds 300 systems.

CONTRACTOR

Ericsson Radio Systems AB, Defence and Space Systems Division, 431 26 Mölndal, Sweden.

3043.193
ERICSSON ARTILLERY LASER RANGEFINDER

The Ericsson artillery laser rangefinder is used by forward observers for range determination of stationary and mobile targets as well as ranging airbursts up to a distance of 5 to 6 km. The rangefinder, weighing less than 10 kg, consists of transceiver unit, goniometer, tripod and battery, and collapses easily for transport in a heavy-duty glass-fibre container. The transceiver unit uses a neodymium-YAG transmitter enabling instant use and no limitation with respect to range measurement rate.

Manoeuvring controls are kept to a minimum in order to secure easy and rapid use which results in controls for three functions only:

(1) trigger button
(2) a button to present blocking range in display and a dial for continuous adjustment of blocking range
(3) a dial for adjustment of reticle illumination.

The rangefinder is equipped with two counters enabling two ranges to be measured simultaneously in the same line of sight. The goniometer is a precision instrument for measuring azimuth and elevation angles within an accuracy of one mrad.

STATUS

In production.

CONTRACTOR

Ericsson Radio Systems AB, Defence and Space Systems Division, 431 26 Mölndal, Sweden.

Ericsson artillery laser rangefinder

3044.193
INTEGRATED LASER FOR MAIN BATTLE TANKS

This integrated laser tank sight uses an advanced miniaturised neodymium-YAG transmitter for maximum repetition rate and temperature independence. Boresighting of the laser to the gun bore is facilitated by the adjustable inner chassis of the laser sight. For operator's convenience the laser sight is equipped with a continuous blocking range. For night fighting purposes a mechanical filter, protecting the operator's eyes from light, is built in and is operated when the laser as well as the gun is triggered.

In addition to the normal eyepiece for gun firing, there is a large field of view sight for observation purposes. The laser rangefinder is designed to operate in co-operation with a ballistic computer. The result from the computer, the aiming mark, is presented in the gunner's sight as a red dot on the target (spot injection).

The laser trigger button is placed on the gunner's control handle.

The Ericsson laser rangefinder sight features:
(1) gunner's sight and laser rangefinder in one unit only
(2) spot injection for computer co-operation
(3) simple alignment of gunner's sight to the main gun of the vehicle
(4) easy and rapid installation in the vehicle.

STATUS

Initially developed for modernisation of the Centurion MBT, this sight is now in production and available for fitting in other tanks requiring updating. Orders have been received from two countries, one being Denmark for retrofit to Centurions.

CONTRACTOR

Ericsson Radio Systems AB, Defence and Space Systems Division, 431 26 Mölndal, Sweden.

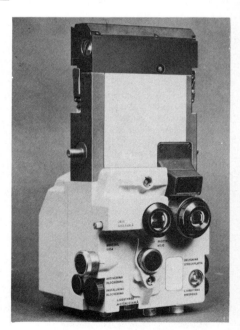

Ericsson gunner's sight for main battle tanks, with integrated laser rangefinder and spot injection

3836.093
ERICSSON LASER TRACKER

The Ericsson laser tracker is being developed for fire control systems. It is of the neodymium-YAG type, and has a wavelength of 1·06 microns. The beamwidth is three milliradians, and the repetition rate 20 pulses per second. The tracker has two main applications. First as a back-up sensor in fire control systems using radar as the main tracking sensor; in this application the tracker will be a solution to the well-known radar multi-path problem, occurring when tracking targets over relatively smooth surfaces. In addition, the laser will give the system a redundant tracking channel, resulting in improved ECCM capability due to the very narrow beam angle.

The laser can also be used as the main tracking sensor in electro-optical fire control systems. The range capability is 7 km at 20 km optical visibility, one-way transmission over 5 km is 50 per cent, target area is 4·5 m² and reflectivity is greater than 0·1.

Angular error signals are generated in a quadrant receiver. The signal processing technique is based on the monopulse principle. The laser tracker uses the same design technology as the Ericsson anti-aircraft laser rangefinder.

STATUS
Pre-production.
CONTRACTOR
Ericsson Radio Systems AB, Defence and Space Systems Division, 431 26 Mölndal, Sweden.

Ericsson laser tracker

3041.153
ERICSSON COAST ARTILLERY LASER RANGEFINDER

A new generation of coast artillery laser rangefinders, successor equipment to the UAL 10102 marine laser rangefinder (**1213.253**), is being delivered to Swedish and Norwegian naval forces. Few details concerning the new system have been revealed apart from the following brief description.

The laser rangefinder consists of three units: the transceiver unit, the display unit, and the trigger pedal. The transceiver uses a high PRF neodymium-YAG air-cooled laser transmitter to permit rapid fall-

of-shot measurements. The display unit, in addition to the main range display, has a memory display to assist in correction of gun fire. This new coast laser rangefinder is designed to interface both electrically and mechanically with the UAL 10102.
STATUS
In production.
CONTRACTOR
Ericsson Radio Systems AB, Defence and Space Systems Division, 431 26 Mölndal, Sweden.

Ericsson coast artillery laser rangefinder

4694.193
ERICSSON INFRA-RED IMAGER

This is an IR imaging system for use on directors in land and naval fire control systems against targets such as aircraft, ships and missiles. The equipment incorporates two characteristics to improve the overall performance:
(1) local dynamic compression which enhances details of the scene so that small objects are not lost against large background variations (sky, clouds, sea and land)

(2) automatic target designation generates markers which are positioned automatically on the detected hot spots in the IR image. This function decreases overall operator workload and minimises the acquisition time.

The system is TV compatible and can be easily integrated with a TV tracker. The IR image is presented on a TV monitor. An electronic "crosshair", which defines the line of sight with high accuracy, is provided to facilitate accurate and rapid boresighting.
CHARACTERISTICS
Spectral region: 8 – 12 μm

Field of view: 6° × 4°
Instantaneous field of view: 0·3 mrad
Frame rate: 25 Hz
Detector: CMT 48 elements
Cooling: 77° K. Joule-Thompson cooler and/or compressed gas
Range: 10 km (jet aircraft); 5 – 7 km (helicopter); 4 – 6 km (sea skimmer)
Dimensions: 60 × 30 × 15 cm
Weight: 25 kg
CONTRACTOR
Ericsson Radio Systems AB, 431 26 Mölndal, Sweden.

3575.083
VTS-800 VIDEO TRACKING EQUIPMENT

The Saab VTS-800 is a new advanced digital correlation tracking equipment introduced by Saab-Scania for various target tracking applications. The tracker embodies the latest technology featuring TV/IR compatibility, centroid tracking and adaptive tracking gate size. It is intended to be used for tracking against target backgrounds of a complexity that goes beyond the ability of conventional contrast trackers.

No technical details have been cleared for publication.

STATUS
In operational service.
CONTRACTOR
Saab Missiles AB, 581 88, Linköping, Sweden.

Monitor picture of VTS-800 target tracker display, showing performance against a surface target

---

3435.193
SAAB IRS-700 IR SURVEILLANCE EQUIPMENT

The Saab IRS-700 is a passive infra-red surveillance equipment developed principally for anti-aircraft defence applications, although also suitable for other roles where an alternative to radar is required. Features emphasised by the manufacturers include passive operation, resistance to jamming, lightweight and small dimensions, high accuracy in bearing and

elevation, and lower cost than comparable radar equipment. The sensor head and display/control unit can be separated by up to 1000 m. The main characteristics are tabulated below. No other technical details have been released.
CHARACTERISTICS
Elevation scan: 27° within −5 and +45°
Azimuth scan: 360°
Rotation rate: 30 rpm

Wavelength: 8 – 13 micron
Weight: Approx 65 kg (sensor head)
STATUS
Prototype developed under a contract from the Swedish Defence Materiel Administration.
CONTRACTOR
Saab Missiles AB, 581 88, Linköping, Sweden.

3813.093
TYPE L AA LASER SIGHT

The Bofors Aerotronics Type L AA fire control system is a day/night laser system, and is designed to be used for anti-aircraft applications. The system can be mounted on a separate tripod or on the gun platform. It can also be mounted on a vehicle or a ship.

The system can be operated at the platform (or the tripod) or be remote controlled by using an optional TV-transmission of the image. The fire control system is based on the principle of the independent line of sight. All optical channels use a common first mirror,

which is servo-controlled in order to make the line of sight independent of gun or platform movements. The sight comprises a day sight and a night vision channel using an image intensifier tube.

The sight also incorporates laser transmitter and receiver channels. There is an optical exit where a standard TV camera can be attached. This interface enables the camera to transmit the day image or the image on the phosphorous screen of the image intensifier tube.

The stabilisation system is of a modular type. For measurement of the angular velocities there are two

gyros on the platform and one gyro on the sub-platform.
CHARACTERISTICS
Day sight
Magnification: ×4 or ×10
Field of view: 15 or 6°
Exit pupil: 6 mm
Night sight
Objective diameter: 160 mm
Magnification: ×7
Field of view: 5°
Exit pupil: 7 mm

Laser rangefinder
Beamwidth, receiver: 1·5 mrad
Pulse repetition rate: 10 Hz
CONTRACTOR
Bofors Aerotronics AB, 181 81 Lidingö 1, Sweden.

Bofors Aerotronics Type L AA day/night laser light

5708.193
PKD-8/KOL-2 SIGHTING SYSTEM FOR ARTILLERY

PKD-8/KOL-2 is an optical sighting system designed to increase the mobility of field artillery by reducing the deployment time for indirect fire. The system combines a PKD-8 panoramic sight on the gun with an indpendent optical collimator (KOL-2) which provides the fixed reference needed for initial alignment and subsequent indirect firing.

The PKD-8 sight is a monocular panoramic instrument for use with either the KOL-2 collimator or conventional aiming references such as pre-surveyed posts or stakes. It has been designed for mounting on the elevation sighting equipment of new guns or retrofitting to existing weapons. Engraved glass scales operated through worm-screws, spring-loaded to eliminate backlash, ensure long-term accuracy.

The KOL-2 is a collimator used in combination with the PKD-8, or other traverse sights, and provides the aiming reference necessary for the initial alignment procedure. The instrument has a built-in traverse scale to allow its use for this purpose and also to allow the gun to be positioned anywhere in a 360° arc around the collimator to simplify deployment. A reticle designed as a symbol plate corresponding to the reticle of the PKD-8 sight is in the objective system of the collimator and is used in the alignment procedure. When the two instruments are used together, the same symbols are seen in the two reticles.

STATUS
In series production.
CONTRACTOR
Bofors Aerotronics AB, 181 81 Lidingö 1, Sweden.

PKD-8 sight in operational use

5709.193
SRS-5 REFLECTING SIGHT

The SRS-5 instrument is an all-purpose reflecting sight for use with automatic guns against air and surface targets and can be used with both land-based and naval anti-aircrat guns. The field of view is 600 mils in azimuth and 300 mils in elevation. A large objective diameter optical system of 96 mm allows the operator to use both eyes for observation. The reticle is projected directly on to the target and is free from parallax.

STATUS
In series production.
CONTRACTOR
Bofors Aerotronics AB, 181 81 Lidingö 1, Sweden.

SRS-5 reflecting sight

SWITZERLAND

4695.193
WILD HEERBRUGG ELECTRO-OPTICAL SYSTEMS
The Wild Heerbrugg organisation, which includes Ernst Leitz Wetzlar of Germany, manufactures a wide range of electro-optical defence orientated equipment. This includes instruments for survey and mapping, boresight and night vision equipment, data based computer systems for survey, gyro equipment for orientation and fixing when deploying missiles, guns, radars, etc, and the design and manufacture of special optical systems and sub-systems. Much of this equipment has been developed for civil applications but brief descriptions are given below of those instruments with specific military applications.
Aiming telescopes
The ZFM1 is a compact aiming telescope, which can

be used for mortars, etc, with an erect image, field of view of 170 mils and a ×1·8 magnification. The ZFR2 is more suited for anti-tank type weapons, with an adjustable tritium illumination, × 2·5 magnification and field of view of 200 mils. The ZFK2 is a more sophisticated version with sliding curves according to ballistics. Field of view is 200 mils with a magnification of × 2·3.
BIG2 night vision goggles
These goggles have high power optics and a second generation image intensifier tube. Weight is only 0·5 kg which includes the face mask and harness. A built-in IR source for short distances can be switched on if required.
FH 155-1 sighting device
This is a sighting device developed by Leitz to

improve the fire performance of howitzers. It combines precise optics and mechanics with digital electronics. The FH-155-1 is in large scale production.
Tank sights and rangefinders
Leitz has developed a number of these equipments, including the FERO Z18 auxiliary telescope sight for the gunner in the Leopard 2 tank. All earlier Marder troop carriers and reconnaissance tanks were fitted with Leitz sighting periscopes for the guns. The company also developed a passive rangefinder for the Leopard 2.
CONTRACTOR
Wild Heerbrugg Ltd, 9435 Heerbrugg, Switzerland.

UNION OF SOVIET SOCIALIST REPUBLICS

3437.193
SOVIET SIGHTS - NOTE
The Soviet Union has developed and deployed a wide range of night vision equipment for all types of equipment ranging from rifles, machine guns, anti-tank launchers, anti-tank guns to armoured vehicles. Most of this equipment is of the infra-red active type, although the APN-2 and NSP-2 can be used both actively and passively. Night vision equipment on the T-62 MBT includes an infra-red searchlight to the right of the main armament (maximum range 800 m), infra-red spotlight on the commander's cupola (maximum range 200 m), and an infra-red driving light for the driver (maximum range 60 m). It is thought that the T-64 (or T-72) MBT (**5112.102**) is provided with passive night vision equipment. The USSR places great emphasis on night actions and spends between 30 and 40 per cent of exercise time on night training. Brief notes on specific types follow:

APN-2
This is mounted on anti-tank guns and has a maximum range of 900 m; it can be used both actively and passively.
APN-3
This infra-red sight is mounted on anti-tank guns and has a maximum range of 2000 m.
APN-57
This infra-red sight is mounted on anti-tank guns and has a maximum range of 700 m.
DAK-1
This is a laser rangefinder which can be used both tripod-mounted and in ACRV-2 vehicles. It is battery powered and about 600 mm long, 300 mm wide and 300 mm deep. Maximum range is 20 km and effective range about 10 km.
NSP-2
This is mounted on weapons such as the AK-47 assault rifle and the RPG-2 anti-tank weapon; it can be used either actively or passively.

PPN-1
This infra-red sight is mounted on machine guns and has a maximum range of 300 m.
PPN-2
This infra-red sight is mounted on machine guns and has a maximum range of 500 m.
TVN-1
This is an infra-red driving aid and is mounted on the glacis plate of MBTs such as the T-55. The driver is provided with a monocular observation piece.
TVN-2
This is an infra-red driving aid and is mounted on the glacis plate of MBTs such as the T-55. The driver is provided with a bi-ocular observation piece.
Infra-red Detection Equipment
The 7·62 mm SVD semi-automatic sniper's rifle and some field binoculars are provided with an infra-red detection system.

UNITED KINGDOM

4784.193
AV 62 COMMANDERS SIGHT
The AV 62 is a surveillance sight designed for fitment to lightweight cupolas in light armoured vehicles such as the Spartan and Striker. It is a daylight viewing monocular instrument with provision for a separate periscopic viewer for daytime which can be

easily and rapidly replaced with an image intensifier device for night surveillance. The main day sight provides ×1 biocular vision and, optionally, by means of a switch, ×10 magnification through the left monocular. A night vision channel, Type L7A1 is a second generation modular unit designed specifically for use with the AV 62. It provides a ×1

magnification through a monocular eyepiece or, alternatively, through a biocular magnifier.
CONTRACTOR
Avimo Limited, Rowbarton, Taunton, Somerset TA2 6HH, England.

4105.193
LH80 HAND-HELD LASER RANGEFINDER
The LH80 hand-held laser rangefinder is a military instrument, completely self-contained in a sturdy waterproof housing and built into the shape of a conventional binocular. Its ergonomic configuration and easily accessible controls allow unrestricted use even by operators with heavily gloved hands. It can range to targets from 150 to 9995 m with a resolution of 5 m. The maximum range is dependent on target size and shape as well as weather conditions. For a vehicle target, ranging can be obtained out to 5 to 6 km. Ranges out to 10 km are possible on large targets (eg buildings). To maintain this performance in all climatic conditions the rangefinder is desiccated, filled with dry nitrogen and fully sealed.

The target is viewed through the right hand ocular via the combined sighting and receiver telescope. This arrangement guarantees that the target seen by the operator is also imaged on to the detector. All

lenses and prisms are manufactured to ensure undistorted viewing with excellent definition, and are anti-reflection coated throughout for maximum light transmission. The optical design incorporates the principle of fixed focus to ensure instant viewing capability and optimum surveillance at all normal ranges through extreme atmospheric conditions. A large exit pupil diameter, providing maximum light gathering qualities, greatly improves vision under low light conditions, while a long eye relief permits full use by observers wearing spectacles, goggles or a respirator. User protection is provided by the incorporation of a laser filter between the graticule and eyepiece. The graticule is illuminated by 'Betalight' for night use.

The transmitter is a miniaturised dye Q-switched neodymium-YAG laser of simple and reliable construction. It has been designed for single shot or low repetition rate operation and requires no special cooling. One short and very intense pulse of infra-red energy is generated for each range measurement. The receiver comprises a silicon avalanche photodiode optimised for the operational wavelength, and hybrid thick film circuitry which includes a programmed gain amplifier to accommodate the wide dynamic range of returned pulses. In addition, the circuitry includes filtering to prevent the registration of reflections from smoke and dust.

Range information is given to the observer to an accuracy of 5 m, by a four-digit light emitting diode (LED) array displayed in the left hand ocular. When viewed this display appears superimposed in the field of view of the sighting telescope.

CHARACTERISTICS
Laser type: Dye Q-switched Nd-YAG
Wavelength: 1·064 microns
Output energy: Nominally 6 mJ
Pulse width: Approx 7×10^{-9} s
Beamwidth: 1·5 mrad (90% energy)
Pulse rate: 12/minute
Receiver field of view: 1·6 mrad
Effective aperture: 42 mm
Type of detector: Silicon avalanche diode
Range accuracy: ±5 m
Range discrimination: 30 m
Range presentation: 4-digit LED display
Minimum/max range: 150/9995 m
Minimum range setting: 150 – 3000 m
Magnification: ×7
Field of view: 7°
Effective aperture: 42 mm
Eyepiece: Fixed focus
Eye relief: 23 mm
Eye protection: Dichroic beam splitter and absorption glass on reticle
Interocular distance: 65 mm
Length: 180 mm
Width: 190 mm
Height: 85 mm
Weight: 2·2 kg (inc battery)
CONTRACTORS
Avimo Limited, Rowbarton, Taunton, Somerset TA2 6HH, England.
  Ferranti plc, Electronic Systems Department, Ferry Road, Edinburgh EH5 2XS, Scotland.

Hand-held laser rangefinder

3091.193
LP3 LASER RANGEFINDER

The LP3 laser rangefinder is a lightweight, man-portable instrument designed for use by artillery forward observers to obtain instantaneous measurements of range, azimuth, and elevation angles to targets. It can range at targets from 200 to 20 000 m with a resolution of 5 m. Azimuth and elevation angles can be determined to an accuracy of one mil.

The equipment consists of a laser transmitter and receiver system which are mounted as a unit with the associated control and counting circuits, and sighting telescope on a goniometer mounting which is supported in use by a tripod. The necessary battery power supply pack is carried on one of the tripod legs.

CHARACTERISTICS
Transmitter
Type: Q-switched Nd-doped glass laser
Wavelength: 1·06 microns
Peak power: 1·5 MW; 45 mJ
Pulse rate: 12/minute (continuous); 30/minute (intermittent)
Beamwidth (90% energy): 1 mrad
Receiver
Field of view: 1 mrad
Detector: PIN diode
Effective aperture: 70 mm
Range: 200 – 20 000 m
Resolution: 5 m
Range discrimination: 30 m
Range presentation: Numeric (LED) displays

Multiple target presentation: 2 ranges displayed
Time variable gain: Included
Optical
Magnification: ×7
Field of view: 7°
Effective aperture: 50 mm
Eye protection: Dichroic beamsplitter plus absorption glass
Quick aiming sight: Included
Total weight: 19·4 kg (with case)
CONTRACTOR
Avimo Limited, Rowbarton, Taunton, Somerset TA2 6HH, England.

4103.193
LP6 LASER RANGEFINDER

The LP6 laser rangefinder can be used for the rapid and accurate determination of target range by forward observers. It has been designed to interface with a variety of tripods, angulation heads and night observation devices. The LP6, used in conjunction with these devices, may be used to determine observer and target positions and to provide data for adjustment of fire even under low light conditions. It can also interface with existing field artillery computing systems. Target ranges can be measured from 200 to 20 000 m with a resolution of ±5 m.
CHARACTERISTICS
Operating temperature: –40 to +55° C
Magnification: ×7
Field of view: 6·5°
Effective aperture: 50 mm
Eye protection: Dichroic beamsplitter and absorption glass in eyepiece
Quick aiming sight: Included
Transmitter
Laser: Q-switched (rotary prism) Nd-doped glass
Wavelength: 1·06 microns
Radiant power: 1·5 MW
Pulse length (half width): 30 × 10⁻⁹ s, nominal

Quantity of radiant energy: 45 mJ
Pump energy (electrical): 15 J
Pulse rate: 12/minute continuous; 30/minute intermittent
Beamwidth (90% energy): 1 mrad
Receiver
Field of view: 1 mrad
Type of detector: PIN photodiode
Effective aperture: 70 mm
Clock frequency of counter: 29 973 MHz
Minimum/max range: 200/20 000 m (determined by range counter)
Resolution: ±5 m
Range discrimination: 30 m
Minimum range setting: 200 – 6000 m continuously
Range presentation: LED displays
Power supply: 24 V Ni-Cd battery
Overall depth: 230 mm
Overall height: 170 mm
Overall width: 120 mm
Weight (total): 15·3 kg (including transit case)
STATUS
Production.
CONTRACTOR
Avimo Limited, Rowbarton, Taunton, Somerset TA2 6HH, England.

LP6 laser rangefinder on angulation head of British Army common mounting system

3092.193
LV2 LASER RANGEFINDER

The Avimo-designed LV2 laser rangefinder is fully interchangeable with the existing Centurion tank gunner's sight and can therefore be readily fitted without modification to this range of armoured vehicle. The instrument is fitted with dual magnification to facilitate target acquisition and gun aiming, in addition to the integrated rangefinder capability. It is a completely self-contained unit, and among the design features of the LV2 are the following:

(1) time variable gain regulator to avoid false registration of unwanted natural phenomena
(2) inbuilt eye protection for the user
(3) remote display facility for use by the tank commander

(4) laser transmitter malfunction, and minimum range setting indicators
(5) additional targets other than first and second echoes indicator.
CHARACTERISTICS
Transmitter
Type: Q-switched Nd-doped glass laser
Wavelength: 1·06 microns
Peak power: 1·5 MW; 45 mJ
Pulse rate: 12/minute (continuous); 30/minute (intermittent)
Exit pupil diameter: 10 mm
Receiver
Field of view: 1 mrad
Detector: PIN diode
Effective aperture: 40 mm
Range: 200 – 20 000 m

Range accuracy: ±5 m up to max range
Range discrimination: 30 m
Range presentation: Numeric (LED) displays
Multiple target presentation: 2 ranges displayed
Time variable gain: Included
Optical
Magnification: ×8 and ×1·6
Field of view: 9° (×8), 45° (×1·6)
Exit pupil diameter: 5 mm
Total weight: 10·2 kg
CONTRACTOR
Avimo Limited, Rowbarton, Taunton, Somerset TA2 6HH, England.

3756.193
LV3 LASER RANGEFINDER

This is a laser rangefinder developed to meet Army requirements for a unit capable of being mounted externally on AFVs. A boresight is built into the LV3 to facilitate accurate boresighting to the carrier vehicle's armament. The control box and display unit is sited in a convenient position for use by the commander or gunner. Ranges on targets between 200 and 20 000 m can be measured with a resolution of 5 m. A continuously variable minimum range gate operative between 200 and 3000 m is incorporated. An additional display can be provided to give the commander and gunner individual information.
CHARACTERISTICS
Transmitter
Laser: Nd-glass
Wavelength: 1·06 micron

LV3 laser rangefinder component units

Output: 1·5 MW nominal
Pulse length: 30 × 10⁻⁹ s nominal
Pulses per minute: 12 continuous, 30 intermittent
Beamwidth (90% energy): 1 mrad

Receiver
Field of view: 0·7 mrad
Detector: PIN diode
Effective aperture: 70 mm
Sensitivity: 120 nW
Clock frequency: 29.973 MHz
Range discrimination: 30 m
Sight
Magnification: ×7
Field of view: 7°
Dimensions: 290 × 180 × 140 mm
Weight: 10 kg
Operating temperature range: –40 to +55° C
STATUS
Production.
CONTRACTOR
Avimo Limited, Rowbarton, Taunton, Somerset TA2 6HH, England.

3757.193
LV10 LASER RANGEFINDER

The Avimo LV10 is an integrated laser rangefinder/gunner's sight which has been designed and developed to provide full interchangeability with the existing gunner's sight on the Scorpion tank without modification to the vehicle. The instrument is capable of measuring the ranges of two targets simultaneously, provided they are both within the laser beam. The distances are displayed instantly in the eyepiece, and ranges can be measured from 200 to 10 000 m with an accuracy of ±5 m over the entire range. A minimum range gate is incorporated, continuously adjustable between 200 and 3000 m.

CHARACTERISTICS
Transmitter
Laser: Nd-glass
Wavelength: 1·06 micron
Power output: 1·5 MW
Pulse length: 30×10^{-9} s
Repetition rate: 12 continuous, 30 intermittent pulses/minute
Beamwidth: < 1 mrad
Receiver
Detector: Avalanche photodiode
Field of view: 1 mrad
Effective aperture: 39 mm
Clock frequency: 29 973 MHz

Resolution: 5 m
Range discrimination: 30 m
Optical data
Magnification: ×10, and separate unit vision system
Field of view: 6·8°
Weight: 11·1 kg
STATUS
Production.
CONTRACTOR
Avimo Limited, Rowbarton, Taunton, Somerset TA2 6HH, England.

3759.193
LV15 LASER RANGEFINDER

The Avimo LV15 is a combined day and night sighting periscope with an integrated laser rangefinding facility. Although initially designed as a direct replacement for M32 periscopes on M48 and M60 tanks it can be readily fitted to a wide range of other AFVs with the minimum of vehicle modification. It provides both visual readouts and ballistic computer data outputs to interface with any desired level of fire control sophistication ranging from manual super-elevation of the gun to a fully computerised fire control system. The sight may be additionally supplied with a spot injection unit (SIU) which provides an illuminated aiming mark when used in conjunction with a fire control computer. The complete instrument is suitable for interfacing with any type of fire control computer system.

The LV15 is a monocular-type instrument comprising three independent modules: a head assembly, a daylight elbow/laser rangefinder assembly and a second-generation passive night vision elbow assembly. These are so designed that the laser rangefinder may be used with either the daylight elbow or the night vision system. A remote control box provides all the necessary controls and readouts required to operate the laser rangefinder with the exception of the laser aiming marks which are contained in the relevant sighting elbows. Facilities can be provided for the injection of a moving aiming mark in the daylight elbow when the sight is used in conjunction with a fire control computer.

The head assembly contains a pivoting mirror, common to both sighting systems, which is driven by a mechanical linkage from the gun mounting via a drive mechanism. A unit power optical system provides the operator with a general observation facility.

The daylight elbow and laser rangefinder is a tri-axial optical system to enable the visible light, laser transmitter and laser receiver to use the same basic optical path. Laser light is separated from the visual by means of dichroic beam splitters and absorption filters at the relevant points. A laser aiming mark and ballistic graticule are displayed in the eyepiece. Both of these may be illuminated for use in low light-level conditions.

The laser is capable of simultaneously measuring two separate ranges provided that the objects are in the line of the laser beam identified by the laser aiming mark. Ranges are displayed on a separate control box within the vehicle and may be duplicated on a remote range readout. Target ranges from 200 to 10 000 m can be measured with an accuracy of ±5 m. Graticules can be supplied with any ballistic pattern.

The night vision elbow incorporates a 25 mm image intensifier tube which amplifies available light (such as moonlight or starlight) and provides the operator with a night fighting capability undetectable by enemy forces. The graticule is illuminated by a light emitting diode which permits a boresighting check at twilight and provides excellent brightness control at all light levels. The separate boresighting controls allow the night vision elbow to be adjusted to coincide with the daylight elbow thus enabling the laser rangefinder to be used in conjunction with the night sight.

CHARACTERISTICS
Depth: 340 mm
Height: 632 mm
Width: 330 mm
Weight: 28 kg
Power supply: 24 V DC (vehicle supply)
Sight head elevation: 18° depression, 22° elevation
Magnification: ×1
Horizontal FoV: 30° 32′
Vertical FoV: 5° 48′
Daylight elbow
Magnification: ×8
Field of view: 8°
Exit pupil: 5 mm
Eye protection: Dichroic B/S and absorption glass in eyepiece
Night vision elbow
Magnification: ×7, ×1
Field of view: 7·3°
Light gain: 1000 minimum
Focus range: 50 m – ∞
Exit pupil: 15 mm
Laser type: Q-switched Nd-doped glass
Wavelength: 1·06 microns
Radiant power: 1·5 MW
Quantity of radiant energy: 45 mJ
Pulse length (half width): 30×10^{-9} s

LV15 laser rangefinder combined day/night periscope sight

Beamwidth (90% energy): 0·7 mrad
Pulse rate: 12/minute continuous; 30/minute intermittent
Receiver FoV: 1 mrad
Detector: Silicon avalanche diode
Effective aperture: 40 mm
Clock frequency: 29·973 MHz
Minimum/max range determined: 200 – 9995 m
Resolution: ±5 m
Range discrimination: 30 m
Minimum range setting: 200 – 6000 m continuously
Range presentation: Numeric display in control box
Multiple target: 2 ranges displayed
STATUS
Production.
CONTRACTOR
Avimo Limited, Rowbarton, Taunton, Somerset TA2 6HH, England.

5714.193
NVL53 DAY/NIGHT SIGHT AND RANGEFINDER

The NVL53 is a combined day and night sighting periscope with an integrated laser rangefinder facility. It is derived from the M32E1 periscope (**4155.193**) used on M48 and M60 battle tanks but is a more compact system suited for light armoured vehicles while still being capable of fitment to larger fighting vehicles. The NVL53 can be installed in both the gunner's and commander's positions, although the commander's sight normally has a daylight elbow fitted in place of the laser rangefinder and is designated NV53.

The instrument provides both visual readout and ballistic computer data outputs to interface with any desired level of fire control ranging from manual super-elevation of the gun to a fully computerised fire control system. The sight may additionally be supplied with a spot injection unit which provides an illuminated aiming mark when used in conjunction with a fire control computer.

The NVL53 is a monocular type instrument comprising three independent modules; a head

assembly, a daylight elbow/laser rangefinder assembly and a passive night vision elbow assembly which incorporates a second-generation image intensifier tube. The laser rangefinder may be used with either the daylight elbow or the night vision system.

The daylight elbow and laser rangefinder is a tri-axial optical system to enable visible light, laser transmitter and laser receiver to use the same basic optical path. Laser light is separated from visual by dichroic beam splitters and absorption filters. A four-digit LED display is projected into the sighting eyepiece and may be duplicated on a remote range readout. Target ranges from 200 up to 9995 m can be measured with a resolution of 5 m.

CHARACTERISTICS
Head assembly
Magnification: ×1
Field of view: 25° horizontal; 8° vertical
Daylight elbow
Magnification: ×8

Day/night sight and rangefinder

Field of view: 8°
Entrance pupil: 35 mm diameter
Exit pupil: 4·375 mm diameter
Laser transceiver
Type: Nd-YAG (dye Q switched)
Wavelength: 1·064 μm

Output: 1 MW typical
Range: 200 to 9995 m
Range accuracy: ± 5 m
Range discrimination: 30 m
Night vision module
Magnification: ×7·1

Field of view: 7·3°
Entrance pupil: 198 mm diameter
Exit pupil: 14 mm diameter
CONTRACTOR
Avimo Limited, Rowbarton, Taunton, Somerset TA2 6HH, England.

5712.193
TL10-T ARTICULATED TELESCOPE LASER RANGEFINDER
The TL10-T laser rangefinder, when integrated into the 'T' series gunner's articulated telescope provides a compact neodymium-YAG laser ranging facility. It replaces the forward objective lens assembly on the existing telescope, thus providing accurate range measurement from under armour without mechanical modification to the vehicle.

The laser assembly incorporates an aiming mark injection facility to enable integration with a computerised fire control system. Range and aiming mark data are displayed in the secondary eyepiece assembly also provided. The basic operating controls are located on a remote panel assembly mounted on the body of the telescope adjacent to the eyepiece. The modified gunner's articulated telescope can then be directly installed in the 'T' series vehicles.
CONTRACTOR
Avimo Limited, Rowbarton, Taunton, Somerset TA2 6HH, England.

TL10-T laser rangefinder

4104.193
DIGITAL GONIOMETER
The Avimo digital goniometer may be used independently or as part of a system with a tripod, battery pack, laser rangefinder or other observation device. Typical functions include various survey tasks, such as those associated with artillery or rocket batteries, and a variety of other tasks such as target indication.

Initial levelling can be accomplished by means of three levelling screws and a bubble, after which switching the unit on puts it in the angle measuring mode. Normally at switch-on the azimuth counter will read 0000, or occasionally 6399 or an arbitrary count, and thus it may be necessary on occasions to reset the count to zero at switch-on by means of the reset button. Moving the adjustable platform through zero starts the elevation counter. The elevation display is not illuminated until the goniometer is traversed through the horizontal position. This is due to the horizontal datum being used to reset the elevation counter to zero. The azimuth counter may be zeroed

Avimo digital goniometer equipment

at any position by actuating the reset button, thus the goniometer may be orientated and zeroed on any desired reference point. The goniometer provides digital readouts of elevation/depression and bearing relative to the original reference points. Fast target acquisition is facilitated by a slipping clutch arrangement incorporated in both elevation/depression and azimuth drives, permitting the user to over-ride the fine controls.

Options available include: an additional display for range information, plus status indicators for multiple target indication and laser power; a mechanical interface to suit customer's mounting requirements; and a computer interface for orientation (and range) information (additional electronics are required to produce serial data interface).
CHARACTERISTICS
Azimuth: 0 – 6399 mrad, ±1 mrad
Elevation: ±250 mrad, ±1 mrad
Display: Digital 4-character LED
Dimensions: 240 × 300 × 210 mm
Weight: 8·0 kg (goniometer), 2·2 kg (tripod), 1·5 kg (battery pack)
Operating temperature range: –30 to +55 C
Power supply: 24 V DC vehicle or Ni-Cd battery, 1 Ah (4 hours' operation)
CONTRACTOR
Avimo Limited, Rowbarton, Taunton, Somerset TA2 6HH, England.

5727.093
GSL 22 GYRO STABILISED LASER RANGEFINDER
This instrument is a development of the LH80 rangefinder (**4105.193**) and is intended for use from mobile platforms such as vehicles, ships and aircraft. It has been developed by Avimo in collaboration with British Aerospace and combines the features of the LH80 with those of the Avimo GSH 21 gyro-stabilised surveillance aid. The equipment will provide a sight line which is stabilised against angular vibrations in pitch and yaw. An automatic steering device allows for intentional movement of the unit during target line-up and follow.

The gyroscopes control the attitude of a gimbal-mounted 45° mirror inserted in front of the objective lens of the laser. The surface area of the mirror is shared between the transmitted laser beam and the combined visual/receiver optics. The front window of the stabiliser module is angled to prevent retro-reflection of the transmitted beam into the receiver.
STATUS
Development.
CONTRACTOR
Avimo Limited, Rowbarton, Taunton, Somerset TA2 6HH, England.

3834.093
IR18 MkII THERMAL SCANNER
The IR18 is a compact, lightweight, high performance thermal imager with television CCIR compatible video output of 625 or 525 lines. This imager, capable of seeing by day or night to a much greater degree than image intensifiers or low light television systems, is wholly passive, independent of ambient light levels, sees through mist, smoke or shadow and is not blinded by sun glare, flares or searchlights.

It is modular in design and consists of a scan head, electronic processor, power supply unit, cooling system and auxiliary telescope.

The scan head contains the line and frame mechanisms, drive circuitry, syncs, detector, pre-amplifiers and bias circuits. It can be separated from the electronic unit. Without an auxiliary telescope it has a field of view of 38° × 25·5° with a 1·73 mrad resolution, and has an afocal optical input which allows it to be coupled to a wide range of telescopes and short periscopes.

The electronic processor houses all the necessary circuitry to provide an output giving a 625 or 525 line display on a TV monitor of any size. Facilities are included to enable alpha-numerics, symbols or graticules to be injected into the output video signal.

The standard system operates with a Joule-Thompson minicooler normally supplied from a remotely located pure air supply unit like the Barr & Stroud QK4 compressor or air bottle. Alternatively the imager can be run using a split Stirling cooling engine. The power supply unit provides all the required IR18 voltage lines when supplied with a nominal 24 volt dc input.

Telescopes have been manufactured with magnifications from × 1·5 to × 14, including dual field of view (typically ×9/×2·5 and ×14/×4). They can have focal athermalisation, remote focus control, an engraved graticule for sighting purposes (an alternative to an electronic graticule), and the external lens surfaces can be given a very hard coating (ARG4) suitable for use with a wiper in sand, mud or salt water conditions. A temperature reference can also be provided. Where an application requires a special telescope the company will undertake design to meet the specific requirements.

The IR18 can be used in two formats: assembled with a suitable telescope it is a thermal imaging scanner producing a TV compatible video output, or as a series of modules it can be incorporated into a large variety of weapon aiming and surveillance systems which employ thermal sensing. It is particularly suited for integration into sighting systems in armoured vehicles, helicopters and ships. It can be used to sight direct-line guns, guided weapons, or to control indirect artillery or mortar fire. The IR18 can also be used for identification at night or in poor visibility to help navigation of ships, hovercraft, aircraft, helicopter and land vehicles.
CHARACTERISTICS
Basic scanner
Field of view: 38° × 25·5°
Resolution: 1·73 mrad
Pupil diameter: 14·5 mm
Detector: Mullard Sprite
MRT (at 0·289 c/mrad): Typically 0·17 – 0·35°C
Spectral bandwidth: 8 – 13 μm
Video output: CCIR compatible (or ETA composite video)
Display: 625/525 lines/frame
Field rate: 50/60 Hz
Frame rate: 25/30 Hz
Weight: 7·4 kg
STATUS
The IR18 has been in serial production since 1981. It is in service with UK MoD and has been sold worldwide. A helicopter version is described under **4785.193**.
CONTRACTOR
Barr & Stroud Ltd, Caxton Street, Anniesland, Glasgow G13 1HZ, Scotland.

IR18 thermal imager with a ×9/×2·5 telescope

4750.193
THERMAL OBSERVATION GUNNERY SIGHT (TOGS)

TOGS is a thermal imaging system, operating in the 8 to 11·75 μm waveband, which completes the day/night gunnery capability of the UK Chieftain and Challenger main battle tanks. It is, however, sufficiently versatile to be fitted to other tanks. The system enables the operator to detect, track and engage potential targets by day and night, and in adverse weather. It provides both the commander and the gunner with a picture of the scene, enabling either to engage a target. A dual field of view telescope provides a target acquisition and vehicle navigation facility in the wide angle, and allows target recognition and gun aiming in the narrow angle. It has been designed for easy retrofit to all tanks and will operate in conjunction with the existing visual sighting system if this is retained.

The TOGS equipment comprises three separate elements; a Thermal Surveillance System (TSS), a Gunnery Sighting System (GSS) and a Test System. The TSS comprises a thermal imager sensor, a processor unit and TV standard displays for both commander and gunner. The thermal sensor is mounted externally on the tank in an armoured barbette and is servo-driven in elevation. When operating in the thermal mode the gunner acquires and engages the target using the display. The GSS element integrates the TSS into the tank fire control system and interfaces with the existing IFCS provision in Chieftain and Challenger. An important component of the GSS is the symbology processor unit which accepts information from the fire control system and generates aiming marks and other symbols for superimposition on the displays.
STATUS

TOGS is in full production and is being fitted to Challenger and retrofitted to Chieftain main battle tanks for the British Army.

TOGS on test

CONTRACTOR
Barr & Stroud Ltd, Caxton Street, Anniesland, Glasgow G13 1HZ, Scotland.

3137.193
BARR & STROUD TANK LASER SIGHT

The tank laser sight, now with Nd-YAG laser rangefinder, has its origin in the Chieftain tank laser sight. Simplicity of design and replacement of off-mounted mini-modules by internally located ones has substantially reduced the mechanical and electrical

Barr & Stroud tank laser sight

problems of installation and made it suitable for a wide range of AFVs. The sight can also be used with thermal imaging systems.

A fundamental feature of the design is the in-built capability to accept a conversion kit which provides a graticule aiming mark projection system for integration within a computer-driven fire control system.

The tank laser sight unit houses the laser transmitter, the receiver system, and the optical sight. The line of sight in elevation is aligned to the axis of the gun by means of a precision parallel linkage, and in azimuth by coincident turret mounting. Boresighting is achieved using controls on the sight unit in conjunction with either a muzzle boresight or the muzzle reference system. Gun laying is achieved through a ballistic graticule or a laying mark provided by a fire control computer.

Laser ranging can be initiated by the gunner or remotely by the tank commander. The range is displayed in the left eyepiece of the sight unit, and remotely at the commander's station on the commander's range read-out unit.

When a target is partially obscured by smoke or other obstacles, the selection of 'last range' on the range unit allows the true range to be obtained by eliminating all received echoes other than the last echo, which comes from the target.
CHARACTERISTICS
System performance
Operating range: 300 – 10 000 m
Accuracy: ±20 m max error (±10 m for 90% of shots)
Read-out: First or last range, display logic, multiple station
Range gate: Preset

Firing rate: 1 pps
Capacitor charging time: <1 s
Optical system
Sighting telescope: ×10
Field of view: 8·5°
Exit pupil: 6 mm
Graticule: Combining laser aiming mark and ballistic data
Boresighting adjustment: ±10 mrad in XY co-ordinates
Acquisition sight: ×1
Transmitter
Power output: 2 MW (nominal)
Pulse width: 6 ns
Beamwidth: 0·5 mrad
Wavelength: 1·064 micron
Receiver: Swept gain
Dimensions
Sight unit: 333 × 289 × 518 mm
Commander's range read-out: 152 × 54 × 60 mm
Weight
Sight unit: 21 kg
Commander's range read-out: 0·68 kg
AMEU: 7 kg
Power supplies
Nominal input voltage: 28 V DC
STATUS
The Barr & Stroud tank laser rangefinder equipment was developed under MoD contract as the standard gunner's laser sight for the British Army Chieftain MBT. It has since been fitted in Centurion, Leopard and Scorpion AFVs.
CONTRACTOR
Barr & Stroud Limited, Caxton Street, Anniesland, Glasgow G13 1HZ, Scotland.

4284.193
PASSIVE INFRA-RED SURVEILLANCE EQUIPMENT

British Aerospace Dynamics Group has been selected to develop passive infra-red surveillance equipment for use in low-level air defence systems to complement active detection systems such as radar. Radiating active surveillance systems will need to become increasingly more complex to counter the effects of jamming and other countermeasures likely to be used by an adversary in the future, and the use of radiating systems also exposes the defender to the risk of detection and location. One low cost solution to these problems has been the development of a passive surveillance system with no detectable emissions, and since 1975 the Dynamics Group has

been researching into the use of infra-red analogues of microwave radar systems.

To undertake the numerous field experiments to prove this concept, the equipment has been installed in a trailer and in the course of a two-week trial to prove its effectiveness, 96 per cent of engageable aircraft targets were observed and located passively at ranges which would have made engagement by a surface-to-air missile system entirely practicable. It was estimated that most of these targets would have been destroyed.
DEVELOPMENT
The company has spent about £3 million on this programme since 1975. The work has been carried out mostly in the Electro-optics Department at

Stevenage with support from the Group's Bristol facilities.
STATUS
Development project. Hardware for the first model of the military version of the equipment was available in 1981 and was compact enough to be mounted on a Land-Rover vehicle. Design, development and manufacture will be carried out using the full facilities of British Aerospace Dynamics Group. The group has also developed a stabiliser, for hand-held laser rangefinders, consisting of a gyro-controlled mirror system.
CONTRACTOR
British Aerospace Dynamics Group, Six Hills Way, Stevenage, Hertfordshire SG1 2DA, England.

5713.193
TYPE 312 LASER BEACON AND TARGET SIMULATOR

A ground-based laser target simulator and navigation and recovery beacon for use with laser seeker equipped aircraft, the Type 312 employs a transmitter module identical with that of the Ferranti Type 306 laser designator/ranger (**1742.193**). Simple optics, which are easily attached to the unit, provide the differing fields of illumination required for the three main applications.

The equipment simulates a laser-designated target giving realistic ranges for airborne seekers operating on a wavelength of 1·06 μm. It may also be used as a navigation beacon to provide accurate updates to an aircraft navigational system and as an aircraft recovery aid to an airfield or landing strip where no navigation aid is available. The Type 312 is rugged, lightweight and man-portable and can be operated from standard army batteries or suitable vehicle power supplies. A data transfer module can be added to enable ground-to-air messages to be passed to the aircraft using the laser receiver in the aircraft.
CONTRACTOR
Ferranti plc, Electro-optics Department, St Andrew's Works, Robertson Avenue, Edinburgh EH11 1PX, Scotland.

Type 312 laser beacon and target simulator

3120.193
FERRANTI TYPE 504 SURFACE-TO-AIR LASER RANGER

The Type 504 is a surface-to-air neodymium-YAG, ten pps, laser ranger. The system has a 1·5 mrad beam divergence and a receiver field of view of 2·5 mrad. The Type 504 weighs approximately 20 kg.

OPERATION

The laser ranger is mounted to the gun and is therefore aligned to the target by the operator's sighting system. Range is derived by measuring the elapsed time between transmitted and received pulses in the normal manner. The accuracy is ±4 m and the system has a maximum range of 10 km. Range information is then used in the BOFI computation process.

STATUS

The first Type 504 equipment for use with the Bofors 40 mm anti-aircraft BOFI gun was delivered in September 1976. The equipment is now in service with a Far Eastern country.

CONTRACTOR

Ferranti plc, Electronic Systems Department, Ferry Road, Edinburgh EH5 2XS, Scotland.

Type 504 surface-to-air laser ranger for Bofors BOFI 40/75

5757.193
TYPE 520 LASER RANGEFINDER

The Type 520 laser rangefinder is a third generation equipment, using a Nd:YAG laser, and is intended for fitment to battle tanks. A combined transmit and receive sightline allows accurate alignment of the transceiver to many sighting systems. The very narrow raw beam divergence gives the instrument a distinct operational advantage since it allows difficult targets at extended ranges to be engaged with a minimum of beam overspill. The narrow beam also overcomes the technical problem of retrofitting on to a sighting system with a very small objective diameter. The Type 520 may be fixed at the rate of one laser pulse every second, keeping the user informed of the ever changing target range.

An Integrated Optical Test System (IOTS), which can be used to test the Type 520 system fully and locate any faulty sub-system, can also be supplied. The test set will perform a full serviceability test of the rangefinder channel when fitted in the AFV sight.

CHARACTERISTICS

Laser type: Nd:YAG
Wavelength: 1·064 μm
Radiant peak power: 2 MW minimum
Emitted energy: 24 millijoules
PRF: 1 pulse/s continuous
Raw beam divergence (90% energy): 4 mrad maximum
Q-switch: Lithium Niobate Pockels cell
Ranging: 300 to 9995 m
Ranging accuracy: 5m
Power supply: 19 to 32V DC (vehicle or battery)

STATUS

In production. The rangefinder is in service with, or has been fitted to and demonstrated in, the Chieftain, Scorpion, Cascavel, M41, M48, M60, T54, T55 and T59 tanks.

CONTRACTOR

Ferranti plc, St Andrews Works, Robertson Avenue, Edinburgh EH11 1PX, Scotland.

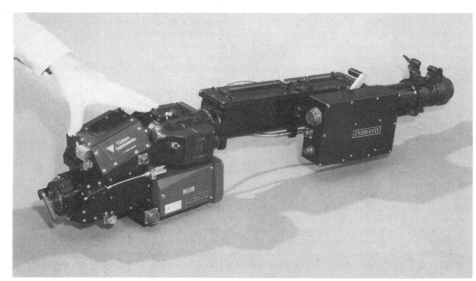

Type 520 B2 laser ranger in Vickers L50 sight

4787.193
TYPE 629 LASER DESIGNATOR/RANGER

The Type 629 laser designator/ranger is modular in design and based on a standard transceiver in production for a number of military products. It has a common transmit/receive path which makes it highly suitable, both mechanically and optically, for integration with existing sighting systems. The equipment can be designed to designate for all existing laser guided weapons and laser spot trackers and is suitable for fitment or retrofit to optical sights.

CHARACTERISTICS

Transmitter: Nd:YAG
Output energy: 90 mJ
Beam divergence: 2 mrad maximum (raw beam)
Range: 300 m to 10 km
Accuracy: 2·5 m
Dimensions; 240 × 183 × 160 mm
Weight: 6 kg

STATUS

In production. A variant is being provided for the British Aerospace Laserfire Rapier.

CONTRACTOR

Ferranti plc, Electric-Optics Department, St Andrew's Works, Robertson Avenue, Edinburgh EH11 1PX, Scotland.

1742.193
FERRANTI LASER TARGET MARKER AND RANGER

The Ferranti laser target marker and ranger (LTMR) has been designed to enable forward air controllers (FACs) to mark ground targets for either co-operating laser seeker equipped ground attack aircraft or for laser guided weapons. Aircraft using the airborne laser seeker counterpart are able to carry out low level, high speed, single pass attacks without the pilot being required to see his target. This concept greatly reduces aircraft exposure to ground defences and, at the same time, very considerably improves weapon delivery accuracy since pilot target tracking errors are eliminated.

The equipment also has built-in laser ranging for artillery or other purposes. When mounted with the Pilkington PE Ltd night observation device, a night operational capability is provided.

The system comprises a main unit weighing approximately 9·5 kg, including cables and a remote firing control, known as the Type 306 laser designator, a nickel-cadmium battery and an angulation head weighing approximately 9 kg and manufactured by Marconi Avionic Systems Ltd. The angulation head provides highly stable support as well as azimuth and elevation control and measurement.

The liquid cooled neodymium-YAG laser target marker and ranger will range out to 10 km with an accuracy of ±5 m and has an endurance to permit target marking for approximately 35 minutes (within a specified duty cycle) before battery recharge is necessary. The PRF during target marking may be 10 or 20 pps.

Overall lightness, compactness, ruggedness, and reliability coupled with high performance are key design features.

OPERATION

The target marker is the ground element of the newly evolved system of close air support.

The FAC aims the marker at the chosen target and calls in ground support aircraft by radio in the conventional manner. When the attacking aircraft approaches, the marker is fired and the airborne marked target seeker acquires and tracks the scattered energy, driving the pilot's head-up display to indicate target position. The pilot may then carry out an attack without ever seeing the target. If laser guided weapons are released, the bomb or missile homes precisely on to the marked target.

Alternatively, LTMR may be used to provide

Target designation by Ferranti laser target marker and ranger (LTMR)

designation for all the current range of NATO laser guided weapons including laser guided bombs and the Copperhead (CLGP) 155 mm shell (**3212.111**).

DEVELOPMENT

The laser target marker has been developed under a UK Government contract as complementary

equipment to the airborne laser ranger and marked target seeker, and for use with laser-guided weapons.

STATUS

In operational service with the British Army and in Oman.

CONTRACTOR

Ferranti plc, Electronic Systems Department, Ferry Road, Edinburgh EH5 2XS, Scotland.

5755.193
FORWARD OBSERVER LASER DESIGNATOR (FOLD)

FOLD is a target designator system built around the Ferranti Type 306 laser designator. This latter system is in use with the British Army and when used with their mount is known as the Laser Target Marker and Ranger (**1742.193**). Its principal use is to designate and mark static targets for aircraft equipped with laser rangers and target seekers.

With the emergence of weapons such as the Hellfire air-to-surface anti-armour missile and the Copperhead cannon-launched guided projectile, the emphasis is more on moving targets' such as battle tanks. To meet this requirement, Ferranti have developed FOLD. The system uses the Type 306

mounted on a Vinten Type 1906 tracking mount which enables the designator to track and designate armoured fighting vehicles. For night use, a thermal imager is added, co-mounted with the designator. Although Ferranti do not stipulate the type of thermal imager it is known that the company has an unofficial agreement with Texas Instruments concerning the AN/TAS-6 (**3826.193**), and is also using the Thorn-EMI imager in trials by the British Army. See also BOLD (**5756.193**) and HELD (**5747.393**). Weight of FOLD, minus the thermal imager, is 22 kg.

STATUS

In development.

CONTRACTOR

Ferranti plc, St. Andrews Works, Robertson Avenue, Edinburgh EH11 1PX, Scotland.

FOLD system using Ferranti Type 306 designator, Vinten Type 1906 mount and Thorn EMI multi-role thermal imager

---

5756.193
BATTLEFIELD OPERATIONS LASER DESIGNATOR (BOLD)

BOLD is a lightweight laser designator for use with laser guided bombs. The experience gained in operating the LMTR system (**1742.193**) during the Falklands campaign highlighted the need for a lightweight, man-portable equipment. As with FOLD (**5755.193**), the system is based on the Type 306 laser designator which is the main unit of the LMTR, mounted on a lightweight, low-cost tracking mount. The BOLD and FOLD tripods are interchangeable. A

third system known as HELD (**5747.393**) is a helicopter mounted version of BOLD and the basic Type 306 can be interchanged easily between ground and air use merely by unbolting from one mount on to the other.

STATUS

In development.

CONTRACTOR

Ferranti plc, St Andrews Works, Robertson Avenue, Edinburgh EH11 1PX, Scotland.

BOLD in field use

3411.193
GSA SERIES GUNSIGHTS

The GSA series of gunsights are designed to replace older fixed reticle gunsights on close-range anti-aircraft guns where the gunner had to judge by eye where to point his gun in order to hit a moving target.

The aiming allowances which have to be considered are for target motion, gravity drop of the ammunition and the effect of crosswind, but by far the most important is that for target motion. This allowance may be formulated in many ways using different parameters, but one that is particularly useful, in the absence of information about the target's speed and direction, is in terms of rate of rotation of the sight line which may be measured by a rate gyro within the gunsight. There is uncertainty about the time of flight of the shell, because of the gunner's limited ability to assess range, but rather than attempt to adjust the range input to the gunsight continuously throughout the attack, the principle adopted is to set into the gunsight a range through which the target must fly and so obtain, with sustained firing, hits at some period of attack – approximately at the time when the actual range equals that set-in. In the case of the GSA 400 series, any one of four ranges may be selected during the course of an attack and that selected is indicated to

the gunner as a number in the collimated reticle pattern. For the GSA 200 series, two ranges are available, a maximum and minimum preset by the operator.

Range rate also appears in the aiming condition, but, in the formulation with sight-line rate of turn as a primary parameter, it does so only in a secondary way. The effect of actual range rate being different from a mean assumed value is merely to alter by a few per cent the range at which hits will be obtained.

The principle of generating the aim-off angle as embodied in gyroscopic gunsights is shown diagrammatically nearby. The gyro rotor is free to deflect in both the horizontal and vertical planes about its suspension and the deflection from the symmetrical position is proportional to the rate of turn (precession) of the rotor axis in space. By attaching a mirror to one end of the rotor and reflecting a reticle from it, the optical system presents this deflection to the gunner as the required aim-off. The other end of the rotor is in the shape of a dome which rotates in a magnetic field produced by a current through the sensitivity windings and the interaction between the induced eddy currents and field provides the torque necessary to precess the gyro rotor in the direction of the target as the gunner tracks the target. By making the current in the sensitivity winding a suitable function of range, the rotor deflection from its position of symmetry as the gunner tracks the target will give a sight-line deflection equal to the aim-off requirement.

The gyro also has gravity windings which enable the rotor to be deflected statically so that the rest position of the sight-line can be compensated for the gravity drop of the ammunition as a function of range.

A lens in the optical path focuses the aiming reticle at infinity making a 'backsight and foresight' unnecessary. The reticle is reflected into the gunner's eye by a semi-reflecting glass through which the target may also be seen and so aligned with the reticle by rotating the gunsight.

The type of prediction embodied in the gunsight is known as 'disturbed sight-line' because the sight-line is not fixed in relation to the body of the gunsight or gun but lags behind it by a variable amount. It can only be moved, however, through the medium of the

Ferranti GSA Mk 3 sight

gun itself, which may create some difficulty for the gunner whose ability to track the target is clearly limited by the combined effect of the sight-line response and the servos which move the gun. Practical trials have shown that with modern gun servos the gunner can quickly learn to cope with the combined response and achieve a good standard of aiming. Moreover, there is the advantage that any errors in the servos do not affect the accuracy of prediction since they are within the aiming control loop.

The GSA is compatible with any gun with a calibre of 20 to 40 mm and the necessary ballistic data is inserted into the computation by means of an adjustment of trim potentiometers on the electronic card module of the unit. This gives the user the flexibility of having one gunsight for a number of guns of different calibre.

STATUS

Oerlikon-Bührle have adopted two variants of this gunsight as standard fit for their equipment – the GSA Mk 3 for field use with the GDF-B and the GSA Mk 3M for their naval GDM-A twin 35 mm AA guns. One African state has adapted the Bofors L40/60 guns in all its navy ships to accept the GSA 302 system. A

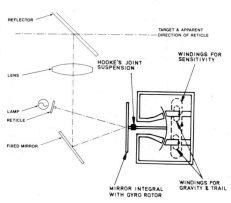

General arrangement of GSA gunsight

REFLECTOR

TARGET & APPARENT DIRECTION OF RETICLE

WINDINGS FOR SENSITIVITY

HOOKE'S JOINT SUSPENSION

LENS

LAMP

RETICLE

FIXED MIRROR

MIRROR INTEGRAL WITH GYRO ROTOR

WINDINGS FOR GRAVITY & TRAIL

South American state fits the GSA 32-JSW (a GSA 200 series type) to its twin 20 mm AA guns. The UK BMARC, a subsidiary of Oerlikon – Bührle, uses the GSA 201 on its GDM-A003 30 mm twin gun mountings. The equipment is now in quantity production for fitment to the Oerlikon-Bührle Type GDF-003 35 mm twin AA field gun and Type GDM-A 35 mm twin AA naval gun. A number of smaller orders have been received for use with optical fire directors and to update Bofors 40/60 40 mm guns for both field and naval applications. Several other countries should soon be fitting the GSA series, either as a stand-by sight or as the prime gunsight. A gunner's trainer, the TA500 series, is also available.

CONTRACTOR
Ferranti plc, Electro-Optics Department, Robertson Avenue, Edinburgh EH11 1PX, Scotland.

4696.093
FERRANTI HELMET POINTING SYSTEM
The Ferranti helmet pointing system (HPS) is a target sighting equipment which directs weapons and sensors towards any target at which the wearer is

Ferranti helmet pointing sight

looking. The HPS provides existing weapon systems with a high-speed visual acquisition mode which can be used when surveillance radar data is unavailable or when passive operation is required.

The HPS is a lightweight, easy-to-use and simple system consisting of the helmet-mounted sight and sensor, a fixed radiator, a signal processing unit, a control unit and a power supply. The observer's sight is light, unobtrusive and compatible with face masks.

When used with tracked Rapier, the commander (or observer) searches for possible targets. The sight has an illuminated aiming mark focused at infinity representing line-of-sight. A tiny sensor, integrated and pre-aligned with the optics, continuously monitors the sightline relative to a radiator fixed to the vehicle. The commander may operate the sight using either right or left eye, or can retract the sight when using binoculars. Once the commander has spotted a target he overlays it with the aiming mark as a means of designating his target. By pressing a button the sightline is transferred to the optical tracker instantaneously, directing it in azimuth and elevation to the target. The tracker operator then follows his normal procedure. In a more general case, the HPS may be adopted to transfer an observer's sightline to a weapon or sensor which is then instantly directed at the target. A variant of the system can be supplied for simultaneous dual observer operation using a common electronics unit.

DEVELOPMENT
The HPS was originally conceived as an aircraft aid and provides unlimited angular coverage and measures line-of-sight angles in azimuth, elevation and roll to an accuracy of 0·5° CEP. It is, however, as a land-based system that it gained its first contract as part of the BAe tracked Rapier missile system for the British Army.

STATUS
Full scale production of the HPS for tracked Rapier is under way. Trials are also being carried out in both fixed-wing aircraft and helicopters.

CONTRACTOR
Ferranti plc, St Andrews Works, Robertson Avenue, Edinburgh EH11 1PX, Scotland.

4707.193
W201 INDIVIDUAL WEAPONSIGHT
The W201 is a lightweight second generation individual weapon sight for infantry use and general surveillance. It has a range in starlight of 500 metres on infantry weapons and up to 5 km for surveillance, depending on light level and terrain.

CHARACTERISTICS
Magnification: ×3
Field of view: 12°

Dimensions: 216 mm × 110 mm diameter
Weight: 1·2 kg
CONTRACTOR
Hall and Watts Ltd, 266 Hatfield Road, St Albans, Hertfordshire AL1 4UN, England.

5711.193
W401 NIGHT OBSERVATION DEVICE
This instrument is a long-range night surveillance sight which has been designed and manufactured to UK MoD standards and specifications. It incorporates a 25 mm second-generation image intensifier tube and an improved optical design to enable the instrument to be produced in a small, lightweight unit.

CHARACTERISTICS
Magnification: ×7
Field of view: 7·8°
Focus range: 20 m – ∞
Dimensions: 420 mm × 240 (diameter) mm
Weight: 8·5 kg
STATUS
In production.
CONTRACTOR
Hall and Watts Ltd, 266 Hatfield Road, St Albans, Hertfordshire AL1 4UN, England.

Hall and Watts night observation device

4131.193
L1A2 ARTILLERY DIRECTOR
Based on the Watts Microptic theodolite ST.190, the L1A2 artillery director is used by the British Army and other forces for artillery survey and gun direction purposes. The director's position is established by normal survey techniques using the instrument to measure angles of prominent features of the landscape, or by reference to the magnetic meridian or astronomical observations. The director then acts as a reference point from which the individual guns of a battery can use their dial sights to set off their bearings to engage a target.

CHARACTERISTICS
Magnification: ×4·2
Field of view: 213 mils
Eyepiece adjustment: –0·5 to 1 dioptre
Graticule: Vertical and horizontal scales divided every 2 mils to ±100 mils figured every 20 mils
Eye relief: 6·6 mm
Weight: 3·63 kg (instrument only); 7·6 kg (instrument in case)
Case dimensions: 317 × 190 × 178 mm
STATUS
Adopted by British Army.
CONTRACTOR
Hall and Watts Ltd, 266 Hatfield Road, St Albans, Hertfordshire AL1 4UN, England.

Hall and Watts L1A2 artillery director instrument as used by British Army

3760.193
LP7 LASER RANGEFINDER

The LP7 is a hand-held portable laser rangefinder equipment for applications in the forward battlefield areas, such as mortar fire control, artillery observation etc.

Among its uses, the LP7 can be mounted on a Lasergage NOD2 night observation device (see photograph) thus enabling the user to obtain ranges by night or day with equal accuracy.

STATUS

Two contracts have been secured from the UK MoD for supply of LP7 equipment to the British Army and Royal Marines. The LP7 is manufactured under licence from Simrad Optronics, Norway and is more fully described under **3155.193**.

CONTRACTOR

Lasergage Ltd, Newtown Road, Hove, East Sussex BN3 7DL, England.

LP7 laser rangefinder on Lasergage NOD2 night observation device

3761.193
LP8 LASER RANGEFINDER

The Lasergage LP8 laser rangefinder is a UK-manufactured version of the SIMRAD LP8 equipment (**3579.193**), described in the Norway entry in this section of *Jane's Weapon Systems*. Details of the LP8 and the major characteristics will be found in that entry, and the appearance and configuration can be seen from the adjacent illustration. The equipment is provided with a mounting bracket so that it can be fitted on to night observation devices, tripods, theodolites etc for applications such as target ranging, survey etc. A typical association is with the Wild T20 telescope, in which the mounting arrangements incorporate a locking device that ensures that the laser rangefinder is correctly boresighted to the telescope. The latter instrument incorporates a filter to protect the user's eyes from laser radiation.

STATUS

No contract details have been revealed for publication.

CONTRACTOR

Lasergage Ltd, Newtown Road, Hove, East Sussex BN3 7DL, England.

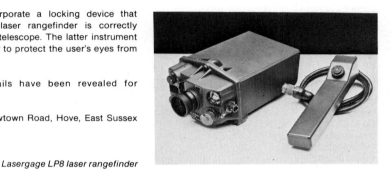

Lasergage LP8 laser rangefinder

4236.193
LP160 LASER RANGEFINDER

The Lasergage LP160 laser rangefinder is a small, compact and lightweight electro-optical instrument designed for use by artillery forward observers and mortar fire controllers. The instrument measures range, azimuth and elevation angle to the target with an accuracy that will facilitate first-round hits. The LP160 fits into modern computerised field artillery fire control systems but can also operate as a self-contained scouting unit for target observation and localisation.

CHARACTERISTICS

Laser: Nd-YAG
Wavelength: 1·064 microns
Output energy: 5 mJ nominal
Pulse width: 10 ns nominal
Pulses per minute: 12 (30 intermittent)
Beamwidth: 1·5 mrad

Q-switch: Saturable dye
Receiver
Field of view: 1·3 mrad nominal
Type of detector: Avalanche photodiode
Minimum/max range: 150/20 000 m
Range resolution: 5 m
Range discrimination: 30 m
Telescope
Aperture: 45 mm
Magnification: ×7
Field of view: 120 mils
Rangefinder and goniometer
Dimensions: 270 × 240 × 230 mm
Weight: 5·8 kg
STATUS
In production.
CONTRACTOR
Lasergage Ltd, Newtown Road, Hove, East Sussex BN3 7DL, England.

LP160 laser rangefinder

4697.193
LT 1065 HAND-HELD THERMAL IMAGER

The LT 1065 hand-held thermal imager is a compact, lightweight instrument intended for use in surveillance, mortar fire control, weapon sighting at night, etc. The operational sensitivity of the equipment is such that differences of less than 1°C are indicated to the operator. The power source is a small battery pack. A range of lens options give differing fields of view and resolutions.

CHARACTERISTICS

Spectral waveband: 3 – 5 µm
Field of view: 21° azimuth; 16° elevation

Resolution: 2·3 mrad
Magnification: × 0·75
Detector: Thermoelectrically cooled CMT
Total number of lines: 96
Temperature sensitivity: 0·3°C
Display: Red LED
Weight: 3 kg
STATUS
In production. An improved version was due to be launched in 1984.
CONTRACTOR
Lasergage Ltd, Newton Road, Hove, East Sussex BN3 7DL, England.

LT 1065 hand-held thermal imager

4780.193
LT 1085 THERMAL IMAGER

The LT 1085 is a lightweight man-portable thermal imager which has been designed for general surveillance purposes. When boresighted with the LP7 laser rangefinder (3760.193), the system is suitable for mortar fire control by day and night. The sight operates in the 8 to 13 μm band and has two fields of view which are optically aligned and switchable. The wide field of view may be used to detect a target and the narrow field of view is employed for recognition. The LT 1085 is designed around a 30-element CMT detector cooled to 77° K with a Joule-Thompson mini-cooler, the high pressure air in a 0·6-litre bottle giving four hours' operation under normal conditions.

CHARACTERISTICS
Detector: CMT cooled to 77° K
Waveband: 8 – 13 μm
Field of view: 12·5° × 9·2° (wide); 5° × 3·7° (narrow)
Resolution: 0·6 mrad (wide); 0·24 mrad (narrow)
Display: Miniature CRT; P21 phosphor
Dimensions: 210 × 225 × 120 mm (excluding battery and gas bottle)
Weight: 3 kg (excluding battery and gas bottle)
CONTRACTOR
Lasergage Ltd, Newtown Road, Hove, East Sussex BN3 7DL, England.

LT 1085 thermal imager

3762.193
LV5 LASER RANGEFINDER

The Lasergage LV5 laser rangefinder is designed for external mounting on armoured fighting vehicles to improve their combat effectiveness by providing accurate range information for weapon aiming. The compact and low profile laser transmitter/receiver is mounted externally and accurately boresighted with the gun. A protective armoured cover with remotely operated front flap can be provided. The control/display unit is located inside the vehicle in a position where it may be seen and used by the gunner or commander. An additional display unit can be provided to give both these crew members range information.

CHARACTERISTICS
Transmitter
Laser: Nd-YAG
Wavelength: 1·054 micron
Pulse length: 10 ns
Output energy: 5 mJ (nominal)
Firing rate: 12 continuous; 30 intermittent pulses/minute
Beamwidth: 1·5 mrad
Receiver
Field of view: 1·3 mrad
Detector: Avalanche photodiode
Effective aperture: 45 mm
Minimum/max range: 200/10 000 m
Range accuracy: 5 m
Range discrimination: 30 m
Minimum range setting: 200 – 300 m continuously variable
Sight
Magnification: ×7
Weight: 2·4 kg (transmitter/receiver); 1·4 kg (control unit)
STATUS
In production.
CONTRACTOR
Lasergage Ltd, Newtown Road, Hove, East Sussex BN3 7DL, England.

Main units of the LV5 vehicle laser rangefinder equipment, with transmitter/receiver unit (right), control/display unit (top) and repeater range display unit (left)

4781.193
LWS 1060 NIGHT SIGHT

The LWS 1060 is a second/third generation small weapons surveillance night sight and is designed for the latest generation of light support infantry weapons. It will accept either second or third generation image intensifiers and will fit most weapons, including SLR, FN, G3, M16 and AK47. An adjustable graticule of contrasting colour is provided for ease of weapon aiming and alternative graticule patterns can be made available. The sight has been tested successfully for identifying and hitting man-sized targets at 300 metres in very low light level conditions.

CONTRACTOR
Lasergage Ltd, Newtown Road, Hove, East Sussex BN3 7DL, England.

4700.193
NOD2 NIGHT OBSERVATION DEVICE

NOD2 is a second generation night observation device for long range surveillance. The instrument uses a 25 mm micro channel plate image intensifier tube for high performance down to very low light levels, and detects active IR devices as if they were white light. The system requires no illumination and when coupled to a laser rangefinder permits engagement at night with an 80 per cent hit probability. A tripod is included with accurately calibrated azimuth and elevation scales.

CHARACTERISTICS
Magnification: × 9·4
Field of view: 5·6°
Focal length of objective: 255 mm
Dimensions: 41·2 cm × 26 cm (diameter)
Weight: 11·62 kg
CONTRACTOR
Lasergage Ltd, Newtown Road, Hove, East Sussex BN3 7DL, England.

NOD2 sight

4698.193
PVS5A NIGHT VISION GOGGLES

The PVS5A second generation passive night vision goggles are intended to bring greater mobility and operational effectiveness to night operations. They include a built-in IR LED light source, and close focus adjustment allowing viewing at ranges from 25 cm to infinity. Muzzle flash protection prevents the tube from being damaged by high intensity short duration light flashes. Image intensification is achieved through 18 mm micro channel wafer image intensifiers.

CHARACTERISTICS
Magnification: × 1
Field of view: 40°
Range: 150 m (man-sized target)
Objective focal length: 26·6 mm
Weight: 0·86 kg
CONTRACTOR
Lasergage Ltd, Newtown Road, Hove, East Sussex BN3 7DL, England.

PVS5A night vision goggles

4699.193
PVS4 and TVS5 WEAPONSIGHTS

These are lightweight passive night vision sights that use a 25 mm micro channel image intensifier tube. Both are second generation instruments using high quality optics, a variable gain tube technology and muzzle flash protection to prevent the tube from damage by high intensity short duration light flashes.

The PVS4 is an individually served weapon sight which is used for close to medium range sighting and can be attached to a number of weapons or hand-held. Typical applications are night fighting and hand-held night surveillance and it can be easily adapted for low-light level photography.

The TVS5 is intended for medium to long range sighting of targets for attachment to a number of crew served weapons such as machine guns and anti-tank weapons. A tripod attachment is fitted for night surveillance and reconnaissance.

CHARACTERISTICS

	PVS4	TVS5
Magnification	× 3·7	× 6·2
Field of view	14·5°	9°
Focus range	25m – ∞	25m – ∞
Weight	1·7 kg	3 kg

CONTRACTOR
Lasergage Ltd, Newtown Road, Hove, East Sussex BN3 7DL, England.

PVS4 weaponsight

4280.193
TICM II THERMAL IMAGING SYSTEMS

TICM II thermal imaging systems are based on modules developed for the UK MoD under the Thermal Imaging Common Module programme. The modules are the 'building bricks' of TICM II systems. They are built to full military standard and use advanced optical and electronic components, including the Mullard 'SPRITE' detector, to give high resolution and sensitivity even at long range. The modular basis gives flexibility in system design coupled with ease of maintenance and repair for cost-effective use in both new weapons and for retrofit. Telescopes and displays can be selected by system designers to meet precise operational requirements.

These indirect view systems are fully television compatible and produce a high-quality video image which can be displayed on television monitors or head-up and head-down displays. Unique among thermal imagers, they are fully automatic in operation and always provide the best possible image, as well as allowing module replacement without any adjustment or set-up time. The systems are particularly suited to applications demanding the highest resolution and reliability such as pilot night vision, target detection and tracking, weapon aiming and surveillance.

CHARACTERISTICS

Spectral bandwidth: 8 – 13 μm
Field of view: 60 × 40° (625-line 50 Hz); 60 × 32·5° (525-line 60 Hz)
Resolution: 2·27 mrad (60° field of view)
Pupil diameter: 10 mm
MRTD: Typically better than 0·1°C
Detector: 8 parallel CMT 'SPRITE'
Video output: CCIR Systems I/EIA-RS170, compatible 625/525-line 50/60 Hz
Weight: 7·2 kg (modules)

STATUS

A major production contract was awarded by the UK MoD for modules to be incorporated in a wide variety of weapon systems for the British armed forces.

TICM II sensors are being supplied for the Thermal Observation and Gunnery System (TOGS) of the British Army's Chieftain and Challenger main battle tanks. Other projects employing TICM II modules include land-based, surface-to-air tracking systems.

Main elements of Marconi Avionics/Rank thermal imager

CONTRACTORS

Marconi Avionics Ltd, Electro-Optical Surveillance Division, Christopher Martin Road, Basildon, Essex SS14 3EL, England.

Rank Taylor Hobson, PO Box 36, Guthlaxton Street, Leicester LE2 05P, England.

4701.193
HHI-8 HAND-HELD THERMAL IMAGER

The HHI-8 hand-held thermal imager is a self-contained, compact equipment of light weight and small size. It is intended for reconnaissance operation in the battlefield by special patrol groups, covert operating groups and other intelligence gathering units.

The instrument functions in the 8 – 12 μm band to avoid normal obscuration (ie total darkness, fog, smoke, etc). It is simple to operate with supplies from readily rechargeable compressed air bottles and replaceable battery packs. The carrying handle serves as the replaceable battery pack and is quickly changed, as is the compressed air bottle.

The HHI-8 is operated by turning on the compressed air and electrical supplies by a single control. The imager is ready for use after a few seconds. The display image, which can be selected to show black-hot or white-hot scene details, is optimised by adjusting the focus by means of the front lens ring, and adjusting window and offset by using indented controls on top of the instrument.

CHARACTERISTICS

Spectral band: 8 – 12 μm
Field of view (fixed): 5° × 3°, magnification ×3·7
Field of view (switched): Wide 9·6° × 5·6°, magnification ×2; narrow 4° × 2·3°, magnification ×4·9
Detector cooling: Joule-Thompson minicooler using compressed air
Battery supply: Self-contained 12V lithium battery in handle. Alternative remote 24V NiCd battery
Air supply: Self-contained 0·24 or 0·6 litre bottle. Alternative remote compressor or bottle
Weight: 3·8 kg (including battery and air bottle)

CONTRACTOR

Marconi Command and Control Systems Ltd, Chobham Road, Frimley, Camberley, Surrey GU16 5PE, England.

HHI-8 hand held-thermal imager

5715.193
THERMAL IMAGER VEHICLE SIGHT

The Thermal Imaging Vehicle Sight (TIVS) is a gunner's sight designed to provide day and night observation and weapon aiming based on the normal thermal energy radiation. It is a plug-in unit suitable for the direct replacement of image intensifier night sights in a range of sight housings currently fitted to a large number of vehicles. For most vehicles, including M-series and T-series battle tanks, armour modifications are not necessary

The TIVS operates in the 8 to 12 μ-band where high energy radiation from an object will penetrate smoke, mist and most fog, and will provide a high thermal contrast picture. The display may be optimised by adjusting the focus, brightness and contrast controls, and the image polarity may be changed from black-on-white to white-on-black. Incorporated within the sight are presettable controls for graticule and aiming marks. The magnification may be changed from ×2 to ×4·9. Suitable periscopic housings can be provided for a range of vehicles.

The display is presented on a CRT, allowing flexibility in layout within the vehicle. A parallel display for the commander can also be fitted.

CHARACTERISTICS

Waveband: 8-12 μ
Optics: Coated lens assembly with two fields of view
Field of view: Wide 9·6° × 5·6° magnification ×2; narrow 3·85 × 2·26° magnification ×4·9
Cooling system: Joule-Thompson mini-cooler, compressed air

CONTRACTOR

Marconi Command and Control Systems Ltd, Chobham Road, Frimley, Camberley, Surrey GU16 5PE, England.

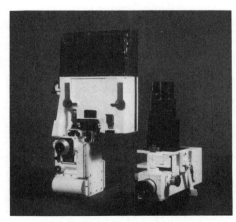

Marconi thermal imager vehicle sight

2403.193
AFV No 52 GUNNER'S SIGHT

This daylight sight has been designed for use on light armoured vehicles and is installed in the British Army Fox (5064.102) and Scimitar vehicles.

AFV No 52 gunner's sight is a binocular instrument giving ×1 and ×10 magnifications and is particularly suitable for use in poor light conditions. In addition to the changeover facility from ×1 to ×10, provision is made for the insertion of a circular graticule into the ×1 field of view which approximately outlines the corresponding ×10 field. Interocular adjustment is provided over the range of 59 to 71 mm. The user can also interpose a laser protection filter into both magnifications, as required.

Care has been taken to ensure that the drive lever which connects the sight to the gun mounting follows the line of sight accurately over the full range of movement in the vertical plane.

A washer/wiper system is fitted to maintain clear vision through the external face and the whole equipment has been designed to a stringent environmental specification.

CHARACTERISTICS

Magnification: ×1 or ×10
Focus: ∞
Eyepiece: Exit pupil diameter: 6·1 mm. Eye clearance: full field 29 mm. Focus: –0·75 dioptre to within 0·25 dioptre (fixed focus)
Eyepiece heaters: 30W, thermostatically controlled
Field range: 14° depression – 41° elevation
High power graticule: In right eye system only. (Graticule adjustable ±10 mils)
Graticule edge illumination: 0·8 A bulb, variable control
Injected graticule in ×1 magnification: 18 W bulb, variable control

CONTRACTOR

MEL, Manor Royal, Crawley, West Sussex RH10 2PZ, England.

2404.193

AFV Nos 68/71/75 COMMANDER'S SIGHTS

These daylight sights have been designed for use on light armoured reconnaissance vehicles. The No 68 sight is fitted to the British Army Fox (**5064.102**), the No 71 to the Scorpion (**5040.102**), and the No 75 to the Scimitar.

AFV Nos 68/71/75 commander's sights are binocular instruments giving both ×1 and ×10 magnifications and are particularly suitable for use under poor light conditions. The change from one magnification to another is by means of a 'flip' control; the user can also interpose a laser protection filter into both magnifications, as required. Interocular adjustment is provided over the range of 59 to 71 mm.

A washer/wiper system is fitted to maintain clear vision through the external face and the whole equipment is designed to a stringent environmental specification.

CHARACTERISTICS

Magnification: ×1 – ×10
Focus: ∞
Eyepiece: Exit pupil diameter: 6·1 mm. Eye clearance: full field 29 mm. Focus: –0·75 dioptre to within 0·25 dioptre (fixed focus)
Eyepiece heaters: 30 W thermostatically controlled

Field range: 14° depression – 41° elevation by top mirror movement
High power graticule: In right eye system only
Graticule edge illumination: 0·8 A bulb, variable control
CONTRACTOR
MEL, Manor Royal, Crawley, West Sussex RH10 2PZ, England.

4101.193

AV No 62 COMMANDERS' SIGHT

The commanders' sight, AV No 62 (Type DC1001 Series) is a surveillance instrument designed to fit lightweight cupolas, such as the AV16 and AV26 fitted to the Spartan and Striker vehicles in the CVR range.

AV No 62 commanders' sight (Type DC1001 Series)

It may also be used for surveillance roles in other types of light armoured vehicles.

AV No 62 is a daylight viewing monocular instrument with provision for a separate, unit power, periscopic viewer to be fitted for daytime use and can be easily and rapidly replaced with an image intensifying monocular sight for night surveillance. The main day sight provides ×1 bi-ocular vision and optionally, by means of a lever, ×10 magnification through the left-hand monocular. The bi-ocular viewers of the AV No 62 sight complement the eight unit power periscopes of the cupola to provide static observation points through 360°.

The main sight and auxiliary day and night periscopic sights share a common head prism and cover a field of view from 10° depression to 55° elevation. Removal and replacement of the auxiliary periscopes is easily carried out from within the vehicle.

The night vision channel Type No DC1002 is a modular unit specifically designed for use with the AV No 62 commanders' day sight. It provides a ×3·1 magnification through a monocular eyepiece or, alternatively, through a bi-ocular magnifier. The brightness of the outside scene may be adjusted to the required level. In addition to an On/Off switch, a focusing control is provided for range. Being detachable, the night vision instrument is itself fully sealed and proofed against environmental pollution.

When mounted in a commanders' cupola, both optical paths of the combination sight share the common head prisms which may be linked to the gun mounting. This enables the sight to follow the gun accurately by day and by night. The head window of AV No 62 sight has a downwards inclination of 20° to avoid reflections which could betray the vehicles' presence or provide a 'target marker'. A wash/wiper incorporated in the cupola system maintains clear vision under adverse weather conditions.

CHARACTERISTICS

AV 62 day sight
Magnification: ×10 or ×1
Field angle: 7° 45' (138 mils)
Eyepiece: Wray 80°
Exit pupil: 4 mm
Eye relief: 22 mm
Ballistics graticule: In ×10 mode with secondary injection into optional passive night-viewing system
Focal length: 256·62 mm
Head prism deviation: 10° depression to 55° elevation (180 – 980 mils)
Height: 584 mm
Width: 304 mm (including drive shaft)
Depth: 190 mm
Weight: 16·7 kg including day viewer
Day vision channel
Magnification: ×1
Height: 216 mm
Diameter: 104 mm
Weight: 0·9 kg
Night vision channel
Magnification: ×3·1
Field of view: 12·2° (217 mils)
Image tube: Mullard 18XX micro-channel plate image intensifier
Power supply: 2·7V mercury battery
Resolution: Starlight 10⁻³ lux 1 mrad/cycle; Moonlight 10⁻¹ lux 0·4 mrad/cycle
Height: 373 mm
Diameter: 104 mm
Weight: 4 kg
CONTRACTOR
MEL, Manor Royal, Crawley, West Sussex RH10 2PZ, England.

4102.193

TYPE DC1032-DC1033 GENERAL-PURPOSE SURVEILLANCE SIGHT

The Type DC1032 general-purpose surveillance day sight provides facilities for a third crew member, usually the gun loader, to assist the vehicle commander in carrying out target acquisition and field surveillance, by both day and night. Two viewing facilities are provided with the day sight via a two-position mirror. The bi-ocular unit power 'window' giving a general view of the scene, while a more specific view can be obtained through the monocular eyepiece which has a magnification factor of eight. The latter instrument's optical system includes a fixed reference graticule to define the centre of the field of view positioned by the azimuth scale.

A feature of the design is the capability for the lower section of the sight body to be pivoted upwards and locked in a stowed position parallel with the vehicle roof. The general-purpose sight is mounted on the cupola or vehicle roof, in a ring mechanism which permits the sight body to be manually rotated through a panoramic 360°. Additionally, the sight's head prism provides for ±10° deviation from the centre of elevation. A simple friction damper enables the selected elevation to be maintained.

The monocular night vision attachment, Type DC1033, may be inserted into the general-purpose sighthead when the day vision system is raised into its 'stowed' position. A simple bayonet, twist and lock fitting permits the attachment to be correctly fitted and securely locked into its position from within the vehicle.

CHARACTERISTICS

Azimuth scan: 360° max (subject to vehicle installation)
Elevation/depression: ±10°
Positional accuracy
Graticule: ±10 mils
Azimuth read-out: ±10 mils
Elevation read-out: ±20 mils
Day vision: Unit power
Azimuth FoV: 15 or 31° with head movement
Elevation FoV: 12 or 31° with head movement
Day vision: Monocular
Magnification: ×8

Field of view: 9°
Objective focal length: 201 mm
Eyepiece focal length: 25 mm
Entrance pupil: 32 mm
Exit pupil: 4 mm
Eye clearance: 22 mm
Night vision: Monocular
Magnification: ×3·1
Field of view: 12·2°
Image intensifier tube: XX1380 (Mullard)
Objective glass: 93·5 mm f1·04 refractor
Resolution
Starlight: 10⁻³ lux – 1 mrad/cycle
Moonlight: 10⁻¹ lux – 0·4 mrad/cycle
Range
Starlight: 650 m
Moonlight: 1600 m
STATUS
This instrument is incorporated in, and forms a part of, the AV No 62 commanders' sight (**4101.193**).
CONTRACTOR
MEL, Manor Royal, Crawley, West Sussex RH10 2PZ, England.

2405.193

PASSIVE NIGHT DRIVING PERISCOPE

The passive binocular night driving periscope has been designed to be used under starlight conditions. It can also be used at illumination levels up to and including daylight, the image brightness being adjustable to suit the user. An automatic electronic limiter device protects the instrument against excessive image brightness.

The sight provides a wide field of true stereoscopic vision, enabling the vehicle to be driven at normal speeds. The objective and eyepiece have both been critically designed and corrected, the objective to give optimum performance in the 0·4 to 0·7 micron wavelength range and the eyepiece to be used with a P20 Phosphor. The exit pupil of the eyepiece is 20 mm. Electrical heating coils are built into each eyepiece assembly to prevent misting and condensation.

The periscope has been designed to facilitate rapid interchange with the normal daylight sights from within the vehicle. It is both dust and waterproof, and in the event of damage the head prism can be replaced without affecting the sealing.

With slight differences this instrument is produced in versions for the Chieftain tank, FV 430 Series of vehicles, and the CVR range.

CHARACTERISTICS
Magnification: ×1
Horizontal field of view: 890 mils (50°)
Vertical field of view: 710 mils (40°)
Illumination range: 10^{-3} to 10^4 lux
Range: 5 – 100 m when focused at 20 m
Exit pupil of eyepiece: 20 mm
Weight: 10 kg approx

DEVELOPMENT
Jointly by MEL and Philips Usfa.
CONTRACTORS
Equipment: MEL, Manor Royal, Crawley, West Sussex RH10 2PZ, England.
  Image intensifier tubes and EHT unit supplied by Philips.

MEL passive night driving periscope

4782.193
MEL WEAPON SIGHTS
MEL produces a range of weapon sights in addition to the systems mentioned previously. The following gives brief outlines of these products:
UA 1116 Weapon Sight
This is a second generation individual weapon sight which is claimed to be one of the smallest and lightest night-sights for portable weapons. It is designed for use with rifles, machine guns, grenade launchers and recoilless guns.
CHARACTERISTICS
Magnification: × 4·2
Field of view: 9·5°
Focus range: 25 mm – ∞
UA 1126 Weapon Sight
This is a lightweight dual purpose weapon sight which provides high performance at target illumination levels down to 0·1 mlux. It has a fixed-focus objective and eyepiece lens, the only control being the On/Off switch. Using a second generation, double proximity tube XX1410, the sight has a magnification of ×4 and a field of view of 9·5 degrees.
UA 1129 Weapon Sight
The UA 1129 is a fixed-focus second generation individual weapon sight which has been developed specifically for use with small lightweight assault

UA 1242 night sight

weapons. Two luminance gain settings are provided for optimum use in differing light levels. A shadow-type aiming mark is fitted and is automatically illuminated in low light conditions. Magnification is ×3·3 and the field of view is 9·5 degrees.
UA 1242 Night Sight
The UA 1242 is a second generation, biocular night sight for surveillance and observation. It has been

UA 1126 weapon sight

designed for use on land, sea and in the air. Magnification is ×5 and the field of view is 7·5 degrees.
CONTRACTOR
MEL, Manor Royal, Crawley, West Sussex RH10 2PZ, England.

3410.193
PPE PASSIVE DRIVING PERISCOPE
Pilkington PE Limited is now producing a new passive driving periscope under contract to the UK MoD. The device enables drivers of armoured fighting vehicles to drive efficiently, hatch down, without the need of artificial illumination. The periscope incorporates a

PPE passive driving periscope, universal model

micro-channel plate intensifier tube manufactured in the UK by Mullard. The tube provides the high gain necessary to achieve good contrast image, particularly in low light-level conditions. In addition it is far less affected by bright lights (eg gun flash, street lights, etc) in the field of view than first generation (cascade tube) systems.
  The optical design features a bi-ocular eyepiece which affords the driver considerable eye relief, minimising the risk of facial injury and reducing eye fatigue over a period of driving. The modular design ensures that the basic periscope fits a variety of armoured fighting vehicles. Assembly is effected by special vehicle mounting brackets and upper casings. The sight is interchangeable with existing day periscopes in a variety of vehicles.
  The device is designed to fit the following range of armoured fighting vehicles, without modification: Leopard, Marder, Chieftain (ARV, AVRV, MBT versions), CVRT, CVRW (Scorpion, Scimitar, Striker, Spartan, Samson, Samaritan), 430 series, and all M series (M107, M109, M110, M113, M60) vehicles. In addition, with some modification to the vehicle, it will fit the French AMX-30 and Panhard AML series.
CHARACTERISTICS
Magnification: ×1 bi-ocular
Field of view: 50° horizontal, 40° vertical
Eye relief: 100 mm
Image tube: Mullard 50/40 mm micro-channel plate
Weight: 7·5 kg

PPE night driving periscope installed in Scorpion light tank

STATUS
In service with the British Army and overseas forces.
CONTRACTOR
Pilkington PE Ltd, Glascoed Road, St Asaph, Clwyd LL17 0LL, Wales.

5710.193
COMMANDER'S DAY/NIGHT SIGHT (CONDOR)
This was designed originally for the Royal Ordnance Factory's main battle tank and provides the tank commander with a 24-hour capability for surveillance, target acquisition and firing of the main armament. It incorporates independent channels for day and night use and interfaces with the main armament via a reticle image projector (PRI) unit. The PRI injects into the sight in line-up a collimated

ballistic graticule to enable the commander to engage the target. The unit will also inject the optimum target engagement data derived from the fire control system, if fitted, to improve probability of first round hit by day and night.
  Condor is designed to fit the Vickers Mk III main battle tank and Centurion, and the ROF main battle tank. Fittings for other vehicles such as the Vickers Valiant, M47, M48, T54 etc, can be made available.

CHARACTERISTICS
Above armour height: 330 × 330 mm
Elevation range: –10 to +35°
Magnification: ×10 day channel; ×4 night channel; ×1 periscope
Field of view: 5° day channel; 8·9° night channel; 56° horizontal/11° vertical (×1 channel)
Weight: 56 kg

STATUS
In production for Vickers and ROF main battle tanks. In December 1980 a contract was awarded for over £6 million for the supply of units to fit in ROF main battle tanks. In March 1983 a further contract worth over $4 million was awarded by the UK MoD for the supply of nearly 1000 PRI units for the Chieftain main battle tank.

CONTRACTOR
Pilkington PE Ltd, Glascoed Road, St Asaph, Clwyd LL17 0LL, Wales.

Condor day/night sight

3403.193
No 63 PASSIVE NIGHT SIGHT (L3A1)
The No 63 sight was designed by PPE for use with the No 62 day sight in the No 16 cupola of the Spartan APC and other vehicles. It is also suitable for use in vehicles and other installations as a straight telescopic sight or as a periscopic sight, as on the 155 mm self-propelled gun.

The sight can be quickly detached from the No 62 sight and fitted to a tripod and periscopic mirror attachment for surveillance on foot.

The wide field of view and excellent range provide very effective surveillance capability coupled with accurate firing of the 7·62 mm cupola machine gun.

CHARACTERISTICS
Magnification: ×1·4 monocular; ×1·1 bi-ocular
Field of view: 20°
Image tube: 25 mm 3-stage cascade
Weight: 4·5 kg (7·5 kg with tripod)
STATUS
In production for the British Army.
CONTRACTOR
Pilkington PE Ltd, Glascoed Road, St Asaph, Clwyd LL17 0LL, Wales.

PPE passive night sight for Spartan shown in dismounted role

3406.193
NIGHT OBSERVATION DEVICE NOD-A
The PPE NOD-A night observation device is a long-range system designed for the British Army for artillery fire control, but the equipment may be used in a number of roles where long-range surveillance is required. The device incorporates a catadioptric lens, 40 mm image intensifier and a bi-ocular eyepiece. This last feature enhances visual comfort by allowing the operator to view the night scene with both eyes simultaneously at a comfortable distance (100 mm) from the eyepiece.

In the British Army the NOD-A will be associated with an LP6 laser rangefinder supplied by Avimo Limited, both devices being carried on a common lightweight mounting, the precision angulation support system (PASS) produced by Marconi Avionics Limited.

CHARACTERISTICS
Magnification: ×5
Field of view: 7·2°
Eye relief: 100 mm
Image tube: 40 mm 3-stage cascade
Weight: 28 kg
Operating temperature: –34 to +70° C
STATUS
In service with the British Army.
CONTRACTOR
Pilkington PE Ltd, Glascoed Road, St Asaph, Clwyd LL17 0LL, Wales.

Night observation device NOD-A

4702.193
EAGLE LONG-RANGE NIGHT SIGHT
Eagle is a second generation night vision equipment developed to meet the increasing need for a lightweight hand-held long range device giving increased performance over first-generation equipment. The instrument acts as a long-range surveillance sight and can also be used in a wide variety of roles including artillery and anti-aircraft fire control systems. Range is such that a main battle tank can be recognised at 1000 metres in starlight conditions.

Eagle uses a binocular eyepiece and incorporates an illuminated graticule suitable for weapon firing and adjustment of fire. The equipment may also be mounted on a tripod. The device is fully compatible with nuclear, biological and chemical (NBC) defence equipment.

CHARACTERISTICS
Magnification: ×8
Field of view: 5°
Weight: Less than 3·5 kg
Power supply: 2 × 1·5V AA size batteries
STATUS
In production.
CONTRACTOR
Pilkington PE Ltd, Glascoed Road, St Asaph, Clwyd LL17 0LL, Wales.

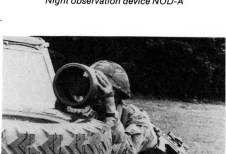

Eagle night sight

3408.193
PPE POCKETSCOPE
The PPE Pocketscope incorporates a second-generation 18 mm micro-channel plate intensifier tube. Weighing only 0·8 kg the sight is designed for hand-held military/paramilitary surveillance duties, is easily stowable in pocket or pouch and effective in a wide range of artificial lighting conditions, eg counter insurgency, border patrol, etc. It also acts as a lightweight individual weapon sight for rifles, machine guns and anti-tank weapons.

CHARACTERISTICS
Magnification: ×2·4
Field of view: 15°
Eye relief: 26 mm
Image tube: 18 mm micro-channel plate
Operating temperature: –40 to +55° C
STATUS
In service with the British Army as a surveillance device and weapon sight.
CONTRACTOR
Pilkington PE Ltd, Glascoed Road, St Asaph, Clwyd LL17 0LL, Wales.

Pocketscope night sight in weapon aiming role

3409.193
PPE NIGHT VISION GOGGLES

The Pilkington PE Nova night vision device has been developed for the UK MoD and employs the cost effective solution of using a single 18 mm microchannel intensifier tube (second generation) with the display being viewed by a specially designed bi-ocular magnifier, affording large eye relief to both eyes simultaneously.

Nova goggles can be worn with a variety of service equipment including helmets, arctic and other combat clothing and are believed to be the first designed specifically for compatibility with nuclear, biological and chemical (NBC) equipment. Developed for a specific British Army requirement for a low cost, lightweight compact head-mounted night surveillance system, the goggles will be used primarily by patrol commanders and AFV commanders. Other roles include night driving of soft skinned vehicles, maintenance, mine laying, construction work, etc.

Power is supplied by a single internal 2·7 V battery (mercury or lithium) which can be easily replaced by the user.

CHARACTERISTICS
Field of view: 40°
Magnification: ×1
Eye relief: 29·5 mm
Weight: Approx 500 g
STATUS
A production contract worth over £1 million and covering more than 1000 goggles was awarded by the UK MoD in February 1983.
CONTRACTOR
Pilkington PE Ltd, Glascoed Road, St Asaph, Clwyd LL17 0LL, Wales.

PPE night vision goggles

3796.093
RANK DAY/NIGHT SIGHT

The Rank day/night sight, also known as Argus in some versions, is of periscopic configuration and is mounted in the roof of the turret giving a very low silhouette. The sight consists of an optical system which provides the operator with a ×10 fixed focus day system, a ×9 night vision with variable focus, and a ×1 fixed focus daylight facility.

The night sight system uses a 25 mm three-stage image intensifier tube. Change from one mode to another is activated by a hand operated lever.

The sight can be supplied for use in the gunner's and/or commander's position. Elevation of the line-of-sight is accomplished by the movement of a tilting head mirror. The gunner's sight is linked to the main armament for control of the elevation mirror, whereas the commander's sight is manually operated and is independent of the gunner's sight.

Either sight can be fitted with a laser rangefinder, as an optional extra. When fitted to the gunner's sight only, range information can be provided for the commander's sight. A thermal pointer device can be provided for up to 360° surveillance with an audible warning signal and an LED target indication signal supplied to the gunner's/commander's sight.

CHARACTERISTICS

Day system	high magnification	unity magnification
Magnification	×10	×1
Field angle	6·4°	25° horizontal 10° vertical
Exit pupil	5 mm dia	—
Eye relief	28 mm	105 mm
Focus	fixed	fixed
Eyepiece	monocular (optional binocular)	viewing window (100 m × 35 mm)

Night system
Magnification: ×9

Gunner's sight, front view

Field angle: 6·5°
Exit pupil: 5 mm dia
Eye relief: 28 mm
Focus: Variable, 50 m – ∞
Eyepiece: As day system
Image intensifier: 25 mm 3-stage
Graticule: As ×10 day system
Common features
Head mirror: –10 to +35°
Laser eye protection: Dichroic beam splitter and glass absorption filters
Height: 680 mm
Width: 230 mm
Depth: 280 mm
Weight: 28 kg
Optional extras
Laser rangefinder: Built-in laser optics suitable for SIMRAD LP6 laser. Range 200 – 15 000 m continuous. Range discrimination 30 m. Digital readout of range information
VARIANTS:

Numerous variants of the Argus sight have been designed for specific vehicles and applications; a summary of the principal ones follows:
SS125: Gunner's day/night sight with elevation link arm suitable for connection with the mantlet on CVR(T) Scorpion, horizontal monocular eyepiece and optical system suitably coated for use with the optional laser rangefinder (laser components may be added later).
SS126: Commander's day/night sight with manual elevation control, angled monocular eyepiece and

Commander's sight, rear view

optical system suitably coated for use with the optical laser rangefinder (laser components may be added later).
SS127: Gunner's day/night sight as SS125, but without provisions for addition of laser rangefinder.
SS128: Commander's day/night sight as SS126, but without provisions for addition of laser rangefinder.
SS129: Laser rangefinder kit, SIMRAD components type LP6, suitable for fitment to SS125 and SS126.
SS111: Plain adaptor for fitment of SS125 or SS127 to gunner's position on CVR(T) Scorpion.
SS117: Azimuth slew ring for fitment of SS126 or SS128 to commander's position on CVR(T) Scorpion.
SS122: A series of day/night sights featuring adaptor plates for fitment to the turret of most armoured vehicles. The SS122 is also available with an integrated laser rangefinder and a fire control computer.
SS123: Gunner's day/night sight as SS125 but complete with laser rangefinder components SS129 installed.
SS124: Commander's day/night sight as SS126 but complete with laser rangefinder SS129 components installed.
STATUS
Specified for the new 105 mm autonomous naval patrol gun (**3659.203**) and other applications.
CONTRACTOR
Rank Pullin Controls Ltd, Langston Road, Debden, Loughton, Essex, England.

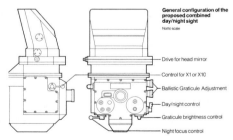

Rank day/night sight

General configuration of the proposed combined day/night sight
Not to scale

Drive for head mirror
Control for X1 or X10
Ballistic Graticule Adjustment
Day/night control
Graticule brightness control
Night focus control

3063.193
SS100/110 NIGHT SIGHT

The designation SS100/110 refers to the two versions of the image intensifier night sight produced for the Fox and Scorpion AFVs. They have the British Army designations of SPAV L2A1 and SPAV L3A1, respectively.

The equipment is turret-mounted in front of the gunner and alongside the main armament. It enables gunners to locate, identify, and engage targets at night without the use of any artificial lighting, and it is also used for general surveillance. A dual role capability is achieved by the use of two objectives, mounted one within the other. The outer objective gives a magnification of ×5·8, while the inner, for surveillance, has a magnification of ×1·6. When high magnification is in use, a shutter isolates the low magnification objective. When the other magnification is selected, an iris diaphragm isolates the high magnification objective.

The image intensifier tube is protected from the effects of gun muzzle flash by a shutter which is operated electrically from the gun firing circuit. An illuminated ballistic graticule with brightness control is injected automatically into the optical system when high magnification is selected, and this is used for laying the main armament. Automatic brightness control for the image intensifier tube is provided.

CHARACTERISTICS
Fox night sight
Magnification: ×5·8 and ×1·6
Field of view: 142 mils (8°) and 498 mils (28°)
Objective focus: Variable 50 m – ∞ and fixed at 30 m

Length: 112 cm
Height: 355 mm
Width: 305 mm
Weight: 59 kg
Scorpion night sight
Magnification: ×5·8 and ×1·6

4791.193
SS120 NIGHT SIGHT
The SS120 is designed for use in the Chieftain tank to provide the commander with night surveillance, target acquisition and assistance in laying the main

3817.193
SS130 DRIVING PERISCOPE
The SS130 periscopic vehicle driver's night vision equipment enables drivers of AFCVs to have passive night vision without needing IR lighting. It is suitable for fitting into the sight aperture of many existing military vehicles and patrol boats. The general configuration can be seen from the photograph.

4792.193
SS141, SS142, AND SS162 COMMANDER SERIES SIGHTS
These are compact periscopic sights designed specifically for the commander's position in small armoured vehicles. The SS141 and SS142 night sights are virtually identical, the only difference being that the head mirror of the latter can be elevated up to 20 degrees for the rapid identification of low flying aircraft. Both sights are based on a second generation

Field of view: 142 mils (8°) and 498 mils (28°)
Objective focus: Variable 50 m – ∞ and fixed at 30 m
Length: 112 cm
Height: 400 mm
Width: 355 mm
Weight: 59 kg

armament. It employs a second generation image intensifier tube which is directly replaceable with a third generation (Gallium Arsenide photocathode) tube when available. The sight is made up of components built up as discreet assemblies which,

The SS130 uses a second-generation intensifier tube, and has a field of view 50° (horizontal) by 40° (vertical).
CONTRACTOR
Rank Pullin Controls Ltd, Langston Road, Debden, Loughton, Essex, England.

image intensifier tube and carry integrated filters to allow daylight use in an emergency. The bi-ocular eyepiece provides × 2·7 magnification which gives a target detection of 1300 metres at night.
The SS162 is a day sight which is interchangeable with the SS142.
CONTRACTOR
Rank Pullin Controls Ltd, Langston Road, Loughton, Essex IG10 3TW, England.

CONTRACTOR
Rank Pullin Controls Ltd, Langston Road, Debden, Loughton, Essex, England.

for ease of maintenance, can easily be broken into four main sub-assemblies.
CONTRACTOR
Rank Pullin Controls Ltd, Langston Road, Loughton, Essex IG10 3TW, England.

SS130 driving periscope

4788.193
SS200 FIRE CONTROL SYSTEM
The SS200 is a computerised fire control system based on the various versions of the Rank Argus day/night sight. It is intended to enhance the fighting capability of armoured vehicles and can be designed to meet customer requirements.
The system incorporates a laser rangefinder and a fire control computer, designed by Rank Pullin, which is coupled to a moving aiming mark within the sight. It takes into account four main parameters: range of target from the laser rangefinder, trunnion tilt of the gun, type of ammunition selected and the crossing speed of the target. The sighting system avoids the

use of a ballistic reticle, thereby preventing a misinterpretation or incorrect interpolation when using the latter. The cross-shaped aiming mark is automatically adjusted by the computer during the complete tracking and firing sequence. The reticle is retained as a reversionary mode.
The fire control system has five elements:
(1) the computer which is the ballistic calculator and provides interface between system, gun, laser, sensors, position encoder, sight displays and crew
(2) the commander's control panel which includes a range display panel and position switches for designation of ammunition type

(3) the trunnion tilt sensor
(4) turret angle sensor which measures the angle turned by the turret over a measured time
(5) the gunner's sight which has a day/night capability with an integral laser rangefinder.
The SS200 is intended primarily for the retrofit market, for both medium and small battle tanks, and also for vehicles such as armoured personnel carriers which mount a gun.
CONTRACTOR
Rank Pullin Controls Ltd, Langston Road, Loughton, Essex IG10 3TW, England.

4790.193
SS500 ARMOURED VEHICLE THERMAL SIGHT
The SS500 is a thermal sight based on the Rank Pullin Argus sight (**3796.0930**), and the thermal imager (**4789.193**) under development by the company. It operates in the commander or gunner position and is instantly switchable from day to thermal imager use to allow 24-hour engagement of targets. A dual

magnification thermal channel is provided with a remote TV display option. An integral laser rangefinder is available.
CHARACTERISTICS
Weight: 36 kg
Thermal imager
Wavelength: 8 – 13 μm
Field of view: 16° × 12° (wide); 5·7° × 4·3° (narrow)

Magnification: ×7 (wide) or ×2·5 (narrow)
Day system
Field of view: 17° × 10° (wide); 6° (narrow)
Magnification: ×1 (wide) or ×9 (narrow)
STATUS
In development.
CONTRACTOR
Rank Pullin Controls Ltd, Langston Road, Loughton, Essex IG10 3TW, England.

4789.193
RANK PULLIN THERMAL IMAGER
The Rank Pullin thermal imager is a mobile, compact lightweight unit designed to operate effectively under battlefield conditions. It uses the SPRITE detector technology to produce a TV/video display with high thermal and spatial resolution.
The imager consist of six basic elements:
(1) the scanner unit containing the scan mechanism

and associated optics, the SPRITE detector and cryogenic cooling head, the scanner drive and detector head amplifier modules
(2) a telescopic unit; a variety of single and dual field of view telescopes are available
(3) the processing electronics unit
(4) a display unit
(5) a control unit (alternatively the controls may be incorporated in the display unit

(6) cooling services for the detector.
The thermal imager is designed for surveillance but alternative configurations are available for vehicle or airborne applications.
CONTRACTOR
Rank Pullin Controls Ltd, Langston Road, Loughton, Essex IG10 3TW, England.

5716.193
RANK PULLIN SIGHTS
In addition to the individual sights manufactured by Rank Pullin Controls which are described in this section, the company has produced a considerable range of optical instruments for military use. These include night and day sights and a brief summary of these devices follows:
SS20 Night Sight
This is a hand-held surveillance night sight with fixed eyepiece focus and simplified controls. It employs a 25 mm cascade image intensifier tube giving a range

in clear starlight of 700 metres for detection, 500 metres for recognition and 300 metres for identification. Weight is 2·78 kg.
SS30 Crew-served Weapon Sight
The SS30 is intended for fitment to anti-tank weapons, howitzers and field artillery. A right angle eyepiece and graticules specific to requirements are available.
SS32 Night Observation Device
The SS32 long-range NOD, also known as 'Twiggy', uses a first generation cascade image intensifier to provide a range out to 1800 metres in clear starlight.

Several thousand SS32 devices are in service throughout the world.
SS59 Crew-served Weapon Sight
This second generation device gives a range out to 1400 metres in clear starlight. It has a fixed eyepiece focus and is intended for fitment to anti-tank weapons, field artillery and howitzers.
SS69 Night Observation Device
The SS69 is a second generation version of the SS32 and provides approximately the same performance. Mechanical construction is very similar but it is about 100 mm shorter.

SS80 Lightweight Night Sight

The SS80 is Rank's latest development in small arms night vision. It weighs less than 1 kg, uses a second generation tube and is suitable for mounting on any automatic weapon or anti-tank gun. Magnification is ×3·8 and recognition range of a standing man in clear starlight is 400 metres.

SS82 Night Pocketscope

A development of the SS80, the SS82 pocketscope can be either hand-held or mounted on a small arms weapon. Magnification is ×2 and the recognition range of a standing man in clear starlight is 210 metres.

CONTRACTOR
Rank Pullin Controls Ltd, Langston Road, Loughton, Essex IG10 3TW, England.

4260.193
THORN EMI MULTI-ROLE THERMAL IMAGER

The Multi-Role Thermal Imager (MRTI) is one of a number of thermal imagers developed by Thorn-EMI under the UK MoD Thermal Imaging Common Modules (TICM) programme. The MRTI uses Class 1 modules from this and has been developed as direct and indirect view systems. Both systems are now in use with the British Army and the Royal Navy. MRTI is suited to a wide range of applications on the battlefield, for offshore patrol, airborne surveillance, weapon aiming and observation of mortar and artillery fire.

Thermal radiation is detected by the cadmium mercury telluride detector array which is scanned across the scene in a series-parallel mode. The detector array operates at 80°K and can be cooled to its working temperature by either a Joule-Thompson cooler using compressed air or by a closed-cycle cooling engine. MRTI is configured to use a 0·6 litre air bottle which, when charged to a pressure of 300 atmospheres, will cool the detector for up to 4·5 hours. The alternative closed cycle cooler has a power consumption of about 40 watts. Power to the rest of the imager can be supplied at voltages between 10 and 30 volts, with a consumption of less than 7 watts.

The system operates in the 8 – 13 μm band and two telescope fields of view are provided. Alternative telescopes are available to give enhanced performances. The equipment maintains focus when switched from one field of view to another. Controls for temperature offset and temperature window are provided and enable the operator to emphasise different temperature ranges within the scene under view. Hot-white or cold-white is switch selectable.

When used in the direct role the thermal scene is reconstructed using a scanned LED array. By adding another module to the direct view system a TV

MRTI in use in the field

Compatible (CCIR) output to a remote display can be obtained to form the indirect view system. The TV monitor can be either mounted on the imager or remoted.

CHARACTERISTICS
Waveband: 8 – 13 μm
Temperature sensitivity: 0·1°K
Field of view: 4·9° × 3·2° narrow; 12·9° × 8° (wide)
Focusing range: 10 m – ∞ (wide); 30 m – ∞ (narrow)
Display: Red LED raster with illuminated graticule and warning symbols for low battery and low air supply.
Dimensions: 480 × 280 × 190 mm
Weight: Thermal imager 10·7 kg (including bottle and battery); remote viewing unit 1·3 kg

STATUS
In production. The equipment is also being developed as a weapon fire control system on helicopters. Trials have been conducted on an Army Air Corps Scout helicopter. British Aerospace are offering the MRTI for use on the Swingfire missile to allow use at night or in poor visibility. Thorn-EMI is co-operating with OIP Optics, Belgium in the production of a thermal imager, based on the MRTI, for integration with the LRS-5 fire control system (**4744.193**).

CONTRACTOR
Thorn EMI Electronics Ltd, Defence Systems Division, Victoria Road, Feltham, Middlesex TW13 7DZ, England.

4703.193
OBSERVER THERMAL IMAGING SYSTEM (OTIS)

OTIS is an adaption of the multi-role thermal imager (MRTI) (**4260.193**) together with a laser rangefinder and angulation head. The MRTI and the laser rangefinder are mutually boresighted. The equipment is man-portable and is intended for application in battlefield surveillance, observation and control of artillery and mortar fire and target tracking for laser guided weapons.

Azimuth and elevation readings are available as

mechanical slipping scales or digital readouts. All other technical characteristics are as given for the MRTI.

STATUS
In production for the UK MoD under a contract worth almost £15 million.

CONTRACTOR
Thorn EMI Electronics Ltd, Defence Systems Division, Victoria Road, Feltham, Middlesex TW13 7DZ, England.

OTIS system in use in the field

4704.193
THORN EMI HAND-HELD THERMAL IMAGER

The Thorn-EMI hand-held thermal imager is a compact lightweight unit intended for use by reconnaissance troops and forward observation officers, as well as a wide range of civil applications. The equipment uses modules developed from the UK Class 1 thermal imaging common module programme and employs a great deal of the technology which led to the MRTI (**4260.193**) and OTIS (**4703.193**) thermal imagers.

It is, however, considerably lighter than either of those equipments, with the electronics having been hybridised to reduce the weight, but maintains considerable commonality to reduce spares holdings and ease maintenance.

CHARACTERISTICS
Waveband: 8 – 12 μm
Detector: Series/parallel Cadmium Mercury Telluride

Field of view: Wide 20° × 8·6° (× 2 magnification); Narrow 8° × 3·4° (×5 magnification)
Focusing range: 5m – ∞
Display: Red LED raster with illuminated graticule and warning symbols for low battery and low air bottle supply
Minimum resolvable temperature difference: 0·3°K
Dimensions: 470 × 210 × 160 mm
Weight: 5 kg (including cooling air bottle and battery)

STATUS
In production. A contract, worth over £13 million, was awarded by the UK MoD in June 1984 for the supply of a large number of this hand-held imager to the British Army.

CONTRACTOR
Thorn EMI Electronics Ltd, Defence Systems Division, Victoria Road, Feltham, Middlesex TW13 7DZ, England.

Thorn EMI hand-held thermal imager

4783.193
UNITED SCIENTIFIC ELECTRO-OPTICAL PRODUCTS

United Scientific Instruments manufactures a number of electro-optical devices. The company is a member of the United Scientific Group and works in collaboration with Avimo, a member of the same group. Brief details are given below of other equipments in the group's range:

LH-83 Hand-held Laser Rangefinder

The LH-83 provides laser rangefinder capability in a hand-held system configuration. The small, lightweight battery operated device is designed to withstand field operating environments.

CHARACTERISTICS
Range: 100 – 4000 m
Range resolution: 5 m
Magnification: ×6
Field of view: 5°
Dimensions: 65 × 165 × 198 mm
Weight: 1·5 kg

VML 23 Vehicle Mounted Laser

The VML 23 is designed for external mounting on armoured fighting vehicles. It is normally mounted on the gun mantlet and protected by an armoured cover. Alignment with the gun bore permits use of the vehicle standard gunner sight for aiming the laser. The instrument is capable of measuring two separate ranges concurrently.

CHARACTERISTICS
Laser: Dye Q-switched Nd:YAG
Wavelength: 1·064 μm
Radiant energy: 45 mJ
Magnification: ×7
Field of view: 7°
Range: 200 – 9995 m
Range resolution: 5 m

NV39T Driver's Night Vision Viewer

The NV39T provides the 'T' series battle tanks with a complete night driving capability. It has been designed to mount in the vehicle as a direct replacement for the daylight periscope and uses a second generation tube.

NV40 Passive Night Vision Periscope

The NV40 night vision periscope comprises a night vision elbow, a periscope head and a mount. The night vision elbow is a modified and improved version of the standard US Army elbow. The persicope head is similar to the existing IR sight but all the optics have high efficiency coatings to prevent glare and improve image contrast.

NV44 Tank Periscope

The NV44 periscope is intended as a replacement for the M20 daylight periscope on the M41 and M47 tanks and provides both day and night fire control by adapting the fire control module of the M60A1 tank. The day body contains a ×9 power telescope with a unit vision window. The passive night elbow mounts onto the day body and uses a second generation image intensifier.

NV46 Passive Night Vision Periscope

The NV46 provides passive night vision for the commander in the T54, T55 and T59 battle tanks. The instrument employs a second generation image intensifier and is directly interchangeable with the existing IR sight. It provides a magnification of ×4·4 and a field of view of 11 degrees.

AN/PAQ-4 IR Laser Aiming Light

The AN/PAQ-4 uses an IR laser to provide an accurate method of convert weapon aiming and target-spotting during night operations. It is mounted directly on the weapon and the pulsed laser light is viewed through night vision goggles or other IR sensitive systems.

AN/PVS-5A Passive Night Vision Goggles

These goggles use 18 mm microchannel wafer second generation image intensifiers to provide night vision for general purpose observation and firing. The user can view at ranges from 25 cm to infinity by means of a focus adjustment.

CONTRACTOR
United Scientific Instruments Ltd, 10 Fitzroy Square, London W1P 6AB, England.

5725.193
VICKERS/MARCONI CO₂ TANK LASER RANGEFINDER

This is a development, by Vickers Instruments and Marconi Avionics, as part of a study to prove the advantages of CO_2 lasers in the penetration of smoke and fog. It is based on the CO_2 TEA laser (transversely-excited laser) which operates at near atmospheric pressure and transmits very short pulses of radiation at high power. The study is intended to provide a laser rangefinder as part of a new battle tank sighting system.

The 10 micron wavelength of the laser rangefinder is compatible with that of thermal imagers and consequently offers advantages in operational use and in optical design. The CO_2 laser is also intrinscially superior in the penetration of smoke, mist and fog compared with the currently used ruby and neodymium-YAG lasers.

The periscopic upper sight has been developed by Vickers Instruments and the laser rangefinder by Marconi Avionics.

DEVELOPMENT
Early research into CO_2 lasers was carried out in the UK by the Royal Signals and Radar Establishment. This latest development is part of a contract placed on Vickers Instruments by the UK MoD for the design of a prototype battle tank sight for the Chieftain and Challenger.

STATUS
In development. Successful trials have been carried out in a main battle tank.

CONTRACTORS
Vickers Instruments, Haxby Road, York YO3 7SD, England.

Marconi Avionics Ltd, Applied Physics Division, Elstree Way, Borehamwood, Hertfordshire, England.

Vickers/Marconi CO₂ tank laser rangefinder

4705.193
L20 LASER RANGEFINDER

The L20 laser rangefinder provides a modular system periscope monocular sight which can be fitted to most main battle tanks. Modules are available for new installation and for retrofit on Chieftain, Challenger, Vickers Mk.3, M41, MBT and CVR(T) Scorpion tanks.

The L20 consists of three interchangeable modules: optics, laser and electronics. The laser and electronics modules can be removed without dismantling the sight, allowing the latter to be used in a reversionary mode should any of the modules be damaged. A Nd:YAG transceiver provides range readout display in the eyepiece. The CRT gives a computer-controlled aiming mark when linked to fire control systems. In addition the CRT displays output from a remote thermal imager or low-light level TV camera. A ×10 sight for gunnery and an integral periscope for general surveillance are incorporated.

CHARACTERISTICS
Type: 2nd generation Nd:YAG
Wavelength: 1·064 μm
Q-switch: Electro-optic
Transmitted energy: 20 mJ
Clock frequency: 30 MHz
Beam divergence: 0·4 mils
Field of view: 0·8 mils
Range limits: 300 to 10 000 m
Range accuracy: 5 m
PRR: 1 pps

STATUS
A £1 million order for L20 sights was received in mid-1984 from an unspecified African country.

CONTRACTOR
Vickers Instruments, Haxby Road, York YO3 7SD, England.

L20 laser rangefinder

4706.193
L50 SIGHT LASER RANGEFINDER

The L50 sight laser rangefinder is a telescopic gunners sight designed and developed for the main battle tanks T55 and T59. The sight is available in two versions: to provide a laser rangefinding capability for conventional mechanical fire control systems, or for laser rangefinding and aiming mark injection for available computer-based fire control systems. The sight rangefinder can be interchanged with the existing telescope, using the turret aperture without modification to armour, turret or eyepiece.

The L50 is modular in construction and consists of an optics or a laser module, range display and control, aiming mark injection and foot firing pedal. A commander's display module is also available.

CHARACTERISTICS
Type: 2nd generation Nd:YAG
Wavelength: 1·064 μm
Beam divergence: 0·4 mils
Field of view: 0·8 mils
Range limits: 300 to 10 000 m
CONTRACTOR
Vickers Instruments, Haxby Road, York YO3 7SD, England.

L50 laser rangefinder

4708.193
WESTON OPTRONICS NIGHT VISION SYSTEMS

Weston Optronics has developed a number of image intensified night vision systems for a variety of applications. These include the LIVE (Low Light Intensified Vision Equipment) series, the WINS 1801 and the Modulux system.

The LIVE series consists of two equipments – LIVE 172 and LIVE 062. Both are designed for military use for general observation and target acquisition/recognition. LIVE 172 is a long-range man-portable device for observation from static locations or vehicles. LIVE 062 is a shorter-range equipment for observation while on foot or when long-range is not required.

The WINS 1801 is an image-intensifier night sight, for use with rifles or, with the addition of a pistol grip, as a hand-held viewer. The sight is 204 mm long, 63 mm in diameter and weighs 1·2 kg. Magnification is ×2·8 giving a field view of 14·6°.

Modulux is a high performance modular night vision equipment intended primarily for security and police forces. It is available with either a first or second generation intensifier tube.
CONTRACTOR
Weston Optronics, 580 Great Cambridge Road, Enfield, Middlesex EN1 3RX, England.

UNITED STATES OF AMERICA

4281.193
LRR-104 Mk IV LASER RANGEFINDERS

The LRR-104 Mark IV is a self-contained, hand-held rangefinder used primarily by artillery forward observers, mortar fire controllers, infantry units and reconnaissance patrols. The Mark IV is rugged, waterproof and fully tested to operate under the most adverse battlefield conditions.

The device operates with any one of three battery types (Alkaline, Lithium or NiCad), all three of which are available worldwide. An optional multi-pin remote connector located below the right eyepiece expands the capabilities to include integration with accessories such as a remote display and control unit, artillery tripod/goniometer, battery charger and computerised fire control systems.

CHARACTERISTICS
Type: Nd:YAG
Wavelength: 1·064 μm
Output energy: 3 mJ
Detector: Silicon avalanche photodiode
Field of view: 2·6 mrad
Range: 50 – 9995 m
Range accuracy: 3 m
Dimensions: 190 × 216 × 79 mm
Weight: 2 kg
CONTRACTOR
International Laser Systems Inc, 3404 N Orange Blossom Trail, Orlando, Florida 32804, USA.

ILS LRR-104 Mk IV hand-held laser rangefinder

4709.193
LRR 104 MARK V LASER RANGEFINDER

The Mark V is the fifth model in the ILS series of LRR-104 hand-held rangefinders. Although smaller and lighter than the Mark IV the latest design retains the critical performance of its predecessor. The Mark V is approximately the size of a pair of 7 × 35 binoculars. In addition to the use by forward observers and artillery units for direct and indirect fire control, the Mark V fills a need of many special forces for an extremely small rangefinder. Instant range operation enables the operator to distinguish moving targets up to 10 km away. Range data and operational indicators are displayed in the sighting optics.

CHARACTERISTICS
Type: Nd:YAG
Wavelength: 1·064 μm
Output energy: 4 mJ nominal
Detector: Silicon avalanche photodiode
Aperture: 35 mm

Field of view: 5 mrad
Range: 50 – 9995 m
Accuracy: 3 m
Dimensions: 127 × 182 × 44 mm
Weight: 2 kg
CONTRACTOR
International Laser Systems Inc, 3404 N Orange Blossom Trail, Orlando, Florida 32804, USA.

4710.193
LRR-104/20 ARTILLERY RANGEFINDER

The LRR-104/20 has been designed using the same basic components as found in the LRR-104 Mark IV (**4281.193**). The unit is identical to the Mark IV in size, weight and durability. The tripod/goniometer assembly features azimuth and elevation indicators to one mil accuracy. The pistol grip handles contain Power and Fire buttons for remote operation of the rangefinder and provide easy manipulation of scan in azimuth and elevation.

CHARACTERISTICS
Type: Nd:YAG
Wavelength: 1·064 μm
Output energy: 12 mJ
Detector: Silicon avalanche photodiode
Field of view: 2·6 mrad
Range: 50 – 199 995 m
Accuracy: 3 m
Dimensions: 190 × 216 × 79 mm
Weight: 2 kg
CONTRACTOR
International Laser Systems Inc, 3404 N Orange Blossom Trail, Orlando, Florida 32804, USA.

LRR-104/20 artillery rangefinder

3200.193
AN/GVS-5 LASER RANGEFINDER

The AN/GVS-5 is a portable, hand-held laser rangefinder resembling, and about the same size as, a pair of binoculars. The unit is completely self-contained and incorporates an internal power supply in the form of a Ni-Cd battery. A neodymium-YAG laser is employed, Q-switched by a chemical Q-switch wafer. The latter consists of a saturable absorbing dye in acrylic plastic which becomes transparent at the correct power level to produce the laser pulse.

The transmitter and receiver optics are combined into a single group comprising the housing, transmitter telescope, and receiver/sighting telescope. This is essentially like one half of a normal binocular assembly with an objective lens and an eyepiece. However, a beam splitter in the optical path provides a means for projection of a reticle and LED range display to the eyepiece, and for providing an optical path to the photodiode detector for the returned laser energy.

CHARACTERISTICS
Type: AN/GVS-5
Laser: Nd-YAG. Q-switched

Wavelength: 1·06 microns
Energy output: <15 mJ
Max range: Classified
Range gate: Continuously adjustable to 5 km
Beam divergence: <1 mrad
Time to range: 1 s
Ranges per battery charge: 700 at 24°C; 350 at 71°C; 200 at -32°C
Operating temperature range: -46 to +71°C
Weight: 2·27 kg
DEVELOPMENT
Development was commenced by the US Army Electronics Command. In 1974 RCA was awarded a $1·5 million contract for development of an initial batch of 20 ED models for test and evaluation; type classification was completed in July 1977 and a production contract was awarded to RCA in December 1977.
STATUS
RCA has been awarded several contracts since 1977 which have totalled over 6000 units.
CONTRACTOR
RCA Automated Systems, Burlington, Massachusetts, USA.

AN/GVS-5 laser rangefinders undergo final inspection

4711.093
TK-640 LASER RANGEFINDER

The TK-640 is readily adaptable for use as an onboard fire control system for battle tanks, assault vehicles and landing craft. It uses a Nd:YAG laser beam to determine accurate range of both day and night targets. The range data determined is provided in the form of electronic signals to drive a 4-digit, 7-segment LED display.

CHARACTERISTICS
Type: Nd:YAG
Wavelength: 1·064 μm

Beam divergence: 0·7 mrad nominal
Output energy: 6 mJ nominal
Detector: Silicon avalanche photodiode
Range: 50 – 9990 m
Range accuracy: 5 m
Dimensions: 190 × 56 × 102 mm
Weight: 2·3 kg
CONTRACTOR
International Laser Systems Inc, 3404 N Orange Blossom Trail, Orlando, Florida 32804, USA.

TK-640 laser rangefinder

4712.093
N-90 SERIES LASER

The N-90 laser was originally designed as a laboratory or industrial system but various options and combinations are available for use in military applications. When combined with an ILS high or medium sensitivity receiver and range counter, the NT-90 becomes a high performance rangefinder with range capabilities out to 20 to 40 km. In this option, the high sensitivity receiver is intended for use against small, long-range targets or when the use of a low laser power is required. The medium sensitivity receiver provides for normal ranging applications.

The addition of an ILS Simulator Module to the basic laser results in a low-cost target simulator for use in verifying aircraft sensor systems and pilot training.

A number of other models are available for specific purposes and various power output options.
CHARACTERISTICS
Wavelength: 1·064 μm
Max energy: 90 mJ
Max repetition rate: 20 pps
Pulse width: 18 ±4 ns
Beam divergence: 2·5 mrads raw beam; 0·5 mrad collimated
Beam diameter: 6·3 mm raw beam; 38 mm collimated
Dimensions: 457 × 254 × 152 mm
Weight: 10 kg
CONTRACTOR
International Laser Systems Inc, 3404 N Orange Blossom Trail, Orlando, Florida 32804, USA.

NT-90 MSR receiver and HRC counter

4112.193
AN/VSG-2 TANK THERMAL SIGHT

The AN/VSG-2 is a thermal imaging infra-red device designed for fitting in US Army M60 tanks as part of an upgrading programme for that series of vehicles. New production M60 tanks have been designated M60A3 since February 1978 when the AN/VVG-2 laser rangefinder and a solid-state ballistics computer were introduced to the tank's fire control system, and the AN/VSG-2 thermal imaging equipment replaced the gunner's passive night vision periscope from mid-1979 onward.

Technical details and performance data have not been released but the latter may reasonably be expected to be no less than those achieved by other land battlefield IR systems based on the range of infra-red 'common modules' developed by Texas Instruments (eg AN/TAS-4, AN/TAS-5, AN/TAS-6).
STATUS
In 1983 total procurement of AN/VSG-2 tank thermal sight equipment had exceeded 7000 units to fulfil M60 tank requirements. The US Army plans to convert all M60A3 passive tank sights to thermal imaging and to upgrade a large number of M60A1 vehicles to the same system.
CONTRACTOR
Texas Instruments Incorporated, PO Box 226015, Dallas, Texas 75266, USA.

Texas Instruments AN/VSG-2 thermal sight for M60 series

1803.193
AN/VVS-1 TANK LASER SYSTEM

This system was developed by Hughes for the US Army M60A1 main battle tank. It consists of a laser rangefinder integrated with a complete fire control system which includes its own computer and the relevant sensors for ballistic calculations. The project was undertaken in the early 1970s to increase the first-round hit capability of the M60A1's 105 mm gun, against both standing and moving targets. Tanks converted by addition of the new fire control system are designated M60A3.

The target range data is processed in the solid-state computer together with crosswind component, gun trunnion cant, bore wear, air temperature, altitude, and tracking rate to provide the correct azimuth and elevation firing values. The computer can provide computation for nine types of ammunition, and the system incorporates self-test facilities.

STATUS
By the end of 1983 Hughes had delivered more than 2000 of these systems for M60A3 tanks. They are now being produced by Kollsman Instrument Company. It was announced in April 1983 that the Spanish Army had selected a version of the M60A3 system for its M48 tanks. The new version uses 70 per cent of the MA60A3 system plus key modules from the M1 rangefinder (**3814.193**).

Kollsman received a contract in January 1984 to produce 461 systems for the US Army M60 tanks. In addition, 94 will be built for tanks for Egypt and 100 will be produced for Saudi Arabia.

CONTRACTORS
Hughes Aircraft Company, PO Box 902, El Segundo, California 90245, USA.

Kollsman Instrument Company, 220 Daniel Webster Highway, Merrimack, New Hampshire 03054, USA.

AN/VVS-1 laser rangefinder for M60A1 tank FCS under test at Hughes Aircraft Company laboratory

3048.193
AN/VVS-2 DRIVER'S NIGHT VISION VIEWER

The VVS-2 is a passive night vision device for drivers of AFVs and has been developed for use by the US Army, initially in M60 tanks. Unlike systems such as the active infra-red M19 and M24 drivers' viewers, the VVS-2 image-intensifier equipment is a totally passive system requiring no active illumination, such as IR searchlights, or headlights. The new system is also claimed to offer a 65 per cent greater field of view than earlier devices. Another advantage is the 'bi-ocular' display which allows the driver to view the scene with both eyes through one, large diameter, eyepiece from a distance of several inches. The oval-shaped field of view of 45° horizontal by 38° vertical is presented with unity magnification. All objects located more than four metres from the tank are presented in focus. The head prism protruding from the tank hull is tilted to prevent reflection of enemy searchlights. There are different versions of the AN/VVS-2 viewer for specific tank models: the AN/VVS-2(V)1A is designed for the

M60A3, the AN/VVS-2(V)2A is designed for the M1, and the AN/VVS-2(V)3 is designed for the M2 and M3 series tanks. These viewers have the 'internal azimuth rotational mount.' This mount is engineered to provide a water-tight seal, easy viewer installation and removal, and a reliable azimuth rotation. These versions are specified by the US Army as standard items for the designated vehicles and fit directly without modifications.

For other US armoured vehicles such as M60A1, M60A2, M48, M47, M41, M113, and LVTP-7, Baird developed the NDS-2 Model 1924. This viewer is an exact replacement for the M19 and M24 active IR viewers. No vehicle modification is required and the viewer installation can be accomplished in the field. All vehicles that use the NDS-2 model 1924 mount can be field retrofitted with a modified tank hatch insert that will accept the 'internal azimuth rotation mount'.

NDS-2
This is the designation given to an export package version of the VVS-2. NDS-2 night driving system packages are configured to suit specific AFV types and consist of a vehicle modification kit and test equipment to support the viewer. Baird has designed NDS-2 packages for both US and foreign vehicles.

CHARACTERISTICS
Field of view: 45 × 38°
Total field coverage: 135° horizontal × 38° vertical
Depth of focus: 4 m – ∞
System resolution: 1·2 mils
System magnification: ×1
Linear distortion: <4%
Image brightness: Variable
Objective lens: f1·09, 33·5 mm focal length
Image intensifier: 25 mm with automatic gain control and bright source protection
Image tube gain: 25 000 minimum
Bi-ocular magnifier: 45°, fixed focus
STATUS
In production. Baird has delivered a modified, requalified version of the AN/VVS-2 to the US Army for use on the M1 tank. Versions have also been engineered for US M2 and M3 armoured vehicles.
CONTRACTOR
Baird Corporation, 125 Middlesex Turnpike, Bedford, Massachusetts 01730, USA.

Three current production versions of Baird Corporation AN/VVS-2(V) night vision driving equipment, (left to right): Model AN/VVS-2(V)1A for M60A3, Model AN/VVS-2(V)2A for M1 tank, and Model 1924 which can be mounted on M60A1/2, M48, M47, M41, M113 and LVTP-7 vehicles

4155.193
M32E1 MODEL 9880 NIGHT VISION ELBOW

The M32E1 Model 9880 passive elbow provides a visually secure night fire control capability for a number of armoured vehicle types. It is designed as an interchangeable replacement for the infra-red M32 and M36 elbows with no vehicle modification required. The configuration and performance of the elbow is in accordance with the current revision of the US Army specification MIL-E-48441.

The equipment uses a 25 mm second-generation image intensifier tube also produced by Varo. Image tube gain and reticle brightness are manually adjustable to compensate for different levels of ambient lighting. Automatic gain control circuitry is employed to maintain automatically the viewed scene illumination at a constant level during periods of changing light level conditions such as the period from sunset to full darkness. This allows the operator of the sight to use the sight without having to re-adjust

the tube gain control every few minutes during this period. The tube features muzzle-flash protection which prevents the tube from being damaged by high intensity short duration flashes of light. The flash protection circuit is designed to recover in time for the observer to see the round hit the target.
CHARACTERISTICS
Optical
Magnification: ×7·2
Field of view: 7·1°

System resolution
At 3 × 10⁻³ ft L: 5·6 lp/mr

At 3×10^{-3} ft L: 5·6 lp/mr
At 3×10^{-5} ft L: 2·7 lp/mr
Objective focal length: 200 mm
Focus range: 50 m – ∞

Eyepiece focal length: 27·9 mm
Eyepiece dioptre focus: +4 to –4
CONTRACTOR
Varo Inc, Integrated Systems Division, 2201 W Walnut St, PO Box 401267, Garland, Texas 75040, USA.

4154.193
MODEL 9891 COMMANDER'S PERISCOPE

The Model 9891 commander's periscope was developed as a direct replacement for the TKN-1 used by the commander in the Soviet-designed T55 and T62 tanks to provide both day and night viewing capability. The image intensifier tube features muzzle-flash protection which prevents the tube from being damaged by high intensity short duration flashes of light. The flash protection circuit is designed to recover in time for the observer to see the round hit the target. Automatic brightness control is a standard feature, and permits viewing during the twilight hours of dusk and dawn and protects the tube against bright flashes of light.

The periscope features a stabilised head mirror to provide the commander with improved on-the-move viewing capability. An illuminated projected reticle permits range information from Varo Model 9897 laser rangefinder (**4151.193**) to be displayed in the field of view.

CHARACTERISTICS
Optical
Magnification: ×4
Field of view: 10·5°
Objective focal length: 135 mm
Objective f number: 1·5
Focus range: 25 m – ∞
Eyepiece dioptre focus: +4 to –4
Eyepiece interpupillary adjustment: 58 ± 5 mm
Electrical power: 18 – 30 V DC
Image intensifier tube
Type: 25 mm micro-channel inverter
Typical resolution: 28 lp/mm
Photocathode response: S-20VR
ABC: Standard

Performance (detection)*	Light Level	
	10⁻¹ lux	10⁻³ lux
Man	763 m	448 m
Jeep	1215 m	715 m
Tank	1863 m	1096 m

*Range is calculated based on a 30% contrast target and 3 resolution elements required for detection

System resolution (100% contrast)
0·001 lux: 2·70 lp/mr
0·1 lux: 3·51 lp/mr
(30% contrast)
0·001 lux: 1·35 lp/mr
0·1 lux: 2·43 lp/mr
CONTRACTOR
Varo Inc, Integrated Systems Division, 2201 W Walnut St, PO Box 401267, Garland, Texas 75040, USA.

4153.193
MODEL 9892 DRIVER'S VIEWER

The Varo Model 9892 driver's viewer was developed to provide night-time operational capability for a wide range of Soviet-designed armoured vehicles such as the T54, T55 and T62. It complements Varo's Model 9894 gunner's periscope to provide an effective night fire control system capability. The periscope was developed as a direct replacement for the TVN-2 IR driver's viewer and mounts interchangeably with the existing daylight vision block. Two-channel binocular viewing provides maximum stereoscopic viewing for added depth perception and increased user comfort.

CHARACTERISTICS
Optical
Magnification: ×1
Field of view: 40°

Objective focal length: 27 mm
Objective f number: 1·2
Focus adjustment: Fixed (4 m – ∞)
Eyepiece dioptre focus: +4 to –4
Eyepiece interpupillary adjustment: 58 ± 5 mm
Image intensifier tube
Type: 18 mm micro-channel
Typical resolution: 28 lp/mm
Photocathode response: S-20VR

Performance (detection)*	Light Level	
	10⁻¹ lux	10⁻³ lux
Man	200 m	117 m
Jeep	295 m	187 m
Tank	452 m	395 m

*Range is calculated based on a 30% contrast target and 3 resolution elements required for detection

System resolution (100% contrast)
0·001 lux: 0·39 lp/mr
0·1 lux: 0·59 lp/mr
(30% contrast)
0·001 lux: 0·25 lp/mr
0·1 lux: 0·49 lp/mr
CONTRACTOR
Varo Inc, Integrated Systems Division, 2201 W Walnut St, PO Box 401267, Garland, Texas 75040, USA.

4150.193
MODEL 9894 GUNNER'S PERISCOPE

The Model 9894 integrated gunner's day/night periscope was developed as a direct replacement for the TPN-1 gunner's periscope used in Soviet-designed T55 and T62 tanks. Installation in these tanks can be accomplished without modification. When integrated with Varo's Model 9895 ballistic computer system (**4156.181**), it provides a full solution fire control system. The major components of the Model 9894 gunner's periscope include: a head/mount assembly with stabilised head mirror for improved viewing and increased ranging accuracy while moving; Model 9880 passive night vision elbow; and a Model 9897 daylight elbow with an integrated laser rangefinder for fast, accurate (±5 m) ranging. Range data is displayed in both day and night fields of view. Apart from the mechanical changes necessary to accommodate the Soviet tank design, this equipment is virtually the same as the Model 9898 (**4149.193**).

CHARACTERISTICS
Magnification: ×7 (night); ×8 (day)
Field of view: 7·5° (night); 8° (day)
Objective focal length: 200 mm (night)
Focus range: 50 m – ∞ (night); fixed (day)
Eyepiece dioptre focus: ±4 (night/day)
Image intensifier tube: 25 mm MCP

Performance (night elbow)*	Light Level	
	10⁻¹ lux	10⁻³ lux
Man	1316 m	626 m
Jeep	2100 m	1000 m
Tank	3220 m	1533 m

*Range is calculated based on a 30% contrast target and 3 resolution elements required for detection

CONTRACTOR
Varo Inc, Integrated Systems Division, 2201 W Walnut St, PO Box 401267, Garland, Texas 75040, USA.

4152.193
MODEL 9896 NIGHT VISION ELBOW

The Model 9896 passive elbow provides fire control capability for armoured vehicles where space is limited and a small compact periscope with high performance is required. It was specifically developed to fulfil the night vision requirements of the M41, M47, and M48 tanks currently using the M20 daylight periscope. The Model 9896 passive elbow can be used with the existing M20 daylight periscope to provide both day and night viewing capability.

The passive elbow features an illuminated projected reticle that is fully adjustable to compensate for varying scene brightness and target contrasts. The standard NATO reticle is provided unless otherwise specified. The tube features muzzle-flash protection which prevents the tube from being damaged by high intensity short duration flashes of light. The flash protection circuit is designed to recover in time for the observer to see the round hit the target. Automatic brightness control is a standard feature. This feature permits viewing during the twilight hours of dusk and dawn and protects the tube against bright flashes of light. The equipment is designed to operate from vehicle power under normal conditions or from a single 2·7 V mercury battery under emergency conditions.

CHARACTERISTICS
Optical
Magnification: ×5·2
Field of view: 10·5°
Objective focal length: 135 mm
Objective f number: 1·5
Focus range: 25 m – ∞

Eyepiece dioptre focus: 2 to +5
Image intensifier tube
Type: 25 mm micro-channel inverter
Typical resolution: 28 lp/mm
Photocathode response: S-20VR

Performance (detection)*	Light Level	
	10⁻¹ lux	10⁻³ lux
Man	763 m	448 m
Jeep	1215 m	715 m
Tank	1863 m	1096 m

*Range is calculated based on a 30% contrast target and 3 resolution elements required for detection

CONTRACTOR
Varo Inc, Integrated Systems Division, 2201 W Walnut St, PO Box 401267, Garland, Texas 75040, USA.

4151.193
MODEL 9897 LASER RANGEFINDER

The Model 9897 daylight elbow/laser rangefinder was developed as a major component of Models 9894 and 9898 (**4150.193** and **4149.193**) gunner's periscopes and is a direct replacement in the US Army's M32 periscope. The elbow features a ×8 visual optical system and a tri-axial laser rangefinder. Range data from the laser rangefinder is automatically displayed in both the day and night elbow fields of view and can be remotely displayed to the commander's periscope.

CHARACTERISTICS
Optical
Magnification: ×8
Field of view: 8°
Range focus: Fixed
Eyepiece dioptre focus: ±4

Laser rangefinder transmitter
Type: Nd-YAG
Beam divergence: ≤5 mil
Logic: First/last pulse
Power: 1 MW, 6 mJ

Laser rangefinder receiver
Field of view: 1 mil
Minimum range: 400 m
Max range: 10 000 m
Range accuracy: ±5 m

CONTRACTOR
Varo Inc, Integrated Systems Division, 2201 W Walnut St, PO Box 401267, Garland, Texas 75040, USA.

4149.193
MODEL 9898 GUNNER'S PERISCOPE

The Model 9898 integrated gunner's day/night periscope was developed as a direct replacement for the M32 gunner's periscope used in the M60 and M48 series tanks. It can be used in many other armoured vehicles, such as the M47 and Centurian tanks, by minor modification to the tank. When integrated with Varo's Model 9895 ballistic computer system, it provides a full solution fire control system (**4156.181**). The major components of the Model 9898 gunner's periscope include: the head/mount assembly with stabilised head mirror for improved viewing and

increased ranging accuracy while moving; passive night vision elbow (Model 9880); and a Model 9897 daylight elbow with an integrated laser rangefinder for fast, accurate (±5 m) ranging. Range data is displayed in both day and night fields of view.

CHARACTERISTICS
Magnification: ×7 (night); ×8 (day)
Field of view: 7·5° (night); 8° (day)
Objective focal length: 200 mm (night)
Focus range: 50 m – ∞ (night); fixed (day)
Eyepiece dioptre focus: ±4 (night/day)
Image intensifier tube: 25 MCP

Performance
(night elbow)*

	Light Level	
	10⁻¹ lux	10⁻³ lux
	10^{-1} lux	10^{-3} lux
Man	1316 m	626 m
Jeep	2100 m	1000 m
Tank	3220 m	1533 m

*Range is calculated based on a 30% contrast target and 3 resolution elements required for detection

CONTRACTOR
Varo Inc, Integrated Systems Division, 2201 W Walnut St, PO Box 401267, Garland, Texas 75040, USA.

5719.193
KOLLMORGEN ELECTRO-OPTICAL SYSTEMS

The Kollmorgen Corporation manufactures a wide variety of land-based electro-optical systems for infantry and armoured vehicle use. Brief details of the main equipments are as follows:

Model 317 M20 Night Vision Kit

The Model 317 night vision kit incorporates a passive night vision channel into the standard M20 sight to provide day/night operation of the periscope. The channel includes an objective lens, a GEN II image intensifier, relay lenses, a day/night mirror assembly and is equipped with a power supply. The kit can also be installed with or without a 1:1 vision block prism.
CHARACTERISTICS
Magnification: ×6
Aperture: 3 cm (day); 4·5 cm (night)
Field of view: 8°

Model 332 Day/Night Viewing Periscope

The Model 332 is for use in those applications which require a high performance sight but which have limited space available. The Model 332 offers a narrow interface which adapts either the M32E1 day elbow telescope with a X1 vision block, or the M36E1 night elbow, to provide, alternately, a day sight and a night sight with quick connect/disconnect interchangeability. The unit uses the full aperture of the night vision elbow for improved low light level performance. The primary application of the Model 332 is as a fire control sight for small to mid-calibre combat vehicle gun arrangements.

Although the M332 is designed for the M32E1 daylight elbow and the M35E11 night elbow, the modular construction of the unit is such that adaptors can be designed for many elbow-type telescopes.

Model 910 Integrated Sight

The Model 910 Integrated Sight is a small stabilised system designed to mount on the turret of a tracked vehicle. The sight supplies a reconnaissance capability, or accurate weapon positioning and

control to the gunner. Gyro stabilised viewing is provided with two magnifications, ×2 and ×8, and with fields of view of 28° and 7° respectively. The unit can be used independently or can be the master or slave to other subsystems on the vehicle. Regardless of mode, boresight information is generated at all times by the periscope.

Model 910 has almost unlimited access to the visible hemisphere above the vehicle. By means of a gimballed prism, the line of sight can be depressed to –10°, elevated to +85°, and rotated continuously 360° in azimuth. The sight is mounted on a separate plate secured to the vehicle deck. A low power laser can be fitted to the sight.

Model 938 Commander's Weapon Station Sight

This is a ×3 power monocular daylight periscope used as a sighting device for the commander's weapon. The instrument is mounted near, and mechanically linked to, the weapon. The line of sight is capable of movement in the vertical plane from –10 to +65°, via a mechanical link to the weapon. A reticle pattern is presented in the field of view.
CHARACTERISTICS
Magnification: ×3
Field of view: 21°
Entrance pupil: 18 mm
Exit pupil: 6 mm

Model 939 Gunner's Auxilliary Sight

The gunner's auxiliary sight is a sealed and pressurised ×8 power optical device that can be used as a primary or back-up sight for the main coaxial armament. The instrument is mounted coaxially with the main gun and is articulated to minimise eyepiece movement when the main/coax weapon is elevated or depressed. A dioptre adjustment is provided to accommodate focal variations between individual observers. Individual reticle patterns may be presented in the field of view. A switchable ND filter is provided to allow use of the sight during high brightness conditions.
CHARACTERISTICS
Magnification: ×8
Field of view: 8°
Entrance pupil: 48 mm
Exit pupil: 6 mm

Model 957 Squad Leader's Search Periscope

This instrument is a sealed single magnification optical device that is used as a target acquisition and vehicle protective surveillance sight for the armoured personnel carrier squad commander. The instrument is mounted on the inside of the top deck of the APC with viewing and control functions internal to the vehicle.
CHARACTERISTICS
Magnification: ×4 minimum
Field of view: 12·5°
Exit pupil: 4·5 mm minimum

Model 972 Gunsight Telescope

The gunsight telescope provides the primary interface with the crew when the mobile gun system is operated in the optical track mode. It also integrates the laser rangefinder to share the optical aperture provided by the stabilised sight unit. The telescope contains both day and night viewing capability,

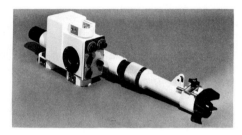
Model 939 gunner's auxiliary sight

Model 973 periscopic telescope

dual eyepieces so that both gunner and squad leader may view the target simultaneously, and relays the image through an interface to a TV scoring camera.
CHARACTERISTICS
Magnification: ×12 (day channel); ×16 (night channel); ×2·5 (laser channel)
Field of view: 5° (day channel); 3° (night channel); 3 mrad (laser channel)
Entrance pupil: 84 mm (day channel); 100 mm (night channel)
Exit pupil: 7 mm

Model 973 Squad Leader's Periscope Telescope

The squad leader's periscope telescope interfaces with a stabilised sight unit to provide visual interface with the crew when the mobile gun system is operated in the optical acquisition mode. The telescope contains both day and night viewing capability.
CHARACTERISTICS
Magnification: ×3 (day) ×4 (night channel)
Field of view: 20° (day); 12° (night channel)
Entrance pupil: 21 mm (day); 50 mm (night channel)
Exit pupil: 7 mm

Model 998 Fire Control Back-up Sight

This is a ballistic periscope fixed-power daylight monocular sight with a range estimating capability. The sight was designed for sighting and firing the primary 25 mm weapon from the electrically stabilised turret of an M2/M3 tracked vehicle. The sight is purely mechanically linked and will allow either the gunner or the commander secondary gun sighting capability in the event of failure of the primary. The sight has laser protection and an armoured head.
CONTRACTOR
Kollmorgen Corporation, Electro-Optical Division, 347 King Street, Northampton, Massachusetts 01060, USA.

Model 317 night vision kit

3571.193
AN/VVS-501 NIGHT DRIVING/OBSERVATION VIEWER

The VVS-501 has been developed for the Canadian Defence Forces for use by the drivers and commanders of AFVs. Similar to the US Army VVS-2 (**3048.193**), the VVS-501 is a passive night vision device employing the 25 mm micro-channel intensifier. Thus it requires no supplementary illumination such as for active IR viewers and provides variable gain within the field not available in viewers based on first-generation tubes. This latter fact is most important when lights or fires appear in the field of view.

The VVS-501 is mounted by replacing the day vision block of the driver's and commander's stations of the Leopard tank and the identical day vision block of the driver's station of the General Motors Canada AVGP. The entrance assembly interfaces with the Leopard windshield wiper and the eyepiece assembly is identical to the VVS-2. A stowage case is provided for the viewer or day vision block when not in use. Vehicle power or batteries may be used.

CHARACTERISTICS
Field of view: 45 × 38°
Total field coverage: 135° horizontal × 38° vertical
Depth of focus: 4 m – ∞
System magnification: ×1
Linear distortion: <4%
Image brightness: Variable
Objective lens: f1·08, 33·6 mm focal length
Image intensifier: 25 mm with automatic gain control and bright source protection
Image tube gain: 25 000 minimum
Bi-ocular magnifier: 45°, fixed focus
STATUS
Contracts with GLS Division of Krause-Maffei, Munich, West Germany for Leopard 1 and 2 tanks and DSS Canada for AVGP. Item fully integrated into NATO logistic systems.
CONTRACTOR
Baird Corporation, 125 Middlesex Turnpike, Bedford, Massachusetts 01730, USA.

Baird Corporation AN/VVS-501 night driving observation viewer for Leopard 2 tank

3822.193
MODEL 350 NIGHT DRIVING SIGHT

The Model 350 night driving viewer is a unity power night vision periscope for the operation of armoured vehicles in total darkness. It is passive in operation, requiring no artificial light sources to generate images on the darkest nights.

Electronically enhanced images are presented to the driver on a large bi-ocular viewer, which provides a 44° field of view. The entire system can be easily rotated left and right to cover a 135° field. The Model 350 can be operated on its own internal battery or connected to the vehicle electrical system. An automatic brightness control maintains constant image brightness despite variations in external illumination. A variable gain control allows the driver to select optimum scene brightness over a wide scale. Bright flash protection circuitry momentarily shuts the unit off during high intensity light bursts or muzzle flashes, with instantaneous restoration of a fully detailed image.

Interchangeable mounts are available for all currently operational combat vehicles.
CHARACTERISTICS
Optical
Magnification: ×1
Field of view: 44° horizontal, 35° vertical
Field coverage: 135° horizontal
Focus range: Fixed focus at 12 m
Depth of field: 4 m – ∞
Weight: 7·27 kg
Image tube gain: 25 000 minimum
Type: 25 mm 2nd generation intensifier
Resolution: 28 lp/mm
Photocathode: S-20R
CONTRACTOR
Javelin Electronics, 6357 Arizona Circle, Los Angeles, California 90045, USA.

Javelin Electronics Model 350 night driving sight

5720.193
LITTON NIGHT VISION POCKETSCOPES

The Litton series of miniature night vision pocketscopes provide passive viewing capabilities under minimal lighting conditions. Amplifying moonlight and starlight up to 600 times, the models use the same second-generation image intensifier.

The Model M-826 contains a ×1 power military lens and housing. It is designed for general observation in military applications where environmental factors can be a concern. For added protection from dust, sand and grime, a special dust cover is available on Litton's M-906 unit. Designed especially for desert and battlefield use, the Model M-906 also contains the ×1 power military lens and housing. Both units allow recognition of a man at approximately 300 m under dark night conditions.

Where longer range observation is necessary, the Model M-907 is available. This unit contains a × 3 power military lens and housing, extending the observation range to approximately 700 m.
CONTRACTOR
Litton Industries, Electron Tube Division, Electro-Optics Department, 1215 South 52nd Street, Tempe, Arizona 85281, USA.

Model M-906 pocketscope

3572.193
BER-40-4 BI-OCULAR EYEPIECE

The BER-40-4 is a new bi-ocular eyepiece lens for image intensification devices and small CRT displays, and is the latest in the Baird family of 25 and 40 mm input format bi-oculars for dual-eyed viewing of a single image. This method of viewing has been proved advantageous for long-term surveillance or viewing normal or low-light television images in physically constrained situations, and for minimising high ambient light reflection problems. The unit is currently being supplied for retrofitting to the AN/TVS-4 night observation device, on which it replaces the original monocular eyepiece. The AN/TVS-4 is a tripod-mounted, medium-range image intensifier surveillance equipment, and the bi-ocular feature allows the observer (or two observers) to view the magnified 40 mm image tube format with both eyes simultaneously. Although the CRT is about 10 cm from the outside glass element of the lens the apparent image is over 40 cm inside the lens. The BER-40-4 lens can be used to magnify one- or two-inch (25 or 50 mm) CRT displays to achieve the apparent equivalent of five- and nine-inch (127 and 228 mm) displays, respectively.
CHARACTERISTICS
Diameter: 97 mm
Weight: 1·5 kg
Resolution: 36 lp/mm
Linear distortion: <4% barrel
Transmission: >85%
Field flatness: 1/8 dioptre
Focal adjustment: Fixed focus
Magnification: ×4·3
Apparent image distance: 406 mm
MTF on axis: 60% at 40 lp/mm
STATUS
In operational use with the US Army and other defence forces.

Baird 40 mm format bi-ocular eyepiece (BER-40-4) on AN/TVS-4 night observation device

CONTRACTOR
Baird Corporation, 125 Middlesex Turnpike, Bedford, Massachusetts 01730, USA.

4122.193
BER-47-1 BI-OCULAR EYEPIECE
The BER-47-1 is a specially designed bi-ocular eyepiece lens for the AN/VVS-2 night vision driver's viewer for US Army AFVs. The AN/VVS-2 is standard equipment on American M60, XM1, M2, and M3 armoured vehicles. The BER-47-1 bi-ocular eyepiece is also used on the AN/VVS-501 night vision driver's viewer for Canadian Leopard I and Mowag series of armoured vehicles and on Baird's NDS-2 night driving systems series of viewers for foreign armoured vehicles.

The BER-47-1 is a 47 mm format bi-ocular eyepiece compatible with a 25 mm format second-generation image intensifier bonded to a fibre optic magnifier that expands the image from 25 mm format to 47 mm format. The bi-ocular eyepiece display permits the operator to view the scene with both eyes simultaneously through one large diameter eyepiece from several inches away. This improves overall performance of the device and provides maximum safety and long-term viewing comfort.
CHARACTERISTICS
Diameter: 100 mm

Weight: 2·6 kg
Resolution: 20 lp/mm
Linear distortion: Varies with application
Transmission: >80%
Field flatness: 1/4 dioptre
Focus adjustment: Fixed focus
Magnification: ×3·75 – 4
Apparent image distance: 482 mm
MTF on axis: 60% at 40 lp/mm
CONTRACTOR
Baird Corporation, 125 Middlesex Turnpike, Bedford, Massachusetts 01730, USA.

4121.193
BER-25 SERIES BI-OCULAR EYEPIECES
The BER-25 is a series of bi-ocular eyepieces designed to be used with first- or second-generation, 25 mm format, image intensifier assemblies. The BER-25 series offers the same long-term viewing comfort and safety as the BER-40-4 (**3572.193**) and the BER-47-1 bi-ocular eyepieces (**4122.193**).

Model BER-25-1 replaces the monocular eyepiece

on AN/PVS-2 individual-served weapon sight and AN/TVS-2 crew-served weapon sight. Model BER-25-2 replaces the monocular eyepiece on AN/PVS-4 individual-served weapon sight and AN/TVS-5 crew-served weapon sight. Model BER-25-5 replaces the monocular eyepiece on the passive elbow (MIL-E-48441) for M32/M35/M36 gunner and commander tank periscopes.
CHARACTERISTICS
Diameter: 84 mm
Weight: 0·8 kg
Resolution: 36 lp/mm
Linear distortion: <4% barrel
Transmission: >85%
Field flatness: 1/8 dioptre
Focus adjustment: Fixed focus
Magnification: ×4·5
Apparent image distance: 406 mm
MTF on axis: 60% at 40 lp/mm
CONTRACTOR
Baird Corporation, 125 Middlesex Turnpike, Bedford, Massachusetts 01730, USA.

Baird 25 mm format bi-ocular eyepiece (BER-25-2) on AN/TVS-5 crew-served weapon sight

Baird 25 mm format bi-ocular eyepiece (BER-25-5) on passive elbow MIL-E-48441 for M32/M35/M36 gunner and commander tank periscopes

4713.193
GP/NVG-1 NIGHT VISION GOGGLES
These small, lightweight night vision goggles are intended for long range observation and surveillance. The goggles consist of two main assemblies, a viewer and a face mask. The viewer can be operated independently or mounted on the face mask or helmet. Included in the view assembly is a three-position switch with ON/OFF/LED for map reading and other tasks requiring auxiliary lighting.

The objective lens has a very large aperture to gather the maximum amount of light to the image intensifier tube which is a Litton second generation 18 mm device. The remainder of the optical chain consists of a collimator lens to gather the output of the image intensifier, mirrors to split this in half, and imager lens and corner mirrors to carry the image to each eyepiece.

A night vision aiming light intended for mounting on an M16 rifle is designed for use with the goggles for night time operation. The aiming light, which

produces a narrow beam of pulsed energy, is boresighted to the weapon and the operator uses the goggles to detect the spot and aim the weapon. The aiming light is also available with different mounts to fit on other weapons.
CHARACTERISTICS
Magnification: ×1
Field of view: 40°
Brightness gain: × 2500
Weight: 643 g (complete assembly of viewer, mask and battery)
Aiming light
Dimensions: 160 × 50 mm
Weight: 170 g
Radiation source: Pulsed diode
STATUS
In production.
CONTRACTOR
Baird Corporation, 125 Middlesex Turnpike, Bedford, Massachusetts 01730, USA.

GP/NVG-1 night vision goggles

4714.193
GP/NVB-4 AND -6 NIGHT VISION BINOCULARS
The GP/NVB-4 and GP/NVB-6 are general purpose night vision binoculars for long range observation and surveillance. The GP/NVB-4 has a 95 mm focal length objective lens and ×4 magnification. The GP/NVB-6 has a 155 mm focal length lens and a ×6 magnification. Both systems provide the high performance of second generation image intensifier tubes. The eyepieces can be individually focused for various eye prescriptions and a focus mechanism allows the operator to refocus quickly on a new target.
CHARACTERISTICS

	GP/NVB-4	GP/NVB-6
Magnification	× 4	× 6
Field of view	10·5°	6·5°
Resolution	0·4 mrads	0·25 mrads
Brightness gain	×1000	×1000
Weight	1·13 kg	3·18 kg
Dimensions	225×145 mm	305×155 mm

CONTRACTOR
Baird Corporation, 125 Middlesex Turnpike, Bedford, Massachusetts 01730, USA.

GP/NVB-6 night vision binoculars

GP/NVB-4 night vision binoculars

3121.193

COMMANDO DAY-NIGHT VISION SYSTEM

The Cadillac Gage Company has developed this equipment as a modular passive day-night main gun sight for fitting to many current AFVs with little modification to existing turrets. The sight will fit all Commando V-150 large turreted vehicles, the LVTP-7, and the M47 and M48 tanks.

Day and night vision capabilities are obtained by the use of interchangeable telescopes. The sight body will accept either a ×8 power day telescope or a ×5·5 power night telescope. These can be changed rapidly without disturbing the sight body or gun zero. The sight also incorporates a unity power periscope with a projected reticle. This offers a wide field of view for such purposes as target acquisition and firing the coaxial machine-gun while on the move.

CHARACTERISTICS
Day sight
Magnification: ×8
True field: 6°
Scan: –10 to +60°
Eyepiece: Adjustment –3 to +3 dioptres. Defogging. Laser safe
Night sight
Magnification: ×5·5
True field: 9°
Scan: –10 to +60°
Eyepiece: –4 to +4 dioptres
Image tube: 25 mm electrostatic
Focusing: 10 m – ∞

Unipower periscope with day sight module

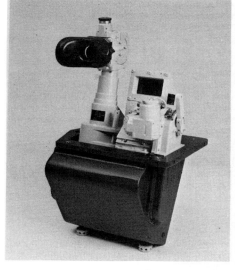
Unipower periscope with night sight module

Unity power periscope
Magnification: ×1
Field: Bi-ocular, 24 (horizontal) × 20° (vertical)
Scan: –10 to +60°
Reticle: Infinity projected, illuminated

CONTRACTOR
Cadillac Gage Company, PO Box 1027, Warren, Michigan 48090, USA.

4256.193

Mk IIIm STEDI-EYE STABILISED MONOCULAR

The Mk IIIm Stedi-eye is a ×8 magnification, lightweight, stabilised monocular that eliminates image motion due to hand movement and platform vibration. It has been designed, like its companions the Mk IIImg and the Mk V, for military applications but is small and light enough to put in a jacket pocket. The optical components are specifically designed to give the observer an extra-wide field of view, long eye-relief, and superior resolution. The instrument is completely passive and does not use electrical power.

CHARACTERISTICS
Magnification: ×8
Objective diameter: 36 mm
Field of view: 10°
Weight: 595 g

STATUS
In service with the USMC, Israeli Air Force, Canadian Forces and South African Air Force.
CONTRACTOR
Fraser-Volpe Corporation, 1025 Thomas Drive, Warminster Industrial Park, Warminster, Pennsylvania 18974, USA.

4257.193

Mk IIImg STEDI-EYE STABILISED MONOCULAR

The Mk IIImg is a ×10 magnification stabilised monocular, also designated the XM-21 by the US Army. It eliminates image motion due to hand movement and platform vibration and, like the Mk V to which it is very similar (**4258.193**), has been designed for military applications. Power is supplied by a standard 'D' cell battery giving 30 hours' operation.

CHARACTERISTICS
Magnification: ×10
Objective diameter: 43 mm

Field of view: 7·7°
Resolution: 6″
Transmission: 65% minimum
Max stabilised scan rate: 5/s with other optional rates
Weight: 1·58 kg
STATUS
The XM-21 has been type tested by the US Army and about 160 units have been supplied for use aboard OH-58 Scout helicopters.
CONTRACTOR
Fraser-Volpe Corporation, 1025 Thomas Drive, Warminster Industrial Park, Warminster, Pennsylvania 18974, USA.

Mk IIImg stabilised monocular

4258.193

Mk V STEDI-EYE STABILISED DAY/NIGHT MONOCULAR

This is a power stabilised monocular that eliminates image motion due to hand movement and platform vibration. It has been designed for day and night military applications and also as a compact low-cost instrument for use from aircraft, boats and surface vehicles.

A gimballed erecting prism array is stabilised by a small internal gyroscope and this removes up to 98 per cent of all input motions. Two controls only are needed: power and stabilisation on/off. There is a choice of an internal battery supply or external 14 to 28 V DC. Use of the monocular at night is achieved by the exchange of eyepieces and can be carried out in less than one minute. The night eyepiece contains a Gen 2, 18 mm image intensifier.

A standard SLR camera can be attached with a simple adaptor allowing hand-held telephoto pictures to be taken from moving platforms. The Mk V used in this fashion increases the focal length of the camera 15 times so that a 50 mm lens becomes effectively 750 mm.

CHARACTERISTICS
Magnification: ×15 (day); ×8·4 (night)

Objective diameter: 55 mm
Field of view: 5·3° (day); 4·5° (night)
Resolution: 5″ (day); 40″ (night)
Transmission: 65% minimum
Max stabilised scan rate: 10°/s
Weight: 1·81 kg
STATUS
In service with US Navy LAMPS helicopters.
CONTRACTOR
Fraser-Volpe Corporation, 1025 Thomas Drive, Warminster Industrial Park, Warminster, Pennsylvania 18974, USA.

4259.193

M61 FIRE CONTROL LEAD COMPUTING SIGHT

The M61 is a visually-aimed lead computing gyro sight for weapon aiming. The sight is a sealed unit containing a lead computing gyro, range magnet, optical system, synchro transmitters and caging device. The range magnet applies the lead computing precession to the gyro while a separate torque motor applies gravity drop corrections. Synchro transmitters provide angular signals to the fire control computer and range-only radar. The fire control computer also supplies signals to the sight to enable it to generate a lead angle and super-elevation.

The main application of the M61 is as part of the Vulcan air defence system (**2850.131**) and the contractor has developed a similar sight for the PIVADS (**4015.131**) product improved Vulcan air defence system.

CHARACTERISTICS
Magnification: ×1
Lead angle: ±25°
Weight: 15·9 kg

Power: 115 V, 400 Hz; 28 V DC
STATUS
In service with US Army and Republic of Korea. More than 800 M61 sights have been manufactured for use in Vulcan and PIVADS.
CONTRACTOR
Fraser-Volpe Corporation, 1025 Thomas Drive, Warminster Industrial Park, Warminster, Pennsylvania 18974, USA.

5717.193
M19A1 DRIVER'S NIGHT PERISCOPE

The M19A1 periscope sight is a sealed unit for night driving. The vehicle is equipped with infra-red or spot lights and the reflected rays are picked up by the periscope. Within the instrument an image converter tube changes the infra-red rays to visible light images which can be seen through the two eyepieces.

The instrument consists of two main parts: the head assembly projecting through the body armour of the vehicle, and the body assembly. The former contains a large prism which directs the incoming infra-red rays down to the body assembly where the objective lens and image converter are situated. The M19A1 has been adapted to all types of vehicle in service with the US Army, including combat tanks, personnel carriers etc. Recent modifications have considerably increased the reliability of the converter tubes.

CHARACTERISTICS

Magnification: ×1
Eyepiece focus: −0·75 to −1 dioptre
Objective focus: ∞
Resolution: 4 minutes arc
Weight: 6·35 kg including head assembly
STATUS
In operational service with the US Army.
CONTRACTOR
Fraser-Volpe Corporation, 1025 Thomas Drive, Warminster Industrial Park, Warminster, Pennsylvania 18974, USA.

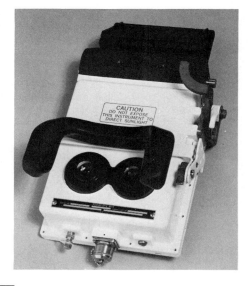

M19A1 night periscope

3814.193
M1 LASER RANGEFINDER

Hughes Aircraft Company has developed a laser rangefinder for the US Army's M1 Abrams main battle tank, this work proceeding in conjunction with the company's development of a thermal imaging system (**3570.193**) for the M1. Both equipments are integrated into the tank's fire control system.

The laser rangefinder consists of a transmitter, receiver, power supply, timing and logic circuitry. It includes a 'safe-switch' that allows the entire fire control system to operate without firing the laser, to guarantee safety during training exercises. Built-in test equipment is used to isolate faults to individual sub-assemblies, which speeds and simplifies maintenance. Designed for extreme reliability, the M1 laser system exceeds 1800 hours mean time between failure.

In action, a tank crew member aims at a target and fires the laser. Its beam travels to the target which reflects the beam back to a receiving telescope. Elapsed time of beam travel to and from the target provides accurate range information to the tank fire control computer almost instantaneously. The computer processes this information in milliseconds, together with other data such as crosswind velocity, air temperature, gun trunnion position, air density, target tracking rate and ammunition ballistics. The computer then delivers correct azimuth and elevation firing commands to the target turret and main gun.

A significant development is a change from a pink ruby as the lasing medium to the more recently developed neodymium-doped yttrium aluminium garnet (Nd-YAG) rods. Not only are the latter significantly smaller and lighter, but their power consumption is lower than ruby lasers because they require less energy to produce a laser beam.

The system is capable of distinguishing between two targets separated by as little as 15 m in range. It also allows the fire control system to differentiate between close-up and far-off targets, by allowing the gunner to select the first reflection (close target) or last reflection (far target).

CHARACTERISTICS

Laser: Nd-YAG
Range: 200 – 7990 m
Range accuracy: ±10 m
Firing rate: 30 pulses/minute
Power supply: 18 – 30 V DC
Weight: 11·3 kg
STATUS
The laser rangefinder programme started in February 1978 and deliveries began in the latter half of 1979. Over 2000 rangefinders and thermal imagers had been delivered by early 1984. M1 Abrams tanks were deployed in Europe for training in 1981 and two went to Switzerland for evaluation by the Swiss Army.
CONTRACTOR
Hughes Aircraft Company, PO Box 902, El Segundo, California 90245, USA.

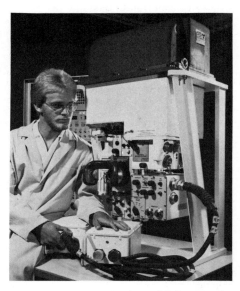

M1 Abrams tank gunner's primary sight incorporating integrated laser rangefinder and thermal imaging systems produced by Hughes

3570.193
M1 THERMAL IMAGING SYSTEM (TIS)

Hughes Aircraft Company developed and is producing the thermal imaging system (TIS) to enable the crews of the new US Army M1 Abrams tank to see through darkness, smoke or haze. It produces an image by sensing the small differences in infra-red heat radiated by objects within view and converting the detected energy into electrical signals which can be displayed on a cathode ray tube similar to a normal television picture. The image displayed is projected into the eyepiece of the M1 tank's gunner.

In addition, light gives the gunner target range information and indicates the existence of more than one target – data which is received from the M1 laser rangefinder (also a Hughes product). Ready-to-fire indication and confirmation that systems are working properly are also provided.

The thermal imaging system generates cross-hairs bore-sighted to the laser rangefinder, as well as computer symbology. This allows the gunner to operate the TIS just as he would the day sight.

The infra-red sight will be housed under armour on the M1 to help it withstand the rigours of the tank environment. However the same system can be packaged for use in lighter vehicles, due to flexibility which allows use of multiple or remote displays. This feature results from replacement of the LED direct-viewing display, commonly used in infra-red imaging systems, with a cathode ray tube.
STATUS
M1 sight development began in late 1976. The first prototype system was delivered nine months after award of the contract. The system is in full production and, as of early 1984, more than 2000 M1 laser rangefinders and thermal imagers had been delivered under contracts with the prime contractor, General Dynamics Corporation and the US Army.
CONTRACTOR
Hughes Aircraft Company, PO Box 902, El Segundo, California 90245, USA.

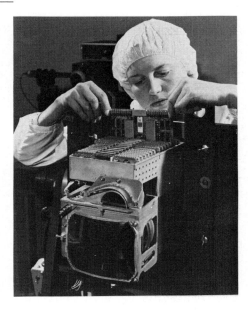

Replacing electronic circuit card of receiver unit of Hughes thermal imaging system for M1 Abrams tank

3051.193
HUGHES GROUND/VEHICULAR LASER LOCATOR DESIGNATOR AN/TVQ-2

Hughes Aircraft Company is producing the AN/TVQ-2 ground/vehicular laser locator designator (G/VLLD) for the US Army Missile Command. It is designed for use by ground troops to enable them to direct laser-guided missiles, bombs, or artillery shells on to targets designated by the ground forces.

The equipment is a lightweight, tripod-mounted unit containing a laser, a rangefinder, a telescopic sight, and a tracking unit. It is man-portable in the field by a crew of two, only one of whom is needed to operate the equipment.

The operational procedure is to use the telescopic sight to scan and search for 'hard' targets such as tanks or bunkers. When a suitable target has been identified, the laser is used to obtain range and bearing data. In co-operation with units deploying laser guided weapons to whom the target has been assigned, the laser is then used to mark the target at the desired impact point to provide guidance for the bomb, missile, or other munition. Provision is made for coding the marking laser energy in wavelength and PRF to permit weapons to differentiate between G/VLLDs.

STATUS
In production and in service with the US Army.
CONTRACTOR
Hughes Aircraft Company, PO Box 902, El Segundo, California 90245, USA.

AN/TVQ-2 ground/vehicular laser locator designator. Picture shows tripod-mounted version but combined laser designator and rangefinder can also be mounted on M113 fire support team armoured vehicles

3157.193
AN/PAQ-1 LASER TARGET DESIGNATOR

The AN/PAQ-1 laser target designator (LTD) is a laser target marker developed as a hand-held instrument for use by ground troops. In addition to its use for target designation to supporting ground attack aircraft and helicopters, the LTD is seen as suitable for such applications as a means of making their position known to rescue or supply aircraft by troops who may have been cut off by opposing ground forces.

The equipment is also compatible with the AN/TVS-5 night vision sight, and so may be used in darkness as well as by day.

The LTD consists of three easily-replaceable modules designed to withstand rough field handling. The transmitter module is a sealed unit which is dry nitrogen purged to provide a clean environment for the laser and optical elements. It can be easily detached without disturbing the optical alignment or the seal.

The electronics module houses the power supply

and control circuitry, code-set panel, external cooling air blower and ducting, heat exchanger and trigger assembly.

A quick detachable battery module completes the basic unit. It is completely sealed and shaped to function as part of the rifle stock, forming the butt end.

When the LTD is operated from an auxiliary power source, the power is supplied through the battery interface connectors, terminated in a module identical to the battery module so that the overall LTD configuration is maintained.

No technical details of the LTD have been released.
STATUS
In production, 177 sets have been delivered to the US armed forces (152 to the Army and 25 to the USAF).
CONTRACTOR
Hughes Aircraft Company, PO Box 902, El Segundo, California 90245, USA.

AN/PAQ-1 laser target designator marking target for aircraft equipped with Pave Penny laser tracker during USAF tests

3816.193
MODULAR UNIVERSAL LASER EQUIPMENT (MULE)

The MULE is based on the AN/PAQ-1 laser target designator (**3157.193**), AN/GVS-5 hand-held laser rangefinder (**3200.193**), plus tripod design concepts from the AN/TVQ-2 ground laser locator designator

Hughes modular universal laser equipment (MULE) deployed in the field

(**3051.193**). This results in significant cost of ownership savings over the life of the equipment, since a large percentage of MULE components are interchangeable, directly, with items from the other programmes. The laser transmitter and electronics from the AN/PAQ-1 are used, with a change in output optics to meet different beam characteristic needs. Rangefinder components carried over from the AN/GVS-5 include detector, video amplifier, range counter/display and low voltage power supply. MULE features built-in test circuits that monitor its own operation automatically. They warn the operator when the battery pack voltage is getting low, when the laser output falls below the laser threshold and certifies other functions. Weighing about 17 kg, the system consists of laser designator/rangefinder and stabilised tracking tripod modules. MULE can be carried readily by two-man forward observer teams over rough terrain into battle areas and set up for use in less than five minutes. For instant target ranging, an observer trains MULE on a target manually, using its telescopic sight for precise aim. He fires a laser beam and MULE measures the time it takes the beam to reach the target and return. The system's computer multiplies half the elapsed time by the speed of light and displays the range immediately on a digital readout. The tripod automatically determines and displays azimuth and elevation co-ordinates. This information, along with range, can be sent quickly in

digital form to a fire control centre via a digital communication terminal, or relayed to an artillery battery by voice channel. To illuminate targets for laser guided weapons, the observer simply trains his sights on the target and triggers the laser beam. Laser-homing missiles, projectiles (and aircraft with laser spot trackers) follow the reflected beam to the target.

Sperry has developed a new lightweight, low cost gyrocompass for use in the MULE system, and known as a north finding module (NFM). It is an automatic gyrocompass with digital readout which uses a micro-computer to determine automatically the angle from true north without pre-orientation or insertion of latitude. The NFM will provide precise azimuth data on targets and this unit is also being evaluated for use with the US Army's AN/TVQ-2 ground/vehicular laser locator designator (G/VLLD) (**3051.193**), the Hughes Firefinder radars (**2848.153** and **1976.153**), and other systems.

The NFM weighs less than 1·8 kg and provides an accuracy of two mils within two minutes and 0·3 mils within ten minutes. There are LED and digital outputs.
STATUS
MULE is in production under a contract for 131 systems for the US Marine Corps.
CONTRACTOR
Hughes Aircraft Company, PO Box 902, El Segundo, California 90245, USA.

3054.053
LASER OPTICAL RANGING AND DESIGNATION SYSTEM (LORADS)

LORADS was originally designed to fulfil the requirement for a one-man portable rangefinder and designator system. The equipment is used primarily by forward observers for indirect fire control and marking of targets for laser seeking weapons. With a

range capability of up to 20 km and a resolution of 5 metres, LORADS can range to or designate any ground target encountered on the battlefield. It is effective against both moving and stationary targets and is compatible with most existing weapon systems.

LORADS consists of a laser designator, range receiver, control panel, tracking mount and tripod.

The control panel has provisions for selectable PRF codes, built-in-test and remote operation up to five km. The tracking mount is a heavy-duty design with exceptionally smooth tracking characteristics. The tripod is all terrain with a standard low silhouette. Range readout is in the eyepiece.

CHARACTERISTICS
Type: Nd:YAG
Wavelength: 1·064 μm
Pulse width: 20 ±5 ns
Output energy: 100 mJoules
Detector: Silicon avalanche photodiode
Maximum range: 20 km
Range accuracy: 5 m

Telescope
Magnification: ×7
Field of view: 7°
STATUS
In production.
CONTRACTOR
International Laser Systems Inc, 3404 N Orange Blossom Trail, Orlando, Florida 32804, USA.

LRR-103 artillery laser rangefinder in tripod-mounted configuration

3823.093
MCTNS MAN-PORTABLE COMMON THERMAL NIGHT SIGHTS

Under US Army sponsorship, American manufacturers have evolved a range of basic elements for night sight equipments used with man-portable weapon systems, such as TOW and Dragon. This system of modular equipment is formally known as the man-portable common thermal night sights family of units. Texas Instruments has designed the basic receiver, based on common modules.

Man-portable common modules are assembled into a chassis to become the basic man-portable receiver. This receiver provides the essential FLIR functions for all of the man-portable night sight equipments.

The AN/TAS-4 sight (**3824.193**) is used on the TOW weapon system and the ground/vehicular laser locator designator (G/VLLD) (**3051.193**) system. For these applications, the basic receiver is inserted into a combination case, a focal telescope, and mount. The basic receiver is inverted and used with a different case (afocal telescope) and mount to provide an AN/TAS-5 (Dragon) night sight (**3825.193**). With its optical display removed, the basic receiver is used with an afocal telescope, cover, mount, and bi-ocular/image intensifier to provide an AN/TAS-6 night observation device, long range (NODLR) (**3826.193**).

The FLIR common modules are the foundation of the commonality concept exemplified by the man-portable sights, but they are also applicable to many other uses for army, air force and navy systems and equipment. The common modules are assembled into the receiver to convert an image formed in the infra-red (IR) spectral band into a visible image displayed to the operator. The modules are:

Mechanical scanner: collects IR energy emitted from a scene or object, and displays visible energy from the LED array to the operator.

IR imager: focuses energy collected by the scanner and transfers it to the detector/dewar module.

Detector dewar: detects IR energy from the image and processes the signals into electronic energy for the amplifiers. This is a 60-element array, 120 or 180 element arrays being available for other applications.

Preamplifiers/postamplifiers: boost the low level electrical signals from the detector array to a level sufficient to drive the LEDs.

LED array: changes the amplified detector signals into a visible image.

Visual collimator: projects the light from the LED display to the operator.

Video auxiliary control: provides the interface function between the controls and the postamplifiers for such functions as brightness and contrast.

30 Hz scan/interface: provides electronic control for the scanner.

Among the non-man-portable sight applications is the AN/VGS-2 tank thermal sight for the M60 MBT which is now in series production by Texas Instruments; for the USN, the AN/AAS-36 IR detecting set uses TI IR technology, as does the USAF's AN/AAQ-9 FLIR equipment. (Both of the latter are airborne equipments).

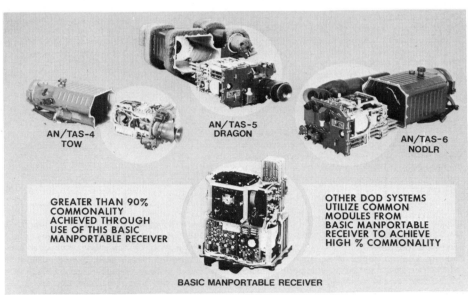

Examples of US Army's thermal imaging night sights and range of man-portable common modules employed in forming these equipments (above and below)

STATUS
Series production by at least two sources (see below) and probably licensed overseas. In February 1983, a contract worth over $24 million was awarded to Kollsman for 300 SU-108 man-portable receivers and 1000 AN/TAS-4 sights for the US Army. Delivery commenced in early 1984.

CONTRACTORS
Texas Instruments Inc, Electro-Optical Division, PO Box 226015, Dallas, Texas 75266, USA. Designers and main contractor.

Kollsman Instrument Company, Daniel Webster Highway South, Merrimack, New Hampshire 03054, USA. Second source manufacturer.

3824.193

AN/TAS-4 TOW NIGHT SIGHT

The AN/TAS-4 night sight provides a night operating capability for the TOW weapon system. The night sight can be rapidly mounted on and removed from the TOW weapon system by simple movement of the interface locking handle. This quick mount/dismount capability allows the soldier to adapt his TOW weapon system to night and degraded visibility conditions rapidly and without modification to existing hardware. The sight is based on the basic man-portable IR receiver (see **3823.093**, US Army designation SU-108/TAS).

A gas bottle provides cryogenic cooling of the detector. The use of compressed air eliminates hazards associated with more exotic coolants. This bottle will provide two hours of system operation and can be replaced rapidly.

System electrical power is provided by a rechargeable battery package which will power the night sight for two hours and is also quickly replaceable. Combining the consumable elements of the AN/TAS-4 into small self-contained, replenishable components allows the night sight to be truly man-portable and virtually self-contained within a weight of less than 7·2 kg.

The AN/TAS-4 when mounted, provides an additional eyeport for the gunner to detect, identify, track and classify targets directly. Since the night sight detects heat energy emissions, it does not depend upon visible light and can 'see' in degraded visual conditions such as smoke, haze, darkness, camouflage, and foliage.

The AN/TAS-4 has been designed and tested to meet the environments encountered by the TOW weapon system and places no special operating constraints upon the use of the TOW.

DEVELOPMENT

Texas Instruments received an Engineering Development Programme (Phase 1) contract from the Night Vision Laboratory in 1973, to provide a FLIR for the TOW weapon system. This equipment was to extend the operating capability of the system to the night environment. Using the 'common-module concept' (developed by TI in conjunction with the Department of Defense), a lightweight (man-portable) self-contained far IR device was developed. Phase 1 of the programme culminated in a Research Development Acceptance Test in which the TI system was field tested in competition. Success in these tests resulted in the Phase II contract award to TI in 1975.

In 1981, Texas Instruments was placed under contract by the US Army to develop improved operational capabilities to accommodate the TOW 2 missile system. This initially involved developing the revisions necessary to provide the night sight to the TOW 2 missile. A subsequent improvement was the elimination of the gas bottle cooling through use of a closed cycle cooler. This improvement has been included in the same configuration. The improved night sight, designated AN/TAS-4A, is in production with Texas Instruments the sole supplier.

STATUS

Production. In February 1983, Kollsman was awarded a $24 million contract by the US Army for the production of almost 1000 AN/TAS-4 sights and over 300 SU-108 receivers. Delivery commenced early 1984.

CONTRACTORS

Texas Instruments Inc, Electro-Optical Division, PO Box 226015, Dallas, Texas 75266, USA.

Kollsman Instrument Company, Daniel Webster Highway South, Merrimack, New Hampshire 03054, USA.

AN/TAS-4A night sight for TOW 2 missile system

3825.193

AN/TAS-5 DRAGON NIGHT SIGHT

The AN/TAS-5 Dragon night sight provides night operating capability for the Dragon weapon system. The night sight can be rapidly mounted on and removed from the missile launch tube. An IR missile tracker is an integral part of the night sight. The equipment is based on the basic man-portable IR receiver (**3823.093**) (US Army designation SU-108/TAS); in this application it is inverted from its usual position, see below.

The night sight AN/TAS-4 gas bottle is located at the centre, and the integral weapon system tracker at the left. To provide the weapon gunner with access to the eyepiece, the basic man-portable receiver is mounted in an inverted position.

Boresighting the AN/TAS-5 in the field is not necessary, since this operation is performed at the depot or factory level. After the weapon is fired, the night sight/weapon system tracker is removed from the launch tube and used on the next missile to be fired.

STATUS

Production.

CONTRACTORS

Texas Instruments Inc, Electro-Optical Division, PO Box 226015, Dallas, Texas 75266, USA.

McDonnell Douglas Astronautics Co, Titusville Division, State Highway 405, Titusville, Florida 32780, USA.

AN/TAS-5 Dragon night sight

3826.193

AN/TAS-6 (AN/UAS-11) NIGHT OBSERVATION DEVICE, LONG RANGE

The AN/TAS-6 night observation device, long range (NODLR) provides night observation post capability to the soldier on the battlefield. This night sight is provided with a tripod, with no need for tools for mounting and dismounting. When used in conjunction with the AN/GVS-5 hand-held laser rangefinder (**3200.193**) this night sight can provide information to supporting artillery in degraded battlefield conditions. The complete system is known as the AN/UAS-11.

The AN/TAS-6, in conjunction with its tripod, the AN/GVS-5 hand-held laser rangefinder, and a boresight mechanism, can provide a two-man team with a versatile man-portable forward observation post, which allows operating capabilities in the presence of degraded conditions such as smoke, haze, darkness, camouflage, and foliage.

The AN/TAS-6 is based on the basic man-portable IR receiver (**3823.093**) and uses the same compressed air gas bottle and rechargeable battery pack as the other man-portable systems (AN/TAS-4, AN/TAS-5). This allows the use of the same logistics supply facilities, thereby increasing support flexibility.

The AN/TAS-6 and the AN/GVS-5, are mounted together with the AN/TAS-6 at the left. The bi-ocular eyepiece is covered with a dual eye shroud which provides visual security for the display. This display is green in colour and is produced by an image intensifier tube.

STATUS

Production.

CONTRACTORS

Texas Instruments Inc, Electro-Optical Division, PO Box 226015, Dallas, Texas 75266, USA. AN/TAS-6.

RCA Automated Systems, Burlington, Massachusetts, USA. AN/GVS-5.

4240.183

TAS TRACKING ADJUNCT SYSTEM (HAWK)

The Tracking Adjunct System (TAS) is an electro-optical tracking system developed as a product improvement for the Hawk surface-to-air missile (**4177.131**) air defence fire control system. It was derived from the TISEO (target identification system, electro-optical) equipment (**1806.363**) which is currently in production and being used by the USAF and a number of foreign countries. TAS provides a passive tracking capability to the Hawk fire control system radar with remote real-time video presentation. It is designed as a complement to the tracking radar. Optical tracking can be coincident or independent of the radar line-of-sight. Manual, automatic acquisition and tracking, rate memory and preferential illumination are key features of the system.

The system also enhances the tracking radar by providing facilities for positive identification, threat assessment, kill assessment, spectre recognition, tracking with minimum doppler, silent tracking and independent tracking. These capabilities represent a positive advantage in a countermeasures environment. More details of the Improved Hawk missile system and its relationship with TAS, along with illustrations of items of TAS hardware, will be found in the entry for that system (**4177.131**) in the Systems Section of this volume. Additional information on the basic TISEO equipment is contained in the Electro-Optical (Air) pages of this section, which follow.

STATUS

Development of the Tracking Adjunct System began

in 1976 and production for the US Army and Marine Corps was started in March 1980. The system is available as a Phase II product improvement for foreign operators of the Hawk missile system.

CONTRACTOR

Northrop Corporation, Electro-Mechanical Division, 500 East Orangethorpe Avenue, Anaheim, California 92801, USA.

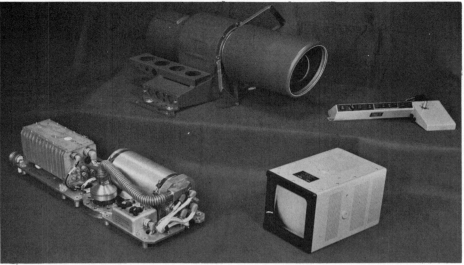

TAS sensor unit mounted with associated electronics unit on Hawk high power illuminator radar, between the two dishes

Hardware of Northrop Tracking Adjunct System used with Hawk surface-to-air missile system

---

5718.193
MINI ELECTRO-OPTICAL IMAGING SYSTEM

This device is for either coastal/border surveillance or for forward control/battle management. It can be used in a fixed ground installation, on a helicopter mast mount, in an RPV or piloted aircraft (side or forward looking). It is intended to complement radar by evaluating targets already detected or to detect 'soft' targets.

The imaging system has a high acquisition rate and

is capable of 1 metre resolution at a range of 15 km. When used with a large aperture F/1 lens, it operates at maximum at light levels equivalent to twilight under overcast skies with visibility as poor as 1 km, or at full moonlight levels with clear skies. A 2·048 element solid-state image detector is used with a variety of lenses from 18 to 70 cm lengths.

CONTRACTOR

Litton Industries, 10 Maguire Road, Lexington, Massachusetts 012173, USA.

Mini electro-optical imaging system

5721.193
SECO ELECTRO-OPTICAL SYSTEMS

The Standard Equipment Company (SECO) produces a wide range of laser, thermal imaging and electro-optical devices for battlefield use. Brief details of the company's systems are as follows:

AIM-1 Infra-red Mini-designator

This is a very small laser designator which provides designation and aiming at ranges up to 800 metres under night conditions. It has an inherent light halo visible to the operator only, to assist in identifying the target, and is designed for boresighting with weapons such as rifles, machine guns, short-range anti-tank missiles, revolvers and pistols by means of elevation and deflection drums.

CHARACTERISTICS

Radiated power: 8 mW
Dimensions: 35 × 42 × 53 mm
Weight: 0·264 kg

LRF-1 Laser Rangefinder

This is a rangefinder for use by artillery forward observers, etc, and is the size of a standard 7 × 50 binocular. It is designed for hand-holding and uses a miniaturised Q-switched Nd-YAG laser transmitter. A four-digit range LED display is provided in the eyepiece.

CHARACTERISTICS

Laser wavelength: 1064 microns
Beamwidth: 1·5 mrad
Range: 8995 m
Accuracy: ± 5 m
Dimensions: 200 × 200 × 90 mm
Weight: 2 kg

Sharp Ray S-8 Target Illuminator

Sharp Ray S-8 is a visible or infra-red illuminator for fast aiming of weapons by spotting the target. It is a self-powered designator which is mounted on the

AIM-1 infra-red mini designator

weapon, being aligned together with it, and is designed for boresighting on rifles, sub-machine guns and shotguns by means of elevation and deflection drums.

SECO Vision 220

This is a portable thermal imaging system comprising an infra-red thermal viewer and a video interface unit. It features four-stage thermo-electric cooling and provides real-time two dimensional images to a standard TV or composite video in 525 or 625 lines.

AD-NDV-2 (AN/VVS-2) Night Vision Driver's Viewer

This is a multi-vehicle passive night vision surveillance and reconnaissance sight which can be mounted in most types of armoured vehicles. It includes a 25 mm second-generation image intensifier with a large diameter binocular display.

CHARACTERISTICS

Magnification: ×1
Field of view: 44° horizontal; 35° vertical
Field coverage: 135° horizontal; 35° vertical

V-NOD-2 Night Observation Device

The V-NOD-2 is a tripod-mounted night vision sight used for long-range surveillance. It uses a 25 mm

micro-channel plate image intensifier tube to allow viewing during the twilight hours of dawn and dusk such that a man can be distinguished at ranges in excess of 1000 metres in light levels of 10^{-3} lux. A laser rangefinder can be supplied as an optional extra.

CHARACTERISTICS

Magnification (optical): × 9·4
Field of view: 5·6°
Performance: At 10^{-3} lux a man can be distinguished at more than 100 metres, a Jeep at more than 1700 metres and a tank at 4000 metres

G2-4 Passive Binocular

The G2-4 is a hand-held passive binocular sight for night observation and long-range viewing. With its high intensity second-generation image intensifier tube the instrument is capable of detecting a man at nearly 1000 metres.

AN/PVS-4 Starlight Scope

This is a second-generation passive night vision sight using a 25 mm micro-channel plate inverter intensifier tube. The sight is intended to be attached

G2-4 passive binocular sight

to a variety of different weapons or may be hand-held for night reconnaissance. An adjustable internally protected reticle and interchangeable reticle patterns allow the sight to be boresighted to various weapons without having to move the sight.

CHARACTERISTICS
Magnification: × 3·7
Field of view: 14·5°
Focus range: 25 m – ∞

AN/TVS-5 Crew Served Weapon Sight

This is a similar equipment to the AN/PVS-4 and is a lightweight passive night vision sight which can be attached to a variety of weapons or can be tripod-mounted for night reconnaissance.

CHARACTERISTICS
Magnification: × 6·2
Field of view: 9°
Focus range: 25 m – ∞

M1A1 Collimator

The M1A1 collimator is used as an infinity reference by artillery gunners to replace aiming posts and lights. It employs a tritium activated light source which requires no batteries or incandescent lamps.

CONTRACTOR
Standard Equipment Company, 9240 No. 107th Street, PO Box 23060, Milwaukee, Wisconsin 53224, USA.

YUGOSLAVIA

3581.093
RLD HAND-HELD LASER RANGEFINDER

The RLD hand-held laser rangefinder can also be goniometer- and/or tripod-mounted, and is intended for forward artillery observation, anti-tank weapons and for infantry use. In use, the operator centres the cross-hair on the target through the right-hand ocular. By pressing the trigger button the laser is fired and the distance is displayed in the left-hand ocular. The display also has two indicator lamps: one shows if there is more than one target in the laser beam; and the other shows the existence of targets within the blocked range. The display is switched off automatically five seconds after laser firing. Continuously adjustable minimum range between 200 and 3000 metres permits selection between various targets.

CHARACTERISTICS
Laser type: Nd-YAG
Peak power: 0·5 – 1 MW
Beam divergence: <1 mrad
Pulse rate: 30/minute
Range (minimum/max): 150/10 000 m
Accuracy: ±5 m
Resolution: Better than 40 m
Blocking: Continuous to 3000 m
Detector: Silicon avalanche diode
Receiver field of view: Approx 1 mrad
Telescope
Magnification: ×7
Field of view: 7°
Eyepiece adjustment: ±5 dioptres
Power supply: 12 V DC
Weight: Approx 2 kg

Iskra RLD hand-held laser rangefinder

STATUS
Production.
CONTRACTOR
Iskra, Centre za Elektrooptiko, Ljublijana, Yugoslavia.

3582.193
T-LMD-2 AND -3 TANK LASER RANGEFINDERS

The T-LMD-2 and -3 laser rangefinders were specially designed for Soviet T-type battle tanks (T-34, T-54, T-55 and T-62 for the -2 version, and T-54, T-55, T-62 and T-72 for the -3), and considerably enhance the fire control capability of these vehicles. The equipments consist of a single unit.

The optical periscope sight is integrated in the laser which is powered from the tank battery. The T-LMD-2 or -3 is mounted in the commander's cupola and the existing commander's periscope is removed from its pivot suspension and replaced by the laser. Connection of a suitable power supply is the only other change necessary. A remote display for the gunner is provided.

CHARACTERISTICS
Laser: Nd-YAG
Max range: Up to 20 000 m, depending upon weather conditions and target.

Range accuracy: ±5 m (-2 version); ±7 m (-3 version)
Radial resolution: 30 m
Number of targets measured: 2
Number of targets displayed: 1
Blocking range: Continuous 200 – 3000 m
Pulse rate: 30/minute
Telescope
Magnification: ×7
Field of view: 5°
Eyepiece adjustment: ±5 dioptres
Power supply: 18 – 29 V DC, approx 20 W
Computer output: BCD code
Weight: Approx 10 kg
CONTRACTOR
Iskra, Centre za Elektrooptiko, Ljublijana, Yugoslavia.

Iskra T-LMD-2 integrated laser rangefinder for tanks

5723.193
SUVOA ARTILLERY FIRE CONTROL SYSTEM

SUVOA is a tripod-mounted optical fire control system for use with coastal or field gun batteries. It is designed to give range to the target from 1000 to 50 000 metres, depending upon the altitude of the observation post. Information on ranges is transmitted to the gun by a transmission system. A radar equipment is co-sited with the instrument in

order to provide range and bearing information in poor visibility or by night.

CHARACTERISTICS
Range: 1000 – 50 000 m
Accuracy: 50 m up to 10 000 m; 200 m up to 20 000 m; 3% up to 50 000 m
Measuring telescope
Magnification: × 18
Field of view: 4°

Observation telescope
Magnification: Variable from ×3 to ×10
Field of view: Variable from 6 – 20°
CONTRACTOR
Federal Directorate of Supply and Procurement, PO Box 308, Knez Mihailova 6, Beograd, Yugoslavia.

5724.193
M61 STEREOSCOPIC RANGEFINDER

The M61 rangefinder is an optical instrument used on artillery observation posts to measure ranges, angles and variation of shot, and for general reconnaissance of the battlefield. It is tripod-mounted and is provided with movable indexes to measure ranges from 400 to 16 000 metres. A co-ordinate computer is normally

combined with the instrument to calculate the X and Y co-ordinates.

CHARACTERISTICS
Magnification: ×14
Inlet pupil diameter: 56 mm; 30 mm with visor for day measuring
Exit pupil diameter: 2·1 mm for day measuring; 4 mm for twilight

Field of view: 4·5° at 1000 m
Weight: 14·5 kg for basic instrument; 73 kg including tripod, computer, night vision accessories and carrying boxes
CONTRACTOR
Federal Directorate of Supply and Procurement, PO Box 308, Knez Mihailova 6, Beograd, Yugoslavia.

3583.193
ALD-M2 LIGHTWEIGHT LASER RANGEFINDER

The ALD-M2 lightweight laser rangefinder provides measurements of range, azimuth, and elevation to targets, and can be used by forward observers for the detection and observation of targets, and to determine the positions of such targets. It can be operated independently or as a component part of a fire control system, and can be mounted on vehicles, night observation devices, weapons, or on its own tripod.

The complete equipment consists of the laser rangefinder with a goniometer, tripod, rechargeable batteries, cables, and transport box. The upper part of the rangefinder is equipped with a coarse sight for rapid aiming at targets that appear only briefly.

CHARACTERISTICS
Laser: Nd-YAG
Wavelength: 1·06 micron
Peak power: 1 – 2 MW
Output beamwidth: Approx 0·7 mrad
Receiver: Silicon avalanche diode

Receiver field of view: 0·9 mrad
Range (minimum/max): 200/20 000 m
Range accuracy: ±5 m
Resolution: Better than 30 m
Pulse rate: 30/minute
Number of measured targets: 2
Number of displayed targets: 2
Blocking: Continuous 200 – 3000 m
Telescope
Field of view: 7°
Magnification: ×8

Eyepiece adjustment: ±5 dioptres
Computer output: BCD
Power supply: 22 – 28 V DC
Weight: Approx 12 kg

CONTRACTOR
Iskra, Centre za Elektrooptiko, Ljubljana, Yugoslavia.

Iskra ALD-M2 artillery laser rangefinder

4715.193
SPDR SIGHTING DEVICES
In addition to the equipment described above, the Yugoslavian Federal Directorate of Supply and Procurement produces sighting devices for various weapons. Brief details of some of these are given below.

Optical Sight ON-M76
This sight is intended for sighting of single stationary, moving, open or camouflaged targets when firing with the M76 7·9 mm rifle, both by day and night. Magnification is ×4, field of view is 5·17 degrees and detection range of an IR source is over 300 metres.

Optical Sighting Device ON-M80
The ON-M80 is used for sighting on targets when firing the RB-44mm M-80 hand launcher, and also for detecting the sources of IR radiation. Magnification is ×3, field of view is 12 degrees and detection of IR source is over 300 metres.

Sighting Device NSB-4A
The NSB-4A is used to sight moving and stationary targets for the M71 128 mm light rocket launcher. Sighting is performed through a right angle telescope. Field of view of the instrument is 150 mil and magnification is ×3·7.

Sighting Device NSB-4B
The NSB-4B serves to sight targets when firing the M75 120 mm light mortar in both day and night conditions. The instrument can also be used with mortars of other calibres. Magnification is ×1·82 and field of view is 8 degrees.

M79 Sighting Device
An optical firing sight for the M79 90 mm hand rocket launcher is available. It can be used both by day and night, has a magnification of ×4 and a field of view of 10 degrees.

Periscope Aiming Circle PB-1 and PB-2
The Periscope Aiming Circle PB-1 and PB-2 are optical instruments used for the measurement of horizontal and vertical angles, magnetic azimuths and ranges. It is normally used on observation posts and firing positions of artillery and mortar units for the correction of fire.

CONTRACTOR
Federal Directorate of Supply and Procurement, PO Box 308, Knez Mihailova 6, Beograd, Yugoslavia.

ELECTRO-OPTICAL EQUIPMENT (SEA)

DENMARK

3857.293
TYPE 771 LOW LIGHT TV CAMERA

The Type 771 low light-level television camera was developed under a Royal Danish Navy contract. It is designed to conform to DEF 133N2 and to be used in conjunction with a television tracking system for automatic fire control applications. A filter wheel permits use over a wide range of ambient lighting conditions, the extremes of attenuation provided being from zero to 10^6. The sensor employed is an ISIT (intensified silicon intensifier target) tube which enables useful pictures to be obtained down to face-plate illumination levels of 5×10^{-4} lux. Lenses are selected to meet user requirements, as are the housings. A window with conductive coating and a washer/wiper are incorporated for protection.

CHARACTERISTICS
Sensor: RCA 4849H, EEV P8065, or Westinghouse WX 32890

Limiting resolution: 550 lines
Scanning: 625 lines 50 Hz 2:1 interlaced CCIR or 525 lines 60 Hz 2:1 interlaced EIA
Black level control: Automatic
AGC amplifier: Normal range 10 dB, max 20 dB
Weight: 11 kg camera with filter wheel; 22 kg lens with housing
STATUS
'Willesmoes' class fast patrol boats of the Royal Danish Navy are equipped with fire control systems that incorporate the Type 771 camera in a target tracking facility and this camera is also known to have been associated with the Sperry Sapphire naval FCS.
CONTRACTOR
JAI (Jorgen Andersen Ingeniorfirma AS), Produktionsvej 1, 2600 Glostrup, Copenhagen, Denmark.

JAI Type 771 low light TV camera

FRANCE

3064.293
FRENCH NAVAL OPTO-ELECTRONIC SYSTEMS

For the French Navy, opto-electronic systems are seen as providing valuable assistance to the present systems for detection, tracking, guidance, display and thermal imaging, and DTCN (the Technical Department for Naval Construction) is energetically continuing R & D along several lines. These include the use of lasers for telemetry, guidance, aiming, illumination, and communications; passive infra-red for guidance, tracking, detection, thermal imaging, and surveillance. Light intensification and low light-level television techniques are being developed and manufactured, as are the uses of thermal imaging for surveillance, target designation, and guidance.

Laser programmes in progress for DTCN consist of rangefinders for naval fire control systems, and two projects concerned with laser tracking and guidance.
LASER RANGEFINDER
The laser rangefinder for ships is designed as a compact and high data rate unit for installation on all old and new rangefinding turrets to provide accurate range information which can be used directly by the gunnery control computer under the supervision of a single operator at the gun fire control console. A fleet-compatible prototype of this laser rangefinder has been built by Compagnie Générale d'Electricité to STCAN specifications. TAON (télémétrie d'artillerie optronique pour navire) equipment is designed for TTAC remote aiming turrets. Its main functions are ranging of air targets and shore targets. Rangefinding is possible between 1·5 and 16 km to an accuracy of ±5 metres. Beamwidth is one milliradian and pulse rate 30 pulses/second. The equipment weighs about 15 kg.
IR RADAR (IRDAR)
DTCN is already considering using a 10·6 micron (ie infra-red) laser source and a heterodyne receiver. This would be a pulse doppler laser radar operating in the infra-red. Although the source and receiver are still at the design stage, the experimental prototype IRDAR equipment was delivered to DTCN by SAT for tests in late 1980 as an exploratory development.

Passive infra-red developments pursued by DTCN include the VAMPIR system for surveillance and detection, and PIRANA for guidance and tracking. The decision to adopt both these equipments for French Navy anti-aircraft corvettes was taken at the beginning of 1980. The final versions are being fitted to the corvettes and were due to be operational in 1984.
INFRA-RED SURVEILLANCE (VAMPIR)
The designation VAMPIR derives from the French for infra-red panoramic air-sea surveillance: veille air mer panoramique infra-rouge. It is a low field and low altitude panoramic detection system intended for the detection of anti-ship missiles at ranges of 10 km or more, even during radar silence (see entry **4106.293**).

A submersible optronic system used in mine disposal operations

INFRA-RED TRACKING (PIRANA)
The PIRANA (pointeur infra-rouge pour l'artillerie navale) is an infra-red aiming unit for naval guns, designed by STCAN and constructed by SAT. The dimensions specified permit simple mounting on existing French Navy gun fire control radars. Its function is to permit these radars to continue accurate tracking at low elevation angles when reflection from the sea surface might degrade radar tracking. This also allows for continued tracking in the face of ECM or under radar silence. The field of view is about 1°, operating wavelength four microns, and the tracking range against a head-on air target is quoted as more than 10 km.

Three versions of PIRANA have evolved, the first two of which were experimental trials equipments, leading to PIRANA 3 which is in production (see entry **3427.293**).
VOLCAN
VOLCAN (viseur optronique leger pour conduite d'arme navale) is an exploratory infra-red bi-spectral sensor for naval surveillance and/or fire control applications. The experimental prototype was built for DTCN by SAGEM, aided by SAT, CILAS, CSEE and SOFRETEC who provided the optronic sensors.

The equipment has been designed to be suitable for mounting on ships of any size, and with sensors weighs about 80 kg. It takes the form of a small turret, within which are housed eight and twelve micron wavelength infra-red cameras, a one-inch vidicon television camera, and a laser rangefinder. The last of these is capable of pulse rates of 2 to 20 Hz using a YAG laser. The equipment also includes an automatic tracking system for night and day optical surveillance, tracking of air targets, aircraft and missile control, particularly low-altitude weapons. The VOLCAN sight includes its own gyroscopic stabilisation.
CONDOR
CONDOR is the French acronym for radar target designation optronic night camera, and its function is to replace turret operators, to enable a target to be designated and identified, and enable a laser to be laid on. In addition, and in the context of comprehensive integration with radar, it can provide sighting facilities or automatic tracking in the event of radar failure, radar silence, loss of track or loss of accuracy at low elevation.

DTCN has designed the operational version of CONDOR. Now in production by SINTRA, it is a TV camera with two different optical paths: one for daylight, a vidicon, and for night use (ISIT). These cameras are to equip all the new French Navy frigates, corvettes and Avisos.

In addition to these lines of research, DTCN is studying potential applications for light amplification and image intensification techniques such as night surveillance from ships and commando operations.
IR PERISCOPE
To increase the capabilities of conventional submarine periscopes, STCAN has designed and is producing a new periscope that permits night vision. PIVAIR (périscope intégré de veille à infra-rouge) has been built by SAGEM in collaboration with SOPELEM to STCAN specifications and is fitted to all new type French Navy submarines and will be retrofitted to others. It provides optical surveillance by night or day, and there is two-axis stabilisation of the optical and IR channels. The former channel provides magnifications of ×1·5 and ×6 and the IR field of view is –3 × 6°. The operating wavelength of PIVAIR is eight to twelve microns.

Thermal imaging by infra-red has appreciable potential, especially where hot-spots and temperature contrasts can be expected, and there is considerable interest in this area of opto-electronics also. A development contract awarded to SAGEM includes a SAT thermal camera operating in the eight to twelve microns band with parallel scanning for target detection over 360° in azimuth in the surveillance mode and target identification in the thermal imaging mode.

3427.293
PIRANA INFRA-RED TRACKER

The PIRANA infra-red tracker has been developed for use on combined electro-optical naval fire control equipments such as the CSEE Totem (**3424.293**), in which it is employed with television and a laser

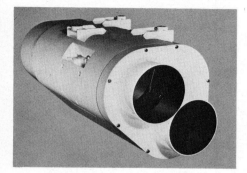

SAT PIRANA III, operational version, IR tracking system (without turret)

rangefinder for the direction of anti-aircraft weapons, or for use on its own as an ancillary to autonomous weapons. The equipment provides a means of passive search, acquisition and target tracking, especially useful in low-altitude low elevation engagements. It has two IR channels for simultaneous tracking at two different wavelengths.

The configuration of the PIRANA equipment can be seen from the nearby illustration and it will be carried on one side of the Totem E-O director unit. The main modules of the infra-red unit are the receiver optical assembly, analysis section, IR detector, cooling, and tracking electronics module. Power supply unit and control panel are located below deck.

CHARACTERISTICS
Optical aperture: 170 mm
Field of view: ±8 mrad
Wavelength: 4 – 5 and 8 – 12 micron bands
Range: 10 – 20 km, depending on type of target
Cooling: Joule Thomson cycle to about 80° K
Dimensions: 75 × 41 × 41 cm
Weight: 70 kg
Power supply: 115 V 400 Hz 1 kVA

DEVELOPMENT
Development was initiated in collaboration with the French Naval authorities in the late 1960s and early 1970s. (See entry **3064.293** at the start of this section for further historical details on this and related naval opto-electronic projects.)
STATUS
Development of the PIRANA I, for the tracking of aircraft targets, has been completed and prototypes of a PIRANA II were given experimental tests during 1977. The latter version has a missile tracking capability in addition to aircraft targets. Experience with the PIRANA I and II trials led to the definition of the PIRANA III version which is now operational with the French Navy. This version is a bi-spectral equipment with two channels working simultaneously together with appropriate signal processing to achieve minimal sensitivity to jamming and environmental noise.
CONTRACTOR
SAT (Société Anonyme de Télécommunications), 41 rue Cantagrel, 75624 Paris Cedex 13, France.

4106.293
VAMPIR SURVEILLANCE EQUIPMENT

VAMPIR (veille air mer panoramique infra-rouge) is a passive infra-red naval surveillance equipment which provides for surveillance and search of both air and surface targets. It is also capable of target designation to either radar or optronic fire control/director systems or equipment.

The configuration of the equipment consists of a cylindrical housing carried on a vertically stabilised mount which is designed to be fixed on the ship's superstructure in a high position to ensure maximum range and freedom from obstruction. Stabilisation of the housing automatically compensates against ship motion, while the optical head rotates at a rate of about 60 rpm to provide all-round scanning of the horizon. The stabilisation horizontal datum can be adjusted up to a maximum elevation of +20°. The equipment is a bi-spectral device operating in two distinct IR bands, thus achieving a very low false alarm rate in the presence of environmental noise. The two separate channels also enable target detection in a variety of meteorological conditions. Signal processing is performed by a sub-system provided by CSEE.

CHARACTERISTICS
Wavelength: 4 – 5 and 8 – 13 micron (simultaneous channels)
Field of view: 360° × 0–20° elevation
Detection range: At least 10 km for frontal attack by missile or aircraft
Target designation accuracy: 1 mrd in elevation and bearing
Sensor cooling: Joule Thomson cycle to about 80° K
Dimensions of stabilised unit: 125 × 60 cm diameter
Rotation rate: 60 rpm
Weight: 400 kg
Power: 115 V 400 Hz 300 VA
STATUS
In production and being fitted to French Navy corvettes.
CONTRACTOR
SAT (Société Anonyme de Télécommunications), 41 rue Cantagrel, 75624 Paris Cedex 13, France.

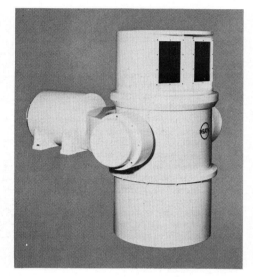

SAT VAMPIR showing stabilised housing for mounting high on ship's superstructure and upper, rotating portion containing bi-spectral sensor units. It provides continuous passive surveillance facilities

---

3566.293
TRS 906 LIGHTWEIGHT ELECTRO-OPTICAL DIRECTOR

This equipment is a line-of-sight stabilised E-O director designed for use aboard warships for surveillance, target indication, fire control or missile guidance purposes.

It comprises a two-axis director stabilised by rate gyros, and a servo control box. The director consists of a fixed pedestal in which is centred a bearing rotating unit which supports the elevation axle actuator. The elevation axle is fitted at both ends with flanges to provide the mechanical interface with the E-O sensor units.

The director is fitted with a joystick, and with a collimated grid sight for local control. The director can be controlled by:
(1) a deck operator, using the joystick
(2) a remote control unit
(3) the elevation and bearing errors signals generated by the E-O equipment.

Slewing speeds and accelerations are 3 rad/s and 7 rad/s² in bearing and 1 rad/s and 3 rad/s² in elevation.

Slewing time for 180° is 1·8 s in bearing. Pointing stability is better than 0·2 mrad rms. Data take-off accuracy is 0·5 mrad peak.

A variety of options exist for using various sensor combinations; in addition to television trackers, infra-red automatic tracking with laser rangefinding or a K-band (millimetric waveband) radar can be employed (see Canopus fire control system **3102.281**).
CHARACTERISTICS
Director (fitted with a TV camera)
Height: 0·77 m
Rotation diameter: 0·8 m
Weight: 120 kg
Servo control box: 0·86 × 0·6 × 0·3 m
Weight: 80 kg
STATUS
In production.
CONTRACTOR
Thomson-CSF, Division Systèmes, Défense et Contrôle, 40 rue Grange Dame Rose, BP34, 92360 Meudon-la-Foret, France.

TRS 906 lightweight naval director with TV and IR cameras

4254.293
TANTALE DIRECTOR TURRET

The Tantale turret is a light support turret, mobile in elevation and bearing, stabilised by an independent gyrometric unit and capable of carrying and aiming the fitted equipment. When used with a control panel located in the operations room, it may be used as a telecommunications antenna support or a high definition optronics detector support (laser, TV, IR).

The Tantale turret is a remote control support system, consisting of, from the bottom upwards: a base mounting on the deck of the vessel; the bearing moving part; an elevation rotating shaft, on which are mounted platforms (two vertical, one horizontal if required) designed to carry the fitted equipment (antenna, detectors, missiles), and the gyro unit. The Tantale turret may be aimed externally (target designation reception), by automatic tracking by an

on-board detector (TV, IR), or by manual control from the operating control panel. The turret is also used as a mounting for a short-range light missile launcher system.
CHARACTERISTICS
Slewing: No bearing limit
Elevation: -30 to +85°
Max speed: 1·5 rad/s for elevation and bearing
Max acceleration: 2 rad/s² for elevation and bearing

Max load: 200 kg or inertia of 80 m²/kg
TV tracking accuracy (on airborne target): 2' peak
Weight: 200 kg (with equipment)
Height: 825 mm
STATUS
Production.

CONTRACTOR
CSEE (Compagnie de Signaux et d'Entreprises
Electriques), 17 place Etienne Pernet, 75738 Paris
Cedex 15, France.

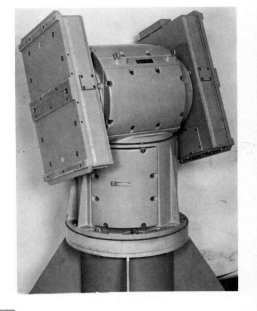

CSEE Tantale director turret (without sensors)

3425.293
PANDA MK2 OPTICAL DIRECTOR
This is a naval optical director equipment capable of
use for weapon control, air and surface target search
and designation, and for practice firing observation. It
is the main optical sight and director of the RADOP 20
naval fire control system (**4049.261**). The general
arrangement of the unit can be seen from the
accompanying illustration. The deck-mounted sight
is provided with power driven azimuth movement and
a stabilised line-of-sight by means of integral rate
gyros. There is also provision for remote control of
the sight to enable it to be laid on from an external
reference.

When operating in the weapon control mode the
sight is used to track the target. The co-ordinates
transmitted by the sight convey all the necessary
firing corrections based on target velocity, weapon
characteristics and parallax between weapon and
sight. In the search mode of operation the sight scans
the surveillance zone in bearing and elevation.
CHARACTERISTICS
Magnification: ×8 and ×2·66
Fields of view: ±3° and ±9°
Azimuth aiming arc: Unlimited
Elevation arc: −25 to +65° (relative to deck)

Max velocity: 1 rad/s (bearing); 0·5 rad/s (elevation)
Weight: <330 kg
The above description applies to the basic optical
version of this director, which is referred to as the
Panda. A more sophisticated version, with additional
facilities such as laser rangefinder, automatic
tracking, local/remote control transfer, multiple
weapon capability etc, is also produced as the Naja
electro-optical director. (**3561.293**).
STATUS
In production for 16 navies.
CONTRACTOR
CSEE (Compagnie de Signaux et d'Entreprises
Electriques), 17 place Etienne Pernet, 75738 Paris
Cedex 15, France.

CSEE Panda Mk2 optical director

3561.293
NAJA ELECTRO-OPTICAL DIRECTOR
This is a naval electro-optical director equipment
usable for air and surface surveillance, automatic TV
tracking at high and low altitude, and accurate fire
control by laser telemetry. The Naja equipment
contributes to the self-defence of surface ships
against aircraft or missile attacks.

In addition to being employed on its own, the Naja
director is the principal fire control element of the
RADOP 30 naval weapon control system (**4049.261**).

The general arrangement of the unit can be seen
from the accompanying illustration.

The deck mounting is provided with a power-driven
azimuth movement and a stabilised line-of-sight by
means of integral rate gyros. The trainable assembly
includes mainly the optical unit, the TV camera, the
laser rangefinder, the training and elevation
kinematic circuits, the analysis unit, the firing
computer and the control and signalling units.

When operating in the fire control mode, the
operator acquires the target which is tracked
automatically by TV. The Naja analogue computer
using the gyro and laser data provides all the
necessary firing adjustments based on target
velocity, angle of elevation, parallax, ballistics and
slope.

The Naja director can be remotely controlled.
CHARACTERISTICS
Optical equipment
Magnification: ×2·5 (field ± 9·5°); ×8 (field ±3°)
Daylight camera or LLTV camera
CILAS laser
Azimuth aiming arc: Unlimited
Elevation arc: −25 to +70°
Max velocity: 60°/s (bearing); 60°/s (elevation)
Weight: 500 kg approx
STATUS
In production. The Naja director has also been
offered as part of a land-based air defence system
based on the Breda twin 40 mm naval system.
CONTRACTOR
CSEE (Compagnie de Signaux et d'Entreprises
Electriques), 17 place Etienne Pernet, 75738 Paris
Cedex 15, France.

CSEE Naja electro-optical director

4255.293
NAJIR ELECTRO-OPTICAL DIRECTOR
The Najir director contributes to the self-defence of
surface ships of any displacement against aircraft or
missile attacks. It can be used against naval or land

targets by night or day. It is unaffected by enemy
jamming.

The Najir director operates as an autonomous unit
with integrated stabilisation and a digital computer. It
is manned by a single operator in two principal

modes: surveillance and target tracking, or fire
control of several weapons of different calibres.

In the former mode the operator can: receive and
re-copy a target designation transmitted by other
surveillance equipment; by means of the auxiliary

sight, immediately acquire a target designated by a watch keeper; quickly identify the target (optical or IR display); decide to select automatic tracking either TV by day or IR by night (or by day in disturbed atmosphere); obtain the target range by laser rangefinder.

In the fire control mode the operator can select the firing mode (against aircraft or floating target), order the simultaneous coupling of two guns, decide to open fire on receipt of 'gun ready' and 'target within range' information and observe the results of firing.

The Najir comprises a fixed structure, a trainable assembly, a tracking system and a remote control station. It can be operated from a remote control station and can be easily integrated with a radar fire control or a centralised tactical data system, due to its digital interface. In the RADOP 40 system, the Najir is associated with a Racal radar.

CHARACTERISTICS
Aiming arcs: unlimited (bearing); –20 to +70° (elevation)
Max velocity: 60°/s (bearing); 60°/s (elevation)
Max acceleration: 60°/s² (bearing); 60°/s² (elevation)
Optical equipment

Binocular telescope: ×2·5 (field ±9·5°); or ×8 (field ±3°)
Daylight TV camera
IR camera
Laser rangefinder
Weight: 550 kg approx
STATUS
Development.
CONTRACTOR
CSEE (Compagnie de Signaux et d'Entreprises Electriques), 17 place Etienne Pernet, 75738 Paris Cedex 15, France.

3426.293
LYNX OPTICAL SIGHT
The CSEE Lynx is a self-contained lightweight optical sight designed for use aboard surface ships of all sizes. It provides for air and surface surveillance and may be used in conjunction with other optical equipments or with a ship's command information centre, and can also be employed for weapon control. In the RADOP 10 naval fire control system (**4049.261**), Lynx is the main sighting element.

Targets are sighted through an optical assembly comprising a binocular sight with choice of two magnifications and a mirror in the elevation plane. A viewer, linked to the scanning mirror, is used to pre-position the sight in the direction of a designated point, thereby aiding rapid acquisition. The mirror is electrically driven in elevation to provide a scan of –25 to +65°. In azimuth, rotation is unlimited, with manual drive. The line-of-sight is stabilised in elevation by means of a rate gyro acting on the mirror.

Relative angular target co-ordinates are transmitted for target designation by a fine and/or coarse precision gyro. Alternatively, angular firing co-ordinates taking into account parallax and elevation corrections can be transmitted by a fine and coarse precision synchro to the controlled weapon. Data and signal links can be provided to other equipment or to the CIC.

The Lynx director may also be equipped with a television camera and a monitor.
CHARACTERISTICS
Magnification: ×2·5 or ×8
Field of view: ±9·5° or ±3°
Scanning field: Unlimited in azimuth, –15 to +75° in elevation
Max speed in elevation: 1 rad/s
Max acceleration: 2 rad/s² (elevation)
Height of eyepieces: Adjustable 1·38 – 1·63 m
Weight: 195 kg
STATUS
In production for Bahrain and Kuwait.
CONTRACTOR
CSEE (Compagnie de Signaux et d'Entreprises Electriques), 17 place Etienne Pernet, 75738 Paris Cedex 15, France.

CSEE Lynx optical director

4052.283
TOUCAN E-O MOUNTING
CSEE is developing a new electro-optical turret called Toucan which is designed for use in naval weapon control applications. The main design requirements are a high payload (up to 200 kg) and high pointing accuracy (of the order of 20 seconds of arc). It is a two-axis turret with provision for stabilisation in three axes. A prototype of the Toucan turret is under trial in the IRDAR programme conducted by DTCN for the French Navy (**3064.293**).

The optical path(s) between the sensor(s) carried on the turret and the below-deck components of the system pass entirely within the turret, and follow a similar path between support and sensor-mounting plates. A remote control operating console is located below deck, incorporating computer assistance for manual operations. Facilities include: speed control by joystick; re-slewing on target designation and execution of a search routine; automatic tracking with three types of tracker (eg IR, TV etc) with automatic acceptance in accordance with priorities selected on the control desk; trajectory extrapolation if target is temporarily lost or masked; automatic sequencing; dialogue or total control by ship's main computer.

Angular position data from the Toucan mounting is transmitted digitally, and the resolver/encoders are stated to have a resolution of three seconds.
CHARACTERISTICS
Weight: 350 kg (bare mounting)
Max payload: 200 kg
Train: Unlimited
Elevation: –25 to +85°
Max acceleration: 4 rad/s² (azimuth and elevation)
Peak overall error: 20″ (dynamic tracking)
CONTRACTOR
CSEE (Compagnie de Signaux et d'Entreprises Electriques), 17 place Etienne Pernet, 75738 Paris Cedex 15, France.

Toucan naval electro-optical head mounting (without sensors)

3424.293
TOTEM NAVAL FIRE CONTROL EQUIPMENT
The Totem electro-optical fire control director has been developed by CSEE to provide naval vessels with a passive means of air defence surveillance, target designation and tracking for use in conjunction with air defence weapons such as anti-aircraft guns. The general arrangement of the above-deck equipment can be seen from the adjacent photograph. A rotating turret carries an elevating head on which are mounted a passive infra-red tracker, a laser rangefinder, and either a normal or low light-level television camera with automatic tracker. Below decks are the servo rack and control and monitoring panels. The former includes three units: one for low-level data processing (ie data representing various parameters from sensor or command transmitters), and servo amplifiers for each axis (vertical and horizontal). The control and monitor panels may be incorporated in the weapon consoles of the related gun or missile systems associated with the Totem director.

The Totem sensor head is provided with stabilisation by means of integral gyros, and the principal mechanical characteristics are tabulated below. The infra-red tracker employed is the SAT PIRANA equipment (**3064.293** and **3427.293**) which is also suitable for mounting on guns or separately. The television sub-system is of SINTRA manufacture, and a CILAS laser rangefinder is employed. Sensors of alternative manufacture may be substituted for the above and CSEE has a combined electro-optical/radar version of the Totem FCS under development; the radar is a Ka-band equipment manufactured by Thomson-CSF, similar to that used in the TRS 906 (**3566.293**).

CHARACTERISTICS
Turret weight: <200 kg (plus weight of sensors)
Max slewing speed: 2 rad/s^2 (elevation and azimuth)
Max slewing acceleration: 2 rad/s (elevation and azimuth)
Angular tracking accuracy: 1′
Power supply: 115 V 3 phase 3 kVA
STATUS
Production.
CONTRACTOR
CSEE (Compagnie de Signaux et d'Entreprises Electriques), 17 place Etienne Pernet, 75738 Paris Cedex 15, France.

CSEE Totem electro-optical fire control system with SAT infra-red tracker (left) and LLTV and laser rangefinder (right)

4716.293
VISON OPTICAL DIRECTOR

As a periscopic optical director, Vison carries out surveillance, target designation and acquisition functions, and automatic tracking of targets. With the incorporation of an optional fire computer it can also be used as a fire control system.

The basic system consists of a periscope providing an optical channel from an exterior-mounted stabilised mobile head. The orientation in bearing and elevation of the mobile head line of sight is controlled from a data processing console at the foot of the periscope. The operator uses a control stick to control the head and an eyepiece which provides optical observation of the surveyed sector (30° or 7·5° according to magnification). In addition to direct optical observation, a TV camera is installed in the optical path and provides a video screen display to the operator. Automatic TV tracking of the target can be used when available.

With the reduced dimensions of Vison, installation of the complete system in the ship structure is relatively simple.
CHARACTERISTICS
Magnification: ×2 or ×8
Field of view: 30° or 7·5°
Bearing scan: Unlimited
Elevation scan: –25 to +70°
Weight: Approx 120 kg (sub-assembly head and periscope); 300 kg (complete system)
STATUS
In development.
CONTRACTOR
CSEE (Compagnie de Signaux et d'Entreprises Electriques), 17 place Etienne Pernet, 75738 Paris, Cedex 15, France.

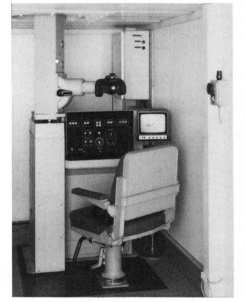

Vison optronic director (interior view)

4717.253
COTOL OPTRONIC FIRE CONTROL SYSTEM

Cotol is a fire control unit capable of performing surveillance on TV or infra-red images, target designation and acquisition, and target automatic tracking. The system is normally installed as part of the ship's overall anti-aircraft defence system, although it can also be used as a control unit against surface targets.

Cotol consists basically of a light turret (Tolcan), manufactured by CSEE, which is directional and stabilised in bearing and elevation. It includes a TV camera, an infra-red camera and a laser rangefinder. A processing console, equipped with two monitors, shows the front panel, any other control units, and the TV and infra-red tracking data, to allow operation from the ship's control room. An electronics unit, incorporating the weapon control computer and the Tolcan remote control unit, completes the system.

Because of its reduced weight and dimensions, Cotol can be easily set up on ships of virtually any tonnage as either the main or secondary fire control system.
CHARACTERISTICS
Bearing scan: Unlimited
Elevation scan: –25 to +85°
Maximum speed: 90°/s in bearing and elevation
Weight: 220 kg (fully equipped turret)
STATUS
In development.
CONTRACTOR
CSEE (Compagnie de Signaux et d'Entreprises Electriques), 17 place Etienne Pernet, 75738 Paris Cedex 15, France.

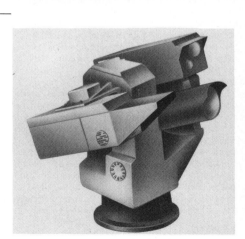

Cotol optronic fire control system

3147.293
TAON TMY83 LASER
RANGEFINDER/ILLUMINATOR

The TMY83 TAON (télémètre d'artillerie optronique pour navire) is a Nd-YAG laser rangefinder developed for naval applications such as integration into electro-optical fire control systems for air defence weapons. The rangefinder and its power supply are housed within a single casing, which is designed for ease of fitting to director mounts or directly on to weapons such as guns. The laser repetition rate is adjustable between ten and twenty pulses per second.
CHARACTERISTICS
Laser type: Nd-YAG, electro-optical Q-switching
Wavelength: 1·06 micron
Pulse duration: ≤20 × 10^{-9} s
Output: >5 MW
Beam divergence: 0·5 mrad
Range: 500 – 20 000 m
Range resolution: ±5 m
Dimensions: 460 × 265 × 160 mm
Weight: 15 kg
DEVELOPMENT
Design and development has been carried out under contract from the French Navy.

The TMY83 replaces the TMV26 naval laser rangefinder (**1799.293**).
CONTRACTOR
CILAS (Compagnie Industrielle des Lasers), route de Nozay, 91460 Marcoussis, France.

TAON TMY83 laser rangefinder

3662.293
TMY113 LASER RANGEFINDER/ILLUMINATOR

The TMY113 is a high repetition rate laser rangefinder designed for integration into the Naja naval electro-optical fire director equipment (**3561.293**). The rangefinder, electronic timing clock, and power supply are all housed within the same casing.
CHARACTERISTICS
Laser material: Nd-YAG
Wavelength: 1·06 micron
Pulse duration: 20 × 10⁻⁹ s
Peak power: >5 MW

PRF: 20 pps
Detector: Avalanche photodiode
Detector field: 2 mrad
Dimensions: 470 × 230 × 170 mm
Weight: <14 kg
Power supply: 115 V/400 Hz, 3-phase
STATUS
Series production.
CONTRACTOR
CILAS (Compagnie Industrielle des Lasers), route de Nozay, 91460 Marcoussis, France.

CILAS TMY113 laser rangefinder/target illuminator for Naja naval electro-optical fire director equipment

4108.493
SOPELEM SUBMARINE PERISCOPES

SOPELEM designs and manufactures all types of submarine periscope, and while details of specific equipments have not been obtained, current production includes the following basic categories:

Surveillance Periscopes
Periscopes of this type provide for observation at fixed navigation periscope depth and can be fitted with a rangefinding radar antenna and a radar search scanner, and several electro-optical sensors. They are designed for day and night observation and may be fitted with a gyro-sextant for star sighting navigational purposes. These periscopes are generally equipped with a recording photographic camera.

Attack Periscopes
With such instruments the crew is able to make an observation of the surface area in all directions from position fixes at all submarine navigation periscope depths. The periscope is completely controlled by hydraulic means giving maximum flexibility and speed of operation. The periscope upper section is of very small cross-section and thus creates minimum wake and also makes detection by radar much more difficult.

All these periscopes are designed and manufactured by SOPELEM which also produces the hydraulic controls and the associated electronic equipment. They equip all submarines of the 'Daphne', '1200 T Agosta' classes, and French nuclear powered submarines.
STATUS
In production.
CONTRACTOR
SOPELEM, 102 rue Chaptal, 92306 Levallois Perret, France.

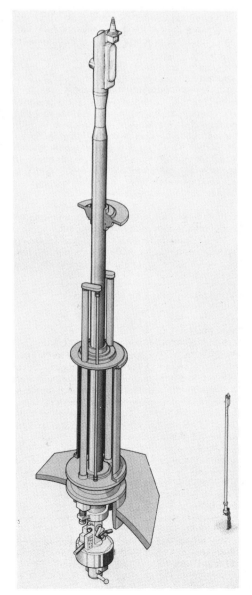

Drawing of typical SOPELEM submarine periscope

ISRAEL

4718.293
GYRO STABILISED SIGHTING SYSTEM

The Gyro Stabilised Sighting System (GSSS) is used for surveillance, identification and target tracking. The system consists of a dual magnification periscope with a gyro-stabilised upper mirror. The mirror coating is effective over a wide spectral range from the visual to near infra-red, and permits optional use of laser or infra-red trackers in parallel with the visual path. High magnification by the stabilised optics enables the observer to identify and lock-on to the target at considerable distances.

The sight is an optical periscope, roof or floor mounted with its rotating viewing head outside. The head includes the upper periscope mirror which is free to rotate in azimuth and elevation. The system can be integrated with a laser rangefinder and/or a low light TV camera.

CHARACTERISTICS
Magnification: × 10 or × 2·5
Field of view: 5° or 20°
Scan: 360° azimuth; –30 to +60° elevation
Tracking rate: 30°/s (azimuth and elevation)
Weight: 65 kg
CONTRACTOR
Israel Aircraft Industries Ltd, Tamam Precision Instruments, Ben Gurion Airport, Israel.

ITALY

3585.293
OGR7/2 OPTICAL DIRECTOR

The optical director Type OGR7 is a shipborne equipment of small size and weight for the control of up to 3 inch calibre guns against air and surface targets. It consists of a tracking system, provided with telescope and open sight, and a computer through which the train and elevation lead angles and the super-elevation are computed with high accuracy. A single gunlayer/operator controls the speed in train and elevation by means of a joystick. The line-of-sight is stabilised so that the operator has only to account for the motion of the target.

The OGR7/2 consists essentially of a revolving platform, supported by a base fixed on the deck, on which is fitted a frame holding the telescope and containing the mechanical, electrical and electronic sub-units of the equipment. The train motion is provided by an electro-hydraulic unit. The motion for the elevation search is provided by a servo which moves the prism of the telescope. The computer is located in the revolving part of the director and consists of transistorised amplifiers and mechanical assemblies including servomotors, potentiometers, resolvers and the control transmitters of gun orders. A high luminosity binocular telescope with fixed eyepieces is used as the optical aiming device. Two concentric aiming circles appear in the left eyepiece.

The telescope is provided with coloured filters that can be inserted by turning a knob. By means of a lever the magnifications can be changed from ×2·3 to ×7. An open sight is located at the left side of the telescope. A servo provides for vertical search motion, keeping it parallel to the line of sight of the telescope.

Stabilisation compensates for the variation of the train and elevation angles due to course alterations or to the pitch and roll of the ship. For this purpose, gyro units are installed. One gyro measures the yaw speed of the ship; two other gyros, located on the director rotating platform, measure the level and cross-level speed, respectively.

The control panel contains: the main switch; the switch to activate the circuit for starting the guns from the director; fire selector for the guns; push-buttons to start and stop the guns; selector for air target or surface target; two knobs and associated dials to introduce the target speed and the cross range of the air target; knob and associated dial to introduce target range in 'surface target'.

OGR7/2-A Optical Director

This is a later development of the basic OGR7 series. Manned by a single operator it consists of a pedestal mounting, an optical head with an integrated image intensifier, an autonomous integrated two-axis stabilisation system and a digital computer for lead angles computation and system management. It is designed for interoperating with naval standard command and control systems. Target range can be tele-transmitted by CIC designation equipment or can be locally introduced by the operator. An integrated laser rangefinder is also available as an option.

CHARACTERISTICS
Telescope
Magnification: ×2·3 and ×7 (×7 at night for OGR7/2-A)
Optical field: 30° and 10°
Max train speed: 100°/s
Max elevation speed: 60°/s; 70°/s for OGR7/2-A
Max train lead angle: ±25°
Max elevation lead angle: ±20°
Crossing range limits: 100 – 2000 m
Target speed limits: 60 – 350 m/s
STATUS
More than 250 sets of the OGR7 series have been supplied to main navies, among them those of West Germany, Greece and Peru. A special version of the OGR7, known as the OGR7 Seacat, has been developed which provides an additional telescope for Seacat missile guidance as well as gunfire direction. This model also bears the designation OG20.
CONTRACTOR
Officine Galileo, 50013 Campi Bisenzio, Florence, Italy.

4262.293
NCS2 SHIPBORNE THERMAL IMAGER

The Officine Galileo NCS2 thermal imaging equipment is designed to detect aerial, surface and missile targets from naval vessels, either independently or integrated with radar and other optical equipments as part of a fire control system. The functions of the NCS2 are summarised as surveillance, acquisition and tracking, and this is achieved by transmitting the thermal image of the target(s) on to an appropriate display on the control console. By converting the imager video into a conventional television signal format, automatic TV tracking techniques can be employed.

The equipment consists of the optics and scanning system, detector, signal processing electronics, and a cooling unit. The optical observation and scanning unit is made up of an array of germanium lenses with an anti-reflection coating in the eight to fourteen micron band. The scanner is of the parallel scan type, interlaced one-to-one and comprising two oscillating mirrors providing 25 frames/s image scanning. The detector employs a mercury-cadmium-telluride linear array of 100 one-to-one spaced elements. The cooling system is of the closed cycle type with one fluid compressor unit and one cooling unit. All major component units of the system are integrated into a single package for installation into a FCS or for mounting as an autonomous equipment.

CHARACTERISTICS
Wavelength: 8 – 14 microns
Detector: MCT
Number of elements: 100 spaced one-to-one
Working temperature: 77° K
Field of view: 50 × 100 mrad
IFOV: 0·25 mrad
Frame rate: 25 Hz
Number of lines: 200
NET: 0·2° K typical
Typical range: 16 km (air target); 18 km (frigate); 6 km (sea skimmer missile)
System weight: Approx 45 kg
STATUS
The NCS2 is now integrated in the electro-optical multi-sensor of the MM-59 fire control system on board the major classes of ships of the Italian Navy.
CONTRACTOR
Officine Galileo, 50013 Campi Bisenzio, Florence, Italy.

NETHERLANDS

3143.293
LIOD LIGHTWEIGHT OPTRONIC DIRECTOR

To offset the increasing use of electronic warfare as a means of degrading radar-based weapon control systems on board ships, Signaal has developed an E-O (electro-optical) sensor system which is passive in operation, insensitive to ECM, and practically undetectable. The LIOD (lightweight optronic director) is an unmanned director for the automatic tracking of air and surface targets.

Tracking is by the optical contrast technique whereby the target is tracked against its background as viewed by a TV or infra-red camera. Range information is provided by a laser rangefinder. Alternatively a 3-D laser-tracker can be fitted. Both the camera and rangefinder are co-mounted on the director head unit, which is provided with appropriate servos and anti-vibration mountings.

The director head is also used as a mounting for combined radar and E-O sensors in the LIROD (3767.281), to provide all-weather capability.

Because of its modular design, LIOD can be used for autonomous or integrated weapon control systems, as an auxiliary sensor for various weapon control or data systems.

The daylight version (illustrated) is fitted with a TV camera and laser, while the high-performance model has a TV camera, infra-red camera and laser rangefinder.

If provided with suitable independent computer capacity and operational control facilities, it could well be used as an autonomous short-range gun control system.

The LIOD sensor, in its basic version, employed as an autonomous weapon control system, is capable of performing the following functions:
(1) optical surveillance for air and surface targets
(2) target designation for anti-air and anti-surface engagements
(3) air or surface fire control

LIOD lightweight optronic director

(4) automatic or rate-aided tracking of one air or surface target

(5) air or surface target gun prediction calculation

(6) simultaneous control of two dual-purpose guns of the same or different calibre

(7) engagement monitoring, kill assessment, and gun fire correction

(8) system status monitoring.

STATUS

In production and delivered to various naval forces.

CONTRACTOR

Hollandse Signaalapparaten BV, PO Box 42, 7550 GD Hengelo, Netherlands.

5722.293
IRSCAN INFRA-RED SURVEILLANCE SYSTEM

IRSCAN is a fast-reaction infra-red surveillance system for air and surface targets. It has been developed for naval applications but can also be used in the land-based role. The scanner is of modular construction with three sensors covering 3 to 5 and 8 to 12 μm wavelengths, and includes elevation drive, self-supporting closed-cycle stirling-type coolers and is mounted on an azimuth drive. In the naval role a stabilisation system is normally provided with shock and vibration isolating mounting.

The system has a dual wavelength capability to cover a variety of infra-red target signatures and environmental conditions, and special techniques for spatial filtering and signal correlation are used to give the system a highly reliable and accurate target detection and tracking performance. A large number of air targets can be auto-tracked while scanning. A display console is equipped with a 15-inch (38 cm) TV monitor, memory supported with alpha-numeric data presentation and light-pen control keys. The console also contains the system computer and all signal processing.

IRSCAN can be used with systems such as LIOD (**3143.293**), LIROD (light-weight radar optronic director) and Goalkeeper (**3616.231**), as well as other anti-missile defence systems.

CHARACTERISTICS

Horizontal coverage: 360°

Elevation scan patterns: Low, medium, high (up to 40°)

System weight: 850 kg

Stabilisation: 2-axis gimbal for roll and pitch

STATUS

The naval version has been developed for the Royal Netherlands Navy and successful sea trials were carried out on HMS Piet Heym, an S-frigate of the RNN.

CONTRACTOR

Hollandse Signaalapparaten BV, PO Box 42, 7550 GD Hengelo, Netherlands.

IRSCAN scanner in naval configuration

3431.293
TYPE UA 9053 THERMAL IMAGING CAMERA

The UA 9053 camera has been designed to enable passive target tracking by both day and night. Its application is either as an auxiliary E-O sensor readily integrated in a radar weapon control system, or as a sensor for an autonomous short-range weapon control system.

The camera produces a standard CCIR video output. Resolution and sensitivity are such that small low-flying targets can be observed and tracked. Tracking of surface targets is also possible. The sensor is equipped with a closed cycle cryo-generator, Philips type UA 7011. The equipment has been designed for application in maritime environments and operates for long periods without maintenance.

CHARACTERISTICS

Field of view: 42 × 23 mrad (azimuth × elevation)

Instantaneous field of view: 0·2 × 0·2 mrad

Detector cooling: Closed cycle type UA 7011

Cool-down time: Approx 10 minutes

Output signal: CCIR compatible

Input power: +24 V DC, –24 V DC

Power consumption: 250 VA

Dimensions: 470 × 275 × 350 mm

Weight: ≤37 kg

CONTRACTOR

Philips Usfa BV, Meerenakkerweg 1, PO Box 218, 5600 MD Eindhoven, Netherlands.

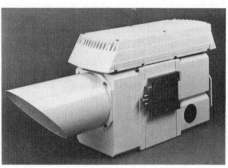

Type UA 9053 infra-red camera

3559.293
TYPE MS7TS MARINE NIGHT SIGHT

The MS7TS marine night observation device is an image intensifier system for medium- and long-range night observation at sea. Unlike radar it gives a visual presentation of a ship's silhouette facilitating discrimination between classes of vessels. It makes unilluminated objects immediately recognisable, for instance a blind fishing boat, a floating trunk, rocks, buoys.

The double-hinged bracket permits fast scanning of the horizon from a pedestal on the bridge or on deck. The night observation device is suitable for use on board all kinds of seagoing ship. Its versatile and sturdy design is well adapted to internal and outside use. The system comprises a high speed mirror objective, a three-stage fibre-coupled image intensifier with power supply, a bi-ocular system for comfortable viewing, or if desired a monocular eyepiece. The nickel cadmium battery can be recharged by a special battery charging unit. It is also possible to feed the observation device from the ship's main supply (optional).

A distortion-compensated image over the entire field of view is offered. The device is provided with an automatic brightness control. Detection of unilluminated ships ranges from 8 to 12 km, depending on ambient conditions. The weight is less than 20 kg.

CHARACTERISTICS

Magnification: ×7

Field of view: 7°

Focus: adjustable, 50 m – infinity

Detection range: 8 – 12 km for unilluminated ships

STATUS

In production.

CONTRACTOR

Oldelft (NV Optische Industrie De Oude Delft), PO Box 72, 2600 MD Delft, Netherlands.

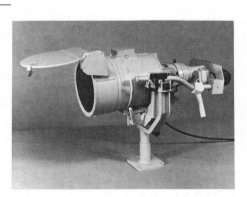

Type MS7TS marine night sight

NORWAY

5728.293
TC10 THERMAL IMAGER

The TC10 is a thermal imager designed specifically for naval applications to provide high penetration of smoke, haze and camouflage. It is a passive system giving high resolution with a minimum resolvable temperature difference of 0·03°C which offers long-range detection and identification. Detection is independent of ambient light and the system will, therefore, operate as efficiently by night as by day. The thermal picture is displayed on a TV monitor.

The TC10 consists of a thermal camera, signal processing unit and a TV monitor. In the shipboard application it is normally mounted on a stabilised platform.

CHARACTERISTICS

Field of view: 1° (vertical); 3° (horizontal)

Resolution: 0·25 mrad

Focusing: 25 m – infinity

Detector: Cadmium mercury telluride

Spectral band: 8 – 12 μm

Mission time: 20 hours with 5 litre cooling bottle at 300 atmospheres

Detector cooling: Compressed gas

Weight: 8 kg (thermal camera); 7·5 kg (signal processing unit)

CONTRACTOR

Simrad Optronics, PO Box 6414, Etterstad, Oslo 6, Norway.

SWEDEN

1231.283
SAAB TVT-300 AUTOMATIC TV TRACKER

The TVT-300 is a system for automatic tracking of objects, in which the optical contrasts of the object against its background as seen by a TV camera are utilised. The basic system consists of a TV camera on a gyro-stabilised platform, a monitor, and an electronics unit containing video processing and servo control circuits. The equipment can be engineered and assembled to serve either fire control or missile guidance applications.

OPERATION

With the target within the view of the TV camera the operator places an electronic 'window' on the target by means of a joystick. The operator then initiates automatic tracking whereby the servo control circuits keep the 'window' centred on the target contrast and also align the target to the centre of the camera field of view.

Signals corresponding to the deviation of the 'window' from the optical axis of the camera are used to control the platform servo motors which, triggered by the deviation signals, train the platform to keep the camera continuously directed towards the selected target. Tracking can be performed on dark or bright contrasts, or on very slight contrast levels. The platform angular positions in bearing and elevation are used for automatic tracking of the guns.

In the Saab TVT-300 the TV camera bearing and elevation values are used to control directly the aiming of AA guns which are slaved to the system. The system replaces the conventional fire direction and correction devices. Target acquisition and corrections are quickly and accurately made from a close-up view of the target seen on the TV monitor.

STATUS

The Saab TVT-300 is operational in several navies.

CONTRACTOR

Saab Missiles AB, 58188 Linköping, Sweden.

Saab TVT-300 automatic TV tracker on board a Swedish fast patrol boat. Other versions are used in the Kalle system and those of other users. Various laser rangefinders are employed

UNITED KINGDOM

1207.293
SHORTS TARGET DESIGNATION SIGHT

The target designation sight is used for visual acquisition and tracking of surface and air targets. The sight consists of a binocular mounted on a sight head fitted to a pedestal which is bolted to the deck. The binocular platform is fitted with handgrips with which the binocular may be rotated and the sight head raised or lowered on an elevating shaft to provide height adjustment.

OPERATION

On acquiring the target in the binocular field of view and centring it on the cross-marking, the operator presses the designated alarm switch on his right hand-grip. The target bearing and elevation information is transmitted automatically to the control centre by two synchro elements, one in the pedestal for bearing, the other in the sight head for elevation.

A number of different versions, fitted with twin and tandem synchros and other variations have been supplied.

DEVELOPMENT

This equipment has been evolved from an element of the Seacat missile system (which see), and is a modification of the pedestal-mounted visual director used with that system.

STATUS

In production.

CONTRACTOR

Short Brothers Limited, PO Box 241, Airport Road, Belfast BT3 9DZ, Northern Ireland.

Shorts target designation sight

3055.293
LSDS OPTICAL FIRE DIRECTOR

The LSDS optical fire director (OFD) is a lightweight, line-of-sight stabilised director fitted with binoculars for operation by a standing operator.

The design concept of the OFD is to produce a low weight, simply constructed director that is easy to install and maintain in ships ranging in size from fast patrol boats to the largest warship. It may be used as a main gun fire/missile control system or as a back-up to more elaborate weapons systems.

The director has duplicate sets of coarse-fine synchro transmissions for both training and elevation and can therefore be used to control two separate weapons or alternatively provide independent transmissions to one weapon for damage control purposes. It may be remotely controlled in either training and elevation or both via coarse-fine synchro transmissions. Stabilisation about the line of sight is controlled by two rate integrating gyroscopes. The director may be operated in an unstabilised mode.

The operator standing on the variable height platform is provided with a safety harness and plug and socket connection for a communications head set and heated suit if required.

OPERATION

The control of the director locally is by means of a thumb-operated two-axis joystick. In the local control mode the operator controls the director from two pistol-type handgrips. The right hand is used to override the deadman's handgrip and to control the two-axis joystick. The left handgrip is used to control a rate selection switch, a rate doubling button, a target acquisition button, and a firing trigger. Having selected a suitable training and elevation rate, operation of the joystick will cause the line of sight to train and elevate smoothly from zero to the rate selected. Velocity or rate-aided tracking is operator selected. If it is necessary to increase momentarily the selected rate this can be achieved by pressing the rate doubling button. Pre-selected controls both for the OFD and the weapons it is controlling are easily accessible on the panel mounted between the two handgrips.

For remote operation the OFD can be controlled by two separate methods:
(1) by synchro drive from the ship's surveillance radar (target indication, training only) or tracking radar (training and elevation)
(2) by a joystick from a below-deck station using a CCTV/IR monitor link for viewing.

In addition to the standard 7 × 50 mm binocular fit, facilities exist for fitting an image intensifier, an infra-red camera for blind-fire capability or a laser rangefinder. A below-decks remote control facility exists employing a CCTV or infra-red camera on the mounting to provide an automatic gun laying capability with the aid of an auto track unit deployed in the CCTV/IR-servo/mount loop. An on-mount digital predictor is available to provide lead angle predictions for enhanced hit probability.

CONSTRUCTION:

The LSDS OFD is constructed from cast aluminium, non-magnetic stainless steel and GRP thus minimising its weight and magnetic signature. The design meets DEF specification 133, Table N2, shipborne equipment – exposed. The director is self-contained apart from a switch/fuse and distribution box which is fitted below deck.

CHARACTERISTICS

Electrical requirements: To DEF standards 61-5 (Part 1)/1
(a) 440 V 3-phase 50-60 Hz or 115 V 3-phase 50-60 Hz, 1 kVA
(b) 115 V/400 Hz, single-phase, 50 VA
(c) 24 V DC, 10 A (including heated suit)
(d) 115 V/50 or 60 Hz conditioning heater supply
Training system performance
Arc: Unlimited
Max velocity: 80°/s
Max acceleration: 150°/s²

LSDS optical fire director

Elevation system performance
Arc: –20 to +70°
Max velocity: 120°/s
Max acceleration: 150°/s²
Weight (including platform): 475 kg
Synchro transmission from the director
Two coarse/fine outputs are available in both training and elevation. Coarse/fine ratios available are: 36:1, 16:1, 9:1, or a combination of these

Synchro-transmission to director
One coarse/fine system on both training and elevation. Coarse/fine ratios: 36:1, 16:1, 9:1, or a combination of these
Open sight
A ring and bead open sight is mounted adjacent to the binoculars
Dimensions
Overall height: 2110 mm

Swept radius: 762 mm
STATUS
Design and development was a private venture project. Recently adopted by the Royal Navy as a director for the GSA7 fire control system, this director has also been selected by ten overseas navies.
CONTRACTOR
Laurence, Scott (Defence Systems) Limited, PO Box 25, Norwich Norfolk NR1 1JD, England.

3829.493
CH84 SUBMARINE ATTACK PERISCOPE

This is one of the periscopes designed for the RN Type 2400 and 'Trafalgar' class submarines. The CH84 periscope incorporates many of the above water sensors available in Barr & Stroud periscopes. The crosshead unit is fitted with a torque drive motor, controlled at the periscope or remotely, which rotates the periscope without physical assistance from the operator. A motorised Olympus OM2 camera is fitted; it has automatic exposure control and the time and date are shown on each of the 250 frames. The optical system includes anti-vibration features and is designed to give maximum resolution in high and low power. It is quasi-binocular to reduce eye strain. Top window heating is controlled by a solid-state unit in the periscope. Bearing transmission is from an optical encoder in the crosshead, and true bearing can be displayed in the left eyepiece. Range from the range estimator is calculated by a microprocessor; estimated target height is set on a unit remote from the periscope.

A laser rangefinder can be fitted. Accurate collimation is maintained with the aiming mark in the optical, image intensification and thermal image systems. Accuracy is ±10 metres. Range to the target is displayed in the eyepiece and can be transmitted to the fire control system. An image intensifier can also be fitted in the optical system. This gives a luminous

gain of up to 30 000 ×, (equivalent to near-starlight) with high resolution. This system uses an additional 110 mm diameter window in the top of the main tube.

A television camera can be fitted at the rear of the ocular box. This can relay the optical, image intensifier or thermal image picture to a remote monitor and/or a video tape recorder, with provision for alpha-numeric insertion of data. A thermal imager can be fitted as an alternative to the image intensifier, and this utilises the 110 mm window (made of germanium) at the top of the main tube. The thermal picture can be viewed in the eyepiece or relayed to a remote monitor and/or video tape recorder.

An active receive antenna can be incorporated in the top tube.

Alternative versions are the CH85 and CH86.
CHARACTERISTICS
Main tube diameter: 254 mm
Top tube diameter: 70 mm nominal
Overall length: 13·5 m approx
Well radius: 356 mm
Magnification: ×1·5, ×6
FOV: 32° × 8°
Laser protection: Filters
TV: 16 mm SIT Vidicon
Image intensifier: Mullard 50/40 mm Type XX 1332
Thermal imager: 8–13 micron band
STATUS
Production.

CH84 submarine attack periscope

CONTRACTOR
Barr & Stroud Ltd, Melrose House, 4-6 Saville Row, London W1X 1AF, England.

3830.493
CK34 SUBMARINE SEARCH PERISCOPE

This is one of the periscopes designed for the RN Type 2400 and 'Trafalgar' class submarines. The CK34 was designed to provide the optical qualities necessary for high resolution photography, the taking of star sights with the artificial horizon sextant and visual observation in poor light conditions. The CK34 periscope shares the following common features with the CH84 torque drive; Olympus camera; anti-vibration optics; top window heater; range estimator and transmission; bearing transmission. (In this case the true bearing is displayed on the front of the ocular box.)

A number of systems which have in the past been operated mechanically are now operated by electro-servo mechanisms. These include: top elevating prism, change power, sextant filters, graticule IN/OUT, and range estimator. They all have 'fail safe' arrangements. All controls and read-outs are now contained in two simplified panels either side of the ocular box. The periscope is quasi-binocular and has three magnifications: ×1·5, ×6 and ×12.

Artificial horizon sextant (AHPS 4): A stabilised mirror slaved to the submarine's compass or SINS system replaces the gyro stabilised platform. All controls have been simplified with the object of taking

a sight within a few seconds. Provision is made for automatically removing errors in the observed altitude caused by the periscope bending or the ship's structure distorting. A print-out provides the observed altitude, bearing and time of observation. An electronic support measures (ESM) antenna can be fitted, the ESM office equipment to be specified by the customer. An active receive antenna can be fitted on top of the ESM array. A television camera can be fitted at the rear of the ocular box to relay the optical picture to a remote monitor and/or video tape recorder, with a facility for alpha-numeric insertion of data.

Alternative versions are the CK35 and CK36.
CHARACTERISTICS
Main tube diameter: 254 mm
Overall length: 13·5 m approx
Well radius: 356 mm
Magnification: ×1·5, ×6, ×12
FOV: 24°, 6°, 3°
Laser protection: Filters
TV: 16 mm SIT vidicon
STATUS
Production.
CONTRACTOR
Barr & Stroud Ltd, Melrose House, 4-6 Saville Row, London W1X 1AF, England.

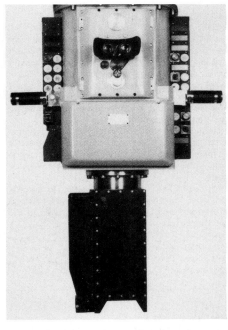

CK34 submarine search periscope

3831.493
SUBMARINE PERISCOPE IMAGE INTENSIFIER

Barr & Stroud has developed a submarine periscope image intensifier equipment which can be retrofitted to existing periscopes such as the CH74, 75, 77, and 81, and others with a tube diameter of 180 mm or more, which can accept a large aperture window, to provide an enhanced night watchkeeping capability. This equipment is offered as a refit package with a complementary laser rangefinder (**3832.493**) for periscope modernisation programmes. A low light television system that can be used with the Attack normal viewing optics or with the image intensifier, is also understood to be available.

The intensifier window near the top of the periscope amplifies the light level of the picture at the phosphor screen to an adequate level for transmission down the periscope. Use of a second-generation intensifier tube produces a high level of amplification and a capability of dealing with bright lights in the field of view. It relays a relatively high light-level image even at low illumination levels. The window being below surface in daylight eliminates unwanted glint. When accurately aligned with a laser rangefinder (if fitted) this enables the rangefinder to be used at night.

A large aperture lens system at the top of the main tube section of the periscope focuses the maximum amount of light which can be gathered with a periscope of this diameter on to the photo cathode of

an image intensifier tube. The resultant image on the tube's phosphor screen is projected via the main optical system which is designed for optimum viewing at the eyepiece(s) with ×6 magnification. The elevation reflector for the image intensification system operates at the same angle of elevation as the main elevation prisms with which it is directly connected.

The electrical supply for the image intensifier tube is derived from the window heating control unit 24 V supply, and the illumination for the graticule is by a light emitting diode (LED) projected into the main optical system. On/off switches for the tube and graticule illumination, together with a dimmer and warning light, are mounted on the faceplate. The tube, with its encapsulated power supply, is in quantity production for the Chieftain tank.

CHARACTERISTICS
Tube type: Mullard 50/40 mm diameter second-generation channel tube with encapsulated power supply

Magnification: ×6 nominal
Angular field: 7° nominal
Line of sight referred to horizon: Elevation ⩾ 15°; depression ⩾ 7½°
Graticule: LED illuminated crossline

CONTRACTOR
Barr & Stroud Ltd, Melrose House, 4-6 Saville Row, London W1X 1AF, England.

3832.493
SUBMARINE LASER RANGEFINDER

This equipment complements the Barr & Stroud submarine image intensifier (**3831.493**) for submarine periscopes. Both equipments are available as an integrated package for updating existing periscopes to provide enhanced capabilities. Used in this way the laser rangefinder provides accuracies of 10 metres over all ranges, with a digital read-out and output to the submarine's fire control system, and day/night capability. False ranges from nearby targets are eliminated.

The range is projected into the eyepiece and uses a LED display. A facility is provided to permit the operator to feed this data to a fire control system.

The main on/off switch is key operated because of the eye hazard posed by lasers. A fire button initiates the laser action for ranging on to the target indicated by the periscope graticule. The first/last range switch normally operates on last range but this gives facility to operate on first range for special situations. A

range cut button removes the range displayed and allows another ranging to proceed.

The laser is a compact Nd-YAG system operating at 1·06 micron. A flashlamp pumps the laser cord and a dye-cell Q-switch allows the generation of the high power laser pulse required for ranging applications. The receiver consists of a silicon avalanche photodiode that converts the reflected 1·06 micron laser energy into an electrical signal which is then amplified by a sensitive, wide-band, low-noise amplifier. The output from the amplifier is fed into a threshold circuit which is set to give a probability of false alarm of 0·1 per cent. With a return signal of 10 nW the amplifier produces a signal which has 99·5 per cent probability of being recorded as a target return.

Power supply, charger and pulse forming network modules convert the ship's supply of 24 V into the voltages required for all the other electronic circuits and also control the sequencing of the rangefinder operation.

The range logic board acts as an electronic stopwatch to determine the time interval from transmission of the laser pulse to reception of the target pulse. The start pulse is provided by sampling a small portion of the laser pulse and the stop pulse is direct from the receiver threshold circuit. The accuracy of timing is determined by the frequency of the internal clock which in this case gives ±10 metres for the displayed target returns (±5 metres can be achieved, if required). A switch on the ocular box allows the logic to determine the time to the first or last pulse within maximum range of the counter.

CHARACTERISTICS
Laser output from periscope window: >30 mJ
Pulse width: <10×10⁻⁹ s
Range accuracy: 10 m
CONTRACTOR
Barr & Stroud Ltd, Melrose House, 4-6 Saville Row, London W1X 1AF, England.

4721.493
BARR & STROUD SUBMARINE OPTRONICS POD

Barr & Stroud is developing a submarine optronics pod which allows a group of sensors to be mounted on a single mast, thus reducing the overall radar signature of the vessel when at periscope depth or when snorting. The pod can be mounted on top of a mast or the search periscope.

The pod is understood to include an IR18 thermal imager, a low-light level TV camera, and ESM and communications antennas. The pod exterior is covered with radar-absorbent material to minimise the reflecting area. Operating equipment includes visual display units and a remote control console for manual or automatic control.

STATUS
Early development.
CONTRACTOR
Barr & Stroud Ltd, Melrose House, 4-6 Saville Row, London W1X 1AF, England.

3405.293
IRCOM

The IRCOM system was developed by PPE to meet the requirement for directional ship to ship covert signalling. A PPE night vision device is used to sight the receiving or transmitting ship and to aim the ship's own Francis signalling lamp. The signal beam is viewed by the night sight which is sensitive to the infra-red light and is visible at up to 6 n miles in daylight and on the horizon at night.

The night sight can be used for general surveillance at night and will enable recognition of a frigate at 3 to 4 n miles under starlight conditions. Targets can be readily detected by their phosphorescent wash or shape.

The signalling light can be used to provide additional illumination for more positive identification of intruders, etc, where the sight is used in the surveillance role.

CHARACTERISTICS
Night vision system
Field of view: 22°
Magnification: ×1·4

Range (moonlight): Frigate at 4 nm
Resolution (starlight): 0·7 mrad
Tube: 3-stage 25 mm extended S20; XX1060/01 Mullard or equivalent; automatic brightness control
Weight: 4·7 kg
Size: 720 × 100 mm
Mounting: Fitted to searchlight
Signalling searchlight
Diameter: 300 mm

Power: 150, 250, or 400 W
Beam divergence: 2 – 3° depending on light source
Mounting: Pintle
Electrical
Sight: 6·7 V battery or 24 V ship supply
Searchlight: 24 V ship supply
CONTRACTOR
Pilkington PE Ltd, Glascoed Road, St Asaph, Clwyd LL17 0LL, Wales.

3794.093
MARCONI AVIONICS V300 SERIES CCTV EQUIPMENT

Marconi Avionics Ltd has designed and produces a wide range of closed-circuit television (CCTV) equipment which is used for a variety of military applications, including missile and weapon control and guidance, target damage assessment, manual or automatic target tracking, surveillance, and security uses. Development of the range began in the early 1960s and variants have been in service for some years. The V323, for example, was supplied to the Royal Navy and other navies for use in Seacat missile guidance and control and this version was described in *Jane's Weapon Systems 1974-75* and earlier editions under entry number **1021.293**.

V334

The V334 is the latest daylight/low light TV camera channel equipment in this series. It is a single unit camera of modular design as described below.

The camera is assembled from a range of modules

Several generations of Marconi V300 Series military television equipment are illustrated in these four typical applications. Top right is the V323 used on an Orion tracker radar for Seacat missile direction; top left is the V0084 low light TV system, on a Marconi ST801 tracker radar; the lower left picture shows a similar radar but this time with the latest V334 TV camera. The lower right photograph is of the V334 fitted to an MRS3 naval director

to form either a daylight or low light camera, using a selection of lenses to provide a wide angle or narrow angle field of view with a suitable aperture. The camera head incorporates the camera and optical assembly within a totally enclosed housing for full environmental protection and electromagnetic shielding.

The front section of the housing is sealed with a special window module having integral heating and wiping facilities. The optical assembly combines the objective lens and elements of the light control system, including neutral density filters, spectral filters, or focal plane apertures. The camera module provides the necessary scanning, processing circuits and supplies for a daylight TV camera. The light control module contains the additional facilities required to operate an intensifier Ebsicon low light sensor tube and allows automatic exposure control over the full range of naturally occurring illumination. Additional features include spectral and polarising filters, each of which offers conditional enhancement of video signal contrast while focal plane apertures of different sizes aid in the rejection of interfering light sources from within the field of view. A simple mechanical interface is provided for attachment of the camera to most director platforms.

Four cameras have been identified:
V3341: Low light; narrow angle field of view
V3342: Daylight; narrow angle field of view
V3343: Daylight; wide angle field of view
V3344: Low light; wide angle field of view
STATUS
The V334 daylight camera is being supplied for the RN lightweight Seawolf system, and for other RN applications. It also forms part of the Ferranti combat weapon system for four new Brazilian corvettes.
CONTRACTOR
Marconi Avionics Limited, Electro-Optical Products Division, Christopher Martin Road, Basildon, Essex SS14 3EL, England.

5729.293
V3800 THERMAL IMAGING SENSOR
The V3800 has been designed specifically for long-range detection and automatic target tracking either in support of naval tracking radars or as the prime sensor in an electro-optical fire control system. It is designed as a 'stand-alone' unit capable of incorporation into various defence systems to give indirect-viewing capability in all weathers.

The sensor is based on the UK Thermal Imaging Common Module programme class II (**4280.193**) and uses a 3° field of view narrow-angle telescope developed by Rank Pullin Controls. The high sensitivity and resolution of the V3800, together with full environmental protection, makes the equipment equally suitable for coastal defence or border surveillance applications.
STATUS
In production. The V3800 has been ordered as part of a fire control system being supplied by Ferranti to equip four new corvettes for Brazil, and by Contraves, Switzerland for its Seaguard close-in-weapon system.
CONTRACTOR
Marconi Avionics Ltd, Electro-Optical Products Division, Christopher Martin Road, Basildon, Essex SS14 3EL, England.

V3800 mounted on the nearside of the EPO 449 director (a Marconi V334 daylight/low light TV camera is on the other side)

3765.093
VINTEN TRACKING MOUNT
The Vinten tracking mount has been designed and developed to military specification to meet UK MoD requirements. It is a compact, robust, portable unit designed for accurate tracking of moving targets. The mount is designed to carry a wide range of sensors and rangefinders including laser rangefinders and target markers, cameras recording either photographic or electronic images, night observation and thermal imaging devices. The mount is designed to accept single or multiple equipments which can be boresighted to each other and to an aiming viewfinder.

The payload can be positioned for convenient operator viewing and the mount adjusted for an imbalance of load up to 690 kg/cm. To allow smooth and accurate tracking at both high and low slew rates, an easily adjustable friction-free drag is incorporated in both axes.

The mount is available with or without data read-out but all equipments are manufactured to accept data. Movement of the equipment pointing angle is measured by an encoder disc on each axis. Angular movement is measured as decimal degrees and can be shown, on a sunlight readable display located in the base of the mount, as either decimal degrees, milliradians or artillery mils (3600/6400). The output, in the form of a digital signal, can be used to operate peripheral equipment for weapon control and guidance or similar applications.

Payloads may be mounted either directly onto the lightweight mounting table or employ the current Army interface assembly. A tripod base, with adjustable feet for levelling on rough terrain, can be supplied with the mount.
CHARACTERISTICS
Bearing system accuracy: Better than 0·5 mrad
Balance to cancel imbalance loads up to 690 kg/cm
Payload: Up to 45 kg
STATUS
Production.
CONTRACTOR
W Vinten Limited, Western Way, Bury St Edmunds, Suffolk IP33 3TB, England.

Vinten tracking mount with typical payload

4109.293
ROD REMOTE OPTRONICS DIRECTOR
A high performance line-of-sight stabilised remotely controlled optronic director (ROD) by Laurence, Scott (Defence Systems) Limited is the result of four years' work on naval stabilised directors and research on the remote optronic director.

The director, which is suitable for fitting to any surface vessel, provides surveillance, tracking and fire control direction. Weighing approximately 155 kg, it can carry a sensor load of up to 75 kg on each side of the training head. It has an excellent field of vision with unlimited azimuth tracking capability.

Control is by joystick from below deck with the dynamic package being suitable for auto-track. The sensor payload capability and dynamic configuration enable the selection of virtually any optronic sensor package. Sensors include low light television and thermal imaging cameras, and laser rangefinders supplied by Marconi, Barr & Stroud and Ericsson, but other types of different manufacture may be fitted.
CHARACTERISTICS: (minus sensors)
Weight: 155 kg
Height: 1080 mm (overall); 880 mm (sensor axis)
Width: 710 mm
Training arc: Unlimited
Elevation arc: –30 to +85°
Training: 150°/s² (acceleration); 120°/s (velocity)
Elevation: 150°/s² (acceleration); 90°/s (velocity)
Shock: 30 gV; 12 gH
Temperature: –20 to +55°C ambient
STATUS
In production.
CONTRACTOR
Laurence, Scott (Defence Systems) Limited, PO Box 25, Norwich, Norfolk NR1 1JD, England.

LSDS remote optronic director (ROD)

4238.293
LROD LIGHTWEIGHT REMOTE OPTRONICS DIRECTOR

The Laurence, Scott lightweight remote optronics director (LROD) has been designed to match the trend toward lower cost, but effective, fire control equipment demanded for surface vessels of all types. It provides surveillance, tracking and fire control direction, and the general principle of operation is similar to that of the company's ROD remote optronic director (**4109.293**, above). Weighing about 60 kg, the LROD can carry a sensor load equal to its own weight and has a capability for two complete turns in azimuth in its standard form, although where required slip-rings can be fitted to permit unlimited traverse.

Control is by a joystick from below deck, although the servo arrangements are suitable for use in automatic tracking systems. Typical sensors are the Marconi televison camera and Ericsson laser rangefinder sight shown in the adjacent illustration.

CHARACTERISTICS
Weight: 60 kg
Height: 620 mm (overall); 525 mm (sensor axis)
Training arc: 2 turns (standard); continuous unlimited optional
Elevation arc: –40 to +85°
Training: 150°/s² (acceleration); 120°/s velocity
Elevation: 150°/s² (acceleration); 90°/s velocity
Shock: 10 g both planes
STATUS
Early production. No details of ship fittings.
CONTRACTOR
Laurence, Scott (Defence Systems) Limited, PO Box 25, Norwich, Norfolk NR1 1JD, England.

4720.293
DIRECTOR AIM STABILISED LOOK-OUT EQUIPMENT

The Director Aim Stabilised Look-out Equipment (DASLE) is a lightweight line-of-sight stabilised unit comprising a deck-mounted pedestal with a rotating head, and a platform which carries a seated operator. A binocular is mounted at eye-level on an elevating arm, and seat height is adjustable. Facilities are also incorporated for fitting additional sensors, ie laser rangers, thermal imagers and TV, which, with the aid of autotrack facilities can provide an advanced system for passive direction and laser rangefinding. On-mount prediction facilities can also be fitted.

Two servo systems are incorporated, one to train the rotating head on to the target, the other to position the binocular arm and sensors in accordance with target elevation. The servo systems can be controlled either locally by the operator or remotely from the associated fire control system (FCS).

Under local control, the director constitutes the principal control point of an FCS. The servo systems are gyro-stabilised to offset random ship motion, and as the operator tracks a target, positional information of the latter, in the form of synchro signals, is fed to other sections of the system as follows:

(1) target training and elevation to the FCS
(2) target training and elevation to the gun mounting and/or missile launcher
(3) target bearing to an indicator.

When the director is set-up for remote control, the training and elevation servo systems are stabilised by a tachogenerator feedback and fed with synchro signals from external sources, eg tracker radar, via the FCS. The director operator acts as an observer, verbally recording fall-of-shot and similar information. Synchro signals are fed to other sections of the system as in the local operating mode.

A further operating mode is incorporated which is used in place of the remote mode permitting elevation to be controlled locally while the director is trained remotely by FCS signals.

CHARACTERISTICS
Overall height: 1820 mm
Weight (without sensors): 615 kg
STATUS
Early development.
CONTRACTOR
Laurence Scott (Defence Systems) Ltd, PO Box 25, Kerrison Road, Norwich, Norfolk NR1 1JD, England.

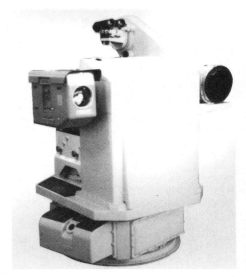

Director Aim Stabilised Look-out Equipment

4129.093
SERIES 2000 PLUS FIRE DIRECTOR

Series 2000 PLUS maritime fire control equipment is designed to locate and follow fast moving targets, providing video and data returns for general surveillance, gun-laying computation, action information and post-mission analysis.

The sensors, normally comprising a TV camera, thermal imager and laser rangefinder, are mounted on a gyro-stabilised electro-optical director. A choice of three basic designs for the director is available, each with a number of options to suit the payload and environment. Pictured here is the EPO429 mount, capable of high positioning accuracy with payloads up to 200 kg. The internal 120-way slip-ring enclosure allows continuous azimuth rotation. Also available are the EPO409 mount for light payloads, and the new EPO449 high-performance unit capable of continuous rotation and velocities in excess of three radians per second. The 409 and 429 can be equipped with binocular sights and local joystick for above-deck training onto the target.

The basic below-deck equipment configuration enables the director to be controlled by joystick for manual tracking and surveillance tasks. At the top end of the Series 2000 PLUS range the equipment is structured as a fully integrated weapons system with closed-loop TV tracking and gun-laying computation. The TV tracker unit enables the director to lock-on to any feature entering a defined 'gate' area within the video field. Lock is held despite target-profile variation; a special 'coast' facility enables immediate re-acquisition after momentary loss, for example, behind clouds.

The company also produces mounts for waveguide-fed antennas, lightweight heads for CCTV surveillance, and X-Y camera tables for presenting graphics.

STATUS
EPO equipment is in service with several of the world's navies and has been specified by two major UK EW system manufacturers.

EPO429 electro-optical director

CONTRACTOR
Evershed Power-Optics Limited, Bridge Road, Chertsey, Surrey KT16 8LJ, England.

4719.293
FERRANTI MULTI-ROLE NAVAL LASERS

Ferranti has developed a number of lasers which can be used in naval applications. The Type 908 rangefinder/designator is modular in concept and is one of a family of naval lasers using common modules. The constituent parts come from the extensive range of successful systems used worldwide in various operational roles. The basic version uses a Type 629 general purpose laser transmitter (**4787.193**) operating at medium power in the wavelength of 1·064 μm and delivering high stability coded pulses.

The Type 908 is a twin aperture equipment, with transmit optics which have a variable beamwidth to allow for rangefinding or illumination. A high sensitivity wide aperture receiver enables rangefinding at extended ranges, the system using the Type 629 transmitter being able to range to 20 km and designate to 9 km. An alternative, the Type 905 high power laser module, is directly interchangeable with the Type 629 and gives the Type 908 a capability of rangefinding out to 35 km and target designation to 16 km.

A simple external attachment to the Type 908 can convert it into a homing beacon for those aircraft which are fitted with either a Ferranti Laser Ranger and Marked Target Seeker (**1196.393**), or a simple infra-red detector with small field of view.

Ferranti is also developing an interchangeable receiver module which will provide angle error information to the director servo system, and thus an auto tracking capability, by the use of a quadrant photodiode in place of the existing ranging diode.

STATUS
In production.
CONTRACTOR
Ferranti plc, St. Andrews Works, Robertson Avenue, Edinburgh EH11 1PX, Scotland.

Type 908 laser rangefinder/designator

UNITED STATES OF AMERICA

4021.293
MODEL 910 STABILISED SIGHT
The Model 910 stabilised naval sight provides viewing for an observer within the pilot house. Two magnifications are provided, ×8 and ×2, with fields of view of 7° and 28° in the object space, respectively. The sight can be used as an entity, completely independent of the fire control system. In addition, the sight can be a master or a slave to the other sub-systems aboard the ship. The system can be used for reconnaissance or to provide position data for slaving a weapon turret. Regardless of the mode, boresight information is generated at all times. The sight has almost unlimited access to the visible hemisphere above the ship. By means of a gimbaled prism, the line of sight can be depressed –10°, elevated to +85°, and rotated continuously 360° about a vertical axis. Within these bounds, the only hindrances to the line of sight are those provided by the ship itself.

CHARACTERISTICS
Optical
Magnification: ×2; ×8
Elevation LOS: –10 to +45°
Fields of view: 28° at ×2 magnification; 7° at ×8 magnification
Eyepiece focus: ±3 dioptres

Electrical
LOS stabilisation: Dual axis ±20° of motion at 0·5 Hz to 2 mrad
Tracking accuracy: ±1 mrad
Slewing rates: Azimuth and/or elevation 100°/s
Output signals: 2-speed resolver with 1 mrad accuracy for elevation and azimuth analogue output
System weight: 100 kg (approx)
STATUS
Initially produced for use on tracked vehicles.
CONTRACTOR
Kollmorgen Corporation, Electro-Optical Division, Northampton, Massachusetts 01060, USA.

4024.293
MODEL 975 OPTRONIC DIRECTOR
The Model 975 optronic director has the function of acquiring and tracking surface or air targets for surveillance or directing the ship's defensive weapons. The platform's line of sight is internally stabilised in two axes to the deck plane. Under control of an operator, automatic tracking and range determination of targets are available using the television system or infra-red target pointer and the laser rangefinder. The ship's weapons can be slaved to the optronic director through the fire control system. The director optical scanning capability can be combined with inputs from an existing ship's fire control system or it can be integrated with the Kollmorgen fire control system (**4019.281**).

The director can be utilised in three modes of operation:
(1) search (surveillance mode)
(2) weapon slave (manual or automatic target tracking mode)
(3) director slaved (external designation).

Operational features include: stabilised line of sight; low light-level television with automatic tracking; infra-red target pointer or thermal imaging; laser rangefinder; optional visual capability.

CHARACTERISTICS
Electrical
Angular coverage: –25 to +70° elevation; n × 360° azimuth
Slew rate: 120°/s² (acceleration); 80°/s (velocity)
Tracking rate: 80°/s² (acceleration); 80°/s (velocity)
Tracking accuracy: ±20 mrad
Television
Field of view (FOV): 30° or 7·5°
Resolution (angular): 1 mrad
Scan rates: 525/60 (other scan rates available)
Video output: 1 V P-P, 75 Ω termination
Thermal imaging sensor
Wavelength: 8 – 12 μm
Field of view: 12° wide; 4° narrow
Detector: MCT (Sprite)
Cooler: Closed cycle (Split Sterling)
Laser
Type: Nd-YAG
Power: 4 mW
Pulse energy (radiated): 60 mJ
Repetition rate: 10 pps/continuous
Range: 12 km (with good visibility)
STATUS
Production.
CONTRACTOR
Kollmorgen Corporation, Electro-Optical Division, Northampton, Massachusetts 01060, USA.

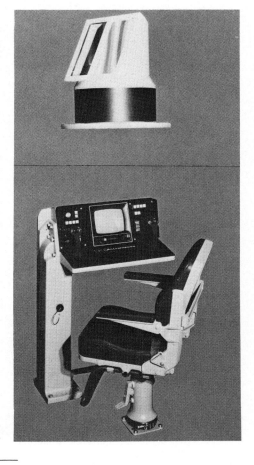

Kollmorgen Model 975 optronic director showing above-deck optical head and operator's console

4023.293
MODEL 985 OPTICAL DIRECTOR
The Model 985 optical director has the function of acquiring and tracking surface and air targets. It is an internally stabilised optical aiming instrument which provides target bearing and elevation signals to the ship's weapon. It consists of:
(1) the director, including all required components for self-stabilisation, power change, and focusing
(2) control console, including all controls, indicators, and read-outs

(3) junction box through which all inputs and outputs are interfaced. Miscellaneous electrical and electronic components are housed in the junction box
(4) cabling to interface the junction box to the console and the director.
CHARACTERISTICS
Angular coverage: –25 to +70° (elevation); n × 360° (azimuth)
Slew rate: 120°/s² (acceleration); 80°/s (velocity)
Tracking rate: 80°/s² (acceleration); 80°/s (velocity)

Tracking accuracy: ±2 mrad
Magnification: ×2, ×8
Field of view: 30°; 7·5°
Focus: 10 m – infinity
STATUS
In production for approximately 50 FPBs.
CONTRACTOR
Kollmorgen Corporation, Electro-Optical Division, Northampton, Massachusetts 01060, USA.

3097.293
Mk 5 LOW LIGHT-LEVEL TV SYSTEM
The Mk 5 LLLTV system can be used for day and night target detection and recognition, extremely long-range detection of faint light sources at night, damage assessment, multiple target discrimination, plus general surveillance and navigation purposes.

The system normally operates at standard line rates, thus permitting easy use with additional remote monitors, video tape recorders, and video trackers, but simple modifications are available for operation at other than standard line rates.

When mounted on the Mk 73 guided missile director, the Mk 5 TV system provides day and night remote viewing capability for the Mk 74 Tartar fire control system.
STATUS
Operational with the USN as part of the Mk 74 Tartar missile fire control system.
CONTRACTOR
General Electric Company, Aircraft Equipment Division, French Road, Utica, New York 13503, USA.

Mk 5 low light-level television system mounted on USN Mk 73 guided missile director

ELECTRO-OPTICAL EQUIPMENT (AIR)

FRANCE

7032.393

APX M334 SERIES GYRO-STABILISED SIGHTS

The APX M334 sight has been designed for the surveillance of land, detection and acquisition of targets, and guidance of missiles in manual remote control.

OPERATION

The equipment consists of a monocular, angularly positioned single lens sight, a body made of a prism correcting the image slanting and a panoramic head including a gyroscope for stabilisation. Two magnifications, ×2·5 and ×10, are provided and the mirror scanning speed is adjustable from 1·5'/s to 13·5°/s at the lower magnification, and from 1·5'/s to 4·5°/s at ×10 magnification. The field of view is 22° at magnification ×2·5 and 5° 30' at magnification ×10; the total scanning field is 262° in azimuth and 72° in elevation.

In the wide field of view, a luminous circle represents the narrow field, and angular differences between the line of sight and the axis of the helicopter can be indicated. For safety reasons the eyepiece is retractable when the equipment is not in use to enable the operator to have normal unobstructed vision outside the aircraft.

The M334 forms the basis of a series of sights; M334-02, M334-04 (**3763.393**), M334-25 (**3763.393**); M397 for HOT, M396 in the Atlantic aircraft and M334-05.

STATUS

In production. In operation on nine types of helicopter and serving with the forces of nine countries. The M334-13 is fitted in WG13 and AB212 helicopters.

CONTRACTOR

SFIM (Société de Fabrication d'Instruments de Mesure), 13 avenue Ramolfo-Garnier, BP 74, 91301 Massy Cedex, France (under DTAT-APX licence).

APX M334 gyro-stabilised sight and control box

3661.393

TCV 115 AIRBORNE LASER RANGEFINDER

The TCV 115 laser rangefinder was designed for integration into the gyro-stabilised APX M334-04 helicopter sight (**3763.393**), and consists of a TCV 80H laser rangefinder and an optical assembly which adapts the rangefinder to the sight and also ensures the projection of the rangefinder cross-hairs in the eyepiece of the sight. The TCV 80H laser rangefinder is also employed in the APX M550 rangefinder/sight (**3414.193**) for land-based use.

CHARACTERISTICS

Wavelength: 1·06 micron
Pulse duration: 25×10^{-9} s
Energy: 100 mJ
Peak power: 4 MW
Divergence of emitted beam: ⩽0·7 mrad
Detector: Avalanche photodiode

Minimum detectable power: ⩽2×10^{-8} W
Receiver field: ⩽0·5 mrad
Operating voltage: Rangefinder 19 – 28V DC; graticule projector 115V/400Hz
Dimensions: 390 × 190 × 180 mm
Weight: 8kg (with optical assembly)
Measurement range: 450 – 19 900 m
Accuracy: ±10 m
Repetition rate: 1 measurement every 2 s for 3 successive shots; 12 measurements/minute

An optical attenuator in the eyepiece ensures protection for the operator's eye during laser firing and provides attenuation of 70 dB at 1·06 micron

STATUS

In series production.

CONTRACTOR

CILAS (Compagnie Industrielle des Lasers), route de Nozay, 91460 Marcoussis, France.

CILAS TCV 115 airborne laser rangefinder

3763.393

APX M334-04 GYRO-STABILISED SIGHT

The APX M334-04 gyro-stabilised sight is an improved model developed from the APX M334 sight (**7032.393**). The main items of the equipment are: the sight itself incorporating a gyro-stabilised mirror allowing the aiming axis to be kept stable irrespective of pitch and yaw movements; an aiming control stick which controls the sight in azimuth and elevation; an optional direction indicator for use by the pilot; and an electronics unit.

The APX M334-04 sight can be fitted if needed with a luminous reticle generator, a fire simulator device, a laser rangefinder, a special eyepiece bearing arm, a TV or cine camera and electronics for sighting assistance.

The APX M334-04 sight is of the monocular type with two magnifications, ×3·2 and ×10·8, the respective fields of view being 300 and 90 mrad. The total scan field is 260° in azimuth and 70° in elevation. The azimuth scan raster can be varied in a stepless

fashion over the range 0·2 to 230 mrad with ×3·2 magnification, and 0·2 to 80 mrad with ×10·8 magnification. Stabilisation and aiming accuracy is better than 0·1 mrad.

The M334-04, equipped with a laser rangefinder, forms the main element of the SFIM OSLOH (Optique Stabilisée de Localisation d'Objectifs sur Hélicoptères) system developed for target detection and localisation by aircraft and helicopters. In this application the nomenclature is M334-25.

STATUS

Production.

CONTRACTOR

SFIM (Société de Fabrication d'Instruments de Mesure), 13 avenue Ramolfo-Garnier, BP 74, 91301 Massy Cedex, France (under DTAT-APX licence).

SFIM APX M334-04 stabilised sight in French military helicopter

---

4239.393

PGS 600 STABILISED OPTRONIC SYSTEMS

PGS 600 systems are designed to add night capability to airborne sighting systems and include a two or three field FLIR, a long focal distance TV and a rangefinder.

PGS 600 systems can be fitted on helicopters in a variety of ways; pod-mounted, chin-mounted as in the Heloise system on the Dauphin or rotor-mast

mounted as the Ophelia system on the BO 105 and the Pharaon system on the Gazelle.

Another version of the PGS 600, Venus, is used on the Dauphin helicopter as a night aiming system for the aircraft HOT anti-tank missile system. The mast-mounted systems allow all-azimuth sighting with the helicopter staying under cover.

DEVELOPMENT

SFIM has developed a lightweight day/night system

for use with the next generation of combat helicopters. It is a third-generation device which can be mounted on the aircraft chin, roof or rotor mast.

CHARACTERISTICS

Diameter of sphere: 600 mm
Angular displacement: 55° elevation; 180° azimuth; for mast-mounted system
Stabilisation: 300 μrad (coarse); fine limits are classified

STATUS
Initial production.
CONTRACTOR
SFIM (Société de Fabrication d'Instruments de Mesure), 13 avenue Ramolfo-Garnier, BP 74, 91301 Massy Cedex, France.

SFIM stabilised optical platform as used in Venus fire control system for Dauphin helicopter

SFIM optronic stabilised platform carrying surveillance and sighting sensors for Ophelia system mounted on top of rotor hub of MBB PAH-1 helicopter

4725.393
SCOTCH WEAPON DELIVERY SYSTEM
The Scotch weapon delivery system is intended specifically for use on helicopters for target tracking and aiming in air-to-air or air-to-ground gun or rocket fire, and presentation of data to the pilot during the target tracking phases. The system consists of a COLTH weapon sight and its associated control unit, and an electronics unit which incorporates a computer. The COLTH sight, which projects a ballistic reticle at infinity, is installed in the upper section of the helicopter cabin and offers a maximum field of view together with minimum masking.

The system is connected to the aircraft sensors which supply the data required, including a rate gyro unit which provides the angular rates of the helicopter. The computer constantly determines the point of impact of the munitions. This point is displayed by the reticle generated by COLTH and superimposed on the landscape. The reticle is slaved to the position of the weapon, with firing corrections superimposed. The computer can be an integral part of the helicopter fire control system.
CHARACTERISTICS
Reticle definition: 140 (±8) mrad in elevation and azimuth
Field of view: azimuth 22°; elevation 20°
Colour of reticle: Blue-green (adjustable brightness)
Accuracy: 1 mrad
Weight: 8 kg
Power supply: 28V dc 120W
STATUS
Pre-production.
CONTRACTOR
SFIM (Société de Fabrication d'Instruments de Mesure), 13 avenue Ramolfo-Garnier, BP 74, 91301 Massy Cedex, France.

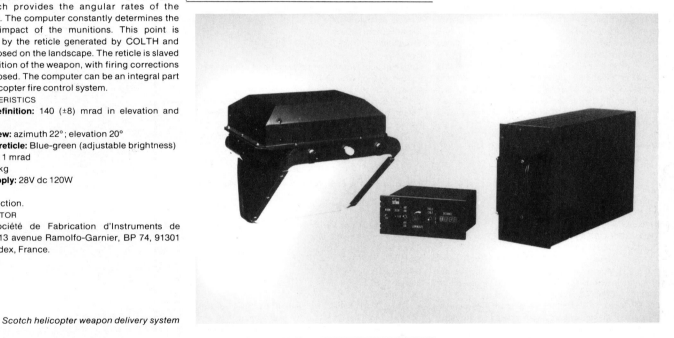

Scotch helicopter weapon delivery system

3856.393
VENUS HOT/HELICOPTER NIGHT SIGHT
The Venus system enables the Dauphin-type helicopters, equipped with HOT anti-armour missiles, to engage tanks in complete darkness (the helicopter is equipped with a night flying system). The Venus system is an adjunct to the standard HOT weapon system, with the same missile and a small modification to the firing post. The night sight and missile IR localising equipments are grouped within a blister located in the nose of the helicopter.

The Venus system is mainly composed of a SFIM gyro-stabilised platform (**4239.393**) supporting a TRT Hector thermal camera (**3854.393**) used to detect, recognise and identify a target from its IR radiation, and a SAT deviation measuring instrument, used to track the missile and supply deviation signals (in relation to the platform axis). There is also a canopy-mounted M 397 stabilised day sight.

A control unit, equipped with a control stick, is provided for the operator, to control the platform axis and, thereby, the line of sight. The platform also accommodates fine stabilising devices. The thermal camera operates in the ten micron band and has two optical fields: one to observe and detect the targets, the other to recognise, identify and track them during the firing sequence. Joule-Thomson effect-type cooling is provided. The received IR image is displayed on a CRT screen located in the eyepiece of the gyro-stabilised sight: the switch-over from day to night observation, and inversely, is thus performed by

Venus HOT/helicopter night sight

a mere switching action. The localiser also has two optical fields, one to capture the missile and the other to track it during the cruising phase.

CHARACTERISTICS

Thermal camera: Large field 8·1 × 5·4°; small field 2·7 × 1·8°
Localiser: Large field ±4°; small field ±0·5°
Platform assembly movement: Azimuth +30 to –20°; elevation 110°
Diameter: 600 mm

Weight: 90 kg
Target detection range: >5000 m
Target engagement range: 4000 m
STATUS
The Venus programme was implemented as a collaborative project and tests of the system's night firing capabilities were concluded successfully in early 1981. More than 50 successful firings have been carried out, even at extreme ranges.

CONTRACTORS
Main contractor: Aerospatiale-Euromissile
   Principal sub-contractors: SFIM, SAT, TRT

3855.393

HADES HELICOPTER LASER ANGLE TRACKER

The HADES system is intended for military helicopters and is used to control missile launching at laser designated targets, under day and night conditions.

The system performs the following functions: target search within a wide angular domain; acquisition of designation targets; automatic target tracking through continuous, accurate aiming of the fire control sight at the illuminated target; enlargement of firing envelope in conjunction with the laser rangefinder.

The HADES equipment consists of two compact modular sub-assemblies: a detection module and an electronic module. The former is associated with the optical unit of the sight, while the latter supplies angular error data to the servomechanisms.

CHARACTERISTICS
Acquisition field: 10° (elevation); ±10° (bearing)
Supply voltage: 28 V DC
Weight: 2 kg
STATUS
Design studies.
CONTRACTOR
Thomson-CSF, Division Equipements Avioniques, 178 boulevard Gabriel-Péri, 92240 Malakoff, Paris, France.

3854.393

HECTOR IMAGING IR EQUIPMENT

The Hector thermal imagery camera is designed for firing the HOT anti-tank missile from the Dauphin helicopter at night and under poor visibility. It allows target detection and identification by converting their infra-red energy into a visible image which is also used for guidance and firing.

This programme is known as Venus (see **3856.393** and **4239.393** above) and a similar programme called Ophelia has been undertaken for the MBB PAH-1 helicopter. In the latter system TRT provides an imaging FLIR named Calipso which has similar characteristics to Hector.

CHARACTERISTICS
Wavelengths: 8, 13 microns
Analysis: Series parallel

Detector: Photovoltaic CdHgTe cooled to 77° K
Cooler: Joule-Thomson effect
Display: Standard miniature TV cathode-ray tube
Integration in gyro stabilised platform (**4239.393**)
Vehicle detection: 4000 m
Identification: 2000 m
Visual field: 10·8 × 6·2° and 2·8 × 1·6°
STATUS
Under experimentation by Aerospatiale. Developed in co-operation with SAT.
CONTRACTORS
TRT (Télécommunications Radioélectriques et Téléphoniques), 88 rue Brillat-Savarin, 75640 Paris, France.
   SAT (Société Anonyme de Télécommunications), 41 rue Cantagrel, 75624 Paris, France.

Hector IR camera mounted on a Dauphin helicopter

3136.393

THOMSON-CSF ATLIS LASER TARGET DESIGNATION POD

ATLIS (automatic-tracking laser illumination system) is a high precision air-to-ground designation system mounted in a pod. It can be mounted on single-seater combat aircraft. The system consists of:

(1) TV/laser fire control pod with TV camera operating with wide or narrow field of view, laser illuminator/rangefinder, automatic two-mode TV tracking, stabilising system, and air-conditioning system
(2) monitoring and control panel and a hand controller in the cockpit, associated with a TV monitor if no TV-type display equipment is already available. The system can be connected to the head-up display, or the radar navigation system or helmet sight for target predesignation.

OPERATION

ATLIS is used for low altitude, high speed, autonomous attack of surface targets with laser-guided weapons; it reduces risks for the attacker

Launch of AS.30 Laser missile from a Jaguar equipped with Thomson-CSF LDP designator pod

owing to the immediate breakaway and long stand-off ranges allowed by the system.

CHARACTERISTICS
Weight: 160 kg
Diameter: 300 mm
Length: 2·52 m
DEVELOPMENT
In 1975 Thomson-CSF awarded a $3·7 million contract to Martin Marietta Aerospace for the development and test of the ATLIS pod. The French company is prime contractor to the French Government, and is responsible for all the cockpit equipment (HUD, video monitor, and controls). The Orlando Division of Martin Marietta is responsible for the pod. The French CILAS company is providing the laser illuminator. Joint arrangements have been concluded between Thomson-CSF and Martin Marietta for the commercial exploitation of the ATLIS pod.

STATUS
Flight tests of an ATLIS prototype system (ATLIS 1) were carried out using a single-seat Jaguar aircraft over a period of five months in late 1976 and early 1977. During that period 44 flights were accomplished by seven different pilots, and favourable results were obtained. About 700 passes against a wide variety of targets were made and these confirmed the ability of the equipment to locate and mark targets for attack by a laser guided missile such as the AS.30 Laser (**3335.311**) from a range of 10 km.

The results of this programme resulted in a French Air Force decision to equip a number of Jaguar aircraft with ATLIS pods and cockpit viewing and control equipment. Development of suitable laser guided bombs and rockets by Matra/Thomson-CSF and Thomson/Brandt is continuing in parallel with AS.30 Laser development by Aerospatiale using the Thomson-CSF Ariel laser seeker.

Laser target designation pod

Following completion of ATLIS pod development, Thomson-CSF and Martin Marietta have developed two new prototypes of an ATLIS 2 (**3820.393**) for use with Jaguar and F-16 type aircraft. The new model weighs 160 kg (compared with the 240 kg of the original ATLIS) and includes a computer capable of directly interfacing with a digital bus-bar as employed in modern aircraft such as the Mirage 2000 and F-16.

By October 1980 ATLIS 2 flight tests had been completed successfully, including firings of AS.30 Laser missiles and laser-guided bombs which all scored direct hits, and production had begun for French Air Force Jaguar aircraft. Thomson-CSF LDP flight tests with Mirage 2000 aircraft were carried out in 1982.

CONTRACTOR
Thomson-CSF, Division Equipements Avioniques, 178 boulevard Gabriel Péri, 92240 Malakoff, Paris, France.

3423.393
THOMSON-CSF VE 110 HEAD-UP DISPLAY
This display comprises two units: a pilot display unit and an electronic unit operating in conjunction with the aircraft nav-attack system. These are described separately in the following paragraphs.
Pilot Display Unit: Collimated images are generated by a pilot display unit which includes: high brilliance and long-life CRT with its deflection control coils, providing stroke written or raster images; the EHT generation circuits; a collimation optical system with a large-diameter lens (110 mm for the VE 110 model

Thomson-CSF VE 110 head-up display

which is a simplified version adapted to light combat or training aircraft); the power supply; and push-button test. A sight recorder mount and pilot controls are provided at the rear part of the pilot display unit. A special mount permits instantaneous replacement of the pilot display unit without any adjustment or re-harmonisation.
Electronic Unit: The symbol generation, ballistic and flight circuits, the interface with the digital data transmission system, and an integrated test system are contained in the electronic unit. The electronic circuitry is of solid-state, integrated circuit type. All circuits are distributed on plug-in cards. The technology used in this equipment gives maximum design flexibility.
OPERATION
The following functions are provided:
(1) Air-to-air:
  (a) All weather interception (operation with a fire control radar such as the Thomson-CSF Cyrano) with display of flight and target information, and flight director.
  (b) Missile launching: missiles of all types can be launched and the HUD may accommodate any type of approach: snap-up or down, head-on, etc.
  (c) Gunfire: with or without radar to provide target range and closing speed, the HUD will provide lead angle and gravity drop

corrections, or it will provide a continuous computation of tracer line generating a synthetic line for snap shooting in dog-fight conditions.
(2) Air-to-ground:
  (a) Conventional armament (gun, rocket, bombs): the HUD provides flight, target, and aiming information in continuous computation of impact point or continuous computation of release point mode for automatic bomb release.
  (b) Special weapons: the HUD is designed to allow operation of a large variety of special weapons, eg missiles of all types including laser or electro-optically guided weapons.
(3) Navigation
  The HUD displays flight and target information, flight director and optionally, TV presentation of FLIR images.
(4) All weather approach and STOL landing.
STATUS
The VE 110 is in production for the modernised Mirage III/IV, the Alpha Jet NG and other light tactical support/trainer aircraft. It is also fitted to the Mirage III G.
CONTRACTOR
Thomson-CSF, Division Equipements Avioniques, 178 boulevard Gabriel Péri, 92240 Malakoff, Paris, France.

1317.393
THOMSON-CSF SERIES 121-196 ATTACK SIGHTS
These displays comprise three units: a collimating head projecting a coloured display; an electronic unit, for signal processing; a pilot's control unit (not required if the head-up display (HUD) is operated through the control unit of the nav/attack system).
Collimating Unit: The coloured display required for an operating mode is obtained with servoed reticles, controlled by signals from the electronic unit. Up to four different sets of reticles may be used. After optical mixing of reticles' images, collimation is effected by a large 120 mm lens.
Electronic Unit: This fulfils the following functions: interface with the nav/attack system associated to the HUD elaboration of the display control signals delivered to the collimating head, according to the operating mode; permanent auto-test of the HUD; power supply.
OPERATION
The following modes may be available:
(1) Air-to-air (operation with a fire control radar, such as the Cyrano)
  (a) All weather interception with display of flight information (horizon, altitude, airspeed), and target information (elevation/azimuth, range, closing speed).
  (b) Missile launching: missiles of all types can be launched, and the HUD may accommodate any type of approach: snap-up or down, head-on etc.

  (c) Gunfire: the HUD is designed to permit automatic gunfire at optimum radar range, in all-weather conditions, with no limitation (such as altitude, speed, etc).
(2) Air-to-ground
  (a) Conventional armament (gun, rocket, bombs): the HUD provides the following display for air-ground attacks: target position, for all-weather approach and ranging (laser or radar, with subsequent display of range to target); bomb impact line roll stabilised, drift corrected, enabling accurate automatic release of low drag and high drag bombs; and altitude levels.
  (b) Special weapons: the HUD is designed to enable operation of a large variety of special weapons, eg missiles of all types, AS.30, Martel, cluster bombs, etc.
(3) Navigation and landing
  (a) Navigation (cruise, terrain following, target approach): the following data can be displayed: horizon; heading and heading commands to keep a selected track; altitude and altitude commands; airspeed (or Mach number) and airspeed commands; flight director.
  (b) All weather approach: this provides for the additional display of the axis of an instrument landing system.
  (c) STOL landing: this is a special display which enables a precise control of flight path angle

Thomson-CSF A 121 attack sight collimating head

and airspeed, resulting in an accurate impact on the runway threshold (within ±30 m), with the proper airspeed.
STATUS
Systems of this type are in production for the French Air Force and for export. The 121 sight is fitted in the Jaguar mainly for air-to-ground missions; the 196 sight is employed in the Mirage F1 principally for air-to-air roles.
CONTRACTOR
Thomson-CSF, Division Equipements Avioniques, 178 boulevard Gabriel Péri, 92240 Malakoff, Paris, France.

3135.393
THOMSON-CSF SERIES VE 120/130 HEAD-UP DISPLAYS
These displays comprise two units: a pilot display unit and an electronic unit operating in connection with the aircraft nav/attack system.
Pilot Display Unit: Collimated images are generated by a pilot display unit which includes: high brilliance and long-life CRT with its deflection control coils, providing stroke written or raster images; the EHT generation circuits; a collimation optical system with a large-diameter lens and combiner giving a large IFOV and a push-button built-in test. A sight recorder mount and pilot controls are provided at the rear part of the pilot display unit. A special mount permits instantaneous replacement of the pilot display unit without any adjustment or pre-harmonisation.
Electronic Unit: The symbol generation, fire computation and navigation computation circuits, the interface with the digital data transmission system, and an integrated test system are contained in the electronic unit. The electronic circuitry is of solid-state, integrated circuit type. All circuits are distributed on plug-in cards. The technology used in

Thomson-CSF VE 120 head-up display unit

this equipment gives maximum design flexibility and allows modifications in symbology. An air-to-air sensor unit, Thomson-CSF AA 120 containing rate gyros, can be added to the system for gyro lead fire control.

OPERATION
The following functions are provided:
(1) Air-to-air
  (a) All weather interception (operation with a fire control radar such as the Thomson-CSF Cyrano) with display of flight and target information, and flight director.
  (b) Missile launching: missiles of all types can be launched and the HUD may accommodate any type of approach snap-up or down, head-on etc.
  (c) Gunfire: with or without radar to provide target range and closing speed the HUD will provide lead angle and gravity drop corrections, or it will provide a continuous computation of tracer line generating a synthetic line for snap shooting in dog-fight conditions.
(2) Air-to-ground
  (a) Conventional armament (gun, rocket, bombs): the HUD provides flight, target and aiming information in continuous computation of impact point or continuous computation of release point mode.

(b) Special weapons: the HUD is designed to allow operation of a large variety of special weapons, eg missiles of all types including laser or electro-optically guided weapons.

(3) Navigation

The HUD displays flight and target information, flight director and TV or FLIR images.

(4) All weather approach and STOL landing.

STATUS

Systems are in production for the Super-Etendard of the French Navy, for Mirage F1 and integrated in an all-electronic multi-display system on the Mirage 2000 (**4723.393**).

CONTRACTOR

Thomson-CSF, Division Equipements Avioniques, 178 boulevard Gabriel Péri, 92240 Malakoff, Paris, France.

Thomson-CSF 130 head-up display unit

4723.393
TMV 980A ELECTRONIC MULTIDISPLAY SYSTEM

The TMV 980A is a highly flexible multimode, multicolour digital display system for the Mirage 2000 aircraft. It consists of an integrated head-up display (HUD), a head-down display (HDD), a complementary HDD in monochrome and an electronics unit/digital computer. The system is intended for use by the pilot in most stages of the mission, using either the HUD or HDD as appropriate. Information on the displays is provided by the various sensors on board and is designed to give the pilot all the information required for a particular phase of his flight.

The VE 130 HUD (**3135.393**) has a large field of view through the windscreen and provides information symbols collimated on the combining glass at infinity. It uses a 3 inch high-resolution, high-brightness, monocolour (green) cathode ray tube associated with the collimating optical system. The 5·1 inch diameter collimating lens gives wide instantaneous field of view which is enlarged in elevation by the use of a twin glass combiner with an optical transmit factor of 80 per cent. An automatic brightness control and manual contrast allows the symbols to be read in ambient light up to 100 000 lux.

The Type VMC 180 HDD is a multifunction unit whereby information is presented in TV raster and/or caligraphic writing with coding and colour for rapid assimilation of the visual data. Two video inputs are provided (radar and TV) plus a link to the electronics unit for generation of coloured alpha-numerics for superimposition on either the radar or TV frame. Information presented includes a radar map, synthetically derived tactical situations, TV raster images (from TV sensors and flight instruments), and tactical data from the system itself or from external sources. The unit uses a 5 × 5 inch multimode cathode ray tube screen with red, amber and green colours. For brightness control, automatic photo cells and manual override are incorporated on the control panel.

Units of the TMV 980A multidisplay system

The complementary Type VMC 65 HDD provides the same information on a 2·5 inch circular monocolour screen.

The electronics unit provides the interface with the aircraft systems, carries out flight and weapon aiming computations, and processes and generates the display symbology.

Weights of the various units are 13 kg for the HUD, 14 kg for the VMC 180 HDD, 4 kg for the VMC 65 HDD and 9 kg for the electronics unit. The latter is of ½ ATR format.

STATUS

In production for the Mirage 2000 multi-role fighter aircraft.

CONTRACTOR

Thomson-CSF, Division Equipements Avioniques, 178 boulevard Gabriel Péri, 92240 Malakoff, Paris, France.

1736.393
TAV-38 LASER RANGEFINDER

The TAV-38 laser rangefinder is designed to provide air-to-ground ranging facilities up to ranges of 10 km in clear-sky conditions. The equipment comprises two units: laser head and power unit. The latter unit weighs 12 kg and has no moving parts. It provides the high energy DC voltage to the flash exciter tube and the auxiliary supplies to the system. The laser head weighs 8·5 kg, and houses the laser cavity, with its neodymium rod, flash exciter, and triggering device. It also contains the receiver circuitry which incorporates an avalanche photodiode, the digital range counter, and transmission/reception optics.

Among the design features contributing to light weight and modest dimensions is an original type of exciter yielding more power to the neodymium rod, thus reducing the heat that needs to be carried away. The laser/internal cooling arrangements make the unit suitable for use under a wide range of ambient temperature conditions.

OPERATION

Ranging is effected by measuring the time interval between the emission of an energy pulse and the return of reflected energy. Measurement is by means of a digital counter, with a clock frequency of 29·98 MHz, which corresponds to a distance increment of five metres. The digital output is converted into serial binary format for output. The wavelength of the emissions is 1·06 micron.

TAV-38 laser rangefinder

The deflector system developed by Thomson-CSF enables the direction of the beam emitted by the laser rangefinder to be referenced to the boresight provided for the pilot by a collimator. The angle of deviation thus obtained is ±10° in both elevation and azimuth.

DEVELOPMENT

The type TAV-38 is the result of collaboration between Thomson-CSF and Marcoussis Laboratories CGE Research Centre, the former being responsible for the beam deflector system and the latter for the TAV-34 laser rangefinder.

STATUS

In operational use with a number of exported Mirage F-1 aircraft and in the French Air Force Jaguar.

CONTRACTORS

Thomson-CSF, Direction Commerciale AVS, 178 boulevard Gabriel Péri, 92240 Malakoff, Paris, France.

CILAS (Compagnie Industrielle des Lasers), route de Nozay, 91460 Marcoussis, France.

5744.393
TMV 630 LASER RANGEFINDER

The TMV 630 laser rangefinder is a second generation equipment developed with the experience gained in the design and manufacture of the TAV-38 (**1736.393**). It is a high performance monobloc compact equipment, especially designed for installation even on board small tactical aircraft. It has a very high performance in angular precision and PRF. Several versions have been designed with a variety of analogue and digital interfaces.

The rangefinder consists of one line-replaceable unit to be fitted on an aircraft mount which is only boresighted once. Its replacement, if necessary, does not require further boresighting. It is composed of two modules integrated into one unit; a laser transmitter/receiver and a beam steerer.

CHARACTERISTICS
Wave length: 1·06 μm
Ranging: Up to 20 km
Length: 530 mm
Weight: 15 kg (33 lb)
STATUS
In production for fitment to the Alpha Jet and modernised Mirage V.
CONTRACTOR
Thomson-CSF, Division Equipements Avioniques, 178 boulevard Gabriel Péri, 92240 Malakoff, Paris, France.

TMV 630 laser rangefinder

3562.393
THOMSON-CSF TYPE 902 GUNSIGHT

The 902 gunsight is the latest model of the series R gunsights (**1518.393**) produced by Thomson-CSF and sold in many countries as well as in France. In its category, the 902 assures maximum performance efficiency in air-to-ground attacks with guns, rockets and clean or retarded bombs and also in the air-to-air gun fire mode with visual stabilised tracking. It is specially adapted to the sighting problem of light strike aircraft.

The 902 gunsight TMV 531 is of monobloc construction and is located directly in front of the pilot's eyes. The nearby illustration shows the general arrangement of the unit. A dove-tail support allows the replacement of the sighting head without realignment.

Two bright graticules (one fixed, one mobile) are collimated on the combining glass, allowing the pilot to view them superimposed upon the outside world without any accommodation problem.
STATUS
In production.
CONTRACTOR
Thomson-CSF, Division Equipements Avioniques, 178 boulevard Gabriel Péri, 92240 Malakoff, Paris, France.

Thomson-CSF Type 902 gunsight

4722.393
CN₂H NIGHT OBSERVATION BINOCULARS

The CN$_2$H binoculars are designed for night observation, night flying and instrument and map reading in helicopters and fixed-wing aircraft. They incorporate either second or third generation light intensifier tubes with the appropriate optics. The binoculars are normally mounted in a fixed position on the pilot's helmet using a special support. The power pack, for supply from the aircraft system, can be fitted at the rear of the helmet. The binoculars are also battery operated in the event of aircraft system failure.
CHARACTERISTICS
Field of view: 40°
Magnification: ×1
Weight: 400 g (binoculars); 850 g (full equipment)
CONTRACTOR
SOPELEM, 102 rue Chaptal, 92306 Levallois Perret, France.

CN$_2$H night observation binoculars

4724.393
HUD SIGHT REPEATER

The Head-up Display (HUD) Sight Repeater is designed for use by the rear seat occupant in two-seat aircraft and provides a televised, collimated image of the display seen through the combiner glass of the pilot's HUD. The rear occupant, normally an instructor pilot, can then follow the symbolic HUD data superimposed on the landscape, control the actions of the front pilot as necessary and check target identification or obstacle avoidance.

The sight repeater consists of two elements:
(1) an electronic scanning unit installed in the front cockpit and consisting of a vidicon pick-up tube, an optical lens, an automatic shutter and a 4-filter filtering unit
(2) the display sub-assembly mounted in the rear cockpit and comprising the display unit itself and a control panel for remote control of the scanning unit operation. The display unit is available in two sizes.
STATUS
In production.

HUD sight repeater

CONTRACTOR
Thomson-CSF, Division Equipements Avioniques, 178 boulevard Gabriel Péri, 92240 Malakoff, Paris, France.

4794.393
ACX DISPLAY SYSTEM

Thomson-CSF, in collaboration with SFENA, is studying an integrated display system intended for the experimental ACX fighter aircraft developed by Marcel Dassault/Breguet Aviation. The proposed system will include three types of display: a wide field-of-view holographic HUD, an 'eye-level' collimated picture display, and a lateral colour 'shadow mask' CRT display.

The holographic and eye-level displays will be provided by Thomson-CSF, with SFENA supplying the lateral colour TV raster display and interfaces to two symbol generators. These latter have been designed by Thomson-CSF and use a new graphic processor, based on LSI integrated circuit technology, to generate all the alpha-numeric information and symbols displayed on the various VDUs.

STATUS
In early design.
CONTRACTORS
Thomson-CSF, Division Equipements Avioniques, 178 boulevard Gabriel Péri, 92240 Malakoff, Paris, France.
SFENA, Controls and Systems Division, Aerodrome de Villacoublay, BP 59, 78141 Velizy-Villacoublay, France.

GERMANY (FEDERAL REPUBLIC)

3853.393
CE626 LASER TRANSMITTER
This unit has been developed for the Panavia Tornado multi-role combat aircraft system.

The transmitter is a nitrogen-cooled neodymium-YAG laser operating with a variable pulse repetition frequency between 9 and 11 Hz and ascertaining together with the receiver the exact range to mobile and stationary targets. The display/operating and control unit and the corresponding power supply units form part of the laser transmitter.

Since its electronics and technology are tailored to system integration, it can be used in many fields, eg ships, aircraft, helicopters, tracked and wheeled vehicles as well as spacecraft. It has been developed for a PRF of 40 Hz.

CONTRACTOR
Eltro GmbH, Postfach 102120, 69 Heidelberg 1, Federal Republic of Germany.

4793.393
MBB NIGHT SIGHT ATTACK SYSTEM
The MBB night sight attack system is an experimental programme being carried out in a modified G91 aircraft. It consists of a head-up display (HUD) mounted in the cockpit and an FLIR camera contained in an externally mounted pod. The image from the FLIR camera is transmitted to the HUD, and also to a ground station by means of a digital data link.

Additional symbols for flight guidance and alpha-numeric information can be added to the picture to give further information concerning the mission to the pilot.

The FLIR camera, supplied by Eltro, and an AEG Telefunken TV system are mounted on a two-axis stabilisation platform housed in a special front section of the pod.

STATUS
In development.
CONTRACTOR
MBB Marine and Special Products Division, Huenfeldstrasse 1-5, 2800 Bremen, Federal Republic of Germany.

ISRAEL

3801.393
WDNS-141 WEAPON DELIVERY SYSTEMS
WDNS-141 is the name of a family of weapon delivery systems produced for fighter/bomber aircraft by Israel Aircraft Industries Ltd. They are designed to assist the pilot by presenting essential data on the head-up display (HUD) for use in navigation, air-to-air and air-to-surface combat missions.

Typically, the system comprises sensors, processors, display and control units. Among the sensors are radar, inertial measuring units, the angle-of-attack systems and a flux-valve compass. In addition to the central processor, computers will include an auxiliary computer and an air data computer. Display equipment may comprise the HUD, horizontal situation indicator, attitude direction indicator and a terminal unit.

The WDNS-141s used by the Israeli Air Force are capable of the following operating modes:
(1) Air-to-air: gunnery, including Hotline (snap shooting), and/or Hotpoint; missile fire; override of air-to-air mode.
(2) Air-to-ground: continuously computed impact point immediate or delayed release; continuously computed release point designated toss bombing (Des-toss), Dive-toss, Toss; manual altitude or range release.

It is possible to use the system to 'mark and store' targets of opportunity.
STATUS
In production and operational.
CONTRACTOR
Israel Aircraft Industries Ltd, Airborne Systems, Ben Gurion Airport, Israel.

4241.383
LOW COST WEAPON DELIVERY SYSTEM (LCWDS)
Based on the company's experience in developing and producing systems for A-4, F-4 and Kfir aircraft operated by the Israeli Forces, Elbit recently introduced a low cost weapon delivery system (LCWDS) equipment which represents a compromise between the expensive, full performance weapon delivery and navigation system and the very low cost, low performance gunsight. The LCWDS is designed to enhance aircraft operational performance capabilities, while the use of digital computation with a head-up display (HUD) improves pilot performance. It is particularly suitable for use on light attack aircraft, advanced trainers and interceptors.

Modes of operation provided include: air-to-ground, air-to-air, and navigation. The navigation mode requires the aircraft to be fitted with a doppler velocity sensor. Facilities provided in the air-to-ground mode are continuously computed impact point, CCRP and manual. There are two uses of the air-to-air mode, Hotline (snap shooting) and LCOS. Computation and display of steering commands for pre-selected waypoints is the main function of the navigation mode.

The LCWDS is based on the installation of three items of equipment in the aircraft and interfacing them with existing aircraft sensors and indicators. The added equipment consists of: the central mission computer (CMC), containing a digital processor, symbol generator and aircraft interface unit; HUD; and the control terminal unit (CTU). Existing aircraft systems interfaced to the LCWDS comprise flux valve, angle of attack, air data computer and gyro reference unit sensors; control facilities such as an armament programmer, and stick and throttle switches; and displays (attitude direction indicator and the horizontal situation indicator).
CHARACTERISTICS
Accuracies: 10 mrad (A/G); 3 mrad (A/A) dependent on accuracy of aircraft gyro reference unit
MTBF: 800 h minimum
Dimensions: CMC 249 × 194 × 140 mm; CTU 167 × 175 × 127 mm; HUD 320 × 120 × 150 mm
Weight: CMC 9 kg; CTU 2·5 kg; HUD 5 kg
Environmental Conditions: CMC MIL-E-5400 Class II; CTU MIL-E-5400 Class IA; HUD MIL-E-5400 Class IA
STATUS
Early production.
CONTRACTOR
Elbit Computers Ltd, PO Box 5390, Haifa 31053, Israel.

Elbit LCWDS units, left to right: central mission computer, head-up display, control terminal unit

4242.383
SYSTEM 81 WDNS
The Elbit weapon delivery and navigation system (WDNS) 81 is a modern IMU-based digital computerised weapon delivery and navigation system for use in advanced combat aircraft for both air-to-air and air-to-ground operations. There are three principal modes of operation provided by the System 81: air-to-air, ground attack, and navigation. In the first of these, the missile launching envelope is computed and displayed to the pilot by a head-up display (HUD) for engaging missiles. When using guns in this mode, Hotline (snap shooting) is the normal method but there is also a lead computing optical sight (LCOS) back-up facility available. For delivering ground attack weapons there are facilities for continuously computed impact point (CCIP), CCRP, toss bombing (toss), release of 'smart bombs', guided munitions etc (special ordnance), and a direct back-up visual delivery capability. The navigation mode computes and displays steering commands for pre-selected destinations, with up to 40 waypoints.

These facilities enable a pilot to navigate to his target accurately and on time, to release a wide range of airborne weapons in 'uncanned' paths, obtain air-to-air missile firing envelope information presented on the HUD, employ 'snap shooting' and LCOS air-to-air firing modes, and to enter before-flight data and control commands. Other features include in-flight position and velocity update, rapid warm-up/alignment, and the design is based on the HOTAS (hands on throttle and stick) principle.

System 81 equipment comprises four main items:

fire control and navigation computer (FCNC), inertial measurement unit, control terminal unit (CTU) and the HUD. The first of these comprises the following five units: central processing unit and program store, converter unit, symbol generator, core store and the power supply unit. The CTU is used for entering data to the central computer and the presentation of certain data from the FCNC to the pilot. The CTU controls system alignment, operation, test, and selection of sub-modes. Its external features can be seen from the nearby illustration. The HUD provides the pilot with all relevant operational information and is designed to employ the minimum number of signals and to have the least possible interference with the pilot's normal viewing. It provides warning information symbology.

Other aircraft systems, indicators and sensors which are linked with the System 81 central computer as peripherals include nose radar (range, range rate and antenna depression data), radar altimeter, inertial measurement unit, flux valve heading reference, air data computer, ADF, attitude direction indicator,

horizontal situation display, armament programmer, 'smart' weapons interface, stick and throttle switches.
CHARACTERISTICS
Central computer: 16-bit with 17 32-bit registers and 7 16-bit registers
Converter: A/D: 28 channels; D/A: 6 channels; S/D: 3 channels; Synchro buffers: 2 channels; Input discrete: 48 channels; Output discrete: 24 channels
Symbol generators: 3000 mrad/20ms, straight lines, scales, digits, letters, circles
Core store: 16 K
Memory: EPROM 48 K × 16 bits; RAM 6 K × 17 bits; Non-volatile RAM 2 K × 17 bits
Dimensions: 273 × 382 × 195 mm
Weight: 20 kg
Control terminal unit
Serial interface to main computer: 1 Mbit/s (16-bit words)
Dimensions: 175 × 167 × 127 mm
Weight: 2·5 kg
STATUS
Production.

Elbit WDNS 81 equipment with head-up display (top), control terminal unit (left) and computer (right)

CONTRACTOR
Elbit Computers Ltd, PO Box 5390, Haifa 31053, Israel.

4002.383
SYSTEM 82 WDNS
The Elbit System 82 weapon delivery and navigation system is an enhanced version of the company's System 81 (**4242.383**, above), providing automated weapon aiming and aircraft navigation facilities for advanced combat aircraft employed on air-to-air and ground attack missions using missiles, guns, conventional bombs, and 'smart' weapons. Compared with the System 81, the WDNS 82 differs in having a stores management sub-system, consisting of an image (TV) display capability for all 'smart' weapons, a separate computer for stores management, a microprocessor-based back-up computer for the fire control and navigation computer (FCNC) and a CRT-based armament control and display panel.

The stores management computer (SMC) manages weapon release with maximum efficiency and safety,

taking into account the conditioning and limiting factors. It includes the following units: dual redundancy, symbol generator, common memory, fault monitor and power supply unit. The back-up computer (BUC) calculates and generates the display of LCOS air-to-air and air-to-ground back-up mode functions to the FCNC. The armament control and display panel (ACDP) is controlled by both the pilot and the SMC. It displays on a TV-type screen continuously updated weapons inventory, video from a variety of sensors (such as forward looking infra-red imaging equipment fitted to the aircraft, or E-O sensors in the homing heads of 'smart' weapons carried by the aircraft), selected program parameters, and warnings in case of erroneous programming.

The extra capacity permits much greater exploitation of the weapons and other related systems and equipment fitted in the aircraft as well as allowing greater flexibility in the choice of weapons

carried and sophistication in their employment. The system is also understood to incorporate a considerable growth potential. Where the System 82 characteristics differ from those of the System 81, they are listed in the table that follows.
CHARACTERISTICS
SMC
Memory: EPROM 58 K; RAM 3 K; Non-volatile RAM 1 K
Inputs: 160 discrete
Outputs: 120 discrete
Real-time clock: 1 kHz
Dimensions: 321 × 194 × 172 mm
Weight: 13·6 kg
ACDP
Scanning: 525 or 875 lines
Bandwidth: 20 MHz
Contrast ratio: 7:1
Dimensions: 172 × 147 × 267 mm
Weight: 7 kg
Back-up computer: Based on 8086 microprocessor
Memory: EPROM 16 K; RAM 1 K
Inputs: 8 analogue, 4 synchro, 10 discrete
Symbol generator: 2300 mrad/20 ms
Dimensions: 241 × 194 × 140 mm
Weight: 9 kg
STATUS
Production.
CONTRACTOR
Elbit Computers Ltd, PO Box 5390, Haifa 31053, Israel.

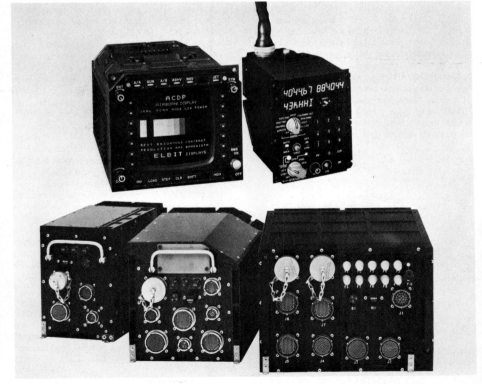

Elbit System 82 WDNS showing (left to right) armament control and display panel and control terminal units (top); back-up computer, stores management computer and fire control and navigation computer (below)

Elbit WDNS System 82 in KFIR C-7 cockpit

SWEDEN

3819.393
HELIOS HELICOPTER SIGHT

Helios is a helicopter roof-mounted sight for use with air/ground weapons. It has magnifications of ×3 and ×12 and provisions for laser target marking and a thermal imaging system for night use. It can accept commands from a helmet sight or from an avionics system and generates accurate position and rate outputs to weapon systems. It can also be slaved to directions from a laser warning receiver, hostile fire indicator or radar warning receiver. Future developments could have a laser illuminator as an easy-add-on feature, and a medium-sized forward-looking infra-red camera would be incorporated if the stabilised optical sight head was replaced by a thermal imaging head.

The use of rate-integrating gyros and the remote location of the electronics has kept the weight of the roof sight down to only 19 kg. The optical design (by Pilkington, UK, which also builds the optical train) is characterised by low vignetting and low field

curvature. The eyepiece arm protruding into the cabin area can be stowed close to the roof when not in use and the eyepiece height is adjustable to suit the operator.

The sight is composed of a number of modules with interfaces to ensure minimal adjustments when a module is changed. The system itself consists of five units: the roof-mounted sight, an electronics unit, control panel, control unit and a line-of-sight indicator.

CHARACTERISTICS

Magnification/field of view: ×3/18° and ×12·4/4·6°
Line-of-sight variation: ±25° elevation; ±120° azimuth
Slew rate: Up to 100°/s
System weight: 27·6 kg
STATUS
In production.
CONTRACTOR
Saab-Scania AB, Box 1017, 551 11, Jönköping, Sweden.

Helios helicopter sight

3818.393
RGS 1 OPTICAL SIGHT

The Saab RGS 1 optical sight is an advanced low cost fixed type sight combining simplicity with accuracy and reliability. Optically the RGS 1 sight displays to the pilot an aiming mark projected at infinity. Deflection of the aiming mark projection is made in azimuth and elevation by manual adjustment of a spherical mirror via turning knobs on either side of the sight unit. The depression and adjustment for the crosswind component are read on indicator scales facing the pilot. The useful width of the RGS 1 optical sight is approximately 100 mm, permitting full two-

eyed viewing, so enhancing pilot efficiency even in turbulent conditions.

In the standard form, the RGS 1 aiming mark includes vertical references intended as ranging aids for stadiametric ranging. The aiming mark appearance and the width of the vertical references can be adapted to customer choice and weapon ranges. The RGS 1 optical sight is designed with a dual lamp arrangement in case of lamp burn-out. The second lamp could be fitted with a coloured filter providing a different aiming mark contrast against a highly illuminated target background. As an additional feature there is also a brightness control

device available for optimisation of the aiming mark illumination for varying brightness conditions. The RGS 1 optical sight is designed to allow the use of a 16 mm recording camera.
STATUS
In production.
CONTRACTORS
Saab-Scania AB, Box 1017, 551 11, Jönköping, Sweden.

Licence manufacture in UK: Avimo Ltd, Taunton, Somerset, England.

1730.393
RGS 2 AIRCRAFT SIGHT

The Saab RGS 2 is a lead computing optical sight developed for use with any type of fighter or attack aircraft. Important design objectives were accuracy, small dimensions and weight, and low price. Its operational function is to display to the pilot a movable aiming mark projected to infinity. The deflection of the aiming mark is controlled in accordance with the characteristics of the preselected weapon, and with certain parameters of the prevailing flight conditions. In the basic configuration, pitch, roll, and yaw rates are measured and all other parameters, such as speed, altitude, and range, are preset manually by the pilot. In more sophisticated configurations, one or more signals are

fed to the system from external sources. This flexibility enables the RGS 2 to be applied to a variety of aircraft types with minimum additional design effort.

The system has provisions for the following attack modes: guns, rockets, and missiles for air-to-air; guns, rockets, and bombs in the air-to-ground role. Stadiametric range (by wing-span setting) measurement is used in the air-to-air gun mode. When bombing, a suitable aiming mark depression (maximum 200 mils) is preset on the control unit. The dynamic range of the aiming mark deflection is plus or minus 140 mils in yaw, and plus 80 to minus 200 mils in pitch. In ground attack modes the RGS 2 system has the optional facility of accepting speed, altitude and attitude data from aircraft sensors, so

automatically deflecting the aiming mark to compensate for actual deviations from the preset values.

The RGS 2 system is comprised of three units: sight head, computer and gyro unit, and control unit. Principal dimensions of these items are as follows:
Sight head: 163 × 136 × 259 mm
Computer and gyro unit: 114 × 175 × 275 mm
Control unit: Size dependent upon system facilities

The sole purpose of the sight head is to generate a moving aiming mark of controllable width. Deflection of the aiming mark is accomplished by a spherical mirror, suspended in gimbals and controlled by a pair of servo systems, comprising torque motors, feed-back pick-offs, and servo amplifiers. The width of the aiming mark is controlled by a reticle mechanism placed in the focal plane of the spherical mirror. The whole optical assembly, with the exception of a fixed plane mirror and an ordinary inclined combining glass, is housed in the base of the sight head.

The computer and gyro unit contains three rate gyros and several circuit boards bearing the computing circuits, signal converters, two identical servo amplifiers, and power supply circuits.

A twin sight arrangement for use in dual control trainer aircraft is simply accomplished by the RGS 2 equipment by having the computer and gyro unit control two sight heads in parallel.

Laser Augmented RGS 2

By incorporating a laser rangefinder and an additional electronics unit, the RGS 2 sighting system will provide considerably improved accuracy in air-to-ground delivery modes, including diving attacks at all angles from level flight and shallow dives to steep attacks.
STATUS
Operational with Royal Netherlands Air Force NF-5A aircraft. In production for Hawk aircraft of the Finnish Air Force and Italian Air Force Aermacchi MB-339 aircraft. Installed in Saab 105G. It has been contracted for the Spanish CASA C-101, Portuguese Air Force Fiat G91R3 aircraft and for others.
CONTRACTORS
Saab-Scania AB, Box 1017, 551 11, Jönköping, Sweden.

Licence manufacture in UK: Avimo Ltd, Taunton, Somerset, England.

Licence manufacture in Italy: Aeritalia Instrumentation Division SpA, Nerviano, Milan, Italy.

Twin installation of Saab RGS 2 sight in Italian Aermacchi 339 jet trainer aircraft

5745.393
ERICSSON LASER RANGEFINDER

A compact airborne high repetition rate laser rangefinder has been developed by Ericsson for easy up-grading of existing systems. It can be integrated into any sighting and weapon delivery system to give higher accuracy and enhanced safety in dive attacks. The rangefinder uses a modular design consisting of transmitter, receiver, range counter and deflection

unit. The laser is aimed at the target by slewing the deflection unit to the aircraft sighting system.

The transmitter is a Nd-YAG type with a PRF of 5 Hz continuously and 10 Hz in bursts. Typical range is 7 km or greater at an optical visibility better than 20 km. The range counter resolution is 5 m.
CONTRACTOR
Ericsson Radio Systems AB, 16380 Stockholm, Sweden.

Ericsson airborne laser rangefinder

3793.393
FFV UNI-FLIR POD

The Swedish FFV (Forenade Fabriksverken) organisation has added a forward-looking IR pod, known as the Uni-FLIR, to its Uni-Pod range of airborne equipment. Other members of the family are the Uni-Gun pod (**5216.303**), Uni-Recce pod (**3386.353**) and the Uni-UV/IR linescanner pod RS18C.

The general configuration of the Uni-FLIR pod can be seen from the photograph of the equipment mounted under the wing of a Saab 105 aircraft, together with a Uni-Gun pod. The Uni-FLIR houses an LM Ericsson imaging IR camera, the associated electronics package and the necessary cooling equipment. The camera is stabilised and views the scene ahead and below the aircraft through an IR optical window in the nose of the pod, which is attached to the aircraft stores hard-points by lugs and braces at standard NATO 14-inch spacing. The IR system is sensitive to radiation in the eight to fourteen micron band and produces real-time thermal images of the terrain ahead of the aircraft. This information is displayed on a cockpit CRT display unit mounted on the aircraft instrument panel.

The FLIR video is TV-compatible and options include automatic target detection, television tracking, and signal processing for image enhancement. Normal functions include day and night vision with some penetration of camouflage, smoke and haze; low altitude flight for ground support etc in darkness; and rapid target detection.
CHARACTERISTICS
Pod diameter: 360 mm
Length: 2015 mm
Weight: 100 kg
FLIR wavelength: 8 – 14 microns
Output: TV compatible to CCIR standard M
Power requirement: 28 V DC, 700 W
CONTRACTOR
FFV Maintenance Division, 581 82 Linköping, Sweden.

General arrangement drawing of FFV Uni-FLIR pod

Saab 105 aircraft equipped with FFV Uni-FLIR pod (left) and Uni-Gun pod (right)

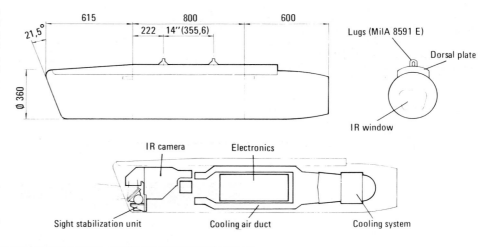

3564.393
RGS 3 AIRCRAFT SIGHT

The RGS 3 is a development of the RGS 2 sight (**1730.393**) and is primarily intended for use with the Martin Marietta advanced laser search and tracking

set (Pave Penny system, **3204.383**). In addition to the functions of the RGS 2, the RGS 3 sight has facilities to produce LSTS line-of-sight information to aid the pilot in identifying targets, and in attack manoeuvres against laser-marked targets in daylight or darkness.

STATUS
Prototype.
CONTRACTOR
Saab-Scania AB, Box 1017, 551 11, Jönköping, Sweden.

UNITED KINGDOM

3057.393
F-16 HUD-SIGHT

The head-up display (HUD) system developed for the F-16 air combat fighter by Marconi Avionics is now in full-scale production. It is essentially an updated version of the very successful digital HUD supplied for US A-7D and A-7E Corsair aircraft. Its 16 K-word electronics unit makes use of the latest MSI technology and EPROM programming to provide a weapon aiming computer and display generator which is readily adaptable to changing weapon technology or new user requirements.

The system accepts inputs of both digital and analogue data from the aircraft sensors and uses these with stored ballistic information to derive weapon aiming solutions which are presented symbolically to the pilot on the combiner glass of the pilot's display unit. The display unit employs a developed and lighter version of the very accurate A-7

Marconi Avionics F-16 HUD sight

optical system and, in versions for the F-16 itself, features an extremely rugged combiner glass to cater for the canopy-off situation. Versions for aircraft with more conventional canopy arrangements employ a much lighter combiner.

Variants of the F-16 system have been adapted for a number of other aircraft types with only minor modifications to system hardware. The major differences between the various versions is in the programming instructions to the electronics unit. The flexibility inherent in this unit allows any symbology format, made up from straight lines and segments of circles, required by the user to be displayed and algorithms suitable for any current air weaponry to be mechanised. The system is also compatible with a raster format in which display symbology is overlaid on a raster presentation of electronic imagery such as radar, forward-looking infra-red or low light-level TV. This feature gives the system day/night and, depending on the sensor employed, all-weather capability. Changes involved in providing this capacity are all electronic in nature and require no additional boxes or changes in system architecture.

A new technology dual-mode HUD has now been

developed and the first production model was delivered to General Dynamics in May 1984. This is the first wide-angle system of its kind, with stroke written symbology operating in both day and night modes. It was produced under a $75 million contract for fitment to F-16C and F-16D aircraft.

STATUS
Now in full production in Marconi Avionics factories at both Rochester, Kent and Atlanta, Georgia. In addition, full-scale production of EUs at Kongsberg Vapenfabrikk of Norway and of PDUs at NV Optische Industrie of the Netherlands has been instituted for

NATO F-16 models. Overall control of all F-16 HUD set production is exercised by a central programme management team at Rochester.
CONTRACTOR
Marconi Avionics Ltd, Airborne Display Division, Airport Works, Rochester, Kent, England.

4314.393
LANTIRN HUD SIGHT

The latest Marconi Avionics HUD system is a wide angle, holographic, day/night HUD on order by the USAF to provide 24-hour attack capability for LANTIRN versions of the F-16 and A-10 aircraft. It makes use of the latest, diffractive optical technology to provide a full 30° by 18° instantaneous field-of-view and combines this with a unique stoke-write-in-raster-flyback technique to superimpose flight and mission symbology on a forward looking infra-red sensor picture of the terrain over which the aircraft is operating.

The electronics unit for this HUD incorporates all three of the basic triad of avionic design standards; MIL-STD-1589B High Order Language, MIL-STD-1750A Airborne Instruction Set Architecture and MIL-STD-1553B Digital Data Bus. This first-ever real application of the three standards will provide

improved adaptability in use, improved performance and reduce life cycle costs.

Although the physical shape and size of the F-16 and A-10 HUDs is considerably different, to accommodate the different cockpit arrangements of the two aircraft, electrical and optical modules are to a large extent common to both, and design studies have shown that the system is readily adapted to most modern tactical aircraft cockpits.
STATUS
Prototype deliveries from Marconi Avionics' Rochester plant began in early 1982 and the sight is now in full production. By July 1984 over 200 day and night missions had been flown successfully as part of the USAF LANTIRN programme.
CONTRACTOR
Marconi Avionics Ltd, Airborne Display Division, Airport Works, Rochester, Kent, England.

Marconi Avionics HUD sight for F-16 LANTIRN aircraft

4726.393
THERMAL CUEING UNIT

The Marconi Avionics Thermal Cueing Unit (TCU) is intended to assist the pilot to detect a potential target at the earliest moment, particularly when flying low and fast over unfamiliar terrain by day or night. Used in conjunction with a forward looking infra-red (FLIR) imaging sensor and a head-up display (HUD), the TCU alerts the pilot to the presence of ground targets that he might otherwise not detect. It extracts the location of potential targets from the FLIR video signal and generates cue symbols for display at the appropriate position on the HUD, overlaying the real scene by day or the synthetic FLIR image by night.

In sophisticated systems, target position coordinates generated by the TCU and designated by the pilot can be further processed to allow automatic target acquisition and weapon handover. Position data can be used to direct a narrow field-of-view imager at a point of interest for target recognition on a head-down display (HDD).

The TCU is fully compatible with the UK Thermal Imager Common Module (TICM) system (**4280.193**) and the Marconi LANTIRN HUD (**4314.393**). Alternative input and output interfaces can be made available to allow the TCU to operate with other types of FLIR sensor and HUD.

In systems where a thermal image is not required on any display, the TCU can operate directly from the FLIR scanner and pre-amplifiers, thus avoiding the need for scan conversion to raster display format.
STATUS
The Thermal Cueing Unit is now in advanced development. It is a repackaged version of trials equipment which was evaluated under UK MoD contract.
CONTRACTOR
Marconi Avionics Ltd, Electro-Optical Advanced Systems Division, Christopher Martin Road, Basildon, Essex SS14 3EL, England.

Thermal Cueing Unit display

5748.393
MARCONI AVIONICS TICM II FLIR POD

This is a joint development by Marconi Avionics and Vinten, to create a flexible and lightweight thermal imaging system which can be attached to a variety of fixed- and rotary-wing aircraft with a minimum of modification. The pod is designed by W Vinten Ltd and accommodates the Marconi Avionics thermal imaging common module (TICM II) (**4280.193**) scanner head and telescope. It provides a TV signal output to cockpit displays on a video monitor or head-up displays (HUDs).

The scanner head and a suitable afocal and athermalised infra-red telescope are boresighted to

TICM II FLIR pod

the pilot's HUD. The telescope magnification is selected to match the field of view of the HUD so that the imagery displayed is in 1:1 registration with the real world. Infra-red radiation reaches the telescope

through an infra-red transmissive window at the front end of the pod. The TICM II processing electronics unit which converts the infra-red signals from the scanner head into TV compatible output, plus a cooling air system to cool the scanner dectector, are incorporated in the pod, which also contains a video cassette recorder to record the FLIR imagery for post flight debriefing and detailed analysis.
STATUS
In production.
CONTRACTOR
Marconi Avionics Ltd, Electro-Optical Systems Group, Christopher Martin Road, Basildon, Essex SS14 3EL, England.

3795.093
MARCONI AVIONICS CCD CAMERAS

Marconi Avionics manufactures a range of TV camera equipment based on the use of solid-state area imaging devices known as charge-coupled devices (CCD). A practical feature of this equipment is the combination of very small dimensions and extreme ruggedness. Among other valuable attributes are low power requirements and long operating life.

CCDs are said to yield an order of magnitude improvement over vidicon camera tubes in dynamic range; they have the broad spectral range of silicon, are free from microphonic effects, have zero lag and

inherent geometric accuracy. Cameras based on CCDs can be used with standard TV monitors and video tape recorders and can be employed as discrete items or as part of a larger system.

A typical application is the AN/AXQ-16V cockpit TV system which provides a real-time recording of gunsight head-up display image data, as well as cockpit audio data, and can provide a real-time presentation of visual data on a rear cockpit display. The system is based on an all-solid-state TV camera which uses a Fairchild 380 × 488 CCD photosensor array to achieve outstanding sensitivity, resolution, and dynamic range. A split camera design minimises

obstruction of the pilot's view, the small camera head being installed on the head-up display.

The use of an on-board video casette recorder (V-1000 AB-R) ensures that a complete video and audio record of engagements is available for immediate replay as soon as the aircraft lands.

Monochrome and colour variants of these systems can be supplied for installation in many aircraft types and fitments.
STATUS
The system is flight proven, qualified and now in production for military aircraft worldwide.

CONTRACTOR
Marconi Avionics Limited, Electro-optical Products Division, Christopher Martin Road, Basildon, Essex SS14 3EL, England.

Typical system for a head-up display, and alternative sensors, showing separation from electronics unit

3056.393
AV-8A HEAD-UP DISPLAY AND WEAPON AIMING COMPUTING SYSTEM

The Smiths Industries HUDWAC system which is currently fitted to the AV-8A aircraft of the USMC and the Matador aircraft of the Spanish Navy provides a comprehensive display of weapon aiming, flight and navigation symbology, as well as performing all the weapon aiming calculations in a separate dedicated computer. The basic system comprises a pilot's display unit (PDU), waveform generator (WFG), interface and weapon aiming computer (IWAC), pilot's control panel (PCP) and extra high tension unit (EHTU).

Pilot's Display Unit: Similar to the Harrier-Jaguar unit, the AV-8A PDU consists essentially of two modules: the optical system and the CRT assembly. The optical system consists of a collimating lens assembly and a combining glass. The 100 mm f0·97 lens assembly provides a total field of view of 25°. All glass-to-air surfaces are treated with an anti-reflective coating to reduce spurious reflections. The CRT assembly consists of a high-brightness CRT, a deflection coil assembly, a focus magnet and a brightness amplifier. The electro-magnetically focused CRT is capable of producing a brightness level which enables the display to be viewed against a background intensity of 35 000 candelas/m² (10 000 ft lamberts).

Waveform Generator: The AV-8A waveform generator is almost identical to that supplied for the Harrier and Jaguar. It generates and controls a comprehensive array of flight, navigation and weapon aiming symbology. The nature and amount of symbology presented to the pilot at any instant, is restricted to those symbols which are relevant to the operating mode selected. This minimises display clutter and enables the pilot to be presented with clear, unambiguous information. The WFG is a

special purpose digital computer which accepts analogue DC signals and discrete control inputs from various sensors and systems on the aircraft. It is of modular construction, housed in a ½ ATR case, and incorporates integrated circuits and multi-layer printed circuit boards.

Interface and Weapon Aiming Computer: The IWAC not only performs all the weapon aiming computing on the AV-8A but also serves as the interface between the Smiths Industries head-up display and the attitude and heading reference system (AHRS). In its latest configuration the IWAC can provide air-to-air, lead-angle aiming and CCIP air-to-ground attacks using rockets, guns and either free-fall, retarded or cluster bombs. It also features a continuously computed break-away warning based on ground avoidance and fragmentation hemisphere criteria.

The IWAC is a hybrid computer performing analogue computation under the control of a central processor. It is housed in a ½ ATR (short) case with a 'dog box' extension.

The original WFG and IWAC are now being replaced by a signal data converter (SDC) and digital interface and weapon aiming computer (DIWAC), both of which have been designed by the company's Clearwater Division in Florida, USA. The new units are 'form, fit and function' replacements of the original units but employ later technology.

Extra High Tension Unit: The EHTU provides a high voltage supply to the CRT in the PDU. To maintain the high level of accuracy required for weapon aiming, the 15 kV output from the EHTU has a very high degree of stabilisation over the full operating temperature range.

STATUS
In production.

CONTRACTORS
Smiths Industries, Aerospace & Defence Systems Company, Cheltenham Division, Bishops Cleeve, Cheltenham, Gloucestershire GL52 4SF, England.

Smiths Industries Inc, St Petersburg/Clearwater Airport, PO Box 5389, Clearwater, Florida 33518, USA.

4130.393
AV-8B HEAD-UP DISPLAY

Smiths Industries (UK) and Smiths Industries Inc (USA) were selected to supply the pilot's display unit (PDU) and the display processor respectively, for the AV-8B version of the Harrier.

The PDU, designed to US MIL specifications, has a 4½ inch lens and is a line replaceable unit. A feature is the precision dual combining glass assembly. There is also an electronically depressible stand-by sight. The high grade optical system and the HUD electronics are housed in separate castings mounted one above the other. This eliminates many of the normal fasteners and mating surfaces and allows easy access to all components for servicing. This construction technique and the use of lighter castings, have made it possible to design a HUD with the same mechanical strength as conventional equipment but weighing 20 per cent less.

The electrostatically focused CRT and electromagnetic deflection yoke are supplied as a fully tested assembly. Together with the bright-up

AV-8B HUD pilot's display unit

circuitry, this forms a shop replaceable assembly (SRA) requiring minimal adjustment on replacement.

Compensation for windshield distortion is applied electronically and optically and can be adjusted to suit the characteristics of the aircraft. The CRT is protected from solar radiation by ultra-violet and infra-red filters in the optical system and CRT brightness, display accuracy and deflection amplifier performance are monitored by a highly reliable BIT system.

All HUD associated controls are mounted on an integral panel at the rear of the HUD. System controls can be mounted on an up-front control panel designed to suit particular aircraft requirements. A connector is provided to enable connecting wires to be routed through the HUD. Provision is made for installing a side-mounted pilot's recording camera which views the symbology and the outside world simultaneously through a precision periscope assembly.

The stand-by sight is a precision LED matrix on a glass substrate. It is electronically depressible and brightness can be adjusted by varying the intensity of the LEDs. This is a simple and highly effective approach that avoids the gear trains and moving parts of mechanical systems.

To prevent salt fog or contamination from the aircraft cooling system, the electronics and optical system are housed in airtight modules cooled by external heat exchangers.

The display processor (computer), designed to full military specifications, generates calligraphic symbology for the HUD and a combination of calligraphic and raster symbology for the head-down multipurpose display in the AV-8B. The display processor is normally controlled by the aircraft's main

avionic mission computer (MC) through the multiplex data bus. It can also receive and process composite video inputs from either the dual mode tracker or various weapon sensors. If the aircraft's main MC fails, the display processor will assume control of sufficient aircraft avionics to provide all essential information for navigation and aircraft attitude control, including data transfer with the engine display panel, the up-front control set, and the all-weather landing system.

Maximum fail operational capability is provided by a combination of redundant circuitry and multiple path data processing. Full utilisation of BIT circuitry provides failure detection and isolation without use of ground support equipment. Periodic and initiated BIT routines provide up to 98 per cent detection of failures. The test mode enables the pilot and ground crew to determine the operational status of the equipment. A high degree of maintainability and human engineering has been incorporated in the design which features a microprocessor and the latest in logic circuits. Positive easy-to-operate module fasteners are provided to facilitate maintenance. Symbol positioning accuracy is achieved using a closed-loop correction technique. All symbols are positioned within one DI (digital increment) for HUD deflection outputs.

STATUS
Initial production.

CONTRACTORS
Smiths Industries, Aerospace & Defence Systems Company, Cheltenham Division, Bishops Cleeve, Cheltenham, Gloucestershire GL52 4SF, England.

Smiths Industries Inc, St Petersburg/Clearwater Airport, PO Box 5389, Clearwater, Florida 33518, USA.

1805.393
TORNADO HEAD-UP DISPLAY

Smiths Industries Ltd, in collaboration with Teldix GmbH and Ottica Mechanica Italiana (OMI), currently supplies the head-up display and weapon aiming computing (HUDWAC) system for the multi-national Tornado programme. The system consists basically of a pilot's display unit (PDU) and an electronic unit (EU). In addition, Smiths Industries is sub-contracted by Litef-Litton Technische Werke for manufacture of the Spirit 3 airborne computer for the Tornado.

Pilot's Display Unit: The PDU is fully line-replaceable and incorporates an integral pilot's control panel, deflection amplifiers, bright-up and power supply modules (including the EHT supply),

Tornado pilot's head-up display unit

and depressible standby sight. It consists essentially of two main sub-assemblies: the electronic (front) module and the optical module. The optical module consists of a combining glass assembly, and a high grade lens group with a 127 mm exit lens providing a total field of view of 25°. All glass-to-air surfaces are treated with an anti-reflective coating to reduce spurious reflections. The electronic module forms the main structure of the PDU and consists of a light, rigid, accurately machined aluminium alloy casting. It houses the deflection amplifiers, CRT assembly, BITE modules and EHT supply. The casting has a machined surface at one end to provide the accurate location of the optical module. The machined end also serves to locate the tube unit accurately relative to the optical module. The electronic module features a removable top metal plate which, when secured, produces a sealed volume enclosing the various modules. Removal of the plate allows access to the modules within.

Electronic Unit: This computer unit is based on a powerful digital on-line processor running on a stored program. Its purpose is to process data, control the generation of the display in the PDU and carry out weapon-aiming computations. It is housed in a compact case. Construction of the computer unit is modular, the main circuits being mounted on 20 multi-layer boards, assembled in pairs to form ten rugged, easily replaceable modules.

The computer unit consists of four main functional areas. The input interface accepts eight channels of serial digital data which it holds in buffer stores until

the information is required by the central processor. The buffer stores are data acquisition devices in the form of MOS circuits designed by Smiths Industries' own Microcircuit Circuit Engineering Company. The central processor is a powerful, high-speed, general-purpose digital computer capable of carrying out extensive weapon-aiming computing tasks, in addition to controlling the generation of a comprehensive display of flight data, navigation information and weapon aiming symbology. The processor is programmed by means of a central memory consisting of semiconductor programmable read only memory (PROM) assemblies which provide high density circuitry and high integrity at low unit cost and power consumption. The output interface generates the waveforms necessary to control the 'cursive' symbology display on the CRT of the PDU in terms of deflection (X and Y) and bright-up (Z) commands. The power supply module accepts 200 V, 400 Hz, 3-phase aircraft supply and 28 V DC.

Built-in test equipment is provided in two forms: continuous in-flight self-monitoring, which checks the internal processes of the computer, and interruptive testing, which allows the checking of symbol generation by the display of test patterns on the PDU.

STATUS
Production.

CONTRACTOR
Smiths Industries, Aerospace & Defence Systems Company, Cheltenham Division, Bishops Cleeve, Cheltenham, Gloucestershire GL52 4SF, England.

3090.393
HEAD-UP DISPLAY FOR HARRIER AND JAGUAR

From inception the Harrier and Jaguar weapon systems have featured a Smiths Industries electronic HUD. The system, which comprises a pilot's display unit (PDU), waveform generator (WFG), pilot's control panel (PCP) and extra high tension unit (EHTU), is designed to provide the pilot with accurate analogue and alpha-numeric symbol displays of primary flight data and navigation and weapon aiming information.

Pilot's Display Unit: This consists essentially of two modules: the optical system and the CRT assembly. The optical system consists of a collimating lens assembly and a combining glass. The 100 mm, f0·97 lens assembly provides a 25° total field of view. The installation provides an instantaneous binocular field of view in the region of 18° in azimuth and 16° in elevation. All glass-to-air surfaces are treated with an anti-reflective coating to reduce spurious reflections.

The CRT assembly consists of a high-brightness CRT, a deflection coil assembly, a focus magnet and a brightness amplifier. The electromagnetically focused CRT, the face of which is coated with a P1 phosphor, is capable of producing a brightness level which enables the display to be viewed against a

background intensity of 35 000 candelas/m² (10 000 ft lamberts). The datum brightness is set by the pilot and thereafter automatically controlled by the action of a solar cell which maintains a constant contrast between the display and the background.

The PDU carries a dual-purpose mounting bracket at the rear, which accepts either a pilot's display recorder (camera) or a crash pad.

Waveform Generator: The symbol generation computer, which forms the heart of the HUD system, is a special purpose digital computer which accepts analogue DC signals and discrete control inputs from various sensors and systems on the aircraft. The analogue signals are converted to digital form at the input stage and thereafter all processing is by digital techniques until the final output stage, where the digital information is converted to analogue waveforms suitable for transmission to the PDU. The entire processing is controlled by a program incorporated during manufacture on MOS storage devices (read-only memories). This system provides high reliability and considerable flexibility of the display content.

The computer is of modular construction, housed in a ½ ATR short case, and incorporates integrated circuits and multi-layer printed circuit boards. The

integral supply operates from the 200 V, 400 Hz, 3-phase aircraft supply. A built-in test facility is provided which allows continuous monitoring of the system and special test modes enable the pilot to perform a confidence check prior to flight or attack.

Pilot's Control Panel (PCP): Manual switching of the HUD system is controlled from the PCP and allows the pilot to select the display required for the particular flight mode in progress. Various alternative symbols or additional symbols can also be selected when required. The panel includes controls for display brightness, target wing-span setting, barometric scale setting and a built-in test facility.

Extra High Tension Unit: The EHTU provides a high voltage supply to the CRT in the PDU. To maintain the high level of accuracy required for weapon aiming, the 15 kV output from the EHTU has a very high degree of stabilisation over the full operating temperature range.

STATUS
Production, with over 600 systems supplied for the Harrier and Jaguar programmes to date.

CONTRACTOR
Smiths Industries, Aerospace & Defence Systems Company, Cheltenham Division, Bishops Cleeve, Cheltenham, Gloucestershire GL52 4SF, England.

3117.393
HEAD-UP DISPLAY FOR SEA HARRIER

The Smiths Industries' head-up display and weapon aiming computing (HUDWAC) system which is currently being supplied for the Sea Harrier, provides a comprehensive display of weapon-aiming, flight and navigation symbology as well as performing all the weapon aiming computations. The system comprises a pilot's display unit (PDU), an electronic unit (EU) and a pilot's control panel (PCP).

Pilot's Display Unit: This is a fully line-replaceable PDU featuring integral deflection amplifiers, bright-up and power supply modules (including EHT) and standby sight. A special feature of this PDU is that it can display symbology and outside world pictures in raster form in addition to traditional cursive symbology. It is of modular construction for ease of maintenance and consists essentially of two main sub-assemblies: the electronic (front) module and the optical module.

The optical module features two optical channels: 'Main' CRT and 'Standby'. In addition it also houses the electronics needed to convert the 28 V aircraft supply to the six volts required to illuminate the quartz halogen lamp used for the standby sight. The combiner glass mounting forms an integral part of the

module and is so arranged that the combiner can hinge downwards to allow both it and the aircraft windscreen to be cleaned. Provision is also made for the mounting of a pilot's display recording camera. The high grade optical system has a 114 mm exit lens providing a total field of view of 22°. Careful design throughout has ensured that optical performance is of a very high standard.

The electronics module forms the main structure of the PDU as well as providing the location for the mounting dowels and bolts from which all datum measurements are taken. Considerable attention has been paid to maintaining the internal packaging and all major modules are plug-in items, accessible through two removable top covers. The case houses the deflection amplifier and power supply boards which are located at the sides of the module to give good thermal characteristics. These boards may be removed easily without the need for special extractors. Two other electronic boards (built-in test and brightness control) are plugged into a separate wiring tray positioned above the CRT assembly. The EHT unit, which provides the stabilised 15 kV supply to the anode of the electrostatically focused CRT, is also easily accessible and is mounted at the front of the electronic module.

Electronic Unit: The EU is centred around a powerful, high-speed, general-purpose digital processor, programmed by a central memory which contains 16 K words of read/write core-store and 6 K words of read-only store. The core-store may be loaded without removing the unit covers by connecting a tape reader to a dedicated plug on the front of the unit. The computer is capable of handling a large number of inputs, both digital and analogue. The analogue signals are multiplexed and then sequentially converted to digital format, while the digital inputs are assembled in data acquisition devices (DADs) of Smiths Industries' own design. The use of DADs enables the input stage to operate asynchronously with respect to the central processor and results in considerable savings in processor time. In addition to the conventional head-up symbol generator, which generates and controls the cursive symbology on the PDU, the computer unit contains a raster symbol generator. This enables raster symbology to be displayed on head-up and head-down display units either independently or combined with raster inputs from radar or E-O sensors. The computer has two integral power supplies, one for the core-store and one for the electronics. Each derives its power from the aircraft 200 V, 400 Hz, 3-phase supply. The functional circuitry is mounted on 32 multi-layer boards, assembled in pairs to form 16 modules which are functionally and electrically interchangeable with modules of the same coding.

Considerable attention has been paid to the integrity of the system. Built-in test equipment continuously monitors the functioning of the system and the validity of the input information, and interruptive testing can be performed by the selection of special test modes.

Pilot's Control Panel: Manual switching of the HUD system is controlled from the PCP and allows the pilot to select the display required for the particular flight mode in progress. Various alternative symbols or additional symbols can also be selected when required. The panel includes controls for display brightness, target wingspan setting, barometric scale setting and a built-in test facility.

STATUS

Production.

CONTRACTOR

Smiths Industries, Aerospace & Defence Systems Company, Cheltenham Division, Bishops Cleeve, Cheltenham, Gloucestershire GL52 4SF, England.

3568.393
SAAB JA37 VIGGEN HEAD-UP DISPLAY

Smiths Industries currently supplies the pilot's display unit (PDU) for the JA37 version of the Viggen. This is a fully line-replaceable PDU consisting essentially of two modules; an electronic or front module and an optical module (with integral control panel).

The optical module consists of a combining glass assembly and a high accuracy 100 mm lens system. The lens system features precision ground input and exit lens groups and a prism, the whole providing a total field of view of 28°. In addition the optical module is provided with a standby sight in order to permit reversionary weapon aiming in the event of a HUD failure.

The electronic module forms the main structure of the PDU and houses the deflection amplifiers, power supplies (including EHT), BITE, CRT assembly, brightness control, combiner servo-amplifier and all the peripheral electronic circuitry. For ease of maintenance the electronics are contained within the PDU in modular form.

STATUS

Production.

CONTRACTOR

Smiths Industries, Aerospace & Defence Systems Company, Cheltenham Division, Bishops Cleeve, Cheltenham, Gloucestershire GL52 4SF, England.

4178.383
FIN 1064 DINAS

The Ferranti FIN 1064 digital inertial navigation and attack system (DINAS) was developed for the RAF Jaguar refit programme to replace the original NAVWASS equipment (**1312.383**).

In the Jaguar, five separate units were replaced by one unit, with a reduction in volume of two-thirds and a weight-saving of some 50 kg compared with the previous system. The FIN 1064 system incorporates the computer, platform, power supply, electronics

FIN 1064 in an aircraft cockpit

and interface modules into the same line replaceable unit (LRU).

FIN 1064 interfaces with all the other weapon-aiming and navigation facilities in the RAF's Jaguars, including the Ferranti LRMTS (laser ranger and marked target seeker) (**1196.393**) which is standard equipment in the single-seat version. Built-in system test software enables the FIN 1064 to self-check automatically, and also to check all the interface signals, thereby indicating to the pilot or ground crew the serviceability of such systems as Tacan, HUD and horizontal situation indicator; this aids assessing the practicability of continuing a mission or in identifying a systems failure for subsequent maintenance action.

For the pilot, the Ferranti FIN 1064 offers significant advantages over older systems, in terms of both ergonomics and performance. Pre-flight alignment times have been minimised and the advanced design of the inertial platform and computer maximises weapon-aiming and navigation accuracy. The control and display unit is mounted on the cockpit coaming, where the pilot can see and operate it easily, without having to go 'head-down' for long periods. Navigation and steering commands are shown on the HUD, providing the pilot with vital data super-imposed on his view of the outside world. With the single-pass, low-level ground attack very much in mind, FIN 1064 has been developed to provide a comprehensive range of 'hands-on-stick and throttle' weapon delivery profiles.

The digital computer is addressable up to 64 K of memory – a large increase on previous systems. System reliability is significantly improved, based on the experience gained by similar Ferranti systems and the early FIN 1064 models.

DEVELOPMENT

FIN 1064 is one of the FIN 1060 family of inertial nav/attack systems derived from the FIN 1000 series. These are in production at Ferranti's Silverknowes,

Three units comprising FIN 1064 for RAF Jaguar (left to right) pilot's display, control unit, and one-box LRU incorporating computer, inertial platform interface, electronics and power supply modules

Edinburgh factory for the Tornado, Sea Harrier, Nimrod MR2 and Mitsubishi F1 aircraft, as well as Jaguar. FIN 1060 can accept PODS (portable data store) for in-cockpit transfer of mission data pre-loaded into PODS by computer-assisted mission planning equipment such as Ferranti Autoplan or Tacplan.

STATUS

The first FIN 1064 was delivered to the BAe Warton factory for rig tests in December 1980. This had been preceded by extensive bench tests at the manufacturer's Edinburgh plant. Flight trials began in 1981. Production equipments were delivered to the RAF in the second quarter of 1983.

CONTRACTOR

Ferranti plc, Navigation Systems Department, Silverknowes, Ferry Road, Edinburgh EH4 4AD, Scotland.

4730.383
FERRANTI FINAS

FINAS (Ferranti Nav/Attack System) is an integrated system which includes the Type 4500 head-up display and weapon aiming computer (HUDWAC), the FIN 2000 inertial navigator and the Type 105D laser rangefinder. It is intended both for new aircraft and as a retrofit package for current types.

The Type 4500 HUDWAC was first displayed in public at the Farnborough Air Show in 1982. It consists of two units, the HUD display itself and a ½ ATR weapon aiming computer. The HUD has an unusually large field of view, 24 × 18, and incorporates its own controls for mode selection. Dual combiners are provided and can be replaced without reharmonisation being necessary. The HUD projects a comprehensive variety of information on to the pilot's line of vision and a number of air-to-air and air-to-ground modes provide data for the automatic or manual release of weapons.

The FIN 2000 inertial navigator is derived from the FIN 1000 fitted to the Nimrod and the Tornado, and also the Sea Harrier NAVHARS system. The Type 105D laser rangefinder has already been produced for the Royal Danish Air Force Draken aircraft and is described under entry **4003.393**.

STATUS

The complete system is on offer for both new aircraft and retrofit programmes. The Type 4500 is undergoing a series of flight trials and has been proposed for a number of aircraft. The FIN 2000 has been on flight trials in both fixed wing aircraft and helicopters of the RAF. The Type 105D laser rangefinder is in operational service with the Danish Draken aircraft.

CONTRACTOR

Ferranti plc, Electro-optics Department, Robertson Avenue, Edinburgh EH11 1PX, Scotland.

1012.393
ISIS WEAPON AIMING SYSTEM

The ISIS (integrated strike and interception systems) series of equipment comprises a range of aircraft sighting systems based on the use of gyro-controlled, lead computing optical techniques. Different versions are available to fulfil air-to-air and air-to-ground missions with varying degrees of complexity, according to operational requirements. Initially intended for the aiming of guns, rockets, missiles and bombs, the ISIS sight can use range information from a laser rangefinder. It can also serve as a low-cost alternative to a CRT type HUD by displaying pointing data from a laser seeker such as the Martin Marietta Pave Penny or the Ferranti LRMTS.

Common to all versions of the ISIS family of weapon aiming sights is the use of a two-axis rate gyro, the movement of which is controlled by variations in the magnetic restraint imposed upon it in accordance with the requirements of the aiming process. The gyro is located in the sighting head, and has two principal parts, concerned with display and control, respectively. The display portion consists of a circular mirror centred on the rotational axis of the gyro. The aiming pattern is reflected from this into the pilot's forward view so that any deflection of the gyro relative to its housing results in a corresponding deflection of the aiming pattern relative to the centre of the field of view. The control portion of the gyro rotates in a controllable magnetic field, the strength of which determines the amount of deflection produced by a given aircraft rate of turn. The control field may also be intentionally unbalanced to produce required deflections of the gyro, and thus the aiming pattern.

OPERATION

Air-to-air (guns): Control of the magnetic restraint of the gyro is particularly applicable to this mode. The constant of proportionality between gyro deflection and aircraft rate of turn is defined as the sensitivity of the sight, which for a given weapon is required to vary with range. This is achieved by coupling the ranging sensor (radar or optical) to a potentiometer which thereby adjusts the field strength operating on the gyro dome. The gyro deflection, and hence the lead angle, is then correct throughout the attack sequence. Fixed range sensitivity operation is possible at a cost in reduced overall accuracy. The effect of gravity upon the projectile is compensated by arranging for a small depression of the sight-line, and the amount of depression is controlled by a similar arrangement for that used to adjust sensitivity, so that the allowance for gravity drop is correct throughout the attack. In tracking the target with the aiming mark, the aircraft is caused to change its heading continuously, and this rate of change of the aircraft axis is a function of the relative speed between the target and fighter. This is measured directly by the two-axis gyro so that the required aim-off angle

ISIS D-195R sight for Hawk aircraft

proportional to range (a measure of the magnetic restraint of the gyro) is determined by the system.

Air-to-surface: In this mode, gravity drop effect assumes greater importance, and a depressed sight-line method of approach is used. The magnetic field controlling the gyro is unbalanced to cause a downward deflection of the aiming pattern, the amount of deflection being dependent upon the aircraft dive angle, speed, and release range. In some versions of ISIS switching is arranged to provide the correct sight-line depression for one fixed speed and one range of dive angles. If continuous speed and pitch angle inputs are available, however, these can be used to provide for continuous variation of sight-line depression.

Manual adjustment of sight-line depression can also be provided. A fixed sensitivity datum is used for each type of weapon in the ground attack mode.

Roll stabilisation of the aiming mark has become a standard feature of many of the ISIS variants where a vertical reference gyro is already installed in the aircraft. This feature reduces the tracking time of the target to a matter of two to three seconds thus limiting the 'exposure time' of the pilot to ground fire.

Additional Facilities: Provisions can be made for the ISIS system to accept inputs from other sources such as doppler drift, laser or radar ranging.

DEVELOPMENT

The basic concept of the ISIS has been developed with the object of enabling the requirements of different users to be met from a range of standard systems, several of which are capable of subsequent extension.

STATUS

The ISIS system first entered operational service in 1968 and current users include the air forces of Argentina, Australia, Austria, Canada, India, Indonesia, Italy, Kenya, Norway, Singapore, UK and Venezuela, and the USMC. Approximately 1500 systems had been ordered as of mid-1982.

ISIS equipment has been fitted to the SAAB 105, (ISIS F-126), Fiat G91Y (ISIS B), Aeromacchi MB 326 (ISIS F-126), McDonnell Douglas A-4S (ISIS D-101), Northrop CF-5A (ISIS N), Northrop NF-5A (ISIS F-195R), BAe Hawk (ISIS D-195R), HAL Ajeet (ISIS

ISIS D-209RM sight for Hunter aircraft

F-195R), HAL HF24 (ISIS F-124) MiG 21FL, Mostar Galeb, and LAS A-4C (D-126R).

The ISIS D-01 has been delivered to the USN for use by the USMC, in conjunction with a USN laser target designator system.

The BAe Hunter aircraft is in service throughout the world, using the GGS MK8S weapon aiming system. As this system was designed in 1953, most of its components are now obsolescent. Ferranti has designed the ISIS D-209RM (three units) weapon aiming system to replace the GGS MK8S (13 units) system in the Hunter so that cockpit modification work is kept to a minimum. The ISIS D-209RM not only embodies latest technology components but also benefits from user Services' experience of ISIS equipment over the last ten years and is designed to incorporate modules for laser target seeker. Laser range and radar range input modules may be incorporated without need to alter the envelope of either the sight head or the electronics unit. The ISIS D-209RM and the Type 106 laser target seeker are combined to form an integrated low-cost head-up air-to-ground target acquisition system for ground attack aircraft.

The ISIS F-195R/3 entered licence production at the Hindustan Aeronautics Ltd, Lucknow plant in 1978, for installation in the HAL Ajeet aircraft.

CONTRACTOR

Ferranti plc, Electro-optics Department, Robertson Avenue, Edinburgh EH11 1PX, Scotland.

4261.393

AF532/AF533/AF580 HELICOPTER ROOF SIGHTS

These Ferranti helicopter sights are designed for use in surveillance, target identification and missile guidance. A built-in interface allows a laser ranger or designator module to be added. Facilities are also provided for the attachment of a recording TV camera. The sight can be adapted for use with night vision equipment, helmet sights and weapons. The AF532 version is in production for the UK Army Air Corps and the AF580 is under evaluation in the United States (see under STATUS below).

The sight provides for two magnifications. For

initial surveillance ×2·5 is provided, with a field of view of 22°, and for target recognition and identification, ×10, with a field of view of 5·5°. The choice of these magnifications are based on optical considerations such as specified identification and recognition criteria as well as the need to achieve a compact and light design.

Every effort has been made in the design to keep

the sight lightweight, simple and reliable. Modular construction eases its maintenance and allows for growth. Built-in first line test facilities are incorporated and dedicated automatic test equipment has been developed for use in servicing at base and overhaul levels.

The sight is installed with its head and most of the optics carried above the normal roof line. Only the

AF533 gyro-stabilised helicopter observation sight installed in Gazelle helicopter

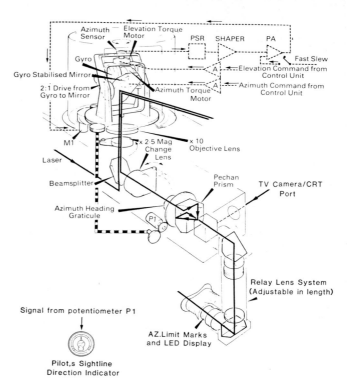

Schematic diagram of the AF533 helicopter sight

down-tube and eyepiece extend down in front of the operator when the sight is in use. The down-tube is adjustable in length which enables the installation to be readily tailored to fit most helicopters. When not required the down-tube is swung up and locked in position, out of the way, against the roof.

The down-tube may be adjusted as necessary for use then pushed aside until required. Also, if the pilot were to be incapacitated, it would be easy for the sight operator to push aside the down-tube and take over control immediately. The control handle is adjustable, both in length and tilt, so that it may always be used with the right forearm resting on the knee for comfortable control. A thumbstick controller on the control handle is used to steer the sightline through ±120° in azimuth and ±30° in elevation, movement of which is achieved by precession of the gyro which directly stabilises the mirror mounted within the rotating head. At ×10 magnification the slew rate is variable up to 5°/s; at ×2·5 magnification the slew rate is progressively variable up to 5°/s but 75°/s fast-slew can be obtained with full deflection of the thumbstick. The two-degree-of-freedom gyro is prevented from toppling under all operational conditions by limit and logic switches associated with a caging mechanism.

CHARACTERISTICS
Weight of installed system: 28 kg (33 kg with laser rangefinder/designator)
Resolution: 20 line pairs/mrad
Magnification: ×2·5, ×10
Field of view: 22° (×2·5 magnification); 5·5° (× 10 magnification)
Total sightline exploration: Azimuth ±120°; elevation ±30°
Exit pupil size: 5 mm diameter
Eye relief: 35 mm
Eyepiece focus: Fixed at –1 dioptre
Vertical adjustment of eyepiece: Variable over 110 mm

DEVELOPMENT
The AF533 sight is developed from the AF530 on which work was commenced in 1970 by Ferranti for use with the BAe Hawkswing missile. Successful trials were carried out before termination of that system's development by the UK MoD in 1975. It is a refined version of the AF530 updated and incorporating improved electronics. Sights with other AF500 designations are being prepared for various helicopters.

Ferranti's first-generation stabilised sight, the AF120, which uses similar stabilisation techniques, is still in service with the British Army.

STATUS
The AF532 is now in production, under a UK MoD contract for fitment to Gazelle helicopters of the Army Air Corps.

The AF580, which is similar to the AF533, has been fitted to two Bell OH58 helicopters of the US Army and is undergoing flight trials in the United States. The sight also incorporates a Ferranti laser rangefinder and designator which is a repackaged version of the Type 629 (**4787.193**) plus a telescope.

CONTRACTORS
Ferranti Instrumentation Ltd, Aircraft Equipment Department, Lily Hill House, Lily Hill Road, Bracknell, Berkshire RG12 2SJ, England, is responsible for the electronics and gyro sub-systems and are the main contractors for the sight. The optical sub-system of this equipment is manufactured by Avimo Ltd, Taunton, Somerset, England.

1196.393
FERRANTI LASER RANGER AND MARKED TARGET SEEKER

This is an aircraft ranging and direction system designed primarily for air-to-surface attacks, when it is used either as a self-contained laser ranger or, when operating in conjunction with a laser target marker (designator), as a simultaneous rangefinder and target seeker. This latter feature, coupled with high accuracy, gives this laser system a distinct advantage over radar ranging equipment. The laser ranger and marked target seeker is specifically intended for use with weapon systems optimised for low level, first pass attack when targets are difficult to detect, tracking time is necessarily short and air-to-surface grazing angles are very low.

OPERATION
The laser ranger operates by directing a pulse of infra-red energy from a YAG laser at the target. Range is then derived by measuring the time interval between transmitting the pulse and receiving the scattered energy returned to the ranger from the target. The laser beam is stabilised against vibration and angular movement to ensure accurate alignment with the target. A high PRF allows continuous range information to be obtained when this is required.

When used in conjunction with a laser target marking system, a forward air controller aims a pulsed laser marker at the designated target and uses a radio link to direct the pilot of the attacking aircraft. As the aircraft approaches the target, the target marker is switched on. The target seeker in the aircraft automatically acquires and tracks the

Ferranti laser ranger and marked target seeker installation in the nose of a Jaguar aircraft

scattered laser energy from the target. The tracking operation generates signals which are translated into director information for presentation to the pilot on a head-up display.

Advantages arising from the latter mode of operation include positive identification of the target by someone who normally has relatively more time available than the pilot; pilot work load is reduced by elimination of the task of searching for the target over a wide field of view; an attack can still be made even though the pilot may not see his target due to poor light or because of camouflage.

The laser beam is fully stabilised against aircraft movements by mounting the transmit and receive optics within a three-axis gimbal head. The head may be used to direct the beam +3 to –20° in elevation, ±12° in azimuth and is roll stabilised to ±90°. The target seeker coverage is considerably more than the limits of head movement. Range is quoted as being greater than pilot's visual range up to 9 km.

The main unit weighs 21·5 kg and is 607 mm long by 269 mm in diameter. The total height, including the heat exchanger, is 300 mm. The electronics unit, weighing 14·5 kg and measuring 432 mm long by 330 mm wide by 127 mm high, contains ranging, seeking, and power supply circuits.

DEVELOPMENT
Development was started in late 1968, under UK Government contract and the first prototype was completed by mid-1970. Prototypes were flown in Canberra, Jaguar, and Harrier aircraft.

In September 1978 a podded version of the LRMTS was proposed by Ferranti and Portsmouth Aviation, enabling the equipment to be retrofitted to other aircraft types. The pod is about 2·3 m long and 37 cm in diameter. It is fitted with a chisel window for the transmission and reception of laser energy. Total weight is 140 kg, inclusive of air conditioning.

STATUS
The equipment is now in service with the RAF and several other air forces. It is operational in Jaguar and Harrier aircraft and a close variant is in production for the RAF Tornado. Over 500 systems have been produced.

CONTRACTOR
Ferranti plc, Electro-optics Department, Robertson Avenue, Edinburgh EH11 1PX, Scotland.

3046.393
FERRANTI TYPE 105 AIR-TO-SURFACE LASER RANGER

The Type 105 system is a low cost, air-to-surface laser ranger aimed at satisfying the all important ranging requirements of ground attack aircraft. The compact, one unit design is ideally suited for installations, on a retrofit basis if necessary, in aircraft when laser ranging is required as an alternative to less accurate radar or other ranging methods. The small size and modular design of the Type 105 may also be used to good advantage in aircraft where, up to now, lack of space has prohibited the inclusion of a range sensor. In particular, two configurations are offered; the in-line Type 105 (illustrated) or the T-shaped Type 105. The latter configuraton is specifically designed for installations with short back to front dimensions.

The Type 105 weighs approximately 9 kg and comprises laser transceiver and beam steerer modules in one unit. The laser is convection cooled Nd-YAG, capable of operation up to at least two pps or at bursts of ten pps. Higher PRFs are available with the simple addition of a liquid cooling block attached to the transceiver module. A photodiode detector for ranging is integrated with the laser transmitter. The beam steerer is simple and of a novel design, permitting roll (±360°) stabilisation of the laser beam which may also be directed over a 20° cone as required by the weapon system.

OPERATION
The Type 105 will provide a range for a wide variety of gunsights (including the Ferranti ISIS series) and weapon systems. It is accurate to better than ±5 m SD and is virtually unjammable. High reliability is a particular feature with a specified figure of not less than 500 hours mean time between failure. A far higher figure is confidently expected by the manufacturers.

STATUS
Prototypes have been flown in the Fairchild two-seat A-10 attack aircraft.

Type 105 air-to-surface laser ranger

CONTRACTOR
Ferranti plc, Electro-optics Department, Robertson Avenue, Edinburgh EH11 1PX, Scotland.

4003.393
FERRANTI TYPE 105D AIR-TO-SURFACE LASER RANGER
The Type 105D is a low cost variant of the earlier private venture Type 105 equipment (**3046.393**). It is a compact single unit system ideally suited for installation, on a retrofit basis if necessary, in aircraft when laser ranging is required as an alternative to less accurate radar or other ranging methods. The small size and modular design of the Type 105D may also be used to good advantage in aircraft where, up to now, lack of space has prohibited the inclusion of a range sensor.

The Type 105D weighs approximately 9 kg and its Nd-YAG laser transceiver operates continuously at ten pps. The beam steerer directs the laser beam within a 20° cone as required by the weapon system. It also provides ±360° roll stabilisation.

OPERATION
The Type 105D is capable of being integrated with a wide variety of weapon systems including gyro gunsights, head-up displays and full inertial nav/attack systems. The equipment is expected to be highly reliable in service with a mean time between failure of the order of 1000 hours. The transceiver concept, where the receiver is incorporated within the transmitter, gives particularly good protection against ranging returns on spurious targets such as dust or smoke, and this is a special operating feature of the Ferranti equipment.
DEVELOPMENT
The equipment was originally a private venture by Ferranti. It was ordered by the Royal Danish Air Force as part of the weapon delivery navigation system (WDNS) refit of their Draken aircraft in June 1980.
STATUS
The Type 105D is being manufactured for the Royal Danish Air Force.

Type 105D laser ranger

CONTRACTOR
Ferranti plc, Electro-optics Department, Robertson Avenue, Edinburgh EH11 1PX, Scotland.

3119.393
FERRANTI TYPE 106
LASER TARGET SEEKER
The Type 106 laser target seeker was conceived in answer to a requirement for a simple laser seeking device for installation in light, ground attack aircraft. It is specifically designed to integrate with the Ferranti ISIS series of gunsights or head-up display systems.

The concept of use is described under the item dealing with the Ferranti laser ranger and marked target seeker (**1196.393**). The incorporation of this system significantly increases the effectiveness of close air support against difficult targets, while reducing the required briefing time between forward air controller and pilot.

The main unit comprises the stabilised optical head of the Ferranti laser ranger and marked target seeker equipment contained in a short, pressurised, canister. An electronics unit contains power supplies and target seeking circuits and is also a variant of the RAF's equipment.

The optical head is roll stabilised ±90° by the aircraft reference and is capable of being directed and stabilised +20 to −25° in elevation, relative to equipment roll axis. The azimuth coverage is ±18° relative to aircraft heading with automatic scanning. This coverage may be further increased by simply manoeuvring the aircraft.

Ferranti Type 106 laser target seeker

OPERATION
The aircraft approaches the target area with the target seeker automatically scanning about a selectable depression angle. When marked target returns are received the seeker locks on and positions an appropriate reticle or gunsight symbol to lie over the target. If the target is outside the field of view of the sight, the pilot is given a direction to steer. The pilot

simply tracks the reticle with his aiming mark and carries out an attack. With this system he need never actually sight the target.

The main and electronics unit weigh approximately 10·5 kg each. The main unit is 312 mm long with a diameter of 247 mm. The total height is 275 mm. The electronics unit is 432 mm long by 330 mm wide by 127 mm high, though it may be repackaged to approximately half this volume if so desired.

In September 1978 a podded version of the Type 106 was announced by Ferranti and Portsmouth Aviation. The pod weighs 125 kg, inclusive of air conditioning, and is about 2·3 m long and 37 cm in diameter.

The Type 106 is also used in combination with the ISIS D-209RM gyro gunsight to form a low-cost head-up air-to-ground target acquisition system for ground attack aircraft.
DEVELOPMENT
The equipment is a private venture variant of similar devices for Jaguar and Harrier.
STATUS
Several other air forces are showing interest in the Type 106 but it is not yet in production other than in its RAF form.
CONTRACTOR
Ferranti plc, Electro-optics Department, Robertson Avenue, Edinburgh EH11 1PX, Scotland.

4727.393
TYPE 117 LASER DESIGNATOR
The Type 117 laser designator/ranger has been designed by Ferranti as an integral part of the forward looking infra-red (FLIR) pod for the US Navy F/A-18 Hornet aircraft. No technical details have been released other than that it is a high power, high-

repetition rate Nd:YAG device with an output power in excess of 100 mJoules.
STATUS
In development under contract to Ford Aerospace and Communications Corporation. The initial contract, worth over $2 million, covers engineering

developments and provision of units for qualification and flight testing.
CONTRACTOR
Ferranti plc, Electro-optics Department, Robertson Avenue, Edinburgh EH11 1PX, Scotland.

5747.393
HELICOPTER LASER DESIGNATOR (HELD)
As with its two ground-based variants, HOLD and FOLD, the Ferranti helicopter laser designator (HELD) is based on the Type 306 designator which has been in service with the British Army since 1980 under the name Laser Target Marker and Ranger (LTMR) (**1742.193**). In the HELD version the Type 306 is fitted to a simple helicopter mount which requires

virtually no modification to the helicopter. A gyro-stabilised mirror is added to the mount to remove the worst of the vibration and motion effects on the laser spot. The system has been successfully tested with laser guided bombs and spot trackers.
CONTRACTOR
Ferranti plc, Electro-optics Department, Robertson Avenue, Edinburgh EH11 1PX, Scotland.

HELD in a Royal Canadian armed forces helicopter

5749.393
TYPE 221 THERMAL SURVEILLANCE SYSTEM
The Type 221 thermal surveillance system has been developed jointly by Ferranti and Barr & Stroud for use in military helicopters. The system incorporates a Barr & Stroud IR18 thermal imager and telescope (**3834.093**) with sightline stabilisation steering through a Ferranti stabilised mirror. The system is passive in operation and provides detection and

recognition of land and sea targets during both day and night in adverse weather conditions.

The stabilisation mirror system is a two-axis device which employs integrating rate gyros as space rate sensors. The mechanism is driven in each axis by direct drive DC torque motor, and steering is achieved by torquing the integrating rate gyro. Angular information is obtained from a resolver fitted to each axis. The Barr & Stroud IR18 is described fully in entry

3834.093. In the Type 221 application it is fitted with a dual field of view (×2·5 and ×9) telescope. The low magnification provides a wide field of view for surveillance, target acquisition and pilot aid while the high magnification allows detailed observation and engagement of targets.

The display can be presented on either 525 or 625 line TV monitors. The output is either to CCIR or EIA composite video formats.

STATUS
In production and operational service.

CONTRACTORS
Barr & Stroud Ltd, Caxton Street, Anniesland, Glasgow G13 1HZ, Scotland.
Ferranti plc, St Andrews Works, Robertson Avenue, Edinburgh EH11 1PX, Scotland.

Type 221 thermal surveillance system

4785.193
HELICOPTER INFRA-RED SYSTEM

The Helicopter Infra-Red System (HIRS) has been developed by Barr & Stroud and Lasergage as a helicopter flying and surveillance aid, based on the former company's IR18 system (**3834.093**). A choice of IR telescopes, depending on the application and range requirements, is available for HIRS and these can be easily fitted and interchanged.

The IR18 thermal imager is housed in a weatherproof pod, aerodynamically designed to ensure minimum drag. The pod is mounted on the exterior of the aircraft via a gimbal and yoke mechanism and is easily transferred from one aircraft to another. The system is also suitable for marine, vehicular or tripod mounting. The controls for the scanner and gimbal are on a single panel in the cockpit. The joystick for the gimbal allows the operator to rotate the pod 100 degrees right and left, 10 degrees above and 100 degrees below level. An LED display indicates the position of the pod.

CHARACTERISTICS
Magnification: ×1, ×1·5 or ×6
Field of view: 38° × 25·5°, 25·3° × 17° or 6·3° × 4·25°
Resolution: 1·73, 1·15 or 0·29 mrad
Weights
Camera pod and gimbals: 20 kg
Control unit: 1·5 kg
Monitor (9″): 4·8 kg
Position indicator: 0·7 kg
Air bottle: 4 kg
Cabling: 4 kg
Optional telescopes: 3·9 kg (×6); 1·2 kg (×1·5)
Compressor (in lieu of air bottle): 18 kg
CONTRACTORS
Barr & Stroud Ltd, Caxton Street, Anniesland, Glasgow G13 1HZ, Scotland.
Lasergage Ltd, Newtown Road, Hove, East Sussex BN3 7DL, England.

4304.363
BAe TARGET DATA ACQUISITION SYSTEM

As part of a continuing research programme concerned with developing passive homing techniques for future ground-to-ground weapons, British Aerospace Dynamics Group has been

Westland Whirlwind helicopter operated by Bristow for British Aerospace equipped with Helitele platform for use in research programme into use of passive infra-red homing for future ground-to-ground weapons

evaluating an automatic target tracking and recording system in a helicopter. Built by the Dynamics Group, the auto-tracking system incorporates many existing items of equipment including the Helitele helicopter gimballed platform (**3356.353**) produced by Marconi.

Infra-red emissions from the ground target being investigated are recorded on magnetic tape from the output of an infra-red camera mounted on the gimbal platform. The infra-red camera is initially pointed at the designated target and then kept accurately aligned on the target by the auto-tracking system, independently of the helicopter's motion. Target tracking accuracies achieved are better than 0·25 milliradians. Both stationary and moving targets can be tracked with equal accuracy. A sodium lamp mounted on the target is used to designate it to the auto-tracking system. A sodium lamp was selected as it provides a suitable high-intensity source for tracking purposes while having a very low infra-red output – low enough not to affect significantly the data being recorded.

A pair of standard industrial TV cameras are mounted on the helicopter's Helitele platform collimated with the infra-red camera sensor. One camera with a wide field-of-view is linked to a TV monitor display and is utilised by the operator to

acquire the designated target. With the aid of a joystick control that is part of the Helitele equipment, the operator aligns the camera on the target. The second TV camera has a narrower field-of-view and is coupled to the servo-system controlling the platform. Following acquisition, the operator switches control over to this camera and the servo-system maintains the target's sodium light source centred in the field-of-view and, hence, the infra-red camera pointing accurately at the target while infra-red emission data is being recorded.

The helicopter was used by British Aerospace Dynamics Group to acquire detailed information of the patterns of infra-red radiation from stationary and moving targets when viewed from all aspects. Apart from utilising this equipment for recording target data (to be used in system modelling and algorithm development) it has recently been developed to demonstrate target tracking in the infra-red wavelength.
STATUS
Development project. Data gathering trials have now been completed and the infra-red camera performance has been further refined.
CONTRACTOR
British Aerospace Dynamics Group, Six Hills Way, Stevenage, Hertfordshire SG1 2DA, England.

3404.393
NIMTAN AIRBORNE NIGHT SIGHT

The PPE Nimtan sight is a modified Spartan battlefield sight (**3403.193**) incorporating a straight eyepiece and pintle mounting. The sight was designed for the MoD for use by the RAF in maritime patrol aircraft. It can also be used in other patrol, supply, and spotter aircraft, helicopters, land vehicles, ships, and hovercraft with or without the pintle.

The sight interfaces with aircraft window shelves provided with bearing potentiometers. The mounting is provided with azimuth locking, horizontal

scanning, and a safety lanyard. Sight controls consist of on-off switch, focus, shutter, and light control setting. Power is obtained from a self-contained battery. The tube is fitted with automatic brightness control.

The sight is of modular construction for ease of maintenance. Both the equipment and storage case meet the environmental requirements of DEF 133.

The range and field of view provide excellent surveillance and reconnaissance capability and the magnification (×1·7) is sufficiently low not to cause vibration of the picture.

CHARACTERISTICS
Magnification: ×1·7
Field of view: 20°
Image tube: 25 mm 3-stage cascade
Weight: 4·5 kg (7·4 kg with support bracket)
STATUS
In service with the RAF.
CONTRACTOR
Pilkington PE Ltd, Glascoed Road, St Asaph, Clwyd LL17 0LL, Wales.

UNITED STATES OF AMERICA

4243.383
TOMAHAWK CCD TV SENSOR

A miniature, solid-state charge-coupled device (CCD) TV camera has been designed and built by Fairchild Imaging Systems Division under contract to McDonnell Douglas Astronautics Corporation for use as the sensor in the Tomahawk cruise missile (**3993.011** and **4197.221**) digital scene matching area correlator (DSMAC) guidance system.

In conjunction with suitable optics and an image intensifier, the CCD TV camera presents real-time video imagery to the processor designed by McDonnell Douglas Astronautics. The latter, using this video information in a correlation mode, supplies final guidance corrections in the terminal phase of the cruise missile flight to its target. The camera uses a CCD sensor developed by Fairchild.

STATUS
In volume production
CONTRACTOR
Fairchild Weston Systems Inc, 300 Robbins Lane, Syosset, New York 11791, USA.

Fairchild CCD TV camera sensor unit for Tomahawk cruise missile programme DSMAC guidance system

1008.393
XM76 ANTI-OSCILLATION SIGHTING SYSTEM

The XM76 is a telescopic target acquisition and identification equipment, providing stabilisation against vibrating environments such as helicopters, vehicles, boats, and ships.
OPERATION
The sighting system senses motion in two axes by means of rate gyros, and the resulting signals are used to control torque motors acting upon a fluid prism optic system to compensate for the sensed motion, thus stabilising the image of the desired field of view. There are separate, and virtually identical, servo-loops for each axis control. The motion signals measured at the optical head are applied to a control module as error signals, and are then demodulated, amplified, and stabilised, power amplified and fed to the torque motors as correction signals. The polarity and magnitude of the corrective signals determines the direction and speed of the torque motors to compensate for the motion of the optical head.

The optical device responsible for effecting motion correction is a fluid prism. This is a variable geometry, liquid-filled prism enclosed by a flexible opaque bellows and two optical flats, front and rear. The flats are movable, transparent windows which serve as the prism faces. There is one flat for each channel, or axis of motion, and each is connected by a linkage to its respective torque motor. Movement of the flat varies the optical geometry of the fluid prism, thereby varying the refraction of light through the prism. These controlled changes result in stabilisation of the image.

The anti-oscillation sighting system has also been adapted to armed helicopter fire control. There have been two applications. The first was to improve the accuracy of the fire by providing the gunner with a stabilised image and ×1·5 to ×12 magnification optics on the gun sight. The second was also to provide a further increase in accuracy by incorporating resolvers into the optical servo loop, and thus slaving the turret to the optical line-of-sight of the XM76 mounted on the sighting station in the cockpit.

The sight also incorporates a monocular zoom lens, controlled by two push-buttons on the unit. These control the direction of the zoom; the ×1·5 for zoom-out (decreased magnification) and the ×12 for zoom-in (increased magnification). Speed of zoom is determined by the detent to which the ×1·5 or ×12 button is pressed: first detent for slow zoom, second detent for fast zoom.
STATUS
Users include the US Army, USAF, USMC, USN, and the Government of Israel. Vehicles fitted with the XM76 sighting system include the OV-2, AHIG, OH6A, OH-58A, and the UH-1 series helicopters for observation, target acquisition, attack and damage assessment.

Stabilised sight head for the M97 20 mm armament system on the Bell AH-1J Twin Cobra

Fixed-wing aircraft include the A-4 and F-4, and other types of vehicle fitted range over AFVs and various types of naval craft. Recent helicopter applications are the stabilisation of laser beams for both target designation and weapon simulation. The Dynalens optical element which corrects for motion has also been incorporated in the pantograph sight of the M97 20/30 mm flexible armament system produced by the General Electric Company (**1288.303**).
CONTRACTOR
Sigma Dynamics Corporation, 827 E Glenside Avenue, Wyncote, Pennsylvania 19095, USA.

1630.393
HONEYWELL VISUALLY COUPLED SYSTEMS

The Honeywell electro-optical and magnetic helmet sights have evolved with the related objectives of simplifying target acquisition for airborne weapons, and also improving this function by utilising the wide search-angle and flexibility of the human eye. This is accomplished by arranging for the pilot's line-of-sight to be determined in relation to aircraft axes. This data can be used as pointing information for a wide range of aircraft systems (AI radar, cameras, infra-red seekers, etc) and for weapon aiming.

The Honeywell helmet sight system consists of the following major elements: helmet-mounted unit (HMU), sensor surveying units (SSU), sensor electronics unit (SEU), and controls mounted on the instrument panel and control stick.

The system operates as follows: two sensor surveying units, rigidly mounted to the airframe and aimed in the pilot's direction emit fan-like beams of infra-red light rotating at constant velocity. The light beams sweep over a reference photo sensor and two pairs of helmet-mounted photo sensors (one pair on each side of the pilot's helmet). The time intervals between the pulses from the helmet photo sensors and the reference pulses are a measure of the angular position of the pilot's head relative to the XYZ reference axes of the aircraft. The photo sensor outputs are transmitted to the sensor electronics unit where the angular computations are performed and converted into azimuth and elevation information. A collimated reticle image, aligned with the sensor pairs, is reflected off the parabolic visor and into the pilot's right eye. Additional digital computations such as fire control and missile launch envelopes may easily be incorporated in the sensor electronics unit with little or no increase in system complexity. In versions being supplied to the USN, a Honeywell HDC-202 digital computer is included.

The advanced magnetic helmet-mounted sight (AMHMS) utilises a system of magnetic fields surrounding the pilot's helmet to determine the direction of the pilot's line-of-sight relative to the aircraft.

VTAS
A total of 500 electro-optical helmet sight systems were supplied to the USN for fitting in F4J aircraft. The visual target acquisition system (VTAS) is used for off-boresight targeting of the Sidewinder air-to-air missile.

IHADSS
The latest version of the Honeywell electro-optical system is the Integrated Helmet and Display Sighting System (IHADSS) which is now in production for the AH-64A advanced attack helicopter. Both the pilot and co-pilot/gunner are provided with helmet units and controls to allow independent and co-operative use of the system. The IHADSS sight component provides off-boresight line-of-sight information to the fire control computer for slaving weapon and sensor to the pilot's head movements. Real world sized video imagery from the slaved and gimballed infra-red sensor is overlaid with targeting as well as flight information symbology, and projected on a combiner glass immediately in front of the pilot's eye. The IHADSS allows night nap-of-the-earth flight at below treetop altitudes without reference to cockpit instruments, and rapid target engagement.

AMHMS
The Advanced Magnetic Helmet Mounted Sight System (AMHMS) has been fully qualified for USAF applications through a contract with the USAF Aeronautical Systems Division and is undergoing flight evaluation in the AFTI-16 aircraft. The system uses a visor projected reticle and a line-of-sight computation, based on magnetic fields, to allow off-boresight target engagement by merely turning the head to place the reticle on the target.

Advanced Concepts
Honeywell is developing advanced helmet-mounted sight and display concepts which include sophisticated displays, 3-D displays, eye tracking, and improved head tracking methods for both aircraft and ground vehicle applications.
STATUS
The company has delivered 500 VTAS systems for the F4J aircraft.

The IHADSS is currently in production for the Hughes AH-64A advanced attack helicopter and is also to be fitted into the CH-53E, HH-60D and A-129 aircraft.

The AMHMS has been military qualified and is undergoing flight evaluation in the AFTI-16 aircraft. It is also in use in the Helmet Mounted Oculometer System for the tactical combat trainer at the US Wright Patterson AFB.
CONTRACTOR
Honeywell Military Avionics Division, 2600 Ridgway Parkway, Minneapolis, Minnesota 55413, USA.

Honeywell IHADSS helmet sight/display

5753.393
SPASYN VISUAL TARGET ACQUISITION SYSTEM
The SPASYN visual target acquisition system is an advanced, ultra-light helmet-mounted sighting system. SPASYN (space synchro) measures the location and orientation of an object in space by means of radiating directional magnetic fields in three orthogonal co-ordinates. Applied to a helmet-mounted sight, this closed-loop transducing system provides a full 6° of freedom in measuring a pilot's line-of-sight to an accuracy of better than 0·5° within a head motion envelope of 5 ft³ (0·14m³). The system enables a pilot to achieve visual acquisition of a given target and lock on automatic tracking systems while remaining in the head-up position and free to perform evasive manoeuvres or other in-flight tasks.

A small transmitter (radiator) mounted on the cockpit frame emits magnetic field vectors which induce voltages (signals) in a sensor mounted in the helmet. These signals are processed by a computer in the system's electronics unit to define the sensor's translation and orientation, ie the operator's line-of-sight angles. The sensor mounted on the helmet weighs approximately ½ ounce (14 grams) and does not encumber the wearer. The SPASYN-based system can be used in both fixed- and rotary-wing aircraft to command weapons and sensors. It can also be used on land or at sea as a target acquisition system, can be vehicle-mounted or can act as an alternative fire-control system in naval vessels.

CHARACTERISTICS
Weight: Sensor ½ oz (14 g); Radiator 1 oz (28 g); Electronics unit 22 lb (10 kg)
Dimensions: Sensor ½ in (1·26 cm) cube; Radiator 1 in (2·54 cm) cube; Electronics unit 13¹⁄₁₀ × 7⅗ × 4⅘ in (33·3 × 19·3 × 12·2 cm)
Accuracy: Nominal head position 0·1°; max error condition 0·5°

SPASYN visual target acquisition sight

CONTRACTOR
Advanced Technology Systems (a division of The Austin Company), PO Box 950, Fair Lawn, New Jersey 07410, USA.

4136.393
AN/ASG-26A LEAD COMPUTING OPTICAL SIGHT
The General Electric Company has developed an improved lead computing optical sight (LCOS) which enables air-to-air attacks to be made without the need for continuous target tracking. This capability is incorporated in the LCOS system for the McDonnell Douglas F-4E aircraft. The complete equipment consists of a pilot's head-up display, a two-axis lead computing gyroscope, gyro mount, and a lead computing amplifier.

Against airborne targets, the equipment displays gun and missile fire control information by means of a servoed aiming reference. Against ground targets, the pilot adjusts the aiming reference manually to control gunnery, rocket firing and bombing displays. An optical path in the centre of the sight-head presents radar aiming data. The head-up display projects the aiming reference by means of a collimated reticle display reflected from the combining glass into the pilot's field of view. The image is focused at infinity.

The aircraft's own manoeuvres generate rate and acceleration signals in the gyro lead computer, range to target is measured by radar, and angle of attack, air density and airspeed data are obtained from the air data computer. Using these parameters, the pilot's aiming reference is displaced in the proper direction to introduce lead angle and gravity corrections. Analogues of the aircraft's roll angle and range information are also projected onto the combining glass. In ground attack modes, other aircraft systems are used to generate corrections for drift, and offset bombing is also possible.

STATUS
GE is, or has been, engaged on lead computing optical sight programmes for the F-101, F-104, F-105, F-111 and F-5 aircraft. The company is supplying the AN/ASG-29 lead computing optical sight (**4137.393**) for the F-5E.

CONTRACTOR
General Electric Company, Aircraft Equipment Division, Binghampton, New York 13902, USA.

4137.393
AN/ASG-29 LEAD COMPUTING OPTICAL SIGHT
General Electric produces the AN/ASG-29 lead computing optical sight (LCOS) for the F-5E aircraft. Compared with the GE AN/ASG-26A, which has a family relationship with the AN/ASG-29, the latter comprises two main units only; a pilot's optical display and a lead computer with its associated mounting base. The equipment provides all weapon delivery modes applicable to the aircraft type, including air-to-air and ground attack engagements with both guns and missiles. Provision is also made for the inclusion of a CCIP bombing mode. In most other respects the AN/ASG-29 is broadly similar to the AN/ASG-26A described in **4136.393**.

CHARACTERISTICS
Total field of view: ±6° azimuth; +2 to –12° elevation
Instantaneous field of view: 7·5°
Collimating lens: 10·4 inches (264 mm) focal length, 4 inches (102 mm) clear aperture

Weights: 6·9 kg (sight head); 7·9 kg (gyro lead computer); 0·8 kg (mounting base)
MTBF: Over 300 h
STATUS
In production for F-5E aircraft.
CONTRACTOR
General Electric Company, Aircraft Equipment Division, Binghampton, New York 13902, USA.

3815.393
LAAT SIGHT
An improved M65 sight known as the laser augmented airborne TOW (LAAT) sight is produced by Hughes for use on US Army AH-15 Cobra attack helicopters. The M65 contains a thermal imaging system comprised of standard US Army common modules, and Hughes has designed and developed a laser transmitter capable of being fitted in the small space between the gimbal assembly and the housing plate of the existing night turret for the TOW anti-tank missile system. This unit is approximately 13 × 13 × 4 cm in size and has a repetition rate of four pulses per second for five seconds on and five seconds off. A multi-pulse laser rangefinder is necessary due to the helicopter's forward motion during target sighting, requiring several range measurements to update the fire control computer.

A novel cooling technique is embodied to reduce size and weight; the laser's flash tube is embedded in a heat conductive and highly reflective layer to avoid the need for more conventional cooling techniques.

STATUS
In operational service.
CONTRACTOR
Hughes Aircraft Company, PO Box 902, El Segundo, California 90245, USA.

The thousandth telescopic sight for the airborne TOW system, at the Hughes plant prior to delivery to the US Army

1806.363
AN/ASX-1 TARGET IDENTIFICATION SYSTEM, ELECTRO-OPTICAL (TISEO)
The target identification system, electro-optical (TISEO) is a high resolution closed-circuit television sensor used for target acquisition, recognition and tracking. The sensor contains a single telescope with two fields of view mounted on a stabilised platform.

TISEO can be slaved to the aircraft radar or operate

TISEO enables the pilot of high speed aircraft to acquire, track, and identify targets at far greater ranges than previously possible. TISEO is installed in recent production F4E Phantoms of the USAF and other air forces

in an independent manual mode. The system is used for air-to-air and air-to-ground target spotting, lock-on and continuous tracking at ranges far beyond the capability of the pilot's unaided eye.

Four line-replaceable-units (LRUs) comprise the total system. The sensor head/stabilised platform is mounted in the left leading edge wing of the F4E aircraft. Separate video processor and power supply units are stored within the aircraft. A control panel is integrated in the F4E rear cockpit. TISEO operator viewing is shared with the F4E radar monitor.
STATUS

TISEO was developed by Northrop under contract to the USAF and is in full production. It is operational as standard equipment on USAF F4E aircraft and is also deployed on F4E aircraft of five other countries. To date, over 540 systems have been delivered.
CONTRACTOR

Northrop Corporation, Electro-Mechanical Division, 500 East Orangethorpe Avenue, Anaheim, California 92801, USA.

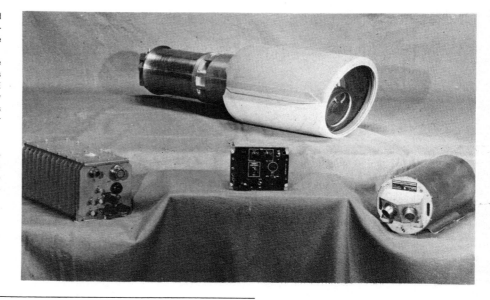

AN/ASX-1 TISEO airborne LRUs

3098.353
AN/ASQ-145 LOW LIGHT-LEVEL TV SYSTEM

A passive TV system, the AN/ASQ-145 is a USAF system utilising dual cameras to provide wide and narrow fields of views simultaneously. In addition to production, General Electric was responsible for system assembly, alignment, and test. The ASQ-145

is a primary sensor of the airborne fire control system used on board the USAF AC-130 aircraft.
STATUS
Operational on board AC-130 aircraft.
CONTRACTOR
General Electric Company, Aircraft Equipment Division, French Road, Utica, New York 13503, USA.

AN/ASQ-145 low light-level television system (without camera heads)

AN/ASQ-145 wide and narrow field of view cameras for the passive LLLTV system

3569.393
VIRTUAL IMAGE DISPLAY

The Virtual Image Display (VID) system is a cockpit TV-display developed to enable fighter aircraft to use the precision-guided Maverick missile (1098.311) or other air-to-surface missiles with TV or imaging infra-red-type guidance.

The display, which uses only a quarter of the space required by a conventional unit, consists of a miniature CRT 2·54 cm in diameter with optics to provide a pilot with a high resolution image more than twice the size of the display unit's lens. This enables the pilot to quickly identify and lock-on to targets at long stand-off ranges.

The optics are designed so that the pilot may look outside the cockpit, then view the display without re-focusing his eyes. A built-in contrast enhancement filter provides a clear display in bright sunlight without using a hood. Remote electronics are used to drive the CRT so that only the optics and the CRT need to be mounted on the cockpit panel. The system

is flexible enough to be modified to fit other applications where a compact remote TV display is needed. The electronics unit does not require special cooling systems and can be located remotely in the aircraft up to a 6·1-metre cable length from the display unit.

The display was designed by Hughes under contract from SRA Communications AB, Stockholm and the Swedish Air Material Department to enable the Swedish Air Force Viggen fighter to carry the Maverick missile without costly and extensive modification to the aircraft's cockpit.
STATUS

Hughes manufactured and delivered 110 sets of the VID system, which is currently operational with the Viggen. The system is also operational with the air forces of Singapore and Switzerland, and is being considered by several other countries.
CONTRACTOR

Hughes Aircraft Company, Radar Systems Group, El Segundo, California 90245, USA.

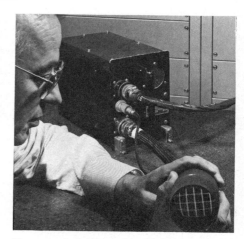

Viggen cockpit TV monitor display for use with Maverick air-to-surface missile system shows test pattern

4215.393
MODEL 200 TISS

The Model 200 thermal imaging sensor set (TISS) provides a passive target imaging capability for naval fire control. The equipment is designed to replace or complement conventional television target sensors on naval fire directors or gimbal sets. Existing video displays, auto-trackers and symbology generators can be used without modification.

The Model 200 incorporates an IR scanner and

two-fields-of-view telescope optics. The IR scanner has 20 mercury cadmium telluride detectors arranged in two arrays which are cooled to between 77 and 90° K. Detector cooling can be provided by either a split-cycle refrigeration machine or a high pressure bottle of nitrogen and a Joule-Thompson cryostat.

Ford Aerospace Model 200 thermal imaging sensor set (TISS)

The equipment is designed to be mounted on a two-axis gimbal without loss of imaging performance. Boresight stability is maintained by an internal raster control circuit. For target recognition and surveillance, a built-in grey scale display is provided, to aid the operator in making control settings for optimum imaging performance.

CHARACTERISTICS
Spectral response: 8 – 11·5 μm
Output: Direct video 625 line 50 Hz
Fields of view: 2·4 × 1·8° (narrow); 9·7 × 7·3° (wide)
Resolution: 0·12 mrad horizontal (narrow field-of-view)
Noise equivalent temperature: 0·3° C

Minimum resolvable temperature: 0·5° C
Power: 115 V AC, 60 Hz
Weight: 28 kg (not including cryo-cooler)
Operating temperature range: –25 to +55° C
CONTRACTOR
Ford Aerospace & Communications Corporation, Ford Road, Newport Beach, California 92660, USA.

3809.363
NORTHROP TCS (TELEVISION SIGHT UNIT)

The Northrop television camera set (TCS), formerly TVSU television sight unit, is an electro-optical tracking system with functional characteristics similar to those of the basic Northrop TISEO (**1806.353**). It features a stabilised closed-circuit television system and precision optics that provide passive target acquisition, identification and tracking at ranges far beyond the capability of the unaided eye. It is packaged in two weapon replaceable assemblies which interface with the avionics and electrical power supply system of the aircraft. TCS interfaces with an on-board video recorder to retain target tracking data. It can operate in an independent manual mode or be slaved to the aircraft radar. The TCS also contains the capability of automatic search and automatic acquisition of airborne targets.
STATUS
TCS was developed by Northrop for installation on the USN F-14 Tomcat fighter to satisfy both air-to-air and air-to-ground missions and an initial production contract was awarded in 1981 to start a multi-year installation programme on new and existing F-14

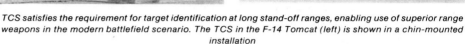

TCS satisfies the requirement for target identification at long stand-off ranges, enabling use of superior range weapons in the modern battlefield scenario. The TCS in the F-14 Tomcat (left) is shown in a chin-mounted installation

aircraft. In mid-1982 the contractor received a continuation award from the US Naval Air Systems Command to produce 31 sets for the F-14. The contract contained an option for 72 additional sets.

First production sets were delivered at the end of 1982.

CONTRACTOR
Northrop Corporation, Electro-Mechanical Division, 500 East Orangethorpe Avenue, Anaheim, California 92801, USA.

4728.393
NORTHROP FOCAL PLANE ARRAY

The Northrop focal plane array system is an experimental infra-red sensor that enables optical target acquisition systems to find distant targets at night and in adverse weather. The system consists of 16 384 sensors, each 0·001 inch in diameter, arranged in a small cluster and linked to a microprocessor. Infra-red radiation detected by the sensors is processed for conversion into a picture display on the host optical unit's television monitor.
STATUS
Flight testing has been carried out successfully in a US Army helicopter. The system is a privately funded venture and no details have yet been disclosed as to its applications, although one possibility is use with the Northrop TCS (**3809.363**).
CONTRACTOR
Northrop Corporation, Electro-Mechanical Division, 500 East Orangethorpe Avenue, Anaheim, California 92801, USA.

4011.383
AQUILA MISSION PAYLOAD SUB-SYSTEM

Under contract to Lockheed Missile and Space Company, Westinghouse has developed the sensor for the US Army's Aquila remotely piloted vehicle (**3168.351**). The system will be used for aerial target acquisition, designation and reconnaissance missions.

The Mission payload sub-system weighs only 43 lb (6·35 kg) and consists of 14 modules that make up the TV camera, target tracker, and laser ranger/designator (**4729.393**), as well as an optical stabilisation system and microprocessor electronics for control and processing. Modular construction of the MPS facilitates adaptation to day/night (FLIR) operation and helps minimise life cycle cost. The Aquila mission payload sub-system embodies previous work carried out by the company in developing the Blue Spot target designator equipment (**3050.383**) described in previous editions of *Jane's Weapon Systems*.
CONTRACTOR
Westinghouse Electric Corporation, Defense and Electronic Systems Center, Box 746, Baltimore, Maryland 21203, USA.

4113.393
ROCKWELL MAST-MOUNTED SIGHT

Rockwell International's Missile Systems Division, working in co-operation with ARRADCOM (US Army Armament Research and Development Command), Dover, New Jersey, has developed and tested a mast-mounted sight and target designator for use on ground attack helicopters. The device is mounted at the rotor hub, above the blades, to permit the helicopter crew maximum observation height while enabling the aircraft to remain behind cover as far as possible.

The mast-mounted sight sensor head contains stabilised optics for target detection and recognition at ranges of 3 to 4 km and laser target designation for weapons such as the Hellfire and Copperhead guided weapons. The equipment has been installed and flown on UH-1M and OH-58C helicopters.

STATUS
In performance tests on a UH-1M the equipment has demonstrated its ability to detect targets at a range of 4 km while remaining undetected by 7 × 10 power optical devices on the ground.
CONTRACTOR
Rockwell International, Missile Systems Division, 4300 East Fifth Avenue, Columbus, Ohio 43216, USA.

5758.393
ILS MAST-MOUNTED LASER RANGEFINDER

International Laser Systems (ILS) has developed a laser rangefinder/target designator for the Northrop mast-mounted sight. Pod-mounted above the rotor, the equipment allows the US Army's Scout helicopter to acquire and illuminate targets at greater stand-off ranges while concealed from the battle area. Hellfire, Copperhead and other laser guided munitions can be guided to their targets by the rangefinder. Northrop is responsible for the integration of all the sensors in the sight on behalf of the prime contractor, McDonnell-Douglas.

The packaging design enables the rangefinder to incorporate all the electronics, power supply, cooling system, range receiver and laser transmitter into one compact lightweight line replaceable unit. The microprocessor system includes a serial, asynchronous digital interface for communication with the sight computer. Internally all sub-assemblies interface via a common bus under control of the main processor which maintains all systems timing through software control. This improves system flexibility for expansion and/or alternative functions.
CONTRACTOR
International Laser Systems Inc, 3404 North Orange Blossom Trail, Orlando, Florida 32804, USA.

4729.393
AQUILA LASER TRANSMITTER ASSEMBLY

This ILS laser transmitter assembly is a subsystem of the US Army Aquila remotely piloted vehicle (**3168.351**). It operates in conjunction with a television camera to provide intelligence gathering, navigation update, range-to-target information and target illumination. It consists of a heat exchanger, cooling system, power supply, pulse forming network, optics and associated electronics in a package weighing approximately 3 kg. Although designed for the Aquila vehicle, the assembly is suitable for installation in other RPVs. See also entry **4011.383**.

STATUS
In production.
CONTRACTOR
International Laser Systems Inc, 3404 North Orange Blossom Trail, Orlando, Florida 32804, USA.

3053.383
ATAFCS EQUIPMENT
The airborne target acquisition and fire control system (ATAFCS) is an advanced electro-optical system containing a television camera for daylight operations, a forward looking infra-red (FLIR) equipment for day/night operations, a laser spot detector for target acquisition, a laser transmitter/receiver for target designation and ranging, and an autotracker with both day and night mission capability. It is designed for installation on both attack and scout helicopters, and is intended to increase the combat effectiveness of US Army helicopters.

Development was undertaken by Ford Aerospace & Communications Corporation, and the project was originally known as ALLD (airborne laser locator designator). In August 1974 the US Army Material Command Precision Designator Project Office, Redstone Arsenal issued a follow-on contract valued at about $3·5 million for the building of another four sets of ATAFCS equipment. This made a total of six sets ordered, two having been called for in the initial award.
STATUS
The first equipment was delivered during 1974 and installed on a US Army Bell Cobra helicopter for flight test and evaluation by the US Army Missile Command. Further deliveries were made in 1974 and in 1975.

The system has been tested successfully in both a pod-mounted version and in a configuration integral with the helicopter nose (as shown).

A helicopter mounted ATAFCS has been used successfully in a night test at the White Sands Missile Range, to acquire and mark a moving tank target for a US Army cannon launched guided projectile (CLGP) fired from a 155 mm howitzer at a range of 5 miles (8 km).
CONTRACTOR
Ford Aerospace & Communications Corporation, Ford Road, Newport Beach, California 92660, USA.

US Army Cobra AH-1G ground attack helicopter showing nose mounting of ATAFCS

3981.393
ALT AIRBORNE LASER TRACKER
The Rockwell airborne laser tracker (ALT) is an automatic laser seeker equipment used to automatically search and track laser marked targets. The ALT is in production for use on the AH-1S Cobra helicopter. In addition ALT components are being produced for the AAH-64A helicopter's target acquisition designation system/pilot night vision system (TADS/PNVS) competition (**3609.393**) and units have also been delivered for other helicopter programmes.

The equipment consists of three units: an electronics unit, a control panel, and a receiver unit. The gimballed optics in the last of the three have a five-inch (127 mm) aperture, and the equipment field of regard is 180° in azimuth and +30° to –60° in elevation.
CHARACTERISTICS
Detector: 4 quadrant silicon
Dynamic range: 120 dB (10⁶)
Instantaneous field of view: 20° azimuth × 10° elevation
Logic: Last pulse

Optics: 5 inches (127 mm) f 0·3
Primary power: 28 V DC and 400 Hz AC
STATUS
In production.
CONTRACTOR
Rockwell International Corporation, Missile Systems Division, 1800 Satellite Boulevard, Duluth, Georgia 30136, USA.

3609.363
TADS/PNVS
The target acquisition designation sight and the pilot night vision sensor (TADS/PNVS) are two independently functioning systems designed and under development for use with US Army advanced attack helicopters (AAH) to enable these aircraft to operate at extended stand-off ranges, day or night, under adverse weather conditions. TADS provides the gunner with a search, detection, and recognition capability with direct view optics, television, or forward looking infra-red (FLIR) sighting systems; these may be used singly, or in combination, depending on tactical, weather, or visibility conditions. Once acquired, targets can be tracked manually or automatically for autonomous attack with 30 mm guns, rockets, or Hellfire missiles. The laser may also be used to designate targets for remote attack by other helicopters or by artillery units firing laser-guided Copperhead munitions. The TADS equipment consists of a rotating turret that mounts on the nose of the helicopter and houses the sensor sub-systems, an optical relay tube (ORT) at the co-pilot/gunner's position, four electronic units in the avionics bay, and cockpit-mounted controls and displays.

PNVS is used by the pilot for night navigation, and consists of an FLIR sensor system packaged in a rotating turret mounted above the TADS; an electronic unit located in the avionics bay; and the pilot's display and controls. The PNVS is slaved to the pilot's helmet display line-of-sight and provides imagery that allows the helicopter to be flown in a 'nap-of-the-earth' fashion at altitudes likely to avoid, or at least minimise, enemy detection.

The laser rangefinder/target designator, provided by International Laser Systems, is integrated with the system and provides navigation and attack capability in low visibility and night conditions.
CHARACTERISTICS
TADS
System coverage: ±120° azimuth; +30 to –60° elevation

TADS/PNVS system on AH-64A Apache advanced attack helicopter

Fields of view (day): TV 0·9° narrow, 4° wide; Direct view 4° narrow (× 16), 18° wide (× 3·5)
Fields of view (night): 3·1° narrow; 10·1° medium; 50° wide
PNVS
System coverage: ±90° azimuth; +20 to –45° elevation
Fields of view: 30× 40°

STATUS
The system is in production under contracts totalling $405 million by the end of 1983.
CONTRACTOR
Martin Marietta Orlando Aerospace, PO Box 5837, Orlando, Florida 32855, USA

3807.353
SEEHAWK SRR FLIR
The lightweight SEEHAWK FLIR (forward looking infra-red) was developed by Northrop under contract to the US Coast Guard. The system provides capability for search and rescue, surveillance, marine patrol, night navigation and a variety of other tasks.

The passive sensor, gimballed with servos, provides complete hemispheric coverage with automatic search, acquisition and target tracking system. Three fields of view (FOV) satisfy a wide range of operational requirements from low level navigation in wide FOV to inspection and identification in the narrow FOV. The servo system provides line-of-sight stabilisation to eliminate vibration and to ensure image quality and resolution. Sensor imagery is displayed on a video monitor in the aircraft with appropriate symbology to aid the operator. A manual control system allows the operator to direct the sensor line-of-sight to any position in the surveillance field. The system can also be slaved to track the radar line-of-sight or other external inputs. Video and audio information may be recorded for either test or record purposes. The SEEHAWK FLIR can be installed on helicopters, fixed wing aircraft or ships.
CHARACTERISTICS
System coverage: Azimuth ±190°; elevation +30 to −105°
Field of view: Wide 30° × 40°; medium 15° × 20°, narrow 5° × 6·7°
STATUS
Over 2000 hours testing on the US Coast Guard HH-52 helicopter and the Beech B-200T special mission aircraft. Production was due to commence in 1984.
CONTRACTOR
Northrop Corporation, Electro-Mechanical Division, 500 East Orangethorpe Avenue, Anaheim, California 92801, USA.

US Coast Guard HH-52 helicopter equipped with test installation of the Northrop SEEHAWK FLIR for operational trials

---

3808.363
AN/AVQ-27 AIRBORNE LASER TARGET DESIGNATOR SET (LTDS)
The AN/AVQ-27 LTDS is rail mounted in the rear cockpit of the Northrop F-5F. The system features small size, light weight, low power, simple operation, and ease of installation and removal. It is packaged and installed so that it does not interfere with other cockpit operations. The LTDS may be installed in most two-seat fighter or fighter-bomber aircraft with only minor wiring modification and without affecting the aircraft's suitability for other missions. The LTDS concept allows the aircraft to be equipped with target designation capability as required by the mission and have it removed when not in use.

The system's principal elements are a stabilised operator sight unit with a retractable periscopic telescope, a laser transmitter, and a 16 mm mission recording camera, all of which are boresighted through common optics in a single self-contained package. The stabilised sighting assembly includes a rate-stabilised mirror that is controlled by a two-axis hand control and provides two tracking modes (rate and rate-aided), a retractable periscopic telescope, and associated optics. The hand control grip contains all the switches necessary to allow for one-hand operation. The laser transmitter consists of a single package that houses a hermetically sealed laser and its associated optics and electronics. The 16 mm mission camera integrated into the LTDS is a version of the same KB-25A/KB-26A standard gun camera now used in the Northrop F-5E/F and other aircraft.
STATUS
LTDS was developed by Northrop to expand the capabilities of F-5B and F-5F aircraft for foreign military sales. Various foreign operators of F-5 aircraft are using, or have awarded contracts for, LTDS.
CONTRACTOR
Northrop Corporation, Electro-Mechanical Division, 500 East Orangethorpe Avenue, Anaheim, California 92801, USA.

LTDS mounted in rear cockpit of F-5F provides a single-package laser designator for laser guided weapons

---

3065.393
PAVE TACK AN/AVQ-26
The Pave Tack system is a 24-hour, adverse weather, electro-optical acquisition, laser designator and weapon delivery system in production for the USAF.

Previous systems such as Pave Knife were used very successfully in South-east Asia by both the USAF and USN to provide target acquisition and laser target designation for the Mk 82, Mk 83 and Mk 84 laser guided bombs from high performance aircraft. The Pave Knife system was used extensively in high threat areas because it allowed the aircraft to manoeuvre and escape throughout designation and weapon delivery. It was limited, however, to clear weather daytime or twilight operations. Other sensor systems used on the B-57G and AC-130 gunships had the capability to deliver ordnance at night but the aircraft were slow and had limited manoeuvrability making them vulnerable to enemy defences and limiting their use to less heavily defended areas.

The Pave Tack system provides 24-hour capability in clear and adverse weather from all altitudes, including extremely low altitude penetration and interdiction. It provides precise target acquisition and laser target designation for a variety of existing and projected laser, electro-optical and IR weapons, against fixed and moving targets. The system additionally provides target location data to the aircraft weapon delivery digital computer to permit more accurate delivery of free-fall conventional ordnance.

The programme employs several key contractors producing major elements of the system under contract to the USAF. Ford Aerospace & Communications Corporation furnishes the pod structure, electronics control, environmental control system and stabilisation systems and is the Pave Tack Pod systems integrator.

The laser and range receiver sub-system is designed and produced by International Laser Systems at Orlando, Florida. It provides target designation capability for the delivery of laser-guided weapons and range to target information for navigation and conventional munition delivery. It is tri-service coded AN/AVQ-25 and is designed for use with existing and projected laser guided weapons.

The forward-looking infra-red (FLIR) sensor is produced by Texas Instruments at Dallas, Texas.

General Electric is producing the virtual image display which is used in the rear cockpit to magnify the image presented on the display. Initially engineered for USAF F-111F aircraft, it is now being applied to expand the weapons delivery capabilities of the RF-4C and F-4E night attack systems.

Basis of the VID design is a multi-element bi-ocular lens system which provides the cockpit observer with a non-distorted, magnified, virtual image of a cluster of small, high resolution CRTs. As developed for the F-111, the VID is directly interchangeable with the AN/APQ-144 indicator/recorder installed in the cockpit, and this was achieved by substituting for the electro-mechanical device that produces a radar scan on a six-inch CRT, a new electronic co-ordinate transformation circuitry. This makes space available for the small CRTs also. Another modification was the addition of an alpha-numeric character generator which enables avionics data to be written on the main CRT electronically, thus eliminating the need for a number of panel dials and indicators. In addition to its ability to display radar information, the VID can present video from TV, FLIR, and weapons.

After successfully completing the F-111 configuration, GE was instructed to produce equipment for the trials of the system in F-4 Pave Tack aircraft. This programme involves a similar conversion for the AN/APQ-120 radar pilot indicator.

The Pave Tack pod is divided into two basic sections, a base section assembly and a head section assembly. The latter contains an optical bench on which are mounted the FLIR, laser, range receiver and the stabilised sight assembly. The optical bench is mounted on the turret structure, which rotates in pitch and is driven by turret servo drive motors. The turret is mounted to the head structure, which rotates in roll with respect to the base section. Roll motion of the head and pitch motion of the turret provide complete unvignetted lower hemisphere coverage and a highly stabilised line-of-sight which is fully controllable over the entire lower hemisphere of the aircraft.

The FLIR is boresighted to (and stabilised with) the laser, and the entire assembly is controlled by the Pave Tack operator aided by a pod-mounted digital aircraft interface unit. The stabilised image and rate-aided tracking mechanisation provide accurate target tracking, laser designation, and weapon delivery throughout a wide spectrum of evasive aircraft manoeuvres. The FLIR has a wide field-of-view

Pave Tack target designation pods are being procured for RAAF F-111 aircraft under a US Foreign Military Sales agreement with the USAF

display for target acquisition. A narrow field-of-view provides high magnification to enhance target identification and allow precise target tracking.

The electronic assemblies to operate the head section are located in the base section. In addition to the power supply and control electronics, the base section contains a digital aircraft interface unit and a CRT display interface unit. The digital aircraft interface unit is integrated with the ARN-101 digital avionics on board the F-4E and RF-4C aircraft as well as with the digital avionics on board the F-111 aircraft. It provides precise target location data to the aircraft weapon delivery digital computer. A special mode designed into the computer permits Pave Tack to be used for terrain avoidance by pointing the line-of-sight along the velocity vector of the aircraft. The computer additionally provides complete built-in testing for all components on the pod.

A video tape recorder records the video displayed in the cockpit for use in bomb damage assessment and location of targets for future missions.

Northrop Corporation is developing a video-augmented tracking system (VATS), under a contract from Ford Aerospace, for retrofit to the Pave Track system. VATS is a next generation, all-digital, dual-mode tracking system using high density packaging

techniques, a micro-processor computer, self-contained power supply and a digital interface to day/night optical sensor systems. VATS allows automatic tracking of ground targets to allow for a reduction in the weapons operator workload. The system has completed DT & E and IOT & E testing for retrofit into Pave Track.

STATUS

149 pods have now been delivered to the USAF, the last of these being accepted into service in July 1982. The number of aircraft converted to accept Pave Track pods is believed to be 60 RF-4Cs, 180 F-4Es and 100 F-111s. Total cost of the 149 systems, plus modifications to the various aircraft is nearly $240 million. In addition, Ford Aerospace has produced pods worth $26·8 million for the RAAF, the last of these being delivered in September 1983, and has a $50 million contract to supply pods, spares & support equipment to South Korea.

CONTRACTORS

Ford Aerospace & Communications Corporation, Ford Road, Newport Beach, California 92663, USA.

Texas Instruments, 13500 North Central Parkway, Dallas, Texas 75222, USA.

International Laser Systems Inc, 3040 North Orange Blossom Trail, Orlando, Florida 32804, USA.

3154.393

PAVE SPIKE LASER TARGET DESIGNATOR

Pave Spike is a day tracking/laser target designator system that provides the F-4D and F-4E aircraft with a self-contained laser-guided ordnance delivery capability. It is being produced by Westinghouse under production contracts monitored by the Aeronautical Systems Division of the USAF. Designated AN/ASQ153(V), the Pave Spike system is able to acquire, track, and designate tactical surface targets from a manoeuvring aircraft at stand-off ranges usual with laser-guided munitions.

The Pave Spike pod contains an optical sub-system, stabilisation and beam pointing sub-system, TV tracking sensor, laser designator/ranger sub-system, environmental control system, and associated electronics. The aircraft-mounted parts of the system comprise line-of-sight indicator, control panel, and range indicator, and a modified radar control handle and weapons release computer.

Dimensions of the pod are: length 366 cm, diameter 25·4 cm, and weight 193 kg. As shown in the adjacent diagram, it is divided into three major sections:

(1) Forward nose/roll section
(2) Umbilical section
(3) Aft electronics section

The forward nose/roll section rotates about the pod's axis, and the rotating assembly contains the electro-optical sensors and the stabilised gimbal. It is sealed and pressurised with nitrogen and temperature controlled for optimum sensor performance. The umbilical section provides physical and electrical interconnections between the rotating

nose section, the aircraft, and the aft electronics section. The last of these contains a thermal cold plate that runs the length of the section. Six major electronic LRUs are mounted on it:

(1) Low-voltage power supply and pod control
(2) Servo electronics

(3) Laser control electronics
(4) Laser power supply
(5) Interface electronics

The AN/ASQ-153(V) designates the Pave Spike system as configured for the F-4D and F-4E aircraft, the pod being mounted in the left front Sparrow

Pave Spike laser target designator pod AN/ASQ-153(V) mounted in one of the Phantom's missile wells

missile well by means of a standard 30 inch (76·2 cm) centre ECM pod adaptor. It has also been integrated with other NATO aircraft. The Pave Spike pod designation is AN/AVQ-23.

STATUS

Delivery of the last Pave Spike pod for the USAF was in August 1977, by which time 327 aircraft had been modified to utilise the pod. Deliveries of pods amounted to 156. In February 1977 it was reported that an undisclosed number of pods had been ordered for use by the Turkish Air Force. This system continues in production for FMS (Foreign Military Sales) requirements.

In August 1978, Ferranti received UK MoD contracts for the provision of technical support for a number of avionic systems in RAF Buccaneer aircraft. Among the equipments are Pave Spike airborne laser designation systems and the associated Pave Way seeker systems mounted on the weapons employed with Pave Spike.

In September 1979 it was disclosed that Westinghouse had supplied 238 ASQ-153 Pave Spike pods, 156 for the USAF and 82 for foreign countries. At that time a developed version, Pave Spike B, was proposed for the USAF F-16 programme, in competition with the ATLIS II pod (**3820.393**), but has not gone into production. Pave Spike B is almost half the length of the orignal Pave Spike (A) model and correspondingly lighter. A Pave Spike C model has also been proposed with 24-hour capability.

CONTRACTOR

Westinghouse Defense and Electronics Center, PO Box 746, Baltimore, Maryland 21203, USA.

4305.393
LANTIRN

LANTIRN (Low Altitude Navigation, Targeting Infrared Night) is a pod-mounted system that will permit attack aircraft to acquire, track, and destroy ground targets with both guided and unguided weapons. It is planned for the single-seat F-16 and A-10 aircraft, but is applicable to other one- or two-seat aircraft in the air-to-ground attack role. With the option to use either or both pods, depending on the particular mission requirement, the system provides operational flexibility and minimises system support impact.

The navigation pod contains a wide field-of-view forward-looking infra-red (FLIR) and a terrain-following radar. The FLIR is displayed to the pilot on a new wide field-of-view head-up display, providing him a night window for low-level flight. The terrain-following radar enables the pilot to operate at very low altitudes with en route weather penetration and blind let-down capability.

The targeting pod contains a stabilised wide and narrow field-of-view targeting FLIR and a laser designator ranger in the nose section, automatic target recogniser and Maverick hand-off unit in the electronics centre section, and an environmental control unit in the tail section. The targeting pod interfaces with the aircraft controls and displays and with the aircraft fire control system to permit low-level, day/night, automatic and manual target acquisition and precision weapon delivery.

The disposition of individual items of equipment can be seen from the illustrations.

In operational use the LANTIRN target acquisition FLIR's two fields-of-view are optimised for target acquisition and recognition. The line-of-sight is cued by the aircraft inertial navigation system or is automatically scanned. The sensor will be properly oriented for the planned attack and selected weapon delivery profile. Previous low altitude target acquisition problems are alleviated by this combination of optimum sensor fields-of-view with automatic cueing or target search. This ensures maximum stand-off and first-pass attack for guided and unguided weapon delivery. The system is particularly effective when used for the delivery of such weapons as the infra-red Maverick missile or laser-guided bombs.

The laser designator/ranger, designed by Intemation Laser Systems, consists of four LRVs: a laser transmitter/receiver, an electronics unit, a power supply and a synchroniser/range computer.

STATUS

The LANTIRN system is in full-scale development by Martin Marietta Orlando Aerospace under a $94 million contract awarded by the USAF in September 1980. The multi-year contract covers the design, development, and test of six prototype units and initial production of the system. Production and deployment is scheduled for the mid-1980s. Initial flight testing began in September 1982 using an F-16B outfitted with a wide field-of-view head-up-display manufactured by Marconi Avionics (UK) (**4314.393**). Flight testing of operational pods began in late 1983 and is scheduled to continue until late 1984.

In July 1982 the USAF and Martin Marietta reworked the contract to reduce the high-risk aspects of the programme; after the US Senate Armed Services Committee directed the USAF not to make a production decision on LANTIRN until there had been a competitive demonstration with the USN F/A-18 FLIR system (**4110.393**). No further information is available on this directive.

CONTRACTORS

Martin Marietta is teamed with Hughes Aircraft, which is responsible for the target recogniser and boresight correlator for Maverick hand-off. Other suppliers include Texas Instruments, (terrain-following radar), Delco Division of General Motors (computers), Sundstrand Aerospace (environmental control systems), and International Laser Systems (laser designator).

The LANTIRN programme is directed by the USAF Aeronautical Systems Division, Deputy for Reconnaissance/Electronic Warfare Systems, Wright Patterson AFB, Ohio, USA.

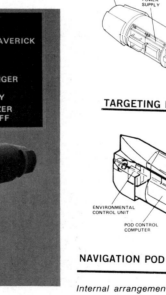

Internal arrangement of components in LANTIRN pods

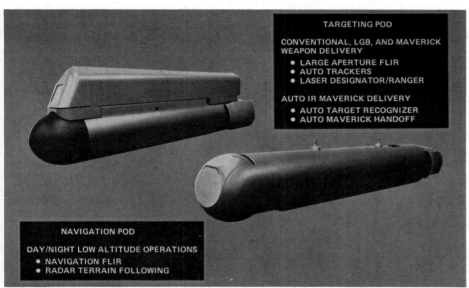

Two pods comprise the LANTIRN system

3203.383
AN/ASB-19 ARBS ANGLE-RATE BOMBING SET

The AN/ASB-19, ARBS, is basically a simple angle-rate system. The tracker, after locking on a target, provides the aircraft-to-target line-of-sight angle and angle rate to the weapon delivery computer (WDC). This information, combined with the true airspeed and altitude (from the air data computer), is processed by the WDC, yielding the weapon delivery solution. Target position, weapon release, and azimuth steering information are generated for display to the pilot via a head-up display (HUD). Unlike most current operational bombing systems neither measurement of range to the target nor inertial quality platform inputs are required for ARBS.

Once the tracker is locked on to the target, in either the laser or TV mode of operation, the pilot is free to manoeuvre within the gimbal limits of 70° nose down, 35° either side of the nose, 10° nose up, and 450° of roll. This freedom allows him to fly an erratic, unpredictable flight path to confuse enemy AAA/SAM tracking, while simultaneously providing target tracking information to the computer. Demonstrated accuracy of ARBS is better than radar or laser trackers. A stand-off, accurate delivery and identification of targets is made possible by the ×6 magnification of the TV tracker.

ARBS is in production for the US Marine Corps A-4M Skyhawk and AV-8B Harrier, the UK GR.Mk 5 Harrier and the Spanish Harrier II.

In the A-4M, ARBS consists of a dual-mode laser/TV tracker (DMT) designed by Hughes, a System/4 Pi Model Sp-1 general purpose digital computer built by IBM Federal Systems Division under US Navy contract, and a control sub-system. Its weight is about 58 kg. The system works in conjunction with the existing cockpit controls and aircraft sensors. An AVQ-24 HUD by Marconi Avionics is used to display steering information to the pilot.

With the AV-8B/GR.Mk 5, Hughes supplies the DMT to McDonnell-Douglas Aircraft Corporation in St Louis where it is integrated into the Harrier's on-board mission computer. ARBS controls, data imagery, video imagery and steering information have been integrated into the HUD, the multi-purpose display (video) and the up-front control set.

The DMT is the main element of the system. A modification of the Hughes STALOC II TV tracker with TV camera shares a common optical element with a laser spot tracker detector on a three-gimbal stabilised platform. Tracking filter electronics, an output signal converter, power supplies, and control logic complete the DMT. A dichroic filter behind the optics separates the laser energy from the visible light for sensing by a four-quadrant laser detector.

The visible light is directed to form an image on the TV vidicon. TV tracking of small, low-contrast, poorly defined moving targets through changes in aspect ratio and in the presence of competing clutter, and even when partially lost to view behind rocks and other obstructions, was demonstrated according to Hughes.

Operating in the laser mode, the sensor automatically acquires the target and, via the WDC, presents steering signals for the pilot on the HUD. After head-up TV acquisition, the pilot is shown a magnified image of the target on the cockpit TV monitor. He may use a hand control to slew the tracker gate to a new track point or to a nearby alternative target. Weapon release in both laser and optical tracking modes is either automatic or manual. A weapon data insert panel provides entry into the weapon delivery computer of weapon characteristics and rack type for ordnance being carried on a particular mission. The necessary ballistic parameters for all weapons are stored in the WDC memory. This unit also provides the computational and control capability for performing the ARBS operational readiness test and fault isolation testing of itself and the dual mode tracker. The system provides automatic tracking of ground targets plus first-pass automatic day/night acquisition of laser-designated targets, providing a useful night-bombing capability.

In addition to the fuselage installation, in the A-4 and the AV-8B/GR.Mk 5, a podded configuration is under consideration to give aircraft with radars or other equipment in the nose an accurate, precise air-to-ground capability. Aircraft such as the F-5E and the F-4 are candidates for the pod.

ARBS can be employed with the complete inventory of guided and unguided weapons. Only software update is required to adapt it to new weapons such as the laser and infra-red guided Maverick air-to-surface missiles.

STATUS

The US Marine Corps is accepting deliveries of ARBS for retrofit into the A-4M. Deliveries from the

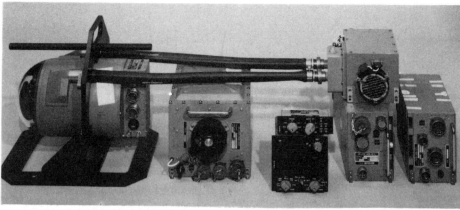

Components of the ARBS showing (from left), receiver/processor, signal data converter, bombing set control (top), control indicator, heat exchanger (top), computer and computer interface

US Marine Corps AV-8B Harrier equipped with ARBS

production line are also being made for the AV-8B/GR.Mk 5 Harrier for the US, UK and Spain. Production is expected to last until the early 1990s with a potential of over 500 units, even without additional orders.

CONTRACTOR

Hughes Aircraft Company, Missile Systems Group, Canoga Park, California 91304, USA.

3982.393
FIREFLY III

Firefly III is the designation of a new integrated fire and flight control (IFFC) system being developed by the Aircraft Equipment Division of General Electric Company. This system will provide a combined air-to-air and air-to-surface weapon delivery capability which will interface with the flight control system and give aircraft control system inputs. The integrated control system will give the USAF a system that is capable of evasive aircraft manoeuvre weapon delivery to ensure significantly increased fighter aircraft survivability coupled with improved weapon delivery accuracy.

Firefly III will employ an electro-optical sensor/tracker system and on-board aircraft sensors to determine target state, using a Kalman filter in the data processing loop. The filter is coupled with gunnery and bombing algorithms to provide commands to the aircraft flight control system to form the overall integrated flight/fire control system.

Under the terms of its contract, GE will be responsible for the design, development, and manufacture of the hardware and related software for the added capability to the fire control system. Flight tests will be carried out in an F-15B aircraft. GE developed and produces the lead computing gyro unit for the F-15, as well as flight controls for this

aircraft and others such as the F-105, F-11, F-4, A-10 and F-18.

STATUS

General Electric was awarded a $3·6 million USAF contract for the design, development and demonstration of the Firefly III integrated fire and flight control system in 1979. No further information has been made available.

CONTRACTOR

General Electric Company, Aircraft Equipment Division, French Road, Utica, New York 13503, USA.

4114.393
OR-89/AA FLIR

The OR-89/AA forward-looking infra-red (FLIR) equipment is a direct derivative of the AN/AAD-4 and AN/AAD-7 FLIR sensors extensively used for the USAF 'gunship' programmes in South-east Asia. The OR-89/AA version is adapted primarily to meet the needs of the S-3A Viking maritime aircraft.

The equipment comprises three main items:
(1) the infra-red sensor package which is designed for gimbal mounting in the aircraft fuselage, with the optical sensor elements projecting below the fuselage underside, and with self-contained stabilisation and servo units
(2) power supply/video converter
(3) infra-red control converter.

Control of the system is via a general purpose digital computer (GPDC) to the FLIR system control converter. The former transmits digital words to the

OR-89/AA FLIR equipment and artist's impression of how the system is employed on S-3A Viking maritime aircraft

FLIR converter which translates the data into set control commands or analogue servo commands. Position data is supplied by the FLIR system control converter, which converts the data into digital format for transmission to the GPDC for status purposes.

The IR sensors employ HgCdTe detectors and there is automatic optical temperature compensation. The output from the system is in television format.

CHARACTERISTICS
Azimuth coverage: ±200°
Elevation coverage: 0 to –84°
Video output: Composite TV, 875-line RS-343
Weight: 120 kg
STATUS
USN fleet introduction of the OR-89/AA began in February 1973 with deployment continuing up to

January 1978. Approximately 400 S-3A systems, or derivatives, had been delivered by 1980. At least 12 other types of aircraft have been fitted with OR-89/AA derivative equipments.
CONTRACTOR
Texas Instruments Incorporated, PO Box 226015, Dallas, Texas 75266, USA.

4120.393
AN/AAR-42 FLIR

The AN/AAR-42 is a pod-mounted forward-looking infra-red (FLIR) equipment, initially designed for use on the A-7E but later modified and used on the A-10

Components of the AN/AAR-42 FLIR produced for pod-mounting on A-7E aircraft

aircraft class. It provides two fields of view displayed on the pilot's head-up display (HUD): the wide FOV gives a 1:1 image of the scene permitting pilot orientation, navigation updating, and target acquisition while the ×4 narrow FOV is employed for

target identification and weapon delivery. This two-axis stabilised FLIR sensor enables the A-7 pilot to carry out close air support, interdiction, and surveillance/recce missions by day or night and in adverse weather conditions.

Other features of the equipment are automatic thermal focus compensation and a slewable line of sight.
CHARACTERISTICS
Azimuth coverage: ±20°
Elevation coverage: +5 to –35°
Video output: Composite TV, 875-line RS-343
Weight: 114 kg
STATUS
Production of the AN/AAR-42 for the A-7E began in 1977, with entry into USN service later that year. In an evaluation programme for the USAF in 1979, the equipment was adapted for use on the two seat N/AW A-10 aircraft. This system was pod-mounted and boresighted with the GAU-8 gun and interfaced via a 1553A data bus. Many evaluation programmes have been carried out at Edwards AFB and Elgin AFB during 1983 with satisfactory results.
CONTRACTOR
Texas Instruments Incorporated, PO Box 226015, Dallas, Texas 75266, USA.

4115.393
OR-5008/AA FLIR

The OR-5008/AA is a special derivative of the OR-89/AA forward-looking infra-red (FLIR) equipment (**4114.393**) adapted for use on the Lockheed CP-140 maritime aircraft used by the Canadian Forces. It is mounted in a similar position to the AN/AAS-36 FLIR (**4116.393**) fitted to American P-3 aircraft. The Canadian version is used for search and rescue, maritime surveillance, mapping, ice reconnaissance and various defence tasks.

Additional requirements beyond the facilities of the OR-89/AA included the use of a USN P-3 interface casting; provision for upward viewing (to +5°);

additional composite video outputs; facilities for retraction and extension of the sensor head; and reduced system maintenance requirements. The equipment comprises three main items, as does the OR-89/AA, and in this and most other respects the version for the CP-140 is essentially the same as the S-3A Viking equipment.
STATUS
The CP-140 FLIR contract was awarded in July 1977 with the first delivery in December 1977.
CONTRACTOR
Texas Instruments Incorporated, PO Box 226015, Dallas, Texas 75266, USA.

OR-5008/AA FLIR equipment as fitted in Canadian CP-140 aircraft

---

4118.393
AN/AAQ-9 FLIR

The AN/AAQ-9 FLIR detecting set was developed for use in the USAF AN/AVQ-26 Pave Tack target designator pod (**3065.393**). The AN/AAQ-9 uses a common module infra-red sensor to provide the aircraft weapon system officer with facilities for location, acquisition, and tracking of enemy targets in day, night, or adverse weather conditions, and to direct weapons against these targets.

The equipment has a two-field-of-view optical system, and there is automatic compensation for aircraft roll movement (derotation). The IR sub-system incorporates automatic thermal and range optical compensation, and has high resolution with very high sensitivity.
CHARACTERISTICS
Magnification: ×2 or ×1
Derotation limits: ±190° to 100°/s
Video output: Composite TV, 525-line RS-170 or 875-line RS-343
Cooling: Forced air
Weight: 48·6 kg (receiver); 12·7 kg (control/electronics)
STATUS
Entered production in 1977. Operationally deployed by USAF on F-4E, RF-4C and F-111 aircraft. The Pave Tack pod with the AN/AAQ-9 has been purchased for use on Australian F-111 aircraft and other countries have disclosed possible applications.

USAF F-111 aircraft with Pave Tack target designator pod on fuselage centre-line. Pod contains AN/AAQ-9 FLIR (inset)

CONTRACTOR
Texas Instruments Incorporated, PO Box 226015, Dallas, Texas 75266, USA.

4117.393
AN/AAQ-10 FLIR

The AN/AAQ-10 is another derivative of the OR-89/AA FLIR (**4114.393**) which has been developed specially for use on helicopters performing search and rescue missions. A single-window turret design was employed to obtain the increased field of regard needed to utilise the helicopter's capability. The vibration characteristics of the vehicle required particular design emphasis on the stabilisation servo elements. The video output is in TV format to EIA standard RS-343A 875-line specification.

The AN/AAQ-10 FLIR configured for use on the HH-53 helicopter consists of an infra-red receiver, power supply, electronic control amplifier, control indicator, and mounting base. All controls are contained in the control indicator, providing the operator with facilities for one-handed control of sensor operation and servo slew commands.

STATUS

Development of the prototype was started in 1974 and it was delivered to the USAF in 1975. In 1978 a production contract for ten systems was awarded, the first production equipment being delivered in December 1978. Production is continuing for various international applications.

CONTRACTOR

Texas Instruments Incorporated, PO Box 226015, Dallas, Texas 75266, USA.

AN/AAQ-10 FLIR as used in HH-53 helicopter

3202.383
AN/AAS-33 TRAM TARGET RECOGNITION AND ATTACK MULTI-SENSOR

The A-6E aircraft TRAM programme incorporates an electro-optical sensor package, AN/AAS-33 TRAM detecting and ranging set, into the basic A-6E. The sensors are contained within a 51 cm diameter stabilised turret, which extends below the aircraft's nose radome. Inside the turret are a forward-looking infra-red receiver (FLIR), a laser ranger/designator, and a separate laser receiver for detecting energy from ground or airborne forward air controller lasers which is reflected by designated targets. The basic operational requirement for TRAM is to improve the USN capability for night surveillance and attack and to deliver laser-guided weapons. Naval applications were foremost in design but the system is capable of all general attack missions.

To fulfil these requirements, the system must have gimbal coverage adequate to permit manoeuvring after weapon release, and stabilisation and pointing accuracies consistent with sensor resolution and weapon performance.

In operation, the operator can simultaneously observe both radar and FLIR displays. For a radar significant target, he would normally use radar for acquisition and hand over to FLIR for identification and attack. The turret can sweep through the full lower hemisphere beneath the aircraft, allowing for free manoeuvre after weapon release.

The FLIR has a continuous optical zoom from a wide field of view with ×2·6 magnification to a narrow ×13 field.

STATUS

In 1976 a $21 million contract for production of 36 TRAM equipments was awarded to Hughes, and an extensive technical and operational evaluation programme took place in 1977. The first production TRAM was delivered in early 1979 and more than 100 systems had been delivered by early 1984. A total of 199 systems have been ordered under current contracts.

CONTRACTOR

Hughes Aircraft Company, PO Box 902, El Segundo, California 90245, USA.

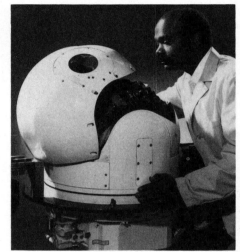

AN/AAS-33 TRAM detecting and ranging set incorporates FLIR, a laser rangefinder/designator and a separate laser receiver

3204.383
PAVE PENNY LASER TRACKER AN/AAS-35

Pave Penny is the code name of a laser tracking pod initially for use on the A-10 close-support attack aircraft and later the A-7D, F-16 and other types. Target designation is accomplished by forward air controllers on the ground or in another aircraft, and the function of the Pave Penny pod is to acquire and track such designated targets, providing outputs to the pilot's head-up display and/or to weapon delivery system avionics.

The pod is 20 cm in diameter and 83 cm long. Weight is about 14·5 kg. It contains optics gimballed in roll and pitch to focus the incident energy on to a silicon PIN diode detector housed within the pitch (inner) gimbal. In a typical installation, this arrangement permits tracking targets within –90 and +15° of the aircraft horizontal datum. Azimuth cover is 90° left or right of the aircraft centre line. The pilot is provided with controls that permit selection of seeker scanning patterns and limits, and choice of various modes of operation.

STATUS

Martin Marietta has been awarded at least six contracts worth a total of more than $80 million for production of Pave Penny pods and associated aircraft and support equipment for the A-10 and A-7 aircraft. In March 1977 the first operational Pave Penny/A-10 was delivered, when it was stated that the USAF intends to equip all of the planned 733 of these aircraft with Pave Penny. The first operational unit of the USAF was the 354th Tactical Fighter Wing, in January 1978.

Production of Pave Penny was completed in 1983 with over 700 pods delivered.

CONTRACTOR

Martin Marietta Orlando Aerospace, PO Box 5837, Orlando, Florida 32855, USA.

Pave Penny sensor mounted below air intake on A-7D aircraft

Pave Penny pod mounted on pylon on USAF A-10 aircraft. Mounts are pre-boresighted so that pods can be installed in a matter of minutes

4116.393
AN/AAS-36 IRDS

The AN/AAS-36 infra-red detecting set (IRDS) is an airborne equipment using IR common modules as the basis of a passive detection system for use on the USN P-3C maritime aircraft. The IR receiver is mounted in an azimuth-over-elevation stabilised gimbal system attached to the underside of the aircraft fuselage to provide extensive lower hemisphere coverage. This permits covert detection of surface ships, surfaced or snorkel-depth submarines, or other targets during darkness or in limited visibility.

In addition to the sensor turret, other items of the equipment include two electronics boxes for control and servo circuitry, and power supplies and video conversion; a video CRT indicator unit; a control panel; and a control stick for target tracking.

CHARACTERISTICS
Azimuth coverage: ±200°
Elevation coverage: +16 to −82°
IR detectors: HgCdTe
Video output: Composite TV, 875-line RS-343
Weight: 136 kg
STATUS
The AN/AAS-36 entered production for USN P-3C aircraft in 1977 and became operational in early 1979. In addition to the USA, numerous other countries equipped with the P-3 aircraft are fitting the AN/AAS-36. Various other FLIRs have evolved from it, such as the AN/AAS-37 (**4119.393**) fitted in the OV-10D aircraft, and the sensor turret has been employed in

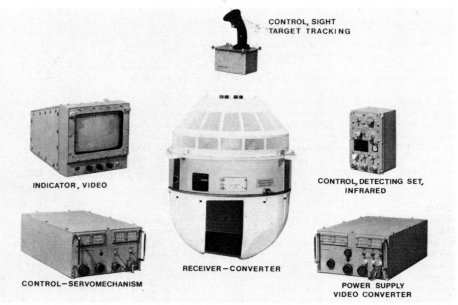

AN/AAS-36 infra-red detecting set (IRDS) system components

various other types, including the CH-53 helicopter, Beechcraft E-90, King Air 200 and Cessna Citation II. Total deliveries of AN/AAS-36 equipments to US and foreign services are expected to exceed 400.

CONTRACTOR
Texas Instruments Incorporated, PO Box 226015, Dallas, Texas 75266, USA.

4119.393
AN/AAS-37 DRTS

The AN/AAS-37 detecting, ranging, and tracking system (DRTS) is a special derivative of the AN/AAS-36 infra-red detecting set (**4116.393**) to which a number of additions have been made to meet the requirements of USMC OV-IOD multiple mission aircraft. Its capabilities include day or night detection and identification of targets and terrain for surveillance, observation and/or interdiction. A laser provides for ranging and designation of ground targets for laser-guided weapons such as Paveway bombs or the Hellfire missile. The electronics are contained in three boxes; there is a separate pilot's video indicator and three small extra control boxes for the additional facilities of this version.

A direct readout of laser ranges is available, and the designation facility uses PRF/PIM coding. There is rate-aided target tracking (adaptive gate or centroid tracker) and offset tracking from the target or a waypoint is possible.

CHARACTERISTICS
Azimuth coverage: ±200°
Elevation coverage: +16 to −82°
Video output: Composite TV, 875-line RS-343
STATUS
In production for USMC since 1978.
CONTRACTOR
Texas Instruments Incorporated, PO Box 226015, Dallas, Texas 75266, USA.

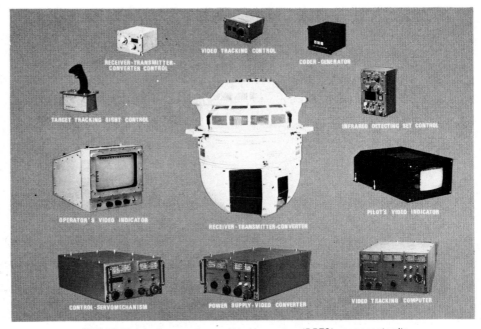

AN/AAS-37 detecting, ranging, and tracking system (DRTS) component units

4110.393
F/A-18 FLIR (AN/AAS-38)

The F/A-18 FLIR equipment AN/AAS-38 will provide the single-seat, twin-engine F/A-18 Hornet with a 24-hour strike capability in support of USN/USMC requirements for attack aircraft to perform interdiction and close air support missions. The FLIR system provides a day, night and adverse weather attack capability by presenting the pilot with real-time passive thermal imagery, in a TV formated display, for locating and identifying targets. Provisions were incorporated in the system design for inclusion of a laser target designator rangefinder which is now in engineering development by Ferranti and is planned for inclusion in the 1986 production deliveries.

The 33 cm diameter, 183 cm long, 170 kg system attaches to the lower left side of the aircraft at the Sparrow missile station. The pilot can select a

AN/AAS-38 FLIR mounted under the fuselage of an F/A-18

displayed field-of-view of 3 × 3° or 12 × 12° and can control the system's precisely stabilised line-of-sight over a field of regard of 30°, –150°, with ±540° of roll freedom. Accuracies are: stabilisation 35 microradians; pointing 400 microradians; and tracking 230 microradians.

The F/A-18 FLIR system interfaces with the aircraft and other on-board avionics systems through the mission computer, receiving commands directly over a MIL-STD-1553A multiplex data bus. The system provides the aircraft mission computer with accurate target line-of-sight pointing angles, angle rates and a complete initiated and periodic BIT evaluation of system readiness. It is the first Navy FLIR attack sensor designed to perform in a supersonic flight

environment. An automatic in-flight boresight compensation for dynamic pod flexure is employed to assure pointing accuracies over the full flight regime.

STATUS
Full-scale development was initiated in March 1978 and the detail design review was completed in that year. Following delivery of six pre-production systems in 1980, formal qualification and flight testing was initiated. Flight testing on the F/A-18 was successfully completed in December 1981 and full scale development was completed in 1983. The system is now in production and the first unit was delivered in December 1983.

A $35 million contract for 12 additional pods,

making a total of 73, was awarded to Ford Aerospace by the US Navy in April 1984.

An advanced fire control pod, based on the AN/AAS-38 design, is under development by Ford and Texas Instruments. It provides increased capability by the inclusion of a laser, an improved FLIR sensor and self-contained cooling. The Ferranti Type 117 laser/designator (**4727.393**) will form part of the pod.

CONTRACTORS
Ford Aerospace & Communications Corporation, Aeronutronic Division, Ford Road, Newport Beach, California 92663, USA.

Texas Instruments Incorporated, PO Box 226015 Dallas, Texas 75266, USA.

5750.383
AIRBORNE INFRA-RED SEARCH AND TRACK SYSTEM

An airborne infra-red search and track system (IRSTS) is under development by General Electric which will conduct the design, fabrication and flight evaluation of the system. The equipment employs modern focal plane array technology and sophisticated signal/clutter processing techniques. Relatively unknown as compared with FLIR technologies, the IRSTS sensors are seen as the key

in combating the threats anticipated from the mid-1980s onwards.

IRSTS is able to track targets of thermal energy at extremely long ranges with high accuracy and represents a significant 'force multiplier' effect in that a multiplicity of targets can be tracked simultaneously so that weapon management can be optimised effectively. The IRSTS sensor is also passive in operation and consequently relatively immune to countermeasures.

STATUS
The project is being funded by the USAF Wright Aeronautical Laboratories. A 16-month design effort has already been carried out.

CONTRACTOR
General Electric Company, Aircraft Equipment Division, French Road, Utica, New York 13503, USA.

3837.093
CONTRAVES DAY/NIGHT REMOTE VIDEO EQUIPMENT

This is a product of the US Contraves Goerz concern which consists of a long range video surveillance system capable of operating under all lighting levels. Its electro-optical system is completely dome-enclosed on an elevation platform that provides a gyro-stabilised line-of-sight together with pan and tilt functions.

The system permits the use of separate electro-optical systems for day and night. A choice of different day or night modes, focal lengths, filtering,

and focusing are controlled remotely from the control console.

There is a portable version which is also remotely operated and battery powered. In this model the TV camera is tripod mounted and controlled from a console which can be located up to 50 m away.

No further installation, sensor, or performance details are available for publication.

STATUS
No details have been made available.

CONTRACTOR
Contraves Goerz Corporation, 610 Epsilon Drive, Pittsburgh, Philadelphia 15238, USA.

Spherical housing of Contraves Goerz day/night remote video surveillance equipment

---

3846.393
AN/AXQ-14 WEAPON CONTROL EQUIPMENT

The AN/AXQ-14 is a two-way data link weapon control and guidance system developed by Hughes Aircraft Company for the GBU-15 precision-guided weapon system (**4190.311**). It consists of three major sub-systems: aircraft data link pod, aircraft data link

AN/AXQ-14 data link pod contains electronics, coder and decoder units, an electronically-scanned antenna for tracking the weapon in normal operations, a forward horn antenna for extended coverage, and recording equipment

control panel, and weapon data link. The aircraft pod, developed by Hughes and certified by the USAF for supersonic flight, contains four line-replaceable units: an electronics unit containing all RF generating and receiving equipment, a de-multiplexer to decode aircraft commands and pod control signals, an encoder, and antenna controls; an electronically phase-scanned antenna which tracks the weapon during normal operation; a forward horn antenna to provide additional antenna coverage; and a mission tape recorder to maintain a permanent record of video data provided by the electro-optical seeker in the weapon. The aircraft data link control panel is used with an existing display in the command aircraft to enable the weapon systems operator to interface with the weapon's guidance system during a mission. The weapon data link mounted on the rear of the GBU-15 provides the link between the weapon and the command aircraft's data link. The system has been successfully flight tested on a variety of USAF and USN aircraft and is compatible with modern high performance aircraft including F-4, F-15, F-16, F/A-18, F-111, A-7 and B-52.

STATUS
The AN/AXQ-14 is currently in production for the USAF and other customers.

AN/AXQ-14 data link system providing two-way video and command link facilities is used for direction of GBU-15 'launch-and-leave' weapon seen beneath this F-4 Phantom's wing. AN/AXQ-14 data link pod is on aircraft fuselage centre-line

CONTRACTOR
Hughes Aircraft Company, Radar Systems Group, El Segundo, California 90245, USA.

5751.393
TIGERSHARK HEAD-UP DISPLAY
The head-up display (HUD) for the F-20 Tigershark is designed to provide the pilot with a reliable display of weapon delivery and navigation information for maximum operational effectivness and survivability. The unit features an instantaneous field-of-view twice that of the F-5 display and the high brightness CRT imagery is visible against a 10 000 foot lambert background. The HUD is the primary flight instrument for the Tigershark and forms part of an integrated avionics and weapon delivery package. An independent standby reticle for backup capability is provided.

CHARACTERISTICS
Field of View: Instantaneous 16° elevation × 19·7° azimuth; total 22° elevation × 22° azimuth
CRT type: Magnetic deflection, P1 phosphor

Power: 81 W continuous
Weight: 24 lb (10·9 kg)
STATUS
In development. Flight trials were due to take place in late 1983/early 1984.
CONTRACTOR
General Electric Company, Aircraft Equipment Division, French Road, Utica, New York 13503, USA.

5752.393
HUGHES HEAD-UP DISPLAY
This latest head-up display (HUD) developed by Hughes uses diffraction optics techniques to provide pilots with a clearer and wider field-of-view. The prime advantage of diffraction optics is that the combiner can be produced with a wide field-of-view such that IR or low-light TV imagery can be displayed on the HUD for high speed low altitude night missions.

The combiner acts as a mirror that reflects only the selected wavelength of light used to produce the symbology on the display. This increases the pilot's ability to see through it to the outside world (transmissivity) to 85 per cent as compared with 50 to 70 per cent for convential HUDs.

Pilot orientated features designed into the HUD include a single piece combiner to avoid bulky support structures, symbology bright enough to be read in very high ambient light conditions, no cockpit reflections and no spillage from the HUD into the cockpit.

STATUS
The new diffraction optics HUD has been selected for the JAS-39 Grippen, Sweden's new multi-role combat aircraft which is due to fly in 1987 and enter service in the 1990s. A full-scale development and production contract was awarded to Hughes by SRA Communications AB, Sweden in January 1983.
CONTRACTOR
Hughes Aircraft Company, Radar Systems Group, El Segundo, California 90245, USA.

ANALYSIS

Italic type indicates that equipment is described in detail in previous editions of Jane's Weapon Systems.

Readers consulting tabular information on land artillery, armoured fighting vehicles, naval vessels, and military aircraft will find illustrations and additional information in the appropriate companion Jane's year book.

2202.114   **Strategic Missiles**

Name or NATO code	Entry no	US code	Number of stages	Propellant	Type of warhead	Single warhead	Alternative warheads	Range	Status	Deployment
Intercontinental Ballistic Missiles (ICBM)										
CHINA, People's Republic										
—	**4210.111**	CSS-3	2	Liquid	Nuclear	Suggested 2 MT	None known	7000 km	Development & reduced-range testing	Limited
DF-5 (provisional)	**4211.111**	CSS-X-4	2	Liquid	Nuclear	Suggested 5 MT	—	c13 000 km	Development & testing	Deployment uncertain
UNION OF SOVIET SOCIALIST REPUBLICS										
Sego	**4207.111**	SS-11	3	Storable	Nuclear	1 MT	MRV (Mods 3 & 4)	c13 000 km	Operational	c500, some converted to SS-17 & SS-19
Savage	**2958.111**	SS-13	3.	Solid	Nuclear	1 MT	None known	8000+ km	Operational	c60
Soviet RS-16	**2991.111**	SS-17	2	Liquid (cold-launch)	Nuclear	1 – 2 MT	MIRV 4 × 200 KT, or 4 × 750 KT	10 000 km	Operational in 1975	150 in converted SS-11 silos
Soviet RS-20	**2992.111**	SS-18	2	Liquid (cold-launch)	Nuclear	20 – 25 MT (Mod 1)	MIRV 8-10 × 500 KT (Mod 2)	10 500 km (Mods 1 & 3) 9250 km (Mod 2)	Operational	c300 in converted SS-9 silos
Soviet RS-18	**2993.111**	SS-19	2	Liquid	Nuclear	5 – 10 MT	MIRV 4 – 6 × 200 KT	9000+ km	Operational	c300
—	**4778.111**	SS-X-24	—	—	Nuclear	—	—	c16 000 km	Development	—
—	**4779.111**	SS-X-25	3	Solid	Nuclear	—	—	—	Development	—
UNITED STATES OF AMERICA										
Titan II	**2826.111**	LGM-25C	2	Liquid	Nuclear	5 MT	None	15 000 km	Phasing out	c40
Minuteman II	**2716.111**	LGM-30F	3	Solid	Nuclear	1 MT	None	11 250 km	Operational	450
Minuteman III	**2717.111**	LGM-30G	3	Solid	Nuclear	1 MT	MIRV 3 × Mk 12 or 12A	11 250 km	Operational	550
Peacekeeper (formerly MX)	**4561.111**	—	4	Solid	Nuclear	—	MIRV 10 × Mk 21	11 100 km	Development	100 planned
Intermediate-range Ballistic Missiles (IRBM)										
CHINA, People's Republic										
—	**2049.111**	CSS-2	1	Liquid	Nuclear	Small	None known	2000-4000 km	Operational	70+
FRANCE										
SSBS S-3	**2163.111**	—	2	Solid	Nuclear	1·2 MT	None known	3000 km	Operational	In 18 converted S-2 silos
UNION OF SOVIET SOCIALIST REPUBLICS										
Skean	**2981.111**	SS-5	1	Liquid	Nuclear	Probably 1 MT	None	3500 km	Operational	SS-4/SS-5 total c320
Scapegoat	**2961.111**	SS-14	2	Solid	Nuclear	1 MT	None known	4000 km	Operational	Mobile Numbers unknown
—	**3219.111**	SS-20	2	Solid	Nuclear	—	MIRV	c5000 km	Operational	1981 c300
—	**4549.111**	SS-22	Not known	—	Nuclear	—	—	700 – 800 km	Operational	Probable replacement for SS-12 Scaleboard
Medium-range Ballistic Missiles (MRBM)										
CHINA, People's Republic										
—	**2010.111**	CCS-1	Not known	Liquid	Nuclear	Possibly 20 KT	None	c1500 km	Possibly operational	c50
UNION OF SOVIET SOCIALIST REPUBLICS										
S&al	**2952.111**	SS-4	1	Liquid	HE or nuclear	Possibly 1 MT if nuclear	None	c1800 km	Obsolescent	Unknown number still deployed but estimated combined SS-4/SS-5 total 320

Name or NATO code	Entry no	US code	Number of stages	Propellant	Type of warhead	Single warhead	Alternative warheads	Range	Status	Deployment
Submarine-launched Ballistic Missiles (SLBM) & Sea-launched Strategic Weapons										
FRANCE										
MSBS	1134.111	M20	2	Solid	Nuclear	1 MT	None	3000 km	Operational	
		M4	3	Solid	Nuclear	6 – 7 × 150 KT	MRV	c4000 km	Development	From 1985
UNION OF SOVIET SOCIALIST REPUBLICS										
Sawfly	1154.411	SSN-6	—	Liquid	Nuclear	?1 MT (Mod 1)	3 × MRV (Mod 3)	c3000 km	Obsolescent	Some 'Y' class submarines
—	3078.411	SSN-8	—	Liquid	Nuclear	—	—	c7800 km	Operational	In 'D' class submarines
Serb	1153.411	SSN-5	—	—	Nuclear	?1 MT	—	1300 km	Obsolescent	Some Hotel II submarines
—	3356.411	SSN-X-17	—	Solid	Nuclear	—	MRV possible	—	Development	Uncertain
Soviet RSM-50	3357.411	SSN-18	—	Liquid	Nuclear	—	MIRV possible	c7000 km	Operational	Some 'D' class submarines
—	4208.411	SSN-20	—	Solid	Nuclear	—	MIRV	c8000 km	Development	'Typhoon' class submarines
—	4975.411	SS-NX-23	—	? Liquid	Nuclear	—	—	—	Development	Possible 'Delta III' submarines
UNITED KINGDOM										
Polaris	2390.411	—	2	Solid	Nuclear	3 × 200 KT	Chevaline MaRV	4600 km	Operational	In 4 RN submarines
UNITED STATES OF AMERICA										
Polaris A-3	1131.411	UGM-27C	2	Solid	Nuclear	—	3 × 200 KT	4600 km	Operational phasing out	
Poseidon C-3	1133.411	UGM-73A	2	Solid	Nuclear	—	MIRV	4600 km	Obsolescent	12 Poseidon submarines converted to Trident C-4 by end 1982
Trident C-4	2840.411	UGM-93A	3	Solid	Nuclear	—	Mk 4 8 × 100 KT or Mk 500	7000 km	Operational	In Ohio-class & converted Poseidon submarines. Larger Trident II (D-5) under development
Tomahawk	3993.001 4197.221	BGM-109	1	Turbojet (solid booster)	Nuclear	—	HE	2400-3200 km	Development	Tactical & land versions also

3229.114 Tactical Land-based Surface-to-surface Missiles

Designation	Entry no	Dimensions l x d – span	Weight	Warhead	Propulsion	Range	Guidance	Deployment
Battlefield support								
FRANCE								
Hades	4777.111	Project for Pluton successor						Project definition
Pluton	2130.111	764 × 65 – 141 cm	2423 kg	Nuclear 25 or 15 KT	Solid	120 km	Inertial	French Army
TAIWAN								
Ching Feng	4547.111	Similar to US Lance						Operational
UNION OF SOVIET SOCIALIST REPUBLICS								
FROG-7	2926.111	900 × 55 cm	c2000 kg	HE or Nuclear	Solid	c60 km	Unguided	USSR & client states
SS-1B (Scud A)	3327.111	c1050 × 85 cm	c4500 kg	HE or nuclear	Storable liquid	80-150 km	Radio command	Warsaw Pact. Possibly obsolescent
SS-1C (Scud B)	3327.111	c1125 × 85 cm	c6300 kg	HE or nuclear	Storable liquid	160-270 km	Simplified inertial	Warsaw Pact, Egypt, Iraq, Syria

Designation	Entry no	Dimensions l x d – span	Weight	Warhead	Propulsion	Range	Guidance	Deployment
USSR cont								
SS-12 (Scaleboard)	2959-111	c1125 × 100 cm	c6800 kg	Presumed nuclear	Probably liquid	c800 km	Probably inertial	USSR. Operational status uncertain
SS-21	2926.111	944 × 46 cm	—	HE or nuclear	Solid	120 km (est)	—	Replacement for FROG-7
SS-22	4549.111	—	—	HE or nuclear	Not known	900 km (est)	—	USSR. Replacement for SS-12
SS-23	4550.111	—	—	HE or nuclear	Solid	500 km (est)	—	Development
UNITED STATES OF AMERICA								
GLCM (BGM-109)	4194.111	640 × 53 – 250 cm	1773 kg	Nuclear	Turbofan	2500 km	Inertial + TERCOM	USA
Lance (MGM-52)	2682.111	614 × 56 cm	c1500 kg	Nuclear Other options	Pre-packed liquid	120 km	Simplified inertial	Belgium, Germany (FR), Italy, Israel, Netherlands, UK
JTACMS	4760.111	Joint tactical missile system. Successor to Lance						Development
Pershing 1a (MGM-31A)	2765.111	c1050 × 100 cm	c4600 kg	Nuclear 60-400 KT	2-stage solid	740 km	Inertial	Germany (FR), USA
Pershing II	2767.111	Improved version of Pershing 1a with terminal guidance.						Deployed in Germany (FR)
Coastal defence								
CHINA, People's Republic								
HY-2 (CSS-N-2)	3984.121	Chinese-built version of Soviet SS-N-2 anti-ship missile						China
FRANCE								
Exocet MM 40	2118.121	578 × 35 – 100 cm	850 kg	165 kg HE	2-stage solid	70 km	Inertial+active radar homing	Early production
INTERNATIONAL								
Otomat	1337.121	438 × 40 – 124 cm	700 kg	210 kg HE	Turbojet+ boosters	100 km	Autopilot+ active radar homing	Egypt, probably Saudi Arabia
NORWAY								
Penguin	3074.121	300 × 28 – 140 cm	340 kg	120 kg SAP	Solid	30 km+	Inertial+IR homing	Development
SWEDEN								
RB 08	2372.121	572 × 66 – 301 cm	900 kg	HE	Turbojet+ boosters	150 km	Autopilot+ active radar homing	Sweden
TAIWAN								
Hsiung Feng	4442.121	Based on coastal defence version of Israeli Gabriel ASM						
UNION OF SOVIET SOCIALIST REPUBLICS								
Samlet (SSC-2B)	2951.121	c700 – 500 cm	c3000 kg	HE	Turbojet+ boosters	c200 km	Command, probably active radar homing	USSR & some client states
Sepal (SSC-1B)	2975.121	c1000 cm	—	HE or nuclear	Air breathing	c450 km	Radio command IR homing	USSR
Anti-tank/Assault								
ARGENTINA								
Mathogo	3677.111	99 × 10 cm	11 kg	HE	Solid	350 – 2100 m	Wire-guided CLOS	Argentina
BRAZIL								
Cobra	4193.111	Brazilian produced version of West German Cobra 2000 (see below)						Production
FRANCE								
ACCP	4552.111	93 × 15 cm	10 kg	HE	Solid	25-600 m	CLOS	Development
ACL-STRIM	2055.111	60 × 9 cm	2·2 kg	0·6 kg	Solid	400-500 m	—	France & 21 other countries
SS-11	2139.111	120 × 16 – 50 cm	30 kg	2·6 kg 3 types	2-stage solid	3000 m	Wire CLOS	More than 20 countries

Designation	Entry no	Dimensions l x d – span	Weight	Warhead	Propulsion	Range	Guidance	Deployment
GERMANY, Federal Republic								
Cobra 2000	2181.111	95 × 10 – 48 cm	10 kg	2·7 kg 3 types	Solid	2000 m	Wire CLOS	Argentina, Brazil, Denmark, Germany (FR), Greece, Israel, Italy, Pakistan, Spain, Turkey
Mamba	2188.111	95 × 12 – 40 cm	11 kg	2·7 kg 3 types	Solid	2000 m	Wire CLOS	Various
INTERNATIONAL								
ADATS	4159.111	205 × 15 cm	51 kg	12 kg+	Solid	8000 m	Laser beam-rider	Swiss/US development
ATEM	3611.111	Anti-tank Euromissile project						France/ Germany (FR)/ UK
EMDG	4545.111	European programme to develop new family of A/T missiles						Project
HOT	2212.111	128 × 14 – 31 cm	23 kg	6 kg HEAT	2-stage solid	4000 m	Wire CLOS	France, Germany (FR) & others
Milan	2215.111	77 × 9 – 27 cm	12 kg	HEAT (K115 introduced in 1984)	Solid	2000 m	Wire automatic CLOS	France, Germany (FR), UK
ISRAEL								
Picket	3991.111	76 × 8 cm	4 kg	HEAT	Solid	500 m	Gyro stabilised LOS	Production Israel
ITALY								
Folgore	2257.111	74 × 8 cm	3	Hollow charge	Solid	1000 m	—	Trials complete
JAPAN								
KAM-3D (Type 64)	2262.111	100 × 12 – 60 cm	16 kg	HEAT	2-stage solid	1800 m	Wire CLOS	Japan
KAM-9 (Type 79)	2263.111	150 × 15 – 33 cm	42 kg	HEAT	Solid	4000 m	SACLOS	Japan
SWEDEN								
Bantam (RB53)	2363.111	85 × 11 – 40 cm	75 kg	1·9 kg hollow charge	2-stage solid	2000 m	Wire CLOS	Sweden, Switzerland
RBS 56 (Bill)	4544.111	90 × 15 – 41 cm	16 kg	HE	Solid	150-2000 m	Wire CLOS	Sweden (1985)
Strix	4557.111	80 × 12 cm	20 kg	HE	Mortar launched	600 m – 8 km	IR homing	Development project
TAIWAN								
Kun-Wu	4438.111	Taiwan produced version of Soviet AT-3 Sagger						Taiwan
UNION OF SOVIET SOCIALIST REPUBLICS								
AT-1 (Snapper)	2983.111	113 × 14 – 75 cm	22 kg	5·2 kg hollow charge	Solid	2300 m	Wire CLOS	Warsaw Pact, Egypt, Syria, Yugoslavia & others
AT-2 (Swatter)	2985.111	116 × 13 – 66 cm	29 kg	HEAT	Solid	3500 m	Wire CLOS possibly with IR homing	Warsaw Pact & others
AT-3 (Sagger)	2950.111	86 × 12 – 47 cm	11 kg	HEAT	Solid	3000 m	Wire CLOS	Warsaw Pact and others
AT-4 (Spigot)	3638.111	c98 × 13 cm	10-12 kg (est)	HEAT	Solid	c2000 m	Semi-automatic CLOS	USSR, Czechoslovakia, Germany (DR), Poland
AT-5 (Spandrel)	3608.111	c100 × 16 cm	12-18 kg	HEAT	Solid	4000 m	CLOS	USSR
AT-6 (Spiral)	3639.111	—	—	HEAT	Solid	—	CLOS	USSR
UNITED KINGDOM								
LAW 80	3986.111	95 × 9 cm	4 kg	HEAT	Solid	500 m	—	UK (1984)
Law mine	4757.111	Unattended automatic weapon development using LAW 80						Development
Merlin	4756.111	81 mm mortar launched anti-armour bomb						Project
Swingfire	2450.111	107 × 17 – 37 cm	34 kg	Hollow charge	Solid	4000 m	Wire CLOS	Belgium, UK
Vigilant	2475.111	107 × 11 – 28 cm	14 kg	6 kg+ hollow charge	2-stage solid	1375 m	Wire manual or auto CLOS	Finland, Kuwait, Libya, Saudi Arabia, UAE, UK

Designation	Entry no	Dimensions l x d – span	Weight	Warhead	Propulsion	Range	Guidance	Deployment
UNITED STATES OF AMERICA								
Dragon (M47) (FGM-77A/ FTM-77A)	2573.111	74 × 13 – 33 cm	12 kg	HE shaped charge	Multiple solid	1000 m	Wire CLOS	USA & others
Gamp	4551.111	Guided anti-armour mortar projectile						Project
Tank Breaker	4472.111	109 × 10 cm	c15 kg	Shaped charge	Solid	—	IR fire-and-forget	Development project
TOW (BGM-71)	2830.111	117 × 15 cm	18 kg	3·6 kg shaped charge	2-stage solid	3500 m	Wire Auto missile tracking CLOS	USA & about 30 others. TOW 2 in development
Copperhead (M712)	3212.111	137 × 15 cm	63 kg	6·4 kg HEAT	Cannon launched	16 km	Laser homing	Production

1763.224   Tactical Shipborne Surface-to-surface Missiles

Designation	Entry no	Dimensions l x d – span	Weight	Warhead	Propulsion	Range	Guidance	Deployment
CHINA, People's Republic								
HY-2 (CSS-N-2)	3973.221	Chinese-built version of Soviet SS-N-2, Styx anti-ship missile						In several classes of Chinese ship
FRANCE								
MM 38 Exocet	1156.221	521 × 35 – 100 cm	735 kg	165 kg HE	2-stage solid	42 km	Inertial + active radar	France & 20 others
SM 39 Exocet	1156.221	580 × 35 – 101 cm	655 kg	165 kg HE	2-stage solid + booster	50 km+	Inertial + active radars	Sub version
MM 40 Exocet	1156.221	578 × 35 – 113 cm	850 kg	165 kg HE	2-stage solid	70 km+	Inertial + active radar	Production
INTERNATIONAL								
ANS	4446.221	Anti-Navires Supersonique project by Aérospatiale and MBB						
Otomat	1336.221	446 × 46 – 135 cm	770 kg	210 kg SAP HE	Solid boosters, turbojet cruise	60-180 km	Autopilot + active radar	Eqypt, Italy, Libya, Peru, Venezuela & others. Mk II & Téséo versions also
ISRAEL								
Gabriel Mk I Gabriel Mk II Gabriel Mk III	6019.221	335 × 34 – 135 cm 341 × 34 – 135 cm 381 × 34 – 135 cm	430 kg 520 kg 560 kg	100 kg HE 100 kg HE 150 kg HE	2-stage solid	18 km 36 km 36 km+	Autopilot/ command + IR or radar	Argentina, Israel, S. Africa, Singapore, Taiwan (as Hsiung Feng) Longer-range Mk II & III in production
ITALY								
Otomach	4195.221	Italian project for successor to Otomat						Study
Sea Killer Mk 2	2253.221	470 × 21 – 100 cm	300 kg	70 kg SAP HE	2-stage solid	25 km	Beam-rider/ radio command CLOS radar	Iran. Used in Marte helicopter anti-ship system
NORWAY								
Penguin	1339.221	300 × 28 – 140 cm	340 kg	120 kg HE	2-stage solid	30 km	Inertial + IR homing	Greece, Norway, Turkey. Coastal-defence & air-launched versions also longer-range Mk 3 in development

Designation	Entry no	Dimensions l x d – span	Weight	Warhead	Propulsion	Range	Guidance	Deployment
SOUTH AFRICA								
Skorpioen	**4444.221**	Believed licence-built version of Israeli Gabriel ASM						S Africa
SWEDEN								
RB 08A	**2366.221**	572 × 66 – 301 cm	1215 kg	c250 kg	2 × solid boosters, turbojet cruise	—	Command/ autopilot + active radar homing	Sweden. Also used for coastal defence
RBS 15	**3976.221**	435 × 50 – 140 cm	600 kg	—	Turbojet solid boosters	150 km (est)	Probably autopilot + active radar homing	Production
TAIWAN								
Hsiung Feng	**4443.221**	Version of Israeli Gabriel ASM						Taiwan
UNION OF SOVIET SOCIALIST REPUBLICS								
SS-N-2 Styx	**1155.221**	625 × 75 – 275 cm (est)	2300 kg	HE 400 kg (2A/2B); 450 kg (2C)	Solid booster + internal cruise motor	40 km max	Probably radio command + IR or active radar homing	Algeria, Bulgaria, China, Cuba, Egypt, Germany (DR), India, Indonesia, N Korea, Poland, Romania, Syria, USSR, Yugoslavia. China has own production
SS-N-3 Shaddock	**2976.221**	1100 × 86 cm (est)	4700 kg	HE or nuclear	Solid boosters + internal cruise motor	180–450 km	Probably radio command	USSR only
SS-N-7	**2987.411**	—	—	HE or nuclear	Probably solid	45-55 km	—	Submarine-launched
SS-N-9 Siren	**1760.221**	—	—	—	Solid	275 km max (est)	Probably radio command	Fitted to 'Nanuchka' missile boats – 6 launchers each
SS-N-12 Sandbox	**4445.221**	1080 × 90 – 200 cm (est)	—	HE or nuclear	—	550 km (est)	—	On 'Kiev' carriers and possibly Echo II subs
SS-N-19	**4196.221**	Vertically-launched anti-ship missile arming *Kirov* and 'Oscar' class submarines						
SS-NX-22	**4761.221**	Anti-ship missile. 16 fitted in 'Slava' class ships						Early deployment
UNITED KINGDOM								
Sea Eagle SL (P5T)	**4447.221**	Ship-launched version of Sea Eagle air-launched ASM						Development
Sea Skua (SL)	**4553.221**	Ship-launched version of air-launched anti-ship missile						Development Ready for production
UNITED STATES OF AMERICA								
Harpoon (RGM-84A)	**2641.221**	457 × 34 – 83 cm	500 kg	HE/nuclear	Solid booster, turbojet cruise	110 km	Programmed inertial + radar	Production for USA & others. Air- & sub-launched versions
Tomahawk (BGM-109)	**4197.221**	Surface- and submarine-launched tactical model of USN Tomahawk sea-launched cruise missile						Production
5-in Guided Projectile	**4213.221**	154 × 13 cm	47·5 kg	13·6 kg	Solid	24 km+	Laser homing	Development

3471.234   **Naval Surface-to-air Missiles**

Designation	Entry no	Dimensions l x d — span	Weight	Warhead	Propulsion	Range	Guidance	Deployment
FRANCE								
Masurca	1177.231	860 × 41 – 150 cm	1850 kg	HE	Solid	40 km	Semi-active radar	On 2 frigates & 1 cruiser
Crotale	2111.231	290 × 15 – 54 cm	80 kg	c15 kg HE	Solid	8·5 km	Radio command	French Navy, Saudi Arabia
SADRAL	4509.231	188 × 9 cm	17 kg	HE 3 kg	Solid	5 km	IR homing	Development
INTERNATIONAL								
NATO Seasparrow (Mk 57)	4775.231	366 × 20 – 102 cm	200 kg	HE	Solid	25 km	Semi-active radar	Belgium, Canada, Denmark, Germany (FR), Italy, Netherlands Norway, USA
ASMD (RAM)	3017.231	279 × 13 cm	70 kg	Anti-ship missile defence system project using rolling airframe missile				USN/Denmark Germany (FR) Development
ISRAEL								
Barak	4200.231	240 × 15 cm (est)	90 kg	HE	Solid	10 km	Semi-active radar	Early fittings
ITALY								
Albatros	2228.231	370 × 20 – 80 cm	220 kg	HE	Solid	c25 km	Semi-active radar	Italy, Greece, Peru, Spain, Venezuela and nine others
SWEDEN								
RBS 70	4546.231	132 × 11 cm	c20 kg	HE	Solid	5 km	Laser beam rider	Development
UNION OF SOVIET SOCIALIST REPUBLICS								
SA-N-1 (Goa)	2939.231	c590 × – 120 cm	—	HE	Solid	c15 km	Beam rider, semi-active homing	Soviet fleet
SA-N-2 (Guideline)	2943.231	1070 × 50 – 170 cm	2300 kg	HE	Solid booster	c45 km	Radio command	1 ship fitted
SA-N-3 (Goblet)	2947.231	c600	c540 kg	40 kg HE	Solid	c30 km	—	On later Soviet ships
SA-N-4	2954.231	320(est)	—	13 kg HE	Solid	c12 km	—	Mostly post-1970 Soviet ships
SA-N-5	4201.231	Quadruple mount of SA-7 man-portable SAM (**2941.131**)						Some AGIs & certain support ships
SA-N-6	4206.231	Thought to be naval version of SA-10 (VLS)						'Kirov' and 'Krasina' classes
SA-N-7	—	New system based on land-based SA-11 SAM or print defence system						'Sovremennyi' class
SA-N-8	4565.231	New VLS short/medium-range system						Development. 'Udaloy' class
UNITED KINGDOM								
Seacat	1019.231	148 × – 65 cm	63 kg	HE	Solid	c5 km	CLOS	Fitted in 16 navies
Sea Dart	6004.231	436 × 42 – 91 cm	550 kg	HE	Solid + ramjet	30 km+	Semi-active radar	Argentina & UK. Lightweight, version designed
Seaslug	6003.231	600 × 41 cm	—	HE	Solid	c45 km	Beam rider	RN, Chile, Pakistan
Seawolf	2442.231	c200 × 24 – 55 cm	80 kg	HE	Solid	—	Command	RN. Lightweight, VLS & container versions developed
UNITED STATES OF AMERICA								
Aegis	2507.231	Area air-defence system using Standard SM-2 missile						USN
Sea Chaparral	3983.231	Naval version of Chaparral land-based air defence system						Export
Standard (MR)	1122.231	457 × 31 cm	c590 kg	HE	Solid	c18 km	Semi-active radar	USN

Designation	Entry no	Dimensions l x d – span	Weight	Warhead	Propulsion	Range	Guidance	Deployment
USA contd (SM-1) (ER)		823 × 31 cm	c1060 kg	HE	Solid	c55 km	Semi-active radar	USN
Standard (MR)	1122.231	457 × 31 cm	—	HE	Solid	c48 km	Inertial reference + command	Development
(SM-2) (ER)	—	823 × 31 cm	—	HE	Solid	c100 km	Semi-active	Development
Tartar	6006.231	460 × 31 cm	680 kg	HE	Solid	16 km	Semi-active radar	Australia, France, Germany (FR), Iran, Italy, Japan, Netherlands, Spain, USA
Terrier	6005.231	800 × 31 cm	1400 kg	HE	Solid	c35 km	Beam rider, semi-active homing	Italy, Netherlands, USA Obsolescent

1756.314   Air Defence Missiles

Designation	Entry no	Dimensions l x d – span	Weight	Warhead	Propulsion	Range	Guidance	Deployment
FRANCE Crotale	2074.131	294 × 16 – 54 cm	80 kg	15 kg HE	Solid	8·5 km	Command	France & others. Cactus version for S Africa, & Shahine for Saudi Arabia
SAM 90	4771.131	Project for 250 kg class land/naval missile system						Feasibility studies
SATCP (Mistral)	4198.131	180 × 9 cm	17 kg	3 kg	Solid	500-5000 m	IR homing	Development
Shahine Sica (TSE 5100)	3972.131	—	—	14 kg HE	Solid	11 km	Command	Saudi Arabia
GERMANY, Federal Republic MFS-2000	4772.131	Design/feasibility study programme for Hawk replacement						Study project
INTERNATIONAL ADATS	4158.131	205 × 15 cm	51 kg	12 kg + HE	Solid	8 km	Laser beam rider	Development
Roland	2218.131	240 × 16 – 50 cm	66 kg	6·5 kg HE	Solid	6 km	Command	Argentina, Brazil, France, Germany (FR), Spain, USA & others
ITALY Aspide	1656.331	370 × 20 – 80 cm	220 kg	HE	Solid	—	Semi-active radar	Italy
JAPAN Tan-SAM	3458.131	270 × 16 cm	100 kg	HE	Solid	7 km	Command + IR homing	Early production
SWEDEN RBS 70	2348.131 3617.131	132 × 11 cm	c20 kg	HE	Solid	5 km	Laser beam rider	Production. Several versions
UNION OF SOVIET SOCIALIST REPUBLICS SA-1 (Guild)	2944.131	c1200 × 71 cm	—	—	Liquid	c32 km	—	USSR
SA-2 (Guideline)	2942.131	c1070 × 70 cm	c2300 kg	130 kg HE	Solid with liquid sustainer	40-50 km	Radio command	USSR & many others
SA-3 (Goa)	2938.131	c670 × 60 cm	636 kg	—	Solid	25-30 km	Probably radio command	USSR & others
SA-4 (Ganef)	2934.131	c880 × 90 – 260 cm	c2500 kg	—	Ramjet+ solid boosters	c70 km	Radio command	USSR, & certain Warsaw Pact states

Designation	Entry no	Dimensions l x d – span	Weight	Warhead	Propulsion	Range	Guidance	Deployment
USSR cont								
SA-5 (Gammon)	**2940.131**	1650 × 100 cm	c10 000 kg	—	Solid	c300 km	—	USSR, Syria
SA-6 (Gainful)	**2930.131**	620 × 33 – 124 cm	c550 kg	c40 kg HE	Rocket ramjet	Up to 60 km	Command + radar homing	USSR & others
SA-7 (Grail)	**2941.131**	129 cm	9·2 kg	—	Solid	9-10 km	IR homing	USSR & others
SA-8 (Gecko)	**3209.131**	c320 × 21 – 60 cm	c190 kg	HE	Solid	12 km	Command	Warsaw Pact
SA-9 (Gaskin)	**3072.131**	200 × 12 cm	30 kg+	HE	Solid	8 km	IR homing	Warsaw Pact
SA-10	**3620.131**	625 × 45 cm (est)	—	—	Prob solid	100 km (est)	—	USSR
SA-11	**4470.131**	Probably new mobile short-range SAM, Mach 3, 3-28 km range						Development probably early deployment
SA-X-12	**4774.131**	New mobile vertical launch long-range SAM						Development trials
SA-13 (Gopher)	**4471.131**	220 × 12 – 40 cm	55 kg	6 kg HE	Solid	10 km	IR homing	USSR
ABM-1B (Galosh)	**2932.131**	c2000 × 275 cm	Anti-ballistic missile					USSR
UNITED KINGDOM								
Bloodhound	**2406.131**	846 × 55 – 283 cm	—	HE	Ramjet + solid boosters	c80 km	Semi-active radar homing	UK, Singapore, Switzerland
Blowpipe	**2409.131**	140 × 7·6 – 27 cm	c81 kg	HE	Solid	Short	Radio command	UK, Canada & others
Guardian	**4524.131**	Land SAM system based on naval Sea Dart (**6004.231**)						Proposal
Javelin	**4533.131**	140 × 8 cm	—	—	Solid	4 km+	SACLOS	Entering production
Landwolf	**4773.131**	Land SAM system based on naval Seawolf (**2442.231**)						Proposal
Rapier	**2424.131**	224 × 13 – 38 cm	c43 kg	HE	Solid	6 km+	CLOS	UK & more than 10 others
Tigercat	**2465.131**	148 × 19 cm	63 kg	HE	Solid	—	Command	UK & 5 others
UNITED STATES OF AMERICA								
Chaparral (MIM-72)	**2542.131**	291 × 13 – 64 cm	c84 kg	HE	Solid	Short	IR homing	USA & c6 others
Hawk	**4177.131**	503 × 36 – 119 cm	627 kg	HE	Solid	40 km	Semi-active homing	USA & over 20 others
Nike-Hercules (MIM-14B)	**2723.131**	1210 × 80 cm	4858 kg	Nuclear/HE	Solid	140 km	Command	NATO & some other states
Patriot (MIM-104)	**2800.131**	531 × 41 cm	—	Nuclear/HE	Solid	—	Command + TVM	Entering service
Redeye	**2784.131**	122 × 7 cm	13 kg	HE	Solid	c3 km	IR homing	Australia, Sweden, USA & others
Saber	**4534.131**	New man-portable SAM project						Demonstrations
Stinger	**2805.131**	152 × 7 cm	15·8 kg	HE	Solid	Short	IR homing	USA

1757.334   **Air-to-air Missiles**

Designation	Entry no	Dimensions l x d – span	Weight	Warhead	Propulsion	Range	Guidance	Deployment
BRAZIL								
Piranha (MAA-1)	**4192.331**	272 × 15 cm	85 kg	12 kg HE	Solid	c10 km	IR homing	Development

Designation	Entry no	Dimensions l x d – span	Weight	Warhead	Propulsion	Range	Guidance	Deployment
FRANCE								
R.530	**1176.331**	328 × 26 – 110 cm	195 kg	27 kg HE	Solid	18 km	Radar & IR versions	France & 14 others. Production ceased
Super 530	**1349.331**	354 × 26 – 90 cm	245 kg	30 kg HE	Solid	36 km	Radar	Operational
R.550 (Magic)	**1348.331**	275 × 16 – 66 cm	91 kg	HE	Solid	200 m-10 km	IR	France & others
INTERNATIONAL								
AMRAAM (AIM-120A)	**3340.331**	365 × 18-53 cm	148 kg	HE	Solid	—	Inertial + radar	Development France, Germany (FR), UK & USA
ASRAAM	**3622.331**	Advanced short-range air-to-air missile project						MoU signed by France, Germany (FR), UK & USA
ISRAEL								
Shafrir	**1659.331**	260 × 16 cm	93 kg	HE	Solid	—	IR	Israel & others
Python 3	**4185.331**	300 × 16 cm	120 kg	11 kg HE	Solid	500 m – 15 km	IR	Entering service
ITALY								
Aspide	**1656.331**	370 × 20 – 100 cm	220 kg	35 kg HE	Solid	—	Semi-active radar	Production
JAPAN								
AAM-1	**1187.331**	c260 cm	70 kg	HE	Solid	7 km	IR	In service JASDF
AAM-2	**1188.331**	Successor to AAM-1 —	—	—	—	—	—	Development
SOUTH AFRICA								
Kukri (V3B)	**4526.331**	294 × 13 – 53 cm	73 kg	HE	Solid	300 m – 4 km	IR	Operational
UNION OF SOVIET SOCIALIST REPUBLICS								
Anab (AA-3)	**1144.331**	360 × 28 – 130 cm	—	—	Solid	16 km+	Radar & IR versions	USSR & client states
Ash (AA-5)	**1145.331**	530 × 30 – 130 cm	—	—	Solid	c30 km	Radar & IR versions	—
Atoll (AA-2)	**1146.331**	280 × 12 – 53 cm	—	HE	Solid	15 km	IR	—
Acrid (AA-6)	**3337.331**	629 × 30 cm	c750 kg	c100 kg	Solid	c37 km	Radar & IR versions	Foxbat
Apex (AA-7)	**3338.331**	430 × 24 – 105 cm	c350 kg	c40 kg	Solid	35/15 km	Radar & IR versions	Flogger, Foxbat
Aphid (AA-8)	**3339.331**	210 × 13 cm	c54 kg	HE	Solid	c8 km	Probably IR	Flogger, Fishbed
AA-9	**4768.331**	Probably long-range 'snap-down' interceptor missile						Foxhound
AA-X-10	**4820.331**	Probably medium-range missile being developed for MiG-29 Fulcrum and Su-27 Flanker						
UNITED KINGDOM								
Red Top	**1080.331**	327 × 22 – 91 cm	160 kg (est)	31 kg	Solid	12 km+	IR	RAF, Kuwait, Saudi Arabia
Sky Flash	**1774.331**	370 × 20 – 102 cm	c192 kg	30 kg	Solid	40 km	Semi-active radar	Production UK, Sweden
UNITED STATES OF AMERICA								
ASAT	**4186.331**	Air-launched anti-satellite weapon project						USAF programme. Research & development
Falcon (AIM-4D)	**1085.331**	198 × 16 – 51 cm	60 kg	HE	Solid	—	IR	USA & others
Falcon (AIM-4E)	**1086.331**	218 × 16 – 61 cm	63.5 kg	HE	Solid	—	Semi-active radar	USA & others
Falcon (AIM-4F)	**1086.331**	218 × 17 – 61 cm	68 kg	HE	Solid	—	Semi-active radar	USA & others
Falcon (AIM-4G)	**1087.331**	218 × 17 – 61 cm	68 kg	HE	Solid	—	IR	USA & others
Phoenix (AIM-54A/C)	**1099.331**	396 × 38 – 91 cm	380 kg	—	Solid	110-165 km	Radar homing	USA, Iran

Designation	Entry no	Dimensions l x d – span	Weight	Warhead	Propulsion	Range	Guidance	Deployment
USA cont								
Sidewinder (AIM-9L)	4767.331	287 × 13 – 62 cm	86 kg	HE	Solid	—	IR	USA & many others. Numerous versions
Sparrow (AIM-7E/F)	1106.331	365 × 20 – 100 cm	200 kg	30 kg HE	Solid	25 km	Semi-active CW radar	USA & others

1756.314   Air-to-surface Missiles

Designation	Entry no	Dimensions l x d – span	Weight	Warhead	Propulsion	Range	Guidance	Deployment
ARGENTINA								
Martin Pescador	3678.311	294 × 22 – 73 cm	140 kg	40 kg HE	Solid	2·5-9 km	Radio command	Production
FRANCE								
AS-15 (TT)	3359.331	230 × 18 – 53 cm	96 kg	30 kg HE	Solid	15 km	Radar command	Ordered by Saudi Arabia
AS.30	*1171.311*	390 × 34 – 100 kg	520 kg	HE	2-stage solid	10-12 km	Radio command	France, Germany (FR), Israel, Switzerland S Africa & others
AS-30L (Laser)	3335.311	365 × 34 – 100 cm	520 kg	HE	Solid	10-20 km	Laser homing	Early production
AS.11	1173.311	120 × 16 – 50 cm	30 kg	A/T, HE, or frag	Solid	3000 m	Wire-guided	France & 21 others
AS.12	1174.311	187 × 21 – 65 cm	76 kg	28 kg various	Solid	600-800 m	Wire-guided	French & UK maritime a/c
ASMP	3635.311	Medium-range project (Air-Sol-Moyenne-Portée)			Ramjet	c100 km		France 1985-86
Exocet (AM 39)	1770.321	470 × 35 – 110 cm	655 kg	165 kg HE	Solid	50-70 km	Inertial + radar homing	France & others
AATCP	4510.311	Helicopter-launched version of Mistral AA missile						Project
Matra LGB	4189.311	Laser guidance packages for use with 400 & 1000 kg bombs					Laser homing	France & others 1985-85
Pegase	4555.311	Modular stand-off ground attack weapon project						Proposal
GERMANY, Federal Republic								
CWS (Container Weapon System)	4449.311	415 × 73 – 200 cm	1200 kg	Multiple	Solid	20 km	—	Development
Kormoran	1180.311	440 × 34 – 100 cm	580 kg	c160 kg HE	Solid	30 nm	Inertial cruise, active/passive radar homing	Germany (FR), Italy
MW-1	3517.311	Multi-purpose sub-munition dispenser tactical weapon						Germany (FR)
VEBAL/SYNDROM	4770.311	Anti-tank weapon project						Development
INTERNATIONAL								
ANS	4450.321	Supersonic anti-ship missile development project						France/ Germany (FR)
Apache CWS	4454.311	Joint stand-off tactical modular weapon development						France/ Germany (FR)
HOT	1771.311	128 × 14 – 31 cm	21 kg	6 kg HE	Solid	4 km	Wire CLOS	—
Martel (AJ 168) Martel (AS 37)	1022.311	390 × 40 – 120 cm 420 × 40 – 120 cm	150 kg 148 kg	HE HE	2-stage solid 2-stage solid	60 km 60 km	Command & TV radiation homing	France & UK
Otomat	1338.311 1336.221	440 × 46 – 119 cm	600 kg	SAP 200 kg	Turbojet	60-80 km	Inertial & active radar homing	—
ISRAEL								
Gabriel III	4529.321	385 × 34 – 110 cm	600 kg	150 kg HE	Solid	60 km+	Inertial + radar homing	Israel
ITALY								
Marte	1651.321	470 × 21 – 100 cm	300 kg	70 kg HE	2-stage solid	20 km	C/LOS radar or optical	Italy

Designation	Entry no	Dimensions l x d – span	Weight	Warhead	Propulsion	Range	Guidance	Deployment
Italy cont Marte Mk 2	1651.321	448 × 31 – 98 cm	330 kg	HE	2-stage solid	20 km	Active radar homing	Development
JAPAN ASM-1	1653.311	—	—	140 kg HE	—	45 km	—	Production
NORWAY Penguin Mk 3	3070.311	318 × 28 – 100 cm	347 kg	120 kg HE	Solid	50 km+	Inertial + IR homing	Development
SWEDEN RB 05A	1190.311	360 × 30 – 80 cm	305 kg	—	Pre-packed liquid	—	Radio command	Sweden Production completed
RB 04E	1189.311	445 × 50 – 200 cm	600 kg	—	Solid	—	Autopilot cruise, active/passive radar homing	Swedish Air Force Production completed
RBS 15F	3975.321	435 × 50 – 140 cm	595 kg	—	Turbojet	150 km (est)	Autopilot+ active radar homing	Ordered for RSAF
RBS 70	4188.311	132 × 12 – 33 cm	15 kg	—	Solid	5 km	Laser beam-rider	Development
UNION OF SOVIET SOCIALIST REPUBLICS								
Kennel (AS1)	1148.311	c844 × – – 480 cm —	—	—	Turbojet	Up to 90 km	Beam riding or command cruise. Passive/active radar homing	Egypt & USSR
Kipper (AS-2)	1150.311	c1000 × 100 – 460 cm —	—	HE	Turbojet	200 km (est)	Programmed autopilot (optional command override) + terminal homing	USSR
Kangaroo (AS-3)	1147.311	1500 × 130 – 900 cm —	—	HE/Nuclear	Turbojet	—	Programmed autopilot + command option	USSR
Kitchen (AS-4)	1151.311	1130 × 95 cm	—	HE/Nuclear	Solid	300-800 km	Inertial + radar homing	USSR
Kelt (AS-5)	1149.311	859 × 430 cm (est)	—	c160 kg	Rocket	Up to 180 km	Autopilot + radar homing	USSR
Kingfish (AS-6)	3633.311	1050 × – 250 cm —	—	HE/Nuclear	Liquid	c200 km	Inertial + radar homing	USSR
Kerry (AS-7)	3634.311	Believed to arm Fencer strike aircraft						USSR
AS-8	3206.311	Provisional designation of new missile on Mi-24 helicopters						
AS-9	3206.311	Possibly anti-radiation missile on Su-19 Fencer aircraft						
AS-X-10	3206.311	Believed to be Mach 0·8 laser-guided weapon						
AS-X-11	3206.311	Possible Soviet equivalent to US Maverick						
AS-X-15	3206.311	Possible air-launched cruise missile development						
UNITED KINGDOM ALARM	4528.311	Anti-radiation missile development programme						RAF & RN late 1980s
Sea Eagle P3T	3630.321	410 × 40 – 120 cm	—	—	Turbojet	c100 km	Inertial + active radar homing	Production for RN & RAF
Sea Skua (CL 834)	1530.321	250 × 28 – 72 cm	145 kg	HE 20 kg	Solid	—	Programmed for command cruise. Semi-active radar homing	Production for RN
UNITED STATES OF AMERICA AGM-130	4190.311	Powered version of GBU-15						Development
ALCM (AGM-86B)	1766.311	630 × 365 cm span	c1270 kg	Nuclear	Turbofan	c2000 km	Inertial + TERCOM	USAF
Bullpup A (AGM-12B)	1280.311	320 × 31 – 95 cm	258 kg	113 kg HE	Pre-packed liquid	11 km	Radio command	NATO Obsolete

Designation	Entry no	Dimensions l x d – span	Weight	Warhead	Propulsion	Range	Guidance	Deployment
USA cont								
Bullpup B (AGM-12C)	1280.311	407 × 44 – 118 cm	812 kg	454 kg HE	Pre-packed liquid	17 km	Radio command	NATO Obsolete
Walleye 1 (AGM-62A)	1129.311	344 × 33 – 116 cm	499 kg	385 kg HE or W72 nuclear	None – guided bomb		TV homing	USAF, USN Obsolete
Walleye 11	1129.311	404 × 46 cm	1061 kg	709 kg HE	None – guided bomb		TV homing	Production for USN
GBU-15(V)	4190.311	Family of guided glide bombs. Various configurations, guidance techniques & payloads						
HVM	4448.311	Hyper velocity missile project						Development
Shrike (AGM-45A)	1102.311	305 × 20 – 91 cm	177 kg	HE	Solid	12-16 km	Radar radiation homing	USAF, USN & some other countries
Maverick (AGM-65)	1098.311	246 × 30 – 71 cm	209 kg	59 kg HE	2-stage solid	—	TV, laser homing, IIR, & scene magnification versions	USA, Greece, Iran, Israel, Saudi Arabia, South Korea, Sweden, Turkey
HARM (AGM-88A)	1769.311	416 × 25 – 113 cm	354 kg	65 kg HE	Solid	20 km+	Anti-radiation homing	Production
Harpoon (AGM-84A)	1301.311	384 × 34 – 91 cm	522 kg	230 kg HE	Turbojet	110 km	Radar homing	Production for USN
Hellfire	1391.311	178 × 18 – 33 cm	43 kg	Solid	—	—	Laser homing	Production for US Army
HOBO(Homing Bombs)	1597.311	Add-on guidance packages for Mk 84 (2000 lb) & Mk 118 (3000 lb) bombs					TV homing	US forces
LAD	4530.311	Modular stand-off ground attack weapon						Development
Paveway (Laser Guided Bombs)	1534.311	Add-on guidance packages for Mk 82 (500 lb), Mk 84 (2000 lb), Mk 117 (750 lb) Mk 118 (3000 lb) demolition, & Mk 20 Mod 2 (Rockeye) cluster bombs					Laser homing	US forces, Australia, Greece, Netherlands, Saudi Arabia, S Korea, Taiwan, Thailand, UK
SRAM (AGM-69A)	1107.311	425 × 45 cm	1000 kg	Nuclear	Solid	60-160 km	Inertial	USAF
Standard ARM (AGM-78B)	1123.311	457 × 34 cm	635 kg	HE	Dual thrust solid	25 km +	Passive radar homing	US forces
TOW	2831.311	116 × 15 cm	19 kg	HE shaped charge	Solid	3750 km	Wire-guided	US & other forces
Wasp	3637.311	152 × – 51 cm span	Anti-armour miniature missile					Development for WAAM programme

1850.314   Air-to-surface Tactical Munitions

Designation	Entry no	Dimensions l x d	Weight	Description
ARGENTINA				
Aircraft rockets				
CBAS-1	3806.303	— × 7 cm	8·7 kg	General purpose rocket
BRAZIL				
Free fall bombs				
AV-BAFG-120	4145.303	—	113 kg	250 lb low-drag general purpose. Equiv to US Mk 81
AV-BAFG-250	4145.303	—	226 kg	500 lb low-drag general purpose. Equiv to US Mk 82
AV-BI-200	4145.303	—	180 kg	400 lb napalm bomb
AV-BI-250	4145.303	—	226 kg	500 lb napalm bomb. Equiv to US BLU-32
AV-BI-375	4145.303	—	340 kg	750 lb napalm bomb. Equiv to US BLU-27
Aircraft rockets				
SBAT-37	4145.303	—	—	37 mm spin stabilised general purpose
SBAT-70	4145.303	—	—	70 mm non -spinning (M1) & spin-stabilised (M2)
SBAT-127	4145.303	—	—	127 mm general purpose
CANADA				
Aircraft rockets				
CRV7	4539.303	104 × 7 cm	11 kg	General purpose

Designation	Entry no	Dimensions l x d	Weight	Description
CHILE				
Free fall bombs				
Cardoen	**4488.303**	—	—	General purpose. 250, 500 & 1000 lb categories
Cluster bombs				
Cardoen	**4487.303**	—	—	500 and 130 lb class cluster bombs
FRANCE				
Free fall bombs				
AN-52	—			Tactical nuclear bomb 15 KT warhead
BL 4	**5214.303**	350 × 46 cm	1000 kg	General purpose
BL 5	**5214.303**	132 × 18 cm	50 kg	General purpose
BL 6	**5214.303**	177 × 23 cm	118 kg	General purpose
BL 7	**5214.303**	166 × 23 cm	115 kg	General purpose for SF 260 aircraft
BL 8	**5215.303**	158 × 19 cm	120 kg	Fragmentation
BL 9	**5215.303**	138 × 19 cm	120 kg	Fragmentation
BL 18	**5215.303**	180 × 19 cm	125 kg	Fragmentation
EU 2	**5214.303**	225 × 27 cm	250 kg	General purpose
EU 3	**5214.303**	285 × 36 cm	452 kg	General purpose
SAMP 25	**5214.303**	212 × 32 cm	247 kg	General purpose
T 15	**5215.303**	75 × 12 cm	15 kg	Fragmentation
T 200	**5214.303**	219 × 40 cm	345 kg	General purpose
Retarded bombs				
BAT 120	**3863.303**	149 × 12 cm	34 kg	Parachute retarded
Durandal	**1999.303**	270 × 22 cm	195 kg	Penetration bomb. Parachute retarded, rocket assisted
Matra Type 200	**1514.393**	—	250 & 400 kg	Used on French & German (FR) aircraft. Tail parachute retarder
TSB	**3152.303**	175 × 10 cm	—	Parachute retarded. Rocked assisted penetration
Cluster bombs and area weapons				
Belouga (BLG 66)	**3150.303**	330 × 58 cm	290 kg	151 bomblets, AT, penetration, or blast
Giboulee	**1509.393**	385 × — cm	490 kg	Bomblet dispenser. 12 or 14 tubes for 60 or 120 0·7 kg anti-personnel or A/T bomblets
Module Bomb	**3865.303**	320 × 32 cm	390 kg	Low level weapon for high value battlefield targets. 2 or 3 modules for 250 kg or 400 kg close bombs
TSB (BAP 100)	**3152.303**	175 × 10 cm	320-710 kg	Tactical support bomb. Penetration or blast cluster
INTERNATIONAL				
Retarded bombs				
LU250 EG-FT	**4541.303**	216 × 27 cm	254 kg	'Ballute' retarder tail
ISRAEL				
Cluster bombs				
TAL 1/2	**4428.303**	234 × 41 cm	250 kg	279 bomblets
SPAIN				
Free fall bombs				
EXPAL	**5244.303**	382 × 46 cm	1000 kg	General purpose, low-drag bombs
		294 × 36 cm	500 kg	
		280 × 33 cm	375 kg	
		215 × 29 cm	250 kg	
		182 × 24 cm	125 kg	
		139 × 18 cm	50 kg	
Retarded bombs				
BRFA	**5207.303**	300 × — cm	330 kg	Parachute retarded. Rocket assisted penetration
EXPAL BRP	**5245.303**	300 × 36 cm	500 kg	Range of low-drag parachute retarded bombs
		285 × 33 cm	375 kg	
		228 × 29 cm	250 kg	
		142 × 18 cm	50 kg	
SWEDEN				
Bombs				
M50 MB	**5224.303**	—	600 kg	HE bomb
M50 SB	**5224.303**	—	250 kg	HE bomb
M51 SB	**5224.303**	—	120 kg	HE bomb
M56 MB	**5224.303**	—	500 kg	HE bomb
M60 LYSB	**5224.303**	—	80 kg	HE fragmentation bomb
M62	**5224.303**	—	75 kg	Flash bomb
Virgo	**7514.393**	158 × 21 cm	123 kg	Used on Lansen, Draken and Viggen. Retarded version also Fragmentation
UNION OF SOVIET SOCIALIST REPUBLICS				
Free fall bombs				
FAB-100	—	—	100 kg	GPLD-HE
FAB-250	—	—	250 kg	GPLD-HE
FAB-500	—	—	500 kg	GPLD-HE
FAB-750	—	—	750 kg	GPLD-HE
FAB-1000	—	—	1000 kg	GPLD-HE
OFAB-250	—	—	250 kg	GPLD-HE/fragmentation
OFAB-500	—	—	500 kg	GPLD-HE/fragmentation
(The above are new series bombs, replacing the older wide-body types: FAB-8, -10, -15, -25, -50, -110, -500 and 1000)				
ZAB-100	—	—	100 kg	LD incendiary bomb
ZAB-250	—	—	250 kg	LD incendiary bomb
ZAB-500	—	—	500 kg	LD incendiary bomb
ZAB-750	—	—	750 kg	LD incendiary bomb
ZAP-200	—	—	200 kg	Incendiary container
(Demolition bombs exist in 100, 250, 750 & 1100 kg models)				
Retarded bombs				
BETAB-250	—	—	250 kg	Boosted concrete demolition bomb

Designation	Entry no	Dimensions l x d	Weight	Description
USSR cont				
BETAB-500	—	—	500 kg	Boosted concrete demolition bomb
M62	3181.303	—	500 kg	Penetration bomb. 250 kg version also
Cluster bombs and area weapons				
—	3181.303	·	—	Range of cluster bombs with incendiary, HE, HEI, Frag & AT bomblets
PTAB-2	—	·	—	Anti-tank bombs using hollow-charge sub-munitions, superseded by PTK-250
PTAB-5	—	—	—	
PTAB-5/1	—	—	—	
PTK-250	—	—	250 kg	LD cluster bomb with shaped-charge A/T projectiles
RPK-180	—	—	180 kg	LD fragmentation cluster bomb
RPK-250	—	—	250 kg	LD fragmentation cluster bomb
RRAB	—	—	—	Thin-walled cluster bomb with incendiary agent
Chemical munitions				
Old series				
AK-2	—	—	250 kg	In-line dispenser for 240 1 kg bomblets filled with mustard-lewisite mixture
CHAB-505	—	—	500 kg	M1942 bomb carrying 180 kg of phosgene
VAP-200	—	—	200 kg	Container for persistent Toxic-B agents
VAP-1000 (BATT)	—	—	1000 kg	Dispenser with 700 litres of stabilised hydrogen-cyanide: 4 per aircraft for low-altitude operations
New series				
PLAB-250	—	—	250 kg	LD napalm bomb
PLAB-500	—	—	500 kg	LD napalm bomb
VAP	—	—	—	Various models of dispenser for persistent toxic-B agents
SOV-AB	—	—	—	Various models. Persistent toxic chemical bombs
NOV-AB	—	—	—	Various models. Non-persistent toxic chemical bombs
FAE	—	—	—	Fuel/air explosive boosted napalm bombs. Introduced 1974-75
Rocket projectiles				
Old series				
ARS-212	—	—	—	212 mm, various models
RS-82	—	—	—	82 mm, M1938
RBS-82	—	—	—	82 mm, M1941
RS-132	—	—	—	132 mm, M1939
RS-132A	—	—	—	132 mm
ROFS-132	—	—	—	132 mm boosted M1941
TRS-190	—	—	—	190 mm, various models
S-5K/S-5MK	—	—	—	57 mm shaped-charge rocket used with UB8, UB16, UB19 & UB32 pods
S-8	—	—	—	80 mm rocket
S-13	—	—	—	130 mm rocket
S-16	—	—	—	160 mm rocket
S-21/S-21M	—	—	—	210 mm rocket, some models with limited visual guidance capability
S-28	—	—	—	280 mm rocket
S-32/S-32M	—	—	—	325 mm rocket, some models with limited visual guidance capability
S-24	—	—	—	240 mm rocket M1976
Miscellaneous				
DAP	—	—	—	Various models. Dispensers for smoke screening agents
DV-AB	—	—	—	Various models. Smoke bomb
FOTAB-250	—	—	250 kg	Photo-flash bomb
PROSAB-250	—	—	250 kg	Parachute flare. Several models
Nuclear munitions				
Bombs	—	—	—	Soviet tactical & stragetic nuclear bombs are stated to be consistently of higher yields than otherwise comparable American weapons. The standard tactical nuclear bomb weighs 1000 kg & has a yield estimated at 350 KT. This is being superseded by a bomb of about 700 kg with a yield of some 250 KT. These weapons may be deployed on Su-17 Fitter A/C/D, MiG-23 Flogger, MiG-27 Flogger D, Su-19 Fencer A, Yak-28 Brewer, MiG-21 Fishbed J/K/L/N, Tu-16 Badger, Tu-22 Blinder & the Tu-26 Backfire. Strategic weapons include bombs of 5, 20, & 50 MT yield carried by Mya A-4 Bison, Tu-20 Bear & the smaller yield strategic bombs on the Tu-16, Tu-22 & Tu-26 also. Nuclear depth bombs are carried by the Tu-20 Bear F, Il-38 May, Be-12 Mail, Ka-25 Hormone A and Mi-14 Haze A on ASW duties.
UNITED KINGDOM				
Free fall bombs				
Mk 1/2	—	—	245 kg	Various aircraft. Battlefield targets
Mk 2	—	—	453 kg	Various aircraft. Battlefield & medium tactical targets
Mk 6	—	—	453 kg	Various aircraft. Battlefield & medium tactical targets
Mk 6*	—	—	453 kg	Various aircraft. Battlefield & medium tactical targets
Mk 7	—	—	453 kg	Various aircraft. Battlefield & medium tactical targets
Mk 7*	—	—	453 kg	Various aircraft. Battlefield & medium tactical targets
Mk 9	—	—	453 kg	Various aircraft. Battlefield & medium tactical targets
Mk 10	—	—	453 kg	Various aircraft. Battlefield & medium tactical targets
Mk 11	—	—	453 kg	Various aircraft. Battlefield & medium tactical targets
Mk 11*	—	—	453 kg	Various aircraft. Battlefield & medium tactical targets
Mk 12*	—	—	453 kg	Various aircraft. Battlefield & medium tactical targets
Mk 13-16	—	—	453 kg	Various aircraft. Battlefield & medium tactical targets
Mk 19	—	—	453 kg	Various aircraft. Battlefield & medium tactical targets

*(Note: Most or all of the above types of bomb can be converted for retarded fall by fitting either Mk 3 or 4 retarder tail type 117, or retarder tail Type 118, See entry no. **1267.393**)

Designation	Entry no	Dimensions l x d	Weight	Description
JP 233	5218.303	—	—	Runway cratering weapon.
Type 117	1267.393	—	453 kg	British Type 117 bomb retarder tails Mk 3 or Mk 4 can be fitted to 1000 lb class UK bombs Mk 6 & Mks 9-19 & US Mk 83, M65, M117
Type 118	1267.393	—	—	British Type 118 bomb retarder tails can be fitted to UK Mk 1/2 & US M64 bombs

Designation	Entry no	Dimensions l x d	Weight	Description
UK cont				
Cluster bombs and area weapons				
BL 755	**1277.303**	245 × 42 cm	277 kg	600 lb bomb No 1 Mk 1. Used by UK & other NATO countries 147 bomblets. Mk 2: shorter delays, Mk 3: 250 mm lugs, Mk 4: 250 mm lugs and Mk 2 delays
UNITED STATES OF AMERICA				
Free fall bombs				
AN-M4A2	—	—	—	Cluster, fragmentation bomb, 100 lb (3 × M40A1)
AN-M30A1	—	—	—	Bomb, GP, 100 lb
AN-M41A1/M41A2	—	—	—	Bomb, fragmentation, 20 lb
AN-M46	—	—	—	Bomb, photoflash, 100 lb
AN-M47A2	—	—	—	Bomb, incendiary, 100 lb
AN-M47A3/M47A4	—	—	—	Bomb, indendiary, 100 lb filling, 40 lb incendiary gel
AN-M47A3/M47A4	—	—	—	Bomb, smoke, 100 lb, filling is 74 lb plasticised WP or 100 lb of WP respectively
AN-M50A2/M50A3	—	—	—	Bomb, incendiary, 4 lb filling 0·6 lb magnesium thermite
AN-M50T A2	—	—	—	Bomb, incendiary 4 lb
AN-M50T X-A3	—	—	—	Bomb, incendiary 4lb
AN-M56A2	—	—	—	Bomb, light case 4000 lb
AN-M57/M57A1	—	—	—	Bomb, GP, 250 lb
AN-M58A2	—	—	—	Bomb, SAP, 500 lb
AN-M59/M59A1/ M59A2	—	—	—	Bomb, SAP, 1000 lb
AN-M64/M64A1	—	—	—	Bomb, GP, 500 lb
AN-M65A1	—	—	—	Bomb, GP, 1000 lb
AN-M66A1/M66A2	—	—	—	Bomb, GP, 2000 lb
AN-M69A1	—	—	—	Bomb, incendiary, 6 lb
AN-M76	—	—	—	Bomb, incendiary, 500 lb, filling 180 lb gasoline and magnesium
AN-M78	—	—	—	Bomb, gas non-persistent, 500 lb
AN-M79	—	—	—	Bomb, gas non-persistent, 1000 lb (various fillings, AC, CK or CG)
AN-M81	—	—	—	Bomb, fragmentation, 260 lb
AN-M88	—	—	—	Bomb, fragmentation, 220 lb
AN-Mk 1 Mod 1/1/3	—	—	—	Bomb, AP, 1600 lb
AN-Mk 23 Mod 1	—	—	—	Bomb, practice miniature, 3 lb
AN-Mk 33	—	—	—	Bomb, AP, 1000 lb
AN-Mk 41	—	—	—	Bomb, depth, 325 lb
AN-Mk 43 Mod 1	—	—	—	Bomb, practice miniature, 3 lb
AN-Mk 47A1	—	—	—	Bomb, GP, 1000 lb
AN-Mk 54	—	—	—	Bomb, depth, 300 lb
AN-Mk 58A2	—	—	—	Bomb, SAP, 500 lb
BDU-27/B	—	—	—	Bomb, fragmentation dummy
BDU-28/B	—	—	—	Bomb, fragmentation dummy
BDU-30B	—	—	—	Bomb, practice
BDU-33B/33A/B	—	—	—	Bomb, practice, 25 lb
BDU-34/B	—	—	—	Bomb, practice
BDU/37B	—	—	—	Bomb, practice
BLU-1/1B/B/1C/B	—	—	—	Bomb, fire, 750 lb, filling 90-100 galls napalm
BLU-3	—	—	0·79 kg	Bomblet, fragmentation anti-materiel. Cylindrical pop-out drag vanes. 0·16 kg cyclotrol filling projecting 250 steel pellets. Called 'Pineapple'
BLU-4	—	—	0·54 kg	Bomblet, anti-materiel, containing spherical fragmentation unit that ejects to height of 3 m on impact & then explodes
BLU-6	—	—	—	Bomb, smoke. Sphere used for payload of TMU 10 smoke tank
BLU-7B/-7A/B	—	—	0·64 kg	Bomblet, anti-tank. Parachute armed & stabilised shaped charge
BLU-7A(D-1)/B	—	—	—	Bomb, anti-tank, dummy
BLU-10A/B/10/B	—	—	—	Bomb, fire, 250 lb, filling 33 galls of napalm
BLU-11/B	—	—	—	Bomb, fire, 500 lb, filling 65 galls of napalm
BLU-14	—	—	—	Bomb, modified MLU-10 for low-level penetration skip bombing
BLU-15	—	—	—	Anti-materiel weapon
BLU-16/B	—	—	0·73 kg	Bomb, smoke. Cylindrical, modified M8 grenade with HC fitting
BLU-17/B	—	—	0·5 kg	Bomb, smoke. Cylindrical, modified M15 grenade with WP filling
BLU-18/B	—	—	0·19 kg	Bomb, fragmentation anti-personnel. Triangular shaped with delay fuze
BLU-19/B23	—	—	—	Bomb, chemical. Explosive burst with GB nerve gas filling
BLU-20/B23	—	—	—	Bomb, chemical. Parachute retarded. Thermal generator for B2 incapacitant gas
BLU-21/B45	—	—	—	Bomb, dry biological agent
BLU-22/B45	—	—	—	Bomb, wet biological agent
BLU-23/B	—	—	—	Bomb, fire, 500 lb, filling 67 galls of napalm
BLU-24/B/24 A/B	—	—	0·73 kg	Bomb, fragmentation, anti-personnel. Spherical with plastic fins & spin delay fuze. Cyclotrol filling. Known as 'Orange'
BLU-25/B	—	—	—	Bomblet, anti-personnel. Cylindrical
BLU-26/B	—	—	0·43 kg	Bomb, fragmentation, anti-personnel/anti-materiel (APAM). 6 cm sphere with varied surface and cyclotrol A3 filling. Detonates on impact throwing out c300 steel pellets. Known as 'Guava'
BLU-27B	—	—	—	Bomb, fire, 750 lb, filling 100 galls napalm B
BLU-28/B	—	—	—	Bomb, containing self-dispersing biological agent
BLU-29/B	—	—	73 kg	Bomb, anti-personnel & anti-materiel (APAM); flame agent canister
BLU-30/B	—	—	—	Bomb, dry chemical agent
BLU-31/B	—	—	—	Bomb, demolition, 750 lb (improved version of MLU-10 land mine with new seismic and acoustic sensor tuned to tanks)
BLU-32/B	—	—	—	Bomb, fire, 500 lb, filling 67 galls of napalm B
BLU-32A/B	—	—	—	Bomb, fire, 595 lb
BLU-33/B	—	—	—	Bomb, demolition, 1500 lb
BLU-34/B	—	—	—	Bomb, demolition, 3000 lb, for hard surface structures
BLU-35/B	—	—	—	Bomb, fire, 250 lb. Modular dispenses 140 kg napalm
BLU-36/B	—	—	0·43 kg	Bomblet APAM, fitted with random relay fuze
BLU-39/B23	—	—	—	Bomb, chemical dummy

Designation	Entry no	Dimensions l x d	Weight	Description
USA cont				
BLU-39 (XM16)	—	—	0·08 kg	Bomblet, chemical. Cylindrical with CS filling that burns as bomb bounces over terrain
BLU-40/B	—	—	0·78 kg	Bomb, fragmentation. Random delay fuze
BLU-41/B	—	—	—	Bomb, fragmentation. Spherical with spin arming & spin delay fuze
BLU-42/B	—	—	—	Mine, anti-personnel. Spherical with varied surface & trip-wired sensors Fitted with anti-disturbance device & self-destruct detonator & fitted with 0·12 kg composition B
BLU-43/B	—	—	0·02 kg	Mine, anti-personnel. Triangular blast mine. Called 'Short Dragontooth'
BLU-44/B	—	—	0·02 kg	Mine, anti-personnel. Triangular blast mine. Called 'Long Dragontooth'
BLU-45/B	—	—	9·1 kg	Mine, land anti-tank. Shaped charge with timed self-destruct
BLU-46/B	—	—	—	Bomb, anti-personnel
BLU-47/B	—	—	—	Bomb, general purpose
BLU-48/B	—	—	—	Bomb, fragmentation. Spherical
BLU-49/B	—	—	6·1 kg	Bomb, fragmentation, cyclotrol 70/30 filling. Ring tail fitted
BLU-50/B	—	—	—	Bomb, chemical, BZ incapacitant gas filling
BLU-51/B	—	—	—	Bomb, fire
BLU-52/B	—	—	—	Bomb, chemical, 700 lb, filling 615 lb of CS gas
BLU-53/B	—	—	9 kg	Bomb, fire. Canister with napalm B filling
BLU-54/B	—	—	—	Mine, anti-personnel. Identical to BLU-42/B but fitted long-life self-destruct timer
BLU-55/B	—	—	—	Mine, anti-personnel
BLU-56/B	—	—	—	Mine, anti-personnel
BLU-57/B	—	—	230 kg	Bomb, fragmentation
BLU-58/B	—	—	230 kg	Bomb, general purpose
BLU-59/B	—	—	0·43 kg	Bomb, fragmentation. Identical to BLU-26 but fitted with shorter random delay fuze.
BLU-60/B	—	—	5·9 kg	Bomb, fragmentation, cyclotrol filling
BLU-61/B	—	—	1 kg	Bomb, fragmentation-incendiary/anti-materiel. Spherical, zirconium/composition B filling
BLU-62/B	—	—	0·43 kg	Bomb, fragmentation APAM, fitted with bounding fragmentation unit & filled with cyclotrol
BLU-63/B	—	—	0·43 kg	Bomb, fragmentation APAM. Spherical scored steel case, spin & impact fuze. Cyclotrol filling
BLU-64/B	—	—	350 kg	Bomb, general purpose FAE, filled with 200 kg hydrocarbon fuel. Combat tested 1967-68 but not adopted for service
BLU-65/B	—	—	—	Bomb, fire, 280 lb
BLU-66/B	—	—	0·73 kg	Bomb, anti-personnel, spherical with plastic tail fins (known as Pineapple)
BLU-67/B	—	—	5 kg	Bomb, cratering
BLU-68/B	—	—	0·42 kg	Bomb, incendiary APAM. Spherical with zirconium sponge filling
BLU-69/B	—	—	0·73 kg	Bomb, incendiary APAM. Spherical
BLU-70/B	—	—	0·4 kg	Bomb, incendiary APAM. Spherical
BLU-71/B	—	—	—	Mine, land
BLU-72/B	—	—	1100 kg	Bomb, FAE, low speed version with retarding drogue chute. 450 kg propane fuel filling. Known as Pave Pat I. Combat tested 1967-68 but not put into service
BLU-73/B	—	—	60 kg	Bomb, FAE. Drogue chute retarded canister containing 33 kg ethylene oxide fuel & fitted with long probe to detonate unit above ground surface
BLU 74/B	—	—	107 kg	Bomb, fire, modular. Napalm B filling
BLU-75/B	—	—	—	Bomb, fire
BLU-76/B	—	—	1200 kg	Bomb, FAE, high speed version but with low speed delivery capability of BLU-72. Known as Pave Pat II.
BLU-77/B	—	—	—	Bomblet, anti-tank fragmentation, APAM with ability to discriminate between hard & soft targets. Fitted with shaped charge that can act as bounding fragmentation unit against personnel
BLU-80	—	—	—	(also known as Bigeye)
BLU-81/B	—	—	—	Mine, anti-vehicle, known as 'Grasshopper'. Cancelled
BLU-82/B	—	—	—	Bomb, GP, 15 000 lb
BLU-82/B	—	—	6800 kg	Bomb, blast, container filled with 5715 kg of gelled slurry blast explosive GSX. 97 cm nose probe to detonate bomb above ground surface. Known as 'Big Blue 82'
BLU-86A/B	—	—	0·45 kg	Bomb, fragmentation, steel case with composition B or cyclotrol filling
BLU-87(D-1)/B	—	—	—	Dummy fragmentation bomb
BLU-87(T-1)/B	—	—	—	Training fragmentation bomb
BLU-89/B	—	—	—	Bomb, GP, blast & fragmentation
BLU-90/B	—	—	—	Bomb, GP, fragmentation case with shaped charge penetration device
BLU-91/B	—	—	—	Mine, anti-tank, Gator
BLU-92/B	—	—	—	Mine, anti-personnel, Gator
BLU-93	—	—	—	No information
BLU-94/B	—	—	—	Mine, riverine/shallow water, anti-ship/anti-tank. Pressure/seismic/magnetic detonation
Briteye	—	—	—	Flare, 5000 candlepower
Bigeye	—	—	—	Bomb, chemical
Deneye	—	—	—	Mine, land
Fireye	—	—	—	Bomb, fire, also known as Mk 122
Gladeye	—	—	—	Bomb
Misteye	—	—	—	Bomb, flare
Weteye	—	—	—	Bomb, chemical, also known as Mk 116
M38A2	—	—	—	Bomb, practice, 100 lb
M40A1	—	—	—	Bomb, Bomb, fragmentation, 23 lb
M42	—	—	—	Grenade, anti-tank/anti-personnel. Ribbon stabilised shaped charge with sideways fragmentation burst able to penetrate 100 mm armour
M47	—	—	—	Bomb, incendiary, 100 lb
M52A1	—	—	—	Bomb, AP, 1000 lb
M69X	—	—	—	Bomb, incendiary, 6 lb
M70/M70A1	—	—	—	Bomb, gas, persistent mustard gas or mustard gas gel re-agent, 115 lb
M74/M74A1	—	—	—	Bomb, incendiary, 10 lb
M82	—	—	—	Bomb, fragmentation, 90 lb

Designation	Entry no	Dimensions l x d	Weight	Description
USA cont				
M83	—	—	—	Bomb, fragmentation, 4 lb (also known as Butterfly bomb)
M84A1	—	—	—	Bomb, target identification, 100 lb
M86	—	—	—	Bomb, fragmentation, 120 lb
M103	—	—	—	Bomb, SAP, 2000 lb
M104	—	—	—	Bomb, leaflet, 100 lb
M105	—	—	—	Bomb, leaflet, 500 lb
M109	—	—	—	Bomb, GP, 12 000 lb
M110	—	—	—	Bomb, GP, 22 000 lb
M113	—	—	—	Bomb, gas persistent, 125 lb
M116	—	—	—	Bomb, fire, 750 lb, filling 80 galls napalm or thickened fuel
M116AA1/A23	—	—	—	Bomb, fire, 750 lb, filling 100 galls napalm or thickened fuel
M117/A1/A1E2	—	—	—	Bomb, GP, 750 lb
M117D	—	—	—	Destructor bomb, high drag, GP (M117 with tail retarding device)
M118E2	—	—	—	Bomb, GP, 3000 lb
M120/M120A1	—	—	—	Bomb, photoflash, 150 lb
M121	—	—	—	Bomb, GP, 10 000 lb
M122	—	—	—	Bomb, photoflash, 100 lb
M124	—	—	—	Bomb, practice, 250 lb
M125A1	—	—	—	Bomb, gas non-persistent, 10 lb (filled with 2·6 lb of GB)
M126	—	—	—	Bomb, incendiary, 4 lb
M129/M129E1/				
M129E2	—	—	—	Bomb, leaflet, 750 lb
MC1	—	—	—	Bomb, gas non-persistent, 750 lb (filling 220 lb of GB)
Mk 1	—	—	—	Bomb, demolition, 2000 lb
Mk 111	—	—	—	Bomb, demolition, 1000 lb
Mk 5 Mods 2 & 3	—	—	—	Bomb, practice miniature, 3 lb
Mk 12	—	—	270 kg	Dispenser 'Padeye' with smoke or BZ incapacitant agent
Mk 15 Mod 2, 3 & 4	—	—	—	Bomb, practice, 100 lb
Mk 17	—	—	—	Dispenser Mk 4 Gladeye with 7 bomblet canisters
Mk 21	—	—	370 kg	Dispenser Mk 5 Sadeye
Mk 22	—	—	370 kg	Dispenser Mk 5 Sadeye
Mk 25	—	—	—	Sea mine, 2000 lb
Mk 36	—	—	—	Sea mine, 1000 lb
Mk 36	—	—	—	Destructor bomb demolition. In Mk 82 fitted with Snakeye Mk 15 tail retarding device & acoustic, seismic & IR detectors to detonate the weapon at approach of vehicle
Mk 39	—	—	—	Sea mine, 2000 lb
Mk 40	—	—	—	Sea mine, 2000 lb
Mk 44	—	—	—	Missile cluster, 550 lb. M16 cluster adaptor with c10 000 'Lazy Dog' shaped iron fragments
Mk 50	—	—	—	Sea mine, 500 lb
Mk 52	—	—	—	Sea mine, 1000 lb
Mk 53	—	—	—	Sea mine, 500 lb
Mk 55	—	—	—	Sea mine, 2000 lb
Mk 56	—	—	—	Sea mine, 2000 lb
Mk 65 Mod 0	—	—	—	Bomb, practice, 500 lb
Mk 66 Mod 0	—	—	—	Bomb, practice, 1000 lb
Mk 76	—	—	—	Bomb, practice, 25 lb
MK 77 Mod 0	—	—	—	Bomb, fire, 750 lb (filling 110 galls gasoline oil)
Mk 77 Mod 1	—	—	—	Bomb, fire, 500 lb (filling 75 galls gasoline oil)
Mk 78 Mods 0, 1 & 2	—	—	—	Bomb, fire, 750 lb (filling 110 galls gasoline oil)
Mk 79 Mod 1	—	—	—	Bomb, fire, 1000 lb (filling 112 galls napalm-gasoline)
Mk 81 Mod 0 & 1	—	—	—	Bomb, 'Slick' low drag, GP, 250 lb
Mk 81 Mod 1	—	—	—	Snakeye bomb, high drag, GP, 150 lb (Mk 81 fitted with Mk 114 tail retarding device)
Mk 82 Mod 0 & 1	—	—	—	Bomb, 'Slick' low drag, GP, 500 lb
Mk 82 Mod 1	—	—	—	Snakeye bomb, high drag, GP, 560 lb (Mk 82 fitted with Mk 15 tail retarding device)
Mk 83 Mod 2 & 3	—	—	—	Bomb, 'Slick' low drag, GP, 1000 lb
Mk 83	—	—	—	Destructor, high drag, GP, 1000 lb (Mk 83 fitted with MAU-91A/B)
Mk 84 Mod 0 & 1	—	—	—	Bomb, 'Slick' low drag, GP, 1970 lb
Mk 86 Mod 0 & 1	—	—	—	Bomb, practice, 250 lb
Mk 87 Mod 0	—	—	—	Bomb, practice, 500 lb
Mk 88 Mod 0	—	—	—	Bomb, practice, 1000 lb
Mk 89 Mod 0 & 1	—	—	—	Bomb, practice, 56 lb
Mk 94 Mod 0	—	—	—	Gas non-persistent, 500 lb (filling is 108 lb of GB)
Mk 106 Mod 0	—	—	—	Bomb, practice, 5 lb
Mk 116 Mod 0	—	—	—	Bomb, chemical, 750 lb (also known as Weteye, filled with 403 lb of GB)
Mk 122	—	—	—	Bomb, fire (also known as Fireye)
Cluster bombs and area weapons				
AN-M1A1/M1A2	—	—	—	Cluster, fragmentation bomb, 100 lb (6 × AN-M41A1)
AN-M1A3/M1A4	—	—	—	Cluster, fragmentation bomb, 100 lb (6 × AN-M41A2)
AN-M4	—	—	—	Cluster, fragmentation bomb, 1000 lb (3 × M40)
CBU-1	—	—	—	Dispenser SUU-7 and 509 × BLU-4 anti-personnel bomblets
CBU-2/A	—	—	—	Dispenser SUU-7 & 360 × BLU-3 anti-materiel bomblets
CBU-2B/A	—	—	—	Dispenser SUU-7 & 409 × BLU-3 anti-materiel bomblets
CBU-3/A	—	—	300 kg	Dispenser SUU-10/A & 352 × BLU-7A/B bomblets
CBU-3A/A	—	—	300 kg	Dispenser SUU-10A/A & 352 × BLU-7A bomblets
CBU-3B/A	—	—	300 kg	Dispenser SUU-10B/A & 371 × BLU-7A/B bomblets
CBU-5	—	—	—	M30 cluster adaptor with 57 × M138 BZ incapacitant gas bomblets
CBU-6	—	—	—	Redesignated CBU-13/A
CBU-7/A	—	—	—	Dispenser SUU-31/A & 1200 × BLU-18/B bomblets

Designation	Entry no	Dimensions l x d	Weight	Description
USA cont				
CBU-8/A	—	—	390 kg	Dispenser SUU-7A/A & 409 BDU-27/B spotting charges
CBU-9/A	—	—	390 kg	Dispenser SUU-7A/A & 406 BDU-28/B dummy bombs
CBU-9A/A	—	—	390 kg	Dispenser SUU-7B/A & 406 BDU-28/B dummy bombs
CBU-10	—	—	—	Dispenser SUU-7. No other details
CBU-11/A	—	—	—	Dispenser SUU-7B/A & 261 BLU-16/B smoke bombs
CBU-12/A	—	—	290 kg	Dispenser SUU-7B/A & 261 BLU-17/B smoke bombs
CBU-12A/A	—	—	290 kg	Dispenser SUU-7C/A & 261 BLU-17B smoke bombs
CBU-13/A	—	—	—	Dispenser SUU-7C/A & 261 BLU-16B & BLU 17-B smoke bombs
CBU-14/A	—	—	—	Dispenser SUU-7B/A & BLU-3/B bombs
CBU-14/A/A	—	—	—	Dispenser SUU-14A/A & BLU-3/B bombs
CBU-15/A	—	—	—	Dispenser SUU-13/A for BLU-19 GB nerve gas bomblets
CBU-16/A	—	—	—	Dispenser SUU-13/A for CDU-9 BZ incapacitant gas cluster
CBU-16A/A	—	—	—	Dispenser SUU-13/A for CDU-9 BZ incapacitant gas cluster
CBU-17/A	—	—	—	Dispenser SUU-13/A & 1200 BLU-34/B practice bomblets
CBU-18/A	—	—	—	Dispenser SUU-13A/A & BLU-25/B anti-personnel bomblet
CBU-19	—	—	—	Twin strongback dispenser with 16 modules each containing 33 BLU-39 bomblets
CBU-22/A	—	—	—	Dispenser SUU-14/A & 72 BLU-17/B smoke bombs
CBU-23/B	—	—	—	Dispenser SUU-31/B & BLU-26/B fragmentation bombs
CBU-24/A	—	—	—	Dispenser SUU-14/A & BLU 24/B fragmentation bombs
CBU-24/B	—	—	—	Dispenser SUU-30/B & 670 BLU-26/B or 670 BLU-36/B fragmentation bombs
CBU-25	—	—	—	Dispenser SUU-14 & BLU-24 bomblets
CBU-26/A	—	—	—	Dispenser SUU-10/A & 352 BDU-37/B dummy fragmentation bombs
CBU-27	—	—	—	Unfilled canister for Type 2 bomblet dispenser, becomes ADU or CDU when filled
CBU-28	—	—	—	Dispenser SUU-13 for 40 × CDU-2 clusters each of 120 × BLU-43 mines
CBU-29/B	—	—	380 kg	Dispenser SUU-30/B & 670 BLU-36/B fragmentation bomblets
CBU-30	—	—	—	Dispenser SUU-13 & 40 × CDU-12 clusters each of 30 × BLU-39 CS incapacitant gas bomblets
CBU-33/A	—	—	350 kg	Dispenser SUU-36/A & 30 BLU-45/B land mines
CBU-34/A	—	—	—	Dispenser SUU-38/A for 10 × CDU-18 or CDU-19 clusters each of 54 × BLU-42 anti-personnel mines
CBU-37/A	—	—	—	Dispenser SUU-13/A for 40 × CDU-3 clusters each of 120 × BLU-44 anti-personnel mines
CBU-38/A	—	—	—	Dispenser SUU-13/A & 40 × BLU-49/B fragmentation bombs
CBU-41/B	—	—	220 kg	Dispenser SUU-51 for 18 × BLU-53 napalm B canisters. Fire bomb cluster
CBU-42/A	—	—	—	Dispenser SUU-38/A for 10 × CDU-20 or CDU-21 clusters each of 54 × BLU-54 anti-personnel mines
CBU-43	—	—	380 kg	Dispenser SUU-37 for CDU-37 clusters of BLU-48 bomblets. Weight 380 kg
CBU-44	—	—	—	Dispenser for anti-personnel bomblets
CBU-45	—	—	—	Dispenser for anti-personnel/materiel bomblets
CBU-46/A	—	—	400 kg	Dispenser SUU-7C/A for 444 × BLU-66/B anti-personnel bomblets
CBU-47	—	—	—	Dispenser SUU-13 for BLU-55 anti-personnel mines
CBU-49/B	—	—	380 kg	Dispenser SUU-30/B & 670 BLU-59/B fragmentation bomblets
CBU-50/A	—	—	—	Dispenser SUU-13 for 40 × BLU-60 fragmentation bomblets
CBU-51/A	—	—	—	Dispenser SUU-13/A & 40 × BLU-67/B cratering bombs
CBU-52/B	—	—	350 kg	Dispenser SUU-30B/B & 254 × BLU-61/B fragmentation bombs
CBU-53/B	—	—	370 kg	Dispenser SUU-30B/B & 670 × BLU-70/B incendiary bomblets
CBU-54/B	—	—	370 kg	Dispenser SUU-30B/B & 670 × BLU-68/B incendiary bomblets
CBU-55/B	—	—	230 kg	Dispenser SUU-49 for 3 × BLU-73 FAE bombs
CBU-57	—	—	—	Dispenser SUU-14A/A for 132 × BLU-69/B incendiary bomblets
CBU-58A/B	—	—	370 kg	Dispenser SUU-30A/B & 650 BLU-63/B fragmentation bombs
CBU-59/B	—	—	—	Dispenser Mk 7 Mod 3 Rockeye for 717 PLU-77/B APAM fragmentation bomblets
CBU-60	—	—	—	Dispenser SUU-50 for 264 × BLU-24 fragmentation bomblets
CBU-61	—	—	—	Dispenser CS incapacitant gas bomblets
CBU-62	—	—	380 kg	Dispenser SUU-30 for 2025 M38 fragmentation grenades
CBU-63	—	—	380 kg	Dispenser SUU-30 for 2025 M40 fragmentation grenades
CBU-66	—	—	—	Dispenser SUU-51/B for CDU-24/B canisters containing BLU-81/B minelets. Cancelled
CBU-68	—	—	—	Dispenser SUU-30 for BLU-48 fragmentation bomblets
CBU-70	—	—	—	Dispenser SUU-30
CBU-71	—	—	370 kg	Dispenser SUU-30 A/B for 670 × BLU-86 A/B fragmentation bomblets
CBU-72	—	—	230 kg	Low drager version of CBU-55 fitted with retarder parachutes
CBU-75A/B	—	—	—	Dispenser SUU-54A/B with 1800 BLU-63/B or BLU-86B fragmentation bombs
CBU-76/B	—	—	—	Dispenser SUU-51B/B for 290 × BLU-61A/B fragmentation/incendiary bomblets
CBU-77/B	—	—	—	Dispenser SUU-51B/B for 790 × BLU-63/B fragmentation bomblets
CBU-78/B	—	—	—	Dispenser SUU-58/B for Gator anti-tank & anti-personnel minelets BLU-91/B & BLU-92/B
CBU-82/B	—	—	—	Dispenser SUU-58/B for BLU-91/B Gator anti-tank mines
CBU-83/B	—	—	—	Dispenser SUU-58/B for BLU-92/B Gator anti-personnel mines
CBU-84/B	—	—	—	Dispenser SUU-54A/B for BLU-91/B & BLU-92/B Gator mines
CBU-85/B	—	—	—	Dispenser SUU-54A/B for BLU-91/B Gator anti-tank mines
CBU-86/B	—	—	—	Dispenser SUU-54A/B for BLU-92/B Gator anti-personnel mines
M12	—	—	—	Cluster, incendiary bomb
M13	—	—	—	Cluster, incendiary bomb, 500 lb
M17	—	—	—	Cluster, incendiary bomb, 500 lb
M19	—	—	—	Cluster, incendiary bomb, 500 lb (36 × M69)
M19A2	—	—	—	Cluster, incendiary bomb, 500 lb
M20/M20A1	—	—	—	Cluster, incendiary bomb, 500 lb
M21	—	—	—	Cluster, incendiary bomb, 500 lb
M22/M22A1	—	—	—	Cluster, incendiary bomb, 500 lb
M26A1	—	—	—	Cluster, fragmentation bomb, 500 lb
M28A2	—	—	—	Cluster, fragmentation bomb, 100 lb (24 × M83)
M31	—	—	—	Cluster, incendiary bomb, 500 lb (38 × M74)
M32	—	—	—	Cluster, gas bomb non-persistent, 1000 lb (76 × M125)
M34A1	—	—	—	Cluster, gas bomb non-persistent, 1000 lb (76 × M125A1)

Designation	Entry no	Dimensions l x d	Weight	Description
USA cont				
M35	—	—	—	Cluster, incendiary bomb, 750 lb (57 × M74A1)
M36	—	—	—	Cluster, incendiary bomb, 750 lb (182 × M50A3)
M43	—	—	—	Cluster, gas bomb incapacitating BZ agent, 750 lb (57 × M138)
M44	—	—	—	Cluster, gas generator incapacitating BZ agent, 175 lb
SUU-7B/A	—	—	—	Dispenser, bomb
SUU-7C/A	—	—	—	Dispenser, bomb
SUU-10/A	—	—	—	Dispenser, bomb
SUU-10A/A	—	—	—	Dispenser, bomb
SUU-10B/A	—	—	—	Dispenser, bomb
SUU-13/A	—	—	—	Dispenser, bomb
SUU-14/A	—	—	—	Dispenser
SUU-20/A	—	—	—	Dispenser, bombs & rockets
SUU-21	—	—	—	Flare launcher
SUU-24/A	—	—	—	Dispenser, bomb, grenades & bomblets
SUU-30/B	—	—	—	Dispenser
SUU-30A/B	—	—	—	Dispenser
SUU-30B/B	—	—	—	Dispenser
SUU-30C/B	—	—	—	Dispenser
SUU-31/B	—	—	—	Dispenser
SUU-36/A	—	—	—	Dispenser, mine
SUU-37/A	—	—	—	Dispenser, bomb
SUU-38/A	—	—	—	Dispenser, high speed tactical fighter munition
SUU-41/A	—	—	—	Dispenser
SUU-41A/A	—	—	—	Dispenser
SUU-42/A	—	—	—	Dispenser, buoy-flare
SUU-43/A	—	—	—	Dispenser, buoy-flare
SUU-44	—	—	—	Dispenser, flare
SUU-45/A	—	—	—	Dispenser, high speed tactical fighter munition
SUU-46/A	—	—	—	Dispenser, bomb
SUU-48/A	—	—	—	Dispenser, bomb
SUU-54/A	—	—	—	Dispenser, bomb
PLU-77/B	—	—	—	Dual purpose anti-tank anti-personnel (APAM) 11 lb fragmentation bomb
MLU-10B	—	—	—	750 lb land mine equipped with seismic, magnetic & IR sensors to detect vehicles & then detonate mine
Rockeye Mk 20	**1534.311** **1998.303**	—	227 kg	Used on A-4, A-6, A-7, F-4 & F-8. About 250 fragmentation bomblets
Grasshopper	—	—	—	Anti-tank mine & aerial dispenser system development programme
Gator	**1849.303**	—	—	Anti-tank & anti-personnel mine dispensing system for US Army, USAF & USN. In early development stage
HSM	**1848.303**	—	—	Hard structure munitions. Development project
M56	—	—	—	Helicopter mining system. 2 SUU-13 dispensers. M15 mine
SUU-54B	**1534.311**	—	907 kg	Cluster bomb. Also guided version (Pave Storm)

(SUU = suspended underwing unit; BLU = bomb live unit; BDU = bomb dummy unit; CBU = cluster bomb unit)

Fuel/air explosive weapons

Designation	Entry no	Dimensions l x d	Weight	Description
BLU-76	—	—	—	For use against pressure-sensitive targets
CBU-55B	**1847.303**	200 × 35 cm	226 kg	Contains 3 separate 45 kg canisters. Used for mine clearance & against pressure-sensitive structures
CBU-72	**1847.303**	—	—	USN development of CBU-55B with retarder parachute
HSF-I	**1847.303**	—	226 kg	FAE bomb development project by USAF
HSF-II	**1847.303**	—	900 kg	FAE bomb development project by USAF
MAD	**1847.303**	—	—	USMC helicopter dispensed FAE project

Guided bombs

Designation	Entry no	Dimensions l x d	Weight	Description
Mk 20 (Rockeye)	**1534.311** **1998.303**	—	226 kg	Laser homing version of Mk 20 (Rockeye) cluster bomb with KMU-420/B guidance package
Mk 82 (Snakeye)	**1534.311**	— × 23 cm	226 kg	Laser homing version of GP Mk 82 bomb KMU-388B/B guidance package
Mk 84	**1534.311**	— × 33 cm	907 kg	Guided versions of GP Mk 84 bomb. KMU-351/A/B laser guidance package, or KMU-353A/B electro-optical guidance package
M117	**1534.311**	—	340 kg	Laser homing. KMU-342/B guidance package
M118E1	**1597.311** **1534.311**	—	1360 kg	Guided versions of M118 demolition bomb. KMU-370B/B laser guidance package, or KMU-390/B electro-optical guidance package
Pave Rocket (RBU-1/A)	**1997.303**	—	—	Guided cluster munition
Pave Storm	**1534.311**	—	907 kg	Laser guided version of SUU-54B cluster bomb
Walleye I	**1129.311**	344 × 33 cm	499 kg	TV-guided
Walleye II	**1129.311**	404 × 46 cm	1061 kg	TV-guided
KMU-420/B	—	—	—	500 lb laser guided bomb (Mk 20 Mod 2 Rockeye II with laser guidance kit)
KMU-342/B	—	—	—	750 lb laser guided bomb (Mk 117 with laser guidance kit)
KMU-351A/B	—	—	—	2000 lb laser guided bomb (Mk 84 with laser guidance kit)
KMU-353A/B	—	—	—	2000 lb electro-guided bomb (Mk 84 with electro-optical guidance kit)
KMU-359/B	—	—	—	2000 lb IR guided bomb (Mk 84 with IR guidance kit)
KMU-370/B	—	—	—	3000 lb laser guided bomb (M118E1 with laser guidance kit)
KMU-388A/B	—	—	—	500 lb laser guided bomb (Mk 82 with laser guidance kit)
KMU-390/B	—	—	—	3000 lb electro-optical guided bomb (M118E1 with electro-optical guidance kit)
KMU-420/B	—	—	—	500 lb laser guided bomb (Mk 20 Mod 2 Rockeye II with laser guidance kit)
KMU-421/B	—	—	—	2000 lb laser guided bomb known as Pave Storm (SUU-54B cluster bomb with laser guidance kit)

Nuclear munitions

Designation	Entry no	Dimensions l x d	Weight	Description
B28	—	—	—	Nuclear free fall bomb. Tactical & strategic versions. Deployed (nos in brackets) on B-52 (4 or 8), A-4(1), F-4 (1), A-6(3), B-1B (20 max). Yields (strategic versions) 1·4 - 28 MT

Designation	Entry no	Dimensions l x d	Weight	Description
USA cont				
B41	—	—	—	Strategic bomb. Obsolete
B43	—	—	—	Tactical/strategic bomb. Deployed (nos in brackets) on A-4(1), A-6(3), A-7(4), F-16(2), F-4(3), F-111(6), B-52(4). At least 5 different yields available, in KT to MT range. Various nose forms employed; parachute retarded or free fall. 'Lay-down' delayed surface burst capability from low-altitude release
B43Y1	—	—	—	Version of B43 under development to similar standard of B77, in lieu of the latter
B57	—	—	—	Tactical. Mods 0/1/2 deployed (nos in brackets) on A-4(1), A-6(3), P-3(3), S-3(4), SH-3(1), F-16(2), F-4(3), FB-111(6). Yields 10-20 KT
B61	—	—	—	Tactical (Mods 0, 2, 3, 4, 5) & strategic (Mod 1) versions produced by Mods 3 & 4 are also strategic. Deployed (nos in brackets) on A-6(3), A-7(4), F-16(2), F-111(6), B-52(4 or 8), FB-111(6), B-1B(38 max). Mods 0/2/3/4/5 yields range 100 - 500 KT; Mod 1 has yield in MT range
B77	—	—	—	FUFO (full fuzing option) bomb. Free fall or retarded, airburst or ground burst. Fitted with lifting aerofoil parachute. Production cancelled, but development continued. Requirement being met by B43Y1, as above
B83	—	—	—	New strategic free fall bomb
BDU8	—	—	—	Probably training version of B43 nuclear bomb
BDU11	—	—	—	Probably training version of nuclear bomb
BDU12	—	—	—	Probably training version of B57 nuclear bomb
BDU38	—	—	—	Probably training version of B61 nuclear bomb
YUGOSLAVIA				
Free fall bombs				
FAB-250	5223.303	—	250 kg	General purpose
FAB-500	5223.303	—	500 kg	General purpose
PLAB 150L	5223.303	—	—	150 litre napalm
RAB	5223.303	—	120 kg	Fragmentation cluster bombs
ZAB-45	5223.303	—	45 kg	Incendiary
Cluster bombs and area weapons				
DPT-150	5223.303	—	—	Cluster bomb unit with 54 × 1·5 kg, 44 × 2·5 kg, or 34 × 3·5 kg bomblets

Land-based Radar

Designation	Entry no	Description	Contractor(s)
BRAZIL			
ASR-BR1	**4133.153**	S-band airport surveillance radar	IPD/PEA
Meteorological radar	**4132.153**	S-band weather and sonde tracking radar	IPD/PEA
CANADA			
CMR-3	**5678.153**	Coastal surveillance radar	Canadian Marconi
CHINA, People's Republic			
Chop Rest	**2019.153**	Early warning radar similar to Soviet Spoon Rest	—
Cross Legs	**2019.153**	Early warning radar used for GCI	—
Cross Slot	**2019.153**	Coastal defence/air search radar	—
Gin Sling	**2019.153**	SAM guidance radar similar to Soviet Fan Song	—
Moon Cone	**2019.153**	Air early warning radar. Stacked dipole arrays	—
Moon Face	**2019.153**	Similar to Moon Cone but only 1 array	—
Moon Mat	**2019.153**	Similar to Moon Cone but only 1 array	—
Moon Plate	**2019.153**	Stacked dipole array on trailer mounting	—
Slot Rest	**2019.153**	Similar to Soviet Spoon Rest. VHF early warning	—
Team Work	**2019.153**	AA gun fire control radar. E-band	—
CZECHOSLOVAKIA			
OPRL-4	3284.153	Surveillance & PAR	Tesla
RL-41	3285.153	Air search & surveillance radar	Tesla
RL-42	**4331.153**	Successor to RL-41	Tesla
RP-4G	**4332.153**	Surveillance & PAR successor to OPRL-4	Tesla
DENMARK			
DR 513	1576.153	Artillery radar	Dannebrog Elektronik
DR 810	2286.153	Ballistic radar	Dannebrog Elektronik
DR 532	1954.153	Ballistics radar for guns or rockets	Dannebrog Elektronik
M/532	1577.153	Doppler radar for projectile velocity measurement	Dannebrog Elektronik
Pointer	1573.153	Portable independent Terma radar I-band	Dannebrog Elektronik
Terma doppler	**5629.163**	Projectile velocity measuring radar	Terma
TSSR	1574.153	Terma splash spotting radar	Dannebrog Elektronik
FRANCE			
Adour	**2056.153**	TH.D 1215 automatic multi-mission missile tracking radar, 200 km range on passive target	Thomson-CSF
Antares	**2060.153**	High precision 3-D E/F-band monopulse radar with electronic scan, in elevation	Thomson-CSF
Aquitaine II	2062.153	Precision missile/satellite tracking monopulse radar	Thomson-CSF
Arabelle	2066.153	Portable transponder	Thomson-CSF
Artois	**2063.153**	(Under development) Missile tracking radar, using electronic scanning techniques, with capacity to track several targets simutaneously	Thomson-CSF
Atlas	**1943.153**	TH.D 2503 G-band monopulse range tracker	Thomson-CSF
Bearn	**2065.153**	Precision missile/satellite tracking radar	Thomson-CSF
Bretagne	2067.153	TH.D 1801 tracking radar	Thomson-CSF
Champagne	2069.153	Missile tracking radar, using 300 km range on 1 m² passive target and to measure target speed to nearest 10 cm/s	Thomson-CSF
Domino 20	2073.153	D-band surveillance radar. Coherent, pulse-doppler; 17 km range; 10° beamwidth; coherent pattern	Thomson-CSF
Domino 30	2083.153	TRS 2101 as Domino 20, but 6·5° beamwidth and 30 km max range	Thomson-CSF
Domino 40N	2084.153	As Domino 20 but 3° pencil beam and 80 km max range	Thomson-CSF
Eldorado	2080.151	I/J-band tracking radar for light anti-aircraft operations against low-flying targets. Associated with MIRADOR surveillance radar as mobile combination	Thomson-CSF
	2082.153		
ER-116-A	**2157.153**	IFF interrogator	Thomson-CSF
LDTR	—	G/H-band scanning radar for special application. Designed to work under high level ECM conditions, has an exceptionally narrow antenna beam	Thomson-CSF
Louxor	3275.153	Experimental electronic scan short-range air defence radar	Thomson-CSF
LP23 (TRS 2050)	2100.153	Long-range D-band surveillance radar	Thomson-CSF
LP23K	**3683.153**	Long-range D-band surveillance radar	Thomson-CSF
Matador	2102.153	3-D E/F-band radar (Mobile and tridimensional air defence operations radar). Range about 250 km. Electronic elevation scan for accurate height measurement	Thomson-CSF
Mirador	2080.151	Pulse-doppler surveillance and target designation radar E/F-band; 18 km range; pencil beam 5·6° wide. Associated with ELDORADO tracking radar for mobile operations for defence against low-flying aircraft	Thomson-CSF
	2116.153		
Mirador II	2080.151	Mobile E/F-band pulse-doppler surveillance radar for defence against low-flying aircraft. Associated with Crotale surface-to-air guided weapons system. Dual, back-to-back, 4° beamwidth antennas. Range 18 km	Thomson-CSF
	2074.131		
	2117.153		
Oeil Noir 1 (DR-VC-1A)	2129.153	D-band pulse-doppler surveillance radar. 10° cosecant pattern beam. Range 15 km. Mounted on AMX-30 tracked AFV with twin 30 mm cannon to form mobile anti-aircraft system	Thomson-CSF
Oeil Vert	3197.153	Later version of Oeil Noir	Thomson-CSF
Olifant	2131.153	Lightweight battlefield radar	Thomson-CSF
Olifant II	2132.153	Lightweight man-portable battlefield patrol radar	Thomson-CSF
ORP-105 (DLM-10-E)	1945.153	E-band meteorological radar	Omera
ORP-310	**1945.153**	I/J-band meteorological radar	Omera
ORP 340	**1945.153**	I-band meteorological radar	Omera
ORV-31	**1945.153**	I/J-band meteorological radar	Omera
Palmier	—	20MW 3-D E/F-band surveillance radar	Thomson-CSF

Designation	Entry no	Description	Contractor(s)
FRANCE cont			
Perceval/Spartiate	**2120.153**	Helicopter recovery radar	Thomson-CSF
Picador	**2119.153**	Mobile 3-D radar	Thomson-CSF
RA 20	*3717.153*	Mobile AA fire control radar	ESD
RA 20S	**5601.153**	Surveillance and target designation radar for low-level air defence	ESD
RA 21	*3718.153*	Mobile AA fire control radar	ESD
Racine	*2136.153*	I/J-band non-recurrent pulsed doppler surveillance and target acquisition radar	LCT
RALF	*2152.153*	Lightweight I/J-band low altitudes surveillance radar using Racine techniques	LCT
Ramsa	**3274.153**	TRS 2140 low-level air defence gap-filler	Thomson-CSF
Rapace	*2137.153*	J-band AFV-mounted surveillance radar	ESD
Rasit	*2142.153*	I/J-band portable medium-range battlefield surveillance radar	ESD
Rasit 72A1 (Rapière)	**2141.153**	I/J-band battlefield surveillance radar. 20 km range	LCT
Rasit 72B	*2153.153*	Lightweight version of Rasit 72A	LCT
Rasit 72C	*2154.153*	Short-range (10 km) version of Rasit 72A	LCT
Rasura	*2143.153*	I/J-band portable or vehicle-mounted battlefield surveillance radar	ESD
Rasura II	*3716.153*	Battlefield surveillance radar	ESD
Ratac	**1528.153**	Battlefield surveillance. Also produced in USA and West Germany	LCT
Rodeo 2	**5602.153**	Fire control radar for low-level air defence	ESD
Rodeo 20	*3719.153*	Anti-aircraft fire control radar	ESD
Siclamen	**3173.153**	Battlefield IFF	LMT
Savoie	**1944.153**	Long-range tracker	Thomson-CSF
Stentor	**3287.153**	Battlefield surveillance radar, I/J-band	LCT
TH.D 1012	*2133.153*	PAR	Thomson-CSF
TH.D 1013	*2098.153*	Light PAR	Thomson-CSF
TH.D 1021	*2058.153*	Airfield surveillance radar	Thomson-CSF
TH.D 1060	—	D-band medium-range surveillance radar. Transportable and suitable for use as gap-filler or as surveillance element of GCA system. 200 km range on small targets; digital MTI system; 2-beam antenna	Thomson-CSF
TH.D 1940	—	Low cost 3-D surveillance radar with electromechanical elevation sweep. Transportable by cargo aircraft, helicopter, or truck	Thomson-CSF
TH.D 1955	*2155.153*	High-power 3-D E/F-band monopulse stacked-beam radar for surveillance or GCI. 400 km range capability	Thomson-CSF
Tiger (TRS 2100)	**2156.153**	E/F-band lightweight surveillance radar for detection of high-flying targets	Thomson-CSF
TRS 2050	*2100.153*	See LP 23	Thomson-CSF
TRS 2052		Successor to TRS 2050	Thomson-CSF
TRS 2053	**3099.153**	Smaller antenna version of TRS 2052 for use as gap-filler	Thomson-CSF
TRS 2055	*2104.153*	2 MW Terminal Area surveillance radar. MTI system. Uses antenna type TH.D-284B	Thomson-CSF
TRS 2056	**3099.153**	Centaure. Transportable recovery radar based on TRS 2052	Thomson-CSF
TRS 2060	**2121.153**	Mobile or static E/F-band surveillance radar	Thomson-CSF
TRS 2065	*2059.153*	ATC approach radar	Thomson-CSF
TRS 2201	**2155.153**	Long-range E/F 3-D air defence radar	Thomson-CSF
TRS 2215	**3272.153**	Transportable version of TRS 2230 E/F-band 3-D radar. TRS 2215D and TRS 22XX are later versions	Thomson-CSF
TRS 2230	**3272.143**	Fixed site 3-D air defence radar. Derived from Satrape	Thomson-CSF
TRS 2310	**3492.153**	PAR	Thomson-CSF
TRS 2600	**4224.153**	E/F-band pulse doppler target designation radar	Thomson-CSF
TRS 2730	**3276.153**	G-band weather radar	Thomson-CSF
TRS 3405	**3100.153**	I-band coastal surveillance radar	Thomson-CSF
TRS 3410	**3273.153**	Transportable version of TRS 3405	Thomson-CSF
Volex III (TRS 2205)	*2160.153*	Medium-range 2-beam 3-D radar. Fast electromechanical elevation sweep with narrow (2×2°) beam	Thomson-CSF
Volex IV	**3271.153**	TRS 2206. Improved version of Volex III	Thomson-CSF
—	—	D-band panoramic radar with double-beam AT 431 HB (9×13 m) antenna; 400 km range; high ECM resistance	Thomson-CSF
—	—	Phased array 3-D radar for air defence and ballistic missile detection. Possible replacement for PALMIER radar	Thomson-CSF
—	—	400-600 MHz surveillance radar for special applications Range better than 1000 km	Thomson-CSF

GERMANY, Federal Republic			
ASR 920	*3707.153*	Mobile radar	AEG-Telefunken
DR 151	**3286.153**	Longer range version of MPDR 30	Siemens
DR 171	**3286.153**	Extended range version of MPDR 45	Siemens
DR 621/641	**3286.153**	Search radar for B2 35 mm Flakpanzer	Siemens
MBVR 120	*3478.153*	Balloon/drone tracking radar	Philips
Meteor 300	**5613.153**	Meteorological radar	Gematronik
MPDR 12	**3286.153**	J-band tracker for B2 35 mm Flakpanzer	Siemens-Albis
MPDR 16	**3286.153**	E/F-band search radar for Roland mobile SAM	Siemens
MPDR 30	**3286.153**	Mobile air search radar. Gap-filler	Siemens
MPDR 3002 S	**3286.153**	Medium-range air search radar	Siemens
MSR 200/MSR 2000	**3286.153**	Lightweight IFF systems	Siemens
MSR 400	**3286.153**	Mobile IFF interrogator	Siemens
OREST	**3706.153**	Mobile electronic scan air defence radar	Siemens
PAR-T4	—	PAR	AEG-Telefunken
SRE-A4	—	10 cm E/F-band medium-range surveillance radar. 500 kW	AEG-Telefunken
SRE-A5	—	Medium-range (60 nm) surveillance radar	AEG-Telefunken
SRE-LL1	—	23 cm D-band long-range surveillance radar. Back-to-back	AEG-Telefunken
—	—	14·5×9 m reflectors 2×0·24 MW. Range 255 nm	
SR-M2B	—	23 cm D-band long-range surveillance radar. IMW. Range 245 nm	AEG-Telefunken
SRT-2	—	SSR	AEG-Telefunken

Designation	Entry no	Description	Contractor(s)
GERMANY, Federal Republic cont			
—	—	Surveillance radar for anti-aircraft fire control system	Siemens
TRMS	3016.153	Transportable electronic scan air defence radar	AEG-Telefunken
1990D	3286.153	IFF interrogator	Siemens
Wimera	4140.153	I-band met balloon tracking radar	Elektro Spezial
INTERNATIONAL			
Zenda	2198.153	Project for SP AFV-mounted battlefield radar	EMI and others
		Believed to have been abandoned	
RATAC	1528.153	Battlefield surveillance radar	LMT/SEL/ITT-Gilfillan
ISRAEL			
EL/M-2106	3646.153	D-band battlefield air warning radar	Elta
EL/M-2108	3647.153	Portable infantry radar	Elta
EL/M-2121	4330.153	Battlefield surveillance radar	Elta
EL/M-2200	1958.153	Range of E/F-band search radars	Elta
EL/M-2205	1958.153	ATC search radar	Elta
EL/M-2206	1958.153	Coastal surveillance radar	Elta
EL/M-2207	3708.153	Shipborne model	Elta
EL/M-2208	3708.153	Shipborne version	Elta
EL/M-2210	1958.153	Mobile search radar	Elta
EL/M-2215	3708.153	Surveillance radar	Elta
EL/M-2216	3708.153	Coastal surveillance radar	Elta
EL/M-2220	4606.153	Mobile air surveillance radar	Elta
Helicapture	4611.153	Tactical radar for helicopter surveillance	Rafael
ITALY			
Alerter	4018.153	I-band search and acquisition radar	Contraves
Argos RAT-5C	2239.153	Coastal defence radar	Selenia
Argos RAT-6L	2243.153	Short-range L-band acquisition radar for AA targets	Selenia
		Suitable for mountainous terrain	
Argos RAT-7S	2282.153	E/F-band 450 W low-coverage radar	Selenia
Argos RAT-8S	1952.153	Mobile coastal surveillance version of RAT-10S	Selenia
Argos RAT-10S	2237.153	Coastal defence radar	Selenia
Argos RAT-15	—	10 cm E/F-band search and surveillance radar. 600 kW	Selenia
Argos RAT-20L	2281.153	D-band long-range surveillance radar	Selenia
Argos RAT-21C	2280.153	C-band high-power low-altitude surveillance radar	Selenia
Argos RAT-31S	1953.153	E/F-band mobile 3-D radar	Selenia
Argos 10	1959.153	D-band high power early warning radar. GE transmitter	Selenia
Argos 800	—	Coastal defence radar	Selenia
ATCR-22	2248.153	High-power D-band civil/military ATC surveillance radar	Selenia
ATCR-33	2248.153	Medium-power E/F-band civil/military ATC surveillance radar	Selenia
ATCR-44	2248.153	Medium-power D-band civil/military ATC surveillance radar	Selenia
Indigo FC Centre (CT40-GM)	2291.153	Missile control system. Italian version of Superfledermaus	Contraves
LPD-20	1529.153	Pulse-doppler and acquisition radar	Contraves
MLV-4	—	Doppler infantry portable battlefield surveillance radar	Selenia
MM/SPQ-3	3278.153	I/J-band multipurpose coastal radar	SMA
Pluto	3277.153	Low-cover surveillance radar for air and coastal defence	Selenia
RIS-3E	2244.153	Monopulse skin or beacon tracking radar	Selenia
RIS-4C/A	2245.153	I/J-band pulsed tracking radar	Selenia
RIS-5X	2246.153	Drone tracking radar	Selenia
Selenia SIR	2248.153	Secondary surveillance radar	Selenia
Sentinel RQT-9X	2249.153	Portable infantry radar	Selenia
RQT-10X	1951.153	Portable infantry radar	Selenia
Shorar	5618.153	Search acquisition and target designation radar	Contraves
SIT 431 (AN/TPX-54)	3279.153	IFF interrogator	Italtel
JAPAN			
JAN/MPQ-N1	4081.153	Type 92 mortar locating radar	—
J/MPQ-P7	4141.153	Artillery locating radar	Toshiba
NPG-360	2297.153	E/F-band surveillance radar	NEC
NPG-434	2297.153	High-power ARSR	NEC
NPG-435	2297.153	PAR	NEC
NPG-454	2297.153	GCA system	NEC
NPG-460	2297.153	E/F-band airport surveillance radar	NEC
NPG-542	2297.153	IFF/SSR system	NEC
NPG-554	2297.153	GCA radar	NEC
NPG-630	2297.153	ARSR	NEC
NPG-864	2297.153	Fixed GCA system	NEC
NPG-880	3702.153	Static 3-D air defence radar, electronic scan	NEC
NPG-905A	2297.153	Secondary surveillance radar	NEC
NPG-1240	2297.153	Airport surveillance radar	NEC
NPM-510	2298.153	Mobile 3-D radar electronic elevation scan	NEC
NPM-554	2297.153	Mobile GCA system	NEC
XJ-FPS	4605.153	Air surveillance radar project	—
NETHERLANDS			
Flycatcher	3283.153	Low-level anti-aircraft fire control system	Signaal
L4/5AA Weapon Control System	—	Weapon control system for use with 40 mm anti-aircraft guns for close air defence. Search and tracking radar antennas on compound mounting which, together with transmitter-receivers computer and displays is mounted on single trailer. Search radar employs FASCAN principle to achieve early detection of very low-flying aircraft	Signaal
LAR, 8GR 200	—	Long-range civil or military air surveillance radar	Signaal
LDTR	—	Long-dwell time radar	Signaal
SLAM	1557.153	Signaal low air-defence module	Signaal

Designation	Entry no	Description	Contractor(s)
NETHERLANDS cont			
Star, 8GR 550	*1556.153*	Terminal area radar with single transmitter-receiver	Signaal
Star, 8GR 552	*1556.153*	Terminal area radar with dual diversity transmitter-receiver	Signaal
Stola	—	Target acquisition system for use against very low flying aircraft. Believed to be I/J-band with back-to-back antenna arrangement. Antennas mounted on telescopic mast which can raise them (apparently) about 10 m to give good low-angle cover and clear obstructions	Signaal
Tank Radar	**2302.153**	Integrated radar system for 35 mm AA tank	Signaal
VI, SGR 104	—	Heightfinding radar	Signaal
VI, 8GR 551	—	Automatic heightfinding and long-range tracking radar	Signaal
—	—	Gap-filling radar	Signaal
POLAND			
AVIA B	**2340.153**	23 cm D-band surveillance radar. 2 1·5 MW transmitter/receivers in frequency diversity. Range 240 km	Industrial Institute of Telecomms, Warsaw
SOUTH AFRICA			
EMVA Mk 10B	**4601.153**	Muzzle velocity measuring radar	Armscor
SWEDEN			
9GR 600	*1549.153*	Frequency-agile 200 kW search radar	PEAB
9KR 400	**4029.153**	Coastal surveillance radar	PEAB
Domti	*2354.153*	Mobile coherent G/H-band pulse doppler search radar for use with AA guns or missiles	L M Ericsson
Ecstra	*2357.153*	I/J-band coherent search and fire control radar for AA gun or missile systems. Separate search and tracking antennas	L M Ericsson
Giraffe (PS-70/R)	**1957.153**	Mobile G/H-band search radar	L M Ericsson
Isidor	*1955.153*	Muzzle velocity measuring radar	SATT
Isidor	*2481.153*	J-band portable intrusion radar	L M Ericsson
Mareld	—	I/J-band coastal defence radar with closed-circuit TV for visual tracking and 30 km range laser rangefinder (by L M Ericsson)	Philips Teleindustri
PE-48/T	*2325.153*	Mobile I/J-band AA fire control radar	L M Ericsson
PE-452/T	*2327.153*	I/J-band range-only AA fire control radar	L M Ericsson
PE-453/T	*2328.153*	Mobile I/J-band AA fire control radar	L M Ericsson
Peder II	*2355.153*	J-band monopulse fire control tracking radar	PEAB
PS-171/R	*2326.153*	Mobile E/F-band search radar	PEAB
TX 745	*1956.153*	Lightweight portable IFF for AA guns and missiles	SATT
UAR 1021	*2357.153* **2377.151**	I/J-band combined search and track pulse doppler radar	PEAB
UAR 1022	*2356.153*	Tracking sub-system of the UAR 1021	PEAB
SWITZERLAND			
CONAR	*2551.153*	Artillery radar fire control system	Contraves
Fieldguard/Skyguard	**2377.151**	Solid-state successor to Superfledermaus; uses separate search and tracking radars whose antennas are concentrically mounted on single pedestal, as with Sea Hunter Shipborne tactical air defence system. Radar is by Ericsson; computer and control circuits by Contraves	Contraves/Ericcson
Superfledermaus	**2376.151**	Anti-aircraft fire control system incorporating tracking radar by Albiswerk with visual attachment. Equipment uses valve circuits and has analogue computer. Latest version has MTI addition by Ericsson	Contraves/Albiswerk/Ericsson
UNION OF SOVIET SOCIALIST REPUBLICS			
Back Net	**2860.153**	Early warning GCI search radar	—
Barlock	**2861.153**	GCI and air search radar. Dual antennas	—
Beam Track	—	Multiple Yagi tracking array	—
Big Bar	**2862.153**	Similar to Barlock but V-beam antennas for heightfinding	—
Big Fred	**4329.153**	Artillery/mortar locating mobile radar	—
Big Mesh	**2863.153**	Similar to Back Net but V-beam antennas	—
Bill Fold	—	Search radar. Transportable	—
Box Brick	—	Trailer-mounted	—
CBR	—	Counter battery radar. E-band 2/300 kW artillery/mortar locating	—
Cheese Brick	—	Truck-mounted	—
Dog House	**2864.153**	Large fixed, phased-array radar for ABM system	—
Dome Glass	—	Trailer-mounted tracker or fire control radar	—
Dry Rack	—	Yagi array	—
Dumbo	—	Compound array of multiple UHF & VHF Yagi arrays	—
End Tray (RMS-1)	—	Parabolic dish tracker. Van-mounted	—
Fan Song	**2866.153**	Series of SAM guidance radars	—
Fan Song B	**2867.153**	E/F-band missile guidance radar	—
Fan Song C	—	Similar to Fan Song B	—
Fan Song E	**2868.153**	G-band missile control radar	—
Fire Can	**2871.153**	E-band trailer-mounted radar similar to US SCR-584	—
Fire Dish	**2872.153**	Similar to Fire Can	—
Fire Wheel	**2873.153**	Conical scan gun fire control radar	—
Flap Track	—	Air search and target acquisition radar	—
Flap Wheel	—	Parabolic dish	—
Flat Face	**2874.153**	Air search and target acquisition radar	—
Fork Rest A	—	Array of 4 VHF Yagi antennas	—
Four Stack	—	Array of 8 co-mounted Yagi antennas	—
Gage	**2875.153**	Acquisition radar. Stacked feeds	—
GS-11	—	Battlefield surveillance radar. J-band, 10 kW, 1·2 km range. Manpack	—
GS-12	—	Battlefield surveillance radar. J-band, 25 kW, 3·5 km range. Manpack or vehicle	—
GS-13	—	Vehicle-mounted battlefield surveillance radar. J-band, 50 kW, 12 km range	—

Designation	Entry no	Description	Contractor(s)
USSR cont			
Gun Dish	**2876.153**	Fire control radar for ZSU-23-4 SP AA tank	—
Hen Egg	**2877.153**	Early warning radar	—
Hen House	**2879.153**	Early warning radar for ABM system	—
Hen Nest	**2877.153**	Early warning radar	—
Hen Roost	**2877.153**	Early warning radar	—
Knife Rest	**2881.153**	VHF early warning radar. Soviet designation P-10	—
	2880.153		
Landfall	—	Coastal warning radar	—
Long Brick	—	Van-mounted array	—
Long Eye	—	Back-to-back dish radars on trailer	—
Long Talk	**3294.153**	Aircraft recovery and GCA search radar	—
Long Track	**2937.153**	Tactical surveillance radar for SAMs	—
Long Trough	—	Trough-shaped air search radar on half-tracked vehicle	—
Low Blow	**2884.153**	I-band radar group for low-level SAMs	—
Mercury Noseband	—	Truck-mounted	—
Mesh Brick	—	Probably mortar locating radar. Offset spiral feeds	—
Mound Brick	—	Trailer-mounted radar with hemispherical dome	—
Nysa B	—	Nodding heightfinder	—
Nysa C	**3296.153**	Long-range air search radar. Probably VHF	—
Odd Lot	—	E-band early warning radar and heightfinder	—
Odd Pair	—	E-band heightfinder	—
One Eye	—	Air search radar with supplementary antenna	—
OR-2	—	Probably airfield surveillance radar	—
OTHR	**3288.153**	Over-the-horizon radar. Pulse type. HF	—
Pat Hand	**2936.153**	H-band missile guidance radar for SA-4 Ganef	—
Patty Cake	**2878.153**	Back-to-back nodding heightfinders	—
Pole Dish	—	—	—
Pork Trough	**4328.153**	Similar to Long Trough on fully tracked vehicle	—
PSNR-1	**4602.153**	Battlefield surveillance radar	—
RL-1	—	Airfield surveillance radar	—
RL-2D	—	Air search radar	—
Rock Cake	—	Transportable nodding heightfinder	—
RP-2E	—	Twin PAR installation	—
Scoreboard	**2974.153**	Broadside array of stacked dipoles. A and B versions	—
Side Net	**3289.153**	Transportable nodding heightfinder	—
Small Yawn	—	Tracker(possibly conical scan) on tracked van	—
Sponge Cake	**2878.153**	Trailer-mounted nodding heightfinder	—
Spoon Rest A	**2889.153**	VHF air warning radar. Vehicle mounted	—
Spoon Rest B	**2899.153**	VHF air warning radar. Semi-fixed version	—
Square Pair	**3290.153**	Target tracking and missile guidance radar for SA-5	—
Squat Eye	**3291.153**	Air search and target acquisition radar	—
Squint Eye	**2891.153**	Target acquisition radar	—
Stone Cake	**2878.153**	Trailer-mounted nodding heightfinder	—
Straight Flush	**2885.153**	Fire control radar group for SA-6	—
Strike Out	—	Similar to Barlock	—
Tachi I	—	Multiple Yagi arrays associated with searchlight	—
Tall King	**3239.153**	Long-range early warning radar. Soviet designation P-14	—
Thin Skin	**3292.153**	H-band nodding heightfinder	—
Token	**2892.153**	E/F-band early warning radar. V-beam antennas	—
Track Dish	—	Dish tracker on tracked van	—
Tub Brick	—	Search radar with radome on trailer	—
Twin Eye	—	Back-to-back dish antennas on building	—
Two Spot	**3295.153**	PAR group	—
Whiff	**2893.153**	Van-mounted fire control radar. E/F-band	—
Whiff Brick	—	Dish-type tracker on trailer van	—
Witch Eight	—	Eight-element dipole-plus-ground-plane array	—
Witch Five	—	Array of five Yagis	—
Witch Four	—	Quadruple dipole array	—
Wood Gage	—	Similar to OR-2	—
Yo Yo	**2895.153**	Early missile guidance radar for SA-1 Guild	—
UNITED KINGDOM			
AA No 3 Mk 7	—	Mobile AA fire control radar. Lock and follow	AEI
ACR-6	—	Medium-range 10 cm search radar. Similar to CR 787 but with additional display and processing facilities	Cossor
ACR-7C	—	Mobile short-range I/J-band surveillance radar	Cossor
ACR 430	2420.153	Series of I-band air search and coastal defence radars	Plessey
AR-1	1140.153	E/F-band medium-range surveillance radar. 650 kW Single or dual transmitter/receivers with frequency diversity. Range 75 nm	Plessey
AR-3D	2484.153	E/F-band 3-D air surveillance radar	Plessey
AR-5	2416.153	D-band long-range surveillance radar. 2 MW Single or dual transmitter/receivers. Range 200 nm	Plessey
AR-15/2	2456.153 and 1141.153	E/F-band medium-range surveillance radar similar to and superseding AR-1. Available in static (**2456.153**) or mobile (**1141.153**) versions	Plessey
AR-320	3649.153	E/F-band surveillance radar. Used in UKADGE update programme	Plessey
AWS-7	3281.153	10 cm primary air and surface search radar	Plessey
AWS-8	3480.153	Coastal surveillance radar	Plessey
CEL 850	**3692.153**	IFF Interrogator	Cossor
Cervantes	5631.153	Mortar and rocket locating radar	Thorn-EMI
Coastal artillery radar	—	3 cm target acquisition and fire control for use with several coastal batteries	Racal
Cossor Monopulse	**4604.153**	Secondary surveillance radar	Cossor
CR 21	—	Medium-range 10 cm surveillance radar. Similar to CR 787 but less microwave preamplifier	Cossor

Designation	Entry no	Description	Contractor(s)
UK cont			
CR-62	**3715.153**	PAR. UK version of FPN-66	Cossor
CR 787	—	Medium-range 10 cm surveillance radar	Cossor
CR 901	—	23 cm long-range high-cover surveillance radar. 2 MW	Cossor
CRI 600	—	Microminiature IFF Mk 10 interrogator	Cossor
CRS 512	**5622.153**	Large aperture IFF/SSR antenna	Cossor
Cymbeline	**1018.153**	Mortar locating radar	EMI
DASR-1	—	10 cm back-to-back long-range/high-cover surveillance radar. 2800 kW transmitter/receivers. Range 110 nm	Plessey, formerly Decca
DASR-3	—	Improved performance version of DASR-1 2·5 MW transmitter/receivers. Range 150 nm	Plessey, formerly Decca
Falconer	**3715.153**	Precision approach radar	Cossor
FCE.AA No. 7	—	Anti-aircraft fire control radar for use with guns or missiles at close range	EMI
Firelight	**2413.153**	Type 86 (which see) target illuminating radar	Ferranti
Green Archer (FA No 8 Mk 1)	*2412.153*	Mortar locating radar	EMI
GS No 14 Mk 1	**2490.153**	See ZB 298	Marconi
GS No 18 Mk 1	*2483.153*	Infantry combat radar. Successor to ZB 298	Marconi
GS No 20	**3490.153**	Claribel hostile fire locating radar	Racal-MESL
Guardsman	**4607.153**	Point defence radar	Plessey
HF-200	*1142.153*	E/F-band height finder radar. 2·5 MW. 10·6×2·4 m antenna	Plessey
IFF 800	**2410.153**	Solid-state military IFF/SIF secondary surveillance radar developed from SSR. 700	Cossor
LC 150	—	10 cm low cover coastal surveillance radar 800 kW. (10·6 m antenna)	Racal
Martello (S713)	**3491.153**	Mobile 3D surveillance radar. Used in UKADGE update programme	Marconi
Martello (S723)	—	New version of S713 Martello. Used in UKADGE and NADGE update programme	Marconi
Mk 10 IFF/SIF	*2418.153*	IFF Mk 10(SIF) interrogation and passive and active decoding equipment	Plessey
Messenger	**4603.153**	Monopulse SSR	Marconi
NIS	**5621.153**	Range of IFF interrogators and transponders for NATO indentification system (NIS)	Cossor
Pacer	*2435.153*	Muzzle velocity measuring radar	Ferranti
Pacer 2	**5627.153**	Muzzle velocity measuring radar	Ferranti
Prowler	*1946.153*	Infantry radar	Marconi
Rapier	**2425.153**	Search and target acquisition radar for Rapier AA missile system	Racal
Rapier (DN 181)	**2439.153**	Tracking radar (Blindfire) for Rapier AA missile system	Marconi
S 105	—	3 cm fixed or mobile harbour and coastal surveillance radar. 70 kW.	Marconi
S 244	—	10 cm heightfinder radar. 2·5 MW 12·2×2·1 m antenna	Marconi
S247/S 266	**2458.153**	Back-to-back early warning radar. Two 2·25 MW transmitter/receivers, one 10 and one 23 cm	Marconi
S 259	*2480.153*	Air-transportable D-band 2 MW tactical radar with limited ground mobility	Marconi
S 264	—	Range of 50 cm long-range surveillance radars	Marconi
S 314	—	10 cm coastal defence radar. 800 kW. 8·8×3 m antenna 40 nm range	Marconi
S 330	**2463.153**	Land mobile tactical surveillance radar. Uses 2 low-profile back-to-back antennas, E/F-band, and D-band plus IFF	Marconi
S 404	**2463.153**	Land mobile G/H-band height finder radar	Marconi
S 500 Series	**5615.153**	Static and tactical surveillance radars. Comprises S511, S512, S513, S525, S531 and S532 operating in the 10 or 23 cm band	Marconi
S 505	—	3 cm harbour and coast watch radar. 20 kW	Marconi
S 513	*5641.153*	Primary surveillance radar	Marconi
S 600 Series	*1168.153*	Modular systems of transmitter/receivers, static and mobile antenna heads, displays and processing equipment capable of deployment to produce wide range of air defence radar systems. Main elements of S 600 Series are as follows:	Marconi
Antenna heads			
S 1006	—	10 cm static heightfinder antenna. 2·4×12·1 m cylindrical parabolic reflector with linear slotted feed	Marconi
S 1010	—	10 cm transportable surveillance antenna, 5·48×1·8 m single curvature parabolic reflector, linear feed, frequency diversity capability	Marconi
S 1011	—	10 cm static surveillance antenna. 13·7×4·57 m parabolic reflector. Can be used in back-to-back configuration	Marconi
S 1012	—	10 cm static surveillance antenna. 13·7×4·57 m cosecant-squared reflector. Can be used in back-to-back configuration	Marconi
S 1013	—	23 cm static surveillance antenna.13·7×4·57 m parabolic reflector. Can be used in back-to-back configuration	Marconi
S 1014	—	23 cm static surveillance antenna 13·7×4·57 m cosecant-squared reflector. Can be used back-to-back	Marconi
S 1015	—	10 m transportable surveillance antenna. 5·48×1·8 m cosecant-squared reflector	Marconi
S 1016	—	23 cm transportable surveillance antenna. 5·48×1·8 m cosecant-squared reflector	Marconi
S 1017	—	5·5 cm transportable heightfinder antenna. 4·27×1·3 m double curvature, point fed reflector	Marconi
S 1061	—	D-band surveillance. 7·6 × 2·4 m	Marconi
Transmitter/receivers			
S 2010	—	1 MW 10 cm transmitter/receiver. Tunable within band	Marconi

Designation	Entry no	Description	Contractor(s)
UK cont			
S 2011	—	2 MW 23 cm transmitter/receiver. Tunable within band	Marconi
S 2012	—	2·5 MW 10 cm transmitter/receiver	Marconi
S 2013	—	1 MW 5·5 cm transmitter/receiver	Marconi
S2018	**2458.153**	E/F-band; 3·3 MW	Marconi
S2019	**2458.153**	D-band; 3·3 MW	Marconi
S 613	**2479.153**	G/H-band mobile/transportable heightfinding radar. 1 MW	Marconi
S 631/S 647	**2458.153**	E/F- and D-band back-to-back 2-plus MW surveillance radars	Marconi
S 650	—	50 cm D-band surveillance radar. 16×3·7 m reflector 500 kW. 150 – 160 nm range	Marconi
S 654	*2459.153*	23 cm surveillance radar 11× 4·6 m reflector 2 MW, 90 nm range	Marconi
S 669	**2462.153**	E/F-band 2·25 MW 150 nm heightfinding radar	Marconi
S 670	—	50 cm surveillance radar 20·7×3·7 m reflector 500 kW. 180 nm range	Marconi
S 690	**2458.153**	E/F-band back-to-back surveillance radar	Marconi
S 700 series	**4630.153**	Family of mobile surveillance radars in D- and E/F-bands. Comprises S704, S705, S706, S711 and S712	Marconi
S 841/S 842	**2464.153**	'800-series' mobile coastal defence I/J-band surveillance radars. Type S 842 has tunable transmitter	Marconi
ST850	**2466.153**	'800-series' I/J-band tracking radar with TV for use with Tigercat AA missile system (**2465.131**)	Marconi
SLA-3C	—	PAR	STC
Scorpion (Type 87)	**2428.153**	Target tracking and illuminating radar for Bloodhound II surface-to-air missile system	Marconi
Sentinel	*5619.153*	Mobile E/F-band tactical radar	Plessey
Shrimp	*2482.153*	J-band surveillance radar	Marconi/RRE
Stingray (Type 83)	—	Target acquisition, tracking, and illuminating mobile radar for use with Bloodhound I and Thunderbird surface-to-air missiles. Used by UK, Swedish, and Australian forces	Marconi
Transportable Watchman	**4631.153**	Mobile version of Watchman	Plessey
Type 13	—	Heightfinder	—
Type 80	—	Long-range surveillance radar. Range 200 nm plus. Probably D-band	Plessey, formerly Decca
Type 82	*2457.153*	'Volumetric', stacked beam 3-D surveillance radar. Used for tactical control of Bloodhound I surface-to-air missiles	Marconi, formerly AEI
Type 83	—	Mobile target tracking and illuminating radar for Bloodhound I	Marconi, formerly AEI
Type 84	*2457.153*	High-power D-band surveillance radar	Marconi, formerly AEI
Type 85	*2457.153*	High-power stacked beam 3-D surveillance radar similar to AEI 4502. Used in Linesman/Mediator UK air defence/ATC system	Marconi, formerly AEI
Type 86 (Firelight)	**2413.153**	Mobile CW target illuminating radar for Bloodhound II surface-to-air missiles	Ferranti
Type 87 (Scorpion)	**2428.153**	Target tracking and illuminating radar for Bloodhound II. CW	Marconi, formerly AEI
Type 200	**1142.153**	E/F-band height finder radar. 2·5 MW. 10·6×2·4 m antenna	Racal
Type 430	**2420.153**	Airfield radar	Plessey
Type 431(M)	**3280.153**	Coastal radar. Fixed and mobile (M) versions	Plessey
Watchman	**5608.153**	E/F-band medium-range surveillance radar	Plessey
ZB 298	**2490.153**	Man-portable non-coherent I/J-band pulsed doppler battlefield surveillance infantry radar for location of men and vehicles out to 10 m	Marconi
870 Series	**3693.153**	IFF interrogators	Cossor
880 Series	**3694.153**	IFF interrogators	Cossor
4502	—	Stacked beam 3-D long range 10 cm surveillance radar 12 lobes. Elliptical parabolic reflector. 17·7×6·6 m. 4 MW	Marconi, formerly AEI
40 Series	*2478.153*	Range of 3-D radars developed from 4502	Marconi, formerly AEI

UNITED STATES OF AMERICA

Designation	Entry no	Description	Contractor(s)
ADAR	*2506.153*	Advanced design array radar. Electronically steered beam for tracking multiple targets	Hughes
AN/-	—	US joint service nomenclature for many systems listed below uses AN/- prefix. For convenience this prefix has been omitted. Thus AN/CPN-6 is listed simply as CPN-6	—
ARBAT	**4079.153**	J-band ballistic testing instrumentation radar	ITT-Gilfillan
ARSR-3/ASR-30	**5623.153**	D-band surveillance radar	Westinghouse
ASR-7	—	E/F-band surveillance radar giving 100 km range on 3 m² target. All digital signal processor. Frequency diversity and 1 MW transmitter available	Texas Instruments
AWCS	**2533.181**	Air weapons control system. Code number 412L, otherwise known as QUICKDRAW. Mobile control and warning system	General Electric
Baltic Approach	**4082.153**	E/F-band Danish coastal defence radar (DCR)	Cardion
BMEWS	**2525.181**	Ballistic missile early warning system to give warning of ICBM/IRBM attacks on USA/UK. Sites at Thule, Greenland (equipped with FPS-49 and FPS-50); Clear, Alaska (equipped with FPS-50 and FPS-92); and Fylingdales Moor, UK (equipped with FPS-49) System code 474L	General Electric, RCA and Western Electric
BPS-1000	**3149.153**	Long-range D-band surveillance radar	Bendix
Cobra Dane (663 A)	**1949.153**	Phased array space tracking radar	Raytheon
Conus OTH-B	**5617.153**	Over-the-horizon surveillance radar	General Electric
CPN-4	—	Mobile GCA	ITT-Gilfillan
CPN-18	—	ATC surveillance radar	Bendix
CPS-1	—	Long-range, semi-transportable early warning radar	General Electric
CPS-5	—	ATC radar	Bendix
CPS-6B	—	Long-range search and heightfinder for early warning	General Electric
CPS-9	—	Weather radar	Raytheon

Designation	Entry no	Description	Contractor(s)
USA cont			
DEW	**2567.181**	Distant early warning system. Code number 413L	Western Electric
DCR	**4082.153**	See Baltic Approach	Cardion
EMS	—	Emergency mission support system. Air transportable, system designed to set up ATC, communications and varied facilities to support operations in areas where such facilities are not available. Code number 842L. Also known as Project FOUR WHEELS. Radars used TPN-14, TPS-35	Chu Associates, ITT-Gilfillan
FAAR	**1526.153**	Forward area alerting radar. Detects very low-flying high-speed aircraft; checks IFF identification; and relays data by VHF link to anti-aircraft sites equipped with Chaparral Redeye or Vulcan. Mobile system with high-mast antenna	Sanders Associates/Sperry
Falcon series (GPS-100)	**4322.153**	Frequency-agile low-coverage netted radar	ITT-Gilfillan
FPN-1A	—	Airfield approach and landing guidance radar system	Bendix
FPN-16	—	GCA-radar. Similar to CPN-4 and MPN-11	ITT-Gilfillan
FPN-28	—	GCA radar	Bendix
FPN-33	—	GCA radar	ITT-Gilfillan
FPN-34	—	Long-range D-band ATC radar	Bendix
FPN-36	**4125.153**	QUAD radar. Tactical GCA system	ITT-Gilfillan
FPN-40	—	GCA radar with IFF capability	ITT-Gilfillan
FPN-47	—	E/F-band medium-range ATC radar (ASR-5)	Texas Instruments
FPN-48	—	Landing Control Central GCA. Similar to MPN-13	ITT-Gilfillan
FPN-50	—	Landing Control Central GCA. Similar to CPN-4A	ITT-Gilfillan
FPN-51	—	E-band airport surveillance radar. Similar to FPN-47 but with ECM capability	Texas Instruments
FPN-52	**4076.153**	GCA PAR system based on FPN-16	ITT-Gilfillan
FPN-55	—	Similar to FPN-47	Texas Instruments
FPN-62	**3714.153**	PAR	Raytheon
FPQ-6	*2508.153* **2846.153**	MIPIR (Missile Precision Instrumentation Radar) G/H-band monopulse missile tracking radar. Transportation version is TPQ-18	RCA
FPQ-13	*2857.153*	G/H-band monopulse missile tracking radar	RCA
FPQ-14	*2508.153*	Modified version of FPQ-6	RCA
FPS-3, 3A	—	D-band long-range radars	Bendix
FPS-5	—	Long-range radar	Hazeltine
FPS-6, 6A, 6B	**2492.153**	E/F-band long-range heightfinding radars. Superseded by FPS-89. Mobile version is MPS-14	General Electric
FPS-7, 7A, 7B, 7C, 7D	**2526.153**	10 MW 3-D search/GCI radar. Cosecant elevation pattern with 7 stacked beams. Search range 500 km. Elevation cover 45 km. MTI, frequency diversity. Part of SAGE system	General Electric
FPS-8	**2493.153**	D-band long-range search radar with MTI. Superseded by FPS-88. Mobile version is MPS-11	General Electric
FPS-10	—	See FPS-27	
FPS-14	*2527.153*	E/F-band 500 kW medium-range (110 km) search radar used in SAGE system	Bendix
FPS-16	**4327.153**	G/H-band monopulse missile-tracking combined primary/ secondary radar. Transportable version is MPS-25	RCA
FPS-17	—	Long range early warning radar for missile detection	General Electric
FPS-18	*2527.153*	1·2 MW E/F-band search radar used in SAGE	
FPS-19	—	DEW LINE radar	Raytheon
FPS-20, 20A, 20B	**2528.153**	Long-range, dual-channel search and GCI radar with MTI 2 MW, D-band; range 350 km. FPS-20 is used in SAGE, FPS-20A in AWCS and FPS-20B in both. GPS-4 is mobile version	Bendix
FPS-23	—	Aircraft alarm system. VHF multiple station doppler aircraft intruder detection system	Motorola and Western Instruments
FPS-24	**2494.153**	Long-range search radar, used in SAGE	General Electric
FPS-26	—	Long-range heightfinder for SAGE. Possible application as early warning radar for SLBM after modification	Avco
FPS-27	—	Replacement for FPS-10. Search radar for SAGE. E-band	Westinghouse
FPS-28	—	Search radar for SAGE	Raytheon
FPS-30	—	Long-range duplex search radar. D-band	Bendix
FPS-33	—	D-band long-range, high-altitude tracker for supersonic targets Includes 2×FPS-8 or 2×MPS-11	General Electric
FPS-35	—	Long-range SAGE or ATC surveillance radar	Sperry
FPS-36	**2723.131**	Nike-Hercules radar. Others are FPS-56, FPS-61, FPS-69-71, FPS-75-76	Raytheon
FPS-37	**2499.153** **2723.131**	High-power acquisition radar for Nike-Hercules	General Electric
FPS-41	—	Long-range meteorological recording radar	Raytheon
FPS-46	—	Long-range electronically steerable array radar (ESAR) See FPS-85	Bendix
FPS-49	**2509.153**	Very long-range tracking for missile early warning (BMEWS) and satellite tracking (SPADATS)	RCA
FPS-50	**2511.153**	BMEWS surveillance radar	General Electric
FPS-56	**2723.131**	See FPS-36	
FPS-59	—	Tracking radar	General Electric
FPS-60	—	SAGE heightfinding radar	—
FPS-61	**2723.131**	See FPS-36	
FPS-63	—	DEW line gap-filler, being modified to FPS-74	Budd
FPS-64, 65, 66, 67, 67A	—	Search radars for SAGE, FPS-67A is also used in AWCS	Bendix
FPS-69, 70, 71	**2723.131**	See FPS-36	
FPS-74	—	See FPS-63	
FPS-75, 76	**2723.131**	See FPS-36	
FPS-77	—	Weather radar	Lear Siegler
FPS-78, 79, 80	—	Tracking radars. FPS-79 and FPS-80 are part of SPACETRACK	General Electric
FPS-85	**2546.153**	D-band 3-D phase array radar for satellite detection, identification and tracking. Based on FPS-46 and part of SPADATS/SPACETRACK	Bendix

Designation	Entry no	Description	Contractor(s)
USA cont			
FPS-87A	—	Long-range D-band surveillance radar. Similar to FPS-91	Bendix
FPS-88, 89	**2512.153**	Modernised versions of FPS-6, FPS-8	General Electric
	2513.153		
FPS-90	—	High-power heightfinder, version of FPS-6 ( ). Similar to APS-507 another version of FPS-6B	General Electric and Canadian Marconi
FPS-91	—	Long-range search and tracking radar. Version of FPS-20	Bendix
FPS-92	**2509.153**	BMEWS scanner/tracker radar. Improved version of FPS-49	RCA
FPS-93	—	Modification of FPS-20	Raytheon
FPS-95	—	Tracking radar	RCA
FPS-100	—	Modernised FPS-20	Bendix
FPS-103	—	Weather radar	Bendix
FPS-105(V)	**2847.153**	G/H-band range instrumentation radar	RCA
FPS-115	**3174.153**	Pave Paws	Raytheon
FPS-117	**4326.153**	Long-range 3-D air defence radar for Seek Igloo programme	General Electric
FPS-507	—	See FPS-90	Canadian Marconi
FPT-5, 7	—	Long-range surveillance and tracking radar transmitters	Ling Temco Vought
FSS-7	2538.153	Radar surveillance central for SLBM system	Avco Cincinnati
GE 592	**4321.153**	Export version of TPS-59	General Electric
GPN-2	—	Mobile ATC radar	Bendix
GPN-6	—	E/F-band ATC surveillance radar 150 km range	LFE
GPN-22	**3713.153**	PAR. Improved TPN-25	Raytheon
GPS-3	—	D-band back-up surveillance radar	General Electric
GPS-4	—	See FPS-20	
GPS-57A	—	Surveillance radar	Bendix
GSN-5	—	Landing Control Central automatic landing system	Bell
GSS-1	—	Mobile gap-filler radar	Raytheon
GSS-7	—	Mobile air defence radar	Raytheon/Hazeltine
HADR	**3721.153**	Electronic scan multi-mode 3-D air defence radar	Hughes
HIPAR	**2499.153**	High-power acquisition radar for Nike Hercules See FPS-37	General Electric
LAADS	**3123.153**	Low-altitude aircraft detection system	Sanders
LASR	**4323.153**	Low-altitude surveillance radar	Hughes
MFR (Multi-function radar)	**5607.153**	Weapon control radar	Hughes
Model 2679	**4632.053**	IFF interrogator	Hazeltine
MPG-1	—	Coastal artillery fire control radar	Bendix
MPN-1, 11, 13, 14, 15	—	Mobile GCA radars	ITT-Gilfillan
MPN-3, 5	—	Mobile GCA radars	Bendix
MPQ-4	**2497.153**	Mortar-locating radar	General Electric
MPQ-10A	**2500.153**	E/F-band mortar locating radar	Sperry
MPQ-12, 18	—	E/F-band 300 km range missile tracking radars	Reeves
MPQ-14	—	Radar Course Directing Central	Advance/Ultrasonic
MPQ-25	—	Trailer-mounted radar for Corporal missile system	ITT-Gilfillan
MPQ-29	—	Drone control radar	Sperry
MPQ-31	—	E/F-band 4000 km range 3-D tracking and guidance radar	Canoga
MPQ-32	—	Field detection and tracking radar	Sylvania
MPQ-33	2640.131	CW illuminator for Hawk missile system. Also MPQ-39	Raytheon
MPQ-34	2640.131	CW target acquisition radar for Hawk	Raytheon
MPQ-35	2640.131	Pulse target acquisition radar for Hawk	Raytheon
MPQ-37	2640.131	Range radar for Hawk	Raytheon
MPQ-39	2640.131	See MPQ-33	
MPQ-43	**2723.131**	HIPIR mobile high-power acquisition radar for Nike Hercules	General Electric
MPQ-49/54	**1526.153**	See FAAR	
MPQ-53	**4478.153**	Multi-function radar group for Patriot air defence missile system	Raytheon
MPQ-501	—	Mortar locating radar. Used in Canada	Raytheon
MPS-3, 4	—	Heightfinding radars	Raytheon
MPS-4, 4A, 4C	—	Heightfinding radars	Hazeltine
MPS-7	—	Long-range D-band search radar	Bendix
MPS-9	—	E/F-band drone and missile control radar. Range 300 km	Reeves
MPS-11, 11A	**2493.153**	See FPS-8	
	2495.153		
MPS-14	**2492.153**	See FPS-6	
	2496.153		
MPS-16	—	Nodding heightfinder for AWCS G/H-band; 300 km range	Crosley
MPS-19	—	Mobile tracking radar. E-band	Reeves
MPS-21	—	3-D search radar. See also TPS-34	Sperry
MPS-23	—	FRESCAN-elevation frequency scanning 3-D search radar	Hughes
MPS-24	—	See TPS-28	
MPS-25	**4327.153**	See FPS-16	
MPS-30	—	Mobile surveillance radar; trailer-mounted TPS-25	Hazeltine, FMC
MPS-36	**2514.153**	Instrumentation tracking radar	RCA
MSG-1	—	Transportable AA artillery director radar	Sperry
MSQ-1A	—	Aircraft ground attack director system	Reeves
MSQ-2	—	Mobile ground attack director system	Reeves
MSQ-4	—	Mobile ATC system	Adler Communication
MSQ-35	—	300 km range I/J-band tracking radar	Reeves
MSQ-39	—	Radar Bomb Scoring Central	Reeves
MSQ-44	—	Radar Bomb Scoring Central	Reeves
MSQ-51	—	Target drone control system	Reeves
MSQ-77	—	Radar Bomb Directing Control	Reeves
MSR	2791.153	Missile site radar for Safeguard ABM system. Phased array type. Prototype at Kwajalein test area	Raytheon
	2798.131		
MSW-1	**2723.131**	Acquisition radar for Nike Ajax and Nike Hercules systems	—
MTTS	—	Mobile target tracking system for drone tracking	Epsco
OTH R	1948.153	Over-the-horizon radars	—
OX-60/FPS-117	**4317.153**	IFF interrogator for FPS-117 Seek Igloo radar	Hazeltine

Designation	Entry no	Description	Contractor(s)
USA cont			
Pave Paws	**1949.153**	Missile warning radars	GE, Raytheon, RCA
	3174.153		
PAR	2790.153	Perimeter Acquisition Radar for Safeguard ABM systems	—
	2798.131	Under development	
PAR 80	**4077.153**	Fixed site J-band PAR	ITT-Gilfillan
PPS-3	—	Portable surveillance radar	Sperry
PPS-4	—	Silent Sentry portable forward area surveillance radar	Sperry
PPS-5/5B	**2540.153**	Transistorised versions of PPS-4	AIL
PPS-6	**5604.153**	Portable battlefield surveillance radar	General Instrument Corp
PPS-9	—	Portable battlefield surveillance radar	RCA
PPS-11/12	**5616.153**	Hand-held battlefield surveillance radar	General Instrument Corp
PPS-15A	**1947.153**	I/J-band infantry radar	General Dynamics
	4324.153		
PPS-55	—	Portable forward area surveillance radar	—
PSS-10	**5605.153**	Miniature battlefield radar receiver	General Instrument Corp
Quadradar Mk V	**4125.153**	Multi-function ATC radar	ITT-Gilfillan
Quadradar Mk VI	**4328.153**	Development of Quadradar Mk 5 with MTI	ITT-Gilfillan
R-200 Series	3640.153	J-band infantry radar	General Instrument Corp
R-2080	4316.153	Battlefield surveillance radar	General Instrument Corp
RCA 2019 M2	2783.153	I/J-band hand-held tactical radar. System weight 4 kg; T/R weight 1 kg; range 500 m on 0·5m² target. Resolution 25 m. Aural output	RCA
RCA 4019 M2	2783.153	I/J-band hand-held tactical radar. System weight 6·35 kg including accessories; T/R weight 3·6 kg; range 1500 m, resolution 25 m. Aural and/or visual output	RCA
Real-time velocimeter	**5628.153**	Transportable artillery tracking radar	Datron
SAGE	**2803.181**	Semi-automatic ground environment system for detecting, identifying and tracking aircraft threats to North America and directing weapon interception. Code number 412L	Western Electric, System Development Corporation Burroughs
SAM-D	**2800.131**	Phased array radar for SAM-D guided missile system now under development	Raytheon
Series 52	**4076.153**	Remote controlled PAR	ITT-Gilfillan
Series 320	**4078.153**	Transportable 3-D E/F-band air defence radar	ITT-Gilfillan
Site Defence Radar	2792.153	Phased-array radar similar in purpose to MSR but smaller	General Electric
SLBM	—	Sea-launched ballistic missile detection system. Purpose is to detect and identify missile attack on North America and warn NORAD and SAC. Code number 474N	Avco
Spacetrack	**2825.181**	USAF world-wide detection, identification, tracking, and reporting system. Records data on all space objects Spacetrack is US section of NORAD SPADATS system Spacetrack code number 496L	General Electric, Philco-Ford, RCA, Bendix, System Development Corporation
SPADATS	**2825.181**	NORAD space object detection and recording system of which SPACETRACK is large part	—
STARTLE	**3648.153**	AFV surveillance and target acquisition radar Development suspended late 1982 for 12 months	Martin Marietta
TMQ-19	3477.153	Meteorological radar	Servo Corps
TPN-8	—	Helicopter-transportable approach radar	ITT-Gilfillan
TPN-12	—	ATC GCA	LFE, Bendix
TPN-14	—	Transportable GCA for EMS	ITT-Gilfillan, RCA
TPN-17	—	Air-transportable landing control central	LFE
TPN-18A	**3129.153**	Lightweight I-band air-transportable ATC radar	ITT-Gilfillan
TPN-19	**2537.153**	All-weather transportable tactical ATC radar with E/F-band terminal area surveillance and I/J-band, dual-mode (search and track) 6 target. PAR. Cassegrain feed antenna	Raytheon
TPN-22	**4075.153**	Automatic all-weather landing radar system	ITT-Gilfillan
TPN-24	**3711.153**	Airfield surveillance radar element of TPN-19 system	Raytheon
TPN-25	**3712.153**	PAR used in TPN-19	Raytheon
TPQ-10	**2498.153**	Transportable radar course direction central for control of close support bombing operations	General Electric
TPQ-14, 15, 16	2640.131	Transportable versions of MPQ-33, 34, 35	Raytheon
TPQ-18	**2846.153**	Transportable version of FPQ-6	RCA
TPQ-19	2640.131	Transportable version of MPQ-39	Raytheon
TPQ-27	3720.153	Radar Course Directing Central	RCA
TPQ-28	—	Omni-directional mortar-locating radar	ITT-Gilfillan
TPQ-31	1950.153	Mortar-locating radar	Raytheon
TPQ-32	**1526.153**	See FAAR	
TPQ-36	**2848.153**	Electronically-scanning mortar locating radar. Used by US and Australia	Hughes
TPQ-37	**1976.153**	Artillery locating radar	Hughes
TPQ-39	**2849.153**	G/H-band digital instrumentation radar	RCA
TPS-1	3128.153	Transportable D-band air search radar. Version of FPS-36	
TPS-10D	—	I/J-band heightfinder. 220 km range	RCA
TPS-21	**2529.153**	Portable I/J-band battlefield surveillance and reconnaissance radar. Range 9 km. Also TPS-33	Admiral
TPS-22	—	Tactical early warning radar for AWCS system Complemented by TPS-27	Westinghouse
TPS-25, 25A	3130.153	Battlefield surveillance radars	Hazeltine
TPS-27	2515.153	3-D tactical radar for AWCS. Complemented by TPS-22	Westinghouse
TPS-31	—	Harbour surveillance radar	Raytheon
TPS-32	**2516.153**	Automatic 3-D tactical long-range surveillance radar	ITT
TPS-33	**2529.153**	See TPS-21	Admiral
TPS-34	**2530.153**	3-D (V-beam) tactical long-range early warning radar	Sperry
TPS-35	—	D-band 500 km surveillance radar for UMS. Modernised version of UPS-1	RCA
TPS-37	—	Transportable version of MPS-16	Avco
TPS-40	—	Long-range heightfinder. Transportable. Similar to MPS-16 and TPS-37	General Electric

Designation	Entry no	Description	Contractor(s)
USA cont			
TPS-43	**2517.153**	Transportable 3-D tactical tracking radar measuring range, altitude, and azimuth plus IFF identification ECM-resistant for forward area operation	Westinghouse
TPS-44	**2518.153**	Transportable tactical surveillance radar (ALERT)	Cardion
TPS-48	*2519.153*	Transportable 3-D tactical radar	Westinghouse
TPS-58	**1528.153**	US designation for RATAC battlefield radar	ITT-Gilfillan
TPS-59	**3282.153**	3-D tactical radar	General Electric
TPS-61	*2520.153*	Tactical surveillance radar	Westinghouse
TPS-63	**3475.153**	Tactical surveillance radar. Operated by USMC	Westinghouse
TPS-65	**3476.153**	Tactical surveillance radar	Westinghouse
TPS-70 (V)-1, -2, -3, -4	**4319.153**	Mobile tactical radar. Air surveillance	Westinghouse
TPX-19, 20, 22	—	Mk X IFF interrogator-responsors	Raytheon
TPX-42	**2535.153**	IFF interrogator system	AIL
TPX-44	—	Interrogator used with TPN-18	ITT-Gilfillan
TPX-45	—	IFF for Hawk missile system	Hazeltine
TPX-46	**3703.153**	IFF interrogator used with various systems	Hazeltine
TPX-50	**3704.153**	IFF interrogator for FAAR system	Hazeltine
TPX-54	**3705.153**	IFF interrogator	Hazeltine
TSQ-81	—	Radar Bomb Directing Central	Reeves
TSQ-96	—	Bomb Directing Central	Reeves
TSW-5	—	Tactical approach radar	RCA
TTQ-28	—	Mortar-locating radar	ITT-Gilfillan
TWS-QR	**4320.153**	Track-while-scan-quiet radar development	Hughes
Type 386	**4325.153**	Battlefield ground surveillance radar	General Dynamics
UPS-1	—	Gap-filler radar for AWCS. See also TPS-35	RCA, Bendix
UPW-1	—	Drone tracking and control radar	Ford, Sperry
UPX-6	—	Mk X IFF interrogator-responsor	Raytheon
VPS-2, 5	**2547.153** *2844.153* **2850.131**	Vulcan air defence system radar	Lockheed
VSTAR	**4080.153**	Transportable E/F-band air defence radar, based on TPQ-37	Hughes

1332.254 　　　　　　　　　　　　　Naval Radar

Designation	Entry no	Description	Contractor(s)
CANADA			
AN/SPS-503	**5677.253**	Naval surveillance radar (see also S1800-entry **3687.253**)	Canadian Marconi
DENMARK			
Scanter Mil	**1575.253**	I-band navigation radar	Terma Elektronik
Scanter Mil Data	**4633.253**	Tactical data system	Terma Elektronik
FRANCE			
ELI 4	**1688.253**	Naval IFF interrogator	LMT
ELR-3	**1934.253**	IFF transponder	LMT
Triton II	**1062.253**	TRS 3030 5 cm air and surface surveillance radar. Used with Castor or Pollux in Vega Series. 205 kW. TRS 3035 is MTI version	Thomson-CSF
Triton C	**3685.253**	TRS 3050 doppler surveillance radar	Thomson-CSF
Triton S	**3254.253**	TRS 3033 pulse doppler version of Triton	Thomson-CSF
Triton X	**3481.253**	TRS 3040 used in Vega-Canopus fire control	Thomson-CSF
Castor II	**1063.253**	TRS 3201-4 I/J-band target tracking radar used in some versions of Vega Series fire control system 20 kW	Thomson-CSF
Pollux	**1064.253**	TRS 3220 I/J-band target tracking radar used in some versions of Vega Series fire control systems. 200 kW	Thomson-CSF
Pollux II	*1686.253*	Improved version of Pollux	Thomson-CSF
Calypso II	*1240.453*	TH.D 1030. I/J-band submarine radar for surveillance and navigation. 70 kW	Thomson-CSF
Calypso III	**1933.253**	TRS 3100 I/J-band submarine radar. Improved version of Calypso II	Thomson-CSF
Calypso IV	**3684.253**	TRS 3110 submarine navigation radar	Thomson-CSF
Jupiter	**1236.253**	TRS 3010 Long-range surveillance radar. D-band. 2MW	Thomson-CSF
Ramses	*1239.253*	TH.D 1022. Short-range navigational and surveillance radar. I/J-band. 35 kW. 60 nm range	Thomson-CSF
Lynx	*1238.153*	Th.D 1051. Dual radar coastal mine-watching system	Thomson-CSF
Saturne	*1237.253*	TRS 3043 E/F-band medium-range air and surface surveillance radar. 1 MW peak	Thomson-CSF
Sea Tiger II	**1687.253**	TRS 3001 surveillance radar. Ordered for new Colombian frigates	Thomson-CSF
DRBC 32	**1894.253**	Series of gun fire control radars. A, B, C, D, and E versions fitted in various classes of French ships	—
DRBI 10	**1593.253**	E/F-band 3-D air surveillance radar. Robinson scanner	Thomson-CSF
DRBJ 11	**3741.253**	Electronic scan naval radar	Thomson-CSF
DRBV 13	**1893.253**	E/F-band pulse-doppler air search radar. Multi-mode operation	—
DRBV 20	**1892.253**	Long range metric air surveillance radar A and C versions in service	—
DRBV 22	**1891.253**	Search radar. A, C, and D versions in service on French and foreign vessels	—
DRBV 23	**1594.253**	D-band long-range air search radar. B and C versions in service	Thomson-CSF
DRBV 26	**1236.253**	See Jupiter	Thomson-CSF
DRBV 27	**1236.253**	Solid-state version of Jupiter. In development	Thomson-CSF
DRBR 51	**1177.231** **1890.253**	I/J-band tracker and target illuminator. 3 scanners Part of Masurca surface-to-air missile system	Thomson-CSF
DRB1 23	**1177.231** **1889.253**	3-D surveillance and target designator radar. D-band 23 cm. Stacked-beam system	Thomson-CSF
3973A	**3255.253**	IFF interrogator antenna system	Thomson-CSF

Designation	Entry no	Description	Contractor(s)
INTERNATIONAL			
Mk 95 Mod O	**3312.253**	Director radar group for NATO Sea Sparrow	NATO Consortium
ISRAEL			
AMDR	**5696.253**	Automatic missile detection radar	Elta
EL/M-2207	**3264.253**	F-band general purpose naval search radar	Elta
EL/M 2208	**4610.253**	Air & surface surveillance radar	Elta
EL/M-2221	**3709.253**	J-band naval fire control radar	Elta
ITALY			
Argus 5000	—	High-power ship's early warning radar. 5 MW peak power	Selenia
MM/BPS-704	**3483.253**	Italian Navy version of 3RM I-band radar for submarine use	SMA
MM/SPN-703	**3482.253**	Italian Navy version of 3RM for surface roles	SMA
MM/SPQ-701	**3262.253**	I-band search and target designation radar	SMA
MM/SPS-702	**3263.253**	Simplified version of MM/SPQ-701	SMA
MM/SPS-768	**1364.253**	Italian Navy version of RAN-3L	Selenia
MM/SPS-774	**1699.253**	Italian Navy version of RAN-10S	Selenia
Orion 250	—	I/J-band fire control radar. Used in NA9 system. Conical scan. 200 kW	Selenia
Orion RTN-10X	**1368.253**	Fire control radar. Used by RN and Brazil	Selenia
Orion RTN-16X	1367.253	I/J-band monopulse fire control radar	Selenia
Orion RTN-20X	**1935.253**	I/J-band fire control radar. Used in DARDO system	Selenia
Orion RTN-30X	**1936.253**	I/J-band fire control radar. Used in Albatros system. Production for Italy 1982	Selenia
RAN-2C	1700.253	G/H-band dual purpose air and surface surveillance radar	Selenia
RAN-3L	**1364.253**	D-band early warning radar. Digital signal processing	Selenia
RAN-7S	1527.253	10 cm air and surface search radar	Selenia
RAN-10S	**1699.253**	E/F-band dual purpose air/sea search radar	Selenia
RAN-IIL/X and 12L/X	**1365.253**	D- and I/J-band system for air warning and weapons control on small ships. Operational Denmark, ordered by Peru and Venezuela	Selenia
RAN-13X	1701.253	I/J-band search radar	Selenia
RAN-14X	1366.253	I/J-band low altitude and surface search radar	Selenia
Sea Hunter	1704.253	Search radar	Contraves
Sea Hunter	1705.253	Tracker radar	Contraves
SPQ-2D	**1703.253**	I/J-band search radar	SMA
3RM	**1702.253**	Series of I-band navigation and surface warning radars	SMA
NETHERLANDS			
DA.05/2	**1554.253**	E/F-band high cover air warning and surface search radar. Medium-range	Signaal
DA.05/3	**1554.253**	STAR, Signaal terminal area radar	Signaal
DA.05/4	**1554.253**	Medium-range air warning and surface search radar. E/F-band	Signaal
DA.08/1	**3479.253**	Medium-range air warning and surface search radar. E/F-band	Signaal
DA.08/2	**3479.253**	High cover version of DA.08/1	Signaal
DA.08/3	**3479.253**	Air warning radar	Signaal
LW.02	**1256.253**	Long-range D-band air surveillance radar	Signaal
LW.04	1553.253	Long-range D-band air search radar	Signaal
LW.08/1	—	Prob D-band	Signaal
LW.08/2	**1973.253**	Long-range air warning and surface search radar. D-band	Signaal
LW.08/3	**1973.253**	Long-range air route surveillance radar (LAR)	Signaal
M40	1591.253	Fire control radars for guns/Seacat missiles	Signaal
SGR-109	1257.253	E/F-band heightfinder	Signaal
SMART	**5626.253**	3-D surveillance radar for data handling and weapon control	Signaal
STIR	**3484.253**	Tracking and illuminating radar. Used in NATO Sea Sparrow and Seawolf VM40 system	Signaal
VM40	**3484.253**	See STIR	
WM20	**1590.253**	Series of small vessel fire control radars	Signaal
ZW.03	1258.253	I-band surface search and navigation radar	Signaal
ZW.06/1	—	Surface search, navigation and helicopter control radar. E/F-band. Operational India, Morocco and Spain; ordered South Korea and Thailand	Signaal
ZW.06/2S & 3/S	**1555.253**	Stabilised surface search, navigation and helicopter control radar. I-band	Signaal
ZW.06/4S	—	Stabilised I-band surface search and navigation radar	Signaal
ZW07/5	**4051.253**	Submarine surface search and navigation radar. I-band	Signaal
ZW08/2S & /3S	**4051.253**	Stabilised I-band surface search, navigation and helicopter control radar	Signaal
			Signaal
ZW08/4S	**4051.253**	Version of ZW.08 with sea-skimmer detection	Signaal
ZW09/1	**4051.253**	Surface search, navigation and helicopter control radar. I-band	Signaal
ZW09/2S & /3S	**4051.253**	Stabilised versions of ZW.09/1	Signaal
ZW09/4S	**4051.253**	Sea skimmer version of ZW.09/3S	Signaal
3D MTTR	**1589.253**	3-D multi-target search and tracking radar	Signaal
SWEDEN			
Sea Giraffe	**4299.253**	Air defence radar. Retrofitting in Spica IIs, to be procured for Spica IIIs	L M Ericsson
Subfar 100	**1545.453**	I/J-band submarine radar	PEAB
9GR 600	**1546.253**	I-band. Frequency-agile 200 kW	PEAB
9LV 200	**1547.253**	J-band monopulse frequence-agile tracking radar	PEAB
UNION OF SOVIET SOCIALIST REPUBLICS			
Ball End	—	High definition surface search radar	—
Ball Gun	**1900.253**	Similar to Ball End	—
Band Stand	**4090.253**	Search radar group on Nanuchka missile corvettes. Housed in large radome. Used with SSN-9 surface-to-surface missile	—
Bass Tilt	**4085.253**	Gun fire control radar. Similar to Drum Tilt, Muff Cob	—
Big Net	**1608.253**	Long-range air surveillance	—
Boat Sail	1507.253	Air search radar for submarine pickets	—
Cylinder Head	1596.253	Gun fire control group on optical director	—

Designation	Entry no	Description	Contractor(s)
USSR cont			
Cross Bird	—	Obsolescent early warning radar	—
Dead Duck	—	IFF system	—
Don	**1900.253**	I/J-band navigation radar	—
Drum Tilt	**1330.253**	I/J-band fire control. Enclosed scanner	—
Egg Cup	—	Splash spotting radar mounted on gun turrets	—
Eye Bowl	**4089.253**	Missile guidance radars on 'Krivak' class destroyers	—
Fan Song E	**1605.253**	Missile control and tracker group for Guideline SAM on *Dzerzhinski*	—
Flat Spin	*1321.353*	Long-range air search radar	—
Front Piece	—	Parabolic cylinder reflector	—
Hair Net	*1607.253*	General purpose E-band search radar	—
Half Bow	—	I/J-band torpedo target designation radar	—
Hawk Screech	**1325.253**	Gun fire control radar	—
Headlight	**1328.253**	Missile fire control group. G/H/I-band operation	—
Head Net A	**1318.253**	Long-range air surveillance radar	—
Head Net B	**1319.253**	Back-to-back installation of 2 Head Net A for low and high cover	—
Head Net C	**1320.253**	Dual V-beam 3-D installation of Head Net A	—
High Lune	*1606.253*	Nodding heightfinder	—
High Pole	—	IFF antenna	—
High Scoop	—	Elliptical paraboloid reflector. Surveillance radar	—
High Sieve	**1900.253**	Surface search radar	—
Horn Spoon	—	Navigation radar	—
Kite Screech	**4084.253**	Gun fire control radar	—
Knife Rest B	**1900.253**	Long wavelength early warning radar	—
Long Bow	—	I/J-band target designation radar for torpedoes or guns	—
Low Sieve	—	Surface search radar	—
Muff Cob	**1611.253**	Gun fire director radar	—
Neptune	—	Navigation radar	—
Owl Screech	**1325.253**	Gun fire control radar	—
Peel Group	**1323.253**	Missile fire control group for Goa	—
Plinth Net	**1609.253**	Medium-range general purpose E-band search radar	—
Pop Group	**1897.253**	Fire control radar group for SAN-4 missile system	—
Post Lamp	—	I/J-band target designation radar	—
Pot Drum	**1612.253**	Short-range surface search radar. H/I-band	—
Pot Head	**1613.253**	Short-range surface search radar	—
Round Top	—	Similar to Wasp Head	—
Scoop Pair	**1324.253**	Twin E-band radar group for SSM	—
Sea Gull	—	P-band long-range air search radar	—
Sheet Bend	—	General purpose navigation and pilotage radar	—
Sheet Curve	—	General purpose navigation and pilotage radar	—
Skin Head	**1614.253**	Surface target detection radar for torpedo boats	—
Ski Pole	—	IFF antenna. On 'Osa' missile boats	—
Slim Net	**1322.253**	High definition surface target radar	—
Snoop Plate	—	Submarine surveillance radar	—
Snoop Slab	—	Submarine surveillance radar	—
Snoop Tray	—	Submarine surveillance radar	—
Square Head	**1595.253**	IFF interrogator array	—
Square Slot	—	Surface detection radar	—
Square Tie	**1329.353**	General purpose search radar	—
Strut Curve	**1331.253**	Lightweight search radar	—
Sun Visor	**1326.253**	Optical director-mounted gun fire control radar	—
Top Bow	**1900.253**	Target acquisition radar for naval guns	—
Top Dome	**4088.253**	SAN-6 missile guidance group	—
Top Pair	**4087.253**	Long-range air surveillance radar	—
Top Sail	**1327.253**	Long-range 3-D air surveillance radar	—
Top Steer	**4086.253**	Air surveillance radar	—
Top Trough	**1610.253**	C-band long-range air search radar	—
Wasp Head	—	Gun fire control radar	—
Witch Five	—	IFF system	—
UNITED KINGDOM			
805 Series	**4302.253**	Naval tracking radar for fire control	Marconi
AWS-1	*1139.253*	Naval version of land-based AR-1	Plessey
AWS-2	**1751.253**	Improved version of AWS-1	Plessey
AWS-3	*3170.253*	Advanced version of AWS-2	Plessey
AWS-4	**3171.253**	Lightweight antenna version of AWS-2. Integrated IFF	Plessey
AWS-5	**3172.253**	Advanced version of ASW-4. Integrated IFF	Plessey
AWS-6	**5620.253**	Search and surveillance radar for naval point defence	Plessey
CEL 850	**3699.253**	Naval IFF interrogator	Cossor
Cossor IFF	*1571.253*	Naval IFF Mk 10 (SIF) 800 Series, 825, 825M	Cossor
Decca	**1941.253**	I/J-band navigation/tactical radars	Decca
Dolphin	*4004.253*	Target detection radar for Seaguard weapon system	Plessey
IFF 877	*3700.253*	Naval IFF interrogator	Cossor
MRS3/GWS 22	**1563.253**	Seacat and gun fire control radar	Sperry
PTR 461	*1896.253*	Shipborne IFF transponder	Plessey
PTR 826	*3259.253*	Shipborne IFF interrogator	Plessey
RRB	**3487.253**	Transponder reply receiver for use with ARI 5983/5954	Microwave Assoc
S604 HN	*1895.253*	Search radar. Fitted Egyptian Ramadan class ships	Marconi
S810	**1754.253**	Surveillance radar. Fitted Egyptian Ramadan class ships	Marconi
S820	**1754.253**	E/F-band surveillance radar	Marconi
S1100	**5632.253**	Radar series for navigation and short-range surveillance	Marconi
S1800	**3687.253**	Series of naval surveillance radars (S1820, S1821 and S1840) based on S810/820	Marconi
SNG 20	—	Fire control system	Marconi
SNW 10	—	Metric wavelength early warning radar	Marconi
SNW-12	—	Early warning radar. 150 cm. 450 kW. 4·28×2·14 m scanner	Marconi

Designation	Entry no	Description	Contractor(s)
UK cont			
SNW-20	—	Early warning radar	—
ST802	**1508.253**	Lightweight fire control radar	Marconi
ST 804	*3686.253*	Naval tracking radar	Marconi
TM626	—	Small navigational radar	Decca
Type 262	—	Short-range anti-aircraft fire control radar	EMI
Type 277	—	Nodding heightfinder radar	—
Type 293	—	General purpose E/F-band search radar	—
Type 294	*3261.253*	Plessey adaptation of RN Type 293	Plessey
Type 901	**1752.253**	Seaslug missile target tracking and guidance radar	Marconi
Type 903	**1563.253**	J-band conical scan tracker used with MRS3 director	Sperry/Plessey
Type 904	**1563.253**	J-band conical scan tracker used with MRS3 director	Sperry/Plessey
Type 909	**1559.253**	Target tracker and illuminating radar for Sea Dart missile system (GWS 30). 8ft cassegrain antenna	Marconi
Type 910	**1562.253**	Tracking radar for Seawolf missile	Marconi
Type 911	**5630.253**	Tracking radar for lightweight Seawolf (previously 805SW)	Marconi
Type 912	**1558.253**	RN designation of Selenia RTN-10X	—
Type 944	—	IFF	—
Type 965	**1560.253**	Primary search radar	Marconi
Type 967	**1561.253**	Compact air surveillance radar. Combined in Sea Wolf system	Marconi
Type 968	**1561.253**	Surface surveillance radar	Marconi
Type 975	**1253.253**	Lightweight I/J-band high definition surface warning radar. 50 kW	Kelvin Hughes
Type 975ZW	**1253.253**	Minehunting version of Type 975. True motion display plus sonar contact working	Kelvin Hughes
Type 978	*1254.253*	3 cm navigational radar. Double-cheese scanner. Successor to Type 974	Decca
Type 979	—	Similar to 978 but with additional B-scope display	—
Type 982	—	Aircraft direction	—
Type 983	—	Nodding heightfinder radar	—
Type 984	*1041.253*	3-D air surveillance long-range radar	Marconi
Type 992	*1255.253*	Long-range surveillance radar. Obsolescent	EMI
Type 992Q	**1753.253**	Solid-state general purpose radar	Marconi
Type 993	—	E/F-band search radar	—
Type 994	*3260.253*	Combination of Type 993 antenna with AWS-2 transmitter/receiver	Plessey
Type 996	**4634.253**	3-D surveillance and target indication radar for Type 23 frigates, Type 42 destroyers and Invincible class carriers	Plessey
Type 1006	**1394.253**	Successor to Type 975. Solid-state. 305mm display Max range 64 nm	Kelvin Hughes
Type 1010	*3698.253*	RN version of Cossor IFF 800	Cossor
Type 1013	*3701.253*	Naval version of Cossor IFF 2750	Cossor
Type 1022	*3486.253*	Replacement for Type 965 long-range radar. Fitted in various classes	Marconi
Type 1030	*3485.253*	Surveillance and target indication radar. Type 992Q replacement	Marconi
Type 1800	**3485.253**	Export version of Type 1030	Marconi
UNITED STATES OF AMERICA			
BPS-1	—	Submarine I-band search and fire control radar	Western Electric
BPS-2	—	Submarine D-band air search radar	Raytheon
BPS-3	—	H-band submarine air search radar	Western Electric
BPS-4	—	Short-range submarine air and surface search radar	Westinghouse
BPS-5	—	Short-range surface search radar for SSN 593 subs	Lockheed Electric
BPS-9	—	Submarine I-band air search radar	Western Electric
BPS-11	—	Submarine surface-search radar for SSB 616 subs	Western Electric
BPS-12	—	Medium range submarine surface-search radar	Fairchild
BPS-13	—	Similar to BPS-12	Fairchild
BPS-14	—	Similar to BPS-12. I/J-band	Fairchild
BPS-15	—	Submarine search and navigation radar. I-band	Sperry
FAST	**4608.253**	C and S-band search radar	General Electric
FLEXAR	*3258.253*	Weapon control system radar	Hughes
HR-76	*3768.253*	I-band combined search and track FCS radar for H-930 system	RCA
MBAR	**4233.253**	Multiple beam acquisition radar	Raytheon
RTN-10	*1245.253*	I/J-band fire control radar for Sea Sparrow III	Raytheon
Ship OTHR	*1937.253*	Shipboard over-the-horizon radar project	—
SPA-72	—	3-D fixed planar array surveillance radar	Hughes
SPG-49	*1749.253*	Guidance radar for Talos and Terrier surface-to-air missiles Used with SPW-2	Sperry
SPG-51	**1247.253**	Tartar missile guidance radar. I/J-band. Part of Mk 73 FCS	Raytheon
SPG-55	**1748.253**	Terrier missile fire control radar. G/H-band	Sperry
SPG-56	*1750.253*	Talos fire control radar. G/H-band	Sperry
SPG-59	—	Typhon missile radar. Performs all functions. Luneberg lens	Westinghouse
SPG-60	**1932.253**	Mk 86 FCS search and track radar	Lockheed
SPQ-5	*1938.253*	Early guidance radar	Sperry
SPQ-9	**1931.253**	Track-while-scan surface fire control radar used in Mk 86 FCS Housed in 300 cm radome	Lockheed
SPQ-11	**4301.253**	Missile space tracking radar. Cobra Judy. Operational	Raytheon/RCA/CSC
SPQ-55	—	Terrier tracking and guidance radar	Sperry
SPQ-60	—	Pulse doppler air target tracking radar used in Mk 86 FCS	—
SPS-3	—	Surveillance radar	Sylvania
SPS-4	—	Air and surface surveillance radar	Raytheon
SPS-5	—	Surface surveillance radar	Raytheon
SPS-6	**1744.253**	Search radar	Westinghouse
SPS-10	**1564.253**	G/H-band surface search radar	Sylvania/Raytheon
SPS-12	*1566.253*	D-band medium/long-range surveillance radar	RCA
SPS-17	—	Long-range surveillance radar	General Electric
SPS-23	—	Heightfinder	General Electric
SPS-29	—	Air surveillance radar for guided missile destroyers	Westinghouse
SPS-30	**1745.253**	Long-range 3-D radar	General Electric

Designation	Entry no.	Description	Contractor(s)
USA cont			
SPS-32	*1250.253*	3-D fixed planar array electronic scanning air and surface search radar	Hughes
SPS-33	*1251.253*	3-D fixed planar array electronic scanning target tracking radar	Hughes
SPS-34	—	Shipborne version of FPS-7 stacked beam 3-D radar	General Electric
SPS-37	**1565.153**	Air search radar	Westinghouse
SPS-39	*1249.253*	'Frescan' hybrid 3-D air target search radar	Hughes
SPS-40	**1746.253**	Air search radar. 'A' version has IFF	Norden
SPS-42	—	Hybrid electronic scanning 3-D radar	Hughes
SPS-43	**1747.253**	Air search radar	Westinghouse
SPS-48	**1252.253**	E/F-band long-range frequency scanned search and target acquisition radar. C and E versions now in production	ITT-Gilfillan
SPS-49	**1939.253**	Long-range air search radar for fitting in 5 Spanish FFGs	—
SPS-52/52A/52B	**1248.253**	Rotating planar (hybrid) 3-D surveillance radar	Hughes
SPS-52C	**5606.253**	Development of SPS-52	Hughes
SPS-55	**1697.253**	I/J-band surface radar	Cardion
SPS-58	**1359.253**	D-band air search radar used in H-930 FCS	Westinghouse
SPS-58LR	**4300.253**	Long-range version of SPS-58	Westinghouse
SPS-59	**3749.281**	Surface search radar used in H-930 FCS	—
SPS-63	**1940.253**	US designation for Italian 3RM series radars (SMA) Used on NATO hydrofoil	—
SPS-65	**1359.253**	Variant of SPS-58	Westinghouse
SPS-67	**3722.253**	Solid-state transmitter/receiver to update SPS-10. New antenna being designed	Norden
SPW-2	—	Talos guidance radar. Used with SPG-49	Sperry
SPY-1	**1570.253**	Multi-function array radar for Aegis system. Electronic scan	RCA/Raytheon
Type 23 TAS	**4609.253**	2-D acquisition radar for NATO Sea Sparrow	Hughes
W-120	**3256.253**	Shipboard version of APQ-120 fire control	Westinghouse
W-160	**4048.253**	J-band fire control radar	Westinghouse
W-611	**3257.253**	Shipboard version of TPS-61 D-band search radar	Westinghouse

1194.354   Airborne Radar

Designation	Entry no	Description	Contractor(s)
CANADA			
APS-504	**3473.353**	ASV search radar	Litton
FRANCE			
Agave	**1672.353**	I/J-band helicopter radar. Fitted French Navy Super Etendards, Jaguar International, all export Mirage FL and 50	Thomson-CSF/ESD
Aida I	—	Boresight ranging radar. Fitted French Navy Etendard IVM. I/J-band	Electronique Serge Dassault
Aida II	**1211.353**	Improved version of Aida I	Electronique Serge Dassault
Antilope	—	All weather strike radar, J-band. 4-lobe cassegrain antenna. Terrain following, mapping, ground attack	Electronique Serge Dassault
Antilope II	—	Simplified version of Antilope for light aircraft	Electronique Serge Dassault
Antilope IV	*1963.353*	Nose radar development for penetrator version of Super-Mirage	ESD/Thomson-CSF
Antilope V TC	**3297.353**	Strike radar for Mirage 2000N	Thomson-CSF
Cobra	—	Low-level strike and terrain following. Experimental system. Some features used in Cyrano III	Thomson-CSF
Cyrano I bis (RA 536)	*1050.353*	Monopulse fire control radar. Used in Mirage IIIC. I/J-band	Thomson-CSF
Cyrano II (RA 537)	**1051.353**	Monopulse fire control radar. Cassegrain antenna. Used in Mirage IIIE. I/J-band	Thomson-CSF
Cyrano III (RA 538)	**3131.353** *1052.353*	9 models in range, providing number of options up to full multi-role capability including air and ground attack and terrain following	Thomson-CSF
Cyrano IV	**1396.353**	Attack radar, air-air/air-ground. French F1s retrofitted with Mk IVM	Thomson-CSF
DRAA-2B	*1961.353*	ASV and navigation radar for Atlantic ASW aircraft	Thomson-CSF
DRAC-25	—	I/J-band fire control radar used in French Vatour fighters	Thomson-CSF
ESD 3300/3400	**1962.353**	IFF transponders	ESD
Heracles	**1960.353**	System of modular tactical radars based on ORB-31	Omera-Segid
Iguane/Agrion/Varan	**3298.253**	ASV radars in production for fixed and rotary wing aircraft	Thomson-CSF
Madrague	—	Pulse doppler early warning radar	Electronique Serge Dassault
Mirage 2000	**3297.353**	Pulse-doppler I/J-band radar for Mirage 2000. Multi-mode RDM version delivered to French AF 1983	Thomson-CSF/ESD
NR-A1-3-A	**1674.353**	Airborne IFF interrogator	LMT
ORB-31	**1793.353**	Helicopter and light aircraft I-band ASV, navigation, and met radar	Omera-Segid
ORB-32	**1960.353**	Sea Heracles	Omera-Segid
Oryx	*1351.353*	J-band terrain following and attack radar	Electronique Serge Dassault
Rafal	—	I/J-band coherent sideways looking radar	Thomson-CSF
RH 370	*1395.353*	I/J-band helicopter ASV radar	Thomson-CSF
Saiga	*1352.353*	Helicopter terrain avoidance radar. K-band	Electronique Serge Dassault
Saiga II	—	Simplified, lightweight version of Saiga	Electronique Serge Dassault
INTERNATIONAL			
APS-503	**1784.353**	Helicopter ASV, search, and navigation radar. I-band	AIL/Litton Canada
APS-504(V)3	**3473.353**	Airborne search radar	Litton Canada/Eaton
NIS	**5621.053**	NATO identification system (IFF). In development	—
ISRAEL			
EL/M-2001B	**3305.353**	I- or J-band ranging radar	Elta
EL/M-2021	**3306.353**	Multi-mode, pulse-doppler, I/J-band attack radar. Believed due for Israeli Lavi light fighter	Elta

Designation	Entry no	Description	Contractor(s)
ITALY			
AN/APX-104/SIT 432	3488.353	Airborne IFF interrogator	Italtel
MM/APQ-706	3309.353	I-band helicopter radar for Marte anti-ship missile system	SMA
MM/APS-705	3307.353	I-band helicopter radar. Dual transmitter/receivers	SMA
MM/APS-707	3308.353	I-band helicopter radar. Single channel version of APS-705	SMA
MM/UPX-709/SIT 421	3489.353	IFF transponder	Italtel
SWEDEN			
DAX-100/200 Series	1741.353	Fire control radars	Ericsson
Ericsson SLAR	4083.353	J-band maritime surveillance radar	Ericsson
PS-03/A (UAP 12)	1208.353	I/J-band AI radar, conical scan. Cassegrain antenna. Used in J35B and J35D Swedish AF Drakens	Ericsson
PS-01/A (UAP 13)	1209.353	Improved version of PS-03/A. Used in J35F Draken	
PS-011/A (UAP 13)	1209.353	Version of PS-01/A used with S71N IR search and track set in J35F	Ericsson
PS-37/A (UAP 1011)	1210.353	I/J-band. Monopulse. Modes include search, ground ranging, mapping, and obstacle avoidance	Ericsson
PS-46A	1964.353	Multi-mode radar for Viggen interceptor	Ericsson
JAS-39	5684.353	Nose radar and AEW radar for JAS-39 Grippen aircraft	Ericsson
UNION OF SOVIET SOCIALIST REPUBLICS			
Bee Hind	—	Tail warning and gun fire control	—
Big Bulge	—	Large ventral radar on Tu-95 Bear bomber	—
Big Nose	—	AI radar used in Tu-28 Fiddler strike aircraft	—
Down Beat	—	Bombing and navigation radar	—
Fan Tail	—	Tail radar for Tu-26 Backfire bomber	—
Fox Fire	—	AI radar. I-band	—
High Lark	—	J-band AI radar. Used in Flogger B/D/F	—
High Fix	—	Airborne ranging radar for Fitter-A and Fitter-C	—
Jay Bird	3311.353	AI radar for MiG-19	—
Look Two	1475.353	I/J-band bombing and navigation radar	—
Mushroom	—	Helicopter ASV radar	—
Puff Ball	1476.343	I/J-band search radar used in Bison aircraft	—
Scan Can	—	AI radar	—
Scan Fix	1477.343	AI radars for MiG-17 and 19 interceptors	—
Scan Odd	1479.353	I-band AI radar for MiG-19	—
Scan Three	1480.353	I-band AI radar for Yak-25	—
Shore Walk	—	Bombing radar for Yak-28 Brewer-B	—
Short Horn	1478.353	J-band bombing and navigation radar	—
Skip Spin	1481.353	I-band AI radars used in Su-11 and Yak 28	—
SLAR	—	Side-looking radar 1MW. J-band	—
Spin Scan	1482.353	Series of AI radars used in Su-9 and MiG-21	—
SRO-1/2	—	IFF transponder. SRO-1 obsolescent	—
SUAWACS	4616.393	Airborne AEW system	—
Toadstool	—	Used on Coke transport aircraft	—
Twin Scan	—	AI radar	—
UNITED KINGDOM			
UK AEW	1971.353	Airborne early warning radar using Nimrod aircraft	Marconi
Airpass I	1031.353	I/J-band AI radar. Search, tracking, and ranging. Used in RAF Lightning interceptors. Produced in 4 versions RAF designation AI23	Ferranti
Airpass II	1033.353	Development of Airpass I with added air-to-ground modes	Ferranti
Airpass III	1032.353	Surface strike radar for Buccaneer aircraft. Multi-mode I/J-band cassegrain antenna	Ferranti
AI-18	—	I/J-band fire control radar for RN Sea Vixen aircraft	GEC (UK)
ARI 5955/5954	1027.353	I-band system for use in ASW helicopters. Enables helicopter to be used as tactical control centre for ASW operation. Secondary radar capability. Fitted RN Sea Kings	MEL
ARI 5983	3310.353	I-band transponder for naval helicopters	Microwave Assoc
ARI 5991	3710.353	Sea Searcher. Replacement for ARI 5955/5954	MEL
ASR 360	5614.353	Maritime surveillance radar for medium sized fixed wing aircraft and helicopters. Developed from Decca Marine systems	Racal
ASV-21D	—	Air-to-surface vessel search radar used in HS 801 Nimrod maritime aircraft	EMI Electronics
Blue Fox	1972.353	Version of Seaspray. Production for RN and Indian Sea Harriers	Ferranti
Blue Kestrel	5685.353	ASV/ASW system in development for EH101 helicopter	Ferranti
Blue Vixen	4615.353	Multi-role pulse doppler system for Sea Harrier update programme. In development	Ferranti
CASTOR	4613.353	Airborne battlefield surveillance radar	Ferranti/Thorn-EMI
Cossor IFF	1572.353	Airborne IFF transponders	Cossor
E290M	1028.353	Combined weather and tactical radar. RCAF	
Foxhunter	1785.353	UK airborne interceptor radar. In production for RAF Tornado ADV aircraft	Marconi
IFF 2720	3695.353	IFF transponder	Cossor
IFF 2743	5603.353	Electronic control unit for use with IFF transponders	Cossor
IFF 3100	3696.353	IFF transponder. Selected for P110	Cossor
IFF 3500	3697.355	IFF airborne interrogator. Selected for P110	Cossor
LRR	1035.353	Lightweight ranging radar. Air and ground ranging Terrain warning	Ferranti
MAREC II	4341.353	Maritime reconnaissance radar	MEL
PTR 820	1224.353	IFF airborne interrogator	Plessey
P111	—	Coherent pulse multi-mode strike. AI and terrain following radar. Developed for classified project	Marconi
P391	1023.353	K-band sideways looking recce radar. Used in UK Phantom recce pod. Licensed to Electronique Serge Dassault	EMI Electronics
SATF	1216.353	Strike and terrain following radar. I/J-band multi-mode	Ferranti
Searchwater	1740.353	ASV and maritime radar. Fitted RAF Nimrods and RN AEW Sea Kings.	EMI

Designation	Entry no.	Description	Contractor(s)
UK cont			
Sea Searcher	**3170.353**	See ARI 5991. Operational	MEL
Seaspray	**1342.353**	I/J-band helicopter ASV radar	Ferranti
Sky Guardian	**4614.353**	Private venture AEW system based on UK AEW radar	Marconi Avionics
Skyranger	**5612.353**	Lightweight weapon control system for small fighter and ground attack aircraft. Aimed at retrofit market	Marconi Avionics
Sky Searcher	**4617.353**	AEW radar based on Sea Searcher	MEL
Super Searcher	**5625.353**	Lightweight maritime surveillance system developed from Sea Searcher	MEL
UNITED STATES OF AMERICA			
APD-7	—	Sideways looking radar. Used RA-5C	Westinghouse
APD-8	—	Sideways looking radar for RF-111A. Not deployed	Westinghouse
APG-22	—	CW ranging radar. USN	Raytheon
APG-31	—	Ranging radar. USAF	Raytheon
APG-43	—	CW AI radar	Raytheon
APG-55	—	AI intercept radar for USAF pulse doppler	Westinghouse
APG-59	—	Fire control radar. USN, USAF	Westinghouse
APG-63	**1765.353**	Multi-mode fire control radar for F-15	Hughes
APG-65	**3302.353**	I/J-band multi-mode radar. Operational in F/A-18 Hornet	Hughes
APG-66	**3303.353**	I/J-band multi-mode F-16 radar	Westinghouse
APG-67	**5610.353**	Multi-mode nose radar for F-5G Tigershark	General Electric
APN-59	—	Search and mapping radar	Sperry
APN-170	*1037.353*	Terrain following radar	General Dynamics
APN-171	*3124.353*	Terrain following radar	General Dynamics
APN-215	**4340.353**	Weather and terrain mapping radar	Bendix
APQ-55	—	Surveillance mapping radar. US Army	
APQ-56	—	Sideways looking radar for RB-47E. USAF	Westinghouse
APQ-67	—	AI radar. USAF	Raytheon
APQ-72	—	I/J-band AI radar. Target illuminator for Sparrow III missile Fitted F-4B	Westinghouse
APQ-81	—	Track-while-scan pulse doppler. USN	Westinghouse
APQ-83	—	Fire control radar for Sidewinder missile	Magnavox
APQ-86	—	Sideways looking battlefield surveillance radar	Texas Instruments
APQ-92	*1489.353*	Search radar used in USN A-6A aircraft	Norden
APQ-94	—	Fitted in F-8D aircraft	Magnavox
APQ-97	*7014.353*	Sideways looking radar. US Army	Westinghouse
APQ-99	**1970.353**	Forward radar for RF-4	Texas Instruments
APQ-100	—	Fire control radar. Used in F-4C. USAF	Westinghouse
APQ-102A	—	Recce radar. Used by USAF, USMC RF-4Cs Modified version fitted to some West German RF-104Gs	Goodyear
APQ-109	—	Fire control radar F-4D. USAF	Westinghouse
APQ-110	—	J-band terrain following and avoidance radar for F-111A Mounted below APQ-113	Texas Instruments
APQ-112	*1490.353*	Tracking radar on A-6A. Used with APQ-92 search radar	Norden
APQ-113	**1966.353**	J-band multi-mode radar for F-111A. Operational USAF and RAAF	General Electric
APQ-114	**1967.353**	Multi-mode nose radar for FB-111A	General Electric
APQ-116	—	Fire control radar. Ground ranging, terrain following AI Used on A-7A	Texas Instruments
APQ-119	—	Modified version of APQ-113. Limited procurement for F-111 programme	General Electric (US)
APQ-120	**1310.353**	AI terrain following radar for F-4E	Westinghouse
APQ-122	**1487.353**	Dual frequency I/J- and K-band radars for AWADS C-130 aircraft	Texas Instruments
APQ-124	—	Doppler AI ranging radar. USN	Magnavox
APQ-125	—	Doppler ranging radar for F-8J	Magnavox
APQ-126	**4334.353**	Used in USN A-7 aircraft	Texas Instruments
APQ-127	—	Forward looking radar	Sperry
APQ-128	—	F-111 terrain following radar	Sperry
APQ-130	—	F-111D attack radar for Mk II avionics	Autonetics
APQ-136	—	Nose radar for AC-119 gunship	Texas Instruments
APQ-137	**1401.353**	K-band MTI radar for detection of ground targets	Emerson
APQ-139	*1486.353*	J-band AMTI terrain avoidance/mapping radar Used in Tropic Moon 3 programme	Texas Instruments
APQ-140	**1488.353**	J-band multi-mode electronic scan radar	Raytheon
APQ-144	**1968.353**	Multi-mode nose radar for F-111F	General Electric
APQ-146	**4335.353**	Forward looking multi-mode nose radar	Texas Instruments
APQ-148/156	**1567.353**	J-band multi-mode radar for A-6E aircraft	Norden
APQ-152	—	All-weather topographic mapping radar set	Goodyear
APQ-153	**1675.353**	Fire control radar	Emerson
APQ-156	**1567.353**	See APQ-148	Norden
APQ-157	**3113.353**	Dual control search and range tracking radar for F-5F	Emerson
APQ-158	**4336.353**	Forward looking multi-mode radar used for Pavelow III	Texas Instruments
APQ-159	**3114.353**	Lightweight multi-mode nose radar. (V)-1 model on F-5E. (V)-2 on F-5F	Emerson
APQ-161	**3301.353**	Update of APS-144 for Pave Tack F-111F	General Electric (US)
APQ-163	**3682.353**	Experimental nose radar for B-1	General Electric
APQ-164	**4647.353**	Navigation and weapon delivery radar for B-1 supersonic bomber	Westinghouse
APS-20	—	Airborne early warning radar	
APS-42	—	Navigation and search radar	Bendix
APS-45	—	Airborne heightfinder radar	Texas Instruments
APS-49	—	High scan-rate ASV	Hazeltine
APS-70	—	Airborne early warning radar	General Electric (US)
APS-73	—	Series of SLARs developed for USAF and flown on C-97, B-58, and C-135 aircraft for test and evaluation of coherent, focused, synthetic aperture side-looking radars	Goodyear
APS-81	—	Nose radar for B-52	—
APS-85	—	Sideways looking MTI radar	Motorola

Designation	Entry no	Description	Contractor(s)
USA cont			
APS-88A	—	ASV search radar for S-2E tracker aircraft	Texas Instruments
APS-91	—	Airborne early warning radar	—
APS-94	**1484.353**	Long-range sideways looking radar. I/J-band	Motorola
APS-96	*1781.353*	Airborne early warning radar for E-2A	General Electric (US)
APS-111 (XN-1)	*1782.353*	Early warning radar for detection of aircraft targets against surface background. Used in E-2A. 2 built	General Electric (US)
APS-113	—	Lightweight helicopter radar	General Electric (US)
APS-115	**1969.353**	ASV search radar for P-3C ASW aircraft. I-band	Texas Instruments
APS-116	**1485.353**	ASV search radar for S-3A ASW aircraft. I-band	Texas Instruments
APS-119 (XN-1)	*1311.353*	Experimental version of APS-96 to provide overland target detection	General Electric
APS-120	**1783.353**	Airborne early warning radar for E-2C aircraft	General Electric
APS-124	**3518.353**	Search radar for LAMPS III helicopter	Texas Instruments
APS-125	**1965.353**	Improved version of APS-120 with ARPS (advanced radar processing sub-system). Fitted E-2C aircraft. Operated US, Israel, Japan etc	General Electric
APS-127	**3519.353**	Search radar for USMC medium-range surveillance aircraft	Texas Instruments
APS-128	**3132.353**	Maritime air search radar. See also DIGITACS (**4612.353**)	AIL
APS-130	**3520.353**	Navigation radar for EA-6B	Norden
APS-133	**4337.353**	Weather and terrain mapping radar	Bendix
APS-134(V)	**4338.353**	ASV/maritime reconnaissance radar for BR-1150	Texas Instruments
APS-137	—	Fire control radar for UH-1 series helicopters with M21 armament sub-system	—
APS-137(V)1	**1485.353**	Update of APS-116 for S-3A ASW aircraft	Texas Instruments
APS-138	**1965.353**	Updated APS-120/125 radar for E-2C	General Electric (US)
APX-72	**3688.353**	Airborne IFF transponder	Hazeltine
APX-76	**3690.353**	Airborne IFF interrogator	Hazeltine
APX-83	**1569.353**	Airborne IFF interrogator for E-2C aircraft	AIL
APX-100(V)	**4339.353**	Airborne IFF transponder	Bendix
APX-103	**3300.353**	IFF interrogator system for E-3A AWACS	AIL
APX-104	**3689.353**	Airborne IFF interrogator	Hazeltine
APY-1	**1585.353**	Airborne warning and control system (AWACS) radar for E-3A	Westinghouse
ASG-14	—	Fire control radar for nuclear armed F-104A	Texas Instruments
ASG-15	—	Rear fire control radar for B-52	Arma
ASG-17	—	Fire control radar. Nuclear weapons	—
ASG-18	—	Fire control radar for AIM-47A and AIM-54 missile Fitted FY-12A	Hughes
ASG-19	—	Fire control radar for F-105D (Thunderstick)	General Electric (US)
ASG-25	—	Fire control radar. Non-nuclear arms	—
ASQ-112	—	MTI radar. USN	Norden
AWG-9	**1100.353**	Missile fire control radar system. F-14	Hughes
AWG-10	**3018.353**	AI-terrain avoidance, mapping radar for F-4J. High prf pulse doppler	Westinghouse
AWG-11	**3018.353**	Version of AWG-10 for RN Phantoms	Westinghouse
AWG-12	**3018.353**	Version of AWG-10 for RAF Phantoms	Westinghouse
DPS-5	**4618.353**	Balloon-borne radar	RCA
UPD-4	**1676.353**	Side-looking radar. Used on USAF RF-4Cs and Japanese RF-4E	Goodyear
UPD-5	—	High resolution side-looking radar with MTI for USAF and West Germany. Development	Westinghouse
UPD-6	*3474.353*	Reconnaissance radar for West German AF	Goodyear
UPD-8	**5686.353**	Side-looking synthetic aperture radar. Update of UPD-4	Goodyear
UPX-709	**3691.353**	Airborne IFF transponder	Hazeltine
AWACS	**1585.353**	Airborne early warning radar for E-3A	Westinghouse
Cobra	*1706.353*	Fire control radar	Hughes
Conformal radar	**5609.353**	Design of surveillance radar embedded in nose and wings with solid-state modules	General Electric
Covert strike radar	**4648.353**	Stand-off radar project	—
DIGITACS	**4612.353**	Improved version of APS-128	Eaton
F-16	**3303.353**	I/J-band pulse-doppler, multi-mode radar for F-16 aircraft	Westinghouse
Egyptian Goose	**3162.353**	Balloon-borne radar project. ARPA	Westinghouse
ESAIRA	*1491.353*	Experimental electronic scanned antenna	Hughes
HOWLS/ULTRA	**3304.353**	Experimental ultra lightweight transmissive array for Hostile Weapons Location Systems programme	General Electric (US)
JSTARS	**5624.353**	Joint USAF/US Army requirement for airborne anti-tank radar. 4 contenders bidding: General Electric, Westinghouse, Hughes, Grumman/Norden	US DoD
MERA	—	Molecular electronics for radar applications Experimental phase scanning system	Texas Instruments
Multibeam Survivable Radar	**5611.353**	Air-to-ground weapon control and battlefield surveillance radar. Contender for JSTARS	General Electric
Project Seek Skyhook	**4618.353**	Balloon-borne radar	RCA
NASARR	*1568.353*	North American search and ranging radar for F-104	Autonetic/NATO
Pocket Veto	**3162.353**	Surveillance radar on ARPA Family II aerostat	Westinghouse
RARF	—	Radome, antenna, RF. Refractive lens phase scanning J-band radar. Experimental	Emerson
RARF	—	Radome, antenna, RF. Reflecting lens phase scanning I- and J-band versions built	Raytheon
Balloon-borne radar	**3162.353**	Improved Pocket Veto radar for surveillance and clutter measurement of USAF	Westinghouse
Tornado nose radar	**4333.353**	Terrain following/mapping radar for strike version of Tornado	Texas Instruments
EC-153	**3299.353**	I/J-band pulse-doppler multi-mode derivative of APQ-153 and APQ-159.	Emerson
WX Series	**1673.353**	Fire control radar series. Developed version selected for F-16	Westinghouse

1521.454   **Sonar Equipment**

Designation	Entry no	Description	Contractor(s)
AUSTRALIA			
Barra (SSQ-801)	**1791.453**	Project Barra. RAAF/RAN project to develop advanced sonobuoy and airborne detection system	Amalgamated Wireless
Mulloka	**1790.453**	Sonar project for RAN	—
SSQ-801	**3998.453**	Barra system passive directional sonobuoy	Amalgamated Wireless
CANADA			
HS-100	**1636.453**	Lightweight search/attack sonar. Hull-mounted and towed versions	Canadian Westinghouse
SBP1-1	**4649.363**	Sonobuoy processor	CDC
SQS-505	**1792.453**	Medium search/attack sonar	Canadian Westinghouse
SQS-507 (Helen)	2038.453	Lightweight variable-depth towed sonar	Canadian Westinghouse
SQS-509	**4000.453**	Lower frequency version of SQS-505	CAE
SSQ-517	3085.453	Passive sonobuoy	Sparton
SSQ-518	3085.453	Passive sonobuoy. Long-life version of SSQ-517	Sparton
SSQ-522	**3086.453**	Active sonobuoy. Canadian version of SSQ-47	Sparton
SSQ-523	**3087.453**	CANCASS, Canadian command-active sonobuoy system	Sparton
SSQ-527	**3780.453**	Improved version of SSQ-517B	Sparton
SSQ-529	**4619.453**	Directional sonobuoy	Sparton
SSQ-530	**4620.453**	Directional passive sonobuoy	Sparton
FRANCE			
Argonaut	**5650.453**	Sonar for RN Type 2400 submarine	Thomson-CSF
Beluga	3774.453	Panoramic sonar	Thomson-CSF
Diodon (TSM 2314)	**1725.253**	Surface vessel sonar. Active	Thomson-CSF
DSRX-61X	**4461.453**	Experimental towed linear array sonar	SINTRA-ALCATEL
DST A 3	1067.453	Active sonobuoy used with DSAA-4 system	SINTRA-ALCATEL
DSTV-4M/DSTV-7Y	**3501.453**	Passive sonobuoys	Thomson-CSF
DUBA-3A	1157.253	Surface vessel attack sonar	SINTRA-ALCATEL
DUBM-20A	1357.253	Active minehunting sonar	Thomson-CSF
DUBM-21B (TSM 2021)	**1977.253**	Mine countermeasures sonar. (Ibis). TSM 2019/2021/2022 variants also	Thomson-CSF
DUBM-40	1358.253	Active minehunting sonar, towed	Thomson-CSF
DUBM-41B (TSM 2050)	**1726.453**	High-resolution side-looking sonar	Thomson-CSF
DUBV-23D	**1159.253**	Active surface vessel search/attack sonar	SINTRA-ALCATEL
DUBV-24C	1217.253	Low-frequency panoramic search/attack sonar	SINTRA-ALCATEL
DUBV-43B	**1334.453**	Variable depth towed sonar. Active or passive. Used with DUBV-23	SINTRA-ALCATEL
DUBY-24C	1355.453	Active submarine sonar. Panoramic, sector or tracking modes	Thomson-CSF
DUUA-1	1161.453	Submarine sonar. A, B and C versions	SINTRA-ALCATEL
DUUA-2A	**1634.453**	Simultaneous search and attack sonar for modernised 'Daphne' class submarines	SINTRA-ALCATEL
DUUA-2B	**3232.453**	Development of DUUA-2A	SINTRA-ALCATEL
DUUX-2	1162.453	Passive submarine detection system	SINTRA-ALCATEL
DUUX-5	**3948.453**	Successor to DUUX-2. Sea Fenelon	SINTRA-ALCATEL
DUAV-4	**1631.353**	HS-71 helicopter sonar	SINTRA-ALCATEL
DUAV-18	1160.353	Helicopter sonar. Superseded by HS.70	SINTRA-ALCATEL
Eledone	**1356.453**	Passive sonar for submarine	Thomson-CSF
Fenelon	**3498.453**	Passive rangefinder for submarines	SINTRA-ALCATEL
HS.12	**4095.453**	Helicopter version of SS12 sonar	SINTRA-ALCATEL
HS.70	1219.353	Helicopter sonar	SINTRA-ALCATEL
IBIS	**4348.453**	Minehunting sonar system	Thomson-CSF
Pascal	1633.253	Surveillance and tracking sonar for small and medium ships	SINTRA-ALCATEL
Piranha (TSM 2140)	1978.253	Small ship attack sonar	Thomson-CSF
Premo	1218.253	Panoramic search/attack sonar	SINTRA-ALCATEL
SS12	**4094.453**	Panoramic sonar for small/medium ships	SINTRA-ALCATEL
SS24	**4096.453**	Panoramic sonar more powerful version of SS12	SINTRA-ALCATEL
SS 24LF	**5633.453**	Passive panoramic sonar	SINTRA-ALCATEL
SS48	**4097.453**	Panoramic surface ship sonar	SINTRA-ALCATEL
SQS-17A	1158.253	Panoramic sonar. Superseded by Premo	SINTRA-ALCATEL
TSM 2019	1977.253	Version of DUBM-21 minehunting family	Thomson-CSF
TSM 2021	1977.253	DUBM-21B minehunting sonar for Triparatite Minehunter (F, NI, B)	Thomson-CSF
TSM 2022	**4349.453**	Derivative of TSM 2021 (above)	Thomson-CSF
TSM 2400/DUBA 25	**1724.253**	Surface vessel sonar (Tarpon)	Thomson-CSF
TSM 2600	5647.253	Lightweight version of TSM 2630	Thomson-CSF
TSM 2630	5646.253	Improved version of Diodon sonar	Thomson-CSF
TSM 2640	5648.253	Passive sonar for patrol craft	Thomson-CSF
TSM 2820	5649.253	Active panoramic sonar (Tarpon)	Thomson-CSF
GERMANY, Federal Republic			
ASO4-2 Mod	—	Active sonar for small vessels. Hull mounted	Krupp Atlas-Elektronik
CSU 3	**4229.453**	Passive/active/intercept sonar for submarines	Krupp Atlas-Elektronik
DSQS-11A	**4230.453**	Hull-mounted mine avoidance sonar for minesweepers	Krupp Atlas-Elektronik
DSQS-11H	**4230.453**	Hull-mounted minehunting sonar	Krupp Atlas-Elektronik
DSQS-21B/C/D	**4228.453**	Series of active panoramic anti-submarine sonar for surface ships Hull-mounted and towed versions	Krupp Atlas-Elektronik
PSU 1-2	**4229.453**	Passive submarine sonar	Krupp Atlas-Elektronik
PRS 3	**4229.453**	Passive ranging sonar for submarines	Krupp Atlas-Elektronik
SIP 3	**4229.453**	Sonar processor for passive classification	Krupp Atlas-Elektronik
ITALY			
BI68	1721.453	Sonobuoy. Double number of RF channels	SELENIA-ELSAG
BIR	1723.453	Miniature sonobuoy for helicopter use	Servomeccanismi
BIT-3	1723.453	Passive sonobuoy	Servomeccanismi
BIT-8	1723.453	Passive sonobuoy	Servomeccanismi
FALCO/GIARDA	3235.453	Submarine detection and location system	SELENIA-ELSAG

Designation	Entry no	Description	Contractor(s)
ITALY cont			
IP64-MD64	**1720.453**	Submarine sonars	SELENIA-ELSAG
IPD-70/S	**3233.453**	Integrated sonar for Sauro submarines	SELENIA-ELSAG
MD 100/S	**3773.453**	Passive submarine sonar	SELENIA-ELSAG
MLS/1A	**3235.453**	Sonar	SELENIA-ELSAG
MSR-810	**4007.453**	Passive sonobuoy	MISAR
SQQ-14	**3234.453**	Mine detection and classification sonar	FIAR
NETHERLANDS			
HSS-15	**4464.453**	Compact panoramic sonar for small ships	Signaal
LW-30	**3141.253**	Passive sonar/intercept system	Signaal
PHS-32	3142.253	Search/attack sonar	Signaal
PHS-34	**5635.453**	Long-range panoramic sonar	Signaal
PHS-36	**4001.453**	Active panoramic sonar	Signaal
SIASS	**5636.453**	Submarine attack and surveillance sonar	Signaal
NORWAY			
SK3D	3644.453	Higher frequency version of SQ-D	Simrad
SQ-D	3644.453	Hull mounted sonar	Simrad
SQ3D/SF	3644.453	Medium range 'searchlight' sonar	Simrad
SS 105	**4128.453**	Coastguard 360° scanning sonar	Simrad
SS 304	**5645.253**	Small ship scanning sonar	Simrad
ST	3644.453	Bulkhead mounted sonar	Simrad
SU	3644.453	Bulkhead mounted version of SU-R	Simrad
SU-R	3644.453	Similar to SU-RS without transducer stabilisation	Simrad
SU-RS	3644.453	Hull mounted long range sonar	Simrad
UNITED KINGDOM			
Bathythermal Buoy	**3770.453**	F-size version of SSQ-36	Dowty
CAMBS (X17255)	**3237.453**	Command Active Multi-Beam Sonobuoy	Dowty
FMS Series	**4625.253**	Family of active and passive sonar systems for surface vessels	Ferranti
G738	**3268.493**	Towed system for decoying active and passive homing torpedoes	Graseby
G750	**3266.453**	Multipurpose all-round active/passive sonar for corvettes and above. Based on RN Type 184. Auto-tracking	Graseby
G768	—	Derived from 750 series for use in smaller ships	Graseby
G777	3267.453	Compact sonar for patrol craft down to 100 tons	Graseby
G780	—	Passive sonar for very small submarines	Graseby
HISOS 1	**5637.353**	Passive/active helicopter sonar (Cormorant)	Plessey Marconi Avionics
Jezebel	**3502.453**	Passive sonobuoy	Dowty
PMS26/27	**7002.253**	Lightweight search/attack sonar	Plessey
PMS32	1221.253	Active panoramic sonar	Plessey
PMS35	3094.253	Small frigate digital sonar	Plessey
PMS40	**5639.253**	Series of modular sonar systems	Plessey
PMS75	**5638.263**	Sidescan sonar equipment	Plessey
MOSAIC	**5654.363**	ASW avionics integration system	Marconi Avionics
MS70	**1374.253**	Solid-state version of Type 193 minehunting sonar	Plessey
Ranger	**3769.453**	SSQ-47B sonobuoy	Dowty
SADE	1788.453	Sensitive Acoustic Detection Equipment. Intruder detection system	Plessey
SSQ-904	**3503.453**	Miniature passive (Jezebel) sonobuoy	Dowty
T17164	1787.453	Mk IC active sonobuoy	Plessey
Type 162M	**1755.453**	Side-looking and bottom profile sonar	Kelvin Hughes
Type 170	—	Surface ship attack sonar	Graseby
Type 176	—	Passive protection sonar for surface ships	Graseby
Type 177	—	Surface ship medium-range searchlight sonar	Graseby
Type 182	**3268.453**	(GI738) towed torpedo decoy sonar	Graseby
Type 183	—	(GI732) emergency underwater communications	Graseby
Type 184M	**3265.453**	RN surface vessel ASW search and attack sonar	Graseby
Type 185	—	Underwater communications sonar	Graseby
Type 186	—	Submarine sonar	EMI
Type 187	—	Submarine sonar	EMI
Type 193	1373.253	Minehunting sonar of RN Mk 1 system	—
Type 193M	**1374.253**	Solid-state improved version of Type 193 minehunting sonar	Plessey
Type 195	**1024.353**	Helicopter sonar based on MS 26/27	Plessey
Type 199	2447.253	Variable depth towed sonar	EMI
Type 719	—	Submarine sonar	EMI
800 Series	**3269.453**	Series of new generation sonars. Modular	Graseby
Type 2001	—	Nuclear submarine sonar	Graseby
Type 2004	—	Conventional/nuclear submarine sonar	Graseby
Type 2007	—	Conventional submarine sonar	Graseby
Type 2008/9	—	Underwater communications sonar	Marconi
Type 2015	**3789.453**	XBT bathythermographic buoy	Plessey
Type 2016	**3787.453**	Advanced fleet escort attack sonar	Plessey
Type 2020	**5651.453**	Passive/active submarine sonar	Plessey
Type 2028	—	Surface ship sonar	Graseby
Type 2034	**4127.453**	Short-range bottom profile sonar	Waverley
Type 2093	4451.453	Minehunting sonar	Plessey
UNITED STATES OF AMERICA			
AMSS	**5652.253**	Advanced minehunting sonar system development	Raytheon/ Thomson-CSF
AQS-13	**1637.353**	Helicopter sonar	Bendix
AQS-14	**4462.353**	Helicopter towed side-looking sonar for mine clearance	Westinghouse
AQS-18	**4456.353**	Helicopter panoramic sonar	Bendix
BQQ-1/4	—	Submarine passive fire control sonars	Sperry/Raytheon
BQQ-1	—	Search and fire control sonars	Raytheon

Designation	Entry no	Description	Contractor(s)
USA cont			
BQQ-2	—	Sonar for Subroc system	Raytheon
BQQ-5	**1983.453**	Nuclear attack submarine sonar	IBM/Raytheon
BQQ-6	**4629.453**	Active/passive sonar for Trident submarines	IBM
BQR-2	—	Submarine passive sonar	EDO/Raytheon
BQR-3	—	Submarine passive sonar	Raytheon
BQR-7	—	Passive sonar. Part of BQQ-2 system. Fitted FBM subs	EDO/Raytheon
BQR-15	**1984.453**	Towed submarine sonar. Fitted FBM subs	Western Electric
BQR-19	—	Submarine sonar	Raytheon
BQR-21	**1985.453**	Submarine passive detection and tracking set (DIMUS). Fitted FBM subs	Honeywell
BQS-4	—	Adds active sonar capability to BQR-2B	EDO
BQS-6	—	Active submarine sonar. Part of BQQ-2 system	Raytheon
BQS-8	—	Under-ice navigation sonar	Hazeltine/EDO
BQS-13	**1986.453**	Submarine search sonar. Passive/active	Raytheon
BQS-14A	—	Submarine navigation sonar for under-ice passage	Hazeltine
BQS-15	—	—	Amtek
BRT-1	*3785.453*	Sonar radio transmitting buoy	Sparton
DE1164	**3115.453**	SQS-56 plus variable depth sonar	Raytheon
DE1167/1191	**3116.453**	Small ship sonar based on SQS-56	Raytheon
Dwarf	**3782.453**	Reduced length, standard diameter miniature passive sonobuoy	Sparton
Dwarf DIFAR	**3782.453**	DIFAR version of Dwarf	Sparton
Dwarf DIFAR(VLAD)	**3782.453**	Vertical line array DIFAR version of Dwarf	Sparton
Dwarf omni	**4458.453**	Dwarf omnidirectional passive sonobuoy	Sparton
Hydroscan	**4460.453**	Towed side-scan seabed mapping sonar	Klein
Micro PUFFS	**3772.453**	Submarine passive ranging sonar	Sperry
Mk 24	**5643.453**	Underwater ordnance location sonar	Klein
PQS-2	**5640.453**	Hand-held active/passive diver sonar	General Instrument Corp
SQA-10	—	Variable depth sonar	Litton
SQA-13	—	Variable depth sonar	EDO/Litton
SQA-14	—	'Searchlight' sonar	Raytheon
SQA-16	—	'Searchlight' sonar	Raytheon
SQA-19	—	Variable depth sonar	Litton
SQG-1	—	Anti-submarine attack sonar	Raytheon
SQQ-14	**1789.453**	Minehunting and classification sonar	GE
SQQ-23	—	Sonar for A/S patrol ships	—
SQQ-30	**4623.253**	Minehunting sonar	General Electric
SQQ-32	**5652.253**	Minehunting sonar	Raytheon
SQR-14	—	Surface sonar	—
SQR-18A	**4622.253**	TACTAS – Tactical Towed Array Sonar	EDO
SQR-19	**4463.253**	Tactical towed array sonar	Gould
SQS-4	—	Short-range active sonar	Sangamo/GE
SQS-23	—	Long-range active sonar	Sangamo
SQS-26	**2536.253**	Bow-mounted, 'bottom bounce' mode sonar to replace SQS-23	EDO/GE
SQS-29/32	—	Surface vessel active sonars. Numbers relate to differing frequencies. 'B' models are associated with variable depth sonar	Sangamo
SQS-35	**2534.253**	Variable depth sonar	EDO
SQS-36	**2534.253**	Medium-range hull sonar	EDO
SQS-38	**2534-253**	Medium-range hull-mounted version of SQS-35	EDO
SQS-53	**2536.253**	Development of SQS-26	GE
SQS-56	**1807.453**	Lightweight sonar for USN PF (Patrol Frigate) ships and other navies (DE1160B)	Raytheon Sparton
SSQ-36	*3781.453*	Bathythermograph sounding buoy	Sparton
SSQ-41	**1987.453**	Sonobuoy, passive	Magnavox/Sparton
SSQ-47	**1988.453**	Sonobuoy, active	Sparton
SSQ-50	*1989.453*	CASS-Command Active Sonobuoy System	Sparton
SSQ-53A	**1990.453**	Sonobuoy, passive directional (DIFAR)	Sparton/Magnavox/Sanders
SSQ-53B	**4457.453**	Successor to SSQ-53A	Sparton
SSQ-57A	**3083.453**	Sound reference sonobuoy	Sparton
SSQ-62	**1991.453**	Sonobuoy, directional version of SSQ-50 (DICASS)	Sparton/Raytheon/Magnavox
SSQ-71	**3786.453**	ATAC, air transportable acoustic communication buoy	Sparton/Sanders
SSQ-77	**3084.453**	VLAD-vertical line array DIFAR passive sonobuoy	Hazeltine/Sparton
SSQ-79	—	Steered vertical line array sonobuoy. Development	Hazeltine
SSQ-86	**4459.453**	Down-link communications sonobuoy	Sparton
SST	**3494.253**	Advanced sonar standard transmitter	Raytheon
UQS-2	—	Minehunting sonar	GE
610	**2580.253**	Long-range hull sonar	EDO
700 Series	**2581.253**	Medium-range. Hull and variable depth versions	EDO
780 Series	**3495.253**	Variable depth sonar. 13 kHz	EDO
786 Series	**3495.253**	Hull-mounted sonar. 13 kHz	EDO
795 Series	**3495.253**	Hull-mounted sonar. 5 kHz	EDO
796 Series	**3495.253**	Hull-mounted sonar. 7 kHz	EDO
900 Series	**5644.453**	Submarine mine avoidance	EDO
910 Series	**5644.453**	Surface ship mine avoidance	EDO
1102/1105 Series	**3496.453**	Submarine active/passive medium range	EDO
7860 Series	**3435.253**	Combined 13 kHz hull sonar with 13 kHz VDS	EDO
7950 Series	**3495.253**	Combined 5 kHz hull sonar with 13 kHz VDS	EDO
7960 Series	**3495.253**	Combined 7 kHz hull sonar with 13 kHz VDS	EDO
TVLAD	**3783.453**	Tuned vertical array omni sonobuoy	Sparton
Widetrac	**3784.453**	Sonar communications buoy	Sparton

4212.454   **Miscellaneous Underwater Detection Equipment**

Designation	Entry no	Description	Contractor(s)
CANADA			
ASA-64	4222.353	Anomaly detection signal processor	CAE
ASA-65	3231.393	Compensator group adapter for ASA 65(V)	CAE
ASA-65(V)	1388.393	Nine-term compensator for MAD system	CAE
ASQ-502	3999.353	Submarine detecting set (MAD)	CAE
ASQ-504(V)	4621.353	Submarine detecting set (MAD)	CAE
OA 5154/ASQ	1980.393	Automatic MAD compensation system	
FRANCE			
Crouzet MAD	*1979.353*	ASW helicopter MAD equipment	Crouzet
DHAX-1	1389.353	Airborne MAD equipment	—
DHAX-3	1390.353	ASW helicopter MAD equipment	—
Lampard (TSM 8210/8220)	4347.363	Airborne digital sonar data processor	Thomson-CSF
PAP 104	1786.453	Mine disposal system	Société ECA
Sonar processor	*1719.263*	Computer for analysis of sonar coverage	SINTRA-ALCATEL
TSM 8200	3791.363	Airborne sonar processing equipment	Thomson-CSF
TSM 9310	3095.263	Sound ray tracer for analysis of sonar equipment performance	Thomson-CSF
ITALY			
CIACIO	3235.453	Torpedo self-homing system	SELENIA-ELSAG
ELT/810	5653.263	Sonar prediction system	Elettronica
FALCO	1722.353	Airborne submarine locating system	SELENIA-ELSAG
FALCO/GIARDA	3235.453	Submarine detection and localisation system	SELENIA-ELSAG
P MICCA	3235.453	Remote-control of deep sea mines	SELENIA-ELSAG
SFM-A	3235.453	Underwater target identification system	SELENIA-ELSAG
NETHERLANDS			
SP1-04	1525.263	Sound ray path analyser	Van der Heem
XSV-01	3493.453	Expendable sound velocimeter for sound ray path measurement	Van der Heem
UNITED KINGDOM			
AQS-901	1981.363	Airborne acoustic data processing and display system	Marconi/Computing Devices
Area defence	4626.453	Passive sonar for area defence	Marconi
ARR-901	4453.363	Airborne sonar data receiver	McMichael
AQS-902 LAPADS	3497.363	Lightweight acoustic processing and display system for ASW helicopters	Marconi
AQS-903	5655.363	Lightweight helicopter processing and display system	Marconi
Deep Mobile target	4680.493	Instrumented ship-launched target	Thorn-EMI
MCM System	*3161.253*	Mine countermeasures system	Plessey/Racal-Decca/Sperry/ Vosper Thornycroft
SACACS	3269.453	Transportable long-range calibration system	Graseby
Nantis-M	4681.273	Action information system	Plessey
SLUTT	3269.453	Underwater transponder target	Graseby
Towed Arrays	4627.463	Towed arrays	Ameeco
UNITED STATES OF AMERICA			
Active processing system	3788.363	Airborne system for processing sonobuoy data	Sparton
AKT-22(V)4	3777.363	Telemetry data transmitting set	EDMAC
ARR-72	3454.363	P-3C Orion sonobuoy receiver system	EDMAC
ARR-75	3455.363	Sonobuoy receiver	EDMAC
ARR-78(V)	3778.363	Advanced sonobuoy communication link (ASCL)	Hazeltine
ASA-66	4013.373	P-3C Orion ASW tactical data cockpit display	Loral
ASA-82	4012.373	S3A Viking ASW tactical data display system	Loral
ASQ-81(V)	3599.253	Airborne MAD system	Texas Instruments
AYA-8B	1982.363	P-3C Orion ASW data processing system	General Electric
DICASS command signal monitor	3788.363	SSQ-50 test equipment in the Directional Command Active Sonobuoy System (DICASS)	Sparton
Directional sonar processor	3788.363	Airborne system for processing DIFAR data	Sparton
OL-5003(–)/ARR	3788.363	Sonobuoy signal processor	Sparton
R-1651/ARA	3776.253	VHF radio receiver for sonobuoy location	EDMAC
RO 308/SSQ-36	1635.453	P-3C Orion bathythermograph data recorder	Western Components
Spectrum analyser	3788.363	Airborne digital processor for real time spectral analysis	Sparton
TD 1135A	3788.363	Demultiplexer processor/display	Sparton
WQC-2A	4455.453	Sonar underwater communications set	General Instruments Corp

2296.444

Torpedoes

Designation	Entry no	Dimensions (d×l)	Description	Contractor(s)
FRANCE				
E14	**1163.441**	21 in×4·29 m	Passive acoustic homing. Contact and magnetic fuze	DTCN/CIT-ALCATEL
E15	**1164.441**	550 mm×6 m	As E14 but 300 kg charge instead of 200 kg	DTCN/CIT-ALCATEL
F17	**3623.441**	21 in×5·9 m	Wire-guided or automatic homing. Surface or submarine targets. F17P multimode version	DTCN
L3	**1165.441**	21 in×4·32 m	Active acoustic homing. Contact and magnetic	DTCN/CIT-ALCATEL
L3 Mod 1	**1165.441**	550 mm×4·3 m	fuze. 200 kg charge 21 in version available for manufacture but not in production	DTCN/CIT-ALCATEL
L4	**2096.441**	21 in×3·13 m	Circular search. Active acoustic homing. Contact and acoustic proximity fuze. Air-launched. Used in Malafon	DTCN
L5 Mod 1	**2128.441**	21 in	Active/passive acoustic homing. Direct attack programmed search. Surface launch weight 1000 kg	DTCN
L5 Mod 3	**2128.441**	21 in	As Mod 1 but submarine launch weight 1300 kg	DTCN
L5 Mod 4	**2128.441**	21 in	Anti-submarine model	DTCN
L5 Mod 4P	**2128.441**	21 in	Multi-purpose model	DTCN
Z16	**2146.441**	550 mm × 7·2 m	Preset course and depth. Runs zig-zag pattern if no target encountered after predetermined distance run. Magnetic and contact fuze. 300 kg charge. Obsolescent	—
GERMANY, Federal Republic				
Seal	**2178.441**	21 in×6·08 m	Wire-guided heavy surface target torpedo. Surface launch Magnetic and impact fuzes. 260 kg warhead	AEG/Krupp Atlas Elektronik
Seeschlange	**2178.441**	21 in×4·15 m	Wire-guided, surface launch, submarine targets. 100 kg warhead	AEG/Krupp Atlas Elektronik
SST-4	**2000.441**	21 in×6·5 m	Wire-guided; active/passive acoustic homing. Torpedo sonar linked to shipborne FCS. 260 kg warhead	AEG
SUT	**2570.441**	21 in×6·1 m	Wire-guided; active/passive acoustic homing. Similar to SST-4 but dual purpose	AEG
ITALY				
A.184	**2003.441**	21 in×6 m	Wire-guided, automatic acoustic homing	Whitehead-Moto Fides
A.244	**2004.441**	324 mm×2·7 m	Acoustic homing. Shallow water and anti-reverberation capabilities	Whitehead-Moto Fides
A.244/S	**2004.441**	324 mm×2·7 m	A.244 with more sophisticated CIACIO homing head	Whitehead-Moto Fides
SWEDEN				
Type 41	*2323.441*	400 mm×2·44 m	Passive homing in azimuth and depth. Shallow water capability Impact and proximity fuze. Electric propulsion. All-up weight 250 kg	Förenade Fabriksverken (FFV)
Type 42	**2474.441**	400 mm×2·44 m	Successor to Type 41 with helicopter-launch capability and optional wire guidance (length then 2·6 m)	FFV
TP 422/423	**2474.441**	-	Swedish Navy versions of Type 42	FFV
TP 427	**2474.441**	-	Export version of Type 42	FFV
TP 61	**2367.441**	21in×6·98 m	Long-range heavyweight passive homing	FFV
TP 613	**2367.441**	-	Swedish Navy version of Type 61	FFV
TP 617	**2367.441**	-	Export version of Type 61	FFV
UNION OF SOVIET SOCIALIST REPUBLICS				
21 in Torpedo	**2995.441**	21 in	Standard fit for submarines. Alternatives available for surface vessel launching	State
Airborne Torpedo	**2996.441**	—	—	State
Light Torpedo	**2997.441**	406 mm×5 m approx	Training deck launchers	State
UNITED KINGDOM				
Mk 8	**2552.441**	21 in×6·7 m	1930s design. Compressed air propulsion, free-running. In RN service until 1973. May still be in service elsewhere	UK MoD
Mk 20	—	21 in×4·11 m	Passive sonar homing (depth and azimuth). Electric propulsion Mechanical course settings. 91 kg charge. 244 m homing depth	UK MoD
Mk 20 (Improved)	*2471.441*	21 in×4·11 m	As standard Mk 20 but with cable-set course angles	UK MoD/Vickers
Mk 23	*3341.441*	21 in	Project abandoned	UK MoD/AUWE
Mk 24	**2472.441**	21 in	Redeveloped as Tigerfish	UK MoD
Tigerfish (Mk 24	**2440.441**	21 in×6·46 m	Wire-guided plus active/passive acoustic homing. Impact and proximity fuze. Torpedo computer coupled to submarine FCS. Electric propulsion	Marconi Space and Defence
Mk 31	**2473.441** (1972/73)	—	Intended replacement for US-designed Mk 44. Project cancelled in 1972 because delays had invalidated design. US Mk 46 bought as stopgap	UK MoD
Spearfish	**4559.441**	21in×6 m(app)	Advanced heavy-weight sub-launched torpedo to meet ASR 7525	MUSL
Stingray	**2448.441**		New acoustic homing lightweight torpedo to replace US Mk 44/46	Marconi Space and Defence
UNITED STATES OF AMERICA				
Mk 14	*2813.441*	21 in×5·25 m	1930s design. Free-running with preset depth and course angles. Compressed air propulsion. Weight 1780 kg. Withdrawn from USN service in 1973 but still in service elsewhere	—
Mk 27 Mod 4	*2165.441*	19 in×3·23 m	Passive acoustic homing. Electric propulsion. Used in USN service as training round prior to Mk 37 introduction but some warshot torpedoes sold elsewhere	—
Mk 32	*3629.441*	2·08 m×483 mm	Acoustic anti-submarine. Operational but obsolescent	—
Mk 37 Mod 0	**2817.441**	19 in×3·52 m	Active/passive acoustic homing. Electric dual-speed propulsion Warshot weight 648 kg. Mod 3 is improved version	Westinghouse
Mk 37 Mod 1	**2818.441**	19 in×4·09 m	Wire-guided. Electric dual-speed propulsion Warshot weight 766 kg. Mod 2 is improved version	Westinghouse
Mk 37 Mod 2	**2818.441**	19 in×4·09 m	Updated version (minor modifications) of Mod 1	Westinghouse
Mk 37 Mod 3	**2817.441**	19 in×3·52 m	Updated version (minor modifications) of Mod 0	Westinghouse
NT 37C Mods 2 & 3	*3971.441*	19 in×3·52 m 19 in×4·09 m	Improved versions of Mk 37 Mods 2 and 3. Better speed, range, and acoustic performance including shallow water capacity. Sold to Canada and Netherlands	Northrop/Honeywell
NT 37D	*4180.441*	19 in×4·5 m (Mod 2) 19 in×3·8m (Mod 3)	Further improvement of NT 37 with Mk 46 OTTO engine and enhanced guidance	Honeywell

Designation	Entry no	Dimensions (d×l)	Description	Contractor(s)
USA cont				
NT 37E	**4762.441**	4·5 m× 483 mm	Latest modernised model of Mk 37	Honeywell
Mk 44	**2820.441**	19 in×2·56 m	2 versions differing slightly in length and both weighing about 233 kg. Active acoustic homing. Electric propulsion. Replaced by Mk 46 in USN and UK service but still in service elsewhere	Several in USA also licence-built overseas
Mk 46 Mod 0	**2822.441**	324 mm×2·67 m	Deep-diving, high-speed, active/passive acoustic homing. Weight about 258 kg. First US torpedo with solid-fuel propulsion	Aerojet-General and others
Mk 46 Mod 1	**2822.441**	324 mm×2·59 m	As Mod 0 but slightly larger and with liquid mono-propellant (OTTO) motor	Aerojet-General and others
CAPTOR	**2541.441**	324 mm×3·7 m	Mk 46 Mod 4 torpedo inserted in a mine casing and released when target detected	Goodyear
Mk 48 Mod 0	**2823.441**	21 in	AS-only version. Superseded during development by Mod 2	Westinghouse
Mk 48 Mod 1	**2823.441**	21 in×5·8 m	Deep-diving (914 m) high-speed (93 km/h) active/passive acoustic homing, wire-guided, long-range (46 km) weapon. Weight about 1600 kg. Said to be most complex torpedo ever designed	Gould (formerly Clevite)
Mk 48 Mod 2	**2823.441**	21 in	Competing against Mod 1 which was selected after comparison at pilot production stage	Westinghouse
Mk 50	**4182.441**	—	Formerly EX-50 Advanced Lightweight Torpedo (ALWT). Successor to Mk 46 (NEARTIP)	Honeywell
Freedom Torpedo	*2618.441*	19 in×4·83 mm	Private-venture development. Wire-guided, pattern-running, electrically propelled. Contact fuze. Warshot weight 1237 kg. Charge 295 kg. Range 11 km Adapts to 21 in tubes	Westinghouse

4234.094   **Electronic Warfare Equipment**

Designation	Entry no	Description	Contractor(s)
CANADA			
Model 100	**1714.253**	Naval direction finder	General Precision
CANEWS	**4161.293**	Naval integrated ESM/ECM system	MEL/Westinghouse
FRANCE			
Type BF	**3374.353**	Airborne radar warning receiver	Thomson-CSF
Dagaie	**3377.293**	Naval countermeasures dispensing system	CSEE
Magaie	**4350.293**	Naval countermeasures decoy system	CSEE
Sagaie	**5656.293**	Naval countermeasures decoy system	CSEE
DB 3141	**3916.393**	Airborne I/J-band jammer pod	Thomson-CSF
DB 3163	**3379.393**	Airborne I/J-band jammer pod	Thomson-CSF
TMV 433	**3533.293**	Naval countermeasures set incorporating DR 2000 receiver, DALIA or ARIAL analysis equipment	Thomson-CSF
TMV 026	**3376.353**	Airborne ESM	Thomson-CSF
TMV 200	**3534.053**	Elisa Elint receiver	Thomson-CSF
BROMURE	**3913.193**	Communications jammer	—
BINOC	**3913.193**	Jammer	—
ELEBORE	**3913.193**	Computer-based HF monitoring system	—
ELFA	**3913.193**	Intercept system	—
ELODEE	**3913.193**	Computer-based communications intercept system	—
EMERAUDE	**3913.193**	Computer-based VHF monitoring system	—
Sapiens	**5657.293**	Naval EW system	Thomson-CSF
TRC 291	**3914.153**	VHF intercept receiver	Thomson-CSF
TRC 294	**3914.153**	VHF/UHF monitoring receiver	Thomson-CSF
TRC 394	**3914.153**	HF monitoring receiver	Thomson-CSF
DR 2000	**3533.293**	Broad-band receiver	Thomson-CSF
DR 4000	**4351.053**	Video/IFM ESM receiver	Thomson-CSF
XR 100	**3535.053**	VHF/UHF communications intelligence receiver system	SINTRA
XR 100 SA	**3535.053**	Automatic receiving system	SINTRA
GERMANY, Federal Republic			
Hot Dog/ Silver Dog	**3643.293**	Naval IR and radar countermeasures dispensing system	Wegmann/Buck
Schalmei	**5659.293**	Naval countermeasures decoy system	AEG Telefunken
E. Series	**4352.053**	Range monitoring receivers	AEG-Telefunken
H. Series	**4636.193**	Range of antenna systems	Rohde & Schwarz
ET 001	*3381.053*	VHF/UHF receiving system	Rohde & Schwarz
Hummel	**4353.153**	VHF jamming transmitters	AEG-Telefunken
ESM 500 Series	**4138.093**	Family of receivers for communications and ESM applications	Rohde & Schwarz
ESP	**4139.093**	Fast scan automatic intercept receiver	Rohde & Schwarz
HE 101	*3531.093*	Active receiving antenna	Rohde & Schwarz
PA 055	**3532.093**	Broad-band doppler direction finder	Rohde & Schwarz
PA 007	**1901.053**	VHF doppler direction finder	Rohde & Schwarz
PA 008	**1901.053**	VHF doppler direction finder	Rohde & Schwarz
PA 009	**1901.053**	UHF doppler direction finder	Rohde & Schwarz
PA 510	**4637.193**	Mobile HF direction finder	Rohde & Schwarz
PA 555	**4637.193**	Mobile version of PA 055	Rohde & Schwarz
PA 010	**3532.093**	HF doppler direction finder	Rohde & Schwarz
AC002	**5658.153**	Directional antenna system	Rohde & Schwarz
EP 1650	**3536.193**	Automatic VHF/UHF radio reconnaissance system	AEG-Telefunken
INTERNATIONAL			
Sibyl	**5683.293**	EW Naval decoy system	BAe/Brandt
ISRAEL			
MN-53	**3461.093**	ESM system for radar intercept	Elbit
EB 41	**4225.093**	Naval ECM system	IAI
EL	**4225.093**	Range of EW systems	IAI
Rafael	**4354.293**	Short-range chaff rocket	Rafael
Rafael	**4355.293**	Long-range chaff rocket	Rafael
Timnex-4CH	**4356.093**	Automatic Elint/ESM system	Elbit
ACDS	**5660.293**	Naval dispenser system	Elbit Computers
CR 274D	**4731.153**	Mobile ELINT system	Elisra
EL/L-8202	**4357.393**	ECM pod	Elta
EL/L-8303	**4225.093**	ESM System	Elta
EL/L-8310	**4225.093**	ELINT/ESM system	Elta
EL/L-8312	**4225.093**	ELINT/ESM system	Elta
EL/K 1150/1160/1250	**4639.193**	COMINT receivers	Elta
EL/K-7001	**4225.093**	Communications monitoring & jamming system	Elta
EL/K-7010	**4225.093**	VHF Communications jammer	Elta
EL/K-7012	**4225.093**	Communications jammer exciters	Elta
EL/K-7020	**4225.093**	EW system	Elta
EL/L-8230	**5730.393**	Airborne ECM system	Elta
RAJ 101	**4638.193**	Land-based jammer	Rafael
SPS20/200	**4640.353**	Airborne radar warning receivers	Elisra
ITALY			
ALQ-X	**4175.093**	Series of airborne jammer pods	Selenia
ALQ-234	**4174.393**	Airborne jammer pod	Selenia
ELT/116	**4173.093**	Naval ESM/ECM system	Elettronica
ELT/128	**4645.093**	Communications direction finder	Elettronica
ELT/132	**4167.193**	Lightweight man-portable radar warning receiver	Elettronica
ELT/211	**4169.293**	Naval ESM equipment	Elettronica
ELT/214	**4173.093**	Naval ESM	Elettronica
ELT/263	**4166.393**	Airborne ESM system (Gufo)	Elettronica
ELT/311	**4173.093**	Jammer	Elettronica

Designation	Entry no	Description	Contractor(s)
ITALY cont			
ELT/318	**4170.293**	Naval noise jammer. Dual-band CW	Elettronica
ELT/457	**4359.393**	Airborne noise jammer pod	Elettronica
ELT/458	**4359.393**	Airborne noise jammer pod	Elettronica
ELT/459	**4359.393**	Airborne noise jammer pod	Elettronica
ELT/460	**4359.393**	Airborne noise jammer pod	Elettronica
ELT/511	**4173.093**	Jammer	Elettronica
ELT/555	**4168.393**	Airborne deception jammer and warning pod	Elettronica
ELT/711	**4173.093**	Naval ESM radar identification module	Elettronica
ELT/712	**4173.093**	Naval EW programming unit	Elettronica
ELT/716	**4173.093**	Naval EW data interface unit	Elettronica
ELT/814	**4172.293**	Naval ECM antenna	Elettronica
ESS-2	**5664.153**	Surveillance & analysis system	Selenia
IGS-1	**3526.193**	Land-mobile ECM system	Selenia
IGS-3	**4175.093**	Computerised mobile integrated ESM/ECM system	Selenia
IHS-6	**3382.393**	Airborne integrated ESM/ECM system	Selenia
INS-1	**4175.093**	Integrated naval EW system for fast patrol boats	Selenia
INS-3	**5663.253**	Computer-assisted naval integrated ESM/ECM system	Selenia
PAW-1	**4175.093**	Radar pulse analyser and warning equipment	Selenia
RQN-1	**3343.253**	Radar intercept equipment	Selenia
RQN-3	**3528.253**	Naval radar intercept equipment	Selenia
TQN-1	**4175.093**	Naval jammer	Selenia
TQN-2	**4175.093**	Modular multi-band airborne jammer	Selenia
TQN-3	**4175.093**	Jammer	Selenia
TQN-4	**4175.093**	Jammer	Selenia
Breda LCRS	**3997.293**	Lightweight chaff rocket launching system	Breda/SNIA Viscosa
Colibri	**4360.353**	Helicopter ECM/ESM system	Elettronica
CO-NEWS	**4644.293**	Naval ESM system	Elettronica
FARAD	**5661.253**	Naval EW system	Elettronica
Fast Jam	**4643.353**	Helicopter-borne jammer	Elettronica
NEWTON	**4172.293**	Naval integrated EW system incorporating ELT/211/318/521	Elettronica
RIDE	*4165.393*	Radio intercept and direction-finding equipment	Elettronica
SCLAR Mk II	**4641.281**	Rocket launching system	Selenia-Elsag
Smart Guard	**4642.353**	VHF/UHF helicopter ESM system	Elettronica
THETIS	**5662.453**	Submarine ESM system	Elettronica
JAPAN			
J/ALQ-2	**4176.093**	Airborne EW used on T-33 aircraft	—
J/ALQ-3	**4176.093**	Airborne EW used on C-46 and YS-11 aircraft	—
J/ALQ-4	**4176.093**	Airborne EW used on F-104 aircraft	—
J/ALQ-5	**4176.093**	Airborne EW used on C-1 aircraft	—
J/ALQ-6	**4176.093**	Airborne EW used on F-4 and ET-2 (F1) aircraft	—
J/ALQ-8	**4176.093**	Airborne countermeasures set used on F-4 aircraft	—
J/APR-1	**4176.093**	Airborne radar warning receiver used on F-104	—
J/APR-2	**4176.093**	Airborne radar warning receiver used on F-4EJ	Tokyo Keiki
J/APR-3	**4176.093**	Radar warning receiver	Tokyo Keiki
J/APR-4	**4176.093**	New airborne RWR for Japanese F-15J aircraft	Tokyo Keiki
NETHERLANDS			
Ramses	**4054.293**	Multi-mode naval ECM system	Signaal
Sphinx	**4055.293**	Naval ESM system	Signaal
RAPIDS	**4056.293**	Radar passive identification system. Naval ESM	Signaal
SPECTRA	**4735.193**	Communications ELINT system	Signaal
NORWAY			
RL 1	**3344.153**	Laser warning receiver	Simrad
SR-1A	**4646.293**	Naval ESM radar warning receiver	Nera
SWEDEN			
BO series	**5666.393**	Pod dispensers for fixed and rotary wing aircraft	Philips
UA 731	**3022.163**	Microwave pulse analyser	SATT
AR 765	**3537.393**	Lightweight RWR for Agusta Bell 206A helicopter	SATT
AR 777	**3904.393**	Airborne computer-controlled ESM receiver	SATT
AR 830	**4733.393**	Airborne warning system	SATT
AQ 800	**4361.393**	Airborne noise jamming pod	SATT
AQ 900	**4734.393**	Airborne pod-mounted jammer	SATT
AQ 31	**3024.393**	Airborne CW jamming pod	SATT
POD KA	**4362.393**	Airborne noise jamming pod	SRA
Lake 2000	**4363.393**	Airborne noise jamming pod	SRA
AR753	**3025.393**	Airborne jammer set-on receiver	SATT
EWS-900	**3538.293**	Naval chaff countermeasures dispenser system	Saab-Scania
Philax	**3133.293**	Naval IR and radar countermeasures system	PEAB
9CM 100/200	**5731.253**	Naval ECM systems	Philips
UNITED KINGDOM			
ARI 23246/1 (Skyshadow)	**3383.393**	ECM pod for RAF Tornado and other strike aircraft	Marconi
ZEUS	**5689.353**	Airborne ECM system	Marconi
HERMES	**5732.053**	ESM system	Marconi
Auditor	**4411.093**	Ground-based ESM	Racal
Stockade	**3911.293**	Naval chaff and IR decoy dispensing system	Wallop
Stockade-Seaflash	**4651.293**	Remotely controlled decoy system	Wallop/Flight Refuelling
Rampart	**4227.193**	Land-based chaff and decoy dispensing system	Wallop
Barricade	**4226.293**	Naval decoy equipment	Wallop
Cascade	**5668.393**	Helicopter decoy system	Wallop
Masquerade	**5667.393**	Airborne decoy system	Wallop
Evade	**4650.393**	Airborne decoy system	Wallop
Kestrel	**4410.393**	Airborne ESM	Racal

Designation	Entry no	Description	Contractor(s)
UK cont			
Hofin	**3369.393**	Hostile fire indicator	MS Instruments
Corvus	**3145.293**	Naval decoy system	Vickers
Cygnus	**5670.293**	Jammer used with Cutlass	Racal
Seafan	**3555.293**	Naval rocket decoy system	Vickers/Plessey
R405	*3371.053*	Multipurpose anti-jamming radar receiver	Plessey
Type 405J	**3372.193**	Transportable land-based radar jammer	Plessey
Type R505	**3373.053**	Anti-jamming radar receiver module	Plessey
PVS 860/1120A	**1712.153**	HF monitoring and direction-finding system	Plessey
PR2250	**3905.153**	HF communications and monitoring receiver 10 kHz – 30 MHz	Plessey
Shield	**5682.293**	Naval missile decoy system	Plessey
CERES	**3370.053**	Computer enhanced radio emission surveillance system	Redifon
RA 1779	**3921.153**	Programmable HF surveillance receiver	Racal
RA 1792	**3922.153**	Programmable synthesised surveillance receiver	Racal
RA 1794	**3919.153**	Tactical receiver used in Racal Series 3000 EW systems	Racal
RA 1795	**5679.153**	ELINT VHF/UHF receiver	Racal
RA 1796	**4737.053**	ELINT HF/VHF/UHF receiver	Racal
RJS 3105	**4738.193**	VHF/UHF jammer	Racal
RJS 3140	**4736.193**	Unattended expendable jammer	Racal
RTA 1470	**3920.153**	Radio direction finding equipment	Racal
CCS 3900	**5681.153**	EW command and control system	Racal
SAT 3311	**5680.153**	HF signal analysis terminal	Racal
System 3000	**3918.193**	Modular EW and radio surveillance system range of equipments	Racal
RJS 3100	**3917.193**	Automatic VHF mobile jamming system	Racal
S373	**4162.193**	Mobile multi-band EW system. Combined ESM and ECM	Marconi
Barbican	**4163.193**	Mobile tactical microwave ESM system	Ferranti/MEL
Fullback	**4411.093**	Radar warning receiver	Racal
Miranda	**3912.193**	Mobile microwave intercept system	MEL
SUSIE	**1707.253**	Series of naval ESM systems	MEL
Scimitar	**3598.293**	Naval jammer	MEL
Manta	**4652.493**	Submarine-borne passive ESM system	MEL
Matilda	**3539.253**	Naval radar threat warning equipment	MEL
Matlock	**5733.153**	Land-based radar warning system	MEL
KATIE	**5734.353**	Airborne radar warning system	MEL
Porpoise	**5671.453**	Submarine equipment	Racal
Prophet	**5673.353**	Radar warning receiver	Racal
Protean	**3193.293**	Naval chaff decoy dispensing system	MEL
Peregrine	**4411.093**	Pod mounted warning receiver	Racal
Pisces	**4411.093**	Submarine ESM system	Racal
Pinemartin	**5695.153**	Land-based tactical ESM system	Racal
Sprat	**5672.453**	Submarine ESM system	Racal
Saviour	**5674.193**	Land-based warning receiver	Racal
Sea Saviour	**5675.293**	Naval radar warning receiver	Racal
SARIE	**1743.263**	Naval selective automatic radar identification equipment	Thorn EMI
Guardian	**4653.293**	Shipborne active & passive ECM system	Thorn EMI
RDL-1	**1341.253**	Tactical ESM system for small ships 2 – 11·25 GHz	Racal
RDL-2	**1341.253**	As RDL-1 plus threat evaluation	Racal
RDL-257	**1341.253**	Frequency range extended to 1 – 18 GHz	Racal
RDL-268	**1341.253**	As RDL-257 but includes frequency measurement also	Racal
RCM-1	**1942.293**	Naval and land-based I-band jammers	Racal
RCM-2	**1942.293**	Jammers with or without stabilised antennas. Various bands	Racal
RWR-1	**4411.093**	Radar warning receiver	Racal
RL1	**4365.193**	Laser warning instrument	Lasergage
RL2	**4365.193**	Laser warning instrument	Lasergage
Cutlass	**3553.293**	Range of computer-based ESM/ECM systems	Racal
MIR-2	**3554.393**	Helicopter or light aircraft ESM equipment	Racal
HWR-2	**1876.053**	Hand-held radar warning receiver	Racal
Weasel	**5669.153**	Classified ground-based system	Racal
EPO	**5737.293**	EPO naval rocket launcher	Evershed
Vicon 77	**5739.353**	Airborne ESM pod	Vinten

UNITED STATES OF AMERICA

AN/AAQ-4	**5742.393**	Airborne infra-red countermeasures (internal)	Northrop
AN/AAQ-8	**5742.393**	Pod-monted infra-red countermeasures systems	Northrop
AN/AAR-34	**4662.393**	IR warning receiver	Cincinnati
AN/AAR-44	**3901.393**	Infra-red warning receiver	Cincinnati Electronics
AN/ALE-1	**3109.393**	Countermeasures dispensing pod	Lundy
AN/ALE-2	**3109.393**	Countermeasures dispensing pod	Lundy
AN/ALE-24	**3109.393**	Chaff dispensing system for B-52G/H aircraft	Lundy
AN/ALE-27	**3109.393**	Chaff dispensing system for B-52C-F aircraft	Lundy
AN/ALE-29A	**3360.393**	Chaff and IR dispensing set for USN tactical aircraft	Lundy
AN/ALE-32	**3109.393**	Chaff dispensing set for EA-6A aircraft	Lundy
AN/ALE-33	**3109.393**	Chaff dispenser used on BQM-34 target drone	Lundy
AN/ALE-36	**4657.393**	Countermeasures dispensing pod	Tracor
AN/ALE-37	**1904.393**	High-capacity chaff dispenser development	—
AN/ALE-38	**4654.393**	Bulk chaff dispenser (USAF)	Tracor
AN/ALE-39	**1905.393**	Expendable countermeasures dispenser for USN/USMC tactical aircraft	Goodyear
AN/ALE-40	**1906.393**	Countermeasures dispenser system for various aircraft	Tracor
AN/ALE-40(V)	**5688.393**	Countermeasures dispenser system	Tracor
AN/ALE-41	**4654.393**	Bulk chaff dispenser (USN)	Tracor
AN/ALE-43	**3110.393**	Chaff cutter/dispenser pod	Lundy
AN/ALE-44	**3111.393**	Countermeasures dispenser pod	Lundy
FAC	**3362.393**	Lightweight countermeasures dispenser system	Lundy
XM-130	**3345.393**	Countermeasures system based on ALE-40 for US Army	Tracor
AN/ALQ-78	**3451.393**	Airborne ESM set used in P-3C aircraft	Loral
AN/ALQ-99	**1908.393**	Tactical noise jamming system for EA-6B	Various
AN/ALQ-100	**1909.393**	Deception jammer	Sanders

Designation	Entry no	Description	Contractor(s)
USA cont			
AN/ALQ-101	**1910.393**	Range of modular jamming pods	Westinghouse
AN/ALQ-119	**1911.393**	Dual-mode jamming pod	Westinghouse
AN/ALQ-123	**1912.393**	Airborne IR deception jammer	Xerox
AN/ALQ-125	**4366.353**	Tactical electronic reconnaissance sensor	Litton
AN/ALQ-126	**1913.393**	Deception jammer developed under USN Charger Blue programme	Sanders
AN/ALQ-128	**4668.393**	Multimode threat warning receiver for USAF F-15	Magnavox
AN/ALQ-130	**1914.393**	Tactical communications jamming equipment for USN aircraft	Eaton Corp
AN/ALQ-131	**1915.393**	Self-protection jamming pod	Westinghouse/Loral
AN/ALQ-133	**1916.393**	Airborne tactical Elint system	United Technology Labs
AN/ALQ-134	**4368.393**	Expendable jammer	Sanders
AN/ALQ-135	**3346.393**	Internal tactical EW system for F-15	Northrop
AN/ALQ-136	**4369.393**	Airborne jammer	ITT
AN/ALQ-137	**4669.393**	Airborne jammer for F/FB-111 and EF-111A aircraft	Sanders
AN/ALQ-140	**3548.393**	Internal IR countermeasures set	Sanders
AN/ALQ-142	**4367.253**	Naval ESM system	Raytheon
AN/ALQ-144	**3546.393**	Deception IR jammer for helicopters	Sanders
AN/ALQ-146	**3550.393**	IR countermeasures set for CH-46D helicopter	Sanders
AN/ALQ-147	**3545.393**	Hot Brick IR countermeasures equipment	Sanders
AN/ALQ-149	**4678.393**	Airborne communications jammer for EA-6B aircraft	Sanders
AN/ALQ-150	**4370.353**	ESM receiver	—
AN/ALQ-151	**4371.393**	Airborne EW system	ESL
AN/ALQ-153	**3384.393**	Radar tail warning set for B-52 aircraft	Westinghouse
AN/ALQ-155	**3552.393**	Computer-managed ECM set for B-52	Northrop
AN/ALQ-156	**3547.393**	Missile detection system for aircraft self-protection	Sanders
AN/ALQ-157	**4375.393**	Infra-red countermeasures system	Xerox
AN/ALQ-162	**4373.393**	Airborne radar jammer	Northrop
AN/ALQ-164	**4740.393**	Airborne pod-mounted jammer for AV-8B	Sanders
AN/ALQ-165	**3894.393**	Airborne self-protection jammer for USN aircraft	Northrop/Sanders/Westinghouse/ITT
AN/ALQ-171	**4374.353**	Conformal countermeasures system	Northrop
AN/ALQ-172	**5693.393**	Noise deception jammer	ITT
AN/ALQ-176(V)	**4100.393**	Lightweight jamming pod system	Sperry
AN/ALQ-178	**4009.393**	Integrated RWR/ECM suite for F-16 aircraft	Loral
AN/ALR-45	**1917.353**	Aircraft RWR	Itek
AN/ALR-46	**3035.353**	Airborne digital threat warning receiver	Itek
AN/ALR-47	**1862.353**	Radar homing and warning set for USN S-3A aircraft	IBM
AN/ALR-50	**1918.353**	Aircraft SAM alert and launch warning receiver	Magnavox
AN/ALR-52	**1919.353**	Multi-band IFM receiver for air or land-mobile applications	ARGO Systems
AN/ALR-56	**3347.353**	Airborne RWR	Loral
AN/ALR-60	**4376.353**	Communications intercept and analysis system	GTE Sylvania
AN/ALR-62(V)	**4377.393**	Radar warning system	Dalmo Victor
AN/ALR-64	**4378.393**	Compass sail warning system	Dalmo Victor
AN/ALR-66	**3642.353**	Programmable airborne RWR	General Instruments Corp
AN/ALR-67(V)	**4372.393**	Radar warning system	Itek
AN/ALR-68	**3525.353**	Airborne digital threat warning receiver	Itek
AN/ALR-69	**4379.353**	Radar warning receiver	Applied Technology
AN/ALR-73	**4164.393**	Airborne ESM for USN E-2C early warning aircraft	Litton Systems
AN/ALR-606	**3908.353**	Aircraft RWR	General Instruments Corp
AN/ALR-646	**3909.353**	Airborne ESM system based on ALR-66	General Instruments Corp
AEL 6040	**4403.093**	ECM universal jammer	American Electronic Labs
AN/ALQ-161B	**3034.393**	Defensive electronics suite for B-1 bomber aircraft	Eaton
AN/ALR-46A	**3892.363**	Airborne digital signal processor	Dalmo Victor
AN/APR-38	**3544.393**	Control indicator set for Wild Weasel II aircraft	Loral
AN/APR-39(V)	**3542.393**	Airborne radar warning system	E-Systems/Loral
AN/APR-43	**4010.393**	RWR developed for USN Compass Sail Clockwise programme	Loral
AN/APR-44	**3365.353**	CMR-500B low-cost RWR	American Electronic Labs
AN/ASQ-171	**4742.393**	Airborne ELINT system for EP-3E ECM aircraft	IBM
AN/GLQ-3A	**4401.193**	HF/VHF communications jammer	Fairchild
AN/KAS-1	**4407.293**	Chemical warfare detection system	Texas
AN/MLQ-33	**4741.193**	Search and jamming system against air/ground communications	GTE Sylvania
AN/MLQ-34	**3895.193**	Mobile tactical communications countermeasures system for US Army (TACJAM)	GTE Sylvania
AN/MLQ-T6	**4664.193**	Communications data link jammer	Cincinnati Electronics
AN/MSQ-103	**4405.193**	TEAM PACK ESM monitoring system	Emerson
AN/SLQ-27	**3349.293**	Shortstop naval defensive EW system. Superseded by SLQ-32	—
AN/SLQ-30	**4388.293**	Naval electronic countermeasures systems (TRUMP)	Kuras-Alterman
AN/SLQ-32	**3349.393**	Naval ESM/ECM system. Replacement for WLR-1. Modular	Raytheon
AN/TLQ-15	**3367.193**	Communications and countermeasures equipment	American Electronic Labs
AN/TLQ-17A	**4406.093**	Countermeasures and jamming set	Fairchild
AN/TSQ-105	**4408.153**	Sigint system (AGTEWS)	Bunker Ramo
AN/TSQ-112	**4409.153**	ECM ground warning and jamming system	GTE Sylvania
AN/ULQ-11	**4384.394**	Airborne jamming system (cefirm header)	—
AN/ULQ-14	**4385.153**	Radar countermeasures system	—
AN/WLR-8	**3082.253**	Naval tactical EW/ESM receiver system	GTE Sylvania
AOCM	*4383.393*	Advanced optical countermeasures pod	Martin Marietta
ARI 18240/1	**4160.393**	ESM suite for UK Nimrod aircraft	Loral
ARJS	**4667.393**	High power stand-off jammer	Grumman
CMR-610A	**4397.053**	Wideband direction-finding receiver	American Electronic Labs
C204/WJ-1140	**4391.053**	Analysis control unit	Watkins-Johnson
DF 8000	**4665.093**	Communications direction-finding system	Cincinnati Electronics
ESCORT	**5743.353**	Airborne Elint system	Raytheon
EW-1017	**4382.353**	Electronic surveillance system	Loral
Guardrail	**4670.353**	Airborne SIGINT system	ESL
HAWCS	**4380.393**	Helicopter all-weather cueing system	Texas Instruments
Jam Pac (V)	**4099.393**	Family of low-cost jammer pods	Sperry
J-3400	**4677.153**	VHF mobile ECM system	GTE Sylvania
LQ-102	**4663.193**	Hand-emplaced expendable jammer	Cincinnati Electronics

Designation	Entry no	Description	Contractor(s)
USA cont			
L6-24	**3875.093**	Direction-finding system	Watkins-Johnson
L-6/A-WJ-1140	**1381.053**	Microwave direction-finder	Watkins-Johnson
MPI-5	**3105.093**	Miniature pulse analyser	American Electronic Labs
MRES	**4658.053**	ECM and C³CM threat generators	Tracor
Piranha	*4402.193*	Applique VHF communications jammer	Fairchild
QRC-259	**4396.053**	Superheterodyne receiver system	Watkins-Johnson
R-281	**1875.153**	Computer-controlled search receiver	Cincinnati Electronics
R-1849	*3033.053*	Remote-controlled HF search receiver	Cincinnati Electronics
R-1850	*3033.053*	Remote-controlled VHF search receiver	Cincinnati Electronics
R-1851	*3033.053*	Remote-controlled UHF search receiver	Cincinnati Electronics
R-5500	**3529.093**	Control and display system for ESM	GTE Sylvania
Rapport II	**3543.393**	ECM system developed for Belgian Mirage V aircraft	Loral
RA-6778	**4676.093**	Communications monitoring equipment	Racal
RA-6793A	**4675.093**	HF monitoring receiver	Racal
RBOC Mk33	**3363.293**	Naval rapid bloom off-board countermeasures decoy system	Hycor/Lundy
RD-280	**1874.153**	HF/VHF surveillance receiver	Cincinnati Electronics
RE-1320A	**4400.093**	Spectrum display unit	Racal
RG Series	**4672.093**	Family of spectrum monitors	Racal
RG-1340	**4399.093**	Spectrum surveillance controller	Racal
RG-5202A	**4673.093**	VHF monitoring receiver	Racal
RG-5540	**4398.053**	VHF/UHF monitor receiver	Racal
RG-5545A	**4674.093**	VHF/UHF monitoring receiver	Racal
S-2150	**4671.353**	Threat warning systems for small ships and submarines	EM Systems
Sea Sentry	**4020.293**	Series of three naval ESM systems	Kollmorgen
Series 2000	**3903.053**	Range of receivers, control and display units for ESM	Norlin
SLR-600 Series	**3910.253**	Range of naval ESM systems based on SLR-600	General Instruments Corp
SN Series	**3037.053**	Range of surveillance receivers for Comint and Elint	Norlin
SPEWS	**4666.393**	Tactical jamming systems for RPVs	Motorola
SRBOC Mk 36	**4656.293**	Naval super rapid bloom off-board countermeasures decoy system	Tracor
SR 200	**4389.293**	Naval ESM system	Sanders
SR 2020	**4659.093**	Tactical ESM receiver	Applied Communications
SR 2152	**4661.093**	VHF/UHF COMINT receiver	Applied Communications
SR 2500	**4660.193**	VHF/UHF monitoring receiver	Applied Communications
TEREC	**4387.153**	Tactical electronic reconnaissance remote terminal (TEREC) & (TRT)	Texas
TN-1000/WJ-1840	**4395.053**	Minceiver TM tuner	Watkins-Johnson
Triton	**4739.293**	Naval threat warning system for small vessels	Dalmo Victor
WJ-927	**4390.053**	Microwave and direction-finding signal analysis system	Watkins-Johnson
WJ-945	**3664.093**	Microwave surveillance and direction-finding system	Watkins-Johnson
WJ-1205B	**3665.093**	Computerised pulse train analyser	Watkins-Johnson
WJ-1240	**1716.053**	Computer-controlled microwave recce system	Watkins-Johnson
WJ-1424	**3666.193**	Microwave ESM equipment	Watkins-Johnson
WJ-1440	**4394.053**	Microwave receiver system	Watkins-Johnson
WJ-1740	**3354.053**	Parallel-scanned digitally controlled microwave receiver	Watkins-Johnson
WJ-1840	**3355.053**	Broadband superhet microwave receiver	Watkins-Johnson
WJ-1920	**4392.093**	Distributed processing system	Watkins-Johnson
WJ-1988	**4393.053**	Direction-finding system	Watkins-Johnson

1505.094   **NATO Designations of Soviet Systems and Equipment**

Designation	Description	Designation	Description	Designation	Description
Acrid	Air-to-air missile	Clank	An-30 survey version of Coke	Fish Net	Pole-mounted twin Yagi array possibly IFF
Alkali	Air-to-air missile	Classic	Il-62 transport aircraft		
Anab	Air-to-air missile	Cleat	Tu-114 transport aircraft	Fishpot	Su-9 interceptor aircraft
Apex	Air-to-air missile	Clobber A	Yak-42 jet transport aircraft	Fitter	Su-7 interceptor aircraft
Aphid	Air-to-air missile	Clod	An-14 general purpose aircraft	Fix Eight	Land-transportable HF Direction-finding system
Ash	Air-to-air missile	Cluster Bay	'Rising' sea mine		
Atoll	Air-to-air missile	Cluster Guard	Anti-sonar hull coating for submarines		
Awl	Air-to-air missile			Fix Four A	Fixed HF direction-finding system
		Cluster Gulf	'Rising' sea mine for deep water	Fix Four B	Fixed HF direction-finding system
Backfire	Tupolev VG bomber	Coach	Il-12 transport aircraft	Fix Four C	Fixed Adcock HF direction-finding system
Back Net	Early warning and GCI radar	Cock	An-22 transport aircraft		
Badger	Tu-16 bomber/reconnaissance aircraft	Cod Eye A/B	Submarine sensors	Fix Four D	Fixed VHF direction-finding system
		Codling	Yak-40 transport aircraft	Fix Six A	Similar to Fix Eight with 6 elements
Ball End	Naval surface warning radar	Coin Grass	Corner reflector land-based VHF array		
Ball Gun	Naval surface warning radar			Flagon-A	Su-11 all-weather fighter aircraft
Band Stand	Naval radar for SSN-9 missile	Coke	An-24/26 transport aircraft	Flagon-B	Sukhoi STOL fighter
Barlock	P-50 Twin scanner land-mobile early warning and GCI radar	Colt	An-2 general purpose aircraft	Flagon-E	Su-15 interceptor aircraft
		Condor	An-400 heavy transport aircraft	Flanker	Su-27 combat/fighter aircraft
Bass Tilt	Naval gun fire control radar. Similar to Drum Tilt and Muff Cob	Cookpot	Tu-124 transport aircraft	Flap Lid	Tracking radar for SA-11
		Coot	Il-18 transport aircraft	Flap Track	Tracking radar mounted on tracked vehicle
Beagle	Twin-jet tactical bomber, recce, EW aircraft	Crab Pot	Microwave communications link antenna		
				Flap Wheel	AA fire control radar
Beam Track	Yagi tracking array. Mobile	Crate	Il-14. Improved Coach	Flashlight	Yak-25 all-weather interceptor
Bean Shell	Aircraft discone VHF antenna	Creek	Yak-12 light aircraft	Flat Face	P-15. Land mobile target acquisition radar
Bear	Tu-20 bomber aircraft	Cross Bird	Naval early warning radar		
Bee Hind	Tail warning radar on Blinder, Bison	Cross Fork	Truck-mounted Yagi array	Flat Spin	Naval air search radar
		Cross Legs	Transportable search radar	Flipper	Experimental fighter
Bell Clout	Naval ECM	Cross Loop A	Naval direction-finder	Flogger	Mikoyan variable-geometry fighter (MiG-23)
Bell Jar	Naval ECM housing	Cross Out	Trailer-mounted search radar		
Bell Tap	Naval ECM	Cross Slot	Ground radar	Foil Two	Ground based IFF
Big Bar A	Early warning and GCI radar	Crown Drum	Aircraft antenna system	Forger	Yak-36 V/STOL carrier aircraft
Big Bulge	Airborne radar on Bear bomber	Crusty	Tu-134 transport aircraft	Fork Rest A	VHF Yagi array
Big Mesh	Early warning and GCI radar	Cub	An-12 transport aircraft	Four Eyes	Naval electro-optical fire control
Big Net	Naval surveillance radar	Cuff	Be-30 transport aircraft	Four Stack	UHF Yagi array
Big Nose	Airborne radar on Fiddler	Curl	An-26 transport aircraft	Foxbat	MiG-25 interceptor aircraft
Bike Pump	Broadband end-fed dipole antenna	Cylinder Head	Ship's gun fire director radar	Fox Fire	I-band AI radar
				Foxhound	'Super-Foxbat' with new look-down radar and AA-9
Bill Fold	Transportable search radar	Dawn	I-band navigation radar		
Bill Spring	Helix radiator with plate reflector	Dead Duck	Naval IFF	Frame Spring	Helical tracking antenna with ground-plane. Shipboard
Bird	Shipboard dipole and Yagi antenna array	Dog House	Phased-array missile and space tracking radar		
				Freehand	Experimental VTOL aircraft
Bison	Mya-4 bomber-reconnaissance aircraft	Dome Glass	Trailer-mounted optical tracker system	Fresco	MiG-17 jet fighter
				Frog-1	Surface-to-surface missile
Blackjack	Long range bomber aircraft	Don A/B/2/ Kay	Naval navigation radars	Frog-2, 3, 4, and 5	Surface-to-surface missiles
Blinder	Tu-22 bomber aircraft				
Boat Sail	Submarine radar	Donets	Series of ship's navigation radars	Frog-7	Surface-to-surface missile
Bob Tail	Naval radio sextant	Down Beat	Navigation/bombing radar for Backfire	Frogfoot	Su-25 ground attack aircraft
Bounder	Prototype bomber			Front Dome	Naval FCS radar for SA-N-7
Bowl Mesh	Shipboard tracking radar	Drum Tilt	AA fire control radar	Front Door	Guidance radar for SS-N-3
Bow Mat	Naval Elint/Sigint antenna	Dry Rack	Pole-mounted quadruple Yagi array	Front Piece	Guidance radar for SS-N-3
Bow Tie	Broadband shipboard antennas			Fulcrum	MiG-29 combat aircraft
Box Brick	Mobile radar	Dumbo	VHF early warning and search radar		
Bread Bin	Trailer-mounted radar			Gage	Ground target acquisition radar
Brewer	Yak-28 attack aircraft	Dustbin	Submarine mast sensor	Gainful	Surface-to-air missile
Brick Group	Submarine ECM system incorporating Brick Pulp and Brick Spit			Galosh	Surface-to-air missile
		Egg Ball	Naval antenna housing	Gammon	Surface-to-air missile
		Egg Cup A/B	Ship's splash spotting radar	Ganef	SA-4 surface-to-air missile
Brick Pulp	Submarine EW antenna	End Tray	Ground radar used with Scud	Gaskin	SA-9 air defence missile
Brick Round	Naval antenna with circular dish reflector	Eye Bowl	Naval missile guidance radar (SS-N-14)	Gecko	Mobile AA missile system
				Gin Pole	Naval ECM
Brick Spit	Submarine EW antenna			Goa	Surface-to-air missile
Brick Spring	High-gain naval helix antenna with ground plane	Fagot	MiG-15 jet fighter	Goblet	SAN-3 naval missile
		Faithless	Mikoyan STOL fighter aircraft	Golf Ball	Submarine mast sensor
Brick Square	Similar to Brick Round but with different feed and reflector	Fan Song A	Tracking radar	Gopher	SA-13 mobile SAM
		Fan Song B	Target tracking radar	Grail	Man-portable AA missile
		Fan Song E	Target tracking radar	Grid Bow	Directional broadband naval communications antenna
Cage Bare	Naval Elint/Sigint antenna	Fan Song Series	Range of electro-mechanically scanned target tracking radars		
Cage Cone A/B	Naval IFF antenna			Grid Shield	Naval Elint/Sigint antenna
		Fan Tail	Tail fire control radar for Backfire B	Griffon	Surface-to-air missile
Cage Stalk	Naval broadband dipole communications antenna			Guideline	Surface-to-air missile
		Farmer	MiG-19 jet fighter	Guild	Surface-to-air missile
Camel	Tu-104 airliner. Civil version of Badger	Farm Loaf	Naval EW antenna housing	Gun Dish	AA fire control radar
		Fencer	New swing-wing fighter		
Camp	An-8 transport aircraft	Feniks	Submarine sonar	Hair Net	Naval search radar
Candid	Il-76 transport aircraft	Fiddler	Tu-28 strike aircraft	Half Bow	Naval target designation radar
Careless	Tu-154 transport aircraft	Fig Jar	Naval ECM antenna housing	Hare	Mi-1 light helicopter
Cat	An-10 transport aircraft	Firebar	Yak-28P all-weather fighter aircraft	Harke	Mi-10 helicopter
Cat House	Missile defence system radar			Hat Rack	Pole-mounted directional antenna
Charger	Tu-144 supersonic transport	Fire Can	Land-mobile AA fire control radar		
Chekhov	ABM system radar	Fire Dish	Trailer-mounted tracking radar	Hawk Screech	Naval fire control radar
Cheese Brick	Truck-mounted version of Box Brick	Fire Iron	Naval gun fire control array of 4 Yagi antennas with reflectors	Hay Pole	Vertically polarised omnidirectional antenna
Chuck Luck	Similar to Cage Stalk but different polarisation	Fire Wheel	AA fire control radar	Hay Rick	Truck-mounted omni array
		Fishbed	MiG-21 interceptor aircraft	Hay Ring	Microwave link relay antenna
Chuck Tube	Naval communications dipole antenna	Fish Bowl	Naval fire control radar	Hay Wain	Omnidirectional discone antenna
				Headlight	Naval fire control radar
Clamshell	3-D acquisition radar for SA-11				

Designation	Description
Head Net A/B/C	Naval long-range air surveillance radar series
Helix	Ka-32 ASW helicopter
Hen Egg	Ballistic missile early-warning radar
Hen House	Ballistic missile early-warning radar
Hen Nest	Ballistic missile early-warning radar
Hen Roost	High power early-warning radar
Hercules	Submarine sonar
High Brick	Truck-mounted radar
High Fix	Ranging radar for Fitter A/C
High Lark	J-band AI radar
High Lune	Ship's nodding heightfinder
High Pole	Naval IFF transponder antenna
High Ring	Naval Elint/Sigint antenna
High Scoop	Naval search radar
High Sieve	Naval search radar
Hind	Mi-24 attack helicopter
Hip	Mi-8 helicopter
Hog	Ka-18. Obsolete development of Hen helicopter
Home Guide	Yagi array for aircraft homing system
Homer	Mi-12 helicopter
Home Talk	Aircraft/ground communications antenna
Hoodlum	Ka-26 helicopter
Hook	Mi-6 helicopter
Hoop	Attack helicopter (poss Mi-29)
Hoplite	Mi-2 helicopter. Enlarged Hare
Hormone	Ka-25 helicopter
Horn Spoon	Ship's navigation radar
Horse	Yak-24. Obsolete military helicopter
Hound	Mi-4 helicopter
Jay Bird	J-band radar used on MiG-25 Foxbat
Kangaroo	Air-to-surface missile
Kelt	Air-to-surface missile
Kennel	Air-to-surface missile
Kerry	Air-to-surface missile
Kingfish	Air-to-surface missile
Kipper	Air-to-surface missile
Kitchen	Air-to-surface missile
Kite Screech	Naval gun fire control radar
Knife Rest A, B, C	P-10 Series. VHF truck-mounted early warning radar
Krug	Very large fixed HF direction-finding system
Land Fall	Coastal surveillance radar
Leningrad	Shipboard high definition surface search radar
Light Bulb	Naval search radar
Long Bow	Naval target designation radar
Long Brick	Small truck-mounted radar/comms system
Long Bull	Target designation radar. Back-to-back antennas
Long Ears	Naval optical fire control system
Long Eye	Land-mobile radar. Back-to-back antennas
Long Talk	Land-mobile multi-radar system
Long Track	Search and acquisition radar for SA-4 and SA-6 missiles
Long Trough	Mortar locating radar
Look Two	Bombing and navigation radar
Loop Three	Trailer-mounted direction-finding system
Low Blow	Radar for SA-3 missile system
Low Sieve	Naval surface search radar
Madge	Be-6 flying boat
Maestro	Trainer for Firebar/Brewer aircraft
Magnum	Yak-30 aerobatic competition aircraft
Maiden	Two-seat version of Fitter
Mail	Be-12 maritime reconnaissance amphibian
Mallow	Be-8/10 jet flying boat
Mandrake	High flying recce aircraft
Mangrove	Yak-26 tactical reconnaissance aircraft

Designation	Description
Mantis	Yak-32 single-seat jet
Mascot	Il-28U trainer version of Beagle
Max	Yak-18 trainer and transport versions
May	Il-38 maritime recce version of Coot
Mercury Grass	Land-mobile system using VHF Yagi arrays
Mercury Noseband	Land-mobile electronic system
Mesh Brick	Land-mobile radar
Midget	MiG-15UTI trainer version of Fagot
Mongol	Trainer version of Fishbed
Moon	Fixed HF direction-finding array
Moon Cone	Large planar array of dipoles with reflector
Moon Face	Similar to Moon Cone
Moon Mat	Similar to Moon Face
Moon Plate	Similar to other Moon systems but land-transportable
Moose	Yak-11 trainer
Moss	AEW version of Cleat
Moujik	Trainer version of Fitter
Mound Brick	Trailer-mounted tracking system
Muff Cob	Naval fire control radar
Mule	Trainer
Mushroom	Helicopter radar
Neptun	Ship's navigation radar
Nysa B	Trailer-mounted radar
Nysa C	Land-transportable radar system
Odd Lot	E-band GCI radar system
Odd Pair	Heightfinder radar. Land-based
Odd Rods	Aircraft multi-band EW antennas
Oka	Ship's navigation radar
One Eye	Surveillance radar. Land-based
OR-2	Semi-fixed search radar
Owl Screech	Naval fire control radar
Paddle Wheel	Shipboard monitoring antenna
Palm Frond	Naval navigation radar
Park Lamp	Submarine mast direction-finding loop antenna
Pat Hand	Radar for SA-4 surface-to-air missile
Patty Cake	Heightfinder radar
Pea Pod	Aircraft antennas
Peel Group	Naval fire control radars for SAN-1 surface-to-air missile
Plank shave	Naval search radar
Port Spring	Submarine mast conical spiral antenna
Plinth Net	Target acquisition radar
Plum Jar	Shipboard EW antenna system
Pole Dish	Possible microwave link antenna
Pop Group	Naval radar for SAN-4 missile
Pork Trough	Mortar locating radar
Post Bow	Naval target designation radar
Post Lamp	Naval target designation radar
Pot Drum	Naval fire control radar
Pot Head	Naval surface search radar
Prong Rest	VHF Yagi array
Puff Ball	Airborne search radar
Punch Bowl	Submarine mast radome
Quint Spring	Navigational tracking antenna
Ram J/K	New Soviet fighter aircraft designs
Ram L	MiG-29 fighter aircraft
Ram M	High altitude reconnaissance aircraft
Ram P	Aircraft thought to be equivalent of US B-1 bomber
Rib Cone	Shipboard broadband omni-directional VHF antenna
Ring Two	Trailer-mounted direction-finding system
Rock Cake	Heightfinder radar
Rod Mat	Ground-based IFF
Round Top	Naval optical fire control system
Saddler	SS-7 ICBM
Sagger	Anti-tank missile
Salish	Coastal defence missile

Designation	Description
Samlet	Surface-to-surface version of Kennel missile
Sandal	Surface-to-surface missile
Sandbox	SS-N-12 anti-ship missile
Sapwood	Rocket booster
Sark	Obsolete SLBM
Sasin	ICBM
Savage	ICBM
Sawfly	Submarine-launched ballistic missile
Scale	IRBM
Scaleboard	Surface-to-surface missile
Scamp	IRBM
Scan Can	Aircraft fire control radar
Scan Fix	AI radar
Scan Odd	AI radar
Scan Three	I/J-band AI radar
Scapegoat	IRBM
Scarp	ICBM
Scoop Pair	Naval target acquisition radars
Score Board	Ground-based IFF
Score Board A	Naval IFF
Scrag	ICBM
Scrooge	IRBM
Scrubber	Naval anti-shipping missile
Scud A and B	Surface-to-surface missiles
Sea Gull	Long-range naval search radar
Sea Net	Naval search radar
Sego	SS-11 ICBM
Sepal	Coastal defence version of Shaddock
Serb	Submarine-launched ballistic missile
Shaddock	Naval surface-to-surface missile
Sheet Bend	Naval search radar
Sheet Curve	Naval search radar
Sheet Nest	Shipboard radar reflector/enhancement system
Shelf	Aircraft antenna
Shika	ZSU-23-4 vehicle with quad-23mm AA system
Ship Globe	Shipborne missile and space tracking radar
Ship Wheel	Shipboard space tracking radar circular reflector
Shore Walk	Communications relay system antenna
Short Horn	K-Band bombing and navigation radar
Shyster	Obsolete ballistic missile
Side Globe	EW housings on large Soviet warships
Side Net	Heightfinder radar
Silex	SS-N-14 ASW missile
Siren	SS-N-9 anti-ship missile
Sirena	Aircraft radar warning set
Skean	IRBM
Skin Head	Target acquisition radar for torpedo boats
Ski Pole	Ship's IFF
Skip Spin	AI radar
Slant Blade	Shipboard broadband VHF antenna
Slim Net	Naval search radar
Small Cross	Rotating dipole direction-finding system
Small Yawn	Artillery locating radar
Snapper	Anti-tank missile
SNAR-6	J-band mortar locating radar
Snoop Plate	Submarine surveillance radar
Snoop Slab	Submarine surface search radar
Snoop Tray	Submarine surveillance radar
Snow Net	Shipboard ring and dipole VHF omni antenna
Snow Shoe	Similar to Snow Net
Spandrel	AT-5 anti-tank missile
Spigot	AT-4 anti-tank missile
Spike Two	Truck-mounted twin dipole array
Spin Scan	AI radar
Spin Trough	Naval IR searchlight or gun director
Spiral	AT-6 anti-tank missile
Sponge Cake	Heightfinder radar
Spoon Rest A	P-12 VHF early warning radar
Sprage Star	Shipboard VHF dipole array
Sprat Star	Shipboard communications array

Designation	Description	Designation	Description	Designation	Description
Square Four	Crossed loop direction-finding array. Land-based	**Tachi 1**	Multiple Yagi arrays associated with searchlight	**Tub Brick**	Trailer-mounted radar
				Tube Tree	Multi-element antenna array
		Tall King	Land-based early warning radar	**Twice Up**	Dipole antenna
Square Head	Naval IFF interrogator antenna	**Tamir**	Submarine sonar	**Twin Eye**	Back-to-back dish antenna array
Square Pair	Target and missile tracking radar for SA-5 missile	**Tee Plinth**	Naval E-O system	**Twin Scan**	I/J-band AI radar
		Thick Eight A	Fixed HF direction-finding array	**Two Spot**	Truck-mounted PAR radar
Square Pick	Array of horizontal and vertical dipoles. Land-based	**Thin Skin**	Heightfinder radar		
		Till Pot	Probably naval ECM	**Vee Cone A/B/C**	Shipboard conical spiral antenna system
Square Slot	Naval search radar	**Toadstool**	Airborne radar on Coke		
Square Tie	Naval GP fire control radar	**Token**	Early warning GCI radar	**Vee Tube**	Naval communications antenna
Square Twin	Sigint/Elint antenna	**Top Bow**	Naval long-range tracking radar		
Squat Eye	Search radar. Land-based	**Top Dome**	Naval SA-N-6 missile guidance group	**Wasp Head**	Naval optical fire control director
Squint Eye	Surveillance radar			**Watch Dog**	ESM multi-band intercept antenna array
Stick Tree	Land-based Yagi array	**Top Hat**	Shipboard EW antenna system		
Stone Cake	Heightfinder radar	**Top Knot**	Naval tactical air navigation radar	**Whiff**	AA fire control radar
Stop Light	Broadband passive ESM	**Top Net**	Naval search radar	**Whiff Brick**	Trailer-mounted dish radar
Straight Flush	Radar for SA-6 missile	**Top Pair**	Naval back-to-back long-range search radar group	**Witch Eight**	8-element dipole array for IFF
Straight Key	Sigint/Elint antenna			**Witch Five**	Naval IFF
Strike Out	Land-mobile search radar similar to Barlock	**Top Sail A/B**	Naval 3-D air search radar	**Witch Four**	Four-element dipole array for IFF
		Top Steer	Naval back-to-back air surveillance radar group	**Wood Gage**	Semi-fixed search radar
Strut Curve	Naval search radar	**Top Trough**	Naval air search radar	**Yard Rake**	Shipboard rotatable Yagi array (IFF)
Stub Brace	Shipboard broadband crossed dipole array	**Track Dish**	Ground tracking radar		
		Trap Door	Naval missile fire control radar	**Yew Loop**	Shipboard radar
Styx	Naval anti-shipping missile	**Tread Mill**	Shipboard Wullenweber VHF dipole array for direction-finding	**Yo Yo**	Target tracking radar
Sun Hat	Pole-mounted antenna				
Sun Visor A/B	Naval fire control radar	**Try Add**	Long-range early warning radar		
Swatter	Anti-tank missile				

Land-based Guns & Artillery

The following five tables contain condensed information from the pages devoted to army ordnance equipment in previous editions of *Jane's Weapon Systems*. This aspect of military technology now forms a major portion of the associated Jane's yearbook, *Jane's Armour and Artillery*, which is published annually and is dedicated to military land fighting vehicles and to tubed artillery; readers seeking detailed treatment of these subjects are directed to that work. Land ordnance was initally incorporated in *Jane's Weapon Systems* as in many instances a gun forms a significant element of one or more of the weapon systems which are the principal concern of this book, but to describe such elements at length can no longer be justified in the context of ever increasing demands on the space available in *Jane's Weapon Systems*, or when the topic has its own Jane's title devoted to it. The tables that follow will be adequate for the understanding and assessment of those weapon systems mentioned in this volume that are concerned with artillery.

4503.114　　　　　　　　　　　　　　**Self-propelled Artillery**

Model	Entry No.	Type	Calibre	Combat weight	Shell weight	Range	Type of ammunition	Engine power/type	Remarks
CANADA									
Sexton	—	Gun-howitzer	87·6 mm	25 885 kg	11·34 kg	12 250 m	HE, AP, smoke	400 hp/P	Obsolete
CZECHOSLOVAKIA									
DANA	—	Howitzer	152 mm	23 000 kg	43·51 kg	18 500 m	HE, APHE, III	345 hp/D	In production
FRANCE									
GCT	5574.103	Gun	155 mm	42 000 kg	43·2 kg	24 000 m	NATO	720 hp/D	In production
Mk F3	5536.103	Gun	155 mm	17 400 kg	43·75 kg	20 040 m	HE, RAP, III	250 hp/P	In production
Mk 61	5537.103	Howitzer	105 mm	16 500 kg	16 kg	15 000 m	HE, HEAT	250 hp/P	Production complete
GERMANY, Federal Republic									
M109G	2192.103	Howitzer	155 mm	24 600 kg	43·18 kg	18 500 m	NATO	420 hp/D	In service
INTERNATIONAL									
SP-70	2196.103	Howitzer	155 mm	43 524 kg	43·4 kg	24 000 m	NATO	987 hp/D	Development
ISRAEL									
L-33	2319.103	Gun-howitzer	155 mm	41 500 kg	43·7 kg	21 000 m	NATO	460 hp/D	Production complete
ITALY									
Palmaria	—	Howitzer	155 mm	46 000 kg	43·5 kg	24 000 m	HE, III, smoke	750 hp/D	In production
M109 (mod)	2193.103	Howitzer	155 mm	—	43·4 kg	24 000 m	NATO	405 hp/D	Conversion
JAPAN									
Type 75	5179.103	Howitzer	155 mm	25 300 kg	43·4 kg	15 000 m	NATO	450 hp/D	In production
Type 74	4035.103	Howitzer	105 mm	16 500 kg	19·06 kg	11 270 m	NATO M1	300 hp/D	Production complete
SOUTH AFRICA									
G6	—	Howitzer	155 mm	36 500 kg	45·5 kg	30 000 m	HE, HE BB, WP	525 hp/D	Development
SWEDEN									
Bandkanon 1A	5527.103	Gun	155 mm	53 000 kg	48 kg	25 600 m	HE	240 hp/D	Production complete
UNION OF SOVIET SOCIALIST REPUBLICS									
M-1975	—	Mortar	240 mm	—	—	—	HE, nuclear	—	In production
—	—	Howitzer	203 mm	—	—	—	HE, nuclear	—	In production
2S5	—	Gun	152 mm	—	43·5 kg	—	HE, HE RAP	520 hp/D	In production
M-1973 (2S3)	5133.103	Gun-howitzer	152 mm	23 000 kg	43·5 kg	18 500 m	HE, HE RAP	520 hp/D	In production
M-1974 (2S1)	5132.103	Howitzer	122 mm	16 000 kg	21·72 kg	15 300 m	HE, HEAT, III	240 hp/D	In production
SU-100	2888.103	Anti-tank gun	100 mm	32 000 kg	16 kg	—	HE, AP, HEAT	520 hp/D	Obsolescent
UNITED KINGDOM									
GBT 155	4342.103	Howitzer	155 mm	14 000 kg (turret)	43·4 kg	24 000 m	NATO	n/a	Turret only
Abbot	5503.103	Gun	105 mm	16 556 kg	16·1 kg	17 100 m	HE, HESH, smoke	240 hp/D	Production complete
UNITED STATES OF AMERICA									
M110A2	5573.103	Howitzer	203 mm	28 350 kg	92·53 kg	21 300 m	HE, chemical, nuclear	405 hp/D	In production
M107	5524.103	Gun	175 mm	28 168 kg	66·78 kg	32 700 m	HE	405 hp/D	Production complete
M109A2	5570.103	Howitzer	155 mm	24 948 kg	42·91 kg	18 100 m	NATO	405 hp/D	In production
M44	5550.103	Howitzer	155 mm	28 350 kg	42·91 kg	14 600 m	NATO	405 hp/D	Production complete
M108	5509.103	Howitzer	105 mm	22 452 kg	18·1 kg	11 500 m	NATO M1	405 hp/D	Production complete
M52	5551.103	Howitzer	105 mm	24 040 kg	18·1 kg	11 270 m	NATO M1	500 hp/P	Production complete
M7	—	Howitzer	105 mm	22 970 kg	21·06 kg	10 500 m	HE, smoke, chemical	350 hp/P	Obsolete

4504.134   **Self-propelled Anti-aircraft Guns**

Model	Entry No.	Type	Calibre	Combat weight	Shell weight	Muzzle velocity	Type of ammunition	Engine power/type	Remarks
CHINA, People's Republic									
Type 63	5529.103	Twin	37 mm	32 000 kg	0·76 kg	880 m/s	FRAG, AP-T	500 hp/D	Conversion
CZECHOSLOVAKIA									
M53/59	2029.103	Twin	30 mm	10 300 kg	0·45 kg	1000 m/s	API, HEI	110 hp/D	Production complete
FRANCE									
AMX-30 DCA	5539.103	Twin	30 mm	—	0·36 kg	1000 m/s	HEI, SAPHEI	720 hp/D	In service
AMX-13 DCA	5539.103	Twin	30 mm	17 200 kg	0·36 kg	1000 m/s	HEI, SAPHEI	250 hp/P	Production complete
VDAA	—	Twin	20 mm	14 200 kg	0·125 kg	1038 m/s	HSS820	235 hp/D	In production
M3 VDA	3669.103	Twin	20 mm	7200 kg	0·125 kg	1038 m/s	HSS820	90 hp/P	In production
GERMANY, Federal Republic									
Wildcat	—	Twin	30 mm	18 500 kg	0·35 kg	1050 m/s	GAU 8/A	320 hp/D	Development complete
INTERNATIONAL									
Gepard	—	Twin	35 mm	47 300 kg	0·55kg	1175 m/s	HEI, SAPHEI. AP	830 hp/D	Production complete
Dragon	—	Twin	30 mm	31 000 kg	0·36 kg	1000 m/s	API, HEI	720 hp/D	Development
ITALY									
OTO 76	—	Single	76·2 mm	46 836 kg	6·4 kg	940 m/s	HE, APFSDS	1000 hp/D	Development
SWITZERLAND									
GDF-CO2	—	Twin	35 mm	18 000 kg	0·55 kg	1175 m/s	HEI, SAPHEI, AP	204 hp/D	Development
UNION OF SOVIET SOCIALIST REPUBLICS									
ZSU-57-2	5514.103	Twin	57 mm	28 100 kg	2·81 kg	1000 m/s	FRAG, APC	520 hp/D	Production complete
ZSU-23-4	5581.103	Quad	23 mm	19 000 kg	0·19 kg	970 m/s	API, HEI	280 hp/D	In production
UNITED STATES OF AMERICA									
Sgt York	—	Twin	40 mm	54 431 kg	0·88 kg	1025 m/s	PFHE, HCHE	810 hp/P	In production
M42	5526.103	Twin	40 mm	22 452 kg	2·15 kg	880 m/s	HE, AP	500 hp/P	Production complete
Eagle	—	Twin	35 mm	14 500 kg	1·58 kg	1175 m/s	HEI, SAPHEI	215 hp/D	Development
M162	5547.103	Rotary	20 mm	12 310 kg	0·1 kg	1030 m/s	HE, AP	215 hp/D	In production
Vulcan-Commando	—	Rotary	20 mm	10 206 kg	0·1 kg	1030 m/s	HE, AP	202 hp/D	In production

4506.134   **Towed Anti-aircraft Guns**

Model	Entry No.	Type	Calibre	Combat weight	Shell weight	Vertical range	Type of ammunition	Rate of fire (cyclic)	Remarks
CANADA									
Boffin	—	Single	40 mm	1770 kg	0·955 kg	4660 m	HE, AP	120 rpm	Obsolete
CHINA, People's Republic									
Type 59	—	Single	100 mm	—	—	—	—	—	Copy of Soviet KS-19
Type 56	—	Single	85 mm	—	—	—	—	—	Copy of Soviet M1939
Type 59	—	Single	57 mm	—	—	—	—	—	Copy of Soviet S-60
Type 55	—	Single	37 mm	—	—	—	—	—	Copy of Soviet M1939
Type 63	—	Twin	37 mm	—	—	—	—	—	Twin version of Type 55
Type 56	—	Quad	14·5 mm	—	—	—	—	—	Copy of Soviet ZPU-4
Type 58	5529.103	Twin	14·5 mm	—	—	—	—	—	Copy of Soviet ZPU-2
CZECHOSLOVAKIA									
—	2311.109	Single	57 mm	5150 kg	2·58 kg	6000 m	APHE, AP	160 rpm	Production complete
M53	2029.103	Twin	30 mm	1750 kg	0·45 kg	6300 m	HEI, API	450-500 rpm	Production complete
M53	2312.103	Quad	12·7 mm	628 kg	0·495 kg	5600 m	API	600 rpm	Production complete

Model	Entry No.	Type	Calibre	Combat weight	Shell weight	Vertical range	Type of ammunition	Rate of fire (cyclic)	Remarks
FRANCE									
53T4	—	Twin	20 mm	2000 kg	0·12 kg	2000 m	HEI, APDS	900 rpm	Development
Cerbere	5233.103	Twin	20 mm	1513 kg	0·12 kg	2000 m	HEI, APDS, API	900 rpm	In production
Centaure	5234.103	Twin	20 mm	994 kg	0·125 kg	2000 m	HSS 820	740 rpm	In production
Tarasque	5187.103	Single	20 mm	660 kg	0·125 kg	2000 m	HSS 820	740 rpm	In production
GERMANY, Federal Republic									
Twin Gun ADS	4266.103	Twin	20 mm	1640 kg	0·12 kg	2000 m	HEI, APDS, API	1000 rpm	In production
M30	—	Single	20 mm	450 kg	0·12 kg	3700 m	AP, HE	280 rpm	Obsolete
M38V	—	Quad	20 mm	1514 kg	0·12 kg	3700 m	AP, HE	480 rpm	Obsolete
GREECE									
Artemis 30	—	Twin	30 mm	6200 kg	0·35 kg	5000 m	GAU-8/A	800 rpm	Ready for production
ISRAEL									
TCM-20	3804.103	Quad	20 mm	1350 kg	0·125 kg	4500 m	HSS 820	1000 rpm	In production
ITALY									
40L70	4343.103	Twin	40 mm	9900 kg	0·96 kg	8700 m	AP, PRE FRAG, HE-T	300 rpm	In production
Breda	2606.103	Single	40 mm	5300 kg	0·96 kg	8700 m	AP, PRE FRAG, HE-T	300 rpm	In production
Breda Twin 30	—	Twin	30 mm	—	0·35 kg	5000 m	GAU-8/A	800 rpm	Prototype
NORWAY									
FK 20-2	—	Single	20 mm	440 kg	0.12 kg	2000 m	HEI, APDS, API	1000 rpm	Production complete
SWEDEN									
M54	2336.103	Single	57 mm	8100 kg	2·6 kg	4000 m	HE	120 rpm	Obsolete
L/70 BOFI	5528.103	Single	40 mm	5500 kg	0·96 kg	4000 m	PFHE, HCHE, HE, APC	120 rpm	In production
L/60	2337.103	Single	40 mm	2400 kg	0.955 kg	2560 m	HE, AP	120 rpm	Obsolescent
SWITZERLAND									
GDF-002	5198.103	Twin	35 mm	6300 kg	0·55 kg	4000 m	HEI, SAPHEI	550 rpm	In production
GCF-BM2	—	Twin	30 mm	5492 kg	0·36 kg	3000 m	HEI, SAPHEI	650 rpm	Production complete
Diana	—	Twin	25 mm	2100 kg	0·18 kg	2500 m	HEI, APDS	8000 rpm	Prototype
GBI-A01	—	Single	25 mm	440 kg	0·18 kg	2500 m	HEI, SAPHEI, APDS	570 rpm	In production
GAI-D01	2384.103	Twin	20 mm	1330 kg	0·125 kg	2000 m	HEI, SAPHEI, AP	1000 rpm	In production
GAI-C01	5587.103	Single	20 mm	370 kg	0·125 kg	2000 m	HEI, SAPHEI, AP	1050 rpm	In production
GAI-B01	5587.103	Single	20 mm	405 kg	0·125 kg	2000 m	HEI, SAPHEI, AP	1000 rpm	In production
UNION OF SOVIET SOCIALIST REPUBLICS									
KS-30	5578.103	Single	130 mm	24 900 kg	33·4 kg	20 000 m	HE, APHE	—	Production complete
KS-19	5579.103	Single	100 mm	9550 kg	15·89 kg	15 000 m	HE, HE-FRAG, AP, APC	—	Production complete
M1944	5580.103	Single	85 mm	5000 kg	15·9 kg	10 000 m	FRAG	—	Production complete
S-60	5514.103	Single	57 mm	4500 kg	2·85 kg	6000 m	FRAG, APC	120 rpm	Production complete
M1939	2887.103	Single	37 mm	2100 kg	0·732 kg	6700 m	FRAG, AP	180 rpm	Production complete
ZU-23	5581.103	Twin	23 mm	950 kg	0·19 kg	5100 m	HEI, API	1000 rpm	Production complete
ZPU-1	5582.103	Single	14·5 mm	413 kg	0·064 kg	5000 m	API	600 rpm	—
ZPU-2	5582.103	Twin	14.5 mm	621 kg	0·064 kg	5000 m	API	600 rpm	—
ZPU-4	5582.103	Quad	14·5 mm	1810 kg	0·064 kg	5000 m	API	600 rpm	—
UNITED KINGDOM									
3·7-inch	2489.103	Single	94 mm	7620 kg	12·7 kg	9000 m	HE, AP	—	Obsolete
40 mm Mk 1	2455.103	Single	40 mm	2034 kg	0·9 kg	2600 m	HE, AP	120 rpm	In limited service

Model	Entry No.	Type	Calibre	Combat weight	Shell weight	Vertical range	Type of ammunition	Rate of fire (cyclic)	Remarks
UNITED STATES OF AMERICA									
M118	—	Single	90 mm	14 650 kg	10·6 kg	8500 m	HE, APHE, HVAP	—	In limited service
M117	—	Single	90 mm	6646 kg	10·6 kg	8500 m	HE, APHE, HVAP	—	In limited service
M51	—	Single	75 mm	8750 kg	5·7 kg	9000 m	HE	45 rpm	Production complete
M1	—	Single	40 mm	2656 kg	0·9 kg	4660 m	HE, HEI, AP	120 rpm	In widespread service
GEMAG-25	—	Rotary	25 mm	1814 kg	0·185 kg	2500 m	HEI, APDS	1000 or 2200 rpm	Prototype
M167	5547.103	Rotary	20 mm	1565 kg	0·103 kg	1200 m	GAU-8/A	3000 rpm	Production complete
YUGOSLAVIA									
M55	2265.103	Triple	20 mm	1100 kg	0·125 kg	2000 m	HSS 820	700 rpm	In production
M75	—	Single	20 mm	260 kg	0·125 kg	2000 m	HSS 820	700 rpm	In production

4505.114   Towed Artillery

Model	Entry no	Type	Calibre	Length of barrel	Combat weight	Shell weight	Range	Type of ammunition	Remarks
ARGENTINA									
Model 77/81	3676.103	Howitzer	155 mm	5·115 m	8000 kg	43 kg	22 000 m	HE, RAP	In service
AUSTRIA									
GH N-45	—	Howitzer	155 mm	6·975 m	8900 kg	45·4 kg	30 000 m	HE, HE BB	In production
BELGIUM									
GC 45	5240.103	Howitzer	155 mm	6·975 m	8222 kg	45·4 kg	30 000 m	HE, HE BB, WP	In production
MECAR 90	2491.103	Anti-tank gun	90 mm	2·898 m	880 kg	5·21 kg	—	HE, HEAP, CAN, smoke	In service
CHINA, People's Republic									
Type 54	—	Howitzer	152 mm	—	—	—	—	—	Copy of Soviet D-1
Type 66	—	Gun-howitzer	152 mm	—	—	—	—	—	Copy of Soviet D-20
Type 59	—	Field gun	130 mm	—	—	—	—	—	Copy of Soviet M-46
Type 59-1	—	Field gun	130 mm	—	—	—	—	—	130 mm barrel of Type 60 carriage
Type 54	—	Howitzer	122 mm	—	—	—	—	—	Copy of Soviet M-30
Type 60	—	Field gun	122 mm	—	—	—	—	—	Copy of Soviet D-74
Type 59	—	Field gun	100 mm	—	—	—	—	—	Copy of Soviet BS-3
Type 56	—	Field gun	85 mm	—	—	—	—	—	Copy of Soviet D-44
Type 54	—	Anti-tank gun	76 mm	—	—	—	—	—	Copy of Soviet Zis-3
Type 55	5529.103	Anti-tank gun	57 mm	—	—	—	—	—	Copy of Soviet Zis-2
CZECHOSLOVAKIA									
M53	2308.103	Field gun	100 mm	6·735 m	4210 kg	15·59 kg	21 000 m	HE, APC-T, HVAPDS, HEAT	Production complete
M-52	2309.103	Field gun	85 mm	5·07 m	2095 m	9·5 kg	16 160 m	HE, AP-T, HEAT, HVAP-T	Production complete
FINLAND									
M-74	3671.103	Gun-howitzer	155 mm	5·99 m	9200 kg	43·6 kg	25 000 m	HE	In production
M-68	3670.103	Howitzer	155 mm	5·115 m	8500 kg	43·6 kg	23 000 m	HE	—
M-60	2037.103	Field gun	122 mm	6·466 m	8500 kg	25 kg	25 000 m	HE	—
M-61/37	2039.103	Howitzer	105 mm	—	1800 kg	14·9 kg	13 400 m	HE	M-37/10 similar
FRANCE									
TR	—	Gun	155 mm	6·2 m	10 680 kg	43·4 kg	24 000 m	NATO	In production
Model 50	—	Howitzer	155 mm	4·41 mm	8100 kg	43 kg	18 000 m	HE	Obsolescent
GERMANY, Federal Republic									
M18 series	—	Howitzer	105 mm	2·941 m	1985 kg	14·81 kg	10 675 m	HE	Obsolete

Model	Entry no	Type	Calibre	Length of barrel	Combat weight	Shell weight	Range	Type of ammunition	Remarks
INDIA									
—	5141.103	Field gun	105 mm	—	—	—	—	—	
INTERNATIONAL									
FH-70	2195.103	Howitzer	155 mm	6·022 m	9300 kg	43·4 kg	24 000 m	NATO	In service
ISRAEL									
Model 839P	—	Howitzer	155 mm	6·67 m	10 850 kg	43·4 kg	24 000 m	NATO	Production
M-71	5151.103	Gun-howitzer	155 mm	6·045 m	9200 kg	43·4 kg	23 500 m	NATO	In service
M-68	2312.103	Gun-howitzer	155 mm	5·18 m	8500 kg	43·7 kg	21 000 m	NATO	Production complete
ITALY									
Model 56	5501.103	Pack howitzer	105 mm	1·478 m	1290 kg	21·06 kg	10 575 m	NATO, M1,	In widespread service
KOREA, Republic (South)									
KH179	—	Howitzer	155 mm	7 m	6860 kg	43·4 kg	22 000 m	NATO	Development
KH178	—	Howitzer	105 mm	4·095 m	2697 kg	21·06 kg	14 700 m	NATO, M1	Development
NETHERLANDS									
M114/39	—	Howitzer	155 mm	6·016 m	7300 kg	43·4 kg	24 600 m	NATO, ERFB	Ready for production
SOUTH AFRICA									
G5	—	Howitzer	155 mm	6·975 m	13 500 kg	45·5 kg	30 000 m	HE, HE BB, WP, smoke	In service
SPAIN									
SC-80	—	Gun	155 mm	6·045 m	9200 kg	43·5 kg	24 000 m	HE	Development
m/26	2031.103	Howitzer	105 mm	3·349 m	1950 kg	15·27 kg	11 450 m	HE, HEAT	Obsolete
SWEDEN									
FH-77A	2332.103	Howitzer	155 mm	5·89 m	11 500 kg	42·4 kg	22 000 m	HE, III	In service
FH-77B	4030.103	Howitzer	155 mm	6·045 m	11 900 kg	42·91 kg	24 000 m	NATO	Export model
Model F	2331.103	Howitzer	155 mm	4·41 m	8150 kg	43 kg	17 700 m	HE	Obsolescent
m/39	—	Howitzer	149·1 mm	3·6 m	5720 kg	41·5 kg	14 600 m	HE	
Type 4140	2335.103	Howitzer	105 mm	3·36 m	2800 kg	15·3 kg	15 600 m	HE	
SWITZERLAND									
M-42	2389.103	Howitzer	150 mm	4·2 m	6500 kg	42 kg	15 000 m	HE	Obsolete
Model 46	2387.103	Howitzer	105 mm	2·31 m	1840 kg	15·1 kg	10 000 m	HE	
Model 35	2388.103	Field gun	105 mm	4·4 m	4540 kg	15·15 kg	21 000 m	HE, AP, III	
Model 50	2393.103	Anti-tank gun	90 mm	2·898 m	556 kg	1·95 kg	3000 m	HEAT	
Model 57	2393.103	Anti-tank gun	90 mm	3·033 m	570 kg	2·7 kg	3000 m	HEAT	
UNION OF SOVIET SOCIALIST REPUBLICS									
S-23	2927.103	Gun	180 mm	8·8 m	21 450 kg	84·09 kg	30 400 m	HE, HE/RAP	Production complete
D-20	5521.103	Gun-howitzer	152·4 mm	5·195 m	5650 kg	43·51 kg	17 410 m	HE, CP, AP-T	In widespread service
M1943(D-1)	5196.103	Howitzer	152·4 mm	4·207 m	3600 kg	40 kg	12 400 m	HE, CP	Production complete
ML-20	2886.103	Gun-howitzer	152·4 mm	4·925 m	7270 kg	43·51 kg	17 265 m	HE, CP, AP-T	Production complete
M-10	—	Howitzer	152·4 mm	3·7 m	4150 kg	40 kg	12 400 m	HE, CP	Production complete
M-46	5554.103	Field gun	130 mm	7·6 m	7700 kg	33·4 kg	27 150 m	HE, APC-T	In widespread service
SM-4-1	5145.103	Coastal gun	130 mm	7·6 m	16 000 kg	33·4 kg	29 500 m	HE, APHE	Production complete
D-74	5519.103	Field gun	121·92 mm	6·45 m	5500 kg	27·3 kg	24 000 m	HE, APC-T	Production complete
D-30	5235.103	Howitzer	121·92 mm	4·875 m	3150 kg	27·3 kg	15 400 m	HE, HEAT-FS	In production and service
M1938(M-30)	5520.103	Howitzer	121·92 mm	2·8 m	2450 kg	21·76 kg	11 800 m	HE, HEAT	In widespread service
M1931/37 (A-19)	2894.103	Field gun	121·92 mm	5·645 m	7250 kg	25 kg	20 800 m	HE, CP, AP-T	In widespread service
T-12	5147.103	Anti-tank gun	100 mm	8·484 m	3000 kg	9·5 kg	8500 m	HEAT, APFSDS	
M1944(BS-3)	5168.103	Field gun	100 mm	6·07 m	3650 kg	15·59 kg	21 000 m	HE, APC-T HEAT, HVAPDS	
SD-44	5517.103	Field gun	85 mm	4·693 m	2250 kg	9·6 kg	15 650 m	HE, AP-T, HVAP-T, HEAT	Uses auxiliary engine
D-44	5517.103	Field gun	85 mm	4·693 m	1725 kg	9·6 kg	15 650 m	as SD-44	

Model	Entry no	Type	Calibre	Length of barrel	Combat weight	Shell weight	Range	Type of ammunition	Remarks
USSR cont									
D-48	5518.103	Anti-tank gun	85 mm	6·49 m	2350 kg	9·7 kg	18 970 m	HE, AP, HVAP	Originally thought to be 85 mm
M1938	—	Mountain gun	76·2 mm	1·63 m	785 kg	6·2 kg	10 100 m	HE	Czech design
M1966	—	Mountain gun	76·2 mm	—	780 kg	6·2 kg	10 500 m	as ZIS-3	Also known as M1969
ZIS-3	5516.103	Field gun	76·2 mm	3·455m	1116 kg	6·2 kg	13 290 m	HE, AP-T, HVAP-T, HEAT	Still in widespread use
CH-26	5238.103	Anti-tank gun	57 mm	4·07 m	1250 kg	3·75 kg	6700 m	HE, AP, HVAP	Uses auxiliary engine
ZIS-2	5516.103	Anti-tank gun	57 mm	4·16 m	1150 kg	3·75 kg	8400 m	HE, AP, HVAP	In widespread service
M-42	2013.103	Anti-tank gun	45 mm	3·087 m	570 kg	2·14 kg	4400 m	HE, AP, HVAP	Production complete
UNITED KINGDOM									
5·5-inch	5546.103	Gun-howitzer	139·7 mm	4·175m	5850 kg	45·35 kg	14 800 m	HE	Production complete
Light Gun	5505.103	Gun	105 mm	—	1858 kg	16·1 kg	17 200 m	HE, HESH, smoke	In production
25-pounder	5502.103	Gun-howitzer	87·6 mm	2·35 m	1800 kg	11·34 kg	12 250 m	HE, AP, smoke	Obsolescent
17-pounder	2486.103	Anti-tank gun	76·2 mm	4·442 m	2923 kg	6·98 kg	9144 m	HE, APC, APDS	Obsolescent
6-pounder	2487.103	Anti-tank gun	57 mm	2·565 m	1224 kg	1·47 kg	8990 m	AP, APDS	Obsolescent
UNITED STATES OF AMERICA									
M115	5549.103	Howitzer	203 mm	5·142 m	13 471 kg	92·53 kg	16 800 m	HE, chemical, nuclear	Production complete
M198	5571.103	Howitzer	155 mm	6·096 m	7076 kg	42.91 kg	22-24 000 m	NATO	In production
M59	5506.103	Gun	155 mm	7·036 m	12 600 kg	43·4 kg	22 000 m	HE, AP, smoke	Production complete
M114	5510.103	Howitzer	155 mm	3·778 m	5760 kg	42·91 kg	14 600 m	NATO	In widespread service
M101	5511.103	Howitzer	105 mm	2·574 m	2030 kg	21·06 kg	11 270 m	NATO M1	In widespread service
M102	5512.103	Howitzer	105 mm	3·382 m	1496 kg	21·06 kg	11 500 m	NATO M1	Production complete
M116	—	Pack howitzer	75 mm	1·195 m	653 kg	8·27 kg	8790 m	HE, HEAT	Production complete
M3	—	Anti-tank gun	37 mm	1·979 m	414 kg	0·73 kg	11 750 m	AP, APC, HE	Production complete
YUGOSLAVIA									
M65	5236.103	Howitzer	155 mm	3·778 m	5791 kg	43 kg	14 995 m	NATO	In production
M56	2267.103	Howitzer	105 mm	3·48 m	2060 kg	15 kg	13 000 m	HE, HESH, AP	In production
M48	2268.103	Mountain gun	76·2 mm	1·178 m	705 kg	6·2 kg	8750 m	HE, HEAT, WP	Several versions

4507.114   AFV Armament

Model	Entry No	Calibre	Length	Muzzle velocity	Weight	Types of ammunition	Remarks
BELGIUM							
Cockerill	—	90 mm	3·248 m	695-900 m/s	462 kg	HE, HEAT, HESH, smoke	In production
Cockerill Mk 4	—	90 mm	4·988 m	730-1000 m/s	923 kg	HE, HESH, HEAT	Development
Cockerill Mk 7	—	90 mm	4·365 m	500-1400 m/s	598 kg	APFSDS, HEAT, HESH, HE	Development complete
Kenerga	—	90 mm	4·67 m	800-1380 m/s	582 kg	APFSDS, HEAT	Development complete
MECAR	2491.103	90 mm	3·13 m	633 m/s	274 kg	HE, HEAT	In production
BRAZIL							
ENGESA EC-90	—	90 mm	3·248 m	—	262 kg	HE, HEAT, HESH, smoke	In production
FRANCE							
GIAT	—	120 mm	7·15 m	1100-1700 m/s	2620 kg	APFSDS	Development
CN105F1	5542.103	105 mm	5·9 m	1000 m/s	2470 kg	HE, HEAT, APFSDS	In production
105/57	2147.103	105 mm	4·622 m	900 m/s	1210 kg	HE, HEAT, APFSDS	In production
F2	—	105 mm	5·04 m	—	720 kg	HE, HEAT, APFSDS	In production

Model	Entry No	Calibre	Length	Muzzle velocity	Weight	Types of ammunition	Remarks
FRANCE cont							
CN90F1	5543.103	90 mm	3 m	650-750 m/s	400 kg	HE, HEAT, Can, smoke	In production
CN90F3	—	90 mm	4·59 m	650-750 m/s	—	HE, HEAT, Can, smoke	In production
CS Super	—	90 mm	4·68 m	—	570 kg	HE, HEAT, APFSDS	In production
CL 81	5171.103	81·4 mm	2·3 m	400 m/s	550 kg	HE, APFSDS	In production
HB 60	5171.103	60·7 mm	1·21 m	—	82 kg	HE, HEAT, APFSDS, Ill, smoke	In production
M621	5589.103	20 mm	2·207 m	975 m/s	45·5 kg	AP, HE	In production
M693	5599.103	20 mm	2·695 m	1100 m/s	70·5 kg	AP, HE	In production
GERMANY, Federal Republic							
Smooth-bore	5170.103	120 mm	5·6 m	—	4290 kg	APFSDS, HEAT-MP	In production
Rh 105-30	4068.103	105 mm	5·345 m	—	1800 kg	APFSDS, HEAT, HESH	Smooth and rifled variants
MK30	—	30 mm	3·35 m	1300 m/s	141·5 kg	GAU-8/A	In production
E 25	—	25 mm	2·85 m	1100-1400 m/s	102 kg	HEI, APDS-T	Development
Rh 202	5600.103	20 mm	2·612 m	1000 m/s	61 kg	APDS, API, HEI	In production
ISRAEL							
HVMS 60	—	60 mm	4·6 m	1620 m/s	700 kg	APFSDS, HE	Development
SWEDEN							
KV 90 S 73	2587.103	90 mm	5·08 m	600-825 m/s	692 kg	HE, HEAT	Production as required
L74	2343.103	105 mm	6·5 m	1500 m/s	—	HE, APDS, smoke	Production complete
SWITZERLAND							
Type KD	4033.103	35 mm	4·74 m	1175 m/s	670 kg	HEI, APDS, SAPHEI	In production
Type KCB	2379.103	30 mm	3·52 m	1080 m/s	135 kg	HEI, SAPHEI	In production
Type KBA	4034.103	25 mm	2·806 m	1100 m/s	112 kg	HEI, SAPHEI, APDS	In production
Type KAA	2649.103	20 mm	2·627 m	1050 m/s	88 kg	HEI, AP, SAPHEI	In production
Type KAD	—	20 mm	2·565 m	1050 m/s	57 kg	HEI, AP, SAPHEI	In production
UNION OF SOVIET SOCIALIST REPUBLICS							
Smooth Bore	—	120 mm	—	—	—	—	In service
U-5TS	2972.103	115 mm	6·325 m	915-1615 m/s	—	HE, HEAT, APFSDS	In service
D-10	2966.103	100 mm	5·608 m	1000 m/s	1948 kg	HE, HEAT, APHE	Production probably complete
D-56	—	76·2 mm	3·455m	—	1150 kg	HE, HEAT	In production
2A28	—	73 mm	—	400 m/s	115 kg	HEAT-FS	In production
UNITED KINGDOM							
EXP 28M1	5178.103	120 mm	5·68 m	1500 m/s (est)	2000 kg	HESH, APDS, DS, smoke	Development
L11	2453.103	120 mm	7·34 m	1370 m/s	1782 kg	HESH, APDS, DS, smoke	In production
L7	5195.103	105 mm	5·89 m	1231 m/s	1282 kg	HESH, APDS, DS, smoke	In production
L23A1	5191.103	76·2 mm	2·156 m	533 m/s	150·59 kg	HESH, HE, Can, smoke	In production
Rarden	5504.103	30 mm	2·959 m	1100 m/s	110 kg	HE, APDS	In production
UNITED STATES OF AMERICA							
M68	2854.103	105 mm	5·55 m	1458 m/s	1128 kg	HE, APDS	In production
M41	2832.103	90 mm	4·908 m	1235 m/s	1076 kg	HE, AP, HVAP, HEAT, Can	Production complete
M36	2855.103	90 mm	5·166 m	914 m/s	1203 kg	HE, AP, APC, HEAT, WP	Production complete
M32	—	76·2 mm	4·75 m	1092 m/s	599 kg	HE, HEAT, HVAP, Can	Production complete
XM274	—	75 mm	5·661 m	—	1144 kg	AP	Development
Talon	—	35 mm	3·15 m	1175 m/s	270 kg	HEI, SAPHEI, APDS	Development
M242	5237.103	25 mm	2·743 m	—	106·8 kg	AP, HE	In production

3179.104   **Land Forces Inventories**

These tables have been designed to help the reader of *Jane's Weapon Systems* to identify quickly the major equipment of all land forces. Equipment covered includes tanks, anti-armour weapons, reconnaissance vehicles, armoured personnel carriers, artillery, and surface-to-surface missiles, and anti-aircraft weapons. Mortars and light anti-tank weapons (including light recoilless rifles) have been omitted. Variants of particular vehicles have also been omitted in certain cases, for example, the M-113 family. In addition some vehicles, eg the AMX-13, can be used in two roles, ie as a reconnaissance vehicle or as a light tank: in these tables they have been included under the heading for which they are normally employed. Finally it should be remembered that some armies use vehicles for different roles than those for which they were designed. A good example is the BMP armoured personnel carrier, which some armies use in its intended role, whilst others use it as a light tank. These tables include equipment that is on order, entering service or in reserve.

User service:	(A)	Army	G	Gun	RCL	Recoilless
	(M)	Marines	GH	Gun howitzer	RR	Recoilless rifle
	(O)	Other, eg air forces ground units	GW	Guided weapon	SPG	Self-propelled gun
	(S)	Internal security role	H	Howitzer	SPH	Self-propelled howitzer
Abbreviations:	ATG	Anti-tank gun	LG	Light gun	SPM	Self-propelled mortar
	CG	Coastal gun	MG	Mountain gun	SSM	Surface-to-surface missile
	FG	Field gun	MRL/S	Multiple rocket launcher/system		
	FH	Field howitzer	PH	Pack howitzer		

Tanks	Anti-armour weapons	Recce	APC	Artillery & SSMs	Anti-air weapons
AFGHANISTAN					
PT-76	85 mm D48 ATG	BRDM-2	BTR-40	76 mm M1942 FG	23 mm ZU-23
T-54/T-55	Snapper GW		BTR-50	100 mm M1944 FG	37 mm M1939
T34/85			BTR-60	100 mm M1955 FG	57 mm S-60
T-62			BRT-152	122 mm M1938 FH	85 mm KS-12
			BMP-1	132 mm MRS	100 mm KS-19
				152 mm D1 FH	23 mm ZSU-23-4
					SA-2(O)
					SA-3
					SA-7
ALBANIA					
T-34/85	45 mm ATG	BA-64	BTR-40	SU-76 SPG	37 mm M1939
T-54/T-55	57 mm ATG	BRDM-1	BTR-50	SU-100 SPG	57 mm S-60
Type 59			BTR-152	76 mm M1942 FG	85 mm KS-12
Type 63			Type 531	85 mm D44 FG	100 mm KS-19
				122 mm M1931/7 FG	SA-2(O)
				122 mm M1938 FH	
				152 mm M1937 GH	
				152 mm D1 FH	
				107 mm Type 63 MRS	
ALGERIA					
T-34/85	Sagger GW	Panhard AML-60	BRT-40	85 mm D44 FG	23 mm ZSU-23-4
T-54/T-55		BRDM-1	BTR-50	105 mm Model 1950 FH	23 mm ZU-23
T-62		BRDM-2	BTR-60	122 mm/240 mm MRL	37 mm M1939
T72			BTR-152	122 mm M1937 FG	37 mm Twin
			Walid	122 mm M1938 FH	57 mm S-60
			BMP-1	122 mm M1974 SPH	57 mm ZSU-57-2
				130 mm M-46 FG	85 mm KS-12
				152 mm M1937 GH	100 mm KS-19
				FROG-4 SSM	SA-6
				SU-100 SPG	SA-7
				ISU-122/IUS-152 SPG	SA-9
ANGOLA					
PT-76	Sagger GW	BRDM-1	BTR-40	76 mm M1942 FG	14·5 mm ZPU-1
T-34/85		BRDM-2	BTR-50	105 mm FH-18	14·5 mm ZPU-4
T-54/T-55		Panhard AML-60	BTR-60	122 mm MRL	20 mm M55
T-62		and 90	BTR-152	122 mm M1974 SPH	23 mm ZSU-23-4
			Panhard M3	130 mm M46 FG	23 mm ZU-23
			OT-62		37 mm M1939
					57 mm ZSU-57-2
					SA-3
					SA-6
					SA-7
ARGENTINA					
AMX-13 FL-12	106 mm RR	VBC 90	AMX VCI	105 mm LFH 18 FH	20 mm Rh 202
Jagdpanzer SK105	Bantam GW	ERC 90 F1 (M)	LVTP-7 (M)	105 mm MRS	30 mm Hispano-Suiza
M41	Cobra GW	AML-90	M113	105 mm PH	40 mm Bofors L/60
Sherman Firefly	Jagdpanzer SK105		MOWAG (S)	105 mm M7 SPG	and L/70
Sherman M4	SS-11 GW		M3 half track	105 mm M101 FH	90 mm M117
TAM	SS-12 GW		Shorland (S)	155 mm CITEFA 77/81	Roland
			VCTP	155 mm M59 G	Tigercat (O,M)
			BDX	155 mm M114 FH	Blowpipe
				155 mm Mk F3 SPH	
AUSTRALIA					
Leopard 1A3	106 mm M40 RR		M113A1	5·5-inch GH	Rapier
	ENTAC GW			105 mm LG	Redeye
				105 mm PH	
				105 mm M101 FH	
				155 mm M198 FH	
AUSTRIA					
M47	106 mm M40 RR		Saurer 4K series	85 mm M52 FG	20 mm Oerlikon
M60A1/A3	Jagdpanzer SK105			105 mm M18/40 FH	35 mm Oerlikon
				105 mm M101 FH	40 mm Bofors L/70

Tanks	Anti-armour weapons	Recce	APC	Artillery & SSMs	Anti-air weapons
AUSTRIA cont				130 mm MRL 155 mm M59 G 155 mm M109 SPH 155 mm M114 FH	40 mm M42
BAHRAIN	120 mm RR TOW GW	Ferret Saladin	AT-105(S) Panhard M3	105 mm LG 155 mm M198 FH	
BANGLADESH M24 T-54/T-55 Type 59	6-pounder ATG 106 mm RCL			25-pounder FG 105 mm PH 105 mm M101 FH	
BELGIUM Leopard 1 M47	90 mm Jagdpanzer ENTAC GW MILAN GW SS-11 GW Striker Swingfire GW	Scorpion FN 4RM (S) Scimitar	AMX VCI M75 BDX (S) AIFV M113 A2 Spartan	105 mm PH 105 mm M101 FH 105 mm M108 SPH 155 mm M44 SPH 155 mm M109 SPH 155 mm M114 FH 203 mm M55 SPH 203 mm M110 SPH 203 mm M115 FH Lance SSM	12·7 mm M55 20 mm M167 Vulcan 35 mm Gepard 40 mm Bofors L/70 57 mm Bofors HAWK (A) Nike Hercules (O)
BENIN PT-76 T-54/T-55		Ferret BRDM-2 M20 M8	M3 half track	105 mm M101 FH 122 mm D30 FH 130 mm M46 FG	14·5 mm ZPU 37 mm M1939 57 mm S-60
BOLIVIA Jagdpanzer SK105		EE-9 Cascavel Commando V-100	M113 MOWAG (S) EE-11 Urutu	75 mm M116 PH 105 mm M101 FH	
BRAZIL M3A1 M41 X1A2/X1A1	106 mm M40 RR Cobra GW	EE-3 Jaraca EE-9 Cascavel M8	EE-11 Urutu (and M) M59 M113	75 mm M116 PH 105 mm PH 105 mm M101 FH 105 mm M102 FH 105 mm M108 SPH 108 mm MRS 155 mm M114 FH 300 mm MRL	35 mm Oerlikon 40 mm Bofors L/60 and L/70 40 mm M1 90 mm M117 90 mm M118 HAWK (O) Roland
BRUNEI		Scorpion	Saracen AT-104 (S) Shorland (S)	105 mm LG	Rapier
BULGARIA T-34/85 T-54/T-55 T-62 T-72	57 mm M1943 ATG 85 mm D48 ATG Sagger GW Snapper GW	BRDM-1 BRDM-2	BTR-40 BTR-50 BTR-60 BTR-152 OT-62 MT-LB PSzH-IV	76 mm M1942 FG 85 mm D44 FG 85 mm SD44 FG 100 mm M1944 FG 122 mm MRS 122 mm D30 FH 122 mm M1937 G 122 mm M1938 FH 130 mm MRS 130 mm M46 FG 152 mm D20 GH 152 mm M1937 GH FROG SSM SCUD SSM	14·5 mm ZPU-2 23 mm ZSU-23-4 23 mm ZU-23 37 mm M1939 57 mm ZSU-57-2 57 mm S-60 57 mm ZSU-57-2 85 mm KS-12 SA-2 (O) SA-6 SA-7
BURMA Comet	6-pounder ATG 17-pounder ATG	Ferret Humber		5·5-inch GH 25-pounder FG 105 mm M101 FH	40 mm M1
BURUNDI	75 mm RCL	Panhard AML-60 and 90	Shorland (S) Walid Panhard M3	75 mm M116 PH	14·5 mm ZPU-4
CAMEROON	6-pounder ATG 106 mm M40 RR	M8/M20 Ferret	Commando V-150 Half track	75 mm M116 PH 85 mm Type 56 FG 105 mm Model 1950 FH	35 mm Oerlikon 37 mm Type 63 40 mm Bofors L/60
CANADA Leopard C1	106 mm M40 RR TOW GW	Lynx M113 C & R	M113 Cougar Grizzly	105 mm PH 105 mm M101 FH 155 mm M109A1 SPH	40 mm Bofors L/60 Boffin Blowpipe
CENTRAL AFRICAN REPUBLIC T-55	106 mm M40 RR	Ferret BRDM-2	BTR-152		

Tanks	Anti-armour weapons	Recce	APC	Artillery & SSMs	Anti-air weapons
CHAD					
		Panhard AML-60 and 90 BRDM-2	M3 half track BTR-60 BTR-152	105 mm M2 FH 122 mm MRS 132 mm MRS	14·5 mm ZPU
CHILE					
AMX-13 AMX-30 M3 Stuart M4 Sherman M41	106 mm M40 RR MILAN GW MAMBA GW	EE-9 Cascavel	MOWAG (S) M113 EE-11 Urutu	105 mm PH 105 mm FH18 FH 105 mm M101 FH 155 mm MkF3 SPH	12·7 mm M55 20 mm Oerlikon 40 mm Bofors L/70 40 mm M1 Crotale twin 20 mm
CHINA, People's Republic					
IS-2 T-34/85 Type 59 Type 60 Type 62 Type 63	57 mm Type 55 ATG 76 mm Type 54 ATG Sagger GW		Type 55 Type 56 Type 531	85 mm Type 56 FG 100 mm Type 59 FG 107 mm/132 mm/140 mm/ 320 mm MRS 122 mm SPH 122 mm M1931 G 122 mm Type 54 FH 122 mm Type 60 FG 130 mm Type 59 FG 130 mm Type 59-1 FG 152 mm Type 54 FH 152 mm Type 66 GH ISU-122/ISU-152 SPG	14·5 mm Type 56 14·5 mm Type 58 37 mm Type 55 37 mm Type 63 57 mm Type 59 85 mm Type 56 100 mm Type 59 CSA-2 (O)
COLOMBIA					
Sherman Stuart	M8 TOW	M8/M20 EE-9 Cascavel	M3 half track M113 EE-11 Urutu	105 mm M101 FH	40 mm Bofors L/60
CONGO					
PT-76 T-62 Type 59 Type 63	6-pounder ATG 57 mm M1943 ATG 85 mm D48 ATG	BRDM-1 BRDM-2	BTR-60 BTR-152	76 mm M1942 FG 100 mm M1944 FG 122 mm MRS 122 mm D30 FH 122 mm M1938 FH 122 mm Type 54 FH 130 mm M46 FG	37 mm M1939 57 mm S-60
CUBA					
PT-76 T-34/85 T-54/T-55 T-62 T-72	57 mm Ch-26 ATG 57 mm M1943 ATG 85 mm D48 ATG Sagger GW Snapper GW	BRDM-1 BRDM-2	BTR-40 BTR-60 BTR-152 BMP-1	75 mm M116 PH 76 mm M1942 FG 85 mm D44 FG 85 mm SD44 FG 122 mm MRS 122 mm D30 FH 122 mm D74 FG 122 mm M1931/7 G 122 mm M1938 FH 130 mm M46 FG 132 mm MRS 152 mm D1 FH 152 mm D20 GH 152 mm M1937 GH 240 mm MRS FROG-4 SSM SU-100 SPG	12·7 mm M53 14·5 mm ZPU-1 14·5 mm ZPU-2 14·5 mm ZPU-4 23 mm ZSU-23-4 23 mm ZU-23 30 mm BTR-60 30 mm M53 37 mm M1939 57 mm S-60 57 mm ZSU-57-2 85 mm KS-12 100 mm KS-19 SA-2 (O) SA-6 SA-7 SA-9
CYPRUS					
T-34/85 T-54/T-55	100 mm ATG	Marmon-Herrington EE-9 Cascavel	BTR-50 BTR-152	25-pounder FG 75 mm M116 PH 105 mm M101 FH 128 mm MRL	3·7-inch 20 mm 40 mm Mk 1
CZECHOSLOVAKIA					
PT-76 T-34/85 T-54/T-55 T-62 T-72	57 mm M1942 ATG Sagger GW Snapper GW	OT-65A BRDM-1	OT-62 OT-64 OT-66 OT-810 BMP-1	76 mm M1942 FG 85 mm M52 FG 100 mm M53 FG 105 mm M18/49 FH 122 mm MRS 122 mm D30 FH 122 mm M1937 G 122 mm M1938 H 122 mm M1974 SPH 130 mm MRS 130 mm M46 FG 152 mm SPH 152 mm D20 GH 152 mm M1937 GH FROG SSM SCUD SSM	14·5 mm ZPU-4 23 mm ZSU-23-4 23 mm ZU-23 30 mm M53 30 mm M53/59 57 mm S-60 57 mm ZSU-57-2 SA-3 SA-4 SA-6 SA-7 SA-9
DENMARK					
Centurion Mk 5/2 Leopard 1 A3 M41	106 mm M40 RR TOW GW		M113	105 mm M101 FH 155 mm M59 G 155 mm M109 SPH	12·7 mm M55 40 mm Bofors L/60 40 mm M1

Tanks	Anti-armour weapons	Recce	APC	Artillery & SSMs	Anti-air weapons
DENMARK cont				155 mm M114 FH 203 mm M115 FH	HAWK (O) Nike Hercules (O) Redeye
DOMINICAN REPUBLIC					
AMX-13 FL-10		Panhard AML	V-150 Commando M3 half track	105 mm M101 FH	40 mm M1
ECUADOR					
AMX-13 FL-12 M3 Stuart M4 Sherman		Panhard AML-60 and 90	AMX-VCI M113 UR-416 VAB Condor	105 mm PH 105 mm M101 FH 155 mm MkF3 SPH	20 mm M163 Vulcan 40 mm Bofors L/70 40 mm M1 Blowpipe M730 Chaparral
EGYPT					
IS-3 Jagdpanzer SK105 M-77 M60A3 PT-76 T-10 T-34/85 T-54/T-55 T-62	57 mm M1943 ATG 76 mm M1942 ATG 100 mm ATG MILAN GW Sagger GW Snapper GW Swingfire GW TOW GW	BRDM-1 BRDM-2	BTR-40 BTR-50 BTR-60 BTR-152 BMP Walid OT-62 OT-64 M113 A2 BMR 600	80 mm/122 mm/130 mm/132 mm/ 140 mm/240 mm MRS 85 mm D44 FG 100 mm M1944 FG 122 mm D30 FH 122 mm D74 FG 122 mm M1937 G 122 mm M1938 FH 130 mm M46 FG 130 mm SM-4 CG 152 mm D1 FH 152 mm M1937 GH 180 mm S-23 G FROG-7 SSM Samlet SSM SCUD SSM SU-100 SPG	12·7 mm M53 14·5 mm ZPU 1 14·5 mm ZPU-2 14·5 mm ZPU-4 23 mm ZSU-23-4 23 mm ZU-23 30 mm LAAG 37 mm M1939 37 mm Twin 40 mm Bofors L/60 57 mm S-60 57 mm ZSU-57-2 85 mm KS-12 100 mm KS-19 SA-2 (O) SA-3 SA-6 SA-7
EL SALVADOR					
AMX-13	75 mm RCL	Panhard AML-90	UR-416 M113	105 mm M101 FH 155 mm M115 FH 105 mm Model M-56 FH	20 mm 40 mm Bofors L/70
ETHIOPIA					
M41 T-34/85 T-54/T-55 T-62 T-72	Sagger GW TOW GW	Panhard AML-60 and 90 BRDM-1 BRDM-2	Commando V-150 M113 BMP-1 BTR-60 BTR-152 UR-416	75 mm M116 PH 105 mm M101 FH 122 mm/200 mm MRS 122 mm D30 FH 130 mm M46 FG 152 mm D1 FH 155 mm M114 FH 180 mm S-23 FG	23 mm ZSU-23-4 23 mm ZU-23 37 mm M1939 57 mm ZSU-57-2 SA-2 SA-3 SA-7
FINLAND					
PT-76 T-54/T-55	95 mm RR SS-11 GW		BMP-1 BTR-50 BTR-60	76 mm m/02 FG 76 mm m/36 FG 105 mm m37/10 FG 105 mm m/41 FG 105 mm m61/37 FG 122 mm D30 FH 122 mm m/38 FH 122 mm M60 FG 130 mm m/54 FG 150 mm m/40 FH 152 mm m/38 FH	23 mm ZU-23 35 mm Oerlikon 40 mm Bofors L/60 and L/70 57 mm S-60 57 mm ZSU-57-2 SA-2 SA-3 SA-7
FRANCE					
AMX-13 FL-10 AMX-30 AMX-30B2	106 mm M40 RR MILAN GW SS-11 GW SS-12 GW HOT GW Harpoon GW ENTAC GW	Panhard AML-60 and 90 Panhard EBR AMX-10RC ERC 90 F4 VBC 90 (S)	AMX VCI AMX-10P VXB-170G(S) VAB	105 mm PH 105 mm M101 FH 105 mm Mk61 SPH 155 mm GCT SPG 155 mm M1950 FH 155 mm MkF3 SPH 155 mm TR FH Pluton SSM	20 mm 30 mm AMX-13 40 mm Bofors L/70 Crotale (O) Roland
GABON					
	106 mm RCL	Eland 60/90 Panhard AML-60 and 90 EE-9 Cascavel	EE-11 Urutu VXB-170 Commando V-150 Panhard M3 ACMAT VBL	76 mm M1942 FG 105 mm M2 FH	37 mm M1937 40 mm Bofors L/60
GERMANY, Democratic Republic					
PT-76 T-35/85 T-54/T-55 T-62 T-72	57 mm Ch-26 ATG 57 mm M1943 ATG 76 mm M1942 ATG 100 mm T12 ATG ASU-85 SP Sagger GW Snapper GW	BRDM-1 BRDM-2	BTR-40 BTR-50 BTR-60 BTR-152 BMP-1 MT-LB PSzH-IV	85 mm D44 FG 85 mm M52 FG 85 mm SD44 FG 122 mm/240 mm MRS 122 mm D30 FH 122 mm M1937 FG 122 mm M1938 PH	14·5 mm ZPU-2 14·5 mm ZPU-4 23 mm ZSU-23-4 23 mm ZU-23 57 mm S-60 57 mm ZSU-57-2 100 mm KS-19

Tanks	Anti-armour weapons	Recce	APC	Artillery & SSMs	Anti-air weapons
GERMANY, Democratic Republic cont				122 mm M1974 SPH	SA-2 (O)
				130 mm M46 FG	SA-3
				152 mm D1 FH	SA-4
				152 mm D20 GH	SA-6
				152 mm M1937 GH	SA-7
				152 mm M1973 SPH	SA-9
				FROG-7 SSM	
				SCUD-B SSM	
GERMANY, Federal Republic					
A2/A2GA2	106 mm M40 RR	Spähpanzer Luchs	M113	90 mm MECAR MG	20 mm FK20-2
Leopard 1 series	HOT GW	SPz 11-2	SPz 12-3	105 mm PH	20 mm Rh 202
Leopard 2	JPZ 90 mm Kanone	Saladin (S)	Marder	105 mm M101 FH	35 mm Gepard
M48 M48A2/A2GA2	JPZ Jaguar 1 (HOT)		MOWAG (S)	110 mm LARS MRS	40 mm Bofors L/70
	JPZ Jaguar 2 (TOW)		UR-416 (S)	155 mm FH-70	HAWK (O)
	JPZ Rakete 2 (SS-11)		Transportpanzer 1	155 mm M109G SPH	Nike Hercules (O)
	MILAN GW			155 mm M114 FH	Redeye
	TOW GW			175 mm M107 SPG	Roland
				203 mm M110A2 SPH	
				Lance SSM	
				Pershing SSM	
GHANA					
		Saladin	MOWAG Piranha	25-pounder FG	
		Ferret		76 mm M1942 FG	
				105 mm LG	
GREECE					
AMX-30	90 mm RCL	M8	M59	25-pounder FG	20 mm Rh.202
Jagdpanzer SK 105	106 mm M40 RR		M113/M113 A2	75 mm M116 PH	30 mm Artemis
Leopard 1	Cobra GW		Half track	105 mm PH	40 mm M1
M24	MILAN GW		AMX-10P	105 mm M52 SPH	75 mm M51
M41	TOW GW		MOWAG Roland (S)	105 mm M101 FH	90 mm M117
M47			UR-416	155 mm M44 SPH	90 mm M118
M48/M48A3/M48A5			Steyr 4K7FA	155 mm M59 G	HAWK (A)
				155 mm M109/M109A2 SPH	Nike Hercules (O)
				155 mm M114 FH	Redeye
				175 mm M107 SPG	
				203 mm M110 SPH	
				203 mm M115 H	
GUATEMALA					
AMX-13		RBY Mk 1	Commando V-150	75 mm M116 PH	40 mm
M3 Stuart		M3A1	M113	105 mm M101 FH	
		M8	Half track		
GUINEA					
PT-76		BRDM-1	BTR-40	76 mm M1942 FG	37 mm M1939
T-34/85		BRDM-2	BTR-50	85 mm D44 FG	57 mm Czechoslovak
T-54/T-55			BTR-60	105 mm Model 1950 FH	57 mm S-60
			BTR-152	122 mm M1931/7 FG	100 mm KS-19
				122 mm M1938 FH	
				130 mm M46 FG	
GUINEA-BISSAU					
PT-76		BRDM-2	BTR-40	85 mm D44 FG	14·5 mm ZPU
T-34/85			BTR-50	105 mm M18 FH	23 mm ZU-23
			BTR-60	122 mm D30 FH	57 mm S-60
			BTR-152	122 mm M1938 FH	SA-7
				130 mm M46 FG	
HAITI					
M3 Stuart	37 mm M3A1 ATG		Commando V-150	75 mm M116 PH	40 mm M1
	57 mm M1 ATG			105 mm M101 FH	
HONDURAS					
	106 mm RCL	RBY Mk1		75 mm M116 PH	
		Scorpion		105 mm M101 FH	
		Staghound			
HUNGARY					
PT-76	57 mm ATG	FUG	BMP	76 mm M1942 FG	14·5 mm ZPU-2
T-34/85	BRDM-2 Sagger		MT-LB	85 mm D44 FG	23 mm ZSU-23-4
T-54/T-55	Sagger GW		PSzH-IV	122 mm/240 mm MRS	57 mm S-60
T-72	Snapper GW			122 mm D30 FH	57 mm ZSU-57-2
	Spigot GW			122 mm M1937 FG	100 mm KS-19
				122 mm M1938 FH	SA-2 (O)
				122 mm M1974 SPH	SA-6
				152 mm D20 GH	SA-7
				FROG SSM	SA-9
				SCUD SSM	
INDIA					
AMX-13	6-pounder ATG		BTR-50	5·5-inch GH	3·7 inch
PT-76	85 mm ATG		BTR-60	25-pounder FG	23 mm ZSU-23-4
T-54/T-55	106 mm M40 RR		BTR-152	75 mm M116 PH	40 mm Bofors L/70
T-62	ENTAC GW		OT-64	76 mm M48 MG	40 mm M1
T-72	MILAN GW		OT-62	100 mm M1944 FG	40 mm Mk1
Vijayanta	Sagger GW		BMP	105 mm FG	SA-2 (O)

Tanks	Anti-armour weapons	Recce	APC	Artillery & SSMs	Anti-air weapons
INDIA cont					
	SS-11 GW			105 mm Abbot SPG 105 mm M56 PH 130 mm SPG 130 mm M46 FG 180 mm S-23 G 203 mm M115 H	SA-3 SA-6 SA-7 Tigercat
INDONESIA					
AMX-13 M3 Stuart PT-76	ENTAC GW	Saladin Ferret AMX-10 PAC 90 VPM 110X	AMX-10P BTR-40 BTR-50 BTR-152 Saracen AMX VCI Commando V-150	76 mm M48 MG 76 mm M1942 FG 105 mm LG 105 mm PH 105 mm M101 FH 122 mm M1938 FH	20 mm Oerlikon 40 mm Bofors L/70 40 mm M1 57 mm S-60
IRAN					
Chieftain Mk3/3(P)/ Mk5/5P M47/M47M M48/M48A5 M60A1 T-54/T-55 T-62	106 mm M40 RR Dragon GW ENTAC GW SS-11 GW SS-12 GW TOW GW	Ferret Scorpion Fox BRDM-2 EE-9 Cascavel	BTR-40 BTR-50 BTR-60 BTR-152 M113 BMP	75 mm M116 PH 85 mm D44 FG 105 mm M101 FH 122 mm MRS 130 mm M46 FG 155 mm M109/M109A1 SPH 155 mm M114 FH 175 mm M107 SPG 203 mm M110 SPH 203 mm M115 FH	23 mm ZSU-23-4 23 mm ZU-23 40 mm Bofors L/70 40 mm M1 57 mm S-60 57 mm ZSU-57-2 85 mm KS-12 HAWK (A) Rapier (O) SA-7 Tigercat (O)
IRAQ					
AMX-30 Jagdpanzer SK 105 PT-76 T-34/85 T-54/T-55 T-62 Type-69 T-72	85 mm ATG HOT GW MILAN GW Sagger GW SS-11 GW	Panhard AML-60 and 90 ERC 90 EE-3 Jaraca EE-9 Cascavel BRDM-2 FUG-70	BTR-50 BTR-60 BTR-152 BMP-1 Panhard M3 Panhard VCR EE-11 Urutu OT-62 OT-64 Walid MOWAG Roland PSzH-IV BMR-600	85 mm D44 FG 105 mm PH 122 mm MRS 122 mm M1937 G 122 mm M1938 FH 122 mm M1974 SPH 130 mm M46 FG 152 mm D-1 FH 152 mm M1937 GH 152 mm M1973 SPH 155 mm GCT SPG FROG SSM SCUD SSM SU-100 SPG	14·5 mm ZPU-1/2/4 23 mm ZSU-23-4 23 mm ZU-23 37 mm M1939 57 mm S-60 57 mm ZSU-57-2 85 mm KS-12 100 mm KS-19 SA-2 (O) SA-3 (O) SA-6 SA-7 SA-9
IRELAND					
Scorpion	90 mm RR MILAN GW	Panhard AML-60 and 90	Panhard M3 Unimog Timoney	25-pounder FG 105 mm LG	40 mm Bofors L/60 and L/70 RBS-70
ISRAEL					
Centurion (upgraded) M48A5 M60/M60A1/M60A3 Merkava Mk 1/Mk2 PT-76 T-54/T-55 T-62	106 mm M40 RR Dragon GW Sagger GW TOW GW	BRDM-2 RBY-1	M3 half track Walid (S) BTR-40 (S) BTR-50 BTR-60 BTR-152 OT-62 M113 series Shoët	105 mm M7 SPH 105 mm M101 FH 122 mm D30 FH 122 mm M1938 FH 130 mm M46 FG 155 mm M109/M109A1 SPH 155 mm M114 FH 155 mm Sherman SP 155 mm Soltam L33 240/290 mm MRS 175 mm M107 SPG 203 mm M110 SPH Lance SSM	20 mm M163 20 mm M167 Vulcan 20 mm TCM-20 20 mm TCM-20 half track 23 mm ZU-23 40 mm Bofors L/70 40 mm M1 Chaparral HAWK Redeye
ITALY					
Leopard I M47 M60A1	106 mm M40 RR Cobra GW Mosquito GW SS-11 GW TOW GW	Fiat 6616 (S)	M113 AMX VCI LVTP-7 (M) Fiat 6614 (S) VCC-1	90 mm MECAR MG 105 mm PH 105 mm M101 FH 155 mm FH-70 155 mm M44 SPH 155 mm M59 G 155 mm M109 SPH 155 mm M114 FH 175 mm M107 SPH 203 mm M110 SPH 203 mm M115 FH Lance SSM	12·7 mm M55 20 mm Rh 202 40 mm Bofors L/70 40 mm M1 HAWK (A) Nike Hercules (O)
IVORY COAST					
AMX-13		Panhard AML-60 and 90 ERC 90 F44	Panhard M3 VAB ACMAT VBL	105 mm M101 FH 105 mm Model 1950 FH	20 mm M3 VDA 40 mm Bofors L/60 and L/70
JAMAICA					
		Ferret	Commando V-150		

Tanks	Anti-armour weapons	Recce	APC	Artillery & SSMs	Anti-air weapons
JAPAN					
M41	105 mm M27 RR		M3 half track	75 mm M116 PH	12·7 mm M16 half track
Type 61	106 mm M40 RR		Type 60	105 mm M52 SPH	12·7 mm M55
Type 74	Type 60 SPRGR		Type 73	105 mm M101 FH	35 mm Oerlikon
	Type 64 GW			105 mm Type 74 SPH	40 mm M1
	KAM-3D			130 mm/300 mm MRS	40 mm M42
				155 mm M44 SPH	75 mm M51
				155 mm M59 G	90 mm M118
				155 mm M114 FH	HAWK (A)
				155 mm Type 75 SPH	Nike Hercules (O)
				203 mm M110 SPH	Redeye
				203 mm M115 FH	
JIBUTI					
	106 mm RCL	BRDM-2	BTR 60	105 mm M56 FH	40 mm Bofors
		Panhard AML 60 and 90			
JORDAN					
Centurion Mk7/2	120 mm RR	Ferret	M113	105 mm M52 SPH	12·7 mm M55
Khalid	106 mm M40 RR	Saladin	Saracen	105 mm M101 FH	20 mm M163 Vulcan
M47	Dragon GW			105 mm M102 FH	20 mm M167 Vulcan
M48	TOW GW			155 mm GC45 FH	40 mm Bofors
M60A1/M60A3				155 mm M59 G	40 mm M42
				155 mm M109/M109A2 SPH	HAWK
				155 mm M114 FH	Javelin
				203 mm M110 SPH	SA-6
				203 mm M115 FH	SA-8
KAMPUCHEA					
Status of equipment uncertain at present					
KENYA					
Vickers Mk3	120 mm RR	Panhard AML-60	Panhard M3	25-pounder FG	20 mm TCM-20
	MILAN GW	and 90	UR-416 (S)	105 mm LG	
	Swingfire GW	Saladin		105 mm M101 FH	
		Ferret		155 mm M109 SPH	
		Fox			
		Shorland			
KOREA, Democratic People's Republic (North)					
PT-76	45 mm M1942 ATG	BA-64	BTR-40	SU-76 SPG	14·5 mm ZPU-2
T-34/85	57 mm M1942 ATG	BRDM-2	BTR-50	SU-100 SPG	14·5 mm ZPU-4
T-54/T-55	85 mm D48 ATG		BTR-60	76 mm M1942 FG	23 mm ZSU-23-4
T-62			BTR-152	85 mm D44 FG	23 mm ZU-23
Type 59			Type 531	100 mm M1944 FG	37 mm M1939
Type 63			BMP-1	122 mm/140 mm/200 mm/	57 mm S-60
				240 mm MRS	57 mm ZSU-57-2
				122 mm M1931/7 G	85 mm KS-12
				122 mm M1938 FH	100 mm KS-19
				130 mm M46 FG	SA-2 (O)
				152 mm M1937 GH	SA-7
KOREA, Republic (South)					
M4 Sherman	76 mm M10 SP	M8	M3 half track	105 mm M52 SPH	12·7 mm M55 SP
M47	90 mm M36 SP		M113	105 mm M101 FH	20 mm M167 Vulcan
M48A2/M48A3/	106 mm M40 RR		Fiat 6614	105 mm M102 FH	35 mm Oerlikon
M48A5	TOW GW		LVTP-7 (M)	155 mm MRS	40 mm Bofors L/60
M60A1				155 mm M59 G	and L/70
				155 mm M109 SPH	40 mm M1
				155 mm M114 FH	HAWK (A)
				175 mm M107 SPG	Nike Hercules (A)
				203 mm M110 SPH	
				203 mm M115 FH	
				Honest John SSM	
KUWAIT					
Centurion Mk 8/1	HOT GW	Ferret	Saracen	25-pounder	HAWK (O)
Chieftain Mk 5/5 (K)	SS-11 GW	Saladin	M113	155 mm M114 FH	SA-6
Vickers Mk-1	TOW GW			155 mm Mk F3 SPH	SA-7
				FROG SSM	
LAOS					
PT-76	106 mm RCL	M8	BTR-40	75 mm M116 PH	37 mm M1939
			BTR-152	105 mm M101 FH	57 mm
			M113	122 mm D30 FH	
				155 mm M114 FH	
LEBANON					
AMX-13	106 mm M40 RR	Saladin	M59	155 mm M114 FH	20 mm M55
M48A5	MILAN GW	Staghound	M113A1/A2	155 mm M1950 FH	20 mm Oerlikon
	TOW GW		Panhard M3		23 mm ZU-23
			Chaimite		30 mm Oerlikon
			Saracen		40 mm Bofors
			VAB		40 mm M42
LIBERIA					
	106 mm RCL	M3A1	M3 half track	75 mm M116 PH	
			MOWAG	105 mm M101 FH	

Tanks	Anti-armour weapons	Recce	APC	Artillery & SSMs	Anti-air weapons
LIBYA					
OF-40	MILAN GW	Ferret	Saracen	105 mm M101 FH	23 mm ZSU-23-4
T-34/85	Sagger GW	Saladin	BTR-40	107 mm/122 mm/130 mm MRS	23 mm ZU-23
T-54/T-55	Vigilant GW	EE-9 Cascavel	BTR-50	122 mm D30 FH	30 mm M53/59
T-62		BRDM-2	BTR-60	122 mm D74 FG	40 mm Bofors L/70
T-72			BMP-1	122 mm M1974 SPH	57 mm S-60
			OT-62	130 mm M46 FG	Crotale (O)
			OT-64	152 mm D1 FH	SA-2 (O)
			Shorland (S)	152 mm D20 GH	SA-3 (O)
			EE-11 Urutu	152 mm M1973 SPH	SA-6 (O)
			Fiat 6614	155 mm M109 SPH	SA-7
			Chaimite	155 mm M114 FH	SA-9
			M113A1	155 mm Palmaria SPH	
LUXEMBOURG					
	106 mm M40 RR		V-150 Commando		
	TOW GW				
MADAGASCAR					
PT-76	106 mm M40 RR	Ferret	M3 half track	76 mm M1942 FG	14·5 mm ZPU-4
		M3A1	UR-416	105 mm M2 FH	
		M8		105 mm M3 FH	
		BRDM-2		122 mm D30 FH	
				122 mm Type 60 FG	
				130 mm M46 FG	
				130 mm Type 59-1 FG	
MALAWI					
		Fox		25-pounder FG	14·5 mm ZPU
		BRDM-2		105 mm LG	Blowpipe
MALAYSIA					
Scorpion 90	120 mm RR	Ferret	Sibmas	105 mm PH	40 mm Bofors L/70
	SS-11 GW	Panhard AML	Commando V-150	5·5-inch GH	40 mm M1
		Commando V-100	Condor		
			Stormer		
			Panhard M3		
			AT-105		
			SB 301 (S)		
			Shorland (S)		
MALI					
T-34/85		BRDM-2	BTR-40	85 mm D44 FG	14·5 mm ZPU
Type 63		M8	BTR-60	100 mm M1944 FG	37 mm M1939
			BTR-152	122 mm D30 FH	57 mm Czechoslovak
				130 mm M46 FG	57 mm S-60
				122 mm/132 mm MRS	SA-3 SAM
MAURITANIA					
		Panhard AML-60 and 90	M3 half track		14·5 mm ZPU
		Panhard EBR 75	Panhard M-3		37 mm M1939
					SA-7 SAM
MEXICO					
M3 Stuart	37 mm M3	M3A1	HWK 11	75 mm M8 SPH	40 mm M1
M5 Stuart		M8	M3 half track	75 mm M116 PH	
		ERC 90 F1	AMX-10P	105 mm M7 SPH	
			Panhard M-3	105 mm M101 FH	
MONGOLIA					
T-34/85	Sagger GW		BTR-60	100 mm M1944 FG	37 mm M1939
T-54/T-55	Snapper GW		BTR-152	122 mm M1938 FH	57 mm S-60
T-62				130 mm M46 FG	SA-2 (O)
				152 mm D1 FH	SA-7
				SU-100 SPG	
MOROCCO					
AMX-13	90 mm M56 SP	Panhard EBR-75	OT-62	SU-100 SPG	14·5 mm ZPU
Jagdpanzer SK105	105 mm M27 RR	Panhard AML-60 and 90	OT-64	75 mm M116 PH	20 mm M163 Vulcan
M48	Dragon GW	M8	Half track	76 mm M1942 FG	20 mm VAB
M60A3	ENTAC GW	AMX-10P	UR-416	85 mm D44 FG	23 mm ZU-23
T-54/T-55	TOW GW	AMX-10RC	VAB	105 mm AMX Mk61 SPH	37 mm M1939
		RAM V-1	Panhard M-3	105 mm M101 FH	57 mm S-60
		Eland 60/90	M113	122 mm MRS	100 mm KS-19
		AML-90	Saurer 4K 7FA	130 mm M46 FG	Chaparral
			Ratel 20/90	152 mm M1937 GH	Crotale
				155 mm M109 SPH	SA-7
				155 mm M114	
				155 mm Mk F3 SPH	
MOZAMBIQUE					
PT-76	85 mm ATG	BRDM-1	BTR-40	76 mm M1942 FG	14·5 mm ZPU
T-34/85	Sagger GW	BRDM-2	BTR-60	85 mm D44 FG	20 mm M55
T-54/T-55			BTR-152	100 mm M1944 FG	23 mm ZSU-23-4
T-62				105 mm M18 FH	23 mm ZU-23
				122 mm MRL	37 mm M1939
				122 mm D30 FH	57 mm S-60
				122 mm M1938 FH	SA-3
				152 mm D1 FH	SA-7

Tanks	Anti-armour weapons	Recce	APC	Artillery & SSMs	Anti-air weapons
NEPAL					
AMX-13				3·7-inch PH	40 mm Bofors L/60
NETHERLANDS					
AMX-13	106 mm M40 RR	M113 C&R	AMX-VCI	105 mm AMX Mk61 SPH	12·7 mm M55
Centurion Mk5/2	TOW GW		AT-104 (S)	105 mm M101 FH	35 mm CA1 SP
Leopard 1			M113	155 mm M109A1/M109A2 SPH	40 mm L/70
Leopard 2			UR-416 (S)	155 mm M114 FH	HAWK (O)
			YP-408	155 mm M198 FH	Nike Hercules (O)
			YPR 765	175 mm M107 SPG	Stinger SAM
				203 mm M110 A2 SPH	
				Lance SSM	
NEW ZEALAND					
	106 mm M40 RR	Ferret	M113	5·5-inch GH	
	120 mm RR	Scorpion		105 mm M56 PH	
NICARAGUA					
M4 Sherman	57 mm M1943	M3A1	BTR-60	105 mm M101 FH	20 mm
PT-76		Staghound		122 mm MRS	40 mm M1
T-54/T-55				152 mm GH	
NIGER					
		Panhard AML-60 and 90	Panhard M-3		20 mm M693
		ERC 60-20	M3 half track		20 mm VDA SP
		M8			37 mm
NIGERIA					
Jagdpanzer SK 105		Scimitar	Saracen	25-pounder FG	14·5 mm ZPU
T-55		Panhard AML-60	Steyr 4K 7FA	76 mm M1942 FG	20 mm
Vickers Mk3		and 90	MOWAG Piranha	105 mm LG	23 mm ZSU-23-4
		Saladin	AMX VTT	105 mm M56 PH	23 mm ZU-23
		Ferret		122 mm D74 FG	37 mm M1939
		Fox		130 mm M46 FG	40 mm Bofors L/70
		Scorpion		122 mm MRS	Blowpipe
		EE-9 Cascavel		155 mm FH-77B FH	Roland
				155 mm Palmaria SPH	
NORWAY					
Leopard 1	106 mm M40 RR	NM 116	M113	105 mm M101 FH	12·7 mm M55
M48	ENTAC GW			120 mm CG	20 mm FK 20-2
	TOW GW			155 mm M109 SPH	40 mm Bofors L/60 and
				155 mm M114 FH	L/70
					40 mm M1
					Nike Hercules (O)
					RBS-70
OMAN					
Chieftain	TOW GW	Saladin	AT-105	25-pounder GH	23 mm ZU-23
M60A1	6-pounder	Ferret	Commando V-150	105 mm LG	Blowpipe
		Scorpion		130 mm M46 FG	Rapier
PAKISTAN					
M4 Sherman	6-pounder	Ferret	M113	5·5-inch GH	3·7-inch
M24	17-pounder		Type 531	25-pounder FG	12·7 mm M55
M41	106 mm M40 RR		UR416	75 mm M116 PH	23 mm ZU-23
M47	Cobra GW			85 mm Type 56 FG	37 mm M1939
M48	M36 SP			100 mm Type 59 FG	40 mm M1
PT-76	TOW GW			105 mm M7 SP	40 mm Mk 1
T-54/T-55	VBC 90 ATG			105 mm M56 PH	57 mm S-60
TAM				105 mm M101 FH	57 mm Type 59
Type 59				130 mm Type 59 FG	90 mm M117
Type 63				155 mm M59 G	Crotale
				155 mm M114 FH	RBS 70
				155 mm M109A2 SPH	
				155 mm M198 FH	
				203 mm M110A2 SPH	
PANAMA					
TAM			Commando V-150		
PARAGUAY					
M3A1 Stuart		M8 (mod)	M3 half track	75 mm M116 PH	20 mm
M4 Sherman				105 mm M101 FH	40 mm M1
PERU					
AMX-13 FL-10/FL-12	SS-11 GW	M3A1	Chaimite	105 mm PH	40 mm Bofors L/60
AMX-30		M8	M113	105 mm M101 FH	and L/70
M4 Sherman		BRDM-2 (A,O)	UR-416 (S)	122 mm D74 FG	23 mm ZSU-23-4
T-54/T-55			MOWAG (S)	130 mm M46 FG	SA-2
TAM			Fiat 6614	155 mm M114 FH	SA-3
			Spz-12-3		SA-7
PHILIPPINES					
M41	106 mm M40 RR	Scorpion	AIFV	105 mm M56 PH	HAWK
			LVTP-7 (M)	105 mm M101 FH	
			LVTP-5 (M)	155 mm M68 GH	
			LVTP-4 (M)	155 mm M114 FH	
			M3 half track		
			M113		

Tanks	Anti-armour weapons	Recce	APC	Artillery & SSMs	Anti-air weapons
PHILIPPINES cont			Chaimite Commando V-150		
POLAND PT-76 (and M) T-34/85 T-54/T-55 T-72	57 mm M1943 ATG 85 mm SD44 ATG ASU-85 SP Sagger GW Snapper GW	BRDM-1 BRDM-2 FUG	BTR-152 BMP-1 OT-62 (and M) OT-64 MT-LB	76 mm M1942 FG 85 mm D44 FG 100 mm M1944 FG 122 mm/140 mm/240 mm MRS 122 mm D30 FH 122 mm M1931/7 FG 122 mm M1938 FH 122 mm M1974 SPH 130 mm M46 FG 152 mm D1 FH 152 mm M1937 GH FROG SSM SCUD SSM	14·5 mm ZPU-2 14·5 mm ZPU-4 23 mm ZSU-23-4 23 mm ZU-23 57 mm S-60 57 mm ZSU-57-2 85 mm KS-12 100 mm KS-19 SA-2 (O) SA-4 SA-6 SA-7 SA-9
PORTUGAL M24 M41 M47 M48/M48A5	106 mm RR SS-11 GW TOW GW	Panhard AML-60 and 90 Saladin	M3 half track M113 Panhard EBR-ETT Panhard M3 Chaimite (and O) Commando Mk3 (S) Shorland	5·5-inch GH 25-pounder FG 57 mm CG 105 mm M7 SP 105 mm M18 FH 105 mm M101 FH 150 mm CG 152 mm CG 155 mm M114 FH 234 mm CG	12·7 mm M55 40 mm Bofors
QATAR AMX-30S		Ferret	Commando AMX VCI VAB AMX-10P Saracen	25-pounder FG 155 mm Mk3 SPH	HAWK
ROMANIA T-34/85 T-54/T-55 T-55 (mod) T-62 T-72	57 mm M1943 ATG 85 mm D48 ATG Sagger GW Snapper GW Swatter GW	BRDM-1 BRDM-2	BTR-50 BTR-60 BTR-152 TAB-72 OT-62	76 mm M48 MG 76 mm M1942 FG 85 mm D44 FG 85 mm SD44 FG 100 mm M1944 FG 122 mm D30 FH 122 mm M1931/7 G 122 mm M1938 FH 130 mm MRS 130 mm SM4-1 CG 152 mm M1937 GH 152 mm M1938 FH FROG SSM SCUD SSM SU-100 SPG	14·5 mm ZPU-2 23 mm ZSU-23-4 30 mm M53 37 mm M1939 57 mm S-60 57 mm ZSU-57-2 85 mm KS-12 100 mm KS-19 SA-2 (O) SA-6
RWANDA	6-pounder ATG	Panhard AML-60/90	Panhard M3	105 mm M101 FH	
SAUDI ARABIA AMX-30S M60/M60A3	Dragon GW Harpoon GW JPz SK-105 SP SS-11 GW TOW GW	Panhard AML-60 and 90 Ferret Fox	M113 Panhard M3 AMX-10P Commando V-150	105 mm M101 FH 105 mm M102 FH 155 mm GCT SPH 155 mm FH-70 FH 155 mm M109 SPH 155 mm M114 FH 155 mm M198 FH 203 mm M110 SPH	20 mm Commando Vulcan 20 mm M163 SPAAG 20 mm M163 Vulcan 20 mm M167 Vulcan 30 mm AMX-30 30 mm Oerlikon Crotale (O) HAWK (O) Redeye Shahine
SENEGAMBIA	MILAN GW	Panhard AML-60 and 90 M8 M20 Ferret (S)	VXB-170 Panhard M3 M3 half track	75 mm PH 105 mm M101 FH 155 mm Model 50 FH	20 mm M693 40 mm Bofors L/60
SIERRA LEONE		Ferret Saladin	MOWAG	25-pounder GH	
SINGAPORE AMX-13 M60	106 mm M40 RR		Commando V-150/ V-200 M113	155 mm M68 FH	20 mm Oerlikon 40 mm Bofors L/70 Bloodhound (O) Rapier (O) RBS-70

Tanks	Anti-armour weapons	Recce	APC	Artillery & SSMs	Anti-air weapons
SOMALIA					
Centurion	85 mm D48 ATG	BRDM-2	BTR-40	76 mm M1942 FG	14·5 mm ZPU-2
M41	MILAN GW	Fiat 6616	BTR-50	85 mm D44 FG	14·5 mm ZPU-4
M47			BTR-60	100 mm M1944 FG	20 mm M167 Vulcan
T-34/85			BTR-152	122 mm D30 FH	23 mm ZSU-23-4
T-54/T-55			Fiat 6614	122 mm M1931/7 FG	23 mm ZU-23
			Commando V-150	122 mm M1938 FH	37 mm M1939
			M113 (TOW)	122 mm Type 60 FG	37 mm Type 63
				130 mm M46 FG	57 mm S-60
				130 mm Type 59-1 FG	100 mm KS-19
				132 mm MRS	SA-2
				152 mm D20 GH	SA-3
				152 mm M1931 G	
				180 mm S23 G	
SOUTH AFRICA					
Centurion/Olifant	6-pounder ATG	Eland 60/90	Saracen	5·5-inch GH	3·7-inch
	17-pounder ATG	Ferret	Ratel 20/60/90	25-pounder FG	20 mm Oerlikon
	90 mm ATG	Staghound	Buffalo	127 mm MRS	35 mm Oerlikon
	ENTAC GW		Hippo	155 mm G5 FH	40 mm Bofors L/60 and L/70
			Rhino		Crotale (A)
					Tigercat (A)
SPAIN					
AMX-30 (A,M)	106 mm M40 RR	Panhard AML-60	M113	105 mm m/26 FH	12·7 mm M55
M41	Dragon GW	and 90 (A,M)	Panhard M3 (A,M)	105 mm M52 SPH (M)	20 mm Oerlikon
M47/M47E	HOT GW		LVTP-7 (M)	105 mm M56 PH	20 mm Rh 202
M48/M48E/	MILAN GW		BMR-600	105 mm M108 SP	35 mm Oerlikon
M48A5 (A,M)	TOW GW		UR-416 (S)	155 mm M44 SP	40 mm Bofors L/70
			BLR	155 mm M109/M109A1/	90 mm M117
				M109A2 SP	HAWK (A)
				155 mm M114 FH	Nike Hercules (A)
				175 mm M107 SP	Chaparral
				203 mm M110 SPH	
				203 mm M115 FH	
				216 mm/300 mm/381 mm MRS	
SRI LANKA					
		Ferret	BTR-152	76 mm M48 MG	3·7-inch
		Saladin		85 mm D44 FG	40 mm
		Daimler			
SUDAN					
M41	85 mm D48 ATG	Saladin	Panhard M3	25-pounder FG	14·5 mm ZPU
M47	Swingfire GW	Ferret	BTR-40	85 mm D44 FG	20 mm M163 Vulcan
M60A1/M60A3		BRDM-1	BTR-50	100 mm M1944 FG	23 mm ZU-23
T-34/85		BRDM-2	BTR-152	105 mm M56 PH	37 mm M1939
T-54/T-55		ERC Guepard	OT-62	105 mm M101 FH	37 mm twin
Type 59			OT-64	122 mm D30 FH	37 mm Type 63
Type 62			Saracen	122 mm M1938 FH	40 mm Bofors L/60
Type 63			Commando V-150	122 mm Type 54 FH	85 mm KS-12
			M113	130 mm Type 59-1 FG	100 mm KS-19
			Walid	AMX 155 mm F Mk3 SPG	SA-2
			Type 531		SA-7
SWEDEN					
Centurion Strv 101/	90 mm RR		Pbv 302	75 mm mobile CG	20 mm Oerlikon
102	Bantam GW		SKPF/VKPF m/42	105 mm 4140 FH	40 mm Bofors m/36
Stridsvagn 103B	BILL			120 mm CG	and L/70
	Ikv-91			150 mm m/39 FH	Bloodhound (O)
	TOW GW			152 mm CG	HAWK (A)
				155 mm Bk 1A SP	RBS-70
				155 mm FH-77A	Redeye
SWITZERLAND					
Centurion Pz.55/60	90 mm Models 50/57 ATG		M113	90 mm MECAR MG	20 mm Oerlikon
Pz.61	106 mm M40 RR		MOWAG	105 mm Model 35 FG	35 mm Oerlikon
Pz.68 Mk1 to 4	Bantam GW			105 mm Model 46 FG	40 mm Bofors L/70
	Dragon GW			155 mm M109/M109A1 SPH	Bloodhound (O)
				155 mm Model 50 FH	Rapier
SYRIA					
PT-76	HOT GW	BRDM-1	BTR-40	85 mm D44 FG	14·5 mm ZPU-2
T-34/85	MILAN GW	BRDM-2	BTR-50	100 mm M1944 FG	14·5 mm ZPU-4
T-54/T-55	Sagger GW		BTR-60	107 mm/122 mm/140 mm/	23 mm ZSU-23-4
T-62	Snapper GW		BTR-152	240 mm MRS	23 mm ZU-23
T-72			BMP-1	122 mm D30 FH	37 mm M1939
			OT-64	122 mm M1931/7 FG	57 mm S-60
				122 mm M1938 FH	57 mm ZSU-57-2
				122 mm M1974 SPH	85 mm KS-12
				122 mm T34 SPG	100 mm KS-19
				130 mm M46 FG	SA-2 (O)
				130 mm SM4-1 CG	SA-6
				152 mm D1 FH	SA-7
				152 mm M1937 GH	SA-8
				180 mm S-23 G	SA-9
				FROG-7 SSM	
				ISU-122/ISU-152 SPG	
				SCUD SSM	
				SU-100 SPG	

Tanks	Anti-armour weapons	Recce	APC	Artillery & SSMs	Anti-air weapons
TAIWAN					
M24 M41 M47 M48	76 mm M18 SP 105 mm M108 SPH 106 mm M40 RR KunWu GW TOW GW	M8	M113 Half track LVT-3C (M) V-150 Commando	75 mm M116 PH 105 mm M101 FH 105 mm T64 FH 127 mm MRS 155 mm SPG 155 mm M59 G 155 mm M109/M109A2 SPH 155 mm M114 FH 155 mm T65 FH 203 mm M110 SPH 203 mm M115 H 240 mm H Honest John SSM	40 mm M1 Chaparral HAWK (A) M42 Nike Hercules (A)
TANZANIA					
T-54 Type 59 Type 62 Type 63	TOW GW	Scorpion BRDM-2	BTR-40 BTR-152 Type 56 Type 531	76 mm M1942 FG 122 mm MRS 122 mm D30 FH 122 mm M1931/7 FG 122 mm Type 54 FH 122 mm Type 60 FG 130 mm M46 FG 130 mm Type 59-1 FG	14·5 mm ZPU-2 14·5 mm ZPU-4 23 mm ZU-23 37 mm M1939 SA-3 SA-6 SA-7
THAILAND					
M41 M48/M48A5 M60A3	106 mm M40 RR TOW GW	EE-9 Cascavel M3A1 M8 M24 Scorpion Commando V-150	M3 half track M113 Saracen (S) LVTP-7 (O) Shorland (S)	105 mm M101 FH 155 mm GC45 GH 155 mm M68 GH (M) 155 mm M114 FH 155 mm M198 FH	12·7 mm M55 20 mm M163 Vulcan 40 mm M1 40 mm M42 HAWK (O)
TOGO					
T-34/85 T-54/T-55		Panhard AML-60 and 90 M8 EE-9 Cascavel	Panhard M3 UR-416 (S) M3 half track	105 mm M2 FH	14·5 mm ZPU
TUNISIA					
AMX-13 FL-10 M41 M48A3 M60A1/M60A3	105 mm Panzerjäger MILAN GW SK105 SS-11 GW TOW GW	Saladin Panhard AML-90 Panhard EBR EE-9 Cascavel	M113-A1 Saurer 4K 7FA VXB-170 Commando V-150 Fiat 6614	105 mm M108 SPH 155 mm M109/M109A2 SPH 155 mm M114 FH 155 mm M1950 FH	20 mm M163 Vulcan Chaparral RBS-70
TURKEY					
Leopard 1A3 M41 M47 M48/M48A1/M48A5	106 mm M40 RR Cobra GW M36 SP MILAN GW SS-11 GW TOW GW		M3 half track M59 M113 Commando V-150 UR-416	75 mm M116 PH 105 mm M7 SP 105 mm M101 FH 105 mm M108 SPH 155 mm M59 G 155 mm M109 SPH 155 mm M114 FH 175 mm M107 SPG 203 mm M110 SPH 203 mm M115 FH Honest John SSM	12·7 mm M55 40 mm Bofors L/70 (A,O) 75 mm M51 90 mm M117 90 mm M118 Nike Hercules Rapier
UGANDA					
Status of equipment uncertain					
UNION OF SOVIET SOCIALIST REPUBLICS					
IS-2 IS-3 IS-4 T-10/T-10M T-34/85 T-54/T-55 T-62 T-64 T-72 T-80	85 mm D48 ATG 100 mm T12 ATG ASU-57 SP ASU-85 SP Sagger GW Spandrel GW Spigot GW Spiral GW Swatter GW	BRDM-1 BRDM-2 PT-76 BMP-R	BTR-40 BTR-50 BTR-60 BTR-70 BTR-80 BTR-152 BMP-1 BMP-80 MT-LB MT-L BMD	ISU-122/ISU-152 SPG SU-100 SPG 76 mm MG 85 mm D44 FG 122/140/240/250 mm MRS SS-21/SS-22/SS-23 SSM 122 mm D30 FH 122 mm M1938 FH 122 mm M1974 SPH 130 mm M46 FG 130 mm SM-4 CG 152 mm D1 FH 152 mm D20 GH 152 mm M1973 SPH 180 mm S-23 203 mm SPH 240 mm SPM FROG SSM Scaleboard SSM SCUD SSM	23 mm ZSU-23-4 23 mm ZU-23 57 mm S-60 57 mm ZSU-57-2 SA-1 SA-2 SA-3 SA-4 SA-5 SA-6 SA-7 SA-8 SA-9 SA-10 SA-11 SA-12 SA-13
UNITED ARAB EMIRATES					
AMX-30 OF-40	120 mm RR TOW Vigilant GW	Scorpion Saladin Ferret Panhard AML-90	Shorland (S) AMX VCI Panhard M3 Saracen	25-pounder FG 105 mm LG 105 mm M56 PH 155 mm MkF3 SPG	20 mm VDA 30 mm Oerlikon Crotale HAWK

Tanks	Anti-armour weapons	Recce	APC	Artillery & SSMs	Anti-air weapons
UNITED ARAB EMIRATES cont		VBC 90 EE-9 Cascavel	VCR VAB AMX-10P		Rapier RBS-70
UNITED KINGDOM Challenger Chieftain	LAW 80 MILAN GW SS-11 GW Swingfire GW TOW GW	Ferret Fox Scorpion Saladin Scimitar	FV432 Saracen Shorland (S) Spartan AT 105 Saxon MCV-80	105 mm Abbot SPG 105 mm LG 155 mm FH-70 155 mm M109A1/ M109A2 SPH 175 mm M107 SPG 203 mm M110A1 SPH Lance SSM	Blowpipe Bloodhound (O) Rapier (A,O) Towed Rapier Track Rapier Javelin
UNITED STATES OF AMERICA M1 M48A5 M60/M60A1/M60A2/ M60A3 (A,M)	106 mm M40 RR Dragon GW Hellfire TOW GW	M2/M3 AIFV	M113 series LVTP-7 (M) M2/M3 M706 (O) Commando Ranger (O) LAV-25	105 mm M101 FH 105 mm M102 FH 105 mm M108 SPH 155 mm M44 SP 155 mm M109A1/M109A2/ M109A3 SPH (A,M) 155 mm M114 FH 155 mm M198 (A,M) 203 mm M110/M110A1/ M110A2 SPH (A,M) Lance SSM MLRS Pershing SSM	20 mm M163 Vulcan 20 mm M167 Vulcan 40 mm DIVADS 40 mm M42 SPG Chaparral HAWK (O) Nike Hercules (O) Patriot Rapier Redeye Roland Stinger
UPPER VOLTA		Panhard AML-60 and 90 Ferret M8 M20	Panhard M3	105 mm M101 FG 105 mm PH	20 mm
URUGUAY M3A1 Stuart M24 M41		M3A1 Scorpion	M113	75 mm G 105 mm M101 FH	
VENEZUELA AMX-30 AMX-13 FL-10	M18 SP SS-11 GW	M8 Panhard AML	AMX VCI UR-416 (S) LVTP-7 (M)	75 mm M116 PH 105 mm M101 FH 105 mm PH 155 mm Mk F3 SPH 160 mm MRL	40 mm Bofors L/60 and L/70
VIET-NAM M41 M48 PT-76 T-34/85 T-54/T-55 Type 59 Type 62 Type 63	Sagger GW SU-76 SPG	BRDM-2	BTR-50 BTR-60 BTR-152 Type 531 Commando V-100 M113 Type 56	76 mm M1942 FG 85 mm D44 FG 100 mm M1944 FG 105 mm M101 FH 105 mm M102 FH 107 mm/122 mm/140 mm MRS 122 mm D30 FH 122 mm D74 FG 122 mm M1931 FG 122 mm M1938 FH 130 mm M46 FG 130 mm Type 59 FG 130 mm Type 59-1 FG 152 mm D1 FH 152 mm M1937 FH 155 mm M109 SPH 155 mm M114 FH ISU-122 SPG SU-76 SPG SU-100 SPG	12·7 mm M53 14·5 mm ZPU-2 14·5 mm ZPU-4 23 mm ZSU-23-4 23 mm ZU-23 30 mm M53 37 mm M1939 37 mm Type 63 40 mm M42 57 mm S-60 57 mm ZSU-57-2 85 mm KS-12 100 mm KS-19 130 mm KS-30 SA-2 (O) SA-3 (O) SA-6 SA-7 SA-9
YEMEN ARAB REPUBLIC (North) M60/M60A1 T-34/85 T-54/T-55	Dragon GW TOW GW Vigilant	Ferret Saladin	M113/M113A1 BTR-40 BTR-60 BTR-152 Walid	76 mm M1942 FG 122 mm MRS 122 mm M1931/7 FG SU-100 SPG	20 mm M163 Vulcan 20 mm M167 Vulcan 23 mm ZSU-23-4 23 mm ZU-23 37 mm M1939 57 mm S-60 SA-6 SA-9 HAWK
YEMEN, PEOPLE'S DEMOCRATIC REPUBLIC (South) T-34/85 T-54/T-55 T-62	Vigilant GW	Ferret Saladin BRDM-2	BTR-40 BTR-60 BTR-152 BMP	25-pounder FG 85 mm D44 FG 122 mm/250 mm MRS 122 mm M1938 FH 130 mm M46 FG	14·5 mm ZPU-2 23 mm ZU-23 23 mm ZSU-23-4 37 mm M1939 57 mm S-60

Tanks	Anti-armour weapons	Recce	APC	Artillery & SSMs	Anti-air weapons
YEMEN, PEOPLE'S DEMOCRATIC REPUBLIC (South) cont					85 mm KS-12
					SA-2
					SA-7
YUGOSLAVIA					
M4 Sherman	57 mm M1943 ATG	M3A1	BTR-40	76 mm M48 MG	3·7-inch
M47	100 mm T12 ATG	M8	BTR-50	76 mm M1942 FG	12·7 mm M55
PT-76	105 mm RR	BRDM-1	BTR-60	88 mm CG	20 mm M30/M38
Sherman Firefly	ASU-57 SP	BRDM-2	BTR-152	105 mm M7 SPG	20 mm M55
T-34/85	M18 SP		M3 half track	105 mm M18 FH	20 mm M75
T-54/T-55	M36 SP		M60	105 mm M18(M) FH	23 mm ZSU-23-4
T-62	Sagger GW		M980	105 mm M18/40 FH	30 mm M53
	Snapper GW		OT-810	105 mm M56 FH	30 mm M53/59
	TOW GW		MT-LB	105 mm M101 FH	37 mm M1939
				122 mm D30 FH	40 mm Bofors L/70
				122 mm M1931/7 FG	40 mm M1
				122 mm M1938 FH	40 mm Mk1
				122 mm M1974 SPH	57 mm S-60
				128 mm MRS	57 mm ZSU-57-2
				130 mm M46 FG	85 mm KS-12
				152 mm D20 GH	90 mm M117
				152 mm M1937 GH	SA-2 (O)
				155 mm M59 G	SA-3
				155 mm M65 FH	SA-6
				155 mm M144 FH	SA-7
				FROG-7 SSM	SA-9
				SU-76 SPG	
				SU-100 SPG	
ZAIRE					
Type 62	57 mm M1943 ATG	Panhard AML-60 and 90	BTR-60	75 mm M116 PH	20 mm
		Ferret	Panhard M3	107 mm MRS	37 mm M1939
			M3 half track	122 mm D30 FH	37 mm Type 63
			M113	122 mm M1938 FH	40 mm Bofors L/60
			Type 531	122 mm Type 60 FG	
				130 mm Type 59-1 FG	
ZAMBIA					
T-54/T-55	Sagger GW	Ferret		25-pounder FG	14·5 mm ZPU
		BRDM-1		105 mm M56 PH	20 mm
		BRDM-2		105 mm M101 FH	85 mm KS-12
				122 mm D30 FH	SA-7
				122 mm MRS	
ZIMBABWE					
T-34/85		Eland 60/90	UR-416	5·5-inch GH	14·5 mm ZPU-1/2/4
T-54/T-55		Ferret	BTR-40	25-pounder FH	20 mm
Type 63		BRDM-2	BTR-152	105 mm LG	23 mm ZU-23
			Buffalo	105 mm PH	SA-7
			Hippo	122 mm Type 60 FG	
			Hyena		
			Leopard		

3871.104

Armoured Fighting Vehicles

Only vehicles of post-Second World War design are included in these tables. Vehicles at a very early stage of development have been excluded.
Abbreviations: AA Anti-aircraft; CA Coaxial; D Diesel; MF Multi-fuel; P Petrol; T Turbine

Designation	Length Hull	Width	Height	Combat weight (tonnes)	Crew	Engine	Armament	Contractor	Notes
AUSTRIA									
Main Battle and Light Tanks									
Jagdpanzer SK 105	5·58 m	2·5 m	2·514 m	17·5 t	3	320 hp D	1 × 105 mm 1 × 7·62 mm CA	Steyr-Daimler-Puch	Classed as tank destroyer, production
Armoured Personnel Carriers, Mechanised Infantry Combat Vehicles and IS Type APCs									
Steyr 4K 7FA	5·87 m	2·5 m	1·69 m	14·8 t	2 + 8	320 hp D	1 × 12·7 mm	Steyr-Daimler-Puch	In production
Steyr 4K 4FA	5·4 m	2·5 m	2·17 m	15 t	2 + 8	250 hp D	1 × 12·7 mm	Steyr-Daimler-Puch	Production complete
BELGIUM									
Reconnaissance Vehicles									
FN 4RM/62F AB	4·5 m	2·26 m	2·52 m	8 t	3	130 hp P	1 × 90 mm 1 × 7·62 mm CA 1 × 7·62 mm AA	FN	Production complete, also MG version
Armoured Personnel Carriers, Mechanised Infantry Combat Vehicles and IS Type APCs									
SIBMAS	7·32 m	2·5 m	2·77 m	16·5 t	3 + 11	320 hp D	Various	SIBMAS	Production complete
BDX	5·05 m	2·5 m	2·84 m	10·7 t	2 + 10	180 hp P	Various	Beherman Demoen	Production complete
Cobra	4·2 m	2·7 m	16·5 m	7·5 t	3 + 9	143 hp D	1 × 12·7 mm 2 × 7·62 mm bow 2 × 106 mm RL	ACEC	Prototype
BRAZIL									
Main Battle and Light Tanks									
X1A2	6·5 m	2·6 m	2·45 m	9 t	3	300 hp D	1 × 90 mm 1 × 7·62 mm CA 1 × 12·7 mm AA	Bernardini	In production
Reconnaissance Vehicles									
ENGESA EE-9	5·19 m	2·59 m	2·36 m	12·2 t	3	190 hp D	1 × 90 mm 1 × 7·62 mm CA 1 × 72 mm AA	ENGESA	In production, also called Cascavel
ENGESA EE-3	4·195 m	2·13 m	1·56 m	5·2 t	3	120 hp D	1 × 12·7 mm AA	ENGESA	In production, also called Jararaca
Armoured Personnel Carriers, Mechanised Infantry Combat Vehicles and IS Type APCs									
ENGESA EE-11	6 m	2·6 m	2·72 m	13 t	2 + 12	212 hp D	Various	ENGESA	In production, also known as Urutu
CHILE									
Armoured Personnel Carriers, Mechanised Infantry Combat Vehicles and IS Type APCs									
VTP-1	6·65 m	2·2 m	2·01 m	9·7 t	2 + 10	172 hp D	Various	Cardoen	Prototype
VTP-2	5·37 m	2·32 m	2·2 m	7·7 t	2 + 10	120 hp D	Various	Cardoen	Prototype
Multi 163	5·057 m	2·23 m	2·1 m	5 t	2 + 8	180 hp P	Various	Makina	In production
CHINA, People's Republic									
Main Battle and Light Tanks									
Type 63	6·1 m	3·35 m	2·19 m	18 t	4	520 hp D	1 × 85 mm 1 × 7·62 mm CA 1 × 12·7mm AA	State factories	In production
Type 62	5·55 m	2·86 m	2·55 m	21 t	4	380 hp D	1 × 85 mm 1 × 7·62 mm CA 1 × 12·7 mm AA	State factories	In production
Armoured Personnel Carriers, Mechanised Infantry Combat Vehicles and IS Type APCs									
Type 531	5·45 m	2·96 m	2·61 m	12·5 t	4 + 10	181 hp D	1 × 12·7 mm	State arsenals	In production
CZECHOSLOVAKIA									
Armoured Personnel Carriers, Mechanised Infantry Combat Vehicles and IS Type APCs									
OT-64C(1)	7·44 m	2·55 m	2·71 m	14·5 t	2 + 15	180 hp D	1 × 14·5 mm	State arsenals	In production, many variants
OT-62B	7·08 m	3·14 m	2·23 m	15 t	2 + 18	300 hp D	1 × 7·62 mm CA 1 × 7·62 mm 1 × 82 mm RL	State arsenals	Production complete, many variants
FRANCE									
Main Battle and Light Tanks									
AMX-40	6·9 m	3·3 m	2·38 m	43 t	4	1100 hp D	1 × 120 mm 1 × 20 mm CA 1 × 7·62 mm AA	ARE, Roanne	Prototype
AMX-32	6·59 m	3·24 m	2·96 m	40 t	4	700 hp MF	1 × 105 mm 1 × 20 mm CA 1 × 7·62 mm AA	ARE, Roanne	Prototype
AMX-30	6·59 m	3·1 m	2·86 m	37 t	4	720 hp MF	1 × 105 mm 1 × 12·7 mm CA 1 × 7·62 mm AA	ARE, Roanne	In production, also built under licence in Spain
AMX-13	4·88 m	2·5 m	2·3 m	15 t	3	250 hp P	1 × 90 mm 1 × 7·62 mm CA 1 × 7·62 mm AA	Creusot-Loire	Production, also 75 mm and 105 mm versions
Reconnaissance Vehicles									
AMX-10RC	6·35 m	2·86 m	2·68 m	15·8 t	4	280 hp D	1 × 105 mm 1 ×7·62 mm CA	ARE, Roanne	In production
Panhard EBR	5·56 m	2·42 m	2·32 m	135 t	4	200 hp P	1 × 90 mm 1 × 7·62 mm CA 2 × 7·62 mm fixed	Panhard	Production complete
Renault VBC 90	5·495 m	2·49 m	2·55 m	12·8 t	3	235 hp D	1 × 90 mm 1 × 7·62 mm CA 1 × 7·62 mm AA	Renault	In production
Panhard ERC 90 F4	5·21 m	2·495 m	1·188 m	7·8 t	3	140 hp P	1 × 90 mm 1 × 7·62 mm CA 1 × 7·62 mm AA	Panhard	In production, other armament installations available
RPX 90	5·2 m	2·65 m	2·52m	10 t	3	250 hp D	1 × 90 mm	LOHR	Prototype
Panhard AML	3·79 m	1·97 m	2·07 m	5·5 t	3	90 hp P	1 × 90 mm 1 × 7·62 mm CA	Panhard	In production, other armament installations available
RPX 6000	4·585 m	2·16 m	1·65 m	7 t	3	180 hp D	1 × 7·62 mm	LOHR	Prototype

Designation	Length Hull	Width	Height	Combat weight (tonnes)	Crew	Engine	Armament	Contractor	Notes
Armoured Personnel Carriers, Mechanised Infantry Combat Vehicles and IS Type APCs									
ACMAT	5·98 m	2·07 m	2·205 m	7·3 t	10/12	125 hp D	Various	ACMAT	In production
AMX-10P	5·778 m	2·78 m	2·57 m	14·2 t	3 + 8	280 hp D	1 × 20 mm 1 × 7·62 mm CA	ARE, Roanne	In production, many variants
VXB-170	5·99 m	2·5 m	2·05 m	12·7 t	1 + 11	170 hp D	Various	Berliet	In production, complete
Renault VAB (4 × 4)	5·98 m	2·49 m	2·06 m	13 t	2 + 10	235 hp D	Various	Saviem/Creusot-Loire	In production, many variants
AMX-VCI	5·7 m	2·51 m	2·41 m	15 t	3 + 10	250 hp D	1 × 20 mm	Creusot-Loire	In production, many variants
Panhard VCR (6 × 6)	4·565 m	2·49 m	2·53 m	7 t	3 + 9	140 hp P	Various	Panhard	In production, many variants
Panhard VCR (4 × 4)	4·565 m	2·49 m	2·03 m	7·6 t	2 + 10		Various	Panhard	In production, many variants
Panhard M3	4·45 m	2·4 m	2·48 m	6·1 t	2 + 10	90 hp P	Various	Panhard	In production, many variants
GERMANY, Federal Republic									
Main Battle and Light Tanks									
Leopard 2	7·72 m	3·7 m	2·79 m	55 t	4	1500 hp MF	1 × 120 mm 1 × 7·62 mm CA 1 × 7·62 mm AA	Krauss-Maffei and Krupp MaK	In production
Leopard 1	7·09 m	3·25 m	2·61 m	40 t	4	830 hp MF	1 × 105 mm 1 × 7·62 mm CA 1 × 7·62 mm AA	Krauss-Maffei and Krupp MaK	In production, also built in Italy
TAM	6·775 m	3·25 m	2·42 m	30·5 t	4	720 hp D	1 × 105 mm 1 × 7·62 mm CA 1 × 7·62 mm AA	Thyssen Henschel	Designed for export, now being built in Argentina
Reconnaissance Vehicles									
Luchs	7·743 m	2·98 m	2·125 m	19·5 t	4	390 hp D	1 × 20 mm 1 × 7·62 mm AA	Thyssen Henschel	Production complete
APE	6·93 m	3·08 m	2·4 m	14·5 t	5	390 hp D	1 × 20 mm	EWK	Prototype
Armoured Personnel Carriers, Mechanised Infantry Combat Vehicles and IS Type APCs									
Marder	6·79 m	3·24 m	2·86 m	28·2 t	4 + 6	600 hp D	1 × 20 mm 1 × 7·62 mm CA 1 × 7·62 mm	Thyssen Henschel, Krupp MaK	Production complete, modified version built in Argentina
Transportpanzer 1	6·76 m	2·98 m	2·3 m	17 t	2 + 10	320 hp D	1 × 20 mm OR 1 × 7·62 mm	Thyssen Henschel	In production
TM 170	6·1 m	2·45 m	2·2 m	9·5 t	2 + 12	168 hp D	Various	Thyssen Maschinenbau	In production, many variants
Condor	6·06 m	2·47 m	2·79 m	9·8 t	3 + 9	368 hp D	1 × 20 mm 1 × 7·62 mm CA	Thyssen Henschel	In production
TM 125	5·54 m	2·46 m	2·015 m	7·6 t	2 + 10	125 hp D	Various	Thyssen Maschinenbau	In production, many variants
UR 416	4·99 m	2·3 m	2·225 m	7·6 t	2 + 8	120 hp D	Various	Thyssen Maschinenbau	In production, many variants
TM 90	4·4 m	2·05 m	1·85 m	4·2 t	1 + 3	90 hp D	Various	Thyssen Maschinenbau	In production, many variants
HUNGARY									
Reconnaissance Vehicles									
FUG	5·79 m	2·5 m	2·25 m	7 t	2 + 4	100 hp D	1 × 7·62 mm	State arsenals	Production complete. Also known as OT-65
Armoured Personnel Carriers, Mechanised Infantry Combat Vehicles and IS Type APCs									
PSzH-1V	5·7 m	2·5 m	2·3 m	7·5 t	3 + 6	100 hp D	1 × 14·5 mm 1 × 7·62 mm CA	State arsenals	Production complete
ISRAEL									
Main Battle and Light Tanks									
Merkava	7·45 m	3·7 m	2·64 m	60 t	4	900 hp D	1 × 105 mm 1 × 7·62 mm CA 2 × 7·62 mm AA	Ordnance factories	In production. Also Mk 2 and 3
Reconnaissance Vehicles									
RBY Mk 1	5·023 m	2·03 m	1·54 m	3·6 t	2 + 6	120 hp P	Various	RAMTA	Production complete
RAM-V1	5·02 m	2·03 m	1·71 m	4·1 t	2 + 4	115 hp D	Various	RAMTA	In production
ITALY									
Main Battle and Light Tanks									
OF-40	6·893 m	3·51 m	2·68 m	43 t	4	830 hp MF	1 × 105 mm 1 × 7·62 mm CA 1 × 7·62 mm AA	OTO Melara	in production, for export
Reconnaissance Vehicles									
FIAT 6616	5·37 m	3·5 m	2·035 m	7·4 t	3	160 hp D	1 × 20 mm 1 × 7·62 mm CA	FIAT/OTO Melara	In production
OTO R3	4·86 m	1·78 m	1·55 m	3·5 t	4/5	95 hp D	Various	OTO Melara	Prototype
ORO R 2·5	4·5 m	1·7 m	1·62 m	3 t	4	95 hp D	Various	OTO Melara	Prototype
F333E	3·3 m	1·7 m	1·42 m	2·6 t	2/3	115 hp P	Various	Ferrari	Prototype
Armoured Personnel Carriers, Mechanised Infantry Combat Vehicles and IS Type APCs									
FIAT 6614	5·86 m	2·5 m	1·75 m	8·5 t	1 + 10	160 hp D	1 × 12·7 mm	OTO Melara/FIAT	In production
OTO C13	5·65 m	2·64 m	1·72 m	13·5 t	2 + 10	390 hp D	Various	OTO Melara	Prototype
IAFV	5·041 m	2·684 m	2·552 m	11·6 t	2 + 7	215 hp D	1 × 12·7 mm 1 × 7·62 mm	OTO Melara	In production, other variants
JAPAN									
Main Battle and Light Tanks									
Type 74	6·7 m	3·18 m	2·67 m	38 t	4	750 hp D	1 × 105 mm 1 × 7·62 mm CA 1 × 12·7 mm AA	Mitsubishi	In production, variable suspension
Type 61	6·3 m	2·95 m	2·49 m	35 t	4	600 hp D	1 × 90 mm 1 × 7·62 mm CA 1 × 12·7 mm AA	Mitsubishi	Production complete
Reconnaissance Vehicles									
Type 82	5·72 m	2·48 m	2·38 m	13· m	8	Diesel	1 × 12·7 mm 1 × 7·62 mm	Komatsu/Mitsubishi	Prototype
Armoured Personnel Carriers, Mechanised Infantry Combat Vehicles and IS Type APCs									
Type 73	5·8 m	2·8 m	2·2 m	13·3 t	3 + 9	300 hp D	3 × 12·7 mm 1 × 7·62 mm bow	Mitsubishi	In production
SU 60	4·85 m	2·4 m	2·31 m	11·8 t	4 + 6	220 hp D	1 × 12·7 mm 1 × 7·62 mm bow	Mitsubishi	Production complete
NETHERLANDS									
Armoured Personnel Carriers, Mechanised Infantry Combat Vehicles and IS Type APCs									
YP-408	6·23 m	2·4 m	2·37 m	12 t	2 + 10	165 hp D	1 × 12·7 mm	DAF	Production complete, many variants

Designation	Length Hull	Width	Height	Combat weight (tonnes)	Crew	Engine	Armament	Contractor	Notes
PORTUGAL									
Armoured Personnel Carriers, Mechanised Infantry Combat Vehicles and IS Type APCs									
Chaimite V-200	5·606 m	2·26 m	2·26 m	7·3 t	11	210 hp D	Various	BRAVIA	In production, many variants
Commando MK III	4·975 m	1·93 m	2·42 m	4·855 t	3 + 5	Various	Various	BRAVIA	In production
ROMANIA									
Armoured Personnel Carriers, Mechanised Infantry Combat Vehicles and IS Type APCs									
TAB-72	7·22 m	2·83 m	2·7m	11 t	3 + 8	2 × 140 hp P	1 × 14·5 mm 1 × 7·62 mm CA	State arsenals	In production. Also 82 mm mortar variant
SOUTH AFRICA									
Armoured Personnel Carriers, Mechanised Infantry Combat Vehicles and IS Type APCs									
Ratel 20	7·21 m	2·5 m	2·91 m	13·5 t	11	282 hp D	1 × 20 mm 1 × 7·62 mm CA 2 × 7·62 mm AA	Sandock-Austral	In production. Also 90 mm gun, 60 mm mortar and 12·7 mm MG Command versions
SPAIN									
Reconnaissance Vehicles									
VEC	6·25 m	2·5 m	2 m	13·75 t	5	306 hp D	Various	ENSA	In production
Armoured Personnel Carriers, Mechanised Infantry Combat Vehicles and IS Type APCs									
BMR-600	6·15 m	2·5 m	2·36 m	13·75 t	2 + 10	306 hp D	1 × 7·62 mm	ENASA	In production other variants
BLR	5·65 m	2·5 m	1·99 m	11·6 t	3 + 12	Various	Various	ENASA	In production
SWEDEN									
Main Battle and Light Tanks									
S tank	7·04 m	3·4 m	2·14 m	39 t	3	240 hp MF 490 hp T	1 × 105 mm 2 × 7·62 mm CA 1 × 7·62 mm AA	Bofors	Production complete
Ikv-91	6·41 m	3 m	2·36 m	16·3 t	4	350 hp D	1 × 90 mm 1 × 7·62 mm CA 1 × 7·62 mm AA	Hägglund & Söner	Production complete
Armoured Personnel Carriers, Mechanised Infantry Combat Vehicles and IS Type APCs									
Pbv 302	5·35 m	2·86 m	2·5 m	13·5 t	2 + 10	280 hp D	1 × 20 mm	Hägglund & Söner	Production complete
SWITZERLAND									
Main Battle and Light Tanks									
Pz.68	6·98 m	3·14 m	2·75 m	39·7 t	4	660 hp D	1 × 105 mm 1 × 7·5 mm CA 1 × 7·5 mm AA	Federal Construction Works, Thun	Production Mk 1 to 4
Pz.61	6·78 m	3·06 m	2·72 m	38 t	4	630 hp D	1 × 105 mm 1 × 20 mm CA 1 × 7·5 mm AA	Federal Construction Works, Thun	Production complete
Reconnaissance Vehicles									
MOWAG Shark	72 m	3 m	1·8 m	21 t	3/4	530 hp D	Various	MOWAG	Development complete, ready for production
MOWAG Spy	4·52 m	2·5 m	1·66 m	7·5 t	3	205 hp D	Various	MOWAG	In production
Armoured Personnel Carriers, Mechanised Infantry Combat Vehicles and IS Type APCs									
MOWAG Tornado	6·7 m	3·15 m	2·94 m	22·3 t	3 + 7	390 hp D	1 × 25 mm 2 × 7·62 mm	MOWAG	Prototype
MOWAG Piranha (6 × 6)	5·97 m	2·5 m	1·85 m	10·5 t	14	300 hp D	Various	MOWAG	In production, also 4 × 4 and 8 × 8 models, many variants, was built in Canada (6 × 6)
MOWAG MR 8	5·31 m	2·2 m	2·22 m	8·2 t	2 + 5	161 hp P	None	MOWAG & others	Production complete, also model with 20 mm turret
MOWAG Grenadier	4·84 m	2·3 m	2·12 m	6·1 t	1 + 8	202 hp P	1 × 20 mm	MOWAG	Production complete
MOWAG Roland	4·44 m	2·01 m	2·03 m	4·7 t	3 + 3	202 hp P	1 × 7·62 mm	MOWAG	In production, many variants
UNION OF SOVIET SOCIALIST REPUBLICS									
Main Battle and Light Tanks									
PT-76	6·91 m	3·14 m	2·195 m	14 t	3	240 hp D	1 × 76 mm 1 × 7·62 mm CA	State arsenals	Production complete
T-72	6·9 m	3·49 m	2·37 m	41 t	3	750 hp D	1 × 125 mm 1 × 7·62 mm CA 1 × 12·7 mm AA	State arsenals	In production, also built in Czechoslovakia and Poland
T-62	6·63 m	3·3 m	2·395 m	40 t	4	580 hp D	1 × 115 mm 1 × 7·62 mm CA 1 × 12·7 mm AA	State arsenals	Production complete
T-55	6·45 m	3·27 m	2·4 m	36 t	4	580 hp D	1 × 100 mm 1 × 7·62 mm CA	State arsenals	Production complete in USSR
T-54	6·45 m	3·27 m	2·4 m	36 t	4	520 hp D	1 × 100 mm 1 × 7·62 mm CA 1 × 7·62 mm bow 1 × 12·7 mm AA	State arsenals	Production complete. Built in China as Type 59
T-64	6·4 m	3·38 m	2·3 m	38 t	3	750 hp D	1 × 125 mm 1 × 7·62 mm CA 1 × 12·7 mm AA	State arsenals	In production
Reconnaissance Vehicles									
BRDM-2	5·75 m	2·35 m	2·31 m	7 t	4	140 hp P	1 × 14·5 mm 1 × 7·62 mm CA	State arsenals	In production, many variants
BRDM-1	5·7 m	2·25 m	1·9 m	5·6 t	5	90 hp P	1 × 7·62 mm	State arsenals	Production complete, many variants
Armoured Personnel Carriers, Mechanised Infantry Combat Vehicles and IS Type APCs									
BTR-70	7·85 m	2·8 m	2·435 m	11 t	2 + 14	2 × D	1 × 14·5 mm 1 × 7·62 mm CA	State arsenals	In production
BTR-60PB	7·56 m	2·825 m	2·31 m	10·3 t	2 + 14	90 hp P (2)	1 × 14·5 mm 1 × 7·62 mm CA	State arsenals	Production complete, many variants
BTR-50	7·08 m	3·14 m	1·97 m	14·2 t	2 + 20	240 hp D	Various	State arsenals	Production complete, many variants
BTR-152V1	6·83 m	2·32 m	2·05 m	8·95 t	2 + 17	110 hp P	1 × 7·62 mm	State arsenals	Production complete, many variants, built in China as Type 56
BMP-1	6·74 m	2·94 m	2·15 m	13·5 t	3 + 8	300 hp D	1 × 73 mm 1 × 7·62 mm CA Sagger	State arsenals	In production, many variants
MT-LB	6·454 m	2·85 m	1·865 m	11·9 t	2 + 11	240 hp D	1 × 7·62 mm	State arsenals	In production, few variants
BMD	5·4 m	2·4 m	1·97 m	6·7 t	2 + 5	240 hp D	1 × 73 mm 1 × 7·62 mm CA 2 × 7·62 mm bow Sagger	State arsenals	In production, many variants
BTR-40	5 m	1·9 m	1·75 m	5·3 t	2 + 8	80 hp P	1 × 7·62 mm	State arsenals	Production complete, many variants, built in China as Type 55

Designation	Length Hull	Width	Height	Combat weight (tonnes)	Crew	Engine	Armament	Contractor	Notes
UNITED KINGDOM									
Main Battle and Light Tanks									
Challenger	8·39 m	3·518 m	2·89 m	62 t	4	1200 hp D	1 × 120 mm 1 × 7·62 mm CA 1 × 7·62 mm AA	ROF Leeds	In production
Khalid	8·39 m	3·518 m	3·012 m	58 t	4	1200 hp D	1 × 120 mm 1 × 7·62 mm CA 1 × 7·62 mm AA	ROF Leeds	In production for Jordan
Centurion Mk 13	7·823 m	3·39 m	3 m	51·82 t	4	650 hp P	1 × 105 mm 1 × 7·62 mm CA 1 × 7·62 mm AA	Various	Production complete
Vickers Mk 3	7·56 m	3·168 m	2·48 m	38·7 t	4	720 hp D	1 × 105 mm 1 × 7·62 mm CA 1 × 7·62 mm AA	Vickers & Madras tank plant	Mk 1 in production in India. Mk 3 in production in UK
Chieftain 900	7·52 m	3·51 m	2·44 m	56 t	4	900 hp D	1 × 120 mm 1 × 7·62 mm CA 1 × 7·62 mm AA	ROF Leeds	Prototype
Chieftain Mk 5	7·52 m	3·66 m	2·89 m	54·1 t	4	730 hp MF	1 × 120 mm 1 × 7·2 mm CA 1 × 7·62 mm AA	Vickers & ROF Leeds	Production complete
Valiant	7·51 m	3·3 m	3·24 m	43·6 t	4	915 hp D	1 × 105 mm 1 × 7·62 mm CA 1 × 7·62 mm AA	Vickers	Prototype, also with 120 mm gun
Reconnaissance Vehicles									
Alvis Saladin	4·93 mm	2·54 m	2·19 m	11·59 t	3	170 hp P	1 × 76 mm 1 × 7·62 mm CA 1 × 7·62 mm AA	Alvis	Production complete
Alvis Scorpion	4·794 m	2·235 m	2·102 m	8 t	3	190 hp P	1 × 76 mm 1 × 7·62 mm CA	Alvis	In production
Shorland	4·597 m	1·778 m	2·286 m	3·36 t	3	91 hp P	1 × 7·62 mm	Shorts	In production
Fox	4·242 m	2·134 m	2·2 m	6·386 t	3	190 hp P	1 × 30 mm 1 × 7·62 mm CA	ROF Leeds	Production complete
Ferret Mk 2/3	3·835 m	1·905 m	1·879 m	4·395 t	2	129 hp P	1 × 7·62 mm	Daimler	Production complete, many variants
Armoured Personnel Carriers, Mechanised Infantry Combat Vehicles and IS Type APCs									
MCV-80	6·34 m	3·04 m	2·74 m	24 t	10	550 hp D	1 × 30 mm 1 × 7·62 mm CA	GKN Sankey	Production from 1985
Valkyri	5·6 m	2·5 m	2·05 m	11 t	2 + 10	180 hp D	Various	Vickers	Prototype
AT-104	5·486 m	2·438 m	2·489 m	8·9 t	2 + 9	Various	Various	GKN Sankey	Production complete
Alvis Stormer	5·28 m	2·31 m	2·49 m	11·6 t	3 + 8	250 hp D	Various	Alvis	In production
Simba	5·26 m	2·49 m	2·1 m	10·18 t	12	210 hp D	Various	GKN Sankey	Prototype
FV432	5·251 m	2·8 m	2·286 m	15·28 t	2 + 10	240 hp MF	1 × 7·62 mm	GKN Sankey	Production complete, many variants
Alvis Saracen	5·233 m	2·539 m	2·463 m	10·17 t	2 + 10	160 hp P	2 × 7·62 mm	Alvis	Production complete, variants
AT-105	5·169 m	2·489 m	2·628 m	10·67 t	2 + 8	Various	Various	GKN Sankey	In production, many variants
Humber 1-ton	4·926 m	2·044 m	2·12 m	5·79 t	2 + 6	120 hp P	None	Various	Production complete
Sandringham	4·445 m	1·69 m	2·083 m	3·7 t	10	92 hp P	Various	Hotspur	In production
SB 401	4·292 m	1·778 m	2·159 m	3·545 t	2 + 6	91 hp P	None	Shorts	In production
UNITED STATES OF AMERICA									
Main Battle and Light Tanks									
M1 Abrams	7·918 m	3·655 m	2·375 m	54·432 t	4	1500 hp T	1 × 105 mm 1 × 7·62 mm CA 1 × 12·7 mm AA 1 × 7·62 mm AA	General Dynamics	In production
M60A1	6·946 m	3·631 m	3·27 m	48·987 t	4	750 hp D	1 × 105 mm 1 × 7·62 mm CA 1 × 12·7 mm AA	General Dynamics	Also M60, current model is M60A3
M48A5	6·87 m	3·631 m	3·086 m	49·987 t	4	750 hp D	1 × 105 mm 1 × 7·62 mm CA 2 × 7·62 mm AA	Various	Originally had 90 mm gun, many now fitted with 105 mm
M47	6·307 m	3·51 m	2·95 m	46·17 t	5	810 hp P	1 × 90 mm 1 × 7·62 mm CA 1 × 7·62 mm bow 1 × 12·7 mm AA	Various	Production complete
M41	5·819 m	3·198 m	2·726 m	23·495 t	4	500 hp P	1 × 76 mm 1 × 7·62 mm CA 1 × 12·7 mm AA	Cadillac	Production complete
Reconnaissance Vehicles									
Commando Scout	4·699 m	2·057 m	2·235 m	6·577 t	2	149 hp D	2 × 7·62 mm	Cadillac Gage	Prototype, other armament installations available
Lynx C & R	4·597 m	2·413 m	2·171 m	8·775 t	3	215 hp D	1 × 12·7 mm 1 × 7·62 mm	FMC	Production as required
Armoured Personnel Carriers, Mechanised Infantry Combat Vehicles and IS Type APCs									
M2, M3	653 m	3·2 m	2·972 m	22·666 t	3 + 7	500 hp D	1 × 25 mm 1 × 7·62mm CA 2 × TOW	FMC	In production, M3 cavalry version
AIFV	5·258 m	2·819 m	2·794 m	13·687 t	3 + 7	264 hp D	1 × 25 mm 1 × 7·62 mm CA	FMC	In production, many variants
M113A1	47 m	2·686 m	2·54 m	11·156 t	2 + 11	215 hp D	1 × 12·7 mm	FMC	In production, many variants
Dragoon	5·588 m	2·438 m	2·642 m	12·7 t	9	300 hp D	1 × 25 mm	Dominion Manufacturing	In production, many variants
Commando V-150	5·689 m	2·26 m	2·54 m	9·888 t	12	202 hp D	1 × 20 mm 1 × 7·62 mm CA 1 × 7·62 mm AA	Cadillac Gage	Production, many variants, also V-100 and V-200
Commando V-300	6·4 m	2·54 m	1·981 m	12·7 t	3 + 9	235 hp D	Various	Cadillac Gage	In production
Commando Ranger	4·699 m	2·019 m	1·981 m	4·536 t	2 + 6	180 hp D	Various	Cadillac Gage	Production, many variants
Lancer	4·42 m	1·792 m	1·727 m	2·812 t	4	150 hp P	Various	VSDC	Ready for production
LVTP7	7·943 m	3·27 m	3·263 m	22·838 t	3 + 25	400 hp D	1 × 12·7 mm	FMC	Production complete, many variants
YUGOSLAVIA									
Armoured Personnel Carriers, Mechanised Infantry Combat Vehicles and IS Type APCs									
M980	6·4 m	2·59 m	2·5 m	13 t	2 + 8	260 hp D	1 × 20 mm 1 × 7·62 mm CA 2 × Sagger	State arsenals	In production
M60	5·02 m	2·77 m	2·38 m	11 t	3 + 10	140 hp D	1 × 12·7 mm 1 × 7·92 mm bow	State arsenals	Production complete, variants

3020.204   Fighting Ships

The following pages list what we believe to be the most important ships of each nation and the equipment carried. Ships are shown in order of completion dates for first of class so that readers may readily see where navies are heading.

The selection of ships as 'important' is somewhat arbitrary. In broad terms all fighting ships of 1000 tons and upwards are included as are smaller craft with missiles. However, other craft, minesweepers, motor torpedo boats, auxiliaries, etc. are generally not significant in terms of their weapon systems.

It will be obvious that there are inevitable gaps in our knowledge of armament and equipment. To those readers seeking more information than can be contained, or justified, in this volume, we would direct their attention to our companion publication, *Jane's Fighting Ships*.

The classification of ships in these tables broadly follows that given in *Jane's Fighting Ships* for the USA section which, in brief, is as follows:

BB	Battleship
CA	Gun cruiser
CG	Guided missile cruiser
CV	Aircraft carrier
DD	Destroyer
FF	Frigate
Corv	Corvette
LHA	Amphibious assault ship (General purpose)
LPH	Amphibious assault ship (Helicopter carrier)
LSD	Dock landing ship
LCC	Amphibious command ship

PHM	Patrol hydrofoil – guided missile
PTF	Fast patrol boat
SS	Submarine

With the following prefixes and suffixes:

A	Auxiliary
B	Ballistic missiles
G	Guided missiles
H	Helicopter carrier
N	Nuclear propelled

Year Built	No	Type	Class	Radar Surveillance	3-D	Data System	SAM	Gunnery Control	Gun	SSM/ASM	Sonar Hull	VDS	A/S weapons	Remarks
ALGERIA														
1967-81	12	PTFG	Osa 1 & 2	Square Tie				Drum Tilt	30 mm	SS-N-2				Being re-armed
1980-82	2	FF	Koni	Strut Curve Don 2			SA-N-4	Hawk Screech Drum Tilt	76 mm 30 mm		Yes		RBU 6000	
1980-83	4	Corv	Nanuchka 2	Square Tie Don 2			SA-N-4	Muff Cob	57 mm	SS-N-2B				More deliveries expected
ANGOLA														
1982-83	6	PTFG	Osa 2						30 mm	SS-N-2				
ARGENTINA														
1944	2	DD	H Bouchard (US Sumner)	SPS 6 or 40 & 10				GFCS 37 GFCS 56 in 1	5 in/38 3 in/50 in 1	Exocet MM38	SQS 30	SQA 10A in 2	Hedgehog Torpedoes (A244S) Helo facility in 2	
1945	1	CV	24 De Mayo (UK Colossus)	Philips LWO 1 & 2 & VI DA.02 ZW.01		CAAIS			40 mm		CWE 10		Sea King helo S2E trackers	
1945	1	DD	Commodoro Py (US Gearing)	SPS 37				GFCS 37	5 in/38	Exocet MM38	SQS 29		Hedgehog Torpedoes (A244S) Helo facility	
1976-81	2	DDG	Hercules (UK Type 42)	965 992 Q 1006		ADAWS 4	Sea Dart/ GWS 30	GSA 1	4·5 in Mk 8 20 mm	Exocet	184 162		Lynx helo Torpedoes (A244S)	
1978-81	3	FF	French A-69	DRBV 51 Decca 202				DRBC 32E Naja optronic Panda	100 mm 40 mm 20 mm	Exocet MM38	Diodon		Torpedoes	
1983-84	4	DDG	Meko 360	DA.08A ZW.06			Aspide	WM 25	5 in 40 mm	Exocet MM40	KAE 80		2 Lynx helo Torpedoes	
1983-87	6	FF	Meko 140	DA.05 Decca surface Decca TM 1226				M20	76 mm OTO-Melara 40 mm	Exocet MM38	AS50-4		Lynx helo Torpedoes (A244S)	
AUSTRALIA														
1961-71	6	FF	River (UK Type 12 modified)	LW.02 M22 SPS55/8GR301			Seacat	M22	4·5 in Mk 6		162 170 in one 177M in one 185 Mulloka to be fitted		Ikara Torpedoes	Being modernised with Mulloka sonar, Mk 44 & 46 torpedoes
1965-67	3	DDG	Perth (US Adams modified)	SPS 10F & 40C 975	SPS 52B	NCDS	Standard RIM 66	GFCS 68	5 in/54		SQS 23F UQC ID UQN 1		Ikara Torpedoes	Modernised 1974-79
1980-84	4	FFG	Oliver Hazard Perry (US Perry modified)	SPS 49 SPS 55		WSP/ WCP	Standard RIM 66	Mk 92 Mod 2 (= WM 28)	76 mm OTO-Melara CIWS in 2	Harpoon	SQS 56		Torpedoes 2 helos	Two of modified type to be built in Australia
BAHRAIN														
1983-84	2	PTFG	TNC-45	WM28?				Panda optical WM28?	76 mm OTO-Melara 40 mm	Exocet				
BANGLADESH														
1958	1	FF	Umar Farooq (UK Type 61)	965 993 278M 986 978				275 radar	4·5 in Mk 6 40 mm		174 164B		Squid	UK frigate Llandaff transferred 1976
1957-59	2	FF	Ali Haider (UK Type 41)	965,993 978				275 radar	4·5 in Mk 6 40 mm		164 174		Squid	UK frigates Jaguar & Lynx transferred 1978/1982

Year Built	No	Type	Class	Radar Surveillance	3-D	Data System	SAM	Gunnery Control	Gun	SSM/ASM	Sonar Hull	VDS	A/S weapons	Remarks
BANGLADESH cont														
1983	4	PTFG	Durbat (Chinese Hegu)						25 mm	Yes				
BELGIUM														
1978	4	FFG	E-71	DA.05 TM-1645/9X		SEWACO 4	NATO Sea Sparrow RIM 7H	WM 25	100 mm	Exocet	SQS 505A		L5 torpedoes 375 mm rocket launchers	
BRAZIL														
1943-45	3	DD	Piaui (US Fletcher)	SPS 6 & 10				GFCS 37 GFCS 63	5 in/38 40 mm		SQS 4 29 or 32		Hedgehog Torpedoes Depth charges	2 in reserve
1944-46	5	DD	Alagoas (US Sumner)	SPS 10 & 6, 37 or 40			Seacat in 1	GFCS 37	5 in/38		SQS 31 or SQA 10 & SQS 40		Torpedoes Hedgehog Depth charges in 1 Wasp helo in 4	
1945	1	CVS	Minais Gerais (UK Majestic)	ZWO-6 MP 1402 SPS-40B				GFCS 29	40 mm				S2E Trackers Sea King helos	
1945	2	DD	Marcilio Dias (US Gearing)	SPS 10 & 40				GFCS 37	5 in/38		SQS 23		Asroc Torpedoes Wasp helo	
1978	2	FF	Niteroi (Vosper Mk 10)	Plessey AWS-2 Signaal ZW.06		CAAIS	Seacat	Selenia RTN-10X WSA-400	4·5 in Mk 8 40 mm/70	Exocet	EDO 610E		Lynx helo Torpedoes Bofors rockets	
1976-79	4	DD	Niteroi (Vosper Mk 10)	Plessey AWS-2 Signaal ZW.06		CAAIS	Seacat	Selenia RTN-10X WSA-400	4·5 in Mk 8 40 mm/70		EDO 610E	EDO 700E	Ikara Lynx helo Torpedoes Bofors rockets Depth charges	
1985	1	FF	Niteroi (Vosper Mk 10)						76 mm OTO-Melara				2 Lynx helos	For training
1985 on	4	FF				CAAIS	Yes	Ferranti WSA 4A20	4·5 in Mk 8 40 mm/70		Yes		Torpedoes Lynx helo	First two ordered 1982. Possible total of 12
BRUNEI														
1978-79	3	PTFG	Waspada	Decca TM 1229				Sea Archer Mk 1	30 mm	Exocet MM 38				
BULGARIA														
1957-58	2	FF	Druzki (USSR Riga)	Slim Net Neptun				Wasp Head/ Sun Visor B	100 mm 37 mm				RBU 1800 Torpedoes Depth charges	
1970-82	6	PTFG	Osa 1 & 2	Square Tie				Drum Tilt	30 mm	SS-N-2				
CAMEROON														
1983	1	PTFG	P48S					Naja	40 mm	Exocet MM 40				
CANADA														
1956-57	6	DDH	St Laurent	SPS 10 & 12				SPG 48 Gunar	3 in/50		SQS 501 502 & 503	SQS 504	Sea King CHSS-2 helo Mk 10 mortar Mk 44/46 torpedoes	
1958-59	4	DD	Improved Restigouche	SPS 10 & 12		UCS 257		SPG 48 GFCS 69	3 in/70		SQS 505 & 501	SQS 505	Asroc Mk 10 mortar	
1958-59	3	DD	Restigouche	SPS 10 & 12				SPG 48 GFCS 69	3 in/70 3 in/50		SQS 10/11 SQS 501 502 & 503		Mk 10 mortar	In reserve
1962-63	4	DD	Mackenzie	SPS 10 & 12				SPG 48 Gunar GFCS 69	3 in/70 in three 3 in/50 in one		SQS 10/11 SQS 501 502 & 503		Mk 10 mortar Mk 44/46 torpedoes	
1964	2	DDH	Annapolis	SPS 10 & 12				SPG 48 Gunar	3 in/50 Mk 33		SQS 10/11 SQS 501 502, 503 504	SQS 504	Sea King CHSS-2 helo Mk 10 mortar Mk 44/46 torpedoes	
1972-73	4	DDH	Tribal	SPQ 2D SPS 501		CCS 280 UCS 280	Sea Sparrow	M22	127 mm (5 in) OTO-Melara		SQS 505 SQS 501	SQS 505	2 Sea King CHSS-2 helos Mk 10 mortar Mk 44/46 torpedoes	
1989-92	6	DDH	Halifax				Sea Sparrow		57 mm CIWS		Towed array & hull		Sea King Torpedoes	
CHILE														
1944	2	DD	Portales (US Sumner)	SPS 10 & 37 or 40				GFCS 37	5 in/38	Exocet MM38	SQS 40V In one		Torpedoes Hedgehog Helo	
1960	2	DDG	Almirante	Plessey AWS-1			Seacat/ GWS22	MM-4 M-4-1-CH	4 in/60 40 mm	Exocet MM38	SQS40V		Squid Mk 44 torpedoes	UK design Modernised early 1970s
1970	2	DLG	Prat (UK County)	965M 992Q			Seaslug Mk 2 Seacat	MRS 3	4·5 in Mk 6 20 mm	Exocet MM38	176 177 182 192		Helo	Transferred from UK 1982 & 1984. Seaslug SAM likely to be replaced

Year Built	No	Type	Class	Radar Surveillance	3-D	Data System	SAM	Gunnery Control	Gun	SSM/ ASM	Sonar Hull	VDS	A/S weapons	Remarks
CHILE cont														
1974	2	DD	Condell (UK Leander)	965, 975 992Q			Seacat/GWS 22	MRS 3	4·5 in Mk 6 20 mm	Exocet MM38	162, 170 177		Helo Torpedoes	
1974	2	PTFG	SAAR IV						76 mm OTO-Melara 20 mm	Gabriel				Purchased 1979 and 1981
CHINA, People's Republic														
1940-42	4	FFG	Anshan (USSR Gordy)	Square Tie Knife Rest A Cross Loop				Mina	130 mm 37 mm	Hai Ying Pegas-2M			Depth charges	
1958-59	4	FF	Chengdu	Slim Net Neptun Square Tie				Sun Visor B	100 mm 37 mm	Hai Ying			Depth charges	Minelaying capability
1967-69	5	FF	Jiangnan	Ball Gun Neptun				Wok Won	100 mm 37 mm				Depth charges RBU 1200	Minelaying capability
1965 on	101	PTFG	Hegu & Hema (USSR Komart type)	Square Tie					25 mm	Hai Ying				Soviet & Chinese built. 1 Hema exists only as hydrofoil version
1965 on	120	PTFG	Osa, Huangfen & Hola	Square Tie in some				Drum Tilt in some	25 mm	Hai Ying				Soviet & Chinese built 1 Hola only as design variation
1971-81	14	DDG	Luda	Knife Rest Square Tie Neptun				Wasp Head Post Lamp or Sun Visor B Rice Lamp	130 mm 37 mm 25 mm	Hai Ying	Yes		FQF 2500 Depth Charges	More building
1976-83	14	FFG	Jianghu	Top Trough Don 2 or Fincurve Square Tie				Sun Visor in some	100 mm 37 mm	Hai Ying	Yes		RBU 1200 Depth charges	More building
1977-78	2	FFG	Jiangdong				Twin SAM	Wasp Head Sun Visor	100 mm 37 mm				RBU 1200 Depth charges	More building

Note: Some further fourteen old escorts have been retained in commission after refitting and modernisation

Year Built	No	Type	Class	Radar Surveillance	3-D	Data System	SAM	Gunnery Control	Gun	SSM/ ASM	Sonar Hull	VDS	A/S weapons	Remarks
COLOMBIA														
1958	2	DD	Siete de Agosto (Swedish Halland modified)	LW.03 DA.02				M20	120 mm 40 mm				Bofors rocket launcher	
1983-84	4	FF	FS 1500	Sea Tiger			Aspide	Castor & Canopus optronic	76 mm OTO-Melara 30 mm	Exocet MM40	ASO 4-2		Helo Torpedoes	
CUBA														
1962-66	14	PTFG	Komar	Square Tie					25 mm	SS-N-2				4 likely to be scrapped
1972-82	18	PTFG	Osa 1 & 2	Square Tie				Drum Tilt	30 mm	SS-N-2				
1981-84	2	FF	USSR Koni						76 mm CIWS				MBU	Minelaying capability
DENMARK														
1962-63	4	FF	Hvidbjornen	AWS-6/CWS-2 NWS-1					3 in		PMS 26		Lynx helo Depth charges	
1966-67	2	FF	Peder Skram	CWS-3, NWS-1 NWS-2			Sea Sparrow	CGS-1 Contraves	5 in/38 40 mm	Harpoon	PMS 26		Depth charges Torpedoes	
1976	1	FF	Beskytterren	AWS-6/CWS-2 NWS-1, NWS-2					3 in		PMS 26		Lynx helo	
1976-78	10	PTFG	Willemoes	NWS-3				9LV 200	76 mm OTO-Melara	Harpoon				Wire-guided torpedoes
1980-82	3	FF	Niels Juel	Plessey AWS-5 Philips Skanter Mk009			Sea Sparrow	Philips 9LV 200 Mk 2	76 mm OTO-Melara	Harpoon	PMS 26		Depth charges Torpedoes	Minelaying Capability
DOMINICAN REPUBLIC														
1944	1	FF	Mella (Canadian River)						100 mm 40 mm 20 mm					Presidential yacht & flagship
ECUADOR														
1943	1	FF	Charles Lawrence	SPS 6 & 10					5 in/38 40 mm				Depth charges Helo facility	
1946	1	DD	US Gearing						5 in/38				Torpedoes	
1976-77	3	PTFG	Quito	Triton				Triton & Pollux with Vega system	76 mm OTO-Melara 35 mm	Exocet MM38				
1971	3	PTFG	Manta						30 mm	Gabriel 2				
1982-84	6	Corv	Esmeraldas	Selenia RAN 10S SMA 3RM20			Aspide	Elsag NA 21 Orion 10X & 20X	76 mm OTO-Melara 40 mm	Exocet MM 40	Diodon		Torpedoes Helo facility	

Year Built	No	Type	Class	Radar Surveillance	3-D	Data System	SAM	Gunnery Control	Gun	SSM/ ASM	Sonar Hull	VDS	A/S weapons	Remarks
EGYPT														
1940	1	FF	Port Said (UK Hunt)						4 in 37 mm 25 mm				Depth charges	
1942	1	FF	Rashid (UK River)						4 in 40 mm 20 mm				Depth charges	Submarine support ship & training. Not sea worthy
1943	1	FF	Tariq (UK Black Swan)						4 in 40 mm 20 mm				Depth charges	
1944	1	DD	El Fateh (UK 'Z')	960 293				275 radar	4·5 in Mk 5 40 mm				Depth charges	
1951	4	DD	Al Nasser (USSR Skory)	High Sieve Cross Bird Don				Various old	130 mm 85 mm 57 mm 37 mm 25 mm	SS-N-2 in 1			Depth charges RBU 2500A in some	Minelaying capability
1962-67	4	PTFG	Komar	Square Tie					25 mm	SS-N-2A				
1966	8	PTFG	Osa 1	1006 & Decca navigation			SA-7	Drum Tilt	30 mm	SS-N-2A				Refitted from Soviet configuration
1975-76	6	PTFG	October	Marconi S810				Marconi/ Sperry Sapphire ST 802	30 mm	Otomat				Modernised Komar type
1980-82	6	PTFG	Ramadan	Marconi S820	CAAIS			Sapphire	76 mm OTO-Melara 40 mm	Otomat				
ETHIOPIA														
1944	1	FF	Ethiopia						5 in/38 40 mm					
1978-81	4	PTFG	Osa 2	Square Tie				Drum Tilt	30 mm	SS-N-2A				
1983	1	FF	Petya 2	Strut Curve Don 2				Hawk Screech	76 mm		Yes		RBU 6000 Depth charges	
FINLAND														
1968	2	Corv	Turunmaa	M20 series				M20 series	120 mm 40 mm 23 mm		Yes		Depth charges A/S rockets	Finnish design
1974-75	4	PTFG	Tuima (Osa 2)						30 mm?					
1979	1	FF	Pohjanmaa	DA 05/2				Philips 9LV 200	120 mm 40 mm 23 mm		Yes		A/S rockets	Minelaying/ training ship Finnish design
1981-86	4	PTFG	Helsinki	Philips 9LV 225				Philips 9LV 225	57 mm 23 mm	RBS 15 -SF	Yes			Finnish design 4 to be completed by 1986
FRANCE														
1956-57	5	DD	Type 47 (ASW)	DRBV 22A & 50 DRBN32				DRBC 32A	100 mm 20 mm		DUBV 23B	DUBV 43A	Malafon 375 mm rocket launcher K2 & L3 torpedoes	
1956-57	2	DDG	Type 47	DRBV 22A & 31	SPS 39A/B	Senit 2	Tartar SM1 or SM1A	DRBC 31E SPG 51C	57 mm		DUBA 1C DUBV 24C		375 mm rocket launcher K2 & L3 torpedoes	
1957	1	DD	Type 53-ASW	DRBV 22A & 51A 2 Decca 1226		Senit 2		DRBC 32E	100 mm	Exocet MM38	DUBV 23D	DUBV 43B	L5 Mod 4 torpedoes Lynx helo To be disposed of in 1990	
1959	1	CG	Colbert	DRBV 20C, 23C, & 50A DRBI 10D Decca RM416		Senit 1	Masurca Mk 2 Mod 3/3A	DRBC 32C DRBC 31A DRBR 51A	100 mm 57 mm	Exocet MM38				
1962	1	DD	Galissoniere (Type 56)	DRBV 22A & 50 DRBN 32				DRBC 32A	100 mm		DUBV 23A	DUBV 43X	Helo Malafon L3 & K2 torpedoes	
1961-63	2	CV	Clemenceau	DRBV 20C, 23B & 50 Decca 1226 NRBA 50 DRBI 10		Senit 2		DRBC 31C/D & 32 A/C	100 mm		SQS 503		Aircraft Helos	
1962-70	9	FF	Commdt Riviere	DRBV 22A Decca 1226				DRBC 32C	100 mm 40 mm	Exocet MM38	DUBA 3A SQS 17A		Helo pad K2 & L3 torpedoes Mortar	
1964	1	CGH	Jeanne d'Arc	DRBV 22D & 50 DRBY 50 DRBN32		Senit 2		DRBC 32A	100 mm	Exocet MM38	SQS 503		8 Lynx helos	Training in peace
1967-70	2	DDG	Suffren	DRBN 32 DRBV 50	DRBI 23	Senit 1	Masurca Mk 2 Mod 2&3	DRBC 32A	100 mm 20 mm	Exocet MM38	DUBV 23A	DUBV 43B	Malafon L5 Mod 4 torpedoes	To be modernised
1973	1	DD	Aconit	DRBV 15 & 22A DRBN 32				DRBC 32B	100 mm		DUBV 23C	DUBV 43B	Malafon L5 Mod 4 torpedoes	

Year Built	No	Type	Class	Radar Surveillance	3-D	Data System	SAM	Gunnery Control	Gun	SSM/ASM	Sonar Hull	VDS	A/S weapons	Remarks
FRANCE cont														
1974-77	3	DDG	Tourville (F 67)	DRBV 26A & 51A Decca 1226		Senit 3	Crotale	DRBC 32D Vega	100 mm 20 mm	Exocet MM38	DUBV 23D	DUBV 43B	Malafon Lynx helos L5 torpedoes	AS 12 missiles in helos
1976-84	17	FF	A 69	DRBV 51A DRBN 32				DRBC 32E Vega	100 mm 20 mm	Exocet MM38 or 40	DUBA 25A		375 mm rocket launcher L3 & L5 torpedoes	
1979-89	7	DDG	C-70 (ASW)	DRBV 51C & 26 Decca 1226		Senit 4	Crotale	DRBC 32D Vega Panda	100 mm 20 mm	Exocet MM38 or 40	DUBV 23D Towed array in some	DUBV 43B	L5 torpedoes Lynx helos with Mk 46 torpedoes	
1979-94	4	DDG	C-70 (AA)	DRBV 26 Decca 1229	DRBJ 11B	Senit 6	Standard MR Sadral	DRBC 32D SPG 51C Vega Naja	100 mm 20 mm	Exocet MM40	DUBA 25/A Towed array		L5 Mod 4 torpedoes Dauphin SA365F helo	
1995 on	2	CVN	PA 88	DRBV15 & 27	DRBV 11B		Sadral or Crotale							About 35 000 tons Design details not yet known
GERMANY, Democratic Republic														
1966	15	PTFG	Osa 1						30 mm	SS-N-2A				
1978-79	2	FF	USSR Koni	Strut Curve Don 2			SA-N-4	Hawk Screech Drum Tilt	76 mm 30 mm		Yes		RBU 6000 Depth charges	Minelaying capability
1981-83	13	Corv	Parchim	Strut Curve TSR 333			SA-N-5		57 mm 30 mm		Yes		RBU 6000 Torpedoes Depth charges	Similar to Soviet Grisha More building to total of 18
GERMANY, Federal Republic														
1961-64	3	DD	Köln (F120)	DA.02				M45	100 mm 40 mm		PAE/ CWE		Bofors D/C mortar Torpedoes Depth charges	Minelaying capability Being phased out as F 122 class completes
1964-68	4	DD	Hamburg	LW.02 DA.02 Decca navigation				M45	100 mm 40 mm	Exocet MM38	ELAC 1 BV		Bofors D/C mortars Depth charges Torpedoes	Minelaying capability Modernised 1975 on
1969-70	3	DDG	Lütjens (US Adams)	SPS 10 & 40	SPS 52	Satir	Tartar SM1 RAM	GFCS 68 GFCS 86 in one	5 in/54	Harpoon	SQS 23		Asroc Torpedoes Depth charges	
1972-75	20	PTFG	148	Triton 3RM 20				Vega-Pollux	76 mm OTO-Melara 40 mm	Exocet MM38				
1976-77	10	PTFG	143	WM27		AGIS	RAM	WM27	76 mm OTO-Melara	Exocet MM38				Wire-guided torpedoes
1982-84	10	PTFG	143A	WM27		AGIS	RAM	WM27	76 mm OTO-Melara	Exocet MM38				Minelaying capability
1982-84	6	FFG	Bremen (F122)	DA.08 3RM 20			NATO Sea Sparrow RAM	WM25	76 mm OTO-Melara	Harpoon	DSQS 21BZ & BO		2 Lynx helos Mk 46 torpedoes	
GREECE														
1942-43	6	DD	Aspis (US Fletcher)	SPS 6 & 10				GFCS 37 GFCS 56 GFCS 63	5 in/38 3 in/55		SQS 39 or 43		Hedgehog Depth charges Torpedoes	Armament varies from ship to ship 3 more from West Germany being used for spares
1943-44	4	FF	Aetos (US Cannon)					GFCS 52	3 in/50 40 mm 20 mm		SQS 51		Hedghog Depth charges Torpedoes	
1944	1	DD	Miaoulis (US Sumner)	SPS 10 & 40				GFCS 37	5 in/38 20 mm		SQS 29	SQA 10	Alouette III helo Hedgehog Mk 44/46 Torpedoes	
1944-46	7	DD	Themistocles (US Gearing)	SPS 10 & 37 or 40				GFCS 37 Argo NA-10	5 in/38 76 mm OTO-Melara in 4 40 mm in 2		SQS 23	SQA 10 in one	Asroc torpedoes	Some variations in armament
1971-72	4	PTFG	La Combattante II	Triton				Vega-Pollux	35 mm	Exocet MM38				Wire-guided torpedoes
1977-78	4	PTFG	La Combattante III	Triton				Vega II-Pollux Panda	76 mm OTO-Melara 30 mm Emerlec	Exocet MM38				Wire-guided torpedoes
1980-81	6	PTFG	La Combattante III	Triton				Vega II-Pollux Panda	76 mm OTO-Melara 30 mm Emerlec	Penguin Mk 2				Wire-guided torpedoes

Year Built	No	Type	Class	Radar Surveillance	3-D	Data System	SAM	Gunnery Control	Gun	SSM/ASM	Sonar Hull	VDS	A/S weapons	Remarks
GREECE cont														
1981-82	2	FF	Kortenaer	LW.08 ZW.06 DA.05		Sewaco 2	Aspide	WM 25	76 mm OTO-Melara	Harpoon	SQS 505		Mk 46 torpedoes Two AB212 helos	
INDIA														
1940	1	CA	Mysore (UK Nigeria)	960, 277 293				274 radar 275 radar	6 in 4 in 40 mm					Immobile & due for disposal
1943	1	FF	Kistna (UK Black Swan)	293				285 radar	4 in 40 mm		149		Depth charges	
1958-60	3	FF	Brahmaputra (UK Leopard)	960, 293				275 radar	4·5 in Mk 6 40 mm		147 162 164		Squid	
1959	2	FF	Kirpan (UK Blackwood)	E-Band					40 mm				Mk 10 mortar	Transferred to Coast Guard
1960	2	FF	Talwar (UK Whitby)	293, 277 Square Tie				FPS 6	40 mm	SS-N-2	170 174		Mk 10 mortar in one. Helo in one	
1961	1	CV	Vikrant (UK Majestic)	LW-05 ZW-06 ZW-10/11					40 mm				Alize helos	Modernised for Sea Harrier
1969-74	12	FF	Arnala (USSR Petya II)	Strut Curve Don 2				Hawk Screech	76 mm		Hercules		RBU 2500 Torpedoes Depth charges	Minelaying capability
1972-80	6	FF	Nilgiri (UK Leander)	HSA W-05 in 5 965 in 1 993 in 1			Seacat GWS 22 or M44	GWS 22 or M40 series	4·5 in Mk 6 20 mm	SS-N-2 may be fitted	184	199 in 4	Mk 10 mortar & Alouette III helo in first 4, Sea King, A244S torpedoes and rocket launcher in remainder	Indian built Many variations
1971-76	16	PTFG	Osa 1 & 2	Square Tie				Drum Tilt	30 mm	SS-N-2B				
1977-78	3	Corv	Nanuchka	Band Stand Don 2			SA-N-4	Muff Cob	57 mm	SS-N-2C				Reported total of 6 expected
1980-82	3	DDG	Kashin 2	Big Net A Don Kay	Head Net C		SA-N-1	Owl Screech Drum Tilt	76 mm 30 mm	SS-N-2C Yes		Yes	Helo RBU 6000	
1983-86	3	FFG	Modified Leander	LW.05/08 978?	Head Net C		SA-N-4	WM25? Drum Tilt	76 mm 30 mm	SS-N-2C	184		Torpedoes (A244S) 2 Sea King helos	3 more being built
INDONESIA														
1955-57	3	FF	Jos Sudarso (USSR Riga)	Slim Net Neptun				Wasp Head/ Sun Visor A	100 mm 37 mm				Depth charges Torpedoes	Minelaying capability
1958	1	FF	Pattimura						76 mm 25 mm				Hedgehog Depth charges	Non-operational
1959-60	4	FF	Samadikun (US Claud Jones)	SPS 4 or 5E Decca navigation				Mk 70	3 in/50 37 mm in 2 25 mm		SQS 39V, 41V, 42V or 45V		Torpedoes Hedgehog	
1979-80	3	FFG	Fatahillah	DA.05 Decca AC 1229				WM 28	120 mm 40 mm 20 mm	Exocet MM38	PHS-32		375 mm rocket launcher Helo on 1 Torpedoes in 2	
1979-80	4	PTFG	PSSM Mk 5	Decca 1226				HSA	57 mm 40 mm	Exocet MM38				4 more ordered in 1982
IRAN														
1944-45	2	DD	Babr (US Sumner)	SPS 10 & 37				GFCS 37	5 in/38	Standard	SQS 29	In 1	Hedgehog Torpedoes Helo	Modernised 1972 In reserve
1946	1	DD	Artemis (UK Battle)	Plessey AWS-1			Seacat	Contraves Sea Hunter	4·5 in Mk 6 40 mm	Standard			Squid	
1964-69	4	FF	Bayandor (US PF type)	SPS 6				GFCS 63 GFCS 51	3 in/50 40 mm 23 mm				Depth charges	
1971-72	4	FF	Saam (Vosper design)	Plessey AWS-1			Seacat	Contraves Sea Hunter	4·5 in Mk 8 35 mm	Sea Killer Mk 1	170 174		Mk 10 mortar	
1977-81	12	PTFG	Kaman (La Combattante II modified)					WM 28	76 mm OTO-Melara 40 mm	Harpoon				Few missiles available. Reported 2 boats sunk
IRAQ														
1972-76	12	PTFG	Osa 1 & 2	Square Tie				Drum Tilt	30 mm	SS-N-2				Four Osa 2 reported sunk
1980	1	FF							57 mm 40 mm 20 mm	If required			Helo pad Torpedoes Mortar Depth charges	Training ship Yugoslavian built
1985-87	4	FF	Italian Lupo				Aspide		127 mm OTO-Melara 40 mm	Otomat Mk 2			Torpedoes Helo	
1984-85	6	Corv	Assad				Aspide		76 mm OTO Melara 40 mm in 4	Otomat			Helo in 2 Torpedoes	

Year Built	No	Type	Class	Radar Surveillance	3-D	Data System	SAM	Gunnery Control	Gun	SSM/ ASM	Sonar Hull	VDS	A/S weapons	Remarks
ISRAEL														
1968-69	12	PTFG	Saar 2 & 3						76 mm OTO-Melara or 40 mm	Gabriel 2	ELAC in 6		Mk 46 torpedoes in 6	Variable armament
1973-80	8	PTFG	Saar 4	Dagan					76 mm OTO-Melara 20 mm CIWS to be fitted	Gabriel 3 Harpoon	ELAC, in 4 boats		Helo pad in 1	
1977	1	PTFG	Dvora	Decca 926					20 mm	Gabriel Mk 1				At 47 tons full load, smallest SSM craft yet built
1980-82	4	PTFG	Saar 4·5						76 mm in 2 30 mm 20 mm CIWS in some	Gabriel 2 Harpoon			Helo in 2	2 more expected
1982 on	2	PHM	US Flagstaff 2						30 mm	Gabriel Harpoon				Possibly 10 more to build in Israel Replacements for Saar 2 & 3 class
?	?	Corv	Saar 5			In GP version			76 mm OTO-Melara 30 mm in some	Gabriel 2 or Harpoon			Helo Bofors rocket launcher Torpedoes	Total number planned not known New design with both A/S & GP versions
ITALY														
1962	2	FF	Bergamini	SPS 12 SPQ-2				Orion OG3	76 mm/62 OTO-Melara		SQS 40		D/C mortar Torpedoes A/B 212 helo	
1963-64	2	DDG	Impavido	SPS 12 SPQ-2 SPN 74B	SPS 39		Standard MR	Orion 10X Argo 10	5 in/38 76 mm/62 OTO-Melara		SQS 39		Torpedoes	
1964	2	CGH	Andrea Doria	SPS 768 SPQ 2D 3RM-20	SPS 39A	SADOC 1	Standard ER	Orion 10X Argo 0	76 mm/62 OTO-Melara		SQS 23-F or SQS 39		Torpedoes 4 A/B 212 helos	
1965-66	4	FF	De Cristofaro	SPQ-2 BX 732				Orion OG3	76 mm/62		SQS 36	SQA 13	Mortar Torpedoes	
1968	2	FF	Alpino	SPS 12 SPQ-2A2 SPN 748				Orion 10X Argo 10	76 mm/62 OTO-Melara		SQS 43V		2 A/B 212 helos D/C mortar Torpedoes	
1969	1	CAH	Vittorio Veneto	SPS 768 SPS 702 SPN 703 3RM-7	SPS 52	SADOC 1	Standard ER	Orion 10X Argo 0 Dardo	76 mm/62 OTO-Melara 40 mm	Otomat Mark 2 (Teseo)	SQS 23		9 A/B 212 helos Torpedoes	
1972-73	2	DDGH	Audace	SPS 768 SPQ-2D	SPS 52		Standard MR	Orion 10X Argo 10	127 mm/ 54 OTO-Melara 76 mm/62 OTO-Melara		CWE 610		2 A/B 212 helos Torpedoes	
1974-82	7	PHM	Sparviero P-420	SPQ 701				Orion 10X Argo 10	76 mm/62 OTO-Melara	Otomat Mk 1 (Teseo)				
1977-80	4	FFG	Lupo	SPS 774 SPQ2F SPN748		SADOC 2	NATO Sea Sparrow	Dardo Orion 10X Argo 10	127 mm/ 54 OTO-Melara 40 mm/ 70 Breda	Otomat Mk 2 (Teseo)	DE 1160B		Torpedoes A/B 212 helo	
1981-84	8	FFG	Maestrale	SPS 774 SPS 702 SPN 703		SADOC 2	Albatros	Dardo Orion 30X Argo 30	127 mm/ 54 OTO-Melara 40 mm/70 Breda	Otomat Mk 2 (Teseo)	DE 1164	DE 1164	2 A/B 212 helos Torpedoes	Similar to Lupo but larger for better A/S weapons
1985	1	CVS	Giuseppe Garibaldi	SPS 768 SPS 774 SPS 702 SPN 749	SPS 52C	SADOC 2	Albatros	Dardo Orion 30X Argo 30	40 mm/70	Otomat Mk 2 (Teseo)	DE 1160LF		16 Sea King helos Torpedoes	
1986-88	4	FF	Minerva	SPS 774 SPN78(V)2		SADOC 2	Albatros	Dardo E Pegaso	76 mm/62 OTO-Melara		DE 1167		Torpedoes	
IVORY COAST														
1978	2	PTFG	Patra						40 mm 20 mm	Exocet MM 40				
JAPAN														
1958-60	7	DD	Ayanami	OPS 1 or 2 OPS 15 or 16				GFCS 57 GFCS 63	3 in/50		OQS 12	OQA 1 in 1	Hedgehog Torpedoes	4 converted to training ships
1959	3	DD	Murasame	OPS 1 OPS 15				GFCS 57 GFCS 63	5 in/54 3 in/50		SQS 29	OQA 1 in 1	Hedgehog Torpedoes Depth charges in 1	
1960	2	DD	Akizuki	OPS 1 OPS 15				GFCS 57 GFCS 63	5 in/54 3 in/50		SQS 29 (J)	OQA 1	Rocket launchers Torpedoes	

Year Built	No	Type	Class	Radar Surveillance	3-D	Data System	SAM	Gunnery Control	Gun	SSM/ASM	Sonar Hull	VDS	A/S weapons	Remarks
JAPAN cont														
1961-64	4	FF	Isuzu	OPS 1 OPS 16 ORD 1				GFCS 63	3 in/50		SQS 29 (J)	OQA 1 in 2	Torpedoes Rocket launcher Depth charges in 2	
1965	1	DDG	Amatsukaze	SPS 29A OPS 16	SPS 39		Standard MR	GFCS 63	3 in/50		SQS 23C		Asroc Hedgehog Torpedoes	
1966-78	6	DD	Yamagumo	OPS 11 & 17				GFCS 56 GFCS 63 GFCS 1 in some	3 in/50		SQS 23 or OQS 3	SQS 35 (J) in 4	Asroc Torpedoes Rocket launcher	
1967-70	4	DD	Takatsuki	OPS 11B & 17				GFCS 56 or GFCS 1	5 in/54		SQS 23 or OQS 3	SQS 35 (J) in 2	Asroc Torpedoes Rocket launcher	2 to be fitted with Harpoon SSM, Sea Sparrow SAM & TASS
1968-70	3	DD	Minegumo	OPS 11 & 17				GFCS-2	3 in/50 76 mm		OQS 3	SQS 35 (J)	Rocket launcher Torpedoes Asroc	
1970-77	11	FF	Chikugo	OPS 14, 19, & 28				GFCS 1 GFCS 51	3 in/50 40 mm		SQS 36	SQS 35 (J) in 5	Asroc Torpedoes	
1973-74	2	DDH	Haruna	OPS 17	SPS 52B		Sea Sparrow to be fitted in 1	GFCS 1	5 in/54		OQS 3		Asroc 3 helos Torpedoes	20 mm CIWS to be fitted in 1
1976-83	3	DDG	Tachikaze	OPS 11B or 28 OPS 17	SPS 52B		Standard MR	GFCS 1	5 in/54	Harpoon in one	OQS 3		Asroc Torpedoes	
1980-81	2	DDH	Shirane	OPS 28 OPS 22	OPS 12		Sea Sparrow	GFCS 1	5 in/54 CIWS in 1		OQS 101 TASS in 1	SQS 35 (J)	Asroc 3 helos Torpedoes	
1981	1	FF	Ishikari	OPS 28 & 19				FCS 2-21	76 mm	Harpoon	SQS 36D		Rocket launcher Torpedoes	
1982-87	12	DDG	Hatsuyuki	OPS 14B & 18			Sea Sparrow	FCS 2-21	76 mm CIWS in 10	Harpoon	OQS 4		Asroc Torpedoes Helo	
1983-84	2	FF	Yubari	OPS 28 & 19				FCS 2-21	76 mm CIWS to be fitted	Harpoon	SQS 36D		Bofors rocket launcher Torpedoes	
1986-88	2	DDG	Improved Sawakaze	OPS 11 & 28	OPS 12		Tartar		5 in/54 CIWS	Harpoon			Asroc Torpedoes	
1988	1	DDG	Improved Hatsuyuki	OPS 28										Similar to Hatsuyuki class
KENYA														
1974-75	4	PTFG	UK built						30 mm	Gabriel 2				
KOREA, Democratic People's Republic (North)														
?	8	PTFG	Komart	Square Tie					25 mm	SS-N-2A				
1968-83	12	PTFG	Osa 1	Square Tie				Drum Tilt	30 mm	SS-N-2A				
?	10	PTFG	Sohung	Square Tie					25 mm	SS-N-2A				Sohung is a local version of Komar
1976-79	2	FF	Najin	Skin Head Pot Head Slim Net					100 mm 57 mm 25 mm	SS-N-2A in 1 or more	Yes	Yes	A/S mortar Depth charges MBU 1800 Torpedoes	
1981 on	8	PTFG	Soju							SS-N-2				Enlarged Osa first built 1981
KOREA, Republic (South)														
1943	2	DD	Chung Mu (US Fletcher)	SPS 6 & 10					5 in/38 40 mm		SQS 20		Hedgehog Torpedoes Depth charges	
1944	1	FF	Chung Nam (US Rudderow)	SPS 5 & 6					5 in/38 40 mm		Yes		Hedgehog Torpedoes Depth charges	
1944	2	DD	Dae Gu (US Sumner)	SPS 10 & 37 or 40					5 in/38 20 mm CIWS in 1	Harpoon	SQS 29	SQA 10	Hedgehog Torpedoes Helo facility	
1944-45	6	FF	Kyong Nam (US Lawrence & Crossley)						5 in/38 40 mm				Depth charges Torpedoes	
1945-46	7	DD	Kwang-Ju (US Gearing)	SPS 10 & 40					5 in/38 CIWS in 1 40 mm in 5 30 mm in 1	Harpoon in 2	SQS 29		Hedgehog Torpedoes Helo	
1970	1	PTFG	Paek Ku 51 (US Asheville)	Raytheon 1645				GFCS 63	3 in/50 40 mm	Standard	None	None	None	
1975-78	8	PTFG	Paek Ku 52-61 (US PSMM 5)						3 in/50 40 mm	Standard or Harpoon				
1981	1	FFG	Ulsan	DA.05 ZW.06				WM 28	76 mm OTO-Melara 30 mm	Harpoon	PAS 32		Torpedoes	Built in Korea Further building programme cancelled
1986 on?	20	PTFG												Reported new programme

Year Built	No	Type	Class	Radar Surveillance	3-D	Data System	SAM	Gunnery Control	Gun	SSM/ ASM	Sonar Hull	VDS	A/S weapons	Remarks
KOREA, Republic (South) cont														
1983 on	4	Corv	HDP 1000						76 mm OTO-Melara 30 mm					7 more planned
KUWAIT														
1982-86	6	PTFG	TNC 45	Decca 1226				Philips 9LV228	76 mm OTO-Melara 40 mm	Exocet MM40				
LIBYA														
1969	1	LPD	Zeltin (Vosper built)	Triton				Vega	40 mm					Support for PTFG and others
1973	1	FF	Dat Assawari (Vosper Mk 7)	RAN 10S RAN 12L/X		IPN 10	Aspide	Argo 10 Orion 10X	4·5 in Mk 8 35 mm	Otomat	Diodon		Torpedoes	
1976-80	12	PTFG	Osa 2	Square Tie				Drum Tilt	30 mm	SS-N-2B				
1979-81	4	Corv	Assad	Selenia RAN 11X Decca TM 1226	IPN 10			Orion 10X Elsag NA10	76 mm OTO-Melara 35 mm	Otomat	Diodon		Torpedoes (A244)	Minelaying capability
1980-83	10	PTFG	La Combattante II G	Triton Castor				Vega Panda	76 mm OTO-Melara 40 mm	Otomat				
1981-84	3	Corv	Nanuchka 2				SA-N-4		57 mm	SS-N-2				1 more expected
MALAYSIA														
1971	1	FF	Rahmat (Yarrow design)	LW.02 Decca 626			Seacat/M44	M20	4·5 in Mk 5 40 mm		170B 174		Mk 10 mortar Helo facility	
1973	1	FF	Hang Tuah (UK Mermaid)	Plessey AWS-1					4 in 40 mm		170 176		Mk 10 mortar	
1972-73	4	PTFG	Perdana (La Combattante II)	Triton				Vega-Pollux	57 mm 40 mm	Exocet MM38				
1979	4	PTFG	Spica M	9GR 600 Decca				9LV 200 Mk 2	57 mm 40 mm	Exocet MM38	Simrad			4 more planned with Exocet MM40
1984	2	FF	FS1500	DA 08				WM 22	100 mm 57 mm 30 mm	Exocet MM38	ASO 84/5		Helo Bofors rocket launcher	
MEXICO														
1943	1	FF	Manuel Azueta (US Edsall)	Kelvin Hughes 14 & 17					3 in/50 40 mm		QCS-1			Training
1943	1	DD	Cuauhtemoc (US Fletcher)	SC & SG 1				GFCS 37 GFCS 51	5 in/38 40 mm				Hedgehog Depth charges	
1943-45	4	FF	Coahuila (US Lawrence & Crosley)	SC				GFCS 51	5 in/38 40 mm 20 mm					
1945	2	DD	US Gearing	SPS 10 & 6 or 12					5 in/38		SQS 23		Torpedoes Helo pad	
MOROCCO														
1976-77	2	PTFG	Okba (French PR 72)					Vega Panda	76 mm OTO-Melara 40 mm	Exocet can be fitted				
1981/82	4	PTFG	Lazaga	ZW.06				WM20 series	76 mm OTO-Melara 40 mm	Exocet MM38				
1983	1	FF	Modified Descubierta	ZW.06 DA.05		Sewaco	Aspide	WM25/41 series	76 mm OTO-Melara 40 mm	Exocet MM40	DE 1160B		Bofors rocket launcher Mk 46 torpedoes	Details uncertain
NETHERLANDS														
1967-68	6	FFG	Van Speijk	LW.03 DA.05 Kelvin Hughes navigation		Sewaco 5	Seacat/M44	M45	76 mm OTO-Melara	Harpoon	CWE 610	DDE 700	Lynx helo Mk 46 torpedoes	Similar to UK Leander but extensively modernised
1975-76	2	FFG	Tromp	Decca navigation	SPO 1	Sewaco 1	Standard NATO Sea Sparrow	WM25	4·7 in	Harpoon	CWE 610		Lynx helo Mk 46 torpedoes	
1978-83	10	FFG	Kortenaer	LW.08 ZW.06		Sewaco 2	NATO Sea Sparrow	WM25 & STIR 18	76 mm OTO-Melara 40 mm	Harpoon	SQS 505 or 509		Lynx helo Mk 46 torpedoes	40 mm guns will be replaced by 'Goalkeeper' CIWS
1990?	4	FFG	'M'		Yes	Sewaco 7	NATO Sea Sparrow	WM 25 STIR 18	76 mm OTO-Melara CIWS	Harpoon	Yes	Possible	Helo Mk 46 torpedoes	Subject to alteration
1985-6	2	FFG	J Van Heemskerck	LW.08 DA.05		Sewaco 6	Standard SM-1 NATO Sea Sparrow	STIR 18 & 24	CIWS	Harpoon	SQS 509		Mk 46 torpedoes	Command ships

Year Built	No	Type	Class	Radar Surveillance	3-D	Data System	SAM	Gunnery Control	Gun	SSM/ASM	Sonar Hull	VDS	A/S weapons	Remarks
NEW ZEALAND														
1963	1	FF	Southland (UK Leander)	994 1006			Seacat/GWS 22		40 mm		170 Graseby G750	199	Wasp helo Ikara GWS 40 Torpedoes	
1966-71	3	FF	Canterbury (UK Leander)	965 993 or 994 1006			Seacat/GWS 22		MRS 3	4·5 in Mk 6 Mod 3		170 177 M		Wasp helo Torpedoes	MRS3 to be replaced by RCA76C5 in 2 Graseby G750 sonar to be fitted in 2 in lieu of 177M
NIGERIA														
1965	1	FF	Obuma (Dutch design)	293 AWS-4					4 in 40 mm	None	Squid Helo pad			Training ship
1980	2	Corv	Erin'mi (Vosper Mk 9)	Plessey AWS 2 Decca TM 1226			Seacat	WM 24	76 mm OTO-Melara 40 mm 20 mm		Plessey PMS 26		Bofors rocket launcher	
1981	3	PTFG	Lurssen FPB-57					WM28	76 mm OTO-Melara 40 mm 30 mm	Otomat				
1982	3	PTFG	Combattante IIIB					Thomson CSF & Panda optical	76 mm OTO-Melara 40 mm 30 mm	Exocet MM38				
1982	1	FF	Aradu	AWS-5 Decca 1226			Aspide	WM25 STIR	127 mm OTO-Melara 40 mm	Otomat Mk 2	KAE80		Lynx helo Torpedoes	
NORWAY														
1965-68	19	PTFG	Storm					M26	3 in 40 mm	Penguin Mk 1			D/C rails	
1966-67	5	FF	Oslo	DRBV 22 Decca 1226			NATO Sea Sparrow	M22	3 in	Penguin Mk 1	SQS 36 Terne III		Terne Torpedoes	
1970-71	6	PTFG	Snogg					Swedish TORI	40 mm	Penguin Mk 1				Anti-ship torpedoes
1977-80	14	PTFG	Hauk					Norwegian MSI-80S	40 mm 20 mm	Penguin Mk 2				Anti-ship torpedoes
OMAN														
1973	1	PTFG	Al Mansur	Decca 1229				Sea Archer	40 mm	Exocet MM38				To be paid off
1982-84	3	PTFG	Province	AWS-4				Sea Archer or Philips 307	76 mm OTO-Melara 40 mm	Exocet MM40				
PAKISTAN														
1945-49	6	DD	Tariq (US Gearing)	SPS 10 & 40					5 in/38		SQS 23		Mk 46 torpedoes Helo facility Asroc	
1946	1	DD	Badr (UK Battle)	293				275 radar	4·5 in 40 mm				Squid	
1963	1	DDG	Babur (UK Country)	965M 992Q 978			Seacat/GWS 22	MRS3	4·5 in Mk 6 20 mm		176 177 182 192		Helo	Seaslug missile system may be removed
1981	4	PTFG	Chinese Hegu						25 mm	SS-N-2				
PERU														
1953	1	CA	Almirante Grau (Dutch De Ruyter)	LW.01 SGR 104 DA.02 ZW.01				M25 M45	6 in 57 mm/60 40 mm/70					
1953	1	CAH	Aguirre (Dutch De Zeven Provincien)	LW.01 DA.02 ZW.01				M25 M45	6 in 57 mm/60 40 mm/70				3 Sea King helos	
1953-54	2	DDG	Ferre (UK Daring)	Plessey AWS-1				TSF	4·5 in Mk 6 40 mm	Exocet			Helo pad	
1954	1	DD	Dutch Holland	LW.03 DA.02				M45	120 mm 40 mm		Signaal MF		Bofors rocket launcher Depth charges	
1956-57	7	DD	Castilla (Dutch Friesland)	LW.03 DA.05				M45	120 mm 40 mm		CWE 10-N PAE 1-N		Bofors rocket launcher Depth charges	
1979-84	3	FFG	Modified Lupo (Italian)				Aspide		127 mm OTO-Melara 40 mm	Otomat Mk 2			A/B 212 helo Torpedoes	1 more Peruvian-built building
1980-81	6	PTFG	French PR 72P	Triton Decca 1226				Vega-Castor II	76 mm OTO-Melara 40 mm 20 mm	Exocet MM38				

Year Built	No	Type	Class	Radar Surveillance	3-D	Data System	SAM	Gunnery Control	Gun	SSM/ ASM	Sonar Hull	VDS	A/S weapons	Remarks
PHILIPPINES														
1942-43	2	FF	Datu Siratuna (US Cannon)	SPS 5 SPS 6C				GFCS 52 GFCS 51	3 in/50 40 mm 20 mm		SQS 17B		Hedgehog Depth charges	
1943	1	FF	Rajah Lakandula (US Savage)	SPS 10 & 28				GFCS 63 GFCS 51	3 in/50 20 mm		SQS 31		Torpedoes Hedgehog (Mk 15) 81 mm mortar	
1943-44	4	FF	A Bonifacio (US Casco)	SPS 53 SPA 34				GFCS 52	5 in/38 40 mm 20 mm				Helo pad to be fitted	
1944-45	2	Corv	Rizal (US Auk)	SPS 5C				GFCS 52 GFCS 51	3 in/50 40 mm 20 mm		SOS-HB TAR- CAN 55 B4-A		Torpedoes Hedgehog Depth charges	
POLAND														
?	13	PTFG	Osa 1	Square Tie				Drum Tilt	30 mm	SS-N-2				
1970	1	DDG	Warszawa (USSR SAM Kotlin)	Head Net A			SA-N-1	Wasp Head/ Sun Visor B Hawk Screech	130 mm 45 mm 30 mm				MBU 6000	
PORTUGAL														
1966-68	3	FF	Da Silva (US Dealey)	MLA 1-B 978 Decca RM 316P				GFCS 63	3 in/50		SQS 30- 32A DUBA 3A	SQA 10A	Bofors rockets Torpedoes	
1967-69	4	FF	Cdte Joao Belo	DRBV 22A DRBV 50 Decca RM 316P				DRBC 31D	100 mm 40 mm		SQS 17A DUBA 3A		12 in mortar Torpedoes	To be modernised
1970-71	6	FF	Joao Coutinho	MLA 1-B Decca TM 626				GFCS 63 GFCS 51	76 mm 40 mm				Depth charges D/C throwers	Modernisation planned
1974-75	4	FF	Baptista de Andrade	AWS-2 Decca TM 626				Pollux Panda	100 mm 40 mm		Diodon		Torpedoes Depth charges	
1986?	3	FF	Kortenaer	DA.05 LW.08 ZW.06		Sewaco	NATO Sea Sparrow	WM 25	76 mm OTO- Melara	Harpoon	SQS 505		Lynx helo Torpedoes	Programme & equipment details to be confirmed
QATAR														
1982-83	3	PTFG	La Combattante III M	Triton				Castor Naja	76 mm OTO- Melara 40 mm 30 mm	Exocet MM40				
ROMANIA														
1964	6	PTFG	Osa 1	Square Tie				Drum Tilt	30 mm	SS-N-2				
1984?	2	DD							76 mm					Approx 4500 ton
1983 on	3	FF							30 mm					
SAUDI ARABIA														
1980-82	9	PTFG	Al Siddiq (US design)	SPS 55 SPS 40B				Mk 92	76 mm OTO- Melara 20 mm CIWS	Harpoon				
1980-83	4	Corv	Badr (US design)	SPS 55 SPS 40B				Mk 92	76 mm OTO- Melara CIWS	Harpoon		SQS 56	Torpedoes	
1984 on	4	FF	F 2000	DRBV 15 Decca 1226		Senit 6	Crotale	Castor II Naja	100 mm 40 mm	Otomat Mk 2 AS 15TT	Diodon TSM 2630	Sorel	Helo F17P & Mk 46 Torpedoes	
SINGAPORE														
1972-75	6	PTFG	Sea Wolf (TNC 45)					WM28	57 mm 40 mm	Gabriel				
SOMALIA														
1975-76	2	PTFG	Osa 2	Square Tie				Drum Tilt	30 mm	SS-N-2				Probably deteriorating since Soviet expulsion
SOUTH AFRICA														
1964	1	FF	President (UK type 12)	Jupiter 293				Elsag NA9C	4·5 in Mk 6 40 mm				Wasp helo Mk 10 mortar Torpedoes	
1977-83	9	PTFG	Minister						76 mm OTO- Melara 20 mm	Skorpioen (Scorpion)				Similar to Israeli Saar 4 class 12 planned. Some in reserve
SPAIN														
1942-44	4	DD	D20 (US Fletcher)	SPS 6C & 10 Raytheon				GFCS 37 GFCS 56 GFCS 63	5 in/38 3 in/50 or 40 mm & 20 mm		SQS 29, 30A, 31, 32		Hedgehog Torpedoes Depth charges	
1943	1	CVS	Dedalo (US Cabot)	SPS 6, 10 & 40A Raytheon				Mk 51 57 & 63	40 mm				20 helos	Modernised 1967 Carries V/STOL & helos
1945	5	DD	D 60 (US Gearing)	SPS 10 & 40 or 37 Raytheon				GFCS 37	5 in/38		SQS 23		Asroc Torpedoes Hughes helo	

Year Built	No	Type	Class	Radar Surveillance	3-D	Data System	SAM	Gunnery Control	Gun	SSM/ ASM	Sonar Hull	VDS	A/S weapons	Remarks
SPAIN cont														
1970	1	DD	Marqués de la Ensenada	SPS 10 & 40 Decca RM 426				GFCS 37 GFCS 56	5 in/38		SQS 32	SQA 10	Helo Torpedoes	
1973-76	5	FFG	Baleares (F-70)	SPS 10 Raytheon	SPS 52A		Standard/ MFCS 74	GFCS 68	5 in/54 Meroka to be fitted	Harpoon	SQS 23	SQS 35V	Asroc Mk 37, 44 & 46 torpedoes	
1975-77	6	PTFG	Lazaga (P-00)	WM-22 Raytheon				WM22 CSEE optical	76 mm OTO-Melara 40 mm	Harpoon to be fitted			Provision for torpedoes & depth charges	Primarily for fishery protection
1976-77	6	PTF	Barcelo (P-10)	Raytheon				CSEE optical	40 mm 20 mm	SSM can be fitted				
1978-82	6	FFG	Descubierta	ZW.06 DA.05/01			Aspide	WM25	76 mm OTO-Melara 40 mm/70	Harpoon to be fitted	Raytheon 1160B	To be fitted	Bofors rocket launcher Mk 44 & 46 torpedoes	
1985-86	3	FFG	F90	SPS 55 SPS 49 RAN 12L			Standard	Mk 92	76 mm Meroka	Harpoon	SQS 56 & TACTAS		Mk 46 torpedoes 2 LAMPS III helos	
1984	1	CVS	P de Asturias	SPS 55 SPN 35A RAN 12L	SPS 52C			VPS-2	Meroka				Helos	To replace Dedalo & carry V/STOL & helos
SWEDEN														
1955-56	2	DD	Halland	Saturne LW.02				WM 20 Philips 9LV 200	120 mm 57 mm 40 mm	RB 08A			Bofors rockets	Non-operational Minelaying capability
1978-82	16	PTFG	Hugin	Skanter 009				Philips 9LV 200 Mk 2	57 mm Bofors	Penguin Mk 2	Simrad SQ 3D/SF			Minelaying capability
1973-76	12	PTFG	Spica 2	Sea Giraffe				Philips 9LV 200	57 mm	RBS 15				Wire-guided torpedoes
1984	2	PTFG	Stockholm	Sea Giraffe				Philips 9LV 200	57 mm 40 mm	RBS 15		Yes		Developed from Spica 2 Minelaying capability
1986 on?	6	PTFG	Göteborg						57 mm 40 mm	RBS 15			Torpedoes	Minelaying capability. Replacements for Spica 1
SYRIA														
1963-66	6	PTFG	Komar	Square Tie					25 mm	SS-N-2				
1966-82	14	PTFG	Osa 1 & 2	Square Tie				Drum Tilt	30 mm	SS-N-2				Some older boats due for disposal
1975	2	FF	USSR Petya 1	Slim Net Don 2				Hawk Screech	76 mm		Yes		RBU 6000 Torpedoes Depth charges	Minelaying capability
TAIWAN														
1943	4	DD	Kun Yang (US Fletcher)	SPS 6C & 10 or 10F			Sea Chaparral	GFCS 37 GFCS 25	5 in/38 3 in/50 40 mm or 20 mm		SQS 40, 41 or 50		Torpedoes Hedgehog Depth charges	Gun armament & A/S weapons vary between ships
1943-45	9	FF	Tien Shan (US Lawrence & Crosley)	SPS 5 in most Decca 707 also in some				GFCS 26 in most	5 in/38 40 mm 20 mm				Torpedoes or Hedgehog Depth charges	Converted to high speed transports
1944	1	FF	Tai Yuan (US Rudderow)	SPSC 6C & 5D					5 in/38 40 mm 20 mm				Torpedoes Hedgehog Depth charges	
1944-45	8	DD	Po Yang (US Sumner)	SPS 10 with SPS 6, 29 or 37				GFCS 37 GFCS 25 GFCS 51	5 in/38 40 mm	Hsiung Feng in 3	SQS 29	SQA 10 in 2	Helo in 2 Torpedoes Hedgehog Depth charges in some	
1945	1	DD	Fu Yang (US Gearing)	SPS 10 & 37				GFCS 25 GFCS 37	5 in/38 40 mm	Hsiung Feng	SQS 29	SQA 10	Torpedoes Hedgehog	
1945-47	13	DD	Kai Yang (US Gearing)	SPS 6, 10, 37, 29 or 40					5 in/38 40 mm	Hsiung Feng 2	SQS 23 or 29		Helo Torpedoes Asroc in 11 Hedgehog Mk 15 in 1	Possibly only 10 operational
1979-83	2	PTFG	Lung Chiang (US PSSM Mk 5)	Selenia RAN 11L/X		IPN 10		Elsag NA 10	76 mm OTO-Melara 30 mm	Hsiung Feng				
1980 on	34	PTFG	Hai Ou						20 mm	Hsiung Feng				Taiwan design of 47 tons In series production
THAILAND														
1943-44	2	FF	Prasae (US Tacoma)	SPS 5 or 10 SPS 6				GFCS 51	3 in/50 40 mm 20 mm		QCU		Torpedoes Depth charges	
1944	1	FF	Pin Klao (US Cannon)	SPS 5 & SC 2				GFCS 52 GFCS 63	3 in/50 40 mm		SQS 42(V)		Torpedoes Depth charges	
1971-74	2	FF	Tapi (US built)	SPS 6		HSA system		GFCS 63	76 mm 40 mm		SQS 179/A		Torpedoes Hedgehog	

Year Built	No	Type	Class	Radar Surveillance	3-D	Data System	SAM	Gunnery Control	Gun	SSM/ ASM	Sonar Hull	VDS	A/S weapons	Remarks
THAILAND con:														
1973	1	FF	Makut Rajakumarn (UK Yarrow design)	LW.04 Decca 626		HSA system	Seacat/M44	WM22	4·5 in Mk 8 40 mm		UK 170B Plessey MS 27 162		Mk 10 mortar Depth charges	
1976-77	3	PTFG	Prabparapak (TNC 45)			HSA system		WM20 series	57 mm 40 mm	Gabriel				
1979-80	3	PTFG	Ratcharit			HSA system		WM20 series	76 mm OTO-Melara 40 mm	Exocet MM 38				
1986-87	2	Corv					Aspide	WM 25	76 mm OTO-Melara 40 mm 20 mm	Harpoon	KAE			Ordered from USA 1983
TUNISIA														
1943	1	FF	P Bourguiba (US Savage)	SPS 10 & 29				GFCS 51 GFCS 63	3 in/50 20 mm		SQS 29		Torpedoes	
1984	3	PTFG	Combattante III M	Sylosat				Naja	76 mm OTO-Melara 40 mm 30 mm	Exocet MM 40				
TURKEY														
1944	1	DD	Muavenet	SPS 6 & 10				GFCS 37	5 in/38 40 mm 20 mm		QCU or QHB			Minelayer Received from US 1971
1945	2	DD	US Carpenter	SPS 10 & 40				GFCS 37	5 in/38		SQS 23		Asroc Torpedoes	Received 1981-82
1945	1	DD	US Sumner	SPS 10 & 29				GFCS 37 GFCS 51	5 in/38 76 mm OTO-Melara 40 mm		SQS 29		Hedgehog Torpedoes	Purchased 1972
1945-46	7	DD	US Gearing (FRAM 1)	SPS 10 & 37/40				GFCS 37	5 in/38 35 mm		SQS 23		Asroc Torpedoes	3 received 1972-73 4 received 1980-82
1945-47	2	DD	US Gearing (FRAM 2)	SPS 6 & 10				GFCS 37	5 in/38 40 mm 35 mm		SQS 29		Hedgehog Torpedoes	Received 1972-74
1961-62	2	FF	German Köln	DA.02				M45	100 mm 40 mm		PAE/CWE		Torpedoes D/C mortars Depth charges	Transferred from Federal Republic of Germany 1983
1967-68	9	PTFG	Kartal	Decca TM 1626				OGR7/2 Galileo	40 mm	Penguin 2			Torpedoes	
1972-75	2	FF	Berk	SPS 10 & 40				GFCS 63	3 in		SQS 29		Torpedoes Depth charges	
1977-83	5	PTFG	Dogan	WM28 Decca TM 1226				WM28	76 mm OTO-Melara 35 mm	Harpoon				
1984 on	4	FF	Meko 200			Serwaco	Aspide	WM 28	5 in CIWS	Harpoon			Torpedoes	Contract signed 1982. Two to be built in Turkey
UNION OF SOVIET SOCIALIST REPUBLICS														
1950 on	9	DD	Skory	Slim Net Don 2				Hawk Screech Top Bow	130 mm 86 mm 57 mm 37 mm 25 mm				Depth charges RBU and torpedoes	10 more in reserve. Many variations between ships Minelaying capabilities
1952-56	9	CA	Sverdlov	Various				Top Bow Egg Cup Sun Visor Drum Tilt in 3	152 mm 100 mm 37 mm 30 mm					Minelaying capability
1952-56	1	CG	Sverdlov	Big Net Slim Net Low Sieve Neptun			SA-N-2	Top Bow Egg Cup Sun Visor	152 mm 100 mm 37 mm					Minelaying capability
1952-56	2	CA	Sverdlov	Top Trough Low Sieve Neptun			SA-N-4	Top Bow Egg Cup Sun Visor Drum Tilt	152 mm 100 mm 37 mm 30 mm				Helo pad	
1952-59	47	FF	Riga	Slim Net Don 2 or Neptun				Sun Visor B Wasp head	100 mm 37 mm 25 mm in some		Yes		RBU 2500 Depth charges	Minelaying capability. About 10 in reserve
1954-56	15	DD	Kotlin	Slim Net Don or Neptun				Sun Visor Egg Cup Hawk Screech	130 mm 45 mm or 25 mm		Yes	In 1	RBU 6000 or RBU 2500 & 6000 Torpedoes Depth charges	Minelaying capability. Some variations between ships 3 more in reserve
1957-58	4	DDG	Kildin	Don 2		Head Net C or Strut Pair		Owl Screech Hawk Screech	76 mm 57 mm 45 mm	SS-N-2C in 3 or SS-N-1 in 1	Yes		RBU 2500 Torpedoes	1 has older radars

Year Built	No	Type	Class	Radar Surveillance	Radar 3-D	Data System	SAM	Gunnery Control	Gunnery Gun	SSM/ ASM	Sonar Hull	Sonar VDS	A/S weapons	Remarks
USSR cont														
1957-62	8	DDG	Kanin	Don Kay	Head Net C		SA-N-1	Hawk Screech Drum Tilt	57 mm 30 mm		Yes		Helo pad RBU 6000 Torpedoes	Krupny conversions made 1968-78
1959 on	65	PTFG	Osa 1	Square Tie			SA-N-5 in some	Drum Tilt	30 mm	SS-N-2B				
1961-72	41	FF	Petya 1 & 2	Strut Curve or Slim Net Neptun or Don 2				Hawk Screech	76 mm		Yes	In some	RBU 2500 or 6000 Torpedoes Depth charges	Minelaying capability in 30
1961-72	8	DDG	Sam Kotlin	Don Kay or Don 2	Head Net C or A		SA-N-1	Sun Visor Hawk Screech Drum Tilt in 4	130 mm 45 mm 30 mm in 4		Hercules?		RBU 6000 or 2500 Torpedoes	
1962-70	12	DDG	Kashin	Big Net	Head Net C or A		SA-N-1	Owl Screech	76 mm		Yes		RBU 6000 RBU 1000 Torpedoes	
1962-70	6	DDG	Modified Kashin	Big Net Don Kay or Don 2	Head Net C		SA-N-1	Owl Screech Bass Tilt	76 mm CIWS	SS-N-2C	Yes	Yes	RBU 6000 Torpedoes Helo pad	1 with new SAM and no SSM
1962-70	1	DDG	Modified Kashin	Don Kay	Top Steer Head Net C		SA-N-7	Owl Screech	76 mm				RBU 6000 Torpedoes	Trials ship for SA-N-7
1962-65	4	CG	Kynda	Head Net A Don 2	Head Net C in 2		SA-N-1	Owl Screech Bass Tilt	76 mm CIWS	SS-N-3B	Tamir/ Hercules		RBU 6000 Torpedoes Helo pad	
1967-68	2	CAH	Moskva	Don 2	Top Sail Head Net C		SA-N-3	Muff Cob	57 mm		Yes	Yes	14 Hormone A helos SUW-N-1 launcher for FRAS-1 missiles RBU 6000	
1964-67	18	FF	Mirka 1 & 2	Slim Net in some Strut Curve Don 2				Hawk Screech	76 mm		Yes	In some	RBU 6000 Torpedoes Depth charges in some	
1967-69	4	CG	Kresta 1	Big Net Plinth Net Don Kay	Head Net C		SA-N-1	Muff Cob Bass Tilt in 1	57 mm CIWS in 1	SS-N-3B	Yes		RBU 6000 RBU 1000 Torpedoes	Has Hormone B helo for missile guidance
1969-77	10	CG	Krestal II	Don Kay	Top Sail Head Net C		SA-N-3	Muff Cob Bass Tilt	57 mm CIWS		Yes		Hormone A helo SS-N-14 Torpedoes RBU 6000 RBU 1000	
1969 on	40	PTFG	Osa II	Square Tie			SA-N-5 in some	Drum Tilt	30 mm	SS-N-2B				
1969 on	17	Corv	Nanuchka 1	Band Stand Peel Pair Spar Stump Don			SA-N-4	Muff Cob	57 mm	SS-N-9				
1970 on	15	FF	Grisha 1	Strut Curve Don 2			SA-N-4	Muff Cob	57 mm		Yes	Yes	Torpedoes RBU 6000 Depth charges	Minelaying capability
????	8	FF	Grisha 2	Strut Curve Don 2				Muff Cob	57 mm		Yes	Yes	Torpedoes RBU 6000 Depth charges	Minelaying capability KGB ships
????	32	FF	Grisha 3	Strut Curve Don 2			SA-N-4	Bass Tilt	57 mm CIWS		Yes	Yes	Torpedoes RBU 6000 Depth charges	Minelaying capability Continuing programme
1970 on	21	FFG	Krivak 1	Don Kay or Palm Frond	Head Net C		SA-N-4	Owl Screech	76 mm		Yes	Yes	SS-N-14 RBU 6000 Torpedoes	Minelaying capability
1971-79	7	CG	Kara	Don 2 Don Kay	Top Sail Head Net C		SA-N-4 SA-N-3	Owl Screech Bass Tilt	76 mm CIWS		Yes	Yes	Hormone A helo SS-N-14 Torpedoes RBU 6000 RBU 1000	
1975	1	PHM	Sarancha	Band Stand			SA-N-4	Bass Tilt	CIWS	SS-N-9				Probably R&D vessel
1975-84	4	CV	Kiev	Top Steer Don 2 Don Kay or Palm Frond	Top Sail		SA-N-4	Owl Bass Tilt	76 mm	SS-N-12	Yes	Yes	RBU 6000 helos SUW-N-1 launcher for FRAS-1 missiles Torpedoes	
1976 on	11	FFG	Krivak II	Don Kay or Palm Frond	Head Net C		SA-N-4	Kite Screech	100 mm		Yes	Yes	SS-N-14 RBU 6000 Torpedoes	Minelaying capability
1976	1	FF	Koni	Strut Curve Don 2			SA-N-4	Owl Screech Drum Tilt	76 mm 30 mm		Yes		RBU 6000 Depth charges	Minelaying capability
1977	1	AOE	Berezina	Strut Curve			SA-N-4	Muff Cob Bass Tilt	57 mm CIWS		Yes		2 Hormone 'A' helos RBU 1000	

Year Built	No	Type	Class	Radar Surveillance	3-D	Data System	SAM	Gunnery Control	Gun	SSM/ ASM	Sonar Hull	VDS	A/S weapons	Remarks
USSR cont														
1978 on	8	Corv	Tarantul I & 2	Band Stand in some Lightbulb or Plank Shave Spin Trough		SA-N-5	Bass Tilt	76 mm CIWS	SS-N-2C or SS-N-22					
1978-82	2	LSD	Ivan Rogov	Don Kay	Head Net C		SA-N-4 SA-N-5 in 1	Owl Screech Bass Tilt	76 mm CIWS BM-21 rocket launcher					
1978 on	7	Corv	Nanuchka III	Band Stand Peel Pair Spar Stump Don			SA-N-4	Bass Tilt	76 mm CIWS	SS-N-9				
1978 on	16	PHM	Matka	Plank Shave				Bass Tilt	76 mm CIWS	SS-N-2C				
1980-87	7	CG	Sovremenny	Top Steer Palm Frond			SA-N-7	Kite Screech Bass Tilt	130 mm CIWS	SS-N-22	Yes		Helix helo RBU 1000 Torpedoes	Minelaying capability
1980-83	2	CGN	Kirov	Top Steer Palm Frond	Top Pair		SA-N-4 or 7 SA-N-6	Kite Screech Bass Tilt	130 mm or 100 mm CIWS	SS-N-19	Yes	Yes	Helos SS-N-14 Torpedoes RBU 6000 RBU 1000 in 1	1 more building
1980-85	8	CG	Udaloy	Strut Pair Palm Frond			SA-N-8	Kite Screech Bass Tilt	100 mm CIWS		Yes	Yes	SS-N-14 2 Helix helos RBU 6000	
1983-85	3	CG	Slava	Top Steer Palm Frond	Top Pair		SA-N-6 SA-N-4? SA-N-7?	Kite Screech Bass Tilt	130 mm CIWS	SS-N-12	Yes	Yes	Helo Torpedoes RBU 600	
1988?	1	CVN												
UNITED ARAB EMIRATES														
1980-81	6	PTFG	Lurssen TNC 45	Decca navigation				Philips 9LV Mk 2 Panda	76 mm OTO-Melara 40 mm	Exocet MM40				
UNITED KINGDOM														
1959	1	CV	Hermes	965, 993, 1006		CAAIS DBA3	Seacat/GWS 22					184		5 Sea Harriers & 9 Sea King, or equivalent	Alternative role as commando carrier LPH. To be disposed of
1960-61	8	FF	Rothesay (modified Type 12)	994, 978			Seacat/GWS 20	MRS 3	4·5 in Mk 6 20 mm in some		170 177		Mk 10 mortar Wasp helo	1 as trials ship with new sonar
1966	2	DDG	County	965M, 992Q, 978 or 1006		ADAWS 1	Seaslug Mk 2 Seacat/GWS 22	MRS 3	4·5 in Mk 6 30 mm 20 mm	Exocet MM38	176, 177, 182, 192		Lynx helo Torpedoes	
1963-65	7	FF	Leander	994, 1006		ADAWS 5	Seacat/GWS 22		40 mm		170 184	199	Ikara GWS 40 Mk 10 mortar Lynx or Wasp helo	
1963-67	8	FFG	Leander	965, 994, 1006		CAAIS	Seacat/GWS 22		40 mm 20 mm	Exocet MM38	184 2024 in some		Torpedoes Lynx or Wasp helo	
1965-67	2	LPD	Fearless	994, 978		CAAIS	Seacat/GWS 20		40 mm					
1968-73	9	FFG	Leander (Broad beam)	965, 994 1006		CAAIS	Sea Wolf/GWS 25 Seacat		4·5 in Mk 6 20 mm	Exocet MM38	2016		Mk 10 mortar or torpedoes Lynx or Wasp helo	Being converted to armament shown
1973	1	DDG	Bristol (Type 82)	965, 992Q, 1006		ADAWS 2	Sea Dart/GWS 30	GSA 1	4·5 in Mk 8 30 mm 20 mm		162, 170 182, 184 185, 189		Ikara GWS 40 Wasp helo pad	
1974-78	6	FFG	Amazon (Type 21)	992Q, 978		CAAIS	Seacat/GWS 24	WSA-4	4·5 in Mk 8 20 mm	Exocet MM38 Sea Skua	184M 162M		Lynx or Wasp helo Mk 46 torpedoes	
1976-84	12	DDG	Sheffield (Type 42)	965R or 1022 1006 992Q or R		ADAWS 4 or 7	Sea Dart/GWS 30	GSA 1	4·5 in Mk 8 30 mm 20 mm	Sea Skua	184M 162M		Lynx helo Torpedoes	
1979-88	12	FFG	Broadsword (Type 22)	967, 968 1006		CAAIS	Sea Wolf/GWS 25		40 mm 20 mm	Exocet MM38 Sea Skua	2016 2008 2031 in some		Torpedoes 2 Lynx helos	Continuing programme. Last 2 to have 4·5 in gun & Harpoon 5SM
1980-84	3	CV	Invincible	1022, 992R 1006		ADAWS 6	Sea Dart/GWS 30		CIWS		2016		9 Sea King helos & 5 Harriers	
1988 on?		FFG	Type 23	996			Sea Wolf		4·5 in Mk 8 CIWS	Harpoon	2016 2031		Lynx helo Torpedoes	

Year Built	No	Type	Class	Radar Surveillance	3-D	Data System	SAM	Gunnery Control	Gun	SSM/ ASM	Sonar Hull	VDS	A/S weapons	Remarks
UNITED STATES OF AMERICA														
	1	AVM	Norton sound	SPS 40	SPY 1	AEGIS	Standard MR							Weapons test ship
1943-50	4	CV	Hancock	SPS 10, 43 & 12 or 30 SPN 10				GFCS 37 GFCS 56	5 in/38 Mk 24 in 3					In reserve
1943-44	2	CV	Essex (modernised)	SPS 10, 30, 43				GFCS 37 GFCS 56	5 in/38 Mk 24		SQS 23		Sea King helo and A/S aircraft	In reserve
1943-44	4	BB	Iowa	SPS 67 & 49				GFCS 37 GFCS 38	16 in/50 5 in/38 Mk 28 CIWS	Tomahawk Harpoon				Fire support ships
1945-46	7	DD	Gearing (Fram I)	SPS 10 & 37 or 40				GFCS 37	5 in/38 Mk 38		SQS 23		Asroc Torpedoes	
1945-47	2	CV	Midway	SPS 10, 30, 43 SPS 49 SPN 41-44	SPS 48	NTDS	Mk 25 Sea Sparrow BPDMS to be fitted in 1		CIWS					
1945-46	2	CG	Albany	SPS 10, 30, 43	SPS 48 or 52	NTDS in 1	Standard MR MFCS 74	GFCS 56	5 in/38 Mk 24		SQS 23		Asroc Torpedoes Helo facility	In reserve
1948-49	2	CA	Des Moines	SPS 6, 8, 10, & 37 in 1				GFCS 37 GFCS 56 GFCS 63 GFCS 39	8 in/55 5 in/38 Mk 32 3 in/50 Mk 33 in 2					In reserve
1955-59	4	CV	Forrestal	SPS 37, 43 SPN 41-43	SPS 48	NTDS	Mk 25 or 29 Sea Sparrow BPDMS		CIWS planned		None	None	A/S aircraft	Varying radar fit
1955-59	14	DD	Forrest Sherman	SPS 10 & 37 or 40				GFCS 56 GFCS 68	5 in/54 Mk 42		SQS 23	In 8	Asroc in 8 Torpedoes	Transferred to inactive fleet
1956-59	4	DDG	Forrest Sherman (Conversion)	SPS 10	SPS 48		Tartar/ MFCS 74	GFCS 68	5 in/54 Mk 42		SQS 23		Asroc Torpedoes	Transferred to inactive fleet
1959-61	10	DDG	Coontz	SPS 10 & 29 or 49	SPS 48	NTDS	Standard ER/ MFCS 76	GFCS 68	5 in/54 Mk 42	Harpoon	SQS 23		Asroc Torpedoes Helo pad	
1960-64	23	DDG	Charles Adams	SPS 10 & 40	SPS 39	SAMID in 1	Tartar/MFCS 76	GFCS 68 (GFCS 86 to be fitted)	5 in/54 Mk 42	Harpoon	SQS 23		Asroc Torpedoes	
1961	1	CVN	Enterprise	SPS 10 & 49, SPN 10, 41-44	SPS 48C	NTDS	Mk 57 Sea Sparrow BPMDS		20 mm CIWS		None	None		
1961	1	CGN	Long Beach	SPS 10 & 49B	SPS 48	NTDS	Standard ER/ MFCS 76	GFCS 56	5 in/38 Mk 30 CIWS	Harpoon	SQS 23		Asroc Torpedoes Utility helo	
1961	2	CV	Kitty Hawk	SPS 10 & 49 SPN 41-44	SPS 48	NTDS	Terrier HT/MFCS 91 or Mk 29 Sea Sparrow BPDMS		CIWS		None	None	A/S aircraft & Sea King helos	Terrier to be replaced by Sea Sparrow
1961-70	7	LPH	Iwo Jima	SPS 10 & 40 SPN 6 & 35 SPS 58			Mk 25 Sea Sparrow		3 in/50 Mk 33 CIWS to be fitted		None	None		
1962	1	CGN	Bainbridge	SPS 10 & 37	SPS 48A	NTDS	Standard ER/ MFCS 76		20 mm	Harpoon	SQS 23		Asroc Torpedoes Helo facility	
1962-64	9	CG	Leahy	SPS 10 & 49	SPS 48C	NTDS	Standard ER/ MFCS 76		CIWS	Harpoon	SQS 23		Asroc Torpedoes	
1963	2	FF	Bronstein	SPS 10B & 40D				GFCS 56	3 in/50 Mk 33		SQS 26 TASS		Asroc Torpedoes Helo facility	
1964-67	9	CG	Belknap	SPS 10 & 49 or 40 or 43	SPS 48	NTDS	Standard ER/ MFCS 76	GFCS 68	5 in/54 Mk 42 3 in/50 CIWS	Harpoon	SQS 26		Asroc Torpedoes LAMPS I helo	
1964-68	10	FF	Garcia	SPS 10C & 40D		Modified ASW/ NTDS in 2		GFCS 56	5 in/38 Mk 30		SQS 26 AXR or SQS 26BX		Asroc Torpedoes LAMPS I helo	
1965	1	FF	Glover	SPS 10 & 40				GFCS 56	5 in/38 Mk 30		SQS 26 AXR SQR 13	SQS 35	Asroc Torpedoes Helo facility	
1965	1	CV	America	SPS 10F & 49 SPN 35, 41 42, 43 & 44	SPS 48C	NTDS	Sea Sparrow in Mk 29 launcher		CIWS				A/S aircraft & Sea King helos	
1966-67	6	FFG	Brooke	SPS 10F	SPS 52A		Tartar/MFCS 74 or Standard MR	GFCS 56	5 in/38		SQS 26 AX SQS 56 in 1		Asroc Torpedoes LAMPS I helo	
1967	1	CGN	Truxtun	SPS 10F & 40D	SPS 48C	NTDS	Standard ER/ MFCS 76	GFCS 68	5 in/54 Mk 42 3 in/50 CIWS planned	Harpoon	SQS 26 SQS 54		Asroc Torpedoes Helo facility	

Year Built	No	Type	Class	Radar Surveillance	3-D	Data System	SAM	Gunnery Control	Gun	SSM/ASM	Sonar Hull	VDS	A/S weapons	Remarks
USA cont														
1968	1	CV	John F Kennedy	SPS 10F, 49 & 65 SPN 41-44	SPS 48	NTDS	Sea Sparrow & Mk 29 launcher		CIWS				A/S aircraft & Sea King helos	
1969-74	46	FF	Knox	SPS 10F & 40 B, C or D			Mk 25 Sea Sparrow BPDMS in 31 NATO Sea Sparrow in 1	GFCS 68	5 in/54 Mk 42 CIWS planned	Harpoon	SQS 26CX SQR 18A TACTAS to be fitted in most	SQS 35 in 19 ships	Asroc Torpedoes LAMPS I helo	
1970-71	2	LCC	Blue Ridge	SPS 10F & 40C	SPS 48C	NTDS ACIS NIPS	Mk 25 Sea Sparrow	GFCS 56	3 in/50 Mk 33				Utility helo facility	
1974-75	2	CGN	California	SPS 10F & 40D	SPS 48C	NTDS	Standard MR/ MFCS 74	GFCS 86	5 in/54 Mk 45 CIWS planned	Harpoon	SQS 26CX		Helo facility Asroc Torpedoes	
1975-87	5	CVN	Nimitz	SPS 10F, 43A SPN 41, 42, 43 & 44	SPS 48C	NTDS	Mk 29 Sea Sparrow		CIWS		None	None	A/S aircraft	
1975-83	31	DD	Spruance	SPS 40B & 55		NTDS	Mk 29 Sea Sparrow	GFCS 86	5 in/54 Mk 45 CIWS in some	Harpoon Tomahawk to be fitted	SQS 53		Asroc Torpedoes 2 LAMPS I helos or 1 Sea King SH-3	
1976-80	5	LHA	Tarawa	SPS 10F & 40B SPN 35	SPS 52	ITAWDS	Mk 25 Sea Sparrow until CIWS fitted	GFCS 86	5 in/54 Mk 45 20 mm CIWS planned					
1976-80	4	CGN	Virginia	SPS 40B & 55	SPS 48C	NTDS	Standard MR/ MFCS 74 Mk 26 launcher	GFCS 86	5 in/54 Mk 45 CIWS planned	Harpoon	SQS 53A		Helo Asroc Torpedoes	
1977-82	6	PHM	Pegasus	SPS-63				GFCS 92 Mod 1	76 mm OTO-Melara	Harpoon				
1977-86	46	FFG	Perry	SPS 49 & 55		NTDS	Standard MR	GFCS 92 Mod 2	76 mm/62 OTO-Melara CIWS planned and some fitted	Harpoon	SQS 56 SQR 19 TACTAS to be fitted	SQR 15	2 LAMPS I helos Torpedoes	Total of 54 planned
1981	4	DDG	Kidd	SPS 55	SPS 48		Standard ER/ MFCS 74	GFCS 86	5 in/54 CIWS		SQS 53 SQR 19 TACTAS to be fitted		Asroc Torpedoes	Originally ordered by Iran
1983	20+	CG	Ticonderoga (CG-47)	SPS 49	SPY 1A	AEGIS	Standard MR	GFCS 86	5 in/54 CIWS	Harpoon Tomahawk in sixth & subsequent ships	TACTAS to be fitted SQS 53		Asroc Torpedoes 2 LAMPS III helos	Continuing programme
1989 on?	?	DDG	Arleigh Burke (DDG-51)	SPY ID	SPY 1A Aegis		Standard MR	Mk 160 Mod 4	5 in/54 CIWS	Harpoon Tomahawk	SQS 53 TACTAS		VL Asroc Mk 46 torpedoes	
URUGUAY														
1943	2	FF	Uruguay (US Cannon)	SPS 6C & 5					3 in/50 40 mm				Hedgehog Depth charges	
1954	1	FF	18 de Julio (US Dealey)	SPS 6E & 5D				GFCS 63	3 in/50				Torpedoes	
VENEZUELA														
1956	2	FF	Almirante Clemente	Plessey AWS-1 Decca 629				Elsag 6 NA10 Mod 0	76 mm OTO-Melara 40 mm		SQS 17B		Depth charges Hedgehog	
1975	3	PTFG	Constitucion (Vosper design)	SPQ 2D					40 mm	Otomat Mk 2				
1974-75	3	PTF	Constitucion (Vosper design)	SPQ 2D				Elsag NA 10 Mod 1 Selenia radar	76 mm OTO-Melara					
1980-82	6	FFG	Italian Lupo	Selenia MM/SPS 74 SMA/SPQ 2F			Aspide	Elsag Mk 10 Mod 0	127 mm OTO-Melara 40 mm	Otomat Mk 2	SQS 29		Torpedoes A/B 212 helo	
VIET-NAM														
1943	1	FF	US Barnegat						5 in/38					Status uncertain
1944	1	FF	US Savage	SPS 10 & 28					3 in/50	SS-N-2 may be fitted			Torpedoes Hedgehog Depth charges	Status uncertain
1977-81	4	FF	USSR Petya	Slim Net Don 2				Hawk Screech	76 mm		Yes		RBU 6000 Torpedoes Depth charges	Minelaying capability
1979-81	8	PTFG	OSA 2	Square Tie				Drum Tilt	30 mm	SS-N-2				

Year Built	No	Type	Class	Radar Surveillance	3-D	Data System	SAM	Gunnery Control	Gun	SSM/ASM	Sonar Hull	VDS	A/S weapons	Remarks
YEMEN, Arab Republic (North)														
1982	2	PTFG	Osa 2	Square Tie					30 mm	SS-N-2				
YEMEN, People's Democratic Republic (South)														
1979-83	8	PTFG	Osa 1	Square Tie				Drum Tilt	30 mm	SS-N-2				
YUGOSLAVIA														
1965-69	10	PTFG	Osa 1	Square Tie				Drum Tilt	30 mm	SS-N-2A				
1977-80	6	PTFG	Koncar (Spica)	Philips TAB				9LV 200	57 mm	SS-N-2B				Built in Yugoslavia
1980-82	2	FF	USSR Koni	Strut Curve			SA-N-4	Owl Screech Drum Tilt Muff Cob	76 mm 30 mm	SS-N-2B	Yes		RBU 6000	Minelaying capability
?	10	PTFG												Reported planned no details available

Submarines

Year Built	No	Type	Class	Displacement (imperial tons) Surf	Dived	Armament	Sonar	Radar	Miscellaneous	Remarks
ALBANIA										
1959 or earlier	3	SS	USSR Whiskey	1080	1350	4 × 21 in bow torpedoes 2 × 16 in stern torpedoes or mines		Snoop Plate		Only 2 operational
ARGENTINA										
1974	2	SS	Salta (Type 209)	1185	1285	8 × 21 in bow torpedoes				
1983 on	6	SS	TR 1700	2100	2300	6 × 21 in bow torpedoes	Active & passive	Periscopic		Some to be built in Argentina
AUSTRALIA										
1967-78	6	SS	Oxley (UK Oberon)	2030	2410	8 × 21 in torpedoes bow & stern (Mark 48) Harpoon	AN/BQG Micropuffs Krupp-Atlas CSU 3-41 2007	1006		Being modernised to fit shown. Harpoon to be added in 1985
BRAZIL										
1945-46	2	SS	Guppy II (US built)		2420	10 × 21 in torpedoes bow & stern				
1946	2	SS	Guppy III (US built)		2450	10 × 21 in torpedoes bow & stern	BQR-2 array BQG-4 (PUFFS)			
1973-77	3	SS	Humaita (UK Oberon)	2030	2410	8 × 21 in torpedoes bow & stern	187 2007	1006		
1985?	3	SS	Type 209	1260	1440	8 × 21 in bow torpedoes	Krupp-Atlas CS 483/1			
BULGARIA										
1972-73	2	SS	USSR Romeo	1400	1800	8 × 21 in torpedoes bow & stern		Snoop Plate		
CANADA										
1965-68	3	SS	UK Oberon	2030	2410	8 × 21 in torpedoes bow & stern	AN/BQG Micropuffs 2007 187C 185 197 2018	1006		Being modernised to fit shown
CHILE										
1976	2	SS	O'Brien (UK Oberon)	2030	2410	8 × 21 in torpedoes bow & stern	Active & passive	1006		
1984-85	2	SS	Chipana (Type 209)	1260	1390	8 × 21 in bow torpedoes				
CHINA, People's Republic										
1956-64	15	SS	USSR Whiskey	1080	1350	4 × 21 in bow torpedoes 2 × 16 in stern torpedoes or mines 25 mm guns in some				5 more in reserve
Continuing	93	SS	USSR Romeo	1400	1800	8 × 21 in torpedoes bow & stern or mines				Chinese building at about 9 a year
1964	1	SSG	USSR Golf	2350	2850	6 × 21 in bow torpedoes 3 tubes for unknown missile				
1974-75	2	SS	Ming	Circa 1500	Circa 1900	Possibly 6 × 21 in torpedoes				
1974 on	6?	SSN	Han		5000?					Possible nuclear. All details uncertain
1982	2	SSBN	Xia		8000?	About 14 CSS-NX3 ballistic missiles				Up to 6 planned

Year Built	No	Type	Class	Displacement (imperial tons)		Armament	Sonar	Radar	Miscellaneous	Remarks
				Surf	Dived					
COLOMBIA										
1972	2	SS	SX-506 Midget (Italian design)	58	70	Swimmers & swimmer delivery vehicles				
1975	2	SS	Type 209	1180	1285	8 × 21 in bow torpedoes	Active & passive			West German built
CUBA										
?	1	SS	USSR Whiskey	1080	1350	4 × 21 bow torpedoes 2 × 16 in stern torpedoes				Received 1979 & probably non-operational
?	3	SS	USSR Foxtrot	1950	2500	6 × 21 in bow torpedoes 4 × 16 in stern torpedoes				Received 1979-84
DENMARK										
1959-64	2	SS	Delfinen	595	643	4 × 21 in torpedoes	Active & passive	Yes		Nearing end of lives
1970	2	SS	Narhvalen	420	450	8 × 21 in bow torpedoes	Active & passive	Yes		
1985-88?	3	SS	UB 80		Circa 750					No decisions yet taken
ECUADOR										
1977-78	2	SS	West German Type 209	1285	1390	8 × 21 in bow torpedoes	Active & passive			
EGYPT										
1957-62	6	SS	USSR Whiskey	1080	1350	4 × 21 in bow torpedoes 2 × 16 in stern torpedoes or mines				Received 1957-62 2 non-operational
1966-84	10	SS	USSR Romeo	1400	1800	8 × 21 in torpedoes bow & stern				8 received 1966-69 & 2 probably cannibalised for spares. 4 more transferred from China 1982-84
FRANCE										
1958-60	5	SS	Narval	1635	1910	6 × 21·7 in bow torpedoes Minelaying capability	DUUX 2A DUUA 2	DRUA 31G		
1964-70	9	SS	Daphne	860	1038	12 × 21·7 in torpedoes bow & stern Minelaying capability	DUUA 2A DUUA 1B DSUV2F DUUX 2A	DRUA 31F		
1966	1	SSB	Gymnote	3340	3870		DUUA 1A DSUV 2D			Trials vessel for M4 missile system
1971-80	5	SSBN	Le Redoutable	8045	8940	M20 missiles 4 × 21 in torpedoes or SM 39 missile	DUUV 23 or 21 DUUX 2	Calypso		4 will be fitted with M4 missiles from 1987-90
1977-78	4	SS	Agosta	1450	1725	4 × 21 in bow torpedoes Exocet SM-39 Minelaying capability	DUUA 1D DUUA 2A DSUV 2H DUUX 2A	DRUA 33C		
1983-92	6	SSN	Rubis	2385	2670	4 × 21 in bow torpedoes or SM39 missile Minelaying capability	DUUA 2B DUUX 2 or 5 DSUV 22	DRUA 33		
1985	1	SSBN	L'Inflexible	8080	8920	M4 missile system L5 & L7 torpedoes or SM39 missile	DSUX 21			
GERMANY, Federal Republic										
1967-69	6	SS	Type 205	419	450	8 × 21 in bow torpedoes Minelaying capability	Active & passive	Thomson-Houston C61		
1973-75	18	SS	Type 206	450	498	8 × 21 in bow torpedoes Minelaying capability	Active & passive	Thomson-Houston C63		
GREECE										
1944	1	SS	Papanikolis (US Guppy 2A)		2445	10 × 21 in torpedoes bow & stern				
1946	1	SS	Katsonis (US Guppy 3)		2450	10 × 21 in torpedoes bow & stern	BQR-2 BQG-4 (PUFFS)			
1971-72	4	SS	Glavkos (West German 209)	1100	1210	8 × 21 in bow torpedoes	Active & passive		Sound ranging UWT	
1979-80	4	SS	Glavkos (West German 209)	1100	1285	8 × 21 in bow torpedoes	Active & passive		Sound ranging UWT	
INDIA										
Received 1968-75	8	SS	USSR Foxtrot	1950	2400	10 × 21 in torpedoes				Unconfirmed reports of more to come
1987 on	4	SS	Type 1500	Circa 1660						2 to be built in Germany
INDONESIA										
1981-83	3	SS	Cakra (Type 1300)	1285	1390	8 × 21 in bow torpedoes			HSA fire control	Total of 4 ordered with 2 more planned
ISRAEL										
1977	3	SS	IKL/Vickers Type 206	420	600	8 × 21 in bow torpedoes			SLAM anti-air missile system?	
ITALY										
1952	2	SS	US Tang	2050	2700	8 × 21 in torpedoes bow & stern	BQS-4C BQR-8	BPS-12	BQG-4 Passive ranging	Likely to be disposed of

Year Built	No	Type	Class	Displacement (imperial tons)		Armament	Sonar	Radar	Miscellaneous	Remarks
				Surf	Dived					
ITALY cont										
1968-69	4	SS	Toti	524	582	4 × 21 in torpedoes	IPD 64	3RM20/SMG	Passive ranging MD 64	
1980-82	4	SS	Sauro	1456	1631	6 × 21 in A 184 bow torpedoes	USEA-Selenia IPD 70	BPS 704	Passive ranging	2 more planned
JAPAN										
1968-69	2	SS	Asashio	2050	2450	6 × 21 in bow torpedoes 2 × 12·7 in stern torpedoes	JQS-3A JQO-2A SQS4	ZPS3		
1971-78	7	SS	Uzushio	1900	2430	6 × 21 in torpedoes amidships				
1980-87	8	SS	Yushio	2200		6 × 21 in torpedoes amidships	ZQQ4 SQS36(J)	ZPS4		1 more ordered. Harpoon to be fitted in later boats
KOREA, Democratic People's Republic (North)										
1960	4	SS	USSR Whiskey	1080	1350	4 × 21 in bow torpedoes 2 × 16 in stern torpedoes Minelaying capability				
1973 on	15	SS	Chinese Romeo	1400	1800	6 × 21 in bow torpedoes 2 × 21 in stern torpedoes or mines	Hercules	Snoop Plate		Part Chinese supplied, part home built
1974 on	?	SS		Circa 50?						
KOREA (Republic)										
1983	1	SS		175						Probably first of class of 4 or 5
LIBYA										
1976-83	6	SS	USSR Foxtrot	1950	2400	6 × 21 in bow torpedoes 4 × 16 in stern torpedoes	Hercules	Snoop Tray		
NETHERLANDS										
1960-61	2	SS	Dolfijn	1520	1830	8 × 21 in torpedoes bow & stern		1001		Will be replaced by Walrus
1965-66	2	SS	Potvis	1509	1831	8 × 21 in torpedoes bow & stern		1001		Will be replaced in late 1980s by Walrus
1972	2	SS	Zwaardvis	2350	2640	6 × 21 in bow torpedoes		1001		
1986 on	6	SS	Walrus	2350	2640	4 × 21 in Mk 48 torpedoes & Harpoon Minelaying capability	Thomson-CSF	Decca navigation		
NORWAY										
1964-67	14	SS	Kobben (West German Type 207)		435	8 × 21 in bow torpedoes	Small active			
1980-94	6	SS			1300	Seal 3 torpedoes	Krupp Atlas			Being built in West Germany. Possibly two more
PAKISTAN										
1969-70	4	SS	Hangor (French Daphne)	869	1043	12 × 21 in torpedoes bow & stern				
1972-73	3	SS	SX 404 (Italian built)	40						12 passenger capacity Clandestine work, etc
1979-80	2	SS	Hashmat (French Agosta)	1450	1725	4 × 21 in bow torpedoes	DUUA-2A DSUV-2H DUUA-1D			
PERU										
1944	2	SS	Guppy 1A		2440	10 × 21 in torpedoes bow & stern				
1954-57	4	SS	Abtao		1400	6 × 21 in torpedoes bow & stern			5 in/25 gun in 2	
1974-82	6	SS	West German (Type 1200)	1185	1290	8 × 21 in torpedoes	Active & passive	Yes	Sound ranging UWT	
POLAND										
	4	SS	USSR Whiskey	1080	1350	4 × 21 in bow torpedoes 2 × 16 in stern torpedoes Mining capability	Tamir	Snoop Plate		
PORTUGAL										
1967-69	3	SS	Albacora (French Daphne)	869	1043	12 × 21·7 in torpedoes bow & stern	Active & passive	DRUA 31E		
SOUTH AFRICA										
1970-71	3	SS	French Daphne	869	1043	12 × 21·7 in torpedoes bow & stern				Refitted with new sonars
SPAIN										
1944	1	SS	S-30 (Guppy IIA)	1837	2416	10 × 21 in torpedoes bow & stern Minelaying capability	BQR-2B BQS-4C	SS-2		Received 1971-74
1973-74	4	SS	S-60 (French Daphne)	865	1042	12 × 21·7 in torpedoes bow & stern Minelaying capability	DUUA 1B DSUV 2F DUUX-2A	DRUA-33A		
1983-85	4	SS	S-70 (French Agosta)	1513	1758	4 × 21 in torpedoes Minelaying capability	DSUV-22A DUUA-2A/2B DUUX-2A DUUX-31	DRUA-33C		

Year Built	No	Type	Class	Displacement (imperial tons)		Armament	Sonar	Radar	Miscellaneous	Remarks
				Surf	Dived					
SWEDEN										
1961-62	4	SS	Draken	835	1110	4 × 21 in bow torpedoes				Likely to be replaced by Näcken & Västergötland Undergoing limited modernisation
1968-69	5	SS	Sjöormen	1125	1400	4 × 21 in bow torpedoes 2 × 16 in torpedoes				
1980-81	3	SS	Näcken	1030	1125	6 × 21 in torpedoes 2 × 16 in torpedoes Minelaying capability				
1987-89	4	SS	Västergötland		1140	6 × 21 in bow torpedoes 3 × 16 in stern torpedoes Minelaying capability				
TAIWAN										
1945-46	2	SS	Hai Shih (US Guppy II)		2420	10 × 21 in torpedoes bow & stern	DUUG 1B BQR 2B BQS 4C	SS-2		Received 1973
1985-86	2	SS	Dutch Improved Zwaardvis							Details not known
TURKEY										
1944-45	8	SS	Guppy IIA & 1A	1848	2440	10 × 21 in torpedoes bow & stern or mines	GQR3 BQR2 BQS2	BPS-9 SS-2		Received 1970-73
1945	2	SS	Guppy III		2540	10 × 21 in torpedoes bow & stern or mines Minelaying capability	BQG4 BQR BQS	SS-2		Received 1973
1951-52	2	SS	US Tang	2100	2700	8 × 21 in torpedoes bow & stern	BQR BQS	BPS-12		Received 1980-83
1975-85	6	SS	West German Type 209	980	1185	8 × 21 in torpedoes	CSU 3-2	S-63/B	Sound ranging UWT	3 boats built in West Germany and 2 in Turkey. Up to 12 planned
UNION OF SOVIET SOCIALIST REPUBLICS										
1951-55	4	SS	Zulu IV	1950	2300	10 × 21 in torpedoes bow & stern Mining capability	Tamir	Snoop Plate or Snoop Tray		Obsolescent & may be disposed of 4 more in reserve
1951-57	50	SS	Whiskey	1080	1350	4 × 21 in bow torpedoes 2 × 16 in stern torpedoes Mining capability	Tamir	Snoop Plate		Possibly another 75 in reserve
1958-61	12	SS	Romeo	1400	1800	8 × 21 in torpedoes bow & stern Mining capability	Hercules Feniks	Snoop Plate		Will probably be deleted. Some used for experimental work
1958-62	5	SSBN	Hotel II		5500	3 × SS-N-5 6 × 21 in bow torpedoes 4 × 16 in stern torpedoes	Hercules Feniks	Snoop Tray		
1958-62	1	SSBN	Hotel III		6000	6 × SS-N-8 6 × 21 in bow torpedoes 4 × 16 in stern torpedoes	Hercules Feniks	Snoop Tray		Test boat for SS-N-8
1958-63	12	SSN	November	4200	5000	8 × 21 in bow torpedoes 2 × 16 in stern torpedoes	Hercules Feniks	Snoop Tray		
1958-71	60	SS	Foxtrot	1950	2500	6 × 21 in bow torpedoes 2 × 16 in stern torpedoes	Hercules Feniks	Snoop Tray		
Converted 1959-63	1	SSR	Whiskey Canvas-bag	1050	1350	4 × 21 in bow torpedoes 2 × 16 in A/S stern torpedoes	Tamir	Boat Sail Snoop Plate		Surveillance picket
1960-62	5	SSN	Echo 1	4300	5200	6 × 21 in bow torpedoes 2 × 16 in stern torpedoes Minelaying capability	Hercules Feniks	Snoop Tray		
1958-62	15	SSB	Golf 2,3 & 5		3000-3500	6 × SS-N-8 (Golf 3) or 3 × SS-N-5 (Golf 2) or 1 × SS-NX-20 (Golf 5) 6 × 21 in bow torpedoes	Hercules Feniks	Snoop Tray or Snoop Plate		
1960?	1	SS	Golf 1		3000	6 × 21 in bow torpedoes	Hercules Feniks	Snoop Tray		As for Golf 2 with missile tubes removed
1961-68	16	SSG	Juliett	3000	3800	4 × SS-N-3A 6 × 21 in bow torpedoes	Hercules Feniks	Snoop Slab		
1961-67	29	SSGN	Echo II	4800	5800	8 × SS-N-3A or SS-N-12 6 × 21 in bow torpedoes 2 × 16 in stern torpedoes	Hercules Feniks	Snoop Tray		About 7 with SS-N-12
1967-74	16	SSN	Victor I		5200	6 × 21 in bow torpedoes SS-N-15	LF bow array MF array	Snoop Tray		
1967-74	34	SSBN/ SSN	Yankee		9300	16 × SS-N-6 Mod 1 or 3 in 23 12 × SS-N-17 in 1 No missiles in 10 6 × 21 in bow torpedoes	MF or LF Bow array	Snoop Tray		10 have been converted to SSN with missiles removed
1967-72	11	SSGN	Charlie I		5000	8 × SS-N-7 6 × 21 in bow torpedoes	Fin sonar	Snoop Tray		
1968 on	4	SS	Bravo	2200	2700	6 × 21 in torpedoes				For training of surface ships
1971	1	SSGN	Papa		7000	10 × SS-N-7 or 9? 6 × 21 in bow torpedoes Possibly SS-N-15	MF/LF	Snoop Tray		
1972-77	16	SSBN	Delta I		10 000	12 × SS-N-8 6 × 21 in bow torpedoes	LF bow array	Snoop Tray		

Year Built	No	Type	Class	Displacement (imperial tons)		Armament	Sonar	Radar	Miscellaneous	Remarks
				Surf	Dived					
USSR cont										
1972 on	7	SSN	Victor II		5800	6 × 21 in bow torpedoes Possibly SS-N-15 Minelaying capability	LF array & MF	Snoop Tray		Enlarged version of Victor I
1973 on	18+	SS	Tango	3000	3700	8 × 21 in torpedoes		Snoop Tray		
1973-80	6	SSN	Charlie II	4400	5500	8 × SS-N-9 6 × 21 in torpedoes	LF array	Snoop Tray		Enlarged version of Charlie I
1975	4	SSBN	Delta II		11 000	16 × SS-N-8 6 × 21 in bow torpedoes	LF bow array	Snoop Tray		
1976 on	6+	SSN	Alfa		3800	6 × 21 in torpedoes Fitted for SS-N-15 Minelaying capability	LF bow array	Snoop Tray		In slow series production
1976 on	15	SSBN	Delta III		11 000	16 × SS-N-18 6 × 21 in torpedoes	LF bow array	Snoop Tray		In series production
1978 on	18+	SSN	Victor III		6000	6 × 21 in bow torpedoes Fitted for SS-N-15	LF bow array & MF	Snoop Tray		
1979 on	6	SS	Kilo	2500	3200	8 × 21 in torpedoes				
1981-85	3	SSGN	Oscar		14 000	24 × SS-N-19 8 × 21 in torpedoes				
1982 on	2+	SSBN	Typhoon		Circa 30 000	20 × SS-N-20 Possibly 6 or 8 × 21 in torpedoes				
1983	1+	SSN	Mike	8000	9700	6 × 21 in torpedoes SS-N-15 or 21				
1983	1+	SSN	Sierra		6500	6 × 21 in torpedoes SS-N-21				
UNITED KINGDOM										
1961-67	15	SS	Porpoise & Oberon	2030	2410	8 × 21 in torpedoes bow & stern	187.2007	1002		
1966-71	5	SSN	Valiant & Churchill		4900	6 × 21 in torpedoes Harpoon	2001.2007 197.183	1006		
1967-69	4	SSBN	Resolution	7500	8400	16 × Polaris A-3 6 × 21 in bow torpedoes	2001.2007 185	I-band		
1973-81	6	SSN	Swiftsure		4500	5 × 21 in torpedoes Harpoon	2001.2007 197.185	1006		
1983-90?	6	SSN	Trafalgar		5208	5 × 21 in torpedoes Harpoon	2001, 2007 2020, 197,183	1006		
1987 on?	1+	SS	2400		2400	6 × 21 in torpedoes	165			
UNITED STATES OF AMERICA										
1956	1	SS	Darter	1720	2388	8 × 21 in torpedoes bow & stern	BQS-4/ BQR-2 BQG-4 (PUFFS)			
1957	1	SSN	Seawolf	3765	4200	6 × 21 in bow torpedoes	SQS-51/ BQR-21			
1957-59	3	SSN	Skate	2570	2861	8 × 21 in torpedoes bow & stern	SQS-49/ BQR-21			
1959	3	SS	Barbel	2145	2640	6 × 21 in bow torpedoes	SQS-49/ BQR-21			
1959-61	5	SSN	Skipjack	3075	3513	6 × 21 in bow torpedoes A/S torpedoes	SQS-49/ BQR-21			
1959	1	SSN	George Washington	6019	6700	6 × 21 in bow torpedoes	BQR-23 BQR-20 BQR-7 BQS-4 BQR-19			Converted from SSBN
1960	1	SSN	Tullibee	2050	2640	4 × 21 in torpedoes	BQQ-3 system BQG-4 BQS-12 BQR-7 BQR-2D BQR-23			
1962-63	3	SSN	Ethan Allen	6955	7880	4 × 21 in bow torpedoes	BQR-15 BQR-2 BQR-7 BQS-4 BQR-20 BQR-23 BQQ-3			Converted from SSBN
1962-68	13	SSN	Permit	3780	4300 to 4470	4 × 21 in torpedoes Subroc Harpoon	BQQ-5 system Towed array			
1963-67	31	SSBN	Lafayette	6650	8250	16 Poseidon C3 or Trident 1 C4 4 × 21 in bow torpedoes	BQR-15/25 BQR-21 BQS-4 BQR-20 BQQ-3			Converted to Poseidon from Polaris Trident 1 missile backfitted in 12 boats 1980-82
1967-75	37	SSN	Sturgeon	4250-4460	4780-4960	4 × 21 in torpedoes Subroc Harpoon	BQQ-5 system BQS-14 Towed array	BPS-14		

Year Built	No	Type	Class	Displacement (imperial tons)		Armament	Sonar	Radar	Miscellaneous	Remarks
				Surf	Dived					
USA cont										
1968	1	AGSS	Dolphin	860	950	No torpedoes	Large bow			Deep diving & research
1969	1	SSN	Narwhal	4800	5350	4 × 21 in torpedoes Subroc Harpoon	BQQ-5 system BQS-14 Towed array			
1974	1	SSN	Glenard P Lipscomb	5900	6480	4 × 21 in bow torpedoes Subroc Harpoon	BQQ-5 system BQS-14 Towed array			
1976-96	71	SSN	Los Angeles	6080	6900	4 × 21 in torpedoes Subroc Harpoon Tomahawk to be fitted	BQS-5 system BQS-15 Towed array	BPS-15		
1981 on	24	SSBN	Ohio	16 600	18 700	24 × Trident 1 C-4 or Trident 2 D-5 4 × 21 in torpedoes	BQQ-6 system Towed array			A majority of these submarines carry A/S Mk 48 torpedoes
VENEZUELA										
1951	1	SS	Picua (US Guppy II)	1870	2420	10 × 21 in torpedoes bow & stern				
1976-77	2	SS	Sabalo (Type 1300)	1285		8 × 21 in bow torpedoes	Krupp active & passive	Thomson-CSF		
YUGOSLAVIA										
1960-62	2	SS	Sutjeska	820	945	6 × 21 in bow torpedoes		Snoop Group		Soviet supplied equipment & armament
1969-70	2	SS	Heroj		1068	6 × 21 in bow torpedoes		Snoop Group		Soviet supplied equipment & armament
1978-81	2	SS	Sava		964	6 × 21 in torpedoes or mines				Soviet supplied equipment & armament

3081.304   Military Aircraft

The following table contains details of the major military aircraft, listed under the country of origin. It is not intended to be exhaustive in either the number of aircraft types listed or in the information given. Similarly, the many individual variants of some aircraft types are not treated separately, entries in most cases being for the main application of a given aircraft type. Readers who require more comprehensive aircraft data are referred to the current edition of the companion volume, *Jane's All the World's Aircraft*. (P), in the 'Contractor' column denotes that the aircraft type is in production.

Model	Name	Contractor(s)	Span	Length	Max TO Wt	Crew	Power plant	Weapons	Remarks
ARGENTINA **Combat**									
IA-58B	Pucará Bravo	FMA (P)	14·5 m	14·25 m	6800 kg	2	2 × Astazou XVI G	4 × 7·62 mm, 2 × 30 mm 1500 kg stores	Improved IA-58 COIN aircraft. Production for Argentinian AF
BRAZIL **Combat**									
AT-26	Xavante	Embraer	10·854 m	10·673 m	5216 kg	2	1 × Viper 20 Mk 540	Underwing bombs, pods etc	Licence assembly of Italian MB 326
CHINA, People's Republic **Combat**									
Q-5	Fantan-A	Nanzhang (P)	10·2 m	15·25 m	10 700 kg	1	2 × R-B-811	2000 kg bombs, rockets, 2 × 30 mm cannon	Tactical strike aircraft, derived from J-6 (MiG-19)
FRANCE **Combat**									
	Super Etendard	Dassault-Breguet (P)	9·6 m	14·31 m	11 500 kg	1	1 × Snecma Atar 8K-50	2 × 30 mm cannon, 2100 kg AAM, ASM, bombs, nuclear weapons	Entered service in 1978
	Mirage III	Dassault-Breguet (P)	8·22 m	15·03 m	13 700 kg	1	1 × Snecma Atar 9C	Sidewinder, Magic, R530, 2 × 30 mm cannon, bombs, rockets, ASM, nuclear weapons	Dimensions are for E version
	Mirage F1	Dassault-Breguet (P)	8·4 m	15 m	15 200 kg	1	1 × Snecma Atar 9K-50	Magic, R530, AS-30, guns, rockets, bombs. 4000 kg ext stores	Dimensions are for C version
	Mirage 5	Dassault-Breguet (P)	8·22 m	15·55 m	13 700 kg	1	1 × Snecma Atar 9C	2 × 30 mm cannon, ASM, bombs, rockets. 4000 kg ext stores	
	Mirage 2000	Dassault-Breguet	9 m	14·35 m	16 500 kg	1	1 × Snecma M53-P2	2 × 30 mm cannon, Super 530, Magic, bombs, rockets, ASM. Up to 6000 kg ext stores	Multi-role fighter
Bombers									
	Mirage IV	Dassault-Breguet	11·85 m	23·5 m	31 600 kg	2	2 × Snecma Atar 9K	1 nuclear weapon. Bombs, rockets, ASM	Medium range
Maritime and ASW									
1150	Atlantic	Dassault-Breguet	36·3 m	31·75 m	43 500 kg	12	2 × RRType Ty20 Mk 21	ASM, bombs, DCs, torpedoes, mines, MAD	ANG with improved systems in development
INDIA **Combat**									
	Ajeet	HAL	6·73 m	9·04 m	4170 kg	1	1 × RR Orpheus 701-01	2 × 30 mm cannon, bombs, rockets	Interceptor/ground attack
INTERNATIONAL **Combat**									
	Alpha Jet	Dassault-Breguet/ Dornier (P)	9·11 m	13·23 m	7500 kg	2	2 × Larzac 04-C5	1 × 27 mm or 30 mm cannon, bombs, rockets, Magic, ASM. 2500 kg ext stores	Jet strike/trainer. Data for strike version
	Jaguar	BAe/Dassault-Breguet (P)	8·69 m	16·83 m	15 700 kg	1	2 × RR/Turboméca Adour	2 × 30 mm cannon, AAM, ASM, bombs, rockets, nuclear weapons. 4535 kg ext stores	In several versions
	Tornado	Aeritalia/BAe/ MBB (P)	8·6 m 13·9 m	16·7 m	26 490 kg	2	2 × RB. 199-34R-04	2 × 27 mm cannon. Sidewinder, bombs, rockets, ASM, nuclear weapons. 8165 kg ext stores	Multi-role combat aircraft. Swing-wing. Data for strike version. Also air defence version
IAR-93	Orao	SOKO/CNIAR (P)	9·63 m	14·88 m	10 500 kg	1	2 × RR Viper Mk 632-41	2 × 23 mm cannon, rockets, bombs. 2500 kg ext stores	
ISRAEL **Combat**									
—	Kfir	Israel Aircraft Industries (P)	8·22 m	15·65 m	14 700 kg	1	1 × J79-JIE	2 × 30 mm cannon, AAM, ASM, bombs, rockets. 4295 kg ext stores	Israeli development of Mirage 5
ITALY **Combat**									
MB-326G		Aermacchi	10·85 m	10·67 m	5216 kg	1-2	1 × RR Viper 20 Mk 540	Up to 1184 kg wing stores	Several versions. Impala in South Africa. Xavante in Brazil
MB-339A		Aermacchi	10·858 m	10·972 m	5895 kg	1-2	1 × RR Viper Mk 632-43	Up to 1815 kg wing stores	Dual trainer-strike

Model	Name	Contractor(s)	Span	Length	Max TO Wt	Crew	Power plant	Weapons	Remarks
JAPAN									
Combat									
F-1	—	Mitsubishi (P)	7·88 m	17·84 m	13 674 kg	1	2 × RR/Turboméca Adour	1 × JM-61 20 mm cannon, bombs, rockets, ASM, AAM. 2721 kg ext stores	Deliveries to JASDF began 1977
Maritime and ASW									
PS-1	—	Shin Meiwa	33·15 m	33·46 m	43 000 kg	9	2 × T64-IHI-10	Rockets, torpedoes, bombs, DCs, MAD	Flying-boat, amphibian
SWEDEN									
Combat									
J35	Draken	Saab-Scania	9·4 m	15·4 m	16 000 kg	1	1 × Sv Flyg RM6C	Missiles, bombs, rockets. 4080 kg stores	Several versions
JA37	Viggen	Saab-Scania (P)	10·6 m	16·3 m	17 000 kg	1	1 × RM8B	1 × 30 mm cannon, AAM, rockets	Several versions, data given for air defence version
UNION OF SOVIET SOCIALIST REPUBLICS									
Combat									
Yak-28	Brewer	Yakovlev	11·73 m	17·98 m	15 875 kg	2	2 × TDR Mk R37F	Guns, bombs, rockets, nuclear weapons	All-weather tactical-bomber
MiG-19	Farmer-C	Mikoyan	9·2 m	14·9 m	8700 kg	1	2 × RB9F	3 × 30 mm cannon, bombs, rockets, AAM	Data given is for J-6, Chinese licence-built version of MiG-19SF
SU-24	Fencer-A	Sukhoi	10·3 m 17·25 m	21·29 m	39 700 kg	2	2 × R-29B	23 mm and 30 mm cannon, bombs, rockets, ASM, nuclear weapons. 8000 kg ext stores	Swing-wing attack aircraft
Yak-28P	Firebar	Yakovlev	12·95 m	21·65 m	15 875 kg	2	2 × Turm RD-11	Anab AAM	All-weather fighter
Yak-36	Forger-A	Yakovlev (P)	7·32 m	15·25 m	11 565 kg	1	1 × Lyulka AL-21 derivative	Gun and rocket pods, ASM, bombs, Aphid, AAM. 2000 kg ext stores	VTOL naval fighter/attack aircraft
MiG-21MF	Fishbed-J	Mikoyan (P)	7·15 m	15·76 m	9400 kg	1	1 × R13-300	2 × 23 mm cannon, Aphid and Atoll AAM, bombs, rockets, nuclear weapons. 2000 kg ext stores	Multi-role fighter
Su-11	Fishpot-C	Sukhoi	8·43 m	17 m	13 600 kg	1	1 × AL-7F-1	Anab AAM	All-weather fighter
Su-7BM	Fitter-A	Sukhoi	8·93 m	17·37 m	13 500 kg	1	1 × AL-7F-1	2 × 30 mm wing cannon, bombs, rockets, nuclear weapons. 1000 kg ext stores	Ground attack fighter
Su-17/20/ 22	Fitter-C	Sukhoi (P)	10·6 m 14 m	18·75 m	17 700 kg	1-2	1 × AL-21F-3	2 × 30 mm cannon, nuclear weapons, Atoll AAM, bombs, rockets, ASM. 3500 kg ext stores	VG tactical combat aircraft. Data for Fitter C. At least eight versions for WARPAC and export
Su-15	Flagon-F	Sukhoi	10·53 m	20·5 m	16 000 kg	1	2 × R-13F2-300	Anab AAM	Several versions. All-weather fighter
Su-25	Frogfoot	Sukhoi	16·75 m	14·95 m	17 237 kg	1	2 × R-13-300	Various	Ground attack, figures estimated
MiG-23	Flogger-B	Mikoyan (P)	8·17 m 14·25 m	16·8 m	20 100 kg	1	1 × R-29B	2 × 23 mm cannon, Atoll, Apex, Aphid, AAM, bombs, rockets. 4500 kg ext stores	Swing-wing interceptor (B/E/G versions) and strike aircraft (F/H versions). Data for Flogger-B
MiG-27	Flogger-D	Mikoyan (P)	14·25 m	16·8 m	20 100 kg	1	1 × R-29B	23 mm Gatling-type gun, rockets, ASM, bombs, nuclear weapons	Ground attack aircraft. Also J version
MiG-25	Foxbat	Mikoyan (P)	13·95 m	23·82 m	36 200 kg	1	2 × R-31	Acrid, Apex, Aphid, AAM	Several versions. Data for Foxbat-A. High performance fighter (Foxbat A/E) and recce (Foxbat B/D)
Bombers									
Tu-26	Backfire	Tupolev (P)	34·45 m 26·21 m	40·23 m	122 500 kg	4	2 × turbofan	Kingfish, Kitchen ASMs, bombs, mines, nuclear weapons	Supersonic long-range strategic bomber
Tu-16	Badger	Tupolev	32·93 m	34·8 m	72 000 kg	—	2 × Mikulin AM-3M	Kelt, Kipper, or Kingfish ASMs, bombs, mines, nuclear weapons	Sub-sonic medium-range strategic bomber. Several versions
Tu-95	Bear	Tupolev	51·1 m	49·5 m	188 000 kg	—	4 × NK-12MV turboprop	Kangaroo ASM, bombs, nuclear weapons	Sub-sonic strategic bomber. Long range. Several versions
MyA-4	Bison	Myasishchev	50·48 m	47·2 m	158 750 kg	—	4 × Mikulin AM-3D	Nuclear weapons, bombs	Sub-sonic strategic bomber. Long range. Several versions
Tu-22	Blinder	Tupolev	27·7 m	40·53 m	83 900 kg	3	2 × turbojet	Kitchen ASM, bombs, mines, nuclear weapons	Supersonic strategic bomber. Medium range. Several versions

Model	Name	Contractor(s)	Span	Length	Max TO Wt	Crew	Power plant	Weapons	Remarks
Maritime and ASW									
Tu-16	Badger D	Tupolev	32·93 m	34·8 m	72 000 kg	—	2 × Mikulin AM-3M	Various sensors	Medium-range maritime reconnaissance version. Also, Badger E/F/K versions. Badger H/J ECM variants
Tu-142	Bear F	Tupolev (P)	51·1 m	49·5 m	188 000 kg	—	4 × NK-12 MV turboprop	Bombs, DCs, ASW torpedoes, sonobuoys, mines, nuclear ASW weapons	Long-range maritime version. Also Bear D recce and missile guidance version and Bear-G ASW variant
Tu-22	Blinder C	Tupolev	27·7 m	40·53 m	83 900 kg	3-4	2 × turbojet	Various sensors	Medium-range maritime reconnaissance version
Be-12	Mail	Beriev	29·71 m	30·17 m	29 483 kg	4	2 × Ivchenko AI-20D	Bombs, DCs, mines, sonobuoys, MAD	Short-range maritime patrol and ASW flying-boat amphibian
Il-38	May	Ilyushin	37·4 m	39·6 m	63 500 kg	—	4 × Ivchenko AI-20	Bombs, DCs, mines, ASW torpedoes, sonobuoys, nuclear ASW weapons, MAD	Medium-range turboprop maritime patrol and ASW
Reconnaissance and Surveillance									
MiG-25	Foxbat-B	Mikoyan	13·4 m	23·82 m	33 400 kg	1	2 × R-31		Long-range, Mach 3+ reconnaissance version of fighter, MiG-25 Foxbat D is ELINT version
Tu-126	Moss	Tupolev	51·2 m	55·2 m	170 000 kg	12	4 × NK-12 MV		Airborne early warning aircraft, limited number built
UNITED KINGDOM									
Combat									
	Buccaneer	British Aerospace	12·9 m	19·33 m	28 123 kg	2	2 × RB 168 Spey	Bullpup, Martel, Sea Eagle, bombs, rockets, nuclear stores	Several versions
GR Mk 3	Harrier	British Aerospace (P)	7·7 m	14·27 m	11 793 kg	1	1 × RR Pegasus 103	Bombs, rockets, 2 × 30 mm cannon, ASM, recce pod, Sidewinder AAM. 2270 kg ext stores	
FRS Mk 1	Sea Harrier	British Aerospace (P)	7·7 m	14·5 m	11 339 kg	1	1 × RR Pegasus 104	Bombs, rockets, 2 × 30 mm cannon, ASM, recce pod, Sidewinder AAM. 3630 kg ext stores	FRS Mk 51 for Indian Navy
1182	Hawk	British Aerospace (P)	9·39 m	11·85 m	7757 kg	1-2	1 × Adour 151	1 × 30 mm cannon, bombs, rokets, Sidewinder AAM. Ext stores 2567 kg	Strike/trainer
167	Strikemaster	British Aerospace	11·23 m	10·27 m	5215 kg	1-2	1 × RR Viper 535	Guns, rockets, bombs	Light attack aircraft
Maritime and ASW									
MR Mk 2	Nimrod	British Aerospace (P)	35 m	38·63 m	80 510 kg	12	4 × Spey Mk 250	ASM, torpedoes, nuclear ASW weapons, bombs, DCs, mines, sonobuoys, MAD	Long-range jet. Mk II with improved systems in service
Reconnaissance and Surveillance									
AEW Mk 3	Nimrod	British Aerospace (P)	35·08 m	41·97 m	—	10	4 × Spey Mk 250		Airborne early warning version of maritime Nimrod
UNITED STATES OF AMERICA									
Combat									
A-4	Skyhawk	McDonnell-Douglas	8·38 m	12·27 m	10 206 kg	1	1 × J52-P-408	2 × 20 mm guns, Sidewinder AAM, ASM, rockets, bombs, nuclear weapons	Many versions
A-6E	Intruder	Grumman (P)	16·15 m	16·69 m	27 397 kg	2	2 × J52-P-8A	Max weapon load 8165 kg. Rockets, bombs, ASM nuclear weapons	Several versions including EW (EA-6B), Carrier deployed
A-7E	Corsair II	LTV (P)	11·8 m	14·06 m	19 050 kg	1	1 × TF-41A-2	Max weapon load 6805 kg. Bombs, rockets, ASM, 1 × 20 mm M-61 gun, Sidewinder AAM, nuclear weapons	USN and USAF versions
AV-8B	Harrier II	McDonnell-Douglas	9·24 m	14·12 m	13 495 kg	1	1 × RR Pegasus 105	Bombs, rockets, 1 × 25 mm cannon, ASM, nuclear weapons, Sidewinder AAM. 4173 kg ext stores	Advanced version Harrier in development
A-10A	Thunderbolt II	Fairchild Republic (P)	17·53 m	16·26 m	22 680 kg	1	2 × TF34-GE-100	1 × GAU-8A 30 mm gun, bombs, rockets, ASM. 7250 kg ext stores	Close support aircraft
A-37B	—	Cessna	10·93 m	8·92 m	6350 kg	1-2	2 × J85-GE-17A	GAU-2B/A 7·62 mm guns. Wing stores	Light strike aircraft
F-4E	Phantom	McDonnell-Douglas	11·77 m	19·2 m	28 030 kg	2	2 × J79-GE-17A	Sparrow, Sidewinder AAM, ASM, bombs, rockets, nuclear weapons. 7250 kg ext stores	Many variants

Model	Name	Contractor(s)	Span	Length	Max TO Wt	Crew	Power plant	Weapons	Remarks
USA cont									
F-5E	Tiger II	Northrop (P)	8·13 m	14·68 m	11 193 kg	1	2 × J85-GE-21	2 × 30 mm guns, Sidewinder AAM, ASM, rockets, bombs. 3175 kg ext stores	Basic export fighter
F-14A	Tomcat	Grumman (P)	11·65 m 19·45 m	18·89 m	33 724 kg	2	2 × TF30-P-412A	Sparrow, Sidewinder, Phoenix AAM, bombs, rockets. 6577 kg ext stores	Swing-wing, all-weather fleet defence fighter
F-15C	Eagle	McDonnell-Douglas (P)	13·05 m	19·43 m	30 845 kg	1	2 × F100-PW-100	Sparrow, Sidewinder AAM, bombs, rockets, ASM, M-61 gun. 7527 kg ext stores	Air superiority fighter. Several versions
F-16A	Fighting Falcon	General Dynamics (P)	9·45 m	14·52 m	16 057 kg	1	1 × F100-PW-200	1 × 20 mm M-61 gun, Sidewinder AAM, bombs, rockets, ASM, nuclear weapons. 5420 kg ext stores	Lightweight fighter
F-18A	Hornet	McDonnell-Douglas	11·43 m	17·07 m	25 400 kg	1	2 × F404-GE-400	1 × 20 mm cannon, Sidewinder, Sparrow AAM, bombs, rockets, nuclear weapons, ASM. 7710 kg ext stores	Also attack version
F-111F	—	General Dynamics	9·74 m 19·2 m	22·4 m	45 359 kg	2	2 × TF30-P-100	Sidewinder AAM, rockets, bombs, 1 × 20 mm cannon pack, nuclear weapons	Swing-wing tactical fighter, several versions
Bombers									
B-52	Stratofortress	Boeing	56·42 m	47·55 m	221 350 kg	6	4 × J57-P-43W	ALCM, SRAM, nuclear weapons, mines, ASM, bombs	Long range strategic bomber. D, G and H versions in USAF service
Maritime and ASW									
P-3C	Orion	Lockheed (P)	30·37 m	35·61 m	64 410 kg	12	4 × T56-A-14	DCs, torpedoes, bombs, mines, sonobuoys, nuclear ASW weapons, MAD. 9071 kg expendable load	Long-range turboprop version produced for Canada as CP-140 Aurora
S-2E	Tracker	Grumman	22·13 m	13·26 m	13 222 kg	4	2 × R-1820-82WA	DCs, bombs, torpedoes	Carrier-borne ASW aircraft
S-3A	Viking	Lockheed	20·92 m	16·25 m	18 597 kg	4	2 × TF-34-2	Torpedoes, bombs, DCs, mines, nuclear ASW weapons, MAD	Carrier-borne jet ASW aircraft
Reconnaissance and Surveillance									
E-2C	Hawkeye	Grumman (P)	24·56 m	17·55 m	23 503 kg	5	2 × T56-A-425		Carrier airborne early warning, surface surveillance and strike control aircraft. Several versions in use
E-3A	Sentry	Boeing (P)	44·42 m	46·61 m	147 420 kg	17	4 × TF33-PW-100A		Long-range airborne warning and control system (AWACS) aircraft
OV-1D	Mohawk	Grumman	12·8 m	12·5 m	6818 kg	2	2 × T53-L-15		Battlefield surveillance and reconnaissance aircraft
OV-10A	Bronco	Rockwell International	12·19 m	12·67 m	6552 kg	2	2 × T76-G-416		Armed observation and ground attack aircraft
U-2R	—	Lockheed	31·39 m	19·20 m	13 154 kg	1	1 × J75-P-13B		High altitude strategic reconnaissance aircraft
TR-1A	—	Lockheed	31·39 m	19·20 m	18 143 kg	1	1 × J75-P-13		High altitude tactical reconnaissance aircraft
SR-71	Blackbird	Lockheed	16·95 m	32·74 m	—	2	2 × J58		Mach 3+ strategic reconnaissance aircraft

Inventory of Aircraft Types

LIST OF ABBREVIATIONS FOR AIRCRAFT MANUFACTURERS

Aer	– Aeritalia	Da	– Dassault	McD	– McDonnell		
Aem	– Aermacchi	DHC	– De Havilland Canada	McD.D	– McDonnell Douglas		
Ae	– Aerospatiale	D	– Douglas	MiG	– Mikoyan Gurevich		
AN	– Antonov	EMB	– Embraer	Mi	– Mil		
BAe	– British Aerospace	F	– Fairchild	MyA	– Myasishchev		
Be	– Bell	G	– Grumman	NA	– North American		
Bee	– Beech	GD	– General Dynamics	N	– Northrop		
BER	– Beriev	HAL	– Hindustan Aeronautics Limited	R	– Rockwell		
BN	– Britten Norman	IAI	– Israel Aircraft Industries	Si	– Sikorsky		
BR	– Breguet	IL	– Ilyushin	Su	– Sukhoi		
BV	– Boeing Vertol	Li	– Lisunov	Tu	– Tupolev		
Can	– Canadair	L	– Lockheed	V	– Vought		
Cess	– Cessna	MBB	– Messerschmitt-Bolkow-Blohm	W	– Westland		
Con	– Convair	MH	– Max Holste	Yak	– Yakolev		

Country	Fighter	Ground Attack and Bombers Anti-Armour Attack/Close Support	Observation Reconnaissance ECM/Early Warning	Maritime	Transport
AFGHANISTAN					
Airforce	MiG 17 Fresco C MiG 19 Farmer MiG 21 Fishbed	Su 17 Fitter C Su 7 Fitter A IL 28 Beagle Mi 24 Hind-A/D			AN 2 AN 24 AN 26 IL 14 IL 18D Mi4 Mi8 Mi24
ALBANIA					
Airforce	Shenyang J2 (MiG 15) Shenyang J4 (MiG 17) Shenyang J6 (MiG 19) Shenyang J7 (MiG 21)				Li 2 AN 2 IL 14 Mi1 Mi4
ALGERIA					
Airforce	MiG 17 Fresco C MiG 21 Fishbed C MiG 23 Flogger E/F MiG 25 Foxbat A	Su 7 Fitter A/B IL 28 Beagle Fouga Magister (Light Attack) Su 20 Fitter C Mi24 Hind-D	Ae Alouette II MiG 25 Foxbat B		AN 12 Fokker F27 IL 14 IL 18 Ae SA 330 Puma Mi4 Mi6 Mi8 L. C130H
ANGOLA					
Airforce	MiG 17 Fresco C MiG 21 Fishbed J		Ae Alouette III	F 27	Noratlas D C47 AN 26 Pilatus Porter Mi8 Tu 134A L-100-30 Lockheed Nord 262 BN Islander
ARGENTINA					

Airforce	Da Mirage IIIEA
	IAI Dagger
		McD.D A-4P
		BAe Canberra B62
		IA58 (Coin)
		IA35 (Coin)
		Be UH1H (Gunship)
		Hughes 500M
		  (Coin)
		MS 760
		  (Light Attack)
			Be 47G/J
			IA 50
					DHC Beaver
					DHC Otter
					D C47
					L C130E/H
					FMA IA50
					DHC Twin Otter
					Fokker F28
					Fokker F27
					Shrike Commander
					B 707-320B
					Be UHID/H
					Si UH19
					Si S61NR
					Ae Lama
					BV CH47C
					LC-47

Navy	Da Super Etendard	McD.D A-4Q
		Aem MB 326G
		  (Light Attack)
		Aem MB339
		  (Light Attack)
		NA T-34C (Coin)
			Be 47G
			Hughes 500M
			Queen Air
			Super King Air
				G S2A/E
				L.SP-2H
				G HU16B
				Ae Alouette III (ASW)
				Si SH3D (ASW)
				W Lynx HAS 23 (ASW)
				Si S-61D (ASW)
					Short Skyvan
					L.LI 88 Electra
					BAe (HS) 125
					F H Porter
					D C47
					DHC Twin Otter
					F.28

Army			Cess Turbo Skywagon Ae Lama Citation 550		Beech Queen Air DHC Twin Otter Be UH 1H Piper Turbo-Navajo Aer G222 Be 212 R Turbo-Commander Swearingen Merlin IIIA Pilatus Turbo-Porter Beech King Air CH 47C R Sabreliner 75E Citation 550 SA 330 Puma

Country	Fighter	Ground Attack and Bombers Anti-Armour Attack/Close Support	Observation Reconnaissance ECM/Early Warning	Maritime	Transport
AUSTRALIA					
Airforce	Da Mirage IIIO McD.D F-18 Hornet	GD F111C Ae MB326H (Light Attack)	BAe Canberra B20 (Recon) GD F111C (Recon)	L P3B/C	Mystère 20 BAe 111 L C130E/H DHC Caribou BAe (HS) 748 Be UH1B/D/H BV CH47C B 707-320C
Navy		Aem MB 326H (Light Attack)	Be 206B-1 BAe (HS) 748 (ECM)	G S2E/G W Sea King Mk 50 W Wessex HAS31B	Be UH1B
Army			Pilatus Turbo-Porter Be 206B-1		GAF Nomad
AUSTRIA					
Airforce		SAAB 105OE	Cess O1E Ae Alouette III Be AB206A OH-58B		Short Skyvan Be AB204B Si S65C Pilatus Turbo-Porter Be AB212B Safir
BANGLADESH					
	MiG 21 Fishbed J Shenyang J6 (MiG 19)	Fouga Magister (Light Attack)			DC-6 AN 12 AN 24 AN 26 Mi 4 Mi 8 Be 212 Ae Alouette III AB 205
BELGIUM					
Airforce	L F104G GD F16A	Da Mirage 5BA/BD Alpha Jet E	DA Mirage 5BR		BAe (HS) 748 Da Falcon 20 W Sea King Mk 48 B 727 L C130H Swearingen Merlin 111A
Navy			Ae Alouette III		
Army			Ae Alouette II		BN Defender
BENIN					
Airforce			Be 47G MH 1521 Ae Alouette II		AN 26 Aero Commander D C47 Fokker F27 SNIAS Corvette
BOLIVIA					
Airforce	Da Mirage 50 NA F.86F Sabre	L T-33AN	Learjet 258D	Cess U206G	D C-47 Convair CV-440/580 D DC-4 D DC-6 L Electra Arava Cess Stationair 6 Cess Centurion Ae Lama
BRAZIL					
Airforce	Da Mirage III EBR N. F5E	EMB 326B (Coin) Be 206 (Gunship) Be UHID (Gunship) Neira T25 (Coin) AT-26 (Coin)	Hughes OH6A F FH1100 Neira L42 Neira T25 EMB 326B (Recce) Be 47G EMB R95 EMB EC95 Be 206	G HU16A/B Con PBY5A G S2 A/E EMB P95 L RC 130E SA 330 Puma EMB 111A/A	B 737-200 BAe Viscount BAe 111 L C130E/H DHC Buffalo BAe (HS) 125 BAe (HS) 748 Be UHID/H Be 206 LKC 130H Be SH1D EMB 110 G S2A EMB 121 EMB 810C
Navy			Be 206B	Si 5-61D-3 W Wasp UH-2 (ASW) W Lynx	W Whirlwind 3 AS-350 Ecureil
BRUNEI					
Army			Be 206B		BAe (HS) 748 Be 205A Be 212 MBB B0105 Si S-76
BULGARIA					
Airforce	MiG 17 Fresco MiG 19 Farmer MiG 21 Fishbed C/J MiG 23 Flogger H	Mi 24 Hind D	MiG 17 Fresco MiG 21 Fishbed H		AN 24 AN 2 IL 14 Tu 134 AN 14 Mi 4 Kamov Ka26 Mi 2 AN 26 Yak 40 Mi 8

Country	Fighter	Ground Attack and Bombers Anti-Armour Attack/Close Support	Observation Reconnaissance ECM/Early Warning	Maritime	Transport
BULGARIA cont					
Navy			Mi 14 Haze A Mi 2 Mi 4		Mi 2 Mi 4
BURMA					
Airforce		L AT33 (Coin) SIA SF260WB (Coin) Pilatus PC-7 Turbo-Trainer	K. Be 47G Ae Alouette III Cess 180		Pilatus Turbo-Porter Be UH1H FH 227 Kawasaki KY-107 DHC 7
CAMEROON					
Airforce		Fouga Magister (Light Attack) Alpha Jet	MH MH1521 Ae Alouette II/III	Do 128 D-6	DHC Buffalo DHC Caribou D C47 Ae SA330 Puma Do 28 Bee Queen Air L C130H BAe (HS) 748 Lama B 737
CANADA					
	Can CF104G Can CF5A Can CF101B/F McD.D CF-18	Can CF104D	Can CT33 (ECM) Da C117 Falcon (ECM) CT133 (ECM)	Si HSS-2 (ASW) L CP140 CP-121 Tracker	DHC Otter DHC Buffalo DHC Twin Otter CH-118 Iroquois CC-109 Cosmopolitan CC-117 Falcon Boeing 737 CC-129 Dakota CC-130E/H Can Challenger CH-135 Huey CH-136 Kiowa CH-137 Chinook CC-132 Dash-7
CENTRAL AFRICAN REPUBLIC					
		la 58 (Coin)	Alouette II		Aem AL60 C-47 DC 3 DC 4 MH 1521M Broussard Caravelle Falcon 20 H. 34
CHAD					
			MH MH1521 Ae Alouette III Reims C337		D C47 D DC4 Nord Noratlas Ae Caravelle Ae Puma Pilatus Turbo-Porter SA 330 Puma
CHILE					
Airforce	N F5E/F Da Mirage 50	HS Hunter FGA71 Cess A37B	Ae Lama Canberra PR9 Learjet 35	G HU-16A	D C-47 L C130H DHC Twin Otter Be UH1H D DC-6A/B Be UH-1D DHC 5D SA 330 Puma
Navy			Be 47G Ae Alouette III	EMB 111N Be Jet Ranger	Be UH1D EMB 110 CASA C212 Piper Navajo Pilatus PC7 Turbo Trainer
Army			Cess 01E Cess 02		Ae SA330 Puma Be UH1H CASA C212 Piper Navajo Piper Cherokee Be Jet Ranger Lama Skymaster II
CHINA, People's Republic					
Airforce	Shenyang J2 Shenyang J4/J5 (MiG 17F/PF) Shenyang J6 (MiG 19S/PF) Shenyang J7 (MiG 21F) Shenyang J8	Hong zhaji-5 (IL-28) Shenyang B6 (Tu16) Nancheng A5 Tu 4 Bull	Shenyang J6 (Recce) Hong zhen-5 (IL-28R)		AN 24 AN 12 AN 26 Y5 Y6 BAe (HS) Trident AN 2 IL 14 IL 18 Li 2 Mi 1 Mi 4 Mi 6 Mi 8 H5 Z6 Ae Super Frelon Curtiss C-46 Tu-124

Country	Fighter	Ground Attack and Bombers Anti-Armour Attack/Close Support	Observation Reconnaissance ECM/Early Warning	Maritime	Transport
CHINA cont					
Navy	Shenyang J4 Shenyang J6	B5 (IL-28)		Ber 6 H 5	Mi 4 Li 2 IL 14
COLOMBIA	IAI Kfir C-2	Da Mirage 5COA L AT33A (Light Attack) Cess A-37B T-37C	Da Mirage 5COR D RB26C Be 47G Hughes OH6A LRT-33A		D C47 D C54 L C130B Fokker F28 BAe (HS) 748 DHC Beaver Be 212 Be UH1B Pilatus Porter Ae Lama DC-3 Cess 404 DC-7 DC-6 IAI Araya Hughes 500C Kaman HH-43B Si TH-55 Hiller H-23
CONGO			MH 1521 Ae Alouette II/III		AN 24 D C47 IL 14 Fokker F28 Nord Fregate SA 330 Puma Corvette
COSTA RICA					DHC Otter Cess 185 Piper Cherokee 6 Cess 180 Hiller FH-1100 Si S-58 ET
CUBA					
Airforce	MiG 17 Fresco MiG 19 Farmer MiG 21 Fishbed C/D/F/J Mig 23 Flogger E/F	Mi 24 Hind D			AN 26 AN 2 AN 24 IL 14 Mi 4 Mi 8
Navy				Mi 4 (ASW)	Mi 4
CZECHOSLOVAKIA					
Airforce	MiG 17 Fresco MiG 21 Fishbed MiG 23 Flogger B/H	Su 7 Fitter A Mi 24 Hind D Su 20 Fitter C	MiG 21 Fishbed H		IL 14 AN 26 Tu 134 AN 24 Mi 4 Mi 8 Avia 14 Let L-410M
DENMARK					
Airforce	L FI04G Can CF104G GD F16A/B	Saab F35	Saab RF35XD S-61A Gulfstream III	Gulfstream III	D C47 L C130H Si S61A
Navy			Ae Alouette III	W Lynx Mk 80	
Army			Hughes 500M SAAB Supporter		
DOMINICAN REPUBLIC					
Airforce	BAe (DH) Vampire FI BAe (DH) Vampire FB50 NA P51D	NA T-28D B 26K	Hughes OH6A Ae Alouette II/III	Con PBY 5A	Curtiss C-46 D C47 DHC Beaver Si UH19 Be 205 Ae Dauphin 2 Hiller UH-12E Aero Commander
ECUADOR					
Airforce	Da Mirage F1 JE N F5E/F	BAe 167 Mk 89 BAe Canberra B6 BAe Sepecat Jaguar Cess A37B	Ae Alouette III Ae Lama		L C130H D DC6B DHC Buffalo BAe (HS) 748 DHC Twin Otter Ae Puma Be 212 L-188 Electra Boeing 727 SA 330 Puma
Navy			Ae Alouette III		IAI Arava Cess 320E Super King Air Cess Citation
Army			Ae Lama Learjet 250		IAI Arava DHC-5D Buffalo Cess 172 Cess 185

Country	Fighter	Ground Attack and Bombers Anti-Armour Attack/Close Support	Observation Reconnaissance ECM/Early Warning	Maritime		Transport
EGYPT						
Airforce	Da Mirage 5SDE MiG 17 Fresco C MiG 19 Farmer MiG 21 Fishbed 　C/E/F/J McD.D F4E Shenyang J6 (MiG 19S/SF) GD F16A/B Da Mirage 2000	Su 7 Fitter A Su 20 Fitter C IL 28 Beagle Tu 16 Badger G Alpha Jet	MiG 21 Fishbed H L EC130H Da Mirage 5SDR G E-2C Hawkeye			Bv CH47C AN 12 IL 14 Mi 4 Mi 6 Mi 8 W Commando II L C130A/H AN 24 Boeing 737 Boeing 707 Falcon 20 DHC Buffalo
Navy				W Sea King Mk 47 (ASW)		Mi 4 Mi 8
Army			Ae Gazelle			W Commando I.II
EL SALVADOR						
	Da Super Mystère	IAI Magister (Coin) Cess A-37	FH 1100 Ae Alouette III Ae Lama Cess O-2			F. C123 D C47 D DC6 IAI Arava Be UH-1H
ETHIOPIA						
Airforce	N F5A/E MiG 21 Fishbed J MiG 23 Flogger F	BAe Canberra B52 NA AT28 (Coin) Mi 24 Hind D (Gunship)	Ae Alouette III			An 26 D C47 D C54 F C119K BAe (HS) Dove Be AB204B Mi 8 IL 14 SA 330 Puma
FINLAND						
	MiG 21 Fishbed N SAAB J35S SAAB J35F	Fouga Magister 　(Light Attack) BAe (HS) Hawk MK 51 　(Light Attack)	Hughes 500 Learjet 35A			D C47 Mi 8 F27 Cess 402B Cherokee Arrow
FRANCE						
Airforce	Da Mirage IIIC/E Da Mirage FIB/C Da Mirage 2000	Sepecat Jaguar Da Mirage 5F Da Mirage IV	Da Mirage F1R Da Mirage IIIR/RD Ae Alouette II/III Da Mirage IV (Recce) L RT33A D DC8F (ECM) Nord Noratlas (ECM/ELINT)			Ae Caravelle B KC135F Nord Fregate Nord Noratlas Transall C160F Ae Puma Falcon 20 Falcon 50 D DC-8 MS 760 Paris MS Broussard DHC Twin Otter SA 330 Puma
Navy	Da Super Etendard VF8E (FN)	Ae Super Frelon	Da Etendard IVP Ae Alouette II/III	BR 1050 Alize BR 1150 Atlantic/NG Ae Super Frelon (ASW) Ae Lynx (ASW) Neptune P-2H Falcon Gardian		Navajo Nord 262 Falcon 10 DC6 D C47 D C54 Nord Fregate Ae Super Frelon
Army		Ae Gazelle/HOT Ae Alouette III/SSII	MH 1521 Cess 01 Ae Alouette II/III Ae Gazelle			Ae Puma
GABON						
	Da Mirage 5G	A-1 Skyraider Fouga Magister	MH 1521M Ae Alouette III Da Mirage 5RG	EMB-III EMB-110P		L L100-20 L L100-30 D C130H Falcon 20E D C47 Nord 262 Ae Puma NAMC YS11A
GERMANY, Democratic Republic						
Airforce	MiG-21 Fishbed D/F/J/L MiG 23 Flogger B	Mi 24 Hind D (Gunship) Su 7BM Fitter				AN 2 AN 26 IL 14 IL 18 Tu 124 Tu 134 Mi 4 Mi 8 L-410
Navy		Mi 8 Hip F		Mi 4 (ASW)		
GERMANY, Federal Republic						
Airforce	McD.D F4F LF104G	Panavia Tornado Alpha Jet A	McD.D RF4E Hansa Jet (ECM)			B 707-320C Transall C160D Do 28D Be UH1D Be 212 VFW 614 L Jetstar Hansa Jet

Country	Fighter	Ground Attack and Bombers Anti-Armour Attack/Close Support	Observation Reconnaissance ECM/Early Warning	Maritime	Transport
GERMANY, Federal cont					
Navy	L F104G	Panavia Tornado	L RF104G BR 1150 (ECM)	BR 1150 Atlantic W Lynx Mk 88 (ASW)	Do 28 W Sea King Mk 41
Army		Bo 105 P (Gunship)	Ae Alouette II/III Bo 105 M		Si CH53G Be UH1D
GHANA					
Airforce		Aem MB 326F/KB	Ae Alouette III	Short Skyvan	Fokker F27 Fokker F28 Be 212
GREECE					
Airforce	McD.D F4E N F5A/B L F104G Da Mirage FICG	V A7H R T2E (Light Attack)	McD.D RF4E Be 206	G HU16B Can CL215 HU-16B	T-33A D C47 L C130H Nord Noratlas Be AB205 NAMC YS11 G Gulfstream Be 212 BV CH 47C Bell 212
Army		Be AH1S (Gunship)	Cess U17 Be 47G		Rockwell Commander Be UH1D Be AB205 Be AB204 BV CH47C Chinook
Navy			Ae Alouette III	Be AB212 ASW	
GUATEMALA					
Airforce		Cess A37B (Coin) Fouga Magister (Coin) L T 33A	Cess U206C Hiller OH23G Cess 172/180		D C47 D C54 D DC6 Be UH1D Si H19 IAI Arava
GUINEA-BISSAU					
Airforce			Ae Alouette III		Do 27 Mi 8 FTB 337 Reims
GUINEA REPUBLIC					
Airforce	MiG 17F Fresco C		Be 47G		AN 14 IL 14 IL 18
GUYANA					
Airforce			Cess U206F Be 206		Bee King Air BN Islander Be 212
HAITI					
Airforce		Cess O-2A (Coin)	Hughes 300 Hughes 500		Si H34 Si S58T D DC3 DHC Beaver Cess 402 Bee Baron
HONDURAS					
Airforce	IAI Super Mystère B2 NA F86K	Cess A37B	Cess U17 L RT33A Cess 180 Cess 185		Si S76 IAI Arava D C47 DC 54 Si H19 Bee C-45 IAI Westwind
HONG KONG					
Police			SA Bulldog 128 SA 365C Dauphin		BN Islander Cess 404 Titan
HUNGARY					
Airforce	MiG 17 Fresco MiG 21 Fishbed/F/PF MiG 23 Flogger B	Su 7B Fitter B Mi 24 Hind D			AN 26 AN 2 AN 24 IL 14 Mi 4 Mi 8 Kamov KA26 Tu 134
INDIA					
Airforce	MiG 23 Flogger G/H HAL Gnat F1 HAL Ajeet HAL Mig 21 FL/M/PFMA/MF bis Da Mirage 2000	HAL HF24 Marut Su 7 Fitter A BAe Canberra B(1) 58/B74/B(1) 12 Sepecat Jaguar Int	Ae Alouette III Ae Cheetah MiG 25 Foxbat B BAe Canberra PR7		AN 12 AN 32 Otter DHC Caribou BAe (HS) 748 Tu 124 Mi 4 Mi 8
Navy	BAe (HS) Sea Hawk BAe Sea Harrier FRS Mk 51		Ae Alouette III	IL 38 May BR 1050 Alize W Sea King Mk 42 Ae Alouette III (ASW) Ka 25 (ASW) Maritime Defender	BAe (DH) Devon BN Islander
INDONESIA					
Airforce	N F5E/F	Rockwell OV 10F (Coin) HS Hawk Mk 53 (Light Attack) McD.D A4E/H	Ae Alouette III Be 47G	L C130H-MP Sh Skyvan	Jetstar 6 Ae Puma GAF Nomad D C47

Country	Fighter	Ground Attack and Bombers Anti-Armour Attack/Close Support	Observation Reconnaissance ECM/Early Warning	Maritime	Transport
INDONESIA cont					
					Fokker F27 L C130B/H/L100-30 CASA C212 Aviocar Short Skyvan DHC Otter Be 204B Si H34 Si 61A Boeing 737
Navy			Be 47G Ae Alouette II/III Bo BO105	Searchmaster HU 16B W Wasp (ASW) B 737MP L C-130H-30MP	D C47 C 212 (ASW) Searchmaster B GAF Nomad
Army			Cess 0-1 Ae Alouette II Cess 185 Bo BO105		DHC Beaver Aero Commander 680 D C47 Be 205 Bee 18 Cess 310P CASA C212 Aviocar
IRAN					
Airforce	McD.D F4D/E N F5E G F14A		McD.D. RF4E Be AB206	LP3F	B 747F Fokker F27 L C130E/H Be AB205 Be AB212 Be 214C AS-61A-4 Aero Commander Falcon 20
Navy			Be AB206	Si SH3D Be AB212 (ASW) Si RH53D (M/S)	Fokker F27 Shrike Commander Be AB205 Falcon 20
Army		Be AH1J	Cess 185 Cess O2A Be AB206		Be 214A BV CH47C Fokker F27 Cess 310 Falcon 20
IRAQ					
Airforce	MiG 17 Fresco C MiG 19 Farmer C MiG 21 Fishbed D/F/J BAe (HS) Hunter FGA59/59A MiG 23 Flogger E/F Da Mirage F1 EQ MiG 25 Foxbat	Su 7 Fitter A IL 28 Beagle Tu 16 Badger A BAe J Provost T52 (Coin) Aero L39Z (Light Attack) Tu 22 Blinder A Su 20 Fitter C Su 22 Fitter E/F Mi 24 Hind D BAe(HS) Hunter FGR9 Da Super Etendard	AB 212 Ae Alouette III Ae Gazelle		AN 26 AN 2 AN 12 AN 24 IL 14 IL 76 Tu 124 Mi 1 Mi 4 Mi 6 Mi 8 W Wessex 52 Ae Super Frelon Ae Puma Falcon 20 SA 330 Puma
IRELAND					
Airforce		SF 260WE Fouga Magister (Light Attack)	Cess 172 Ae Alouette III	Bee Super King Air	BAe (HS) 125 SA 365 Dauphin
ISRAEL					
Airforce	Da Mirage IIICJ IAI Kfir/Kfir C2 McD.D F4E McD.D F15A GD F16A IAI Lavi	McD.D A4E/F/H/N Be AH1G/S Hughes Defender	McD.D RF4E G E2C Cess U206C Do 27 Be 206 G EV1 (ELINT) Boeing 707 (ELINT) Bee RU21 (ELINT) B C-97 (ELINT) IAI Arava (ELINT)		B707 D C47 B KC 97G/J L C130E/H L. KC130H BN Islander Be AB 205 Si CH53D Ae Super Frelon Do 28 Bee Queen Air Be 212 Skywagon
Navy				IAI 1124 N	Bell 206
ITALY					
Airforce	L F104G Aer F104S	Aer G91Y Panavia Tornado MB 339	L RF104G F EC119 L EC130 Fokker F27 (ECM) Piaggio PD808 (ECM) Be AB47G/J Be AB206 Fiat G222 (ECM) MB 326 (ECM) MB 339 (ECM)		L C130H D DC6 D DC9 Piaggio P166M Piaggio PD 808 Aer G222 Be AB204B AB 212 AS 6ITS SM 208M
Navy			Be AB47G/J	BR 1150 Atlantic Be AB204AS (ASW) Be AB212AS (ASW) Si SH3D (ASW) G S-2 Tracker	
Army		A 109 Hirundo A129 Mangusta	Cess O1E Piper L18/21 SIAI SM1019 Be AB47G/J Be AB206		Be AB204B Be AB205A BV CH47C

Country	Fighter	Ground Attack and Bombers Anti-Armour Attack/Close Support	Observation Reconnaissance ECM/Early Warning	Maritime	Transport
IVORY COAST					
Airforce		Alpha Jet (Coin)	Ae Alouette II/III Reims F337 SA 365 Dauphin		Fokker F27 Fokker F28 Ae Puma Gulfstream II/III Cess 421 Bee King Air
JAMAICA					
			Be 206B Cess Super Skymaster		BN Islander Bee King Air Be 206B Be 212 Cess 210
JAPAN					
Airforce	L F104J McD.D F4EJ McD.D F15EJ	Mitsubishi F1	McD.D RF4EJ NAMC YS11E (ECM)	G E-2C Hawkeye Mu-2J/S (ASW)	Mitsubishi MU 2S Kawasaki CIA NAMC YS11 BV KV107 Si S62A Bee Queen Air
Navy				L P3C Orion L P2J/V G S2A/F Si SH3A/B (ASW) BV KV107 (M/S)	Si S61A Si S62 NAMC YS11M US-1
Army		Be AH-1J	Mitsubishi LR1 Hughes OH6J/D Cess 0-1AE		Be UH1B/H BV KV107 BV CH-47 Chinook
JORDAN					
Airforce	N F5A/E Da Mirage F1CJ/BJ	AH-IS Cobra	Ae Alouette III		L C130B/H CASA 212 Aviocar Riley Dove Boeing 727 Sabreliner 75A Si S-76
KAMPUCHEA					
Data uncertain due to internal situation. Includes two Mi8 helicopters					
KENYA					
	N F5E	BAe 167 Mk 87 BAe (HS) Hawk Mk 52 (Light Attack) Hughes 500MD (Gunship)	Be 47G Ae Alouette II Hughes 500MD Ae Gazelle		Do 28 DHC Beaver DHC Buffalo DHC Caribou Ae Puma SA 330 Puma Navajo Chieftain
KOREA, People's Democratic Republic (North)					
Airforce	MiG 17 Fresco MiG 21 Fishbed MiG 19 Farmer	Su 7 Fitter A IL 28 Beagle			AN 2 IL 14 IL 18 Mi 4 Mi 8 Tu 154B AN 24
KOREA, Republic (South)					
Airforce	McD.D F4D/E NA F86D/F N F5E/F GD F-16A/B	R OV10G Cess A37B	N RF5A Cess O1 Cess U17 Cess O2A		L C130H DHC Beaver Curtiss C46 D C54 F C123 F C123K Be UH1D/N Be 212 Si H19 BAe HS 748 Aero Commander
Army		Hughes 500MD (gunship)			Be UH1N OH23
Navy				G S2A/F Hughes 500MD (ASW)	
KUWAIT					
Airforce	Da Mirage F1CK	BAe 167 Mk 83 McD.D A4KU SA 342	Ae Gazelle		D DC-9 McD.D DC9B L L100-20 Ae Puma
LAOS					
Airforce	MiG 21 Fishbed	D AC47 NA AT28A/D (Coin)			AN 2 AN 24 Mi 8 D C47 Si UH34
LEBANON					
Airforce	Da Mirage IIIEL/BL BAe (HS) Hunter F70/FGA70	Ae Gazelle (Gunship)	Ae Alouette II/III		Be AB212 Shrike Commander Dove 6 Ae Puma
LESOTHO					
Police Air Wing					Short Skyvan 3M MBB B0105 Do 27 Do 28

Country	Fighter	Ground Attack and Bombers Anti-Armour Attack/Close Support	Observation Reconnaissance ECM/Early Warning	Maritime	Transport
LIBERIA					
Army					D C47 Cess 172/185/207/337
LIBYA					
Airforce	MiG 23 Flogger E/F/H Da Mirage F1AD/ED Da Mirage 5DE MiG 25 Foxbat A MiG 21 Fishbed	Da Mirage 5D Su 20 Fitter E/F/J Tu 22 Blinder A Mi 24 Hind D	Da Mirage 5DR Ae Alouette II/III Be AB 47G MiG 25 Foxbat B/D		Fiat G.222 D C47 L C130H Ae Super Frelon Mi 8 Bv CH47C Falcon 20 Jetstar Be AB212
Army			Cess O1 Be AB206 Ae Alouette III Ae Gazelle		
MADAGASCAR					
Airforce	MiG 21 Fishbed D/FL		Reims 337 Be 47G Alouette II/III BN Defender		AN 26 D C47 D C53D Yak 40 BAe 748 Cess 172M Mi 8
MALAWI					
Airforce		BN Defender (Coin)	Ae Alouette III		Do 27 Ae SA330L Puma Do 28 D C47 HS 125 Short Skyvan
MALAYSIA					
Airforce	N F5E McD.D A4C/L	CAN CL41G (Light Attack) D A-4L Skyhawk	Be 47G Ae Alouette III N RF5E MBB Bo105	C 130H-MP	Cess 402B DHC Caribou BAe (HS) 125 Fokker F28 Si S61A L C130H
MALI					
Airforce	MiG 17 Fresco				AN 2 SN 60 Corvette AN 24 AN 26 Mi 8
MALTA					
Armed forces			AB 204 AB 206 Be 47G		
MAURITANIA					
Airforce		BN Defender (Coin)	Reims F337 MH 1521M Piper Cheyenne II		BN Islander Ae Caravelle D HC Buffalo D DC4 Short Skyvan 3M
MEXICO					
Airforce	N F5E/F	L AT33A (Light Attack) NA AT6G (Coin) NA AT28D (Coin)	Be 47 Be 206 Ae Alouette III LASA-60 Hiller 12E		Aero Commander D C47 D C54 D DC7 D C118 IAI Arava BN Islander Be 205 Be 212 Ae Puma DHC 5D Boeing 727/737 L Electra HS 125 BAe 111 Sabreliner Augusta A109 L Jetstar
Navy			Be 47 Ae Alouette II	G HU16A	D C47 F FH227 DHC 5D Learjet 25D Bee Bonanza Cess 150/337/402
MONGOLIA					
Airforce	MiG 21 Fishbed D/J	MiG 17 Fresco			AN 2 AN 24 IL 14 Mi 8 Mi 4
MOROCCO					
Airforce	N F5A/E Da Mirage F1CH/EH	Fouga Magister (Light Attack) Alpha Jet (Light Strike) OV-10A (Coin) Hughes 500 Defender (Gunship) Be AH1S (Gunship)	Falcon 20 (ECM) Do 28 MH 1521 Ae Alouette II Be AB206A Ae Gazelle Ae Lama		L C130H/KC-130H Be AB205 Ae Puma Be AB212 BV CH47C Falcon 20/50 Gulfstream 2 King Air 100 BV CH-47C Chinook

Country	Fighter	Ground Attack and Bombers Anti-Armour Attack/Close Support	Observation Reconnaissance ECM/Early Warning	Maritime	Transport
MOZAMBIQUE					
Airforce	MiG 21 Fishbed J MiG 17 Fresco C				Mi 8 Noratlas D C47 PA 32 AN 26 Tu 134
NATO					
			Boeing E3A		
NEPAL					
Airforce			Ae Alouette III		Turbo Porter BAe (HS) 748 Short Skyvan Ae Puma
NETHERLANDS					
Airforce	L F104G N NF5A F 16A		L RF104G Ae Alouette III MBB Bo105	Fokker F27	Fokker F27
Navy				BR 1150 Atlantic L SP2H W Lynx SH14B/C (ASW) L P3C	Fokker F27 W Lynx UH14A
NEW ZEALAND					
Airforce		McD.D A4K BAC 167 Mk 88	Be 47G	L P3B W Wasp	Boeing 727 Cess 421C L C130H BAe (HS) Andover Be UH1D/H
Navy				W Wasp (ASW)	
NICARAGUA					
Airforce		NA AT28 (Coin) L AT33A (Light Attack)	Piper Super Cub Hughes OH6A Cess 180 Cess O2A Ae Alouette III		D C47 Bee C45 Si CH34 CASA C212 IAI Arava
NIGER					
Airforce			MH 1521 Reims F337		D C47 C 54B Aero Commander Do 28 Nord Noratlas L C130H B 737-200C
NIGERIA					
Airforce	MiG 21 Fishbed J	Alpha Jet Sepecat Jaguar Int.	Do 27 MBB BO 105 Ae Alouette II	Fokker F27 Maritime	Do 28 Fokker F27 Fokker F28 L C130H W Whirlwind Ae Puma Gulfstream Piper Navajo Piper Navajo Chieftain Hughes 300C
NORWAY					
Airforce	N F5A L F104G Can CF 104G GD F16A		N RF5A Cess 01E Piper L18C Da Falcon 20C (ECM)	L P3B W Lynx Mk 86	DHC Twin Otter L C130H Be UH1B W Sea King Mk 439
OMAN					
Airforce	BAe (HS) Hunter FGA73	BAe 167 Mk 82/82A Sepecat Jaguar BAe Hawk	Be AB206	BN Defender	BAe 111 Short Skyvan Be AB205 Be 212 Be AB214B D C130H Falcon 20
PAKISTAN					
Airforce	Shenyang F6 Da Mirage IIIEP Da Mirage 5 GD F-16	M B57B Nancheng A5	Da Mirage IIIRP L RT33A Ae Alouette III HH-43B		L C130 B/E L L100-20 Ae Puma Fokker F27 Cess 172 Twin Bonanza Baron Falcon 20 Piper Seneca II Aero Commander
Navy			Ae Alouette III	W Sea King Mk 45 Fokker F27	
Army		AH-15 Cobra	Cess O1E Be 47G Ae Alouette III MFI 17 Mishak		Ae Puma Mi 8 FTR 337
PANAMA					
Airforce			BE UH-B/D/H Cess U-17 Cess 172		D C47 DHC Twin Otter BN Islander L Electra Short Skyvan Falcon 20 CASA Aviocar

Country	Fighter	Ground Attack and Bombers Anti-Armour Attack/Close Support	Observation Reconnaissance ECM/Early Warning	Maritime	Transport
PAPUA NEW GUINEA					
Defence Force			Nomad		D C47
PARAGUAY					
Airforce		NA AT6G (Coin) Cess A37B (Coin) EMB 326GB (Coin)	Cessna 185 Hiller 12E Cess 421 Cess 337RG	PBY-5A	CV 340 DHC Twin Otter DHC Otter D C47 D C54 D DC6B EMB 110
Navy			Be 47G		D C47
PERU					
Airforce	Da Mirage 5P Da Mirage 2000	BAe Canberra Cess A37B Su 22 Fitter E/J MB 339	Pilatus Turbo-Porter Be 47G Ae Alouette III Ae Lama	G UH 16B	DHC Buffalo DHC Twin Otter D C47 D C54 D DC6 Curtiss C46 L L100-20 Mi 8 Be 212 AN 26 Mi 6
Navy			Ae Alouette III Be 47G Be 206	G S2A/E Fokker F27MPA Be AB212 (ASW) Si SH3D (ASW)	D C47 Be UH1D/H
Army			Be 47G Ae Alouette III Cess 185		Helio Courier Mi-8
PHILIPPINES					
Airforce	N F5A/B/E LTV F8H	SIAI SF260MX (Light Attack) D AC47A NA AT28A/D (Coin) L AT 33A Bee T34A (Coin) Gr OV-10A	Cess 0-1 Cess U17A/B F FH 1100 MBB B0105 L RT33A	G HU16B Fokker F27 MPA	BN Islander L C130H F C123K D C47 Fokker F27 GAF Nomad L L100 NAMC YS11 Be UH1D/H/N Si CH19 Si H34 Si S62 Si S76 Si S70
Army			Hughes 500D		Be UH-1H Bo105C
Navy			MBB BO105	BN Defender	
POLAND					
Airforce	MiG 17/LIM6 Fresco MiG 21 Fishbed MiG 23 Flogger H	Su 7 Fitter A Su 20 Fitter C TS 11 Iskra Mi 2 (Gunship) Mi 24 Hind D	IL 28R Beagle MiG 21 Fishbed H Wilga		AN 2 AN 12 AN 26 IL 14 IL 18 Tu 134 Yak 40 Mi 2 Mi 4 Mi 8
Navy	MiG 17/LIM6 Fresco MiG 21 Fishbed		IL 28R Beagle	Mi 4 (ASW)	Mi 2 Mi 4 Mi 8
PORTUGAL					
Airforce	Fiat G91R3/4	Reims 337 (Coin) V A-7P	Ae Alouette III Cess 185 Reims 337		L C130H CASA Aviocar Ae Puma
QATAR					
Airforce	Da Mirage F1 BAe (HS) Hunter FGA78	Alpha Jet Hunter FGA78	W Lynx Mk 28		W Commando 2A/C W Whirlwind B707 B727 BN Islander
ROMANIA					
Airforce	MiG 17 Fresco C MiG 19 Farmer MiG 21 Fishbed C/D	Su 7 Fitter A IAR 93 Orao IL28 Beagle Alouette III	Ae Alouette III AN 30 IL28 Beagle		Ae Puma Boeing 707 AN 24 AN 26 IL 14 IL 18 IL 62 Mi 2 Mi 4 Mi 8 Li 2
Navy				Mi 4	Mi 4
RWANDA					
		Fouga Magister	AM 3C Ae Alouette III		D C47 BN Islander BN Defender Caravelle

Country	Fighter	Ground Attack and Bombers Anti-Armour Attack/Close Support	Observation Reconnaissance ECM/Early Warning	Maritime	Transport
SAUDI ARABIA					
Airforce	N F5E BAe Lightning F53 McD.D F15C/D	BAe 167 Mk 80/80A	Be AB206 Ae Alouette III B E-3A Ae SA365F Dauphin KV-107-11 (SAR) N RF-5E		CASA 212 L C130H/E L KC130H Be AB205 Be AB212 Boeing 707/KC707 Jet Star Be AB 206 Learjet Boeing 747
SENEGAMBIA					
Airforce		Fouga Magister (Coin) Reims 337 (Coin)	MH 1521 Ae Alouette II Ae Gazelle		Ae Puma D C47 B 727 Fokker F27 Short Skyvan BN Defender DHC Twin Otter Caravelle
SINGAPORE					
Airforce	BAe (HS) Hunter F6A74 N F5E	McD.D A4E/S BAe (HS) Hunter FGA74	HS Hunter FR74		Be UH-1H L C130B/H Short Skyvan Be 212
SOMALIA					
Airforce	MiG 17 Fresco MiG 21 Fishbed	IL 28 Beagle SF 260W	SM 1019		Aer G222 AN 2 AN 24 AN 26 D C47 Mi 4 Mi 8 Be AB204 AB 212 Bee C45 Do 28
SOUTH AFRICA					
Airforce	Da Mirage IIICZ/EZ Da Mirage F1CZ	BAe (HS) Buccaneer S50 BAe Canberra B12 Impala II Da Mirage F1AZ	Da Mirage IIIRZ Aem AM3C Cessna 185 Ae Alouette III	BAe (HS) Shackleton MR3 Piaggio P166S W Wasp (ASW)	Viscount 781 Transall C160Z D C47 L C130B D DC4 BAe (HS) 125 Ae Puma Ae Super Frelon Merlin IVA Atlas Kudu
SPAIN					
Airforce	McD.D F4C Da Mirage IIIEE Da Mirage FI/CE/EE McD.D F-18A	SRF5A Hispano HA200/220	Cess 01E Do 27 Be 47G McD. D RF4C Ae Alouette III SRF5A	L P3A Fokker F27MPA	Do 28 C 207 Azor D DC8 Falcon 20 Navajo Be LH-1H AB A7J L C130H L KC130H CASA 212 Aviocar DHC Caribou Be AB205 Be UH1H Ae Puma
Navy	BAe (HS) AV8A Matador	Be AH1G (Gunship)		Si SH3D (ASW) Be AB212 (ASW) Hughes 500M (ASW) Si SH60B(ASW)	Comanche Twin Comanche
Army		Be AH1S (Gunship) OH 58A	Be AB47G Be AB206 Ae Alouette III MBB Bo 105		Be UH1C/H BV CH47C Be AB 205
SRI LANKA					
Airforce			Be 47G Be 206 Ae Dauphin		BAe (DH) Dove BAe (DH) Heron Con 440 Riley Heron Cess Super Skymaster BAe HS748 D DC3 Cess 421C
SUDAN					
Airforce	Shenyang J4 MiG 21 Fishbed D N F5E/F	BAe 145 (Coin)	Pilatus Turbo-Porter Bo 105		DHC Buffalo Mi 8 DHC Twin Otter L C130H Ae SA330 Puma
SWEDEN					
Airforce	SAAB J35 D/F SAAB JA 37	SAAB Sk60B SAAB AJ37	SAAB J32D (ECM) SAAB SF37 SAAB Sk60C SAAB Sk50	KV-107 SAAB SH37	D C47 L C130EH Ae Caravelle
Navy			Ae AB206 Ae Alouette II	Be AB206 (ASW)	Bv 107

Country	Fighter	Ground Attack and Bombers Anti-Armour Attack/Close Support	Observation Reconnaissance ECM/Early Warning	Maritime	Transport
SWEDEN cont					
Army			Piper Super Cub Do 27 Be AB206 Ae Alouette II HS Bulldog		Be AB204B
SWITZERLAND					
Airforce	Da Mirage IIIS/B BAe (HS) Hunter F58A N F5E/F	BAe (DH) Venom FB50	Da Mirage IIIRS Ae Alouette II/III		Do 27 Pilatus Porter Pilatus Turbo-Porter T Bonanza S S70A4
SYRIA					
Airforce	MiG 21 Fishbed D/F/J/L MiG 23 Flogger E/F MiG 25 Foxbat A	Su 7 Fitter A Su 22 Fitter E/F Mi 24 Hind D Ae Gazelle	MiG 25 Foxbat B	Ka 25 Hormone A (ASW)	D C47 Ae Super Frelon Piper Navajo Falcon 20 AN 12 AN 24 AN 26 D C47 IL 14 IL 18 IL 76 Mi 4 Mi 8 Mi 6 AB 212
TAIWAN					
Airforce	N F5A/B/E/F L F104G/D		L RF104G Be 47G DC47 (ECM)	G HU16B G S2A Hughes 500MD (ASW)	D C47 Hughes 500 DC 54 Curtiss C46 F C119 F C123 Be UH1D/H Si UH19 B 720B
Army					Be UH1H Si CH34 Kawasaki KH4 Hughes 500
TANZANIA					
Airforce	Shenyang F4 Shenyang F6 Shenyang F7		Be AB206 Be 47G		Fokker F28 Cess 310 Cess 404 B CH-47 AN 2 DHC Buffalo HS 748 BV CH47C Chinook
THAILAND					
Airforce	N F5A/E	NA AT28D (Coin) F AU23A (Coin) R OV10C (Coin) NA AT6G (Coin) Cess A37B	L RT33A Helio U10 N RF5E		D C47 F C123B/K BAe (HS) 748 Be UH1H Si S58T L C130 GAF Nomad CASA C212 Aviocar
Navy		Cess 337		Can CL215 (SAR) G HU16B G S2A/F Fokker F27MP	Be 212
Army			Cess 0-1 Be 206 FH 1100 Hiller OH23F		Be UH1B/D BV CH-47A Bee 99
TOGO					
Airforce		Fouga Magister (Light Attack) EMB 326G Alpha Jet (Light Attack)	Reims 337 MH 1521		D DC8 B 720 Gulfstream II DHC Buffalo Fokker F28 Ae Puma
TUNISIA					
Airforce	N F5E/F	Aer MB325B/K/L (Light Attack)	Ae Alouette II/III		Flamant AB 205 Be UH-1H Ae Puma
TURKEY					
Airforce	McD.D F4E N F5A/B Aerit F104S L F104G	McD.D F-4E NA F100	N RF5A McD.D. RF4E Be UH-1H(ECM)		BAC Viscount D C47 D C54 L C130E C 160 Be AB204 Bé UH1D Si H19 BN Islander
Navy				G S2A/E Be AB212 (ASW)	Be AB205A
Army			Do 27 Be AB206		Do 27 Do 28D

Country	Fighter	Ground Attack and Bombers Anti-Armour Attack/Close Support	Observation Reconnaissance ECM/Early Warning	Maritime	Transport
TURKEY cont					Cess 421B Be AB 205 Be AB204 DHC Beaver Cess 206
UGANDA Airforce	MiG 21 Fishbed	MiG 17 Fresco Fouga Magister			Gulfstream II Piper Aztec Piper Super Cub AB 212 AB 206 Mi 8

UNION OF SOVIET SOCIALIST REPUBLICS
Airforce
	MiG 21 Fishbed D/F/J/K/L/N
	MiG 23 Flogger B/G/H
	MiG 25 Foxbat A/E
	Tu 28P Fiddler
	Yak 28P Firebar
	Su 11 Fishpot C
	Su 15 Flagon B/D/E/F .
	MiG 27 Flogger
	MiG 29 Fulcrum
	MiG 31 Foxhound
	Su 24 Fencer
		Su 7 Fitter A
		Su 17 Fitter C/D/G/H
		Su 24 Fencer A
		MyA Bison A/B/C
		Tu 16 Badger A/B/C/C mod/
		  G/G mod
		Tu 22 Blinder A/B
		Tu 95 Bear A/B
		Tu 26 Backfire B
		Yak 28 Brewer A/B/C
		Mi 24 Hind A/C/D/E/F
		MiG 27 Flogger D/J
		Su 25 Frogfoot
			AN 12 Cub B (ELINT)
			AN 12 Cub C (ECM)
			Tu 126 Moss
			MiG 25 Foxbat B/D
			Yak 28R Brewer D
			Tu 16 Badger D/E/F/J
			Yak 28 Brewer E
			  (ECM)
			IL 18 Coot-A
			  (ELINT)
			IL 14 (ELINT)
			IL Mainstay
					AN 14 Clod
					AN 12 Cub
					AN 22 Cock
					AN 24 Coke
					AN 26 Curl
					AN 32 Cline
					AN 72 Coaler
					IL 14 Crate
					IL 18 Coot
					IL 76 Candid
					Yak 40 Codling
					Tu 134 Crusty
					Mi 1 Hare
					Mi 2 Hoplite
					Mi 4 Hound
					Mi 6 Hook
					Mi 8 Hip
					Mi 10 Harke
					Mi 26 Halo

Navy	Yak 36 Forger A	Tu 16 Badger C/C mod/
		  G/G Mod
		Tu 22 Blinder A
		Tu 26 Backfire B
		Su 17 Fitter C/D
			Ka 25 Hormone B
			  (ELINT)
			Ka 32 Helix B (ELINT)
			Tu 16 Badger D/E/F/K
			Tu 22 Blinder C
			Tu 142 Bear D
			Tu 16 Badger H/J (ECM)
			AN 12 Cub B (ELINT)
				Be 12 Mail
				IL 38 May
				Tu 142 Bear F/G (ASW)
				Ka 25 Hormone A (ASW)
				Ka-32 Helix-A (ASW)
				Mi 14 Haze A (ASW)
					Mi 4 Hound
					Mi 6 Hook
					Mi 8 Hip
					Ka 25 Hormone C
					IL 14 Crate
					IL 18 Coot
					AN 12 Cub A
					AN 24 Coke

UNITED ARAB EMIRATES	Da Mirage 5AD/EAD	Da Mirage 5AD BAe (HS) Hunter FGA 56 Ae Gazelle MB326K	Da Mirage 5RAD BAe (HS) Hunter FR 76A Ae Alouette III We Lynx		L L100 Be AB205A Gulfstream II BAe (HS) 125 Mystère 20F B 207 DHC Buffalo DHC Caribou BN Islander L C130H Ae Puma Be 205 B 720-023B Aer G-222 Be AB 206 Be AB 212 CASA C212 Aviocar

UNITED KINGDOM
Airforce
	Lightning F2A/3/6
	McD.D FG1 (F4K)
	McD.D FGR2 (F4M)
	BAe Hawk
	Tornado F2
		BAe Buccaneer
		  S2A/B/C/D
		BAe Harrier GR3
		Sepecat Jaguar GR1
		BAe Hunter FGA9
		Panavia Tornado GR1
			BAe Canberra PR7/9
			BAe Nimrod R1
			BAe Shackleton AEW2
			BAe Canberra B6
			  (ELINT)
			BAe Canberra T17
			  (ECM)
			BAe Nimrod AEW3
				Nimrod MR1/MR2	BAe 146
					BAe VC10
					BAe Pembroke
					BAe Andover
					BAe 125
					L C130 Mk 1/Mk 3
					W Wessex HC2
					BV Chinook HC Mk 1
					W Puma HC1
					W Sea King
					  HAR Mk 3

Navy/Marines	BAe (HS) Sea Harrier FSR1			W Wessex HAS3 (ASW) W Sea King HAS2/2A/5 (ASW) W Wasp HAS1 (ASW) W Lynx HAS2/3 (ASW)	W Wessex HU5
Army			Ae Alouette II W Gazelle AH 1 W Scout AH1 W Lynx AH Mk1		DHC Beaver

UNITED STATES OF AMERICA
Airforce
	Con F106A
	McD.D F101B
	McD.D F4C/D/E
	McD.D F15C/D
	N F5A/E
	GD F16A
		McD.D F4G
		Cess A37B
		V A7D
		F A10 A
		GD F111A/D/E/F
		GD FB111A
		B 52D/G/H
		L AC130A/E/H
		McD.D F4G
			B E3A
			Cess OA 37
			GD EFIIIA
			Cess O2A/B
			R OV10A
			McD.D RF4C
			L SR71
			L U2/R
			L. TR 1A
			B RC135C/D/R/T/
			  M/S/U/V/W
			L E3A
			L E4A/B
			B EC135C/G/H/K/
			  P/J/NPL
			L DC130E/H
			L EC130E
					McD. D KC 10A
					Si CH 53
					C 12A
					VC 9C
					Bee C12
					B C134A/B
					B KC135A/Q/R
					B VC137B/C
					L C5A
					L C130A/B/D/E/H
					L HC130H/N/P
					L VC140A/B
					L C141A/B
					McD.D C9A
					Be UH1F/H
					Be HH 1H/N
					S CH3E
					S HH3E
					S HH53B/C
					DHC 4 (C7A)

Country	Fighter	Ground Attack and Bombers Anti-Armour Attack/Close Support	Observation Reconnaissance ECM/Early Warning	Maritime	Transport
USA cont					
Navy and Marine Corps	G F14A McD.D F4J/N/S McD.D F18A	G A6E BAe (HS) AV8A/B McD.D A4 F/M V A7B/E Be AH1J/T	R OV10A/D McD.D RF4B V RF8G D EA3B D EKA3B L EP3E L EC130G/Q G EA6A/B/E G E2A/B/C	L P3A/B/C L S3A Si SH3D/H Si RH53D	D C118 F C119 D C9B G C1A G C2A L C130F/R L KC130F/R Bell UH1E/N Bell HH1K BV CH46A/D/F BV UH46 K HH2D S CH53D/E KA 6D CT39 Bee UC12A
Army		Be AH1G/Q/S Hughes AH64A	G OVIA/B/C/D Bee RU21 A/B/C/D/E Hughes OH6A Be OH58A		Be UH1H BV CH47A/B/C Si CH54 Bee C12A/D Pilatus Turbo-Porter H 34 H 13 UH 19 Bee 421A Bee U8 Si UH60A
UPPER VOLTA					
Airforce			MH 1521 Reims 337		Aero Commander 500 D C47 Nord 262 BAe (HS) 748 SA365N Dauphin
URUGUAY					
Airforce		L AT33A (Coin) Cess A37B Pucara IA8B	T-6G Cess U17		Cess 182 Queen Air Hiller H23F CASA C 212 Super Club EMB 110 D C47 F FH227 Fokker F27 Be UH1H/B
Navy			G S2A/G	Bee Super King Air G S2A/G	NA SNJ4/6 Be 222 Si SH34
VENEZUELA					
Airforce	Can CF5A NA F86K Da Mirage IIIEV GD F16A N F5E/F	Da Mirage 5V R OV10E (Coin) BAe Canberra B82/88 R T2D (Coin)	BAe Canberra PR83 Ae Alouette III Be 206B/L		Ae G222 D C47 F C123B L C130H Be UH1D/H/N BAe HS 748 B 737 D DC9 Cess 182 Bee Queen Air BN Islander Bee King Air Be 412 Agusta A109 Be 206 B/C
Navy			Be 47G	Be AB212 (ASW) G S2E G HU16A	BAe (HS) 748 D C47 Cess 310 Bee King Air Piper Aztec DHC Dash 7
Army			Ae Alouette III Be 47G		Be 205 Merlin IAI Arava BN Islander Bee King Air Bee Queen Air Be UH1D/H
VIET-NAM					
Airforce	MiG 17 Fresco MiG 19 Farmer Mig 21 Fishbed N F5A/E MiG 23 Flogger F	IL 28 Beagle Cess A37B Su 20 Fitter C			L C130A/B BV CH47C AN 2 AN 24 AN 26 IL 14 IL 18 LI 2 Mi 4 Mi 6 Be UH1 Mi 8
Navy				Mi 4	Mi 4

Country	Fighter	Ground Attack and Bombers Anti-Armour Attack/Close Support	Observation Reconnaissance ECM/Early Warning	Maritime	Transport
YEMEN, Arab Republic (North)					
Airforce	MiG 17 Fresco C MiG 21 Fishbed N F5E	IL 28 Beagle Su 22 Fitter F			L C130E Short Skyvan D C47 IL 14 Mi 4 Mi 8 AN 24 AN 26 Be AB205 Be AB212
YEMEN, People's Democratic Republic (South)					
Airforce	MiG 17 Fresco C MiG 21 Fishbed	Su 22 Fitter F IL 28 Beagle Mi 24 Hind			AN 24 D C47 IL 14 Mi 4 Mi 8
YUGOSLAVIA					
Airforce	MiG 21 Fishbed C/D/J	SOKO Jastreb SOKO Kraguj Ae Gazelle	L RT33A Ae Alouette III Ae Gazelle UTVA-66	CL215(SAR)	Learjet 25B Falcon 50 B 727 AN 26 AN 12 D DC6 IL 14 IL 18 Yak 40 Be AB205 Mi 4 Mi 8 W Whirlwind Pilatus Turbo-Porter
Navy				KA 25 Hormone A (ASW)	Mi 8 Ae Gazelle
ZAIRE					
	Da Mirage 5M/DM	Aem MB326GB (Light Attack) NA AT6 (Coin) NA AT28D (Coin) Reims C337 (Coin)	Be AB47 Ae Alouette III		D C47 Ae Puma Ae Super Frelon DHC Caribou D C54 D DC6 DHC Buffalo L C130H Fokker F27
ZAMBIA					
	Shenyang F6 MiG 21 Fishbed	Aem MB326GB (Light Attack) SOKO Jastreb SIAI SF260MZ (Light Attack)	Ae Alouette III Be 47G		D C47 DHC Beaver DHC Caribou DHC Buffalo Do 28 BAe (HS) 748 Be AB212 Be AB205A Yak 40 Mi 8
ZIMBABWE					
Airforce	BAe (DH) Vampire FB9 BAe (HS) Hunter FGA9	S1A1 SF260W (Coin) BAe Canberra B2 Cess/Reims 337 (Coin) BAe Hawk	Ae Alouette II/III		D C47 BN Islander AB 250A Cheetah Cess 185 CASA 212 Aviocar Cess 421C

ADDENDA

CHINA (PEOPLE'S REPUBLIC)

4818.181
GM-09 TANK FCS

The GM-09 tank fire control system (FCS) is produced and offered by the People's Republic of China for export to nations wishing to update the FCS of their existing AFV inventory. It is also suitable for installation as original equipment in new tanks.

Modular design has been employed and the system is comprised of a number of small units. These include:

(1) central control unit, based on an 8080 microprocessor computer and incorporating input/output circuits and control panel etc. This is used to insert data manually into the system, and the processor computes firing data

(2) azimuth rate sensor which employs a photoelectric angular transducer to measure turret rate

(3) elevation sensor. An ammunition selector is also mounted on this unit

(4) gun trunion tilt sensor

(5) power supply unit

(6) modified gun control handle which is used to control the gun in azimuth and elevation for tracking and sighting. The control also includes the firing button and the interface for automatic gun laying

(7) laser rangefinder

(8) modified gunner's telescope. On its side are mounted an optical system to inject the aiming point on a miniature CRT into the eyepiece, and the connecting cable. It is used to display the computed lead angle to the gunner by means of an aiming light spot. The gunner lays this aiming spot onto the target and fires the gun.

OPERATION

In combat the gunner temporarily stops the vehicle when a target is detected. He sights and tracks the target for three seconds, after which the laser is fired. The computer calculates the target motion parameters, based on range and angular increments and derives the output data for firing, based on ballistic computations and the other input data. These outputs are presented to the gunner via the CRT and displayed in the eyepiece as azimuth and elevation lead angles. The same data is used to generate signals for the automatic gun-laying device to bring the gun to bear. The gunner aims at the target by bringing the aiming spot to the target centre in the eyepiece and then fires. In this way a first round hit can be obtained in under ten seconds from target detection, according to the contractor.

CHARACTERISTICS

Target range: 300 – 6000 m

Tracking speed: At least 40 mils/s (azimuth); 10 mils/s (elevation)

Crosswind: –20 to +25 m/s

MV deviation: 0 – 5%

Gun trunnion tilt: –250 to +250 mils

Elevation lead: –10 to +60 mils

Azimuth lead: –32 to +32 mils

System weight: 53 kg

STATUS

Production.

CONTRACTOR

China Electronics Import & Export Corp, PO Box 45, Taiyuan, People's Republic of China.

4816.153
TYPE 311-A FIRE CONTROL RADAR

The Type 311-A fire control radar is for use with anti-aircraft guns and is normally employed with batteries of either 37 mm or 57 mm calibres. It operates on X-band frequencies and is capable of both search and target tracking functions and is generally used with a computer and an optical rangefinder.

The Type 311-A consists of an operations trailer with the main electronic and mechanical elements of the radar, and a towing vehicle in which the operators are carried together with a power generating set, tools and spare parts. The complete system can be set up or dismantled to move within about 15 minutes and the weight of the radar trailer is less than four tons. The towing vehicle with equipment weighs under eight tons.

Detection range on a fighter-size aircraft target in the search mode is at least 30 km, with a maximum tracking range of 25 km. Minimum reliable tracking range is about 500 metres. The radar can be switched to any one of three pre-programmed operating frequencies by the operator, and target position data in the tracking mode can be fed to the computer in either rectangular or spherical co-ordinates. In the search mode, the radar beam is oscillated in the vertical plane at a rate of 4 Hz to broaden the effective beam. A target within this beam that subsequently deviates in either elevation or azimuth by 20 mils or more from the radar boresight axis can then be tracked automatically.

CHARACTERISTICS

Operating frequencies: X-band, 3 switchable

Peak power: 200 KW (0·3 µs pulse); 180 KW (0·9 µs pulse)

Pulse width: 0·3 µs (narrow); 0·9 µs (broad)

PRF: 2500 Hz (narrow pulse); 833 Hz (broad pulse)

Antenna gain: At least 35 dB

Horizontal beamwidth: 2·6°

Vertical beamwidth: 2·4°

Sidelobe: –18 dB (max)

Receiver sensitivity: –92 dB/mW (CW)

Max range: 30 km (detection); 25 km (tracking)

STATUS

Production

CONTRACTOR

Chuanbei Electronics Company, People's Republic of China.

4814.153
TYPE 404A COAST SURVEILLANCE RADAR

The Type 404A is an X-band surveillance radar for use by coastal defence forces. There are two receiver channels operating in frequency diversity and comprehensive signal processing facilities are provided. The elliptical antenna is equipped with a remotely adjustable circular polarising device to reject rain and other clutter. Display arrangements include a PPI, and A- and B-scope presentations.

CHARACTERISTICS

Frequency: X-band

Range: To radar horizon

Antenna gain: 39 dB

Accuracy: 100 m (range); 0·35° (bearing)

Resolution: Better than 200 m (range); 0·8° (bearing)

STATUS

Production.

CONTRACTOR

China Electronics Import & Export Corp, 49 Fuxing Road, Beijing, People's Republic of China.

Type 404A coast surveillance radar

4811.153
TYPE 581 AIR WARNING RADAR

The Type 581 is a medium and low altitude air warning radar for tactical applications. It is a transportable system with the 9·7 metre span scanner mounted on turning gear that is carried on a wheeled trailer, which is stabilised for operational use by large folding legs with screw-jacks at their ends.

The operating frequency is in the L-band, giving a detection range of up to 190 km against a fighter aircraft target. There are two units in a Type 581 mobile convoy, one consisting of the scanner and turning gear (and probably the diesel-electric generator unit also), and an electronics vehicle which includes the transmitter/receiver and operators' cabin.

CHARACTERISTICS

Frequency: L-band

Peak power: 500 W

Pulse width: 4 ms/2 ms

PRF: 300 Hz/600 Hz

Noise figure: 3 dB

Antenna: 9·7 × 3 m

Polarisation: Linear

Gain: 34 dB
Range: 190 km (fighter target)
Accuracy: 1 km (range); 4° (bearing)
MTI: 20 dB (clutter visibility); 34 dB (cancellation ratio)
Displays: PPI (12-inch); A/R (7-inch)

STATUS
Production.
CONTRACTOR
China Electronics Import & Export Corp, 49 Fuxing Road, Beijing, People's Republic of China.

Type 581 air warning radar

4804.153
TYPE 701 WIND FINDING RADAR

The Type 701 is a wind finding radar for tracking meteorological radio sondes to obtain wind velocities, temperatures, pressures, and relative humidities at different levels of the atmosphere. It can be employed in either a fixed role or mounted on a four-wheeled trailer for mobile applications. An engine-driven generator is provided for use without main electrical supplies. A rectangular array of multiple Yagi antenna elements is mounted on the roof of the mobile version, the array being steerable in azimuth and elevation.

CHARACTERISTICS
Frequency range: 400 MHz + 3 MHz
Receiver sensitivity: < 5μV
Max detection range: 150 – 200 km
Max height: 20 – 30 km
Transmitter power: 20 kw (peak)
Weight: approx 2 tons (trailer version)
STATUS
Production.
CONTRACTOR
China Electronics Import & Export Corp, 49 Fuxing Road, Beijing, People's Republic of China.

Type 701 wind finding radar

4803.153
TYPE 714 METEOROLOGICAL RADAR

The Type 714 meteorological radar is a modern S-band equipment for the detection and location of precipitation and related cloud formations, and provides a variety of display facilities in addition to digital readout and recording facilities.

The design incorporates solid-state components with the exceptions of magnetron, thyratron and CRTs, and the circuitry provides for automatic noise monitoring, automatic power monitoring, IF and video normalisation facilities. The antenna is a high precision dish reflector, housed within a protective radome and illuminated by a front-feed horn. A desktop display gives four operational modes: PPI, slant range/height indicator (RHI), horizontal range/height indicator (DHI), and also drives a photographic display which can record selected or random pictures of the displayed data in accordance with automatic programming.

CHARACTERISTICS
Frequency: S-band
Peak power: 1 MW
Antenna diameter: 4 m
Noise factor: Better than 3 dB
Receiver dynamic range: 70 dB
Operating range: 600 km
Operating height: 24 km
STATUS
In production.
CONTRACTOR
China Electronics Import & Export Corp, 49 Fuxing Road, Beijing, People's Republic of China.

Type 714 meteorological radar

4807.153

TYPE 791-A PRECISION APPROACH RADAR

The Type 719-A precision approach radar (PAR) is a typical military mobile radar equipment. It is mounted on a six-wheeled truck, although the manufacturers state that both mobile and fixed installations are available.

This Chinese-manufactured system closely resembles the Soviet RSP-7 PAR, known to NATO as Two Spot (**3295.153**), and it could well be a licence-made version although there are slight differences. For example, in the Soviet version the PAR antenna heads are located between the driver's cab and the radar cab, whereas in the Chinese model the antennas are at the rear end of the whole assembly.

However, this could be nothing more significant than the fact that the equipment was designed as a cabin-housed equipment meant to be carried on a flat-bed truck, and capable of being loaded either way round. There are similar slight differences in the scanner outlines.

Operation is in the X-band and dual transmitter/receivers are provided to ensure continuity of service; for the same reason the display indicators are also duplicated.

The two scanners, for search and azimuth guidance and for elevation guidance, are co-located on a mounting at the rear of the vehicle. There is an operators' cab in front of this which also contains communications facilities. Circular polarisation is provided to combat weather clutter and the receiver includes a logarithmic IF amplifier.

CHARACTERISTICS

Frequency: X-band

Range: 35 km (15 km in rain)

Coverage: 1 – 8° (elevation); 20° (azimuth)

Accuracy: 0·35° (elevation); 0·5° (azimuth)

Range accuracy: approx 60 m

Resolution: 200 m (range); 1·2° (angular)

Type 791-A PAR

STATUS

Production.

CONTRACTOR

China Electronics Import & Export Corp, 49 Fuxing Road, Beijing, People's Republic of China.

4805.153

TYPE 793 TERMINAL AREA RADAR

The Type 793 radar system is an integrated air surveillance and approach radar for the control of air traffic in terminal areas. S- and X-band radars are combined in a single system using a large elliptical paraboloid antenna illuminated by multiple horn feeds carried on a boom extending from under the lower edge of the scanner.

The surveillance function is performed by the S-band radar. This incorporates variable circular polarisation, a low-noise parametric amplifier, and DMTI facilities. It is a solid-state equipment apart from the transmitter and CRT tubes, and ICs are used extensively. Facilities included in the X-band approach section of the Type 793 include adjustable circular polarisation, log IF amplifier, DMTI, digital techniques in range and angular measurements, and single-tube dual B-scope data presentation is provided.

CHARACTERISTICS	Search	Approach
Frequency	S-band	X-band
Range (max)	100 km	35 km
Range (medium rain)	80 km	15 km
Azimuth cover	360°	20°
Elevation cover	40° cosec	–1 to +9°
Max altitude	10 000 m	
Range accuracy	± 2%	± 2%
Azimuth accuracy	± 1·5°	± 0·5°
Elevation accuracy		± 0·35°

It has been stated that both fixed and mobile versions of this equipment have been produced.

STATUS

Production.

CONTRACTOR

China Electronics Import & Export Corp, 49 Fuxing Road, Beijing, People's Republic of China.

Type 793 terminal area radar

4806.153

TYPE 796 AIR ROUTE SURVEILLANCE RADAR

The Type 796 long range air route surveillance radar is a modern high-power solid-state L-band equipment that uses a large double curvature antenna and dual beam operation to provide good coverage at low and high altitudes for surveillance of air traffic over wide areas. It is claimed to have very good anti-clutter performance and low cover by virtue of an advanced DMTI technique and the adoption of a dual beam with a large vertical dimension to give a vertical

pattern that provides a sharp cut-off at the horizon. Circular polarisation is employed to reduce precipitation clutter, and target detection is improved by means of frequency diversity operation.

Except for magnetrons, thyratrons and CRTs, circuitry is all solid-state, and for reliability of operation the electronics are duplicated.

CHARACTERISTICS

Frequency: L-band

Frequency separation: Over 80 MHz

Transmitter pulse power: At least 2·2 MW

PRF: 360 Hz (mean)

Receiver noise: 2·5 dB

Antenna: 15·5 m wide (8·7 m²)

Polarisation: Linear/circular

Gain: At least 35 dB (low beam); at least 33·6 dB (high beam)

Sidelobe level: ≤ –25 dB

Beamwidth (3 dB): 1·1°

Rotation rate: 6 rpm

Max range: 350 km

STATUS
Production.
CONTRACTOR
China Electronics Import & Export Corp, 49 Fuxing
Road, Beijing, People's Republic of China.

Type 796 air route surveillance radar

4810.153
EAGLE COASTAL RADAR

Under the name of 'Eagle' the Chinese authorities are
offering for export a Ku-band mobile radar designed
for use by coastal artillery units, presumably for target
detection and location as well as for fire correction by
means of splash-spotting techniques, although this is
not categorically stated.

The general arrangement consists of a small (1- to
2-ton) four-wheeled van with a modestly sized mesh
antenna unit with its turning gear mounted on the roof
of the cab. The latter houses the transmitter/receiver
and display equipment in addition to providing
working space for the operating crew. Power for the
radar is derived from a small portable engine-driven
electrical generator that can be located a short
distance from the vehicle which is equipped with
corner jacks for stability on site.

CHARACTERISTICS
Frequency: Ku-band
Range: 50 km (1000 – 3000 t ship target); 27 km (75 t
craft)
Accuracy: 0·09° (bearing); 15 m (range)
Weight: 300 kg (radar only)
STATUS
Production. Available for export.
CONTRACTOR
China Electronics Import & Export Corp, 49 Fuxing
Road, Beijing, People's Republic of China.

Eagle coastal radar

4809.153
CHEETAH ARTILLERY RADAR

Cheetah is the name given by the Chinese authorities
to a Ku-band mobile radar that is stated to be for
battlefield use by artillery formations for surveillance
and gun fire correction purposes. The complete unit,
except for a small engine-driven portable electrical
generator that is apparently located a short distance
from the radar unit, is carried on a six-wheeled
military truck.

The complete system is probably a Chinese version
of the Soviet SNAR-2 radar known to NATO as Pork
Trough (**4328.153**), except that in Soviet Army service
the equipment is carried on a tracked vehicle.

The Cheetah system is mounted on a flat-bed truck
in a cab that contains the electronic equipment and
also serves as the operators' cabin. A low-profile
rotating antenna is mounted on the roof of the cab
with part of the turning gear probably protruding
below into the working space. The operational
function of the Cheetah radar is battlefield
surveillance for targets such as tanks and armoured
concentrations, and for correction of artillery gun fire.

Although performance details are sparse, there are
claims of some relevance, as indicated in the table
below, and references to a two-colour display which
shows moving targets in a different colour to the main
picture, anti-jamming facilities, and MTI.

CHARACTERISTICS
Frequency: Ku-band
Detection range: 300 m – 16 km (tank target)
Elevation coverage: ± 10°
Accuracy: 5 m (range); 1 mil (azimuth)
STATUS
Production and available for export.
CONTRACTOR
China Electronics Import & Export Corp, 49 Fuxing
Road, Beijing, People's Republic of China.

Cheetah artillery radar

4813.153
JLG-43 HEIGHTFINDING RADAR
The JLG-43 is a nodding heightfinder which follows
the pattern of the well-known Soviet 'Cake' series of
equipments. It is a mobile system inasmuch as it is
readily transportable by military road vehicles, and
the complete system can probably be carried in a
two-truck load.

Operating frequencies are in the S-band and a
2 MW transmitter provides for coverage out to a range
of 200 km and gives a height coverage of up to 25 000
metres.
CHARACTERISTICS
Frequency: S-band
Pulse width: 3 µs
Peak power: 2 MW
Range: 200 km
Height: 25 000 m
Elevation coverage: 0 – 30°
Accuracy: 300 m (height); 2° (azimuth)
STATUS
Production.
CONTRACTOR
China Electronics Import & Export Corp, 49 Fuxing
Road, Beijing, People's Republic of China.

JLG-43 heightfinding radar

4812.153
JLP-40 SURVEILLANCE RADAR
The JLP-40 is a tactical air defence radar designed for
use with heightfinder radar(s) for GCI or similar
applications. It is similar in design to the Soviet Bar
Lock radar (2861.153) from which it may well have
been derived, and features the same arrangement of
two large scanners attached to front and rear sides of
a rotating cabin that houses the transmitter/receivers.

Operation is in the S- and L-bands, each parabolic
scanner being illuminated by stacked horn feeds to
generate families of multiple beams. There are five
S-band transmitter/receivers and these are thought to
operate with the lower of the two antennas, while the
L-band feeds illuminate the upper scanner. An IFF
interrogator is incorporated in the system also. Three
PPI displays are provided, and one azimuth/range
display, plus between two to four additional PPIs. MTI
facilities are provided in the L-band transmitter/
receiver chains.

The whole system is transportable, though hardly
'mobile' despite the use of wheeled trailers for much
of the equipment, and clearly preparing such a large
and complex system for operation must occupy
several hours from the time of arrival at a surveyed
site.
CHARACTERISTICS
Operating frequencies: L- and S-bands
Range: 270 km
Height: 20 000 m
Azimuth coverage: 360°
Elevation coverage: 0·5 – 30°
Accuracy: 500 m (range); + 0·5° (bearing)

JLP-40 surveillance radar

4815.153
MW-5 FIRE CONTROL RADAR

The MW-5 is a mobile artillery fire control radar
operating on X-band and S-band frequencies. It is
similar to the Soviet Fire Can radar (**2871.153**) and
may well be either a copy or a derivative of that
equipment. All the main elements of the equipment
are housed in or on a four-wheeled trailer that
consists of a container which also serves a cabin for
the operating crew.

A circular dish antenna for target search and
tracking is mounted on the roof of the cabin. The
S-band is employed for target detection and
acquisition, possibly with designation by a different
long-range search/air warning radar associated with
the military unit, and X-band will be used for target
tracking. The conical scan technique is probably
employed for the latter function. Good ECCM
characteristics are claimed for the MW-5 by its
manufacturer.

CHARACTERISTICS
Frequencies: S-band (search); X-band (tracking)
Detection range: 55 km (bomber)
Max tracking range: 35 km
Tracking accuracy: 20 m (range); 1·6 mil (azimuth);
1·8 mil (elevation)
STATUS
Production.
CONTRACTOR
China Electronics Import & Export Corp, 49 Fuxing
Road, Beijing, People's Republic of China.

MW-5 fire control radar

4817.153
SW CHINA MOBILE TACTICAL 3-D RADAR

The South-west China Research Institute of Radar
Technology has revealed brief details of a mobile, or
transportable, 3-D tactical air surveillance radar that
is now being offered for export. From artists'
impressions issued by the Institute it can be gathered
that the system broadly follows the Soviet pattern for
equipment of this type, with the antenna,
transmitter(s), receiver(s), turning gear and support
structure, displays and operating facilities, etc being
configured as a series of individual trailer or container
loads, for assembly on site into the complete system.

The 3-D radar is shown as comprising a large
double curvature scanner located on the rear of a cab

that presumably contains the main transmitter/
receiver electronic units, which is mounted on turning
gear that forms the basis of a towed chassis. Stacked
feed horns are located at the opposite end of the cabin
to illuminate the scanner to generate a multi-lobe
radar beam pattern. Connected to this unit by cables
are a number of containers or shelters that are
assumed to house the operating crew and other
electronic equipment.

No detailed specifications have been released by
the manufacturer, but features that have been
disclosed include the following:
(1) an all solid-state multi-channel receiving system
is used
(2) automatic 3-D tracking is provided

(3) comprehensive ECCM facilities include very low
far-field sidelobe levels, PRF stagger, fast
frequency jump, an adaptive threshold, digital
cancellation, CFAR, frequency diversity
operation, and multi-beam disconnection.
STATUS
Unconfirmed, but prototypes are presumed to have
been built and tested.
CONTRACTOR
South-west China Research Institute of Radar
Technology, PO Box 501, Duyun, Guizhou Province,
People's Republic of China.

4808.253
TYPE 756 NAVAL RADAR

The Type 756 (Kaige 756 Series) naval radar is a marine navigation radar that offers dual band operation in the X- and S-bands. Of modern design, this equipment offers such facilities as inter-switching, dual displays, automatic plotting, etc. The system is designed to meet IMCO regulations and is of solid-state modular construction.

Design features include AFC, digital defruiter and performance monitor, 40 and 31 cm dual displays, and the inter-switching unit permits six different operating modes: either of the two radars can be operated independently, or both can be operated simultaneously. Two sizes of X-band slotted waveguide antenna are available (2 or 3 metres), and the S-band unit is 3·8 metres long. Separate (unstabilised) turning gear is provided for both.

CHARACTERISTICS
Antenna: Slotted waveguide
Rotation rate: 18 – 22 rpm

Frequency band	X	X	S
Length	2 m	3 m	3·8 m
Horizontal beamwidth	1·3°	0·8°	2°
Vertical beamwidth	20°	18°	22°
Gain	30 dB	32 dB	27 dB

Transmitter/receiver
Peak power: 50 kW
Noise figure: 10 dB
STATUS
Production.
CONTRACTOR
Fourth Shanghai Radio Factory, 1001 Zhao Jia Bang Road, Shanghai, People's Republic of China.

Type 756 naval radar

FRANCE

4797.353
RAPHAEL TH AIRBORNE SURVEILLANCE RADAR

Raphael TH is a sideways-looking airborne radar employing techniques based on the Iguane family (3298.353). It was originally designed for land area surveillance but is also capable of use in the maritime surveillance role. The system is pod-mounted and employs pulse compression techniques to provide accurate and sharp mapping. Radar information is transmitted by a high-speed radio link to a ground or ship-based command centre, which can be up to several hundreds of kilometres away, where the information is processed and displayed in real time.

STATUS
The Raphael radar has been ordered under two contracts with the first systems due for delivery in 1986.
CONTRACTOR
Thomson-CSF, Avionics Division, 178 boulevard Gabriel Péri, 92240 Malakoff, France.

4802.393
ALKAN SONOBUOY LAUNCHERS

Alkan is developing a range of sonobuoy launchers designed to fit into various fixed- and rotary-wing aircraft. This range includes the Types 8020, 8025 and 8030 launchers which meet a number of operational requirements and allow for easy installation in the cabin or stores bay. The Type 8020 is a cylindrical launcher capable of carrying 8 size A or 16 size F sonobuoys and has an in-flight reloading capability. The Type 8025 carries only one size A or size F buoy but has facilities for release from a pressurised cabin. The Type 8030 launcher is designed specifically for the Bregeut Atlantic Mk 1 and ATL2 aircraft.

The power for buoy ejection is provided by compressed gas stored in a vessel at the top of the buoy. Each buoy is packed in a container-launcher which provides for its storage and ejection.
STATUS
In development.
CONTRACTOR
SAR Alkan & Cie, Equipements Aeronautiques, Rue du 8 mai 1945, 944600 Valenton, France.

Alkan 8020 sonobuoy launcher unit

UNITED KINGDOM

4798.153
S723 MARTELLO 3-D SURVEILLANCE RADAR

The S723 Martello radar is a later version of the earlier S713 system (3491.153) and differs considerably in both physical appearance and technical characteristics. Physically, the S723 presents a different appearance having a wider horizontal but shorter vertical aperture. Technically, the new planar array antenna incorporates integral solid-state transmitters giving a 'fail-soft' capability, combined with high performance receiver modules. Two versions of the S723 are available, S723A and 723C, the latter having six elevation beams as opposed to eight for the S723A.

The S723 is a 3-D stacked beam radar with a parallel receiving system for height finding. Bearing, range and height are available on every target on each revolution of the antenna. The planar antenna is a vertical stack of array elements each fed from solid-state transmitters housed in the antenna spine. Each element has its own high performance receiver. The transmitted RF power is fed to each array with appropriate phase and amplitude relationship to obtain a cosecant squared vertical cover with narrow azimuth beamwidth and low sidelobes.

Returns from the targets are received by all arrays. The individual receiver outputs are then combined in a passive beam-forming network which synthesises either eight or six elevation beams matched to the required elevation cover. All beams have pulse compression and full adaptive signal processing is provided out to maximum range. Target bearing and range are automatically extracted from a series of individual returns by the plot forming system and monopulse measurement of returns in adjacent beams yield corresponding height data.

The trailer-mounted antenna accommodates the solid-state transmitters, the receivers, the beam-forming network, and the IFF/SSR interrogator and its co-mounted antenna. The electronics container houses the eight or six adaptive signal processors, the 3-D plot extraction system, the IFF/SSR data extractor, the plot correlation and digital data link equipment, and a radar management console.
CHARACTERISTICS
Instrumented range: 270 nm
Instrumented height: 200 000 ft
Instrumented azimuth: 360° at 6 rpm
Range accuracy: 525 ft
Height accuracy: 1700 ft (S723A); 2000 ft (S723C)
Azimuth accuracy: 0·13°
Detection range: 270 nm (S723A); 230 nm (S723C) (for small aircraft)

In production. Four S723 systems have been ordered, two for the UK and two for Denmark under NATO ground defence update requirements. The first UK system was scheduled for delivery in late 1984.

This series feature in a joint bid by Marconi and US companies for a $500 million contract for CONUS MAR, a civil/military radar network of 48 minimally attended radars for the US Joint Surveillance System (JSS).

CONTRACTOR
Marconi Radar Systems Ltd, Writtle Road Works, Chelmsford, Essex CM1 3BN, England.

S723 Marconi Martello 3-D radar's new planar array antenna is noticeably smaller than the earlier S713 Martello

---

4600.153
FASTAR BATTLEFIELD SURVEILLANCE RADAR
FASTAR is a man-portable radar for use in the battlefield forward area as a surveillance and target acquisition aid. It consists of an I-band, non-coherent pulse doppler radar, based on the ZB 298 equipment (**2490.153**), and an operator's control and display unit.

Moving targets, at ranges of up to 20 km, can be detected automatically and presented on the display unit at the same 1:50 000 scale as a military map. Any target can be selected by the operator using a joystick control to obtain an immediate display of the target's range, bearing and grid reference. The display incorporates an electro-luminescent flat panel, which is activated and controlled by the joystick, and presents simple instructions to guide the operator through the setting-up procedure. The radar memory stores moving target positions and the display can show target trails over a period of time.

STATUS
In early production.

CONTRACTOR
Marconi Avionics Ltd, Elstree Way, Borehamwood, Hertfordshire WD6 1RX, England.

4801.193
SENTRY ESM SYSTEM
Sentry is a family of mobile land-based ESM systems designed for intercept and analysis of the high and low frequency bands used by radars employed in battlefield surveillance, mortar locating, forward SAM and airborne applications. The family is based on a modular design such that systems ranging from simple radar intercept equipments to full ESM systems comprising land-mobile individual and slave/master radar information gathering units can be provided.

The Sentry equipment consists of:
(1) radome-mounted antennas
(2) ESM receivers, processors and recording facilities in sealed compartments
(3) control and display units
(4) radio links
(5) power generators and air conditioning.

The system is normally installed in a Land-Rover type vehicle but can be configured for other vehicles. In the larger systems facilities can be included to feed in radar information collected by aircraft and other sources.

STATUS
In development.

CONTRACTOR
Marconi Defence Systems Ltd, The Grove, Warren Lane, Stanmore, Middlesex HA7 4LY, England.

Marconi Sentry mobile ESM system

4799.393
APOLLO AIRBORNE ECM SYSTEM
Apollo is a version of the Zeus system (**5689.353**) and is a comprehensive ECM equipment for both passive and active countermeasures on strike aircraft. The radar warning capability is provided by the Marconi Guardian receiver and, using the radar warning receiver processor for management, a transmitter is added to provide a jamming system capable of countering SAM, AAM and radar controlled gun systems. Apollo can be fitted conformally, as a complete on-board system, or can be pod-mounted, depending on the aircraft type. The system also provides facilities for the control of additional countermeasures such as IR flares and chaff dispensers.

CONTRACTOR
Marconi Defence Systems Ltd, The Gove, Warren Lane, Stanmore, Middlesex HA7 4LY, England.

4800.393
GUARDIAN AIRBORNE RADAR WARNING RECEIVER
The Guardian radar warning receiver is a lightweight crystal video equipment based on the ARI 18223/228 systems which are in service with a variety of aircraft. The system is designed to combine accurate analysis and threat warning with the high probability of signal interception provided by a crystal video receiver.

Parameters of the intercepted signal are measured and passed to a software-controlled digital processor which analyses and identifies the threat. Information is displayed to the aircraft crew by one of several types of display, alpha-numeric presentation on a CRT display, LED display, central warning display, or on the head-up display. The processor also has sufficient capacity to manage a range of countermeasures such as jammers, chaff dispensers, IR flares, etc (see Apollo system).

CONTRACTOR
Marconi Defence Systems Ltd, The Gove, Warren Lane, Stanmore, Middlesex HA7 4LY, England.

NUMERICAL LIST OF ENTRIES

*Deleted entries appear in italics, the date given shows the edition in which the entry last appeared

Index

Printed by Eyre & Spottiswoode Ltd, Thanet Press, Margate